An
OXFORD ANTHOLOGY
of ENGLISH POETRY

Second Edition

An OXFORD ANTHOLOGY *of* ENGLISH POETRY

CHOSEN AND EDITED BY

HOWARD FOSTER LOWRY

The College of Wooster

AND

WILLARD THORP

Princeton University

WITH THE ASSISTANCE OF

HOWARD C. HORSFORD

Princeton University

Second 

Edition

New York OXFORD UNIVERSITY PRESS *1956*

Library of Congress Catalogue Card Number: 56-8008

Fourth printing, 1969

PRINTED IN THE UNITED STATES OF AMERICA

Acknowledgments

To Professor Carleton Brown and the Clarendon Press, Oxford, for 'Ubi Sount Qui Ante Nos Fuerount' and 'Say me, wiit in the brom' from *English Lyrics of the Thirteenth Century,* edited by Carleton Brown.

To the Clarendon Press, Oxford, for the eleven poems of Robert Bridges.

To Walter de la Mare for 'The End' from *O Lovely England.*

To Doubleday and Company and Mrs. George Bambridge for 'Recessional' and 'Chant-Pagan' from *The Five Nations* by Rudyard Kipling, copyright 1903 by Rudyard Kipling; 'Equality of Sacrifice,' 'The Coward,' 'A Dead Statesman,' and 'Salonikan Grave' from 'Epitaphs of the Great War' from *The Years Between* by Rudyard Kipling, copyright 1911 by Rudyard Kipling; 'Danny Deever,' 'The Widow at Windsor,' and 'Shillin' a Day' from *Departmental Ditties and Ballads and Barrack-Room Ballads* by Rudyard Kipling; 'Follow me 'Ome' from *The Seven Seas* by Rudyard Kipling; 'Harp Song of the Dane Women' from *Puck of Pook's Hill* by Rudyard Kipling, copyright 1905, 1906 by Rudyard Kipling; 'Road Song of the Bandar-Log' from 'Kaa's Hunting' from *The Jungle Book* by Rudyard Kipling; 'A St. Helena Lullaby' from *Rewards and Fairies* by Rudyard Kipling, copyright 1910 by Rudyard Kipling.

To Harcourt, Brace and Company for 'The Love Song of J. Alfred Prufrock,' 'Gerontion,' 'Sweeney Among the Nightingales,' 'The Waste Land,' and 'The Journey of the Magi' from *Collected Poems, 1909–1935* by T. S. Eliot, copyright 1936 by Harcourt, Brace and Company; 'Little Gidding' from *Four Quartets* by T. S. Eliot, copyright 1943 by T. S. Eliot.

To Harold Matson Company for 'Tempt me no more' from *Collected Poems, 1929–1933* by C. Day Lewis, copyright 1933 by C. Day Lewis; 'Second Chorus' from 'Noah and the Waters' included in *A Time To Dance* by C. Day Lewis, copyright 1936 by The Modern Library.

To Harper and Brothers for the poems of Algernon Charles Swinburne.

To Henry Holt and Company for 'All That's Past,' 'The Listeners,' 'The Ghost,' 'An Epitaph,' and 'Song of the Mad Prince' from *Collected Poems 1901–1918* by Walter de la Mare, copyright 1920 by Henry Holt and Company, copyright 1948 by Walter de la Mare; 'The Old Angler' and 'The Stranger' from *Poems, 1919–1934* by Walter de la Mare, copyright 1936 by Henry Holt and Company; and for the selections from *Collected Poems* by A. E. Housman, copyright 1940 by Henry Holt and Company.

To Longmans, Green and Company and the Trustees of the late William Morris for 'A Day is Coming' from *Chants for Socialists* by William Morris.

To The Macmillan Company for the poems of Matthew Arnold, Alfred Lord Tennyson, Robert Browning, and Christina Rossetti; for the poems here included from *Collected Poems,* New Complete American Edition, 1926, by Thomas Hardy, copyright 1925 by The Macmillan Company; and for the selections from *Collected Poems* (Second Edition, 1951), by William Butler Yeats, copyright 1935 by The Macmillan Company.

To New Directions for the selections from *Poems* by Wilfred Owen, all rights reserved; and for the selections from *Collected Poems of Dylan Thomas,* copyright 1953 by Dylan Thomas, and *Selected Writings* by Dylan Thomas, copyright 1946 by New Directions.

To Oxford University Press for 'One and One' from *Short Is the Time* by C. Day Lewis, copyright 1940, 1943 by Oxford University Press, Inc.; for the selections from *Poems of Gerard Manley Hopkins,* Third Edition, 1948, reprinted by permission of the poet's family and Oxford University Press.

To Random House for 'Musée des Beaux Arts,' 'In Memory of W. B. Yeats,' 'September 1, 1939,' 'Herman Melville,' and 'As I walked out one evening,' from *Another Time* by W. H. Auden, copyright 1940 by W. H. Auden; 'Something is Bound to Happen,' 'Perhaps,' 'Spring,' and 'Petition' from *The Collected Poetry* by W. H. Auden, copyright 1945 by W. H. Auden; 'Look, stranger, on this island' and 'Oh, for doors to be open' from *On This Island* by W. H. Auden, copyright 1937 by Random House; 'Alone, alone, about a dreadful wood' and 'The Flight into Egypt' from *For the Time Being* by W. H. Auden, copyright 1944 by W. H. Auden; 'The Shield of Achilles' from *The Shield of Achilles* by W. H. Auden, copyright 1952 by W. H. Auden; for 'Bagpipe Music' and 'The Sunlight on the Garden' from *Poems, 1925–1940* by Louis MacNeice, copyright 1937 by Louis MacNeice; 'Prayer Before Birth' and 'Brother Fire' from *Springboard* by Louis MacNeice, copyright 1945 by Random House; for 'My parents kept me,' 'What I expected,' 'I think continually,' and 'Landscape near an Aerodrome' from *Poems* by Stephen Spender, copyright 1934 by The Modern Library, and 'An Elementary School Classroom' and 'To a Spanish Poet' from *Ruins and Visions* by Stephen Spender, copyright 1942 by Stephen Spender (as revised for *Collected Poems* by Stephen Spender, copyright 1955 by Stephen Spender).

To the Vanguard Press for the selections from *Collected Poems of Edith Sitwell,* copyright 1954 by Edith Sitwell.

To The Viking Press for 'Piano,' 'Gloire de Dijon,' 'Snake,' and 'The North Country' from *Collected Poems* by D. H. Lawrence, copyright 1929 by Jonathan Cape and Harrison Smith, Inc.; 'City-Life,' 'Lucifer,' 'Shadows,' 'Bavarian Gentians,' and 'The Ship of Death' from *Last Poems* by D. H. Lawrence, copyright 1933 by Frieda Lawrence.

Preface

In the more than twenty years that have elapsed since this anthology was first published, it has become increasingly clear that the first half of the twentieth century will rank, without apologies, beside other great ages of poetry. The original edition of this collection drew a reluctant line approximately at 1900; this is no longer either desirable or even possible. Consequently we have not only considerably expanded the original representation of Hardy, Housman, and Hopkins more nearly in accord with their modern significance, but we have also added twelve new poets. Altogether, there are one hundred and forty new poems here, ranging in length from a few stanzas of Hardy to *The Waste Land* of Eliot.

In making our choices, we have surveyed the whole range of modern English poetry. We believe that these selections of the best and most representative poems, from the most significant poets whose body of work is substantial, fairly characterize the work of the last fifty years. Thus, despite their exchanged citizenships, we have not hesitated to include both the American Eliot and the English Auden because of their importance in the tradition of modern British poetry. Inevitably, of course, others will have different preferences in both poems and poets. But, apart from taking into account a very few copyright restrictions, we can only say that this choice represents our best considered judgment.

The book is intended for the general course in English literature or English poetry commonly offered in colleges and universities, and for that wider company of readers outside academic walls who may wish to discover or review some of the best of their heritage. The editors have merely tried to give the fullest possible measure of the best in English poetry as they see it.

Our standard of choice has been quite simple. We have tried to collect only that literature which in itself seemed most worth reading and in itself most worth returning upon. Naturally we want the serious student to be able to trace in our selections the exciting connections between books and a living society. Thc intellectual, social, religious, scientific, and political history of England — 'the flavor of the centuries' — is reflected in these pages even more than we had at first thought it would be. But, even so, we have stubbornly tried to remember that books are in only a secondary way the product of influences and tendencies. Primarily they are the work of men and women, of minds and spirits that in any time or province would somehow effect their right to live.

We have, of course, not shrunk from reprinting much that men have long thought excellent. The trite is usually not half so trite as in our pride we believe it to be, and at the worst may be better than the falsely original. On the other hand, we do hope that the reader may discover some slight touches of sequence, arrangement, and relationship which will be fresh enough to give him pleasure. Certainly the student will come upon frequent suggestions for reading that will tempt him to go far beyond the covers of this volume.

The teacher of literature will find some departures from the form and method of good anthologies he may already know. These experiments need perhaps some explanation. First of all, we believe that an anthology covering nearly five hundred years should not attempt to be, at the same time, a manual of literary criticism. We have refrained, therefore — with possibly a few exceptions where zeal got the better of discretion — from general criticism of authors and from analyses of literary periods. We prefer to use the space gained thereby for additional selections and for notes, often in the author's own words, that may clarify or embellish a particular poem. Perhaps the practice may be approved by teachers who will enjoy the freedom of presenting criticism in their own way or who may wish to use one of the several good histories of English literature now available. We should like to feel, moreover, that in our own small way we have protested against a current vice in education, namely, the exalting of books-about-books above the books themselves. The one concession we have made — the brief biographical sketches at the end of the volume — will not tell a student one whit of what he ought to think and say about a given author. If he gets anything at all from this book, he must read the author's own words. After this salutary exercise he may go on as he pleases to discover what he thinks — even what he should think! — about him.

However unwarranted the contemporary fashion of decrying modern poems as 'obscure,' it remains true that many of these poems are not, on first trying, easy to read. But in keeping with our editorial principle we have sought through the notes only to 'clarify' the particular poem rather than to interpret it. Each instance, however, presents different problems. For example, Hopkins and Eliot are probably about equally 'difficult.' But in addition for Eliot, many historical and poetic associations must be elucidated before the interpretive act can be performed by the reader. Therefore, in the one case, the notes are relatively few; in the other, extensive. Even so we trust that in elucidation we have not trespassed too far on interpretation.

There is more matter here than can be formally studied and discussed within an academic year. The book supplies, consequently, much of that collateral reading which must too often be the breathless nibbling from reserved shelves. Anyone who will read all that is here will have a solid accomplishment to his credit, and surely no mean acquaintance with English poetry. He will observe that some authors are represented by brief selections, given as extra measure and chosen either because they round off a particular period or line of thought, or because we had not the heart to pass them by. On the whole, however, our business was with authors of major importance and of the highest quality, and these are shown in full and adequate selection. We have not hesitated to extract important units from longer works. It is, of course, not pleasant to dismember Wordsworth's *Prelude,* to take only one example. But this is less painful, infinitely more suggestive, and even fairer than to cut Wordsworth himself by allowing only his short lyrics and narrative bits to stand for him and to pass by *The Prelude* altogether.

We begin with selections from Middle English, not because we wish to minimize the importance of earlier writing, but because Old English can be studied in a survey only in translation, which is not Old English at all. It has seemed best to allow the earlier poets as much of the color of their original text as we reasonably could. The Middle English verse is in the old spelling, and so is Spenser — for to modernize Spenser would destroy his deliberate archaism. In general, however, the spelling of the sixteenth-century poets has been modernized, as has also, but to a limited degree, their punctuation. To punctuate Drayton, for example, according to the rules of modern handbooks is to put the Elizabethan muse in a strait jacket. Much of the subtlety of Tudor and Stuart poetry is gained by the intentional ambiguity which the rhetorical punctuation of the day allowed. It has been kept here except in places where it would completely mislead one who has been taught the modern rules. Likewise, the post-Elizabethan poets have been generally allowed to spell, though not to capitalize, as they please. We have observed that the practice which a student is compelled to have in reading by ear rather than by eye more than compensates for the occasional difficulty he may have with an antique form. The date after a poem, unless otherwise specified, indicates the year of publication.

The biographical sketches which have been retained from the first edition are by Margaret Farrand Thorp. Howard C. Horsford has provided the new ones. We are pleased to recognize on the title page, and here, his other contributions to this revision.

HOWARD FOSTER LOWRY
The College of Wooster
WILLARD THORP
Princeton University

Contents

Thomas Campion [1567–1620]

Sir Walter Raleigh [1552?–1618]

Sir Philip Sidney [1554–1586]

Samuel Daniel [1562–1619]

Edmund Spenser [1552?–1599]

Michael Drayton [1563–1631]

Christopher Marlowe [1564–1593]

William Shakespeare [1564–1616]

Ben Jonson [1573?–1637]

John Donne [1572–1631]

Robert Herrick [1591–1674]

George Herbert [1593–1633]

Richard Crashaw [1613?–1649]

Henry Vaughan [1622–1695]

Thomas Carew [1595?–1639?]

Richard Lovelace [1618–1657]

Edmund Waller [1606–1687]

Abraham Cowley [1618–1667]

Andrew Marvell [1621–1678]

John Milton [1608–1674]

Songs from Restoration Plays

John Dryden [1631–1700]

Alexander Pope [1688–1744]

James Thomson [1700–1748]

Thomas Gray [1716–1771]

William Collins [1721–1759]

Oliver Goldsmith [1730–1774]

William Cowper [1731–1800]

William Blake [1757–1827]

Ballads

Robert Burns [1759–1796]

William Wordsworth [1770–1850]

Samuel Taylor Coleridge [1772–1834]

Thomas Moore [1779–1852]

Sir Walter Scott [1771–1832]

Lord Byron [1788–1824]

Percy Bysshe Shelley [1792–1822]

John Keats [1795–1821]

Walter Savage Landor [1775–1864]

Alfred Lord Tennyson [1809–1892]

Robert Browning [1812–1889]

Elizabeth Barrett Browning [1806–1861]

Emily Brontë [1818–1848]

Arthur Hugh Clough [1819–1861]

Matthew Arnold [1822–1888]

Dante Gabriel Rossetti [1828–1882]

Christina Rossetti [1830–1894]

William Morris [1834–1896]

Algernon Charles Swinburne [1837–1909]

James Thomson [1834–1882]

George Meredith [1828–1909]

Francis Thompson [1859–1907]

Thomas Hardy [1840–1928]

Gerard Manley Hopkins [1844–1889]

Robert Bridges [1844–1930]

A. E. Housman [1859–1936]

Rudyard Kipling [1865–1936]

Walter de la Mare [1873–]

Wilfred Owen [1893–1918]

David Herbert Lawrence [1885–1930]

William Butler Yeats [1865–1939]

Edith Sitwell [1887–]

Thomas Stearns Eliot [1888–]

Cecil Day Lewis [1904–]

Wystan Hugh Auden [1907–]

Louis MacNeice [1907–]

Stephen Spender [1909–]

Dylan Thomas [1914–1953]

Index of Authors

Medieval Lyrics

Ubi Sount Qui Ante Nos Fueroun[1]

Were beth[2] they biforen us weren,
Houndės ladden and hauekės beren
And hadden feld and wode?
The richė levedies[3] in hoere bour,[4]
That wereden gold in hoere tressour
With hoere brighttė rode;[5]

Eten and drounken and maden hem[6] glad;
Hoere lif was al with gamen i-lad,
Men keneleden hem biforen,
They beren hem wel swithe heye —[7]
And in a twincling of on eye
Hoere soulės weren forloren.

Were is that lawing[8] and that song,
That trayling[9] and that proudė gong,[10]
Tho hauekės and tho houndės?
Al that joye is went away,
That wele is comen to weylaway,[11]
To manie hardė stoundės.[12]

Hoere paradis hy nomen[13] here,
And nou they lien in helle i-fere,[14]
The fuir[15] hit brennės hevere.
Long is ay and long is ho,
Long is wy and long is wo —
Thennės ne cometh they nevere.

Dreghy[16] here, man, thenne if thou wilt
A luitel pine,[17] that me[18] the bit,[19]
Withdrau thine eysės[20] ofte,
They[21] thi pinė be oun-rede;[22]
And[23] thou thenkė on thi mede
Hit sal the thinken[24] softe.

If that fend, that foulė thing,
Thorou wikkė roun,[25] thorou fals egging,[26]
Nethere the haveth i-cast,
Oup and be god chaunpioun!
Stond, ne fal namore adoun
For a luytel blast.

Thou tak the rodė[27] to thi staf,
And thenk on him that thereonne yaf
His lif that was so lef.
He hit yaf for the, thou yelde hit him
Again his fo; that staf thou nim[28]
And wrek him of that thef.

Of rightte bileve, thou nim that sheld,
The wiles that thou best in that feld
Thin hond to strenkthen fonde,
And kep thy fo with stavės ord,[29]
And do that traytre seien[30] that word.
Biget that murie londe,[31]

Ther-inne is day with-houten night,
With-outen endė strenkthe and might,
And wreche of everich fo,
Mid god him-selwen echė lif,
And pes and rest withoutė strif,
Welė with-outen wo.

Mayden moder, hevenė quene,
Thou might and const and owest[32] to bene
Oure sheld agein the fende;
Help ous sunne[33] for to flen,
That we moten thi sone i-seen
In joye with-outen hende. Amen.

---

1 Where are those who before us lived?
2 are
3 ladies
4 their bower
5 complexion
6 them
7 so proudly
8 laughing
9 trailing of gowns
10 going
11 woe
12 pains
13 they took
14 gone away
15 fire
16 suffer
17 pain
18 one
19 bids
20 'eases,' pleasures

21 though
22 bitter
23 if
24 seem
25 charm
26 incitement
27 'rood' (cross)
28 take
29 point
30 say
31 *i.e.*, heaven
32 ought
33 sin

'Say me, wiit in the brom'

'Say me, wiit[34] in the brom,[35]
Teche me wou[36] I sule don
That min hosebonde
Me lovien wolde.'

'Hold thine tunke[37] stille
And hawe[38] al thine wille.'

Adam lay ibowndyn[39]

Adam lay ibowndyn,
 Bowndyn in a bond;
Fowr thowsand wynter
 Thowt he not to long;
And al was for an appil,
 An appil that he tok,
As clerkės[40] fyndyn
 Wretyn in here[41] book.
Ne hadde the appil take ben,
 The appil taken ben,
Ne hadde never our lady
 A ben hevene qwen.
Blyssid be the tyme
 That appil take was.
Therfore we mown[42] syngyn:
 Deo gracias.

I syng of a mayden

I syng of a mayden
 That is makeles;[43]
Kyng of alle kynges
 To here sone che ches.[44]

He cam also stylle
 Ther[45] his moder was,
As dew in aprylle
 That fallyt on the gras.

He cam also stylle
 To his moderes bowr
As dew in aprille
 That fallyt on the flour.

He cam also stylle
 Ther his moder lay,
As dew in aprille
 That fallyt on the spray.

Moder and maydyn
 Was never non but che;
Wel may swych a lady
 Godes moder be.

Thys endris nygth

Thys endris[46] nygth
I saw a sygth,
 A stare as brygt as day;
And ever among
A mayden song
 'Lullay, by, by, lullay.'

This lovely lady sat and song, and to hyr
 chyld con[47] say,
'My sone, my broder, my fader der, why
 lyest thou thus in hay?
My swete bryd,
Thus it ys betyde,[48]
 Thow thou be kyng veray;
But nevertheles
I wyl not ses[49]
 To syng, by, by, lullay.'

The chyld than spak in hys talkyng, and
 to hys moder sayd,
'I bekydde[50] am for heven kyng, in crybbe
 thow I be layd.
For aungeiles brygt
Done to me lygt,
 Thou knowest it ys no nay;
And of that sygt
Thou mayst be lygt
 To syng, by, by, lullay.'

---

34 creature
35 The broom-plant. It is useful in magic.
36 how
37 tongue
38 have
39 According to the medieval legend Adam lay bound in limbo from the time of his death until Christ released him and all the worthies of Jewry at the Harrowing of Hell.
40 scholars
41 their
42 may
43 without a mate
44 she chose
45 where

46 last
47 began
48 happened
49 cease
50 proclaimed

'Now, swet son, syn thou art kyng, why art thou layd in stall?
Why ne thou ordende thi beddyng in sum gret kyngės hall?
Me thynkyth it is rygt,
That kyng or knyght
Shuld ly in good aray;
And than among
It wer no wrong
To syng, by, by, lullay.'

'Mary moder, I am thi chyld, thow I be layd in stall,
Lordės and dukes shal worsshyp me and so shall kyngės all.
Ye shall well se
That kyngės thre
Shal come the xii day,
For this behest
Yefe me thi brest,
And syng, by, by, lullay.'

'Now tell me, swet son, I the pray, thou art me leve and dere,
How shuld I kepe the to thy pay [51] and mak the glad of chere.
For all thi wyll
I wold fullfyll,
Thou wetyste [52] full well in fay,[53]
And for all thys,
I wyll the kys,
And syng, by, by, lullay.'

'My der moder, whan tym it be, thou take me up on loft,
And set me upon thi kne, and handyll me full soft,
And in thi arme
Thou hyl [54] me warme,
And kepė nygt and day;
If I wepe,
And may not slepe,
Thou syng, by, by, lullay.'

'Now, swet son, syn it is so, that all thyng is at thi wyll,
I pray the grauntė me a bone,[55] yf it be both rygt and skyll.[56]
That chyld or man
That wyl or kan
Be mery upon my day,
To blyse hem bryng,
And I shal syng,
Lullay, by, by, lullay.'

[51] liking
[52] knowest
[53] faith
[54] protect
[55] boon
[56] reason

The lytyll prety nyghtyngale

The lytyll prety nyghtyngale
Among the levys grene,
I wold I were wyth her all nyght.
But yet ye wete not whome I mene.

The nyghtyngale sat one [57] a brere
Among the thornys sherpe and keyn,
And comfort me wyth mery cher.
But yet ye wot not whome I mene.

She dyd aper all on hur keynde [58]
A lady ryght well beseyne;
With wordys of loff tolde me hur mynde.
But yet ye wot not whome I mene.

Hyt dyd me goode upon hur to loke;
Hur corse was closyd [59] all in grene;
Away fro me hur hert she toke.
But yet ye wot not whome I mene.

'Lady,' I cryed wyth rufull mone,
'Have mynd of me that true hath bene;
For I love none but you alone.'
But yet ye wot not whome I mene.

Lully, lulley [60]

Lully, lulley, lully, lulley,
The faucon hath borne my make [61] away.

He bare hym up, he bare hym down,
He bare hym into an orchard browne.

In that orchard there was an halle,
That was hangéd with purpill and pall.

[57] on
[58] by nature
[59] dressed
[60] Behind the allegory and symbolism of this poem lie the holy mystery of the death of Christ and the medieval worship of His Body in the Blessed Sacrament.
[61] mate

And in that hall there was a bede,
It was hangéd with gold so rede.

And in that bed there lythe [62] a knyght,
His woundis bledyng day and nyght.

By that bede side kneleth a may,[63]
And she wepeth both nyght and day.

And by that bede side there stondith a ston,
Corpus Christi wretyn there on.

[62] lieth [63] maiden

Geoffrey Chaucer

1340?–1400

THE CANTERBURY TALES *

The Prologue

Here biginneth the Book of the Tales of Caunterbury

WHAN that Aprille with his shoures sote
The droghte of Marche hath perced to the rote,
And bathed every veyne in swich licour,
Of which vertu engendred is the flour;
Whan Zephirus eek with his swete breeth
Inspired hath in every holt and heeth
The tendre croppes, and the yonge sonne
Hath in the Ram [1] his halfe cours y-ronne,
And smale fowles maken melodye,
That slepen al the night with open yë,
(So priketh hem nature in hir corages):
Than longen folk to goon on pilgrimages
(And palmers for to seken straunge strondes)
To ferne halwes, couthe in sondry londes;
And specially, from every shires ende
Of Engelond, to Caunterbury they wende,
The holy blisful martir [2] for to seke,
That hem hath holpen, whan that they were seke.
Bifel that, in that seson on a day,
In Southwerk [3] at the Tabard as I lay
Redy to wenden on my pilgrimage
To Caunterbury with ful devout corage,
At night was come in-to that hostelrye
Wel nyne and twenty in a companye,
Of sondry folk, by aventure y-falle
In felawshipe, and pilgrims were they alle,
That toward Caunterbury wolden ryde;
The chambres and the stables weren wyde,
And wel we weren esed atte beste.
And shortly, whan the sonne was to reste,
So hadde I spoken with hem everichon,
That I was of hir felawshipe anon,
And made forward erly for to ryse,
To take our wey, ther as I yow devyse.
But natheles, whyl I have tyme and space,
Er that I ferther in this tale pace,
Me thinketh it acordaunt to resoun,
To telle yow al the condicioun
Of ech of hem, so as it semed me,
And whiche they weren, and of what degree;
And eek in what array that they were inne:
And at a knight than wol I first biginne.
A KNIGHT ther was, and that a worthy man,
That fro the tyme that he first bigan
To ryden out, he loved chivalrye,
Trouthe [4] and honour, fredom [5] and curteisye.
Ful worthy was he in his lordes werre,
And therto hadde he riden (no man ferre)

* Several of the stories which Chaucer included in *The Canterbury Tales* were written before he conceived, probably in 1387, the idea of the pilgrimage. He worked on the series intermittently from then until the time of his death in 1400.

A Chaucer Glossary will be found at the end of this book.

[1] Early in April the sun is in the second half of the zodiacal sign of the Ram.

[2] St. Thomas à Becket of Canterbury, buried in the cathedral after his murder in 1170 by four of the knights of Henry II.

[3] Across London Bridge on the south side of the City. Here inns offered hospitality to the pilgrims.

[4] Here, fidelity.

[5] liberality

As wel in Cristendom as hethenesse,
And ever honoured for his worthinesse.
At Alisaundre he was, whan it was wonne;
Ful ofte tyme he hadde the bord bigonne [6]
Aboven alle naciouns in Pruce.[7]
In Lettow [8] hadde he reysed and in Ruce,
No Cristen man so ofte of his degree.
In Gernade [9] at the sege eek hadde he be
Of Algezir, and riden in Belmarye.[10]
At Lyeys [11] was he, and at Satalye,
Whan they were wonne; and in the Grete See [12]
At many a noble armee hadde he be.
At mortal batailles hadde he been fiftene,
And foughten for our feith at Tramissene [13]
In listes thryes, and ay slayn his fo.
This ilke worthy knight had been also
Somtyme with the lord of Palatye,[14]
Ageyn another hethen in Turkye:
And evermore he hadde a sovereyn prys.
And though that he were worthy, he was wys,
And of his port as meke as is a mayde.
He never yet no vileinye ne sayde
In al his lyf, un-to no maner wight.
He was a verray parfit gentil knight.
But for to tellen yow of his array,
His hors were gode, but he was nat gay.
Of fustian he wered a gipoun
Al bismotered with his habergeoun;
For he was late y-come from his viage,
And wente for to doon his pilgrimage.
With him ther was his sone, a yong SQUYER,
A lovyere, and a lusty bacheler,
With lokkes crulle, as they were leyd in presse.
Of twenty yeer of age he was, I gesse.
Of his stature he was of evene lengthe,
And wonderly deliver, and greet of strengthe.
And he had been somtyme in chivachye,
In Flaundres, in Artoys, and Picardye,
And born him wel, as of so litel space,
In hope to stonden in his lady [15] grace.
Embrouded was he, as it were a mede
Al ful of fresshe floures, whyte and rede.
Singinge he was, or floytinge, al the day;
He was as fresh as is the month of May.
Short was his goune, with sleves longe and wyde.
Wel coude he sitte on hors, and faire ryde.
He coude songes make and wel endyte,
Juste and eek daunce, and wel purtreye and wryte.
So hote he lovede, that by nightertale
He sleep namore than dooth a nightingale.
Curteys he was, lowly, and servisable,
And carf biforn his fader at the table.
A YEMAN hadde he, and servaunts namo
At that tyme, for him liste ryde so;
And he was clad in cote and hood of grene;
A sheef of pecok-arwes brighte and kene
Under his belt he bar ful thriftily;
(Wel coude he dresse his takel yemanly:
His arwes drouped noght with fetheres lowe),
And in his hand he bar a mighty bowe.
A not-heed hadde he, with a broun visage.
Of wode-craft wel coude he al the usage.
Upon his arm he bar a gay bracer,
And by his syde a swerd and a bokeler,
And on that other syde a gay daggere,
Harneised wel, and sharp as point of spere;
A Cristofre [16] on his brest of silver shene.
An horn he bar, the bawdrik was of grene;
A forster was he, soothly, as I gesse.
Ther was also a Nonne, a PRIORESSE,
That of hir smyling was ful simple and coy;
Hir gretteste ooth was but by sëynt Loy,[17]
And she was cleped madame Eglentyne.
Ful wel she song the service divyne,
Entuned in hir nose ful semely;
And Frensh she spak ful faire and fetisly,

---

[6] Sat at the head of the table.
[7] Prussia
[8] Lithuania
[9] Grenada
[10] In north Africa.
[11] Lyeys, *etc.* In Asia Minor.
[12] The Mediterranean.
[13] In north Africa.
[14] Palatia in Asia Minor.

[15] lady's
[16] A medal with an image of St. Christopher, the patron saint of voyagers.
[17] A Breton saint, Eligius or Loy, popular in England at the time.

After the scole of Stratford atte Bowe,[18]
For Frensh of Paris was to hir unknowe.
At mete wel y-taught was she with-alle;
She leet no morsel from hir lippes falle,
Ne wette hir fingres in hir sauce depe.
Wel coude she carie a morsel, and wel kepe,
That no drope ne fille up-on hir brest.
In curteisye was set ful muche hir lest.
Hir over lippe wyped she so clene,
That in hir coppe was no ferthing sene
Of grece, whan she dronken hadde hir draughte.
Ful semely after hir mete she raughte,
And sikerly she was of greet disport,
And ful plesaunt, and amiable of port,
And peyned hir to countrefete chere
Of court, and been estatlich of manere,
And to ben holden digne of reverence.
But, for to speken of hir conscience,
She was so charitable and so pitous,
She wolde wepe, if that she sawe a mous
Caught in a trappe, if it were deed or bledde.
Of smale houndes had she, that she fedde
With rosted flesh, or milk and wastel-breed.
But sore weep she if oon of hem were deed,
Or if men smoot it with a yerde smerte:
And al was conscience and tendre herte.
Ful semely hir wimpel pinched was;
Hir nose tretys; hir eyen greye as glas;
Hir mouth ful smal, and ther-to softe and reed;
But sikerly she hadde a fair forheed;
It was almost a spanne brood, I trowe;
For, hardily, she was nat undergrowe.
Ful fetis was hir cloke, as I was war.
Of smal coral aboute hir arm she bar
A peire of bedes, gauded al with grene;
And ther-on heng a broche of gold ful shene,
On which ther was first write a crowned A,
And after, *Amor vincit omnia.*

Another NONNE with hir hadde she,
That was hir chapeleyne, and PREESTES THREE.

A MONK ther was, a fair for the maistrye,
An out-rydere, that lovede venerye;
A manly man, to been an abbot able.
Ful many a deyntee hors hadde he in stable:
And, whan he rood, men mighte his brydel here
Ginglen in a whistling wind as clere,
And eek as loude as dooth the chapel-belle
Ther as this lord was keper of the celle.
The reule of seint Maure or of seint Beneit,[19]
By-cause that it was old and som-del streit,
This ilke monk leet olde thinges pace,
And held after the newe world the space.
He yaf nat of that text a pulled hen,
That seith, that hunters been nat holy men;
Ne that a monk, whan he is cloisterlees,
Is lykned til a fish that is waterlees;
This is to seyn, a monk out of his cloistre.
But thilke text held he nat worth an oistre;
And I seyde, his opinioun was good.
What sholde he studie, and make him-selven wood,
Upon a book in cloistre alwey to poure,
Or swinken with his handes, and laboure,
As Austin [20] bit? How shal the world be served?
Lat Austin have his swink to him reserved.
Therfore he was a pricasour aright;
Grehoundes he hadde, as swifte as fowel in flight;
Of priking and of hunting for the hare
Was al his lust, for no cost wolde he spare.
I seigh his sleves purfiled at the hond
With grys, and that the fyneste of a lond;

---

[18] A village to the east of London where the prioress's nunnery was.

[19] seint Maure, *etc.* Founders of the great and, in their intention, strict order of the Benedictines.

[20] St. Augustine

And, for to festne his hood under his chin,
He hadde of gold y-wroght a curious pin:
A love-knotte in the gretter ende ther was.
His heed was balled, that shoon as any glas,
And eek his face, as he had been anoint.
He was a lord ful fat and in good point;[21]
His eyen stepe, and rollinge in his heed,
That stemed as a forneys of a leed;
His botes souple, his hors in greet estat.
Now certeinly he was a fair prelat;
He was nat pale as a for-pyned goost.
A fat swan loved he best of any roost.
His palfrey was as broun as is a berye.
  A Frere ther was, a wantown and a merye,
A limitour, a ful solempne man.
In alle the ordres foure[22] is noon that can
So muche of daliaunce and fair langage.
He hadde maad ful many a mariage
Of yonge wommen, at his owne cost.
Un-to his ordre he was a noble post.
Ful wel biloved and famulier was he
With frankeleyns over-al in his contree,
And eek with worthy wommen of the toun:
For he had power of confessioun,
As seyde him-self, more than a curat,
For of his ordre he was licentiat.
Ful swetely herde he confessioun,
And plesaunt was his absolucioun;
He was an esy man to yeve penaunce
Ther as he wiste to han a good pitaunce;
For unto a povre ordre for to yive
Is signe that a man is wel y-shrive.
For if he yaf, he dorste make avaunt,
He wiste that a man was repentaunt.
For many a man so hard is of his herte,
He may nat wepe al-thogh him sore smerte.
Therfore, in stede of weping and preyeres,
Men moot yeve silver to the povre freres.
His tipet was ay farsed ful of knyves
And pinnes, for to yeven faire wyves.
And certeinly he hadde a mery note;
Wel coude he singe and pleyen on a rote.
Of yeddinges he bar utterly the prys.
His nekke whyt was as the flour-de-lys;
Ther-to he strong was as a champioun.
He knew the tavernes wel in every toun,
And everich hostiler and tappestere
Bet than a lazar or a beggestere;
For un-to swich a worthy man as he
Acorded nat, as by his facultee,
To have with seke lazars aqueyntaunce.
It is nat honest, it may nat avaunce
For to delen with no swich poraille,
But al with riche and sellers of vitaille.
And over-al, ther as profit sholde aryse,
Curteys he was, and lowly of servyse.
Ther nas no man no-wher so vertuous.
He was the beste beggere in his hous;
And yaf a certeyn ferme for the graunt;
Noon of his bretheren cam ther in his haunt;
For thogh a widwe hadde noght a sho,
So plesaunt was his '*In principio*,'[23]
Yet wolde he have a ferthing, er he wente.
His purchas was wel bettre than his rente.[24]
And rage he coude, as it were right a whelpe.
In love-dayes ther coude he muchel helpe.
For there he was nat lyk a cloisterer,
With a thredbar cope, as is a povre scoler,
But he was lyk a maister or a pope.
Of double worsted was his semi-cope,
That rounded as a belle out of the presse.
Somwhat he lipsed, for his wantownesse,
To make his English swete up-on his tonge;
And in his harping, whan that he had songe,
His eyen twinkled in his heed aright,
As doon the sterres in the frosty night.
This worthy limitour was cleped Huberd.

---

[21] *en bon point*, stout.

[22] Dominican, Franciscan, Carmelite, and Augustinian.

[23] The opening phrase in the Gospel of St. John — a favorite greeting with friars.

[24] His purchas, *etc.* His begging brought more than he collected in rent.

A Marchant was ther with a forked berd,
In mottelee, and hye on horse he sat,
Up-on his heed a Flaundrish bever hat;
His botes clasped faire and fetisly.
His resons he spak ful solempnely,
Souninge alway th'encrees of his winning.
He wolde the see were kept for any thing[25]
Bitwixe Middelburgh and Orewelle.
Wel coude he in eschaunge sheeldes selle.[26]
This worthy man ful wel his wit bisette;
Ther wiste no wight that he was in dette,
So estatly was he of his governaunce,
With his bargaynes, and with his chevisaunce.
For sothe he was a worthy man with-alle,
But sooth to seyn, I noot how men him calle.

A Clerk ther was of Oxenford also,
That un-to logik hadde longe y-go.
As lene was his hors as is a rake,
And he nas nat right fat, I undertake;
But loked holwe, and ther-to soberly.
Ful thredbar was his overest courtepy;
For he had geten him yet no benefyce,
Ne was so worldly for to have offyce.
For him was lever have at his beddes heed
Twenty bokes, clad in blak or reed,
Of Aristotle and his philosophye,
Than robes riche, or fithele, or gay sautrye.
But al be that he was a philosophre,[27]
Yet hadde he but litel gold in cofre;
But al that he mighte of his freendes hente,
On bokes and on lerninge he it spente,
And bisily gan for the soules preye
Of hem that yaf him wher-with to scoleye.
Of studie took he most cure and most hede.
Noght o word spak he more than was nede,
And that was seyd in forme and reverence,
And short and quik, and ful of hy sentence.
Souninge in moral vertu was his speche,
And gladly wolde he lerne, and gladly teche.

A Sergeant[28] of the Lawe, war and wys,
That often hadde been at the parvys,
Ther was also, ful riche of excellence.
Discreet he was, and of greet reverence:
He semed swich, his wordes weren so wyse.
Justyce he was ful often in assyse,
By patente, and by pleyn commissioun;
For his science, and for his heigh renoun
Of fees and robes hadde he many oon.
So greet a purchasour was no-wher noon.
Al was fee simple[29] to him in effect,
His purchasing mighte nat been infect.
No-wher so bisy a man as he ther nas,
And yet he semed bisier than he was.
In termes hadde he caas and domes alle,
That from the tyme of king William were falle.
Therto he coude endyte, and make a thing,
Ther coude no wight pinche at his wryting;
And every statut coude he pleyn by rote.
He rood but hoomly in a medlee cote
Girt with a ceint of silk, with barres smale;[30]
Of his array telle I no lenger tale.

A Frankeleyn was in his companye;
Whyt was his berd, as is the dayesye.
Of his complexioun he was sangwyn.
Wel loved he by the morwe a sop in wyn.
To liven in delyt was ever his wone,
For he was Epicurus owne sone,
That heeld opinioun, that pleyn delyt
Was verraily felicitee parfyt.
An housholdere, and that a greet, was he;
Seint Julian[31] he was in his contree.

---

[25] He wolde, *etc.* He wished the sea-route between these ports kept open at all costs.

[26] Only the royal money changers were allowed to make profits in exchange. He is acting illegally.

[27] An alchemist was also termed a 'philosophre.'

[28] A royal judge, of importance. There were only twenty.

[29] unrestricted possession

[30] The official dress for a sergeant was of brown and green stripes.

[31] The patron saint of hospitality.

His breed, his ale, was alwey after oon;
A bettre envyned man was no-wher noon.
With-oute bake mete was never his hous,
Of fish and flesh, and that so plentevous,
It snewed in his hous of mete and drinke,
Of alle deyntees that men coude thinke.
After the sondry sesons of the yeer,
So chaunged he his mete and his soper.
Ful many a fat partrich hadde he in mewe,
And many a breem and many a luce in stewe.
Wo was his cook, but-if his sauce were
Poynaunt and sharp, and redy al his gere.
His table dormant in his halle alway
Stood redy covered al the longe day.
At sessiouns ther was he lord and sire;
Ful ofte tyme he was knight of the shire.[32]
An anlas and a gipser al of silk
Heng at his girdel, whyt as morne milk.
A shirreve hadde he been, and a countour;
Was no-wher such a worthy vavasour.
An HABERDASSHER and a CARPENTER,
A WEBBE, a DYERE, and a TAPICER,
Were with us eek, clothed in o liveree,
Of a solempne and greet fraternitee.
Ful fresh and newe hir gere apyked was;
Hir knyves were y-chaped noght with bras,
But al with silver, wroght ful clene and weel,
Hir girdles and hir pouches every-deel.
Wel semed ech of hem a fair burgeys,
To sitten in a yeldhalle on a deys.
Everich, for the wisdom that he can,
Was shaply for to been an alderman.
For catel hadde they y-nogh and rente,
And eek hir wyves wolde it wel assente;
And elles certein were they to blame.
It is ful fair to been y-clept '*ma dame*,'
And goon to vigilyës al bifore,
And have a mantel royalliche y-bore.
A COOK they hadde with hem for the nones,
To boille the chiknes with the mary-bones,
And poudre-marchant tart, and galingale.

[32] Member of Parliament for his county.

Wel coude he knowe a draughte of London ale.
He coude roste, and sethe, and broille, and frye,
Maken mortreux, and wel bake a pye.
But greet harm was it, as it thoughte me,
That on his shine a mormal hadde he;
For blankmanger, that made he with the beste.
A SHIPMAN was ther, woning fer by weste:
For aught I woot, he was of Dertemouthe.
He rood up-on a rouncy, as he couthe,
In a gowne of falding to the knee.
A daggere hanging on a laas hadde he
Aboute his nekke under his arm adoun.
The hote somer had maad his hewe al broun;
And, certeinly, he was a good felawe.
Ful many a draughte of wyn had he y-drawe [33]
From Burdeux-ward, whyl that the chapman sleep.
Of nyce conscience took he no keep.
If that he faught, and hadde the hyer hond,
By water he sente hem hoom [34] to every lond.
But of his craft to rekene wel his tydes,
His stremes and his daungers him bisydes,
His herberwe and his mone, his lodemenage,
Ther nas noon swich from Hulle to Cartage.[35]
Hardy he was, and wys to undertake;
With many a tempest hadde his berd been shake.
He knew wel alle the havenes, as they were,
From Gootlond [36] to the cape of Finistere,[37]
And every cryke in Britayne and in Spayne;
His barge y-cleped was the Maudelayne.

[33] The shipman stole wine which he was bringing over for others.
[34] He drowned his prisoners pirate-fashion.
[35] Probably not Carthage but a Spanish port.
[36] Perhaps Gotland, off Sweden.
[37] A cape in Brittany.

With us ther was a Doctour of Phisyk,
In al this world ne was ther noon him lyk
To speke of phisik and of surgerye;
For he was grounded in astronomye.
He kepte his pacient a ful greet del
In houres, by his magik naturel.[38]
Wel coude he fortunen the ascendent
Of his images for his pacient.
He knew the cause of everich maladye,
Were it of hoot or cold, or moiste, or drye,
And where engendred, and of what humour;[39]
He was a verrey parfit practisour.
The cause y-knowe, and of his harm the rote,
Anon he yaf the seke man his bote.
Ful redy hadde he his apothecaries,
To sende him drogges and his letuaries,
For ech of hem made other for to winne;
Hir frendschipe nas nat newe to biginne.
Wel knew he th'olde Esculapius,
And Deiscorides, and eek Rufus,
Old Ypocras, Haly, and Galien;
Serapion, Razis, and Avicen;
Averrois, Damascien, and Constantyn;
Bernard, and Gatesden, and Gilbertyn.[40]
Of his diete mesurable was he,
For it was of no superfluitee,
But of greet norissing and digestible.
His studie was but litel on the bible.
In sangwin and in pers he clad was al,
Lyned with taffata and with sendal;
And yet he was but esy of dispence;
He kepte that he wan in pestilence.
For gold in phisik is a cordial,[41]
Therfore he lovede gold in special.

A good Wyf was ther of bisyde Bathe,
But she was som-del deef, and that was scathe.
Of clooth-making she hadde swiche an haunt,
She passed hem of Ypres and of Gaunt.
In al the parisshe wyf ne was ther noon
That to th' offring bifore hir sholde goon;
And if ther dide, certeyn, so wrooth was she,
That she was out of alle charitee.
Hir coverchiefs ful fyne were of ground;
I dorste swere they weyeden ten pound
That on a Sonday were upon hir heed.
Hir hosen weren of fyn scarlet reed,
Ful streite y-teyd, and shoos ful moiste and newe.
Bold was hir face, and fair, and reed of hewe.
She was a worthy womman al hir lyve,
Housbondes at chirche-dore she hadde fyve,
Withouten other companye in youthe;
But therof nedeth nat to speke as nouthe.
And thryes hadde she been at Jerusalem;
She hadde passed many a straunge streem;
At Rome she hadde been, and at Boloigne,
In Galice at seint Jame,[42] and at Coloigne.
She coude muche of wandring by the weye:
Gat-tothed was she, soothly for to seye.
Up-on an amblere esily she sat,
Y-wimpled wel, and on hir heed an hat
As brood as is a bokeler or a targe;
A foot-mantel aboute hir hipes large,
And on hir feet a paire of spores sharpe.
In felawschip wel coude she laughe and carpe.
Of remedyes of love she knew perchaunce,
For she coude of that art the olde daunce.

A good man was ther of religioun,
And was a povre Persoun of a toun;
But riche he was of holy thoght and werk.
He was also a lerned man, a clerk,
That Cristes gospel trewely wolde preche;
His parisshens devoutly wolde he teche.
Benigne he was, and wonder diligent,
And in adversitee ful pacient;
And swich he was y-preved ofte sythes.
Ful looth were him to cursen for his tythes,

[38] As opposed to black magic which was unlawful. The physician was versed in astrology and knew the right 'hours' for making images of his patients which could be used as charms in treating them.

[39] The four 'humours' or liquids of the body were supposed to be hot, cold, moist, and dry.

[40] All well-known medical authorities. The last two were Englishmen.

[41] Tincture of gold was used as a stimulant, but Chaucer refers here, as well, to the physician's avarice.

[42] Saint James, whose shrine at Compostella in Spain was important.

But rather wolde he yeven, out of doute,
Un-to his povre parisshens aboute
Of his offring, and eek of his substaunce.
He coude in litel thing han suffisaunce.
Wyd was his parisshe, and houses fer a-sonder,
But he ne lafte nat, for reyn ne thonder,
In siknes nor in meschief, to visyte
The ferreste in his parisshe, muche and lyte,[43]
Up-on his feet, and in his hand a staf.
This noble ensample to his sheep he yaf,
That first he wroghte, and afterward he taughte;
Out of the gospel he tho wordes caughte;
And this figure he added eek ther-to,
That if gold ruste, what shal iren do?
For if a preest be foul, on whom we truste,
No wonder is a lewed man to ruste;
And shame it is, if a preest take keep,
A shiten shepherde and a clene sheep.
Wel oghte a preest ensample for to yive,
By his clennesse, how that his sheep shold live.
He sette nat his benefice to hyre,
And leet his sheep encombred in the myre,
And ran to London, un-to sëynt Poules,
To seken him a chaunterie[44] for soules,
Or with a bretherhed to been withholde;
But dwelte at hoom, and kepte wel his folde,
So that the wolf ne made it nat miscarie;
He was a shepherde and no mercenarie.
And though he holy were, and vertuous,
He was to sinful man nat despitous,
Ne of his speche daungerous ne digne,
But in his teching discreet and benigne.
To drawen folk to heven by fairnesse
By good ensample, was his bisinesse:
But it were any persone obstinat,
What-so he were, of heigh or lowe estat,
Him wolde he snibben sharply for the nones.
A bettre preest, I trowe that nowher noon is.
He wayted after no pompe and reverence,
Ne maked him a spyced conscience,

[43] high and low
[44] A chantry is an endowment to pay for the perpetual saying of masses for the person who leaves the endowment.

But Cristes lore, and his apostles twelve,
He taughte, and first he folwed it him-selve.
With him ther was a PLOWMAN, was his brother,
That hadde y-lad of dong ful many a fother,
A trewe swinker and a good was he,
Livinge in pees and parfit charitee.
God loved he best with al his hole herte
At alle tymes, thogh him gamed or smerte,
And thanne his neighebour right as him-selve.
He wolde thresshe, and ther-to dyke and delve,
For Cristes sake, for every povre wight,
Withouten hyre, if it lay in his might.
His tythes payed he ful faire and wel,
Bothe of his propre swink and his ca-tel.
In a tabard he rood upon a mere.
Ther was also a Reve and a Millere,
A Somnour and a Pardoner also,
A Maunciple, and my-self; ther were namo.
The MILLER was a stout carl, for the nones,
Ful big he was of braun, and eek of bones;
That proved wel,[45] for over-al ther he cam,
At wrastling he wolde have alwey the ram.[46]
He was short-sholdred, brood, a thikke knarre,
Ther nas no dore that he nolde heve of harre,
Or breke it, at a renning, with his heed.
His berd as any sowe or fox was reed,
And ther-to brood, as though it were a spade.
Up-on the cop right of his nose he hade
A werte, and ther-on stood a tuft of heres,
Reed as the bristles of a sowes eres;
His nose-thirles blake were and wyde.
A swerd and bokeler bar he by his syde;
His mouth as greet was as a greet forneys.

[45] That was certainly so.
[46] prize

He was a janglere and a goliardeys,
And that was most of sinne and harlotryes.
Wel coude he stelen corn, and tollen thryes;[47]
And yet he hadde a thombe of gold,[48] pardee.
A whyt cote and a blew hood wered he.
A baggepype wel coude he blowe and sowne,
And ther-with-al he broghte us out of towne.

A gentil Maunciple was ther of a temple,
Of which achatours mighte take exemple
For to be wyse in bying of vitaille
For whether that he payde or took by taille,
Algate he wayted so in his achat,
That he was ay biforn and in good stat.
Now is nat that of God a ful fair grace,
That swich a lewed mannes wit shal pace
The wisdom of an heep of lerned men?
Of maistres hadde he mo than thryes ten,
That were of lawe expert and curious;
Of which ther were a doseyn in that hous
Worthy to been stiwardes of rente and lond
Of any lord that is in Engelond,
To make him live by his propre good,
In honour dettelees, but he were wood,
Or live as scarsly as him list desire;
And able for to helpen al a shire
In any cas that mighte falle or happe;
And yit this maunciple sette hir aller cappe.[49]

The Reve was a sclendre colerik man,
His berd was shave as ny as ever he can.
His heer was by his eres round y-shorn.
His top was dokked lyk a preest biforn.
Ful longe were his legges, and ful lene,
Y-lyk a staf, ther was no calf y-sene.
Wel coude he kepe a gerner and a binne;
Ther was noon auditour coude on him winne.
Wel wiste he, by the droghte, and by the reyn,
The yelding of his seed, and of his greyn.
His lordes sheep, his neet, his dayerye,
His swyn, his hors, his stoor, and his pultrye,
Was hoolly in this reves governing,
And by his covenaunt yaf the rekening,
Sin that his lord was twenty yeer of age;
Ther coude no man bringe him in arrerage.
Ther nas baillif, ne herde, ne other hyne,
That he ne knew his sleighte and his covyne;
They were adrad of him, as of the deeth.
His woning was ful fair up-on an heeth,
With grene treës shadwed was his place.
He coude bettre than his lord purchace.
Ful riche he was astored prively,
His lord wel coude he plesen subtilly,
To yeve and lene him of his owne good,
And have a thank, and yet a cote and hood.
In youthe he lerned hadde a good mister;
He was a wel good wrighte, a carpenter.
This reve sat up-on a ful good stot,
That was al pomely grey, and highte Scot.
A long surcote of pers up-on he hade,
And by his syde he bar a rusty blade.
Of Northfolk was this reve, of which I telle,
Bisyde a toun men clepen Baldeswelle.
Tukked he was, as is a frere, aboute,
And ever he rood the hindreste of our route.

A Somnour was ther with us in that place,
That hadde a fyr-reed cherubinnes face,
For sawcefleem he was, with eyen narwe.
As hoot he was, and lecherous, as a sparwe;
With scalled browes blake, and piled berd;
Of his visage children were aferd.
Ther nas quik-silver, litarge, ne brimstoon,
Boras, ceruce, ne oille of tartre noon,
Ne oynement that wolde clense and byte,
That him mighte helpen of his whelkes whyte,

---

47 take triple toll

48 Refers to the proverb 'An honest miller hath a golden thumb.' As millers go, he was honest, and he was expert in judging flour.

49 sette hir, *etc.*, fooled them all

Nor of the knobbes sittinge on his chekes.
Wel loved he garleek, oynons, and eek lekes,
And for to drinken strong wyn, reed as blood.
Than wolde he speke, and crye as he were wood.
And whan that he wel dronken hadde the wyn,
Than wolde he speke no word but Latyn.
A fewe termes hadde he, two or three,
That he had lerned out of som decree;
No wonder is, he herde it al the day;
And eek ye knowen wel, how that a jay
Can clepen 'Watte,' as well as can the pope.
But who-so coude in other thing him grope,
Thanne hadde he spent al his philosophye;
Ay '*Questio quid iuris*'[50] wolde he crye.
He was a gentil harlot and a kinde;
A bettre felawe sholde men noght finde.
He wolde suffre, for a quart of wyn,
A good felawe to have his concubyn
A twelf-month, and excuse him atte fulle:
Ful prively a finch eek coude he pulle.[51]
And if he fond o-wher a good felawe,
He wolde techen him to have non awe,
In swich cas, of the erchedeknes[52] curs,
But-if a mannes soule were in his purs;
For in his purs he sholde y-punisshed be.
'Purs is the erchedeknes helle,' seyde he.
But wel I woot he lyed right in dede;
Of cursing oghte ech gilty man him drede—
For curs wol slee, right as assoilling saveth—
And also war him of a *significavit*.[53]
In daunger hadde he at his owne gyse
The yonge girles[54] of the diocyse,
And knew hir counseil, and was al hir reed.
A gerland hadde he set up-on his heed,
As greet as it were for an ale-stake;
A bokeler hadde he maad him of a cake.
With him ther rood a gentil PARDONER
Of Rouncival,[55] his freend and his compeer,
That streight was comen fro the court of Rome.
Ful loude he song, 'Com hider, love, to me.'
This somnour bar to him a stif burdoun,
Was never trompe of half so greet a soun.
This pardoner hadde heer as yelow as wex,
But smothe it heng, as dooth a strike of flex;
By ounces henge his lokkes that he hadde,
And ther-with he his shuldres overspradde;
But thinne it lay, by colpons oon and oon;
But hood, for jolitee, ne wered he noon,
For it was trussed up in his walet.
Him thoughte, he rood al of the newe jet;
Dischevele, save his cappe, he rood al bare.
Swiche glaringe eyen hadde he as an hare.
A vernicle[56] hadde he sowed on his cappe.
His walet lay biforn him in his lappe,
Bret-ful of pardoun come from Rome al hoot.
A voys he hadde as smal as hath a goot.
No berd hadde he, ne never sholde have,
As smothe it was as it were late y-shave;
I trowe he were a gelding or a mare.
But of his craft, fro Berwik into Ware,
Ne was ther swich another pardoner.
For in his male he hadde a pilwe-beer,
Which that, he seyde, was our lady veyl:
He seyde, he hadde a gobet of the seyl
That sëynt Peter hadde, whan that he wente
Up-on the see, til Jesu Crist him hente.
He hadde a croys of latoun, ful of stones,
And in a glas he hadde pigges bones.
But with thise relikes, whan that he fond
A povre person dwelling up-on lond,
Up-on a day he gat him more moneye

[50] 'What's the law here?'
[51] Ful prively, *etc.* He treated women as he allowed others to do.
[52] The archdeacon dealt with cases of fornication.
[53] A writ against an excommunicated person.
[54] Used of both sexes.
[55] A hospital in London, near Charing Cross.
[56] A handkerchief with the face of Christ painted on it

Than that the person gat in monthes tweye.
And thus, with feyned flaterye and japes,
He made the person and the peple his apes.
But trewely to tellen, atte laste,
He was in chirche a noble ecclesiaste.
Wel coude he rede a lessoun or a storie,
But alderbest he song an offertorie;
For wel he wiste, whan that song was songe,
He moste preche, and wel affyle his tonge,
To winne silver, as he ful wel coude;
Therefore he song so meriely and loude.
Now have I told you shortly, in a clause,
Th'estat, th'array, the nombre, and eek the cause
Why that assembled was this companye
In Southwerk, at this gentil hostelrye,
That highte the Tabard, faste by the Belle.
But now is tyme to yow for to telle
How that we baren us that ilke night,
Whan we were in that hostelrye alight.
And after wol I telle of our viage,
And al the remenaunt of our pilgrimage.
But first I pray yow, of your curteisye,
That ye n'arette it nat my vileinye,[57]
Thogh that I pleynly speke in this matere,
To telle yow hir wordes and hir chere;
Ne thogh I speke hir wordes properly.
For this ye knowen al-so wel as I,
Who-so shal telle a tale after a man,
He moot reherce, as ny as ever he can,
Everich a word, if it be in his charge,
Al speke he never so rudeliche and large;
Or elles he moot telle his tale untrewe,
Or feyne thing, or finde wordes newe.
He may nat spare, al-thogh he were his brother;
He moot as wel seye o word as another.
Crist spak him-self ful brode in holy writ,
And wel ye woot, no vileinye is it.
Eek Plato seith, who-so that can him rede,
The wordes mote be cosin to the dede.
Also I prey yow to foryeve it me,
Al have I nat set folk in hir degree
Here in this tale, as that they sholde stonde;
My wit is short, ye may wel understonde.
Greet chere made our hoste us everichon,
And to the soper sette us anon;
And served us with vitaille at the beste.
Strong was the wyn, and wel to drinke us leste.
A semely man our hoste was with-alle
For to han been a marshal in an halle;
A large man he was with eyen stepe,
A fairer burgeys is ther noon in Chepe:[58]
Bold of his speche, and wys, and wel y-taught,
And of manhod him lakkede right naught.
Eek therto he was right a mery man,
And after soper pleyen he bigan,
And spak of mirthe amonges othere thinges,
Whan that we hadde maad our rekeninges;
And seyde thus: 'Now, lordinges, trewely,
Ye been to me right welcome hertely:
For by my trouthe, if that I shal nat lye,
I ne saugh this yeer so mery a companye
At ones in this herberwe as is now.
Fayn wolde I doon yow mirthe, wiste I how.
And of a mirthe I am right now bithoght,
To doon yow ese, and it shal coste noght.
Ye goon to Caunterbury; God yow spede,
The blisful martir quyte yow your mede.
And wel I woot, as ye goon by the weye,
Ye shapen yow to talen and to pleye;
For trewely, confort ne mirthe is noon
To ryde by the weye doumb as a stoon;
And therfore wol I maken yow disport,
As I seyde erst, and doon yow som confort.
And if yow lyketh alle, by oon assent,
Now for to stonden at my jugement,
And for to werken as I shal yow seye,
To-morwe, whan ye ryden by the weye,
Now, by my fader soule,[59] that is deed,

[57] rudeness

[58] Cheapside, the mercantile street of London.

[59] father's soul

But ye be merye, I wol yeve yow myn heed.
Hold up your hond, withouten more speche.'
  Our counseil was nat longe for to seche;
Us thoughte it was noght worth to make it wys,
And graunted him withouten more avys,
And bad him seye his verdit, as him leste.
  'Lordinges,' quod he, 'now herkneth for the beste;
But tak it not, I prey yow, in desdeyn;
This is the poynt, to speken short and pleyn,
That ech of yow, to shorte with your weye,
In this viage, shal telle tales tweye,
To Caunterbury-ward, I mene it so,
And hom-ward he shal tellen othere two,
Of aventures that whylom han bifalle.
And which of yow that bereth him best of alle,
That is to seyn, that telleth in this cas
Tales of best sentence and most solas,
Shal have a soper at our aller cost[60]
Here in this place, sitting by this post,
Whan that we come agayn fro Caunterbury.
And for to make yow the more mery,
I wol my-selven gladly with yow ryde,
Right at myn owne cost, and be your gyde.
And who-so wol my jugement withseye
Shal paye al that we spenden by the weye.
And if ye vouche-sauf that it be so,
Tel me anon, with-outen wordes mo,
And I wol erly shape me therfore.'
  This thing was graunted, and our othes swore
With ful glad herte, and preyden him also
That he wold vouche-sauf for to do so,
And that he wolde been our governour,
And of our tales juge and reportour,
And sette a soper at a certeyn prys;
And we wold reuled been at his devys,
In heigh and lowe;[61] and thus, by oon assent,
We been acorded to his jugement.
And ther-up-on the wyn was fet anon;
We dronken, and to reste wente echon,
With-outen any lenger taryinge.
  A-morwe, whan that day bigan to springe,
Up roos our host, and was our aller cok,[62]
And gadrede us togidre, alle in a flok,
And forth we riden, a litel more than pas,
Un-to the watering of seint Thomas.[63]
And there our host bigan his hors areste,
And seyde; 'Lordinges, herkneth, if yow leste.
Ye woot your forward, and I it yow recorde.
If even-song and morwe-song acorde,
Lat see now who shal telle the firste tale.
As ever mote I drinke wyn or ale,
Who-so be rebel to my jugement
Shal paye for al that by the weye is spent.
Now draweth cut, er that we ferrer twinne;
He which that hath the shortest shal biginne.
Sire knight,' quod he, 'my maister and my lord,
Now draweth cut, for that is myn acord.
Cometh neer,' quod he, 'my lady prioresse;
And ye, sir clerk, lat be your shamfastnesse,
Ne studieth noght; ley hond to, every man.'
  Anon to drawen every wight bigan,
And shortly for to tellen, as it was,
Were it by aventure, or sort, or cas,
The sothe is this, the cut fil to the knight,
Of which ful blythe and glad was every wight;
And telle he moste his tale, as was resoun,
By forward and by composicioun,
As ye han herd; what nedeth wordes mo?
And whan this gode man saugh it was so,
As he that wys was and obedient
To kepe his forward by his free assent,
He seyde: 'Sin I shal beginne the game,

[60] cost of us all
[61] in all respects

[62] cock of us all
[63] A watering place for horses two miles along the road

What, welcome be the cut, a Goddes name!
Now lat us ryde, and herkneth what I seye.'
  And with that word we riden forth our weye;
And he bigan with right a mery chere
His tale anon, and seyde in this manere.

Here endeth the prolog of this book

The Franklin's Prologue

The Prologe of the Frankeleyns Tale

THISE olde gentil Britons [64] in hir dayes
Of diverse aventures maden layes,
Rymeyed in hir firste Briton tonge;
Which layes with hir instruments they songe,
Or elles redden hem for hir plesaunce;
And oon of hem have I in remembraunce,
Which I shal seyn with good wil as I can.
  But, sires, by-cause I am a burel man,
At my biginning first I yow biseche
Have me excused of my rude speche;
I lerned never rethoryk certeyn;
Thing that I speke, it moot be bare and pleyn.
I sleep never on the mount of Pernaso,
Ne lerned Marcus Tullius Cithero.
Colours ne knowe I none, with-outen drede,
But swiche colours as growen in the mede,
Or elles swiche as men dye or peynte.
Colours of rethoryk ben me to queynte;
My spirit feleth noght of swich matere.
But if yow list, my tale shul ye here.

The Franklin's Tale

Here biginneth the Frankeleyns Tale

IN Armorik, that called is Britayne,
Ther was a knight that loved and dide his payne
To serve a lady in his beste wyse;
And many a labour, many a greet empryse
He for his lady wroghte, er she were wonne.
For she was oon, the faireste under sonne,
And eek therto come of so heigh kinrede,
That wel unnethes dorste this knight, for drede,
Telle hir his wo, his peyne, and his distresse.
But atte laste, she, for his worthinesse,
And namely for his meke obeysaunce,
Hath swich a pitee caught of his penaunce,
That prively she fil of his accord [65]
To take him for hir housbonde and hir lord,
Of swich lordshipe as men han over hir wyves;
And for to lede the more in blisse hir lyves,
Of his free wil he swoor hir as a knight,
That never in al his lyf he, day ne night,
Ne sholde up-on him take no maistrye
Agayn hir wil, ne kythe hir jalousye,
But hir obeye, and folwe hir wil in al
As any lovere to his lady shal;
Save that the name of soveraynetee,
That wolde he have for shame of his degree.
  She thanked him, and with ful greet humblesse
She seyde, 'sire, sith of your gentillesse
Ye profre me to have so large a reyne,
Ne wolde never god bitwixe us tweyne,
As in my gilt, were outher werre or stryf,
Sir, I wol be your humble trewe wyf,
Have heer my trouthe, til that myn herte breste.'
Thus been they bothe in quiete and in reste.
  For o thing, sires, saufly dar I seye,
That frendes everich other moot obeye,
If they wol longe holden companye.
Love wol nat ben constreyned by maistrye;
Whan maistrie comth, the god of love anon
Beteth hise winges, and farewel! he is gon!
Love is a thing as any spirit free;
Wommen of kinde desiren libertee,

[64] Inhabitants of French Brittany.

[65] agreed

And nat to ben constreyned as a thral;
And so don men, if I soth seyen shal.
Loke who that is most pacient in love,
He is at his avantage al above.
Pacience is an heigh vertu certeyn;
For it venquisseth, as thise clerkes seyn,
Thinges that rigour sholde never atteyne.
For every word men may nat chyde or pleyne.
Lerneth to suffre, or elles, so moot I goon,
Ye shul it lerne, wher-so ye wole or noon.
For in this world, certein, ther no wight is,
That he ne dooth or seith som-tyme amis.
Ire, siknesse, or constellacioun,
Wyn, wo, or chaunginge of complexioun
Causeth ful ofte to doon amis or speken.
On every wrong a man may nat be wreken;
After the tyme, moste be temperaunce
To every wight that can on governaunce.
And therfore hath this wyse worthy knight,
To live in ese, suffrance hir bihight,
And she to him ful wisly gan to swere
That never sholde ther be defaute in here.
Heer may men seen an humble wys accord;
Thus hath she take hir servant and hir lord,
Servant in love, and lord in mariage;
Than was he bothe in lordship and servage;
Servage? nay, but in lordshipe above,
Sith he hath bothe his lady and his love;
His lady, certes, and his wyf also,
The which that lawe of love acordeth to.
And whan he was in this prosperitee,
Hoom with his wyf he gooth to his contree,
Nat fer fro Penmark, ther his dwelling was,
Wher-as he liveth in blisse and in solas.
Who coude telle, but he had wedded be,
The joye, the ese, and the prosperitee
That is bitwixe an housbonde and his wyf?
A yeer and more lasted this blissful lyf,
Til that the knight of which I speke of thus,
That of Kayrrud was cleped Arveragus,
Shoop him to goon, and dwelle a yeer or tweyne
In Engelond, that cleped was eek Briteyne,
To seke in armes worship and honour;
For al his lust he sette in swich labour;
And dwelled ther two yeer, the book seith thus.
Now wol I stinte of this Arveragus,
And speken I wole of Dorigene his wyf,
That loveth hir housbonde as hir hertes lyf.
For his absence wepeth she and syketh,
As doon thise noble wyves whan hem lyketh.
She moorneth, waketh, wayleth, fasteth, pleyneth;
Desyr of his presence hir so distreyneth,
That al this wyde world she sette at noght.
Hir frendes, whiche that knewe hir hevy thoght,
Conforten hir in al that ever they may;
They prechen hir, they telle hir night and day,
That causelees she sleeth hir-self, allas!
And every comfort possible in this cas
They doon to hir with al hir bisinesse,
Al for to make hir leve hir heavinesse.
By proces, as ye knowen everichoon,
Men may so longe graven in a stoon,
Til som figure ther-inne emprented be.
So longe han they conforted hir, til she
Receyved hath, by hope and by resoun,
Th'emprenting of hir consolacioun,
Thurgh which hir grete sorwe gan aswage;
She may nat alwey duren in swich rage.
And eek Arveragus, in al this care,
Hath sent hir lettres hoom of his welfare,
And that he wol come hastily agayn;
Or elles hadde this sorwe hir herte slayn.
Hir freendes sawe hir sorwe gan to slake,
And preyede hir on knees, for goddes sake,
To come and romen hir in companye,
Awey to dryve hir derke fantasye.
And finally, she graunted that requeste;
For wel she saugh that it was for the beste.
Now stood hir castel faste by the see,

And often with hir freendes walketh she
Hir to disporte up-on the bank an heigh,
Wher-as she many a ship and barge seigh
Seilinge hir cours, wher-as hem liste go;
But than was that a parcel of hir wo.
For to hir-self ful ofte 'allas!' seith she,
'Is ther no ship, of so manye as I see,
Wol bringen hom my lord? than were myn herte
Al warisshed of his bittre peynes smerte.'
  Another tyme their wolde she sitte and thinke,
And caste hir eyen dounward fro the brinke.
But whan she saugh the grisly rokkes blake,
For verray fere so wolde hir herte quake,
That on hir feet she mighte hir noght sustene.
Than wolde she sitte adoun upon the grene,
And pitously in-to the see biholde,
And seyn right thus, with sorweful sykes colde:
  'Eterne god, that thurgh thy purveyaunce
Ledest the world by certein governaunce,
In ydel, as men seyn, ye no-thing make;
But, lord, thise grisly feendly rokkes blake,
That semen rather a foul confusioun
Of werk than any fair creacioun
Of swich a parfit wys god and a stable,
Why han ye wroght this werk unresonable?
For by this werk, south, north, ne west, ne eest,
Ther nis y-fostred man, ne brid, ne beest;
It dooth no good, to my wit, but anoyeth.
See ye nat, lord, how mankinde it destroyeth?
An hundred thousand bodies of mankinde
Han rokkes slayn, al be they nat in minde,
Which mankinde is so fair part of thy werk
That thou it madest lyk to thyn owene merk.
Than semed it ye hadde at greet chiertee
Toward mankinde; but how than may it be
That ye swiche menes make it to destroyen,
Whiche menes do no good, but ever anoyen?
I woot wel clerkes wol seyn, as hem leste,
By arguments, that al is for the beste,
Though I ne can the causes nat y-knowe.
But thilke god, that made wind to blowe,
As kepe my lord! this my conclusioun;
To clerkes lete I al disputisoun.
But wolde god that alle thise rokkes blake
Were sonken in-to helle for his sake!
Thise rokkes sleen myn herte for the fere.'
Thus wolde she seyn, with many a pitous tere.
  Hir freendes sawe that it was no disport
To romen by the see, but disconfort;
And shopen for to pleyen somwher elles.
They leden hir by riveres and by welles,
And eek in othere places delitables;
They dauncen, and they pleyen at ches and tables.
  So on a day, right in the morwe-tyde,
Un-to a gardin that was ther bisyde,
In which that they had maad hir ordinaunce
Of vitaille and of other purveyaunce,
They goon and pleye hem al the longe day.
And this was on the sixte morwe of May,
Which May had peynted with his softe shoures
This gardin ful of leves and of floures;
And craft of mannes hand so curiously
Arrayed hadde this gardin, trewely,
That never was ther gardin of swich prys,
But-if it were the verray paradys.
Th' odour of floures and the fresshe sighte
Wolde han maad any herte for to lighte
That ever was born, but-if to gret siknesse,
Or to gret sorwe helde it in distresse;
So ful it was of beautee with plesaunce.
At-after diner gonne they to daunce,
And singe also, save Dorigen allone,

Which made alwey hir compleint and hir mone;
For she ne saugh him on the daunce go,
That was hir housbonde and hir love also.
But nathelees she moste a tyme abyde,
And with good hope lete hir sorwe slyde.
Up-on this daunce, amonges othere men,
Daunced a squyer biforen Dorigen,
That fressher was and jolyer of array,
As to my doom, than is the monthe of May.
He singeth, daunceth, passinge any man
That is, or was, sith that the world bigan.
Ther-with he was, if men sholde him discryve,
Oon of the beste faringe [66] man on-lyve;
Yong, strong, right vertuous, and riche and wys,
And wel biloved, and holden in gret prys.
And shortly, if the sothe I tellen shal,
Unwiting of this Dorigen at al,
This lusty squyer, servant to Venus,
Which that y-cleped was Aurelius,
Had loved hir best of any creature
Two yeer and more, as was his aventure,
But never dorste he telle hir his grevaunce;
With-outen coppe [67] he drank al his penaunce.
He was despeyred, no-thing dorste he seye,
Save in his songes somwhat wolde he wreye
His wo, as in a general compleyning;
He seyde he lovede, and was biloved no-thing.
Of swich matere made he manye layes,
Songes, compleintes, roundels, virelayes,
How that he dorste nat his sorwe telle,
But languissheth, as a furie dooth in helle;
And dye he moste, he seyde, as dide Ekko [68]
For Narcisus, that dorste nat telle hir wo.
In other manere than ye here me seye,
Ne dorste he nat to hir his wo biwreye;
Save that, paraventure, som-tyme at daunces,
Ther yonge folk kepen hir observaunces,
It may wel be he loked on hir face
In swich a wyse, as man that asketh grace;
But no-thing wiste she of his entente.
Nathelees, it happed, er they thennes wente,
By-cause that he was hir neighebour,
And was a man of worship and honour,
And hadde y-knowen him of tyme yore,
They fille in speche; and forth more and more
Un-to his purpos drough Aurelius,
And whan he saugh his tyme, he seyde thus:
'Madame,' quod he, 'by god that this world made,
So that I wiste it mighte your herte glade,
I wolde, that day that your Arveragus
Wente over the see, that I, Aurelius,
Had went ther never I sholde have come agayn;
For wel I woot my service is in vayn.
My guerdon is but bresting of myn herte;
Madame, reweth upon my peynes smerte;
For with a word ye may me sleen or save,
Heer at your feet god wolde that I were grave!
I ne have as now no leyser more to seye;
Have mercy, swete, or ye wol do me deye!'
She gan to loke up-on Aurelius:
'Is this your wil,' quod she, 'and sey ye thus?
Never erst,' quod she, 'ne wiste I what ye mente.
But now, Aurelie, I knowe your entente,
By thilke god that yaf me soule and lyf,
Ne shal I never been untrewe wyf
In word ne werk, as fer as I have wit:
I wol ben his to whom that I am knit;
Tak this for fynal answer as of me.'
But after that in pley thus seyde she:
'Aurelie,' quod she, 'by heighe god above,
Yet wolde I graunte yow to been your love,
Sin I yow see so pitously complayne;
Loke what day that, endelong Britayne,

66 handsomest
67 In full measure.
68 Echo is said to have pined away for love of Narcissus until only her voice remained.

Ye remoeve alle the rokkes, stoon by stoon,
That they ne lette ship ne boot to goon —
I seye, whan ye han maad the coost so clene
Of rokkes, that ther nis no stoon y-sene,
Than wol I love yow best of any man;
Have heer my trouthe in al that ever I can.'
'Is ther non other grace in yow?' quod he.
'No, by that lord,' quod she, 'that maked me!
For wel I woot that it shal never bityde.
Lat swiche folies out of your herte slyde.
What deyntee sholde a man han in his lyf
For to go love another mannes wyf,
That hath hir body whan so that him lyketh?'
  Aurelius ful ofte sore syketh;
Wo was Aurelie, whan that he this herde,
And with a sorweful herte he thus answerde:
  'Madame,' quod he, 'this were an inpossible!
Than moot I dye of sodein deth horrible.'
And with that word he turned him anoon.
Tho come hir othere freendes many oon,
And in the aleyes romeden up and doun,
And no-thing wiste of this conclusioun,
But sodeinly bigonne revel newe
Til that the brighte sonne loste his hewe;
For th'orisonte hath reft the sonne his light;
This is as muche to seye as it was night.
And hoom they goon in joye and in solas,
Save only wrecche Aurelius, allas!
He to his hous is goon with sorweful herte;
He seeth he may nat fro his deeth asterte.
Him semed that he felte his herte colde;
Up to the hevene his handes he gan holde,
And on his knowes bare he sette him doun,
And in his raving seyde his orisoun.
For verray wo out of his wit he breyde.
He niste what he spak, but thus he seyde;
With pitous herte his pleynt hath he bigonne
Un-to the goddes, and first un-to the sonne:
  He seyde, 'Appollo, god and governour
Of every plaunte, herbe, tree and flour,
That yevest, after thy declinacioun,
To ech of hem his tyme and his sesoun,
As thyn herberwe chaungeth lowe or hye,
Lord Phebus, cast thy merciable yë
On wrecche Aurelie, which that am but lorn.
Lo, lord! my lady hath my deeth y-sworn
With-oute gilt, but thy benignitee
Upon my dedly herte have some pitee!
For wel I woot, lord Phebus, if yow lest,
Ye may me helpen, save my lady, best.
Now voucheth sauf that I may yow devyse
How that I may been holpe and in what wyse.
  Your blisful suster, Lucina the shene,
That of the see is chief goddesse and quene,
Though Neptunus have deitee in the see,
Yet emperesse aboven him is she:
Ye knowen wel, lord, that right as hir desyr
Is to be quiked and lightned of your fyr,
For which she folweth yow ful bisily,
Right so the see desyreth naturelly
To folwen hir, as she that is goddesse
Bothe in the see and riveres more and lesse.
Wherfore, lord Phebus, this is my requeste —
Do this miracle, or do myn herte breste —
That now, next at this opposicioun,[69]
Which in the signe shal be of the Leoun,
As preyeth hir so greet a flood to bringe,
That fyve fadme at the leeste it overspringe
The hyeste rokke in Armorik Briteyne;
And lat this flood endure yeres tweyne;
Than certes to my lady may I seye:
"Holdeth your heste, the rokkes been aweye."
  Lord Phebus, dooth this miracle for me;
Preye hir she go no faster cours than ye;
I seye, preyeth your suster that she go
No faster cours than ye thise yeres two.
Than shal she been evene atte fulle alway,
And spring-flood laste bothe night and day.
And, but she vouche-sauf in swiche manere

[69] When the moon is full, a time of high tides.

To graunte me my sovereyn lady dere,
Prey hir to sinken every rok adoun
In-to hir owene derke regioun
Under the ground, ther Pluto dwelleth inne,
Or never-mo shal I my lady winne.
Thy temple in Delphos wol I barefoot seke;
Lord Phebus, see the teres on my cheke,
And of my peyne have som compassioun.'
And with that word in swowne he fil adoun,
And longe tyme he lay forth in a traunce.
His brother, which that knew of his penaunce,
Up caughte him and to bedde he hath him broght.
Dispeyred in this torment and this thoght
Lete I this woful creature lye;
Chese he, for me, whether he wol live or dye.
Arveragus, with hele and greet honour,
As he that was of chivalrye the flour,
Is comen hoom, and othere worthy men.
O blisful artow now, thou Dorigen,
That hast thy lusty housbonde in thyne armes,
The fresshe knight, the worthy man of armes,
That loveth thee, as his owene hertes lyf.
No-thing list him to been imaginatyf
If any wight had spoke, whyl he was oute,
To hire of love; he hadde of it no doute.
He noght entendeth to no swich matere,
But daunceth, justeth, maketh hir good chere;
And thus in joye and blisse I lete hem dwelle,
And of the syke Aurelius wol I telle.
In langour and in torment furious
Two yeer and more lay wrecche Aurelius,
Er any foot he mighte on erthe goon;
Ne confort in this tyme hadde he noon,
Save of his brother, which that was a clerk;
He knew of al this wo and al this werk.
For to non other creature certeyn
Of this matere he dorste no word seyn.
Under his brest he bar it more secree
Than ever dide Pamphilus [70] for Galathee.
His brest was hool, with-oute for to sene,
But in his herte ay was the arwe kene.
And wel ye knowe that of a sursanure
In surgerye is perilous the cure,
But men mighte touche the arwe, or come therby.
His brother weep and wayled prively,
Til atte laste him fil in remembraunce,
That whyl he was at Orliens [71] in Fraunce,
As yonge clerkes, that been likerous
To reden artes that been curious,
Seken in every halke and every herne
Particuler sciences for to lerne,
He him remembred that, upon a day,
At Orliens in studie a book he say
Or magik naturel, which his felawe,
That was that tyme a bacheler of lawe,
Al were he ther to lerne another craft,
Had prively upon his desk y-laft;
Which book spak muchel of the operaciouns,
Touchinge the eighte and twenty mansiouns [72]
That longen to the mone, and swich folye,
As in our dayes is nat worth a flye;
For holy chirches feith in our bileve
Ne suffreth noon illusion us to greve.
And whan this book was in his remembraunce,
Anon for joye his herte gan to daunce,
And to him-self he seyde prively:
'My brother shal be warisshed hastily;
For I am siker that ther be sciences,
By whiche men make diverse apparences
Swiche as thise subtile tregetoures pleye.
For ofte at festes have I wel herd seye,
That tregetours, with-inne an halle large,
Have maad come in a water and a barge,
And in the halle rowen up and doun.
Somtyme hath semed come a grim leoun;
And somtyme floures springe as in a mede;
Somtyme a vyne, and grapes whyte and rede;
Somtyme a castel, al of lym and stoon;

[70] A medieval poet who wrote a Latin poem in praise of Galatea.
[71] Orléans, where he had studied at the University.
[72] The positions of the moon during a lunar month.

And whan hem lyked, voyded it anoon.
Thus semed it to every mannes sighte.
Now than conclude I thus, that if I mighte
At Orliens som old felawe y-finde,
That hadde this mones mansions in minde,
Or other magik naturel above,
He sholde wel make my brother han his love.
For with an apparence a clerk may make
To mannes sighte, that alle the rokkes blake
Of Britaigne weren y-voyded everichon,
And shippes by the brinke comen and gon,
And in swich forme endure a day or two;
Than were my brother warisshed of his wo.
Than moste she nedes holden hir biheste,
Or elles he shal shame hir atte leste.'
What sholde I make a lenger tale of this?
Un-to his brotheres bed he comen is,
And swich comfort he yaf him for to gon
To Orliens, that he up stirte anon,
And on his wey forthward thanne is he fare,
In hope for to ben lissed of his care.
Whan they were come almost to that citee,
But-if it were a two furlong or three,
A yong clerk rominge by him-self they mette,
Which that in Latin thriftily hem grette,
And after that he seyde a wonder thing:
'I knowe,' quod he, 'the cause of your coming';
And er they ferther any fote wente,
He tolde hem al that was in hir entente.
This Briton clerk him asked of felawes
The whiche that he had knowe in olde dawes;
And he answerde him that they dede were,
For whiche he weep ful ofte many a tere.
Doun of his hors Aurelius lighte anon,
And forth with this magicien is he gon
Hoom to his hous, and made hem wel at ese.
Hem lakked no vitaille that mighte hem plese;
So wel arrayed hous as ther was oon
Aurelius in his lyf saugh never noon.
He shewed him, er he wente to sopeer,
Forestes, parkes ful of wilde deer;
Ther saugh he hertes with hir hornes hye,
The gretteste that ever were seyn with yë.
He saugh of hem an hondred slayn with houndes,
And somme with arwes blede of bittre woundes.
He saugh, whan voided were thise wilde deer,
Thise fauconers upon a fair river,
That with hir haukes han the heron slayn.
Tho saugh he knightes justing in a playn;
And after this, he dide him swich plesaunce,
That he him shewed his lady on a daunce
On which him-self he daunced, as him thoughte.
And whan this maister, that this magik wroughte,
Saugh it was tyme, he clapte his handes two,
And farewel! al our revel was ago.
And yet remoeved they never out of the hous,
Whyl they saugh al this sighte merveillous,
But in his studie, ther-as his bookes be,
They seten stille, and no wight but they three.
To him this maister called his squyer,
And seyde him thus: 'is redy our soper?
Almost an houre it is, I undertake,
Sith I yow bad our soper for to make,
Whan that thise worthy men wenten with me
In-to my studie, ther-as my bookes be.'
'Sire,' quod this squyer, 'whan it lyketh yow,
It is al redy, though ye wol right now.'
'Go we than soupe,' quod he, 'as for the beste;
This amorous folk som-tyme mote han reste.'
At-after soper fille they in tretee,

What somme sholde this maistres guerdon be,
To remoeven alle the rokkes of Britayne,
And eek from Gerounde to the mouth of Sayne.[73]
He made it straunge, and swoor, so god him save,
Lasse than a thousand pound he wolde nat have,
Ne gladly for that somme he wolde nat goon.
Aurelius, with blisful herte anoon,
Answerde thus, 'fy on a thousand pound!
This wyde world, which that men seye is round,
I wolde it yeve, if I were lord of it.
This bargayn is ful drive, for we ben knit.
Ye shal be payed trewely, by my trouthe!
But loketh now, for no necligence or slouthe,
Ye tarie us heer no lenger than to-morwe.'
'Nay,' quod this clerk, 'have heer my feith to borwe.'
To bedde is goon Aurelius whan him leste,
And wel ny al that night he hadde his reste;
What for his labour and his hope of blisse,
His woful herte of penaunce hadde a lisse.
Upon the morwe, whan that it was day,
To Britaigne toke they the righte way,
Aurelius, and this magicien bisyde,
And been descended ther they wolde abyde;
And this was, as the bokes me remembre,
The colde frosty seson of Decembre.
Phebus wex old, and hewed lyk latoun,
That in his hote declinacioun
Shoon as the burned gold with stremes brighte;
But now in Capricorn adoun he lighte,
Wher-as he shoon ful pale, I dar wel seyn.
The bittre frostes, with the sleet and reyn,
Destroyed hath the grene in every yerd.
Janus sit by the fyr, with double berd,
And drinketh of his bugle-horn the wyn.
Biforn him stant braun of the tusked swyn,
And 'Nowel' cryeth every lusty man.
Aurelius, in al that ever he can,
Doth to his maister chere and reverence,
And preyeth him to doon his diligence
To bringen him out of his peynes smerte,
Or with a swerd that he wolde slitte his herte.
This subtil clerk swich routhe had of this man,
That night and day he spedde him that he can,
To wayte a tyme of his conclusioun;
This is to seye, to make illusioun,
By swich an apparance or jogelrye,
I ne can no termes of astrologye,
That she and every wight sholde wene and seye,
That of Britaigne the rokkes were aweye,
Or elles they were sonken under grounde.
So atte laste he hath his tyme y-founde
To maken his japes and his wrecchednesse
Of swich a supersticious cursednesse.
His tables Toletanes [74] forth he broght,
Ful wel corrected, ne ther lakked noght,
Neither his collect ne his expans yeres,[75]
Ne his rotes [76] ne his othere geres,
As been his centres [77] and his arguments,
And his proporcionels convenients [78]
For his equacions in every thing.
And, by his eighte spere [79] in his wirking,
He knew ful wel how fer Alnath was shove
Fro the heed of thilke fixe Aries above
That in the ninthe speere considered is;
Ful subtilly he calculed al this.
Whan he had founde his firste mansioun,
He knew the remenant by proporcioun;

[73] from Gerounde, *etc.* The rivers Gironde and Seine.

[74] Astronomical tables.

[75] Computations for a number of years or for single years.

[76] Basic astronomical figures for use in his computations.

[77] Points on his instrument representing stars.

[78] Tables for computing the movements of planets in fractions of the year.

[79] The sphere of the fixed stars. The point of this passage, which is highly technical, is to show that the astrologer knew how to determine the procession of the equinoxes.

And knew the arysing of his mone weel,
And in whos face, and terme,[80] and every-deel;
And knew ful weel the mones mansioun
Acordaunt to his operacioun,
And knew also his othere observaunces
For swiche illusiouns and swiche meschaunces
As hethen folk used in thilke dayes;
For which no lenger maked he delayes,
But thurgh his magik, for a wyke or tweye,
It semed that alle the rokkes were aweye.
Aurelius, which that yet despeired is
Wher he shal han his love or fare amis,
Awaiteth night and day on this miracle;
And whan he knew that ther was noon obstacle,
That voided were thise rokkes everichon,
Doun to his maistres feet he fil anon,
And seyde, 'I woful wrecche, Aurelius,
Thanke yow, lord, and lady myn Venus,
That me han holpen fro my cares colde:'
And to the temple his wey forth hath he holde,
Wher-as he knew he sholde his lady see.
And whan he saugh his tyme, anon-right he,
With dredful herte and with ful humble chere,
Salewed hath his sovereyn lady dere:
'My righte lady,' quod this woful man,
'Whom I most drede and love as I best can,
And lothest were of al this world displese,
Nere it that I for yow have swich disese,[81]
That I moste dyen heer at your foot anon,
Noght wolde I telle how me is wo bigon;
But certes outher moste I dye or pleyne;
Ye slee me giltelees for verray peyne.
But of my deeth, thogh that ye have no routhe,
Avyseth yow, er that ye breke your trouthe.
Repenteth yow, for thilke god above,
Er ye me sleen by-cause that I yow love.
For, madame, wel ye woot what ye han hight;
Nat that I chalange any thing of right
Of yow my sovereyn lady, but your grace;
But in a gardin yond, at swich a place,
Ye woot right wel what ye bihighten me;
And in myn hand your trouthe plighten ye
To love me best, god woot, ye seyde so,
Al be that I unworthy be therto.
Madame, I speke it for the honour of yow,
More than to save myn hertes lyf right now;
I have do so as ye comanded me;
And if ye vouche-sauf, ye may go see.
Doth as yow list, have your biheste in minde,
For quik or deed, right ther ye shul me finde;
In yow lyth al, to do me live or deye;—
But wel I woot the rokkes been aweye!'
He taketh his leve, and she astonied stood,
In al hir face nas a drope of blood;
She wende never han come in swich a trappe:
'Allas!' quod she, 'that ever this sholde happe!
For wende I never, by possibilitee,
That swich a monstre or merveille mighte be!
It is agayns the proces of nature:'
And hoom she gooth a sorweful creature.
For verray fere unnethe may she go,
She wepeth, wailleth, al a day or two,
And swowneth, that it routhe was to see;
But why it was, to no wight tolde she;
For out of toune was goon Arveragus.
But to hir-self she spak, and seyde thus,
With face pale and with ful sorweful chere,
In hir compleynt, as ye shul after here:
'Allas,' quod she, 'on thee, Fortune, I pleyne,
That unwar wrapped hast me in thy cheyne;
For which, t'escape, woot I no socour
Save only deeth or elles dishonour;
Oon of thise two bihoveth me to chese.

[80] The signs of the zodiac were divided into parts so designated.
[81] suffering

But nathelees, yet have I lever lese
My lyf than of my body have a shame,
Or knowe my-selven fals, or lese my name,
And with my deth I may be quit, y-wis.
Hath ther nat many a noble wyf, er this,
And many a mayde y-slayn hir-self, allas!
Rather than with hir body doon trespas?
Yis, certes, lo, thise stories beren witnesse;
Whan thretty tyraunts, ful of cursednesse,
Had slayn Phidoun in Athenes, atte feste,
They comanded his doghtres for t'areste,
And bringen hem biforn hem in despyt
Al naked, to fulfille hir foul delyt,
And in hir fadres blood they made hem daunce
Upon the pavement, god yeve hem mischaunce!
For which thise woful maydens, ful of drede,
Rather than they wolde lese hir maydenhede,
They prively ben stirt in-to a welle,
And dreynte hem-selven, as the bokes telle.
They of Messene lete enquere and seke
Of Lacedomie fifty maydens eke,
On whiche they wolden doon hir lecherye;
But was ther noon of al that companye
That she nas slayn, and with a good entente
Chees rather for to dye than assente
To been oppressed of hir maydenhede.
Why sholde I thanne to dye been in drede?
Lo, eek, the tiraunt Aristoclides
That loved a mayden, heet Stimphalides,
Whan that hir fader slayn was on a night,
Un-to Dianes temple goth she right,
And hente the image in hir handes two,
Fro which image wolde she never go.
No wight ne mighte hir handes of it arace,
Til she was slayn right in the selve place.
Now sith that maydens hadden swich despyt
To been defouled with mannes foul delyt,
Wel oghte a wyf rather hir-selven slee
Than be defouled, as it thinketh me.
What shal I seyn of Hasdrubales wyf,
That at Cartage birafte hir-self hir lyf?
For whan she saugh that Romayns wan the toun,
She took hir children alle, and skipte adoun
In-to the fyr, and chees rather to dye
Than any Romayn dide hir vileinye.
Hath nat Lucresse y-slayn hir-self, allas!
At Rome, whanne she oppressed was
Of Tarquin, for hir thoughte it was a shame
To liven whan she hadde lost hir name?
The sevene maydens of Milesie also
Han slayn hem-self, for verray drede and wo,
Rather than folk of Gaule hem sholde oppresse.
Mo than a thousand stories, as I gesse,
Coude I now telle as touchinge this matere.
Whan Habradate was slayn, his wyf so dere
Hirselven slow, and leet hir blood to glyde
In Habradates woundes depe and wyde,
And seyde, "my body, at the leeste way,
Ther shal no wight defoulen, if I may."
What sholde I mo ensamples heer-of sayn,
Sith that so manye han hem-selven slayn
Wel rather than they wolde defouled be?
I wol conclude, that it is bet for me
To sleen my-self, than been defouled thus.
I wol be trewe un-to Arveragus,
Or rather sleen my-self in som manere,
As dide Demociones doghter dere,
By-cause that she wolde nat defouled be.
O Cedasus! it is ful greet pitee,
To reden how thy doghtren deyde, allas!
That slowe hem-selven for swich maner cas.
As greet a pitee was it, or wel more,
The Theban mayden, that for Nichanore
Hir-selven slow, right for swich maner wo.

Another Theban mayden dide right so;
For oon of Macedoine hadde hir oppressed,
She with hir deeth hir maydenhede redressed.
What shal I seye of Nicerates wyf,
That for swich cas birafte hir-self hir lyf?
How trewe eek was to Alcebiades
His love, that rather for to dyen chees
Than for to suffre his body unburied be!
Lo which a wyf was Alcestė,' quod she.
'What seith Omer of gode Penalopee?
Al Grece knoweth of hir chastitee.
Pardee, of Laodomya is writen thus,
That whan at Troye was slayn Prothe-selaus,
No lenger wolde she live after his day.
The same of noble Porcia telle I may;
With-oute Brutus coude she nat live,
To whom she hadde al hool hir herte yive.
The parfit wyfhod of Arthemesye
Honoured is thurgh al the Barbarye.
O Teuta, queen! thy wyfly chastitee
To alle wyves may a mirour be.
The same thing I seye of Bilia,
Of Rodogone, and eek Valeria.'
Thus pleyned Dorigene a day or tweye,
Purposinge ever that she wolde deye.
But nathelees, upon the thridde night,
Hom cam Arveragus, this worthy knight,
And asked hir, why that she weep so sore?
And she gan wepen ever lenger the more.
'Allas!' quod she, 'that ever was I born!
Thus have I seyd,' quod she, 'thus have I sworn'—
And told him al as ye han herd bifore;
It nedeth nat reherce it yow na-more.
This housbond with glad chere, in freendly wyse,
Answerde and seyde as I shal yow devyse:
'Is ther oght elles, Dorigen, but this?'
'Nay, nay,' quod she, 'god help me so, as wis;
This is to muche, and it were goddes wille.'
'Ye, wyf,' quod he, 'lat slepen that is stille;
It may be wel, paraventure, yet to-day.
Ye shul your trouthe holden, by my fay!
For god so wisly have mercy on me,
I hadde wel lever y-stiked for to be,
For verray love which that I to yow have,
But-if ye sholde your trouthe kepe and save.
Trouthe is the hyeste thing that man may kepe:'—
But with that word he brast anon to wepe,
And seyde, 'I yow forbede, up peyne of deeth,
That never, whyl thee lasteth lyf ne breeth,
To no wight tel thou of this aventure.
As I may best, I wol my wo endure,
Ne make no contenance of hevinesse,
That folk of yow may demen harm or gesse.'
And forth he cleped a squyer and a mayde:
'Goth forth anon with Dorigen,' he sayde,
'And bringeth hir to swich a place anon.'
They take hir leve, and on hir wey they gon;
But they ne wiste why she thider wente.
He nolde no wight tellen his entente.
Paraventure an heep of yow, y-wis,
Wol holden him a lewed man in this,
That he wol putte his wyf in jupartye;
Herkneth the tale, er ye up-on hir crye.
She may have bettre fortune than yow semeth;
And whan that ye han herd the tale, demeth.
This squyer, which that highte Aurelius,
On Dorigen that was so amorous,
Of aventure happed hir to mete
Amidde the toun, right in the quikkest strete,
As she was boun to goon the wey forth-right
Toward the gardin ther-as she had hight
And he was to the gardinward also;
For wel he spyed, whan she wolde go
Out of hir hous to any maner place.

But thus they mette, of aventure or grace;
And he saleweth hir with glad entente,
And asked of hir whiderward she wente?
And she answerde, half as she were mad,
'Un-to the gardin, as myn housbond bad,
My trouthe for to holde, allas! allas!'
Aurelius gan wondren on this cas,
And in his herte had greet compassioun
Of hir and of hir lamentacioun,
And of Arveragus, the worthy knight,
That bad hir holden al that she had hight,
So looth him was his wyf sholde breke hir trouthe;
And in his herte he caughte of this greet routhe,
Consideringe the beste on every syde,
That fro his lust yet were him lever abyde
Than doon so heigh a cherlish wrecched-nesse
Agayns franchyse and alle gentillesse;
For which in fewe wordes seyde he thus:
'Madame, seyth to your lord Arveragus,
That sith I see his grete gentillesse
To yow, and eek I see wel your dis-tresse,
That him were lever han shame (and that were routhe)
Than ye to me sholde breke thus your trouthe,
I have wel lever ever to suffre wo
Than I departe the love bitwix yow two.
I yow relesse, madame, in-to your hond
Quit every surement and every bond,
That ye han maad to me as heer-biforn,
Sith thilke tyme which that ye were born.
My trouthe I plighte, I shal yow never repreve
Of no biheste, and here I take my leve,
As of the treweste and the beste wyf
That ever yet I knew in al my lyf.
But every wyf be-war of hir biheste,
On Dorigene remembreth atte leste.
Thus can a squyer doon a gentil dede,
As well as can a knight, with-outen drede.'
She thonketh him up-on hir knees al bare,
And hoom un-to hir housbond is she fare,
And tolde him al as ye han herd me sayd;
And be ye siker, he was so weel apayd,
That it were inpossible me to wryte;
What sholde I lenger of this cas endyte?
Arveragus and Dorigene his wyf
In sovereyn blisse leden forth hir lyf.
Never eft ne was ther angre hem bitwene;
He cherisseth hir as though she were a quene;
And she was to him trewe for evermore.
Of thise two folk ye gete of me na-more.
Aurelius, that his cost hath al forlorn,
Curseth the tyme that ever he was born:
'Allas,' quod he, 'allas! that I bihighte
Of pured gold a thousand pound of wighte
Un-to this philosophre! how shal I do?
I see na-more but that I am fordo.
Myn heritage moot I nedes selle,
And been a begger; heer may I nat dwelle,
And shamen al my kinrede in this place,
But I of him may gete bettre grace.
But nathelees, I wol of him assaye,
At certeyn dayes, yeer by yeer, to paye,
And thanke him of his grete curteisye;
My trouthe wol I kepe, I wol nat lye.'
With herte soor he gooth un-to his cofre,
And broghte gold un-to this philosophre,
The value of fyve hundred pound, I gesse,
And him bisecheth, of his gentillesse,
To graunte him dayes of the remenaunt,
And seyde, 'maister, I dar wel make avaunt,
I failled never of my trouthe as yit;
For sikerly my dette shal be quit
Towardes yow, how-ever that I fare
To goon a-begged in my kirtle bare.
But wolde ye vouche-sauf, up-on seurtee,
Two yeer or three for to respyten me,
Than were I wel; for elles moot I selle
Myn heritage; ther is na-more to telle.'
This philosophre sobrely answerde,
And seyde thus, whan he thise wordes herde:
'Have I nat holden covenant un-to thee?'
'Yes, certes, wel and trewely,' quod he.
'Hastow nat had thy lady as thee lyketh?'

'No, no,' quod he, and sorwefully he syketh.
'What was the cause? tel me if thou can.'
Aurelius his tale anon bigan,
And tolde him al, as ye han herd bifore;
It nedeth nat to yow reherce it more.
He seide, 'Arveragus, of gentillesse,
Had lever dye in sorwe and in distresse
Than that his wyf were of hir trouthe fals.'
The sorwe of Dorigen he tolde him als,
How looth hir was to been a wikked wyf,
And that she lever had lost that day hir lyf,
And that hir trouthe she swoor, thurgh innocence:
'She never erst herde speke of apparence;
That made me han of hir so greet pitee.
And right as frely as he sente hir me,
As frely sente I hir to him ageyn.
This al and som, ther is na-more to seyn.'
This philosophre answerde, 'leve brother,
Everich of yow dide gentilly til other.
Thou art a squyer, and he is a knight;
But god forbede, for his blisful might,
But-if a clerk coude doon a gentil dede
As wel as any of yow, it is no drede!
Sire, I relesse thee thy thousand pound,
As thou right now were cropen out of the ground,[82]
Ne never er now ne haddest knowen me.
For sire, I wol nat take a peny of thee
For al my craft, ne noght for my travaille.
Thou hast y-payed wel for my vitaille;
It is y-nogh, and farewel, have good day:'
And took his hors, and forth he gooth his way.
Lordinges, this question wolde I aske now,
Which was the moste free, as thinketh yow?
Now telleth me, er that ye ferther wende.
I can na-more, my tale is at an ende.

Here is ended the Frankeleyns Tale

[82] As thou right now, *etc.* As if you had just crept out of the ground.

The wordes of the Host to the Phisicien and the Pardoner

Our Hoste gan to swere as he were wood,[83]
'Harrow!' quod he, 'by nayles and by blood!
This was a fals cherl and a fals justyse!
As shamful deeth as herte may devyse
Come to thise juges and hir advocats!
Algate this sely mayde is slayn, allas!
Allas! to dere boghte she beautee!
Wherfore I seye al day, as men may see,
That yiftes of fortune or of nature
Ben cause of deeth to many a creature.
Hir beautee was hir deeth, I dar wel sayn;
Allas! so pitously as she was slayn!
Of bothe yiftes that I speke of now
Men han ful ofte more harm than prow.
But trewely, myn owene mayster dere,
This is a pitous tale for to here.
But natheles, passe over, is no fors;
I prey to god, so save thy gentil cors,
And eek thyne urinals and thy jordanes,
Thyn Ypocras, and eek thy Galianes,
And every boist ful of thy letuarie;
God blesse hem, and our lady seinte Marie!
So mot I theen,[84] thou art a propre man,
And lyk a prelat, by seint Ronyan![85]
Seyde I nat wel? I can nat speke in terme;
But wel I woot, thou doost my herte to erme,
That I almost have caught a cardiacle.
By corpus bones! but I have triacle,
Or elles a draught of moyste and corny ale,
Or but I here anon a mery tale,
Myn herte is lost for pitee of this mayde.
Thou bel amy, thou Pardoner,' he seyde,
'Tel us som mirthe or japes right anon.'
'It shall be doon,' quod he, 'by seint Ronyon!
But first,' quod he, 'heer at this ale-stake
I wol both drinke, and eten of a cake.'

[83] Our Hoste gan, *etc.* The Physician has just told the pitiful tale of the wicked judge Appius who tried to force Virginia to do his will. The Host is greatly moved.
[84] So may I thrive
[85] There is no such saint. The Host may mean Ronan

But right anon thise gentils gonne to crye,
'Nay! lat him telle us of no ribaudye;
Tel us som moral thing, that we may lere
Som wit, and thanne wol we gladly here.'
'I graunte, y-wis,' quod he, 'but I mot thinke
Up-on som honest thing, whyl that I drinke.'

The Prologue of the Pardoner's Tale

Here folweth the Prologe of the Pardoners Tale

Radix malorum est Cupiditas: Ad Thimotheum, sexto.[86]

'Lordings,' quod he, 'in chirches whan I preche,
I peyne me to han an hauteyn speche,
And ringe it out as round as gooth a belle,
For I can al by rote that I telle.
My theme is alwey oon, and ever was—
"*Radix malorum est Cupiditas.*"
First I pronounce whennes that I come,
And than my bulles shewe I, alle and somme.
Our lige lordes seel on my patente,
That shewe I first, my body to warente,
That no man be so bold, ne preest ne clerk,
Me to destourbe of Cristes holy werk;
And after that than telle I forth my tales,
Bulles of popes and of cardinales,
Of patriarkes, and bishoppes I shewe;
And in Latyn I speke a wordes fewe,
To saffron with my predicacioun,
And for to stire men to devocioun.
Than shewe I forth my longe cristal stones,
Y-crammed ful of cloutes and of bones;
Reliks been they, as wenen they echoon.
Than have I in latoun a sholder-boon
Which that was of an holy Jewes shepe.
"Good men," seye I, "tak of my wordes kepe;
If that this boon be wasshe in any welle,
If cow, or calf, or sheep, or oxe swelle
That any worm hath ete, or worm y-stonge,
Tak water of that welle, and wash his tonge,
And it is hool anon; and forthermore,
Of pokkes and of scabbe, and everysore
Shal every sheep be hool, that of this welle
Drinketh a draughte; tak kepe eek what I telle.
If that the good-man, that the bestes oweth,
Wol every wike, er that the cok him croweth,
Fastinge, drinken of this welle a draughte,
As thilke holy Jewe our eldres taughte,
His bestes and his stoor shal multiplye.
And, sirs, also it heleth jalousye;
For, though a man be falle in jalous rage,
Let maken with this water his potage,
And never shal he more his wyf mistriste,
Though he the sooth of hir defaute wiste;
Al had she taken prestes two or three.
Heer is a miteyn eek, that ye may see.
He that his hond wol putte in this miteyn,
He shal have multiplying of his greyn,
Whan he hath sowen, be it whete or otes,
So that he offre pens, or elles grotes.
Good men and wommen, o thing warne I yow,
If any wight be in this chirche now,
That hath doon sinne horrible, that he
Dar nat, for shame, of it y-shriven be,
Or any womman, be she yong or old,
That hath y-maad hir housbond cokewold,
Swich folk shul have no power ne no grace
To offren to my reliks in this place.
And who-so findeth him out of swich blame,
He wol com up and offre in goddes name,
And I assoille him by the auctoritee
Which that by bulle y-graunted was to me."
By this gaude have I wonne, yeer by yeer,
An hundred mark sith I was Pardoner.
I stonde lyk a clerk in my pulpet,
And whan the lewed peple is doun y-set,
I preche, so as ye han herd bifore,
And telle an hundred false japes more.

[86] The love of money is the root of all evil. *I Timothy*, *vi*, 10.

Than peyne I me to strecche forth the nekke,
And est and west upon the peple I bekke,
As doth a dowve sitting on a berne.
Myn hondes and my tonge goon so yerne,
That it is joye to see my bisinesse.
Of avaryce and of swich cursednesse
Is al my preching, for to make hem free
To yeve her pens, and namely un-to me.
For my entente is nat but for to winne,
And no-thing for correccioun of sinne.
I rekke never, whan that they ben beried,
Though that her soules goon a-blake-beried!
For certes, many a predicacioun
Comth ofte tyme of yvel entencioun;
Som for plesaunce of folk and flaterye,
To been avaunced by ipocrisye,
And som for veyne glorie, and som for hate.
For, whan I dar non other weyes debate,
Than wol I stinge him with my tonge smerte
In preching, so that he shal nat asterte
To been defamed falsly, if that he
Hath trespased to my brethren or to me.
For, though I telle noght his propre name,
Men shal wel knowe that it is the same
By signes and by othere circumstances.
Thus quyte I folk that doon us displesances;
Thus spitte I out my venim under hewe
Of holynesse, to seme holy and trewe.
But shortly myn entente I wol devyse;
I preche of no-thing but for coveityse.
Therfor my theme is yet, and ever was —
"*Radix malorum est cupiditas.*"
Thus can I preche agayn that same vyce
Which that I use, and that is avaryce.
But, though my-self be gilty in that sinne,
Yet can I maken other folk to twinne
From avaryce, and sore to repente.
But that is nat my principal entente.
I preche no-thing but for coveityse;
Of this matere it oughte y-nogh suffyse.
Than telle I hem ensamples many oon
Of olde stories, longe tyme agoon:
For lewed peple loven tales olde;
Swich thinges can they wel reporte and holde.
What? trowe ye, the whyles I may preche,
And winne gold and silver for I teche,
That I wol live in povert wilfully?
Nay, nay, I thoghte it never trewely!
For I wol preche and begge in sondry londes;
I wol not do no labour with myn hondes,
Ne make baskettes, and live therby,
Because I wol nat beggen ydelly.
I wol non of the apostles counterfete;
I wol have money, wolle, chese, and whete,
Al were it yeven of the povrest page,
Or of the povrest widwe in a village,
Al sholde hir children sterve for famyne.
Nay! I wol drinke licour of the vyne,
And have a joly wenche in every toun.
But herkneth, lordings, in conclusioun;
Your lyking is that I shal telle a tale.
Now, have I dronke a draughte of corny ale,
By god, I hope I shal yow telle a thing
That shal, by resoun, been at your lyking.
For, though myself be a ful vicious man,
A moral tale yet I yow telle can,
Which I am wont to preche, for to winne.
Now holde your pees, my tale I wol beginne.'

The Pardoner's Tale

Here biginneth the Pardoners Tale

In Flaundres whylom was a companye
Of yonge folk, that haunteden folye,
As ryot, hasard, stewes, and tavernes,
Wher-as, with harpes, lutes, and giternes,
They daunce and pleye at dees bothe day and night,
And ete also and drinken over hir might,
Thurgh which they doon the devel sacrifyse
With-in that develes temple, in cursed wyse,
By superfluitee abhominable;

Hir othes been so grete and so dampnable,
That it is grisly for to here hem swere;
Our blissed lordes body they to-tere;
Hem thoughte Jewes rente him noght y-nough;
And ech of hem at otheres sinne lough.
And right anon than comen tombesteres
Fetys and smale, and yonge fruytesteres,
Singers with harpes, baudes, wafereres,
Whiche been the verray develes officeres
To kindle and blowe the fyr of lecherye,
That is annexed un-to glotonye;
The holy writ take I to my witnesse,
That luxurie is in wyn and dronkenesse.
Lo, how that dronken Loth, unkindely,
Lay by his doghtres two, unwitingly;
So dronke he was, he niste what he wroghte.
Herodes, (who-so wel the stories soghte)
Whan he of wyn was replet at his feste,
Right at his owene table he yaf his heste
To sleen the Baptist John ful giltelees.
Senek seith eek a good word doutelees;
He seith, he can no difference finde
Bitwix a man that is out of his minde
And a man which that is dronkelewe,
But that woodnesse, y-fallen in a shrewe,
Persevereth lenger than doth dronkenesse.
O glotonye, ful of cursednesse,
O cause first of our confusioun,
O original of our dampnacioun,
Til Crist had boght us with his blood agayn!
Lo, how dere, shortly for to sayn,
Aboght was thilke cursed vileinye;
Corrupt was al this world for glotonye!
Adam our fader, and his wyf also,
Fro Paradys to labour and to wo
Were driven for that vyce, it is no drede;
For whyl that Adam fasted, as I rede,
He was in Paradys; and whan that he
Eet of the fruyt defended on the tree,
Anon he was out-cast to wo and peyne.
O glotonye, on thee wel oghte us pleyne!
O, wiste a man how many maladyes
Folwen of excesse and of glotonyes,
He wolde been the more mesurable
Of his diete, sittinge at his table.
Allas! the shorte throte, the tendre mouth,
Maketh that, Est and West, and North and South,
In erthe, in eir, in water men to-swinke
To gete a glotoun deyntee mete and drinke!
Of this matere, o Paul, wel canstow trete,
'Mete un-to wombe, and wombe eek un-to mete,
Shal god destroyen bothe,' as Paulus seith.[87]
Allas! a foul thing is it, by my feith,
To seye this word, and fouler is the dede,
Whan man so drinketh of the whyte and rede,[88]
That of his throte he maketh his privee,
Thurgh thilke cursed superfluitee.
The apostel weping seith ful pitously,[89]
'Ther walken many of whiche yow told have I,
I seye it now weping with pitous voys,
[That] they been enemys of Cristes croys,
Of whiche the ende is deeth, wombe is her god.'
O wombe! O bely! O stinking cod,
Fulfild of donge and of corrupcioun!
At either ende of thee foul is the soun.
How greet labour and cost is thee to finde!
Thise cokes, how they stampe, and streyne, and grinde,
And turnen substaunce in-to accident,[90]
To fulfille al thy likerous talent!
Out of the harde bones knokke they
The mary, for they caste noght a-wey
That may go thurgh the golet softe and swote;
Of spicerye, of leef, and bark, and rote
Shal been his sauce y-maked by delyt,
To make him yet a newer appetyt.
But certes, he that haunteth swich delyces
Is deed, whyl that he liveth in tho vyces.
A lecherous thing is wyn, and dronkenesse

---

[87] *I Corinthians*, vi, 13.
[88] White and red wines.
[89] *Philippians*, iii, 18–19.
[90] turnen substaunce, *etc.* A term in scholastic philosophy, meaning here to change the very nature of the food

Is ful of stryving and of wrecchednesse.
O dronke man, disfigured is thy face,
Sour is thy breeth, foul artow to embrace,
And thurgh thy dronke nose semeth the soun
As though thou seydest ay 'Sampsoun, Sampsoun';
And yet, god wot, Sampsoun drank never no wyn.
Thou fallest, as it were a stiked swyn;
Thy tonge is lost, and al thyn honest cure;
For dronkenesse is verray sepulture
Of mannes wit and his discrecioun.
In whom that drinke hath dominacioun,
He can no conseil kepe, it is no drede.
Now kepe yow fro the whyte and fro the rede,
And namely fro the whyte wyn of Lepe,[91]
That is to selle in Fish-strete or in Chepe.
This wyn of Spayne crepeth subtilly
In othere wynes, growing faste by,
Of which ther ryseth swich fumositee,
That whan a man hath dronken draughtes three,
And weneth that he be at hoom in Chepe,
He is in Spayne, right at the toune of Lepe,
Nat at the Rochel, ne at Burdeux toun;[92]
And thanne wol he seye, 'Sampsoun, Sampsoun.'
But herkneth, lordings, o word, I yow preye,
That alle the sovereyn actes, dar I seye,
Of victories in th'olde testament,
Thurgh verray god, that is omnipotent,
Were doon in abstinence and in preyere;
Loketh the Bible, and ther ye may it lere.
Loke, Attila, the grete conquerour,
Deyde in his sleep, with shame and dishonour,
Bledinge ay at his nose in dronkenesse;
A capitayn shoulde live in sobrenesse.
And over al this, avyseth yow right wel
What was comaunded un-to Lamuel[93] —
Nat Samuel, but Lamuel, seye I —
Redeth the Bible, and finde it expresly
Of wyn-yeving to hem that han justyse.
Na-more of this, for it may wel suffyse.
And now that I have spoke of glotonye,
Now wol I yow defenden hasardrye.
Hasard is verray moder of lesinges,
And of deceite, and cursed forsweringes,
Blaspheme of Crist, manslaughtre, and wast also
Of catel and of tyme; and forthermo,
It is repreve and contrarie of honour
For to ben holde a commune hasardour.
And ever the hyër he is of estaat,
The more is he holden desolaat.
If that a prince useth hasardrye,
In alle governaunce and policye
He is, as by commune opinioun,
Y-holde the lasse in reputacioun.
Stilbon,[94] that was a wys embassadour,
Was sent to Corinthe, in ful greet honour,
Fro Lacidomie, to make hir alliaunce.
And whan he cam, him happede, par chaunce,
That alle the grettest that were of that lond,
Pleyinge atte hasard he hem fond.
For which, as sone as it mighte be,
He stal him hoom agayn to his contree,
And seyde, 'ther wol I nat lese my name;
N' I wol nat take on me so greet defame,
Yow for to allye un-to none hasardours.
Sendeth othere wyse embassadours;
For, by my trouthe, me were lever dye,
Than I yow sholde to hasardours allye.
For ye that been so glorious in honours
Shul nat allyen yow with hasardours
As by my wil, ne as by my tretee.'
This wyse philosophre thus seyde he.
Loke eek that, to the king Demetrius
The king of Parthes, as the book[95] seith us,
Sente him a paire of dees of gold in scorn,
For he hadde used hasard ther-biforn;
For which he heeld his glorie or his renoun

[91] Near Cadiz. This wine may be sherry.
[92] Nat at the Rochel, *etc.* The French wines were milder than those of Spain, with which they were often adulterated.
[93] Lemuel. See *Proverbs*, xxxi, 4.
[94] The Pardoner means Chilon. The story is in John of Salisbury's *Policraticus*, I, 5.
[95] *Policraticus.*

At no value or reputacioun.
Lordes may finden other maner pley
Honeste y-nough to dryve the day awey.
Now wol I speke of othes false and grete
A word or two, as olde bokes trete.
Gret swering is a thing abhominable,
And false swering is yet more reprevable.
The heighe god forbad swering at al,
Witnesse on Mathew; [96] but in special
Of swering seith the holy Jeremye,[97]
'Thou shalt seye sooth thyn othes, and nat lye,
And swere in dome, and eek in rightwisnesse;'
But ydel swering is a cursednesse.
Bihold and see, that in the firste table
Of heighe goddes hestes honurable,[98]
How that the seconde heste of him is this—
'Tak nat my name in ydel or amis.'
Lo, rather he forbedeth swich swering
Than homicyde or many a cursed thing;
I seye that, as by ordre, thus it stondeth;
This knowen, that his hestes understondeth,
How that the second heste of god is that.
And forther over, I wol thee telle al plat,
That vengeance shal nat parten from his hous,
That of his othes is to outrageous.
'By goddes precious herte, and by his nayles,
And by the blode of Crist, that it is in Hayles,[99]
Seven is my chaunce, and thyn is cink and treye;
By goddes armes, if thou falsly pleye,
This dagger shal thurgh-out thyn herte go'—
This fruyt cometh of the bicched bones two,
Forswering, ire, falsnesse, homicyde.
Now, for the love of Crist that for us dyde,
Leveth your othes, bothe grete and smale;
But, sirs, now wol I telle forth my tale.

THISE ryotoures three, of whiche I telle,
Longe erst er pryme rong of any belle,
Were set hem in a taverne for to drinke;
And as they satte, they herde a belle clinke
Biforn a cors, was caried to his grave;
That oon of hem gan callen to his knave,
'Go bet,' quod he, 'and axe redily,
What cors is this that passeth heer forby;
And look that thou reporte his name wel.'
'Sir,' quod this boy, 'it nedeth never-a-del.
It was me told, er ye cam heer, two houres;
He was, pardee, an old felawe of youres;
And sodeynly he was y-slayn to-night,
For-dronke, as he sat on his bench upright;
Ther cam a privee theef, men clepeth Deeth,
That in this contree al the peple sleeth,
And with his spere he smoot his herte a-two,
And wente his wey with-outen wordes mo.
He hath a thousand slayn this pestilence:
And, maister, er ye come in his presence,
Me thinketh that it were necessarie
For to be war of swich an adversarie:
Beth redy for to mete him evermore.
Thus taughte me my dame, I sey na-more.'
'By seinte Marie,' seyde this taverner,
'The child seith sooth, for he hath slayn this yeer,
Henne over a myle, with-in a greet village,
Both man and womman, child and hyne, and page.
I trowe his habitacioun be there;
To been avysed greet wisdom it were,
Er that he dide a man a dishonour.'
'Ye, goddes armes,' quod this ryotour,
'Is it swich peril with him for to mete?
I shal him seke by wey and eek by strete,
I make avow to goddes digne bones!
Herkneth, felawes, we three been al ones;
Lat ech of us holde up his hond til other,
And ech of us bicomen otheres brother,

---

[96] *St. Matthew*, v, 34.
[97] *Jeremiah*, iv, 2.
[98] The commandments were divided into two tables, the first concerned with man's duty to God, the second with his duty toward other men. Our third commandment was the second in the medieval list, from the fact that they counted the first two as one.
[99] A phial of Christ's blood was shown at this abbey in Gloucestershire.

And we wol sleen this false traytour Deeth;
He shal be slayn, which that so many sleeth,
By goddes dignitee, er it be night.'
Togidres han thise three her trouthes plight,
To live and dyen ech of hem for other,
As though he were his owene y-boren brother.
And up they sterte al dronken, in this rage,
And forth they goon towardes that village,
Of which the taverner had spoke biforn,
And many a grisly ooth than han they sworn,
And Cristes blessed body they to-rente —
'Deeth shal be deed, if that they may him hente.'
Whan they han goon nat fully half a myle,
Right as they wolde han troden over a style,
An old man and a povre with hem mette.
This olde man ful mekely hem grette,
And seyde thus, 'now, lordes, god yow see!'
The proudest of thise ryotoures three
Answerde agayn, 'what? carl, with sory grace,[100]
Why artow al forwrapped save thy face?
Why livestow so longe in so greet age?'
This olde man gan loke in his visage,
And seyde thus, 'for I ne can nat finde
A man, though that I walked in-to Inde,
Neither in citee nor in no village,
That wolde chaunge his youthe for myn age;
And therfore moot I han myn age stille,
As longe time as it is goddes wille.
Ne deeth, allas! ne wol nat han my lyf;
Thus walke I, lyk a restelees caityf,
And on the ground, which is my modres gate,
I knokke with my staf, bothe erly and late,
And seye, "leve moder, leet me in!
Lo, how I vanish, flesh, and blood, and skin!
Allas! whan shul my bones been at reste?
Moder, with yow wolde I chaunge my cheste,
That in my chambre longe tyme hath be,
Ye! for an heyre clout[101] to wrappe me!"
But yet to me she wol nat do that grace,
For which ful pale and welked is my face.
But, sirs, to yow it is no curteisye
To speken to an old man vileinye,
But he trespasse in worde, or elles in dede.
In holy writ[102] ye may your-self wel rede,
"Agayns an old man, hoor upon his heed,
Ye sholde aryse;" wherfor I yeve yow reed,
Ne dooth un-to an old man noon harm now,
Na-more than ye wolde men dide to yow
In age, if that ye so longe abyde;
And god be with yow, wher ye go or ryde.
I moot go thider as I have to go.'
'Nay, olde cherl, by god, thou shalt nat so,'
Seyde this other hasardour anon;
'Thou partest nat so lightly, by seint John!
Thou spak right now of thilke traitour Deeth,
That in this contree alle our frendes sleeth.
Have heer my trouthe, as thou art his aspye,
Tel wher he is, or thou shalt it abye,
By god, and by the holy sacrament!
For soothly thou art oon of his assent,
To sleen us yonge folk, thou false theef!'
'Now, sirs,' quod he, 'if that yow be so leef
To finde Deeth, turne up this croked wey,
For in that grove I lafte him, by my fey,
Under a tree, and ther he wol abyde;
Nat for your boost he wol him no-thing hyde.

[100] An oath.

[101] A hair cloth; in this case, a shroud.

[102] *Leviticus*, xix, 32.

See ye that ook? right ther ye shul him finde.
God save yow, that boghte agayn man-kinde,
And yow amende!' — thus seyde this olde man.
And everich of thise ryotoures ran,
Til he cam to that tree, and ther they founde
Of florins fyne of golde y-coyned rounde
Wel ny an eighte busshels, as hem thoughte.
No lenger thanne after Deeth they soughte,
But ech of hem so glad was of that sighte,
For that the florins been so faire and brighte,
That doun they sette hem by this precious hord.
The worste of hem he spake the firste word.
'Brethren,' quod he, 'tak kepe what I saye;
My wit is greet, though that I bourde and pleye.
This tresor hath fortune un-to us yiven,
In mirthe and jolitee our lyf to liven,
And lightly as it comth, so wol we spende.
Ey! goddes precious dignitee! who wende
To-day, that we sholde han so fair a grace?
But mighte this gold be caried fro this place
Hoom to myn hous, or elles un-to youres —
For wel ye woot that al this gold is oures —
Than were we in heigh felicitee.
But trewely, by daye it may nat be;
Men wolde seyn that we were theves stronge,
And for our owene tresor doon us honge.
This tresor moste y-caried be by nighte
As wysly and as slyly as it mighte.
Wherfore I rede that cut among us alle
Be drawe, and lat see wher the cut wol falle;
And he that hath the cut with herte blythe
Shal renne to the toune, and that ful swythe,
And bringe us breed and wyn ful prively.
And two of us shul kepen subtilly
This tresor wel; and, if he wol nat tarie,
Whan it is night, we wol this tresor carie
By oon assent, wher-as us thinketh best.'
That oon of hem the cut broughte in his fest,
And bad hem drawe, and loke wher it wol falle;
And it fil on the yongeste of hem alle;
And forth toward the toun he wente anon.
And al-so sone as that he was gon,
That oon of hem spak thus un-to that other,
'Thou knowest wel thou art my sworne brother,
Thy profit wol I telle thee anon.
Thou woost wel that our felawe is agon;
And heer is gold, and that ful greet plentee,
That shal departed been among us three.
But natheles, if I can shape it so
That it departed were among us two
Hadde I nat doon a freendes torn to thee?'
That other answerde, 'I noot how that may be;
He woot how that the gold is with us tweye,
What shal we doon, what shal we to him seye?'
'Shal it be conseil?' seyde the firste shrewe,
'And I shal tellen thee, in wordes fewe,
What we shal doon, and bringe it wel aboute.'
'I graunte,' quod that other, 'out of doute,
That, by my trouthe, I wol thee nat biwreye.'
'Now,' quod the firste, 'thou woost wel we be tweye,
And two of us shul strenger be than oon.
Look whan that he is set, and right anoon
Arys, as though thou woldest with him pleye;
And I shal ryve him thurgh the sydes tweye

Whyl that thou strogelest with him as in game,
And with thy dagger look thou do the same;
And than shal al this gold departed be,
My dere freend, bitwixen me and thee;
Than may we bothe our lustes al fulfille,
And pleye at dees right at our owene wille.'
And thus acorded been thise shrewes tweye
To sleen the thridde, as ye han herd me seye.

This yongest, which that wente un-to the toun,
Ful ofte in herte he rolleth up and doun
The beautee of thise florins newe and brighte.
'O lord!' quod he, 'if so were that I mighte
Have al this tresor to my-self allone,
Ther is no man that liveth under the trone
Of god, that sholde live so mery as I!'
And atte laste the feend, our enemy,
Putte in his thought that he shold poyson beye,
With which he mighte sleen his felawes tweye;
For-why the feend fond him in swich lyvinge,
That he had leve him to sorwe bringe,
For this was outrely his fulle entente
To sleen hem bothe, and never to repente.
And forth he gooth, no lenger wolde he tarie,
Into the toun, un-to a pothecarie,
And preyed him, that he him wolde selle
Som poyson, that he mighte his rattes quelle;
And eek ther was a polcat in his hawe,
That, as he seyde, his capouns hadde y-slawe,
And fayn he wolde wreke him, if he mighte,
On vermin, that destroyed him by nighte.

The pothecarie answerde, 'and thou shalt have
A thing that, al-so god my soule save,
In al this world ther nis no creature,
That ete or dronke hath of this confiture
Noght but the mountance of a corn of whete,
That he ne shal his lyf anon forlete;
Ye, sterve he shal, and that in lasse whyle
Than thou wolt goon a paas nat but a myle;
This poyson is so strong and violent.'

This cursed man hath in his hond y-hent
This poyson in a box, and sith he ran
In-to the nexte strete, un-to a man,
And borwed [of] him large botels three;
And in the two his poyson poured he;
The thridde he kepte clene for his drinke.
For al the night he shoop him for to swinke
In caryinge of the gold out of that place.
And whan this ryotour, with sory grace,
Had filled with wyn his grete botels three,
To his felawes agayn repaireth he.

What nedeth it to sermone of it more?
For right as they had cast his deeth bifore,
Right so they han him slayn, and that anon.
And whan that this was doon, thus spak that oon,
'Now lat us sitte and drinke, and make us merie,
And afterward we wol his body berie.'
And with that word it happed him, par cas,
To take the botel ther the poyson was,
And drank, and yaf his felawe drinke also,
For which anon they storven bothe two.

But, certes, I suppose that Avicen [103]
Wroot never in no canon, ne in no fen,
Mo wonder signes of empoisoning
Than hadde thise wrecches two, er hir ending.
Thus ended been thise homicydes two,
And eek the false empoysoner also.

O cursed sinne, ful of cursednesse!
O traytours homicyde, o wikkednesse!
O glotonye, luxurie, and hasardrye!

---

[103] This Arab physician wrote a medical treatise called the *Canon*. Its chapters were termed fens.

Thou blasphemour of Crist with vileinye
And othes grete, of usage and of pryde!
Allas! mankinde, how may it bityde,
That to thy creatour which that thee wroghte,
And with his precious herte-blood thee boghte,
Thou are so fals and so unkinde, allas!
Now, goode men, god forgeve yow your trespas,
And ware yow fro the sinne of avaryce.
Myn holy pardoun may yow alle waryce,
So that ye offre nobles or sterlinges,
Or elles silver broches, spones, ringes.
Boweth your heed under this holy bulle!
Cometh up, ye wyves, offreth of your wolle!
Your name I entre heer in my rolle anon;
In-to the blisse of hevene shul ye gon;
I yow assoile, by myn heigh power,
Yow that wol offre, as clene and eek as cleer
As ye were born; and, lo, sirs, thus I preche.
And Jesu Crist, that is our soules leche,
So graunte yow his pardon to receyve;
For that is best; I wol yow nat deceyve.
But sirs, o word forgat I in my tale,
I have relikes and pardon in my male,
As faire as any man in Engelond,
Whiche were me yeven by the popes hond.
If any of yow wol, of devocioun,
Offren, and han myn absolucioun,
Cometh forth anon, and kneleth heer adoun,
And mekely receyveth my pardoun:
Or elles, taketh pardon as ye wende,
Al newe and fresh, at every tounes ende,
So that ye offren alwey newe and newe
Nobles and pens, which that be gode and trewe.
It is an honour to everich that is heer,
That ye mowe have a suffisant pardoneer
T'assoille yow, in contree as ye ryde,
For aventures which that may bityde.
Peraventure ther may falle oon or two
Doun of his hors, and breke his nekke atwo.
Look which a seuretee is it to yow alle
That I am in your felaweship y-falle,
That may assoille yow, bothe more and lasse,
Whan that the soule shal fro the body passe.
I rede that our hoste heer shal biginne,
For he is most envoluped in sinne.
Com forth, sir hoste, and offre first anon,
And thou shalt kisse the reliks everichon,
Ye, for a grote! unbokel anon thy purs.'
'Nay, nay,' quod he, 'than have I Cristes curs!
Lat be,' quod he, 'it shal nat be, so thee'ch![104]
Thou woldest make me kisse thyn old breech,
And swere it were a relik of a seint,
Thogh it were with thy fundement depeint!
But by the croys which that seint Eleyne fond,[105]
I wolde I hadde thy coillons in myn hond
In stede of relikes or of seintuarie;
Lat cutte hem of, I wol thee helpe hem carie;
They shul be shryned in an hogges tord.'
This pardoner answerde nat a word;
So wrooth he was, no word ne wolde he seye.
'Now,' quod our host, 'I wol no lenger pleye
With thee, ne with noon other angry man.'
But right anon the worthy Knight bigan,
Whan that he saugh that al the peple lough,
'Na-more of this, for it is right y-nough;
Sir Pardoner, be glad and mery of chere;
And ye, sir host, that been to me so dere,
I prey yow that ye kisse the Pardoner.
And Pardoner, I prey thee, drawe thee neer,

[104] As I may prosper.

[105] Saint Helen, mother of the emperor Constantine, is said to have discovered the place where the true cross was concealed.

And, as we diden, lat us laughe and pleye.'
Anon they kiste, and riden forth hir weye.

Here is ended the Pardoners Tale

The Prioress's Prologue

Bihold the mery wordes of the Host to the Shipman and to the lady Prioresse

'Wel seyd,[106] by *corpus dominus,'*[107] quod our hoste,
'Now longe moot thou sayle by the coste,
Sir gentil maister, gentil marineer!
God yeve this monk a thousand last quad yeer![108]
A ha! felawes! beth ware of swiche a jape!
The monk putte in the mannes hood an ape,
And in his wyves eek, by seint Austin!
Draweth no monkes more un-to your in.
But now passe over, and lat us seke aboute,
Who shal now telle first, of al this route,
Another tale;' and with that word he sayde,
As curteisly as it had been a mayde,
'My lady Prioresse, by your leve,
So that I wiste I sholde yow nat greve,
I wolde demen that ye tellen sholde
A tale next, if so were that ye wolde.
Now wol ye vouche-sauf, my lady dere?'
'Gladly,' quod she, and seyde as ye shal here.

Explicit

The Prioress's Tale

The Prologe of the Prioresses Tale

Domine, dominus noster.[109]

O Lord our lord, thy name how merveillous
Is in this large worlde y-sprad—quod she:—
For noght only thy laude precious
Parfourned is by men of dignitee,
But by the mouth of children thy bountee
Parfourned is, for on the brest soukinge
Som tyme shewen they thyn heryinge.

Wherfor in laude, as I best can or may,
Of thee, and of the whyte lily flour
Which that thee bar, and is a mayde alway,
To telle a storie I wol do my labour;
Not that I may encresen hir honour;
For she hir-self is honour, and the rote
Of bountee, next hir sone, and soules bote.—

O moder mayde! o mayde moder free!
O bush unbrent, brenninge in Moyses sighte,
That ravisedest doun fro the deitee,
Thurgh thyn humblesse, the goost that in th'alighte,
Of whos vertu, whan he thyn herte lighte,
Conceived was the fadres sapience,
Help me to telle it in thy reverence!

Lady! thy bountee, thy magnificence,
Thy vertu, and thy grete humilitee
Ther may no tonge expresse in no science;
For som-tyme, lady, er men praye to thee,
Thou goost biforn of thy benignitee,
And getest us the light, thurgh thy preyere,
To gyden us un-to thy sone so dere.

My conning is so wayk, o blisful quene,
For to declare thy grete worthinesse,
That I ne may the weighte nat sustene,
But as a child of twelf monthe old, or lesse,
That can unnethes any word expresse,
Right so fare I, and therfor I yow preye,
Gydeth my song that I shal of yow seye.

Explicit

Here biginneth the Prioresses Tale

Ther was in Asie, in a greet citee,
Amonges Cristen folk, a Jewerye,[110]
Sustened by a lord of that contree

[106] The Shipman's Tale of the lecherous Dan John has just been finished and the Host turns to thank the teller.
[107] Bad Latin for 'By the body of our Lord.'
[108] Cartloads of bad years.
[109] O Lord, our Lord.
[110] Jewish quarter

For foule usure and lucre of vilanye,[111]
Hateful to Crist and to his companye;
And thurgh the strete men mighte ryde or wende,
For it was free, and open at either ende.

A litel scole of Cristen folk ther stood
Doun at the ferther ende, in which ther were
Children an heep, y-comen of Cristen blood,
That lerned in that scole yeer by yere
Swich maner doctrine as men used there,
This is to seyn, to singen and to rede,
As smale children doon in hir childhede.

Among thise children was a widwes sone,
A litel clergeon, seven yeer of age,
That day by day to scole was his wone,
And eek also, wher-as he saugh th'image
Of Cristes moder, hadde he in usage,
As him was taught, to knele adoun and seye
His *Ave Marie,* as he goth by the weye.

Thus hath this widwe hir litel sone y-taught
Our blisful lady, Cristes moder dere,
To worshipe ay, and he forgat it naught,
For sely child wol alday sone lere;
But ay, whan I remembre on this matere,
Seint Nicholas[112] stant ever in my presence,
For he so yong to Crist did reverence.

This litel child, his litel book lerninge,
As he sat in the scole at his prymer,
He *Alma redemptoris*[113] herde singe,
As children lerned hir antiphoner;
And, as he dorste, he drough him ner and ner,
And herkned ay the wordes and the note,
Til he the firste vers coude al by rote.

Noght wiste he what this Latin was to seye,
For he so yong and tendre was of age;
But on a day his felaw gan he preye
T'expounden him this song in his langage,
Or telle him why this song was in usage;
This preyde he him to construe and declare
Ful ofte tyme upon his knowes bare.

His felaw, which that elder was than he,
Answerde him thus: 'this song, I have herd seye,
Was maked of our blisful lady free,
Hir to salue, and eek hir for to preye
To been our help and socour whan we deye.
I can no more expounde in this matere;
I lerne song, I can but smal grammere.'

'And is this song maked in reverence
Of Cristes moder?' seyde this innocent;
'Now certes, I wol do my diligence
To conne it al, er Cristemasse is went;
Though that I for my prymer shal be shent,
And shal be beten thryës in an houre,
I wol it conne, our lady for to honoure.'

His felaw taughte him homward prively,
Fro day to day, til he coude it by rote,
And than he song it wel and boldely
Fro word to word, acording with the note;
Twyës a day it passed thurgh his throte,
To scoleward and homward whan he wente;
On Cristes moder set was his entente.

As I have seyd, thurgh-out the Jewerye
This litel child, as he cam to and fro,
Ful merily than wolde he singe, and crye
O Alma redemptoris ever-mo.
The swetnes hath his herte perced so
Of Cristes moder, that, to hir to preye,
He can nat stinte of singing by the weye.

Our firste fo, the serpent Sathanas,
That hath in Jewes herte his waspes nest,
Up swal, and seide, 'O Hebraik peple, allas!
Is this to yow a thing that is honest,

---

111 filthy lucre
112 The patron saint of schoolboys. As a baby he would be suckled only once on Wednesdays and Fridays.
113 A medieval anthem beginning 'Cherishing mother of the redeemer.'

That swich a boy shal walken as him lest
In your despyt, and singe of swich sentence,
Which is agayn your lawes reverence?'

Fro thennes forth the Jewes han conspyred
This innocent out of this world to chace;
An homicyde ther-to han they hyred,
That in an aley hadde a privee place;
And as the child gan for-by for to pace,
This cursed Jew him hente and heeld him faste,
And kitte his throte, and in a pit him caste.

I seye that in a wardrobe they him threwe
Wher-as these Jewes purgen hir entraille.
O cursed folk of Herodes al newe,
What may your yvel entente yow availle?
Mordre wol out, certein, it wol nat faille,
And namely ther th'onour of god shal sprede,
The blood out cryeth on your cursed dede.

'O martir, souded to virginitee,
Now maystou singen, folwing ever in oon
The whyte lamb celestial,' quod she,
'Of which the grete evangelist, seint John,
In Pathmos wroot, which seith that they that goon
Biforn this lamb, and singe a song al newe,
That never, fleshly, wommen they ne knewe.'

This povre widwe awaiteth al that night
After hir litel child, but he cam noght;
For which, as sone as it was dayes light,
With face pale of drede and bisy thoght,
She hath at scole and elles-wher him soght,
Til finally she gan so fer espye
That he last seyn was in the Jewerye.

With modres pitee in hir brest enclosed,
She gooth, as she were half out of hir minde,
To every place wher she hath supposed
By lyklihede hir litel child to finde;
And ever on Cristes moder meke and kinde
She cryde, and atte laste thus she wroghte,
Among the cursed Jewes she him soghte.

She frayneth and she preyeth pitously
To every Jew that dwelte in thilke place,
To telle hir, if hir child wente oght for-by.
They seyde, 'nay'; but Jesu, of his grace,
Yaf in hir thought, inwith a litel space,
That in that place after hir sone she cryde,
Wher he was casten in a pit bisyde.

O grete god, that parfournest thy laude
By mouth of innocents, lo heer thy might!
This gemme of chastitee, this emeraude,
And eek of martirdom the ruby bright,
Ther he with throte y-corven lay upright,
He '*Alma redemptoris*' gan to singe
So loude, that al the place gan to ringe.

The Cristen folk, that thurgh the streete wente,
In coomen, for to wondre up-on this thing,
And hastily they for the provost sente;
He cam anon with-outen tarying,
And herieth Crist that is of heven king,
And eek his moder, honour of mankinde,
And after that, the Jewes leet he binde.

This child with pitous lamentacioun
Up-taken was, singing his song alway;
And with honour of greet processioun
They carien him un-to the nexte abbay.
His moder swowning by the bere lay;
Unnethe might the peple that was there
This newe Rachel bringe fro his bere.

With torment and with shamful deth echon
This provost dooth thise Jewes for to sterve
That of this mordre wiste, and that anon;
He nolde no swich cursednesse observe.
Yvel shal have, that yvel wol deserve.
Therfor with wilde hors he dide hem drawe,
And after that he heng hem by the lawe.

Up-on his bere ay lyth this innocent
Biforn the chief auter, whyl masse laste,
And after that, the abbot with his covent
Han sped hem for to burien him ful faste;
And whan they holy water on him caste,
Yet spak this child, whan spreyned was holy water,
And song—'*O Alma redemptoris mater!*'

This abbot, which that was an holy man
As monkes been, or elles oghten be,
This yonge child to conjure he bigan,
And seyde, 'o dere child, I halse thee,
In vertu of the holy Trinitee,
Tel me what is thy cause for to singe,
Sith that thy throte is cut, to my seminge?'[114]

'My throte is cut un-to my nekke-boon,'
Seyde this child, 'and, as by wey of kinde,
I sholde have deyed, ye, longe tyme agoon,
But Jesu Crist, as ye in bokes finde,
Wil that his glorie laste and be in minde;
And, for the worship of his moder dere,
Yet may I singe, "*O Alma*" loude and clere.

This welle of mercy, Cristes moder swete,
I lovede alwey, as after my conninge;
And whan that I my lyf sholde forlete,
To me she cam, and bad me for to singe
This antem verraily in my deyinge.
As ye han herd, and, whan that I had songe,
Me thoughte, she leyde a greyn up-on my tonge.

Wherfor I singe, and singe I moot certeyn
In honour of that blisful mayden free,
Til fro my tonge of-taken is the greyn;
And afterward thus seyde she to me,
"My litel child, now wol I fecche thee
Whan that the greyn is fro thy tonge y-take;
Be nat agast, I wol thee nat forsake."'

[114] As it seems to me.

This holy monk, this abbot, him mene I,
His tonge out-caughte, and took a-wey the greyn,
And he yaf up the goost ful softely.
And whan this abbot had this wonder seyn,
His salte teres trikled doun as reyn,
And gruf he fil al plat up-on the grounde,
And stille he lay as he had been y-bounde.

The covent eek lay on the pavement
Weping, and herien Cristes moder dere,
And after that they ryse, and forth ben went,
And toke awey this martir fro his bere,
And in a tombe of marbul-stones clere
Enclosen they his litel body swete;
Ther he is now, god leve us for to mete.

O yonge Hugh of Lincoln,[115] slayn also
With cursed Jewes, as it is notable,
For it nis but a litel whyle ago;
Preye eek for us, we sinful folk unstable,
That, of his mercy, god so merciable
On us his grete mercy multiplye,
For reverence of his moder Marye. Amen.

Here is ended the Prioresses Tale

The Nun's Priest's Tale

Here biginneth the Nonne Preestes Tale of the Cok and Hen, Chauntecleer and Pertelote

A POVRE widwe, somdel stape in age,
Was whylom dwelling in a narwe cotage,
Bisyde a grove, standing in a dale.
This widwe, of which I telle yow my tale,
Sin thilke day that she was last a wyf,
In pacience ladde a ful simple lyf,
For litel was hir catel and hir rente;
By housbondrye, of such as God hir sente,
She fond[116] hir-self, and eek hir doghtren two.
Three large sowes hadde she, and namo,
Three kyn, and eek a sheep that highte Malle,
Ful sooty was hir bour, and eek hir halle,

[115] According to a church historian, he was murdered by the Jews in 1255.
[116] kept

In which she eet ful many a sclendre meel.
Of poynaunt sauce hir neded never a deel.
No deyntee morsel passed thurgh hir throte;
Hir dyete was accordant to hir cote.
Repleccioun ne made hir never syk;
Attempree dyete was al hir phisyk,
And exercyse, and hertes suffisaunce.
The goute lette hir no-thing[117] for to daunce,
N'apoplexye shente nat hir heed;
No wyn ne drank she, neither whyt ne reed;
Hir bord was served most with whyt and blak,
Milk and broun breed, in which she fond no lak,
Seynd bacoun, and somtyme an ey or tweye,
For she was as it were a maner deye.
A yerd she hadde, enclosed al aboute
With stikkes, and a drye dich with-oute,
In which she hadde a cok, hight Chauntecleer,
In al the land of crowing nas his peer.
His vois was merier than the mery orgon
On messe-dayes that in the chirche gon;
Wel sikerer was his crowing in his logge,
Than is a clokke, or an abbey orlogge.
By nature knew he ech ascencioun
Of equinoxial in thilke toun;
For whan degrees fiftene were ascended,
Thanne crew he, that it mighte nat ben amended.
His comb was redder than the fyn coral,
And batailed, as it were a castel-wal.
His bile was blak, and as the jeet it shoon;
Lyk asur were his legges, and his toon;
His nayles whytter than the lilie flour,
And lyk the burned gold was his colour.
This gentil cok hadde in his governaunce
Sevene hennes, for to doon al his plesaunce,
Whiche were his sustres and his paramours,
And wonder lyk to him, as of colours.
Of whiche the faireste hewed on hir throte
Was cleped faire damoysele Pertelote.
Curteys she was, discreet, and debonaire,

[117] Hindered her not at all.

And compaignable, and bar hir-self so faire,
Sin thilke day that she was seven night old,
That trewely she hath the herte in hold
Of Chauntecleer loken in every lith;
He loved hir so, that wel was him therwith.
But such a joye was it to here hem singe,
Whan that the brighte sonne gan to springe,
In swete accord, 'my lief is faren in londe.'
For thilke tyme, as I have understonde,
Bestes and briddes coude speke and singe.
And so bifel, that in a daweninge,
As Chauntecleer among his wyves alle
Sat on his perche, that was in the halle,
And next him sat this faire Pertelote,
This Chauntecleer gan gronen in his throte,
As man that in his dreem is drecched sore.
And whan that Pertelote thus herde him rore,
She was agast, and seyde, 'O herte dere,
What eyleth yow, to grone in this manere?
Ye been a verray sleper, fy for shame!'
And he answerde and seyde thus, 'madame,
I pray yow, that ye take it nat a-grief:
By god, me mette I was in swich meschief
Right now, that yet myn herte is sore afright.
Now god,' quod he, 'my swevene recche aright,
And keep my body out of foul prisoun!
Me mette, how that I romed up and doun
Withinne our yerde, wher-as I saugh a beste,
Was lyk an hound, and wolde han maad areste
Upon my body, and wolde han had me deed.
His colour was bitwixe yelwe and reed;
And tipped was his tail, and bothe his eres,
With blak, unlyk the remenant of his heres;
His snowte smal, with glowinge eyen tweye.
Yet of his look for fere almost I deye;
This caused me my groning, doutelees.'

'Avoy!' quod she, 'fy on yow, hertelees!
Allas!' quod she, 'for, by that god above,
Now han ye lost myn herte and al my love;
I can nat love a coward, by my feith.
For certes, what so any womman seith,
We alle desyren, if it mighte be,
To han housbondes hardy, wyse, and free,
And secree, and no nigard, ne no fool,
Ne him that is agast of every tool,
Ne noon avauntour, by that god above!
How dorste ye seyn for shame unto your love,
That any thing mighte make yow aferd?
Have ye no mannes herte, and han a berd?
Allas! and conne ye been agast of swevenis?
No-thing, god wot, but vanitee, in sweven is.
Swevenes engendren of replecciouns,
And ofte of fume, and of complecciouns,
Whan humours been to habundant in a wight.
Certes this dreem, which ye han met to-night,
Cometh of the grete superfluitee
Of youre rede *colera,*[118] pardee,
Which causeth folk to dreden in here dremes
Of arwes, and of fyr with rede lemes,
Of grete bestes, that they wol hem byte,
Of contek, and of whelpes grete and lyte;
Right as the humour of malencolye
Causeth ful many a man, in sleep, to crye,
For fere of blake beres, or boles blake,
Or elles, blake develes wole hem take.
Of othere humours coude I telle also,
That werken many a man in sleep ful wo;
But I wol passe as lightly as I can.
Lo Catoun,[119] which that was so wys a man,
Seyde he nat thus, ne do no fors of dremes?[120]
Now, sire,' quod she, 'whan we flee fro the bemes,
For Goddes love, as tak som laxatyf;
Up peril of my soule, and of my lyf,
I counseille yow the beste, I wol nat lye,
That bothe of colere and of malencolye
Ye purge yow; and for ye shul nat tarie,
Though in this toun is noon apotecarie,
I shal my-self to herbes techen yow,
That shul ben for your hele, and for your prow;
And in our yerd tho herbes shal I finde,
The whiche han of hir propertee, by kinde,
To purgen yow binethe, and eek above.
Forget not this, for goddes owene love!
Ye been ful colerik of compleccioun.
Ware the sonne in his ascencioun
Ne fynde yow nat repleet of humours hote;
And if it do, I dar wel leye a grote,
That ye shul have a fevere terciane,
Or an agu, that may be youre bane.
A day or two ye shul have digestyves
Of wormes, er ye take your laxatyves,
Of lauriol, centaure, and fumetere,
Or elles of ellebor, that groweth there,
Of catapuce, or of gaytres beryis,
Of erbe yve, growing in our yerd, that mery is;
Pekke hem up right as they growe, and ete hem in.
Be mery, housbond, for your fader kin!
Dredeth no dreem; I can say yow namore.'
'Madame,' quod he, '*graunt mercy* of your lore.
But nathelees, as touching daun Catoun,
That hath of wisdom such a greet renoun,
Though that he bad no dremes for to drede,
By god, men may in olde bokes rede
Of many a man, more of auctoritee
Than ever Catoun was, so mote I thee,
That al the revers seyn of his sentence,
And han wel founden by experience,
That dremes ben significaciouns,
As wel of joye as tribulaciouns
That folk enduren in this lyf present.
Ther nedeth make of this noon argument;
The verray preve sheweth it in dede.
Oon of the gretteste auctours that men rede

118 The red bile, the humour which engendered anger.
119 The medieval Dionysius Cato.
120 do no fors, *etc.* Pay no attention to dreams.

Seith thus, that whylom two felawes wente
On pilgrimage, in a ful good entente;
And happed so, they come into a toun,
Wher-as ther was swich congregacioun
Of peple, and eek so streit of herbergage
That they ne founde as muche as o cotage
In which they bothe mighte y-logged be.
Wherfor thay mosten, of necessitee,
As for that night, departen compaignye;
And ech of hem goth to his hostelrye,
And took his logging as it wolde falle.
That oon of hem was logged in a stalle,
Fer in a yerd, with oxen of the plough;
That other man was logged wel y-nough,
As was his aventure, or his fortune,
That us governeth alle as in commune.
And so bifel, that, longe er it were day,
This man mette in his bed, ther-as he lay,
How that his felawe gan up-on him calle,
And seyde, "allas! for in an oxes stalle
This night I shal be mordred ther I lye.
Now help me, dere brother, er I dye;
In alle haste com to me," he sayde.
This man out of his sleep for fere abrayde;
But whan that he was wakned of his sleep,
He turned him, and took of this no keep;
Him thoughte his dreem nas but a vanitee.
Thus twyës in his sleping dremed he.
And atte thridde tyme yet his felawe
Cam, as him thoughte, and seide, "I am now slawe;
Bihold my blody woundes, depe and wyde!
Arys up erly in the morwe-tyde,
And at the west gate of the toun," quod he,
"A carte ful of dong ther shaltow see,
In which my body is hid ful prively;
Do thilke carte aresten boldely.
My gold caused my mordre, sooth to sayn;"
And tolde him every poynt how he was slayn,
With a ful pitous face, pale of hewe.
And truste wel, his dreem he fond ful trewe;
For on the morwe, as sone as it was day,
To his felawes in he took the way;
And whan that he cam to this oxes stalle,
After his felawe he bigan to calle.
The hostiler answered him anon,
And seyde, "sire, your felawe is agon,
As sone as day he wente out of the toun."
This man gan fallen in suspecioun,
Remembring on his dremes that he mette,
And forth he goth, no lenger wolde he lette,
Unto the west gate of the toun, and fond
A dong-carte, as it were to donge lond,
That was arrayed in the same wyse
As ye han herd the dede man devyse;
And with an hardy herte he gan to crye
Vengeaunce and justice of this felonye: —
"My felawe mordred is this same night,
And in this carte he lyth gapinge upright.
I crye out on the ministres," quod he,
"That sholden kepe and reulen this citee;
Harrow! allas! her lyth my felawe slayn!"
What sholde I more un-to this tale sayn?
The peple out-sterte, and caste the cart to grounde,
And in the middel of the dong they founde
The dede man, that mordred was al newe.
O blisful god, that art so just and trewe!
Lo, how that thou biwreyest mordre alway!
Mordre wol out, that see we day by day.
Mordre is so wlatsom and abhominable
To god, that is so just and resonable,
That he ne wol nat suffre it heled be;
Though it abyde a yeer, or two, or three,
Mordre wol out, this my conclusioun.
And right anoon, ministres of that toun
Han hent the carter, and so sore him pyned,
And eek the hostiler so sore engyned,
That thay biknewe hir wikkednesse anoon,
And were an-hanged by the nekke-boon.
Here may men seen that dremes been to drede.
And certes, in the same book I rede,
Right in the nexte chapitre after this,
(I gabbe nat, so have I joye or blis,)
Two men that wolde han passed over see,
For certeyn cause, in-to a fer contree,
If that the wind ne hadde been contrarie,
That made hem in a citee for to tarie,

That stood ful mery upon an haven-syde.
But on a day, agayn the even-tyde,
The wind gan chaunge, and blew right as hem leste.
Jolif and glad they wente un-to hir reste,
And casten hem ful erly for to saille;
But to that oo man fil a greet mervaille.
That oon of hem, in sleping as he lay,
Him mette a wonder dreem, agayn the day;
Him thoughte a man stood by his beddes syde,
And him comaunded, that he sholde abyde,
And seyde him thus, "if thou to-morwe wende,
Thou shalt be dreynt; my tale is at an ende."
He wook, and tolde his felawe what he mette,
And preyde him his viage for to lette;
As for that day, he preyde him to abyde.
His felawe, that lay by his beddes syde,
Gan for to laughe, and scorned him ful faste.
"No dreem," quod he, "may so myn herte agaste,
That I wol lette for to do my thinges.
I sette not a straw by thy dreminges,
For swevenes been but vanitees and japes.
Men dreme al-day of owles or of apes,
And eke of many a mase ther withal;
Men dreme of thing that never was ne shal.
But sith I see that thou wolt heer abyde,
And thus for-sleuthen wilfully thy tyde,
God wot it reweth me; and have good day."
And thus he took his leve, and wente his way.
But er that he hadde halfe his cours y-seyled,
Noot I nat why, ne what mischaunce it eyled,
But casuelly the shippes botme rente,
And ship and man under the water wente
In sighte of othere shippes it byside,
That with hem seyled at the same tyde.
And therfor, faire Pertelote so dere,
By swiche ensamples olde maistow lere,
That no man sholde been to recchelees
Of dremes, for I sey thee, doutelees,
That many a dreem ful sore is for to drede.
Lo, in the lyf of seint Kenelm, I rede,
That was Kenulphus sone, the noble king
Of Mercenrike,[121] how Kenelm mette a thing;
A lyte er he was mordred, on a day,
His mordre in his avisioun he say.
His norice him expouned every del
His sweven, and bad him for to kepe him wel
For traisoun; but he nas but seven yeer old,
And therfore litel tale hath he told
Of any dreem, so holy was his herte.
By god, I hadde lever than my sherte
That ye had rad his legende, as have I.
Dame Pertelote, I sey yow trewely,
Macrobeus, that writ th'avisioun[122]
In Affrike of the worthy Cipioun,
Affermeth dremes, and seith that they been
Warning of thinges that men after seen.
And forther-more, I pray yow loketh wel
In th'olde testament, of Daniel,
If he held dremes any vanitee.
Reed eek of Joseph, and ther shul ye see
Wher dremes ben somtyme (I sey nat alle)
Warning of thinges that shul after falle.
Loke of Egipt the king, daun Pharao,
His bakere and his boteler also,
Wher they ne felte noon effect in dremes.
Who-so wol seken actes of sondry remes,
May rede of dremes many a wonder thing.
Lo Cresus, which that was of Lyde king,
Mette he nat that he sat upon a tree,
Which signified he sholde anhanged be?
Lo heer Andromacha, Ectores wyf,
That day that Ector sholde lese his lyf,
She dremed on the same night biforn,
How that the lyf of Ector sholde be lorn,
If thilke day he wente in-to bataille;
She warned him, but it mighte nat availle;
He wente for to fighte nathelees,
But he was slayn anoon of Achilles.
But thilke tale is al to long to telle,

[121] Mercia, in the central part of England.
[122] Macrobius's commentary on Cicero's *Dream of Scipio*

And eek it is ny day, I may nat dwelle.
Shortly I seye, as for conclusioun,
That I shal han of this avisioun
Adversitee; and I seye forther-more,
That I ne telle [123] of laxatyves no store,
For they ben venimous, I woot it wel;
I hem defye, I love hem never a del.
  Now let us speke of mirthe, and stinte al this;
Madame Pertelote, so have I blis,
Of o thing god hath sent me large grace;
For whan I see the beautee of your face,
Ye ben so scarlet-reed about your yën,
It maketh al my drede for to dyen;
For, also siker as *In principio,*[124]
Mulier est hominis confusio;
Madame, the sentence of this Latin is —
Womman is mannes joye and al his blis.
For whan I fele a-night your softe syde,
Al-be-it that I may nat on you ryde,
For that our perche is maad so narwe, alas!
I am so ful of joye and of solas
That I defye bothe sweven and dreem.'
And with that word he fley doun fro the beem,
For it was day, and eek his hennes alle;
And with a chuk he gan hem for to calle,
For he had founde a corn, lay in the yerd.
Royal he was, he was namore aferd;
He fethered Pertelote twenty tyme,
And trad as ofte, er that it was pryme.
He loketh as it were a grim leoun;
And on his toos he rometh up and doun,
Him deyned not to sette his foot to grounde.
He chukketh, whan he hath a corn y-founde,
And to him rennen thanne his wyves alle.
Thus royal, as a prince is in his halle,
Leve I this Chauntecleer in his pasture;
And after wol I telle his aventure.
  Whan that the month in which the world bigan,
That highte March, whan god first maked man,
Was complet, and [y]-passed were also,
Sin March bigan, thritty dayes and two,
Bifel that Chauntecleer, in al his pryde,
His seven wyves walking by his syde,
Caste up his eyen to the brighte sonne,
That in the signe of Taurus hadde y-ronne
Twenty degrees and oon, and somwhat more;
And knew by kynde, and by noon other lore,
That it was pryme, and crew with blisful stevene.
'The sonne,' he sayde, 'is clomben up on hevene
Fourty degrees and oon, and more, y-wis.
Madame Pertelote, my worldes blis,
Herkneth thise blisful briddes how they singe,
And see the fresshe floures how they springe;
Ful is myn herte of revel and solas.'
But sodeinly him fil a sorweful cas;
For ever the latter ende of joye is wo.
God woot that worldly joye is sone ago;
And if a rethor coude faire endyte,
He in a cronique saufly mighte it wryte,
As for a sovereyn notabilitee.
Now every wys man, lat him herkne me;
This storie is al-so trewe, I undertake,
As is the book of Launcelot de Lake,[125]
That wommen holde in ful gret reverence.
Now wol I torne agayn to my sentence.
  A col-fox, ful of sly iniquitee,
That in the grove hadde woned yeres three,
By heigh imaginacioun forn-cast,
The same night thurgh-out the hegges brast
Into the yerd, ther Chauntecleer the faire
Was wont, and eek his wyves, to repaire;
And in a bed of wortes stille he lay,
Til it was passed undern of the day,
Wayting his tyme on Chauntecleer to falle,
As gladly doon thise homicydes alle,
That in awayt liggen to mordre men.
O false mordrer, lurking in thy den!
O newe Scariot,[126] newe Genilon! [127]

[123] Set no store by.
[124] The first phrase in St. John's Gospel.
[125] An interminable romance.
[126] Judas Iscariot. [127] Roland's betrayer.

False dissimilour, O Greek Sinon,[128]
That broghtest Troye al outrely to sorwe!
O Chauntecleer, acursed be that morwe,
That thou into that yerd flough fro the bemes!
Thou were ful wel y-warned by thy dremes,
That thilke day was perilous to thee.
But what that god forwoot mot nedes be,
After the opinioun of certeyn clerkis.
Witnesse on him, that any perfit clerk is,
That in scole is gret altercacioun
In this matere, and greet disputisoun,
And hath ben of an hundred thousand men.
But I ne can not bulte it to the bren,
As can the holy doctour Augustyn,
Or Boëce,[129] or the bishop Bradwardyn,[130]
Whether that goddes worthy forwiting
Streyneth me nedely for to doon a thing,
(Nedely clepe I simple necessitee);
Or elles, if free choys be graunted me
To do that same thing, or do it noght,
Though god forwoot it, er that it was wroght;
Or if his witing streyneth nevere a del
But by necessitee condicionel.
I wol not han to do of swich matere;
My tale is of a cok, as ye may here,
That took his counseil of his wyf, with sorwe,
To walken in the yerd upon that morwe
That he had met the dreem, that I yow tolde.
Wommennes counseils been ful ofte colde;
Wommannes counseil broghte us first to wo,
And made Adam fro paradys to go,
Ther-as he was ful mery, and wel at ese.—
But for I noot, to whom it mighte displese,
If I counseil of wommen wolde blame,
Passe over, for I seyde it in my game.
Rede auctours, wher they trete of swich matere,
And what thay seyn of wommen ye may here.
Thise been the cokkes wordes, and nat myne;
I can noon harm of no womman divyne.—
Faire in the sond, to bathe hir merily,
Lyth Pertelote, and alle hir sustres by,
Agayn the sonne; and Chauntecleer so free
Song merier than the mermayde in the see;
For Phisiologus[131] seith sikerly,
How that they singen wel and merily.
And so bifel that, as he caste his yë,
Among the wortes, on a boterflye,
He was war of this fox that lay ful lowe.
No-thing ne liste him thanne for to crowe,
But cryde anon, 'cok, cok,' and up he sterte,
As man that was affrayed in his herte.
For naturelly a beest desyreth flee
Fro his contrarie, if he may it see,
Though he never erst had seyn it with his yë.
This Chauntecleer, whan he gan him espye,
He wolde han fled, but that the fox anon
Seyde, 'Gentil sire, allas! wher wol ye gon?
Be ye affrayed of me that am your freend?
Now certes, I were worse than a feend,
If I to yow wolde harm or vileinye.
I am nat come your counseil for t'espye;
But trewely, the cause of my cominge
Was only for to herkne how that ye singe.
For trewely ye have as mery a stevene
As eny aungel hath, that is in hevene;
Therwith ye han in musik more felinge
Than hadde Boëce, or any that can singe.
My lord your fader (god his soule blesse!)
And eek your moder, of hir gentilesse,
Han in myn hous y-been, to my gret ese;
And certes, sire, ful fayn wolde I yow plese.
But for men speke of singing, I wol saye,
So mote I brouke wel myn eyen tweye,
Save yow, I herde never man so singe,

[128] The deviser of the Trojan horse.
[129] Boethius, a late Roman philosopher much read in medieval times.
[130] English theologian of the fourteenth century.
[131] A collection of fabulous descriptions of beasts.

As dide your fader in the morweninge;
Certes, it was of herte, al that he song.
And for to make his voys the more strong,
He wolde so peyne him, that with bothe his yën
He moste winke, so loude he wolde cryen,
And stonden on his tiptoon ther-with-al,
And strecche forth his nekke long and smal.
And eek he was of swich discrecioun,
That ther nas no man in no regioun
That him in song or wisdom mighte passe.
I have wel rad in daun Burnel the Asse,[132]
Among his vers, how that ther was a cok,
For that a preestes sone yaf him a knok
Upon his leg, whyl he was yong and nyce,
He made him for to lese his benefyce.
But certeyn, ther nis no comparisoun
Bitwix the wisdom and discrecioun
Of youre fader, and of his subtiltee.
Now singeth, sire, for seinte Charitee,
Let see, conne ye your fader countrefete?'
This Chauntecleer his winges gan to bete,
As man that coude his tresoun nat espye,
So was he ravisshed with his flaterye.

Allas! ye lordes, many a fals flatour
Is in your courtes, and many a losengeour,
That plesen yow wel more, by my feith,
Than he that soothfastnesse unto yow seith.
Redeth Ecclesiaste[133] of flaterye;
Beth war, ye lordes, of hir trecherye.

This Chauntecleer stood hye up-on his toos,
Strecching his nekke, and heeld his eyen cloos,
And gan to crowe loude for the nones;
And daun Russel the fox sterte up at ones,
And by the gargat hente Chauntecleer,
And on his bak toward the wode him beer,
For yet ne was ther no man that him sewed.
O destinee, that mayst nat been eschewed!
Allas, that Chauntecleer fleigh fro the bemes!
Allas, his wyf ne roghte nat of dremes!
And on a Friday fil al this meschaunce.

O Venus, that art goddesse of plesaunce,
Sin that thy servant was this Chauntecleer,
And in thy service dide al his poweer,
More for delyt, than world to multiplye,
Why woldestow suffre him on thy day to dye?
O Gaufred,[134] dere mayster soverayn,
That, whan thy worthy king Richard was slayn
With shot, compleynedest his deth so sore,
Why ne hadde I now thy sentence and thy lore,
The Friday for to chyde, as diden ye?
(For on a Friday soothly slayn was he.)
Than wolde I shewe yow how that I coude pleyne
For Chauntecleres drede, and for his peyne.

Certes, swich cry ne lamentacioun
Was never of ladies maad, whan Ilioun
Was wonne, and Pirrus with his streite swerd,
Whan he hadde hent king Priam by the berd,
And slayn him (as saith us *Eneydos*),
As maden alle the hennes in the clos,
Whan they had seyn of Chauntecleer the sighte.
But sovereynly dame Pertelote shrighte,
Ful louder than dide Hasdrubales wyf,
Whan that hir housbond hadde lost his lyf,
And that the Romayns hadde brend Cartage;
She was so ful of torment and of rage,
That wilfully into the fyr she sterte,
And brende hir-selven with a stedfast herte.
O woful hennes, right so cryden ye,
As, whan that Nero brende the citee
Of Rome, cryden senatoures wyves,
For that hir housbondes losten alle hir lyves;
Withouten gilt this Nero hath hem slayn.
Now wol I torne to my tale agayn: —

This sely widwe, and eek hir doghtres two,
Herden thise hennes crye and maken wo,

---

[132] An Anglo-Latin satirical poem of the 12th century.
[133] The book of *Ecclesiasticus* in the *Apocrypha*.
[134] Geoffrey de Vinsauf, who wrote a bombastic lament for the death of Richard I.

And out at dores sterten they anoon,
And syen the fox toward the grove goon,
And bar upon his bak the cok away;
And cryden, 'Out! harrow! and weyla-way!
Ha, ha, the fox!' and after him they ran,
And eek with staves many another man;
Ran Colle our dogge, and Talbot, and Gerland,
And Malkin, with a distaf in hir hand;
Ran cow and calf, and eek the verray hogges
So were they fered for berking of the dogges
And shouting of the men and wimmen eke,
They ronne so, hem thoughte hir herte breke.
They yelleden as feendes doon in helle;
The dokes cryden as men wolde hem quelle;
The gees for fere flowen over the trees;
Out of the hyve cam the swarm of bees;
So hidous was the noyse, a! *benedicite!*
Certes, he Jakke Straw,[135] and his meynee,
Ne made never shoutes half so shrille,
Whan that they wolden any Fleming kille,
As thilke day was maad upon the fox.
Of bras thay broghten bemes, and of box,
Of horn, of boon, in whiche they blewe and pouped,
And therwithal thay shryked and they houped;
It semed as that heven sholde falle.
Now, gode men, I pray yow herkneth alle!
Lo, how fortune turneth sodeinly
The hope and pryde eek of hir enemy!
This cok, that lay upon the foxes bak,
In al his drede, un-to the fox he spak,
And seyde, 'sire, if that I were as ye,
Yet sholde I seyn (as wis god helpe me),
Turneth agayn, ye proude cherles alle!
A verray pestilence up-on yow falle!
Now am I come un-to this wodes syde,
Maugree your heed, the cok shal heer abyde;
I wol him ete in feith, and that anon.'—
The fox answerde, 'in feith, it shal be don,'—
And as he spak that word, al sodeinly
This cok brak from his mouth deliverly,
And heighe up-on a tree he fleigh anon.
And whan the fox saugh that he was y-gon,
'Allas!' quod he, 'O Chauntecleer, allas!
I have to yow,' quod he, 'y-doon trespas,
In-as-muche as I maked yow aferd,
Whan I yow hente, and broghte out of the yerd;
But, sire, I dide it in no wikke entente;
Com doun, and I shal telle yow what I mente.
I shal seye sooth to yow, god help me so.'
'Nay than,' quod he, 'I shrewe us bothe two,
And first I shrewe my-self, bothe blood and bones,
If thou bigyle me ofter than ones.
Thou shalt na-more, thurgh thy flaterye,
Do me to singe and winke with myn yë.
For he that winketh, whan he sholde see,
Al wilfully, god lat him never thee!'
'Nay,' quod the fox, 'but god yeve him meschaunce,
That is so undiscreet of governaunce,
That jangleth whan he sholde holde his pees.'
Lo, swich it is for to be recchelees,
And necligent, and truste on flaterye.
But ye that holden this tale a folye,
As of a fox, or of a cok and hen,
Taketh the moralitee, good men.
For seint Paul seith,[136] that al that writen is,
To our doctryne it is y-write, y-wis.
Taketh the fruyt, and lat the chaf be stille.
Now, gode god, if that it be thy wille,
As seith my lord, so make us alle good men;
And bringe us to his heighe blisse. Amen.

Here is ended the Nonne Preestes Tale

[135] Leader of the Peasants' Revolt in 1381.

[136] *II Timothy*, iii, 16.

Thomas Hoccleve

1370?–1450?

Hoccleve's Lament for Chaucer and Gower

from The Regement of Princes [1]

[Stanzas 281–283, 297–301]

'O, MAISTER deere, and fadir reverent!
Mi maister Chaucer, flour of eloquence,
Mirour of fructuous entendement,[2]
O, universel fadir in science![3]
Allas! that thou thyn excellent prudence
In thi bed mortel mightist naght byqwethe;
What eiled Deth? Allas! whi wolde he sle[4] the?

'O Deth! thou didest naght harme singuleer
In slaghtere of him; but al this land it smertith;
But nathelees, yit hast thou no power
His name sle; his hy vertu astertith[5]
Unslayn fro the, which ay us lyfly hertyth,[6]
With bookes of his ornat endytyng,
That is to al this land enlumynyng.

'Hast thou nat eeke my maister Gower slayn,
Whos vertu I am insufficient
For to descreyve?[7] I wote wel in certayn,
For to sleen al this world thou haast yment;
But syn our lorde Crist was obedient
To the, in feith I can no ferther seye;
His creatures mosten the obeye.'

. . .

Simple is my goost,[8] and scars my letterure,[9]
Unto your excellence for to write
Myn inward love, and yit in aventure[10]
Wyle I me putte, thogh I can but lyte.[11]
Mi dere maistir — God his soule quyte! —[12]
And fadir, Chaucer, fayn wolde han me taght;
But I was dul, and lerned lite or naght.

Allas! my worthi maister honorable,
This landes verray tresor and richesse,
Deth, by thi deth, hath harme irreparable
Unto us doon; hir vengeable duresse[13]
Despoiled hath this land of the swetnesse
Of rethorik; for unto Tullius[14]
Was never man so lyk amonges us.

Also, who was hier[15] in philosophie
To Aristotle, in our tonge, but thow?
The steppes of Virgile in poesie
Thow filwedist[16] eeke, men wot wel ynow.[17]
That combre-world,[18] that the, my maistir, slow,
Wold I slayn were! deth was to hastyf
To renne on the, and reve the thi lyf.

Deth hath but smal consideracioun
Unto the vertuous, I have espied,
No more, as shewith the probacioun,
Than to a vicious maistir losel[19] tried;
Among an heep, every man is maistried;
With hire, as wel the porre as is the riche;
Lered[20] and lewde[21] eeke standen al yliche.[22]

She myghte han taried hir vengeance awhile,
Til that sum man had egal to the be.
Nay, lat be that! sche knew wel that this yle[23]

[1] Hoccleve wrote the *Regement* (*i.e.*, Government) in 1411–1412 to curry favor with the Prince of Wales, later Henry V. It is a vast moral poem which discusses everything from the reasons why women must be better than men to the reasons why Henry ought to provide for poets.
[2] intelligence
[3] knowledge
[4] slay
[5] escapeth
[6] enheartens
[7] describe
[8] spirit
[9] learning
[10] venture
[11] little
[12] requite
[13] cruelty
[14] Marcus Tullius Cicero
[15] heir
[16] didst follow
[17] enough
[18] useless thing
[19] vicious maister, *etc.* One proved to be a vicious master-rogue.
[20] learned
[21] lowly
[22] alike
[23] isle

May never man forth brynge lyk to the,
And hir office [24] needes so mot she;
God bad hir so, I truste as for thi beste;
O maister, maister, god thi soule reste!

Hoccleve's Humorous Praise of his Lady [25]

Of my lady, wel me rejoise I may:
Hir golden forheed is ful narw [26] and smal;
Hir browes been lyk to dym reed coral;
And as the jeet [27] hir yen [28] glistren ay.

Hir bowgy [29] cheekes been as softe as clay,
With large jowes [30] and substancial.
Of my lady, wel me rejoise I may:
Hir golden forheed is ful narw and smal;

[24] appointed task
[25] Hoccleve is satirising the extravagant lady-worship of his time. The form of the poem, the roundel, was introduced from France and extensively practised by Chaucer and his successors in the making of love poems.
[26] narrow
[27] jet
[28] eyes
[29] puffy
[30] jaws

Hir browes been lyk to dym reed coral;
And as the jeet hir yen glistren ay.

Hir nose a pentice [31] is, that it ne shal
Reyne [32] in hir mowth thogh shee uprightes lay.
Of my lady, wel me rejoise I may:
Hir golden forheed is ful narw and smal;
Hir browes been lyk to dym reed coral;
And as the jeet hir yen glistren ay.

Hir mowth is nothyng scant with lippes gray;
Hir chin unnethe [33] may be seen at al;
Hir comly body shape as a foot-bal:
And shee syngith ful lyk a papejay.[34]
Of my lady, wel me rejoise I may:
Hir golden forheed is ful narw and smal;
Hir browes been lyk to dym reed coral;
And as the jeet hir yen glistren ay.

[31] penthouse — the projecting roof of a building
[32] rain
[33] hardly
[34] parrot

Robert Henryson

1430?–1506?

Robin and Makin

Robene sat on gud grene hill,
Kepand a flok of fe,[1]
Mirry Makyne said him till,[2]
'Robene, thow rew [3] on me;
I haif the luvit lowd and still,[4]
Thir yeiris two or thre;
My dule in dern bot gif thow dill,
Doutless but dreid I de.' [5]

Robene answerit, 'Be the rude,[6]
Nathing of lufe I knaw,
Bot keipis my scheip undir yone wid,[7]

[1] sheep
[2] to
[3] have pity
[4] openly and secretly
[5] My dule, *etc.* Unless you soothe my secret sorrow, surely I shall die.
[6] By the cross
[7] wood

Lo quhair [8] thay raik on raw: [9]
Quhat hes marrit [10] the in thy mude,
Makyne, to me thow schaw;
Or quhat is lufe, or to be lude? [11]
Fane wald I leir [12] that law.'

'At luvis lair [13] gife [14] thow will leir,
Tak thair ane a, b, c;
Be heynd,[15] courtass, and fair of feir,[16]
Wyse, hardy, and fre; [17]
So that no denger do the deir,[18]
Quhat dule in dern thow dre; [19]
Preiss the [20] with pane at all poweir,
Be patient and previe.'

[8] where. (In the Scots dialect *qu* is equivalent to *w.*)
[9] move in a row
[10] undone
[11] loved
[12] learn
[13] lore
[14] if
[15] gentle
[16] demeanor
[17] bold and lavish
[18] harm
[19] suffer
[20] strive

Robene answerit hir agane,
'I wait [21] nocht quhat is luve;
But I haif mervell in certane
Quhat makis the this wanrufe: [22]
The weddir is fair, and I am fane,
My scheip gois haill aboif; [23]
And [24] we wald play us in this plane,
Thay wald us bayth reproif.'

'Robene, tak tent [25] unto my taill,
And wirk all as I reid,
And thow sall haif my hairt all haill,
Eik and my maidenheid.
Sen [26] God sendis bute for baill [27]
And for murnyng remeid,
In dern with the, bot gif I daill,[28]
Dowtles I am bot deid.'

'Makyne, to morne this ilk a tyde,[29]
And ye will meet me heir,
Peraventure my scheip may gang besyd,[30]
Quhill we haif liggit [31] full neir;
Bot mawgre haif I and I byd,
Fra thay begin to steir; [32]
Quhat lyis on hairt I will nocht hyd;
Makyn, than mak gud cheir.'

'Robene, thow reivis me roif [33] and rest;
I luve bot the allone.'
'Makyne, adew, the sone gois west,
The day is neir hand gone.'
'Robene, in dule I am so drest,[34]
That lufe wilbe my bone.'
'Ga lufe, Makyne, quhair evir thow list,
For lemman [35] I lue nane.'

'Robene, I stand in sic a styll; [36]
I sicht,[37] and that full sair.'
'Makyne, I haif bene heir this quhyle;
At hame God gif I wair.' [38]
'My huny, Robene, talk ane quhill,
Gif thow will do na mair.'

'Makyne, sum uthir man begyle,
For hamewart I will fair.'

Robene on his wayis went,
Als licht [39] as leif of tre;
Mawkin murnit in hir intent,[40]
And trowd him nevir to se.
Robene brayd atour the bent; [41]
Than Mawkyne cryit on hie,
'Now ma thow sing, for I am schent.[42]
Quhat alis lufe at me?' [43]

Mawkyne went hame withowttin faill,
Full wery eftir cowth weip: [44]
Than Robene in a ful fair daill
Assemblit all his scheip.
Be that sum pairte of Mawkynis aill
Outthrow his hairt cowd creip;
He fallowit hir fast thair till assaill,
And till hir tuke gude keip.

'Abyd, abyd, thow fair Makyne,
A word for ony thing;
For all my luve it sal be thyne,
Withowttin depairting.
All haill thy harte for till haif myne [45]
Is all my cuvating;
My scheip to morne quhill [46] houris nyne
Will neid of no keping.'

'Robene, thow hes hard soung and say,
In gestis and storeis auld,
"The man that will nocht quhen he may
Sall haif nocht quhen he wald."
I pray to Jesu every day
Mot eik [47] thair cairis cauld,
That first preissis [48] with the to play,
Be firth,[49] forrest, or fawld.'

'Makyne, the nicht is soft and dry,
The wedder is warme and fair,
And the grene woid [50] rycht neir us by
To walk attour all quhair;

[21] wot
[22] unhappiness
[23] together up the hill
[24] if
[25] heed (attention)
[26] since
[27] recompense for harm
[28] In dern with, *etc.* In secret with thee unless I deal.
[29] same time
[30] astray
[31] lain
[32] Bot mawgre, *etc.* But an uneasy feeling have I, if I stay when they begin to stir.
[33] bereavest me of quiet
[34] in sorrow I am so fixed
[35] lover
[36] state
[37] sigh
[38] God grant I were.

[39] light
[40] thought
[41] hurried over the field
[42] lost
[43] What has love against me?
[44] did weep
[45] All haill, *etc.* Wholly thy heart for to have mine.
[46] till
[47] increase
[48] try
[49] wood
[50] wood

Thair ma na janglour [51] us espy,
  That is to lufe contrair;
Thairin, Makyne, bath ye and I
  Unsene we ma repair.'

'Robene, that warld is all away
  And quyt brocht till ane end,
And nevir agane thairto perfay [52]
  Sall it be as thow wend; [53]
For of my pane thow maid it play,
  And all in vane I spend;
As thow hes done, sa sall I say,
  Murne on, I think to mend.'

'Mawkyne, the howp of all my heill,[54]
  My hairt on the is sett,

[51] gossip
[52] *par foi*
[53] thought (weened)
[54] hope of all my health

And evirmair to the be leill,[55]
  Quhill I may leif but lett; [56]
Nevir to faill, as utheris feill,
  Quhat grace that evir I gett.'
'Robene, with the I will nocht deill;
  Adew, for thus we mett.'

Malkyne went hame blyth annewche,[57]
  Attour the holttis hair; [58]
Robene murnit, and Malkyne lewche,[59]
  Scho sang, he sichit sair;
And so left him, bayth wo and wrewche,[60]
  In dolour and in cair,
Kepand his hird under a huche,[61]
  Amangis the holtis hair.

[55] loyal
[56] live without ceasing
[57] enough
[58] hoary woods
[59] laughed
[60] woeful and wretched
[61] cliff

William Dunbar

1465?–1530?

Lament for the Makaris [1] *Quhen* [2] *He Wes Seik*

I THAT in heill [3] wes and glaidnes,
Am trublit now with gret seiknes,
And feblit with infirmitie;
  Timor Mortis conturbat me.[4]

Our plesance heir is all vane glory,
This fals warld is bot transitory,
The flesche is brukle,[5] the Fend is sle; [6]
  Timor Mortis conturbat me.

The stait of man dois change et vary,
Now sound, now seik, now blyth, now
    sary,
Now dansand mirry, now like to dee;
  Timor Mortis conturbat me.

No stait in erd heir standis sickir; [7]
As with the wynd wavis the wickir,[8]
So wavis this warldis vanite;
  Timor Mortis conturbat me.

[1] poets
[2] when
[3] health
[4] Fear of Death disquiets me.
[5] brittle
[6] sly
[7] sure
[8] willow-branch

Onto the ded gois all Estatis,
Princis, Prelotis, and Potestatis,
Baith riche et pur of all degre;
  Timor Mortis conturbat me.

He takis the knychtis in to feild,
Anarmit [9] under helme et scheild;
Wictour he is at all melle; [10]
  Timor Mortis conturbat me.

That strang unmercifull tyrand
Takis on the moderis breist sowkand
The bab, full of benignite;
  Timor Mortis conturbat me.

He takis the campion [11] in the stour,[12]
The capitane closit in the tour,
The lady in bour full of bewte;
  Timor Mortis conturbat me.

He spairis no lord for his piscence,[13]
Na clerk for his intelligence;
His awfull strak may no man fle;
  Timor Mortis conturbat me.

[9] armed
[10] contest
[11] champion, warrior
[12] battle
[13] power

Art, magicianis, and astrologgis,
Rethoris, logicianis, et theologgis,
Thame helpis no conclusions sle;
  Timor Mortis conturbat me.

In medicyne the most practicianis,
Lechis, surrigianis, et phisicianis,
Thame self fra ded may not supple; [14]
  Timor Mortis conturbat me.

I see that makaris amang the laif [15]
Playis heir ther pageant, syne [16] gois to graif;
Sparit is nocht ther faculte; [17]
  Timor Mortis conturbat me.

He hes done petuously devour,
The noble Chaucer, of makaris flouir,
The Monk [18] of Berry, and Gower, all thre;
  Timor Mortis conturbat me.

The gude Syr Hew of Eglintoun,[19]
Et eik, Heryot, et Wyntoun,
He hes tane out of this cuntre;
  Timor Mortis conturbat me.

That scorpioun fell hes done infek
Maister Johne Clerk, and James Afflek,
Fra balat making et trigide;
  Timor Mortis conturbat me.

Holland et Barbour he has berevit;
Allace! that he nought with us levit [20]
Schir Mungo Lokert of the Le;
  Timor Mortis conturbat me.

Clerk of Tranent eik he has tane,
That maid the anteris [21] of Gawane;
Schir Gilbert Hay endit has he;
  Timor Mortis conturbat me.

[14] help
[15] left (rest)
[16] then
[17] profession
[18] Lydgate
[19] Syr Hew, *etc.* Dunbar reviews the great names of Scottish song, from Barbour, who died in 1395, to men who were contemporary with himself.
[20] leaves
[21] adventures

He has Blind Hary, et Sandy Traill
Slaine with his schour of mortall haill,
Quhilk [22] Patrik Johnestoun myght nought fle;
  Timor Mortis conturbat me.

He hes reft Merseir his endite,[23]
That did in luf so lifly write,
So schort, so quyk, of sentence [24] hie;
  Timor Mortis conturbat me.

He hes tane Roull of Aberdene,
And gentill Roull of Corstorphine;
Two bettir fallowis did no man se;
  Timor Mortis conturbat me.

In Dumfermelyne he has done roune [25]
With Maister Robert Henrisoun;
Schir Johne the Ros embrast hes he;
  Timor Mortis conturbat me.

And he has now tane, last of aw,
Gud gentill Stobo et Quintyne Schaw,
Of quham [26] all wichtis [27] hes pete:
  Timor Mortis conturbat me.

Gud Maister Walter Kennedy,
In poynt of dede lyis veraly,
Gret reuth [28] it wer that so suld be;
  Timor Mortis conturbat me.

Sen he has all by brether tane,
He will naught lat me lif alane,
On forse I man [29] his nyxt pray be;
  Timor Mortis conturbat me.

Sen for the deid remeid is non,
Best is that we for dede dispone.
Eftir our deid that lif may we;
  Timor Mortis conturbat me.

Quod Dunbar quhen he wes seik, etc.

[22] which
[23] writing
[24] meaning
[25] ruin
[26] whom
[27] wights (men)
[28] pity
[29] must

Followis How Dumbar Wes Desyrd to be Ane Freir[30]

THIS nycht befoir the dawing cleir,
Me thocht Sanct Francis did to me appeir,
With ane religiouss abbeit[31] in his hand,
And said, 'In thiss go cleith[32] the my serwand;
Reffuss the warld, for thow mon be a freir.'

With him and with his abbeit bayth I skarrit,[33]
Lyk to ane man that with a gaist wes marrit:[34]
Me thocht on bed he layid it me abone,
Bot on the flure delyverly[35] and sone
I lap thairfra, and nevir wald cum nar it.

Quoth he, 'Quhy skarris thow with this holy weid?[36]
Cleith the thairin, for weir it thow most neid;
Thow, that hes lang done Venus lawis teiche,
Sall now be freir, and in this abbeit preiche;
Delay it nocht, it mon be done but dreid.'[37]

Quod I, 'Sanct Francis, loving be the till,[38]
And thankit mot thow be of thy gude will
To me, that of thy clayis[39] ar so kynd;
Bot thame to weir it nevir come in my mynd;
Sweit Confessour, thow tak it nocht in ill.

In haly legendis haif I hard allevin,[40]
Ma[41] sanctis of bischoppis, nor[42] freiris, be sic sevin;[43]
Off full few freiris that hes bene sanctis I reid;
Quhairfoir ga bring to me ane bischopis weid,
Gife evir thow wald my saule gaid unto Hevin.

My brethir oft hes maid the supplicationis,
Be epistillis, sermonis, and relationis,
To tak the abyte, bot thow did postpone;
But ony process,[44] cum on thairfoir annone,
All sircumstance put by and excusationis.

Gif evir my fortoun wes to be a freir,
The dait thairof is past full mony a yeir;
For into every lusty toun and place
Off all Yngland, frome Berwick to Kalice,
I haif in to thy habeit maid gud cheir.

In freiris weid full fairly haif I fleichit,[45]
In it haif I in pulpet gon and preichit
In Derntoun kirk, and eik in Canterberry;
In it I past at Dover our[46] the ferry
Throw Piccardy, and thair the peple teichit.

Als lang as I did beir the freiris style,
In me, God wait, wes mony wrink[47] and wyle;
In me wes falset[48] with every wicht to flatter,
Quhilk mycht be flemit[49] with na haly watter;
I wes ay reddy all men to begyle.

This freir that did Sanct Francis thair appeir,
Ane fieind he wes in liknes of ane freir;
He vaneist away with stynk and fyrie smowk;
With him me thocht all the houshend[50] he towk,
And I awoik as wy[51] that wes in weir.[52]

Quod Dumbar.

---

[30] Dunbar had actually been a novice of the Franciscan order. When he speaks, in lines 34–40, of his journeys in the habit of the order, he is telling the truth.
[31] monk's habit (robe)
[32] clothe
[33] was frightened
[34] astonished
[35] quickly
[36] garment
[37] without fear
[38] to
[39] clothes
[40] alleged
[41] more
[42] than
[43] seven, *i.e.*, a great many
[44] without more ado
[45] flattered
[46] over
[47] trick
[48] falsehood
[49] banished
[50] gable
[51] man
[52] doubt

To a Ladye

Sweit roiss of vertew and of gentilnes,
Delytsum lyllie of everie lustynes,[53]
Richest in bontie,[54] and in bewtie cleir,
And everie vertew that is held most deir,
Except onlie that ye ar mercyless.

In to your garthe [55] this day I did persew,
Thair saw I flowris that fresche wer of hew;
Baithe quhyte and reid moist [56] lusty wer to seyne,
And halsum herbis upone stalkis grene;
Yit leif nor flour fynd could I nane of rew.

I dout that Merche, with his cauld blastis keyne,
Hes slane this gentill herbe, that I of mene;
Quhois petewous [57] deithe dois to my hart sic pane
That I wald mak to plant his rute agane,
So confortand his levis unto me bene.

Quod Dumbar.

[53] pleasure
[54] goodness (French *bonté*)
[55] garden
[56] most
[57] whose piteous

John Skelton

1460?–1529

To Mistress Isabel Pennell

from A ryght delectable tratyse upon a goodly Garland or Chapelet of Lawrell, 1523 [1]

By Saint Mary, my lady,
Your mammy and your daddy
Brought forth a goodly baby!

My maiden Isabel,
Reflaring rosabel,[2]
The fragrant camomel;
The ruddy rosary,
The sovereign rosemary,
The pretty strawberry;
The columbine, the nept,
The gillyflower [3] well set,
The proper violet:
Ennewéd [4] your colour
Is like the daisy flower
After the April shower;
Star of the morrow gray,
The blossom on the spray,
The freshest flower of May;
Maidenly demure,
Of womanhood the lure;
Wherefore I make you sure
It were an heavenly health,
It were an endless wealth,
A life for God himself,
To hear this nightingale
Among the birdes smale
Warbeling in the vale,
Dug, dug,
Jug, jug,
Good year and good luck,
With chuck, chuck, chuck, chuck!

[1] In the vision poem from which this and the following lyrics are taken Skelton describes magniloquently how he was allowed to thrust himself among the great poets of the past in their 'college above the starry sky.' He is there commanded to give poetical thanks to various ladies who have been weaving the garland for him.
[2] fragrant fair rose
[3] pink or carnation
[4] freshened

To Mistress Margaret Hussey

Merry Margaret,
As midsummer flower,
Gentle as falcon
Or hawk of the tower: [5]
With solace and gladness,
Much mirth and no madness,
All good and no badness;
So joyously,
So maidenly,
So womanly
Her demeaning
In every thing,
Far, far passing
That I can indite,
Or suffice to write
Of Merry Margaret

[5] The tower-hawk was specially bred to fly high.

As midsummer flower,
Gentle as falcon
Or hawk of the tower.
As patient and still
And as full of good will
As fair Isaphill,[6]
Coliander,[7]
Sweet pomander,[8]
Good Cassander,[9]
Steadfast of thought,
Well made, well wrought,
Far may be sought
Ere that he can find
So courteous, so kind
As Merry Margaret,
This midsummer flower,
Gentle as falcon
Or hawk of the tower.

To Mistress Gertrude Statham

Though ye were hard-hearted,
And I with you thwarted

[6] Hypsipyle, of Lemnos, renowned for her beauty.
[7] coriander (an aromatic herb)
[8] A ball of sweet herbs worn against infection.
[9] Cassandra, daughter of Priam.

With wordes that smarted,
Yet now doubtless ye give me cause
To write of you this goodly clause,
Mistress Gertrude,
With womanhood endued,
With virtue well renewed.
I will that ye shall be
In all benignity
Like to Dame Pasiphae;[10]
For now doubtless ye give me cause
To write of you this goodly clause,
Mistress Gertrude,
With womanhood endued,
With virtue well renewed.
Partly by your counsel,
Garnished with laurel
Was my fresh coronal;
Wherefore doubtless ye give me cause
To write of you this goodly clause,
Mistress Gertrude,
With womanhood endued,
With virtue well renewed.

[10] The wife of Minos of Crete.

Sir Thomas Wyatt

1503?–1542

Description of the Contrarious Passions in a Lover

I find no peace, and all my war is done;
I fear and hope; I burn, and freeze like ice;
I fly aloft, yet can I not arise;
And nought I have, and all the world I season.[1]
That locks nor looseth holdeth me in prison,
And holds me not, yet can I 'scape no wise;
Nor lets me live, nor die, at my devise,
And yet of death it giveth me occasion.
Without eye, I see; without tongue, I plain;
I wish to perish, yet I ask for health;
I love another, and thus I hate myself;
I feed me in sorrow, and laugh in all my pain.
Lo, thus displeaseth me both death and life,
And my delight is causer of this strife.

[Tottel's *Songs and Sonetts,* 1557]

[1] seize upon, as a hawk its prey

A Renouncing of Love

Farewell, love, and all thy laws for ever,
Thy baited hooks shall tangle me no more;
Senec[2] and Plato call me from thy lore
To perfect wealth, my wit for to endeavour;
In blinde error when I did persévere,

[2] Seneca, the Latin writer of tragedies, was a favorite author with Wyatt.

Thy sharp repulse that pricketh aye so sore
Taught me in trifles that I set no store,
But scape forth thence, since liberty is lever.
Therefore, farewell! Go trouble younger hearts,
And in me claim no more authority;
With idle youth go use thy property,
And thereon spend thy many brittle darts.
For hitherto though I have lost my time,
Me list no longer rotten boughs to climb.

[Tottel's *Songs and Sonetts,* 1557]

Unstable dream, according to the place

UNSTABLE dream, according to the place,
Be steadfast once: or else at least be true:
By tasted sweetness make me not to rue
The sudden loss of thy false feignéd grace.
By good respect, in such a dangerous case,
Thou brought'st not her into these tossing seas,
But madest my sprite to live my care t'encrease,
My body in tempest her delight t'embrace.
The body dead, the sprite had his desire;
Painless was th' one: the other in delight;
Why then, alas! did it not keep it right,
But thus return to leap into the fire?
And where it was at wish could not remain.
Such mocks of dreams do turn to deadly pain.

[Tottel's *Songs and Sonetts,* 1557]

Divers doth use, as I have heard and know

DIVERS doth use, as I have heard and know,
(When that to change their ladies do begin),
To moan and wail, and never for to lin,[3]
Hoping thereby to pease[4] their painful woe.
And some there be, that when it chanceth so
That women change, and hate where love hath been,
They call them false, and think with words to win
The hearts of them which otherwhere doth go.
But as for me, though that by chance indeed
Change hath outworn the favour that I had,
I will not wail, lament, nor yet be sad,
Nor call her false that falsely did me feed;
But let it pass, and think it is of kind[5]
That often change doth please a woman's mind.

Alas! madam, for stealing of a kiss

ALAS! madam, for stealing of a kiss,
Have I so much your mind therein offended?
Or have I done so grievously amiss,
That by no means it may be amended?
Revenge you then; the readiest way is this:
Another kiss, my life it shall have ended.
For to my mouth the first my heart did suck,
The next shall clean out of my breast it pluck.

[Tottel's *Songs and Sonetts,* 1557]

The Lover Showeth How He is Forsaken of Such as He Sometime Enjoyed

THEY flee from me, that sometime did me seek,
With naked foot stalking within my chamber.
Once have I seen them gentle, tame, and meek,
That now are wild, and do not once remember
That sometime they have put themselves in danger

[3] cease [4] appease [5] nature

To take bread at my hand; and now they range,
Busily seeking in continual change.
Thanked be fortune it hath been otherwise,
Twenty times better; but once especial,
In thin array, after a pleasant guise,
When her loose gown did from her shoulders fall,
And she me caught in her arms long and small,
And therewithal so sweetly did me kiss
And softly said, 'Dear heart, how like you this?'
It was no dream, for I lay broad awaking.
But all is turned now, through my gentleness,
Into a bitter fashion of forsaking;
And I have leave to go, of her goodness,
And she also to use newfangleness.[6]
But since that I unkindly so am served,
How like you this? what hath she now deserved?

[Tottel's *Songs and Sonetts*, 1557]

Forget not yet the tried intent

Forget not yet the tried intent
Of such a truth as I have meant,
My great travail, so gladly spent,
Forget not yet.

Forget not yet when first began
The weary life ye know, since when
The suit, the service none tell can,
Forget not yet.

Forget not yet the great assays,
The cruel wrong, the scornful ways;
The painful patience in denays,
Forget not yet.

Forget not yet, forget not this,
How long ago hath been, and is,
The mind that never meant amiss,
Forget not yet.

Forget not, then, thine own approved,
The which so long hath thee so loved,
Whose steadfast faith yet never moved;
Forget not this.

The Lover Complaineth the Unkindness of his Love

My lute, awake, perform the last
Labour that thou and I shall waste,
And end that I have now begun;
And when this song is sung and past,
My lute, be still, for I have done.
As to be heard where ear is none,
As lead to grave in marble stone,
My song may pierce her heart as soon.
Should we then sigh, or sing, or moan?
No, no, my lute, for I have done.
The rocks do not so cruelly
Repulse the waves continually,
As she my suit and affection;
So that I am past remedy,
Whereby my lute and I have done.
Proud of the spoil that thou hast got
Of simple hearts, through lovè's shot;
By whom unkind thou hast them won,
Think not he hath his bow forgot,
Although my lute and I have done.
Vengeance shall fall on thy disdain,
That makest but game on earnest pain;
Think not alone under the sun
Unquit to cause thy lovers plain,
Although my lute and I have done.
May chance thee lie withered and old,
In winter nights that are so cold,
Plaining in vain unto the moon;
Thy wishes then dare not be told.
Care then who list, for I have done.
And then may chance thee to repent
The time that thou hast lost and spent
To cause thy lovers sigh and swoon;
Then shalt thou know beauty but lent,
And wish and want as I have done.
Now cease, my lute, this is the last
Labour that thou and I shall waste,
And ended is that we begun.
Now is this song both sung and past,
My lute, be still, for I have done.

[Tottel's *Songs and Sonetts*, 1557]

[6] inconstancy

And wilt thou leave me thus?

And wilt thou leave me thus?
Say nay, say nay, for shame,
To save thee from the blame
Of all my grief and grame; [7]
And wilt thou leave me thus!
Say nay, say nay!

And wilt thou leave me thus,
That hath loved thee so long,
In wealth and woe among?
And is thy heart so strong
As for to leave me thus?
Say nay, say nay!

And wilt thou leave me thus,
That hath given thee my heart,
Never for to depart,
Neither for pain or smart;
And wilt thou leave me thus!
Say nay, say nay!

And wilt thou leave me thus,
And have no more pitý
Of him that loveth thee?
Alas, thy cruelty!
And wilt thou leave me thus!
Say nay, say nay!

[7] anger

Henry Howard, Earl of Surrey

1517?–1547

Description of Spring, wherein Each Thing Renews Save Only the Lover [1]

The soote [2] season that bud and bloom forth brings
With green hath clad the hill and eke the vale,
The nightingale with feathers new she sings,
The turtle to her make [3] hath told her tale.
Summer is come, for every spray now springs,
The hart hath hung his old head on the pale,
The buck in brake his winter coat he flings,
The fishes float with new repairéd scale,
The adder all her slough away she slings,
The swift swallow pursueth the flyės smale,
The busy bee her honey now she mings,—
Winter is worn, that was the flowers' bale:
And thus I see, among these pleasant things
Each care decays—and yet my sorrow springs.

[Tottel's *Songs and Sonetts*, 1557]

[1] Surrey adapted this sonnet from one of Petrarch's beginning: *Zefiro torna, e 'l bel tempo rimena*, but he makes the spring an English spring. [2] sweet [3] mate

Complaint of a Lover Rebuked

Love that doth reign and live within my thought,
And built his seat within my captive breast,
Clad in the arms wherein with me he fought,
Oft in my face he doth his banner rest.
But she that taught me love and suffer pain,
My doubtful hope and eke my hot desire
With shamefast look to shadow and refrain,
Her smiling grace converteth straight to ire.
And coward Love, then, to the heart apace
Taketh his flight, where he doth lurke and plain
His purpose lost, and dare not shew his face.
For my lord's guilt thus faultless bide I pain;
Yet from my lord shall not my foot remove:
Sweet is the death that taketh end by love.

Description and Praise of his Love Geraldine [4]

From Tuscan came my lady's worthy race;
Fair Florence was sometime her ancient seat;
The western isle, whose pleasant shore doth face
Wild Camber's cliffs, did give her lively heat;
Fostered she was with milk of Irish breast;
Her sire an earl, her dame of princes' blood;
From tender years in Britain she doth rest,
With king's child, where she tasteth costly food;
Hunsdon did first present her to mine eyne;
Bright is her hue, and Geraldine she hight;
Hampton me taught to wish her first for mine,
And Windsor, alas! doth chase me from her sight.
Beauty, of kind; her virtues, from above;
Happy is he that can obtain her love.

[Tottel's *Songs and Sonetts,* 1557]

Prisoned in Windsor, he Recounteth his Pleasure there Passed

So cruel prison how could betide, alas,
As proud Windsor? Where I in lust and joy
With a king's son my childish years did pass
In greater feast than Priam's sons of Troy;
Where each sweet place returns a taste full sour:
The large green courts where we were wont to hove
With eyes cast up into the maidens' tower,
And easy sighs, such as folk draw in love;
The stately seats, the ladies bright of hue,
The dances short, long tales of great delight;
With words and looks that tigers could but rue,
Where each of us did plead the other's right;
The palm play [5] where, despoiléd for the game,
With dazéd eyes oft we by gleams of love
Have missed the ball and got sight of our dame,
To bait her eyes, which kept the leads [6] above;
The gravel ground, with sleeves tied on the helm,
On foaming horse, with swords and friendly hearts,
With cheer, as though one should another whelm,
Where we have fought, and chaséd oft with darts;
With silver drops the mead yet spread for ruth,
In active games of nimbleness and strength,
Where we did strain, trainéd with swarms of youth,
Our tender limbs that yet shot up in length;
The secret groves which oft we made resound
Of pleasant plaint and of our ladies' praise,
Recording oft what grace each one had found,
What hope of speed,[7] what dread of long delays;
The wild forest, the clothéd holts [8] with green,
With reins avaled,[9] and swift ybreathéd horse,
With cry of hounds and merry blasts between,
Where we did chase the fearful hart of force;
The wild vales eke that harboured us each night,
Wherewith, alas! reviveth in my breast

---

[4] The little daughter of Gerald Fitzgerald, Earl of Kildare, is the subject of this poem. Surrey had seen the Irish girl, we suppose, for the first time at Hunsdon House. Since she was nine at the time, this could hardly have been a serious affair. If the poem was written in July 1537, Surrey was then confined at Windsor Castle.

[5] An old form of tennis, rather like modern handball.
[6] leaded roofs
[7] fortune
[8] woods
[9] slackened

The sweet accord; such sleeps as yet delight,
The pleasant dreams, the quiet bed of rest;
The secret thoughts imparted with such trust,
The wanton talk, the divers change of play,
The friendship sworn, each promise kept so just,
Wherewith we passed the winter night away.
And with this thought the blood forsakes the face,
The tears berain my cheeks of deadly hue,
The which as soon as sobbing sighs, alas!
Upsuppéd have, thus I my plaint renew:
'O place of bliss! renewer of my woes!
Give me account—where is my noble fere?[10]
Whom in thy walls thou dost each night enclose,
To other lief, but unto me most dear!'
Echo, alas! that doth my sorrow rue,
Returns thereto a hollow sound of plaint.
Thus I alone, where all my freedom grew,
In prison pine with bondage and restraint;
And with remembrance of the greater grief
To banish the less, I find my chief relief.

[Tottel's *Songs and Sonetts,* 1557]

London, hast thou accuséd me[11]

LONDON, hast thou accuséd me
Of breach of laws, the root of strife?
Within whose breast did boil to see,
So fervent hot, thy dissolute life,
That even the hate of sins that grow
Within thy wicked walls so rife,
For to break forth did convert so
That terror could not it repress.
The which, by words, since preachers know
What hope is left for to redress,
By unknown means it likéd me
My hidden burden to express,
Whereby it might appear to thee
That secret sin hath secret spite,
From justice' rod no fault is free;
But that all such as work unright
In most quiet are next ill rest.
In secret silence of the night
This made me, with a reckless breast,
To wake thy sluggards with my bow—
A figure of the Lord's behest,
Whose scourge for sin the Scriptures show.
That, as the fearful thunder-clap
By sudden flame at hand we know,
Of pebble-stones the soundless rap
The dreadful plague might make thee see
Of God's wrath that doth thee enwrap;
That pride might know, from conscience free
How lofty works may her defend;
And envy find, as he hath sought
How other seek him to offend;
And wrath taste of each cruel thought,
The just shapp[12] higher in the end;
And idle sloth, that never wrought,
To heaven his spirit lift may begin;
And greedy lucre live in dread
To see what hate ill-got goods win;
The lechers, ye that lusts do feed,
Perceive what secrecy is in sin;
And gluttons' hearts for sorrow bleed,
Awakéd, when their fault they find:
In loathsome vice each drunken wight[13]
To stir to God, this was my mind.
Thy windows had done me no spite,
But proud people that dread no fall,
Clothéd with falsehood and unright,
Bred in the closures of thy wall;
But wrested to wrath in fervent zeal,
Thou haste to strife, my secret call.
Enduréd hearts no warning feel;
O shameless whore, is dread then gone
By such thy foes as meant thy weal?
O member of false Babylon!
The shop of craft! the den of ire!
Thy dreadful doom draws fast upon;
Thy martyrs' blood, by sword and fire,
In heaven and earth for justice call.
The Lord shall hear their just desire,

---

[10] companion; Henry Fitzroy, Duke of Richmond, natural son of Henry VIII by Elizabeth Blount.

[11] This violent invective was hardly deserved by the action of the city constables in locking up in the Fleet prison Surrey, the younger Sir Thomas Wyatt, son of the poet, and their companions. Their window-breaking escapade took place in April 1543.

[12] This may be read from the manuscript 'shall be.'

[13] man

The flame of wrath shall on thee fall,
With famine and pest lamentably
Stricken shall be thy lechers all;
Thy proud towers and turrets high,
Enemies to God, beat stone from stone,
Thine idols burnt that wrought iniquity;
When none thy ruin shall bemoan,
But render unto the right wise Lord
That so hath judgéd Babylon,
Immortal praise with one accord.

Elizabethan Miscellanies

In the sixteenth century courtly poets usually did not publish their work as soon as it was written. Copies of their verses circulated among their friends, and often manuscript collections made up by their admirers got into the hands of enterprising printers. These miscellanies were then issued with such fanciful names as *A Gorgeous Gallery of Gallant Inventions* (1578), *The Forest of Fancy* (1579), *The Phoenix Nest* (1593), *A Poetical Rhapsody* (1602). Many of the poems by authors of this period, here printed under their names, were first read by the public in these miscellanies.

The aged Lover renounceth Love [1]

I loathe that I did love,
  In youth that I thought sweet,
As time requires for my behove,
  Methinks they are not meet.

My lusts they do me leave,
  My fancies all be fled,
And tract of time begins to weave
  Grey hairs upon my head.

For age with stealing steps
  Hath clawed me with his crutch,
And lusty life away she leaps
  As there had been none such.

My Muse doth not delight
  Me as she did before;
My hand and pen are not in plight,
  As they have been of yore.

For reason me denies
  This youthly idle rhyme;
And day by day to me she cries,
  'Leave off these toys in time.'

The wrinkles in my brow,
  The furrows in my face,
Say limping age will hedge him now
  Where youth must give him place.

The harbinger of death,
  To me I see him ride,
The cough, the cold, the gasping breath
  Doth bid me to provide

A pickaxe and a spade,
  And eke a shrouding sheet,
A house of clay for to be made
  For such a guest most meet.

Methinks I hear the clark
  That knolls the careful [2] knell,
And bids me leave my woeful wark,
  Ere nature me compel.

My keepers knit the knot
  That youth did laugh to scorn,
Of me that clean shall be forgot
  As I had not been born.

Thus must I youth give up,
  Whose badge I long did wear;
To them I yield the wanton cup
  That better may it bear.

Lo, here the baréd skull,
  By whose bald sign I know
That stooping age away shall pull
  Which youthful years did sow.

For beauty with her band
  These crooked cares hath wrought,

[1] The First Gravedigger sings snatches of this popular lyric in *Hamlet*, V, 2.

[2] full of care

And shippéd me into the land
  From whence I first was brought.

And ye that bide behind,
  Have ye none other trust:
As ye of clay were cast by kind,
  So shall ye waste to dust.

[Lord Vaux, Tottel's *Songs and Sonetts*, 1557]

The Lullaby of a Lover

Sing lullaby, as women do,
  Wherewith they bring their babes to rest;
And lullaby can I sing too,
  As womanly as can the best.
With lullaby they still the child;
And, if I be not much beguiled,
Full many wanton babes have I,
Which must be stilled with lullaby.

First, lullaby my youthful years,
  It is now time to go to bed;
For crooked age and hoary hairs
  Have won the haven within my head.
With lullaby, then, youth be still!
With lullaby content thy will!
Since courage quails and comes behind,
Go sleep, and so beguile thy mind!

Next, lullaby my gazing eyes,
  Which wonted were to glance apace;
For every glass may now suffice
  To show the furrows in my face.
With lullaby, then, wink [3] awhile!
With lullaby your looks beguile!
Let no fair face, nor beauty bright,
Entice you eft [4] with vain delight.

And lullaby my wanton will;
  Let reason's rule now reign thy thought,
Since all too late I find by skill
  How dear I have thy fancies bought.
With lullaby now take thine ease!
With lullaby thy doubts appease!
For trust to this, if thou be still,
My body shall obey thy will.

Eke lullaby my loving boy;
  My little Robin, take thy rest!
Since age is cold and nothing coy,
  Keep close thy coin, for so is best.
With lullaby be thou content!
With lullaby thy lusts relent!
Let others pay which have mo [5] pence,
Thou art too poor for such expense.

Thus, lullaby my youth, mine eyes,
  My will, my ware, and all that was:
I can no mo delays devise;
  But welcome pain, let pleasure pass.
With lullaby now take your leave!
With lullaby your dreams deceive!
And when you rise with waking eye,
Remember Gascoigne's lullaby!

[George Gascoigne, *A Hundreth Sundry Flowers*, 1573]

A new Courtly Sonnet of the Lady Greensleeves

Greensleeves was all my joy,
  Greensleeves was my delight;
Greensleeves was my heart of gold,
  And who but Lady Greensleeves?

Alas, my Love! ye do me wrong
  To cast me off discourteously:
And I have lovéd you so long,
  Delighting in your company.
    Greensleeves was all my joy, &c.

I have been ready at your hand,
  To grant whatever you would crave.
I have both wagéd [6] life and land,
  Your love and goodwill for to have.
    Greensleeves was all my joy, &c.

I bought thee kerchers to thy head,
  That were wrought fine and gallantly:
I kept thee both at board and bed,
  Which cost my purse well favouredly,[7]
    Greensleeves was all my joy, &c.

I bought thee petticoats of the best,
  The cloth so fine as fine might be:

[3] close the eyes
[4] again
[5] more
[6] staked
[7] handsomely

I gave thee jewels for thy chest,
And all this cost I spent on thee.
Greensleeves was all my joy, &c.

Thy smock of silk, both fair and white,
With gold embroidered gorgeously:
Thy petticoat of sendal[8] right:
And thus I bought thee gladly.
Greensleeves was all my joy, &c.

Thy girdle of gold so red,
With pearls bedeckéd sumptuously:
The like no other lasses had,
And yet thou wouldst not love me.
Greensleeves was all my joy, &c.

Thy purse and eke thy gay gilt knives,
Thy pincase gallant to the eye,
No better wore the burgess' wives,
And yet thou wouldst not love me.
Greensleeves was all my joy, &c.

Thy crimson stockings all of silk,
With gold all wrought above the knee;
Thy pumps as white as was the milk,
And yet thou wouldst not love me.
Greensleeves was all my joy, &c.

Thy gown was of the grossy green,[9]
Thy sleeves of satin hanging by,
Which made thee be our harvest queen,
And yet thou wouldst not love me.
Greensleeves was all my joy, &c.

Thy garters fringéd with the gold,
And silver aglets[10] hanging by,
Which made thee blithe for to behold,
And yet thou wouldst not love me.
Greensleeves was all my joy, &c.

My gayest gelding I thee gave,
To ride wherever likéd thee;
No lady ever was so brave,
And yet thou wouldst not love me.
Greensleeves was all my joy, &c.

[8] A thin rich silk.
[9] The color of a vigorous plant.
[10] pendants

My men were clothéd all in green,
And they did ever wait on thee:
All this was gallant to be seen,
And yet thou wouldst not love me.
Greensleeves was all my joy, &c.

They set thee up, they took thee down,
They served thee with humility;
Thy foot might not once touch the ground,
And yet thou wouldst not love me.
Greensleeves was all my joy, &c.

For every morning when thou rose,
I sent thee dainties orderly,
To cheer thy stomack from all woes,
And yet thou wouldst not love me.
Greensleeves was all my joy, &c.

Thou couldst desire no earthly thing
But still thou hadst it readily:
Thy music[11] still to play and sing,
And yet thou wouldst not love me.
Greensleeves was all my joy, &c.

And who did pay for all this gear
That thou didst spend when pleaséd thee?
Even I that am rejected here,
And thou disdain'st to love me.
Greensleeves was all my joy, &c.

Well, I pray to God on high,
That thou my constancy may'st see,
And that yet once before I die,
Thou wilt vouchsafe to love me.
Greensleeves was all my joy, &c.

Greensleeves, now farewell! adieu!
God I pray to prosper thee:
For I am still thy lover true—
Come once again and love me.
Greensleeves was all my joy,
Greensleeves was my delight;
Greensleeves was my heart of gold,
And who but Lady Greensleeves.

[*A Handful of Pleasant Delights*, 1584]

[11] Private band of musicians.

A proper Song, entitled: Fain would I have a pretty Thing to give unto my Lady

FAIN would I have a pretty thing
  To give unto my lady:
I name no thing, nor mean no thing,
But as pretty a thing as may be.

Twenty journeys would I make,
  And twenty ways would hie me,
To make adventure for her sake
  To set some matter by me.
    But I would fain have, &c.

Some do long for pretty knacks,
  And some for strange devices;
God send me that my lady lacks,
  I care not what the price is.
    Thus fain would I have, &c.

Some go here and some go there
  Where gazes be not geason,[12]
And I go gaping everywhere,
  But still come out of season.
    Yet fain would I have, &c.

I walk the town and tread the street,
  In every corner seeking:
The pretty thing I cannot meet
  That's for my lady's liking.
    Fain would I have, &c.

The mercers pull me going by;
  The silk-wives say, 'What lack ye?'
'The thing you have not,' then say I,
  'Ye foolish fools, go pack ye!'
    But fain would I have, &c.

It is not all the silk in Cheap,[13]
  Nor all the golden treasure,
Nor twenty bushels on a heap,
  Can do my lady pleasure.
    But fain would I have, &c.

The gravers of the golden shows
  With jewels do beset me;
The shemsters[14] in the shops, that sews,
  They do nothing but let me.
    But fain would I have, &c.

But were it in the wit of man
  By any means to make it,
I could for money buy it than,
  And say, 'Fair lady, take it!'
    Thus fain would I have, &c.

O lady, what a luck is this,
  That my good willing misseth
To find what pretty thing it is
  That my good lady wisheth!
    Thus fain would I have had this pretty thing
      To give unto my lady:
    I said no harm, nor I meant no harm,
      But as pretty a thing as may be.

[*A Handful of Pleasant Delights*, 1584]

To Colin Clout

BEAUTY sat bathing by a spring
  Where fairest shades did hide her;
The winds blew calm, the birds did sing,
  The cool streams ran beside her.
My wanton thoughts enticed mine eye
  To see what was forbidden:
But better memory said, fie!
  So vain desire was chidden.
    Hey nonny, nonny, &c.

Into a slumber then I fell,
  When fond imagination
Seemèd to see, but could not tell
  Her feature or her fashion.
But even as babes in dreams do smile,
  And sometime fall a-weeping,
So I awaked, as wise this while
  As when I fell a-sleeping.
    Hey nonny, nonny, &c.

[Anthony Munday, *England's Helicon*, 1600]

[12] uncommon
[13] Cheapside, the principal mercantile street in old London.
[14] sempstresses

Lyrics from Elizabethan Plays and Entertainments

Back and side go bare, go bare

BACK and side go bare, go bare,
  Both foot and hand go cold;
But, belly, God send thee good ale enough,
  Whether it be new or old.

I cannot eat but little meat,
  My stomach is not good;
But sure I think that I can drink
  With him that wears a hood.
Though I go bare, take ye no care,
  I am nothing a-cold;
I stuff my skin so full within
  Of jolly good ale and old.

Back and side go bare, go bare,
  Both foot and hand go cold;
But, belly, God send thee good ale enough,
  Whether it be new or old.

I love no roast but a nutbrown toast,
  And a crab[1] laid in the fire;
A little bread shall do me stead,
  Much bread I not desire.
No frost nor snow, no wind, I trow,
  Can hurt me if I would,
I am so wrapped, and throughly lapped
  Of jolly good ale and old.

Back and side go bare, &c.

And Tib my wife, that as her life
  Loveth well good ale to seek,
Full oft drinks she, till ye may see
  The tears run down her cheeks.
Then doth she troll[2] to me the bowl,
  Even as a maltworm[3] should,
And saith, Sweetheart, I took my part
  Of this jolly good ale and old.

Back and side go bare, &c.

Now let them drink, till they nod and
    wink,
  Even as good fellows should do;
They shall not miss to have the bliss
  Good ale doth bring men to;
And all poor souls that have scoured bowls
  Or have them lustily trolled,
God save the lives of them and their wives,
  Whether they be young or old.

Back and side go bare, &c.

[William Stevenson, *Gammer Gurton's Needle,* ?1560] [4]

Cupid and my Campaspe played

CUPID and my Campaspe played
At cards for kisses; Cupid paid.
He stakes his quiver, bow, and arrows,
His mother's doves and team of sparrows,
Loses them too; then down he throws
The coral of his lip, the rose
Growing on's cheek (but none knows
    how),
With these the crystal of his brow,
And then the dimple of his chin:
All these did my Campaspe win.
At last he set her both his eyes;
She won, and Cupid blind did rise.
  O Love! has she done this to thee?
  What shall, alas, become of me?

[John Lyly,[5] *Campaspe,* ?1580]

Song by Fairies

Omnes. Pinch him, pinch him, black and
    blue,
  Saucy mortals must not view
  What the queen of stars is doing,
  Nor pry into our fairy wooing.
1 *Fairy.* Pinch him blue.

[1] Roasted crab-apples were put in the drink.
[2] send round
[3] toper

[4] The date after each play refers to the probable year of production.
[5] It is possible that the songs in Lyly's plays are not of his making.

2 *Fairy.* And pinch him black.
3 *Fairy.* Let him not lack
Sharp nails to pinch him blue and red,
Till sleep has rocked his addle-head.
4 *Fairy.* For the trespass he hath done,
Spots all o'er his flesh shall run.
Kiss Endymion, kiss his eyes,
Then to our midnight haydegyes.[6]

[John Lyly, *Endymion,* ?1586]

Phyllida and Corydon

In the merry month of May,
In a morn by break of day,
Forth I walked by the woodside,
Whenas May was in his pride.
There I spiéd all alone
Phyllida and Corydon.
Much ado there was, God wot,
He would love and she would not.
She said, never man was true;
He said, none was false to you.
He said, he had loved her long;
She said, love should have no wrong.
Corydon would kiss her then;
She said, maids must kiss no men
Till they did for good and all.
Then she made the shepherd call
All the heavens to witness truth,
Never loved a truer youth.
Thus with many a pretty oath,
Yea and nay, and faith and troth,
Such as silly shepherds use
When they will not love abuse;
Love, which had been long deluded,
Was with kisses sweet concluded.
And Phyllida with garlands gay
Was made the Lady of the May.

[Nicholas Breton, *The Honourable Entertainment given to the Queen's Majesty in Progress at Elvetham,*[7] 1591]

[6] country dances

[7] Queen Elizabeth was in the habit of making extended visits to her courtiers. They were obliged to entertain her extravagantly and often provided in her honor elaborate pageants and shows. This song was sung in an entertainment on the third day of her visit to the Earl of Hertford in 1591.

What thing is love?

What thing is love? for, well I wot, love is a thing.
It is a prick, it is a sting,
It is a pretty, pretty thing;
It is a fire, it is a coal,
Whose flame creeps in at ev'ry hole;
And as my wit doth best devise,
Love's dwelling is in ladies' eyes;
From whence do glance love's piercing darts,
That make such holes into our hearts;
And all the world herein accord
Love is a great and mighty lord;
And when he list to mount so high,
With Venus he in heaven doth lie,
And evermore hath been a god
Since Mars and she played even and odd.

[George Peele, *The Hunting of Cupid,* 1591]

Adieu, farewell earth's bliss

Adieu, farewell earth's bliss,
This world uncertain is;
Fond are life's lustful joys,
Death proves them all but toys,
None from his darts can fly.
I am sick, I must die.
Lord, have mercy on us!

Rich men, trust not in wealth,
Gold cannot buy you health;
Physic himself must fade,
All things to end are made.
The plague [8] full swift goes by;
I am sick, I must die.
Lord, have mercy on us!

Beauty is but a flower
Which wrinkles will devour:
Brightness falls from the air,
Queens have died young and fair,
Dust has closed Helen's eye.
I am sick, I must die.
Lord, have mercy on us!

[8] The plague made an almost annual assault on London, necessitating the closing of the theatres and sending into the country all who could afford to go.

Strength stoops unto the grave,
Worms feed on Hector brave,
Swords may not fight with fate.
Earth still holds ope her gate;
Come! come! the bells do cry.
I am sick, I must die.
Lord, have mercy on us!

Wit with his wantonness
Tasteth death's bitterness;
Hell's executioner
Hath no ears for to hear
What vain art can reply.
I am sick, I must die.
Lord, have mercy on us!

Haste, therefore, each degree,
To welcome destiny.
Heaven is our heritage,
Earth but a player's stage;
Mount we unto the sky.
I am sick, I must die.
Lord, have mercy on us!

[Thomas Nashe, *Summer's Last Will and Testament,* 1593]

Art thou poor, yet hast thou golden slumbers?

Art thou poor, yet hast thou golden slumbers?
Oh, sweet content!
Art thou rich, yet is thy mind perplexed?
Oh, punishment!
Dost thou laugh to see how fools are vexed
To add to golden numbers, golden numbers?
Oh, sweet content, oh, sweet, &c.

Work apace, apace, apace, apace;
Honest labour bears a lovely face,
Then hey noney, noney, hey noney, noney.

Canst drink the waters of the crispéd spring?
Oh, sweet content!
Swim'st thou in wealth, yet sink'st in thine own tears?
Oh, punishment!
Then he that patiently want's burden bears,
No burden bears, but is a king, a king.
Oh, sweet content, &c.
Work apace, apace, &c.

[Thomas Dekker, *The Pleasant Comedy of Patient Grissill,* 1600]

Lay a garland on my hearse

Lay a garland on my hearse
Of the dismal yew;
Maidens, willow branches bear,
Say I diéd true.

My Love was false, but I was firm
From my hour of birth.
Upon my buried body lay
Lightly, gently, earth.

[Beaumont and Fletcher, *The Maid's Tragedy,* ?1609]

Beauty clear and fair

Beauty clear and fair,
Where the air
Rather like a perfume dwells;
Where the violet and the rose
Their blue veins and blush disclose,
And come to honour nothing else;

Where to live near,
And planted there,
Is to live, and still live new;
Where to gain a favour is
More than life, perpetual bliss,
Make me live by serving you.

Dear, again back recall
To this light,
A stranger to himself and all;
Both the wonder and the story
Shall be yours, and eke the glory;
I am your servant, and your thrall.

[Massinger and Fletcher, *The Elder Brother,* ?1635]

Hear, ye ladies that despise

Hear, ye ladies that despise,
What the mighty Love has done;
Fear examples, and be wise:
Fair Calisto was a nun;
Leda, sailing on the stream
To deceive the hopes of man,
Love accounting but a dream,
Doted on a silver swan;
Danaë,[9] in a brazen tower,
Where no love was, lov'd a shower.

Hear, ye ladies that are coy,
What the mighty Love can do;
Fear the fierceness of the boy:
The chaste moon he makes to woo;
Vesta, kindling holy fires,
Circled round about with spies,
Never dreaming loose desires,
Doting at the altar dies;
Ilion, in a short hour, higher
He can build, and once more fire.

[John Fletcher, *Valentinian*, ?1610]

Hence, all you vain delights

Hence, all you vain delights,
As short as are the nights
Wherein you spend your folly;
There's nought in this life sweet,
If man were wise to see't,
But only melancholy,
Oh, sweetest melancholy.
Welcome, folded arms and fixéd eyes,
A sigh that piercing mortifies,
A look that's fastened to the ground,
A tongue chained up without a sound.
Fountain-heads, and pathless groves,
Places which pale passion loves,
Moonlight walks, when all the fowls
Are warmly housed, save bats and owls,
A midnight bell, a parting groan,
These are the sounds we feed upon;
Then stretch our bones in a still gloomy valley,
Nothing's so dainty sweet as lovely melancholy.

[John Fletcher, *The Nice Valour*, ?1613]

Care-charming Sleep, thou easer of all woes

Care-charming Sleep,[10] thou easer of all woes,
Brother to Death, sweetly thyself dispose
On this afflicted prince; fall like a cloud
In gentle showers; give nothing that is loud
Or painful to his slumbers; easy, sweet,
And as a purling stream, thou son of Night,
Pass by his troubled senses; sing his pain,
Like hollow murmuring wind or silver rain;
Into this prince gently, oh, gently slide,
And kiss him into slumbers like a bride.

[John Fletcher, *Valentinian*, ?1610]

[9] These fair ladies were all encountered by Zeus.
[10] Probably suggested by Daniel's sonnet (see p. 90).

Drink to-day, and drown all sorrow

Drink to-day, and drown all sorrow,
You shall perhaps not do it to-morrow.
Best, while you have it, use your breath;
There is no drinking after death.

Wine works the heart up, wakes the wit;
There is no cure 'gainst age but it.
It helps the headache, cough, and tisic,[11]
And is for all diseases physic.

Then let us swill, boys, for our health;
Who drinks well, loves the commonwealth,
And he that will to bed go sober
Falls with the leaf still in October.

[Massinger, Field, and Fletcher, *The Bloody Brother*, ?1613]

[11] consumption

Call for the robin redbreast

CALL for the robin redbreast and the wren,
Since o'er shady groves they hover,
And with leaves and flowers do cover
The friendless bodies of unburied men.
Call unto his funeral dole
The ant, the field-mouse, and the mole,
To rear him hillocks that shall keep him warm,
And, when gay tombs are robbed, sustain no harm;
But keep the wolf far thence, that's foe to men,
For with his nails he'll dig them up again.

[John Webster, *The White Devil,* 1611]

Trip it gipsies, trip it fine

TRIP it gipsies, trip it fine,
Show tricks and lofty capers;
At threading needles [12] we repine,
And leaping over rapiers.
Pindy-pandy rascal toyes,
We scorn cutting purses,
Though we live by making noise,
For cheating none can curse us.

Over high ways, over low,
And over stones and gravel,
Though we trip it on the toe,
And thus for silver travel;
Though our dances waste our backs,
At night fat capons mend them;
Eggs well brew'd in butter'd sack,
Our wenches say befriend them.

Oh that all the world were mad!
Then should we have fine dancing,
Hobby-horses would be had,
And brave girls keep a-prancing.
Beggars would on cock-horse ride,
And boobies fall a-roaring,
And cuckolds, though no horns be spied,
Be one another goring.

Welcome, poet, to our ging,[13]
Make rimes, we'll give thee reason;
Canary bees thy brain shall sting,
Mull-sack did ne'er speak treason.
Peter-see-me [14] shall wash thy noll,[15]
And Malaga glasses fox thee,
If, poet, thou toss not bowl for bowl,
Thou shalt not kiss a doxy.[16]

[Thomas Middleton, *The Spanish Gipsy,* 1623]

[12] A chain dance.

Can you paint a thought

CAN you paint a thought, or number
Every fancy in a slumber?
Can you count soft minutes roving
From a dial's point by moving?
Can you grasp a sigh, or lastly,
Rob a virgin's honour chastely?
No, oh no; yet you may
Sooner do both that and this,
This and that, and never miss,
Than by any praise display
Beauty's beauty; such a glory
As (beyond all fate, all story)
All arms, all arts,
All loves, all hearts,
Greater than those or they,
Do, shall, and must obey.

[John Ford, *The Broken Heart,* ?1633]

[13] gang
[14] A corruption of the name of a Spanish wine called Pedro Ximenes.
[15] noddle
[16] wench

Elizabethan Song Books

One of the necessary accomplishments of Elizabethan gentlemen and ladies, as indeed of the folk of all classes, was the ability to sing well. Lutes hung in the barber shops for the patrons to finger while they waited. In every gathering the latest new song was demanded and performed by amateurs with professional skill. Merry England was really merry and rightly called a nest of singing birds because it abounded in poets and composers whose work was understood and loved.

A charming picture of the universal devotion to music in the age appears in the *Plaine and Easie Introduction to Practicall Musicke,* a text book written by one of the great composers of the day. It proves that a man must not only be able to sing well at sight but also to argue learnedly about musical theory.

'Among the rest of the guests, by chance, master *Aphron* came thither also, who falling to discourse of Musicke, was in an argument so quickly taken up and hotly pursued by *Eudoxus* and *Calergus,* two kinsmen of *Sophobulus,* as in his own art he was overthrowen. But he still sticking in his opinion, the two gentlemen requested me to examine his reasons and confute them. But I refusing and pretending ignorance, the whole company condemned me of discurtesie, being fully perswaded, that I had beene as skilfull in that art, as they tooke me to be learned in others. But supper being ended, and Musick bookes (according to the custome) being brought to the tables, the mistresse of the house presented me with a part, earnestly requesting me to sing. But when, after many excuses I protested unfainedly that I could not: every one began to wonder. Yea, some whispered to others, demaunding how I was brought up.'

The songs were of two kinds: airs for a single voice, sung to the most sensitive and sympathetic of stringed instruments, the lute, and part-songs which were composed under such names as madrigal, canzonet, motet, and glee. The music for the part-songs is difficult, which makes its performance by amateurs the more remarkable, but extraordinarily beautiful and varied. It has only recently been recovered after a neglect of three centuries. The words alone, fine poetry though they are, give no idea of the effect of the music combined with them. It is a kind of sacrilege to separate them as we have here.

Though Amaryllis dance in green

THOUGH Amaryllis dance in green
Like Fairy Queen,
And sing full clear;
Corinna can, with smiling, cheer.
Yet since their eyes make heart so sore,
Hey ho! 'chill [1] love no more.

My sheep are lost for want of food,
And I so wood [2]
That all the day
I sit and watch a herd-maid gay,
Who laughs to see me sigh so sore;
Hey ho! 'chill love no more.

Her loving looks, her beauty bright,
Is such delight
That all in vain
I love to like, and lose my gain
For her, that thanks me not therefor.
Hey ho! 'chill love no more.

Ah, wanton eyes! my friendly foes
And cause of woes,
Your sweet desire
Breeds flames of ice, and freezing fire.
Ye scorn to see me weep so sore:
Hey ho! 'chill love no more.

Love ye who list, I force him not:
Sith, God it wot,
The more I wail,
The less my sighs and tears prevail:
What shall I do, but say therefore,
Hey ho! 'chill love no more.

[W. Byrd's *Psalms, Sonets, and Songs,* 1588]

[1] A dialect form of 'I will.'
[2] mad

If women could be fair

IF women could be fair, and never fond,[3]
Or that their beauty might continue still,
I would not marvel though they made men bond
By service long to purchase their good will;
But when I see how frail these creatures are
I laugh that men forget themselves so far.

To mark what choice they make, and how they change;
How, leaving best, the worst they choose out still;
And how, like haggards [4] wild, about they range,
Scorning after reason to follow will:

[3] foolish
[4] wild hawks

Who would not shake such buzzards from the fist,
And let them fly (fair fools) which way they list?

Yet for our sport we fawn and flatter both,
To pass the time when nothing else can please,
And train them on to yield by subtle oath
The sweet content that gives such humour ease.
And then we say, when we their follies try,
To play with fools, O what a fool was I.

[Edward Vere, Earl of Oxford, W. Byrd's *Psalms, Sonets, and Songs,* 1588]

Come away, come, sweet love!

Come away, come, sweet love! The golden morning breaks;
All the earth, all the air of love and pleasure speaks.
Teach thine arms then to embrace,
And sweet
Roseate
Lips to kiss,
And mix our souls in mutual bliss;
Eyes were made for beauty's grace,
Viewing,
Rueing
Love-long pain
Procured by beauty's rude disdain.

Come away, come, sweet love! The golden morning wastes,
While the sun from his sphere his fiery arrows casts
Making all the shadows fly,
Playing,
Staying
In the grove
To entertain the stealth of love.
Thither, sweet love, let us hie,
Flying,
Dying
In desire
Winged with hopes and heavenly fire.

Come away, come, sweet love! Do not in vain adorn
Beauty's grace, that should rise like to the naked morn.
Lilies on the riverside
And fair
Cyprian
Flowers new-blown
Desire no beauties but their own,
Ornament is nurse of pride;
Pleasure
Measure
Love's delight.
Haste then, sweet love, our wishéd flight!

[John Dowland, *The First Booke of Songes or Ayres,* 1597]

Among the daffadillies

Among the daffadillies
And fair white splendent lilies
The god of Love came creeping,
Where Dian's nymphs lay sleeping.
He bent his bow but missed his footing,
And loosing, lost both labour, shaft, and shooting.

[Giles Farnaby, *Canzonets to Fowre Voyces,* 1598]

Farewell, dear Love!

Farewell, dear Love! since thou wilt needs be gone:
Mine eyes do show my life is almost done.
Nay, I will never die
So long as I can spy;
There be many moe
Though that she do go.
There be many moe, I fear not.
Why then, let her go, I care not.

Farewell, farewell! since this I find is true,
I will not spend more time in wooing you.
But I will seek elsewhere
If I may find her there.
Shall I bid her go?
What and if I do?

Shall I bid her go, and spare not?
Oh, no, no, no, no, I dare not.

Ten thousand times farewell! Yet stay awhile;
Sweet, kiss me once; sweet kisses time beguile.
I have no power to move:
How now am I in love!
Wilt thou needs be gone?
Go then, all in one.
Wilt thou needs be gone? Oh, hie thee!
Nay; stay, and do no more deny me.

Once more farewell! I see 'loth to depart'
Bids oft adieu to her that holds my heart.
But, seeing I must lose
Thy love which I did choose,
Go thy ways for me,
Since it may not be.
Go thy ways for me. But whither?
Go, oh, but where I may come thither.

What shall I do? My Love is now departed.
She is as fair as she is cruel-hearted:
She would not be entreated
With prayers oft repeated.
If she come no more,
Shall I die therefore?
If she come no more, what care I?
Faith, let her go, or come, or tarry!

[Robert Jones's *The Firste Booke of Songes and Ayres*, 1600]

And would you see my mistress' face?

And would you see my mistress' face?
It is a flowery garden place
Where knots of beauties have such grace
That all is work and nowhere space.

It is a sweet delicious morn
Where day is breeding, never born.
It is a meadow yet unshorn
Whom thousand flowers do adorn.

It is the heavens' bright reflex,
Weak eyes to dazzle and to vex;
It is the Idæa of her sex,
Envy of whom doth world perplex.

It is a face of death that smiles,
Pleasing though it kills the whiles,
Where death and love in pretty wiles
Each other mutually beguiles.

It is fair beauty's freshest youth,
It is the feigned Elysium's truth,
The Spring that wintered hearts reneweth;
And this is that my soul pursueth.

[Philip Rosseter, *A Booke of Ayres*, 1601]

As Vesta was from Latmos hill descending

As Vesta was from Latmos hill descending,
She spied a maiden queen the same ascending,
Attended on by all the shepherds' swain,
To whom Diana's darlings, running down amain,
First two by two, then three by three together,
Alone their goddess leaving, hasted thither;
And mingling with the shepherds of her train,
With mirthful tunes her presence did entertain.
Then sang the shepherds and nymphs of Diana:
Long live fair Oriana.

[Thomas Weelkes, *The Triumphes of Oriana*,[5] 1601]

Weep you no more, sad fountains

Weep you no more, sad fountains;
What need you flow so fast?
Look how the snowy mountains
Heaven's sun doth gently waste.

[5] *The Triumphs of Oriana* was the most famous of the Elizabethan music collections. The madrigals which it contained were all made in praise of 'Oriana,' that is, the illustrious virgin queen Elizabeth. All the important composers of the day contributed to the book.

But my sun's heavenly eyes
View not your weeping,
That now lies sleeping
Softly, now softly lies
Sleeping.

Sleep is a reconciling,
A rest that peace begets.
Doth not the sun rise smiling
When fair at ev'n he sets?
Rest you then, rest, sad eyes,
Melt not in weeping
While she lies sleeping
Softly, now softly lies
Sleeping.

[John Dowland, *The Third and Last Booke of Songs or Aires*, 1603]

There is a lady sweet and kind

THERE is a lady sweet and kind,
Was never face so pleased my mind;
I did but see her passing by,
And yet I love her till I die.

Her gesture, motion and her smiles,
Her wit, her voice, my heart beguiles;
Beguiles my heart, I know not why,
And yet I love her till I die.

Her free behaviour, winning looks,
Will make a lawyer burn his books.
I touched her not, alas, not I,
And yet I love her till I die.

Had I her fast betwixt mine arms,
Judge you that think such sports were harms,
Wer't any harm? No, no, fie, fie!
For I will love her till I die.

Should I remain confinéd there,
So long as Phoebus in his sphere,
I to request, she to deny,
Yet would I love her till I die.

Cupid is wingéd and doth range
Her country so my love doth change;
But change she earth, or change she sky,
Yet will I love her till I die.

[Thomas Ford, *Musicke of Sundrie Kindes*, 1607]

Come, sirrah Jack, ho!

COME, sirrah Jack, ho!
Fill some tobacco.
Bring a wire
And some fire!
Haste away,
Quick I say!
Do not stay!
Shun delay!
For I drank none good to-day.

I swear that this tobacco
It's perfect Trinidado.
By the Mass
Never was
Better gear[6]
Than is here.
By the rood
For the blood
It is very very good.

Fill the pipe once more,
My brains dance trenchmore.[7]
It is heady,
I am giddy.
Head and brains,
Back and reins,
Joints and veins
From all pains
It doth well purge and make clean.

For those that do condemn it,
Or such as not commend it,
Never were so wise to learn
Good tobacco to discern;
Let them go
Pluck a crow,
And not know,
As I do,
The sweet of Trinidado.

[Thomas Weelkes, *Ayeres or Phantasticke Spirites*, 1608]

[6] business

[7] A lively old English dance.

The silver swan

The silver swan, who living had no note,
When death approached unlocked her silent throat;
Leaning her breast against the reedy shore,
Thus sung her first and last, and sung no more:
Farewell, all joys; O death, come close mine eyes;
More geese than swans now live, more fools than wise.

[Orlando Gibbons, *The First Set of Madrigals and Mottets*, 1612]

O softly singing lute

O softly singing lute,
See with my tears thou time do keep.
Yet softly, gentle strings,
Agree with love that cannot sleep.
Sorrow hist whenas it sings.
When tears do fall then sighs arise.
So grief oft shines in most sad eyes,
Yea, love through heart it dies — it dies.

[Francis Pilkington, *The Second Set of Madrigals and Pastorals*, 1624]

Thomas Campion

1567–1620

Hark, all you ladies that do sleep

Hark, all you ladies that do sleep;
The fairy queen Proserpina
Bids you awake and pity them that weep.
You may do in the dark
What the day doth forbid;
Fear not the dogs that bark,
Night will have all hid.

But if you let your lovers moan,
The fairy queen Proserpina
Will send abroad her fairies ev'ry one,
That shall pinch black and blue
Your white hands and fair arms
That did not kindly rue
Your paramours' harms.

In myrtle arbours on the downs
The fairy queen Proserpina,
This night by moon-shine leading merry rounds
Holds a watch with sweet love,
Down the dale, up the hill;
No plaints or groans may move
Their holy vigil.

All you that will hold watch with love,
The fairy queen Proserpina
Will you make fairer than Dione's [1] dove;
Roses red, lilies white,
And the clear damask hue,
Shall on your cheeks alight:
Love will adorn you.

All you that love, or loved before,
The fairy queen Proserpina
Bids you increase that loving humour more:
They that yet have not fed
On delight amorous,
She vows that they shall lead
Apes in Avernus.[2]

[*Astrophel and Stella*, 1591]

[1] The mother of the goddess of love.

[2] We are asked to believe that old maids suffer this indignity in Hades.

I care not for these ladies

I care not for these ladies,
That must be wooed and prayed,
Give me kind Amarillis
The wanton country maid;
Nature art disdaineth,
Her beauty is her own;
Her when we court and kiss,
She cries, forsooth, let go.
But when we come where comfort is,
She never will say no.

If I love Amarillis,
She gives me fruit and flowers,

But if we love these ladies,
We must give golden showers,
Give them gold that sell love,
Give me the nutbrown lass,
Who when we court and kiss,
She cries, forsooth, let go.
But when we come where comfort is,
She never will say no.

These ladies must have pillows,
And beds by strangers wrought,
Give me a bower of willows,
Of moss and leaves unbought,
And fresh Amarillis,
With milk and honey fed,
Who, when we court and kiss,
She cries, forsooth, let go.
But when we come where comfort is,
She never will say no.

[*A Booke of Ayres*, 1601]

Follow thy fair sun

Follow thy fair sun, unhappy shadow,
Though thou be black as night,
And she made all of light,
Yet follow thy fair sun, unhappy shadow.

Follow her whose light thy light depriveth,
Though here thou liv'st disgraced,
And she in heaven is placed,
Yet follow her whose light the world reviveth.

Follow those pure beams whose beauty burneth,
That so have scorchéd thee,
As thou still black must be,
Till her kind beams thy black to brightness turneth.

Follow her while yet her glory shineth:
There comes a luckless night,
That will dim all her light;
And this the black unhappy shade divineth.

Follow still since so thy fates ordainéd;
The sun must have his shade,
Till both at once do fade,
The sun still proud, the shadow still disdainéd.

[*A Booke of Ayres*, 1601]

The man of life upright

The man of life upright,
Whose guiltless heart is free
From all dishonest deeds,
Or thought of vanity,

The man whose silent days
In harmless joys are spent,
Whom hopes cannot delude,
Nor sorrow discontent;

That man needs neither towers
Nor armour for defence,
Nor secret vaults to fly
From thunder's violence.

He only can behold
With unaffrighted eyes
The horrors of the deep
And terrors of the skies.

Thus, scorning all the cares
That fate, or fortune brings,
He makes the heaven his book,
His wisdom heav'nly things,

Good thoughts his only friends,
His wealth a well-spent age,
The earth his sober inn
And quiet pilgrimage.

[*A Booke of Ayres*, 1601]

Jack and Joan they think no ill

Jack and Joan they think no ill,
But loving live, and merry still;
Do their week-day's work, and pray
Devoutly on the holy day:
Skip and trip it on the green,

And help to choose the Summer Queen:
Lash out,[3] at a country feast,
Their silver penny with the best.

Well can they judge of nappy[4] ale,
And tell at large a winter tale;
Climb up to the apple loft,
And turn the crabs[5] till they be soft.
Tib is all the father's joy,
And little Tom the mother's boy.
All their pleasure is content;
And care, to pay the yearly rent.

Joan can call by name her cows,
And deck her windows with green boughs;
She can wreaths and tutties[6] make,
And trim with plums a bridal cake.
Jack knows what brings gain or loss;
And his long flail can stoutly toss:
Make the hedge, which others break,
And ever thinks what he doth speak.

Now, you courtly dames and knights,
That study only strange delights;
Though you scorn the home-spun gray,
And revel in your rich array:
Though your tongues dissemble deep,
And can your heads from danger keep;
Yet, for all your pomp and train,
Securer lives the silly swain.

[*Two Bookes of Ayres*, ?1613]

Shall I come, sweet Love, to thee

SHALL I come, sweet Love, to thee,
  When the ev'ning beams are set?
Shall I not excluded be?
  Will you find no feignéd let?[7]
Let me not, for pity, more,
Tell the long hours at your door.

Who can tell what thief or foe,
  In the covert of the night,
For his prey will work my woe,
  Or through wicked foul despite:
So may I die unredressed,
Ere my long love be possessed.

But to let such dangers pass,
  Which a lover's thoughts disdain,
'Tis enough in such a place
  To attend love's joys in vain.
Do not mock me in thy bed,
While these cold nights freeze me dead.

[*The Third and Fourth Booke of Ayres*, ?1617]

There is a garden in her face

THERE is a garden in her face,
Where roses and white lilies grow;
  A heav'nly paradise is that place,
Wherein all pleasant fruits do flow.
  There cherries grow, which none may buy
  Till 'Cherry-ripe'[8] themselves do cry.

  Those cherries fairly do enclose
Of orient pearl a double row;
  Which when her lovely laughter shows,
They look like rose-buds filled with snow.
  Yet them nor peer nor prince can buy,
  Till 'Cherry-ripe' themselves do cry.

  Her eyes like angels watch them still;
Her brows like bended bows do stand,
  Threatening with piercing frowns to kill
All that attempt with eye or hand
  Those sacred cherries to come nigh,
  Till 'Cherry-ripe' themselves do cry.

[*The Third and Fourth Booke of Ayres*, ?1617]

Thou joy'st, fond boy

THOU joy'st, fond boy, to be by many lovéd:
To have thy beauty of most dames approvéd;
For this dost thou thy native worth disguise

[3] squander
[4] strong
[5] apples
[6] nosegays
[7] hindrance

[8] A London street-cry.

And play'st the sycophant t'observe their eyes;
Thy glass thou counsel'st more t'adorn thy skin,
That first should school thee to be fair within.

'Tis childish to be caught with pearl, or amber,
And woman-like too much to cloy the chamber;
Youths should the field affect, heat their rough steeds,
Their hardened nerves to fit for better deeds.
Is't not more joy strong holds to force with swords
Than women's weakness take with looks or words?

Men that do noble things all purchase glory:
One man for one brave act have proved a story:
But if that one ten thousand dames o'ercame,
Who would record it, if not to his shame?
'Tis far more conquest with one to live true
Than every hour to triumph lord of new.

[*The Third and Fourth Booke of Ayres*, ?1617]

The Writer to his Book[9]

'Whither thus hastes my little book so fast?'
'To Paul's[10] Churchyard.' 'What! in those cells to stand,
With one leaf like a rider's cloak put up
To catch a termer?[11] or lie musty there
With rimes a term set out, or two, before?'
'Some will redeem me.' 'Few.' 'Yes, read me too.'
'Fewer.' 'Nay, love me.' 'Now thou dot'st, I see.'
'Will not our English Athens art defend?'
'Perhaps.' 'Will lofty courtly wits not aim
Still at perfection?' 'If I grant?' 'I fly.'
'Whither?' 'To Paul's.' 'Alas, poor book, I rue
Thy rash self-love; go, spread thy pap'ry wings:
Thy lightness can not help or hurt my fame.'

[9] This tender address is made by Campion to his 'book', *Observations in the Art of English Poesie*, 1602, one of the most acute treatises on verse-making ever written.
[10] Booksellers displayed their wares in stalls around the cathedral of St. Paul's in London.

Rose-cheeked Laura, come

Rose-cheeked Laura, come
Sing thou smoothly with thy beauties
Silent music, either other
Sweetly gracing.

Lovely forms do flow
From consent divinely framèd;
Heav'n is music, and thy beauty's
Birth is heavenly.

These dull notes we sing
Discords need for helps to grace them;
Only beauty purely loving
Knows no discord,

But still moves delight
Like clear springs renewed by flowing,
Ever perfect, ever in them-
Selves eternal.

[*Observations in the Art of English Poesie*, 1602]

[11] Anyone come to London to do business in the Law Terms which were held three times a year.

Sir Walter Raleigh

1552?–1618

Sir Walter Raleigh to the Queen

Our passions are most like to floods and streams;
The shallow murmur; but the deep are dumb.
So when affections yield discourse, it seems
The bottom is but shallow whence they come.
They that are rich in words must needs discover
That they are poor in that which makes a lover.

Wrong not, dear empress of my heart,
The merit of true passion,
With thinking that he feels no smart,
That sues for no compassion;
Since, if my plaints serve not to prove
The conquest of your beauty,
It comes not from defect of love,
But from excess of duty.

For knowing that I sue to serve
A saint of such perfection,
As all desire, but none deserve,
A place in her affection;
I rather choose to want relief
Than venture the revealing;
When glory recommends the grief,
Despair distrusts the healing.

Thus those desires that aim too high,
For any mortal lover,
When reason cannot make them die,
Discretion will them cover.
Yet when discretion doth bereave
The plaints that they should utter,
Then your discretion may perceive,
That silence is a suitor.

Silence in love bewrays more woe,
Than words, though ne'er so witty,
A beggar that is dumb, ye know,
Deserveth double pity.
Then misconceive not (dearest heart)
My true, though secret passion,
He smarteth most that hides his smart,
And sues for no compassion.

The Nymph's Reply to the Shepherd [1]

If all the world and love were young,
And truth in every shepherd's tongue,
These pretty pleasures might me move,
To live with thee, and be thy love.

Time drives the flocks from field to fold,
When rivers rage and rocks grow cold,
And Philomel becometh dumb,
The rest complains of care to come.

The flowers do fade, and wanton fields,
To wayward winter reckoning yields,
A honey tongue, a heart of gall,
Is fancy's spring, but sorrow's fall.

Thy gowns, thy shoes, thy beds of roses,
Thy cap, thy kirtle, and thy posies,
Soon break, soon wither, soon forgotten:
In folly ripe, in reason rotten.

Thy belt of straw and ivy buds,
Thy coral clasps and amber studs,
All these in me no means can move,
To come to thee, and be thy love.

---

[1] In the collection from which this poem is taken it follows Marlowe's *Come live with me, and be my love* (see p. 247).

But could youth last, and love still breed,
Had joys no date, nor age no need,
Then these delights my mind might move,
To live with thee, and be thy love.

[*England's Helicon,* 1600]

The Passionate Man's Pilgrimage

Supposed to be written by one at the point of death [2]

Give me my scallop shell [3] of quiet,
My staff of faith to walk upon,
My scrip [4] of joy, immortal diet,
My bottle of salvation:
My gown of glory, hope's true gage,
And thus I'll make my pilgrimage.

Blood must be my body's balmer,
No other balm will there be given
Whilst my soul like a white palmer
Travels to the land of heaven,
Over the silver mountains,
Where spring the nectar fountains;
And there I'll kiss
The bowl of bliss,
And drink my eternal fill
On every milken hill.
My soul will be a-dry before,
But after it, will ne'er thirst more.

And by the happy blissful way
More peaceful pilgrims I shall see,
That have shook off their gowns of clay,
And go apparelled fresh like me.
I'll bring them first
To slake their thirst,
And then to taste those nectar suckets
At the clear wells
Where sweetness dwells,
Drawn up by saints in crystal buckets.

And when our bottles and all we
Are filled with immortality;
Then the holy paths we'll travel
Strewed with rubies thick as gravel,
Ceilings of diamonds, sapphire floors,
High walls of coral and pearl bowers.

From thence to heaven's bribeless hall
Where no corrupted voices brawl,
No conscience molten into gold,
Nor forg'd accusers bought and sold,
No cause deferred, nor vain-spent journey,
For there Christ is the King's Attorney:
Who pleads for all without degrees,
And he hath angels,[5] but no fees.

When the grand twelve million jury
Of our sins with sinful fury,
Gainst our souls black verdicts give,
Christ pleads his death, and then we live.
Be thou my speaker, taintless pleader,
Unblotted lawyer, true proceeder,
Thou movest salvation even for alms,
Not with a bribéd lawyer's palms.

And this is my eternal plea,
To him that made heaven, earth and sea,
Seeing my flesh must die so soon,
And want a head to dine next noon,
Just at the stroke when my veins start and spread
Set on my soul an everlasting head.
Then am I ready like a palmer fit,
To tread those blest paths which before I writ.

[*Daiphantus,* 1604]

The Lie

Go, soul, the body's guest,
Upon a thankless arrant.[6]
Fear not to touch the best;
The truth shall be thy warrant.
Go, since I needs must die,
And give the world the lie.

Say to the court, it glows
And shines like rotten wood;
Say to the church, it shows
What's good, and doth no good:

[2] In November 1603 Raleigh was condemned to die. The poem seems to refer to his trial and his approaching execution which did not arrive.
[3] The badge worn by pilgrims.
[4] The pilgrim's wallet.

[5] A pun on the angel-noble, an Elizabethan coin.
[6] errand

If church and court reply,
Then give them both the lie.

Tell potentates, they live
Acting by others' action,
Not loved unless they give,
Not strong but by affection:
If potentates reply,
Give potentates the lie.

Tell men of high condition
That manage the estate,
Their purpose is ambition,
Their practice only hate:
And if they once reply,
Then give them all the lie.

Tell them that brave it most,
They beg for more by spending,
Who, in their greatest cost,
Like nothing but commending:
And if they make reply,
Then give them all the lie.

Tell zeal it wants devotion;
Tell love it is but lust;
Tell time it meets but motion;
Tell flesh it is but dust:
And wish them not reply,
For thou must give the lie.

Tell age it daily wasteth;
Tell honour how it alters;
Tell beauty how she blasteth;
Tell favour how it falters:
And as they shall reply,
Give every one the lie.

Tell wit how much it wrangles
In tickle point of niceness;
Tell wisdom she entangles
Herself in over-wiseness:
And when they do reply,
Straight give them both the lie.

Tell physic of her boldness;
Tell skill it is prevention;
Tell charity of coldness;
Tell law it is contention:
And as they do reply,
So give them still the lie.

Tell fortune of her blindness;
Tell nature of decay;
Tell friendship of unkindness;
Tell justice of delay;
And if they will reply,
Then give them all the lie.

Tell arts they have no soundness,
But vary by esteeming;
Tell schools they want profoundness,
And stand too much on seeming:
If arts and schools reply,
Give arts and schools the lie.

Tell faith it's fled the city;
Tell how the country erreth;
Tell, manhood shakes off pity,
Tell, virtue least preferréd:
And if they do reply,
Spare not to give the lie.

So when thou hast, as I
Commanded thee, done blabbing,
Because to give the lie
Deserves no less than stabbing,
Stab at thee he that will—
No stab thy soul can kill.

[Davison's *A Poetical Rhapsody*, 1608]

On the Life of Man

WHAT is our life? a play of passion,
Our mirth the music of division,
Our mothers' wombs the tiring houses be,
Where we are dressed for this short comedy,
Heaven the judicious sharp spectator is,
That sits and marks still who doth act amiss,
Our graves that hide us from the searching sun,
Are like drawn curtains when the play is done,
Thus march we playing to our latest rest,
Only we die in earnest, that's no jest.

[Orlando Gibbons's *The First Set of Madrigals and Mottets*, 1612]

The Author's Epitaph, made by Himself[7]

EVEN such is time, which takes in trust
Our youth, our joys, and all we have,
And pays us but with age and dust,
Who in the dark and silent grave,
When we have wandered all our ways,
Shuts up the story of our days:
And from which earth, and grave, and dust,
The Lord shall raise me up I trust.

[*The Prerogative of Parliaments in England*, 1628]

[7] Tradition says that Raleigh wrote this the night before he was beheaded.

Sir Philip Sidney

1554–1586

ASTROPHEL AND STELLA[1]

I

LOVING in truth, and fain my love in verse to show,
That the dear she might take some pleasure of my pain:
Pleasure might cause her read, reading might make her know,
Knowledge might pity win, and pity grace obtain —
I sought fit words, to paint the blackest face of woe,
Studying inventions fine, her wits to entertain,
Oft turning others' leaves, to see if thence would flow
Some fresh and fruitful shower, upon my sun-burnt brain.
But words came halting out, wanting invention's stay,
Invention, nature's child, fled stepdame study's blows,
And others' feet still seemed but strangers in my way.
Thus great with child to speak, and helpless in my throes,
Biting my tongue and pen, beating myself for spite:
Fool said my muse to me, look in thy heart and write.

XXIV

Rich[2] fools there be, whose base and filthy heart
Lies hatching still the goods wherein they flow,
Damning themselves to Tantalus his smart,
Wealth breeding want, more rich, more wretched grow.
Yet to those fools heaven doth such wit impart,
As what their hands do hold, their heads do know.
And knowing, love; and loving, lay apart
As scattered things, far from all danger's show.
But that rich fool, who by blind Fortune's lot,
The richest gem of love and life enjoys,
And can with foul abuse such beauties blot,
Let him, deprived of sweet but unfelt joys
Exiled for aye from those high treasures which
He knows not, grow, in only folly rich.

XXXI

With how sad steps, O moon, thou climb'st the skies,
How silently, and with how mean a face,
What! may it be that even in heavenly place

[1] This group of sonnets is taken from the sequence written by Sidney in honor of his lady Stella and published, after his death, in 1591 under the title *Syr P. S. His Astrophel and Stella*. The poems hide a real affair, differing in this respect from the 'literary exercises' in Petrarchan style which many Elizabethan poets wrote. Stella has been identified as Penelope Devereux, whom Sidney first saw when she was a child. She married Lord Rich against her will, and the misfortune of this marriage seems to have increased Sidney's love for her. The most passionate of the sonnets refer to this period of their lives.

[2] The punning sonnet was a form of wit practised by the sonneteers. Lord Rich was Stella's husband.

That busy archer his sharp arrows tries?
Sure, if that long with love acquainted eyes
Can judge of love, thou feel'st a lover's case;
I read within thy looks thy languished grace.
To me that feel the like, my state descries.
Then even of fellowship, O moon, tell me,
Is constant love deemed there but want of wit?
Are beauties there as proud as here there be?
Do they above love to be lov'd, and yet
Those lovers scorn whom that love doth possess?
Do they call virtue there ungratefulness?

XXXIX

Come sleep! O sleep, the certain knot of peace,
The bathing place of wits,[3] the balm of woe,
The poor man's wealth, the prisoner's release,
The indifferent judge between the high and low,
With shield of proof, shield me from out the press
Of these fierce darts, despair at me doth throw;
O make in me those civil wars to cease:
I will good tribute pay if thou do so.
Take thou of me smooth pillows, sweetest bed,
A chamber deaf of noise, and blind of light,
A rosy garland, and a weary head.
And if these things (as being thine in right)
Move not thy heavy grace, thou shalt in me,
(Livelier than else) rare Stella's image see.

[3] bathing, *etc.* The version of the sonnets which Sidney's sister published in 1598, to wipe away 'those spots wherewith the beauties thereof were unworthily blemished' in the edition of 1591, prints for this *baiting place of wit.* To bait a horse meant to stop at an inn and give him oats.

XLI

Having this day,[4] my horse, my hand, my lance
Guided so well, that I obtained the prize,
Both by the judgment of the English eyes,
And of some sent by that sweet enemy France;
Horsemen my skill in horsemanship advance,
Townfolk my strength; a daintier judge applies
His praise to slight which from good use doth rise;
Some lucky wits impute it but to chance:
Others, because from both sides I do take
My blood from them that do excel in this,
Think nature me a man at arms did make.
How far they shoot awry! the true cause is,
Stella looked on, and from her heavenly face,
Sent forth her beams, which made so fair a race.

LIV

Because I breathe not love to every one,
Nor do not use set colours for to wear,
Nor nourish special locks[5] with vowéd hair,
Nor give each speech a full point[6] of a groan,
The courtly nymphs, acquainted with the moan
Of them which in their lips love's standard bear,
What, he! (say they of me) No, I dare swear
He cannot love: no, no, let him alone.
And think so still, so Stella know my mind.
Protest indeed, I know not Cupid's dart;
But how fair maids, at length this true shall find,

[4] Elizabeth's courtiers revived the pageantry of the medieval tourney to do her honor. This particular joust probably took place in 1581 when French ambassadors were in England to arrange a marriage with the English queen.

[5] Sidney's contemporary Greene says: 'Will you be Frenchefied with a love lock downe to your shoulders, wherein you may weare your mistresse favour?'

[6] stop

That his right badge is learnéd[7] in the heart.
Dumb swans, not chattering pies,[8] do lovers prove,
They love indeed who dare not say they love.

LIX

Dear, why make you more of a dog than me?
If he do love, alas, I burn in love;
If he wait well, I never thence would move;
If he be fair, yet but a dog can be;
Little he is, so little worth is he:
He barks, my songs in one voice oft doth prove;
Bidden, (perhaps) he fetcheth thee a glove;
But I unbid, fetch even my soul to thee.
Yet while I languish, him that bosom clips,
That lap doth lap, nay lets in spite of spite
This fawning mate taste of those sugared lips;
Alas, if you grant only such delight
To witless things, then love I hope, (since wit
Becomes a clog) will soon ease me of it.

LXXIII

Love still a boy, and oft a wanton is,
Schooled only by his mother's tender eye;
What wonder then if he his lesson miss,
When for so soft a rod dear play he try.
And yet my star, because a sugared kiss,
In sport I suck, while she asleep doth lie,
Doth lower, nay chide, nay threat for only this;
Sweet, it was saucy love that pressed so nigh.
But no 'scuse serves, she makes her wrath appear
In beauty's throne; see now who dares come near
Those scarlet judges, threatening bloody pain.

[7] The 1598 edition has *worn*.
[8] magpies

O heavenly fool, thy most kiss-worthy face
Anger invests with such a lovely grace,
That anger's self I needs must kiss again.

LXXXIV

Highway, since you my chief Parnassus be,
And that my muse, to some ears not unmeet,
Tempers her words to trampling horses' feet
More often than a chamber melody,
Now blessed you bear onwards blessed me,
To her where my heart safeliest shall meet;
My muse and I must you of duty greet,
With thanks and wishes wishing thankfully;
Be you still carefully kept by public heed,
By no encroachment wronged, nor time forgot,
Nor blamed for blood, nor shamed for sinful deed,
And that you know I envy you no whit,
Of highest wish, I wish you so much bliss,
Hundreds of years you Stella's feet may kiss.

The Eighth Sonnet[9]

In a grove most rich of shade,
Where birds wanton music made,
May, then young, his pied weeds[10] showing,
New perfumes with flowers fresh growing,

Astrophel with Stella sweet,
Did for mutual confort meet;
Both within themselves oppressed,
But either in each other blessed.

Him great harms had taught much care,[11]

[9] In the sixteenth century the word *sonnet* was loosely used by poets.
[10] variegated dress
[11] sorrow

Her fair neck a foul yoke bare;
But her sight his cares did banish,
In his sight her yoke did vanish.

Wept they had, alas, the while;
But now tears themselves did smile,
While their eyes by love directed,
Interchangeably reflected.

Sighed they had; but now betwixt
Sighs of woe were glad sighs mixed;
With arms crossed, yet testifying
Restless rest, and living dying.

Their ears hungry of each word
Which the dear tongue would afford,
But their tongues restrained from walking,
Till their hearts had ended talking.

But when their tongues could not speak,
Love itself did silence break;
Love did set his lips asunder,
Thus to speak in love and wonder.

Stella, sovereign of my joy,
Fair triumphress in annoy:
Stella, star of heavenly fire,
Stella, loadstar of desire.

Stella, in whose shining eyes
Are the lights of Cupid's skies,
Whose beams where they are once darted
Love therewith is straight imparted.

Stella, whose voice when it speaks,
Senses all asunder breaks;
Stella, whose voice when it singeth,
Angels to acquaintance bringeth.

Stella, in whose body is
Writ the characters [12] of bliss;
Whose sweet face all beauty passeth,
Save the mind which it surpasseth.

Grant, Oh grant, but speech (alas)
Fails me, fearing on to pass;
Grant to me, what am I saying?
But no sin there is in praying.

Grant (O dear) on knees I pray
(Knees on ground he then did stay)
That not I, but since I prove you,
Time and place for me near move you.

Never season was more fit,
Never room more apt for it;
Smiling air allows my reason;
These birds sing; now use the season.

This small wind which so sweet is,
See how it the leaves doth kiss;
Each tree in his best attiring,
Sense of love to love inspiring.

Love makes earth the water drink,
Love to earth makes water sink;
And if dumb things be so witty,
Shall a heavenly Grace want pity?

There his hands (in their speech) fain
Would have made tongue's language plain;
But her hands his hands compelling,
Gave repulse, all grace expelling.

Therewithal, away she went,
Leaving him with passion rent,
With what she had done and spoken,
That therewith my song is broken.

[12] marks

Who hath his fancy pleaséd

Who hath his fancy pleaséd
With fruits of happy sight,
Let here his eyes be raiséd
On nature's sweetest light,
A light which doth dissever
And yet unite the eyes,
A light which dying never
Is cause the looker dies.

She never dies, but lasteth
In life of lover's heart;
He ever dies that wasteth
In love his chiefest part.

Thus is her life still guarded
In never dying faith;
Thus is his death rewarded,
Since she lives in his death.

Look then and die, the pleasure
Doth answer well the pain:
Small loss of mortal treasure
Who may immortal gain.
Immortal be her graces,
Immortal is her mind;
They, fit for heavenly places;
This, heaven in it doth bind.

But eyes these beauties see not,
Nor sense that grace descries,
Yet eyes deprivéd be not
From sight of her fair eyes,
Which, as of inward glory
They are the outward seal;
So may they live still sorry
Which die not in that weal.

But who hath fancies pleaséd
With fruits of happy sight,
Let here his eyes be raiséd
On nature's sweetest light.

[*Certaine Sonets,* 1598]

Leave me, O love which reachest

LEAVE me, O love which reachest but to dust,
And thou, my mind, aspire to higher things;
Grow rich in that which never taketh rust:
Whatever fades, but fading pleasure brings.

Draw in thy beams, and humble all thy might,
To that sweet yoke, where lasting freedoms be;
Which breaks the clouds and opens forth the light,
That doth both shine and give us sight to see.

O take fast hold; let that light be thy guide
In this small course which birth draws out to death,
And think how evil becometh him to slide,
Who seeketh heav'n, and comes of heav'nly breath.
Then farewell world; thy uttermost I see;
Eternal love, maintain thy life in me.

[*Certaine Sonets,* 1598]

Dispraise of a Courtly Life

WALKING in bright Phoebus' blaze,
Where with heat oppressed I was,
I got to a shady wood,
Where green leaves did newly bud
And of grass was plenty dwelling,
Decked with pied flowers sweetly smelling.

In this wood a man I met,
On lamenting wholly set;
Ruing change of wonted state,
Whence he was transforméd late,
Once to shepherd's god retaining,
Now in servile court remaining.

There he, wandering malcontent,
Up and down perplexéd went,
Daring not to tell to me,
Spake unto a senseless tree,
One amongst the rest electing
These same words, or this effecting.

My old mates, I grieve to see,
Void of me in field to be,
Where we once our lovely sheep,
Lovingly like friends did keep,
Oft each other's friendship proving,
Never striving, but in loving.

But may love abiding be
In poor shepherd's base degree?
It belongs to such alone
To whom art of love is known;
Silly shepherds are not witting
What in art of love is fitting.

Nay, what need the art to those,
To whom we our love disclose?
It is to be uséd then,
When we do but flatter men;
Friendship true in heart assuréd,
Is by nature's gifts procuréd.

Therefore shepherds wanting skill,
Can love's duties best fulfill,
Since they know not how to feign,
Nor with love to cloak disdain;
Like the wiser sort, whose learning
Hides their inward skill of harming.

Well was I, while under shade
Oaken reeds me music made,
Striving with my mates in song;
Mixing mirth our songs among,
Greater was the shepherd's treasure,
Than this false, fine, courtly pleasure.

Where, how [13] many creatures be,
So many puffed in mind I see,
Like to Juno's bird of pride,
Scarce each other can abide;
Friends like to black swans appearing
Sooner these than those in hearing.

Therefore Pan, if thou mayest be
Made to listen unto me,
Grant, I say (if silly man
May make treaty to god Pan)
That I, without thee denying,
May be still to thee relying.

Only for my two loves' [14] sake,
In whose love I pleasure take,
Only two do me delight
With their ever pleasing sight,
Of all men to thee retaining.
Grant me with those two remaining.

So shall I to thee always,
With my reeds sound mighty praise,
And first lamb that shall befall,
Yearly deck thine altar shall,
If it please thee to be reflected,
And I from thee not rejected.

So I left him in that place,
Taking pity on his case,
Learning this among the rest
That the mean estate is best,
Better filléd with contenting
Void of wishing and repenting.

[Davison's *A Poetical Rhapsody*, 1602]

[13] so

[14] This is the second of two pastorals made by Sidney 'upon his meeting with his two worthy Friends and fellow-poets, Sir Edward Dier, and Maister Fulke Grevill.'

My true love hath my heart

My true love hath my heart, and I have his,
By just exchange, one for the other given.
I hold his dear, and mine he cannot miss:
There never was a better bargain driven.

His heart in me, keeps me and his in one,
My heart in him, his thoughts and senses guides:
He loves my heart, for once it was his own:
I cherish his, because in me it bides.

His heart his wound receivéd from my sight:
My heart was wounded, with his wounded heart,
For as from me, on him his hurt did light,
So still me thought in me his hurt did smart:
Both equall hurt, in this change sought our bliss:
My true love hath my heart and I have his.

[*The Countesse of Pembrokes Arcadia*, 1593]

Since nature's works be good

Since nature's works be good, and death doth serve
As nature's work, why should we fear to die?

Since fear is vain, but when it may preserve,
Why should we fear that which we cannot fly?

Fear is more pain, than is the pain it fears,
Disarming human minds of native might:
While each conceit an ugly figure bears,
Which were not evil, well view'd in reason's light.
Our owly eyes, which dimm'd with passions be,
And scarce discern the dawn of coming day,
Let them be cleared, and now begin to see,
Our life is but a step, in dusty way.
Then let us hold the bliss of peaceful mind,
Since this we feel, great loss we cannot find.

[*The Countesse of Pembrokes Arcadia*, 1593]

Samuel Daniel

1562–1619

SONNETS

To Delia [1]

UNTO the boundless ocean of thy beauty
Runs this poor river, charged with streams of zeal,
Returning thee the tribute of my duty,
Which here my love, my youth, my plaints reveal.
Here I unclasp the book of my charged soul,
Where I have cast the accounts of all my care;
Here have I summed my sighs, here I enroll
How they were spent for thee. Look what they are;
Look on the dear expenses of my youth,
And see how just I reckon with thine eyes;
Examine well thy beauty with my truth,
And cross my cares ere greater sums arise.
Read it, sweet maid, though it be done but slightly;
Who can shew all his love doth love but lightly.

FAIR is my love, and cruel as she's fair;
Her brow shades frowns, although her eyes are sunny,
Her smiles are lightning, though her pride despair,
And her disdains are gall, her favours honey;
A modest maid, decked with a blush of honour,
Whose feet do tread green paths of youth and love,
The wonder of all eyes that look upon her,
Sacred on earth, designed a saint above.
Chastity and beauty, which were deadly foes,
Live, reconciléd friends, within her brow;
And, had she pity to conjoin with those,
Then who had heard the plaints I utter now?
For had she not been fair and thus unkind,
My muse had slept, and none had known my mind.

AND yet I cannot reprehend the flight,
Or blame the attempt presuming so to soar;
The mounting venture for a high delight
Did make the honour of the fall the more.
For who gets wealth that puts not from the shore?
Danger hath honour, great designs their fame;
Glory doth follow, courage goes before;
And though the event oft answers not the same,

[1] Daniel's Delia is probably his patroness, the Countess of Pembroke. These sonnets are then less personal than Sidney's or Drayton's. After their first publication in 1592 additions were made in subsequent editions.

Suffice that high attempts have never shame.
The mean observer, whom base safety keeps,
Lives without honour, dies without a name,
And in eternal darkness ever sleeps.
  And therefore, Delia, 'tis to me no blot
  To have attempted though attained thee not.

THOU canst not die whilst any zeal abound
In feeling hearts that can conceive these lines;
Though thou, a Laura,[2] hast no Petrarch found,
In base attire yet clearly beauty shines.
And I, though born within a colder clime,
Do feel mine inward heat as great (I know it);
He never had more faith, although more rhyme;
I love as well, though he could better show it.
But I may add one feather to thy fame,
To help her flight throughout the fairest isle;
And if my pen could more enlarge thy name,
Then shouldst thou live in an immortal style.
  For though that Laura better limnéd be,
  Suffice, thou shalt be loved as well as she.

CARE-CHARMER Sleep, son of the sable night,
Brother to death, in silent darkness born,
Relieve my languish and restore the light,
With dark forgetting of my care's return;
And let the day be time enough to mourn
The shipwreck of my ill-adventured youth,
Let waking eyes suffice to wail their scorn,
Without the torment of the night's untruth.
Cease, dreams, the images of day-desires,
To model forth the passions of the morrow,
Never let rising sun approve you liars,
To add more grief to aggravate my sorrow.
  Still let me sleep, embracing clouds in vain,
  And never wake to feel the day's disdain.

LET others sing of knights and paladins
In agéd accents and untimely words,
Paint shadows in imaginary lines
Which well the reach of their high wits records.
But I must sing of thee, and those fair eyes
Authentic shall my verse in time to come,
When yet the unborn shall say, 'Lo, where she lies,
Whose beauty made him speak that else was dumb.'
These are the arks, the trophies I erect,
That fortify thy name against old age,
And these thy sacred virtues must protect
Against the dark and time's consuming rage.
  Though the error of my youth in them appear,
  Suffice they show I lived and loved thee dear.

LIKE as the lute delights or else dislikes,[3]
As is his art that plays upon the same,
So sounds my Muse according as she strikes
On my heart-strings high-tuned unto her fame.
Her touch doth cause the warble of the sound,
Which here I yield in lamentable wise,
A wailing descant[4] on the sweetest ground,[5]
Whose due reports give honour to her eyes.
Else harsh my style, untunable my Muse,
Hoarse sounds the voice that praiseth not her name;

[2] The lady of Petrarch's sonnets.

[3] displeases
[4] A counter-tune.
[5] The fundamental melody.

If any pleasing relish here I use,
Then judge the world her beauty gives the same;
For no ground else could make the music such,
Nor other hand could give so true a touch.

Love is a sickness full of woes

Love is a sickness full of woes,
All remedies refusing;
A plant that with most cutting grows,
Most barren with best using.
Why so?
More we enjoy it, more it dies;
If not enjoyed it sighing cries,
Hey ho.
Love is a torment of the mind,
A tempest everlasting;
And Jove hath made it of a kind,
Not well, nor full, nor fasting.
Why so?
More we enjoy it, more it dies;
If not enjoyed it sighing cries,
Hey ho.

[*Hymen's Triumph*, 1615]

THE COMPLAINT OF ROSAMOND[6]

Out from the horror of infernal deeps
My poor afflicted ghost comes here to plain it,
Attended with my shame that never sleeps,
The spot wherewith my kind[7] and youth did stain it;
My body found a grave where to contain it,
A sheet could hide my face, but not my sin,
For fame finds never tomb t'inclose it in.

And which is worse, my soul is now denied
Her transport to the sweet Elysian rest,
The joyful bliss for ghosts repurified,
The ever-springing gardens of the blest;
Charon denies me waftage with the rest,
And says my soul can never pass the river,
Till lovers' sighs on earth shall it deliver.

So shall I never pass, for how should I
Procure this sacrifice amongst the living?
Time hath long since worn out the memory
Both of my life and life's unjust depriving;
Sorrow for me is dead for aye reviving.
Rosamond hath little left her but her name,
And that disgraced, for time hath wronged the same.

No muse suggests the pity of my case;
Each pen doth overpass my just complaint,
Whilst others are preferred, though far more base;
Shore's wife[8] is graced, and passes for a saint;
Her legend justifies her foul attaint.
Her well-told tale did such compassion find
That she is passed, and I am left behind.

Which seen with grief, my miserable ghost
(Whilom invested in so fair a veil,
Which whilst it lived was honoured of the most,
And being dead, gives matter to bewail)
Comes to solicit thee, since others fail,
To take this task, and in thy woful song
To form my case, and register my wrong.

[6] The poem was published in 1592 but received additions, chiefly of moralizing stanzas. Rosamond was the mistress of Henry II, but the story that his queen poisoned her is a legend. So too, we hope, is the tradition that on her tomb in Godstow nunnery was carved:
Hic jacet in tumba Rosa mundi, non rosa munda:
Non redolet, sed olet, quae redolere solet.

[7] sex

[8] Jane Shore, the mistress of Edward IV.

Although I know thy just lamenting muse,
Toiled in th'affliction of thine own distress,
In others' care hath little time to use,
And therefore mayst esteem of mine the less;
Yet as thy hopes attend happy redress,
The joys depending on a woman's grace,
So move thy mind a woeful woman's case.

Delia [9] may hap to deign to read our story,
And offer up her sighs among the rest,
Whose merit would suffice for both our glory,
Whereby thou might'st be graced and I be blest;
That indulgence would profit me the best.
Such power she hath by whom thy youth is led,
To joy the living and to bless the dead.

So I, through beauty made the woeful'st wight,
By beauty might have comfort after death;
That dying fairest, by the fairest might
Find life above on earth, and rest beneath.
She that can bless us with one happy breath,
Give comfort to thy muse to do her best,
That thereby thou mayst joy and I might rest.

Thus said, forthwith moved with a tender care
And pity, which myself could never find,
What she desired, my muse deigned to declare,
And therefore willed her boldly tell her mind;
And I, more willing took this charge assigned
Because her griefs were worthy to be known,
And telling hers, might hap forget mine own.

Then write, quoth she, the ruin of my youth,
Report the down-fall of my slipp'ry state;
Of all my life reveal the simple truth,
To teach to others what I learnt too late.
Exemplify my frailty, tell how fate
Keeps in eternal dark our fortunes hidden,
And ere they come, to know them 'tis forbidden.

For whilst the sunshine of my fortune lasted,
I joyed the happiest warmth, the sweetest heat
That ever yet imperious beauty tasted;
I had what glory ever flesh could get,
But this fair morning had a shameful set.
Disgrace darked honour, sin did cloud my brow,
As note the sequel, and I'll tell thee how.

The blood I stained was good and of the best,
My birth had honour and my beauty fame;
Nature and fortune joined to make me blest,
Had I had grace t'have known to use the same.
My education showed from whence I came,
And all concurred to make me happy first,
That so great hope might make me more accursed.

Happy lived I whilst parents' eye did guide
The indiscretion of my feeble ways,
And country home kept me from being eyed,
Where best unknown I spent my sweetest days;
Till that my friends mine honour sought to raise
To higher place, which greater credit yields,

[9] Sidney's sister, the Countess of Pembroke, is probably meant.

Deeming such beauty was unfit for fields.

From country then to court I was preferred,
From calm to storms, from shore into the deeps;
There where I perished, where my youth first erred;
There where I lost the flower which honour keeps;
There where the worser thrives, the better weeps.
Ah me, poor wench, on this unhappy shelf
I grounded me and cast away myself.

There whereas frail and tender beauty stands
With all assaulting powers environéd;
Having but prayers and weak feeble hands
To hold their honour's fort unvanquishéd;
There where to stand and be unconqueréd
Is to b'above the nature of our kind,
That cannot long for pity be unkind.

For thither comed (when years had armed my youth
With rarest proof of beauty ever seen,
When my reviving eye had learnt the truth
That it had power to make the winter green,
And flower affections whereas none had been),
Soon could I teach my brow to tyrannize,
And make the world do homage to mine eyes.

. . . .

Ah, beauty! siren! fair enchanting good!
Sweet silent rhetoric of persuading eyes!
Dumb eloquence, whose power doth move the blood
More than the words or wisdom of the wise!
Still harmony, whose diapason[10] lies
Within a brow, the key which passions move
To ravish sense and play a world in love!

What might I then not do whose power was such?
What cannot women do that know their power?
What woman knows it not (I fear too much)
How bliss or bale lies in their laugh or lour,
Whilst they enjoy their happy blooming flower,
Whilst nature decks them in their best attires
Of youth and beauty, which the world admires?

Such one was I, my beauty was mine own,
No borrowed blush which bankrupt beauties seek;
That new-found shame, a sin to us unknown,
Th'adulterate beauty of a falséd cheek,
Vile stain to honour and to women eke,
Seeing that time our fading must detect,
Thus with defect to cover our defect.

Impiety of times, chastity's abater,
Falsehood, wherein thyself thyself deniest,
Treason to counterfeit the seal of nature,
The stamp of heaven, impresséd by the highest,
Disgrace unto the world, to whom thou liest,
Idol unto thyself, shame to the wise,
And all that honour thee idolatrize.

Far was that sin from us whose age was pure,
When simple beauty was accounted best,
The time when women had no other lure
But modesty, pure cheeks, a virtuous breast,
This was the pomp wherewith my youth was blest;

[10] concord of sounds

These were the weapons which mine honour won
In all the conflicts which my eyes begun;

Which were not small, I wrought on no mean object;
A crown was at my feet, scepters obeyed me;
Whom fortune made my king, love made my subject;
Who did command the land most humbly prayed me;
Henry the second, that so highly weighed me,
Found well, by proof, the privilege of beauty,
That it had power to countermand all duty.

For after all his victories in France,
And all the triumphs of his honour won,
Unmatched by sword, was vanquished by a glance,
And hotter wars within his breast begun —
Wars whom whole legions of desires drew on,
Against all which my chastity contends
With force of honour, which my shame defends.

. . . .

And safe mine honour stood, till that in truth
One of my sex, of place and nature bad,
Was set in ambush to entrap my youth,
One in the habit of like frailty clad,
One who the liv'ry of like weakness had,
A seeming matron, yet a sinful monster,
As by her words the chaster sort may conster.[11]

She set upon me with the smoothest speech
That court and age could cunningly devise;
Th'one authentic made her fit to teach,
The other learned her how to subtilize.
Both were enough to circumvent the wise,
A document that well might teach the sage
That there's no trust in youth, nor hope in age.

. . . .

So well the golden balls cast down before me
Could entertain my course, hinder my way;
Whereat my retchless[12] youth, stooping to store me,
Lost me the goal, the glory, and the day.
Pleasure had set my well-schooled thoughts to play,
And bade me use the virtue of mine eyes,
For sweetly it fits the fair to wantonise.

Thus wrought to sin, soon was I trained from court
T'a solitary grange, there to attend
The time the king should thither make resort,
Where he love's long-desiréd work should end.
Thither he daily messages doth send,
With costly jewels, orators of love,
Which (ah, too well men know) do women move.

The day before the night of my defeature
He greets me with a casket richly wrought,
So rare that art did seem to strive with nature
T'express the cunning workman's curious thought;
The mystery whereof I prying sought,
And found engraven on the lid above
Amymone, how she with Neptune strove.

There might I see describéd how she lay,
At those proud feet not satisfied with prayer;

[11] construe

[12] reckless

Wailing her heavy hap, cursing the day,
In act so piteous to express despair.
And by how much more grieved, so much more fair;
Her tears upon her cheeks, poor careful[13] girl,
Did seem, against the sun, crystal and pearl.

. . . .

These precedents presented to my view,
Wherein the presage of my fall was shown,
Might have forewarned me well what would ensue,
And others' harms have made me shun mine own;
But fate is not prevented, though foreknown,
For that must hap, decreed by heavenly powers
Who work our fall yet make the fault still ours.

. . . .

I saw the sin wherein my foot was en-t'ring,
I saw how that dishonour did attend it,
I saw the shame whereon my flesh was vent'ring,
Yet had I not the power for to defend it.
So weak is sense, when error hath condemned it;
We see what's good, and thereto we consent,
But yet we choose the worst, and soon repent.

And now I come to tell the worst of illness,
Now draws the date of mine affliction near;
Now when the dark had wrapt up all in stillness,
And dreadful black had dispossessed the clear,
Comed was the night, mother of sleep and fear,
Who with her sable mantle friendly covers
The sweet stolen sports of joyful meeting lovers.

When lo! I joyed my lover, not my love,
And felt the hand of lust most undesired;
Enforced, th'unprovéd bitter-sweet to prove,
Which yields no mutual pleasure when 'tis hired.
Love's not constrain'd, nor yet of due required:
Judge they who are unfortunately wed
What 'tis to come unto a loathéd bed.

. . . .

What greater torment ever could have been,
Than to enforce the fair to live retired?
For what is beauty if it be not seen?
Or what is't to be seen if not admired,
And though admired, unless in love desired?
Never were cheeks of roses, locks of amber,
Ordained to live imprisoned in a chamber.

Nature created beauty for the view,
Like as the fire for heat, the sun for light;
The fair do hold this privilege as due
By ancient charter, to live most in sight,
And she that is debarred it, hath not right.
In vain our friends from this do us dehort,
For beauty will be where is most resort.

. . . .

Yet would to God my foot had never moved
From country safety, from the fields of rest,
To know the danger to be highly loved,
And live in pomp to brave among the best;

[13] full of care

Happy for me, better had I been blest,
If I unluckily had never strayed,
But lived at home a happy country maid,

Whose unaffected innocency thinks
No guileful fraud, as doth the courtly liver;
She's decked with truth; the river where she drinks
Doth serve her for her glass, her counsel-giver;
She loves sincerely, and is lovéd ever;
Her days are peace, and so she ends her breath —
True life, that knows not what's to die till death.

So should I never have been regist'red
In the black book of the unfortunate,
Nor had my name enrolled with maids misled,
Which bought their pleasures at so high a rate;
Nor had I taught, through my unhappy fate,
This lesson, which myself learnt with expense,
How most it hurts that most delights the sense.

Shame follows sin, disgrace is duly given,
Impiety will out, never so closely done;
No walls can hide us from the eye of heaven,
For shame must end what wickedness begun;
Forth breaks reproach when we least think thereon,
And this is ever proper unto courts,
That nothing can be done but fame reports.

Fame doth explore what lies most secret hidden,
Ent'ring the closet of the palace dweller,
Abroad revealing what is most forbidden;
Of truth and falsehood both an equal teller,
'Tis not a guard can serve for to expel her.
The sword of justice cannot cut her wings,
Nor stop her mouth from utt'ring secret things.

And this our stealth she could not long conceal
From her whom such a forfeit most concerned,
The wrongéd queen, who could so closely deal
That she the whole of all our practice learned,
And watched a time when least it was discerned,
In absence of the king, to wreak her wrong
With such revenge as she desiréd long.

The labyrinth [14] she entered by that thread
That served a conduct to my absent lord,
Left there by chance, reserved for such a deed,
Where she surprised me whom she so abhorred.
Enraged with madness, scarce she speaks a word,
But flies with eager fury to my face,
Off'ring me most unwomanly disgrace.

Look how a tigress that hath lost her whelp
Runs fiercely ranging through the woods astray,
And seeing herself deprived of hope or help,
Furiously assaults what's in her way,
To satisfy her wrath, not for a prey;
So fell she on me in outrageous wise,
As could disdain and jealousy devise.

And after all her vile reproaches used,
She forced me take the poison she had brought
To end the life that had her so abused,

[14] Henry is supposed to have built Rosamond a house as intricate in design as the Cretan labyrinth.

And free her fears and ease her jealous thought.
No cruelty her wrath could leave unwrought,
No spiteful act that to revenge is common,
No beast being fiercer than a jealous woman.

Here take, saith she, thou impudent, unclean,
Base, graceless strumpet, take this next your heart;
Your love-sick heart, that overcharged hath been
With pleasure's surfeit, must be purged with art.
This potion hath a power that will convert
To nought those humors that oppress you so;
And, girl, I'll see you take it ere I go.

What, stand you now amazed, retire you back?
Tremble you, minion? Come, dispatch with speed;
There is no help, your champion now you lack,
And all these tears you shed will nothing stead;
Those dainty fingers needs must do the deed.
Take it, or I will drench[15] you else by force,
And trifle not, lest that I use you worse.

Having this bloody doom from hellish breath,
My woeful eyes on every side I cast,
Rigour about me, in my hand my death,
Presenting me the horror of my last,
All hope of pity and of comfort past.
No means, no power, no forces to contend,
My trembling hands must give myself my end.

[15] make you drink

Those hands that beauty's ministers had been,
They must give death, that me adorned of late;
That mouth that newly gave consent to sin,
Must now receive destruction in thereat;
That body which my lust did violate,
Must sacrifice itself t'appease the wrong:
So short is pleasure, glory lasts so long.

And she no sooner saw I had it taken,
But forth she rushes, proud with victory,
And leaves m'alone, of all the world forsaken,
Except of death, which she had left with me;
Death and myself alone together be,
To whom she did her full revenge refer;
Oh, poor weak conquest, both for him and her.

Then straight my conscience summons up my sin
T'appear before me in a hideous face;
Now doth the terror of my soul begin,
When ev'ry corner of that hateful place
Dictates mine error and reveals disgrace;
Whilst I remain oppressed in every part,
Death in my body, horror at my heart.

Down on my bed my loathsome self I cast,
The bed that likewise gives in evidence
Against my soul, and tells I was unchaste,
Tells I was wanton, tells I followed sense;
And therefore cast by guilt of mine offence,
Must here the right of heaven needs satisfy,
And where I wanton lay, must wretched die.

Here I began to wail my hard mishap,
My sudden, strange, unlooked-for misery;
Accusing them that did my youth entrap,

To give me such a fall of infamy.
And, Poor distresséd Rosamond, said I,
Is this thy glory got, to die forlorn
In deserts where no ear can hear thee mourn?

Nor any eye of pity to behold
The woeful end of my sad tragedy?
But that thy wrongs unseen, thy tale untold,
Must here in secret silence buried lie,
And with thee thine excuse together die.
Thy sin revealed, but thy repentance hid,
Thy shame alive, but dead what thy death did.

. . . .

This, and much more, I would have uttered then,
A testament to be recorded still,
Signed with my blood, subscribed with conscience' pen,
To warn the fair and beautiful from ill.
Though I could wish, by th'example of my will,
I had not left this note unto the fair,
But died intestate to have had no heir.

But now the poison spread through all my veins
Gan dispossess my living senses quite,
And nought-respecting death, the last of pains,
Placed his pale colors, th'ensign of his might,
Upon his new-got spoil before his right;
Thence chased my soul, setting my day ere noon,
When I least thought my joys could end so soon.

And as conveyed t'untimely funerals,
My scarce-cold corpse not suffered longer stay,
Behold, the king, by chance returning, falls
T'encounter with the same upon the way,
As he repaired to see his dearest joy;
Not thinking such a meeting could have been,
To see his love, and seeing been unseen.

. . . .

Amazed he stands, nor voice nor body steers,
Words had no passage, tears no issue found,
For sorrow shut up words, wrath kept in tears;
Confused affects each other do confound,
Oppressed with grief his passions had no bound.
Striving to tell his woes, words would not come,
For light cares speak, when mighty griefs are dumb.

At length extremity breaks out a way,
Through which th'imprisoned voice with tears attended
Wails out a sound that sorrows do bewray,
With arms a-cross and eyes to heaven bended,
Vapouring out sighs that to the skies ascended —
Sighs, the poor ease calamity affords,
Which serve for speech when sorrow wanteth words.

O heavens, quoth he, why do mine eyes behold
The hateful rays of this unhappy sun?
Why have I light to see my sins controlled,
With blood of mine own shame thus vilely done?
How can my sight endure to look thereon?
Why doth not black eternal darkness hide
That from mine eyes my heart cannot abide?

. . . .

Pitiful mouth, saith he, that living gavest
The sweetest comfort that my soul could wish,

Oh, be it lawful now, that dead thou havest
This sorrowful farewell of a dying kiss;
And you, fair eyes, containers of my bliss,
Motives of love, born to be matchéd never,
Entombed in your sweet circles, sleep forever.

Ah, now methinks I see death dallying seeks
To entertain itself in love's sweet place;
Decayéd roses of discoloured cheeks
Do yet retain dear notes of former grace,
And ugly death sits fair within her face;
Sweet remnants resting of vermilion red,
That death itself doubts whether she be dead.

Wonder of beauty, O receive these plaints,
These obsequies, the last that I shall make thee;
For lo, my soul that now already faints,
That loved thee living, dead will not forsake thee,
Hastens her speedy course to overtake thee.
I'll meet my death, and free myself thereby,
For, ah, what can he do that cannot die?

Yet ere I die, this much my soul doth vow,
Revenge shall sweeten death with ease of mind,
And I will cause posterity shall know
How fair thou wert above all women-kind,
And after-ages monuments shall find
Showing thy beauty's title, not thy name,
Rose of the world, that sweetened so the same.

This said, though more desirous yet to say,
For sorrow is unwilling to give over,
He doth repress what grief would else bewray,
Lest he too much his passions should discover;
And yet respect scarce bridles such a lover,
So far transported that he knows not whither,
For love and majesty dwell ill together.

Then were my funerals not long deferred,
But done with all the rites pomp could devise,
At Godstow, where my body was interred,
And richly tombed in honourable wise,
Where yet as now scarce any note descries
Unto these times the memory of me,
Marble and brass so little lasting be.

. . . .

But here an end, I may no longer stay,
I must return t'attend at Stygian flood;
Yet ere I go, this one word more I pray,
Tell Delia now her sigh may do me good,
And will her note the frailty of our blood;
And if I pass unto those happy banks,
Then she must have her praise, thy pen her thanks.

So vanished she, and left me to return
To prosecute the tenor of my woes,
Eternal matter for my muse to mourn;
But yet the world hath heard too much of those,
My youth such errors must no more disclose.
I'll hide the rest, and grieve for what hath been;
Who made me known must make me live unseen.

Edmund Spenser

1552?–1599

THE SHEPHERD'S CALENDAR *

Note: **In general, English printers did not make any distinction between i and j, u and v. The reader will observe that in these poems of Spenser we have followed the Elizabethan printer in this practice, which was already old-fashioned on the Continent.**

August

ARGVMENT

In this Æglogue is set forth a delectable controuersie, made in imitation of that in Theocritus: whereto also Virgile fashioned his third and seuenth Æglogue. They choose for vmpere of their strife, Cuddie, a neatheards boye, who hauing ended their cause, reciteth also himselfe a proper song, whereof Colin he sayth was Authour.

WILLYE. PERIGOT. CVDDIE.

TELL me *Perigot,* what shalbe the game,[1]
Wherefore with myne thou dare thy musick matche?
Or bene thy Bagpypes renne farre out of frame?
Or hath the Crampe thy ioynts benomd with ache?

PERIGOT

Ah *Willye,* when the hart is ill assayde,
How can Bagpipe, or ioynts be well apayd?

WILLYE

What the foule euill hath thee so bestadde? [2]
Whilom thou was peregall to the best,
And wont to make the iolly shepeheards gladde
With pyping and dauncing, didst passe the rest.

PERIGOT

Ah *Willye* now I haue learnd a newe daunce:
My old musick mard by a newe mischaunce.

WILLYE

Mischiefe mought [3] to that newe mischaunce befall,
That so hath raft vs of our meriment.
But reede me, what payne doth thee so appall?
Or louest thou, or bene thy younglings miswent?

PERIGOT

Loue hath misled both my younglings, and mee:
I pyne for payne, and they my payne to see.

WILLYE

Perdie and wellawaye: ill may they thriue:
Neuer knewe I louers sheepe in good plight.
But and if in rymes with me thou dare striue,
Such fond fantsies shall soone be put to flight.

PERIGOT

That shall I doe, though mochell worse I fared:
Neuer shall be sayde that *Perigot* was dared.

WILLYE

Then loe *Perigot* the Pledge, which I plight:
A mazer [4] ywrought of the Maple warre:
Wherein is enchased many a fayre sight
Of Beres and Tygres, that maken fiers warre:
And ouer them spred a goodly wild vine,
Entrailed with a wanton Yuie twine.

---

* The author of the eclogues which make up the 'Calendar' signed himself 'Immerito' in the first edition, 1579. The secret of Spenser's authorship was well kept, in spite of the curiosity which the mysteries of the book aroused, and was not fully revealed until the publication of three books of *The Faerie Queene* in 1590.

[1] stake

[2] What the devil has put you in this state?

[3] may mischief

[4] bowl

Thereby is a Lambe in the Wolues iawes:
But see, how fast renneth the shepheard swayne,
To saue the innocent from the beastes pawes:
And here with his shepehooke hath him slayne.
Tell me, such a cup hast thou euer sene?
Well mought it beseme any haruest Queene.

PERIGOT

Thereto will I pawne yonder spotted Lambe,
Of all my flocke there nis sike another:
For I brought him vp without the Dambe.
But *Colin Clout* rafte me of his brother,
That he purchast of me in the playne field:[5]
Sore against my will was I forst to yield.

WILLYE

Sicker make like account of his brother.
But who shall iudge the wager wonne or lost?

PERIGOT

That shall yonder heardgrome, and none other,
Which ouer the pousse hetherward doth post.

WILLYE

But for the Sunnebeame so sore doth vs beate,
Were not better, to shunne the scortching heate?

PERIGOT

Well agreed *Willy:* then sitte thee downe swayne:
Sike a song neuer heardest thou, but *Colin* sing.

CVDDIE

Gynne, when ye lyst, ye iolly shepheards twayne:
Sike a iudge, as *Cuddie,* were for a king.

[5] open contest

Perigot. It fell vpon a holly[6] eue,
Willye. hey ho hollidaye,
Per. When holly fathers wont to shrieue:
Wil. now gynneth this roundelay.
Per. Sitting vpon a hill so hye
Wil. hey ho the high hyll,
Per. The while my flocke did feede thereby,
Wil. the while the shepheard selfe did spill:
Per. I saw the bouncing Bellibone,
Wil. hey ho Bonibell,
Per. Tripping ouer the dale alone,
Wil. she can trippe it very well:
Per. Well decked in a frocke of gray,
Wil. hey ho gray is greete,
Per. And in a Kirtle of greene saye,[7]
Wil. the greene is for maydens meete:
Per. A chapelet on her head she wore,
Wil. hey ho chapelet,
Per. Of sweete Violets therein was store,
Wil. she sweeter then the Violet.
Per. My sheepe did leaue theyr wonted foode,
Wil. hey ho seely sheepe,
Per. And gazd on her, as they were wood,[8]
Wil. woode as he, that did them keepe.
Per. As the bonilasse passed bye,
Wil. hey ho bonilasse,
Per. She roude at me with glauncing eye,
Wil. as cleare as the christall glasse:
Per. All as the Sunnye beame so bright,
Wil. hey ho the Sunne beame,
Per. Glaunceth from *Phœbus* face forthright,
Wil. so loue into thy hart did streame:
Per. Or as the thonder cleaues the cloudes,
Wil. hey ho the Thonder,

[6] holy
[7] serge
[8] crazy

Per. Wherein the lightsome leuin shroudes,
Wil. so cleaues thy soule a sonder:
Per. Or as Dame *Cynthias* siluer raye
Wil. hey ho the Moonelight,
Per. Vpon the glyttering waue doth playe:
Wil. such play is a pitteous plight.
Per. The glaunce into my heart did glide,
Wil. hey ho the glyder,
Per. Therewith my soule was sharply gryde,
Will. such woundes soone wexen wider.
Per. Hasting to raunch the arrow out,
Wil. hey ho Perigot.
Per. I left the head in my hart roote:
Wil. it was a desperate shot.
Per. There it ranckleth ay more and more,
Wil. hey ho the arrowe,
Per. Ne can I find salue for my sore:
Wil. loue is a curelesse sorrowe.
Per. And though my bale with death I bought,
Wil. hey ho heauie cheere,
Per. Yet should thilk lasse not from my thought:
Wil. so you may buye gold to deare.
Per. But whether in paynefull loue I pyne,
Wil. hey ho pinching payne,
Per. Or thriue in welth, she shalbe mine.
Wil. but if thou can her obteine.
Per. And if for gracelesse greefe I dye,
Wil. hey ho gracelesse griefe,
Per. Witnesse, shee slewe me with her eye:
Wil. let thy follye be the priefe.
Per. And you, that sawe it, simple shepe,
Wil. hey ho the fayre flocke,
Per. For priefe thereof, my death shall weepe,
Wil. and mone with many a mocke.
Per. So learnd I loue on a hollye eue,
Wil. hey ho holidaye,
Per. That euer since my hart did greue.
Wil. now endeth our roundelay.

CVDDYE

Sicker sike[9] a roundle neuer heard I none.
Little lacketh *Perigot* of the best.
And *Willye* is not greatly ouergone,
So weren his vndersongs well addrest.

WILLYE

Herdgrome, I feare me, thou haue a squint eye:
Areede vprightly,[10] who has the victorye?

CVDDIE

Fayth of my soule, I deeme ech haue gayned.
For thy let the Lambe be *Willye* his owne:
And for *Perigot* so well hath hym payned,
To him be the wroughten mazer alone.

PERIGOT

Perigot is well pleased with the doome:
Ne can *Willye* wite the witelesse herdgroome.

WILLYE

Neuer dempt more right of beautye I weene,
The shepheard of *Ida,* that iudged beauties Queene.

CVDDIE

But tell me shepherds, should it not yshend
Your roundels fresh, to heare a doolefull verse
Of Rosalend (who knowes not Rosalend?)
That Colin made, ylke can I you rehearse.

PERIGOT

Now say it *Cuddie,* as thou art a ladde:
With mery thing its good to medle sadde.

WILLYE

Fayth of my soule, thou shalt ycrouned be
In *Colins* stede, if thou this song areede:
For neuer thing on earth so pleaseth me,
As him to heare, or matter of his deede.[11]

---

[9] surely such
[10] justly
[11] songs of his making

CVDDIE

Then listneth ech vnto my heauy laye,
And tune your pypes as ruthful, as ye may.

Ye wastefull woodes beare witnesse of my woe,
Wherein my plaints did oftentimes resound:
Ye carelesse byrds are priuie to my cryes,
  Which in your songs were wont to make a part:
  Thou pleasaunt spring hast luld me oft a sleepe,
  Whose streames my tricklinge teares did ofte augment.
Resort of people doth my greefs augment,
  The walled townes do worke my greater woe:
  The forest wide is fitter to resound
  The hollow Echo of my carefull cryes,
  I hate the house, since thence my loue did part,
  Whose waylefull want debarres myne eyes from sleepe.
Let stremes of teares supply the place of sleepe:
  Let all that sweete is, voyd:[12] and all that may augment
  My doole, drawe neare. More meete to wayle my woe,
  Bene the wild woddes my sorrowes to resound,
  Then bedde, or bowre, both which I fill with cryes,
  When I them see so waist, and fynd no part
Of pleasure past. Here will I dwell apart
  In gastful groue therefore, till my last sleepe
  Doe close mine eyes: so shall I not augment
  With sight of such a chaunge my restlesse woe:
  Helpe me, ye baneful byrds, whose shrieking sound
  Ys signe of dreery death, my deadly cryes
Most ruthfully to tune. And as my cryes
  (Which of my woe cannot bewray least part)
  You heare all night, when nature craueth sleepe,
  Increase, so let your yrksome yells augment.
  Thus all the night in plaints, the daye in woe
  I vowed haue to wayst, till safe and sound
She home returne, whose voyces siluer sound
  To cheerefull songs can chaunge my cherelesse cryes.
  Hence with the Nightingale will I take part,
  That blessed byrd, that spends her time of sleepe
  In songs and plaintiue pleas, the more taugment
  The memory of hys misdeede, that bred her woe:
And you that feele no woe, | when as the sound
  Of these my nightly cryes | ye heare apart,
  Let breake your sounder sleepe | and pitie augment.

PERIGOT

O *Colin, Colin,* the shepheards ioye,
  How I admire ech turning of thy verse:
And *Cuddie,* fresh *Cuddie* the liefest boye,
  How dolefully his doole thou didst rehearse.

CUDDIE

Then blowe your pypes shepheards, til you be at home:
The night nigheth fast, yts time to be gone.

Perigot his Embleme.
Vincenti gloria victi.

[12] depart

Willyes Embleme.

Vinto non vitto.

Cuddies Embleme.

Felice chi può.

GLOSSE [13]

Bestadde) disposed, ordered.
Peregall) equall.
Whilome) once.
Rafte) bereft, depriued.
Miswent) gon a straye.
Ill may) according to Virgile.

Infelix o semper ouis pecus.

A mazer) So also do Theocritus and Virgile feigne pledges of their strife.
Enchased) engrauen. Such pretie descriptions euery where vseth Theocritus, to bring in his Idyllia. For which speciall cause indede he by that name termeth his Æglogues: for Idyllion in Greke signifieth the shape or picture of any thyng, wherof his booke is ful. And not, as I haue heard some fondly guesse, that they be called not Idyllia, but Hædilia, of the Goteheards in them.
Entrailed) wrought betwene.
Haruest Queene) The manner of country folke in haruest tyme.
Pousse.) Pease.
It fell vpon) Perigot maketh hys song in prayse of his loue, to whom Willy answereth euery vnder verse. By Perigot who is meant, I can not vprightly say. but if it be, who is supposed, his love deserueth no lesse prayse, then he giueth her.
Greete) weeping and complaint.
Chaplet) a kind of Garlond lyke a crowne.
Leuen) Lightning.
Cynthia) was sayd to be the Moone.
Gryde) perced.
But if) not vnlesse.
Squint eye) partiall iudgement.
Ech haue) so saith Virgile.

Et vitula tu dignus, et hic &c.

So by enterchaunge of gyfts Cuddie pleaseth both partes.
Doome) iudgement.
Dempt) for deemed, iudged.
Wite the witelesse) blame the blamelesse.
The shepherd of Ida) was sayd to be Paris.
Beauties Queene) Venus, to whome Paris adiudged the golden Apple, as the pryce of her beautie.

Embleme.

The meaning hereof is very ambiguous: for Perigot by his poesie claming the conquest, and Willye not yeelding, Cuddie the arbiter of theyr cause, and Patron of his own, semeth to chalenge it, as his dew, saying, that he is happy which can, so abruptly ending but hee meaneth eyther him, that can win the beste, or moderate him selfe being best, and leaue of with the best.

AMORETTI [14]

III

THE souerayne beauty which I doo admyre,
witnesse the world how worthy to be prayzed:
the light wherof hath kindled heauenly fyre,
in my fraile spirit by her from basenesse raysed.
That being now with her huge brightnesse dazed,
base thing I can no more endure to view:
But looking still on her I stand amazed,
at wondrous sight of so celestiall hew.
So when my toung would speak her praises dew,
it stopped is with thoughts astonishment:
and when my pen would write her titles true,
it rauisht is with fancies wonderment:
Yet in my hart I then both speake and write
the wonder that my wit cannot endite.

VIII

MORE then most faire, full of the liuing fire,
Kindled aboue vnto the maker neere:
no eies but ioyes, in which al powers conspire,
that to the world naught else be counted deare.
Thrugh your bright beames doth not the blinded guest,
shoot out his darts to base affections wound:
but Angels come to lead fraile mindes to rest
in chast desires on heauenly beauty bound.
You frame my thoughts and fashion me within,
you stop my toung, and teach my hart to speake,
you calme the storme that passion did begin,

---

[13] The gloss was supplied to *The Shepherd's Calendar* by 'E. K.' who is probably Spenser's friend Edward Kirke.

[14] These sonnets are the record of Spenser's courtship of his wife, Elizabeth Boyle. They were published with the *Epithalamion* (see p. 107) in 1595.

strong thrugh your cause, but by your vertue weak.
Dark is the world, where your light shined neuer;
well is he borne, that may behold you euer.

XLI

Is it her nature or is it her will,
to be so cruell to an humbled foe?
if nature, then she may it mend with skill,
if will, then she at will may will forgoe.
But if her nature and her wil be so,
that she will plague the man that loues her most:
and take delight t'encrease a wretches woe,
then all her natures goodly guifts are lost.
And that same glorious beauties ydle boast,
is but a bayt such wretches to beguile:
as being long in her loues tempest tost,
she meanes at last to make her piteous spoyle.
O fayrest fayre let neuer it be named,
that so fayre beauty was so fowly shamed.

LXIII

After long stormes and tempests sad assay,
Which hardly I endured heretofore:
in dread of death and daungerous dismay,
with which my silly barke was tossed sore:
I doe at length descry the happy shore,
in which I hope ere long for to arryue;
fayre soyle it seemes from far and fraught with store
of all that deare and daynty is alyue.
Most happy he that can at last atchyue
the ioyous safety of so sweet a rest:
whose least delight sufficeth to depriue
remembrance of all paines which him opprest.
All paines are nothing in respect of this,
all sorrowes short that gaine eternall blisse.

LXVII

Lyke as a huntsman after weary chace,
Seeing the game from him escapt away,
sits downe to rest him in some shady place,
with panting hounds beguiled of their pray:
So after long pursuit and vaine assay,
when I all weary had the chace forsooke,
the gentle deare returnd the selfe-same way,
thinking to quench her thirst at the next brooke.
There she beholding me with mylder looke,
sought not to fly, but fearelesse still did bide:
till I in hand her yet halfe trembling tooke,
and with her owne goodwill hir fyrmely tyde.
Strange thing me seemd to see a beast so wyld,
so goodly wonne with her owne will beguyld.

LXXII

Oft when my spirit doth spred her bolder winges,
In mind to mount vp to the purest sky:
it down is weighd with thoght of earthly things
and clogd with burden of mortality,
Where when that souerayne beauty it doth spy,
resembling heauens glory in her light:
drawne with sweet pleasures bayt, it back doth fly,
and vnto heauen forgets her former flight.
There my fraile fancy fed with full delight,
doth bath in blisse and mantleth most at ease:
ne thinks of other heauen, but how it might

her harts desire with most contentment please.
Hart need not with none other happinesse,
but here on earth to haue such heuens blisse.

LXXV

One day I wrote her name vpon the strand,
but came the waues and washed it away:
agayne I wrote it with a second hand,
but came the tyde, and made my paynes his pray.
Vayne man, sayd she, that doest in vaine assay,
a mortall thing so to immortalize,
for I my selue shall lyke to this decay,
and eek my name bee wyped out lykewize.
Not so, (quod I) let baser things deuize
to dy in dust, but you shall liue by fame:
my verse your vertues rare shall eternize,
and in the heuens wryte your glorious name.
Where whenas death shall all the world subdew,
our loue shall liue, and later life renew.

Upon a day

Vpon a day as loue lay sweetly slumbring,
all in his mothers lap:
A gentle Bee with his loud trumpet murm'ring,
about him flew by hap.
Whereof when he was wakened with the noyse,
and saw the beast so small:
Whats this (quoth he) that giues so great a voyce,
that wakens men withall?
In angry wize he flyes about,
and threatens all with corage stout.

To whom his mother closely smiling sayd,
twixt earnest and twixt game:
See thou thy selfe likewise art lyttle made,
if thou regard the same.
And yet thou suffrest neyther gods in sky,
nor men in earth to rest:
But when thou art disposed cruelly,
theyr sleepe thou doost molest.
Then eyther change thy cruelty,
or giue lyke leaue vnto the fly.

Nathlesse the cruell boy not so content,
would needs the fly pursue:
And in his hand with heedlesse hardiment,
him caught for to subdue.
But when on it he hasty hand did lay,
the Bee him stung therefore:
Now out alasse (he cryde) and wel-away,
I wounded am full sore:
The fly that I so much did scorne,
hath hurt me with his little horne.

Vnto his mother straight he weeping came,
and of his griefe complayned:
Who could not chose but laugh at his fond game,
though sad to see him pained.
Think now (quod she) my sonne how great the smart
of those whom thou dost wound:
Full many thou hast pricked to the hart,
that pitty neuer found:
Therefore henceforth some pitty take,
when thou doest spoyle of louers make.

She tooke him streight full pitiously lamenting,
and wrapt him in her smock:
She wrapt him softly, all the while repenting,
that he the fly did mock.
She drest his wound and it embaulmed wel
with salue of soueraigne might:
And then she bath'd him in a dainty well
the well of deare delight.
Who would not oft be stung as this,
to be so bath'd in Venus blis?

The wanton boy was shortly wel recured,
of that his malady:
But he soone after fresh againe enured,
his former cruelty.
And since that time he wounded hath my selfe
with his sharpe dart of loue:
And now forgets the cruell carelesse elfe,
his mothers heast to proue.
So now I languish, till he please
my pining anguish to appease.

EPITHALAMION [15]

YE learned sisters [16] which haue oftentimes
Beene to me ayding, others to adorne:
Whom ye thought worthy of your gracefull rymes,
That euen the greatest did not greatly scorne
To heare theyr names sung in your simple layes,
But ioyed in theyr prayse.
And when ye list your owne mishaps to mourne,
Which death, or loue, or fortunes wreck did rayse,
Your string could soone to sadder tenor turne,
And teach the woods and waters to lament
Your dolefull dreriment.
Now lay those sorrowfull complaints aside,
And hauing all your heads with girland crownd,
Helpe me mine owne loues prayses to resound,
Ne let the same of any be enuide:
So Orpheus did for his owne bride,
So I vnto my selfe alone will sing,
The woods shall to me answer and my Eccho ring.

Early before the worlds light giuing lampe,
His golden beame vpon the hils doth spred,
Hauing disperst the nights vnchearefull dampe,
Doe ye awake, and with fresh lusty hed,
Go to the bowre of my beloued loue,
My truest turtle doue,
Bid her awake; for Hymen is awake,
And long since ready forth his maske to moue,
With his bright Tead [17] that flames with many a flake,
And many a bachelor to waite on him,
In theyr fresh garments trim.
Bid her awake therefore and soone her dight,
For lo the wished day is come at last,
That shall for al the paynes and sorrowes past,
Pay to her vsury of long delight:
And whylest she doth her dight,
Doe ye to her of ioy and solace sing,
That all the woods may answer and your eccho ring.

Bring with you all the Nymphes that you can heare
Both of the riuers and the forrests greene:
And of the sea that neighbours to her neare,
Al with gay girlands goodly wel beseene.
And let them also with them bring in hand,
Another gay girland
For my fayre loue of lillyes and of roses,
Bound trueloue wize with a blew silke riband.
And let them make great store of bridale poses,
And let them eeke bring store of other flowers
To deck the bridale bowers.
And let the ground whereas her foot shall tread,

[15] Written for Spenser's own marriage in 1594.
[16] the Muses

[17] torch

For feare the stones her tender foot should wrong
Be strewed with fragrant flowers all along,
And diapred lyke the discolored mead.
Which done, doe at her chamber dore awayt,
For she will waken strayt,
The whiles doe ye this song vnto her sing,
The woods shall to you answer and your Eccho ring.

Ye Nymphes of Mulla [18] which with carefull heed,
The siluer scaly trouts doe tend full well,
And greedy pikes which vse therein to feed,
(Those trouts and pikes all others doo excell)
And ye likewise which keepe the rushy lake,[19]
Where none doo fishes take,
Bynd vp the locks the which hang scatterd light,
And in his waters which your mirror make,
Behold your faces as the christall bright,
That when you come whereas my loue doth lie,
No blemish she may spie.
And eke ye lightfoot mayds which keepe the deere,
That on the hoary mountayne vse to towre,
And the wylde wolues which seeke them to deuoure,
With your steele darts doo chace from comming neer
Be also present heere,
To helpe to decke her and to help to sing,
That all the woods may answer and your eccho ring.

Wake, now my loue, awake; for it is time,
The Rosy Morne long since left Tithones bed,
All ready to her siluer coche to clyme,

[18] The river Awbeg, south of Kilcolman, where Spenser lived in Ireland. [19] Kilcolman Castle was beside a lake.

And Phœbus gins to shew his glorious hed.
Hark how the cheerefull birds do chaunt theyr laies
And carroll of loues praise.
The merry Larke hir mattins sings aloft,
The thrush replyes, the Mauis descant playes,
The Ouzell shrills, the Ruddock warbles soft,
So goodly all agree with sweet consent,
To this dayes merriment.
Ah my deere loue why doe ye sleepe thus long,
When meeter were that ye should now awake,
T'awayt the comming of your ioyous make,[20]
And hearken to the birds louelearned song,
The deawy leaues among.
For they of ioy and pleasance to you sing,
That all the woods them answer and theyr eccho ring.

My loue is now awake out of her dreame,
And her fayre eyes like stars that dimmed were
With darksome cloud, now shew theyr goodly beams
More bright then Hesperus his head doth rere.
Come now ye damzels, daughters of delight,
Helpe quickly her to dight,
But first come ye fayre houres which were begot
In Ioues sweet paradice, of Day and Night,
Which doe the seasons of the yeare allot,
And al that euer in this world is fayre
Doe make and still repayre.
And ye three handmayds [21] of the Cyprian Queene,
The which doe still adorne her beauties pride,

[20] mate [21] the Graces

Helpe to addorne my beautifullest bride:
And as ye her array, still throw betweene
Some graces to be seene,
And as ye vse to Venus, to her sing,
The whiles the woods shal answer and your eccho ring.

Now is my loue all ready forth to come,
Let all the virgins therefore well awayt,
And ye fresh boyes that tend vpon her groome
Prepare your selues; for he is comming strayt.
Set all your things in seemely good aray
Fit for so ioyfull day,
The ioyfulst day that euer sunne did see.
Faire Sun, shew forth thy fauourable ray,
And let thy lifull heat not feruent be
For feare of burning her sunshyny face,
Her beauty to disgrace.
O fayrest Phœbus, father of the Muse,
If euer I did honour thee aright,
Or sing the thing, that mote thy mind delight,
Doe not thy seruants simple boone refuse,
But let this day let this one day be myne,
Let all the rest be thine.
Then I thy souerayne prayses loud wil sing,
That all the woods shal answer and theyr eccho ring.

Harke how the Minstrels gin to shrill aloud
Their merry Musick that resounds from far,
The pipe, the tabor, and the trembling Croud,[22]
That well agree withouten breach or iar.
But most of all the Damzels doe delite,
When they their tymbrels smyte,
And thereunto doe daunce and carrol sweet,
That all the sences they doe rauish quite,
The whyles the boyes run vp and downe the street,
Crying aloud with strong confused noyce,
As if it were one voyce.
Hymen io Hymen, Hymen they do shout,
That euen to the heauens theyr shouting shrill
Doth reach, and all the firmament doth fill,
To which the people standing all about,
As in approuance doe thereto applaud
And loud aduaunce her laud,
And euermore they Hymen Hymen sing,
That al the woods them answer and theyr eccho ring.

Loe where she comes along with portly pace
Lyke Phœbe from her chamber of the East,
Arysing forth to run her mighty race,
Clad all in white, that seemes a virgin best.
So well it her beseemes that ye would weene
Some angell she had beene.
Her long loose yellow locks lyke golden wyre,
Sprinckled with perle, and perling flowres a tweene,
Doe lyke a golden mantle her attyre,
And being crowned with a girland greene,
Seeme lyke some mayden Queene.
Her modest eyes abashed to behold
So many gazers, as on her do stare,
Vpon the lowly ground affixed are.
Ne dare lift vp her countenance too bold,
But blush to heare her prayses sung so loud,
So farre from being proud.
Nathlesse doe ye still loud her prayses sing.
That all the woods may answer and your eccho ring.

Tell me ye merchants daughters did ye see
So fayre a creature in your towne before,
So sweet, so louely, and so mild as she,
Adorned with beautyes grace and vertues store

[22] fiddle

Her goodly eyes lyke Saphyres shining bright,
Her forehead yuory white,
Her cheekes lyke apples which the sun hath rudded,
Her lips lyke cherryes charming men to byte,
Her brest like to a bowle of creame vncrudded,
Her paps lyke lyllies budded,
Her snowie necke lyke to a marble towre,
And all her body like a pallace fayre,
Ascending vppe with many a stately stayre,
To honors seat and chastities sweet bowre.
Why stand ye still ye virgins in amaze,
Vpon her so to gaze,
Whiles ye forget your former lay to sing,
To which the woods did answer and your eccho ring.

But if ye saw that which no eyes can see,
The inward beauty of her liuely spright,[23]
Garnisht with heauenly guifts of high degree,
Much more then would ye wonder at that sight,
And stand astonisht lyke to those which red
Medusaes mazeful hed.
There dwels sweet loue and constant chastity,
Vnspotted fayth and comely womanhood,
Regard of honour and mild modesty,
There vertue raynes as Queene in royal throne,
And giueth lawes alone.
The which the base affections doe obay,
And yeeld theyr seruices vnto her will,
Ne thought of thing vncomley euer may
Thereto approch to tempt her mind to ill.
Had ye once seene these her celestial threasures,
And vnreuealed pleasures,
Then would ye wonder and her prayses sing,
That al the woods should answer and your echo ring.

[23] spirit

Open the temple gates vnto my loue,
Open them wide that she may enter in,
And all the postes adorne as doth behoue,
And all the pillours deck with girlands trim,
For to recyue this Saynt with honour dew,
That commeth in to you.
With trembling steps and humble reuerence,
She commeth in, before th'almighties vew,
Of her ye virgins learne obedience,
When so ye come into those holy places,
To humble your proud faces:
Bring her vp to th'high altar, that she may
The sacred ceremonies there partake,
The which do endlesse matrimony make,
And let the roring Organs loudly play
The praises of the Lord in liuely notes,
The whiles with hollow throates
The Choristers the ioyous Antheme sing,
That al the woods may answere and their eccho ring.

Behold whiles she before the altar stands
Hearing the holy priest that to her speakes
And blesseth her with his two happy hands,
How the red roses flush vp in her cheekes,
And the pure snow with goodly vermill stayne,
Like crimsin dyde in grayne,[24]
That euen th'Angels which continually,
About the sacred Altare doe remaine,
Forget their seruice and about her fly,
Ofte peeping in her face that seemes more fayre,
The more they on it stare.
But her sad[25] eyes still fastened on the ground,
Are gouerned with goodly modesty,
That suffers not one looke to glaunce awry,
Which may let in a little thought vnsownd.
Why blush ye loue to giue to me your hand,
The pledge of all our band?[26]
Sing ye sweet Angels, Alleluya sing,

[24] fast dye [25] serious [26] tie

That all the woods may answere and your eccho ring.

Now al is done; bring home the bride againe,
Bring home the triumph of our victory,
Bring home with you the glory of her gaine,
With ioyance bring her and with iollity.
Neuer had man more ioyfull day then this,
Whom heauen would heape with blis.
Make feast therefore now all this liue long day,
This day for euer to me holy is,
Poure out the wine without restraint or stay,
Poure not by cups, but by the belly full,
Poure out to all that wull,
And sprinkle all the postes and wals with wine,
That they may sweat, and drunken be withall.
Crowne ye God Bacchus with a coronall,
And Hymen also crowne with wreathes of vine,
And let the Graces daunce vnto the rest;
For they can doo it best:
The whiles the maydens doe theyr carroll sing,
To which the woods shal answer and theyr eccho ring

Ring ye the bels, ye yong men of the towne,
And leaue your wonted labors for this day:
This day is holy; doe ye write it downe,
That ye for euer it remember may.
This day [27] the sunne is in his chiefest hight,
With Barnaby the bright,
From whence declining daily by degrees,
He somewhat loseth of his heat and light,
When once the Crab behind his back he sees.
But for this time it ill ordained was,
To chose the longest day in all the yeare,
And shortest night, when longest fitter weare:
Yet neuer day so long, but late would passe.
Ring ye the bels, to make it weare away,
And bonefiers make all day,
And daunce about them, and about them sing:
That all the woods may answer, and your eccho ring.

Ah when will this long weary day haue end,
And lende me leaue to come vnto my loue?
How slowly do the houres theyr numbers spend?
How slowly does sad Time his feathers moue?
Hast thee O fayrest Planet to thy home
Within the Westerne fome:
Thy tyred steedes long since haue need of rest.
Long though it be, at last I see it gloome,
And the bright euening star with golden creast
Appeare out of the East.
Fayre childe of beauty, glorious lampe of loue
That all the host of heauen in rankes doost lead,
And guydest louers through the nightes dread,
How chearefully thou lookest from aboue,
And seemst to laugh atweene thy twinkling light
As ioying in the sight
Of these glad many which for ioy doe sing,
That all the woods them answer and their echo ring.

Now ceasse ye damsels your delights forepast;
Enough is it, that all the day was youres:
Now day is doen, and night is nighing fast:
Now bring the Bryde into the brydall boures.

[27] St. Barnabas' Day, 11 June, was, according to the old calendar, the longest day of the year.

Now night is come, now soone her disaray,
And in her bed her lay;
Lay her in lillies and in violets,
And silken courteins ouer her display,
And odourd sheetes, and Arras couerlets.
Behold how goodly my faire loue does ly
In proud humility;
Like vnto Maia, when as Ioue her tooke,
In Tempe, lying on the flowry gras,
Twixt sleepe and wake, after she weary was,
With bathing in the Acidalian brooke.
Now it is night, ye damsels may be gon,
And leaue my loue alone,
And leaue likewise your former lay to sing:
The woods no more shal answere, nor your echo ring.

Now welcome night, thou night so long expected,
That long daies labour doest at last defray,
And all my cares, which cruell loue collected,
Hast sumd in one, and cancelled for aye:
Spread thy broad wing ouer my loue and me,
That no man may vs see,
And in thy sable mantle vs enwrap,
From feare of perrill and foule horror free.
Let no false treason seeke vs to entrap,
Nor any dread disquiet once annoy
The safety of our ioy:
But let the night be calme and quietsome,
Without tempestuous storms or sad afray:
Lyke as when Ioue with fayre Alcmena lay,
When he begot the great Tirynthian groome:
Or lyke as when he with thy selfe did lie,
And begot Maiesty.
And let the mayds and yongmen cease to sing:
Ne let the woods them answer, nor theyr eccho ring.

Let no lamenting cryes, nor dolefull teares,
Be heard all night within nor yet without:
Ne let false whispers, breeding hidden feares,
Breake gentle sleepe with misconceiued dout.
Let no deluding dreames, nor dreadful sights
Make sudden sad affrights;
Ne let housefyres, nor lightnings helpelesse harmes,
Ne let the Pouke,[28] nor other euill sprights,
Ne let mischiuous witches with theyr charmes,
Ne let hob Goblins, names whose sence we see not,
Fray vs with things that be not.
Let not the shriech Oule, nor the Storke be heard:
Nor the night Rauen that still deadly yels,
Nor damned ghosts cald vp with mighty spels,
Nor griesly vultures make vs once affeard:
Ne let th'unpleasant Quyre of Frogs still croking
Make vs to wish theyr choking.
Let none of these theyr drery accents sing;
Ne let the woods them answer, nor theyr eccho ring.

Bvt let stil Silence trew night watches keepe,
That sacred peace may in assurance rayne,
And tymely sleep, when it is tyme to sleepe,
May poure his limbs forth on your pleasant playne,
The whiles an hundred little winged loues,
Like diuers fethered doues,
Shall fly and flutter round about your bed,
And in the secret darke, that none reproues,
Their prety stealthes shal worke, and snares shal spread
To filch away sweet snatches of delight,
Conceald through couert night.
Ye sonnes of Venus, play your sports at will,

[28] Puck

For greedy pleasure, carelesse of your toyes,
Thinks more vpon her paradise of ioyes,
Then what ye do, albe it good or ill.
All night therefore attend your merry play,
For it will soone be day:
Now none doth hinder you, that say or sing,
Ne will the woods now answer, nor your Eccho ring.

Who is the same, which at my window peepes?
Or whose is that faire face, that shines so bright,
Is it not Cinthia,[29] she that neuer sleepes,
But walkes about high heauen al the night?
O fayrest goddesse, do thou not enuy
My loue with me to spy:
For thou likewise didst loue, though now vnthought,
And for a fleece of woll, which priuily,
The Latmian shephard[30] once vnto thee brought,
His pleasures with thee wrought.
Therefore to vs be fauorable now;
And sith of wemens labours thou hast charge,
And generation goodly dost enlarge,
Encline thy will t'effect our wishfull vow,
And the chast wombe informe with timely seed,
That may our comfort breed:
Till which we cease our hopefull hap to sing,
Ne let the woods vs answere, nor our Eccho ring.

And thou great Iuno, which with awful might
The lawes of wedlock still dost patronize,
And the religion of the faith first plight
With sacred rites hast taught to solemnize:
And eeke for comfort often called art
Of women in their smart,

[29] the moon
[30] Endymion

Eternally bind thou this louely band,
And all thy blessings vnto vs impart.
And thou glad Genius, in whose gentle hand,
The bridale bowre and geniall bed remaine,
Without blemish or staine,
And the sweet pleasures of theyr loues delight
With secret ayde doest succour and supply,
Till they bring forth the fruitfull progeny,
Send vs the timely fruit of this same night.
And thou fayre Hebe, and thou Hymen free,
Grant that it may so be.
Til which we cease your further prayse to sing,
Ne any woods shal answer, nor your Eccho ring.

And ye high heauens, the temple of the gods,
In which a thousand torches flaming bright
Doe burne, that to vs wretched earthly clods,
In dreadful darknesse lend desired light;
And all ye powers which in the same remayne,
More then we men can fayne,[31]
Poure out your blessing on vs plentiously,
And happy influence vpon vs raine,
That we may raise a large posterity,
Which from the earth, which they may long possesse,
With lasting happinesse,
Vp to your haughty pallaces may mount,
And for the guerdon of theyr glorious merit
May heauenly tabernacles there inherit,
Of blessed Saints for to increase the count.
So let vs rest, sweet loue, in hope of this,
And cease till then our tymely ioyes to sing,
The woods no more vs answer, nor our eccho ring.

[31] imagine

Song made in lieu of many ornaments,
With which my loue should duly haue bene dect,
Which cutting off through hasty accidents,[32]
Ye would not stay your dew time to expect,
But promist both to recompens,
Be vnto her a goodly ornament,
And for [33] short time an endlesse moniment.

THE FAERIE QVEENE.

Disposed into twelue bookes,

Fashioning

XII. Morall vertues.

TO

THE MOST HIGH,
MIGHTIE
And
MAGNIFICENT
EMPRESSE RENOVV-
MED FOR PIETIE, VER-
TVE, AND ALL GRATIOVS
GOVERNMENT ELIZABETH BY
THE GRACE OF GOD QVEENE
OF ENGLAND FRAVNCE AND
IRELAND AND OF VIRGI-
NIA, DEFENDOVR OF THE
FAITH, &C. HER MOST
HVMBLE SERVAVNT
EDMVND SPENSER
DOTH IN ALL HV-
MILITIE DEDI-
CATE, PRE-
SENT
AND CONSECRATE THESE
HIS LABOVRS TO LIVE
VVITH THE ETERNI-
TIE OF HER
FAME.

[32] accidents of haste. The marriage date had perhaps been put ahead. [33] instead of

A
Letter of the Authors expounding his

whole intention in the course of this worke: which for that it giueth great light to the Reader, for the better vnderstanding is hereunto annexed.

To the Right noble, and Valorous, Sir Walter Raleigh knight, Lo. Wardein of the Stanneryes, and her Maiesties liefetenaunt of the County of Cornewayll.

Sir, knowing how doubtfully all Allegories may be construed, and this booke of mine, which I haue entituled the Faery Queene, being a continued Allegory, or darke conceit, I haue thought good aswell for auoyding of gealous opinions and misconstructions, as also for your better light in reading therof, (being so by you commanded,) to discouer vnto you the general intention and meaning, which in the whole course thereof I haue fashioned, without expressing of any particular purposes or by-accidents therein occasioned. The generall end therefore of all the booke is to fashion a gentleman or noble person in vertuous and gentle discipline: Which for that I conceiued shoulde be most plausible and pleasing, being coloured with an historicall fiction, the which the most part of men delight to read, rather for variety of matter, then for profite of the ensample, I chose the historye of king Arthure, as most fitte for the excellency of his person, being made famous by many mens former workes, and also furthest from the daunger of enuy, and suspition of present time. In which I haue followed all the antique Poets historicall; first Homere, who in the Persons of Agamemnon and Vlysses hath ensampled a good gouernour and a vertuous man, the one in his Ilias, the other in his Odysseis: then Virgil, whose like intention was to doe in the person of Aeneas: after him Ariosto comprised them both in his Orlando: and lately Tasso disseuered them againe, and formed both parts in two persons, namely that part which they in Philosophy call Ethice, or vertues of a priuate man, coloured in his Rinaldo: the other named Politice in his Godfredo. By ensample of which excellente Poets, I labour to pourtraict in Arthure, before he was king, the image of a braue knight, perfected in the twelue priuate morall vertues, as Aristotle hath deuised, the which is the purpose of these first twelue bookes [34]: which if I finde to be well accepted, I may be perhaps encoraged, to frame the other part of pollliticke vertues in his person, after that hee came to be king.

To some I know this Methode will seeme displeasaunt, which had rather haue good discipline

[34] Spenser completed only six books and part of a seventh.

diliuered plainly in way of precepts, or sermoned at large, as they vse, then thus clowdily enwrapped in Allegoricall deuises. But such, me seeme, should be satisfide with the vse of these dayes, seeing all things accounted by their showes, and nothing esteemed of, that is not delightfull and pleasing to commune sence. For this cause is Xenophon preferred before Plato, for that the one in the exquisite depth of his iudgement, formed a Commune welth such as it should be, but the other in the person of Cyrus and the Persians fashioned a gouernement such as might best be: So much more profitable and gratious is doctrine by ensample, then by rule. So haue I laboured to doe in the person of Arthure: whome I conceiue after his long education by Timon, to whom he was by Merlin deliuered to be brought vp, so soone as he was borne of the Lady Igrayne, to haue seene in a dream or vision the Faery Queen, with whose excellent beauty rauished, he awaking resolued to seeke her out; and so being by Merlin armed, and by Timon throughly instructed, he went to seeke her forth in Faerye land. In that Faery Queene I meane glory in my generall intention, but in my particular I conceiue the most excellent and glorious person of our soueraine the Queene, and her kingdome in Faery land. And yet in some places els, I doe otherwise shadow her. For considering she beareth two persons, the one of a most royall Queene or Empresse, the other of a most vertuous and beautifull Lady, this latter part in some places I doe expresse in Belphœbe, fashioning her name according to your owne excellent conceipt of Cynthia, (Phœbe and Cynthia being both names of Diana.) So in the person of Prince Arthure I sette forth magnificence in particular, which vertue for that (according to Aristotle and the rest) it is the perfection of all the rest, and conteineth in it them all; therefore in the whole course I mention the deedes of Arthure applyable to that vertue, which I write of in that booke. But of the xii. other vertues, I make xii. other knights the patrones, for the more variety of the history: Of which these three [35] bookes contayn three.

The first of the knight of the Redcrosse, in whome I expresse Holynes: The seconde of Sir Guyon, in whome I sette forth Temperaunce: The third of Britomartis, a Lady knight, in whome I picture Chastity. But because the beginning of the whole worke seemeth abrupte and as depending vpon other antecedents, it needs that ye know the occasion of these three knights seuerall aduentures. For the Methode of a Poet historical is not such, as of an Historiographer. For an Historiographer discourseth of affayres orderly as they were donne, accounting as well the times as the actions, but a Poet thrusteth into the middest, euen where it most concerneth him, and there recoursing to the thinges forepaste, and diuining of thinges to come, maketh a pleasing Analysis of all.

The beginning therefore of my history, if it were to be told by an Historiographer, should be the twelfth booke, which is the last, where I deuise that the Faery Queene kept her Annuall feaste xii. dayes, vppon which xii. seuerall dayes, the occasions of the xii. seuerall aduentures hapned, which being vndertaken by xii. seuerall knights, are in these xii books seuerally handled and discoursed. The first was this. In the beginning of the feast, there presented him selfe a tall clownishe younge man, who falling before the Queen of Faries desired a boone (as the manner then was) which during that feast she might not refuse: which was that hee might haue the atchieuement of any aduenture, which during that feaste should happen. That being graunted, he rested him on the floore, vnfitte through his rusticity for a better place. Soone after entred a faire Ladye in mourning weedes, riding on a white Asse, with a dwarfe behind her leading a warlike steed, that bore the Armes of a knight, and his speare in the dwarfes hand. Shee falling before the Queene of Faeries, complayned that her father and mother, an ancient King and Queene, had bene by an huge dragon many years shut vp in a brasen Castle, who thence suffred them not to yssew; and therefore besought the Faery Queene to assygne her some one of her knights to take on him that exployt. Presently that clownish person vpstarting, desired that aduenture: whereat the Queene much wondering, and the Lady much gainesaying, yet he earnestly importuned his desire. In the end the Lady told him that vnlesse that armour which she brought, would serue him (that is the armour of a Christian man specified by Saint Paul vi Ephes.) that he could not succeed in that enterprise, which being forthwith put vpon him with dewe furnitures thereunto, he seemed the goodliest man in al that company, and was well liked of the Lady. And eftesoones taking on him knighthood, and mounting on that straunge Courser, he went forth with her on that aduenture: where beginneth the first booke, vz.

A gentle knight was pricking on the playne. &c.

The second day ther came in a Palmer bearing an Infant with bloody hands, whose Parents he complained to haue bene slayn by an Enchaunteresse called Acrasia; and therfore craued of the Faery Queene, to appoint him some knight, to performe that aduenture, which being assigned to Sir Guyon, he presently went forth with that same Palmer: which is the beginning of the second booke and the whole subiect thereof. The third day there came in a Groome who complained before the Faery Queene, that a vile Enchaunter called Busirane had in hand a most faire Lady called Amoretta, whom he kept in most grieuous torment, because she would not yield him the pleasure of her body. Whereupon Sir Scudamour the louer of that Lady presently tooke on him that aduenture. But being vnable to performe it by reason of the hard Enchauntments, after long sorrow, in the end met with Britomartis, who succoured him, and reskewed his loue.

But by occasion hereof, many other aduentures are intermedled, but rather as Accidents, then intendments: as the loue of Britomart, the ouer-

[35] In the 1590 edition of *The Faerie Queene,* in which this letter appeared, the first three books were printed.

throw of Marinell, the misery of Florimell, the vertuousnes of Belphœbe, the lasciuiousnes of Hellenora, and many the like.

Thus much, Sir, I haue briefly ouerronne to direct your vnderstanding to the wel-head of the History, that from thence gathering the whole intention of the conceit, ye may as in a handfull gripe al the discourse, which otherwise may happily seeme tedious and confused. So humbly crauing the continuance of your honorable fauour towards me, and th'eternall establishment of your happines, I humbly take leaue.

23. Ianuary. 1589.
Yours most humbly affectionate.
Ed. Spenser.

THE FIRST
BOOKE OF THE
FAERIE QVEENE.

Contayning
THE LEGENDE OF THE KNIGHT OF THE RED CROSSE,
OR
OF HOLINESSE.

1

Lo I the man, whose Muse whilome did maske,
As time her taught, in lowly Shepheards weeds,[36]
Am now enforst a far vnfitter taske,
For trumpets sterne to chaunge mine Oaten reeds,
And sing of Knights and Ladies gentle deeds;
Whose prayses hauing slept in silence long,
Me, all too meane, the sacred Muse areeds[37]
To blazon broad emongst her learned throng:
Fierce warres and faithfull loues shall moralize my song.

2

Helpe then, O holy Virgin chiefe of nine,[38]
Thy weaker Nouice to performe thy will,
Lay forth out of thine euerlasting scryne[39]
The antique rolles, which there lye hidden still,
Of Faerie knights and fairest *Tanaquill*,[40]
Whom that most noble Briton Prince[41] so long
Sought through the world, and suffered so much ill,
That I must rue his vndeserued wrong:
O helpe thou my weake wit, and sharpen my dull tong.

3

And thou most dreaded impe of highest *Ioue*,
Faire *Venus* sonne, that with thy cruell dart
At that good knight so cunningly didst roue,
That glorious fire it kindled in his hart,
Lay now thy deadly Heben[42] bow apart,
And with thy mother milde come to mine ayde:
Come both, and with you bring triumphant *Mart*,[43]
In loues and gentle iollities arrayd,
After his murdrous spoiles and bloudy rage allayd.

4

And with them eke, O Goddesse[44] heauenly bright,
Mirrour of grace and Maiestie diuine,
Great Lady of the greatest Isle, whose light
Like *Phœbus* lampe throughout the world doth shine,
Shed thy faire beames into my feeble eyne,
And raise my thoughts too humble and too vile,

[36] garments. A reference to Spenser's pastoral poem, *The Shepherd's Calendar*, 1579.
[37] commands
[38] Clio, the Muse of history, or possibly Calliope, the Muse of epic poetry.

[39] chest
[40] An Etruscan queen, who is meant here to represent Queen Elizabeth.
[41] Arthur [42] ebony [43] Mars [44] Queen Elizabeth

To thinke of that true glorious type of thine,
The argument of mine afflicted stile:
The which to heare, vouchsafe, O dearest dred[45] a-while.

Canto I

The Patron of true Holinesse,
Foule Errour doth defeate:
Hypocrisie him to entrappe,
Doth to his home entreate.

1

A Gentle Knight was pricking[46] on the plaine,
Y cladd in mightie armes and siluer shielde,
Wherein old dints of deepe wounds did remaine,
The cruell markes of many' a bloudy fielde;
Yet armes till that time did he neuer wield:
His angry steede did chide his foming bitt,
As much disdayning to the curbe to yield:
Full iolly[47] knight he seemd, and faire did sitt,
As one for knightly giusts and fierce encounters fitt.

2

But on his brest a bloudie Crosse he bore,
The deare remembrance of his dying Lord,
For whose sweete sake that glorious badge he wore,
And dead as liuing euer him ador'd:
Vpon his shield the like was also scor'd,
For soueraine hope, which in his helpe he had:
Right faithfull true he was in deede and word,
But of his cheere[48] did seeme too solemne sad;
Yet nothing did he dread, but euer was ydrad.[49]

3

Vpon a great aduenture he was bond,
That greatest *Gloriana*[50] to him gaue,
That greatest Glorious Queene of *Faerie* lond,
To winne him worship, and her grace to haue,
Which of all earthly things he most did craue;
And euer as he rode, his hart did earne[51]
To proue his puissance in battell braue
Vpon his foe, and his new force to learne;
Vpon his foe, a Dragon horrible and stearne.

4

A louely Ladie rode him faire beside,
Vpon a lowly Asse more white then snow,
Yet she much whiter, but the same did hide
Vnder a vele, that wimpled was full low,
And ouer all a blacke stole she did throw,
As one that inly mournd: so was she sad,
And heauie sat vpon her palfrey slow:
Seemed in heart some hidden care she had,
And by her in a line a milke white lambe she lad.

5

So pure an innocent, as that same lambe,
She was in life and euery vertuous lore,
And by descent from Royall lynage came
Of ancient Kings and Queenes, that had of yore
Their scepters stretcht from East to Western shore,
And all the world in their subiection held;

[45] loved yet feared
[46] spurring his horse
[47] handsome
[48] countenance
[49] dreaded
[50] Queen Elizabeth
[51] yearn

Till that infernall feend with foule vprore
Forwasted[52] all their land, and them expeld:
Whom to auenge, she had this Knight from far compeld.

6

Behind her farre away a Dwarfe did lag,
That lasie seemd in being euer last,
Or wearied with bearing of her bag
Of needments at his backe. Thus as they past,
The day with cloudes was suddeine ouercast,
And angry *Ioue* an hideous storme of raine
Did poure into his Lemans[53] lap so fast,
That euery wight to shrowd it did constrain,
And this faire couple eke to shroud themselues were fain.

7

Enforst to seeke some couert nigh at hand,
A shadie groue not far away they spide,
That promist ayde the tempest to withstand:
Whose loftie trees yclad with sommers pride,
Did spred so broad, that heauens light did hide,
Not perceable with power of any starre:
And all within were pathes and alleies wide,
With footing worne, and leading inward farre:
Faire harbour that them seemes; so in they entred arre.

8

And foorth they passe, with pleasure forward led,
Ioying to heare the birdes sweete harmony,
Which therein shrouded from the tempest dred,
Seemd in their song to scorne the cruell sky.
Much can they prayse the trees so straight and hy,
The sayling Pine, the Cedar proud and tall,
The vine-prop Elme, the Poplar neuer dry,
The builder Oake, sole king of forrests all,
The Aspine good for staues, the Cypresse funerall.

9

The Laurell, meed of mightie Conquerours
And Poets sage, the Firre that weepeth still,
The Willow worne of forlorne Paramours,
The Eugh obedient to the benders will,
The Birch for shaftes, the Sallow for the mill,
The Mirrhe sweete bleeding in the bitter wound,
The warlike Beech, the Ash for nothing ill,
The fruitfull Oliue, and the Platane round,
The caruer Holme,[54] the Maple seeldom inward sound.

10

Led with delight, they thus beguile the way,
Vntill the blustring storme is ouerblowne;
When weening[55] to returne, whence they did stray,
They cannot finde that path, which first was showne,
But wander too and fro in wayes vnknowne,
Furthest from end then, when they neerest weene,
That makes them doubt, their wits be not their owne:

[52] completely laid waste
[53] lover's (*i.e.*, the earth)
[54] evergreen oak
[55] thinking

So many pathes, so many turnings seene,
That which of them to take, in diuerse doubt they been.

11

At last resoluing forward still to fare,
Till that some end they finde or in or out,
That path they take, that beaten seemd most bare,
And like to lead the labyrinth about;
Which when by tract they hunted had throughout,
At length it brought them to a hollow caue,
Amid the thickest woods. The Champion stout
Eftsoones[56] dismounted from his courser braue,
And to the Dwarfe a while his needlesse spere he gaue.

12

Be well aware, quoth then that Ladie milde,
Least suddaine mischiefe ye too rash prouoke:
The danger hid, the place vnknowne and wilde,
Breedes dreadfull doubts: Oft fire is without smoke,
And perill, without show: therefore your stroke
Sir knight with-hold, till further triall made.
Ah Ladie (said he) shame were to reuoke
The forward footing for an hidden shade:
Vertue giues her selfe light, through darkenesse for to wade.

13

Yea but (quoth she) the perill of this place
I better wot then you, though now too late
To wish you backe returne with foule disgrace,
Yet wisedome warnes, whilest foot is in the gate,[57]
To stay the steppe, ere forced to retrate.
This is the wandring wood, this *Errours den,*
A monster vile, whom God and man does hate:
Therefore I read[58] beware. Fly fly (quoth then
The fearefull Dwarfe:) this is no place for liuing men.

14

But full of fire and greedy hardiment,
The youthfull knight could not for ought be staide,
But forth vnto the darksome hole he went,
And looked in: his glistring armor made
A litle glooming light, much like a shade,
By which he saw the vgly monster plaine,
Halfe like a serpent horribly displaide,
But th'other halfe did womans shape retaine,
Most lothsom, filthie, foule, and full of vile disdaine.

15

And as she lay vpon the durtie ground,
Her huge long taile her den all ouerspred,
Yet was in knots and many boughtes[59] vpwound,
Pointed with mortall sting. Of her there bred
A thousand yong ones, which she dayly fed,
Sucking vpon her poisonous dugs, eachone
Of sundry shapes, yet all ill fauored:
Soone as that vncouth light vpon them shone,

[56] at once

[57] path [58] advise [59] folds

Into her mouth they crept, and suddain all were gone.

16

Their dam vpstart, out of her den effraide,
And rushed forth, hurling her hideous taile
About her cursed head, whose folds displaid
Were stretcht now forth at length without entraile.[60]
She lookt about, and seeing one in mayle
Armed to point, sought backe to turne againe;
For light she hated as the deadly bale,
Ay wont in desert darknesse to remaine,
Where plaine none might her see, nor she see any plaine.

17

Which when the valiant Elfe [61] perceiu'd, he lept
As Lyon fierce vpon the flying pray,
And with his trenchand blade her boldly kept
From turning backe, and forced her to stay:
Therewith enrag'd she loudly gan to bray,
And turning fierce, her speckled taile aduaunst,
Threatning her angry sting, him to dismay:
Who nought aghast, his mightie hand enhaunst: [62]
The stroke down from her head vnto her shoulder glaunst.

18

Much daunted with that dint, her sence was dazd,
Yet kindling rage, her selfe she gathered round,
And all attonce her beastly body raizd
With double forces high aboue the ground:
Tho wrapping vp her wrethed sterne arownd,
Lept fierce vpon his shield, and her huge traine
All suddenly about his body wound,
That hand or foot to stirre he stroue in vaine:
God helpe the man so wrapt in *Errours* endlesse traine.

19

His Lady sad to see his sore constraint,
Cride out, Now now Sir knight, shew what ye bee,
Add faith vnto your force, and be not faint:
Strangle her, else she sure will strangle thee.
That when he heard, in great perplexitie,
His gall did grate for griefe [63] and high disdaine,
And knitting all his force got one hand free,
Wherewith he grypt her gorge with so great paine,
That soone to loose her wicked bands did her constraine.

20

Therewith she spewd out of her filthy maw
A floud of poyson horrible and blacke,
Full of great lumpes of flesh and gobbets [64] raw,
Which stunck so vildly, that it forst him slacke
His grasping hold, and from her turne him backe:
Her vomit full of bookes and papers [65] was,
With loathly frogs and toades, which eyes did lacke,
And creeping sought way in the weedy gras:

[60] uncoiled
[61] The knight was the son of an elf.
[62] raised
[63] pain
[64] lumps
[65] The reference is to the scurrilous pamphlet attacks by the Jesuits and others on Elizabeth and her Protestant church.

Her filthy parbreake[66] all the place defiled has.

21

As when old father *Nilus* gins to swell
With timely pride aboue the *Aegyptian* vale,
His fattie waues do fertile slime outwell,
And ouerflow each plaine and lowly dale:
But when his later spring gins to avale,[67]
Huge heapes of mudd he leaues, wherein there breed
Ten thousand kindes of creatures, partly male
And partly female of his fruitfull seed;
Such vgly monstrous shapes elswhere may no man reed.[68]

22

The same so sore annoyed has the knight,
That welnigh choked with the deadly stinke,
His forces faile, ne can no longer fight.
Whose corage when the feend perceiu'd to shrinke,
She poured forth out of her hellish sinke
Her fruitfull cursed spawne of serpents small,
Deformed monsters, fowle, and blacke as inke,
Which swarming all about his legs did crall,
And him encombred sore, but could not hurt at all.

23

As gentle Shepheard in sweete euen-tide,
When ruddy *Phœbus* gins to welke[69] in west,
High on an hill, his flocke to vewen wide,
Markes which do byte their hasty supper best;
A cloud of combrous gnattes do him molest,
All striuing to infixe their feeble stings,
That from their noyance he no where can rest,
But with his clownish hands their tender wings
He brusheth oft, and oft doth mar their murmurings.

24

Thus ill bestedd, and fearefull more of shame,
Then of the certaine perill he stood in,
Halfe furious vnto his foe he came,
Resolv'd in minde all suddenly to win,
Or soone to lose, before he once would lin;[70]
And strooke at her with more then manly force,
That from her body full of filthie sin
He raft her hatefull head without remorse;
A streame of cole black bloud forth gushed from her corse.

25

Her scattred brood, soone as their Parent deare
They saw so rudely falling to the ground,
Groning full deadly, all with troublous feare,
Gathred themselues about her body round,
Weening their wonted entrance to haue found
At her wide mouth: but being there withstood
They flocked all about her bleeding wound,
And sucked vp their dying mothers blood,
Making her death their life, and eke her hurt their good.

26

That detestable sight him much amazde,
To see th'vnkindly[71] Impes of heauen accurst,

[66] vomit [67] sink [68] perceive [69] fade

[70] cease [71] unnatural

Deuoure their dam; on whom while so he gazd,
Hauing all satisfide their bloudy thurst,
Their bellies swolne he saw with fulnesse burst,
And bowels gushing forth: well worthy end
Of such as drunke her life, the which them nurst;
Now needeth him no lenger labour spend,
His foes haue slaine themselues, with whom he should contend.

27

His Ladie seeing all, that chaunst, from farre
Approcht in hast to greet his victorie,
And said, Faire knight, borne vnder happy starre,
Who see your vanquisht foes before you lye;
Well worthy be you of that Armorie,
Wherein ye haue great glory wonne this day,
And proou'd your strength on a strong enimie,
Your first aduenture: many such I pray,
And henceforth euer wish, that like succeed it may.

28

Then mounted he vpon his Steede againe,
And with the Lady backward sought to wend;
That path he kept, which beaten was most plaine,
Ne euer would to any by-way bend,
But still did follow one vnto the end,
The which at last out of the wood them brought.
So forward on his way (with God to frend)
He passed forth, and new aduenture sought;
Long way he trauelled, before he heard of ought.

29

At length they chaunst to meet vpon the way
An aged Sire, in long blacke weedes yclad,
His feete all bare, his beard all hoarie gray,
And by his belt his booke he hanging had;
Sober he seemde, and very sagely sad,
And to the ground his eyes were lowly bent,
Simple in shew, and voyde of malice bad,
And all the way he prayed, as he went,
And often knockt his brest, as one that did repent.

30

He faire the knight saluted, louting low,
Who faire him quited, as that courteous was:
And after asked him, if he did know
Of straunge aduentures, which abroad did pas.
Ah my deare Sonne (quoth he) how should, alas,
Silly[72] old man, that liues in hidden cell,
Bidding[73] his beades all day for his trespas,
Tydings of warre and worldly trouble tell?
With holy father sits not with such things to mell.[74]

31

But if of daunger which hereby doth dwell,
And homebred euill ye desire to heare,
Of a straunge man I can you tidings tell,
That wasteth all his countrey farre and neare.
Of such (said he) I chiefly do inquere,
And shall you well reward to shew the place,

[72] simple [73] telling [74] meddle

In which that wicked wight his dayes doth weare:
For to all knighthood it is foule disgrace,
That such a cursed creature liues so long a space.

32

Far hence (quoth he) in wastfull wildernesse
His dwelling is, by which no liuing wight
May euer passe, but thorough great distresse.
Now (sayd the Lady) draweth toward night,
And well I wote, that of your later fight
Ye all forwearied be: for what so strong,
But wanting rest will also want of might?
The Sunne that measures heauen all day long,
At night doth baite [75] his steedes the *Ocean* waues emong.

33

Then with the Sunne take Sir, your timely rest,
And with new day new worke at once begin:
Vntroubled night they say giues counsell best.
Right well Sir knight ye haue aduised bin,
(Quoth then that aged man;) the way to win
Is wisely to aduise: now day is spent;
Therefore with me ye may take vp your In
For this same night. The knight was well content:
So with that godly father to his home they went.

34

A little lowly Hermitage it was,
Downe in a dale, hard by a forests side,
Far from resort of people, that did pas
In trauell to and froe: a little wyde [76]
There was an holy Chappell edifyde,
Wherein the Hermite dewly wont to say
His holy things each morne and euentyde:
Thereby a Christall streame did gently play,
Which from a sacred fountaine welled forth alway.

35

Arriued there, the little house they fill,
Ne looke for entertainement, where none was:
Rest is their feast, and all things at their will;
The noblest mind the best contentment has.
With faire discourse the euening so they pas:
For that old man of pleasing wordes had store,
And well could file his tongue as smooth as glas;
He told of Saintes and Popes, and euermore
He strowd an *Aue-Mary* after and before.

36

The drouping Night thus creepeth on them fast,
And the sad [77] humour loading their eye liddes,
As messenger of *Morpheus* on them cast
Sweet slombring deaw, the which to sleepe them biddes.
Vnto their lodgings then his guestes he riddes: [78]
Where when all drownd in deadly sleepe he findes,
He to his study goes, and there amiddes
His Magick bookes and artes of sundry kindes,

[75] refresh

[76] a short distance off
[77] heavy
[78] dispatches

He seekes out mighty charmes, to trouble sleepy mindes.

37

Then choosing out few wordes most horrible,
(Let none them read) thereof did verses frame,
With which and other spelles like terrible,
He bad awake blacke *Plutoes* griesly Dame,[79]
And cursed heauen, and spake reprochfull shame
Of highest God, the Lord of life and light;
A bold bad man, that dar'd to call by name
Great *Gorgon*,[80] Prince of darknesse and dead night,
At which *Cocytus* quakes, and *Styx* is put to flight.

38

And forth he cald out of deepe darknesse dred
Legions of Sprights, the which like little flyes
Fluttring about his euer damned hed,
A-waite whereto their seruice he applyes,
To aide his friends, or fray [81] his enimies:
Of those he chose out two, the falsest twoo,
And fittest for to forge true-seeming lyes;
The one of them he gaue a message too,
The other by him selfe staide other worke to doo.

39

He making speedy way through spersed ayre,
And through the world of waters wide and deepe,
To *Morpheus* house doth hastily repaire.
Amid the bowels of the earth full steepe,
And low, where dawning day doth neuer peepe,
His dwelling is; there *Tethys* [82] his wet bed
Doth euer wash, and *Cynthia* [83] still doth steepe
In siluer deaw his euer-drouping hed,
Whiles sad Night ouer him her mantle black doth spred.

40

Whose double gates he findeth locked fast,
The one faire fram'd of burnisht Yuory,
The other all with siluer ouercast;
And wakefull dogges before them farre do lye,
Watching to banish Care their enimy,
Who oft is wont to trouble gentle Sleepe.
By them the Sprite doth passe in quietly,
And vnto *Morpheus* comes, whom drowned deepe
In drowsie fit he findes: of nothing he takes keepe.[84]

41

And more, to lulle him in his slumber soft,
A trickling streame from high rocke tumbling downe
And euer-drizling raine vpon the loft,
Mixt with a murmuring winde, much like the sowne
Of swarming Bees, did cast him in a swowne:
No other noyse, nor peoples troublous cryes,
As still are wont t'annoy the walled towne,
Might there be heard: but carelesse Quiet lyes,
Wrapt in eternall silence farre from enemyes.

---

[79] Proserpine
[80] Demogorgon, so evil a deity that even his name is fearful.
[81] frighten
[82] the ocean
[83] the moon
[84] heed

42

The messenger approching to him spake,
But his wast wordes returnd to him in vaine:
So sound he slept, that nought mought him awake.
Then rudely he him thrust, and pusht with paine,
Whereat he gan to stretch: but he againe
Shooke him so hard, that forced him to speake.
As one then in a dreame, whose dryer [85] braine
Is tost with troubled sights and fancies weake,
He mumbled soft, but would not all his silence breake.

43

The Sprite then gan more boldly him to wake,
And threatned vnto him the dreaded name
Of *Hecate:* whereat he gan to quake,
And lifting vp his lumpish head, with blame
Halfe angry asked him, for what he came.
Hither (quoth he) me *Archimago* sent,
He that the stubborne Sprites can wisely tame,
He bids thee to him send for his intent
A fit false dreame, that can delude the sleepers sent.[86]

44

The God obayde, and calling forth straight way
A diuerse dreame out of his prison darke,
Deliuered it to him, and downe did lay
His heauie head, deuoide of carefull carke [87]
Whose sences all were straight benumbd and starke.
He backe returning by the Yuorie dore,
Remounted vp as light as chearefull Larke,
And on his litle winges the dreame he bore
In hast vnto his Lord, where he him left afore.

45

Who all this while with charmes and hidden artes,
Had made a Lady of that other Spright,
And fram'd of liquid ayre her tender partes
So liuely, and so like in all mens sight,
That weaker sence it could haue rauisht quight:
The maker selfe for all his wondrous witt,
Was nigh beguiled with so goodly sight:
Her all in white he clad, and ouer it
Cast a blacke stole, most like to seeme for *Vna* fit.

46

Now when that ydle dreame was to him brought,
Vnto that Elfin knight he bad him fly,
Where he slept soundly void of euill thought,
And with false shewes abuse his fantasy,
In sort as he him schooled priuily:
And that new creature borne without her dew,[88]
Full of the makers guile, with vsage sly
He taught to imitate that Lady trew,
Whose semblance she did carrie vnder feigned hew.

47

Thus well instructed, to their worke they hast,
And comming where the knight in slomber lay,
The one vpon his hardy head him plast,

[85] The possessor of a dry brain is prone to dream as wits and poets do.
[86] sense
[87] care
[88] unduly, *i.e.*, unnaturally born

And made him dreame of loues and lustfull play,
That nigh his manly hart did melt away,
Bathed in wanton blis and wicked ioy:
Then seemed him his Lady by him lay,
And to him playnd, how that false winged boy
Her chast hart had subdewd, to learne Dame pleasures toy.

48

And she her selfe of beautie soueraigne Queene,
Faire *Venus* seemde vnto his bed to bring
Her, whom he waking euermore did weene
To be the chastest flowre, that ay did spring
On earthly braunch, the daughter of a king,
Now a loose Leman to vile seruice bound:
And eke the *Graces* seemed all to sing,
Hymen io Hymen, dauncing all around,
Whilst freshest *Flora* her with Yuie girlond crownd.

49

In this great passion of vnwonted lust,
Or wonted feare of doing ought amis,
He started vp, as seeming to mistrust
Some secret ill, or hidden foe of his:
Lo there before his face his Lady is,
Vnder blake stole hyding her bayted hooke,
And as halfe blushing offred him to kis,
With gentle blandishment and louely looke,
Most like that virgin true, which for her knight him took.

50

All cleane dismayd to see so vncouth sight,
And halfe enraged at her shamelesse guise,
He thought haue slaine her in his fierce despight:
But hasty heat tempring with sufferance wise,
He stayde his hand, and gan himselfe aduise
To proue his sense, and tempt her faigned truth.
Wringing her hands in wemens pitteous wise,
Tho can she[89] weepe, to stirre vp gentle ruth,
Both for her noble bloud, and for her tender youth.

51

And said, Ah Sir, my liege Lord and my loue,
Shall I accuse the hidden cruell fate,
And mightie causes wrought in heauen aboue,
Or the blind God, that doth me thus amate,[90]
For hoped loue to winne me certaine hate?
Yet thus perforce he bids me do, or die.
Die is my dew: yet rew my wretched state
You, whom my hard auenging destinie
Hath made iudge of my life or death indifferently.

52

Your owne deare sake forst me at first to leaue
My Fathers kingdome, There she stopt with teares;
Her swollen hart her speach seemd to bereaue,
And then againe begun, My weaker yeares
Captiu'd to fortune and frayle worldly feares,
Fly to your faith for succour and sure ayde:
Let me not dye in languor and long teares.
Why Dame (quoth he) what hath ye thus dismayd?

[89] then she did [90] cast down

What frayes ye, that were wont to comfort me affrayd?

53

Loue of your selfe, she said, and deare constraint
Lets me not sleepe, but wast the wearie night
In secret anguish and vnpittied plaint,
Whiles you in carelesse sleepe are drowned quight.
Her doubtfull words made that redoubted knight
Suspect her truth: yet since no'vntruth he knew,
Her fawning loue with foule disdainefull spight
He would not shend,[91] but said, Deare dame I rew,
That for my sake vnknowne such griefe vnto you grew.

54

Assure your selfe, it fell not all to ground;
For all so deare as life is to my hart,
I deeme your loue, and hold me to you bound;
Ne let vaine feares procure your needlesse smart,
Where cause is none, but to your rest depart.
Not all content, yet seemd she to appease
Her mournefull plaintes, beguiled of her art,
And fed with words, that could not chuse but please,
So slyding softly forth, she turnd as to her ease.

55

Long after lay he musing at her mood,
Much grieu'd to thinke that gentle Dame so light,
For whose defence he was to shed his blood.
At last dull wearinesse of former fight
Hauing yrockt a sleepe his irkesome spright,
That troublous dreame gan freshly tosse his braine,
With bowres, and beds, and Ladies deare delight:
But when he saw his labour all was vaine,
With that misformed spright he backe returnd againe.

[91] scold

Canto II

The guilefull great Enchaunter parts
The Redcrosse Knight from Truth:
Into whose stead faire falshood steps,
And workes him wofull ruth.

1

By this the Northerne wagoner [92] had set
His seuenfold teme [93] behind the stedfast starre,[94]
That was in Ocean waues yet neuer wet,
But firme is fixt, and sendeth light from farre
To all, that in the wide deepe wandring arre:
And chearefull Chaunticlere with his note shrill
Had warned once, that *Phœbus* fiery carre
In hast was climbing vp the Easterne hill,
Full enuious that night so long his roome did fill.

2

When those accursed messengers of hell,
That feigning dreame, and that faireforged Spright
Came to their wicked maister, and gan tell
Their bootelesse paines, and ill succeeding night:
Who all in rage to see his skilfull might
Deluded so, gan threaten hellish paine

[92] Boötes
[93] Charles' Wain
[94] the North Star

And sad *Proserpines* wrath, them to affright.
But when he saw his threatning was but vaine,
He cast about, and searcht his balefull bookes againe.

3

Eftsoones he tooke that miscreated faire,
And that false other Spright, on whom he spred
A seeming body of the subtile aire,
Like a young Squire, in loues and lustyhed
His wanton dayes that euer loosely led,
Without regard of armes and dreaded fight:
Those two he tooke, and in a secret bed,
Couered with darknesse and misdeeming night,
Them both together laid, to ioy in vaine delight.

4

Forthwith he runnes with feigned faithfull hast
Vnto his guest, who after troublous sights
And dreames, gan now to take more sound repast,
Whom suddenly he wakes with fearefull frights,
As one aghast with feends or damned sprights,
And to him cals, Rise rise vnhappy Swaine,
That here wex old in sleepe, whiles wicked wights
Haue knit themselues in *Venus* shamefull chaine;
Come see, where your false Lady doth her honour staine.

5

All in amaze he suddenly vp start
With sword in hand, and with the old man went;
Who soone him brought into a secret part,
Where that false couple were full closely ment[95]
In wanton lust and lewd embracement:
Which when he saw, he burnt with gealous fire,
The eye of reason was with rage yblent,[96]
And would haue slaine them in his furious ire,
But hardly was restreined of that aged sire.

6

Returning to his bed in torment great,
And bitter anguish of his guiltie sight,
He could not rest, but did his stout heart eat,
And wast his inward gall with deepe despight,
Yrkesome of life, and too long lingring night.
At last faire *Hesperus* in highest skie
Had spent his lampe, and brought forth dawning light
Then vp he rose, and clad him hastily;
The Dwarfe him brought his steed: so both away do fly.

7

Now when the rosy-fingred Morning faire,
Weary of aged *Tithones*[97] saffron bed,
Had spred her purple robe through deawy aire,
And the high hils *Titan*[98] discouered,
The royall virgin shooke off drowsy-hed,
And rising forth out of her baser bowre,
Lookt for her knight, who far away was fled,
And for her Dwarfe, that wont to wait each houre;
Then gan she waile and weepe, to see that woefull stowre.[99]

8

And after him she rode with so much speede

---

[95] joined
[96] blinded
[97] Loved by the goddess of the dawn, who gave him immortality but forgot to add ete nal youth.
[98] the sun
[99] time of turmoil

As her slow beast could make; but all in vaine:
For him so far had borne his light-foot steede,
Pricked with wrath and fiery fierce disdaine,
That him to follow was but fruitlesse paine;
Yet she her weary limbes would neuer rest,
But euery hill and dale, each wood and plaine
Did search, sore grieued in her gentle brest,
He so vngently left her, whom she loued best.

9

But subtill *Archimago,* when his guests
He saw diuided into double parts,
And *Vna* wandring in woods and forrests,
Th'end of his drift, he praisd his diuelish arts,
That had such might ouer true meaning harts;
Yet rests not so, but other meanes doth make,
How he may worke vnto her further smarts:
For her he hated as the hissing snake,
And in her many troubles did most pleasure take.

10

He then deuisde himselfe how to disguise;
For by his mightie science he could take
As many formes and shapes in seeming wise,
As euer *Proteus*[100] to himselfe could make:
Sometime a fowle, sometime a fish in lake,
Now like a foxe, now like a dragon fell,
That of himselfe he oft for feare would quake,
And oft would flie away. O who can tell
The hidden power of herbes, and might of Magicke spell?

11

But now seemde best, the person to put on
Of that good knight, his late beguiled guest:
In mighty armes he was yclad anon,
And siluer shield: vpon his coward brest
A bloudy crosse, and on his crauen crest
A bounch of haires discolourd diuersly:
Full iolly knight he seemde, and well addrest,
And when he sate vpon his courser free,
Saint George himself ye would haue deemed him to be.

12

But he the knight, whose semblaunt he did beare,
The true *Saint George* was wandred far away,
Still flying from his thoughts and gealous feare;
Will was his guide, and griefe led him astray.
At last him chaunst to meete vpon the way
A faithlesse Sarazin[101] all arm'd to point,
In whose great shield was writ with letters gay
Sans foy: full large of limbe and euery ioint
He was, and cared not for God or man a point.

13

He had a faire companion of his way,
A goodly Lady clad in scarlot red,
Purfled[102] with gold and pearle of rich assay,
And like a *Persian* mitre on her hed
She wore, with crownes and owches[103] garnished,

100 A sea-god.

101 A general designation for all pagans.
102 ornamented
103 jewels

The which her lauish louers to her gaue;
Her wanton palfrey all was ouerspred
With tinsell trappings, wouen like a waue,
Whose bridle rung with golden bels and bosses braue.

14

With faire disport and courting dalliaunce
She intertainde her louer all the way:
But when she saw the knight his speare aduaunce,
She soone left off her mirth and wanton play,
And bad her knight addresse him to the fray:
His foe was nigh at hand. He prickt with pride
And hope to winne his Ladies heart that day,
Forth spurred fast: adowne his coursers side
The red bloud trickling staind the way, as he did ride.

15

The knight of the *Redcrosse* when him he spide,
Spurring so hote with rage dispiteous,
Gan fairely couch[104] his speare, and towards ride:
Soone meete they both, both fell and furious,
That daunted with their forces hideous,
Their steeds do stagger, and amazed stand,
And eke themselues too rudely rigorous,
Astonied with the stroke of their owne hand,
Do backe rebut, and each to other yeeldeth land.

16

As when two rams stird with ambitious pride,
Fight for the rule of the rich fleeced flocke,
Their horned fronts so fierce on either side
Do meete, that with the terrour of the shocke
Astonied both, stand sencelesse as a blocke,
Forgetfull of the hanging victory:
So stood these twaine, vnmoued as a rocke,
Both staring fierce, and holding idely
The broken reliques of their former cruelty.

17

The *Sarazin* sore daunted with the buffe
Snatcheth his sword, and fiercely to him flies;
Who well it wards, and quyteth[105] cuff with cuff:
Each others equall puissaunce enuies,
And through their iron sides with cruell spies
Does seeke to perce: repining courage yields
No foote to foe. The flashing fier flies
As from a forge out of their burning shields,
And streames of purple bloud new dies the verdant fields.

18

Curse on that Crosse (quoth then the *Sarazin*)
That keepes thy body from the bitter fit,[106]
Dead long ygoe I wote thou haddest bin,
Had not that charme from thee forwarned it:
But yet I warne thee now assured sitt,
And hide thy head. Therewith vpon his crest
With rigour so outrageous he smitt,
That a large share it hewd out of the rest,
And glauncing downe his shield, from blame[107] him fairely blest.[108]

---

[104] put in position

[105] requiteth

[106] mortal crisis

[107] injury

[108] delivered

19

Who thereat wondrous wroth, the sleeping spark
Of natiue vertue gan eftsoones reuiue,
And at his haughtie helmet making mark,
So hugely stroke, that it the steele did riue,
And cleft his head. He tumbling downe aliue,
With bloudy mouth his mother earth did kis,
Greeting his graue: his grudging ghost did striue
With the fraile flesh; at last it flitted is,
Whither the soules do fly of men, that liue amis.

20

The Lady when she saw her champion fall,
Like the old ruines of a broken towre,
Staid not to waile his woefull funerall,
But from him fled away with all her powre;
Who after her as hastily gan scowre,
Bidding the Dwarfe with him to bring away
The *Sarazins* shield, signe of the conqueroure.
Her soone he ouertooke, and bad to stay,
For present cause was none of dread her to dismay.

21

She turning backe with ruefull countenaunce,
Cride, Mercy mercy Sir vouchsafe to show
On silly Dame, subiect to hard mischaunce,
And to your mighty will. Her humblesse low
In so ritch weedes and seeming glorious show,
Did much emmoue his stout heroïcke heart,
And said, Deare dame, your suddein ouerthrow
Much rueth me; but now put feare apart,
And tell, both who ye be, and who that tooke your part.

22

Melting in teares, then gan she thus lament;
The wretched woman, whom vnhappy howre
Hath now made thrall to your commandement,
Before that angry heauens list[109] to lowre,
And fortune false betraide me to your powre
Was, (O what now auaileth that I was!)
Borne the sole daughter of an Emperour,[110]
He that the wide West vnder his rule has,
And high hath set his throne, where *Tiberis* doth pas.

23

He in the first flowre of my freshest age,
Betrothed me vnto the onely haire
Of a most mighty king, most rich and sage;
Was neuer Prince so faithfull and so faire,
Was neuer Prince so meeke and debonaire;
But ere my hoped day of spousall shone,
My dearest Lord fell from high honours staire,
Into the hands of his accursed fone,[111]
And cruelly was slaine, that shall I euer mone.

24

His blessed body spoild of liuely breath,
Was afterward, I know not how, conuaid
And fro me hid: of whose most innocent death

---

[109] were pleased [110] the Pope [111] foes

When tidings came to me vnhappy maid,
O how great sorrow my sad soule assaid.[112]
Then forth I went his woefull corse to find,
And many yeares throughout the world I straid,
A virgin widow, whose deepe wounded mind
With loue, long time did languish as the striken hind.

25

At last it chaunced this proud *Sarazin*
To meete me wandring, who perforce me led
With him away, but yet could neuer win
The Fort, that Ladies hold in soueraigne dread.
There lies he now with foule dishonour dead.
Who whiles he liu'de, was called proud *Sans foy,*
The eldest of three brethren, all three bred
Of one bad sire, whose youngest is *Sans ioy,*
And twixt them both was borne the bloudy bold *Sans loy.*

26

In this sad plight, friendlesse, vnfortunate,
Now miserable I *Fidessa* dwell,
Crauing of you in pitty of my state,
To do none ill, if please ye not do well.
He in great passion all this while did dwell,
More busying his quicke eyes, her face to view,
Then his dull eares, to heare what she did tell;
And said, Faire Lady hart of flint would rew
The vndeserued woes and sorrowes, which ye shew.

27

Henceforth in safe assuraunce may ye rest,
Hauing both found a new friend you to aid,
And lost an old foe, that did you molest:
Better new friend then an old foe is said.
With chaunge of cheare the seeming simple maid
Let fall her eyen, as shamefast to the earth,
And yeelding soft, in that she nought gain-said,
So forth they rode, he feining seemely merth,
And she coy lookes: so dainty they say maketh derth.[113]

28

Long time they thus together traueiled,
Till weary of their way, they came at last,
Where grew two goodly trees, that faire did spred
Their armes abroad, with gray mosse ouercast,
And their greene leaues trembling with euery blast,
Made a calme shadow far in compasse round:
The fearefull Shepheard often there aghast
Vnder them neuer sat, ne wont there sound
His mery oaten pipe, but shund th'vnlucky ground.

29

But this good knight soone as he them can spie,
For the coole shade him thither hastly got:
For golden *Phœbus* now ymounted hie,
From fiery wheeles of his faire chariot
Hurled his beame so scorching cruell hot,
That liuing creature mote it not abide;
And his new Lady it endured not.

112 assailed

113 so dainty, *etc.* Coyness causes desire.

There they alight, in hope themselues to hide
From the fierce heat, and rest their weary limbs a tide.[114]

30

Faire seemely pleasaunce each to other makes,
With goodly purposes there as they sit:
And in his falsed fancy he her takes
To be the fairest wight, that liued yit;
Which to expresse, he bends his gentle wit,
And thinking of those braunches greene to frame
A girlond for her dainty forehead fit,
He pluckt a bough; out of whose rift there came
Small drops of gory bloud, that trickled downe the same.

31

Therewith a piteous yelling voyce was heard,
Crying, O spare with guilty hands to teare
My tender sides in this rough rynd embard,[115]
But fly, ah fly far hence away, for feare
Least to you hap, that happened to me heare,
And to this wretched Lady, my deare loue,
O too deare loue, loue bought with death too deare.
Astond he stood, and vp his haire did houe,
And with that suddein horror could no member moue.

32

At last whenas the dreadfull passion
Was ouerpast, and manhood well awake,
Yet musing at the straunge occasion,
And doubting much his sence, he thus bespake;
What voyce of damned Ghost from *Limbo* lake,[116]
Or guilefull spright wandring in empty aire,
Both which fraile men do oftentimes mistake,
Sends to my doubtfull eares these speaches rare,
And ruefull plaints, me bidding guiltlesse bloud to spare?

33

Then groning deepe, Nor damned Ghost, (quoth he,)
Nor guilefull sprite to thee these wordes doth speake,
But once a man *Fradubio,*[117] now a tree,
Wretched man, wretched tree; whose nature weake,
A cruell witch her cursed will to wreake,
Hath thus transformd, and plast in open plaines,
Where *Boreas* doth blow full bitter bleake,
And scorching Sunne does dry my secret vaines:
For though a tree I seeme, yet cold and heat me paines.

34

Say on *Fradubio* then, or man, or tree,
Quoth then the knight, by whose mischieuous arts
Art thou misshaped thus, as now I see?
He oft finds med'cine, who his griefe imparts;
But double griefs afflict concealing harts,
As raging flames who striueth to suppresse.
The author then (said he) of all my smarts,
Is one *Duessa* a false sorceresse,
That many errant knights hath brought to wretchednesse.

35

In prime of youthly yeares, when corage hot

---

[114] time
[115] imprisoned

[116] On the border of hell. [117] Of doubtful faith.

The fire of loue and ioy of cheualree
First kindled in my brest, it was my lot
To loue this gentle Lady, whom ye see,
Now not a Lady, but a seeming tree;
With whom as once I rode accompanyde,
Me chaunced of a knight encountred bee,
That had a like faire Lady by his syde,
Like a faire Lady, but did fowle *Duessa* hyde.

36

Whose forged beauty he did take in hand,[118]
All other Dames to haue exceeded farre;
I in defence of mine did likewise stand,
Mine, that did then shine as the Morningstarre:
So both to battell fierce arraunged arre,
In which his harder fortune was to fall
Vnder my speare: such is the dye of warre:
His Lady left as a prise martiall,
Did yield her comely person, to be at my call.

37

So doubly lou'd of Ladies vnlike faire,
Th'one seeming such, the other such indeede,
One day in doubt I cast for to compare,
Whether in beauties glorie did exceede;
A Rosy girlond was the victors meede:
Both seemde to win, and both seemde won to bee,
So hard the discord was to be agreede.
Frælissa was as faire, as faire mote bee,
And euer false *Duessa* seemde as faire as shee.

38

The wicked witch now seeing all this while
The doubtfull ballaunce equally to sway,
What not by right, she cast to win by guile,
And by her hellish science raisd streight way
A foggy mist, that ouercast the day,

[118] maintain

And a dull blast, that breathing on her face,
Dimmed her former beauties shining ray,
And with foule vgly forme did her disgrace:
Then was she faire alone, when none was faire in place.

39

Then cride she out, Fye, fye, deformed wight,
Whose borrowed beautie now appeareth plaine
To haue before bewitched all mens sight;
O leaue her soone, or let her soone be slaine.
Her loathly visage viewing with disdaine,
Eftsoones I thought her such, as she me told,
And would haue kild her; but with faigned paine,
The false witch did my wrathfull hand withhold;
So left her, where she now is turnd to treen mould.[119]

40

Thens forth I tooke *Duessa* for my Dame,
And in the witch vnweeting ioyd long time,
Ne euer wist, but that she was the same,
Till on a day (that day is euery Prime,[120]
When Witches wont do penance for their crime)
I chaunst to see her in her proper hew,
Bathing her selfe in origane[121] and thyme:
A filthy foule old woman I did view,
That euer to haue toucht her, I did deadly rew.

41

Her neather partes misshapen, monstruous,
Were hidd in water, that I could not see,

[119] shape
[120] springtime
[121] 'Organie healeth scabs, itchings, and scurvinesse being used in bathes.' (Girard's *Herball*)

But they did seeme more foule and hideous,
Then womans shape man would beleeue to bee.
Thens forth from her most beastly companie
I gan refraine, in minde to slip away,
Soone as appeard safe opportunitie:
For danger great, if not assur'd decay
I saw before mine eyes, if I were knowne to stray.

42

The diuelish hag by chaunges of my cheare
Perceiu'd my thought, and drownd in sleepie night,
With wicked herbes and ointments did besmeare
My bodie all, through charmes and magicke might,
That all my senses were bereaued quight:
Then brought she me into this desert waste,
And by my wretched louers side me pight,[122]
Where now enclosd in wooden wals full faste,
Banisht from liuing wights, our wearie dayes we waste.

43

But how long time, said then the Elfin knight,
Are you in this misformed house to dwell?
We may not chaunge (quoth he) this euil plight,
Till we be bathed in a liuing well;
That is the terme prescribed by the spell.
O how, said he, mote I that well out find,
That may restore you to your wonted well[123]?
Time and suffised fates to former kynd[124]
Shall vs restore, none else from hence may vs vnbynd.

44

The false *Duessa*, now *Fidessa* hight,
Heard how in vaine *Fradubio* did lament,
And knew well all was true. But the good knight
Full of sad feare and ghastly dreriment,
When all this speech the liuing tree had spent,
The bleeding bough did thrust into the ground,
That from the bloud he might be innocent,
And with fresh clay did close the wooden wound:
Then turning to his Lady, dead with feare her found.

45

Her seeming dead he found with feigned feare,
As all vnweeting of that well she knew,
And paynd himselfe with busie care to reare
Her out of carelesse swowne. Her eylids blew
And dimmed sight with pale and deadly hew
At last she vp gan lift: with trembling cheare
Her vp he tooke, too simple and too trew,
And oft her kist. At length all passed feare,
He set her on her steede, and forward forth did beare.

Canto III

Forsaken Truth long seekes her loue,
And makes the Lyon mylde,
Marres blind Deuotions mart,[125] ***and fals***
In hand of leachour vylde.

I

Nought is there vnder heau'ns wide hollownesse,
That moues more deare compassion of mind,

[122] placed [123] well-being [124] nature

[125] trade

Then beautie brought t'vnworthy wretchednesse
Through enuies snares or fortunes freakes vnkind:
I, whether lately through her brightnesse blind,
Or through alleageance and fast fealtie,
Which I do owe vnto all woman kind,
Feele my heart perst with so great agonie,
When such I see, that all for pittie I could die.

2

And now it is empassioned so deepe,
For fairest *Vnaes* sake, of whom I sing,
That my fraile eyes these lines with teares do steepe,
To thinke how she through guilefull handeling,
Though true as touch, though daughter of a king,
Though faire as ever living wight was faire,
Though nor in word nor deede ill meriting,
Is from her knight diuorced in despaire
And her due loues deriu'd [126] to that vile witches share.

3

Yet she most faithfull Ladie all this while
Forsaken, wofull, solitarie mayd
Farre from all peoples prease,[127] as in exile,
In wildernesse and wastfull deserts strayd,
To seeke her knight; who subtilly betrayd
Through that late vision, which th'Enchaunter wrought,
Had her abandond. She of nought affrayd,
Through woods and wastnesse wide him daily sought;
Yet wished tydings none of him vnto her brought.

4

One day nigh wearie of the yrkesome way,
From her vnhastie beast she did alight,
And on the grasse her daintie limbes did lay
In secret shadow, farre from all mens sight:
From her faire head her fillet she vndight,
And laid her stole aside. Her angels face
As the great eye of heauen shyned bright,
And made a sunshine in the shadie place;
Did neuer mortall eye behold such heauenly grace.

5

It fortuned out of the thickest wood
A ramping Lyon rushed suddainly,
Hunting full greedie after saluage [128] blood;
Soone as the royall virgin he did spy,
With gaping mouth at her ran greedily,
To haue attonce deuour'd her tender corse:
But to the pray when as he drew more ny,
His bloudie rage asswaged with remorse,
And with the sight amazd, forgat his furious forse.

6

In stead thereof he kist her wearie feet,[129]
And lickt her lilly hands with fawning tong,
As he her wronged innocence did weet.
O how can beautie maister the most strong,
And simple truth subdue auenging wrong?
Whose yeelded pride and proud submission,
Still dreading death, when she had marked long,
Her hart gan melt in great compassion,

[126] drawn away
[127] press

[128] savage
[129] The lion is said to reverence virgins and those of royal blood. Here he probably typifies reason.

And drizling teares did shed for pure affection.

7

The Lyon Lord of euerie beast in field,
Quoth she, his princely puissance doth abate,
And mightie proud to humble weake does yield,
Forgetfull of the hungry rage, which late
Him prickt, in pittie of my sad estate:
But he my Lyon, and my noble Lord,
How does he find in cruell hart to hate
Her that him lou'd, and euer most adord,
As the God of my life? why hath he me abhord?

8

Redounding teares did choke th'end of her plaint,
Which softly ecchoed from the neighbour wood;
And sad to see her sorrowfull constraint
The kingly beast vpon her gazing stood;
With pittie calmd, downe fell his angry mood.
At last in close hart shutting vp her paine,
Arose the virgin borne of heauenly brood,
And to her snowy Palfrey got againe,
To seeke her strayed Champion, if she might attaine.

9

The Lyon would not leaue her desolate,
But with her went along, as a strong gard
Of her chast person, and a faithfull mate
Of her sad troubles and misfortunes hard:
Still when she slept, he kept both watch and ward,
And when she wakt, he waited diligent,
With humble seruice to her will prepard:
From her faire eyes he tooke commaundement,
And euer by her lookes conceiued her intent.

10

Long she thus traueiled through deserts wyde,
By which she thought her wandring knight shold pas,
Yet neuer shew of liuing wight espyde;
Till that at length she found the troden gras,
In which the tract of peoples footing was,
Vnder the steepe foot of a mountaine hore;
The same she followes, till at last she has
A damzell[130] spyde slow footing her before,
That on her shoulders sad[131] a pot of water bore.

11

To whom approching she to her gan call,
To weet, if dwelling place were nigh at hand;
But the rude wench her answer'd nought at all,
She could not heare, nor speake, nor vnderstand;
Till seeing by her side the Lyon stand,
With suddaine feare her pitcher downe she threw,
And fled away: for neuer in that land
Face of faire Ladie she before did vew,
And that dread Lyons looke her cast in deadly hew.

12

Full fast she fled, ne euer lookt behynd,
As if her life vpon the wager lay,
And home she came, whereas her mother[132] blynd
Sate in eternall night: nought could she say,
But suddaine catching hold, did her dismay

---

[130] Abessa, representing Superstition.
[131] heavily laden
[132] Corceca, or Blind Devotion.

With quaking hands, and other signes of feare:
Who full of ghastly fright and cold affray,
Gan shut the dore. By this arriued there
Dame *Vna,* wearie Dame, and entrance did requere.

13

Which when none yeelded, her vnruly Page
With his rude clawes the wicket open rent,
And let her in; where of his cruell rage
Nigh dead with feare, and faint astonishment,
She found them both in darkesome corner pent;
Where that old woman day and night did pray
Vpon her beades deuoutly penitent;
Nine hundred *Pater nosters* euery day,
And thrise nine hundred *Aues* she was wont to say.

14

And to augment her painefull pennance more,
Thrise euery weeke in ashes she did sit,
And next her wrinkled skin rough sackcloth wore,
And thrise three times did fast from any bit:
But now for feare her beads she did forget.
Whose needlesse dread for to remoue away,
Faire *Vna* framed words and count'nance fit:
Which hardly doen, at length she gan them pray,
That in their cotage small, that night she rest her may.

15

The day is spent, and commeth drowsie night,
When euery creature shrowded is in sleepe;
Sad *Vna* downe her laies in wearie plight,
And at her feet the Lyon watch doth keepe:
In stead of rest, she does lament, and weepe
For the late losse of her deare loued knight,
And sighes, and grones, and euermore does steepe
Her tender brest in bitter teares all night,
All night she thinks too long, and often lookes for light.

16

Now when *Aldeboran*[133] was mounted hie
Aboue the shynie *Cassiopeias* chaire,
And all in deadly sleepe did drowned lie,
One[134] knocked at the dore, and in would fare;
He knocked fast, and often curst, and sware,
That readie entrance was not at his call:
For on his backe a heauy load he bare
Of nightly stelths and pillage seuerall,[135]
Which he had got abroad by purchase criminall.

17

He was to weete a stout and sturdie thiefe,
Wont to robbe Churches of their ornaments,
And poore mens boxes of their due reliefe,
Which giuen was to them for good intents;
The holy Saints of their rich vestiments
He did disrobe, when all men carelesse slept,
And spoild the Priests of their habiliments,
Whiles none the holy things in safety kept;
Then he by cunning sleights in at the window crept.

---

[133] A bright, red star in Taurus.
[134] Kirkrapine, or the Church-robber.
[135] of different kinds

18

And all that he by right or wrong could find,
Vnto this house he brought, and did bestow
Vpon the daughter of this woman blind,
Abessa daughter of *Corceca* slow,
With whom he whoredome vsd, that few did know,
And fed her fat with feast of offerings,
And plentie, which in all the land did grow;
Ne spared he to giue her gold and rings:
And now he to her brought part of his stolen things.

19

Thus long the dore with rage and threats he bet,[136]
Yet of those fearefull women none durst rize,
The Lyon frayed [137] them, him in to let:
He would no longer stay him to aduize,
But open breakes the dore in furious wize,
And entring is; when that disdainfull beast
Encountring fierce, him suddaine doth surprize,
And seizing cruell clawes on trembling brest,
Vnder his Lordly foot him proudly hath supprest.

20

Him booteth not resist, nor succour call,
His bleeding hart is in the vengers hand,
Who streight him rent in thousand peeces small,
And quite dismembred hath: the thirstie land
Drunke vp his life; his corse left on the strand.
His fearefull friends weare out the wofull night,
Ne dare to weepe, nor seeme to vnderstand
The heauie hap, which on them is alight,
Affraid, least to themselues the like mishappen might.

21

Now when broad day the world discouered has,
Vp *Vna* rose, vp rose the Lyon eke;
And on their former iourney forward pas,
In wayes vnknowne, her wandring knight to seeke,
With paines farre passing that long wandring *Greeke*,[138]
That for his loue refused deitie;
Such were the labours of this Lady meeke,
Still seeking him, that from her still did flie,
Then furthest from her hope, when most she weened nie.

22

Soone as she parted thence, the fearefull twaine,
That blind old woman and her daughter deare
Came forth, and finding *Kirkrapine* there slaine,
For anguish great they gan to rend their heare,
And beat their brests, and naked flesh to teare.
And when they both had wept and wayld their fill,
Then forth they ranne like two amazed deare,
Halfe mad through malice, and reuenging will,
To follow her, that was the causer of their ill.

23

Whom ouertaking, they gan loudly bray,
With hollow howling, and lamenting cry,
Shamefully at her rayling all the way,
And her accusing of dishonesty,

136 beat
137 frightened
138 Ulysses

[illegible] the flowre of faith and chastity;
[illegible] amidst her rayling, she did
[illegible]
[illegible]gues, and mischiefs, and long misery
Might fall on her, and follow all the way,
And that in endlesse error she might euer stray.

24

But when she saw her prayers nought preuaile,
She backe returned with some labour lost;
And in the way as she did weepe and waile,
A knight her met in mighty armes embost,
Yet knight was not for all his bragging bost,
But subtill *Archimag,* that *Vna* sought
By traynes[139] into new troubles to haue tost:
Of that old woman tydings he besought,
If that of such a Ladie she could tellen ought.

25

Therewith she gan her passion to renew,
And cry, and curse, and raile, and rend her heare,
Saying, that harlot she too lately knew,
That causd her shed so many a bitter teare,
And so forth told the story of her feare:
Much seemed he to mone her haplesse chaunce,
And after for that Ladie did inquere;
Which being taught, he forward gan aduaunce
His fair enchaunted steed, and eke his charmed launce.

26

Ere long he came, where *Vna* traueild slow,
And that wilde Champion wayting her besyde:
Whom seeing such, for dread he durst not show
Himselfe too nigh at hand, but turned wyde
Vnto an hill; from whence when she him spyde,
By his like seeming shield, her knight by name
She weend it was, and towards him gan ryde:
Approching nigh, she wist it was the same,
And with faire fearefull humblesse towards him shee came.

27

And weeping said, Ah my long lacked Lord,
Where haue ye bene thus long out of my sight?
Much feared I to haue bene quite abhord,
Or ought[140] haue done, that ye displeasen might,
That should as death vnto my deare hart light:
For since mine eye your ioyous sight did mis,
My chearefull day is turnd to chearelesse night,
And eke my night of death the shadow is;
But welcome now my light, and shining lampe of blis.

28

He thereto meeting said, My dearest Dame,
Farre be it from your thought, and fro my will,
To thinke that knighthood I so much should shame,
As you to leaue, that haue me loued still,
And chose in Faery court of meere goodwill,
Where noblest knights were to be found on earth:

[139] tricks

[140] aught

The earth shall sooner leaue her kindly skill
To bring forth fruit, and make eternall derth,
Then I leaue you, my liefe,[141] yborne of heauenly berth.

29

And sooth to say, why I left you so long,
Was for to seeke aduenture in strange place,
Where *Archimago* said a felon strong
To many knights did daily worke disgrace;
But knight he now shall neuer more deface:
Good cause of mine excuse,[142] that mote[143] ye please
Well to accept, and euermore embrace
My faithfull seruice, that by land and seas
Haue vowd you to defend, now then your plaint appease.

30

His louely words her seemd due recompence
Of all her passed paines: one louing howre
For many yeares of sorrow can dispence:
A dram of sweet is worth a pound of sowre:
She has forgot, how many a wofull stowre[144]
For him she late endur'd; she speakes no more
Of past: true is, that true loue hath no powre
To looken backe; his eyes be fixt before.
Before her stands her knight, for whom she toyld so sore.

31

Much like, as when the beaten marinere,
That long hath wandred in the *Ocean* wide,
Oft soust in swelling *Tethys* saltish teare,
And long time hauing tand his tawney hide
With blustring breath of heauen, that none can bide,
And scorching flames of fierce *Orions* hound,[145]
Soone as the port from farre he has espide,
His chearefull whistle merrily doth sound,
And *Nereus* crownes[146] with cups; his mates him pledg around.

32

Such ioy made *Vna,* when her knight she found;
And eke th'enchaunter ioyous seemd no lesse,
Then the glad marchant, that does vew from ground
His ship farre come from watrie wildernesse,
He hurles out vowes, and *Neptune* oft doth blesse:
So forth they past, and all the way they spent
Discoursing of her dreadfull late distresse,
In which he askt her, what the Lyon ment:
Who told her all that fell in iourney as she went.

33

They had not ridden farre, when they might see
One pricking towards them with hastie heat,
Full strongly armd, and on a courser free,
That through his fiercenesse fomed all with sweat,
And the sharpe yron did for anger eat,
When his hot ryder spurd his chauffed[147] side;

---

[141] dear
[142] good cause for my excuse
[143] may
[144] danger
[145] the dog-star
[146] Drinks in honor of Nereus, the sea god.
[147] heated

His looke was sterne, and seemed still to threat
Cruell reuenge, which he in hart did hyde,
And on his shield *Sans loy* in bloudie lines was dyde.

34

When nigh he drew vnto this gentle payre
And saw the Red-crosse, which the knight did beare,
He burnt in fire, and gan eftsoones prepare
Himselfe to battell with his couched speare.
Loth was that other, and did faint through feare,
To taste th'vntryed dint of deadly steele;
But yet his Lady did so well him cheare,
That hope of new good hap he gan to feele;
So bent [148] his speare, and spurnd his horse with yron heele.

35

But that proud Paynim forward came so fierce,
And full of wrath, that with his sharp-head speare
Through vainely crossed shield he quite did pierce,
And had his staggering steede not shrunke for feare,
Through shield and bodie eke he should him beare:
Yet so great was the puissance of his push,
That from his saddle quite he did him beare:
He tombling rudely downe to ground did rush,
And from his gored wound a well of bloud did gush.

36

Dismounting lightly from his loftie steed,
He to him lept, in mind to reaue his life,
And proudly said, Lo there the worthie meed
Of him, that slew *Sansfoy* with bloudie knife;
Henceforth his ghost freed from repining strife,
In peace may passen ouer *Lethe* [149] lake,
When mourning altars purgd with enemies life,
The blacke infernall *Furies* doen aslake:
Life from *Sansfoy* thou tookst, *Sansloy* shall from thee take.

37

Therewith in haste his helmet gan vnlace,
Till *Vna* cride, O hold that heauie hand,
Deare Sir, what euer that thou be in place:
Enough is, that thy foe doth vanquisht stand
Now at thy mercy: Mercie not withstand:
For he is one the truest knight aliue,
Though conquered now he lie on lowly land,
And whilest him fortune fauourd, faire did thriue
In bloudie field: therefore of life him not depriue.

38

Her piteous words might not abate his rage,
But rudely rending vp his helmet, would
Haue slaine him straight: but when he sees his age,
And hoarie head of *Archimago* old,
His hastie hand he doth amazed hold,
And halfe ashamed, wondred at the sight:
For the old man well knew he, though vntold,
In charmes and magicke to haue wondrous might,
Ne euer wont in field, ne in round lists [150] to fight.

39

And said, Why *Archimago*, lucklesse syre,
What doe I see? what hard mishap is this,

---

[148] levelled for action

[149] The river of forgetfulness in Hades.

[150] Tournaments held in enclosed arenas.

That hath thee hither brought to taste mine yre?
Or thine the fault, or mine the error is,
In stead of foe to wound my friend amis?
He answered nought, but in a traunce still lay,
And on those guilefull dazed eyes of his
The cloud of death did sit. Which doen [151] away,
He left him lying so, ne would no lenger stay.

40

But to the virgin comes, who all this while
Amased stands, her selfe so mockt to see
By him, who has the guerdon of his guile,
For so misfeigning her true knight to bee:
Yet is she now in more perplexitie,
Left in the hand of that same Paynim bold,
From whom her booteth not at all to flie;
Who by her cleanly garment catching hold,
Her from her Palfrey pluckt, her visage to behold.

41

But her fierce seruant full of kingly awe
And high disdaine, whenas his soueraine Dame
So rudely handled by her foe he sawe,
With gaping iawes full greedy at him came,
And ramping on his shield, did weene the same
Haue reft away with his sharpe rending clawes.
But he was stout, and lust did now inflame
His corage more, that from his griping pawes
He hath his shield redeem'd, and foorth his swerd he drawes.

42

O then too weake and feeble was the forse
Of saluage beast, his puissance to withstand:
For he was strong, and of so mightie corse,
As euer wielded speare in warlike hand,
And feates of armes did wisely vnderstand.
Eftsoones he perced through his chaufed chest
With thrilling [152] point of deadly yron brand,
And launcht [153] his Lordly hart: with death opprest
He roar'd aloud, whiles life forsooke his stubborne brest.

43

Who now is left to keepe the forlorne maid
From raging spoile of lawlesse victors will?
Her faithfull gard remou'd, her hope dismaid,
Her selfe a yeelded pray to saue or spill.[154]
He now Lord of the field, his pride to fill,
With foule reproches, and disdainfull spight
Her vildly entertaines, and will or nill,
Beares her away vpon his courser light:
Her prayers nought preuaile, his rage is more of might.

44

And all the way, with great lamenting paine,
And piteous plaints she filleth his dull eares,
That stony hart could riuen haue in twaine,
And all the way she wets with flowing teares:
But he enrag'd with rancor, nothing heares.

---

[151] passed

[152] piercing [153] pierced [154] destroy

Her seruile beast yet would not leaue her so,
But followes her farre off, ne ought he feares,
To be partaker of her wandring woe,
More mild in beastly kind, then that her beastly foe.

Canto IIII

To sinfull house of Pride, Duessa guides the faithfull knight,
Where brothers death to wreak Sansioy doth chalenge him to fight.

1

Young knight, what euer that dost armes professe,
And through long labours huntest after fame,
Beware of fraud, beware of ficklenesse,
In choice, and change of thy deare loued Dame,
Least thou of her beleeue too lightly blame,
And rash misweening doe thy hart remoue:
For vnto knight there is no greater shame,
Then lightnesse and inconstancie in loue;
That doth this *Redcrosse* knights ensample plainly proue.

2

Who after that he had faire *Vna* lorne,
Through light misdeeming of her loialtie,
And false *Duessa* in her sted had borne,
Called *Fidess'*, and so supposd to bee;
Long with her traueild, till at last they see
A goodly building,[155] brauely garnished,
The house of mightie Prince it seemd to bee:
And towards it a broad high way that led,
All bare through peoples feet, which thither traueiled.

3

Great troupes of people traueild thitherward
Both day and night, of each degree and place,
But few returned, hauing scaped hard,
With balefull beggerie, or foule disgrace,
Which euer after in most wretched case,
Like loathsome lazars, by the hedges lay.
Thither *Duessa* bad him bend his pace:
For she is wearie of the toilesome way,
And also nigh consumed is the lingring day.

4

A stately Pallace built of squared bricke,
Which cunningly was without morter laid,
Whose wals were high, but nothing strong, nor thick,
And golden foile all ouer them displaid,
That purest skye with brightnesse they dismaid:
High lifted vp were many loftie towres,
And goodly galleries farre ouer laid,
Full of faire windowes, and delightfull bowres;
And on the top a Diall told the timely howres.

5

It was a goodly heape for to behould,
And spake the praises of the workmans wit;
But full great pittie, that so faire a mould
Did on so weake foundation euer sit:
For on a sandie hill, that still did flit,[156]
And fall away, it mounted was full hie,
That euery breath of heauen shaked it:
And all the hinder parts, that few could spie,
Were ruinous and old, but painted cunningly.

6

Arriued there they passed in forth right;
For still to all the gates stood open wide,

155 The House of Pride.

156 move

Yet charge of them was to a Porter hight[157]
Cald *Maluenù,* who entrance none denide:
Thence to the hall, which was on euery side
With rich array and costly arras dight:
Infinite sorts of people did abide
There waiting long, to win the wished sight
Of her, that was the Lady of that Pallace bright.

7

By them they passe, all gazing on them round,
And to the Presence mount; whose glorious vew
Their frayle amazed senses did confound:
In liuing Princes court none euer knew
Such endlesse richesse, and so sumptuous shew;
Ne *Persia* selfe, the nourse of pompous pride
Like euer saw. And there a noble crew
Of Lordes and Ladies stood on euery side,
Which with their presence faire, the place much beautifide.

8

High aboue all a cloth of State was spred,
And a rich throne, as bright as sunny day,
On which there sate most braue embellished
With royall robes and gorgeous array,
A mayden Queene, that shone as *Titans* ray,
In glistring gold, and peerelesse pretious stone:
Yet her bright blazing beautie did assay
To dim the brightnesse of her glorious throne,
As enuying her selfe, that too exceeding shone.

[157] committed

9

Exceeding shone, like *Phœbus* fairest childe,[158]
That did presume his fathers firie wayne,
And flaming mouthes of steedes vnwonted wilde
Through highest heauen with weaker hand to rayne;
Proud of such glory and aduancement vaine,
While flashing beames do daze his feeble eyen,
He leaues the welkin way most beaten plaine,
And rapt with whirling wheeles, inflames the skyen,
With fire not made to burne, but fairely for to shyne.

10

So proud she shyned in her Princely state,
Looking to heauen; for earth she did disdayne,
And sitting high; for lowly she did hate:
Lo vnderneath her scornefull feete, was layne
A dreadfull Dragon with an hideous trayne,
And in her hand she held a mirrhour bright,
Wherein her face she often vewed fayne,[159]
And in her selfe-lou'd semblance tooke delight;
For she was wondrous faire, as any liuing wight.

11

Of griesly *Pluto* she the daughter was,
And sad *Proserpina* the Queene of hell;
Yet did she thinke her pearelesse worth to pas
That parentage, with pride so did she swell,
And thundring *Ioue,* that high in heauen doth dwell,

[158] Phaeton, who attempted to drive the chariot of the sun.
[159] gladly

And wield the world, she claymed for her syre,
Or if that any else did *Ioue* excell:
For to the highest she did still aspyre,
Or if ought higher were then that, did it desyre.

12

And proud *Lucifera*[160] men did her call,
That made her selfe a Queene, and crownd to be,
Yet rightfull kingdome she had none at all,
Ne heritage of natiue soueraintie,
But did vsurpe with wrong and tyrannie
Vpon the scepter, which she now did hold:
Ne ruld her Realmes with lawes, but pollicie,
And strong aduizement of six wisards[161] old,
That with their counsels bad her kingdome did vphold.

13

Soone as the Elfin knight in presence came,
And false *Duessa* seeming Lady faire,
A gentle Husher, *Vanitie* by name
Made rowme, and passage for them did prepaire:
So goodly brought them to the lowest staire
Of her high throne, where they on humble knee
Making obeyssance, did the cause declare,
Why they were come, her royall state to see,
To proue the wide report of her great Maiestee.

14

With loftie eyes, halfe loth to looke so low,
She thanked them in her disdainefull wise,
Ne other grace vouchsafed them to show
Of Princesse worthy, scarse them bad arise.
Her Lordes and Ladies all this while deuise
Themselues to setten forth to straungers sight:
Some frounce their curled haire in courtly guise,
Some prancke their ruffes, and others trimly dight
Their gay attire: each others greater pride does spight.

15

Goodly they all that knight do entertaine,
Right glad with him to haue increast their crew:
But to *Duess'* each one himselfe did paine
All kindnesse and faire courtesie to shew;
For in that court whylome[162] her well they knew:
Yet the stout Faerie mongst the middest crowd
Thought all their glorie vaine in knightly vew,
And that great Princesse too exceeding prowd,
That to strange knight no better countenance allowd.

16

Suddein vpriseth from her stately place
The royall Dame, and for her coche doth call:
All hurtlen forth, and she with Princely pace,
As faire *Aurora* in her purple pall,
Out of the East the dawning day doth call:
So forth she comes: her brightnesse brode doth blaze;
The heapes of people thronging in the hall,
Do ride each other, vpon her to gaze:
Her glorious glitterand light doth all mens eyes amaze.

---

160 Pride
161 The remaining six of the Seven Deadly Sins.
162 formerly

17

So forth she comes, and to her coche does clyme,
Adorned all with gold, and girlonds gay,
That seemd as fresh as *Flora* in her prime,
And stroue to match, in royall rich array,
Great *Iunoes* golden chaire, the which they say
The Gods stand gazing on, when she does ride
To *Ioues* high house through heauens bras-paued way
Drawne of faire Pecocks, that excell in pride,
And full of *Argus*[163] eyes their tailes dispredden wide.

18

But this was drawne of six vnequall beasts,
On which her six sage Counsellours did ryde,
Taught to obay their bestiall beheasts,
With like conditions to their kinds applyde:
Of which the first, that all the rest did guyde,
Was sluggish *Idlenesse* the nourse of sin;
Vpon a slouthfull Asse he chose to ryde,
Arayd in habit blacke, and amis[164] thin,
Like to an holy Monck, the seruice to begin.

19

And in his hand his Portesse[165] still he bare;
That much was worne, but therein little red,
For of deuotion he had little care,
Still drownd in sleepe, and most of his dayes ded;
Scarse could he once vphold his heauie hed,
To looken, whether it were night or day:
May seeme the wayne was very euill led,
When such an one had guiding of the way,
That knew not, whether right he went, or else astray.

20

From worldly cares himselfe he did esloyne,[166]
And greatly shunned manly exercise,
From euery worke he chalenged essoyne,
For contemplation sake: yet otherwise,
His life he led in lawlesse riotise;
By which he grew to grieuous malady;
For in his lustlesse limbs through euill guise
A shaking feuer raignd continually:
Such one was *Idlenesse,* first of this company.

21

And by his side rode loathsome *Gluttony,*
Deformed creature, on a filthie swyne,
His belly was vp-blowne with luxury,
And eke with fatnesse swollen were his eyne,
And like a Crane his necke was long and fyne,
With which he swallowd vp excessiue feast,
For want whereof poore people oft did pyne;
And all the way, most like a brutish beast,
He spued vp his gorge, that all did him deteast.

22

In greene vine leaues he was right fitly clad;
For other clothes he could not weare for heat,
And on his head an yuie girland had,
From vnder which fast trickled downe the sweat:
Still as he rode, he somewhat still did eat,
And in his hand did beare a bouzing can,

[163] Hera put the hundred eyes of Argos into the peacock's tail.
[164] Amice, a fold of white linen worn about the neck by a celebrant priest.
[165] breviary
[166] remove

Of which he supt so oft, that on his seat
His dronken corse he scarse vpholden can,
In shape and life more like a monster, then a man.

23

Vnfit he was for any worldly thing,
And eke vnhable once to stirre or go,
Not meet to be of counsell to a king,
Whose mind in meat and drinke was drowned so,
That from his friend he seldome knew his fo:
Full of diseases was his carcas blew,
And a dry dropsie through his flesh did flow:
Which by misdiet daily greater grew:
Such one was *Gluttony,* the second of that crew.

24

And next to him rode lustfull *Lechery,*
Vpon a bearded Goat, whose rugged haire,
And whally[167] eyes (the signe of gelosy,)
Was like the person selfe, whom he did beare:
Who rough, and blacke, and filthy did appeare,
Vnseemely man to please faire Ladies eye;
Yet he of Ladies oft was loued deare,
When fairer faces were bid standen by:
O who does know the bent of womens fantasy?

25

In a greene gowne he clothed was full faire,
Which vnderneath did hide his filthinesse,
And in his hand a burning hart he bare,
Full of vaine follies, and new fanglenesse:
For he was false, and fraught with ficklenesse,
And learned had to loue with secret lookes,

[167] streaked

And well could daunce, and sing with ruefulnesse,
And fortunes tell, and read in louing bookes,
And thousand other wayes, to bait his fleshly hookes.

26

Inconstant man, that loued all he saw,
And lusted after all, that he did loue,
Ne would his looser life be tide to law,
But ioyd weake wemens hearts to tempt and proue
If from their loyall loues he might then moue;
Which lewdnesse fild him with reprochfull paine
Of that fowle euill, which all men reproue,
That rots the marrow, and consumes the braine:
Such one was *Lecherie,* the third of all this traine.

27

And greedy *Auarice* by him did ride,
Vpon a Camell loaden all with gold;
Two iron coffers hong on either side,
With precious mettall full, as they might hold,
And in his lap an heape of coine he told;
For of his wicked pelfe his God he made,
And vnto hell him selfe for money sold;
Accursed vsurie was all his trade,
And right and wrong ylike in equall ballaunce waide.

28

His life was nigh vnto deaths doore yplast,
And thred-bare cote, and cobled shoes he ware,
Ne scarse good morsell all his life did tast,
But both from backe and belly still did spare,
To fill his bags, and richesse to compare;[168]

[168] gather

Yet chylde ne kinsman liuing had he none
To leaue them to; but thorough daily care
To get, and nightly feare to lose his owne,
He led a wretched life vnto him selfe vnknowne.

29

Most wretched wight, whom nothing might suffise,
Whose greedy lust did lacke in greatest store,
Whose need had end, but no end couetise,
Whose wealth was want, whose plenty made him pore,
Who had enough, yet wished euer more;
A vile disease, and eke in foote and hand
A grieuous gout tormented him full sore,
That well he could not touch, nor go, nor stand:
Such one was *Auarice,* the fourth of this faire band.

30

And next to him malicious *Enuie* rode,
Vpon a rauenous wolfe, and still did chaw
Betweene his cankred teeth a venemous tode,
That all the poison ran about his chaw;[169]
But inwardly he chawed his owne maw
At neighbours wealth, that made him euer sad;
For death it was, when any good he saw,
And wept, that cause of weeping none he had,
But when he heard of harme, he wexed wondrous glad.

31

All in a kirtle of discolourd say[170]
He clothed was, ypainted full of eyes;
And in his bosome secretly there lay
An hatefull Snake, the which his taile vptyes
In many folds, and mortall sting implyes.[171]
Still as he rode, he gnasht his teeth, to see
Those heapes of gold with griple[172] Couetyse,
And grudged at the great felicitie
Of proud *Lucifera,* and his owne companie.

32

He hated all good workes and vertuous deeds,
And him no lesse, that any like did vse,
And who with gracious bread the hungry feeds,
His almes for want of faith he doth accuse;
So euery good to bad he doth abuse:
And eke the verse of famous Poets witt
He does backebite, and spightfull poison spues
From leprous mouth on all, that euer writt:
Such one vile *Enuie* was, that fifte in row did sitt.

33

And him beside rides fierce reuenging *Wrath,*
Vpon a Lion, loth for to be led;
And in his hand a burning brond he hath,
The which he brandisheth about his hed;
His eyes did hurle forth sparkles fiery red,
And stared sterne on all, that him beheld,
As ashes pale of hew and seeming ded;
And on his dagger still his hand he held,
Trembling through hasty rage, when choler in him sweld.

34

His ruffin raiment all was staind with blood,

[169] jaw
[170] varicolored woolen cloth
[171] encloses
[172] greedy

Which he had spilt, and all to rags yrent,
Through vnaduized rashnesse woxen wood;
For of his hands he had no gouernement,
Ne car'd for bloud in his auengement:
But when the furious fit was ouerpast,
His cruell facts[173] he often would repent;
Yet wilfull man he neuer would forecast,
How many mischieues should ensue his heedlesse hast.

35

Full many mischiefes follow cruell *Wrath;*
Abhorred bloudshed, and tumultuous strife,
Vnmanly murder, and vnthrifty scath,[174]
Bitter despight, with rancours rusty knife,
And fretting griefe the enemy of life;
All these, and many euils moe haunt ire,
The swelling Splene, and Frenzy raging rife,
The shaking Palsey, and Saint *Fraunces* fire.[175]
Such one was *Wrath,* the last of this vngodly tire.[176]

36

And after all, vpon the wagon beame
Rode *Sathan,* with a smarting whip in hand,
With which he forward lasht the laesie teme,
So oft as *Slowth* still in the mire did stand.
Huge routs of people did about them band,
Showting for ioy, and still before their way
A foggy mist had couered all the land;
And vnderneath their feet, all scattered lay
Dead sculs and bones of men, whose life had gone astray.

[173] deeds
[174] harm
[175] erysipelas
[176] crew

37

So forth they marchen in this goodly sort,
To take the solace of the open aire,
And in fresh flowring fields themselues to sport;
Emongst the rest rode that false Lady faire,
The fowle *Duessa,* next vnto the chaire
Of proud *Lucifera,* as one of the traine:
But that good knight would not so nigh repaire,
Him selfe estraunging from their ioyaunce vaine,
Whose fellowship seemd far vnfit for warlike swaine.

38

So hauing solaced themselues a space
With pleasaunce of the breathing fields yfed,
They backe returned to the Princely Place;
Whereas an errant knight in armes ycled,
And heathnish shield, wherein with letters red
Was writ *Sans ioy,* they new arriued find:
Enflam'd with fury and fiers hardyhed,
He seemd in hart to harbour thoughts vnkind,
And nourish bloudy vengeaunce in his bitter mind.

39

Who when the shamed shield of slaine *Sans foy*
He spide with that same Faery champions page,
Bewraying him, that did of late destroy
His eldest brother, burning all with rage
He to him leapt, and that same enuious gage[177]
Of victors glory from him snatcht away:

[177] pledge of battle

But th'Elfin knight, which ought[178] that warlike wage,
Disdaind to loose the meed he wonne in fray,
And him rencountring fierce, reskewd the noble pray.

40

Therewith they gan to hurtlen greedily,
Redoubted battaile ready to darrayne,[179]
And clash their shields, and shake their swords on hy,
That with their sturre they troubled all the traine;
Till that great Queene vpon eternall paine
Of high displeasure, that ensewen might,
Commaunded them their fury to refraine,
And if that either to that shield had right,
In equall lists they should the morrow next it fight.

41

Ah dearest Dame, (quoth then the Paynim bold,)
Pardon the errour of enraged wight,
Whom great griefe made forget the raines to hold
Of reasons rule, to see this recreant knight,
No knight, but treachour full of false despight
And shamefull treason, who through guile hath slayn
The prowest knight, that euer field did fight,
Euen stout *Sans foy* (O who can then refrayn?)
Whose shield he beares renuerst, the more to heape disdayn.

42

And to augment the glorie of his guile,
His dearest loue the faire *Fidessa* loe
Is there possessed of the traytour vile,
Who reapes the haruest sowen by his foe,
Sowen in bloudy field, and bought with woe:
That brothers hand shall dearely well requight
So be, O Queene, you equall fauour showe.
Him litle answerd th'angry Elfin knight;
He neuer meant with words, but swords to plead his right.

43

But threw his gauntlet as a sacred pledge,
His cause in combat the next day to try:
So been they parted both, with harts on edge,
To be aueng'd each on his enimy.
That night they pas in ioy and iollity,
Feasting and courting both in bowre and hall;
For Steward was excessiue *Gluttonie,*
That of his plenty poured forth to all;
Which doen, the Chamberlain *Slowth* did to rest them call.

44

Now whenas darkesome night had all displayd
Her coleblacke curtein ouer brightest skye,
The warlike youthes on dayntie couches layd,
Did chace away sweet sleepe from sluggish eye,
To muse on meanes of hoped victory.
But whenas *Morpheus* had with leaden mace
Arrested all that courtly company,
Vp-rose *Duessa* from her resting place,
And to the Paynims lodging comes with silent pace.

45

Whom broad awake she finds, in troublous fit,
Forecasting, how his foe he might annoy,

178 owned
179 decide by combat

And him amoues with speaches seeming fit:
Ah deare *Sans ioy,* next dearest to *Sans foy,*
Cause of my new griefe, cause of my new ioy,
Ioyous, to see his ymage in mine eye,
And greeu'd, to thinke how foe did him destroy,
That was the flowre of grace and cheualrye;
Lo his *Fidessa* to thy secret faith I flye.

46

With gentle wordes he can her fairely greet,
And bad say on the secret of her hart.
Then sighing soft, I learne that litle sweet
Oft tempred is (quoth she) with muchell smart:
For since my brest was launcht with louely dart
Of deare *Sansfoy,* I neuer ioyed howre,
But in eternall woes my weaker hart
Haue wasted, louing him with all my powre,
And for his sake haue felt full many an heauie stowre.

47

At last when perils all I weened past,
And hop'd to reape the crop of all my care,
Into new woes vnweeting I was cast,
By this false faytor,[180] who vnworthy ware
His worthy shield, whom he with guilefull snare
Entrapped slew, and brought to shamefull graue.
Me silly maid away with him he bare,
And euer since hath kept in darksome caue,
For that I would not yeeld, that to *Sans-foy* I gaue.

180 deceiver

48

But since faire Sunne hath sperst that lowring clowd,
And to my loathed life now shewes some light,
Vnder your beames I will me safely shrowd,
From dreaded storme of his disdainfull spight:
To you th'inheritance belongs by right
Of brothers prayse, to you eke longs his loue.
Let not his loue, let not his restlesse spright
Be vnreung'd, that calles to you aboue
From wandring *Stygian* shores, where it doth endlesse moue.

49

Thereto said he, Faire Dame be nought dismaid
For sorrowes past; their griefe is with them gone:
Ne yet of present perill be affraid;
For needlesse feare did neuer vantage none,
And helplesse hap it booteth not to mone.
Dead is *Sans-foy,* his vitall paines are past,
Though greeued ghost for vengeance deepe do grone:
He liues, that shall him pay his dewties last,
And guiltie Elfin bloud shall sacrifice in hast.

50

O but I feare the fickle freakes (quoth shee)
Of fortune false, and oddes of armes in field.
Why dame (quoth he) what oddes can euer bee,
Where both do fight alike, to win or yield?
Yea but (quoth she) he beares a charmed shield,
And eke enchaunted armes, that none can perce,

Ne none can wound the man, that does them wield.
Charmd or enchaunted (answerd he then ferce)
I no whit reck, ne you the like need to reherce.

51

But faire *Fidessa,* sithens [181] fortunes guile,
Or enimies powre hath now captiued you,
Returne from whence ye came, and rest a while
Till morrow next, that I the Elfe subdew,
And with *Sans-foyes* dead dowry you endew.
Ay me, that is a double death (she said)
With proud foes sight my sorrow to renew:
Where euer yet I be, my secrete aid
Shall follow you. So passing forth she him obaid.

Canto V

The faithfull knight in equall field
subdewes his faithlesse foe,
Whom false Duessa saues, and for
his cure to hell does goe.

1

The noble hart, that harbours vertuous thought,
And is with child of glorious great intent,
Can neuer rest, vntill it forth haue brought
Th'eternall brood of glorie excellent:
Such restlesse passion did all night torment
The flaming corage of that Faery knight,
Deuizing, how that doughtie turnament
With greatest honour he atchieuen might;
Still did he wake, and still did watch for dawning light.

2

At last the golden Orientall gate
Of greatest heauen gan to open faire,
And *Phœbus* fresh, as bridegrome to his mate,
Came dauncing forth, shaking his deawie haire:
And hurld his glistring beames through gloomy aire.
Which when the wakeful Elfe perceiu'd, streight way
He started vp, and did him selfe prepaire,
In sun-bright armes, and battailous array:
For with that Pagan proud he combat will that day.

3

And forth he comes into the commune hall,
Where earely waite him many a gazing eye,
To weet what end to straunger knights may fall.
There many Minstrales maken melody,
To driue away the dull melancholy,
And many Bardes, that to the trembling chord
Can tune their timely voyces cunningly,
And many Chroniclers, that can record
Old loues, and warres for Ladies doen by many a Lord.

4

Soone after comes the cruell Sarazin,
In wouen maile all armed warily,
And sternly lookes at him, who not a pin
Does care for looke of liuing creatures eye.
They bring them wines of *Greece* and *Araby,*
And daintie spices fetcht from furthest *Ynd,*
To kindle heat of corage priuily:
And in the wine a solemne oth they bynd

---

181 since

T'obserue the sacred lawes of armes, that are assynd.

5

At last forth comes that far renowmed Queene,
With royall pomp and Princely maiestie;
She is ybrought vnto a paled greene,[182]
And placed vnder stately canapee,
The warlike feates of both those knights to see.
On th'other side in all mens open vew
Duessa placed is, and on a tree
Sans-foy his shield is hangd with bloudy hew:
Both those the lawrell girlonds to the victor dew.

6

A shrilling trompet sownded from on hye,
And vnto battaill bad them selues addresse:
Their shining shieldes about their wrestes they tye,
And burning blades about their heads do blesse,[183]
The instruments of wrath and heauinesse:
With greedy force each other doth assayle,
And strike so fiercely, that they do impresse
Deepe dinted furrowes in the battred mayle;
The yron walles to ward their blowes are weake and fraile.

7

The Sarazin was stout, and wondrous strong,
And heaped blowes like yron hammers great:
For after bloud and vengeance he did long.
The knight was fiers, and full of youthly heat:
And doubled strokes, like dreaded thunders threat:
For all for prayse and honour he did fight.
Both stricken strike, and beaten both do beat,
That from their shields forth flyeth firie light,
And helmets hewen deepe, shew marks of eithers might.

8

So th'one for wrong, the other striues for right:
As when a Gryfon seized of his pray,
A Dragon fiers encountreth in his flight,
Through widest ayre making his ydle way,
That would his rightfull rauine[184] rend away:
With hideous horrour both together smight,
And souce[185] so sore, that they the heauens affray:
The wise Southsayer seeing so sad sight,
Th'amazed vulgar tels of warres and mortall fight.

9

So th'one for wrong, the other striues for right,
And each to deadly shame would driue his foe:
The cruell steele so greedily doth bight
In tender flesh, that streames of bloud down flow,
With which the armes, that earst so bright did show,
Into a pure vermillion now are dyde:
Great ruth in all the gazers harts did grow,
Seeing the gored woundes to gape so wyde,
That victory they dare not wish to either side.

10

At last the Paynim chaunst to cast his eye,
His suddein eye, flaming with wrathfull fyre,

[182] The lists enclosed with palings.
[183] brandish
[184] spoil
[185] attack

Vpon his brothers shield, which hong thereby:
Therewith redoubled was his raging yre,
And said, Ah wretched sonne of wofull syre,
Doest thou sit wayling by black *Stygian* lake,
Whilest here thy shield is hangd for victors hyre,
And sluggish german[186] doest thy forces slake,
To after-send his foe, that him may ouertake?

11

Goe caytiue Elfe, him quickly ouertake,
And soone redeeme from his long wandring woe;
Goe guiltie ghost, to him my message make,
That I his shield haue quit[187] from dying foe.
Therewith vpon his crest he stroke him so,
That twise he reeled, readie twise to fall;
End of the doubtfull battell deemed tho
The lookers on, and lowd to him gan call
The false *Duessa,* Thine the shield, and I, and all.

12

Soone as the Faerie heard his Ladie speake,
Out of his swowning dreame he gan awake,
And quickning faith, that earst was woxen weake,
The creeping deadly cold away did shake:
Tho mou'd with wrath, and shame, and Ladies sake,
Of all attonce he cast[188] auengd to bee,
And with so'exceeding furie at him strake,
That forced him to stoupe vpon his knee;
Had he not stouped so, he should haue clouen bee,

[186] brother [187] redeemed [188] devised how

13

And to him said, Goe now proud Miscreant,
Thy selfe thy message doe to german deare,
Alone he wandring thee too long doth want:
Goe say, his foe thy shield with his doth beare.
Therewith his heauie hand he high gan reare,
Him to haue slaine; when loe a darkesome clowd
Vpon him fell: he no where doth appeare,
But vanisht is. The Elfe him cals alowd,
But answer none receiues: the darknes him does shrowd.

14

In haste *Duessa* from her place arose,
And to him running said, O prowest knight,
That euer Ladie to her loue did chose,
Let now abate the terror of your might,
And quench the flame of furious despight,
And bloudie vengeance; lo th'infernall powres
Couering your foe with cloud of deadly night,
Haue borne him hence to *Plutoes* balefull bowres.
The conquest yours, I yours, the shield, and glory yours.

15

Not all so satisfide, with greedie eye
He sought all round about, his thirstie blade
To bath in bloud of faithlesse enemy;
Who all that while lay hid in secret shade:
He standes amazed, how he thence should fade.
At last the trumpets Triumph sound on hie,

And running Heralds humble homage made,
Greeting him goodly with new victorie,
And to him brought the shield, the cause of enmitie.

16

Wherewith he goeth to that soueraine Queene,
And falling her before on lowly knee,
To her makes present of his seruice seene:
Which she accepts, with thankes, and goodly gree,[189]
Greatly aduauncing[190] his gay cheualree.
So marcheth home, and by her takes the knight,
Whom all the people follow with great glee,
Shouting, and clapping all their hands on hight,
That all the aire it fils, and flyes to heauen bright.

17

Home is he brought, and laid in sumptuous bed:
Where many skilfull leaches him abide,
To salue his hurts, that yet still freshly bled.
In wine and oyle they wash his woundes wide,
And softly can embalme on euery side.
And all the while, most heauenly melody
About the bed sweet musicke did diuide,[191]
Him to beguile of griefe and agony:
And all the while *Duessa* wept full bitterly.

18

As when a wearie traueller that strayes
By muddy shore of broad seuen-mouthed *Nile,*
Vnweeting of the perillous wandring wayes,
Doth meet a cruell craftie Crocodile,
Which in false griefe hyding his harmefull guile,
Doth weepe full sore, and sheddeth tender teares:
The foolish man, that pitties all this while
His mournefull plight, is swallowed vp vnwares,
Forgetfull of his owne, that mindes anothers cares.

19

So wept *Duessa* vntill euentide,
That shyning lampes in *Ioues* high house were light:
Then forth she rose, ne lenger would abide,
But comes vnto the place, where th'Hethen knight
In slombring swownd nigh voyd of vitall spright,
Lay couer'd with inchaunted cloud all day:
Whom when she found, as she him left in plight,
To wayle his woefull case she would not stay,
But to the easterne coast of heauen makes speedy way.

20

Where griesly *Night,* with visage deadly sad,
That *Phœbus* chearefull face durst neuer vew,
And in a foule blacke pitchie mantle clad,
She findes forth comming from her darkesome mew,[192]
Where she all day did hide her hated hew.
Before the dore her yron charet stood,
Alreadie harnessed for iourney new;
And coleblacke steedes yborne of hellish brood,
That on their rustie bits did champ, as they were wood.

---

[189] will
[190] praising
[191] Play brilliantly in parts
[192] place of confinement

21

Who when she saw *Duessa* sunny bright,
Adornd with gold and iewels shining cleare,
She greatly grew amazed at the sight,
And th'vnacquainted[193] light began to feare:
For neuer did such brightnesse there appeare,
And would haue backe retyred to her caue,
Vntill the witches speech she gan to heare,
Saying, Yet O thou dreaded Dame, I craue
Abide, till I haue told the message, which I haue.

22

She stayd, and foorth *Duessa* gan proceede,
O thou most auncient Grandmother[194] of all,
More old then *Ioue*, whom thou at first didst breede,
Or that great house of Gods cælestiall,
Which wast begot in *Dæmogorgons* hall,
And sawst the secrets of the world vnmade,
Why suffredst thou thy Nephewes deare to fall
With Elfin sword, most shamefully betrade?
Lo where the stout *Sansioy* doth sleepe in deadly shade.

23

And him before, I saw with bitter eyes
The bold *Sansfoy* shrinke vnderneath his speare;
And now the pray of fowles in field he lyes,
Nor wayld of friends, nor laid on groning beare,
That whylome was to me too dearely deare.
O what of Gods then boots it to be borne,
If old *Aveugles*[195] sonnes so euill heare?
Or who shall not great *Nightes* children scorne,
When two of three her Nephews are so fowle forlorne.

24

Vp then, vp dreary Dame, of darknesse Queene,
Go gather vp the reliques of thy race,
Or else goe them auenge, and let be seene,
That dreaded *Night* in brightest day hath place,
And can the children of faire light deface.
Her feeling speeches some compassion moued
In hart, and chaunge in that great mothers face:
Yet pittie in her hart was neuer proued
Till then: for euermore she hated, neuer loued.

25

And said, Deare daughter rightly may I rew
The fall of famous children borne of mee,
And good successes, which their foes ensew:[196]
But who can turne the streame of destinee,
Or breake the chayne of strong necessitee,
Which fast is tyde to *Ioues* eternall seat?
The sonnes of Day he fauoureth, I see,
And by my ruines thinkes to make them great:
To make one great by others losse, is bad excheat.[197]

26

Yet shall they not escape so freely all;
For some shall pay the price of others guilt:

[193] strange
[194] Night was the daughter of Chaos and so older than any of the gods.

[195] The Blind, the father of the three Paynims.
[196] befall
[197] exchange

And he the man that made *Sansfoy* to fall,
Shall with his owne bloud price[198] that he hath spilt.
But what art thou, that telst of Nephews kilt?
I that do seeme not I, *Duessa* am,
(Quoth she) how euer now in garments gilt,
And gorgeous gold arayd I to thee came;
Duessa I, the daughter of Deceipt and Shame.

27

Then bowing downe her aged backe, she kist
The wicked witch, saying; In that faire face
The false resemblance of Deceipt, I wist
Did closely lurke; yet so true-seeming grace
It carried, that I scarse in darkesome place
Could it discerne, though I the mother bee
Of falshood, and root of *Duessaes* race.
O welcome child, whom I haue longd to see,
And now haue seene vnwares. Lo now I go with thee.

28

Then to her yron wagon she betakes,
And with her beares the fowle welfauourd witch:
Through mirkesome aire her readie way she makes.
Her twyfold Teme, of which two blacke as pitch,
And two were browne, yet each to each vnlich,[199]
Did softly swim away, ne euer stampe,
Vnlesse she chaunst their stubborne mouths to twitch;
Then foming tarre, their bridles they would champe,
And trampling the fine element, would fiercely rampe.

29

So well they sped, that they be come at length
Vnto the place, whereas the Paynim lay,
Deuoid of outward sense, and natiue strength,
Couerd with charmed cloud from vew of day,
And sight of men, since his late luckelesse fray.
His cruell wounds with cruddy[200] bloud congealed,
They binden vp so wisely, as they may,
And handle softly, till they can be healed:
So lay him in her charet, close in night concealed.

30

And all the while she stood vpon the ground,
The wakefull dogs did neuer cease to bay,
As giuing warning of th'vnwonted sound,
With which her yron wheeles did them affray,
And her darke griesly looke them much dismay;
The messenger of death, the ghastly Owle
With drearie shriekes did also her bewray;
And hungry Wolues continually did howle,
At her abhorred face, so filthy and so fowle.

31

Thence turning backe in silence soft they stole,
And brought the heauie corse with easie pace
To yawning gulfe of deepe *Auernus* hole.
By that same hole an entrance darke and bace
With smoake and sulphure hiding all the place,

[198] pay

[199] unlike

[200] curdled, *i.e.*, coagulated

Descends to hell: there creature neuer past,
That backe returned without heauenly grace;
But dreadfull *Furies,* which their chaines haue brast,
And damned sprights sent forth to make ill men aghast.

32

By that same way the direfull dames doe driue
Their mournefull charet, fild with rusty blood,
And downe to *Plutoes* house are come biliue:
Which passing through, on euery side them stood
The trembling ghosts with sad amazed mood,
Chattring their yron teeth, and staring wide
With stonie eyes; and all the hellish brood
Of feends infernall flockt on euery side,
To gaze on earthly wight, that with the Night durst ride.

33

They pas the bitter waues of *Acheron,*
Where many soules sit wailing woefully,
And come to fiery flood of *Phlegeton,*[201]
Whereas the damned ghosts in torments fry,
And with sharpe shrilling shriekes doe bootlesse cry,
Cursing high *Ioue,* the which them thither sent.
The house of endlesse paine is built thereby,
In which ten thousand sorts of punishment
The cursed creatures doe eternally torment.

[201] Acheron and Phlegeton are rivers in Hades.

34

Before the threshold dreadfull *Cerberus*
His three deformed heads did lay along,
Curled with thousand adders venemous,
And lilled forth his bloudie flaming tong:
At them he gan to reare his bristles strong,
And felly gnarre,[202] vntill dayes enemy
Did him appease; then downe his taile he hong
And suffered them to passen quietly:
For she in hell and heauen had power equally.

35

There was *Ixion* turned on a wheele,
For daring tempt the Queene of heauen to sin;
And *Sisyphus* an huge round stone did reele
Against an hill, ne might from labour lin;[203]
There thirstie *Tantalus* hong by the chin;
And *Tityus* fed a vulture on his maw;
Typhœus ioynts were stretched on a gin,
Theseus condemned to endlesse slouth by law,
And fifty sisters[204] water in leake vessels draw.

36

They all beholding worldly wights in place,
Leaue off their worke, vnmindfull of their smart,
To gaze on them; who forth by them doe pace,
Till they be come vnto the furthest part:
Where was a Caue ywrought by wondrous art,
Deepe, darke, vneasie, dolefull, comfortlesse,
In which sad *Æsculapius* farre a part

[202] fiercely snarled
[203] cease
[204] The Danaides, who slew their husbands and were thus punished.

Emprisond was in chaines remedilesse,
For that *Hippolytus* rent corse he did redresse.[205]

37

Hippolytus a iolly huntsman was,
That wont in charet chace the foming Bore;
He all his Peeres in beautie did surpas,
But Ladies loue as losse of time forbore:
His wanton stepdame loued him the more,
But when she saw her offred sweets refused
Her loue she turnd to hate, and him before
His father fierce of treason false accused,
And with her gealous termes his open eares abused.

38

Who in all rage his Sea-god syre besought,
Some cursed vengeance on his sonne to cast:
From surging gulf two monsters straight were brought,
With dread whereof his chasing steedes aghast,
Both charet swift and huntsman ouercast.
His goodly corps on ragged cliffs yrent,
Was quite dismembred, and his members chast
Scattered on euery mountaine, as he went,
That of *Hippolytus* was left no moniment.

39

His cruell stepdame seeing what was donne,
Her wicked dayes with wretched knife did end,
In death auowing th'innocence of her sonne.
Which hearing his rash Syre, began to rend
His haire, and hastie tongue, that did offend:
Tho gathering vp the relicks[206] of his smart
By *Dianes* meanes, who was *Hippolyts* frend,
Them brought to *Æsculape,* that by his art
Did heale them all againe, and ioyned euery part.

40

Such wondrous science in mans wit to raine
When *Ioue* auizd, that could the dead reuiue,
And fates expired could renew againe,
Of endlesse life he might him not depriue,
But vnto hell did thrust him downe aliue,
With flashing thunderbolt ywounded sore:
Where long remaining, he did alwaies striue
Himselfe with salues to health for to restore,
And slake the heauenly fire, that raged euermore.

41

There auncient Night arriuing, did alight
From her nigh wearie waine, and in her armes
To *Æsculapius* brought the wounded knight:
Whom hauing softly disarayd of armes,
Tho gan to him discouer all his harmes,
Beseeching him with prayer, and with praise,
If either salues, or oyles, or herbes, or charmes
A fordonne wight from dore of death mote raise,
He would at her request prolong her nephews daies.

42

Ah Dame (quoth he) thou temptest me in vaine,

---

[205] heal
[206] The pieces of Hippolytus' body.

To dare the thing, which daily yet I rew,
And the old cause of my continued paine
With like attempt to like end to renew.
Is not enough, that thrust from heauen dew
Here endlesse penance for one fault I pay,
But that redoubled crime with vengeance new
Thou biddest me to eeke?[207] Can Night defray
The wrath of thundring *Ioue,* that rules both night and day?

43

Not so (quoth she) but sith that heauens king
From hope of heauen hath thee excluded quight,
Why fearest thou, that canst not hope for thing,
And fearest not, that more thee hurten might,
Now in the powre of euerlasting Night?
Goe to then, O thou farre renowmed sonne
Of great *Apollo,* shew thy famous might
In medicine, that else hath to thee wonne
Great paines, and greater praise, both neuer to be donne.[208]

44

Her words preuaild: And then the learned leach
His cunning hand gan to his wounds to lay,
And all things else, the which his art did teach:
Which hauing seene, from thence arose away
The mother of dread darknesse, and let stay
Aueugles sonne there in the leaches cure,
And backe returning tooke her wonted way,
To runne her timely race, whilst *Phœbus* pure
In westerne waues his wearie wagon did recure.

45

The false *Duessa* leauing noyous Night,
Returnd to stately pallace of dame Pride;
Where when she came, she found the Faery knight
Departed thence, albe his woundes wide
Not throughly heald, vnreadie were to ride.
Good cause he had to hasten thence away;
For on a day his wary Dwarfe had spide,
Where in a dongeon deepe huge numbers lay
Of caytiue wretched thrals, that wayled night and day.

46

A ruefull sight, as could be seene with eie;
Of whom he learned had in secret wise
The hidden cause of their captiuitie,
How mortgaging their liues to *Couetise,*
Though wastfull Pride, and wanton Riotise,
They were by law of that proud Tyrannesse
Prouokt with *Wrath,* and *Enuies* false surmise,
Condemned to that Dongeon mercilesse,
Where they should liue in woe, and die in wretchednesse.

47

There was that great proud king of *Babylon,*[209]
That would compell all nations to adore,
And him as onely God to call vpon,
Till through celestiall doome throwne out of dore,
Into an Oxe he was transform'd of yore:
There also was king *Crœsus,* that enhaunst

[207] increase
[208] therefore eternal
[209] Nebuchadnezzar

His heart too high through his great riches store;
And proud *Antiochus,*[210] the which aduaunst
His cursed hand gainst God, and on his altars daunst.

48

And them long time before, great *Nimrod* was,
That first the world with sword and fire warrayd;
And after him old *Ninus*[211] farre did pas
In princely pompe, of all the world obayd;
There also was that mightie Monarch[212] layd
Low vnder all, yet aboue all in pride,
That name of natiue syr did fowle vpbrayd,
And would as *Ammons* sonne be magnifide,
Till scornd of God and man a shamefull death he dide.[213]

49

All these together in one heape were throwne,
Like carkases of beasts in butchers stall.
And in another corner wide were strowne
The antique ruines of the *Romaines* fall:
Great *Romulus* the Grandsyre of them all,
Proud *Tarquin,* and too lordly *Lentulus,*
Stout *Scipio,* and stubborne *Hanniball,*
Ambitious *Sylla,* and sterne *Marius,*
High *Cæsar,* great *Pompey,* and fierce *Antonius.*

50

Amongst these mighty men were wemen mixt,
Proud wemen, vaine, forgetfull of their yoke;
The bold *Semiramis,* whose sides transfixt
With sonnes owne blade, her fowle reproches spoke;
Faire *Sthenobœa,*[214] that her selfe did choke
With wilfull cord, for wanting of her will;
High minded *Cleopatra,* that with stroke
Of Aspes sting her selfe did stoutly kill;
And thousands moe the like, that did that dongeon fill.

51

Besides the endlesse routs of wretched thralles,
Which thither were assembled day by day,
From all the world after their wofull falles,
Through wicked pride, and wasted wealthes decay.
But most of all, which in that Dongeon lay
Fell from high Princes courts, or Ladies bowres,
Where they in idle pompe, or wanton play,
Consumed had their goods, and thriftlesse howres,
And lastly throwne themselues into these heauy stowres.

52

Whose case when as the careful Dwarfe had tould,
And made ensample of their mournefull sight
Vnto his maister, he no lenger would
There dwell in perill of like painefull plight,
But early rose, and ere that dawning light
Discouered had the world to heauen wyde,
He by a priuie Posterne tooke his flight,

[210] King of Syria
[211] Legendary founder of Nineveh.
[212] Alexander the Great
[213] Alexander was reputed to have died of drunkenness.
[214] Who killed herself for love of Bellerophon.

That of no enuious eyes he mote be spyde:
For doubtlesse death ensewd, if any him descryde.

53

Scarse could he footing find in that fowle way,
For many corses, like a great Lay-stall,[215]
Of murdred men which therein strowed lay,
Without remorse, or decent funerall:
Which all through that great Princesse pride did fall
And came to shamefull end. And them beside
Forth ryding vnderneath the castell wall,
A donghill of dead carkases he spide,
The dreadfull spectacle of that sad house of *Pride.*

Canto VI

From lawlesse lust by wondrous grace
fayre Vna is releast:
Whom saluage nation does adore,
and learnes her wise beheast.

1

As when a ship, that flyes faire vnder saile,
An hidden rocke escaped hath vnwares,
That lay in waite her wrack for to bewaile,
The Marriner yet halfe amazed stares
At perill past, and yet in doubt ne dares
To ioy at his foole-happie oversight: [216]
So doubly is distrest twixt ioy and cares
The dreadlesse courage of this Elfin knight,
Hauing escapt so sad ensamples in his sight.

2

Yet sad he was that his too hastie speed
The faire *Duess'* had forst him leaue behind;
And yet more sad, that *Vna* his deare dreed [217]
Her truth had staind with treason so vnkind;
Yet crime in her could neuer creature find,
But for his loue, and for her owne selfe sake,
She wandred had from one to other *Ynd,*
Him for to seeke, ne euer would forsake,
Till her vnwares the fierce *Sansloy* did ouertake.

3

Who after *Archimagoes* fowle defeat,
Led her away into a forrest wilde,
And turning wrathfull fire to lustfull heat,
With beastly sin thought her to haue defilde,
And made the vassall of his pleasures vilde.
Yet first he cast by treatie, and by traynes,
Her to perswade, that stubborne fort to yilde:
For greater conquest of hard loue he gaynes,
That workes it to his will, then he that it constraines.

4

With fawning wordes he courted her a while,
And looking louely, and oft sighing sore,
Her constant hart did tempt with diuerse guile:
But wordes, and lookes, and sighes she did abhore,
As rocke of Diamond stedfast euermore.
Yet for to feed his fyrie lustfull eye,
He snatcht the vele, that hong her face before;
Then gan her beautie shine, as brightest skye,
And burnt his beastly hart t'efforce her chastitye.

5

So when he saw his flatt'ring arts to fayle,
And subtile engines bet from batteree,

---

[215] pile of filth
[216] escape
[217] An object loved and reverenced.

With greedy force he gan the fort assayle,
Whereof he weend possessed soone to bee,
And win rich spoile of ransackt chastetee.
Ah heauens, that do this hideous act behold,
And heauenly virgin thus outraged see,
How can ye vengeance iust so long withhold,
And hurle not flashing flames vpon that Paynim bold?

6

The pitteous maiden carefull comfortlesse,
Does throw out thrilling shriekes, and shrieking cryes,
The last vaine helpe of womens great distresse,
And with loud plaints importuneth the skyes,
That molten starres do drop like weeping eyes;
And *Phœbus* flying so most shamefull sight,
His blushing face in foggy cloud implyes,
And hides for shame. What wit of mortall wight
Can now deuise to quit a thrall from such a plight?

7

Eternall prouidence exceeding thought,
Where none appeares can make her selfe a way:
A wondrous way it for this Lady wrought,
From Lyons clawes to pluck the griped pray.
Her shrill outcryes and shriekes so loud did bray,
That all the woodes and forestes did resownd;
A troupe of *Faunes* and *Satyres* [218] far away
Within the wood were dauncing in a rownd,
Whiles old *Syluanus* slept in shady arber sownd.

8

Who when they heard that pitteous strained voice,
In hast forsooke their rurall meriment,
And ran towards the far rebownded noyce,
To weet, what wight so loudly did lament.
Vnto the place they come incontinent:
Whom when the raging Sarazin espide,
A rude, misshapen, monstrous rablement,
Whose like he neuer saw, he durst not bide,
But got his ready steed, and fast away gan ride.

9

The wyld woodgods arriued in the place,
There find the virgin dolefull desolate,
With ruffled rayments, and faire blubbred face,
As her outrageous foe had left her late,
And trembling yet through feare of former hate;
All stand amazed at so vncouth sight,
And gin to pittie her vnhappie state,
All stand astonied at her beautie bright,
In their rude eyes vnworthie of so wofull plight.

10

She more amaz'd, in double dread doth dwell;
And euery tender part for feare does shake:
As when a greedie Wolfe through hunger fell
A seely Lambe farre from the flocke does take,
Of whom he meanes his bloudie feast to make,
A Lyon spyes fast running towards him,
The innocent pray in hast he does forsake,

[218] Wood-gods, but in the allegory representing the common people.

Which quit from death yet quakes in euery lim
With chaunge of feare, to see the Lyon looke so grim.

11

Such fearefull fit assaid her trembling hart,
Ne word to speake, ne ioynt to moue she had:
The saluage nation feele her secret smart,
And read her sorrow in her count'nance sad;
Their frowning forheads with rough hornes yclad,
And rusticke horror [219] all a side doe lay,
And gently grenning, shew a semblance glad
To comfort her, and feare to put away,
Their backward bent knees teach her humbly to obay.

12

The doubtfull Damzell dare not yet commit
Her single person to their barbarous truth,
But still twixt feare and hope amazd does sit,
Late learnd what harme to hastie trust ensu'th,
They in compassion of her tender youth,
And wonder of her beautie soueraine,
Are wonne with pitty and vnwonted ruth,
And all prostrate vpon the lowly plaine,
Do kisse her feete, and fawne on her with count'nance faine.

13

Their harts she ghesseth by their humble guise,
And yieldes her to extremitie of time; [220]
So from the ground she fearelesse doth arise,
And walketh forth without suspect of crime:
They all as glad, as birdes of ioyous Prime,[221]
Thence lead her forth, about her dauncing round,
Shouting, and singing all a shepheards ryme,
And with greene braunches strowing all the ground,
Do worship her, as Queene, with oliue girlond cround.

14

And all the way their merry pipes they sound,
That all the woods with doubled Eccho ring,
And with their horned feet do weare the ground,
Leaping like wanton kids in pleasant Spring.
So towards old *Syluanus* they her bring;
Who with the noyse awaked, commeth out,
To weet the cause, his weake steps gouerning,
And aged limbs on Cypresse stadle [222] stout,
And with an yuie twyne his wast is girt about.

15

Far off he wonders, what them makes so glad,
Or *Bacchus* merry fruit they did inuent,[223]
Or *Cybeles* franticke rites haue made them mad;
They drawing nigh, vnto their God present
That flowre of faith and beautie excellent.
The God himselfe vewing that mirrhour rare,
Stood long amazd, and burnt in his intent;

[219] roughness [220] her condition

[221] spring [222] staff [223] find

His owne faire *Dryope*[224] now he thinkes not faire,
And *Pholoe*[225] fowle, when her to this he doth compaire.

16

The woodborne people fall before her flat,
And worship her as Goddesse of the wood;
And old *Syluanus* selfe bethinkes not, what
To thinke of wight so faire, but gazing stood,
In doubt to deeme her borne of earthly brood;
Sometimes Dame *Venus* selfe he seemes to see,
But *Venus* neuer had so sober mood;
Sometimes *Dianà* he her takes to bee,
But misseth bow, and shaftes, and buskins to her knee.

17

By vew of her he ginneth to reuiue
His ancient loue, and dearest *Cyparisse,*
And calles to mind his pourtraiture aliue,
How faire he was, and yet not faire to this,
And how he slew with glauncing dart amisse
A gentle Hynd, the which the louely boy
Did loue as life, aboue all worldly blisse;
For griefe whereof the lad n'ould after ioy,
But pynd away in anguish and selfe-wild annoy.

18

The wooddy Nymphes, faire *Hamadryades*
Her to behold do thither runne apace,
And all the troupe of light-foot *Naiades,*
Flocke all about to see her louely face:
But when they vewed haue her heauenly grace,
They enuie her in their malitious mind,
And fly away for feare of fowle disgrace:
But all the *Satyres* scorne their woody kind,
And henceforth nothing faire, but her on earth they find.

19

Glad of such lucke, the luckelesse lucky maid,
Did her content to please their feeble eyes,
And long time with that saluage people staid,
To gather breath in many miseries.
During which time her gentle wit she plyes,
To teach them truth, which worshipt her in vaine,
And made her th'Image of Idolatryes;
But when their bootlesse zeale she did restraine
From her own worship, they her Asse would worship fayn.

20

It fortuned a noble warlike knight[226]
By iust occasion to that forrest came,
To seeke his kindred, and the lignage right,
From whence he tooke his well deserued name:
He had in armes abroad wonne muchell fame,
And fild far landes with glorie of his might,
Plaine, faithfull, true, and enimy of shame,
And euer lou'd to fight for Ladies right,
But in vaine glorious frayes he litle did delight.

21

A Stayres sonne yborne in forrest wyld,
By straunge aduenture as it did betyde,
And there begotten of a Lady myld,
Faire *Thyamis* the daughter of *Labryde,*

[224] Stolen by the Hamadryads from her father, King Dryops.
[225] a nymph

[226] Sir Satyrane

That was in sacred bands of wedlocke tyde
To *Therion,* a loose vnruly swayne;
Who had more ioy to raunge the forrest wyde,
And chase the saluage beast with busie payne,
Then serue his Ladies loue, and wast in pleasures vayne.

22

The forlorne mayd did with loues longing burne,
And could not lacke her louers company,
But to the wood she goes, to serue her turne,
And seeke her spouse, that from her still does fly,
And followes other game and venery:
A Satyre chaunst her wandring for to find,
And kindling coles of lust in brutish eye,
The loyall links of wedlocke did vnbind,
And made her person thrall vnto his beastly kind.

23

So long in secret cabin there he held
Her captiue to his sensuall desire,
Till that with timely fruit her belly sweld,
And bore a boy vnto that saluage sire:
Then home he suffred her for to retire,
For ransome leauing him the late borne childe;
Whom till to ryper yeares he gan aspire,
He noursled vp in life and manners wilde,
Emongst wild beasts and woods, from lawes of men exilde.

24

For all he taught the tender ymp, was but
To banish cowardize and bastard feare;
His trembling hand he would him force to put
Vpon the Lyon and the rugged Beare,
And from the she Beares teats her whelps to teare;
And eke wyld roring Buls he would him make
To tame, and ryde their backs not made to beare;
And the Robuckes in flight to ouertake,
That euery beast for feare of him did fly and quake.

25

Thereby so fearelesse, and so fell he grew,
That his owne sire and maister of his guise [227]
Did often tremble at his horrid vew,
And oft for dread of hurt would him aduise,
The angry beasts not rashly to despise,
Nor too much to prouoke; for he would learne
The Lyon stoup to him in lowly wise,
(A lesson hard) and make the Libbard sterne
Leaue roaring, when in rage he for reuenge did earne.

26

And for to make his powre approued more,
Wyld beasts in yron yokes he would compell;
The spotted Panther, and the tusked Bore,
The Pardale [228] swift, and the Tigre cruell;
The Antelope, and Wolfe both fierce and fell;
And them constraine in equall teme to draw.
Such ioy he had, their stubborne harts to quell,
And sturdie courage tame with dreadfull aw,
That his beheast they feared, as a tyrans law.

27

His louing mother came vpon a day
Vnto the woods, to see her little sonne;

[227] course of life

[228] panther

And chaunst vnwares to meet him in the way,
After his sportes, and cruell pastime donne,
When after him a Lyonesse did runne,
That roaring all with rage, did lowd requere
Her children deare, whom he away had wonne:
The Lyon whelpes she saw how he did beare,
And lull in rugged armes, withouten childish feare.

28

The fearefull Dame all quaked at the sight,
And turning backe, gan fast to fly away,
Vntill with loue reuokt from vaine affright,
She hardly yet perswaded was to stay,
And then to him these womanish words gan say;
Ah *Satyrane,* my dearling, and my ioy,
For loue of me leaue off this dreadfull play;
To dally thus with death, is no fit toy,
Go find some other play-fellowes, mine own sweet boy.

29

In these and like delights of bloudy game
He trayned was, till ryper yeares he raught,[229]
And there abode, whilst any beast of name
Walkt in that forest, whom he had not taught
To feare his force: and then his courage haught
Desird of forreine foemen to be knowne,
And far abroad for straunge aduentures sought:
In which his might was neuer ouerthrowne,
But through all Faery lond his famous worth was blown.

30

Yet euermore it was his manner faire,
After long labours and aduentures spent,
Vnto those natiue woods for to repaire,
To see his sire and ofspring auncient.
And now he thither came for like intent;
Where he vnwares the fairest *Una* found,
Straunge Lady, in so straunge habiliment,
Teaching the Satyres, which her sat around,
Trew sacred lore, which from her sweet lips did redound.

31

He wondred at her wisedome heauenly rare,
Whose like in womens wit he neuer knew;
And when her curteous deeds he did compare,
Gan her admire, and her sad sorrowes rew,
Blaming of Fortune, which such troubles threw,
And ioyd to make proofe of her crueltie
On gentle Dame, so hurtlesse, and so trew:
Thenceforth he kept her goodly company,
And learnd her discipline of faith and veritie.

32

But she all vowd vnto the *Redcrosse* knight,
His wandring perill closely did lament,
Ne in this new acquaintaunce could delight,
But her deare heart with anguish did torment,
And all her wit in secret counsels spent,
How to escape. At last in priuie wise
To *Satyrane* she shewed her intent;
Who glad to gain such fauour, gan deuise,

---

229 reached

How with that pensiue Maid he best might thence arise.

33

So on a day when Satyres all were gone,
To do their seruice to *Syluanus* old,
The gentle virgin left behind alone
He led away with courage stout and bold.
Too late it was, to Satyres to be told,
Or euer hope recouer her againe:
In vaine he seekes that hauing cannot hold.
So fast he carried her with carefull paine,
That they the woods are past, and come now to the plaine.

34

The better part now of the lingring day,
They traueild had, when as they farre espide
A wearie wight forwandring by the way,
And towards him they gan in hast to ride,
To weet of newes, that did abroad betide,
Or tydings of her knight of the *Redcrosse*.
But he them spying, gan to turne aside,
For feare as seemd, or for some feigned losse;
More greedy they of newes, fast towards him do crosse.

35

A silly man, in simple weedes forworne,
And soild with dust of the long dried way;
His sandales were with toilesome trauell torne,
And face all tand with scorching sunny ray,
As he had traueild many a sommers day,
Through boyling sands of *Arabie* and *Ynde;*
And in his hand a *Iacobs* staffe,[230] to stay
His wearie limbes vpon: and eke behind,
His scrip did hang, in which his needments he did bind.

36

The knight approching nigh, of him inquerd
Tydings of warre, and of aduentures new;
But warres, nor new aduentures none he herd.
Then *Vna* gan to aske, if ought he knew,
Or heard abroad of that her champion trew,
That in his armour bare a croslet red.
Aye me, Deare dame (quoth he) well may I rew
To tell the sad sight, which mine eies haue red:
These eyes did see that knight both liuing and eke ded.

37

That cruell word her tender hart so thrild,
That suddein cold did runne through euery vaine,
And stony horrour all her sences fild
With dying fit, that downe she fell for paine.
The knight her lightly reared vp againe,
And comforted with curteous kind reliefe:
Then wonne from death, she bad him tellen plaine
The further processe of her hidden griefe;[231]
The lesser pangs can beare, who hath endur'd the chiefe.

38

Then gan the Pilgrim thus, I chaunst this day,

---

[230] pilgrim's staff
[231] The events which were as yet hidden from her.

This fatall day, that shall I euer rew,
To see two knights in trauell on my way
(A sory sight) arraung'd in battell new,
Both breathing vengeaunce, both of wrathfull hew:
My fearefull flesh did tremble at their strife,
To see their blades so greedily imbrew,
That drunke with bloud, yet thristed after life:
What more? the *Redcrosse* knight was slaine with Paynim knife.

39

Ah dearest Lord (quoth she) how might that bee,
And he the stoutest knight, that euer wonne?
Ah dearest dame (quoth he) how might I see
The thing, that might not be, and yet was donne?
Where is (said *Satyrane*) that Paynims sonne,
That him of life, and vs of ioy hath reft?
Not far away (quoth he) he hence doth wonne [232]
Foreby a fountaine, where I late him left
Washing his bloudy wounds, that through the steele were cleft.

40

Therewith the knight thence marched forth in hast,
Whiles *Vna* with huge heauinesse opprest,
Could not for sorrow follow him so fast;
And soone he came, as he the place had ghest,
Whereas that *Pagan* proud him selfe did rest,
In secret shadow by a fountaine side:
Euen he it was, that earst would haue supprest
Faire *Vna*: whom when *Satyrane* espide,
With fowle reprochfull words he boldly him defide.

41

And said, Arise thou cursed Miscreaunt,
That hast with knightlesse guile and trecherous train
Faire knighthood fowly shamed, and doest vaunt
That good knight of the *Redcrosse* to haue slain:
Arise, and with like treason now maintain
Thy guilty wrong, or else thee guilty yield.
The Sarazin this hearing, rose amain,
And catching vp in hast his three square shield,
And shining helmet, soone him buckled to the field.

42

And drawing nigh him said, Ah misborne Elfe,
In euill houre thy foes thee hither sent,
Anothers wrongs to wreake vpon thy selfe:
Yet ill thou blamest me, for hauing blent
My name with guile and traiterous intent;
That *Redcrosse* knight, perdie, I neuer slew,
But had he beene, where earst his armes were lent,
Th'enchaunter vaine his errour should not rew:
But thou his errour shalt, I hope now prouen trew.

43

Therewith they gan, both furious and fell,
To thunder blowes, and fiersly to assaile
Each other bent his enimy to quell,
That with their force they perst both plate and maile,

232 dwell

And made wide furrowes in their fleshes fraile,
That it would pitty any liuing eie.
Large floods of bloud adowne their sides did raile;
But floods of bloud could not them satisfie:
Both hungred after death: both chose to win, or die.

44

So long they fight, and fell reuenge pursue,
That fainting each, themselues to breathen let,
And oft refreshed, battell oft renue:
As when two Bores with rancling malice met,
Their gory sides fresh bleeding fiercely fret,
Til breathlesse both them selues aside retire,
Where foming wrath, their cruell tuskes they whet,
And trample th'earth, the whiles they may respire;
Then backe to fight againe, new breathed and entire.

45

So fiersly, when these knights had breathed once,
They gan to fight returne, increasing more
Their puissant force, and cruell rage attonce,
With heaped strokes more hugely, then before,
That with their drerie wounds and bloudy gore
They both deformed, scarsely could be known.
By this sad *Vna* fraught with anguish sore,
Led with their noise, which through the aire was thrown,
Arriu'd, where they in erth their fruitles bloud had sown.

46

Whom all so soone as that proud Sarazin
Espide, he gan reuiue the memory
Of his lewd lusts, and late attempted sin,
And left the doubtfull battell hastily,
To catch her, newly offred to his eie:
But *Satyrane* with strokes him turning, staid,
And sternely bad him other businesse plie,
Then hunt the steps of pure vnspotted Maid:
Wherewith he all enrag'd, these bitter speaches said.

47

O foolish faeries sonne, what furie mad
Hath thee incenst, to hast thy dolefull fate?
Were it not better, I that Lady had,
Then that thou hadst repented it too late?
Most sencelesse man he, that himselfe doth hate,
To loue another. Lo then for thine ayd
Here take thy louers token on thy pate.
So they to fight; the whiles the royall Mayd
Fled farre away, of that proud Paynim sore afrayd.

48

But that false *Pilgrim,* which that leasing [233] told,
Being in deed old *Archimage,* did stay
In secret shadow, all this to behold,
And much reioyced in their bloudy fray:
But when he saw the Damsell passe away
He left his stond, and her pursewd apace,
In hope to bring her to her last decay.
But for to tell her lamentable cace,
And eke this battels end, will need another place.

233 lie

Canto VII

The Redcrosse knight is captiue made
By Gyaunt proud opprest,
Prince Arthur meets with Vna great-
ly with those newes distrest.

I

WHAT man so wise, what earthly wit so ware,
As to descry the crafty cunning traine,
By which deceipt doth maske in visour faire,
And cast her colours dyed deepe in graine,[234]
To seeme like Truth, whose shape she well can faine,
And fitting gestures to her purpose frame,
The guiltlesse man with guile to entertaine?
Great maistresse of her art was that false Dame,
The false *Duessa,* cloked with *Fidessaes* name.

2

Who when returning from the drery *Night,*
She fownd not in that perilous house of *Pryde,*
Where she had left, the noble *Redcrosse* knight,
Her hoped pray, she would no lenger bide,
But forth she went, to seeke him far and wide.
Ere long she fownd, whereas he wearie sate,
To rest him selfe, foreby a fountaine side,
Disarmed all of yron-coted Plate,
And by his side his steed the grassy forage ate.

3

He feedes vpon the cooling shade, and bayes[235]
His sweatie forehead in the breathing wind,
Which through the trembling leaues full gently playes
Wherein the cherefull birds of sundry kind
Do chaunt sweet musick, to delight his mind:
The Witch approching gan him fairely greet,
And with reproch of carelesnesse vnkind
Vpbrayd, for leauing her in place vnmeet,
With fowle words tempring faire, soure gall with hony sweet.

4

Vnkindnesse past, they gan of solace treat,
And bathe in pleasaunce of the ioyous shade,
Which shielded them against the boyling heat,
And with greene boughes decking a gloomy glade,
About the fountaine like a girlond made;
Whose bubbling waue did euer freshly well,
Ne euer would through feruent sommer fade:
The sacred Nymph, which therein wont to dwell,
Was out of *Dianes* fauour, as it then befell.

5

The cause was this: one day when *Phœbe*[236] fayre
With all her band was following the chace,
This Nymph, quite tyr'd with heat of scorching ayre
Sat downe to rest in middest of the race:
The goddesse wroth gan fowly her disgrace,
And bad the waters, which from her did flow,
Be such as she her selfe was then in place.

[234] fast dye

[235] bathes

[236] One of the names of Diana.

Thenceforth her waters waxed dull and slow,
And all that drunke thereof, did faint and feeble grow.

6

Hereof this gentle knight vnweeting was,
And lying downe vpon the sandie graile,[237]
Drunke of the streame, as cleare as cristall glas;
Eftsoones his manly forces gan to faile,
And mightie strong was turnd to feeble fraile.
His chaunged powres at first them selues not felt,
Till crudled cold his corage gan assaile,
And chearefull bloud in faintnesse chill did melt,
Which like a feuer fit through all his body swelt.[238]

7

Yet goodly court he made still to his Dame,
Pourd out in loosnesse on the grassy grownd,
Both carelesse of his health, and of his fame:
Till at the last he heard a dreadfull sownd,
Which through the wood loud bellowing, did rebownd,
That all the earth for terrour seemd to shake,
And trees did tremble. Th'Elfe therewith astownd,
Vpstarted lightly from his looser make,[239]
And his vnready weapons gan in hand to take.

8

But ere he could his armour on him dight,
Or get his shield, his monstrous enimy
With sturdie steps came stalking in his sight,
An hideous Geant[240] horrible and hye,
That with his talnesse seemd to threat the skye,
The ground eke groned vnder him for dreed;
His liuing like saw neuer liuing eye,
Ne durst behold: his stature did exceed
The hight of three the tallest sonnes of mortall seed.

9

The greatest Earth his vncouth mother was,
And blustring *Æolus* his boasted sire,
Who with his breath, which through the world doth pas,
Her hollow womb did secretly inspire,
And fild her hidden caues with stormie yre,
That she conceiu'd; and trebling the dew time,
In which the wombes of women do expire,
Brought forth this monstrous masse of earthly slime,
Puft vp with emptie wind, and fild with sinfull crime.

10

So growen great through arrogant delight
Of th'high descent, whereof he was yborne,
And through presumption of his matchlesse might,
All other powres and knighthood he did scorne.
Such now he marcheth to this man forlorne,
And left to losse: his stalking steps are stayde
Vpon a snaggy Oke, which he had torne
Out of his mothers bowelles, and it made
His mortall mace, wherewith his foemen he dismayde.

11

That when the knight he spide, he gan aduance
With huge force and insupportable mayne,

[237] gravel
[238] burned
[239] mate
[240] Orgoglio, or Pride.

And towardes him with dreadfull fury praunce;
Who haplesse, and eke hopelesse, all in vaine
Did to him pace, sad battaile to darrayne,[241]
Disarmd, disgrast, and inwardly dismayde,
And eke so faint in euery ioynt and vaine,
Through that fraile fountaine, which him feeble made,
That scarsely could he weeld his bootlesse single blade.

12

The Geaunt strooke so maynly mercilesse,
That could haue ouerthrowne a stony towre,
And were not heauenly grace, that him did blesse,
He had beene pouldred [242] all, as thin as flowre:
But he was wary of that deadly stowre,
And lightly lept from vnderneath the blow:
Yet so exceeding was the villeins powre,
That with the wind it did him ouerthrow,
And all his sences stound, that still he lay full low.

13

As when that diuelish yron Engin wrought
In deepest Hell, and framd by *Furies* skill,
With windy Nitre and quick Sulphur fraught,
And ramd with bullet round, ordaind to kill,
Conceiueth fire, the heauens it doth fill
With thundring noyse, and all the ayre doth choke,
That none can breath, nor see, nor heare at will,
Through smouldry cloud of duskish stincking smoke,
That th'onely breath him daunts, who hath escapt the stroke.

14

So daunted when the Geaunt saw the knight,
His heauie hand he heaued vp on hye,
And him to dust thought to haue battred quight,
Vntill *Duessa* loud to him gan crye;
O great *Orgoglio,* greatest vnder skye,
O hold thy mortall hand for Ladies sake,
Hold for my sake, and do him not to dye,
But vanquisht thine eternall bondslaue make,
And me thy worthy need vnto thy Leman take.

15

He hearkned, and did stay from further harmes,
To gayne so goodly guerdon,[243] as she spake:
So willingly she came into his armes,
Who her as willingly to grace did take,
And was possessed of his new found make.
Then vp tooke the slombred sencelesse corse,
And ere he could out of his swowne awake,
Him to his castle brought with hastie forse,
And in a Dongeon deepe him threw without remorse.

16

From that day forth *Duessa* was his deare,
And highly honourd in his haughtie eye,
He gaue her gold and purple pall to weare,
And triple crowne set on her head full hye,

---

[241] decide
[242] powdered
[243] reward

And her endowd with royall maiestye:
Then for to make her dreaded more of men,
And peoples harts with awfull terrour tye,
A monstrous beast ybred in filthy fen
He chose, which he had kept long time in darksome den.

17

Such one it was, as that renowmed Snake
Which great *Alcides*[244] in *Stremona* slew,
Long fostred in the filth of *Lerna* lake,
Whose many heads out budding euer new,
Did breed him endlesse labour to subdew:
But this same Monster much more vgly was;
For seuen great heads out of his body grew,
An yron brest, and backe of scaly bras,
And all embrewd in bloud, his eyes did shine as glas.

18

His tayle was stretched out in wondrous length,
That to the house of heauenly gods it raught,
And with extorted powre, and borrow'd strength,
The euer-burning lamps from thence it brought,
And prowdly threw to ground, as things of nought;
And vnderneath his filthy feet did tread
The sacred things, and holy heasts[245] foretaught.
Vpon this dreadfull Beast with seuenfold head
He set the false *Duessa*, for more aw and dread.

19

The wofull Dwarfe, which saw his maisters fall,
Whiles he had keeping of his grasing steed,
And valiant knight become a caytiue thrall,
When all was past, tooke vp his forlorne weed,[246]
His mightie armour, missing most at need;
His siluer shield, now idle maisterlesse;
His poynant speare, that many made to bleed,
The ruefull moniments of heauinesse,
And with them all departes, to tell his great distresse.

20

He had not trauaild long, when on the way
He wofull Ladie, wofull *Vna* met,
Fast flying from the Paynims greedy pray,
Whilest *Satyrane* him from pursuit did let:[247]
Who when her eyes she on the Dwarfe had set,
And saw the signes, that deadly tydings spake,
She fell to ground for sorrowfull regret,
And liuely[248] breath her sad brest did forsake,
Yet might her pitteous hart be seene to pant and quake.

21

The messenger of so vnhappie newes
Would faine haue dyde: dead was his hart within,
Yet outwardly some little comfort shewes:
At last recouering hart, he does begin
To rub her temples, and to chaufe her chin,
And euery tender part does tosse and turne:
So hardly he the flitted life does win,
Vnto her natiue prison to retourne:
Then gins her grieued ghost thus to lament and mourne.

---

244 Hercules
245 instructions

246 abandoned clothing
247 hinder
248 life-giving

22

Ye dreary instruments of dolefull sight,
That doe this deadly spectacle behold,
Why do ye lenger feed on loathed light,
Or liking find to gaze on earthly mould,
Sith cruell fates the carefull threeds vnfould,
The which my life and loue together tyde?
Now let the stony dart of senselesse cold
Perce to my hart, and pas through euery side,
And let eternall night so sad sight fro me hide.

23

O lightsome day, the lampe of highest *Ioue,*
First made by him, mens wandring wayes to guyde,
When darknesse he in deepest dongeon droue,
Henceforth thy hated face for euer hyde,
And shut vp heauens windowes shyning wyde:
For earthly sight can nought but sorrow breed,
And late repentance, which shall long abyde.
Mine eyes no more on vanitie shall feed,
But seeled vp with death, shall haue their deadly meed.

24

Then downe againe she fell vnto the ground;
But he her quickly reared vp againe:
Thrise did she sinke adowne in deadly swownd,
And thrise he her reviu'd with busie paine:
At last when life recouer'd had the raine,
And ouer-wrestled his strong enemie,
With foltring tong, and trembling euery vaine,
Tell on (quoth she) the wofull Tragedie,
The which these reliques sad present vnto mine eie.

25

Tempestuous fortune hath spent all her spight,
And thrilling sorrow throwne his vtmost dart;
Thy sad tongue cannot tell more heauy plight,
Then that I feele, and harbour in mine hart:
Who hath endur'd the whole, can beare each part.
If death it be, it is not the first wound,
That launched [249] hath my brest with bleeding smart.
Begin, and end the bitter balefull stound; [250]
If lesse, then that I feare, more fauour I haue found.

26

Then gan the Dwarfe the whole discourse declare,
The subtill traines of *Archimago* old;
The wanton loues of false *Fidessa* faire,
Bought with the bloud of vanquisht Paynim bold:
The wretched payre transform'd to treen mould;
The house of Pride, and perils round about;
The combat, which he with *Sansioy* did hould;
The lucklesse conflict with the Gyant stout,
Wherein captiu'd, of life or death he stood in doubt.

27

She heard with patience all vnto the end,
And stroue to maister sorrowfull assay,
Which greater grew, the more she did contend,
And almost rent her tender hart in tway;
And loue fresh coles vnto her fire did lay:
For greater loue, the greater is the losse.
Was neuer Ladie loued dearer day,[251]

---

[249] pierced [250] moment
[251] No Lady ever loved day more dearly.

Then she did loue the knight of the *Redcrosse*;
For whose deare sake so many troubles her did tosse.

28

At last when feruent sorrow slaked was,
She vp arose, resoluing him to find
Aliue or dead: and forward forth doth pas,
All as the Dwarfe the way to her assynd:
And euermore in constant carefull mind
She fed her wound with fresh renewed bale;
Long tost with stormes, and bet with bitter wind,
High ouer hils, and low adowne the dale,
She wandred many a wood, and measurd many a vale.

29

At last she chaunced by good hap to meet
A goodly knight, faire marching by the way
Together with his Squire, arayed meet:
His glitterand armour shined farre away,
Like glauncing light of *Phœbus* brightest ray;
From top to toe no place appeared bare,
That deadly dint of steele endanger may:
Athwart his brest a bauldrick [252] braue he ware,
That shynd, like twinkling stars, with stons most pretious rare.

30

And in the midst thereof one pretious stone
Of wondrous worth, and eke of wondrous mights,
Shapt like a Ladies head, exceeding shone,
Like *Hesperus* emongst the lesser lights,
And stroue for to amaze the weaker sights;
Thereby his mortall blade full comely hong
In yuory sheath, ycaru'd with curious slights,[253]
Whose hilts were burnisht gold, and handle strong
Of mother pearle, and buckled with a golden tong.

31

His haughtie helmet, horrid all with gold,
Both glorious brightnesse, and great terrour bred;
For all the crest a Dragon did enfold
With greedie pawes, and ouer all did spred
His golden wings: his dreadfull hideous hed
Close couched on the beuer,[254] seem'd to throw
From flaming mouth bright sparkles fierie red,
That suddeine horror to faint harts did show;
And scaly tayle was stretcht adowne his backe full low.

32

Vpon the top of all his loftie crest,
A bunch of haires discolourd diuersly,
With sprincled pearle, and gold full richly drest,
Did shake, and seem'd to daunce for iollity,
Like to an Almond tree ymounted hye
On top of greene *Selinis* [255] all alone,
With blossomes braue bedecked daintily;
Whose tender locks do tremble euery one
At euery little breath, that vnder heauen is blowne.

33

His warlike shield all closely couer'd was,
Ne might of mortall eye be euer seene;
Not made of steele, nor of enduring bras,
Such earthly mettals soone consumed bene:

---

252 Belt worn over the shoulder.
253 devices
254 Lower part of the helmet.
255 Possibly Selinus in Sicily.

But all of Diamond perfect pure and cleene
It framed was, one massie entire mould,
Hewen out of Adamant rocke with engines keene,
That point of speare it neuer percen could,
Ne dint of direfull sword diuide the substance would.

34

The same to wight he neuer wont disclose,
But when as monsters huge he would dismay,
Or daunt vnequall armies of his foes,
Or when the flying heauens he would affray;
For so exceeding shone his glistring ray,
That *Phœbus* golden face it did attaint,
As when a cloud his beames doth ouerlay;
And siluer *Cynthia* wexed pale and faint,
As when her face is staynd with magicke arts constraint.

35

No magicke arts hereof had any might,
Nor bloudie wordes of bold Enchaunters call,
But all that was not such, as seemd in sight,
Before that shield did fade, and suddeine fall:
And when him list the raskall routes appall,
Men into stones therewith he could transmew,
And stones to dust, and dust to nought at all;
And when him list the prouder lookes subdew,
He would them gazing, blind, or turne to other hew.

36

Ne let it seeme, that credence this exceedes,
For he that made the same, was knowne right well
To haue done much more admirable deedes.
It *Merlin* was, which whylome did excell
All liuing wightes in might of magicke spell:
Both shield, and sword, and armour all he wrought
For this young Prince, when first to armes he fell;
But when he dyde, the Faerie Queene it brought
To Faerie lond, where yet it may be seene, if sought.

37

A gentle youth, his dearely loued Squire
His speare of heben wood behind him bare,
Whose harmefull head, thrice heated in the fire,
Had riuen many a brest with pikehead square;
A goodly person, and could menage faire
His stubborne steed with curbed canon[256] bit,
Who vnder him did trample as the aire,
And chauft, that any on his backe should sit;
The yron rowels into frothy fome he bit.

38

When as this knight nigh to the Ladie drew,
With louely court he gan her entertaine;
But when he heard her answeres loth, he knew
Some secret sorrow did her heart distraine:[257]
Which to allay, and calme her storming paine,
Faire feeling words he wisely gan display,
And for her humour fitting purpose faine,
To tempt the cause it selfe for to bewray;

[256] A small round bit.
[257] oppress

Wherewith emmou'd, these bleeding words she gan to say.

39

What worlds delight, or ioy of liuing speach
Can heart, so plung'd in sea of sorrowes deepe,
And heaped with so huge misfortunes, reach?
The carefull cold beginneth for to creepe,
And in my heart his yron arrow steepe,
Soone as I thinke vpon my bitter bale:
Such helplesse harmes yts better hidden keepe,
Then rip vp griefe, where it may not auaile,
My last left comfort is, my woes to weepe and waile.

40

Ah Ladie deare, quoth then the gentle knight,
Well may I weene, your griefe is wondrous great;
For wondrous great griefe groneth in my spright,
Whiles thus I heare you of your sorrowes treat.
But wofull Ladie let me you intrete,
For to vnfold the anguish of your hart:
Mishaps are maistred by aduice discrete,
And counsell mittigates the greatest smart;
Found neuer helpe, who neuer would his hurts impart.

41

O but (quoth she) great griefe will not be tould,
And can more easily be thought, then said.
Right so; (quoth he) but he, that neuer would,
Could neuer: will to might giues greatest aid.
But griefe (quoth she) does greater grow displaid,
If then it find not helpe, and breedes despaire.
Despaire breedes not (quoth he) where faith is staid.
No faith so fast (quoth she) but flesh does paire.[258]
Flesh may empaire (quoth he) but reason can repaire.

42

His goodly reason, and well guided speach
So deepe did settle in her gratious thought,
That her perswaded to disclose the breach,
Which loue and fortune in her heart had wrought,
And said; Faire Sir, I hope good hap hath brought
You to inquire the secrets of my griefe,
Or that your wisedome will direct my thought,
Or that your prowesse can me yield reliefe:
Then heare the storie sad, which I shall tell you briefe.

43

The forlorne Maiden, whom your eyes haue seene
The laughing stocke of fortunes mockeries,
And th'only daughter of a King and Queene,
Whose parents deare, whilest equall destinies
Did runne about, and their felicities
The fauourable heauens did not enuy,
Did spread their rule through all the territories,
Which *Phison* and *Euphrates* floweth by,
And *Gehons*[259] golden waues doe wash continually.

[258] impair
[259] These three rivers are in Paradise.

44

Till that their cruell cursed enemy,
An huge great Dragon horrible in sight,
Bred in the loathly lakes of *Tartary*,[260]
With murdrous rauine, and deuouring might
Their kingdome spoild, and countrey wasted quight:
Themselues, for feare into his iawes to fall,
He forst to castle strong to take their flight,
Where fast embard in mightie brasen wall,
He has them now foure yeres besiegd to make them thrall.

45

Full many knights aduenturous and stout
Haue enterprizd that Monster to subdew;
From euery coast that heauen walks about,
Haue thither come the noble Martiall crew,
That famous hard atchieuements still pursew,
Yet neuer any could that girlond win,
But all still shronke, and still he greater grew:
All they for want of faith, or guilt of sin,
The pitteous pray of his fierce crueltie haue bin.

46

At last yledd with farre reported praise,
Which flying fame throughout the world had spred,
Of doughtie knights, whom Faery land did raise,
That noble order hight of Maidenhed,
Forthwith to court of *Gloriane* I sped,
Of *Gloriane* great Queene of glory bright,
Whose kingdomes seat *Cleopolis* is red,[261]
There to obtaine some such redoubted knight,
That Parents deare from tyrants powre deliuer might.

47

It was my chance (my chance was faire and good)
There for to find a fresh vnproued knight,
Whose manly hands imbrew'd in guiltie blood
Had neuer bene, ne euer by his might
Had throwne to ground the vnregarded right:
Yet of his prowesse proofe he since hath made
(I witnesse am) in many a cruell fight;
The groning ghosts of many one dismaide
Haue felt the bitter dint of his auenging blade.

48

And ye the forlorne reliques of his powre,
His byting sword, and his deuouring speare,
Which haue endured many a dreadfull stowre,
Can speake his prowesse, that did earst you beare,
And well could rule: now he hath left you heare,
To be the record of his ruefull losse,
And of my dolefull disauenturous deare:[262]
O heauie record of the good *Redcrosse*,
Where haue you left your Lord, that could so well you tosse?

49

Well hoped I, and faire beginnings had,
That he my captiue langour should redeeme,
Till all vnweeting, an Enchaunter bad
His sence abusd, and made him to misdeeme
My loyalty, not such as it did seeme;

[260] Hell
[261] 'The city of glory (London) is called.'

[262] injury

That rather death desire, then such despight.
Be iudge ye heauens, that all things right esteeme,
How I him lou'd, and loue with all my might,
So thought I eke of him, and thinke I thought aright.

50

Thenceforth me desolate he quite forsooke,
To wander, where wilde fortune would me lead,
And other bywaies he himselfe betooke,
Where neuer foot of liuing wight did tread,
That brought not backe the balefull body dead;
In which him chaunced false *Duessa* meete,
Mine onely foe, mine onely deadly dread,
Who with her witchcraft and misseeming sweete,
Inueigled him to follow her desires vnmeete.

51

At last by subtill sleights she him betraid
Vnto his foe, a Gyant huge and tall,
Who him disarmed, dissolute, dismaid,
Vnwares surprised, and with mightie mall[263]
The monster mercilesse him made to fall,
Whose fall did neuer foe before behold;
And now in darkesome dungeon, wretched thrall,
Remedilesse, for aie he doth him hold;
This is my cause of griefe, more great, then may be told.

52

Ere she had ended all, she gan to faint:
But he her comforted and faire bespake,
Certes, Madame, ye haue great cause of plaint,
That stoutest heart, I weene, could cause to quake.
But be of cheare, and comfort to you take:
For till I haue acquit your captiue knight,
Assure your selfe, I will you not forsake.
His chearefull words reuiu'd her chearelesse spright,
So forth they went, the Dwarfe them guiding euer right.

Canto VIII

Faire virgin to redeeme her deare
brings Arthur to the fight:
Who slayes the Gyant, wounds the beast,
and strips Duessa quight.

1

Ay me, how many perils doe enfold
The righteous man, to make him daily fall?
Were not, that heauenly grace doth him vphold,
And stedfast truth acquite him out of all.
Her loue is firme, her care continuall,
So oft as he through his owne foolish pride,
Or weaknesse is to sinfull bands made thrall:
Else should this *Redcrosse* knight in bands haue dyde,
For whose deliuerance she this Prince doth thither guide.

2

They sadly traueild thus, vntill they came
Nigh to a castle builded strong and hie:
Then cryde the Dwarfe, lo yonder is the same,
In which my Lord my liege doth lucklesse lie,
Thrall to that Gyants hatefull tyrannie:
Therefore, deare Sir, your mightie powres assay.
The noble knight alighted by and by
From loftie steede, and bad the Ladie stay,

[263] club

To see what end of fight should him befall that day.

3

So with the Squire, th'admirer of his might,
He marched forth towards that castle wall;
Whose gates he found fast shut, ne liuing wight
To ward the same, nor answere commers call.
Then tooke that Squire an horne of bugle[264] small,
Which hong adowne his side in twisted gold,
And tassels gay. Wyde wonders ouer all
Of that same hornes great vertues weren told,
Which had approued bene in vses manifold.

4

Was neuer wight, that heard that shrilling sound,
But trembling feare did feele in euery vaine;
Three miles it might be easie heard around,
And Ecchoes three answerd it selfe againe:
No false enchauntment, nor deceiptfull traine
Might once abide the terror of that blast,
But presently was voide and wholly vaine:
No gate so strong, no locke so firme and fast,
But with that percing noise flew open quite, or brast.

5

The same before the Geants gate he blew,
That all the castle quaked from the ground,
And euery dore of freewill open flew.
The Gyant selfe dismaied with that sownd,
Where he with his *Duessa* dalliance fownd,
In hast came rushing forth from inner bowre,
With staring countenance sterne, as one astownd,
And staggering steps, to weet, what suddein stowre
Had wrought that horror strange, and dar'd his dreaded powre.

6

And after him the proud *Duessa* came,
High mounted on her manyheaded beast,
And euery head with fyrie tongue did flame,
And euery head was crowned on his creast,
And bloudie mouthed with late cruell feast.
That when the knight beheld, his mightie shild
Vpon his manly arme he soone addrest,
And at him fiercely flew, with courage fild,
And eger greedinesse through euery member thrild.

7

Therewith the Gyant buckled him to fight,
Inflam'd with scornefull wrath and high disdaine,
And lifting vp his dreadfull club on hight,
All arm'd with ragged snubbs[265] and knottie graine,
Him thought at first encounter to haue slaine.
But wise and warie was that noble Pere,
And lightly leaping from so monstrous maine,
Did faire auoide the violence him nere;
It booted nought, to thinke, such thunderbolts to beare.

8

Ne shame he thought to shunne so hideous might:

264 ox

265 knobs

The idle stroke, enforcing furious way,
Missing the marke of his misaymed sight
Did fall to ground, and with his heauie sway
So deepely dinted in the driuen clay,
That three yardes deepe a furrow vp did throw:
The sad earth wounded with so sore assay,
Did grone full grieuous vnderneath the blow,
And trembling with strange feare, did like an earthquake show.

9

As when almightie *Ioue* in wrathfull mood,
To wreake the guilt of mortall sins is bent,
Hurles forth his thundring dart with deadly food,[266]
Enrold in flames, and smouldring dreriment,
Though riuen cloudes and molten firmament;
The fierce threeforked engin making way,
Both loftie towres and highest trees hath rent,
And all that might his angrie passage stay,
And shooting in the earth, casts vp a mount of clay.

10

His boystrous [267] club, so buried in the ground,
He could not rearen vp againe so light,
But that the knight him at auantage found,
And whiles he stroue his combred clubbe to quight
Out of the earth, with blade all burning bright
He smote off his left arme, which like a blocke
Did fall to ground, depriu'd of natiue might;
Large streames of bloud out of the truncked stocke
Forth gushed, like fresh water streame from riuen rocke.

11

Dismaied with so desperate deadly wound,
And eke impatient of vnwonted paine,
He loudly brayd with beastly yelling sound,
That all the fields rebellowed againe;
As great a noyse, as when in Cymbrian plaine [268]
An heard of Bulles, whom kindly [269] rage doth sting,
Do for the milkie mothers want complaine,
And fill the fields with troublous bellowing,
The neighbour woods around with hollow murmur ring.

12

That when his deare *Duessa* heard, and saw
The euill stownd, that daungerd her estate,
Vnto his aide she hastily did draw
Her dreadfull beast, who swolne with bloud of late
Came ramping forth with proud presumpteous gate,
And threatned all his heads like flaming brands.
But him the Squire made quickly to retrate,
Encountring fierce with single sword in hand,
And twixt him and his Lord did like a bulwarke stand.

13

The proud *Duessa* full of wrathfull spight,
And fierce disdaine, to be affronted so,

[266] feud

[267] rough

[268] Possibly the Crimea.

[269] natural

Enforst her purple beast with all her might
That stop out of the way to ouerthroe,
Scorning the let of so vnequall foe:
But nathemore would that courageous swayne
To her yeeld passage, gainst his Lord to goe,
But with outrageous strokes did him restraine,
And with his bodie bard the way atwixt them twaine.

14

Then tooke the angrie witch her golden cup,
Which still she bore, replete with magick artes;
Death and despeyre did many thereof sup,
And secret poyson through their inner parts,
Th'eternall bale of heauie wounded harts;
Which after charmes and some enchauntments said,
She lightly sprinkled on his weaker parts;
Therewith his sturdie courage soone was quayd,[270]
And all his senses were with suddeine dread dismayd.

15

So downe he fell before the cruell beast,
Who on his necke his bloudie clawes did seize,
That life nigh crusht out of his panting brest:
No powre he had to stirre, nor will to rize.
That when the carefull knight gan well auise.
He lightly left the foe, with whom he fought,
And to the beast gan turne his enterprise;
For wondrous anguish in his hart it wrought,
To see his loued Squire into such thraldome brought.

16

And high aduauncing his bloud-thirstie blade,
Stroke one of those deformed heads so sore,
That of his puissance proud ensample made;
His monstrous scalpe downe to his teeth it tore,
And that misformed shape mis-shaped more:
A sea of bloud gusht from the gaping wound,
That her gay garments staynd with filthy gore,
And ouerflowed all the field around;
That ouer shoes in bloud he waded on the ground.

17

Thereat he roared for exceeding paine,
That to haue heard, great horror would haue bred,
And scourging th'emptie ayre with his long traine,
Through great impatience of his grieued hed
His gorgeous ryder from her loftie sted
Would haue cast downe, and trod in durtie myre,
Had not the Gyant soone her succoured;
Who all enrag'd with smart and franticke yre,
Came hurtling in full fierce, and forst the knight retyre.

18

The force, which wont in two to be disperst,
In one alone left hand he now vnites,
Which is through rage more strong then both were erst;
With which his hideous club aloft he dites,[271]

[270] subdued

[271] raises

And at his foe with furious rigour smites,
That strongest Oake might seeme to ouerthrow:
The stroke vpon his shield so heauie lites,
That to the ground it doubleth him full low:
What mortall wight could euer beare so monstrous blow?

19

And in his fall his shield, that couered was,
Did loose his vele[272] by chaunce, and open flew:
The light whereof, that heauens light did pas,
Such blazing brightnesse through the aier threw,
That eye mote not the same endure to vew.
Which when the Gyant spyde with staring eye,
He downe let fall his arme, and soft withdrew
His weapon huge, that heaued was on hye
For to haue slaine the man, that on the ground did lye.

20

And eke the fruitfull-headed[273] beast, amaz'd
At flashing beames of that sunshiny shield,
Became starke blind, and all his senses daz'd,
That downe he tumbled on the durtie field,
And seem'd himselfe as conquered to yield.
Whom when his maistresse proud perceiu'd to fall,
Whiles yet his feeble feet for faintnesse reeld,
Vnto the Gyant loudly she gan call,
O helpe *Orgoglio,* helpe, or else we perish all.

[272] covering [273] many-headed

21

At her so pitteous cry was much amoou'd
Her champion stout, and for to ayde his frend,
Againe his wonted angry weapon proou'd:
But all in vaine: for he has read his end
In that bright shield, and all their forces spend
Themselues in vaine: for since that glauncing sight,
He hath no powre to hurt, nor to defend;
As where th'Almighties lightning brond does light,
It dimmes the dazed eyen, and daunts the senses quight.

22

Whom when the Prince, to battell new addrest,
And threatning high his dreadfull stroke did see,
His sparkling blade about his head he blest,
And smote off quite his right leg by the knee,
That downe he tombled; as an aged tree,
High growing on the top of rocky clift,
Whose hartstrings with keene steele nigh hewen be,
The mightie trunck halfe rent, with ragged rift
Doth roll adowne the rocks, and fall with fearefull drift.

23

Or as a Castle reared high and round,
By subtile engins and malitious slight
Is vndermined from the lowest ground,
And her foundation forst, and feebled quight,
At last downe falles, and with her heaped hight
Her hastie ruine does more heauie make,
And yields it selfe vnto the victours might;

Such was this Gyaunts fall, that seemd to shake
The stedfast globe of earth, as it for feare did quake.

24

The knight then lightly leaping to the pray,
With mortall steele him smot againe so sore,
That headlesse his vnweldy bodie lay,
All wallowd in his owne fowle bloudy gore,
Which flowed from his wounds in wondrous store.
But soone as breath out of his breast did pas,
That huge great body, which the Gyaunt bore,
Was vanisht quite, and of that monstrous mas
Was nothing left, but like an emptie bladder was.

25

Whose grieuous fall, when false *Duessa* spide,
Her golden cup she cast vnto the ground,
And crowned mitre[274] rudely threw aside;
Such percing griefe her stubborne hart did wound,
That she could not endure that dolefull stound,
But leauing all behind her, fled away:
The light-foot Squire her quickly turnd around,
And by hard meanes enforcing her to stay,
So brought vnto his Lord, as his deserued pray.

26

The royall Virgin, which beheld from farre,
In pensiue plight, and sad perplexitie.
The whole atchieuement of this doubtfull warre,
Came running fast to greet his victorie,
With sober gladnesse, and myld modestie,
And with sweet ioyous cheare him thus bespake;
Faire braunch of noblesse, flowre of cheualrie,
That with your worth the world amazed make,
How shall I quite the paines, ye suffer for my sake?

27

And you fresh bud of vertue springing fast,
Whom these sad eyes saw nigh vnto deaths dore,
What hath poore Virgin for such perill past,
Wherewith you to reward? Accept therefore
My simple selfe, and seruice euermore;
And he that high does sit, and all things see
With equall eyes,[275] their merites to restore,
Behold what ye this day haue done for mee,
And what I cannot quite, requite with vsuree.

28

But sith the heauens, and your faire handeling
Haue made you maister of the field this day,
Your fortune maister eke with gouerning,
And well begun end all so well, I pray,
Ne let that wicked woman scape away;
For she it is, that did my Lord bethrall,
My dearest Lord, and deepe in dongeon lay,
Where he his better dayes hath wasted all.
O heare, how piteous he to you for ayd does call.

---

[274] The papal tiara.

[275] impartially

29

Forthwith he gaue in charge vnto his Squire,
That scarlot whore to keepen carefully;
Whiles he himselfe with greedie great desire
Into the Castle entred forcibly,
Where liuing creature none he did espye;
Then gan he lowdly through the house to call:
But no man car'd to answere to his crye.
There raignd a solemne silence ouer all,
Nor voice was heard, nor wight was seene in bowre or hall.

30

At last with creeping crooked pace forth came
An old old man,[276] with beard as white as snow,
That on a staffe his feeble steps did frame,
And guide his wearie gate both too and fro:
For his eye sight him failed long ygo,
And on his arme a bounch of keyes he bore,
The which vnused rust did ouergrow:
Those were the keyes of euery inner dore,
But he could not them vse, but kept them still in store.

31

But very vncouth sight was to behold,
How he did fashion his vntoward pace,
For as he forward moou'd his footing old,
So backward still was turnd his wrincled face,
Vnlike to men, who euer as they trace,
Both feet and face one way are wont to lead.
This was the auncient keeper of that place,
And foster father of the Gyant dead;
His name *Ignaro* did his nature right aread.

32

His reuerend haires and holy grauitie
The knight much honord, as beseemed well,
And gently askt, where all the people bee,
Which in that stately building wont to dwell.
Who answerd him full soft, he could not tell.
Againe he askt, where that same knight was layd,
Whom great *Orgoglio* with his puissaunce fell
Had made his caytiue thrall; againe he sayde,
He could not tell: ne euer other answere made.

33

Then asked he, which way he in might pas:
He could not tell, againe he answered.
Thereat the curteous knight displeased was,
And said, Old sire, it seemes thou hast not red[277]
How ill it sits with that same siluer hed
In vaine to mocke, or mockt in vaine to bee:
But if thou be, as thou art pourtrahed
With natures pen, in ages graue degree,
Aread[278] in grauer wise, what I demaund of thee.

34

His answere likewise was, he could not tell.
Whose sencelesse speach, and doted ignorance
When as the noble Prince had marked well,
He ghest his nature by his countenance,
And calmd his wrath with goodly temperance.

---

[276] Ignorance

[277] noticed

[278] answer

Then to him stepping, from his arme did reach
Those keyes, and made himselfe free enterance.
Each dore he opened without any breach;
There was no barre to stop, nor foe him to empeach.

35

There all within full rich arayd he found,
With royall arras and resplendent gold.
And did with store of euery thing abound,
That greatest Princes presence might behold.
But all the floore (too filthy to be told)
With bloud of guiltlesse babes, and innocents trew,
Which there were slaine, as sheepe out of the fold,
Defiled was, that dreadfull was to vew,
And sacred [279] ashes ouer it was strowed new.

36

And there beside of marble stone was built
An Altare, caru'd with cunning imagery,
On which true Christians bloud was often spilt,
And holy Martyrs often doen to dye,
With cruell malice and strong tyranny:
Whose blessed sprites from vnderneath the stone
To God for vengeance cryde continually,
And with great griefe were often heard to grone,
That hardest heart would bleede, to heare their piteous mone.

37

Through euery rowme he sought, and euery bowr,
But no where could he find that wofull thrall:
At last he came vnto an yron dore,
That fast was lockt, but key found not at all
Emongst that bounch, to open it withall;
But in the same a little grate was pight,[280]
Through which he sent his voyce, and lowd did call
With all his powre, to weet, if liuing wight
Were housed therewithin, whom he enlargen might.

38

Therewith an hollow, dreary, murmuring voyce
These piteous plaints and dolours did resound;
O who is that, which brings me happy choyce
Of death, that here lye dying euery stound,
Yet liue perforce in balefull darkenesse bound?
For now three Moones haue changed thrice their hew,
And haue been thrice hid vnderneath the ground,
Since I the heauens chearefull face did vew,
O welcome thou, that doest of death bring tydings trew.

39

Which when that Champion heard, with percing point
Of pitty deare his hart was thrilled sore,
And trembling horrour ran through euery ioynt,
For ruth of gentle knight so fowle forlore:
Which shaking off, he rent that yron dore,
With furious force, and indignation fell;
Where entred in, his foot could find no flore,
But all a deepe descent, as darke as hell,
That breathed euer forth a filthie banefull smell.

279 accursed

280 placed

40

But neither darkenesse fowle, nor filthy bands,
Nor noyous smell his purpose could withhold,
(Entire affection hateth nicer[281] hands)
But that with constant zeale, and courage bold,
After long paines and labours manifold,
He found the meanes that Prisoner vp to reare;
Whose feeble thighes, vnhable to vphold
His pined corse, him scarse to light could beare,
A ruefull spectacle of death and ghastly drere.

41

His sad dull eyes deepe sunck in hollow pits,
Could not endure th'vnwonted sunne to view;
His bare thin cheekes for want of better bits,[282]
And empty sides deceiued of their dew,[283]
Could make a stony hart his hap to rew;
His rawbone armes, whose mighty brawned bowrs[284]
Were wont to riue steele plates, and helmets hew,
Were cleane consum'd, and all his vitall powres
Decayd, and all his flesh shronk vp like withered flowres.

42

Whom when his Lady saw, to him she ran
With hasty ioy: to see him made her glad,
And sad to view his visage pale and wan,
Who earst in flowres of freshest youth was clad.
Tho when her well of teares she wasted had,
She said, Ah dearest Lord, what euill starre
On you hath fround, and pourd his influence bad,
That of your selfe ye thus berobbed arre,
And this misseeming hew your manly looks doth marre?

43

But welcome now my Lord, in wele or woe,
Whose presence I haue lackt too long a day;
And fie on Fortune mine auowed foe,
Whose wrathfull wreakes them selues do now alay.
And for these wrongs shall treble penaunce pay
Of treble good: good growes of euils priefe.[285]
The chearelesse man, whom sorrow did dismay,
Had no delight to treaten of his griefe;
His long endured famine needed more reliefe.

44

Faire Lady, then said that victorious knight,
The things, that grieuous were to do, or beare,
Them to renew, I wote, breeds no delight;
Best musicke breeds delight in loathing eare:
But th'onely good, that growes of passed feare,
Is to be wise, and ware of like agein.
This dayes ensample hath this lesson deare
Deepe written in my heart with yron pen,
That blisse may not abide in state of mortall men.

45

Henceforth sir knight, take to you wonted strength,
And maister these mishaps with patient might;

[281] too nice
[282] bites of food
[283] due
[284] muscles
[285] experience

Loe where your foe lyes stretcht in monstrous length,
And loe that wicked woman in your sight,
The roote of all your care, and wretched plight,
Now in your powre, to let her liue, or dye.
To do her dye (quoth *Vna*) were despight,
And shame t'auenge so weake an enimy;
But spoile her of her scarlot robe, and let her fly.

46

So as she bad, that witch they disaraid,
And robd of royall robes, and purple pall,
And ornaments that richly were displaid;
Ne spared they to strip her naked all.
Then when they had despoild her tire and call,[286]
Such as she was, their eyes might her behold,
That her misshaped parts did them appall,
A loathly, wrinckled hag, ill fauoured, old,
Whose secret filth good manners biddeth not be told.

47

Her craftie head was altogether bald,
And as in hate of honorable eld,
Was ouergrowne with scurfe and filthy scald;
Her teeth out of her rotten gummes were feld,
And her sowre breath abhominably smeld;
Her dried dugs, like bladders lacking wind,
Hong downe, and filthy matter from them weld;
Her wrizled skin as rough, as maple rind,
So scabby was, that would haue loathd all womankind.

48

Her neather parts, the shame of all her kind,
My chaster Muse for shame doth blush to write;
But at her rompe she growing had behind
A foxes taile, with dong all fowly dight;
And eke her feete most monstrous were in sight;
For one of them was like an Eagles claw,
With griping talaunts armd to greedy fight,
The other like a Beares vneuen paw:
More vgly shape yet neuer liuing creature saw.

49

Which when the knights beheld, amazd they were,
And wondred at so fowle deformed wight.
Such then (said *Vna*) as she seemeth here,
Such is the face of falshood, such the sight
Of fowle *Duessa,* when her borrowed light
Is laid away, and counterfesaunce knowne.
Thus when they had the witch disrobed quight,
And all her filthy feature open showne,
They let her goe at will, and wander wayes vnknowne.

50

She flying fast from heauens hated face,
And from the world that her discouered wide,
Fled to the wastfull wildernesse apace,
From liuing eyes her open shame to hide,
And lurkt in rocks and caues long vnespide.
But that faire crew of knights, and *Vna* faire
Did in that castle afterwards abide,

---

[286] cap

To rest them selues, and weary powres repaire,
Where store they found of all, that dainty was and rare.

Canto IX

His loues and lignage Arthur tells:
The knights knit friendly bands:
Sir Treuisan flies from Despayre,
Whom Redcrosse knight withstands.

1

O GOODLY golden chaine, wherewith yfere[287]
The vertues linked are in louely wize:
And noble minds of yore allyed were,
In braue poursuit of cheualrous emprize,
That none did others safety despize,
Nor aid enuy to him, in need that stands,
But friendly each did others prayse deuize
How to aduaunce with fauourable hands,
As this good Prince redeemd the *Redcrosse* knight from bands.

2

Who when their powres, empaird through labour long,
With dew repast they had recured well,
And that weake captiue wight now wexed strong,
Them list no lenger there at leasure dwell,
But forward fare, as their aduentures fell,
But ere they parted, *Vna* faire besought
That straunger knight his name and nation tell;
Least so great good, as he for her had wrought,
Should die vnknown, and buried be in thanklesse thought.

3

Faire virgin (said the Prince) ye me require
A thing without the compas of my wit:
For both the lignage and the certain Sire,
From which I sprong, from me are hidden yit.
For all so soone as life did me admit
Into this world, and shewed heauens light,
From mothers pap I taken was vnfit:
And streight deliuered to a Faery knight,
To be vpbrought in gentle thewes[288] and martiall might.

4

Vnto old *Timon* he me brought byliue,[289]
Old *Timon,* who in youthly yeares hath beene
In warlike feates th'expertest man aliue,
And is the wisest now on earth I weene;
His dwelling is low in a valley greene,
Vnder the foot of *Rauran* mossy hore,
From whence the riuer *Dee* as siluer cleene
His tombling billowes rolls with gentle rore:
There all my dayes he traind me vp in vertuous lore.

5

Thither the great Magicien *Merlin* came,
As was his vse, ofttimes to visit me:
For he had charge my discipline to frame,
And Tutours nouriture to ouersee.
Him oft and oft I askt in priuitie,
Of what loines and what lignage I did spring:
Whose aunswere bad me still assured bee,
That I was sonne and heire vnto a king,
As time in her iust terme the truth to light should bring.

6

Well worthy impe, said then the Lady gent,[290]

[287] together. The chain symbolizes Prince Arthur who, as Magnificence, unites in himself all the virtues.

[288] habits

[289] immediately

[290] gentle

And Pupill fit for such a Tutours hand.
But what aduenture, or what high intent
Hath brought you hither into Faery land,
Aread Prince *Arthur,* crowne of Martiall band?
Full hard it is (quoth he) to read aright
The course of heauenly cause, or vnderstand
The secret meaning of th'eternall might,
That rules mens wayes, and rules the thoughts of liuing wight.

7

For whither he through fatall deepe foresight
Me hither sent, for cause to me vnghest,
Or that fresh bleeding wound, which day and night
Whilome doth rancle in my riuen brest,
With forced fury following his[291] behest,
Me hither brought by wayes yet neuer found,
You to haue helpt I hold my selfe yet blest.
Ah curteous knight (quoth she) what secret wound
Could euer find, to grieue the gentlest hart on ground?

8

Deare Dame (quoth he) you sleeping sparkes awake,
Which troubled once, into huge flames will grow,
Ne euer will their feruent fury slake
Till liuing moysture into smoke do flow,
And wasted life do lye in ashes low.
Yet sithens silence lesseneth not my fire,
But told it flames, and hidden it does glow,
I will reuele, what ye so much desire:
Ah Loue, lay downe thy bow, the whiles I may respire.

[291] its

9

It was in freshest flowre of youthly yeares,
When courage first does creepe in manly chest,
Then first the coale of kindly heat appeares
To kindle loue in euery liuing brest;
But me had warnd old *Timons* wise behest,
Those creeping flames by reason to subdew,
Before their rage grew to so great vnrest,
As miserable louers vse to rew,
Which still wex old in woe, whiles woe still wexeth new.

10

That idle name of loue, and louers life,
As losse of time, and vertues enimy
I euer scornd, and ioyd to stirre vp strife,
In middest of their mournfull Tragedy,
Ay wont to laugh, when them I heard to cry,
And blow the fire, which them to ashes brent:
Their God himselfe, grieu'd at my libertie,
Shot many a dart at me with fiers intent,
But I them warded all with wary gouernment.[292]

11

But all in vaine: no fort can be so strong,
Ne fleshly brest can armed be so sound,
But will at last be wonne with battrie long,
Or vnawares at disauantage found;
Nothing is sure, that growes on earthly ground:
And who most trustes in arme of fleshly might,
And boasts, in beauties chaine not to be bound,
Doth soonest fall in disauentrous fight,
And yeeldes his caytiue neck to victours most despight.

[292] control

12

Ensample make of him your haplesse ioy,[293]
And of my selfe now mated,[294] as ye see;
Whose prouder vaunt that proud aueng-ing boy
Did soone pluck downe, and curbd my libertie.
For on a day prickt forth with iollitie
Of looser life, and heat of hardiment,
Raunging the forest wide on courser free,
The fields, the floods, the heauens with one consent
Did seeme to laugh on me, and fauour mine intent.

13

For-wearied with my sports, I did alight
From loftie steed, and downe to sleepe me layd;
The verdant gras my couch did goodly dight,
And pillow was my helmet faire dis-playd:
Whiles euery sence the humour sweet embayd,[295]
And slombring soft my hart did steale away,
Me seemed, by my side a royall Mayd
Her daintie limbes full softly down did lay:
So faire a creature yet saw neuer sunny day.

14

Most goodly glee and louely blandishment
She to me made, and bad me loue her deare,
For dearely sure her loue was to me bent,
As when iust time expired should ap-peare.
But whether dreames delude, or true it were,
Was neuer hart so rauisht with delight,
Ne liuing man like words did euer heare,
As she to me deliuered all that night;
And at her parting said, She Queene of Faeries hight.

[293] *i.e.*, the Redcross Knight
[294] defeated
[295] bathed

15

When I awoke, and found her place de-uoyd,
And nought but pressed gras, where she had lyen,
I sorrowed all so much, as earst I ioyd,
And washed all her place with watry eyen.
From that day forth I lou'd that face diuine;
From that day forth I cast in carefull mind,
To seeke her out with labour, and long tyne,[296]
And neuer vow to rest, till her I find,
Nine monethes I seeke in vaine yet ni'll that vow vnbind.

16

Thus as he spake, his visage wexed pale,
And chaunge of hew great passion did bewray;
Yet still he stroue to cloke his inward bale,
And hide the smoke, that did his fire display,
Till gentle *Vna* thus to him gan say;
O happy Queene of Faeries, that hast found
Mongst many, one that with his prowesse may
Defend thine honour, and thy foes con-found:
True Loues are often sown, but seldom grow on ground.

17

Thine, O then, said the gentle *Redcrosse* knight,

[296] grief

Next to that Ladies loue, shalbe the place,
O fairest virgin, full of heauenly light,
Whose wondrous faith, exceeding earthly race,
Was firmest fixt in mine extremest case.
And you, my Lord, the Patrone of my life,
Of that great Queene may well gaine worthy grace:
For onely worthy you through prowes priefe
Yf liuing man mote worthy be, to be her liefe.

18

So diuersly discoursing of their loues,
The golden Sunne his glistring head gan shew,
And sad remembraunce now the Prince amoues,
With fresh desire his voyage to pursew:
Als *Vna* earnd her traueill to renew.
Then those two knights, fast friendship for to bynd,
And loue establish each to other trew,
Gaue goodly gifts, the signes of gratefull mynd,
And eke as pledges firme, right hands together ioynd.

19

Prince *Arthur* gaue a boxe of Diamond sure,
Embowd with gold and gorgeous ornament,
Wherein were closd few drops of liquor pure,
Of wondrous worth, and vertue excellent,
That any wound could heale incontinent:
Which to requite, the *Redcrosse* knight him gaue
A booke, wherein his Saueours testament
Was writ with golden letters rich and braue;
A worke of wondrous grace, and able soules to saue.

20

Thus beene they parted, *Arthur* on his way
To seeke his loue, and th'other for to fight
With *Vnaes* foe, that all her realme did pray.[297]
But she now weighing the decayed plight,
And shrunken synewes of her chosen knight,
Would not a while her forward course pursew,
Ne bring him forth in face of dreadfull fight,
Till he recouered had his former hew:
For him to be yet weake and wearie well she knew.

21

So as they traueild, lo they gan espy
An armed knight towards them gallop fast,
That seemed from some feared foe to fly,
Or other griesly thing, that him agast.
Still as he fled, his eye was backward cast,
As if his feare still followed him behind;
Als flew his steed, as he his bands had brast,
And with his winged heeles did tread the wind,
As he had beene a fole of *Pegasus* his kind.

22

Nigh as he drew, they might perceiue his head
To be vnarmd, and curld vncombed heares
Vpstaring stiffe, dismayd with vncouth dread;
Nor drop of bloud in all his face appeares
Nor life in limbe: and to increase his feares,

[297] ravage

In fowle reproch of knighthoods faire degree,
About his neck an hempen rope he weares,
That with his glistring armes does ill agree;[298]
But he of rope or armes has now no memoree.

23

The *Redcrosse* knight toward him crossed fast,
To weet, what mister wight[299] was so dismayd:
There him he finds all sencelesse and aghast,
That of him selfe he seemd to be afrayd;
Whom hardly he from flying forward stayd,
Till he these wordes to him deliuer might;
Sir knight, aread who hath ye thus arayd,
And eke from whom make ye this hasty flight:
For neuer knight I saw in such misseeming plight.

24

He answered nought at all, but adding new
Feare to his first amazment, staring wide
With stony eyes, and hartlesse hollow hew,
Astonisht stood, as one that had aspide
Infernall furies, with their chaines vntide.
Him yet againe, and yet againe bespake
The gentle knight; who nought to him replide,
But trembling euery ioynt did inly quake,
And foltring tongue at last these words seemd forth to shake.

25

For Gods deare loue, Sir knight, do me not stay;
For loe he comes, he comes fast after mee.
Eft[300] looking backe would faine haue runne away;
But he him forst to stay, and tellen free
The secret cause of his perplexitie:
Yet nathemore by his bold hartie speach,
Could his bloud-frosen hart emboldned bee,
But through his boldnesse rather feare did reach,
Yet forst, at last he made through silence suddein breach.

26

And am I now in safetie sure (quoth he)
From him, that would haue forced me to dye?
And is the point of death now turnd fro mee,
That I may tell this haplesse history?
Feare nought: (quoth he) no daunger now is nye.
Then shall I you recount a ruefull cace,
(Said he) the which with this vnlucky eye
I late beheld, and had not greater grace
Me reft from it, had bene partaker of the place.

27

I lately chaunst (Would I had neuer chaunst)
With a faire knight to keepen companee,
Sir *Terwin* hight, that well himselfe aduaunst
In all affaires, and was both bold and free,
But not so happie as mote happie bee:
He lou'd, as was his lot, a Ladie gent,
That him againe lou'd in the least degree:

[298] Hanging is a shameful death fit only for rogues.
[299] kind of person

[300] again

For she was proud, and of too high intent,
And ioyd to see her louer languish and lament.

28

From whom returning sad and comfortlesse,
As on the way together we did fare,
We met that villen (God from him me blesse)[301]
That cursed wight, from whom I scapt whyleare,[302]
A man of hell, that cals himselfe *Despaire*:
Who first vs greets, and after faire areedes
Of tydings strange, and of aduentures rare:
So creeping close, as Snake in hidden weedes,
Inquireth of our states, and of our knightly deedes.

29

Which when he knew, and felt our feeble harts
Embost[303] with bale, and bitter byting griefe,
Which loue had launched with his deadly darts,
With wounding words and termes of foule repriefe
He pluckt from vs all hope of due reliefe,
That earst vs held in loue of lingring life;
Then hopelesse hartlesse, gan the cunning thiefe
Perswade vs die, to stint all further strife:
To me he lent this rope, to him a rustie knife.

30

With which sad instrument of hastie death,
That wofull louer, loathing lenger light,
A wide way made to let forth liuing breath.
But I more fearefull, or more luckie wight,
Dismayd with that deformed dismall sight,
Fled fast away, halfe dead with dying feare:
Ne yet assur'd of life by you, Sir knight,
Whose like infirmitie like chaunce may beare:
But God you neuer let his charmed speeches heare.

31

How may a man (said he) with idle speach
Be wonne, to spoyle the Castle[304] of his health?
I wote (quoth he) whom triall late did teach,
That like would not for all this worldes wealth:
His subtill tongue, like dropping honny, mealt'th
Into the hart, and searcheth euery vaine,
That ere one be aware, by secret stealth
His powre is reft, and weaknesse doth remaine.
O neuer Sir desire to try his guilefull traine.

32

Certes (said he) hence shall I neuer rest,
Till I that treachours art haue heard and tride;
And you Sir knight, whose name mote I request,
Of grace do me vnto his cabin guide.
I that hight *Treuisan* (quoth he) will ride
Against my liking backe, to doe you grace:
But nor for gold nor glee will I abide
By you, when ye arriue in that same place;
For leuer had I die, then see his deadly face.

33

Ere long they come, where that same wicked wight

---

[301] protect
[302] just now
[303] overwhelmed
[304] the body

His dwelling has, low in an hollow caue,
Farre vnderneath a craggie clift ypight,
Darke, dolefull, drearie, like a greedie graue,
That still for carrion carcases doth craue:
On top whereof aye dwelt the ghastly Owle,
Shrieking his baleful note, which euer draue
Farre from that haunt all other chearefull fowle;
And all about it wandring ghostes did waile and howle.

34

And all about old stockes and stubs of trees,
Whereon nor fruit, nor leafe was euer seene,
Did hang vpon the ragged rocky knees;[305]
On which had many wretches hanged beene,
Whose carcases were scattered on the greene,
And throwne about the cliffs. Arriued there,
That bare-head knight for dread and dolefull teene,[306]
Would faine haue fled, ne durst approachen neare,
But th'other forst him stay, and comforted in feare.

35

That darkesome caue they enter, where they find
That cursed man, low sitting on the ground,
Musing full sadly in his sullein mind;
His griesie lockes, long growen, and vnbound,
Disordred hong about his shoulders round,
And hid his face; through which his hollow eyne
Lookt deadly dull, and stared as astound;
His raw-bone cheekes through penurie and pine,
Were shronke into his iawes, as he did neuer dine.

36

His garment nought but many ragged clouts,
With thornes together pind and patched was,
The which his naked sides he wrapt abouts;
And him beside there lay vpon the gras
A drearie corse, whose life away did pas,
All wallowd in his owne yet lukewarme blood,
That from his wound yet welled fresh alas;
In which a rustie knife fast fixed stood,
And made an open passage for the gushing flood.

37

Which piteous spectacle, approuing trew
The wofull tale that *Treuisan* had told,
When as the gentle *Redcrosse* knight did vew,
With firie zeale he burnt in courage bold,
Him to auenge, before his bloud were cold,
And to the villein said, Thou damned wight,
The author of this fact, we here behold,
What iustice can but iudge against thee right,
With thine owne bloud to price his bloud here shed in sight?

38

What franticke fit (quoth he) hath thus distraught
Thee, foolish man, so rash a doome to giue?
What iustice euer other iudgement taught,

---
305 projections
306 grief

But he should die, who merites not to liue?
None else to death this man despayring driue,
But his owne guiltie mind deseruing death.
Is then vniust to each his due to giue?
Or let him die, that loatheth liuing breath?
Or let him die at ease, that liueth here vneath? [307]

39

Who trauels by the wearie wandring way,
To come vnto his wished home in haste,
And meetes a flood, that doth his passage stay,
Is not great grace to helpe him ouer past,
Or free his feet, that in the myre sticke fast?
Most enuious man, that grieues at neighbours good,
And fond, that ioyest in the woe thou hast,
Why wilt not let him passe, that long hath stood
Vpon the banke, yet wilt thy selfe not passe the flood? [308]

40

He there does now enioy eternall rest
And happie ease, which thou doest want and craue,
And further from it daily wanderest:
What if some litle paine the passage haue,
That makes fraile flesh to feare the bitter waue?
Is not short paine well borne, that brings long ease,
And layes the soule to sleepe in quiet graue?
Sleepe after toyle, port after stormie seas,
Ease after warre, death after life does greatly please.

[307] with difficulty
[308] yet wilt, *etc.* Even if you yourself will not.

41

The knight much wondred at his suddeine wit,
And said, The terme of life is limited,
Ne may a man prolong, nor shorten it;
The souldier may not moue from watchfull sted,
Nor leaue his stand, vntill his Captaine bed.
Who life did limit by almightie doome,
(Quoth he) knowes best the termes established;
And he, that points the Centonell his roome,
Doth license him depart at sound of morning droome.

42

Is not his deed, what euer thing is donne,
In heauen and earth? did not he all create
To die againe? all ends that was begonne.
Their times in his eternall booke of fate
Are written sure, and haue their certaine date.
Who then can striue with strong necessitie,
That holds the world in his still chaunging state,
Or shunne the death ordaynd by destinie?
When houre of death is come, let none aske whence, nor why.

43

The lenger life, I wote the greater sin,
The greater sin, the greater punishment:
All those great battels, which thou boasts to win,
Through strife, and bloud-shed, and auengement,
Now praysd, hereafter deare thou shalt repent:
For life must life, and bloud must bloud repay.

Is not enough thy euill life forespent? [309]
For he, that once hath missed the right way,
The further he doth goe, the further he doth stray.

44

Then do no further goe, no further stray,
But here lie downe, and to thy rest betake,
Th'ill to preuent, that life ensewen may.
For what hath life, that may it loued make,
And giues not rather cause it to forsake?
Feare, sicknesse, age, losse, labour, sorrow, strife,
Paine, hunger, cold, that makes the hart to quake;
And euer fickle fortune rageth rife,
All which, and thousands mo do make a loathsome life.

45

Thou wretched man, of death hast greatest need,
If in true ballance thou wilt weigh thy state:
For neuer knight, that dared warlike deede,
More lucklesse disauentures did amate: [310]
Witnesse the dongeon deepe, wherein of late
Thy life shut vp, for death so oft did call;
And though good lucke prolonged hath thy date,
Yet death then, would the like mishaps forestall,
Into the which hereafter thou maiest happen fall.

46

Why then doest thou, O man of sin, desire
To draw thy dayes forth to their last degree?
Is not the measure of thy sinfull hire
High heaped vp with huge iniquitie,
Against the day of wrath, to burden thee?
Is not enough, that to this Ladie milde
Thou falsed hast thy faith with periurie,
And sold thy selfe to serue *Duessa* vilde,
With whom in all abuse thou hast thy selfe defilde?

47

Is not he iust, that all this doth behold
From highest heauen, and beares an equall eye?
Shall he thy sins vp in his knowledge fold,
And guiltie be of thine impietie?
Is not his law, Let euery sinner die:
Die shall all flesh? what then must needs be donne,
Is it not better to doe willinglie,
Then linger, till the glasse be all out ronne?
Death is the end of woes: die soone, O faeries sonne.

48

The knight was much enmoued with his speach,
That as a swords point through his hart did perse,
And in his conscience made a secret breach,
Well knowing true all, that he did reherse
And to his fresh remembrance did reuerse
The vgly vew of his deformed crimes,
That all his manly powres it did disperse,
As he were charmed with inchaunted rimes,
That oftentimes he quakt, and fainted oftentimes.

49

In which amazement, when the Miscreant
Perceiued him to wauer weake and fraile,
Whiles trembling horror did his conscience dant,

[309] wasted
[310] dishearten

And hellish anguish did his soule assaile,
To driue him to despaire, and quite to quaile,
He shew'd him painted in a table[311] plaine,
The damned ghosts, that doe in torments waile,
And thousand feends that doe them endlesse paine
With fire and brimstone, which for euer shall remaine.

50

The sight whereof so throughly him dismaid,
That nought but death before his eyes he saw,
And euer burning wrath before him laid,
By righteous sentence of th'Almighties law:
Then gan the villein him to ouercraw,[312]
And brought vnto him swords, ropes, poison, fire,
And all that might him to perdition draw;
And bad him choose, what death he would desire:
For death was due to him, that had prouokt Gods ire.

51

But when as none of them he saw him take,
He to him raught a dagger sharpe and keene,
And gaue it him in hand: his hand did quake,
And tremble like a leafe of Aspin greene,
And troubled bloud through his pale face was seene
To come, and goe with tydings from the hart,
As it a running messenger had beene.
At last resolu'd to worke his finall smart,
He lifted vp his hand, that backe againe did start.

52

Which when as *Vna* saw, through euery vaine
The crudled cold ran to her well of life,
As in a swowne: but soone reliu'd againe,
Out of his hand she snatcht the cursed knife,
And threw it to the ground, enraged rife,
And to him said, Fie, fie, faint harted knight,
What meanest thou by this reprochfull strife?
Is this the battell, which thou vauntst to fight
With that fire-mouthed Dragon, horrible and bright?

53

Come, come away, fraile, feeble, fleshly wight,
Ne let vaine words bewitch thy manly hart,
Ne diuelish thoughts dismay thy constant spright.
In heauenly mercies hast thou not a part?
Why shouldst thou then despeire, that chosen art?
Where iustice growes, there grows eke greater grace,
The which doth quench the brond of hellish smart,
And that accurst hand-writing doth deface.
Arise, Sir knight arise, and leaue this cursed place.

54

So vp he rose, and thence amounted streight.
Which when the carle beheld, and saw his guest
Would safe depart, for all his subtill sleight,

[311] canvas
[312] exult over

He chose an halter from among the rest,
And with it hung himselfe, vnbid[313] vnblest.
But death he could not worke himselfe thereby;
For thousand times he so himselfe had drest,
Yet nathelesse it could not doe him die,
Till he should die his last, that is eternally.

Canto X

Her faithfull knight faire Vna brings
to house of Holinesse,
Where he is taught repentance, and
the way to heauenly blesse.

1

WHAT man is he, that boasts of fleshly might,
And vaine assurance of mortality,
Which all so soone, as it doth come to fight,
Against spirituall foes, yeelds by and by,
Or from the field most cowardly doth fly?
Ne let the man ascribe it to his skill,
That thorough grace hath gained victory.
If any strength we haue, it is to ill,
But all the good is Gods, both power and eke will.

2

By that, which lately hapned, *Vna* saw,
That this her knight was feeble, and too faint;
And all his sinews woxen weake and raw,
Through long enprisonment, and hard constraint,
Which he endured in his late restraint,
That yet he was vnfit for bloudie fight:
Therefore to cherish him with diets daint,
She cast to bring him, where he chearen might,
Till he recouered had his late decayed plight.

3

There was an auntient house not farre away,
Renowmd throughout the world for sacred lore,
And pure vnspotted life: so well they say
It gouernd was, and guided euermore,
Through wisedome of a matrone graue and hore;
Whose onely ioy was to relieue the needes
Of wretched soules, and helpe the helpelesse pore:
All night she spent in bidding of her bedes,
And all the day in doing good and godly deedes.

4

Dame *Cœlia*[314] men did her call, as thought
From heauen to come, or thither to arise,
The mother of three daughters, well vpbrought
In goodly thewes, and godly exercise:
The eldest two most sober, chast, and wise,
Fidelia and *Speranza* virgins were,
Though spousd, yet wanting wedlocks solemnize;
But faire *Charissa* to a louely fere[315]
Was lincked, and by him had many pledges dere.

5

Arriued there, the dore they find fast lockt;
For it was warely watched night and day,
For feare of many foes: but when they knockt,
The Porter opened vnto them streight way:
He was an aged syre, all hory gray,
With lookes full lowly cast, and gate full slow,

[313] without prayer

[314] The Heavenly

[315] companion

Wont on a staffe his feeble steps to stay,
Hight *Humiltá*. They passe in stouping low;
For streight and narrow was the way, which he did show.

6

Each goodly thing is hardest to begin,
But entred in a spacious court they see,
Both plaine, and pleasant to be walked in,
Where them does meete a francklin[316] faire and free,
And entertaines with comely courteous glee,
His name was *Zele,* that him right well became,
For in his speeches and behauiour hee
Did labour liuely to expresse the same,
And gladly did them guide, till to the Hall they came.

7

There fairely them receiues a gentle Squire,
Of milde demeanure, and rare courtesie,
Right cleanly clad in comely sad attire;
In word and deede that shew'd great modestie,
And knew his good[317] to all of each degree,
Hight *Reuerence*. He them with speeches meet
Does faire entreat; no courting nicetie,
But simple true, and eke vnfained sweet,
As might become a Squire so great persons to greet.

8

And afterwards them to his Dame he leades,
That aged Dame, the Ladie of the place:
Who all this while was busie at her beades:
Which doen, she vp arose with seemely grace,
And toward them full matronely did pace.
Where when that fairest *Vna* she beheld,
Whom well she knew to spring from heauenly race,
Her hart with ioy vnwonted inly sweld,
As feeling wondrous comfort in her weaker eld.

9

And her embracing said, O happie earth,
Whereon thy innocent feet doe euer tread,
Most vertuous virgin borne of heauenly berth,
That to redeeme thy woefull parents head,
From tyrans rage, and euer-dying dread,
Hast wandred through the world now long a day;
Yet ceasest not thy wearie soles to lead,
What grace hath thee now hither brought this way?
Or doen thy feeble feet vnweeting hither stray?

10

Strange thing it is an errant knight to see
Here in this place, or any other wight,
That hither turnes his steps. So few there bee,
That chose the narrow path, or seeke the right:
All keepe the broad high way, and take delight
With many rather for to go astray,
And be partakers of their euill plight,
Then with a few to walke the rightest way;
O foolish men, why haste ye to your owne decay?

11

Thy selfe to see, and tyred limbs to rest,
O matrone sage (quoth she) I hither came,
And this good knight his way with me addrest,
Led with thy prayses and broad-blazed fame,

[316] a freeman
[317] proper behavior

That vp to heauen is blowne. The auncient Dame
Him goodly greeted in her modest guise,
And entertaynd them both, as best became,
With all the court'sies, that she could deuise.
Ne wanted ought, to shew her bounteous or wise.

12

Thus as they gan of sundry things deuise,
Loe two most goodly virgins came in place,
Ylinked arme in arme in louely wise,
With countenance demure, and modest grace,
They numbred euen steps and equall pace:
Of which the eldest, that *Fidelia* hight,
Like sunny beames threw from her Christall face,
That could haue dazed the rash beholders sight,
And round about her head did shine like heauens light.

13

She was araied all in lilly white,
And in her right hand bore a cup of gold,
With wine and water filled vp to the hight,
In which a Serpent did himselfe enfold,
That horrour made to all, that did behold;
But she no whit did chaunge her constant mood:
And in her other hand she fast did hold
A booke, that was both signd and seald with blood,
Wherein darke things were writ, hard to be vnderstood.

14

Her younger sister, that *Speranza* hight,
Was clad in blew, that her beseemed well;
Not all so chearefull seemed she of sight,
As was her sister; whether dread did dwell,
On anguish in her hart, is hard to tell:
Vpon her arme a siluer anchor lay,
Whereon she leaned euer, as befell:
And euer vp to heauen, as she did pray,
Her steadfast eyes were bent, ne swarued other way.

15

They seeing *Vna,* towards her gan wend,
Who them encouuters with like courtesie;
Many kind speeches they betwene them spend,
And greatly ioy each other well to see:
Then to the knight with shamefast modestie
They turne themselves, at *Vnaes* meeke request,
And him salute with well beseeming glee;
Who faire them quites, as him beseemed best,
And goodly gan discourse of many a noble gest.[318]

16

Then *Vna* thus; But she your sister deare;
The deare *Charissa* where is she become?
Or wants she health, or busie is elsewhere?
Ah no, said they, but forth she may not come:
For she of late is lightned of her wombe,
And hath encreast the world with one sonne more,
That her to see should be but troublesome.
Indeede (quoth she) that should her trouble sore,
But thankt be God, and her encrease so euermore.

---

[318] chivalric act

17

Then said the aged *Cœlia,* Deare dame,
And you good Sir, I wote that of your toyle,
And labours long, through which ye hither came,
Ye both forwearied be: therefore a whyle
I read [319] you rest, and to your bowres recoyle.
Then called she a Groome, that forth him led
Into a goodly lodge, and gan despoile
Of puissant armes, and laid in easie bed;
His name was meeke *Obedience* rightfully ared.[320]

18

Now when their wearie limbes with kindly rest,
And bodies were refresht with due repast,
Faire *Vna* gan *Fidelia* faire request,
To haue her knight into her schoolehouse plaste,
That of her heauenly learning he might taste,
And heare the wisedome of her words diuine.
She graunted, and that knight so much agraste,[321]
That she him taught celestiall discipline,
And opened his dull eyes, that light mote in them shine.

19

And that her sacred Booke, with bloud ywrit,
That none could read, except she did them teach,
She vnto him disclosed euery whit,
And heauenly documents thereout did preach,
That weaker wit of man could neuer reach,
Of God, of grace, of iustice, of free will,
That wonder was to heare her goodly speach:
For she was able, with her words to kill,
And raise againe to life the hart, that she did thrill.[322]

20

And when she list poure out her larger spright,
She would commaund the hastie Sunne to stay,
Or backward turne his course from heauens hight;
Sometimes great hostes of men she could dismay,
Dry-shod to passe, she parts the flouds in tway;
And eke huge mountaines from their natiue seat
She would commaund, themselues to beare away,
And throw in raging sea with roaring threat.
Almightie God her gaue such powre, and puissance great.

21

The faithfull knight now grew in litle space,
By hearing her, and by her sisters lore,
To such perfection of all heauenly grace,
That wretched world he gan for to abhore,
And mortall life gan loath, as thing forlore,
Greeu'd with remembrance of his wicked wayes,
And prickt with anguish of his sinnes so sore,
That he desirde to end his wretched dayes:
So much the dart of sinfull guilt the soule dismayes.

22

But wise *Speranza* gaue him comfort sweet,
And taught him how to take assured hold
Vpon her siluer anchor, as was meet;

[319] advise
[320] made known
[321] favored
[322] pierce

Else had his sinnes so great, and manifold
Made him forget all that *Fidelia* told.
In this distressed doubtfull agonie,
When him his dearest *Vna* did behold,
Disdeining life, desiring leaue to die,
She found her selfe assayld with great perplexitie.

23

And came to *Cœlia* to declare her smart,
Who well acquainted with that commune plight,
Which sinfull horror workes in wounded hart,
Her wisely comforted all that she might,
With goodly counsell and aduisement right;
And streightway sent with carefull diligence,
To fetch a Leach, the which had great insight
In that disease of grieued conscience,
And well could cure the same; His name was *Patience.*

24

Who comming to that soule-diseased knight,
Could hardly him intreat, to tell his griefe:
Which knowne, and all that noyd his heauie spright
Well searcht, eftsoones he gan apply reliefe
Of salues and med'cines, which had passing priefe,[323]
And thereto added words of wondrous might:
By which to ease he him recured briefe,
And much asswag'd the passion [324] of his plight,
That he his paine endur'd, as seeming now more light.

25

But yet the cause and root of all his ill,
Inward corruption, and infected sin,
Not purg'd nor heald, behind remained still,
And festring sore did rankle yet within,
Close creeping twixt the marrow and the skin.
Which to extirpe, he laid him priuily
Downe in a darkesome lowly place farre in,
Whereas he meant his corrosiues to apply,
And with streight diet tame his stubborne malady.

26

In ashes and sackcloth he did array
His daintie corse, proud humors to abate,
And dieted with fasting euery day,
The swelling of his wounds to mitigate,
And made him pray both earely and eke late:
And euer as superfluous flesh did rot
Amendment readie still at hand did wayt,
To pluck it out with pincers firie whot,
That soone in him was left no one corrupted iot.

27

And bitter *Penance* with an yron whip,
Was wont him once to disple euery day:
And sharpe *Remorse* his hart did pricke and nip,
That drops of bloud thence like a well did play;
And sad *Repentance* vsed to embay
His bodie in salt water smarting sore,
The filthy blots of sinne to wash away.
So in short space they did to health restore
The man that would not liue, but earst lay at deathes dore.

28

In which his torment often was so great,
That like a Lyon he would cry and rore,
And rend his flesh, and his owne synewes eat.
His owne deare *Vna* hearing euermore

[323] power
[324] suffering

His ruefull shriekes and gronings, often tore
Her guiltlesse garments, and her golden heare,
For pitty of his paine and anguish sore;
Yet all with patience wisely she did beare;
For well she wist, his crime could else be neuer cleare.

29

Whom thus recouer'd by wise Patience,
And trew *Repentance* they to *Vna* brought:
Who ioyous of his cured conscience,
Him dearely kist, and fairely eke besought
Himselfe to chearish, and consuming thought
To put away out of his carefull brest.
By this *Charissa,* late in child-bed brought,
Was woxen strong, and left her fruitfull nest;
To her faire *Vna* brought this vnacquainted guest.

30

She was a woman in her freshest age,
Of wondrous beauty, and of bountie rare,
With goodly grace and comely personage,
That was on earth not easie to compare;
Full of great loue, but *Cupids* wanton snare
As hell she hated, chast in worke and will;
Her necke and breasts were euer open bare,
That ay thereof her babes might sucke their fill;
The rest was all in yellow robes arayed still.

31

A multitude of babes about her hong,
Playing their sports, that ioyd her to behold,
Whom still she fed, whiles they were weake and young,
But thrust them forth still, as they wexed old:
And on her head she wore a tyre of gold,
Adornd with gemmes and owches wondrous faire,
Whose passing price vneath was to be told;
And by her side there sate a gentle paire
Of turtle doues, she sitting in an yuorie chaire.

32

The knight and *Vna* entring, faire her greet,
And bid her ioy of that her happie brood;
Who them requites with court'sies seeming meet,
And entertaines with friendly chearefull mood.
Then *Vna* her besought, to be so good,
As in her vertuous rules to schoole her knight,
Now after all his torment well withstood,
In that sad house of *Penaunce,* where his spright
Had past the paines of hell, and long enduring night.

33

She was right ioyous of her iust request,
And taking by the hand that Faeries sonne,
Gan him instruct in euery good behest,
Of loue, and righteousnesse, and well to donne,[325]
And wrath, and hatred warely to shonne,
That drew on men Gods hatred, and his wrath,
And many soules in dolours had fordonne:
In which when him she well instructed hath,
From thence to heauen she teacheth him the ready path.

[325] well-doing

34

Wherein his weaker wandring steps to guide,
An auncient matrone she to her does call,
Whose sober lookes her wisedome well descride:[326]
Her name was *Mercie,* well knowne ouer all,
To be both gratious, and eke liberall:
To whom the carefull charge of him she gaue,
To lead aright, that he should neuer fall
In all his wayes through this wide worldes waue,
That Mercy in the end his righteous soule might saue.

35

The godly Matrone by the hand him beares
Forth from her presence, by a narrow way,
Scattred with bushy thornes, and ragged breares,
Which still before him she remou'd away,
That nothing might his ready passage stay:
And euer when his feet encombred were,
Or gan to shrinke, or from the right to stray,
She held him fast, and firmely did vpbeare,
As carefull Nourse her child from falling oft does reare.

36

Eftsoones vnto an holy Hospitall,
That was fore by the way, she did him bring,
In which seuen Bead-men[327] that had vowed all
Their life to seruice of high heauens king
Did spend their dayes in doing godly thing:
Their gates to all were open euermore,
That by the wearie way were traueiling,
And one sate wayting euer them before,
To call in commers-by, that needy were and pore.

37

The first of them that eldest was, and best,
Of all the house had charge and gouernement,
As Guardian and Steward of the rest:
His office was to giue entertainment
And lodging, vnto all that came, and went:
Not vnto such, as could him feast againe,
And double quite, for that he on them spent,
But such, as want of harbour did constraine:
Those for Gods sake his dewty was to entertaine.

38

The second was as Almner[328] of the place,
His office was, the hungry for to feed,
And thristy giue to drinke, a worke of grace:
He feard not once him selfe to be in need,
Ne car'd to hoord for those, whom he did breede:
The grace of God he layd vp still in store,
Which as a stocke he left vnto his seede;
He had enough, what need him care for more?
And had he lesse, yet some he would giue to the pore.

39

The third had of their wardrobe custodie,
In which were not rich tyres, nor garments gay,
The plumes of pride, and wings of vanitie,
But clothes meet to keepe keene could away,
And naked nature seemely to aray;

[326] revealed
[327] men of prayer
[328] An official distributor of alms.

With which bare wretched wights he dayly clad,
The images of God in earthly clay;
And if that no spare cloths to giue he had,
His owne coate he would cut, and it distribute glad.

40

The fourth appointed by his office was,
Poore prisoners to relieue with gratious ayd,
And captiues to redeeme with price of bras,
From Turkes and Sarazins, which them had stayd;
And though they faultie were, yet well he wayd,
That God to vs forgiueth euery howre
Much more then that, why they in bands were layd,
And he[329] that harrowd hell with heauie stowre,
The faultie soules from thence brought to his heauenly bowre.

41

The fift had charge sicke persons to attend,
And comfort those, in point of death which lay;
For them most needeth comfort in the end,
When sin, and hell, and death do most dismay
The feeble soule departing hence away.
All is but lost, that liuing we bestow,
If not well ended at our dying day.
O man haue mind of that last bitter throw;
For as the tree does fall, so lyes it euer low.

42

The sixt had charge of them now being dead,
In seemely sort their corses to engraue,
And deck with dainty flowres their bridall bed,
That to their heauenly spouse both sweet and braue
They might appeare, when he their soules shall saue.
The wondrous workemanship of Gods owne mould,
Whose face he made, all beasts to feare, and gaue
All in his hand, euen dead we honour should.
Ah dearest God me graunt, I dead be not defould.

43

The seuenth now after death and buriall done,
Had charge the tender Orphans of the dead
And widowes ayd, least they should be vndone:
In face of iudgement he their right would plead,
Ne ought the powre of mighty men did dread
In their defence, nor would for gold or fee
Be wonne their rightfull causes downe to tread:
And when they stood in most necessitee,
He did supply their want, and gaue them euer free.

44

There when the Elfin knight arriued was,
The first and chiefest of the seuen, whose care
Was guests to welcome, towardes him did pas:
Where seeing *Mercie,* that his steps vp bare,
And alwayes led, to her with reuerence rare
He humbly louted in meeke lowlinesse,
And seemely welcome for her did prepare:
For of their order she was Patronesse,
Albe *Charissa* were their chiefest founderesse.

---

[329] Christ who, after his death, descended into Hell and freed the patriarchs from the rule of Satan.

45

There she awhile him stayes, him selfe to rest,
That to the rest more able he might bee:
During which time, in euery good behest
And godly worke of Almes and charitee
She him instructed with great industree;
Shortly therein so perfect he became,
That from the first vnto the last degree,
His mortall life he learned had to frame
In holy righteousnesse, without rebuke or blame.

46

Thence forward by that painfull way they pas,
Forth to an hill, that was both steepe and hy;
On top whereof a sacred chappell was,
And eke a litle Hermitage thereby,
Wherein an aged holy man did lye,
That day and night said his deuotion,
Ne other worldly busines did apply;
His name was heauenly *Contemplation;*
Of God and goodnesse was his meditation.

47

Great grace that old man to him giuen had;
For God he often saw from heauens hight,
All[330] were his earthly eyen both blunt and bad,
And through great age had lost their kindly sight,
Yet wondrous quick and persant was his spright,[331]
As Eagles eye, that can behold the Sunne:
That hill they scale with all their powre and might,
That his frayle thighes nigh wearie and fordonne
Gan faile, but by her helpe the top at last he wonne.

[330] although
[331] spirit

48

There they do finde that godly aged Sire,
With snowy lockes adowne his shoulders shed,
As hoarie frost with spangles doth attire
The mossy braunches of an Oke halfe ded.
Each bone might through his body well be red,
And euery sinew seene through his long fast:
For nought he car'd his carcas long vnfed;
His mind was full of spirituall repast,
And pyn'd his flesh, to keepe his body low and chast.

49

Who when these two approching he aspide,
At their first presence grew agrieued sore,
That forst him lay his heauenly thoughts aside;
And had he not that Dame respected more,
Whom highly he did reuerence and adore,
He would not once haue moued for the knight.
They him saluted standing far afore;
Who well them greeting, humbly did requight,
And asked, to what end they clomb that tedious height.

50

What end (quoth she) should cause vs take such paine,
But that same end, which euery liuing wight
Should make his marke, high heauen to attaine?
Is not from hence the way, that leadeth right
To that most glorious house, that glistreth bright
With burning starres, and euerliuing fire,

Whereof the keyes are to thy hand behight[332]
By wise *Fidelia*? she doth thee require,
To shew it to this knight, according his desire.

51

Thrise happy man, said then the father graue,
Whose staggering steps thy steady hand doth lead,
And shewes the way, his sinfull soule to saue.
Who better can the way to heauen aread,
Then thou thy selfe, that was both borne and bred
In heauenly throne, where thousand Angels shine?
Thou doest the prayers of the righteous sead
Present before the maiestie diuine,
And his auenging wrath to clemencie incline.

52

Yet since thou bidst, thy pleasure shalbe donne.
Then come thou man of earth, and see the way,
That neuer yet was seene of Faeries sonne,
That neuer leads the traueiler astray,
But after labours long, and sad delay,
Brings them to ioyous rest and endlesse blis.
But first thou must a season fast and pray,
Till from her bands the spright assoiled[333] is,
And haue her strength recur'd from fraile infirmitis.

53

That done, he leads him to the highest Mount;
Such one, as that same mighty man of God,[334]
That bloud-red billowes like a walled front
On either side disparted with his rod,
Till that his army dry-foot through them yod,[335]
Dwelt fortie dayes vpon; where writ in stone
With bloudy letters by the hand of God,
The bitter doome of death and balefull mone
He did receiue, whiles flashing fire about him shone.

54

Or like that sacred hill, whose head full hie,
Adornd with fruitfull Oliues all arownd,
Is, as it were for endlesse memory
Of that deare Lord, who oft thereon was fownd,
For euer with a flowring girlond crownd:
Or like that pleasaunt Mount,[336] that is for ay
Through famous Poets verse each where renownd,
On which the thrise three learned Ladies play
Their heauenly notes, and make full many a louely lay.

55

From thence, far off he vnto him did shew
A litle path, that was both steepe and long,
Which to a goodly Citie led his vew;
Whose wals and towres were builded high and strong
Of perle and precious stone, that earthly tong
Cannot describe, nor wit of man can tell;
Too high a ditty for my simple song;
The Citie of the great king hight it well,
Wherein eternall peace and happinesse doth dwell.

56

As he thereon stood gazing, he might see
The blessed Angels to and fro descend

[332] entrusted [333] absolved [334] Moses

[335] went
[336] Parnassus, the home of the Muses.

From highest heauen, in gladsome companee,
And with great ioy into that Citie wend,
As commonly as friend does with his frend.
Whereat he wondred much, and gan enquere,
What stately building durst so high extend
Her loftie towres vnto the starry sphere,
And what vnknowen nation there empeopled were.

57

Faire knight (quoth he) *Hierusalem* that is,
The new *Hierusalem,* that God has built
For those to dwell in, that are chosen his,
His chosen people purg'd from sinfull guilt,
With pretious bloud, which cruelly was spilt
On cursed tree, of that vnspotted lam,
That for the sinnes of all the world was kilt:
Now are they Saints all in that Citie sam,[337]
More deare vnto their God, then younglings to their dam.

58

Till now, said then the knight, I weened well,
That great *Cleopolis,* where I haue beene,
In which that fairest *Faerie Queene* doth dwell,
The fairest Citie was, that might be seene;
And that bright towre all built of christall cleene,
Panthea, seemd the brightest thing, that was:
But now by proofe all otherwise I weene;
For this great Citie that does far surpas,
And this bright Angels towre quite dims that towre of glas.

[337] together

59

Most trew, then said the holy aged man;
Yet is *Cleopolis* for earthly frame,
The fairest peece, that eye beholden can:
And well beseemes all knights of noble name,
That couet in th'immortall booke of fame
To be eternized, that same to haunt,
And doen their seruice to that soueraigne Dame,
That glorie does to them for guerdon graunt:
For she is heauenly borne, and heauen may iustly vaunt.

60

And thou faire ymp, sprong out from English race,
How euer now accompted Elfins sonne,
Well worthy doest thy seruice for her grace,
To aide a virgin desolate foredonne.
But when thou famous victorie hast wonne,
And high emongst all knights hast hong thy shield,
Thenceforth the suit of earthly conquest shonne,
And wash thy hands from guilt of bloudy field:
For bloud can nought but sin, and wars but sorrowes yield.

61

Then seeke this path, that I to thee presage,
Which after all to heauen shall thee send;
Then peaceably thy painefull pilgrimage
To yonder same *Hierusalem* do bend,
Where is for thee ordaind a blessed end:
For thou emongst those Saints, whom thou doest see,
Shalt be a Saint, and thine owne nations frend
And Patrone: thou Saint *George* shalt called bee,

Saint *George* of mery England, the signe of victoree.

62

Vnworthy wretch (quoth he) of so great grace,
How dare I thinke such glory to attaine?
These that haue it attaind, were in like cace
(Quoth he) as wretched, and liu'd in like paine.
But deeds of armes must I at last be faine,
And Ladies loue to leaue so dearely bought?
What need of armes, where peace doth ay remaine,
(Said he) and battailes none are to be fought?
As for loose loues are vaine, and vanish into nought.

63

O let me not (quoth he) then turne againe
Backe to the world, whose ioyes so fruitlesse are;
But let me here for aye in peace remaine,
Or streight way on that last long voyage fare,
That nothing may my present hope empare.
That may not be (said he) ne maist thou yit
Forgo that royall maides bequeathed care,
Who did her cause into thy hand commit,
Till from her cursed foe thou haue her freely quit.

64

Then shall I soone, (quoth he) so God me grace,
Abet that virgins cause disconsolate,
And shortly backe returne vnto this place,
To walke this way in Pilgrims poore estate.
But now aread, old father, why of late
Didst thou behight me borne of English blood,
Whom all a Faeries sonne doen nominate?
That word shall I (said he) auouchen good,
Sith to thee is vnknowne the cradle of thy brood.

65

For well I wote, thou springst from ancient race
Of *Saxon* kings, that haue with mightie hand
And many bloudie battailes fought in place
High reard their royall throne in *Britane* land,
And vanquisht them, vnable to withstand:
From thence a Faerie thee vnweeting reft,
There as thou slepst in tender swadling band,
And her base Elfin brood there for thee left.
Such men do Chaungelings call, so chaungd by Faeries theft.

66

Thence she thee brought into this Faerie lond,
And in an heaped furrow did thee hyde,
Where thee a Ploughman all vnweeting fond,
As he his toylesome teme that way did guyde,
And brought thee vp in ploughmans state to byde,
Whereof *Georgos* [338] he thee gaue to name;
Till prickt with courage, and thy forces pryde,
To Faery court thou cam'st to seeke for fame,
And proue thy puissaunt armes, as seemes thee best became.

---

338 γεωργός, farmer

67

O holy Sire (quoth he) how shall I quight
The many fauours I with thee haue found,
That hast my name and nation red aright,
And taught the way that does to heauen bound?
This said, adowne he looked to the ground,
To haue returnd, but dazed were his eyne,
Through passing brightnesse, which did quite confound
His feeble sence, and too exceeding shyne.
So darke are earthly things compard to things diuine.

68

At last whenas himselfe he gan to find,
To *Vna* back he cast him to retire;
Who him awaited still with pensiue mind.
Great thankes and goodly meed to that good syre,
He thence departing gaue for his paines hyre.
So came to *Vna,* who him ioyd to see,
And after litle rest, gan him desire,
Of her aduenture mindfull for to bee.
So leaue they take of *Cœlia,* and her daughters three.

Canto XI

The knight with that old Dragon fights
two dayes incessantly:
The third him ouerthrowes, and gayns
most glorious victory.

1

High time now gan it wex for *Vna* faire,
To thinke of those her captiue Parents deare,
And their forwasted kingdome to repaire:
Whereto whenas they now approched neare,
With hartie words her knight she gan to cheare,
And in her modest manner thus bespake;
Deare knight, as deare, as euer knight was deare,
That all these sorrowes suffer for my sake,
High heauen behold the tedious toyle, ye for me take.

2

Now are we come vnto my natiue soyle,
And to the place, where all our perils dwell;
Here haunts that feend, and does his dayly spoyle,
Therefore henceforth be at your keeping well,
And euer ready for your foeman fell:
The sparke of noble courage now awake,
And striue your excellent selfe to excell;
That shall ye euermore renowmed make,
Aboue all knights on earth, that batteill vndertake.

3

And pointing forth, lo yonder is (said she)
The brasen towre in which my parents deare
For dread of that huge feend emprisond be,
Whom I from far see on the walles appeare,
Whose sight my feeble soule doth greatly cheare:
And on the top of all I do espye
The watchman wayting tydings glad to heare,
That O my parents might I happily
Vnto you bring, to ease you of your misery.

4

With that they heard a roaring hideous sound,
That all the ayre with terrour filled wide,
And seemd vneath to shake the stedfast ground.

Eftsoones that dreadfull Dragon they espide,
Where stretcht he lay vpon the sunny side
Of a great hill, himselfe like a great hill.
But all so soone, as he from far descride
Those glistring armes, that heauen with light did fill,
He rousd himselfe full blith, and hastned them vntill.

5

Then bad the knight his Lady yede[339] aloofe,
And to an hill her selfe with draw aside,
From whence she might behold that battailles proof
And eke be safe from daunger far descryde:
She him obayd, and turnd a little wyde.
Now O thou sacred Muse,[340] most learned Dame,
Faire ympe of *Phœbus,* and his aged bride,[341]
The Nourse of time, and euerlasting fame,
That warlike hands ennoblest with immortall name;

6

O gently come into my feeble brest,
Come gently, but not with that mighty rage,
Wherewith the martiall troupes thou doest infest,
And harts of great Heroës doest enrage,
That nought their kindled courage may aswage,
Soone as thy dreadfull trompe begins to sownd;
The God of warre with his fiers equipage
Thou doest awake, sleepe neuer he so sownd,
And scared nations doest with horrour sterne astownd.

[339] pass on
[340] Clio, or Calliope
[341] Memory. The Muses were the children of Jove and Mnemosyne (Memory). Spenser, following another tradition, makes Phoebus Apollo their father.

7

Faire Goddesse lay that furious fit[342] aside,
Till I of warres and bloudy *Mars* do sing,
And Briton fields with Sarazin bloud bedyde,
Twixt that great faery Queene and Paynim king,
That with their horrour heauen and earth did ring,
A worke of labour long, and endlesse prayse:
But now a while let downe that haughtie string,
And to my tunes thy second tenor rayse,
That I this man of God his godly armes may blaze.

8

By this the dreadfull Beast drew nigh to hand,
Halfe flying, and halfe footing in his hast,
That with his largenesse measured much land,
And made wide shadow vnder his huge wast;
As mountaine doth the valley ouercast.
Approching nigh, he reared high afore
His body monstrous, horrible, and vast,
Which to increase his wondrous greatnesse more,
Was swolne with wrath, and poyson, and with bloudy gore.

9

And ouer all with brasen scales was armd,
Like plated coate of steele, so couched neare,
That nought mote perce, ne might his corse be harmd
With dint of sword, nor push of pointed speare;
Which as an Eagle, seeing pray appeare,
His aery plumes doth rouze, full rudely dight,

[342] passage of music

So shaked he, that horrour was to heare,
For as the clashing of an Armour bright,
Such noyse his rouzed scales did send vnto the knight.

10

His flaggy wings when forth he did display,
Were like two sayles, in which the hollow wynd
Is gathered full, and worketh speedy way:
And eke the pennes,[343] that did his pineons bynd,
Were like mayne-yards, with flying canuas lynd,
With which whenas him list the ayre to beat,
And there by force vnwonted passage find,
The cloudes before him fled for terrour great,
And all the heauens stood still amazed with his threat.

11

His huge long tayle wound vp in hundred foldes,
Does ouerspred his long bras-scaly backe,
Whose wreathed boughts when euer he vnfoldes,
And thick entangled knots adown does slacke,
Bespotted as with shields of red and blacke,
It sweepeth all the land behind him farre,
And of three furlongs does but little lacke;
And at the point two stings in-fixed arre,
Both deadly sharpe, that sharpest steele exceeden farre.

12

But stings and sharpest steele did far exceed
The sharpnesse of his cruell rending clawes;
Dead was it sure, as sure as death in deed,
Whateuer thing does touch his rauenous pawes,
Or what within his reach he euer drawes.
But his most hideous head my toung to tell
Does tremble: for his deepe deuouring iawes
Wide gaped, like the griesly mouth of hell,
Through which into his darke abisse all rauin fell.

13

And that more wondrous was, in either iaw
Three ranckes of yron teeth enraunged were,
In which yet trickling bloud and gobbets raw
Of late deuoured bodies did appeare,
That sight thereof bred cold congealed feare:
Which to increase, and all atonce to kill,
A cloud of smoothering smoke and sulphur seare
Out of his stinking gorge forth steemed still,
That all the ayre about with smoke and stench did fill.

14

His blazing eyes, like two bright shining shields,
Did burne with wrath, and sparkled liuing fyre;
As two broad Beacons, set in open fields,
Send forth their flames farre off to euery shyre,
And warning giue, that enemies conspyre,
With fire and sword the region to inuade;

343 feathers

So flam'd his eyne with rage and rancorous yre:
But farre within, as in a hollow glade,
Those glaring lampes were set, that made a dreadfull shade.

15

So dreadfully he towards him did pas,
Forelifting vp aloft his speckled brest,
And often bounding on the brused gras,
As for great ioyance of his newcome guest.
Eftsoones he gan aduance his haughtie crest,
As chauffed Bore his bristles doth vpreare,
And shoke his scales to battell readie drest;
That made the *Redcrosse* knight nigh quake for feare,
As bidding bold defiance to his foeman neare.

16

The knight gan fairely couch his steadie speare,
And fiercely ran at him with rigorous might.
The pointed steele arriuing rudely theare,
His harder hide would neither perce, nor bight,
But glauncing by forth passed forward right;
Yet sore amoued with so puissant push,
The wrathfull beast about him turned light,
And him so rudely passing by, did brush
With his long tayle, that horse and man to ground did rush.

17

Both horse and man vp lightly rose againe,
And fresh encounter towards him addrest:
But th'idle stroke yet backe recoyld in vaine,
And found no place his deadly point to rest.
Exceeding rage enflam'd the furious beast,
To be auenged of so great despight;
For neuer felt his imperceable brest
So wondrous force, from hand of liuing wight;
Yet had he prou'd the powre of many a puissant knight.

18

Then with his wauing wings displayed wyde,
Himselfe vp high he lifted from the ground,
And with strong flight did forcibly diuide
The yielding aire, which nigh too feeble found
Her flitting partes, and element vnsound,
To beare so great a weight: he cutting way
With his broad sayles, about him soared round:
At last low stouping with vnweldie sway,
Snatcht vp both horse and man, to beare them quite away.

19

Long he them bore aboue the subiect [344] plaine,
So farre as Ewghen bow a shaft may send,
Till struggling strong did him at last constraine,
To let them downe before his flightes end:
As hagard [345] hauke presuming to contend
With hardie fowle, aboue his hable might,
His wearie pounces [346] all in vaine doth spend,
To trusse [347] the pray too heauie for his flight;
Which comming downe to ground, does free it selfe by fight.

[344] lying beneath
[345] wild
[346] claws
[347] grip

20

He so disseized of his gryping grosse,[348]
The knight his thrillant speare againe assayd
In his bras-plated body to embosse,
And three mens strength vnto the stroke he layd;
Wherewith the stiffe beame quaked, as affrayd,
And glauncing from his scaly necke, did glyde
Close vnder his left wing, then broad displayd.
The percing steele there wrought a wound full wyde,
That with the vncouth [349] smart the Monster lowdly cryde.

21

He cryde, as raging seas are wont to rore,
When wintry storme his wrathfull wreck does threat,
The rolling billowes beat the ragged shore,
As they the earth would shoulder from her seat,
And greedie gulfe does gape, as he would eat
His neighbour element in his reuenge:
Then gin the blustring brethren boldly threat,
To moue the world from off his stedfast henge,
And boystrous battell make, each other to auenge.

22

The steely head stucke fast still in his flesh,
Till with his cruell clawes he snatcht the wood,
And quite a sunder broke. Forth flowed fresh
A gushing riuer of blacke goarie blood,
That drowned all the land, whereon he stood;
The streame thereof would driue a water-mill.
Trebly augmented was his furious mood
With bitter sense of his deepe rooted ill,
That flames of fire he threw forth from his large nosethrill.

23

His hideous tayle then hurled he about,
And therewith all enwrapt the nimble thyes
Of his froth-fomy steed, whose courage stout
Striuing to loose the knot, that fast him tyes,
Himselfe in streighter bandes too rash implyes,
That to the ground he is perforce constraynd
To throw his rider: who can quickly ryse
From off the earth, with durty bloud distaynd,[350]
For that reprochfull fall right fowly he disdaynd.

24

And fiercely tooke his trenchand blade in hand,
With which he stroke so furious and so fell,
That nothing seemd the puissance could withstand:
Vpon his crest the hardned yron fell,
But his more hardned crest was armd so well,
That deeper dint therein it would not make;
Yet so extremely did the buffe him quell,
That from thenceforth he shund the like to take,
But when he saw them come, he did them still [351] forsake.

25

The knight was wrath to see his stroke beguyld,

---

348 heavy
349 unaccustomed
350 stained
351 ever

And smote againe with more outrageous might;
But backe againe the sparckling steele recoyld,
And left not any marke, where it did light;
As if in Adamant rocke it had bene pight.
The beast impatient of his smarting wound,
And of so fierce and forcible despight,
Thought with his wings to stye [352] aboue the ground;
But his late wounded wing vnseruiceable found.

26

Then full of griefe and anguish vehement,
He lowdly brayd, that like was neuer heard,
And from his wide deuouring ouen sent
A flake of fire, that flashing in his beard,
Him all amazd, and almost made affeard:
The scorching flame sore swinged [353] all his face,
And through his armour all his bodie seard,
That he could not endure so cruell cace,
But thought his armes to leaue, and helmet to vnlace.

27

Not that great Champion [354] of the antique world,
Whom famous Poetes verse so much doth vaunt,
And hath for twelue huge labours high extold,
So many furies and sharpe fits did haunt,
When him the poysoned garment did enchaunt
With *Centaures* bloud, and bloudie verses charm'd,
As did this knight twelue thousand dolours daunt,
Whom fyrie steele now burnt, that earst him arm'd,
That erst him goodly arm'd, now most of all him harm'd.

28

Faint, wearie, sore, emboyled, grieued, brent
With heat, toyle, wounds, armes, smart, and inward fire
That neuer man such mischiefes did torment;
Death better were, death did he oft desire,
But death will neuer come, when needes require.
Whom so dismayd when that his foe beheld,
He cast to suffer him no more respire,
But gan his sturdie sterne about to weld,
And him so strongly stroke, that to the ground him feld.

29

It fortuned (as faire it then befell)
Behind his backe vnweeting, where he stood,
Of auncient time there was a springing well,
From which fast trickled forth a siluer flood,
Full of great vertues, and for med'cine good.
Whylome, before that cursed Dragon got
That happie land, and all with innocent blood
Defyld those sacred waues, it rightly hot [355]
The well of life, ne yet his vertues had forgot.

30

For vnto life the dead it could restore,
And guilt of sinfull crimes cleane wash away,
Those that with sicknesse were infected sore,
It could recure, and aged long decay

[352] mount [353] burnt [354] Hercules

[355] was called

Renew, as one were borne that very day.
But *Silo*[356] this, and *Iordan* did excell,
And th'English *Bath,* and eke the German *Spau,*
Ne can *Cephise,* nor *Hebrus*[357] match this well:
Into the same the knight backe ouerthrowen, fell.

31

Now gan the golden *Phœbus* for to steepe
His fierie face in billowes of the west,
And his faint steedes watred in Ocean deepe,
Whiles from their iournall labours they did rest,
When that infernall Monster, hauing kest
His wearie foe into that liuing well,
Can high aduance his broad discoloured brest,
Aboue his wonted pitch, with countenance fell,
And clapt his yron wings, as victor he did dwell.

32

Which when his pensiue Ladie saw from farre,
Great woe and sorrow did her soule assay,
As weening that the sad ende of the warre,
And gan to highest God entirely pray,
That feared chance from her to turne away;
With folded hands and knees full lowly bent
All night she watcht, ne once adowne would lay
Her daintie limbs in her sad dreriment,
But praying still did wake, and waking did lament.

33

The morrow next gan early to appeare,
That *Titan* rose to runne his daily race;
But early ere the morrow next gan reare
Out of the sea faire *Titans* deawy face,
Vp rose the gentle virgin from her place,
And looked all about, if she might spy
Her loued knight to moue his manly pace:
For she had great doubt of his safety,
Since late she saw him fall before his enemy.

34

At last she saw, where he vpstarted braue
Out of the well, wherein he drenched lay;
As Eagle fresh out of the Ocean waue,
Where he hath left his plumes all hoary gray,
And deckt himselfe with feathers youthly gay,
Like Eyas hauke vp mounts vnto the skies,
His newly budded pineons to assay,
And marueiles at himselfe, still as he flies:
So new this new-borne knight to battell new did rise.

35

Whom when the damned feend so fresh did spy,
No wonder if he wondred at the sight,
And doubted, whether his late enemy
It were, or other new supplied knight.
He, now to proue his late renewed might,
High brandishing his bright deaw-burning blade,
Vpon his crested scalpe so sore did smite,
That to the scull a yawning wound it made:
The deadly dint his dulled senses all dismaid.

36

I wote not, whether the reuenging steele
Were hardned with that holy water dew,
Wherein he fell, or sharper edge did feele,

[356] The pool of Siloam (*St. John*, ix, 7).
[357] Cephisus is a river near Athens; Hebrus a river in Thrace.

Or his baptized hands now greater grew;
Or other secret vertue did ensew;
Else neuer could the force of fleshly arme,
Ne molten mettall in his bloud embrew:[358]
For till that stownd could neuer wight him harme,
By subtilty, nor slight, nor might, nor mighty charme.

37

The cruell wound enraged him so sore,
That loud he yelled for exceeding paine;
As hundred ramping Lyons seem'd to rore,
Whom rauenous hunger did thereto constraine:
Then gan he tosse aloft his stretched traine,
And therewith scourge the buxome[359] aire so sore,
That to his force to yeelden it was faine;
Ne ought his sturdie strokes might stand afore,
That high trees ouerthrew, and rocks in peeces tore.

38

The same aduauncing high aboue his head,
With sharpe intended[360] sting so rude him smot,
That to the earth him droue, as stricken dead,
Ne liuing wight would haue him life behot:[361]
The mortall sting his angry needle shot
Quite through his shield, and in his shoulder seasd,
Where fast it stucke, ne would there out be got:
The griefe thereof him wondrous sore diseasd,
Ne might his ranckling paine with patience be appeasd.

39

But yet more mindfull of his honour deare,
Then of the grieuous smart, which him did wring,
From loathed soile he can him lightly reare,
And stroue to loose the farre infixed sting:
Which when in vaine he tryde with struggeling,
Inflam'd with wrath, his raging blade he heft,
And strooke so strongly, that the knotty string
Of his huge taile he quite a sunder cleft,
Fiue ioynts thereof he hewd, and but the stump him left.

40

Hart cannot thinke, what outrage, and what cryes,
With foule enfouldred[362] smoake and flashing fire,
The hel-bred beast threw forth vnto the skyes,
That all was couered with darknesse dire:
Then fraught with rancour, and engorged ire,
He cast at once him to auenge for all,
And gathering vp himselfe out of the mire,
With his vneuen wings did fiercely fall
Vpon his sunne-bright shield, and gript it fast withall.

41

Much was the man encombred with his hold,
In feare to lose his weapon in his paw,
Ne wist yet, how his talants to vnfold;
Nor harder was from *Cerberus* greedie iaw
To plucke a bone, then from his cruell claw
To reaue by strength the griped gage away:

[358] plunge
[359] yielding
[360] extended
[361] promised
[362] hurled like thunder

Thrise he assayd it from his foot to draw,
And thrise in vaine to draw it did assay,
It booted nought to thinke, to robbe him of his pray.

42

Tho when he saw no power might preuaile,
His trustie sword he cald to his last aid,
Wherewith he fiercely did his foe assaile,
And double blowes about him stoutly laid,
That glauncing fire out of the yron plaid;
As sparckles from the Anduile vse to fly,
When heauie hammers on the wedge are swaid;
Therewith at last he forst him to vnty
One of his grasping feete, him to defend thereby.

43

The other foot, fast fixed on his shield,
Whenas no strength, nor stroks mote him constraine
To loose, ne yet the warlike pledge to yield,
He smot thereat with all his might and maine,
That nought so wondrous puissance might sustaine;
Vpon the ioynt the lucky steele did light,
And made such way, that hewd it quite in twaine;
The paw yet missed not his minisht might,
But hong still on the shield, as it at first was pight.

44

For griefe thereof, and diuelish despight,
From his infernall fournace forth he threw
Huge flames, that dimmed all the heauens light,
Enrold in duskish smoke and brimstone blew;
As burning *Aetna* from his boyling stew
Doth belch out flames, and rockes in peeces broke,
And ragged ribs of mountaines molten new,
Enwrapt in coleblacke clouds and filthy smoke,
That all the land with stench, and heauen with horror choke.

45

The heate whereof, and harmefull pestilence
So sore him noyd, that forst him to retire
A little backward for his best defence,
To saue his bodie from the scorching fire,
Which he from hellish entrailes did expire.
It chaunst (eternall God that chaunce did guide)
As he recoyled backward, in the mire
His nigh forwearied feeble feet did slide,
And downe he fell, with dread of shame sore terrifide.

46

There grew a goodly tree him faire beside,
Loaden with fruit and apples rosie red,
As they in pure vermilion had beene dide,
Whereof great vertues ouer all were red:
For happie life to all, which thereon fed,
And life eke euerlasting did befall:
Great God it planted in that blessed sted
With his almightie hand, and did it call
The tree of life, the crime of our first fathers fall.

47

In all the world like was not to be found,
Saue in that soile, where all good things did grow,
And freely sprong out of the fruitfull ground,
As incorrupted Nature did them sow,

Till that dread Dragon all did ouerthrow.
Another like faire tree eke grew thereby,
Whereof who so did eat, eftsoones did know
Both good and ill: O mornefull memory:
That tree through one mans fault hath doen vs all to dy.

48

From that first tree forth flowd, as from a well,
A trickling streame of Balme, most soueraine
And daintie deare,[363] which on the ground still fell,
And ouerflowed all the fertill plaine,
As it had deawed bene with timely raine:
Life and long health that gratious ointment gaue,
And deadly woundes could heale, and reare againe
The senselesse corse appointed for the graue.
Into that same he fell: which did from death him saue.

49

For nigh thereto the euer damned beast
Durst not approch, for he was deadly made,[364]
And all that life preserued, did detest:
Yet he it oft aduentur'd to inuade.
By this the drouping day-light gan to fade,
And yeeld his roome to sad succeeding night,
Who with her sable mantle gan to shade
The face of earth, and wayes of liuing wight,
And high her burning torch set vp in heauen bright.

50

When gentle *Vna* saw the second fall
Of her deare knight, who wearie of long fight,
And faint through losse of bloud, mou'd not at all,
But lay as in a dreame of deepe delight,
Besmeard with pretious Balme, whose vertuous might
Did heale his wounds, and scorching heat alay,
Againe she stricken was with sore affright,
And for his safetie gan deuoutly pray;
And watch the noyous night, and wait for ioyous day.

51

The ioyous day gan early to appeare,
And faire *Aurora* from the deawy bed
Of aged *Tithone* gan her selfe to reare,
With rosie cheekes, for shame as blushing red;
Her golden lockes for haste were loosely shed
About her eares, when *Vna* her did marke
Clymbe to her charet, all with flowers spred,
From heauen high to chase the chearelesse darke:
With merry note her loud salutes the mounting larke.

52

Then freshly vp arose the doughtie knight,
All healed of his hurts and woundes wide,
And did himselfe to battell readie dight;
Whose early foe awaiting him beside
To haue deuourd, so soone as day he spyde,
When now he saw himselfe so freshly reare,
As if late fight had nought him damnifyde,
He woxe dismayd, and gan his fate to feare;
Nathlesse with wonted rage he him aduanced neare.

363 very delicate

364 born of death

53

And in his first encounter, gaping wide,
He thought attonce him to haue swallowd quight,
And rusht vpon him with outragious pride;
Who him r'encountring fierce, as hauke in flight,
Perforce rebutted backe. The weapon bright
Taking aduantage of his open iaw,
Ran through his mouth with so importune might,
That deepe emperst his darksome hollow maw,
And back retyrd, his life bloud forth with all did draw.

54

So downe he fell, and forth his life did breath,
That vanisht into smoke and cloudes swift;
So downe he fell, that th'earth him vnderneath
Did grone, as feeble so great load to lift;
So downe he fell, as an huge rockie clift,
Whose false foundation waues haue wast away,
With dreadfull poyse[365] is from the mayneland rift,
And rolling downe, great *Neptune* doth dismay;
So downe he fell, and like an heaped mountaine lay.

55

The knight himselfe euen trembled at his fall,
So huge and horrible a masse it seem'd;
And his deare Ladie, that beheld it all,
Durst not approch for dread, which she misdeem'd,
But yet at last, when as the direfull feend
She saw not stirre, off-shaking vaine affright,
She nigher drew, and saw that ioyous end:
Then God she praysd, and thankt her faithfull knight,
That had atchieu'd so great a conquest by his might.

[365] force

Canto XII

Faire Vna to the Redcrosse knight
betrouthed is with ioy:
Though false Duessa it to barre
her false sleights doe imploy.

1

Behold I see the hauen nigh at hand,
To which I meane my wearie course to bend;
Vere the maine shete, and bare vp with the land,
The which afore is fairely to be kend,[366]
And seemeth safe from stormes, that may offend;
There this faire virgin wearie of her way
Must landed be, now at her iourneyes end:
There eke my feeble barke a while may stay,
Till merry wind and weather call her thence away.

2

Scarsely had *Phœbus* in the glooming East
Yet harnessed his firie-footed teeme,
Ne reard aboue the earth his flaming creast,
When the last deadly smoke aloft did steeme,
That signe of last outbreathed life did seeme
Vnto the watchman on the castle wall;
Who thereby dead that balefull Beast did deeme,
And to his Lord and Ladie lowd gan call,
To tell, how he had seene the Dragons fatall fall.

[366] known

3

Vprose with hastie ioy, and feeble speed
That aged Sire, the Lord of all that land,
And looked forth, to weet, if true indeede
Those tydings were, as he did vnderstand,
Which whenas true by tryall he out fond,
He bad to open wyde his brazen gate,
Which long time had bene shut, and out of hond[367]
Proclaymed ioy and peace through all his state;
For dead now was their foe, which them forrayed late.

4

Then gan triumphant Trompets sound on hie,
That sent to heauen the ecchoed report
Of their new ioy, and happie victorie
Gainst him, that had them long opprest with tort,[368]
And fast imprisoned in sieged fort.
Then all the people, as in solemne feast,
To him assembled with one full consort,
Reioycing at the fall of that great beast,
From whose eternall bondage now they were releast.

5

Forth came that auncient Lord and aged Queene,
Arayd in antique robes downe to the ground,
And sad habiliments right well beseene;
A noble crew about them waited round
Of sage and sober Peres, all grauely gownd;
Whom farre before did march a goodly band
Of tall young men, all hable armes to sownd,[369]
But now they laurell braunches bore in hand;
Glad signe of victorie and peace in all their land.

6

Vnto that doughtie Conquerour they came,
And him before themselues prostrating low,
Their Lord and Patrone loud did him proclame,
And at his feet their laurell boughes did throw.
Soone after them all dauncing on a row
The comely virgins came, with girlands dight,
As fresh as flowres in medow greene do grow,
When morning deaw vpon their leaues doth light:
And in their hands sweet Timbrels all vpheld on hight.

7

And them before, the fry of children young
Their wanton sports and childish mirth did play,
And to the Maydens sounding tymbrels sung
In well attuned notes, a ioyous lay,
And made delightfull musicke all the way,
Vntill they came, where that faire virgin stood;
As faire *Diana* in fresh sommers day
Beholds her Nymphes, enraung'd in shadie wood,
Some wrestle, some do run, some bathe in christall flood.

8

So she beheld those maydens meriment
With chearefull vew; who when to her they came,
Themselues to ground with gratious humblesse bent,
And her ador'd by honorable name,
Lifting to heauen her euerlasting fame:

[367] immediately
[368] wrong
[369] bear

Then on her head they set a girland greene,
And crowned her twixt earnest and twixt game;
Who in her selfe-resemblance well beseene,
Did seeme such, as she was, a goodly maiden Queene.

9

And after, all the raskall many [370] ran,
Heaped together in rude rablement,
To see the face of that victorious man:
Whom all admired, as from heauen sent,
And gazd vpon with gaping wonderment.
But when they came, where that dead Dragon lay,
Stretcht on the ground in monstrous large extent,
The sight with idle feare did them dismay,
Ne durst approch him nigh, to touch, or once assay.

10

Some feard, and fled; some feard and well it faynd;
One that would wiser seeme, then all the rest,
Warnd him not touch, for yet perhaps remaynd
Some lingring life within his hollow brest,
Or in his wombe might lurke some hidden nest
Of many Dragonets, his fruitfull seed;
Another said, that in his eyes did rest
Yet sparckling fire, and bad thereof take heed;
Another said, he saw him moue his eyes indeed.

11

One mother, when as her foolehardie chyld
Did come too neare, and with his talants play,
Halfe dead through feare, her litle babe reuyld,
And to her gossips gan in counsell say;
How can I tell, but that his talants may
Yet scratch my sonne, or rend his tender hand?
So diuersly themselues in vaine they fray; [371]
Whiles some more bold, to measure him nigh stand,
To proue how many acres he did spread of land.

12

Thus flocked all the folke him round about,
The whiles that hoarie king, with all his traine,
Being arriued, where that champion stout
After his foes defeasance did remaine,
Him goodly greetes, and faire does entertaine,
With princely gifts of yourie and gold,
And thousand thankes him yeelds for all his paine.
Then when his daughter deare he does behold,
Her dearely doth imbrace, and kisseth manifold.

13

And after to his Pallace he them brings,
With shaumes, and trompets, and with Clarions sweet;
And all the way the ioyous people sings,
And with their garments strowes the paued street:
Whence mounting vp, they find purueyance meet
Of all, that royall Princes court became,
And all the floore was vnderneath their feet
Bespred with costly scarlot of great name,[372]
On which they lowly sit, and fitting purpose frame.

---

[370] common herd

[371] frighten

[372] value

14

What needs me tell their feast and goodly guize,
In which was nothing riotous nor vaine?
What needs of daintie dishes to deuize,
Of comely seruices, or courtly trayne?
My narrow leaues cannot in them containe
The large discourse of royall Princes state.
Yet was their manner then but bare and plaine:
For th'antique world excesse and pride did hate;
Such proud luxurious pompe is swollen vp but late.

15

Then when with meates and drinkes of euery kinde
Their feruent appetites they quenched had,
That auncient Lord gan fit occasion finde,
Of straunge aduentures, and of perils sad,
Which in his trauell him befallen had,
For to demaund of his renowmed guest:
Who then with vtt'rance, graue, and count'nance sad,
From point to point, as is before exprest,
Discourst his voyage long, according his request.

16

Great pleasure mixt with pittifull regard,
That godly King and Queene did passionate,[373]
Whiles they his pittifull aduentures heard,
That oft they did lament his lucklesse state,
And often blame the too importune fate,
That heapd on him so many wrathfull wreakes:
For neuer gentle knight, as he of late,
So tossed was in fortunes cruell freakes;
And all the while salt teares bedeawd the hearers cheaks.

17

Then said that royall Pere in sober wise;
Deare Sonne, great beene the euils, which ye bore
From first to last in your late enterprise,
That I note,[374] whether prayse, or pitty more:
For neuer liuing man, I weene, so sore
In sea of deadly daungers was distrest;
But since now safe ye seised haue the shore,
And well arriued are, (high God be blest)
Let vs deuize of ease and euerlasting rest.

18

Ah dearest Lord, said then that doughty knight,
Of ease or rest I may not yet deuize,
For by the faith, which I to armes haue plight,
I bounden am streight after this emprize,
As that your daughter can ye well aduize,
Backe to returne to that great Faerie Queene,
And her to serue six yeares in warlike wize,
Gainst that proud Paynim king, that workes her teene:
Therefore I ought craue pardon, till I there haue beene.

19

Vnhappie falles that hard necessitie,
(Quoth he) the troubler of my happie peace,
And vowed foe of my felicitie;
Ne I against the same can iustly preace:[375]
But since that band ye cannot now release,

[373] express with feeling

[374] ne wot, *i.e.*, know not
[375] press

Nor doen vndo; (for vowes may not be vaine)
Soone as the terme of those six yeares shall cease,
Ye then shall hither backe returne againe,
The marriage to accomplish vowd betwixt you twain.

20

Which for my part I couet to performe,
In sort as through the world I did proclame,
That who so kild that monster most deforme,
And him in hardy battaile ouercame,
Should haue mine onely daughter to his Dame,[376]
And of my kingdome heire apparaunt bee:
Therefore since now to thee perteines the same,
By dew desert of noble cheualree,
Both daughter and eke kingdome, lo I yield to thee.

21

Then forth he called that his daughter faire,
The fairest *Vn'* his onely daughter deare,
His onely daughter, and his onely heyre;
Who forth proceeding with sad sober cheare,
As bright as doth the morning starre appeare
Out of the East, with flaming lockes bedight,
To tell that dawning day is drawing neare,
And to the world does bring long wished light;
So faire and fresh that Lady shewd her selfe in sight.

22

So faire and fresh, as freshest flowre in May;
For she had layd her mournefull stole aside,
And widow-like sad wimple throwne away,
Wherewith her heauenly beautie she did hide,
Whiles on her wearie iourney she did ride;
And on her now a garment she did weare,
All lilly white, withoutten spot, or pride,
That seemd like silke and siluer wouen neare,[377]
But neither silke nor siluer therein did appeare.

23

The blazing brightnesse of her beauties beame,
And glorious light of her sunshyny face
To tell, were as to striue against the streame.
My ragged rimes are all too rude and bace,
Her heauenly lineaments for to enchace.
Ne wonder; for her owne deare loued knight,
All were she dayly with himselfe in place,
Did wonder much at her celestiall sight:
Oft had he seene her faire, but neuer so faire dight.

24

So fairely dight, when she in presence came,
She to her Sire made humble reuerence,
And bowed low, that her right well became,
And added grace vnto her excellence:
Who with great wisedome, and graue eloquence
Thus gan to say. But eare he thus had said,
With flying speede, and seeming great pretence,

[376] as his wife

[377] closely

Came running in, much like a man dismaid,
A Messenger with letters, which his message said.

25

All in the open hall amazed stood,
At suddeinnesse of that vnwarie sight,
And wondred at his breathlesse hastie mood.
But he for nought would stay his passage right[378]
Till fast before the king he did alight;
Where falling flat, great humblesse he did make,
And kist the ground, whereon his foot was pight;[379]
Then to his hands that writ he did betake,
Which he disclosing, red thus, as the paper spake.

26

To thee, most mighty king of *Eden* faire,
Her greeting sends in these sad lines addrest,
The wofull daughter, and forsaken heire
Of that great Emperour[380] of all the West;
And bids thee be aduized for the best,
Ere thou thy daughter linck in holy band
Of wedlocke to that new vnknowen guest:
For he already plighted his right hand
Vnto another loue, and to another land.

27

To me sad mayd, or rather widow sad,
He was affiaunced long time before,
And sacred pledges he both gaue, and had,
False erraunt knight, infamous, and forswore:
Witnesse the burning Altars, which he swore,
And guiltie heauens of his bold periury,
Which though he hath polluted oft of yore,
Yet I to them for iudgement iust do fly,
And them coniure t'auenge this shamefull iniury.

28

Therefore since mine he is, or free or bond,
Or false or trew, or liuing or else dead,
Withhold, O soueraine Prince, your hasty hond
From knitting league with him, I you aread;
Ne weene my right with strength adowne to tread,
Through weakenesse of my widowhed, or woe:
For truth is strong, her rightfull cause to plead,
And shall find friends, if need requireth soe,
So bids thee well to fare, Thy neither friend, nor foe, *Fidessa.*

29

When he these bitter byting words had red,
The tydings straunge did him abashed make,
That still he sate long time astonished
As in great muse, ne word to creature spake.
At last his solemne silence thus he brake,
With doubtfull eyes fast fixed on his guest;
Redoubted knight, that for mine onely sake
Thy life and honour late aduenturest,
Let nought be hid from me, that ought to be exprest.

30

What meane these bloudy vowes, and idle threats,
Throwne out from womanish impatient mind?
What heauens? what altars? what enraged heates

378 forward   379 placed   380 the Pope

Here heaped vp with termes of loue vnkind,
My conscience cleare with guilty bands would bind?
High God be witnesse, that I guiltlesse ame.
But if your selfe, Sir knight, ye faultie find,
Or wrapped be in loues of former Dame,
With crime do not it couer, but disclose the same.

31

To whom the *Redcrosse* knight this answere sent,
My Lord, my King, be nought hereat dismayd,
Till well ye wote by graue intendiment,[381]
What woman, and wherefore doth me vpbrayd
With breach of loue, and loyalty betrayd.
It was in my mishaps, as hitherward
I lately traueild, that vnwares I strayd
Out of my way, through perils straunge and hard;
That day should faile me, ere I had them all declard.

32

There did I find, or rather I was found
Of this false woman, that *Fidessa* hight,
Fidessa hight the falsest Dame on ground,
Most false *Duessa,* royall richly dight,
That easie was t' inuegle weaker sight:
Who by her wicked arts, and wylie skill,
Too false and strong for earthly skill or might,
Vnwares me wrought vnto her wicked will,
And to my foe betrayd, when least I feared ill.

33

Then stepped forth the goodly royall Mayd,
And on the ground her selfe prostrating low,
With sober countenaunce thus to him sayd;
O pardon me, my soueraigne Lord, to show
The secret treasons, which of late I know
To haue bene wroght by that false sorceresse.
She onely she it is, that earst did throw
This gentle knight into so great distresse,
That death him did awaite in dayly wretchednesse.

34

And now it seems, that she suborned hath
This craftie messenger with letters vaine,
To worke new woe and improuided[382] scath,
By breaking of the band betwixt vs twaine;
Wherein she vsed hath the practicke paine
Of this false footman, clokt with simplenesse,
Whom if ye please for to discouer plaine,
Ye shall him *Archimago* find, I ghesse,
The falsest man aliue; who tries shall find no lesse.

35

The king was greatly moued at her speach,
And all with suddein indignation fraight,[383]
Bad on that Messenger rude hands to reach.
Eftsoones the Gard, which on his state did wait,
Attacht that faitor[384] false, and bound him strait:
Who seeming sorely chauffed at his band,
As chained Beare, whom cruell dogs do bait,
With idle force did faine them to withstand,

[381] attention

[382] unforeseen

[383] fraught

[384] deceiver

And often semblaunce made to scape out of their hand.

36

But they him layd full low in dungeon deepe,
And bound him hand and foote with yron chains.
And with continuall watch did warely keepe;
Who then would thinke, that by his subtile trains
He could escape fowle death or deadly paines?
Thus when that Princes wrath was pacifide,
He gan renew the late forbidden banes,[385]
And to the knight his daughter deare he tyde,
With sacred rites and vowes for euer to abyde.

37

His owne two hands the holy knots did knit,
That none but death for euer can deuide;
His owne two hands, for such a turne most fit,
The housling [386] fire did kindle and prouide,
And holy water thereon sprinckled wide;
At which the bushy Teade [387] a groome did light,
And sacred lampe in secret chamber hide,
Where it should not be quenched day nor night,
For feare of euill fates, but burnen euer bright.

38

Then gan they sprinckle all the posts with wine,
And made great feast to solemnize that day;
They all perfumde with frankencense diuine,
And precious odours fetcht from far away,
That all the house did sweat with great aray:
And all the while sweete Musicke did apply
Her curious skill, the warbling notes to play,
To driue away the dull Melancholy;
The whiles one sung a song of loue and iollity.

39

During the which there was an heauenly noise
Heard sound through all the Pallace pleasantly,
Like as it had bene many an Angels voice,
Singing before th'eternall maiesty,
In their trinall triplicities [388] on hye;
Yet wist no creature, whence that heauenly sweet
Proceeded, yet each one felt secretly
Himselfe thereby reft of his sences meet,
And rauished with rare impression in his sprite.

40

Great ioy was made that day of young and old,
And solemne feast proclaimd throughout the land,
That their exceeding merth may not be told:
Suffice it heare by signes to vnderstand
The vsuall ioyes at knitting of loues band.
Thrise happy man the knight himselfe did hold,
Possessed of his Ladies hart and hand,
And euer, when his eye did her behold,
His heart did seeme to melt in pleasures manifold.

41

Her ioyous presence and sweet company
In full content he there did long enioy,

[385] marriage banns [386] sacramental [387] torch

[388] The nine Orders of the Angels.

Ne wicked enuie, ne vile gealosy
His deare delights were able to annoy:
Yet swimming in that sea of blisfull ioy,
He nought forgot, how he whilome had sworne,
In case he could that monstrous beast destroy,
Vnto his Farie Queene backe to returne:
The which he shortly did, and *Vna* left to mourne.

42

Now strike your sailes ye iolly Mariners,
For we be come vnto a quiet rode,[389]
Where we must land some of our passengers,
And light this wearie vessell of her lode.
Here she a while may make her safe abode,
Till she repaired haue her tackles spent,
And wants supplide. And then againe abroad
On the long voyage whereto she is bent:
Well may she speede and fairely finish her intent.

[389] anchorage

Michael Drayton

1563–1631

IDEA [1]

XX

An evil spirit, your beauty, haunts me still,
Wherewith, alas, I have been long possessed,
Which ceaseth not to tempt me to each ill,
Nor gives me once but one poor minute's rest;
In me it speaks, whether I sleep or wake,
And when by means to drive it out I try,
With greater torments then it me doth take,
And tortures me in most extremity;
Before my face it lays down my despairs,
And hastes me on unto a sudden death,
Now tempting me to drown myself in tears,
And then in sighing to give up my breath.
Thus am I still provoked to every evil
By this good wicked spirit, sweet angel devil.

XXIV

I hear some say, this man is not in love,
Who, can he love? a likely thing they say;
Read but his verse, and it will easily prove;
O judge not rashly (gentle Sir) I pray,
Because I loosely trifle in this sort,
As one that fain his sorrows would beguile:
You now suppose me all this time in sport,
And please yourself with this conceit the while.
You shallow censors, sometimes see you not
In greatest perils some men pleasant be,
Where fame by death is only to be got,
They resolute? so stands the case with me;
Where other men, in depth of passion cry,
I laugh at fortune, as in jest to die.

XXIX

When conquering love did first my heart assail,
Unto mine aid I summoned every sense,
Doubting,[2] if that proud tyrant should prevail,
My heart should suffer for mine eyes offence;
But he with beauty first corrupted sight,
My hearing bribed with her tongue's harmony,
My taste, by her sweet lips drawn with delight,
My smelling won with her breath's spicery;
But when my touching came to play his part,
(The king of senses, greater than the rest)

[1] Drayton's sonnets went through many editions. The best text is that of 1619.

[2] fearing

He yields love up the keys unto my heart,
And tells the other how they should be blest;
And thus by those of whom I hoped for aid,
To cruel love my soul was first betrayed.

XXXVII

Dear, why should you command me to my rest,
When now the night doth summon all to sleep?
Methinks this time becometh lovers best;
Night was ordained together friends to keep.
How happy are all other living things,
Which though the day disjoin by sev'ral flight,
The quiet evening yet together brings,
And each returns unto his love at night!
O thou that art so courteous else to all,
Why shouldst thou, Night, abuse me only thus,
That ev'ry creature to his kind dost call,
And yet 'tis thou dost only sever us?
Well could I wish it would be ever day,
If when night comes you bid me go away.

LXI

Since there's no help, come let us kiss and part;
Nay, I have done, you get no more of me,
And I am glad, yea glad with all my heart
That thus so cleanly I myself can free;
Shake hands forever, cancel all our vows,
And when we meet at any time again,
Be it not seen in either of our brows
That we one jot of former love retain.
Now at the last gasp of love's latest breath,
When, his pulse failing, passion speechless lies,
When faith is kneeling by his bed of death,
And innocence is closing up his eyes,
Now if thou wouldst, when all have given him over,
From death to life thou mightst him yet recover.

The Crier

Good folk, for gold or hire,
But help me to a crier;
For my poor heart is run astray
After two eyes that passed this way.
Oyes,[3] oyes, oyes,
If there be any man
In town or country can
Bring me my heart again,
I'll please him for his pain;
And by these marks I will you show
That only I this heart do owe.[4]
It is a wounded heart,
Wherein yet sticks the dart;
Ev'ry piece sore hurt throughout it,
Faith and troth writ round about it;
It was a tame heart, and a dear,
And never used to roam;
But having got this haunt, I fear
'Twill hardly stay at home.
For God's sake, walking by the way,
If you my heart do see,
Either impound it for a stray,
Or send it back to me.

The Ninth Eclogue[5]

Batt. Gorbo, as thou cam'st this way
By yonder little hill,
Or as thou through the fields didst stray,
Saw'st thou my Daffodil?

She's in a frock of Lincoln green,
Which colour likes her sight,
And never hath her beauty seen
But through a veil of white;

Than roses, richer to behold,
That trim up lovers' bowers,
The pansy and the marigold,
Though Phœbus' paramours.

Gorbo. Thou well describ'st the daffodill;
It is not full an hour
Since by the spring, near yonder hill,
I saw that lovely flower.

---

[3] The word with which the court crier summons court.
[4] own
[5] Drayton's *Eclogues*, first published in 1606, were an expansion of his *Idea, the Shepherd's Garland* of 1593.

Batt. Yet my fair flower thou didst not meet,
Nor news of her didst bring,
And yet my Daffodil's more sweet
Than that by yonder spring.

Gorbo. I saw a shepherd that doth keep
In yonder field of lilies,
Was making, as he fed his sheep,
A wreath of daffodillies.

Batt. Yet, Gorbo, thou delud'st me still,
My flower thou didst not see,
For know, my pretty Daffodil
Is worn of none but me.

To show itself but near her seat
No lily is so bold,
Except to shade her from the heat,
Or keep her from the cold.

Gorbo. Through yonder vale as I did pass,
Descending from the hill,
I met a smirking bonny lass,
They call her Daffodil;

Whose presence, as along she went,
The pretty flowers did greet,
As though their heads they downward bent
With homage to her feet.

And all the shepherds that were nigh,
From top of every hill,
Unto the valleys loud did cry,
There goes sweet Daffodil.

Batt. Ay, gentle shepherd, now with joy
Thou all my flocks dost fill,
That's she alone, kind shepherd's boy,
Let us to Daffodil.

To the Virginian Voyage[6]

You brave heroic minds
Worthy your country's name,
That honour still pursue,
Go, and subdue,
Whilst loit'ring hinds
Lurk here at home, with shame.

Britons, you stay too long;
Quickly aboard bestow you,
And with a merry gale
Swell your stretched sail,
With vows as strong
As the winds that blow you.

Your course securely steer,
West and by south forth keep,
Rocks, lee-shores, nor shoals,
When Æolus scowls,
You need not fear,
So absolute the deep.

And cheerfully at sea,
Success you still entice,
To get the pearl and gold,
And ours to hold,
Virginia,
Earth's only paradise,

Where nature hath in store
Fowl, venison, and fish,
And the fruitful'st soil
Without your toil
Three harvests more,
All greater than your wish.

And the ambitious vine
Crowns with his purple mass,
The cedar reaching high
To kiss the sky,
The cypress, pine,
And useful sassafras.

To whom the golden age
Still nature's laws doth give,
No other cares that tend,
But them to defend
From winter's age,
That long there doth not live.

Whenas the luscious smell
Of that delicious land,

[6] First published in 1606. The preparations made by the London Company in 1606 for the colonizing of Virginia were eagerly followed by the poets. The new lands, teeming with every kind of riches, promised an earthly paradise.

Above the seas that flows,
The clear wind throws,
Your hearts to swell
Approaching the dear strand,

In kenning of the shore,
(Thanks to God first given,)
O you, the happi'st men,
Be frolic then,
Let cannons roar,
Frighting the wide heaven.

And in regions far
Such heroes bring ye forth
As those from whom we came,
And plant our name
Under that star
Not known unto our north.

And as there plenty grows
Of laurel everywhere,
Apollo's sacred tree,
You it may see
A poet's brows
To crown, that may sing there.

Thy voyages attend,
Industrious Hakluyt,[7]
Whose reading shall enflame
Men to seek fame,
And much commend
To after-times thy wit.

To my most dearly-loved friend, Henry Reynolds, Esquire, of Poets and Poesy[8]

My dearly lovéd friend, how oft have we
In winter evenings, meaning to be free,
To some well-chosen place used to retire,
And there with moderate meat,[9] and wine, and fire,
Have passed the hours contentedly with chat;
Now talked of this, and then discoursed of that,
Spoke our own verses 'twixt ourselves; if not,
Other men's lines which we by chance had got,
Or some stage pieces famous long before,
Of which your happy memory had store;
And I remember you much pleaséd were
Of those who livéd long ago to hear,
As well as of those of these latter times
Who have enriched our language with their rhymes,
And in succession how still up they grew,
Which is the subject that I now pursue.
For from my cradle you must know that I
Was still inclined to noble poesy,
And when that once *Pueriles*[10] I had read,
And newly had my Cato[11] construéd,
In my small self I greatly marveled then,
Amongst all other, what strange kind of men
These poets were; and pleaséd with the name,
To my mild tutor merrily I came,
(For I was then a proper[12] goodly page,
Much like a pigmy, scarce ten years of age)
Clasping my slender arms about his thigh,
O my dear master! cannot you, quoth I,
Make me a poet? Do it if you can,
And you shall see I'll quickly be a man.
Who me thus answered smiling: Boy, quoth he,
If you'll not play the wag, but I may see
You ply your learning, I will shortly read
Some poets to you. Phœbus[13] be my speed,
To 't hard went I, when shortly he began
And first read to me honest Mantuan,[14]
Then Virgil's *Eclogues;* being entered thus,

---

[7] Hakluyt's *Principall Navigations, Voiages, and Discoveries of the English Nation* (1589–1600) had awakened the nation to the heroic attempts of the earlier group of explorers to establish the claim of England to the new world.

[8] Drayton's metrical recollections of the poets, alive and dead, that he had known and loved were first printed in 1627.

[9] food

[10] *Sententiae Pueriles* was the Latin primer used by schoolboys.

[11] Erasmus' edition of Dionysius Cato's *Disticha de Moribus* was a school text.

[12] handsome

[13] The god of inspired poetry.

[14] The *Eclogues* of Baptista Spagnuoli Mantuanus were among the required reading of the schools.

Methought I straight had mounted Pegasus,
And in his full career could make him stop
And bound upon Parnassus' bi-clift[15] top.
I scorned your ballad then, though it were done
And had for finis, William Elderton.[16]
But soft, in sporting with this childish jest
I from my subject have too long digressed;
Then to the matter that we took in hand,
Jove and Apollo for the Muses stand.

Then noble Chaucer, in those former times
The first enriched our English with his rhymes,
And was the first of ours that ever brake
Into the Muses' treasure, and first spake
In weighty numbers,[17] delving in the mine
Of perfect knowledge, which he could refine
And coin for current; and as much as then
The English language could express to men,
He made it do, and by his wondrous skill,
Gave us much light from his abundant quill.

And honest Gower,[18] who in respect of him
Had only sipped at Aganippe's[19] brim,
And though in years this last was him before,
Yet fell he far short of the other's store.

When after those, four ages very near,
They with the Muses which conversèd were:
That princely Surrey, early in the time
Of the eight Henry, who was then the prime
Of England's noble youth; with him there came
Wyatt, with reverence whom we still do name
Amongst our poets; Bryan[20] had a share
With the two former, which accompted are
The time's best makers, and the authors were
Of those small poems which the title bear
Of *Songs and Sonnets,*[21] wherein oft they hit
On many dainty passages of wit.

Gascoigne and Churchyard[22] after them again
In the beginning of Eliza's reign,
Accompted were great meterers many a day,
But not inspirèd with brave fire; had they
Lived but a little longer they had seen
Their works before them to have buried been.

Grave moral Spenser after these came on,
Than whom I am persuaded there was none
Since the blind bard his *Iliads* up did make
Fitter a task like that to undertake,
To set down boldly, bravely to invent,
In all high knowledge surely excellent.

The noble Sidney with this last arose,
That heroë for numbers and for prose,
That throughly paced our language as to show
The plenteous English hand in hand might go
With Greek or Latin; and did first reduce
Our tongue from Lyly's[23] writing, then in use:
Talking of stones, stars, plants, of fishes, flies,
Playing with words and idle similes;
As th' English apes and very zanies be,
Of everything that they do hear and see,
So imitating his ridiculous tricks,
They spake and writ all like mere lunatics.

Then Warner,[24] though his lines were not so trimmed,

---

15 Parnassus is reputed to be twin-peaked.

16 The broadside ballads were sold in the streets and described in lurid language the latest murder or calamity. Elderton was one of the most notorious of the ballad-makers.

17 verses

18 Chaucer's contemporary.

19 The fountain of the Muses.

20 His name is known but not his poetry.

21 Tottel's famous miscellany.

22 Once page to the Earl of Surrey and a poet himself.

23 The author of the court-romance *Euphues*, noted for its fantastic style.

24 His chief work was a metrical history of England.

Nor yet his poem so exactly limned
And neatly jointed, but the critic may
Easily reprove him, yet this let me say
For my old friend: some passages there be
In him which I protest have taken me
With almost wonder, so fine, clear, and new
As yet they have been equallèd by few.
  Neat Marlowe, bathèd in the Thespian springs,
Had in him those brave translunary things
That the first poets had; his raptures were
All air and fire, which made his verses clear,
For that fine madness still he did retain
Which rightly should possess a poet's brain.
  And surely Nashe,[25] though he a proser were,
A branch of laurel yet deserves to bear;
Sharply satiric was he, and that way
He went, since that his being to this day
Few have attempted, and I surely think
Those words shall hardly be set down with ink,
Shall scorch and blast so as his could, where he
Would inflict vengeance. And be it said of thee,
Shakespeare, thou hadst as smooth a comic vein,
Fitting the sock, and in thy natural brain
As strong conception and as clear a rage
As anyone that trafficked with the stage.
  Amongst these, Samuel Daniel, whom if I
May speak of, but to censure do deny,
Only have heard some wise men him rehearse
To be too much historian in verse;
His rhymes were smooth, his meters well did close,
But yet his manner better fitted prose.
Next these, learn'd Jonson in this list I bring,
Who had drunk deep of the Pierian spring,

[25] The satirist and playwright.

Whose knowledge did him worthily prefer,
And long was lord here of the theater;
Who in opinion made our learn'st to stick,
Whether in poems rightly dramatic,
Strong Seneca or Plautus, he or they
Should bear the buskin or the sock away.
Others again here livèd in my days
That have of us deservèd no less praise
For their translations than the daintiest wit
That on Parnassus thinks he high'st doth sit,
And for a chair may 'mongst the muses call
As the most curious maker of them all;
As reverent Chapman,[26] who hath brought to us
Musæus, Homer, and Hesiodus
Out of the Greek, and by his skill hath reared
Them to that height, and to our tongues endeared,
That were those poets at this day alive
To see their books thus with us to survive,
They would think, having neglected them so long,
They had been written in the English tongue.
  And Sylvester,[27] whom from the French more weak
Made Bartas of his six days' labour speak
In natural English; who, had he there stayed
He had done well, and never had bewrayed[28]
His own invention to have been so poor,
Who still wrote less in striving to write more.
  Then dainty Sandys, that hath to English done
Smooth sliding Ovid, and hath made him run
With so much sweetness and unusual grace,
As though the neatness of the English pace

[26] The most learned, after Jonson, of the poets and dramatists.
[27] He translated Bartas' *Semaines* and so popularized it in England.
[28] revealed

Should tell the jetting [29] Latin that it came
But slowly after, as though stiff and lame,
So Scotland sent us hither, for our own,
That man whose name I ever would have known
To stand by mine, that most ingenious knight,
My Alexander, to whom in his right
I want extremely, yet in speaking thus
I do but show the love that was 'twixt us,
And not his numbers which were brave and high,
So like his mind was his clear poesy;
And my dear Drummond, to whom much I owe
For his much love, and proud I was to know
His poesy; for which two worthy men,
I Menstry still shall love, and Hawthornden.[30]
Then the two Beaumonts [31] and my Browne [32] arose,
My dear companions whom I freely chose
My bosom friends, and in their several ways
Rightly born poets, and in these last days
Men of much note and no less nobler parts,
Such as have freely told to me their hearts,
As I have mine to them; but if you shall
Say in your knowledge that these be not all
Have writ in numbers, be informed that I
Only myself to these few men do tie,
Whose works oft printed, set on every post,[33]
To public censure subject have been most;
For such whose poems, be they ne'er so rare,
In private chambers that encloistered are,
And by transcription daintily must go,
As though the world unworthy were to know
Their rich composures, let those men that keep
These wondrous relics in their judgment deep,
And cry them up so, let such pieces be
Spoke of by those that shall come after me;
I pass not for them, nor do mean to run
In quest of these that them applause have won
Upon our stages in these latter days,
That are so many—let them have their bays
That do deserve it; let those wits that haunt
Those public circuits,[34] let them freely chant
Their fine composures, and their praise pursue;
And so, my dear friend, for this time adieu.

Nymphidia, the Court of Fairy

OLD Chaucer doth of Thopas [35] tell,
Mad Rab'lais of Pantagruel,[36]
A latter third of Dowsabell,[37]
With such poor trifles playing;
Others the like have laboured at,
Some of this thing and some of that,
And many of they know not what,
But that they must be saying.

Another sort there be that will
Be talking of the fairies still,
Nor never can they have their fill,
As they were wedded to them;
No tales of them their thirst can slake,
So much delight therein they take,
And some strange thing they fain would make,
Knew they the way to do them.

Then since no muse hath been so bold,
Or of the later, or the old,
Those elvish secrets to unfold,
Which lie from others' reading,

[29] strutting
[30] Alexander's home was at Menstry, Drummond's at Hawthornden.
[31] These are Sir John and Francis, the poetical twin of Fletcher.
[32] A pastoralist.
[33] Books were advertised by displaying their title-pages.
[34] playhouses
[35] The hero of Chaucer's mock-romance in the *Canterbury Tales*.
[36] The son of Gargantua in Rabelais' tale.
[37] Drayton's own ballad on this subject.

My active muse to light shall bring
The court of that proud fairy king,
And tell there of the reveling;
Jove prosper my proceeding.

And thou, Nymphidia, gentle fay,
Which meeting me upon the way
These secrets didst to me bewray,
Which now I am in telling,
My pretty light fantastic maid,
I here invoke thee to my aid
That I may speak what thou hast said,
In numbers smoothly swelling.

This palace standeth in the air,
By necromancy placéd there,
That it no tempests needs to fear,
Which way soe'er it blow it.
And somewhat southward toward the noon,
Whence lies a way up to the moon,
And thence the fairy can as soon
Pass to the earth below it.

The walls of spiders' legs are made,
Well mortiséd and finely laid;
He was the master of his trade,
It curiously that buildéd;
The windows of the eyes of cats,
And for the roof, instead of slats,
Is covered with the skins of bats,
With moonshine that are gilded.

Hence Oberon him sport to make,
Their rest when weary mortals take,
And none but only fairies wake,
Descendeth for his pleasure.
And Mab, his merry queen, by night
Bestrides young folks that lie upright,
(In elder times the Mare[38] that hight)
Which plagues them out of measure.

Hence shadows, seeming idle shapes,
Of little frisking elves and apes,
To earth do make their wanton scapes,
As hope of pastime hastes them;
Which maids think on the hearth they see
When fires well ne'er consuméd be,
There dancing hays[39] by two and three,
Just as their fancy casts them.

These make our girls their sluttery rue
By pinching them both black and blue,
And put a penny in their shoe,
The house for cleanly sweeping;
And in their courses make that round,
In meadows and in marshes found,
Of them so called the fairy ground,
Of which they have the keeping.

These, when a child haps to be got
Which after proves an idiot,
When folk perceive it thriveth not,
The fault therein to smother,
Some silly doting brainless calf
That understands things by the half,
Say that the fairy left this auf[40]
And took away the other.

But listen and I shall you tell
A chance in fairy that befell,
Which certainly may please some well,
In love and arms delighting:
Of Oberon that jealous grew
Of one of his own fairy crew,
Too well, he feared, his queen that knew,
His love but ill requiting.

Pigwiggen was this fairy knight,
One wondrous gracious in the sight
Of fair Queen Mab, which day and night
He amorously observéd;
Which make King Oberon suspect
His service took too good effect,
His sauciness and often checked,
And could have wished him starvéd.

Pigwiggen gladly would commend
Some token to Queen Mab to send,
If sea or land him aught could lend,
Were worthy of her wearing;
At length this lover doth devise
A bracelet made of emmets' eyes,
A thing he thought that she would prize,
No whit her state impairing.

[38] This goblin sits on the chest of a sleeper and bothers his dreams.

[39] rustic dances

[40] awkward oaf

And to the queen a letter writes,
Which he most curiously indites,
Conjuring her by all the rites
  Of love, she would be pleaséd
To meet him, her true servant, where
They might without suspect or fear
Themselves to one another clear,
  And have their poor hearts easéd.

At midnight the appointed hour,
And for the queen a fitting bower,
Quoth he, is that fair cowslip flower,
  On Hipcut hill that groweth;
In all your train there's not a fay
That ever went to gather May
But she hath made it in her way,
  The tallest there that groweth.

When by Tom Thumb, a fairy page,
He sent it, and doth him engage,
By promise of a mighty wage,
  It secretly to carry;
Which done, the queen her maids doth call,
And bids them to be ready all;
She would go see her summer hall,
  She could no longer tarry.

Her chariot ready straight is made,
Each thing therein is fitting laid
That she by nothing might be stayed,
  For nought must her be letting;
Four nimble gnats the horses were,
Their harnesses of gossamer,
Fly Cranion, her charioteer,
  Upon the coach-box getting.

Her chariot of a snail's fine shell,
Which for the colours did excel,
The fair Queen Mab becoming well,
  So lively was the limning;
The seat the soft wool of the bee;
The cover, gallantly to see,
The wing of a pied butterflee,
  I trow, 'twas simple trimming.

The wheels composed of crickets' bones,
And daintily made for the nonce;
For fear of rattling on the stones
  With thistle-down they shod it;
For all her maidens much did fear,
If Oberon had chanced to hear
That Mab his queen should have been there,
  He would not have abode it.

She mounts her chariot with a trice,
Nor would she stay for no advice,
Until her maids, that were so nice,
  To wait on her were fitted,
But ran herself away alone;
Which when they heard, there was not one
But hasted after to be gone,
  As she had been diswitted.

Hop and Mop and Drop so clear,
Pip and Trip and Skip that were
To Mab, their sovereign, ever dear,
  Her special maids of honour;
Fib and Tib and Pink and Pin,
Tick and Quick and Jill and Jin,
Tit and Nit and Wap and Win,
  The train that wait upon her.

Upon a grasshopper they got,
And what with amble and with trot,
For hedge nor ditch they sparéd not,
  But after her they hie them.
A cobweb over them they throw,
To shield the wind if it should blow;
Themselves they wisely could bestow,
  Lest any should espy them.

But let us leave Queen Mab a while,
Through many a gate, o'er many a stile,
That now had gotten by this wile,
  Her dear Pigwiggen kissing,
And tell how Oberon doth fare,
Who grew as mad as any hare,
When he had sought each place with care
  And found his queen was missing.

By grisly Pluto he doth swear,
He rent his clothes and tore his hair,
And as he runneth here and there
  An acorn cup he greeteth;
Which soon he taketh by the stalk,
About his head he lets it walk,
Nor doth he any creature balk,
  But lays on all he meeteth.

The Tuscan poet[41] doth advance
The frantic Paladin of France,
And those more ancient do enhance
Alcides in his fury;
And others, Ajax, Telamon;
But to this time there hath been none
So bedlam[42] as our Oberon,
Of which I dare assure you.

And first encount'ring with a wasp,
He in his arms the fly doth clasp
As though his breath he forth would grasp,
Him for Pigwiggen taking.
Where is my wife, thou rogue? quoth he,
Pigwiggen, she is come to thee,
Restore her or thou di'st by me.
Whereat the poor wasp quaking,

Cries, Oberon, great Fairy King,
Content thee I am no such thing;
I am a wasp, behold my sting.
At which the fairy started;
When soon away the wasp doth go,
Poor wretch was never frighted so,
He thought his wings were much too slow,
O'erjoyed they so were parted.

He next upon a glow-worm light,
(You must suppose it now was night),
Which for her hinder part was bright,
He took to be a devil.
And furiously doth her assail
For carrying fire in her tail;
He thrashed her rough coat with his flail,
The mad king feared no evil.

O, quoth the glow-worm, hold thy hand,
Thou puissant King of Fairyland,
Thy mighty strokes who may withstand;
Hold, or of life despair I!
Together then herself doth roll,
And tumbling down into a hole,
She seemed as black as any coal,
Which vexed away the fairy.

From thence he ran into a hive,
Amongst the bees he letteth drive,
And down their combs begins to rive,
All likely to have spoiléd;
Which with their wax his face besmeared,
And with their honey daubed his beard;
It would have made a man afeared
To see how he was moiléd.

A new adventure him betides,
He met an ant, which he bestrides,
And post thereon away he rides,
Which with his haste doth stumble
And came full over on her snout,
Her heels so threw the dirt about,
For she by no means could get out,
But over him doth tumble.

And being in this piteous case,
And all beslurried, head and face,
On runs he in this wild-goose chase;
As here and there he rambles
Half blind, against a molehill hit,
And for a mountain taking it,
For all he was out of his wit,
Yet to the top he scrambles.

And being gotten to the top,
Yet there himself he could not stop,
But down on th' other side doth chop,
And to the foot came rumbling,
So that the grubs therein that bred,
Hearing such turmoil overhead,
Thought surely they had all been dead,
So fearful was the jumbling.

And falling down into a lake,
Which him up to the neck doth take,
His fury somewhat it doth slake,
He calleth for a ferry;
Where you may some recovery note,
What was his club he made his boat,
And in his oaken cup doth float
As safe as in a wherry.

Men talk of the adventures strange
Of Don Quishott,[43] and of their change
Through which he arméd oft did range,
Of Sancho Panchas's travel;

[41] Ariosto, whose Orlando was one of the twelve Paladins of France.
[42] mad

[43] Don Quishott (Quixote) and Sancho Panza, his squire, are the chief figures in Cervantes' romance.

But should a man tell everything
Done by this frantic fairy king,
And them in lofty numbers sing,
It well his wits might gravel.

Scarce set on shore, but therewithal
He meeteth Puck, which most men call
Hobgoblin, and on him doth fall
With words from frenzy spoken.
Ho, ho, quoth Hob, God save thy grace,
Who dressed thee in this piteous case?
He thus that spoiled my sovereign's face
I would his neck were broken.

This Puck seems but a dreaming dolt,
Still walking like a ragged colt,
And oft out of a bush doth bolt,
Of purpose to deceive us.
And leading us, make us to stray,
Long winter's nights, out of the way,
And when we stick in mire and clay,
Hob doth with laughter leave us.

Dear Puck, quoth he, my wife is gone;
As e'er thou lov'st King Oberon,
Let everything but this alone,
With vengeance and pursue her;
Bring her to me alive or dead,
Or that vile thief Pigwiggen's head.
That villain hath defiled my bed,
He to this folly drew her.

Quoth Puck, My liege, I'll never lin,[44]
But I will thorough thick and thin
Until at length I bring her in,
My dearest lord, ne'er doubt it.
Thorough brake, thorough brier,
Thorough muck, thorough mire,
Thorough water, thorough fire,
And this goes Puck about it.

This thing Nymphidia overheard,
That on this mad king had a guard,
Not doubting of a great reward
For first this business broaching;
And through the air away doth go,
Swift as an arrow from the bow,
To let her sovereign Mab to know
What peril was approaching.

[44] cease

The queen, bound with love's powerful'st charm,
Sat with Pigwiggen, arm in arm;
Her merry maids that thought no harm
About the room were skipping.
A humble-bee, their minstrel, played
Upon his hautboy; [45] ev'ry maid
Fit for this revels was arrayed,
The hornpipe neatly tripping.

In comes Nymphidia and doth cry:
My sovereign, for your safety fly,
For there is danger but too nigh,
I posted to forewarn you;
The king hath sent Hobgoblin out
To seek you all the fields about,
And of your safety you may doubt,
If he but once discern you.

When like an uproar in a town,
Before them everything went down;
Some tore a ruff and some a gown,
'Gainst one another justling.
They flew about like chaff i' th' wind,
For haste some left their masks behind,
Some could not stay their gloves to find,
There never was such bustling.

Forth ran they by a secret way
Into a brake that near them lay,
Yet much they doubted there to stay
Lest Hob should hap to find them;
He had a sharp and piercing sight,
All one to him the day and night,
And therefore were resolved by flight
To leave this place behind them.

At length one chanced to find a nut
In th' end of which a hole was cut,
Which lay upon a hazel root,
There scattered by a squirrel
Which out the kernel gotten had;
Whence quoth this fay, Dear Queen, be glad,
Let Oberon be ne'er so mad,
I'll set you safe from peril.

Come all into this nut, quoth she,
Come closely in, be ruled by me,

[45] The ancestor of the oboe.

Each one may here a chooser be,
For room ye need not wrastle,
Nor need ye be together heaped.
So one by one therein they crept,
And lying down they soundly slept,
As safe as in a castle.

Nymphidia, that this while doth watch,
Perceived if Puck the queen should catch,
That he would be her over-match,
Of which she well bethought her.
Found it must be some powerful charm,
The queen against him that must arm,
Or surely he would do her harm,
For thoroughly he had sought her.

And list'ning if she aught could hear
That her might hinder, or might fear,
But finding still the coast was clear,
Nor creature had descried her;
Each circumstance and having scanned,
She came thereby to understand
Puck would be with them out of hand,
When to her charms she hied her.

And first her fern seed doth bestow,
The kernel of the mistletoe,
And here and there as Puck should go,
With terror to affright him,
She nightshade straws to work him ill,
Therewith her vervain and her dill,
That hind'reth witches of their will,
Of purpose to despite him.

Then sprinkles she the juice of rue
That groweth underneath the yew,
With nine drops of the midnight dew,
From lunary distilling;
The molewarp's brain mixed therewithal,
And with the same the pismire's gall,
For she in nothing short would fall,
The fairy was so willing.

Then thrice under a brier doth creep,
Which at both ends was rooted deep,
And over it three times she leap,
Her magic much availing;
Then on Proserpina doth call,
And so upon her spell doth fall,
Which here to you repeat I shall,
Not in one tittle failing:

By the croaking of the frog,
By the howling of the dog,
By the crying of the hog,
Against the storm arising;
By the evening curfew bell,
By the doleful dying knell,
Oh, let this my direful spell,
Hob, hinder thy surprising.

By the mandrake's dreadful groans,
By the lubrican's [46] sad moans,
By the noise of dead men's bones
In charnel houses rattling;
By the hissing of the snake,
The rustling of the fire-drake,
I charge thee thou this place forsake,
Nor of Queen Mab be pratling.

By the whirlwind's hollow sound,
By the thunder's dreadful stound,
Yells of spirits under ground,
I charge thee not to fear us;
By the screech-owl's dismal note,
By the black night-raven's throat,
I charge thee, Hob, to tear thy coat
With thorns, if thou come near us.

Her spell thus spoke, she stepped aside,
And in a chink herself doth hide
To see thereof what would betide,
For she doth only mind him;
When presently she Puck espies,
And well she marked his gloating eyes,
How under every leaf he pries,
In seeking still to find them.

But once the circle got within,
The charms to work do straight begin,
And he was caught as in a gin;
For as he thus was busy,
A pain he in his head-piece feels,
Against a stubbéd tree he reels,
And up went poor Hobgoblin's heels,
Alas, his brain was dizzy.

[46] Leprechaun, a pigmy sprite in Irish folk-lore.

At length upon his feet he gets,
Hobgoblin fumes, Hobgoblin frets,
And as again he forward sets,
  And through the bushes scrambles,
A stump doth trip him in his pace,
Down comes poor Hob upon his face,
And lamentably tore his case
  Amongst the briers and brambles.

A plague upon Queen Mab, quoth he,
And all her maids, where'er they be,
I think the devil guided me
  To seek her so provokéd.
Where stumbling at a piece of wood
He fell into a ditch of mud,
Where to the very chin he stood
  In danger to be chokéd.

Now worse than e'er he was before,
Poor Puck doth yell, poor Puck doth roar,
That waked Queen Mab, what doubted sore
  Some treason had been wrought her,
Until Nymphidia told the queen
What she had done, what she had seen,
Who then had well-near cracked her spleen
  With very extreme laughter.

But leave we Hob to clamber out,
Queen Mab and all her fairy rout,
And come again to have about
  With Oberon, yet madding;
And with Pigwiggen now distraught,
Who much was troubled in his thought,
That he so long the queen had sought,
  And through the fields was gadding.

And as he runs he still doth cry:
King Oberon, I thee defy,
And dare thee here in arms to try
  For my dear lady's honour;
For that she is a queen right good,
In whose defence I'll shed my blood,
And that thou in this jealous mood
  Hast laid this slander on her.

And quickly arms him for the field,
A little cockle-shell his shield,
Which he could very bravely wield,
  Yet it could not be piercéd;
His spear, a bent both stiff and strong,
And well near of two inches long;
The pile was of a horsefly's tongue,
  Whose sharpness nought reverséd.

And puts him on a coat of mail,
Which was of a fish's scale,
That when his foe should him assail,
  No point should be prevailing;
His rapier was a hornet's sting,
It was a very dangerous thing,
For if he chanced to hurt the king
  It would be long in healing.

His helmet was a beetle's head,
Most horrible and full of dread,
That able was to strike one dead,
  Yet did it well become him;
And for a plume a horse's hair,
Which being tosséd with the air
Had force to strike his foe with fear,
  And turn his weapon from him.

Himself he on an earwig set,
Yet scarce he on his back could get,
So oft and high he did curvet
  Ere he himself could settle;
He made him turn, and stop, and bound,
To gallop, and to trot the round,
He scarce could stand on any ground,
  He was so full of mettle.

When soon he met with Tomalin,
One that a valiant knight had been,
And to King Oberon of kin;
  Quoth he, Thou manly fairy,
Tell Oberon I come prepared,
Then bid him stand upon his guard,
This hand his baseness shall reward,
  Let him be ne'er so wary.

Say to him thus, that I defy
His slanders and his infamy,
And as a mortal enemy
  Do publicly proclaim him;
Withal, that if I had mine own
He should not wear the fairy crown,

But with a vengeance should come down,
  Nor we a king should name him.

This Tomalin could not abide
To hear his sovereign vilified,
But to the fairy court him hied,
  Full furiously he posted,
With ev'ry thing Pigwiggen said:
How title to the crown he laid,
And in what arms he was arrayed,
  And how himself he boasted.

'Twixt head and foot, from point to point,
He told th' arming of each joint,
In every piece how neat and quaint,
  For Tomalin could do it;
How fair he sat, how sure he rid,
As of the courser he bestrid,
How managed, and how well he did.
  The king which listened to it,

Quoth he, Go, Tomalin, with speed,
Provide me arms, provide my steed,
And everything that I shall need,
  By thee I will be guided.
To strait account call thou thy wit,
See there be wanting not a whit,
In everything see thou me fit,
  Just as my foe's provided.

Soon flew this news through fairyland,
Which gave Queen Mab to understand
The combat that was then in hand
  Betwixt those men so mighty;
Which greatly she began to rue,
Perceiving that all fairy knew
The first occasion from her grew,
  Of these affairs so weighty.

Wherefore, attended with her maids,
Through fogs and mists and damps she wades,
To Proserpine, the Queen of Shades,
  To treat that it would please her
The cause into her hands to take,
For ancient love and friendship's sake,
And soon thereof an end to make,
  Which of much care would ease her.

A while there let we Mab alone,
And come we to King Oberon,
Who armed to meet his foe is gone,
  For proud Pigwiggen crying;
Who sought the fairy king as fast,
And had so well his journeys cast
That he arrivéd at the last,
  His puissant foe espying.

Stout Tomalin came with the king,
Tom Thumb doth on Pigwiggen bring,
That perfect were in everything
  To single fights belonging.
And therefore they themselves engage
To see them exercise their rage
With fair and comely equipage,
  Not one the other wronging.

So like in arms these champions were
As they had been a very pair,
So that a man would almost swear
  That either had been either;
Their furious steeds began to neigh,
That they were heard a mighty way;
Their staves upon their rests they lay,
  Yet ere they flew together

Their seconds minister an oath,
Which was indifferent to them both,
That on their knightly faith and troth
  No magic them suppliéd;
And sought them that they had no charms
Wherewith to work each other's harms,
But came with simple open arms
  To have their causes triéd.

Together furiously they ran,
That to the ground came horse and man,
The blood out of their helmets span,
  So sharp were their encounters;
And though they to the earth were thrown
Yet quickly they regained their own,
Such nimbleness was never shown,
  They were two gallant mounters.

When in a second course again
They forward came with might and main,

Yet which had better of the twain
The seconds could not judge yet;
Their shields were into pieces cleft,
Their helmets from their heads were reft,
And to defend them nothing left,
These champions would not budge yet.

Away from them their staves they threw,
Their cruel swords they quickly drew,
And freshly they the fight renew,
They every stroke redoubled;
Which made Proserpina take heed,
And make to them the greater speed,
For fear lest they too much should bleed,
Which wondrously her troubled.

When to th' infernal Styx she goes,
She takes the fogs from thence that rose
And in a bag doth them enclose;
When well she had them blended,
She hies her then to Lethe spring,
A bottle and thereof doth bring,
Wherewith she meant to work the thing
Which only she intended.

Now Proserpine with Mab is gone
Unto the place where Oberon
And proud Pigwiggen, one to one,
Both to be slain were likely;
And there themselves they closely hide,
Because they would not be espied,
For Proserpine meant to decide
The matter very quickly.

And suddenly unties the poke,
Which out of it sent such a smoke
As ready was them all to choke,
So grievous was the pother;
So that the knights each other lost,
And stood as still as any post,
Tom Thumb nor Tomalin could boast
Themselves of any other.

But when the mist gan somewhat cease,
Proserpina commandeth peace,
And that awhile they should release
Each other of their peril;
Which here, quoth she, I do proclaim
To all, in dreadful Pluto's name,
That as ye will eschew his blame,
You let me hear the quarrel.

But here yourselves you must engage,
Somewhat to cool your spleenish rage,
Your grievous thirst and to assuage,
That first you drink this liquor,
Which shall your understanding clear,
As plainly shall to you appear,
Those things from me that you shall hear
Conceiving much the quicker.

This Lethe water, you must know,
The memory destroyeth so,
That of our weal or of our woe
It all remembrance blotted;
Of it nor can you ever think,
For they no sooner took this drink,
But nought into their brains could sink
Of what had them besotted.

King Oberon forgotten had
That he for jealousy ran mad;
But of his queen was wondrous glad,
And asked how they came thither.
Pigwiggen likewise doth forget
That he Queen Mab had ever met,
Or that they were so hard beset
When they were found together.

Nor neither of them both had thought
That e'er they had each other sought,
Much less that they a combat fought,
But such a dream were loathing.
Tom Thumb had got a little sup,
And Tomalin scarce kissed the cup,
Yet had their brains so sure locked up
That they remembered nothing.

Queen Mab and her light maids the while
Amongst themselves do closely smile
To see the king caught with this wile,
With one another jesting.
And to the fairy court they went,
With mickle joy and merriment,
Which thing was done with good intent,
And thus I left them feasting.

[*The Battle of Agincourt*, 1627]

To the Cambro-Britons and their Harp, his Ballad of Agincourt [47]

FAIR stood the wind for France,
When we our sails advance,
Nor now to prove our chance,
  Longer will tarry;
But putting to the main
At Kaux, the mouth of Seine,
With all his martial train,
  Landed King Harry.

And taking many a fort,
Furnished in warlike sort,
Marcheth towards Agincourt,
  In happy hour;
Skirmishing day by day
With those that stopped his way,
Where the French gen'ral lay
  With all his power.

Which in his height of pride,
King Henry to deride,
His ransom to provide
  To the King sending;
Which he neglects the while
As from a nation vile,
Yet with an angry smile
  Their fall portending.

And turning to his men,
Quoth our brave Henry then:
Though they to one be ten,
  Be not amazéd.
Yet have we well begun,
Battles so bravely won
Have ever to the sun
  By fame been raiséd.

And for myself, quoth he,
This my full rest shall be,
England ne'er mourn for me,
  Nor more esteem me;
Victor I will remain,
Or on this earth lie slain,
Never shall she sustain
  Loss to redeem me.

Poitiers and Crécy tell,
When most their pride did swell,
Under our swords they fell;
  No less our skill is
Than when our grandsire [48] great,
Claiming the regal seat
By many a warlike feat,
  Lopped the French lilies.

The Duke of York so dread
The eager vaward [49] led;
With the main Henry sped
  Amongst his henchmen.
Excester had the rear,
A braver man not there,
O Lord, how hot they were
  On the false Frenchmen!

They now to fight are gone,
Armor on armor shone,
Drum now to drum did groan,
  To hear was wonder,
That with the cries they make
The very earth did shake,
Trumpet to trumpet spake,
  Thunder to thunder.

Well it thine age became,
O noble Erpingham,
Which didst the signal aim
  To our hid forces;
When from a meadow by,
Like a storm suddenly,
The English archery
  Stuck the French horses.

With Spanish yew so strong,
Arrows a cloth-yard long,
That like to serpents stung,
  Piercing the weather;
None from his fellow starts,
But playing manly parts,
And like true English hearts,
  Stuck close together.

When down their bows they threw,
And forth their bilboes [50] drew,

---

[47] The famous battle of Agincourt, in which Henry V of England defeated a superior force of French, took place on 25 October 1415.

[48] His great-grandfather Edward III, victor of Crécy.
[49] vanward
[50] swords

And on the French they flew,
  Not one was tardy;
Arms were from shoulders sent,
Scalps to the teeth were rent,
Down the French peasants went;
  Our men were hardy.

This while our noble King,
His broad sword brandishing,
Down the French host did ding,
  As to o'erwhelm it;
And many a deep wound lent,
His arms with blood besprent,
And many a cruel dent
  Bruiséd his helmet.

Gloster, that Duke so good,
Next of the royal blood,
For famous England stood
  With his brave brother;
Clarence, in steel so bright,
Though but a maiden knight,
Yet in that furious fight,
  Scarce such another.

Warwick in blood did wade,
Oxford the foe invade,
And cruel slaughter made,
  Still as they ran up;
Suffolk his axe did ply,
Beaumont and Willoughby
Bare them right doughtily,
  Ferrers and Fanhope.

Upon Saint Crispin's day
Fought was this noble fray,
Which fame did not delay
  To England to carry;
Oh, when shall English men
With such acts fill a pen,
Or England breed again
  Such a King Harry?

[*Poems*, 1619]

Christopher Marlowe

1564–1593

The Passionate Shepherd to his Love

Come live with me, and be my love,
And we will all the pleasures prove,
That valleys, groves, hills and fields,
Woods, or steepy mountain yields.

And we will sit upon the rocks,
Seeing the shepherds feed their flocks
By shallow rivers, to whose falls
Melodious birds sing madrigals.

And I will make thee beds of roses,
And a thousand fragrant poesies,
A cap of flowers, and a kirtle,
Embroidred all with leaves of myrtle.

A gown made of the finest wool,
Which from our pretty lambs we pull,
Fair linéd slippers for the cold,
With buckles of the purest gold.

A belt of straw and ivy buds,
With coral clasps and amber studs,
And if these pleasures may thee move,
Come live with me, and be my love.

The shepherds' swains shall dance and sing
For thy delight each May-morning.
If these delights thy mind may move,
Then live with me, and be my love.

[*England's Helicon*, 1600]

Hero and Leander

THE ARGUMENT OF THE FIRST SESTIAD

Hero's description and her loves,
The fane of Venus; where he moves
His worthy love-suit, and attains;
Whose bliss the wrath of Fates restrains,
For Cupid's grace to Mercury,
Which tale the Author doth imply.

On Hellespont, guilty of true-love's blood,
In view and opposite, two cities stood,

Seaborderers, disjoined by Neptune's might:
The one Abydos, the other Sestos hight.
At Sestos, Hero dwelt; Hero the fair,
Whom young Apollo courted for her hair,
And offred as a dower his burning throne,
Where she should sit for men to gaze upon.
The outside of her garments were of lawn,
The lining purple silk, with gilt stars drawn,
Her wide sleeves green, and bordered with a grove,
Where Venus in her naked glory strove
To please the careless and disdainful eyes
Of proud Adonis that before her lies.
Her kirtle blue, whereon was many a stain,
Made with the blood of wretched lovers slain.
Upon her head she wore a myrtle wreath,
From whence her veil reached to the ground beneath.
Her veil was artificial flowers and leaves,
Whose workmanship both man and beast deceives.
Many would praise the sweet smell as she passed,
When 'twas the odour which her breath forth cast,
And there for honey bees have sought in vain,
And beat from thence, have lighted there again.
About her neck hung chains of pebble stone,
Which, lightened by her neck, like diamonds shone.
She wore no gloves, for neither sun nor wind
Would burn or parch her hands, but to her mind,
Or warm or cool them, for they took delight
To play upon those hands, they were so white.
Buskins of shells all silvered uséd she,
And branched with blushing coral to the knee;
Where sparrows perched, of hollow pearl and gold,
Such as the world would wonder to behold;
Those with sweet water oft her handmaid fills,
Which as she went would chirrup through the bills.
Some say, for her the fairest Cupid pined,
And looking in her face, was strooken blind.
But this is true, so like was one the other,
As he imagined Hero was his mother.
And oftentimes into her bosom flew,
About her naked neck his bare arms threw,
And laid his childish head upon her breast,
And with still panting rocked, there took his rest.
So lovely fair was Hero, Venus' nun,
As nature wept, thinking she was undone;
Because she took more from her than she left,
And of such wondrous beauty her bereft:
Therefore in sign her treasure suffered wrack,
Since Hero's time, hath half the world been black.
Amorous Leander, beautiful and young,
(Whose tragedy divine Musæus [1] sung)
Dwelt at Abydos: since him dwelt there none,
For whom succeeding times make greater moan.
His dangling tresses that were never shorn,
Had they been cut, and unto Colchis [2] born,
Would have allured the vent'rous youth of Greece
To hazard more than for the golden fleece.
Fair Cynthia wished his arms might be her sphere;
Grief made her pale, because she moves not there.
His body was as straight as Circe's wand,
Jove might have sipped out nectar from his hand.
Even as delicious meat is to the taste,
So was his neck in touching and surpassed

---

[1] A Greek grammarian who wrote a poem on Hero and Leander.
[2] According to legend, the location of the Golden Fleece

The white of Pelop's [3] shoulder. I could tell ye,
How smooth his breast was, and how white his belly,
And whose immortal fingers did imprint
That heavenly path, with many a curious dint,
That runs along his back; but my rude pen
Can hardly blazen forth the loves of men,
Much less of powerful gods: let it suffice,
That my slack muse sings of Leander's eyes,
Those orient cheeks and lips, exceeding his [4]
That leapt into the water for a kiss
Of his own shadow, and despising many,
Died ere he could enjoy the love of any.
Had wild Hippolytus [5] Leander seen,
Enamoured of his beauty had he been;
His presence made the rudest peasant melt,
That in the vast uplandish country dwelt;
The barbarous Thracian soldier, moved with nought,
Was moved with him, and for his favour sought.
Some swore he was a maid in man's attire,
For in his looks were all that men desire,
A pleasant smiling cheek, a speaking eye,
A brow for love to banquet royally;
And such as knew he was a man would say,
Leander, thou art made for amorous play:
Why art thou not in love, and loved of all?
Though thou be fair, yet be not thine own thrall.
  The men of wealthy Sestos, every year,
(For his sake whom their goddess held so dear,
Rose-cheeked Adonis) kept a solemn feast.
Thither resorted many a wand'ring guest,
To meet their loves; such as had none at all,
Came lovers home from this great festival.
For every street, like to a firmament,
Glistered with breathing stars, who where they went,
Frighted the melancholy earth, which deemed
Eternal heaven to burn, for so it seemed,
As if another Phaeton had got
The guidance of the sun's rich chariot.
But far above the loveliest Hero shined,
And stole away th' enchanted gazer's mind;
For like sea-nymphs' inveigling harmony,
So was her beauty to the standers by.
Nor that night-wand'ring pale and watery star [6]
(When yawning dragons draw her thirling [7] car
From Latmos' mount up to the gloomy sky,
Where, crowned with blazing light and majesty,
She proudly sits) more over-rules the flood,
Than she the hearts of those that near her stood.
Even as when gaudy nymphs pursue the chase,
Wretched Ixion's shaggy-footed race,[8]
Incensed with savage heat, gallop amain
From steep pine-bearing mountains to the plain:
So ran the people forth to gaze upon her,
And all that viewed her were enamoured on her.
And as in fury of a dreadful fight,
Their fellows being slain or put to flight,
Poor soldiers stand with fear of death dead strooken,
So at her presence all, surprised and tooken,
Await the sentence of her scornful eyes:
He whom she favours lives, the other dies.
There might you see one sigh, another rage,
And some (their violent passions to assuage)
Compile sharp satires; but alas too late,
For faithful love will never turn to hate.
And many, seeing great princes were denied,

[3] Demeter gave Pelops an ivory shoulder in place of the one eaten by her.
[4] *i.e.*, Narcissus'
[5] Hippolytus refused the love of his stepmother Phaedra.

[6] The moon.
[7] (cloud) piercing
[8] the Centaurs.

Pined as they went, and thinking on her died.
On this feast day, O curséd day and hour,
Went Hero thorough Sestos, from her tower
To Venus' temple, where unhappily,
As after chanced, they did each other spy.
So fair a church as this had Venus none;
The walls were of discoloured [9] jasper stone,
Wherein was Proteus [10] carvéd, and o'er head,
A lively vine of green sea-agate spread;
Where by one hand, light headed Bacchus hung,
And with the other, wine from grapes out-wrung.
Of crystal shining fair the pavement was;
The town of Sestos called it Venus' glass.
There might you see the gods in sundry shapes,
Committing heady riots, incest, rapes:
For know, that underneath this radiant floor
Was Danaë's statue in a brazen tower,
Jove slyly stealing from his sister's bed,
To dally with Idalian Ganymed,
And for his love Europa bellowing loud,
And tumbling with the Rainbow in a cloud:
Blood-quaffing Mars heaving the iron net,
Which limping Vulcan and his Cyclops set;
Love kindling fire, to burn such towns as Troy,
Sylvanus weeping for the lovely boy [11]
That now is turned into a cypress tree,
Under whose shade the wood-gods love to be.
And in the midst a silver altar stood;
There Hero sacrificing turtles' [12] blood,
Vailed to the ground, veiling her eye-lids close,
And modestly they opened as she rose:
Thence flew Love's arrow with the golden head,
And thus Leander was enamouréd.
Stone still he stood, and evermore he gazed,
Till with the fire that from his count'nance blazed,
Relenting Hero's gentle heart was strook,
Such force and virtue hath an amorous look.
It lies not in our power to love, or hate,
For will in us is over-ruled by fate.
When two are stript long ere the course begin,
We wish that one should lose, the other win;
And one especially do we affect
Of two gold ingots like in each respect.
The reason no man knows, let it suffice,
What we behold is censured by our eyes.
Where both deliberate, the love is slight,
Who ever loved, that loved not at first sight?
He kneeled, but unto her devoutly prayed;
Chaste Hero to herself thus softly said:
Were I the saint he worships, I would hear him,
And as she spake those words, came somewhat near him.
He started up, she blushed as one ashamed;
Wherewith Leander much more was inflamed.
He touched her hand, in touching it she trembled;
Love deeply grounded, hardly is dissembled.
These lovers parléd by the touch of hands,
True love is mute, and oft amazéd stands.
Thus while dumb signs their yielding hearts entangled,
The air with sparks of living fire was spangled,
And night deep drenched in mystic Acheron [13]
Heaved up her head, and half the world upon
Breathed darkness forth (dark night is Cupid's day).
And now begins Leander to display

[9] varicolored
[10] An old man of the sea who had the power of changing his shape.
[11] Cyparissus
[12] *I.e.*, turtle doves', birds sacred to Venus.
[13] A river in Hades.

Love's holy fire, with words, with sighs and tears,
Which like sweet music entered Hero's ears;
And yet at every word she turned aside,
And always cut him off as he replied.
At last, like to a bold sharp sophister,
With cheerful hope thus he accosted her.
Fair creature, let me speak without offence;
I would my rude words had the influence,
To lead thy thoughts as thy fair looks do mine,
Then shouldst thou be his prisoner who is thine,
Be not unkind and fair; misshapen stuff
Are of behaviour boisterous and rough.
O shun me not, but hear me ere you go,
God knows I cannot force love, as you do.
My words shall be as spotless as my youth,
Full of simplicity and naked truth.
This sacrifice (whose sweet perfume descending,
From Venus' altar to your footsteps bending)
Doth testify that you exceed her far,
To whom you offer, and whose nun you are.
Why should you worship her? her you surpass,
As much as sparkling diamonds flaring glass.
A diamond set in lead his worth retains,
A heavenly nymph, beloved of human swains,
Receives no blemish, but oft-times more grace,
Which makes me hope, although I am but base,
Base in respect of thee, divine and pure,
Dutiful service may thy love procure,
And I in duty will excell all other,
As thou in beauty dost exceed Love's mother.
Nor heaven, nor thou, were made to gaze upon;
As heaven preserves all things, so save thou one.
A stately builded ship, well rigged and tall,
The ocean maketh more majestical:
Why vowest thou then to live in Sestos here,
Who on love's seas more glorious wouldst appear?
Like untuned golden strings all women are,
Which long time lie untouched, will harshly jar.
Vessels of brass oft handled, brightly shine;
What difference betwixt the richest mine
And basest mold, but use? for both, not used,
Are of like worth. Then treasure is abused,
When misers keep it; being put to loan,
In time it will return us two for one.
Rich robes themselves and others do adorn;
Neither themselves nor others, if not worn.
Who builds a palace and rams up the gate,
Shall see it ruinous and desolate.
Ah, simple Hero, learn thyself to cherish,
Lone women like to empty houses perish.
Less sins the poor rich man that starves himself,
In heaping up a mass of drossy pelf,
Than such as you: his golden earth remains,
Which after his decease, some other gains.
But this fair gem, sweet in the loss alone,
When you fleet hence, can be bequeathed to none.
Or if it could, down from th'enameled sky
All heaven would come to claim this legacy,
And with intestine broils the world destroy,
And quite confound nature's sweet harmony.
Well therefore by the gods decreed it is,
We human creatures should enjoy that bliss.
One is no number, maids are nothing then,
Without the sweet society of men.
Wilt thou live single still? one shalt thou be,

Though never-singling Hymen couple thee.
Wild savages, that drink of running springs,
Think water far excels all earthly things:
But they that daily taste neat wine, despise it.
Virginity, albeit some highly prize it,
Compared with marriage, had you tried them both,
Differs as much as wine and water doth.
Base bullion for the stamp's sake we allow;
Even so for men's impression do we you,
By which alone our reverend fathers say,
Women receive perfection every way.
This idol which you term virginity
Is neither essence subject to the eye,
No, nor to any one exterior sense,
Nor hath it any place of residence,
Nor is't of earth or mold celestial,
Or capable of any form at all.
Of that which hath no being do not boast;
Things that are not at all are never lost.
Men foolishly do call it virtuous;
What virtue is it that is born with us?
Much less can honour be ascribed thereto;
Honour is purchased by the deeds we do.
Believe me, Hero, honour is not won
Until some honourable deed be done.
Seek you for chastity, immortal fame,
And know that some have wronged Diana's name?
Whose name is it, if she be false or not,
So she be fair, but some vile tongues will blot?
But you are fair (ay me) so wondrous fair,
So young, so gentle, and so debonair,
As Greece will think, if thus you live alone,
Some one or other keeps you as his own.
Then, Hero, hate me not, nor from me fly,
To follow swiftly blasting infamy.
Perhaps thy sacred priesthood makes thee loath;
Tell me, to whom mad'st thou that heedless oath?

To Venus, answered she, and as she spake,
Forth from those two tralucent cisterns brake
A stream of liquid pearl, which down her face
Made milk-white paths, whereon the gods might trace[14]
To Jove's high court. He thus replied: The rites
In which love's beauteous empress most delights,
Are banquets, Doric[15] music, midnight-revel,
Plays, masques, and all that stern age counteth evil.
Thee as a holy idiot doth she scorn,
For thou in vowing chastity hast sworn
To rob her name and honour, and thereby
Commit'st a sin far worse than perjury,
Even sacrilege against her deity,
Through regular and formal purity.
To expiate which sin, kiss and shake hands;
Such sacrifice as this Venus demands.

Thereat she smiled, and did deny him so,
As put thereby, yet might he hope for mo.
Which makes him quickly re-enforce his speech,
And her in humble manner thus beseech.

Though neither gods nor men may thee deserve,
Yet for her sake whom you have vowed to serve,
Abandon fruitless cold virginity,
The gentle queen of love's sole enemy.
Then shall you most resemble Venus' nun,
When Venus' sweet rites are performed and done.
Flint-breasted Pallas joys in single life,
But Pallas and your mistress are at strife.
Love, Hero, then, and be not tyrannous,
But heal the heart that thou hast wounded thus,
Nor stain thy youthful years with avarice;
Fair fools delight to be accounted nice.
The richest corn dies, if it be not reaped,

[14] follow the track [15] strong, warlike

Beauty alone is lost, too warily kept.
These arguments he used, and many more,
Wherewith she yielded, that was won before.
Hero's looks yielded, but her words made war;
Women are won when they begin to jar.
Thus having swallowed Cupid's golden hook,
The more she strived, the deeper was she strook.
Yet evilly feigning anger, strove she still,
And would be thought to grant against her will.
So having paused a while, at last she said:
Who taught thee rhetoric to deceive a maid?
Ay me, such words as these should I abhor,
And yet I like them for the orator.
With that Leander stoopt, to have embraced her,
But from his spreading arms away she cast her,
And thus bespake him: Gentle youth forbear
To touch the sacred garments which I wear.
Upon a rock, and underneath a hill,
Far from the town (where all is whist and still,
Save that the sea playing on yellow sand,
Sends forth a rattling murmur to the land,
Whose sound allurs the golden Morpheus
In silence of the night to visit us,)
My turret stands, and there, God knows, I play
With Venus' swans and sparrows all the day.
A dwarfish beldame bears me company,
That hops about the chamber where I lie,
And spends the night (that might be better spent)
In vain discourse, and apish merriment.
Come thither. As she spake this, her tongue tript,
For unawares (*Come thither*) from her slipt,
And suddenly her former colour changed,
And here and there her eyes through anger ranged.
And like a planet, moving several ways,
At one self instant, she, poor soul, assays,
Loving, not to love at all, and every part
Strove to resist the motions of her heart.
And hands so pure, so innocent, nay such
As might have made heaven stoop to have a touch,
Did she uphold to Venus, and again
Vowed spotless chastity, but all in vain.
Cupid beats down her prayers with his wings,
Her vows above the empty air he flings;
And deep enraged, his sinewy bow he bent,
And shot a shaft that burning from him went;
Wherewith she, strooken, looked so dolefully,
As made Love sigh, to see his tyranny.
And as she wept, her tears to pearl he turned,
And wound them on his arm, and for her mourned.
Then towards the palace of the Destinies,
Laden with languishment and grief, he flies,
And to those stern nymphs humbly made request,
Both might enjoy each other, and be blest.
But with a ghastly dreadful countenance,
Threatening a thousand deaths at every glance,
They answered Love, nor would vouchsafe so much
As one poor word, their hate to him was such.
Harken a while, and I will tell you why:
Heaven's wingéd herald, Jove-born Mercury,
The self-same day that he asleep had laid
Enchanted Argus,[16] spied a country maid,
Whose careless hair, instead of pearl t'adorn it,
Glist'red with dew, as one that seemed to scorn it:

[16] By order of Jove, Mercury lulled Argus asleep and slew him.

Her breath as fragrant as the morning rose,
Her mind pure, and her tongue untaught to gloze.
Yet proud she was, (for lofty pride that dwells
In towered courts, is oft in shepherds' cells.)
And too too well the fair vermillion knew,
And silver tincture of her cheeks, that drew
The love of every swain. On her this god
Enamoured was, and with his snaky rod,
Did charm her nimble feet, and made her stay,
The while upon a hillock down he lay,
And sweetly on his pipe began to play,
And with smooth speech her fancy to assay,
Till in his twining arms he locked her fast,
And then he wooed with kisses, and at last,
As shepherds do, her on the ground he laid,
And tumbling in the grass, he often strayed
Beyond the bounds of shame, in being bold
To eye those parts which no eye should behold.
And like an insolent commanding lover,
Boasting his parentage, would needs discover
The way to new Elysium; but she,
Whose only dower was her chastity,
Having striven in vain, was now about to cry,
And crave the help of shepherds that were nigh.
Herewith he stayed his fury, and began
To give her leave to rise; away she ran;
After went Mercury, who used such cunning,
As she to hear his tale, left off her running.
Maids are not won by brutish force and might,
But speeches full of pleasure and delight.
And knowing Hermes courted her, was glad
That she such loveliness and beauty had
As could provoke his liking, yet was mute,
And neither would deny, nor grant his suit.
Still vowed he love, she wanting no excuse
To feed him with delays, as women use,
Or thirsting after immortality—
All women are ambitious naturally—
Imposed upon her lover such a task,
As he ought not perform, nor yet she ask.
A draught of flowing nectar she requested,
Wherewith the king of gods and men is feasted.
He, ready to accomplish what she willed,
Stole some from Hebe (Hebe Jove's cup filled,)
And gave it to his simple rustic love,
Which being known (as what is hid from Jove?)
He inly stormed, and waxed more furious
Than for the fire filched by Prometheus,
And thrusts him down from heaven; he wand'ring here,
In mournful terms, with sad and heavy cheer
Complained to Cupid. Cupid, for his sake,
To be revenged on Jove did undertake,
And those on whom heaven, earth, and hell relies,
I mean the adamantine Destinies,
He wounds with love, and forced them equally
To dote upon deceitful Mercury.
They offred him the deadly fatal knife
That shears the slender threads of human life;
At his fair feathered feet the engines laid,
Which th'earth from ugly Chaos' den upweighed:
These he regarded not, but did entreat,
That Jove, usurper of his father's seat,
Might presently be banished into hell,
And aged Saturn in Olympus dwell.
They granted what he craved, and once again
Saturn and Ops began their golden reign.
Murder, rape, war, lust and treachery,
Were with Jove closed in Stygian empery.
But long this blessèd time continued not:
As soon as he his wishèd purpose got,
He, reckless of his promise, did despise
The love of th'everlasting Destinies.
They seeing it, both Love and him abhorred.

And Jupiter unto his place restored.
And but that learning, in despite of fate,
Will mount aloft, and enter heaven gate,
And to the seat of Jove itself advance,
Hermes had slept in hell with ignorance;
Yet as a punishment they added this,
That he and poverty should always kiss.
And to this day is every scholar poor,
Gross gold from them runs headlong to the boor.
Likewise the angry sisters thus deluded,
To venge themselves on Hermes, have concluded
That Midas' brood shall sit in honour's chair,
To which the Muses' sons are only heir:
And fruitful wits that in aspiring are,
Shall, discontent, run into regions far;
And few great lords in virtuous deeds shall joy,
But be surprised with every garish toy;
And still enrich the lofty servile clown,
Who with encroaching guile keeps learning down.
Then muse not Cupid's suit no better sped,
Seeing in their loves the Fates were injuréd.

THE ARGUMENT OF THE SECOND SESTIAD [17]

Hero of love takes deeper sense,
And doth her love more recompense.
Their first night's meeting, where sweet kisses
Are th'only crowns of both their blisses.
He swims t' Abydos, and returns;
Cold Neptune with his beauty burns,
Whose suit he shuns, and doth aspire
Hero's fair tower, and his desire.

[17] Marlowe completed the second sestiad but no more. The dramatist Chapman finished the story, which was published in 1598.

William Shakespeare 1564–1616

SONGS FROM THE PLAYS

ARIEL *sings*

FULL fathom five thy father lies;
Of his bones are coral made:
Those are pearls that were his eyes:
Nothing of him that doth fade,
But doth suffer a sea-change
Into something rich and strange.
Sea-nymphs hourly ring his knell:
[*Burden:* ding-dong.
Hark! now I hear them,— ding-dong, bell.

[*The Tempest,* 1611]

Who is Silvia? what is she?
That all our swains commend her?
Holy, fair, and wise is she;
The heaven such grace did lend her,
That she might admired be.

Is she kind as she is fair?
For beauty lives with kindness:
Love doth to her eyes repair,
To help him of his blindness;
And, being help'd, inhabits there.

Then to Silvia let us sing,
That Silvia is excelling;
She excels each mortal thing
Upon the dull earth dwelling;
To her let us garlands bring.

[*The Two Gentlemen of Verona,* 1591]

Enter MARIANA *and a* Boy: Boy *sings*

Take, O take those lips away,
That so sweetly were forsworn;
And those eyes, the break of day,
Lights that do mislead the morn:
But my kisses bring again,
bring again,
Seals of love, but seal'd in vain,
seal'd in vain.

[*Measure for Measure,* 1603]

BALTHAZAR *sings*

Sigh no more, ladies, sigh no more,
Men were deceivers ever;
One foot in sea, and one on shore,
To one thing constant never.
Then sigh not so,
But let them go,
And be you blithe and bonny,
Converting all your sounds of woe
Into Hey nonny, nonny.

Sing no more ditties, sing no mo
Of dumps so dull and heavy;
The fraud of men was ever so,
Since summer first was leavy.
Then sigh not so,
But let them go,
And be you blithe and bonny,
Converting all your sounds of woe
Into Hey nonny, nonny.

[*Much Ado about Nothing,* 1599]

[*A Song, whilst* BASSANIO *comments on the caskets to himself*

Tell me where is fancy bred,
Or in the heart or in the head?
How begot, how nourished?
Reply, reply.

It is engender'd in the eyes,
With gazing fed; and fancy dies
In the cradle where it lies.
Let us all ring fancy's knell:
I'll begin it,—Ding, dong, bell.
All. Ding, dong, bell.

[*The Merchant of Venice,* 1596]

Enter AMIENS, JAQUES, *and Others*

SONG

Ami. Under the greenwood tree
Who loves to lie with me,
And turn his merry note
Unto the sweet bird's throat,
Come hither, come hither, come hither:
Here shall he see
No enemy
But winter and rough weather.

Who doth ambition shun,
[*All together here.*
And loves to live i' the sun,
Seeking the food he eats,
And pleas'd with what he gets,
Come hither, come hither, come hither:
Here shall he see
No enemy
But winter and rough weather.

[*As You Like It,* 1599]

Ami. Blow, blow, thou winter wind,
Thou art not so unkind
As man's ingratitude;
Thy tooth is not so keen,
Because thou art not seen,
Although thy breath be rude.
Heigh-ho! sing, heigh-ho! unto the green holly:
Most friendship is feigning, most loving mere folly.
Then heigh-ho! the holly!
This life is most jolly.

Freeze, freeze, thou bitter sky,
That dost not bite so nigh
As benefits forgot:
Though thou the waters warp,
Thy sting is not so sharp
As friend remember'd not.
Heigh-ho! sing, heigh-ho! unto the green holly:
Most friendship is feigning, most loving mere folly.
Then heigh-ho! the holly!
This life is most jolly.

[*As You Like It,* 1599]

Clown. O mistress mine! Where are you roaming?
O! stay and hear; your true love's coming,
That can sing both high and low.
Trip no further, pretty sweeting;
Journeys end in lovers meeting,
Every wise man's son doth know.

Sir Andrew. Excellent good, i' faith.

Sir Toby. Good, good.

Clo. What is love? 'tis not hereafter;
Present mirth hath present laughter;
What's to come is still unsure:
In delay there lies no plenty;
Then come kiss me, sweet and twenty,
Youth's a stuff will not endure.

[*Twelfth Night,* 1601]

Clo. Come away, come away, death,
And in sad cypress let me be laid;
Fly away, fly away, breath;
I am slain by a fair cruel maid.
My shroud of white, stuck all with yew,
O! prepare it.
My part of death, no one so true
Did share it.

Not a flower, not a flower sweet,
On my black coffin let there be strown;
Not a friend, not a friend greet
My poor corse, where my bones shall be thrown.
A thousand thousand sighs to save,
Lay me, O! where
Sad true lover never find my grave,
To weep there.

[*Twelfth Night,* 1601]

Clo. When that I was and a little tiny boy,
With hey, ho, the wind and the rain;
A foolish thing was but a toy,
For the rain it raineth every day.

But when I came to man's estate,
With hey, ho, the wind and the rain;
'Gainst knaves and thieves men shut their gates,
For the rain it raineth every day.

But when I came, alas! to wive,
With hey, ho, the wind and the rain;
By swaggering could I never thrive,
For the rain it raineth every day.

But when I came unto my beds,
With hey, ho, the wind and the rain;
With toss-pots still had drunken heads,
For the rain it raineth every day.

A great while ago the world begun,
With hey, ho, the wind and the rain;
But that's all one, our play is done,
And we'll strive to please you every day.

[*Twelfth Night,* 1601]

Enter AUTOLYCUS, *singing*

Lawn as white as driven snow;
Cyprus black as e'er was crow;
Gloves as sweet as damask roses;
Masks for faces and for noses;
Bugle-bracelet, necklace-amber,
Perfume for a lady's chamber;
Golden quoifs and stomachers,
For my lads to give their dears;
Pins and poking-sticks of steel;
What maids lack from head to heel:
Come buy of me, come; come buy, come buy;
Buy, lads, or else your lasses cry:
Come buy.

[*The Winter's Tale,* 1611]

Orpheus with his lute made trees,
And the mountain tops that freeze,
Bow themselves, when he did sing:
To his music plants and flowers
Ever sprung; as sun and showers
There had made a lasting spring.

Every thing that heard him play,
Even the billows of the sea,
Hung their heads, and then lay by.
In sweet music is such art,
Killing care and grief of heart
Fall asleep, or hearing, die.

[*King Henry the Eighth,* 1612] [1]

[1] John Fletcher wrote a large part of *Henry the Eighth* and may therefore be the author of this song.

Come, thou monarch of the vine,
Plumpy Bacchus, with pink eyne!
In thy fats our cares be drown'd,
With thy grapes our hairs be crown'd:
Cup us, till the world go round,
Cup us, till the world go round!

[*Antony and Cleopatra*, 1607]

Guiderius. Fear no more the heat o' the sun,
Nor the furious winter's rages;
Thou thy worldly task hast done,
Home art gone, and ta'en thy wages;
Golden lads and girls all must,
As chimney-sweepers, come to dust.

Arviragus. Fear no more the frown o' the great,
Thou art past the tyrant's stroke:
Care no more to clothe and eat;
To thee the reed is as the oak;
The sceptre, learning, physic, must
All follow this, and come to dust

Gui. Fear no more the lightning-flash,
Arv. Nor the all-dreaded thunder-stone;
Gui. Fear not slander, censure rash;
Arv. Thou hast finish'd joy and moan:
Both. All lovers young, all lovers must
Consign to thee, and come to dust.

Gui. No exorciser harm thee!
Arv. Nor no witchcraft charm thee!
Gui. Ghost unlaid forbear thee!
Arv. Nothing ill come near thee!
Both. Quiet consummation have;
And renowned be thy grave!

[*Cymbeline*, 1610]

SONNETS

TO THE · ONLIE · BEGETTER · OF ·
THESE · INSUING · SONNETS,
MR. W. H.,[2] ALL HAPPINESSE
AND · THAT · ETERNITIE ·
PROMISED ·
BY ·
OUR EVER-LIVING POET ·
WISHETH ·
THE WELL-WISHING ·
ADVENTURER · IN
SETTING ·
FORTH

T. T.

I

FROM fairest creatures we desire increase,
That thereby beauty's rose might never die,
But as the riper should by time decease,
His tender heir might bear his memory:
But thou, contracted to thine own bright eyes,
Feed'st thy light's flame with self-substantial fuel,
Making a famine where abundance lies,
Thyself thy foe, to thy sweet self too cruel.
Thou that art now the world's fresh ornament
And only herald to the gaudy spring,
Within thine own bud buriest thy content
And, tender churl, mak'st waste in niggarding.
Pity the world, or else this glutton be,
To eat the world's due, by the grave and thee.

XIII

O! that you were yourself; but, love, you are
No longer yours than you yourself here live:
Against this coming end you should prepare,
And your sweet semblance to some other give:

[2] Who the 'Mr. W. H.' is who was the 'begetter' of Shakespeare's sonnets no one knows, though many a man has made a guess. The two likeliest candidates are William Herbert, third Earl of Pembroke, and Henry Wriothesley, third Earl of Southampton. It may be that begetter means simply 'obtainer.' In that case the mysterious Mr. W. H. could be either a printer's agent or some friend of Shakespeare who passed his sonnets on to the printer Thomas Thorpe, who issued them in 1609, probably without Shakespeare's consent.

So should that beauty which you hold in lease
Find no determination; then you were
Yourself again, after yourself's decease,
When your sweet issue your sweet form should bear.
Who lets so fair a house fall to decay,
Which husbandry in honour might uphold
Against the stormy gusts of winter's day
And barren rage of death's eternal cold?
O! none but unthrifts. Dear my love, you know
You had a father: let your son say so.

XV

When I consider every thing that grows
Holds in perfection but a little moment,
That this huge stage presenteth nought but shows
Whereon the stars in secret influence comment;
When I perceive that men as plants increase,
Cheered and check'd e'en by the self-same sky,
Vaunt in their youthful sap, at height decrease,
And wear their brave state out of memory;
Then the conceit of this inconstant stay
Sets you most rich in youth before my sight,
Where wasteful Time debateth with Decay,
To change your day of youth to sullied night;
And, all in war with Time for love of you,
As he takes from you, I engraft you new.

XVIII

Shall I compare thee to a summer's day?
Thou art more lovely and more temperate:
Rough winds do shake the darling buds of May,
And summer's lease hath all too short a date:
Sometime too hot the eye of heaven shines,
And often is his gold complexion dimm'd;
And every fair from fair sometime declines,
By chance, or nature's changing course untrimm'd;
But thy eternal summer shall not fade,
Nor lose possession of that fair thou ow'st,
Nor shall death brag thou wander'st in his shade,
When in eternal lines to time thou grow'st;
So long as men can breathe, or eyes can see,
So long lives this, and this gives life to thee.

XXIII

As an unperfect actor on the stage,
Who with his fear is put besides his part,
Or some fierce thing replete with too much rage,
Whose strength's abundance weakens his own heart;
So I, for fear of trust, forget to say
The perfect ceremony of love's rite,
And in mine own love's strength seem to decay,
O'ercharg'd with burden of mine own love's might.
O! let my books be then the eloquence
And dumb presagers of my speaking breast,
Who plead for love, and look for recompense,
More than that tongue that more hath more express'd.
O! learn to read what silent love hath writ:
To hear with eyes belongs to love's fine wit.

XXIX

When in disgrace with fortune and men's eyes
I all alone beweep my outcast state,
And trouble deaf heaven with my bootless cries,
And look upon myself, and curse my fate,
Wishing me like to one more rich in hope,
Featur'd like him, like him with friends possess'd,

Desiring this man's art, and that man's scope,
With what I most enjoy contented least;
Yet in these thoughts myself almost despising,
Haply I think on thee, — and then my state,
Like to the lark at break of day arising
From sullen earth, sings hymns at heaven's gate;
For thy sweet love remember'd such wealth brings
That then I scorn to change my state with kings.

XXX

When to the sessions of sweet silent thought
I summon up remembrance of things past,
I sigh the lack of many a thing I sought,
And with old woes new wail my dear times' waste:
Then can I drown an eye, unus'd to flow,
For precious friends hid in death's dateless[3] night,
And weep afresh love's long since cancell'd woe,
And moan the expense of many a vanish'd sight:
Then can I grieve at grievances foregone,
And heavily from woe to woe tell o'er
The sad account of fore-bemoaned moan,
Which I new pay as if not paid before.
But if the while I think on thee, dear friend,
All losses are restor'd and sorrows end.

XXXIII

Full many a glorious morning have I seen
Flatter the mountain-tops with sovereign eye,
Kissing with golden face the meadows green,
Gilding pale streams with heavenly alchymy;
Anon permit the basest clouds to ride
With ugly rack[4] on his celestial face,
And from the forlorn world his visage hide,
Stealing unseen to west with this disgrace:
Even so my sun one early morn did shine,
With all-triumphant splendour on my brow;
But, out! alack! he was but one hour mine,
The region cloud hath mask'd him from me now.
Yet him for this my love no whit disdaineth;
Suns of the world may stain when heaven's sun staineth.

XXXVI

Let me confess that we two must be twain,
Although our undivided loves are one:
So shall those blots that do with me remain,
Without thy help, by me be borne alone.
In our two loves there is but one respect,
Though in our lives a separable spite,
Which, though it alter not love's sole effect,
Yet doth it steal sweet hours from love's delight.
I may not evermore acknowledge thee,
Lest my bewailéd guilt should do thee shame,
Nor thou with public kindness honour me,
Unless thou take that honour from thy name:
But do not so; I love thee in such sort
As thou being mine, mine is thy good report.

LIII

What is your substance, whereof are you made,
That millions of strange shadows on you tend?
Since every one hath, every one, one shade,
And you, but one, can every shadow lend.
Describe Adonis, and the counterfeit
Is poorly imitated after you;
On Helen's cheek all art of beauty set,
And you in Grecian tires are painted new:
Speak of the spring and foison of the year,
The one doth shadow of your beauty show,
The other as your bounty doth appear;

[3] endless
[4] mass

And you in every blessed shape we know.
In all external grace you have some part,
But you like none, none you, for constant heart.

LV

Not marble, nor the gilded monuments
Of princes, shall outlive this powerful rime;
But you shall shine more bright in these contents
Than unswept stone, besmear'd with sluttish time.
When wasteful war shall statues overturn,
And broils root out the work of masonry,
Nor Mars his sword nor war's quick fire shall burn
The living record of your memory.
'Gainst death and all-oblivious enmity
Shall you pace forth; your praise shall still find room
Even in the eyes of all posterity
That wear this world out to the ending doom.
So, till the judgment that yourself arise,
You live in this, and dwell in lovers' eyes.

LXXI

No longer mourn for me when I am dead
Than you shall hear the surly sullen bell
Give warning to the world that I am fled
From this vile world, with vilest worms to dwell:
Nay, if you read this line, remember not
The hand that writ it; for I love you so,
That I in your sweet thoughts would be forgot,
If thinking on me then should make you woe.
O! if,—I say, you look upon this verse,
When I perhaps compounded am with clay,
Do not so much as my poor name rehearse,
But let your love even with my life decay;
Lest the wise world should look into your moan,
And mock you with me after I am gone.

LXXIII

That time of year thou mayst in me behold
When yellow leaves, or none, or few, do hang
Upon those boughs which shake against the cold,
Bare ruin'd choirs, where late the sweet birds sang.
In me thou see'st the twilight of such day
As after sunset fadeth in the west;
Which by and by black night doth take away,
Death's second self, that seals up all in rest.
In me thou see'st the glowing of such fire,
That on the ashes of his youth doth lie,
As the death-bed whereon it must expire
Consum'd with that which it was nourish'd by.
This thou perceiv'st, which makes thy love more strong,
To love that well which thou must leave ere long.

LXXXI

Or I shall live your epitaph to make,
Or you survive when I in earth am rotten;
From hence your memory death cannot take,
Although in me each part will be forgotten.
Your name from hence immortal life shall have,
Though I, once gone, to all the world must die:
The earth can yield me but a common grave,
When you entombéd in men's eyes shall lie.
Your monument shall be my gentle verse,
Which eyes not yet created shall o'er-read;
And tongues to be your being shall rehearse,
When all the breathers of this world are dead;
You still shall live,—such virtue hath my pen,—
Where breath most breathes,—even in the mouths of men.

LXXXVI

Was it the proud full sail of his great verse,
Bound for the prize of all too precious you,
That did my ripe thoughts in my brain inhearse,
Making their tomb the womb wherein they grew?
Was it his spirit, by spirits taught to write
Above a mortal pitch, that struck me dead?
No, neither he, nor his compeers by night
Giving him aid, my verse astonished.
He, nor that affable familiar ghost
Which nightly gulls him with intelligence,
As victors of my silence cannot boast;
I was not sick of any fear from thence:
But when your countenance fill'd up his line,
Then lack'd I matter; that enfeebled mine.

LXXXVII

Farewell! thou art too dear for my possessing,
And like enough thou know'st thy estimate:
The charter of thy worth gives thee releasing;
My bonds in thee are all determinate.
For how do I hold thee but by thy granting?
And for that riches where is my deserving?
The cause of this fair gift in me is wanting,
And so my patent back again is swerving.
Thyself thou gav'st, thy own worth then not knowing,
Or me, to whom thou gav'st it, else mistaking;
So thy great gift, upon misprision growing,
Comes home again, on better judgment making.
Thus have I had thee, as a dream doth flatter,
In sleep a king, but, waking, no such matter.

LXXXIX

Say that thou didst forsake me for some fault,
And I will comment upon that offence:
Speak of my lameness, and I straight will halt,
Against thy reasons making no defence.
Thou canst not, love, disgrace me half so ill,
To set a form upon desired change,
As I'll myself disgrace; knowing thy will,
I will acquaintance strangle, and look strange;
Be absent from thy walks; and in my tongue
Thy sweet beloved name no more shall dwell,
Lest I, too much profane, should do it wrong,
And haply of our old acquaintance tell.
For thee, against myself I'll vow debate,
For I must ne'er love him whom thou dost hate.

XCIX

The forward violet thus did I chide:
Sweet thief, whence didst thou steal thy sweet that smells,
If not from my love's breath? The purple pride
Which on thy soft cheek for complexion dwells
In my love's veins thou hast too grossly dy'd.
The lily I condemnéd for thy hand,
And buds of marjoram had stol'n thy hair;
The roses fearfully on thorns did stand,
One blushing shame, another white despair;
A third, nor red nor white, had stol'n of both,
And to his robbery had annex'd thy breath;
But, for his theft, in pride of all his growth
A vengeful canker eat him up to death.
More flowers I noted, yet I none could see
But sweet or colour it had stol'n from thee.

CII

My love is strengthen'd, though more weak in seeming;

I love not less, though less the show appear:
That love is merchandiz'd whose rich esteeming
The owner's tongue doth publish every where.
Our love was new, and then but in the spring,
When I was wont to greet it with my lays;
As Philomel in summer's front doth sing,
And stops her pipe in growth of riper days:
Not that the summer is less pleasant now
Than when her mournful hymns did hush the night,
But that wild music burthens every bough,
And sweets grown common lose their dear delight.
Therefore, like her, I sometimes hold my tongue,
Because I would not dull you with my song.

CIV

To me, fair friend, you never can be old,
For as you were when first your eye I ey'd,
Such seems your beauty still. Three winters cold
Have from the forests shook three summers' pride,
Three beauteous springs to yellow autumn turn'd
In process of the seasons have I seen,
Three April perfumes in three hot Junes burn'd,
Since first I saw you fresh, which yet are green.
Ah! yet doth beauty, like a dial-hand,
Steal from his figure, and no pace perceiv'd;
So your sweet hue, which methinks still doth stand,
Hath motion, and mine eye may be deceiv'd:
For fear of which, hear this, thou age unbred:
Ere you were born was beauty's summer dead.

CVI

When in the chronicle of wasted time
I see descriptions of the fairest wights,
And beauty making beautiful old rime,
In praise of ladies dead and lovely knights,
Then, in the blazon of sweet beauty's best,
Of hand, of foot, of lip, of eye, of brow,
I see their antique pen would have express'd
Even such a beauty as you master now.
So all their praises are but prophecies
Of this our time, all you prefiguring;
And, for they look'd but with divining eyes,
They had not skill enough your worth to sing:
For we, which now behold these present days,
Have eyes to wonder, but lack tongues to praise.

CVII

Not mine own fears, nor the prophetic soul
Of the wide world dreaming on things to come,
Can yet the lease of my true love control,
Suppos'd as forfeit to a confin'd doom.
The mortal moon hath her eclipse endur'd,
And the sad augurs mock their own presage;
Incertainties now crown themselves assur'd,
And peace proclaims olives of endless age.
Now with the drops of this most balmy time
My love looks fresh, and Death to me subscribes,
Since, spite of him, I'll live in this poor rime,
While he insults o'er dull and speechless tribes:
And thou in this shalt find thy monument,
When tyrants' crests and tombs of brass are spent.

CX

Alas! 'tis true I have gone here and there,
And made myself a motley to the view,

Gor'd mine own thoughts, sold cheap what is most dear,
Made old offences of affections new;
Most true it is that I have look'd on truth
Askance and strangely; but, by all above,
These blenches [5] gave my heart another youth,
And worse essays prov'd thee my best of love.
Now all is done, save what shall have no end:
Mine appetite I never more will grind
On newer proof, to try an older friend,
A god in love, to whom I am confin'd.
Then give me welcome, next my heaven the best,
Even to thy pure and most most loving breast.

CXVI

Let me not to the marriage of true minds
Admit impediments. Love is not love
Which alters when it alteration finds,
Or bends with the remover to remove:
O, no! it is an ever-fixed mark,
That looks on tempests and is never shaken;
It is the star to every wandering bark,
Whose worth's unknown, although his height be taken.
Love's not Time's fool, though rosy lips and cheeks
Within his bending sickle's compass come;
Love alters not with his brief hours and weeks,
But bears it out even to the edge of doom.
If this be error, and upon me prov'd,
I never writ, nor no man ever lov'd.

CXXIII

No, Time, thou shalt not boast that I do change:
Thy pyramids built up with newer might
To me are nothing novel, nothing strange;
They are but dressings of a former sight.
Our dates are brief, and therefore we admire
What thou dost foist upon us that is old;
And rather make them born to our desire
Than think that we before have heard them told.
Thy registers and thee I both defy,
Not wondering at the present nor the past,
For thy records and what we see doth lie,
Made more or less by thy continual haste.
This I do vow, and this shall ever be;
I will be true, despite thy scythe and thee.

CXXX

My mistress' eyes are nothing like the sun;
Coral is far more red than her lips' red:
If snow be white, why then her breasts are dun;
If hairs be wires, black wires grow on her head.
I have seen roses damask'd, red and white,
But no such roses see I in her cheeks;
And in some perfumes is there more delight
Than in the breath that from my mistress reeks.
I love to hear her speak, yet well I know
That music hath a far more pleasing sound:
I grant I never saw a goddess go,—
My mistress, when she walks, treads on the ground:
And yet, by heaven, I think my love as rare
As any she belied with false compare.

CXXXII

Thine eyes I love, and they, as pitying me,
Knowing thy heart torments me with disdain,
Have put on black and loving mourners be,
Looking with pretty ruth upon my pain.
And truly not the morning sun of heaven
Better becomes the grey cheeks of the east,
Nor that full star that ushers in the even,
Doth half that glory to the sober west,
As those two mourning eyes become thy face:

[5] side-glances

O! let it then as well beseem thy heart
To mourn for me, since mourning doth thee grace,
And suit thy pity like in every part.
Then will I swear beauty herself is black,
And all they foul that thy complexion lack.

CXXXVIII

When my love swears that she is made of truth,
I do believe her, though I know she lies,
That she might think me some untutor'd youth,
Unlearnéd in the world's false subtleties.
Thus vainly thinking that she thinks me young,
Although she knows my days are past the best,
Simply I credit her false-speaking tongue:
On both sides thus is simple truth supprest.
But wherefore says she not she is unjust?
And wherefore say not I that I am old?
O! love's best habit is in seeming trust,
And age in love loves not to have years told:
Therefore I lie with her, and she with me,
And in our faults by lies we flatter'd be.

CXLIII

Lo, as a careful housewife runs to catch
One of her feather'd creatures broke away,
Sets down her babe, and makes all quick dispatch
In pursuit of the thing she would have stay;
Whilst her neglected child holds her in chase,
Cries to catch her whose busy care is bent
To follow that which flies before her face,
Not prizing her poor infant's discontent:
So runn'st thou after that which flies from thee,
Whilst I thy babe chase thee afar behind;
But if thou catch thy hope, turn back to me,
And play the mother's part, kiss me, be kind;
So will I pray that thou mayst have thy *Will*,
If thou turn back and my loud crying still.

CXLIV

Two loves I have of comfort and despair,
Which like two spirits do suggest me still:
The better angel is a man right fair,
The worser spirit a woman, colour'd ill.
To win me soon to hell, my female evil
Tempteth my better angel from my side,
And would corrupt my saint to be a devil,
Wooing his purity with her foul pride.
And whether that my angel be turn'd fiend
Suspect I may, but not directly tell;
But being both from me, both to each friend,
I guess one angel in another's hell:
Yet this shall I ne'er know, but live in doubt,
Till my bad angel fire my good one out.

Ben Jonson*

1573?–1637

Why I Write not of Love

Some act of Love's bound to reherse,
I thought to bind him, in my verse:
Which when he felt, Away (quoth he)
Can poets hope to fetter me?
It is enough they once did get
Mars, and my mother, in their net:
I weare not these my wings in vaine.
With which he fled me; and againe,
Into my rimes could ne're be got
By any art. Then wonder not,
That since, my numbers are so cold,
When Love is fled, and I grow old.

[*The Forest*]

* The text of the selections from Jonson, unless otherwise stated, is that of the 1641 folio of the *Works*.

EPIGRAMS

To the Reader

Pray thee, take care, that tak'st my book in hand,
To read it well: that is, to understand.

To my Book

It will be look'd for, book, when some but see
Thy title, Epigrammes, and nam'd of mee,
Thou should'st be bold, licentious, full of gall;
Wormewood, and sulphure, sharp, and tooth'd withall,
Become a petulant thing, hurle inke and wit
As mad-men stones, not caring whom they hit.
Deceive their malice, who could wish it so.
And by thy wiser temper, let men know
Thou art not covetous of least self-fame
Made from the hazard of anothers shame.
Much lesse, with lewd, prophane, and beastly phrase,
To catch the worlds loose laughter, or vaine gaze.
He that departs with his own honesty
For vulgar praise, doth it too dearely buy.

To King James

How, best of kings, dost thou a scepter beare!
How, best of poets,[1] dost thou laurell weare!
But two things rare the Fates had in their store,
And gave thee both, to shew they could no more.
For such a poet, while thy daies were greene,
Thou wert, as chiefe of them are said t'have been.
And such a prince thou art we daily see,
As chiefe of those still promise they will bee.
Whom should my Muse then flye to, but the best
Of kings for grace; of poets, for my test?

[1] King James was not only a poet but also the compiler of a book of rules 'to be observit in Scottis Poesie.'

To John Donne

Donne, the delight of Phœbus and each muse,
Who, to thy one, all other braines refuse;
Whose every work, of thy most early wit,
Came forth example, and remaines so, yet:
Longer a knowing, than most wits do live;
And which no affection praise enough can give!
To it, thy language, letters, arts, best life,
Which might with halfe mankind maintaine a strife;
All which I meane to praise, and yet I would;
But leave, because I cannot as I should!

To the Ghost of Martial

Martial, thou gav'st farre nobler epigrammes
To thy Domitian, than I can my James;
But in my royall subject I passe thee,
Thou flattered'st thine, mine cannot flatter'd bee.

On my first Son [2]

Farewell, thou child of my right hand, and joy;
My sinne was too much hope of thee, lov'd boy.
Seven yeares tho'wert lent to me, and I thee pay,
Exacted by thy fate, on the just day.

[2] The boy was born in 1596 and died in 1603 of the plague then raging in London. Jonson was in the country at the time, but had a vision of the boy 'of manly shape and of the growth that he 'shall be at the resurrection.'

O, could I lose all father, now. For why
Will man lament the state he should envié?
To have so soone scap'd worlds and fleshes rage,
And, if no other miserie, yet age?
Rest in soft peace, and, ask'd, say, Here doth lye
Ben. Jonson his best piece of poetrie.
For whose sake, hence-forth, all his vowes be such,
As what hee loves may never like too much.

To Francis Beaumont[3]

How I doe love thee, Beaumont, and thy Muse,
That unto me dost such religion use!
How I doe feare my selfe, that am not worth
The least indulgent thought thy pen drops forth!
At once thou mak'st me happie, and unmak'st;
And giving largely to me, more thou tak'st.
What fate is mine, that so it selfe bereaves?
What art is thine, that so thy friend deceives?
When even there, where most thou praisest mee,
For writing better, I must envie thee.

On Lucy, Countess of Bedford[4]

This morning, timely rapt with holy fire,
I thought to forme unto my zealous Muse
What kinde of creature I could most desire,
To honour, serve, and love; as poets use.
I meant to make her faire, and free, and wise,
Of greatest blood, and yet more good than great;
I meant the day-starre should not brighter rise,
Nor lend like influence from his lucent seat.
I meant she should be courteous, facile, sweet,
Hating that solemn vice of greatnesse, pride;
I meant each softest vertue, there should meet,
Fit in that softer bosome to reside.
Only a learnéd, and a manly soule
I purpos'd her; that should, with even powers,
The rock,[5] the spindle, and the sheeres controule
Of Destiny, and spin her owne free houres.
Such when I meant to faine, and wish'd to see,
My Muse bade, Bedford write, and that was shee.

To Edward Allen[6]

If Rome so great, and in her wisest age,
Fear'd not to boast the glories of her stage,
As skilfull Roscius, and grave Æsope, men
Yet crown'd with honors, as with riches, then;
Who had no lesse a trumpet of their name,
Than Cicero, whose every breath was fame:
How can so great example dye in me,
That Allen, I should pause to publish thee?
Who both their graces in thy selfe hast more
Out-stript than they did all that went before:
And present worth in all dost so contract,
As others speak, but only thou dost act.
Weare this renowne. 'Tis just, that who did give
So many poets life, by one should live.

---

[3] The dramatist.
[4] The patroness of many poets.
[5] distaff
[6] A great actor, creator of the chief rôles in Marlowe's plays.

Inviting a Friend to Supper

To night, grave sir, both my poore house and I
 Doe equally desire your company;
Not that we think us worthy such a ghest,
 But that your worth will dignifie our feast,
With those that come; whose grace may make that seeme
 Something, which else could hope for no esteeme.
It is the faire acceptance, Sir, creates
 The entertaynment perfect, not the cates.
Yet shall you have, to rectifie your palate,
 An olive, capers, or some better sallad
Ushring the mutton; with a short-leg'd hen,
 If we can get her, full of eggs, and then,
Limons, and wine for sauce: to these, a coney [7]
 Is not to be despair'd of, for our money;
And, though fowle, now, be scarce, yet there are clarks,
 The skie not falling, think we may have larks.
I'le tell you of more, and lye, so you will come;
 Of partrich, phesant, wood-cock, of which some
May yet be there; and godwit, if we can:
 Knat, raile, and ruffe [8] too. How so ere, my man
Shall reade a peece of Virgil, Tacitus,
 Livie, or of some better booke to us,
Of which wee'll speake our minds, amidst our meate;
 And I'le professe no verses to repeate;
To this, if ought appeare, which I know not of,
 That will the pastrie, not my paper, show of.
Digestive cheese, and fruit there sure will bee;
 But that which most doth take my muse, and mee,
Is a pure cup of rich Canary-wine,
 Which is the Mermaids,[9] now, but shall bee mine;
Of which had Horace, or Anacreon [10] tasted,
 Their lives, as doe their lines, till now had lasted.
Tabacco, nectar, or the Thespian spring,
 Are all but Luthers beere to this I sing.
Of this we will sup free, but moderately,
 And wee will have no Pooly,[11] or Parrot by;
Nor shall our cups make any guiltie men:
 But at our parting, we will be, as when
We innocently met. No simple word,
 That shall be utter'd at our mirthfull boord,
Shall make us sad next morning, or affright
 The libertie that wee'le enjoy to night.

An Epitaph on S. P.,[12] a Child of Q. El.'s Chapel

Weep with me, all you that read
 This little story:
And know, for whom a teare you shed,
 Death's selfe is sorry.
'Twas a child that so did thrive
 In grace, and feature,
As Heaven and Nature seem'd to strive
 Which own'd the creature.
Yeares he numbred scarce thirteene
 When Fates turn'd cruell,
Yet three fill'd zodiackes had he been
 The stages jewell;
And did act (what now we moane)
 Old men so duely,
As, sooth, the Parcae thought him one,
 He plai'd so truely.
So, by error, to his fate
 They all consented;
But viewing him since (alas, too late)
 They have repented;

[7] rabbit
[8] The first three are birds. The ruffe is a small perch.

[9] The Mermaid Tavern was the gathering place of the 'Tribe of Ben.'
[10] Greek amatory poet, a favorite with Jonson.
[11] Poll-parrot
[12] Salathiel Pavy, one of the Children of the Chapel Royal. He had begun acting at the age of ten and died at thirteen.

And have sought (to give new birth)
In bathes to steep him;
But being so much too good for earth,
Heaven vows to keep him.

SONGS FROM THE PLAYS AND MASQUES

Slow, slow, fresh fount

Slow, slow, fresh fount, keep time with my salt teares;
Yet slower, yet, O faintly, gentle springs;
List to the heavy part the musick beares,
Woe weeps out her division,[13] when shee sings.
Droup hearbs and flowres;
Fall griefe in showres;
Our beauties are now ours:
O, I could still
(Like melting snow upon some craggy hill,)
drop, drop, drop, drop,
Since natures pride is now a wither'd daffodil.

[*Cynthia's Revels*]

Queene and Huntresse

Queene and Huntresse,[14] chaste and faire,
Now the sunne is laid to sleepe,
Seated, in thy silver chaire,
State in wonted manner keepe;
Hesperus intreats thy light,
Goddesse excellently bright.

Earth, let not thy envious shade
Dare itself to interpose;
Cynthia's shining orbe was made
Heaven to cleere, when day did close;
Blesse us then with wishéd sight,
Goddesse excellently bright.

Lay thy bow of pearle apart,
And thy crystall-shining quiver;
Give unto the flying hart
Space to breathe, how short soever:
Thou that mak'st a day of night,
Goddesse excellently bright.

[*Cynthia's Revels*]

To Celia

Come, my Celia, let us prove,
While wee can, the sports of love,
Time will not be ours, for ever:
He, at length, our good will sever.
Spend not then his gifts in vaine.
Sunnes that set may rise againe;
But, if once wee lose this light,
'Tis, with us, perpetuall night.
Why should we deferre our joyes?
Fame and rumor are but toies.
Cannot wee delude the eyes
Of a few poore houshold spyes?
Or his easier eares beguile,
So removéd by our wile?
'Tis no sinne loves fruit to steele;
But the sweet thefts to reveale:
To bee taken, to be seene,
These have crimes accounted beene.

[*Volpone*]

Still to be neat

Still to be neat, still to be drest,
As you were going to a feast;
Still to bee pou'dred, still perfum'd:
Lady, it is to be presum'd,
Though arts hid causes are not found,
All is not sweet, all is not sound.

Give me a look, give me a face,
That makes simplicity a grace;
Robes loosely flowing, hayre as free:
Such sweet neglect more taketh me
Than all th'adulteries of art;
They strike mine eyes, but not my heart.

[*The Silent Woman*]

Beauties, have ye seen this toy

I *Grace*

Beauties, have ye seen this toy,
Calléd Love, a little boy,
Almost naked, wanton, blind,

[13] musical part
[14] Diana

Cruell now; and then as kind?
If he be amongst ye, say;
He is Venus' run-away.

2 *Grace*

She that will but now discover
Where the wingéd wag doth hover,
Shall, to night, receive a kisse,
How or where her selfe would wish:
But, who brings him to his mother,
Shall have that kisse, and another.

3 *Grace*

H'hath of markes about him plenty:
You shall know him among twenty.
All his body is a fire,
And his breath a flame entire,
That being shot, like lightning, in,
Wounds the heart, but not the skin.

1 *Grace*

At his sight, the sun hath turned,
Neptune in the waters, burned;
Hell hath felt a greater heat;
Jove himselfe forsook his seat;
From the center, to the skie
Are his trophæes rearéd hie.

2 *Grace*

Wings he hath, which though yee clip,
He will leape from lip, to lip,
Over liver, lights, and heart,
But not stay in any part;
And if chance his arrow misses,
He will shoot himselfe, in kisses.

3 *Grace*

He doth beare a golden bow,
And a quiver, hanging low,
Full of arrows that out-brave
Dian's shafts; where if he have
Any head more sharp than other,
With that first he strikes his mother.

1 *Grace*

Still the fairest are his fuell.
When his dayes are to be cruell,
Lovers hearts are all his food;
And his bathes their warmest blood:
Nought but wounds his hand doth season,
And he hates none like to Reason.

2 *Grace*

Trust him not; his words, though sweet,
Seldome with his heart do meet.
All his practise is deceit;
Every gift it is a bait;
Not a kisse but poyson beares;
And most treason in his teares.

3 *Grace*

Idle minutes are his raign;
Then the straggler makes his gaine,
By presenting maids with toyes,
And would have ye think 'hem joyes;
'Tis the ambition of the elfe,
To 'have all children as himselfe.

1 *Grace*

If by these ye please to know him,
Beauties, be not nice, but show him.

2 *Grace*

Though ye had a will to hide him,
Now, we hope, ye'le not abide him.

3 *Grace*

Since yee heare his falser play;
And that he is Venus' run-away.

[*The Hue and Cry after Cupid*]

Hymn to Comus [15]

Roome, roome, make roome for the bouncing bellie,
First father of sauce and deviser of jellie;
Prime master of arts and the giver of wit,
That found out the excellent engine, the spit;
The plough, and the flaile, the mill, and the hopper,

[15] The god of the belly.

The hutch, and the boulter, the furnace and copper,
The oven, the baven,[16] the mawkin,[17] the peele,[18]
The harth, and the range, the dogge, and the wheele,[19]
He, he first invented the hogshead and tun,
The gimlet and vice too, and taught 'em to run,
And since with the funnell and Hippocras bag,[20]
H'as made of himselfe, that now he cries swag; [21]
Which showes though the pleasure be but of foure inches,
Yet he is a weesell, the gullet that pinches
Of any delight, and not spares from this backe,
What ever to make of the bellie a sacke!
Haile, haile, plump paunch! O the founder of taste,
For fresh-meats, or powlder'd, or pickle, or paste,
Devourer of broyl'd, back'd, roasted, or sod; [22]
And emptier of cups, be they even or odd;
All which have now made thee so wide i'the waste,
As scarce with no pudding thou art to be lac'd,
But eating and drinking untill thou dost nod,
Thou break'st all thy girdles and break'st forth a god.

[*Pleasure Reconciled to Virtue*]

Though I am young

Though I am young, and cannot tell,
Either that Death or Love is well,
Yet I have heard they both beare darts,
And both doe ayme at humane hearts.
And then againe, I have beene told
Love wounds with heat, as Death with cold;
So that I feare they doe but bring
Extreames to touch, and meane one thing.

As in a ruine we it call
One thing to be blowne up, or fall;
Or to our end, like way may have,
By a flash of lightning, or a wave;
So Loves inflaméd shaft or brand
May kill as soone as Deaths cold hand;
Except Loves fires the vertue have
To fright the frost out of the grave.

[*The Sad Shepherd*]

To the Memory of my beloved the Author, Mr. William Shakespeare: and what he hath left us

To draw no envy (Shakespeare) on thy name,
Am I thus ample to thy booke, and fame;
While I confesse thy writings to be such
As neither man, nor muse, can praise too much.
'Tis true, and all mens suffrage. But these wayes
Were not the paths I meant unto thy praise;
For seeliest ignorance on these may light,
Which, when it sounds at best, but eccho's right;
Or blind affection, which doth ne're advance
The truth, but gropes, and urgeth all by chance;
Or crafty malice might pretend this praise,
And think to ruine, where it seem'd to raise.
These are, as some infamous baud, or whore,
Should praise a matron. What could hurt her more?
But thou art proofe against them, and indeed

[16] a bundle of sticks
[17] mop
[18] baker's shovel
[19] for turning the spit
[20] Hippocras, a sweet wine flavored with spices, was filtered through a bag.
[21] belly
[22] boiled

Above th'ill fortune of them, or the need.
I, therefore, will begin. Soule of the age!
The applause! delight! the wonder of our stage!
My Shakespeare, rise; I will not lodge thee by
Chaucer, or Spenser, or bid Beaumont lye
A little further, to make thee a roome;
Thou art a moniment, without a tombe,
And art alive still, while thy booke doth live,
And we have wits to reade, and praise to give.
That I not mixe thee so, my braine excuses;
I meane with great, but disproportion'd muses:
For, if I thought my judgement were of yeeres,
I should commit thee surely with thy peeres,
And tell how farre thou didst our Lily outshine,
Or sporting Kid, or Marlowes mighty line.
And though thou hadst small Latine, and lesse Greeke,
From thence to honour thee I would not seeke
For names; but call forth thundring Æschilus,
Euripides, and Sophocles to us,
Paccuvius, Accius,[23] him of Cordova[24] dead,
To life againe, to heare thy buskin tread
And shake a stage: or, when thy sockes were on,
Leave thee alone for the comparison
Of all that insolent Greece or haughtie Rome
Sent forth, or since did from their ashes come.
Triumph, my Britaine, thou hast one to showe
To whom all scenes of Europe homage owe.
He was not of an age, but for all time!
And all the Muses still were in their prime,
When like Apollo he came forth to warme
Our eares, or like a Mercury to charme!
Nature her selfe was proud of his designes,
And joy'd to weare the dressing of his lines,
Which were so richly spun, and woven so fit,
As, since, she will vouchsafe no other wit.
The merry Greeke, tart Aristophanes,
Neat Terence, witty Plautus, now not please,
But antiquated and deserted lye
As they were not of natures family.
Yet must I not give nature all; thy art,
My gentle Shakespeare, must enjoy a part;
For though the poet's matter nature be,
His art doth give the fashion. And that he
Who casts to write a living line, must sweat,
(Such as thine are) and strike the second heat
Upon the Muses anvile, turne the same,
(And himselfe with it) that he thinkes to frame;
Or for the lawrell he may gaine a scorne,
For a good poet's made, as well as borne;
And such wert thou. Looke how thy fathers face
Lives in his issue; even so the race
Of Shakespeares minde and manners brightly shines
In his well tornéd, and true-filéd lines;
In each of which he seemes to shake a lance,
As brandish't at the eyes of ignorance.
Sweet swan of Avon! what a sight it were
To see thee in our waters yet appeare,
And make those flights upon the bankes of Thames,
That so did take Eliza,[25] and our James!

[23] Pacuvius and Accius were Roman tragic poets.
[24] Seneca, the Roman tragic poet, was born in Spain.
[25] Queen Elizabeth.

But stay, I see thee in the hemisphere
Advanc'd, and made a constellation there!
Shine forth, thou starre of poets, and with rage
Or influence, chide, or cheere the drooping stage;
Which, since thy flight from hence, hath mourn'd like night,
And despaires day, but for thy volumes light.

[*Mr. William Shakespeares Comedies, Histories, & Tragedies*, 1623]

from A CELEBRATION OF CHARIS

How he saw her

I BEHELD her, on a day,
When her looke out-flourisht May:
And her dressing did out-brave
All the pride the fields then have:
Farre I was from being stupid,
For I ran and call'd on Cupid;
Love if thou wilt ever see
Marke of glorie, come with me;
Where's thy quiver? bend thy bow:
Here's a shaft, thou art to slow!
And (withall) I did untie
Every cloud about his eye;
But, he had not gain'd his sight
Sooner, than he lost his might,
Or his courage; for away
Strait hee ran, and durst not stay,
Letting bow and arrow fall,
Nor for any threat, or call,
Could be brought once back to looke,
I foole-hardie, there up tooke
Both the arrow he had quit,
And the bow: which thought to hit
This my object. But she threw
Such a lightning (as I drew)
At my face, that tooke my sight,
And my motion from me quite;
So that there, I stood a stone,
Mock'd of all: and call'd of one
(Which with griefe and wrath I heard)
Cupids statue with a beard,
Or else one that plaid his ape,
In a Hercules-his shape.

Her triumph

SEE the chariot at hand here of Love,
Wherein my lady rideth!
Each that drawes is a swan, or a dove,
And well the carre Love guideth.
As she goes, all hearts doe duty
Unto her beauty;
And enamour'd, doe wish, so they might
But enjoy such a sight,
That they still were to run by her side,
Through swords, through seas, whether she would ride.

Doe but looke on her eyes; they doe light
All that Loves world compriseth!
Doe but looke on her haire; it is bright
As Loves starre when it riseth!
Doe but marke, her forhead's smoother
Then words that sooth her!
And from her arched browes, such a grace
Sheds it selfe through the face,
As alone there triumphs to the life
All the gaine, all the good, of the elements strife.

Have you seene but a bright lillie grow,
Before rude hands have touch'd it?
Ha'you mark'd but the fall o'the snow
Before the soyle hath smutch'd it?
Ha'you felt the wooll of bever?
Or swans downe ever?
Or have smelt o'the bud o'the brier?
Or the nard [26] in the fire?
Or have tasted the bag of the bee?
O so white! O so soft! O so sweet is she!

Begging another, on colour of mending the former

FOR loves-sake, kisse me once againe;
I long, and should not beg in vaine,

[26] An aromatic balsam.

Here's none to spie, or see;
Why doe you doubt, or stay?
I'll taste as lightly as the bee
That doth but touch his flower, and flies away.
Once more, and (faith) I will be gone;
Can he that loves, aske lesse then one?
Nay, you may erre in this,
And all your bountie wrong:
This could be call'd but halfe a kisse.
What w'are but once to doe, we should doe long;
I will but mend the last, and tell
Where, how it would have relish'd well;
Joyne lip to lip, and try:
Each suck others breath.
And whilst our tongues perplexéd lie,
Let who will, thinke us dead, or wish our death.

[*Underwoods*]

An Ode to himself

Where do'st thou carelesse lie
Buried in ease and sloth?
Knowledge, that sleepes, doth die;
And this securitie,
It is the common moth,
That eats on wits, and arts, and destroyes them both.

Are all th'Aonian[27] springs
Dri'd up? Lyes Thespia wast?
Doth Clarius[28] harp want strings,
That not a nymph now sings?
Or droop they as disgrac't,
To see their seats and bowers by chattring pies defac't?

If hence thy silence be,
As 'tis too just a cause,
Let this thought quicken thee:
Minds that are great and free
Should not on fortune pause;
'Tis crowne enough to vertue still, her owne applause.

What though the greedie frie
Be taken with false baytes
Of worded balladrie,
And think it poesie?
They die with their conceits,
And only pitious scorne upon their folly waites.

Then take in hand thy lyre,
Strike in thy proper straine,
With Japhets[29] lyne aspire
Sols chariot for new fire,
To give the world againe:
Who aided him, will thee, the issue of Joves braine.

And since our daintie age
Cannot indure reproofe.
Make not thy selfe a page
To that strumpet, the stage,
But sing high and aloofe,
Safe from the wolves black jaw, and the dull asses hoofe.

[*Underwoods*]

An Epigram

To King Charles for an hundred pounds he sent me in my Sickness. 1629

Great Charles, among the holy gifts of grace
Annexéd to thy person, and thy place,
'Tis not enough (thy pietie is such)
To cure the call'd kings evill[30] with thy touch;
But thou wilt yet a kinglier mastrie trie,
To cure the poets evill, povertie:
And, in these cures, do'st so thy selfe enlarge,
As thou dost cure our evill, at thy charge.
Nay, and in this, thou show'st to value more
One poet, then of other folke ten score.
O pietie, so to weigh the poores estates!

[27] The Muses have their home in Aonia.
[28] Apollo, from his temple at Clarus.

[29] Prometheus was the son of Jepetus.
[30] scrofula. It was thought that the touch of the royal hand would cure the disease. Anne was the last English sovereign to 'touch' for it. Dr. Johnson was taken to London for her ministration.

O bountie, so to difference the rates!
What can the poet wish his king may doe,
But that he cure the peoples evill too?

[*Underwoods*]

An Epistle

Answering to one that asked to be sealed of the Tribe of Ben

Men that are safe, and sure, in all they doe,
Care not what trials they are put unto;
They meet the fire, the test, as martyrs would;
And though opinion stampe them not, are gold.
I could say more of such, but that I flie
To speake my selfe out too ambitiously,
And shewing so weake an act to vulgar eyes
Put conscience and my right to comprimise.
Let those that meerely talke, and never thinke,
That live in the wild anarchie of drinke,
Subject to quarrell only, or else such
As make it their proficiencie, how much
They'ave glutted in, and letcher'd out that weeke,
That never yet did friend, or friendship, seeke
But for a sealing: let these men protest.
Or th'other on their borders, that will jeast
On all soules that are absent, even the dead,
Like flies, or wormes, which mans corrupt parts fed;
That to speake well, thinke it above all sinne,
Of any companie but that they are in,
Call every night to supper in these fitts,
And are receiv'd for the covey of witts;
That censure all the towne, and all th'affaires,
And know whose ignorance is more then theirs;
Let these men have their wayes, and take their times
To vent their libels, and to issue rimes;
I have no portion in them, nor their deale
Of newes they get, to strew out the long meale;
I studie other friendships, and more one,
Then these can ever be; or else wish none.
What is't to me whether the French designe
Be, or be not, to get the Val-telline?[31]
Or the States ships sent forth belike to meet
Some hopes of Spaine in their West-Indian fleet?
Whether the dispensation yet be sent,
Or that the match[32] from Spaine was ever meant?
I wish all well, and pray high heaven conspire
My princes safetie,[33] and my kings desire;
But if for honour we must draw the sword,
And force back that which will not be restor'd,[34]
I have a body, yet, that spirit drawes
To live, or fall a carkasse in the cause.
So farre without inquirie what the States,
Brunsfield,[35] and Mansfield[36] doe this yeare, my fates
Shall carry me at call; and I'le be well,
Though I doe neither heare these newes, nor tell
Of Spaine or France; or were not prick'd downe one
Of the late mysterie of reception,[37]
Although my fame, to his,[38] not under-heares,
That guides the motions, and directs the beares.
But that's a blow by which in time I may

---

[31] A valley near the Lake of Como which France in 1623 was seeking to recover.

[32] Between the Prince of Wales and the Infanta of Spain. The Pope delayed giving the necessary dispensation.

[33] The Prince was then in Spain.

[34] The Elector Palatine, husband of the king's daughter, Elizabeth, had been driven from his territory.

[35] Jonson means Brunswick. The ruler was a cousin of the Princess Elizabeth.

[36] Commander of the Elector Palatine's army.

[37] For the Prince on his return. Jonson was not asked to devise a masque for the occasion.

[38] The reference is probably to Inigo Jones, Jonson's great rival in the production of masques at court.

Lose all my credit with my Christmas clay,
And animated porc'lane of the court;
Ay, and for this neglect, the courser sort
Of earthen jarres there may molest me too.
Well, with mine owne fraile pitcher, what to doe
I have decreed; keepe it from waves, and presse,
Lest it be justled, crack'd, made nought, or lesse;
Live to that point I will for which I am man,
And dwell as in my center, as I can,
Still looking to, and ever loving heaven;
With reverence using all the gifts then given.
'Mongst which, if I have any friendships sent
Such as are square, wel-tagde, and permanent,
Not built with canvasse, paper, and false lights
As are the glorious scenes at the great sights,[39]
And that there be no fev'ry heats, nor colds,
Oylie expansions, or shrunke durtie folds,
But all so cleare, and led by reasons flame,
As but to stumble in her sight were shame:
These I will honour, love, embrace, and serve,
And free it from all question to preserve.
So short you read my character, and theirs
I would call mine, to which not many staires
Are asked to climbe. First give me faith, who know
My selfe a little. I will take you so,
As you have writ your selfe. Now stand, and then
Sir, you are sealéd of the Tribe of Ben.

[*Underwoods*]

[39] masques

John Donne

1572–1631

Song [1]

Goe, and catche a falling starre,
Get with child a mandrake [2] roote,
Tell me, where all past yeares are,
Or who cleft the divels foot,
Teach me to heare mermaides singing,
Or to keep off envies stinging,
And finde
What winde
Serves to advance an honest minde.

If thou beest borne to strange sights,
Things invisible to see,
Ride ten thousand daies and nights,
Till age snow white haires on thee,
Thou, when thou retorn'st, wilt tell mee
All strange wonders that befell thee,
And sweare
No where
Lives a woman true, and faire.

If thou findst one, let mee know,
Such a pilgrimage were sweet;
Yet doe not, I would not goe,
Though at next doore wee might meet,
Though shee were true, when you met her,
And last, till you write your letter,
Yet shee
Will bee
False, ere I come, to two, or three.

[1] Donne's poems were first published in 1633, two years after his death.
[2] The root of the mandrake suggests the shape of the human body.

The Sun Rising

Busie old foole, unruly sunne,
Why dost thou thus,

Through windowes, and through curtaines call on us?
Must to thy motions lovers seasons run?

Sawcy pedantique wretch, goe chide
Late schoole boyes, and sowre prentices,
Goe tell court-huntsmen, that the king will ride,
Call countrey ants to harvest offices;
Love, all alike, no season knowes, nor clyme,
Nor houres, dayes, moneths, which are the rags of time.

Thy beames, so reverend, and strong
Why shouldst thou thinke?
I could eclipse and cloud them with a winke,
But that I would not lose her sight so long;
If her eyes have not blinded thine,
Looke, and to morrow late, tell mee,
Whether both the Indias of spice and myne [3]
Be where thou leftst them, or lie here with mee.
Aske for those kings whom thou saw'st yesterday,
And thou shalt heare, all here in one bed lay.

She is all states, and all princes, I;
Nothing else is.
Princes doe but play us; compar'd to this,
All honor's mimique; all wealth alchimie.
Thou, sunne, art halfe as happy as wee,
In that the world's contracted thus;
Thine age askes ease, and since thy duties bee
To warme the world, that's done in warming us.
Shine here to us, and thou art every where;
This bed thy center is, these walls, thy spheare.

[3] The East and West Indies.

The Indifferent

I CAN love both faire and browne,
Her whom abundance melts, and her whom want betraies,
Her who loves lonenesse best, and her who maskes and plaies,
Her whom the country form'd, and whom the town,
Her who beleeves, and her who tries,
Her who still weepes with spungie eyes,
And her who is dry corke, and never cries;
I can love her, and her, and you and you,
I can love any, so she be not true.

Will no other vice content you?
Wil it not serve your turn to do, as did your mothers?
Or have you all old vices spent, and now would finde out others?
Or doth a feare, that men are true, torment you?
Oh we are not, be not you so,
Let mee, and doe you, twenty know.
Rob mee, but binde me not, and let me goe.
Must I, who came to travaile thorow you,
Grow your fixt subject, because you are true?

Venus heard me sigh this song,
And by loves sweetest part, variety, she swore,
She heard not this till now, and that it should be so no more.
She went, examin'd, and return'd ere long,
And said, alas, Some two or three
Poore heretiques in love there bee,
Which thinke to stablish dangerous constancie.
But I have told them, since you will be true,
You shall be true to them, who are false to you.

The triple Fool

I AM two fooles, I know,
For loving, and for saying so
In whining poetry;

But where's that wiseman, that would not be I,
If she would not deny?
Then as th'earths inward narrow crooked lanes
Do purge sea waters fretfull salt away,
I thought, if I could draw my paines,
Through rimes vexation, I should them allay.
Griefe brought to numbers cannot be so fierce,
For, he tames it, that fetters it in verse.

But when I have done so,
Some man, his art and voice to show,
Doth set [4] and sing my paine,
And, by delighting many, frees againe
Griefe, which verse did restraine.
To love and griefe tribute of verse belongs,
But not of such as pleases when'tis read;
Both are increaséd by such songs,
For both their triumphs so are publishéd,
And I, which was two fooles, do so grow three;
Who are a little wise, the best fooles bee.

Song

Sweetest love, I do not goe,
For wearinesse of thee,
Nor in hope the world can show
A fitter love for mee;
But since that I
Must dye at last, 'tis best,
To use my selfe in jest
Thus by fain'd deaths to dye;

Yesternight the sunne went hence,
And yet is here to day,
He hath no desire nor sense,
Nor halfe so short a way;
Then feare not mee,
But beleeve that I shall make
Speedier journeyes, since I take
More wings and spurres then hee.

O how feeble is mans power,
That if good fortune fall,
Cannot adde another houre,
Nor a lost houre recall!
But come bad chance,
And wee joyne to it our strength,
And wee teach it art and length,
It selfe o'r us to advance.

When thou sigh'st, thou sigh'st not winde,
But sigh'st my soule away,
When thou weep'st, unkindly kinde,
My lifes blood doth decay.
It cannot bee
That thou lov'st mee, as thou say'st,
If in thine my life thou waste,
Thou art the best of mee.

Let not thy divining heart
Forethinke me any ill,
Destiny may take thy part,
And may thy feares fulfill;
But thinke that wee
Are but turn'd aside to sleepe;
They who one another keepe
Alive, ne'r parted bee.

The Anniversary

All kings, and all their favorites,
All glory of honors, beauties, wits,
The sun it selfe, which makes times as they passe,
Is elder by a yeare, now, then it was
When thou and I first one another saw;
All other things to their destruction draw,
Only our love hath no decay;
This, no to morrow hath, nor yesterday,
Running, it never runs from us away,
But truly keepes his first, last, everlasting day.

Two graves must hide thine and my coarse;
If one might, death were no divorce.
Alas, as well as other princes, wee,
(Who prince enough in one another bee,)

[4] set to music

Must leave at last in death, these eyes, and eares,
Oft fed with true oathes, and with sweet salt teares;
But soules where nothing dwells but love
(All other thoughts being inmates) then shall prove
This, or a love increaséd there above,
When bodies to their graves, soules from their graves, remove.

And then wee shall be throughly blest,
But wee no more, then all the rest;
Here upon earth, we are kings, and none but wee
Can be such kings, nor of such subjects bee;
Who is so safe as wee where none can doe
Treason to us, except one of us two?
True and false feares let us refraine,
Let us love nobly, and live, and adde againe
Yeares and yeares unto yeares, till we attaine
To write threescore; this is the second of our raigne.

The Dream

Deare love, for nothing lesse then thee
Would I have broke this happy dreame;
It was a theame
For reason, much too strong for phantasie,
Therefore thou wakd'st me wisely; yet
My dreame thou brok'st not, but continued'st it,
Thou art so truth, that thoughts of thee suffice
To make dreames truths; and fables histories;
Enter these armes, for since thou thoughtst it best,
Not to dreame all my dreame, let's act the rest.

As lightning, or a tapers light,
Thine eyes, and not thy noise wak'd mee;
Yet I thought thee
(For thou lovest truth) an angell, at first sight,
But when I saw thou sawest my heart,
And knew'st my thoughts, beyond an angels art,
When thou knew'st what I dreamt, when thou knew'st when
Excesse of joy would wake me, and cam'st then,
I must confesse, it could not chuse but bee
Prophane, to thinke thee any thing but thee.

Comming and staying show'd thee, thee,
But rising makes me doubt, that now,
Thou are not thou.
That love is weake, where feare's as strong as hee;
'Tis not all spirit, pure, and brave,
If mixture it of feare, shame, honor, have.
Perchance as torches which must ready bee,
Men light and put out,[5] so thou deal'st with mee;
Thou cam'st to kindle, goest to come; then I
Will dreame that hope againe, but else would die.

Love's Alchemy

Some that have deeper digg'd loves myne then I,
Say, where his centrique happinesse doth lie.
I have lov'd, and got, and told,
But should I love, get, tell, till I were old,
I should not finde that hidden mysterie;
Oh, 'tis imposture all.
And as no chymique yet th'elixar got,
But glorifies his pregnant pot,
If by the way to him befall
Some odoriferous thing, or medicinall,
So, lovers dreame a rich and long delight,
But get a winter-seeming summers night.

[5] Grierson quotes from Donne's *Fifty Sermons*, 36, p. 332: 'If it [a torch] have never been lighted, it does not easily take light, but it must be bruised and beaten first; if it have been lighted and put out . . . it does easily conceive fire.'

Our ease, our thrift, our honor, and our day,
Shall we, for this vaine bubles shadow pay?
Ends love in this, that my man
Can be as happy as I can, if he can
Endure the short scorne of a bridegroomes play?
That loving wretch that sweares,
'Tis not the bodies marry, but the mindes,
Which he in her angelique findes,
Would sweare as justly, that he heares,
In that dayes rude hoarse minstralsey, the spheares.
Hope not for minde in women; at their best
Sweetnesse and wit, they are but mummy, possest.

The Curse

Who ever guesses, thinks, or dreames he knowes
Who is my mistris, wither by this curse;
His only, and only his purse
May some dull heart to love dispose,
And shee yeeld then to all that are his foes;
May he be scorn'd by one, whom all else scorne,
Forsweare to others, what to her he hath sworne,
With feare of missing, shame of getting, torne.

Madnesse his sorrow, gout his cramp, may hee
Make, by but thinking who hath made him such;
And may he feele no touch
Of conscience, but of fame, and bee
Anguish'd, not that 'twas sinne, but that 'twas shee;
In early and long scarcenesse may he rot,
For land which had been his, if he had not
Himselfe incestuously an heire begot.

May he dreame treason, and beleeve that hee
Meant to performe it, and confesse, and die,
And no record tell why;
His sonnes, which none of his may bee,
Inherite nothing but his infamie;
Or may he so long parasites have fed,
That he would faine be theirs, whom he hath bred,
And at the last be circumcis'd [6] for bread.

The venom of all stepdames, gamsters gall,
What tyrans, and their subjects interwish,
What plants, mynes, beasts, foule, fish,
Can cóntribute, all ill which all
Prophets, or poets spake, and all which shall
Be annex'd in schedules unto this by mee,
Fall on that man; for if it be a shee
Nature before hand hath out-curséd mee.

The Bait [7]

Come live with mee, and bee my love,
And we will some new pleasures prove
Of golden sands, and christall brookes,
With silken lines, and silver hookes.

There will the river whispering runne
Warm'd by thy eyes, more then the sunne.
And there the inamor'd fish will stay,
Begging themselves they may betray.

When thou wilt swimme in that live bath,
Each fish, which every channell hath,
Will amorously to thee swimme,
Gladder to catch thee, then thou him.

If thou, to be so seene, beest loath,
By sunne, or moone, thou darknest both,
And if my selfe have leave to see,
I need not their light, having thee.

Let others freeze with angling reeds,
And cut their legges, with shells and weeds,

[6] and so stigmatized
[7] One of the imitations, of which there were many, of Marlowe's poem. See p. 247.

Or treacherously poore fish beset,
With strangling snare, or windowie net;

Let coarse bold hands, from slimy nest
The bedded fish in banks out-wrest,
Or curious traitors, sleavesilke flies
Bewitch poore fishes wandring eyes.

For thee, thou needst no such deceit,
For thou thy selfe art thine owne bait;
That fish, that is not catch'd thereby,
Alas, is wiser farre then I.

A Valediction: forbidding mourning [8]

As virtuous men passe mildly away,
And whisper to their soules, to goe,
Whilst some of their sad friends doe say,
The breath goes now, and some say, no:

So let us melt, and make no noise,
No teare-floods, nor sigh-tempests move,
T'were prophanation of our joyes
To tell the layetie our love.

Moving of th'earth brings harmes and feares;
Men reckon what it did and meant,
But trepidation [9] of the spheares,
Though greater farre, is innocent.

Dull sublunary lovers love
(Whose soule is sense) cannot admit
Absence, because it doth remove
Those things which elemented it.

But we by a love so much refin'd,
That our selves know not what it is,
Inter-assurèd of the mind,
Care lesse, eyes, lips, and hands to misse.

Our two soules therefore, which are one,
Though I must goe, endure not yet
A breach, but an expansion,
Like gold to ayery thinnesse beate.

If they be two, they are two so
As stiffe twin compasses are two;
Thy soule the fixt foot, makes no show
To move, but doth, if the other doe.

And though it in the center sit,
Yet when the other far doth rome,
It leanes, and hearkens after it,
And growes erect, as that comes home.

Such wilt thou be to mee, who must
Like th'other foot, obliquely runne;
Thy firmnes makes my circle just,
And makes me end, where I begunne.

[8] Written when Donne parted from his wife to go into France in 1612. The song 'Sweetest love' relates to the same event. See p. 278.

[9] According to the Ptolemaic astronomy, a slow movement of the ninth sphere.

Love's Deity

I LONG to talke with some old lovers ghost,
Who dyed before the god of love was borne;
I cannot thinke that hee, who then lov'd most,
Sunke so low, as to love one which did scorne.
But since this god produc'd a destinie,
And that vice-nature, custome, lets it be,
I must love her, that loves not mee.

Sure, they which made him god, meant not so much,
Nor he, in his young godhead practis'd it;
But when an even flame two hearts did touch,
His office was indulgently to fit
Actives to passives. Correspondencie
Only his subject was; it cannot bee
Love, till I love her, that loves mee.

But every moderne god will now extend
His vast prerogative, as far as Jove.
To rage, to lust, to write to, to commend,
All is the purlewe of the god of love.
Oh were wee wak'ned by this tyrannie
To ungod this child againe, it could not bee
I should love her, who loves not mee.

Rebell and atheist too, why murmure I,
  As though I felt the worst that love could doe?
Love might make me leave loving, or might trie
  A deeper plague, to make her love me too;
Which, since she loves before, I am loth to see;
Falshood is worse then hate; and that must bee,
  If shee whom I love, should love mee.

Love's Diet

To what a combersome unwieldinesse
And burdenous corpulence my love had growne,
  But that I did, to make it lesse,
  And keepe it in proportion,
Give it a diet, made it feed upon
That which love worst endures, discretion.

Above one sigh a day I allow'd him not,
Of which my fortune, and my faults had part;
  And if sometimes by stealth he got
  A she sigh from my mistresse heart,
And thought to feast on that, I let him see
'Twas neither very sound, nor meant to mee.

If he wroung from mee a teare, I brin'd it so
With scorne or shame, that him it nourish'd not;
  If he suck'd hers, I let him know
  'Twas not a teare, which hee had got;
His drinke was counterfeit, as was his meat;
For, eyes which rowle towards all, weepe not, but sweat.

What ever he would dictate, I writ that,
But burnt my letters; when she writ to me,
  And that that favour made him fat,
  I said, if any title bee
Convey'd by this, Ah, what doth it availe,
To be the fortieth name in an entaile?

Thus I reclaim'd my buzard [10] love, to flye
At what, and when, and how, and where I chuse;
  Now negligent of sport I lye,
  And now as other fawkners use,
I spring a mistresse, sweare, write, sigh and weepe;
And the game kill'd, or lost, goe talke, and sleepe.

The Will

  Before I sigh my last gaspe, let me breath,
  Great Love, some legacies; here I bequeath
  Mine eyes to Argus, if mine eyes can see;
  If they be blinde, then Love, I give them thee;
  My tongue to Fame; to embassadours mine eares;
    To women or the sea, my teares.
  Thou, Love, has taught mee heretofore
  By making me serve her who had twenty more,
That I should give to none, but such as had too much before.

  My constancie I to the planets give;
  My truth to them, who at the court doe live;
  Mine ingenuity and opennesse,
  To Jesuites; to buffones my pensivenesse;
  My silence to any, who abroad hath beene;
    My mony to a Capuchin.
  Thou, Love, taught'st me, by appointing mee
  To love there, where no love receiv'd can be,
Onely to give to such as have an incapacitie.

  My faith I give to Roman Catholiques;
  All my good works unto the Schismaticks [11]
  Of Amsterdam; my best civility

[10] The buzzard was a useless kind of hawk.
[11] Puritan extremists.

And courtship, to an universitie;
My modesty I give to souldiers bare;
My patience let gamesters share.
Thou, Love, taughtst mee, by making mee
Love her that holds my love disparity,
Onely to give to those that count my gifts indignity.

I give my reputation to those
Which were my friends; mine industrie to foes;
To schoolemen I bequeath my doubtfulnesse;
My sicknesse to physitians, or excesse;
To nature, all that I in ryme have writ;
And to my company my wit.
Thou, Love, by making mee adore
Her, who begot this love in mee before,
Taughtst me to make, as though I gave, when I did but restore.

To him for whom the passing bell next tolls,
I give my physick bookes; my written rowles
Of morall counsels, I to Bedlam [12] give;
My brazen medals, unto them which live
In want of bread; to them which passe among
All forrainers, mine English tongue.
Thou, Love, by making mee love one
Who thinkes her friendship a fit portion
For yonger lovers, dost my gifts thus disproportion.

Therefore I'll give no more; but I'll undoe
The world by dying; because love dies too.
Then all your beauties will bee no more worth
Then gold in mines, where none doth draw it forth;
And all your graces no more use shall have

[12] Bethlehem Hospital, a London asylum for the insane.

Then a sun dyall in a grave.
Thou, Love, taughtst mee, by making mee
Love her who doth neglect both mee and thee,
To invent, and practise this one way, to annihilate all three.

The Relique

When my grave is broke up againe
Some second ghest to entertaine,
(For graves have learn'd that womanhead
To be to more then one a bed)
And he that digs it, spies
A bracelet of bright haire about the bone,
Will he not let us alone,
And thinke that there a loving couple lies,
Who thought that this device might be some way
To make their soules, at the last busie day,
Meet at this grave, and make a little stay?

If this fall in a time, or land,
Where mis-devotion [13] doth command,
Then, he that digges us up, will bring
Us to the bishop, and the king,
To make us reliques; [14] then
Thou shalt be a Mary Magdalen, and I
A something else thereby;
All women shall adore us, and some men;
And since at such time, miracles are sought,
I would have that age by this paper taught
What miracles wee harmlesse lovers wrought.

First, we lov'd well and faithfully,
Yet knew not what wee lov'd, nor why;
Difference of sex no more wee knew,
Then our guardian angells doe;
Comming and going, wee

[13] Donne defines this as 'praying for the dead.'

[14] Donne is referring to the veneration of the relics of saints, a practice which the Reformation decried.

Perchance might kisse,[15] but not between
those meales;
Our hands ne'r toucht the seales,
Which nature, injur'd by late law, sets
free.
These miracles wee did; but now alas,
All measure, and all language, I should
passe,
Should I tell what a miracle shee was.

The Dissolution

Shee is dead; and all which die
To their first elements resolve;
And wee were mutuall elements to us,
And made of one another.
My body then doth hers involve,
And those things whereof I consist, hereby
In me abundant grow, and burdenous,
And nourish not, but smother.
My fire of passion, sighes of ayre,
Water of teares, and earthly sad despaire,
Which my materialls bee,
But neere worne out by loves securitie,
Shee, to my losse, doth by her death repaire,
And I might live long wretched so
But that my fire doth with my fuell grow.
Now as those active kings
Whose foraine conquest treasure brings,
Receive more, and spend more, and soon-
est breake,
This (which I am amaz'd that I can
speake)
This death, hath with my store
My use encreas'd.
And so my soule more earnestly releas'd,
Will outstrip hers; as bullets flowen before
A latter bullet may o'rtake, the pouder
being more.

The Computation

For the first twenty yeares, since yesterday,
I scarce beleev'd thou could'st be gone
away;
For forty more I fed on favours past,
And forty on hopes, that thou would'st
they might last.
Teares drown'd one hundred, and sighes
blew out two;
A thousand, I did neither thinke, nor
doe,
Or not divide, all being one thought of
you;
Or in a thousand more, forgot that too.
Yet call not this long life; but thinke that I
Am, by being dead, immortall; can ghosts
die?

The Paradox

No lover saith, I love, nor any other
Can judge a perfect lover;
Hee thinkes that else none can nor will
agree
That any loves but hee;
I cannot say I lov'd, for who can say
Hee was kill'd yesterday?
Love with excesse of heat, more yong then
old,
Death kills with too much cold;
Wee dye but once, and who lov'd last did
die,
Hee that saith twice, doth lye;
For though hee seeme to move, and stirre
a while,
It doth the sense beguile.
Such life is like the light which bideth yet
When the lights life is set,
Or like the heat, which fire in solid matter
Leaves behinde, two houres after.
Once I lov'd and dy'd; and am now become
Mine epitaph and tombe.
Here dead men speake their last, and so
do I;
Love-slaine, loe, here I lye.

Elegy IX: The Autumnal[16]

No spring, nor summer beauty hath such
grace
As I have seen in one autumnall face.

[15] In England in Donne's time it was the habit to kiss on meeting and parting. Erasmus, when he came to England, was enchanted with the custom and recommended it as a good cure for the gout.

[16] Written to honor Mrs. Magdalen Herbert, mother of the poet and the ambassador. Walton describes her char-

Yong beauties force our love, and that's a rape;
This doth but counsaile, yet you cannot scape.
If t'were a shame to love, here t'were no shame;
Affection here takes reverences name.
Were her first yeares the Golden Age? That's true,
But now shee's gold oft tried, and ever new.
That was her torrid and inflaming time,
This is her tolerable tropique clyme.
Faire eyes, who askes more heate then comes from hence,
He in a fever wishes pestilence.
Call not these wrinkles, graves; if graves they were,
They were Loves graves; for else he is no where.
Yet lies not Love dead here, but here doth sit
Vow'd to this trench, like an anchorit.[17]
And here, till hers, which must be his death, come,
He doth not digge a grave, but build a tombe.
Here dwells he; though he sojourne ev'ry where,
In progresse,[18] yet his standing house is here.
Here, where still evening is; not noone, nor night;
Where no voluptuousnesse, yet all delight.
In all her words, unto all hearers fit,
You may at revels,[19] you at counsaile, sit.
This is Loves timber, youth his underwood;
There he, as wine in June, enrages blood,
Which then comes seasonabliest, when our tast
And appetite to other things, is past.
Xerxes' strange Lydian love, the platane tree,
Was lov'd for age, none being so large as shee,
Or else because, being yong, nature did blesse
Her youth with ages glory, barrennesse.
If we love things long sought, age is a thing
Which we are fifty yeares in compassing;
If transitory things, which soone decay,
Age must be lovelyest at the latest day.
But name not winter-faces, whose skin's slacke,
Lanke, as an unthrifts purse, but a soules sacke;
Whose eyes seeke light within, for all here's shade;
Whose mouthes are holes, rather worne out, then made;
Whose every tooth to a severall place is gone,
To vexe their soules at resurrection;
Name not these living deaths-heads unto mee,
For these, not ancient, but antique be.
I hate extreames; yet I had rather stay
With tombs, then cradles, to weare out a day.
Since such loves motion naturall is, may still
My love descend, and journey downe the hill,
Not panting after growing beauties, so,
I shall ebbe out with them, who homeward goe.

acter during the time she lived at Oxford: 'her great and harmless wit, her cheerful gravity, and her obliging behaviour, gained her an acquaintance and friendship with most of any eminent worth or learning, that were at that time in or near that University.' Walton adds that this poem was written then, but the date would probably be too early (1596–1600).

17 hermit

18 a state journey made by royalty

19 courtly entertainments

Satire I [20]

Away thou fondling motley humorist,
Leave mee, and in this standing woodden chest,
Consorted with these few bookes, let me lye
In prison, and here be coffin'd, when I dye;

20 Donne's satires, in which he was opening a new vein of poetry, were written between 1593 and 1597.

Here are Gods conduits, grave divines; and here
Natures secretary, the philosopher;[21]
And jolly[22] statesmen, which teach how to tie
The sinewes of a cities mistique bodie;
Here gathering chroniclers, and by them stand
Giddie fantastique poets of each land.
Shall I leave all this constant company,
And follow headlong, wild uncertaine thee?
First sweare by thy best love in earnest
(If thou which lov'st all, canst love any best)
Thou wilt not leave mee in the middle street,
Though some more spruce companion thou dost meet;
Not though a captaine do come in thy way
Bright parcell gilt, with forty dead mens pay;[23]
Not though a briske perfum'd piert courtier
Deigne with a nod, thy courtesie to answer.
Nor come a velvet justice with a long
Great traine of blew coats, twelve, or fourteen strong,
Wilt thou grin or fawne on him, or prepare
A speech to court his beautious sonne and heire?
For better or worse take mee, or leave mee;
To take and leave mee is adultery.
Oh monstrous, superstitious puritan,
Of refin'd manners, yet ceremoniall man,
That when thou meet'st one, with enquiring eyes
Dost search, and like a needy broker prize
The silke and gold he weares, and to that rate,
So high or low, dost raise thy formall hat;
That wilt consort none, untill thou have knowne
What lands hee hath in hope, or of his owne,
As though all thy companions should make thee
Jointures, and marry thy deare company.
Why should'st thou (that dost not onely approve,
But in ranke itchie lust, desire, and love
The nakednesse and barenesse to enjoy,
Of thy plumpe muddy whore, or prostitute boy)
Hate vertue, though shee be naked, and bare?
At birth, and death, our bodies naked are;
And till our soules be unapparrelléd
Of bodies, they from blisse are banishéd.
Mans first blest state was naked, when by sinne
Hee lost that, yet hee was cloath'd but in beasts skin;
And in this course attire, which I now weare,
With God, and with the Muses I conferre.
But since thou like a contrite penitent,
Charitably warn'd of thy sinnes, dost repent
These vanities, and giddinesses, loe,
I shut my chamber doore, and come, lets goe.
But sooner may a cheape whore, who hath beene
Worne by as many severall men in sinne,
As are black feathers, or musk-colour hose,
Name her childs right true father 'mongst all those;
Sooner may one guesse, who shall beare away
The infanta of London,[24] heire to an India;
And sooner may a gulling weather spie
By drawing forth heavens scheme,[25] tell certainly
What fashioned hats, or ruffes, or suits next yeare
Our subtile-witted antique youths will weare,

[21] Aristotle was 'the philosopher.' [22] haughty
[23] A captain of a company was allowed to claim the pay of a certain number of dead soldiers. Apparently it was frequently spent on gilt armor.

[24] The reference is to the wealth of the City of London represented by its great guilds and merchant princes.
[25] a horoscope

Then thou, when thou depart'st from mee, canst show
Whither, why, when, or with whom thou wouldst go.
But how shall I be pardon'd my offence
That thus have sinn'd against my conscience?
Now we are in the street; he first of all,
Improvidently proud, creepes to the wall;
And so imprisoned, and hem'd in by mee,
Sells for a little state his libertie.
Yet though he cannot skip forth now to greet
Every fine silken painted foole we meet,
He them to him with amorous smiles allures,
And grins, smacks, shrugs, and such an itch endures,
As prentises, or schoole-boyes which doe know
Of some gay sport abroad, yet dare not goe.
And as fidlers stop lowest, at highest sound,
So to the most brave, stoops hee nigh'st the ground.
But to a grave man, he doth move no more
Then the wise politique horse[26] would heretofore,
Or thou, O elephant, or ape, wilt doe,
When any names the King of Spaine to you.
Now leaps he upright, joggs me, and cryes, Do you see
Yonder well favoured youth? Which? Oh, 'tis hee
That dances so divinely; Oh, said I,
Stand still, must you dance here for company?
Hee droopt, wee went, till one (which did excell
Th'Indians, in drinking his tobacco well)
Met us; they talk'd; I whispered, let us goe,
'T may be you smell him not, truely I doe;
He heares not mee, but, on the other side
A many-coloured peacock having spide,
Leaves him and mee; I for my lost sheep stay;
He followes, overtakes, goes on the way,
Saying, Him whom I last left, all repute
For his device in hansoming a sute,
To judge of lace, pinke, panes, print, cut, and pleite,
Of all the court, to have the best conceit;
Our dull comedians want him, let him goe;
But Oh, God strengthen thee, why stoop'st thou so?
Why? he hath travayld; Long? No; But to me
(Which understand none,) he doth seeme to be
Perfect French, and Italian; I replyed,
So is the poxe; he answered not, but spy'd
More men of sort, of parts, and qualities;
At last his love he in a windowe spies,
And like light dew exhal'd, he flings from mee
Violently ravish'd to his lechery.
Many were there; he could command no more;
Hee quarrell'd, fought, bled; and turn'd out of dore
  Directly came to mee hanging the head,
  And constantly a while must keepe his bed.

[26] A famous performing horse, exhibited in London, as were the elephant and ape referred to in the next line.

HOLY SONNETS[27]

I

Thou hast made me, and shall thy worke decay?
Repaire me now, for now mine end doth haste;
I runne to death, and death meets me as fast,
And all my pleasures are like yesterday;
I dare not move my dimme eyes any way,
Despaire behind, and death before doth cast
Such terrour, and my feeble flesh doth waste
By sinne in it, which it t'wards hell doth weigh;
Onely thou art above, and when towards thee

[27] The *Holy Sonnets* were composed after the death of Donne's wife in 1617.

By thy leave I can looke, I rise againe;
But our old subtle foe so tempteth me,
That not one houre my selfe I can sustaine;
Thy grace may wing me to prevent his art,
And thou like adamant draw mine iron heart.

VI

THIS is my playes last scene; here heavens appoint
My pilgrimages last mile; and my race
Idly, yet quickly runne, hath this last pace;
My spans last inch, my minutes latest point,
And gluttonous death, will instantly unjoynt
My body, and soule, and I shall sleepe a space;
But my ever-waking part shall see that face,
Whose feare already shakes my every joynt.
Then, as my soule to heaven her first seate, takes flight,
And earth-borne body, in the earth shall dwell,
So fall my sinnes, that all may have their right,
To where they are bred, and would presse me, to hell.
Impute me righteous, thus purg'd of evill,
For thus I leave the world, the flesh, the devill.

VII

AT the round earths imagin'd corners, blow
Your trumpets, Angells, and arise, arise
From death, you numberlesse infinities
Of soules, and to your scattred bodies goe;
All whom the flood did, and fire shall o'erthrow,
All whom warre, dearth, age, agues, tyrannies,
Despaire, law, chance, hath slaine, and you whose eyes,
Shall behold God, and never tast deaths woe.
But let them sleepe, Lord, and mee mourne a space,
For, if above all these, my sinnes abound,
'Tis late to aske abundance of thy grace,
When wee are there; here on this lowly ground,
Teach mee how to repent; for that's as good
As if thou hadst seal'd my pardon, with thy blood.

X

DEATH be not proud, though some have callèd thee
Mighty and dreadfull, for, thou art not soe;
For those, whom thou think'st thou dost overthrow,
Die not, poore death, nor yet canst thou kill mee.
From rest and sleepe, which but thy pictures bee,
Much pleasure, then from thee, much more must flow,
And soonest our best men with thee doe goe,
Rest of their bones, and soules deliverie.
Thou art slave to fate, chance, kings, and desperate men,
And dost with poyson, warre, and sicknesse dwell,
And poppie, or charmes can make us sleepe as well,
And better then thy stroake; why swell'st thou then?
One short sleepe past, wee wake eternally,
And death shall be no more; death, thou shalt die.

XIII

WHAT if this present were the worlds last night?
Marke in my heart, O soule, where thou dost dwell,
The picture of Christ crucified, and tell
Whether that countenance can thee affright,
Teares in his eyes quench the amasing light,
Blood fills his frownes, which from his pierc'd head fell.
And can that tongue adjudge thee unto hell,

Which pray'd forgivenesse for his foes fierce spight?
No, no; but as in my idolatrie
I said to all my profane mistresses,
Beauty, of pitty, foulnesse onely is
A signe of rigour: so I say to thee,
To wicked spirits are horrid shapes assign'd,
This beauteous forme assures a pitious minde.

XIV

BATTER my heart, three person'd God; for, you
As yet but knocke, breathe, shine, and seeke to mend;
That I may rise, and stand, o'erthrow mee, and bend
Your force, to breake, blowe, burn and make me new.
I, like an usurpt towne, to another due,
Labour to admit you, but Oh, to no end.
Reason, your viceroy in mee, mee should defend,
But is captiv'd, and proves weake or untrue.
Yet dearely I love you, and would be lovéd faine,
But am betroth'd unto your enemie;
Divorce mee, untie, or breake that knot againe,
Take mee to you, imprison mee, for I
Except you enthrall mee, never shall be free,
Nor ever chast, except you ravish mee.

XVII

SINCE she [28] whom I lov'd hath payd her last debt
To nature, and to hers, and my good is dead,
And her soule early into heaven ravishéd,
Wholly on heavenly things my mind is sett.
Here the admyring her my mind did whett
To seeke thee, God; so streames do shew their head;
But though I have found thee, and thou my thirst hast fed,
A holy thirsty dropsy melts mee yett.
But why should I begg more love, when as thou
Dost wooe my soule for hers, offring all thine;
And dost not only feare least I allow
My love to saints and angels, things divine,
But in thy tender jealosy dost doubt
Least the world, fleshe, yea devill putt thee out.

XVIII

SHOW me, deare Christ, thy spouse, so bright and clear.[29]
What! is it she, which on the other shore
Goes richly painted? or which, rob'd and tore,
Laments and mournes in Germany and here?
Sleepes she a thousand, then peepes up one yeare?
Is she selfe truth and errs? now new, now outwore?
Doth she, and did she, and shall she evermore
On one, on seaven, or on no hill appeare?
Dwells she with us, or like adventuring knights
First travaile we to seeke and then make love?
Betray, kind husband, thy spouse to our sights,
And let myne amorous soule court thy mild dove,
Who is most trew, and pleasing to thee, then
When she is embrac'd and open to most men.

A Hymn to Christ, at the Author's last going into Germany [30]

IN what torne ship soever I embarke,
That ship shall be my embleme of thy arke;

[28] Donne's wife

[29] An important autobiographical sonnet. Donne was no fanatic believer in the supremacy of one church. He could see good in the three branches, Roman, Anglican, and Calvinist.

[30] The date of the voyage was 1619.

What sea soever swallow mee, that flood
Shall be to mee an embleme of thy blood;
Though thou with clouds of anger do disguise
Thy face, yet through that maske I know those eyes,
Which, though they turne away sometimes,
They never will despise.

I sacrifice this iland unto thee,
And all whom I lov'd there, and who lov'd mee;
When I have put our seas twixt them and mee,
Put thou thy sea [31] betwixt my sinnes and thee.
As the trees sap doth seeke the root below
In winter, in my winter now I goe
Where none but thee, th'eternall root
Of true love, I may know.

Nor thou nor thy religion dost controule
The amorousnesse of an harmonious soule,
But thou would'st have that love thy selfe: as thou
Art jealous, Lord, so I am jealous now;
Thou lov'st not, till from loving more, thou free
My soule: who ever gives, takes libertie;
O, if thou car'st not whom I love,
Alas, thou lov'st not mee.

Seale then this bill of my divorce to all
On whom those fainter beames of love did fall;
Marry those loves, which in youth scattered bee
On fame, wit, hopes (false mistresses) to thee.
Churches are best for prayer that have least light:
To see God only, I goe out of sight;
And to scape stormy dayes, I chuse
An everlasting night.

[31] Some seventeenth century editions read 'blood,' which explains the passage.

Hymn to God my God, in my Sickness [32]

Since I am comming to that holy roome
Where, with thy quire of saints for evermore,
I shall be made thy musique; as I come
I tune the instrument here at the dore,
And what I must doe then, thinke here before.

Whilst my physitians by their love are growne
Cosmographers, and I their mapp, who lie
Flat on this bed, that by them may be showne
That this is my south-west discoverie,
Per fretum febris,[33] by these streights to die,

I joy, that in these straits I see my west;
For, though theire currants yeeld returne to none,
What shall my west hurt me? As west and east
In all flatt maps (and I am one) are one,[34]
So death doth touch the resurrection.

Is the pacifique sea my home? Or are
The easterne riches? Is Jerusalem?
Anyan,[35] and Magellan, and Gibraltare,
All streights, and none but streights, are wayes to them,
Whether where Japhet dwelt, or Cham, or Sem.
We thinke that Paradise and Calvarie,
Christs crosse, and Adams tree, stood in one place;
Looke, Lord, and finde both Adams met in me;
As the first Adams sweat surrounds my face,

[32] This hymn was written eight days before Donne's death, according to Walton.
[33] Through the straits of fever.
[34] On a map of the world the points on the right edge correspond to those on the left.
[35] Behring Strait

May the last Adams blood my soule embrace.
So, in his purple wrapp'd, receive mee, Lord;
By these, his thornes, give me his other crowne;
And as to others soules I preach'd thy word,
Be this my text, my sermon to mine owne,
Therfore that he may raise, the Lord throws down.

Robert Herrick

1591–1674

The Argument of his Book [1]

I sing of brooks, of blossomes, birds, and bowers:
Of April, May, of June, and July-flowers.
I sing of May-poles, hock-carts,[2] wassails, wakes,
Of bride-grooms, brides, and of their bridall-cakes.
I write of youth, of love, and have accesse
By these, to sing of cleanly-wantonnesse.
I sing of dewes, of raines, and piece by piece
Of balme, of oyle, of spice, and amber-greece.
I sing of times trans-shifting; and I write
How roses first came red, and lillies white.
I write of groves, of twilights, and I sing
The Court of Mab, and of the Fairie-King.
I write of Hell; I sing (and ever shall)
Of Heaven, and hope to have it after all.

To his Muse

Whither, mad maiden, wilt thou roame?
Farre safer 'twere to stay at home:
Where thou mayst sit, and piping please
The poore and private cottages.
Since coats,[3] and hamlets, best agree
With this thy meaner minstralsie.
There with the reed, thou mayst expresse
The shepherds fleecie happinesse:
And with thy eclogues intermixe
Some smooth, and harmlesse beucolicks.
There on a hillock thou mayst sing
Unto a handsome shephardling;
Or to a girle (that keeps the neat[4])
With breath more sweet than violet.
There, there, (perhaps) such lines as these
May take the simple villages.
But for the court, the country wit
Is despicable unto it.
Stay then at home, and doe not goe
Or flie abroad to seeke for woe.
Contempts in courts and cities dwell;
No critick haunts the poore man's cell:
Where thou mayst hear thine own lines read
By no one tongue, there, censuréd.
That man's unwise will search for ill,
And may prevent it, sitting still.

To the sour Reader

If thou dislik'st the piece thou light'st on first;
Thinke that of all, that I have writ, the worst:
But if thou read'st my booke unto the end,
And still do'st this, and that verse, reprehend:
O perverse man! If all disgustfull be,
The extreame scabbe [5] take thee, and thine, for me.

When he would have his verses read

In sober mornings, doe not thou reherse
The holy incantation of a verse;

[1] *Hesperides*, 1648, from which all but the last two of the poems printed here have been taken. Herrick was not a lover of order, and the poems in his book keep no sequence or theme. They are given here in his arrangement.
[2] harvest-home carts, *i. e.*, the last loaded
[3] cots

[4] cattle
[5] A filthy skin disease.

But when that men have both well drunke, and fed,
Let my enchantments then be sung, or read.
When laurell spirits i' th' fire, and when the hearth
Smiles to it selfe, and guilds the roofe with mirth;
When up the Thyrse [6] is rais'd, and when the sound
Of sacred orgies flyes, A round,[7] A round;
When the rose raignes, and locks with ointments shine,
Let rigid Cato read these lines of mine.

Upon the loss of his Mistresses

I HAVE lost, and lately, these
Many dainty mistresses:
Stately Julia, prime of all;
Sapho next, a principall:
Smooth Anthea, for a skin
White, and heaven-like chrystalline:
Sweet Electra, and the choice
Myrha, for the lute, and voice.
Next, Corinna, for her wit,
And the graceful use of it:
With Perilla: all are gone;
Onely Herrick's left alone,
For to number sorrow by
Their departures hence, and die.

Cherry-pit [8]

JULIA and I did lately sit
Playing for sport, at cherry-pit:
She threw; I cast; and having thrown,
I got the pit, and she the stone.

Discontents in Devon

MORE discontents I never had
Since I was born, then here;
Where I have been, and still am sad,
In this dull Devon-shire:
Yet justly too I must confesse;
I ne'r invented such
Ennobled numbers for the presse,
Then where I loath'd so much.

[6] A javelin twined with ivy.
[7] A part-song like 'Three Blind Mice.'
[8] A game in which cherry stones were thrown into a small hole.

To Anthea

Now is the time, when all the lights wax dim;
And thou (Anthea) must withdraw from him
Who was thy servant. Dearest, bury me
Under that holy-oke, or Gospel-tree:
Where (though thou see'st not) thou may think upon
Me, when thou yeerly go'st procession:
Or for mine honour, lay me in that tombe
In which thy sacred reliques shall have roome.
For my embalming (Sweetest) there will be
No spices wanting, when I'm laid by thee.

Delight in Disorder

A SWEET disorder in the dresse
Kindles in cloathes a wantonnesse:
A lawne about the shoulders thrown
Into a fine distraction:
An erring lace, which here and there
Enthralls the crimson stomacher:
A cuffe neglectfull, and thereby
Ribbands to flow confusedly:
A winning wave (deserving note)
In the tempestuous petticote:
A carelesse shooe-string, in whose tye
I see a wilde civility:
Doe more bewitch me, then when art
Is too precise in every part.

The Bag of the Bee

ABOUT the sweet bag of a Bee,
Two cupids fell at odds;
And whose the pretty prize shu'd be,
They vow'd to ask the gods.

Which Venus hearing, thither came,
  And for their boldness stript them:
And taking thence from each his flame;
  With rods of mirtle whipt them.

Which done, to still their wanton cries,
  When quiet grown sh'ad seen them,
She kist, and wip'd thir dove-like eyes;
  And gave the bag between them.

His Farewell to Sack [9]

Farewell thou Thing, time-past so knowne, so deare
To me, as blood to life and spirit: neare,
Nay, thou more neare then kindred, friend, man, wife,
Male to the female, soule to body: life
To quick action, or the warme soft side
Of the resigning, yet resisting bride.
The kisse of virgins; first-fruits of the bed;
Soft speech, smooth touch, the lips, the maidenhead:
These, and a thousand sweets, co'd never be
So neare, or deare, as thou wast once to me.
O thou the drink of gods, and angels! Wine
That scatter'st spirit and lust; whose purest shine,
More radiant then the summers sun-beams shows;
Each way illustrious, brave; and like to those
Comets we see by night; whose shagg'd portents
Fore-tell the comming of some dire events:
Or some full flame, which with a pride aspires,
Throwing about his wild, and active fires.
'Tis thou, above nectar, O divinest soule!
(Eternall in thy self) that canst controule
That, which subverts whole nature, grief and care;
Vexation of the mind, and damn'd despaire.
'Tis thou, alone, who with thy mistick fan,[10]
Work'st more then wisdome, art, or nature can,
To rouze the sacred madnesse; and awake
The frost-bound-blood, and spirits; and to make
Them frantick with thy raptures, flashing through
The soule, like lightning, and as active too.
'Tis not Apollo can, or those thrice three
Castalian sisters,[11] sing, if wanting thee.
Horace, Anacreon both had lost their fame,
Hadst thou not fill'd them with thy fire and flame.
Phæbean splendour! and thou Thespian spring!
Of which, sweet swans must drink, before they sing
Their true-pac'd numbers, and their holy-layes,
Which makes them worthy cedar, and the bayes.
But why? why longer doe I gaze upon
Thee with the eye of admiration?
Since I must leave thee; and enforc'd, must say
To all thy witching beauties, Goe! Away!
But if thy whimpring looks doe ask me why?
Then know, that Nature bids thee goe, not I.
'Tis her erroneous self has made a braine
Uncapable of such a soveraigne,
As is thy powerfull selfe. Prethee not smile;
Or smile more inly; lest thy looks beguile
My vowes denounc'd in zeale, which thus much show thee,
That I have sworn, but by thy looks to know thee.
Let others drink thee freely; and desire
Thee and their lips espous'd; while I admire,
And love thee; but not taste thee. Let my Muse

[9] A dry Spanish wine, a favorite drink of the Elizabethans.

[10] Used in Bacchic festivals.

[11] the Muses

Faile of thy former helps: and onely use
Her inadult'rate strength: what's done by me
Hereafter, shall smell of the lamp, not thee.

Corinna's going A-Maying

Get up, get up for shame, the blooming morne
Upon her wings presents the god unshorne.
See how Aurora throwes her faire
Fresh-quilted colours through the aire:
Get up, sweet slug-a-bed, and see
The dew-bespangling herbe and tree.
Each flower has wept, and bow'd toward the east,
Above an houre since; yet you not drest,
Nay! not so much as out of bed?
When all the birds have mattens seyd,
And sung their thankfull hymnes: 'tis sin,
Nay, profanation to keep in,
Whenas a thousand virgins on this day,
Spring, sooner then the lark, to fetch in may.

Rise; and put on your foliage, and be seene
To come forth, like the spring-time, fresh and greene;
And sweet as Flora. Take no care
For jewels for your gowne, or haire:
Feare not; the leaves will strew
Gemms in abundance upon you:
Besides, the childhood of the day has kept,
Against you come, some orient pearls unwept:
Come, and receive them while the light
Hangs on the dew-locks of the night:
And Titan [12] on the eastern hill
Retires himselfe, or else stands still
Till you come forth. Wash, dresse, be briefe in praying:
Few beads are best, when once we goe a Maying.

Come, my Corinna, come; and comming, marke
How each field turns a street; each street a parke
Made green, and trimm'd with trees: see how
Devotion gives each house a bough,
Or branch: each porch, each doore, ere this,
An arke a tabernacle is
Made up of white-thorn neatly enterwove;
As if here were those cooler shades of love.
Can such delights be in the street,
And open fields, and we not see 't?
Come, we'll abroad; and let's obay
The proclamation made for May:
And sin no more, as we have done, by staying:
But my Corinna, come, let's goe a Maying.

There's not a budding boy, or girle, this day,
But is got up, and gone to bring in May.
A deale of youth, ere this, is come
Back, and with white-thorn laden home.
Some have dispatcht their cakes and creame,
Before that we have left [13] to dreame:
And some have wept, and woo'd, and plighted troth.
And chose their priest, ere we can cast off sloth:
Many a green-gown has been given; [14]
Many a kisse, both odde and even:
Many a glance too has been sent
From out the eye, love's firmament:
Many a jest told of the keyes betraying
This night, and locks pickt, yet w'are not a Maying.

Come, let us goe, while we are in our prime;
And take the harmlesse follie of the time.
We shall grow old apace, and die
Before we know our liberty.
Our life is short; and our dayes run
As fast away as do's the sunne:

[12] the sun

[13] ceased

[14] Many a girl has been tumbled on the grass.

And as a vapour, or a drop of raine
Once lost, can ne'er be found againe:
  So when or you or I are made
  A fable, song, or fleeting shade;
  All love, all liking, all delight
  Lies drown'd with us in endlesse night.
Then while time serves, and we are but decaying;
Come, my Corinna, come, let's goe a Maying.

To his dying Brother, Master William Herrick

Life of my life, take not so soone thy flight,
But stay the time till we have bade good night.
Thou hast both wind and tide with thee; thy way
As soone dispatcht is by the night, as day.
Let us not then so rudely henceforth goe
Till we have wept, kist, sigh't, shook hands, or so.
There's paine in parting; and a kind of hell,
When once true-lovers take their last farewell.
What? shall we two our endlesse leaves take here
Without a sad looke, or a solemne teare?
He knowes not love, that hath not this truth proved,
Love is most loth to leave the thing beloved.
Pay we our vowes, and goe; yet when we part
Then, even then, I will bequeath my heart
Into thy loving hands: for Ile keep none
To warme my breast, when thou my pulse art gone.
No, here Ile last, and walk (a harmless shade)
About this urne, wherein thy dust is laid,
To guard it so, as nothing here shall be
Heavy, to hurt those sacred seeds of thee.

To the Virgins, to make much of Time

Gather ye rose-buds while ye may,
  Old Time is still a flying:
And this same flower that smiles to day,
  To morrow will be dying.

The glorious lamp of heaven, the sun,
  The higher he's a getting;
The sooner will his race be run,
  And neerer he's to setting.

That age is best, which is the first,
  When youth and blood are warmer;
But being spent, the worse, and worst
  Times, still succeed the former.

Then be not coy, but use your time;
  And while ye may, goe marry;
For having lost but once your prime,
  You may for ever tarry.

The Hock-cart, or Harvest home:

TO THE RIGHT HONOURABLE MILDMAY, EARL OF WESTMORLAND

Come, sons of summer, by whose toile,
We are the lords of wine and oile;
By whose tough labours, and rough hands,
We rip up first, then reap our lands.
Crown'd with the eares of corne, now come,
And, to the pipe, sing harvest home.
Come forth, my lord, and see the cart
Drest up with all the country art.
See, here a maukin,[15] there a sheet,
As spotlesse pure, as it is sweet:
The horses, mares, and frisking fillies,
(Clad, all, in linnen, white as lillies.)
The harvest swaines, and wenches bound
For joy, to see the hock-cart crown'd.
About the cart, heare, how the rout
Of rurall younglings raise the shout;
Pressing before, some coming after,
Those with a shout, and these with laughter.
Some blesse the cart; some kisse the sheaves;
Some prank them up with oaken leaves:
Some crosse the fill-horse; some with great

[15] cloth

Devotion, stroak the home-borne wheat:
While other rusticks, lesse attent
To prayers, then to merryment,
Run after with their breeches rent.
Well, on, brave boyes, to your lord's hearth,
Glitt'ring with fire; where, for your mirth,
Ye shall see first the large and cheefe
Foundation of your feast, fat beefe:
With upper stories, mutton, veale
And bacon, (which makes full the meale)
With sev'rall dishes standing by,
As here a custard, there a pie,
And here all-tempting frumentie.
And for to make the merry cheere,
If smirking wine be wanting here,
There's that, which drowns all care, stout beere;
Which freely drink to your lords health,
Then to the plough, (the common-wealth)
Next to your flailes, your fanes,[16] your fatts;[17]
Then to the maids with wheaten hats:
To the rough sickle, and crookt sythe,
Drink, frollick, boyes, till all be blythe.
Feed, and grow fat; and as ye eat,
Be mindfull, that the lab'ring neat[18]
(As you) may have their fill of meat.
And know, besides, ye must revoke
The patient oxe unto the yoke,
And all goe back unto the plough
And harrow, (though they'r hang'd up now.)
And, you must know, your lords words true,
Feed him ye must, whose food fils you.
And that this pleasure is like raine,
Not sent ye for to drowne your paine,
But for to make it spring againe.

Not to love

He that will not love, must be
My scholar, and learn this of me:
There be in love as many feares,
As the summers corne has eares;
Sighs, and sobs, and sorrowes more
Then the sand, that makes the shore;
Freezing cold, and firie heats,
Fainting swoones, and deadly sweats;
Now an ague, then a fever,
Both tormenting lovers ever.
Wods't thou know, besides all these,
How hard a woman 'tis to please?
How crosse, how sullen, and how soone
She shifts and changes like the moone.
How false, how hollow she's in heart;
And how she is her owne least part;
How high she's priz'd, and worth but small;
Little thou 'lt love, or not at all.

To Anthea, who may Command him any Thing

Bid me to live, and I will live
Thy Protestant to be;
Or bid me love, and I will give
A loving heart to thee.

A heart as soft, a heart as kind,
A heart as sound and free,
As in the whole world thou canst find,
That heart Ile give to thee.

Bid that heart stay, and it will stay,
To honour thy decree;
Or bid it languish quite away,
And 't shall doe so for thee.

Bid me to weep, and I will weep
While I have eyes to see;
And having none, yet I will keep
A heart to weep for thee.

Bid me despaire, and Ile despaire,
Under that cypresse tree;
Or bid me die, and I will dare
E'en death, to die for thee.

Thou art my life, my love, my heart,
The very eyes of me;
And hast command of every part,
To live and die for thee.

[16] winnowing fans
[17] casks
[18] cattle

Oberon's Feast

Shapcot![19] *to thee the fairy state*
I with discretion, dedicate.
Because thou prizest things that are
Curious, and un-familiar.
Take first the feast; these dishes gone;
Wee'l see the fairy-court anon.

A LITTLE mushroome-table spred,
After short prayers, they set on bread;
A moon-parcht grain of purest wheat,
With same small glit'ring gritt, to eate
His choyce bitts with; then in a trice
They make a feast lesse great then nice.
But all this while his eye is serv'd,
We must not thinke his eare was sterv'd
But that there was in place to stir
His spleen, the chirring grasshopper;
The merry cricket, puling flie,
The piping gnat for minstralcy.
And now, we must imagine first,
The elves present to quench his thirst
A pure seed-pearle of infant dew,
Brought and besweetned in a blew
And pregnant violet; which done,
His kitling eyes begin to runne
Quite through the table, where he spies
The hornes of paperie butterflies;
Of which he eates, and tastes a little
Of that we call the cuckoes spittle.
A little fuz-ball pudding stands
By, yet not blessèd by his hands,
That was too coorse; but then forthwith
He ventures boldly on the pith
Of sugred rush, and eates the sagge[20]
And well bestrutted[21] bees sweet bagge:
Gladding his pallat with some store
Of emits eggs; what wo'd he more?
But beards of mice, a newt's stew'd thigh,
A bloated earewig, and a flie;
With the red-capt worme, that's shut
Within the concave of a nut,
Browne as his tooth. A little moth,
Late fatned in a piece of cloth:
With withered cherries; mandrakes eares;
Moles eyes; to these, the slain-stags teares
The unctuous dewlaps of a snaile;
The broke-heart of a nightingale
Ore-come in musicke; with a wine,
Ne're ravisht from the flattering vine,
But gently prest from the soft side
Of the most sweet and dainty bride,[22]
Brought in a dainty daizie, which
He fully quaffs up to bewitch
His blood to height; this done, commended
Grace by his priest; *the feast is ended.*

[19] A lawyer and a friend of Herrick.
[20] sagging [21] swollen
[22] rose

Upon Prudence Baldwin her Sickness

PRUE, my dearest maid, is sick,
Almost to be lunatick.
Æsculapius! come and bring
Means for her recovering;
And a gallant cock shall be
Offer'd up by her, to thee.

To Daffodils

FAIRE daffadills, we weep to see
You haste away so soone;
As yet the early-rising sun
Has not attain'd his noone.
Stay, stay,
Until the hasting day
Has run
But to the even-song;
And, having pray'd together, we
Will go with you along.

We have short time to stay, as you,
We have as short a spring;
As quick a growth to meet decay,
As you, or any thing.
We die,
As your hours doe, and drie
Away,
Like to the summers raine;
Or as the pearles of mornings dew
Ne'r to be found againe.

Upon M. Ben Jonson — Epigram

AFTER the rare arch-poet JOHNSON dy'd,
The sock grew loathsome, and the buskin's pride,

Together with the stage's glory, stood
Each like a poore and pitied widowhood.
The cirque prophan'd was; and all postures rackt;
For men did strut, and stride, and stare, not act.
Then temper flew from words; and men did squeake,
Looke red, and blow, and bluster, but not speake;
No holy-rage, or frantick-fires did stirre,
Or flash about the spacious theater.
No clap of hands, or shout, or praises proofe
Did crack the play-house sides, or cleave her roofe.
Artlesse the sceane was; and that monstrous sin
Of deep and arrant ignorance came in;
Such ignorance as theirs was, who once hist
At thy unequal'd play, the Alchymist.[23]
Oh fie upon 'em! Lastly too, all witt
In utter darkenes did, and still will sit
Sleeping the lucklesse age out, till that she
Her resurrection ha's again with thee.

The Willow Garland[24]

A willow Garland thou did'st send
Perfum'd (last day) to me,
Which did but only this portend,
I was forsooke by thee.

Since so it is, Ile tell thee what,
To morrow thou shalt see
Me weare the willow; after that,
To die upon the tree.

As beasts unto the altars go
With garlands drest, so I
Will, with my willow-wreath also,
Come forth and sweetly dye.

Kissing and Bussing

Kissing and bussing differ both in this;
We busse our wantons, but our wives we kiss.

[23] Acted in 1610. [24] Symbolic of unrequited love.

To Phillis to Love, and Live with him

Live, live with me, and thou shalt see
The pleasures Ile prepare for thee:
What sweets the country can afford
Shall blesse thy bed, and blesse thy board.
The soft sweet mosse shall be thy bed,
With crawling woodbine over-spread,
By which the silver-shedding streames
Shall gently melt thee into dreames.
Thy clothing next, shall be a gowne
Made of the fleeces' purest downe.
The tongues of kids shall be thy meate;
Their milke thy drinke; and thou shalt eate
The paste of filberts for thy bread
With cream of cowslips butteréd;
Thy feasting-tables shall be hills
With daisies spread, and daffadils;
Where thou shalt sit, and red-brest by,
For meat, shall give thee melody.
Ile give thee chaines and carkanets[25]
Of primroses and violets.
A bag and bottle thou shalt have,
That richly wrought, and this as brave;
So that as either shall expresse
The wearer's no meane shepheardesse.
At sheering-times, and yearely wakes,
When Themilis his pastime makes,
There thou shalt be; and be the wit,
Nay more, the feast, and grace of it.
On holy-dayes, when virgins meet
To dance the heyes[26] with nimble feet,
Thou shalt come forth and then appeare
The queen of roses for that yeere.
And having danc't ('bove all the best)
Carry the garland from the rest.
In wicker-baskets maids shal bring
To thee, (my dearest Shephardling)
The blushing apple, bashfull peare,
And shame-fac't plum, (all simp'ring there).
Walk in the groves, and thou shalt find
The name of Phillis in the rind
Of every straight, and smooth-skin tree,
Where kissing that, Ile twice kisse thee.
To thee a sheep-hook I will send,
Be-pranckt with ribbands, to this end,

[25] necklaces [26] rustic dances

This, this alluring hook might be
Lesse for to catch a sheep, then me.
Thou shalt have possets, wassails fine,
Not made of ale, but spicéd wine;
To make thy maids and selfe free mirth,
All sitting neer the glitt'ring hearth.
Thou sha't have ribbands, roses, rings,
Gloves, garters, stockings, shooes, and strings
Of winning colours, that shall move
Others to lust, but me to love.
These (nay) and more, thine own shal be,
If thou wilt love, and live with me.

Anacreontic

Born I was to be old,
And for to die here;
After that, in the mould
Long for to lye here.
But before that day comes,
Still I be bousing:
For I know, in the tombs
There's no carousing.

His Prayer to Ben Jonson

When I a verse shall make,
Know I have praid thee,
For old religion's sake,
Saint Ben to aide me.

Make the way smooth for me,
When I, thy Herrick,
Honouring thee, on my knee
Offer my lyrick.

Candles Ile give to thee,
And a new altar;
And thou Saint Ben, shalt be
Writ in my Psalter.

The bad Season makes the Poet sad

Dull to my selfe, and almost dead to these
My many fresh and fragrant mistresses,
Lost to all musick now, since every thing
Puts on the semblance here of sorrowing.
Sick is the land to th' heart; and doth endure
More dangerous faintings by her desp'rate cure.
But if that golden age wo'd come again,
And Charles here rule, as he before did raign,
If smooth and unperplext the seasons were,
As when the sweet Maria [27] livéd here,
I sho'd delight to have my curles halfe drown'd
In Tyrian dewes, and head with roses crown'd.
And once more yet (ere I am laid out dead)
Knock at the Starre with my exalted Head.

The Night-piece, to Julia

Her eyes the glow-worme lend thee,
The shooting starres attend thee;
And the elves also,
Whose little eyes glow
Like the sparks of fire, befriend thee.

No will-o'-th'-wispe mis-light thee,
Nor snake, or slow-worme bite thee;
But on, on thy way
Not making a stay,
Since ghost ther's none to affright thee.

Let not the darke thee cumber;
What though the moon do's slumber?
The starres of the night
Will lend thee their light,
Like tapers cleare without number.

Then Julia let me wooe thee,
Thus, thus to come unto me;
And when I shall meet
Thy silv'ry feet,
My soule I'le poure into thee.

To his lovely Mistresses

One night i' th' yeare, my dearest beauties, come

[27] Henrietta Maria, the queen of Charles I.

And bring those dew-drink-offerings to my tomb.
When thence ye see my reverend ghost to rise,
And there to lick th' effuséd sacrifice,
Though paleness be the livery that I weare,
Looke ye not wan, or colourlesse for feare.
Trust me, I will not hurt ye; or once shew
The least grim looke, or cast a frown on you;
Nor shall the tapers when I'm there, burn blew.
This I may do (perhaps) as I glide by,
Cast on my girles a glance, and loving eye;
Or fold mine armes and sigh, because I've lost
The world so soon, and in it, you the most.
Then [28] these, no feares more on your fancies fall,
Though then I smile, and speake no words at all.

His Grange, or private Wealth

Though clock,
To tell how night drawes hence, I've none,
A cock,
I have, to sing how day drawes on.
I have
A maid (my Prew) by good luck sent,
To save
That little fates me gave or lent.
A hen
I keep, which creeking day by day,
Tells when
She goes her long white egg to lay.
A goose
I have, which, with a jealous eare,
Lets loose
Her tongue, to tell what danger's neare.
A lamb
I keep (tame) with my morsells fed,
Whose dam
An orphan left him (lately dead).
A cat
I keep, that playes about my house,
Grown fat
With eating many a miching [29] mouse.
To these
A Trasy [30] I do keep, whereby
I please
The more my rurall privacie;
Which are
But toyes, to give my heart some ease:
Where care
None is, slight things do lightly please.

[28] than

Upon Julia's Clothes

Whenas in silks my Julia goes,
Then, then (me thinks) how sweetly flowes
That liquefaction of her clothes.

Next, when I cast mine eyes and see
That brave vibration each way free;
O how that glittering taketh me!

Upon Prue his Maid

In this little urne is laid
Prewdence Baldwin (once my maid)
From whose happy spark here let
Spring the purple violet.

The Invitation

To sup with thee thou didst me home invite,
And mad'st a promise that mine appetite
Sho'd meet and tire, on such lautitious [31] meat,
The like not Heliogabalus did eat;
And richer wine wo'dst give to me (thy guest)
Then Roman Sylla pour'd out at his feast.
I came; ('tis true) and lookt for fowle of price,
The bastard phenix; bird of Paradice;
And for no less then aromatick wine
Of maydens'-blush, commixt with jessimine.

[29] thieving
[30] his spaniel
[31] sumptuous

Cleane was the herth, the mantle larded jet;
Which wanting Lar, and smoke, hung weeping wet;
At last, i' th' noone of winter, did appeare
A rag'd-soust-neats-foot [32] with sick vinegar;
And in a burnisht flagonet stood by
Beere small [33] as comfort, dead as charity.
At which amaz'd, and pondring on the food,
How cold it was, and how it chil'd my blood,
I curst the master; and I damn'd the souce; [34]
And swore I'de got the ague of the house.
Well, when to eat thou dost me next desire,
I'le bring a fever; since thou keep'st no fire.

To M. Henry Lawes,[35] the excellent Composer, of his Lyrics

Touch but thy lire (my Harrie) and I heare
From thee some raptures of the rare Gotire.
Then if thy voice commingle with the string,
I heare in thee the rare Laniere to sing;

Or curious Wilson. Tell me, canst thou be
Less then Apollo, that usurp'st such three?
Three, unto whom the whole world give applause;
Yet their three praises, praise but one; that's Lawes.

Ceremonies for Candlemas [36] Eve

Down with the rosemary and bayes,
Down with the misleto;
Instead of holly, now up-raise
The greener box (for show.)

The holly hitherto did sway;
Let box now domineere,
Untill the dancing Easter-day,
Or Easters Eve appeare.

Then youthfull box which now hath grace,
Your houses to renew,
Grown old, surrender must his place,
Unto the crispéd yew.

When yew is out, then birch comes in,
And many flowers beside;
Both of a fresh and fragrant kinne
To honour Whitsontide.

Green rushes then, and sweetest bents,
With cooler oken boughs,
Come in for comely ornaments,
To re-adorn the house.
Thus times do shift; each thing his turne do's hold;
New things succeed, as former things grow old.

The Ceremonies for Candlemas Day

Kindle the Christmas brand and then
Till sunne-set, let it burne;
Which quencht, then lay it up agen,
Till Christmas next returne.

Part must be kept wherewith to teend
The Christmas log next yeare;
And where 'tis safely kept, the fiend,
Can do no mischiefe (there.)

Upon Ben Jonson

Here lyes Johnson with the rest
Of the poets; but the best.
Reader, wo'dst thou more have known?
Aske his story, not this stone.
That will speake what this can't tell
Of his glory. *So farewell.*

[32] Ox-foot, formerly used as food.
[33] weak beer
[34] souse (pickled meat)
[35] Henry Lawes was the most gifted of the composers at the court of Charles I. It was possibly at his suggestion that Milton wrote *Comus*, for which Lawes made the music. The other musicians mentioned here were contemporaries of Lawes.
[36] The feast of the purification of the Virgin.

An Ode for him

Ah Ben!
Say how, or when
Shall we thy guests
Meet at those lyrick feasts,
Made at the Sun,
The Dog, the triple Tunne? [37]
Where we such clusters had,
As made us nobly wild, not mad;
And yet each verse of thine
Out-did the meate, out-did the frolick wine.

My Ben!
Or come agen,
Or send to us
Thy wit's great over-plus;
But teach us yet
Wisely to husband it,
Lest we that tallent spend;
And having once brought to an end
That precious stock, the store
Of such a wit the world sho'd have no more.

His Tears to Thamesis [38]

I send, I send here my supremest kiss
To thee, my silver-footed Thamasis.
No more shall I reiterate [39] thy Strand,
Whereon so many stately structures stand;
Nor in the summers sweeter evenings go,
To bath in thee (as thousand others doe,)
No more shall I along thy christall glide,
In barge (with boughes and rushes beautifi'd)
With soft-smooth virgins (for our chast disport)
To Richmond, Kingstone, and to Hampton-Court;
Never againe shall I with finnie-ore
Put from, or draw unto the faithfull shore;
And landing here, or safely landing there,
Make way to my belovéd Westminster;
Or to the golden-Cheap-side, where the earth
Of Julia Herrick gave to me my Birth.
May all clean nimphs and curious water dames,
With swan-like-state, flote up and down thy streames;
No drought upon thy wanton waters fall
To make them leane, and languishing at all.
No ruffling winds come hither to decease [40]
Thy pure, and silver-wristed Naides.
Keep up your state, ye streams; and as ye spring,
Never make sick your banks by surfeiting.
Grow young with tydes, and though I see ye never,
Receive this vow, so fare-ye-well for ever.

His Desire

Give me a man that is not dull,
When all the world with rifts is full;
But unamaz'd dares clearely sing,
Whenas the roof's a-tottering;
And, though it falls, continues still
Tickling the citterne with his quill.

His Litany, to the Holy Spirit [41]

In the houre of my distresse,
When temptations me oppresse,
And when I my sins confesse,
Sweet Spirit comfort me!

When I lie within my bed,
Sick in heart and sick in head,
And with doubts discomforted,
Sweet Spirit comfort me!

When the house doth sigh and weep,
And the world is drown'd in sleep,
Yet mine eyes the watch do keep;
Sweet Spirit comfort me!

When the artlesse doctor sees
No one hope, but of his fees,
And his skill runs on the lees;
Sweet Spirit comfort me!

---

[37] Three taverns where Jonson and his 'sons' caroused.
[38] The river Thames. [39] go along

[40] disease, *i.e.*, trouble
[41] These last two poems are taken from Herrick's *Noble Numbers: or, His Pious Pieces*, 1647.

When his potion and his pill,
Has, or none, or little skill,
Meet for nothing, but to kill;
Sweet Spirit comfort me!

When the passing-bell doth tole,
And the furies in a shole
Come to fright a parting soule;
Sweet Spirit comfort me!

When the tapers now burne blew,
And the comforters are few,
And that number more then true;
Sweet Spirit comfort me!

When the priest his last hath praid,
And I nod to what is said,
'Cause my speech is now decaid;
Sweet Spirit comfort me!

When (God knowes) I'm tost about,
Either with despaire, or doubt;
Yet before the glasse be out,
Sweet Spirit comfort me!

When the tempter me pursu'th
With the sins of all my youth,
And halfe damns me with untruth;
Sweet Spirit comfort me!

When the flames and hellish cries
Fright mine eares, and fright mine eyes,
And all terrors me surprise;
Sweet Spirit comfort me!

When the Judgment is reveal'd,
And that open'd which was seal'd,
When to Thee I have appeal'd;
Sweet Spirit comfort me!

Grace for a Child

Here a little child I stand,
Heaving up my either hand;
Cold as paddocks though they be,
Here I lift them up to Thee,
For a benizon to fall
On our meat, and on us all. *Amen.*

George Herbert

1593–1633

The Dedication [1]

Lord, my first-fruits present themselves to thee;
Yet not mine neither; for from thee they came,
And must return. Accept of them and me,
And make us strive who shall sing best thy name.
Turn their eyes hither who shall make a gain;
Theirs who shall hurt themselves or me, refrain.

The Second Thanksgiving, or The Reprisal

I have consider'd it, and finde
There is no dealing with thy mighty passion;
For though I die for thee, I am behinde;
My sinnes deserve the condemnation.

O, make me innocent, that I
May give a disentangled state and free;
And yet thy wounds still my attempts defie,
For by thy death I die for thee.

Ah, was it not enough that thou
By thy eternall glorie didst outgo me?
Couldst thou not grief's sad conquests me allow,
But in all vict'ries overthrow me?

Yet by confession will I come
Into thy conquest. Though I can do nought
Against thee, in thee I will overcome
The man who once against thee fought.

[1] Most of Herbert's short poems, including all of those printed here, were issued in *The Temple; Sacred Poems and Private Ejaculations*, 1633.

Easter Wings

Lord, who createdst man in wealth and store,
Though foolishly he lost the same,
Decaying more and more,
Till he became
Most poore;

With thee
O let me rise,
As larks, harmoniously,
And sing this day thy victories;
Then shall the fall further the flight in me.

My tender age in sorrow did beginne;
And still with sicknesses and shame
Thou didst so punish sinne,
That I became
Most thinne.

With thee
Let me combine,
And feel this day thy victorie;
For, if I imp [2] my wing on thine,
Affliction shall advance the flight in me.

Nature

Full of rebellion, I would die,
Or fight, or travell, or denie
That thou hast ought to do with me.
O, tame my heart;
It is thy highest art,
To captivate strongholds to thee.

If thou shalt let this venome lurk,
And in suggestions fume and work,
My soul will turn to bubbles straight,
And thence, by kinde,
Vanish into a winde,
Making thy workmanship deceit.

O, smooth my rugged heart, and there
Engrave thy rev'rend law and fear;
Or make a new one, since the old
Is saplesse grown,
And a much fitter stone
To hide my dust then thee to hold.

[2] To mend the damaged wing of a hawk by grafting to it feathers from another bird.

Repentance

Lord, I confesse my sin is great;
Great is my sinne. O, gently treat
With thy quick flow'r thy momentanie [3] bloom,
Whose life still pressing
Is one undressing,
A steadie aiming at a tombe.

Man's age is two houres' work, or three;
Each day doth round about us see.
Thus are we to delights, but we are all
To sorrows old,
If life be told
From what life feeleth, Adam's fall.

O, let thy height of mercie, then,
Compassionate short-breathéd men;
Cut me not off for my most foul transgression.
I do confesse
My foolishnesse;
My God, accept of my confession.

Sweeten at length this bitter bowl
Which thou hast pour'd into my soul;
Thy wormwood turn to health, windes to fair weather;
For if thou stay,
I and this day,
As we did rise, we die together.

When thou for sinne rebukest man,
Forthwith he waxeth wo and wan;
Bitternesse fills our bowels, all our hearts
Pine and decay
And drop away,
And carrie with them th' other parts.

But thou wilt sinne and grief destroy;
That so the broken bones may joy,

[3] momentary

And tune together in a well-set song,
Full of his praises
Who dead men raises.
Fractures well cur'd make us more strong.

The Windows

LORD, how can man preach thy eternall word?
He is a brittle crazie glasse;
Yet in thy temple thou dost him afford
This glorious and transcendent place,
To be a window through thy grace.

But when thou dost anneal in glasse thy storie,
Making thy life to shine within
The holy preachers, then the light and glorie
More rev'rend grows, and more doth win;
Which else shows watrish, bleak, and thin.

Doctrine and life, colours and light, in one
When they combine and mingle, bring
A strong regard and aw; but speech alone
Doth vanish like a flaring thing,
And in the eare, not conscience, ring.

Man

MY God, I heard this day
That none doth build a stately habitation
But he that means to dwell therein.
What house more stately hath there been,
Or can be, then is man to whose creation
All things are in decay?

For man is ev'ry thing,
And more: he is a tree, yet bears mo fruit;
A beast, yet is, or should be, more;
Reason and speech we onely bring;
Parrats may thank us, if they are not mute,
They go upon the score.

Man is all symmetrie,
Full of proportions, one limbe to another,
And all to all the world besides;
Each part may call the farthest brother,
For head with foot hath private amitie,
And both with moons and tides.

Nothing hath got so farre
But man hath caught and kept it as his prey;
His eyes dismount the highest starre;
He is in little all the sphere;
Herbs gladly cure our flesh, because that they
Finde their acquaintance there.

For us the windes do blow,
The earth resteth, heav'n moveth, fountains flow;
Nothing we see but means our good,
As our delight or as our treasure;
The whole is either our cupboard of food
Or cabinet of pleasure.

The starres have us to bed;
Night draws the curtain, which the sunne withdraws;
Musick and light attend our head,
All things unto our flesh are kinde
In their descent and being; to our minde
In their ascent and cause.

Each thing is full of dutie:
Waters united are our navigation;
Distinguishéd, our habitation;
Below, our drink; above, our meat;
Both are our cleanlinesse. Hath one such beautie?
Then how are all things neat!

More servants wait on man
Than he'l take notice of; in ev'ry path
He treads down that which doth befriend him
When sicknesse makes him pale and wan.
Oh mightie love! Man is one world, and hath
Another to attend him.

Since then, my God, thou hast
So brave a palace built, O dwell in it,
That it may dwell with thee at last!
Till then afford us so much wit,
That, as the world serves us, we may serve thee,
And both thy servants be.

Mortification

How soon doth man decay!
When clothes are taken from a chest of sweets [4]
To swaddle infants, whose young breath
Scarce knows the way,
Those clouts are little winding-sheets,
Which do consign and send them unto death.

When boyes go first to bed,
They step into their voluntarie graves;
Sleep binds them fast; onely their breath
Makes them not dead.
Successive nights, like rolling waves,
Convey them quickly who are bound for death.

When youth is frank and free,
And calls for musick, while his veins do swell,
All day exchanging mirth and breath
In companie,
That musick summons to the knell
Which shall befriend him at the house of death.

When man grows staid and wise,
Getting a house and home, where he may move
Within the circle of his breath,
Schooling his eyes,
That dumbe inclosure maketh love
Unto the coffin that attends his death.

When age grows low and weak,
Marking his grave, and thawing ev'ry year,
Till all do melt and drown his breath
When he would speak,

[4] sweet scents

A chair or litter shows the biere
Which shall convey him to the house of death.

Man, ere he is aware,
Hath put together a solemnitie,
And drest his hearse, while he has breath
As yet to spare;
Yet, Lord, instruct us so to die,
That all these dyings may be life in death.

The Quip

THE merrie World did on a day
With his train-bands and mates agree
To meet together where I lay,
And all in sport to geere at me.

First Beautie crept into a rose,
Which when I pluckt not, 'Sir,' said she,
'Tell me, I pray, whose hands are those?'
But thou shalt answer, Lord, for me.

Then Money came, and chinking still,
'What tune is this, poore man?' said he;
'I heard in musick you had skill';
But thou shalt answer, Lord, for me.

Then came brave Glorie puffing by
In silks that whistled, who but he!
He scarce allowed me half an eie;
But thou shalt answer, Lord, for me.

Then came quick Wit and Conversation,
And he would needs a comfort be,
And, to be short, make an oration;
But thou shalt answer, Lord, for me.

Yet when the houre of thy designe
To answer these fine things shall come,
Speak not at large, say, I am thine,
And then they have their answer home.

The Collar

I STRUCK the board, and cry'd, 'No more;
I will abroad.'
What, shall I ever sigh and pine?

My lines and life are free; free as the road,
Loose as the winde, as large as store.
Shall I be still in suit?
Have I no harvest but a thorn
To let me bloud, and not restore
What I have lost with cordiall fruit?
Sure there was wine
Before my sighs did drie it; there was corn
Before my tears did drown it;
Is the yeare onely lost to me?
Have I no bayes to crown it,
No flowers, no garlands gay? all blasted,
All wasted?
Not so, my heart; but there is fruit,
And thou hast hands.
Recover all thy sigh-blown age
On double pleasures; leave thy cold dispute
Of what is fit and not; forsake thy cage,
Thy rope of sands
Which pettie thoughts have made; and made to thee
Good cable, to enforce and draw,
And be thy law,
While thou didst wink and wouldst not see.
Away! take heed;
I will abroad.
Call in thy death's-head there, tie up thy fears;
He that forbears
To suit and serve his need
Deserves his load.
But as I rav'd and grew more fierce and wilde
At every word,
Methought I heard one calling, 'Childe';
And I reply'd, 'My Lord.'

The Pulley

When God at first made man,
Having a glasse of blessings standing by,
'Let us,' said he, 'poure on him all we can;
Let the world's riches, which disperséd lie,
Contract into a span.'

So strength first made a way,
Then beautie flow'd, then wisdome, honour, pleasure;
When almost all was out, God made a stay,
Perceiving that, alone of all his treasure,
Rest in the bottome lay.

'For if I should,' said he,
'Bestow this jewell also on my creature,
He would adore my gifts in stead of me,
And rest in Nature, not the God of Nature;
So both should losers be.

Yet let him keep the rest,
But keep them with repining restlessnesse;
Let him be rich and wearie, that at least,
If goodnesse leade him not, yet wearinesse
May tosse him to my breast.'

Aaron [5]

Holinesse on the head,
Light and perfections on the breast,
Harmonious bells below, raising the dead
To leade them unto life and rest:
Thus are true Aarons drest.

Profaneness in my head,
Defects and darknesse in my breast,
A noise of passions ringing me for dead
Unto a place where is no rest:
Poore priest, thus am I drest.

Onely another head
I have, another heart and breast,
Another musick, making live, not dead,
Without whom I could have no rest:
In him I am well drest.

---

[5] Aaron is the perfect type of priest. Herbert's own devotion to his priestly office is shown in Walton's account of his assumption of his duties at Bemerton. 'When at his induction he was shut into Bemerton Church, being left there alone to toll the bell, — as the Law requires him, — he staid so much longer than an ordinary time, before he returned to those friends that staid expecting him at the Church-door, that his friend Mr. Woodnot looked in at the Church-window, and saw him lie prostrate on the ground before the Altar; at which time and place — as he after told Mr. Woodnot — he set some rules to himself, for the future manage of his life; and then and there made a vow to labour to keep them.'

Christ is my onely head,
My alone-onely heart and breast,
My onely musick, striking me ev'n dead,
That to the old man I may rest,
And be in him new-drest.

So, holy in my head,
Perfect and light in my deare breast,
My doctrine tun'd by Christ, who is not dead,
But lives in me while I do rest,
Come, people; Aaron's drest.

Richard Crashaw

1613?–1649

Wishes

To his (supposed) Mistress

Who ere shee bee,
That not impossible shee
That shall command my heart and mee;

Where ere shee lye,
Lock't up from mortall eye,
In shady leaves of destiny,

Till that ripe birth
Of studied fate stand forth,
And teach her faire steps to our earth;

Till that divine
Idæa, take a shrine
Of chrystall flesh, through which to shine;

Meet you her, my wishes,
Bespeake her to my blisses,
And bee yee call'd my absent kisses.

I wish her beauty,
That owes not all his duty
To gaudy tire, or glistring shoo-ty.

Something more than
Taffata or tissew can,
Or rampant feather, or rich fan.

More then the spoyle
Of shop, or silkewormes toyle,
Or a bought blush, or a set smile.

A face that's best
By its owne beauty drest,
And can alone commend the rest.

A face made up
Out of no other shop,
Then what nature's white hand sets ope.

A cheeke where youth,
And blood, with pen of truth
Write, what the reader sweetly ru'th.

A cheeke where growes
More then a morning rose,
Which to no boxe his being owes.

Lipps, where all day
A lover's kisse may play,
Yet carry nothing thence away.

Lookes that oppresse
Their richest tires, but dresse
And cloathe their simplest nakednesse.

Eyes, that displaces
The neighbour diamond, and out faces
That sunshine by their owne sweet graces.

Tresses, that weare
Jewells but to declare
How much themselves more pretious are,

Whose native ray,
Can tame the wanton day
Of gems, that in their bright shades play.

Each ruby there,
Or pearl that dare appeare,
Bee its owne blush, bee its owne teare.

A well tam'd heart,
For whose more noble smart,
Love may bee long chusing a dart.

Eyes, that bestow
Full quivers on love's bow,
Yet pay lesse arrowes then they owe.

Smiles, that can warme
The blood, yet teach a charme,
That chastity shall take no harme.

Blushes, that bin
The burnish of no sin,
Nor flames of ought too hot within.

Joyes, that confesse
Vertue their mistresse,
And have no other head to dresse.

Feares, fond and flight,[1]
As the coy bride's, when night
First does the longing lover right.

Teares, quickly fled,
And vaine, as those are shed
For a dying maydenhead.

Dayes, that need borrow
No part of their good morrow,
From a forespent night of sorrow.

Dayes, that in spight
Of darkenesse, by the light
Of a cleere mind are day all night.

Nights, sweet as they,
Made short by lovers' play,
Yet long by th'absence of the day.

Life, that dares send
A challenge to his end,
And when it comes say, Welcome friend.

Sydnæan [2] showers
Of sweet discourse, whose powers
Can crowne old winter's head with flowers,

Soft silken houres,
Open sunnes; shady bowers,
Bove all; nothing within that lowres.

What ere delight
Can make daye's forehead bright;
Or give downe to the wings of night.

In her whole frame,
Have nature all the name,
Art and ornament the shame.

Her flattery,
Picture and poesy,
Her counsell her owne vertue bee.

I wish her store
Of worth may leave her poore
Of wishes; and I wish — no more.

Now if time knowes
That her whose radiant browes
Weave them a garland of my vowes;

Her whose just bayes
My future hopes can raise,
A trophie to her present praise;

Her that dares bee,
What these lines wish to see:
I seeke no further, it is shee.

'Tis shee, and heere,
Lo, I uncloath and cleare
My wishes' cloudy character.

May she enjoy it,
Whose merit dare apply it,
But modesty dares still deny it.

Such worth as this is,
Shall fixe my flying wishes,
And determine them to kisses.

Let her full glory,
My fancyes, fly before yee;
Bee ye my fictions; but her story.

[*The Delights of the Muses,* 1646]

---

[1] fleeting
[2] *I.e.,* of Sir Philip Sidney, whose prose romance, *Arcadia,* is probably meant.

An Epitaph upon a Young Married Couple Dead and Buried Together

To these, whom death again did wed,
This grave's their second marriage-bed.
For though the hand of fate could force
'Twixt soul and body a divorce,
It could not sunder man and wife,
'Cause they both livéd but one life.
Peace, good reader. Doe not weep.
Peace, the lovers are asleep.
They, sweet turtles, folded ly
In the last knott love could ty.
And though they ly as they were dead,
Their pillow stone, their sheetes of lead,
(Pillow hard, and sheetes not warm)
Love made the bed; they'l take no harm;
Let them sleep; let them sleep on.
Till this stormy night be gone,
Till the'aeternall morrow dawn;
Then the curtaines will be drawn
And they wake into a light,
Whose day shall never dy in night.

[*The Delights of the Muses*, 1646;
text from *Carmen Deo Nostro*, 1652]

The Tear

WHAT bright soft thing is this?
Sweet Mary,[3] thy faire eyes expence?
A moist sparke it is,
A watry diamond; from whence
The very terme, I think, was found,
The water of a diamond.

O 'tis not a teare,
'Tis a starre about to drop
From thine eye its spheare;
The sunne will stoope and take it up.
Proud will his sister be to weare
This, thine eyes jewell, in her eare.

O 'tis a teare,
Too true a teare; for no sad eyne,
How sad so e're,
Raine so true a teare as thine;
Each drop leaving a place so deare,
Weeps for it selfe, is its owne teare.

Such a pearle as this is,
(Slipt from Aurora's dewy brest)
The rose bud's sweet lip kisses;
And such the rose its selfe when vext
With ungentle flames, does shed,
Sweating in too warme a bed.

Such the maiden gemme
By the wanton spring put on,
Peeps from her parent stemme,
And blushes on the manly sun;
This watry blossome of thy eyne
Ripe, will make the richer wine.

Faire drop, why quak'st thou so?
'Cause thou streight must lay thy head
In the dust? O no;
The dust shall never bee thy bed;
A pillow for thee will I bring,
Stuft with downe of angels wing.

Thus carryed up on high,
(For to heaven thou must goe)
Sweetly shalt thou lye,
And in soft slumbers bath thy woe;
Till the singing orbes awake thee,
And one of their bright chorus make thee.

There thy selfe shalt bee
An eye, but not a weeping one;
Yet I doubt of thee,
Whither th'hadst rather there have shone
An eye of heaven; or still shine here
In th'heaven of Mary's eye, a teare.

[*Steps to the Temple*, 1646]

[3] St. Mary Magdalene

On the Blessed Virgin's Bashfulness

THAT on her lap she casts her humble eye,
'Tis the sweet pride of her humility.
The faire starre is well fixt, for where, O where
Could she have fixt it on a fairer speare?
'Tis heav'n, 'tis heaven she sees, heavens God there lyes;

She can see heaven, and ne're lift up her eyes:
This new guest to her eyes new lawes hath given,
'Twas once looke up, 'tis now looke downe to heaven.

[*Steps to the Temple*, 1646]

I am the Door

And now th'art set wide ope, the speare's sad art,
Lo! hath unlockt thee at the very heart;
Hee to himselfe (I feare the worst)
And his owne hope,
Hath shut these doores of heaven that durst
Thus set them ope.

[*Steps to the Temple*, 1646]

Upon the Body of our Blessed Lord, Naked and Bloody

They have left thee naked, Lord; O that they had!
This garment too I would they had deny'd.

Thee with thy self they have too richly clad,
Opening the purple wardrobe in thy side.

O never could there be garment too good
For thee to wear, but this, of thine owne blood.

[*Carmen Deo Nostro*, 1652]

A Hymn to the Name and Honour of the Admirable Saint Teresa[4]

Love, thou art absolute sole lord
Of life and death. To prove the word,
Wee'l now appeal to none of all
Those thy old souldiers, great and tall,
Ripe men of martyrdom, that could reach down
With strong arms their triumphant crown;
Such as could with lusty breath
Speak lowd into the face of death
Their great Lord's glorious name; to none
Of those whose spatious bosomes spread a throne
For love at larg to fill: spare blood and sweat;
And see him take a private seat,
Making his mansion in the mild
And milky soul of a soft child.
Scarse has she learn't to lisp the name
Of martyr; yet she thinks it shame
Life should so long play with that breath
Which spent can buy so brave a death.
She never undertook to know
What death with love should have to doe;
Nor has she e're yet understood
Why to show love, she should shed blood;
Yet though she cannot tell you why,
She can love, and she can dy.
Scarse has she blood enough to make
A guilty sword blush for her sake;
Yet has she a heart dares hope to prove
How much lesse strong is death then love.
Be love but there; let poor six yeares
Be pos'd with the maturest feares
Man trembles at, you straight shall find
Love knows no nonage, nor the mind.
'Tis love, not yeares or limbs that can
Make the martyr, or the man.
Love touch't her heart, and lo it beates
High, and burnes with such brave heates,
Such thirsts to dy, as dares drink up
A thousand cold deaths in one cup.
Good reason, for she breathes all fire.
Her weake brest heaves with strong desire
Of what she may with fruitles wishes
Seek for amongst her mother's kisses.
Since 'tis not to be had at home
She'l travail to a martyrdom.
No home for hers confesses she
But where she may a martyr be.
Sh'el to the Moores, and trade with them,

[4] St. Teresa exerted a great influence on Crashaw. He had probably become acouainted with her life and works through her autobiography, translated into English in 1642. Another of his finest poems, *The Flaming Heart*, is a rhapsody in honor of the saint, evoked by a picture of her 'with a seraphim beside her'.

For this unvalued diadem.
She'l offer them her dearest breath,
With Christ's name in't, in change for death.
Sh'el bargain with them, and will give
Them God; teach them how to live
In him: or, if they this deny,
For him she'l teach them how to dy.
So shall she leave amongst them sown
Her Lord's blood; or at lest her own.
  Farewel then, all the world! Adieu.
Teresa is no more for you.
Farewell, all pleasures, sports, and joyes,
(Never till now esteemèd toyes)
Farewell what ever deare may bee,
Mother's armes or father's knee;
Farewell house, and farewell home!
She's for the Moores, and martyrdom.
  Sweet, not so fast! lo, thy fair spouse
Whom thou seekst with so swift vowes,
Calls thee back, and bidds thee come
T'embrace a milder martyrdom.
  Blest powres forbid thy tender life
Should bleed upon a barborous knife;
Or some base hand have power to race [5]
Thy brest's chast cabinet, and uncase
A soul kept there so sweet; O no;
Wise heavn will never have it so;
Thou art love's victime, and must dy
A death more mysticall and high.
Into love's arms thou shalt let fall
A still-surviving funerall.
His is the dart [6] must make the death
Whose stroke shall tast thy hallow'd breath;
A dart thrice dip't in that rich flame
Which writes thy spouse's radiant name
Upon the roof of heav'n; where ay
It shines, and with a soveraign ray
Beates bright upon the burning faces
Of soules which in that name's sweet graces
Find everlasting smiles. So rare,
So spirituall, pure, and fair
Must be th'immortall instrument
Upon whose choice point shall be sent
A life so lov'd; and that there be
Fitt executioners for thee,
The fair'st and first-born sons of fire
Blest Seraphim, shall leave their quire
And turn love's souldiers, upon thee
To exercise their archerie.
  O how oft shalt thou complain
Of a sweet and subtle pain.
Of intolerable joyes;
Of a death, in which who dyes
Loves his death, and dyes again.
And would for ever so be slain.
And lives, and dyes; and knowes not why
To live, but that he thus may never leave to dy.
  How kindly will thy gentle heart
Kiss the sweetly-killing dart!
And close in his embraces keep
Those delicious wounds, that weep
Balsom to heal themselves with. Thus
When these thy deaths, so numerous,
Shall all at last dy into one,
And melt thy soul's sweet mansion,
Like a soft lump of incense, hasted
By too hott a fire, and wasted
Into perfuming clouds, so fast
Shalt thou exhale to heavn at last
In a resolving sigh, and then,
O what? Ask not the tongues of men.
Angells cannot tell; suffice,
Thy selfe shall feel thine own full joyes
And hold them fast for ever. There
So soon as thou shalt first appear,
The moon of maiden stars, thy white
Mistress, attended by such bright
Soules as thy shining self, shall come
And in her first ranks make thee room;
Where 'mongst her snowy family
Immortall wellcomes wait for thee.
  O what delight, when reveal'd life shall stand
And teach thy lipps heav'n with his hand;
On which thou now maist to thy wishes
Heap up thy consecrated kisses.
What joyes shall seize thy soul, when she
Bending her blessed eyes on thee
(Those second smiles of heav'n) shall dart
Her mild rayes through thy melting heart!

[5] cut away
[6] St. Teresa, in a vision, saw and felt herself pierced with a long dart of gold.

Angels, thy old freinds, there shall greet thee,
Glad at their own home now to meet thee.
All thy good workes which went before
And waited for thee, at the door,
Shall own thee there; and all in one
Weave a constellation
Of crowns, with which the king thy spouse
Shall build up thy triumphant browes.
All thy old woes shall now smile on thee
And thy paines sitt bright upon thee.
All thy sorrows here shall shine,
All thy suffrings be divine.
Tears shall take comfort, and turn gemms,
And wrongs repent to diadems.
Ev'n thy deaths shall live; and new
Dresse the soul that erst they slew.
Thy wounds shall blush to such bright scarres
As keep account of the Lamb's warres.
Those rare workes, where thou shal leave writt,
Love's noble history, with witt
Taught thee by none but him, while here
They feed our soules, shall cloth thine there.
Each heavnly word by whose hid flame
Our hard hearts shall strike fire, the same
Shall flourish on thy browes, and be
Both fire to us and flame to thee;
Whose light shall live bright in thy face
By glory, in our hearts by grace.
Thou shalt look round about, and see
Thousands of crown'd soules throng to be
Themselves thy crown. Sons of thy vowes,
The virgin-births with which thy sovereign spouse
Made fruitfull thy fair soul, goe now
And with them all about thee, bow
To Him. Put on (hee'l say) put on
(My rosy love) that thy rich zone
Sparkling with the sacred flames
Of thousand soules whose happy names
Heav'n keeps upon thy score. (Thy bright
Life brought them first to kisse the light
That kindled them to starrs.) And so
Thou with the Lamb, thy Lord, shalt goe;
And whereso 'ere he setts his white
Stepps, walk with Him those wayes of light
Which who in death would live to see,
Must learn in life to dy like thee.

[*Carmen Deo Nostro*, 1652 [7]]

[7] An earlier version is found in *Steps to the Temple*, 1646.

Henry Vaughan

1622–1695

Idle Verse [1]

Go, go, queint folies, sugred sin,
Shadow no more my door;
I will no longer cobwebs spin,
I'm too much on the score.

For since amidst my youth and night
My great preserver smiles,
Wee'l make a match, my only light,
And joyn against their wiles;

Blind, desp'rate fits, that study how
To dresse and trim our shame,
That gild rank poyson and allow
Vice in a fairer name;

The purles of youthful bloud and bowles,
Lust in the robes of love,
The idle talk of feav'rish souls
Sick with a scarf, or glove;

Let it suffice my warmer days
Simper'd, and shin'd on you,
Twist not my cypresse with your bays,
Or roses wth my yewgh;

Go, go, seek out some greener thing,
It snows and freezeth here;
Let nightingales attend the spring,
Winter is all my year.

[1] Vaughan's great collection of religious poetry, *Silex Scintillans*, from which all the poems here have been taken, came out in two parts, 1650 and 1655.

The Pursuit

Lord! what a busie, restles thing
Hast thou made man!
Each day and houre he is on wing,
Rest not a span;
Then having lost the sunne and light,
By clouds surpriz'd,
He keeps a commerce in the night
With aire disguis'd;
Hadst thou given to this active dust
A state untir'd,
The lost sonne [2] had not left the huske
Nor home desir'd;
That was thy secret, and it is
Thy mercy too,
For when all failes to bring to blisse,
Then, this must doe.
Ah! Lord! and what a purchase will that be,
To take us sick, that sound would not take thee?

The Retreat

Happy those early dayes when I
Shin'd in my angell-infancy!
Before I understood this place
Appointed for my second race,
Or taught my soul to fancy ought
But a white, celestiall thought;
When yet I had not walkt above
A mile, or two, from my first love,
And looking back (at that short space,)
Could see a glimpse of his bright-face;
When on some gilded cloud or flowre
My gazing soul would dwell an houre,
And in those weaker glories spy
Some shadows of eternity;
Before I taught my tongue to wound
My conscience with a sinfull sound,
Or had the black art to dispence
A sev'rall sinne to ev'ry sence;
But felt through all this fleshly dresse
Bright shootes of everlastingnesse.
O how I long to travell back
And tread again that ancient track!
That I might once more reach that plaine,

[2] the Prodigal Son

Where first I left my glorious traine,
From whence th'inlightned spirit sees
That shady city of palme trees;
But (ah!) my soul with too much stay
Is drunk, and staggers in the way.
Some men a forward motion love,
But I by backward steps would move,
And when this dust falls to the urn,
In that state I came, return.

Peace

My soul, there is a countrie
Far beyond the stars,
Where stands a wingéd centrie
All skilfull in the wars;
There above noise and danger
Sweet peace sits crown'd with smiles,
And one born in a manger
Commands the beauteous files;
He is thy gracious friend,
And (O my soul, awake!)
Did in pure love descend
To die here for thy sake.
If thou canst get but thither,
There growes the flowre of peace,
The rose that cannot wither,
Thy fortresse, and thy ease;
Leave then thy foolish ranges:
For none can thee secure,
But one, who never changes,
Thy God, thy life, thy cure.

The Burial of an Infant

Blest infant bud, whose blossome-life
Did only look about, and fal,
Wearyed out in a harmles strife
Of tears, and milk, the food of all;

Sweetly didst thou expire; thy soul
Flew home unstain'd by his new kin,
For ere thou knew'st how to be foul,
Death wean'd thee from the world and sin.

Softly rest all thy virgin-crums,[3]
Lapt in the sweets of thy young breath,

[3] the body

Expecting till thy Saviour comes
To dress them, and unswadle death.

The World

I SAW Eternity the other night
Like a great ring of pure and endless light,
All calm, as it was bright;
And round beneath it, Time in hours, days, years,
Driv'n by the spheres
Like a vast shadow mov'd, in which the world
And all her train were hurl'd;
The doting lover in his queintest strain
Did there complain,
Neer him, his lute, his fancy, and his flights,
Wits sour delights,
With gloves and knots, the silly snares of pleasure,
Yet his dear treasure
All scatter'd lay, while he his eyes did pour
Upon a flowr.

The darksome states-man, hung with weights and woe,
Like a thick midnight-fog mov'd there so slow
He did not stay, nor go;
Condemning thoughts (like sad ecclipses) scowl
Upon his soul,
And clouds of crying witnesses without
Pursued him with one shout.
Yet dig'd the mole, and lest his ways be found
Workt under ground,
Where he did clutch his prey, but one did see
That policie;
Churches and altars fed him, perjuries
Were gnats and flies;
It rain'd about him bloud and tears, but he
Drank them as free.

The fearfull miser on a heap of rust
Sate pining all his life there, did scarce trust
His own hands with the dust,
Yet would not place one peece above, but lives
In feare of theeves.
Thousands there were as frantick as himself
And hug'd each one his pelf,
The down-right epicure plac'd heav'n in sense
And scorned pretence,
While others slipt into a wide excesse,
Said little lesse;
The weaker sort slight triviall wares inslave,
Who think them brave,
And poor, despiséd truth sate counting by
Their victory.

Yet some, who all this while did weep and sing,
And sing, and weep, soar'd up into the Ring;
But most would use no wing.
O fools (said I,) thus to prefer dark night
Before true light,
To live in grots and caves, and hate the day
Because it shews the way,
The way which from this dead and dark abode
Leads up to God,
A way where you might tread the sun, and be
More bright than he.
But as I did their madness so discusse,
One whisper'd thus:
This Ring the bride-groome did for none provide
But for his bride.

They are all gone into the world of light

THEY are all gone into the world of light!
And I alone sit lingring here;
Their very memory is fair and bright
And my sad thoughts doth clear.

It glows and glitters in my cloudy brest
Like stars upon some gloomy grove,
Or those faint beams in which this hill is drest,
After the sun's remove.

I see them walking in an air of glory,
Whose light doth trample on my days:
My days, which are at best but dull and hoary,
Meer glimering and decays.

O holy hope and high humility,
High as the heavens above!
These are your walks, and you have shew'd them me
To kindle my cold love.

Dear, beauteous death! the jewel of the just!
Shining no where but in the dark;
What mysteries do lie beyond thy dust,
Could man outlook that mark!

He that hath found some fledg'd birds nest may know,
At first sight, if the bird be flown;
But what fair well or grove he sings in now,
That is to him unknown.

And yet, as angels in some brighter dreams
Call to the soul, when man doth sleep,
So some strange thoughts transcend our wonted theams,
And into glory peep.

If a star were confin'd into a tomb,
Her captive flames must needs burn there;
But when the hand that lockt her up gives room,
She'l shine through all the sphaere.

O Father of eternal life, and all
Created glories under thee,
Resume thy spirit from this world of thrall
Into true liberty!

Either disperse these mists which blot and fill
My perspective (still) as they pass,
Or else remove me hence unto that hill,
Where I shall need no glass.

Midnight

When to my eyes
(Whilst deep sleep others catches,)
Thine hoast of spyes,
The starres, shine in their watches,
I doe survey
Each busie ray,
And how they work, and wind,
And wish each beame
My soul doth streame,
With the like ardour shin'd;
What emanations,
Quick vibrations
And bright stirs are there!
What thin ejections,
Cold affections,
And slow motions here!

Thy heav'ns (some say,)
Are a firie-liquid light
Which, mingling, aye
Streames and flames thus to the sight.
Come then, my god!
Shine on this bloud,
And water in one beame,
And thou shalt see
Kindled by thee
Both liquors burne and streame.
O what bright quicknes,
Active brightnes,
And celestiall flowes
Will follow after
On that water,
Which thy spirit blowes!

The Waterfall

With what deep murmurs through times silent stealth
Doth thy transparent, cool and watry wealth

Here flowing fall,
And chide, and call,
As if his liquid, loose retínue staid
Lingring, and were of this steep place afraid,
The common pass
Where, clear as glass,
All must descend
Not to an end,
But quickned by this deep and rocky grave,
Rise to a longer course more bright and brave.

Dear stream! dear bank, where often I
Have sate, and pleas'd my pensive eye,
Why, since each drop of thy quick store
Runs thither, whence it flow'd before,
Should poor souls fear a shade or night,
Who came (sure) from a sea of light?
Or since those drops are all sent back
So sure to thee, that none doth lack,
Why should frail flesh doubt any more
That what God takes, hee'l not restore?
O useful element and clear!
My sacred wash and cleanser here,
My first consigner unto those
Fountains of life where the Lamb goes!
What sublime truths and wholesome themes
Lodge in thy mystical, deep streams!
Such as dull man can never finde
Unless that spirit lead his minde
Which first upon thy face did move,
And hatch'd all with his quickning love.
As this loud brooks incessant fall
In streaming rings restagnates all,
Which reach by course the bank, and then
Are no more seen, just so pass men.
O my invisible estate,
My glorious liberty, still late!
Thou art the channel my soul seeks,
Not this with cataracts and creeks.

Thomas Carew

1595?–1639?

Ask me no more where Jove bestows [1]

Ask me no more where Jove bestows,
When June is past, the fading rose;
For in your beauties orient deep,
These flow'rs as in their causes sleep.

Ask me no more whither doe stray
The golden atomes of the day;
For in pure love heaven did prepare
Those powders to inrich your hair.

Ask me no more whither doth haste
The nightingale, when May is past;
For in your sweet dividing [2] throat
She winters, and keeps warm her note.

Ask me no more where those stars light
That downwards fall in dead of night;
For in your eyes they sit, and there
Fixéd become as in their sphere.

Ask me no more if east or west,
The phenix builds her spicy nest;
For unto you at last she flies,
And in your fragrant bosome dies.

[1] The first printed edition of Carew's poems appeared in 1640, one year after his death. All the poems given here appeared in that edition. [2] singing

Celia Singing

Hark, how my Celia, with the choice
Musick of her hand and voice
Stils the loud wind; and makes the wild
Insenséd bore and panther mild;
Mark how these statues like men move,
Whilst men with wonder, statues prove!
This stiff rock bends to worship her,
That idol turns idolater.

Now see how all the new inspir'd
Images with love are fir'd;

Hark how the tender marble groans,
And all the late transforméd stones
Court the fair nymph with many a tear,
Which she (more stony than they were)
Beholds with unrelenting mind;
Whilst they, amaz'd to see combin'd
Such matchless beauty with disdain,
Are all turn'd into stones again.

Murdering Beauty

I'L gaze no more on her bewitching face,
Since ruine harbours there in every place;
For my enchanted soul alike she drowns
With calmes and tempests of her smiles and frowns.
I'l love no more those cruel eyes of hers,
Which pleas'd, or anger'd, still are murderers;
For if she dart (like lightning) through the air
Her beams of wrath, she kills me with despair;
If she behold me with a pleasing eye,
I surfet with excess of joy, and dye.

A Deposition from Love

I WAS foretold, your rebel sex
Nor love nor pity knew;
And with what scorn you use to vex
Poor hearts that humbly sue;
Yet I believ'd to crown our pain,
Could we the fortress win,
The happy lover sure should gain
A paradise within;
I thought loves plagues like dragons sate
Only to fright us at the gate.

But I did enter, and enjoy
What happy lovers prove;
For I could kiss, and sport, and toy,
And taste those sweets of love;
Which, had they but a lasting state,
Or if in Celia's brest
The force of love might not abate,
Jove were too mean a guest.
But now her breach of faith far more
Afflicts, than did her scorn before.

Hard fate! to have been once possest,
As victor, of a heart
Atchiev'd with labor and unrest,
And then forc'd to depart.
If the stout foe will not resigne
When I besiege a town,
I lose but what was never mine;
But he that is cast down
From enjoy'd beauty, feels a woe,
Only deposéd kings can know.

Secrecy Protested

FEAR not (dear Love) that I'l reveal
Those houres of pleasure we two steal;
No eye shall see, nor yet the sun
Descry, what thou and I have done;
No ear shall hear our love, but we
Silent as the night will be;
The god of love himself (whose dart
Did first wound mine, and then thy heart)
Shall never know, that we can tell,
What sweets in stoln embraces dwell:
This only meanes may find it out,
If when I die, physicians doubt
What caus'd my death, and there to view
Of all their judgments which was true,
Rip up my heart, O then, I fear,
The world will see thy picture there.

Epitaph on the Lady Mary Villiers [3]

THE Lady Mary Villiers lies
Under this stone; with weeping eyes
The parents that first gave her breath,
And their sad friends laid her in earth;
If any of them (reader) were
Known unto thee, shed a tear;
Or if thy self possess a gem,
As dear to thee, as this to them,
Though a stranger to this place,
Bewail in theirs thine own hard case;
For thou perhaps at thy return
Mayst find thy darling in an urn.

[3] Who this lady is, we do not know. She must have been of the family of the Dukes of Buckingham.

Richard Lovelace

1618–1657

To Lucasta, going beyond the Seas[1]

If to be absent were to be
Away from thee;
Or that when I am gone,
You or I were alone;
Then, my Lucasta, might I crave
Pity from blustring winde, or swallowing wave.

But I'le not sigh one blast or gale
To swell my saile,
Or pay a teare to swage
The foaming blew-gods rage;
For whether he will let me passe
Or no, I'm still as happy as I was.

Though seas and land betwixt us both,
Our faith and troth,
Like separated soules,
All time and space controules:
Above the highest sphere wee meet
Unseene, unknowne, and greet as angels greet.

So then we doe anticipate
Our after-fate,
And are alive i'th'skies,
If this our lips and eyes
Can speake like spirits unconfin'd
In Heav'n, their earthy bodies left behind.

To Lucasta, going to the Wars

Tell me not (Sweet) I am unkinde,
That from the nunnerie
Of thy chaste breast and quiet minde,
To warre and armes I flie.

True; a new mistresse now I chase,
The first foe in the field;
And with a stronger faith imbrace
A sword, a horse, a shield.

Yet this inconstancy is such
As you too shall adore;
I could not love thee (Deare) so much,
Lov'd I not honour more.

Gratiana dancing and singing

See! with what constant motion,
Even, and glorious, as the sunne,
Gratiana steeres that noble frame,
Soft as her breast, sweet as her voyce
That gave each winding law and poyze,
And swifter then the wings of fame.

She beat the happy pavement
By such a starre made firmament
Which now no more the roofe envies;
But swells up high with Atlas ev'n,
Bearing the brighter, nobler Heav'n,
And in her, all the dieties.

Each step trod out a lovers thought
And the ambitious hopes he brought,
Chain'd to her brave feet with such arts,
Such sweet command, and gentle awe,
As when she ceas'd, we fighting saw
The floore lay pav'd with broken hearts.

So did she move; so did she sing
Like the harmonious spheres that bring
Unto their rounds their musick's ayd;
Which she performéd such a way,
As all th'inamour'd world will say
The Graces dauncéd, and Apollo play'd.

To Althea, from Prison[2]

When Love with unconfinéd wings
Hovers within my gates,
And my divine Althea brings
To whisper at the grates;
When I lye tangled in her haire,
And fetterd to her eye,
The Gods that wanton in the aire,
Know no such liberty.

[1] With the exception of a few lines, the whole of Lovelace's poetry is contained in two small volumes, *Lucasta*, 1649, and *Lucasta, Posthume Poems*, 1659. The first four of the following poems are taken from the first of these volumes; the last is from the second.

[2] Written in 1642 when Lovelace was imprisoned in the Gatehouse for having presented a 'Kentish Petition' to the House of Commons.

When flowing cups run swiftly round
With no allaying Thames,
Our carelesse heads with roses bound,
Our hearts with loyall flames;
When thirsty griefe in wine we steepe,
When healths and draughts go free,
Fishes that tipple in the deepe,
Know no such libertie.

When (like committed linnets) I
With shriller throat shall sing
The sweetness, mercy, majesty,
And glories of my king;
When I shall voyce aloud, how good
He is, how great should be;
Inlargéd winds that curle the flood,
Know no such liberty.

Stone walls do not a prison make,
Nor iron bars a cage;
Mindes innocent and quiet take
That for an hermitage;
If I have freedome in my love
And in my soule am free,
Angels alone that sore above,
Injoy such liberty.

Strive not, vain lover, to be fine

Strive not, vain lover, to be fine,
Thy silk's the silk-worms, and not thine;
You lessen to a fly your mistris thought,
To think it may be in a cobweb caught.
What though her thin transparent lawn
Thy heart in a strong net hath drawn?
Not all the arms the god of fire ere made,
Can the soft bulwarks of nak'd love invade.

Be truly fine then, and your self dress
In her fair souls immac'late glass:
Then by reflection you may have the bliss,
Perhaps, to see what a true fineness is;
When all your gawderies will fit
Those only that are poor in wit:
She that a *clinquant* outside doth adore,
Dotes on a gilded statue, and no more.

Edmund Waller

1606–1687

An Apology for having Loved before[1]

They that never had the use
Of the grapes surprizing juyce;
To the first delicious cup,
All their reason render up;

Neither do not care to know,
Whether it be best or no.
So they that are to love inclin'd;
Sway'd by chance, not choice or art,

To the first that's fair or kind,
Make a present of their heart;
'Tis not she that first we love,
But whom dying we approve.

To man that was i'th' evening made,
Stars gave the first delight;
Admiring, in the gloomy shade,
Those little drops of light.

Then at Aurora, whose fair hand
Remov'd them from the skies,
He gazing toward the east did stand,
She entertain'd his eyes;

But when the bright sun did appear,
All those he 'gan despise,
His wonder was determin'd there,
And could no higher rise;

He neither might, nor wisht to know
A more refulgent light;
For that (as mine your beauties now)
Imploy'd his utmost sight.

[1] Waller's poems were first collected in 1645. All those printed here, except the last, are from that edition.

To my young Lady Lucy Sidney

Why came I so untimely forth
Into a world which, wanting thee,
Could entertain us with no worth
Or shadow of felicity,
That time should me so far remove
From that which I was born to love?

Yet, fairest blossom, do not slight
That age which you may know so soon;
The rosie morn resigns her light,
And milder glory to the noon;
And then what wonders shall you do,
Whose dawning beauty warms us so?

Hope waits upon the flowry prime,
And summer, though it be less gay,
Yet is not lookt on as a time
Of declination or decay.
For with a full hand that does bring
All that was promis'd by the spring.

At Penshurst [2]

While in the park I sing, the listning deer
Attend my passion, and forget to fear.
When to the beeches I report my flame,
They bow their heads as if they felt the same;
To gods appealing, when I reach their bowrs
With loud complaints, they answer me in showrs.
To thee a wild and cruel soul is given,
More deaf than trees, and prouder than the heav'n.
Love's foe profest, why dost thou falsly feign
Thy self a Sidney? from which noble strain
He sprung, that could so far exalt the name
Of love and warm our nation with his flame,
That all we can of love or high desire,
Seems but the smoak of am'rous Sidneys fire.
Nor call her mother, who so well do's prove,
One breast may hold both chastity and love.
Never can she, that so exceeds the spring
In joy and bounty, be suppos'd to bring
One so destructive; to no humane stock
We owe this fierce unkindness, but the rock,
That cloven rock produc'd thee, by whose side
Nature to recompence the fatal pride
Of such stern beauty, plac'd those healing springs,[3]
Which not more help, than that destruction brings.
Thy heart no ruder than the rugged stone,
I might, like Orpheus, with my numerous moan
Melt to compassion; now my trait'rous song,
With thee conspires to do the singer wrong;
While thus I suffer not my self to lose
The memory of what augments my woes;
But with my own breath still foment the fire,
Which flames as high as fancy can aspire.
This last complaint th'indulgent ears did pierce
Of just Apollo, president of verse:
Highly concernéd, that the muse should bring
Damage to one whom he had taught to sing,
Thus he advis'd me, On yon agéd tree,
Hang up thy lute, and hye thee to the sea,
That there with wonders thy diverted mind
Some truce at least may with this passion find.
Ah cruel nymph! from whom her humble swain
Flies for relief unto the raging main;
And from the winds and tempests do's expect

---

[2] The family seat of the Sidneys. Waller was a poetical lover — not too ardent — of Dorothy Sidney.

[3] The mineral waters which supply Tunbridge Wells.

A milder fate, than from her cold neglect;
Yet there he'll pray that the unkind may prove
Blest in her choice; and vows this endless love
Springs from no hope of what she can confer,
But from those gifts which heav'n has heap'd on her.

To Phillis

Phillis, why should we delay
Pleasures shorter than the day?
Could we (which we never can)
Stretch our lives beyond their span;
Beauty like a shadow flies,
And our youth before us dies;
Or would youth and beauty stay,
Love hath wings, and will away.
Love hath swifter wings than time;
Change in love to heaven does clime.
Gods that never change their state,
Vary oft their love and hate.
Phillis, to this truth we owe,
All the love betwixt us two:
Let not you and I require,
What has been our past desire;
On what shepherds you have smil'd,
Or what nymphs I have beguil'd;
Leave it to the planets too,
What we shall hereafter do;
For the joys we now may prove,
Take advice of present love.

Say, lovely dream

Say, lovely dream, where couldst thou find
Shadows to counterfeit that face?
Colours of this glorious kind,
Come not from any mortal place.

In heaven it self thou sure wer't drest
With that angel-like disguise;
Thus deluded am I blest,
And see my joy with closéd eyes.

But, ah, this image is too kind
To be other than a dream!
Cruel Sacharissa's mind
Never put on that sweet extreme.

Fair dream, if thou intend'st me grace,
Change that heavenly face of thine;
Paint despis'd love in thy face,
And make it to appear like mine.

Pale, wan, and meager let it look,
With a pity-moving shape,
Such as wander by the brook
Of Lethe, or from graves escape.

Then to that matchless nymph appear,
In whose shape thou shinest so,
Softly in her sleeping ear,
With humble words express my wo.

Perhaps from greatness, state, and pride,
Thus surpriséd she may fall:
Sleep does disproportion hide,
And, death resembling, equals all.

On a Girdle

That which her slender waste confin'd
Shall now my joyful temples bind;
No monarch but would give his crown,
His arms might do what this has done.

It was my heaven's extreamest sphear,
The pale which held that lovely dear;
My joy, my grief, my hope, my love,
Did all within this circle move.

A narrow compass, and yet there
Dwelt all that's good, and all that's fair:
Give me but what this riban bound,
Take all the rest the sun goes round.

Go, lovely rose

Go, lovely rose,
Tell her that wastes her time and me,
That now she knows,
When I resemble her to thee,
How sweet and fair she seems to be.

Tell her that's young,
And shuns to have her graces spy'd,
That hadst thou sprung
In desarts, where no men abide,
Thou must have uncommended dy'd.

Small is the worth
Of beauty from the light retir'd;
Bid her come forth,
Suffer her self to be desir'd,
And not blush so to be admir'd.

Then die, that she,
The common fate of all things rare,
May read in thee;
How small a part of time they share,
That are so wondrous sweet and fair.

Of the last Verses in the Book

When we for age could neither read nor write,
The subject made us able to indite.
The soul with nobler resolutions deckt,
The body stooping, does herself erect:
No mortal parts are requisite to raise
Her that, unbody'd, can her maker praise.

The seas are quiet, when the winds give o're;
So calm are we, when passions are no more;
For then we know how vain it was to boast
Of fleeting things, so certain to be lost.
Clouds of affection from our younger eyes
Conceal that emptiness which age descries.

The soul's dark cottage, batter'd and decay'd,
Lets in new light thro chinks that time has made;
Stronger by weakness, wiser men become
As they draw near to their eternal home:
Leaving the old, both worlds at once they view,
That stand upon the threshold of the new.

[*Poems, &c Written upon Several Occasions,* 1686]

Abraham Cowley

1618–1667

Of Myself [1]

This only grant me, that my means may lye
Too low for envy, for contempt too high.
Some honor I would have,
Not from great deeds, but good alone;
The unknown are better than ill known:
Rumour can ope' the grave.
Acquaintance I would have, but when't depends
Not on the number, but the choice, of friends.

Books should, not business, entertain the light,
And sleep, as undisturbed as death, the night.
My house a cottage more
Than palace, and should fitting be
For all my use, no luxury.
My garden painted o'er
With Natures hand, not Arts, and pleasures yield,
Horace might envy in his Sabine field.

Thus would I double my lifes fading space;
For he, that runs it well, twice runs his race.
And in this true delight,
These unbought sports, this happy state,
I would not fear nor wish my fate;
But boldly say each night,
Tomorrow let my sun his beams display,
Or in clouds hide them; I have liv'd to-day.

[1] In printing this in his essay *Of My Self* in 1668, Cowley remarked that it is the 'latter end of an Ode which I made when I was but thirteen years old. . . . The Beginning of it is Boyish, but of this part which I here set down (if a very little were corrected) I should hardly now be much ashamed.'

The Wish

Well then; I now do plainly see
This busie world and I shall ne'er agree.

The very honey of all earthly joy
Does, of all meats, the soonest cloy;
And they, methinks, deserve my pity
Who for it can endure the stings,
The crowd, and buz, and murmurings
Of this great hive, the city.

Ah yet, e're I descend to the grave,
May I a small house and large garden have;
And a few friends, and many books, both true,
Both wise, and both delightful too!
And since love ne'er will from me flee,
A mistress moderately fair,
And good as guardian-angels are,
Only belov'd, and loving me!

O fountains! when in you shall I
Myself eas'd of unpeaceful thoughts espy?
O fields! Oh woods! when, when shall I be made
The happy tenant of your shade?
Here's the spring-head of pleasure's flood;
Here's wealthy Nature's treasury,
Where all the riches lie that she
Has coyn'd and stampt for good.

Pride and ambition here
Only in far-fetched metaphors appear;
Here nought but winds can hurtful murmurs scatter,
And nought but echo flatter.
The gods, when they descended, hither
From heav'n did always choose their way;
And therefore we may boldly say
That 'tis the way too thither.

How happy here should I
And one dear she live, and embracing dye!
She who is all the world, and can exclude
In deserts, solitude.
I should have then this only fear:
Lest men, when they my pleasure see,
Should hither throng to live like me,
And so make a city here.

[*The Mistress*, 1647; text 1656]

The Thief

Thou rob'st my days of bus'ness and delights
Of sleep thou rob'st my nights;
Ah, lovely thief, what wilt thou do?
What? rob me of Heaven too?
Thou even my prayers dost steal from me:
And I, with wild idolatry,
Begin, to God, and end them all, to thee.

Is it a sin to love, that it should thus
Like an ill conscience torture us?
Whate'er I do, where'er I go
(None guiltless e'er was haunted so)
Still, still, methinks, thy face I view,
And still thy shape does me pursue,
As if, not you me, but I had murthered you.

From books I strive some remedy to take,
But thy name all the letters make;
Whate'er 'tis writ, I find that there.
Like points and commas everywhere.
Me blest for this let no man hold;
For I, as Midas did of old,
Perish by turning ev'ry thing to gold.

What do I seek, alas, or why do I
Attempt in vain from thee to fly?
For, making thee my deity,
I gave thee then ubiquity.
My pains resemble hell in this:
The divine presence there too is,
But to torment men, not to give them bliss.

[*The Mistress*, 1647; text 1656]

Ode, Of Wit [2]

Tell me, O tell, what kind of thing is wit,
Thou who master art of it.
For the first matter [3] loves variety less;
Less women lov't, either in love or dress.
A thousand different shapes it bears,
Comely in thousand shapes appears.

---

[2] This poem, first published in 1656, attempts to define that element in writing which is different from the controlled and reasoned part. We should call it imagination rather than wit, which now has a narrowed meaning.
[3] matter before the creation

Yonder we saw it plain; and here 'tis now,
Like spirits in a place, we know not how.

London that vents of false ware so much store,
In no ware deceives us more.
For men led by the colour, and the shape,
Like Zeuxes' birds fly to the painted grape;
Some things do through our judgment pass
As through a multiplying glass.
And sometimes, if the object be too far,
We take a falling meteor for a star.

Hence 'tis a wit, that greatest word of fame,
Grows such a common name.
And wits by our creation they become,
Just so, as titular bishops [4] made at Rome.
'Tis not a tale, 'tis not a jest
Admired with laughter at a feast,
Nor florid talk which can that title gain;
The proofs of wit for ever must remain.

'Tis not to force some lifeless verses meet
With their five gowty feet.
All ev'ry where, like man's, must be the soul,
And reason the inferior powers controul.
Such were the numbers [5] which could call
The stones into the Theban wall.
Such miracles are ceast; and now we see
No towns or houses rais'd by poetrie.

Yet 'tis not to adorn, and gild each part;
That shows more cost, then art.
Jewels at nose and lips but ill appeare;
Rather then all things wit, let none be there.
Several lights will not be seen,
If there be nothing else between.
Men doubt, because they stand so thick i' th' skie,
If those be stars which paint the galaxie.

[4] Roman Catholic bishops in countries hostile to Catholicism, as England was in Cowley's time.
[5] The music of Amphion.

'Tis not when two like words make up one noise;
Jests for Dutch men, and English boys.
In which who finds out wit, the same may see
In an'grams and acrostiques poetrie.
Much less can that have any place
At which a virgin hides her face,
Such dross the fire must purge away; 'tis just
The author blush, where there the reader must.

'Tis not such lines as almost crack the stage
When Bajazet [6] begins to rage.
Nor a tall metaphor in the bombast way,
Nor the dry chips of short lung'd Seneca.
Nor upon all things to obtrude,
And force some odd similitude.[7]
What is it then, which like the power divine
We only can by negatives define?

In a true piece of wit all things must be,
Yet all things there agree.
As in the ark, joyn'd without force or strife,
All creatures dwelt; all creatures there had life.
Or as the primitive forms of all
(If we compare great things with small)
Which without discord or confusion lie,
In that strange mirror of the Deitie.

But love that moulds one man up out of two,
Makes me forget and injure you.
I took you for my self sure when I thought
That you in any thing were to be taught.
Correct my error with thy pen;
And if any ask me then,
What thing right wit, and height of genius is,
I'll onely shew your lines, and say, 'Tis this.

[6] The ranting villain-king in Marlowe's *Tamburlaine.*
[7] exaggerated simile

Andrew Marvell

1621–1678

Bermudas [1]

WHERE the remote Bermudas ride
In th' oceans bosome unespy'd,
From a small boat, that row'd along,
The listning winds receiv'd this song.
What should we do but sing his praise
That led us through the watry maze,
Unto an isle so long unknown,
And yet far kinder than our own?
Where he the huge sea-monsters wracks,
That lift the deep upon their backs.
He lands us on a grassy stage,
Safe from the storms, and prelat's rage.
He gave us this eternal spring,
Which here enamells every thing;
And sends the fowls to us in care,
On daily visits through the air.
He hangs in shades the orange bright,
Like golden lamps in a green night.
And does in the pomgranates close,
Jewels more rich than Ormus shows.
He makes the figs our mouths to meet;
And throws the melons at our feet.
But apples [2] plants of such a price,
No tree could ever bear them twice.
With cedars, chosen by his hand,
From Lebanon, he stores the land.
And makes the hollow seas that roar,
Proclaim the ambergris on shoar.
He cast (of which we rather boast)
The gospels pearl upon our coast.
And in these rocks for us did frame
A temple, where to sound his name.
Oh, let our voice his praise exalt,
Till it arrive at heavens vault:
Which thence (perhaps) rebounding, may
Eccho beyond the Mexique bay.
Thus sung they, in the English boat,
An holy and a chearful note,
And all the way, to guide their chime,
With falling oars they kept the time.

[1] All the poems of Marvell printed here are included in the *Miscellaneous Poems*, 1681.
[2] pineapples

To his coy Mistress

HAD we but world enough, and time,
This coyness, lady, were no crime.
We would sit down, and think which way
To walk, and pass our long loves day.
Thou by the Indian Ganges side
Should'st rubies find; I by the tide
Of Humber would complain. I would
Love you ten years before the flood:
And you should, if you please, refuse
Till the conversion of the Jews.
My vegetable love should grow
Vaster then empires, and more slow.
An hundred years should go to praise
Thine eyes, and on thy forehead gaze.
Two hundred to adore each breast;
But thirty thousand to the rest.
An age at least to every part,
And the last age should show your heart.
For, lady, you deserve this state;
Nor would I love at lower rate.
But at my back I alwaies hear
Times wingéd charriot hurrying near;
And yonder all before us lye
Desarts of vast eternity.
Thy beauty shall no more be found;
Nor in thy marble vault shall sound
My echoing song; then worms shall try
That long preserv'd virginity;
And your quaint honour turn to dust;
And into ashes all my lust.
The grave's a fine and private place,
But none I think do there embrace.
Now therefore, while the youthful hew
Sits on thy skin like morning lew,[3]
And while thy willing soul transpires
At every pore with instant fires,
Now let us sport us while we may;
And now, like am'rous birds of prey,
Rather at once our time devour,
Than languish in his slow-chapt [4] pow'r.
Let us roll all our strength, and all
Our sweetness, up into one ball;

[3] warmth
[4] slow-jawed

And tear our pleasures with rough strife,
Thorough the iron gates of life.
Thus, though we cannot make our sun
Stand still, yet we will make him run.

The Definition of Love

My love is of a birth as rare
As 'tis for object strange and high;
It was begotten by despair
Upon impossibility.

Magnanimous despair alone
Could show me so divine a thing,
Where feeble hope could ne'r have flown
But vainly flapt its tinsel wing.

And yet I quickly might arrive
Where my extended soul is fixt,
But fate does iron wedges drive,
And alwaies crouds it self betwixt.

For fate with jealous eye does see
Two perfect loves, nor lets them close;
Their union would her ruine be,
And her tyrannick pow'r depose.

And therefore her decrees of steel
Us as the distant poles have plac'd,
(Though loves whole world on us doth wheel)
Not by themselves to be embrac'd.

Unless the giddy heaven fall,
And earth some new convulsion tear;
And, us to joyn, the world should all
Be cramp'd into a planisphere.[5]

As lines, so loves, oblique may well
Themselves in every angle greet;
But ours so truly paralel,
Though infinite, can never meet.

Therefore the love which us doth bind,
But fate so enviously debarrs,
Is the conjunction of the mind,
And opposition of the stars.

[5] Projection of a sphere on a plane.

The Mower against Gardens

Luxurious man, to bring his vice in use,
Did after him the world seduce;
And from the fields the flow'rs and plants allure,
Where nature was most plain and pure.
He first enclos'd within the gardens square
A dead and standing pool of air;
And a more luscious earth for them did knead,
Which stupifi'd them while it fed.
The pink grew then as double as his mind;
The nutriment did change the kind.
With strange perfumes he did the roses taint;
And flow'rs themselves were taught to paint.
The tulip, white, did for complexion seek,
And learn'd to interline its cheek;
Its onion root [6] they then so high did hold,
That one was for a meadow sold.
Another world was search'd, through oceans new,
To find the marvel of Peru.[7]
And yet these rarities might be allow'd,
To man, that sov'raign thing and proud,
Had he not dealt between the bark and tree,
Forbidden mixtures there to see.
No plant now knew the stock from which it came;
He grafts upon the wild the tame,
That the uncertain and adult'rate fruit
Might put the palate in dispute.
His green seraglio has its eunuchs too,
Lest any tyrant him out-doe.
And in the cherry he does nature vex,
To procreate without a sex.
'Tis all enforc'd, the fountain and the grot,
While the sweet fields do lye forgot;
Where willing nature does to all dispence
A wild and fragrant innocence;
And fauns and faryes do the meadows till,
More by their presence then their skill.

[6] During the craze for tulips, bulbs were sold like precious stones.
[7] A flowering herb of great beauty.

Their statues polish'd by some ancient hand,
May to adorn the gardens stand;
But howso'ere the figures do excel,
The gods themselves with us do dwell.

The Garden

How vainly men themselves amaze
To win the palm, the oke, or bayes;
And their uncessant labours see
Crown'd from some single herb or tree,
Whose short and narrow vergéd [8] shade
Does prudently their toyles upbraid;
While all flow'rs and all trees do close
To weave the garlands of repose.

Fair quiet, have I found thee here,
And innocence thy sister dear!
Mistaken long, I sought you then
In busie companies of men.
Your sacred plants, if here below,
Only among the plants will grow.
Society is all but rude,
To this delicious solitude.

No white nor red was ever seen
So am'rous as this lovely green.
Fond lovers, cruel as their flame,
Cut in these trees their mistress name.
Little, alas, they know, or heed,
How far these beauties hers exceed!
Fair trees! where s'eer your barkes I wound,
No name shall but your own be found.

When we have run our passions heat,
Love hither makes his best retreat.
The gods, that mortal beauty chase,
Still in a tree did end their race.
Apollo hunted Daphne so,
Only that she might laurel grow.
And Pan did after Syrinx speed,
Not as a nymph, but for a reed.

What wond'rous life in this I lead!
Ripe apples drop about my head;
The luscious clusters of the vine
Upon my mouth do crush their wine;

[8] margined

The nectaren, and curious [9] peach,
Into my hands themselves do reach;
Stumbling on melons, as I pass,
Insnar'd with flow'rs, I fall on grass.

Mean while the mind, from pleasure less,
Withdraws into its happiness:
The mind, that ocean where each kind
Does streight its own resemblance find;
Yet it creates, transcending these,
Far other worlds, and other seas;
Annihilating all that's made
To a green thought in a green shade.

Here at the fountains sliding foot,
Or at some fruit-trees mossy root,
Casting the bodies vest aside,
My soul into the boughs does glide;
There like a bird it sits, and sings,
Then whets, and combs its silver wings;
And till prepar'd for longer flight,
Waves in its plumes the various light.

Such was that happy garden-state,
While man there walk'd without a mate;
After a place so pure, and sweet,
What other help could yet be meet!
But 'twas beyond a mortal's share
To wander solitary there;
Two paradises 'twere, in one
To live in paradise alone.

How well the skilful gardner drew
Of flow'rs and herbes this dial new,
Where, from above, the milder sun
Does through a fragrant zodiack run;
And, as it works, th' industrious bee
Computes its time as well as we.
How could such sweet and wholsome hours
Be reckon'd but with herbs and flow'rs!

On Mr. Milton's Paradise Lost [10]

When I beheld the poet blind, yet bold,
In slender book his vast design unfold,

[9] choice

[10] Marvell's lines were first published in the second edition of Milton's poem, 1674.

Messiah crown'd, Gods reconcil'd decree,
Rebelling angels, the forbidden tree,
Heav'n, hell, earth, chaos, all; the argument
Held me a while misdoubting[11] his intent,
That he would ruine (for I saw him strong)
The sacred truths to fable and old song,
(So Sampson[12] groap'd the temples posts in spight)
The world o'rewhelming to revenge his sight.
Yet as I read, soon growing less severe,
I lik'd his project, the success did fear;
Through that wide field how he his way should find
O're which lame faith leads understanding blind;
Lest he perplext the things he would explain,
And what was easie he should render vain.
Or if a work so infinite he spann'd,
Jealous I was that some less skilful hand
(Such as disquiet alwayes what is well,
And by ill imitating would excell)
Might hence presume the whole creations day
To change in scenes, and show it in a play.[13]
Pardon me, mighty poet, nor despise
My causeless, yet not impious, surmise.
But I am now convinc'd, and none will dare
Within thy labours to pretend a share.
Thou has not miss'd one thought that could be fit,
And all that was improper dost omit:
So that no room is here for writers left,
But to detect their ignorance or theft.
That majesty which through thy work doth reign,
Draws the devout, deterring the profane.
And things divine thou treatst of in such state
As them preserves, and thee, inviolate.
At once delight and horrour on us seize,
Thou singst with so much gravity and ease;
And above humane flight dost soar aloft,
With plume so strong, so equal, and so soft.
The bird nam'd from that paradise you sing
So never flags, but alwaies keeps on wing.
Where couldst thou words of such a compass find?
Whence furnish such a vast expense of mind?
Just Heav'n thee, like Tiresias, to requite,
Rewards with prophesie thy loss of sight.
Well mightst thou scorn thy readers to allure
With tinkling rhime, of thy own sense secure;
While the Town-Bays[14] writes all the while and spells,
And like a pack-horse tires without his bells.
Their fancies like our bushy points[15] appear,
The poets tag them; we for fashion wear.
I too transported by the mode offend,
And while I mean to praise thee, must commend.
Thy verse created like thy theme sublime,
In number, weight, and measure, needs not rhime.

---

[11] with misgivings about

[12] Milton's *Samson Agonistes* had appeared in 1671.

[13] Aubrey, the biographer, records that Dryden asked permission to put *Paradise Lost* 'into a drama in rhymme. Mr. Milton recieved him civilly, and told him he would give him leave to tagge his verses.'

[14] Dryden was satirized under the name of Bays in Buckingham's *Rehearsal*.

[15] For lacing hose. Their ends were 'bushy' or 'tagged'.

John Milton

1608–1674

On Shakespear [1]

What needs my Shakespear for his honour'd bones,
The labour of an age in pilèd stones,
Or that his hallow'd reliques should be hid
Under a star-ypointing pyramid?
Dear son of memory, great heir of fame,
What need'st thou such weak witnes of thy name?
Thou in our wonder and astonishment
Hast built thy self a live-long monument.
For whilst to th'shame of slow-endeavouring art,
Thy easie numbers flow, and that each heart
Hath from the leaves of thy unvalu'd book,
Those Delphick lines with deep impression took,
Then thou our fancy of it self bereaving,
Dost make us marble with too much conceaving;
And so sepulcher'd in such pomp dost lie,
That kings for such a tomb would wish to die.

At a Solemn Music

Blest pair of Sirens, pledges of Heav'ns joy,
Sphear-born harmonious sisters, Voice, and Vers,
Wed your divine sounds, and mixt power employ
Dead things with inbreath'd sense able to pierce;
And to our high-rais'd phantasie present
That undisturbèd song of pure content,[2]
Ay sung before the saphire-colour'd throne
To him that sits theron
With saintly shout, and solemn jubily,
Where the bright Seraphim in burning row
Their loud up-lifted Angel trumpets blow,
And the Cherubick host in thousand quires
Touch their immortal harps of golden wires,
With those just Spirits that wear victorious palms,
Hymns devout and holy psalms
Singing everlastingly;
That we on Earth with undiscording voice
May rightly answer that melodious noise;
As once we did, till disproportion'd sin
Jarr'd against natures chime, and with harsh din
Broke the fair musick that all creatures made
To their great Lord, whose love their motion sway'd
In perfect diapason,[3] whilst they stood
In first obedience, and their state of good.
O may we soon again renew that song,
And keep in tune with Heav'n, till God ere long
To his celestial consort us unite,
To live with him, and sing in endles morn of light.

[*Poems of Mr. John Milton,* 1645; written 1633–1634]

SONNETS

How soon hath Time

How soon hath Time, the suttle theef of youth,
  Stoln on his wing my three and twentith yeer!
  My hasting dayes flie on with full career,
  But my late spring no bud or blossom shew'th.
Perhaps my semblance might deceive the truth,

[1] Contributed to the group of commendatory verses, by various authors, prefixed to the 1632 folio of Shakespeare's works.

[2] This should perhaps read *consent, i.e.,* harmony.

[3] The perfect interval of an octave.

That I to manhood am arriv'd so near,
And inward ripenes doth much less appear,
That som more timely-happy spirits indu'th.
Yet be it less or more, or soon or slow,
It shall be still in strictest measure eev'n,
To that same lot, however mean, or high,
Toward which Time leads me, and the will of Heav'n;
All is, if I have grace to use it so,
As ever in my great task Masters eye.

On the late Massacre in Piedmont[4]

Avenge, O Lord, thy slaughter'd saints, whose bones
Lie scatter'd on the Alpine mountains cold,
Ev'n them who kept thy truth so pure of old
When all our fathers worship't stocks and stones.[5]
Forget not: in thy book record their groanes
Who were thy sheep and in their antient fold
Slayn by the bloody Piemontese that roll'd
Mother with infant down the rocks. Their moans
The vales redoubl'd to the hills, and they
To Heav'n. Their martyr'd blood and ashes sow
O're all th'Italian fields where still doth sway
The triple tyrant:[6] that from these may grow
A hunder'd-fold, who having learnt thy way,
Early may fly the Babylonian[7] wo.

[4] The Count of Turin in 1655 persecuted the Protestants in the Piedmont.
[5] When England was a Catholic country.
[6] the Pope
[7] The Puritans identified the Church of Rome with the Babylon of the Book of Revelation.

When I consider how my light is spent[8]

When I consider how my light is spent,
E're half my days, in this dark world and wide,
And that one talent which is death to hide,
Lodg'd with me useless, though my soul more bent
To serve therewith my Maker, and present
My true account, lest he returning chide;
Doth God exact day-labour, light deny'd,
I fondly ask. But patience to prevent
That murmur, soon replies, God doth not need
Either man's work or his own gifts; who best
Bear his milde yoak, they serve him best, his state
Is kingly. Thousands at his bidding speed
And post o're land and ocean without rest:
They also serve who only stand and waite.

COMUS[9]

A MASK

Presented at Ludlow-Castle

The Persons

The attendant Spirit afterwards in the habit of Thyrsis.
Comus with his crew.
The Lady.
1. Brother.
2. Brother.
Sabrina the Nymph.

The cheif persons which presented, were

The Lord Bracly,
Mr. Thomas Egerton his Brother,
The Lady Alice Egerton.

The first Scene discovers a wilde Wood.

The attendant Spirit descends or enters.

[8] Written in 1655.
[9] Written in 1634 at the request of the composer Henry Lawes, to celebrate the Earl of Bridgewater's accession to the presidency of Wales and the Marches. In the performance, the parts of the Lady and the two Brothers were taken by the Earl's children, the Lady Alice Egerton, Lord Brackley, and Mr. Thomas Egerton. Lawes, who was music-tutor in the family, composed the music and produced the masque.

Before the starry threshold of Joves court
My mansion is, where those immortal shapes
Of bright aëreal Spirits live insphear'd
In regions milde of calm and serene ayr,
Above the smoak and stirr of this dim spot,
Which men call Earth, and with low-thoughted care
Confin'd, and pester'd[10] in this pin-fold here,
Strive to keep up a frail, and feaverish being
Unmindfull of the crown that Vertue gives,
After this mortal change, to her true servants
Amongst the enthron'd gods on sainted seats.
Yet som there be that by due steps aspire
To lay their just hands on that golden key
That ope's the Palace of Eternity:
To such my errand is, and but for such,
I would not soil these pure ambrosial weeds
With the rank vapours of this sin-worn mould.
But to my task. Neptune besides the sway
Of every salt flood, and each ebbing stream,
Took in by lot 'twixt high, and neather Jove,
Imperial rule of all the sea-girt Iles
That, like to rich, and various gemms, inlay
The unadornéd boosom of the Deep;
Which he to grace his tributary gods
By course commits to severall government,
And gives them leave to wear their saphire crowns,
And weild their little tridents. But this Ile,
The greatest and the best of all the main,
He quarters to his blu-hair'd[11] deities;
And all this tract that fronts the falling sun
A noble peer of mickle trust and power
Has in his charge, with temper'd awe to guide
An old and haughty nation, proud in arms:

[10] shut up
[11] Sea gods were so wigged in the masques of the time.

Where his fair off-spring nurs't in princely lore,
Are coming to attend their fathers state,
And new-entrusted scepter. But their way
Lies through the pérplex't paths of this drear wood,
The nodding horror of whose shady brows
Threats the forlorn and wandring passinger.
And here their tender age might suffer perill,
But that by quick command from soveran Jove
I was dispacht for their defence, and guard;
And listen why, for I will tell ye now
What never yet was heard in tale or song
From old, or modern bard, in hall, or bowr.
Bacchus that first from out the purple grape,
Crush't the sweet poyson of mis-uséd wine,
After the Tuscan mariners transform'd[12]
Coasting the Tyrrhene shore, as the winds listed,
On Circes Iland fell. (Who knows not Circe
The daughter of the sun, whose charméd cup
Whoever tasted, lost his upright shape,
And downward fell into a groveling swine?)
This Nymph that gaz'd upon his clustring locks,
With ivy berries wreath'd, and his blithe youth,
Had by him, ere he parted thence, a son
Much like his father, but his mother more,
Whom therfore she brought up and Comus nam'd,
Who ripe, and frolick of his full grown age,
Roaving the Celtick, and Iberian fields,
At last betakes him to this ominous wood,
And in thick shelter of black shades imbowr'd,
Excells his mother at her mighty art;
Offring to every weary travailer
His orient liquor in a crystal glasse,

[12] Bacchus, when kidnapped by Tyrrhenian pirates, transformed his captors into dolphins.

To quench the drouth of Phœbus, which as they taste
(For most do taste through fond intemperate thirst)
Soon as the potion works, their human count'nance,
Th' express resemblance of the gods, is chang'd
Into som brutish form of woolf, or bear,
Or ounce, or tiger, hog, or bearded goat,
All other parts remaining as they were.
And they, so perfect is their misery,
Not once perceive their foul disfigurement,
But boast themselves more comely then before
And all their friends, and native home forget,
To roule with pleasure in a sensual stie.
Therfore when any favour'd of high Jove,
Chances to pass through this adventrous glade,
Swift as the sparkle of a glancing star
I shoot from Heav'n to give him safe convoy,
As now I do. But first I must put off
These my skie robes spun out of Iris wooff,
And take the weeds and likenes of a swain
That to the service of this house belongs,
Who with his soft pipe, and smooth-dittied song,
Well knows to still the wilde winds when they roar,
And hush the waving woods, nor of lesse faith,[13]
And in this office of his mountain watch,
Likeliest, and neerest to the present ayd
Of this occasion. But I hear the tread
Of hatefull steps; I must be viewles now.

Comus *enters with a charming-rod in one hand, his glass in the other; with him a rout of Monsters, headed like sundry sorts of wilde beasts, but otherwise like men and women, their apparel glistring. They com in making a riotous and unruly noise, with torches in their hands.*

Comus. The star that bids the shepherd fold
Now the top of Heav'n doth hold,
And the gilded car of day,
His glowing axle doth allay
In the steep Atlantick stream;
And the slope sun his upward beam
Shoots against the dusky pole,
Pacing toward the other gole
Of his chamber in the east.
Mean while welcom joy, and feast,
Midnight shout, and revelry,
Tipsie dance, and jollity.
Braid your locks with rosie twine,
Dropping odours, dropping wine.
Rigor now is gon to bed,
And Advice with scrupulous head,
Strict Age, and sowre Severity,
With their grave saws, in slumber ly.
We that are of purer fire
Imitate the starry quire,
Who in their nightly watchfull sphears,
Lead in swift round the months and years.
The sounds and seas with all their finny drove
Now to the moon in wavering morrice[14] move;
And on the tawny sands and shelves
Trip the pert Fairies and the dapper Elves;
By dimpled brook, and fountain brim,
The Wood-Nymphs deckt with daisies trim,
Their merry wakes and pastimes keep:
What hath night to do with sleep?
Night hath better sweets to prove,
Venus now wakes, and wak'ns Love.
Com, let us our rites begin;
'Tis onely day-light that makes sin
Which these dun shades will ne're report.
Hail goddesse of nocturnal sport,
Dark vaild Cotytto,[15] t' whom the secret flame
Of mid-night torches burns; mysterious dame
That ne're art call'd, but when the dragon woom
Of Stygian darknes spets her thickest gloom,
And makes one blot of all the ayr.
Stay thy cloudy ebon chair,

[13] not less faithful (than skilful)

[14] A grotesque folk-dance.

[15] A Thracian goddess whose rites were particularly licentious.

Wherin thou rid'st with Hecat, and befriend
Us thy vow'd priests, til utmost end
Of all thy dues be done, and none left out,
Ere the blabbing eastern scout,
The nice morn on th' Indian steep,
From her cabin'd loop hole peep,
And to the tel-tale sun discry
Our conceal'd solemnity.
Com, knit hands, and beat the ground,
In a light fantastick round.

The Measure.

Break off, break off. I feel the different pace,
Of som chast footing neer about this ground.
Run to your shrouds, within these brakes and trees;
Our number may affright. Som virgin sure
(For so I can distinguish by mine art)
Benighted in these woods. Now to my charms,
And to my wily trains,[16] I shall e're long
Be well stock't with as fair a herd as graz'd
About my mother Circe. Thus I hurl
My dazling spells into the spungy ayr,
Of power to cheat the eye with blear illusion,
And give it false presentments, lest the place
And my quaint habits [17] breed astonishment,
And put the damsel to suspicious flight;
Which must not be, for that's against my course.
I under fair pretence of friendly ends,
And well plac't words of glozing courtesie
Baited with reasons not unplausible,
Wind me into the easie-hearted man,
And hugg him into snares. When once her eye
Hath met the vertue of this magick dust,
I shall appear som harmles villager
Whom thrift keeps up about his country gear.
But here she comes; I fairly step aside,
And hearken, if I may, her busines here.

The Lady enters.

Lady. This way the noise was, if mine ear be true,
My best guide now; me thought it was the sound
Of riot, and ill manag'd merriment,
Such as the jocond flute, or gamesom pipe
Stirs up among the loose unleter'd hinds,
When for their teeming flocks, and granges full,
In wanton dance they praise the bounteous Pan,
And thank the gods amiss. I should be loath
To meet the rudenesse, and swill'd insolence
Of such late wassailers; yet O where els
Shall I inform my unacquainted feet
In the blind mazes of this tangl'd wood?
My brothers, when they saw me wearied out
With this long way, resolving here to lodge
Under the spreading favour of these pines,
Stept as they se'd to the next thicket side
To bring me berries, or such cooling fruit
As the kind hospitable woods provide.
They left me then, when the gray-hooded Eev'n
Like a sad votarist in palmers weed
Rose from the hindmost wheels of Phœbus wain.
But where they are, and why they came not back,
Is now the labour of my thoughts; 'tis likeliest
They had ingag'd their wandring steps too far,
And envious darknes, e're they could return,
Had stole them from me. Els, O theevish Night,
Why shouldst thou, but for som fellonious end,
In thy dark lantern thus close up the stars,
That nature hung in Heav'n, and fill'd their lamps

---

16 tricks
17 garments

With everlasting oil, to give due light
To the misled and lonely travailer?
This is the place, as well as I may guess,
Whence eev'n now the tumult of loud mirth
Was rife, and perfet in my list'ning ear,
Yet nought but single darknes do I find.
What might this be? A thousand fantasies
Begin to throng into my memory
Of calling shapes, and beckning shadows dire,
And airy tongues, that syllable mens names
On sands, and shoars, and desert wildernesses.
These thoughts may startle well, but not astound
The vertuous mind, that ever walks attended
By a strong siding champion, Conscience. —
O welcom pure-ey'd Faith, white-handed Hope,
Thou hovering Angel girt with golden wings,
And thou unblemish't form of Chastity;
I see ye visibly, and now beleeve
That he, the Supreme Good, t' whom all things ill
Are but as slavish officers of vengeance,
Would send a glistring guardian, if need were,
To keep my life and honour unassail'd.
Was I deceiv'd, or did a sable cloud
Turn forth her silver lining on the night?
I did not err; there does a sable cloud
Turn forth her silver lining on the night,
And casts a gleam over this tufted grove.
I cannot hallow to my brothers, but
Such noise as I can make to be heard farthest
Ile venter, for my new enliv'nd spirits
Prompt me; and they perhaps are not far off.

Song

Sweet Echo, sweetest Nymph that liv'st unseen
Within thy airy shell
By slow Meander's *margent green,*
And in the violet imbroider'd vale
Where the love-lorn nightingale
Nightly to thee her sad song mourneth well:
Canst thou not tell me of a gentle pair
That likest thy Narcissus *are?*
O if thou have
Hid them in som flowry cave,
Tell me but where,
Sweet Queen of Parly,[18] *Daughter of the Sphear,*
So maist thou be translated to the skies,
And give resounding grace to all Heav'ns harmonies.

Com. Can any mortal mixture of earths mould
Breath such divine inchanting ravishment?
Sure somthing holy lodges in that brest,
And with these raptures moves the vocal air
To testifie his hidd'n residence;
How sweetly did they float upon the wings
Of silence, through the empty-vaulted night
At every fall smoothing the raven doune
Of darknes till it smil'd: I have oft heard
My mother Circe with the Sirens three,
Amid'st the flowry-kirtl'd Naiades,
Culling their potent hearbs and balefull drugs,
Who as they sung, would take the prison'd soul,
And lap it in Elysium; Scylla wept,
And chid her barking waves into attention,
And fell Charybdis murmur'd soft applause.
Yet they in pleasing slumber lull'd the sense,
And in sweet madnes rob'd it of it self;
But such a sacred, and home-felt delight,
Such sober certainty of waking bliss
I never heard till now. Ile speak to her
And she shall be my queen. Hail forren wonder
Whom certain these rough shades did never breed
Unlesse the goddes that in rurall shrine
Dwell'st here with Pan, or Silvan, by blest song

[18] Discourse. In *At a Solemn Music* Milton addresses Voice and Verse as 'sphere-born harmonious sisters.'

Forbidding every bleak unkindly fog
To touch the prosperous growth of this tall wood.
La. Nay, gentle shepherd, ill is lost that praise
That is addrest to unattending ears;
Not any boast of skill, but extreme shift
How to regain my sever'd company
Compell'd me to awake the courteous Echo
To give me answer from her mossie couch.
Co. What chance, good Lady, hath bereft you thus?
La. Dim darknes, and this leavy labyrinth.
Co. Could that divide you from neer-ushering guides?
La. They left me weary on a grassie terf.
Co. By falshood, or discourtesie, or why?
La. To seek i'th vally som cool friendly spring.
Co. And left your fair side all unguarded, Lady?
La. They were but twain, and purpos'd quick return.
Co. Perhaps fore-stalling night prevented them.
La. How easie my misfortune is to hit!
Co. Imports their loss, beside the present need?
La. No less then if I should my brothers loose.
Co. Were they of manly prime, or youthful bloom?
La. As smooth as Hebe's their unrazor'd lips.
Co. Two such I saw, what time the labour'd oxe
In his loose traces from the furrow came,
And the swink't[19] hedger at his supper sate;
I saw them under a green mantling vine
That crawls along the side of yon small hill,
Plucking ripe clusters from the tender shoots,
Their port was more then human, as they stood;
I took it for a faëry vision
Of som gay creatures of the element
That in the colours of the rainbow live
And play i'th plighted clouds. I was awstrook,
And as I past, I worshipt: if those you seek
It were a journey like the path to Heav'n,
To help you find them. *La.* Gentle villager,
What readiest way would bring me to that place?
Co. Due west it rises from this shrubby point.
La. To find out that, good shepherd, I suppose,
In such a scant allowance of star-light,
Would overtask the best land-pilots art,
Without the sure guess of well-practiz'd feet.
Co. I know each lane, and every alley green,
Dingle, or bushy dell of this wilde wood,
And every bosky bourn from side to side,
My daily walks and ancient neighbourhood;
And if your stray attendance be yet lodg'd,
Or shroud within these limits, I shall know
Ere morrow wake, or the low roosted lark
From her thatch't pallat rowse, if otherwise
I can conduct you, Lady, to a low
But loyal cottage, where you may be safe
Till further quest. *La.* Shepherd, I take thy word,
And trust thy honest offer'd courtesie,
Which oft is sooner found in lowly sheds
With smoaky rafters, then in tapstry halls
And courts of princes, where it first was nam'd,
And yet is most pretended. In a place
Less warranted then this, or less secure,
I cannot be, that I should fear to change it.
Eie me, blest Providence, and square my triall
To my proportion'd strength. Shepherd, lead on.—

[19] work-wearied

The Two Brothers.

Eld. Bro. Unmuffle, ye faint stars, and thou, fair Moon
That wontst to love the travailers benizon,
Stoop thy pale visage through an amber cloud,
And disinherit Chaos, that raigns here
In double night of darknes, and of shades;
Or if your influence be quite damm'd up
With black usurping mists, som gentle taper
Though a rush candle from the wicker hole
Of som clay habitation visit us
With thy long levell'd rule of streaming light,
And thou shalt be our star of Arcady,
Or Tyrian Cynosure.[20] 2. *Bro.* Or if our eyes
Be barr'd that happines, might we but hear
The folded flocks pen'd in their watled cotes,
Or sound of pastoral reed with oaten stops,
Or whistle from the lodge, or village cock
Count the night watches to his feathery dames,
'Twould be som solace yet, som little chearing
In this close dungeon of innumerous boughs.
But O that haples virgin, our lost sister,
Where may she wander now, whether betake her
From the chill dew, amongst rude burrs and thistles?
Perhaps som cold bank is her boulster now
Or 'gainst the rugged bark of som broad elm
Leans her unpillow'd head fraught with sad fears.
What if in wild amazement, and affright,
Or while we speak, within the direfull grasp
Of savage hunger, or of savage heat?
Eld. Bro. Peace, brother, be not over-exquisite
To cast the fashion of uncertain evils;
For grant they be so, while they rest unknown,
What need a man forestall his date of grief,
And run to meet what he would most avoid?
Or if they be but false alarms of fear,
How bitter is such self-delusion?
I do not think my sister so to seek,
Or so unprincipl'd in vertues book,
And the sweet peace that goodnes boosoms ever,
As that the single want of light and noise
(Not being in danger, as I trust she is not)
Could stir the constant mood of her calm thoughts,
And put them into mis-becoming plight.
Vertue could see to do what Vertue would
By her own radiant light, though sun and moon
Were in the flat sea sunk. And Wisdoms self
Oft seeks to sweet retiréd solitude,
Where with her best nurse, Contemplation,
She plumes her feathers, and lets grow her wings
That in the various bussle of resort
Were all to ruffl'd and sometimes impair'd.
He that has light within his own cleer brest
May sit i'th center, and enjoy bright day,
But he that hides a dark soul, and foul thoughts,
Benighted walks under the mid-day sun;
Himself is his own dungeon.
2. *Bro.* Tis most true
That musing meditation most affects
The pensive secrecy of desert cell,
Far from the cheerfull haunt of men, and herds,
And sits as safe as in a senat house;
For who would rob a hermit of his weeds,
His few books, or his beads, or maple dish,
Or do his gray hairs any violence?
But beauty like the fair Hesperian tree
Laden with blooming gold, had need the guard
Of dragon watch with uninchanted eye,

[20] The Greek sailors steered by the star of Arcady, the Great Bear. The Phoenician mariners used the Lesser Bear, whence called the 'Tyrian Cynosure'.

To save her blossoms, and defend her fruit
From the rash hand of bold Incontinence.
You may as well spred out the unsun'd heaps
Of misers treasure by an out-laws den,
And tell me it is safe, as bid me hope
Danger will wink [21] on Opportunity,
And let a single helpless maiden pass
Uninjur'd in this wilde surrounding wast.
Of night, or loneliness it recks me not,
I fear the dred events that dog them both,
Lest som ill greeting touch attempt the person
Of our unownéd sister.
Eld. Bro. I do not, brother,
Inferr, as if I thought my sisters state
Secure without all doubt, or controversie:
Yet where an equall poise of hope and fear
Does arbitrate th'event, my nature is
That I encline to hope, rather then fear,
And gladly banish squint suspicion.
My sister is not so defenceless left
As you imagine, she has a hidden strength
Which you remember not.
2. *Bro.* What hidden strength,
Unless the strength of Heav'n, if you mean that?
Eld. Bro. I mean that too, but yet a hidden strength
Which if Heav'n gave it, may be term'd her own:
'Tis chastity, my brother, chastity:
She that has that, is clad in compleat steel,
And like a quiver'd nymph with arrows keen,
May trace huge forests, and unharbour'd [22] heaths,
Infamous hills, and sandy perilous wildes,
Where through the sacred rayes of chastity,
No savage fierce, bandite, or mountaneer
Will dare to soyl her virgin purity.
Yea there, where very desolation dwels
By grots, and caverns shag'd with horrid shades,
She may pass on with unblench't [23] majesty,
Be it not don in pride, or in presumption.
Som say no evil thing that walks by night
In fog, or fire, by lake, or moorish fen,
Blew meager hag, or stubborn unlaid ghost,
That breaks his magick chains at curfeu time,
No goblin, or swart faëry of the mine,
Hath hurtfull power o're true virginity.
Do ye beleeve me yet, or shall I call
Antiquity from the old schools of Greece
To testifie the arms of Chastity?
Hence had the huntress Dian her dred bow,
Fair silver-shafted Queen for ever chaste,
Wherwith she tam'd the brinded lioness
And spotted mountain pard, but set at nought
The frivolous bolt of Cupid; gods and men
Fear'd her stern frown, and she was queen oth' woods.
What was that snaky-headed Gorgon sheild
That wise Minerva wore, unconquer'd virgin,
Wherwith she freez'd her foes to congeal'd stone,
But rigid looks of chast austerity,
And noble grace that dash't brute violence
With sudden adoration, and blank aw.
So dear to Heav'n is saintly chastity,
That when a soul is found sincerely so,
A thousand liveried Angels lacky her,
Driving far off each thing of sin and guilt,
And in cleer dream, and solemn vision
Tell her of things that no gross ear can hear,
Till oft convérs with heav'nly habitants
Begin to cast a beam on th'outward shape,
The unpolluted temple of the mind,
And turns it by degrees to the souls essence,
Till all be made immortal. But when lust,
By unchaste looks, loose gestures, and foul talk,
But most by leud and lavish act of sin,
Lets in defilement to the inward parts,
The soul grows clotted by contagion,
Imbodies, and imbrutes, till she quite loose
The divine property of her first being.

[21] shut the eye
[22] unharboring
[23] free from blemish

Such are those thick and gloomy shadows damp
Oft seen in charnell vaults, and sepulchers
Lingering, and sitting by a new made grave,
As loath to leave the body that it lov'd,
And link't it self by carnal sensuality
To a degenerate and degraded state.
2. *Bro.* How charming is divine Philosophy!
Not harsh, and crabbed as dull fools suppose,
But musical as is Apollo's lute,
And a perpetual feast of nectar'd sweets,
Where no crude [24] surfet raigns. *Eld. Bro.* List, list, I hear
Som far off hallow break the silent air.
2. *Bro.* Me thought so too; what should it be?
Eld. Bro. For certain
Either som one, like us, night-founder'd [25] here,
Or els som neighbour wood-man, or at worst,
Som roaving robber calling to his fellows.
2. *Bro.* Heav'n keep my sister. Agen, agen, and neer,
Best draw, and stand upon our guard.
Eld. Bro. Ile hallow,
If he be friendly, he comes well; if not,
Defence is a good cause, and Heav'n be for us.

The attendant Spirit habited like a Shepherd.

That hallow I should know, what are you? speak;
Com not too neer, you fall on iron stakes else.
Spir. What voice is that, my young Lord? speak agen.
2. *Bro.* O brother, 'tis my father shepherd sure.
Eld. Bro. Thyris? whose artful strains have oft delaid
The huddling brook to hear his madrigal,
And sweeten'd every muskrose of the dale;
How cam'st thou here, good swain? Hath any ram
Slip't from the fold, or young kid lost his dam,
Or straggling weather the pen't flock forsook?
How couldst thou find this dark sequester'd nook?
Spir. O my lov'd masters heir, and his next joy,
I came not here on such a trivial toy
As a stray'd ewe, or to pursue the stealth
Of pilfering woolf; not all the fleecy wealth
That doth enrich these downs is worth a thought
To this my errand, and the care it brought.
But O, my virgin Lady, where is she?
How chance she is not in your company?
Eld. Bro. To tell thee sadly,[26] shepherd, without blame,
Or our neglect, we lost her as we came.
Spir. Ay me unhappy, then my fears are true.
Eld. Bro. What fears good Thyrsis? Prethee briefly shew.
Spir. Ile tell ye, 'tis not vain or fabulous,
(Though so esteem'd by shallow ignorance)
What the sage poets taught by th' heav'nly Muse,
Storied of old in high immortal vers
Of dire Chimera's and inchanted iles,
And rifted rocks whose entrance leads to hell,
For such there be, but unbelief is blind.
Within the navil of this hideous wood,
Immur'd in cypress shades a sorcerer dwels
Of Bacchus, and of Circe born, great Comus,
Deep skill'd in all his mothers witcheries,
And here to every thirsty wanderer,
By sly enticement gives his banefull cup,
With many murmurs mixt, whose pleasing poison
The visage quite transforms of him that drinks,
And the inglorious likenes of a beast

[24] sour and unripe [25] night-bound

[26] seriously

Fixes instead, unmoulding reasons mintage
Character'd in the face; this have I learn't
Tending my flocks hard by i'th hilly crofts,
That brow this bottom glade, whence night by night
He and his monstrous rout are heard to howl
Like stabl'd wolves, or tigers at their prey,
Doing abhorréd rites to Hecate
In their obscuréd haunts of inmost bowres.
Yet have they many baits, and guilefull spells
To inveigle and invite th'unwary sense
Of them that pass unweeting by the way.
This evening late by then the chewing flocks
Had ta'n their supper on the savoury herb
Of knot-grass dew-besprent, and were in fold,
I sate me down to watch upon a bank
With ivy canopied, and interwove
With flaunting hony-suckle, and began,
Wrapt in a pleasing fit of melancholy,
To meditate my rural minstrelsie,
Till fancy had her fill, but ere a close
The wonted roar was up amidst the woods,
And fill'd the air with barbarous dissonance,
At which I ceas't, and listen'd them a while,
Till an unusuall stop of sudden silence
Gave respit to the drowsie frighted steeds
That draw the litter of close-curtain'd sleep.
At last a soft and solemn breathing sound
Rose like a steam of rich distill'd perfumes,
And stole upon the air, that even silence
Was took e're she was ware, and wish't she might
Deny her nature, and be never more
Still to be so displac't. I was all eare,
And took in strains that might create a soul
Under the ribs of Death, But, O, ere long
Too well I did perceive it was the voice
Of my most honour'd Lady, your dear sister.
Amaz'd I stood, harrow'd with grief and fear,
And, O poor hapless nightingale, thought I,
How sweet thou sing'st, how neer the deadly snare!
Then down the lawns I ran with headlong hast
Through paths, and turnings oft'n trod by day,
Till guided by mine ear, I found the place
Where that damn'd wisard hid in sly disguise
(For so by certain signes I knew) had met
Already, ere my best speed could prævent,
The aidless innocent Lady, his wish't prey,
Who gently ask't if he had seen such two,
Supposing him som neighbour villager.
Longer I durst not stay, but soon I guess't
Ye were the two she mean't; with that I sprung
Into swift flight, till I had found you here,
But furder know I not. 2. *Bro.* O night and shades,
How are ye joyn'd with hell in triple knot
Against th'unarméd weakness of one virgin
Alone, and helpless! Is this the confidence
You gave me, Brother? *Eld. Bro.* Yes, and keep it still;
Lean on it safely, not a period
Shall be unsaid for me. Against the threats
Of malice or of sorcery, or that power
Which erring men call Chance, this I hold firm:
Vertue may be assail'd, but never hurt,
Surpriz'd by unjust force, but not enthrall'd,
Yea even that which mischief meant most harm,
Shall in the happy trial prove most glory.
But evil on it self shall back recoyl,
And mix no more with goodness, when at last
Gather'd like scum, and setl'd to it self,
It shall be in eternal restless change
Self-fed, and self-consum'd; if this fail,
The pillar'd firmament is rott'nness,

And earths base built on stubble. But com, let's on.
Against th' opposing will and arm of Heav'n
May never this just sword be lifted up,
But for that damn'd magician, let him be girt
With all the greisly legions that troop
Under the sooty flag of Acheron,
Harpyies and Hydra's, or all the monstrous forms
'Twixt Africa and Inde, Ile find him out,
And force him to restore his purchase [27] back,
Or drag him by the curls, to a foul death,
Curs'd as his life.
Spir. Alas, good ventrous youth,
I love thy courage yet, and bold emprise,
But here thy sword can do thee little stead.
Farr other arms, and other weapons, must
Be those that quell the might of hellish charms;
He with his bare wand can unthred thy joynts,
And crumble all thy sinews.
Eld. Bro. Why prethee, Shepherd,
How durst thou then thy self approach so neer
As to make this relation?
Spir. Care and utmost shifts
How to secure the Lady from surprisal,
Brought to my mind a certain shepherd lad
Of small regard to see to, yet well skill'd
In every vertuous plant and healing herb
That spreds her verdant leaf to th'morning ray;
He lov'd me well, and oft would beg me sing,
Which when I did, he on the tender grass
Would sit, and hearken even to extasie,
And in requitall ope his leather'n scrip,
And shew me simples of a thousand names
Telling their strange and vigorous faculties.
Amongst the rest a small unsightly root,
But of divine effect, he cull'd me out;

[27] plunder

The leaf was darkish, and had prickles on it,
But in another countrey, as he said,
Bore a bright golden flowre, but not in this soyl:
Unknown, and like esteem'd, and the dull swayn
Treads on it daily with his clouted shoon,
And yet more med'cinal is it then that moly
That Hermes once to wise Ulysses gave.
He call'd it hæmony, and gave it me,
And bad me keep it as of sov'ran use
'Gainst all inchantments, mildew blast, or damp
Or gastly furies apparition.
I purs't it up, but little reck'ning made,
Till now that this extremity compell'd,
But now I find it true; for by this means
I knew the foul inchanter, though disguis'd,
Enter'd the very lime-twigs [28] of his spells,
And yet came off. If you have this about you
(As I will give you when we go) you may
Boldly assault the necromancers hall;
Where if he be, with dauntless hardihood,
And brandish't blade rush on him, break his glass,
And shed the lushious liquor on the ground;
But sease his wand. Though he and his curst crew
Feirce signe of battail make, and menace high,
Or like the sons of Vulcan vomit smoak,
Yet will they soon retire, if he but shrink.
Eld. Bro. Thyrsis, lead on apace; Ile follow thee,
And som good angel bear a sheild before us.

The Scene changes to a stately palace, set out with all manner of deliciousness; soft musick, tables spred with all dainties. Comus *appears with his rabble, and the Lady set in an inchanted chair, to whom he offers his glass, which she puts by, and goes about to rise.*

[28] Twigs smeared with bird-lime for catching birds.

Comus. Nay, Lady, sit; if I but wave this wand,
Your nerves are all chain'd up in alabaster,
And you a statue; or as Daphne [29] was
Root-bound, that fled Apollo.
La. Fool, do not boast.
Thou canst not touch the freedom of my minde
With all thy charms, although this corporal rinde
Thou haste immanacl'd, while Heav'n sees good.
Co. Why are you vext, Lady? why do you frown?
Here dwell no frowns, nor anger; from these gates
Sorrow flies farr. See here be all the pleasures
That fancy can beget on youthfull thoughts,
When the fresh blood grows lively, and returns
Brisk as the April buds in primrose-season.
And first behold this cordial julep here
That flames, and dances in his crystal bounds,
With spirits of balm, and fragrant syrops mixt.
Not that nepenthes which the wife of Thone
In Egypt gave to Jove-born Helena
Is of such power to stir up joy as this,
To life so friendly, or so cool to thirst.
Why should you be so cruel to your selfe,
And to those dainty limms which nature lent
For gentle usage, and soft delicacy?
But you invert the cov'nants of her trust,
And harshly deal like an ill borrower
With that which you receiv'd on other terms,
Scorning the unexempt condition
By which all mortal frailty must subsist,
Refreshment after toil, ease after pain,
That have been tir'd all day without repast,
And timely rest have wanted; but, fair virgin,
This will restore all soon.
La. 'Twill not, false traitor,
'Twill not restore the truth and honesty
That thou hast banish't from thy tongue with lies.
Was this the cottage, and the safe abode
Thou told'st me of? What grim aspects are these,
These oughly-headed monsters? Mercy guard me!
Hence with thy brew'd inchantments, foul deceiver,
Hast thou betrai'd my credulous innocence
With visor'd falshood, and base forgery,
And wouldst thou seek again to trap me here
With lickerish [30] baits fit to ensnare a brute?
Were it a draft for Juno when she banquets,
I would not taste thy treasonous offer; none
But such as are good men can give good things,
And that which is not good, is not delicious
To a well-govern'd and wise appetite.
Co. O foolishnes of men! that lend their ears
To those budge doctors of the Stoick furr,[31]
And fetch their precepts from the cynick tub,[32]
Praising the lean and shallow Abstinence.
Wherefore did Nature powre her bounties forth,
With such a full and unwithdrawing hand,
Covering the earth with odours, fruits, and flocks,
Thronging the seas with spawn innumerable,
But all to please, and sate the curious taste?
And set to work millions of spinning worms,
That in their green shops weave the smooth-hair'd silk
To deck her sons; and that no corner might
Be vacant of her plenty, in her own loyns

---

[29] Daphne when pursued by Apollo prayed to be changed into a laurel-tree.

[30] tempting

[31] Solemn philosophers of the Stoic persuasion. Budge fur is lamb's wool.

[32] The tub of Diogenes, the Cynic philosopher.

So hutch't th'all-worshipt ore, and precious gems
To store her children with. If all the world
Should in a pet of temperance feed on pulse,
Drink the clear stream, and nothing wear but freize,[33]
Th'all-giver would be unthank't, would be unprais'd,
Not half his riches known, and yet despis'd,
And we should serve him as a grudging master,
As a penurious niggard of his wealth,
And live like Natures bastards, not her sons,
Who would be quite surcharged with her own weight,
And strangl'd with her waste fertility;
Th'earth cumber'd, and the wing'd air dark't with plumes,
The herds would over-multitude their lords,
The sea o'refraught would swell, and th'unsought diamonds
Would so emblaze the forhead of the deep,
And so bestudd with stars, that they below
Would grow inur'd to light, and com at last
To gaze upon the sun with shameless brows.
List, Lady, be not coy, and be not cosen'd
With that same vaunted name virginity.
Beauty is natures coyn, must not be hoorded,
But must be currant, and the good thereof
Consists in mutual and partak'n bliss,
Unsavoury in th'injoyment of it self;
If you let slip time, like a neglected rose
It withers on the stalk with languish't head.
Beauty is Natures brag, and must be shown
In courts, at feasts, and high solemnities
Where most may wonder at the workmanship;

[33] coarse cloth

It is for homely features to keep home,
They had their name thence; course complexions
And cheeks of sorry grain [34] will serve to ply
The sampler, and to teize the huswifes wooll.
What need a vermeil-tinctured lip for that,
Love-darting eyes, or tresses like the morn?
There was another meaning in these gifts;
Think what, and be adviz'd; you are but young yet.

La. I had not thought to have unlockt my lips
In this unhallow'd air, but that this jugler
Would think to charm my judgement, as mine eyes,
Obtruding false rules pranckt in reasons garb.
I hate when vice can bolt [35] her arguments,
And vertue has no tongue to check her pride:
Impostor, do not charge most innocent Nature,
As if she would her children should be riotous
With her abundance. She, good cateress,
Means her provision onely to the good
That live according to her sober laws,
And holy dictate of spare Temperance:
If every just man that now pines with want
Had but a moderate and beseeming share
Of that which lewdly-pamper'd Luxury
Now heaps upon som few with vast excess,
Natures full blessings would be well dispenc't
In unsuperfluous eeven proportion,
And she no whit encomber'd with her store;
And then the giver would be better thank't,
His praise due paid, for swinish gluttony
Ne're looks to Heav'n amidst his gorgeous feast,
But with besotted base ingratitude
Cramms, and blasphemes his feeder. Shall I go on?

[34] drab color
[35] gift

Or have I said anough? To him that dares
Arm his profane tongue with contemptuous words
Against the sun-clad power of Chastity,
Fain would I somthing say, yet to what end?
Thou hast nor eare, nor soul to apprehend
The sublime notion, and high mystery
That must be utter'd to unfold the sage
And serious doctrine of Virginity;
And thou art worthy that thou shouldst not know
More happiness then this thy present lot.
Enjoy your deer wit, and gay rhetorick
That hath so well been taught her dazling fence;
Thou art not fit to hear thy self convinc't;
Yet should I try, the uncontrouléd worth
Of this pure cause would kindle my rap't spirits
To such a flame of sacred vehemence,
That dumb things would be mov'd to sympathize,
And the brute Earth would lend her nerves, and shake,
Till all thy magick structures rear'd so high,
Were shatter'd into heaps o're thy false head.

Co. She fables not. I feel that I do fear
Her words set off by som superior power;
And though not mortal, yet a cold shuddring dew
Dips me all o're, as when the wrath of Jove [36]
Speaks thunder, and the chains of Erebus
To som of Saturns crew. I must dissemble,
And try her yet more strongly. Com, no more,
This is meer moral bable, and direct
Against the canon laws of our foundation;
I must not suffer this, yet 'tis but the lees
And setlings of a melancholy blood.
But this will cure all streight; one sip of this
Will bathe the drooping spirits in delight
Beyond the bliss of dreams. Be wise, and taste.—

The Brothers rush in with swords drawn, wrest his glass out of his hand, and break it against the ground; his rout make signe of resistance, but are all driven in; the attendant Spirit comes in.

Spir. What, have you let the false enchanter scape?
O ye mistook; ye should have snatcht his wand
And bound him fast; without his rod revers't,
And backward mutters of dissevering power,
We cannot free the Lady that sits here
In stony fetters fixt, and motionless.
Yet stay, be not disturb'd; now I bethink me,
Som other means I have which may be us'd,
Which once of Melibœus old I learnt,
The soothest shepherd that ere pip't on plains.
There is a gentle nymph not farr from hence,
That with moist curb sways the smooth Severn stream;
Sabrina is her name, a virgin pure,
Whilom she was the daughter of Locrine,
That had the scepter from his father Brute.
The guiltless damsel, flying the mad pursuit
Of her enragéd stepdam Guendolen,
Commended her fair innocence to the flood
That stay'd her flight with his cross-flowing course.
The water nymphs that in the bottom plaid,
Held up their pearléd wrists and took her in,
Bearing her straight to aged Nereus hall,
Who, piteous of her woes, rear'd her lank head,
And gave her to his daughters to imbathe
In nectar'd lavers strew'd with asphodil,
And through the porch and inlet of each sense
Dropt in ambrosial oils till she reviv'd,
And underwent a quick immortal change,

[36] The reference is to the war between Jove and the Titans.

Made Goddess of the River. Still she retains
Her maid'n gentlenes, and oft at eeve
Visits the herds along the twilight meadows,
Helping all urchin blasts,[37] and ill luck signes
That the shrewd[38] medling elfe delights to make,
Which she with pretious viold liquors heals.
For which the shepherds at their festivals
Carrol her goodnes lowd in rustick layes,
And throw sweet garland wreaths into her stream
Of pancies, pinks, and gaudy daffadils.
And, as the old swain said, she can unlock
The clasping charm, and thaw the mumming spell,
If she be right invok't in warbled song,
For maid'nhood she loves, and will be swift
To aid a virgin, such as was her self,
In hard besetting need; this will I try
And adde the power of som adjouring verse.

Song

Sabrina fair,
Listen where thou art sitting
Under the glassie, cool, translucent wave,
In twisted braids of lillies knitting
The loose train of thy amber-dropping hair;
Listen for dear honour's sake,
Goddess of the silver lake,
Listen and save.

Listen and appear to us
In name of great Oceanus,[39]
By the earth-shaking Neptune's mace,
And Tethys grave majestick pace,
By hoary Nereus wrincled look,
And the Carpathian wisards hook,
By scaly Tritons winding shell,
And old sooth-saying Glaucus spell,
By Leucothea's lovely hands,
And her son that rules the strands,
By Thetis tinsel-slipper'd feet,
And the songs of Sirens sweet,
By dead Parthenope's dear tomb,
And fair Ligea's golden comb,
Wherwith she sits on diamond rocks
Sleeking her soft alluring locks,
By all the Nymphs that nightly dance
Upon thy streams with wily glance,
Rise, rise, and heave thy rosie head
From thy coral-pav'n bed,
And bridle in thy headlong wave,
Till thou our summons answered have.
Listen and save.

Sabrina *rises, attended by water-nymphes, and sings.*

By the rushy-fringéd bank,
Where grows the willow and the osier dank,
My sliding chariot stayes,
Thick set with agat, and the azurn sheen
Of turkis blew, and emrauld green
That in the channell strayes;
Whilst from off the waters fleet
Thus I set my printless feet
O're the cowslips velvet head,
That bends not as I tread,
Gentle swain at thy request
I am here.

Spir. Goddess dear,
We implore thy powerful hand
To undo the charméd band
Of true virgin here distrest,
Through the force, and through the wile
Of unblest inchanter vile
Sab. Shepherd 'tis my office best
To help insnaréd chastity;
Brightest Lady, look on me,
Thus I sprinkle on thy brest
Drops that from my fountain pure,
I have kept of pretious cure,
Thrice upon thy fingers tip,
Thrice upon thy rubied lip,
Next this marble venom'd seat
Smear'd with gumms of glutenous heat,
I touch with chaste palms moist and cold
Now the spell hath lost his hold;

[37] blights sent by evil spirits
[38] malicious
[39] Milton has collected here the deities of the sea, from Oceanus and Tethys, god and goddess of the ocean-stream, to the Siren Ligea.

And I must haste ere morning hour
To wait in Amphitrite's bowr.

Sabrina descends, and the Lady rises out of her seat.

Spir. Virgin, daughter of Locrine
Sprung of old Anchises line,
May thy brimméd waves for this
Their full tribute never miss
From a thousand petty rills,
That tumble down the snowy hills:
Summer drouth, or singéd air
Never scorch thy tresses fair,
Nor wet Octobers torrent flood
Thy molten crystal fill with mudd;
May thy billows rowl ashoar
The beryl, and the golden ore,
May thy lofty head be crown'd
With many a tower and terrass round,
And here and there thy banks upon
With groves of myrrhe, and cinnamon.

Com, Lady; while Heaven lends us grace,
Let us fly this curséd place,
Lest the Sorcerer us intice
With som other new device.
Not a waste, or needless sound
Till we com to holier ground.
I shall be your faithfull guide
Through this gloomy covert wide,
And not many furlongs thence
Is your fathers residence,
Where this night are met in state
Many a friend to gratulate
His wish't presence, and beside
All the swains that there abide,
With jiggs, and rural dance resort.
We shall catch them at their sport,
And our sudden coming there
Will double all their mirth and chere;
Com let us haste, the stars grow high,
But night sits monarch yet in the mid sky.

The Scene changes, presenting Ludlow *Town and the Presidents Castle; then com in countrey-dancers, after them the attendant Spirit, with the two Brothers and the Lady.*

Song

Spir. *Back shepherds, back, anough your play,*
Till next sun-shine holiday.
Here be without duck or nod
Other trippings to be trod
Of lighter toes, and such court guise
As Mercury *did first devise*
With the mincing Dryades
On the lawns, and on the leas.

This second Song presents them to their father and mother.

Noble Lord, and Lady bright,
I have brought ye new delight.
Here behold so goodly grown
Three fair branches of your own,
Heav'n hath timely tri'd their youth,
Their faith, their patience, and their truth.
And sent them here through hard assays
With a crown of deathless praise,
To triumph in victorious dance
O're sensual Folly, and Intemperance.

The dances ended, the Spirit epiloguizes.

Spir. To the ocean now I fly,
And those happy climes that ly
Where day never shuts his eye,
Up in the broad fields of the sky:
There I suck the liquid ayr
All amidst the gardens fair
Of Hesperus, and his daughters three
That sing about the golden tree:
Along the crispéd shades and bowres
Revels the spruce and jocond spring,
The Graces, and the rosie-boosom'd Howres
Thither all their bounties bring,
That there eternal summer dwels,
And west winds, with musky wing
About the cedar'n alleys fling
Nard, and cassia's balmy smels.
Iris there with humid bow,
Waters the odorous banks that blow
Flowers of more mingled hew
Then her purfl'd scarf can shew,
And drenches with Elysian dew
(List mortals, if your ears be true)
Beds of hyacinth, and roses
Where young Adonis oft reposes,
Waxing well of his deep wound
In slumber soft; and on the ground

Sadly sits th' Assyrian queen,[40]
But far above in spangled sheen
Celestial Cupid her fam'd son advanc't,
Holds his dear Psyche sweet intranc't
After her wandring labours long,
Till free consent the gods among
Make her his eternal bride,
And from her fair unspotted side
Two blissful twins are to be born,
Youth and Joy; so Jove hath sworn.
But now my task is smoothly don,
I can fly, or I can run
Quickly to the green earths end,
Where the bow'd welkin slow doth bend,
And from thence can soar as soon
To the corners of the moon.
Mortals that would follow me,
Love Vertue, she alone is free;
She can teach ye how to clime
Higher than the spheary chime;[41]
Or if Vertue feeble were,
Heav'n it self would stoop to her.

LYCIDAS

In this Monody the Author bewails a learned Friend, unfortunatly drown'd in his Passage from Chester on the Irish Seas, 1637. And by occasion foretels the ruine of our corrupted clergy then in their height.

YET once more, O ye laurels, and once more
Ye myrtles brown, with ivy never-sear,
I com to pluck your berries harsh and crude,
And with forc'd fingers rude,
Shatter your leaves before the mellowing year.[42]
Bitter constraint, and sad occasion dear,
Compels me to disturb your season due:
For Lycidas is dead, dead ere his prime,
Young Lycidas, and hath not left his peer.
Who would not sing for Lycidas? He knew
Himself to sing, and build the lofty rhyme.
He must not flote upon his watry bear[43]
Unwept, and welter to the parching wind,
Without the meed of som melodious tear.
Begin then, Sisters[44] of the sacred well,
That from beneath the seat of Jove doth spring;
Begin, and somewhat loudly sweep the string.
Hence with denial vain, and coy excuse,
So may som gentle Muse
With lucky words favour my destin'd urn,
And as he passes turn,
And bid fair peace be to my sable shrowd.
For we were nurst upon the self-same hill,
Fed the same flock, by fountain, shade, and rill.
Together both, ere the high lawns appear'd
Under the opening eye-lids of the morn,
We drove a field, and both together heard
What time the gray-fly winds her sultry horn,
Batt'ning our flocks with the fresh dews of night,
Oft till the star that rose, at ev'ning, bright
Toward Heav'ns descent had slop'd his westering wheel.
Mean while the rural ditties were not mute,
Temper'd to th'oaten flute;
Rough Satyrs danc'd, and Fauns with clov'n heel,
From the glad sound would not be absent long,
And old Damætas[45] lov'd to hear our song.
But O the heavy change, now thou art gon,
Now thou art gon, and never must return!
Thee shepherd, thee the woods, and desert caves,
With wilde thyme and the gadding vine o'regrown,
And all their echoes mourn.
The willows, and the hazle copses green,
Shall now no more be seen,
Fanning their joyous leaves to thy soft layes.

---

[40] Venus
[41] The music of the spheres.
[42] Milton had resolved not to compose more poetry until his gift was fully ripe.
[43] bier
[44] the Muses
[45] Possibly Milton's tutor at Cambridge.

As killing as the canker to the rose,
Or taint-worm to the weanling herds that graze,
Or frost to flowers, that their gay wardrop [46] wear,
When first the white thorn blows;
Such, Lycidas, thy loss to shepherds ear.
Where were ye, Nymphs, when the remorseless deep
Clos'd o're the head of your lov'd Lycidas?
For neither were ye playing on the steep,
Where your old bards, the famous Druids ly,
Nor on the shaggy top of Mona high,
Nor yet where Deva spreads her wisard stream:
Ay me, I fondly dream!
Had ye bin there — for what could that have don?
What could the Muse [47] her self that Orpheus bore,
The Muse her self, for her inchanting son
Whom universal nature did lament,
When by the rout that made the hideous roar,
His goary visage down the stream was sent,
Down the swift Hebrus to the Lesbian shore?
Alas! What boots it with uncessant care
To tend the homely slighted shepherds trade,
And strictly meditate the thankles Muse?
Were it not better don as others use,
To sport with Amaryllis in the shade,
Or with the tangles of Neæra's hair?
Fame is the spur that the clear spirit doth raise
(That last infirmity of noble mind)
To scorn delights, and live laborious dayes;
But the fair guerdon when we hope to find,
And think to burst out into sudden blaze,
Comes the blind Fury with th'abhorréd shears,
And slits the thin spun life. But not the praise,
Phœbus repli'd, and touch'd my trembling ears;
Fame is no plant that grows on mortal soil,
Nor in the glistering foil
Set off to th'world, nor in broad rumour lies,
But lives and spreds aloft by those pure eyes,
And perfet witnes of all judging Jove;
As he pronounces lastly on each deed,
Of so much fame in Heav'n expect thy meed.
O fountain Arethuse,[48] and thou honour'd floud,
Smooth-sliding Mincius, crown'd with vocall reeds,
That strain I heard was of a higher mood.
But now my oate [49] proceeds,
And listens to the Herald [50] of the Sea
That came in Neptune's plea,
He ask'd the waves, and ask'd the fellon winds,
What hard mishap hath doom'd this gentle swain?
And question'd every gust of rugged wings
That blows from off each beakéd promontory,
They knew not of his story,
And sage Hippotades [51] their answer brings,
That not a blast was from his dungeon stray'd,
The ayr was calm, and on the level brine,
Sleek Panope [52] with all her sisters play'd.
It was that fatall and perfidious bark
Built in th'eclipse, and rigg'd with curses dark,
That sunk so low that sacred head of thine.
Next Camus,[53] reverend Sire, went footing slow,
His mantle hairy, and his bonnet sedge,
Inwrought with figures dim, and on the edge

[46] wardrobe
[47] Calliope bore Orpheus, who was torn to pieces by the Thracian women for his slight to them.

[48] A well in Sicily, representing here the Greek tradition of pastoral poetry, as Mincius does the Latin.
[49] shepherd's pipe
[50] Triton
[51] Aeolus
[52] a Nereid
[53] The river Cam, which flows through Cambridge.

Like to that sanguine flower inscrib'd with woe.[54]
Ah, who hath reft (quoth he) my dearest pledge?
Last came, and last did go,
The Pilot [55] of the Galilean lake,
Two massy keyes he bore of metals twain,
(The golden opes, the iron shuts amain).
He shook his miter'd locks, and stern bespake:
How well could I have spar'd for thee, young swain,
Anow of such as for their bellies sake,
Creep and intrude, and climb into the fold!
Of other care they little reck'ning make,
Then how to scramble at the shearers feast,
And shove away the worthy bidden guest.
Blind mouthes! that scarce themselves know how to hold
A sheep-hook, or have learn'd ought els the least
That to the faithfull herdmans art belongs!
What recks it them? What need they? They are sped;
And when they list, their lean and flashy songs
Grate on their scrannel [56] pipes of wretched straw;
The hungry sheep look up, and are not fed,
But swoln with wind, and the rank mist they draw,
Rot inwardly, and foul contagion spread:
Besides what the grim woolf with privy paw
Daily devours apace, and nothing sed,
But that two-handed engine [57] at the door,
Stands ready to smite once, and smite no more.
Return Alpheus,[58] the dread voice is past,
That shrunk thy streams. Return Sicilian Muse,
And call the vales, and bid them hither cast
Their bels, and flourets of a thousand hues.
Ye valleys low where the milde whispers use,
Of shades and wanton winds, and gushing brooks,
On whose fresh lap the swart star [59] sparely looks,
Throw hither all your quaint enameld eyes,
That on the green terf suck the honied showres,
And purple all the ground with vernal flowres.
Bring the rathe primrose that forsaken dies,
The tufted crow-toe, and pale gessamine,
The white pink, and the pansie freakt with jeat,
The glowing violet.
The musk-rose, and the well attir'd woodbine.
With cowslips wan that hang the pensive hed,
And every flower that sad embroidery wears;
Bid amaranthus all his beauty shed,
And daffadillies fill their cups with tears,
To strew the laureat herse where Lycid lies.
For so to interpose a little ease,
Let our frail thoughts dally with false surmise.
Ay me! Whilst thee the shores, and sounding seas
Wash far away, where ere thy bones are hurld,
Whether beyond the stormy Hebrides,
Where thou perhaps under the whelming tide
Visit'st the bottom of the monstrous world;
Or whether thou to our moist vows deny'd,

---

[54] The hyacinth is said to be marked *ai, ai* (woe! woe!) in memory of Hyacinthus.
[55] St. Peter, who holds the keys of the Kingdom of Heaven.
[56] thin
[57] This passage has not been satisfactorily explained. It may refer to the two-handed sword of Revelation, to the two houses of Parliament, the sword of St. Michael, *etc.*
[58] A river in Arcadia.
[59] The dog-star, supposedly injurious to plants.

Sleep'st by the fable of Bellerus [60] old,
Where the great vision of the guarded Mount [61]
Looks toward Namancos and Bayona's hold; [62]
Look homeward Angel, now, and melt with ruth.
And, O ye Dolphins, waft the haples youth.
  Weep no more, woful shepherds weep no more,
For Lycidas, your sorrow, is not dead,
Sunk though he be beneath the watry floar;
So sinks the day-star in the ocean bed,
And yet anon repairs his drooping head,
And tricks his beams, and with new spangled ore,[63]
Flames in the forehead of the morning sky:
So Lycidas sunk low, but mounted high,
Through the dear might of him that walk'd the waves
Where, other groves, and other streams along,
With nectar pure his oozy locks he laves,
And hears the unexpressive [64] nuptiall song,
In the blest kingdoms meek of joy and love.
There entertain him all the Saints above,
In solemn troops, and sweet societies
That sing, and singing in their glory move,
And wipe the tears for ever from his eyes.
Now Lycidas the shepherds weep no more;
Hence forth thou art the Genius of the shore,
In thy large recompense, and shalt be good
To all that wander in that perilous flood.
  Thus sang the uncouth swain to th'okes and rills,
While the still morn went out with sandals gray;
He touch'd the tender stops of various quills,
With eager thought warbling his Dorick [65] lay:
And now the sun had stretch'd out all the hills,
And now was dropt into the western bay.
At last he rose, and twitch'd his mantle blew:
To morrow to fresh woods, and pastures new.

[*Justa Edouardo King naufrago, ab amicis mœrentibus*,[66] 1638]

PARADISE LOST

BOOK I [67]

THE ARGUMENT

THIS first book proposes first in brief the whole subject, Mans disobedience, and the loss thereupon of Paradise wherein he was plac't: then touches the prime cause of his fall, the Serpent, or rather Satan in the Serpent; who revolting from God, and drawing to his side many legions of Angels, was by the command of God driven out of Heaven with all his crew into the great Deep. Which action past over, the poem hasts into the midst of things, presenting Satan with his Angels now fallen into Hell, describ'd here, not in the center (for Heaven and Earth may be suppos'd as yet not made, certainly not yet accurst) but in a place of utter darknesse, fitliest call'd Chaos: Here Satan with his Angels lying on the burning lake, thunder-struck and astonisht, after a certain space recovers, as from confusion, calls up him who next in order and dignity lay by him; they confer of thir miserable fall. Satan awakens all his legions, who lay till then in the same manner confounded. They rise: thir numbers, array of battel, thir chief leaders nam'd, according to the idols known afterwards in Canaan and the countries adjoyning. To these Satan directs his speech, comforts them with hope yet of regaining Heaven, but tells them lastly of a new world and new kind of creature to be created, according to an ancient prophesie or report in Heaven; for that Angels were long before this visible creation was the opinion of many ancient Fathers. To find out the truth of this prophesie, and what to determin thereon, he refers to a full councell. What

[60] Land's End
[61] St. Michael's Mount, off Penzance.
[62] *i.e.*, towards Spain [63] gold [64] inexpressible
[65] The dialect of the Greek pastoral poets.
[66] The memorial volume containing verses by friends of King. Milton had known him at Cambridge, though their acquaintanceship was hardly more than casual. The invitation to contribute to the volume of memorial verses gave the young poet an opportunity to try his hand at a poetic form in vogue during the Renaissance—the pastoral elegy.
[67] The ten books of *Paradise Lost*, published in 1667 were in the edition of 1674 expanded to twelve.

his associates thence attempt. Pandemonium the palace of Satan rises, suddenly built out of the Deep: the infernal Peers there sit in counsel.

Of Mans first disobedience, and the fruit
Of that forbidden tree, whose mortal tast
Brought death into the World, and all our woe,
With loss of Eden, till one greater Man
Restore us, and regain the blissful Seat,
Sing, Heav'nly Muse,[68] that on the secret top
Of Oreb, or of Sinai, didst inspire
That shepherd, who first taught the chosen seed,
In the beginning how the Heav'ns and Earth
Rose out of Chaos: or if Sion hill
Delight thee more, and Siloa's brook that flow'd
Fast by the oracle of God,[69] I thence
Invoke thy aid to my adventrous song,
That with no middle flight intends to soar
Above th' Aonian mount,[70] while it pursues
Things unattempted yet in prose or rhime.
And chiefly Thou O Spirit, that dost prefer
Before all temples th' upright heart and pure,
Instruct me, for Thou know'st; Thou from the first
Wast present, and with mighty wings outspread
Dove-like satst brooding on the vast Abyss
And mad'st it pregnant: what in me is dark
Illumine, what is low raise and support;
That to the highth of this great argument
I may assert Eternal Providence,
And justifie the wayes of God to men.
  Say first, for Heav'n hides nothing from thy view,
Nor the deep tract of Hell, say first what cause
Mov'd our Grand [71] Parents in that happy state,
Favour'd of Heav'n so highly, to fall off
From their Creator, and transgress his will
For one restraint, lords of the World besides?
Who first seduc'd them to that fowl revolt?
Th' infernal Serpent; he it was, whose guile
Stird up with envy and revenge, deceiv'd
The mother of mankinde, what time his pride
Had cast him out from Heav'n, with all his host
Of rebel Angels, by whose aid aspiring
To set himself in glory above his peers,
He trusted to have equal'd the most High,
If he oppos'd; and with ambitious aim
Against the throne and monarchy of God
Rais'd impious war in Heav'n and battel proud
With vain attempt. Him the Almighty Power
Hurld headlong flaming from th' ethereal skie
With hideous ruine and combustion down
To bottomless perdition, there to dwell
In adamantine chains and penal fire,
Who durst defie th' Omnipotent to arms.
Nine times the space that measures day and night
To mortal men, he with his horrid crew
Lay vanquisht, rowling in the fiery gulfe,
Confounded though immortal. But his doom
Reserv'd him to more wrath; for now the thought
Both of lost happiness and lasting pain
Torments him; round he throws his baleful eyes
That witness'd huge affliction and dismay,
Mixt with obdurate pride and stedfast hate.
At once as far as Angels kenn he views
The dismal situation waste and wilde,
A dungeon horrible, on all sides round
As one great furnace flam'd; yet from those flames
No light, but rather darkness visible
Serv'd only to discover sights of woe,
Regions of sorrow, doleful shades, where peace
And rest can never dwell, hope never comes
That comes to all; but torture without end

68 The power that inspired Moses on Mt. Sinai.
69 The Temple of Jerusalem.
70 Mt. Helicon, sacred to the Muses.
71 original.

Still urges, and a fiery deluge, fed
With ever-burning sulphur unconsum'd.
Such place Eternal Justice had prepar'd
For those rebellious, here their prison ordain'd
In utter [72] darkness, and their portion set
As far remov'd from God and light of Heav'n
As from the center thrice to th' utmost pole.[73]
O how unlike the place from whence they fell!
There the companions of his fall, o'rewhelm'd
With floods and whirlwinds of tempestuous fire,
He soon discerns and weltring by his side
One next himself in power, and next in crime,
Long after known in Palestine, and nam'd
Beëlzebub. To whom th' Arch-Enemy,[74]
And thence in Heav'n call'd Satan, with bold words
Breaking the horrid silence thus began.
  If thou beest he; but O how fall'n! how chang'd
From him, who in the happy realms of light
Cloth'd with transcendent brightness didst outshine
Myriads though bright. If he whom mutual league,
United thoughts and counsels, equal hope,
And hazard in the glorious enterprize,
Joynd with me once, now misery hath joynd
In equal ruin: into what pit thou seest
From what highth fal'n, so much the stronger provd
He with his thunder: and till then who knew
The force of those dire arms? Yet not for those
Nor what the potent Victor in his rage
Can else inflict do I repent or change,
Though chang'd in outward lustre, that fixt mind
And high disdain, from sence of injur'd merit,
That with the mightiest rais'd me to contend,
And to the fierce contention brought along
Innumerable force of Spirits arm'd
That durst dislike his reign, and me preferring,
His utmost power with adverse power oppos'd
In dubious battel on the plains of Heav'n,
And shook his throne. What though the field be lost?
All is not lost; the unconquerable will,
And study of revenge, immortal hate,
And courage never to submit or yield;
And what is else not to be overcome?
That glory never shall his wrath or might
Extort from me. To bow and sue for grace
With suppliant knee, and deifie his power
Who from the terrour of this arm so late
Doubted his empire, that were low indeed,
That were an ignominy and shame beneath
This downfall; since by Fate the strength of gods
And this empyreal substance cannot fail;
Since through experience of this great event
In arms not worse, in foresight much advanc't,
We may with more successful hope resolve
To wage by force or guile eternal warr
Irreconcileable, to our grand Foe,
Who now triumphs, and in th' excess of joy
Sole reigning holds the tyranny of Heav'n.
  So spake th' apostate Angel, though in pain,
Vaunting aloud, but rackt with deep despare;

[72] outer

[73] According to the Ptolemaic system of astronomy, which Milton followed, the earth is the center of the universe. The other heavenly bodies revolve around it in concentric spheres made of a transparent substance. The globe which these ten spheres form is suspended from heaven by a chain, so Milton says. In this passage he pictures the poles of the earth as projecting beyond the outmost sphere. Above and below the starry universe is chaos, and the place into which the angels fell is the specially prepared hell at the bottom of chaos.

[74] Satan in Hebrew means adversary.

And him thus answer'd soon his bold Compeer.
O Prince, O Chief of many thronéd Powers,
That led th' imbattelld Seraphim to warr
Under thy conduct, and in dreadful deeds
Fearless, endanger'd Heav'ns perpetual King;
And put to proof his high supremacy,
Whether upheld by strength, or chance, or Fate,
Too well I see and rue the dire event,
That with sad overthrow and foul defeat
Hath lost us Heav'n, and all this mighty host
In horrible destruction laid thus low,
As far as gods and heav'nly essences
Can perish: for the mind and spirit remains
Invincible, and vigour soon returns,
Though all our glory extinct, and happy state
Here swallow'd up in endless misery.
But what if he our Conqueror, (whom I now
Of force believe almighty, since no less
Then such could hav orepow'rd such force as ours)
Have left us this our spirit and strength intire
Strongly to suffer and support our pains,
That we may so suffice his vengeful ire,
Or do him mightier service as his thralls
By right of warr, what e're his business be
Here in the heart of Hell to work in fire,
Or do his errands in the gloomy deep?
What can it then avail though yet we feel
Strength undiminisht, or eternal being
To undergo eternal punishment?
Whereto with speedy words th' Arch-fiend reply'd.
Fall'n Cherube, to be weak is miserable
Doing or suffering: but of this be sure,
To do ought good never will be our task,
But ever to do ill our sole delight,
As being the contrary to his high will
Whom we resist. If then his providence
Out of our evil seek to bring forth good,
Our labour must be to pervert that end,
And out of good still to find means of evil;
Which oft times may succeed, so as perhaps
Shall grieve him, if I fail [75] not, and disturb
His inmost counsels from their destind aim.
But see, the angry Victor hath recall'd
His ministers of vengeance and pursuit
Back to the gates of Heav'n; the sulphurous hail
Shot after us in storm, oreblown hath laid
The fiery surge, that from the precipice
Of Heav'n receiv'd us falling, and the thunder,
Wing'd with red lightning and impetuous rage,
Perhaps hath spent his shafts, and ceases now
To bellow through the vast and boundless Deep.
Let us not slip th' occasion, whether scorn,
Or satiate fury yield it from our Foe.
Seest thou yon dreary plain, forlorn and wilde,
The seat of desolation, voyd of light,
Save what the glimmering of these livid flames
Casts pale and dreadful? Thither let us tend
From off the tossing of these fiery waves,
There rest, if any rest can harbour there,
And reassembling our afflicted powers,
Consult how we may henceforth most offend
Our Enemy, our own loss how repair,
How overcome this dire calamity,
What reinforcement we may gain from hope,
If not what resolution from despare.
Thus Satan talking to his neerest mate,
With head up-lift above the wave, and eyes
That sparkling blaz'd, his other parts besides
Prone on the flood, extended long and large
Lay floating many a rood, in bulk as huge

[75] mistake

As whom the fables name of monstrous size,
Titanian, or Earth-born, that warr'd on Jove,
Briarios or Typhon,[76] whom the den
By ancient Tarsus held, or that sea-beast
Leviathan, which God of all his works
Created hugest that swim th' ocean stream.
Him haply slumbring on the Norway foam,
The pilot of some small night-founder'd[77] skiff,
Deeming some island, oft, as sea-men tell,
With fixéd anchor in his skaly rind,
Moors by his side under the lee, while night
Invests the sea, and wishéd morn delayes.
So stretcht out huge in length the Arch-fiend lay
Chain'd on the burning lake, nor ever thence
Had ris'n or heav'd his head, but that the will
And high permission of all-ruling Heaven
Left him at large to his own dark designs,
That with reiterated crimes he might
Heap on himself damnation, while he sought
Evil to others, and enrag'd might see
How all his malice serv'd but to bring forth
Infinite goodness, grace and mercy shewn
On Man by him seduc't, but on himself
Treble confusion, wrath and vengeance pour'd.
Forthwith upright he rears from off the pool
His mighty stature; on each hand the flames
Drivn backward slope their pointing spires, and rowld
In billows, leave i' th' midst a horrid vale.
Then with expanded wings he stears his flight
Aloft, incumbent on the dusky air
That felt unusual weight, till on dry land
He lights, if it were land that ever burn'd
With solid, as the lake with liquid fire;
And such appear'd in hue, as when the force
Of subterranean wind transports a hill
Torn from Pelorus, or the shatter'd side
Of thundring Ætna, whose combustible
And fewel'd entrals thence conceiving fire,
Sublim'd with mineral fury, aid the winds,
And leave a singéd bottom all involv'd
With stench and smoak. Such resting found the sole
Of unblest feet. Him followed his next mate,
Both glorying to have scap't the Stygian flood
As gods, and by their own recover'd strength,
Not by the sufferance of supernal power.
Is this the region, this the soil, the clime,
Said then the lost Arch Angel, this the seat
That we must change for Heav'n, this mournful gloom
For that celestial light? Be it so, since hee
Who now is sovran can dispose and bid
What shall be right: fardest from him is best,
Whom reason hath equald, force hath made supream
Above his equals. Farewel happy fields
Where joy for ever dwells. Hail horrours, hail
Infernal world, and thou profoundest Hell
Receive thy new possessor: one who brings
A mind not to be chang'd by place or time.
The mind is its own place, and in it self
Can make a Heav'n of Hell, a Hell of Heav'n.
What matter where, if I be still the same,
And what I should be, all but less then[78] hee
Whom thunder hath made greater? Here at least
We shall be free; th' Almighty hath not built
Here for his envy, will not drive us hence:
Here we may reign secure, and in my choyce,
To reign is worth ambition though in Hell:

[76] Briarios was a Titan; Typhon, a giant. Both were the offspring of Ge (Earth). The giants tried to dethrone Jove.

[77] overtaken by night

[78] only less than

Better to reign in Hell, then serve in Heav'n.
But wherefore let we then our faithful friends,
Th' associates and copartners of our loss,
Lye thus astonisht on th' oblivious [79] pool,
And call them not to share with us their part
In this unhappy mansion, or once more
With rallied arms to try what may be yet
Regained in Heav'n, or what more lost in Hell?
So Satan spake, and him Beëlzebub
Thus answer'd. Leader of those armies bright,
Which but th' Omnipotent none could have foyld,
If once they hear that voyce, their liveliest pledge
Of hope in fears and dangers, heard so oft
In worst extreams, and on the perilous edge
Of battel when it rag'd, in all assaults
Their surest signal, they will soon resume
New courage and revive, though now they lye
Groveling and prostrate on yon lake of fire,
As we erewhile, astounded and amaz'd;
No wonder, fall'n such a pernicious highth.
He scarce had ceas't when the superiour Fiend
Was moving toward the shore; his ponderous shield,
Ethereal temper, massy, large and round,
Behind him cast; the broad circumference
Hung on his shoulders like the moon, whose orb
Through optic glass the Tuscan artist [80] views
At ev'ning from the top of Fesole,
Or in Valdarno, to descry new lands,
Rivers or mountains in her spotty globe.
His spear, to equal which the tallest pine
Hewn on Norwegian hills, to be the mast
Of some great ammiral,[81] were but a wand,

[79] causing forgetfulness
[80] Galileo, whom Milton had met at Florence, improved the telescope. Fiesole is on a hill overlooking Florence, which lies in the valley of the Arno.
[81] Admiral, the flagship of a fleet.

He walkt with, to support uneasie steps
Over the burning marle, not like those steps
On Heavens azure; and the torrid clime
Smote on him sore besides, vaulted with fire.
Nathless he so endur'd, till on the beach
Of that inflaméd sea, he stood and call'd
His legions, Angel forms, who lay intrans't
Thick as autumnal leaves that strow the brooks
In Vallombrosa,[82] where th' Etrurian shades
High overarch't imbowr; or scatterd sedge
Afloat, when with fierce winds Orion arm'd
Hath vext the Red-Sea [83] coast, whose waves orethrew
Busiris [84] and his Memphian[85] chivalrie,
While with perfidious hatred they pursu'd
The sojourners of Goshen, who beheld
From the safe shore their floating carkases
And broken chariot wheels; so thick bestrown
Abject and lost lay these, covering the flood,
Under amazement of their hideous change.
He call'd so loud, that all the hollow Deep
Of Hell resounded. Princes, Potentates,
Warriers, the flowr of Heav'n, once yours, now lost,
If such astonishment as this can sieze
Eternal spirits; or have ye chos'n this place
After the toyl of battel to repose
Your wearied vertue, for the ease you find
To slumber here, as in the vales of Heav'n?
Or in this abject posture have ye sworn
To adore the Conquerour who now beholds
Cherube and Seraph rowling in the flood
With scatter'd arms and ensigns, till anon
His swift pursuers from Heav'n gates discern

[82] A 'shady valley' eighteen miles from Florence. Milton is said to have passed several days at a monastery there.
[83] The Hebrew name means 'Sea of Sedge.'
[84] Though Busiris was an earlier ruler than the Pharaoh who was drowned in the Red Sea, Milton identifies him with that oppressor of the Israelites. [85] Egyptian

Th' advantage, and descending tread us down
Thus drooping, or with linkéd thunder-bolts
Transfix us to the bottom of this gulfe?
Awake, arise, or be for ever fall'n.
They heard, and were abasht, and up they sprung
Upon the wing, as when men wont to watch
On duty, sleeping found by whom they dread,
Rouse and bestir themselves ere well awake.
Nor did they not perceave the evil plight
In which they were, or the fierce pains not feel;
Yet to their Generals voyce they soon obeyd
Innumerable. As when the potent rod
Of Amrams son [86] in Egypts evill day
Wav'd round the coast, up call'd a pitchy cloud
Of locusts, warping on the eastern wind,
That ore the realm of impious Pharaoh hung
Like night, and darken'd all the land of Nile;
So numberless were those bad Angels seen
Hovering on wing under the cope of Hell
'Twixt upper, néther, and surrounding fires;
Till, as a signal giv'n, th' uplifted spear
Of their great Sultan waving to direct
Thir course, in even ballance down they light
On the firm brimstone, and fill all the plain;
A multitude, like which the populous North
Pour'd never from her frozen loyns, to pass
Rhene or the Danaw,[87] when her barbarous sons
Came like a deluge on the South, and spread
Beneath Gibraltar to the Lybian sands.
Forthwith from every squadron and each band
The heads and leaders thither hast where stood
Their great Commander; godlike shapes and forms
Excelling human, princely Dignities,
And Powers that earst in Heaven sat on thrones;
Though of their names in heav'nly records now
Be no memorial, blotted out and ras'd
By thir rebellion, from the Books of Life.
Nor had they yet among the sons of Eve
Got them new names, till wandring ore the Earth,
Through Gods high sufferance for the tryal of man,
By falsities and lyes the greatest part
Of mankind they corrupted to forsake
God their Creator, and th' invisible
Glory of him, that made them, to transform
Oft to the image of a brute, adorn'd
With gay religions full of pomp and gold,
And devils to adore for deities:
Then were they known to men by various names,
And various idols through the heathen world.
Say, Muse, their names then known, who first, who last,
Rous'd from the slumber, on that fiery couch,
At thir great Emperors call, as next in worth
Came singly where he stood on the bare strand,
While the promiscuous croud stood yet aloof?
The chief were those who from the pit of Hell
Roaming to seek their prey on Earth, durst fix
Their seats, long after, next the seat of God,
Their altars by his altar, gods ador'd
Among the nations round, and durst abide
Jehovah thundring out of Sion, thron'd
Between the Cherubim; yea, often plac'd
Within his sanctuary it self their shrines,
Abominations; and with curséd things

[86] Moses
[87] Rhine or the Danube

His holy rites, and solemn feasts profan'd,
And with their darkness durst affront his light.
First Moloch,[88] horrid King, besmear'd with blood
Of human sacrifice, and parents tears,
Though for the noyse of drums and timbrels loud
Their childrens cries unheard, that past through fire
To his grim idol. Him the Ammonite
Worshipt in Rabba and her watry plain,
In Argob and in Basan, to the stream
Of utmost Arnon. Nor content with such
Audacious neighbourhood, the wisest heart
Of Solomon he led by fraud to build
His temple right against the temple of God
On that opprobrious hill,[89] and made his grove
The pleasant vally of Hinnom, Tophet thence
And black Gehenna call'd, the type of Hell.
Next Chemos,[90] th' obscene dread of Moabs sons,
From Aroer to Nebo, and the wild
Of southmost Abarim; in Hesebon
And Horonaim, Seons realm, beyond
The flowry dale of Sibma clad with vines,
And Eleale to th' Asphaltick Pool.[91]
Peor his other name, when he entic'd
Israel in Sittim on their march from Nile
To do him wanton rites, which cost them woe.
Yet thence his lustful orgies he enlarg'd
Even to that hill of scandal, by the grove
Of Moloch homicide, lust hard by hate;
Till good Josiah drove them thence to Hell.
With these came they, who from the bordring flood
Of old Euphrates to the brook that parts
Egypt from Syrian ground, had general names
Of Baalim and Ashtaroth, those male,
These feminine. For spirits when they please
Can either sex assume, or both; so soft
And uncompounded is their essence pure,
Not ti'd or manacl'd with joynt or limb,
Nor founded on the brittle strength of bones,
Like cumbrous flesh; but in what shape they choose
Dilated or condens't, bright or obscure,
Can execute their aerie purposes,
And works of love or enmity fulfill.
For those the race of Israel oft forsook
Their living strength, and unfrequented left
His righteous altar, bowing lowly down
To bestial gods; for which their heads as low
Bow'd down in battel, sunk before the spear
Of despicable foes. With these in troop
Came Astoreth, whom the Phœnicians call'd
Astarte, queen of heav'n, with crescent horns;
To whose bright image nightly by the moon
Sidonian virgins paid their vows and songs;
In Sion also not unsung, where stood
Her temple on th' offensive mountain, built
By that uxorious king,[92] whose heart though large,
Beguil'd by fair idolatresses, fell
To idols foul. Thammuz [93] came next behind,
Whose annual wound in Lebanon allur'd
The Syrian damsels to lament his fate
In amorous dittyes all a summers day,
While smooth Adonis [94] from his native rock
Ran purple to the sea, suppos'd with blood

[88] A sun god, demanding child-sacrifice.
[89] The Mount of Olives, later called, because of these pagan rites, the Mount of Offense.
[90] Actually Moloch, as worshipped among the Moabites.
[91] The Dead Sea, near which these towns and hills lie.
[92] Solomon
[93] The Phoenician Adonis, slain by a boar in Lebanon. He dies each year and goes to the regions below, leaving all nature dead and sterile. In the spring he is allowed to return to the world.
[94] A Phoenician river.

Of Thammuz yearly wounded: the love-tale
Infected Sions daughters with like heat,
Whose wanton passions in the sacred porch
Ezekiel saw, when by the vision led
His eye survay'd the dark idolatries
Of alienated Judah. Next came one
Who mourn'd in earnest, when the captive Ark
Maim'd his brute image, head and hands lopt off
In his own temple, on the grunsel [95] edge,
Where he fell flat, and sham'd his worshipers:
Dagon his name, sea monster, upward man
And downward fish; yet had his temple high
Rear'd in Azotus, dreaded through the coast
Of Palestine, in Gath and Ascalon,
And Accaron and Gaza's frontier bounds.
Him follow'd Rimmon,[96] whose delightful seat
Was fair Damascus, on the fertil banks
Of Abbana and Pharphar, lucid streams.
He also against the house of God was bold:
A leper once he lost and gain'd a king,
Ahaz his sottish conquerour, whom he drew
Gods altar to disparage and displace
For one of Syrian mode, whereon to burn
His odious offrings, and adore the gods
Whom he had vanquisht. After these appear'd
A crew who under names of old renown,
Osiris, Isis, Orus and their train
With monstrous shapes and sorceries abus'd
Fanatic Egypt and her priests, to seek
Thir wandring gods disguis'd in brutish forms
Rather then human. Nor did Israel scape
Th' infection when their borrow'd [97] gold compos'd
The calf in Oreb: and the rebel king
Doubl'd that sin [98] in Bethel and in Dan,
Lik'ning his Maker to the grazéd ox,
Jehovah, who in one night when he pass'd
From Egypt marching, equal'd [99] with one stroke
Both her first born and all her bleating gods.
Belial [100] came last, then whom a Spirit more lewd
Fell not from Heaven, or more gross to love
Vice for it self. To him no temple stood
Or altar smoak'd; yet who more oft then hee
In temples and at altars, when the priest
Turns atheist, as did Elys sons, who fill'd
With lust and violence the house of God.
In courts and palaces he also reigns,
And in luxurious cities, where the noyse
Of riot ascends above thir loftiest towrs,
And injury and outrage; and when night
Darkens the streets, then wander forth the sons
Of Belial, flown [101] with insolence and wine.
Witness the streets of Sodom, and that night
In Gibeah, when hospitable dores
Yielded thir matrons to prevent worse rape.
These were the prime in order and in might;
The rest were long to tell, though far renown'd,
Th' Ionian gods, of Javan's issue [102] held
Gods, yet confest later then Heav'n and Earth
Thir boasted parents; Titan,[103] Heav'ns first born
With his enormous brood, and birthright seis'd

[95] threshold
[96] An Assyrian deity. See *II Kings*, v and xvi.
[97] As one 'borrows' the enemy's goods,
[98] Jeroboam made two golden calves.
[99] Struck down in the tenth plague.
[100] Belial was not a heathen god but an abstraction meaning wickedness. Milton uses the word to personify the excesses of such a society as that of Restoration England.
[101] flushed
[102] *i.e.*, the Ionians
[103] One of the Titans, sons of Uranus (Heaven) and Ge (Earth) was Cronos (Saturn). He took the throne from his father, but was in turn dethroned by Zeus (Jove), whose mother was Rhea.

By younger Saturn, he from mightier Jove
His own and Rhea's son like measure found;
So Jove usurping reign'd. These first in Creet
And Ida known, thence on the snowy top
Of cold Olympus rul'd the middle air,
Thir highest Heav'n; or on the Delphian cliff,
Or in Dodona, and through all the bounds
Of Doric land; or who with Saturn old
Fled over Adria to th' Hesperian fields,
And ore the Celtic roam'd the utmost isles.
All these and more came flocking; but with looks
Down cast and damp; [104] yet such wherein appear'd
Obscure som glimps of joy to have found thir chief
Not in despair, to have found themselves not lost
In loss it self; which on his count'nance cast
Like doubtful hue. But he, his wonted pride
Soon recollecting, with high words, that bore
Semblance of worth not substance, gently rais'd
Their fainted courage, and dispel'd their fears.
Then strait commands that at the warlike sound
Of trumpets loud and clarions be upreard
His mighty standard; that proud honour claim'd
Azazel as his right, a Cherube tall:
Who forthwith from the glittering staff unfurld
Th' imperial ensign, which full high advanc't,
Shon like a meteor streaming to the wind
With gemms and golden lustre rich imblaz'd,
Seraphic arms and trophies; all the while
Sonorous mettal blowing martial sounds:
At which the universal host upsent
A shout that tore Hells concave, and beyond
Frighted the reign of Chaos and old Night.
All in a moment through the gloom were seen
Ten thousand banners rise into the air
With orient colours waving: with them rose
A forrest huge of spears; and thronging helms
Appear'd, and serried shields in thick array
Of depth immeasurable. Anon they move
In perfect phalanx to the Dorian mood [105]
Of flutes and soft recorders; [106] such as rais'd
To highth of noblest temper heros old
Arming to battel, and in stead of rage
Deliberate valour breath'd, firm and unmov'd
With dread of death to flight or foul retreat,
Nor wanting power to mitigate and swage
With solemn touches, troubl'd thoughts, and chase
Anguish and doubt and fear and sorrow and pain
From mortal or immortal minds. Thus they
Breathing united force with fixéd thought
Mov'd on in silence to soft pipes that charm'd
Thir painful steps o're the burnt soyle; and now
Advanc't in view they stand, a horrid [107] front
Of dreadful length and dazling arms, in guise
Of warriers old with order'd spear and shield,
Awaiting what command thir mighty Chief
Had to impose. He through the arméd files

---

[104] depressed

[105] The Greek musical mode which is the 'strain of courage.'

[106] Wooden flutes used in Milton's time for solemn music.

[107] bristling

Darts his experienc't eye, and soon traverse
The whole battalion views, thir order due,
Thir visages and stature as of gods,
Thir number last he summs. And now his heart
Distends with pride, and hardning in his strength
Glories: for never since created man,
Met such imbodied force, as nam'd wth these
Could merit more then that small infantry [108]
Warr'd on by cranes; though all the giant brood
Of Phlegra [109] with th' heroic race were joyn'd
That fought at Theb's and Ilium, on each side
Mixt with auxiliar gods; and what resounds
In fable or romance of Uthers son [110]
Begirt with British and Armoric [111] knights;
And all who since, baptiz'd or infidel
Jousted in Aspramont or Montalban,
Damasco, or Marocco, or Trebisond,
Or whom Biserta sent from Afric shore
When Charlemain with all his peerage fell
By Fontarabbia. Thus far these beyond
Compare of mortal prowess, yet observ'd
Thir dread Commander. He above the rest
In shape and gesture proudly eminent,
Stood like a towr; his form had yet not lost
All her original brightness, nor appear'd
Less then Arch Angel ruind, and th' excess
Of glory obscur'd: as when the sun new ris'n
Looks through the horizontal misty air
Shorn of his beams, or from behind the moon
In dim eclips disastrous twilight sheds
On half the nations, and with fear of change
Perplexes monarchs. Dark'n'd so, yet shon
Above them all th' Arch Angel: but his face
Deep scars of thunder had intrencht, and care
Sat on his faded cheek, but under browes
Of dauntless courage, and considerate [112] pride
Waiting revenge. Cruel his eye, but cast
Signs of remorse and passion [113] to behold
The fellows of his crime, the followers rather
(Far other once beheld in bliss) condemn'd
For ever now to have their lot in pain,
Millions of Spirits for his fault amerc't
Of Heav'n, and from eternal splendors flung
For his revolt, yet faithfull how they stood,
Thir glory witherd. As when Heavens fire
Hath scath'd the forrest oaks, or mountain pines,
With singéd top their stately growth though bare
Stands on the blasted heath. He now prepar'd
To speak; whereat their doubl'd ranks they bend
From wing to wing, and half enclose him round
With all his Peers: attention held them mute.
Thrice he assayd, and thrice in spite of scorn,
Tears such as Angels weep, burst forth: at last
Words interwove with sighs found out their way.
O myriads of immortal Spirits, O Powers
Matchless, but with th' Almighty, and that strife
Was not inglorious, though th' event was dire,
As this place testifies, and this dire change
Hateful to utter. But what power of mind
Foreseeing or presaging, from the depth

[108] the pigmies
[109] In Macedonia, where the wars between the giants and the gods took place.
[110] King Arthur
[111] Breton
[112] considering
[113] deep feeling

Of knowledge past or present, could have fear'd,
How such united force of gods, how such
As stood like these, could ever know repulse?
For who can yet beleeve, though after loss,
That all these puissant legions, whose exile
Hath emptied Heav'n, shall faile to re-ascend
Self-rais'd, and repossess their native seat?
For me, be witness all the host of Heav'n,
If counsels different, or danger shun'd
By me, have lost our hopes. But he who reigns
Monarch in Heav'n, till then as one secure
Sat on his throne, upheld by old repute,
Consent of custome, and his regal state
Put forth at full, but still his strength conceal'd,
Which tempted our attempt, and wrought our fall.
Henceforth his might we know, and know our own
So as not either to provoke, or dread
New warr, provok't; our better part remains
To work in close design, by fraud or guile
What force effected not: that he no less
At length from us may find, who overcomes
By force, hath overcome but half his foe.
Space may produce new worlds; whereof so rife
There went a fame in Heav'n that he ere long
Intended to create, and therein plant
A generation, whom his choice regard
Should favour equal to the Sons of Heaven.
Thither, if but to prie, shall be perhaps
Our first eruption, thither or elsewhere;
For this infernal pit shall never hold
Cælestial Spirits in bondage, nor th' Abysse
Long under darkness cover. But these thoughts
Full counsel must mature. Peace is despaird,
For who can think submission! Warr then, warr
Open or understood must be resolv'd.
He spake; and to confirm his words, outflew
Millions of flaming swords, drawn from the thighs
Of mighty Cherubim; the sudden blaze
Far round illumin'd Hell. Highly they rag'd
Against the Highest, and fierce with graspéd arms
Clash'd on their sounding shelds the din of war,
Hurling defiance toward the vault of Heav'n.
There stood a hill not far whose griesly top
Belch'd fire and rowling smoak; the rest entire
Shon with a glossie scurff, undoubted sign
That in his womb was hid metallic ore,
The work of sulphur.[114] Thither wing'd with speed
A numerous brigad hasten'd, as when bands
Of pioners with spade and pickaxe arm'd
Forerun the royal camp, to trench a field,
Or cast a rampart. Mammon led them on,
Mammon, the least erected Spirit that fell
From heav'n, for ev'n in heav'n his looks and thoughts
Were always downward bent, admiring more
The riches of Heav'ns pavement, trod'n gold,
Then aught divine or holy else enjoy'd
In vision beatific. By him first
Men also, and by his suggestion taught,
Ransack'd the Center,[115] and with impious hands
Rifl'd the bowels of their mother Earth
For treasures better hid. Soon had his crew
Op'nd into the hill a spacious wound
And dig'd out ribs of gold. Let none admire
That riches grow in Hell; that soyle may best

---

[114] Metals were once supposed to be compounded of sulphur and mercury.
[115] the earth

Deserve the pretious bane. And here let those
Who boast in mortal things, and wondring tell
Of Babel, and the works[116] of Memphian kings,
Learn how thir greatest monuments of fame,
And strength and art are easily outdone
By spirits reprobate, and in an hour
What in an age they with incessant toyle
And hands innumerable scarce perform.
Nigh on the plain in many cells prepar'd,
That underneath had veins of liquid fire
Sluc'd from the lake, a second multitude
With wondrous art founded the massie ore,
Severing each kinde, and scum'd the bullion dross;
A third as soon had form'd within the ground
A various mould, and from the boyling cells
By strange conveyance fill'd each hollow nook,
As in an organ from one blast of wind
To many a row of pipes the sound-board breaths.
Anon out of the earth a fabrick huge
Rose like an exhalation, with the sound
Of dulcet symphonies and voices sweet,
Built like a temple, where pilasters round
Were set, and Doric pillars overlaid
With golden architrave; nor did there want
Cornice or freeze, with bossy sculptures grav'n;
The roof was fretted gold. Not Babilon,
Nor great Alcairo such magnificence
Equal'd in all thir glories, to inshrine
Belus or Serapis thir gods, or seat
Thir kings, when Ægypt with Assyria strove
In wealth and luxurie. Th' ascending pile
Stood fixt her stately highth, and strait the dores
Op'ning thir brazen foulds discover wide
Within, her ample spaces o're the smooth
And level pavement: from the archéd roof
Pendant by suttle magic, many a row
Of starry lamps and blazing cressets fed
With naphtha and asphaltus yeilded light
As from a sky. The hasty multitude
Admiring enter'd, and the work some praise
And some the architect: his hand was known
In Heav'n by many a towred structure high,
Where scepter'd Angels held thir residence,
And sat as Princes, whom the supreme King
Exalted to such power, and gave to rule,
Each in his herarchie, the Orders[117] bright.
Nor was his name[118] unheard or unador'd
In ancient Greece; and in Ausonian[119] land
Men called him Mulciber; and how he fell
From Heav'n, they fabl'd, thrown by angry Jove
Sheer o're the chrystal battlements: from morn
To noon he fell, from noon to dewy eve,
A summers day; and with the setting sun
Dropt from the zenith like a falling star,
On Lemnos th' Ægæan ile. Thus they relate,
Erring; for he with his rebellious rout
Fell long before; nor aught avail'd him now
To have built in Heav'n high towrs; nor did he scape
By all his engins, but was headlong sent
With his industrious crew to build in hell.
Mean while the wingéd haralds by command
Of sovran power, with awful ceremony
And trumpets sound throughout the host proclaim
A solemn councel forthwith to be held
At Pandæmonium, the high capital
Of Satan and his Peers. Thir summons call'd

[116] the pyramids

[117] The Angels are divided into three Hierarchies, each consisting of three Orders.

[118] Vulcan

[119] Italian

From every band and squaréd regiment
By place or choice the worthiest; they anon
With hundreds and with thousands trooping came
Attended; all access was throng'd, the gates
And porches wide, but chief the spacious hall
(Though like a cover'd field, where champions bold
Wont ride in arm'd, and at the Soldans chair
Defi'd the best of Panim chivalry
To mortal combat or career with lance)
Thick swarm'd, both on the ground and in the air,
Brusht with the hiss of russling wings. As bees
In spring time, when the sun with Taurus rides,
Poure forth thir populous youth about the hive
In clusters; they among fresh dews and flowers
Flie to and fro, or on the smoothéd plank,
The suburb of thir straw-built cittadel,
New rub'd with baume, expatiate and confer
Thir state affairs. So thick the aerie crowd
Swarm'd and were straitn'd; till the signal giv'n,
Behold a wonder! They but now who seemd
In bigness to surpass Earths giant sons,
Now less then smallest dwarfs, in narrow room
Throng numberless, like that pigmean race
Beyond the Indian Mount, or faerie elves,
Whose midnight revels, by a forrest side
Or fountain, some belated peasant sees,
Or dreams he sees, while over head the moon
Sits arbitress, and neerer to the earth
Wheels her pale course, they on thir mirth and dance
Intent, with jocond music charm his ear;
At once with joy and fear his heart rebounds.
Thus incorporeal Spirits to smallest forms
Reduc'd thir shapes immense, and were at large,
Though without number still amidst the hall
Of that infernal court. But far within
And in thir own dimensions like themselves
The great Seraphic Lords and Cherubim
In close recess and secret conclave sat
A thousand demy-gods on golden seats,
Frequent and full. After short silence then
And summons read, the great consult began.

BOOK II

THE ARGUMENT

The consultation begun, Satan debates whether another battel be to be hazarded for the recovery of Heaven: some advise it, others dissuade. A third proposal is prefer'd, mention'd before by Satan, to search the truth of that prophesie or tradition in Heaven concerning another world, and another kind of creature equal or not much inferiour to themselves, about this time to be created. Thir doubt who shall be sent on this difficult search. Satan, thir chief, undertakes alone the voyage, is honourd and applauded. The councel thus ended, the rest betake them several wayes and to several imployments, as thir inclinations lead them, to entertain the time till Satan return. He passes on his journey to Hell gates, finds them shut, and who sat there to guard them, by whom at length they are op'nd, and discover to him the great gulf between Hell and Heaven; with what difficulty he passes through, directed by Chaos, the Power of that place, to the sight of this new World which he sought.

High on a throne of royal state, which far
Outshon the wealth of Ormus [120] and of Ind,
Or where the gorgeous East with richest hand
Showrs on her kings barbaric pearl and gold,
Satan exalted sat, by merit rais'd
To that bad eminence; and from despair
Thus high uplifted beyond hope, aspires
Beyond thus high, insatiate to pursue

[120] An island in the Persian gulf.

Vain warr with Heav'n, and by success [121] untaught
His proud imaginations thus displaid.
Powers and Dominions, Deities of Heav'n,
For since no deep within her gulf can hold
Immortal vigor, though opprest and fall'n,
I give not Heav'n for lost. From this descent
Celestial vertues rising, will appear
More glorious and more dread then from no fall,
And trust themselves to fear no second fate.
Mee though just right, and the fixt laws of Heav'n
Did first create your leader, next, free choice,
With what besides, in counsel or in fight
Hath bin achievd of merit, yet this loss
Thus farr at least recover'd, hath much more
Establisht in a safe unenvied throne
Yielded with full consent. The happier state
In Heav'n, which follows dignity, might draw
Envy from each inferior; but who here
Will envy whom the highest place exposes
Formost to stand against the Thunderers aime
Your bulwark, and condemns to greatest share
Of endless pain? Where there is then no good
For which to strive, no strife can grow up there
From faction; for none sure will claim in hell
Precedence, none, whose portion is so small
Of present pain, that with ambitious mind
Will covet more. With this advantage then
To union, and firm faith, and firm accord,
More then can be in Heav'n, we now return
To claim our just inheritance of old,
Surer to prosper then prosperity
Could have assur'd us; and by what best way,
Whether of open warr or covert guile,
We now debate; who can advise, may speak.
He ceas'd, and next him Moloc, scepter'd king
Stood up, the strongest and the fiercest Spirit
That fought in Heav'n; now fiercer by despair.
His trust was with th' Eternal to be deem'd
Equal in strength, and rather then be less
Car'd not to be at all; with that care lost
Went all his fear: of God, or Hell, or worse
He reckd not, and these words thereafter spake.
My sentence is for open warr. Of wiles,
More unexpert, I boast not: them let those
Contrive who need, or when they need, not now.
For while they sit contriving, shall the rest,
Millions that stand in arms, and longing wait
The signal to ascend, sit lingring here
Heav'ns fugitives, and for thir dwelling place
Accept this dark opprobrious den of shame,
The prison of his tyranny who reigns
By our delay? No, let us rather choose
Arm'd with Hell flames and fury all at once
O're Heav'ns high towrs to force resistless way,
Turning our tortures into horrid arms
Against the Torturer; when to meet the noise
Of his almighty engin he shall hear
Infernal thunder, and for lightning see
Black fire and horror shot with equal rage
Among his Angels; and his throne it self
Mixt with Tartarean sulphur, and strange fire,
His own invented torments. But perhaps
The way seems difficult and steep to scale
With upright wing against a higher foe.
Let such bethink them, if the sleepy drench

[121] experience

Of that forgetful lake benumme not still,
That in our proper [122] motion we ascend
Up to our native seat: descent and fall
To us is adverse. Who but felt of late
When the fierce foe hung on our brok'n rear
Insulting, and pursu'd us through the Deep,
With what compulsion and laborious flight
We sunk thus low? Th' ascent is easie then;
Th' event is fear'd; should we again provoke
Our stronger, some worse way his wrath may find
To our destruction, if there be in Hell
Fear to be worse destroy'd. What can be worse
Then to dwell here, driv'n out from bliss, condemn'd
In this abhorréd deep to utter woe;
Where pain of unextinguishable fire
Must exercise us without hope of end
The vassals of his anger, when the scourge
Inexorably, and the torturing houre
Calls us to penance? More destroy'd then thus
We should be quite abolisht and expire.
What fear we then? what doubt we to incense
His utmost ire? which to the highth enrag'd,
Will either quite consume us, and reduce
To nothing this essential,[123] happier farr
Then miserable to have eternal being:
Or if our substance be indeed divine,
And cannot cease to be, we are at worst
On this side nothing; and by proof we feel
Our power sufficient to disturb his Heav'n,
And with perpetual inrodes to allarme,
Though inaccessible, his fatal throne:
Which if not victory is yet revenge.
He ended frowning, and his look denounc'd [124]
Desperate revenge, and battel dangerous
To less then gods. On th' other side up rose
Belial, in act more graceful and humane;
A fairer person lost not Heav'n; he seemd
For dignity compos'd and high exploit:
But all was false and hollow; though his tongue
Dropt manna, and could make the worse appear
The better reason, to perplex and dash
Maturest counsels: for his thoughts were low;
To vice industrious, but to nobler deeds
Timorous and slothful: yet he pleas'd the eare,
And with perswasive accent thus began.
I should be much for open warr, O Peers,
As not behind in hate; if what was urg'd
Main reason to perswade immediate warr,
Did not disswade me most, and seem to cast
Ominous conjecture on the whole success;
When he who most excels in fact of arms,
In what he counsels and in what excels
Mistrustful, grounds his courage on despair
And utter dissolution, as the scope
Of all his aim, after some dire revenge.
First, what revenge? The towrs of Heav'n are fill'd
With arméd watch, that render all access
Impregnable; oft on the bordering Deep
Encamp thir legions, or with obscure wing
Scout farr and wide into the realm of night,
Scorning surprize. Or could we break our way
By force, and at our heels all Hell should rise
With blackest insurrection, to confound
Heav'ns purest light, yet our great Enemie,
All incorruptible, would on his throne
Sit unpolluted, and th' ethereal mould
Incapable of stain would soon expel
Her mischief, and purge off the baser fire
Victorious. Thus repuls'd, our final hope
Is flat despair; we must exasperate

---

[122] natural
[123] essence (adjective for noun)
[124] proclaimed

Th' Almighty Victor to spend all his rage,
And that must end us, that must be our cure,
To be no more; sad cure; for who would loose,
Though full of pain, this intellectual being,
Those thoughts that wander through Eternity,
To perish rather, swallowd up and lost
In the wide womb of uncreated night,
Devoid of sense and motion? And who knows,
Let this be good, whether our angry Foe
Can give it, or will ever? How he can
Is doubtful; that he never will is sure.
Will he, so wise, let loose at once his ire,
Belike through impotence, or unaware,
To give his enemies thir wish, and end
Them in his anger, whom his anger saves
To punish endless? Wherefore cease we then?
Say they who counsel warr, we are decreed,
Reserv'd and destin'd to eternal woe;
Whatever doing, what can we suffer more,
What can we suffer worse? Is this then worst,
Thus sitting, thus consulting, thus in arms?
What when we fled amain, pursu'd and strook
With Heav'ns afflicting thunder, and besought
The Deep to shelter us? This Hell then seem'd
A refuge from those wounds: or when we lay
Chain'd on the burning lake? That sure was worse.
What if the breath that kindl'd those grim fires
Awak'd should blow them into sevenfold rage
And plunge us in the flames? Or from above
Should intermitted vengeance arme again
His red right hand to plague us? What if all
Her stores were op'n'd, and this firmament
Of Hell should spout her cataracts of fire,
Impendent horrors, threatning hideous fall
One day upon our heads; while we perhaps
Designing or exhorting glorious warr,
Caught in a fierie tempest shall be hurl'd
Each on his rock transfixt, the sport and prey
Of racking whirlwinds, or for ever sunk
Under yon boyling ocean, wrapt in chains,
There to converse with everlasting groans,
Unrespited, unpitied, unrepreevd,
Ages of hopeless end; this would be worse.
Warr therefore, open or conceal'd, alike
My voice disswades; for what can force or guile
With him, or who deceive his mind, whose eye
Views all things at one view? He from Heav'ns highth
All these our motions vain, sees and derides;
Not more almighty to resist our might
Then wise to frustrate all our plots and wiles.
Shall we then live thus vile, the race of Heav'n
Thus trampl'd, thus expell'd to suffer here
Chains and these torments? Better these then worse
By my advice; since fate inevitable
Subdues us, and omnipotent decree
The Victors will. To suffer, as to doe,
Our strength is equal, nor the law unjust
That so ordains: this was at first resolv'd,
If we were wise, against so great a foe
Contending, and so doubtful what might fall.
I laugh, when those who at the spear are bold
And vent'rous, if that fail them, shrink and fear
What yet they know must follow, to endure
Exile, or ignominy, or bonds, or pain,
The sentence of thir Conquerour. This is now
Our doom; which if we can sustain and bear,

Our Supream Foe in time may much remit
His anger, and perhaps thus farr remov'd,
Not mind us not offending, satisfi'd
With what is punish't; whence these raging fires
Will slack'n, if his breath stir not thir flames.
Our purer essence then will overcome
Thir noxious vapour, or enur'd not feel,
Or chang'd at length, and to the place conformd
In temper and in nature, will receive
Familiar the fierce heat, and void of pain;
This horror will grow milde, this darkness light,
Besides what hope the never-ending flight
Of future days may bring, what chance, what change
Worth waiting, since our present lot appeers
For happy though but ill, for ill not worst,
If we procure not to our selves more woe.

Thus Belial, with words cloath'd in reasons garb,
Counsel'd ignoble ease, and peaceful sloath,
Not peace; and after him thus Mammon spake.

Either to disinthrone the King of Heav'n
We warr, if warr be best, or to regain
Our own right lost. Him to unthrone we then
May hope, when everlasting Fate shall yeild
To fickle Chance, and Chaos judge the strife.
The former vain to hope argues as vain
The latter; for what place can be for us
Within Heav'ns bound, unless Heav'ns Lord supream
We overpower? Suppose he should relent
And publish grace to all, on promise made
Of new subjection; with what eyes could we
Stand in his presence humble, and receive
Strict laws impos'd, to celebrate his throne
With warbl'd hymns, and to his Godhead sing
Forc't Halleluiahs, while he lordly sits
Our envied sovran, and his altar breathes
Ambrosial odours and ambrosial flowers,
Our servile offerings? This must be our task
In Heav'n, this our delight; how wearisom
Eternity so spent in worship paid
To whom we hate. Let us not then pursue
By force impossible, by leave obtain'd
Unacceptable, though in Heav'n, our state
Of splendid vassalage, but rather seek
Our own good from our selves, and from our own
Live to our selves, though in this vast recess,
Free, and to none accountable, preferring
Hard liberty before the easie yoke
Of servile pomp. Our greatness will appear
Then most conspicuous, when great things of small,
Useful of hurtful, prosperous of adverse
We can create, and in what place so e're
Thrive under evil, and work ease out of pain
Through labour and endurance. This deep world
Of darkness do we dread? How oft amidst
Thick clouds and dark doth Heav'ns all-ruling Sire
Choose to reside, his glory unobscur'd,
And with the majesty of darkness round
Covers his throne; from whence deep thunders roar
Must'ring thir rage, and Heav'n resembles Hell!
As he our darkness, cannot we his light
Imitate when we please? This desart soile
Wants not her hidden lustre, gemms and gold;
Nor want we skill or art, from whence to raise
Magnificence; and what can Heav'n shew more?
Our torments also may in length of time
Become our elements, these piercing fires
As soft as now severe, our temper chang'd

Into their temper; which must needs remove
The sensible [125] of pain. All things invite
To peaceful counsels, and the settl'd state
Of order, how in safety best we may
Compose our present evils, with regard
Of what we are and where, dismissing quite
All thoughts of warr; ye have what I advise.
He scarce had finisht, when such murmur filld
Th' assembly, as when hollow rocks retain
The sound of blustring winds, which all night long
Had rous'd the sea, now with hoarse cadence lull
Sea-faring men orewatcht, whose bark by chance
Or pinnace anchors in a craggy bay
After the tempest. Such applause was heard
As Mammon ended, and his sentence pleas'd,
Advising peace: for such another field
They dreaded worse then Hell; so much the fear
Of thunder and the sword of Michael
Wrought still within them; and no less desire
To found this nether empire, which might rise
By pollicy, and long process of time,
In emulation opposite to Heav'n.
Which when Beëlzebub perceiv'd, then whom,
Satan except, none higher sat, with grave
Aspect he rose, and in his rising seem'd
A pillar of state; deep on his front engraven
Deliberation sat and publick care;
And princely counsel in his face yet shon,
Majestick though in ruin. Sage he stood
With Atlantean shoulders fit to bear
The weight of mightiest monarchies; his look
Drew audience and attention still as night
Or summers noon-tide air, while thus he spake.
Thrones and imperial Powers, off-spring of Heav'n,
Ethereal Vertues; or these titles now
Must we renounce, and changing stile be call'd
Princes of Hell? for so the popular vote
Inclines, here to continue, and build up here
A growing empire. Doubtless. While we dream,
And know not that the King of Heav'n hath doom'd
This place our dungeon, not our safe retreat
Beyond his potent arm, to live exempt
From Heav'ns high jurisdiction, in new league
Banded against his throne, but to remaine
In strictest bondage, though thus far remov'd,
Under th' inevitable curb, reserv'd
His captive multitude. For he, be sure,
In highth or depth, still first and last will reign
Sole king, and of his kingdom loose no part
By our revolt, but over Hell extend
His empire, and with iron scepter rule
Us here, as with his golden those in Heav'n.
What sit we then projecting peace and warr?
Warr hath determin'd us, and foild with loss
Irreparable; tearms of peace yet none
Voutsaf't or sought; for what peace will be giv'n
To us enslav'd, but custody severe,
And stripes, and arbitrary punishment
Inflicted? And what peace can we return,
But, to our power, hostility and hate,
Untam'd reluctance, and revenge though slow,
Yet ever plotting how the Conquerour least
May reap his conquest, and may least rejoyce

[125] sense

In doing what we most in suffering feel?
Nor will occasion want, nor shall we need
With dangerous expedition to invade
Heav'n, whose high walls fear no assault or siege,
Or ambush from the Deep. What if we find
Some easier enterprize? There is a place
(If ancient and prophetic fame in Heav'n
Err not) another World, the happy seat
Of som new race call'd Man, about this time
To be created like to us, though less
In power and excellence, but favour'd more
Of him who rules above; so was his will
Pronounc'd among the gods, and by an oath,
That shook Heav'ns whol circumference, confirm'd.
Thither let us bend all our thoughts, to learn
What creatures there inhabit, of what mould,
Or substance, how endu'd, and what thir power,
And where thir weakness, how attempted best,
By force or suttlety. Though Heav'n be shut,
And Heav'ns high Arbitrator sit secure
In his own strength, this place may lye expos'd
The utmost border of his kingdom, left
To their defence who hold it: here perhaps
Som advantagious act may be achiev'd
By sudden onset, either with Hell fire
To waste his whole Creation, or possess
All as our own, and drive as we were driven,
The punie habitants; or if not drive,
Seduce them to our party, that thir God
May prove thir foe, and with repenting hand
Abolish his own works. This would surpass
Common revenge, and interrupt his joy
In our confusion, and our joy upraise
In his disturbance; when his darling sons
Hurl'd headlong to partake with us, shall curse
Thir frail originals,[126] and faded bliss,
Faded so soon. Advise if this be worth
Attempting, or to sit in darkness here
Hatching vain empires. Thus Beëlzebub
Pleaded his devilish counsel, first devis'd
By Satan, and in part propos'd: for whence,
But from the author of all ill could spring
So deep a malice, to confound the race
Of mankind in one root, and Earth with Hell
To mingle and involve, done all to spite
The great Creatour? But thir spite still serves
His glory to augment. The bold design
Pleas'd highly those infernal States, and joy
Sparkl'd in all thir eyes; with full assent
They vote: whereat his speech he thus renews.
Well have ye judg'd, well ended long debate,
Synod of gods, and like to what ye are,
Great things resolv'd; which from the lowest deep
Will once more lift us up, in spight of Fate,
Neerer our ancient seat; perhaps in view
Of those bright confines, whence, with neighbouring arms
And opportune excursion, we may chance
Re-enter Heav'n; or else in some milde zone
Dwell not unvisited of Heav'ns fair light
Secure, and at the brightning orient beam
Purge off this gloom; the soft delicious air,
To heal the scarr of these corrosive fires,
Shall breath her balme. But first whom shall we send
In search of this new world, whom shall we find
Sufficient? Who shall tempt with wandring feet
The dark unbottom'd infinite Abyss
And through the palpable obscure find out

[126] parents, *i.e.*, Adam and Eve

His uncouth way, or spread his aerie flight
Upborn with indefatigable wings
Over the vast abrupt, ere he arrive
The happy ile; what strength, what art can then
Suffice, or what evasion bear him safe
Through the strict senteries and stations thick
Of Angels watching round? Here he had need
All circumspection, and wee now no less
Choice in our suffrage; for on whom we send,
The weight of all and our last hope relies.
  This said, he sat; and expectation held
His look suspence, awaiting who appeer'd
To second, or oppose, or undertake
The perilous attempt. But all sat mute,
Pondering the danger with deep thoughts; and each
In others count'nance red his own dismay
Astonisht: none among the choice and prime
Of those Heav'n-warring champions could be found
So hardie as to proffer or accept
Alone the dreadful voyage; till at last
Satan, whom now transcendent glory rais'd
Above his fellows, with monarchal pride
Conscious of highest worth, unmov'd thus spake.
  O Progeny of Heav'n, Empyreal Thrones,
With reason hath deep silence and demurr
Seis'd us, though undismaid. Long is the way
And hard, that out of Hell leads up to light;
Our prison strong, this huge convex of fire,
Outrageous to devour, immures us round
Ninefold, and gates of burning adamant
Barr'd over us prohibit all egress.
These past, if any pass, the void profound
Of unessential [127] Night receives him next
Wide gaping, and with utter loss of being
Threatens him, plung'd in that abortive gulf.
If thence he scape into what ever world,
Or unknown region, what remains him less
Then [128] unknown dangers and as hard escape?
But I should ill become this throne, O Peers,
And this imperial sov'ranty, adorn'd
With splendor, arm'd with power, if aught propos'd
And judg'd of public moment, in the shape
Of difficulty or danger, could deterre
Me from attempting. Wherefore do I assume
These royalties, and not refuse to reign,
Refusing to accept as great a share
Of hazard as of honour, due alike
To him who reigns, and so much to him due
Of hazard more, as he above the rest
High honourd sits? Go therfore mighty Powers,
Terror of Heav'n, though fall'n; intend [129] at home,
While here shall be our home, what best may ease
The present misery, and render Hell
More tollerable; if there be cure or charm
To respite or deceive, or slack the pain
Of this ill mansion: intermit no watch
Against a wakeful foe, while I abroad
Through all the coasts of dark destruction seek
Deliverance for us all. This enterprize
None shall partake with me. Thus saying rose
The Monarch, and prevented all reply,
Prudent, least from his resolution rais'd
Others among the chief might offer now
(Certain to be refus'd) what erst they feard;
And so refus'd might in opinion stand
His rivals, winning cheap the high repute
Which he through hazard huge must earn. But they

127 without essence or being

128 than

129 consider

Dreaded not more th' adventure then his voice
Forbidding; and at once with him they rose;
Thir rising all at once was as the sound
Of thunder heard remote. Towards him they bend
With awful reverence prone; and as a god
Extoll him equal to the highest in Heav'n.
Nor fail'd they to express how much they prais'd,
That for the general safety he despis'd
His own: for neither do the Spirits damn'd
Loose all thir vertue; least bad men should boast
Thir specious deeds on earth, which glory excites,
Or close ambition varnisht o're with zeal.
Thus they thir doubtful consultations dark
Ended, rejoycing in thir matchless Chief:
As when from mountain tops the dusky clouds
Ascending, while the north wind sleeps, o'respread
Heavn's chearful face, the lowring element
Scowls ore the dark'nd lantskip snow, or showre;
If chance the radiant sun with farewell sweet
Extend his ev'ning beam, the fields revive,
The birds thir notes renew, and bleating herds
Attest thir joy, that hill and valley rings.
O shame to men! Devil with devil damn'd
Firm concord holds; men onely disagree
Of creatures rational, though under hope
Of heavenly grace; and God proclaiming peace,
Yet live in hatred, enmitie, and strife
Among themselves, and levie cruel warres,
Wasting the Earth, each other to destroy:
As if (which might induce us to accord)
Man had not hellish foes anow besides,
That day and night for his destruction waite.

The Stygian councel thus dissolv'd; and forth
In order came the grand infernal Peers;
Midst came thir mighty Paramount, and seemd
Alone th' Antagonist of Heav'n, nor less
Then Hells dread Emperour with pomp supream,
And god-like imitated state; him round
A globe of fierie Seraphim inclos'd
With bright imblazonrie, and horrent[130] arms.
Then of thir session ended, they bid cry
With trumpets regal sound the great result:
Toward the four winds four speedy Cherubim
Put to thir mouths the sounding alchymie[131]
By haralds voice explain'd: the hollow Abyss
Heard farr and wide, and all the host of Hell
With deafning shout, return'd them loud acclaim.
Thence more at ease thir minds and somwhat rais'd
By false presumptuous hope, the rangéd powers
Disband, and wandring, each his several way
Pursues, as inclination or sad choice
Leads him perplext, where he may likeliest find
Truce to his restless thoughts, and entertain
The irksome hours, till his great Chief return.
Part on the plain, or in the air sublime
Upon the wing, or in swift race contend,
As at th' Olympian Games or Pythian fields;
Part curb thir fierie steeds, or shun the goal
With rapid wheels, or fronted brigads form.
As when to warn proud cities, warr appears
Wag'd in the troubl'd skie, and armies rush

[130] bristling
[131] Trumpets of 'alchemy gold,' *i.e.*, brass.

To battel in the clouds; before each van
Pric forth the aerie knights, and couch thir spears
Till thickest legions close; with feats of arms
From either end of Heav'n the welkin burns.
Others with vast Typhœan[132] rage more fell,
Rend up both rocks and hills, and ride the air
In whirlwind; Hell scarce holds the wilde uproar.
As when Alcides[133] from Oealia crown'd
With conquest, felt th' envenom'd robe, and tore
Through pain up by the roots Thessalian pines,
And Lichas from the top of Oeta threw
Into th' Euboic Sea. Others more milde,
Retreated in a silent valley, sing
With notes angelical to many a harp
Thir own heroic deeds and hapless fall
By doom of battel; and complain that Fate
Free Vertue should enthrall to Force or Chance.
Thir song was partial, but the harmony
(What could it less when Spirits immortal sing?)
Suspended Hell, and took with ravishment
The thronging audience. In discourse more sweet
(For eloquence the soul, song charms the sense,)
Others apart sat on a hill retir'd,
In thoughts more elevate, and reason'd high
Of Providence, Foreknowledge, Will, and Fate,
Fixt fate, free will, foreknowledge absolute,
And found no end, in wandring mazes lost.
Of good and evil much they argu'd then,
Of happiness and final misery,
Passion and apathie, and glory and shame,
Vain wisdom all, and false philosophie:
Yet with a pleasing sorcerie could charm
Pain for a while or anguish, and excite
Fallacious hope, or arm th' obduréd brest
With stubborn patience as with triple steel.
Another part in squadrons and gross bands
On bold adventure to discover wide
That dismal World, if any clime perhaps
Might yeild them easier habitation, bend
Four ways thir flying march, along the banks
Of four infernal rivers that disgorge
Into the burning lake thir baleful streams;
Abhorréd Styx, the flood of deadly hate,
Sad Acheron of sorrow, black and deep;
Cocytus, nam'd of lamentation loud
Heard on the ruful stream; fierce Phlegeton
Whose waves of torrent fire inflame with rage.
Farr off from these a slow and silent stream,
Lethe, the river of oblivion, roules
Her watrie labyrinth, whereof who drinks,
Forthwith his former state and being forgets,
Forgets both joy and grief, pleasure and pain.
Beyond this flood a frozen continent
Lies dark and wilde, beat with perpetual storms
Of whirlwind and dire hail, which on firm land
Thaws not, but gathers heap, and ruin seems
Of ancient pile; all else deep snow and ice,
A gulf profound as that Serbonian Bog
Betwixt Damiata and mount Casius old,
Where armies whole have sunk: the parching air
Burns frore, and cold performs th' effect of fire.
Thither by harpy-footed furies hail'd,
At certain revolutions all the damn'd
Are brought; and feel by turns the bitter change
Of fierce extreams, extreams by change more fierce,

[132] Like Typhon in the war with Jove.
[133] Hercules. His wife obtained from Nessus a poisoned shirt which was brought to Hercules by Lichas.

From beds of raging fire to starve in ice
Thir soft ethereal warmth, and there to pine
Immovable, infixt, and frozen round,
Periods of time, thence hurried back to fire.
They ferry over this Lethean sound
Both to and fro, thir sorrow to augment,
And wish and struggle, as they pass, to reach
The tempting stream, with one small drop to loose
In sweet forgetfulness all pain and woe,
All in one moment, and so neer the brink;
But Fate withstands, and to oppose th' attempt
Medusa with Gorgonian terror guards
The ford, and of it self the water flies
All taste of living wight, as once it fled
The lip of Tantalus. Thus roving on
In confus'd march forlorn, th' adventrous bands
With shuddring horror pale, and eyes agast,
View'd first thir lamentable lot, and found
No rest. Through many a dark and drearie vaile
They pass'd, and many a region dolorous,
O're many a frozen, many a fierie Alpe,
Rocks, caves, lakes, fens, bogs, dens, and shades of death,
A universe of death, which God by curse
Created evil, for evil only good,
Where all life dies, death lives, and nature breeds,
Perverse, all monstrous, all prodigious things,
Abominable, inutterable, and worse
Then fables yet have feign'd, or fear conceiv'd,
Gorgons and Hydras, and Chimeras dire.
Mean while the Adversary of God and Man,
Satan with thoughts inflam'd of highest design,
Puts on swift wings, and toward the gates of Hell
Explores his solitary flight; som times
He scours the right hand coast, som times the left,
Now shaves with level wing the Deep, then soares
Up to the fiery concave touring high.
As when farr off at sea a fleet descri'd
Hangs in the clouds, by æquinoctial winds
Close sailing from Bengala, or the Iles
Of Ternate and Tidore, [134] whence merchants bring
Thir spicie drugs: they on the trading flood
Through the wide Ethiopian [135] to the Cape
Ply stemming nightly toward the pole. So seem'd
Farr off the flying Fiend. At last appeer
Hell bounds high reaching to the horrid roof,
And thrice threefold the gates; three folds were brass,
Three iron, three of adamantine rock,
Impenitrable, impal'd with circling fire,
Yet unconsum'd. Before the gates there sat
On either side a formidable shape;
The one seem'd woman to the waste, and fair,
But ended foul in many a scaly fould
Voluminous and vast, a serpent arm'd
With mortal sting. About her middle round
A cry of Hell hounds never ceasing bark'd
With wide Cerberean mouths full loud, and rung
A hideous peal; yet, when they list, would creep,
If aught disturb'd thir noyse, into her woomb,
And kennel there, yet there still bark'd and howl'd
Within unseen. Farr less abhorrd then these
Vex'd Scylla bathing in the sea that parts
Calabria from the hoarce Trinacrian shore:
Nor uglier follow the night-hag, when call'd
In secret, riding through the air she comes

[134] Two of the Spice Islands in the Malay Archipelago
[135] Indian Ocean

Lur'd with the smell of infant blood, to dance
With Lapland[136] witches, while the labouring moon
Eclipses at thir charms. The other shape,
If shape it might be call'd that shape had none
Distinguishable in member, joynt, or limb,
Or substance might be call'd that shadow seem'd,
For each seem'd either; black it stood as night,
Fierce as ten furies, terrible as Hell,
And shook a dreadful dart; what seem'd his head
The likeness of a kingly crown had on.
Satan was now at hand, and from his seat
The monster moving onward came as fast,
With horrid strides; Hell trembled as he strode.
Th' undaunted Fiend what this might be admir'd,[137]
Admir'd, not fear'd; God and his Son except,
Created thing naught vallu'd he nor shun'd;
And with disdainful look thus first began.
  Whence and what art thou, execrable shape,
That dar'st, though grim and terrible, advance
Thy miscreated front athwart my way
To yonder gates? Through them I mean to pass,
That be assured, without leave askt of thee:
Retire, or taste thy folly, and learn by proof,
Hell-born, not to contend with Spirits of Heav'n.
  To whom the Goblin[138] full of wrauth reply'd,
Art thou that Traitor Angel, art thou hee,
Who first broke peace in Heav'n and faith, till then
Unbrok'n, and in proud rebellious arms
Drew after him the third part of Heav'ns sons
Conjur'd against the highest, for which both thou
And they outcast from God, are here condemn'd
To waste eternal daies in woe and pain?
And reck'n'st thou thy self with Spirits of Heav'n,
Hell-doomd, and breath'st defiance here and scorn,
Where I reign king, and to enrage thee more,
Thy king and lord? Back to thy punishment,
False fugitive, and to thy speed add wings,
Least with a whip of scorpions I pursue
Thy lingring, or with one stroke of this dart
Strange horror seise thee, and pangs unfelt before.
  So spake the grieslie terrour, and in shape,
So speaking and so threatning, grew ten fold
More dreadful and deform: on th' other side
Incenc't with indignation Satan stood
Unterrifi'd, and like a comet burn'd,
That fires the length of Ophiucus[139] huge
In th' Artick sky, and from his horrid hair
Shakes pestilence and warr. Each at the head
Level'd his deadly aime; thir fatall hands
No second stroke intend, and such a frown
Each cast at th' other, as when two black clouds
With Heav'ns artillery fraught, come rattling on
Over the Caspian, then stand front to front
Hov'ring a space, till winds the signal blow
To joyn thir dark encounter in mid air.
So frownd the mighty combatants, that Hell

---

[136] A favorite meeting place of witches.
[137] wondered
[138] demon
[139] A constellation of the northern hemisphere.

Grew darker at thir frown, so matcht they stood;
For never but once more was either like
To meet so great a foe:[140] and now great deeds
Had been achiev'd, whereof all Hell had rung,
Had not the snakie Sorceress that sat
Fast by Hell gate, and kept the fatal key,
Ris'n, and with hideous outcry rush'd between.
O father, what intends thy hand, she cry'd,
Against thy only son? What fury, O son,
Possesses thee to bend that mortal dart
Against thy fathers head? And know'st for whom;
For him who sits above and laughs the while
At thee ordain'd his drudge, to execute
What e're his wrath, which he calls justice, bids,
His wrath which one day will destroy ye both.
She spake, and at her words the hellish Pest
Forbore, then these to her Satan return'd:
So strange thy outcry, and thy words so strange
Thou interposest, that my sudden hand
Prevented, spares to tell thee yet by deeds
What it intends; till first I know of thee,
What thing thou art, thus double-form'd, and why
In this infernal vaile first met thou call'st
Me father, and that fantasm call'st my son.
I know thee not, nor ever saw till now
Sight more detestable then him and thee.
T' whom thus the Portress of Hell gate reply'd;
Hast thou forgot me then, and do I seem
Now in thine eye so foul, once deemd so fair
In Heav'n, when at th' assembly, and in sight
Of all the Seraphim with thee combin'd
In bold conspiracy against Heav'ns King,
All on a sudden miserable pain
Surpris'd thee, dim thine eyes, and dizzie swumm
In darkness, while thy head flames thick and fast
Threw forth, till on the left side op'ning wide,
Likest to thee in shape and count'nance bright,
Then shining heav'nly fair, a goddess arm'd
Out of thy head I sprung. Amazement seis'd
All th' Host of Heav'n. Back they recoild affraid
At first, and call'd me Sin, and for a sign
Portentous held me; but familiar grown,
I pleas'd, and with attractive graces won
The most averse, thee chiefly, who full oft
Thy self in me thy perfect image viewing
Becam'st enamour'd, and such joy thou took'st
With me in secret, that my womb conceiv'd
A growing burden. Mean while warr arose,
And fields were fought in Heav'n; wherein remaind
(For what could else) to our Almighty Foe
Cleer victory, to our part loss and rout
Through all the Empyrean. Down they fell
Driv'n headlong from the pitch of Heaven, down
Into this Deep, and in the general fall
I also; at which time this powerful key
Into my hand was giv'n, with charge to keep
These gates for ever shut, which none can pass
Without my op'ning. Pensive here I sat
Alone; but long I sat not, till my womb
Pregnant by thee, and now excessive grown
Prodigious motion felt and rueful throes.

140 *i.e.*, Christ

At last this odious offspring whom thou seest
Thine own begotten, breaking violent way
Tore through my entrails, that with fear and pain
Distorted, all my nether shape thus grew
Transform'd: but he my inbred enemie
Forth issu'd, brandishing his fatal dart
Made to destroy. I fled, and cry'd out Death;
Hell trembl'd at the hideous name, and sigh'd
From all her caves, and back resounded Death.
I fled, but he pursu'd (though more, it seems,
Inflam'd with lust then rage) and swifter far,
Me overtook, his mother all dismaid,
And in embraces forcible and foule
Ingendring with me, of that rape begot
These yelling monsters that with ceasless cry
Surround me, as thou sawst, hourly conceiv'd
And hourly born, with sorrow infinite
To me; for when they list, into the womb
That bred them they return, and howle and gnaw
My bowels, their repast; then bursting forth
Afresh with conscious terrours vex me round,
That rest or intermission none I find.
Before mine eyes in opposition sits
Grim Death, my son and foe, who sets them on,
And me, his parent, would full soon devour
For want of other prey, but that he knows
His end with mine involvd; and knows that I
Should prove a bitter morsel, and his bane,
When ever that shall be; so Fate pronounc'd.
But thou, O father, I forewarn thee, shun
His deadly arrow; neither vainly hope
To be invulnerable in those bright arms,
Though temper'd heav'nly, for that mortal dint,
Save he who reigns above, none can resist.
She finish'd, and the suttle Fiend his lore
Soon learnd, now milder, and thus answerd smooth.
Dear daughter, since thou claim'st me for thy sire,
And my fair son here showst me, the dear pledge
Of dalliance had with thee in Heav'n, and joys
Then sweet, now sad to mention, through dire change
Befalln us unforeseen, unthought of, know
I come no enemie, but to set free
From out this dark and dismal house of pain,
Both him and thee, and all the heav'nly Host
Of Spirits that in our just pretenses arm'd
Fell with us from on high: from them I go
This uncouth [141] errand sole, and one for all
My self expose, with lonely steps to tread
Th' unfounded Deep, and through the void immense
To search with wandring quest a place foretold
Should be, and, by concurring signs, ere now
Created vast and round, a place of bliss
In the pourlieues of Heav'n, and therein plac't
A race of upstart creatures, to supply
Perhaps our vacant room, though more remov'd,
Least Heav'n surcharg'd with potent multitude
Might hap to move new broiles. Be this or aught
Then this more secret, now design'd, I haste
To know, and this once known, shall soon return,

[141] unknown

And bring ye to the place where thou and Death
Shall dwell at ease, and up and down unseen
Wing silently the buxom [142] air, imbalm'd
With odours. There ye shall be fed and fill'd
Immeasurably; all things shall be your prey.
He ceas'd, for both seemd highly pleasd, and Death
Grinnd horrible a gastly smile, to hear
His famine should be fill'd, and blest his mawe
Destin'd to that good hour: no less rejoyc'd
His mother bad, and thus bespake her sire.
  The key of this infernal Pit by due,
And by command of Heav'ns all-powerful King
I keep, by him forbidden to unlock
These adamantine gates; against all force
Death ready stands to interpose his dart,
Fearless to be o'rematcht by living might.
But what ow I to his commands above
Who hates me, and hath hither thrust me down
Into this gloom of Tartarus profound,
To sit in hateful office here confin'd,
Inhabitant of Heav'n, and heav'nlie-born,
Here in perpetual agonie and pain,
With terrors and with clamors compasst round
Of mine own brood, that on my bowels feed?
Thou art my father, thou my author, thou
My being gav'st me; whom should I obey
But thee, whom follow? Thou wilt bring me soon
To that new world of light and bliss, among
The gods who live at ease, where I shall reign
At thy right hand voluptuous, as beseems
Thy daughter and thy darling, without end
  Thus saying, from her side the fatal key,
Sad instrument of all our woe, she took;

[142] yielding

And towards the gate rouling her bestial train,
Forthwith the huge portcullis high up drew,
Which but her self not all the Stygian powers
Could once have mov'd; then in the key-hole turns
Th' intricate wards, and every bolt and bar
Of massie iron or sollid rock with ease
Unfast'ns. On a sudden op'n flie
With impetuous recoile and jarring sound
Th' infernal dores, and on thir hinges grate
Harsh thunder, that the lowest bottom shook
Of Erebus. She op'nd, but to shut
Excel'd her power; the gates wide op'n stood,
That with extended wings a bannerd host
Under spread ensigns marching might pass through
With horse and chariots rankt in loose array;
So wide they stood, and like a furnace mouth
Cast forth redounding [143] smoak and ruddy flame.
Before thir eyes in sudden view appear
The secrets of the hoarie deep, a dark
Illimitable ocean without bound,
Without dimension, where length, breadth, and highth,
And time and place are lost; where eldest Night
And Chaos, ancestors of Nature, hold
Eternal anarchie, amidst the noise
Of endless warrs, and by confusion stand.
For hot, cold, moist, and dry, four champions fierce
Strive here for maistrie, and to battel bring
Thir embryon atoms; they around the flag
Of each his faction, in thir several clanns,
Light-arm'd or heavy, sharp, smooth, swift or slow,

[143] rolling in clouds

Swarm populous, unnumber'd as the sands
Of Barca or Cyrene's [144] torrid soil,
Levied to side with warring winds, and poise
Thir lighter wings. To whom these most adhere,
Hee rules a moment; Chaos umpire sits,
And by decision more imbroiles the fray
By which he reigns: next him high arbiter
Chance governs all. Into this wilde Abyss,
The womb of Nature and perhaps her grave,
Of neither sea, nor shore, nor air, nor fire,
But all these in thir pregnant causes mixt
Confus'dly, and which thus must ever fight,
Unless th' Almighty Maker them ordain
His dark materials to create more worlds,
Into this wild Abyss the warie Fiend
Stood on the brink of Hell and look'd a while,
Pondering his voyage: for no narrow frith
He had to cross. Nor was his eare less peal'd
With noises loud and ruinous (to compare
Great things with small) then when Bellona [145] storms,
With all her battering engines bent to rase
Som capital city, or less then if this frame
Of Heav'n were falling, and these elements
In mutinie had from her axle torn
The stedfast Earth. At last his sail-broad vannes [146]
He spreads for flight, and in the surging smoak
Uplifted spurns the ground; thence many a league
As in a cloudy chair ascending rides
Audacious, but that seat soon failing, meets
A vast vacuitie: all unawares
Fluttring his pennons vain plumb down he drops
Ten thousand fadom deep, and to this hour
Down had been falling, had not by ill chance
The strong rebuff of som tumultuous cloud
Instinct with fire and nitre hurried him
As many miles aloft: that furie stay'd,
Quencht in a boggie Syrtis,[147] neither sea,
Nor good dry land: nigh founderd on he fares,
Treading the crude consistence, half on foot,
Half flying; behoves him now both oare and saile.
As when a gryfon through the wilderness
With wingéd course ore hill or moarie dale,
Pursues the Arimaspian [148] who by stelth
Had from his wakeful custody purloind
The guarded gold. So eagerly the fiend
Ore bog or steep, through strait, rough, dense, or rare,
With head, hands, wings, or feet pursues his way,
And swims or sinks, or wades, or creeps, or flyes.
At length a universal hubbub wilde
Of stunning sounds and voices all confus'd
Born through the hollow dark, assaults his eare
With loudest vehemence. Thither he plyes,
Undaunted to meet there what ever power
Or spirit of the nethermost Abyss
Might in that noise reside, of whom to ask
Which way the neerest coast of darkness lyes
Bordering on light; when strait behold the throne
Of Chaos, and his dark pavilion spread
Wide on the wasteful Deep; with him enthron'd
Sat sable-vested Night, eldest of things,
The consort of his reign; and by them stood
Orcus and Ades, and the dreaded name
Of Demogorgon; Rumor next and Chance,

[144] Cities in northern Africa.
[145] goddess of war
[146] wings

[147] Quicksands of the north coast of Africa.
[148] The one-eyed Arimaspi, living near the North Pole, were wont to steal gold from the gryphons whose particular business it was to guard it.

And Tumult and Confusion all imbroild,
And Discord with a thousand various mouths.
T' whom Satan turning boldly, thus. Ye Powers
And Spirits of this nethermost Abyss,
Chaos and ancient Night, I come no spie,
With purpose to explore or to disturb
The secrets of your realm, but by constraint
Wandring this darksome desart, as my way
Lies through your spacious empire up to light,
Alone, and without guide, half lost, I seek
What readiest path leads where your gloomie bounds
Confine with Heav'n; or if som other place
From your dominion won, th' Ethereal King
Possesses lately, thither to arrive
I travel this profound. Direct my course;
Directed, no mean recompence it brings
To your behoof, if I that region lost,
All usurpation thence expell'd, reduce
To her original darkness and your sway
(Which is my present journey) and once more
Erect the standerd there of ancient Night;
Yours be th' advantage all, mine the revenge.
Thus Satan; and him thus the Anarch old
With faultring speech and visage incompos'd
Answer'd. I know thee, stranger, who thou art,
That mighty leading Angel, who of late
Made head against Heav'ns King, though overthrown.
I saw and heard, for such a numerous host
Fled not in silence through the frighted deep
With ruin upon ruin, rout on rout,
Confusion worse confounded; and Heav'n gates
Pourd out by millions her victorious bands
Pursuing. I upon my frontieres here
Keep residence; if all I can will serve,
That little which is left so to defend
Encroacht on still through our intestine broiles
Weakning the scepter of old Night: first Hell
Your dungeon stretching far and wide beneath;
Now lately Heaven and Earth, another World
Hung ore my realm, link'd in a golden chain
To that side Heav'n from whence your legions fell.
If that way be your walk, you have not farr;
So much the neerer danger; goe and speed;
Havock and spoil and ruin are my gain.
He ceas'd; and Satan staid not to reply,
But glad that now his sea should find a shore,
With fresh alacritie and force renew'd
Springs upward like a pyramid of fire
Into the wilde expanse, and through the shock
Of fighting elements, on all sides round
Environ'd wins his way; harder beset
And more endanger'd, then when Argo [149] pass'd
Through Bosporus betwixt the justling rocks:
Or when Ulysses on the larbord shunnd
Charybdis, and by th' other whirlpool steard.
So he with difficulty and labour hard
Mov'd on, with difficulty and labour hee;
But hee once past, soon after when man fell,
(Strange alteration!) Sin and Death amain
Following his track, such was the will of Heav'n,
Pav'd after him a broad and beat'n way
Over the dark Abyss, whose boiling gulf
Tamely endur'd a bridge of wondrous length

[149] The boat in which Jason sailed to search for the golden fleece.

From Hell continu'd reaching th' utmost Orbe[150]
Of this frail World; by which the Spirits perverse
With easie intercourse pass to and fro
To tempt or punish mortals, except whom
God and good Angels guard by special grace.
But now at last the sacred influence
Of light appears, and from the walls of Heav'n
Shoots farr into the bosom of dim Night
A glimmering dawn; here Nature first begins
Her fardest verge, and Chaos to retire
As from her outmost works a brok'n foe
With tumult less and with less hostile din,
That Satan with less toil, and now with ease
Wafts on the calmer wave by dubious light
And like a weather-beaten vessel holds
Gladly the port, though shrouds and tackle torn;
Or in the emptier waste, resembling air,
Weighs his spread wings, at leasure to behold
Farr off extended th' empyreal Heav'n, wide
In circuit, undetermind square or round,
With opal towrs and battlements adorn'd
Of living saphire, once his native seat;
And fast by, hanging in a golden chain,
This pendant World, in bigness as a starr
Of smallest magnitude close by the moon.
Thither full fraught with mischievous revenge,
Accurst, and in a cursèd hour, he hies.

BOOK III

THE ARGUMENT

God sitting on his throne sees Satan flying towards this world, then newly created; shews him to the Son who sat at his right hand; foretells the success of Satan in perverting mankind; clears his own justice and wisdom from all imputation, having created Man free and able enough to have withstood his Tempter; yet declares his purpose of grace towards him, in regard he fell not of his own malice, as did Satan, but by him seduc't. The Son of God renders praises to his Father for the manifestation of his gracious purpose towards Man; but God again declares, that grace cannot be extended towards Man without the satisfaction of divine justice; Man hath offended the majesty of God by aspiring to Godhead, and therefore with all his progeny devoted to death must dye, unless some one can be found sufficient to answer for his offence, and undergoe his punishment. The Son of God freely offers himself a ransome for Man: the Father accepts him, ordains his incarnation, pronounces his exaltation above all names in Heaven and Earth; commands all the Angels to adore him; they obey, and hymning to their harps in full quire, celebrate the Father and the Son. Mean while Satan alights upon the bare convex of this Worlds outermost Orb; where wandring he first finds a place since call'd the Lymbo of Vanity. What persons and things fly up thither. Thence comes to the gate of Heaven, describ'd ascending by stairs, and the waters above the Firmament that flow about it. His passage thence to the Orb of the Sun; he finds there Uriel, the regent of that orb, but first changes himself into the shape of a meaner Angel; and pretending a zealous desire to behold the new creation and Man whom God had plac't here, inquires of him the place of his habitation, and is directed; alights first on Mount Niphates.

Hail holy light, ofspring of Heav'n first born,
Or of th' Eternal Coeternal beam
May I express thee unblam'd? Since God is light,
And never but in unapproachèd light
Dwelt from Eternitie, dwelt then in thee,
Bright effluence of bright essence increate.
Or hear'st[151] thou rather pure ethereal stream,
Whose fountain who shall tell? Before the Sun,
Before the Heavens thou wert, and at the voice
Of God, as with a mantle didst invest
The rising world of waters dark and deep,
Won from the void and formless infinite.
Thee I re-visit now with bolder wing,
Escap't the Stygian Pool, though long detain'd
In that obscure sojourn, while in my flight
Through utter and through middle darkness borne

[150] The outermost of the ten spheres surrounding the earth.

[151] likest to be called

With other notes then to th' Orphean lyre
I sung of Chaos and eternal Night,
Taught by the heav'nly Muse to venture down
The dark descent, and up to reascend,
Though hard and rare: thee I revisit safe,
And feel thy sovran vital lamp; but thou
Revisit'st not these eyes, that rowle in vain
To find thy piercing ray, and find no dawn;
So thick a drop serene hath quencht thir orbs,
Or dim suffusion veild. Yet not the more
Cease I to wander where the Muses haunt
Cleer spring, or shadie grove, or sunnie hill,
Smit with the love of sacred song; but chief
Thee Sion and the flowrie brooks beneath
That wash thy hallowd feet, and warbling flow,
Nightly I visit: nor somtimes forget
Those other two equal'd with me in Fate,
So were I equal'd with them in renown,
Blind Thamyris and blind Mæonides,
And Tiresias and Phineaus,[152] prophets old.
Then feed on thoughts, that voluntarie move
Harmonious numbers; as the wakeful bird
Sings darkling, and in shadiest covert hid
Tunes her nocturnal note. Thus with the year
Seasons return, but not to me returns
Day, or the sweet approach of ev'n or morn,
Or sight of vernal bloom, or summers rose,
Or flocks, or herds, or human face divine;
But cloud in stead, and ever-during dark
Surrounds me, from the chearful waies of men
Cut off, and for the book of knowledg fair
Presented with a universal blanc
Of Natures works to mee expung'd and ras'd,[153]
And wisdome at one entrance quite shut out.
So much the rather thou celestial light
Shine inward, and the mind through all her powers
Irradiate; there plant eyes; all mist from thence
Purge and disperse, that I may see and tell
Of things invisible to mortal sight.

. . .

BOOK IV

THE ARGUMENT

Satan now in prospect of Eden, and nigh the place where he must now attempt the bold enterprize which he undertook alone against God and Man, falls into many doubts with himself, and many passions, fear, envy, and despare; but at length confirms himself in evil, journeys on to Paradise, whose outward prospect and scituation is described, overleaps the bounds, sits in the shape of a cormorant on the Tree of Life, as highest in the Garden to look about him. The Garden describ'd; Satans first sight of Adam and Eve; his wonder at thir excellent form and happy state, but with resolution to work thir fall; overhears thir discourse, thence gathers that the Tree of Knowledge was forbidden them to eat of, under penalty of death; and thereon intends to found his temptation, by seducing them to transgress: then leaves them a while, to know further of thir state by some other means. Mean while Uriel descending on a sun-beam warns Gabriel, who had in charge the gate of Paradise, that some evil spirit had escap'd the Deep, and past at noon by his sphere in the shape of a good Angel down to Paradise, discovered after by his furious gestures in the Mount. Gabriel promises to find him out ere morning. Night coming on, Adam and Eve discourse of going to thir rest: thir bower describ'd; thir evening worship. Gabriel drawing forth his bands of night-watch to walk the round of Paradise, appoints two strong Angels to Adams bower, least the evill spirit should be there doing some harm to Adam or Eve sleeping; there they find him at the ear of Eve, tempting her in a dream, and bring him, though unwilling, to Gabriel; by whom question'd, he scornfully answers, prepares resistance, but hinder'd by a sign from Heaven, flies out of Paradise.

BOOK V

THE ARGUMENT

Morning approach't, Eve relates to Adam her troublesome dream; he likes it not, yet comforts her. They come forth to thir day labours. Their morning hymn at the door of their bower. God, to render Man inexcusable, sends Raphael to admonish him of his obedience, of his free estate,

[152] Poets of antiquity who, like Milton, were stricken with blindness. Maeonides is Homer. [153] erased

of his energy near at hand; who he is, and why his enemy, and whatever else may avail Adam to know. Raphael comes down to Paradise; his appearance describ'd; his coming discern'd by Adam afar off sitting at the door of his bower. He goes out to meet him, brings him to his lodge, entertains him with the choycest fruits of Paradise got together by Eve; their discourse at table. Raphael performs his message, minds Adam of his state and of his enemy; relates at Adams request who that enemy is, and how he came to be so, beginning from his first revolt in Heaven, and the occasion thereof; how he drew his legions after him to the parts of the north, and there incited them to rebel with him, perswading all but only Abdiel, a Seraph, who in argument diswades and opposes him, then forsakes him.

BOOK VI

THE ARGUMENT

Raphael continues to relate how Michael and Gabriel were sent forth to battel against Satan and his Angels. The first fight describ'd: Satan and his Powers retire under night. He calls a councel, invents devilish engines, which in the second dayes fight put Michael and his Angels to some disorder. But they at length pulling up mountains overwhelm'd both the force and machins of Satan. Yet the tumult not so ending, God on the third day sends Messiah, his Son, for whom he had reserv'd the glory of that victory. Hee in the power of his Father coming to the place, and causing all his legions to stand still on either side, with his chariot and thunder driving into the midst of his enemies, pursues them unable to resist towards the wall of Heaven; which opening, they leap down with horrour and confusion into the place of punishment prepar'd for them in the Deep. Messiah returns with triumph to his Father.

BOOK VII

THE ARGUMENT

Raphael, at the request of Adam, relates how and wherefore this world was first created; that God, after the expelling of Satan and his Angels out of Heaven, declar'd his pleasure to create another World and other creatures to dwell therein; sends his Son with glory and attendance of Angels to perform the work of creation in six dayes: the Angels celebrate with hymns the performance thereof, and his reascention into Heaven.

BOOK VIII

THE ARGUMENT

Adam inquires concerning celestial motions, is doubtfully answer'd, and exhorted to search rather things more worthy of knowledg. Adam assents, and still desirous to detain Raphael, relates to him what he remember'd since his own creation, his placing in Paradise, his talk with God concerning solitude and fit society, his first meeting and nuptials with Eve, his discourse with the Angel thereupon; who after admonitions repeated, departs.

BOOK IX

THE ARGUMENT

Satan having compast the Earth, with meditated guile returns as a mist by night into Paradise, enters into the Serpent sleeping. Adam and Eve in the morning go forth to thir labours, which Eve proposes to divide in several places, each labouring apart. Adam consents not, alledging the danger, lest that Enemy, of whom they were forewarn'd, should attempt her found alone. Eve loath to be thought not circumspect or firm enough, urges her going apart, the rather desirous to make tryal of her strength; Adam at last yields. The Serpent finds her alone; his subtle approach, first gazing, then speaking, with much flattery extolling Eve above all other creatures. Eve wondring to hear the Serpent speak, asks how he attain'd to human speech and such understanding not till now; the Serpent answers, that by tasting of a certain tree in the Garden he attain'd both to speech and reason, till then void of both. Eve requires him to bring her to that tree, and finds it to be the Tree of Knowledge forbidden. The Serpent now grown bolder, with many wiles and arguments, induces her at length to eat. She pleas'd with the taste deliberates awhile whether to impart thereof to Adam or not; at last brings him of the fruit; relates what persuaded her to eat thereof. Adam at first amaz'd, but perceiving her lost, resolves through vehemence of love to perish with her; and extenuating the trespass, eats also of the fruit. The effects thereof in them both; they seek to cover thir nakedness; then fall to variance and accusation of one another.

BOOK X

THE ARGUMENT

Mans transgression known, the Guardian Angels forsake Paradise and return up to Heaven to approve thir vigilance, and are approv'd, God declaring that the entrance of Satan could not be by them prevented. He sends his Son to judge the transgressors, who descends and gives sentence accordingly; then in pity cloaths them both, and reascends. Sin and Death, sitting till then at the gates of Hell, by wondrous sympathie feeling the success of Satan in this new World, and the sin by Man there committed, resolve to sit no longer confin'd in Hell, but to follow Satan, thir sire, up to the place of Man. To make the way easier from Hell to this World to and fro, they pave a broad highway or bridge over Chaos, according to the track that Satan first made; then preparing for Earth, they meet him, proud of his success, returning to Hell; thir mutual gratulation. Satan arrives at Pandemonium; in full assembly relates with boasting his success against Man; instead of applause is entertained with a general hiss by all his audience, transform'd with himself also suddenly into serpents, according to his doom giv'n in Paradise; then deluded with a shew of the forbidden Tree springing up before them, they greedily reaching to take of the fruit, chew dust and bitter ashes. The proceedings of Sin and Death. God foretels the final victory of his Son over them, and the renewing of all things; but for the present commands his Angels to make several alterations in the heavens and elements. Adam more and more perceiving his fall'n condition, heavily bewailes, rejects the condolement of Eve; she persists and at length appeases him: then to evade the curse likely to fall on thir ofspring, proposes to Adam violent wayes, which he approves not, but conceiving better hope, puts her in mind of the late promise made them, that her seed should be reveng'd on the Serpent, and exhorts her with him to seek peace of the offended Deity, by repentance and supplication.

BOOK XI

THE ARGUMENT

The Son of God presents to his Father the prayers of our first parents now repenting, and intercedes for them. God accepts them, but declares that they must no longer abide in Paradise; sends Michael with a band of Cherubim to dispossess them; but first to reveal to Adam future things. Michaels coming down. Adam shews to Eve certain ominous signs; he discerns Michaels approach, goes out to meet him. The Angel denounces [154] thir departure. Eve's lamentation. Adam pleads, but submits. The Angel leads him up to a high hill, sets before him in vision what shall happ'n till the flood.

BOOK XII

THE ARGUMENT

The Angel Michael continues from the flood to relate what shall succeed; then, in the mention of Abraham, comes by degrees to explain, who that Seed of the Woman shall be, which was promised Adam and Eve in the Fall; his Incarnation, Death, Resurrection, and Ascention; the state of the Church till his second coming. Adam greatly satisfied and recomforted by these relations and promises, descends the hill with Michael; wakens Eve, who all this while had slept, but with gentle dreams compos'd to quietness of mind and submission. Michael in either hand leads them out of Paradise, the fiery sword waving behind them, and the Cherubim taking thir stations to guard the place.

[154] proclaims

Songs from Restoration Plays

Ah Cloris! that I now could sit

Ah Cloris! that I now could sit
  As unconcern'd, as when
Your infant beauty cou'd beget
  No pleasure, nor no pain.

When I the dawn us'd to admire,
  And prais'd the coming day;
I little thought the growing fire
  Must take my rest away.

Your charms in harmless childhood lay,
  Like metals in the mine,
Age from no face took more away,
  Than youth conceal'd in thine.

But as your charms insensibly
  To their perfection prest,
Fond love as unperceiv'd did flye,
  And in my bosom rest.

My passion with your beauty grew,
  And Cupid at my heart,
Still as his mother favour'd you,
  Threw a new flaming dart.

Each glori'd in their wanton part,
  To make a lover he
Employ'd the utmost of his art,
  To make a beauty she.

Though now I slowly bend to love,
  Uncertain of my fate,
If your fair self my chains approve,
  I shall my freedom hate.

Lovers, like dying men, may well
  At first disorder'd be,
Since none alive can truly tell
  What fortune they must see.

[Sir Charles Sedley, *The Mulberry-Garden*, 1668]

A spouse I do hate

A SPOUSE I do hate,
For either she's false or she's jealous;
But give us a mate,
Who nothing will ask us, or tell us.

She stands on no terms,
Nor chaffers, by way of indenture,
Her love for your farms;
But takes her kind man at a venture.

If all prove not right,
Without an act, process, or warning,
From wife for a night,
You may be divorc'd in the morning.

When parents are slaves,
Their bratts cannot be any other;
Great wits and great braves,
Have always a punk to their mother.

[William Wycherley, *Love in a Wood,* 1671]

Love in fantastic triumph sat

LOVE in fantastic triumph sat,
Whilst bleeding hearts around him flowed,
From which fresh pains he did create,
And strange tyrannic power he showed.
From thy bright eyes he took his fire,
Which round about in sport he hurled;
But 'twas from mine he took desire
Enough to undo the amorous world.

From me he took his sighs and tears,
From thee his pride and cruelty;
From me his languishments and fears,
And every killing dart from thee:
Thus thou and I the god have armed,
And set him up a deity;
But my poor heart alone is harmed,
Whilst thine the victor is, and free.

[Mrs. Aphra Behn, *Abdelazer,* 1676]

Sawney was tall

SAWNEY was tall, and of noble race,
And lov'd me better then any yen,[1]
But noo he liggs by another lasse,
And Sawney will nere be my love agen.
I gave him a fine Scotch sarke and band,
I put um on with my awn hand;
I gave him house, and I gave him land,
Yet Sawney will ne'ere be my love agen.

I rob'd the groves of all their store,
And nosegays made to give Sawney yen;
He kist my breast, and fain would do more,
Gude feth methought he was a bonny yen:
He squeez'd my fingers, grasp'd my knee,
And carv'd my name on each green tree;
And sigh'd and languisht to ligg by me;
But now he ne'ere will be my love agen.

My bongrace,[2] and my sun-burnt face
He prais'd; and also my russet gown;
But now he dotes on the copper lace,
Of some lew'd quean of London-town.
He gangs and gives her curds and creame,
Whilst I poor saule sit sighing at heam; [3]
And ne're joye Sawney unless in a dreame;
For now he ne're will be my love agen.

[Thomas D'Urfey, *The Virtuous Wife,* 1679]

Come, all ye youths

COME, all ye youths, whose hearts e're bled
By cruel beauties pride,
Bring each a garland on his head,
Let none his sorrows hide,
But hand in hand around me move,
Singing the saddest tales of love;
And see, when your complaints ye joyn,
If all your wrongs can equal mine.

The happyest mortal once was I,
My heart no sorrows knew.
Pity the pain with which I dye,
But ask not whence it grew.
Yet if a tempting fair you find
That's very lovely, very kind,

[1] one

[2] sunbonnet

[3] home

Though bright as heaven whose stamp she bears,
Think of my fate, and shun her snares.

[Thomas Otway, *The Orphan*, 1680]

Let some great joys pretend to find

Let some great joys pretend to find
In empty whimsies of the mind;
And nothing to the soul can come,
Till th'ushering senses make it room.
Nor can the mind be e'r at ease,
Unless you first the body please.

Life is, what e're vain man may doubt,
But taking in and putting out.
Since life's but a span,
Live as much as you can;
Let none of it pass without pleasure;
But push on your strength
Of what life wants in length:
In the breadth you must make up the measure.

All solid pleasures, fops lay by;
And seek they know not what, nor why:
Imperfect images th'enjoy,
Which fancy makes, and can destroy.
Wh' in immaterial things delight,
Dream in the day as well as night:
In that how can they pleasure take,
Of which no image thought can make.

In vain no moment then be spent,
Fill up the little life that's lent;
Feasts, musick, wine the day possess;
The night, love, youth and beauty bless.
The senses now in parcels treat,
Then all together by the great;
No empty space in life be found,
But one continued joy go round.

[Thomas Shadwell, *The Woman-Captain*, 1679]

The Expostulation

Still wilt thou sigh, and still in vain
A cold neglectful nymph adore;
No longer fruitlessly complain,
But to thy self, thy self restore.
In youth thou caught'st this fond disease,
And shouldst abandon it in age;
Some other nymph as well may please,
Absence or bus'ness disingage.

On tender hearts the wounds of love,
Like those imprinted on young trees,
Or kill at first, or else they prove
Larger b'insensible degrees.
Business I try'd, she fill'd my mind;
On others lips my dear I kist;
But never solid joy could find,
When I my charming Sylvia mist.

Long absence, like a Greenland night,
Made me but wish for sun the more;
And that inimitable light,
She, none but she, could e're restore.
She never once regards thy fire,
Nor ever vents one sigh for thee,
I must the glorious sun admire,
Though he can never look on me.

Look well, you'll find she's not so rare,
Much of her former beauty's gone;
My love her shadow larger far
Is made by her declining sun.
What if her glories faded be,
My former wounds I must indure;
For should the bow unbended be,
Yet that can never help the cure.

[Thomas Shadwell, *The Squire of Alsatia*, 1688]

A Souldier and a Sailor

A Souldier and a Sailor,
A Tinker, and a Tailor,
Had once a doubtful strife, sir,
To make a maid a wife, sir,
Whose name was Buxom Joan.
For now the time was ended,
When she no more intended,
To lick her lips at men, sir,
And gnaw the sheets in vain, sir,
And lie o' nights alone.

The Souldier swore like thunder,
He lov'd her more than plunder;
And shew'd her many a scar, sir,
That he had brought from far, sir
With fighting for her sake.
The Tailor thought to please her,
With off'ring her his measure.
The Tinker too with mettle,
Said he could mend her kettle,
And stop up ev'ry leak.

But while these three were prating,
The Sailor slily waiting,
Thought if it came about, sir,
That they should all fall out, sir:
He then might play his part.
And just e'en as he meant, sir,
To loggerheads they went, sir,
And then he let fly at her,
A shot 'twixt wind and water,
That won this fair maids heart.

[William Congreve, *Love for Love,* 1695]

Slaves to London

Slaves to London, I'll deceive you;
For the country now I leave you.
Who can bear, and not be mad
Wine so dear, and yet so bad?
Such a noise, an air so smoaky,
That to stun yee, this to choak yee,
Men so selfish false and rude,
Nymphs so young, and yet so lewd?

If we play, we're sure of losing;
If we love, our doom we're chusing.
At the playhouse tedious sport,
Cant in City, cringe at Court,
Dirt in streets, and dirty bullies,
Jolting coaches, whores and cullies,[4]
Knaves and coxcombs ev'ry where.
Who that's wise wou'd tarry here?

Quiet harmless country pleasure
Shall at home engross my leisure.
Farewell, London, I'll repair
To my native country air:
I leave all thy plagues behind me —
But at home my wife will find me?
O yee Gods! 'Tis ten times worse!
London is a milder curse.

[Peter Motteux, *Love's a Jest,* 1696]

[4] simpletons

John Dryden

1631–1700

ABSALOM AND ACHITOPHEL [1]

In pious times, e'r priest-craft did begin,
Before polygamy was made a sin;
When Man on many multipli'd his kind,
E'r one to one was cursedly confin'd,
When Nature prompted and no law deni'd
Promiscuous use of concubine and bride;
Then Israel's monarch,[2] after Heavens own heart,
His vigorous warmth did, variously, impart
To wives and slaves: and, wide as his command,
Scatter'd his Maker's image through the land.
Michal,[3] of royal blood, the crown did wear,
A soil ungrateful to the tiller's care:
Not so the rest; for several mothers bore
To god-like David several sons before.
But since like slaves his bed they did ascend,
No true succession could their seed attend.
Of all this numerous progeny was none

[1] Published in 1681, Dryden's poem, based on the story of the revolt of Absalom (*II Samuel,* xiii–xviii), is a satire on recent events at the court of Charles II. Dryden was, as the poem of course shows, a defender of the king and the Tories.

[2] Charles II (David)

[3] Catherine of Portugal, Charles's queen, who bore him no children.

So beautiful so brave as Absalon.[4]
Whether, inspird by some diviner lust,
His father got him with a greater gust,
Or that his conscious destiny made way
By manly beauty to imperial sway,
Early in foreign fields he won renown
With kings and states allied to Israel's crown:
In peace the thoughts of war he coud remove
And seem'd as he were onely born for love.
What e'r he did was done with so much ease,
In him alone, 'twas natural to please;
His motions all accompanied with grace;
And Paradise was open'd in his face.
With secret joy, indulgent David view'd
His youthful image in his son renew'd;
To all his wishes nothing he deni'd
And made the charming Annabel[5] his bride.
What faults he had (for who from faults is free?)
His father coud not or he woud not see.
Some warm excesses, which the law forbore,
Were constru'd youth that purg'd by boiling o'r:
And Amnon's murther,[6] by a specious name,
Was call'd a just revenge for injur'd fame.
Thus prais'd and lov'd, the noble youth remain'd,
While David, undisturb'd, in Sion reign'd.
But life can never be sincerely blest:
Heav'n punishes the bad, and proves the best.
The Jews, a headstrong, moody, murm'ring race
As ever tri'd th' extent and stretch of grace;
God's pamper'd people, whom, debauch'd with ease,
No king could govern nor no god could please;
(Gods they had tri'd of every shape and size
That god-smiths could produce or priests devise:)
These Adam-wits, too fortunately free,
Began to dream they wanted liberty;
And when no rule, no president was found
Of men, by laws less circumscrib'd and bound;
They led their wild desires to woods and caves;
And thought that all but savages were slaves.
They who, when Saul[7] was dead, without a blow
Made foolish Ishbosheth[8] the crown forgo;
Who banisht David did from Hebron bring,
And, with a general shout, proclaim'd him King:
Those very Jews who at their very best
Their humour more than loyalty exprest,
Now wondred why so long they had obey'd
An idol-monarch which their hands had made;
Thought they might ruine him they could create
Or melt him to that golden calf, a State.
But these were random bolts: No form'd design
No interest made the factious croud to join:
The sober part of Israel, free from stain,
Well knew the value of a peaceful reign;
And, looking backward with a wise afright,
Saw seams of wounds, dishonest to the sight:
In contemplation of whose ugly scars,
They curst the memory of civil wars.
The moderate sort of men, thus qualifi'd,
Inclin'd the ballance to the better side;
And David's mildness manag'd it so well,
The bad found no occasion to rebel.
But, when to sin our byast nature leans,

[4] The Duke of Monmouth, Charles's son by the low-born Lucy Walter. Earlier in his father's favor, he had incurred the royal anger by his opposition to his Catholic uncle, James, Duke of York, and his intimacy with the great leader of the Whigs, the Earl of Shaftesbury. The Whigs were intent on preventing James from succeeding his brother, and openly championed the cause of the illegitimate Monmouth.

[5] Anne Scott, Countess of Buccleuch

[6] Probably the assault made on Sir John Coventry in 1673.

[7] Oliver Cromwell

[8] Richard Cromwell

The careful Devil is still at hand with means;
And providently pimps for ill desires:
The Good Old Cause,[9] reviv'd, a plot requires,
Plots, true or false, are necessary things,
To raise up common-wealths and ruin kings.
  Th' inhabitants of old Jerusalem,
Were Jebusites; [10] the town so call'd from them;
And their's the native right ——
But when the chosen people grew more strong,
The rightful cause at length became the wrong;
And every loss the men of Jebus bore,
They still were thought God's enemies the more.
Thus, worn and weaken'd, well or ill content,
Submit they must to David's government:
Impoverish't and depriv'd of all command,
Their taxes doubled as they lost their land;
And, what was harder yet to flesh and blood,
Their gods disgrac'd, and burnt like common wood.
This set the heathen priesthood in a flame,
For priests of all religions are the same:
Of whatsoe'er descent their godhead be,
Stock, stone, or other homely pedigree,
In his defence his servants are as bold,
As if he had been born of beaten gold.
The Jewish Rabbins,[11] though their enemies,
In this conclude them honest men and wise:
For 'twas their duty, all the learned think,
T' espouse his cause by whom they eat and drink.
From hence began that plot,[12] the nations curse,
Bad in itself, but represented worse,
Rais'd in extremes, and in extremes decri'd,
With oaths affirm'd, with dying vows deni'd,
Nor weigh'd or winnow'd by the multitude,
But swallow'd in the mass, unchewed and crude.
Some truth there was, but dashed and brew'd with lies;
To please the fools, and puzzle all the wise.
Succeeding times did equal folly call
Believing nothing or believing all.
The Egyptian rites [13] the Jebusites embrac'd,
Where gods were recommended by their taste.
Such sav'ry deities must needs be good
As serv'd at once for worship and for food.
By force they could not introduce these gods,
For ten to one in former days was odds.
So fraud was us'd, (the sacrificers trade,)
Fools are more hard to conquer than persuade.
Their busie teachers mingled with the Jews
And rak'd for converts even the court and stews:
Which Hebrew priests the more unkindly took,
Because the fleece accompanies the flock.
Some thought they God's Anointed meant to slay
By guns, invented since full many a day:
Our author swears it not; but who can know
How far the Devil and Jebusites may go?
This plot, which fail'd for want of common sense,
Had yet a deep and dangerous consequence;
For as, when raging fevers boil the blood
The standing lake soon floats into a floud;
And ev'ry hostile humour which before
Slept quiet in its channels bubbles o're:
So, several factions from this first ferment

[9] The Puritan cause.
[10] Roman Catholics
[11] The Anglican clergy.
[12] The Popish Plot, largely manufactured by the infamous Titus Oates. Charles and the court party took little stock in it, but the Whigs were, or pretended to be, in a frenzy of fear.
[13] Roman Catholic ceremonies and dogmas, in particular that of transubstantiation.

Work up to foam, and threat the government.
Some by their friends, more by themselves thought wise,
Oppos'd the pow'r to which they could not rise.
Some had in courts been great and, thrown from thence,
Like fiends were hardened in impenitence.
Some, by their monarch's fatal mercy grown,
From pardon'd rebels, kinsmen to the throne
Were raised in pow'r and publick office high;
Strong bands, if bands ungrateful men coud tie.
Of these the false Achitophel[14] was first,
A name to all succeeding ages curst.
For close designs and crooked counsels fit,
Sagacious, bold, and turbulent of wit,
Restless, unfixt in principles and place,
In pow'r unpleased, impatient of disgrace;
A fiery soul, which working out its way,
Fretted the pigmy body to decay:
And o'r informed the tenement of clay.
A daring pilot in extremity;
Pleas'd with the danger, when the waves went high
He sought the storms; but, for a calm unfit,
Would steer too nigh the sands to boast his wit.
Great wits are sure to madness near alli'd
And thin partitions do their bounds divide;
Else, why should he, with wealth and honour blest,
Refuse his age the needful hours of rest?
Punish a body which he coud not please,
Bankrupt of life, yet prodigal of ease?
And all to leave what with his toil he won
To that unfeather'd two-legg'd thing, a son:
Got, while his soul did huddled notions trie;
And born a shapeless lump, like anarchy.
In friendship false, implacable in hate,
Resolv'd to ruine or to rule the state;
To compass this the triple bond he broke;
The pillars of the publick safety shook,
And fitted Israel for a foreign yoke;[15]
Then, seiz'd with fear, yet still affecting fame,
Usurp'd a patriot's all-attoning name.
So easie still it proves in factious times
With publick zeal to cancel private crimes:
How safe is treason and how sacred ill,
Where none can sin against the peoples will,
Where crouds can wink; and no offence be known,
Since in anothers guilt they find their own.
Yet, fame deserv'd, no enemy can grudge;
The statesman we abhor, but praise the judge.
In Israels courts ne'er sat an Abbethdin[16]
With more discerning eyes or hands more clean,
Unbrib'd, unsought, the wretched to redress;
Swift of dispatch and easie of access.
Oh, had he been content to serve the crown
With vertues onely proper to the gown,
Or had the rankness of the soil been freed
From cockle that opprest the noble seed,
David for him his tuneful harp had strung,
And Heav'n had wanted one immortal song.
But wild ambition loves to slide, not stand,
And Fortunes ice prefers to Vertues land.
Achitophel, grown weary to possess
A lawful fame, and lazie happiness,
Disdain'd the golden fruit to gather free
And lent the crowd his arm to shake the tree.
Now, manifest of crimes, contriv'd long since,
He stood at bold defiance with his prince:
Held up the buckler of the peoples cause
Against the crown; and sculk'd behind the laws.
The wish'd occasion of the Plot he takes;

[14] The Earl of Shaftesbury, once a trusted minister of Charles, now his avowed opponent.

[15] In 1667 England made a 'triple bond' with Sweden and Holland against France. This was broken in 1670 when England allied herself with France against Holland. Dryden accuses Shaftesbury unjustly here.

[16] Judge. Shaftesbury had been Lord Chancellor.

Some circumstances finds, but more he makes.
By buzzing emissaries, fills the ears
Of listening crouds, with jealousies and fears
Of arbitrary counsels brought to light,
And proves the king himself a Jebusite.
Weak arguments! which yet he knew full well,
Were strong with people easie to rebel.
For, govern'd by the moon, the giddy Jews
Tread the same track when she the prime renews:
And once in twenty years, their scribes record,
By natural instinct they change their lord.
Achitophel still wants a chief, and none
Was found so fit as warlike Absalon:
Not, that he wish'd his greatness to create,
(For politicians neither love nor hate:)
But, for he knew his title not allow'd,
Would keep him still depending on the croud,
That kingly pow'r, thus ebbing out, might be
Drawn to the dregs of a democracie.
Him he attempts with studied arts to please
And sheds his venome in such words as these.
  Auspicious Prince! at whose nativity
Some royal planet rul'd the southern sky;
Thy longing countries darling and desire,
Their cloudy pillar, and their guardian fire,
Their second Moses, whose extended wand
Divides the seas and shows the promis'd land,
Whose dawning day, in every distant age,
Has exercised the sacred prophets rage,
The peoples pray'r, the glad diviners theam,
The young mens vision and the old mens dream!
Thee, Saviour, thee the nations vows confess;
And, never satisfi'd with seeing, bless:
Swift, unbespoken pomps, thy steps proclaim,
And stammering babes are taught to lisp thy name.
How long wilt thou the general joy detain;
Starve, and defraud the people of thy reign?
Content ingloriously to pass thy days,
Like one of vertues fools that feeds on praise;
Till thy fresh glories, which now shine so bright,
Grow stale and tarnish with our dayly sight.
Believe me, royal youth, thy fruit must be
Or gather'd ripe, or rot upon the tree.
Heav'n has to all allotted, soon or late,
Some lucky revolution of their fate:
Whose motions, if we watch and guide with skill,
(For humane good depends on humane will,)
Our fortune rolls as from a smooth descent
And, from the first impression, takes the bent;
But, if unseiz'd, she glides away like wind;
And leaves repenting folly far behind.
Now, now she meets you with a glorious prize
And spreads her locks before her as she flies.
Had thus old David, from whose loins you spring,
Not dar'd, when Fortune call'd him, to be king,
At Gath [17] an exile he might still remain,
And Heavens anointing oil had been in vain.
Let his successful youth your hopes engage,
But shun th' example of declining age.
Behold him setting in his western skies,
The shadows lengthening as the vapours rise.
He is not now, as when, on Jordan's [18] sand,
The joyful people throng'd to see him land,
Cov'ring the beach and blackning all the strand:

[17] Brussels
[18] The reference is to Charles's triumphant landing at Dover in May 1660.

But like the Prince of Angels, from his height,
Comes tumbling downward with diminish'd light:
Betray'd by one poor plot to publick scorn,
(Our onely blessing since his curst return,)
Those heaps of people which one sheaf did bind,
Blown off and scatter'd by a puff of wind.
What strength can he to your designs oppose,
Naked of friends, and round beset with foes?
If Pharaoh's [19] doubtful succour he should use,
A foreign aid would more incense the Jews:
Proud Egypt would dissembled friendship bring;
Foment the war, but not support the King:
Nor woud the royal party e'r unite
With Pharaoh's arms t' assist the Jebusite;
Or if they shoud, their interest soon would break,
And, with such odious aid, make David weak.
All sorts of men, by my successful arts
Abhorring kings, estrange their altered hearts
From David's rule: and 'tis the general cry,
Religion, Common-wealth, and Liberty.
If you, as champion of the publique good,
Add to their arms a chief of royal blood;
What may not Israel hope, and what applause
Might such a general gain by such a cause?
Not barren praise alone, that gaudy flow'r,
Fair onely to the sight, but solid pow'r:
And nobler is a limited command,
Giv'n by the love of all your native land;
Than a successive title, long, and dark,
Drawn from the mouldy rolls of Noah's ark.

What cannot praise effect in mighty minds,
When flattery sooths and when ambition blinds!
Desire of pow'r, on earth a vitious weed,
Yet, sprung from high is of cœlestial seed;
In God 'tis glory: and when men aspire,
'Tis but a spark too much of heavenly fire.
Th' ambitious youth, too covetous of fame,
Too full of angels metal in his frame,
Unwarily was led from vertues ways,
Made drunk with honour, and debauch'd with praise.
Half loath and half consenting to the ill,
(For loyal blood within him strugled still,)
He thus repli'd—And what pretence have I
To take up arms for publick liberty?
My father governs with unquestion'd right;
The Faiths Defender and mankinds delight,
Good, gracious, just, observant of the laws;
And Heav'n by wonders has espous'd his cause.
Whom has he wrong'd in all his peaceful reign?
Who sues for justice to his throne in vain?
What millions has he pardoned of his foes
Whom just revenge did to his wrath expose?
Mild, easie, humble, studious of our good,
Enclin'd to mercy, and averse from blood.
If mildness ill with stubborn Israel suit,
His crime is God's belovéd attribute.
What could he gain, his people to betray
Or change his right, for arbitrary sway?
Let haughty Pharaoh curse with such a reign
His fruitful Nile, and yoak a servile train.
If David's rule Jerusalem displease,
The dog-star heats their brains to this disease.
Why then should I, encouraging the bad,
Turn rebel and run popularly mad?
Were he a tyrant who, by lawless might,
Opprest the Jews and rais'd the Jebusite,
Well might I mourn; but Nature's holy bands
Would curb my spirits, and restrain my hands;
The people might assert their liberty;

———

[19] Louis XIV, to whom Charles was actually obligated for vast sums which allowed him freedom from the exactions of Parliament.

But what was right in them, were crime in me.
His favour leaves me nothing to require;
Prevents my wishes and out-runs desire
What more can I expect while David lives?
All but his kingly diadem he gives:
And that: but there he paus'd; then sighing, said,
Is justly destin'd for a worthier head.
For when my father from his toyls shall rest
And late augment the number of the blest:
His lawful issue shall the throne ascend,
Or the collat'ral line, where that shall end.
His brother, though opprest with vulgar spight,
Yet dauntless and secure of native right,
Of every royal vertue stands possest;
Still dear to all the bravest and the best.
His courage foes, his friends his truth proclaim;
His loyalty the king, the world his fame.
His mercy ev'n th' offending croud will find,
For sure he comes of a forgiving kind.
Why should I then repine at heavens decree
Which gives me no pretence to royalty?
Yet oh that Fate, propitiously inclin'd,
Had rais'd my birth, or had debas'd my mind;
To my large soul, not all her treasure lent,
And then betrai'd it to a mean descent.
I find, I find my mounting spirits bold,
And David's part disdains my mothers mold.
Why am I scanted by a niggard birth?
My soul disclaims the kindred of her earth:
And, made for empire, whispers me within;
Desire of greatness is a god-like sin.

Him staggering so when Hells dire agent found,
While fainting vertue scarce maintain'd her ground,
He pours fresh forces in, and thus replies:
Th' eternal God, supreamly good and wise,
Imparts not these prodigious gifts in vain;
What wonders are reserv'd to bless your reign?
Against your will your arguments have shown,
Such vertue's only giv'n to guide a throne.
Not that your father's mildness I contemn,
But manly force becomes the diadem.
'Tis true he grants the people all they crave;
And more perhaps than subjects ought to have:
For lavish grants suppose a monarch tame
And more his goodness than his wit proclaim.
But when should people strive their bonds to break,
If not when kings are negligent or weak?
Let him give on till he can give no more,
The thrifty Sanhedrin[20] shall keep him poor:
And every sheckle which he can receive
Shall cost a limb of his prerogative.
To ply him with new plots shall be my care;
Or plunge him deep in some expensive war;
Which, when his treasure can no more supply,
He must, with the remains of kingship, buy.
His faithful friends our jealousies and fears
Call Jebusites; and Pharaoh's pensioners,
Whom, when our fury from his aid has torn,
He shall be naked left to publick scorn.
The next successor, whom I fear and hate,
My arts have made obnoxious to the State;
Turn'd all his vertues to his overthrow,
And gain'd our elders to pronounce a foe.
His right, for sums of necessary gold,
Shall first be pawn'd, and afterwards be sold;
Till time shall ever-wanting David draw,
To pass your doubtful title into law.

[20] Parliament

If not; the people have a right supreme
To make their kings; for kings are made for them.
All empire is no more than pow'r in trust,
Which, when resum'd, can be no longer just.
Succession, for the general good design'd,
In its own wrong a nation cannot bind:
If altering that, the people can relieve,
Better one suffer, than a nation grieve.
The Jews well know their pow'r: e'r Saul they chose
God was their King, and God they durst depose.
Urge now your piety, your filial name,
A father's right and fear of future fame;
The publick good, that universal call,
To which even Heav'n submitted, answers all.
Nor let his love enchant your generous mind;
'Tis Natures trick to propagate her kind.
Our fond begetters, who would never die,
Love but themselves in their posterity.
Or let his kindness by th' effects be tried
Or let him lay his vain pretence aside.
God said he loved your father; coud he bring
A better proof than to anoint him king?
It surely shew'd, He lov'd the shepherd well
Who gave so fair a flock as Israel.
Would David have you thought his darling son?
What means he then, to alienate the crown?
The name of godly he may blush to bear:
'Tis after Gods own heart to cheat his heir.
He to his brother gives supreme command;
To you a legacie of barren land:
Perhaps th' old harp on which he thrums his lays:
Or some dull Hebrew ballad in your praise.
Then the next heir, a prince, severe and wise,
Already looks on you with jealous eyes,
Sees through the thin disguises of your arts,
And marks your progress in the peoples hearts.
Though now his mighty soul its grief contains;
He meditates revenge who least complains.
And like a lion, slumb'ring in the way,
Or sleep dissembling, while he waits his prey,
His fearless foes within his distance draws,
Constrains his roaring, and contracts his paws:
Till at the last, his time for fury found,
He shoots with sudden vengeance from the ground:
The prostrate vulgar, passes o'r and spares;
But with a lordly rage, his hunters tears;
Your case no tame expedients will afford;
Resolve on death, or conquest by the sword,
Which for no less a stake than life, you draw,
And self-defence is Natures eldest law.
Leave the warm people no considering time;
For then rebellion may be thought a crime.
Prevail your self of what occasion gives,
But trie your title while your father lives;
And, that your arms may have a fair pretence,
Proclaim, you take them in the king's defence;
Whose sacred life each minute woud expose,
To plots, from seeming friends and secret foes.
And who can sound the depth of David's soul?
Perhaps his fear, his kindness may controul.
He fears his brother, though he loves his son,
For plighted vows too late to be undone.
If so, by force he wishes to be gain'd,
Like womens leachery to seem constrain'd:
Doubt not; but, when he most affects the frown,
Commit a pleasing rape upon the crown.
Secure his person to secure your cause;

They who possess the prince, possess the laws.

He said, and this advice above the rest
With Absalom's mild nature suited best;
Unblamed of life (ambition set aside,)
Not stain'd with cruelty, nor puft with pride.
How happy had he been, if destiny
Had higher placed his birth, or not so high!
His kingly vertues might have claim'd a throne
And blest all other countries but his own:
But charming greatness, since so few refuse;
'Tis juster to lament him, than accuse.
Strong were his hopes a rival to remove,
With blandishments to gain the publick love,
To head the faction while their zeal was hot,
And popularly prosecute the plot.
To farther this, Achitophel unites
The malecontents of all the Israelites:
Whose differing parties he could wisely join
For several ends, to serve the same design.
The best, and of the princes some were such,
Who thought the pow'r of monarchy too much:
Mistaken men, and patriots in their hearts;
Not wicked, but seduc'd by impious arts.
By these the springs of property were bent,
And wound so high, they crack'd the government.
The next for interest sought t' embroil the State,
To sell their duty at a dearer rate;
And make their Jewish markets of the throne;
Pretending publick good, to serve their own.
Others thought kings an useless heavy load,
Who cost too much, and did too little good.
These were for laying honest David by
On principles of pure good husbandry.
With them join'd all th' haranguers of the throng
That thought to get preferment by the tongue.
Who follow next, a double danger bring,
Not onely hating David, but the king;
The Solymæan rout; [21] well vers'd of old
In godly faction, and in treason bold;
Cowring and quaking at a conqu'ror's sword,
But lofty to a lawful prince restored;
Saw with disdain an ethnick plot begun
And scorned by Jebusites to be out-done.
Hot Levites [22] headed these; who pul'd before
From th' Ark, which in the Judges days they bore,
Resum'd their cant, and with a zealous crie
Pursu'd their old belov'd theocracie.
Where Sanhedrin and priest enslav'd the nation
And justifi'd their spoils by inspiration:
For who so fit for reign as Aaron's race,[23]
If once dominion they could found in grace?
These led the pack; though not of surest scent,
Yet deepest mouth'd against the government.
A numerous host of dreaming saints succeed;
Of the true old enthusiastick breed:
'Gainst form and order they their pow'r imploy.
Nothing to build, and all things to destroy.
But far more numerous was the herd of such,
Who think too little, and who talk too much.
These, out of meer instinct, they knew not why,
Adored their fathers' God, and property:
And, by the same blind benefit of fate,
The Devil and the Jebusite did hate:
Born to be sav'd, even in their own despight;

---

[21] The citizens of London, with whom Shaftesbury was a great hero. He had deliberately gone down to live among them and knew how to make himself appear their champion.

[22] The Presbyterian ministers.

[23] *i.e.*, the clergy

Because they could not help believing right.
Such were the tools; but a whole hydra more
Remains, of sprouting heads too long to score:
Some of their chiefs were princes of the land;
In the first rank of these did Zimri [24] stand:
A man so various, that he seem'd to be
Not one, but all mankind's epitome.
Stiff in opinions, always in the wrong;
Was every thing by starts, and nothing long:
But, in the course of one revolving moon,
Was chymist, fidler, states-man, and buffoon;
Then all for women, painting, rhiming, drinking,
Besides ten thousand freaks that died in thinking.
Blest madman, who coud every hour employ,
With something new to wish, or to enjoy!
Railing and praising were his usual theams;
And both (to shew his judgment) in extreams:
So over violent, or over civil,
That every man, with him, was god or devil.
In squandring wealth was his peculiar art:
Nothing went unrewarded, but desert.
Begger'd by fools, whom still he found too late:
He had his jest, and they had his estate.
He laugh'd himself from court; then sought relief
By forming parties, but could ne'r be chief:
For, spight of him, the weight of business fell
On Absalom and wise Achitophel:
Thus wicked but in will, of means bereft,
He left not faction, but of that was left.
  Titles and names 'twere tedious to reherse
Of lords, below the dignity of verse.

[24] The Duke of Buckingham, a mercurial statesman and the literary enemy of Dryden.

Wits, warriors, commonwealths-men were the best:
Kind husbands and meer nobles all the rest
And, therefore in the name of dulness, be
The well-hung Balaam [25] and cold Caleb [26] free;
And canting Nadab [27] let oblivion damn,
Who made new porridge for the Paschal Lamb.
Let friendships holy band some names assure,
Some their own worth, and some let scorn secure.
Nor shall the rascal rabble here have place,
Whom kings no titles gave, and God no grace:
Not bull-fac'd Jonas,[28] who coud statutes draw
To mean rebellion, and make treason law.
But he, though bad, is follow'd by a worse,
The wretch, who Heav'ns Anointed dar'd to curse.
Shimei,[29] whose youth did early promise bring
Of zeal to God, and hatred to his king;
Did wisely from expensive sins refrain,
And never broke the Sabbath, but for gain:
Nor ever was he known an oath to vent,
Or curse, unless against the government.
Thus, heaping wealth, by the most ready way
Among the Jews, which was to cheat and pray;
The City, to reward his pious hate
Against his master, chose him magistrate:
His hand a vare of justice did uphold;
His neck was loaded with a chain of gold.
During his office, treason was no crime.
The Sons of Belial had a glorious time:
For Shimei, though not prodigal of pelf,
Yet lov'd his wicked neighbour as himself:

[25] The Earl of Huntingdon.

[26] Lord Grey, one of the greatest cowards who ever lived.

[27] Lord Howard of Escrick. It was told that he had drunk the sacrament in ale poured over roasted apples, a drink known as 'lamb's wool'.

[28] Sir William Jones, the Attorney-General.

[29] Slingsby Bethel, sheriff of London in 1680. His invention of the packed jury was useful to Shaftesbury's cause.

When two or three were gather'd to declaim
Against the monarch of Jerusalem,
Shimei was always in the midst of them.
And, if they curst the King when he was by,
Woud rather curse, than break good company.
If any durst his factious friends accuse,
He pact a jury of dissenting Jews:
Whose fellow-feeling, in the godly cause
Would free the suff'ring saint from humane laws,
For laws are onely made to punish those
Who serve the King, and to protect his foes.
If any leisure time he had from pow'r,
(Because 'tis sin to misimploy an hour;)
His bus'ness was by writing to persuade
That kings were useless, and a clog to trade:
And that his noble stile he might refine,
No Rechabite more shund the fumes of wine.
Chaste were his cellars; and his shrieval board
The grossness of a City feast abhor'd:
His cooks, with long disuse, their trade forgot;
Cool was his kitchin, though his brains were hot.
Such frugal vertue malice may accuse;
But sure 'twas necessary to the Jews:
For towns once burnt, such magistrates require
As dare not tempt Gods Providence by fire.
With spiritual food he fed his servants well,
But free from flesh that made the Jews rebel:
And Moses's laws he held in more account,
For forty days of fasting in the Mount.
To speak the rest, who better are forgot,
Would tire a well-breath'd witness of the Plot:
Yet, Corah,[30] thou shalt from oblivion pass;
Erect thyself thou monumental brass:
High as the serpent of thy metal made,
While nations stand secure beneath thy shade.
What though his birth were base, yet comets rise
From earthly vapours, e'r they shine in skies.
Prodigious actions may as well be done
By weaver's issue as by prince's son.
This arch-attestor for the publick good
By that one deed enobles all his bloud.
Who ever ask'd the witnesses high race
Whose oath with martyrdom did Stephen grace?
Ours was a Levite, and as times went then,
His tribe were God-almighties gentlemen.
Sunk were his eyes, his voice was harsh and loud,
Sure signs he neither cholerick was, nor proud:
His long chin prov'd his wit; his saint-like grace
A church vermilion, and a Moses's face.
His memory, miraculously great,
Coud plots, exceeding mans belief, repeat;
Which, therefore cannot be accounted lies,
For humane wit coud never such devise.
Some future truths are mingled in his book;
But where the witness fail'd, the prophet spoke:
Some things like visionary flights appear;
The spirit caught him up, the Lord knows where:
And gave him his Rabinical degree,[31]
Unknown to foreign university.
His judgment yet his mem'ry did excel,
Which piec'd his wondrous evidence so well:
And suited to the temper of the times;
Then groaning under Jebusitick crimes.
Let Israels foes suspect his heav'nly call,
And rashly judge his writ apocryphal;
Our laws for such affronts have forfeits made:
He takes his life, who takes away his trade.
Were I myself in witness Corah's place,
The wretch who did me such a dire disgrace

[30] Titus Oates, the perjured inventor of the Popish plot.

[31] Oates pretended to be a Doctor of Divinity from Salamanca.

Should whet my memory, though once forgot,
To make him an appendix of my plot.
His zeal to Heav'n, made him his prince despise,
And load his person with indignities:
But zeal peculiar priviledge affords,
Indulging latitude for deeds and words:
And Corah might for Agag's [32] murther call,
In terms as coarse as Samuel us'd to Saul.
What others in his evidence did join,
(The best that coud be had for love or coin,)
In Corah's own predicament will fall
For witness is a common name to all.

Surrounded thus with friends of every sort,
Deluded Absalom forsakes the court:
Impatient of high hopes, urg'd with renown,
And fir'd with near possession of a crown.
The admiring croud are dazled with surprize
And on his goodly person feed their eyes:
His joy conceal'd, he sets himself to show;
On each side bowing popularly low:
His looks, his gestures, and his words he frames
And with familiar ease repeats their names.
Thus, form'd by Nature, furnished out with arts,
He glides unfelt into their secret hearts:
Then with a kind compassionating look,
And sighs, bespeaking pity e'r he spoke,
Few words he said, but easie those and fit,
More slow than Hybla drops, and far more sweet.
I mourn, my country-men, your lost estate,
Though far unable to prevent your fate:
Behold a banish'd [33] man, for your dear cause
Expos'd a prey to arbitrary laws!
Yet oh! that I alone coud be undone
Cut off from empire, and no more a son!
Now all your liberties a spoil are made;
Egypt and Tyrus [34] intercept your trade,
And Jebusites your sacred rites invade.
My father, whom with reverence yet I name,
Charm'd into ease, is careless of his fame:
And, brib'd with petty sums of foreign gold,
Is grown in Bathsheba's [35] embraces old:
Exalts his enemies, his friends destroys,
And all his pow'r against himself imploys.
He gives, and let him give my right away;
But why should he his own and yours betray?
He onely, he can make the nation bleed,
And he alone from my revenge is freed.
Take then my tears (with that he wiped his eyes)
'Tis all the aid my present pow'r supplies:
No court-informer can these arms accuse;
These arms may sons against their fathers use;
And, 'tis my wish, the next successor's reign
May make no other Israelite complain.

Youth, beauty, graceful action seldom fail:
But common interest always will prevail:
And pity never ceases to be shown
To him, who makes the peoples wrongs his own.
The croud, (that still believe their kings oppress,)
With lifted hands their young Messiah bless:
Who now begins his progress to ordain
With chariots, horsemen, and a num'rous train;
From east to west his glories he displays:
And, like the sun, the Promis'd Land surveys.
Fame runs before him as the morning-star,
And shouts of joy salute him from afar:
Each house receives him as a guardian god;

[32] Sir Edmund Bury Godfrey, a justice of the peace before whom Oates made a deposition in regard to the plot. He was shortly after found dead in a ditch with a sword wound through his heart.

[33] The king had sent Monmouth from England in 1679.

[34] France and Holland

[35] The Duchess of Portsmouth, Charles's French mistress.

And consecrates the place of his abode:
But hospitable treats did most commend
Wise Issachar,[36] his wealthy western friend.
This moving court that caught the peoples eyes,
And seem'd but pomp, did other ends disguise:
Achitophel had form'd it, with intent
To sound the depths, and fathom where it went,
The peoples hearts distinguish friends from foes;
And trie their strength before they came to blows.
Yet all was colour'd with a smooth pretence
Of specious love, and duty to their prince.
Religion, and redress of grievances,
Two names, that always cheat and always please,
Are often urg'd; and good King David's life
Endanger'd by a brother and a wife.
Thus, in a pageant shew, a plot is made;
And peace it self is war in masquerade.
Oh foolish Israel! never warn'd by ill:
Still the same bait, and circumvented still!
Did ever men forsake their present ease,
In midst of health imagine a disease;
Take pains contingent mischiefs to foresee,
Make heirs for monarchs, and for God decree?
What shall we think! Can people give away
Both for themselves and sons their native sway?
Then they are left defenceless, to the sword
Of each unbounded, arbitrary lord:
And laws are vain, by which we right enjoy,
If kings unquestion'd can those laws destroy.
Yet if the croud be judge of fit and just,
And kings are onely officers in trust,
Then this resuming cov'nant was declar'd
When kings were made, or is for ever bar'd:
If those who gave the scepter, coud not tie
By their own deed their own posterity,
How then coud Adam bind his future race?
How coud his forfeit on mankind take place?
Or how coud heavenly Justice damn us all
Who ne'r consented to our fathers fall?
Then kings are slaves to those whom they command,
And tenants to their peoples pleasure stand.
Add that the pow'r, for property allow'd,
Is mischievously seated in the croud;
For who can be secure of private right,
If sovereign sway may be dissolv'd by might?
Nor is the peoples judgment always true:
The most may err as grosly as the few.
And faultless kings run down, by common cry,
For vice, oppression, and for tyranny.
What standard is there in a fickle rout,
Which, flowing to the mark, runs faster out?
Nor onely crouds, but Sanhedrins may be
Infected with this publick lunacy:
And share the madness of rebellious times,
To murther monarchs for imagin'd crimes.
If they may give and take when e'r they please,
Not kings alone, (the Godheads images,)
But government it self at length must fall
To Natures state, where all have right to all.
Yet, grant our lords the people, kings can make,
What prudent men a setled throne woud shake?
For whatsoe'r their sufferings were before,
That change they covet makes them suffer more.
All other errors but disturb a state;
But innovation is the blow of fate.
If ancient fabricks nod, and threat to fall,
To patch the flaws, and buttress up the wall,
Thus far 'tis duty; but here fix the mark:
For all beyond it is to touch our ark.
To change foundations, cast the frame anew,
Is work for rebels who base ends pursue:

[36] Thomas Thynne of Longleat (in southwest England).

At once divine and humane laws controul,
And mend the parts by ruine of the whole.
The tamp'ring world is subject to this curse,
To physick their disease into a worse.

Now what relief can righteous David bring?
How fatal 'tis to be too good a king!
Friends he has few, so high the madness grows;
Who dare be such, must be the people's foes:
Yet some there were ev'n in the worst of days;
Some let me name, and naming is to praise.

In this short file Barzillai [37] first appears;
Barzillai crown'd with honour and with years:
Long since, the rising rebels he withstood
In regions waste, beyond the Jordans flood:
Unfortunately brave to buoy the State;
But sinking underneath his master's fate:
In exile with his god-like prince he mourn'd,
For him he suffer'd, and with him return'd.
The court he practis'd, not the courtier's art:
Large was his wealth, but larger was his heart:
Which, well the noblest objects knew to chuse,
The fighting warriour, and recording muse.
His bed coud once a fruitful issue boast:
Now more than half a father's name is lost.
His eldest hope, with every grace adorn'd,
By me (so Heav'n will have it) always mourn'd
And always honour'd, snatch'd in manhoods prime
B' unequal fates and providences crime:
Yet not before the goal of honour won,
All parts fulfill'd of subject and of son;
Swift was the race, but short the time to run.
Oh narrow circle, but of pow'r divine,
Scanted in space, but perfect in thy line!
By sea, by land, thy matchless worth was known;
Arms thy delight, and war was all thy own:
Thy force, infus'd, the fainting Tyrians prop'd;
And haughty Pharaoh found his fortune stop'd.
Oh ancient honour, Oh unconquered hand,
Whom foes unpunish'd never coud withstand!
But Israel was unworthy of thy name:
Short is the date of all immoderate fame.
It looks as Heav'n our ruine had design'd,
And durst not trust thy fortune and thy mind.
Now, free from earth, thy disencumbred soul
Mounts up, and leaves behind the clouds and starry pole:
From thence thy kindred legions maist thou bring,
To aid the Guardian Angel of thy king.
Here stop my Muse, here cease thy painful flight;
No pinions can pursue immortal height:
Tell good Barzillai thou canst sing no more,
And tell thy soul she should have fled before;
Or fled she with his life, and left this verse
To hang on her departed patron's herse?
Now take thy steepy flight from Heav'n, and see
If thou canst find on earth another he;
Another he would be too hard to find;
See then whom thou canst see not far behind.
Zadock [38] the priest, whom, shunning pow'r and place,
His lowly mind advanc'd to David's grace:
With him the Sagan [39] of Jerusalem,

[37] The Duke of Ormond. Cromwell was victorious over him at Drogheda. He fled to France and remained firm in Charles's cause during all the years of the Commonwealth.

[38] Sancroft, the Archbishop of Canterbury.

[39] Compton, the Bishop of London.

Of hospitable soul and noble stem;
Him [40] of the western dome whose weighty sense
Flows in fit words and heavenly eloquence.
The prophets sons, by such example led,
To learning and to loyalty were bred:
For colleges on bounteous kings depend,
And never rebel was to arts a friend.
To these succeed the pillars of the laws,
Who best coud plead, and best can judge a cause.
Next them a train of loyal peers ascend:
Sharp judging Adriel,[41] the Muses friend,
Himself a Muse: — In Sanhedrins debate
True to his prince, but not a slave of State.
Whom David's love with honours did adorn,
That from his disobedient son were torn.
Jotham [42] of piercing wit and pregnant thought,
Endew'd by nature and by learning taught
To move assemblies, who but onely tri'd
The worse a while, then chose the better side;
Nor chose alone, but turned the balance too;
So much the weight of one brave man can do.
Hushai [43] the friend of David in distress,
In publick storms of manly stedfastness;
By foreign treaties he inform'd his youth;
And join'd experience to his native truth.
His frugal care suppli'd the wanting throne;
Frugal for that, but bounteous of his own:
'Tis easie conduct when exchequers flow;
But hard the task to manage well the low:
For sovereign power is too deprest or high,
When kings are forced to sell, or crouds to buy.
Indulge one labour more, my weary Muse,
For Amiel,[44] who can Amiel's praise refuse?
Of ancient race by birth, but nobler yet
In his own worth, and without title great:
The Sanhedrin long time as chief he rul'd,
Their reason guided, and their passion cool'd:
So dextrous was he in the crown's defence,
So form'd to speak a loyal nations sense,
That, as their band was Israels tribes in small,
So fit was he to represent them all.
Now rasher charioteers the seat ascend,
Whose loose carriers his steady skill commend:
They, like th' unequal ruler of the day,
Misguide the seasons, and mistake the way;
While he withdrawn at their mad labour smiles
And safe enjoys the sabbath of his toils.

These were the chief; a small but faithful band
Of worthies in the breach who dar'd to stand
And tempt th' united fury of the land.
With grief they view'd such powerful engines bent
To batter down the lawful government.
A numerous faction with pretended frights,
In Sanhedrins to plume the regal rights.
The true successor from the court removed:
The plot, by hireling witnesses improv'd.
These ills they saw, and, as their duty bound,
They shew'd the King the danger of the wound:
That no concessions from the throne woud please;
But lenitives fomented the disease;
That Absalom, ambitious of the crown,
Was made the lure to draw the people down:
That false Achitophel's pernitious hate
Had turn'd the Plot to ruine Church and State;
The council violent, the rabble worse:
That Shimei taught Jerusalem to curse.

---

[40] Dolben, Dean of Westminster Abbey, the 'western dome'.
[41] The Earl of Mulgrave, a poet and a patron of poets—in particular of Dryden.
[42] The Marquis of Halifax, a moderate man.
[43] Lawrence Hyde, ambassador and Lord High Treasurer.
[44] Seymour, Speaker of the House of Commons from 1673–1679.

With all these loads of injuries opprest,
And long revolving in his careful brest
Th' event of things; at last his patience tir'd,
Thus from his royal throne, by Heav'n inspir'd,
The god-like David spoke; with awful fear
His train their Maker in their master hear.

Thus long have I by native mercy sway'd,
My wrongs dissembl'd, my revenge delay'd;
So willing to forgive th' offending age;
So much the father did the king asswage.
But now so far my clemency they slight,
Th' offenders question my forgiving right.
That one was made for many, they contend;
But 'tis to rule, for that's a monarch's end.
They call my tenderness of blood, my fear,
Though manly tempers can the longest bear.
Yet since they will divert my native course,
'Tis time to show I am not good by force.
Those heap'd affronts that haughty subjects bring,
Are burdens for a camel, not a king:
Kings are the publick pillars of the state,
Born to sustain and prop the nations weight:
If my young Sampson will pretend a call
To shake the column, let him share the fall:
But oh that yet he woud repent and live!
How easie 'tis for parents to forgive!
With how few tears a pardon might be won
From nature, pleading for a darling son!
Poor pitied youth, by my paternal care,
Rais'd up to all the height his frame coud bear:
Had God ordain'd his fate for empire born,
He woud have giv'n his soul another turn.
Gull'd with a patriot's name, whose modern sense
Is one that woud by law supplant his prince:
The peoples brave, the politicians tool;
Never was patriot yet, but was a fool.
Whence comes it that religion and the laws
Should more be Absalom's than David's cause?
His old instructor, e'r he lost his place,
Was never thought indu'd with so much grace.
Good heav'ns, how faction can a patriot paint!
My rebel ever proves my peoples saint:
Woud they impose an heir upon the throne?
Let Sanhedrins be taught to give their own.
A king's at least a part of government;
And mine as requisite as their consent:
Without my leave a future king to choose,
Infers a right the present to depose:
True, they petition me t' approve their choice:
But Esau's hands suit ill with Jacob's voice.
My pious subjects for my safety pray,
Which to secure, they take my pow'r away.
From plots and treasons Heav'n preserve my years,
But save me most from my petitioners.
Unsatiate as the barren womb or grave;
God cannot grant so much as they can crave.
What then is left but with a jealous eye
To guard the small remains of royalty?
The law shall still direct my peaceful sway,
And the same law teach rebels to obey:
Votes shall no more established pow'r controul,
Such votes as make a part exceed the whole:
No groundless clamours shall my friends remove
Nor crouds have pow'r to punish e'r they prove;
For gods and god-like kings their care express,
Still to defend their servants in distress.
Oh that my pow'r to saving were confin'd:
Why am I forc'd, like Heav'n, against my mind,
To make examples of another kind?

Must I at length the sword of justice draw?
Oh curst effects of necessary law!
How ill my fear they by my mercy scan,
Beware the fury of a patient man.
Law they require, let law then shew her face;
They could not be content to look on Grace,
Her hinder parts, but with a daring eye
To tempt the terror of her front, and die.
By their own arts 'tis righteously decreed,
Those dire artificers of death shall bleed.
Against themselves their witnesses will swear,
Till, viper-like, their mother plot they tear,
And suck for nutriment that bloudy gore
Which was their principle of life before.
Their Belial with their Belzebub will fight;
Thus on my foes, my foes shall do me right.
Nor doubt th' event; for factious crouds engage
In their first onset, all their brutal rage;
Then let 'em take an unresisted course;
Retire and traverse, and delude their force:
But when they stand all breathless, urge the fight,
And rise upon 'em with redoubled might:
For lawful pow'r is still superiour found,
When long driv'n back, at length it stands the ground.

He said. Th' Almighty, nodding, gave consent;
And peals of thunder shook the firmament.
Henceforth a series of new time began,
The mighty years in long procession ran:
Once more the God-like David was restor'd,
And willing nations knew their lawful lord.

MAC FLECKNOE

or, A Satire upon the True-blue Protestant Poet T. S.[45] *(1682)*

ALL humane things are subject to decay,
And, when Fate summons, monarchs must obey:
This Fleckno[46] found, who, like Augustus, young
Was call'd to empire and had govern'd long:
In prose and verse was own'd, without dispute
Through all the realms of Non-sense, absolute.
This aged prince now flourishing in peace,
And blest with issue of a large increase,
Worn out with business, did at length debate
To settle the succession of the State;
And pond'ring which of all his sons was fit
To reign, and wage immortal war with wit,
Cry'd, 'tis resolv'd; for Nature pleads that he
Should onely rule, who most resembles me:
Sh—— alone my perfect image bears,
Mature in dullness from his tender years;
Sh—— alone of all my sons is he
Who stands confirm'd in full stupidity.
The rest to some faint meaning make pretence,
But *Sh*—— never deviates into sense.
Some beams of wit on other souls may fall,
Strike through and make a lucid intervall;
But *Sh*——'s genuine night admits no ray,
His rising fogs prevail upon the day:
Besides, his goodly fabrick fills the eye
And seems design'd for thoughtless majesty:
Thoughtless as monarch oakes that shade the plain,
And, spread in solemn state, supinely reign.
Heywood and Shirley[47] were but types of thee,

[45] Thomas Shadwell the poet, at whom the satire is aimed. He had earlier been a friend of Dryden, but the two men were now in opposite camps. In 1682 Dryden published *The Medal*, a satire on the Whig leader Shaftesbury. Shadwell, as the official Whig poet, answered it with *The Medal of John Bayes*. Dryden countered with *Mac Flecknoe* so brilliantly that Shadwell, who was by no means a dull fellow, has ever since had the reputation which his enemy here gives him.

[46] An Irish poet of no importance whom Dryden uses here as the archetype of dullness.

[47] Dramatists of the preceding age.

Thou last great prophet of tautology:
Even I, a dunce of more renown than they,
Was sent before but to prepare thy way:
And coarsely clad in Norwich drugget [48] came
To teach the nations in thy greater name.
My warbling lute, the lute I whilom strung,
When to King John of Portugal I sung,
Was but the prelude to that glorious day,
When thou on silver Thames did'st cut thy way,
With well tim'd oars before the royal barge,
Swelled with the pride of thy celestial charge;
And, big with hymn, commander of an host,
The like was ne'er in *Epsom* [49] blankets tost.
Methinks I see the new Arion sail,
The lute [50] still trembling underneath thy nail.
At thy well sharpned thumb from shore to shore
The treble squeaks for fear, the bases roar:
Echoes from Pissing-Ally, *Sh*—— call,
And *Sh*—— they resound from Aston Hall,
About thy boat the little fishes throng,
As at the morning toast that floats along.
Sometimes, as prince of thy harmonious band,
Thou wield'st thy papers in thy threshing hand.
St. André's [51] feet ne'er kept more equal time,
Not ev'n the feet of thy own *Psyche's* [52] rhime:
Though they in number as in sense excell,
So just, so like tautology they fell
That, pale with envy, Singleton forswore
The lute and sword which he in triumph bore,
And vow'd he ne'er would act Villerius [53] more.
Here stopt the good old syre; and wept for joy,
In silent raptures of the hopefull boy.
All arguments, but most his plays, perswade
That for anointed dulness he was made.
  Close to the walls which fair Augusta [54] bind,
(The fair Augusta much to fears inclin'd)
An ancient fabrick raised t' inform the sight,
There stood of yore, and Barbican it hight:
A watch tower once, but now, so fate ordains,
Of all the pile an empty name remains.
From its old ruins brothel-houses rise,
Scenes of lewd loves, and of polluted joys,
Where their vast courts the mother-strumpets keep,
And, undisturb'd by watch, in silence sleep.
Near these a Nursery [55] erects its head,
Where queens are formed, and future hero's bred;
Where unfledged actors learn to laugh and cry,
Where infant punks their tender voices try,
And little Maximins [56] the gods defy.
Great Fletcher never treads in Buskins here,
Nor greater Johnson dares in socks appear.
But gentle Simkin [57] just reception finds
Amidst this monument of vanisht minds;
Pure clinches,[58] the suburbian muse affords;
And Panton [59] waging harmless war with words.
Here Flecknoe, as a place to fame well known,
Ambitiously design'd his *Sh*——'s throne.
For ancient Decker [60] prophesi'd long since,
That in this pile should reign a mighty prince,

[48] A coarse cloth.
[49] A reference to Shadwell's play *Epsom Wells*. In his *Virtuoso* a character is tossed in a blanket
[50] Shadwell was a good amateur musician and was very proud of his skill on the lute. [51] A French dancing-master.
[52] Shadwell's opera, an important landmark in the history of music-drama.
[53] A character in Davenant's *Siege of Rhodes*.
[54] London. Her 'fears' are of Catholic plots.
[55] Lady Davenant (widow of the dramatist) had established this theater in the old Barbican in 1671.
[56] A character in Dryden's *Tyrannic Love*.
[57] clown [58] puns
[59] Possibly an actor of pantomime.
[60] An Elizabethan dramatist.

Born for a scourge of wit, and flayle of sense,
To whom true dulness should some *Psyches* owe,
But worlds of *Misers* [61] from his pen should flow;
Humorists and hypocrites it should produce,
Whole Raymond families and tribes of Bruce.
  Now Empress Fame had publisht the renown
Of *Sh* ——'s coronation through the town.
Rows'd by report of fame, the nations meet,
From near Bun-hill and distant Watling-street.
No Persian carpets spread th' imperial way,
But scatter'd limbs of mangled poets lay;
From dusty shops neglected authors come,
Martyrs of pies and reliques of the bum.
Much Heywood, Shirley, Ogleby there lay,
But loads of *Sh* —— almost choakt the way.
Bilk'd stationers for yeomen stood prepar'd
And *H* —— [62] was Captain of the Guard.
The hoary Prince in majesty appear'd,
High on a throne of his own labours rear'd.
At his right hand our young Ascanius sat
Rome's other hope and pillar of the State.
His brows thick fogs, instead of glories, grace,
And lambent dullness plaid around his face.
As Hannibal did to the altars come,
Swore by his syre a mortal foe to Rome;
So *Sh* —— swore, nor should his vow bee vain,
That he till death true dullness would maintain;
And, in his father's right, and realms defence,
Ne'er to have peace with wit, nor truce with sense.
The king himself the sacred unction made,
As king by office, and as priest by trade:
In his sinister hand, instead of ball,
He placed a mighty mug of potent ale;
Love's Kingdom [63] to his right he did convey,
At once his sceptre and his rule of sway;
Whose righteous lore the Prince had practis'd young
And from whose loyns recorded *Psyche* sprung.
His temples, last, with poppies were o'erspread,
That nodding seem'd to consecrate his head:
Just at that point of time, if Fame not lye,
On his left hand twelve reverend owls did fly.
So Romulus, 'tis sung, by Tyber's brook,
Presage of sway from twice six vultures took.
Th' admiring throng loud acclamations make
And omens of his future empire take.
The syre then shook the honours of his head,
And from his brows damps of oblivion shed
Full on the filial dullness: long he stood,
Repelling from his breast the raging god;
At length burst out in this prophetick mood:
  Heavens bless my son, from Ireland let him reign
To far Barbadoes on the western main;
Of his dominion may no end be known,
And greater than his father's be his throne.
Beyond loves kingdom let him stretch his pen;
He paused, and all the people cry'd Amen.
Then thus continued he, my son, advance
Still in new impudence, new ignorance.
Success let others teach, learn thou from me
Pangs without birth, and fruitless industry.
Let *Virtuoso's* in five years [64] be writ;
Yet not one thought accuse thy toyl of wit.
Let gentle George [65] in triumph tread the stage,

[61] Among Shadwell's plays are *The Miser* and *The Humorists*. Raymond is a character in the latter; Bruce a character in his *Virtuoso*. [62] Herringman, a publisher.

[63] A play by Flecknoe.

[64] A reference to Shadwell's slowness of composition.

[65] Etherege, a comic dramatist. The names which follow are of characters in his plays.

Make Dorimant betray, and Loveit rage;
Let Cully, Cockwood, Fopling, charm the pit,
And in their folly show the writers wit.
Yet still thy fools shall stand in thy defence
And justifie their author's want of sense.
Let 'em be all by thy own model made
Of dulness and desire no foreign aid,
That they to future ages may be known,
Not copies drawn, but issue of thy own.
Nay let thy men of wit too be the same,
All full of thee, and differing but in name;
But let no alien *S-dl-ly* [66] interpose
To lard with wit thy hungry *Epsom* prose.
And when false flowers of rhetorick thou would'st cull,
Trust Nature, do not labour to be dull;
But write thy best, and top; and in each line
Sir Formal's [67] oratory will be thine.
Sir Formal, though unsought, attends thy quill,
And does thy northern [68] dedications fill.
Nor let false friends seduce thy mind to fame,
By arrogating Johnson's [69] hostile name.
Let Father Flecknoe fire thy mind with praise
And Uncle Ogleby [70] thy envy raise.
Thou art my blood, where Johnson has no part:
What share have we in Nature or in Art?
Where did his wit on learning fix a brand
And rail at arts he did not understand?
Where made he love in Prince Nicander's [71] vein,
Or swept the dust in *Psyche's* humble strain?
Where sold he bargains, whip-stich, kiss my arse,
Promis'd a play and dwindled to a farce?
When did his Muse from Fletcher scenes purloin,
As thou whole Eth'ridg dost transfuse to thine?
But so transfused as oyls on waters flow,
His always floats above, thine sinks below.
This is thy province, this thy wondrous way,
New humours to invent for each new play:
This is that boasted byas of thy mind,
By which one way, to dullness, 'tis inclined,
Which makes thy writings lean on one side still,
And, in all changes, that way bends thy will.
Nor let thy mountain belly make pretence
Of likeness; thine's a tympany of sense.
A tun of man in thy large bulk is writ,
But sure thou'rt but a kilderkin of wit.
Like mine thy gentle numbers feebly creep;
Thy tragick muse gives smiles, thy comick sleep.
With whate'er gall thou settst thy self to write,
Thy inoffensive satyrs never bite.
In thy fellonious heart though venom lies,
It does but touch thy Irish pen, and dyes.
Thy genius calls thee not to purchase fame
In keen iambicks, but mild anagram:
Leave writing plays, and chuse for thy command
Some peacefull province in Acrostick Land.
There thou maist wings display, and altars raise,
And torture one poor word ten thousand ways;
Or, if thou would'st thy diff'rent talents suit,
Set thy own songs, and sing them to thy lute.
He said, but his last words were scarcely heard,
For Bruce and Longvil [72] had a trap prepar'd,
And down they sent the yet declaiming bard.

[66] Sir Charles Sedley, who assisted Shadwell in some of his scenes. [67] Sir Formal is in Shadwell's *Virtuoso*.

[68] A reference to Shadwell's patron, the Duke of Newcastle.

[69] Shadwell rather self-consciously felt himself to be the perpetuator of Jonson's genius.

[70] A dancing-master turned poet, who is also referred to in line 102.

[71] A character in *Psyche*.

[72] Bruce and Longvil. In *The Virtuoso* these gentlemen so treat Sir Formal Trifle.

Sinking he left his drugget robe behind,
Borne upwards by a subterranean wind.
The mantle fell to the young prophet's part
With double portion of his father's art.

A Song for St. Cecilia's Day [78]

NOVEMBER 22, 1687

1

FROM harmony, from heav'nly harmony
This universal frame began;
When Nature underneath a heap
Of jarring atomes lay,
And cou'd not heave her head,
The tuneful voice was heard from high,
Arise, ye more than dead.
Then cold and hot and moist and dry
In order to their stations leap,
And musick's pow'r obey.
From harmony, from heavenly harmony
This universal frame began:
From harmony to harmony
Through all the compass of the notes it ran,
The diapason closing full in man.

2

What passion cannot musick raise and quell?
When Jubal struck the corded shell,
His listening brethren stood around,
And, wond'ring, on their faces fell
To worship that celestial sound:
Less than a god they thought there could not dwell
Within the hollow of that shell,
That spoke so sweetly, and so well.
What passion cannot musick raise and quell?

3

The trumpets loud clangor
Excites us to arms
With shrill notes of anger
And mortal alarms.
The double double double beat
Of the thund'ring drum
Cryes, heark the foes come;
Charge, charge, 'tis too late to retreat.

4

The soft complaining flute
In dying notes discovers
The woes of hopeless lovers,
Whose dirge is whisper'd by the warbling lute.

5

Sharp violins proclaim
Their jealous pangs and desperation,
Fury, frantick indignation,
Depth of pains and height of passion,
For the fair, disdainful dame.

6

But oh! what art can teach
What human voice can reach
The sacred organs praise?
Notes inspiring holy love,
Notes that wing their heavenly ways
To mend the choires above.

7

Orpheus cou'd lead the savage race,
And trees unrooted left their place,
Sequacious of the lyre;
But bright Cecilia rais'd the wonder high'r:
When to her organ vocal breath was given,
An angel heard, and straight appear'd
Mistaking earth for Heav'n.

GRAND CHORUS

As from the pow'r of sacred lays
The spheres began to move,
And sung the great Creator's praise
To all the bless'd above;
So, when the last and dreadful hour
This crumbling pageant shall devour,
The trumpet shall be heard on high,
The dead shall live, the living die,
And musick shall untune the sky.

[78] A musical society had been formed in London in 1683 for the performance annually of an ode in honor of the patron saint of music. In the course of the next twenty years the greatest composers and poets of the time joined their talents in the preparation of the odes. Dryden in 1687 collaborated with the court musician, Baptista Draghi. He was again the poet selected in 1697.

ALEXANDER'S FEAST;

Or, the Power of Music

AN ODE IN HONOUR OF ST. CECILIA'S DAY: 1697

'TWAS at the royal feast, for Persia won,
By Philip's warlike son:
Aloft in awful state
The god-like heroe sate
On his imperial throne;
His valiant peers were plac'd around;
Their brows with roses and with myrtles bound.
(So should desert in arms be crown'd:)
The lovely Thais by his side,
Sate like a blooming Eastern bride
In flow'r of youth and beauty's pride.
Happy, happy, happy pair!
None but the brave,
None but the brave,
None but the brave deserves the fair.

CHORUS

Happy, happy, happy pair!
None but the brave,
None but the brave,
None but the brave deserves the fair.

Timotheus [74] plac'd on high
Amid the tuneful quire,
With flying fingers touch'd the lyre:
The trembling notes ascend the sky,
And heav'nly joys inspire.
The song began from Jove;
Who left his blissful seats above,
(Such is the pow'r of mighty love.)
A dragon's fiery form bely'd the god:
Sublime on radiant spires he rode,
When he to fair Olympia press'd:
And while he sought her snowy breast:
Then, round her slender waist he curl'd,
And stamp'd an image of himself, a sov'raign of the world.
The list'ning crowd admire the lofty sound,
A present deity, they shout around:
A present deity, the vaulted roofs rebound.

With ravish'd ears
The monarch hears,
Assumes the god,
Affects to nod,
And seems to shake the spheres.

CHORUS

With ravish'd ears
The monarch hears,
Assumes the god,
Affects to nod,
And seems to shake the spheres.

The praise of Bacchus then the sweet musician sung,
Of Bacchus ever fair, and ever young:
The jolly god in triumph comes;
Sound the trumpets; beat the drums;
Flush'd with a purple grace
He shows his honest face:
Now give the hautboys breath; he comes, He comes.
Bacchus ever fair and young
Drinking joys did first ordain;
Bacchus blessings are a treasure;
Drinking is the soldiers pleasure;
Rich the treasure;
Sweet the pleasure;
Sweet is pleasure after pain.

CHORUS

Bacchus blessings are a treasure,
Drinking is the soldier's pleasure;
Rich the treasure,
Sweet the pleasure,
Sweet is pleasure after pain.

Sooth'd with the sound the king grew vain;
Fought all his battails o'er again;
And thrice he routed all his foes, and thrice he slew the slain.
The master saw the madness rise,

---

[74] Alexander's favorite musician.

His glowing cheeks, his ardent eyes;
And while he heav'n and earth defy'd,
Chang'd his hand, and check'd his pride.
He chose a mournful muse,
Soft pity to infuse;
He sung Darius great and good,
By too severe a fate,
Fallen, fallen, fallen, fallen,
Fallen from his high estate,
And weltring in his blood:

Deserted at his utmost need
By those his former bounty fed;
On the bare earth expos'd he lies,
With not a friend to close his eyes.
With down-cast looks the joyless victor sate,
Revolving in his alter'd soul
The various turns of chance below;
And, now and then, a sigh he stole,
And tears began to flow.

CHORUS

Revolving in his alter'd soul
The various turns of chance below;
And, now and then, a sigh he stole,
And tears began to flow.

The mighty master smil'd to see
That love was in the next degree;
'Twas but a kindred-sound to move,
For pity melts the mind to love.
Softly sweet, in Lydian measures,
Soon he sooth'd his soul to pleasures.
War, he sung, is toil and trouble;
Honour but an empty bubble.
Never ending, still beginning,
Fighting still, and still destroying,
If the world be worth thy winning,
Think, O think, it worth enjoying.
Lovely Thais sits beside thee,
Take the good the gods provide thee.
The many rend the skies, with loud applause;
So love was crown'd, but musique won the cause.
The prince, unable to conceal his pain,
Gaz'd on the fair
Who caus'd his care,
And sigh'd and look'd, sigh'd and look'd,
Sigh'd and look'd, and sigh'd again:
At length, with love and wine at once oppress'd,
The vanquish'd victor sunk upon her breast.

CHORUS

The prince, unable to conceal his pain,
Gaz'd on the fair
Who caus'd his care,
And sigh'd and look'd, sigh'd and look'd,
Sigh'd and look'd, and sigh'd again;
At length, with love and wine at once oppress'd,
The vanquish'd victor sunk upon her breast.

Now strike the golden lyre again;
A lowder yet, and yet a lowder strain.
Break his bands of sleep asunder,
And rouze him, like a rattling peal of thunder.
Hark, hark, the horrid sound
Has rais'd up his head;
As awak'd from the dead,
And amaz'd he stares around.
Revenge, revenge, Timotheus cries,
See the Furies arise!
See the snakes that they rear,
How they hiss in their hair,
And the sparkles that flash from their eyes!
Behold a ghastly band,
Each a torch in his hand!
Those are Grecian ghosts, that in battail were slain,
And unbury'd remain
Inglorious on the plain:
Give the vengeance due
To the valiant crew.
Behold how they toss their torches on high,

How they point to the Persian abodes,
And glitt'ring temples of their hostile gods.
The princes applaud with a furious joy;
And the king seized a flambeau with zeal to destroy;
Thais led the way,
To light him to his prey,
And, like another Hellen, fir'd another Troy.

CHORUS

And the king seiz'd a flambeau with zeal to destroy;
Thais led the way,
To light him to his prey,
And, like another Hellen, fir'd another Troy.

Thus long ago,
'Ere heaving bellows learn'd to blow,
While organs yet were mute,
Timotheus, to his breathing flute
And sounding lyre,
Cou'd swell the soul to rage, or kindle soft desire.
At last divine Cecelia came,
Inventress of the vocal frame;
The sweet enthusiast, from her sacred store,
Enlarg'd the former narrow bounds,
And added length to solemn sounds,
With Nature's mother-wit, and arts unknown before.
Let old Timotheus yield the prize,
Or both divide the crown:
He rais'd a mortal to the skies;
She drew an angel down.

GRAND CHORUS

At last divine Cecilia came,
Inventress of the vocal frame;
The sweet enthusiast, from her sacred store,
Enlarg'd the former narrow bounds,
And added length to solemn sounds,
With Nature's mother-wit, and arts unknown before.
Let old Timotheus yield the prize,
Or both divide the crown:
He rais'd a mortal to the skies;
She drew an angel down.

Prologue and Epilogue to Tyrannick Love, or The Royal Martyr[75]

PROLOGUE

SELF-LOVE (which never rightly understood)
Makes poets still conclude their plays are good,
And malice in all criticks raigns so high,
That for small errors, they whole plays decry;
So that to see this fondness, and that spite,
You'd think that none but mad-men judge or write.
Therefore our Poet, as he thinks not fit
T' impose upon you what he writes for wit
So hopes that, leaving you your censures free,
You equal judges of the whole will be:
They judge but half, who only faults will see.
Poets, like lovers, should be bold and dare,
They spoil their business with an over-care;
And he, who servilely creeps after sence,
Is safe, but ne're will reach an excellence.
Hence 'tis, our Poet, in his conjuring,
Allow'd his fancy the full scope and swing.
But when a tyrant for his theme he had,
He loos'd the reins, and bid his Muse run mad;
And though he stumbles in a full career,
Yet rashness is a better fault than fear.
He saw his way; but in so swift a pace,
To chuse the ground might be to lose the race.
They then, who of each trip th' advantage take,
Find but those faults, which they want wit to make.

[75] Produced in 1669.

EPILOGUE

Spoken by Mrs. Ellen[76] *when she was to be carried off by the Bearers*

To the Bearer. Hold! are you mad? you damn'd, confounded dog!
I am to rise, and speak the epilogue.
To the Audience. I come, kind Gentlemen, strange news to tell ye;
I am the ghost of poor departed Nelly.
Sweet Ladies, be not frighted; I'le be civil;
I'm what I was, a little harmless devil.
For, after death, we sprights have just such natures,
We had, for all the world, when humane creatures;
And, therefore, I, that was an actress here,
Play all my tricks in Hell, a goblin there.
Gallants, look to 't, you say there are no sprights;
But I'll come dance about your beds at nights;
And faith you'll be in a sweet kind of taking,
When I surprise you between sleep and waking.
To tell you true, I walk, because I dye
Out of my calling, in a tragedy.
O Poet, damn'd dull Poet, who could prove
So senseless, to make Nelly dye for love!
Nay, what's yet worse, to kill me in the prime
Of Easter-term, in tart and cheese-cake time!
I'le fit the fopp; for I'le not one word say,
T' excuse his godly, out of fashion play;
A play, which, if you dare but twice sit out,
You'll all be slander'd, and be thought devout.[77]
But, farewel, Gentlemen, make haste to me,
I'm sure e're long to have your company.
As for my epitaph when I am gone,
I'le trust no poet, but will write my own.

Here Nelly lies, who, though she lived a slater'n,
Yet dy'd a princess, acting in S. Cathar'n.

[76] Nell Gwyn

[77] *Tyrannic Love* is based on the story of St. Catherine of Alexandria.

Epilogue To Mithridates, King of Pontus[78]

You've seen a pair of faithful lovers die:
And much you care, for most of you will cry,
'Twas a just judgment on their constancy.
For, Heaven be thank'd, we live in such an age,
When no man dies for love, but on the stage:
And ev'n those martyrs are but rare in plays;
A cursed sign how much true faith decays:
Love is no more a violent desire;
'Tis a meer metaphor, a painted fire.
In all our sex, the name examin'd well,
Is pride to gain, and vanity to tell.
In woman, 'tis of subtil int'rest made;
Curse on the punk that made it first a trade!
She first did wits prerogative remove,
And made a fool presume to prate of love.
Let honour and preferment go for gold,
But glorious beauty is not to be sold;
Or, if it be, 'tis at a rate so high,
That nothing but adoring it shou'd buy.
Yet the rich cullies may their boasting spare;
They purchase but sophisticated ware.
'Tis prodigality that buys deceit,
Where both the giver, and the taker cheat.
Men but refine on the old half-crown way;
And women fight, like Swizzers, for their pay.

SONGS FROM THE PLAYS

Ah fading joy

Ah fading joy, how quickly art thou past!
  Yet we thy ruine haste:
As if the cares of humane life were few,
  We seek out new,
And follow fate that does too fast pursue.

See how on ev'ry bough the birds express
  In their sweet notes their happiness.

[78] A tragedy by Lee, produced in 1678. Dryden's prologues and epilogues were so much in demand by other dramatists that he could ask as much as seven guineas for one.

They all enjoy and nothing spare;
But on their mother Nature lay their care:
Why then should man, the lord of all below,
Such troubles chuse to know,
As none of all his subjects undergo?

Hark, hark, the waters fall, fall, fall
And with a murmuring sound
Dash, dash, upon the ground,
To gentle slumbers call.

[*The Indian Emperor*, 1665]

After the pangs of a desperate lover

After the pangs of a desperate lover,
When day and night I have sigh'd all in vain,
Ah what a pleasure it is to discover
In her eyes pity, who causes my pain!

When with unkindness our love at a stand is,
And both have punish'd our selves with the pain,
Ah what a pleasure the touch of her hand is,
Ah what a pleasure to press it again!

When the denial comes fainter and fainter,
And her eyes give what her tongue does deny,
Ah what a trembling I feel when I venture,
Ah what a trembling does usher my joy!

When, with a sigh, she accords me the blessing,
And her eyes twinkle 'twixt pleasure and pain;
Ah what a joy 'tis, beyond all expressing,
Ah what a joy to hear, shall we again!

[*An Evening's Love*, 1668]

Calm was the even

Calm was the even, and clear was the sky,
And the new-budding flowers did spring,
When all alone went Amyntas and I
To hear the sweet nightingal sing;
I sate, and he laid him down by me;
But scarcely his breath he could draw;
For when with a fear, he began to draw near,
He was dash'd with A ha ha ha ha!

He blush'd to himself, and lay still for a while,
And his modesty curb'd his desire;
But straight I convinc'd all his fear with a smile,
Which added new flames to his fire.
O Sylvia, said he, you are cruel,
To keep your poor lover in awe;
Then once more he prest with his hand to my brest
But was dash'd with A ha ha ha ha.

I knew 'twas his passion that caus'd all his fear;
And therefore I pity'd his case:
I whisper'd him softly, there's no body here
And laid my cheek close to his face:
But as he grew bolder and bolder,
A shepheard came by us and saw;
And just as our bliss we began with a kiss,
He laugh'd out with A ha ha ha ha.

[*An Evening's Love*, 1668]

Song of the Zambra Dance

Beneath a myrtle shade
Which Love for none but happy lovers made,
I slept, and straight my love before me brought
Phillis the object of my waking thought;
Undres'd she came my flames to meet,
While love strow'd flow'rs beneath her feet;
Flow'rs, which so press'd by her, became more sweet.

From the bright visions head
A careless vail of lawn was loosely spread:

From her white temples fell her shaded hair,
Like cloudy sunshine not too brown nor fair:
Her hands, her lips did love inspire;
Her ev'ry grace my heart did fire:
But most her eyes which languish'd with desire.

Ah, charming fair, said I,
How long can you my bliss and yours deny?
By Nature and by love this lonely shade
Was for revenge of suffring lovers made:
Silence and shades with love agree:
Both shelter you and favour me;
You cannot blush because I cannot see.

No, let me dye, she said,
Rather than loose the spotless name of maid:
Faintly methought she spoke, for all the while
She bid me not believe her, with a smile.
Then dye, said I, she still deny'd:
And is it thus, thus, thus she cry'd
You use a harmless maid, and so she dy'd!

I wak'd, and straight I knew
I lov'd so well it made my dream prove true:
Fancy, the kinder mistress of the two,
Fancy had done what Phillis wou'd not do!
Ah, cruel nymph, cease your disdain,
While I can dream you scorn in vain;
Asleep or waking you must ease my pain.

[*The Conquest of Granada*, 1670]

Why should a foolish marriage vow

Why should a foolish marriage vow
Which long ago was made,
Oblige us to each other now
When passion is decay'd?
We lov'd, and we lov'd, as long as we cou'd,
Till our love was lov'd out in us both:
But our marriage is dead, when the pleasure is fled:
'Twas pleasure first made it an oath.

If I have pleasures for a friend,
And farther love in store,
What wrong has he whose joys did end,
And who cou'd give no more?
'Tis a madness that he
Shou'd be jealous of me,
Or that I shou'd bar him of another:
For all we can gain is to give our selves pain,
When neither can hinder the other.

[*Marriage a la Mode*, 1672]

Alexander Pope 1688–1744

Ode on Solitude [1]

Happy the man whose wish and care
A few paternal acres bound,
Content to breathe his native air
In his own ground.

Whose herds with milk, whose fields with bread,
Whose flocks supply him with attire,
Whose trees in summer yield him shade,
In winter fire.

Bless'd who can unconcern'dly find
Hours, days, and years slide soft away,
In health of body, peace of mind,
Quiet by day;

Sound sleep by night: study and ease
Together mix'd; sweet recreation;
And innocence, which most does please,
With meditation.

Thus let me live, unseen, unknown,
Thus unlamented let me die;
Steal from the world, and not a stone
Tell where I lie.

[1] Although Pope's own statement that this was written when he was about twelve years old is probably untrue, it is apparently his earliest remaining poem.

from AN ESSAY ON CRITICISM[2]

PART I

INTRODUCTION. That it is as great a fault to judge ill as to write ill, and a more dangerous one to the public. That a true Taste is as rare to be found as a true Genius. That most men are born with some Taste, but spoiled by false education. The multitude of Critics, and causes of them. That we are to study our own Taste, and know the limits of it. Nature the best guide of judgment. Improved by Art and rules, which are but methodized Nature. Rules derived from the practice of the ancient poets. That therefore the ancients are necessary to be studied by a Critic, particularly Homer and Virgil. Of licenses, and the use of them by the ancients. Reverence due to the ancients, and praise of them.

'T IS hard to say if greater want of skill
Appear in writing or in judging ill;
But of the two less dangerous is th' offence
To tire our patience than mislead our sense:
Some few in that, but numbers err in this;
Ten censure wrong for one who writes amiss;
A fool might once himself alone expose;
Now one in verse makes many more in prose.
'T is with our judgments as our watches, none
Go just alike, yet each believes his own.
In Poets as true Genius is but rare,
True Taste as seldom is the Critic's share;
Both must alike from Heav'n derive their light,
These born to judge, as well as those to write.
Let such teach others who themselves excel,
And censure freely who have written well;
Authors are partial to their wit, 't is true,
But are not Critics to their judgment too?
Yet if we look more closely, we shall find
Most have the seeds of judgment in their mind:
Nature affords at least a glimm'ring light;
The lines, tho' touch't but faintly, are drawn right:
But as the slightest sketch, if justly traced,
Is by ill col'ring but the more disgraced,
So by false learning is good sense defaced:
Some are bewilder'd in the maze of schools,
And some made coxcombs Nature meant but fools:
In search of wit these lose their common sense,
And then turn Critics in their own defence:
Each burns alike, who can or cannot write,
Or with a rival's or an eunuch's spite,
All fools have still an itching to deride,
And fain would be upon the laughing side.
If Mævius[3] scribble in Apollo's spite,
There are who judge still worse than he can write.
Some have at first for Wits, then Poets pass'd;
Turn'd Critics next, and prov'd plain Fools at last.
Some neither can for Wits nor Critics pass,
As heavy mules are neither horse nor ass.
Those half-learn'd witlings, numerous in our isle,
As half-form'd insects on the banks of Nile;
Unfinish'd things, one knows not what to call,
Their generation's so equivocal;
To tell them would a hundred tongues require,
Or one vain Wit's, that might a hundred tire.
But you who seek to give and merit fame,
And justly bear a Critic's noble name,
Be sure yourself and your own reach to know,
How far your Genius, Taste, and Learning go,

[2] Written between 1707 and 1709; published in 1711.

[3] An uninspired Roman poet.

Launch not beyond your depth, but be discreet,
And mark that point where Sense and Dulness meet.
Nature to all things fix'd the limits fit,
And wisely curb'd proud man's pretending wit.
As on the land while here the ocean gains,
In other parts it leaves wide sandy plains;
Thus in the soul while Memory prevails,
The solid power of Understanding fails;
Where beams of warm Imagination play,
The Memory's soft figures melt away.
One Science only will one genius fit;
So vast is Art, so narrow human wit:
Not only bounded to peculiar arts,
But oft in those confin'd to single parts.
Like Kings we lose the conquests gain'd before,
By vain ambition still to make them more:
Each might his sev'ral province well command,
Would all but stoop to what they understand.
First follow Nature, and your judgment frame
By her just standard, which is still the same;
Unerring Nature, still divinely bright,
One clear, unchanged, and universal light,
Life, force, and beauty must to all impart,
At once the source, and end, and test of Art.
Art from that fund each just supply provides,
Works without show, and without pomp presides.
In some fair body thus th' informing soul
With spirits feeds, with vigour fills the whole;
Each motion guides, and every nerve sustains,
Itself unseen, but in th' effects remains.
Some, to whom Heav'n in wit has been profuse,
Want as much more to turn it to its use;
For Wit and Judgment often are at strife,
Tho' meant each other's aid, like man and wife.
'T is more to guide than spur the Muse's steed,
Restrain his fury than provoke his speed:
The winged courser, like a gen'rous horse,
Shows most true mettle when you check his course.
Those rules of old, discover'd, not devised,
Are Nature still, but Nature methodized;
Nature, like Liberty, is but restrain'd
By the same laws which first herself ordain'd.
Hear how learn'd Greece her useful rules indites
When to repress and when indulge our flights:
High on Parnassus' top her sons she show'd,
And pointed out those arduous paths they trod;
Held from afar, aloft, th' immortal prize,
And urged the rest by equal steps to rise.
Just precepts thus from great examples giv'n,
She drew from them what they derived from Heav'n.
The gen'rous Critic fann'd the poet's fire,
And taught the world with reason to admire.
Then Criticism the Muse's handmaid prov'd,
To dress her charms, and make her more belov'd:
But following Wits from that intention stray'd:
Who could not win the mistress woo'd the maid;
Against the Poets their own arms they turn'd,
Sure to hate most the men from whom they learn'd.
So modern 'pothecaries, taught the art
By doctors' bills to play the doctor's part,
Bold in the practice of mistaken rules,
Prescribe, apply, and call their masters fools.
Some on the leaves of ancient authors prey;

Nor time nor moths e'er spoil'd so much as they;
Some drily plain, without invention's aid,
Write dull receipts how poems may be made;
These leave the sense, their learning to display,
And those explain the meaning quite away.
  You then whose judgment the right course would steer,
Know well each ancient's proper character;
His fable, subject, scope in every page;
Religion, country, genius of his age:
Without all these at once before your eyes,
Cavil you may, but never criticise.
Be Homer's works your study and delight,
Read them by day, and meditate by night;
Thence form your judgment, thence your maxims bring,
And trace the Muses upward to their spring.
Still with itself compared, his text peruse;
And let your comment be the Mantuan Muse.[4]
  When first young Maro in his boundless mind
A work t' outlast immortal Rome design'd,
Perhaps he seem'd above the critic's law,
And but from Nature's fountains scorn'd to draw;
But when t' examine ev'ry part he came,
Nature and Homer were, he found, the same.
Convinced, amazed, he checks the bold design,
And rules as strict his labour'd work confine
As if the Stagyrite [5] o'erlook'd each line.
Learn hence for ancient rules a just esteem;
To copy Nature is to copy them.
  Some beauties yet no precepts can declare,
For there's a happiness as well as care.
Music resembles poetry; in each
Are nameless graces which no methods teach,
And which a master-hand alone can reach.
If, where the rules not far enough extend,
(Since rules were made but to promote their end)
Some lucky license answer to the full
Th' intent proposed, that license is a rule.
Thus Pegasus, a nearer way to take,
May boldly deviate from the common track.
Great Wits sometimes may gloriously offend,
And rise to faults true Critics dare not mend;
From vulgar bounds with brave disorder part,
And snatch a grace beyond the reach of Art,
Which, without passing thro' the judgment, gains
The heart, and all its end at once attains.
In prospects thus some objects please our eyes,
Which out of Nature's common order rise,
The shapeless rock, or hanging precipice.
But tho' the ancients thus their rules invade,
(As Kings dispense with laws themselves have made)
Moderns, beware! or if you must offend
Against the precept, ne'er transgress its end;
Let it be seldom, and compell'd by need;
And have at least their precedent to plead;
The Critic else proceeds without remorse,
Seizes your fame, and puts his laws in force.
  I know there are to whose presumptuous thoughts
Those freer beauties, ev'n in them, seem faults.
Some figures monstrous and misshaped appear,
Consider'd singly, or beheld too near,

[4] Virgil
[5] Aristotle

Which, but proportion'd to their light or place,
Due distance reconciles to form and grace.
A prudent chief not always must display
His powers in equal ranks and fair array,
But with th' occasion and the place comply,
Conceal his force, nay, seem sometimes to fly.
Those oft are stratagems which errors seem,
Nor is it Homer nods, but we that dream.
  Still green with bays each ancient altar stands
Above the reach of sacrilegious hands,
Secure from flames, from Envy's fiercer rage,
Destructive War, and all-involving Age.
See from each clime the learn'd their incense bring!
Hear in all tongues consenting pæans ring!
In praise so just let ev'ry voice be join'd,
And fill the gen'ral chorus of mankind.
Hail, Bards triumphant! born in happier days,
Immortal heirs of universal praise!
Whose honours with increase of ages grow,
As streams roll down, enlarging as they flow;
Nations unborn your mighty names shall sound,
And worlds applaud that must not yet be found!
O may some spark of your celestial fire
The last, the meanest of your sons inspire,
(That on weak wings, from far, pursues your flights,
Glows while he reads, but trembles as he writes)
To teach vain Wits a science little known,
T' admire superior sense, and doubt their own.

PART II

Causes hindering a true judgment. Pride. Imperfect learning. Judging by parts, and not by the whole. Critics in wit, language, versification only. Being too hard to please, or too apt to admire. Partiality — too much love to a sect — to the ancients or moderns. Prejudice or prevention. Singularity. Inconstancy. Party spirit. Envy. Against envy, and in praise of good nature. When severity is chiefly to be used by critics.

Of all the causes which conspire to blind
Man's erring judgment, and misguide the mind,
What the weak head with strongest bias rules,
Is Pride, the never failing vice of fools.
Whatever Nature has in worth denied
She gives in large recruits of needful Pride:
For as in bodies, thus in souls, we find
What wants in blood and spirits swell'd with wind:
Pride, where Wit fails, steps in to our defence,
And fills up all the mighty void of Sense:
If once right Reason drives that cloud away,
Truth breaks upon us with resistless day.
Trust not yourself; but your defects to know,
Make use of ev'ry friend — and ev'ry foe.
  A little learning is a dangerous thing;
Drink deep, or taste not the Pierian spring: [6]
There shallow draughts intoxicate the brain,
And drinking largely sobers us again.
Fired at first sight with what the Muse imparts,
In fearless youth we tempt the heights of arts,
While from the bounded level of our mind
Short views we take, nor see the lengths behind:
But more advanc'd, behold with strange surprise
New distant scenes of endless science rise!
So pleas'd at first the tow'ring Alps we try,
Mount o'er the vales, and seem to tread the sky;
Th' eternal snows appear already past,
And the first clouds and mountains seem the last:
But those attain'd, we tremble to survey

[6] Pieria was counted the birthplace of the Muses.

The growing labours of the lengthen'd way;
Th' increasing prospect tires our wand'ring eyes,
Hills peep o'er hills, and Alps on Alps arise!
A perfect judge will read each work of wit.
With the same spirit that its author writ;
Survey the whole, nor seek slight faults to find
Where Nature moves, and Rapture warms the mind:
Nor lose, for that malignant dull delight,
The gen'rous pleasure to be charm'd with wit.
But in such lays as neither ebb nor flow,
Correctly cold, and regularly low,
That shunning faults one quiet tenor keep,
We cannot blame indeed — but we may sleep.
In Wit, as Nature, what affects our hearts
Is not th' exactness of peculiar parts;
'T is not a lip or eye we beauty call,
But the joint force and full result of all.
Thus when we view some well proportion'd dome,
(The world's just wonder, and ev'n thine, O Rome!) [7]
No single parts unequally surprise,
All comes united to th' admiring eyes;
No monstrous height, or breadth, or length, appear;
The whole at once is bold and regular.
Whoever thinks a faultless piece to see,
Thinks what ne'er was, nor is, nor e'er shall be.
In every work regard the writer's end,
Since none can compass more than they intend;
And if the means be just, the conduct true,
Applause, in spite of trivial faults, is due.
As men of breeding, sometimes men of wit,
T' avoid great errors must the less commit;
Neglect the rules each verbal critic lays,
For not to know some trifles is a praise.
Most critics, fond of some subservient art,
Still make the whole depend upon a part:
They talk of Principles, but Notions prize,
And all to one lov'd folly sacrifice.
Once on a time La Mancha's Knight,[8] they say,
A certain bard encount'ring on the way,
Discours'd in terms as just, with looks as sage,
As e'er could Dennis,[9] of the Grecian Stage;
Concluding all were desperate sots and fools
Who durst depart from Aristotle's rules.
Our author, happy in a judge so nice,
Produced his play, and begg'd the knight's advice;
Made him observe the Subject and the Plot,
The Manners, Passions, Unities; what not?
All which exact to rule were brought about,
Were but a combat in the lists left out.
'What! leave the combat out?' exclaims the knight.
'Yes, or we must renounce the Stagyrite.'
'Not so, by Heaven! (he answers in a rage)
Knights, squires, and steeds must enter on the stage.'
'So vast a throng the stage can ne'er contain.'
'Then build a new, or act it in a plain.'
Thus critics of less judgment than caprice,
Curious, not knowing, not exact, but nice,
Form short ideas, and offend in Arts
(As most in Manners), by a love to parts.
Some to Conceit alone their taste confine,
And glitt'ring thoughts struck out at every line;
Pleas'd with a work where nothing's just or fit,
One glaring chaos and wild heap of wit.
Poets, like painters, thus unskill'd to trace

7 St. Peter's

8 Don Quixote

9 John Dennis, critic and dramatist, one of Pope's contemporaries.

The naked nature and the living grace,
With gold and jewels cover every part,
And hide with ornaments their want of Art.
True Wit is Nature to advantage dress'd,
What oft was thought, but ne'er so well express'd;
Something whose truth convinced at sight we find,
That gives us back the image of our mind.
As shades more sweetly recommend the light,
So modest plainness sets off sprightly wit:
For works may have more wit than does them good,
As bodies perish thro' excess of blood.
Others for language all their care express,
And value books, as women men, for dress:
Their praise is still — the Style is excellent;
The Sense they humbly take upon content.
Words are like leaves; and where they most abound,
Much fruit of sense beneath is rarely found.
False eloquence, like the prismatic glass,
Its gaudy colours spreads on every place;
The face of Nature we no more survey,
All glares alike, without distinction gay;
But true expression, like th' unchanging sun,
Clears and improves whate'er it shines upon;
It gilds all objects, but it alters none.
Expression is the dress of thought, and still
Appears more decent as more suitable.
A vile Conceit in pompous words express'd
Is like a clown in regal purple dress'd:
For diff'rent styles with diff'rent subjects sort,
As sev'ral garbs with country, town, and court.
Some by old words to fame have made pretence,
Ancients in phrase, mere moderns in their sense;
Such labour'd nothings, in so strange a style,
Amaze th' unlearn'd, and make the learned smile;
Unlucky as Fungoso in the play,[10]
These sparks with awkward vanity display
What the fine gentleman wore yesterday;
And but so mimic ancient wits at best,
As apes our grandsires in their doublets drest.
In words as fashions the same rule will hold,
Alike fantastic if too new or old:
Be not the first by whom the new are tried,
Nor yet the last to lay the old aside.
But most by Numbers judge a poet's song,
And smooth or rough with them is right or wrong.
In the bright Muse tho' thousand charms conspire,
Her voice is all these tuneful fools admire;
Who haunt Parnassus but to please their ear,
Not mend their minds; as some to church repair,
Not for the doctrine, but the music there.
These equal syllables alone require,
Tho' oft the ear the open vowels tire,
While expletives their feeble aid do join,
And ten low words oft creep in one dull line:
While they ring round the same unvaried chimes,
With sure returns of still expected rhymes;
Where'er you find 'the cooling western breeze,'
In the next line, it 'whispers thro' the trees;'
If crystal streams 'with pleasing murmurs creep,'
The reader's threaten'd (not in vain) with 'sleep;'
Then, at the last and only couplet, fraught
With some unmeaning thing they call a thought,

[10] In Ben Jonson's *Every Man out of His Humour.*

A needless Alexandrine ends the song,
That, like a wounded snake, drags its slow length along.
Leave such to tune their own dull rhymes, and know
What's roundly smooth, or languishingly slow;
And praise the easy vigour of a line
Where Denham's strength and Waller's sweetness join.[11]
True ease in writing comes from Art, not Chance,
As those move easiest who have learn'd to dance.
'T is not enough no harshness gives offence;
The sound must seem an echo to the sense.
Soft is the strain when zephyr gently blows,
And the smooth stream in smoother numbers flows;
But when loud surges lash the sounding shore,
The hoarse rough verse should like the torrent roar.
When Ajax strives some rock's vast weight to throw,
The line, too, labours, and the words move slow:
Not so when swift Camilla scours the plain,
Flies o'er th' unbending corn, and skims along the main.
Hear how Timotheus' varied lays surprise,
And bid alternate passions fall and rise! [12]
While at each change the son of Libyan Jove
Now burns with glory, and then melts with love;
Now his fierce eyes with sparkling fury glow,
Now sighs steal out, and tears begin to flow:
Persians and Greeks like turns of nature found,
And the world's Victor stood subdued by sound!
The power of music all our hearts allow,
And what Timotheus was is Dryden now.
  Avoid extremes, and shun the fault of such
Who still are pleas'd too little or too much.
At ev'ry trifle scorn to take offence;
That always shows great pride or little sense:
Those heads, as stomachs, are not sure the best
Which nauseate all, and nothing can digest.
Yet let not each gay turn thy rapture move;
For fools admire, but men of sense approve:
As things seem large which we thro' mist descry,
Dulness is ever apt to magnify.
  Some foreign writers, some our own despise;
The ancients only, or the moderns prize.
Thus Wit, like Faith, by each man is applied
To one small sect, and all are damn'd beside.
Meanly they seek the blessing to confine,
And force that sun but on a part to shine,
Which not alone the southern wit sublimes,
But ripens spirits in cold northern climes;
Which from the first has shone on ages past,
Enlights the present, and shall warm the last;
Tho' each may feel increases and decays,
And see now clearer and now darker days.
Regard not then if wit be old or new,
But blame the False and value still the True.
  Some ne'er advance a judgment of their own,
But catch the spreading notion of the town;
They reason and conclude by precedent,
And own stale nonsense which they ne'er invent.
Some judge of authors' names, not works, and then

---

[11] Poets of the mid-seventeenth century, who used the closed couplet.

[12] Refers, as do the following lines, to Dryden's *Alexander's Feast.*

Nor praise nor blame the writings, but the men.
Of all this servile herd, the worst is he
That in proud dulness joins with Quality;
A constant critic at the great man's board,
To fetch and carry nonsense for my lord.
What woeful stuff this madrigal would be
In some starv'd hackney sonneteer or me!
But let a lord once own the happy lines,
How the Wit brightens! how the Style refines!
Before his sacred name flies every fault,
And each exalted stanza teems with thought!
  The vulgar thus thro' imitation err,
As oft the learn'd by being singular;
So much they scorn the crowd, that if the throng
By chance go right, they purposely go wrong.
So schismatics the plain believers quit,
And are but damn'd for having too much wit.
Some praise at morning what they blame at night,
But always think the last opinion right.
A Muse by these is like a mistress used,
This hour she's idolized, the next abused;
While their weak heads, like towns unfortified,
'Twixt sense and nonsense daily change their side.
Ask them the cause; they're wiser still, they say;
And still to-morrow's wiser than to-day.
We think our fathers fools, so wise we grow;
Our wiser sons, no doubt, will think us so.
Once school-divines this zealous isle o'erspread;
Who knew most sentences, was deepest read.
Faith, Gospel, all seem'd made to be disputed,
And none had sense enough to be confuted.
Scotists and Thomists [13] now in peace remain
Amidst their kindred cobwebs in Ducklane.[14]
If Faith itself has diff'rent dresses worn,
What wonder modes in Wit should take their turn?
Oft, leaving what is natural and fit,
The current Folly proves the ready Wit;
And authors think their reputation safe,
Which lives as long as fools are pleas'd to laugh.
  Some, valuing those of their own side or mind,
Still make themselves the measure of mankind:
Fondly we think we honour merit then,
When we but praise ourselves in other men.
Parties in wit attend on those of state,
And public faction doubles private hate.
Pride, Malice, Folly, against Dryden rose,
In various shapes of parsons, critics, beaux:
But sense survived when merry jests were past;
For rising merit will buoy up at last.
Might he return and bless once more our eyes,
New Blackmores and new Milbournes [15] must arise.
Nay, should great Homer lift his awful head,
Zoilus [16] again would start up from the dead.
Envy will Merit as its shade pursue,
But like a shadow proves the substance true;
For envied Wit, like Sol eclips'd, makes known
Th' opposing body's grossness, not its own.
When first that sun too powerful beams displays,
It draws up vapours which obscure its rays;
But ev'n those clouds at last adorn its way,
Reflect new glories, and augment the day.
  Be thou the first true merit to befriend;

[13] Followers of the thirteenth century scholastics, Duns Scotus and St. Thomas Aquinas.

[14] Second-hand books were sold there.

[15] Both Blackmore, a physician and poet of a sort, and Milbourn, a clergyman, attacked Dryden.

[16] A Greek critic of the fourth century who attacked Homer.

His praise is lost who stays till all commend.
Short is the date, alas! of modern rhymes,
And 't is but just to let them live betimes.
No longer now that Golden Age appears,
When patriarch wits survived a thousand years:
Now length of fame (our second life) is lost,
And bare threescore is all ev'n that can boast:
Our sons their fathers' failing language see,
And such as Chaucer is shall Dryden be.
So when the faithful pencil has design'd
Some bright idea of the master's mind,
Where a new world leaps out at his command,
And ready Nature waits upon his hand;
When the ripe colours soften and unite,
And sweetly melt into just shade and light;
When mellowing years their full perfection give,
And each bold figure just begins to live,
The treach'rous colours the fair art betray,
And all the bright creation fades away!

Unhappy Wit, like most mistaken things,
Atones not for that envy which it brings:
In youth alone its empty praise we boast,
But soon the short-lived vanity is lost;
Like some fair flower the early Spring supplies,
That gaily blooms, but ev'n in blooming dies.
What is this Wit, which must our cares employ?
The owner's wife that other men enjoy;
Then most our trouble still when most admired,
And still the more we give, the more required;
Whose fame with pains we guard, but lose with ease,
Sure some to vex, but never all to please;
'T is what the vicious fear, the virtuous shun,
By fools 't is hated, and by knaves undone!

If wit so much from Ignorance undergo,
Ah, let not Learning too commence its foe!
Of old those met rewards who could excel,
And such were prais'd who but endeavour'd well;
Tho' triumphs were to gen'rals only due,
Crowns were reserv'd to grace the soldiers too.
Now they who reach Parnassus' lofty crown
Employ their pains to spurn some others down;
And while self-love each jealous writer rules,
Contending wits become the sport of fools;
But still the worst with most regret commend,
For each ill author is as bad a friend.
To what base ends, and by what abject ways,
Are mortals urged thro' sacred lust of praise!
Ah, ne'er so dire a thirst of glory boast,
Nor in the critic let the man be lost!
Good nature and good sense must ever join;
To err is human, to forgive divine.

But if in noble minds some dregs remain,
Not yet purged off, of spleen and sour disdain,
Discharge that rage on more provoking crimes,
Nor fear a dearth in these flagitious times.
No pardon vile obscenity should find,
Tho' Wit and Art conspire to move your mind;
But dulness with obscenity must prove
As shameful sure as impotence in love.
In the fat age of pleasure, wealth, and ease
Sprung the rank weed, and thrived with large increase:
When love was all an easy monarch's care,
Seldom at council, never in a war;

Jilts ruled the state, and statesmen farces writ;
Nay wits had pensions, and young lords had wit;
The Fair sat panting at a courtier's play,
And not a mask went unimprov'd away;
The modest fan was lifted up no more,
And virgins smil'd at what they blush'd before.
The following license of a foreign reign
Did all the dregs of bold Socinus [17] drain;
Then unbelieving priests reform'd the nation,
And taught more pleasant methods of salvation;
Where Heav'n's free subjects might their rights dispute,
Lest God himself should seem too absolute;
Pulpits their sacred satire learn'd to spare,
And vice admired to find a flatt'rer there!
Encouraged thus, Wit's Titans braved the skies,
And the press groan'd with licens'd blasphemies.
These monsters, Critics! with your darts engage,
Here point your thunder, and exhaust your rage!
Yet shun their fault, who, scandalously nice,
Will needs mistake an author into vice:
All seems infected that th' infected spy,
As all looks yellow to the jaundic'd eye.

THE RAPE OF THE LOCK [18]

An Heroi-Comical Poem

Nolueram, Belinda, tuos violare capillos;
Sed juvat, hoc precibus me tribuisse tuis.
— *Mart.*

TO MRS. ARABELLA FERMOR

MADAM, — It will be in vain to deny that I have some regard for this piece, since I dedicate it to You. Yet you may bear me witness it was intended only to divert a few young ladies, who have good sense and good humour enough to laugh not only at their sex's little unguarded follies, but at their own. But as it was communicated with the air of a secret, it soon found its way into the world. An imperfect copy having been offer'd to a bookseller, you had the good-nature for my sake, to consent to the publication of one more correct: this I was forced to, before I had executed half my design, for the Machinery was entirely wanting to complete it.

The Machinery, Madam, is a term invented by the critics, to signify that part which the Deities, Angels, or Dæmons, are made to act in a poem: for the ancient poets are in one respect like many modern ladies; let an action be never so trivial in itself, they always make it appear of the utmost importance. These Machines I determined to raise on a very new and odd foundation, the Rosicrucian doctrine of Spirits.

I know how disagreeable it is to make use of hard words before a lady; but it is so much the concern of a poet to have his works understood, and particularly by your sex, that you must give me leave to explain two or three difficult terms. The Rosicrucians are a people I must bring you acquainted with. The best account I know of them is in a French book called *La Comte de Gabalis,* which, both in its title and size, is so like a novel, that many of the fair sex have read it for one by mistake. According to these gentlemen, the four elements are inhabited by Spirits, which they call Sylphs, Gnomes, Nymphs, and Salamanders. The Gnomes, or Dæmons of earth, delight in mischief; but the Sylphs, whose habitation is in the air, are the best-conditioned creatures imaginable; for, they say, any mortal may enjoy the most intimate familiarities with these gentle spirits, upon a condition very easy to all true adepts, — an inviolate preservation of chastity.

As to the following cantos, all the passages of them are as fabulous as the Vision at the beginning, or the Transformation at the end (except the loss of your hair, which I always mention with reverence). The human persons are as fictitious as the airy ones; and the character of Belinda, as it is now managed, resembles you in nothing but in beauty.

If this poem had as many graces as there are in your person or in your mind, yet I could never hope it should pass thro' the world half so uncen-

[17] Lilio and Fausto Sozzini (Socinus) revived in the sixteenth century the Arian heresy that Jesus was not God but his prophet.

[18] First written in 1711, and published in 1712 in *Lintot's Miscellanies;* the present enlarged form of the poem, with the added 'machinery' of gnomes and sylphs, appeared in 1714. Pope wrote the mock epic at his friend John Caryll's suggestion, in order to heal a quarrel by reducing it to an absurdity. Lord Petre had in fun cut off a lock of Miss Arabella Fermor's hair. The maiden's anger grew into a family feud, whose possible serious consequences were averted, it is said, by Pope's amusing intervention.

The epigram from Martial reads: 'I desired not, Belinda, to do violence to your locks; but I am happy to pay this tribute to your prayers.'

sured as You have done. But let its fortune be what it will, mine is happy enough, to have given me this occasion of assuring you that I am, with the truest esteem, Madam,

Your most obedient, humble servant,

A. Pope.

CANTO I

What dire offence from am'rous causes springs,
What mighty contests rise from trivial things,
I sing — This verse to *Caryll,* muse! is due:
This, ev'n Belinda may vouchsafe to view:
Slight is the subject, but not so the praise,
If she inspire, and he approve my lays.
Say what strange motive, Goddess! could compel
A well-bred Lord t' assault a gentle Belle?
O say what stranger cause, yet unexplor'd,
Could make a gentle Belle reject a Lord?
In tasks so bold can little men engage,
And in soft bosoms dwells such mighty rage?
Sol thro' white curtains shot a tim'rous ray,
And oped those eyes that must eclipse the day.
Now lapdogs give themselves the rousing shake,
And sleepless lovers just at twelve awake:
Thrice rung the bell, the slipper knock'd the ground,[19]
And the press'd watch return'd a silver sound.
Belinda still her downy pillow prest,
Her guardian Sylph prolong'd the balmy rest.
'Twas he had summon'd to her silent bed
The morning-dream that hover'd o'er her head;
A youth more glitt'ring than a Birthnight Beau
(That ev'n in slumber caus'd her cheek to glow)
Seem'd to her ear his winning lips to lay,
And thus in whispers said, or seem'd to say:
'Fairest of mortals, thou distinguish'd care
Of thousand bright Inhabitants of Air!
If e'er one vision touch'd thy infant thought,
Of all the nurse and all the priest have taught —
Of airy elves by moonlight shadows seen,
The silver token, and the circled green,
Or virgins visited by Angel-powers,
With golden crowns and wreaths of heav'nly flowers;
Hear and believe! thy own importance know,
Nor bound thy narrow views to things below.
Some secret truths, from learned pride conceal'd,
To maids alone and children are reveal'd:
What tho' no credit doubting Wits may give?
The fair and innocent shall still believe.
Know, then, unnumber'd Spirits round thee fly,
The light militia of the lower sky:
These, tho' unseen, are ever on the wing,
Hang o'er the Box, and hover round the Ring.
Think what an equipage thou hast in air,
And view with scorn two pages and a chair.
As now your own, our beings were of old,
And once inclosed in woman's beauteous mould;
Thence, by a soft transition, we repair
From earthly vehicles to these of air.
Think not, when woman's transient breath is fled,
That all her vanities at once are dead;
Succeeding vanities she still regards,
And, tho' she plays no more, o'erlooks the cards.
Her joy in gilded chariots, when alive,
And love of Ombre, after death survive.
For when the Fair in all their pride expire,
To their first elements their souls retire.
The sprites of fiery termagants in flame

---

[19] As a fourth summons.

Mount up, and take a Salamander's name.
Soft yielding minds to water glide away,
And sip, with Nymphs, their elemental tea.
The graver prude sinks downward to a Gnome
In search of mischief still on earth to roam.
The light coquettes in Sylphs aloft repair,
And sport and flutter in the fields of air.
'Know further yet: whoever fair and chaste
Rejects mankind, is by some Sylph embraced;
For spirits, freed from mortal laws, with ease
Assume what sexes and what shapes they please.
What guards the purity of melting maids,
In courtly balls, and midnight masquerades,
Safe from the treach'rous friend, the daring spark,
The glance by day, the whisper in the dark;
When kind occasion prompts their warm desires,
When music softens, and when dancing fires?
'Tis but their Sylph, the wise Celestials know,
Tho' Honour is the word with Men below.
'Some nymphs there are, too conscious of their face,
For life predestin'd to the Gnome's embrace.
These swell their prospects and exalt their pride,
When offers are disdain'd, and love denied:
Then gay ideas crowd the vacant brain,
While peers, and dukes, and all their sweeping train,
And garters, stars, and coronets appear,
And in soft sounds, 'Your Grace' salutes their ear.
'Tis these that early taint the female soul,
Instruct the eyes of young coquettes to roll,
Teach infant cheeks a bidden blush to know,
And little hearts to flutter at a Beau.
'Oft, when the world imagine women stray,
The Sylphs thro' mystic mazes guide their way;
Thro' all the giddy circle they pursue,
And old impertinence expel by new.
What tender maid but must a victim fall
To one man's treat, but for another's ball?
When Florio speaks, what virgin could withstand,
If gentle Damon did not squeeze her hand?
With varying vanities, from every part,
They shift the moving toyshop of their heart;
Where wigs with wigs, with sword-knots sword-knots strive,
Beaux banish beaux, and coaches coaches drive.
This erring mortals Levity may call;
Oh blind to truth! the Sylphs contrive it all.
'Of these am I, who thy protection claim,
A watchful sprite, and Ariel is my name.
Late, as I ranged the crystal wilds of air,
In the clear mirror of thy ruling star
I saw, alas! some dread event impend,
Ere to the main this morning sun descend,
But Heav'n reveals not what, or how, or where.
Warn'd by the Sylph, O pious maid, beware!
This to disclose is all thy guardian can:
Beware of all, but most beware of Man!'
He said; when Shock, who thought she slept too long,
Leap'd up, and waked his mistress with his tongue.
'Twas then, Belinda, if report say true,
Thy eyes first open'd on a billet-doux;
Wounds, charms, and ardours were no sooner read,
But all the vision vanish'd from thy head.
And now, unveil'd, the toilet stands display'd,
Each silver vase in mystic order laid.

First, robed in white, the nymph intent adores,
With head uncover'd the Cosmetic powers.
A heav'nly image in the glass appears;
To that she bends, to that her eyes she rears.
Th' inferior priestess, at her altar's side,
Trembling begins the sacred rites of Pride.
Unnumber'd treasures ope at once, and here
The various off'rings of the world appear;
From each she nicely culls with curious toil,
And decks the Goddess with the glitt'ring spoil.
This casket India's glowing gems unlocks,
And all Arabia breathes from yonder box.
The tortoise here and elephant unite,
Transform'd to combs, the speckled, and the white.
Here files of pins extend their shining rows,
Puffs, powders, patches, bibles, billet-doux.
Now awful Beauty puts on all its arms;
The Fair each moment rises in her charms,
Repairs her smiles, awakens every grace,
And calls forth all the wonders of her face;
Sees by degrees a purer blush arise,
And keener lightnings quicken in her eyes.
The busy Sylphs surround their darling care,
These set the head, and those divide the hair,
Some fold the sleeve, whilst others plait the gown;
And Betty's [20] prais'd for labours not her own.

CANTO II

Not with more glories, in th' ethereal plain,
The sun first rises o'er the purpled main,
Than, issuing forth, the rival of his beams
Launch'd on the bosom of the silver Thames.
Fair nymphs, and well-dress'd youths around her shone,
But every eye was fix'd on her alone.
On her white breast a sparkling cross she wore,
Which Jews might kiss, and infidels adore.
Her lively looks a sprightly mind disclose,
Quick as her eyes, and as unfix'd as those:
Favours to none, to all she smiles extends;
Oft she rejects, but never once offends.
Bright as the sun, her eyes the gazers strike,
And, like the sun, they shine on all alike.
Yet graceful ease, and sweetness void of pride,
Might hide her faults, if belles had faults to hide;
If to her share some female errors fall,
Look on her face, and you'll forget 'em all.

This nymph, to the destruction of mankind,
Nourish'd two locks, which graceful hung behind
In equal curls, and well conspired to deck
With shining ringlets the smooth iv'ry neck.
Love in these labyrinths his slaves detains,
And mighty hearts are held in slender chains.
With hairy springes we the birds betray,
Slight lines of hair surprise the finny prey,
Fair tresses man's imperial race ensnare,
And beauty draws us with a single hair.

Th' adventurous Baron the bright locks admired;
He saw, he wish'd, and to the prize aspired.
Resolv'd to win, he meditates the way,
By force to ravish, or by fraud betray;
For when success a lover's toil attends,
Few ask if fraud or force attain'd his ends.

For this, ere Phœbus rose, he had implor'd
Propitious Heav'n, and every Power ador'd,
But chiefly Love — to Love an altar built

[20] Belinda's maid

Of twelve vast French romances, neatly gilt.
There lay three garters, half a pair of gloves,
And all the trophies of his former loves;
With tender billet-doux he lights the pyre,
And breathes three am'rous sighs to raise the fire.
Then prostrate falls, and begs with ardent eyes
Soon to obtain, and long possess the prize:
The Powers gave ear, and granted half his prayer,
The rest the winds dispers'd in empty air.

But now secure the painted vessel glides,
The sunbeams trembling on the floating tides;
While melting music steals upon the sky,
And soften'd sounds along the waters die:
Smooth flow the waves, the zephyrs gently play,
Belinda smil'd, and all the world was gay.
All but the Sylph — with careful thoughts opprest
Th' impending woe sat heavy on his breast.
He summons straight his denizens of air;
The lucid squadrons round the sails repair:
Soft o'er the shrouds aërial whispers breathe
That seem'd but zephyrs to the train beneath.
Some to the sun their insect-wings unfold,
Waft on the breeze, or sink in clouds of gold;
Transparent forms too fine for mortal sight,
Their fluid bodies half dissolv'd in light,
Loose to the wind their airy garments flew,
Thin glitt'ring textures of the filmy dew,
Dipt in the richest tincture of the skies,
Where light disports in ever-mingling dyes,
While ev'ry beam new transient colours flings,
Colours that change whene'er they wave their wings.
Amid the circle, on the gilded mast,
Superior by the head was Ariel placed;
His purple pinions opening to the sun,
He raised his azure wand, and thus begun:

'Ye Sylphs and Sylphids, to your chief give ear.
Fays, Fairies, Genii, Elves, and Dæmons, hear!
Ye know the spheres and various tasks assign'd
By laws eternal to th' aërial kind.
Some in the fields of purest ether play,
And bask and whiten in the blaze of day:
Some guide the course of wand'ring orbs on high,
Or roll the planets thro' the boundless sky:
Some, less refin'd, beneath the moon's pale light
Pursue the stars that shoot athwart the night,
Or suck the mists in grosser air below,
Or dip their pinions in the painted bow,
Or brew fierce tempests on the wintry main,
Or o'er the glebe distil the kindly rain.
Others, on earth, o'er human race preside,
Watch all their ways, and all their actions guide:
Of these the chief the care of nations own,
And guard with arms divine the British Throne.

'Our humbler province is to tend the Fair,
Not a less pleasing, tho' less glorious care;
To save the Powder from too rude a gale;
Nor let th' imprison'd Essences exhale;
To draw fresh colours from the vernal flowers;
To steal from rainbows ere they drop in showers
A brighter Wash; to curl their waving hairs,
Assist their blushes and inspire their airs;
Nay oft, in dreams invention we bestow,
To change a Flounce, or add a Furbelow.

'This day black omens threat the brightest Fair,

That e'er deserv'd a watchful spirit's care;
Some dire disaster, or by force or slight;
But what, or where, the Fates have wrapt in night.
Whether the nymph shall break Diana's law,
Or some frail China jar receive a flaw;
Or stain her honour, or her new brocade,
Forget her prayers, or miss a masquerade,
Or lose her heart, or necklace, at a ball;
Or whether Heav'n has doom'd that Shock must fall.
Haste, then, ye Spirits! to your charge repair:
The flutt'ring fan be Zephyretta's care;
The drops [21] to thee, Brillante, we consign;
And, Momentilla, let the watch be thine;
Do thou, Crispissa, tend her fav'rite Lock;
Ariel himself shall be the guard of Shock.
'To fifty chosen sylphs, of special note,
We trust th' important charge, the petticoat;
Oft have we known that sev'n-fold fence to fail,
Tho' stiff with hoops, and arm'd with ribs of whale:
Form a strong line about the silver bound,
And guard the wide circumference around.
'Whatever spirit, careless of his charge,
His post neglects, or leaves the Fair at large,
Shall feel sharp vengeance soon o'ertake his sins:
Be stopp'd in vials, or transfix'd with pins,
Or plunged in lakes of bitter washes lie,
Or wedg'd whole ages in a bodkin's eye;
Gums and pomatums shall his flight restrain,
While clogg'd he beats his silken wings in vain,
Or alum styptics with contracting power
Shrink his thin essence like a rivell'd flower:
Or, as Ixion fix'd, the wretch shall feel
The giddy motion of the whirling mill,
In fumes of burning chocolate shall glow,
And tremble at the sea that froths below!'

[21] earrings

He spoke; the spirits from the sails descend;
Some, orb in orb, around the nymph extend;
Some thread the mazy ringlets of her hair;
Some hang upon the pendants of her ear;
With beating hearts the dire event they wait,
Anxious, and trembling for the birth of Fate.

CANTO III

Close by those meads, for ever crown'd with flowers,
Where Thames with pride surveys his rising towers
There stands a structure [22] of majestic frame,
Which from the neighb'ring Hampton takes its name.
Here Britain's statesmen oft the fall foredoom
Of foreign tyrants, and of nymphs at home;
Here, thou, great Anna! whom three realms obey,
Dost sometimes counsel take — and sometimes tea.
Hither the Heroes and the Nymphs resort,
To taste awhile the pleasures of a court;
In various talk th' instructive hours they past,
Who gave the ball, or paid the visit last;
One speaks the glory of the British Queen,
And one describes a charming Indian screen;
A third interprets motions, looks, and eyes;
At every word a reputation dies.
Snuff, or the fan, supply each pause of chat,
With singing, laughing, ogling, *and all that*.
Meanwhile, declining from the noon of day,

[22] Hampton Court, a royal palace.

The sun obliquely shoots his burning ray;
The hungry judges soon the sentence sign,
And wretches hang that jurymen may dine;
The merchant from th' Exchange returns in peace,
And the long labours of the toilet cease.
Belinda now, whom thirst of fame invites,
Burns to encounter two adventurous knights,
At Ombre[23] singly to decide their doom,
And swells her breast with conquests yet to come.
Straight the three bands prepare in arms to join,
Each band the number of the sacred Nine.
Soon as she spreads her hand, th' aërial guard
Descend, and sit on each important card:
First Ariel perch'd upon a Matadore,
Then each according to the rank they bore;
For Sylphs, yet mindful of their ancient race,
Are, as when women, wondrous fond of place.
  Behold four Kings in majesty revered,
With hoary whiskers and a forky beard;
And four fair Queens, whose hands sustain a flower
Th' expressive emblem of their softer power;
Four Knaves, in garbs succinct, a trusty band,
Caps on their heads, and halberts in their hand
And party-colour'd troops, a shining train,
Draw forth to combat on the velvet plain.
  The skilful nymph reviews her force with care;
'Let Spades be trumps!' she said, and trumps they were.
  Now move to war her sable Matadores,
In show like leaders of the swarthy Moors.
Spadillio first, unconquerable lord!
Led off two captive trumps, and swept the board.
As many more Manillio forced to yield,
And march'd a victor from the verdant field.
Him Basto follow'd, but his fate more hard
Gain'd but one trump and one plebeian card.
With his broad sabre next, a chief in years,
The hoary Majesty of Spades appears,
Puts forth one manly leg, to sight reveal'd;
The rest his many colour'd robe conceal'd.
The rebel Knave, who dares his prince engage,
Proves the just victim of his royal rage.
Ev'n mighty Pam,[24] that Kings and Queens o'erthrew,
And mow'd down armies in the fights of Loo,
Sad chance of war! now destitute of aid,
Falls undistinguish'd by the victor Spade.
  Thus far both armies to Belinda yield;
Now to the Baron Fate inclines the field.
His warlike amazon her host invades,
Th' imperial consort of the crown of Spades.
The Club's black tyrant first her victim died,
Spite of his haughty mien and barb'rous pride:
What boots the regal circle on his head,
His giant limbs, in state unwieldy spread;
That long behind he trails his pompous robe,
And, of all monarchs, only grasps the globe?
  The Baron now his Diamonds pours apace;
Th' embroider'd King who shows but half his face,
And his refulgent Queen, with powers combin'd,
Of broken troops an easy conquest find.
Clubs, Diamonds, Hearts, in wild disorder seen,

[23] A card game, usually for three players, each of whom received nine cards. The 'ombre' who declared the trump was defeated (the loss was termed 'codille') if one of the other two took more tricks than he. 'Matadores' were the three highest cards: 'Spadillio,' the ace of spades, 'Manillio' (the two of trumps when trumps were black; the seven of trumps when red), and 'Basto,' the ace of clubs.

[24] The knave of clubs, the highest card in loo.

With throngs promiscuous strew the level green.
Thus when dispers'd a routed army runs,
Of Asia's troops, and Afric's sable sons,
With like confusion diff'rent nations fly,
Of various habit, and of various dye;
The pierced battalions disunited fall
In heaps on heaps; one fate o'erwhelms them all.
The Knave of Diamonds tries his wily arts,
And wins (oh shameful chance!) the Queen of Hearts.
At this, the blood the virgin's cheek forsook,
A livid paleness spreads o'er all her look;
She sees, and trembles at th' approaching ill,
Just in the jaws of ruin, and Codille.
And now (as oft in some distemper'd state)
On one nice trick depends the gen'ral fate!
An Ace of Hearts steps forth: the King unseen
Lurk'd in her hand, and mourn'd his captive Queen.
He springs to vengeance with an eager pace,
And falls like thunder on the prostrate Ace.
The nymph, exulting, fills with shouts the sky;
The walls, the woods, and long canals reply.
Oh thoughtless mortals! ever blind to fate,
Too soon dejected, and too soon elate:
Sudden these honours shall be snatch'd away,
And curs'd for ever this victorious day.
For lo! the board with cups and spoons is crown'd,
The berries crackle, and the mill turns round;
On shining Altars of Japan they raise
The silver lamp; the fiery spirits blaze:
From silver spouts the grateful liquors glide,
While China's earth receives the smoking tide.
At once they gratify their scent and taste,
And frequent cups prolong the rich repast.
Straight hover round the Fair her airy band;
Some, as she sipp'd, the fuming liquor fann'd,
Some o'er her lap their careful plumes display'd,
Trembling, and conscious of the rich brocade.
Coffee (which makes the politician wise,
And see thro' all things with his half-shut eyes)
Sent up in vapors to the Baron's brain
New stratagems, the radiant Lock to gain.
Ah, cease, rash youth! desist ere 't is too late,
Fear the just Gods, and think of Scylla's fate!
Changed to a bird, and sent to flit in air,
She dearly pays for Nisus' injured hair!
But when to mischief mortals bend their will,
How soon they find fit instruments of ill!
Just then, Clarissa drew with tempting grace
A two-edg'd weapon from her shining case:
So ladies in romance assist their knight,
Present the spear, and arm him for the fight.
He takes the gift with rev'rence, and extends
The little engine on his fingers' ends;
This just behind Belinda's neck he spread,
And o'er the fragrant steams she bends her head.
Swift to the Lock a thousand sprites repair;
A thousand wings, by turns, blow back the hair;
And thrice they twitch'd the diamond in her ear;
Thrice she look'd back, and thrice the foe drew near.
Just in that instant, anxious Ariel sought

The close recesses of the virgin's thought:
As on the nosegay in her breast reclin'd,
He watch'd th' Ideas rising in her mind,
Sudden he view'd, in spite of all her art,
An earthly Lover lurking at her heart.
Amazed, confused, he found his power expired,
Resign'd to fate, and with a sigh retired.

The Peer now spreads the glitt'ring forfex wide,
T' inclose the Lock; now joins it, to divide.
Ev'n then, before the fatal engine closed,
A wretched Sylph too fondly interposed;
Fate urged the shears, and cut the Sylph in twain
(But airy substance soon unites again).[25]
The meeting points the sacred hair dissever
From the fair head, for ever, and for ever!

Then flash'd the living lightning from her eyes,
And screams of horror rend th' affrighted skies.
Not louder shrieks to pitying Heav'n are cast,
When husbands, or when lapdogs breathe their last;
Or when rich China vessels, fall'n from high,
In glitt'ring dust and painted fragments lie!
'Let wreaths of triumph now my temples twine,'
The Victor cried, 'the glorious prize is mine!
While fish in streams, or birds delight in air,
Or in a coach and six the British Fair,
As long as Atalantis [26] shall be read,
Or the small pillow grace a lady's bed,
While visits shall be paid on solemn days,
When numerous wax-lights in bright order blaze:
While nymphs take treats, or assignations give,
So long my honour, name, and praise shall live!
What Time would spare, from Steel receives its date,
And monuments, like men, submit to Fate!
Steel could the labour of the Gods destroy,
And strike to dust th' imperial towers of Troy;
Steel could the works of mortal pride confound
And hew triumphal arches to the ground.
What wonder, then, fair Nymph! thy hairs should feel
The conquering force of unresisted steel?'

CANTO IV

But anxious cares the pensive nymph opprest
And secret passions labour'd in her breast.
Not youthful kings in battle seiz'd alive,
Not scornful virgins who their charms survive,
Not ardent lovers robb'd of all their bliss,
Not ancient ladies when refused a kiss,
Not tyrants fierce that unrepenting die,
Not Cynthia when her mantua's pinn'd awry,
E'er felt such rage, resentment, and despair,
As thou, sad Virgin! for thy ravish'd hair.

For, that sad moment, when the Sylphs withdrew,
And Ariel weeping from Belinda flew,
Umbriel, a dusky, melancholy sprite
As ever sullied the fair face of light,
Down to the central earth, his proper scene,
Repair'd to search the gloomy cave of Spleen.

Swift on his sooty pinions flits the Gnome,
And in a vapour reach'd the dismal dome.
No cheerful breeze this sullen region knows,

---

[25] Milton, curiously enough, is responsible for this touch. Pope cites *Paradise Lost*, vi, 330–334:

'But the ethereal substance closed,
Not long divisible: and from the gash
A stream of nectarous humor issuing flowed
Sanguine, such as celestial spirits may bleed.'

[26] Mrs. Manley's *The New Atalantis*, 1709, a very Baedeker of contemporary gossip and scandal.

The dreaded East is all the wind that blows.
Here in a grotto shelter'd close from air,
And screen'd in shades from day's detested glare,
She sighs for ever on her pensive bed,
Pain at her side, and Megrim [27] at her head.
Two handmaids wait the throne; alike in place,
But diff'ring far in figure and in face.
Here stood Ill-nature, like an ancient maid,
Her wrinkled form in black and white array'd!
With store of prayers for mornings, nights, and noons,
Her hand is fill'd; her bosom with lampoons.
There Affectation, with a sickly mien,
Shows in her cheek the roses of eighteen,
Practis'd to lisp, and hang the head aside,
Faints into airs, and languishes with pride;
On the rich quilt sinks with becoming woe,
Wrapt in a gown for sickness and for show.
The fair ones feel such maladies as these,
When each new night-dress gives a new disease.

A constant vapour o'er the palace flies
Strange phantoms rising as the mists arise;
Dreadful as hermits' dreams in haunted shades,
Or bright as visions of expiring maids:
Now glaring fiends, and snakes on rolling spires,
Pale spectres, gaping tombs, and purple fires;
Now lakes of liquid gold, Elysian scenes,
And crystal domes, and angels in machines.

Unnumber'd throngs on ev'ry side are seen,
Of bodies changed to various forms by Spleen.
Here living Teapots stand, one arm held out,
One bent; the handle this, and that the spout:
A Pipkin [28] there, like Homer's Tripod [29] walks;
Here sighs a Jar, and there a Goose-pie [30] talks;
Men prove with child, as powerful fancy works,
And maids turn'd bottles call aloud for corks.

Safe pass'd the Gnome thro' this fantastic band,
A branch of healing spleenwort in his hand.
Then thus address'd the Power — 'Hail, wayward Queen!
Who rule the sex to fifty from fifteen:
Parent of Vapours and of female wit,
Who give th' hysteric or poetic fit,
On various tempers act by various ways,
Make some take physic, others scribble plays;
Who cause the proud their visits to delay,
And send the godly in a pet to pray.
A nymph there is that all your power disdains,
And thousands more in equal mirth maintains.
But oh! if e'er thy Gnome could spoil a grace,
Or raise a pimple on a beauteous face,
Like citron-waters matrons' cheeks inflame,
Or change complexions at a losing game;
If e'er with airy horns I planted heads,
Or rumpled petticoats, or tumbled beds,
Or caused suspicion when no soul was rude,
Or discomposed the head-dress of a prude,
Or e'er to costive lapdog gave disease,
Which not the tears of brightest eyes could ease,
Hear me, and touch Belinda with chagrin;
That single act gives half the world the spleen.'

The Goddess, with a discontented air,
Seems to reject him tho' she grants his prayer.

---

27 Literally 'headache,' but in Pope's time it often meant 'the blues' or melancholy.

28 small jar

29 See *Iliad*, xviii, 372–381.

30 Alludes to a real fact; a lady of distinction imagined herself in this condition. [Pope.]

A wondrous Bag with both her hands she binds,
Like that where once Ulysses held the winds;
There she collects the force of female lungs,
Sighs, sobs, and passions, and the war of tongues.
A Vial next she fills with fainting fears,
Soft sorrows, melting griefs, and flowing tears.
The Gnome rejoicing bears her gifts away,
Spreads his black wings, and slowly mounts to day.
  Sunk in Thalestris'[31] arms the nymph he found,
Her eyes dejected, and her hair unbound.
Full o'er their heads the swelling Bag he rent,
And all the Furies issued at the vent.
Belinda burns with more than mortal ire,
And fierce Thalestris fans the rising fire.
'O wretched maid!' she spread her hands, and cried
(While Hampton's echoes, 'Wretched maid!' replied),
Was it for this you took such constant care
The bodkin, comb, and essence to prepare?
For this your locks in paper durance bound?
For this with torturing irons wreathed around?
For this with fillets strain'd your tender head,
And bravely bore the double loads of lead?
Gods! shall the ravisher display your hair,
While the fops envy, and the ladies stare!
Honour forbid! at whose unrivall'd shrine
Ease, Pleasure, Virtue, all, our sex resign.
Methinks already I your tears survey,
Already hear the horrid things they say,
Already see you a degraded toast,
And all your honour in a whisper lost!
How shall I, then, your hapless fame defend?
'T will then be infamy to seem your friend!
And shall this prize, th' inestimable prize,
Exposed thro' crystal to the gazing eyes,
And heighten'd by the diamond's circling rays,
On that rapacious hand for ever blaze?
Sooner shall grass in Hyde Park Circus grow,
And Wits take lodgings in the sound of Bow;[32]
Sooner let earth, air, sea, to chaos fall,
Men, monkeys, lapdogs, parrots, perish all!'
  She said; then raging to Sir Plume[33] repairs,
And bids her beau demand the precious hairs
(Sir Plume, of amber snuff-box justly vain,
And the nice conduct of a clouded cane):
With earnest eyes, and round unthinking face,
He first the snuff-box open'd, then the case,
And thus broke out—'My lord, why, what the devil!
Z—ds! damn the Lock! 'fore Gad, you must be civil!
Plague on 't! 't is past a jest—nay, prithee, pox!
Give her the hair.'—He spoke, and rapp'd his box.
  'It grieves me much,' replied the Peer again,
'Who speaks so well should ever speak in vain:
But by this Lock, this sacred Lock, I swear
(Which never more shall join its parted hair;
Which never more its honours shall renew,
Clipp'd from the lovely head where late it grew),
That, while my nostrils draw the vital air,
This hand, which won it, shall for ever wear.'
He spoke, and speaking, in proud triumph spread

---

[31] A friend of Belinda's, supposedly a Mrs. Morley.

[32] The bells of St. Mary le Bow, in Cheapside, the unfashionable section. Grub Street was well within hearing distance. A London 'cockney' is one born 'within the sound of Bow's bells.'

[33] Sir George Brown, brother of Mrs. Morley, 'Thalestris.' He was very angry that Pope put only nonsense in his mouth in the sketch that follows.

The long-contended honours of her head.
  But Umbriel, hateful Gnome, forbears not so;
He breaks the Vial whence the sorrows flow.
Then see! the nymph in beauteous grief appears,
Her eyes half-languishing, half drown'd in tears;
On her heav'd bosom hung her drooping head,
Which with a sigh she rais'd, and thus she said:
  'For ever curs'd be this detested day,
Which snatch'd my best, my fav'rite curl away!
Happy! ah, ten times happy had I been,
If Hampton Court these eyes had never seen!
Yet am not I the first mistaken maid,
By love of courts to numerous ills betray'd.
O had I rather unadmired remain'd
In some lone isle, or distant northern land;
Where the gilt chariot never marks the way,
Where none learn Ombre, none e'er taste Bohea![34]
There kept my charms conceal'd from mortal eye,
Like roses, that in deserts bloom and die.
What mov'd my mind with youthful lords to roam?
O had I stay'd, and said my prayers at home;
'Twas this the morning omens seem'd to tell,
Thrice from my trembling hand the patch[35]-box fell;
The tott'ring china shook without a wind;
Nay, Poll sat mute, and Shock was most unkind!
A Sylph, too, warn'd me of the threats of fate,
In mystic visions, now believ'd too late!
See the poor remnants of these slighted hairs!
My hands shall rend what ev'n thy rapine spares.
These, in two sable ringlets taught to break,
Once gave new beauties to the snowy neck;
The sister-lock now sits uncouth alone,
And in its fellow's fate foresees its own;
Uncurl'd it hangs, the fatal shears demands,
And tempts once more thy sacrilegious hands.
O hadst thou, cruel! been content to seize
Hairs less in sight, or any hairs but these!'

CANTO V

SHE said: the pitying audience melt in tears;
But Fate and Jove had stopp'd the Baron's ears.
In vain Thalestris with reproach assails,
For who can move when fair Belinda fails?
Not half so fix'd the Trojan[36] could remain,
While Anna begg'd and Dido raged in vain.
Then grave Clarissa graceful waved her fan;
Silence ensued, and thus the nymph began:
  'Say, why are beauties prais'd and honour'd most,
The wise man's passion, and the vain man's toast?
Why deck'd with all that land and sea afford,
Why angels call'd, and angel-like ador'd?
Why round our coaches crowd the white-glov'd beaux?
Why bows the side-box from its inmost rows?
How vain are all these glories, all our pains,
Unless Good Sense preserve what Beauty gains;

[34] tea
[35] 'Beauty spot' of sticking plaster for the face.
[36] Aeneas

That men may say when we the front-box grace,
" Behold the first in virtue as in face! "
Oh! if to dance all night, and dress all day,
Charm'd the smallpox, or chased old age away;
Who would not scorn what housewife's cares produce,
Or who would learn one earthly thing of use?
To patch, nay, ogle, might become a saint,
Nor could it sure be such a sin to paint.
But since, alas! frail beauty must decay,
Curl'd or uncurl'd, since locks will turn to gray;
Since painted, or not painted, all shall fade,
And she who scorns a man must die a maid;
What then remains, but well our power to use,
And keep good humour still whate'er we lose?
And trust me, dear, good humour can prevail,
When airs, and flights, and screams, and scolding fail.
Beauties in vain their pretty eyes may roll;
Charms strike the sight, but merit wins the soul.'

So spoke the dame, but no applause ensued;
Belinda frown'd, Thalestris call'd her prude.
'To arms, to arms!' the fierce virago cries,
And swift as lightning to the combat flies.
All side in parties, and begin th' attack;
Fans clap, silks rustle, and tough whalebones crack;
Heroes' and heroines' shouts confusedly rise,
And bass and treble voices strike the skies.
No common weapons in their hands are found,
Like Gods they fight nor dread a mortal wound.

So when bold Homer makes the Gods engage,
And heav'nly breasts with human passions rage;
'Gainst Pallas, Mars; Latona, Hermes arms;
And all Olympus rings with loud alarms;
Jove's thunder roars, Heav'n trembles all around,
Blue Neptune storms, the bell'wing deeps resound:
Earth shakes her nodding towers, the ground gives way,
And the pale ghosts start at the flash of day!

Triumphant Umbriel, on a sconce's height,
Clapp'd his glad wings, and sat to view the fight:
Propp'd on their bodkin-spears, the sprites survey
The growing combat, or assist the fray.

While thro' the press enraged Thalestris flies,
And scatters death around from both her eyes,
A Beau and Witling perish'd in the throng,
One died in metaphor, and one in song:
'O cruel Nymph! a living death I bear,'
Cried Dapperwit, and sunk beside his chair.
A mournful glance Sir Fopling upwards cast,
'Those eyes are made so killing'—was his last.
Thus on Mæander's flowery margin lies
Th' expiring swan, and as he sings he dies.

When bold Sir Plume had drawn Clarissa down,
Chloe stepp'd in, and kill'd him with a frown;
She smiled to see the doughty hero slain,
But, at her smile, the beau revived again.
Now Jove suspends his golden scales in air,
Weighs the men's wits against the lady's hair;
The doubtful beam long nods from side to side;

At length the wits mount up, the hairs subside.
See fierce Belinda on the Baron flies,
With more than usual lightning in her eyes;
Nor fear'd the chief th' unequal fight to try,
Who sought no more than on his foe to die.
But this bold lord, with manly strength endued,
She with one finger and a thumb subdued:
Just where the breath of life his nostrils drew,
A charge of snuff the wily virgin threw;
The Gnomes direct, to every atom just,
The pungent grains of titillating dust.
Sudden, with starting tears each eye o'erflows,
And the high dome reëchoes to his nose.
'Now meet thy fate,' incens'd Belinda cried,
And drew a deadly bodkin from her side.
(The same, his ancient personage to deck,
Her great-great-grandsire wore about his neck,
In three seal-rings; which after, melted down,
Form'd a vast buckle for his widow's gown:
Her infant grandame's whistle next it grew,
The bells she jingled, and the whistle blew;
Then in a bodkin graced her mother's hairs,
Which long she wore and now Belinda wears.)
'Boast not my fall,' he cried, 'insulting foe!
Thou by some other shalt be laid as low;
Nor think to die dejects my lofty mind:
All that I dread is leaving you behind!
Rather than so, ah, let me still survive,
And burn in Cupid's flames — but burn alive.'
'Restore the Lock!' she cries; and all around
'Restore the Lock!' the vaulted roofs rebound.
Not fierce Othello in so loud a strain
Roar'd for the handkerchief that caus'd his pain.
But see how oft ambitious aims are cross'd,
And chiefs contend till all the prize is lost!
The lock, obtain'd with guilt, and kept with pain,
In ev'ry place is sought, but sought in vain:
With such a prize no mortal must be blest.
So Heav'n decrees! with Heav'n who can contest?
Some thought it mounted to the lunar sphere,
Since all things lost on earth are treasured there.
There heroes' wits are kept in pond'rous vases,
And beaux' in snuffboxes and tweezer-cases.
There broken vows, and deathbed alms are found,
And lovers' hearts with ends of riband bound,
The courtier's promises, and sick man's prayers,
The smiles of harlots, and the tears of heirs,
Cages for gnats, and chains to yoke a flea,
Dried butterflies, and tomes of casuistry.
But trust the Muse — she saw it upward rise,
Tho' mark'd by none but quick poetic eyes
(So Rome's great founder [37] to the heav'ns withdrew,
To Proculus alone confess'd in view):
A sudden star, it shot thro' liquid air,
And drew behind a radiant trail of hair.
Not Berenice's [38] locks first rose so bright,
The heav'ns bespangling with dishevell'd light.
The Sylphs behold it kindling as it flies,
And pleas'd pursue its progress thro' the skies.
This the beau monde shall from the Mall survey,

[37] Romulus. See Livy, I, xvi.
[38] An Egyptian queen whose lock of hair, dedicated for her husband's return from war, is supposed to have become a constellation.

And hail with music its propitious ray;
This the blest lover shall for Venus take,
And send up vows from Rosamonda's lake;[39]
This Partridge[40] soon shall view in cloudless skies,
When next he looks thro' Galileo's eyes;
And hence th' egregious wizard shall foredoom
The fate of Louis, and the fall of Rome.
  Then cease, bright Nymph! to mourn thy ravish'd hair,
Which adds new glory to the shining sphere!
Not all the tresses that fair head can boast
Shall draw such envy as the Lock you lost.
For after all the murders of your eye,
When, after millions slain, yourself shall die;
When those fair suns shall set, as set they must,
And all those tresses shall be laid in dust,
This Lock the Muse shall consecrate to fame,
And 'midst the stars inscribe Belinda's name.

ELOISA TO ABELARD[41]

ARGUMENT

Abelard and Eloisa flourished in the twelfth century; they were two of the most distinguished persons of their age in Learning and Beauty, but for nothing more famous than for their unfortunate passion. After a long course of calamities, they retired each to a several convent, and consecrated the remainder of their days to Religion. It was many years after this separation that a letter of Abelard's to a friend, which contained the history of his misfortune, fell into the hands of Eloisa. This, awakening all her tenderness, occasioned those celebrated letters (out of which the following is partly extracted), which give so lively a picture of the struggles of Grace and Nature, Virtue and Passion.

In these deep solitudes and awful cells,
Where heav'nly-pensive Contemplation dwells,
And ever-musing Melancholy reigns,
What means this tumult in a vestal's veins?
Why rove my thoughts beyond this last retreat?
Why feels my heart its long-forgotten heat?
Yet, yet I love!—From Abelard it came,
And Eloisa yet must kiss the name.
  Dear fatal name! rest ever unreveal'd,
Nor pass these lips, in holy silence seal'd:
Hide it, my heart, within that close disguise,
Where, mix'd with God's, his lov'd idea lies:
O write it not, my hand—the name appears
Already written—wash it out, my tears!
In vain lost Eloisa weeps and prays,
Her heart still dictates, and her hand obeys.
  Relentless walls! whose darksome round contains
Repentant sighs, and voluntary pains:
Ye rugged rocks, which holy knees have worn;
Ye grots and caverns shagg'd with horrid thorn!
Shrines! where their vigils pale-eyed virgins keep,
And pitying saints, whose statues learn to weep!
Tho' cold like you, unmov'd and silent grown,
I have not yet forgot myself to stone.
All is not Heav'n's while Abelard has part,
Still rebel Nature holds out half my heart;
Nor prayers nor fasts its stubborn pulse restrain,
Nor tears, for ages taught to flow in vain.

---

39 In St. James's Park.

40 John Partridge was a ridiculous star-gazer, who in his almanacks every year never failed to predict the downfall of the Pope and the King of France, then at war with the English. [Pope.] He had been the victim in 1707 of Swift's famous hoax in the 'Bickerstaff' papers, which foretold his death and later pretended that death had come at the hour predicted.

41 The poem was partly inspired by Pope's somewhat self-attentive grief in his separation from Lady Mary Wortley Montagu, who, after having become his friend in 1715, left England the following year. He commended the piece to her in a letter of June 1717, suggesting a personal application. Published in *Works*, 3 June 1717.

Soon as thy letters trembling I unclose,
That well-known name awakens all my woes.
Oh name for ever sad! for ever dear!
Still breathed in sighs, still usher'd with a tear.
I tremble too, where'er my own I find,
Some dire misfortune follows close behind.
Line after line my gushing eyes o'erflow,
Led thro' a safe variety of woe:
Now warm in love, now with'ring in my bloom,
Lost in a convent's solitary gloom!
There stern religion quench'd th' unwilling flame,
There died the best of passions, Love and Fame.

Yet write, O write me all, that I may join
Griefs to thy griefs, and echo sighs to thine.
Nor foes nor fortune take this power away;
And is my Abelard less kind than they?
Tears still are mine, and those I need not spare;
Love but demands what else were shed in prayer.
No happier task these faded eyes pursue;
To read and weep is all they now can do.

Then share thy pain, allow that sad relief;
Ah, more than share it, give me all thy grief.
Heav'n first taught letters for some wretch's aid,
Some banish'd lover, or some captive maid;
They live, they speak, they breathe what love inspires,
Warm from the soul, and faithful to its fires;
The virgin's wish without her fears impart,
Excuse the blush, and pour out all the heart,
Speed the soft intercourse from soul to soul,
And waft a sigh from Indus to the Pole.

Thou know'st how guiltless first I met thy flame,
When Love approach'd me under Friendship's name;
My fancy form'd thee of angelic kind,
Some emanation of th' all-beauteous Mind.
Those smiling eyes, attemp'ring every ray,
Shone sweetly lambent with celestial day,
Guiltless I gazed; Heav'n listen'd while you sung;
And truths divine came mended from that tongue.
From lips like those what precept fail'd to move?
Too soon they taught me 't was no sin to love:
Back thro' the paths of pleasing sense I ran,
Nor wish'd an angel whom I loved a man.
Dim and remote the joys of saints I see;
Nor envy them that Heav'n I lose for thee.

How oft, when press'd to marriage, have I said,
Curse on all laws but those which Love has made!
Love, free as air, at sight of human ties,
Spreads his light wings, and in a moment flies.
Let Wealth, let Honour, wait the wedded dame,
August her deed, and sacred be her fame;
Before true passion all those views remove;
Fame, Wealth, and Honour! what are you to Love?
The jealous God, when we profane his fires,
Those restless passions in revenge inspires,
And bids them make mistaken mortals groan,
Who seek in love for aught but love alone.
Should at my feet the world's great master fall,
Himself, his throne, his world, I'd scorn 'em all:
Not Cæsar's empress would I deign to prove;
No, make me mistress to the man I love;
If there be yet another name more free,
More fond than mistress, make me that to thee!
O happy state! when souls each other draw,
When Love is liberty, and Nature law:
All then is full, possessing and possess'd,

No craving void left aching in the breast:
Ev'n thought meets thought, ere from the lips it part,
And each warm wish springs mutual from the heart.
This sure is bliss (if bliss on earth there be),
And once the lot of Abelard and me.

Alas, how changed! what sudden horrors rise!
A naked lover bound and bleeding lies!
Where, where was Eloise? her voice, her hand,
Her poniard had opposed the dire command.
Barbarian, stay! that bloody stroke restrain;
The crime was common, common be the pain.
I can no more; by shame, by rage suppress'd,
Let tears and burning blushes speak the rest.

Canst thou forget that sad, that solemn day,
When victims at yon altar's foot we lay?
Canst thou forget what tears that moment fell,
When, warm in youth, I bade the world farewell?
As with cold lips I kiss'd the sacred veil,
The shrines all trembled, and the lamps grew pale:
Heav'n scarce believ'd the conquest it survey'd,
And saints with wonder heard the vows I made.
Yet then, to those dread altars as I drew,
Not on the cross my eyes were fix'd, but you:
Not grace, or zeal, love only was my call,
And if I lose thy love, I lose my all.
Come! with thy looks, thy words, relieve my woe;
Those still at least are left thee to bestow.
Still on that breast enamour'd let me lie,
Still drink delicious poison from thy eye,
Pant on thy lip, and to thy heart be press'd;
Give all thou canst — and let me dream the rest.
Ah, no! instruct me other joys to prize,
With other beauties charm my partial eyes!
Full in my view set all the bright abode,
And make my soul quit Abelard for God.

Ah, think at least thy flock deserves thy care,
Plants of thy hand, and children of thy prayer.
From the false world in early youth they fled,
By thee to mountains, wilds, and deserts led.
You raised these hallow'd walls; the desert smil'd,
And Paradise was open'd in the wild.
No weeping orphan saw his father's stores
Our shrines irradiate or emblaze the floors;
No silver saints, by dying misers giv'n,
Here bribed the rage of ill-requited Heav'n;
But such plain roofs as piety could raise,
And only vocal with the Maker's praise.
In these lone walls (their day's eternal bound),
These moss-grown domes with spiry turrets crown'd,
Where awful arches make a noonday night,
And the dim windows shed a solemn light,
Thy eyes diffused a reconciling ray,
And gleams of glory brighten'd all the day.
But now no face divine contentment wears,
'T is all blank sadness, or continual tears.
See how the force of others' prayers I try,
(O pious fraud of am'rous charity!)
But why should I on others' prayers depend?
Come thou, my father, brother, husband, friend!
Ah, let thy handmaid, sister, daughter, move,
And all those tender names in one, thy love!
The darksome pines, that o'er yon rocks reclin'd,
Wave high, and murmur to the hollow wind,

The wand'ring streams that shine between the hills,
The grots that echo to the tinkling rills,
The dying gales that pant upon the trees,
The lakes that quiver to the curling breeze —
No more these scenes my meditation aid,
Or lull to rest the visionary maid:
But o'er the twilight groves and dusky caves,
Long-sounding aisles and intermingled graves,
Black Melancholy sits, and round her throws
A death-like silence, and a dread repose:
Her gloomy presence saddens all the scene,
Shades every flower, and darkens every green,
Deepens the murmur of the falling floods,
And breathes a browner horror on the woods.
Yet here for ever, ever must I stay;
Sad proof how well a lover can obey!
Death, only Death can break the lasting chain;
And here, ev'n then shall my cold dust remain;
Here all its frailties, all its flames resign,
And wait till 't is no sin to mix with thine.
Ah, wretch! believ'd the spouse of God in vain,
Confess'd within the slave of Love and man.
Assist me, Heav'n! but whence arose that prayer?
Sprung it from piety or from despair?
Ev'n here, where frozen Chastity retires,
Love finds an altar for forbidden fires.
I ought to grieve, but cannot what I ought;
I mourn the lover, not lament the fault;
I view my crime, but kindle at the view,
Repent old pleasures, and solicit new;
Now turn'd to Heav'n, I weep my past offence,
Now think of thee, and curse my innocence.
Of all affliction taught a lover yet,
'T is sure the hardest science to forget!
How shall I lose the sin, yet keep the sense,
And love th' offender, yet detest th' offence?
How the dear object from the crime remove,
Or how distinguish Penitence from Love?
Unequal task! a passion to resign,
For hearts so touch'd, so pierced, so lost as mine:
Ere such a soul regains its peaceful state,
How often must it love, how often hate!
How often hope, despair, resent, regret,
Conceal, disdain — do all things but forget!
But let Heav'n seize it, all at once 't is fired;
Not touch'd, but rapt; not waken'd, but inspired!
O come! O teach me Nature to subdue,
Renounce my love, my life, myself — and You:
Fill my fond heart with God alone, for he
Alone can rival, can succeed to thee.
How happy is the blameless vestal's lot!
The world forgetting, by the world forgot;
Eternal sunshine of the spotless mind,
Each prayer accepted, and each wish resign'd;
Labour and rest, that equal periods keep;
Obedient slumbers that can wake and weep;
Desires composed, affections ever ev'n;
Tears that delight, and sighs that waft to Heav'n.
Grace shines around her with serenest beams,
And whisp'ring angels prompt her golden dreams.
For her th' unfading rose of Eden blooms,
And wings of seraphs shed divine perfumes;
For her the spouse prepares the bridal ring;
For her white virgins hymeneals sing;
To sounds of heav'nly harps she dies away,
And melts in visions of eternal day.
Far other dreams my erring soul employ,
Far other raptures of unholy joy.
When at the close of each sad, sorrowing day,

Fancy restores what vengeance snatch'd away,
Then conscience sleeps, and leaving Nature free,
All my loose soul unbounded springs to thee!
Oh curst, dear horrors of all-conscious night!
How glowing guilt exalts the keen delight!
Provoking demons all restraint remove,
And stir within me every source of love.
I hear thee, view thee, gaze o'er all thy charms,
And round thy phantom glue my clasping arms.
I wake: — no more I hear, no more I view,
The phantom flies me, as unkind as you.
I call aloud; it hears not what I say:
I stretch my empty arms; it glides away.
To dream once more I close my willing eyes;
Ye soft illusions, dear deceits, arise!
Alas, no more! methinks we wand'ring go
Thro' dreary wastes, and weep each other's woe,
Where round some mould'ring tower pale ivy creeps,
And low-brow'd rocks hang nodding o'er the deeps.
Sudden you mount, you beckon from the skies;
Clouds interpose, waves roar, and winds arise.
I shriek, start up, the same sad prospect find,
And wake to all the griefs I left behind.
For thee the Fates, severely kind, ordain
A cool suspense from pleasure and from pain;
Thy life a long dead calm of fix'd repose;
No pulse that riots, and no blood that glows.
Still as the sea, ere winds were taught to blow,
Or moving spirit bade the waters flow;
Soft as the slumbers of a saint forgiv'n,
And mild as opening gleams of promised Heav'n.
Come, Abelard! for what hast thou to dread?
The torch of Venus burns not for the dead.
Nature stands check'd; Religion disapproves;
Ev'n thou art cold — yet Eloisa loves.
Ah, hopeless, lasting flames; like those that burn
To light the dead, and warm th' unfruitful urn!
What scenes appear where'er I turn my view;
The dear ideas, where I fly, pursue;
Rise in the grove, before the altar rise,
Stain all my soul, and wanton in my eyes.
I waste the matin lamp in sighs for thee,
Thy image steals between my God and me:
Thy voice I seem in every hymn to hear,
With every bead I drop too soft a tear.
When from the censer clouds of fragrance roll,
And swelling organs lift the rising soul,
One thought of thee puts all the pomp to flight,
Priests, tapers, temples, swim before my sight:
In seas of flame my plunging soul is drown'd,
While altars blaze, and angels tremble round.
While prostrate here in humble grief I lie,
Kind virtuous drops just gath'ring in my eye,
While praying, trembling, in the dust I roll,
And dawning grace is opening on my soul:
Come, if thou dar'st, all charming as thou art!
Oppose thyself to Heav'n; dispute my heart;
Come, with one glance of those deluding eyes
Blot out each bright idea of the skies;
Take back that grace, those sorrows and those tears,
Take back my fruitless penitence and prayers;
Snatch me, just mounting, from the blest abode:

Assist the fiends, and tear me from my God!
No, fly me, fly me, far as pole from pole;
Rise Alps between us! and whole oceans roll!
Ah, come not, write not, think not once of me,
Nor share one pang of all I felt for thee.
Thy oaths I quit, thy memory resign;
Forget, renounce me, hate whate'er was mine.
Fair eyes, and tempting looks (which yet I view),
Long lov'd, ador'd ideas, all adieu!
O Grace serene! O Virtue heav'nly fair!
Divine Oblivion of low-thoughted care!
Fresh blooming Hope, gay daughter of the sky!
And Faith, our early immortality!
Enter each mild, each amicable guest;
Receive, and wrap me in eternal rest!
See in her cell sad Eloisa spread,
Propt on some tomb, a neighbour of the dead.
In each low wind methinks a spirit calls,
And more than echoes talk along the walls.
Here, as I watch'd the dying lamps around,
From yonder shrine I heard a hollow sound:
'Come, sister, come! (it said, or seem'd to say)
Thy place is here, sad sister, come away;
Once, like thyself, I trembled, wept, and pray'd,
Love's victim then, tho' now a sainted maid:
But all is calm in this eternal sleep;
Here grief forgets to groan, and love to weep;
Ev'n superstition loses ev'ry fear:
For God, not man, absolves our frailties here.'
I come, I come! prepare your roseate bowers,
Celestial palms, and ever-blooming flowers.
Thither, where sinners may have rest, I go,
Where flames refin'd in breasts seraphic glow;
Thou, Abelard! the last sad office pay,
And smooth my passage to the realms of day:
See my lips tremble, and my eyeballs roll,
Suck my last breath, and catch my flying soul!
Ah, no — in sacred vestments mayst thou stand,
The hallow'd taper trembling in thy hand,
Present the cross before my lifted eye,
Teach me at once, and learn of me, to die.
Ah then, thy once lov'd Eloisa see!
It will be then no crime to gaze on me.
See from my cheek the transient roses fly!
See the last sparkle languish in my eye!
Till ev'ry motion, pulse, and breath be o'er,
And ev'n my Abelard be lov'd no more.
O Death, all-eloquent! you only prove
What dust we doat on, when 't is man we love.
Then too, when Fate shall thy fair frame destroy
(That cause of all my guilt, and all my joy),
In trance ecstatic may thy pangs be drown'd,
Bright clouds descend, and angels watch thee round;
From opening skies may streaming glories shine,
And saints embrace thee with a love like mine.
May one kind grave [42] unite each hapless name,
And graft my love immortal on thy fame!
Then, ages hence, when all my woes are o'er,
When this rebellious heart shall beat no more;
If ever chance two wand'ring lovers brings,
To Paraclete's white walls and silver springs,
O'er the pale marble shall they join their heads,
And drink the falling tears each other sheds;
Then sadly say, with mutual pity mov'd,
'O may we never love as these have lov'd!'

[42] Abelard and Eloisa were interred in the same grave or in monuments adjoining, in the Monastery of the Paraclete; he died in the year 1142, she in 1163. [Pope.]

From the full choir, when loud hosannas rise,
And swell the pomp of dreadful sacrifice,
Amid that scene if some relenting eye
Glance on the stone where our cold relics lie,
Devotion's self shall steal a thought from Heav'n,
One human tear shall drop, and be forgiv'n.
And sure if Fate some future bard shall join
In sad similitude of griefs to mine,
Condemn'd whole years in absence to deplore,
And image charms he must behold no more, —
Such if there be, who loves so long, so well,
Let him our sad, our tender story tell;
The well-sung woes will soothe my pensive ghost;
He best can paint them who shall feel them most.

Ode to Quinbus Flestrin [43]

THE MAN MOUNTAIN, BY TITTY TIT, POET LAUREATE TO HIS MAJESTY OF LILLIPUT. TRANSLATED INTO ENGLISH

In amaze
Lost I gaze!
Can our eyes
Reach thy size!
May my lays
Swell with praise,
Worthy thee!
Worthy me!
Muse, inspire
All thy fire!
Bards of old
Of him told,
When they said
Atlas' head
Propp'd the skies:
See! and believe your eyes!
See him stride
Valleys wide,
Over woods,
Over floods!
When he treads,
Mountains' heads
Groan and shake,
Armies quake;
Lest his spurn
Overturn
Man and steed:
Troops, take heed!
Left and right,
Speed your flight!
Lest an host
Beneath his foot be lost;
Turn'd aside
From his hide
Safe from wound,
Darts rebound.
From his nose
Clouds he blows!
When he speaks,
Thunder breaks!
When he eats,
Famine threats!
When he drinks,
Neptune shrinks!
Nigh thy ear
In mid air,
On thy hand
Let me stand;
So shall I,
Lofty poet! touch the sky.

[43] This 'Ode' was written by Pope after reading *Gulliver's Travels*, and published in the *Miscellanies* of Pope and Swift in 1727; *Poems occasioned by reading the Travels of Captain Lemuel Gulliver explanatory and commendatory*, 1727.

Intended for Sir Isaac Newton [44]

IN WESTMINSTER ABBEY

ISAACUS NEWTONUS

QUEM IMMORTALEM TESTANTUR TEMPUS, NATURA, CŒLUM: MORTALEM HOC MARMOR FATETUR

Nature and Nature's laws lay hid in Night:
God said, *Let* Newton *be!* and all was Light.

[44] Published in *The Grub-street Journal*, 16 July 1730.

AN ESSAY ON MAN[45]

In Four Epistles to H. St. John, Lord Bolingbroke

EPISTLE I

OF THE NATURE AND STATE OF MAN, WITH RESPECT TO THE UNIVERSE

ARGUMENT

Of Man in the abstract. I. That we can judge only with regard to our own system, being ignorant of the relations of systems and things, verse 17, etc. II. That Man is not to be deemed imperfect, but a being suited to his place and rank in the creation, agreeable to the general order of things, and conformable to ends and relations to him unknown, verse 35, etc. III. That it is partly upon his ignorance of future events, and partly upon the hope of a future state, that all his happiness in the present depends, verse 77, etc. IV. The pride of aiming at more knowledge, and pretending to more perfection, the cause of Man's error and misery. The impiety of putting himself in the place of God, and judging of the fitness or unfitness, perfection or imperfection, justice or injustice, of his dispensations, verse 113, etc. V. The absurdity of conceiting himself the final cause of the creation, or expecting that perfection in the moral world which is not in the natural, verse 131, etc. VI. The unreasonableness of his complaints against Providence, while, on the one hand, he demands the perfections of the angels, and, on the other, the bodily qualifications of the brutes; though to possess any of the sensitive faculties in a higher degree would render him miserable, verse 173, etc. VII. That throughout the whole visible world a universal order and gradation in the sensual and mental faculties is observed, which causes a subordination of creature to creature, and of all creatures to Man. The gradations of Sense, Instinct, Thought, Reflection, Reason: that Reason alone countervails all the other faculties, verse 207, etc. VIII. How much further this order and subordination of living creatures may extend above and below us; were any part of which broken, not that part only, but the whole connected creation must be destroyed, verse 233, etc. IX. The extravagance, madness, and pride of such a desire, verse 259, etc. X. The consequence of all, the absolute submission due to Providence, both as to our present and future state, verse 281, etc., to the end.

Awake, my St. John! leave all meaner things
To low ambition and the pride of Kings.
Let us, since life can little more supply
Than just to look about us and to die,
Expatiate free o'er all this scene of Man;
A mighty maze! but not without a plan;[46]
A wild, where weeds and flowers promiscuous shoot,
Or garden, tempting with forbidden fruit.
Together let us beat this ample field,
Try what the open, what the covert yield;
The latent tracts, the giddy heights, explore
Of all who blindly creep or sightless soar;
Eye Nature's walks, shoot Folly as it flies,
And catch the manners living as they rise;
Laugh where we must, be candid where we can,
But vindicate the ways of God to Man.
I. Say first, of God above or Man below
What can we reason but from what we know?
Of Man what see we but his station here,
From which to reason, or to which refer?
Thro' worlds unnumber'd tho' the God be known,
'T is ours to trace him only in our own.
He who thro' vast immensity can pierce,
See worlds on worlds compose one universe,
Observe how system into system runs,
What other planets circle other suns,
What varied being peoples every star,
May tell why Heav'n has made us as we are:
But of this frame, the bearings and the ties,
The strong connexions, nice dependencies,

[45] The first epistle was written in 1732; the complete work was finished and published, in four epistles, in 1734. Lord Bolingbroke, Pope's intimate friend, had discussed many of the ideas with him. A 'Design' to the poem reads in part: 'I chose verse, and even rhyme, for two reasons. The one will appear obvious; that principles, maxims, or precepts, so written, both strike the reader more strongly at first, and are more easily retained by him afterwards: the other may seem odd, but it is true: I found I could express them more shortly this way than in prose itself; and nothing is more certain than that much of the force as well as grace of arguments or instructions depends on their conciseness.'

[46] The last verse, as it stood in the original editions, was —

'A mighty maze of walks without a plan;'

and perhaps this came nearer Pope's real opinion than the verse he substituted for it. [Lowell.]

Gradations just, has thy pervading soul
Look'd thro'; or can a part contain the whole?
  Is the great chain that draws all to agree,
And drawn supports, upheld by God or thee?
  II. Presumptuous Man! the reason wouldst thou find,
Why form'd so weak, so little, and so blind?
First, if thou canst, the harder reason guess,
Why form'd no weaker, blinder, and no less!
Ask of thy mother earth why oaks are made
Taller or stronger than the weeds they shade!
Or ask of yonder argent fields above
Why Jove's satellites are less than Jove!
  Of systems possible, if 't is confest
That wisdom infinite must form the best,
Where all must fall or not coherent be,
And all that rises rise in due degree;
Then in the scale of reas'ning life 't is plain
There must be, somewhere, such a rank as Man:
And all the question (wrangle e'er so long)
Is only this,—if God has placed him wrong?
  Respecting Man, whatever wrong we call,
May, must be right, as relative to all.
In human works, tho' labour'd on with pain,
A thousand movements scarce one purpose gain;
In God's, one single can its end produce,
Yet serve to second too some other use:
So Man, who here seems principal alone,
Perhaps acts second to some sphere unknown,
Touches some wheel, or verges to some goal:
'T is but a part we see, and not a whole.
  When the proud steed shall know why Man restrains
His fiery course, or drives him o'er the plains;
When the dull ox, why now he breaks the clod,
Is now a victim, and now Egypt's God;
Then shall Man's pride and dulness comprehend
His actions', passions', being's, use and end;
Why doing, suff'ring, check'd, impell'd; and why
This hour a Slave, the next a Deity.
  Then say not Man's imperfect, Heav'n in fault;
Say rather Man's as perfect as he ought;
His knowledge measured to his state and place,
His time a moment, and a point his space.
If to be perfect in a certain sphere,
What matter soon or late, or here or there?
The blest to-day is as completely so
As who began a thousand years ago.
  III. Heav'n from all creatures hides the book of Fate,
All but the page prescribed, their present state;
From brutes what men, from men what spirits know;
Or who could suffer Being here below?
The lamb thy riot dooms to bleed to-day,
Had he thy Reason would he skip and play?
Pleas'd to the last he crops the flowery food,
And licks the hand just rais'd to shed his blood.
O blindness to the future! kindly giv'n,
That each may fill the circle mark'd by Heav'n;
Who sees with equal eye, as God of all,
A hero perish or a sparrow fall,
Atoms or systems into ruin hurl'd,
And now a bubble burst, and now a world.
  Hope humbly then; with trembling pinions soar;
Wait the great teacher Death, and God adore.
What future bliss He gives not thee to know,
But gives that hope to be thy blessing now.

Hope springs eternal in the human breast:
Man never is, but always to be, blest.
The soul, uneasy and confin'd from home,
Rests and expatiates in a life to come.
Lo, the poor Indian! whose untutor'd mind
Sees God in clouds, or hears him in the wind;
His soul proud Science never taught to stray
Far as the solar walk or milky way;
Yet simple nature to his hope has giv'n,
Behind the cloud-topt hill, an humbler Heav'n,
Some safer world in depth of woods embraced,
Some happier island in the wat'ry waste,
Where slaves once more their native land behold,
No fiends torment, no Christians thirst for gold.
To be, contents his natural desire;
He asks no Angel's wing, no Seraph's fire;
But thinks, admitted to that equal sky,
His faithful dog shall bear him company.
IV. Go, wiser thou! and in thy scale of sense
Weigh thy opinion against Providence;
Call imperfection what thou fanciest such;
Say, here he gives too little, there too much;
Destroy all creatures for thy sport or gust,
Yet cry, if Man's unhappy, God's unjust;
If Man alone engross not Heav'n's high care,
Alone made perfect here, immortal there:
Snatch from his hand the balance and the rod,
Rejudge his justice, be the god of God.
In pride, in reas'ning pride, our error lies;
All quit their sphere, and rush into the skies!
Pride still is aiming at the bless'd abodes,
Men would be Angels, Angels would be Gods.
Aspiring to be Gods if Angels fell,
Aspiring to be Angels men rebel:
And who but wishes to invert the laws
Of order, sins against th' Eternal Cause.
V. Ask for what end the heav'nly bodies shine,
Earth for whose use,—Pride answers, ''T is for mine:
For me kind Nature wakes her genial power,
Suckles each herb, and spreads out ev'ry flower;
Annual for me the grape, the rose, renew
The juice nectareous and the balmy dew;
For me the mine a thousand treasures brings;
For me health gushes from a thousand springs;
Seas roll to waft me, suns to light me rise;
My footstool earth, my canopy the skies.'
But errs not Nature from this gracious end,
From burning suns when livid deaths descend,
When earthquakes swallow, or when tempests sweep
Towns to one grave, whole nations to the deep?
'No,' 't is replied, 'the first Almighty Cause
Acts not by partial but by gen'ral laws;
Th' exceptions few; some change since all began
And what created perfect?'—Why then Man?
If the great end be human happiness,
Then Nature deviates; and can Man do less?
As much that end a constant course requires
Of showers and sunshine, as of Man's desires;
As much eternal springs and cloudless skies,
As Men for ever temp'rate, calm, and wise.
If plagues or earthquakes break not Heav'n's design,
Why then a Borgia or a Catiline?

Who knows but He, whose hand the lightning forms,
Who heaves old ocean, and who wings the storms;
Pours fierce Ambition in a Cæsar's mind,
Or turns young Ammon [47] loose to scourge mankind?
From pride, from pride, our very reas'ning springs;
Account for moral as for natural things:
Why charge we Heav'n in those, in these acquit?
In both, to reason right is to submit.

Better for us, perhaps, it might appear,
Were there all harmony, all virtue here;
That never air or ocean felt the wind,
That never passion discomposed the mind:
But all subsists by elemental strife;
And passions are the elements of life.
The gen'ral order, since the whole began,
Is kept in Nature, and is kept in Man.

VI. What would this Man? Now upward will he soar,
And little less than Angel, would be more;
Now looking downwards, just as griev'd appears
To want the strength of bulls, the fur of bears.
Made for his use all creatures if he call,
Say what their use, had he the powers of all?
Nature to these without profusion kind,
The proper organs, proper powers assign'd;
Each seeming want compensated of course,
Here with degrees of swiftness, there of force;
All in exact proportion to the state;
Nothing to add, and nothing to abate;
Each beast, each insect, happy in its own:
Is Heav'n unkind to Man, and Man alone?
Shall he alone, whom rational we call,
Be pleas'd with nothing if not bless'd with all?

The bliss of Man (could pride that blessing find)
Is not to act or think beyond mankind;
No powers of body or of soul to share,
But what his nature and his state can bear.
Why has not Man a microscopic eye?
For this plain reason, Man is not a fly.
Say, what the use, were finer optics giv'n,
T' inspect a mite, not comprehend the Heav'n?
Or touch, if tremblingly alive all o'er,
To smart and agonize at every pore?
Or quick effluvia darting thro' the brain,
Die of a rose in aromatic pain?
If Nature thunder'd in his opening ears,
And stunn'd him with the music of the spheres,
How would he wish that Heav'n had left him still
The whisp'ring zephyr and the purling rill?
Who finds not Providence all good and wise,
Alike in what it gives and what denies?

VII. Far as creation's ample range extends,
The scale of sensual, mental powers ascends.
Mark how it mounts to Man's imperial race
From the green myriads in the peopled grass:
What modes of sight betwixt each wide extreme,
The mole's dim curtain and the lynx's beam:
Of smell, the headlong lioness [48] between
And hound sagacious on the tainted green:
Of hearing, from the life that fills the flood
To that which warbles thro' the vernal wood.
The spider's touch, how exquisitely fine,
Feels at each thread, and lives along the line:
In the nice bee what sense so subtly true,
From pois'nous herbs extracts the healing dew!
How instinct varies in the grovelling swine,
Compared, half-reas'ning elephant, with thine!

[47] Alexander the Great, whom the priests of the Libyan Jupiter Ammon saluted as the son of their god.

[48] The manner of the lion's hunting is this: at their first going out in the night-time, they set up a loud roar, and then listen to the noise made by the beasts in their flight, pursuing them by the ear, and not by the nostril. [Pope.]

'Twixt that and reason what a nice barrier!
For ever separate, yet for ever near!
Remembrance and reflection how allied!
What thin partitions Sense from Thought divide!
And middle natures how they long to join,
Yet never pass th' insuperable line!
Without this just gradation could they be
Subjected, these to those, or all to thee!
The powers of all subdued by thee alone,
Is not thy Reason all these powers in one?
VIII. See thro' this air, this ocean, and this earth
All matter quick, and bursting into birth:
Above, how high progressive life may go!
Around, how wide! how deep extend below!
Vast chain of Being! which from God began;
Natures ethereal, human, angel, man,
Beast, bird, fish, insect, who no eye can see,
No glass can reach; from infinite to thee;
From thee to nothing.—On superior powers
Were we to press, inferior might on ours;
Or in the full creation leave a void,
Where, one step broken, the great scale's destroy'd:
From Nature's chain whatever link you like,
Tenth, or ten thousandth, breaks the chain alike.
And if each system in gradation roll,
Alike essential to th' amazing Whole,
The least confusion but in one, not all
The system only, but the Whole must fall.
Let earth unbalanced from her orbit fly,
Planets and stars run lawless thro' the sky;
Let ruling angels from their spheres be hurl'd,
Being on being wreck'd, and world on world;
Heav'n's whole foundations to their centre nod,
And Nature tremble to the throne of God!
All this dread order break—for whom? for thee?
Vile worm!—O madness! pride! impiety!
IX. What if the foot, ordain'd the dust to tread,
Or hand to toil, aspired to be the head?
What if the head, the eye, or ear repin'd
To serve mere engines to the ruling mind?
Just as absurd for any part to claim
To be another in this gen'ral frame;
Just as absurd to mourn the tasks or pains
The great directing Mind of All ordains.
All are but parts of one stupendous Whole,
Whose body Nature is, and God the soul;
That, changed thro' all, and yet in all the same,
Great in the earth as in th' ethereal frame,
Warms in the sun, refreshes in the breeze,
Glows in the stars, and blossoms in the trees;
Lives thro' all life, extends thro' all extent,
Spreads undivided, operates unspent;
Breathes in our soul, informs our mortal part,
As full, as perfect, in a hair as heart;
As full, as perfect, in vile Man that mourns,
As the rapt Seraph that adores and burns.
To him no high, no low, no great, no small;
He fills, he bounds, connects, and equals all!
X. Cease, then, nor Order imperfection name;
Our proper bliss depends on what we blame.
Know thy own point: this kind, this due degree
Of blindness, weakness, Heav'n bestows on thee.
Submit: in this or any other sphere,
Secure to be as bless'd as thou canst bear;
Safe in the hand of one disposing Power,
Or in the natal or the mortal hour.
All Nature is but Art unknown to thee;
All Chance, Direction, which thou canst not see;
All Discord, Harmony not understood;
All partial Evil, universal Good:
And spite of Pride, in erring Reason's spite,
One truth is clear, *Whatever is, is right.*

EPISTLE TO DR. ARBUTHNOT [49]

BEING THE PROLOGUE TO THE SATIRES

ADVERTISEMENT

This paper is a sort of bill of complaint, begun many years since, and drawn up by snatches, as the several occasions offered. I had no thoughts of publishing it, till it pleased some Persons of Rank and Fortune (the authors of 'Verses to the Imitator of Horace,' and of an 'Epistle to a Doctor of Divinity from a Nobleman at Hampton Court') to attack, in a very extraordinary manner, not only my Writings (of which, being public, the Public is judge), but my Person, Morals, and Family; whereof, to those who know me not, a truer information may be requisite. Being divided between the necessity to say something of myself, and my own laziness to undertake so awkward a task, I thought it the shortest way to put the last hand to this epistle. If it have any thing pleasing, it will be that by which I am most desirous to please, the Truth and the Sentiment; and if any thing offensive, it will be only to those I am least sorry to offend, the vicious or the ungenerous.

Many will know their own pictures in it, there being not a circumstance but what is true; but I have, for the most part, spared their names, and they may escape being laughed at if they please.

I would have some of them know it was owing to the request of the learned and candid Friend to whom it is inscribed, that I make not as free use of theirs as they have done of mine. However, I shall have this advantage and honour on my side, that whereas, by their proceeding, any abuse may be directed at any man, no injury can possibly be done by mine, since a nameless character can never be found out but by its truth and likeness.

P. 'SHUT, shut the door, good John!' [50] fatigued, I said;
'Tie up the knocker, say I'm sick, I'm dead.'
The Dog-star rages! nay, 't is past a doubt
All Bedlam or Parnassus is let out:
Fire in each eye, and papers in each hand,
They rave, recite, and madden round the land.
What walls can guard me, or what shades can hide?
They pierce my thickets, thro' my grot [51] they glide,
By land, by water, they renew the charge,
They stop the chariot, and they board the barge.
No place is sacred, not the church is free,
Ev'n Sunday shines no Sabbath-day to me:
Then from the Mint [52] walks forth the man of rhyme,
Happy to catch me just at dinner time.
Is there a Parson much bemused in beer,
A maudlin Poetess, a rhyming Peer,
A clerk foredoom'd his father's soul to cross,
Who pens a stanza when he should engross?
Is there who, lock'd from ink and paper, scrawls
With desp'rate charcoal round his darken'd walls?
All fly to TWIT'NAM, and in humble strain
Apply to me to keep them mad or vain,
Arthur,[53] whose giddy son neglects the laws,
Imputes to me and my damn'd works the cause:
Poor Cornus [54] sees his frantic wife elope,
And curses Wit and Poetry, and Pope.
Friend to my life (which did not you prolong,
The world had wanted many an idle song)!
What Drop or Nostrum can this plague remove?
Or which must end me, a fool's wrath or love?
A dire dilemma! either way I'm sped;
If foes, they write, if friends, they read me dead.
Seiz'd and tied down to judge, how wretched I!

---

[49] The occasion for the poem actually was the attacks on Pope mentioned in the 'Advertisement.' The first was supposedly by Lady Mary Wortley Montagu and Lord John Hervey; the second by Hervey alone. A few passages had been written earlier, but the satire dates, on the whole, from 1734. It was published 2 January 1735. The 'dialogue' is between Pope and Dr. John Arbuthnot, physician, literary man, and Pope's close friend. Arbuthnot died in 1735, a short time after the *Epistle* was printed. Like *The Dunciad* and the other satires, the poem shows Pope's remarkable gift for *personal* abuse in an age when such a talent was often sorely needed.

[50] John Searl, for many years Pope's body-servant.

[51] An artificial grotto, built under a road, was one of the prides of Pope's estate at Twickenham.

[52] A district in London where debtors were safe from arrest; on Sundays they were safe anywhere.

[53] Arthur Moore, politician and father of James Moore Smythe, of whom Pope often made fun.

[54] Robert Walpole

Who can't be silent, and who will not lie.
To laugh were want of goodness and of grace,
And to be grave exceeds all power of face.
I sit with sad civility, I read
With honest anguish and an aching head,
And drop at last, but in unwilling ears,
This saving counsel, 'Keep your piece nine years.'[55]
'Nine years!' cries he, who, high in Drury lane,
Lull'd by soft zephyrs thro' the broken pane,
Rhymes ere he wakes, and prints before Term[56] ends,
Obliged by hunger and request of friends:
The piece, you think, is incorrect? why, take it!
I'm all submission: what you'd have it — make it.'
Three things another's modest wishes bound,
'My friendship, and a Prologue, and ten pound.'
Pitholeon[57] sends to me: "You know his Grace,
I want a patron; ask him for a place.'
Pitholeon libell'd me — 'But here's a letter
Informs you, Sir, 'twas when he knew no better.
Dare you refuse him? Curll[58] invites to dine,
He'll write a *Journal,* or he'll turn Divine.'
Bless me! a packet. — 'T is a stranger sues,
A Virgin Tragedy, an Orphan Muse.
If I dislike it, 'Furies, death, and rage!'
If I approve, 'Commend it to the stage.'
There (thank my stars) my whole commission ends,
The players[59] and I are, luckily, no friends.
Fired that the house rejects him, ''Sdeath, I'll print it,
And shame the fools — your int'rest, Sir, with Lintot.'[60]
Lintot, dull rogue, will think your price too much:
'Not, Sir, if you revise it, and retouch.'
All my demurs but double his attacks;
At last he whispers, 'Do, and we go snacks.'
Glad of a quarrel, straight I clap the door;
'Sir, let me see your works and you no more.'
'T is sung, when Midas' ears began to spring
(Midas, a sacred person and a king),
His very Minister who spied them first
(Some say his Queen) was forc'd to speak or burst.
And is not mine, my friend, a sorer case,
When ev'ry coxcomb perks them in my face?
A. Good friend, forbear! you deal in dangerous things;
I'd never name Queens, Ministers, or Kings;
Keep close to ears, and those let asses prick,
'T is nothing — *P.* Nothing! if they bite and kick?
Out with it, DUNCIAD! let the secret pass,
That secret to each fool, that he's an ass:
The truth once told (and wherefore should we lie?)
The Queen of Midas slept, and so may I.
You think this cruel? take it for a rule,
No creature smarts so little as a fool.
Let peals of laughter, Codrus! round thee break,
Thou unconcern'd canst hear the mighty crack:
Pit, Box, and Gall'ry in convulsions hurl'd,
Thou stand'st unshook amidst a bursting world.
Who shames a Scribbler? break one cobweb thro',
He spins the slight self-pleasing thread anew:

[55] Horace, *De Arte Poetica*, l. 388.

[56] The London 'season'; strictly, the months when the courts of law are in session.

[57] The name taken from a foolish poet of Rhodes, who pretended much to Greek. [Pope.]

[58] Edmund Curll, piratical book-seller and enemy of Pope, whose name he had often signed to poor material. He had printed Pope's private letters in 1727.

[59] The first edition reads 'Cibber.' Colley Cibber, who had made fun of Pope's play, *Three Hours after Marriage*, done in collaboration with Gay and Arbuthnot, was pilloried by Pope in *The Dunciad*.

[60] Bernard Lintot published much of Pope's writing.

Destroy his fib, or sophistry — in vain!
The creature's at his dirty work again,
Throned in the centre of his thin designs,
Proud of a vast extent of flimsy lines.
Whom have I hurt? has Poet yet or Peer
Lost the arch'd eyebrow or Parnassian sneer?
And has not Colley[61] still his lord and whore?
His butchers Henley? his freemasons Moore?
Does not one table Bavius still admit?
Still to one Bishop Philips[62] seem a wit?
Still Sappho[63]— *A.* Hold! for God's sake — you'll offend.
No names — be calm — learn prudence of a friend.
I too could write, and I am twice as tall;
But foes like these — *P.* One flatt'rer's worse than all.
Of all mad creatures, if the learn'd are right,
It is the slaver kills, and not the bite.
A fool quite angry is quite innocent:
Alas! 't is ten times worse when they repent.
One dedicates in high heroic prose,
And ridicules beyond a hundred foes;
One from all Grub-street will my fame defend,
And, more abusive, calls himself my friend:
This prints my *Letters,* that expects a bribe,
And others roar aloud, 'Subscribe, subscribe!'
There are who to my person pay their court:
I cough like Horace; and tho' lean, am short;
Ammon's great son one shoulder had too high,
Such Ovid's nose, and 'Sir! you have an eye —'
Go on, obliging creatures! make me see
All that disgraced my betters met in me.
Say, for my comfort, languishing in bed,
'Just so immortal Maro held his head:'
And when I die, be sure you let me know
Great Homer died three thousand years ago.
Why did I write? what sin to me unknown
Dipp'd me in ink, my parents', or my own?
As yet a child, nor yet a fool to fame,
I lisp'd in numbers, for the numbers came:
I left no calling for this idle trade,
No duty broke, no father disobey'd:
The Muse but serv'd to ease some friend, not wife,
To help me thro' this long disease my life,
To second, ARBUTHNOT! thy art and care,
And teach the being you preserv'd, to bear.
A. But why then publish? *P.* Granville[64] the polite,
And knowing Walsh, would tell me I could write;
Well-natured Garth inflamed with early praise,
And Congreve lov'd, and Swift endured my lays;
The courtly Talbot, Somers, Sheffield,[65] read;
Ev'n mitred Rochester[66] would nod the head,
And St. John's self (great Dryden's friends before)
With open arms receiv'd one poet more.
Happy my studies, when by these approv'd!
Happier their author, when by these belov'd!
From these the world will judge of men and books,
Not from the Burnets, Oldmixons, and Cookes.[67]
Soft were my numbers; who could take offence
While pure description held the place of sense?
Like gentle Fanny's[68] was my flowery theme,

[61] Cibber
[62] Ambrose Philips, who had Bishop Boulter for a patron.
[63] Lady Mary Wortley Montagu

[64] George Granville, afterwards Lord Lansdowne. He, Dr. Garth, a physician, and particularly William Walsh were the first to encourage Pope as a writer.
[65] All patrons of literature.
[66] Francis Atterbury, Bishop of Rochester.
[67] Authors of secret and scandalous history. [Pope.]
[68] Lord Hervey, the 'Sporus' of lines 305–333 below.

'A painted mistress, or a purling stream.'
Yet then did Gildon draw his venal quill;
I wish'd the man a dinner, and sat still:
Yet then did Dennis[69] rave in furious fret;
I never answer'd; I was not in debt.
If want provoked, or madness made them print,
I waged no war with Bedlam or the Mint.
Did some more sober critic come abroad;
If wrong, I smiled, if right, I kiss'd the rod.
Pains, reading, study, are their just pretence,
And all they want is spirit, taste, and sense.
Commas and points they set exactly right,
And 't were a sin to rob them of their mite.
Yet ne'er one sprig of laurel graced these ribalds,
From slashing Bentleys down to piddling Tibbalds.[70]
Each wight who reads not, and but scans and spells,
Each word-catcher that lives on syllables,
Ev'n such small critics some regard may claim,
Preserv'd in Milton's or in Shakspeare's name.
Pretty! in amber to observe the forms
Of hairs, or straws, or dirt, or grubs, or worms!
The things, we know, are neither rich nor rare,
But wonder how the devil they got there.
Were others angry: I excused them too;
Well might they rage, I gave them but their due.
A man's true merit 't is not hard to find;
But each man's secret standard in his mind,
That casting-weight Pride adds to emptiness,
This, who can gratify? for who can guess?
The bard[71] whom pilfer'd pastorals renown,
Who turns a Persian tale for half-a-crown,
Just writes to make his barrenness appear,
And strains from hard-bound brains eight lines a year;
He who still wanting, tho' he lives on theft,
Steals much, spends little, yet has nothing left;
And he who now to sense, now nonsense, leaning,
Means not, but blunders round about a meaning:
And he whose fustian's so sublimely bad,
It is not poetry, but prose run mad:
All these my modest satire bade translate,
And own'd that nine such poets made a Tate.[72]
How did they fume, and stamp, and roar, and chafe!
And swear not ADDISON himself was safe.
Peace to all such! but were there one whose fires
True Genius kindles, and fair Fame inspires,
Bless'd with each talent and each art to please,
And born to write, converse, and live with ease;
Should such a man, too fond to rule alone,
Bear, like the Turk, no brother near the throne;
View him with scornful, yet with jealous eyes,
And hate for arts that caus'd himself to rise;
Damn with faint praise, assent with civil leer,
And without sneering teach the rest to sneer;
Willing to wound, and yet afraid to strike,
Just hint a fault, and hesitate dislike;
Alike reserv'd to blame or to commend,
A tim'rous foe, and a suspicious friend;
Dreading ev'n fools; by flatterers besieged,

---

[69] Charles Gildon and John Dennis, critics who had drawn Pope's fire.

[70] Bentley was a classical scholar, whose last effort had been a not too worthy edition of *Paradise Lost;* Theobald was the editor of Shakespeare.

[71] Ambrose Philips

[72] Nahum Tate, then poet laureate.

And so obliging that he ne'er obliged;
Like Cato, give his little Senate laws,
And sit attentive to his own applause:
While Wits and Templars ev'ry sentence raise,
And wonder with a foolish face of praise —
Who but must laugh if such a man there be?
Who would not weep, if Atticus [73] were he?
  What tho' my name stood rubric [74] on the walls,
Or plaster'd posts, with claps,[75] in capitals?
Or smoking forth, a hundred hawkers load,
On wings of winds came flying all abroad?
I sought no homage from the race that write;
I kept, like Asian Monarchs, from their sight:
Poems I heeded (now berhymed so long)
No more than thou, great George! a birth-day song.
I ne'er with Wits or Witlings pass'd my days
To spread about the itch of verse and praise;
Nor like a puppy daggled thro' the town
To fetch and carry sing-song up and down;
Nor at rehearsals sweat, and mouth'd, and cried,
With handkerchief and orange at my side;
But sick of fops, and poetry, and prate,
To Bufo [76] left the whole Castalian state.
  Proud as Apollo on his forked hill
Sat full-blown Bufo, puff'd by ev'ry quill:
Fed with soft dedication all day long,
Horace and he went hand in hand in song.
His library (where busts of poets dead,
And a true Pindar stood without a head)
Receiv'd of Wits an undistinguish'd race,
Who first his judgment ask'd, and then a place:

[73] Addison
[74] On the walls of Lintot's shop the names of new books were posted in red letters.
[75] posters
[76] Probably Lord Halifax.

Much they extoll'd his pictures, much his seat,
And flatter'd ev'ry day, and some days eat:
Till grown more frugal in his riper days,
He paid some bards with port, and some with praise;
To some a dry rehearsal was assign'd,
And others (harder still) he paid in kind.
Dryden alone (what wonder?) came not nigh;
Dryden alone escaped this judging eye:
But still the great have kindness in reserve;
He help'd to bury whom he help'd to starve.
May some choice patron bless each gray goose quill!
May every Bavius have his Bufo still!
So when a statesman wants a day's defence,
Or Envy holds a whole week's war with Sense,
Or simple Pride for flatt'ry makes demands,
May dunce by dunce be whistled off my hands!
Bless'd be the great! for those they take away,
And those they left me — for they left me Gay; [77]
Left me to see neglected Genius bloom,
Neglected die, and tell it on his tomb:
Of all thy blameless life the sole return
My Verse, and Queensb'ry weeping o'er thy urn!
  Oh let me live my own, and die so too
(To live and die is all I have to do)!
Maintain a poet's dignity and ease,
And see what friends, and read what books I please;
Above a Patron, tho' I condescend
Sometimes to call a minister my Friend.
I was not born for courts or great affairs;
I pay my debts, believe, and say my prayers;
Can sleep without a poem in my head,

[77] John Gay, the poet, one of Pope's closest friends.

Nor know if Dennis be alive or dead.
Why am I ask'd what next shall see the light?
Heav'ns! was I born for nothing but to write?
Has life no joys for me? or (to be grave)
Have I no friend to serve, no soul to save?
'I found him close with Swift'—'Indeed? no doubt
(Cries prating Balbus) something will come out.'
'T is all in vain, deny it as I will;
'No, such a genius never can lie still:'
And then for mine obligingly mistakes
The first lampoon Sir Will or Bubo [78] makes.
Poor guiltless I! and can I choose but smile,
When ev'ry coxcomb knows me by my style?
Curst be the verse, how well soe'er it flow,
That tends to make one worthy man my foe,
Give Virtue scandal, Innocence a fear,
Or from the soft-eyed virgin steal a tear!
But he who hurts a harmless neighbour's peace,
Insults fall'n Worth, or Beauty in distress,
Who loves a lie, lame Slander helps about,
Who writes a libel, or who copies out;
That fop whose pride affects a patron's name,
Yet absent, wounds an author's honest fame;
Who can your merit selfishly approve,
And show the sense of it without the love;
Who has the vanity to call you friend,
Yet wants the honour, injured, to defend;
Who tells whate'er you think, whate'er you say,
And, if he lie not, must at least betray;
Who to the Dean and Silver Bell can swear,
And sees at Canons what was never there;
Who reads but with a lust to misapply,
Make satire a lampoon, and fiction, lie:
A lash like mine no honest man shall dread,
But all such babbling blockheads in his stead.
Let Sporus [79] tremble—*A.* What? that thing of silk,
Sporus, that mere white curd of Ass's milk?
Satire or sense, alas! can Sporus feel?
Who breaks a butterfly upon a wheel?
P. Yet let me flap this bug with gilded wings,
This painted child of dirt, that stinks and stings;
Whose buzz the witty and the fair annoys,
Yet Wit ne'er tastes, and Beauty ne'er enjoys;
So well-bred spaniels civilly delight
In mumbling of the game they dare not bite.
Eternal smiles his emptiness betray,
As shallow streams run dimpling all the way,
Whether in florid impotence he speaks,
And, as the prompter breathes, the puppet squeaks,
Or at the ear of Eve, familiar toad,
Half froth, half venom, spits himself abroad,
In puns, or politics, or tales, or lies,
Or spite, or smut, or rhymes, or blasphemies;
His wit all see-saw between *that* and *this,*
Now high, now low, now master up, now miss,
And he himself one vile Antithesis.
Amphibious thing! that acting either part,
The trifling head, or the corrupted heart;
Fop at the toilet, flatt'rer at the board,
Now trips a lady, and now struts a lord.
Eve's tempter thus the Rabbins have exprest,
A cherub's face, a reptile all the rest;
Beauty that shocks you, Parts that none will trust,
Wit that can creep, and Pride that licks the dust.

[78] Sir William Yonge and Bubb Doddington.

[79] Lord Hervey. Sporus was the name of a eunuch, favorite at the court of Nero.

Not Fortune's worshipper, nor Fashion's fool,
Not Lucre's madman, nor Ambition's tool,
Not proud nor servile; — be one poet's praise,
That if he pleas'd, he pleas'd by manly ways:
That flatt'ry ev'n to Kings, he held a shame,
And thought a lie in verse or prose the same;
That not in fancy's maze he wander'd long,
But stoop'd to truth, and moralized his song;
That not for Fame, but Virtue's better end,
He stood the furious foe, the timid friend,
The damning critic, half approving wit,
The coxcomb hit, or fearing to be hit;
Laugh'd at the loss of friends he never had,
The dull, the proud, the wicked, and the mad;
The distant threats of vengeance on his head,
The blow unfelt, the tear he never shed;
The tale revived, the lie so oft o'erthrown,
Th' imputed trash and dulness not his own;
The morals blacken'd when the writings 'scape,
The libell'd person, and the pictured shape;
Abuse on all he lov'd, or lov'd him, spread,
A friend in exile, or a father dead;
The whisper, that, to greatness still too near,
Perhaps yet vibrates on his Sov'reign's ear —
Welcome for thee, fair Virtue! all the past:
For thee, fair Virtue! welcome ev'n the last!
A. But why insult the poor? affront the great?
P. A knave's a knave to me in ev'ry state;
Alike my scorn, if he succeed or fail,
Sporus at court, or Japhet [80] in a jail;
A hireling scribbler, or a hireling peer,
Knight of the post corrupt, or of the shire;
If on a Pillory, or near a Throne,
He gain his prince's ear, or lose his own.
Yet soft by nature, more a dupe than wit,
Sappho can tell you how this man was bit:
This dreaded Satirist Dennis will confess
Foe to his pride, but friend to his distress:
So humble, he has knock'd at Tibbald's door,
Has drunk with Cibber, nay, has rhymed for Moore.
Full ten years slander'd, did he once reply?
Three thousand suns went down on Welsted's [81] lie.
To please a mistress one aspers'd his life;
He lash'd him not, but let her be his wife:
Let Budgell [82] charge low Grub-street on his quill,
And write whate'er he pleased, except his will;
Let the two Curlls [83] of town and court abuse
His father, mother, body, soul, and muse:
Yet why? that father held it for a rule,
It was a sin to call our neighbour fool;
That harmless mother thought no wife a whore:
Hear this, and spare his family, James Moore!
Unspotted names, and memorable long,
If there be force in Virtue, or in Song.
Of gentle blood (part shed in honour's cause,
While yet in Britain honour had applause)
Each parent sprung — *A.* What fortune, pray? —
P. Their own;
And better got than Bestia's from the throne.
Born to no pride, inheriting no strife,
Nor marrying discord in a noble wife,
Stranger to civil and religious rage,

[80] Japhet Crooke, a forger.

[81] This man had the impudence to tell in print that Mr. P. had occasioned a lady's death, and to name a person he never heard of. [Pope.]

[82] Charged with forging a will, to his own advantage.

[83] The bookseller, Edmund Curll, and Lord Hervey.

The good man walk'd innoxious thro' his age.
No courts he saw, no suits would ever try,
Nor dared an oath, nor hazarded a lie.
Unlearn'd, he knew no schoolman's subtle art,
No language but the language of the heart.
By Nature honest, by Experience wise,
Healthy by Temp'rance and by Exercise;
His life, tho' long, to sickness pass'd unknown,
His death was instant and without a groan.
O grant me thus to live, and thus to die!
Who sprung from kings shall know less joy than I.
  O friend! may each domestic bliss be thine!
Be no unpleasing melancholy mine:
Me, let the tender office long engage
To rock the cradle of reposing Age,
With lenient arts extend a Mother's breath,
Make Languor smile, and smooth the bed of Death;
Explore the thought, explain the asking eye,
And keep a while one parent from the sky!
On cares like these if length of days attend,
May Heav'n, to bless those days, preserve my friend!
Preserve him social, cheerful, and serene,
And just as rich as when he serv'd a Queen.[84]
  A. Whether that blessing be denied or giv'n,
Thus far was right; — the rest belongs to Heav'n.

Universal Prayer [85]

DEO OPT. MAX.

FATHER of all! in ev'ry age,
  In ev'ry clime ador'd,
By saint, by savage, and by sage,
  Jehovah, Jove, or Lord!

Thou Great First Cause, least understood,
  Who all my sense confin'd
To know but this, that thou art good,
  And that myself am blind:

Yet gave me, in this dark estate,
  To see the good from ill;
And binding Nature fast in Fate,
  Left free the human Will.

What Conscience dictates to be done,
  Or warns me not to do;
This teach me more than Hell to shun,
  That more than Heav'n pursue.

What blessings thy free bounty gives
  Let me not cast away;
For God is paid when man receives;
  T' enjoy is to obey.

Yet not to earth's contracted span
  Thy goodness let me bound,
Or think thee Lord alone of man,
  When thousand worlds are round.

Let not this weak unknowing hand
  Presume thy bolts to throw,
And deal damnation round the land
  On each I judge thy foe.

If I am right, thy grace impart,
  Still in the right to stay;
If I am wrong, O teach my heart
  To find that better way.

Save me alike from foolish Pride
  Or impious Discontent,
At aught thy wisdom has denied,
  Or aught thy goodness lent.

Teach me to feel another's woe,
  To hide the fault I see:
That mercy I to others show,
  That mercy show to me.

Mean tho' I am, not wholly so,
  Since quicken'd by thy breath;
O lead me, whereso'er I go,
  Thro' this day's life or death!

This day be bread and peace my lot:
  All else beneath the sun
Thou know'st if best bestow'd or not,
  And let thy will be done.

[84] Arbuthnot had been Queen Anne's physician.

[85] Published 22 June 1738. It was written to correct the current impression of Pope's fatalism and naturalism.

To Thee, whose temple is all Space,
  Whose altar earth, sea, skies,
One chorus let all Being raise,
  All Nature's incense rise!

On a Certain Lady at Court [86]

I KNOW the thing that's most uncommon;
(Envy, be silent, and attend!)
I know a reasonable Woman,
Handsome and witty, yet a friend:

Not warp'd by Passion, awed by Rumour,
Not grave thro' Pride, nor gay thro' Folly,
An equal mixture of Good-humour,
And sensible soft Melancholy.

'Has she no faults then (Envy says), sir?'
Yes, she has one, I must aver:
When all the world conspires to praise her,
The woman's deaf and does not hear.

[86] Published in *Works*, 1751. Written for Catharine Howard, one of Queen Caroline's waiting-women, afterward Countess of Suffolk and mistress to George II.

James Thomson

1700–1748

THE SEASONS: A POEM [1]

from *Autumn*

FLED is the blasted verdure of the fields;
And, shrunk into their beds, the flowery race
Their sunny robes resign. Even what remained
Of bolder fruits falls from the naked tree;
And — woods, fields, gardens, orchards, all around —
The desolated prospect thrills the soul.
  He comes! he comes! in every breeze the Power
Of Philosophic Melancholy comes!
His near approach the sudden-starting tear,
The glowing cheek, the mild dejected air,
The softened feature, and the beating heart,
Pierced deep with many a virtuous pang, declare.
O'er all the soul his sacred influence breathes;
Inflames imagination; through the breast
Infuses every tenderness; and far
Beyond dim earth exalts the swelling thought.
Ten thousand thousand fleet ideas, such
As never mingled with the vulgar dream,
Crowd fast into the mind's creative eye.
As fast the correspondent passions rise,
As varied, and as high — devotion raised
To rapture, and divine astonishment;
The love of nature unconfined, and, chief,
Of human race; the large ambitious wish
To make them blest; the sigh for suffering worth
Lost in obscurity; the noble scorn
Of tyrant pride; the fearless great resolve;
The wonder which the dying patriot draws,
Inspiring glory through remotest time;
The awakened throb for virtue and for fame;
The sympathies of love and friendship dear,
With all the social offspring of the heart.
  Oh! bear me then to vast embowering shades,
To twilight groves, and visionary vales,
To weeping grottoes, and prophetic glooms;
Where angel forms athwart the solemn dusk,

[1] *The Seasons*, in composition and particularly in revision, has a considerable history. *Winter* was begun in 1725 and published in March 1726, a thin folio of 405 lines. This was later increased to 1069 lines in successive editions, the last in Thomson's own life-time appearing in 1746. *Summer* was printed in 1727, *Spring* in 1728, and *Autumn* in 1730. The entire poem finally came to 5541 lines. Never before had a poem of such length been primarily devoted to natural description — certainly not in the age of Pope. The chief selection here, from *Winter*, is preceded by the interesting if brief passage from *Autumn* on 'Philosophic Melancholy.'

Tremendous, sweep, or seem to sweep along;
And voices more than human, through the void
Deep-sounding, seize the enthusiastic ear.
 Or is this gloom too much? Then lead, ye Powers
That o'er the garden and the rural seat
Preside, which, shining through the cheerful land
In countless numbers, blest Britannia sees —
Oh! lead me to the wide extended walks,
The fair majestic paradise of Stowe!
Not Persian Cyrus on Ionia's shore
E'er saw such sylvan scenes, such various art
By genius fired, such ardent genius tamed
By cool judicious art, that in the strife
All-beauteous Nature fears to be outdone.

from *Winter*

THE ARGUMENT

The subject proposed. Address to the Earl of Wilmington. First approach of Winter. According to the natural course of the season, various storms described. Rain. Wind. Snow. The driving of the snows: a man perishing among them; *whence reflection on the wants and miseries of human life*. The wolves descending from the Alps and the Apennines. A winter evening described: as spent by philosophers; by the country people; in the city. Frost. A view of Winter within the polar circle. A thaw. The whole concluding with moral reflections on a future state.

SEE, Winter comes to rule the varied year,
Sullen and sad, with all his rising train —
Vapours, and clouds, and storms. Be these my theme;
These, that exalt the soul to solemn thought
And heavenly musing. Welcome, kindred glooms!
Cogenial [2] horrors, hail! With frequent foot,
Pleased have I, in my cheerful morn of life,
When nursed by careless solitude I lived
And sung of Nature with unceasing joy,
Pleased have I wandered through your rough domain;
Trod the pure virgin-snows, myself as pure;
Heard the winds roar, and the big torrent burst;
Or seen the deep-fermenting tempest brewed
In the grim evening-sky. Thus passed the time,
Till through the lucid chambers of the south
Looked out the joyous Spring — looked out and smiled.

 To thee, the patron of this first essay,
The Muse, O Wilmington! [3] renews her song.
Since has she rounded the revolving year:
Skimm'd the gay Spring; on eagle-pinions borne,
Attempted through the Summer-blaze to rise;
Then swept o'er Autumn with the shadowy gale.
And now among the Wintry clouds again,
Rolled in the doubling storm, she tries to soar,
To swell her note with all the rushing winds,
To suit her sounding cadence to the floods;
As is her theme, her numbers wildly great.
Thrice happy, could she fill thy judging ear
With bold description and with manly thought!
Nor art thou skilled in awful schemes alone,
And how to make a mighty people thrive;
But equal goodness, sound integrity,
A firm, unshaken, uncorrupted soul
Amid a sliding age, and burning strong,
Not vainly blazing, for thy country's weal,
A steady spirit, regularly free —

[2] known from birth

[3] *Winter* was originally dedicated to Sir Spencer Compton, Speaker of the House of Commons. He was made Earl of Wilmington in 1730.

These, each exalting each, the statesman light
Into the patriot; these, the public hope
And eye to thee converting, bid the Muse
Record what envy dares not flattery call.

Now, when the cheerless empire of the sky
To Capricorn the Centaur-Archer yields,
And fierce Aquarius stains the inverted year[4] —
Hung o'er the farthest verge of heaven, the sun
Scarce spreads o'er ether the dejected day.
Faint are his gleams, and ineffectual shoot
His struggling rays in horizontal lines
Through the thick air; as clothed in cloudy storm,
Weak, wan, and broad, he skirts the southern sky;
And, soon descending, to the long dark night,
Wide-shading all, the prostrate world resigns.
Nor is the night unwished; while vital heat,
Light, life, and joy the dubious day forsake.
Meantime, in sable cincture, shadows vast,
Deep-tinged and damp, and congregated clouds,
And all the vapoury turbulence of heaven
Involve the face of things. Thus Winter falls,
A heavy gloom oppressive o'er the world,
Through Nature shedding influence malign,
And rouses up the seeds of dark disease.
The soul of man dies in him, loathing life,
And black with more than melancholy views.
The cattle droop; and o'er the furrowed land,
Fresh from the plough, the dun discoloured flocks,
Untended spreading, crop the wholesome root.
Along the woods, along the moorish fens,
Sighs the sad genius of the coming storm;
And up among the loose disjointed cliffs
And fractured mountains wild, the brawling brook
And cave, presageful, send a hollow moan,
Resounding long in listening fancy's ear.
Then comes the father of the tempest forth,
Wrapt in black glooms. First, joyless rains obscure
Drive through the mingling skies with vapour foul,
Dash on the mountain's brow, and shake the woods
That grumbling wave below. The unsightly plain
Lies a brown deluge; as the low-bent clouds
Pour flood on flood, yet unexhausted still
Combine, and, deepening into night, shut up
The day's fair face. The wanderers of heaven,
Each to his home, retire; save those that love
To take their pastime in the troubled air,
Or skimming flutter round the dimply pool.
The cattle from the untasted fields return
And ask, with meaning low, their wonted stalls,
Or ruminate in the contiguous shade.
Thither the household feathery people crowd,
The crested cock, with all his female train,
Pensive and dripping; while the cottage-hind
Hangs o'er the enlivening blaze, and taleful there
Recounts his simple frolic: much he talks,
And much he laughs, nor recks the storm that blows
Without, and rattles on his humble roof.
Wide o'er the brim, with many a torrent swelled,

[4] The sun leaves the sign of Sagittarius (the 'Centaur-Archer') on 21 December and enters that of Capricorn. A month later it enters the sign of Aquarius.

And the mixed ruin of its banks o'erspread,
At last the roused-up river pours along:
Resistless, roaring, dreadful, down it comes,
From the rude mountain and the mossy wild,
Tumbling through rocks abrupt, and sounding far;
Then o'er the sanded valley floating spreads,
Calm, sluggish, silent; till again, constrained
Between two meeting hills, it bursts a way
Where rocks and woods o'erhang the turbid stream;
There, gathering triple force, rapid and deep,
It boils, and wheels, and foams, and thunders through.

Nature! great parent! whose unceasing hand
Rolls round the Seasons of the changeful year,
How mighty, how majestic are thy works!
With what a pleasing dread they swell the soul,
That sees astonished, and astonished sings!
Ye too, ye winds! that now begin to blow
With boisterous sweep, I raise my voice to you.
Where are your stores, ye powerful beings! say,
Where your aerial magazines reserved
To swell the brooding terrors of the storm?
In what far-distant region of the sky,
Hushed in deep silence, sleep you when 'tis calm?

When from the pallid sky the Sun descends,
With many a spot, that o'er his glaring orb
Uncertain wanders, stained; red fiery streaks
Begin to flush around. The reeling clouds
Stagger with dizzy poise, as doubting yet
Which master to obey; while, rising slow,
Blank in the leaden-coloured east, the moon
Wears a wan circle round her blunted horns.
Seen through the turbid, fluctuating air,
The stars obtuse emit a shivering ray;
Or frequent seem to shoot athwart the gloom,
And long behind them trail the whitening blaze.
Snatched in short eddies, plays the withered leaf;
And on the flood the dancing feather floats.
With broadened nostrils to the sky upturned,
The conscious heifer snuffs the stormy gale.
Even, as the matron, at her nightly task,
With pensive labour draws the flaxen thread,
The wasted taper and the crackling flame
Foretell the blast. But chief the plumy race,
The tenants of the sky, its changes speak.
Retiring from the downs, where all day long
They picked their scanty fare, a blackening train
Of clamorous rooks thick-urge their weary flight,
And seek the closing shelter of the grove.
Assiduous, in his bower, the wailing owl
Plies his sad song. The cormorant on high
Wheels from the deep, and screams along the land.
Loud shrieks the soaring hern; and with wild wing
The circling sea-fowl cleave the flaky clouds.
Ocean, unequal pressed, with broken tide
And blind commotion heaves; while from the shore,
Eat into caverns by the restless wave,
And forest-rustling mountain comes a voice
That, solemn-sounding, bids the world prepare.
Then issues forth the storm with sudden burst,

And hurls the whole precipitated air
Down in a torrent. On the passive main
Descends the ethereal force, and with strong gust
Turns from its bottom the discoloured deep.
Through the black night that sits immense around,
Lashed into foam, the fierce-conflicting brine
Seems o'er a thousand raging waves to burn.
Meantime the mountain-billows, to the clouds
In dreadful tumult swelled, surge above surge,
Burst into chaos with tremendous roar,
And anchored navies from their stations drive
Wild as the winds, across the howling waste
Of mighty waters: now the inflated wave
Straining they scale, and now impetuous shoot
Into the secret chambers of the deep,
The wintry Baltic thundering o'er their head.
Emerging thence again, before the breath
Of full-exerted heaven they wing their course,
And dart on distant coasts — if some sharp rock
Or shoal insidious break not their career,
And in loose fragments fling them floating round.

Nor less at land the loosened tempest reigns.
The mountain thunders, and its sturdy sons
Stoop to the bottom of the rocks they shade.
Lone on the midnight steep, and all aghast,
The dark wayfaring stranger breathless toils,
And, often falling, climbs against the blast.
Low waves the rooted forest, vexed, and sheds
What of its tarnished honours yet remain —
Dashed down and scattered, by the tearing wind's
Assiduous fury, its gigantic limbs.
Thus struggling through the dissipated grove,
The whirling tempest raves along the plain;
And, on the cottage thatched or lordly roof
Keen-fastening, shakes them to the solid base.
Sleep frighted flies; and round the rocking dome,
For entrance eager, howls the savage blast.
Then too, they say, through all the burdened air
Long groans are heard, shrill sounds, and distant sighs,
That, uttered by the demon of the night,
Warn the devoted wretch of woe and death.

Huge uproar lords it wide. The clouds, commixed
With stars swift-gliding, sweep along the sky.
All Nature reels: till Nature's King, who oft
Amid tempestuous darkness dwells alone,
And on the wings of the careering wind
Walks dreadfully serene, commands a calm;
Then straight air, sea, and earth are hushed at once.

As yet 'tis midnight deep. The weary clouds,
Slow-meeting, mingle into solid gloom.
Now, while the drowsy world lies lost in sleep,
Let me associate with the serious Night,
And Contemplation, her sedate compeer;
Let me shake off the intrusive cares of day,
And lay the meddling senses all aside.

Where now, ye lying vanities of life!
Ye ever-tempting, ever-cheating train!
Where are you now? and what is your amount?

Vexation, disappointment, and remorse.
Sad, sickening thought! and yet deluded man,
A scene of crude disjointed visions past,
And broken slumbers, rises still resolved,
With new-flushed hopes, to run the giddy round.

Father of light and life! thou Good Supreme!
O teach me what is good! teach me Thyself!
Save me from folly, vanity, and vice,
From every low pursuit; and feed my soul
With knowledge, conscious peace, and virtue pure —
Sacred, substantial, never-fading bliss!

The keener tempests come: and, fuming dun
From all the livid east or piercing north,
Thick clouds ascend, in whose capacious womb
A vapoury deluge lies, to snow congealed.
Heavy they roll their fleecy world along,
And the sky saddens with the gathered storm.
Through the hushed air the whitening shower descends,
At first thin-wavering; till at last the flakes
Fall broad and wide and fast, dimming the day
With a continual flow. The cherished fields
Put on their winter-robe of purest white.
'Tis brightness all; save where the new snow melts
Along the mazy current. Low the woods
Bow their hoar head; and, ere the languid sun
Faint from the west emits his evening ray,
Earth's universal face, deep-hid and chill,
Is one wild dazzling waste, that buries wide
The works of man. Drooping, the labourer-ox
Stands covered o'er with snow, and then demands
The fruit of all his toil. The fowls of heaven,
Tamed by the cruel season, crowd around
The winnowing store, and claim the little boon
Which Providence assigns them. One alone,
The redbreast, sacred to the household gods,
Wisely regardful of the embroiling sky,
In joyless fields and thorny thickets leaves
His shivering mates, and pays to trusted man
His annual visit. Half afraid, he first
Against the window beats; then brisk alights
On the warm hearth; then, hopping o'er the floor,
Eyes all the smiling family askance,
And pecks, and starts, and wonders where he is —
Till, more familiar grown, the table-crumbs
Attract his slender feet. The foodless wilds
Pour forth their brown inhabitants. The hare,
Though timorous of heart, and hard beset
By death in various forms, dark snares, and dogs,
And more unpitying men, the garden seeks,
Urged on by fearless want. The bleating kind
Eye the bleak heaven, and next the glistening earth,
With looks of dumb despair; then, sad-dispersed,
Dig for the withered herb through heaps of snow.

Now, shepherds, to your helpless charge be kind:
Baffle the raging year, and fill their pens
With food at will; lodge them below the storm,
And watch them strict: for, from the bellowing east,
In this dire season, oft the whirlwind's wing
Sweeps up the burden of whole wintry plains

In one wide waft, and o'er the hapless flocks,
Hid in the hollow of two neighbouring hills,
The billowy tempest whelms; till, upward urged,
The valley to a shining mountain swells,
Tipt with a wreath high-curling in the sky.
As thus the snows arise, and, foul and fierce,
All Winter drives along the darkened air,
In his own loose-revolving fields the swain
Disastered stands; sees other hills ascend,
Of unknown joyless brow; and other scenes,
Of horrid prospect, shag the trackless plain;
Nor finds the river nor the forest, hid
Beneath the formless wild; but wanders on
From hill to dale, still more and more astray —
Impatient flouncing through the drifted heaps,
Stung with the thoughts of home: the thoughts of home
Rush on his nerves and call their vigour forth
In many a vain attempt. How sinks his soul!
What black despair, what horror fills his heart,
When, for the dusky spot which fancy feigned
His tufted cottage rising through the snow,
He meets the roughness of the middle waste,
Far from the track and blest abode of man;
While round him night resistless closes fast,
And every tempest, howling o'er his head,
Renders the savage wilderness more wild.
Then throng the busy shapes into his mind
Of covered pits, unfathomably deep,
A dire descent! beyond the power of frost;
Of faithless bogs; of precipices huge,
Smoothed up with snow; and (what is land unknown,
What water) of the still unfrozen spring,
In the loose marsh or solitary lake,
Where the fresh fountain from the bottom boils.
These check his fearful steps; and down he sinks
Beneath the shelter of the shapeless drift,
Thinking o'er all the bitterness of death,
Mixed with the tender anguish nature shoots
Through the wrung bosom of the dying man —
His wife, his children, and his friends unseen.
In vain for him the officious wife prepares
The fire fair-blazing and the vestment warm;
In vain his little children, peeping out
Into the mingling storm, demand their sire
With tears of artless innocence. Alas!
Nor wife nor children more shall he behold,
Nor friends, nor sacred home. On every nerve
The deadly Winter seizes, shuts up sense,
And, o'er his inmost vitals creeping cold,
Lays him along the snows a stiffened corse,
Stretched out, and bleaching in the northern blast.

. . .

To thy loved haunt return,[5] my happy muse:
For now, behold! the joyous Winter days,
Frosty, succeed; and through the blue serene,
For sight too fine, the ethereal nitre flies,
Killing infectious damps, and the spent air
Storing afresh with elemental life.
Close crowds the shining atmosphere; and binds
Our strengthened bodies in its cold embrace,
Constringent; feeds, and animates our blood;

[5] After a long description of the philosopher regaling his winter evenings in 'high converse with the mighty dead' — all good classical subjects — and of the same winter evening as passed by country people and those in town.

Refines our spirits, through the new-strung nerves
In swifter sallies darting to the brain —
Where sits the soul, intense, collected, cool,
Bright as the skies, and as the season keen.
All nature feels the renovating force
Of Winter — only to the thoughtless eye
In ruin seen. The frost-concocted glebe
Draws in abundant vegetable soul,
And gathers vigour for the coming year;
A stronger glow sits on the lively cheek
Of ruddy fire; and luculent along
The purer rivers flow: their sullen deeps,
Transparent, open to the shepherd's gaze,
And murmur hoarser at the fixing frost.

What art thou, frost? and whence are thy keen stores
Derived, thou secret all-invading power,
Whom even the illusive fluid cannot fly?
Is not thy potent energy, unseen,
Myriads of little salts, or hooked, or shaped
Like double wedges, and diffused immense
Through water, earth, and ether? Hence at eve,
Steamed eager from the red horizon round,
With the fierce rage of Winter deep suffused,
An icy gale, oft shifting, o'er the pool
Breathes a blue film, and in its mid-career
Arrests the bickering stream. The loosened ice,
Let down the flood and half dissolved by day,
Rustles no more; but to the sedgy bank
Fast grows, or gathers round the pointed stone,
A crystal pavement, by the breath of heaven
Cemented firm; till, seized from shore to shore,
The whole imprisoned river growls below.
Loud rings the frozen earth, and hard reflects
A double noise; while, at his evening watch,
The village-dog deters the nightly thief;
The heifer lows; the distant waterfall
Swells in the breeze; and with the hasty tread
Of traveller the hollow-sounding plain
Shakes from afar. The full ethereal round,
Infinite worlds disclosing to the view,
Shines out intensely keen, and, all one cope
Of starry glitter, glows from pole to pole.
From pole to pole the rigid influence falls
Through the still night incessant, heavy, strong,
And seizes nature fast. It freezes on.
Till morn, late-rising o'er the drooping world,
Lifts her pale eye unjoyous. Then appears
The various labour of the silent night —
Prone from the dripping eave, and dumb cascade,
Whose idle torrents only seem to roar,
The pendent icicle; the frost-work fair,
Where transient hues and fancied figures rise;
Wide-spouted o'er the hill the frozen brook,
A livid tract, cold-gleaming on the morn;
The forest bent beneath the plumy wave;
And by the frost refined the whiter snow
Incrusted hard, and sounding to the tread
Of early shepherd, as he pensive seeks
His pining flock, or from the mountain top,
Pleased with the slippery surface, swift descends.

On blithesome frolics bent, the youthful swains,
While every work of man is laid at rest,
Fond o'er the river crowd, in various sport
And revelry dissolved; where, mixing glad,
Happiest of all the train! the raptured boy
Lashes the whirling top. Or, where the Rhine
Branched out in many a long canal extends,
From every province swarming, void of care,
Batavia rushes forth; and, as they sweep
On sounding skates a thousand different ways
In circling poise swift as the winds along,
The then gay land is maddened all to joy.
Nor less the northern courts, wide o'er the snow,
Pour a new pomp. Eager, on rapid sleds,

Their vigorous youth in bold contention wheel
The long-resounding course. Meantime, to raise
The manly strife, with highly blooming charms,
Flushed by the season, Scandinavia's dames
Or Russia's buxom daughters glow around.
Pure, quick, and sportful is the wholesome day;
But soon elapsed. The horizontal sun
Broad o'er the south hangs at his utmost noon;
And ineffectual strikes the gelid cliff.
His azure gloss the mountain still maintains,
Nor feels the feeble touch. Perhaps the vale
Relents awhile to the reflected ray;
Or from the forest falls the clustered snow,
Myriads of gems, that in the waving gleam
Gay-twinkle as they scatter. Thick around
Thunders the sport of those who with the gun,
And dog impatient bounding at the shot,
Worse than the season desolate the fields,
And, adding to the ruins of the year,
Distress the footed or the feathered game.
But what is this? Our infant Winter sinks
Divested of his grandeur should our eye
Astonished shoot into the frigid zone,
Where for relentless months continual night
Holds o'er the glittering waste her starry reign.
There, through the prison of unbounded wilds,
Barred by the hand of nature from escape,
Wide roams the Russian exile. Naught around
Strikes his sad eye but deserts lost in snow,
And heavy-loaded groves, and solid floods
That stretch athwart the solitary vast
Their icy horrors to the frozen main,
And cheerless towns far distant — never blessed,
Save when its annual course the caravan
Bends to the golden coast of rich Cathay,[6]
With news of human-kind. Yet there life glows;
Yet, cherished there, beneath the shining waste
The furry nations harbour — tipt with jet,
Fair ermines spotless as the snows they press;
Sables of glossy black; and, dark-embrowned,
Or beauteous freakt with many a mingled hue,
Thousands besides, the costly pride of courts.
There, warm together pressed, the trooping deer
Sleep on the new-fallen snows; and, scarce his head
Raised o'er the heapy wreath, the branching elk
Lies slumbering sullen in the white abyss.
The ruthless hunter wants nor dogs nor toils,
Nor with the dread of sounding bows he drives
The fearful flying race — with ponderous clubs,
As weak against the mountain-heaps they push
Their beating breast in vain, and piteous bray,
He lays them quivering on the ensanguined snows,
And with loud shouts rejoicing bears them home.
There, through the piny forest half-absorpt,
Rough tenant of these shades, the shapeless bear,
With dangling ice all horrid, stalks forlorn;
Slow-paced, and sourer as the storms increase,
He makes his bed beneath the inclement drift,

---

[6] The old name of China. [Thomson.]

And, with stern patience, scorning weak complaint,
Hardens his heart against assailing want.
Wide o'er the spacious regions of the north
That see Boötes urge his tardy wain,
A boisterous race, by frosty Caurus[7] pierced,
Who little pleasure know and fear no pain,
Prolific swarm. They once relumed the flame
Of lost mankind in polished slavery sunk;
Drove martial horde on horde, with dreadful sweep
Resistless rushing o'er the enfeebled south,
And gave the vanquished world another form.

. . .

Muttering, the winds at eve with blunted point
Blow hollow-blustering from the south. Subdued,
The frost resolves into a trickling thaw.
Spotted the mountains shine: loose sleet descends,
And floods the country round. The rivers swell,
Of bonds impatient. Sudden from the hills,
O'er rocks and woods, in broad brown cataracts,
A thousand snow-fed torrents shoot at once;
And, where they rush, the wide-resounding plain
Is left one slimy waste. Those sullen seas,
That wash'd the ungenial pole, will rest no more
Beneath the shackles of the mighty north,
But, rousing all their waves, resistless heave.
And, hark! the lengthening roar continuous runs
Athwart the rifted deep: at once it bursts,
And piles a thousand mountains to the clouds.
Ill fares the bark, with trembling wretches charged,
That, tossed amid the floating fragments, moors
Beneath the shelter of an icy isle,
While night o'erwhelms the sea, and horror looks
More horrible. Can human force endure
The assembled mischiefs that besiege them round? —
Heart-gnawing hunger, fainting weariness,
The roar of winds and waves, the crush of ice,
Now ceasing, now renewed with louder rage,
And in dire echoes bellowing round the main.
More to embroil the deep, Leviathan
And his unwieldy train in dreadful sport
Tempest the loosened brine; while through the gloom
Far from the bleak inhospitable shore,
Loading the winds, is heard the hungry howl
Of famished monsters, there awaiting wrecks.
Yet Providence, that ever-waking Eye,
Looks down with pity on the feeble toil
Of mortals lost to hope, and lights them safe
Through all this dreary labyrinth of fate.

'Tis done! Dread Winter spreads his latest glooms,
And reigns tremendous o'er the conquered year.
How dead the vegetable kingdom lies!
How dumb the tuneful! Horror wide extends
His desolate domain. Behold, fond man!
See here thy pictured life; pass some few years,
Thy flowering Spring, thy Summer's ardent strength,
Thy sober Autumn fading into age,
And pale concluding Winter comes at last
And shuts the scene. Ah! whither now are fled

[7] The north-west wind. [Thomson.]

Those dreams of greatness? those unsolid hopes
Of happiness? those longings after fame?
Those restless cares? those busy bustling days?
Those gay-spent festive nights? those veering thoughts,
Lost between good and ill, that shared thy life?
All now are vanished! Virtue sole survives —
Immortal, never-failing friend of man,
His guide to happiness on high. And see!
'Tis come, the glorious morn! the second birth
Of heaven and earth! awakening nature hears
The new-creating word, and starts to life
In every heightened form, from pain and death
For ever free. The great eternal scheme,
Involving all, and in a perfect whole
Uniting, as the prospect wider spreads,
To reason's eye refined clears up apace.
Ye vainly wise! ye blind presumptuous! now,
Confounded in the dust, adore that Power
And Wisdom — oft arraigned: see now the cause
Why unassuming worth in secret lived
And died neglected: why the good man's share
In life was gall and bitterness of soul:
Why the lone widow and her orphans pined
In starving solitude; while luxury
In palaces lay straining her low thought
To form unreal wants: why heaven-born truth
And moderation fair wore the red marks
Of superstition's scourge; why licensed pain,
That cruel spoiler, that embosomed foe,
Embittered all our bliss. Ye good distressed!
Ye noble few! who here unbending stand
Beneath life's pressure, yet bear up a while,
And what your bounded view, which only saw
A little part, deemed evil is no more:
The storms of wintry time will quickly pass,
And one unbounded Spring encircle all.

Rule, Britannia! [8]

When Britain first, at Heaven's command,
Arose from out the azure main,
This was the charter of the land,
And guardian angels sung this strain —
'Rule, Britannia, rule the waves;
Britons never will be slaves.'

The nations, not so blest as thee,
Must in their turns to tyrants fall;
While thou shalt flourish great and free,
The dread and envy of them all.
'Rule,' &c.

Still more majestic shalt thou rise,
More dreadful from each foreign stroke;
As the loud blast that tears the skies
Serves but to root thy native oak.
'Rule,' &c.

Thee haughty tyrants ne'er shall tame;
All their attempts to bend thee down
Will but arouse thy generous flame,
But work their woe and thy renown.
'Rule,' &c.

To thee belongs the rural reign;
Thy cities shall with commerce shine;
All thine shall be the subject main,
And every shore it circles thine.
'Rule,' &c.

The Muses, still with freedom found,
Shall to thy happy coast repair:
Blest isle! with matchless beauty crowned,
And manly hearts to guard the fair.
'Rule, Britannia, rule the waves;
Britons never will be slaves.'

---

[8] Published in 1740 in *Alfred: A Masque*, Act ii, scene 5 — in which David Mallet collaborated with Thomson.

Thomas Gray

1716–1771

Ode on a Distant Prospect of Eton College [1]

Ἄνθρωπος ἱκανὴ πρόφασις εἰς τὸ δυστυχεῖν.[2]
— MENANDER.

YE distant spires, ye antique towers,
That crown the watry glade,
Where grateful Science still adores
Her Henry's [3] holy Shade;
And ye, that from the stately brow
Of Windsor's [4] heights th' expanse below
Of grove, of lawn, of mead survey,
Whose turf, whose shade, whose flowers
among
Wanders the hoary Thames along
His silver-winding way.

Ah happy hills, ah pleasing shade,
Ah fields belov'd in vain,
Where once my careless childhood stray'd,
A stranger yet to pain!
I feel the gales, that from ye blow,
A momentary bliss bestow,
As waving fresh their gladsome wing,
My weary soul [5] they seem to sooth,
And, redolent of joy and youth,
To breathe a second spring.

Say, Father Thames, for thou hast seen
Full many a sprightly race
Disporting on thy margent green
The paths of pleasure trace,
Who foremost now delight to cleave
With pliant arm thy glassy wave?
The captive linnet which enthrall?
What idle progeny succeed
To chase the rolling circle's speed,
Or urge the flying ball?

While some on earnest business bent
Their murm'ring labours ply
'Gainst graver hours, that bring constraint
To sweeten liberty:
Some bold adventurers disdain
The limits of their little reign,
And unknown regions dare descry:
Still as they run they look behind,
They hear a voice in every wind,
And snatch a fearful joy.

Gay hope is theirs by fancy fed,
Less pleasing when possest;
The tear forgot as soon as shed,
The sunshine of the breast:
Theirs buxom health of rosy hue,
Wild wit, invention ever-new,
And lively cheer of vigour born;
The thoughtless day, the easy night,
The spirits pure, the slumbers light,
That fly th' approach of morn.

Alas, regardless of their doom,
The little victims play!
No sense have they of ills to come,
Nor care beyond to-day:
Yet see how all around 'em wait
The Ministers of human fate,
And black Misfortune's baleful train!
Ah, shew them where in ambush stand
To seize their prey the murth'rous band!
Ah, tell them, they are men!

These shall the fury Passions tear,
The vultures of the mind,
Disdainful Anger, pallid Fear,
And Shame that skulks behind;
Or pining Love shall waste their youth,
Or Jealousy with rankling tooth,
That inly gnaws the secret heart,
And Envy wan, and faded Care,
Grim-visag'd comfortless Despair,
And Sorrow's piercing dart.

Ambition this shall tempt to rise,
Then whirl the wretch from high,
To bitter Scorn a sacrifice,
And grinning Infamy.

[1] Written in 1742; first published in folio pamphlet by Dodsley in 1747.
[2] A human being: cause enough for misery.
[3] King Henry the Sixth, Founder of the College. [Gray.]
[4] Windsor Castle, a royal palace, on the opposite side of the Thames from Eton.
[5] Gray's friend, Richard West, had recently died. Two other Eton friends, Thomas Ashton and Horace Walpole, were for the time being estranged from him.

The stings of Falshood those shall try,
And hard Unkindness' alter'd eye,
That mocks the tear it forc'd to flow;
And keen Remorse with blood defil'd,
And moody Madness laughing wild
Amid severest woe.

Lo, in the vale of years beneath
A grisly troop are seen,
The painful family of Death,
More hideous than their Queen:
This racks the joints, this fires the veins,
That every labouring sinew strains,
Those in the deeper vitals rage:
Lo, Poverty, to fill the band,
That numbs the soul with icy hand,
And slow-consuming Age.

To each his suff'rings: all are men,
Condemn'd alike to groan;
The tender for another's pain,
Th' unfeeling for his own.
Yet ah! why should they know their fate?
Since sorrow never comes too late,
And happiness too swiftly flies.
Thought would destroy their paradise.
No more; where ignorance is bliss,
'Tis folly to be wise.

Ode on the Death of a Favourite Cat,

Drowned in a Tub of Gold Fishes[6]

'Twas on a lofty vase's side,
Where China's gayest art had dy'd
The azure flowers, that blow;
Demurest of the tabby kind,
The pensive Selima reclin'd,
Gazed on the lake below.

Her conscious tail her joy declar'd;
The fair round face, the snowy beard,
The velvet of her paws,
Her coat, that with the tortoise vies,
Her ears of jet, and emerald eyes,
She saw; and purr'd applause.

Still had she gaz'd; but 'midst the tide
Two angel forms were seen to glide,
The Genii of the stream:
Their scaly armour's Tyrian hue
Thro' richest purple to the view
Betray'd a golden gleam.

The hapless Nymph with wonder saw:
A whisker first and then a claw,
With many an ardent wish,
She stretch'd in vain to reach the prize.
What female heart can gold despise?
What Cat's averse to fish?

Presumptuous Maid! with looks intent
Again she stretch'd, again she bent,
Nor knew the gulf between.
(Malignant Fate sat by, and smil'd)
The slipp'ry verge her feet beguil'd,
She tumbled headlong in.

Eight times emerging from the flood
She mew'd to ev'ry watry God,
Some speedy aid to send.
No Dolphin came, no Nereid stirr'd
Nor cruel *Tom,* nor *Susan* heard.
A Fav'rite has no friend!

From hence, ye Beauties, undeceiv'd,
Know, one false step is ne'er retriev'd,
And be with caution bold.
Not all that tempts your wand'ring eyes
And heedless hearts, is lawful prize;
Nor all, that glisters, gold.

Elegy Written in a Country Church-Yard[7]

The Curfew tolls the knell of parting day,
The lowing herd wind slowly o'er the lea,
The plowman homeward plods his weary way,
And leaves the world to darkness and to me.

[6] The verses were sent to Walpole, the owner of the cat, in a letter dated 1 March 1747. They were published in Dodsley's *Collection,* 1748 (first edition).

[7] Begun in August 1742, but the main portion was written between 1746 and 1750. It was finished 12 June 1750, one hundred years before Tennyson's *In Memoriam* appeared. When the editors of the *Magazine of Magazines* asked permission to print it, Gray requested Horace Walpole to publish the *Elegy* anonymously. It was issued on 16 February 1751.

Now fades the glimmering landscape on the sight,
And all the air a solemn stillness holds,
Save where the beetle wheels his droning flight,
And drowsy tinklings lull the distant folds;

Save that from yonder ivy-mantled tow'r [8]
The moping owl does to the moon complain
Of such, as wand'ring near her secret bow'r,
Molest her ancient solitary reign.

Beneath those rugged elms, that yew-tree's shade,
Where heaves the turf in many a mould'ring heap,
Each in his narrow cell for ever laid,
The rude Forefathers of the hamlet sleep.

The breezy call of incense-breathing Morn,
The swallow twitt'ring from the straw-built shed,
The cock's shrill clarion, or the echoing horn,
No more shall rouse them from their lowly bed.

For them no more the blazing hearth shall burn,
Or busy housewife ply her evening care:
No children run to lisp their sire's return,
Or climb his knees the envied kiss to share.

Oft did the harvest to their sickle yield,
Their furrow oft the stubborn glebe has broke;
How jocund did they drive their team afield!
How bow'd the woods beneath their sturdy stroke!

Let not Ambition mock their useful toil,
Their homely joys, and destiny obscure;
Nor Grandeur hear with a disdainful smile,
The short and simple annals of the poor.

The boast of heraldry, the pomp of pow'r,
And all that beauty, all that wealth e'er gave,
Awaits alike th' inevitable hour.
The paths of glory lead but to the grave.

Nor you, ye Proud, impute to These the fault,
If Mem'ry o'er their Tomb no Trophies raise,
Where thro' the long-drawn isle and fretted vault
The pealing anthem swells the note of praise.

Can storied urn or animated bust
Back to its mansion call the fleeting breath?
Can Honour's voice provoke the silent dust,
Or Flatt'ry sooth the dull cold ear of Death?

Perhaps in this neglected spot is laid
Some heart once pregnant with celestial fire;
Hands, that the rod of empire might have sway'd,
Or wak'd to ecstasy the living lyre.

But Knowledge to their eyes her ample page
Rich with the spoils of time did ne'er unroll;
Chill Penury repress'd their noble rage,
And froze the genial current of the soul.

Full many a gem of purest ray serene,
The dark unfathom'd caves of ocean bear:
Full many a flower is born to blush unseen,
And waste its sweetness on the desert air.

Some village-Hampden,[9] that with dauntless breast
The little Tyrant of his fields withstood;

[8] The scene is probably that of the churchyard at Stoke Poges. Gray himself is buried there beside his mother.

[9] John Hampden, leader of the opposition to Charles I's attempt to levy ship-money.

Some mute inglorious Milton here may rest,
Some Cromwell guiltless of his country's blood.

Th' applause of list'ning senates to command,
The threats of pain and ruin to despise,
To scatter plenty o'er a smiling land,
And read their hist'ry in a nation's eyes,

Their lot forbad: nor circumscrib'd alone
Their growing virtues, but their crimes confin'd;
Forbad to wade through slaughter to a throne,
And shut the gates of mercy on mankind,

The struggling pangs of conscious truth to hide,
To quench the blushes of ingenuous shame,
Or heap the shrine of Luxury and Pride
With incense kindled at the Muse's flame.

Far from the madding crowd's ignoble strife,
Their sober wishes never learn'd to stray;
Along the cool sequester'd vale of life
They kept the noiseless tenor of their way.

Yet ev'n these bones from insult to protect
Some frail memorial still erected nigh,
With uncouth rhimes and shapeless sculpture deck'd,
Implores the passing tribute of a sigh.

Their name, their years, spelt by th' unletter'd muse,
The place of fame and elegy supply:
And many a holy text around she strews,
That teach the rustic moralist to die.

For who to dumb Forgetfulness a prey,
This pleasing anxious being e'er resign'd,
Left the warm precincts of the cheerful day,
Nor cast one longing ling'ring look behind?

On some fond breast the parting soul relies,
Some pious drops the closing eye requires;
Ev'n from the tomb the voice of Nature cries,
Ev'n in our Ashes live their wonted Fires.

For thee, who mindful of th' unhonour'd Dead
Dost in these lines their artless tale relate;
If chance, by lonely contemplation led,
Some kindred Spirit shall inquire thy fate,

Haply some hoary-headed Swain may say,
'Oft have we seen him at the peep of dawn
'Brushing with hasty steps the dews away
'To meet the sun upon the upland lawn.

'There at the foot of yonder nodding beech
'That wreathes its old fantastic roots so high,
'His listless length at noontide would he stretch,
'And pore upon the brook that babbles by.

'Hard by yon wood, now smiling as in scorn,
'Mutt'ring his wayward fancies he would rove,
'Now drooping, woeful wan, like one forlorn,
'Or craz'd with care, or cross'd in hopeless love.

'One morn I miss'd him on the custom'd hill,
'Along the heath and near his fav'rite tree;
'Another came; nor yet beside the rill,
'Nor up the lawn, nor at the wood was he;

'The next with dirges due in sad array
'Slow thro' the church-way path we saw him born.
'Approach and read (for thou can'st read) the lay,
'Grav'd on the stone beneath yon aged thorn.'

THE EPITAPH

Here rests his head upon the lap of Earth
A Youth to Fortune and to Fame unknown.
Fair Science frown'd not on his humble birth,
And Melancholy mark'd him for her own.

Large was his bounty, and his soul sincere,
Heav'n did a recompense as largely send:
He gave to Mis'ry all he had, a tear,
He gain'd from Heav'n ('twas all he wish'd) a friend.

No farther seek his merits to disclose,
Or draw his frailties from their dread abode,
(There they alike in trembling hope repose,)
The bosom of his Father and his God.

The Progress of Poesy

A PINDARIC ODE [10]

Φωνᾶντα συνετοῖσιν· ἐς
Δὲ τὸ πᾶν ἑρμηνέων χατίζει.[11]

—Pindar, Olymp. II.

I. 1

Awake, Æolian lyre, awake,
And give to rapture all thy trembling strings.
From Helicon's harmonious springs
A thousand rills their mazy progress take:
The laughing flowers, that round them blow,
Drink life and fragrance as they flow.
Now the rich stream of music winds along
Deep, majestic, smooth, and strong,
Thro' verdant vales, and Ceres' golden reign:
Now rolling down the steep amain,
Headlong, impetuous, see it pour:
The rocks, and nodding groves rebellow to the roar.

I. 2

[12] Oh! Sovereign of the willing soul,
Parent of sweet and solemn-breathing airs,
Enchanting shell! [13] the sullen Cares,
And frantic Passions hear thy soft controul.
On Thracia's hills the Lord of War,
Has curb'd the fury of his car,
And drop'd his thirsty lance at thy command.
Perching on the scept'red hand
Of Jove, thy magic lulls the feather'd king [14]
With ruffled plumes, and flagging wing:
Quench'd in dark clouds of slumber lie
The terror of his beak, and light'nings of his eye.

I. 3

[15] Thee the voice, the dance, obey,
Temper'd to thy warbled lay.
O'er Idalia's [16] velvet-green
The rosy-crowned Loves are seen
On Cytherea's day
With antic Sports, and blue-eyed Pleasures,
Frisking light in frolic measures;
Now pursuing, now retreating,
Now in circling troops they meet:

---

[10] Written in 1754; first published, together with 'The Bard' in 1757, in *Odes*, the first book to be printed by Horace Walpole's Press at Strawberry Hill.

[11] A voice full of meaning to the wise, but one requiring interpreters for the general sort; or, as Gray himself suggested in a letter, 'Vocal to the intelligent alone.'

[12] Power of harmony to calm the turbulent sallies of the soul. The thoughts are borrowed from the first Pythian of Pindar. [Gray.]

[13] The lyre was supposedly fashioned by Hermes from a tortoise shell.

[14] the eagle

[15] Power of harmony to produce all the graces of motion in the body. [Gray.]

[16] A town in Cyprus where there is a temple to Venus or Cytherea.

To brisk notes in cadence beating
Glance their many-twinkling feet.
Slow melting strains their Queen's approach declare:
Where'er she turns the Graces homage pay.
With arms sublime,[17] that float upon the air,
In gliding state she wins her easy way:
O'er her warm cheek, and rising bosom, move
The bloom of young Desire, and purple light of Love.

II. 1

Man's feeble race what Ills await,
Labour, and Penury, the racks of Pain,
Disease, and Sorrow's weeping train,
And Death, sad refuge from the storms of Fate!
The fond complaint, my Song, disprove,
And justify the laws of Jove.
Say, has he giv'n in vain the heav'nly Muse?
Night, and all her sickly dews,
Her Spectres wan, and Birds of boding cry,
He gives to range the dreary sky:
Till down the eastern cliffs afar
Hyperion's march they spy, and glitt'ring shafts of war.

II. 2

[18] In climes beyond the solar road,
Where shaggy forms o'er ice-built mountains roam,
The Muse has broke the twilight-gloom
To cheer the shiv'ring Native's dull abode.
And oft, beneath the od'rous shade
Of Chili's boundless forests laid,
She deigns to hear the savage Youth repeat
In loose numbers wildly sweet
Their feather-cinctured Chiefs, and dusky Loves.
Her track, where'er the Goddess roves,
Glory pursue, and generous Shame,
Th' unconquerable Mind, and Freedom's holy flame.

II. 3

[19] Woods, that wave o'er Delphi's steep,
Isles, that crown th' Egæan deep,
Fields, that cool Ilissus laves,
Or where Mæander's amber waves
In lingering Lab'rinths creep,
How do your tuneful Echos languish,
Mute, but to the voice of Anguish?
Where each old poetic Mountain
Inspiration breath'd around:
Ev'ry shade and hallow'd Fountain
Murmur'd deep a solemn sound:
Till the sad Nine in Greece's evil hour
Left their Parnassus for the Latian plains.
Alike they scorn the pomp of tyrant-Power,
And coward Vice, that revels in her chains.
When Latium had her lofty spirit lost,
They sought, oh Albion! next thy sea-encircled coast.

III. 1

Far from the sun and summer-gale,
In thy green lap was Nature's Darling [20] laid,
What time, where lucid Avon stray'd,
To Him the mighty Mother did unveil
Her aweful face: The dauntless Child
Stretch'd forth his little arms, and smiled.
This pencil take (she said) whose colours clear
Richly paint the vernal year:
Thine too these golden keys, immortal Boy!

---

[17] upraised

[18] Extensive influence of poetic Genius over the remotest and most uncivilized nations: its connection with liberty, and the virtues that naturally attend on it. [Gray.]

[19] Progress of Poetry from Greece to Italy, and from Italy to England. Chaucer was not unacquainted with the writings of Dante or of Petrarch. The Earl of Surrey and Sir Tho. Wyatt had travelled in Italy, and formed their taste there; Spenser imitated the Italian writers; Milton improved on them: but this School expired soon after the Restoration, and a new one arose on the French model, which has subsisted ever since. [Gray.]

[20] Shakespear. [Gray.]

This can unlock the gates of Joy;
Of Horrour that, and thrilling Fears,
Or ope the sacred source of sympathetic
Tears.

III. 2

Nor second He,[21] that rode sublime
Upon the seraph-wings of Ecstasy,
The secrets of th' Abyss to spy.
He pass'd the flaming bounds of Place and
Time:
The living Throne, the saphire-blaze,
Where Angels tremble, while they gaze,
He saw; but blasted with excess of light,
Closed his eyes in endless night.
Behold, where Dryden's less presumptuous
car,
Wide o'er the fields of Glory bear
Two Coursers of ethereal race,[22]
With necks in thunder cloath'd, and long-
resounding pace.

III. 3

Hark, his hands the lyre explore!
Bright-eyed Fancy hovering o'er
Scatters from her pictured urn
Thoughts that breath, and words that
burn.
But ah! 'tis heard no more ——
Oh! Lyre divine, what daring Spirit
Wakes thee now? Tho' he inherit
Nor the pride nor ample pinion,
That the Theban Eagle [23] bear
Sailing with supreme dominion
Thro' the azure deep of air:
Yet oft before his infant eyes would run
Such forms, as glitter in the Muse's ray
With orient hues, unborrow'd of the
Sun:
Yet shall he mount, and keep his distant
way
Beyond the limits of a vulgar fate,
Beneath the Good how far — but far above
the Great.

---

[21] Milton. [Gray.]
[22] Meant to express the stately march and sounding energy of Dryden's rhimes. [Gray.]
[23] Pindar compares himself to that bird, and his enemies to ravens that croak and clamour in vain below, while it pursues its flight, regardless of their noise. [Gray.]

The Bard

A Pindaric Ode [24]

ADVERTISEMENT

The following Ode is founded on a Tradition current in Wales, that Edward the First, when he completed the conquest of that country, ordered all the Bards that fell into his hands to be put to death.

I. 1

'Ruin seize thee, ruthless King!
'Confusion on thy banners wait,
'Tho' fann'd by Conquest's crimson wing
'They mock the air with idle state.
'Helm, nor Hauberk's twisted mail,
'Nor even thy virtues, Tyrant, shall avail
'To save thy secret soul from nightly fears,
'From Cambria's [25] curse, from Cambria's
tears!'
Such were the sounds, that o'er the crested
pride
Of the first Edward scatter'd wild dis-
may,
As down the steep of Snowdon's [26] shaggy
side
He wound with toilsome march his long
array.
Stout Glo'ster [27] stood aghast in speechless
trance:
To arms! cried Mortimer,[28] and couch'd his
quiv'ring lance.

I. 2

On a rock, whose haughty brow
Frowns o'er Conway's foaming flood,
Robed in the sable garb of woe,
With haggard eyes the Poet stood;
(Loose his beard, and hoary hair [29]

---

[24] Begun in December 1754, partly completed and then laid aside until May 1757, when Gray was inspired by hearing Parry, a Welsh harper; published in 1757 with *The Progress of Poesy* in *Odes*. [25] Wales
[26] *Snowdon* was a name given by the Saxons to that mountainous tract, which the Welch themselves call *Craigian-eryri:* it included all the highlands of Caernarvonshire and Merionethshire, as far east as the river Conway. [Gray.]
[27] Gilbert de Clare, surnamed the Red, Earl of Gloucester and Hertford, son-in-law to King Edward. [Gray.]
[28] Edmond de Mortimer, Lord of Wigmore. They both [he and Gilbert de Clare] were *Lords-Marchers*, whose lands lay on the borders of Wales, and probably accompanied the King in this expedition. [Gray.]
[29] The image was taken from a well-known picture of Raphaël, representing the Supreme Being in the vision of Ezekiel: there are two of these paintings (both believed original), one at Florence, the other at Paris. [Gray.]

Stream'd, like a meteor, to the troubled air)
And with a Master's hand, and Prophet's fire,
Struck the deep sorrows of his lyre.
'Hark, how each giant-oak, and desert cave,
'Sighs to the torrent's aweful voice beneath!
'O'er thee, oh King! their hundred arms they wave,
'Revenge on thee in hoarser murmurs breath;
'Vocal no more, since Cambria's fatal day,
'To high-born Hoel's harp, or soft Llewellyn's lay.

I. 3

'Cold is Cadwallo's tongue,
'That hush'd the stormy main:
'Brave Urien sleeps upon his craggy bed:
'Mountains, ye mourn in vain
'Modred, whose magic song
'Made huge Plinlimmon [30] bow his cloud-top'd head.
'On dreary Arvon's [31] shore they lie,
'Smear'd with gore, and ghastly pale:
'Far, far aloof th' affrighted ravens fail;
'The famish'd Eagle screams, and passes by.
'Dear lost companions of my tuneful art,
'Dear, as the light that visits these sad eyes,
'Dear, as the ruddy drops that warm my heart,
'Ye died amidst your dying country's cries —
'No more I weep. They do not sleep.
'On yonder cliffs, a grisly band,
'I see them sit, they linger yet,
'Avengers of their native land:
'With me in dreadful harmony they join,
'And weave with bloody hands the tissue of thy line.'

[30] A mountain in Wales.
[31] The shores of Caernarvonshire opposite to the isle of Anglesey. [Gray.]

II. 1

"Weave the warp, and weave the woof,
"The winding-sheet of Edward's race.
"Give ample room, and verge enough
"The characters of hell to trace.
"Mark the year, and mark the night,
"When Severn shall re-echo with affright
"The shrieks of death, thro' Berkley's roofs that ring,
"Shrieks of an agonizing King! [32]
"She-Wolf [33] of France, with unrelenting fangs,
"That tear'st the bowels of thy mangled Mate,
"From thee be born, who o'er thy country hangs
"The scourge of Heav'n.[34] What Terrors round him wait!
"Amazement in his van, with Flight combined,
"And Sorrow's faded form, and Solitude behind.

II. 2

"Mighty Victor, mighty Lord,
"Low on his funeral couch he lies! [35]
"No pitying heart, no eye, afford
"A tear to grace his obsequies.
"Is the sable Warriour [36] fled?
"Thy son is gone. He rests among the Dead.
"The Swarm, that in thy noon-tide beam were born?
"Gone to salute the rising Morn.
"Fair [37] laughs the Morn, and soft the Zephyr blows,
"While proudly riding o'er the azure realm
"In gallant trim the gilded Vessel goes;
"Youth on the prow, and Pleasure at the helm;

[32] Edward the Second, cruelly butchered in Berkley-Castle. [Gray.]
[33] Isabel of France, Edward the Second's adulterous Queen. [Gray.]
[34] Triumphs of Edward the Third in France. [Gray.]
[35] Death of that King, abandoned by his Children, and even robbed in his last moments by his Courtiers and his Mistress. [Gray.]
[36] Edward, the Black Prince, dead some time before his Father. [Gray.]
[37] Magnificence of Richard the Second's reign. [Gray.]

"Regardless of the sweeping Whirlwind's sway,
"That, hush'd in grim repose, expects his evening-prey.

II. 3

"Fill high the sparkling bowl
"The rich repast prepare,
"Reft of a crown, he yet may share the feast:
"Close by the regal chair
"Fell Thirst and Famine scowl
"A baleful smile upon their baffled Guest.[38]
"Heard ye the din of battle [39] bray,
"Lance to lance, and horse to horse?
"Long Years of havock urge their destined course,
"And thro' the kindred squadrons mow their way.
"Ye Towers of Julius,[40] London's lasting shame,
"With many a foul and midnight murther fed,
"Revere his Consort's [41] faith, his Father's [42] fame,
"And spare the meek Usurper's [43] holy head.
"Above, below, the rose [44] of snow,
"Twined with her blushing foe, we spread:
"The bristled Boar [45] in infant-gore
"Wallows beneath the thorny shade.
"Now, Brothers, bending o'er th' accursed loom
"Stamp we our vengeance deep, and ratify his doom.

III. 1

"Edward, lo! to sudden fate
"(Weave we the woof. The thread is spun)
"Half of thy heart we consecrate.[46]
"(The web is wove. The work is done.)"
'Stay, ah stay! nor thus forlorn
'Leave me unbless'd, unpitied, here to mourn:
'In yon bright track, that fires the western skies,
'They melt, they vanish from my eyes.
'But oh! what solemn scenes on Snowdon's height
'Descending slow their glitt'ring skirts unroll?
'Visions of glory, spare my aching sight,
'Ye unborn Ages, crowd not on my soul!
'No more our long-lost Arthur [47] we bewail.
'All-hail, ye genuine Kings,[48] Britannia's Issue, hail!

III. 2

'Girt with many a Baron bold
'Sublime their starry fronts they rear;
'And gorgeous Dames, and Statesmen old
'In bearded majesty, appear.
'In the midst a Form divine!
'Her eye proclaims her of the Briton-Line;
'Her lyon-port,[49] her awe-commanding face,
'Attemper'd sweet to virgin-grace.
'What strings symphonious tremble in the air,

---

[38] Richard the Second was starved to death. [Gray.]

[39] Ruinous civil wars of York and Lancaster. [Gray.]

[40] Henry the Sixth, George Duke of Clarence, Edward the Fifth, Richard Duke of York, *&c.* believed to be murthered secretly in the Tower of London. The oldest part of that structure is vulgarly attributed to Julius Cæsar. [Gray.]

[41] Margaret of Anjou, a woman of heroic spirit, who struggled hard to save her Husband and her Crown. [Gray.]

[42] Henry the Fifth. [Gray.]

[43] Henry the Sixth very near being canonized. The line of Lancaster had no right of inheritance to the Crown. [Gray.]

[44] The white and red roses, devices of York and Lancaster. [Gray.]

[45] The silver Boar was the badge of Richard the Third; whence he was usually known in his own time by the name of *the Boar*. [Gray.]

[46] Eleanor of Castile died a few years after the conquest of Wales. The heroic proof she gave of her affection for her Lord is well known. The monuments of his regret, and sorrow for the loss of her, are still to be seen at Northampton, Geddington, Waltham, and other places. [Gray.]

[47] It was the common belief of the Welch nation, that King Arthur was still alive in Fairy-Land, and should return again to reign over Britain. [Gray.]

[48] Both Merlin and Taliessin had prophesied, that the Welch should regain their sovereignty over this island; which seemed to be accomplished in the House of Tudor. [Gray.]

[49] Speed relating an audience given by Queen Elizabeth to Paul Dzialinski, Ambassadour of Poland, says, 'And 'thus she, lion-like rising, daunted the malapert Orator no 'less with her stately port and majestical deporture, than 'with the tartnesse of her princelie checkes.' [Gray.]

'What strains of vocal transport round her play!
'Hear from the grave, great Taliessin,[50] hear;
'They breathe a soul to animate thy clay.
'Bright Rapture calls, and soaring, as she sings,
'Waves in the eye of Heav'n her many-colour'd wings.

III. 3

'The verse adorn again
'Fierce War, and faithful Love,[51]
'And Truth severe, by fairy Fiction drest.
'In buskin'd measures [52] move
'Pale Grief, and pleasing Pain,
'With Horrour, Tyrant of the throbbing breast.
'A Voice,[53] as of the Cherub-Choir,
'Gales from blooming Eden bear;
'And distant warblings lessen on my ear,
'That lost in long futurity expire. [54]
'Fond impious Man, think'st thou, yon sanguine cloud,
'Rais'd by thy breath, has quench'd the Orb of day?
'To-morrow he repairs the golden flood,
'And warms the nations with redoubled ray.
'Enough for me: With joy I see
'The different doom our Fates assign.
'Be thine Despair, and scept'red Care,
'To triumph, and to die, are mine.'
He spoke, and headlong from the mountain's height
Deep in the roaring tide he plung'd to endless night.[55]

[50] Taliessin, Chief of the Bards, flourished in the VIth Century. His works are still preserved, and his memory held in high veneration among his Countrymen. [Gray.]

[51] Fierce wars and faithful loves shall moralize my song. *Spenser's Proëme to the Fairy Queen.* [Gray.]

[52] Shakespear. [Gray.]

[53] Milton. [Gray.]

[54] The succession of Poets after Milton's time. [Gray.]

[55] 'Mr. Fox, supposing the bard sung his song but once over, does not wonder if Edward the First did not understand him. This last criticism is rather unhappy, for though it had been sung a hundred times under his window, it was absolutely impossible King Edward should understand him; but that is no reason for Mr. Fox, who lives almost 500 years after him. It is very well; the next thing I print shall be in Welch — that's all.' [Gray, in letter to Mason, undated, No. 148 in Tovey's edition.]

The Fatal Sisters

An Ode [56]

PREFACE

In the Eleventh Century *Sigurd,* Earl of the Orkney-Islands, went with a fleet of ships and a considerable body of troops into Ireland, to the assistance of *Sictryg with the silken beard,* who was then making war on his father-in-law *Brian,* King of Dublin: [57] the Earl and all his forces were cut to pieces, and *Sictryg* was in danger of a total defeat; but the enemy had a greater loss by the death of *Brian,* their King, who fell in the action. On Christmas-day, (the day of the battle,) a Native of *Caithness* in Scotland saw at a distance a number of persons on horseback riding full speed towards a hill, and seeming to enter into it. Curiosity led him to follow them, till looking through an opening in the rocks he saw twelve gigantic figures resembling women: [58] they were all employed about a loom; and as they wove, they sung the following dreadful Song; which when they had finished, they tore the web into twelve pieces, and (each taking her portion) galloped Six to the North and as many to the South.

Now the storm begins to lower,
(Haste, the loom of Hell prepare,)
Iron-sleet of arrowy shower
Hurtles in the darken'd air.

Glitt'ring lances are the loom,
Where the dusky warp we strain,
Weaving many a Soldier's doom,
Orkney's woe, and Randver's bane.

See the grisly texture grow,
('Tis of human entrails made,)
And the weights, that play below,
Each a gasping Warriour's head.

Shafts for shuttles, dipt in gore,
Shoot the trembling cords along.
Sword, that once a Monarch bore,
Keep the tissue close and strong.

Mista black, terrific Maid,
Sangrida, and Hilda see,

[56] Written in 1761; published in *Poems,* 1768. Professor Kittredge has shown that Gray's version is from a Latin translation of an old Norse poem. The Norse text, with a prose translation, may be found in Vigfusson and Powell's *Corpus Poeticum Boreale,* I, 281–283. The poem celebrates the Battle of Clontarf, fought, not as Gray says, on Christmas day, but on Good Friday, 1014.

[57] Actually Sictryg was King of Dublin, and Brian, King of Ireland. Brian was Sictryg's stepfather.

[58] The Valkyries, some of the names of whom appear in stanzas 5 and 8.

Join the wayward work to aid:
'Tis the woof of victory.

Ere the ruddy sun be set,
Pikes must shiver, javelins sing,
Blade with clattering buckler meet,
Hauberk crash, and helmet ring.

(Weave the crimson web of war)
Let us go, and let us fly,
Where our Friends the conflict share,
Where they triumph, where they die.

As the paths of fate we tread,
Wading thro' th' ensanguin'd field:
Gondula, and Geira, spread
O'er the youthful King[59] your shield.

We the reins to slaughter give,
Ours to kill, and ours to spare:
Spite of danger he shall live.
(Weave the crimson web of war.)

They, whom once the desert-beach
Pent within its bleak domain,
Soon their ample sway shall stretch
O'er the plenty of the plain.

Low the dauntless Earl is laid,
Gor'd with many a gaping wound:
Fate demands a nobler head,
Soon a King[60] shall bite the ground.

Long his loss shall Eirin weep,
Ne'er again his likeness see;
Long her strains in sorrow steep,
Strains of Immortality!

Horror covers all the heath,
Clouds of carnage blot the sun.
Sisters, weave the web of death;
Sisters, cease, the work is done.

Hail the task, and hail the hands!
Songs of joy and triumph sing!
Joy to the victorious bands;
Triumph to the younger King.

Mortal, thou that hear'st the tale,
Learn the tenour of our song.
Scotland, thro' each winding vale
Far and wide the notes prolong.

Sisters, hence with spurs of speed:
Each her thundering faulchion wield;
Each bestride her sable steed.
Hurry, hurry to the field.

Sonnet

On the Death of Richard West[61]

In vain to me the smiling Mornings shine,
And redning Phœbus lifts his golden Fire:
The Birds in vain their amorous Descant join;
Or cheerful Fields resume their green Attire:
These Ears, alas! for other Notes repine,
A different Object do these Eyes require.
My lonely Anguish melts no Heart, but mine;
And in my Breast the imperfect Joys expire.
Yet Morning smiles the busy Race to cheer,
And new-born Pleasure brings to happier Men:
The Fields to all their wonted Tribute bear:
To warm their little Loves the Birds complain:
I fruitless mourn to him that cannot hear,
And weep the more because I weep in vain.

Song[62]

Thyrsis, when we parted, swore
Ere the spring he would return —
Ah! what means yon violet flower!
And the buds that deck the thorn!
'Twas the Lark that upward sprung!
'Twas the Nightingale that sung!

Idle notes! untimely green!
Why this unavailing haste?
Western gales and skies serene
Speak not always winter past.
Cease, my doubts, my fears to move,
Spare the honour of my Love.

---

59 Sictryg

60 Brian

61 The Pembroke MS. is dated 'at Stoke, Aug. 1742': first published in 1775. West, the friend of Gray from the Eton days, had died on 1 June 1742, at the age of twenty-six. See Wordsworth's criticism of the sonnet in his Preface to the *Lyrical Ballads*.

62 Written October 1761, to an old air of Geminiani first published in *European Magazine*, February 1791.

William Collins

1721–1759

A Song from Shakespeare's Cymbeline [1]

SUNG BY GUIDERUS AND ARVIRAGUS OVER FIDELE, SUPPOS'D TO BE DEAD

I

To fair Fidele's grassy tomb
  Soft maids and village hinds shall bring
Each op'ning sweet, of earliest bloom,
  And rifle all the breathing Spring.

II

No wailing ghost shall dare appear
  To vex with shrieks this quiet grove:
But shepherd lads assemble here,
  And melting virgins own their love.

III

No wither'd witch shall here be seen,
  No goblins lead their nightly crew:
The female fays shall haunt the green,
  And dress thy grave with pearly dew!

IV

The redbreast oft at ev'ning hours
  Shall kindly lend his little aid:
With hoary moss, and gather'd flow'rs,
  To deck the ground where thou art laid.

V

When howling winds, and beating rain,
  In tempests shake the sylvan cell:
Or midst the chace on ev'ry plain,
  The tender thought on thee shall dwell.

VI

Each lonely scene shall thee restore,
  For thee the tear be duly shed:
Belov'd, till life could charm no more;
  And mourn'd, till Pity's self be dead.

[1] Published in 1744, with the second edition of the *Epistle to Sir Thomas Hanmer.*

Ode to Fear [2]

THOU, to whom the World unknown
With all its shadowy shapes is shown;
Who see'st appall'd th' unreal scene,
While Fancy lifts the veil between:
    Ah Fear! Ah frantic Fear!
    I see, I see Thee near.
I know thy hurried step, thy haggard eye!
Like Thee I start, like Thee disorder'd fly,
For lo what monsters in thy train appear!
Danger, whose limbs of giant mold
What mortal eye can fix'd behold?
Who stalks his round, an hideous form,
Howling amidst the midnight storm,
Or throws him on the ridgy steep
Of some loose hanging rock to sleep:
And with him thousand phantoms join'd,
Who prompt to deeds accurs'd the mind:
And those, the Fiends, who near allied,
O'er Nature's wounds, and wrecks preside;
Whilst Vengeance, in the lurid air,
Lifts her red arm, expos'd and bare:
On whom that rav'ning Brood of Fate,[3]
Who lap the blood of Sorrow, wait;
Who, Fear, this ghastly train can see,
And look not madly wild, like Thee?

Epode

In earliest Greece to Thee with partial choice,
  The grief-full Muse addrest her infant tongue;
The maids and matrons, on her awful voice,
  Silent and pale in wild amazement hung.

Yet he, the bard [4] who first invok'd thy name,
  Disdain'd in Marathon its pow'r to feel:

[2] This and the three following poems were published in *Odes on Several Descriptive and Allegoric Subjects*, 1747 (the actual date of publication was December 1746).
[3] 'The hounds whom none may escape' of Sophocles' *Electra*, l. 1388.
[4] Aeschylus, who fought at Marathon.

For not alone he nurs'd the poet's flame,
But reach'd from virtue's hand the patriot's steel.

But who is he[5] whom later garlands grace,
Who left a-while o'er Hybla's dews to rove,
With trembling eyes thy dreary steps to trace,
Where Thou and Furies shar'd the baleful Grove?[6]

Wrapt in thy cloudy veil th' Incestuous Queen
Sigh'd the sad call her son and husband hear'd,[7]
When once alone it broke the silent scene,
And he the wretch of Thebes no more appear'd.

O Fear, I know Thee by my throbbing heart,
Thy with'ring pow'r inspir'd each mournful line,
Tho' gentle Pity claim her mingled part,
Yet all the thunders of the scene are thine!

Antistrophe

Thou who such weary lengths hast past,
Where wilt thou rest, mad Nymph, at last?
Say, wilt thou shroud in haunted cell,
Where gloomy Rape and Murder dwell?
Or, in some hollow'd seat,
'Gainst which the big waves beat,
Hear drowning sea-men's cries in tempests brought!
Dark pow'r, with shudd'ring meek submitted thought
Be mine, to read the visions old,
Which thy awak'ning bards have told:
And lest thou meet my blasted view,
Hold each strange tale devoutly true;

[5] Sophocles, whose sweet lines suggest Hybla, the Sicilian city celebrated for the honey produced nearby.
[6] The scene of *Oedipus Coloneus* is a grove dedicated to the Furies.
[7] See *Oedipus Coloneus*, ll. 1622–1625. It was not Jocasta who called Oedipus, but a god.

Ne'er be I found, by Thee o'eraw'd,
In that thrice-hallow'd eve abroad,
When ghosts, as cottage-maids believe,
Their pebbled beds permitted leave,
And gobblins haunt from fire, or fen,
Or mine, or flood, the walks of men!
O Thou whose spirit most possest
The sacred seat of Shakespear's breast!
By all that from thy prophet broke,
In thy divine emotions spoke:
Hither again thy Fury deal,
Teach me but once like him to feel:
His cypress wreath my meed decree,
And I, O Fear, will dwell with Thee!

Ode on the Poetical Character

I

As once (if not with light regard,
I read aright that gifted bard,[8]
(Him whose school above the rest
His loveliest Elfin Queen has blest.)
One, only one, unrival'd fair,[9]
Might hope the magic girdle wear,
At solemn turney hung on high,
The wish of each love-darting eye;

Lo! to each other nymph in turn applied,
As if, in air unseen, some hov'ring hand,
Some chaste and angel-friend to virgin-fame,
With whisper'd spell had burst the starting band,
If left unblest her loath'd dishonour'd side;
Happier hopeless fair, if never
Her baffled hand with vain endeavour
Had touch'd that fatal zone to her denied!
Young Fancy thus, to me divinest name,
To whom, prepar'd and bath'd in heav'n,
The cest[10] of amplest pow'r is giv'n:
To few the god-like gift assigns,
To gird their blest prophetic loins,
And gaze her visions wild, and feel unmix'd her flame!

[8] Spenser
[9] Amoret; not Florimel, as Collins erroneously thought See *The Faerie Queene*, IV, 5, stanzas 16–19.
[10] girdle

2

The band, as fairy legends say,
Was wove on that creating day,
When He who call'd with thought to birth
Yon tented sky, this laughing earth,
And drest with springs, and forests tall,
And pour'd the main engirting all,
Long by the lov'd enthusiast woo'd,
Himself in some diviner mood,
Retiring, sate with her alone,
And plac'd her on his saphire throne,
The whiles, the vaulted shrine around,
Seraphic wires were heard to sound,
Now sublimest triumph swelling,
Now on love and mercy dwelling;
And she, from out the veiling cloud,
Breath'd her magic notes aloud:
And thou, thou rich-hair'd Youth of Morn,
And all thy subject life was born!
The dang'rous Passions kept aloof,
Far from the sainted growing woof:
But near it sate ecstatic Wonder,
List'ning the deep applauding thunder:
And Truth, in sunny vest array'd,
By whose the tarsel's[11] eyes were made;
All the shad'wy tribes of Mind,
In braided dance their murmurs join'd,
And all the bright uncounted Pow'rs
Who feed on heav'n's ambrosial flow'rs.
Where is the bard whose soul can now
Its high presuming hopes avow?
Where he who thinks, with rapture blind,
This hallow'd work for him design'd?

3

High on some cliff, to heav'n up-pil'd,
Of rude access, of prospect wild,
Where, tangled round the jealous steep,
Strange shades o'erbrow the valleys deep,
And holy genii guard the rock,
Its Glooms embrown, its springs unlock,
While on its rich ambitious head,
An Eden, like his own, lies spread.
I view that oak, the fanciest glades among,
By which as Milton lay, his ev'ning ear,
From many a cloud that drop'd ethereal dew,
Nigh spher'd in heav'n its native strains could hear:
On which that ancient trump he reach'd was hung;
Thither oft his glory greeting,
From Waller's myrtle shades retreating,
With many a vow from Hope's aspiring tongue,
My trembling feet his guiding steps pursue;
In vain — such bliss to one alone
Of all the sons of soul was known,
And Heav'n, and Fancy, kindred pow'rs,
Have now o'erturn'd th' inspiring bow'rs,
Or curtain'd close such scene from ev'ry future view.

[11] male falcon

Ode

Written in the beginning of the Year 1746[12]

1

How sleep the brave, who sink to rest,
By all their country's wishes blest!
When Spring, with dewy fingers cold,
Returns to deck their hallow'd mold,
She there shall dress a sweeter sod,
Than Fancy's feet have ever trod.

2

By fairy hands their knell is rung,
By forms unseen their dirge is sung;
There Honour comes, a pilgrim grey,
To bless the turf that wraps their clay,
And Freedom shall awhile repair,
To dwell a weeping hermit there!

[12] On 11 May 1745 the English incurred heavy losses in a battle with the French at Fontenoy, Belgium; on 21 September 1745, at Prestonpans, Scotland, and again on 17 January 1746, at Falkirk, many fell in fighting the army of the Young Pretender.

Ode to Evening

IF aught of oaten stop, or pastoral song,
May hope, chaste Eve, to soothe thy modest ear,
Like thy own solemn springs,
Thy springs, and dying gales,

O nymph reserv'd, while now the bright-hair'd sun
Sits in yon western tent, whose cloudy skirts,
With brede [13] ethereal wove,
O'erhang his wavy bed:

Now air is hush'd, save where the weak-ey'd bat,
With short shrill shriek flits by on leathern wing,
Or where the beetle winds
His small but sullen horn,

As oft he rises 'midst the twilight path,
Against the Pilgrim borne in heedless hum:
Now teach me, maid compos'd,
To breathe some soften'd strain,

Whose numbers, stealing thro' thy darkning vale,
May not unseemly with its stillness suit,
As, musing slow, I hail
Thy genial lov'd return!

For when thy folding-star arising shews
His paly circlet, at his warning lamp
The fragrant Hours, and elves
Who slept in flowers the day,

And many a nymph who wreaths her brows with sedge,
And sheds the fresh'ning dew, and lovelier still,
The pensive Pleasures sweet
Prepare thy shadowy car.

Then lead, calm vot'ress, where some sheety lake
Cheers the lone heath, or some time-hallow'd pile,
Or upland fallows grey
Reflect its last cool gleam.

But when chill blust'ring winds, or driving rain,
Forbid my willing feet, be mine the hut
That from the mountain's side,
Views wilds, and swelling floods,

And hamlets brown, and dim-discover'd spires,
And hears their simple bell, and marks o'er all
Thy dewy fingers draw
The gradual dusky veil.

While Spring shall pour his show'rs, as oft he wont,
And bathe thy breathing tresses, meekest Eve!
While Summer loves to sport,
Beneath thy ling'ring light;

While sallow Autumn fills thy lap with leaves,
Or Winter yelling thro' the troublous air,
Affrights thy shrinking train,
And rudely rends thy robes;

So long, sure-found beneath the sylvan shed,
Shall Fancy, Friendship, Science, rose-lip'd Health
Thy gentlest influence own,
And hymn thy fav'rite name!

[13] embroidery (braid)

An Ode [14]
on the Popular Superstitions of the Highlands of Scotland,

CONSIDERED AS THE SUBJECT OF POETRY

I

H——,[15] thou return'st from Thames, whose Naiads long

[14] Written about 1749; published posthumously in *The Transactions of the Royal Society of Edinburgh*, 1788. Soon after this first — and incomplete — edition, what was printed as a 'perfect' copy appeared in London. The text here given is that of the first edition.

Lowell wrote in his essay on Pope in *My Study Windows*: 'The whole Romantic School, in its germ, no doubt, but yet unmistakably foreshadowed, lies already in the "Ode on the Superstitions of the Highlands." He [Collins] was the first to bring back into poetry something of the antique fervor, and found again the long-lost secret of being classically elegant without being pedantically cold.'

[15] John Home (1722–1808). Scotch clergyman and dramatist, author of *Douglas*. His tragedy, *Agis*, had just been refused by Garrick in London.

Have seen thee ling'ring, with a fond delay,
Mid those soft friends, whose hearts, some future day,
Shall melt, perhaps, to hear thy tragic song.
Go, not unmindful of that cordial youth,[16]
Whom, long endear'd, thou leav'st by Lavant's side;
Together let us wish him lasting truth,
And joy untainted with his destin'd bride.
Go! nor regardless, while these numbers boast
My short-liv'd bliss, forget my social name;
But think far off how, on the southern coast,
I met thy friendship with an equal flame!
Fresh to that soil thou turn'st, whose ev'ry vale
Shall prompt the poet, and his song demand:
To thee thy copious subjects ne'er shall fail;
Thou need'st but take the pencil to thy hand,
And paint what all believe who own thy genial land.

II

There must thou wake perforce thy Doric [17] quill,
'Tis Fancy's land to which thou sett'st thy feet;
Where still, 'tis said, the fairy people meet
Beneath each birkin shade on mead or hill.
There each trim lass that skims the milky store
To the swart tribes [18] their creamy bowl allots;
By night they sip it round the cottage-door,
While airy minstrels warble jocund notes.
There every herd, by sad experience, knows
How, wing'd with fate, their elf-shot arrows fly;
When the sick ewe her summer food foregoes,
Or, stretch'd on earth, the heart-smit heifers lie.
Such airy beings awe th' untutor'd swain:
Nor thou, though learn'd, his homelier thoughts neglect;
Let thy sweet muse the rural faith sustain:
These are the themes of simple, sure effect,
That add new conquests to her boundless reign,
And fill, with double force, her heart-commanding strain.

III

Ev'n yet preserv'd, how often may'st thou hear,
Where to the pole the Boreal mountains run,
Taught by the father to his list'ning son
Strange lays, whose power had charm'd a Spenser's ear.
At ev'ry pause, before thy mind possest,
Old Runic bards shall seem to rise around,
With uncouth lyres, in many-coloured vest,
Their matted hair with boughs fantastic crown'd:
Whether thou bid'st the well-taught hind repeat
The choral dirge that mourns some chieftain brave,
When ev'ry shrieking maid her bosom beat,
And strew'd with choicest herbs his scented grave;
Or whether, sitting in the shepherd's shiel,[19]
Thou hear'st some sounding tale of war's alarms;

---

[16] John Barrow, who had introduced Home and Collins.
[17] *i.e.*, simple, natural
[18] The Brownies. See Milton's *L'Allegro*, ll. 105–106:
'— how the drudging goblin sweat
To earn his cream bowl, duly set.'

[19] temporary shelter

When, at the bugle's call, with fire and steel,
The sturdy clans pour'd forth their bony swarms,
And hostile brothers met to prove each other's arms.

IV

'Tis thine to sing, how framing hideous spells
In Sky's lone isle the gifted wizard seer,
Lodged in the wintry cave with ———,
Or in the depth of Uist's dark forests dwells:
How they, whose sight such dreary dreams engross,
With their own visions oft astonish'd droop,
When o'er the wat'ry strath [20] or quaggy moss
They see the gliding ghosts unbodied troop.
Or if in sports, or on the festive green,
Their ——— glance some fated youth descry,
Who, now perhaps in lusty vigour seen
And rosy health, shall soon lamented die.
For them the viewless forms of air obey,
Their bidding heed, and at their beck repair.
They know what spirit brews the stormful day,
And heartless, oft like moody madness stare
To see the phantom train their secret work prepare.

[25 lines lost]

VI

What though far off, from some dark dell espied
His [21] glimm'ring mazes cheer th' excursive sight,
Yet turn, ye wand'rers, turn your steps aside,
Nor trust the guidance of that faithless light;
For watchful, lurking 'mid th' unrustling reed,
At those mirk hours the wily monster lies,
And listens oft to hear the passing steed,
And frequent round him rolls his sullen eyes,
If chance his savage wrath may some weak wretch surprise.

VII

Ah, luckless swain, o'er all unblest indeed!
Whom late bewilder'd in the dank, dark fen,
Far from his flocks and smoking hamlet then!
To that sad spot ———————:
On him, enrag'd, the fiend, in angry mood,
Shall never look with pity's kind concern,
But instant, furious, raise the whelming flood
O'er its drown'd bank, forbidding all return.
Or, if he meditate his wish'd escape
To some dim hill that seems uprising near,
To his faint eye the grim and grisly shape,
In all its terrors clad, shall wild appear.
Meantime, the wat'ry surge shall around him rise,
Pour'd sudden forth from ev'ry swelling source.
What now remains but tears and hopeless sighs?
His fear-shook limbs have lost their youthly force,
And down the waves he floats, a pale and breathless corse.

VIII

For him, in vain, his anxious wife shall wait,
Or wander forth to meet him on his way;

[20] river valley
[21] Will-o'-the -wisp's

For him, in vain, at to-fall [22] of the day,
His babes shall linger at th' unclosing gate!
Ah, ne'er shall he return! Alone, if night
Her travell'd limbs in broken slumbers steep,
With dropping willows drest, his mournful sprite
Shall visit sad, perchance, her silent sleep:
Then he, perhaps, with moist and wat'ry hand,
Shall fondly seem to press her shudd'ring cheek
And with his blue swoln face before her stand,
And, shiv'ring cold, these piteous accents speak:
Pursue, dear wife, thy daily toils pursue
At dawn or dusk, industrious as before;
Nor e'er of me one hapless thought renew,
While I lie welt'ring on the ozier'd [23] shore,
Drown'd by the Kaelpie's [24] wrath, nor e'er shall aid thee more!

IX

Unbounded is thy range; with varied style
Thy muse may, like those feath'ry tribes which spring
From their rude rocks, extend her skirting wing
Round the moist marge of each cold Hebrid isle,
To that hoar pile which still its ruin shows:
In whose small vaults [25] a pigmy-folk is found,
Whose bones the delver with his spade upthrows,
And culls them, wond'ring, from the hallow'd ground!
Or thither where beneath the show'ry west
The mighty kings of three fair realms are laid: [26]
Once foes, perhaps, together now they rest.
No slaves revere them, and no wars invade:
Yet frequent now, at midnight's solemn hour,
The rifted mounds their yawning cells unfold,
And forth the monarchs stalk with sov'reign pow'r
In pageant robes, and wreath'd with sheeny gold,
And on their twilight tombs aerial council hold.

X

But O! o'er all, forget not Kilda's race,
On whose bleak rocks, which brave the wasting tides,
Fair Nature's daughter, Virtue, yet abides.
Go, just, as they, their blameless manners trace!
Then to my ear transmit some gentle song
Of those whose lives are yet sincere and plain,
Their bounded walks the rugged cliffs along,
And all their prospect but the wintry main.
With sparing temp'rance, at the needful time,
They drain the sainted spring, or, hunger-prest,
Along th' Atlantic rock undreading climb,
And of its eggs despoil the Solan's [27] nest.
Thus blest in primal innocence they live,
Suffic'd and happy with that frugal fare
Which tasteful toil and hourly danger give.
Hard is their shallow soil, and bleak and bare;
Nor ever vernal bee was heard to murmur there!

XI

Nor need'st thou blush, that such false themes engage

---

[22] closing
[23] willow-covered
[24] water-spirit's
[25] The small bones contained in a stone vault in the Island of Benbecula are believed by the natives to be those of pigmies.
[26] The tombs of the kings of Norway, Ireland, and Scotland were supposedly on the Island of Iona.
[27] gannet's (a wild goose)

Thy gentle[28] mind, of fairer stores possest;
For not alone they touch the village breast,
But fill'd in elder time th' historic page,
There Shakespeare's self, with ev'ry garland crown'd,
In musing hour, his wayward sisters[29] found,
And with their terrors drest the magic scene.
From them he sung, when mid his bold design,
Before the Scot afflicted and aghast,
The shadowy kings of Banquo's fated line,
Through the dark cave in gleamy pageant past.
Proceed, nor quit the tales which, simply told,
Could once so well my answ'ring bosom pierce;
Proceed, in forceful sounds and colours bold
The native legends of thy land rehearse;
To such adapt thy lyre and suit thy powerful verse.

XII

In scenes like these, which, daring to depart
From sober truth, are still to nature true,
And call forth fresh delight to fancy's view,
Th' heroic muse employ'd her Tasso's art![30]
How have I trembled, when at Tancred's stroke,
Its gushing blood the gaping cypress pour'd;
When each live plant with mortal accents spoke,
And the wild blast up-heav'd the vanish'd sword!
How have I sat, when pip'd the pensive wind,
To hear his harp, by British Fairfax strung.
Prevailing poet, whose undoubting mind
Believ'd the magic wonders which he sung!
Hence at each sound imagination glows;
Hence his warm lay with softest sweetness flows;
Melting it flows, pure, num'rous, strong and clear,
And fills th' impassion'd heart, and wins th' harmonious ear.

XIII

All hail, ye scenes that o'er my soul prevail,
Ye ——— friths[31] and lakes which, far away,
Are by smooth Annan fill'd or past'ral Tay,
Or Don's romantic springs, at distance, hail!
The time shall come when I, perhaps, may tread
Your lowly glens, o'erhung with spreading broom,
Or o'er your stretching heaths by fancy led:
Then will I dress once more the faded bow'r,
Where Johnson sat in Drummond's[32] ——— shade;
Or crop from Tiviots dale each ———,
And mourn on Yarrow's banks ———
Meantime, ye Pow'rs, that on the plains which bore
The cordial youth, on Lothian's plains attend,
Where'er he dwell, on hill, or lowly muir,
To him I lose, your kind protection lend,
And, touch'd with love like mine, preserve my absent friend.

---

[28] cultivated [29] The 'weird' sisters in *Macbeth.*
[30] See Tasso, *Jerusalem Delivered,* canto xiii, stanzas 41–43, 46. Edward Fairfax's English translation was made in 1600.

[31] bays
[32] In 1619 Ben Jonson visited the poet William Drummond at Hawthornden, near Edinburgh. Drummond has recorded the conversation.

Oliver Goldsmith

1730–1774

On a Beautiful Youth Struck Blind with Lightning[1]

[*Imitated from the Spanish*]

Sure 'twas by Providence design'd,
Rather in pity, than in hate,
That he should be, like Cupid, blind,
To save him from Narcissus' fate.

An Elegy on that Glory of her Sex, Mrs. Mary Blaize[2]

Good people all, with one accord,
Lament for Madam Blaize,
Who never wanted a good word—
From those who spoke her praise.

The needy seldom pass'd her door,
And always found her kind;
She freely lent to all the poor,—
Who left a pledge behind.

She strove the neighbourhood to please,
With manners wond'rous winning,
And never follow'd wicked ways,—
Unless when she was sinning.

At church, in silks and satins new,
With hoop of monstrous size,
She never slumber'd in her pew,—
But when she shut her eyes.

Her love was sought, I do aver,
By twenty beaux and more;
The king himself has follow'd her,—
When she has walk'd before.[3]

But now her wealth and finery fled,
Her hangers-on cut short all;
The doctors found, when she was dead,—
Her last disorder mortal.

Let us lament, in sorrow sore,
For Kent-street[4] well may say,
That had she liv'd a twelve-month more,—
She had not died to-day.

THE TRAVELLER
or
A Prospect of Society[5]

DEDICATION

TO THE REV. HENRY GOLDSMITH

Dear Sir,

I am sensible that the friendship between us can acquire no new force from the ceremonies of a Dedication; and perhaps it demands an excuse thus to prefix your name to my attempts, which you decline giving with your own. But as a part of this Poem was formerly written to you from Switzerland, the whole can now, with propriety, be only inscribed to you. It will also throw a light upon many parts of it, when the reader understands, that it is addressed to a man, who, despising Fame and Fortune, has retired early to Happiness and Obscurity, with an income of forty pounds a year.[6]

I now perceive, my dear brother, the wisdom of your humble choice. You have entered upon a sacred office, where the harvest is great, and the labourers are but few; while you have left the field of Ambition, where the labourers are many, and the harvest not worth carrying away. But of all kinds of ambition, what from the refinement of the times, from different systems of criti-

---

[1] First published in *The Bee*, 6 October 1759.

[2] Published in *The Bee*, 27 October 1759. Goldsmith resented the endless imitations of Gray's *Elegy*. He had written in *The Critical Review*, vii, 263: 'If an hero or a poet happens to die with us, the whole band of elegiac poets raise the dismal chorus, adorn his hearse with all the paltry escutcheons of flattery, rise into bombast, paint him at the head of his thundering legions, or reigning Pegasus in his most rapid career; they are sure to strew cypress enough upon the bier, dress up all the muses in mourning, and look themselves every whit as dismal and sorrowful as an undertaker's shop.' Goldsmith drew partly for his poem upon an old French popular song of Monsieur de la Palisse (or Palice).

[3] The French song has this:

On dit que dans ses amours
Il fut caressé des belles,
Qui le suivirent toujours,
Tant qu'il marcha devant elles.

[4] A poor street in Southwark.

[5] The poem was conceived and partly written during Goldsmith's wanderings on the Continent, February 1755–1756. It was not published until 19 December 1764 The present text is that of the ninth edition, issued in 1774 the year of Goldsmith's death.

[6] See *The Deserted Village*, ll. 141–142.

cism, and from the divisions of party, that which pursues poetical fame is the wildest.

Poetry makes a principal amusement among unpolished nations; but in a country verging to the extremes of refinement, Painting and Music come in for a share. As these offer the feeble mind a less laborious entertainment, they at first rival Poetry, and at length supplant her; they engross all that favour once shown to her, and though but younger sisters, seize upon the elder's birthright.

Yet, however this art may be neglected by the powerful, it is still in greater danger from the mistaken efforts of the learned to improve it. What criticisms have we not heard of late in favour of blank verse, and Pindaric odes, choruses, anapæsts and iambics, alliterative care and happy negligence! Every absurdity has now a champion to defend it; and as he is generally much in the wrong, so he has always much to say; for error is ever talkative.

But there is an enemy to this art still more dangerous, I mean Party. Party entirely distorts the judgment, and destroys the taste. When the mind is once infected with this disease, it can only find pleasure in what contributes to increase the distemper. Like the tiger, that seldom desists from pursuing man after having once preyed upon human flesh, the reader, who has once gratified his appetite with calumny, makes, ever after, the most agreeable feast upon murdered reputation. Such readers generally admire some half-witted thing, who wants to be thought a bold man, having lost the character of a wise one. Him they dignify with the name of poet; his tawdry lampoons are called satires, his turbulence is said to be force, and his frenzy fire.

What reception a Poem may find, which has neither abuse, party, nor blank verse [7] to support it, I cannot tell, nor am I solicitous to know. My aims are right. Without espousing the cause of any party, I have attempted to moderate the rage of all. I have endeavoured to show, that there may be equal happiness in states, that are differently governed from our own; that every state has a particular principle of happiness, and that this principle in each may be carried to a mischievous excess. There are few can judge, better than yourself, how far these positions are illustrated in this Poem.

I am, dear Sir,
Your most affectionate Brother,
OLIVER GOLDSMITH.

REMOTE, unfriended, melancholy, slow,
Or by the lazy Scheldt, or wandering Po;
Or onward, where the rude Carinthian boor
Against the houseless stranger shuts the door;
Or where Campania's [8] plain forsaken lies,
A weary waste expanding to the skies:
Where'er I roam, whatever realms to see,
My heart untravell'd fondly turns to thee;
Still to my brother turns with ceaseless pain,
And drags at each remove a lengthening chain.

Eternal blessings crown my earliest friend,
And round his dwelling guardian saints attend:
Bless'd be that spot, where cheerful guests retire
To pause from toil, and trim their ev'ning fire;
Bless'd that abode, where want and pain repair,
And every stranger finds a ready chair;
Bless'd be those feasts with simple plenty crown'd,
Where all the ruddy family around
Laugh at the jests or pranks that never fail,
Or sigh with pity at some mournful tale,
Or press the bashful stranger to his food,
And learn the luxury of doing good.

But me, not destin'd such delights to share,
My prime of life [9] in wand'ring spent and care,
Impell'd, with steps unceasing, to pursue
Some fleeting good, that mocks me with the view;
That, like the circle bounding earth and skies,
Allures from far, yet, as I follow, flies;
My fortune leads to traverse realms alone,
And find no spot of all the world my own.

E'en now, where Alpine solitudes ascend,
I sit me down a pensive hour to spend;
And, plac'd on high above the storm's career,

[7] Goldsmith, like Johnson and Gay, disliked blank verse, thinking it suitable only to the 'greatest sublimity of subject.'

[8] The Roman Campagna.

[9] He was twenty-seven when he returned from his tour in 1756.

Look downward where a hundred realms appear;
Lakes, forests, cities, plains, extending wide,
The pomp of kings, the shepherd's humbler pride.

When thus Creation's charms around combine,
Amidst the store, should thankless pride repine?
Say, should the philosophic mind disdain
That good, which makes each humbler bosom vain?
Let school-taught pride dissemble all it can,
These little things are great to little man;
And wiser he, whose sympathetic mind
Exults in all the good of all mankind.
Ye glitt'ring towns, with wealth and splendour crown'd,
Ye fields, where summer spreads profusion round,
Ye lakes, whose vessels catch the busy gale,
Ye bending swains, that dress the flow'ry vale,
For me your tributary stores combine;
Creation's heir, the world, the world is mine!

As some lone miser visiting his store,
Bends at his treasure, counts, re-counts it o'er;
Hoards after hoards his rising raptures fill,
Yet still he sighs, for hoards are wanting still:
Thus to my breast alternate passions rise,
Pleas'd with each good that heaven to man supplies:
Yet oft a sigh prevails, and sorrows fall,
To see the hoard of human bliss so small;
And oft I wish, amidst the scene, to find
Some spot to real happiness consign'd,
Where my worn soul, each wand'ring hope at rest,
May gather bliss to see my fellows bless'd.

But where to find that happiest spot below,
Who can direct, when all pretend to know?
The shudd'ring tenant of the frigid zone
Boldly proclaims that happiest spot his own,
Extols the treasures of his stormy seas,
And his long nights of revelry and ease;
The naked negro, panting at the line,
Boasts of his golden sands and palmy wine,
Basks in the glare, or stems the tepid wave,
And thanks his gods for all the good they gave.
Such is the patriot's boast, where'er we roam,
His first, best country ever is, at home.
And yet, perhaps, if countries we compare,
And estimate the blessings which they share,
Though patriots flatter, still shall wisdom find
An equal portion dealt to all mankind,
As different good, by Art or Nature given,
To different nations makes their blessings even.

Nature, a mother kind alike to all,
Still grants her bliss at Labour's earnest call;
With food as well the peasant is supplied
On Idra's [10] cliffs as Arno's shelvy side;
And though the rocky-crested summits frown,
These rocks, by custom, turn to beds of down.
From Art more various are the blessings sent;
Wealth, commerce, honour, liberty, content.
Yet these each other's power so strong contest,
That either seems destructive of the rest.
Where wealth and freedom reign, contentment fails,
And honour sinks where commerce long prevails.
Hence every state to one lov'd blessing prone,

[10] Idria, in Carniola, noted for its mines.

Conforms and models life to that alone.
Each to the favourite happiness attends,
And spurns the plan that aims at other ends;
Till, carried to excess in each domain,
This favourite good begets peculiar pain.

But let us try these truths with closer eyes,
And trace them through the prospect as it lies:
Here for a while my proper cares resign'd,
Here let me sit in sorrow for mankind,
Like yon neglected shrub at random cast,
That shades the steep, and sighs at every blast.

Far to the right where Apennine ascends,
Bright as the summer, Italy extends;
Its uplands sloping deck the mountain's side,
Woods over woods in gay theatric pride;
While oft some temple's mould'ring tops between
With venerable grandeur mark the scene.

Could Nature's bounty satisfy the breast,
The sons of Italy were surely blest.
Whatever fruits in different climes were found,
That proudly rise, or humbly court the ground;
Whatever blooms in torrid tracts appear,
Whose bright succession decks the varied year;
Whatever sweets salute the northern sky
With vernal lives that blossom but to die;
These here disporting own the kindred soil,
Nor ask luxuriance from the planter's toil;
While sea-born gales their gelid wings expand
To winnow [11] fragrance round the smiling land.

But small the bliss that sense alone bestows,
And sensual bliss is all the nation knows.
In florid beauty groves and fields appear,
Man seems the only growth that dwindles here.
Contrasted faults through all his manners reign;
Though poor, luxurious; though submissive, vain;
Though grave, yet trifling; zealous, yet untrue;
And e'en in penance planning sins anew.
All evils here contaminate the mind,
That opulence departed leaves behind;
For wealth was theirs, not far remov'd the date,
When commerce proudly flourish'd through the state;
At her command the palace learn'd to rise,
Again the long-fall'n column sought the skies;
The canvas glow'd beyond e'en Nature warm,
The pregnant quarry teem'd with human form;
Till, more unsteady than the southern gale,
Commerce on other shores display'd her sail;
While nought remain'd of all that riches gave,
But towns unmann'd, and lords without a slave;
And late the nation found, with fruitless skill,
Its former strength was but plethoric ill.

Yet still the loss of wealth is here supplied
By arts, the splendid wrecks of former pride;
From these the feeble heart and long-fall'n mind
An easy compensation seem to find.
Here may be seen, in bloodless pomp array'd,
The paste-board triumph and the cavalcade;
Processions form'd for piety and love,

[11] Here 'waft.'

A mistress or a saint in every grove.[12]
By sports like these are all their cares beguil'd,
The sports of children satisfy the child;
Each nobler aim, repress'd by long control,
Now sinks at last, or feebly mans the soul;
While low delights, succeeding fast behind,
In happier meanness occupy the mind:
As in those domes, where Caesars once bore sway,
Defac'd by time and tottering in decay,
There in the ruin, heedless of the dead,
The shelter-seeking peasant builds his shed,
And, wond'ring man could want the larger pile,
Exults, and owns his cottage with a smile.

My soul, turn from them; turn we to survey
Where rougher climes a nobler race display,
Where the bleak Swiss their stormy mansions tread,
And force a churlish soil for scanty bread;
No product here the barren hills afford,
But man and steel, the soldier and his sword;
No vernal blooms their torpid rocks array,
But winter ling'ring chills the lap of May;
No Zephyr fondly sues the mountain's breast,
But meteors glare, and stormy glooms invest.

Yet still, e'en here, content can spread a charm,
Redress the clime, and all its rage disarm.
Though poor the peasant's hut, his feasts though small,
He sees his little lot the lot of all;
Sees no contiguous palace rear its head
To shame the meanness of his humble shed;
No costly lord the sumptuous banquet deal
To make him loathe his vegetable meal;
But calm, and bred in ignorance and toil,
Each wish contracting, fits him to the soil.
Cheerful at morn he wakes from short repose,
Breasts the keen air, and carols as he goes;
With patient angle trolls the finny deep,
Or drives his vent'rous plough-share to the steep;
Or seeks the den where snow-tracks mark the way,
And drags the struggling savage into day.
At night returning, every labour sped,
He sits him down the monarch of a shed;
Smiles by his cheerful fire, and round surveys
His children's looks, that brighten at the blaze;
While his lov'd partner, boastful of her hoard,
Displays her cleanly platter on the board:
And haply too some pilgrim, thither led,
With many a tale repays the nightly bed.

Thus every good his native wilds impart,
Imprints the patriot passion on his heart,
And e'en those ills, that round his mansion rise,
Enhance the bliss his scanty fund supplies.
Dear is that shed to which his soul conforms,
And dear that hill which lifts him to the storms;
And as a child, when scaring sounds molest,
Clings close and closer to the mother's breast,
So the loud torrent, and the whirlwind's roar,
But bind him to his native mountains more.

Such are the charms to barren states assign'd;

---

[12] In his *Present State of Polite Learning*, 1759, pp. 50–51, Goldsmith says: 'Happy Country [Italy], where the pastoral age begins to revive! Where the wits even of Rome are united into a rural groupe of nymphs and swains, under the appellation of modern Arcadians [refers to the Bolognese Academy of the *Arcadi*]. Where in the midst of porticos, processions, and cavalcades, abbés turned into shepherds, and shepherdesses without sheep, indulge their innocent *divertimenti*.'

Their wants but few, their wishes all confin'd.
Yet let them only share the praises due,
If few their wants, their pleasures are but few;
For every want that stimulates the breast,
Becomes a source of pleasure when redrest.
Whence from such lands each pleasing science flies,
That first excites desire, and then supplies;
Unknown to them, when sensual pleasures cloy,
To fill the languid pause with finer joy;
Unknown those powers that raise the soul to flame,
Catch every nerve, and vibrate through the frame.
Their level life is but a smould'ring fire,
Unquench'd by want, unfann'd by strong desire;
Unfit for raptures, or, if raptures cheer
On some high festival of once a year,
In wild excess the vulgar breast takes fire,
Till, buried in debauch, the bliss expire.

But not their joys alone thus coarsely flow:
Their morals, like their pleasures, are but low;
For, as refinement stops, from sire to son
Unalter'd, unimprov'd the manners run;
And love's and friendship's finely pointed dart
Fall blunted from each indurated heart.
Some sterner virtues o'er the mountain's breast
May sit, like falcons cow'ring on the nest;
But all the gentler morals, such as play
Through life's more cultur'd walks, and charm the way,
These far dispers'd, on timorous pinions fly,
To sport and flutter in a kinder sky.

To kinder skies, where gentler manners reign,
I turn; and France displays her bright domain.
Gay sprightly land of mirth and social ease,
Pleas'd with thyself, whom all the world can please,
How often have I led thy sportive choir,
With tuneless pipe,[13] beside the murmuring Loire!
Where shading elms along the margin grew,
And freshen'd from the wave the Zephyr flew;
And haply, though my harsh touch falt'ring still,
But mock'd all tune, and marr'd the dancer's skill;
Yet would the village praise my wondrous power,
And dance, forgetful of the noon-tide hour.
Alike all ages. Dames of ancient days
Have led their children through the mirthful maze,
And the gay grandsire, skill'd in gestic[14] lore,
Has frisk'd beneath the burthen of three-score.

So bless'd a life these thoughtless realms display,
Thus idly busy rolls their world away:
Theirs are those arts that mind to mind endear,
For honour forms the social temper here:
Honour, that praise which real merit gains,
Or e'en imaginary worth obtains,
Here passes current; paid from hand to hand,
It shifts in splendid traffic round the land:
From courts, to camps, to cottages it strays,
And all are taught an avarice of praise;
They please, are pleas'd, they give to get esteem,
Till, seeming bless'd, they grow to what they seem.

But while this softer art their bliss supplies,

---

[13] On his tour in 1755, Goldsmith won many a night's lodging by his playing.
[14] Traditional gestures or movements.

It gives their follies also room to rise;
For praise too dearly lov'd, or warmly sought,
Enfeebles all internal strength of thought;
And the weak soul, within itself unblest,
Leans for all pleasure on another's breast.
Hence ostentation here, with tawdry art,
Pants for the vulgar praise which fools impart;
Here vanity assumes her pert grimace,
And trims her robes of frieze with copper lace;
Here beggar pride defrauds her daily cheer,
To boast one splendid banquet once a year;
The mind still turns where shifting fashion draws,
Nor weighs the solid worth of self-applause.

To men of other minds my fancy flies,
Embosom'd in the deep where Holland lies.
Methinks her patient sons before me stand,
Where the broad ocean leans against the land,
And sedulous to stop the coming tide,
Lift the tall rampire's artificial pride.
Onward, methinks, and diligently slow,
The firm-connected bulwark seems to grow;
Spreads its long arms amidst the wat'ry roar,
Scoops out an empire, and usurps the shore;
While the pent ocean rising o'er the pile,
Sees an amphibious world beneath him smile;
The slow canal, the yellow-blossom'd vale,
The willow-tufted bank, the gliding sail,
The crowded mart, the cultivated plain,
A new creation rescu'd from his reign.

Thus, while around the wave-subjected soil
Impels the native to repeated toil,
Industrious habits in each bosom reign,
And industry begets a love of gain.
Hence all the good from opulence that springs,
With all those ills superfluous treasure brings,
Are here displayed. Their much-lov'd wealth imparts
Convenience, plenty, elegance, and arts;
But view them closer, craft and fraud appear,
E'en liberty itself is barter'd here.[15]
At gold's superior charms all freedom flies,
The needy sell it, and the rich man buys;
A land of tyrants, and a den of slaves,
Here wretches seek dishonourable graves,
And calmly bent, to servitude conform,
Dull as their lakes that slumber in the storm.

Heavens! how unlike their Belgic sires of old!
Rough, poor, content, ungovernably bold;
War in each breast, and freedom on each brow;
How much unlike the sons of Britain now!

Fir'd at the sound, my genius spreads her wing,
And flies where Britain courts the western spring;
Where lawns extend that scorn Arcadian pride,
And brighter streams than fam'd Hydaspes glide.
There all around the gentlest breezes stray,
There gentle music melts on ev'ry spray;
Creation's mildest charms are there combin'd,
Extremes are only in the master's mind!
Stern o'er each bosom reason holds her state,
With daring aims irregularly great;
Pride in their port, defiance in their eye,
I see the lords of human kind pass by,
Intent on high designs, a thoughtful band,
By forms unfashion'd, fresh from Nature's hand;
Fierce in their native hardiness of soul,
True to imagin'd right, above control,

[15] Slavery was frequent and the victims were often children, sold by their parents for definite periods.

While e'en the peasant boasts these rights to scan,
And learns to venerate himself as man.

Thine, Freedom, thine the blessings pictur'd here,
Thine are those charms that dazzle and endear;
Too bless'd, indeed, were such without alloy,
But foster'd e'en by Freedom, ills annoy:
That independence Britons prize too high,
Keeps man from man, and breaks the social tie;
The self-dependent lordlings stand alone,
All claims that bind and sweeten life unknown;
Here by the bonds of nature feebly held,
Minds combat minds, repelling and repell'd.
Ferments arise, imprison'd factions roar,
Repress'd ambition struggles round her shore,
Till over-wrought, the general system feels
Its motions stop, or frenzy fire the wheels.

Nor this the worst. As nature's ties decay,
As duty, love, and honour fail to sway,
Fictitious bonds, the bonds of wealth and law,
Still gather strength, and force unwilling awe.
Hence all obedience bows to these alone,
And talent sinks, and merit weeps unknown;
Till time may come, when stripp'd of all her charms,
The land of scholars, and the nurse of arms,
Where noble stems transmit the patriot flame,
Where kings have toil'd, and poets wrote for fame,[16]
One sink of level avarice shall lie,
And scholars, soldiers, kings, unhonour'd die.

Yet think not, thus when Freedom's ills I state,
I mean to flatter kings, or court the great;
Ye powers of truth, that bid my soul aspire,
Far from my bosom drive the low desire;
And thou, fair Freedom, taught alike to feel[17]
The rabble's rage, and tyrant's angry steel;
Thou transitory flower, alike undone
By proud contempt, or favour's fostering sun,
Still may thy blooms the changeful clime endure,
I only would repress them to secure:
For just experience tells, in every soil,
That those who think must govern those that toil;
And all that freedom's highest aims can reach,
Is but to lay proportion'd loads on each.
Hence, should one order disproportioned grow,
Its double weight must ruin all below.

O then how blind to all that truth requires,
Who think it freedom when a part aspires!
Calm is my soul, nor apt to rise in arms,
Except when fast-approaching danger warms:
But when contending chiefs blockade the throne,
Contracting regal power to stretch their own;
When I behold a factious band agree
To call it freedom when themselves are free;
Each wanton judge new penal statutes draw,
Laws grind the poor, and rich men rule the law;
The wealth of climes, where savage nations roam,
Pillag'd from slaves to purchase slaves at home;
Fear, pity, justice, indignation start,
Tear off reserve, and bare my swelling heart;

[16] In the first edition the line significantly read:
'And monarchs toil, and poets pant for fame.'

[17] Lines 365–380 are not in the first edition.

Till half a patriot, half a coward grown,
I fly from petty tyrants to the throne.

Yes, brother, curse with me that baleful hour,
When first ambition struck at regal power;
And thus polluting honour in its source,
Gave wealth to sway the mind with double force.
Have we not seen, round Britain's peopled shore,
Her useful sons exchang'd for useless ore?
Seen all her triumphs but destruction haste,
Like flaring tapers bright'ning as they waste;
Seen opulence, her grandeur to maintain,
Lead stern depopulation in her train,
And over fields where scatter'd hamlets rose,
In barren solitary pomp repose?
Have we not seen, at pleasure's lordly call,
The smiling long-frequented village fall? [18]
Beheld the duteous son, the sire decay'd,
The modest matron, and the blushing maid,
Forc'd from their homes, a melancholy train,
To traverse climes beyond the western main;
Where wild Oswego spreads her swamps around,
And Niagara stuns with thund'ring sound?

E'en now, perhaps, as there some pilgrim strays
Through tangled forests, and through dangerous ways;
Where beasts with man divided empire claim,
And the brown Indian marks with murd'rous aim;
There, while above the giddy tempest flies,
And all around distressful yells arise,
The pensive exile, bending with his woe,
To stop too fearful, and too faint to go,[19]
Casts a long look where England's glories shine,
And bids his bosom sympathise with mine.

Vain, very vain, my weary search to find
That bliss which only centres in the mind:
Why have I stray'd from pleasure and repose,
To seek a good each government bestows?
In every government, though terrors reign,
Though tyrant kings, or tyrant laws restrain,
How small, of all that human hearts endure,[20]
That part which laws or kings can cause or cure.
Still to ourselves in every place consign'd,
Our own felicity we make or find:
With secret course, which no loud storms annoy,
Glides the smooth current of domestic joy.
The lifted axe, the agonising wheel,
Luke's [21] iron crown, and Damiens' [22] bed of steel,
To men remote from power but rarely known,
Leave reason, faith, and conscience, all our own.

Elegy on the Death of a Mad Dog [23]

Good people all, of every sort,
Give ear unto my song;
And if you find it wond'rous short,
It cannot hold you long.

In Islington there was a man,
Of whom the world might say,
That still a godly race he ran,
Whene'er he went to pray.

---

[18] These lines are the germ of *The Deserted Village* (see page 495).

[19] This line, according to Boswell, was written by Dr. Johnson. Goldsmith's original line read:
'And faintly fainter, fainter seems to go.'

[20] Johnson wrote ll. 429–434 and ll. 437–438.

[21] George and Luke Dosa, or Doscha, headed a rebellion in Hungary in 1513, the former — not Luke — being proclaimed king by the peasants. It was he, therefore, who was tortured later, with a red-hot iron crown.

[22] Robert-François Damiens, 1714–1757, tortured and executed for attempting to assassinate Louis XV.

[23] First published in *The Vicar of Wakefield*, 1766.

A kind and gentle heart he had,
To comfort friends and foes;
The naked every day he clad,
When he put on his clothes.

And in that town a dog was found,
As many dogs there be,
Both mongrel, puppy, whelp, and hound,
And curs of low degree.

This dog and man at first were friends;
But when a pique began,
The dog, to gain some private ends,
Went mad and bit the man.

Around from all the neighbouring streets
The wond'ring neighbours ran,
And swore the dog had lost his wits,
To bite so good a man.

The wound it seem'd both sore and sad
To every Christian eye;
And while they swore the dog was mad,
They swore the man would die.

But soon a wonder came to light,
That show'd the rogues they lied:
The man recover'd of the bite,
The dog it was that died.

THE DESERTED VILLAGE [24]

DEDICATION

TO SIR JOSHUA REYNOLDS

DEAR SIR,

I can have no expectations in an address of this kind, either to add to your reputation, or to establish my own. You can gain nothing from my admiration, as I am ignorant of that art in which you are said to excel; and I may lose much by the severity of your judgment, as few have a juster taste in poetry than you. Setting interest therefore aside, to which I never paid much attention, I must be indulged at present in following my affections. The only dedication I ever made was to my brother, because I loved him better than most other men. He is since dead. Permit me to inscribe this Poem to you.

How far you may be pleased with the versification and mere mechanical parts of this attempt, I don't pretend to enquire; but I know you will object (and indeed several of our best and wisest friends concur in the opinion) that the depopulation it deplores is no where to be seen, and the disorders it laments are only to be found in the poet's own imagination. To this I can scarce make any other answer than that I sincerely believe what I have written; that I have taken all possible pains, in my country excursions, for these four or five years past, to be certain of what I allege; and that all my views and enquiries have led me to believe those miseries real, which I here attempt to display. But this is not the place to enter into an enquiry, whether the country be depopulating, or not; the discussion would take up much room, and I should prove myself, at best, an indifferent politician, to tire the reader with a long preface, when I want his unfatigued attention to a long poem.

In regretting the depopulation of the country, I inveigh against the increase of our luxuries; and here also I expect the shout of modern politicians against me. For twenty or thirty years past, it has been the fashion to consider luxury as one of the greatest national advantages; and all the wisdom of antiquity in that particular, as erroneous. Still however, I must remain a professed ancient on that head, and continue to think those luxuries prejudicial to states, by which so many vices are introduced, and so many kingdoms have been undone. Indeed so much has been poured out of late on the other side of the question, that, merely for the sake of novelty and variety, one would sometimes wish to be in the right.

I am, Dear Sir,
Your sincere friend, and ardent admirer,
OLIVER GOLDSMITH.

SWEET AUBURN! [25] loveliest village of the plain,
Where health and plenty cheer'd the labouring swain,
Where smiling spring its earliest visit paid,
And parting summer's lingering blooms delay'd:
Dear lovely bowers of innocence and ease,
Seats of my youth, when every sport could please,
How often have I loiter'd o'er thy green,
Where humble happiness endear'd each scene;
How often have I paus'd on every charm,
The shelter'd cot, the cultivated farm,
The never-failing brook, the busy mill,
The decent church that topp'd the neighbouring hill,

[24] Published 26 May 1770.

[25] Memories of Lissoy, home of Goldsmith's youth in Ireland, seem to be blended with happier pictures of English village life.

The hawthorn bush, with seats beneath the shade,
For talking age and whisp'ring lovers made;
How often have I bless'd the coming day,
When toil remitting lent its turn to play,
And all the village train, from labour free,
Led up their sports beneath the spreading tree;
While many a pastime circled in the shade,
The young contending as the old survey'd;
And many a gambol frolick'd o'er the ground,
And sleights of art and feats of strength went round;
And still as each repeated pleasure tir'd,
Succeeding sports the mirthful band inspir'd;
The dancing pair that simply sought renown,
By holding out to tire each other down;
The swain mistrustless of his smutted face,
While secret laughter titter'd round the place;
The bashful virgin's side-long looks of love,
The matron's glance that would those looks reprove:
These were thy charms, sweet village; sports like these,
With sweet succession, taught e'en toil to please;
These round thy bowers their cheerful influence shed,
These were thy charms — But all these charms are fled.

Sweet smiling village, loveliest of the lawn,
Thy sports are fled, and all thy charms withdrawn;
Amidst thy bowers the tyrant's hand is seen,
And desolation saddens all thy green:
One only master[26] grasps the whole domain,
And half a tillage stints thy smiling plain:
No more thy glassy brook reflects the day,
But chok'd with sedges, works its weedy way.
Along thy glades, a solitary guest,
The hollow-sounding bittern guards its nest;
Amidst thy desert walks the lapwing flies,
And tires their echoes with unvaried cries.
Sunk are thy bowers in shapeless ruin all,
And the long grass o'ertops the mould'ring wall;
And trembling, shrinking from the spoiler's hand,
Far, far away, thy children leave the land.

Ill fares the land, to hast'ning ills a prey,
Where wealth accumulates, and men decay:
Princes and lords may flourish, or may fade;
A breath can make them, as a breath has made;
But a bold peasantry, their country's pride,
When once destroy'd, can never be supplied.

A time there was, ere England's griefs began,
When every rood of ground maintain'd its man;
For him light labour spread her wholesome store,
Just gave what life requir'd, but gave no more:
His best companions, innocence and health;
And his best riches, ignorance of wealth.

But times are alter'd; trade's unfeeling train
Usurp the land and dispossess the swain;
Along the lawn, where scatter'd hamlets rose,

---

[26] By the repeated Enclosure Acts landlords could enclose common land in order to improve their holdings. Naturally there were many harsh expulsions.

Unwieldy wealth, and cumbrous pomp repose;
And every want to opulence allied,
And every pang that folly pays to pride.
Those gentle hours that plenty bade to bloom,
Those calm desires that ask'd but little room,
Those healthful sports that grac'd the peaceful scene,
Liv'd in each look, and brighten'd all the green;
These, far departing, seek a kinder shore,
And rural mirth and manners are no more.

Sweet AUBURN! parent of the blissful hour,
Thy glades forlorn confess the tyrant's power.
Here as I take my solitary rounds,
Amidst thy tangling walks, and ruin'd grounds,
And, many a year elaps'd, return to view
Where once the cottage stood, the hawthorn grew,
Remembrance wakes with all her busy train,
Swells at my breast, and turns the past to pain.

In all my wand'rings round this world of care,
In all my griefs — and GOD has given my share —
I still had hopes my latest hours to crown,
Amidst these humble bowers to lay me down;
To husband out life's taper at the close,
And keep the flame from wasting by repose.
I still had hopes, for pride attends us still,
Amidst the swains to show my book-learn'd skill,
Around my fire an evening group to draw,
And tell of all I felt, and all I saw;
And, as a hare, whom hounds and horns pursue,
Pants to the place from whence at first she flew,
I still had hopes, my long vexations pass'd,
Here to return — and die at home at last.

O blest retirement, friend to life's decline,
Retreats from care, that never must be mine,
How happy he who crowns in shades like these,
A youth of labour with an age of ease;
Who quits a world where strong temptations try
And, since 'tis hard to combat, learns to fly!
For him no wretches, born to work and weep,
Explore the mine, or tempt the dangerous deep;
No surly porter stands in guilty state
To spurn imploring famine from the gate;
But on he moves to meet his latter end,
Angels around befriending Virtue's friend;
Bends to the grave with unperceiv'd decay,
While Resignation gently slopes the way;
And, all his prospects bright'ning to the last,
His Heaven commences ere the world be pass'd!

Sweet was the sound, when oft at evening's close
Up yonder hill the village murmur rose;
There, as I pass'd with careless steps and slow,
The mingling notes came soften'd from below;
The swain responsive as the milk-maid sung,
The sober herd that low'd to meet their young;
The noisy geese that gabbled o'er the pool,
The playful children just let loose from school;
The watchdog's voice that bay'd the whisp'ring wind
And the loud laugh that spoke the vacant mind;

These all in sweet confusion sought the shade,
And fill'd each pause the nightingale had made.
But now the sounds of population fail,
No cheerful murmurs fluctuate in the gale,
No busy steps the grass-grown foot-way tread,
For all the bloomy flush of life is fled.
All but yon widow'd, solitary thing
That feebly bends beside the plashy spring;
She, wretched matron, forc'd, in age, for bread,
To strip the brook with mantling cresses spread,
To pick her wintry faggot from the thorn,
To seek her nightly shed, and weep till morn;
She only left of all the harmless train,
The sad historian of the pensive plain.

Near yonder copse, where once the garden smil'd,
And still where many a garden flower grows wild;
There, where a few torn shrubs the place disclose,
The village preacher's [27] modest mansion rose.
A man he was to all the country dear,
And passing rich with forty pounds a year;
Remote from towns he ran his godly race,
Nor e'er had chang'd, nor wished to change his place;
Unpractis'd he to fawn, or seek for power,
By doctrines fashion'd to the varying hour;
Far other aims his heart had learned to prize,
More skill'd to raise the wretched than to rise.
His house was known to all the vagrant train,
He chid their wand'rings, but reliev'd their pain;
The long-remember'd beggar was his guest,
Whose beard descending swept his aged breast;
The ruin'd spendthrift, now no longer proud,
Claim'd kindred there, and had his claims allow'd;
The broken soldier, kindly bade to stay,
Sat by his fire, and talk'd the night away;
Wept o'er his wounds, or tales of sorrow done,
Shoulder'd his crutch, and show'd how fields were won.
Pleas'd with his guests, the good man learn'd to glow,
And quite forgot their vices in their woe;
Careless their merits, or their faults to scan,
His pity gave ere charity began.

Thus to relieve the wretched was his pride,
And e'en his failings lean'd to Virtue's side;
But in his duty prompt at every call,
He watch'd and wept, he pray'd and felt, for all.
And, as a bird each fond endearment tries
To tempt its new-fledg'd offspring to the skies,
He tried each art, reprov'd each dull delay,
Allur'd to brighter worlds, and led the way.

Beside the bed where parting life was laid,
And sorrow, guilt, and pain, by turns dismay'd,
The reverend champion stood. At his control,
Despair and anguish fled the struggling soul;
Comfort came down the trembling wretch to raise,
And his last falt'ring accents whisper'd praise.

---

[27] Both Goldsmith's father and brother (see the allusion to 'forty pounds a year' in the Dedication to *The Traveller*, p. 486) were models for this portrait.

At church, with meek and unaffected grace,
His looks adorn'd the venerable place;
Truth from his lips prevail'd with double sway,
And fools, who came to scoff, remain'd to pray.
The service pass'd, around the pious man,
With steady zeal, each honest rustic ran;
Even children follow'd with endearing wile,
And pluck'd his gown, to share the good man's smile.
His ready smile a parent's warmth express'd,
Their welfare pleas'd him, and their cares distress'd;
To them his heart, his love, his griefs were given,
But all his serious thoughts had rest in Heaven.
As some tall cliff, that lifts its awful form,
Swells from the vale, and midway leaves the storm,
Though round its breast the rolling clouds are spread,
Eternal sunshine settles on its head.

Beside yon straggling fence that skirts the way,
With blossom'd furze unprofitably gay,
There, in his noisy mansion, skill'd to rule,
The village master taught his little school;
A man severe he was, and stern to view;
I knew him well, and every truant knew;
Well had the boding tremblers learn'd to trace
The day's disasters in his morning face;
Full well they laugh'd, with counterfeited glee,
At all his jokes, for many a joke had he;
Full well the busy whisper, circling round,
Convey'd the dismal tidings when he frown'd;
Yet he was kind; or if severe in aught,
The love he bore to learning was in fault;
The village all declar'd how much he knew;
'Twas certain he could write, and cypher too;
Lands he could measure, terms and tides presage,
And e'en the story ran that he could gauge.
In arguing too, the parson own'd his skill,
For e'en though vanquish'd, he could argue still;
While words of learned length and thund'ring sound
Amazed the gazing rustics rang'd around,
And still they gaz'd, and still the wonder grew,
That one small head could carry all he knew.

But past is all his fame. The very spot
Where many a time he triumph'd, is forgot.
Near yonder thorn, that lifts its head on high,
Where once the sign-post caught the passing eye,
Low lies that house where nut-brown draughts inspir'd,
Where grey-beard mirth and smiling toil retir'd,
Where village statesmen talk'd with looks profound,
And news much older than their ale went round.
Imagination fondly stoops to trace
The parlour splendours of that festive place;
The white-wash'd wall, the nicely sanded floor,
The varnish'd clock that click'd behind the door;
The chest contriv'd a double debt to pay,
A bed by night, a chest of drawers by day;
The pictures plac'd for ornament and use,
The twelve good rules,[28] the royal game of goose;[29]

---

[28] King Charles I's 'Twelve Good Rules,' the wall-motto of many a house, were supposedly found in his study after his death.

[29] A game played with dice.

The hearth, except when winter chill'd the day,
With aspen boughs, and flowers, and fennel gay;
While broken tea-cups, wisely kept for show,
Rang'd o'er the chimney, glistn'd in a row.

Vain, transitory splendours! Could not all
Reprieve the tottering mansion from its fall!
Obscure it sinks, nor shall it more impart
An hour's importance to the poor man's heart;
Thither no more the peasant shall repair
To sweet oblivion of his daily care;
No more the farmer's news, the barber's tale,
No more the wood-man's ballad shall prevail;
No more the smith his dusky brow shall clear,
Relax his pond'rous strength, and lean to hear;
The host himself no longer shall be found
Careful to see the mantling bliss go round;
Nor the coy maid, half willing to be press'd,
Shall kiss the cup to pass it to the rest.

Yes! let the rich deride, the proud disdain,
These simple blessings of the lowly train;
To me more dear, congenial to my heart,
One native charm, than all the gloss of art;
Spontaneous joys, where Nature has its play,
The soul adopts, and owns their first-born sway;
Lightly they frolic o'er the vacant mind,
Unenvied, unmolested, unconfin'd:
But the long pomp, the midnight masquerade,
With all the freaks of wanton wealth array'd,
In these, ere triflers half their wish obtain,
The toiling pleasure sickens into pain;
And, e'en while fashion's brightest arts decoy,
The heart distrusting asks, if this be joy.

Ye friends to truth, ye statesmen, who survey
The rich man's joys increase, the poor's decay,
'Tis yours to judge, how wide the limits stand
Between a splendid and a happy land.
Proud swells the tide with loads of freighted ore,
And shouting Folly hails them from her shore;
Hoards, e'en beyond the miser's wish abound,
And rich men flock from all the world around.
Yet count our gains. This wealth is but a name
That leaves our useful products still the same.
Not so the loss. The man of wealth and pride
Takes up a space that many poor supplied;
Space for his lake, his park's extended bounds,
Space for his horses, equipage, and hounds;
The robe that wraps his limbs in silken sloth
Has robb'd the neighbouring fields of half their growth,
His seat, where solitary sports are seen,
Indignant spurns the cottage from the green;
Around the world each needful product flies,
For all the luxuries the world supplies:
While thus the land adorn'd for pleasure, all
In barren splendour feebly waits the fall.

As some fair female unadorn'd and plain,
Secure to please while youth confirms her reign,
Slights every borrow'd charm that dress supplies,

Nor shares with art the triumph of her eyes:
But when those charms are pass'd, for charms are frail,
When time advances, and when lovers fail,
She then shines forth, solicitous to bless,
In all the glaring impotence of dress.
Thus fares the land, by luxury betray'd,
In nature's simplest charms at first array'd;
But verging to decline, its splendours rise,
Its vistas strike, its palaces surprise;
While scourg'd by famine from the smiling land,
The mournful peasant leads his humble band;
And while he sinks, without one arm to save,
The country blooms — a garden, and a grave.

Where then, ah! where, shall poverty reside,
To 'scape the pressure of contiguous pride?
If to some common's fenceless limits stray'd,
He drives his flock to pick the scanty blade,
Those fenceless fields the sons of wealth divide,
And e'en the bare-worn common is denied.

If to the city sped — What waits him there?
To see profusion that he must not share;
To see ten thousand baneful arts combin'd
To pamper luxury, and thin mankind;
To see those joys the sons of pleasure know
Extorted from his fellow creature's woe.
Here, while the courtier glitters in brocade,
There the pale artist[30] plies the sickly trade;
Here, while the proud their long-drawn pomps display,
There the black gibbet glooms beside the way.[31]
The dome where Pleasure holds her midnight reign
Here, richly deck'd, admits the gorgeous train;
Tumultuous grandeur crowds the blazing square,
The rattling chariots clash, the torches glare.
Sure scenes like these no troubles e'er annoy!
Sure these denote one universal joy!
Are these thy serious thoughts? — Ah, turn thine eyes
Where the poor houseless shiv'ring female lies.
She once, perhaps, in village plenty bless'd,
Has wept at tales of innocence distress'd;
Her modest looks the cottage might adorn,
Sweet as the primrose peeps beneath the thorn;
Now lost to all; her friends, her virtue fled,
Near her betrayer's door she lays her head,
And, pinch'd with cold, and shrinking from the shower,
With heavy heart deplores that luckless hour,
When idly first, ambitious of the town,
She left her wheel and robes of country brown.

Do thine, sweet AUBURN, thine, the loveliest train,
Do thy fair tribes participate her pain?
E'en now, perhaps, by cold and hunger led,
At proud men's doors they ask a little bread!

Ah, no. To distant climes, a dreary scene,
Where half the convex world intrudes between,
Through torrid tracts with fainting steps they go,
Where wild Altama[32] murmurs to their woe.
Far different there from all that charm'd before,

---

30 artisan

31 Even shop-lifting was then punishable by death.

32 Altamaha, a river in Georgia.

The various terrors of that horrid shore;
Those blazing suns that dart a downward ray,
And fiercely shed intolerable day;
Those matted woods where birds forget to sing,
But silent bats in drowsy clusters cling;
Those pois'nous fields with rank luxuriance crown'd,
Where the dark scorpion gathers death around;
Where at each step the stranger fears to wake
The rattling terrors of the vengeful snake;
Where crouching tigers[33] wait their hapless prey,
And savage men more murd'rous still than they;
While oft in whirls the mad tornado flies,
Mingling the ravag'd landscape with the skies.
Far different these from every former scene,
The cooling brook, the grassy-vested green,
The breezy covert of the warbling grove,
That only shelter'd thefts of harmless love.

Good heaven! what sorrows gloom'd that parting day,
That call'd them from their native walks away;
When the poor exiles, every pleasure pass'd,
Hung round their bowers, and fondly look'd their last,
And took a long farewell, and wish'd in vain
For seats like these beyond the western main;
And shudd'ring still to face the distant deep,
Return'd and wept, and still return'd to weep.
The good old sire, the first prepar'd to go
To new-found worlds, and wept for others' woe;
But for himself, in conscious virtue brave,
He only wish'd for worlds beyond the grave.
His lovely daughter, lovelier in her tears,
The fond companion of his helpless years,
Silent went next, neglectful of her charms,
And left a lover's for a father's arms.
With louder plaints the mother spoke her woes,
And bless'd the cot where every pleasure rose
And kiss'd her thoughtless babes with many a tear,
And clasp'd them close, in sorrow doubly dear;
Whilst her fond husband strove to lend relief
In all the silent manliness of grief.

O Luxury! thou curs'd by Heaven's decree,
How ill exchang'd are things like these for thee!
How do thy potions, with insidious joy
Diffuse their pleasures only to destroy!
Kingdoms, by thee, to sickly greatness grown,
Boast of a florid vigour not their own;
At every draught more large and large they grow,
A bloated mass of rank unwieldy woe;
Till sapp'd their strength, and every part unsound,
Down, down they sink, and spread a ruin round.

E'en now the devastation is begun,
And half the business of destruction done;
E'en now, methinks, as pond'ring here I stand,
I see the rural virtues leave the land:
Down where yon anchoring vessel spreads the sail,
That idly waiting flaps with ev'ry gale,
Downward they move, a melancholy band,

[33] It has been pointed out that Goldsmith apparently defends himself in his *Animated Nature*, 1774, iii, 244: 'There is an animal in America, which is usually called the Red Tiger, but Mr. Buffon calls it the Cougar, which, no doubt, is very different from the tiger of the east. Some, however, have thought proper to rank both together, and I will take leave to follow their example.'

Pass from the shore, and darken all the strand.
Contented toil, and hospitable care,
And kind connubial tenderness, are there;
And piety, with wishes plac'd above,
And steady loyalty, and faithful love.
And thou, sweet Poetry, thou loveliest maid,
Still first to fly where sensual joys invade;
Unfit in these degenerate times of shame,
To catch the heart, or strike for honest fame;
Dear charming nymph, neglected and decried,
My shame in crowds, my solitary pride;
Thou source of all my bliss, and all my woe,
That found'st me poor at first, and keep'st me so;
Thou guide by which the nobler arts excel,
Thou nurse of every virtue, fare thee well!
Farewell, and Oh! where'er thy voice be tried,
On Torno's [34] cliffs, or Pambamarca's [35] side,
Whether where equinoctial [36] fervours glow,
Or winter wraps the polar world in snow,
Still let thy voice, prevailing over time,
Redress the rigours of th' inclement clime;
Aid slighted truth; with thy persuasive strain
Teach erring man to spurn the rage of gain;
Teach him, that states of native strength possess'd,
Though very poor, may still be very bless'd;
That trade's proud empire hastes to swift decay,
As ocean sweeps the labour'd mole away;
While self-dependent power can time defy,
As rocks resist the billows and the sky.[37]

Song

from 'She Stoops to Conquer' [38]

Let school-masters puzzle their brain,
With grammar, and nonsense, and learning;
Good liquor, I stoutly maintain,
Gives *genus* a better discerning.
Let them brag of their heathenish gods,
Their Lethes, their Styxes, and Stygians:
Their Quis, and their Quaes, and their Quods,
They're all but a parcel of Pigeons.
Toroddle, toroddle, toroll.

When Methodist preachers come down
A-preaching that drinking is sinful,
I'll wager the rascals a crown
They always preach best with a skinful.
But when you come down with your pence,
For a slice of their scurvy religion,
I'll leave it to all men of sense,
But you, my good friend, are the pigeon.
Toroddle, toroddle, toroll.

Then come, put the jorum about,
And let us be merry and clever;
Our hearts and our liquors are stout;
Here's the Three Jolly Pigeons for ever.
Let some cry up woodcock or hare,
Your bastards, your ducks, and your widgeons;
But of all the birds in the air,
Here's a health to the Three Jolly Pigeons.
Toroddle, toroddle, toroll.

[34] Tornea, a river which flows into the Gulf of Bothnea, Sweden.
[35] Mountain in Ecuador.
[36] equatorial
[37] The last four lines are attributed by Boswell to Dr. Johnson.

[38] Published in 1773. It is sung by Tony Lumpkin at 'The Three Pigeons' ale-house, in honor of which he claimed to have composed it, in spite of his own magnificent illiteracy.

Retaliation[39]

A Poem

INCLUDING EPITAPHS ON THE MOST DISTINGUISHED WITS OF THIS METROPOLIS

OF old, when Scarron[40] his companions invited,
Each guest brought his dish, and the feast was united;
If our landlord[41] supplies us with beef, and with fish,
Let each guest bring himself, and he brings the best dish:
Our Dean shall be venison, just fresh from the plains;
Our Burke shall be tongue, with a garnish of brains;
Our Will shall be wild-fowl, of excellent flavour,
And Dick with his pepper shall heighten their savour:
Our Cumberland's sweet-bread its place shall obtain,
And Douglas is pudding, substantial and plain:
Our Garrick's a salad; for in him we see
Oil, vinegar, sugar, and saltness agree:
To make out the dinner, full certain I am,
That Ridge is anchovy, and Reynolds is lamb;
That Hickey's a capon, and by the same rule,
Magnanimous Goldsmith a gooseberry fool.
At a dinner so various, at such a repast,
Who'd not be a glutton, and stick to the last?
Here, waiter! more wine, let me sit while I'm able,
Till all my companions sink under the table;
Then, with chaos and blunders encircling my head,
Let me ponder, and tell what I think of the dead.

Here lies the good Dean, re-united to earth,
Who mix'd reason with pleasure, and wisdom with mirth:
If he had any faults, he has left us in doubt,
At least, in six weeks, I could not find 'em out;
Yet some have declar'd, and it can't be denied 'em,
That sly-boots was cursedly cunning to hide 'em.

Here lies our good Edmund, whose genius was such,
We scarcely can praise it, or blame it too much;
Who, born for the Universe, narrow'd his mind,

---

[39] Published as a pamphlet on 19 April 1774, fifteen days after Goldsmith's death. There was an anonymous prefatory letter to the publisher, which ended: 'Dr. Goldsmith belonged to a Club of Beaux Esprits, where Wit sparkled sometimes at the Expence of Good-nature. It was proposed to write Epitaphs on the Doctor; his Country, Dialect and Person, furnished Subjects of Witticism. — The Doctor was called on for Retaliation, and at their next Meeting produced the following Poem which I think adds one Leaf to his immortal Wreath.' The reference is to the contest between Goldsmith and Garrick, in which each was to say the other's epitaph. Garrick spoke the now famous lines:

'Here lies Nolly Goldsmith, for shortness call'd Noll,
Who wrote like an angel, but talk'd like poor Poll.'

Unable, according to the story, to produce a reply at the time, Goldsmith later offered his 'Retaliation.'

[40] Paul Scarron (1610–1660), French writer and member of a brilliant set of great ladies, courtesans, and men of letters.

[41] In the first edition of the poem appeared the notes of identification here quoted. The first was on the landlord, 'The Master of the St. James's Coffee-house, where the Doctor [Goldsmith], and the Friends he has characterized in this poem, held an occasional Club.'

'Doctor Barnard, Dean of Derry in Ireland, author of many ingenious pieces.'

'Mr. Edmund Burke, member for Wendover, and one of the greatest orators in this kingdom.'

'Mr. William Burke, late secretary to General Conway, and member for Bedwin.'

'Mr. Richard Burke, collector of Granada, no less remarkable in the walks of wit and humour than his brother Edmund Burke is justly distinguished in all the branches of useful and polite literature.'

'Author of The West Indian, Fashionable Lover, the Brothers, and other dramatic pieces.'

'Doctor Douglas, Canon of Windsor, an ingenious Scotch gentleman, who has no less distinguished himself as a *Citizen of the World*, than a *sound Critic* in detecting several literary mistakes (or rather *forgeries*) of his countrymen; particularly Lauder on Milton and *Bower's History of the Popes*.'

'David Garrick, Esq.; joint Patentee and acting Manager of the Theatre-Royal, Drury-Lane. For the *other parts* of his character, *vide* the Poem.'

'Counsellor John Ridge, a gentleman belonging to the Irish bar, the *relish* of whose agreeable and pointed conversation is admitted, by all his acquaintance, to be very properly compared to the above sauce.'

'Sir Joshua Reynolds, President of the Royal Academy.'

'An eminent Attorney, whose hospitality and good humour have acquired him in this Club, the title of "honest Tom Hickey."'

'Mr. T. Townshend, Member for Whitchurch' [afterwards first Viscount Sydney. He had attacked Johnson's pension in Parliament.].

And to party gave up what was meant for mankind.
Though fraught with all learning, yet straining his throat
To persuade Tommy Townshend to lend him a vote;
Who, too deep for his hearers, still went on refining
And thought of convincing, while they thought of dining; [42]
Though equal to all things, for all things unfit,
Too nice for a statesman, too proud for a wit:
For a patriot, too cool; for a drudge, disobedient;
And too fond of the *right* to pursue the *expedient.*
In short, 'twas his fate, unemploy'd, or in place, Sir,
To eat mutton cold, and cut blocks with a razor.

Here lies honest William, whose heart was a mint,
While the owner ne'er knew half the good that was in't;
The pupil of impulse, it forc'd him along,
His conduct still right, with his argument wrong;
Still aiming at honour, yet fearing to roam,
The coachman was tipsy, the chariot drove home;
Would you ask for his merits? alas! he had none;
What was good was spontaneous, his faults were his own.

Here lies honest Richard, whose fate I must sigh at;
Alas, that such frolic should now be so quiet!
What spirits were his! what wit and what whim!
Now breaking a jest, and now breaking a limb; [43]
Now wrangling and grumbling to keep up the ball,
Now teasing and vexing, yet laughing at all!
In short, so provoking a devil was Dick,
That we wish'd him full ten times a day at Old Nick;
But, missing his mirth and agreeable vein,
As often we wish'd to have Dick back again.

Here Cumberland [44] lies, having acted his parts,
The Terence of England, the mender of hearts;
A flattering painter, who made it his care
To draw men as they ought to be, not as they are.
His gallants are all faultless, his women divine,
And comedy wonders at being so fine;
Like a tragedy queen he has dizen'd her out,
Or rather like tragedy giving a rout.
His fools have their follies so lost in a crowd
Of virtues and feelings, that folly grows proud;
And coxcombs, alike in their failings alone,
Adopting his portraits, are pleas'd with their own.
Say, where has our poet this malady caught?
Or, wherefore his characters thus without fault?
Say, was it that vainly directing his view
To find out men's virtues, and finding them few,
Quite sick of pursuing each troublesome elf,
He grew lazy at last, and drew from himself?

---

[42] Burke's — for some — too lofty utterances had secured him the nickname of the 'Dinner Bell.'

[43] 'The above Gentleman having slightly fractured one of his arms and legs, at different times, the Doctor has rallied him on those accidents, as a kind of *retributive* justice for breaking his jests on other people.'

[44] Cumberland is said (one can hardly believe it) to have accepted this ironical portrait 'with gratitude'! As an exponent of Sentimental Comedy he was bound to attract the satire of Goldsmith, who feared the new drama would banish humor and character from the theatre — and 'all spectators too.'

Here Douglas retires, from his toils to relax,
The scourge of imposters, the terror of quacks:
Come, all ye quack bards, and ye quacking divines,
Come, and dance on the spot where your tyrant reclines:
When Satire and Censure encircl'd his throne,
I fear'd for your safety, I fear'd for my own;
But now he is gone, and we want a detector,
Our Dodds [45] shall be pious, our Kenricks [46] shall lecture;
Macpherson [47] write bombast, and call it a style,
Our Townshend make speeches, and I shall compile;
New Lauders and Bowers the Tweed shall cross over,
No countryman living their tricks to discover;
Detection her taper shall quench to a spark,
And Scotchman meet Scotchman, and cheat in the dark.

Here lies David Garrick, describe me, who can,
An abridgment of all that was pleasant in man;
As an actor, confess'd without rival to shine:
As a wit, if not first, in the very first line:
Yet, with talents like these, and an excellent heart,
The man had his failings, a dupe to his art.
Like an ill-judging beauty, his colours he spread,
And beplaster'd with rouge his own natural red.
On the stage he was natural, simple, affecting;
'Twas only that when he was off he was acting.
With no reason on earth to go out of his way,
He turn'd and he varied full ten times a day.
Though secure of our hearts, yet confoundedly sick
If they were not his own by finessing and trick,
He cast off his friends, as a huntsman his pack,
For he knew when he pleas'd he could whistle them back.
Of praise a mere glutton, he swallow'd what came,
And the puff of a dunce he mistook it for fame;
Till his relish grown callous, almost to disease,
Who pepper'd the highest was surest to please.
But let us be candid, and speak out our mind,
If dunces applauded, he paid them in kind.
Ye Kenricks, ye Kellys,[48] and Woodfalls [49] so grave,
What a commerce was yours, while you got and you gave!
How did Grub-street re-echo the shouts that you rais'd,
While he was be-Roscius'd, and you were be-prais'd!
But peace to his spirit, wherever it flies,
To act as an angel, and mix with the skies:
Those poets, who owe their best fame to his skill,
Shall still be his flatterers, go where he will.
Old Shakespeare, receive him, with praise and with love,
And Beaumonts and Bens be his Kellys above.

[45] Dr. William Dodd, who three years later was hanged for forgery, in spite of Dr. Johnson's efforts to save him.

[46] Dr. William Kenrick, who 'lately read lectures at the Devil Tavern, under the Title of "The School of Shakespeare."' He had the year before written a scurrilous attack on Goldsmith in *The London Packet.*

[47] James Macpherson, author of 'Ossian,' who, as the contemporary note craftily says, 'lately, from the mere *force of his style*, wrote down the first poet of all antiquity.' He had published more recently a bad prose translation of Homer.

[48] Hugh Kelley (1739–1777), a 'sentimental' dramatist, advanced by Garrick himself as a popular rival of Goldsmith.

[49] 'Mr. William Woodfall, Printer of the Morning Chronicle' and dramatic critic.

Here Hickey reclines, a most blunt, pleasant creature,
And slander itself must allow him good nature:
He cherish'd his friend, and he relish'd a bumper;
Yet one fault he had, and that one was a thumper.
Perhaps you may ask if the man was a miser?
I answer, no, no, for he always was wiser:
Too courteous, perhaps, or obligingly flat?
His very worst foe can't accuse him of that:
Perhaps he confided in men as they go,
And so was too foolishly honest? Ah no!
Then what was his failing? come, tell it, and, burn ye!
He was, could he help it? — a special attorney.[50]

Here Reynolds [51] is laid, and, to tell you my mind,
He has not left a wiser or better behind:
His pencil was striking, resistless, and grand;
His manners were gentle, complying, and bland;
Still born to improve us in every part,
His pencil our faces, his manners our heart:
To coxcombs averse, yet most civilly steering,
When they judg'd without skill he was still hard of hearing:
When they talk'd of their Raphaels, Correggios, and stuff,
He shifted his trumpet, and only took snuff.[52]

POSTSCRIPT

After the Fourth Edition of this Poem was printed, the Publisher received an Epitaph on Mr. Whitefoord,[53] from a friend of the late Doctor Goldsmith, inclosed in a letter, of which the following is an abstract: —

'I have in my possession a sheet of paper, containing near forty lines in the Doctor's own handwriting: there are many scattered, broken verses, on Sir Jos. Reynolds, Counsellor Ridge, Mr. Beauclerk, and Mr. Whitefoord. The Epitaph on the last-mentioned gentleman is the only one that is finished, and therefore I have copied it, that you may add it to the next edition. It is a striking proof of Doctor Goldsmith's good-nature. I saw this sheet of paper in the Doctor's room, five or six days before he died; and, as I had got all the other Epitaphs, I asked him if I might take it. *"In truth you may, my Boy,"* (replied he,) *"for it will be of no use to me where I am going."*'

Here Whitefoord reclines, and deny it who can,
Though he *merrily* liv'd, he is now a *grave* man; [54]
Rare compound of oddity, frolic, and fun!
Who relish'd a joke, and rejoic'd in a pun;
Whose temper was generous, open, sincere;
A stranger to flatt'ry, a stranger to fear;
Who scatter'd around wit and humour at will;
Whose daily *bons mots* half a column might fill;
A Scotchman, from pride and from prejudice free;
A scholar, yet surely no pedant was he.

What pity, alas! that so lib'ral a mind
Should so long be to news-paper essays confin'd;
Who perhaps to the summit of science could soar,
Yet content 'if the table he set on a roar';
Whose talents to fill any station were fit,
Yet happy if Woodfall [55] confess'd him a wit.

Ye news-paper witlings! ye pert scribbling folks

---

[50] One practising in one court only.

[51] Goldsmith loved Reynolds; note the absence of any satire such as that given to Burke and Garrick.

[52] 'Sir Joshua Reynolds is so remarkably deaf as to be under the necessity of using an ear trumpet in company; he is, at the same time, equally remarkable for taking a great quantity of snuff. . . .'

[53] Caleb Whitefoord, Scotch wine-merchant and art connoisseur. He has been suspected of writing the lines himself.

[54] The pun comes from *Romeo and Juliet*, iii, 1.

[55] Henry Sampson Woodfall, printer of *The Public Advertiser* and editor of Junius's *Letters* (not the *William* Woodfall of line 115).

Who copied his squibs, and re-echoed his jokes;
Ye tame imitators, ye servile herd, come,
Still follow your master, and visit his tomb:
To deck it, bring with you festoons of the vine,
And copious libations bestow on his shrine:
Then strew all around it (you can do no less)
Cross-readings [56], *Ship-news,* and *Mistakes of the Press.*

Merry Whitefoord, farewell! for *thy* sake I admit
That a Scot may have humour, I had almost said wit:
This debt to thy mem'ry I cannot refuse,
'Thou best humour'd man with the worst humour'd muse.'

[56] Witticisms derived by reading two or three columns of a newspaper horizontally across instead of vertically and downwards. Goldsmith once said it would have given him more pleasure to be the author of Whitefoord's 'lucky inventions' than of all his own works; Johnson praised them and Horace Walpole laughed over them till he cried.

William Cowper

1731–1800

Walking with God

Gen. v. 24 [1]

OH! for a closer walk with GOD,
A calm and heav'nly frame;
A light to shine upon the road
That leads me to the Lamb!

Where is the blessedness I knew
When first I saw the LORD?
Where is the soul-refreshing view
Of JESUS, and his word?

What peaceful hours I once enjoy'd!
How sweet their mem'ry still!
But they have left an aching void,
The world can never fill.

Return, O holy Dove, return,
Sweet messenger of rest;
I hate the sins that made thee mourn,
And drove thee from my breast.

The dearest idol I have known,
Whate'er that idol be;
Help me to tear it from thy throne,
And worship only thee.

So shall my walk be close with GOD,
Calm and serene my frame;
So purer light shall mark the road
That leads me to the Lamb.

[1] The sixty-seven 'Olney Hymns' composed by Cowper were mostly written during 1771 and 1772; the remaining 281 hymns are the work of the Reverend John Newton. It was during his residence at Olney that Cowper came under Newton's influence. Published in 1779.

On the Loss of the Royal George [2]

WRITTEN WHEN THE NEWS ARRIVED,

by desire of Lady Austen, who wanted words to the March in Scipio.

TOLL for the brave —
The brave! that are no more:
All sunk beneath the wave,
Fast by their native shore.
Eight hundred of the brave,
Whose courage well was tried,
Had made the vessel heel
And laid her on her side;
A land-breeze shook the shrouds,
And she was overset;
Down went the Royal George,
With all her crew complete.

Toll for the brave —
Brave Kempenfelt is gone,
His last sea-fight is fought,
His work of glory done.
It was not in the battle,

[2] In August 1782 the *Royal George*, flagship of Admiral Kempenfelt, suddenly went down while being repaired at Portsmouth. Eight hundred men were lost, including the admiral, who had recently won a victory over the French. The poem was published in Hayley's *Life and Posthumous Writings*, 1803.

No tempest gave the shock,
She sprang no fatal leak,
She ran upon no rock;
His sword was in the sheath,
His fingers held the pen,
When Kempenfelt went down
With twice four hundred men.

Weigh the vessel up,
Once dreaded by our foes,
And mingle with your cup
The tears that England owes;
Her timbers yet are sound,
And she may float again,
Full charg'd with England's thunder,
And plough the distant main;
But Kempenfelt is gone,
His victories are o'er;
And he and his Eight hundred
Must plough the wave no more.

THE TASK [3]

from BOOK I

THE SOFA

ARGUMENT OF THE FIRST BOOK. — Historical deduction of seats, from the stool to the Sofa — A School-boy's ramble — A walk in the country — The scene described — Rural sounds as well as sights delightful — Another walk — Mistake concerning the charms of solitude corrected — Colonnades commended — Alcove, and the view from it — The wilderness — The grove — The thresher — The necessity and the benefits of exercise — The works of nature superior to, and in some instances inimitable by, art — The wearisomeness of what is commonly called a life of pleasure — Change of scene sometimes expedient — A common described, and the character of crazy Kate introduced — Gipsies — The blessings of civilized life — That state most favourable to virtue — The South Sea islanders compassionated, but chiefly Omai — His present state of mind supposed — Civilized life friendly to virtue, but not great cities — Great cities, and London in particular, allowed their due praise, but censured — Fete champetre — The book concludes with a reflection on the fatal effects of dissipation and effeminacy upon our public measures.

I SING the SOFA. I, who lately sang
Truth, Hope, and Charity,[4] and touch'd with awe
The solemn chords, and with a trembling hand,
Escap'd with pain from that advent'rous flight,
Now seek repose upon an humbler theme;
The theme though humble, yet august and proud
Th' occasion — for the Fair commands the song.
Time was, when clothing sumptuous or for use,
Save their own painted skins, our sires had none.
As yet black breeches were not; satin smooth,
Or velvet soft, or plush with shaggy pile:
The hardy chief upon the rugged rock
Wash'd by the sea, or on the grav'ly bank
Thrown up by wintry torrents roaring loud,
Fearless of wrong, repos'd his weary strength.
Those barb'rous ages past, succeeded next
The birth-day of invention; weak at first,
Dull in design, and clumsy to perform.
Joint-stools were then created; on three legs
Upborn they stood. Three legs upholding firm
A massy slab, in fashion square or round.
On such a stool immortal Alfred sat,
And sway'd the sceptre of his infant realms:
And such in ancient halls and mansions drear
May still be seen; but perforated sore,
And drill'd in holes, the solid oak is found,
By worms voracious eating through and through.
At length a generation more refin'd

[3] Cowper prefixed this advertisement to the first edition: 'The history of the following production is briefly this: — A lady, fond of blank verse, demanded a poem of that kind from the author, and gave him the SOFA for a subject. He obeyed; and, having much leisure, connected another subject with it; and, pursuing the train of thought to which his situation and turn of mind led him, brought forth at length, instead of the trifle which he at first intended, a serious affair — a Volume!' Cowper began his work, at Lady Austen's suggestion, probably in July 1783, and finished six books which were published in 1785.

[4] Titles of three poems in Cowper's first volume of 1782.

Improv'd the simple plan; made three legs four,
Gave them a twisted form vermicular,
And o'er the seat, with plenteous wadding stuff'd,
Induc'd a splendid cover, green and blue,
Yellow and red, of tap'stry richly wrought,
And woven close, or needle-work sublime.
There might ye see the piony spread wide,
The full-blown rose, the shepherd and his lass,
Lap-dog and lambkin with black staring eyes,
And parrots with twin cherries in their beak.

Now came the cane from India, smooth and bright
With Nature's varnish; sever'd into stripes
That interlac'd each other, these supplied
Of texture firm a lattice-work, that brac'd
The new machine, and it became a chair.
But restless was the chair; the back erect
Distress'd the weary loins, that felt no ease;
The slipp'ry seat betray'd the sliding part
That press'd it, and the feet hung dangling down,
Anxious in vain to find the distant floor.
These for the rich: the rest, whom fate had plac'd
In modest mediocrity, content
With base materials, sat on well-tann'd hides,
Obdurate and unyielding, glassy smooth,
With here and there a tuft of crimson yarn,
Or scarlet crewel,[5] in the cushion fixt;
If cushion might be call'd, what harder seem'd
Than the firm oak of which the frame was form'd.
No want of timber then was felt or fear'd
In Albion's happy isle. The lumber stood
Pond'rous and fixt by its own massy weight.
But elbows still were wanting; these, some say,
An alderman of Cripplegate contriv'd:
And some ascribe th' invention to a priest
Burly and big, and studious of his ease.
But, rude at first, and not with easy slope
Receding wide, they press'd against the ribs,
And bruis'd the side; and, elevated high,
Taught the rais'd shoulders to invade the ears.
Long time elaps'd or e'er our rugged sires
Complain'd, though incommodiously pent in,
And ill at ease behind. The ladies first
'Gan murmur, as became the softer sex.
Ingenious fancy, never better pleas'd
Than when employ'd t' accommodate the fair,
Heard the sweet moan with pity, and devis'd
The soft settee; one elbow at each end,
And in the midst an elbow it receiv'd,
United yet divided, twain at once.
So sit two kings of Brentford on one throne;
And so two citizens who take the air,
Close pack'd, and smiling, in a chaise and one.
But relaxation of the languid frame,
By soft recumbency of outstretch'd limbs,
Was bliss reserv'd for happier days. So slow
The growth of what is excellent; so hard
T' attain perfection in this nether world.
Thus first necessity invented stools,
Convenience next suggested elbow-chairs,
And luxury th' accomplish'd Sofa last.

The nurse sleeps sweetly, hir'd to watch the sick,
Whom snoring she disturbs. As sweetly he,
Who quits the coach-box at the midnight hour
To sleep within the carriage more secure,
His legs depending at the open door.
Sweet sleep enjoys the curate in his desk,
The tedious rector drawling o'er his head;
And sweet the clerk below. But neither sleep
Of lazy nurse, who snores the sick man dead,

[5] Worsted yarn twisted slackly or knotted.

Nor his who quits the box at midnight hour
To slumber in the carriage more secure,
Nor sleep enjoy'd by curate in his desk,
Nor yet the dozings of the clerk, are sweet,
Compar'd with the repose the Sofa yields.
Oh may I live exempted (while I live
Guiltless of pamper'd appetite obscene)
From pangs arthritic, that infest the toe
Of libertine excess. The Sofa suits
The gouty limb, 'tis true; but gouty limb,
Though on a Sofa, may I never feel:
For I have lov'd the rural walk through lanes
Of grassy swarth, close cropt by nibbling sheep,
And skirted thick with intertexture firm
Of thorny boughs; have lov'd the rural walk
O'er hills, through valleys, and by rivers' brink,
E'er since a truant boy I pass'd my bounds
T' enjoy a ramble on the banks of Thames;
And still remember, nor without regret
Of hours that sorrow since has much endear'd,
How oft, my slice of pocket store consum'd,
Still hung'ring, pennyless and far from home,
I fed on scarlet hips [6] and stony haws,[7]
Or blushing crabs,[8] or berries, that emboss
The bramble, black as jet, or sloes austere.
Hard fare! but such as boyish appetite
Disdains not; nor the palate, undeprav'd
By culinary arts, unsav'ry deems.
No Sofa then awaited my return;
Nor Sofa then I needed. Youth repairs
His wasted spirits quickly, by long toil
Incurring short fatigue; and, though our years
As life declines speed rapidly away,
And not a year but pilfers as he goes
Some youthful grace that age would gladly keep;
A tooth or auburn lock, and by degrees
Their length and colour from the locks they spare;
Th' elastic spring of an unwearied foot
That mounts the stile with ease, or leaps the fence,
That play of lungs, inhaling and again
Respiring freely the fresh air, that makes
Swift pace or steep ascent no toil to me,
Mine have not pilfer'd yet; nor yet impair'd
My relish of fair prospect; scenes that sooth'd
Or charm'd me young, no longer young, I find
Still soothing and of pow'r to charm me still.
And witness, dear companion of my walks,[9]
Whose arm this twentieth winter I perceive
Fast lock'd in mine, with pleasure such as love,
Confirm'd by long experience of thy worth
And well-tried virtues, could alone inspire —
Witness a joy that thou hast doubled long.
Thou know'st my praise of nature most sincere,
And that my raptures are not conjur'd up
To serve occasions of poetic pomp,
But genuine, and art partner of them all.
How oft upon yon eminence our pace
Has slacken'd to a pause, and we have born
The ruffling wind, scarce conscious that it blew,
While admiration, feeding at the eye,
And still unsated, dwelt upon the scene.
Thence with what pleasure have we just discern'd
The distant plough slow moving, and beside
His lab'ring team, that swerv'd not from the track,
The sturdy swain diminish'd to a boy!

[6] Ripe fruit of the rosebush.
[7] Fruit of the hawthorn.
[8] crab-apples

[9] Mary Unwin, from whom he was never separated from 1765 until 1796, the year of her death. She doubtless would have become his wife but for his third attack of madness brought on by the harmful religious fanaticism of his friend the Reverend John Newton, co-author of the *Olney Hymns*.

Here Ouse, slow winding through a level plain
Of spacious meads with cattle sprinkled o'er,
Conducts the eye along its sinuous course
Delighted. There, fast rooted in their bank,
Stand, never overlook'd, our fav'rite elms,
That screen the herdsman's solitary hut;
While far beyond, and overthwart the stream
That, as with molten glass, inlays the vale,
The sloping land recedes into the clouds;
Displaying on its varied side the grace
Of hedge-row beauties numberless, square tow'r,
Tall spire, from which the sound of cheerful bells
Just undulates upon the list'ning ear,
Groves, heaths, and smoking villages, remote.
Scenes must be beautiful, which, daily view'd,[10]
Please daily, and whose novelty survives
Long knowledge and the scrutiny of years.
Praise justly due to those that I describe.
  Nor rural sights alone, but rural sounds,
Exhilarate the spirit, and restore
The tone of languid Nature. Mighty winds,
That sweep the skirt of some far-spreading wood
Of ancient growth, make music not unlike
The dash of ocean on his winding shore,
And lull the spirit while they fill the mind;
Unnumber'd branches waving in the blast,
And all their leaves fast flutt'ring, all at once.
Nor less composure waits upon the roar
Of distant floods, or on the softer voice
Of neighb'ring fountain, or of rills that slip
Through the cleft rock, and, chiming as they fall
Upon loose pebbles, lose themselves at length
In matted grass, that with a livelier green
Betrays the secret of their silent course.
Nature inanimate employs sweet sounds,
But animated nature sweeter still,
To sooth and satisfy the human ear.
Ten thousand warblers cheer the day, and one
The live-long night: nor these alone, whose notes
Nice finger'd art must emulate in vain,
But cawing rooks, and kites that swim sublime
In still repeated circles, screaming loud,
The jay, the pie, and ev'n the boding owl
That hails the rising moon, have charms for me.
Sounds inharmonious in themselves and harsh,
Yet heard in scenes where peace for ever reigns,
And only there, please highly for their sake.

. . .

  Blest he, though undistinguish'd from the crowd
By wealth or dignity, who dwells secure,
Where man, by nature fierce, has laid aside
His fierceness, having learnt, though slow to learn,
The manners and the arts of civil life.
His wants, indeed, are many; but supply
Is obvious, plac'd within the easy reach
Of temp'rate wishes and industrious hands.
Here virtue thrives as in her proper soil;
Not rude and surly, and beset with thorns,
And terrible to sight, as when she springs
(If e'er she spring spontaneous) in remote
And barb'rous climes, where violence prevails,
And strength is lord of all; but gentle, kind,
By culture tam'd, by liberty refresh'd,
And all her fruits by radiant truth matur'd.

[10] The familiar scenes were those found between Olney and Weston. Cowper wrote to the Reverend William Unwin: 'My descriptions are all from nature: not one of them second-hand. My delineations of the heart are from my own experience: not one of them borrowed from books.'

War and the chase engross the savage whole;
War follow'd for revenge, or to supplant
The envied tenants of some happier spot,
The chase for sustenance, precarious trust!
His hard condition with severe constraint
Binds all his faculties, forbids all growth
Of wisdom, proves a school in which he learns
Sly circumvention, unrelenting hate,
Mean self-attachment, and scarce aught beside.
Thus fare the shiv'ring natives of the north,
And thus the rangers of the western world,
Where it advances far into the deep,
Towards th' antarctic. Ev'n the favour'd isles,
So lately found,[11] although the constant sun
Cheer all their seasons with a grateful smile,
Can boast but little virtue; and, inert
Through plenty, lose in morals what they gain
In manners — victims of luxurious ease.
These therefore I can pity, plac'd remote
From all that science traces, art invents,
Or inspiration teaches; and enclosed
In boundless oceans, never to be pass'd
By navigators uninform'd as they,
Or plough'd perhaps by British bark again:
But, far beyond the rest, and with most cause,
Thee, gentle savage! [12] whom no love of thee
Or thine, but curiosity perhaps,
Or else vain glory, prompted us to draw
Forth from thy native bow'rs, to show thee here
With what superior skill we can abuse
The gifts of Providence, and squander life.
The dream is past; and thou hast found again
Thy cocoas and bananas, palms and yams,
And homestall thatch'd with leaves. But hast thou found
Their former charms? And, having seen our state,
Our palaces, our ladies, and our pomp
Of equipage, our gardens, and our sports,
And heard our music; are thy simple friends,
Thy simple fare, and all thy plain delights,
As dear to thee as once? And have thy joys
Lost nothing by comparison with our's?
Rude as thou art, (for we return'd thee rude
And ignorant, except of outward show)
I cannot think thee yet so dull of heart
And spiritless, as never to regret
Sweets tasted here, and left as soon as known.
Methinks I see thee straying on the beach,
And asking of the surge that bathes thy foot
If ever it has wash'd our distant shore.
I see thee weep, and thine are honest tears,
A patriot's for his country: thou art sad
At thought of her forlorn and abject state,
From which no pow'r of thine can raise her up.
Thus fancy paints thee, and, though apt to err,
Perhaps errs little when she paints thee thus.
She tells me, too, that duly ev'ry morn
Thou climb'st the mountain top, with eager eye
Exploring far and wide the wat'ry waste
For sight of ship from England. Ev'ry speck
Seen in the dim horizon turns thee pale

---

[11] The Society and Friendly Islands, first discovered by the Spaniards in 1606, but visited by Captain Cook in 1769 and subsequent years.

[12] Omai, a young native of Otaheite, one of the Friendly Islands, who was brought to England in 1774 to satisfy the new — partly Rousseauistic — craze for the 'noble savage.' He was painted by Reynolds and lesser artists, presented at court and generally shown to the 'great world,' though educated scarcely at all. Dr. Johnson was charmed with his good manners and gentleness. He remained simple enough to call ice 'stone water' and snow 'white rain'; in declining snuff he could say simply, 'No tank you, Sir, me nose be no hungry.' Yet, as Cowper suggests, a taste of civilisation, without making him over, spoiled him for life in the South Seas. He is said to have died about 1780, before Cowper's sympathetic lines were written. For an entertaining treatment of the eighteenth century's 'return to the primitive' see Chauncey Brewster Tinker's *Nature's Simple Plan*, 1922.

With conflict of contending hopes and fears.
But comes at last the dull and dusky eve,
And sends thee to thy cabin, well-prepar'd
To dream all night of what the day denied.
Alas! expect it not. We found no bait
To tempt us in thy country. Doing good,
Disinterested good, is not our trade.
We travel far, 'tis true, but not for nought;
And must be brib'd, to compass earth again,
By other hopes and richer fruits than your's.
But, though true worth and virtue in the mild
And genial soil of cultivated life
Thrive most, and may perhaps thrive only there,
Yet not in cities oft: in proud and gay
And gain-devoted cities. Thither flow,
As to a common and most noisome sew'r,
The dregs and feculence of ev'ry land.
In cities foul example on most minds
Begets its likeness. Rank abundance breeds
In gross and pamper'd cities sloth and lust,
And wantonness and gluttonous excess.
In cities vice is hidden with most ease,
Or seen with least reproach; and virtue, taught
By frequent lapse, can hope no triumph there
Beyond th' achievement of successful flight.
I do confess them nurs'ries of the arts,
In which they flourish most; where, in the beams
Of warm encouragement, and in the eye
Of public note, they reach their perfect size.
Such London is, by taste and wealth proclaim'd
The fairest capital of all the world,
By riot and incontinence the worst.
There, touch'd by Reynolds, a dull blank becomes
A lucid mirror, in which Nature sees
All her reflected features. Bacon[13] there
Gives more than female beauty to a stone,
And Chatham's eloquence to marble lips.
Nor does the chissel occupy alone
The pow'rs of sculpture, but the style as much;
Each province of her art her equal care.
With nice incision of her guided steel
She ploughs a brazen field, and clothes a soil
So sterile with what charms soe'er she will,
The richest scen'ry and the loveliest forms.
Where finds philosophy her eagle eye,
With which she gazes at yon burning disk
Undazzled, and detects and counts his spots?
In London: where her implements exact,
With which she calculates, computes, and scans,
All distance, motion, magnitude, and now
Measures an atom, and now girds a world?
In London. Where has commerce such a mart,
So rich, so throng'd, so drain'd, and so supplied,
As London — opulent, enlarg'd, and still
Increasing, London? Babylon of old
Not more the glory of the earth than she,
A more accomplish'd world's chief glory now.
She has her praise. Now mark a spot or two,
That so much beauty would do well to purge;
And show this queen of cities, that so fair
May yet be foul; so witty, yet not wise.
It is not seemly, nor of good report,
That she is slack in discipline; more prompt
T' avenge than to prevent the breach of law:
That she is rigid in denouncing death
On petty robbers, and indulges life
And liberty, and oft-times honour too,
To peculators of the public gold:
That thieves at home must hang; but he, that puts

[13] John Bacon (1740–1799), sculptor, who had admired Cowper's first volume and sent him a print of his own monument of Chatham.

Into his overgorg'd and bloated purse
The wealth of Indian provinces, escapes.[14]
Nor is it well, nor can it come to good,
That, through profane and infidel contempt
Of holy writ, she has presum'd t' annul
And abrogate, as roundly as she may,
The total ordinance and will of God;
Advancing fashion to the post of truth,
And cent'ring all authority in modes
And customs of her own, till sabbath rites
Have dwindled into unrespected forms,
And knees and hassocks are well-nigh divorc'd.
God made the country, and man made the town.
What wonder then that health and virtue, gifts
That can alone make sweet the bitter draught
That life holds out to all, should most abound
And least be threaten'd in the fields and groves?
Possess ye, therefore, ye, who, borne about
In chariots and sedans, know no fatigue
But that of idleness, and taste no scenes
But such as art contrives, possess ye still
Your element; there only can ye shine,
There only minds like your's can do no harm.
Our groves were planted to console at noon
The pensive wand'rer in their shades. At eve
The moon-beam, sliding softly in between
The sleeping leaves, is all the light they wish,
Birds warbling all the music. We can spare
The splendour of your lamps; they but eclipse
Our softer satellite. Your songs confound
Our more harmonious notes: the thrush departs
Scar'd, and th' offended nightingale is mute.
There is a public mischief in your mirth;
It plagues your country. Folly such as your's,
Grac'd with a sword, and worthier of a fan,
Has made, what enemies could ne'er have done,
Our arch of empire, stedfast but for you,
A mutilated structure, soon to fall.

[14] A hit at Warren Hastings, or perhaps the general practises of the East India Company.

from BOOK II

THE TIMEPIECE

Oh for a lodge in some vast wilderness,
Some boundless contiguity of shade,
Where rumour of oppression and deceit,
Of unsuccessful or successful war,
Might never reach me more. My ear is pain'd,
My soul is sick, with ev'ry day's report
Of wrong and outrage with which earth is fill'd.
There is no flesh in man's obdurate heart,
It does not feel for man; the nat'ral bond
Of brotherhood is sever'd as the flax
That falls asunder at the touch of fire.
He finds his fellow guilty of a skin
Not colour'd like his own; and, having pow'r
T' enforce the wrong, for such a worthy cause
Dooms and devotes him as his lawful prey.
Lands intersected by a narrow frith
Abhor each other. Mountains interpos'd
Make enemies of nations, who had else,
Like kindred drops, been mingled into one.
Thus man devotes his brother, and destroys;
And, worse than all, and most to be deplor'd,
As human nature's broadest, foulest blot,
Chains him, and tasks him, and exacts his sweat
With stripes, that mercy, with a bleeding heart,
Weeps when she sees inflicted on a beast.
Then what is man? And what man, seeing this,

And having human feelings, does not blush,
And hang his head, to think himself a man?
I would not have a slave to till my ground,
To carry me, to fan me while I sleep,
And tremble when I wake, for all the wealth
That sinews bought and sold have ever earn'd.
No: dear as freedom is, and in my heart's
Just estimation priz'd above all price,
I had much rather be myself the slave,
And wear the bonds, than fasten them on him.
We have no slaves at home. — Then why abroad?
And they themselves, once ferried o'er the wave
That parts us, are emancipate and loos'd.
Slaves cannot breathe in England;[15] if their lungs
Receive our air, that moment they are free;
They touch our country, and their shackles fall.
That's noble, and bespeaks a nation proud
And jealous of the blessing. Spread it then,
And let it circulate through ev'ry vein
Of all your empire; that where Britain's pow'r
Is felt, mankind may feel her mercy too.

. . .

England, with all thy faults, I love thee still —
My country! and, while yet a nook is left
Where English minds and manners may be found,
Shall be constrain'd to love thee. Though thy clime
Be fickle, and thy year most part deform'd
With dripping rains, or wither'd by a frost,
I would not yet exchange thy sullen skies,
And fields without a flow'r, for warmer France
With all her vines; nor for Ausonia's groves
Of golden fruitage, and her myrtle bow'rs.
To shake thy senate, and from heights sublime
Of patriot eloquence to flash down fire
Upon thy foes, was never meant my task:
But I can feel thy fortunes, and partake
Thy joys and sorrows, with as true a heart
As any thund'rer there. And I can feel
Thy follies, too; and with a just disdain
Frown at effeminates, whose very looks
Reflect dishonour on the land I love.
How, in the name of soldiership and sense,
Should England prosper, when such things, as smooth
And tender as a girl, all essenc'd o'er
With odours, and as profligate as sweet;
Who sell their laurel for a myrtle wreath,
And love when they should fight; when such as these
Presume to lay their hand upon the ark
Of her magnificent and awful cause?
Time was when it was praise and boast enough
In ev'ry clime, and travel where we might,
That we were born her children. Praise enough
To fill th' ambition of a private man,
That Chatham's language was his mother tongue,
And Wolfe's great name compatriot with his own.
Farewell those honours, and farewell with them
The hope of such hereafter! They have fall'n
Each in his field of glory; one in arms,
And one in council — Wolfe upon the lap
Of smiling victory that moment won,
And Chatham heart-sick of his country's shame!
They made us many soldiers. Chatham, still
Consulting England's happiness at home,
Secur'd it by an unforgiving frown,
If any wrong'd her. Wolfe, where'er he fought,
Put so much of his heart into his act,

[15] Lord Mansfield gave in 1772 the court decision that 'slaves cannot breathe in England.' In 1811 the slave trade was abolished.

That his example had a magnet's force,
And all were swift to follow whom all lov'd.
Those suns are set. Oh, rise some other such!
Or all that we have left is empty talk
Of old achievements, and despair of new.

. . .

from BOOK III

THE GARDEN

I was a stricken deer, that left the herd
Long since;[16] with many an arrow deep infixt
My panting side was charg'd, when I withdrew
To seek a tranquil death in distant shades.
There was I found by one who had himself
Been hurt by th' archers. In his side he bore,
And in his hands and feet, the cruel scars.
With gentle force soliciting the darts,
He drew them forth, and heal'd, and bade me live.
Since then, with few associates, in remote
And silent woods I wander, far from those
My former partners of the peopled scene;
With few associates, and not wishing more.
Here much I ruminate, as much I may,
With other views of men and manners now
Than once, and others of a life to come.
I see that all are wand'rers, gone astray
Each in his own delusions; they are lost
In chase of fancied happiness, still woo'd
And never won. Dream after dream ensues;
And still they dream that they shall still succeed.
And still are disappointed. Rings the world
With the vain stir. I sum up half mankind,
And add two thirds of the remaining half,
And find the total of their hopes and fears
Dreams, empty dreams. . . .

[16] Cowper's first break-down came in London in 1763, where he made several attempts at suicide. He went to an asylum, remaining there until June 1765. His melancholy and religious fears made him think that he was eternally damned. The last thirty-five years of his life were spent in peaceful villages—Huntingdon, Olney, Weston, and East Dereham in Norfolk.

BOOK IV

THE WINTER EVENING

Argument of the Fourth Book.—The post comes in—The newspaper is read—The world contemplated at a distance—Address to winter—The rural amusements of a winter evening compared with the fashionable ones—Address to evening—A brown study—Fall of snow in the evening—The waggoner—A poor family-piece—The rural thief—Public houses—The multitude of them censured—The farmer's daughter: what she was—what she is—The simplicity of country manners almost lost—Causes of the change—Desertion of the country by the rich—Neglect of magistrates—The militia principally in fault—The new recruit and his transformation—Reflection on bodies corporate—The love of rural objects natural to all, and never to be totally extinguished.

Hark! 'tis the twanging horn o'er yonder bridge,
That with its wearisome but needful length
Bestrides the wintry flood, in which the moon
Sees her unwrinkled face reflected bright;—
He comes, the herald of a noisy world,
With spatter'd boots, strapp'd waist, and frozen locks;
News from all nations lumb'ring at his back.
True to his charge, the close-pack'd load behind,
Yet careless what he brings, his one concern
Is to conduct it to the destin'd inn:
And, having dropp'd th' expected bag, pass on.
He whistles as he goes, light-hearted wretch,
Cold and yet cheerful: messenger of grief
Perhaps to thousands, and of joy to some;
To him indiff'rent whether grief or joy.
Houses in ashes, and the fall of stocks,
Births, deaths, and marriages, epistles wet

With tears, that trickled down the writer's cheeks
Fast as the periods from his fluent quill,
Or charg'd with am'rous sighs of absent swains,
Or nymphs responsive, equally affect
His horse and him, unconscious of them all.
But oh th' important budget! usher'd in
With such heart-shaking music, who can say
What are its tidings? have our troops awak'd?
Or do they still, as if with opium drugg'd,
Snore to the murmurs of th' Atlantic wave?
Is India free? and does she wear her plum'd
And jewell'd turban with a smile of peace,
Or do we grind her still? The grand debate,
The popular harangue, the tart reply,
The logic, and the wisdom, and the wit,
And the loud laugh — I long to know them all;
I burn to set th' imprison'd wranglers free,
And give them voice and utt'rance once again.
Now stir the fire, and close the shutters fast,
Let fall the curtains, wheel the sofa round,
And, while the bubbling and loud-hissing urn,
Throws up a steamy column, and the cups,
That cheer but not inebriate, wait on each,
So let us welcome peaceful ev'ning in.
Not such his ev'ning, who with shining face
Sweats in the crowded theatre, and, squeez'd
And bor'd with elbow-points through both his sides,
Out-scolds the ranting actor on the stage:
Nor his, who patient stands till his feet throb,
And his head thumps, to feed upon the breath
Of patriots, bursting with heroic rage,
Or placemen, all tranquillity and smiles.
This folio of four pages, happy work!
Which not ev'n critics criticise; that holds
Inquisitive attention, while I read,
Fast bound in chains of silence, which the fair,
Though eloquent themselves, yet fear to break;
What is it, but a map of busy life,
Its fluctuations, and its vast concerns?
Here runs the mountainous and craggy ridge
That tempts ambition. On the summit see
The seals of office glitter in his eyes;
He climbs, he pants, he grasps them! At his heels,
Close at his heels, a demagogue ascends,
And with a dext'rous jerk soon twists him down,
And wins them, but to lose them in his turn.
Here rills of oily eloquence in soft
Meanders lubricate the course they take;
The modest speaker is asham'd and griev'd
T' engross a moment's notice, and yet begs,
Begs a propitious ear for his poor thoughts,
However trivial all that he conceives.
Sweet bashfulness! it claims at least this praise,
The dearth of information and good sense
That it foretells us always comes to pass.
Cat'racts of declamation thunder here;
There forests of no meaning spread the page,
In which all comprehension wanders, lost;
While fields of pleasantry amuse us there
With merry descants on a nation's woes.
The rest appears a wilderness of strange
But gay confusion; roses for the cheeks,
And lilies for the brows of faded age,
Teeth for the toothless, ringlets for the bald,
Heav'n, earth, and ocean, plunder'd of their sweets,
Nectareous essences, Olympian dews,
Sermons, and city feasts, and fav'rite airs,
Æthereal journies, submarine exploits,
And Katterfelto,[17] with his hair on end

[17] A sleight-of-hand expert whose popular catch-phrase was, 'Wonders! Wonders! Wonders!'

At his own wonders, wond'ring for his bread.

'Tis pleasant through the loop-holes of retreat
To peep at such a world; to see the stir
Of the great Babel, and not feel the crowd;
To hear the roar she sends through all her gates
At a safe distance, where the dying sound
Falls a soft murmur on th' uninjur'd ear.
Thus sitting, and surveying thus at ease
The globe and its concerns, I seem advanc'd
To some secure and more than mortal height,
That lib'rates and exempts me from them all.
It turns submitted to my view, turns round
With all its generations; I behold
The tumult, and am still. The sound of war
Has lost its terrors ere it reaches me;
Grieves, but alarms me not. I mourn the pride
And av'rice that make man a wolf to man;
Hear the faint echo of those brazen throats
By which he speaks the language of his heart,
And sigh, but never tremble at the sound.
He travels and expatiates, as the bee
From flow'r to flow'r, so he from land to land;
The manners, customs, policy of all
Pay contribution to the store he gleans;
He sucks intelligence in ev'ry clime,
And spreads the honey of his deep research
At his return — a rich repast for me.
He travels, and I too. I tread his deck,
Ascend his topmast, through his peering eyes
Discover countries, with a kindred heart
Suffer his woes, and share in his escapes;
While fancy, like the finger of a clock,
Runs the great circuit, and is still at home.

Oh Winter, ruler of th' inverted year,
Thy scatter'd hair with sleet like ashes fill'd,
Thy breath congeal'd upon thy lips, thy cheeks
Fring'd with a beard made white with other snows
Than those of age, thy forehead wrapt in clouds,
A leafless branch thy sceptre, and thy throne
A sliding car, indebted to no wheels,
But urg'd by storms along its slipp'ry way,
I love thee, all unlovely as thou seem'st,
And dreaded as thou art! Thou hold'st the sun
A pris'ner in the yet undawning east,
Short'ning his journey between morn and noon,
And hurrying him, impatient of his stay,
Down to the rosy west; but kindly still
Compensating his loss with added hours
Of social converse and instructive ease,
And gath'ring, at short notice, in one group
The family dispers'd, and fixing thought,
Not less dispers'd by day-light and its cares.
I crown thee king of intimate delights,
Fire-side enjoyments, home-born happiness,
And all the comforts that the lowly roof
Of undisturb'd retirement, and the hours
Of long uninterrupted ev'ning, know.
No rattling wheels stop short before these gates;
No powder'd pert, proficient in the art
Of sounding an alarm, assaults these doors
Till the street rings; no stationary steeds
Cough their own knell, while, heedless of the sound,
The silent circle fan themselves, and quake:
But here the needle plies its busy task,
The pattern grows, the well-depicted flow'r,
Wrought patiently into the snowy lawn,
Unfolds its bosom; buds, and leaves, and sprigs,
And curling tendrils, gracefully dispos'd,
Follow the nimble finger of the fair;
A wreath that cannot fade, of flow'rs that blow

With most success when all besides decay.
The poet's or historian's page, by one
Made vocal for th' amusement of the rest;
The sprightly lyre, whose treasure of sweet sounds
The touch from many a trembling chord shakes out;
And the clear voice symphonious, yet distinct,
And in the charming strife triumphant still;
Beguile the night, and set a keener edge
On female industry: the threaded steel
Flies swiftly, and, unfelt, the task proceeds.
The volume clos'd, the customary rites
Of the last meal commence. A Roman meal;
Such as the mistress of the world once found
Delicious, when her patriots of high note,
Perhaps by moonlight, at their humble doors,
And under an old oak's domestic shade,
Enjoy'd — spare feast! — a radish and an egg!
Discourse ensues, not trivial, yet not dull,
Nor such as with a frown forbids the play
Of fancy, or proscribes the sound of mirth:
Nor do we madly, like an impious world,
Who deem religion frenzy, and the God
That made them an intruder on their joys,
Start at his awful name, or deem his praise
A jarring note. Themes of a graver tone,
Exciting oft our gratitude and love,
While we retrace with mem'ry's pointing wand,
That calls the past to our exact review,
The dangers we have 'scap'd, the broken snare,
The disappointd foe, deliv'rance found
Unlook'd for, life preserv'd and peace restor'd —
Fruits of omnipotent eternal love.
Oh ev'nings worthy of the gods! exclaim'd
The Sabine bard.[18] Oh ev'nings, I reply,
More to be priz'd and coveted than yours,
As more illumin'd, and with nobler truths,
That I, and mine, and those we love, enjoy.
  Is winter hideous in a garb like this?
Needs he the tragic fur, the smoke of lamps,
The pent-up breath of an unsav'ry throng,
To thaw him into feeling; or the smart
And snappish dialogue, that flippant wits
Call comedy, to prompt him with a smile?
The self-complacent actor, when he views
(Stealing a side-long glance at a full house)
The slope of faces, from the floor to th' roof,
(As if one master-spring controul'd them all)
Relax'd into an universal grin,
Sees not a count'nance there that speaks of joy
Half so refin'd or so sincere as our's.
Cards were superfluous here, with all the tricks
That idleness has ever yet contriv'd
To fill the void of an unfurnish'd brain,
To palliate dulness, and give time a shove.
Time, as he passes us, has a dove's wing,
Unsoil'd, and swift, and of a silken sound;
But the world's time is time in masquerade!
Their's, should I paint him, has his pinions fledg'd
With motley plumes; and, where the peacock shows
His azure eyes, is tinctur'd black and red
With spots quadrangular of di'mond form,
Ensanguin'd hearts, clubs typical of strife,
And spades, the emblem of untimely graves.
What should be and what was an hourglass once,
Becomes a dice-box, and a billiard mast
Well does the work of his destructive scythe.

[18] Horace: *Satires*, Bk. II, vi, l. 65.

Thus deck'd, he charms a world whom fashion blinds
To his true worth, most pleas'd when idle most;
Whose only happy are their wasted hours.
Ev'n misses, at whose age their mothers wore
The back-string and the bib, assume the dress
Of womanhood, sit pupils in the school
Of card-devoted time, and, night by night,
Plac'd at some vacant corner of the board,
Learn ev'ry trick, and soon play all the game.
But truce with censure. Roving as I rove,
Where shall I find an end, or how proceed?
As he that travels far oft turns aside
To view some rugged rock or mould'ring tow'r,
Which, seen, delights him not; then, coming home,
Describes and prints it, that the world may know
How far he went for what was nothing worth;
So I, with brush in hand and pallet spread,
With colours mix'd for a far diff'rent use,
Paint cards and dolls, and ev'ry idle thing
That fancy finds in her excursive flights.
Come, Ev'ning, once again, season of peace;
Return, sweet Ev'ning, and continue long!
Methinks I see thee in the streaky west,
With matron-step slow-moving, while the night
Treads on thy sweeping train; one hand employ'd
In letting fall the curtain of repose
On bird and beast, the other charg'd for man
With sweet oblivion of the cares of day:
Not sumptuously adorn'd, nor needing aid,
Like homely featur'd night, of clust'ring gems;
A star or two, just twinkling on thy brow,
Suffices thee; save that the moon is thine
No less than her's, not worn indeed on high
With ostentatious pageantry, but set
With modest grandeur in thy purple zone,
Resplendent less, but of an ampler round.
Come then, and thou shalt find thy vot'ry calm,
Or make me so. Composure is thy gift:
And, whether I devote thy gentle hours
To books, to music, or the poet's toil;
To weaving nets for bird-alluring fruit;
Or twining silken threads round iv'ry reels,
When they command whom man was born to please;
I slight thee not, but make thee welcome still.
Just when our drawing-rooms begin to blaze
With lights, by clear reflection multiplied
From many a mirror, in which he of Gath,
Goliath, might have seen his giant bulk
Whole, without stooping, tow'ring crest and all,
My pleasures, too, begin. But me, perhaps,
The glowing hearth may satisfy awhile
With faint illumination, that uplifts
The shadow to the ceiling, there by fits
Dancing uncouthly to the quiv'ring flame.
Not undelightful is an hour to me
So spent in parlour twilight: such a gloom
Suits well the thoughtful or unthinking mind,
The mind contemplative, with some new theme
Pregnant, or indispos'd alike to all.
Laugh ye, who boast your more mercurial pow'rs,
That never feel a stupor, know no pause,
Nor need one; I am conscious, and confess,
Fearless, a soul that does not always think.
Me oft has fancy, ludicrous and wild,
Sooth'd with a waking dream of houses, tow'rs,
Trees, churches, and strange visages, express'd
In the red cinders, while with poring eye
I gaz'd, myself creating what I saw.
Nor less amus'd have I quiescent watch'd

The sooty films that play upon the bars,
Pendulous, and foreboding, in the view
Of superstition, prophesying still,
Though still deceiv'd, some stranger's near approach.
'Tis thus the understanding takes repose
In indolent vacuity of thought,
And sleeps and is refresh'd. Meanwhile the face
Conceals the mood lethargic with a mask
Of deep deliberation, as the man
Were task'd to his full strength, absorb'd and lost.
Thus oft, reclin'd at ease, I lose an hour
At ev'ning, till at length the freezing blast,
That sweeps the bolted shutter, summons home
The recollected pow'rs; and, snapping short
The glassy threads, with which the fancy weaves
Her brittle toys, restores me to myself.
How calm is my recess; and how the frost,
Raging abroad, and the rough wind, endear
The silence and the warmth enjoy'd within!
I saw the woods and fields, at close of day,
A variegated show; the meadows green,
Though faded; and the lands, where lately wav'd
The golden harvest, of a mellow brown,
Upturn'd so lately by the forceful share.
I saw far off the weedy fallows smile
With verdure not unprofitable, graz'd
By flocks, fast feeding, and selecting each
His fav'rite herb; while all the leafless groves,
That skirt th' horizon, wore a sable hue,
Scarce notic'd in the kindred dusk of eve.
To-morrow brings a change, a total change!
Which even now, though silently perform'd,
And slowly, and by most unfelt, the face
Of universal nature undergoes.
Fast falls a fleecy show'r: the downy flakes,
Descending, and with never-ceasing lapse,
Softly alighting upon all below,
Assimilate all objects. Earth receives
Gladly the thick'ning mantle; and the green
And tender blade, that fear'd the chilling blast,
Escapes unhurt beneath so warm a veil.
In such a world; so thorny, and where none
Finds happiness unblighted; or, if found,
Without some thistly sorrow at its side;
It seems the part of wisdom, and no sin
Against the law of love, to measure lots
With less distinguish'd than ourselves; that thus
We may with patience bear our mod'rate ills,
And sympathise with others, suff'ring more.
Ill fares the trav'ller now, and he that stalks
In pond'rous boots beside his reeking team.
The wain goes heavily, impeded sore
By congregated loads adhering close
To the clogg'd wheels; and in its sluggish pace,
Noiseless, appears a moving hill of snow.
The toiling steeds expand the nostril wide,
While ev'ry breath, by respiration strong
Forc'd downward, is consolidated soon
Upon their jutting chests. He, form'd to bear
The pelting brunt of the tempestuous night,
With half-shut eyes, and pucker'd cheeks, and teeth
Presented bare against the storm, plods on.
One hand secures his hat, save when with both
He brandishes his pliant length of whip,
Resounding oft, and never heard in vain.
Oh happy; and, in my account, denied
That sensibility of pain with which
Refinement is endued, thrice happy thou!
Thy frame, robust and hardy, feels indeed
The piercing cold, but feels it unimpair'd.
The learned finger never need explore
Thy vig'rous pulse; and the unhealthful east,

That breathes the spleen, and searches ev'ry bone
Of the infirm, is wholesome air to thee.
Thy days roll on, exempt from household care;
The waggon is thy wife; and the poor beasts,
That drag the dull companion to and fro,
Thine helpless charge, dependent on thy care.
Ah, treat them kindly! rude as thou appear'st,
Yet show that thou hast mercy! which the great,
With needless hurry whirl'd from place to place,
Humane as they would seem, not always show.
Poor, yet industrious, modest, quiet, neat;
Such claim compassion in a night like this,
And have a friend in ev'ry feeling heart.
Warm'd, while it lasts, by labour, all day long
They brave the season, and yet find at eve,
Ill clad and fed but sparely, time to cool.
The frugal housewife trembles when she lights
Her scanty stock of brush-wood, blazing clear,
But dying soon, like all terrestrial joys.
The few small embers left she nurses well;
And, while her infant race, with outspread hands
And crowded knees, sit cow'ring o'er the sparks,
Retires, content to quake, so they be warm'd.
The man feels least, as more inur'd than she
To winter, and the current in his veins
More briskly mov'd by his severer toil;
Yet he, too, finds his own distress in their's
The taper soon extinguish'd, which I saw
Dangled along at the cold finger's end
Just when the day declin'd, and the brown loaf
Lodg'd on the shelf, half eaten, without sauce
Of sav'ry cheese, or butter, costlier still;
Sleep seems their only refuge: for, alas,
Where penury is felt the thought is chain'd,
And sweet colloquial pleasures are but few!
With all this thrift they thrive not. All the care
Ingenious parsimony takes but just
Saves the small inventory, bed, and stool,
Skillet, and old carv'd chest, from public sale.
They live, and live without extorted alms
From grudging hands; but other boast have none
To sooth their honest pride, that scorns to beg,
Nor comfort else, but in their mutual love.
I praise you much, ye meek and patient pair,
For ye are worthy; choosing rather far
A dry but independent crust, hard earn'd,
And eaten with a sigh, than to endure
The rugged frowns and insolent rebuffs
Of knaves in office, partial in the work
Of distribution; lib'ral of their aid
To clam'rous importunity in rags,
But oft-times deaf to suppliants, who would blush
To wear a tatter'd garb however coarse,
Whom famine cannot reconcile to filth:
These ask with painful shyness, and, refus'd
Because deserving, silently retire!
But be ye of good courage! Time itself
Shall much befriend you. Time shall give increase;
And all your num'rous progeny, well-train'd,
But helpless, in few years shall find their hands,
And labour too. Meanwhile ye shall not want
What, conscious of your virtues, we can spare,
Nor what a wealthier than ourselves may send.

I mean the man, who, when the distant poor
Need help, denies them nothing but his name.
But poverty, with most who whimper forth
Their long complaints, is self-inflicted woe;
Th' effect of laziness or sottish waste.
Now goes the nightly thief prowling abroad
For plunder; much solicitous how best
He may compensate for a day of sloth
By works of darkness and nocturnal wrong.
Woe to the gard'ner's pale, the farmer's hedge,
Plash'd neatly, and secur'd with driven stakes
Deep in the loamy bank. Uptorn by strength,
Resistless in so bad a cause, but lame
To better deeds, he bundles up the spoil —
An ass's burden — and, when laden most
And heaviest, light of foot, steals fast away.
Nor does the boarded hovel better guard
The well-stack'd pile of riven logs and roots
From his pernicious force. Nor will he leave
Unwrench'd the door, however well secur'd,
Where Chanticleer amidst his haram sleeps
In unsuspecting pomp. Twitch'd from the perch,
He gives the princely bird, with all his wives,
To his voracious bag, struggling in vain,
And loudly wond'ring at the sudden change. —
Nor this to feed his own! 'Twere some excuse
Did pity of their suff'rings warp aside
His principle, and tempt him into sin
For their support, so destitute. — But they
Neglected pine at home; themselves, as more
Expos'd than others, with less scruple made
His victims, robb'd of their defenceless all.
Cruel is all he does. 'Tis quenchless thirst
Of ruinous ebriety that prompts
His ev'ry action, and imbrutes the man.
Oh for a law to noose the villain's neck
Who starves his own; who persecutes the blood
He gave them in his children's veins, and hates
And wrongs the woman he has sworn to love!
Pass where we may, through city or through town,
Village, or hamlet, of this merry land,
Though lean and beggar'd, ev'ry twentieth pace
Conducts th' unguarded nose to such a whiff
Of stale debauch, forth-issuing from the styes
That law has licens'd, as makes temp'rance reel.
There sit, involv'd and lost in curling clouds
Of Indian fume, and guzzling deep, the boor,
The lackey, and the groom: the craftsman there
Takes a Lethean leave of all his toil;
Smith, cobbler, joiner, he that plies the shears,
And he that kneads the dough; all loud alike,
All learned, and all drunk! The fiddle screams
Plaintive and piteous, as it wept and wail'd
Its wasted tones and harmony unheard:
Fierce the dispute, whate'er the theme; while she,
Fell Discord, arbitress of such debate,
Perch'd on the sign-post, holds with even hand
Her undecisive scales. In this she lays
A weight of ignorance; in that, of pride;
And smiles, delighted with th' eternal poise.

Dire is the frequent curse, and its twin sound
The cheek-distending oath, not to be prais'd
As ornamental, musical, polite,
Like those which modern senators employ,
Whose oath is rhet'ric, and who swear for fame!
Behold the schools in which plebeian minds,
Once simple, are initiated in arts
Which some may practise with politer grace,
But none with readier skill! — 'tis here they learn
The road that leads, from competence and peace,
To indigence and rapine; till at last
Society, grown weary of the load,
Shakes her encumber'd lap, and casts them out.
But censure profits little: vain th' attempt
To advertise in verse a public pest,
That, like the filth with which the peasant feeds
His hungry acres, stinks, and is of use.
Th' excise is fatten'd with the rich result
Of all this riot; and ten thousand casks,
For ever dribbling out their base contents,
Touch'd by the Midas finger of the state,
Bleed gold for ministers to sport away.
Drink, and be mad, then; 'tis your country bids!
Gloriously drunk, obey th' important call!
Her cause demands th' assistance of your throats; —
Ye all can swallow, and she asks no more.
  Would I had fall'n upon those happier days
That poets celebrate; those golden times,
And those Arcadian scenes, that Maro sings,
And Sidney, warbler of poetic prose.
Nymphs were Dianas then, and swains had hearts
That felt their virtues: innocence, it seems,
From courts dismiss'd, found shelter in the groves;
The footsteps of simplicity, impress'd
Upon the yielding herbage, (so they sing)
Then were not all effac'd: then speech profane,
And manners profligate, were rarely found;
Observ'd as prodigies, and soon reclaim'd.
Vain wish! those days were never: airy dreams
Sat for the picture; and the poet's hand,
Imparting substance to an empty shade,
Impos'd a gay delirium for a truth.
Grant it: — I still must envy them an age
That favour'd such a dream; in days like these
Impossible, when virtue is so scarce,
That to suppose a scene where she presides,
Is tramontane, and stumbles all belief.
No: we are polish'd now! the rural lass,
Whom once her virgin modesty and grace,
Her artless manners, and her neat attire,
So dignified, that she was hardly less
Than the fair shepherdess of old romance,
Is seen no more. The character is lost!
Her head, adorn'd with lappets pinn'd aloft,
And ribbands streaming gay, superbly rais'd,
And magnified beyond all human size,
Indebted to some smart wig-weaver's hand
For more than half the tresses it sustains;
Her elbows ruffled, and her tott'ring form
Ill propp'd upon French heels, she might be deem'd
(But that the basket dangling on her arm
Interprets her more truly) of a rank
Too proud for dairy work, or sale of eggs.
Expect her soon with foot-boy at her heels,
No longer blushing for her awkward load,
Her train and her umbrella all her care!
  The town has ting'd the country; and the stain
Appears a spot upon a vestal's robe,
The worse for what it soils. The fashion runs

Down into scenes still rural; but, alas,
Scenes rarely grac'd with rural manners now!
Time was when, in the pastoral retreat,
Th' unguarded door was safe; men did not watch
T' invade another's right, or guard their own.
Then sleep was undisturb'd by fear, unscar'd
By drunken howlings; and the chilling tale
Of midnight murder was a wonder heard
With doubtful credit, told to frighten babes.
But farewell now to unsuspicious nights,
And slumbers unalarm'd! Now, ere you sleep,
See that your polish'd arms be prim'd with care,
And drop the night-bolt; — ruffians are abroad;
And the first larum of the cock's shrill throat
May prove a trumpet, summoning your ear
To horrid sounds of hostile feet within.
Ev'n day-light has its dangers; and the walk
Through pathless wastes and woods, unconscious once
Of other tenants than melodious birds,
Or harmless flocks, is hazardous and bold.
Lamented change! to which full many a cause
Invet'rate, hopeless of a cure, conspires.
The course of human things from good to ill,
From ill to worse, is fatal, never fails.
Increase of pow'r begets increase of wealth;
Wealth luxury, and luxury excess;
Excess, the scrofulous and itchy plague
That seizes first the opulent, descends
To the next rank contagious, and in time
Taints downward all the graduated scale
Of order, from the chariot to the plough.
The rich, and they that have an arm to check
The license of the lowest in degree,
Desert their office; and themselves, intent
On pleasure, haunt the capital, and thus
To all the violence of lawless hands
Resign the scenes their presence might protect.
Authority herself not seldom sleeps,
Though resident, and witness of the wrong.
The plump convivial parson often bears
The magisterial sword in vain, and lays
His rev'rence and his worship both to rest
On the same cushion of habitual sloth.
Perhaps timidity restrains his arm;
When he should strike he trembles, and sets free,
Himself enslav'd by terror of the band,
Th' audacious convict, whom he dares not bind.
Perhaps, though by profession ghostly pure,
He too may have his vice, and sometimes prove
Less dainty than becomes his grave outside
In lucrative concerns. Examine well
His milk-white hand; the palm is hardly clean —
But here and there an ugly smutch appears.
Foh! 'twas a bribe that left it: he has touch'd
Corruption! Whoso seeks an audit here
Propitious, pays his tribute, game or fish,
Wild-fowl or ven'son; and his errand speeds.

But faster far, and more than all the rest,
A noble cause, which none who bears a spark
Of public virtue ever wish'd remov'd,
Works the deplor'd and mischievous effect.
'Tis universal soldiership has stabb'd
The heart of merit in the meaner class.
Arms, through the vanity and brainless rage
Of those that bear them, in whatever cause,
Seem most at variance with all moral good,
And incompatible with serious thought.

The clown, the child of nature, without guile,
Blest with an infant's ignorance of all
But his own simple pleasures; now and then
A wrestling-match, a foot-race, or a fair;
Is ballotted, and trembles at the news:
Sheepish he doffs his hat, and, mumbling, swears
A bible-oath to be whate'er they please,
To do he knows not what! The task perform'd,
That instant he becomes the serjeant's care,
His pupil, and his torment, and his jest.
His awkward gait, his introverted toes,
Bent knees, round shoulders, and dejected looks,
Procure him many a curse. By slow degrees,
Unapt to learn, and form'd of stubborn stuff,
He yet by slow degrees puts off himself,
Grows conscious of a change, and likes it well:
He stands erect; his slouch becomes a walk;
He steps right onward, martial in his air,
His form and movement; is as smart above
As meal and larded locks can make him; wears
His hat, or his plum'd helmet, with a grace;
And, his three years of heroship expir'd,
Returns indignant to the slighted plough.
He hates the field, in which no fife or drum
Attends him; drives his cattle to a march;
And sighs for the smart comrades he has left.
'Twere well if his exterior change were all—
But with his clumsy port the wretch has lost
His ignorance and harmless manners too!
To swear, to game, to drink; to show at home
By lewdness, idleness, and sabbath-breach,
The great proficiency he made abroad;
T' astonish and to grieve his gazing friends,
To break some maiden's and his mother's heart;
To be a pest where he was useful once;
Are his sole aim, and all his glory, now!
Man in society is like a flow'r
Blown in its native bed: 'tis there alone
His faculties, expanded in full bloom,
Shine out; there only reach their proper use.
But man, associated and leagu'd with man
By regal warrant, or self-join'd by bond
For int'rest-sake, or swarming into clans
Beneath one head for purposes of war,
Like flow'rs selected from the rest, and bound
And bundled close to fill some crowded vase,
Fades rapidly, and, by compression marr'd,
Contracts defilement not to be endur'd.
Hence charter'd boroughs are such public plagues;
And burghers, men immaculate perhaps
In all their private functions, once combin'd,
Become a loathsome body, only fit
For dissolution, hurtful to the main.
Hence merchants, unimpeachable of sin
Against the charities of domestic life,
Incorporated, seem at once to lose
Their nature; and, disclaiming all regard
For mercy and the common rights of man,
Build factories with blood, conducting trade
At the sword's point, and dyeing the white robe
Of innocent commercial justice red.
Hence, too, the field of glory, as the world
Misdeems it, dazzled by its bright array,
With all its majesty of thund'ring pomp,
Enchanting music, and immortal wreaths,
Is but a school where thoughtlessness is taught
On principle, where foppery atones
For folly, gallantry for ev'ry vice.
But, slighted as it is, and by the great
Abandon'd, and, which still I more regret,
Infected with the manners and the modes
It knew not once, the country wins me still.

I never fram'd a wish, or form'd a plan,
That flatter'd me with hopes of earthly bliss,
But there I laid the scene. There early stray'd
My fancy, ere yet liberty of choice
Had found me, or the hope of being free.
My very dreams were rural; rural, too,
The first-born efforts of my youthful muse,
Sportive, and jingling her poetic bells
Ere yet her ear was mistress of their pow'rs.
No bard could please me but whose lyre was tun'd
To Nature's praises. Heroes and their feats
Fatigued me, never weary of the pipe
Of Tityrus, assembling, as he sang,
The rustic throng beneath his fav'rite beech.
Then Milton had indeed a poet's charms:
New to my taste, his Paradise surpass'd
The struggling efforts of my boyish tongue
To speak its excellence. I danced for joy.
I marvell'd much that, at so ripe an age
As twice sev'n years, his beauties had then first
Engag'd my wonder; and, admiring still,
And still admiring, with regret suppos'd
The joy half lost because not sooner found.
Thee too, enamour'd of the life I lov'd,
Pathetic in its praise, in its pursuit
Determin'd, and possessing it at last
With transports such as favour'd lovers feel,
I studied, priz'd, and wish'd that I had known,
Ingenious Cowley! and, though now reclaim'd
By modern lights from an erroneous taste,
I cannot but lament thy splendid wit
Entangled in the cobwebs of the schools.
I still revere thee, courtly though retir'd;
Though stretch'd at ease in Chertsey's silent bow'rs,
Not unemploy'd; and finding rich amends
For a lost world in solitude and verse.
'Tis born with all: the love of Nature's works
Is an ingredient in the compound man,
Infus'd at the creation of the kind.
And, though th' Almighty Maker has throughout
Discriminated each from each, by strokes
And touches of his hand, with so much art
Diversified, that two were never found
Twins at all points — yet this obtains in all,
That all discern a beauty in his works,
And all can taste them: minds that have been form'd
And tutor'd, with a relish more exact,
But none without some relish, none unmov'd.
It is a flame that dies not even there,
Where nothing feeds it: neither business, crowds,
Nor habits of luxurious city-life;
Whatever else they smother of true worth
In human bosoms; quench it, or abate.
The villas with which London stands begirt,
Like a swarth Indian with his belt of beads,
Prove it. A breath of unadult'rate air,
The glimpse of a green pasture, how they cheer
The citizen, and brace his languid frame!
Ev'n in the stifling bosom of the town,
A garden, in which nothing thrives, has charms
That soothe the rich possessor; much consol'd,
That here and there some sprigs of mournful mint,
Of nightshade, or valerian, grace the well
He cultivates. These serve him with a hint
That nature lives; that sight-refreshing green
Is still the liv'ry she delights to wear,
Though sickly samples of th' exub'rant whole.
What are the casements lin'd with creeping herbs,
The prouder sashes fronted with a range
Of orange, myrtle, or the fragrant weed,

The Frenchman's darling? are they not all proofs
That man, immur'd in cities, still retains
His inborn inextinguishable thirst
Of rural scenes, compensating his loss
By supplemental shifts, the best he may?
The most unfurnish'd with the means of life,
And they that never pass their brick-wall bounds
To range the fields and treat their lungs with air,
Yet feel the burning instinct: over head
Suspend their crazy boxes, planted thick,
And water'd duly. There the pitcher stands
A fragment, and the spoutless tea-pot there;
Sad witnesses how close-pent man regrets
The country, with what ardour he contrives
A peep at nature, when he can no more.
Hail, therefore, patroness of health, and ease,
And contemplation, heart-consoling joys
And harmless pleasures, in the throng'd abode
Of multitudes unknown! hail, rural life!
Address himself who will to the pursuit
Of honours, or emolument, or fame;
I shall not add myself to such a chase,
Thwart his attempts, or envy his success.
Some must be great. Great offices will have
Great talents. And God gives to ev'ry man
The virtue, temper, understanding, taste,
That lifts him into life; and lets him fall
Just in the niche he was ordain'd to fill.
To the deliv'rer of an injur'd land
He gives a tongue t' enlarge upon, an heart
To feel, and courage to redress her wrongs;
To monarchs dignity; to judges sense;
To artists ingenuity and skill;
To me an unambitious mind, content
In the low vale of life, that early felt
A wish for ease and leisure, and ere long
Found here that leisure and that ease I wish'd.

The Dog and the Water-lily[19]

NO FABLE

THE noon was shady, and soft airs
Swept Ouse's silent tide,
When, 'scap'd from literary cares,
I wander'd on his side.

My spaniel, prettiest of his race,
And high in pedigree,
(Two nymphs,[20] adorn'd with ev'ry grace,
That spaniel found for me)

Now wanton'd lost in flags and reeds,
Now starting into sight
Pursued the swallow o'er the meads
With scarce a slower flight.

It was the time when Ouse display'd
His lilies newly blown;
Their beauties I intent survey'd;
And one I wish'd my own.

With cane extended far I sought
To steer it close to land;
But still the prize, though nearly caught,
Escap'd my eager hand.

Beau marked my unsuccessful pains
With fixt consid'rate face,
And puzzling set his puppy brains
To comprehend the case.

But with a chirrup clear and strong,
Dispersing all his dream,
I thence withdrew, and follow'd long
The windings of the stream.

My ramble finish'd, I return'd.
Beau trotting far before
The floating wreath again discern'd,
And plunging left the shore.

I saw him with that lily cropp'd
Impatient swim to meet
My quick approach, and soon he dropp'd
The treasure at my feet.

---

[19] Written in August 1788; published in *The Gentleman's Magazine*, December 1791.
[20] Sir Robert Gunning's daughters. [Cowper.]

Charm'd with the sight, the world, I cried,
Shall hear of this thy deed,
My dog shall mortify the pride
Of man's superior breed;

But, chief, myself I will enjoin,
Awake at duty's call,
To show a love as prompt as thine
To Him who gives me all.

On the Receipt of My Mother's Picture out of Norfolk[21]

The Gift of My Cousin Ann Bodham

Oh that those lips had language! Life has pass'd
With me but roughly since I heard thee last.
Those lips are thine — thy own sweet smiles I see,
The same that oft in childhood solaced me;
Voice only fails, else, how distinct they say,
"Grieve not, my child, chase all thy fears away!"
The meek intelligence of those dear eyes
(Blest be the art that can immortalize,
The art that baffles time's tyrannic claim
To quench it) here shines on me still the same.
Faithful remembrancer of one so dear,
Oh welcome guest, though unexpected, here!
Who bidd'st me honour with an artless song,
Affectionate, a mother lost so long,
I will obey, not willingly alone,
But gladly, as the precept were her own;
And, while that face renews my filial grief,
Fancy shall weave a charm for my relief —
Shall steep me in Elysian reverie,
A momentary dream, that thou art she.
My mother! when I learn'd that thou wast dead,
Say, wast thou conscious of the tears I shed?
Hover'd thy spirit o'er thy sorrowing son,
Wretch even then, life's journey just begun?
Perhaps thou gav'st me, though unseen, a kiss;
Perhaps a tear, if souls can weep in bliss —
Ah that maternal smile! it answers — Yes.
I heard the bell toll'd on thy burial day,
I saw the hearse that bore thee slow away,
And, turning from my nurs'ry window, drew
A long, long sigh, and wept a last adieu!
But was it such? — It was. — Where thou art gone
Adieus and farewells are a sound unknown.
May I but meet thee on that peaceful shore,
The parting sound shall pass my lips no more!
Thy maidens griev'd themselves at my concern,
Oft gave me promise of a quick return.
What ardently I wish'd, I long believ'd,
And, disappointed still, was still deceiv'd;
By disappointment every day beguil'd,
Dupe of *to-morrow* even from a child.
Thus many a sad to-morrow came and went,
Till, all my stock of infant sorrow spent,
I learn'd at last submission to my lot;
But, though I less deplor'd thee, ne'er forgot.
Where once we dwelt our name is heard no more,
Children not thine have trod my nurs'ry floor;
And where the gard'ner Robin, day by day,
Drew me to school along the public way,
Delighted with my bauble coach, and wrapt
In scarlet mantle warm, and velvet capt,
'Tis now become a history little known,
That once we call'd the past'ral house[22] our own.
Short-liv'd possession! but the record fair
That mem'ry keeps of all thy kindness there,

[21] Written in February 1790; published in a pamphlet together with *The Dog and the Water-Lily* — but without Cowper's sanction — in 1798. Cowper's mother died on 12 November 1737, when he was not quite six years old.

[22] The rectory of Great Berkhampstead, Hertfordshire, Cowper's birthplace.

Still outlives many a storm that has effac'd
A thousand other themes less deeply trac'd.
Thy nightly visits to my chamber made,
That thou might'st know me safe and warmly laid;
Thy morning bounties ere I left my home,
The biscuit, or confectionary plum;
The fragrant waters on my cheeks bestow'd
By thy own hand, till fresh they shone and glow'd;
All this, and more endearing still than all,
Thy constant flow of love, that knew no fall,
Ne'er roughen'd by those cataracts and brakes
That humour interpos'd too often makes;
All this still legible in mem'ry's page,
And still to be so, to my latest age,
Adds joy to duty, makes me glad to pay
Such honours to thee as my numbers may;
Perhaps a frail memorial, but sincere,
Not scorn'd in heav'n, though little notic'd here.

Could time, his flight revers'd, restore the hours,
When, playing with thy vesture's tissued flow'rs,
The violet, the pink, and jessamine,
I prick'd them into paper with a pin,
(And thou wast happier than myself the while,
Would'st softly speak, and stroke my head and smile)
Could those few pleasant hours again appear,
Might one wish bring them, would I wish them here?
I would not trust my heart — the dear delight
Seems so to be desir'd, perhaps I might. —
But no — what here we call our life is such,
So little to be lov'd, and thou so much,
That I should ill requite thee to constrain
Thy unbound spirit into bonds again.

Thou, as a gallant bark from Albion's coast
(The storms all weather'd and the ocean cross'd)
Shoots into port at some well-haven'd isle,
Where spices breathe and brighter seasons smile,
There sits quiescent on the floods that show
Her beauteous forms reflected clear below,
While airs impregnated with incense play
Around her, fanning light her streamers gay;
So thou, with sails how swift! hast reach'd the shore
" Where tempests never beat nor billows roar,"
And thy lov'd consort [23] on the dang'rous tide
Of life, long since, has anchor'd at thy side.
But me, scarce hoping to attain that rest,
Always from port withheld, always distress'd —
Me howling winds drive devious, tempest toss'd,
Sails ript, seams op'ning wide, and compass lost,
And day by day some current's thwarting force
Sets me more distant from a prosp'rous course.
But oh the thought, that thou art safe, and he!
That thought is joy, arrive what may to me.
My boast is not that I deduce my birth
From loins enthron'd, and rulers of the earth; [24]
But higher far my proud pretensions rise —
The son of parents pass'd into the skies.
And now, farewell — time, unrevok'd, has run
His wonted course, yet what I wish'd is done.
By contemplation's help, not sought in vain,

[23] Cowper's father died in 1756.
[24] His mother was descended by four separate lines from Henry III.

I seem t' have liv'd my childhood o'er again;
To have renew'd the joys that once were mine,
Without the sin of violating thine:
And, while the wings of fancy still are free,
And I can view this mimic shew of thee,
Time has but half succeeded in his theft —
Thyself remov'd, thy power to sooth me left.

Sonnet to William Wilberforce, Esq.[25]

Thy country, Wilberforce, with just disdain,
Hears thee, by cruel men and impious, call'd
Fanatic, for thy zeal to loose th' enthrall'd
From exile, public sale, and slav'ry's chain.
Friend of the poor, the wrong'd, the fetter-gall'd,
Fear not lest labour such as thine be vain!
Thou hast achiev'd a part; hast gain'd the ear
Of Britain's senate to thy glorious cause;
Hope smiles, joy springs, and tho' cold caution pause
And weave delay, the better hour is near,
That shall remunerate thy toils severe
By peace for Afric, fenc'd with British laws.
  Enjoy what thou hast won, esteem and love
  From all the just on earth, and all the blest above!

Sonnet to Mrs. Unwin[26]

Mary! I want a lyre with other strings;
Such aid from Heaven as some have feign'd they drew!
An eloquence scarce given to mortals, new,
And undebas'd by praise of meaner things!
That, ere through age or woe I shed my wings,
I may record thy worth, with honour due,
In verse as musical as thou art true, —
Verse, that immortalizes whom it sings!
But thou hast little need: there is a book,
By seraphs writ with beams of heav'nly light,
On which the eyes of God not rarely look;
A chronicle of actions just and bright!
  There all thy deeds, my faithful Mary, shine,
  And since thou own'st that praise, I spare thee mine.

To Mary[27]

The twentieth year is well-nigh past,
Since first our sky was overcast;
Ah would that this might be the last!
My Mary!

Thy spirits have a fainter flow,
I see thee daily weaker grow —
'Twas my distress that brought thee low,
My Mary!

Thy needles, once a shining store,
For my sake restless heretofore,
Now rust disus'd, and shine no more,
My Mary!

For though thou gladly wouldst fulfil
The same kind office for me still,
Thy sight now seconds not thy will,
My Mary!

But well thou play'd'st the housewife's part,
And all thy threads with magic art
Have wound themselves about this heart,
My Mary!

Thy indistinct expressions seem
Like language utter'd in a dream;
Yet me they charm, whate'er the theme,
My Mary!

---

[25] Written in April 1792, and straightway published in *Northampton Mercury*.
[26] Written in 1796; published in 1803.
[27] Written in the autumn of 1793; published in 1803, with the exception of the tenth stanza, first printed in 1900. The opening stanza refers to the year 1773 when Cowper's engagement to Mrs. Unwin was broken, because of a recurrence of his madness.

Thy silver locks, once auburn bright,
Are still more lovely in my sight
Than golden beams of orient light,
My Mary!

For could I view nor them nor thee,
What sight worth seeing could I see?
The sun would rise in vain for me,
My Mary!

Partakers of thy sad decline,
Thy hands their little force resign;
Yet, gently prest, press gently mine,
My Mary!

And then I feel that still I hold
A richer store ten thousandfold
Than misers fancy in their gold,
My Mary!

Such feebleness of limbs thou prov'st,
That now at every step thou mov'st
Upheld by two; yet still thou lov'st,
My Mary!

And still to love, though prest with ill,
In wintry age to feel no chill,
With me is to be lovely still,
My Mary!

But ah! by constant heed I know,
How oft the sadness that I show
Transforms thy smiles to looks of woe,
My Mary!

And should my future lot be cast
With much resemblance of the past,
Thy worn-out heart will break at last,
My Mary!

The Castaway [28]

OBSCUREST night involv'd the sky,
Th' Atlantic billows roar'd,
When such a destin'd wretch as I,
Wash'd headlong from on board,
Of friends, of hope, of all bereft,
His floating home for ever left.

No braver chief could Albion boast
Than he with whom he went,
Nor ever ship left Albion's coast,
With warmer wishes sent.
He lov'd them both, but both in vain,
Nor him beheld, nor her again.

Not long beneath the whelming brine,
Expert to swim, he lay;
Nor soon he felt his strength decline,
Or courage die away;
But wag'd with death a lasting strife,
Supported by despair of life.

He shouted: nor his friends had fail'd
To check the vessel's course,
But so the furious blast prevail'd,
That, pitiless perforce,
They left their outcast mate behind,
And scudded still before the wind.

Some succour yet they could afford;
And, such as storms allow,
The cask, the coop, the floated cord,
Delay'd not to bestow.
But he (they knew) nor ship, nor shore,
Whate'er they gave, should visit more.

Nor, cruel as it seem'd, could he
Their haste himself condemn,
Aware that flight, in such a sea,
Alone could rescue them;
Yet bitter felt it still to die
Deserted, and his friends so nigh.

He long survives, who lives an hour
In ocean, self-upheld;
And so long he, with unspent pow'r,
His destiny repell'd;
And ever, as the minutes flew,
Entreated help, or cried — Adieu!

At length, his transient respite past,
His comrades, who before
Had heard his voice in ev'ry blast,
Could catch the sound no more.
For then, by toil subdued, he drank
The stifling wave, and then he sank.

[28] Written 20 March 1799; published by Hayley in 1803. The castaway's story is told in Lord Anson's *Voyage round the World* (1748).

No poet wept him: but the page
  Of narrative sincere,
That tells his name, his worth, his age,
  Is wet with Anson's tear.
And tears by bards or heroes shed
Alike immortalize the dead.

I therefore purpose not, or dream,
  Descanting on his fate,
To give the melancholy theme
  A more enduring date:
But misery still delights to trace
Its 'semblance in another's case.

No voice divine the storm allay'd,
  No light propitious shone;
When, snatch'd from all effectual aid,
  We perish'd, each alone:
But I beneath a rougher sea,
And whelm'd in deeper gulphs than he.

William Blake

1757–1827

To the Evening Star[1]

Thou fair-hair'd angel of the evening,
Now, whilst the sun rests on the mountains, light
Thy bright torch of love; thy radiant crown
Put on, and smile upon our evening bed!
Smile on our loves, and while thou drawest the
Blue curtains of the sky, scatter thy silver dew
On every flower that shuts its sweet eyes
In timely sleep. Let thy west wind sleep on
The lake; speak silence with thy glimmering eyes,
And wash the dusk with silver. Soon, full soon,
Dost thou withdraw; then the wolf rages wide,
And the lion glares thro' the dun forest:
The fleeces of our flocks are cover'd with
Thy sacred dew: protect them with thine influence.

Song

How sweet I roam'd from field to field
And tasted all the summer's pride,
Till I the Prince of Love beheld
Who in the sunny beams did glide!

He show'd me lilies for my hair,
And blushing roses for my brow;
He led me through his gardens fair
Where all his golden pleasures grow.

With sweet May dews my wings were wet,
And Phoebus fir'd my vocal rage;
He caught me in his silken net,
And shut me in his golden cage.

He loves to sit and hear me sing,
Then, laughing, sports and plays with me;
Then stretches out my golden wing,
And mocks my loss of liberty.

Song

My silks and fine array,
My smiles and languish'd air,
By love are driv'n away;
And mournful lean Despair
Brings me yew to deck my grave;
Such end true lovers have.

His face is fair as heav'n
When springing buds unfold;
O why to him was't giv'n
Whose heart is wintry cold?
His breast is love's all-worshipp'd tomb,
Where all love's pilgrims come.

Bring me an axe and spade,
Bring me a winding-sheet;
When I my grave have made
Let winds and tempests beat:
Then down I'll lie as cold as clay.
True love doth pass away!

[1] This and the three following poems were published in *Poetical Sketches*, 1783.

To the Muses

WHETHER on Ida's shady brow,
Or in the chambers of the East,
The chambers of the sun, that now
From ancient melody have ceas'd;

Whether in Heaven ye wander fair,
Or the green corners of the earth,
Or the blue regions of the air
Where the melodious winds have birth;

Whether on crystal rocks ye rove,
Beneath the bosom of the sea
Wand'ring in many a coral grove,
Fair Nine, forsaking Poetry!

How have you left the ancient love
That bards of old enjoy'd in you!
The languid strings do scarcely move!
The sound is forc'd, the notes are few!

SONGS OF INNOCENCE[2]

Introduction

PIPING down the valleys wild,
Piping songs of pleasant glee,
On a cloud I saw a child,
And he laughing said to me:

'Pipe a song about a Lamb!'
So I piped with merry cheer.
'Piper, pipe that song again;'
So I piped: he wept to hear.

'Drop thy pipe, thy happy pipe;
Sing thy songs of happy cheer:'
So I sang the same again,
While he wept with joy to hear.

'Piper, sit thee down and write
In a book, that all may read.'
So he vanish'd from my sight,
And I pluck'd a hollow reed,

And I made a rural pen,
And I stain'd the water clear,
And I wrote my happy songs
Every child may joy to hear.

[2] Published in 1789.

The Lamb

LITTLE Lamb, who made thee?
Dost thou know who made thee?
Gave thee life, and bid thee feed,
By the stream and o'er the mead;
Gave thee clothing of delight,
Softest clothing, woolly, bright;
Gave thee such a tender voice,
Making all the vales rejoice?
Little Lamb, who made thee?
Dost thou know who made thee?

Little Lamb, I'll tell thee,
Little Lamb, I'll tell thee:
He is callèd by thy name,
For He calls Himself a Lamb.
He is meek, and He is mild;
He became a little child.
I a child, and thou a lamb,
We are callèd by His name.
Little Lamb, God bless thee!
Little Lamb, God bless thee!

The Little Black Boy

MY mother bore me in the southern wild,
And I am black, but O! my soul is white;
White as an angel is the English child,
But I am black, as if bereav'd of light.

My mother taught me underneath a tree,
And, sitting down before the heat of day,
She took me on her lap and kissèd me,
And, pointing to the east, began to say:

'Look on the rising sun,—there God does live,
And gives His light, and gives His heat away;
And flowers and trees and beasts and men receive
Comfort in morning, joy in the noonday.

'And we are put on earth a little space,
That we may learn to bear the beams of love;
And these black bodies and this sunburnt face
Is but a cloud, and like a shady grove.

'For when our souls have learn'd the heat to bear,
The cloud will vanish; we shall hear His voice,
Saying: "Come out from the grove, My love and care,
And round My golden tent like lambs rejoice."'

Thus did my mother say, and kissèd me;
And thus I say to little English boy.
When I from black and he from white cloud free,
And round the tent of God like lambs we joy,

I'll shade him from the heat, till he can bear
To lean in joy upon our Father's knee;
And then I'll stand and stroke his silver hair,
And be like him, and he will then love me.

A Cradle Song

SWEET dreams, form a shade
O'er my lovely infant's head;
Sweet dreams of pleasant streams
By happy, silent, moony beams.

Sweet sleep, with soft down
Weave thy brows an infant crown.
Sweet sleep, Angel mild,
Hover o'er my happy child.

Sweet smiles, in the night
Hover over my delight;
Sweet smiles, mother's smiles,
All the livelong night beguiles.

Sweet moans, dovelike sighs,
Chase not slumber from thy eyes.
Sweet moans, sweeter smiles,
All the dovelike moans beguiles.

Sleep, sleep, happy child,
All creation slept and smil'd;
Sleep, sleep, happy sleep,
While o'er thee thy mother weep.

Sweet babe, in thy face
Holy image I can trace.
Sweet babe, once like thee,
Thy Maker lay and wept for me,

Wept for me, for thee, for all,
When He was an infant small.
Thou His image ever see,
Heavenly face that smiles on thee,

Smiles on thee, on me, on all;
Who became an infant small.
Infant smiles are His own smiles;
Heaven and earth to peace beguiles.

Holy Thursday

'TWAS on a Holy Thursday, their innocent faces clean,
The children walking two and two, in red and blue and green,
Grey-headed beadles walk'd before, with wands as white as snow,
Till into the high dome of Paul's they like Thames' waters flow.

O what a multitude they seem'd, these flowers of London town!
Seated in companies they sit with radiance all their own.
The hum of multitudes was there, but multitudes of lambs,
Thousands of little boys and girls raising their innocent hands.

Now like a mighty wind they raise to Heaven the voice of song,
Or like harmonious thunderings the seat of Heaven among.
Beneath them sit the agèd men, wise guardians of the poor;
Then cherish pity, lest you drive an angel from your door.

The Divine Image

To Mercy, Pity, Peace, and Love
All pray in their distress;
And to these virtues of delight
Return their thankfulness.

For Mercy, Pity, Peace, and Love
Is God, our Father dear,

And Mercy, Pity, Peace, and Love
Is man, His child and care.

For Mercy has a human heart,
Pity a human face,
And Love, the human form divine,
And Peace, the human dress.

Then every man, of every clime,
That prays in his distress,
Prays to the human form divine,
Love, Mercy, Pity, Peace.

And all must love the human form,
In heathen, Turk, or Jew;
Where Mercy, Love, and Pity dwell
There God is dwelling too.

SONGS OF EXPERIENCE[3]

Introduction

Hear the voice of the Bard!
Who present, past, and future, sees;
Whose ears have heard
The Holy Word
That walk'd among the ancient trees,

Calling the lapséd soul,
And weeping in the evening dew;
That might control
The starry pole,
And fallen, fallen light renew!

'O Earth, O Earth, return!
Arise from out the dewy grass;
Night is worn,
And the morn
Rises from the slumberous mass.

'Turn away no more;
Why wilt thou turn away.
The starry floor,
The wat'ry shore,
Is giv'n thee till the break of day.'

The Tiger

Tiger! Tiger! burning bright
In the forests of the night,
What immortal hand or eye
Could frame thy fearful symmetry?

In what distant deeps or skies
Burnt the fire of thine eyes?
On what wings dare he aspire?
What the hand dare seize the fire?

And what shoulder, and what art,
Could twist the sinews of thy heart?
And when thy heart began to beat,
What dread hand? and what dread feet?

What the hammer? what the chain?
In what furnace was thy brain?
What the anvil? what dread grasp
Dare its deadly terrors clasp?

When the stars threw down their spears,
And water'd heaven with their tears,
Did he smile his work to see?
Did he who made the Lamb make thee?

Tiger! Tiger! burning bright
In the forests of the night,
What immortal hand or eye,
Dare frame thy fearful symmetry?

The Clod and the Pebble

'Love seeketh not itself to please,
Nor for itself hath any care,
But for another gives its ease,
And builds a Heaven in Hell's despair.'

So sung a little Clod of Clay,
Trodden with the cattle's feet,
But a Pebble of the brook
Warbled out these metres meet:

'Love seeketh only Self to please,
To bind another to its delight,
Joys in another's loss of ease,
And builds a Hell in Heaven's despite.'

Holy Thursday

Is this a holy thing to see
In a rich and fruitful land,
Babes reduc'd to misery,
Fed with cold and usurous hand?

[3] Published in 1794.

Is that trembling cry a song?
Can it be a song of joy?
And so many children poor?
It is a land of poverty!

And their sun does never shine,
And their fields are bleak and bare,
And their ways are fill'd with thorns:
It is eternal winter there.

For where'er the sun does shine,
And where'er the rain does fall,
Babe can never hunger there,
Nor poverty the mind appall.

A Poison Tree

I was angry with my friend:
I told my wrath, my wrath did end.
I was angry with my foe:
I told it not, my wrath did grow.

And I water'd it in fears,
Night and morning with my tears;
And I sunnéd it with smiles,
And with soft deceitful wiles.

And it grew both day and night,
Till it bore an apple bright;
And my foe beheld it shine,
And he knew that it was mine,

And into my garden stole
When the night had veil'd the pole:
In the morning glad I see
My foe outstretch'd beneath the tree.

The Sick Rose

O Rose, thou art sick!
The invisible worm,
That flies in the night,
In the howling storm,

Has found out thy bed
Of crimson joy;
And his dark secret love
Does thy life destroy.

Ah! Sun-flower

Ah! Sun-flower! weary of time,
Who countest the steps of the sun;
Seeking after that sweet golden clime,
Where the traveller's journey is done;

Where the Youth pined away with desire,
And the pale Virgin shrouded in snow,
Arise from their graves, and aspire
Where my Sun-flower wishes to go.

The Garden of Love

I went to the Garden of Love,
And saw what I never had seen:
A Chapel was built in the midst,
Where I used to play on the green.

And the gates of this Chapel were shut,
And 'Thou shalt not' writ over the door;
So I turn'd to the Garden of Love
That so many sweet flowers bore;

And I saw it was filléd with graves,
And tomb-stones where flowers should be;
And priests in black gowns were walking their rounds,
And binding with briars my joys and desires.

A Little Boy Lost

'Nought loves another as itself,
Nor venerates another so,
Nor is it possible to Thought
A greater than itself to know:

'And, Father, how can I love you
Or any of my brothers more?
I love you like the little bird
That picks up crumbs around the door.'

The Priest sat by and heard the child,
In trembling zeal he seiz'd his hair:
He led him by his little coat,
And all admir'd the priestly care.

And standing on the altar high,
'Lo! what a fiend is here,' said he,
'One who sets reason up for judge
Of our most holy Mystery.'

The weeping child could not be heard,
The weeping parents wept in vain;
They stripp'd him to his little shirt,
And bound him in an iron chain;

And burn'd him in a holy place,
Where many had been burn'd before:
The weeping parents wept in vain.
Are such things done on Albion's shore?

Never seek to tell thy love [4]

NEVER seek to tell thy love,
Love that never told can be;
For the gentle wind does move
Silently, invisibly.

I told my love, I told my love,
I told her all my heart;
Trembling, cold, in ghastly fears,
Ah! she doth depart.

Soon as she was gone from me,
A traveller came by,
Silently, invisibly:
He took her with a sigh.

Mock on, mock on, Voltaire, Rousseau [5]

MOCK on, mock on, Voltaire, Rousseau;
Mock on, mock on; 'tis all in vain!
You throw the sand against the wind,
And the wind blows it back again.

And every sand becomes a gem
Reflected in the beams divine;
Blown back they blind the mocking eye,
But still in Israel's paths they shine.

The Atoms of Democritus
And Newton's Particles of Light
Are sands upon the Red Sea shore,
Where Israel's tents do shine so bright.

Auguries of Innocence [6]

To see a World in a grain of sand,
And a Heaven in a wild flower,
Hold Infinity in the palm of your hand,
And Eternity in an hour.
A robin redbreast in a cage
Puts all Heaven in a rage.
A dove-house fill'd with doves and pigeons
Shudders Hell thro' all its regions.
A dog starv'd at his master's gate
Predicts the ruin of the State.
A horse misus'd upon the road
Calls to Heaven for human blood.
Each outcry of the hunted hare
A fibre from the brain does tear.
A skylark wounded in the wing,
A cherubim does cease to sing.
The game-cock clipt and arm'd for fight
Does the rising sun affright.
Every wolf's and lion's howl
Raises from Hell a Human soul.
The wild deer, wandering here and there,
Keeps the Human soul from care.
The lamb misus'd breeds public strife,
And yet forgives the butcher's knife.
The bat that flits at close of eve
Has left the brain that won't believe.
The owl that calls upon the night
Speaks the unbeliever's fright.
He who shall hurt the little wren
Shall never be belov'd by men.
He who the ox to wrath has mov'd
Shall never be by woman lov'd.
The wanton boy that kills the fly
Shall feel the spider's enmity.
He who torments the chafer's sprite
Weaves a bower in endless night.

[4] From the earlier poems of the Rossetti MS., written *circa* 1793–1811; published by Rossetti in the second volume of Gilchrist's *Life*, 1863.

[5] From later poems in Rossetti MS., *circa* 1800–1810.

[6] From poems in Pickering MS., written *circa* 1801–1803; also published by Rossetti, 1863. 'The title "Auguries of Innocence" probably, as Mr. Yeats conjectures, refers only to the opening quatrain, although the MS. itself has no space or line separating it from the couplets which follow. These proverbs are here placed in the sequence in which they appear in the MS., where they were doubtless transcribed from scattered jottings elsewhere.' [John Sampson, editor of Oxford edition, wherein his own rearrangement is appended to the reading here used.]

The caterpillar on the leaf
Repeats to thee thy mother's grief.
Kill not the moth nor butterfly,
For the Last Judgement draweth nigh.
He who shall train the horse to war
Shall never pass the polar bar.
The beggar's dog and widow's cat,
Feed them, and thou wilt grow fat.
The gnat that sings his summer's song
Poison gets from Slander's tongue.
The poison of the snake and newt
Is the sweat of Envy's foot.
The poison of the honey-bee
Is the artist's jealousy.
The prince's robes and beggar's rags
Are toadstools on the miser's bags.
A truth that's told with bad intent
Beats all the lies you can invent.
It is right it should be so;
Man was made for joy and woe;
And when this we rightly know,
Thro' the world we safely go.
Joy and woe are woven fine,
A clothing for the soul divine;
Under every grief and pine
Runs a joy with silken twine.
The babe is more than swaddling-bands;
Throughout all these human lands
Tools were made, and born were hands,
Every farmer understands.
Every tear from every eye
Becomes a babe in Eternity;
This is caught by Females bright,
And return'd to its own delight.
The bleat, the bark, bellow, and roar
Are waves that beat on Heaven's shore.
The babe that weeps the rod beneath
Writes revenge in realms of death.
The beggar's rags, fluttering in air,
Does to rags the heavens tear.
The soldier, arm'd with sword and gun,
Palsied strikes the summer's sun.
The poor man's farthing is worth more
Than all the gold on Afric's shore.
One mite wrung from the labourer's hands
Shall buy and sell the miser's lands
Or, if protected from on high,
Does that whole nation sell and buy.
He who mocks the infant's faith
Shall be mock'd in Age and Death.
He who shall teach the child to doubt
The rotting grave shall ne'er get out.
He who respects the infant's faith
Triumphs over Hell and Death.
The child's toys and the old man's reasons
Are the fruits of the two seasons.
The questioner, who sits so sly,
Shall never know how to reply.
He who replies to words of Doubt
Doth put the light of knowledge out.
The strongest poison ever known
Came from Caesar's laurel crown.
Nought can deform the human race
Like to the armour's iron brace.
When gold and gems adorn the plough
To peaceful arts shall Envy bow.
A riddle, or the cricket's cry,
Is to Doubt a fit reply.
The emmet's inch and eagle's mile
Make lame Philosophy to smile.
He who doubts from what he sees
Will ne'er believe, do what you please.
If the Sun and Moon should doubt,
They'd immediately go out.
To be in a passion you good may do,
But no good if a passion is in you.
The whore and gambler, by the state
Licensed, build that nation's fate.
The harlot's cry from street to street
Shall weave Old England's winding-sheet.
The winner's shout, the loser's curse,
Dance before dead England's hearse.
Every night and every morn
Some to misery are born.
Every morn and every night
Some are born to sweet delight.
Some are born to sweet delight,
Some are born to endless night.
We are led to believe a lie
When we see not thro' the eye,
Which was born in a night, to perish in a night,
When the Soul slept in beams of light.
God appears, and God is Light,
To those poor souls who dwell in Night;
But does a Human Form display
To those who dwell in realms of Day.

from 'Milton' [7]

AND did those feet in ancient time
Walk upon England's mountains green?
And was the holy Lamb of God
On England's pleasant pastures seen?

And did the Countenance Divine
Shine forth upon our clouded hills?
And was Jerusalem builded here
Among these dark Satanic Mills?

Bring me my bow of burning gold!
Bring me my arrows of desire!
Bring me my spear! Oh clouds, unfold!
Bring me my chariot of fire!

I will not cease from mental fight,
Nor shall my sword sleep in my hand,
Till we have built Jerusalem
In England's green and pleasant land.

[7] *Milton*, one of the 'prophetic books,' was begun between 1800 and 1803. Blake's engravings for it were not completed until 1808–1809.

Ballads[1]

Lady Isabel and the Elf-knight

FAIR lady Isabel sits in her bower sewing,
Aye as the gowans [2] grow gay
There she heard an elf-knight blawing his horn.
The first morning in May.

'If I had yon horn that I hear blawing,
An yon elf-knight to sleep in my bosom.'

This maiden had scarcely these words spoken,
Till in at her window the elf-knight has luppen.[3]

'It's a very strange matter, fair maiden,' said he,
'I canna blaw my horn but ye call on me.

'But will ye go to yon greenwood side?
If ye canna gang, I will cause you to ride.'

He leapt on a horse, and she on another,
And they rode on to the greenwood together.

'Light down, light down, lady Isabel,' said he,
'We are come to the place where ye are to die.'

'Hae mercy, hae mercy, kind sir, on me,
Till ance my dear father and mother I see.'

'Seven king's-daughters here hae I slain,
And ye shall be the eighth o them.'

'O sit down a while, lay your head on my knee,
That we may hae some rest before that I die.'

She stroak'd him sae fast, the nearer he did creep,
Wi a sma charm she lull'd him fast asleep.

Wi his ain sword-belt sae fast as she ban [4] him,
Wi his ain dag-durk [5] sae sair as she dang him.

'If seven kings-daughters here ye hae slain,
Lye ye here, a husband to them a'.'

[1] The custom in anthologies of this sort of placing the popular ballads at the end of the medieval period has a sanction from usage not too well justified from their history. Though the ballad form is medieval, many of the specimens we possess are related to events of the sixteenth and seventeenth centuries. Moreover, interest in them as a literary form and the collecting and comparing of variants really begins, of course, in the eighteenth century. It seems most logical, therefore, to introduce the ballads here in the time of Bishop Percy, whose rescue of the folio manuscript (published as Percy's *Reliques of Ancient English Poetry*, 1765), before its complete extinction as a fire-lighter in the mansion of Humphrey Pitt, is certainly the most important event in ballad history.

[2] daisies [3] leapt

[4] bound [5] dagger

Edward

'Why dois your brand sae drap wi bluid,
Edward, Edward,
Why dois your brand sae drap wi bluid,
And why sae sad gang yee O?'
'O I hae killed my hauke[6] sae guid,
Mither, mither,
O I hae killed my hauke sae guid,
And I had nae mair bot hee O.'

'Your haukis bluid was nevir sae reid,
Edward, Edward,
Your haukis bluid was nevir sae reid,
My deir son I tell thee O.'
'O I hae killed my reid-roan steid,
Mither, mither,
O I hae killed my reid-roan steid,
That erst was sae fair and frie O.'

'Your steid was auld, and ye hae gat mair,
Edward, Edward,
Your steid was auld, and ye hae gat mair,
Sum other dule ye drie[7] O.
'O I hae killed my fadir deir,
Mither, mither,
O I hae killed my fadir deir,
Alas, and wae is mee O!'

'And whatten penance wul ye drie for that,
Edward, Edward?
And whatten penance will ye drie for that?
My deir son, now tell me O.'
'Ile set my feit in yonder boat,
Mither, mither,
Ile set my feit in yonder boat,
And Ile fare ovir the sea O.'

'And what wul ye doe wi your towirs and your ha,[8]
Edward, Edward?
And what wul ye doe wi your towirs and your ha,
That were sae fair to see O?'
'Ile let thame stand tul they doun fa,
Mither, mither,
Ile let thame stand tul they doun fa,
For here nevir mair maun I bee O.'

'And what wul ye leive to your bairns and your wife,
Edward, Edward?
And what wul ye leive to your bairns and your wife,
Whan ye gang ovir the sea O?'
'The warldis room, late them beg thrae[9] life,
Mither, mither,
The warldis room, late them beg thrae life,
For thame nevir mair wul I see O.'

'And what wul ye leive to your ain mither deir,
Edward, Edward?
And what wul ye leive to your ain mither deir?
My deir son, now tell me O.'
'The curse of hell frae me sall ye beir,
Mither, mither,
The curse of hell frae me sall ye beir,
Sic counseils ye gave to me O.'

[6] hawk [7] grief you suffer [8] hall [9] through

The Three Ravens

There were three ravens sat on a tree,
Downe a downe, hay down, hay downe
There were three ravens sat on a tree,
With a downe
There were three ravens sat on a tree,
They were as blacke as they might be.
With a downe derrie, derrie, derrie, downe, downe

The one of them said to his mate,
'Where shall we our breakfast take?'

'Downe in yonder greene field,
There lies a knight slain under his shield.

'His hounds they lie downe at his feete,
So well they can their master keepe.

'His haukes they flie so eagerly,
There's no fowle dare him come nie.'

Downe there comes a fallow doe,
As great with yong as she might goe.

She lift up his bloudy hed,
And kist his wounds that were so red.

She got him up upon her backe,
And carried him to earthen lake.[10]

She buried him before the prime,
She was dead herselfe ere even-song time.

God send every gentleman,
Such haukes, such hounds, and such a leman.[11]

Thomas Rymer[12]

TRUE THOMAS lay oer yond grassy bank,
  And he beheld a ladie gay,
A ladie that was brisk and bold,
  Come riding oer the fernie brae.

Her skirt was of the grass-green silk,
  Her mantel of the velvet fine,
At ilka tett[13] of her horse's mane
  Hung fifty silver bells and nine.

True Thomas he took off his hat,
  And bowed him low down till[14] his knee:
'All hail, thou mighty Queen of Heaven!
  For your peer on earth I never did see.'

'O no, O no, True Thomas,' she says,
  'That name does not belong to me;
I am but the queen of fair Elfland,
  And I'm come here for to visit thee.

. . .

'But ye maun go wi me now, Thomas,
  True Thomas, ye maun go wi me,
For ye maun serve me seven years,
  Thro weel or wae as may chance to be.'

She turned about her milk-white steed,
  And took True Thomas up behind,
And aye wheneer her bridle rang,
  The steed flew swifter than the wind.

For forty days and forty nights
  He wade thro red blude to the knee,
And he saw neither sun nor moon,
  But heard the roaring of the sea.

O they rade on, and further on,
  Until they came to a garden green:
'Light down, light down, ye ladie free,
  Some of that fruit let me pull to thee.'

'O no, O no, True Thomas,' she says,
  'That fruit maun not be touched by thee,
For a' the plagues that are in hell
  Light on the fruit of this countrie.

'But I have a loaf here in my lap,
  Likewise a bottle of claret wine,
And now ere we go farther on,
  We'll rest a while, and ye may dine.'

When he had eaten and drunk his fill,
  'Lay down your head upon my knee,'
The lady sayd, 'ere we climb yon hill,
  And I will show you fairlies[15] three.

'O see not ye yon narrow road,
  So thick beset wi thorns and briers?
That is the path of righteousness,
  Tho after it but few enquires.

'And see not ye that braid braid road,
  That lies across yon lillie leven?[16]
That is the path of wickedness,
  Tho some call it the road to heaven.

'And see not ye that bonny road,
  Which winds about the fernie brae?
That is the road to fair Elfland,
  Where you and I this night maun gae.

'But Thomas, ye maun hold your tongue,
  Whatever you may hear or see,

---

[10] pit
[11] lover
[12] Thomas of Erceldoune lived in Scotland in the thirteenth century. In the next hundred years he acquired a great reputation as a soothsayer. His powers were obtained, as this ballad shows, from the queen of the elves herself.
[13] tuft
[14] to

[15] marvels
[16] lawn

For gin ae word you should chance to speak,
  You will neer get back to your ain countrie.'

He has gotten a coat of the even cloth,
  And a pair of shoes of velvet green,
And till seven years were past and gone
  True Thomas on earth was never seen.

The Cherry-tree Carol

JOSEPH was an old man,
  and an old man was he,
When he wedded Mary,
  in the land of Galilee.

Joseph and Mary walked
  through an orchard good,
Where was cherries and berries,
  so red as any blood.

Joseph and Mary walked
  through an orchard green,
Where was berries and cherries,
  as thick as might be seen.

O then bespoke Mary,
  so meek and so mild:
'Pluck me one cherry, Joseph,
  for I am with child.'

O then bespoke Joseph,
  with words most unkind:
'Let him pluck thee a cherry
  that brought thee with child.'

O then bespoke the babe,
  within his mother's womb:
'Bow down then the tallest tree,
  for my mother to have some.'

Then bowed down the highest tree
  unto his mother's hand;
Then she cried, 'See, Joseph,
  I have cherries at command.'

O then bespoke Joseph:
  'I have done Mary wrong;
But cheer up, my dearest,
  and be not cast down.'

Then Mary plucked a cherry,
  as red as the blood,
Then Mary went home
  with her heavy load.

Then Mary took her babe,
  and sat him on her knee,
Saying, 'My dear son, tell me
  what this world will be.'

'O I shall be as dead, mother,
  as the stones in the wall;
O the stones in the streets, mother,
  shall mourn for me all.

'Upon Easter-day, mother,
  my uprising shall be;
O the sun and the moon, mother,
  shall both rise with me.'

Sir Patrick Spens

THE king sits in Dumferling toune,
  Drinking the blude-reid wine:
'O whar will I get guid sailor,
  To sail this schip of mine?'

Up and spak an eldern knicht,[17]
  Sat at the kings richt kne:
'Sir Patrick Spence is the best sailor
  That sails upon the se.'

The king has written a braid letter,
  And signd it wi his hand,
And sent it to Sir Patrick Spence,
  Was walking on the sand.

The first line that Sir Patrick red,
  A loud lauch lauched he;
The next line that Sir Patrick red,
  The teir blinded his ee.

[17] knight

'O wha is this has don this deid,
This ill deid don to me,
To send me out this time o' the yeir,
To sail upon the se!

'Mak hast, mak haste, my mirry men all,
Our guid schip sails the morne: '
'O say na sae, my master deir,
For I feir a deadlie storme.

'Late late yestreen I saw the new moone,
Wi the auld moone in hir arme,
And I feir, I feir, my deir master
That we will cum to harme.'

O our Scots nobles wer richt laith [18]
To weet their cork-heild schoone;
But lang owre [19] a' the play wer playd,
Thair hats they swam aboone.[20]

O lang, lang may their ladies sit,
Wi thair fans into their hand,
Or eir they se Sir Patrick Spence
Cum sailing to the land.

O lang, lang may the ladies stand,
Wi thair gold kems in their hair,
Waiting for thair ain deir lords,
For they'll se thame na mair.

Haf-owre,[21] haf-owre to Aberdour,
It's fiftie fadom deip,
And thair lies guid Sir Patrick Spence,
Wi the Scots lords at his feit.

Child Waters

Childe Watters in his stable stoode,
And stroaket his milke-white steede;
To him came a faire young ladye
As ere did weare womans weede.[22]

Saies, 'Christ you save, good Chyld Waters!'
Sayes, 'Christ you save and see! [23]
My girdle of gold, which was too longe,
Is now to short for mee.

'And all is with one chyld of yours,
I feele sturre at my side;
My gowne of greene, it is to strayght;
Before it was to wide.'

'If the child be mine, Faire Ellen,' he sayd,
'Be mine, as you tell mee,
Take you Cheshire and Lancashire both,
Take them your owne to bee.

'If the child be mine, Faire Ellen,' he said,
'Be mine, as you doe sweare,
Take you Cheshire and Lancashire both,
And make that child your heyre.'

Shee saies, 'I had rather have one kisse,
Child Waters, of thy mouth,
Then I wold have Cheshire and Lancashire both,
That lyes by north and south.

'And I had rather have a twinkling,
Child Waters, of your eye,
Then I wold have Cheshire and Lancashire both,
To take them mine oune to bee.'

'To-morrow, Ellen, I must forth ryde
Soe far into the north countrye;
The fairest lady that I can find,
Ellen, must goe with mee.'
'And ever I pray you, Child Watters,
Your foot-page let me bee!'

'If you will my footpage be, Ellen,
As you doe tell it mee,
Then you must cut your gowne of greene
An inche above your knee.

'Soe must you doe your yellow lockes,
Another inch above your eye;
You must tell noe man what is my name;
My footpage then you shall bee.'

All this long day Child Waters rode,
Shee ran bare foote by his side;
Yet was he never soe curteous a knight
To say, Ellen, will you ryde?

[18] loath
[19] ere
[20] above
[21] half-over
[22] clothes
[23] protect

But all this day Child Waters rode,
She ran bar foote thorow the broome;
Yet was he never soe curteous a knight
As to say, ‘ Put on your shoone.’

‘ Ride softlye,’ she said, ‘ Child Watters;
Why doe you ryde soe fast?
The child which is no mans but yours
My bodye it will burst.’

He sayes, ‘ Sees thou yonder water, Ellen,
That flowes from banke to brim? ’
‘ I trust to God, Child Waters,’ she said,
‘ You will never see mee swime.’

But when shee came to the waters side,
She sayled to the chinne:
‘ Except the lord of heaven be my speed,
Now must I learne to swime.’

The salt waters bare up Ellens clothes,
Our Ladye bare up her chinne,
And Child Waters was a woe man, good Lord,
To see Faire Ellen swime.

And when shee over the water was,
Shee then came to his knee:
He said, ‘ Come hither, Faire Ellen,
Loe yonder what I see!

‘ Seest thou not yonder hall, Ellen?
Of red gold shine the gates;
There’s four and twenty fayre ladyes,
The fairest is my wordlye make.[24]

‘ Seest thou not yonder hall, Ellen?
Of red gold shineth the tower;
There is four and twenty faire ladyes,
The fairest is my paramoure.’

‘ I doe see the hall now, Child Waters,
That of red gold shineth the gates;
God give good then of your selfe,
And of your wordlye make!

‘ I doe see the hall, now Child Waters,
That of red gold shineth the tower;
God give good then of your selfe,
And of your paramoure! ’

There were four and twenty ladyes,
Were playing at the ball,
And Ellen was the fairest ladye,
Must bring his steed to the stall.

There were four and twenty faire ladyes
Was playing at the chesse;
And Ellen, shee was the fairest ladye,
Must bring his horsse to grasse.

And then bespake Child Waters sister,
And these were the words said shee:
‘ You have the prettyest footpage, brother,
That ever I saw with mine eye;

‘ But that his belly it is soe bigg,
His girdle goes wonderous hye;
And ever I pray you, Child Waters,
Let him goe into the chamber with mee.’

‘ It is more meete for a little footpage,
That has run through mosse and mire,
To take his supper upon his knee
And sit downe by the kitchin fyer,
Then to goe into the chamber with any ladye
That weares soe rich attyre.’

But when they had suppéd every one,
To bed they took the way;
He sayd, ‘ Come hither, my little footpage,
Hearken what I doe say.

‘ And goe thee downe into yonder towne,
And low into the street;
The fairest ladye that thou can find,
Hyer her in mine armes to sleepe,
And take her up in thine armes two,
For filinge [25] of her feete.’

Ellen is gone into the towne,
And low into the streete;
The fairest ladye that shee cold find
Shee hyred in his armes to sleepe,
And took her in her armes two,
For filing of her feete.

[24] mate

[25] defiling

'I pray you now, good Child Waters,
That I may creepe in at your beds feete;
For there is noe place about this house
Where I may say a sleepe.'

This night and it drove on afterward
Till it was neere the day:
He sayd, 'Rise up, my little foote-page,
And give my steed corne and hay;
And soe doe thou the good blacke oates,
That he may carry me the better away.'

And up then rose Faire Ellen,
And gave his steed corne and hay,
And soe shee did and the good blacke oates,
That he might carry him the better away.

Shee layned her backe to the manger side,
And greivouslye did groane;
And that beheard his mother deere,
And heard her make her moane.

Shee said, 'Rise up, thou Child Waters,
I thinke thou art a cursed man;
For yonder is a ghost in thy stable,
That greivouslye doth groane,
Or else some woman laboures of child,
Shee is soe woe begone.'

But up then rose Child Waters,
And did on his shirt of silke;
Then he put on his other clothes
On his body as white as milke.

And when he came to the stable-dore,
Full still that hee did stand,
That hee might heare now Faire Ellen,
How shee made her monand.

She said, 'Lullabye, my owne deere child!
Lullabye, deere child, deere!
I wold thy father were a king,
Thy mother layd on a beere!'

'Peace now,' he said, 'good Faire Ellen,
And be of good cheere, I thee pray,
And the bridal and the churching both,
They shall bee upon one day.'

Clerk Saunders

Clark Sanders and May Margret
Walkt ower yon graveld green,
And sad and heavy was the love,
I wat, it fell this twa between.

'A bed, a bed,' Clark Sanders said,
'A bed, a bed for you and I;
'Fye no, fye no,' the lady said,
'Until the day we married be.

'For in it will come my seven brothers,
'And a' their torches burning bright;
They'll say, We hae but ae sister,
And here her lying wi a knight.'

'Ye'l take the sourde fray my scabbord,
And lowly, lowly lift the gin,[26]
And you may say, your oth to save,
You never let Clark Sanders in.

'Yele take a napken in your hand,
And ye'l ty up baith your een,
An ye may say, your oth to save,
That ye saw na Sandy sen late yestreen.

'Yele take me in your armes twa,
Yele carrey me ben [27] into your bed,
And ye may say, your oth to save,
In your bower-floor I never tread.'

She has taen the sourde fray his scabbord,
And lowly, lowly lifted the gin;
She was to swear, her oth to save,
She never let Clerk Sanders in.

She has tain a napkin in her hand,
And she ty'd up baith her eeen;
She was to swear, her oth to save,
She saw na him sene late yestreen.

She has taen him in her armes twa,
And carried him ben into her bed;
She was to swear, her oth to save,
He never in her bower-floor tread.

[26] latch
[27] in

In and came her seven brothers,
And all their torches burning bright;
Says they, 'We hae but ae sister
And see there her lying wi a knight.'

Out and speaks the first of them,
'A [28] wat they hay been lovers dear;'
Out and speaks the next of them,
'They hay been in love this many a year.'

Out and speaks the third of them,
'It wear great sin this twa to twain;' [29]
Out an speaks the fourth of them,
'It wear a sin to kill a sleeping man.'

Out and speaks the fifth of them,
'A wat they'll near be twained by me;'
Out and speaks the sixt of them,
'We'l tak our leave an gae our way.'

Out and speaks the seventh of them,
'Altho there wear no a man but me,

. . .

I bear the brand, I'le gar [30] him die.'

Out he has taen a bright long brand,
And he has striped it throw the straw,
And throw and throw Clarke Sanders' body
A wat he has gard cold iron gae.

Sanders he started, and Margret she lapt,
Intill his arms whare she lay,
And well and wellsom was the night,
A wat it was between these twa.

And they lay still, and sleeped sound,
Untill the day began to daw;
And kindly till him she did say
'It's time, trew-love, ye wear awa.'

They lay still, and sleeped sound,
Untill the sun began to shine;
She lookt between her and the wa,
And dull and heavy was his eeen.

[28] I [29] separate [30] cause

She thought it had been a loathsome sweat,
A wat it had fallen this twa between;
But it was the blood of his fair body,
A wat his life days wair na lang.

'O Sanders, I'le do for your sake
What other ladys would na thoule; [31]
When seven years is come and gone,
There's near a shoe go on my sole.

'O Sanders, I'le do for your sake
What other ladies would think mare;
When seven years is come an gone,
Ther's nere a comb go in my hair.

'O Sanders, I'le do for your sake
What other ladies would think lack;
When seven years is come and gone,
I'le wear nought but dowy [32] black.'

The bells gaed clinking throw the towne,
To carry the dead corps to the clay,
An sighing says her May Margret,
'A wat I bide a doulfou day.'

In an come her father dear,
Stout steping on the floor;

. . .

'Hold your toung, my doughter dear,
Let all your mourning a bee;
I'le carry the dead corps to the clay,
And I'le come back an comfort thee.'

'Comfort well your seven sons,
For comforted will I never bee;
For it was neither lord nor loune [33]
That was in bower last night wi mee.'

The Wife of Usher's Well

THERE lived a wife at Usher's Well,
And a wealthy wife was she;
She had three stout and stalwart sons,
And sent them oer the sea.

[31] suffer
[32] doleful
[33] lout, low fellow

They hadna been a week from her,
A week but barely ane,
When word came to the carline wife [34]
That her three sons were gane.

They hadna been a week from her,
A week but barely three,
When word came to the carlin wife
That her sons she'd never see.

'I wish the wind may never cease,
Nor fashes [35] in the flood,
Till my three sons come hame to me,
In earthly flesh and blood.'

It fell about the Martinmass,[36]
When nights are lang and mirk,
The carlin wife's three sons came hame,
And their hats were o the birk.[37]

It neither grew in syke [38] nor ditch,
Nor yet in ony sheugh; [39]
But at the gates o Paradise,
That birk grew fair eneugh.

. . .

'Blow up the fire, my maidens,
Bring water from the well;
For a' my house shall feast this night,
Since my three sons are well.'

And she has made to them a bed,
She's made it large and wide,
And she's taen her mantle her about,
Set down at the bed-side.

. . .

Up then crew the red, red cock,
And up and crew the gray;
The eldest to the youngest said,
'Tis time we were away.

The cock he hadna crawd but once,
And clappd his wings at a',
When the youngest to the eldest said,
Brother, we must awa.

'The cock doth craw, the day doth daw,
The channerin [40] worm doth chide;
Gin we be mist out o our place,
A sair pain we maun bide.

'Fare ye well, my mother dear!
Fareweel to barn and byre! [41]
And fare ye weel, the bonny lass,
That kindles my mother's fire!'

[34] old woman
[35] troubles
[36] 11 November
[37] birch
[38] trench
[39] furrow

The Bailiff's Daughter of Islington

There was a youth, and a well belovd youth,
And he was a esquire's son,
He loved the bayliff's daughter dear,
That lived in Islington.

She was coy, and she would not believe
That he did love her so,
No, nor at any time she would
Any countenance to him show.

But when his friends did understand
His fond and foolish mind,
They sent him up to fair London,
An apprentice for to bind.

And when he had been seven long years,
And his love he had not seen,
'Many a tear have I shed for her sake
When she little thought of me.'

All the maids of Islington
Went forth to sport and play;
All but the bayliff's daughter dear;
She secretly stole away.

She put off her gown of gray,
And put on her puggish [42] attire;
She's up to fair London gone,
Her true-love to require.

As she went along the road,
The weather being hot and dry,
There was she aware of her true-love,
At length came riding by.

[40] grumbling
[41] cow-house
[42] ragged

She stept to him, as red as any rose,
And took him by the bridle-ring:
'I pray you, kind sir, give me one penny,
To ease my weary limb.'

'I prithee, sweetheart, canst thou tell me
Where that thou wast born?'
'At Islington, kind sir,' said she,
'Where I have had many a scorn.'

'I prithee, sweetheart, canst thou tell me
Whether thou dost know
The baliff's daughter of Islington?'
'She's dead, sir, long ago.'

'Then will I sell my goodly steed,
My saddle and my bow;
I will into some far countrey,
Where no man doth me know.'

'O stay, O stay, thou goodly youth!
She's alive, she is not dead;
Here she standeth by thy side,
And is ready to be thy bride.'

'O farewel grief, and welcome joy,
Ten thousand times and more!
For now I have seen my own true-love,
That I thought I should have seen no more.'

Robin Hood and Guy of Gisborne [43]

When shawes [44] beene sheene, and shrads [45] fyll fayre,
And leeves both large and longe,
It is merry, walking in the fayre forrest,
To heare the small birds songe.

The woodweele sang, and wold not cease,
Amongst the leaves a lyne: [46]
And it is by two wight yeomen,
By deare God, that I meane.

. . .

'Me thought they did mee beate and binde,
And tooke my bow mee froe;
If I bee Robin a-live in this lande,
I'le be wrocken on both them towe.'

'Sweavens [47] are swift, master,' quoth John,
'As the wind that blowes ore a hill;
For if it be never soe lowde this night,
To-morrow it may be still.'

'Buske yee, bowne yee,[48] my merry men all,
For John shall goe with mee;
For I'le goe seeke yond wight yeomen
In greenwood where they bee.'

They cast on their gowne of greene,
A shooting gone are they,
Until they came to the merry greenwood,
Where they had gladdest bee;
There were they ware of a wight yeoman,
His body leaned to a tree.

A sword and a dagger he wore by his side,
Had beene many a mans bane,
And he was clad in his capull-hyde,[49]
Top, and tayle, and mayne.

'Stand you still, master,' quoth Litle John,
'Under this trusty tree,
And I will goe to yond wight yeoman,
To know his meaning trulye.'

'A, John, by me thou sets noe store,
And that's a farley [50] thinge;
How oft send I my men before,
And tarry my-selfe behinde?

'It is noe cunning a knave to ken,
And a man but heare him speake;

[43] Robin Hood seems to be the invention of the ballad-makers, though tradition assigns his deeds to the fourteenth century. In forty ballads concerned with his depredations on the richer orders and his friendly acts in behalf of the needy, they have built up his character and supplied him with a life-history.

In this ballad some derangement of the story has taken place. At the start, a few verses are missing. Robin has been dreaming that two yeoman beat and bind him, and he goes to seek them out. One is Sir Guy and the other the sheriff of Nottingham. How Robin knew that the sheriff had attacked his camp we are never informed.

[44] woods

[45] groves

[46] of linden

[47] dreams

[48] make ready

[49] horsehide

[50] marvellous

And it were not for bursting of my bowe,
John, I wold thy head breake.'

But often words they breeden bale,
That parted Robin and John;
John is gone to Barnesdale,
The gates [51] he knowes eche one.

And when hee came to Barnesdale,
Great heavinesse there hee had;
He found two of his fellowes
Were slaine both in a slade,[52]

And Scarlett a foote flyinge was,
Over stockes and stone,
For the sheriffe with seven score men
Fast after him is gone.

'Yet one shoote I'le shoote,' sayes Litle John,
'With Crist his might and mayne;
I'le make yond fellow that flyes soe fast
To be both glad and faine.'

John bent up a good veiwe [53] bow,
And fetteled him to shoote;
The bow was made of a tender boughe,
And fell downe to his foote.

'Woe worth thee, wicked wood,' sayd Litle John,
'That ere thou grew on a tree!
For this day thou art my bale,
My boote when thou shold bee!'

This shoote it was but looselye shot,
The arrowe flew in vaine,
And it met one of the sheriffes men;
Good William a Trent was slaine.

It had beene better for William a Trent
To hange upon a gallowe
Then for to lye in the greenwoode,
There slaine with an arrowe.

And it is sayd, when men be met,
Six can doe more than three:

[51] paths [52] valley [53] yew

And they have tane Litle John,
And bound him fast to a tree.

'Thou shalt be drawen by dale and downe,' quoth the sheriffe,
'And hanged hye on a hill:'
'But thou may fayle,' quoth Litle John,
'If it be Christs owne will.'

Let us leave talking of Litle John,
For hee is bound fast to a tree,
And talke of Guy and Robin Hood,
In the green woode where they bee.

How these two yeomen together they met,
Under the leaves of lyne,
To see what marchandise they made
Even at that same time.

'Good morrow, good fellow,' quoth Sir Guy;
'Good morrow, good fellow,' quoth hee;
'Methinkes by this bow thou beares in thy hand
A good archer thou seems to bee.'

'I am wilfull of my way,' quoth Sir Guye,
'And of my morning tyde:'
'I'le lead thee through the wood,' quoth Robin,
'Good fellow, I'le be thy guide.'

'I seeke an outlaw,' quoth Sir Guye,
'Men call him Robin Hood;
I had rather meet with him upon a day
Then forty pounds of golde.'

'If you tow met, it wold be seene whether were better
Afore yee did part awaye;
Let us some other pastime find,
Good fellow, I thee pray.

'Let us some other masteryes [54] make,
And wee will walke in the woods even;
Wee may chance meet with Robin Hoode
At some unset steven.' [55]

[54] deeds
[55] time

They cut them downe the summer shroggs [56]
  Which grew both under a bryar,
And set them three score rood in twin,[57]
  To shoote the prickes full neare.

'Leade on, good fellow,' sayd Sir Guye,
  'Lead on, I doe bid thee:'
'Nay, by my faith,' quoth Robin Hood,
  'The leader thou shalt bee.'

The first good shoot that Robin led
  Did not shoote an inch the pricke froe;
Guy was an archer good enoughe,
  But he cold neere shoote soe.

The second shoote Sir Guy shot,
  He shot within the garlande;
But Robin Hoode shot it better then hee,
  For he clove the good pricke-wande.

'Gods blessing in thy heart!' sayes Guye,
  'Good fellow, thy shooting is goode;
For an thy hart be as good as thy hands,
  Thou were better then Robin Hood.

'Tell me thy name, good fellow,' quoth Guy,
  'Under the leaves of lyne:'
'Nay, by my faith,' quoth good Robin,
  'Till thou have told me thine.'

'I dwell by dale and downe,' quoth Guye,
  'And I have done many a curst turne;
And he that calles me by my right name
  Calls me Guye of good Gysborne.'

'My dwelling is in the wood,' sayes Robin;
  'By thee I set right nought;
My name is Robin Hood of Barnesdale,
  A fellow thou has long sought.'

He that had neither beene a kithe nor kin
  Might have seene a full fayre sight,
To see how together these yeomen went,
  With blades both browne and bright.

To have seene how these yeomen together fought,
  Two howers of a summers day;
It was neither Guy nor Robin Hood
  That fettled them to flye away.

Robin was reacheles [58] on a roote,
  And stumbled at that tyde,
And Guy was quicke and nimble withall,
  And hit him ore the left side.

'Ah, deere Lady!' sayd Robin Hoode,
  'Thou art both mother and may!
I thinke it was never mans destinye
  To dye before his day.'

Robin thought on Our Lady deere,
  And soone leapt up againe,
And thus he came with an awkwarde stroke;
  Good Sir Guy hee has slayne.

He tooke Sir Guys head by the hayre,
  And sticked it on his bowes end:
'Thou hast been traytor all thy life,
  Which thing must have an ende.'

Robin pulled forth an Irish knife,
  And nicked Sir Guy in the face,
That hee was never on a woman borne
  Cold tell who Sir Guy was.

Saies 'Lye there, lye there, good Sir Guye,
  And with me be not wrothe;
If thou have had the worse stroakes at my hand,
  Thou shalt have the better cloathe.'

Robin did off his gowne of greene,
  Sir Guye hee did it throwe;
And hee put on that capull-hyde,
  That clad him top to toe.

'The bowe, the arrowes, and little horne,
  And with me now I'le beare;
For now I will goe to Barnesdale,
  To see how my men doe fare.'

[56] wands
[57] twain
[58] reckless

Robin set Guyes horne to his mouth,
A lowd blast in it he did blow;
That beheard the sheriffe of Nottingham,
As he leaned under a lowe.[59]

'Hearken! hearken!' sayd the sheriffe,
'I heard noe tydings but good;
For yonder I heare Sir Guyes horne blowe,
For he hath slaine Robin Hoode.

'For yonder I hear Sir Guyes horne blow,
It blowes soe well in tyde,
For yonder comes that wighty yeoman,
Clad in his capull-hyde.

'Come hither, thou good Sir Guy,
Aske of mee what thou wilt have:'
'I'le none of thy gold,' sayes Robin Hood,
'Nor I'le none of it have.

'But now I have slaine the master,' he sayd,
'Let me goe strike the knave;
This is all the reward I aske,
Nor noe other will I have.'

'Thou art a madman,' said the shiriffe,
'Thou sholdest have had a knights fee;
Seeing thy asking hath beene soe bad,
Well granted it shall be.'

But Litle John heard his master speake,
Well he knew that was his steven;[60]
'Now shall I be loset,' quoth Litle John,
'With Christs might in heaven.'

But Robin hee hyed him towards Litle John,
Hee thought hee wold loose him belive;[61]
The sheriffe and all his companye
Fast after him did drive.

'Stand abacke! stand abacke!' sayd Robin;
'Why draw you mee soe neere?
It was never the use in our countrye
One's shrift another shold heere.'

But Robin pulled forth an Irish knife,
And losed John hand and foote,
And gave him Sir Guyes bow in his hand,
And bade it be his boote.

But John tooke Guyes bow in his hand —
His arrowes were rawstye by the roote —;[62]
The sherriffe saw Litle John draw a bow
And fettle him to shoote.

Towards his house in Nottingam
He fled full fast away,
And soe did all his companye,
Not one behind did stay.

But he cold neither soe fast goe,
Nor away soe fast run,
But Litle John, with an arrow broade,
Did cleave his heart in twin.

[59] lay concealed under a hill
[60] voice
[61] soon

The Hunting of the Cheviot [63]

[CHEVY CHASE]

God prosper long our noble king,
our liffes and saftyes all!
A woeful hunting once there did
in Chevy Chase befall.

To drive the deere with hound and horne
Erle Pearcy took the way:
The child may rue that is unborne
the hunting of that day!

The stout Erle of Northumberland
a vow to God did make
His pleasure in the Scottish woods
three sommers days to take,

The cheefest harts in Chevy Chase
to kill and beare away:
These tydings to Erle Douglas came
in Scottland, where he lay.

[62] Possibly, 'rusty at the end, with blood.'
[63] This poem is a late broadside version of the traditional ballad which celebrates a fight that took place in 1388. Addison said of it (*Spectator*, 70 and 74) that it was the favorite ballad of the common people of England. Ben Jonson would rather have been the author of *Chevy Chase* than of all his works. Sidney says he never heard the old song but that 'I found not my heart moved more than with a trumpet.'

Who sent Erle Pearcy present word
 he wold prevent his sport;
The English erle, not fearing that,
 did to the woods resort,

With fifteen hundred bowmen bold,
 all chosen men of might,
Who knew full well in time of neede
 to ayme their shafts arright.

The gallant greyhounds swiftly ran
 to chase the fallow deere;
On Munday they began to hunt,
 ere daylight did appeare.

And long before high noone they had
 a hundred fat buckes slaine;
Then having dined, the drovyers went
 to rouze the deare againe.

The bowmen mustered on the hills,
 well able to endure;
Their backsids all with speciall care
 that day were guarded sure.

The hounds ran swiftly through the woods
 the nimble deere to take,
That with their cryes the hills and dales
 an eccho shrill did make.

Lord Pearcy to the querry went
 to veiw the tender deere;
Quoth he, 'Erle Douglas promised once
 this day to meete me heere;

But if I thought he wold not come,
 noe longer wold I stay.'
With that a brave younge gentlman
 thus to the erle did say:

'Loe, yonder doth Erle Douglas come,
 hys men in armour bright;
Full twenty hundred Scottish speres
 all marching in our sight.

'All men of pleasant Tivydale,
 fast by the river Tweede:'
'O ceaze your sports!' Erle Pearcy said,
 'and take your bowes with speede.

'And now with me, my countrymen,
 your courage forth advance!
For there was never champion yet,
 in Scottland nor in France,

'That ever did on horsbacke come,
 but, and if my hap it were,
I durst encounter man for man,
 with him to breake a spere.'

Erle Douglas on his milke-white steede,
 most like a baron bold,
Rode formost of his company,
 whose armor shone like gold.

'Shew me,' sayd hee, 'whose men you bee
 that hunt soe boldly heere,
That without my consent doe chase
 and kill my fallow deere.'

The first man that did answer make
 was noble Pearcy hee,
Who sayd, 'Wee list not to declare
 nor shew whose men wee bee;

'Yet wee will spend our deerest blood
 thy cheefest harts to slay.'
Then Douglas swore a solempne oathe,
 and this in rage did say:

'Ere thus I will outbraved bee,
 one of us tow shall dye;
I know thee well, an erle thou art;
 Lord Pearcy, soe am I.

'But trust me, Pearcye, pittye it were,
 and great offence, to kill
Then any of these our guiltlesse men,
 for they have done none ill.

'Let thou and I the battell trye,
 and set our men aside:'
'Accurst bee he!' Erle Pearcye sayd,
 'by whome it is denyed.'

Then stept a gallant squire forth —
 Witherington was his name —
Who said, 'I wold not have it told
 to Henry our king, for shame,

'That ere my captaine fought on foote,
and I stand looking on.
You bee two Erles,' quoth Witherington,
'and I a squier alone;

'I'le doe the best that doe I may,
while I have power to stand;
While I have power to weeld my sword,
I'le fight with hart and hand.'

Our English archers bent their bowes;
their harts were good and trew;
At the first flight of arrowes sent,
full foure score Scotts they slew.

To drive the deere with hound and horne,
Douglas bade on the bent,[64]
Two captaines moved with mickle might,
their speres to shivers went.

They closed full fast on every side,
noe slacknes there was found,
But many a gallant gentleman
lay gasping on the ground.

O Christ! it was great greeve to see
how eche man chose his spere,
And how the blood out of their brests
did gush like water cleare.

At last these two stout erles did meet,
like captaines of great might;
Like lyons woode [65] they layd on lode; [66]
they made a cruell fight.

They fought untill they both did sweat,
with swords of tempered steele,
Till blood downe their cheekes like raine
the trickling downe did feele.

'O yeeld thee, Pearcye!' Douglas sayd,
'And in faith I will thee bringe
Where thou shall high advanced bee
by James our Scottish king.

'Thy ransome I will freely give,
and this report of thee,
Thou art the most couragious knight,
that ever I did see.'

[64] field [65] mad [66] *i.e.*, heartily

'Noe, Douglas!' quoth Erle Percy then,
'thy profer I doe scorne;
I will not yeelde to any Scott
that ever yet was borne!'

With that there came an arrow keene,
out of an English bow,
Which stroke Erle Douglas on the brest
a deepe and deadlye blow.

Who never sayd more words then these;
'Fight on, my merry men all!
For why, my life is at an end,
lord Pearcy sees my fall.'

Then leaving life, Erle Pearcy tooke
the dead man by the hand;
Who said, 'Erle Dowglas, for thy life,
wold I had lost my land!

'O Christ! my verry hart doth bleed
for sorrow for thy sake,
For sure, a more redoubted knight
mischance cold never take.'

A knight amongst the Scotts there was
which saw Erle Douglas dye,
Who streight in hart did vow revenge
upon the Lord Pearcye.

Sir Hugh Mountgomerye was he called,
who, with a spere full bright,
Well mounted on a gallant steed,
ran feircly through the fight,

And past the English archers all,
without all dread or feare,
And through Erle Percyes body then
he thrust his hatfull spere.

With such a vehement force and might
his body he did gore,
The staff ran through the other side
a large cloth-yard and more.

Thus did both those nobles dye,
whose courage none cold staine;
An English archer then perceived
the noble erle was slaine.

He had a good bow in his hand,
made of a trusty tree;
An arrow of a cloth-yard long
to the hard head haled hee.

Against Sir Hugh Mountgomerye
his shaft full right he set;
The grey-goose-winge that was there-on
in his harts bloode was wet.

This fight from breake of day did last
till setting of the sun,
For when they rung the evening-bell
the battel scarse was done.

With stout Erle Percy there was slaine
Sir John of Egerton,
Sir Robert Harcliffe and Sir William,
Sir James, that bold barron.

And with Sir George and Sir James,
both knights of good account,
Good Sir Raphe Rebbye there was slaine,
whose prowesse did surmount.

For Witherington needs must I wayle
as one in dolefull dumpes,
For when his leggs were smitten of,
he fought upon his stumpes.

And with Erle Dowglas there was slaine
Sir Hugh Mountgomerye,
And Sir Charles Morrell, that from feelde
one foote wold never flee;

Sir Roger Hever of Harcliffe tow,
his sisters sonne was hee;
Sir David Lambwell, well esteemed,
but saved he cold not bee.

And the Lord Maxwell, in like case,
with Douglas he did dye;
Of twenty hundred Scottish speeres,
scarce fifty-five did flye.

Of fifteen hundred Englishmen
went home but fifty-three;
The rest in Chevy Chase were slaine,
under the greenwoode tree.

Next day did many widdowes come
their husbands to bewayle;
They washt their wounds in brinish teares,
but all wold not prevayle.

Theyr bodyes, bathed in purple blood,
they bore with them away;
They kist them dead a thousand times
ere they were cladd in clay.

The newes was brought to Eddenborrow,
where Scottlands king did rayne,
That brave Erle Douglas soddainlye
was with an arrow slaine.

'O heavy newes!' King James can say;
'Scottland may wittenesse bee
I have not any captaine more
of such account as hee.'

Like tydings to King Henery came,
within as short a space,
That Pearcy of Northumberland
was slaine in Chevy Chase.

'Now God be with him!' said our king,
'sith it will noe better bee;
I trust I have within my realme
five hundred as good as hee.

'Yett shall not Scotts nor Scottland say
but I will vengeance take,
And be revengéd on them all
for brave Erle Percyes sake.'

This vow the king did well performe
after on Humble-downe;
In one day fifty knights were slayne,
with lords of great renowne.

And of the rest, of small account,
did many hundreds dye:
Thus endeth the hunting in Chevy Chase,
made by the Erle Pearcye.

God save our king, and blesse this land
with plentye, joy, and peace,
And grant henceforth that foule debate
twixt noble men may ceaze!

Mary Hamilton [67]

Word's gane to the kitchen,
  And word's gane to the ha,
That Marie Hamilton gangs wi bairn
  To the hichest Stewart of a'.

He's courted her in the kitchen,
  He's courted her in the ha,
He's courted her in the laigh [68] cellar,
  And that was warst of a'.

She's tyed it in her apron
  And she's thrown it in the sea;
Says, 'Sink ye, swim ye, bonny wee babe!
  You'll neer get mair o me.'

Down then came the auld queen,
  Goud tassels tying her hair:
'O Marie, where's the bonny wee babe
  That I heard greet [69] sae sair?'

'There was never a babe intill [70] my room,
  As little designs to be;
It was but a touch o my sair side,
  Come oer my fair bodie.'

'O Marie, put on your robes o black,
  Or else your robes o brown,
For ye maun gang wi me the night,
  To see fair Edinbro town.'

'I winna put on my robes o black,
  Nor yet my robes o brown;
But I'll put on my robes o white,
  To shine through Edinbro town.'

When she gaed up the Cannogate,
  She laughd loud laughters three;
But when she cam down the Cannogate
  The tear blinded her ee.

When she gaed up the Parliament stair,
  The heel cam aff her shee;
And lang or she cam down again
  She was condemned to dee.

When she cam down the Cannogate,
  The Cannogate sae free,
Many a ladie lookd oer her window,
  Weeping for this ladie.

'Ye need nae weep for me,' she says,
  'Ye need nae weep for me;
For had I not slain mine own sweet babe,
  This death I wadna dee.

'Bring me a bottle of wine,' she says,
  'The best that eer ye hae,
That I may drink to my weil-wishers,
  And they may drink to me.

'Here's a health to the jolly sailors,
  That sail upon the main;
Let them never let on to my father and mother
  But what I'm coming hame.

'Here's a health to the jolly sailors,
  That sail upon the sea;
Let them never let on to my father and mother
  That I cam here to dee.

'Oh little did my mother think,
  The day she cradled me,
What lands I was to travel through,
  What death I was to dee.

'Oh little did my father think,
  The day he held up me,
What lands I was to travel through,
  What death I was to dee.

'Last night I washd the queen's feet,
  And gently laid her down;
And a' the thanks I've gotten the nicht
  To be hangd in Edinbro town!

'Last nicht there was four Maries,
  The nicht there'l be but three;
There was Marie Seton, and Marie Beton,
  And Marie Carmichael, and me.'

[67] Mary Stuart had four Maries among her ladies-in-waiting, but there is no official record that one of them came to Mary Hamilton's sad end.
[68] low
[69] weep
[70] into

Captain Car[71]

It befell at Martynmas,[72]
When wether waxéd colde,
Captaine Care said to his men,
We must go take a holde.[73]

Syck, sike, and to-towe[74] sike,
And sike and like to die;
The sikest night that ever I abode,
God lord have mercy on me!

'Haille, master, and wether you will,
And wether ye like it best;'
'To the castle of Crecrynbroghe,
And there we will take our reste.

'I knowe wher is a gay castle,
Is builded of lyme and stone;
Within their is a gay ladie,
Her lord is riden and gone.'

The ladie she lend on her castle-walle,
She loked upp and downe;
There was she ware of an host of men,
Come riding to the towne.

'Se yow, my meri men all,
And se yow what I see?
Yonder I see an host of men,
I muse who they bee.'

She thought he had ben her wed lord,
As he comd riding home;
Then was it traitur Captaine Care,
The lord of Ester-towne.

They wer no soner at supper sett,
Then after said the grace,
Or Captaine Care and all his men
Wer lighte aboute the place.

'Gyve over thi howsse, thou lady gay,
And I will make the a bande;
To-nighte thou shall ly within my armes,
To-morrowe thou shall ere[75] my lande.'

Then bespacke the eldest sonne,
That was both whitt and redde:
'O mother dere, geve over your howsse,
Or elles we shalbe deade.'

'I will not geve over my hous,' she saithe,
'Not for feare of my lyffe;
It shalbe talked throughout the land,
The slaughter of a wyffe.

'Fetch me my pestilett,
And charge me my gonne,
That I may shott at yonder bloddy butcher,
The lord of Easter-towne.'

Styfly upon her wall she stode,
And lett the pellettes flee;
But then she myst the blody bucher,
And she slew other three.

'I will not geve over my hous,' she saithe,
'Neither for lord nor lowne;
Nor yet for traitour Captaine Care,
The lord of Easter-towne.

'I desire of Captine Care,
And all his bloddye band,
That he would save my eldest sonne,
The eare of all my lande.

'Lap him in a shete,' he sayth,
'And let him downe to me,
And I shall take him in my armes,
His waran shall I be.'

The captayne sayd unto him selfe:
Wyth sped, before the rest,
He cut his tonge out of his head,
His hart out of his brest.

He lapt them in a handkerchef,
And knet it of knotes three,
And cast them over the castell-wall,
At that gay ladye.

'Fye upon the, Captayne Care,
And all thy bloddy band!
For thou hast slayne my eldest sonne,
The ayre of all my land.'

[71] The events of this ballad took place in 1571, when Captain Car was sent by Adam Gordon to reduce the house of Towie.
[72] 11 November
[73] stronghold [74] too-too [75] till

Then bespake the yongest sonne,
That sat on the nurses knee,
Sayth, 'Mother gay, geve over your house;
It smoldereth me.

'I wold geve my gold,' she saith,
'And so I wolde my fee,
For a blaste of the westryn wind,
To dryve the smoke from thee.

'Fye upon the, John Hamleton,
That ever I paid the hyre!
For thou hast broken my castle-wall,
And kyndled in the fyre.'

The lady gate to her close parler,
The fire fell aboute her head;
She toke up her children thre,
Seth, 'Babes, we are all dead.'

Then bespake the hye steward,
That is of hye degree;
Saith, 'Ladie gay, you are in close,
Wether ye fighte or flee.'

Lord Hamleton dremd in his dream,
In Carvall where he laye,
His halle were all of fyre,
His ladie slayne or daye.

'Busk and bowne,[76] my mery men all,
Even and go ye with me;
For I dremd that my haal was on fyre,
My lady slayne or day.'

He buskt him and bownd hym,
And like a worthi knighte;
And when he saw his hall burning,
His harte was no dele lighte.

He sett a trumpet till his mouth,
He blew as it plesd his grace;
Twenty score of Hamlentons
Was light aboute the place.

'Had I knowne as much yesternighte
As I do to-daye,
Captaine Care and all his men
Should not have gone so quite.

[76] make ready

'Fye upon the, Captaine Care,
And all thy blody bande!
Thou haste slayne my lady gay,
More wurth then all thy lande.

'If thou had ought eny ill will,' he saith,
'Thou shoulde have taken my lyffe,
And have saved my children thre,
All and my lovesome wyffe.'

The Bitter Withy[77]

As it fell out on a Holy day
The drops of rain did fall, did fall,
Our Saviour asked leave of His mother Mary
If He might go play at ball.

'To play at ball my own dear Son,
It's time You was going or gone,
But be sure let me hear no complaint of You
At night when You do come home.'

It was upling scorn and downling scorn,
Oh, there He met three jolly jerdins.[78]
Oh, there He asked the three jolly jerdins
If they would go play at ball.

'Oh, we are lords' and ladies' sons,
Born in bower or in hall,
And You are but some poor maid's child
Born'd in an ox's stall.'

'If you are lords' and ladies' sons,
Born'd in bower or in hall,
Then at the very last I'll make it appear
That I am above you all.'

Our Saviour built a bridge with the beams of the sun,
And over He gone, He gone He.
And after followed the three jolly jerdins,
And drownded they were all three.

[77] willow
[78] children

It was upling scorn and downling scorn,
The mothers of them did whoop and call,
Crying out, 'Mary mild, call back your Child,
For ours are drownded all.'

Mary mild, Mary mild, called home her Child,
And laid our Saviour across her knee,
And with a whole handful of bitter withy
She gave Him slashes three.

Then He says to His mother, 'Oh! the withy, oh! the withy,
The bitter withy that causes me to smart, to smart,
Oh! the withy it shall be the very first tree
That perishes at the heart.'

Robert Burns

1759–1796

Mary Morison[1]

O Mary, at thy window be,
It is the wish'd, the trysted hour!
Those smiles and glances let me see,
That make the miser's treasure poor:
How blythely wad I bide the stoure,[2]
A weary slave frae sun to sun,
Could I the rich reward secure,
The lovely Mary Morison.

Yestreen, when to the trembling string
The dance gaed thro' the lighted ha',
To thee my fancy took its wing,
I sat, but neither heard nor saw:
Tho' this was fair, and that was braw,[3]
And yon the toast of a' the town,
I sigh'd, and said amang them a',
'Ye are na Mary Morison.'

O Mary, canst thou wreck his peace,
Wha for thy sake wad gladly die?
Or canst thou break that heart of his,
Whase only faut is loving thee?
If love for love thou wilt na gie,[4]
At least be pity to me shown!
A thought ungentle canna be
The thought o' Mary Morison.

[1] Written in 1780 or 1781, and sent to Thomson in a letter of 20 March 1793; published in *Works*, 1800.
[2] suffer hardship, or struggle
[3] handsome, fine
[4] not give

Epistle to John Lapraik, an old Scottish Bard[5]

While briers an' woodbines budding green,
An' paitricks[6] scraichin' loud at e'en,
An' morning poussie[7] whiddin[8] seen,
Inspire my Muse,
This freedom, in an unknown frien',
I pray excuse.

On Fasten-een[9] we had a rockin',
To ca' the crack[10] and weave our stockin';
And there was muckle fun and jokin',
Ye need na doubt;
At length we had a hearty yokin'
At sang about.[11]

There was ae sang, amang the rest,
Aboon[12] them a' it pleas'd me best,
That some kind husband had addrest
To some sweet wife:
It thirl'd the heart-strings thro' the breast,
A' to the life.

I've scarce heard ought describ'd sae weel,
What gen'rous, manly bosoms feel;

[5] Dated 1 April 1785; published in the Kilmarnock edition of *Poems*, 1786. Lapraik (1727–1807), a poet of Ayrshire, had been ruined by the failure of the Ayr Bank in 1772. The song which Burns praises in lines 12 f. is 'When I upon thy bosom lean,' later published with Burns's aid.
[6] partridges
[7] hare
[8] scudding
[9] The evening before Lent.
[10] carry on the conversation
[11] 'turn-about' at a song for each one
[12] above

Thought I 'Can this be Pope, or Steele,
Or Beattie's wark!'
They tauld me 'twas an odd kind chiel [13]
About Muirkirk.[14]

It pat me fidgin' fain [15] to hear 't,
And sae about him there I spier'd; [16]
Then a' that kenn'd him round declar'd
He had ingine,[17]
That nane excell'd it, few cam near 't,
It was sae fine.

That, set him to a pint of ale,
An' either douce [18] or merry tale,
Or rhymes an' sangs he'd made himsel,
Or witty catches,
'Tween Inverness and Teviotdale,
He had few matches.

Then up I gat, an' swoor an aith,
Tho' I should pawn my pleugh and graith,[19]
Or die a cadger pownie's [20] death,
At some dyke-back,[21]
A pint an' gill I'd gie them baith
To hear your crack.[22]

But, first an' foremost, I should tell,
Amaist as soon as I could spell,
I to the crambo-jingle [23] fell;
Tho' rude an' rough,
Yet crooning to a body's sel,
Does weel eneugh.

I am nae poet, in a sense,
But just a rhymer, like, by chance,
An' hae to learning nae pretence,
Yet what the matter?
Whene'er my Muse does on me glance,
I jingle at her.

Your critic-folk may cock their nose,
And say 'How can you e'er propose,
You wha ken hardly verse frae prose,
To mak a sang?'

[13] fellow
[14] Where Lapraik lived before he lost his money.
[15] tingling with pleasure
[16] asked
[17] genius
[18] serious
[19] tools
[20] hawker's pony's
[21] back of a fence
[22] talk
[23] rhyming-game

But, by your leaves, my learnéd foes,
Ye're maybe wrang.

What's a' your jargon o' your schools,
Your Latin names for horns an' stools;
If honest nature made you fools,
What sairs [24] your grammars?
Ye'd better ta'en up spades and shools,[25]
Or knappin'-hammers.[26]

A set o' dull conceited hashes
Confuse their brains in college classes!
They gang in stirks,[27] and come out asses,
Plain truth to speak;
An' syne [28] they think to climb Parnassus
By dint o' Greek!

Gie me ae spark o' Nature's fire,
That's a' the learning I desire;
Then tho' I drudge thro' dub [29] an' mire
At pleugh or cart,
My Muse, though hamely in attire,
May touch the heart.

O for a spunk [30] o' Allan's glee,
Or Fergusson's,[31] the bauld an' slee,[32]
Or bright Lapraik's, my friend to be,
If I can hit it!
That would be lear [33] eneugh for me,
If I could get it.

Now, sir, if ye hae friends enow,
Tho' real friends, I b'lieve, are few,
Yet, if your catalogue be fou,
I'se no insist;
But gif ye want ae friend that's true,
I'm on your list.

I winna blaw about mysel,
As ill I like my fauts to tell;
But friends, an' folks that wish me well,
They sometimes roose [34] me;
Tho' I maun own, as mony still
As far abuse me.

[24] serves
[25] shovels
[26] hammers for breaking stones
[27] young bullocks
[28] then
[29] puddle
[30] spark
[31] Allan Ramsay (1686–1758) and Robert Fergusson (1750–1774), Scotch poets.
[32] bold and ingenious
[33] lore
[34] praise

There's ae wee faut they whiles lay to me,
I like the lasses — Gude forgie me!
For mony a plack [35] they wheedle frae me,
At dance or fair;
Maybe some ither thing they gie me
They weel can spare.

But Mauchline [36] race, or Mauchline fair,
I should be proud to meet you there;
We'se gie a night's discharge to care,
If we forgather,
An' hae a swap o' rhymin'-ware
Wi' ane anither.

The four-gill chap,[37] we'se gar [38] him clatter,
An' kirsen [39] him wi' reekin [40] water;
Syne we'll sit down an' tak our whitter,[41]
To cheer our heart;
An' faith, we'se be acquainted better
Before we part.

Awa, ye selfish warly [42] race,
Wha think that havins,[43] sense, an' grace,
Ev'n love an' friendship, should give place
To catch-the-plack! [44]
I dinna like to see your face,
Nor hear your crack.

But ye whom social pleasure charms,
Whose hearts the tide of kindness warms,
Who hold your being on the terms,
'Each aid the others,'
Come to my bowl, come to my arms,
My friends, my brothers!

But to conclude my lang epistle,
As my auld pen's worn to the gristle;
Twa lines frae you wad gar me fissle,[45]
Who am, most fervent,
While I can either sing, or whistle,
Your friend and servant.

[35] a small coin
[36] A town not far from Mossgiel farm, which Burns and his brother Gilbert had taken in 1784.
[37] cup
[38] we'll make
[39] christen
[40] steaming
[41] hearty draught
[42] worldly
[43] good manners
[44] hunt-the-coin
[45] would make me tingle (with delight)

The Jolly Beggars [46]

When lyart [47] leaves bestrow the yird [48]
Or, wavering like the baukie bird,[49]
Bedim cauld Boreas' blast;
When hailstanes drive wi' bitter skyte,[50]
And infant frosts begin to bite,
In hoary cranreuch [51] drest;
Ae night at e'en a merry core [52]
O' randie gangrel bodies [53]
In Poosie Nansie's held the splore,[54]
To drink their orra duddies.[55]
Wi' quaffing and laughing,
They ranted [56] and they sang;
Wi' jumping and thumping
The very girdle rang.

First, niest [57] the fire, in auld red rags,
Ane sat, weel brac'd wi' mealy bags,
And knapsack a' in order;
His doxy [58] lay within his arm;
Wi' usquebae [59] and blankets warm,
She blinket [60] on her sodger;
An' aye he gies the tosy [61] drab
The tither skelpin' kiss,[62]
While she held up her greedy gab,[63]
Just like an aumous [64] dish:
Ilk smack still did crack still
Just like a cadger's [65] whip;
Then staggering, and swaggering,
He roar'd this ditty up —

I am a son of Mars, who have been in many wars,
And show my cuts and scars wherever I come;
This here was for a wench, and that other in a trench,
When welcoming the French at the sound of the drum.
Lal de daudle, &c.

[46] Written in 1785; published in Stewart and Meikle's *Poetical Miscellany*, 1799. It was suggested by a chance visit of Burns, with two friends, to a 'doss-house' of 'Poosie Nansie's' in Mauchline, where they found a company of roisterers. Burns immediately began his cantata. See Carlyle's praise of the poem in his essay on Burns.
[47] faded
[48] earth
[49] bat
[50] spirt
[51] hoar-frost
[52] company
[53] lawless vagabonds
[54] carousal
[55] spare clothes, or rather rags
[56] roistered
[57] next
[58] wench
[59] whiskey
[60] smirked
[61] tipsy
[62] another smacking kiss
[63] mouth
[64] alms
[65] hawker's

My 'prenticeship I pass'd where my leader breath'd his last,
When the bloody die was cast on the heights of Abrám; [66]
And I servéd out my trade when the gallant game was play'd,
And the Moro [67] low was laid at the sound of the drum.

I lastly was with Curtis, among the floating batt'ries,[68]
And there I left for witness an arm and a limb:
Yet let my country need me, with Elliot [69] to head me,
I'd clatter on my stumps at the sound of a drum.

And now tho' I must beg, with a wooden arm and leg,
And many a tatter'd rag hanging over my bum,
I'm as happy with my wallet, my bottle, and my callet,[70]
As when I used in scarlet to follow a drum.

What tho' with hoary locks I must stand the winter shocks,
Beneath the woods and rocks oftentimes for a home?
When the t'other bag I sell, and the t'other bottle tell,
I could meet a troop of hell at the sound of the drum.

He ended; and the kebars [71] sheuk
Aboon the chorus roar;
While frighted rattons [72] backward leuk,
And seek the benmost bore.[73]
A fairy fiddler frae the neuk,[74]
He skirled [75] out *Encore!*
But up arose the martial chuck,
And laid the loud uproar.

I once was a maid, tho' I cannot tell when,
And still my delight is in proper young men;
Some one of a troop of dragoons was my daddie,
No wonder I'm fond of a sodger laddie.
Sing, Lal de dal, &c.

The first of my loves was a swaggering blade,
To rattle the thundering drum was his trade;
His leg was so tight, and his cheek was so ruddy,
Transported I was with my sodger laddie.

But the godly old chaplain left him in the lurch;
The sword I forsook for the sake of the church;
He ventur'd the soul, and I riskéd the body, —
'Twas then I prov'd false to my sodger laddie.

Full soon I grew sick of my sanctified sot,
The regiment at large for a husband I got;
From the gilded spontoon [76] to the fife I was ready,
I askéd no more but a sodger laddie.

But the peace it reduced me to beg in despair,
Till I met my old boy at a Cunningham fair;
His rags regimental they flutter'd so gaudy,
My heart it rejoiced at a sodger laddie.

And now I have liv'd — I know not how long,
And still I can join in a cup or a song;
But whilst with both hands I can hold the glass steady,
Here's to thee, my hero, my sodger laddie!

Poor Merry Andrew in the neuk
Sat guzzling wi' a tinkler hizzie; [77]

[66] At Quebec in 1759.
[67] At Santiago de Cuba, where the British stormed the fortress in 1762.
[68] At Gibraltar in 1782.
[69] Sir George Elliot, who defended Gibraltar against the French and Spanish, 1779–1783.
[70] wench
[71] rafters
[72] rats
[73] inmost hole
[74] corner
[75] shrilled

[76] A weapon carried by officers.
[77] tinker-wench

They mind't na wha the chorus teuk,
Between themselves they were sae busy.
At length, wi' drink and courting dizzy,
He stoitered [78] up an' made a face;
Then turn'd, an' laid a smack on Grizzy,
Syne [79] tun'd his pipes wi' grave grimace.

Sir Wisdom's a fool when he's fou,[80]
Sir Knave is a fool in a session;
He's there but a 'prentice I trow,
But I am a fool by profession.

My grannie she bought me a beuk,
And I held awa to the school;
I fear I my talent misteuk,
But what will ye hae of a fool?

For drink I would venture my neck;
A hizzie's the half o' my craft;
But what could ye other expect,
Of ane that's avowedly daft?

I ance was tied up like a stirk,[81]
For civilly swearing and quaffing;
I ance was abused i' the kirk,
For touzling a lass i' my daffin.[82]

Poor Andrew that tumbles for sport,
Let naebody name wi' a jeer;
There's even, I'm tauld, i' the Court,
A tumbler ca'd the Premier.

Observ'd ye yon reverend lad
Maks faces to tickle the mob?
He rails at our mountebank squad —
It's rivalship just i' the job.

And now my conclusion I'll tell,
For, faith! I'm confoundedly dry;
The chiel [83] that's a fool for himsel',
Gude Lord! he's far dafter than I.

Then niest outspak a raucle carlin,[84]
Wha kent fu' weel to cleek [85] the sterling,
For mony a pursie she had hookit,
And had in mony a well been dookit;
Her love had been a Highland laddie,
But weary fa' the waefu' woodie!
Wi' sighs and sobs, she thus began
To wail her braw John Highlandman: —

A Highland lad my love was born,
The Lawlan' laws he held in scorn;
But he still was faithfu' to his clan,
My gallant braw John Highlandman.

CHORUS

Sing hey, my braw John Highlandman!
Sing ho, my braw John Highlandman!
There's no a lad in a' the lan'
Was match for my John Highlandman.

With his philibeg [86] an' tartan plaid,
And gude claymore [87] down by his side,
The ladies' hearts he did trepan,
My gallant braw John Highlandman.

We rangéd a' from Tweed to Spey,
And lived like lords and ladies gay;
For a Lawlan' face he fearéd nane,
My gallant braw John Highlandman.

They banish'd him beyond the sea;
But ere the bud was on the tree,
Adown my cheeks the pearls ran,
Embracing my John Highlandman.

But oh! they catch'd him at the last,
And bound him in a dungeon fast;
My curse upon them every one!
They've hang'd my braw John Highlandman.

And now a widow I must mourn
The pleasures that will ne'er return;
No comfort but a hearty can,
When I think on John Highlandman.

A pigmy scraper wi' his fiddle,
Wha used at trysts [88] and fairs to driddle,[89]

78 staggered
79 then
80 full
81 young bullock
82 fun
83 young fellow
84 sturdy old woman
85 snatch

86 kilt
87 sword
88 cattle-markets
89 toddle

Her strappin' limb and gaucy [90] middle
(He reach'd nae higher)
Had holed his heartie like a riddle,[91]
And blawn't on fire.

Wi' hand on haunch, and upward ee,
He croon'd his gamut, one, two, three,
Then, in an arioso key,
The wee Apollo
Set aff, wi' allegretto glee,
His giga solo.

Let me ryke [92] up to dight [93] that tear,
And go wi' me and be my dear,
And then your every care and fear
May whistle owre the lave [94] o't.

CHORUS

I am a fiddler to my trade,
And a' the tunes that e'er I play'd,
The sweetest still to wife or maid,
Was whistle owre the lave o't.

At kirns [95] and weddings we'se be there,
And oh! sae nicely's we will fare;
We'll bouse about, till Daddie Care
Sings whistle owre the lave o't.

Sae merrily's the banes we'll pyke,[96]
And sun oursels about the dyke,
And at our leisure, when ye like,
We'll whistle owre the lave o't.

But bless me wi' your heav'n o' charms,
And while I kittle hair on thairms,[97]
Hunger and cauld, and a' sic harms,
May whistle owre the lave o't.

Her charms had struck a sturdy caird,[98]
As well as poor gut-scraper;
He taks the fiddler by the beard,
And draws a roosty rapier —

He swoor, by a' was swearing worth,
To spit him like a pliver,[99]
Unless he would from that time forth
Relinquish her for ever.

Wi' ghastly ee, poor tweedle-dee
Upon his hunkers [100] bended,
And pray'd for grace wi' ruefu' face,
And sae the quarrel ended.

But tho' his little heart did grieve
When round the tinkler prest her,
He feign'd to snirtle [101] in his sleeve,
When thus the caird address'd her: —

My bonnie lass, I work in brass,
A tinkler is my station;
I've travell'd round all Christian ground
In this my occupation;
I've ta'en the gold, I've been enroll'd
In many a noble squadron;
But vain they search'd, when off I march'd
To go and clout [102] the cauldron.

Despise that shrimp, that wither'd imp,
Wi' a' his noise and caperin';
And tak a share wi' those that bear
The budget [103] and the apron;
And, by that stoup, my faith and houp!
And by that dear Kilbaigie,[104]
If e'er ye want, or meet wi' scant,
May I ne'er weet my craigie.[105]

The caird prevail'd — th' unblushing fair
In his embraces sunk,
Partly wi' love o'ercome sae sair,
And partly she was drunk.
Sir Violino, with an air
That show'd a man o' spunk,
Wish'd unison between the pair,
And made the bottle clunk
To their health that night.

But urchin Cupid shot a shaft
That play'd a dame a shavie; [106]
The fiddler rak'd her fore and aft,
Behint the chicken cavie.[107]

---

90 buxom
91 sieve
92 reach
93 wipe
94 rest
95 harvest-homes
96 bones we'll pick
97 tickle hair on guts, *i.e.*, to fiddle
98 tinker
99 plover
100 hams
101 snigger
102 patch
103 A tinker's bag of tools.
104 A brand of whiskey.
105 throat
106 trick
107 coop

Her lord, a wight of Homer's craft,
  Tho' limpin' wi' the spavie,[108]
He hirpled [109] up, and lap like daft,[110]
  And shor'd them *Dainty Davie*
    O' boot [111] that night.

He was a care-defying blade
  As ever Bacchus listed;
Tho' Fortune sair upon him laid,
  His heart she ever miss'd it.
He had nae wish, but to be glad,
  Nor want but when he thirsted;
He hated nought but to be sad,
  And thus the Muse suggested
    His sang that night.

I am a bard of no regard
  Wi' gentlefolks, and a' that;
But Homer-like, the glowrin' byke,[112]
  Frae town to town I draw that.

CHORUS

For a' that, and a' that,
  And twice as meikle's a' that;
I've lost but ane, I've twa behin',
  I've wife eneugh for a' that.

I never drank the Muses' stank,[113]
  Castalia's burn,[114] and a' that;
But there it streams, and richly reams! [115]
  My Helicon I ca' that.

Great love I bear to a' the fair,
  Their humble slave, and a' that;
But lordly will, I hold it still
  A mortal sin to thraw [116] that.

In raptures sweet this hour we meet
  Wi' mutual love, and a' that;
But for how lang the flee may stang,
  Let inclination law that.

Their tricks and craft hae put me daft,
  They've ta'en me in, and a' that;
But clear your decks, and *Here's the sex!*
  I like the jads for a' that.

[108] spavin
[109] hobbled
[110] leaped like mad
[111] gratis, 'to boot'
[112] staring crowd
[113] pool, or ditch
[114] brook
[115] foams
[116] thwart

For a' that, and a' that,
  And twice as meikle's a' that,
My dearest bluid, to do them guid,
  They're welcome till't, for a' that.

So sung the bard — and Nansie's wa's
Shook with a thunder of applause,
  Re-echo'd from each mouth;
They toom'd their pocks,[117] an' pawn'd their duds,
They scarcely left to co'er their fuds,[118]
  To quench their lowin' [119] drouth.

Then owre again the jovial thrang
  The poet did request
To lowse [120] his pack, an' wale [121] a sang,
  A ballad o' the best;
    He rising, rejoicing,
      Between his twa Deborahs,
    Looks round him, an' found them
      Impatient for the chorus.

See the smoking bowl before us,
  Mark our jovial ragged ring;
Round and round take up the chorus,
  And in raptures let us sing —

CHORUS

A fig for those by laws protected!
  Liberty's a glorious feast!
Courts for cowards were erected,
  Churches built to please the priest.

What is title? what is treasure?
  What is reputation's care?
If we lead a life of pleasure,
  'Tis no matter how or where!

With the ready trick and fable,
  Round we wander all the day;
And at night, in barn or stable,
  Hug our doxies on the hay.

Does the train-attended carriage
  Thro' the country lighter rove?
Does the sober bed of marriage
  Witness brighter scenes of love?

[117] emptied their pouches
[118] cover their tails
[119] burning
[120] open
[121] choose

Life is all a variorum,
  We regard not how it goes;
Let them cant about decorum
  Who have characters to lose.

Here's to budgets, bags, and wallets!
  Here's to all the wandering train!
Here's our ragged brats and callets! [122]
  One and all cry out *Amen!*

CHORUS

A fig for those by law protected!
  Liberty's a glorious feast!
Courts for cowards were erected,
  Churches built to please the priest.

The Holy Fair [123]

A robe of seeming truth and trust
Hid crafty observation;
And secret hung, with poison'd crust,
The dirk of defamation:
A mask that like the gorget show'd,
Dye-varying on the pigeon;
And for a mantle large and broad,
He wrapt him in religion.

HYPOCRISY À LA MODE.

UPON a simmer Sunday morn,
  When Nature's face is fair,
I walkéd forth to view the corn,
  An' snuff the caller [124] air.
The risin' sun, owre Galston muirs,
  Wi' glorious light was glintin';
The hares were hirplin' [125] down the furrs,[126]
  The lav'rocks [127] they were chantin'
    Fu' sweet that day.

As lightsomely I glowr'd [128] abroad,
  To see a scene sae gay,
Three hizzies,[129] early at the road,
  Cam skelpin' [130] up the way.
Twa had manteeles o' dolefu' black,
  But ane wi' lyart [131] lining;

[122] wenches
[123] Written in 1785; published in *Poems*, 1786. The satire is directed against the 'tent-preaching' which went on in the churchyard while the Communion was being held in the church. At Mauchline the preaching-tent adjoined a tavern.
[124] cool
[125] limping
[126] furrows
[127] larks
[128] stared
[129] wenches
[130] hastening
[131] gray

The third, that gaed a wee a-back,
  Was in the fashion shining
    Fu' gay that day.

The twa appear'd like sisters twin,
  In feature, form, an' claes;
Their visage wither'd, lang an' thin,
  An' sour as ony slaes.[132]
The third cam up, hap-stap-an'-lowp,[133]
  As light as ony lambie,
An' wi' a curchie low did stoop,
  As soon as e'er she saw me,
    Fu' kind that day.

Wi' bonnet aff, quoth I, 'Sweet lass,
  I think ye seem to ken me;
I'm sure I've seen that bonnie face,
  But yet I canna name ye.'
Quo' she, an' laughin' as she spak,
  An' taks me by the hands,
'Ye, for my sake, hae gi'en the feck [134]
  Of a' the ten commands
    A screed [135] some day.

My name is Fun — your crony dear,
  The nearest friend ye hae;
An' this is Superstition here,
  An' that's Hypocrisy.
I'm gaun to Mauchline Holy Fair,
  To spend an hour in daffin'.[136]
Gin [137] ye'll go there, yon runkled [138] pair,
  We will get famous laughin'
    At them this day.'

Quoth I, 'Wi' a' my heart, I'll do't;
  I'll get my Sunday's sark [139] on,
An' meet you on the holy spot;
  Faith, we'se hae fine remarkin'!'
Then I gaed hame at crowdie-time,[140]
  An' soon I made me ready;
For roads were clad, frae side to side,
  Wi' mony a wearie bodie
    In droves that day.

Here farmers gash [141] in ridin' graith [142]
  Gaed hoddin' by their cotters;

[132] sloe berries
[133] hop, step and leap
[134] bulk
[135] rip
[136] fun
[137] if
[138] wrinkled
[139] shirt
[140] breakfast, or 'porridge-time
[141] spruce
[142] garb

There swankies young [143] in braw braid-claith
Are springin' owre the gutters.
The lasses, skelpin' barefit, thrang,
In silks an' scarlets glitter,
Wi' sweet-milk cheese, in mony a whang,
An' farls [144] bak'd wi' butter,
Fu' crump [145] that day.

When by the plate we set our nose,
Weel heapéd up wi' ha'pence,
A greedy glow'r [146] Black Bonnet [147] throws,
An' we maun draw our tippence.
Then in we go to see the show:
On ev'ry side they're gath'rin';
Some carryin' deals, some chairs an' stools,
An' some are busy bleth'rin' [148]
Right loud that day.

Here stands a shed to fend the show'rs,
An' screen our country gentry;
There racer Jess an' twa-three whores
Are blinkin' at the entry.
Here sits a raw o' tittlin' jades,
Wi' heavin' breasts an' bare neck,
An' there a batch o' wabster lads,
Blackguardin' frae Kilmarnock
For fun this day.

Here some are thinkin' on their sins,
An' some upo' their claes;
Ane curses feet that fyl'd his shins,
Anither sighs an' prays:
On this hand sits a chosen swatch,[149]
Wi' screw'd up, grace-proud faces;
On that a set o' chaps, at watch,
Thrang [150] winkin' on the lasses
To chairs that day.

O happy is that man an' blest! [151]
Nae wonder that it pride him!
Wha's ain dear lass, that he likes best,
Comes clinkin' [152] down beside him!
Wi' arm repos'd on the chair-back
He sweetly does compose him;
Which, by degrees, slips round her neck,
An's loof [153] upon her bosom,
Unkenn'd [154] that day.

Now a' the congregation o'er
Is silent expectation;
For Moodie [155] speels the holy door,[156]
Wi' tidings o' damnation.
Should Hornie, as in ancient days,
'Mang sons o' God present him,
The very sight o' Moodie's face
To's ain het hame had sent him
Wi' fright that day.

Hear how he clears the points o' faith
Wi' rattlin' an' wi' thumpin'!
Now meekly calm, now wild in wrath,
He's stampin' an' he's jumpin'!
His lengthen'd chin, his turned-up snout,
His eldritch [157] squeal an' gestures,
O how they fire the heart devout,
Like cantharidian plaisters,
On sic a day!

But, hark! the tent has chang'd its voice;
There's peace an' rest nae langer;
For a' the real judges rise,
They canna sit for anger.
Smith [158] opens out his cauld harangues,
On practice and on morals;
An' aff the godly pour in thrangs
To gie the jars an' barrels
A lift that day.

What signifies his barren shine
Of moral pow'rs an' reason?
His English style an' gesture fine
Are a' clean out o' season.
Like Socrates or Antonine,
Or some auld pagan Heathen,

[143] young blades
[144] oat-cakes
[145] crisp
[146] look
[147] The black bonnet was worn by the elder who took collection at the door.
[148] chattering
[149] sample
[150] busily
[151] *Psalm* cxlvi, 5 (Scotch metrical version).
[152] moving smartly
[153] hand
[154] unknown
[155] Alexander Moodie (1722–1799), the fiery minister of Riccarton.
[156] climbs the open-air pulpit
[157] unearthly
[158] George Smith, minister of Galston, a 'moderate.'

The moral man he does define,
  But ne'er a word o' faith in
        That's right that day.

In guid time comes an antidote
  Against sic poison'd nostrum;
For Peebles,[159] frae the water-fit,[160]
  Ascends the holy rostrum:
See, up he's got the word o' God,
  An' meek an' mim [161] has view'd it,
While Common Sense [162] has ta'en the road,
  An' aff, an' up the Cowgate
        Fast, fast, that day.

Wee Miller,[163] neist, the Guard relieves,
  An' Orthodoxy raibles,[164]
Tho' in his heart he weel believes,
  An' thinks it auld wives' fables:
But, faith! the birkie [165] wants a Manse,
  So cannilie he hums them;
Altho' his carnal wit an' sense
  Like hafflins-wise o'ercomes him [166]
        At times that day.

Now, butt an' ben,[167] the Change-house fills,
  Wi' yill-caup [168] Commentators;
Here's crying out for bakes an' gills,
  An' there the pint-stowp clatters;
While thick an' thrang, an' loud an' lang,
  Wi' logic, an' wi' Scripture,
They raise a din, that in the end
  Is like to breed a rupture
        O' wrath that day.

Leeze me on drink! [169] it gi'es us mair
  Than either school or college;
It kindles wit, it waukens lair,[170]
  It pangs us fou o' knowledge.

159 William Peebles, orthodox minister of Newton-on-Ayr.
160 river-mouth
161 prim
162 Refers to the 'New Light' party, but here probably to Burns's friend, Dr. Mackenzie.
163 Alexander Millar, the short, plump assistant minister of St. Michael's.
164 gabbles
165 fellow
166 nearly half overcomes him
167 kitchen and parlor
168 ale-cup
169 Dear to me is drink!
170 learning

Be't whisky gill, or penny wheep,
  Or ony stronger potion,
It never fails, on drinkin' deep,
  To kittle [171] up our notion
        By night or day.

The lads an' lasses, blythely bent
  To mind baith saul an' body,
Sit round the table, weel content,
  An' steer about the toddy.
On this ane's dress, an' that ane's leuk,
  They're makin observations;
While some are cosy i' the neuk,
  An' formin' assignations
        To meet some day.

But now the Lord's ain trumpet touts,
  Till a' the hills are rairin',
An' echoes back return the shouts;
  Black Russel [172] is na sparin':
His piercing words, like Highlan' swords,
  Divide the joints an' marrow;
His talk o' Hell, where devils dwell,
  Our very 'sauls does harrow'
        Wi' fright that day!

A vast, unbottom'd, boundless pit,
  Fill'd fou o' lowin [173] brunstane,
Wha's ragin' flame, an' scorchin' heat,
  Wad melt the hardest whun-stane!
The half-asleep start up wi' fear
  An' think they hear it roarin',
When presently it does appear
  'Twas but some neebor snorin'
        Asleep that day.

'Twad be owre lang a tale to tell
  How mony stories past,
An' how they crowded to the yill,[174]
  When they were a' dismist;
How drink gaed round, in cogs [175] an' caups,
  Amang the furms and benches;
An' cheese an' bread, frae women's laps,
  Was dealt about in lunches,
        An' dawds [176] that day.

171 tickle
172 John Russel, dark-visaged and stern Calvinist minister at Kilmarnock, with a voice to wake the dead.
173 burning
174 ale
175 wooden mugs
176 lumps

In comes a gawsie, gash guidwife,[177]
  An' sits down by the fire,
Syne draws her kebbuck [178] an' her knife;
  The lasses they are shyer.
The auld guidmen, about the grace,
  Frae side to side they bother,
Till some ane by his bonnet lays,
  An' gi'es them't like a tether.
      Fu' lang that day.

Waesucks! [179] for him that gets nae lass,
  Or lasses that hae naething!
Sma' need has he to say a grace,
  Or melvie [180] his braw claithing!
O wives, be mindfu', ance yoursel
  How bonnie lads ye wanted,
An' dinna for a kebbuck-heel
  Let lasses be affronted
      On sic a day!

Now Clinkumbell,[181] wi' rattlin' tow,
  Begins to jow an' croon,[182]
Some swagger hame the best they dow,[183]
  Some wait the afternoon.
At slaps [184] the billies [185] halt a blink,[186]
  Till lasses strip their shoon:
Wi' faith an' hope, an' love an' drink,
  They're a' in famous tune
      For crack [187] that day.

How mony hearts this day converts
  O' sinners and o' lasses!
Their hearts o' stane, gin night, are gane
  As saft as ony flesh is.
There's some are fou o' love divine,
  There's some are fou o' brandy;
An' mony jobs that day begin
  May end in houghmagandie [188]
      Some ither day.

[177] buxom, keen goodwife
[178] cheese
[179] alas
[180] dust with meal
[181] church-bell
[182] peal and hum
[183] are able
[184] breaches in fences
[185] young men
[186] short time
[187] talk
[188] fornication

The Cotter's Saturday Night [189]

MY lov'd, my honour'd, much respected friend!
  No mercenary bard his homage pays:
With honest pride I scorn each selfish end,
  My dearest meed a friend's esteem and praise:
  To you I sing, in simple Scottish lays,
The lowly train in life's sequester'd scene;
  The native feelings strong, the guileless ways;
What Aiken in a cottage would have been —
Ah! tho' his worth unknown, far happier there, I ween.

November chill blaws loud wi' angry sough;
  The short'ning winter-day is near a close;
The miry beasts retreating frae the pleugh;
  The black'ning trains o' craws to their repose:
  The toil-worn Cotter frae his labour goes,
This night his weekly moil is at an end,
  Collects his spades, his mattocks, and his hoes,
Hoping the morn in ease and rest to spend,
And weary, o'er the moor, his course does hameward bend.

At length his lonely cot appears in view,
  Beneath the shelter of an agéd tree;
Th' expectant wee things, toddlin', stacher [190] through
  To meet their Dad, wi' flichterin' [191] noise an' glee.
  His wee bit ingle,[192] blinkin bonnilie,
His clean hearth-stane, his thrifty wifie's smile,
  The lisping infant prattling on his knee,

[189] Written in 1785; published in 1786. The motto for the poem, addressed to Robert Aiken, an Ayrshire solicitor, was the stanza from Gray's *Elegy* beginning, 'Let not Ambition mock their useful toil' (see p. 469). Burns greatly reflects the poetry of the eighteenth century, particularly of the Spenserian imitators, for he had not read *The Faerie Queene* at the time.
[190] totter
[191] fluttering
[192] fire-place

Does a' his weary kiaugh [193] and care beguile,
An' makes him quite forget his labour an' his toil.

Belyve,[194] the elder bairns come drapping in,
At service out, amang the farmers roun';
Some ca' the pleugh, some herd, some tentie rin [195]
A cannie errand to a neibor town:
Their eldest hope, their Jenny, woman-grown,
In youthfu' bloom, love sparkling in her e'e,
Comes hame, perhaps to shew a braw new gown,
Or deposite her sair-won penny-fee,
To help her parents dear, if they in hardship be.

With joy unfeign'd, brothers and sisters meet,
An' each for other's weelfare kindly spiers.[196]
The social hours, swift-wing'd, unnoticed fleet;
Each tells the uncos [197] that he sees or hears;
The parents, partial, eye their hopeful years;
Anticipation forward points the view.
The mother, wi' her needle an' her sheers,
Gars [198] auld claes look amaist as weel's the new;
The father mixes a' wi' admonition due.

Their master's an' their mistress's command,
The younkers a' are warnéd to obey;
An' mind their labours wi' an eydent [199] hand,
An' ne'er, tho' out o' sight, to jauk or play:
'And O! be sure to fear the Lord alway,
An' mind your duty, duly, morn an' night!
Lest in temptation's path ye gang astray,
Implore His counsel and assisting might:
They never sought in vain that sought the Lord aright!'

But hark! a rap comes gently to the door;
Jenny, wha kens the meaning o' the same,
Tells how a neibor lad cam o'er the moor,
To do some errands, and convoy her hame.
The wily mother sees the conscious flame
Sparkle in Jenny's e'e, and flush her cheek;
Wi' heart-struck anxious care, inquires his name,
While Jenny hafflins [200] is afraid to speak;
Weel pleased the mother hears it's nae wild worthless rake.

Wi' kindly welcome, Jenny brings him ben;[201]
A strappin' youth; he takes the mother's eye;
Blythe Jenny sees the visit's no ill ta'en;
The father cracks [202] of horses, pleughs, and kye.
The youngster's artless heart o'erflows wi' joy,
But blate and laithfu',[203] scarce can weel behave;
The mother, wi' a woman's wiles, can spy
What makes the youth sae bashfu' an' sae grave;
Weel-pleased to think her bairn's respected like the lave.[204]

---

193 anxiety
194 by-and-by
195 heedful to run
196 asks
197 news
198 makes
199 diligent

200 half
201 in
202 talks
203 bashful and sheepish
204 rest

O happy love! where love like this is found;
O heart-felt raptures! bliss beyond compare!
I've pacéd much this weary mortal round,
And sage experience bids me this declare —
'If Heaven a draught of heavenly pleasure spare,
One cordial in this melancholy vale,
'Tis when a youthful, loving, modest pair
In other's arms breathe out the tender tale,
Beneath the milk-white thorn that scents the evening gale.'

Is there, in human form, that bears a heart —
A wretch, a villain, lost to love and truth —
That can, with studied, sly, ensnaring art,
Betray sweet Jenny's unsuspecting youth?
Curse on his perjur'd arts, dissembling smooth!
Are honour, virtue, conscience, all exil'd?
Is there no pity, no relenting ruth,
Points to the parents fondling o'er their child?
Then paints the ruin'd maid, and their distraction wild?

But now the supper crowns their simple board,
The halesome parritch, chief of Scotia's food:
The sowpe [205] their only hawkie [206] does afford,
That 'yont the hallan [207] snugly chows her cood;
The dame brings forth in complimental mood,
To grace the lad, her weel-hain'd kebbuck,[208] fell; [209]
And aft he's prest, and aft he ca's it good;
The frugal wifie, garrulous, will tell
How 'twas a towmond [210] auld sin' lint was i' the bell.[211]

The cheerfu' supper done, wi' serious face
They round the ingle form a circle wide;
The sire turns o'er, wi' patriarchal grace,
The big ha'-bible,[212] ance his father's pride:
His bonnet rev'rently is laid aside,
His lyart haffets [213] wearing thin an' bare;
Those strains that once did sweet in Zion glide —
He wales [214] a portion with judicious care,
And 'Let us worship God!' he says with solemn air.

They chant their artless notes in simple guise;
They tune their hearts, by far the noblest aim:
Perhaps Dundee's wild warbling measures rise,
Or plaintive Martyrs, worthy of the name;
Or noble Elgin beets [215] the heav'nward flame,
The sweetest far of Scotia's holy lays:
Compared with these, Italian trills are tame;
The tickled ears no heartfelt raptures raise;
Nae unison hae they with our Creator's praise.

The priest-like father reads the sacred page,
How Abram was the friend of God on high;

---

205 milk
206 cow
207 beyond the partition
208 well-saved cheese
209 pungent

210 twelve-month
211 since flax was in flower
212 The 'Hall-Bible' once used in the noble's hall for general services.
213 gray temples
214 chooses
215 kindles

Or Moses bade eternal warfare wage
With Amalek's ungracious progeny;
Or how the royal bard [216] did groaning lie
Beneath the stroke of Heaven's avenging ire;
Or Job's pathetic plaint, and wailing cry;
Or rapt Isaiah's wild seraphic fire;
Or other holy seers that tune the sacred lyre.

Perhaps the Christian volume is the theme,
How guiltless blood for guilty man was shed;
How He who bore in Heaven the second name
Had not on earth whereon to lay His head;
How His first followers and servants sped;
The precepts sage they wrote to many a land:
How he,[217] who lone in Patmos banishéd,
Saw in the sun a mighty angel stand,
And heard great Bab'lon's doom pronounced by Heaven's command.

Then kneeling down to Heaven's Eternal King
The saint, the father, and the husband prays:
Hope 'springs exulting on triumphant wing,' [218]
That thus they all shall meet in future days:
There ever bask in uncreated rays,
No more to sigh, or shed the bitter tear,
Together hymning their Creator's praise,
In such society, yet still more dear;
While circling Time moves round in an eternal sphere.

Compared with this, how poor Religion's pride,
In all the pomp of method and of art,
When men display to congregations wide
Devotion's every grace, except the heart!
The Power, incensed, the pageant will desert,
The pompous strain, the sacerdotal stole;
But haply, in some cottage far apart,
May hear, well pleased, the language of the soul;
And in His Book of Life the inmates poor enrol.

Then homeward all take off their several way;
The youngling cottagers retire to rest:
The parent-pair their secret homage pay,
And proffer up to Heav'n the warm request,
That He who stills the raven's clamorous nest,
And decks the lily fair in flowery pride,
Would, in the way His wisdom sees the best,
For them and for their little ones provide;
But chiefly in their hearts with grace divine preside.

From scenes like these old Scotia's grandeur springs,
That makes her loved at home, revered abroad:
Princes and lords are but the breath of kings,
'An honest man's the noblest work of God;' [219]
And certes, in fair virtue's heavenly road,
The cottage leaves the palace far behind;
What is a lordling's pomp? a cumbrous load,

[216] David
[217] John
[218] Inexact quotation of Pope, *Windsor Forest*, l. 112.

[219] Pope, *Essay on Man*, Epistle iv, 248.

Disguising oft the wretch of human kind,
Studied in arts of hell, in wickedness refin'd!

O Scotia! my dear, my native soil!
For whom my warmest wish to Heaven is sent!
Long may thy hardy sons of rustic-toil
Be blest with health, and peace, and sweet content!
And O may Heaven their simple lives prevent
From luxury's contagion, weak and vile;
Then, howe'er crowns and coronets be rent,
A virtuous populace may rise the while,
And stand a wall of fire around their much-loved isle.

O Thou! who poured the patriotic tide
That streamed thro' Wallace's undaunted heart,
Who dared to nobly stem tyrannic pride,
Or nobly die — the second glorious part,
(The patriot's God, peculiarly thou art,
His friend, inspirer, guardian, and reward!)
O never, never, Scotia's realm desert;
But still the patriot, and the patriot-bard,
In bright succession raise, her ornament and guard!

To a Mouse [220]

ON TURNING HER UP IN HER NEST WITH THE PLOUGH, NOVEMBER, 1785

Wee, sleekit,[221] cow'rin', tim'rous beastie,
O what a panic's in thy breastie!
Thou need na start awa sae hasty,
Wi' bickering brattle! [222]
I wad be laith to rin an' chase thee
Wi' murd'ring pattle! [223]

[220] Published in 1786.
[221] sleek
[222] with hasty scamper
[223] plow-staff

I'm truly sorry man's dominion
Has broken Nature's social union,
An' justifies that ill opinion
Which makes thee startle
At me, thy poor earth-born companion,
An' fellow-mortal!

I doubt na, whiles, but thou may thieve;
What then? poor beastie, thou maun live!
A daimen-icker in a thrave [224]
'S a sma' request:
I'll get a blessin' wi' the lave,
And never miss 't!

Thy wee bit housie, too, in ruin!
Its silly wa's the win's are strewin'!
An' naething, now, to big [225] a new ane
O' foggage green! [226]
An' bleak December's winds ensuin',
Baith snell [227] an' keen!

Thou saw the fields laid bare and waste,
An' weary winter comin' fast,
An' cozie here, beneath the blast,
Thou thought to dwell,
Till crash! the cruel coulter past
Out-thro' thy cell.

That wee bit heap o' leaves an' stibble
Has cost thee mony a weary nibble!
Now thou's turn'd out, for a' thy trouble,
But house or hald,[228]
To thole [229] the winter's sleety dribble,
An' cranreuch [230] cauld!

But, Mousie, thou art no thy lane,[231]
In proving foresight may be vain:
The best laid schemes o' mice an' men
Gang aft a-gley,[232]
An' lea'e us nought but grief an' pain
For promis'd joy.

Still thou art blest compar'd wi' me!
The present only toucheth thee:

[224] An occasional ear in twenty-four sheaves.
[225] build
[226] coarse grass
[227] bitter
[228] without house or possession
[229] endure
[230] hoar-frost
[231] not alone
[232] astray

But oh! I backward cast my e'e
On prospects drear!
An' forward tho' I canna see,
I guess an' fear!

Address to the Deil[233]

O THOU! whatever title suit thee,
Auld Hornie, Satan, Nick, or Clootie,[234]
Wha in yon cavern grim an' sootie,
Clos'd under hatches,
Spairges[235] about the brunstane cootie,[236]
To scaud poor wretches!

Hear me, auld Hangie, for a wee,
An' let poor damnéd bodies be;
I'm sure sma' pleasure it can gie,
Ev'n to a deil,
To skelp[237] an' scaud poor dogs like me,
An' hear us squeal!

Great is thy pow'r, an' great thy fame;
Far kenn'd an' noted is thy name;
An', tho' yon lowin heugh's[238] thy hame,
Thou travels far;
An' faith! thou's neither lag nor lame,
Nor blate nor scaur.[239]

Whyles[240] rangin' like a roarin' lion
For prey, a' holes an' corners tryin';
Whyles on the strong-wing'd tempest flyin',
Tirlin'[241] the kirks;
Whyles, in the human bosom pryin',
Unseen thou lurks.

I've heard my reverend grannie say,
In lanely glens ye like to stray;
Or, where auld ruin'd castles gray
Nod to the moon.
Ye fright the nightly wand'rer's way,
Wi' eldritch[242] croon.

When twilight did my grannie summon
To say her pray'rs, douce,[243] honest woman!
Aft yont the dyke[244] she's heard you bummin,[245]
Wi' eerie drone;
Or, rustlin', thro' the boortrees[246] comin',
Wi' heavy groan.

Ae dreary windy winter night
The stars shot down wi' sklentin'[247] light,
Wi' you mysel I gat a fright
Ayont the lough;[248]
Ye like a rash-buss[249] stood in sight
Wi' waving sough.

The cudgel in my nieve[250] did shake,
Each bristled hair stood like a stake,
When wi' an eldritch stoor[251] 'quaick, quaick,'
Amang the springs,
Awa ye squatter'd[252] like a drake
On whistlin' wings.

Let warlocks[253] grim an' wither'd hags
Tell how wi' you on ragweed nags
They skim the muirs, an' dizzy crags
Wi' wicked speed;
And in kirk-yards renew their leagues
Owre howkit[254] dead.

Thence country wives, wi' toil an' pain,
May plunge an' plunge the kirn[255] in vain;
For oh! the yellow treasure's taen
By witchin' skill;
An' dawtit twal-pint Hawkie's gane
As yell's the bill.[256]

Thence mystic knots mak great abuse
On young guidmen, fond, keen, an' crouse;[257]
When the best wark-lume[258] i' the house,
By cantrip[259] wit,
Is instant made no worth a louse,
Just at the bit.

---

233 Written in 1785; published in 1786. For a motto Burns chose lines 128–129 of *Paradise Lost*, Book I:
'O Prince, O Chief of many thronéd pow'rs!
That led th' embattl'd seraphim to war.'
234 little hoof
235 splashes
236 tub
237 smack
238 flaming pit
239 shy nor timid
240 sometimes
241 unroofing
242 unearthly
243 grave
244 oft beyond the wall
245 humming
246 shrub-elders
247 slanting
248 beyond the lake
249 clump of rushes
250 fist
251 unearthly hoarse
252 fluttered on the water
253 wizards
254 dug up
255 churn
256 And the petted, twelve-pint cow is gone as dry as the bull.
257 bold
258 work-loom, or tool
259 magic

When thowes [260] dissolve the snawy hoord,
An' float the jinglin' icy-boord,
Then water-kelpies [261] haunt the foord,
By your direction,
An' 'nighted trav'llers are allur'd
To their destruction.

An' aft your moss-traversing spunkies [262]
Decoy the wight that late an' drunk is:
The bleezin, curst, mischievous monkies
Delude his eyes,
Till in some miry slough he sunk is,
Ne'er mair to rise.

When masons' mystic word an' grip
In storms an' tempests raise you up,
Some cock or cat your rage maun stop,[263]
Or, strange to tell!
The youngest brither ye wad whip
Aff straught to hell.

Lang syne, in Eden's bonnie yard,
When youthfu' lovers first were pair'd,
And all the soul of love they shar'd,
The raptur'd hour,
Sweet on the fragrant flow'ry swaird,
In shady bow'r;

Then you, ye auld snick-drawing [264] dog!
Ye cam to Paradise incog.
An' play'd on man a cursed brogue,[265]
(Black be your fa!)
An' gied the infant warld a shog.[266]
'Maist ruin'd a'.

D'ye mind that day, when in a bizz,[267]
Wi' reekit [268] duds, an' reestit gizz,[269]
Ye did present your smoutie phiz
'Mang better folk,
An' sklented [270] on the man of Uz [271]
Your spitefu' joke?

An' how ye gat him i' your thrall,
An' brak him out o' house an' hal',
While scabs an' blotches did him gall
Wi' bitter claw,
An' lows'd his ill-tongu'd wicked scawl,[272]
Was warst ava?

But a' your doings to rehearse,
Your wily snares an' fechtin' [273] fierce,
Sin' that day Michael did you pierce,
Down to this time,
Wad ding a' Lallan tongue, or Erse,[274]
In prose or rhyme.

An' now, auld Cloots, I ken ye're thinkin',
A certain Bardie's rantin', drinkin',
Some luckless hour will send him linkin' [275]
To your black pit;
But faith! he'll turn a corner jinkin',[276]
An' cheat you yet.

But fare you weel, auld Nickie-ben!
O wad ye tak a thought an' men'!
Ye aiblins [277] might — I dinna ken —
Still hae a stake:
I'm wae [278] to think upo' yon den,
Ev'n for your sake!

Address to the Unco Guid, or the Rigidly Righteous [279]

My son, these maxims make a rule,
And lump them aye thegither:
The rigid righteous is a fool,
The rigid wise anither:
The cleanest corn that e'er was dight,[280]
May hae some pyles o' caff in;
So ne'er a fellow-creature slight
For random fits o' daffin.
SOLOMON (Eccles. vii. 16).

O YE wha are sae guid yoursel,
Sae pious and sae holy,
Ye've nought to do but mark and tell
Your neibour's fauts and folly!
Whase life is like a weel-gaun [281] mill,
Supplied wi' store o' water:
The heapéd happer's [282] ebbing still,
And still the clap plays clatter:

---

260 thaws
261 river-demons
262 will-o-the-wisp
263 *I.e.*, by being made a sacrificial offering.
264 scheming
265 trick
266 shock
267 flurry
268 smoky
269 singed wig
270 turned, squinted
271 Job

272 scold
273 fighting
274 would outdo a Lowland tongue or Gaelic
275 tripping
276 dodging
277 perhaps
278 sad
279 Written in 1786; published in *Poems, Chiefly in the Scottish Dialect*, 1787.
280 winnowed
281 well-going
282 hopper's

Hear me, ye venerable core,[283]
As counsel for poor mortals,
That frequent pass douce [284] Wisdom's door,
For glaikit [285] Folly's portals;
I, for their thoughtless careless sakes,
Would here propone [286] defences, —
Their donsie [287] tricks, their black mistakes,
Their failings and mischances.

Ye see your state wi' their's compar'd,
And shudder at the niffer; [288]
But cast a moment's fair regard —
What makes the mighty differ?
Discount what scant occasion gave,
That purity ye pride in,
And (what's aft mair than a' the lave [289])
Your better art o' hidin'.

Think, when your castigated pulse
Gies now and then a wallop,
What ragings must his veins convulse,
That still eternal gallop!
Wi' wind and tide fair i' your tail,
Right on ye scud your sea-way;
But in the teeth o' baith to sail,
It maks an unco [290] leeway.

See Social life and Glee sit down,
All joyous and unthinking,
Till, quite transmogrified,[291] they're grown
Debauchery and Drinking:
O would they stay to calculate
Th' eternal consequences;
Or your more dreaded hell to state,
Damnation of expenses!

Ye high, exalted, virtuous Dames,
Tied up in godly laces,
Before ye gie poor Frailty names,
Suppose a change o' cases;
A dear lov'd lad, convenience snug,
A treacherous inclination —
But, let me whisper i' your lug,[292]
Ye're aiblins [293] nae temptation.

Then gently scan your brother man,
Still gentler sister woman;
Tho' they may gang a kennin wrang,
To step aside is human.
One point must still be greatly dark,
The moving why they do it;
And just as lamely can ye mark
How far perhaps they rue it.

Who made the heart, 'tis He alone
Decidedly can try us;
He knows each chord, its various tone,
Each spring, its various bias.
Then at the balance let's be mute,
We never can adjust it;
What's done we partly may compute,
But know not what's resisted.

To a Mountain Daisy [294]

ON TURNING ONE DOWN WITH THE PLOUGH, IN APRIL, 1786

Wee modest crimson-tippéd flow'r,
Thou's met me in an evil hour;
For I maun crush amang the stoure [295]
Thy slender stem:
To spare thee now is past my pow'r,
Thou bonnie gem.

Alas! it's no thy neibor sweet,
The bonnie lark, companion meet,
Bending thee 'mang the dewy weet
Wi' spreckl'd breast,
When upward springing, blythe to greet
The purpling east.

Cauld blew the bitter-biting north
Upon thy early humble birth;
Yet cheerfully thou glinted forth
Amid the storm,
Scarce rear'd above the parent-earth
Thy tender form.

The flaunting flow'rs our gardens yield
High shelt'ring woods and wa's [296] maun shield,

---

[283] corps, company
[284] grave
[285] giddy
[286] propose
[287] restive
[288] exchange
[289] rest
[290] uncommon
[291] transformed
[292] ear
[293] perhaps

[294] Published in 1786.
[295] dust
[296] walls

But thou, beneath the random bield [297]
O' clod or stane,
Adorns the histie [298] stibble-field,
Unseen, alane.

There, in thy scanty mantle clad,
Thy snawy bosom sun-ward spread,
Thou lifts thy unassuming head
In humble guise;
But now the share uptears thy bed,
And low thou lies!

Such is the fate of artless maid,
Sweet flow'ret of the rural shade,
By love's simplicity betray'd,
And guileless trust,
Till she like thee, all soil'd, is laid
Low i' the dust.

Such is the fate of simple bard,
On life's rough ocean luckless starr'd:
Unskilful he to note the card
Of prudent lore,
Till billows rage, and gales blow hard,
And whelm him o'er!

Such fate to suffering worth is giv'n,
Who long with wants and woes has striv'n,
By human pride or cunning driv'n
To mis'ry's brink,
Till wrench'd of ev'ry stay but Heav'n,
He ruin'd, sink!

Ev'n thou who mourn'st the Daisy's fate,
That fate is thine — no distant date;
Stern Ruin's ploughshare drives elate
Full on thy bloom,
Till crush'd beneath the furrow's weight
Shall be thy doom!

To a Louse [299]

ON SEEING ONE ON A LADY'S BONNET AT CHURCH

HA! wh'are ye gaun, ye crowlin' ferlie! [300]
Your impudence protects you sairly:
I canna say but ye strunt [301] rarely,
Owre gauze and lace;

[297] shelter
[298] bare
[299] Written and published in 1786.
[300] crawling wonder
[301] strut

Tho' faith! I fear ye dine but sparely
On sic a place.

Ye ugly, creepin' blastit [302] wonner,
Detested, shunn'd by saunt an' sinner!
How dare ye set your fit upon her,
Sae fine a lady?
Gae somewhere else, and seek your dinner
On some poor body.

Swith,[303] in some beggar's haffet [304] squattle; [305]
There ye may creep, and sprawl, and sprattle [306]
Wi' ither kindred jumping cattle,
In shoals and nations;
Where horn nor bane ne'er dare unsettle
Your thick plantations.

Now haud [307] ye there, ye're out o' sight,
Below the fatt'rels,[308] snug and tight;
Na, faith ye yet! ye'll no be right
Till ye've got on it,
The very tapmost tow'ring height
O' Miss's bonnet.

My sooth! right bauld [309] ye set your nose out,
As plump and gray as onie grozet,[310]
O for some rank mercurial rozet,[311]
Or fell red smeddum! [312]
I'd gie you sic a hearty doze o't,
Wad dress your droddum! [313]

I wad na been surpris'd to spy
You on an auld wife's flannen toy; [314]
Or aiblins [315] some bit duddie [316] boy,
On's wyliecoat; [317]
But Miss's fine Lunardi! fie,
How daur ye do't?

O Jenny, dinna toss your head,
An' set your beauties a' abread!

[302] blasted
[303] haste
[304] temple
[305] settle
[306] scramble
[307] hold
[308] ribbon-ends
[309] bold
[310] gooseberry
[311] rosin
[312] powder
[313] breech
[314] flannel head-dress
[315] perhaps
[316] ragged
[317] undervest

Ye little ken what curséd speed
The blastie's makin'!
Thae winks and finger-ends, I dread,
Are notice takin'!

O wad some Pow'r the giftie [318] gie us
To see oursels as others see us!
It wad frae mony a blunder free us,
And foolish notion:
What airs in dress an' gait wad lea'e us,
And ev'n devotion!

Of a' the Airts [319]

Of a' the airts [320] the wind can blaw,
I dearly like the west,
For there the bonnie lassie lives,
The lassie I lo'e best:
There's wild woods grow, and rivers row,[321]
And mony a hill between;
But day and night my fancy's flight
Is ever wi' my Jean.

I see her in the dewy flowers,
I see her sweet and fair:
I hear her in the tunefu' birds,
I hear her charm the air:
There's not a bonnie flower that springs
By fountain, shaw,[322] or green;
There's not a bonnie bird that sings,
But minds me o' my Jean.

Auld Lang Syne [323]

Should auld acquaintance be forgot,
And never brought to min'?
Should auld acquaintance be forgot,
And auld lang syne?

For auld lang syne, my dear.
For auld lang syne,
We'll tak a cup o' kindness yet,
For auld lang syne.

And surely ye'll be your pint-stowp,
And surely I'll be mine;
And we'll tak a cup o' kindness yet
For auld lang syne.

We twa hae run about the braes,
And pu'd the gowans [324] fine;
But we've wander'd mony a weary foot
Sin' auld lang syne.

We twa hae paidled i' the burn,[325]
From morning sun till dine;
But seas between us braid hae roar'd
Sin' auld lang syne.

And there's a hand, my trusty fiere,[326]
And gie's a hand o' thine;
And we'll tak a right guid-willie waught,[327]
For auld lang syne.

John Anderson my Jo [328]

John Anderson my jo,[329] John,
When we were first acquent,
Your locks were like the raven,
Your bonnie brow was brent; [330]
But now your brow is beld, John,
Your locks are like the snow;
But blessings on your frosty pow,[331]
John Anderson, my jo.

John Anderson my jo, John,
We clamb the hill thegither;
And mony a canty [332] day, John,
We've had wi' ane anither:
Now we maun totter down, John,
And hand in hand we'll go,
And sleep thegither at the foot,
John Anderson, my jo.

---

[318] small gift
[319] Written in 1788; published in 1790. In that year Burns had married Jean Armour and taken a farm at Ellisland, where shortly after his arrival he wrote this lyric for his wife, who was still in Ayrshire.
[320] directions
[321] roll
[322] wood
[323] Written in 1788; published in *The Scots Musical Museum*, V, in 1796.

[324] pulled the wild daisies
[325] brook
[326] friend
[327] good-will draught
[328] Written in 1788–1789; published in *The Scots Musical Museum*, III, in 1790.
[329] sweetheart
[330] straight
[331] head
[332] jolly

Afton Water [333]

Flow gently, sweet Afton, among thy green braes,[334]
Flow gently, I'll sing thee a song in thy praise;
My Mary's asleep by thy murmuring stream,
Flow gently, sweet Afton, disturb not her dream.

Thou stock-dove whose echo resounds thro' the glen,
Ye wild whistling blackbirds in yon thorny den,
Thou green-crested lapwing, thy screaming forbear,
I charge you disturb not my slumbering fair.

How lofty, sweet Afton, thy neighbouring hills,
Far mark'd with the courses of clear winding rills;
There daily I wander as noon rises high,
My flocks and my Mary's sweet cot in my eye.

How pleasant thy banks and green valleys below,
Where wild in the woodlands the primroses blow;
There oft as mild ev'ning weeps over the lea,
The sweet-scented birk [335] shades my Mary and me.

Thy crystal stream, Afton, how lovely it glides,
And winds by the cot where my Mary resides;
How wanton thy waters her snowy feet lave,
As gathering sweet flow'rets she stems thy clear wave.

Flow gently, sweet Afton, among thy green braes,
Flow gently, sweet river, the theme of my lays;
My Mary's asleep by thy murmuring stream,
Flow gently, sweet Afton, disturb not her dream.

[333] Written in 1789; published in *The Scots Musical Museum*, IV, in 1792.
[334] hills
[335] birch

Willie Brewed [336]

O Willie brew'd a peck o' maut,
  And Rob and Allan cam to see;
Three blyther hearts, that lee-lang [337] night,
  Ye wad na found in Christendie.

We are na fou',[338] we're no that fou,
  But just a drappie in our ee;
The cock may craw, the day may daw,
  And aye we'll taste the barley bree.

Here are we met, three merry boys,
  Three merry boys, I trow, are we;
And mony a night we've merry been,
  And mony mae we hope to be!

It is the moon, I ken her horn,
  That's blinkin' in the lift [339] sae hie;
She shines sae bright to wyle us hame,
  But, by my sooth! she'll wait a wee.

Wha first shall rise to gang awa,
  A cuckold, coward loun is he!
Wha first beside his chair shall fa',
  He is the King among us three!

[336] Written in 1789; published in *The Scots Musical Museum*, III, in 1790. 'The air is Masterton's; the song mine. The occasion of it was this: Mr. Wm. Nicol, of the High School, Edinburgh, during the autumn vacation being at Moffat, honest Allan (who was at that time on a visit to Dalswinton) and I went to pay Nicol a visit. We had such a joyous meeting that Mr. Masterton and I agreed, each in our own way, that we should celebrate the business.'
[337] live-long
[338] full
[339] sky

To Mary in Heaven[340]

Thou lingering star, with lessening ray,
That lov'st to greet the early morn,
Again thou usherest in the day
My Mary from my soul was torn.
O Mary! dear departed shade!
Where is thy place of blissful rest?
Seest thou thy lover lowly laid?
Hear'st thou the groans that rend his breast?

That sacred hour can I forget?
Can I forget the hallow'd grove,
Where by the winding Ayr we met,
To live one day of parting love?
Eternity will not efface
Those records dear of transports past;
Thy image at our last embrace —
Ah! little thought we 'twas our last!

Ayr gurgling kiss'd his pebbled shore,
O'erhung with wild woods, thickening green;
The fragrant birch, and hawthorn hoar,
Twin'd amorous round the raptur'd scene.
The flowers sprang wanton to be prest,
The birds sang love on ev'ry spray,
Till too too soon, the glowing west
Proclaim'd the speed of wingéd day.

Still o'er these scenes my memory wakes,
And fondly broods with miser care!
Time but the impression deeper makes,
As streams their channels deeper wear.
My Mary, dear departed shade!
Where is thy place of blissful rest?
Seest thou thy lover lowly laid?
Hear'st thou the groans that rend his breast?

[340] Written in 1789; published in 1790. The subject of the song was Mary Campbell, a sailor's daughter at Clyde. She is supposed to have died in the autumn of 1788. About this 'Highland Lassie' Burns wrote the following note: '[She] was a warm-hearted, charming young creature as ever blessed a man with generous love. After a pretty long tract of the most ardent reciprocal attachment we met by appointment on the second Sunday of May, in a sequestered spot by the Banks of Ayr, where we spent the day in taking farewell, before she should embark for the Western Highlands to arrange matters for our projected change of life. At the close of the Autumn following she crossed the sea to meet me at Greenock, where she had scarce landed when she was seized with a malignant fever, which hurried my dear girl to the grave in a few days, before I could even hear of her illness.'

Tam Glen[341]

My heart is a breaking, dear Tittie,[342]
Some counsel unto me come len',
To anger them a' is a pity;
But what will I do wi' Tam Glen?

I'm thinking, wi' sic a braw fellow,
In poortith[343] I might mak a fen';[344]
What care I in riches to wallow,
If I maunna marry Tam Glen?

There's Lowrie the laird o' Dumeller,
'Guid-day to you, brute!' he comes ben:[345]
He brags and he blaws o' his siller,
But when will he dance like Tam Glen?

My minnie[346] does constantly deave[347] me,
And bids me beware o' young men;
They flatter, she says, to deceive me;
But wha can think sae o' Tam Glen?

My daddie says, gin[348] I'll forsake him,
He'll gie me guid hunder marks[349] ten:
But, if it's ordain'd I maun take him,
O wha will I get but Tam Glen?

Yestreen at the Valentine's dealing,
My heart to my mou[350] gied a sten:[351]
For thrice I drew one without failing,
And thrice it was written, Tam Glen.

The last Halloween I was waukin'
My droukit sark-sleeve,[352] as ye ken;
His likeness cam up the house stalkin' —
And the very gray breeks o' Tam Glen!

[341] Written in 1788–1789; published in 1790.
[342] sister
[343] poverty
[344] shift
[345] in
[346] mother
[347] deafen
[348] if
[349] Scotch coins worth a little over twenty-six cents.
[350] mouth
[351] leap
[352] Was watching my drenched shirt-sleeve. Burns has a note to *Halloween*, line 25: 'You go out, one or more — for this is a social spell — to a south-running spring, or rivulet, where "three lairds' lands meet," and dip your left shirt-sleeve. Go to bed in sight of a fire, and hang your wet sleeve before it to dry. Lie awake; and, some time near midnight, an apparition, having the exact figure of the grand object in question [a future husband], will come and turn the sleeve, as if to dry the other side of it.'

Come, counsel, dear Tittie, don't tarry;
  I'll gie you my bonnie black hen,
Gif ye will advise me to marry
  The lad I lo'e dearly, Tam Glen.

Tam o' Shanter[353]

When chapman billies[354] leave the street,
And drouthy[355] neibors neibors meet,
As market-days are wearing late,
An' folk begin to tak the gate;
While we sit bousing at the nappy,[356]
An' getting fou[357] and unco happy,
We think na on the lang Scots miles,
The mosses, waters, slaps,[358] and styles,
That lie between us and our hame,
Where sits our sulky sullen dame,
Gathering her brows like gathering storm,
Nursing her wrath to keep it warm.
  This truth fand honest Tam o' Shanter,
As he frae Ayr ae night did canter —
(Auld Ayr, wham ne'er a town surpasses
For honest men and bonnie lasses).
  O Tam! hadst thou but been sae wise
As ta'en thy ain wife Kate's advice!
She tauld thee weel thou was a skellum,[359]
A bletherin', blusterin', drunken blellum;[360]
That frae November till October,
Ae market-day thou was na sober;
That ilka melder[361] wi' the miller
Thou sat as lang as thou had siller;
That every naig was ca'd[362] a shoe on,
The smith and thee gat roarin' fou on;
That at the Lord's house, even on Sunday,
Thou drank wi' Kirkton Jean till Monday.
She prophesied that, late or soon,
Thou would be found deep drown'd in Doon;
Or catch'd wi' warlocks[363] in the mirk
By Alloway's auld haunted kirk.
  Ah, gentle dames! it gars me greet[364]
To think how mony counsels sweet,
How mony lengthen'd sage advices,
The husband frae the wife despises!
  But to our tale: Ae market night,
Tam had got planted unco right,
Fast by an ingle,[365] bleezing[366] finely,
Wi' reaming swats,[367] that drank divinely;
And at his elbow, Souter[368] Johnny,
His ancient, trusty, drouthy crony;
Tam lo'ed him like a very brither;
They had been fou for weeks thegither.
The night drave on wi' sangs and clatter,
And aye the ale was growing better:
The landlady and Tam grew gracious,
Wi' favours secret, sweet, and precious;
The souter tauld his queerest stories;
The landlord's laugh was ready chorus:
The storm without might rair and rustle,
Tam did na mind the storm a whistle.
  Care, mad to see a man sae happy,
E'en drown'd himsel amang the nappy.
As bees flee hame wi' lades o' treasure,
The minutes wing'd their way wi' pleasure;
Kings may be blest, but Tam was glorious,
O'er a' the ills o' life victorious!
  But pleasures are like poppies spread —
You seize the flow'r, its bloom is shed;
Or like the snow falls in the river —
A moment white, then melts for ever;
Or like the borealis race,
That flit ere you can point their place;
Or like the rainbow's lovely form
Evanishing amid the storm.
Nae man can tether time nor tide;
The hour approaches Tam maun ride;
That hour, o' night's black arch the keystane,
That dreary hour, he mounts his beast in;
And sic a night he taks the road in,

---

[353] Written in 1790; published in *The Edinburgh Magazine*, March 1791. The poem is based upon legends centering about Alloway Kirk, a ruin within a mile of Burns's birth-place, and the nearby bridge over the river Doon. Tam o' Shanter himself perhaps recalls stories current of a non-teetotaler farmer, Douglas Graham (1739–1811), who was a tenant of the farm of Shanter. He owned a boat named *Tam o' Shanter*, as well as a shrewish wife. It was told that once when, after he had lingered at a tavern and some wags plucked his horse's tail to a stump, he maintained that witches at Alloway Kirk had done the trick. Burns held the poem to be 'my standard performance in the poetical line.'

[354] comrade pedlars
[355] thirsty
[356] drinking the ale
[357] full
[358] fence-holes
[359] good-for-nothing
[360] babbler
[361] every grinding
[362] nailed
[363] wizards
[364] makes me weep
[365] fire-place
[366] blazing
[367] foaming, new ale
[368] cobbler

As ne'er poor sinner was abroad in.
  The wind blew as 'twad blawn its last;
The rattling show'rs rose on the blast;
The speedy gleams the darkness swallow'd;
Loud, deep, and lang, the thunder bellow'd:
That night, a child might understand,
The Deil had business on his hand.
  Weel mounted on his gray mare, Meg,
A better never lifted leg,
Tam skelpit [369] on thro' dub [370] and mire,
Despising wind, and rain, and fire;
Whiles [371] holding fast his gude blue bonnet;
Whiles crooning o'er some auld Scots sonnet;
Whiles glow'ring round wi' prudent cares,
Lest bogles [372] catch him unawares.
Kirk-Alloway was drawing nigh,
Whare ghaists and houlets [373] nightly cry.
  By this time he was cross the ford,
Where in the snaw the chapman smoor'd; [374]
And past the birks [375] and meikle stane,[376]
Where drunken Charlie brak's neck-bane;
And thro' the whins,[377] and by the cairn,
Where hunters fand the murder'd bairn;
And near the thorn, aboon [378] the well,
Where Mungo's mither hang'd hersel.
Before him Doon pours all his floods;
The doubling storm roars thro' the woods;
The lightnings flash from pole to pole;
Near and more near the thunders roll:
When, glimmering thro' the groaning trees,
Kirk-Alloway seem'd in a bleeze;
Thro' ilka bore [379] the beams were glancing;
And loud resounded mirth and dancing.
  Inspiring bold John Barleycorn!
What dangers thou canst make us scorn!
Wi' tippenny,[380] we fear nae evil;
Wi' usquebae,[381] we'll face the devil!
The swats sae ream'd in Tammie's noddle,
Fair play, he car'd na deils a boddle! [382]
But Maggie stood right sair astonish'd,
Till, by the heel and hand admonish'd,
She ventur'd forward on the light;
And, vow! Tam saw an unco sight!
Warlocks and witches in a dance!
Nae cotillon brent new [383] frae France,
But hornpipes, jigs, strathspeys, and reels,[384]
Put life and mettle in their heels.
A winnock-bunker [385] in the east,
There sat auld Nick, in shape o' beast —
A touzie tyke,[386] black, grim, and large!
To gie them music was his charge:
He screw'd the pipes and gart them skirl.[387]
Till roof and rafters a' did dirl.[388]
Coffins stood round like open presses,
That shaw'd the dead in their last dresses;
And by some devilish cantraip sleight [389]
Each in its cauld hand held a light,
By which heroic Tam was able
To note upon the haly table
A murderer's banes in gibbet-airns;
Twa span-lang, wee, unchristen'd bairns;
A thief new-cutted frae the rape —
Wi his last gasp his gab [390] did gape;
Five tomahawks, wi' blude red rusted;
Five scymitars, wi' murder crusted;
A garter, which a babe had strangled;
A knife, a father's throat had mangled,
Whom his ain son o' life bereft —
The gray hairs yet stack to the heft;
Wi' mair of horrible and awfu',
Which even to name wad be unlawfu'.
  As Tammie glowr'd,[391] amaz'd, and curious,
The mirth and fun grew fast and furious:
The piper loud and louder blew;
The dancers quick and quicker flew;
They reel'd, they set, they cross'd, they cleekit,[392]

---

[369] clattered
[370] puddle
[371] now
[372] hobgoblins
[373] owls
[374] smothered
[375] birches
[376] great stone
[377] furze
[378] above
[379] every chink
[380] two-penny ale
[381] A brand of whiskey.
[382] farthing
[383] brand-new
[384] Scottish dances
[385] window-seat
[386] shaggy dog
[387] made them scream
[388] ring
[389] magic trick
[390] mouth
[391] stared
[392] caught (each other)

Till ilka carlin swat and reekit,[393]
And coost her duddies to the wark,[394]
And linkit[395] at it in her sark![396]
  Now Tam, O Tam! had thae been queans,[397]
A' plump and strapping in their teens;
Their sarks, instead o' creeshie flannen,[398]
Been snaw-white seventeen hunder linen![399]
Thir breeks[400] o' mine, my only pair,
That ance were plush, o' gude blue hair,
I wad hae gi'en them off my hurdies,[401]
For ae blink o' the bonnie burdies![402]
  But wither'd beldams, auld and droll,
Rigwoodie[403] hags wad spean[404] a foal,
Louping and flinging on a crummock,[405]
I wonder didna turn thy stomach.
  But Tam kent what was what fu' brawlie:[406]
There was ae winsome wench and walie[407]
That night enlisted in the core,[408]
Lang after kent on Carrick shore!
(For mony a beast to dead she shot,
And perish'd mony a bonnie boat,
And shook baith meikle corn and bear,[409]
And kept the country-side in fear.)
Her cutty[410] sark, o' Paisley harn;[411]
That while a lassie she had worn,
In longitude tho' sorely scanty,
It was her best, and she was vauntie.[412]
Ah! little kent thy reverend grannie
That sark she coft[413] for her wee Nannie
Wi' twa pund Scots[414] ('twas a' her riches)
Wad ever grac'd a dance of witches!
  But here my muse her wing maun cour:[415]
Sic flights are far beyond her pow'r —
To sing how Nannie lap and flang,[416]
(A souple jade she was, and strang);
And how Tam stood, like ane bewitch'd,
And thought his very een enrich'd;
Even Satan glowr'd, and fidg'd fu' fain,[417]
And hotch'd[418] and blew wi' might and main:
Till first ae caper, syne[419] anither,
Tam tint[420] his reason a' thegither,
And roars out 'Weel done, Cutty-sark!'
And in an instant all was dark!
And scarcely had he Maggie rallied,
When out the hellish legion sallied.
  As bees bizz out wi' angry fyke[421]
When plundering herds assail their byke,[422]
As open[423] pussie's[424] mortal foes
When pop! she starts before their nose,
As eager runs the market-crowd,
When 'Catch the thief!' resounds aloud.
So Maggie runs; the witches follow,
Wi' mony an eldritch[425] skriech and hollow.
  Ah, Tam! ah, Tam! thou'll get thy fairin'!
In hell they'll roast thee like a herrin'!
In vain thy Kate awaits thy comin'!
Kate soon will be a woefu' woman!
Now do thy speedy utmost, Meg,
And win the key-stane o' the brig:[426]
There at them thou thy tail may toss,
A running stream they darena cross.
But ere the key-stane she could make,
The fient a tail she had to shake!
For Nannie, far before the rest,
Hard upon noble Maggie prest,
And flew at Tam wi' furious ettle;[427]
But little wist she Maggie's mettle!
Ae spring brought off her master hale,
But left behind her ain gray tail:
The carlin claught her by the rump,
And left poor Maggie scarce a stump.
  Now, wha this tale o' truth shall read,
Each man and mother's son, take heed;

---

393 till each witch sweat and steamed
394 threw off her rags to the work
395 danced
396 shirt
397 young wenches
398 greasy flannel
399 fine linen — 1700 threads (to a width)
400 these breeches
401 buttocks
402 maidens
403 old lean
404 wean
405 leaping and capering on a staff
406 full well
407 buxom
408 company
409 barley
410 short
411 coarse linen
412 vain
413 bought
414 A total of about eighty cents.
415 lower
416 jumped and kicked
417 fidgeted with pleasure
418 jerked
419 then
420 lost
421 fuss
422 hive
423 *i.e.*, begin to bark
424 the hare's
425 unearthly
426 bridge
427 aim

Whene'er to drink you are inclin'd,
Or cutty-sarks rin in your mind,
Think! ye may buy the joys o'er dear;
Remember Tam o' Shanter's mare.

Ye Flowery Banks o' Bonnie Doon[428]

Ye flowery banks o' bonnie Doon,
How can ye blume sae[429] fair?
How can ye chant, ye little birds,
And I sae fu' o' care?

Thou'll break my heart, thou bonnie bird,
That sings upon the bough;
Thou minds me o' the happy days,
When my fause luve was true.

Thou'll break my heart, thou bonnie bird,
That sings beside thy mate;
For sae I sat, and sae I sang,
And wist[430] na o' my fate.

Aft hae I rov'd by bonnie Doon,
To see the wood-bine twine,
And ilka[431] bird sang o' its love,
And sae did I o' mine.

Wi' lightsome heart I pu'd[432] a rose
Frae off its thorny tree:
And my fause luver staw my rose,
But left the thorn wi' me.

Ae Fond Kiss[433]

Ae fond kiss, and then we sever!
Ae fareweel, alas, for ever!
Deep in heart-wrung tears I'll pledge thee,
Warring sighs and groans I'll wage[434] thee.
Who shall say that fortune grieves him
While the star of hope she leaves him?
Me, nae cheerfu' twinkle lights me,
Dark despair around benights me.

I'll ne'er blame my partial fancy,
Naething could resist my Nancy;

[428] Written probably early in 1791; published in *S.M.M.*, IV, in 1792.
[429] so
[430] knew
[431] every
[432] stole
[433] Written in 1791; published in 1792.
[434] pledge

But to see her was to love her,
Love but her, and love for ever.
Had we never lov'd sae kindly,
Had we never lov'd sae blindly,
Never met — or never parted,
We had ne'er been broken-hearted.

Fare thee weel, thou first and fairest!
Fare thee weel, thou best and dearest!
Thine be ilka joy and treasure,
Peace, enjoyment, love, and pleasure.
Ae fond kiss, and then we sever;
Ae fareweel, alas, for ever!
Deep in heart-wrung tears I'll pledge thee,
Warring sighs and groans I'll wage thee.

The De'il's awa' wi' the Exciseman[435]

The De'il cam fiddling thro' the town,
And danced awa wi' the Exciseman;
And ilka[436] wife cried 'Auld Mahoun,[437]
We wish you luck o' your prize, man.'

We'll mak our maut, and brew our drink,
We'll dance, and sing, and rejoice, man;
And mony thanks to the muckle[438] black De'il
That danced awa wi' the Exciseman.

There's threesome reels, and foursome reels,
There's hornpipes and strathspeys, man;
But the ae best dance e'er cam to our lan',
Was — the De'il's awa wi' the Exciseman.

Highland Mary[439]

Ye banks, and braes,[440] and streams around
The castle o' Montgomery,
Green be your woods, and fair your flowers,

[435] Written and published in 1792.
[436] every
[437] Old Mahomet; 'the devil' here.
[438] great
[439] Written in 1792; published in *Select Collections of Original Scotch Airs*, II, in 1799. The song concerns Mary Campbell; see *To Mary in Heaven*, p. 581.
[440] hill-slopes

Your waters never drumlie![441]
There simmer first unfauld her robes,
And there the langest tarry;
For there I took the last fareweel
O' my sweet Highland Mary.

How sweetly bloom'd the gay green birk,[442]
How rich the hawthorn's blossom,
As underneath their fragrant shade
I clasp'd her to my bosom!
The golden hours on angel wings
Flew o'er me and my dearie;
For dear to me as light and life
Was my sweet Highland Mary.

Wi' mony a vow, and lock'd embrace,
Our parting was fu' tender;
And, pledging aft to meet again,
We tore oursels asunder;
But oh! fell death's untimely frost,
That nipt my flower sae early!
Now green's the sod, and cauld's the clay,
That wraps my Highland Mary!

O pale, pale now, those rosy lips,
I aft have kiss'd sae fondly!
And closed for aye the sparkling glance,
That dwelt on me sae kindly!
And mould'ring now in silent dust,
That heart that lo'ed me dearly!
But still within my bosom's core
Shall live my Highland Mary.

Scots Wha Hae[443]

ROBERT BRUCE'S ADDRESS TO HIS ARMY, BEFORE THE BATTLE OF BANNOCKBURN

Scots, wha hae wi' Wallace bled,
Scots, wham Bruce has aften led,
Welcome to your gory bed,
Or to victorie.

Now's the day, and now's the hour;
See the front o' battle lour!
See approach proud Edward's power—
Chains and slaverie!

Wha will be a traitor knave?
Wha can fill a coward's grave?
Wha sae base as be a slave?
Let him turn and flee!

Wha for Scotland's King and law
Freedom's sword will strongly draw,
Freeman stand, or freeman fa'?
Let him follow me!

By oppression's woes and pains!
By your sons in servile chains!
We will drain our dearest veins,
But they shall be free!

Lay the proud usurpers low!
Tyrants fall in every foe!
Liberty's in every blow!
Let us do or die!

My love is like a red red rose[444]

My love is like a red red rose
That's newly sprung in June:
My love is like the melodie
That's sweetly play'd in tune.

So fair art thou, my bonnie lass,
So deep in love am I:
And I will love thee still, my dear,
Till a' the seas gang dry.

Till a' the seas gang dry, my dear,
And the rocks melt wi' the sun:
And I will love thee still, my dear,
While the sands o' life shall run.

And fare thee weel, my only love,
And fare thee weel awhile!
And I will come again, my love,
Tho' it were ten thousand mile.

---

441 muddy, troubled 442 birch

443 Written in 1793; published in *The Morning Chronicle*, 8 May 1794. Burns once wrote that, thinking upon the tradition that the air *Hey Tutti Taiti* was Robert Bruce's march at the battle of Bannockburn, 24 June 1314, he was moved to compose a kind of Scottish ode, fitted to the tune, such as might have been 'the gallant royal Scot's address to his heroic followers on that eventful morning.' Apparently some thoughts of the newer Revolution in France were mingled with Burns's memory of the old fight for Scottish freedom. He acknowledged that the story of William Wallace, the national hero, 'poured a Scottish prejudice into my veins which will boil along there till the flood-gates of life shut in eternal rest.'

444 Written in 1794; published in 1796.

For a' that and a' that [445]

Is there, for honest poverty,
That hangs his head, and a' that?
The coward-slave, we pass him by,
We dare be poor for a' that!
For a' that, and a' that,
Our toils obscure, and a' that;
The rank is but the guinea stamp;
The man's the gowd [446] for a' that.

What tho' on hamely fare we dine,
Wear hodden-gray,[447] and a' that;
Gie fools their silks, and knaves their wine,
A man's a man for a' that.
For a' that, and a' that,
Their tinsel show, and a' that;
The honest man, tho' e'er sae poor,
Is King o' men for a' that.

Ye see yon birkie,[448] ca'd a lord,
Wha struts, and stares, and a' that;
Tho' hundreds worship at his word,
He's but a coof [449] for a' that:
For a' that, and a' that,
His riband, star, and a' that,
The man of independent mind,
He looks and laughs at a' that.

A prince can mak a belted knight,
A marquis, duke, and a' that;
But an honest man's aboon [450] his might,
Guid faith he mauna fa' [451] that!
For a' that, and a' that,
Their dignities, and a' that,
The pith o' sense, and pride o' worth,
Are higher rank than a' that.

Then let us pray that come it may
As come it will for a' that,
That sense and worth o'er a' the earth,
Shall bear the gree [452] and a' that;
For a' that, and a' that,
It's comin' yet for a' that,
That man to man, the world o'er,
Shall brithers be for a' that.

[445] Written in 1794; published in *The Glasgow Magazine*, August 1795.
[446] gold
[447] coarse gray woolen
[448] conceited fellow
[449] fool, ninny
[450] above
[451] claim

O, wert thou in the cauld blast [453]

O, WERT thou in the cauld blast,
On yonder lea, on yonder lea,
My plaidie to the angry airt,[454]
I'd shelter thee, I'd shelter thee.
Or did misfortune's bitter storms
Around thee blaw, around thee blaw,
Thy bield [455] should be my bosom,
To share it a', to share it a'.

Or were I in the wildest waste,
Sae black and bare, sae black and bare,
The desert were a paradise,
If thou wert there, if thou wert there.
Or were I monarch o' the globe,
Wi' thee to reign, wi' thee to reign,
The brightest jewel in my crown
Wad be my queen, wad be my queen.

[452] have the prize
[453] Written in 1796; published in *Works*, 1800. The poem was composed during Burns's last illness, in appreciation of the kindness he and his family had received from Jessie Lewars. A favorite melody which she played on the piano for him gave the framework for the lyric.
[454] quarter
[455] shelter

William Wordsworth

1770–1850

Lines Written in Early Spring [1]

I HEARD a thousand blended notes,
While in a grove I sate reclined,
In that sweet mood when pleasant thoughts
Bring sad thoughts to the mind.

To her fair works did Nature link
The human soul that through me ran;

[1] This and the three following poems were published in *Lyrical Ballads*, 1798, having been written the same year. 'Actually composed while I was sitting by the side of the brook that runs down from the Comb, in which stands the village of Alford, through the grounds of Alfoxden. It was a chosen resort of mine.' [Wordsworth.]

And much it grieved my heart to think
What man has made of man.

Through primrose tufts, in that green bower,
The periwinkle trailed its wreaths;
And 'tis my faith that every flower
Enjoys the air it breathes.

The birds around me hopped and played,
Their thoughts I cannot measure: —
But the least motion which they made,
It seemed a thrill of pleasure.

The budding twigs spread out their fan,
To catch the breezy air;
And I must think, do all I can,
That there was pleasure there.

If this belief from heaven be sent,
If such be Nature's holy plan,
Have I not reason to lament
What man has made of man?

Expostulation and Reply [2]

'Why, William, on that old grey stone,
Thus for the length of half a day,
Why, William, sit you thus alone,
And dream your time away?

'Where are your books? — that light bequeathed
To Beings else forlorn and blind!
Up! up! and drink the spirit breathed
From dead men to their kind.

'You look round on your Mother Earth,
As if she for no purpose bore you;
As if you were her first-born birth,
And none had lived before you!'

One morning thus, by Esthwaite lake,
When life was sweet, I knew not why,
To me my good friend Matthew spake,
And thus I made reply:

'The eye — it cannot choose but see;
We cannot bid the ear be still;
Our bodies feel, where'er they be,
Against or with our will.

'Nor less I deem that there are Powers
Which of themselves our minds impress;
That we can feed this mind of ours
In a wise passiveness.

'Think you, 'mid all this mighty sum
Of things for ever speaking,
That nothing of itself will come,
But we must still be seeking?

'— Then ask not wherefore, here, alone,
Conversing as I may,
I sit upon this old grey stone,
And dream my time away.'

The Tables Turned [3]

AN EVENING SCENE ON THE SAME SUBJECT

Up! up! my Friend, and quit your books;
Or surely you'll grow double:
Up! up! my Friend, and clear your looks;
Why all this toil and trouble?

The sun, above the mountain's head,
A freshening lustre mellow
Through all the long green fields has spread,
His first sweet evening yellow.

Books! 'tis a dull and endless strife:
Come, hear the woodland linnet,
How sweet his music! on my life,
There's more of wisdom in it.

And hark! how blithe the throstle sings!
He, too, is no mean preacher:
Come forth into the light of things,
Let Nature be your Teacher.

[2] In the first edition of *Lyrical Ballads*, Wordsworth says that this poem and the one which follows grew out of his talks 'with a friend who was somewhat unreasonably attached to modern books of Moral Philosophy.' The poet was often told, he says, that the piece was a high favorite among the Quakers.

[3] This mild little poem, particularly the sixth stanza, has been taken very desperately by some modern Humanists and by others who deplore Wordsworth's 'philosophy of nature.' For an interesting comparison see Arnold's *In Harmony with Nature* (p. 1079).

She has a world of ready wealth,
Our minds and hearts to bless —
Spontaneous wisdom breathed by health,
Truth breathed by cheerfulness.

One impulse from a vernal wood
May teach you more of man,
Of moral evil and of good,
Than all the sages can.

Sweet is the lore which Nature brings;
Our meddling intellect
Mis-shapes the beauteous forms of things: —
We murder to dissect.

Enough of Science and of Art;
Close up those barren leaves;
Come forth, and bring with you a heart
That watches and receives.

Lines

COMPOSED A FEW MILES ABOVE TINTERN ABBEY, ON REVISITING THE BANKS OF THE WYE DURING A TOUR. JULY 13, 1798.[4]

Five years have past; five summers, with the length
Of five long winters! and again I hear
These waters, rolling from their mountain-springs
With a soft inland murmur. — Once again
Do I behold these steep and lofty cliffs,
That on a wild secluded scene impress
Thoughts of more deep seclusion; and connect
The landscape with the quiet of the sky.
The day is come when I again repose
Here, under this dark sycamore, and view
These plots of cottage-ground, these orchard-tufts,
Which at this season, with their unripe fruits,
Are clad in one green hue, and lose themselves
'Mid groves and copses. Once again I see
These hedge-rows, hardly hedge-rows, little lines
Of sportive wood run wild: these pastoral farms,
Green to the very door; and wreaths of smoke
Sent up, in silence, from among the trees!
With some uncertain notice, as might seem
Of vagrant dwellers in the houseless woods,
Or of some Hermit's cave, where by his fire
The Hermit sits alone.

These beauteous forms,
Through a long absence, have not been to me
As is a landscape to a blind man's eye:
But oft, in lonely rooms, and 'mid the din
Of towns and cities, I have owed to them,
In hours of weariness, sensations sweet,
Felt in the blood, and felt along the heart;
And passing even into my purer mind,
With tranquil restoration: — feelings too
Of unremembered pleasure: such, perhaps,
As have no slight or trivial influence
On that best portion of a good man's life,
His little, nameless, unremembered, acts
Of kindness and of love. Nor less, I trust,
To them I may have owed another gift,
Of aspect more sublime; that blessed mood,
In which the burthen of the mystery,
In which the heavy and the weary weight
Of all this unintelligible world,
Is lightened: — that serene and blessed mood,
In which the affections gently lead us on, —
Until, the breath of this corporeal frame
And even the motion of our human blood

[4] 'No poem of mine was composed under circumstances more pleasant for me to remember than this. I began it upon leaving Tintern, after crossing the Wye, and concluded it just as I was entering Bristol in the evening, after a ramble of four or five days with my sister. Not a line of it was altered, and not any part of it written down till I reached Bristol. It was published almost immediately after in the Lyrical Ballads.' [Wordsworth.] The poem might well be called 'the little *Prelude*,' and it should be carefully compared with the longer work (p. 602 f.).

Almost suspended, we are laid asleep
In body, and become a living soul:
While with an eye made quiet by the power
Of harmony, and the deep power of joy,
We see into the life of things.
                                        If this
Be but a vain belief, yet, oh! how oft —
In darkness and amid the many shapes
Of joyless daylight; when the fretful stir
Unprofitable, and the fever of the world,
Have hung upon the beatings of my heart —
How oft, in spirit, have I turned to thee,
O sylvan Wye! thou wanderer thro' the woods,
How often has my spirit turned to thee!

And now, with gleams of half-extinguished thought,
With many recognitions dim and faint,
And somewhat of a sad perplexity,
The picture of the mind revives again:
While here I stand, not only with the sense
Of present pleasure, but with pleasing thoughts
That in this moment there is life and food
For future years. And so I dare to hope,
Though changed, no doubt, from what I was when first
I came among these hills; when like a roe
I bounded o'er the mountains, by the sides
Of the deep rivers, and the lonely streams,
Wherever nature led: more like a man
Flying from something that he dreads than one
Who sought the thing he loved. For nature then
(The coarser pleasures of my boyish days,
And their glad animal movements all gone by)
To me was all in all. — I cannot paint
What then I was. The sounding cataract
Haunted me like a passion: the tall rock,
The mountain, and the deep and gloomy wood,
Their colours and their forms, were then to me
An appetite; a feeling and a love,
That had no need of a remoter charm,
By thought supplied, nor any interest
Unborrowed from the eye. — That time is past,
And all its aching joys are now no more,
And all its dizzy raptures. Not for this
Faint I, nor mourn nor murmur; other gifts
Have followed; for such loss, I would believe,
Abundant recompense. For I have learned
To look on nature, not as in the hour
Of thoughtless youth; but hearing oftentimes
The still, sad music of humanity,
Nor harsh nor grating, though of ample power
To chasten and subdue. And I have felt
A presence that disturbs me with the joy
Of elevated thoughts; a sense sublime
Of something far more deeply interfused,
Whose dwelling is the light of setting suns,
And the round ocean and the living air,
And the blue sky, and in the mind of man:
A motion and a spirit, that impels
All thinking things, all objects of all thought,
And rolls through all things. Therefore am I still
A lover of the meadows and the woods,
And mountains; and of all that we behold
From this green earth; of all the mighty world
Of eye, and ear, — both what they half create,
And what perceive; well pleased to recognise
In nature and the language of the sense
The anchor of my purest thoughts, the nurse,
The guide, the guardian of my heart, and soul
Of all my moral being.
                                        Nor perchance,
If I were not thus taught, should I the more
Suffer my genial spirits to decay:
For thou art with me here upon the banks
Of this fair river; thou my dearest Friend,

My dear, dear Friend;[5] and in thy voice I catch
The language of my former heart, and read
My former pleasures in the shooting lights
Of thy wild eyes. Oh! yet a little while
May I behold in thee what I was once,
My dear, dear Sister! and this prayer I make,
Knowing that Nature never did betray
The heart that loved her; 'tis her privilege,
Through all the years of this our life, to lead
From joy to joy: for she can so inform
The mind that is within us, so impress
With quietness and beauty, and so feed
With lofty thoughts, that neither evil tongues,
Rash judgments, nor the sneers of selfish men,
Nor greetings where no kindness is, nor all
The dreary intercourse of daily life,
Shall e'er prevail against us, or disturb
Our cheerful faith, that all which we behold
Is full of blessings. Therefore let the moon
Shine on thee in thy solitary walk;
And let the misty mountain-winds be free
To blow against thee: and, in after years,
When these wild ecstasies shall be matured
Into a sober pleasure; when thy mind
Shall be a mansion for all lovely forms,
Thy memory be as a dwelling-place
For all sweet sounds and harmonies; oh! then,
If solitude, or fear, or pain, or grief,
Should be thy portion, with what healing thoughts
Of tender joy wilt thou remember me,
And these my exhortations! Nor, perchance —
If I should be where I no more can hear
Thy voice, nor catch from thy wild eyes these gleams
Of past existence — wilt thou then forget
That on the banks of this delightful stream
We stood together; and that I, so long
A worshipper of Nature, hither came
Unwearied in that service: rather say
With warmer love — oh! with far deeper zeal
Of holier love. Nor wilt thou then forget
That after many wanderings, many years
Of absence, these steep woods and lofty cliffs,
And this green pastoral landscape, were to me
More dear, both for themselves and for thy sake!

Strange fits of passion have I known [6]

STRANGE fits of passion have I known:
And I will dare to tell,
But in the Lover's ear alone,
What once to me befell.

When she I loved looked every day
Fresh as a rose in June,
I to her cottage bent my way,
Beneath an evening-moon.

Upon the moon I fixed my eye,
All over the wide lea;
With quickening pace my horse drew nigh
Those paths so dear to me.

And now we reached the orchard-plot;
And, as we climbed the hill,
The sinking moon to Lucy's cot
Came near, and nearer still.

In one of those sweet dreams I slept,
Kind Nature's gentlest boon!
And all the while my eyes I kept
On the descending moon.

[5] His sister, Dorothy, who is also praised in *The Prelude* as the source, not merely of Wordsworth's poetic inspiration and insight, but of much of the best in his own life. See pp. 629 f., 632, 641 f.

[6] The second edition of *Lyrical Ballads*, with additions and in two volumes, was published in 1800. In that year appeared the 'Lucy' poems, with the exception of the third, all composed in Germany in 1799, and here printed in succession. Wordsworth never said who 'Lucy' was.

My horse moved on; hoof after hoof
He raised, and never stopped:
When down behind the cottage roof,
At once, the bright moon dropped.

What fond and wayward thoughts will slide
Into a Lover's head!
'O mercy!' to myself I cried,
'If Lucy should be dead!'

She dwelt among the untrodden ways

She dwelt among the untrodden ways
Beside the springs of Dove,
A Maid whom there were none to praise
And very few to love:

A violet by a mossy stone
Half hidden from the eye!
— Fair as a star, when only one
Is shining in the sky.

She lived unknown, and few could know
When Lucy ceased to be;
But she is in her grave, and, oh,
The difference to me!

I travelled among unknown men

I travelled among unknown men,
In lands beyond the sea;
Nor, England! did I know till then
What love I bore to thee.

'Tis past, that melancholy dream!
Nor will I quit thy shore
A second time; for still I seem
To love thee more and more.

Among thy mountains did I feel
The joy of my desire;
And she I cherished turned her wheel
Beside an English fire.

Thy mornings showed, thy nights concealed,
The bowers where Lucy played;
And thine too is the last green field
That Lucy's eyes surveyed.

[1807]

Three years she grew in sun and shower [7]

Three years she grew in sun and shower,
Then Nature said, 'A lovelier flower
On earth was never sown;
This Child I to myself will take;
She shall be mine, and I will make
A Lady of my own.

'Myself will to my darling be
Both law and impulse: and with me
The Girl, in rock and plain,
In earth and heaven, in glade and bower,
Shall feel an overseeing power
To kindle or restrain.

'She shall be sportive as the fawn
That wild with glee across the lawn
Or up the mountain springs;
And hers shall be the breathing balm,
And hers the silence and the calm
Of mute insensate things.

'The floating clouds their state shall lend
To her; for her the willow bend;
Nor shall she fail to see
Even in the motions of the Storm
Grace that shall mould the Maiden's form
By silent sympathy.

'The stars of midnight shall be dear
To her; and she shall lean her ear
In many a secret place
Where rivulets dance their wayward round,
And beauty born of murmuring sound
Shall pass into her face.

'And vital feelings of delight
Shall rear her form to stately height,
Her virgin bosom swell;

[7] Composed in the Harz Forest in Germany.

Such thoughts to Lucy I will give
While she and I together live
Here in this happy dell.'

Thus Nature spake — The work was done —
How soon my Lucy's race was run!
She died, and left to me
This heath, this calm, and quiet scene;
The memory of what has been,
And never more will be.

A slumber did my spirit seal

A slumber did my spirit seal;
 I had no human fears:
She seemed a thing that could not feel
 The touch of earthly years.

No motion has she now, no force;
 She neither hears nor sees;
Rolled round in earth's diurnal course,
 With rocks, and stones, and trees.

Lucy Gray [8]

OR, SOLITUDE

Oft I had heard of Lucy Gray:
And, when I crossed the wild,
I chanced to see at break of day
The solitary child.

No mate, no comrade Lucy knew;
She dwelt on a wide moor,
— The sweetest thing that ever grew
Beside a human door!

You yet may spy the fawn at play,
The hare upon the green;
But the sweet face of Lucy Gray
Will never more be seen.

'To-night will be a stormy night —
You to the town must go;
And take a lantern, Child, to light
Your mother through the snow.'

'That, Father! will I gladly do:
'Tis scarcely afternoon —
The minster-clock has just struck two,
And yonder is the moon!'

At this the Father raised his hook,
And snapped a faggot-band;
He plied his work; — and Lucy took
The lantern in her hand.

Not blither is the mountain roe:
With many a wanton stroke
Her feet disperse the powdery snow,
That rises up like smoke.

The storm came on before its time:
She wandered up and down;
And many a hill did Lucy climb:
But never reached the town.

The wretched parents all that night
Went shouting far and wide;
But there was neither sound nor sight
To serve them for a guide.

At day-break on a hill they stood
That overlooked the moor;
And thence they saw the bridge of wood,
A furlong from their door.

They wept — and, turning homeward, cried,
'In heaven we all shall meet;'
— When in the snow the mother spied
The print of Lucy's feet.

Then downwards from the steep hill's edge
They tracked the footmarks small;
And through the broken hawthorn hedge,
And by the long stone-wall;

And then an open field they crossed:
The marks were still the same;

---

[8] Written in 1799; published in 1800. The tale 'was founded on a circumstance told me by my sister, of a little girl who, not far from Halifax in Yorkshire, was bewildered in a snow storm. . . . The way in which the incident was treated, and the spiritualizing of the character, might furnish hints for contrasting the imaginative influences which I have endeavored to throw over common life with Crabbe's matter-of-fact style of [treatment]. This is not spoken to his disparagement, far from it, but to direct the attention of thoughtful readers . . . to a comparison that may enlarge the circle of their sensibilities, and tend to produce in them a catholic judgement.' [Wordsworth.]

They tracked them on, nor ever lost;
And to the bridge they came.

They followed from the snowy bank
Those footmarks, one by one,
Into the middle of the plank;
And further there were none!

— Yet some maintain that to this day
She is a living child;
That you may see sweet Lucy Gray
Upon the lonesome wild.

O'er rough and smooth she trips along,
And never looks behind;
And sings a solitary song
That whistles in the wind.

Michael [9]

A PASTORAL POEM

If from the public way you turn your steps
Up the tumultuous brook of Green-head Ghyll,
You will suppose that with an upright path
Your feet must struggle; in such bold ascent,
The pastoral mountains front you, face to face.
But, courage! for around that boisterous brook
The mountains have all opened out themselves,
And made a hidden valley of their own.
No habitation can be seen; but they
Who journey thither find themselves alone
With a few sheep, with rocks and stones, and kites
That overhead are sailing in the sky.
It is in truth an utter solitude;
Nor should I have made mention of this Dell
But for one object which you might pass by,
Might see and notice not. Beside the brook
Appears a straggling heap of unhewn stones!
And to that simple object appertains
A story — unenriched with strange events,
Yet not unfit, I deem, for the fireside,
Or for the summer shade. It was the first
Of those domestic tales that spake to me
Of Shepherds, dwellers in the valleys, men
Whom I already loved; — not verily
For their own sakes, but for the fields and hills
Where was their occupation and abode.
And hence this Tale, while I was yet a Boy
Careless of books, yet having felt the power
Of Nature, by the gentle agency
Of natural objects, led me on to feel
For passions that were not my own, and think
(At random and imperfectly indeed)
On man, the heart of man, and human life.
Therefore, although it be a history
Homely and rude, I will relate the same
For the delight of a few natural hearts; [10]
And, with yet fonder feeling, for the sake
Of youthful Poets, who among these hills
Will be my second self when I am gone.

Upon the forest-side in Grasmere Vale
There dwelt a Shepherd, Michael was his name;
An old man, stout of heart, and strong of limb.
His bodily frame had been from youth to age
Of an unusual strength: his mind was keen,
Intense, and frugal, apt for all affairs,
And in his shepherd's calling he was prompt
And watchful more than ordinary men.
Hence had he learned the meaning of all winds,

[9] Written and published in 1800. Wordsworth's note reads: 'Written at Town-end, Grasmere, about the same time as *The Brothers*. The Sheepfold, on which so much of the poem turns, remains, or rather the ruins of it. The character and circumstances of Luke were taken from a family to whom had belonged, many years before, the house we lived in at Town-end, along with some fields and woodlands on the eastern shore of Grasmere. The name of the Evening Star was not in fact given to this house, but to another on the same side of the valley, more to the north.'

[10] Wordsworth wrote to his friend Poole: 'I have attempted to give a picture of a man, of strong mind and lively sensibility, agitated by two of the most powerful affections of the human heart — the parental affection, and the love of property, *landed* property, including the feelings of inheritance, home, and personal and family independence.'

Of blasts of every tone; and oftentimes,
When others heeded not, He heard the South
Make subterraneous music, like the noise
Of bagpipers on distant Highland hills.
The Shepherd, at such warning, of his flock
Bethought him, and he to himself would say,
'The winds are now devising work for me!'
And, truly, at all times, the storm, that drives
The traveller to a shelter, summoned him
Up to the mountains: he had been alone
Amid the heart of many thousand mists,
That came to him, and left him, on the heights.
So lived he till his eightieth year was past.
And grossly that man errs, who should suppose
That the green valleys, and the streams and rocks,
Were things indifferent to the Shepherd's thoughts.
Fields, where with cheerful spirits he had breathed
The common air; hills, which with vigorous step
He had so often climbed; which had impressed
So many incidents upon his mind
Of hardship, skill or courage, joy or fear;
Which, like a book, preserved the memory
Of the dumb animals, whom he had saved,
Had fed or sheltered, linking to such acts
The certainty of honourable gain;
Those fields, those hills — what could they less? had laid
Strong hold on his affections, were to him
A pleasurable feeling of blind love,
The pleasure which there is in life itself.

His days had not been passed in singleness.
His Helpmate was a comely matron, old —
Though younger than himself full twenty years.
She was a woman of a stirring life,
Whose heart was in her house: two wheels she had
Of antique form; this large, for spinning wool;
That small, for flax; and, if one wheel had rest,
It was because the other was at work.
The Pair had but one inmate in their house,
An only Child, who had been born to them
When Michael, telling o'er his years, began
To deem that he was old, — in shepherd's phrase,
With one foot in the grave. This only Son,
With two brave sheep-dogs tried in many a storm,
The one of an inestimable worth,
Made all their household. I may truly say,
That they were as a proverb in the vale
For endless industry. When day was gone,
And from their occupations out of doors
The Son and Father were come home, even then,
Their labour did not cease; unless when all
Turned to the cleanly supper-board, and there,
Each with a mess of pottage and skimmed milk,
Sat round the basket piled with oaten cakes,
And their plain home-made cheese. Yet when the meal
Was ended, Luke (for so the Son was named)
And his old Father both betook themselves
To such convenient work as might employ
Their hands by the fire-side; perhaps to card
Wool for the Housewife's spindle, or repair
Some injury done to sickle, flail, or scythe,
Or other implement of house or field.

Down from the ceiling, by the chimney's edge
That in our ancient uncouth country style

With huge and black projection over-browed
Large space beneath, as duly as the light
Of day grew dim the Housewife hung a lamp;
An aged utensil, which had performed
Service beyond all others of its kind.
Early at evening did it burn — and late,
Surviving comrade of uncounted hours,
Which, going by from year to year, had found,
And left, the couple neither gay perhaps
Nor cheerful, yet with objects and with hopes,
Living a life of eager industry.
And now, when Luke had reached his eighteenth year,
There by the light of this old lamp they sate,
Father and Son, while far into the night
The Housewife plied her own peculiar work,
Making the cottage through the silent hours
Murmur as with the sound of summer flies.
This light was famous in its neighbourhood,
And was a public symbol of the life
That thrifty Pair had lived. For, as it chanced,
Their cottage on a plot of rising ground
Stood single, with large prospect, north and south,
High into Easedale, up to Dunmail-Raise,
And westward to the village near the lake;
And from this constant light, so regular,
And so far seen, the House itself, by all
Who dwelt within the limits of the vale,
Both old and young, was named The Evening Star.

Thus living on through such a length of years,
The Shepherd, if he loved himself, must needs
Have loved his Helpmate; but to Michael's heart
This son of his old age was yet more dear —
Less from instinctive tenderness, the same
Fond spirit that blindly works in the blood of all —
Than that a child, more than all other gifts
That earth can offer to declining man,
Brings hope with it, and forward-looking thoughts,
And stirrings of inquietude, when they
By tendency of nature needs must fail.
Exceeding was the love he bare to him,
His heart and his heart's joy! For oftentimes
Old Michael, while he was a babe in arms,
Had done him female service, not alone
For pastime and delight, as is the use
Of fathers, but with patient mind enforced
To acts of tenderness; and he had rocked
His cradle, as with a woman's gentle hand.

And in a later time, ere yet the Boy
Had put on boy's attire, did Michael love,
Albeit of a stern unbending mind,
To have the Young-one in his sight, when he
Wrought in the field, or on his shepherd's stool
Sate with a fettered sheep before him stretched
Under the large old oak, that near his door
Stood single, and, from matchless depth of shade,
Chosen for the Shearer's covert from the sun,
Thence in our rustic dialect was called
The Clipping Tree,[11] a name which yet it bears.
There, while they two were sitting in the shade,
With others round them, earnest all and blithe,
Would Michael exercise his heart with looks
Of fond correction and reproof bestowed
Upon the Child, if he disturbed the sheep

[11] Clipping is the word used in the North of England for shearing. [Wordsworth.]

By catching at their legs, or with his shouts
Scared them, while they lay still beneath the shears.

And when by Heaven's good grace the boy grew up
A healthy Lad, and carried in his cheek
Two steady roses that were five years old;
Then Michael from a winter coppice cut
With his own hand a sapling, which he hooped
With iron, making it throughout in all
Due requisites a perfect shepherd's staff,
And gave it to the Boy; wherewith equipt
He as a watchman oftentimes was placed
At gate or gap, to stem or turn the flock;
And, to his office prematurely called,
There stood the urchin, as you will divine,
Something between a hindrance and a help;
And for this cause not always, I believe,
Receiving from his Father hire of praise;
Though nought was left undone which staff, or voice,
Or looks, or threatening gestures, could perform.

But soon as Luke, full ten years old, could stand
Against the mountain blasts; and to the heights,
Not fearing toil, nor length of weary ways,
He with his Father daily went, and they
Were as companions, why should I relate
That objects which the Shepherd loved before
Were dearer now? that from the Boy there came
Feelings and emanations — things which were
Light to the sun and music to the wind;
And that the old Man's heart seemed born again?

Thus in his Father's sight the Boy grew up:
And now, when he had reached his eighteenth year,
He was his comfort and his daily hope.

While in this sort the simple household lived
From day to day, to Michael's ear there came
Distressful tidings. Long before the time
Of which I speak, the Shepherd had been bound
In surety for his brother's son, a man
Of an industrious life, and ample means;
But unforeseen misfortunes suddenly
Had prest upon him; and old Michael now
Was summoned to discharge the forfeiture,
A grievous penalty, but little less
Than half his substance. This unlooked-for claim,
At the first hearing, for a moment took
More hope out of his life than he supposed
That any old man ever could have lost.
As soon as he had armed himself with strength
To look his trouble in the face, it seemed
The Shepherd's sole resource to sell at once
A portion of his patrimonial fields.
Such was his first resolve; he thought again,
And his heart failed him. 'Isabel,' said he,
Two evenings after he had heard the news,
'I have been toiling more than seventy years,
And in the open sunshine of God's love
Have we all lived; yet, if these fields of ours
Should pass into a stranger's hand, I think
That I could not lie quiet in my grave.
Our lot is a hard lot; the sun himself
Has scarcely been more diligent than I;
And I have lived to be a fool at last
To my own family. An evil man
That was, and made an evil choice, if he
Were false to us; and, if he were not false,
There are ten thousand to whom loss like this
Had been no sorrow. I forgive him; — but
'Twere better to be dumb than to talk thus.

When I began, my purpose was to speak
Of remedies and of a cheerful hope.
Our Luke shall leave us, Isabel; the land

Shall not go from us, and it shall be free;
He shall possess it, free as is the wind
That passes over it. We have, thou know'st,
Another kinsman — he will be our friend
In this distress. He is a prosperous man,
Thriving in trade — and Luke to him shall go,
And with his kinsman's help and his own thrift
He quickly will repair this loss, and then
He may return to us. If here he stay,
What can be done? Where every one is poor,
What can be gained? '
At this the old Man paused,
And Isabel sat silent, for her mind
Was busy, looking back into past times.
There's Richard Bateman, thought she to herself,
He was a parish-boy — at the church-door
They made a gathering for him, shillings, pence,
And halfpennies, wherewith the neighbours bought
A basket, which they filled with pedlar's wares;
And, with this basket on his arm, the lad
Went up to London, found a master there,
Who, out of many, chose the trusty boy
To go and overlook his merchandise
Beyond the seas; where he grew wondrous rich,
And left estates and monies to the poor,
And, at his birth-place, built a chapel floored
With marble, which he sent from foreign lands.
These thoughts, and many others of like sort,
Passed quickly through the mind of Isabel,
And her face brightened. The old Man was glad,
And thus resumed: — ' Well, Isabel! this scheme
These two days has been meat and drink to me.
Far more than we have lost is left us yet.
We have enough — I wish indeed that I
Were younger; — but this hope is a good hope.
Make ready Luke's best garments, of the best
Buy for him more, and let us send him forth
To-morrow, or the next day, or to-night:
If he *could* go, the Boy should go to-night.'

Here Michael ceased, and to the fields went forth
With a light heart. The Housewife for five days
Was restless morn and night, and all day long
Wrought on with her best fingers to prepare
Things needful for the journey of her son.
But Isabel was glad when Sunday came
To stop her in her work: for, when she lay
By Michael's side, she through the last two nights
Heard him, how he was troubled in his sleep:
And when they rose at morning she could see
That all his hopes were gone. That day at noon
She said to Luke, while they two by themselves
Were sitting at the door, ' Thou must not go:
We have no other Child but thee to lose,
None to remember — do not go away,
For if thou leave thy Father he will die.'
The Youth made answer with a jocund voice;
And Isabel, when she had told her fears,
Recover'd heart. That evening her best fare
Did she bring forth, and all together sat
Like happy people round a Christmas fire.

With daylight Isabel resumed her work;
And all the ensuing week the house appeared

As cheerful as a grove in Spring: at length
The expected letter from their kinsman came,
With kind assurances that he would do
His utmost for the welfare of the Boy;
To which, requests were added, that forthwith
He might be sent to him. Ten times or more
The letter was read over; Isabel
Went forth to show it to the neighbours round;
Nor was there at that time on English land
A prouder heart than Luke's. When Isabel
Had to her house returned, the old Man said,
'He shall depart to-morrow.' To this word
The Housewife answered, talking much of things
Which, if at such short notice he should go,
Would surely be forgotten. But at length
She gave consent, and Michael was at ease.

Near the tumultuous brook of Green-head Ghyll,
In that deep valley, Michael had designed
To build a Sheep-fold; and, before he heard
The tidings of his melancholy loss,
For this same purpose he had gathered up
A heap of stones, which by the streamlet's edge
Lay thrown together, ready for the work.
With Luke that evening thitherward he walked:
And soon as they had reached the place he stopped,
And thus the old Man spake to him:—'My son,
To-morrow thou wilt leave me: with full heart
I look upon thee, for thou art the same
That wert a promise to me ere thy birth,
And all thy life hast been my daily joy.
I will relate to thee some little part
Of our two histories; 'twill do thee good
When thou art from me, even if I should touch
On things thou can'st not know of.—After thou
First cam'st into the world—as oft befalls
To new-born infants—thou didst sleep away
Two days, and blessings from thy Father's tongue
Then fell upon thee. Day by day passed on,
And still I loved thee with increasing love.
Never to living ear came sweeter sounds
Than when I heard thee by our own fire-side
First uttering, without words, a natural tune;
While thou, a feeding babe, didst in thy joy
Sing at thy Mother's breast. Month followed month,
And in the open fields my life was passed
And on the mountains; else I think that thou
Hadst been brought up upon thy Father's knees.
But we were playmates, Luke: among these hills,
As well thou knowest, in us the old and young
Have played together, nor with me didst thou
Lack any pleasure which a boy can know.'
Luke had a manly heart; but at these words
He sobbed aloud. The old Man grasped his hand,
And said, 'Nay, do not take it so—I see
That these are things of which I need not speak.
—Even to the utmost I have been to thee
A kind and a good Father: and herein
I but repay a gift which I myself
Received at others' hands; for, though now old

Beyond the common life of man, I still
Remember them who loved me in my youth.
Both of them sleep together: here they lived,
As all their Forefathers had done; and, when
At length their time was come, they were not loth
To give their bodies to the family mould.
I wished that thou shouldst live the life they lived,
But 'tis a long time to look back, my Son,
And see so little gain from threescore years.
These fields were burthened when they came to me;
Till I was forty years of age, not more
Than half of my inheritance was mine.
I toiled and toiled; God blessed me in my work,
And till these three weeks past the land was free.
— It looks as if it never could endure
Another Master. Heaven forgive me, Luke,
If I judge ill for thee, but it seems good
That thou shouldst go.'
At this the old Man paused;
Then, pointing to the stones near which they stood,
Thus, after a short silence, he resumed:
'This was a work for us; and now, my Son,
It is a work for me. But, lay one stone —
Here, lay it for me, Luke, with thine own hands.
Nay, Boy, be of good hope; — we both may live
To see a better day. At eighty-four
I still am strong and hale; — do thou thy part;
I will do mine. — I will begin again
With many tasks that were resigned to thee:
Up to the heights, and in among the storms,
Will I without thee go again, and do
All works which I was wont to do alone,
Before I knew thy face. — Heaven bless thee, Boy!
Thy heart these two weeks has been beating fast
With many hopes; it should be so — yes — yes —
I knew that thou couldst never have a wish
To leave me, Luke: thou hast been bound to me
Only by links of love: when thou art gone,
What will be left to us! — But I forget
My purposes. Lay now the corner-stone,
As I requested; and hereafter, Luke,
When thou art gone away, should evil men
Be thy companions, think of me, my Son,
And of this moment; hither turn thy thoughts,
And God will strengthen thee: amid all fear
And all temptation, Luke, I pray that thou
May'st bear in mind the life thy Fathers lived,
Who, being innocent, did for that cause
Bestir them in good deeds. Now, fare thee well —
When thou return'st, thou in this place wilt see
A work which is not here: a covenant
'Twill be between us; but, whatever fate
Befall thee, I shall love thee to the last,
And bear thy memory with me to the grave.'

The Shepherd ended here; and Luke stooped down,
And, as his Father had requested, laid
The first stone of the Sheep-fold. At the sight
The old Man's grief broke from him; to his heart
He pressed his Son, he kisséd him and wept;
And to the house together they returned.
— Hushed was that House in peace, or seeming peace,
Ere the night fell: — with morrow's dawn the Boy

Began his journey, and, when he had reached
The public way, he put on a bold face;
And all the neighbours, as he passed their doors,
Came forth with wishes and with farewell prayers,
That followed him till he was out of sight.

A good report did from their Kinsman come,
Of Luke and his well-doing: and the Boy
Wrote loving letters, full of wondrous news,
Which, as the Housewife phrased it, were throughout
'The prettiest letters that were ever seen.'
Both parents read them with rejoicing hearts.
So, many months passed on: and once again
The Shepherd went about his daily work
With confident and cheerful thoughts; and now
Sometimes when he could find a leisure hour
He to that valley took his way, and there
Wrought at the Sheep-fold. Meantime Luke began
To slacken in his duty; and, at length,
He in the dissolute city gave himself
To evil courses: ignominy and shame
Fell on him, so that he was driven at last
To seek a hiding-place beyond the seas.

There is a comfort in the strength of love;
'Twill make a thing endurable, which else
Would overset the brain, or break the heart:
I have conversed with more than one who well
Remember the old Man, and what he was
Years after he had heard this heavy news.
His bodily frame had been from youth to age
Of an unusual strength. Among the rocks
He went, and still looked up to sun and cloud,
And listened to the wind; and, as before,
Performed all kinds of labour for his sheep,
And for the land, his small inheritance.
And to that hollow dell from time to time
Did he repair, to build the Fold of which
His flock had need. 'Tis not forgotten yet
The pity which was then in every heart
For the old Man — and 'tis believed by all
That many and many a day he thither went,
And never lifted up a single stone.

There, by the Sheep-fold, sometimes was he seen
Sitting alone, or with his faithful Dog,
Then old, beside him, lying at his feet.
The length of full seven years, from time to time,
He at the building of this Sheep-fold wrought,
And left the work unfinished when he died.
Three years, or little more, did Isabel
Survive her Husband: at her death the estate
Was sold, and went into a stranger's hand.
The Cottage which was named the Evening Star
Is gone — the ploughshare has been through the ground
On which it stood; great changes have been wrought
In all the neighbourhood: — yet the oak is left
That grew beside their door; and the remains
Of the unfinished Sheep-fold may be seen
Beside the boisterous brook of Green-head Ghyll.

THE PRELUDE

OR, GROWTH OF A POET'S MIND

AN AUTOBIOGRAPHICAL POEM [12]

ADVERTISEMENT

[By the Editor of 1850]

The following poem was commenced in the beginning of the year 1799, and completed in the summer of 1805.

The design and occasion of the work are described by the Author in his Preface to the 'Excursion,' first published in 1814, where he thus speaks: —

'Several years ago, when the Author retired to his native mountains with the hope of being enabled to construct a literary work that might live, it was a reasonable thing that he should take a review of his own mind, and examine how far Nature and Education had qualified him for such an employment.

'As subsidiary to this preparation, he undertook to record, in verse, the origin and progress of his own powers, as far as he was acquainted with them.

'That work, addressed to a dear friend, most distinguished for his knowledge and genius, and to whom the Author's intellect is deeply indebted, has been long finished; and the result of the investigation which gave rise to it, was a determination to compose a philosophical Poem, containing views of Man, Nature, and Society, and to be entitled the "Recluse"; as having for its principal subject the sensation and opinions of a poet living in retirement.

'The preparatory poem is biographical, and conducts the history of the Author's mind to the point where he was emboldened to hope that his faculties were sufficiently matured for entering upon the arduous labour which he had proposed to himself; and the two works have the same kind of relation to each other, if he may so express himself, as the Ante-chapel has to the body of a Gothic Church. Continuing this allusion, he may be permitted to add, that his minor pieces, which have been long before the public, when they shall be properly arranged, will be found by the attentive reader to have such connection with the main work as may give them claim to be likened to the little cells, oratories, and sepulchral recesses, ordinarily included in those edifices.'

Such was the Author's language in the year 1814.

It will thence be seen, that the present Poem was intended to be introductory to the 'Recluse,' and that the 'Recluse,' if completed, would have consisted of Three Parts. Of these, the Second Part alone, viz. the 'Excursion,' was finished, and given to the world by the Author.

The First Book of the First Part of the 'Recluse' still [1850] remains in manuscript; but the Third Part was only planned. The materials of which it would have been formed have, however, been incorporated, for the most part, in the Author's other Publications, written subsequently to the 'Excursion.'

The Friend, to whom the present Poem is addressed, was the late SAMUEL TAYLOR COLERIDGE, who was resident in Malta, for the restoration of his health, when the greater part of it was composed.

Mr. Coleridge read a considerable portion of the Poem while he was abroad; and his feelings, on hearing it recited by the Author (after his return to his own country) are recorded in his Verses, addressed to Mr. Wordsworth, which will be found in the 'Sibylline Leaves,' p. 197, ed. 1817, or 'Poetical Works, by S. T. Coleridge,' vol. i., p. 206.

RYDAL MOUNT,
July 13th, 1850.

from BOOK I

CHILDHOOD AND SCHOOL-TIME

FAIR seed-time had my soul, and I grew up 301
Fostered alike by beauty and by fear:
Much favoured in my birthplace, and no less
In that belovéd Vale [13] to which erelong
We were transplanted — there were we let loose
For sports of wider range. Ere I had told
Ten birth-days, when among the mountain-slopes
Frost, and the breath of frosty wind, had snapped
The last autumnal crocus, 'twas my joy

[12] Begun in 1798, not 1799, as stated in the advertisement (the Preamble in 1795), and completed in 1805. It was not published until after Wordsworth's death, in 1850. For thirty-five years it was in continual revision. Professor Ernest de Selincourt's notable critical edition edited from the manuscripts (Oxford, 1926) now gives us, in a new sense, 'the growth of a poet's mind' — and of his art as well. Not merely does the 1850 edition show, by comparison with the earlier text, many changes in ideas — a growing conservatism, a leaning toward dogmatic Christianity that departs from his earlier mysticism and naturalistic rapture — but it also proves that, contrary to the legend, the poetic faculty did not die in Wordsworth's later years. The revisions moved often toward a higher level of poetry. Some samples of the first draft are given in the notes. The text used here is that of 1850.

[13] Esthwaite, at the northwest end of which is Hawkshead, where Wordsworth spent his schooldays. He entered the Grammar-school in 1779 with his elder brother Richard

With store of springes o'er my shoulder hung
To range the open heights where woodcocks run
Among the smooth green turf. Through half the night,
Scudding away from snare to snare, I plied
That anxious visitation; — moon and stars
Were shining o'er my head. I was alone,
And seemed to be a trouble to the peace
That dwelt among them. Sometimes it befell
In these night wanderings, that a strong desire
O'erpowered my better reason, and the bird
Which was the captive of another's toil
Became my prey; and when the deed was done
I heard among the solitary hills
Low breathings coming after me, and sounds
Of undistinguishable motion, steps
Almost as silent as the turf they trod.

Nor less when spring had warmed the cultured Vale,
Moved we as plunderers where the mother-bird
Had in high places built her lodge; though mean
Our object and inglorious, yet the end
Was not ignoble. Oh! when I have hung
Above the raven's nest, by knots of grass
And half-inch fissures in the slippery rock
But ill sustained, and almost (so it seemed)
Suspended by the blast that blew amain,
Shouldering the naked crag, oh, at that time
While on the perilous ridge I hung alone,
With what strange utterance did the loud dry wind
Blow through my ear! the sky seemed not a sky
Of earth — and with what motion moved the clouds!

Dust as we are, the immortal spirit grows
Like harmony in music; [14] there is a dark
Inscrutable workmanship that reconciles
Discordant elements, makes them cling together
In one society. How strange that all
The terrors, pains, and early miseries,
Regrets, vexations, lassitudes interfused
Within my mind, should e'er have borne a part,
And that a needful part, in making up
The calm existence that is mine when I
Am worthy of myself! Praise to the end!
Thanks to the means which Nature deigned to employ;
Whether her fearless visitings, or those
That came with soft alarm, like hurtless light
Opening the peaceful clouds; or she may use
Severer interventions, ministry
More palpable, as best might suit her aim.

One summer evening (led by her) I found
A little boat tied to a willow tree
Within a rocky cave, its usual home.
Straight I unloosed her chain, and stepping in
Pushed from the shore. It was an act of stealth
And troubled pleasure, nor without the voice
Of mountain-echoes did my boat move on;
Leaving behind her still, on either side,
Small circles glittering idly in the moon,
Until they melted all into one track
Of sparkling light. But now, like one who rows,
Proud of his skill, to reach a chosen point
With an unswerving line, I fixed my view
Upon the summit of a craggy ridge,
The horizon's utmost boundary; far above

[14] It is instructive to compare this with the earlier version:
'The mind of Man is fram'd even like the breath
And harmony of music.'

Was nothing but the stars and the grey sky.
She was an elfin pinnace; lustily
I dipped my oars into the silent lake,
And, as I rose upon the stroke, my boat
Went heaving through the water like a swan;
When, from behind that craggy steep till then
The horizon's bound, a huge peak, black and huge,
As if with voluntary power instinct
Upreared its head. I struck and struck again,
And growing still in stature the grim shape
Towered up between me and the stars, and still,
For so it seemed, with purpose of its own
And measured motion like a living thing,
Strode after me. With trembling oars I turned,
And through the silent water stole my way
Back to the covert of the willow tree;
There in her mooring-place I left my bark, —
And through the meadows homeward went, in grave
And serious mood; but after I had seen
That spectacle, for many days, my brain
Worked with a dim and undetermined sense
Of unknown modes of being; o'er my thoughts
There hung a darkness, call it solitude
Or blank desertion. No familiar shapes
Remained, no pleasant images of trees,
Of sea or sky, no colours of green fields;
But huge and mighty forms, that do not live
Like living men, moved slowly through the mind [15]
By day, and were a trouble to my dreams.

Wisdom and Spirit of the universe!
Thou Soul that art the eternity of thought,
Thou givest to forms and images a breath
And everlasting motion, not in vain
By day or star-light thus from my first dawn
Of childhood didst thou intertwine for me
The passions that build up our human soul;
Not with the mean and vulgar works of man,
But with high objects, with enduring things —
With life and nature — purifying thus
The elements of feeling and of thought,
And sanctifying, by such discipline,
Both pain and fear, until we recognise
A grandeur in the beatings of the heart.
Nor was this fellowship vouchsafed to me
With stinted kindness. In November days,
When vapours rolling down the valley made
A lonely scene more lonesome, among woods,
At noon and 'mid the calm of summer nights,
When, by the margin of the trembling lake,
Beneath the gloomy hills homeward I went
In solitude, such intercourse was mine;
Mine was it in the fields both day and night,
And by the waters, all the summer long.

And in the frosty season, when the sun
Was set, and visible for many a mile
The cottage windows blazed through twilight gloom,
I heeded not their summons: happy time
It was indeed for all of us — for me
It was a time of rapture! Clear and loud
The village clock tolled six, — I wheeled about,
Proud and exulting like an untired horse
That cares not for his home. All shod with steel,
We hissed along the polished ice in games
Confederate, imitative of the chase
And woodland pleasures, — the resounding horn,

[15] Professor Garrod suggests that these lines be punctuated thus:
'But huge and mighty forms that do not live,
Like living men moved slowly through the mind.'

The pack loud chiming, and the hunted hare.
So through the darkness and the cold we flew,
And not a voice was idle; with the din
Smitten, the precipices rang aloud;
The leafless trees and every icy crag
Tinkled like iron; while far distant hills
Into the tumult sent an alien sound
Of melancholy not unnoticed, while the stars
Eastward were sparkling clear, and in the west
The orange sky of evening died away.
Not seldom from the uproar I retired
Into a silent bay, or sportively
Glanced sideway, leaving the tumultuous throng,
To cut across the reflex of a star
That fled, and, flying still before me, gleamed
Upon the glassy plain; and oftentimes,
When we had given our bodies to the wind,
And all the shadowy banks on either side
Came sweeping through the darkness, spinning still
The rapid line of motion, then at once
Have I, reclining back upon my heels,
Stopped short; yet still the solitary cliffs
Wheeled by me — even as if the earth had rolled
With visible motion her diurnal round!
Behind me did they stretch in solemn train,
Feebler and feebler, and I stood and watched
Till all was tranquil as a dreamless sleep.

. . .

Nor, sedulous as I have been to trace
How Nature by extrinsic passion first
Peopled the mind with forms sublime or fair,
And made me love them, may I here omit
How other pleasures have been mine, and joys
Of subtler origin; how I have felt,
Not seldom even in that tempestuous time,
Those hallowed and pure motions of the sense
Which seem, in their simplicity, to own
An intellectual charm; that calm delight
Which, if I err not, surely must belong
To those first-born affinities that fit
Our new existence to existing things,
And, in our dawn of being, constitute
The bond of union between life and joy.

Yes, I remember when the changeful earth,
And twice five summers on my mind had stamped
The faces of the moving year, even then
I held unconscious intercourse with beauty
Old as creation, drinking in a pure
Organic pleasure from the silver wreaths
Of curling mist, or from the level plain
Of waters coloured by impending clouds.

The sands of Westmoreland, the creeks and bays
Of Cumbria's rocky limits, they can tell
How, when the Sea threw off his evening shade
And to the shepherd's hut on distant hills
Sent welcome notice of the rising moon,
How I have stood, to fancies such as these
A stranger, linking with the spectacle
No conscious memory of a kindred sight,
And bringing with me no peculiar sense
Of quietness or peace; yet have I stood,
Even while mine eye hath moved o'er many a league
Of shining water, gathering as it seemed,
Through every hair-breadth in that field of light,
New pleasure like a bee among the flowers.

. . .

from BOOK II

SCHOOL-TIME — [continued]

Midway on long Winander's [16] eastern shore,

[16] Windermere's

Within the crescent of a pleasant bay,
A tavern[17] stood; no homely-featured house,
Primeval like its neighbouring cottages,
But 'twas a splendid place, the door beset
With chaises, grooms, and liveries, and within
Decanters, glasses, and the blood-red wine.
In ancient times, and ere the Hall was built
On the large island, had this dwelling been
More worthy of a poet's love, a hut,
Proud of its own bright fire and sycamore shade.
But — though the rhymes were gone that once inscribed
The threshold, and large golden characters,
Spread o'er the spangled sign-board, had dislodged
The old Lion and usurped his place, in slight
And mockery of the rustic painter's hand —
Yet, to this hour, the spot to me is dear
With all its foolish pomp. The garden lay
Upon a slope surmounted by a plain
Of a small bowling-green; beneath us stood
A grove, with gleams of water through the trees
And over the tree-tops; nor did we want
Refreshment, strawberries and mellow cream.
There, while through half an afternoon we played
On the smooth platform, whether skill prevailed
Or happy blunder triumphed, bursts of glee
Made all the mountains ring. But, ere nightfall,
When in our pinnace we returned at leisure
Over the shadowy lake, and to the beach
Of some small island steered our course with one,
The Minstrel of the Troop,[18] and left him there,
And rowed off gently, while he blew his flute
Alone upon the rock — oh, then, the calm
And dead still water lay upon my mind
Even with a weight of pleasure, and the sky,
Never before so beautiful, sank down
Into my heart, and held me like a dream!
Thus were my sympathies enlarged, and thus
Daily the common range of visible things
Grew dear to me: already I began
To love the sun; a boy I loved the sun,
Not as I since have loved him, as a pledge
And surety of our earthly life, a light
Which we behold and feel we are alive;
Nor for his bounty to so many worlds —
But for this cause, that I had seen him lay
His beauty on the morning hills, had seen
The western mountain touch his setting orb,
In many a thoughtless hour, when, from excess
Of happiness, my blood appeared to flow
For its own pleasure, and I breathed with joy.
And, from like feelings, humble though intense,
To patriotic and domestic love
Analogous, the moon to me was dear;
For I could dream away my purposes,
Standing to gaze upon her while she hung
Midway between the hills, as if she knew
No other region, but belonged to thee,
Yea, appertained by a peculiar right
To thee and thy grey huts, thou one dear Vale!

Those incidental charms which first attached
My heart to rural objects, day by day
Grew weaker, and I hasten on to tell
How Nature, intervenient till this time
And secondary, now at length was sought
For her own sake.

. . .

Many are our joys
In youth, but oh! what happiness to live

[17] The White Lion at Bowness.
[18] 'Robert Greenwood, afterwards Senior Fellow of Trinity College, Cambridge.' [Wordsworth's *Memoirs*.]

When every hour brings palpable access
Of knowledge, when all knowledge is delight,
And sorrow is not there! The seasons came,
And every season wheresoe'er I moved
Unfolded transitory qualities,
Which, but for this most watchful power of love,
Had been neglected; left a register
Of permanent relations, else unknown.
Hence life, and change, and beauty, solitude
More active even than 'best society'[19]—
Society made sweet as solitude
By silent inobtrusive sympathies,
And gentle agitations of the mind
From manifold distinctions, difference
Perceived in things, where, to the unwatchful eye,
No difference is, and hence, from the same source,
Sublimer joy; for I would walk alone,
Under the quiet stars, and at that time
Have felt whate'er there is of power in sound
To breathe an elevated mood, by form
Or image unprofaned; and I would stand,
If the night blackened with a coming storm,
Beneath some rock, listening to notes that are
The ghostly language of the ancient earth,
Or make their dim abode in distant winds.
Thence did I drink the visionary power;
And deem not profitless those fleeting moods
Of shadowy exultation: not for this,
That they are kindred to our purer mind
And intellectual life; but that the soul,
Remembering how she felt, but what she felt
Remembering not, retains an obscure sense
Of possible sublimity, whereto
With growing faculties she doth aspire,
With faculties still growing, feeling still
That whatsoever point they gain, they yet
Have something to pursue.
And not alone,
'Mid gloom and tumult, but no less 'mid fair
And tranquil scenes, that universal power
And fitness in the latent qualities
And essences of things, by which the mind
Is moved with feelings of delight, to me
Came strengthened with a superadded soul,
A virtue not its own.

. . .

'Twere long to tell
What spring and autumn, what the winter snows,
And what the summer shade, what day and night,
Evening and morning, sleep and waking, thought
From sources inexhaustible, poured forth
To feed the spirit of religious love
In which I walked with Nature. But let this
Be not forgotten, that I still retained
My first creative sensibility;
That by the regular action of the world
My soul was unsubdued. A plastic power
Abode with me; a forming hand, at times
Rebellious, acting in a devious mood;
A local spirit of his own, at war
With general tendency, but, for the most,
Subservient strictly to external things
With which it communed. An auxiliar light
Came from my mind, which on the setting sun
Bestowed new splendour; the melodious birds,
The fluttering breezes, fountains that run on
Murmuring so sweetly in themselves, obeyed
A like dominion, and the midnight storm
Grew darker in the presence of my eye:
Hence my obeisance, my devotion hence,
And hence my transport.

. . .

[19] 'For solitude sometimes is best society.' [*Paradise Lost*, ix, 249.]

Yet were I grossly destitute of all
Those human sentiments that make this earth
So dear, if I should fail with grateful voice
To speak of you, ye mountains, and ye lakes
And sounding cataracts, ye mists and winds
That dwell among the hills where I was born.
If in my youth I have been pure in heart,
If, mingling with the world, I am content
With my own modest pleasures, and have lived
With God and Nature communing, removed
From little enmities and low desires,
The gift is yours; if in these times of fear [20]
This melancholy waste of hopes o'erthrown,
If, 'mid indifference and apathy,
And wicked exultation when good men
On every side fall off, we know not how,
To selfishness, disguised in gentle names
Of peace and quiet and domestic love,
Yet mingled not unwillingly with sneers
On visionary minds; if, in this time
Of dereliction and dismay, I yet
Despair not of our nature, but retain
A more than Roman confidence, a faith
That fails not, in all sorrow my support,
The blessing of my life; the gift is yours,
Ye winds and sounding cataracts! 'tis yours,
Ye mountains! thine, O Nature! Thou hast fed
My lofty speculations; and in thee,
For this uneasy heart of ours, I find
A never-failing principle of joy
And purest passion.
Thou, my Friend! [21] wert reared
In the great city, 'mid far other scenes;
But we, by different roads, at length have gained
The self-same bourne. And for this cause to thee
I speak, unapprehensive of contempt,
The insinuated scoff of coward tongues,
And all that silent language which so oft
In conversation between man and man
Blots from the human countenance all trace
Of beauty and of love. For thou hast sought
The truth in solitude, and, since the days
That gave thee liberty, full long desired,
To serve in Nature's temple, thou hast been
The most assiduous of her ministers;
In many things my brother, chiefly here
In this our deep devotion.
Fare thee well!
Health and the quiet of a healthful mind
Attend thee! seeking oft the haunts of men,
And yet more often living with thyself,
And for thyself, so haply shall thy days
Be many, and a blessing to mankind.

from BOOK III

RESIDENCE AT CAMBRIDGE

The Evangelist St. John [22] my patron was:
Three Gothic courts are his, and in the first
Was my abiding-place, a nook obscure;
Right underneath, the College kitchens made
A humming sound, less tuneable than bees.
But hardly less industrious; with shrill notes
Of sharp command and scolding intermixed.
Near me hung Trinity's loquacious clock,
Who never let the quarters, night or day,
Slip by him unproclaimed, and told the hours
Twice over with a male and female voice.
Her pealing organ was my neighbour too;
And from my pillow, looking forth by light
Of moon or favouring stars, I could behold
The antechapel where the statue stood
Of Newton with his prism and silent face,

[20] *I.e.*, in 1799, after the failure of the French Revolution.

[21] Coleridge, as so throughout the poem. He had been brought up at Christ's Hospital, London; see his *Frost at Midnight*, p. 684.

[22] Wordsworth entered St. John's College, Cambridge in October 1787.

The marble index of a mind for ever
Voyaging through strange seas of Thought, alone.[23]

. . .

Oft when the dazzling show no longer new
Had ceased to dazzle, ofttimes did I quit
My comrades, leave the crowd, buildings and groves,
And as I paced alone the level fields
Far from those lovely sights and sounds sublime
With which I had been conversant, the mind
Drooped not; but there into herself returning,
With prompt rebound seemed fresh as heretofore.
At least I more distinctly recognised
Her native instincts: let me dare to speak
A higher language, say that now I felt
What independent solaces were mine,
To mitigate the injurious sway of place
Or circumstance, how far soever changed
In youth, or *to* be changed in after years.
As if awakened, summoned, roused, constrained,
I looked for universal things; perused
The common countenance of earth and sky:
Earth, nowhere unembellished by some trace
Of that first Paradise whence man was driven;
And sky, whose beauty and bounty are expressed
By the proud name she bears — the name of Heaven.
I called on both to teach me what they might;
Or turning the mind in upon herself,
Pored, watched, expected, listened, spread my thoughts
And spread them with a wider creeping; felt
Incumbencies more awful, visitings
Of the Upholder of the tranquil soul,
That tolerates the indignities of Time,
And, from the centre of Eternity
All finite motions overruling, lives
In glory immutable. But peace! enough
Here to record that I was mounting now
To such community with highest truth —
A track pursuing, not untrod before,
From strict analogies by thought supplied
Or consciousnesses not to be subdued.
To every natural form, rock, fruit, or flower,
Even the loose stones that cover the highway,
I gave a moral life: I saw them feel,
Or linked them to some feeling: the great mass
Lay bedded in a quickening soul, and all
That I beheld respired with inward meaning.
Add that whate'er of Terror or of Love
Or Beauty, Nature's daily face put on
From transitory passion, unto this
I was as sensitive as waters are
To the sky's influence in a kindred mood
Of passion; was obedient as a lute
That waits upon the touches of the wind.
Unknown, unthought of, yet I was most rich —
I had a world about me — 'twas my own;
I made it, for it only lived to me,
And to the God who sees into the heart.

. . .

Companionships,
Friendships, acquaintances, were welcome all.
We sauntered, played, or rioted; we talked
Unprofitable talk at morning hours;
Drifted about along the streets and walks,
Read lazily in trivial books, went forth
To gallop through the country in blind zeal
Of senseless horsemanship, or on the breast
Of Cam sailed boisterously, and let the stars
Come forth, perhaps without one quiet thought.

[23] These last two famous lines were not in the first draft, but were added when Wordsworth was over sixty years old.

Such was the tenour of the second act
In this new life. Imagination slept,
And yet not utterly. I could not print
Ground where the grass had yielded to the steps
Of generations of illustrious men,
Unmoved. I could not always lightly pass
Through the same gateways, sleep where they had slept,
Wake where they waked, range that inclosure old,
That garden of great intellects, undisturbed.
Place also by the side of this dark sense
Of noble feeling, that those spiritual men,
Even the great Newton's own ethereal self,
Seemed humbled in these precincts thence to be
The more endeared. Their several memories here
(Even like their persons in their portraits clothed
With the accustomed garb of daily life)
Put on a lowly and a touching grace
Of more distinct humanity, that left
All genuine admiration unimpaired.

Beside the pleasant Mill of Trompington [24]
I laughed with Chaucer [25] in the hawthorn shade;
Heard him, while birds were warbling, tell his tales
Of amorous passion. And that gentle Bard,
Chosen by the Muses for their Page of State —
Sweet Spenser, moving through his clouded heaven
With the moon's beauty and the moon's soft pace,
I called him Brother, Englishman, and Friend!
Yea, our blind Poet, who, in his later day,
Stood almost single; uttering odious truth —
Darkness before, and danger's voice behind,
Soul awful — if the earth has ever lodged
An awful soul — I seemed to see him here
Familiarly, and in his scholar's dress
Bounding before me, yet a stripling youth —
A boy, no better, with his rosy cheeks
Angelical, keen eye, courageous look,
And conscious step of purity and pride.
Among the band of my compeers was one
Whom chance had stationed in the very room
Honoured by Milton's name. O temperate Bard!
Be it confest that, for the first time, seated
Within thy innocent lodge and oratory,
One of a festive circle, I poured out
Libations, to thy memory drank, till pride
And gratitude grew dizzy in a brain
Never excited by the fumes of wine
Before that hour, or since.

. . .

I did not love,
Judging not ill perhaps, the timid course
Of our scholastic studies; could have wished
To see the river flow with ampler range
And freer pace; but more, far more, I grieved
To see displayed among an eager few,
Who in the field of contest persevered,
Passions unworthy of youth's generous heart
And mounting spirit, pitiably repaid,
When so disturbed, whatever palms are won.
From these I turned to travel with the shoal
Of more unthinking natures, easy minds
And pillowy; yet not wanting love that makes
The day pass lightly on, when foresight sleeps,
And wisdom and the pledges interchanged
With our own inner being are forgot.

---

[24] Near Cambridge; scene of Chaucer's *Reve's Tale*.

[25] 'When I began to give myself up to the profession of a poet for life, I was impressed with a conviction, that there were four poets whom I must have continually before me as examples — Chaucer, Shakespeare, Spenser, and Milton. These I must study, and equal *if I could*; and I need not think of the rest.' [Wordsworth's *Memoirs*.]

Yet was this deep vacation not given up
To utter waste. Hitherto I had stood
In my own mind remote from social life,
(At least from what we commonly so name,)
Like a lone shepherd on a promontory
Who lacking occupation looks far forth
Into the boundless sea, and rather makes
Than finds what he beholds.

. . .

from BOOK IV

SUMMER VACATION

When first I made
Once more the circuit of our little lake,
If ever happiness hath lodged with man,
That day consummate happiness was mine,
Wide-spreading, steady, calm, contemplative.
The sun was set, or setting, when I left
Our cottage door, and evening soon brought on
A sober hour, not winning or serene,
For cold and raw the air was, and untuned;
But as a face we love is sweetest then
When sorrow damps it, or, whatever look
It chance to wear, is sweetest if the heart
Have fulness in herself; even so with me
It fared that evening. Gently did my soul
Put off her veil, and, self-transmuted, stood
Naked, as in the presence of her God.
While on I walked, a comfort seemed to touch
A heart that had not been disconsolate:
Strength came where weakness was not known to be,
At least not felt; and restoration came
Like an intruder knocking at the door
Of unacknowledged weariness. I took
The balance, and with firm hand weighed myself.
— Of that external scene which round me lay,
Little, in this abstraction, did I see;
Remembered less; but I had inward hopes
And swellings of the spirit, was rapt and soothed,
Conversed with promises, had glimmering views
How life pervades the undecaying mind;
How the immortal soul with God-like power
Informs, creates, and thaws the deepest sleep
That time can lay upon her; how on earth
Man, if he do but live within the light
Of high endeavours, daily spreads abroad
His being armed with strength that cannot fail.

. . .

'Mid a throng
Of maids and youths, old men, and matrons staid,
A medley of all tempers, I had passed
The night in dancing, gaiety, and mirth,
With din of instruments and shuffling feet,
And glancing forms, and tapers glittering,
And unaimed prattle flying up and down;
Spirits upon the stretch, and here and there
Slight shocks of young love-liking interspersed,
Whose transient pleasure mounted to the head,
And tingled through the veins. Ere we retired,
The cock had crowed, and now the eastern sky
Was kindling, not unseen, from humble copse
And open field, through which the pathway wound,
And homeward led my steps. Magnificent
The morning rose, in memorable pomp,
Glorious as e'er I had beheld — in front,
The sea lay laughing at a distance; near,
The solid mountains shone, bright as the clouds,
Grain-tinctured, drenched in empyrean light;
And in the meadows and the lower grounds

Was all the sweetness of a common dawn —
Dews, vapours, and the melody of birds,
And labourers going forth to till the fields.
Ah! need I say, dear Friend! that to the brim
My heart was full; I made no vows, but vows
Were then made for me; bond unknown to me
Was given, that I should be, else sinning greatly,
A dedicated Spirit. On I walked
In thankful blessedness, which yet survives.

. . .

When from our better selves we have too long
Been parted by the hurrying world, and droop,
Sick of its business, of its pleasures tired,
How gracious, how benign, is Solitude;
How potent a mere image of her sway;
Most potent when impressed upon the mind
With an appropriate human centre — hermit,
Deep in the bosom of the wilderness;
Votary (in vast cathedral, where no foot
Is treading, where no other face is seen)
Kneeling at prayers; or watchman on the top
Of lighthouse, beaten by Atlantic waves;
Or as the soul of that great Power is met
Sometimes embodied on a public road,
When, for the night deserted, it assumes
A character of quiet more profound
Than pathless wastes.
Once, when those summer months
Were flown, and autumn brought its annual show
Of oars with oars contending, sails with sails,
Upon Winander's spacious breast, it chanced
That — after I had left a flower-decked room
(Whose in-door pastime, lighted up, survived
To a late hour), and spirits overwrought
Were making night do penance for a day
Spent in a round of strenuous idleness —
My homeward course led up a long ascent,
Where the road's watery surface, to the top
Of that sharp rising, glittered to the moon
And bore the semblance of another stream
Stealing with silent lapse to join the brook
That murmured in the vale. All else was still;
No living thing appeared in earth or air,
And, save the flowing water's peaceful voice,
Sound there was none — but, lo! an uncouth shape,
Shown by a sudden turning of the road,
So near that, slipping back into the shade
Of a thick hawthorn, I could mark him well,
Myself unseen. He was of stature tall,
A span above man's common measure, tall,
Stiff, lank, and upright; a more meagre man
Was never seen before by night or day.
Long were his arms, pallid his hands; his mouth
Looked ghastly in the moonlight: from behind,
A mile-stone propped him; I could also ken
That he was clothed in military garb,
Though faded, yet entire. Companionless,
No dog attending, by no staff sustained,
He stood, and in his very dress appeared
A desolation, a simplicity,
To which the trappings of a gaudy world
Make a strange back-ground. From his lips, ere long,
Issued low muttered sounds, as if of pain
Or some uneasy thought; yet still his form
Kept the same awful steadiness — at his feet
His shadow lay, and moved not. From self-blame
Not wholly free, I watched him thus; at length

Subduing my heart's specious cowardice,
I left the shady nook where I had stood
And hailed him. Slowly from his resting-place
He rose, and with a lean and wasted arm
In measured gesture lifted to his head
Returned my salutation; then resumed
His station as before; and when I asked
His history, the veteran, in reply,
Was neither slow nor eager; but, unmoved,
And with a quiet uncomplaining voice,
A stately air of mild indifference,
He told in few plain words a soldier's tale —
That in the Tropic Islands he had served,
Whence he had landed scarcely three weeks past;
That on his landing he had been dismissed,
And now was travelling towards his native home.
This heard, I said, in pity, 'Come with me.'
He stooped, and straightway from the ground took up
An oaken staff by me yet unobserved —
A staff which must have dropt from his slack hand
And lay till now neglected in the grass.
Though weak his step and cautious, he appeared
To travel without pain, and I beheld,
With an astonishment but ill suppressed,
His ghostly figure moving at my side;
Nor could I, while we journeyed thus, forbear
To turn from present hardships to the past,
And speak of war, battle, and pestilence,
Sprinkling this talk with questions, better spared,
On what he might himself have seen or felt.
He all the while was in demeanour calm,
Concise in answer; solemn and sublime
He might have seemed, but that in all he said
There was a strange half-absence, as of one
Knowing too well the importance of his theme,
But feeling it no longer. Our discourse
Soon ended, and together on we passed
In silence through a wood gloomy and still.
Up-turning, then, along an open field,
We reached a cottage. At the door I knocked,
And earnestly to charitable care
Commended him as a poor friendless man,
Belated and by sickness overcome.
Assured that now the traveller would repose
In comfort, I entreated that henceforth
He would not linger in the public ways,
But ask for timely furtherance and help
Such as his state required. At this reproof,
With the same ghastly mildness in his look,
He said, 'My trust is in the God of Heaven,
And in the eye of him who passes me!'

The cottage door was speedily unbarred,
And now the soldier touched his hat once more
With his lean hand, and in a faltering voice,
Whose tone bespake reviving interests
Till then unfelt, he thanked me; I returned
The farewell blessing of the patient man,
And so we parted. Back I cast a look,
And lingered near the door a little space,
Then sought with quiet heart my distant home.

from BOOK V

BOOKS

Here must we pause: this only let me add,
From heart-experience, and in humblest sense
Of modesty, that he, who in his youth
A daily wanderer among woods and fields
With living Nature hath been intimate,
Not only in that raw unpractised time

Is stirred to ecstasy, as others are,
By glittering verse; but further, doth receive,
In measure only dealt out to himself,
Knowledge and increase of enduring joy
From the great Nature that exists in works
Of mighty Poets. Visionary power
Attends the motions of the viewless winds,
Embodied in the mystery of words:
There, darkness makes abode, and all the host
Of shadowy things work endless changes, — there,
As in a mansion like their proper home,
Even forms and substances are circumfused
By that transparent veil with light divine,
And, through the turnings intricate of verse,
Present themselves as objects recognised,
In flashes, and with glory not their own.

from BOOK VI

CAMBRIDGE AND THE ALPS[26]

When from the Vallais we had turned, and clomb
Along the Simplon's steep and rugged road,
Following a band of muleteers, we reached
A halting-place, where all together took
Their noon-tide meal. Hastily rose our guide,
Leaving us at the board; awhile we lingered,
Then paced the beaten downward way that led
Right to a rough stream's edge, and there broke off;
The only track now visible was one
That from the torrent's further brink held forth
Conspicuous invitation to ascend
A lofty mountain. After brief delay
Crossing the unbridged stream, that road we took,
And clomb with eagerness, till anxious fears
Intruded, for we failed to overtake
Our comrades gone before. By fortunate chance,
While every moment added doubt to doubt,
A peasant met us, from whose mouth we learned
That to the spot which had perplexed us first
We must descend, and there should find the road,
Which in the stony channel of the stream
Lay a few steps, and then along its banks;
And, that our future course, all plain to sight,
Was downwards, with the current of that stream.
Loth to believe what we so grieved to hear,
For still we had hopes that pointed to the clouds,
We questioned him again, and yet again;
But every word that from the peasant's lips
Came in reply, translated by our feelings,
Ended in this, — *that we had crossed the Alps.*

Imagination — here the Power so called
Through sad incompetence of human speech,
That awful Power rose from the mind's abyss
Like an unfathomed vapour that enwraps,
At once, some lonely traveller. I was lost;
Halted without an effort to break through;
But to my conscious soul I now can say —
'I recognise thy glory: ' in such strength
Of usurpation, when the light of sense
Goes out, but with a flash that has revealed
The invisible world, doth greatness make abode,
There harbours; whether we be young or old,
Our destiny, our being's heart and home,
Is with infinitude, and only there;

---

[26] With his friend Robert Jones, Wordsworth spent his third 'long vacation' from Cambridge, in 1790, walking through France and Switzerland.

With hope it is, hope that can never die,
Effort, and expectation, and desire,
And something evermore about to be.
Under such banners militant, the soul
Seeks for no trophies, struggles for no spoils
That may attest her prowess, blest in thoughts
That are their own perfection and reward,
Strong in herself and in beatitude
That hides her, like the mighty flood of Nile
Poured from his fount of Abyssinian clouds
To fertilise the whole Egyptian plain.

The melancholy slackening that ensued
Upon those tidings by the peasant given
Was soon dislodged. Downwards we hurried fast,
And, with the half-shaped road which we had missed,
Entered a narrow chasm. The brook and road
Were fellow-travellers in this gloomy strait,
And with them did we journey several hours
At a slow pace. The immeasurable height
Of woods decaying, never to be decayed,
The stationary blasts of waterfalls,
And in the narrow rent at every turn
Winds thwarting winds, bewildered and forlorn,
The torrents shooting from the clear blue sky,
The rocks that muttered close upon our ears,
Black drizzling crags that spake by the way-side
As if a voice were in them, the sick sight
And giddy prospect of the raving stream,
The unfettered clouds and region of the Heavens,
Tumult and peace, the darkness and the light —
Were all like workings of one mind, the features
Of the same face, blossoms upon one tree;
Characters of the great Apocalypse,
The types and symbols of Eternity,
Of first, and last, and midst, and without end.

. . .

from BOOK VII

RESIDENCE IN LONDON[27]

Genius of Burke![28] forgive the pen seduced
By specious wonders, and too slow to tell
Of what the ingenuous, what bewildered men,
Beginning to mistrust their boastful guides,
And wise men, willing to grow wiser, caught,
Rapt auditors! from thy most eloquent tongue —
Now mute, for ever mute in the cold grave.
I see him, — old, but vigorous in age, —
Stand like an oak whose stag-horn branches start
Out of its leafy brow, the more to awe
The younger brethren of the grove. But some —
While he forewarns, denounces, launches forth,
Against all systems built on abstract rights,
Keen ridicule; the majesty proclaims
Of Institutes and Laws, hallowed by time;
Declares the vital power of social ties
Endeared by Custom; and with high disdain,
Exploding upstart Theory, insists
Upon the allegiance to which men are born —
Some — say at once a froward multitude —
Murmur (for truth is hated, where not loved)
As the winds fret within the Æolian cave,
Galled by their monarch's chain. The times were big
With ominous change, which, night by night, provoked

[27] In 1791, after taking his degree at Cambridge. It is a realistic and varied description of the city.

[28] Not written before 1820, this impression of Burke shows the growing conservatism of Wordsworth's later years, just as lines 544–550, also a late addition to the text, illustrate his ecclesiasticism.

Keen struggles, and black clouds of passion raised;
But memorable moments intervened,
When Wisdom, like the Goddess from Jove's brain,
Broke forth in armour of resplendent words,
Startling the Synod. Could a youth, and one
In ancient story versed, whose breast had heaved
Under the weight of classic eloquence,
Sit, see, and hear, unthankful, uninspired?

Nor did the Pulpit's oratory fail
To achieve its higher triumph. Not unfelt
Were its admonishments, nor lightly heard
The awful truths delivered thence by tongues
Endowed with various power to search the soul;
Yet ostentation, domineering, oft
Poured forth harangues, how sadly out of place! —
There have I seen a comely bachelor,
Fresh from a toilette of two hours, ascend
His rostrum, with seraphic glance look up,
And, in a tone elaborately low
Beginning, lead his voice through many a maze
A minuet course; and, winding up his mouth,
From time to time, into an orifice
Most delicate, a lurking eyelet, small,
And only not invisible, again
Open it out, diffusing thence a smile
Of rapt irradiation, exquisite.
Meanwhile the Evangelists, Isaiah, Job,
Moses, and he [29] who penned, the other day,
The Death of Abel, Shakspeare, and the Bard [30]
Whose genius spangled o'er a gloomy theme
With fancies thick as his inspiring stars,
And Ossian (doubt not — 'tis the naked truth)
Summoned from streamy Morven — each and all
Would, in their turns, lend ornaments and flowers
To entwine the crook of eloquence that helped
This pretty Shepherd, pride of all the plains,
To rule and guide his captivated flock.

. . .

Oh, blank confusion! [31] true epitome
Of what the mighty City is herself,
To thousands upon thousands of her sons,
Living amid the same perpetual whirl
Of trivial objects, melted and reduced
To one identity, by differences
That have no law, no meaning, and no end —
Oppression, under which even highest minds
Must labour, whence the strongest are not free.
But though the picture weary out the eye,
By nature an unmanageable sight,
It is not wholly so to him who looks
In steadiness, who hath among least things
An under-sense of greatest; sees the parts
As parts, but with a feeling of the whole.
This, of all acquisitions, first awaits
On sundry and most widely different modes
Of education, nor with least delight
On that through which I passed. Attention springs,
And comprehensiveness and memory flow,
From early converse with the works of God
Among all regions; chiefly where appear
Most obviously simplicity and power.
Think, how the everlasting streams and woods,
Stretched and still stretching far and wide, exalt

[29] Gessner, whose *Tod Abels*, 1758, ran through many English editions in translation.
[30] The reference is to Young's *Night Thoughts*, 1742–1745.

[31] St. Bartholomew's Fair, typical of the city, which he contrasted unfavorably with the simpler rural fair of the Lake district.

The roving Indian, on his desert sands:
What grandeur not unfelt, what pregnant show
Of beauty, meets the sun-burnt Arab's eye:
And, as the sea propels, from zone to zone,
Its currents; magnifies its shoals of life
Beyond all compass; spreads, and sends aloft
Armies of clouds, — even so, its powers and aspects
Shape for mankind, by principles as fixed,
The views and aspirations of the soul
To majesty. Like virtue have the forms
Perennial of the ancient hills; nor less
The changeful language of their countenances
Quickens the slumbering mind, and aids the thoughts,
However multitudinous, to move
With order and relation. This, if still,
As hitherto, in freedom I may speak,
Not violating any just restraint,
As may be hoped, of real modesty, —
This did I feel, in London's vast domain.
The Spirit of Nature was upon me there;
The soul of Beauty and enduring Life [32]
Vouchsafed her inspiration, and diffused,
Through meagre lines and colours, and the press
Of self-destroying, transitory things,
Composure, and ennobling Harmony.

from BOOK VIII

RETROSPECT. — LOVE OF NATURE LEADING TO LOVE OF MAN

Yet, hail to you
Moors, mountains, headlands, and ye hollow vales,
Ye long deep channels for the Atlantic's voice,
Powers of my native region! Ye that seize
The heart with firmer grasp! Your snows and streams
Ungovernable, and your terrifying winds,
That howl so dismally for him who treads
Companionless your awful solitudes!
There, 'tis the shepherd's task the winter long
To wait upon the storms: of their approach
Sagacious, into sheltering coves he drives
His flock, and thither from the homestead bears
A toilsome burden up the craggy ways,
And deals it out, their regular nourishment
Strewn on the frozen snow. And when the spring
Looks out, and all the pastures dance with lambs,
And when the flock, with warmer weather, climbs
Higher and higher, him his office leads
To watch their goings, whatsoever track
The wanderers choose. For this he quits his home
At day-spring, and no sooner doth the sun
Begin to strike him with a fire-like heat,
Than he lies down upon some shining rock,
And breakfasts with his dog. When they have stolen,
As is their wont, a pittance from strict time,
For rest not needed or exchange of love,
Then from his couch he starts; and now his feet
Crush out a livelier fragrance from the flowers
Of lowly thyme, by Nature's skill enwrought
In the wild turf: the lingering dews of morn
Smoke round him, as from hill to hill he hies,
His staff protending like a hunter's spear,
Or by its aid leaping from crag to crag,
And o'er the brawling beds of unbridged streams.
Philosophy, methinks, at Fancy's call,
Might deign to follow him through what he does

[32] Wordsworth had felt this 'absent ministration' first when he was at Cambridge, now in London. He has yet to make a third and greater test of it.

Or sees in his day's march; himself he feels,
In those vast regions where his service lies,
A freeman, wedded to his life of hope
And hazard, and hard labour interchanged
With that majestic indolence so dear
To native man. A rambling schoolboy, thus
I felt his presence in his own domain,
As of a lord and master, or a power,
Or genius, under Nature, under God,
Presiding; and severest solitude
Had more commanding looks when he was there.
When up the lonely brooks on rainy days
Angling I went, or trod the trackless hills
By mists bewildered, suddenly mine eyes
Have glanced upon him distant a few steps,
In size a giant, stalking through thick fog,
His sheep like Greenland bears; or, as he stepped
Beyond the boundary line of some hill-shadow,
His form hath flashed upon me, glorified
By the deep radiance of the setting sun:
Or him have I descried in distant sky,
A solitary object and sublime,
Above all height! like an aerial cross
Stationed alone upon a spiry rock
Of the Chartreuse, for worship. Thus was man
Ennobled outwardly before my sight,
And thus my heart was early introduced
To an unconscious love and reverence
Of human nature; hence the human form
To me became an index of delight,
Of grace and honour, power and worthiness.
Meanwhile this creature — spiritual almost
As those of books, but more exalted far;
Far more of an imaginative form
Than the gay Corin of the groves, who lives
For his own fancies, or to dance by the hour,
In coronal, with Phyllis in the midst —
Was, for the purposes of kind, a man
With the most common; husband, father; learned,
Could teach, admonish; suffered with the rest
From vice and folly, wretchedness and fear;
Of this I little saw, cared less for it,
But something must have felt.
Call ye these appearances —
Which I beheld of shepherds in my youth,
This sanctity of Nature given to man —
A shadow, a delusion, ye who pore
On the dead letter, miss the spirit of things;
Whose truth is not a motion or a shape
Instinct with vital functions, but a block
Or waxen image which yourselves have made,
And ye adore! But blessèd be the God
Of Nature and of Man that this was so;
That men before my inexperienced eyes
Did first present themselves thus purified,
Removed, and to a distance that was fit:
And so we all of us in some degree
Are led to knowledge, wheresoever led,
And howsoever; were it otherwise,
And we found evil fast as we find good
In our first years, or think that it is found,
How could the innocent heart bear up and live!
But doubly fortunate my lot; not here
Alone, that something of a better life
Perhaps was round me than it is the privilege
Of most to move in, but that first I looked
At man through objects that were great or fair;
First communed with him by their help. And thus
Was founded a sure safeguard and defence
Against the weight of meanness, selfish cares,
Coarse manners, vulgar passions, that beat in
On all sides from the ordinary world
In which we traffic. Starting from this point

I had my face turned toward the truth, began
With an advantage furnished by that kind
Of prepossession, without which the soul
Receives no knowledge that can bring forth good,
No genuine insight ever comes to her.
From the restraint of over-watchful eyes
Preserved, I moved about, year after year,
Happy, and now most thankful that my walk
Was guarded from too early intercourse
With the deformities of crowded life,
And those ensuing laughters and contempts,
Self-pleasing, which, if we would wish to think
With a due reverence on earth's rightful lord,
Here placed to be the inheritor of heaven,
Will not permit us; but pursue the mind,
That to devotion willingly would rise,
Into the temple and the temple's heart.

Yet deem not, Friend! that human kind with me
Thus early took a place pre-eminent;
Nature herself was, at this unripe time,
But secondary to my own pursuits
And animal activities, and all
Their trivial pleasures; and when these had drooped
And gradually expired, and Nature, prized
For her own sake, became my joy, even then —
And upwards through late youth, until not less
Than two-and-twenty summers had been told —
Was Man in my affections and regards
Subordinate to her, her visible forms
And viewless agencies: a passion, she,
A rapture often, and immediate love
Ever at hand; he, only a delight
Occasional, an accidental grace,
His hour being not yet come.

. . .

Nor shall we not be tending towards that point
Of sound humanity to which our Tale
Leads, though by sinuous ways, if here I show
How Fancy, in a season when she wove
Those slender cords, to guide the unconscious Boy
For the Man's sake, could feed at Nature's call
Some pensive musings which might well beseem
Maturer years.
A grove there is whose boughs
Stretch from the western marge of Thurston-mere,
With length of shade so thick, that whoso glides
Along the line of low-roofed water, moves
As in a cloister. Once — while, in that shade
Loitering, I watched the golden beams of light
Flung from the setting sun, as they reposed
In silent beauty on the naked ridge
Of a high eastern hill — thus flowed my thoughts
In a pure stream of words fresh from the heart:
Dear native Regions, wheresoe'er shall close
My mortal course, there will I think on you;
Dying, will cast on you a backward look;
Even as this setting sun (albeit the Vale
Is no where touched by one memorial gleam)
Doth with the fond remains of his last power
Still linger, and a farewell lustre sheds
On the dear mountain-tops where first he rose.

Enough of humble arguments; recall,
My Song! those high emotions which thy voice
Has heretofore made known; that bursting forth
Of sympathy, inspiring and inspired,

When everywhere a vital pulse was felt,
And all the several frames of things, like stars,
Through every magnitude distinguishable,
Shone mutually indebted, or half lost
Each in the other's blaze, a galaxy
Of life and glory. In the midst stood Man,
Outwardly, inwardly contemplated,
As, of all visible natures, crown, though born
Of dust, and kindred to the worm; a Being,
Both in perception and discernment, first
In every capability of rapture,
Through the divine effect of power and love;
As, more than anything we know, instinct
With godhead, and, by reason and by will,
Acknowledging dependency sublime.

. . .

From all sides, when whate'er was in itself
Capacious found, or seemed to find, in me
A correspondent amplitude of mind;
Such is the strength and glory of our youth!
The human nature unto which I felt
That I belonged, and reverenced with love,
Was not a punctual presence, but a spirit
Diffused through time and space, with aid derived
Of evidence from monuments, erect,
Prostrate, or leaning towards their common rest
In earth, the widely scattered wreck sublime
Of vanished nations, or more clearly drawn
From books and what they picture and record.

'Tis true, the history of our native land,
With those of Greece compared and popular Rome,
And in our high-wrought modern narratives
Stript of their harmonising soul, the life
Of manners and familiar incidents,
Had never much delighted me. And less
Than other intellects had mine been used
To lean upon extrinsic circumstance
Of record or tradition; but a sense
Of what in the Great City had been done
And suffered, and was doing, suffering, still,
Weighed with me, could support the test of thought;
And, in despite of all that had gone by,
Or was departing never to return,
There I conversed with majesty and power
Like independent natures. Hence the place
Was thronged with impregnations like the Wilds
In which my early feelings had been nursed —
Bare hills and valleys, full of caverns, rocks,
And audible seclusions, dashing lakes,
Echoes and waterfalls, and pointed crags
That into music touch the passing wind.
Here then my young imagination found
No uncongenial element; could here
Among new objects serve or give command,
Even as the heart's occasions might require,
To forward reason's else too scrupulous march.
The effect was, still more elevated views
Of human nature. Neither vice nor guilt,
Debasement undergone by body or mind,
Nor all the misery forced upon my sight,
Misery not lightly passed, but sometimes scanned
Most feelingly, could overthrow my trust
In what we *may* become; induce belief
That I was ignorant, had been falsely taught,
A solitary, who with vain conceits
Had been inspired, and walked about in dreams.

From those sad scenes when meditation turned,
Lo! everything that was indeed divine
Retained its purity inviolate,
Nay brighter shone, by this portentous gloom
Set off; such opposition as aroused
The mind of Adam, yet in Paradise
Though fallen from bliss, when in the East he saw
Darkness ere day's mid course, and morning light
More orient in the western cloud, that drew
O'er the blue firmament a radiant white,
Descending slow with something heavenly fraught.

Add also, that among the multitudes
Of that huge city, oftentimes was seen
Affectingly set forth, more than elsewhere
Is possible, the unity of man,
One spirit over ignorance and vice
Predominant in good and evil hearts;
One sense for moral judgments, as one eye
For the sun's light. The soul when smitten thus
By a sublime *idea*, whencesoe'er
Vouchsafed for union or communion, feeds
On the pure bliss, and takes her rest with God.

Thus from a very early age, O Friend!
My thoughts by slow gradations had been drawn
To human-kind, and to the good and ill
Of human life: Nature had led me on;
And oft amid the "busy hum" I seemed
To travel independent of her help,
As if I had forgotten her; but no,
The world of human-kind outweighed not hers
In my habitual thoughts; the scale of love,
Though filling daily, still was light, compared
With that in which *her* mighty objects lay.

from BOOK IX

RESIDENCE IN FRANCE [33]

France lured me forth; the realm that I had crossed
So lately, journeying toward the snow-clad Alps.
But now, relinquishing the scrip and staff,
And all enjoyment which the summer sun
Sheds round the steps of those who meet the day
With motion constant as his own, I went
Prepared to sojourn in a pleasant town,[34]
Washed by the current of the stately Loire.

Through Paris lay my readiest course, and there
Sojourning a few days, I visited
In haste, each spot of old or recent fame,
The latter chiefly; from the field of Mars [35]
Down to the suburbs of St. Antony,
And from Mont Martre southward to the Dome
Of Geneviève.[36] In both her clamorous Halls,
The National Synod and the Jacobins,
I saw the Revolutionary Power
Toss like a ship at anchor, rocked by storms;
The Arcades I traversed, in the Palace huge
Of Orleans; coasted round and round the line
Of Tavern, Brothel, Gaming-house, and Shop,
Great rendezvous of worst and best, the walk
Of all who had a purpose, or had not;
I stared and listened, with a stranger's ears,
To Hawkers and Haranguers, hubbub wild!
And hissing Factionists with ardent eyes,
In knots, or pairs, or single. Not a look
Hope takes, or Doubt or Fear is forced to wear,

---

[33] Wordsworth went there at the end of 1791.

[34] He left Orléans for Blois in the early months of 1792.

[35] Scene of the Federation Oath, 14 July 1790, to celebrate the anniversary of the fall of the Bastille.

[36] The Panthéon.

But seemed there present; and I scanned them all,
Watched every gesture uncontrollable,
Of anger, and vexation, and despite,
All side by side, and struggling face to face,
With gaiety and dissolute idleness.

Where silent zephyrs sported with the dust
Of the Bastille, I sate in the open sun,
And from the rubbish gathered up a stone,
And pocketed the relic, in the guise
Of an enthusiast; yet, in honest truth,
I looked for something that I could not find,
Affecting more emotion than I felt;
For 'tis most certain, that these various sights,
However potent their first shock, with me
Appeared to recompense the traveller's pains
Less than the painted Magdalene of Le Brun,
A beauty exquisitely wrought, with hair
Dishevelled, gleaming eyes, and rueful cheek
Pale and bedropped with everflowing tears.

. . .

Even here, though less than with the peaceful house
Religious, 'mid those frequent monuments
Of Kings, their vices and their better deeds,
Imagination, potent to inflame
At times with virtuous wrath and noble scorn,
Did also often mitigate the force
Of civic prejudice, the bigotry,
So call it, of a youthful patriot's mind;
And on these spots with many gleams I looked
Of chivalrous delight. Yet not the less,
Hatred of absolute rule, where will of one
Is law for all, and of that barren pride
In them who, by immunities unjust,
Between the sovereign and the people stand,
His helper and not theirs, laid stronger hold
Daily upon me, mixed with pity too
And love; for where hope is, there love will be
For the abject multitude. And when we[37] chanced
One day to meet a hunger-bitten girl,
Who crept along fitting her languid gait
Unto a heifer's motion, by a cord
Tied to her arm, and picking thus from the lane
Its sustenance, while the girl with pallid hands
Was busy knitting in a heartless mood
Of solitude, and at the sight my friend
In agitation said, ''Tis against *that*
That we are fighting,' I with him believed
That a benignant spirit was abroad
Which might not be withstood, that poverty
Abject as this would in a little time
Be found no more, that we should see the earth
Unthwarted in her wish to recompense
The meek, the lowly, patient child of toil,
All institutes for ever blotted out
That legalised exclusion, empty pomp
Abolished, sensual state and cruel power,
Whether by edict of the one or few;
And finally, as sum and crown of all,
Should see the people having a strong hand
In framing their own laws; whence better days
To all mankind.

. . .

from BOOK X

RESIDENCE IN FRANCE— [continued][38]

Lamentable crimes,
'Tis true, had gone before this hour, dire work

[37] Wordsworth and Michel Armand Beaupuy, fifteen years his elder, partly the model of Wordsworth's own 'Happy Warrior.' Though of a noble family, Beaupuy favored the Revolution and fired the zeal of others in the cause.

[38] Wordsworth returned to Paris from the provinces in

Of massacre, in which the senseless sword
Was prayed to as a judge; but these were past,
Earth free from them for ever, as was thought, —
Ephemeral monsters, to be seen but once!
Things that could only show themselves and die.

Cheered with this hope, to Paris I returned,
And ranged, with ardour heretofore unfelt,
The spacious city, and in progress passed
The prison where the unhappy Monarch lay,
Associate with his children and his wife
In bondage; and the palace, lately stormed
With roar of cannon by a furious host.
I crossed the square (an empty area then!)
Of the Carrousel, where so late had lain
The dead, upon the dying heaped, and gazed
On this and other spots, as doth a man
Upon a volume whose contents he knows
Are memorable, but from him locked up,
Being written in a tongue he cannot read,
So that he questions the mute leaves with pain,
And half upbraids their silence. But that night
I felt most deeply in what world I was,
What ground I trod on, and what air I breathed.
High was my room and lonely, near the roof
Of a large mansion or hotel, a lodge
That would have pleased me in more quiet times;
Nor was it wholly without pleasure then.
With unextinguished taper I kept watch,
Reading at intervals; the fear gone by
Pressed on me almost like a fear to come.
I thought of those September massacres,
Divided from me by one little month,
Saw them and touched: the rest was conjured up
From tragic fictions or true history,
Remembrances and dim admonishments.
The horse is taught his manage, and no star
Of wildest course but treads back his own steps;
For the spent hurricane the air provides
As fierce a successor; the tide retreats
But to return out of its hiding-place
In the great deep; all things have second birth;
The earthquake is not satisfied at once;
And in this way I wrought upon myself,
Until I seemed to hear a voice that cried,
To the whole city, 'sleep no more.' The trance
Fled with the voice to which it had given birth;
But vainly comments of a calmer mind
Promised soft peace and sweet forgetfulness.
The place, all hushed and silent as it was,
Appeared unfit for the repose of night,
Defenceless as a wood where tigers roam.

. . .

Amid the depth
Of those enormities,[39] even thinking minds
Forgot, at seasons, whence they had their being;
Forgot that such a sound was ever heard
As Liberty upon earth: yet all beneath
Her innocent authority was wrought,
Nor could have been, without her blessèd name.
The illustrious wife of Roland, in the hour
Of her composure, felt that agony,
And gave it vent in her last words. O Friend!
It was a lamentable time for man,
Whether a hope had e'er been his or not;
A woeful time for them whose hopes survived

October 1792. Meantime the Tuileries had been stormed by the mob, the King deposed and imprisoned, and the September Massacres had taken place. Over three thousand Royalist suspects were killed.

[39] Of the Reign of Terror, September 1793, to the fall of Robespierre, 26 July 1794. Wordsworth had returned to England in January 1793, still hopeful that good might come of the Revolution, and shocked when his own country went to war with France in February 1793.

The shock; most woeful for those few who still
Were flattered, and had trust in human kind:
They had the deepest feeling of the grief.
Meanwhile the Invaders fared as they deserved:
The Herculean Commonwealth had put forth her arms,
And throttled with an infant godhead's might
The snakes about her cradle; that was well,
And as it should be; yet no cure for them
Whose souls were sick with pain of what would be
Hereafter brought in charge against mankind.
Most melancholy at that time, O Friend!
Were my day-thoughts, — my nights were miserable;
Through months, through years, long after the last beat
Of those atrocities, the hour of sleep
To me came rarely charged with natural gifts,
Such ghastly visions had I of despair
And tyranny, and implements of death;
And innocent victims sinking under fear,
And momentary hope, and worn-out prayer,
Each in his separate cell, or penned in crowds
For sacrifice, and struggling with fond mirth
And levity in dungeons, where the dust
Was laid with tears. Then suddenly the scene
Changed, and the unbroken dream entangled me
In long orations, which I strove to plead
Before unjust tribunals, — with a voice
Labouring, a brain confounded, and a sense,
Death-like, of treacherous desertion, felt
In the last place of refuge — my own soul.

. . .

Yet not the less,
For those examples, in no age surpassed,
Of fortitude and energy and love,
And human nature faithful to herself
Under worst trials, was I driven to think
Of the glad times when first I traversed France
A youthful pilgrim; [40] above all reviewed
That eventide, when under windows bright
With happy faces and with garlands hung,
And through a rainbow-arch that spanned the street,
Triumphal pomp for liberty confirmed,
I paced, a dear companion at my side,
The town of Arras, whence with promise high
Issued, on delegation to sustain
Humanity and right, *that* Robespierre,
He who thereafter, and in how short time!
Wielded the sceptre of the Atheist crew.
When the calamity spread far and wide —
And this same city, that did then appear
To outrun the rest in exultation, groaned
Under the vengeance of her cruel son,
As Lear reproached the winds — I could almost
Have quarrelled with that blameless spectacle
For lingering yet an image in my mind
To mock me under such a strange reverse.

O Friend! few happier moments have been mine
Than that which told the downfall of this Tribe
So dreaded, so abhorred. The day [41] deserves
A separate record. Over the smooth sands
Of Leven's ample estuary lay
My journey, and beneath a genial sun,
With distant prospect among gleams of sky
And clouds, and intermingling mountain-tops,
In one inseparable glory clad,
Creatures of one ethereal substance met
In consistory, like a diadem

[40] In 1790 with Robert Jones. They passed through Arras on 16 July. [41] In August 1794.

Or crown of burning seraphs as they sit
In the empyrean. Underneath that pomp
Celestial, lay unseen the pastoral vales
Among whose happy fields I had grown up
From childhood. On the fulgent spectacle,
That neither passed away nor changed, I gazed
Enrapt; but brightest things are wont to draw
Sad opposites out of the inner heart,
As even their pensive influence drew from mine.
How could it otherwise? for not in vain
That very morning had I turned aside
To seek the ground where, 'mid a throng of graves,
An honoured teacher of my youth [42] was laid,
And on the stone were graven by his desire
Lines from the churchyard elegy of Gray.
This faithful guide, speaking from his death-bed,
Added no farewell to his parting counsel,
But said to me, 'My head will soon lie low;'
And when I saw the turf that covered him,
After the lapse of full eight years, those words,
With sound of voice and countenance of the Man,
Came back upon me, so that some few tears
Fell from me in my own despite. But now
I thought, still traversing that widespread plain,
With tender pleasure of the verses graven
Upon his tombstone, whispering to myself:
He loved the Poets, and, if now alive,
Would have loved me, as one not destitute
Of promise, nor belying the kind hope
That he had formed, when I, at his command,
Began to spin, with toil, my earliest songs.

[42] The Reverend William Taylor, master at Hawkshead, who had died in 1786.

As I advanced, all that I saw or felt
Was gentleness and peace. Upon a small
And rocky island near, a fragment stood
(Itself like a sea rock) the low remains
(With shells encrusted, dark with briny weeds)
Of a dilapidated structure, once
A Romish chapel, where the vested priest
Said matins at the hour that suited those
Who crossed the sands with ebb of morning tide.
Not far from that still ruin all the plain
Lay spotted with a variegated crowd
Of vehicles and travellers, horse and foot,
Wading beneath the conduct of their guide
In loose procession through the shallow stream
Of inland waters; the great sea meanwhile
Heaved at safe distance, far retired. I paused,
Longing for skill to paint a scene so bright
And cheerful, but the foremost of the band
As he approached, no salutation given
In the familiar language of the day,
Cried, "Robespierre is dead!"—nor was a doubt,
After strict question, left within my mind
That he and his supporters all were fallen.

Great was my transport, deep my gratitude
To everlasting Justice, by this fiat
Made manifest. 'Come now, ye golden times,'
Said I forth-pouring on those open sands
A hymn of triumph: 'as the morning comes
From out the bosom of the night, come ye:
Thus far our trust is verified; behold!
They who with clumsy desperation brought
A river of Blood, and preached that nothing else
Could cleanse the Augean stable, by the might
Of their own helper have been swept away;
Their madness stands declared and visible;

Elsewhere will safety now be sought, and earth
March firmly towards righteousness and peace.' —
Then schemes I framed more calmly, when and how
The madding factions might be tranquillised,
And how through hardships manifold and long
The glorious renovation would proceed.
Thus interrupted by uneasy bursts
Of exultation, I pursued my way
Along that very shore which I had skimmed
In former days, when — spurring from the Vale
Of Nightshade, and St. Mary's mouldering fane,
And the stone abbot, after circuit made
In wantonness of heart, a joyous band
Of schoolboys hastening to their distant home
Along the margin of the moonlight sea —
We beat with thundering hoofs the level sand.

from BOOK XI

FRANCE — [concluded] [43]

From that time forth, Authority in France
Put on a milder face; Terror had ceased,
Yet everything was wanting that might give
Courage to them who looked for good by light
Of rational Experience, for the shoots
And hopeful blossoms of a second spring:
Yet, in me, confidence was unimpaired;
The Senate's language, and the public acts
And measures of the Government, though both
Weak, and of heartless omen, had not power
To daunt me; in the People was my trust,
And in the virtues which mine eyes had seen.
I knew that wound external could not take
Life from the young Republic; that new foes
Would only follow, in the path of shame,
Their brethren, and her triumphs be in the end
Great, universal, irresistible.
This intuition led me to confound
One victory with another, higher far, —
Triumphs of unambitious peace at home,
And noiseless fortitude. Beholding still
Resistance strong as heretofore, I thought
That what was in degree the same was likewise
The same in quality, — that, as the worse
Of the two spirits then at strife remained
Untired, the better, surely, would preserve
The heart that first had roused him. Youth maintains,
In all conditions of society,
Communion more direct and intimate
With Nature, — hence, ofttimes, with reason too —
Than age or manhood, even. To Nature, then,
Power had reverted: habit, custom, law,
Had left an interregnum's open space
For *her* to move about in, uncontrolled.
Hence could I see how Babel-like their task,
Who, by the recent deluge stupefied,
With their whole souls went culling from the day
Its petty promises, to build a tower
For their own safety; laughed with my compeers
At gravest heads, by enmity to France
Distempered, till they found, in every blast
Forced from the street-disturbing newsman's horn,
For her great cause record or prophecy
Of utter ruin. How might we believe
That wisdom could, in any shape, come near
Men clinging to delusions so insane?
And thus, experience proving that no few

[43] Wordsworth here goes back over the ground of the two preceding books, to describe his feelings from his arrival in France in 1791 till his return to England in 1793.

Of our opinions had been just, we took
Like credit to ourselves where less was due,
And thought that other notions were as sound,
Yea, could not but be right, because we saw
That foolish men opposed them. . . .
It hath been told
That I was led to take an eager part
In arguments of civil polity,
Abruptly, and indeed before my time:
I had approached, like other youths, the shield
Of human nature from the golden side,
And would have fought, even to the death, to attest
The quality of the metal which I saw.
What there is best in individual man,
Of wise in passion, and sublime in power,
Benevolent in small societies,
And great in large ones, I had oft revolved,
Felt deeply, but not thoroughly understood
By reason: nay, far from it; they were yet,
As cause was given me afterwards to learn,
Not proof against the injuries of the day;
Lodged only at the sanctuary's door,
Not safe within its bosom. Thus prepared,
And with such general insight into evil,
And of the bounds which sever it from good,
As books and common intercourse with life
Must needs have given — to the inexperienced mind,
When the world travels in a beaten road,
Guide faithful as is needed — I began
To meditate with ardour on the rule
And management of nations; what it is
And ought to be; and strove to learn how far
Their power or weakness, wealth or poverty,
Their happiness or misery, depends
Upon their laws, and fashion of the State.

O pleasant exercise of hope and joy!
For mighty were the auxiliars which then stood
Upon our side, us who were strong in love!
Bliss was it in that dawn to be alive,
But to be young was very Heaven! O times,
In which the meagre, stale, forbidding ways
Of custom, law, and statute, took at once
The attraction of a country in romance!
When Reason seemed the most to assert her rights
When most intent on making of herself
A prime enchantress — to assist the work,
Which then was going forward in her name!
Not favoured spots alone, but the whole Earth,
The beauty wore of promise — that which sets
(As at some moments might not be unfelt
Among the bowers of Paradise itself)
The budding rose above the rose full blown.
What temper at the prospect did not wake
To happiness unthought of? The inert
Were roused, and lively natures rapt away!
They who had fed their childhood upon dreams,
The play-fellows of fancy, who had made
All powers of swiftness, subtilty, and strength
Their ministers, — who in lordly wise had stirred
Among the grandest objects of the sense,
And dealt with whatsoever they found there
As if they had within some lurking right
To wield it; — they, too, who of gentle mood
Had watched all gentle motions, and to these
Had fitted their own thoughts, schemers more mild,
And in the region of their peaceful selves; —
Now was it that *both* found, the meek and lofty
Did both find, helpers to their hearts' desire,

And stuff at hand, plastic as they could wish, —
Were called upon to exercise their skill,
Not in Utopia, — subterranean fields,—
Or some secreted island, Heaven knows where!
But in the very world, which is the world
Of all of us, — the place where, in the end,
We find our happiness, or not at all!

. . .

This was the time,[44] when, all things tending fast
To depravation, speculative schemes —
That promised to abstract the hopes of Man
Out of his feelings, to be fixed thenceforth
For ever in a purer element —
Found ready welcome. Tempting region *that*
For Zeal to enter and refresh herself,
Where passions had the privilege to work,
And never hear the sound of their own names.
But, speaking more in charity, the dream
Flattered the young, pleased with extremes, nor least
With that which makes our Reason's naked self
The object of its fervour. What delight!
How glorious! in self-knowledge and self-rule,
To look through all the frailties of the world,
And, with a resolute mastery shaking off
Infirmities of nature, time, and place,
Build social upon personal Liberty.
Which, to the blind restraints of general laws
Superior, magisterially adopts
One guide, the light of circumstances, flashed
Upon an independent intellect.
Thus expectation rose again; thus hope,
From her first ground expelled,[45] grew proud once more.
Oft, as my thoughts were turned to human kind,
I scorned indifference; but, inflamed with thirst
Of a secure intelligence, and sick
Of other longing, I pursued what seemed
A more exalted nature; wished that Man
Should start out of his earthly, worm-like state,
And spread abroad the wings of Liberty,
Lord of himself, in undisturbed delight —
A noble aspiration! *yet* I feel
(Sustained by worthier as by wiser thoughts)
The aspiration, nor shall ever cease
To feel it; — but return we to our course.

Enough, 'tis true — could such a plea excuse
Those aberrations — had the clamorous friends
Of ancient Institutions said and done
To bring disgrace upon their very names;
Disgrace, of which, custom and written law,
And sundry moral sentiments as props
Or emanations of those institutes,
Too justly bore a part. A veil had been
Uplifted; why deceive ourselves? in sooth,
'Twas even so; and sorrow for the man
Who either had not eyes wherewith to see,
Or, seeing, had forgotten! A strong shock
Was given to old opinions; all men's minds
Had felt its power, and mine was both let loose,
Let loose and goaded. After what hath been
Already said of patriotic love,
Suffice it here to add, that, somewhat stern
In temperament, withal a happy man,
And therefore bold to look on painful things,

[44] In February 1793 William Godwin's *Enquiry concerning Political Justice* was published. For a time Wordsworth felt the spell of its doctrine of the *rationalistic* perfectibility of man, just as Shelley did a few years later.

[45] *i.e.*, by the failure of the Revolution, and by England's own enmity with France.

Free likewise of the world, and thence more bold,
I summoned my best skill, and toiled, intent
To anatomise the frame of social life;
Yea, the whole body of society
Searched to its heart. Share with me, Friend! the wish
That some dramatic tale, endued with shapes
Livelier, and flinging out less guarded words
Than suit the work we fashion, might set forth
What then I learned, or think I learned, of truth,
And the errors into which I fell, betrayed
By present objects, and by reasonings false
From their beginnings, inasmuch as drawn
Out of a heart that had been turned aside
From Nature's way by outward accidents,
And which was thus confounded, more and more
Misguided, and misguiding. So I fared,
Dragging all precepts, judgments, maxims, creeds,
Like culprits to the bar; calling the mind,
Suspiciously, to establish in plain day
Her titles and her honours; now believing,
Now disbelieving; endlessly perplexed
With impulse, motive, right and wrong, the ground
Of obligation, what the rule and whence
The sanction; till, demanding formal *proof*,
And seeking it in everything, I lost
All feeling of conviction, and, in fine,
Sick, wearied out with contrarieties,
Yielded up moral questions in despair.

This was the crisis of that strong disease,
This the soul's last and lowest ebb; I drooped,
Deeming our blessèd reason of least use
Where wanted most: 'The lordly attributes
Of will and choice,' I bitterly exclaimed,
'What are they but a mockery of a Being
Who hath in no concerns of his a test
Of good and evil; knows not what to fear
Or hope for, what to covet or to shun;
And who, if those could be discerned, would yet
Be little profited, would see, and ask
Where is the obligation to enforce?
And, to acknowledged law rebellious, still,
As selfish passion urged, would act amiss;
The dupe of folly, or the slave of crime.'

Depressed, bewildered thus, I did not walk
With scoffers, seeking light and gay revenge
From indiscriminate laughter, nor sate down
In reconcilement with an utter waste
Of intellect; such sloth I could not brook,
(Too well I loved, in that my spring of life,
Pains-taking thoughts, and truth, their dear reward)
But turned to abstract science, and there sought
Work for the reasoning faculty enthroned
Where the disturbances of space and time —
Whether in matters various, properties
Inherent, or from human will and power
Derived — find no admission. Then it was —
Thanks to the bounteous Giver of all good! —
That the belovéd Sister [46] in whose sight
Those days were passed, now speaking in a voice
Of sudden admonition — like a brook
That did but *cross* a lonely road, and now
Is seen, heard, felt, and caught at every turn,
Companion never lost through many a league —
Maintained for me a saving intercourse
With my true self; for, though bedimmed and changed

[46] Dorothy Wordsworth

Much, as it seemed, I was no further changed
Than as a clouded and a waning moon:
She whispered still that brightness would return,
She, in the midst of all, preserved me still
A Poet, made me seek beneath that name,
And that alone, my office upon earth;
And, lastly, as hereafter will be shown,
If willing audience fail not, Nature's self,
By all varieties of human love
Assisted, led me back through opening day
To those sweet counsels between head and heart
Whence grew that genuine knowledge, fraught with peace,
Which, through the later sinkings of this cause,
Hath still upheld me, and upholds me now
In the catastrophe (for so they dream,
And nothing less), when, finally to close
And seal up all the gains of France, a Pope
Is summoned in to crown an Emperor[47]—
This last opprobrium, when we see a people,
That once looked up in faith, as if to Heaven
For manna, take a lesson from the dog
Returning to his vomit; when the sun
That rose in splendour, was alive, and moved
In exultation with a living pomp
Of clouds—his glory's natural retinue—
Hath dropped all functions by the gods bestowed,
And, turned into a gewgaw, a machine,
Sets like an Opera phantom.
Thus, O Friend!
Through times of honour and through times of shame
Descending, have I faithfully retraced
The perturbations of a youthful mind
Under a long-lived storm of great events—
A story destined for thy ear, who now,
Among the fallen of nations, dost abide[48]
Where Etna, over hill and valley, casts
His shadow stretching towards Syracuse,
The city of Timoleon! Righteous Heaven!
How are the mighty prostrated! They first,
They first of all that breathe should have awaked
When the great voice was heard from out the tombs
Of ancient heroes. If I suffered grief
For ill-requited France, by many deemed
A trifler only in her proudest day;
Have been distressed to think of what she once
Promised, now is; a far more sober cause
Thine eyes must see of sorrow in a land,
To the reanimating influence lost
Of memory, to virtue lost and hope,
Though with the wreck of loftier years bestrewn.

But indignation works where hope is not,
And thou, O Friend! wilt be refreshed. There is
One great society alone on earth:
The noble Living and the noble Dead.[49]

. . .

from BOOK XII

IMAGINATION AND TASTE, HOW IMPAIRED AND RESTORED

Long time have human ignorance and guilt
Detained us, on what spectacles of woe
Compelled to look, and inwardly oppressed
With sorrow, disappointment, vexing thoughts,

[47] On 2 December 1802 Pope Pius VII was to crown Napoleon. But Napoleon took the crown from the altar and put it on.

[48] Coleridge was in Sicily from early August to November 1804.

[49] See Wordsworth's *Convention of Cintra*, 1809: 'There is a spiritual community binding together the living and the dead; the good, the brave and the wise, of all ages. We would not be rejected from that community: and therefore do we hope.'

Confusion of the judgment, zeal decayed,
And, lastly, utter loss of hope itself
And things to hope for! Not with these began
Our song, and not with these our song must end.—
Ye motions of delight, that haunt the sides
Of the green hills; ye breezes and soft airs,
Whose subtle intercourse with breathing flowers,
Feelingly watched, might teach Man's haughty race
How without injury to take, to give
Without offence; ye who, as if to show
The wondrous influence of power gently used,
Bend the complying heads of lordly pines,
And, with a touch, shift the stupendous clouds
Through the whole compass of the sky; ye brooks,
Muttering along the stones, a busy noise
By day, a quiet sound in silent night;
Ye waves, that out of the great deep steal forth
In a calm hour to kiss the pebbly shore,
Not mute, and then retire, fearing no storm;
And you, ye groves, whose ministry it is
To interpose the covert of your shades,
Even as a sleep, between the heart of man
And outward troubles, between man himself,
Not seldom, and his own uneasy heart:
Oh! that I had a music and a voice
Harmonious as your own, that I might tell
What ye have done for me. The morning shines,
Nor heedeth Man's perverseness; Spring returns,—
I saw the Spring return, and could rejoice,
In common with the children of her love,
Piping on boughs, or sporting on fresh fields,
Or boldly seeking pleasure nearer heaven
On wings that navigate cerulean skies.
So neither were complacency, nor peace,
Nor tender yearnings, wanting for my good
Through these distracted times; in Nature still
Glorying, I found a counterpoise in her,
Which, when the spirit of evil reached its height,
Maintained for me a secret happiness.

. . .

O Soul of Nature! excellent and fair!
That didst rejoice with me, with whom I, too,
Rejoiced through early youth, before the winds
And roaring waters, and in lights and shades
That marched and countermarched about the hills
In glorious apparition, Powers on whom
I daily waited, now all eye and now
All ear; but never long without the heart
Employed, and man's unfolding intellect:
O Soul of Nature! that, by laws divine
Sustained and governed, still dost overflow
With an impassioned life, what feeble ones
Walk on this earth! how feeble have I been
When thou wert in thy strength! Nor this through stroke
Of human suffering, such as justifies
Remissness and inaptitude of mind,
But through presumption; even in pleasure pleased
Unworthily, disliking here, and there
Liking; by rules of mimic art transferred
To things above all art; but more,—for this,
Although a strong infection of the age,
Was never much my habit—giving way
To a comparison of scene with scene,
Bent overmuch on superficial things,
Pampering myself with meagre novelties
Of colour and proportion; to the moods
Of time and season, to the moral power,
The affections and the spirit of the place,
Insensible. Nor only did the love
Of sitting thus in judgment interrupt
My deeper feelings, but another cause,

More subtle and less easily explained,
That almost seems inherent in the creature,
A twofold frame of body and of mind.
I speak in recollection of a time
When the bodily eye, in every stage of life
The most despotic of our senses, gained
Such strength in *me* as often held my mind
In absolute dominion. Gladly here,
Entering upon abstruser argument,
Could I endeavour to unfold the means
Which Nature studiously employs to thwart
This tyranny, summons all the senses each
To counteract the other, and themselves,
And makes them all, and the objects with which all
Are conversant, subservient in their turn
To the great ends of Liberty and Power.
But leave we this: enough that my delights
(Such as they were) were sought insatiably.
Vivid the transport, vivid though not profound;
I roamed from hill to hill, from rock to rock,
Still craving combinations of new forms,
New pleasure, wider empire for the sight,
Proud of her own endowments, and rejoiced
To lay the inner faculties asleep.
Amid the turns and counterturns, the strife
And various trials of our complex being,
As we grow up, such thraldom of that sense
Seems hard to shun. And yet I knew a maid,[50]
A young enthusiast, who escaped these bonds;
Her eye was not the mistress of her heart;
Far less did rules prescribed by passive taste,
Or barren intermeddling subtleties,
Perplex her mind; but, wise as women are
When genial circumstance hath favoured them,
She welcomed what was given, and craved no more;
Whate'er the scene presented to her view
That was the best, to that she was attuned
By her benign simplicity of life,
And through a perfect happiness of soul,
Whose variegated feelings were in this
Sisters, that they were each some new delight.
Birds in the bower, and lambs in the green field,
Could they have known her, would have loved; methought
Her very presence such a sweetness breathed,
That flowers, and trees, and even the silent hills,
And everything she looked on, should have had
An intimation how she bore herself
Towards them and to all creatures. God delights
In such a being; for, her common thoughts
Are piety, her life is gratitude.

Even like this maid, before I was called forth
From the retirement of my native hills,
I loved whate'er I saw: nor lightly loved,
But most intensely; never dreamt of aught
More grand, more fair, more exquisitely framed
Than those few nooks to which my happy feet
Were limited. I had not at that time
Lived long enough, nor in the least survived
The first diviner influence of this world,
As it appears to unaccustomed eyes.
Worshipping then among the depth of things,
As piety ordained; could I submit
To measured admiration, or to aught
That should preclude humility and love?
I felt, observed, and pondered; did not judge,
Yea, never thought of judging; with the gift

[50] Dorothy

Of all this glory filled and satisfied.
And afterwards, when through the gorgeous Alps
Roaming, I carried with me the same heart:
In truth, the degradation — howsoe'er
Induced, effect, in whatsoe'er degree,
Of custom that prepares a partial scale
In which the little oft outweighs the great;
Or any other cause that hath been named;
Or lastly, aggravated by the times
And their impassioned sounds, which well might make
The milder minstrelsies of rural scenes
Inaudible — was transient; I had known
Too forcibly, too early in my life,
Visitings of imaginative power
For this to last: I shook the habit off
Entirely and for ever, and again
In Nature's presence stood, as now I stand,
A sensitive being, a *creative* soul.

There are in our existence spots of time,
That with distinct pre-eminence retain
A renovating virtue, whence, depressed
By false opinion and contentious thought,
Or aught of heavier or more deadly weight,
In trivial occupations, and the round
Of ordinary intercourse, our minds
Are nourished and invisibly repaired;
A virtue, by which pleasure is enhanced,
That penetrates, enables us to mount,
When high, more high, and lifts us up when fallen.
This efficacious spirit chiefly lurks
Among those passages of life that give
Profoundest knowledge to what point, and how,
The mind is lord and master — outward sense
The obedient servant of her will. Such moments
Are scattered everywhere, taking their date
From our first childhood. I remember well,
That once, while yet my inexperienced hand
Could scarcely hold a bridle, with proud hopes
I mounted, and we journeyed towards the hills:
An ancient servant of my father's house
Was with me, my encourager and guide:
We had not travelled long, ere some mischance
Disjoined me from my comrade; and, through fear
Dismounting, down the rough and stony moor
I led my horse, and, stumbling on, at length
Came to a bottom, where in former times
A murderer had been hung in iron chains.
The gibbet-mast had mouldered down, the bones
And iron case were gone; but on the turf,
Hard by, soon after that fell deed was wrought,
Some unknown hand had carved the murderer's name.
The monumental letters were inscribed
In times long past; but still, from year to year,
By superstition of the neighbourhood,
The grass was cleared away, and to this hour
The characters are fresh and visible: [51]
A casual glance had shown them, and I fled,
Faltering and faint, and ignorant of the road:
Then, reascending the bare common, saw
A naked pool that lay beneath the hills,
The beacon on the summit, and, more near,
A girl, who bore a pitcher on her head,
And seemed with difficult steps to force her way
Against the blowing wind. It was, in truth,
An ordinary sight; but I should need
Colours and words that are unknown to man,
To paint the visionary dreariness

[51] 'T.P.M.' (Thomas Parker murdered); the initials, at the Cowdrake Quarry, near Penrith, were those of the victim, not the murderer.

Which, while I looked all round for my lost guide,
Invested moorland waste, and naked pool,
The beacon crowning the lone eminence,
The female and her garments vexed and tossed
By the strong wind. When, in the blessèd hours
Of early love, the loved one at my side,
I roamed, in daily presence of this scene,
Upon the naked pool and dreary crags,
And on the melancholy beacon, fell
A spirit of pleasure and youth's golden gleam;
And think ye not with radiance more sublime
For these remembrances, and for the power
They had left behind? So feeling comes in aid
Of feeling, and diversity of strength
Attends us, if but once we have been strong.
Oh! mystery of man, from what a depth
Proceed thy honours. I am lost, but see
In simple childhood something of the base
On which thy greatness stands; but this I feel,
That from thyself it comes, that thou must give,
Else never canst receive. The days gone by
Return upon me almost from the dawn
Of life: the hiding-places of man's power
Open; I would approach them, but they close.
I see by glimpses now; when age comes on,
May scarcely see at all; and I would give,
While yet we may, as far as words can give,
Substance and life to what I feel, enshrining,
Such is my hope, the spirit of the Past
For future restoration. — Yet another
Of these memorials: —
One Christmas-time,[52]
On the glad eve of its dear holidays,
Feverish, and tired, and restless, I went forth
Into the fields, impatient for the sight
Of those led palfreys that should bear us home;
My brothers and myself. There rose a crag,
That, from the meeting-point of two highways
Ascending, overlooked them both, far stretched;
Thither, uncertain on which road to fix
My expectation, thither I repaired,
Scout-like, and gained the summit; 'twas a day
Tempestuous, dark, and wild, and on the grass
I sate half-sheltered by a naked wall;
Upon my right hand couched a single sheep,
Upon my left a blasted hawthorn stood;
With those companions at my side, I watched,
Straining my eyes intensely, as the mist
Gave intermitting prospect of the copse
And plain beneath. Ere we to school returned, —
That dreary time, — ere we had been ten days
Sojourners in my father's house, he died,
And I and my three brothers, orphans then,
Followed his body to the grave. The event,
With all the sorrow that it brought, appeared
A chastisement; and when I called to mind
That day so lately past, when from the crag
I looked in such anxiety of hope;
With trite reflections of morality,
Yet in the deepest passion, I bowed low
To God, Who thus corrected my desires;
And, afterwards, the wind and sleety rain,
And all the business of the elements,
The single sheep, and the one blasted tree,
And the bleak music from that old stone wall,
The noise of wood and water, and the mist
That on the line of each of those two roads
Advanced in such indisputable shapes;
All these were kindred spectacles and sounds

[52] December 1783.

To which I oft repaired, and thence would drink,
As at a fountain; and on winter nights,
Down to this very time, when storm and rain
Beat on my roof, or, haply, at noon-day,
While in a grove I walk, whose lofty trees,
Laden with summer's thickest foliage, rock
In a strong wind, some working of the spirit,
Some inward agitations thence are brought,
Whate'er their office, whether to beguile
Thoughts over busy in the course they took,
Or animate an hour of vacant ease.

from BOOK XIII

IMAGINATION AND TASTE, HOW IMPAIRED AND RESTORED — [concluded]

From Nature doth emotion come, and moods
Of calmness equally are Nature's gift:
This is her glory; these two attributes
Are sister horns that constitute her strength.
Hence Genius, born to thrive by interchange
Of peace and excitation, finds in her
His best and purest friend; from her receives
That energy by which he seeks the truth,
From her that happy stillness of the mind
Which fits him to receive it when unsought.

Such benefit the humblest intellects
Partake of, each in their degree; 'tis mine
To speak, what I myself have known and felt;
Smooth task! for words find easy way, inspired
By gratitude, and confidence in truth.
Long time in search of knowledge did I range
The field of human life, in heart and mind
Benighted; but, the dawn beginning now
To re-appear, 'twas proved that not in vain
I had been taught to reverence a Power
That is the visible quality and shape
And image of right reason; that matures
Her processes by steadfast laws; gives birth
To no impatient or fallacious hopes,
No heat of passion or excessive zeal,
No vain conceits; provokes to no quick turns
Of self-applauding intellect; but trains
To meekness, and exalts by humble faith;
Holds up before the mind intoxicate
With present objects, and the busy dance
Of things that pass away, a temperate show
Of objects that endure; and by this course
Disposes her, when over-fondly set
On throwing off incumbrances, to seek
In man, and in the frame of social life,
Whate'er there is desirable and good
Of kindred permanence, unchanged in form
And function, or, through strict vicissitude
Of life and death, revolving. Above all
Were re-established now those watchful thoughts
Which, seeing little worthy or sublime
In what the Historian's pen so much delights
To blazon — power and energy detached
From moral purpose — early tutored me
To look with feelings of fraternal love
Upon the unassuming things that hold
A silent station in this beauteous world.

Thus moderated, thus composed, I found
Once more in Man an object of delight,
Of pure imagination, and of love;
And, as the horizon of my mind enlarged,
Again I took the intellectual eye
For my instructor, studious more to see
Great truths, than touch and handle little ones.
Knowledge was given accordingly; my trust
Became more firm in feelings that had stood
The test of such a trial; clearer far

My sense of excellence — of right and wrong:
The promise of the present time retired
Into its true proportion; sanguine schemes,
Ambitious projects, pleased me less; I sought
For present good in life's familiar face,
And built thereon my hopes of good to come.

. . .

For, the time
Had never been when throes of mighty Nations
And the world's tumult unto me could yield,
How far soe'er transported and possessed,
Full measure of content; but still I craved
An intermingling of distinct regards
And truths of individual sympathy
Nearer ourselves. Such often might be gleaned
From the great City, else it must have proved
To me a heart-depressing wilderness;
But much was wanting: therefore did I turn
To you, ye pathways, and ye lonely roads;
Sought you enriched with everything I prized,
With human kindnesses and simple joys.

Oh! next to one dear state of bliss, vouchsafed
Alas! to few in this untoward world,
The bliss of walking daily in life's prime
Through field or forest with the maid we love,
While yet our hearts are young, while yet we breathe
Nothing but happiness, in some lone nook,
Deep vale, or anywhere, the home of both,
From which it would be misery to stir:
Oh! next to such enjoyment of our youth,
In my esteem, next to such dear delight,
Was that of wandering on from day to day
Where I could meditate in peace, and cull
Knowledge that step by step might lead me on
To wisdom; or, as lightsome as a bird
Wafted upon the wind from distant lands,
Sing notes of greeting to strange fields or groves,
Which lacked not voice to welcome me in turn:
And, when that pleasant toil had ceased to please,
Converse with men, where if we meet a face
We almost meet a friend, on naked heaths
With long long ways before, by cottage bench,
Or well-spring where the weary traveller rests.

Who doth not love to follow with his eye
The windings of a public way? the sight,
Familiar object as it is, hath wrought
On my imagination since the morn
Of childhood, when a disappearing line,
One daily present to my eyes, that crossed
The naked summit of a far-off hill
Beyond the limits that my feet had trod,
Was like an invitation into space
Boundless, or guide into eternity.
Yes, something of the grandeur which invests
The mariner who sails the roaring sea
Through storm and darkness, early in my mind
Surrounded, too, the wanderers of the earth;
Grandeur as much, and loveliness far more.
Awed have I been by strolling Bedlamites;
From many other uncouth vagrants (passed
In fear) have walked with quicker step; but why
Take note of this? When I began to enquire,
To watch and question those I met, and speak
Without reserve to them, the lonely roads
Were open schools in which I daily read
With most delight the passions of mankind,

Whether by words, looks, sighs, or tears, revealed;
There saw into the depth of human souls,
Souls that appear to have no depth at all
To careless eyes. And — now convinced at heart
How little those formalities, to which
With overweening trust alone we give
The name of Education, have to do
With real feeling and just sense; how vain
A correspondence with the talking world
Proves to the most; and called to make good search
If man's estate, by doom of Nature yoked
With toil, be therefore yoked with ignorance;
If virtue be indeed so hard to rear,
And intellectual strength so rare a boon —
I prized such walks still more, for there I found
Hope to my hope, and to my pleasure peace
And steadiness, and healing and repose
To every angry passion. There I heard,
From mouths of men obscure and lowly, truths
Replete with honour; sounds in unison
With loftiest promises of good and fair.

. . .

Here, calling up to mind what then I saw,
A youthful traveller, and see daily now
In the familiar circuit of my home,
Here might I pause, and bend in reverence
To Nature, and the power of human minds,
To men as they are men within themselves.
How oft high service is performed within,
When all the external man is rude and show, —
Not like a temple rich with pomp and gold,
But a mere mountain-chapel, that protects
Its simple worshippers from sun and shower.
Of these, said I, shall be my song; of these,
If future years mature me for the task,
Will I record the praises, making verse
Deal boldly with substantial things; in truth
And sanctity of passion, speak of these,
That justice may be done, obeisance paid
Where it is due: thus haply shall I teach,
Inspire; through unadulterated ears
Pour rapture, tenderness, and hope, — my theme
No other than the very heart of man,
As found among the best of those who live —
Not unexalted by religious faith,
Nor uninformed by books, good books, though few —
In Nature's presence: thence may I select
Sorrow, that is not sorrow, but delight;
And miserable love, that is not pain
To hear of, for the glory that redounds
Therefrom to human kind, and what we are.
Be mine to follow with no timid step
Where knowledge leads me: it shall be my pride
That I have dared to tread this holy ground,
Speaking no dream, but things oracular;
Matter not lightly to be heard by those
Who to the letter of the outward promise
Do read the invisible soul; by men adroit
In speech, and for communion with the world
Accomplished; minds whose faculties are then
Most active when they are most eloquent,
And elevated most when most admired.
Men may be found of other mould than these,
Who are their own upholders, to themselves
Encouragement, and energy, and will,
Expressing liveliest thoughts in lively words
As native passion dictates. Others, too,
There are among the walks of homely life
Still higher, men for contemplation framed,
Shy, and unpractised in the strife of phrase;
Meek men, whose very souls perhaps would sink

Beneath them, summoned to such intercourse:
Theirs is the language of the heavens, the power,
The thought, the image, and the silent joy:
Words are but under-agents in their souls;
When they are grasping with their greatest strength,
They do not breathe among them: this I speak
In gratitude to God, Who feeds our hearts
For His own service; knoweth, loveth us,
When we are unregarded by the world.

Also, about this time did I receive
Convictions still more strong than heretofore,
Not only that the inner frame is good,
And graciously composed, but that, no less,
Nature for all conditions wants not power
To consecrate, if we have eyes to see,
The outside of her creatures, and to breathe
Grandeur upon the very humblest face
Of human life. I felt that the array
Of act and circumstance, and visible form,
Is mainly to the pleasure of the mind
What passion makes them; that meanwhile the forms
Of Nature have a passion in themselves,
That intermingles with those works of man
To which she summons him; although the works
Be mean, have nothing lofty of their own;
And that the Genius of the Poet hence
May boldly take his way among mankind
Wherever Nature leads; that he hath stood
By Nature's side among the men of old,
And so shall stand for ever. Dearest Friend!
If thou partake the animating faith
That Poets, even as Prophets, each with each
Connected in a mighty scheme of truth,
Have each his own peculiar faculty,
Heaven's gift, a sense that fits him to perceive
Objects unseen before, thou wilt not blame
The humblest of this band who dares to hope
That unto him hath also been vouchsafed
An insight that in some sort he possesses,
A privilege whereby a work of his,
Proceeding from a source of untaught things,
Creative and enduring, may become
A power like one of Nature's. To a hope
Not less ambitious once among the wilds
Of Sarum's Plain, my youthful spirit was raised; [53]
There, as I ranged at will the pastoral downs
Trackless and smooth, or paced the bare white roads
Lengthening in solitude their dreary line,
Time with his retinue of ages fled
Backwards, nor checked his flight until I saw
Our dim ancestral Past in vision clear;
Saw multitudes of men, and, here and there,
A single Briton clothed in wolf-skin vest,
With shield and stone-axe, stride across the wold;
The voice of spears was heard, the rattling spear
Shaken by arms of mighty bone, in strength,
Long mouldered, of barbaric majesty.
I called on Darkness — but before the word
Was uttered, midnight darkness seemed to take
All objects from my sight; and lo! again
The Desert visible by dismal flames;
It is the sacrificial altar, fed
With living men — how deep the groans! the voice
Of those that crowd the giant wicker thrills
The monumental hillocks, and the pomp
Is for both worlds, the living and the dead.
At other moments — (for through that wide waste
Three summer days I roamed) where'er the Plain

[53] In 1793 Wordsworth spent three days on Salisbury Plain.

Was figured o'er with circles, lines, or mounds,
That yet survive, a work, as some divine,
Shaped by the Druids, so to represent
Their knowledge of the heavens, and image forth
The constellations — gently was I charmed
Into a waking dream, a reverie
That, with believing eyes, where'er I turned,
Beheld long-bearded teachers, with white wands
Uplifted, pointing to the starry sky,
Alternately, and plain below, while breath
Of music swayed their motions, and the waste
Rejoiced with them and me in those sweet sounds.

This for the past, and things that may be viewed
Or fancied in the obscurity of years
From monumental hints: and thou, O Friend!
Pleased with some unpremeditated strains
That served those wanderings to beguile, hast said
That then and there my mind had exercised
Upon the vulgar forms of present things,
The actual world of our familiar days,
Yet higher power; had caught from them a tone,
An image, and a character, by books
Not hitherto reflected. Call we this
A partial judgment — and yet why? for *then*
We were as strangers; and I may not speak
Thus wrongfully of verse, however rude,
Which on thy young imagination, trained
In the great City, broke like light from far.
Moreover, each man's Mind is to herself
Witness and judge; and I remember well
That in life's every-day appearances
I seemed about this time to gain clear sight
Of a new world — a world, too, that was fit
To be transmitted, and to other eyes
Made visible; as ruled by those fixed laws
Whence spiritual dignity originates,
Which do both give it being and maintain
A balance, an ennobling interchange
Of action from without and from within;
The excellence, pure function, and best power
Both of the object seen, and eye that sees.

from BOOK XIV

CONCLUSION

It was a close, warm, breezeless summer night,[54]
Wan, dull, and glaring, with a dripping fog
Low-hung and thick that covered all the sky;
But, undiscouraged, we began to climb
The mountain-side. The mist soon girt us round,
And, after ordinary travellers' talk
With our conductor, pensively we sank
Each into commerce with his private thoughts:
Thus did we breast the ascent, and by myself
Was nothing either seen or heard that checked
Those musings or diverted, save that once
The shepherd's lurcher, who, among the crags,
Had to his joy unearthed a hedgehog, teased
His coiled-up prey with barkings turbulent.
This small adventure, for even such it seemed
In that wild place and at the dead of night,
Being over and forgotten, on we wound
In silence as before. With forehead bent
Earthward, as if in opposition set
Against an enemy, I panted up
With eager pace, and no less eager thoughts.
Thus might we wear a midnight hour away,

[54] In the summer of 1793, when Wordsworth was on a tour with his friend Robert Jones.

Ascending at loose distance each from each,
And I, as chanced, the foremost of the band;
When at my feet the ground appeared to brighten,
And with a step or two seemed brighter still;
Nor was time given to ask or learn the cause,
For instantly a light upon the turf
Fell like a flash, and lo! as I looked up,
The Moon hung naked in a firmament
Of azure without cloud, and at my feet
Rested a silent sea of hoary mist.
A hundred hills their dusky backs upheaved
All over this still ocean; and beyond,
Far, far beyond, the solid vapours stretched,
In headlands, tongues, and promontory shapes,
Into the main Atlantic, that appeared
To dwindle, and give up his majesty,
Usurped upon far as the sight could reach.
Not so the ethereal vault; encroachment none
Was there, nor loss; only the inferior stars
Had disappeared, or shed a fainter light
In the clear presence of the full-orbed Moon,
Who, from her sovereign elevation, gazed
Upon the billowy ocean, as it lay
All meek and silent, save that through a rift —
Not distant from the shore whereon we stood,
A fixed, abysmal, gloomy, breathing-place —
Mounted the roar of waters, torrents, streams
Innumerable, roaring with one voice!
Heard over earth and sea, and, in that hour,
For so it seemed, felt by the starry heavens.

When into air had partially dissolved
That vision, given to spirits of the night
And three chance human wanderers, in calm thought
Reflected, it appeared to me the type
Of a majestic intellect, its acts
And its possessions, what it has and craves,
What in itself it is, and would become.
There I behold the emblem of a mind
That feeds upon infinity, that broods
Over the dark abyss, intent to hear
Its voices issuing forth to silent light
In one continuous stream; a mind sustained
By recognitions of transcendent power,
In sense conducting to ideal form,
In soul of more than mortal privilege.
One function, above all, of such a mind
Had Nature shadowed there, by putting forth,
'Mid circumstances awful and sublime,
That mutual domination which she loves
To exert upon the face of outward things,
So moulded, joined, abstracted, so endowed
With interchangeable supremacy,
That men, least sensitive, see, hear, perceive,
And cannot choose but feel. The power, which all
Acknowledge when thus moved, which Nature thus
To bodily sense exhibits, is the express
Resemblance of that glorious faculty
That higher minds bear with them as their own.
This is the very spirit in which they deal
With the whole compass of the universe:
They from their native selves can send abroad
Kindred mutations; for themselves create
A like existence; and, whene'er it dawns
Created for them, catch it, or are caught
By its inevitable mastery,
Like angels stopped upon the wing by sound
Of harmony from Heaven's remotest spheres.
Them the enduring and the transient both
Serve to exalt; they build up greatest things
From least suggestions; ever on the watch,
Willing to work and to be wrought upon,
They need not extraordinary calls
To rouse them; in a world of life they live,

By sensible impressions not enthralled,
But by their quickening impulse made more prompt
To hold fit converse with the spiritual world,
And with the generations of mankind
Spread over time, past, present, and to come,
Age after age, till Time shall be no more.
Such minds are truly from the Deity,
For they are Powers; and hence the highest bliss
That flesh can know is theirs — the consciousness
Of Whom they are, habitually infused
Through every image and through every thought,
And all affections by communion raised
From earth to heaven, from human to divine;
Hence endless occupation for the Soul,
Whether discursive or intuitive;
Hence cheerfulness for acts of daily life,
Emotions which best foresight need not fear,
Most worthy then of trust when most intense.
Hence, amid ills that vex and wrongs that crush
Our hearts — if here the words of Holy Writ
May with fit reverence be applied — that peace
Which passeth understanding, that repose
In moral judgments which from this pure source
Must come, or will by man be sought in vain.

. . .

This spiritual Love acts not nor can exist
Without Imagination, which, in truth,
Is but another name for absolute power
And clearest insight, amplitude of mind,
And Reason in her most exalted mood.
This faculty hath been the feeding source
Of our long labour: we have traced the stream
From the blind cavern whence is faintly heard
Its natal murmur; followed it to light
And open day; accompanied its course
Among the ways of Nature, for a time
Lost sight of it bewildered and engulphed;
Then given it greeting as it rose once more
In strength, reflecting from its placid breast
The works of man and face of human life;
And lastly, from its progress have we drawn
Faith in life endless, the sustaining thought
Of human Being, Eternity, and God.

Imagination having been our theme,
So also hath that intellectual Love,
For they are each in each, and cannot stand
Dividually.

. . .

Child of my parents! Sister of my soul!
Thanks in sincerest verse have been elsewhere
Poured out for all the early tenderness
Which I from thee imbibed: and 'tis most true
That later seasons owed to thee no less;
For, spite of thy sweet influence and the touch
Of kindred hands that opened out the springs
Of genial thought in childhood, and in spite
Of all that unassisted I had marked
In life or nature of those charms minute
That win their way into the heart by stealth,
Still (to the very going-out of youth)
I too exclusively esteemed *that* love,
And sought *that* beauty, which, as Milton sings,
Hath terror in it.[55] Thou didst soften down
This over-sternness; but for thee, dear Friend!
My soul, too reckless of mild grace, had stood

[55] See *Paradise Lost*, ix, 489–91.

In her original self too confident,
Retained too long a countenance severe;
A rock with torrents roaring, with the clouds
Familiar, and a favourite of the stars:
But thou didst plant its crevices with flowers,
Hang it with shrubs that twinkle in the breeze,
And teach the little birds to build their nests
And warble in its chambers. At a time
When Nature, destined to remain so long
Foremost in my affections, had fallen back
Into a second place, pleased to become
A handmaid to a nobler than herself,
When every day brought with it some new sense
Of exquisite regard for common things,
And all the earth was budding with these gifts
Of more refined humanity, thy breath,
Dear Sister! was a kind of gentler spring
That went before my steps. Thereafter came
One[56] whom with thee friendship had early paired;
She came, no more a phantom to adorn
A moment, but an inmate of the heart,
And yet a spirit, there for me enshrined
To penetrate the lofty and the low;
Even as one essence of pervading light
Shines, in the brightest of ten thousand stars,
And, the meek worm that feeds her lonely lamp
Couched in the dewy grass.

. . .

Oh! yet a few short years of useful life,
And all will be complete, thy race be run,
Thy monument of glory will be raised;
Then, though (too weak to tread the ways of truth)
This age fall back to old idolatry,
Though men return to servitude as fast
As the tide ebbs, to ignominy and shame
By nations sink together, we shall still
Find solace — knowing what we have learnt to know,
Rich in true happiness if allowed to be
Faithful alike in forwarding a day
Of firmer trust, joint labourers in the work
(Should Providence such grace to us vouchsafe)
Of their deliverance, surely yet to come.
Prophets of Nature, we to them will speak
A lasting inspiration, sanctified
By reason, blest by faith: what we have loved,
Others will love, and we will teach them how;
Instruct them how the mind of man becomes
A thousand times more beautiful than the earth
On which he dwells, above this frame of things
(Which, 'mid all revolution in the hopes
And fears of men, doth still remain unchanged)
In beauty exalted, as it is itself
Of quality and fabric more divine.

My heart leaps up[57]

My heart leaps up when I behold
A rainbow in the sky:
So was it when my life began;
So is it now I am a man;
So be it when I shall grow old,
Or let me die!
The Child is father of the Man;
And I could wish my days to be
Bound each to each by natural piety.

Resolution and Independence[58]

I

There was a roaring in the wind all night:
The rain came heavily and fell in floods;

[56] Mary Hutchinson, Wordsworth's wife. Actually she had no influence on Wordsworth during the years *The Prelude* covers.

[57] Composed 26 March 1802; published in *Poems in Two Volumes*, 1807.

[58] Written in 1802; published in 1807. 'Written at Town-end, Grasmere. This old Man I met a few hundred

But now the sun is rising calm and bright;
The birds are singing in the distant woods;
Over his own sweet voice the Stock-dove broods;
The Jay makes answer as the Magpie chatters;
And all the air is filled with pleasant noise of waters.

II

All things that love the sun are out of doors;
The sky rejoices in the morning's birth;
The grass is bright with rain-drops; — on the moors
The hare is running races in her mirth;
And with her feet she from the plashy earth
Raises a mist; that, glittering in the sun,
Runs with her all the way, wherever she doth run.

III

I was a Traveller then upon the moor;
I saw the hare that raced about with joy;
I heard the woods and distant waters roar;
Or heard them not, as happy as a boy:
The pleasant season did my heart employ:
My old remembrances went from me wholly;
And all the ways of men, so vain and melancholy.

IV

But, as it sometimes chanceth, from the might
Of joy in minds that can no further go,
As high as we have mounted in delight
In our dejection do we sink as low;
To me that morning did it happen so;
And fears and fancies thick upon me came;
Dim sadness — and blind thoughts, I knew not, nor could name.

yards from my cottage; and the account of him is taken from his own mouth. I was in the state of feeling described in the beginning of the poem, while crossing over Barton Fell from Mr. Clarkson's, at the foot of Ullswater, toward Askham. The image of the hare I then observed on the ridge of the Fell.' [Wordsworth.] In a letter Wordsworth also wrote: '. . . I cannot conceive a figure more impressive than that of an old man like this, the survivor of a wife and ten children, travelling alone among the mountains and all lonely places, carrying with him his own fortitude and the necessities which an unjust state of society has laid upon him.'

V

I heard the skylark warbling in the sky;
And I bethought me of the playful hare:
Even such a happy child of earth am I;
Even as these blissful creatures do I fare;
Far from the world I walk, and from all care;
But there may come another day to me —
Solitude, pain of heart, distress, and poverty.

VI

My whole life I have lived in pleasant thought,
As if life's business were a summer mood;
As if all needful things would come unsought
To genial faith, still rich in genial good;
But how can He expect that others should
Build for him, sow for him, and at his call
Love him, who for himself will take no heed at all?

VII

I thought of Chatterton,[59] the marvellous Boy,
The sleepless Soul that perished in his pride;
Of Him [60] who walked in glory and in joy
Following his plough, along the mountain-side:
By our own spirits are we deified:
We Poets in our youth begin in gladness;
But thereof come in the end despondency and madness.

VIII

Now, whether it were by peculiar grace,
A leading from above, a something given,
Yet it befell that, in this lonely place,
When I with these untoward thoughts had striven,
Beside a pool bare to the eye of heaven
I saw a Man before me unawares:
The oldest man he seemed that ever wore grey hairs.

59 Thomas Chatterton (1752–1770), who, in desperate poverty, poisoned himself.
60 Robert Burns

IX

As a huge stone is sometimes seen to lie
Couched on the bald top of an eminence;
Wonder to all who do the same espy,
By what means it could thither come, and whence;
So that it seems a thing endued with sense:
Like a sea-beast crawled forth, that on a shelf
Of rock or sand reposeth, there to sun itself;

X

Such seemed this Man, not all alive nor dead,
Nor all asleep — in his extreme old age:
His body was bent double, feet and head
Coming together in life's pilgrimage;
As if some dire constraint of pain, or rage
Of sickness felt by him in times long past,
A more than human weight upon his frame had cast.

XI

Himself he propped, limbs, body, and pale face,
Upon a long grey staff of shaven wood:
And, still as I drew near with gentle pace,
Upon the margin of that moorish flood
Motionless as a cloud the old Man stood,
That heareth not the loud winds when they call;
And moveth all together, if it move at all.

XII

At length, himself unsettling, he the pond
Stirred with his staff, and fixedly did look
Upon the muddy water, which he conned,
As if he had been reading in a book:
And now a stranger's privilege I took;
And, drawing to his side, to him did say,
'This morning gives us promise of a glorious day.'

XIII

A gentle answer did the old Man make,
In courteous speech which forth he slowly drew:
And him with further words I thus bespake,
'What occupation do you there pursue?
This is a lonesome place for one like you.'
Ere he replied, a flash of mild surprise
Broke from the sable orbs of his yet-vivid eyes.

XIV

His words came feebly, from a feeble chest,
But each in solemn order followed each,
With something of a lofty utterance drest —
Choice word and measured phrase, above the reach
Of ordinary men; a stately speech;
Such as grave Livers do in Scotland use,
Religious men, who give to God and man their dues.

XV

He told, that to these waters he had come
To gather leeches, being old and poor:
Employment hazardous and wearisome!
And he had many hardships to endure:
From pond to pond he roamed, from moor to moor;
Housing, with God's good help, by choice or chance;
And in this way he gained an honest maintenance.

XVI

The old Man still stood talking by my side;
But now *his* voice to me was like a stream
Scarce heard; nor word from word could I divide;
And the whole body of the Man did seem
Like one whom I had met with in a dream;
Or like a man from some far region sent,
To give me human strength, by apt admonishment.

XVII

My former thoughts returned: the fear that kills;
And hope that is unwilling to be fed;
Cold, pain, and labour, and all fleshly ills;
And mighty Poets in their misery dead.
— Perplexed, and longing to be comforted,

My question eagerly did I renew,
'How is it that you live, and what is it you do?'

XVIII

He with a smile did then his words repeat;
And said that, gathering leeches, far and wide
He travelled; stirring thus about his feet
The waters of the pools where they abide.
'Once I could meet with them on every side;
But they have dwindled long by slow decay;
Yet still I persevere, and find them where I may.'

XIX

While he was talking thus, the lonely place,
The old Man's shape, and speech — all troubled me:
In my mind's eye I seemed to see him pace
About the weary moors continually,
Wandering about alone and silently.
While I these thoughts within myself pursued,
He, having made a pause, the same discourse renewed.

XX

And soon with this he other matter blended,
Cheerfully uttered, with demeanour kind,
But stately in the main; and, when he ended,
I could have laughed myself to scorn to find
In that decrepit Man so firm a mind.
'God,' said I, 'be my help and stay secure;
I'll think of the Leech-gatherer on the lonely moor!'

Composed upon Westminster Bridge,

SEPTEMBER 3, 1802[61]

EARTH has not anything to show more fair:
Dull would he be of soul who could pass by
A sight so touching in its majesty:
This City now doth, like a garment, wear
The beauty of the morning; silent, bare,
Ships, towers, domes, theatres, and temples lie
Open unto the fields, and to the sky;
All bright and glittering in the smokeless air.
Never did sun more beautifully steep
In his first splendour, valley, rock, or hill;
Ne'er saw I, never felt, a calm so deep!
The river glideth at his own sweet will:
Dear God! the very houses seem asleep;
And all that mighty heart is lying still!

Composed by the Sea-side, near Calais

AUGUST 1802[62]

FAIR Star of evening, Splendour of the west,
Star of my Country! — on the horizon's brink
Thou hangest, stooping, as might seem, to sink
On England's bosom; yet well pleased to rest,
Meanwhile, and be to her a glorious crest
Conspicuous to the Nations. Thou, I think,
Shouldst be my Country's emblem; and shouldst wink,
Bright Star! with laughter on her banners, drest
In thy fresh beauty. There! that dusky spot
Beneath thee, that is England; there she lies.
Blessings be on you both! one hope, one lot,
One life, one glory! — I, with many a fear
For my dear Country, many heartfelt sighs,
Among men who do not love her, linger here.

[61] Written 31 July 1802; published 1807.
[62] Published 1807.

It is a beauteous evening, calm and free [63]

It is a beauteous evening, calm and free,
The holy time is quiet as a Nun
Breathless with adoration; the broad sun
Is sinking down in its tranquillity;
The gentleness of heaven broods o'er the Sea:
Listen! the mighty Being is awake,
And doth with his eternal motion make
A sound like thunder — everlastingly.
Dear Child! [64] dear Girl! that walkest with me here,
If thou appear untouched by solemn thought,
Thy nature is not therefore less divine:
Thou liest in Abraham's bosom all the year;
And worshipp'st at the Temple's inner shrine,
God being with thee when we know it not.

On the Extinction of the Venetian Republic [65]

Once did She hold the gorgeous east in fee;
And was the safeguard of the west: the worth
Of Venice did not fall below her birth,
Venice, the eldest Child of Liberty.
She was a maiden City, bright and free;
No guile seduced, no force could violate;
And, when she took unto herself a Mate,
She must espouse the everlasting Sea.[66]
And what if she had seen those glories fade,
Those titles vanish, and that strength decay;
Yet shall some tribute of regret be paid
When her long life hath reached its final day:
Men are we, and must grieve when even the Shade
Of that which once was great is passed away.

To Toussaint l'Ouverture [67]

Toussaint, the most unhappy man of men!
Whether the whistling Rustic tend his plough
Within thy hearing, or thy head be now
Pillowed in some deep dungeon's earless den; —
O miserable Chieftain! where and when
Wilt thou find patience! Yet die not; do thou
Wear rather in thy bonds a cheerful brow:
Though fallen thyself, never to rise again,
Live, and take comfort. Thou hast left behind
Powers that will work for thee; air, earth, and skies;
There's not a breathing of the common wind
That will forget thee; thou hast great allies;
Thy friends are exultations, agonies,
And love, and man's unconquerable mind.

September, 1802

NEAR DOVER [68]

Inland, within a hollow vale, I stood;
And saw, while sea was calm and air was clear,
The coast of France — the coast of France how near!
Drawn almost into frightful neighbourhood.
I shrunk; for verily the barrier flood

---

[63] Written in August 1802; published 1807.
[64] Caroline, Wordsworth's French daughter.
[65] Written in 1802; published in 1807. The particular glory of Venice dates from the conquest of Constantinople in 1202, when the state began its long history as 'safeguard of the West' against the Turks. Founded in the fifth century, Venice had owned more than a thousand years of independence until 1797, when, by the treaty of Campo Formio, its territory was divided between France and Austria.
[66] 'The Wedding of the Adriatic,' an annual ceremony, dating as a sacred rite from 1177, was performed by the Doge's dropping a ring into the sea. It came to symbolize the maritime power of Venice.
[67] Written in August(?) 1802; published in *The Morning Post*, 2 February 1803, and in *Poems*, 1807. Toussaint was the Negro liberator and governor of St. Domingo. Upon Napoleon's edict of 1801, re-establishing slavery in St. Domingo, Toussaint resisted, was treacherously arrested, and sent to Paris, where, after ten months in prison he died in April 1803.
[68] Published 1807.

Was like a lake, or river bright and fair,
A span of waters; yet what power is there!
What mightiness for evil and for good!
Even so doth God protect us if we be
Virtuous and wise. Winds blow, and waters roll,
Strength to the brave, and Power, and Deity;
Yet in themselves are nothing! One decree
Spake laws to *them,* and said that by the soul
Only, the Nations shall be great and free.

London, 1802 [69]

MILTON! thou shouldst be living at this hour:
England hath need of thee: she is a fen
Of stagnant waters: altar, sword, and pen,
Fireside, the heroic wealth of hall and bower,
Have forfeited their ancient English dower
Of inward happiness. We are selfish men;
Oh! raise us up, return to us again;
And give us manners, virtue, freedom, power.
Thy soul was like a Star, and dwelt apart;
Thou hadst a voice whose sound was like the sea:
Pure as the naked heavens, majestic, free,
So didst thou travel on life's common way,
In cheerful godliness; and yet thy heart
The lowliest duties on herself did lay.

She was a Phantom of delight [70]

SHE was a Phantom of delight
When first she gleamed upon my sight;
A lovely Apparition, sent
To be a moment's ornament;
Her eyes as stars of Twilight fair;
Like Twilight's, too, her dusky hair;
But all things else about her drawn
From May-time and the cheerful Dawn;
A dancing Shape, an Image gay,
To haunt, to startle, and way-lay.

I saw her upon nearer view,
A Spirit, yet a Woman too!
Her household motions light and free,
And steps of virgin-liberty;
A countenance in which did meet
Sweet records, promises as sweet;
A Creature not too bright or good
For human nature's daily food;
For transient sorrows, simple wiles,
Praise, blame, love, kisses, tears, and smiles.

And now I see with eye serene
The very pulse of the machine; [71]
A Being breathing thoughtful breath,
A Traveller between life and death;
The reason firm, the temperate will,
Endurance, foresight, strength, and skill;
A perfect Woman, nobly planned,
To warn, to comfort, and command;
And yet a Spirit still, and bright
With something of angelic light.

The Solitary Reaper [72]

BEHOLD her, single in the field,
Yon solitary Highland Lass!
Reaping and singing by herself;
Stop here, or gently pass!
Alone she cuts and binds the grain,
And sings a melancholy strain;
O listen! for the Vale profound
Is overflowing with the sound.

---

69 Written in September 1802; published 1807.

70 Written in 1804; published in 1807. 'Written at Town-end, Grasmere. The germ of this poem was four lines composed as a part of the verses on the *Highland Girl.* Though beginning in this way, it was written from my heart, as is sufficiently obvious.' [Wordsworth.] Wordsworth's wife was Mary Hutchinson.

71 Wordsworth's sense of this word has fallen, with other things, before the Industrial Revolution.

72 Written between 1803 and 1805; published in 1807. In her entry of 13 September 1803 in *Recollections of a Tour Made in Scotland,* Dorothy Wordsworth describes the reapers and goes on to say, 'It is not uncommon in the more lonely parts of the Highlands to see a single person so employed. The following poem was suggested to William by a beautiful sentence in Thomas Wilkinson's "Tour in Scotland."' Wordsworth himself pointed out the entry in Wilkinson: 'Passed a female who was reaping alone: she sung in Erse, as she bended over her sickle; the sweetest human voice I ever heard: her strains were tenderly melancholy, and felt delicious, long after they were heard no more.'

No Nightingale did ever chaunt
More welcome notes to weary bands
Of travellers in some shady haunt,
Among Arabian sands:
A voice so thrilling ne'er was heard
In spring-time from the Cuckoo-bird,
Breaking the silence of the seas
Among the farthest Hebrides.

Will no one tell me what she sings? —
Perhaps the plaintive numbers flow
For old, unhappy, far-off things,
And battles long ago:
Or is it some more humble lay,
Familiar matter of to-day?
Some natural sorrow, loss, or pain,
That has been, and may be again?

Whate'er the theme, the Maiden sang
As if her song could have no ending;
I saw her singing at her work,
And o'er the sickle bending; —
I listened, motionless and still;
And, as I mounted up the hill,
The music in my heart I bore,
Long after it was heard no more.

I wandered lonely as a cloud[73]

I WANDERED lonely as a cloud
That floats on high o'er vales and hills,
When all at once I saw a crowd,
A host, of golden daffodils;
Beside the lake, beneath the trees,
Fluttering and dancing in the breeze.

Continuous as the stars that shine
And twinkle on the milky way,
They stretched in never-ending line
Along the margin of a bay:
Ten thousand saw I at a glance,
Tossing their heads in sprightly dance.

The waves beside them danced; but they
Out-did the sparkling waves in glee:
A poet could not but be gay,
In such a jocund company:
I gazed — and gazed — but little thought
What wealth the show to me had brought:

For oft, when on my couch I lie
In vacant or in pensive mood,
They flash upon that inward eye
Which is the bliss of solitude;
And then my heart with pleasure fills,
And dances with the daffodils.

Elegiac Stanzas

SUGGESTED BY A PICTURE OF PEELE CASTLE, IN A STORM, PAINTED BY SIR GEORGE BEAUMONT[74]

I WAS thy neighbour once, thou rugged Pile!
Four summer weeks I dwelt in sight of thee:
I saw thee every day; and all the while
Thy Form was sleeping on a glassy sea.

So pure the sky, so quiet was the air!
So like, so very like, was day to day!
Whene'er I looked, thy Image still was there;
It trembled, but it never passed away.
How perfect was the calm! it seemed no sleep;
No mood, which season takes away, or brings:
I could have fancied that the mighty Deep
Was even the gentlest of all gentle Things.

Ah! THEN, if mine had been the Painter's hand,
To express what then I saw; and add the gleam,
The light that never was, on sea or land,
The consecration, and the Poet's dream;

[73] Written in 1804; published in 1807. 'The two best lines in it are by Mary [ll. 21–22]. The daffodils grew, and still grow, on the margin of Ullswater, and probably may be seen to this day as beautiful in the month of March, nodding their golden heads beside the dancing and foaming waves.' [Wordsworth.]

[74] Written in 1805; published in 1807. Wordsworth visited his cousin during a summer vacation in the neighborhood of this Peele Castle, which is in Lancashire. Beaumont, the poet's friend, painted two pictures of the castle, one of which, except for Lady Beaumont's interference, would have been given to Mrs. Wordsworth. The painting went, upon Sir George's death, to Sir Uvedale Price.

I would have planted thee, thou hoary Pile
Amid a world how different from this!
Beside a sea that could not cease to smile;
On tranquil land, beneath a sky of bliss.

Thou shouldst have seemed a treasure-house divine
Of peaceful years; a chronicle of heaven;—
Of all the sunbeams that did ever shine
The very sweetest had to thee been given.

A Picture had it been of lasting ease,
Elysian quiet, without toil or strife;
No motion but the moving tide, a breeze,
Or merely silent Nature's breathing life.

Such, in the fond illusion of my heart,
Such Picture would I at that time have made:
And seen the soul of truth in every part,
A steadfast peace that might not be betrayed.

So once it would have been,—'tis so no more;
I have submitted to a new control:
A power is gone, which nothing can restore;
A deep distress hath humanised my Soul.

Not for a moment could I now behold
A smiling sea, and be what I have been:
The feeling of my loss will ne'er be old;
This, which I know, I speak with mind serene.

Then, Beaumont, Friend! who would have been the Friend,
If he had lived, of Him whom I deplore,
This work of thine I blame not, but commend;
This sea in anger, and that dismal shore.

O 'tis a passionate Work!—yet wise and well,
Well chosen is the spirit that is here;
That Hulk which labours in the deadly swell,
This rueful sky, this pageantry of fear!

And this huge Castle, standing here sublime,
I love to see the look with which it braves,
Cased in the unfeeling armour of old time,
The lightning, the fierce wind, and trampling waves.

Farewell, farewell the heart that lives alone,
Housed in a dream, at distance from the Kind!
Such happiness, wherever it be known,
Is to be pitied; for 'tis surely blind.

But welcome fortitude, and patient cheer,
And frequent sights of what is to be borne!
Such sights, or worse, as are before me here.—
Not without hope we suffer and we mourn.

Nuns fret not at their convent's narrow room [75]

I

Nuns fret not at their convent's narrow room;
And hermits are contented with their cells;
And students with their pensive citadels;
Maids at the wheel, the weaver at his loom,
Sit blithe and happy; bees that soar for bloom,
High as the highest Peak of Furness-fells,[76]
Will murmur by the hour in foxglove bells:
In truth the prison, unto which we doom
Ourselves, no prison is: and hence for me,
In sundry moods, 'twas pastime to be bound
Within the Sonnet's scanty plot of ground;
Pleased if some Souls (for such there needs must be)

---

[75] Written in 1806; published in 1807.

[76] Then the inclusive name for all the hills east of the Duddon, south of the Brathay, and west of Windermere.

Who have felt the weight of too much liberty,
Should find brief solace there, as I have found.

The world is too much with us[77]

The world is too much with us; late and soon,
Getting and spending, we lay waste our powers:
Little we see in Nature that is ours;
We have given our hearts away, a sordid boon!
This Sea that bares her bosom to the moon;
The winds that will be howling at all hours,
And are up-gathered now like sleeping flowers;
For this, for everything, we are out of tune;
It moves us not. — Great God! I'd rather be
A Pagan suckled in a creed outworn;
So might I, standing on this pleasant lea,
Have glimpses that would make me less forlorn;
Have sight of Proteus rising from the sea;
Or hear old Triton blow his wreathèd horn.

ODE

INTIMATIONS OF IMMORTALITY FROM RECOLLECTIONS OF EARLY CHILDHOOD[78]

The Child is father of the Man;
And I could wish my days to be
Bound each to each by natural piety.

I

There was a time when meadow, grove, and stream,
The earth, and every common sight,
To me did seem
Apparelled in celestial light,
The glory and the freshness of a dream.
It is not now as it hath been of yore; —
Turn wheresoe'er I may,
By night or day,
The things which I have seen I now can see no more.

---

[77] Published 1807.

[78] Written in the period between 1803 (1802?) and 1806; published in 1807. It is exceedingly important to realize that the poem is, in effect, an 'answer' to Coleridge's *Ode on Dejection* (see p. 691). A comparison of the two pieces, with respect to ideas, form, and verbal echoes, is illuminating. Wordsworth's own note is as follows:

'This was composed during my residence at Town-end, Grasmere. Two years at least passed between the writing of the four first stanzas and the remaining part. To the attentive and competent reader the whole sufficiently explains itself; but there may be no harm in adverting here to particular feelings or *experiences* of my own mind on which the structure of the poem partly rests. Nothing was more difficult for me in childhood than to admit the notion of death as a state applicable to my own being. I have said elsewhere —

A simple child,
That lightly draws its breath,
And feels its life in every limb,
What should it know of death! —

But it was not so much from feelings of animal vivacity that *my* difficulty came as from a sense of the indomitableness of the Spirit within me. I used to brood over the stories of Enoch and Elijah, and almost to persuade myself that, whatever might become of others, I should be translated, in something of the same way, to heaven. With a feeling congenial to this, I was often unable to think of external things as having external existence, and I communed with all that I saw as something not apart from, but inherent in, my own immaterial nature. Many times while going to school have I grasped at a wall or tree to recall myself from this abyss of idealism to the reality. At that time I was afraid of such processes. In later periods of life I have deplored, as we have all reason to do, a subjugation of an opposite character, and have rejoiced over the remembrances, as is expressed in the lines —

Obstinate questionings
Of sense and outward things,
Fallings from us, vanishings, etc.

To that dream-like vividness and splendour which invest objects of sight in childhood, every one, I believe, if he would look back, could bear testimony, and I need not dwell upon it here: but having in the poem regarded it as presumptive evidence of a prior state of existence, I think it right to protest against a conclusion, which has given pain to some good and pious persons, that I meant to inculcate such a belief. It is far too shadowy a notion to be recommended to faith, as more than an element in our instincts of immortality. But let us bear in mind that, though the idea is not advanced in revelation, there is nothing there to contradict it, and the fall of Man presents an analogy in its favor. Accordingly, a pre-existent state has entered into the popular creeds of many nations; and, among all persons acquainted with classic literature, is known as an ingredient in Platonic philosophy. Archimedes said that he could move the world if he had a point whereon to rest his machine. Who has not felt the same aspirations as regards the world of his own mind? Having to wield some of its elements when I was impelled to write this poem on the "Immortality of the Soul," I took hold of the notion of pre-existence as having sufficient foundation in humanity for authorising me to make for my purpose the best use of it I could as a poet.'

II

The Rainbow comes and goes,
And lovely is the Rose,
The Moon doth with delight
Look round her when the heavens are bare,
Waters on a starry night
Are beautiful and fair;
The sunshine is a glorious birth;
But yet I know, where'er I go,
That there hath past away a glory from the earth.

III

Now, while the birds thus sing a joyous song,
And while the young lambs bound
As to the tabor's sound,
To me alone there came a thought of grief:
A timely utterance gave that thought relief,
And I again am strong:
The cataracts blow their trumpets from the steep;
Nor more shall grief of mine the season wrong;
I hear the Echoes through the mountains throng,
The Winds come to me from the fields of sleep,
And all the earth is gay;
Land and sea
Give themselves up to jollity,
And with the heart of May
Doth every Beast keep holiday;—
Thou Child of Joy,
Shout round me, let me hear thy shouts, thou happy Shepherd-boy!

IV

Ye blesséd Creatures, I have heard the call
Ye to each other make; I see
The heavens laugh with you in your jubilee;
My heart is at your festival,
My head hath its coronal,
The fulness of your bliss, I feel—I feel it all.
Oh evil day! if I were sullen
While Earth herself is adorning,
This sweet May-morning,
And the Children are culling
On every side,
In a thousand valleys far and wide,
Fresh flowers; while the sun shines warm,
And the Babe leaps up on his Mother's arm:—
I hear, I hear, with joy I hear!
—But there's a Tree, of many, one,
A single Field which I have looked upon,
Both of them speak of something that is gone:
The Pansy at my feet
Doth the same tale repeat:
Whither is fled the visionary gleam?
Where is it now, the glory and the dream?

V

Our birth is but a sleep and a forgetting:
The Soul that rises with us, our life's Star,
Hath had elsewhere its setting,
And cometh from afar:
Not in entire forgetfulness,
And not in utter nakedness,
But trailing clouds of glory do we come
From God, who is our home:
Heaven lies about us in our infancy!
Shades of the prison-house begin to close
Upon the growing Boy,
But He beholds the light, and whence it flows,
He sees it in his joy;
The Youth, who daily farther from the east
Must travel, still is Nature's Priest,
And by the vision splendid
Is on his way attended;
At length the Man perceives it die away,
And fade into the light of common day.

VI

Earth fills her lap with pleasures of her own;
Yearnings she hath in her own natural kind,

And, even with something of a Mother's mind,
And no unworthy aim,
The homely Nurse doth all she can
To make her Foster-child, her Inmate Man,
Forget the glories he hath known,
And that imperial palace whence he came.

VII

Behold the Child among his new-born blisses,
A six years' Darling of a pigmy size!
See, where 'mid work of his own hand he lies,
Fretted by sallies of his mother's kisses,
With light upon him from his father's eyes!
See, at his feet, some little plan or chart,
Some fragment from his dream of human life,
Shaped by himself with newly-learned art;
A wedding or a festival,
A mourning or a funeral;
And this hath now his heart,
And unto this he frames his song:
Then will he fit his tongue
To dialogues of business, love, or strife;
But it will not be long
Ere this be thrown aside,
And with new joy and pride
The little Actor cons another part;
Filling from time to time his " humorous stage " [79]
With all the Persons, down to palsied Age,
That Life brings with her in her equipage;
As if his whole vocation
Were endless imitation.

VIII

Thou, whose exterior semblance doth belie
Thy Soul's immensity;
Thou best Philosopher, who yet dost keep
Thy heritage, thou Eye among the blind,
That, deaf and silent, read'st the eternal deep,
Haunted for ever by the eternal mind, —
Mighty Prophet! Seer blest!
On whom those truths do rest,
Which we are toiling all our lives to find,
In darkness lost, the darkness of the grave;
Thou, over whom thy Immortality
Broods like the Day, a Master o'er a Slave,
A Presence which is not to be put by;
Thou little Child yet glorious in the might
Of heaven-born freedom on thy being's height,
Why with such earnest pains dost thou provoke
The years to bring the inevitable yoke,
Thus blindly with thy blessedness at strife?
Full soon thy Soul shall have her earthly freight,
And custom lie upon thee with a weight,
Heavy as frost, and deep almost as life!

IX

O joy! that in our embers
Is something that doth live,
That nature yet remembers
What was so fugitive!
The thought of our past years in me doth breed
Perpetual benediction: not indeed
For that which is most worthy to be blest;
Delight and liberty, the simple creed
Of Childhood, whether busy or at rest,
With new-fledged hope still fluttering in his breast: —
Not for these I raise
The song of thanks and praise;
But for those obstinate questionings
Of sense and outward things,
Fallings from us, vanishings;
Blank misgivings of a Creature
Moving about in worlds not realised,
High instincts before which our mortal Nature
Did tremble like a guilty Thing surprised:
But for those first affections,
Those shadowy recollections,
Which, be they what they may,
Are yet the fountain-light of all our day,
Are yet a master-light of all our seeing;

[79] See *As You Like It*, II, vii, 139–166, the speech of Jacques, beginning 'All the world's a stage.'

Uphold us, cherish, and have power to make
Our noisy years seem moments in the being
Of the eternal Silence: truths that wake,
To perish never:
Which neither listlessness, nor mad endeavour,
Nor Man nor Boy,
Nor all that is at enmity with joy,
Can utterly abolish or destroy!
Hence in a season of calm weather
Though inland far we be,
Our Souls have sight of that immortal sea
Which brought us hither,
Can in a moment travel thither,
And see the Children sport upon the shore,
And hear the mighty waters rolling evermore.

X

Then sing, ye Birds, sing, sing, a joyous song!
And let the young Lambs bound
As to the tabor's sound!
We in thought will join your throng,
Ye that pipe and ye that play,
Ye that through your hearts today
Feel the gladness of the May!
What though the radiance which was once so bright
Be now for ever taken from my sight,
Though nothing can bring back the hour
Of splendour in the grass, of glory in the flower;
We will grieve not, rather find
Strength in what remains behind;
In the primal sympathy
Which having been must ever be;
In the soothing thoughts that spring
Out of human suffering;
In the faith that looks through death,
In years that bring the philosophic mind.

XI

And O, ye Fountains, Meadows, Hills, and Groves,
Forebode not any severing of our loves!
Yet in my heart of hearts I feel your might;
I only have relinquished one delight
To live beneath your more habitual sway.
I love the Brooks which down their channels fret,
Even more than when I tripped lightly as they;
The innocent brightness of a new-born Day
Is lovely yet;
The Clouds that gather round the setting sun
Do take a sober colouring from an eye
That hath kept watch o'er man's mortality;
Another race hath been, and other palms are won.
Thanks to the human heart by which we live,
Thanks to its tenderness, its joys, and fears,
To me the meanest flower that blows can give
Thoughts that do often lie too deep for tears.

Laodamia [80]

'With sacrifice before the rising morn
Vows have I made by fruitless hope inspired;
And from the infernal Gods, 'mid shades forlorn
Of night, my slaughtered Lord have I required:
Celestial pity I again implore; —
Restore him to my sight — great Jove, restore!'

So speaking, and by fervent love endowed
With faith, the Suppliant heavenward lifts her hands;
While, like the sun emerging from a cloud,

---

[80] Written in 1814; published in *Poems*, 1815. 'The incident of the trees growing and withering [see ll. 169 f.] put the subject into my thoughts, and I wrote with the hope of giving it a loftier tone than, so far as I know, has been given to it by any of the Ancients who have treated of it. It cost me more trouble than almost anything of equal length I have ever written.' [Wordsworth.]

Her countenance brightens — and her eye expands;
Her bosom heaves and spreads, her stature grows;
And she expects the issue in repose.

O terror! what hath she perceived? — O joy!
What doth she look on? — whom doth she behold?
Her Hero slain upon the beach of Troy?
His vital presence? his corporeal mould?
It is — if sense deceive her not — 'tis He!
And a God leads him, wingéd Mercury!

Mild Hermes spake — and touched her with his wand
That calms all fear; 'Such grace hath crowned thy prayer,
Laodamía! that at Jove's command
Thy Husband walks the paths of upper air:
He comes to tarry with thee three hours' space;
Accept the gift, behold him face to face!'

Forth sprang the impassioned Queen her Lord to clasp;
Again that consummation she essayed;
But unsubstantial Form eludes her grasp
As often as that eager grasp was made.
The Phantom parts — but parts to re-unite,
And re-assume his place before her sight.

'Protesiláus, lo! thy guide is gone!
Confirm, I pray, the vision with thy voice:
This is our palace, — yonder is thy throne;
Speak, and the floor thou tread'st on will rejoice.
Not to appal me have the gods bestowed
This precious boon; and blest a sad abode.'

'Great Jove, Laodamía! doth not leave
His gifts imperfect: — Spectre though I be,
I am not sent to scare thee or deceive;
But in reward of thy fidelity.
And something also did my worth obtain;
For fearless virtue bringeth boundless gain.

'Thou knowest, the Delphic oracle foretold
That the first Greek who touched the Trojan strand
Should die; but me the threat could not withhold:
A generous cause a victim did demand;
And forth I leapt upon the sandy plain;
A self-devoted chief — by Hector slain.'

'Supreme of Heroes — bravest, noblest, best!
Thy matchless courage I bewail no more,
Which then, when tens of thousands were depressed
By doubt, propelled thee to the fatal shore;
Thou found'st — and I forgive thee — here thou art —
A nobler counsellor than my poor heart.

'But thou, though capable of sternest deed,
Wert kind as resolute, and good as brave;
And he, whose power restores thee, hath decreed
Thou shouldst elude the malice of the grave:
Redundant are thy locks, thy lips as fair
As when their breath enriched Thessalian air.

'No Spectre greets me, — no vain Shadow this;
Come, blooming Hero, place thee by my side!
Give, on this well-known couch, one nuptial kiss
To me, this day, a second time thy bride!'
Jove frowned in heaven: the conscious Parcæ threw
Upon those roseate lips a Stygian hue.

'This visage tells thee that my doom is past:
Nor should the change be mourned, even if the joys
Of sense were able to return as fast

And surely as they vanish. Earth destroys
Those raptures duly — Erebus disdains:
Calm pleasures there abide — majestic pains.

'Be taught, O faithful Consort, to control
Rebellious passion: for the Gods approve
The depth, and not the tumult, of the soul;
A fervent, not ungovernable, love.
Thy transports moderate; and meekly mourn
When I depart, for brief is my sojourn —'

'Ah wherefore? — Did not Hercules by force
Wrest from the guardian Monster of the tomb
Alcestis, a reanimated corse,
Given back to dwell on earth in vernal bloom?[81]
Medea's spells dispersed the weight of years,
And Æson stood a youth 'mid youthful peers.[82]

'The Gods to us are merciful — and they
Yet further may relent: for mightier far
Than strength of nerve and sinew, or the sway
Of magic potent over sun and star,
Is love, though oft to agony distrest,
And though his favourite seat be feeble woman's breast.

'But if thou goest, I follow —' 'Peace!' he said, —
She looked upon him and was calmed and cheered;
The ghastly colour from his lips had fled;
In his deportment, shape, and mien, appeared
Elysian beauty, melancholy grace,
Brought from a pensive though a happy place.

[81] As told in the *Alcestis* of Euripides.
[82] See Ovid, *Metamorphoses*, VII, 159–293.

He spake of love, such love as Spirits feel
In worlds whose course is equable and pure;
No fears to beat away — no strife to heal —
The past unsighed for, and the future sure;
Spake of heroic arts in graver mood
Revived, with finer harmony pursued;

Of all that is most beauteous — imaged there
In happier beauty; more pellucid streams,
An ampler ether, a diviner air,
And fields invested with purpureal gleams;
Climes which the sun, who sheds the brightest day
Earth knows, is all unworthy to survey.

Yet there the Soul shall enter which hath earned
That privilege by virtue. — 'Ill,' said he,
'The end of man's existence I discerned,
Who from ignoble games and revelry
Could draw, when we had parted, vain delight,
While tears were thy best pastime, day and night;

'And while my youthful peers before my eyes
(Each hero following his peculiar bent)
Prepared themselves for glorious enterprise
By martial sports, — or, seated in the tent,
Chieftains and kings in council were detained;
What time the fleet at Aulis[83] lay enchained.

'The wished-for wind was given: — I then revolved
The oracle, upon the silent sea;
And, if no worthier led the way, resolved
That, of a thousand vessels, mine should be

[83] The Greek fleet was becalmed there until Iphigenia, daughter of Agamemnon, was sacrificed to secure the favor of Artemis.

The foremost prow in pressing to the strand, —
Mine the first blood that tinged the Trojan sand.

'Yet bitter, oft-times bitter, was the pang
When of thy loss I thought, belovéd Wife!
On thee too fondly did my memory hang,
And on the joys we shared in mortal life, —
The paths which we had trod — these fountains, flowers;
My new-planned cities, and unfinished towers.

'But should suspense permit the Foe to cry,
"Behold they tremble! — haughty their array,
Yet of their number no one dares to die?"
In soul I swept the indignity away:
Old frailties then recurred: — but lofty thought,
In act embodied, my deliverance wrought.

'And Thou, though strong in love, art all too weak
In reason, in self-government too slow;
I counsel thee by fortitude to seek
Our blest re-union in the shades below.
The invisible world with thee hath sympathised;
Be thy affections raised and solemnised.

'Learn, by a mortal yearning, to ascend —
Seeking a higher object. Love was given,
Encouraged, sanctioned, chiefly for that end;
For this the passion to excess was driven —
That self might be annulled: her bondage prove
The fetters of a dream opposed to love.' —

Aloud she shrieked! for Hermes reappears!
Round the dear Shade she would have clung — 'tis vain:
The hours are past — too brief had they been years;
And him no mortal effort can detain:
Swift, toward the realms that know not earthly day,
He through the portal takes his silent way,
And on the palace-floor a lifeless corse She lay.

Thus, all in vain exhorted and reproved,
She perished; and, as for a wilful crime,
By the just Gods whom no weak pity moved,
Was doomed to wear out her appointed time,
Apart from happy Ghosts, that gather flowers
Of blissful quiet 'mid unfading bowers.

— Yet tears to human suffering are due;
And mortal hopes defeated and o'erthrown
Are mourned by man, and not by man alone,
As fondly he believes. — Upon the side
Of Hellespont (such faith was entertained)
A knot of spiry trees for ages grew
From out the tomb of him for whom she died;
And ever, when such stature they had gained
That Ilium's walls were subject to their view,
The trees' tall summits withered at the sight;
A constant interchange of growth and blight![84]

After-thought to 'The River Duddon'[85]

I THOUGHT of Thee, my partner and my guide,
As being past away. — Vain sympathies!
For, backward, Duddon! as I cast my eyes,
I see what was, and is, and will abide;

[84] For the account of these long-lived trees, see Pliny's 'Natural History,' lib. xvi. cap. 44 . . . [Wordsworth.]

[85] This is the final sonnet of a series, *The River Duddon*, published in 1820. Rising on the borders of Westmoreland, Cumberland, and Lancashire, the river flows southwest to the Irish Sea. Wordsworth knew the stream from boyhood.

Still glides the Stream, and shall for ever glide;
The Form remains, the Function never dies;
While we, the brave, the mighty, and the wise,
We Men, who in our morn of youth defied
The elements, must vanish;[86] — be it so!
Enough, if something from our hands have power
To live, and act, and serve the future hour;
And if, as toward the silent tomb we go,
Through love, through hope, and faith's transcendent dower,
We feel that we are greater than we know.

To a Skylark[87]

Ethereal minstrel! pilgrim of the sky!
Dost thou despise the earth where cares abound?
Or, while the wings aspire, are heart and eye
Both with thy nest upon the dewy ground?
Thy nest which thou canst drop into at will,
Those quivering wings composed, that music still!

Leave to the nightingale her shady wood;
A privacy of glorious light is thine;
Whence thou dost pour upon the world a flood
Of harmony, with instinct more divine;
Type of the wise who soar, but never roam;
True to the kindred points of Heaven and Home!

Inside of King's College Chapel, Cambridge[88]

Tax not the royal Saint with vain expense,
With ill-matched aims the Architect who planned —
Albeit labouring for a scanty band
Of white-robed Scholars only — this immense
And glorious Work of fine intelligence!
Give all thou canst; high Heaven rejects the lore
Of nicely-calculated less or more;
So deemed the man who fashioned for the sense
These lofty pillars, spread that branching roof
Self-poised, and scooped into ten thousand cells,
Where light and shade repose, where music dwells
Lingering — and wandering on as loth to die;
Like thoughts whose very sweetness yieldeth proof
That they were born for immortality.

Scorn not the Sonnet[89]

Scorn not the Sonnet; Critic, you have frowned,
Mindless of its just honours; with this key
Shakspeare unlocked his heart; the melody
Of this small lute gave ease to Petrarch's wound;
A thousand times this pipe did Tasso sound;
With it Camöens[90] soothed an exile's grief;
The Sonnet glittered a gay myrtle leaf
Amid the cypress with which Dante crowned
His visionary brow: a glow-worm lamp,
It cheered mild Spenser, called from Faery-land
To struggle through dark ways; and when a damp
Fell round the path of Milton, in his hand
The Thing became a trumpet; whence he blew
Soul-animating strains — alas, too few!

86 These lines were suggested by similar ones in the lament for Bion by Moschus.
87 Written in 1825; published in *Poems*, 1827.
88 Published in *Ecclesiastical Sketches*, 1822.
89 Published 1827.
90 A Portuguese poet (1524–1580).

Samuel Taylor Coleridge 1772–1834

THE RIME OF THE ANCIENT MARINER [1]

Part I

An ancient Mariner meeteth three Gallants bidden to a wedding-feast, and detaineth one.

It is an ancient Mariner,
And he stoppeth one of three.
'By thy long grey beard and glittering eye,
Now wherefore stopp'st thou me?

The Bridegroom's doors are opened wide,
And I am next of kin;
The guests are met, the feast is set:
May'st hear the merry din.'

He holds him with his skinny hand,
'There was a ship,' quoth he.
'Hold off! unhand me, grey-beard loon!'
Eftsoons [2] his hand dropt he.

The Wedding-Guest is spellbound by the eye of the old seafaring man, and constrained to hear his tale.

He holds him with his glittering eye—
The Wedding-Guest stood still,
And listens like a three years' child:
The Mariner hath his will.

The Wedding-Guest sat on a stone:
He cannot choose but hear;
And thus spake on that ancient man,
The bright-eyed Mariner.

'The ship was cheered, the harbour cleared,
Merrily did we drop
Below the kirk, below the hill,
Below the lighthouse top.

The Mariner tells how the ship sailed southward with a good wind and fair weather, till it reached the line.

The Sun came up upon the left,
Out of the sea came he!
And he shone bright, and on the right
Went down into the sea.

---

[1] Written 1797–1798; published in the first edition of the *Lyrical Ballads*, 1798. It was much altered for the second edition in 1800, chiefly in the removal of many archaic expressions. The marginal gloss, added in 1815–1816, was published in *Sibylline Leaves*, 1817, when Coleridge's name appeared with it. For Coleridge's description of the origins of the poem and his general scheme with Wordsworth, see *Biographia Literaria*, chapter XIV. The Reverend Alexander Dyce was authority for the following statement by Wordsworth: 'I had very little share in the composition of it [the poem], for I soon found that the style of Coleridge and myself would not assimilate. Besides the lines (in the fourth part):

"And thou art long, and lank, and brown,
As is the ribbed sea sand"—

I wrote the stanza in the first part [ll. 13–16] and four or five lines more in different parts of the poem which I could not now point out. The idea of "*shooting an albatross*" *was mine, for I had been reading Shelvocke's Voyages, which probably Coleridge never saw.* I also suggested the reanimation of the dead bodies, to work the ship.'

[2] straightway

Higher and higher every day,
Till over the mast at noon—'
The Wedding-Guest here beat his breast,
For he heard the loud bassoon.

The Wedding-Guest heareth the bridal music; but the Mariner continueth his tale.

The bride hath paced into the hall,
Red as a rose is she;
Nodding their heads before her goes
The merry minstrelsy.

The Wedding-Guest he beat his breast,
Yet he cannot choose but hear;
And thus spake on that ancient man,
The bright-eyed Mariner.

The ship driven by a storm toward the south pole.

'And now the STORM-BLAST came, and he
Was tyrannous and strong:
He struck with his o'ertaking wings,
And chased us south along.

With sloping masts and dipping prow,
As who pursued with yell and blow
Still treads the shadow of his foe,
And forward bends his head,
The ship drove fast, loud roared the blast,
And southward aye we fled.

And now there came both mist and snow,
And it grew wondrous cold:
And ice, mast-high, came floating by,
As green as emerald.

The land of ice, and of fearful sounds where no living thing was to be seen.

And through the drifts the snowy clifts
Did send a dismal sheen:
Nor shapes of men nor beasts we ken—
The ice was all between.

The ice was here, the ice was there,
The ice was all around:
It cracked and growled, and roared and howled,
Like noises in a swound!

Till a great sea-bird, called the Albatross, came through the snow-fog, and was received with great joy and hospitality.

At length did cross an Albatross,
Thorough the fog it came;
As if it had been a Christian soul,
We hailed it in God's name.

It ate the food it ne'er had eat,
And round and round it flew.

The ice did split with a thunder-fit;
The helmsman steered us through!

And lo! the Albatross proveth a bird of good omen, and followeth the ship as it returned northward through fog and floating ice.

And a good south wind sprung up behind;
The Albatross did follow,
And every day, for food or play,
Came to the mariners' hollo!

In mist or cloud, on mast or shroud,
It perched for vespers nine;
Whiles all the night, through fog-smoke white,
Glimmered the white Moon-shine.'

The ancient Mariner inhospitably killeth the pious bird of good omen.

'God save thee, ancient Mariner!
From the fiends, that plague thee thus!—
Why look'st thou so?'—With my cross-bow
I shot the ALBATROSS.

PART II

The Sun now rose upon the right:
Out of the sea came he,
Still hid in mist, and on the left
Went down into the sea.

And the good south wind still blew behind,
But no sweet bird did follow,
Nor any day for food or play
Came to the mariners' hollo!

His shipmates cry out against the ancient Mariner, for killing the bird of good luck.

And I had done a hellish thing,
And it would work 'em woe:
For all averred, I had killed the bird
That made the breeze to blow.
Ah wretch! said they, the bird to slay,
That made the breeze to blow!

But when the fog cleared off, they justify the same, and thus make themselves accomplices in the crime.

Nor dim nor red, like God's own head,
The glorious Sun uprist:
Then all averred, I had killed the bird
That brought the fog and mist.
'Twas right, said they, such birds to slay,
That bring the fog and mist.

The fair breeze continues; the ship enters the Pacific Ocean, and sails northward, even till it reaches the Line.

The fair breeze blew, the white foam flew,
The furrow followed free;
We were the first that ever burst
Into that silent sea.

The ship hath been suddenly becalmed.

Down dropt the breeze, the sails dropt down,
'Twas sad as sad could be;
And we did speak only to break
The silence of the sea!

All in a hot and copper sky,
The bloody Sun, at noon,
Right up above the mast did stand,
No bigger than the Moon.

Day after day, day after day,
We stuck, nor breath nor motion;
As idle as a painted ship
Upon a painted ocean.

And the Albatross begins to be avenged.

Water, water, every where,
And all the boards did shrink;
Water, water, every where,
Nor any drop to drink.

The very deep did rot: O Christ!
That ever this should be!
Yea, slimy things did crawl with legs
Upon the slimy sea.

About, about, in reel and rout
The death-fires danced at night;
The water, like a witch's oils,
Burnt green, and blue and white.

A Spirit had followed them; one of the invisible inhabitants of this planet, neither departed souls nor angels; concerning whom the learned Jew, Josephus, and the Platonic Constantinopolitan, Michael Psellus, may be consulted. They are very numerous, and there is no climate or element without one or more.

And some in dreams assuréd were
Of the Spirit that plagued us so;
Nine fathoms deep he had followed us
From the land of mist and snow.

And every tongue, through utter drought,
Was withered at the root;
We could not speak, no more than if
We had been choked with soot.

The shipmates, in their sore distress, would fain throw the whole guilt on the ancient Mariner: in sign whereof they hang the dead sea-bird round his neck.

Ah! well a-day! what evil looks
Had I from old and young!
Instead of the cross, the Albatross
About my neck was hung.

Part III

There passed a weary time. Each throat
Was parched, and glazed each eye.
A weary time! a weary time!
How glazed each weary eye,
When looking westward, I beheld
A something in the sky.

The ancient Mariner beholdeth a sign in the element afar off.

At first it seemed a little speck,
And then it seemed a mist;
It moved and moved, and took at last
A certain shape, I wist.[3]

A speck, a mist, a shape, I wist!
And still it neared and neared:
As if it dodged a water-sprite,
It plunged and tacked and veered.

At its nearer approach, it seemeth him to be a ship; and at a dear ransom he freeth his speech from the bonds of thirst.

With throats unslaked, with black lips baked,
We could nor laugh nor wail;
Through utter drought all dumb we stood!
I bit my arm, I sucked the blood,
And cried, A sail! a sail!

With throats unslaked, with black lips baked,
Agape they heard me call:
Gramercy! they for joy did grin,
And all at once their breath drew in,
As they were drinking all.

A flash of joy;

And horror follows. For can it be a ship that comes onward without wind or tide?

See! see! (I cried) she tacks no more!
Hither to work us weal;
Without a breeze, without a tide,
She steadies with upright keel!

The western wave was all a-flame.
The day was well nigh done!
Almost upon the western wave
Rested the broad bright Sun;
When that strange shape drove suddenly
Betwixt us and the Sun.

It seemeth him but the skeleton of a ship.

And straight the Sun was flecked with bars,
(Heaven's Mother send us grace!)
As if through a dungeon-grate he peered
With broad and burning face.

[3] believed, knew

And its ribs are seen as bars on the face of the setting Sun.

Alas! (thought I, and my heart beat loud)
How fast she nears and nears!
Are those *her* sails that glance in the Sun,
Like restless gossameres?

The Spectre-Woman and her Death-mate, and no other on board the skeleton ship.

Are those *her* ribs through which the Sun
Did peer, as through a grate?
And is that Woman all her crew?
Is that a DEATH? and are there two?
Is DEATH that woman's mate?

Like vessel, like crew!

Death and Life-in-Death have diced for the ship's crew, and she (the latter) winneth the ancient Mariner.

Her lips were red, *her* looks were free,
Her locks were yellow as gold:
Her skin was as white as leprosy,
The Night-mare LIFE-IN-DEATH was she,
Who thicks man's blood with cold.

The naked hulk alongside came,
And the twain were casting dice;
'The game is done! I've won! I've won!'
Quoth she, and whistles thrice.

No twilight within the courts of the Sun.

The Sun's rim dips; the stars rush out:
At one stride comes the dark;
With far-heard whisper, o'er the sea,
Off shot the spectre-bark.

At the rising of the Moon,

We listened and looked sideways up!
Fear at my heart, as at a cup,
My life-blood seemed to sip!
The stars were dim, and thick the night,
The steersman's face by his lamp gleamed white;
From the sails the dew did drip —
Till clomb above the eastern bar
The hornéd Moon, with one bright star
Within the nether tip.

One after another,

One after one, by the star-dogged Moon,
Too quick for groan or sigh,
Each turned his face with a ghastly pang,
And cursed me with his eye.

His shipmates drop down dead.

Four times fifty living men,
(And I heard nor sigh nor groan)
With heavy thump, a lifeless lump,
They dropped down one by one.

But Life-in-Death begins her work on the ancient Mariner.

The souls did from their bodies fly, —
They fled to bliss or woe!
And every soul, it passed me by,
Like the whizz of my cross-bow!

Part IV

The Wedding-Guest feareth that a Spirit is talking to him;

'I fear thee, ancient Mariner!
I fear thy skinny hand!
And thou art long, and lank, and brown,
As is the ribbed sea-sand.[4]

I fear thee and thy glittering eye,
And thy skinny hand, so brown.' —

But the ancient Mariner assureth him of his bodily life, and proceedeth to relate his horrible penance.

Fear not, fear not, thou Wedding-Guest!
This body dropt not down.

Alone, alone, all, all alone,
Alone on a wide wide sea!
And never a saint took pity on
My soul in agony.

He despiseth the creatures of the calm,

The many men, so beautiful!
And they all dead did lie:
And a thousand thousand slimy things
Lived on; and so did I.

And envieth that they should live, and so many lie dead.

I looked upon the rotting sea,
And drew my eyes away;
I looked upon the rotting deck,
And there the dead men lay.

I looked to heaven, and tried to pray;
But or ever a prayer had gusht,
A wicked whisper came, and made
My heart as dry as dust.

I closed my lids, and kept them close,
And the balls like pulses beat;
For the sky and the sea, and the sea and the sky
Lay like a load on my weary eye,
And the dead were at my feet.

But the curse liveth for him in the eye of the dead men.

The cold sweat melted from their limbs,
Nor rot nor reek did they:
The look with which they looked on me
Had never passed away.

[4] For the last two lines of this stanza, I am indebted to Mr. Wordsworth. It was on a delightful walk from Nether Stowey to Dulverton, with him and his sister, in the Autumn of 1797, that this Poem was planned, and in part composed. [Coleridge.]

An orphan's curse would drag to hell
A spirit from on high;
But oh! more horrible than that
Is the curse in a dead man's eye!
Seven days, seven nights, I saw that curse,
And yet I could not die.

In his loneliness and fixedness he yearneth towards the journeying Moon, and the stars that still sojourn, yet still move onward; and every where the blue sky belongs to them, and is their appointed rest, and their native country and their own natural homes, which they enter unannounced, as lords that are certainly expected and yet there is a silent joy at their arrival.

The moving Moon went up the sky,
And no where did abide:
Softly she was going up,
And a star or two beside —

Her beams bemocked the sultry main,
Like April hoar-frost spread;
But where the ship's huge shadow lay,
The charméd water burnt alway
A still and awful red.

By the light of the Moon he beholdeth God's creatures of the great calm.

Beyond the shadow of the ship,
I watched the water-snakes:
They moved in tracks of shining white,
And when they reared, the elfish light
Fell off in hoary flakes.

Within the shadow of the ship
I watched their rich attire:
Blue, glossy green, and velvet black,
They coiled and swam; and every track
Was a flash of golden fire.

Their beauty and their happiness.

O happy living things! no tongue
Their beauty might declare:
A spring of love gushed from my heart,

He blesseth them in his heart.

And I blessed them unaware:
Sure my kind saint took pity on me,
And I blessed them unaware.

The spell begins to break.

The self-same moment I could pray;
And from my neck so free
The Albatross fell off, and sank
Like lead into the sea.

Part V

Oh sleep! it is a gentle thing,
Beloved from pole to pole!
To Mary Queen the praise be given!
She sent the gentle sleep from Heaven,
That slid into my soul.

By grace of the holy Mother, the ancient Mariner is refreshed with rain.

The silly buckets on the deck,
That had so long remained,
I dreamt that they were filled with dew;
And when I awoke, it rained.

My lips were wet, my throat was cold,
My garments all were dank;
Sure I had drunken in my dreams,
And still my body drank.

I moved, and could not feel my limbs:
I was so light — almost
I thought that I had died in sleep,
And was a blesséd ghost.

He heareth sounds and seeth strange sights and commotions in the sky and the element.

And soon I heard a roaring wind:
It did not come anear;
But with its sound it shook the sails,
That were so thin and sere.

The upper air burst into life!
And a hundred fire-flags sheen,[5]
To and fro they were hurried about!
And to and fro, and in and out,
The wan stars danced between.

And the coming wind did roar more loud,
And the sails did sigh like sedge;
And the rain poured down from one black cloud;
The Moon was at its edge.

The thick black cloud was cleft, and still
The Moon was at its side:
Like waters shot from some high crag,
The lightning fell with never a jag,
A river steep and wide.

The bodies of the ship's crew are inspired [inspirited, S.L.] *and the ship moves on;*

The loud wind never reached the ship,
Yet now the ship moved on!
Beneath the lightning and the Moon
The dead men gave a groan.

They groaned, they stirred, they all uprose,
Nor spake, nor moved their eyes;
It had been strange, even in a dream,
To have seen those dead men rise.

[5] bright

The helmsman steered, the ship moved on;
Yet never a breeze up-blew;
The mariners all 'gan work the ropes,
Where they were wont to do;
They raised their limbs like lifeless tools—
We were a ghastly crew.

The body of my brother's son
Stood by me, knee to knee:
The body and I pulled at one rope,
But he said nought to me.[6]

But not by the souls of the men, nor by dæmons of earth or middle air, but by a blessed troop of angelic spirits, sent down by the invocation of the guardian saint.

'I fear thee, ancient Mariner!'
Be calm, thou Wedding-Guest!
'Twas not those souls that fled in pain,
Which to their corses came again,
But a troop of spirits blest:

For when it dawned—they dropped their arms,
And clustered round the mast;
Sweet sounds rose slowly through their mouths,
And from their bodies passed.

Around, around, flew each sweet sound,
Then darted to the Sun;
Slowly the sounds came back again,
Now mixed, now one by one.

Sometimes a-dropping from the sky
I heard the sky-lark sing;
Sometimes all little birds that are,
How they seemed to fill the sea and air
With their sweet jargoning!

And now 'twas like all instruments,
Now like a lonely flute;
And now it is an angel's song,
That makes the heavens be mute.

It ceased; yet still the sails made on
A pleasant noise till noon,
A noise like of a hidden brook
In the leafy month of June,
That to the sleeping woods all night
Singeth a quiet tune.

---

[6] After l. 344 there originally followed these two lines:
'And I quak'd to think of my own voice
How frightful it would be!'

Till noon we quietly sailed on,
Yet never a breeze did breathe:
Slowly and smoothly went the ship,
Moved onward from beneath.

The lonesome Spirit from the south-pole carries on the ship as far as the Line, in obedience to the angelic troop, but still requireth vengeance.

Under the keel nine fathom deep,
From the land of mist and snow,
The spirit slid: and it was he
That made the ship to go.
The sails at noon left off their tune,
And the ship stood still also.

The Sun, right up above the mast,
Had fixed her to the ocean:
But in a minute she 'gan stir,
With a short uneasy motion —
Backwards and forwards half her length
With a short uneasy motion.

Then like a pawing horse let go,
She made a sudden bound:
It flung the blood into my head,
And I fell down in a swound.

The Polar Spirit's fellow-dæmons, the invisible inhabitants of the element, take part in his wrong; and two of them relate, one to the other, that penance long and heavy for the ancient Mariner hath been accorded to the Polar Spirit, who returneth southward.

How long in that same fit I lay,
I have not to declare;
But ere my living life returned,
I heard and in my soul discerned
Two voices in the air.

'Is it he?' quoth one, 'Is this the man?
By him who died on cross,
With his cruel bow he laid full low
The harmless Albatross.

The spirit who bideth by himself
In the land of mist and snow,
He loved the bird that loved the man
Who shot him with his bow.'

The other was a softer voice,
As soft as honey-dew:
Quoth he, 'The man hath penance done,
And penance more will do.'

Part VI

FIRST VOICE

'But tell me, tell me! speak again,
Thy soft response renewing —
What makes that ship drive on so fast?
What is the ocean doing?'

SECOND VOICE

'Still as a slave before his lord,
The ocean hath no blast;
His great bright eye most silently
Up to the Moon is cast —

If he may know which way to go;
For she guides him smooth or grim.
See, brother, see! how graciously
She looketh down on him.'

FIRST VOICE

The Mariner hath been cast into a trance; for the angelic power causeth the vessel to drive northward faster than human life could endure.

'But why drives on that ship so fast,
Without or wave or wind?'

SECOND VOICE

'The air is cut away before,
And closes from behind.

Fly, brother, fly! more high, more high!
Or we shall be belated:
For slow and slow that ship will go,
When the Mariner's trance is abated.'

The supernatural motion is retarded; the Mariner awakes, and his penance begins anew.

I woke, and we were sailing on
As in a gentle weather:
'Twas night, calm night, the moon was high;
The dead men stood together.

All stood together on the deck,
For a charnel-dungeon fitter:
All fixed on me their stony eyes,
That in the Moon did glitter.

The pang, the curse, with which they died,
Had never passed away:
I could not draw my eyes from theirs,
Nor turn them up to pray.

The curse is finally expiated.

And now this spell was snapt: once more
I viewed the ocean green,
And looked far forth, yet little saw
Of what had else been seen —

Like one, that on a lonesome road
Doth walk in fear and dread,
And having once turned round walks on,

And turns no more his head;
Because he knows, a frightful fiend
Doth close behind him tread.

But soon there breathed a wind on me,
Nor sound nor motion made:
Its path was not upon the sea,
In ripple or in shade.

It raised my hair, it fanned my cheek
Like a meadow-gale of spring —
It mingled strangely with my fears,
Yet it felt like a welcoming.

Swiftly, swiftly flew the ship,
Yet she sailed softly too:
Sweetly, sweetly blew the breeze —
On me alone it blew.

And the ancient Mariner beholdeth his native country.

Oh! dream of joy! is this indeed
The light-house top I see?
Is this the hill? is this the kirk?
Is this mine own countree?

We drifted o'er the harbour-bar,
And I with sobs did pray —
O let me be awake, my God!
Or let me sleep alway.

The harbour-bay was clear as glass,
So smoothly it was strewn!
And on the bay the moonlight lay,
And the shadow of the Moon.

The rock shone bright, the kirk no less,
That stands above the rock:
The moonlight steeped in silentness
The steady weathercock.

The angelic spirits leave the dead bodies,

And the bay was white with silent light,
Till rising from the same,
Full many shapes, that shadows were,
In crimson colours came.

And appear in their own forms of light.

A little distance from the prow
Those crimson shadows were:
I turned my eyes upon the deck —
Oh, Christ! what saw I there!

Each corse lay flat, lifeless and flat,
And, by the holy rood!
A man all light, a seraph-man,
On every corse there stood.

This seraph-band, each waved his hand:
It was a heavenly sight!
They stood as signals to the land,
Each one a lovely light;

This seraph-band, each waved his hand,
No voice did they impart —
No voice; but oh! the silence sank
Like music on my heart.

But soon I heard the dash of oars,
I heard the Pilot's cheer;
My head was turned perforce away
And I saw a boat appear.

The Pilot and the Pilot's boy,
I heard them coming fast:
Dear Lord in Heaven! it was a joy
The dead men could not blast.

I saw a third — I heard his voice:
It is the Hermit good!
He singeth loud his godly hymns
That he makes in the wood.
He'll shrieve my soul, he'll wash away
The Albatross's blood.

Part VII

The Hermit of the Wood,

This Hermit good lives in that wood
Which slopes down to the sea.
How loudly his sweet voice he rears!
He loves to talk with marineres
That come from a far countree.

He kneels at morn, and noon, and eve —
He hath a cushion plump:
It is the moss that wholly hides
The rotted old oak-stump.

The skiff-boat neared: I heard them talk,
'Why, this is strange, I trow!
Where are those lights so many and fair,
That signal made but now?'

Approacheth the ship with wonder.

'Strange, by my faith!' the Hermit said—
'And they answered not our cheer!
The planks looked warped! and see those sails,
How thin they are and sere!
I never saw aught like to them,
Unless perchance it were

Brown skeletons of leaves that lag
My forest-brook along;
When the ivy-tod [7] is heavy with snow,
And the owlet whoops to the wolf below,
That eats the she-wolf's young.'

'Dear Lord! it hath a fiendish look—
(The Pilot made reply)
I am a-feared'—'Push on, push on!'
Said the Hermit cheerily.

The boat came closer to the ship,
But I nor spake nor stirred;
The boat came close beneath the ship,
And straight a sound was heard.

The ship suddenly sinketh.

Under the water it rumbled on,
Still louder and more dread:
It reached the ship, it split the bay;
The ship went down like lead.

The ancient Mariner is saved in the Pilot's boat.

Stunned by that loud and dreadful sound,
Which sky and ocean smote,
Like one that hath been seven days drowned
My body lay afloat;
But swift as dreams, myself I found
Within the Pilot's boat.

Upon the whirl, where sank the ship,
The boat spun round and round;
And all was still, save that the hill
Was telling of the sound.

I moved my lips—the Pilot shrieked
And fell down in a fit;
The holy Hermit raised his eyes,
And prayed where he did sit.

I took the oars: the Pilot's boy,
Who now doth crazy go,
Laughed loud and long, and all the while

[7] ivy-bush

His eyes went to and fro.
'Ha! ha!' quoth he, 'full plain I see,
The Devil knows how to row.'

And now, all in my own countree,
I stood on the firm land!
The Hermit stepped forth from the boat,
And scarcely he could stand.

The ancient Mariner earnestly entreateth the Hermit to shrieve him; and the penance of life falls on him.

'O shrieve me, shrieve me, holy man!'
The Hermit crossed his brow.
'Say quick,' quoth he, 'I bid thee say —
What manner of man art thou?'

Forthwith this frame of mine was wrenched
With a woful agony,
Which forced me to begin my tale;
And then it left me free.

And ever and anon through out his future life an agony constraineth him to travel from land to land;

Since then, at an uncertain hour,
That agony returns:
And till my ghastly tale is told,
This heart within me burns.

I pass, like night, from land to land;
I have strange power of speech;
That moment that his face I see,
I know the man that must hear me:
To him my tale I teach.

What loud uproar bursts from that door!
The wedding-guests are there:
But in the garden-bower the bride
And bride-maids singing are:
And hark the little vesper bell,
Which biddeth me to prayer!

O Wedding-Guest! this soul hath been
Alone on a wide wide sea:
So lonely 'twas, that God himself
Scarce seemèd there to be.

O sweeter than the marriage-feast,
'Tis sweeter far to me,
To walk together to the kirk
With a goodly company! —

To walk together to the kirk,
And all together pray,

While each to his great Father bends,
Old men, and babes, and loving friends
And youths and maidens gay!

And to teach, by his own example, love and reverence to all things that God made and loveth.

Farewell, farewell! but this I tell
To thee, thou Wedding-Guest!
He prayeth well, who loveth well
Both man and bird and beast.

He prayeth best, who loveth best
All things both great and small;
For the dear God who loveth us,
He made and loveth all.

The Mariner, whose eye is bright,
Whose beard with age is hoar,
Is gone: and now the Wedding-Guest
Turned from the bridegroom's door.

He went like one that hath been stunned,
And is of sense forlorn:
A sadder and a wiser man,
He rose the morrow morn.[8]

CHRISTABEL [9]

Part I

'Tis the middle of night by the castle clock,
And the owls have awakened the crowing cock;
Tu — whit! —— Tu — whoo!
And hark, again! the crowing cock,
How drowsily it crew.

Sir Leoline, the Baron rich,
Hath a toothless mastiff bitch;
From her kennel beneath the rock
She maketh answer to the clock,
Four for the quarters, and twelve for the hour;
Ever and aye, by shine and shower,
Sixteen short howls, not over loud;
Some say, she sees my lady's shroud.

[8] In his *Table Talk*, 31 May 1830, Coleridge has: 'Mrs. Barbauld once told me that she admired the Ancient Mariner very much, but that there were two faults in it, it was improbable, and had no moral. As for the probability, I owned that that might admit some question; but as to the want of a moral, I told her that in my own judgment the poem had too much; and that the only, or chief fault, if I might say so, was the obtrusion of the moral sentiment so openly on the reader as a principle or cause of action in a work of such pure imagination. It ought to have had no more moral than the Arabian Night's tale of the merchant's sitting down to eat dates by the side of a well, and throwing the shells aside, and lo! a genie starts up, and says he *must* kill the aforesaid merchant, *because* one of the date shells had, it seems, put out the eye of the genie's son.'

Professor John Livingston Lowes, whose remarkable book *The Road to Xanadu* is the manifest destiny of any good reader of Coleridge, thinks Charles Lamb, in a letter to Wordsworth, has given the touchstone of *The Ancient Mariner:* 'For me, I was never so affected with any human tale. After first reading it, I was totally possessed with it for many days — I dislike all the miraculous part of it, but the feelings of the man under the operation of such scenery dragged me along like Tom Piper's magic whistle.'

[9] The first part was written in 1797, the second in 1800. The conclusion to the second part was done probably in 1801. First published, with *Kubla Khan* and *The Pains of Sleep*, in 1816. Coleridge wrote to De Quincey that the fragment would not have been published but for the distress of the Morgans, with whom he was living at the time. He received £80 for the poem.

The original Preface reads in part: 'Since the latter date [1800], my poetic powers have been, till very lately, in a state of suspended animation. But as, in my very first conception of the tale, I had the whole present to my mind, with the wholeness, no less than the liveliness of a vision; I trust that I shall be able to embody in verse the three parts yet to come, in the course of the present year . . . I have only to add that the metre of Christabel is not, properly speaking, irregular, though it may seem so from its being founded on a new principle: namely, that of counting in each line the accents, not the syllables. Though the latter may vary from seven to twelve, yet in each line the accents will be found to be only four. Nevertheless, this occasional variation in number of syllables is not introduced wantonly, or for the mere ends of convenience, but in correspondence with some transition in the nature of the imagery or passion.'

Is the night chilly and dark?
The night is chilly, but not dark.
The thin gray cloud is spread on high,
It covers but not hides the sky.
The moon is behind, and at the full;
And yet she looks both small and dull.
The night is chill, the cloud is gray:
'Tis a month before the month of May,
And the Spring comes slowly up this way.

The lovely lady, Christabel,
Whom her father loves so well,
What makes her in the wood so late,
A furlong from the castle gate?
She had dreams all yesternight
Of her own betrothéd knight;
And she in the midnight wood will pray
For the weal of her lover that's far away.

She stole along, she nothing spoke,
The sighs she heaved were soft and low,
And naught was green upon the oak
But moss and rarest mistletoe:
She kneels beneath the huge oak tree,
And in silence prayeth she.

The lady sprang up suddenly,
The lovely lady, Christabel!
It moaned as near, as near can be,
But what it is she cannot tell.—
On the other side it seems to be,
Of the huge, broad-breasted, old oak tree.

The night is chill; the forest bare;
Is it the wind that moaneth bleak?
There is not wind enough in the air
To move away the ringlet curl
From the lovely lady's cheek—
There is not wind enough to twirl
The one red leaf, the last of its clan,
That dances as often as dance it can,
Hanging so light, and hanging so high,
On the topmost twig that looks up at the sky.

Hush, beating heart of Christabel!
Jesu, Maria, shield her well!
She folded her arms beneath her cloak,
And stole to the other side of the oak.
What sees she there?

There she sees a damsel bright,
Drest in a silken robe of white,
That shadowy in the moonlight shone:
The neck that made that white robe wan,
Her stately neck, and arms were bare;
Her blue-veined feet unsandal'd were,
And wildly glittered here and there
The gems entangled in her hair.
I guess, 'twas frightful there to see
A lady so richly clad as she—
Beautiful exceedingly!

Mary mother, save me now!
(Said Christabel,) And who art thou?

The lady strange made answer meet,
And her voice was faint and sweet:—
Have pity on my sore distress,
I scarce can speak for weariness:
Stretch forth thy hand, and have no fear!
Said Christabel, How camest thou here?
And the lady, whose voice was faint and sweet,
Did thus pursue her answer meet:—

My sire is of a noble line,
And my name is Geraldine:
Five warriors seized me yestermorn,
Me, even me, a maid forlorn:
They choked my cries with force and fright,
And tied me on a palfrey white.
The palfrey was as fleet as wind,
And they rode furiously behind.
They spurred amain, their steeds were white:
And once we crossed the shade of night.
As sure as Heaven shall rescue me,
I have no thought what men they be;
Nor do I know how long it is
(For I have lain entranced I wis)
Since one, the tallest of the five,
Took me from the palfrey's back,
A weary woman, scarce alive.
Some muttered words his comrades spoke:
He placed me underneath this oak;
He swore they would return with haste:
Whither they went I cannot tell—
I thought I heard, some minutes past,

Sounds as of a castle bell.
Stretch forth thy hand (thus ended she),
And help a wretched maid to flee.

Then Christabel stretched forth her hand,
And comforted fair Geraldine:
O well, bright dame! may you command
The service of Sir Leoline;
And gladly our stout chivalry
Will he send forth and friends withal
To guide and guard you safe and free
Home to your noble father's hall.

She rose: and forth with steps they passed
That strove to be, and were not, fast.
Her gracious stars the lady blest,
And thus spake on sweet Christabel:
All our household are at rest,
The hall as silent as the cell;
Sir Leoline is weak in health,
And may not well awakened be,
But we will move as if in stealth,
And I beseech your courtesy,
This night, to share your couch with me.

They crossed the moat, and Christabel
Took the key that fitted well;
A little door she opened straight,
All in the middle of the gate;
The gate that was ironed within and without,
Where an army in battle array had marched out.
The lady sank, belike through pain,
And Christabel with might and main
Lifted her up, a weary weight,
Over the threshold of the gate: [10]
Then the lady rose again,
And moved, as she were not in pain.

So free from danger, free from fear,
They crossed the court: right glad they were.
And Christabel devoutly cried
To the lady by her side,
Praise we the Virgin all divine
Who hath rescued thee from thy distress!
Alas, alas! said Geraldine,
I cannot speak for weariness.
So free from danger, free from fear,
They crossed the court: right glad they were.

Outside her kennel, the mastiff old
Lay fast asleep, in moonshine cold.
The mastiff old did not awake,
Yet she an angry moan did make!
And what can ail the mastiff bitch?
Never till now she uttered yell
Beneath the eye of Christabel.
Perhaps it is the owlet's scritch:
For what can ail the mastiff bitch?

They passed the hall, that echoes still,
Pass as lightly as you will!
The brands were flat, the brands were dying,
Amid their own white ashes lying;
And when the lady passed, there came
A tongue of light, a fit of flame;
And Christabel saw the lady's eye,
And nothing else saw she thereby,
Save the boss of the shield of Sir Leoline tall,
Which hung in a murky old niche in the wall.
O softly tread, said Christabel,
My father seldom sleepeth well.

Sweet Christabel her feet doth bare,
And jealous of the listening air
They steal their way from stair to stair,
Now in glimmer, and now in gloom,
And now they pass the Baron's room,
As still as death, with stifled breath!
And now have reached her chamber door;
And now doth Geraldine press down
The rushes of the chamber floor.

The moon shines dim in the open air,
And not a moonbeam enters here.
But they without its light can see
The chamber carved so curiously,
Carved with figures strange and sweet,

[10] For the first time we have the clue to Geraldine, for the threshold had been blessed to keep evil spirits away. Note also the details that follow: her unwillingness to praise the Virgin, and the premonition of the dog and even of the fire that an evil spirit is near.

All made out of the carver's brain,
For a lady's chamber meet:
The lamp with twofold silver chain
Is fastened to an angel's feet.

The silver lamp burns dead and dim;
But Christabel the lamp will trim.
She trimmed the lamp, and made it bright,
And left it swinging to and fro,
While Geraldine, in wretched plight,
Sank down upon the floor below.

O weary lady, Geraldine,
I pray you, drink this cordial wine!
It is a wine of virtuous powers;
My mother made it of wild flowers.

And will your mother pity me,
Who am a maiden most forlorn?
Christabel answered — Woe is me!
She died the hour that I was born.
I have heard the grey-haired friar tell
How on her death-bed she did say,
That she should hear the castle-bell
Strike twelve upon my wedding-day.
O mother dear! that thou wert here!
I would, said Geraldine, she were!

But soon with altered voice, said she —
'Off, wandering mother! Peak and pine!
I have power to bid thee flee.'
Alas! what ails poor Geraldine?
Why stares she with unsettled eye?
Can she the bodiless dead espy?
And why with hollow voice cries she,
'Off, woman, off! this hour is mine —
Though thou her guardian spirit be,
Off, woman, off! 'tis given to me.'

Then Christabel knelt by the lady's side,
And raised to heaven her eyes so blue —
Alas! said she, this ghastly ride —
Dear lady! it hath wildered you!
The lady wiped her moist cold brow,
And faintly said, 'tis over now!'

Again the wild-flower wine she drank:
Her fair large eyes 'gan glitter bright,
And from the floor whereon she sank,
The lofty lady stood upright:
She was most beautiful to see
Like a lady of a far countrée.

And thus the lofty lady spake —
'All they who live in the upper sky,
Do love you, holy Christabel!
And you love them, and for their sake
And for the good which me befel,
Even I in my degree will try,
Fair maiden, to requite you well.
But now unrobe yourself; for I
Must pray, ere yet in bed I lie.'

Quoth Christabel, So let it be!
And as the lady bade, did she.
Her gentle limbs did she undress,
And lay down in her loveliness.

But through her brain of weal and woe
So many thoughts moved to and fro,
That vain it were her lids to close;
So half-way from the bed she rose,
And on her elbow did recline
To look at the lady Geraldine.

Beneath the lamp the lady bowed,
And slowly rolled her eyes around;
Then drawing in her breath aloud,
Like one that shuddered, she unbound
The cincture from beneath her breast:
Her silken robe, and inner vest,
Dropt to her feet, and full in view,
Behold! her bosom and half her side ——
A sight to dream of, not to tell!
O shield her! shield sweet Christabel!

Yet Geraldine nor speaks nor stirs;
Ah! what a stricken look was hers!
Deep from within she seems half-way
To lift some weight with sick assay,
And eyes the maid and seeks delay;
Then suddenly, as one defied,
Collects herself in scorn and pride,
And lay down by the Maiden's side! —
And in her arms the maid she took,
Ah wel-a-day!
And with low voice and doleful look
These words did say:

'In the touch of this bosom there worketh a spell,
Which is lord of thy utterance, Christabel!
Thou knowest to-night, and wilt know to-morrow,
This mark of my shame, this seal of my sorrow;
But vainly thou warrest,
For this is alone in
Thy power to declare,
That in the dim forest
Thou heard'st a low moaning,
And found'st a bright lady, surpassingly fair;
And didst bring her home with thee in love and in charity,
To shield her and shelter her from the damp air.'

The Conclusion to Part I

It was a lovely sight to see
The lady Christabel, when she
Was praying at the old oak tree.
Amid the jaggéd shadows
Of mossy leafless boughs,
Kneeling in the moonlight,
To make her gentle vows;
Her slender palms together prest,
Heaving sometimes on her breast;
Her face resigned to bliss or bale —
Her face, oh call it fair not pale,
And both blue eyes more bright than clear,
Each about to have a tear.

With open eyes (ah woe is me!)
Asleep, and dreaming fearfully,
Fearfully dreaming, yet, I wis,[11]
Dreaming that alone, which is —
O sorrow and shame! Can this be she,
The lady, who knelt at the old oak tree?
And lo! the worker of these harms,
That holds the maiden in her arms,
Seems to slumber still and mild,
As a mother with her child.

A star hath set, a star hath risen,
O Geraldine! since arms of thine
Have been the lovely lady's prison.
O Geraldine! one hour was thine —
Thou'st had thy will! By tairn [12] and rill,
The night-birds all that hour were still.
But now they are jubilant anew,
From cliff and tower, tu — whoo! tu — whoo!
Tu — whoo! tu — whoo! from wood and fell!

And see! the lady Christabel
Gathers herself from out her trance;
Her limbs relax, her countenance
Grows sad and soft; the smooth thin lids
Close o'er her eyes; and tears she sheds —
Large tears that leave the lashes bright!
And oft the while she seems to smile
As infants at a sudden light!

Yea, she doth smile, and she doth weep,
Like a youthful hermitess,
Beauteous in a wilderness,
Who, praying always, prays in sleep.
And, if she move unquietly,
Perchance, 'tis but the blood so free
Comes back and tingles in her feet.
No doubt, she hath a vision sweet.
What if her guardian spirit 'twere,
What if she knew her mother near?
But this she knows, in joys and woes,
That saints will aid if men will call:
For the blue sky bends over all!

Part II

Each matin bell, the Baron saith,
Knells us back to a world of death.
These words Sir Leoline first said,
When he rose and found his lady dead:
These words Sir Leoline will say
Many a morn to his dying day!

And hence the custom and law began
That still at dawn the sacristan,
Who duly pulls the heavy bell,
Five and forty beads must tell
Between each stroke — a warning knell,

[11] think

[12] tarn, or mountain pool

Which not a soul can choose but hear
From Bratha Head [13] to Wyndermere.

Saith Bracy the bard, So let it knell!
And let the drowsy sacristan
Still count as slowly as he can!
There is no lack of such, I ween,
As well fill up the space between.
In Langdale Pike and Witch's Lair,
And Dungeon-ghyll so foully rent,
With ropes of rock and bells of air
Three sinful sextons' ghosts are pent,
Who all give back, one after t'other,
The death-note to their living brother;
And oft too, by the knell offended,
Just as their one! two! three! is ended,
The devil mocks the doleful tale
With a merry peal from Borodale.

The air is still! through mist and cloud
That merry peal comes ringing loud;
And Geraldine shakes off her dread,
And rises lightly from the bed;
Puts on her silken vestments white,
And tricks her hair in lovely plight,
And nothing doubting of her spell
Awakens the lady Christabel.
'Sleep you, sweet lady Christabel?
I trust that you have rested well.'

And Christabel awoke and spied
The same who lay down by her side —
O rather say, the same whom she
Raised up beneath the old oak tree!
Nay, fairer yet! and yet more fair!
For she belike hath drunken deep
Of all the blessedness of sleep!
And while she spake, her looks, her air
Such gentle thankfulness declare,
That (so it seemed) her girded vests
Grew tight beneath her heaving breasts.
'Sure I have sinn'd!' said Christabel,
'Now heaven be praised if all be well!'
And in low faltering tones, yet sweet,
Did she the lofty lady greet
With such perplexity of mind
As dreams too lively leave behind.

So quickly she rose, and quickly arrayed
Her maiden limbs, and having prayed
That He, who on the cross did groan,
Might wash away her sins unknown,
She forthwith led fair Geraldine
To meet her sire, Sir Leoline.

The lovely maid and the lady tall
Are pacing both into the hall,
And pacing on through page and groom,
Enter the Baron's presence-room.

The Baron rose, and while he prest
His gentle daughter to his breast,
With cheerful wonder in his eyes
The lady Geraldine espies,
And gave such welcome to the same,
As might beseem so bright a dame!

But when he heard the lady's tale,
And when she told her father's name,
Why waxed Sir Leoline so pale,
Murmuring o'er the name again,
Lord Roland de Vaux of Tryermaine?

Alas! they had been friends in youth;
But whispering tongues can poison truth;
And constancy lives in realms above;
And life is thorny; and youth is vain;
And to be wroth with one we love
Doth work like madness in the brain.
And thus it chanced, as I divine,
With Roland and Sir Leoline.
Each spake words of high disdain
And insult to his heart's best brother:
They parted — ne'er to meet again!
But never either found another
To free the hollow heart from paining —
They stood aloof, the scars remaining,
Like cliffs which had been rent asunder;
A dreary sea now flows between; —
But neither heat, nor frost, nor thunder,
Shall wholly do away, I ween,
The marks of that which once hath been.[14]

Sir Leoline, a moment's space,
Stood gazing on the damsel's face:

[13] The Brathay River flows into Lake Windermere. These and the following details are of the Lake district.

[14] Coleridge thought that these lines were 'the best and sweetest passage' he ever wrote. They have been thought to refer to his temporary quarrel with Southey.

And the youthful Lord of Tryermaine
Came back upon his heart again.

O then the Baron forgot his age,
His noble heart swelled high with rage;
He swore by the wounds in Jesu's side
He would proclaim it far and wide,
With trump and solemn heraldry,
That they, who thus had wronged the dame,
Were base as spotted infamy!
'And if they dare deny the same,
My herald shall appoint a week,
And let the recreant traitors seek
My tourney court — that there and then
I may dislodge their reptile souls
From the bodies and forms of men!'
He spake: his eye in lightning rolls!
For the lady was ruthlessly seized; and he kenned
In the beautiful lady the child of his friend!

And now the tears were on his face,
And fondly in his arms he took
Fair Geraldine, who met the embrace,
Prolonging it with joyous look.
Which when she viewed, a vision fell
Upon the soul of Christabel,
The vision of fear, the touch and pain!
She shrunk and shuddered, and saw again —
(Ah, woe is me! Was it for thee,
Thou gentle maid! such sights to see?)

Again she saw that bosom old,
Again she felt that bosom cold,
And drew in her breath with a hissing sound:
Whereat the Knight turned wildly round,
And nothing saw, but his own sweet maid
With eyes upraised, as one that prayed.

The touch, the sight, had passed away,
And in its stead that vision blest,
Which comforted her after-rest
While in the lady's arms she lay,
Had put a rapture in her breast,
And on her lips and o'er her eyes
Spread smiles like light!
With new surprise,
'What ails then my belovéd child?'
The Baron said — His daughter mild
Made answer, 'All will yet be well!'
I ween, she had no power to tell
Aught else: so mighty was the spell.

Yet he, who saw this Geraldine,
Had deemed her sure a thing divine:
Such sorrow with such grace she blended,
As if she feared she had offended
Sweet Christabel, that gentle maid!
And with such lowly tones she pray'd
She might be sent without delay
Home to her father's mansion.
'Nay!
Nay, by my soul!' said Leoline.
'Ho! Bracy the bard, the charge be thine!
Go thou, with music sweet and loud,
And take two steeds with trappings proud,
And take the youth whom thou lov'st best
To bear thy harp, and learn thy song,
And clothe you both in solemn vest,
And over the mountains haste along,
Lest wandering folk, that are abroad,
Detain you on the valley road.

'And when he has crossed the Irthing flood,
My merry bard! he hastes, he hastes
Up Knorren Moor, through Halegarth Wood,
And reaches soon that castle good
Which stands and threatens Scotland's wastes.

'Bard Bracy! bard Bracy! your horses are fleet,
Ye must ride up the hall, your music so sweet,
More loud than your horses' echoing feet!
And loud and loud to Lord Roland call,
Thy daughter is safe in Langdale hall!
Thy beautiful daughter is safe and free —
Sir Leoline greets thee thus through me!
He bids thee come without delay
With all thy numerous array

And take thy lovely daughter home:
And he will meet thee on the way
With all his numerous array
White with their panting palfreys' foam:
And, by mine honour! I will say,
That I repent me of the day
When I spake words of fierce disdain
To Roland de Vaux of Tryermaine! —
— For since that evil hour hath flown,
Many a summer's sun hath shone;
Yet ne'er found I a friend again
Like Roland de Vaux of Tryermaine.

The lady fell, and clasped his knees,
Her face upraised, her eyes o'erflowing;
And Bracy replied, with faltering voice,
His gracious Hail on all bestowing! —
'Thy words, thou sire of Christabel,
Are sweeter than my harp can tell;
Yet might I gain a boon of thee,
This day my journey should not be,
So strange a dream hath come to me,
That I had vowed with music loud
To clear yon wood from thing unblest,
Warned by a vision in my rest!
For in my sleep I saw that dove,
That gentle bird, whom thou dost love,
And call'st by thy own daughter's name —
Sir Leoline! I saw the same
Fluttering, and uttering fearful moan,
Among the green herbs in the forest alone.
Which when I saw and when I heard,
I wonder'd what might ail the bird;
For nothing near it could I see,
Save the grass and green herbs underneath the old tree.

'And in my dream methought I went
To search out what might there be found;
And what the sweet bird's trouble meant,
That thus lay fluttering on the ground.
I went and peered, and could descry
No cause for her distressful cry;
But yet for her dear lady's sake
I stooped, methought, the dove to take,
When lo! I saw a bright green snake
Coiled around its wings and neck.
Green as the herbs on which it couched,
Close by the dove's its head it crouched;
And with the dove it heaves and stirs,
Swelling its neck as she swelled hers!
I woke; it was the midnight hour,
The clock was echoing in the tower;
But though my slumber was gone by,
This dream it would not pass away —
It seems to live upon my eye!
And thence I vowed this self-same day
With music strong and saintly song
To wander through the forest bare,
Lest aught unholy loiter there.'

Thus Bracy said: the Baron, the while,
Half-listening heard him with a smile;
Then turned to Lady Geraldine,
His eyes made up of wonder and love;
And said in courtly accents fine,
'Sweet maid, Lord Roland's beauteous dove,
With arms more strong than harp or song,
Thy sire and I will crush the snake!'
He kissed her forehead as he spake,
And Geraldine in maiden wise
Casting down her large bright eyes,
With blushing cheek and courtesy fine
She turned her from Sir Leoline;
Softly gathering up her train,
That o'er her right arm fell again;
And folded her arms across her chest,
And couched her head upon her breast,
And looked askance at Christabel ——
Jesu, Maria, shield her well!

A snake's small eye blinks dull and shy;
And the lady's eyes they shrunk in her head,
Each shrunk up to a serpent's eye,
And with somewhat of malice, and more of dread,
At Christabel she looked askance! —
One moment — and the sight was fled!
But Christabel in dizzy trance
Stumbling on the unsteady ground
Shuddered aloud, with a hissing sound;
And Geraldine again turned round,
And like a thing, that sought relief,
Full of wonder and full of grief,

She rolled her large bright eyes divine
Wildly on Sir Leoline.

The maid, alas! her thoughts are gone,
She nothing sees — no sight but one!
The maid, devoid of guile and sin,
I know not how, in fearful wise,
So deeply had she drunken in
That look, those shrunken serpent eyes,
That all her features were resigned
To this sole image in her mind:
And passively did imitate
That look of dull and treacherous hate!
And thus she stood, in dizzy trance,
Still picturing that look askance
With forced unconscious sympathy
Full before her father's view ——
As far as such a look could be
In eyes so innocent and blue!

And when the trance was o'er, the maid
Paused awhile, and inly prayed:
Then falling at the Baron's feet,
'By my mother's soul do I entreat
That thou this woman send away!'
She said: and more she could not say:
For what she knew she could not tell,
O'er-mastered by the mighty spell.

Why is thy cheek so wan and wild,
Sir Leoline? Thy only child
Lies at thy feet, thy joy, thy pride,
So fair, so innocent, so mild;
The same, for whom thy lady died!
O by the pangs of her dear mother
Think thou no evil of thy child!
For her, and thee, and for no other,
She prayed the moment ere she died:
Prayed that the babe for whom she died,
Might prove her dear lord's joy and pride!
That prayer her deadly pangs beguiled,
Sir Leoline!
And wouldst thou wrong thy only child,
Her child and thine?

Within the Baron's heart and brain
If thoughts, like these, had any share,
They only swelled his rage and pain,
And did but work confusion there.
His heart was cleft with pain and rage,
His cheeks they quivered, his eyes were wild,
Dishonoured thus in his old age;
Dishonoured by his only child,
And all his hospitality
To the wronged daughter of his friend
By more than woman's jealousy
Brought thus to a disgraceful end —
He rolled his eye with stern regard
Upon the gentle minstrel bard,
And said in tones abrupt, austere —
'Why, Bracy! dost thou loiter here?
I bade thee hence!' The bard obeyed;
And turning from his own sweet maid,
The agéd knight, Sir Leoline,
Led forth the lady Geraldine!

1800

The Conclusion to Part II [15]

A little child, a limber elf,
Singing, dancing to itself,
A fairy thing with red round cheeks,
That always finds, and never seeks,
Makes such a vision to the sight
As fills a father's eyes with light;

[15] The lines were sent to Southey in a letter of 6 May 1801. Coleridge never finished the poem, giving as his reason the fear that he could not properly execute the subtle and difficult idea. James Gillman, who cared for Coleridge during the latter years, tells of a conclusion which the poet used to outline for his friends: 'The following relation was to have occupied a third and fourth canto, and to have closed the tale. Over the mountains, the Bard, as directed by Sir Leoline, hastes with his disciple; but in consequence of one of those inundations supposed to be common to this country, the spot only where the castle once stood is discovered — the edifice itself being washed away. He determines to return. Geraldine, being acquainted with all that is passing, like the weird sisters in *Macbeth*, vanishes. Reappearing, however, she waits the return of the Bard, exerting in the meantime, by her wily arts, all the anger she could rouse in the Baron's breast, as well as that jealousy of which he is described to have been susceptible. The old Bard and the youth at length arrive, and therefore she can no longer personate the character of Geraldine, the daughter of Lord Roland de Vaux, but changes her appearance to that of the accepted though absent lover of Christabel. Next ensues a courtship most distressing to Christabel, who feels, she knows not why, great disgust for her once favoured knight. This coldness is very painful to the Baron, who has no more conception than herself of the supernatural transformation. She at last yields to her father's entreaties, and consents to approach the altar with this hated suitor. The real lover, returning, enters at this moment, and produces the ring which she had once given him in sign of her betrothment. Thus defeated, the supernatural being Geraldine disappears. As predicted, the castle bell tolls, the mother's voice is heard, and, to the exceeding great joy of the parties, the rightful marriage takes place, after which follows a reconciliation and explanation between the father and daughter.'

And pleasures flow in so thick and fast
Upon his heart, that he at last
Must needs express his love's excess
With words of unmeant bitterness.
Perhaps 'tis pretty to force together
Thoughts so all unlike each other;
To mutter and mock a broken charm,
To dally with wrong that does no harm.
Perhaps 'tis tender too and pretty
At each wild word to feel within
A sweet recoil of love and pity.
And what, if in a world of sin
(O sorrow and shame should this be true!)
Such giddiness of heart and brain
Comes seldom save from rage and pain,
So talks as it's most used to do.

Kubla Khan[16]

In Xanadu did Kubla Khan
A stately pleasure-dome decree:
Where Alph, the sacred river, ran
Through caverns measureless to man
Down to a sunless sea.
So twice five miles of fertile ground
With walls and towers were girdled round:
And there were gardens bright with sinuous rills,
Where blossomed many an incense-bearing tree;
And here were forests ancient as the hills,
Enfolding sunny spots of greenery.

But oh! that deep romantic chasm which slanted
Down the green hill athwart a cedarn cover!
A savage place! as holy and enchanted
As e'er beneath a waning moon was haunted
By woman wailing for her demon-lover!
And from this chasm, with ceaseless turmoil seething,
As if this earth in fast thick pants were breathing,
A mighty fountain momently was forced:
Amid whose swift half-intermitted burst
Huge fragments vaulted like rebounding hail,
Or chaffy grain beneath the thresher's flail:
And 'mid these dancing rocks at once and ever
It flung up momently the sacred river.
Five miles meandering with a mazy motion
Through wood and dale the sacred river ran,
Then reached the caverns measureless to man,
And sank in tumult to a lifeless ocean:
And 'mid this tumult Kubla heard from far
Ancestral voices prophesying war!

The shadow of the dome of pleasure
Floated midway on the waves;
Where was heard the mingled measure
From the fountain and the caves.
It was a miracle of rare device,
A sunny pleasure-dome with caves of ice!

A damsel with a dulcimer
In a vision once I saw:
It was an Abyssinian maid,

[16] Written in 1798 (not 1797, as Coleridge erroneously stated); published with *Christabel* and *The Pains of Sleep*, 1816. A preface by the author explains the genesis and composition of the poem: 'In the summer of the year 1797 [1798], the Author, then in ill health, had retired to a lonely farm-house. . . . In consequence of a slight indisposition, an anodyne had been prescribed, from the effects of which he fell asleep in his chair at the moment that he was reading the following sentence, or words of the same substance, in "Purchas's Pilgrimage": "Here the Khan Kubla commanded a palace to be built, and a stately garden thereunto. And thus ten miles of fertile ground were inclosed with a wall." The Author continued for about three hours in a profound sleep, at least of the external senses, during which time he has the most vivid confidence, that he could not have composed less than from two to three hundred lines; if that indeed can be called composition in which all the images rose up before him as *things*, with a parallel production of the correspondent expressions, without any sensation or consciousness of effort. On awaking he appeared to himself to have a distinct recollection of the whole, and taking his pen, ink, and paper, instantly and eagerly wrote down the lines that are here preserved. At this moment he was unfortunately called out by a person on business from Porlock, and detained by him above an hour, and on his return to his room, found, to his no small surprise and mortification, that though he still retained some vague and dim recollection of the general purport of the vision, yet, with the exception of some eight or ten scattered lines and images, all the rest had passed away like the images on the surface of a stream into which a stone has been cast, but, alas! without the after restoration of the latter!'

And on her dulcimer she played,
Singing of Mount Abora.[17]
Could I revive within me
Her symphony and song,
To such a deep delight 'twould win me,
That with music loud and long,
I would build that dome in air,
That sunny dome! those caves of ice!
And all who heard should see them there,
And all should cry, Beware! Beware!
His flashing eyes, his floating hair!
Weave a circle round him thrice,
And close your eyes with holy dread,
For he on honey-dew hath fed,
And drunk the milk of Paradise.

Frost at Midnight [18]

THE Frost performs its secret ministry,
Unhelped by any wind. The owlet's cry
Came loud — and hark, again! loud as before.
The inmates of my cottage, all at rest,
Have left me to that solitude, which suits
Abstruser musings: save that at my side
My cradled infant [19] slumbers peacefully.
'Tis calm indeed! so calm, that it disturbs
And vexes meditation with its strange
And extreme silentness. Sea, hill, and wood,
This populous village! Sea, and hill, and wood,
With all the numberless goings-on of life,
Inaudible as dreams! the thin blue flame
Lies on my low-burnt fire, and quivers not;
Only that film,[20] which fluttered on the grate,
Still flutters there, the sole unquiet thing.
Methinks, its motion in this hush of nature
Gives it dim sympathies with me who live,
Making it a companionable form,
Whose puny flaps and freaks the idling Spirit
By its own moods interprets, every where
Echo or mirror seeking of itself,
And makes a toy of Thought.

But O! how oft,
How oft, at school,[21] with most believing mind,
Presageful, have I gazed upon the bars,
To watch that fluttering *stranger!* and as oft
With unclosed lids, already had I dreamt
Of my sweet birth-place,[22] and the old church-tower,
Whose bells, the poor man's only music, rang
From morn to evening, all the hot Fair-day,
So sweetly, that they stirred and haunted me
With a wild pleasure, falling on mine ear
Most like articulate sounds of things to come!
So gazed I, till the soothing things, I dreamt,
Lulled me to sleep, and sleep prolonged my dreams!
And so I brooded all the following morn,
Awed by the stern preceptor's [23] face, mine eye
Fixed with mock study on my swimming book:
Save if the door half opened, and I snatched
A hasty glance, and still my heart leaped up,
For still I hoped to see the *stranger's* face,
Townsman, or aunt, or sister more beloved,
My play-mate when we both were clothed alike!

---

[17] The suggestion, made by Professor Lane Cooper, that this is really Milton's 'Mount Amara', an 'earthly paradise' in Abyssinia, is accepted, with interesting elaborations, in *The Road to Xanadu* (pp. 374 f.).

[18] First published in a pamphlet, 1798, the year in which it was written.

[19] His son Hartley, born in 1796.

[20] In all parts of the kingdom these films are called *strangers* and supposed to portend the arrival of some absent friend. [Coleridge.]

[21] Christ's Hospital, where he remained from 1782 to 1791.

[22] Ottery St. Mary, Devonshire, where his father was rector.

[23] Boyer, master at Christ's Hospital, notorious for his floggings, with whom Coleridge had one severe encounter (see *Table Talk*, 27 May 1830).

Dear Babe, that sleepest cradled by my side,
Whose gentle breathings, heard in this deep calm,
Fill up the interspersèd vacancies
And momentary pauses of the thought!
My babe so beautiful! it thrills my heart
With tender gladness, thus to look at thee,
And think that thou shalt learn far other lore,
And in far other scenes! For I was reared
In the great city, pent 'mid cloisters dim,
And saw nought lovely but the sky and stars.
But *thou,* my babe! shalt wander like a breeze
By lakes and sandy shores,[24] beneath the crags
Of ancient mountain, and beneath the clouds,
Which image in their bulk both lakes and shores
And mountain crags: so shalt thou see and hear
The lovely shapes and sounds intelligible
Of that eternal language, which thy God
Utters, who from eternity doth teach
Himself in all, and all things in himself.
Great universal Teacher! he shall mould
Thy spirit, and by giving make it ask.

Therefore all seasons shall be sweet to thee,
Whether the summer clothe the general earth
With greenness, or the redbreast sit and sing
Betwixt the tufts of snow on the bare branch
Of mossy apple-tree, while the nigh thatch
Smokes in the sun-thaw; whether the eave-drops fall
Heard only in the trances of the blast,
Or if the secret ministry of frost
Shall hang them up in silent icicles,
Quietly shining to the quiet Moon.

[24] In 1800 Coleridge moved to Keswick in the Lake district.

France: an Ode [25]

I

Ye Clouds! that far above me float and pause,[26]
Whose pathless march no mortal may controul!
Ye Ocean-Waves! that, wheresoe'er ye roll,
Yield homage only to eternal laws!
Ye Woods! that listen to the night-birds singing,
Midway the smooth and perilous slope reclined,
Save when your own imperious branches swinging,
Have made a solemn music of the wind!
Where, like a man beloved of God,
Through glooms, which never woodman trod,
How oft, pursuing fancies holy,
My moonlight way o'er flowering weeds I wound,
Inspired beyond the guess of folly,
By each rude shape and wild unconquerable sound!
O ye loud Waves! and O ye Forests high!
And O ye Clouds that far above me soared!
Thou rising Sun! thou blue rejoicing Sky!
Yea, every thing that is and will be free!
Bear witness for me, wheresoe'er ye be,
With what deep worship I have still adored
The spirit of divinest Liberty.

II

When France in wrath her giant-limbs upreared,
And with that oath, which smote air, earth, and sea,
Stamped her strong foot and said she would be free,

[25] First published in *The Morning Post,* 16 April 1798. It was inspired by the French invasion of Switzerland in that year.

[26] 'An invocation to those objects in Nature the contemplation of which had inspired the Poet with a devotional love of Liberty.' [Coleridge's 'Argument' for the first stanza.]

Bear witness for me, how I hoped and feared! [27]
With what a joy my lofty gratulation
Unawed I sang, amid a slavish band:
And when to whelm the disenchanted nation,
Like fiends embattled by a wizard's wand,
The Monarchs marched in evil day,
And Britain joined the dire array;
Though dear her shores and circling ocean,
Though many friendships, many youthful loves
Had swoln the patriot emotion
And flung a magic light o'er all her hills and groves;
Yet still my voice, unaltered, sang defeat
To all that braved the tyrant-quelling lance,
And shame too long delayed and vain retreat!
For ne'er, O Liberty! with partial aim
I dimmed thy light or damped thy holy flame;
But blessed the paeans of delivered France,
And hung my head and wept at Britain's name.

III

'And what,' I said, 'though Blasphemy's loud scream [28]
With that sweet music of deliverance strove!
Though all the fierce and drunken passions wove
A dance more wild than e'er was maniac's dream!
Ye storms, that round the dawning East assembled,
The Sun was rising, though ye hid his light!'
And when, to soothe my soul, that hoped and trembled,
The dissonance ceased, and all seemed calm and bright;
When France her front deep-scarr'd and gory
Concealed with clustering wreaths of glory;
When, insupportably advancing,
Her arm made mockery of the warrior's ramp;
While timid looks of fury glancing,
Domestic treason, crushed beneath her fatal stamp,
Writhed like a wounded dragon in his gore;
Then I reproached my fears that would not flee;
'And soon,' I said, 'shall Wisdom teach her lore
In the low huts of them that toil and groan!
And, conquering by her happiness alone,
Shall France compel the nations to be free,
Till Love and Joy look round, and call the Earth their own.'

IV

Forgive me, Freedom! O forgive those dreams!
I hear thy voice, I hear thy loud lament,
From bleak Helvetia's icy caverns sent —
I hear thy groans upon her blood-stained streams!
Heroes, that for your peaceful country perished,
And ye that, fleeing, spot your mountain-snows
With bleeding wounds; forgive me, that I cherished
One thought that ever blessed your cruel foes!

---

[27] 'The exultation of the Poet at the commencement of the French Revolution [compare Wordsworth], and his unqualified abhorrence of the Alliance against the Republic [France at war with Prussia and Austria, in 1792; with Holland and England, in 1793].' [Argument, second stanza.]

[28] 'The blasphemies and horrors during the domination of the Terrorists regarded by the Poet as a transient storm, and as the natural consequence of the former despotism and of the foul superstition of Popery. Reason, indeed, began to suggest many apprehensions; yet still the Poet struggled to retain the hope that France would make conquests by no other means than by presenting to the observation of Europe a people more happy and better instructed than under other forms of Government.' [Argument, third stanza.]

To scatter rage, and traitorous guilt,
Where Peace her jealous home had built;
A patriot-race to disinherit
Of all that made their stormy wilds so dear;
And with inexpiable spirit
To taint the bloodless freedom of the mountaineer —
O France, that mockest Heaven, adulterous, blind,
And patriot only in pernicious toils!
Are these thy boasts, Champion of human kind?
To mix with Kings in the low lust of sway,
Yell in the hunt, and share the murderous prey;
To insult the shrine of Liberty with spoils
From freemen torn; to tempt and to betray?

V

The Sensual and the Dark rebel in vain,[29]
Slaves by their own compulsion! In mad game
They burst their manacles and wear the name
Of Freedom, graven on a heavier chain!
O Liberty! with profitless endeavour
Have I pursued thee, many a weary hour;
But thou nor swell'st the victor's strain, nor ever
Didst breathe thy soul in forms of human power.
Alike from all, howe'er they praise thee,
(Nor prayer, nor boastful name delays thee)
Alike from Priestcraft's harpy minions,
And factious Blasphemy's obscener slaves,
Thou speedest on thy subtle pinions,
The guide of homeless winds, and playmate of the waves!
And there I felt thee! — on that sea-cliff's verge,
Whose pines, scarce travelled by the breeze above,
Had made one murmur with the distant surge!
Yes, while I stood and gazed, my temples bare,
And shot my being through earth, sea, and air,
Possessing all things with intensest love,
O Liberty! my spirit felt thee there.

Love [30]

ALL thoughts, all passions, all delights,
Whatever stirs this mortal frame,
All are but ministers of Love,
And feed his sacred flame.

Oft in my waking dreams do I
Live o'er again that happy hour,
When midway on the mount I lay,
Beside the ruined tower.

The moonshine, stealing o'er the scene
Had blended with the lights of eve;
And she was there, my hope, my joy,
My own dear Genevieve!

She leant against the armèd man,
The statue of the armèd knight;[31]
She stood and listened to my lay,
Amid the lingering light.

---

[29] 'An address to Liberty, in which the Poet expresses his conviction that those feelings and that grand *ideal* of Freedom which the mind attains by its contemplation of its individual nature, and of the sublime surrounding objects (see Stanza the First) do not belong to men, as a society, nor can possibly be either gratified or realised, under any form of human government; but belong to the individual man, so far as he is pure, and inflamed with the love and adoration of God in Nature.' [Argument, fifth stanza.]

[30] First published in *The Morning Post*, 21 December 1799. It was probably written during or shortly after a visit which Coleridge made to Wordsworth's friends, the Hutchinsons, at Sockburn. Sarah Hutchinson, later Wordsworth's sister-in-law, whom Coleridge met here for the first time, became a devoted friend. Coleridge had, of course, previously made his unhappy marriage with Sara Fricker.

[31] There is such a statue in the church at Sockburn, of a knight whose slaying of a monstrous wyverne or 'worme' is commemorated by a stone in a field nearby.

Few sorrows hath she of her own,
My hope! my joy! my Genevieve!
She loves me best, whene'er I sing
The songs that make her grieve.

I played a soft and doleful air,
I sang an old and moving story —
An old rude song, that suited well
That ruin wild and hoary.

She listened with a flitting blush,
With downcast eyes and modest grace;
For well she knew, I could not choose
But gaze upon her face.

I told her of the Knight that wore
Upon his shield a burning brand;
And that for ten long years he wooed
The Lady of the Land.

I told her how he pined: and ah!
The deep, the low, the pleading tone
With which I sang another's love,
Interpreted my own.

She listened with a flitting blush,
With downcast eyes, and modest grace;
And she forgave me, that I gazed
Too fondly on her face!

But when I told the cruel scorn
That crazed that bold and lovely Knight,
And that he crossed the mountain-woods,
Nor rested day nor night;

That sometimes from the savage den,
And sometimes from the darksome shade,
And sometimes starting up at once
In green and sunny glade, —

There came and looked him in the face
An angel beautiful and bright;
And that he knew it was a Fiend,
This miserable Knight!

And that unknowing what he did,
He leaped amid a murderous band,
And saved from outrage worse than death
The Lady of the Land!

And how she wept, and clasped his knees;
And how she tended him in vain —
And ever strove to expiate
The scorn that crazed his brain; —

And that she nursed him in a cave;
And how his madness went away,
When on the yellow forest-leaves
A dying man he lay; —

His dying words — but when I reached
That tenderest strain of all the ditty,
My faultering voice and pausing harp
Disturbed her soul with pity!

All impulses of soul and sense
Had thrilled my guileless Genevieve;
The music and the doleful tale,
The rich and balmy eve;

And hopes, and fears that kindle hope,
An undistinguishable throng,
And gentle wishes long subdued,
Subdued and cherished long!

She wept with pity and delight,
She blushed with love, and virgin-shame;
And like the murmur of a dream,
I heard her breathe my name.

Her bosom heaved — she stepped aside,
As conscious of my look she stepped —
Then suddenly, with timorous eye
She fled to me and wept.

She half enclosed me with her arms,
She pressed me with a meek embrace;
And bending back her head, looked up,
And gazed upon my face.

'Twas partly love, and partly fear,
And partly 'twas a bashful art,
That I might rather feel, than see,
The swelling of her heart.

I calmed her fears, and she was calm,
And told her love with virgin pride;
And so I won my Genevieve,
My bright and beauteous Bride.

Hymn before Sun-rise

IN THE VALE OF CHAMOUNI [32]

Hast thou a charm to stay the morning-star
In his steep course? So long he seems to pause
On thy bald awful head, O sovran Blanc.
The Arve and Arveiron [33] at thy base
Rave ceaselessly; but thou, most awful Form!
Risest from forth thy silent sea of pines,
How silently! Around thee and above
Deep is the air and dark, substantial, black,
An ebon mass: methinks thou piercest it,
As with a wedge! But when I look again,
It is thine own calm home, thy crystal shrine,
Thy habitation from eternity!
O dread and silent Mount! I gazed upon thee,
Till thou, still present to the bodily sense,
Didst vanish from my thought: entranced in prayer
I worshipped the Invisible alone.

Yet, like some sweet beguiling melody,
So sweet, we know not we are listening to it,
Thou, the meanwhile, wast blending with my Thought,
Yea, with my Life and Life's own secret joy:
Till the dilating Soul, enrapt, transfused,
Into the mighty vision passing — there
As in her natural form, swelled vast to Heaven!

Awake, my soul! not only passive praise
Thou owest! not alone these swelling tears,
Mute thanks and secret ecstasy! Awake,
Voice of sweet song! Awake, my heart, awake!
Green vales and icy cliffs, all join my Hymn.

Thou first and chief, sole sovereign of the Vale!
O struggling with the darkness all the night,
And visited all night by troops of stars,
Or when they climb the sky or when they sink:
Companion of the morning-star at dawn,
Thyself Earth's rosy star, and of the dawn
Co-herald: wake, O wake, and utter praise!
Who sank thy sunless pillars deep in Earth?
Who filled thy countenance with rosy light?
Who made thee parent of perpetual streams?

And you, ye five wild torrents fiercely glad!
Who called you forth from night and utter death,
From dark and icy caverns called you forth,
Down those precipitous, black, jaggéd rocks,
For ever shattered and the same for ever?
Who gave you your invulnerable life,
Your strength, your speed, your fury, and your joy,
Unceasing thunder and eternal foam?
And who commanded (and the silence came),
Here let the billows stiffen, and have rest?

Ye Ice-falls! ye that from the mountain's brow
Adown enormous ravines slope amain —
Torrents, methinks, that heard a mighty voice,
And stopped at once amid their maddest plunge!
Motionless torrents! silent cataracts!
Who made you glorious as the Gates of Heaven

---

[32] First printed in *The Morning Post*, 11 September 1802. Coleridge never was at Chamouni, one of the high mountains of the Savoy Alps. As De Quincey pointed out, the poem is based upon an ode to Chamouni by a German poet, Friederika Brun. 'On the other hand,' says De Quincey, 'by a judicious amplification of some topics, and by its far deeper tone of lyrical enthusiasm, the dry bones of the German outline have been created by Coleridge into the fullness of life. It is not, therefore, a paraphrase, but a recast of the original.'

[33] Rivers

Beneath the keen full moon? Who bade the sun
Clothe you with rainbows? Who, with living flowers [34]
Of loveliest blue, spread garlands at your feet? —
God! let the torrents, like a shout of nations,
Answer! and let the ice-plains echo, God!
God! sing ye meadow-streams with gladsome voice!
Ye pine-groves, with your soft and soul-like sounds!
And they too have a voice, yon piles of snow,
And in their perilous fall shall thunder, God!

Ye living flowers that skirt the eternal frost!
Ye wild goats sporting round the eagle's nest!
Ye eagles, play-mates of the mountain-storm!
Ye lightnings, the dread arrows of the clouds!
Ye signs and wonders of the element!
Utter forth God, and fill the hills with praise!

Thou too, hoar Mount! with thy sky-pointing peaks,
Oft from whose feet the avalanche, unheard,
Shoots downward, glittering through the pure serene
Into the depth of clouds, that veil thy breast —
Thou too again, stupendous Mountain! thou
That as I raise my head, awhile bowed low
In adoration, upward from thy base
Slow travelling with dim eyes suffused with tears,
Solemnly seemest, like a vapoury cloud,
To rise before me — Rise, O ever rise,
Rise like a cloud of incense from the Earth!
Thou kingly Spirit throned among the hills,
Thou dread ambassador from Earth to Heaven,
Great Hierarch! tell thou the silent sky,
And tell the stars, and tell yon rising sun
Earth, with her thousand voices, praises God.

[34] The beautiful *Gentiana major*, or greater gentian, with blossoms of the brightest blue, grows in large companies a few steps from the never-melted ice of the glaciers. I thought it an affecting emblem of the boldness of human hope, venturing near, and, as it were, leaning over the brink of the grave. . . . Who *would* be, who *could* be an Atheist in this valley of wonders! [Coleridge.]

Inscription for a Fountain on a Heath [35]

This Sycamore, oft musical with bees, —
Such tents the Patriarchs loved! O long unharmed
May all its agéd boughs o'er-canopy
The small round basin, which this jutting stone
Keeps pure from falling leaves! Long may the Spring,
Quietly as a sleeping infant's breath,
Send up cold waters to the traveller
With soft and even pulse! Nor ever cease
Yon tiny cone of sand its soundless dance,
Which at the bottom, like a Fairy's Page,
As merry and no taller, dances still,
Nor wrinkles the smooth surface of the Fount.
Here Twilight is and Coolness: here is moss,
A soft seat, and a deep and ample shade.
Thou may'st toil far and find no second tree.
Drink, Pilgrim, here; Here rest! and if thy heart
Be innocent, here too shalt thou refresh
Thy spirit, listening to some gentle sound,
Or passing gale or hum of murmuring bees!

[35] Published in *The Morning Post*, 24 September 1802.

Dejection: an Ode [36]

Late, late yestreen I saw the new Moon,
With the old Moon in her arms;
And I fear, I fear, my Master dear!
We shall have a deadly storm.
Ballad of Sir Patrick Spence.

I

Well! If the Bard was weather-wise, who made
The grand old ballad of Sir Patrick Spence,
This night, so tranquil now, will not go hence
Unroused by winds, that ply a busier trade
Than those which mould yon cloud in lazy flakes,
Or the dull sobbing draft, that moans and rakes
Upon the strings of this Æolian lute,
Which better far were mute.
For lo! the New-moon winter-bright!
And overspread with phantom light,
(With swimming phantom light o'erspread
But rimmed and circled by a silver thread)
I see the old Moon in her lap, foretelling
The coming-on of rain and squally blast.
And oh! that even now the gust were swelling,
And the slant night-shower driving loud and fast!
Those sounds which oft have raised me, whilst they awed,
And sent my soul abroad,
Might now perhaps their wonted impulse give,
Might startle this dull pain, and make it move and live!

II

A grief without a pang, void, dark, and drear,
A stifled, drowsy, unimpassioned grief,
Which finds no natural outlet, no relief,
In word, or sigh, or tear —
O Lady! in this wan and heartless mood,
To other thoughts by yonder throstle woo'd,
All this long eve, so balmy and serene,
Have I been gazing on the western sky,
And its peculiar tint of yellow green:
And still I gaze — and with how blank an eye!
And those thin clouds above, in flakes and bars,
That give away their motion to the stars;
Those stars, that glide behind them or between,
Now sparkling, now bedimmed, but always seen:
Yon crescent Moon, as fixed as if it grew
In its own cloudless, starless lake of blue;
I see them all so excellently fair,
I see, not feel, how beautiful they are!

III

My genial spirits fail;
And what can these avail
To lift the smothering weight from off my breast?
It were a vain endeavour,
Though I should gaze for ever
On that green light that lingers in the west:
I may not hope from outward forms to win
The passion and the life, whose fountains are within.

IV

O Lady! we receive but what we give,
And in our life alone does Nature live:
Ours is her wedding garment, ours her shroud!
And would we aught behold, of higher worth,
Than that inanimate cold world allowed
To the poor loveless ever-anxious crowd,
Ah! from the soul itself must issue forth
A light, a glory, a fair luminous cloud
Enveloping the Earth —

---

[36] Written 4 April 1802, and first published in *The Morning Post* on 4 October of the same year — the wedding-day of Wordsworth, to whom it was addressed. For the important connection between this and the *Ode on the Intimations of Immortality*, see p. 650, note 78. In an early version, the name 'William' occurred where 'Lady' is used in this text.

And from the soul itself must there be sent
A sweet and potent voice, of its own birth,
Of all sweet sounds the life and element!

V

O pure of heart! thou need'st not ask of me
What this strong music in the soul may be!
What, and wherein it doth exist,
This light, this glory, this fair luminous mist,
This beautiful and beauty-making power.
Joy, virtuous Lady! Joy that ne'er was given,
Save to the pure, and in their purest hour,
Life, and Life's effluence, cloud at once and shower,
Joy, Lady! is the spirit and the power,
Which wedding Nature to us gives in dower
A new Earth and new Heaven,
Undreamt of by the sensual and the proud —
Joy is the sweet voice, Joy the luminous cloud —
We in ourselves rejoice!
And thence flows all that charms or ear or sight,
All melodies the echoes of that voice,
All colours a suffusion from that light.

VI

There was a time when, though my path was rough,
This joy within me dallied with distress,
And all misfortunes were but as the stuff
Whence Fancy made me dreams of happiness:
For hope grew round me, like the twining vine,
And fruits, and foliage not my own, seemed mine.
But now afflictions bow me down to earth:
Nor care I that they rob me of my mirth;
But oh! each visitation
Suspends what nature gave me at my birth,
My shaping spirit of Imagination.
For not to think of what I needs must feel,
But to be still and patient, all I can;
And haply by abstruse research to steal
From my own nature all the natural man —
This was my sole resource, my only plan:
Till that which suits a part infects the whole,
And now is almost grown the habit of my soul.

VII

Hence, viper thoughts, that coil around my mind,
Reality's dark dream!
I turn from you, and listen to the wind,
Which long has raved unnoticed. What a scream
Of agony by torture lengthened out
That lute sent forth! Thou Wind, that rav'st without,
Bare crag, or mountain-tairn, or blasted tree,
Or pine-grove whither woodman never clomb,
Or lonely house, long held the witches' home,
Methinks were fitter instruments for thee,
Mad Lutanist! who in this month of showers,
Of dark-brown gardens, and of peeping flowers,
Mak'st Devils' yule, with worse than wintry song,
The blossoms, buds, and timorous leaves among.
Thou Actor, perfect in all tragic sounds!
Thou mighty Poet, e'en to frenzy bold!
What tell'st thou now about?
'Tis of the rushing of an host in rout,
With groans, of trampled men, with smarting wounds —
At once they groan with pain, and shudder with the cold!
But hush! there is a pause of deepest silence!
And all that noise, as of a rushing crowd,

With groans, and tremulous shudderings — all is over —
It tells another tale, with sounds less deep and loud!
A tale of less affright,
And tempered with delight,
As Otway's [37] self had framed the tender lay, —
'Tis of a little child
Upon a lonesome wild,
Not far from home, but she hath lost her way:
And now moans low in bitter grief and fear,
And now screams loud, and hopes to make her mother hear.

VIII

'Tis midnight, but small thoughts have I of sleep:
Full seldom may my friend such vigils keep!
Visit her, gentle Sleep! with wings of healing,
And may this storm be but a mountain-birth,
May all the stars hang bright above her dwelling,
Silent as though they watched the sleeping Earth!
With light heart may she rise,
Gay fancy, cheerful eyes,
Joy lift her spirit, joy attune her voice;
To her may all things live, from pole to pole,
Their life the eddying of her living soul!
O simple spirit, guided from above,
Dear Lady! friend devoutest of my choice,
Thus mayest thou ever, evermore rejoice.

The Pains of Sleep [38]

Ere on my bed my limbs I lay,
It hath not been my use to pray
With moving lips or bended knees;
But silently, by slow degrees,
My spirit I to Love compose,
In humble trust mine eye-lids close,
With reverential resignation,
No wish conceived, no thought exprest,
Only a sense of supplication;
A sense o'er all my soul imprest
That I am weak, yet not unblest,
Since in me, round me, every where
Eternal Strength and Wisdom are.

But yester-night I prayed aloud
In anguish and in agony,
Up-starting from the fiendish crowd
Of shapes and thoughts that tortured me:
A lurid light, a trampling throng,
Sense of intolerable wrong,
And whom I scorned, those only strong!
Thirst of revenge, the powerless will
Still baffled, and yet burning still!
Desire with loathing strangely mixed
On wild or hateful objects fixed.
Fantastic passions! maddening brawl!
And shame and terror over all!
Deeds to be hid which were not hid,
Which all confused I could not know
Whether I suffered, or I did:
For all seemed guilt, remorse or woe,
My own or others still the same
Life-stifling fear, soul-stifling shame.

So two nights passed: the night's dismay
Saddened and stunned the coming day.
Sleep, the wide blessing, seemed to me
Distemper's worst calamity.
The third night, when my own loud scream
Had waked me from the fiendish dream,
O'ercome with sufferings strange and wild,
I wept as I had been a child;
And having thus by tears subdued
My anguish to a milder mood,
Such punishments, I said, were due
To natures deepliest stained with sin, —
For aye entempesting anew

[37] Earlier version: 'thou [Wordsworth] thyself.' What follows is obviously a reference to Wordsworth's own *Lucy Gray*. Thomas Otway, 1652–1685, the dramatist, whose masterpiece is *Venice Preserved*.

[38] Written in 1803, after Coleridge had begun to feel the effects of his taking opium; published in 1816. In a letter to Thomas Poole, 3 October 1803, Coleridge said that he would not wish upon his worst enemy the benightmared sleep he had been having. — 'My dreams become the substances of my life.'

The unfathomable hell within,
The horror of their deeds to view,
To know and loathe, yet wish and do!
Such griefs with such men well agree,
But wherefore, wherefore fall on me?
To be beloved is all I need,
And whom I love, I love indeed.[39]

The Exchange [40]

We pledged our hearts, my love and I,—
I in my arms the maiden clasping;
I could not guess the reason why,
But, oh! I trembled like an aspen.

Her father's love she bade me gain;
I went, but shook like any reed!
I strove to act the man — in vain!
We had exchanged our hearts indeed.

An Invocation [41]

From *Remorse* [Act III, Scene i, ll. 69–82.]

Hear, sweet Spirit, hear the spell,
Lest a blacker charm compel!
So shall the midnight breezes swell
With thy deep long-lingering knell.

And at evening evermore,
In a chapel on the shore,
Shall the chaunter, sad and saintly,
Yellow tapers burning faintly,
Doleful masses chaunt for thee,
Miserere Domine!

Hush! the cadence dies away
On the quiet moonlight sea:
The boatmen rest their oars and say,
Miserere Domine!

On Donne's Poetry [42]

With Donne, whose muse on dromedary trots,
Wreathe iron pokers into true-love knots;
Rhyme's sturdy cripple, fancy's maze and clue,
Wit's forge and fire-blast, meaning's press and screw.

Epitaph [43]

Stop, Christian passer-by!—Stop, child of God,
And read with gentle breast. Beneath this sod
A poet lies, or that which once seem'd he.
O, lift one thought in prayer for S. T. C.;
That he who many a year with toil of breath
Found death in life, may here find life in death!
Mercy for praise — to be forgiven for fame
He ask'd, and hoped, through Christ. Do thou the same!

[39] The same year he had written to a friend: 'Me, who from my childhood have had no avarice, no ambition, whose very vanity, in my vainest moments was, nine-tenths of it, the desire and delight, and necessity of loving and of being loved!'
[40] First published in *The Courier*, 16 April 1804.
[41] First published in *Remorse*, 1813.
[42] Written probably in 1818; published in *Literary Remains*, 1836.
[43] Written in 1833; published the following year.

Thomas Moore

1779–1852

The harp that once through Tara's halls [1]

The harp that once through Tara's [2] halls
The soul of music shed,
Now hangs as mute on Tara's walls,
As if that soul were fled.—
So sleeps the pride of former days,
So glory's thrill is o'er,
And hearts, that once beat high for praise,
Now feel that pulse no more.

[1] This and the following five poems are from *Irish Melodies*, published 1808–1834.
[2] Tara, near Dublin, was a residence of the early Irish kings.

No more to chiefs and ladies bright
  The harp of Tara swells;
The chord alone, that breaks at night,
  Its tale of ruin tells.
Thus Freedom now so seldom wakes,
  The only throb she gives,
Is when some heart indignant breaks,
  To show that still she lives.

The young May moon

The young May moon is beaming, love,
The glow-worm's lamp is gleaming, love,
    How sweet to rove
    Through Morna's grove,
When the drowsy world is dreaming, love!
Then awake! — the heavens look bright, my dear,
'Tis never too late for delight, my dear,
    And the best of all ways
    To lengthen our days,
Is to steal a few hours from the night, my dear!

Now all the world is sleeping, love,
But the Sage, his star-watch keeping, love,
    And I, whose star,
    More glorious far,
Is the eye from that casement peeping, love.
Then awake! — till rise of sun, my dear,
The Sage's glass we'll shun, my dear,
    Or, in watching the flight
    Of bodies of light,
He might happen to take thee for one, my dear.

The Minstrel Boy

The Minstrel Boy to the war is gone,
  In the ranks of death you'll find him;
His father's sword he has girded on,
  And his wild harp slung behind him. —
'Land of song!' said the warrior-bard,
  'Though all the world betrays thee,
One sword, at least, thy rights shall guard,
  One faithful harp shall praise thee!'

The Minstrel fell! — but the foeman's chain
  Could not bring his proud soul under;
The harp he lov'd ne'er spoke again,
  For he tore its chords asunder;
And said, 'No chains shall sully thee,
  Thou soul of love and bravery!
Thy songs were made for the pure and free,
  They shall never sound in slavery.'

Farewell! — but whenever you welcome the hour

Farewell! — but whenever you welcome the hour,
That awakens the night-song of mirth in your bower,
Then think of the friend who once welcom'd it too,
And forgot his own griefs to be happy with you.
His griefs may return, not a hope may remain
Of the few that have brighten'd his pathway of pain,
But he ne'er will forget the short vision, that threw
Its enchantment around him, while ling'ring with you.

And still on that evening, when pleasure fills up
To the highest top sparkle each heart and each cup,
Where'er my path lies, be it gloomy or bright,
My soul, happy friends, shall be with you that night;
Shall join in your revels, your sports, and your wiles,
And return to me, beaming all o'er with your smiles —
Too blest, if it tells me that, 'mid the gay cheer,
Some kind voice had murmur'd, 'I wish he were here!'

Let Fate do her worst, there are relics of joy,

Bright dreams of the past, which she cannot destroy;
Which come in the night-time of sorrow and care,
And bring back the features that joy used to wear.
Long, long be my heart with such memories fill'd!
Like the vase, in which roses have once been distill'd —
You may break, you may shatter the vase, if you will,
But the scent of the roses will hang round it still.

The time I've lost in wooing

The time I've lost in wooing,
In watching and pursuing
The light, that lies
In woman's eyes,
Has been my heart's undoing.
Though Wisdom oft has sought me,
I scorn'd the lore she brought me,
My only books
Were woman's looks,
And folly's all they've taught me.

Her smile when Beauty granted,
I hung with gaze enchanted,
Like him, the sprite,
Whom maids by night
Oft meet in glen that's haunted.
Like him, too, Beauty won me,
But while her eyes were on me,
If once their ray
Was turn'd away,
O! winds could not outrun me.

And are those follies going?
And is my proud heart growing
Too cold or wise
For brilliant eyes
Again to set it glowing?
No, vain, alas! th' endeavour
From bonds so sweet to sever;
Poor Wisdom's chance
Against a glance
Is now as weak as ever.

Dear Harp of my Country

Dear Harp of my Country! in darkness I found thee,
The cold chain of silence had hung o'er thee long,
When proudly, my own Island Harp, I unbound thee,
And gave all thy chords to light, freedom, and song!
The warm lay of love and the light note of gladness
Have waken'd thy fondest, thy liveliest thrill;
But, so oft hast thou echo'd the deep sigh of sadness,
That ev'n in thy mirth it will steal from thee still.

Dear Harp of my Country! farewell to thy numbers,
This sweet wreathe of song is the last we shall twine!
Go, sleep with sunshine of Fame on thy slumbers,
Till touched by some hand less unworthy than mine;
If the pulse of the patriot, soldier, or lover,
Have throbb'd at our lay, 'tis thy glory alone;
I was *but* as the wind, passing heedlessly over,
And all the wild sweetness I wak'd was thy own.

At the mid hour of night [3]

At the mid hour of night, when stars are weeping, I fly
To the lone vale we lov'd, when life shone warm in thine eye;

[3] This and the following poem are from *National Airs*, published 1815. The Advertisement read: 'It is Cicero, I believe, who says "*natura ad modos ducimur*"; and the abundance of wild indigenous airs, which almost every country except England possesses, sufficiently proves the truth of his assertion. . . . A pretty air without words resembles one of those *half* creatures of Plato, which are described as wandering, in search of the remainder of themselves, through the world. To supply this other half, by uniting with congenial words the many fugitive melodies which have hitherto had none, or only such as are unintelligible to the generality of their hearers, is the object and ambition of the present work.'

And I think oft, if spirits can steal from the regions of air,
To revisit past scenes of delight, thou wilt come to me there,
And tell me our love is remember'd, even in the sky.

Then I sing the wild song 'twas once such pleasure to hear!
When our voices commingling breath'd, like one, on the ear;
And, as Echo far off through the vale my sad orison rolls,
I think, oh my love! 'tis thy voice from the Kingdom of Souls,
Faintly answering still the notes that once were so dear.

Oft, in the stilly night

[Scotch Air]

Oft, in the stilly night,
Ere Slumber's chain has bound me,
Fond Memory brings the light
Of other days around me;
The smiles, the tears,
Of boyhood's years,
The words of love then spoken;
The eyes that shone,
Now dimm'd and gone,
The cheerful hearts now broken!
Thus, in the stilly night,
Ere Slumber's chain has bound me,
Sad Memory brings the light
Of other days around me.

When I remember all
The friends, so link'd together,
I've seen around me fall,
Like leaves in wintry weather;
I feel like one
Who treads alone
Some banquet-hall deserted,
Whose lights are fled,
Whose garlands dead,
And all but he departed!
Thus, in the stilly night,
Ere Slumber's chain has bound me,
Sad Memory brings the light
Of other days around me.

Sir Walter Scott

1771–1832

William and Helen[1]

From heavy dreams fair Helen rose,
And eyed the dawning red:
'Alas, my love, thou tarriest long!
O art thou false or dead?'

With gallant Fred'rick's[2] princely power
He sought the bold Crusade;
But not a word from Judah's wars
Told Helen how he sped.

With Paynim and with Saracen
At length a truce was made,
And every knight return'd to dry
The tears his love had shed.

Our gallant host was homeward bound
With many a song of joy;
Green waved the laurel in each plume,
The badge of victory.

And old and young, and sire and son,
To meet them crowd the way,
With shouts, and mirth, and melody,
The debt of love to pay.

Full many a maid her true-love met,
And sobb'd in his embrace,
And flutt'ring joy in tears and smiles
Array'd full many a face.

Nor joy nor smile for Helen sad;
She sought the host in vain;
For none could tell her William's fate,
If faithless, or if slain.

[1] Written in 1795; published in 1796. It is a translation or imitation of Bürger's *Lenore*. Scott's interest had been aroused by hearing a report of a reading of William Taylor's unpublished rendering of the tale.

[2] Frederick Barbarossa; on the Third Crusade, 1189–1192.

The martial band is past and gone;
She rends her raven hair,
And in distraction's bitter mood
She weeps with wild despair.

'O rise, my child,' her mother said,
'Nor sorrow thus in vain;
A perjured lover's fleeting heart
No tears recall again.'

'O mother, what is gone, is gone,
What's lost for ever lorn:
Death, death alone can comfort me;
O had I ne'er been born!

'O break, my heart — O break at once!
Drink my life-blood, Despair!
No joy remains on earth for me,
For me in heaven no share.'

'O enter not in judgment, Lord!'
The pious mother prays;
'Impute not guilt to thy frail child!
She knows not what she says.

'O say thy pater noster, child!
O turn to God and grace!
His will, that turn'd thy bliss to bale,
Can change thy bale to bliss.'

'O mother, mother, what is bliss?
O mother, what is bale?
My William's love was heaven on earth,
Without it earth is hell.

'Why should I pray to ruthless Heaven,
Since my loved William's slain?
I only pray'd for William's sake,
And all my prayers were vain.'

'O take the sacrament, my child,
And check these tears that flow;
By resignation's humble prayer,
O hallow'd be thy woe!'

'No sacrament can quench this fire,
Or slake this scorching pain;
No sacrament can bid the dead
Arise and live again.

'O break, my heart — O break at once!
Be thou my god, Despair!
Heaven's heaviest blow has fallen on me,
And vain each fruitless prayer.'

'O enter not in judgment, Lord,
With thy frail child of clay!
She knows not what her tongue has spoke;
Impute it not, I pray!

'Forbear, my child, this desperate woe,
And turn to God and grace;
Well can devotion's heavenly glow
Convert thy bale to bliss.'

'O mother, mother, what is bliss?
O mother, what is bale?
Without my William what were heaven,
Or with him what were hell?'

Wild she arraigns the eternal doom,
Upbraids each sacred power,
Till, spent, she sought her silent room,
All in the lonely tower.

She beat her breast, she wrung her hands,
Till sun and day were o'er,
And through the glimmering lattice shone
The twinkling of the star.

Then, crash! the heavy drawbridge fell
That o'er the moat was hung;
And, clatter! clatter! on its boards
The hoof of courser rung.

The clank of echoing steel was heard
As off the rider bounded;
And slowly on the winding stair
A heavy footstep sounded.

And hark! and hark! a knock — tap! tap!
A rustling stifled noise;
Door-latch and tinkling staples ring;
At length a whispering voice:

'Awake, awake, arise, my love!
How, Helen, dost thou fare?
Wak'st thou, or sleep'st? laugh'st thou, or weep'st?
Hast thought on me, my fair?'

'My love! my love! — so late by night!
I waked, I wept for thee:
Much have I borne since dawn of morn;
Where, William couldst thou be?'

'We saddle late — from Hungary
I rode since darkness fell;
And to its bourne we both return
Before the matin-bell.'

'O rest this night within my arms,
And warm thee in their fold!
Chill howls through hawthorn bush the wind:
My love is deadly cold.'

'Let the wind howl through hawthorn bush!
This night we must away;
The steed is wight,[3] the spur is bright;
I cannot stay till day.

'Busk, busk, and boune! [4] thou mount'st behind
Upon my black barb [5] steed:
O'er stock and stile,[6] a hundred miles,
We haste to bridal bed.'

'To-night — to-night a hundred miles?
O dearest William, stay!
The bell strikes twelve — dark, dismal hour!
O wait, my love, till day!'

'Look here, look here — the moon shines clear —
Full fast I ween we ride;
Mount and away! for ere the day
We reach our bridal bed.

'The black barb snorts, the bridle rings;
Haste, busk, and boune, and seat thee!
The feast is made, the chamber spread,
The bridal guests await thee.'

Strong love prevail'd. She busks, she bounes,
She mounts the barb behind,
And round her darling William's waist
Her lily arms she twined.

And, hurry! hurry! off they rode,
As fast as fast might be;
Spurn'd from the courser's thundering heels
The flashing pebbles flee.

And on the right, and on the left,
Ere they could snatch a view,
Fast, fast each mountain, mead, and plain,
And cot, and castle flew.

'Sit fast — dost fear? The moon shines clear;
Fleet goes my barb — keep hold!
Fear'st thou?' 'O no!' she faintly said;
'But why so stern and cold?

'What yonder rings? what yonder sings?
Why shrieks the owlet grey?'
''Tis death-bells' clang, 'tis funeral song,
The body to the clay.

'With song and clang, at morrow's dawn,
Ye may inter the dead:
To-night I ride, with my young bride,
To deck our bridal bed.

'Come with thy choir, thou coffin'd guest,
To swell our nuptial song!
Come, priest, to bless our marriage feast!
Come all, come all along!'

Ceased clang and song; down sunk the bier;
The shrouded corpse arose:
And, hurry! hurry! all the train
The thundering steed pursues.

And, forward! forward! on they go;
High snorts the straining steed;
Thick pants the rider's labouring breath,
As headlong on they speed.

---

[3] powerful
[4] Dress and get ready.
[5] Barbary
[6] stump

'O William, why this savage haste?
  And where thy bridal bed?'
''Tis distant far, low, damp, and chill,
  And narrow, trustless maid.'

'No room for me?' 'Enough for both;
  Speed, speed, my barb, thy course!'
O'er thundering bridge, through boiling surge
  He drove the furious horse.

Tramp! tramp! along the land they rode,
  Splash! splash! along the sea;
The scourge is wight, the spur is bright,
  The flashing pebbles flee.

Fled past on right and left how fast
  Each forest, grove, and bower!
On right and left fled past how fast
  Each city, town, and tower!

'Dost fear? dost fear? The moon shines clear,
  Dost fear to ride with me?
Hurrah! hurrah! the dead can ride!'
  'O William, let them be!

'See there, see there! What yonder swings,
  And creaks 'mid whistling rain?'
'Gibbet and steel, th' accursed wheel;
  A murderer in his chain.

'Hollo! thou felon, follow here:
  To bridal bed we ride;
And thou shalt prance a fetter dance
  Before me and my bride.'

And, hurry! hurry! clash! clash! clash!
  The wasted form descends;
And fleet as wind through hazel bush
  The wild career [7] attends.

Tramp! tramp! along the land they rode,
  Splash! splash! along the sea;
The scourge is red, the spur drops blood,
  The flashing pebbles flee.

How fled what moonshine faintly show'd!
  How fled what darkness hid!
How fled the earth beneath their feet,
  The heaven above their head!

'Dost fear! dost fear! The moon shines clear,
  And well the dead can ride;
Does faithful Helen fear for them?'
  'O leave in peace the dead!'

'Barb! barb! methinks I hear the cock;
  The sand will soon be run:
Barb! barb! I smell the morning air;
  The race is wellnigh done.'

Tramp! tramp! along the land they rode,
  Splash! splash! along the sea;
The scourge is red, the spur drops blood,
  The flashing pebbles flee.

'Hurrah! hurrah! well ride the dead;
  The bride, the bride is come;
And soon we reach the bridal bed,
  For, Helen, here's my home.'

Reluctant on its rusty hinge
  Revolved an iron door,
And by the pale moon's setting beam
  Were seen a church and tower.

With many a shriek and cry, whiz round
  The birds of midnight, scared;
And rustling like autumnal leaves
  Unhallow'd ghosts were heard.

O'er many a tomb and tombstone pale
  He spurr'd the fiery horse,
Till sudden at an open grave
  He check'd the wondrous course.

The falling gauntlet quits the rein,
  Down drops the casque of steel,
The cuirass leaves his shrinking side,
  The spur his gory heel.

[7] gallop

The eyes desert the naked skull,
  The mould'ring flesh the bone,
Till Helen's lily arms entwine
  A ghastly skeleton.

The furious barb snorts fire and foam,
  And, with a fearful bound,
Dissolves at once in empty air,
  And leaves her on the ground.

Half seen by fits, by fits half heard,
  Pale spectres flit along,
Wheel round the maid in dismal dance,
  And howl the funeral song;

'E'en when the heart's with anguish cleft,
  Revere the doom of Heaven!
Her soul is from her body reft;
  Her spirit be forgiven!'

To a Lady [8]

WITH FLOWERS FROM THE ROMAN WALL

Take these flowers which, purple waving,
  On the ruin'd rampart grew,
Where, the sons of freedom braving,
  Rome's imperial standards flew.

Warriors from the breach of danger
  Pluck no longer laurels there;
They but yield the passing stranger
  Wild-flower wreaths for Beauty's hair.

The Lay of the Last Minstrel [9]

Canto VI, I

Breathes there the man with soul so dead,
Who never to himself hath said,
  This is my own, my native land!
Whose heart hath ne'er within him burn'd,
As home his footsteps he hath turn'd,
  From wandering on a foreign strand!
If such there breathe, go, mark him well;
For him no Minstrel raptures swell;
High though his titles, proud his name,
Boundless his wealth as wish can claim;
Despite those titles, power, and pelf,
The wretch, concentred all in self,
Living, shall forfeit fair renown,
And, doubly dying, shall go down
To the vile dust, from whence he sprung,
Unwept, unhonour'd, and unsung.

[8] Written in 1797.
[9] Published 1805.

Hunting Song [10]

Waken, lords and ladies gay,
On the mountain dawns the day,
All the jolly chase is here,
With hawk, and horse, and hunting-spear!
Hounds are in their couples yelling,
Hawks are whistling, horns are knelling,
Merrily, merrily, mingle they,
'Waken, lords and ladies gay.'

Waken, lords and ladies gay,
The mist has left the mountain grey,
Springlets in the dawn are steaming,
Diamonds on the brake are gleaming:
And foresters have busy been,
To track the buck in thicket green;
Now we come to chant our lay,
'Waken, lords and ladies gay.'

Waken, lords and ladies gay,
To the greenwood haste away;
We can show you where he lies,
Fleet of foot, and tall of size;
We can show the marks he made,
When 'gainst the oak his antlers fray'd;
You shall see him brought to bay,
'Waken, lords and ladies gay.'

Louder, louder chant the lay,
Waken, lords and ladies gay!
Tell them youth, and mirth, and glee,
Run a course as well as we;
Time, stern huntsman! who can baulk,
Stanch as hound, and fleet as hawk:
Think of this, and rise with day,
Gentle lords and ladies gay.

[10] Published in *Edinburgh Annual Register*, 1808.

Marmion[11]

Canto V, 12, Lochinvar

O, young Lochinvar is come out of the west,
Through all the wide Border his steed was the best;
And save his good broadsword he weapons had none,
He rode all unarm'd, and he rode all alone.
So faithful in love, and so dauntless in war,
There never was knight like the young Lochinvar.

He staid not for brake, and he stopp'd not for stone,
He swam the Eske river where ford there was none;
But ere he alighted at Netherby gate,
The bride had consented, the gallant came late:
For a laggard in love, and a dastard in war,
Was to wed the fair Ellen of brave Lochinvar.

So boldly he enter'd the Netherby Hall,
Among bride's-men, and kinsmen, and brothers, and all:
Then spoke the bride's father, his hand on his sword,
(For the poor craven bridegroom said never a word,)
'O come ye in peace here, or come ye in war,
Or to dance at our bridal, young Lord Lochinvar?'

'I long woo'd your daughter, my suit you denied; —
Love swells like the Solway, but ebbs like its tide —
And now am I come, with this lost love of mine,
To lead but one measure, drink one cup of wine.
There are maidens in Scotland more lovely by far,
That would gladly be bride to the young Lochinvar.'

The bride kiss'd the goblet: the knight took it up,
He quaff'd off the wine, and he threw down the cup.
She look'd down to blush, and she look'd up to sigh,
With a smile on her lips and a tear in her eye.
He took her soft hand, ere her mother could bar, —
'Now tread we a measure!' said young Lochinvar.

So stately his form, and so lovely her face,
That never a hall such a galliard[12] did grace;
While her mother did fret, and her father did fume,
And the bridegroom stood dangling his bonnet and plume;
And the bride-maidens whisper'd, ''Twere better by far,
To have match'd our fair cousin with young Lochinvar.'

One touch to her hand, and one word in her ear,
When they reach'd the hall-door, and the charger stood near;
So light to the croupe the fair lady he swung,
So light to the saddle before her he sprung!
'She is won! we are gone, over bank, bush, and scaur;
They'll have fleet steeds that follow,' quoth young Lochinvar.

There was mounting 'mong Græmes of the Netherby clan;
Forsters, Fenwicks, and Musgraves, they rode and they ran:
There was racing and chasing on Cannobie Lee,
But the lost bride of Netherby ne'er did they see.

[11] Published 1808.

[12] gay dance

So daring in love, and so dauntless in war,
Have ye e'er heard of gallant like young Lochinvar? —

The Lady of the Lake[13]

Canto I, Invocation

Harp of the North![14] that mouldering long hast hung
On the witch-elm that shades Saint Fillan's spring,
And down the fitful breeze thy numbers flung,
Till envious ivy did around thee cling,
Muffling with verdant ringlet every string, —
O minstrel Harp, still must thine accents sleep?
'Mid rustling leaves and fountains murmuring,
Still must thy sweeter sounds their silence keep,
Nor bid a warrior smile, nor teach a maid to weep?

Not thus, in ancient days of Caledon,
Was thy voice mute amid the festal crowd,
When lay of hopeless love, or glory won,
Aroused the fearful, or subdued the proud.
At each according pause was heard aloud
Thine ardent symphony sublime and high!
Fair dames and crested chiefs attention bow'd;
For still the burden of thy minstrelsy
Was Knighthood's dauntless deed, and Beauty's matchless eye.

O wake once more! how rude soe'er the hand
That ventures o'er thy magic maze to stray;
O wake once more! though scarce my skill command
Some feeble echoing of thine earlier lay:
Though harsh and faint, and soon to die away,
And all unworthy of thy nobler strain,
Yet if one heart throb higher at its sway,
The wizard note has not been touch'd in vain.
Then silent be no more! Enchantress, wake again!

I, 31, Song

'Soldier, rest! thy warfare o'er,
Sleep the sleep that knows not breaking;
Dream of battled fields no more,
Days of danger, nights of waking.
In our isle's enchanted hall,
Hands unseen thy couch are strewing,
Fairy strains of music fall,
Every sense in slumber dewing.
Soldier, rest! thy warfare o'er,
Dream of fighting fields no more:
Sleep the sleep that knows not breaking,
Morn of toil, nor night of waking.

'No rude sound shall reach thine ear,
Armour's clang, or war-steed champing,
Trump nor pibroch summon here
Mustering clan, or squadron tramping,
Yet the lark's shrill fife may come
At the day-break from the fallow,
And the bittern sound his drum,
Booming from the sedgy shallow.
Ruder sounds shall none be near,
Guards nor warders challenge here,
Here's no war-steed's neigh and champing,
Shouting clans, or squadrons stamping.'

Canto II, 19, Boat Song

'Hail to the Chief who in triumph advances!
Honour'd and bless'd be the evergreen Pine!
Long may the tree, in his banner that glances,
Flourish, the shelter and grace of our line!
Heaven send it happy dew,
Earth lend it sap anew,

---

[13] Published 1810.
[14] The old Scottish minstrelsy.

Gayly to bourgeon,[15] and broadly to grow,
While every Highland glen
Sends our shout back agen,
Roderigh Vich Alpine dhu, ho! ieroe!

'Ours is no sapling, chance-sown by the fountain,
Blooming at Beltane,[16] in winter to fade;
When the whirlwind has stripp'd every leaf on the mountain,
The more shall Clan-Alpine exult in her shade.
Moor'd in the rifted rock,
Proof to the tempest's shock,
Firmer he roots him the ruder it blow;
Menteith and Breadalbane, then,
Echo his praise agen,
Roderigh Vich Alpine dhu, ho! ieroe!

II, 20

'Proudly our pibroch has thrill'd in Glen Fruin,
And Bannochar's groans to our slogan replied;
Glen Luss and Ross-dhu, they are smoking in ruin,
And the best of Loch Lomond lie dead on her side.
Widow and Saxon maid
Long shall lament our raid,
Think of Clan-Alpine with fear and with woe;
Lennox and Leven-glen
Shake when they hear agen,
Roderigh Vich Alpine dhu, ho! ieroe!

'Row, vassals, row, for the pride of the Highlands!
Stretch to your oars, for the evergreen Pine!
O! that the rose-bud that graces yon islands
Were wreathed in a garland around him to twine!
O that some seedling gem,
Worthy such noble stem,

[15] bud
[16] May-day

Honour'd and bless'd in their shadow might grow!
Loud should Clan-Alpine then
Ring from her deepmost glen,
Roderigh Vich Alpine dhu, ho! ieroe!'

Canto III, 16, CORONACH [17]

'HE is gone on the mountain,
He is lost to the forest,
Like a summer-dried fountain,
When our need was the sorest.
The font, reappearing,
From the rain-drops shall borrow,
But to us comes no cheering,
To Duncan no morrow!

The hand of the reaper
Takes the ears that are hoary,
But the voice of the weeper
Wails manhood in glory.
The autumn winds rushing
Waft the leaves that are searest,
But our flower was in flushing,
When blighting was nearest.

Fleet foot on the correi,
Sage counsel in cumber,
Red hand in the foray,
How sound is thy slumber!
Like the dew on the mountain,
Like the foam on the river,
Like the bubble on the fountain,
Thou art gone, and for ever!'

Canto VI, CONCLUSION

HARP of the North, farewell! The hills grow dark,
On purple peaks a deeper shade descending;
In twilight copse the glow-worm lights her spark,
The deer, half-seen, are to the covert wending.
Resume thy wizard elm! the fountain lending,
And the wild breeze, thy wilder minstrelsy;

[17] Lament

Thy numbers sweet with nature's vespers blending,
With distant echo from the fold and lea,
And herd-boy's evening pipe, and hum of housing bee.

Yet once again farewell, thou Minstrel harp!
Yet once again forgive my feeble sway,
And little reck I of the censure sharp
May idly cavil at an idle lay.
Much have I owed thy strains on life's long way,
Through secret woes the world has never known,
When on the weary night dawn'd wearier day,
And bitterer was the grief devour'd alone.
That I o'erlive such woes, Enchantress! is thine own.

Hark! as my lingering footsteps slow retire,
Some Spirit of the Air has waked thy string!
'Tis now a seraph bold, with touch of fire,
'Tis now the brush of Fairy's frolic wing.
Receding now, the dying numbers ring
Fainter and fainter down the rugged dell,
And now the mountain breezes scarcely bring
A wandering witch-note of the distant spell —
And now, 'tis silent all! — Enchantress, fare thee well!

Rokeby[18]

Canto III, 16, Song

O, Brignal banks are wild and fair,
And Greta woods are green,
And you may gather garlands there
Would grace a summer queen.
And as I rode by Dalton-hall,
Beneath the turrets high,
A maiden on the castle wall
Was singing merrily, —
'O, Brignal banks are fresh and fair,
And Greta woods are green;
I'd rather rove with Edmund there,
Than reign our English queen.'

'If, maiden, thou wouldst wend with me,
To leave both tower and town,
Thou first must guess what life lead we,
That dwell by dale and down.
And if thou canst that riddle read,
As read full well you may,
Then to the greenwood shalt thou speed,
As blithe as Queen of May.'
Yet sung she, 'Brignal banks are fair,
And Greta woods are green;
I'd rather rove with Edmund there,
Than reign our English queen.

III, 17

I read you, by your bugle-horn,
And by your palfrey good,
I read you for a ranger sworn,
To keep the king's greenwood.'
'A ranger, lady, winds his horn,
And 'tis at peep of light;
His blast is heard at merry morn,
And mine at dead of night.'
Yet sung she, 'Brignal banks are fair,
And Greta woods are gay;
I would I were with Edmund there,
To reign his Queen of May!

With burnish'd brand and musketoon,
So gallantly you come,
I read you for a bold dragoon,
That lists the tuck of drum.'
'I list no more the tuck of drum,
No more the trumpet hear;
But when the beetle sounds his hum,
My comrades take the spear.
And O! though Brignal banks be fair,
And Greta woods be gay,
Yet mickle must the maiden dare,
Would reign my Queen of May!

[18] Published 1813.

III, 18

Maiden! a nameless life I lead,
  A nameless death I'll die;
The fiend, whose lantern lights the mead,
  Were better mate than I!
And when I'm with my comrades met
  Beneath the greenwood bough,
What once we were we all forget,
  Nor think what we are now.
Yet Brignal banks are fresh and fair,
  And Greta woods are green,
And you may gather garlands there
  Would grace a summer queen.'

Jock of Hazeldean [19]

'Why weep ye by the tide, ladie?
  Why weep ye by the tide?
I'll wed ye to my youngest son,
  And ye sall be his bride:
And ye sall be his bride, ladie,
  Sae comely to be seen'—
But aye she loot the tears down fa'
  For Jock of Hazeldean.

'Now let this wilfu' grief be done,
  And dry that cheek so pale;
Young Frank is chief of Errington,
  And lord of Langley-dale;
His step is first in peaceful ha',
  His sword in battle keen'—
But aye she loot the tears down fa'
  For Jock of Hazeldean.

'A chain of gold ye sall not lack,
  Nor braid to bind your hair;
Nor mettled hound, nor managed hawk,
  Nor palfrey fresh and fair;
And you, the foremost o' them a',
  Shall ride our forest queen'—
But aye she loot the tears down fa'
  For Jock of Hazeldean.

The kirk was deck'd at morning-tide,
  The tapers glimmer'd fair;
The priest and bridegroom wait the bride,
  And dame and knight are there.
They sought her baith by bower and ha';
  The ladie was not seen!
She's o'er the Border, and awa'
  Wi' Jock of Hazeldean.

from *The Antiquary* [20]

THE AGED CARLE [21]

'Why sit'st thou by that ruin'd hall,
  Thou aged carle so stern and grey?
Dost thou its former pride recall,
  Or ponder how it pass'd away?'—

'Know'st thou not me?' the Deep Voice cried;
  'So long enjoy'd, so oft misused—
Alternate, in thy fickle pride,
  Desired, neglected, and accused!

'Before my breath, like blazing flax,
  Man and his marvels pass away!
And changing empires wane and wax,
  Are founded, flourish, and decay.

'Redeem mine hours—the space is brief—
While in my glass the sand-grains shiver,
And measureless thy joy or grief
  When Time and thou shall part for ever!'

[Chap. x.]

from *Old Mortality* [22]

Sound, sound the clarion, fill the fife!
  To all the sensual world proclaim,
One crowded hour of glorious life
  Is worth an age without a name.

[Chap. xxxiii.]

Anonymous.[23]

[19] Written (except for the first stanza, which is ancient) in 1816; published in Campbell Albyn's *Anthology*, 1816.

[20] Published 1816.

[21] churl, or peasant

[22] Published 1816.

[23] Really by Scott himself. One day, while correcting proof-sheets of *The Antiquary*, Scott asked his friend Ballantyne to hunt a passage in Beaumont and Fletcher. 'Hang it, Johnnie!' Scott said, 'I believe I can make a motto sooner than you will find one.' From then on, according to Lockhart, 'whenever memory failed to suggest

from *The Heart of Midlothian*[24]

PROUD MAISIE

PROUD Maisie is in the wood,
Walking so early;
Sweet Robin sits on the bush,
Singing so rarely.

'Tell me, thou bonny bird,
When shall I marry me?'
'When six braw gentlemen
Kirkward shall carry ye.'

'Who makes the bridal bed,
Birdie, say truly?'
'The grey-headed sexton
That delves the grave duly.

'The glow-worm o'er grave and stone
Shall light thee steady.
The owl from the steeple sing,
"Welcome, proud lady."'

[Chaps. XIV–XXXIX.]

from *The Pirate*[25]

THE SONG OF THE REIM-KENNAR

STERN eagle of the far north-west,
Thou that bearest in thy grasp the thunder-bolt,
Thou whose rushing pinions stir ocean to madness,
Thou the destroyer of herds, thou the scatterer of navies,
Amidst the scream of thy rage,
Amidst the rushing of thy onward wings,
Though thy scream be loud as the cry of a perishing nation,
Though the rushing of thy wings be like the roar of ten thousand waves,
Yet hear, in thine ire and thy haste,
Hear thou the voice of the Reim-kennar.

Thou hast met the pine-trees of Drontheim,
Their dark-green heads lie prostrate beside their up-rooted stems;
Thou hast met the rider of the ocean,
The tall, the strong bark of the fearless rover,
And she has struck to thee the topsail
That she had not veil'd to a royal armada.
Thou hast met the tower that bears its crest among the clouds,
The battled massive tower of the Jarl[26] of former days,
And the cope-stone of the turret
Is lying upon its hospitable hearth;
But thou too shalt stoop, proud compeller of clouds,
When thou hearest the voice of the Reim-kennar.

There are verses that can stop the stag in the forest,
Ay, and when the dark-colour'd dog is opening on his track;
There are verses can make the wild hawk pause on the wing,
Like the falcon that wears the hood and the jesses,
And who knows the shrill whistle of the fowler.
Thou who canst mock at the scream of the drowning mariner,
And the crash of the ravaged forest,
And the groan of the overwhelmed crowds,
When the church hath fallen in the moment of prayer;
There are sounds which thou also must list,
When they are chanted by the voice of the Reim-kennar.

Enough of woe hast thou wrought on the ocean.
The widows wring their hands on the beach;
Enough of woe hast thou wrought on the land,
The husbandman folds his arms in despair;
Cease thou the waving of thy pinions,
Let the ocean repose in her dark strength;

---

an appropriate epigraph, he had recourse to the inexhaustible mines of "*old play*" or "*old ballad*" to which we owe some of the most exquisite verses that ever flowed from his pen.'

[24] Published 1818.

[25] Published 1821. The Norwegian 'Song of the Tempest' is sung by the witch Norna after she has stared long at the sky. 'Reim-kennar' means a sorceress, one who can read magic rimes or incantations.

[26] Norse chief

Cease thou the flashing of thine eye,
Let the thunderbolt sleep in the armoury of Odin;
Be thou still at my bidding, viewless racer of the north-western heaven,—
Sleep thou at the voice of Norna the Reim-kennar.

Eagle of the far north-western waters,
Thou hast heard the voice of the Reim-kennar,
Thou hast closed thy wide sails at her bidding,
And folded them in peace by thy side.
My blessing be on thy retiring path;
When thou stoopest from thy place on high,
Soft be thy slumbers in the caverns of the unknown ocean,
Rest till destiny shall again awaken thee;
Eagle of the north-west, thou hast heard the voice of the Reim-kennar.

[Chap. VI.]

from *Quentin Durward*[27]

COUNTY GUY

AH! County Guy, the hour is nigh,
The sun has left the lea,
The orange flower perfumes the bower,
The breeze is on the sea.
The lark, his lay who thrill'd all day,
Sits hush'd his partner nigh;
Breeze, bird, and flower, confess the hour,
But where is County Guy?

The village maid steals through the shade,
Her shepherd's suit to hear;
To beauty shy, by lattice high,
Sings high-born Cavalier.
The star of Love, all stars above,
Now reigns o'er earth and sky;
And high and low the influence know—
But where is County Guy?

[Chap. IV.]

[27] Published 1823.

George Noel Gordon, Lord Byron

1788–1824

Maid of Athens, ere we part[1]

Ζώη μοῦ, σᾶς ἀγαπῶ.[2]

MAID of Athens, ere we part,
Give, oh give me back my heart!
Or, since that has left my breast,
Keep it now, and take the rest!
Hear my vow before I go,
Ζώη μοῦ, σᾶς ἀγαπῶ.

By those tresses unconfined,
Woo'd by each Ægean wind;
By those lids whose jetty fringe
Kiss thy soft cheeks' blooming tinge;
By those wild eyes like the roe,
Ζώη μοῦ, σᾶς ἀγαπῶ.

By that lip I long to taste;
By that zone-encircled waist;
By all the token-flowers that tell
What words can never speak so well;
By love's alternate joy and woe,
Ζώη μοῦ, σᾶς ἀγαπῶ.

Maid of Athens! I am gone:
Think of me, sweet! when alone.
Though I fly to Istambol,
Athens holds my heart and soul:
Can I cease to love thee? No!
Ζώη μοῦ, σᾶς ἀγαπῶ.

[1] Written at Athens in 1810; first published with *Childe Harold,* 1812. The girl is supposedly Theresa Macri, with whose mother Byron and his friend Hobhouse lodged.

[2] My life, I love thee.

CHILDE HAROLD'S PILGRIMAGE [3]

CANTO III

'Afin que cette application vous forçât de penser à autre chose; il n'y a en vérité de remède que celui-là et le temps.' [4]

Lettre du Roi de Prusse à D'Alembert, Sept. 7, 1776.

I

Is thy face like thy mother's, my fair child!
Ada! sole daughter of my house and heart? [5]
When last I saw thy young blue eyes they smiled,
And then we parted,—not as now we part,
But with a hope.—
Awaking with a start,
The waters heave around me; and on high
The winds lift up their voices: I depart,
Whither I know not; but the hour's gone by,
When Albion's lessening shores could grieve or glad mine eye.

II

Once more upon the waters! yet once more!
And the waves bound beneath me as a steed
That knows his rider. Welcome to their roar!
Swift be their guidance, wheresoe'er it lead!
Though the strain'd mast should quiver as a reed,
And the rent canvas fluttering strew the gale,
Still must I on; for I am as a weed,
Flung from the rock, on Ocean's foam to sail
Where'er the surge may sweep, the tempest's breath prevail.

III

In my youth's summer I did sing of One,[6]
The wandering outlaw of his own dark mind;
Again I seize the theme, then but begun,
And bear it with me, as the rushing wind
Bears the cloud onwards: in that Tale I find
The furrows of long thought, and dried-up tears,
Which, ebbing, leave a sterile track behind,
O'er which all heavily the journeying years
Plod the last sands of life,—where not a flower appears.

IV

Since my young days of passion—joy, or pain,
Perchance my heart and harp have lost a string,
And both may jar: it may be, that in vain
I would essay as I have sung to sing.
Yet, though a dreary strain, to this I cling;
So that it wean me from the weary dream
Of selfish grief or gladness—so it fling
Forgetfulness around me—it shall seem
To me, though to none else, a not ungrateful theme.

[3] The first two cantos were published in 1812 with instant success. Byron 'awoke to find himself famous,' the social and romantic sensation of London. The scandal that broke upon his separation from Anne Milbanke, whom he had married in January 1815, caused him to sail from Dover on 25 April 1816, an 'exile' never to return. Proud, and scornful of the idolaters who had turned so swiftly against him, Byron now felt the pitch of 'Titan agony' and revolt which, however touched by theatricality it may have been, evoked his true genius. He went to Geneva, where he lingered and where he met Shelley, whose influence is reflected in the third canto of *Childe Harold*. This part of the poem was written in May and June 1816, and brought back by Shelley to England for publication the same year.

[4] In order that this task may force you to think of something else; there is truly no remedy except that and time.

[5] Byron never saw Ada after she was five weeks old.

[6] Childe Harold

V

He, who grown aged in this world of woe,
In deeds, not years, piercing the depths of life,
So that no wonder waits him; nor below
Can love or sorrow, fame, ambition, strife,
Cut to his heart again with the keen knife
Of silent, sharp endurance: he can tell
Why thought seeks refuge in lone caves, yet rife
With airy images, and shapes which dwell
Still unimpair'd, though old, in the soul's haunted cell.

VI

'T is to create, and in creating live
A being more intense that we endow
With form our fancy, gaining as we give
The life we image, even as I do now.
What am I? Nothing: but not so art thou,
Soul of my thought! with whom I traverse earth,
Invisible but gazing, as I glow
Mix'd with thy spirit, blended with thy birth,
And feeling still with thee in my crush'd feelings' dearth.

VII

Yet must I think less wildly: — I *have* thought
Too long and darkly, till my brain became,
In its own eddy boiling and o'erwrought,
A whirling gulf of phantasy and flame:
And thus, untaught in youth my heart to tame,
My springs of life were poison'd. 'T is too late!
Yet am I changed; though still enough the same
In strength to bear what time cannot abate,
And feed on bitter fruits without accusing Fate.

VIII

Something too much of this; — but now 't is past,
And the spell closes with its silent seal.
Long absent Harold re-appears at last;
He of the breast which fain no more would feel,
Wrung with the wounds which kill not, but ne'er heal;
Yet Time, who changes all, had alter'd him
In soul and aspect as in age: years steal
Fire from the mind as vigour from the limb;
And life's enchanted cup but sparkles near the brim.

IX

His had been quaff'd too quickly, and he found
The dregs were wormwood; but he fill'd again,
And from a purer fount, on holier ground,
And deem'd its spring perpetual; but in vain!
Still round him clung invisibly a chain
Which gall'd for ever, fettering though unseen,
And heavy though it clank'd not; worn with pain,
Which pined although it spoke not, and grew keen,
Entering with every step he took through many a scene.

X

Secure in guarded coldness, he had mix'd
Again in fancied safety with his kind,
And deem'd his spirit now so firmly fix'd
And sheath'd with an invulnerable mind,
That, if no joy, no sorrow lurk'd behind;

And he, as one, might 'midst the many stand
Unheeded, searching through the crowd to find
Fit speculation; such as in strange land
He found in wonder-works of God and Nature's hand.

XI

But who can view the ripen'd rose, nor seek
To wear it? who can curiously behold
The smoothness and the sheen of beauty's cheek,
Nor feel the heart can never all grow old?
Who can contemplate Fame through clouds unfold
The star which rises o'er her steep, nor climb?
Harold, once more within the vortex, roll'd
On with the giddy circle, chasing Time,
Yet with a nobler aim than in his youth's fond prime.

XII

But soon he knew himself the most unfit
Of men to herd with Man; with whom he held
Little in common; untaught to submit
His thoughts to others, though his soul was quell'd
In youth by his own thoughts; still uncompell'd,
He would not yield dominion of his mind
To spirits against whom his own rebell'd;
Proud though in desolation; which could find
A life within itself, to breathe without mankind.

XIII

Where rose the mountains, there to him were friends;
Where roll'd the ocean, thereon was his home;
Where a blue sky, and glowing clime, extends,
He had the passion and the power to roam;
The desert, forest, cavern, breaker's foam,
Were unto him companionship; they spake
A mutual language, clearer than the tome
Of his land's tongue, which he would oft forsake
For Nature's pages glass'd by sunbeams on the lake.

XIV

Like the Chaldean, he could watch the stars,
Till he had peopled them with beings bright
As their own beams; and earth, and earth-born jars,
And human frailties, were forgotten quite:
Could he have kept his spirit to that flight
He had been happy; but this clay will sink
Its spark immortal, envying it the light
To which it mounts, as if to break the link
That keeps us from yon heaven which woos us to its brink.

XV

But in Man's dwellings he became a thing
Restless and worn, and stern and wearisome,
Droop'd as a wild-born falcon with clipt wing,
To whom the boundless air alone were home:
Then came his fit again, which to o'ercome,
As eagerly the barr'd-up bird will beat
His breast and beak against his wiry dome

Till the blood tinge his plumage, so the heat
Of his impeded soul would through his bosom eat.

XVI

Self-exiled Harold wanders forth again,
With nought of hope left, but with less of gloom;
The very knowledge that he lived in vain,
That all was over on this side the tomb,
Had made Despair a smilingness assume,
Which, though 't were wild, — as on the plunder'd wreck
When mariners would madly meet their doom
With draughts intemperate on the sinking deck, —
Did yet inspire a cheer, which he forbore to check.

XVII

Stop! — for thy tread is on an Empire's dust!
An Earthquake's spoil is sepulchred below!
Is the spot mark'd with no colossal bust?
Nor column trophied for triumphal show?
None; but the moral's truth tells simpler so,
As the ground was before, thus let it be; —
How that red rain hath made the harvest grow!
And is this all the world has gain'd by thee,
Thou first and last of fields! king-making Victory?

XVIII

And Harold stands upon this place of skulls,
The grave of France, the deadly Waterloo!
How in an hour the power which gave annuls
Its gifts, transferring fame as fleeting too!
In 'pride of place'[7] here last the eagle flew,
Then tore with bloody talon the rent plain,
Pierced by the shaft of banded nations through;
Ambition's life and labours all were vain;
He wears the shatter'd links of the world's broken chain.

XIX

Fit retribution! Gaul may champ the bit
And foam in fetters; — but is Earth more free?
Did nations combat to make *One* submit;
Or league to teach all kings true sovereignty?
What! shall reviving Thraldom again be
The patch'd-up idol of enlighten'd days?
Shall we, who struck the Lion down, shall we
Pay the Wolf homage? proffering lowly gaze
And servile knees to thrones? No; *prove* before ye praise!

XX

If not, o'er one fallen despot boast no more!
In vain fair cheeks were furrow'd with hot tears
For Europe's flowers long rooted up before
The trampler of her vineyards; in vain years
Of death, depopulation, bondage, fears,
Have all been borne, and broken by the accord
Of roused-up millions; all that most endears
Glory, is when the myrtle wreathes a sword

[7] A term in falconry, meaning 'the highest pitch of flight.'

Such as Harmodius [8] drew on Athens' tyrant lord.

XXI

There was a sound of revelry by night,
And Belgium's capital had gather'd then
Her Beauty and her Chivalry, and bright
The lamps shone o'er fair women and brave men;
A thousand hearts beat happily; and when
Music arose with its voluptuous swell,
Soft eyes look'd love to eyes which spake again,
And all went merry as a marriage bell;
But hush! hark! a deep sound strikes like a rising knell!

XXII

Did ye not hear it? — No; 't was but the wind,
Or the car rattling o'er the stony street;
On with the dance! let joy be unconfined;
No sleep till morn, when Youth and Pleasure meet
To chase the glowing Hours with flying feet —
But hark! — that heavy sound breaks in once more,
As if the clouds its echo would repeat;
And nearer, clearer, deadlier than before!
Arm! Arm! it is — it is — the cannon's opening roar!

XXIII

Within a window'd niche of that high hall
Sate Brunswick's fated chieftain; [9] he did hear
That sound the first amidst the festival,
And caught its tone with Death's prophetic ear;
And when they smiled because he deem'd it near,
His heart more truly knew that peal too well
Which stretch'd his father on a bloody bier,
And roused the vengeance blood alone could quell;
He rush'd into the field, and, foremost fighting, fell.

XXIV

Ah! then and there was hurrying to and fro,
And gathering tears, and tremblings of distress,
And cheeks all pale, which but an hour ago
Blush'd at the praise of their own loveliness;
And there were sudden partings, such as press
The life from out young hearts, and choking sighs
Which ne'er might be repeated; who could guess
If ever more should meet those mutual eyes,
Since upon night so sweet such awful morn could rise!

XXV

And there was mounting in hot haste: the steed,
The mustering squadron, and the clattering car,
Went pouring forward with impetuous speed,
And swiftly forming in the ranks of war;
And the deep thunder peal on peal afar;
And near, the beat of the alarming drum
Roused up the soldier ere the morning star;
While thronged the citizens with terror dumb,
Or whispering, with white lips — 'The foe! they come! they come!'

---

[8] He slew the tyrant Hipparchus with a sword concealed in myrtle leaves.

[9] Frederick William, Duke of Brunswick, who fell in the first part of the battle. His father had been killed in 1806.

XXVI

And wild and high the 'Cameron's gathering'[10] rose!
The war-note of Lochiel, which Albyn's hills
Have heard, and heard, too, have her Saxon foes: —
How in the noon of night that pibroch thrills,
Savage and shrill! But with the breath which fills
Their mountain-pipe, so fill the mountaineers
With the fierce native daring which instils
The stirring memory of a thousand years,
And Evan's, Donald's fame rings in each clansman's ears!

XXVII

And Ardennes[11] waves above them her green leaves,
Dewy with nature's tear-drops as they pass,
Grieving, if aught inanimate e'er grieves,
Over the unreturning brave, — alas!
Ere evening to be trodden like the grass
Which now beneath them, but above shall grow
In its next verdure, when this fiery mass
Of living valour, rolling on the foe
And burning with high hope shall moulder cold and low.

XXVIII

Last noon beheld them full of lusty life,
Last eve in Beauty's circle proudly gay,
The midnight brought the signal-sound of strife,
The morn the marshalling in arms, — the day
Battle's magnificently stern array!
The thunder-clouds close o'er it, which when rent
The earth is cover'd thick with other clay,
Which her own clay shall cover, heap'd and pent,
Rider and horse, — friend, foe, — in one red burial blent!

XXIX

Their praise is hymn'd by loftier harps than mine:
Yet one I would select from that proud throng,
Partly because they blend me with his line,
And partly that I did his sire some wrong,
And partly that bright names will hallow song;
And his was of the bravest, and when shower'd
The death-bolts deadliest the thinn'd files along,
Even where the thickest of war's tempest lower'd,
They reach'd no nobler breast than thine, young gallant Howard![12]

XXX

There have been tears and breaking hearts for thee,
And mine were nothing had I such to give;
But when I stood beneath the fresh green tree,
Which living waves where thou didst cease to live,
And saw around me the wide field revive
With fruits and fertile promise, and the Spring
Came forth her work of gladness to contrive,
With all her reckless birds upon the wing,

[10] The war song of the Clan Cameron, whose chief was called by the name of his estate, Lochiel.

[11] Woods near the battlefield, supposedly Shakespeare's 'Forest of Arden.'

[12] Major Frederick Howard, son of the Earl of Carlisle, Byron's guardian and distant relative. Byron had satirized the Earl in *English Bards and Scotch Reviewers* (1809).

I turn'd from all she brought to those she could not bring.

XXXI

I turn'd to thee, to thousands, of whom each
And one as all a ghastly gap did make
In his own kind and kindred, whom to teach
Forgetfulness were mercy for their sake;
The Archangel's trump, not Glory's, must awake
Those whom they thirst for; though the sound of Fame
May for a moment soothe, it cannot slake
The fever of vain longing, and the name
So honour'd but assumes a stronger, bitterer claim.

XXXII

They mourn, but smile at length; and, smiling, mourn:
The tree will wither long before it fall;
The hull drives on, though mast and sail be torn;
The roof-tree sinks, but moulders on the hall
In massy hoariness; the ruin'd wall
Stands when its wind-worn battlements are gone;
The bars survive the captive they enthral;
The day drags through, though storms keep out the sun;
And thus the heart will break, yet brokenly live on:

XXXIII

Even as a broken mirror, which the glass
In every fragment multiplies; and makes
A thousand images of one that was,
The same, and still the more, the more it breaks;
And thus the heart will do which not forsakes,
Living in shatter'd guise; and still, and cold,
And bloodless, with its sleepless sorrow aches,
Yet withers on till all without is old,
Showing no visible sign, for such things are untold.

XXXIV

There is a very life in our despair,
Vitality of poison, — a quick root
Which feeds these deadly branches; for it were
As nothing did we die; but Life will suit
Itself to Sorrow's most detested fruit,
Like to the apples on the Dead Sea's shore,
All ashes to the taste: Did man compute
Existence by enjoyment, and count o'er
Such hours 'gainst years of life, — say, would he name threescore?

XXXV

The Psalmist number'd out the years of man:
They are enough; and if thy tale be *true,*
Thou, who didst grudge him even that fleeting span,
More than enough, thou fatal Waterloo!
Millions of tongues record thee, and anew
Their children's lips shall echo them, and say —
'Here, where the sword united nations drew,
Our countrymen were warring on that day!'
And this is much, and all which will not pass away.

XXXVI

There sunk the greatest, nor the worst of men,[13]
Whose spirit, antithetically mixt,
One moment of the mightiest, and again
On little objects with like firmness fixt;
Extreme in all things! hadst thou been betwixt,
Thy throne had still been thine, or never been;

[13] Napoleon

For daring made thy rise as fall: thou seek'st
Even now to re-assume the imperial mien,
And shake again the world, the Thunderer of the scene!

XXXVII

Conqueror and captive of the earth art thou!
She trembles at thee still, and thy wild name
Was ne'er more bruited in men's minds than now
That thou art nothing, save the jest of Fame,
Who woo'd thee once, thy vassal, and became
The flatterer of thy fierceness, till thou wert
A god unto thyself; nor less the same
To the astounded kingdoms all inert,
Who deem'd thee for a time whate'er thou didst assert.

XXXVIII

Oh, more or less than man — in high or low,
Battling with nations, flying from the field;
Now making monarchs' necks thy footstool, now
More than thy meanest soldier taught to yield;
An empire thou couldst crush, command, rebuild,
But govern not thy pettiest passion, nor,
However deeply in men's spirits skill'd,
Look through thine own, nor curb the lust of war,
Nor learn that tempted Fate will leave the loftiest star.

XXXIX

Yet well thy soul hath brook'd the turning tide
With that untaught innate philosophy,
Which, be it wisdom, coldness, or deep pride,
Is gall and wormwood to an enemy.
When the whole host of hatred stood hard by,
To watch and mock thee shrinking, thou hast smiled
With a sedate and all-enduring eye; —
When Fortune fled her spoil'd and favourite child,
He stood unbow'd beneath the ills upon him piled.

XL

Sager than in thy fortunes; for in them
Ambition steel'd thee on too far to show
That just habitual scorn, which could contemn
Men and their thoughts; 't was wise to feel, not so
To wear it ever on thy lip and brow,
And spurn the instruments thou wert to use
Till they were turn'd unto thine overthrow:
'Tis but a worthless world to win or lose;
So hath it proved to thee, and all such lot who choose.

XLI

If, like a tower upon a headland rock,
Thou hadst been made to stand or fall alone,
Such scorn of man had help'd to brave the shock;
But men's thoughts were the steps which paved thy throne,
Their admiration thy best weapon shone;
The part of Philip's son [14] was thine, not then
(Unless aside thy purple had been thrown)
Like stern Diogenes to mock at men;
For sceptred cynics earth were far too wide a den.

[14] Alexander the Great

XLII

But quiet to quick bosoms is a hell,
And *there* hath been thy bane; there is a fire
And motion of the soul which will not dwell
In its own narrow being, but aspire
Beyond the fitting medium of desire;
And, but once kindled, quenchless evermore,
Preys upon high adventure, nor can tire
Of aught but rest; a fever at the core,
Fatal to him who bears, to all who ever bore.

XLIII

This makes the madmen who have made men mad
By their contagion; Conquerors and Kings,
Founders of sects and systems, to whom add
Sophists, Bards, Statesmen, all unquiet things
Which stir too strongly the soul's secret springs,
And are themselves the fools to those they fool;
Envied, yet how unenviable! what stings
Are theirs! One breast laid open were a school
Which would unteach mankind the lust to shine or rule:

XLIV

Their breath is agitation, and their life
A storm whereon they ride, to sink at last,
And yet so nursed and bigoted to strife,
That should their days, surviving perils past,
Melt to calm twilight, they feel overcast
With sorrow and supineness, and so die;
Even as a flame unfed, which runs to waste
With its own flickering, or a sword laid by,
Which eats into itself, and rusts ingloriously.

XLV

He who ascends to mountain-tops, shall find
The loftiest peaks most wrapt in clouds and snow;
He who surpasses or subdues mankind,
Must look down on the hate of those below.
Though high *above* the sun of glory glow,
And far *beneath* the earth and ocean spread,
Round him are icy rocks, and loudly blow
Contending tempests on his naked head,
And thus reward the toils which to those summits led.

XLVI

Away with these! true Wisdom's world will be
Within its own creation, or in thine,
Maternal Nature! for who teems like thee,
Thus on the banks of thy majestic Rhine?
There Harold gazes on a work divine,
A blending of all beauties; streams and dells,
Fruit, foliage, crag, wood, cornfield, mountain, vine,
And chiefless castles breathing stern farewells
From gray but leafy walls, where Ruin greenly dwells.

XLVII

And there they stand, as stands a lofty mind,
Worn, but unstooping to the baser crowd,
All tenantless, save to the crannying wind,
Or holding dark communion with the cloud.

There was a day when they were young and proud;
Banners on high, and battles pass'd below;
But they who fought are in a bloody shroud,
And those which waved are shredless dust ere now,
And the bleak battlements shall bear no future blow.

XLVIII

Beneath these battlements, within those walls,
Power dwelt amidst her passions; in proud state
Each robber chief upheld his armed halls,
Doing his evil will, nor less elate
Than mightier heroes of a longer date.
What want these outlaws conquerors should have
But history's purchased page to call them great?
A wider space, an ornamented grave?
Their hopes were not less warm, their souls were full as brave.

XLIX

In their baronial feuds and single fields,
What deeds of prowess unrecorded died!
And Love, which lent a blazon to their shields,
With emblems well devised by amorous pride,
Through all the mail of iron hearts would glide;
But still their flame was fierceness, and drew on
Keen contest and destruction near allied,
And many a tower for some fair mischief won,
Saw the discolour'd Rhine beneath its ruin run.

L

But Thou, exulting and abounding river!
Making thy waves a blessing as they flow
Through banks whose beauty would endure for ever
Could man but leave thy bright creation so,
Nor its fair promise from the surface mow
With the sharp scythe of conflict, — then to see
Thy valley of sweet waters, were to know
Earth paved like Heaven; and to seem such to me,
Even now what wants thy stream? — that it should Lethe be.

LI

A thousand battles have assail'd thy banks,
But these and half their fame have pass'd away,
And Slaughter heap'd on high his weltering ranks;
Their very graves are gone, and what are they?
Thy tide wash'd down the blood of yesterday,
And all was stainless, and on thy clear stream
Glass'd, with its dancing light, the sunny ray;
But o'er the blacken'd memory's blighting dream
Thy waves would vainly roll, all sweeping as they seem.

LII

Thus Harold inly said, and pass'd along,
Yet not insensible to all which here
Awoke the jocund birds to early song
In glens which might have made even exile dear:
Though on his brow were graven lines austere,
And tranquil sternness, which had ta'en the place
Of feelings fierier far but less severe,

Joy was not always absent from his face,
But o'er it in such scenes would steal with transient trace.

LIII

Nor was all love shut from him, though his days
Of passion had consumed themselves to dust.
It is in vain that we would coldly gaze
On such as smile upon us; the heart must
Leap kindly back to kindness, though disgust
Hath wean'd it from all worldlings: thus he felt,
For there was soft remembrance, and sweet trust
In one fond breast,[15] to which his own would melt,
And in its tenderer hour on that his bosom dwelt.

LIV

And he had learn'd to love, — I know not why,
For this in such as him seems strange of mood, —
The helpless looks of blooming infancy,
Even in its earliest nurture; what subdued,
To change like this, a mind so far imbued
With scorn of man, it little boots to know;
But thus it was; and though in solitude
Small power the nipp'd affections have to grow,
In him this glow'd when all beside had ceased to glow.

LV

And there was one soft breast, as hath been said,
Which unto his was bound by stronger ties
Than the church links withal; and, though unwed,
That love was pure, and, far above disguise,
Had stood the test of mortal enmities
Still undivided, and cemented more
By peril, dreaded most in female eyes;
But this was firm, and from a foreign shore
Well to that heart might his these absent greetings pour!

1

The castled crag of Drachenfels
Frowns o'er the wide and winding Rhine,
Whose breast of waters broadly swells
Between the banks which bear the vine,
And hills all rich with blossom'd trees,
And fields which promise corn and wine,
And scatter'd cities crowning these,
Whose far white walls along them shine,
Have strew'd a scene, which I should see
With double joy wert *thou* with me.

2

And peasant girls, with deep blue eyes,
And hands which offer early flowers,
Walk smiling o'er this paradise;
Above, the frequent feudal towers
Through green leaves lift their walls of gray;
And many a rock which steeply lowers,
And noble arch in proud decay,
Look o'er this vale of vintage-bowers;
But one thing want these banks of Rhine, —
Thy gentle hand to clasp in mine!

3

I send the lilies given to me;
Though long before thy hand they touch,

---

15 Refers to Byron's half-sister Augusta.

I know that they must wither'd be,
But yet reject them not as such;
For I have cherish'd them as dear,
Because they yet may meet thine eye,
And guide thy soul to mine even here,
When thou behold'st them drooping nigh,
And know'st them gather'd by the Rhine,
And offer'd from my heart to thine!

4

The river nobly foams and flows,
The charm of this enchanted ground,
And all its thousand turns disclose
Some fresher beauty's varying round:
The haughtiest breast its wish might bound
Through life to dwell delighted here;
Nor could on earth a spot be found
To nature and to me so dear,
Could thy dear eyes in following mine
Still sweeten more these banks of Rhine!

LVI

By Coblentz, on a rise of gentle ground,
There is a small and simple pyramid,
Crowning the summit of the verdant mound;
Beneath its base are heroes' ashes hid,
Our enemy's — but let not that forbid
Honour to Marceau! [16] o'er whose early tomb
Tears, big tears, gush'd from the rough soldier's lid,
Lamenting and yet envying such a doom,
Falling for France, whose rights he battled to resume.

LVII

Brief, brave, and glorious was his young career, —
His mourners were two hosts, his friends and foes;
And fitly may the stranger lingering here
Pray for his gallant spirit's bright repose;
For he was Freedom's champion, one of those,
The few in number, who had not o'erstept
The charter to chastise which she bestows
On such as wield her weapons; he had kept
The whiteness of his soul, and thus men o'er him wept.

LVIII

Here Ehrenbreitstein,[17] with her shatter'd wall
Black with the miner's blast, upon her height
Yet shows of what she was, when shell and ball
Rebounding idly on her strength did light:
A tower of victory! from whence the flight
Of baffled foes was watch'd along the plain:
But Peace destroy'd what War could never blight,
And laid those proud roofs bare to Summer's rain —
On which the iron shower for years had pour'd in vain.

LIX

Adieu to thee, fair Rhine! How long delighted
The stranger fain would linger on his way!
Thine is a scene alike where souls united
Or lonely Contemplation thus might stray;
And could the ceaseless vultures cease to prey
On self-condemning bosoms, it were here,

[16] A general of the French Revolutionary armies, who was killed in 1796, aged twenty-seven.

[17] A fortress on the Rhine, captured in 1799 by the French, who later demolished it.

Where Nature, nor too sombre nor too gay,
Wild but not rude, awful yet not austere,
Is to the mellow Earth as Autumn to the year.

LX

Adieu to thee again! a vain adieu!
There can be no farewell to scene like thine;
The mind is colour'd by thy every hue;
And if reluctantly the eyes resign
Their cherish'd gaze upon thee, lovely Rhine!
'Tis with the thankful heart of parting praise;
More mighty spots may rise, more glaring shine,
But none unite in one attaching maze
The brilliant, fair, and soft, — the glories of old days.

LXI

The negligently grand, the fruitful bloom
Of coming ripeness, the white city's sheen,
The rolling stream, the precipice's gloom,
The forest's growth, and Gothic walls between,
The wild rocks shaped as they had turrets been,
In mockery of man's art; and these withal
A race of faces happy as the scene,
Whose fertile bounties here extend to all,
Still springing o'er thy banks, though Empires near them fall.

LXII

But these recede. Above me are the Alps,
The palaces of Nature, whose vast walls
Have pinnacled in clouds their snowy scalps,
And throned Eternity in icy halls
Of cold sublimity, where forms and falls
The avalanche — the thunderbolt of snow!
All that expands the spirit, yet appals,
Gather around these summits, as to show
How Earth may pierce to Heaven, yet leave vain man below.

LXIII

But ere these matchless heights I dare to scan,
There is a spot should not be pass'd in vain, —
Morat! [18] the proud, the patriot field! where man
May gaze on ghastly trophies of the slain,
Nor blush for those who conquer'd on that plain;
Here Burgundy bequeath'd his tombless host,
A bony heap, through ages to remain,
Themselves their monument; — the Stygian coast
Unsepulchred they roam'd, and shriek'd each wandering ghost.

LXIV

While Waterloo with Cannæ's [19] carnage vies,
Morat and Marathon twin names shall stand;
They were true Glory's stainless victories,
Won by the unambitious heart and hand
Of a proud, brotherly, and civic band,
All unbought champions in no princely cause
Of vice entail'd Corruption; they no land
Doom'd to bewail the blasphemy of laws
Making kings' rights divine, by some Draconic [20] clause.

LXV

By a lone wall a lonelier column rears
A gray and grief-worn aspect of old days;

[18] The town and lake, near Neufchâtel. The Swiss there defeated Charles the Bold, Duke of Burgundy, in 1476.

[19] Hannibal there defeated the Romans in 216 B.C.

[20] Draco, earliest of the lawmakers of Athens, drew up a code famous for its severity.

'Tis the last remnant of the wreck of years,
And looks as with the wild-bewilder'd gaze
Of one to stone converted by amaze,
Yet still with consciousness; and there it stands
Making a marvel that it not decays,
When the coeval pride of human hands,
Levell'd Adventicum,[21] hath strew'd her subject lands.

LXVI

And there — oh! sweet and sacred be the name! —
Julia [22] — the daughter, the devoted — gave
Her youth to Heaven; her heart, beneath a claim
Nearest to Heaven's, broke o'er a father's grave.
Justice is sworn 'gainst tears, and hers would crave
The life she lived in; but the judge was just,
And then she died on him she could not save.
Their tomb was simple, and without a bust,
And held within their urn one mind, one heart, one dust.

LXVII

But these are deeds which should not pass away,
And names that must not wither, though the earth
Forgets her empires with a just decay,
The enslavers and the enslaved, their death and birth;
The high, the mountain-majesty of worth
Should be, and shall, survivor of its woe,
And from its immortality look forth
In the sun's face, like yonder Alpine snow,
Imperishably pure beyond all things below.

LXVIII

Lake Leman [23] woos me with its crystal face,
The mirror where the stars and mountains view
The stillness of their aspect in each trace
Its clear depth yields of their far height and hue:
There is too much of man here, to look through
With a fit mind the might which I behold;
But soon in me shall Loneliness renew
Thoughts hid, but not less cherish'd than of old,
Ere mingling with the herd had penn'd me in their fold.

LXIX

To fly from, need not be to hate, mankind:
All are not fit with them to stir and toil,
Nor is it discontent to keep the mind
Deep in its fountain, lest it overboil
In the hot throng, where we become the spoil
Of our infection, till too late and long
We may deplore and struggle with the coil,
In wretched interchange of wrong for wrong
Midst a contentious world, striving where none are strong.

LXX

There, in a moment we may plunge our years
In fatal penitence, and in the blight
Of our own soul turn all our blood to tears,
And colour things to come with hues of Night;
The race of life becomes a hopeless flight

[21] The capital of Roman Switzerland.
[22] A young priestess of Aventicum who, according to a monumental inscription now proved a forgery, died after a vain effort to save her father. condemned for treason.

[23] Lake Geneva

To those that walk in darkness: on the sea
The boldest steer but where their ports invite;
But there are wanderers o'er Eternity
Whose bark drives on and on, and anchor'd ne'er shall be.

LXXI

Is it not better, then, to be alone,
And love Earth only for its earthly sake?
By the blue rushing of the arrowy Rhone,
Or the pure bosom of its nursing lake,
Which feeds it as a mother who doth make
A fair but froward infant her own care,
Kissing its cries away as these awake;—
Is it not better thus our lives to wear,
Than join the crushing crowd, doom'd to inflict or bear?

LXXII

I live not in myself, but I become
Portion of that around me; and to me
High mountains are a feeling, but the hum
Of human cities torture: I can see
Nothing to loathe in nature, save to be
A link reluctant in a fleshly chain,
Class'd among creatures, when the soul can flee,
And with the sky, the peak, the heaving plain
Of ocean, or the stars, mingle, and not in vain.

LXXIII

And thus I am absorb'd, and this is life:
I look upon the peopled desert past,
As on a place of agony and strife,
Where, for some sin, to sorrow I was cast,
To act and suffer, but remount at last
With a fresh pinion; which I feel to spring,
Though young, yet waxing vigorous as the blast
Which it would cope with, on delighted wing,
Spurning the clay-cold bonds which round our being cling.

LXXIV

And when, at length, the mind shall be all free
From what it hates in this degraded form,
Reft of its carnal life, save what shall be
Existent happier in the fly and worm,—
When elements to elements conform,
And dust is as it should be, shall I not
Feel all I see, less dazzling, but more warm?
The bodiless thought? the Spirit of each spot?
Of which, even now, I share at times the immortal lot?

LXXV

Are not the mountains, waves, and skies, a part
Of me and of my soul, as I of them?
Is not the love of these deep in my heart
With a pure passion? should I not contemn
All objects, if compared with these? and stem
A tide of suffering, rather than forego
Such feelings for the hard and worldly phlegm
Of those whose eyes are only turn'd below,
Gazing upon the ground, with thoughts which dare not glow?

LXXVI

But this is not my theme; and I return
To that which is immediate, and require
Those who find contemplation in the urn,
To look on One,[24] whose dust was once all fire,
A native of the land where I respire
The clear air for a while—a passing guest,

[24] Jean Jacques Rousseau (1712–1778), born in Geneva, where he spent his early years.

Where he became a being, — whose desire
Was to be glorious; 't was a foolish quest,
The which to gain and keep, he sacrificed all rest.

LXXVII

Here the self-torturing sophist, wild Rousseau,
The apostle of affliction, he who threw
Enchantment over passion, and from woe
Wrung overwhelming eloquence, first drew
The breath which made him wretched; yet he knew
How to make madness beautiful, and cast
O'er erring deeds and thoughts a heavenly hue
Of words, like sunbeams, dazzling as they past
The eyes, which o'er them shed tears feelingly and fast.

LXXVIII

His love was passion's essence: — as a tree
On fire by lightning, with ethereal flame
Kindled he was, and blasted; for to be
Thus, and enamour'd, were in him the same.
But his was not the love of living dame,
Nor of the dead who rise upon our dreams,
But of ideal beauty, which became
In him existence, and o'erflowing teems
Along his burning page, distemper'd though it seems.

LXXIX

This breathed itself to life in Julie,[25] *this*
Invested her with all that's wild and sweet;
This hallow'd, too, the memorable kiss
Which every morn his fever'd lip would greet,
From hers, who but with friendship his would meet;[26]
But to that gentle touch through brain and breast
Flash'd the thrill'd spirit's love-devouring heat;
In that absorbing sigh perchance more blest
Than vulgar minds may be with all they seek possest.

LXXX

His life was one long war with self-sought foes,
Or friends by him self-banish'd; for his mind
Had grown Suspicion's sanctuary, and chose,
For its own cruel sacrifice, the kind,
'Gainst whom he raged with fury strange and blind.
But he was phrensied, — wherefore, who may know?
Since cause might be which skill could never find;
But he was phrensied by disease or woe,
To that worst pitch of all, which wears a reasoning show.

LXXXI

For then he was inspired, and from him came,
As from the Pythian's mystic cave of yore,
Those oracles which set the world in flame,
Nor ceased to burn till kingdoms were no more:
Did he not this for France? which lay before
Bow'd to the inborn tyranny of years?
Broken and trembling to the yoke she bore,

[25] Heroine of Rousseau's novel, *Julie, ou la nouvelle Héloïse.*

[26] This refers to the account in his *Confessions* of his passion for the Comtesse d'Houdetot [the mistress of St. Lambert], and his long walk every morning for the sake of the single kiss which was the common salutation of French acquaintance. [Byron.]

Till by the voice of him and his compeers
Roused up to too much wrath, which follows o'ergrown fears?

LXXXII

They made themselves a fearful monument!
The wreck of old opinions — things which grew,
Breathed from the birth of time: the veil they rent,
And what behind it lay, all earth shall view.
But good with ill they also overthrew,
Leaving but ruins, wherewith to rebuild
Upon the same foundation, and renew
Dungeons and thrones, which the same hour refill'd,
As heretofore, because ambition was self-will'd.

LXXXIII

But this will not endure, nor be endured!
Mankind have felt their strength, and made it felt.
They might have used it better, but, allured
By their new vigour, sternly have they dealt
On one another; pity ceased to melt
With her once natural charities. But they,
Who in oppression's darkness caved had dwelt;
They were not eagles, nourish'd with the day;
What marvel then, at times, if they mistook their prey?

LXXXIV

What deep wounds ever closed without a scar?
The heart's bleed longest, and but heal to wear
That which disfigures it; and they who war
With their own hopes, and have been vanquish'd, bear
Silence, but not submission: in his lair
Fix'd Passion holds his breath, until the hour
Which shall atone for years; none need despair:
It came, it cometh, and will come, — the power
To punish or forgive — in *one* we shall be slower.

LXXXV

Clear, placid Leman! thy contrasted lake,
With the wild world I dwelt in, is a thing
Which warns me, with its stillness, to forsake
Earth's troubled waters for a purer spring.
This quiet sail is as a noiseless wing
To waft me from distraction; once I loved
Torn ocean's roar, but thy soft murmuring
Sounds sweet as if a Sister's voice reproved,
That I with stern delights should e'er have been so moved.

LXXXVI

It is the hush of night, and all between
Thy margin and the mountains, dusk, yet clear,
Mellow'd and mingling, yet distinctly seen,
Save darken'd Jura, whose capt heights appear
Precipitously steep; and drawing near,
There breathes a living fragrance from the shore,
Of flowers yet fresh with childhood; on the ear
Drops the light drip of the suspended oar,
Or chirps the grasshopper one good-night carol more;

LXXXVII

He is an evening reveller, who makes
His life an infancy, and sings his fill;
At intervals, some bird from out the brakes
Starts into voice a moment, then is still.
There seems a floating whisper on the hill,
But that is fancy, for the starlight dews
All silently their tears of love instil,
Weeping themselves away, till they infuse
Deep into nature's breast the spirit of her hues.

LXXXVIII

Ye stars! which are the poetry of heaven!
If in your bright leaves we would read the fate
Of men and empires, — 't is to be forgiven,
That in our aspirations to be great,
Our destinies o'erleap their mortal state,
And claim a kindred with you; for ye are
A beauty and a mystery, and create
In us such love and reverence from afar,
That fortune, fame, power, life, have named themselves a star.

LXXXIX

All heaven and earth are still — though not in sleep,
But breathless, as we grow when feeling most;
And silent, as we stand in thoughts too deep: —
All heaven and earth are still: From the high host
Of stars, to the lull'd lake and mountain-coast,
All is concenter'd in a life intense,
Where not a beam, nor air, nor leaf is lost,
But hath a part of being, and a sense
Of that which is of all Creator and Defence.

XC

Then stirs the feeling infinite, so felt
In solitude, where we are *least* alone;
A truth, which through our being then doth melt,
And purifies from self: it is a tone,
The soul and source of music, which makes known
Eternal harmony, and sheds a charm
Like to the fabled Cytherea's zone,[27]
Binding all things with beauty; — t' would disarm
The spectre Death, had he substantial power to harm.

XCI

Not vainly did the early Persian make
His altar the high places, and the peak
Of earth-o'ergazing mountains, and thus take
A fit and unwall'd temple, there to seek
The Spirit, in whose honour shrines are weak,
Uprear'd of human hands. Come, and compare
Columns and idol-dwellings, Goth or Greek,
With Nature's realms of worship, earth and air,
Nor fix on fond abodes to circumscribe thy pray'r!

XCII

The sky is changed! — and such a change! Oh night,
And storm, and darkness, ye are wondrous strong,
Yet lovely in your strength, as is the light
Of a dark eye in woman! Far along,
From peak to peak, the rattling crags among
Leaps the live thunder! Not from one lone cloud,
But every mountain now hath found a tongue,
And Jura answers, through her misty shroud,

[27] The girdle of Venus, which drew love to its wearer.

Back to the joyous Alps, who call to her aloud!

XCIII

And this is in the night: — Most glorious night!
Thou wert not sent for slumber! let me be
A sharer in thy fierce and far delight, —
A portion of the tempest and of thee!
How the lit lake shines, a phosphoric sea,
And the big rain comes dancing to the earth!
And now again 't is black, — and now, the glee
Of the loud hills shakes with its mountain-mirth,
As if they did rejoice o'er a young earthquake's birth.

XCIV

Now, where the swift Rhone cleaves his way between
Heights which appear as lovers who have parted
In hate, whose mining depths so intervene,
That they can meet no more, though broken-hearted;
Though in their souls, which thus each other thwarted,
Love was the very root of the fond rage
Which blighted their life's bloom, and then departed:
Itself expired, but leaving them an age
Of years all winters, — war within themselves to wage.

XCV

Now, where the quick Rhone thus hath cleft his way,
The mightiest of the storms hath ta'en his stand:
For here, not one, but many, make their play,
And fling their thunder-bolts from hand to hand,
Flashing and cast around; of all the band,
The brightest through these parted hills hath fork'd
His lightnings, — as if he did understand,
That in such gaps as desolation work'd,
There the hot shaft should blast whatever therein lurk'd.

XCVI

Sky, mountains, river, winds, lake, lightnings! ye!
With night, and clouds, and thunder, and a soul
To make these felt and feeling, well may be
Things that have made me watchful; the far roll
Of your departing voices, is the knoll[28]
Of what in me is sleepless, — if I rest.
But where of ye, O tempests! is the goal?
Are ye like those within the human breast?
Or do ye find, at length, like eagles, some high nest?

XCVII

Could I embody and unbosom now
That which is most within me, — could I wreak
My thoughts upon expression, and thus throw
Soul, heart, mind, passions, feelings, strong or weak,
All that I would have sought, and all I seek,
Bear, know, feel, and yet breathe — into *one* word,
And that one word were Lightning, I would speak;
But as it is, I live and die unheard,
With a most voiceless thought, sheathing it as a sword.

XCVIII

The morn is up again, the dewy morn,
With breath all incense, and with cheek all bloom,

---

[28] knell

Laughing the clouds away with playful scorn,
And living as if earth contain'd no tomb,—
And glowing into day: we may resume
The march of our existence: and thus I,
Still on thy shores, fair Leman! may find room
And food for meditation, nor pass by
Much, that may give us pause, if ponder'd fittingly.

XCIX

Clarens![29] sweet Clarens, birthplace of deep Love!
Thine air is the young breath of passionate thought;
Thy trees take root in Love; the snows above
The very Glaciers have his colours caught,
And sun-set into rose-hues sees them wrought
By rays which sleep there lovingly: the rocks,
The permanent crags, tell here of Love, who sought
In them a refuge from the worldly shocks,
Which stir and sting the soul with hope that woos, then mocks.

C

Clarens! by heavenly feet thy paths are trod,—
Undying Love's, who here ascends a throne
To which the steps are mountains; where the god
Is a pervading life and light,—so shown
Not on those summits solely, nor alone
In the still cave and forest; o'er the flower
His eye is sparkling, and his breath hath blown,
His soft and summer breath, whose tender power
Passes the strength of storms in their most desolate hour.

CI

All things are here of *him;* from the black pines,
Which are his shade on high, and the loud roar
Of torrents, where he listeneth, to the vines
Which slope his green path downward to the shore,
Where the bow'd waters meet him, and adore,
Kissing his feet with murmurs; and the wood,
The covert of old trees, with trunks all hoar,
But light leaves, young as joy, stands where it stood,
Offering to him, and his, a populous solitude.

CII

A populous solitude of bees and birds,
And fairy-form'd and many-colour'd things,
Who worship him with notes more sweet than words,
And innocently open their glad wings,
Fearless and full of life: the gush of springs,
And fall of lofty fountains, and the bend
Of stirring branches, and the bud which brings
The swiftest thought of beauty, here extend,
Mingling, and made by Love, unto one mighty end.

CIII

He who hath loved not, here would learn that lore,
And make his heart a spirit; he who knows
That tender mystery, will love the more;

[29] Village on Lake Geneva, favorite rendezvous of the lovers in Rousseau's *Julie*.

For this is Love's recess, where vain men's woes,
And the world's waste, have driven him far from those,
For 'tis his nature to advance or die;
He stands not still, but or decays, or grows
Into a boundless blessing, which may vie
With the immortal lights, in its eternity!

CIV

'T was not for fiction chose Rousseau this spot,
Peopling it with affections; but he found
It was the scene which Passion must allot
To the mind's purified beings; 't was the ground
Where early Love his Psyche's zone unbound,
And hallow'd it with loveliness: 't is lone,
And wonderful, and deep, and hath a sound,
And sense, and sight of sweetness; here the Rhone
Hath spread himself a couch, the Alps have rear'd a throne.

CV

Lausanne! and Ferney![30] ye have been the abodes
Of names which unto you bequeath'd a name;
Mortals, who sought and found, by dangerous roads,
A path to perpetuity of fame:
They were gigantic minds, and their steep aim
Was, Titan-like, on daring doubts to pile
Thoughts which should call down thunder, and the flame
Of Heaven again assail'd, if Heaven the while
On man and man's research could deign do more than smile.

CVI

The one[31] was fire and fickleness, a child
Most mutable in wishes, but in mind
A wit as various, — gay, grave, sage, or wild, —
Historian, bard, philosopher, combined;
He multiplied himself among mankind,
The Proteus of their talents: But his own
Breathed most in ridicule, — which, as the wind,
Blew where it listed, laying all things prone, —
Now to o'erthrow a fool, and now to shake a throne.

CVII

The other, deep and slow, exhausting thought,
And hiving wisdom with each studious year,
In meditation dwelt, with learning wrought,
And shaped his weapon with an edge severe,
Sapping a solemn creed with solemn sneer;
The lord of irony, — that master-spell,
Which stung his foes to wrath, which grew from fear,
And doom'd him to the zealot's ready Hell,
Which answers to all doubts so eloquently well.

CVIII

Yet, peace be with their ashes, — for by them,
If merited, the penalty is paid;
It is not ours to judge, — far less condemn;
The hour must come when such things shall be made
Known unto all, or hope and dread allay'd
By slumber, on one pillow, in the dust,
Which, thus much we are sure, must lie decay'd;

[30] At the former Gibbon finished his *Decline and Fall of the Roman Empire* in 1788; Voltaire spent his last years at Ferney.

[31] Voltaire

And when it shall revive, as is our trust,
'T will be to be forgiven, or suffer what is just.

CIX

But let me quit man's works, again to read
His Maker's, spread around me, and suspend
This page, which from my reveries I feed,
Until it seems prolonging without end.
The clouds above me to the white Alps tend,
And I must pierce them, and survey whate'er
May be permitted, as my steps I bend
To their most great and growing region, where
The earth to her embrace compels the powers of air.

CX

Italia! too, Italia! looking on thee,
Full flashes on the soul the light of ages,
Since the fierce Carthaginian almost won thee,
To the last halo of the chiefs and sages
Who glorify thy consecrated pages;
Thou wert the throne and grave of empires; still,
The fount at which the panting mind assuages
Her thirst of knowledge, quaffing there her fill,
Flows from the eternal source of Rome's imperial hill.

CXI

Thus far have I proceeded in a theme
Renew'd with no kind auspices: — to feel
We are not what we have been, and to deem
We are not what we should be, and to steel
The heart against itself; and to conceal,
With a proud caution, love, or hate, or aught, —
Passion or feeling, purpose, grief or zeal, —
Which is the tyrant spirit of our thought,
Is a stern task of soul: — No matter, — it is taught.

CXII

And for these words, thus woven into song,
It may be that they are a harmless wile, —
The colouring of the scenes which fleet along,
Which I would seize, in passing, to beguile
My breast, or that of others, for a while.
Fame is the thirst of youth, but I am not
So young as to regard men's frown or smile,
As loss or guerdon of a glorious lot;
I stood and stand alone, — remember'd or forgot.

CXIII

I have not loved the world, nor the world me;
I have not flatter'd its rank breath, nor bow'd
To its idolatries a patient knee,
Nor coin'd my cheek to smiles, nor cried aloud
In worship of an echo; in the crowd
They could not deem me one of such; I stood
Among them, but not of them; in a shroud
Of thoughts which were not their thoughts, and still could,
Had I not filed [32] my mind, which thus itself subdued.

CXIV

I have not loved the world, nor the world me, —
But let us part fair foes; I do believe,
Though I have found them not, that there may be
Words which are things, hopes which will not deceive,

[32] defiled

And virtues which are merciful, nor weave
Snares for the failing; I would also deem
O'er others' griefs that some sincerely grieve;
That two, or one, are almost what they seem,
That goodness is no name, and happiness no dream.

CXV

My daughter! with thy name this song begun;
My daughter! with thy name thus much shall end;
I see thee not, I hear thee not, but none
Can be so wrapt in thee; thou art the friend
To whom the shadows of far years extend:
Albeit my brow thou never shouldst behold,
My voice shall with thy future visions blend,
And reach into thy heart, when mine is cold,
A token and a tone, even from thy father's mould.

CXVI

To aid thy mind's development, to watch
Thy dawn of little joys, to sit and see
Almost thy very growth, to view thee catch
Knowledge of objects, — wonders yet to thee!
To hold thee lightly on a gentle knee,
And print on thy soft cheek a parent's kiss, —
This, it should seem, was not reserved for me;
Yet this was in my nature: as it is,
I know not what is there, yet something like to this.

CXVII

Yet, though dull Hate as duty should be taught,
I know that thou wilt love me; though my name
Should be shut from thee, as a spell still fraught
With desolation, and a broken claim:
Though the grave closed between us, — 't were the same,
I know that thou wilt love me; though to drain
My blood from out thy being were an aim,
And an attainment, — all would be in vain, —
Still thou wouldst love me, still that more than life retain.

CXVIII

The child of love, though born in bitterness,
And nurtured in convulsion. Of thy sire
These were the elements, and thine no less.
As yet such are around thee, but thy fire
Shall be more temper'd, and thy hope far higher.
Sweet be thy cradled slumbers! O'er the sea
And from the mountains where I now respire,
Fain would I waft such blessing upon thee,
As, with a sigh, I deem thou might'st have been to me.

CANTO IV[33]

I

I STOOD in Venice, on the Bridge of Sighs;[34]
A palace and a prison on each hand:

[33] In the autumn of 1816, after Shelley's departure for England, Byron went into Italy with his friend Hobhouse. He made Venice his headquarters for the next three years. The following spring he made the journey over Italy which furnished him material for Canto IV of *Childe Harold*. It was published in 1818.

[34] The *Ponte dei Suspiri*, which connects the palace of the Doge to the state prisons, its name arising from the custom of conducting condemned prisoners across it for execution.

I saw from out the wave her structures rise
As from the stroke of the enchanter's wand:
A thousand years their cloudy wings expand
Around me, and a dying Glory smiles
O'er the far times, when many a subject land
Look'd to the winged Lion's marble piles,
Where Venice sate in state, throned on her hundred isles!

II

She looks a sea Cybele, fresh from ocean,
Rising with her tiara of proud towers
At airy distance, with majestic motion,
A ruler of the waters and their powers:
And such she was; — her daughters had their dowers
From spoils of nations, and the exhaustless East
Pour'd in her lap all gems in sparkling showers.
In purple was she robed, and of her feast
Monarchs partook, and deem'd their dignity increased.

III

In Venice Tasso's echoes are no more,
And silent rows the songless gondolier;[35]
Her palaces are crumbling to the shore,
And music meets not always now the ear:
Those days are gone — but Beauty still is here.
States fall, arts fade — but Nature doth not die,
Nor yet forget how Venice once was dear,
The pleasant place of all festivity,
The revel of the earth, the masque of Italy!

IV

But unto us she hath a spell beyond
Her name in story, and her long array
Of mighty shadows, whose dim forms despond
Above the dogeless city's vanish'd sway;
Ours is a trophy which will not decay
With the Rialto; Shylock and the Moor,
And Pierre, cannot be swept or worn away —
The keystones of the arch! though all were o'er,
For us repeopled were the solitary shore.

V

The beings of the mind are not of clay;
Essentially immortal, they create
And multiply in us a brighter ray
And more beloved existence: that which Fate
Prohibits to dull life, in this our state
Of mortal bondage, by these spirits supplied,
First exiles, then replaces what we hate;
Watering the heart whose early flowers have died,
And with a fresher growth replenishing the void.

. . .

XIII

Before St. Mark still glow his steeds of brass,
Their gilded collars glittering in the sun;
But is not Doria's[36] menace come to pass?
Are they not *bridled?* — Venice, lost and won,
Her thirteen hundred years of freedom done,
Sinks, like a seaweed, into whence she rose!
Better be whelm'd beneath the waves, and shun,
Even in destruction's depth, her foreign foes,

[35] Before Napoleon's capture of Venice in 1797, the gondoliers used to sing stanzas from Tasso's *Jerusalem Delivered.*

[36] Doria, the Genoese commander, said in 1379 that he would bridle the horses of St. Mark before giving peace to Venice.

From whom submission wrings an infamous repose.

XIV

In youth she was all glory, — a new Tyre;
Her very by-word sprung from victory,
The 'Planter of the Lion,'[37] which through fire
And blood she bore o'er subject earth and sea;
Though making many slaves, herself still free,
And Europe's bulwark 'gainst the Ottomite;
Witness Troy's rival, Candia![38] Vouch it, ye
Immortal waves that saw Lepanto's fight!
For ye are names no time nor tyranny can blight.

XV

Statues of glass — all shiver'd — the long file
Of her dead Doges are declined to dust;
But where they dwelt, the vast and sumptuous pile
Bespeaks the pageant of their splendid trust;
Their sceptre broken, and their sword in rust,
Have yielded to the stranger: empty halls,
Thin streets, and foreign aspects, such as must
Too oft remind her who and what enthrals,
Have flung a desolate cloud o'er Venice' lovely walls.

XVI

When Athens' armies fell at Syracuse,[39]
And fetter'd thousands bore the yoke of war,
Redemption rose up in the Attic Muse,
Her voice their only ransom from afar:
See! as they chant the tragic hymn, the car
Of the o'ermaster'd victor stops, the reins
Fall from his hands, his idle scimitar
Starts from its belt — he rends his captive's chains,
And bids him thank the bard for freedom and his strains.

XVII

Thus, Venice, if no stronger claim were thine,
Were all thy proud historic deeds forgot,
Thy choral memory of the Bard divine,
Thy love of Tasso, should have cut the knot
Which ties thee to thy tyrants; and thy lot
Is shameful to the nations, — most of all,
Albion! to thee: the Ocean queen should not
Abandon Ocean's children; in the fall
Of Venice think of thine, despite thy watery wall.

XVIII

I loved her from my boyhood; she to me
Was as a fairy city of the heart,
Rising like water-columns from the sea,
Of joy the sojourn, and of wealth the mart;
And Otway, Radcliffe, Schiller, Shakspeare's art,[40]
Had stamp'd her image in me, and even so,
Although I found her thus, we did not part;
Perchance even dearer in her day of woe,
Than when she was a boast, a marvel, and a show.

XIX

I can repeople with the past — and of
The present there is still for eye and thought,

[37] The Lion of St. Mark, emblem of the Republic of Venice.

[38] Candia, in Crete, was defended against the Turks by the Venetians for twenty-four years.

[39] Plutarch, in his Life of Nicias, tells how, after the defeat of the Athenians at Syracuse in 413 B.C., some captives gained freedom by reciting passages from Euripides.

[40] The reference is to Otway's *Venice Preserved*, Ann Radcliffe's *The Mysteries of Udolpho*, Schiller's *Der Geisterseher*, and, of course, Shakespeare's *Othello* and *The Merchant of Venice*.

And meditation chasten'd down, enough;
And more, it may be, than I hoped or sought;
And of the happiest moments which were wrought
Within the web of my existence, some
From thee, fair Venice! have their colours caught:
There are some feelings Time cannot benumb,
Nor Torture shake, or mine would now be cold and dumb.

. . .

XXV

But my soul wanders; I demand it back
To meditate amongst decay, and stand
A ruin amidst ruins; there to track
Fall'n states and buried greatness, o'er a land
Which *was* the mightiest in its old command,
And *is* the loveliest, and must ever be
The master-mould of Nature's heavenly hand;
Wherein were cast the heroic and the free,
The beautiful, the brave, the lords of earth and sea,

XXVI

The commonwealth of kings, the men of Rome!
And even since, and now, fair Italy!
Thou art the garden of the world, the home
Of all Art yields, and Nature can decree;
Even in thy desert, what is like to thee?
Thy very weeds are beautiful, thy waste
More rich than other climes' fertility;
Thy wreck a glory, and thy ruin graced
With an immaculate charm which cannot be defaced.

XXVII

The moon is up, and yet it is not night;
Sunset divides the sky with her; a sea
Of glory streams along the Alpine height
Of blue Friuli's mountains; Heaven is free
From clouds, but of all colours seems to be, —
Melted to one vast Iris of the West, —
Where the Day joins the past Eternity,
While, on the other hand, meek Dian's crest
Floats through the azure air — an island of the blest!

XXVIII

A single star is at her side, and reigns
With her o'er half the lovely heaven; but still
Yon sunny sea heaves brightly, and remains
Roll'd o'er the peak of the far Rhætian hill,
As Day and Night contending were, until
Nature reclaim'd her order: — gently flows
The deep-dyed Brenta, where their hues instil
The odorous purple of a new-born rose,
Which streams upon her stream, and glass'd within it glows,

XXIX

Fill'd with the face of heaven, which, from afar,
Comes down upon the waters; all its hues,
From the rich sunset to the rising star,
Their magical variety diffuse:
And now they change; a paler shadow strews
Its mantle o'er the mountains; parting day
Dies like the dolphin, whom each pang imbues
With a new colour as it gasps away,
The last still loveliest, — till — 't is gone — and all is gray.

. . .

LXXVIII

Oh Rome! my country! city of the soul!
The orphans of the heart must turn to thee,
Lone mother of dead empires! and control
In their shut breasts their petty misery.
What are our woes and sufferance? Come and see
The cypress, hear the owl, and plod your way
O'er steps of broken thrones and temples, Ye!
Whose agonies are evils of a day —
A world is at our feet as fragile as our clay.

LXXIX

The Niobe of nations! there she stands,
Childless and crownless, in her voiceless woe;
An empty urn within her wither'd hands,
Whose holy dust was scatter'd long ago;
The Scipios' tomb contains no ashes now;
The very sepulchres lie tenantless
Of their heroic dwellers: dost thou flow,
Old Tiber! through a marble wilderness?
Rise, with thy yellow waves, and mantle her distress.

LXXX

The Goth, the Christian, Time, War, Flood, and Fire,
Have dealt upon the seven-hill'd city's pride;
She saw her glories star by star expire,
And up the steep barbarian monarchs ride,
Where the car climb'd the Capitol; far and wide
Temple and tower went down, nor left a site:
Chaos of ruins! who shall trace the void,
O'er the dim fragments cast a lunar light,
And say, 'here was, or is,' where all is doubly night?

LXXXI

The double night of ages, and of her,
Night's daughter, Ignorance, hath wrapt and wrap
All round us: we but feel our way to err:
The ocean hath its chart, the stars their map,
And Knowledge spreads them on her ample lap;
But Rome is as the desert, where we steer
Stumbling o'er recollections; now we clap
Our hands, and cry 'Eureka!' it is clear —
When but some false mirage of ruin rises near.

. . .

CXXVIII

Arches on arches! as it were that Rome,
Collecting the chief trophies of her line,
Would build up all her triumphs in one dome,
Her Coliseum stands; the moonbeams shine
As 't were its natural torches, for divine
Should be the light which streams here to illume
This long-explored but still exhaustless mine
Of contemplation; and the azure gloom
Of an Italian night, where the deep skies assume

CXXI

Hues which have words, and speak to ye of heaven,
Floats o'er this vast and wondrous monument,
And shadows forth its glory. There is given
Unto the things of earth, which Time hath bent,
A spirit's feeling, and where he hath leant

His hand, but broke his scythe, there is a power
And magic in the ruin'd battlement,
For which the palace of the present hour
Must yield its pomp, and wait till ages are its dower.

CXXX

Oh Time! the beautifier of the dead,
Adorner of the ruin, comforter
And only healer when the heart hath bled;
Time! the corrector where our judgments err,
The test of truth, love — sole philosopher,
For all beside are sophists — from thy thrift,
Which never loses though it doth defer —
Time, the avenger! unto thee I lift
My hands, and eyes, and heart, and crave of thee a gift:

CXXXI

Amidst this wreck, where thou hast made a shrine
And temple more divinely desolate,
Among thy mightier offerings here are mine,
Ruins of years, though few, yet full of fate:
If thou hast ever seen me too elate,
Hear me not; but if calmly I have borne
Good, and reserved my pride against the hate
Which shall not whelm me, let me not have worn
This iron in my soul in vain — shall *they* not mourn?

CXXXII

And thou, who never yet of human wrong
Left the unbalanced scale, great Nemesis!
Here, where the ancient paid thee homage long —
Thou who didst call the Furies from the abyss,
And round Orestes bade them howl and hiss
For that unnatural retribution — just,
Had it but been from hands less near — in this
Thy former realm, I call thee from the dust!
Dost thou not hear my heart? — Awake! thou shalt, and must.

CXXXIII

It is not that I may not have incurr'd
For my ancestral faults or mine the wound
I bleed withal, and, had it been conferr'd
With a just weapon, it had flow'd unbound;
But now my blood shall not sink in the ground;
To thee I do devote it — *thou* shalt take
The vengeance, which shall yet be sought and found,
Which if *I* have not taken for the sake ——
But let that pass — I sleep, but thou shalt yet awake.

CXXXIV

And if my voice break forth, 't is not that now
I shrink from what is suffer'd: let him speak
Who hath beheld decline upon my brow,
Or seen my mind's convulsion leave it weak;
But in this page a record will I seek.
Not in the air shall these my words disperse,
Though I be ashes; a far hour shall wreak
The deep prophetic fulness of this verse,
And pile on human heads the mountain of my curse!

CXXXV

That curse shall be Forgiveness. — Have I not —
Hear me, my mother Earth! behold it, Heaven!
Have I not had to wrestle with my lot?
Have I not suffer'd things to be forgiven?
Have I not had my brain sear'd, my heart riven,
Hopes sapp'd, name blighted, Life's life lied away?
And only not to desperation driven,
Because not altogether of such clay
As rots into the souls of those whom I survey.

CXXXVI

From mighty wrongs to petty perfidy
Have I not seen what human things could do?
From the loud roar of foaming calumny
To the small whisper of the as paltry few,
And subtler venom of the reptile crew,
The Janus glance of whose significant eye,
Learning to lie with silence, would *seem* true,
And without utterance, save the shrug or sigh,
Deal round to happy fools its speechless obloquy.

CXXXVII

But I have lived, and have not lived in vain:
My mind may lose its force, my blood its fire,
And my frame perish even in conquering pain;
But there is that within me which shall tire
Torture and Time, and breathe when I expire;
Something unearthly, which they deem not of,
Like the remember'd tone of a mute lyre,
Shall on their soften'd spirits sink, and move
In hearts all rocky now the late remorse of love.

CXXXVIII

The seal is set. — Now welcome, thou dread power!
Nameless, yet thus omnipotent, which here
Walk'st in the shadow of the midnight hour
With a deep awe, yet all distinct from fear;
Thy haunts are ever where the dead walls rear
Their ivy mantles, and the solemn scene
Derives from thee a sense so deep and clear
That we become a part of what has been,
And grow unto the spot, all-seeing but unseen.

CXXXIX

And here the buzz of eager nations ran,
In murmur'd pity, or loud-roar'd applause,
As man was slaughter'd by his fellow-man.
And wherefore slaughter'd? wherefore, but because
Such were the bloody Circus' genial laws,
And the imperial pleasure. — Wherefore not?
What matters where we fall to fill the maws
Of worms — on battle-plains or listed spot?
Both are but theatres where the chief actors rot.

CXL

I see before me the Gladiator lie: [41]
He leans upon his hand — his manly brow
Consents to death, but conquers agony,
And his droop'd head sinks gradually low —

---

[41] Suggested by the statue of *The Dying Gladiator* (now called *The Dying Gaul*) in the Capitoline Museum.

And through his side the last drops, ebbing slow
From the red gash, fall heavy, one by one,
Like the first of a thunder-shower; and now
The arena swims around him — he is gone,
Ere ceased the inhuman shout which hail'd the wretch who won.

CXLI

He heard it, but he heeded not — his eyes
Were with his heart, and that was far away;
He reck'd not of the life he lost nor prize,
But where his rude hut by the Danube lay,
There were his young barbarians all at play,
There was their Dacian [42] mother — he, their sire,
Butcher'd to make a Roman holiday —
All this rush'd with his blood — Shall he expire
And unavenged? Arise! ye Goths, and glut your ire!

CXLII

But here, where Murder breathed her bloody steam;
And here, where buzzing nations choked the ways,
And roar'd or murmur'd like a mountain stream
Dashing or winding as its torrent strays;
Here, where the Roman million's blame or praise
Was death or life, the playthings of a crowd,
My voice sounds much — and fall the stars' faint rays
On the arena void — seats crush'd — walls bow'd —
And galleries, where my steps seem echoes strangely loud.

CXLIII

A ruin — yet what ruin! from its mass
Walls, palaces, half-cities, have been rear'd;
Yet oft the enormous skeleton ye pass,
And marvel where the spoil could have appear'd.
Hath it indeed been plunder'd, or but clear'd?
Alas! developed, opens the decay,
When the colossal fabric's form is near'd:
It will not bear the brightness of the day,
Which streams too much on all years, man, have reft away.

CXLIV

But when the rising moon begins to climb
Its topmost arch, and gently pauses there;
When the stars twinkle through the loops of time,
And the low night-breeze waves along the air
The garland-forest, which the gray walls wear,
Like laurels on the bald first Cæsar's head;
When the light shines serene but doth not glare,
Then in this magic circle raise the dead:
Heroes have trod this spot — 't is on their dust ye tread.

CXLV

'While stands the Coliseum, Rome shall stand;
'When falls the Coliseum, Rome shall fall;
'And when Rome falls — the World.' [43] From our own land

[42] Trajan carried to Rome thousands of captives from the Roman province of Dacia, north of the Danube, and made them join combats in the arena.

[43] This is quoted in the *Decline and Fall of the Roman Empire*, as a proof that the Coliseum was entire, when seen by the Anglo-Saxon pilgrims at the end of the seventh, or the beginning of the eighth, century. [Byron.] Gibbon cites Bede's *Glossarium* as his source.

Thus spake the pilgrims o'er this mighty wall
In Saxon times, which we are wont to call
Ancient; and these three mortal things are still
On their foundations, and unalter'd all;
Rome and her Ruin past Redemption's skill,
The World, the same wide den — of thieves, or what ye will.

. . .

CLXXV

But I forget. — My Pilgrim's shrine is won,
And he and I must part, — so let it be, —
His task and mine alike are nearly done;
Yet once more let us look upon the sea;
The midland ocean breaks on him and me,
And from the Alban Mount we now behold
Our friend of youth, that Ocean, which when we
Beheld it last by Calpe's rock [44] unfold
Those waves, we follow'd on till the dark Euxine roll'd

CLXXVI

Upon the blue Symplegades: long years —
Long, though not very many — since have done
Their work on both; some suffering and some tears
Have left us nearly where we had begun:
Yet not in vain our mortal race hath run;
We have had our reward, and it is here, —
That we can yet feel gladden'd by the sun,
And reap from earth, sea, joy almost as dear
As if there were no man to trouble what is clear.

CLXXVII

Oh! that the Desert were my dwelling-place,
With one fair Spirit [45] for my minister,
That I might all forget the human race,
And, hating no one, love but only her!
Ye elements! — in whose ennobling stir
I feel myself exalted — Can ye not
Accord me such a being? Do I err
In deeming such inhabit many a spot?
Though with them to converse can rarely be our lot.

CLXXVIII

There is a pleasure in the pathless woods,
There is a rapture on the lonely shore,
There is society, where none intrudes,
By the deep Sea, and music in its roar:
I love not Man the less, but Nature more,
From these our interviews, in which I steal
From all I may be, or have been before,
To mingle with the Universe, and feel
What I can ne'er express, yet cannot all conceal.

CLXXIX

Roll on, thou deep and dark blue Ocean — roll!
Ten thousand fleets sweep over thee in vain;
Man marks the earth with ruin — his control
Stops with the shore; upon the watery plain
The wrecks are all thy deed, nor doth remain
A shadow of man's ravage, save his own,
When, for a moment, like a drop of rain,
He sinks into thy depths with bubbling groan,
Without a grave, unknell'd, uncoffin'd, and unknown.

CLXXX

His steps are not upon thy paths, — thy fields

[44] Gibraltar, last seen by Byron in 1811.

[45] Augusta

Are not a spoil for him, — thou dost arise
And shake him from thee; the vile strength he wields
For earth's destruction thou dost all despise,
Spurning him from thy bosom to the skies,
And send'st him, shivering in thy playful spray
And howling, to his Gods, where haply lies
His petty hope in some near port or bay,
And dashest him again to earth: — there let him lay.

CLXXXI

The armaments which thunderstrike the walls
Of rock-built cities, bidding nations quake,
And monarchs tremble in their capitals,
The oak leviathans, whose huge ribs make
Their clay creator the vain title take
Of lord of thee, and arbiter of war —
These are thy toys, and, as the snowy flake,
They melt into thy yeast of waves, which mar
Alike the Armada's pride or spoils of Trafalgar.

CLXXXII

Thy shores are empires, changed in all save thee —
Assyria, Greece, Rome, Carthage, what are they?
Thy waters wash'd them power while they were free,
And many a tyrant since; their shores obey
The stranger, slave, or savage; their decay
Has dried up realms to deserts: — not so thou; —
Unchangeable, save to thy wild waves' play,
Time writes no wrinkle on thine azure brow:
Such as creation's dawn beheld, thou rollest now.

CLXXXIII

Thou glorious mirror, where the Almighty's form
Glasses itself in tempests; in all time, —
Calm or convulsed, in breeze, or gale, or storm,
Icing the pole, or in the torrid clime
Dark-heaving — boundless, endless, and sublime,
The image of eternity, the throne
Of the Invisible; even from out thy slime
The monsters of the deep are made; each zone
Obeys thee; thou goest forth, dread, fathomless, alone.

CLXXXIV

And I have loved thee, Ocean! and my joy
Of youthful sports was on thy breast to be
Borne, like thy bubbles, onward: from a boy
I wanton'd with thy breakers — they to me
Were a delight; and if the freshening sea
Made them a terror — 't was a pleasing fear,
For I was as it were a child of thee,
And trusted to thy billows far and near,
And laid my hand upon thy mane — as I do here.

CLXXXV

My task is done, my song hath ceased, my theme
Has died into an echo; it is fit
The spell should break of this protracted dream.
The torch shall be extinguish'd which hath lit

My midnight lamp — and what is writ, is writ;
Would it were worthier! but I am not now
That which I have been — and my visions flit
Less palpably before me — and the glow
Which in my spirit dwelt is fluttering, faint, and low.

CLXXXVI

Farewell! a word that must be, and hath been —
A sound which makes us linger; — yet — farewell!
Ye! who have traced the Pilgrim to the scene
Which is his last, if in your memories dwell
A thought which once was his, if on ye swell
A single recollection, not in vain
He wore his sandal-shoon and scallop-shell;
Farewell! with *him* alone may rest the pain,
If such there were — with *you,* the moral of his strain.

Darkness [46]

I HAD a dream, which was not all a dream.
The bright sun was extinguish'd, and the stars
Did wander darkling in the eternal space,
Rayless, and pathless, and the icy earth
Swung blind and blackening in the moonless air;
Morn came and went — and came, and brought no day,
And men forgot their passions in the dread
Of this their desolation; and all hearts
Were chill'd into a selfish prayer for light:
And they did live by watchfires — and the thrones,
The palaces of crowned kings — the huts,
The habitations of all things which dwell,
Were burnt for beacons; cities were consumed,
And men were gather'd round their blazing homes
To look once more into each other's face;
Happy were those who dwelt within the eye
Of the volcanos, and their mountain-torch:
A fearful hope was all the world contain'd;
Forests were set on fire — but hour by hour
They fell and faded — and the crackling trunks
Extinguish'd with a crash — and all was black.
The brows of men by the despairing light
Wore an unearthly aspect, as by fits
The flashes fell upon them; some lay down
And hid their eyes and wept; and some did rest
Their chins upon their clenched hands, and smiled;
And others hurried to and fro, and fed
Their funeral piles with fuel, and look'd up
With mad disquietude on the dull sky,
The pall of a past world; and then again
With curses cast them down upon the dust,
And gnash'd their teeth and howl'd: the wild birds shriek'd
And, terrified, did flutter on the ground,
And flap their useless wings; the wildest brutes
Came tame and tremulous; and vipers crawl'd
And twined themselves among the multitude,
Hissing, but stingless — they were slain for food!
And War, which for a moment was no more,
Did glut himself again: — a meal was bought
With blood, and each sate sullenly apart
Gorging himself in gloom: no love was left;

[46] Written in July 1816; published with *The Prisoner of Chillon* the same year.

All earth was but one thought — and that was death
Immediate and inglorious; and the pang
Of famine fed upon all entrails — men
Died, and their bones were tombless as their flesh;
The meagre by the meagre were devour'd,
Even dogs assail'd their masters, all save one,
And he was faithful to a corse, and kept
The birds and beasts and famish'd men at bay,
Till hunger clung[47] them, or the dropping dead
Lured their lank jaws; himself sought out no food,
But with a piteous and perpetual moan,
And a quick desolate cry, licking the hand
Which answer'd not with a caress — he died.
The crowd was famish'd by degrees; but two
Of an enormous city did survive,
And they were enemies: they met beside
The dying embers of an altar-place
Where had been heap'd a mass of holy things
For an unholy usage; they raked up,
And shivering scraped with their cold skeleton hands
The feeble ashes, and their feeble breath
Blew for a little life, and made a flame
Which was a mockery; then they lifted up
Their eyes as it grew lighter, and beheld
Each other's aspects — saw, and shriek'd, and died —
Even of their mutual hideousness they died,
Unknowing who he was upon whose brow
Famine had written Fiend. The world was void,
The populous and the powerful was a lump,
Seasonless, herbless, treeless, manless, lifeless,
A lump of death — a chaos of hard clay.
The rivers, lakes, and ocean all stood still,
And nothing stirr'd within their silent depths;
Ships sailorless lay rotting on the sea,
And their masts fell down piecemeal: as they dropp'd
They slept on the abyss without a surge —
The waves were dead; the tides were in their grave,
The moon, their mistress, had expired before;
The winds were wither'd in the stagnant air,
And the clouds perish'd; Darkness had no need
Of aid from them — She was the Universe.

THE BRIDE OF ABYDOS:[48]

A TURKISH TALE

'Had we never loved so kindly,
Had we never loved so blindly,
Never met or never parted,
We had ne'er been broken-hearted.' — Burns

CANTO I

I

Know ye the land[49] where the cypress and myrtle
Are emblems of deeds that are done in their clime?
Where the rage of the vulture, the love of the turtle,[50]
Now melt into sorrow, now madden to crime!
Know ye the land of the cedar and vine,

[47] dried them up

[48] Taking advantage of the popular reputation won for him in 1812 by the first two cantos of *Childe Harold*, Byron rapidly produced a series of oriental tales. He outdid Sir Walter Scott, who had established the romantic narrative poem. Writing to calm an impossible love he had conceived for the wife of a friend, Byron says that he completed *The Bride of Abydos*, first entitled *Zuleika*, in four nights. It was published in 1813.

[49] See Goethe's 'Kennst du das Land wo die Citronen blühn?'

[50] turtle-dove

Where the flowers ever blossom, the beams ever shine;
Where the light wings of Zephyr, oppress'd with perfume,
Wax faint o'er the gardens of Gúl [51] in her bloom;
Where the citron and olive are fairest of fruit,
And the voice of the nightingale never is mute:
Where the tints of the earth, and the hues of the sky,
In colour though varied, in beauty may vie,
And the purple of ocean is deepest in dye;
Where the virgins are soft as the roses they twine,
And all, save the spirit of man, is divine?
'T is the clime of the East; 't is the land of the Sun —
Can he smile on such deeds as his children have done?
Oh! wild as the accents of lovers' farewell
Are the hearts which they bear, and the tales which they tell.

II

Begirt with many a gallant slave,
Apparell'd as becomes the brave,
Awaiting each his lord's behest
To guide his steps, or guard his rest,
Old Giaffir sate in his Divan: [52]
Deep thought was in his aged eye;
And though the face of Mussulman
Not oft betrays to standers by
The mind within, well skill'd to hide
All but unconquerable pride,
His pensive cheek and pondering brow
Did more than he was wont avow.

III

'Let the chamber be clear'd.' — The train disappear'd. —
'Now call me the chief of the Haram guard.'
With Giaffir is none but his only son,
And the Nubian awaiting the sire's award.
'Haroun — when all the crowd that wait
Are pass'd beyond the outer gate,
(Woe to the head whose eye beheld
My child Zuleika's face unveil'd!)
Hence, lead my daughter from her tower;
Her fate is fix'd this very hour:
Yet not to her repeat my thought;
By me alone be duty taught!'

'Pacha! to hear is to obey.'
No more must slave to despot say —
Then to the tower had ta'en his way,
But here young Selim silence brake,
First lowly rendering reverence meet;
And downcast look'd, and gently spake,
Still standing at the Pacha's feet:
For son of Moslem must expire,
Ere dare to sit before his sire!

'Father! for fear that thou shouldst chide
My sister, or her sable guide,
Know — for the fault, if fault there be,
Was mine, then fall thy frowns on me —
So lovelily the morning shone,
That — let the old and weary sleep —
I could not; and to view alone
The fairest scenes of land and deep,
With none to listen and reply
To thoughts with which my heart beat high
Were irksome — for whate'er my mood,
In sooth I love not solitude;
I on Zuleika's slumber broke,
And, as thou knowest that for me
Soon turns the Haram's grating key,
Before the guardian slaves awoke
We to the cypress groves had flown,
And made earth, main, and heaven our own!
There linger'd we, beguiled too long
With Mejnoun's tale, or Sadi's song;
Till I, who heard the deep tambour

[51] The rose.
[52] State council

Beat thy Divan's approaching hour,
To thee, and to my duty true,
Warn'd by the sound, to greet thee flew:
But there Zuleika wanders yet —
Nay, Father, rage not — nor forget
That none can pierce that secret bower
But those who watch the women's tower.'

IV

'Son of a slave' — the Pacha said —
'From unbelieving mother bred,
Vain were a father's hope to see
Aught that beseems a man in thee.
Thou, when thine arm should bend the bow,
And hurl the dart, and curb the steed,
Thou, Greek in soul if not in creed,
Must pore where babbling waters flow,
And watch unfolding roses blow.
Would that yon orb, whose matin glow
Thy listless eyes so much admire,
Would lend thee something of his fire!
Thou, who wouldst see this battlement
By Christian cannon piecemeal rent;
Nay, tamely view old Stambol's wall
Before the dogs of Moscow fall,
Nor strike one stroke for life and death
Against the curs of Nazareth!
Go — let thy less than woman's hand
Assume the distaff — not the brand.
But, Haroun! — to my daughter speed;
And hark — of thine own head take heed —
If thus Zuleika oft takes wing —
Thou see'st yon bow — it hath a string!'

V

No sound from Selim's lip was heard,
At least that met old Giaffir's ear,
But every frown and every word
Pierced keener than a Christian's sword.
'Son of a slave! — reproach'd with fear!
Those gibes had cost another dear.
Son of a slave! — and *who* my sire?'
Thus held his thoughts their dark career;
And glances ev'n of more than ire
Flash forth, then faintly disappear.
Old Giaffir gazed upon his son
And started; for within his eye
He read how much his wrath had done;
He saw rebellion there begun:
'Come hither, boy — what, no reply?
I mark thee — and I know thee too;
But there be deeds thou dar'st not do:
But if thy beard had manlier length,
And if thy hand had skill and strength,
I'd joy to see thee break a lance,
Albeit against my own perchance.'

As sneeringly these accents fell,
On Selim's eye he fiercely gazed:
That eye return'd him glance for glance,
And proudly to his sire's was raised,
Till Giaffir's quail'd and shrunk askance —
And why — he felt, but durst not tell.
'Much I misdoubt this wayward boy
Will one day work me more annoy:
I never loved him from his birth,
And — but his arm is little worth,
And scarcely in the chase could cope
With timid fawn or antelope,
Far less would venture into strife
Where man contends for fame and life —
I would not trust that look or tone:
No — nor the blood so near my own.
That blood — he hath not heard — no more —
I'll watch him closer than before.
He is an Arab to my sight,
Or Christian crouching in the fight —
But hark! — I hear Zuleika's voice;
Like Houris' hymn it meets mine ear:
She is the offspring of my choice;
Oh! more than ev'n her mother dear,
With all to hope, and nought to fear —
My Peri! ever welcome here!
Sweet, as the desert fountain's wave
To lips just cool'd in time to save —
Such to my longing sight art thou;
Nor can they waft to Mecca's shrine

More thanks for life, than I for thine,
Who blest thy birth and bless thee now.'

VI

Fair, as the first that fell of womankind,
When on that dread yet lovely serpent smiling,
Whose image then was stamp'd upon her mind —
But once beguil'd — and ever more beguiling;
Dazzling, as that, oh! too transcendent vision
To Sorrow's phantom-peopled slumber given,
When heart meets heart again in dreams Elysian,
And paints the lost on Earth revived in Heaven;
Soft, as the memory of buried love;
Pure, as the prayer which Childhood wafts above,
Was she — the daughter of that rude old Chief,
Who met the maid with tears — but not of grief.

Who hath not proved how feebly words essay
To fix one spark of Beauty's heavenly ray?
Who doth not feel, until his failing sight
Faints into dimness with its own delight,
His changing cheek, his sinking heart confess
The might, the majesty of Loveliness?
Such was Zuleika, such around her shone
The nameless charms unmark'd by her alone —
The light of love, the purity of grace,
The mind, the Music breathing from her face,
The heart whose softness harmonized the whole,
And oh! that eye was in itself a Soul!

Her graceful arms in meekness bending
Across her gently-budding breast;
At one kind word those arms extending
To clasp the neck of him who blest
His child caressing and carest,
Zuleika came — and Giaffir felt
His purpose half within him melt:
Not that against her fancied weal
His heart though stern could ever feel;
Affection chain'd her to that heart;
Ambition tore the links apart.

VII

'Zuleika! child of gentleness!
How dear this very day must tell,
When I forget my own distress,
In losing what I love so well,
To bid thee with another dwell:
Another! and a braver man
Was never seen in battle's van.
We Moslem reck not much of blood;
But yet the line of Carasman
Unchanged, unchangeable hath stood
First of the bold Timariot bands [53]
That won and well can keep their lands.
Enough that he who comes to woo
Is kinsman of the Bey Oglou:
His years need scarce a thought employ;
I would not have thee wed a boy.
And thou shalt have a noble dower:
And his and my united power
Will laugh to scorn the death-firman,
Which others tremble but to scan,
And teach the messenger what fate
The bearer of such boon may wait.
And now thou know'st thy father's will:
All that thy sex hath need to know:
'T was mine to teach obedience still —
The way to love, thy lord may show.'

VIII

In silence bow'd the virgin's head;
And if her eye was fill'd with tears
That stifled feeling dare not shed,
And changed her cheek from pale to red,
And red to pale, as through her ears
Those winged words like arrows sped,
What could such be but maiden fears?
So bright the tear in Beauty's eye,

[53] Turkish cavalry

Love half regrets to kiss it dry;
So sweet the blush of Bashfulness,
Even Pity scarce can wish it less!

Whate'er it was the sire forgot;
Or if remember'd, mark'd it not;
Thrice clapp'd his hands, and call'd his steed,
Resign'd his gem-adorn'd chibouque,[54]
And mounting featly for the mead,
With Maugrabee [55] and Mamaluke,[56]
His way amid his Delis [57] took,
To witness many an active deed
With sabre keen, or blunt jerreed.[58]
The Kislar [59] only and his Moors
Watch well the Haram's massy doors.

IX

His head was leant upon his hand,
His eye look'd o'er the dark blue water
That swiftly glides and gently swells
Between the winding Dardanelles;
But yet he saw nor sea nor strand,
Nor even his Pacha's turban'd band
Mix in the game of mimic slaughter,
Careering cleave the folded felt,
With sabre stroke right sharply dealt;
Nor mark'd the javelin-darting crowd
Nor heard their Ollahs [60] wild and loud —
He thought but of old Giaffir's daughter!

X

No word from Selim's bosom broke;
One sigh Zuleika's thought bespoke:
Still gazed he through the lattice grate,
Pale, mute, and mournfully sedate.
To him Zuleika's eye was turn'd,
But little from his aspect learn'd:
Equal her grief, yet not the same;
Her heart confess'd a gentler flame:

[54] pipe
[55] Moorish hired soldiers.
[56] Soldiers once slaves.
[57] cavalrymen
[58] javelin
[59] Chief of the black eunuchs.
[60] shouts of battle

But yet that heart, alarm'd or weak,
She knew not why, forbade to speak.
Yet speak she must — but when essay?
'How strange he thus should turn away!
Not thus we e'er before have met;
Nor thus shall be our parting yet.'
Thrice paced she slowly through the room,
And watch'd his eye — it still was fix'd:
She snatch'd the urn wherein was mix'd
The Persian Atar-gul's perfume,
And sprinkled all its odours o'er
The pictured roof and marble floor:
The drops, that through his glittering vest
The playful girl's appeal address'd,
Unheeded o'er his bosom flew,
As if that breast were marble too.
'What, sullen yet? it must not be —
Oh! gentle Selim, this from thee!'
She saw in curious order set
The fairest flowers of eastern land —
'He loved them once; may touch them yet,
If offer'd by Zuleika's hand.'
The childish thought was hardly breathed
Before the rose was pluck'd and wreathed;
The next fond moment saw her seat
Her fairy form at Selim's feet:
'This rose to calm my brother's cares
A message from the Bulbul [61] bears;
It says to-night he will prolong
For Selim's ear his sweetest song;
And though his note is somewhat sad,
He'll try for once a strain more glad,
With some faint hope his alter'd lay
May sing these gloomy thoughts away.

XI

'What! not receive my foolish flower?
Nay then I am indeed unblest:

[61] nightingale

On me can thus thy forehead lower?
And know'st thou not who loves thee best?
Oh, Selim dear! oh, more than dearest!
Say, is it me thou hat'st or fearest?
Come, lay thy head upon my breast,
And I will kiss thee into rest,
Since words of mine, and songs must fail,
Ev'n from my fabled nightingale.
I knew our sire at times was stern,
But this from thee had yet to learn:
Too well I know he loves thee not;
But is Zuleika's love forgot?
Ah! deem I right? the Pacha's plan —
This kinsman Bey of Carasman
Perhaps may prove some foe of thine.
If so, I swear by Mecca's shrine, —
If shrines that ne'er approach allow
To woman's step admit her vow, —
Without thy free consent, command,
The Sultan should not have my hand!
Think'st thou that I could bear to part
With thee, and learn to halve my heart?
Ah! were I sever'd from thy side,
Where were thy friend — and who my guide?
Years have not seen, Time shall not see,
The hour that tears my soul from thee:
Ev'n Azrael, from his deadly quiver
When flies that shaft, and fly it must,
That parts all else, shall doom for ever
Our hearts to undivided dust!'

XII

He lived, he breathed, he moved, he felt;
He raised the maid from where she knelt;
His trance was gone, his keen eye shone
With thoughts that long in darkness dwelt;
With thoughts that burn — in rays that melt.
As the stream late conceal'd
By the fringe of its willows,
When it rushes reveal'd
In the light of its billows;
As the bolt bursts on high
From the black cloud that bound it,
Flash'd the soul of that eye
Through the long lashes round it.
A war-horse at the trumpet's sound,
A lion roused by heedless hound,
A tyrant waked to sudden strife
By graze of ill-directed knife,
Starts not to more convulsive life
Than he, who heard that vow, display'd,
And all, before repress'd, betray'd:
'Now thou art mine, for ever mine,
With life to keep, and scarce with life resign;
Now thou art mine, that sacred oath,
Though sworn by one, hath bound us both.
Yes, fondly, wisely hast thou done;
That vow hath saved more heads than one:
But blench not thou — thy simplest tress
Claims more from me than tenderness;
I would not wrong the slenderest hair
That clusters round thy forehead fair,
For all the treasures buried far
Within the caves of Istakar.
This morning clouds upon me lower'd,
Reproaches on my head were show-er'd,
And Giaffir almost call'd me coward!
Now I have motive to be brave;
The son of his neglected slave,
Nay, start not, 't was the term he gave,
May show, though little apt to vaunt,
A heart his words nor deeds can daunt.
His son, indeed! — yet, thanks to thee,
Perchance I am, at least shall be;
But let our plighted secret vow
Be only known to us as now.
I know the wretch who dares demand
From Giaffir thy reluctant hand;
More ill-got wealth, a meaner soul
Holds not a Musselim's [62] control:
Was he not bred in Egripo?
A viler race let Israel show!
But let that pass — to none be told
Our oath; the rest shall time unfold.
To me and mine leave Osman Bey;
I've partisans for peril's day:

62 governor's

Think not I am what I appear;
I've arms, and friends, and vengeance near.'

XIII

'Think not thou art what thou appearest!
  My Selim, thou art sadly changed:
This morn I saw thee gentlest, dearest;
  But now thou'rt from thyself estranged.
My love thou surely knew'st before,
It ne'er was less, nor can be more.
To see thee, hear thee, near thee stay,
  And hate the night I know not why,
Save that we meet not but by day;
  With thee to live, with thee to die,
  I dare not to my hope deny:
Thy cheek, thine eyes, thy lips to kiss,
Like this — and this — no more than this;
For, Allah! sure thy lips are flame:
  What fever in thy veins is flushing?
My own have nearly caught the same,
  At least I feel my cheek, too, blushing.
To soothe thy sickness, watch thy health,
Partake, but never waste thy wealth,
Or stand with smiles unmurmuring by,
And lighten half thy poverty;
Do all but close thy dying eye,
For that I could not live to try;
To these alone my thoughts aspire:
More can I do? or thou require?
But, Selim, thou must answer why
We need so much of mystery?
The cause I cannot dream nor tell,
But be it, since thou say'st 't is well;
Yet what thou mean'st by " arms " and " friends,"
Beyond my weaker sense extends.
I meant that Giaffir should have heard
  The very vow I plighted thee;
His wrath would not revoke my word:
  But surely he would leave me free.
  Can this fond wish seem strange in me,
To be what I have ever been?
What other hath Zuleika seen
From simple childhood's earliest hour?
  What other can she seek to see
Than thee, companion of her bower,
  The partner of her infancy?
These cherish'd thoughts with life begun,
  Say, why must I no more avow?
What change is wrought to make me shun
  The truth; my pride, and thine till now?
To meet the gaze of stranger's eyes
Our law, our creed, our God denies;
Nor shall one wandering thought of mine
At such, our Prophet's will, repine:
No! happier made by that decree,
He left me all in leaving thee.
Deep were my anguish, thus compell'd
To wed with one I ne'er beheld:
This wherefore should I not reveal?
Why wilt thou urge me to conceal?
I know the Pacha's haughty mood
To thee hath never boded good;
And he so often storms at nought,
Allah! forbid that e'er he ought!
And why I know not, but within
My heart concealment weighs like sin.
If then such secrecy be crime,
  And such it feels while lurking here;
Oh, Selim! tell me yet in time,
  Nor leave me thus to thoughts of fear.
Ah! yonder see the Tchocadar,[63]
My father leaves the mimic war;
I tremble now to meet his eye —
Say, Selim, canst thou tell me why?'

XIV

'Zuleika — to thy tower's retreat
Betake thee — Giaffir I can greet:
And now with him I fain must prate
Of firmans,[64] imposts, levies, state.
There's fearful news from Danube's banks,
Our Vizier [65] nobly thins his ranks,

---

[63] An attendant who ushers an official.
[64] royal edicts
[65] High Mohammedan official.

For which the Giaour [66] may give him thanks!
Our Sultan hath a shorter way
Such costly triumph to repay.
But, mark me, when the twilight drum
  Hath warn'd the troops to food and sleep,
Unto thy cell will Selim come:
  Then softly from the Haram creep
  Where we may wander by the deep:
  Our garden battlements are steep;
Nor these will rash intruder climb
To list our words, or stint our time;
And if he doth, I want not steel
Which some have felt, and more may feel.
Then shalt thou learn of Selim more
Than thou hast heard or thought before:
Trust me, Zuleika — fear not me!
Thou know'st I hold a Haram key.'
'Fear thee, my Selim! ne'er till now
Did word like this ——'
                    'Delay not thou;
I keep the key — and Haroun's guard
Have *some,* and hope of *more* reward.
To-night, Zuleika, thou shalt hear
My tale, my purpose, and my fear:
I am not, love! what I appear.'

CANTO II

I

THE winds are high on Helle's wave,
  As on that night of stormy water
When Love, who sent, forgot to save
The young, the beautiful, the brave,
  The lonely hope of Sestos' daughter.[67]
Oh! when alone along the sky
Her turret-torch was blazing high,
Though rising gale, and breaking foam,
And shrieking sea-birds warn'd him home;
And clouds aloft and tides below,
With signs and sounds, forbade to go,
He could not see, he would not hear,
Or sound or sign foreboding fear;
His eye but saw that light of love,
The only star it hail'd above;
His ear but rang with Hero's song,
'Ye waves, divide not lovers long!' —
That tale is old, but love anew
May nerve young hearts to prove as true.

II

The winds are high, and Helle's tide
  Rolls darkly heaving to the main;
And Night's descending shadows hide
  That field with blood bedew'd in vain,
The desert of old Priam's pride;
  The tombs, sole relics of his reign,
All — save immortal dreams that could beguile
The blind old man of Scio's rocky isle!

III

Oh! yet — for there my steps have been;
  These feet have press'd the sacred shore,
These limbs that buoyant wave hath borne — [68]
Minstrel! with thee to muse, to mourn,
  To trace again those fields of yore,
Believing every hillock green
  Contains no fabled hero's ashes,
And that around the undoubted scene
  Thine own 'broad Hellespont' still dashes,
Be long my lot! and cold were he
Who there could gaze denying thee!

IV

The night hath closed on Helle's stream,
  Nor yet hath risen on Ida's hill
That moon, which shone on his high theme:
No warrior chides her peaceful beam,
  But conscious shepherds bless it still.
Their flocks are grazing on the mound
  Of him [69] who felt the Dardan's arrow:

66 Any non-Mohammedan, particularly a Christian.
67 Hero, native of the city of Sestos.
68 Byron swam the Hellespont on 3 May 1810, and never forgot the fact.
69 Achilles

That mighty heap of gather'd ground
Which Ammon's son[70] ran proudly round,
By nations raised, by monarchs crown'd,
Is now a lone and nameless barrow!
Within — thy dwelling-place how narrow!
Without — can only strangers breathe
The name of him that *was* beneath:
Dust long outlasts the storied stone;
But Thou — thy very dust is gone!

V

Late, late to-night will Dian cheer
The swain, and chase the boatman's fear;
Till then — no beacon on the cliff
May shape the course of struggling skiff;
The scatter'd lights that skirt the bay,
All, one by one, have died away;
The only lamp of this lone hour
Is glimmering in Zuleika's tower.
Yes! there is light in that lone chamber,
And o'er her silken ottoman
Are thrown the fragrant beads of amber,
O'er which her fairy fingers ran;
Near these, with emerald rays beset,
(How could she thus that gem forget?)
Her mother's sainted amulet,
Whereon engraved the Koorsee text,
Could smooth this life, and win the next;
And by her comboloio[71] lies
A Koran of illumined dyes;
And many a bright emblazon'd rhyme
By Persian scribes redeem'd from time;
And o'er those scrolls, not oft so mute,
Reclines her now neglected lute;
And round her lamp of fretted gold
Bloom flowers in urns of China's mould;
The richest work of Iran's loom,
And Sheeraz' tribute of perfume;
All that can eye or sense delight
Are gather'd in that gorgeous room:
But yet it hath an air of gloom.
She, of this Peri cell the sprite,
What doth she hence, and on so rude a night?

VI

Wrapt in the darkest sable vest,
Which none save noblest Moslem wear,
To guard from winds of heaven the breast
As heaven itself to Selim dear,
With cautious steps the thicket threading,
And starting oft, as through the glade
The gust its hollow moanings made,
Till on the smoother pathway treading,
More free her timid bosom beat,
The maid pursued her silent guide;
And though her terror urged retreat,
How could she quit her Selim's side?
How teach her tender lips to chide?

VII

They reach'd at length a grotto, hewn
By nature, but enlarged by art,
Where oft her lute she wont to tune,
And oft her Koran conn'd apart;
And oft in youthful reverie
She dream'd what Paradise might be:
Where woman's parted soul shall go
Her Prophet had disdain'd to show;[72]
But Selim's mansion was secure,
Nor deem'd she, could he long endure
His bower in other worlds of bliss
Without *her*, most beloved in this!
Oh! who so dear with him could dwell?
What Houri soothe him half so well?

VIII

Since last she visited the spot
Some change seem'd wrought within the grot:
It might be only that the night
Disguised things seen by better light:
That brazen lamp but dimly threw
A ray of no celestial hue;

[70] Alexander
[71] A Turkish rosary.
[72] The Koran allots at least a third of Paradise to well-behaved women. [Byron.]

But in a nook within the cell
Her eye on stranger objects fell.
There arms were piled, not such as wield
The turban'd Delis in the field;
But brands of foreign blade and hilt,
And one was red — perchance with guilt!
Ah! how without can blood be spilt?
A cup too on the board was set
That did not seem to hold sherbet.
What may this mean? she turn'd to see
Her Selim — 'Oh! can this be he?'

IX

His robe of pride was thrown aside,
His brow no high-crown'd turban bore,
But in its stead a shawl of red,
Wreathed lightly round, his temples wore:
That dagger, on whose hilt the gem
Were worthy of a diadem,
No longer glitter'd at his waist,
Where pistols unadorn'd were braced;
And from his belt a sabre swung,
And from his shoulder loosely hung
The cloak of white, the thin capote [73]
That decks the wandering Candiote; [74]
Beneath — his golden plated vest
Clung like a cuirass to his breast;
The greaves below his knee that wound
With silvery scales were sheathed and bound.
But were it not that high command
Spake in his eye, and tone, and hand,
All that a careless eye could see
In him was some young Galiongée.[75]

X

'I said I was not what I seem'd;
And now thou see'st my words were true:
I have a tale thou hast not dream'd,
If sooth — its truth must others rue.
My story now 't were vain to hide,
I must not see thee Osman's bride:
But had not thine own lips declared
How much of that young heart I shared,
I could not, must not, yet have shown
The darker secret of my own.
In this I speak not now of love;
That, let time, truth, and peril prove:
But first — Oh! never wed another —
Zuleika! I am not thy brother!'

XI

'Oh! not my brother! — yet unsay —
God! am I left alone on earth
To mourn — I dare not curse — the day
That saw my solitary birth?
Oh! thou wilt love me now no more!
My sinking heart foreboded ill;
But know *me* all I was before,
Thy sister — friend — Zuleika still.
Thou led'st me here perchance to kill;
If thou hast cause for vengeance, see!
My breast is offer'd — take thy fill!
Far better with the dead to be
Than live thus nothing now to thee!
Perhaps far worse, for now I know
Why Giaffir always seem'd thy foe;
And I, alas! am Giaffir's child,
For whom thou wert contemn'd, reviled.
If not thy sister — wouldst thou save
My life, oh! bid me be thy slave!'

XII

'My slave, Zuleika! — nay, I'm thine:
But, gentle love, this transport calm.
Thy lot shall yet be link'd with mine;
I swear it by our Prophet's shrine,
And be that thought thy sorrow's balm.
So may the Koran verse display'd
Upon its steel direct my blade,
In danger's hour to guard us both,
As I preserve that awful oath!
The name in which thy heart hath prided
Must change; but, my Zuleika, know,
That tie is widen'd, not divided,
Although thy Sire's my deadliest foe.
My father was to Giaffir all

[73] long cloak
[74] Cretan
[75] Turkish sailor.

That Selim late was deem'd to thee:
That brother wrought a brother's fall,
But spared, at least, my infancy;
And lull'd me with a vain deceit
That yet a like return may meet.
He rear'd me, not with tender help,
But like the nephew of a Cain;
He watch'd me like a lion's whelp,
That gnaws and yet may break his chain.
My father's blood in every vein
Is boiling; but for thy dear sake
No present vengeance will I take;
Though here I must no more remain.
But first, beloved Zuleika! hear
How Giaffir wrought this deed of fear.

XIII

'How first their strife to rancour grew,
If love or envy made them foes,
It matters little if I knew;
In fiery spirits, slights, though few
And thoughtless, will disturb repose.
In war Abdallah's arm was strong,
Remember'd yet in Bosniac song,
And Paswan's rebel hordes attest
How little love they bore such guest:
His death is all I need relate,
The stern effect of Giaffir's hate;
And how my birth disclosed to me,
Whate'er beside it makes, hath made me free.

XIV

'When Paswan, after years of strife,
At last for power, but first for life,
In Widdin's walls too proudly sate,
Our Pachas rallied round the state;
Nor last nor least in high command,
Each brother led a separate band;
They gave their horse-tails [76] to the wind,
And mustering in Sophia's plain
Their tents were pitch'd, their post assign'd;
To one, alas! assign'd in vain!
What need of words! the deadly bowl,
By Giaffir's order drugged and given,
With venom subtle as his soul,
Dismiss'd Abdallah's hence to heaven.
Reclined and feverish in the bath,
He, when the hunter's sport was up,
But little deem'd a brother's wrath
To quench his thirst had such a cup:
The bowl a bribed attendant bore;
He drank one draught, nor needed more!
If thou my tale, Zuleika, doubt,
Call Haroun — he can tell it out.

XV

'The deed once done, and Paswan's feud
In part suppress'd, though ne'er subdued,
Abdallah's Pachalick [77] was gain'd: —
Thou know'st not what in our Divan
Can wealth procure for worse than man —
Abdallah's honours were obtain'd
By him a brother's murder stain'd;
'T is true, the purchase nearly drain'd
His ill got treasure, soon replaced.
Wouldst question whence? Survey the waste,
And ask the squalid peasant how
His gains repay his broiling brow! —
Why me the stern usurper spared,
Why thus with me his palace shared,
I know not. Shame, regret, remorse,
And little fear from infant's force;
Besides, adoption as a son
By him whom Heaven accorded none,
Or some unknown cabal, caprice,
Preserved me thus; — but not in peace:
He cannot curb his haughty mood,
Nor I forgive a father's blood.

XVI

'Within thy father's house are foes;
Not all who break his bread are true:
To these should I my birth disclose,
His days, his very hours were few:
They only want a heart to lead,
A hand to point them to the deed.
But Haroun only knows, or knew,

[76] A Pasha's standard.

[77] Territory ruled by a Pasha.

This tale, whose close is almost nigh:
He in Abdallah's palace grew,
And held that post in his Serai [78]
Which holds he here — he saw him die:
But what could single slavery do?
Avenge his lord? alas! too late;
Or save his son from such a fate?
He chose the last, and when elate
With foes subdued, or friends betray'd,
Proud Giaffir in high triumph sate,
He led me helpless to his gate,
And not in vain it seems essay'd
To save the life for which he pray'd.
The knowledge of my birth secured
From all and each, but most from me;
Thus Giaffir's safety was insured.
Removed he too from Roumelie
To this our Asiatic side,
Far from our seats by Danube's tide,
With none but Haroun, who retains
Such knowledge — and that Nubian feels
A tyrant's secrets are but chains,
From which the captive gladly steals,
And this and more to me reveals:
Such still to guilt just Alla sends —
Slaves, tools, accomplices — no friends!

XVII

'All this, Zuleika, harshly sounds;
But harsher still my tale must be:
Howe'er my tongue thy softness wounds,
Yet I must prove all truth to thee.
I saw thee start this garb to see,
Yet is it one I oft have worn,
And long must wear: this Galiongée,
To whom thy plighted vow is sworn,
Is leader of those pirate hordes,
Whose laws and lives are on their swords;
To hear whose desolating tale
Would make thy waning cheek more pale:
Those arms thou see'st my band have brought,
The hands that wield are not remote;
This cup too for the rugged knaves
Is fill'd — once quaff'd, they ne'er repine:
Our Prophet might forgive the slaves;
They're only infidels in wine.

XVIII

'What could I be? Proscribed at home,
And taunted to a wish to roam;
And listless left — for Giaffir's fear
Denied the courser and the spear —
Though oft — Oh, Mahomet! how oft! —
In full Divan the despot scoff'd,
As if *my* weak unwilling hand
Refused the bridle or the brand:
He ever went to war alone,
And pent me here untried — unknown;
To Haroun's care with women left,
By hope unblest, of fame bereft,
While thou — whose softness long endear'd,
Though it unmann'd me, still had cheer'd —
To Brusa's walls for safety sent,
Awaited'st there the field's event.
Haroun, who saw my spirit pining
Beneath inaction's sluggish yoke,
His captive, though with dread resigning,
My thraldom for a season broke,
On promise to return before
The day when Giaffir's charge was o'er.
'T is vain — my tongue cannot impart
My almost drunkenness of heart,
When first this liberated eye
Survey'd Earth, Ocean, Sun, and Sky,
As if my spirit pierced them through,
And all their inmost wonders knew!
One word alone can paint to thee
That more than feeling — I was Free!
E'en for thy presence ceased to pine;
The World — nay, Heaven itself was mine!

[78] Harem

XIX

'The shallop of a trusty Moor
Convey'd me from this idle shore;
I long'd to see the isles that gem
Old Ocean's purple diadem:
I sought by turns, and saw them all;
But when and where I join'd the crew,
With whom I'm pledged to rise or fall,
When all that we design to do
Is done, 't will then be time more meet
To tell thee, when the tale's complete.

XX

''T is true, they are a lawless brood,
But rough in form, nor mild in mood;
And every creed, and every race,
With them hath found — may find a place;
But open speech, and ready hand,
Obedience to their chief's command;
A soul for every enterprise,
That never sees with terror's eyes;
Friendship for each, and faith to all,
And vengeance vow'd for those who fall,
Have made them fitting instruments
For more than ev'n my own intents.
And some — and I have studied all
Distinguish'd from the vulgar rank,
But chiefly to my council call
The wisdom of the cautious Frank —
And some to higher thoughts aspire,
The last of Lambro's patriots there
Anticipated freedom share;
And oft around the cavern fire
On visionary schemes debate,
To snatch the Rayahs [79] from their fate.
So let them ease their hearts with prate
Of equal rights, which man ne'er knew;
I have a love for freedom too.
Ay! let me like the ocean-Patriarch roam,
Or only know on land the Tartar's home!
My tent on shore, my galley on the sea,
Are more than cities and Serais to me:
Borne by my steed, or wafted by my sail,
Across the desert, or before the gale,
Bound where thou wilt, my barb! [80] or glide, my prow!
But be the star that guides the wanderer, Thou!
Thou, my Zuleika, share and bless my bark;
The Dove of peace and promise to mine ark!
Or, since that hope denied in worlds of strife,
Be thou the rainbow to the storms of life!
The evening beam that smiles the clouds away,
And tints to-morrow with prophetic ray!
Blest — as the Muezzin's strain from Mecca's wall
To pilgrims pure and prostrate at his call;
Soft — as the melody of youthful days,
That steals the trembling tear of speechless praise;
Dear — as his native song to Exile's ears,
Shall sound each tone thy long-loved voice endears.
For thee in those bright isles is built a bower
Blooming as Aden [81] in its earliest hour.
A thousand swords, with Selim's heart and hand,
Wait — wave — defend — destroy — at thy command!
Girt by my band, Zuleika at my side,
The spoil of nations shall bedeck my bride.
The Haram's languid years of listless ease
Are well resign'd for cares — for joys like these:
Not blind to fate, I see, where'er I rove,
Unnumber'd perils — but one only love!
Yet well my toils shall that fond breast repay,
Though fortune frown, or falser friends betray.
How dear the dream in darkest hours of ill,
Should all be changed, to find thee faithful still!
Be but thy soul, like Selim's, firmly shown;
To thee be Selim's tender as thine own;

[79] Male unbelievers who pay a special tax.

[80] Barbary horse

[81] Mohammedan paradise

To soothe each sorrow, share in each delight,
Blend every thought, do all — but disunite!
Once free, 't is mine our horde again to guide;
Friends to each other, foes to aught beside:
Yet there we follow but the bent assign'd
By fatal Nature to man's warring kind:
Mark! where his carnage and his conquests cease!
He makes a solitude, and calls it — peace!
I, like the rest, must use my skill or strength,
But ask no land beyond my sabre's length:
Power sways but by division — her resource
The blest alternative of fraud or force!
Ours be the last; in time deceit may come
When cities cage us in a social home:
There ev'n thy soul might err — how oft the heart
Corruption shakes which peril could not part!
And woman, more than man, when death or woe,
Or even Disgrace, would lay her lover low,
Sunk in the lap of Luxury will shame —
Away suspicion! — *not* Zuleika's name!
But life is hazard at the best; and here
No more remains to win, and much to fear:
Yes, fear! the doubt, the dread of losing thee,
By Osman's power, and Giaffir's stern decree.
That dread shall vanish with the favouring gale,
Which Love to-night hath promised to my sail:
No danger daunts the pair his smile hath blest,
Their steps still roving, but their hearts at rest.
With thee all toils are sweet, each clime hath charms;
Earth — sea alike — our world within our arms!
Ay — let the loud winds whistle o'er the deck,
So that those arms cling closer round my neck:
The deepest murmur of this lip shall be,
No sigh for safety, but a prayer for thee!
The war of elements no fears impart
To Love, whose deadliest bane is human Art:
There lie the only rocks our course can check;
Here moments menace — *there* are years of wreck!
But hence ye thoughts that rise in Horror's shape!
This hour bestows, or ever bars escape.
Few words remain of mine my tale to close;
Of thine but *one* to waft us from our foes;
Yea — foes — to me will Giaffir's hate decline?
And is not Osman, who would part us, thine?

XXI

'His head and faith from doubt and death
Return'd in time my guard to save;
Few heard, none told, that o'er the wave
From isle to isle I roved the while;
And since, though parted from my band
Too seldom now I leave the land,
No deed they 've done, nor deed shall do,
Ere I have heard and doom'd it too:
I form the plan, decree the spoil,
'T is fit I oftener share the toil.
But now too long I've held thine ear;
Time presses, floats my bark, and here
We leave behind but hate and fear.
To-morrow Osman with his train
Arrives — to-night must break thy chain:
And wouldst thou save that haughty Bey, —
Perchance *his* life who gave thee thine, —
With me this hour away — away!
But yet, though thou art plighted mine,
Wouldst thou recall thy willing vow,

Appall'd by truths imparted now,
Here rest I — not to see thee wed:
But be that peril on *my* head!'

XXII

Zuleika, mute and motionless,
Stood like that statue of distress,
When, her last hope for ever gone,
The mother harden'd into stone:
All in the maid that eye could see
Was but a younger Niobé.
But ere her lip, or even her eye,
Essay'd to speak, or look reply,
Beneath the garden's wicket porch
Far flash'd on high a blazing torch!
Another—and another—and another—
'Oh! fly — no more — yet now my more than brother!'
Far, wide, through every thicket spread
The fearful lights are gleaming red;
Nor these alone — for each right hand
Is ready with a sheathless brand.
They part, pursue, return, and wheel
With searching flambeau, shining steel;
And last of all, his sabre waving,
Stern Giaffir in his fury raving:
And now almost they touch the cave —
Oh! must that grot be Selim's grave?

XXIII

Dauntless he stood — ''T is come — soon past —
One kiss, Zuleika — 't is my last:
But yet my band not far from shore
May hear this signal, see the flash;
Yet now too few — the attempt were rash:
No matter — yet one effort more.'
Forth to the cavern mouth he stept;
His pistol's echo rang on high,
Zuleika started not, nor wept,
Despair benumb'd her breast and eye! —
'They hear me not, or if they ply
Their oars, 't is but to see me die;
That sound hath drawn my foes more nigh.
Then forth my father's scimitar,
Thou ne'er hast seen less equal war!
Farewell, Zuleika! — sweet! retire:
Yet stay within — here linger safe,
At thee his rage will only chafe.
Stir not — lest even to thee perchance
Some erring blade or ball should glance.
Fear'st thou for him? — may I expire
If in this strife I seek thy sire!
No — though by him that poison pour'd;
No — though again he call me coward!
But tamely shall I meet their steel?
No — as each crest save *his* may feel!'

XXIV

One bound he made, and gain'd the sand:
Already at his feet hath sunk
The foremost of the prying band,
A gasping head, a quivering trunk:
Another falls — but round him close
A swarming circle of his foes;
From right to left his path he cleft,
And almost met the meeting wave:
His boat appears — not five oars' length —
His comrades strain with desperate strength —
Oh! are they yet in time to save?
His feet the foremost breakers lave;
His band are plunging in the bay,
Their sabres glitter through the spray;
Wet — wild — unwearied to the strand
They struggle — now they touch the land!
They come — 't is but to add to slaughter —
His heart's best blood is on the water.

XXV

Escaped from shot, unharm'd by steel,
Or scarcely grazed its force to feel,
Had Selim won, betray'd, beset,
To where the strand and billows met;
There as his last step left the land —
And the last death-blow dealt his hand —
Ah! wherefore did he turn to look

For her his eye but sought in vain?
That pause, that fatal gaze he took,
Hath doom'd his death, or fix'd his chain.
Sad proof, in peril and in pain,
How late will Lover's hope remain!
His back was to the dashing spray;
Behind, but close, his comrades lay,
When, at the instant, hiss'd the ball —
'So may the foes of Giaffir fall!'
Whose voice is heard? whose carbine rang?
Whose bullet through the night-air sang,
Too nearly, deadly aim'd to err?
'T is thine — Abdallah's Murderer!
The father slowly rued thy hate,
The son hath found a quicker fate:
Fast from his breast the blood is bubbling,
The whiteness of the sea-foam troubling —
If aught his lips essay'd to groan,
The rushing billows choked the tone!

XXVI

Morn slowly rolls the clouds away;
Few trophies of the fight are there:
The shouts that shook the midnight-bay
Are silent; but some signs of fray
That strand of strife may bear,
And fragments of each shiver'd brand;
Steps stamp'd; and dash'd into the sand
The print of many a struggling hand
May there be mark'd; nor far remote
A broken torch, an oarless boat;
And tangled on the weeds that heap
The beach where shelving to the deep
There lies a white capote!
'T is rent in twain — one dark-red stain
The wave yet ripples o'er in vain;
But where is he who wore?
Ye! who would o'er his relics weep,
Go, seek them where the surges sweep
Their burthen round Sigæum's steep
And cast on Lemnos' shore;
The sea-birds shriek above the prey,
O'er which their hungry beaks delay,
As shaken on his restless pillow,
His head heaves with the heaving billow;
That hand, whose motion is not life,
Yet feebly seems to menace strife,
Flung by the tossing tide on high,
Then levell'd with the wave —
What recks it, though that corse shall lie
Within a living grave?
The bird that tears that prostrate form
Hath only robb'd the meaner worm;
The only heart, the only eye
Had bled or wept to see him die,
Had seen those scatter'd limbs composed,
And mourn'd above his turban-stone,
That heart hath burst — that eye was closed —
Yea — closed before his own!

XXVII

By Helle's stream there is a voice of wail!
And woman's eye is wet — man's cheek is pale:
Zuleika! last of Giaffir's race,
Thy destined lord is come too late:
He sees not — ne'er shall see thy face!
Can he not hear
The loud Wul-wulleh [82] warn his distant ear?
Thy handmaids weeping at the gate,
The Koran-chanters of the hymn of fate,
The silent slaves with folded arms that wait,
Sighs in the hall, and shrieks upon the gale,
Tell him thy tale!
Thou didst not view thy Selim fall!
That fearful moment when he left the cave
Thy heart grew chill:
He was thy hope — thy joy — thy love — thine all,
And that last thought on him thou couldst not save
Sufficed to kill;
Burst forth in one wild cry — and all was still.
Peace to thy broken heart, and virgin grave!

---

[82] Death-song of Turkish women.

Ah! happy! but of life to lose the worst!
That grief — though deep — though fatal — was thy first!
Thrice happy ne'er to feel nor fear the force
Of absence, shame, pride, hate, revenge, remorse!
And, oh! that pang where more than madness lies!
The worm that will not sleep — and never dies;
Thought of the gloomy day and ghastly night,
That dreads the darkness, and yet loathes the light,
That winds around, and tears the quivering heart!
Ah! wherefore not consume it — and depart!
Woe to thee, rash and unrelenting chief!
Vainly thou heap'st the dust upon thy head,
Vainly the sackcloth o'er thy limbs dost spread:
By that same hand Abdallah — Selim bled.
Now let it tear thy beard in idle grief:
Thy pride of heart, thy bride for Osman's bed,
She, whom thy sultan had but seen to wed,
Thy Daughter's dead!
Hope of thine age, thy twilight's lonely beam,
The Star hath set that shone on Helle's stream.
What quench'd its ray? — the blood that thou hast shed!
Hark! to the hurried question of Despair:
'Where is my child?' — an Echo answers — 'Where?'

XXVIII

Within the place of thousand tombs
That shine beneath, while dark above
The sad but living cypress glooms
And withers not, though branch and leaf
Are stamp'd with an eternal grief,
Like early unrequited Love,
One spot exists, which ever blooms,
Ev'n in that deadly grove —
A single rose is shedding there
Its lonely lustre, meek and pale:
It looks as planted by Despair —
So white — so faint — the slightest gale
Might whirl the leaves on high;
And yet, though storms and blight assail,
And hands more rude than wintry sky
May wring it from the stem — in vain —
To-morrow sees it bloom again:
The stalk some spirit gently rears,
And waters with celestial tears;
For well may maids of Helle deem
That this can be no earthly flower,
Which mocks the tempest's withering hour,
And buds unshelter'd by a bower;
Nor droops though Spring refuse her shower,
Nor woos the summer beam:
To it the livelong night there sings
A bird unseen — but not remote:
Invisible his airy wings,
But soft as harp that Houri strings
His long entrancing note!
It were the Bulbul; but his throat,
Though mournful, pours not such a strain:
For they who listen cannot leave
The spot, but linger there and grieve,
As if they loved in vain!
And yet so sweet the tears they shed,
'T is sorrow so unmix'd with dread,
They scarce can bear the morn to break
That melancholy spell,
And longer yet would weep and wake,
He sings so wild and well!
But when the day-blush bursts from high
Expires that magic melody.
And some have been who could believe,
(So fondly youthful dreams deceive
Yet harsh be they that blame,)
That note so piercing and profound

Will shape and syllable its sound
  Into Zuleika's name.
'T is from her cypress summit heard,
That melts in air the liquid word:
'T is from her lowly virgin earth
That white rose takes its tender birth.
There late was laid a marble stone;
Eve saw it placed — the Morrow gone!
It was no mortal arm that bore
That deep-fix'd pillar to the shore;
For there, as Helle's legends tell,
Next morn 't was found where Selim fell;
Lash'd by the tumbling tide, whose wave
Denied his bones a holier grave:
And there by night, reclined, 't is said,
Is seen a ghastly turban'd head:
  And hence extended by the billow,
  'T is named the ' Pirate-phantom's pillow! '
  Where first it lay that mourning flower
  Hath flourish'd; flourisheth this hour,
Alone and dewy, coldly pure and pale;
As weeping Beauty's cheek at Sorrow's tale!

Sonnet on Chillon [83]

Eternal Spirit of the chainless Mind!
  Brightest in dungeons, Liberty! thou art,
  For there thy habitation is the heart —
The heart which love of thee alone can bind;
And when thy sons to fetters are consign'd —
  To fetters, and the damp vault's dayless gloom,
  Their country conquers with their martyrdom,
And Freedom's fame finds wings on every wind.
Chillon! thy prison is a holy place,
  And thy sad floor an altar — for 't was trod,
Until his very steps have left a trace
  Worn, as if thy cold pavement were a sod,
By Bonnivard! [84] May none those marks efface!
  For they appeal from tyranny to God.

She walks in beauty [85]

I

She walks in beauty, like the night
  Of cloudless climes and starry skies;
And all that 's best of dark and bright
  Meet in her aspect and her eyes:
Thus mellow'd to that tender light
  Which heaven to gaudy day denies.

II

One shade the more, one ray the less,
  Had half impair'd the nameless grace
Which waves in every raven tress,
  Or softly lightens o'er her face;
Where thoughts serenely sweet express
  How pure, how dear their dwelling-place.

III

And on that cheek, and o'er that brow,
  So soft, so calm, yet eloquent,
The smiles that win, the tints that glow,
  But tell of days in goodness spent,
A mind at peace with all below,
  A heart whose love is innocent!

The Destruction of Sennacherib [86]

I

The Assyrian came down like the wolf on the fold,
And his cohorts were gleaming in purple and gold;
And the sheen of their spears was like stars on the sea,
When the blue wave rolls nightly on deep Galilee.

---

[83] Written in June 1816, as was *The Prisoner of Chillon*, after a visit with Shelley to the Castle on the shore of Lake Geneva; published the same year.

[84] François Bonivard (1493–1570), Swiss republican, imprisoned by the Duke of Savoy for six years, 1530–1536, in the Castle of Chillon. He is Byron's famous 'prisoner.'

[85] Written in 1814; published in *Hebrew Melodies*, 1815.

[86] Written and published, in *Hebrew Melodies*, 1815 See *II Kings*, xviii–xix.

II

Like the leaves of the forest when Summer is green,
That host with their banners at sunset were seen:
Like the leaves of the forest when Autumn hath blown,
That host on the morrow lay wither'd and strown.

III

For the Angel of Death spread his wings on the blast,
And breathed in the face of the foe as he pass'd;
And the eyes of the sleepers wax'd deadly and chill,
And their hearts but once heaved, and for ever grew still!

IV

And there lay the steed with his nostril all wide,
But through it there roll'd not the breath of his pride;
And the foam of his gasping lay white on the turf,
And cold as the spray of the rock-beating surf.

V

And there lay the rider distorted and pale,
With the dew on his brow, and the rust on his mail:
And the tents were all silent, the banners alone,
The lances unlifted, the trumpet unblown.

VI

And the widows of Ashur [87] are loud in their wail,
And the idols are broke in the temple of Baal;
And the might of the Gentile, unsmote by the sword,
Hath melted like snow in the glance of the Lord!

[87] Assyria

When we two parted [88]

When we two parted
In silence and tears,
Half broken-hearted
To sever for years,
Pale grew thy cheek and cold,
Colder thy kiss;
Truly that hour foretold
Sorrow to this.

The dew of the morning
Sunk chill on my brow —
It felt like the warning
Of what I feel now.
Thy vows are all broken,
And light is thy fame:
I hear thy name spoken,
And share in its shame.

They name thee before me,
A knell to mine ear;
A shudder comes o'er me —
Why wert thou so dear?
They know not I knew thee,
Who knew thee too well: —
Long, long shall I rue thee,
Too deeply to tell.

In secret we met —
In silence I grieve,
That thy heart could forget,
Thy spirit deceive.
If I should meet thee
After long years,
How should I greet thee? —
With silence and tears.

Stanzas for Music [89]

There's not a joy the world can give like that it takes away,
When the glow of early thought declines in feeling's dull decay;
'T is not on youth's smooth cheek the blush alone, which fades so fast,

[88] Written in 1808; published in *Poems*, 1816.
[89] Written in 1815; published in *Poems*, 1816.

But the tender bloom of heart is gone, ere youth itself be past.

Then the few whose spirits float above the wreck of happiness
Are driven o'er the shoals of guilt or ocean of excess:
The magnet of their course is gone, or only points in vain
The shore to which their shiver'd sail shall never stretch again.

Then the mortal coldness of the soul like death itself comes down;
It cannot feel for others' woes, it dare not dream its own;
That heavy chill has frozen o'er the fountain of our tears,
And though the eye may sparkle still, 't is where the ice appears.

Though wit may flash from fluent lips, and mirth distract the breast,
Through midnight hours that yield no more their former hope of rest;
'T is but as ivy-leaves around the ruin'd turret wreath,
All green and wildly fresh without, but worn and grey beneath.

Oh could I feel as I have felt, — or be what I have been,
Or weep as I could once have wept o'er many a vanish'd scene;
As springs in deserts found seem sweet, all brackish though they be,
So, midst the wither'd waste of life, those tears would flow to me.

Stanzas for Music [90]

There be none of Beauty's daughters
With a magic like thee;
And like music on the waters
Is thy sweet voice to me:
When, as if its sound were causing
The charmed ocean's pausing,
The waves lie still and gleaming,
And the lull'd winds seem dreaming:

And the midnight moon is weaving
Her bright chain o'er the deep;
Whose breast is gently heaving,
As an infant's asleep:
So the spirit bows before thee,
To listen and adore thee;
With a full but soft emotion,
Like the swell of Summer's ocean.

[90] Written in 1816; published in *Poems* the same year.

To Thomas Moore [91]

I

My boat is on the shore,
And my bark is on the sea;
But, before I go, Tom Moore,
Here 's a double health to thee!

II

Here 's a sigh to those who love me,
And a smile to those who hate;
And, whatever sky 's above me,
Here 's a heart for every fate.

III

Though the ocean roar around me,
Yet it still shall bear me on;
Though a desert should surround me,
It hath springs that may be won.

IV

Were 't the last drop in the well,
As I gasp'd upon the brink,
Ere my fainting spirit fell,
'T is to thee that I would drink.

V

With that water, as this wine,
The libation I would pour

[91] The first stanza was written in 1816, the rest in 1817 and sent to Moore; first published in *The Traveller*, 8 January 1821.

Should be — peace with thine and mine,
  And a health to thee, Tom Moore.

So, we'll go no more a roving [92]

I

So, we 'll go no more a roving
  So late into the night,
Though the heart be still as loving,
  And the moon be still as bright.

II

For the sword outwears its sheath,
  And the soul wears out the breast,
And the heart must pause to breathe,
  And love itself have rest.

III

Though the night was made for loving,
  And the day returns too soon,
Yet we 'll go no more a roving
  By the light of the moon.

from DON JUAN [93]

FRAGMENT

On the back of the Poet's MS. of Canto I.

I WOULD to heaven that I were so much clay,
  As I am blood, bone, marrow, passion, feeling —
Because at least the past were pass'd away —
  And for the future — (but I write this reeling,
Having got drunk exceedingly to-day,
  So that I seem to stand upon the ceiling)
I say — the future is a serious matter —
And so — for God's sake — hock and sodawater!

DEDICATION

I

BOB SOUTHEY! You're a poet — Poet-laureate,
  And representative of all the race;
Although 't is true that you turn'd out a Tory [94] at
  Last, — yours has lately been a common case;
And now, my Epic Renegade! what are ye at?
  With all the Lakers, in and out of place?
A nest of tuneful persons, to my eye
Like 'four and twenty Blackbirds in a pye;

II

'Which pye being open'd they began to sing'
  (This old song and new simile holds good),
'A dainty dish to set before the King,'
  Or Regent; [95] who admires such kind of food; —
And Coleridge,[96] too, has lately taken wing,

[92] Written in 1817; published in *Letters and Journals*, 1830.

[93] Written at various intervals between 1818 and 1823; published between 1819 and 1824, except for the incomplete seventeenth canto, which was not printed until 1903. About all that the Spanish traditional libertine Don Juan de Tenorio contributed to Byron's poem was the name and a touch of his leading passion. As the story grew it became one of the great satires of all time, finally moving from the East to become an indictment of English society. The amazing scope — and the gusto — of the work is best summarized in Byron's famous letter to John Murray, his publisher, after the fifth canto was done: 'The 5th is so far from being the last of *D. J.* that it is hardly the beginning. I meant to take him the tour of Europe, with a proper mixture of siege, battle, and adventure, and to make him finish [*i.e.*, be executed] as Anacharsis Cloots in the French Revolution. To how many cantos this may extend, I know not, nor whether (even if I live) I shall complete it; but this was my notion: I meant to have made him a *Cavalier Servente* in Italy, and a cause for a divorce in England and a Sentimental "Werther-faced man" in Germany, so as to show the different ridicules of the society in each of those countries, and to have displayed him gradually *gâté* and *blasé* as he grew older, as is natural. But I had not quite fixed whether to make him end in Hell, or in an unhappy marriage, not knowing which would be the severest. The Spanish tradition says Hell: but it is probably only an Allegory of the other state.' Byron had finished sixteen cantos and had begun a seventeenth when he died.

[94] Like Wordsworth and Coleridge, Southey had been driven by the excesses of the French Revolution from his republican enthusiasm.

[95] The Prince of Wales, later George IV, was made Regent when his father became insane in 1811. Southey became poet laureate in 1813.

[96] In his prose writing.

But like a hawk encumber'd with his hood, —
Explaining metaphysics to the nation —
I wish he would explain his Explanation.

III

You, Bob! are rather insolent, you know,
At being disappointed in your wish
To supersede all warblers here below,
And be the only Blackbird in the dish;
And then you overstrain yourself, or so,
And tumble downward like the flying fish
Gasping on deck, because you soar too high, Bob,
And fall, for lack of moisture quite a-dry, Bob!

IV

And Wordsworth, in a rather long 'Excursion'
(I think the quarto holds five hundred pages),
Has given a sample from the vasty version
Of his new system to perplex the sages;
'T is poetry — at least by his assertion,
And may appear so when the dog-star rages —
And he who understands it would be able
To add a story to the Tower of Babel.

V

You — Gentlemen! by dint of long seclusion
From better company, have kept your own
At Keswick, and, through still continued fusion
Of one another's minds, at last have grown
To deem as a most logical conclusion,
That Poesy has wreaths for you alone:
There is a narrowness in such a notion,
Which makes me wish you'd change your lakes for ocean.

. . .

CANTO I

I

I WANT a hero: an uncommon want,
When every year and month sends forth a new one,
Till, after cloying the gazettes with cant,
The age discovers he is not the true one:
Of such as these I should not care to vaunt,
I 'll therefore take our ancient friend Don Juan —
We all have seen him, in the pantomime,[97]
Sent to the devil somewhat ere his time.

. . .

V

Brave men were living before Agamemnon
And since, exceeding valorous and sage,
A good deal like him too, though quite the same none;
But then they shone not on the poet's page,
And so have been forgotten: — I condemn none,
But can't find any in the present age
Fit for my poem (that is, for my new one);
So, as I said, I 'll take my friend Don Juan.

VI

Most epic poets plunge 'in medias res'
(Horace makes this the heroic turnpike road),
And then your hero tells, whene'er you please,
What went before — by way of episode,
While seated after dinner at his ease,
Beside his mistress in some soft abode,
Palace, or garden, paradise, or cavern,
Which serves the happy couple for a tavern.

VII

That is the usual method, but not mine —
My way is to begin with the beginning;

[97] *Don Juan; or The Libertine*, derived from Shadwell's play. In the omitted stanzas a number of possible heroes are rejected.

The regularity of my design
  Forbids all wandering as the worst of sinning,
And therefore I shall open with a line
  (Although it cost me half an hour in spinning)
Narrating somewhat of Don Juan's father,
And also of his mother, if you 'd rather.

VIII

In Seville was he born, a pleasant city,
  Famous for oranges and women — he
Who has not seen it will be much to pity,
  So says the proverb — and I quite agree;
Of all the Spanish towns is none more pretty,
  Cadiz, perhaps — but that you soon may see: —
Don Juan's parents lived beside the river,
A noble stream, and call'd the Guadalquivir.

IX

His father's name was Jóse — *Don,* of course,
  A true Hidalgo, free from every stain
Of Moor or Hebrew blood, he traced his source
  Through the most Gothic gentlemen of Spain;
A better cavalier ne'er mounted horse,
  Or, being mounted, e'er got down again,
Than Jóse, who begot our hero, who
Begot — but that's to come —— Well, to renew:

X

His mother was a learned lady, famed
  For every branch of every science known —
In every Christian language ever named,
  With virtues equall'd by her wit alone:
She made the cleverest people quite ashamed,
  And even the good with inward envy groan,
Finding themselves so very much exceeded
In their own way by all the things that she did.

XI

Her memory was a mine: she knew by heart
  All Calderon and greater part of Lopé,
So that if any actor miss'd his part
  She could have served him for the prompter's copy;
For her Feinagle's [98] were an useless art,
  And he himself obliged to shut up shop — he
Could never make a memory so fine as
That which adorn'd the brain of Donna Inez.

XII

Her favourite science was the mathematical,
  Her noblest virtue was her magnanimity;
Her wit (she sometimes tried at wit) was Attic all,
  Her serious sayings darken'd to sublimity;
In short, in all things she was fairly what I call
  A prodigy — her morning dress was dimity,
Her evening silk, or, in the summer, muslin,
And other stuffs, with which I won't stay puzzling.

XIII

She knew the Latin — that is, 'the Lord's prayer,'
  And Greek — the alphabet — I'm nearly sure;
She read some French romances here and there,
  Although her mode of speaking was not pure;
For native Spanish she had no great care,
  At least her conversation was obscure;
Her thoughts were theorems, her words a problem,
As if she deem'd that mystery would ennoble 'em.

---

[98] Gregor von Feinagle, inventor of a system of memorizing founded on the ancients. He had lectured in 1811 at the Royal Institution.

XIV

She liked the English and the Hebrew tongue,
And said there was analogy between 'em;
She proved it somehow out of sacred song,
But I must leave the proofs to those who've seen 'em,
But this I heard her say, and can't be wrong,
And all may think which way their judgments lean 'em,
' 'T is strange — the Hebrew noun which means " I am,"
The English always use to govern d — n.'

. . .

XXXVIII

Sagest of women, even of widows, she
Resolved that Juan [99] should be quite a paragon,
And worthy of the noblest pedigree:
(His sire was of Castile, his dam from Aragon).
Then for accomplishments of chivalry,
In case our lord the king should go to war again,
He learned the arts of riding, fencing, gunnery,
And how to scale a fortress — or a nunnery.

XXXIX

But that which Donna Inez most desired,
And saw into herself each day before all
The learned tutors whom for him she hired,
Was, that his breeding should be strictly moral:
Much into all his studies she inquired,
And so they were submitted first to her, all,
Arts, sciences, no branch was made a mystery
To Juan's eyes, excepting natural history.

[99] After the death of his father.

XL

The languages, especially the dead,
The sciences, and most of all the abstruse,
The arts, at least all such as could be said
To be the most remote from common use,
In all these he was much and deeply read:
But not a page of anything that's loose,
Or hints continuation of the species,
Was ever suffer'd, lest he should grow vicious.

XLI

His classic studies made a little puzzle,
Because of filthy loves of gods and goddesses,
Who in the earlier ages raised a bustle,
But never put on pantaloons or bodices;
His reverend tutors had at times a tussle,
And for their Æneids, Iliads, and Odysseys,
Were forced to make an odd sort of apology,
For Donna Inez dreaded the Mythology.

XLII

Ovid's a rake, as half his verses show him,
Anacreon's morals are a still worse sample,
Catullus scarcely has a decent poem,
I don't think Sappho's Ode a good example,
Although Longinus tells us there is no hymn
Where the sublime soars forth on wings more ample;
But Virgil's songs are pure, except that horrid one [100]
Beginning with 'Formosum Pastor Corydon.'

XLIII

Lucretius' irreligion is too strong
For early stomachs, to prove wholesome food;
I can't help thinking Juvenal was wrong,

[100] *Eclogues*, 2.

Although no doubt his real intent was good,
For speaking out so plainly in his song,
So much indeed as to be downright rude;
And then what proper person can be partial
To all those nauseous epigrams of Martial?

XLIV

Juan was taught from out the best edition,
Expurgated by learned men, who place,
Judiciously, from out the schoolboy's vision,
The grosser parts; but, fearful to deface
Too much their modest bard by this omission,
And pitying sore his mutilated case,
They only add them all in an appendix,
Which saves, in fact, the trouble of an index;

XLV

For there we have them all 'at one fell swoop,'
Instead of being scatter'd through the pages;
They stand forth marshall'd in a handsome troop,
To meet the ingenuous youth of future ages,
Till some less rigid editor shall stoop
To call them back into their separate cages,
Instead of standing staring all together,
Like garden gods — and not so decent either.

XLVI

The Missal too (it was the family Missal)
Was ornamented in a sort of way
Which ancient mass-books often are, and this all
Kinds of grotesques illumined; and how they,
Who saw those figures on the margin kiss all,
Could turn their optics to the text and pray,
Is more than I know — But Don Juan's mother
Kept this herself, and gave her son another.

XLVII

Sermons he read, and lectures he endured,
And homilies, and lives of all the saints;
To Jerome and to Chrysostom inured,
He did not take such studies for restraints;
But how faith is acquired, and then insured,
So well not one of the aforesaid paints
As Saint Augustine in his fine Confessions,
Which make the reader envy his transgressions.

XLVIII

This, too, was a seal'd book to little Juan —
I can't but say that his mamma was right,
If such an education was the true one.
She scarcely trusted him from out her sight;
Her maids were old, and if she took a new one,
You might be sure she was a perfect fright,
She did this during even her husband's life —
I recommend as much to every wife.

XLIX

Young Juan wax'd in godliness and grace;
At six a charming child, and at eleven
With all the promise of as fine a face
As e'er to man's maturer growth was given.
He studied steadily and grew apace,
And seem'd, at least, in the right road to heaven,
For half his days were pass'd at church, the other
Between his tutors, confessor, and mother

L

At six, I said, he was a charming child,
At twelve he was a fine, but quiet boy;
Although in infancy a little wild,
They tamed him down amongst them: to destroy
His natural spirit not in vain they toil'd,
At least it seem'd so; and his mother's joy
Was to declare how sage, and still, and steady,
Her young philosopher was grown already.

. . .

CXC

But Donna Inez (to divert the train
Of one of the most circulating scandals [101]
That had for centuries been known in Spain,
At least since the retirement of the Vandals,
First vow'd (and never had she vow'd in vain)
To Virgin Mary several pounds of candles;
And then, by the advice of some old ladies,
She sent her son to be shipp'd off from Cadiz.

CXCI

She had resolved that he should travel through
All European climes, by land or sea,
To mend his former morals, and get new,
Especially in France and Italy
(At least this is the thing most people do).
Julia was sent into a convent: she
Grieved, but, perhaps, her feelings may be better
Shown in the following copy of her Letter: —

CXCII

'They tell me 't is decided you depart:
'T is wise — 't is well, but not the less a pain;
I have no further claim on your young heart,
Mine is the victim, and would be again:
To love too much has been the only art
I used; — I write in haste, and if a stain
Be on this sheet, 't is not what it appears;
My eyeballs burn and throb, but have no tears.

CXCIII

'I loved, I love you, for this love have lost
State, station, heaven, mankind's, my own esteem,
And yet cannot regret what it hath cost,
So dear is still the memory of that dream;
Yet, if I name my guilt, 't is not to boast,
None can deem harshlier of me than I deem:
I trace this scrawl because I cannot rest —
I've nothing to reproach or to request.

CXCIV

'Man's love is of man's life a thing apart,
'T is woman's whole existence; man may range
The court, camp, church, the vessel, and the mart;
Sword, gown, gain, glory offer in exchange
Pride, fame, ambition, to fill up his heart,
And few there are whom these cannot estrange;
Men have all these resources, we but one,
To love again, and be again undone.

CXCV

'You will proceed in pleasure, and in pride,
Beloved and loving many; all is o'er
For me on earth, except some years to hide
My shame and sorrow deep in my heart's core:
These I could bear, but cannot cast aside
The passion which still rages as before, —
And so farewell — forgive me, love me — No,
That word is idle now — but let it go.

[101] Don Juan meantime has fallen in love with Donna Julia, a married woman.

CXCVI

'My breast has been all weakness, is so yet;
But still I think I can collect my mind;
My blood still rushes where my spirit's set,
As roll the waves before the settled wind;
My heart is feminine, nor can forget —
To all, except one image, madly blind;
So shakes the needle, and so stands the pole,
As vibrates my fond heart to my fix'd soul.

CXCVII

'I have no more to say, but linger still,
And dare not set my seal upon this sheet,
And yet I may as well the task fulfil,
My misery can scarce be more complete:
I had not lived till now, could sorrow kill;
Death shuns the wretch who fain the blow would meet,
And I must even survive this last adieu,
And bear with life to love and pray for you!'

CXCVIII

This note was written upon gilt-edged paper
With a neat little crow-quill, slight and new;
Her small white hand could hardly reach the taper,
It trembled as magnetic needles do,
And yet she did not let one tear escape her;
The seal a sun-flower; '*Elle vous suit partout,*'
The motto, cut upon a white cornelian;
The wax was superfine, its hue vermilion.

. . .

CCXIII

But now at thirty years my hair is gray —[102]
(I wonder what it will be like at forty?
I thought of a peruke the other day —)
My heart is not much greener; and, in short, I
Have squander'd my whole summer while 't was May,
And feel no more the spirit to retort; I
Have spent my life, both interest and principal,
And deem not, what I deem'd, my soul invincible.

CCXIV

No more — no more — Oh! never more on me
The freshness of the heart can fall like dew,
Which out of all the lovely things we see
Extracts emotions beautiful and new;
Hived in our bosoms like the bag o' the bee.
Think'st thou the honey with those objects grew?
Alas! 't was not in them, but in thy power
To double even the sweetness of a flower.

CCXV

No more — no more — Oh! never more, my heart,
Canst thou be my sole world, my universe!
Once all in all, but now a thing apart,
Thou canst not be my blessing or my curse:
The illusion's gone forever, and thou art
Insensible, I trust, but none the worse,
And in thy stead I've got a deal of judgment,
Though heaven knows how it ever found a lodgment.

CCXVI

My days of love are over; me no more
The charms of maid, wife, and still less of widow,
Can make the fool of which they made before, —

[102] This talk of himself with which Byron closes the first canto is a far cry from 'the pageant of his bleeding heart' in *Childe Harold*.

In short, I must not lead the life I did do;
The credulous hope of mutual minds is o'er,
The copious use of claret is forbid too,
So for a good old-gentlemanly vice,
I think I must take up with avarice.

CCXVII

Ambition was my idol, which was broken
Before the shrines of Sorrow, and of Pleasure;
And the two last have left me many a token
O'er which reflection may be made at leisure;
Now, like Friar Bacon's brazen head,[103] I've spoken,
'Time is, Time was, Time's past:' — a chymic treasure
Is glittering youth, which I have spent betimes —
My heart in passion, and my head on rhymes.

CCXVIII

What is the end of fame? 't is but to fill
A certain portion of uncertain paper:
Some liken it to climbing up a hill,
Whose summit, like all hills, is lost in vapour;
For this men write, speak, preach, and heroes kill,
And bards burn what they call their 'midnight taper,'
To have, when the original is dust,
A name, a wretched picture, and worse bust.

CCXIX

What are the hopes of man? Old Egypt's King
Cheops erected the first pyramid
And largest, thinking it was just the thing
To keep his memory whole, and mummy hid:
But somebody or other rummaging,
Burglariously broke his coffin's lid

[103] In Greene's play, *The Honourable History of Friar Bacon and Friar Bungay*, II, 58 f.

Let not a monument give you or me hopes,
Since not a pinch of dust remains of Cheops.

CCXX

But I, being fond of true philosophy,
Say very often to myself, 'Alas!
All things that have been born were born to die,
And flesh (which Death mows down to hay) is grass;
You 've pass'd your youth not so unpleasantly,
And if you had it o'er again — 't would pass —
So thank your stars that matters are no worse,
And read your Bible, sir, and mind your purse.'

CCXXI

But for the present, gentle reader! and
Still gentler purchaser! the bard — that's I —
Must, with permission, shake you by the hand,
And so your humble servant, and goodbye!
We meet again, if we should understand
Each other; and if not, I shall not try
Your patience further than by this short sample —
'T were well if others follow'd my example.

CCXXII

'Go, little book, from this my solitude!
I cast thee on the waters — go thy ways!
And if, as I believe, thy vein be good,
The world will find thee after many days.'
When Southey's read, and Wordsworth understood,
I can't help putting in my claim to praise —
The four first rhymes are Southey's, every line:
For God's sake, reader! take them not for mine!

CANTO III

LXXXII[104]

Their poet, a sad trimmer, but no less
In company a very pleasant fellow,
Had been the favourite of full many a mess
Of men, and made them speeches when half mellow;
And though his meaning they could rarely guess,
Yet still they deign'd to hiccup or to bellow
The glorious meed of popular applause,
Of which the first ne'er knows the second cause.

LXXXIII

But now being lifted into high society,
And having pick'd up several odds and ends
Of free thoughts in his travels, for variety,
He deem'd, being in a lone isle, among friends,
That without any danger of a riot, he
Might for long lying make himself amends;
And singing as he sung in his warm youth,
Agree to a short armistice with truth.

LXXXIV

He had travell'd 'mongst the Arabs, Turks, and Franks,
And knew the self-loves of the different nations;
And having lived with people of all ranks,
Had something ready upon most occasions —
Which got him a few presents and some thanks.
He varied with some skill his adulations;
To 'do at Rome as Romans do,' a piece
Of conduct was which he observed in Greece.

[104] Juan, having survived shipwreck on his way to Italy, came ashore on an island and is cared for by Haidée, the beautiful daughter of Lambro, a pirate then away at sea. Juan and Haidée, deeply in love and believing Lambro dead, were holding a great feast. After dwarfs, dancing girls, and others have contributed to the revelry, a poet is introduced.

LXXXV

Thus, usually, when he was asked to sing,
He gave the different nations something national;
'T was all the same to him — 'God save the king,'
Or '*Ça ira,*' according to the fashion all:
His muse made increment of anything,
From the high lyric down to the low rational:
If Pindar sang horse-races, what should hinder
Himself from being as pliable as Pindar?

LXXXVI

In France, for instance, he would write a chanson;
In England a six canto quarto tale;
In Spain he'd make a ballad or romance on
The last war — much the same in Portugal;
In Germany, the Pegasus he'd prance on
Would be old Goethe's — (see what says De Staël);[105]
In Italy he'd ape the 'Trecentisti;'[106]
In Greece, he'd sing some sort of hymn like this t' ye:

I

The isles of Greece, the isles of Greece!
Where burning Sappho loved and sung,
Where grew the arts of war and peace,
Where Delos[107] rose, and Phœbus sprung!
Eternal summer gilds them yet,
But all, except their sun, is set.

2

This Scian and the Teian muse,[108]
The hero's harp, the lover's lute,
Have found the fame your shores refuse:
Their place of birth alone is mute
To sounds which echo further west
Than your sires' 'Islands of the Blest.'

[105] Madame de Staël in her book on Germany had said that Goethe represented the entire of his country's literature.

[106] Writers in the style of the fourteenth century.

[107] The island of Delos had supposedly risen from the sea to become the birthplace of Apollo.

[108] The island of Scio claimed to be the birthplace of Homer; Teos, in Asia Minor, that of Anacreon.

3

The mountains look on Marathon —
  And Marathon looks on the sea;
And musing there an hour alone,
  I dream'd that Greece might still be free;
For standing on the Persians' grave,
I could not deem myself a slave.

4

A king [109] sate on the rocky brow
  Which looks o'er sea-born Salamis;
And ships, by thousands, lay below,
  And men in nations; — all were his!
He counted them at break of day —
And when the sun set where were they?

5

And where are they? and where art thou,
  My country? On thy voiceless shore
The heroic lay is tuneless now —
  The heroic bosom beats no more!
And must thy lyre, so long divine,
Degenerate into hands like mine?

6

'T is something, in the dearth of fame,
  Though link'd among a fetter'd race,
To feel at least a patriot's shame,
  Even as I sing, suffuse my face;
For what is left the poet here?
  For Greeks a blush — for Greece a tear.

7

Must *we* but weep o'er days more blest?
  Must *we* but blush? — Our fathers bled.
Earth! render back from out thy breast
  A remnant of our Spartan dead!
Of the three hundred grant but three,
To make a new Thermopylæ!

8

What, silent still? and silent all?
  Ah! no; — the voices of the dead
Sound like a distant torrent's fall,
  And answer, 'Let one living head,
But one arise, — we come, we come!'
'T is but the living who are dumb.

9

In vain — in vain: strike other chords;
  Fill high the cup with Samian wine!
Leave battles to the Turkish hordes,
  And shed the blood of Scio's vine!
Hark! rising to the ignoble call —
How answers each bold Bacchanal!

10

You have the Pyrrhic dance as yet;
  Where is the Pyrrhic phalanx gone?
Of two such lessons, why forget
  The nobler and the manlier one?
You have the letters Cadmus gave — [110]
Think ye he meant them for a slave?

11

Fill high the bowl with Samian wine!
  We will not think of themes like these!
It made Anacreon's song divine:
  He served — but served Polycrates —
A tyrant; but our masters then
Were still, at least, our countrymen.

12

The tyrant of the Chersonese
  Was freedom's best and bravest friend;
That tyrant was Miltiades!
  Oh! that the present hour would lend
Another despot of the kind!
Such chains as his were sure to bind.

13

Fill high the bowl with Samian wine!
  On Suli's rock, and Parga's shore,[111]
Exists the remnant of a line
  Such as the Doric mothers bore;
And there, perhaps, some seed is sown,
The Heracleidan blood might own.

---

[109] Xerxes, King of Persia, whose fleet was defeated at Salamis by the Greeks.

[110] Cadmus was said to have introduced the alphabet from Phoenicia into Greece.

[111] Both places in Albania.

14

Trust not for freedom to the Franks —
They have a king who buys and sells;
In native swords, and native ranks,
The only hope of courage dwells:
But Turkish force, and Latin fraud,
Would break your shield, however broad.

15

Fill high the bowl with Samian wine!
Our virgins dance beneath the shade —
I see their glorious black eyes shine;
But gazing on each glowing maid,
My own the burning tear-drop laves,
To think such breasts must suckle slaves.

16

Place me on Sunium's marbled steep,
Where nothing, save the waves and I,
May hear our mutual murmurs sweep;
There, swan-like, let me sing and die:
A land of slaves shall ne'er be mine —
Dash down yon cup of Samian wine!

LXXXVII

Thus sung, or would, or could, or should have sung,
The modern Greek, in tolerable verse;
If not like Orpheus quite, when Greece was young,
Yet in these times he might have done much worse:
His strain display'd some feeling — right or wrong;
And feeling, in a poet, is the source
Of others' feeling; but they are such liars,
And take all colours — like the hands of dyers.

. . .

CI

T' our tale. — The feast was over, the slaves gone,
The dwarfs and dancing girls had all retired;
The Arab lore and poet's song were done,
And every sound of revelry expired;
The lady and her lover, left alone,
The rosy flood of twilight's sky admired; —
Ave Maria! o'er the earth and sea,
That heavenliest hour of Heaven is worthiest thee!

CII

Ave Maria! blessed be the hour!
The time, the clime, the spot, where I so oft
Have felt that moment in its fullest power
Sink o'er the earth so beautiful and soft,
While swung the deep bell in the distant tower,
Or the faint dying day-hymn stole aloft,
And not a breath crept through the rosy air,
And yet the forest leaves seem'd stirr'd with prayer.

CIII

Ave Maria! 't is the hour of prayer!
Ave Maria! 't is the hour of love!
Ave Maria! may our spirits dare
Look up to thine and to thy Son's above!
Ave Maria! oh that face so fair!
Those downcast eyes beneath the Almighty dove —
What though 't is but a pictured image strike,
That painting is no idol, — 't is too like.

CIV

Some kinder casuists are pleased to say,
In nameless print — that I have no devotion;
But set those persons down with me to pray,
And you shall see who has the properest notion
Of getting into heaven the shortest way;
My altars are the mountains and the ocean,
Earth, air, stars, — all that springs from the great Whole,
Who hath produced, and will receive the soul.

CV

Sweet hour of twilight! — in the solitude
Of the pine forest, and the silent shore
Which bounds Ravenna's immemorial wood,
Rooted where once the Adrian wave flow'd o'er,
To where the last Cæsarean fortress stood,
Evergreen forest! which Boccaccio's lore
And Dryden's lay[112] made haunted ground to me,
How have I loved the twilight hour and thee!

CVI

The shrill cicalas, people of the pine,
Making their summer lives one ceaseless song,
Were the sole echoes, save my steed's and mine,
And vesper bell's that rose the boughs along;
The spectre huntsman of Onesti's line,
His hell-dogs, and their chase, and the fair throng
Which learn'd from this example not to fly
From a true lover, — shadow'd my mind's eye.

CVII

Oh, Hesperus! thou bringest all good things —
Home to the weary, to the hungry cheer,
To the young bird the parent's brooding wings,
The welcome stall to the o'erlabour'd steer;
Whate'er of peace about our hearthstone clings,
Whate'er our household gods protect of dear,
Are gather'd round us by thy look of rest;
Thou bring'st the child, too, to the mother's breast.

[112] Dryden's *Theodore and Honoria*, adapted from the eighth tale of the fifth day of Boccaccio's *Decameron*, is the story of a ghostly huntsman of the district near Ravenna. Dryden's Theodore is Boccaccio's Onesti.

CVIII

Soft hour! which wakes the wish and melts the heart
Of those who sail the seas, on the first day
When they from their sweet friends are torn apart;
Or fills with love the pilgrim on his way
As the far bell of vesper makes him start,
Seeming to weep the dying day's decay;
Is this a fancy which our reason scorns?
Ah! surely nothing dies but something mourns!

. . .

CANTO IV

XII

'Whom the gods love die young' was said of yore,
And many deaths do they escape by this:
The death of friends, and that which slays even more —
The death of friendship, love, youth, all that is,
Except mere breath; and since the silent shore
Awaits at last even those who longest miss
The old archer's shafts, perhaps the early grave
Which men weep over may be meant to save.

XIII

Haidée and Juan thought not of the dead.
The heavens, and earth, and air, seem'd made for them:
They found no fault with Time, save that he fled;
They saw not in themselves aught to condemn;
Each was the other's mirror, and but read
Joy sparkling in their dark eyes like a gem,
And knew such brightness was but the reflection
Of their exchanging glances of affection.

XIV

The gentle pressure, and the thrilling touch,
The least glance better understood than words,
Which still said all, and ne'er could say too much;
A language, too, but like to that of birds,
Known but to them, at least appearing such
As but to lovers a true sense affords;
Sweet playful phrases, which would seem absurd
To those who have ceased to hear such, or ne'er heard.

XV

All these were theirs, for they were children still,
And children still they should have ever been;
They were not made in the real world to fill
A busy character in the dull scene,
But like two beings born from out a rill,
A nymph and her beloved, all unseen
To pass their lives in fountains and on flowers,
And never know the weight of human hours.

XVI

Moons changing had roll'd on, and changeless found
Those their bright rise had lighted to such joys
As rarely they beheld throughout their round;
And these were not of the vain kind which cloys,
For theirs were buoyant spirits, never bound
By the mere senses; and that which destroys
Most love, possession, unto them appear'd
A thing which each endearment more endear'd.

XVII

Oh beautiful! and rare as beautiful!
But theirs was love in which the mind delights
To lose itself, when the old world grows dull,
And we are sick of its hack sounds and sights,
Intrigues, adventures of the common school,
Its petty passions, marriages, and flights,
Where Hymen's torch but brands one strumpet more,
Whose husband only knows her not a wh—re.

XVIII

Hard words; harsh truth; a truth which many know.
Enough.—The faithful and the fairy pair,
Who never found a single hour too slow,
What was it made them thus exempt from care?
Young innate feelings all have felt below,
Which perish in the rest, but in them were
Inherent; what we mortals call romantic,
And always envy, though we deem it frantic.

XIX

This is in others a factitious state,
An opium dream of too much youth and reading,
But was in them their nature or their fate:
No novels e'er had set their young hearts bleeding,
For Haidée's knowledge was by no means great,
And Juan was a boy of saintly breeding;
So that there was no reason for their loves
More than for those of nightingales or doves.

XX

They gazed upon the sunset; 't is an hour
Dear unto all, but dearest to *their* eyes,
For it had made them what they were: the power

Of love had first o'erwhelm'd them from such skies,
When happiness had been their only dower,
And twilight saw them link'd in passion's ties;
Charm'd with each other, all things charm'd that brought
The past still welcome as the present thought.

XXI

I know not why, but in that hour to-night,
Even as they gazed, a sudden tremor came,
And swept, as 't were, across their hearts' delight,
Like the wind o'er a harp-string, or a flame,
When one is shook in sound, and one in sight:
And thus some boding flash'd through either frame,
And call'd from Juan's breast a faint low sigh,
While one new tear arose in Haidée's eye.

XXII

That large black prophet eye seem'd to dilate
And follow far the disappearing sun,
As if their last day of a happy date
With his broad, bright, and dropping orb were gone.
Juan gazed on her as to ask his fate —
He felt a grief, but knowing cause for none,
His glance inquired of hers for some excuse
For feelings causeless, or at least abstruse.

XXIII

She turn'd to him, and smiled, but in that sort
Which makes not others smile; then turn'd aside:
Whatever feeling shook her, it seem'd short,
And master'd by her wisdom or her pride;
When Juan spoke, too — it might be in sport —
Of this their mutual feeling, she replied —
'If it should be so, — but — it cannot be —
Or I at least shall not survive to see.'

XXIV

Juan would question further, but she press'd
His lip to hers, and silenced him with this,
And then dismiss'd the omen from her breast,
Defying augury with that fond kiss;
And no doubt of all methods 't is the best:
Some people prefer wine — 't is not amiss;
I have tried both; so those who would a part take
May choose between the headache and the heartache.

XXV

One of the two according to your choice,
Woman or wine, you'll have to undergo;
Both maladies are taxes on our joys:
But which to choose, I really hardly know;
And if I had to give a casting voice,
For both sides I could many reasons show,
And then decide, without great wrong to either,
It were much better to have both than neither.

XXVI

Juan and Haidée gazed upon each other
With swimming looks of speechless tenderness,
Which mix'd all feelings, friend, child, lover, brother;
All that the best can mingle and express
When two pure hearts are pour'd in one another,
And love too much, and yet cannot love less;

But almost sanctify the sweet excess
By the immortal wish and power to bless.

XXVII

Mix'd in each other's arms, and heart in heart,
Why did they not then die? — they had lived too long
Should an hour come to bid them breathe apart;
Years could but bring them cruel things or wrong;
The world was not for them, nor the worlds' art
For beings passionate as Sappho's song;
Love was born *with* them, *in* them, so intense,
It was their very spirit — not a sense.

XXVIII

They should have lived together deep in woods,
Unseen as sings the nightingale; they were
Unfit to mix in these thick solitudes
Call'd social, haunts of Hate, and Vice, and Care;
How lonely every freeborn creature broods!
The sweetest song-birds nestle in a pair;
The eagle soars alone; the gull and crow
Flock o'er their carrion, just like men below.

XXIX

Now pillow'd cheek to cheek, in loving sleep,
Haidée and Juan their siesta took,
A gentle slumber, but it was not deep,
For ever and anon a something shook
Juan, and shuddering o'er his frame would creep;
And Haidée's sweet lips murmur'd like a brook
A wordless music, and her face so fair
Stirr'd with her dream, as rose-leaves with the air;

XXX

Or as the stirring of a deep clear stream
Within an Alpine hollow, when the wind
Walks o'er it, was she shaken by the dream,
The mystical usurper of the mind —
O'erpowering us to be whate'er may seem
Good to the soul which we no more can bind:
Strange state of being! (for 't is still to be),
Senseless to feel, and with seal'd eyes to see.

XXXI

She dream'd of being alone on the sea-shore,
Chain'd to a rock; she knew not how, but stir
She could not from the spot, and the loud roar
Grew, and each wave rose roughly, threatening her;
And o'er her upper lip they seem'd to pour,
Until she sobb'd for breath, and soon they were
Foaming o'er her lone head, so fierce and high —
Each broke to drown her, yet she could not die.

XXXII

Anon — she was released, and then she stray'd
O'er the sharp shingles with her bleeding feet,
And stumbled almost every step she made;
And something roll'd before her in a sheet,
Which she must still pursue howe'er afraid:
'T was white and indistinct, nor stopp'd to meet
Her glance nor grasp, for still she gazed and grasp'd,
And ran, but it escaped her as she clasp'd.

XXXIII

The dream changed: — in a cave she stood, its walls

Were hung with marble icicles; the work
Of ages on its water-fretted halls,
Where waves might wash, and seals might breed and lurk;
Her hair was dripping, and the very balls
Of her black eyes seem'd turn'd to tears, and mirk
The sharp rocks look'd below each drop they caught,
Which froze to marble as it fell, — she thought.

XXXIV

And wet, and cold, and lifeless at her feet,
Pale as the foam that froth'd on his dead brow,
Which she essay'd in vain to clear, (how sweet
Were once her cares, how idle seem'd they now!)
Lay Juan, nor could aught renew the beat
Of his quench'd heart; and the sea dirges low
Rang in her sad ears like a mermaid's song,
And that brief dream appear'd a life too long.

XXXV

And gazing on the dead, she thought his face
Faded, or alter'd into something new —
Like to her father's features, till each trace
More like and like to Lambro's aspect grew —
With all his keen worn look and Grecian grace;
And starting, she awoke, and what to view?
Oh! Powers of Heaven! what dark eye meets she there?
'T is — 't is her father's — fix'd upon the pair!

XXXVI

Then shrieking, she arose, and shrieking fell,
With joy and sorrow, hope and fear, to see
Him whom she deem'd a habitant where dwell
The ocean-buried, risen from death, to be
Perchance the death of one she loved too well:
Dear as her father had been to Haidée,
It was a moment of that awful kind ——
I have seen such — but must not call to mind.

XXXVII

Up Juan sprang to Haidée's bitter shriek,
And caught her falling, and from off the wall
Snatch'd down his sabre, in hot haste to wreak
Vengeance on him who was the cause of all:
Then Lambro, who till now forebore to speak,
Smiled scornfully, and said, 'Within my call,
A thousand scimitars await the word;
Put up, young man, put up your silly sword.'

XXXVIII

And Haidée clung around him; 'Juan, 't is —
'T is Lambro — 't is my father! Kneel with me —
He will forgive us — yes — it must be — yes.
Oh! dearest father, in this agony
Of pleasure and of pain — even while I kiss
Thy garment's hem with transport, can it be
That doubt should mingle with my filial joy?
Deal with me as thou wilt, but spare this boy.'

XXXIX

High and inscrutable the old man stood,
Calm in his voice, and calm within his eye —
Not always signs with him of calmest mood:
He look'd upon her, but gave no reply;
Then turn'd to Juan, in whose cheek the blood
Oft came and went, as there resolved to die;

In arms, at least, he stood, in act to spring
On the first foe whom Lambro's call might bring.

XL

'Young man, your sword;' so Lambro once more said:
Juan replied, 'Not while this arm is free.'
The old man's cheek grew pale, but not with dread,
And drawing from his belt a pistol, he
Replied, 'Your blood be then on your own head.'
Then look'd close at the flint, as if to see
'T was fresh — for he had lately used the lock —
And next proceeded quietly to cock.

XLI

It has a strange quick jar upon the ear,
That cocking of a pistol, when you know
A moment more will bring the sight to bear
Upon your person, twelve yards off, or so;
A gentlemanly distance, not too near,
If you have got a former friend for foe;
But after being fired at once or twice,
The ear becomes more Irish, and less nice.

XLII

Lambro presented, and one instant more
Had stopp'd this Canto, and Don Juan's breath,
When Haidée threw herself her boy before;
Stern as her sire: 'On me,' she cried, 'let death
Descend — the fault is mine; this fatal shore
He found — but sought not. I have pledged my faith;
I love him — I will die with him: I knew
Your nature's firmness — know your daughter's too.'

XLIII

A minute past, and she had been all tears,
And tenderness, and infancy; but now
She stood as one who champion'd human fears —
Pale, statue-like, and stern, she woo'd the blow;
And tall beyond her sex, and their compeers,
She drew up to her height, as if to show
A fairer mark; and with a fix'd eye scann'd
Her father's face — but never stopp'd his hand.

XLIV

He gazed on her, and she on him; 't was strange
How like they look'd! the expression was the same;
Serenely savage, with a little change
In the large dark eye's mutual-darted flame;
For she, too, was as one who could avenge,
If cause should be — a lioness, though tame;
Her father's blood before her father's face
Boil'd up, and proved her truly of his race.

XLV

I said they were alike, their features and
Their stature, differing but in sex and years:
Even to the delicacy of their hand
There was resemblance, such as true blood wears;
And now to see them, thus divided, stand
In fix'd ferocity, when joyous tears,
And sweet sensations, should have welcomed both,
Shows what the passions are in their full growth.

XLVI

The father paused a moment, then withdrew
His weapon, and replaced it; but stood still,
And looking on her, as to look her through,

'Not *I*,' he said, 'have sought this stranger's ill;
Not *I* have made this desolation: few
Would bear such outrage, and forbear to kill;
But I must do my duty — how thou hast
Done thine, the present vouches for the past.

XLVII

'Let him disarm; or, by my father's head,
His own shall roll before you like a ball!'
He raised his whistle as the word he said,
And blew; another answer'd to the call,
And rushing in disorderly, though led,
And arm'd from boot to turban, one and all,
Some twenty of his train came, rank on rank;
He gave the word, 'Arrest or slay the Frank.'

XLVIII

Then, with a sudden movement, he withdrew
His daughter; while compress'd within his clasp,
'Twixt her and Juan interposed the crew;
In vain she struggled in her father's grasp —
His arms were like a serpent's coil: then flew
Upon their prey, as darts an angry asp,
The file of pirates: save the foremost, who
Had fallen, with his right shoulder half cut through.

XLIX

The second had his cheek laid open; but
The third, a wary, cool old sworder, took
The blows upon his cutlass, and then put
His own well in; so well, ere you could look,
His man was floor'd, and helpless at his foot,
With the blood running like a little brook
From two smart sabre gashes, deep and red —
One on the arm, the other on the head.

L

And then they bound him where he fell, and bore
Juan from the apartment: with a sign
Old Lambro bade them take him to the shore,
Where lay some ships which were to sail at nine.
They laid him in a boat, and plied the oar
Until they reach'd some galliots, placed in line;
On board of one of these, and under hatches,
They stow'd him, with strict orders to the watches.

LI

The world is full of strange vicissitudes,
And here was one exceedingly unpleasant:
A gentleman so rich in the world's goods,
Handsome and young, enjoying all the present,
Just at the very time when he least broods
On such a thing, is suddenly to sea sent,
Wounded and chain'd, so that he cannot move,
And all because a lady fell in love.

LII

Here I must leave him, for I grow pathetic,
Moved by the Chinese nymph of tears, green tea!
Than whom Cassandra was not more prophetic;
For if my pure libations exceed three,
I feel my heart become so sympathetic,
That I must have recourse to black Bohea:[113]
'Tis pity wine should be so deleterious,
For tea and coffee leave us much more serious,

[113] Another kind of tea.

LIII

Unless when qualified with thee, Cogniac!
Sweet Naïad of the Phlegethontic rill[114]
Ah! why the liver wilt thou thus attack,
And make, like other nymphs, thy lovers ill?
I would take refuge in weak punch, but *rack*
(In each sense[115] of the word), whene'er I fill
My mild and midnight beakers to the brim,
Wakes me next morning with its synonym.

LIV

I leave Don Juan for the present, safe —
Not sound, poor fellow, but severely wounded;
Yet could his corporal pangs amount to half
Of those with which his Haidée's bosom bounded!
She was not one to weep, and rave, and chafe,
And then give way, subdued because surrounded;
Her mother was a Moorish maid from Fez,
Where all is Eden, or a wilderness.

LV

There the large olive rains its amber store
In marble fonts; there grain, and flour, and fruit,
Gush from the earth until the land runs o'er;
But there, too, many a poison-tree has root,
And midnight listens to the lion's roar,
And long, long deserts scorch the camel's foot,
Or heaving whelm the helpless caravan;
And as the soil is, so the heart of man.

[114] This river of Hades runs not water, but fire.
[115] *i.e., punch* and *disturbance*

LVI

Afric is all the sun's, and as her earth
Her human clay is kindled; full of power
For good or evil, burning from its birth,
The Moorish blood partakes the planet's hour,
And like the soil beneath it will bring forth:
Beauty and love were Haidée's mother's dower;
But her large dark eye show'd deep Passion's force,
Though sleeping like a lion near a source.

LVII

Her daughter, temper'd with a milder ray,
Like summer clouds all silvery, smooth, and fair,
Till slowly charged with thunder they display
Terror to earth, and tempest to the air,
Had held till now her soft and milky way;
But overwrought with passion and despair,
The fire burst forth from her Numidian veins,
Even as the Simoom[116] sweeps the blasted plains.

LVIII

The last sight which she saw was Juan's gore,
And he himself o'ermaster'd and cut down;
His blood was running on the very floor
Where late he trod, her beautiful, her own;
Thus much she view'd an instant and no more, —
Her struggles ceased with one convulsive groan;
On her sire's arm, which until now scarce held
Her writhing, fell she like a cedar fell'd.

[116] A scorching wind.

LIX

A vein had burst, and her sweet lips' pure dyes
Were dabbled with the deep blood which ran o'er;
And her head droop'd, as when the lily lies
O'ercharged with rain: her summon'd handmaids bore
Their lady to her couch with gushing eyes;
Of herbs and cordials they produced their store,
But she defied all means they could employ,
Like one life could not hold, nor death destroy.

LX

Days lay she in that state unchanged, though chill —
With nothing livid, still her lips were red;
She had no pulse, but death seem'd absent still;
No hideous sign proclaim'd her surely dead;
Corruption came not in each mind to kill
All hope; to look upon her sweet face bred
New thoughts of life, for it seem'd full of soul —
She had so much, earth could not claim the whole.

LXI

The ruling passion, such as marble shows
When exquisitely chisell'd, still lay there,
But fix'd as marble's unchanged aspect throws
O'er the fair Venus, but for ever fair;
O'er the Laocoön's all eternal throes,
And ever-dying Gladiator's air,
Their energy like life forms all their fame,
Yet looks not life, for they are still the same.

LXII

She woke at length, but not as sleepers wake,
Rather the dead, for life seem'd something new,
A strange sensation which she must partake
Perforce, since whatsoever met her view
Struck not on memory, though a heavy ache
Lay at her heart, whose earliest beat still true
Brought back the sense of pain without the cause,
For, for a while, the furies made a pause.

LXIII

She look'd on many a face with vacant eye,
On many a token without knowing what;
She saw them watch her without asking why,
And reck'd not who around her pillow sat;
Not speechless, though she spoke not; not a sigh
Relieved her thoughts; dull silence and quick chat
Were tried in vain by those who served; she gave
No sign, save breath, of having left the grave.

LXIV

Her handmaids tended, but she heeded not;
Her father watch'd, she turn'd her eyes away;
She recognised no being, and no spot,
However dear or cherish'd in their day;
They changed from room to room, but all forgot,
Gentle, but without memory she lay;
At length those eyes, which they would fain be weaning
Back to old thoughts, wax'd full of fearful meaning.

LXV

And then a slave bethought her of a harp;
The harper came, and tuned his instrument;

At the first notes, irregular and sharp,
On him her flashing eyes a moment bent,
Then to the wall she turn'd as if to warp
Her thoughts from sorrow through her heart re-sent;
And he began a long low island song
Of ancient days, ere tyranny grew strong.

LXVI

Anon her thin wan fingers beat the wall
In time to his old tune; he changed the theme,
And sung of love; the fierce name struck through all
Her recollection; on her flash'd the dream
Of what she was, and is, if ye could call
To be so being; in a gushing stream
The tears rush'd forth from her o'er-clouded brain,
Like mountain mists at length dissolved in rain.

LXVII

Short solace, vain relief! — thought came too quick,
And whirl'd her brain to madness; she arose
As one who ne'er had dwelt among the sick,
And flew at all she met, as on her foes;
But no one ever heard her speak or shriek,
Although her paroxysm drew towards its close; —
Hers was a phrensy which disdain'd to rave,
Even when they smote her, in the hope to save.

LXVIII

Yet she betray'd at times a gleam of sense;
Nothing could make her meet her father's face,
Though on all other things with looks intense
She gazed, but none she ever could retrace;
Food she refused, and raiment; no pretence
Avail'd for either; neither change of place,
Nor time, nor skill, nor remedy, could give her
Senses to sleep — the power seem'd gone for ever.

LXIX

Twelve days and nights she wither'd thus; at last,
Without a groan, or sigh, or glance, to show
A parting pang, the spirit from her passed:
And they who watch'd her nearest could not know
The very instant, till the change that cast
Her sweet face into shadow, dull and slow,
Glazed o'er her eyes — the beautiful, the black —
Oh! to possess such lustre — and then lack!

LXX

She died, but not alone; she held within
A second principle of life, which might
Have dawn'd a fair and sinless child of sin;
But closed its little being without light,
And went down to the grave unborn, wherein
Blossom and bough lie wither'd with one blight;
In vain the dews of Heaven descend above
The bleeding flower and blasted fruit of love.

LXXI

Thus lived — thus died she; never more on her
Shall sorrow light, or shame. She was not made
Through years or moons the inner weight to bear,
Which colder hearts endure till they are laid
By age in earth: her days and pleasures were
Brief, but delightful — such as had not staid

Long with her destiny; but she sleeps well
By the sea-shore, whereon she loved to dwell.

LXXII

That isle is now all desolate and bare,
Its dwellings down, its tenants pass'd away;
None but her own and father's grave is there,
And nothing outward tells of human clay;
Ye could not know where lies a thing so fair,
No stone is there to show, no tongue to say,
What was; no dirge, except the hollow sea's,
Mourns o'er the beauty of the Cyclades.

LXXIII

But many a Greek maid in a loving song
Sighs o'er her name; and many an islander
With her sire's story makes the night less long;
Valour was his, and beauty dwelt with her;
If she loved rashly, her life paid for wrong —
A heavy price must all pay who thus err,
In some shape; let none think to fly the danger,
For soon or late Love is his own avenger.

. . .

CANTO XI

VIII [117]

Don Juan had got out on Shooter's Hill;
Sunset the time, the place the same declivity
Which looks along that vale of good and ill
Where London streets ferment in full activity;
While everything around was calm and still,
Except the creak of wheels, which on their pivot he
Heard, — and that bee-like, bubbling, busy hum
Of cities, that boil over with their scum: —

IX

I say, Don Juan, wrapt in contemplation,
Walk'd on behind his carriage, o'er the summit,
And lost in wonder of so great a nation,
Gave way to 't, since he could not overcome it.
'And here,' he cried, 'is Freedom's chosen station;
Here peal's the people's voice, nor can entomb it
Racks, prisons, inquisitions; resurrection
Awaits it, each new meeting or election.

X

'Here are chaste wives, pure lives; here people pay
But what they please; and if that things be dear,
'T is only that they love to throw away
Their cash, to show how much they have a year.
Here laws are all inviolate; none lay
Traps for the traveller; every highway's clear;
Here' — he was interrupted by a knife,
With — 'Damn your eyes! your money or your life!' —

XI

These freeborn sounds proceeded from four pads
In ambush laid, who had perceived him loiter
Behind his carriage; and, like handy lads,
Had seized the lucky hour to reconnoitre,

[117] Meantime Juan, sent as a captive slave to a market in Turkey, was bought by the Sultana. He escaped, fought with the Russians before Ismail, carried the news of victory to Catherine the Great, and finally became a great favorite at the Russian Court. He at last has set out to England as envoy, and now draws near London.

In which the heedless gentleman who gads
  Upon the road, unless he prove a fighter,
May find himself within that isle of riches
Exposed to lose his life as well as breeches.

XII

Juan, who did not understand a word
  Of English, save their shibboleth, 'God damn!'
And even that he had so rarely heard,
  He sometimes thought 't was only their 'Salām,'
Or 'God be with you!' — and 't is not absurd
  To think so: for half English as I am
(To my misfortune), never can I say
I heard them wish 'God with you,' save that way; —

XIII

Juan yet quickly understood their gesture,
  And being somewhat choleric and sudden,
Drew forth a pocket-pistol from his vesture,
  And fired it into one assailant's pudding —
Who fell, as rolls an ox o'er in his pasture,
  And roar'd out, as he writhed his native mud in,
Unto his nearest follower or henchman,
'Oh Jack! I'm floor'd by that 'ere bloody Frenchman!'

XIV

On which Jack and his train set off at speed,
  And Juan's suite, late scatter'd at a distance,
Came up, all marvelling at such a deed,
  And offering, as usual, late assistance.
Juan, who saw the moon's late minion bleed
  As if his veins would pour out his existence,
Stood calling out for bandages and lint,
And wish'd he had been less hasty with his flint.

XV

'Perhaps,' thought he, 'it is the country's wont
  To welcome foreigners in this way: now
I recollect some innkeepers who don't
  Differ, except in robbing with a bow,
In lieu of a bare blade and brazen front.
  But what is to be done? I can't allow
The fellow to lie groaning on the road:
So take him up; I'll help you with the load.'

XVI

But ere they could perform this pious duty,
  The dying man cried, 'Hold! I've got my gruel!
Oh! for a glass of *max!* We 've miss'd our booty;
  Let me die where I am!' And as the fuel
Of life shrunk in his heart, and thick and sooty
  The drops fell from his death-wound, and he drew ill
His breath, — he from his swelling throat untied
A kerchief, crying 'Give Sal that!' — and died.

. . .

XLV

In the great world, — which, being interpreted,
  Meaneth the west or worst end of a city,
And about twice two thousand people bred
  By no means to be very wise or witty,
But to sit up while others lie in bed,
  And look down on the universe with pity, —
Juan, as an inveterate patrician,
Was well received by persons of condition.

XLVI

He was a bachelor, which is a matter
  Of import both to virgin and to bride,
The former's hymeneal hopes to flatter;
  And (should she not hold fast by love or pride)

'T is also of some moment to the latter:
  A rib 's a thorn in a wed gallant's side,
Requires decorum, and is apt to double
The horrid sin — and what 's still worse, the trouble.

XLVII

But Juan was a bachelor — of arts,
  And parts, and hearts: he danced and sung, and had
An air as sentimental as Mozart's
  Softest of melodies; and could be sad
Or cheerful, without any ' flaws or starts,'
  Just at the proper time: and though a lad,
Had seen the world — which is a curious sight,
And very much unlike what people write.

XLVIII

Fair virgins blush'd upon him; wedded dames
  Bloom'd also in less transitory hues;
For both commodities dwell by the Thames,
  The painting and the painted; youth, ceruse,
Against his heart preferr'd their usual claims,
  Such as no gentleman can quite refuse;
Daughters admired his dress, and pious mothers
Inquired his income, and if he had brothers.

XLIX

The milliners who furnish ' drapery Misses '
  Throughout the season, upon speculation
Of payment ere the honey-moon's last kisses
  Have waned into a crescent's coruscation,
Thought such an opportunity as this is,
  Of a rich foreigner's initiation,
Not to be overlook'd — and gave such credit,
That future bridegrooms swore, and sigh'd, and paid it.

L

The Blues, that tender tribe, who sigh o'er sonnets,
  And with the pages of the last Review
Line the interior of their heads or bonnets,
  Advanced in all their azure's highest hue:
They talk'd bad French or Spanish, and upon its
  Late authors ask'd him for a hint or two;
And which was softest, Russian or Castilian?
And whether in his travels he saw Ilion?

LI

Juan, who was a little superficial,
  And not in literature a great Drawcansir,[118]
Examined by this learned and especial
  Jury of matrons, scarce knew what to answer:
His duties warlike, loving, or official,
  His steady application as a dancer,
Had kept him from the brink of Hippocrene,
Which now he found was blue instead of green.

LII

However, he replied at hazard, with
  A modest confidence and calm assurance,
Which lent his learned lucubrations pith,
  And pass'd for arguments of good endurance.
That prodigy, Miss Araminta Smith
  (Who at sixteen translated ' Hercules Furens '
Into as furious English), with her best look,
Set down his sayings in her common-place book.

[118] The satiric portrait of a 'critic' (Dryden) in *The Rehearsal*, a play by George Villiers.

LIII

Juan knew several languages — as well
He might — and brought them up with skill, in time
To save his fame with each accomplish'd belle,
Who still regretted that he did not rhyme.
There wanted but this requisite to swell
His qualities (with them) into sublime:
Lady Fitz-Frisky, and Miss Mævia Mannish,
Both long'd extremely to be sung in Spanish.

LIV

However, he did pretty well, and was
Admitted as an aspirant to all
The coteries, and, as in Banquo's glass,
At great assemblies or in parties small,
He saw ten thousand living authors pass,
That being about their average numeral;
Also the eighty 'greatest living poets,'
As every paltry magazine can show *it's*.

LV

In twice five years the 'greatest living poet,'
Like to the champion in the fisty ring,
Is call'd on to support his claim, or show it,
Although 't is an imaginary thing.
Even I — albeit I'm sure I did not know it,
Nor sought of foolscap subjects to be king, —
Was reckon'd, a considerable time,
The grand Napoleon of the realms of rhyme.

. . . .

On This Day I Complete My Thirty-sixth Year

Missolonghi,[119] Jan. 22, 1824.

'T is time this heart should be unmoved,
Since others it hath ceased to move:
Yet, though I cannot be beloved,
Still let me love!

My days are in the yellow leaf;
The flowers and fruits of love are gone;
The worm, the canker, and the grief
Are mine alone!

The fire that on my bosom preys
Is lone as some volcanic isle;
No torch is kindled at its blaze —
A funeral pile.

The hope, the fear, the jealous care,
The exalted portion of the pain
And power of love, I cannot share,
But wear the chain.

But 't is not *thus* — and 't is not *here* —
Such thoughts should shake my soul, nor *now*,
Where glory decks the hero's bier,
Or binds his brow.

The sword, the banner, and the field,
Glory and Greece, around me see!
The Spartan, borne upon his shield,
Was not more free.

Awake! (not Greece — she *is* awake!)
Awake, my spirit! Think through *whom*
Thy life-blood tracks its parent lake,
And then strike home!

Tread those reviving passions down,
Unworthy manhood! — unto thee
Indifferent should the smile or frown
Of beauty be.

If thou regrett'st thy youth, *why live?*
The land of honourable death
Is here: — up to the field, and give
Away thy breath!

Seek out — less often sought than found —
A soldier's grave, for thee the best;
Then look around, and choose thy ground,
And take thy rest.

[119] Byron had gone there to assist the war for Greek independence. He contracted a fever and died on 19 April of the same year.

Percy Bysshe Shelley

1792–1822

Stanzas — April 1814 [1]

AWAY! the moor is dark beneath the moon,
Rapid clouds have drank the last pale beam of even:
Away! the gathering winds will call the darkness soon.
And profoundest midnight shroud the serene lights of heaven.

Pause not! The time is past! Every voice cries, Away!
Tempt not with one last tear thy friend's ungentle mood:
Thy lover's eye, so glazed and cold, dares not entreat thy stay:
Duty and dereliction guide thee back to solitude.

Away, away! to thy sad and silent home;
Pour bitter tears on its desolated hearth;
Watch the dim shades as like ghosts they go and come,
And complicate strange webs of melancholy mirth.

The leaves of wasted autumn woods shall float around thine head:
The blooms of dewy spring shall gleam beneath thy feet:
But thy soul or this world must fade in the frost that binds the dead,
Ere midnight's frown and morning's smile, ere thou and peace may meet.

The cloud shadows of midnight possess their own repose,
For the weary winds are silent, or the moon is in the deep:
Some respite to its turbulence unresting ocean knows;
Whatever moves, or toils, or grieves, hath its appointed sleep.

Thou in the grave shalt rest — yet till the phantoms flee
Which that house and heath and garden made dear to thee erewhile,
Thy remembrance, and repentance, and deep musings are not free
From the music of two voices and the light of one sweet smile.

ALASTOR

OR

THE SPIRIT OF SOLITUDE [2]

PREFACE

THE poem entitled *Alastor* may be considered as allegorical of one of the most interesting situations of the human mind. It represents a youth of uncorrupted feelings and adventurous genius led forth by an imagination inflamed and purified through familiarity with all that is excellent and majestic, to the contemplation of the universe. He drinks deep of the fountains of knowledge, and is still insatiate. The magnificence and beauty of the external world sinks profoundly into the frame of his conceptions, and affords to their modifications a variety not to be exhausted. So long as it is possible for his desires to point towards objects thus infinite and unmeasured, he is joyous, and tranquil, and self-possessed. But the period arrives when these objects cease to suffice. His mind is at length suddenly awakened and thirsts for intercourse with an intelligence similar to itself. He

[1] Written in April 1814; published with *Alastor*, 1816.

[2] Written in 1815; published in 1816. The title was suggested by Thomas Love Peacock, from the Greek 'Ἀλάστωρ, 'an evil genius' (here the 'spirit of solitude'). The best comment on the poem is Mrs. Shelley's note:

'*Alastor* is written in a very different tone from *Queen Mab*. In the latter, Shelley poured out all the cherished speculations of his youth — all the irrepressible emotions of sympathy, censure, and hope, to which the present suffering, and what he considers the proper destiny, of his fellow-creatures, gave birth. *Alastor*, on the contrary, contains an individual interest only. A very few years, with their attendant events, had checked the ardour of Shelley's hopes, though he still thought them well grounded, and that to advance their fulfilment was the noblest task man could achieve.

'This is neither the time nor place to speak of the misfortunes that chequered his life. It will be sufficient to images to himself the Being whom he loves. Conversant with speculations of the sublimest and most perfect natures, the vision in which he embodies his own imaginations unites all of wonderful, or wise, or beautiful, which the poet, the philosopher, or the lover could depicture. The intellectual faculties, the imagination, the functions of sense, have their respective requisitions on the sympathy of corresponding powers in other human beings. The Poet is represented as uniting these requisitions, and attaching them to a single image. He seeks in vain for a prototype of his conception. Blasted by his disappointment, he descends to an untimely grave.

The picture is not barren of instruction to actual men. The Poet's self-centred seclusion was avenged by the furies of an irresistible passion pursuing him to speedy ruin. But that Power which strikes the luminaries of the world with sudden darkness and extinction, by awakening them to too exquisite a perception of its influences, dooms to a slow and poisonous decay those meaner spirits that dare to abjure its dominion. Their destiny is more abject and inglorious as their delinquency is more contemptible and pernicious. They who, deluded by no generous error, instigated by no sacred thirst of doubtful knowledge, duped by no illustrious superstition, loving nothing on this earth, and cherishing no hopes beyond, yet keep aloof from sympathies with their kind, rejoicing neither in human joy nor mourning with human grief; these, and such as they, have their apportioned curse. They languish, because none feel with them their common nature. They are morally dead. They are neither friends, nor lovers, nor fathers, nor citizens of the world, nor benefactors of their country. Among those who attempt to exist without human sympathy, the pure and tender-hearted perish through the intensity and passion of their search after its communities, when the vacancy of their spirit suddenly makes itself felt. All else, selfish, blind, and torpid, are those unforeseeing multitudes who constitute, together with their own, the lasting misery and loneliness of the world. Those who love not their fellow-beings live unfruitful lives, and prepare for their old age a miserable grave.

'The good die first,
And those whose hearts are dry as summer dust,
Burn to the socket!' [3]

December 14, 1815.

Nondum amabam, et amare amabam, quaerebam quid amarem, amans amare.

— *Confess. St. August.*

Earth, ocean, air, belovéd brotherhood!
If our great Mother [4] has imbued my soul
With aught of natural piety to feel
Your love, and recompense the boon with mine;
If dewy morn, and odorous noon, and even,
With sunset and its gorgeous ministers,
And solemn midnight's tingling silentness;
If autumn's hollow sighs in the sere wood,
And winter robing with pure snow and crowns
Of starry ice the grey grass and bare boughs;
If spring's voluptuous pantings when she breathes
Her first sweet kisses, have been dear to me;
If no bright bird, insect, or gentle beast
I consciously have injured, but still loved
And cherished these my kindred; then forgive

say that, in all he did, he at the time of doing it believed himself justified to his own conscience; while the various ills of poverty and loss of friends brought home to him the sad realities of life. Physical suffering had also considerable influence in causing him to turn his eyes inward; inclining him rather to brood over the thoughts and emotions of his own soul than to glance abroad, and to make, as in *Queen Mab*, the whole universe the object and subject of his song. In the Spring of 1815 an eminent physician pronounced that he was dying rapidly of a consumption; abscesses were formed on his lungs, and he suffered acute spasms. Suddenly a complete change took place; and, though through life he was a martyr to pain and debility, every symptom of pulmonary disease vanished. His nerves, which nature had formed sensitive to an unexampled degree, were rendered still more susceptible by the state of his health.

'As soon as the peace of 1814 had opened the Continent, he went abroad. He visited some of the more magnificent scenes of Switzerland, and returned to England from Lucerne, by the Reuss and the Rhine. The river-navigation enchanted him. In his favourite poem of *Thalaba*, his imagination had been excited by a description of such a voyage. In the summer of 1815, after a tour along the southern coast of Devonshire and a visit to Clifton, he rented a house on Bishopgate Heath, on the borders of Windsor Forest, where he enjoyed several months of comparative health and tranquil happiness. The later summer months were warm and dry. Accompanied by a few friends, he visited the source of the Thames, making a voyage in a wherry from Windsor to Cricklade. His beautiful stanzas in the churchyard of Lechlade were written on that occasion. *Alastor* was composed on his return. He spent his days under the oak-shades of Windsor Great Park; and the magnificent woodland was a fitting study to inspire the various descriptions of forest-scenery we find in the poem.

'None of Shelley's poems is more characteristic than this. The solemn spirit that reigns throughout, the worship of the majesty of nature, the broodings of a poet's heart in solitude — the mingling of the exulting joy which the various aspects of the visible universe inspires with the sad and struggling pangs which human passion imparts — give a touching interest to the whole. The death which he had often contemplated during the last months as certain and near he here represented in such colours as had, in his lonely musings, soothed his soul to peace. The versification sustains the solemn spirit which breathes throughout: it is peculiarly melodious. The poem ought rather to be considered didactic than narrative: it was the outpouring of his own emotions, embodied in the purest form he could conceive, painted in the ideal hues which his brilliant imagination inspired, and softened by the recent anticipation of death.'

[3] Wordsworth, *The Excursion*, I, 500–502.

[4] Nature

This boast, belovéd brethren, and withdraw
No portion of your wonted favour now!

Mother of this unfathomable world!
Favour my solemn song, for I have loved
Thee ever, and thee only; I have watched
Thy shadow, and the darkness of thy steps,
And my heart ever gazes on the depth
Of thy deep mysteries. I have made my bed
In charnels and on coffins, where black death
Keeps record of the trophies won from thee,
Hoping to still these obstinate questionings
Of thee and thine, by forcing some lone ghost
Thy messenger, to render up the tale
Of what we are. In lone and silent hours,
When night makes a weird sound of its own stillness,
Like an inspired and desperate alchymist
Staking his very life on some dark hope,
Have I mixed awful talk and asking looks
With my most innocent love, until strange tears
Uniting with those breathless kisses, made
Such magic as compels the charméd night
To render up thy charge: . . . and, though ne'er yet
Thou hast unveiled thy inmost sanctuary,
Enough from incommunicable dream,
And twilight phantasms, and deep noonday thought,
Has shone within me, that serenely now
And moveless, as a long-forgotten lyre
Suspended in the solitary dome
Of some mysterious and deserted fane,
I wait thy breath, Great Parent, that my strain
May modulate with murmurs of the air,
And motions of the forests and the sea,
And voice of living beings, and woven hymns
Of night and day, and the deep heart of man.

There was a Poet whose untimely tomb
No human hands with pious reverence reared,
But the charmed eddies of autumnal winds
Built o'er his mouldering bones a pyramid
Of mouldering leaves in the waste wilderness: —
A lovely youth, — no mourning maiden decked
With weeping flowers, or votive cypress wreath,
The lone couch of his everlasting sleep: —
Gentle, and brave, and generous, — no lorn bard
Breathed o'er his dark fate one melodious sigh:
He lived, he died, he sung, in solitude.
Strangers have wept to hear his passionate notes,
And virgins, as unknown he passed, have pined
And wasted for fond love of his wild eyes.
The fire of those soft orbs has ceased to burn,
And Silence, too enamoured of that voice,
Locks its mute music in her rugged cell.

By solemn vision, and bright silver dream,
His infancy was nurtured. Every sight
And sound from the vast earth and ambient air,
Sent to his heart its choicest impulses.
The fountains of divine philosophy
Fled not his thirsting lips, and all of great,
Or good, or lovely, which the sacred past
In truth or fable consecrates, he felt
And knew. When early youth had passed, he left
His cold fireside and alienated home
To seek strange truths in undiscovered lands.
Many a wide waste and tangled wilderness
Has lured his fearless steps; and he has bought
With his sweet voice and eyes, from savage men,

His rest and food. Nature's most secret steps
He like her shadow has pursued, where'er
The red volcano overcanopies
Its fields of snow and pinnacles of ice
With burning smoke, or where bitumen lakes
On black bare pointed islets ever beat
With sluggish surge, or where the secret caves
Rugged and dark, winding among the springs
Of fire and poison, inaccessible
To avarice or pride, their starry domes
Of diamond and of gold expand above
Numberless and immeasurable halls,
Frequent with crystal column, and clear shrines
Of pearl, and thrones radiant with chrysolite.
Nor had that scene of ampler majesty
Than gems or gold, the varying roof of heaven
And the green earth lost in his heart its claims
To love and wonder; he would linger long
In lonesome vales, making the wild his home,
Until the doves and squirrels would partake
From his innocuous hand his bloodless food,
Lured by the gentle meaning of his looks,
And the wild antelope, that starts whene'er
The dry leaf rustles in the brake, suspend
Her timid steps to gaze upon a form
More graceful than her own.

His wandering step
Obedient to high thoughts, has visited
The awful ruins of the days of old:
Athens, and Tyre, and Balbec, and the waste
Where stood Jerusalem, the fallen towers
Of Babylon, the eternal pyramids,
Memphis and Thebes, and whatsoe'er of strange
Sculptured on alabaster obelisk,
Or jasper tomb, or mutilated sphynx,
Dark Æthiopia in her desert hills
Conceals. Among the ruined temples there,
Stupendous columns, and wild images
Of more than man, where marble dæmons watch
The Zodiac's brazen mystery,[5] and dead men
Hang their mute thoughts on the mute walls around,
He lingered, poring on memorials
Of the world's youth, through the long burning day
Gazed on those speechless shapes, nor, when the moon
Filled the mysterious halls with floating shades
Suspended he that task, but ever gazed
And gazed, till meaning on his vacant mind
Flashed like strong inspiration, and he saw
The thrilling secrets of the birth of time.

Meanwhile an Arab maiden brought his food,
Her daily portion, from her father's tent,
And spread her matting for his couch, and stole
From duties and repose to tend his steps: —
Enamoured, yet not daring for deep awe
To speak her love: — and watched his nightly sleep,
Sleepless herself, to gaze upon his lips
Parted in slumber, whence the regular breath
Of innocent dreams arose: then, when red morn
Made paler the pale moon, to her cold home
Wildered, and wan, and panting, she returned.

The Poet wandering on, through Arabie
And Persia, and the wild Carmanian waste,

[5] On the walls and columns of the temple of Denderah, a city in Upper Egypt, mythological figures are set in the fashion of the zodiac.

And o'er the aërial mountains which pour down
Indus and Oxus from their icy caves,
In joy and exultation held his way;
Till in the vale of Cashmire, far within
Its loneliest dell, where odorous plants entwine
Beneath the hollow rocks a natural bower,
Beside a sparkling rivulet he stretched
His languid limbs. A vision on his sleep
There came, a dream of hopes that never yet
Had flushed his cheek. He dreamed a veilèd maid
Sate near him, talking in low solemn tones.
Her voice was like the voice of his own soul
Heard in the calm of thought; its music long,
Like woven sounds of streams and breezes, held
His inmost sense suspended in its web
Of many-coloured woof and shifting hues.
Knowledge and truth and virtue were her theme,
And lofty hopes of divine liberty,
Thoughts the most dear to him, and poesy,
Herself a poet. Soon the solemn mood
Of her pure mind kindled through all her frame
A permeating fire: wild numbers then
She raised, with voice stifled in tremulous sobs
Subdued by its own pathos: her fair hands
Were bare alone, sweeping from some strange harp
Strange symphony, and in their branching veins
The eloquent blood told an ineffable tale.
The beating of her heart was heard to fill
The pauses of her music, and her breath
Tumultuously accorded with those fits
Of intermitted song. Sudden she rose,
As if her heart impatiently endured
Its bursting burthen: at the sound he turned,
And saw by the warm light of their own life
Her glowing limbs beneath the sinuous veil
Of woven wind, her outspread arms now bare,
Her dark locks floating in the breath of night,
Her beamy bending eyes, her parted lips
Outstretched, and pale, and quivering eagerly.
His strong heart sunk and sickened with excess
Of love. He reared his shuddering limbs and quelled
His gasping breath, and spread his arms to meet
Her panting bosom: . . . she drew back a while,
Then, yielding to the irresistible joy,
With frantic gesture and short breathless cry
Folded his frame in her dissolving arms.
Now blackness veiled his dizzy eyes, and night
Involved and swallowed up the vision; sleep,
Like a dark flood suspended in its course,
Rolled back its impulse on his vacant brain.

Roused by the shock he started from his trance —
The cold white light of morning, the blue moon
Low in the west, the clear and garish hills,
The distinct valley and the vacant woods,
Spread round him where he stood. Whither have fled
The hues of heaven that canopied his bower
Of yesternight? The sounds that soothed his sleep,
The mystery and the majesty of Earth,
The joy, the exultation? His wan eyes
Gaze on the empty scene as vacantly
As ocean's moon looks on the moon in heaven.
The spirit of sweet human love has sent

A vision [6] to the sleep of him who spurned
Her choicest gifts. He eagerly pursues
Beyond the realms of dream that fleeting shade;
He overleaps the bounds. Alas! Alas!
Were limbs, and breath, and being intertwined
Thus treacherously? Lost, lost, for ever lost,
In the wide pathless desert of dim sleep,
That beautiful shape! Does the dark gate of death
Conduct to thy mysterious paradise,
O Sleep? Does the bright arch of rainbow clouds,
And pendent mountains seen in the calm lake,
Lead only to a black and watery depth,
While death's blue vault, with loathliest vapours hung,
Where every shade which the foul grave exhales
Hides its dead eye from the detested day,
Conducts, O Sleep, to thy delightful realms?
This doubt with sudden tide flowed on his heart,
The insatiate hope which it awakened, stung
His brain even like despair.

While daylight held
The sky, the Poet kept mute conference
With his still soul. At night the passion came,
Like the fierce fiend of a distempered dream,
And shook him from his rest, and led him forth
Into the darkness. — As an eagle grasped
In the folds of the green serpent, feels her breast
Burn with the poison, and precipitates
Through night and day, tempest, and calm, and cloud,
Frantic with dizzying anguish, her blind flight
O'er the wide aëry wilderness: thus driven
By the bright shadow of that lovely dream,
Beneath the cold glare of the desolate night,
Through tangled swamps and deep precipitous dells,
Startling with careless step the moonlight snake,
He fled. Red morning dawned upon his flight,
Shedding the mockery of its vital hues
Upon his cheek of death. He wandered on
Till vast Aornos seen from Petra's steep
Hung o'er the low horizon like a cloud;
Through Balk, and where the desolated tombs
Of Parthian kings scatter to every wind
Their wasting dust,[7] wildly he wandered on,
Day after day a weary waste of hours,
Bearing within his life the brooding care
That ever fed on its decaying flame.
And now his limbs were lean; his scattered hair
Sered by the autumn of strange suffering
Sung dirges in the wind; his listless hand
Hung like dead bone within its withered skin;
Life, and the lustre that consumed it, shone
As in a furnace burning secretly
From his dark eyes alone. The cottagers,
Who ministered with human charity
His human wants, beheld with wondering awe
Their fleeting visitant. The mountaineer,
Encountering on some dizzy precipice
That spectral form, deemed that the Spirit of wind
With lightning eyes, and eager breath, and feet
Disturbing not the drifted snow, had paused
In its career: the infant would conceal

[6] The Alastor or evil genius of solitude, sent as an Avenger by the 'spirit of sweet human love.'

[7] At Arbela, in Assyria; Caracallus violated the royal tombs.

His troubled visage in his mother's robe
In terror at the glare of those wild eyes,
To remember their strange light in many a dream
Of after-times; but youthful maidens, taught
By nature, would interpret half the woe
That wasted him, would call him with false names
Brother, and friend, would press his pallid hand
At parting, and watch, dim through tears, the path
Of his departure from their father's door.

At length upon the lone Chorasmian [8] shore
He paused, a wide and melancholy waste
Of putrid marshes. A strong impulse urged
His steps to the sea-shore. A swan was there,
Beside a sluggish stream among the reeds.
It rose as he approached, and with strong wings
Scaling the upward sky, bent its bright course
High over the immeasurable main.
His eyes pursued its flight.—'Thou hast a home,
Beautiful bird; thou voyagest to thine home,
Where thy sweet mate will twine her downy neck
With thine, and welcome thy return with eyes
Bright in the lustre of their own fond joy.
And what am I that I should linger here,
With voice far sweeter than thy dying notes,
Spirit more vast than thine, frame more attuned
To beauty, wasting these surpassing powers
In the deaf air, to the blind earth, and heaven
That echoes not my thoughts?' A gloomy smile
Of desperate hope wrinkled his quivering lips.
For sleep, he knew, kept most relentlessly
Its precious charge, and silent death exposed,
Faithless perhaps as sleep, a shadowy lure,
With doubtful smile mocking its own strange charms.

Startled by his own thoughts he looked around.
There was no fair fiend near him, not a sight
Or sound of awe but in his own deep mind.
A little shallop floating near the shore
Caught the impatient wandering of his gaze.
It had been long abandoned, for its sides
Gaped wide with many a rift, and its frail joints
Swayed with the undulations of the tide.
A restless impulse urged him to embark
And meet lone Death on the drear ocean's waste;
For well he knew that mighty Shadow loves
The slimy caverns of the populous deep.

The day was fair and sunny, sea and sky
Drank its inspiring radiance, and the wind
Swept strongly from the shore, blackening the waves.
Following his eager soul, the wanderer
Leaped in the boat, he spread his cloak aloft
On the bare mast, and took his lonely seat,
And felt the boat speed o'er the tranquil sea
Like a torn cloud before the hurricane.

As one that in a silver vision floats
Obedient to the sweep of odorous winds
Upon resplendent clouds, so rapidly
Along the dark and ruffled waters fled
The straining boat.—A whirlwind swept it on,
With fierce gusts and precipitating force,

[8] Would be properly the Aral Sea, but Shelley evidently means the Caspian Sea.

Through the white ridges of the chaféd sea.
The waves arose. Higher and higher still
Their fierce necks writhed beneath the tempest's scourge
Like serpents struggling in a vulture's grasp.
Calm and rejoicing in the fearful war
Of wave ruining on wave, and blast on blast
Descending, and black flood on whirlpool driven
With dark obliterating course, he sate:
As if their genii were the ministers
Appointed to conduct him to the light
Of those belovéd eyes, the Poet sate
Holding the steady helm. Evening came on,
The beams of sunset hung their rainbow hues
High 'mid the shifting domes of sheeted spray
That canopied his path o'er the waste deep;
Twilight, ascending slowly from the east,
Entwined in duskier wreaths her braided locks
O'er the fair front and radiant eyes of day;
Night followed, clad with stars. On every side
More horribly the multitudinous streams
Of ocean's mountainous waste to mutual war
Rushed in dark tumult thundering, as to mock
The calm and spangled sky. The little boat
Still fled before the storm; still fled, like foam
Down the steep cataract of a wintry river;
Now pausing on the edge of the riven wave;
Now leaving far behind the bursting mass
That fell, convulsing ocean: safely fled —
As if that frail and wasted human form,
Had been an elemental god.

At midnight
The moon arose: and lo! the ethereal cliffs
Of Caucasus, whose icy summits shone
Among the stars like sunlight, and around
Whose caverned base the whirlpools and the waves
Bursting and eddying irresistibly
Rage and resound for ever. — Who shall save? —
The boat fled on, — the boiling torrent drove, —
The crags closed round with black and jaggéd arms
The shattered mountain overhung the sea,
And faster still, beyond all human speed,
Suspended on the sweep of the smooth wave,
The little boat was driven. A cavern there
Yawned, and amid its slant and winding depths
Ingulfed the rushing sea. The boat fled on
With unrelaxing speed. — 'Vision and Love!'
The Poet cried aloud, 'I have beheld
The path of thy departure. Sleep and death
Shall not divide us long!'

The boat pursued
The windings of the cavern. Daylight shone
At length upon that gloomy river's flow;
Now, where the fiercest war among the waves
Is calm, on the unfathomable stream
The boat moved slowly. Where the mountain, riven,
Exposed those black depths to the azure sky,
Ere yet the flood's enormous volume fell
Even to the base of Caucasus, with sound
That shook the everlasting rocks, the mass
Filled with one whirlpool all that ample chasm;
Stair above stair the eddying waters rose,
Circling immeasurably fast, and laved
With alternating dash the gnarlèd roots
Of mighty trees, that stretched their giant arms

In darkness over it. I' the midst was left,
Reflecting, yet distorting every cloud,
A pool of treacherous and tremendous calm.
Seized by the sway of the ascending stream,
With dizzy swiftness, round, and round, and round,
Ridge after ridge the straining boat arose,
Till on the verge of the extremest curve,
Where, through an opening of the rocky bank,
The waters overflow, and a smooth spot
Of glassy quiet mid those battling tides
Is left, the boat paused shuddering.—Shall it sink
Down the abyss? Shall the reverting stress
Of that resistless gulf embosom it?
Now shall it fall?—A wandering stream of wind,
Breathed from the west, has caught the expanded sail,
And, lo! with gentle motion, between banks
Of mossy slope, and on a placid stream,
Beneath a woven grove it sails, and, hark!
The ghastly torrent mingles its far roar,
With the breeze murmuring in the musical woods.
Where the embowering trees recede, and leave
A little space of green expanse, the cove
Is closed by meeting banks, whose yellow flowers
For ever gaze on their own drooping eyes,
Reflected in the crystal calm. The wave
Of the boat's motion marred their pensive task,
Which nought but vagrant bird, or wanton wind,
Or falling spear-grass, or their own decay
Had e'er disturbed before. The Poet longed
To deck with their bright hues his withered hair,
But on his heart its solitude returned,
And he forbore. Not the strong impulse hid
In those flushed cheeks, bent eyes, and shadowy frame
Had yet performed its ministry: it hung
Upon his life, as lightning in a cloud
Gleams, hovering ere it vanish, ere the floods
Of night close over it.

The noonday sun
Now shone upon the forest, one vast mass
Of mingling shade, whose brown magnificence
A narrow vale embosoms. There, huge caves,
Scooped in the dark base of their aëry rocks
Mocking its moans, respond and roar for ever.
The meeting boughs and implicated[9] leaves
Wove twilight o'er the Poet's path, as led
By love, or dream, or god, or mightier Death,
He sought in Nature's dearest haunt, some bank,
Her cradle, and his sepulchre. More dark
And dark the shades accumulate. The oak,
Expanding its immense and knotty arms,
Embraces the light beech. The pyramids
Of the tall cedar overarching, frame
Most solemn domes within, and far below,
Like clouds suspended in an emerald sky,
The ash and the acacia floating hang
Tremulous and pale. Like restless serpents, clothed
In rainbow and in fire, the parasites,
Starred with ten thousand blossoms, flow around
The grey trunks, and, as gamesome infants' eyes,
With gentle meanings, and most innocent wiles,
Fold their beams round the hearts of those that love,
These twine their tendrils with the wedded boughs

[9] interwoven

Uniting their close union; the woven leaves
Make net-work of the dark blue light of day,
And the night's noontide clearness, mutable
As shapes in the weird clouds. Soft mossy lawns
Beneath these canopies extend their swells,
Fragrant with perfumed herbs, and eyed with blooms
Minute yet beautiful. One darkest glen
Sends from its woods of musk-rose, twined with jasmine,
A soul-dissolving odour, to invite
To some more lovely mystery. Through the dell,
Silence and Twilight here, twin-sisters, keep
Their noonday watch, and sail among the shades
Like vaporous shapes half seen; beyond, a well,
Dark, gleaming, and of most translucent wave,
Images all the woven boughs above,
And each depending leaf, and every speck
Of azure sky, darting between their chasms;
Nor aught else in the liquid mirror laves
Its portraiture, but some inconstant star
Between one foliaged lattice twinkling fair,
Or, painted bird, sleeping beneath the moon,
Or gorgeous insect floating motionless,
Unconscious of the day, ere yet his wings
Have spread their glories to the gaze of noon.

Hither the Poet came. His eyes beheld
Their own wan light through the reflected lines
Of his thin hair, distinct in the dark depth
Of that still fountain; as the human heart,
Gazing in dreams over the gloomy grave,
Sees its own treacherous likeness there. He heard
The motion of the leaves, the grass that sprung
Startled and glanced and trembled even to feel
An unaccustomed presence, and the sound
Of the sweet brook that from the secret springs
Of that dark fountain rose. A Spirit [10] seemed
To stand beside him — clothed in no bright robes
Of shadowy silver or enshrining light.
Borrowed from aught the visible world affords
Of grace, or majesty, or mystery; —
But, undulating woods, and silent well,
And leaping rivulet, and evening gloom
Now deepening the dark shades, for speech assuming,
Held commune with him, as if he and it
Were all that was, — only . . . when his regard
Was raised by intense pensiveness, . . . two eyes,
Two starry eyes, hung in the gloom of thought,
And seemed with their serene and azure smiles
To beckon him.

Obedient to the light
That shone within his soul, he went, pursuing
The windings of the dell. — The rivulet
Wanton and wild, through many a green ravine
Beneath the forest flowed. Sometimes it fell
Among the moss with hollow harmony
Dark and profound. Now on the polished stones
It danced; like childhood laughing as it went:
Then, through the plain in tranquil wanderings crept,
Reflecting every herb and drooping bud
That overhung its quietness. — ' O stream!

[10] Of Nature, that here answers the Poet's own melancholy and absorption with the thought of death.

Whose source is inaccessibly profound,
Whither do thy mysterious waters tend?
Thou imagest my life. Thy darksome stillness,
Thy dazzling waves, thy loud and hollow gulfs,
Thy searchless fountain, and invisible course
Have each their type in me: and the wide sky,
And measureless ocean may declare as soon
What oozy cavern or what wandering cloud
Contains thy waters, as the universe
Tell where these living thoughts reside, when stretched
Upon thy flowers my bloodless limbs shall waste
I' the passing wind!'

Beside the grassy shore
Of the small stream he went; he did impress
On the green moss his tremulous step, that caught
Strong shuddering from his burning limbs. As one
Roused by some joyous madness from the couch
Of fever, he did move; yet, not like him,
Forgetful of the grave, where, when the flame
Of his frail exultation shall be spent,
He must descend. With rapid steps he went
Beneath the shade of trees, beside the flow
Of the wild babbling rivulet; and now
The forest's solemn canopies were changed
For the uniform and lightsome evening sky.
Grey rocks did peep from the spare moss, and stemmed
The struggling brook: tall spires of windlestrae
Threw their thin shadows down the rugged slope,
And nought but gnarled roots of ancient pines
Branchless and blasted, clenched with grasping roots
The unwilling soil. A gradual change was here,
Yet ghastly. For, as fast years flow away,
The smooth brow gathers, and the hair grows thin
And white, and where irradiate dewy eyes
Had shone, gleam stony orbs: — so from his steps
Bright flowers departed, and the beautiful shade
Of the green groves, with all their odorous winds
And musical motions. Calm, he still pursued
The stream, that with a larger volume now
Rolled through the labyrinthine dell; and there
Fretted a path through its descending curves
With its wintry speed. On every side now rose
Rocks, which, in unimaginable forms,
Lifted their black and barren pinnacles
In the light of evening, and, its precipice
Obscuring the ravine, disclosed above,
Mid toppling stones, black gulfs and yawning caves,
Whose windings gave ten thousand various tongues
To the loud stream. Lo! where the pass expands
Its stony jaws, the abrupt mountain breaks,
And seems, with its accumulated crags,
To overhang the world: for wide expand
Beneath the wan stars and descending moon
Islanded seas, blue mountains, mighty streams,
Dim tracts and vast, robed in the lustrous gloom
Of leaden-coloured even, and fiery hills
Mingling their flames with twilight, on the verge
Of the remote horizon. The near scene,

In naked and severe simplicity,
Made contrast with the universe. A pine,
Rock-rooted, stretched athwart the vacancy
Its swinging boughs, to each inconstant blast
Yielding one only response, at each pause
In most familiar cadence, with the howl
The thunder and the hiss of homeless streams
Mingling its solemn song, whilst the broad river,
Foaming and hurrying o'er its rugged path,
Fell into that immeasurable void
Scattering its waters to the passing winds.

Yet the grey precipice and solemn pine
And torrent, were not all; — one silent nook
Was there. Even on the edge of that vast mountain,
Upheld by knotty roots and fallen rocks,
It overlooked in its serenity
The dark earth, and the bending vault of stars.
It was a tranquil spot, that seemed to smile
Even in the lap of horror. Ivy clasped
The fissured stones with its entwining arms,
And did embower with leaves for ever green,
And berries dark, the smooth and even space
Of its inviolated floor, and here
The children of the autumnal whirlwind bore,
In wanton sport, those bright leaves, whose decay,
Red, yellow, or ethereally pale,
Rivals the pride of summer. 'Tis the haunt
Of every gentle wind, whose breath can teach
The wilds to love tranquillity. One step,
One human step alone, has ever broken
The stillness of its solitude: — one voice
Alone inspired its echoes; — even that voice
Which hither came, floating among the winds,
And led the loveliest among human forms
To make their wild haunts the depository
Of all the grace and beauty that endued
Its motions, render up its majesty,
Scatter its music on the unfeeling storm,
And to the damp leaves and blue cavern mould,
Nurses of rainbow flowers and branching moss,
Commit the colours of that varying cheek,
That snowy breast, those dark and drooping eyes.

The dim and hornéd moon hung low, and poured
A sea of lustre on the horizon's verge
That overflowed its mountains. Yellow mist
Filled the unbounded atmosphere, and drank
Wan moonlight even to fulness: not a star
Shone, not a sound was heard; the very winds,
Danger's grim playmates, on that precipice
Slept, clasped in his embrace. — O, storm of death!
Whose sightless speed divides this sullen night:
And thou, colossal Skeleton, that, still
Guiding its irresistible career
In thy devastating omnipotence,
Art king of this frail world, from the red field
Of slaughter, from the reeking hospital,
The patriot's sacred couch, the snowy bed
Of innocence, the scaffold and the throne,
A mighty voice invokes thee. Ruin calls
His brother Death. A rare and regal prey
He hath prepared, prowling around the world;
Glutted with which thou mayst repose, and men
Go to their graves like flowers or creeping worms,

Nor ever more offer at thy dark shrine
The unheeded tribute of a broken heart.

When on the threshold of the green recess
The wanderer's footsteps fell, he knew that death
Was on him. Yet a little, ere it fled,
Did he resign his high and holy soul
To images of the majestic past,
That paused within his passive being now,
Like winds that bear sweet music, when they breathe
Through some dim latticed chamber. He did place
His pale lean hand upon the rugged trunk
Of the old pine. Upon an ivied stone
Reclined his languid head, his limbs did rest,
Diffused and motionless, on the smooth brink
Of that obscurest chasm; — and thus he lay,
Surrendering to their final impulses
The hovering powers of life. Hope and despair,
The torturers, slept; no mortal pain or fear
Marred his repose, the influxes of sense,
And his own being unalloyed by pain,
Yet feebler and more feeble, calmly fed
The stream of thought, till he lay breathing there
At peace, and faintly smiling: — his last sight
Was the great moon, which o'er the western line
Of the wide world her mighty horn suspended,
With whose dun beams inwoven darkness seemed
To mingle. Now upon the jaggéd hills
It rests, and still as the divided frame
Of the vast meteor sunk, the Poet's blood,
That ever beat in mystic sympathy
With nature's ebb and flow, grew feebler still:
And when two lessening points of light alone
Gleamed through the darkness, the alternate gasp
Of his faint respiration scarce did stir
The stagnate night: — till the minutest ray
Was quenched, the pulse yet lingered in his heart.
It paused — it fluttered. But when heaven remained
Utterly black, the murky shades involved
An image, silent, cold, and motionless,
As their own voiceless earth and vacant air.
Even as a vapour fed with golden beams
That ministered on sunlight, ere the west
Eclipses it, was now that wondrous frame —
No sense, no motion, no divinity —
A fragile lute, on whose harmonious strings
The breath of heaven did wander — a bright stream
Once fed with many-voicéd waves — a dream
Of youth, which night and time have quenched for ever,
Still, dark, and dry, and unremembered now.

O, for Medea's wondrous alchemy,
Which wheresoe'er it fell made the earth gleam
With bright flowers, and the wintry boughs exhale
From vernal blooms fresh fragrance! O, that God,
Profuse of poisons, would concede the chalice
Which but one living man has drained, who now,
Vessel of deathless wrath, a slave that feels
No proud exemption in the blighting curse
He bears, over the world wanders for ever,
Lone as incarnate death! O, that the dream

Of dark magician in his visioned cave,
Raking the cinders of a crucible
For life and power, even when his feeble hand
Shakes in its last decay, were the true law
Of this so lovely world! But thou art fled
Like some frail exhalation; which the dawn
Robes in its golden beams, — ah! thou hast fled!
The brave, the gentle, and the beautiful,
The child of grace and genius. Heartless things
Are done and said i' the world, and many worms
And beasts and men live on, and mighty Earth
From sea and mountain, city and wilderness,
In vesper low or joyous orison,
Lifts still its solemn voice: — but thou art fled —
Thou canst no longer know or love the shapes
Of this phantasmal scene, who have to thee
Been purest ministers, who are, alas!
Now thou art not. Upon those pallid lips
So sweet even in their silence, on those eyes
That image sleep in death, upon that form
Yet safe from the worm's outrage, let no tear
Be shed — not even in thought. Nor, when those hues
Are gone, and those divinest lineaments,
Worn by the senseless wind, shall live alone
In the frail pauses of this simple strain,
Let not high verse, mourning the memory
Of that which is no more, or painting's woe
Or sculpture, speak in feeble imagery
Their own cold powers. Art and eloquence,
And all the shows o' the world are frail and vain
To weep a loss that turns their lights to shade.
It is a woe too 'deep for tears,' when all
Is reft at once, when some surpassing Spirit,
Whose light adorned the world around it, leaves
Those who remain behind, not sobs or groans,
The passionate tumult of a clinging hope;
But pale despair and cold tranquillity,
Nature's vast frame, the web of human things,
Birth and the grave, that are not as they were.

Hymn to Intellectual Beauty[11]

I

THE awful shadow of some unseen Power
  Floats though unseen among us, — visiting
  This various world with as inconstant wing
As summer winds that creep from flower to flower, —
Like moonbeams that behind some piny mountain shower,
    It visits with inconstant glance
    Each human heart and countenance;
Like hues and harmonies of evening, —
    Like clouds in starlight widely spread, —
    Like memory of music fled, —
    Like aught that for its grace may be
Dear, and yet dearer for its mystery.

II

Spirit of BEAUTY, that dost consecrate
  With thine own hues all thou dost shine upon

[11] Written in 1816; published in Leigh Hunt's *Examiner*, 19 January 1817. According to Mrs. Shelley, it was conceived during Shelley's voyage on Lake Geneva with Lord Byron. Material beauty as observed on earth shows but 'broken lights' of that ideal or 'intellectual' beauty, which is perfect, immaterial, and eternal, and in itself the peak of human contemplation. This Platonic concept is so frequent and important in English poetry that the first 'vocation of the scholar' is to read of it at first hand in Plato's own work, chiefly in *The Symposium*, 211–212 (appropriately, in Shelley's translation, if possible). This 'intellectual beauty' is, of course, prefigured in Shelley's own *Alastor*.

Of human thought or form, — where art thou gone?
Why dost thou pass away and leave our state,
This dim vast vale of tears, vacant and desolate?
Ask why the sunlight not for ever
Weaves rainbows o'er yon mountain-river,
Why aught should fail and fade that once is shown,
Why fear and dream and death and birth
Cast on the daylight of this earth
Such gloom, — why man has such a scope
For love and hate, despondency and hope?

III

No voice from some sublimer world hath ever
To sage or poet these responses given —
Therefore the names of Demon, Ghost, and Heaven,
Remain the records of their vain endeavour,
Frail spells — whose uttered charm might not avail to sever,
From all we hear and all we see,
Doubt, chance, and mutability.
Thy light alone — like mist o'er mountains driven,
Or music by the night-wind sent
Through strings of some still instrument,
Or moonlight on a midnight stream,
Gives grace and truth to life's unquiet dream.

IV

Love, Hope, and Self-esteem, like clouds depart
And come, for some uncertain moments lent.
Man were immortal, and omnipotent,
Didst thou, unknown and awful as thou art,
Keep with thy glorious train firm state within his heart.
Thou messenger of sympathies,
That wax and wane in lovers' eyes —
Thou — that to human thought art nourishment,
Like darkness to a dying flame!
Depart not as thy shadow came,
Depart not — lest the grave should be,
Like life and fear, a dark reality.

V

While yet a boy I sought for ghosts, and sped
Through many a listening chamber, cave and ruin,
And starlight wood, with fearful steps pursuing
Hopes of high talk with the departed dead.
I called on poisonous names with which our youth is fed;
I was not heard — I saw them not —
When musing deeply on the lot
Of life, at that sweet time when winds are wooing
All vital things that wake to bring
News of birds and blossoming, —
Sudden, thy shadow fell on me;
I shrieked, and clasped my hands in ecstasy!

VI

I vowed that I would dedicate my powers
To thee and thine — have I not kept the vow? [12]
With beating heart and streaming eyes, even now
I call the phantoms of a thousand hours
Each from his voiceless grave: they have in visioned bowers
Of studious zeal or love's delight
Outwatched with me the envious night —
They know that never joy illumed my brow
Unlinked with hope that thou wouldst free

[12] *Cf.* Wordsworth's 'dedication' of spirit in *The Prelude.*

This world from its dark slavery,
That thou — O awful Loveliness,
Wouldst give whate'er these words cannot express.

VII

The day becomes more solemn and serene
When noon is past — there is a harmony
In autumn, and a lustre in its sky,
Which through the summer is not heard or seen,
As if it could not be, as if it had not been!
Thus let thy power, which like the truth
Of nature on my passive youth
Descended, to my onward life supply
Its calm — to one who worships thee,
And every form containing thee,
Whom, Spirit fair, thy spells did bind
To fear himself, and love all human kind.

Ozymandias [13]

I met a traveller from an antique land
Who said: Two vast and trunkless legs of stone
Stand in the desert . . . Near them, on the sand,
Half sunk, a shattered visage lies, whose frown,
And wrinkled lip, and sneer of cold command,
Tell that its sculptor well those passions read
Which yet survive, stamped on these lifeless things,
The hand that mocked them, and the heart that fed:
And on the pedestal these words appear:
'My name is Ozymandias, king of kings:
Look on my works, ye Mighty, and despair!'
Nothing beside remains. Round the decay
Of that colossal wreck, boundless and bare
The lone and level sands stretch far away.

[13] Written in 1817; published in Hunt's *Examiner*, 11 January 1818.

Stanzas

WRITTEN IN DEJECTION NEAR NAPLES [14]

I

The sun is warm, the sky is clear,
The waves are dancing fast and bright,
Blue isles and snowy mountains wear
The purple noon's transparent might,
The breath of the moist earth is light,
Around its unexpanded buds;
Like many a voice of one delight,
The winds, the birds, the ocean floods,
The City's voice itself, is soft like Solitude's.

II

I see the Deep's untrampled floor
With green and purple seaweeds strown;
I see the waves upon the shore,
Like light dissolved in star-showers, thrown:
I sit upon the sands alone, —
The lightning of the noontide ocean
Is flashing round me, and a tone
Arises from its measured motion,
How sweet! did any heart now share in my emotion.

III

Alas! I have nor hope nor health,
Nor peace within nor calm around,
Nor that content surpassing wealth
The sage in meditation found,
And walked with inward glory crowned —
Nor fame, nor power, nor love, nor leisure.
Others I see whom these surround —
Smiling they live, and call life pleasure; —

[14] Written, according to Mrs. Shelley, in December 1818 published in *Posthumous Poems*, 1824.

To me that cup has been dealt in another
measure.

IV

Yet now despair itself is mild,
Even as the winds and waters are;
I could lie down like a tired child,
And weep away the life of care
Which I have borne and yet must
bear,
Till death like sleep might steal on me,
And I might feel in the warm air
My cheek grow cold, and hear the sea
Breathe o'er my dying brain its last monotony.

V

Some might lament that I were cold,
As I, when this sweet day is gone,
Which my lost heart, too soon grown
old,
Insults with this untimely moan;
They might lament — for I am one
Whom men love not, — and yet regret,
Unlike this day, which, when the sun
Shall on its stainless glory set,
Will linger, though enjoyed, like joy in
memory yet.

Sonnet: England in 1819[15]

AN old, mad, blind, despised, and dying
king,[16] —
Princes, the dregs of their dull race, who
flow
Through public scorn, — mud from a
muddy spring, —
Rulers who neither see, nor feel, nor
know,
But leech-like to their fainting country
cling,
Till they drop, blind in blood, without a
blow, —
A people starved and stabbed in the untilled field, —
An army, which liberticide and prey
Makes as a two-edged sword to all who
wield, —
Golden and sanguine laws which tempt
and slay;
Religion Christless, Godless — a book
sealed;
A Senate, — Time's worst statute unrepealed, —
Are graves, from which a glorious Phantom may
Burst, to illumine our tempestuous day.

[15] First published by Mrs. Shelley in her first collected edition, 1839. Shelley, who had been aroused by the Manchester Massacre of 16 August and felt that a civil overturn was certain to come in England, had sent the poem to Hunt in 1819. It was not published then because of fear of the libel laws. [16] George III

from *Prometheus Unbound,*
Act IV[17]

Panthea.[18] Peace! peace! A mighty
Power, which is as darkness,
Is rising out of Earth, and from the sky
Is showered like night, and from within
the air
Bursts, like eclipse which had been
gathered up
Into the pores of sunlight: the bright visions,
Wherein the singing spirits rode and
shone,
Gleam like pale meteors through a watery
night.
Ione. There is a sense of words upon
mine ear.
Panthea. An universal sound like
words: Oh, list!

Demogorgon

Thou, Earth, calm empire of a happy soul,
Sphere of divinest shapes and harmonies,
Beautiful orb! gathering as thou dost roll

[17] Written in four acts between September 1818 and December 1819; published in 1820. Aeschylus had represented the Titan Prometheus, chained to a rock by Zeus in punishment for the theft of fire in man's behalf, as being reconciled to the god by disclosing the secret danger to Zeus's empire. Shelley, however, was averse to 'reconciling the Champion with the Oppressor of Mankind.' In his version, through the ultimate power of Demogorgon, or Eternal Fate, surpassing even the Olympians, Zeus is overthrown and Prometheus is freed. All the spirits of the universe chant their hymn of rejoicing.

[18] Panthea and Ione are Oceanides; they represent the spirits of faith and hope.

The love which paves thy path along the skies:

The Earth

I hear: I am as a drop of dew that dies.

Demogorgon

Thou, Moon, which gazest on the nightly Earth
With wonder, as it gazes upon thee;
Whilst each to men, and beasts, and the swift birth
Of birds, is beauty, love, calm, harmony:

The Moon

I hear: I am a leaf shaken by thee!

Demogorgon

Ye Kings of suns and stars, Dæmons and Gods,
Aetherial Dominations, who possess
Elysian, windless, fortunate abodes
Beyond Heaven's constellated wilderness:

A Voice from above

Our great Republic hears, we are blest, and bless.

Demogorgon

Ye happy Dead, whom beams of brightest verse
Are clouds to hide, not colours to portray,
Whether your nature is that universe
Which once ye saw and suffered —

A Voice from beneath

Or as they
Whom we have left, we change and pass away.

Demogorgon

Ye elemental Genii, who have homes
From man's high mind even to the central stone
Of sullen lead; from heaven's star-fretted domes
To the dull weed some sea-worm battens on:

A confused Voice

We hear: thy words waken Oblivion.

Demogorgon

Spirits, whose homes are flesh: ye beasts and birds,
Ye worms, and fish; ye living leaves and buds;
Lightning and wind; and ye untameable herds,
Meteors and mists, which throng air's solitudes: —

A Voice

Thy voice to us is wind among still woods.

Demogorgon

Man, who wert once a despot and a slave;
A dupe and a deceiver; a decay;
A traveller from the cradle to the grave
Through the dim night of this immortal day:

All

Speak: thy strong words may never pass away.

Demogorgon

This is the day, which down the void abysm
At the Earth-born's spell yawns for Heaven's despotism,
And Conquest is dragged captive through the deep:
Love, from its awful throne of patient power
In the wise heart, from the last giddy hour
Of dread endurance, from the slippery, steep,
And narrow verge of crag-like agony, springs
And folds over the world its healing wings.

Gentleness, Virtue, Wisdom, and Endurance,
These are the seals of that most firm assurance
Which bars the pit over Destruction's strength;
And if, with infirm hand, Eternity,
Mother of many acts and hours, should free
The serpent that would clasp her with his length;
These are the spells by which to reassume
An empire o'er the disentangled doom.

To suffer woes which Hope thinks infinite;
To forgive wrongs darker than death or night;
To defy Power, which seems omnipotent;
To love, and bear; to hope till Hope creates
From its own wreck the thing it contemplates;
Neither to change, nor falter, nor repent;
This, like thy glory, Titan, is to be
Good, great and joyous, beautiful and free;
This is alone Life, Joy, Empire, and Victory.

Ode to the West Wind [19]

I

O WILD West Wind, thou breath of Autumn's being,
Thou, from whose unseen presence the leaves dead
Are driven, like ghosts from an enchanter fleeing,

Yellow, and black, and pale, and hectic red,
Pestilence-stricken multitudes: O thou,
Who chariotest to their dark wintry bed

The wingéd seeds, where they lie cold and low,
Each like a corpse within its grave, until
Thine azure sister of the Spring shall blow

Her clarion o'er the dreaming earth, and fill
(Driving sweet buds like flocks to feed in air)
With living hues and odours plain and hill:

Wild Spirit, which art moving everywhere;
Destroyer and preserver; hear, oh, hear!

II

Thou on whose stream, mid the steep sky's commotion,
Loose clouds like earth's decaying leaves are shed,
Shook from the tangled boughs of Heaven and Ocean,

Angels of rain and lightning: there are spread
On the blue surface of thine aëry surge,
Like the bright hair uplifted from the head

Of some fierce Maenad, even from the dim verge
Of the horizon to the zenith's height,
The locks of the approaching storm. Thou dirge

Of the dying year, to which this closing night
Will be the dome of a vast sepulchre,
Vaulted with all thy congregated might

[19] Written in 1819; published with *Prometheus Unbound*, 1820. 'This poem was conceived and chiefly written in a wood that skirts the Arno, near Florence, and on a day when that tempestuous wind, whose temperature is at once mild and animating, was collecting the vapours which pour down the autumnal rains. They began, as I foresaw, at sunset with a violent tempest of hail and rain, attended by that magnificent thunder and lightning peculiar to the Cisalpine regions. The phenomenon alluded to at the conclusion of the third stanza is well known to naturalists. The vegetation at the bottom of the sea, of rivers, and of lakes, sympathizes with that of the land in the change of seasons, and is consequently influenced by the winds which announce it.' [Shelley.]

Observe that Shelley gives the *terza rima* of Dante (properly, continuous verse with rhyme *a-b-a*, *b-c-b*, *c-d-c*, etc.) stanzaic form by concluding each division with a couplet. The whole poem is a technical masterpiece.

Of vapours, from whose solid atmosphere
Black rain, and fire, and hail will burst: oh, hear!

III

Thou who didst waken from his summer dreams
The blue Mediterranean, where he lay,
Lulled by the coil of his crystálline streams,

Beside a pumice isle in Baiae's [20] bay,
And saw in sleep old palaces and towers
Quivering within the wave's intenser day,

All overgrown with azure moss and flowers
So sweet, the sense faints picturing them! Thou
For whose path the Atlantic's level powers

Cleave themselves into chasms, while far below
The sea-blooms and the oozy woods which wear
The sapless foliage of the ocean, know

Thy voice, and suddenly grow gray with fear,
And tremble and despoil themselves: oh, hear!

IV

If I were a dead leaf thou mightest bear;
If I were a swift cloud to fly with thee;
A wave to pant beneath thy power, and share

The impulse of thy strength, only less free
Than thou, O uncontrollable! If even
I were as in my boyhood, and could be

The comrade of thy wanderings over Heaven,
As then, when to outstrip thy skiey speed
Scarce seemed a vision; I would ne'er have striven

As thus with thee in prayer in my sore need.
Oh, lift me as a wave, a leaf, a cloud!
I fall upon the thorns of life! I bleed!

A heavy weight of hours has chained and bowed
One too like thee: tameless, and swift, and proud.

V

Make me thy lyre, even as the forest is:
What if my leaves are falling like its own!
The tumult of thy mighty harmonies

Will take from both a deep, autumnal tone,
Sweet though in sadness. Be thou, Spirit fierce,
My spirit! Be thou me, impetuous one!

Drive my dead thoughts over the universe
Like withered leaves to quicken a new birth!
And, by the incantation of this verse,

Scatter, as from an unextinguished hearth
Ashes and sparks, my words among mankind!
Be through my lips to unawakened earth

The trumpet of a prophecy! O, Wind,
If Winter comes, can Spring be far behind?

The Indian Serenade [21]

I

I ARISE from dreams of thee
In the first sweet sleep of night,
When the winds are breathing low,
And the stars are shining bright:
I arise from dreams of thee,
And a spirit in my feet

[20] A town by the sea, near Naples.

[21] Written in 1819; published in *The Liberal*, 1822

Hath led me — who knows how?
To thy chamber window, Sweet!

II

The wandering airs they faint
On the dark, the silent stream —
The Champak [22] odours fail
Like sweet thoughts in a dream;
The nightingale's complaint,
It dies upon her heart; —
As I must on thine,
Oh, belovéd as thou art!

III

Oh lift me from the grass!
I die! I faint! I fail!
Let thy love in kisses rain
On my lips and eyelids pale.
My cheek is cold and white, alas!
My heart beats loud and fast; —
Oh! press it to thine own again,
Where it will break at last.

Love's Philosophy [23]

I

THE fountains mingle with the river
And the rivers with the Ocean,
The winds of Heaven mix for ever
With a sweet emotion;
Nothing in the world is single;
All things by a law divine
In one spirit meet and mingle.
Why not I with thine? —

II

See the mountains kiss high Heaven
And the waves clasp one another;
No sister-flower would be forgiven
If it disdained its brother;
And the sunlight clasps the earth
And the moonbeams kiss the sea:
What is all this sweet work worth
If thou kiss not me?

[22] Hindu word for a species of magnolia tree.
[23] Written in 1819; published in Leigh Hunt's *Indicator* of 22 December the same year.

The Cloud [24]

I BRING fresh showers for the thirsting flowers,
From the seas and the streams;
I bear light shade for the leaves when laid
In their noonday dreams.
From my wings are shaken the dews that waken
The sweet buds every one,
When rocked to rest on their mother's breast,
As she dances about the sun.
I wield the flail of the lashing hail,
And whiten the green plains under,
And then again I dissolve it in rain,
And laugh as I pass in thunder.

I sift the snow on the mountains below,
And their great pines groan aghast;
And all the night 'tis my pillow white,
While I sleep in the arms of the blast.
Sublime on the towers of my skiey bowers,
Lightning my pilot sits;
In a cavern under is fettered the thunder,
It struggles and howls at fits;
Over earth and ocean, with gentle motion,
This pilot is guiding me,
Lured by the love of the genii that move
In the depths of the purple sea;
Over the rills, and the crags, and the hills,
Over the lakes and the plains,
Wherever he dream, under mountain or stream,
The Spirit he loves remains;
And I all the while bask in Heaven's blue smile,
Whilst he is dissolving in rains.

The sanguine Sunrise, with his meteor eyes,
And his burning plumes outspread,
Leaps on the back of my sailing rack,
When the morning star shines dead;
As on the jag of a mountain crag,
Which an earthquake rocks and swings,
An eagle alit one moment may sit
In the light of its golden wings.

[24] Written at Pisa, and published (with *Prometheus Unbound*) in 1820.

And when Sunset may breathe, from the lit sea beneath,
Its ardours of rest and of love,
And the crimson pall of eve may fall
From the depth of Heaven above,
With wings folded I rest, on mine aëry nest,
As still as a brooding dove.

That orbéd maiden with white fire laden,
Whom mortals call the Moon,
Glides glimmering o'er my fleece-like floor,
By the midnight breezes strewn;
And wherever the beat of her unseen feet,
Which only the angels hear,
May have broken the woof of my tent's thin roof,
The stars peep behind her and peer;
And I laugh to see them whirl and flee,
Like a swarm of golden bees,
When I widen the rent in my wind-built tent,
Till the calm rivers, lakes, and seas,
Like strips of the sky fallen through me on high,
Are each paved with the moon and these.

I bind the Sun's throne with a burning zone,
And the Moon's with a girdle of pearl;
The volcanoes are dim, and the stars reel and swim,
When the whirlwinds my banner unfurl.
From cape to cape, with a bridge-like shape,
Over a torrent sea,
Sunbeam-proof, I hang like a roof,—
The mountains its columns be.
The triumphal arch through which I march
With hurricane, fire, and snow,
When the Powers of the air are chained to my chair,
Is the million-coloured bow;
The sphere-fire above its soft colours wove,
While the moist Earth was laughing below.

I am the daughter of Earth and Water,
And the nursling of the Sky;
I pass through the pores of the ocean and shores;
I change, but I cannot die.
For after the rain when with never a stain
The pavilion of Heaven is bare,
And the winds and sunbeams with their convex gleams
Build up the blue dome of air,
I silently laugh at my own cenotaph,[25]
And out of the caverns of rain,
Like a child from the womb, like a ghost from the tomb,
I arise and unbuild it again.

To a Skylark [26]

Hail to thee, blithe Spirit!
Bird thou never wert,
That from Heaven, or near it,
Pourest thy full heart
In profuse strains of unpremeditated art.

Higher still and higher
From the earth thou springest
Like a cloud of fire;
The blue deep thou wingest,
And singing still dost soar, and soaring ever singest.

In the golden lightning
Of the sunken sun,
O'er which clouds are bright'ning,
Thou dost float and run;
Like an unbodied joy whose race is just begun.

The pale purple even
Melts around thy flight;

[25] A cenotaph (here 'the blue dome of air') is an empty tomb or a monument which honors one lost or buried elsewhere.

[26] Written at Leghorn in 1820; published, with *Prometheus Unbound*, the same year. Compare this with Wordsworth's poem, p. 657.

Like a star of Heaven,
In the broad daylight
Thou art unseen, but yet I hear thy shrill delight,

Keen as are the arrows
Of that silver sphere,
Whose intense lamp narrows
In the white dawn clear
Until we hardly see — we feel that it is there.

All the earth and air
With thy voice is loud,
As, when night is bare,
From one lonely cloud
The moon rains out her beams, and Heaven is overflowed.

What thou art we know not;
What is most like thee?
From rainbow clouds there flow not
Drops so bright to see
As from thy presence showers a rain of melody.

Like a Poet hidden
In the light of thought,
Singing hymns unbidden,
Till the world is wrought
To sympathy with hopes and fears it heeded not:

Like a high-born maiden
In a palace-tower,
Soothing her love-laden
Soul in secret hour
With music sweet as love, which overflows her bower:

Like a glow-worm golden
In a dell of dew,
Scattering unbeholden
Its aëreal hue
Among the flowers and grass, which screen it from the view!

Like a rose embowered
In its own green leaves,
By warm winds deflowered,
Till the scent it gives
Makes faint with too much sweet those heavy-wingéd thieves:

Sound of vernal showers
On the twinkling grass,
Rain-awakened flowers,
All that ever was
Joyous, and clear, and fresh, thy music doth surpass:

Teach us, Sprite or Bird,
What sweet thoughts are thine:
I have never heard
Praise of love or wine
That panted forth a flood of rapture so divine.

Chorus Hymeneal,
Or triumphal chant,
Matched with thine would be all
But an empty vaunt,
A thing wherein we feel there is some hidden want.

What objects are the fountains
Of thy happy strain?
What fields, or waves, or mountains?
What shapes of sky or plain?
What love of thine own kind? what ignorance of pain?

With thy clear keen joyance
Languor cannot be:
Shadow of annoyance
Never came near thee:
Thou lovest — but ne'er knew love's sad satiety.

Waking or asleep,
Thou of death must deem
Things more true and deep
Than we mortals dream,
Or how could thy notes flow in such a crystal stream?

We look before and after,
And pine for what is not:
Our sincerest laughter
With some pain is fraught;
Our sweetest songs are those that tell of saddest thought.

Yet if we could scorn
Hate, and pride, and fear;
If we were things born
Not to shed a tear,
I know not how thy joy we ever should come near.

Better than all measures
Of delightful sound,
Better than all treasures
That in books are found,
Thy skill to poet were, thou scorner of the ground!

Teach me half the gladness
That thy brain must know,
Such harmonious madness
From my lips would flow
The world should listen then — as I am listening now.

Hymn of Apollo [27]

I

THE sleepless Hours who watch me as I lie,
Curtained with star-inwoven tapestries
From the broad moonlight of the sky,
Fanning the busy dreams from my dim eyes, —
Waken me when their Mother, the gray Dawn,
Tells them that dreams and that the moon is gone.

II

Then I arise, and climbing Heaven's blue dome,
I walk over the mountains and the waves,
Leaving my robe upon the ocean foam;
My footsteps pave the clouds with fire; the caves
Are filled with my bright presence, and the air
Leaves the green Earth to my embraces bare.

III

The sunbeams are my shafts, with which I kill
Deceit, that loves the night and fears the day;
All men who do or even imagine ill
Fly me, and from the glory of my ray
Good minds and open actions take new might,
Until diminished by the reign of Night.

IV

I feed the clouds, the rainbows and the flowers
With their aethereal colours; the moon's globe
And the pure stars in their eternal bowers
Are cinctured with my power as with a robe;
Whatever lamps on Earth or Heaven may shine
Are portions of one power, which is mine.

V

I stand at noon upon the peak of Heaven,
Then with unwilling steps I wander down
Into the clouds of the Atlantic even;
For grief that I depart they weep and frown:
What look is more delightful than the smile
With which I soothe them from the western isle?

VI

I am the eye with which the Universe
Beholds itself and knows itself divine;
All harmony of instrument or verse,
All prophecy, all medicine is mine,
All light of art or nature; — to my song
Victory and praise in its own right belong.

[27] Written in 1820; published in 1824. This poem and the one following were written to be inserted in *Midas*, a projected drama by Shelley's friend, Edward Williams. The first scene shows Apollo and Pan contending for a prize in music before Tmolus, god of the mountain, and Midas. Apollo, the sun-god, was also the patron of medicine and music.

Hymn of Pan[28]

I

From the forests and highlands
We come, we come;
From the river-girt islands,
Where loud waves are dumb
Listening to my sweet pipings.
The wind in the reeds and the rushes,
The bees on the bells of thyme,
The birds on the myrtle bushes,
The cicale[29] above in the lime,
And the lizards below in the grass,
Were as silent as ever old Tmolus was,
Listening to my sweet pipings.

II

Liquid Peneus was flowing,
And all dark Tempe lay
In Pelion's shadow, outgrowing
The light of the dying day,
Speeded by my sweet pipings.
The Sileni, and Sylvans, and Fauns,
And the Nymphs of the woods and the waves,
To the edge of the moist river-lawns,
And the brink of the dewy caves,
And all that did then attend and follow,
Were silent with love, as you now, Apollo,
With envy of my sweet pipings.

III

I sang of the dancing stars,
I sang of the daedal[30] Earth,
And of Heaven — and the giant wars,
And Love, and Death, and Birth, —
And then I changed my pipings, —
Singing how down the vale of Maenalus
I pursued a maiden and clasped a reed.[31]
Gods and men, we are all deluded thus!
It breaks in our bosom and then we bleed:
All wept, as I think both ye now would,
If envy or age had not frozen your blood,
At the sorrow of my sweet pipings.

[28] Written in 1820; published in 1824. See note to previous poem. Pan, the god of flocks and shepherds, invented the flute which he made from a reed (see Mrs. Browning's *A Musical Instrument*, p. 1060).
[29] locust
[30] Rich, variegated, ingeniously formed.
[31] Just as Pan was about to embrace the fleeing nymph Syrinx she was transformed into reeds.

To Night[32]

I

Swiftly walk o'er the western wave,
Spirit of Night!
Out of the misty eastern cave,
Where, all the long and lone daylight,
Thou wovest dreams of joy and fear,
Which make thee terrible and dear, —
Swift be thy flight!

II

Wrap thy form in a mantle gray,
Star-inwrought!
Blind with thine hair the eyes of Day;
Kiss her until she be wearied out,
Then wander o'er city, and sea, and land,
Touching all with thine opiate wand —
Come, long-sought!

III

When I arose and saw the dawn,
I sighed for thee;
When light rode high, and the dew was gone,
And noon lay heavy on flower and tree,
And the weary Day turned to his rest,
Lingering like an unloved guest,
I sighed for thee.

IV

Thy brother Death came, and cried,
Wouldst thou me?
Thy sweet child Sleep, the filmy-eyed,
Murmured like a noontide bee,
Shall I nestle near thy side?
Wouldst thou me? — And I replied,
No, not thee!

V

Death will come when thou art dead,
Soon, too soon —

[32] Written in 1821; published in *Posthumous Poems*, 1824.

Sleep will come when thou art fled;
Of neither would I ask the boon
I ask of thee, belovéd Night —
Swift be thine approaching flight,
Come soon, soon!

To —— [33]

Music, when soft voices die,
Vibrates in the memory —
Odours, when sweet violets sicken,
Live within the sense they quicken.

Rose leaves, when the rose is dead,
Are heaped for the belovéd's bed;
And so thy thoughts, when thou art gone,
Love itself shall slumber on.

Song

I

Rarely, rarely, comest thou,
Spirit of Delight!
Wherefore hast thou left me now
Many a day and night?
Many a weary night and day
'Tis since thou art fled away.

II

How shall ever one like me
Win thee back again?
With the joyous and the free
Thou wilt scoff at pain.
Spirit false! thou hast forgot
All but those who need thee not.

III

As a lizard with the shade
Of a trembling leaf,
Thou with sorrow art dismayed;
Even the sighs of grief
Reproach thee, that thou art not near,
And reproach thou wilt not hear.

IV

Let me set my mournful ditty
To a merry measure;
Thou wilt never come for pity,
Thou wilt come for pleasure;
Pity then will cut away
Those cruel wings, and thou wilt stay.

V

I love all that thou lovest,
Spirit of Delight!
The fresh Earth in new leaves dressed,
And the starry night;
Autumn evening, and the morn
When the golden mists are born.

VI

I love snow, and all the forms
Of the radiant frost;
I love waves, and winds, and storms,
Everything almost
Which is Nature's, and may be
Untainted by man's misery.

VII

I love tranquil solitude,
And such society
As is quiet, wise, and good;
Between thee and me
What difference? but thou dost possess
The things I seek, not love them less.

VIII

I love Love — though he has wings,
And like light can flee,
But above all other things,
Spirit, I love thee —
Thou art love and life! Oh, come,
Make once more my heart thy home.

A Lament

I

O world! O life! O time!
On whose last steps I climb,
Trembling at that where I had stood before;
When will return the glory of your prime?
No more — Oh, never more!

[33] Written in 1821 and published in 1824, as were also the three following poems.

II

Out of the day and night
A joy has taken flight;
  Fresh spring, and summer, and winter hoar,
Move my faint heart with grief, but with delight
    No more — Oh, never more!

To ——

I

One word is too often profaned
  For me to profane it,
One feeling too falsely disdained
  For thee to disdain it;
One hope is too like despair
  For prudence to smother,
And pity from thee more dear
  Than that from another.

II

I can give not what men call love,
  But wilt thou accept not
The worship the heart lifts above
  And the Heavens reject not, —
The desire of the moth for the star,
  Of the night for the morrow,
The devotion to something afar
  From the sphere of our sorrow?

ADONAIS [34]

AN ELEGY ON THE DEATH OF JOHN KEATS, AUTHOR OF ENDYMION, HYPERION, ETC.

'Αστὴρ πρὶν μὲν ἔλαμπες ἐνὶ ζωοῖσιν Ἑῷος·
νῦν δὲ θανὼν λάμπεις Ἕσπερος ἐν φθιμένοις. [35] — Plato.

PREFACE

Φάρμακον ἦλθε, Βίων, ποτὶ σὸν στόμα, φάρμακον εἶδες.
πῶς τευ τοῖς χείλεσσι ποτέδραμε, κοὐκ ἐγλυκάνθη;
τίς δὲ βροτὸς τοσσοῦτον ἀνάμερος, ἢ κεράσαι τοι,
ἢ δοῦναι λαλέοντι τὸ φάρμακον; ἔκφυγεν ᾠδάν. [36]

— Moschus, Epitaph. Bion.

It is my intention to subjoin to the London edition of this poem a criticism upon the claims of its lamented object to be classed among the writers of the highest genius who have adorned our age. My known repugnance to the narrow principles of taste on which several of his earlier compositions were modelled prove at least that I am an impartial judge. I consider the fragment of *Hyperion* as second to nothing that was ever produced by a writer of the same years.

John Keats died at Rome of a consumption, in his twenty-fourth year, on the —— of —— 1821; and was buried in the romantic and lonely cemetery of the Protestants in that city, under the pyramid which is the tomb of Cestius, and the massy walls and towers, now mouldering and desolate, which formed the circuit of ancient Rome. The cemetery is an open space among the ruins, covered in winter with violets and daisies. It might make one in love with death, to think that one should be buried in so sweet a place.

The genius of the lamented person to whose memory I have dedicated these unworthy verses was not less delicate and fragile than it was beautiful; and where cankerworms abound, what wonder if its young flower was blighted in the bud? The savage criticism on his *Endymion,* which appeared in the *Quarterly Review,* produced

---

[34] Written at Pisa during early June 1821; printed in Pisa by 13 July of the same year. Copies reached England in December. There was actually no 'London edition' during Shelley's lifetime. Keats and Shelley had known each other pleasantly at Leigh Hunt's, but *Adonais* is not the tribute of a devoted friend. It is rather a lament for the ideal rejected by the world, for poetry, and, still more, for a poet in whose life Shelley read the lineaments of his own. When he wrote the Preface he did not know the exact date of Keats's death; and he shared the unworthy and untrue belief that Keats had 'been killed by the reviewers,' notably by the attack of *The Quarterly Review* upon *Endymion.* The form is that of the Greek pastoral elegy, done in Spenserian stanzas. The title, the general theme, the refrain, minor devices, the grief of nature for the dead, the images of death, and the renewal of the departed in new cycles of forms reflect Bion's *Lament for Adonis.* As a model of a poet's grief for a brother poet there was Moschus' *Elegy on the Death of Bion.* 'The *Adonais,*' wrote Shelley, 'in spite of its mysticism, is the least imperfect of my compositions, and, as the image of my regret and honour for poor Keats, I wish it to be so.'

[35] Thou wert the morning star among the living,
  Ere thy fair light had fled; —
Now, having died, thou art as Hesperus, giving
  New splendour to the dead. [Shelley's translation.]

[36] Poison came, Bion, to thy mouth — thou didst know poison. To such lips as thine did it come, and was not sweetened? What mortal was so cruel that could mix poison for thee, or who could give thee the venom that heard thy voice? Surely he had no music in his soul [Andrew Lang's translation.]

the most violent effect on his susceptible mind; the agitation thus originated ended in the rupture of a blood-vessel in the lungs; a rapid consumption ensued, and the succeeding acknowledgements from more candid critics of the true greatness of his powers were ineffectual to heal the wound thus wantonly inflicted.

It may be well said that these wretched men know not what they do. They scatter their insults and their slanders without heed as to whether the poisoned shaft lights on a heart made callous by many blows or one like Keats's composed of more penetrable stuff. One of their associates is, to my knowledge, a most base and unprincipled calumniator. As to *Endymion,* was it a poem, whatever might be its defects, to be treated contemptuously by those who had celebrated, with various degrees of complacency and panegyric, *Paris,* and *Woman,* and a *Syrian Tale,* and Mrs. Lefanu, and Mr. Barrett, and Mr. Howard Payne, and a long list of the illustrious obscure? Are these the men who in their venal good nature presumed to draw a parallel between the Rev. Mr. Milman and Lord Byron? What gnat did they strain at here, after having swallowed all those camels? Against what woman taken in adultery dares the foremost of these literary prostitutes to cast his opprobrious stone? Miserable man! you, one of the meanest, have wantonly defaced one of the noblest specimens of the workmanship of God. Nor shall it be your excuse, that, murderer as you are, you have spoken daggers, but used none.

The circumstances of the closing scene of poor Keats's life were not made known to me until the *Elegy* was ready for the press. I am given to understand that the wound which his sensitive spirit had received from the criticism of *Endymion* was exasperated by the bitter sense of unrequited benefits; the poor fellow seems to have been hooted from the stage of life, no less by those on whom he had wasted the promise of his genius, than those on whom he had lavished his fortune and his care. He was accompanied to Rome, and attended in his last illness by Mr. Severn, a young artist of the highest promise, who, I have been informed, 'almost risked his own life, and sacrificed every prospect to unwearied attendance upon his dying friend.' Had I known these circumstances before the completion of my poem, I should have been tempted to add my feeble tribute of applause to the more solid recompense which the virtuous man finds in the recollection of his own motives. Mr. Severn can dispense with a reward from 'such stuff as dreams are made of.' His conduct is a golden augury of the success of his future career — may the unextinguished Spirit of his illustrious friend animate the creations of his pencil, and plead against Oblivion for his name!

I

I WEEP for Adonais — he is dead!
O, weep for Adonais! though our tears
Thaw not the frost which binds so dear a head!
And thou, sad Hour, selected from all years
To mourn our loss, rouse thy obscure compeers,
And teach them thine own sorrow, say: 'With me
Died Adonais; till the Future dares
Forget the Past, his fate and fame shall be
An echo and a light unto eternity!'

II

Where wert thou, mighty Mother,[37] when he lay,
When thy Son lay, pierced by the shaft which flies
In darkness? where was lorn Urania
When Adonais died? With veilèd eyes,
'Mid listening Echoes, in her Paradise
She sate, while one, with soft enamoured breath,
Rekindled all the fading melodies,
With which, like flowers that mock the corse beneath,
He had adorned and hid the coming bulk of Death.

III

Oh, weep for Adonais — he is dead!
Wake, melancholy Mother, wake and weep!
Yet wherefore? Quench within their burning bed
Thy fiery tears, and let thy loud heart keep
Like his, a mute and uncomplaining sleep;
For he is gone, where all things wise and fair
Descend; — oh, dream not that the amorous Deep
Will yet restore him to the vital air;
Death feeds on his mute voice, and laughs at our despair.

IV

Most musical of mourners, weep again!
Lament anew, Urania! — He died,

[37] Urania, the heavenly muse; see Milton's *Paradise Lost*, the opening of Book VII.

Who was the Sire[38] of an immortal strain,
Blind, old, and lonely, when his country's pride,
The priest, the slave, and the liberticide,
Trampled and mocked with many a loathéd rite
Of lust and blood; he went, unterrified,
Into the gulf of death; but his clear Sprite
Yet reigns o'er earth; the third among the sons of light.[39]

V

Most musical of mourners, weep anew!
Not all to that bright station dared to climb;
And happier they their happiness who knew,
Whose tapers yet burn through that night of time
In which suns perished; others more sublime,
Struck by the envious wrath of man or god,
Have sunk, extinct in their refulgent prime;
And some yet live, treading the thorny road,
Which leads, through toil and hate, to Fame's serene abode.

VI

But now, thy youngest, dearest one, has perished —
The nursling of thy widowhood, who grew,
Like a pale flower by some sad maiden cherished,
And fed with true-love tears, instead of dew;[40]
Most musical of mourners, weep anew!
Thy extreme hope, the loveliest and the last,
The bloom, whose petals nipped before they blew
Died on the promise of the fruit, is waste;
The broken lily lies — the storm is overpast.

VII

To that high Capital,[41] where kingly Death
Keeps his pale court in beauty and decay,
He came; and bought, with price of purest breath,
A grave among the eternal. — Come away!
Haste, while the vault of blue Italian day
Is yet his fitting charnel-roof! while still
He lies, as if in dewy sleep he lay;
Awake him not! surely he takes his fill
Of deep and liquid rest, forgetful of all ill.

VIII

He will awake no more, oh, never more! —
Within the twilight chamber spreads apace
The shadow of white Death, and at the door
Invisible Corruption waits to trace
His extreme way to her dim dwelling-place;
The eternal Hunger sits, but pity and awe
Soothe her pale rage, nor dares she to deface
So fair a prey, till darkness, and the law
Of change, shall o'er his sleep the mortal curtain draw.

IX

Oh, weep for Adonais! — The quick Dreams,
The passion-wingéd Ministers of thought,
Who were his flocks, whom near the living streams

38 Milton
39 If *epic* poets are intended, Homer and Dante were the first and second, according to Shelley's own *Defence of Poetry*.
40 A reference to Keats's *Isabella; or The Pot of Basil.*
41 Rome

Of his young spirit he fed, and whom he taught
The love which was its music, wander not,—
Wander no more, from kindling brain to brain,
But droop there, whence they sprung; and mourn their lot
Round the cold heart, where, after their sweet pain,
They ne'er will gather strength, or find a home again.

X

And one with trembling hands clasps his cold head,
And fans him with her moonlight wings, and cries;
'Our love, our hope, our sorrow, is not dead;
See, on the silken fringe of his faint eyes,
Like dew upon a sleeping flower, there lies
A tear some Dream has loosened from his brain.'
Lost Angel of a ruined Paradise!
She knew not 'twas her own; as with no stain
She faded, like a cloud which had outwept its rain.

XI

One from a lucid urn of starry dew
Washed his light limbs as if embalming them;
Another clipped her profuse locks, and threw
The wreath upon him, like an anadem,[42]
Which frozen tears instead of pearls begem;
Another in her wilful grief would break
Her bow and wingéd reeds, as if to stem
A greater loss with one which was more weak;
And dull the barbéd fire against his frozen cheek.

XII

Another Splendour on his mouth alit,
That mouth, whence it was wont to draw the breath
Which gave it strength to pierce the guarded wit,
And pass into the panting heart beneath
With lightning and with music: the damp death
Quenched its caress upon his icy lips;
And, as a dying meteor stains a wreath
Of moonlight vapour, which the cold night clips,[43]
It flushed through his pale limbs, and passed to its eclipse.

XIII

And others came . . . Desires and Adorations,
Wingéd Persuasions and veiled Destinies,
Splendours, and Glooms, and glimmering Incarnations
Of hopes and fears, and twilight Phantasies;
And Sorrow, with her family of Sighs,
And Pleasure, blind with tears, led by the gleam
Of her own dying smile instead of eyes,
Came in slow pomp;—the moving pomp might seem
Like pageantry of mist on an autumnal stream.

XIV

All he had loved, and moulded into thought,
From shape, and hue, and odour, and sweet sound,
Lamented Adonais. Morning sought
Her eastern watch-tower, and her hair unbound,
Wet with the tears which should adorn the ground,
Dimmed the aëreal eyes that kindle day;
Afar the melancholy thunder moaned,
Pale Ocean in unquiet slumber lay,

[42] crown or garland

[43] embraces

And the wild Winds flew round, sobbing
in their dismay.

XV

Lost Echo sits amid the voiceless mountains,
And feeds her grief with his remembered lay,
And will no more reply to winds or fountains,
Or amorous birds perched on the young green spray,
Or herdsman's horn, or bell at closing day;
Since she can mimic not his lips, more dear
Than those [44] for whose disdain she pined away
Into a shadow of all sounds: — a drear
Murmur, between their songs, is all the woodmen hear.

XVI

Grief made the young Spring wild, and she threw down
Her kindling buds, as if she Autumn were,
Or they dead leaves; since her delight is flown,
For whom should she have waked the sullen year?
To Phoebus was not Hyacinth [45] so dear
Nor to himself Narcissus,[46] as to both
Thou, Adonais: wan they stand and sere
Amid the faint companions of their youth,
With dew all turned to tears; odour, to sighing ruth.

XVII

Thy spirit's sister, the lorn nightingale
Mourns not her mate with such melodious pain;
Not so the eagle, who like thee could scale
Heaven, and could nourish in the sun's domain
Her mighty youth with morning, doth complain,
Soaring and screaming round her empty nest,
As Albion wails for thee: the curse of Cain
Light on his [47] head who pierced thy innocent breast,
And scared the angel soul that was its earthly guest!

XVIII

Ah, woe is me! Winter is come and gone,
But grief returns with the revolving year;
The airs and streams renew their joyous tone;
The ants, the bees, the swallows reappear;
Fresh leaves and flowers deck the dead Seasons' bier;
The amorous birds now pair in every brake,
And build their mossy homes in field and brere; [48]
And the green lizard, and the golden snake,
Like unimprisoned flames, out of their trance awake.

XIX

Through wood and stream and field and hill and Ocean
A quickening life from the Earth's heart has burst
As it has ever done, with change and motion,
From the great morning of the world when first
God dawned on Chaos; in its stream immersed,

[44] Of Narcissus, for whom Echo pined away into a mere voice.
[45] A youth changed upon his death into a flower, by Apollo, who loved him dearly.
[46] Narcissus fell in love with his own image reflected in a fountain. He also was changed into a flower.

[47] The author (J. W. Croker) of the supposedly fatal anonymous review of *Endymion* in *The Quarterly Review* April 1818.
[48] briar

The lamps of Heaven flash with a softer light;
All baser things pant with life's sacred thirst;
Diffuse themselves; and spend in love's delight,
The beauty and the joy of their renewéd might.

XX

The leprous corpse, touched by this spirit tender,
Exhales itself in flowers of gentle breath;
Like incarnations of the stars, when splendour
Is changed to fragrance, they illumine death
And mock the merry worm that wakes beneath;
Nought we know, dies. Shall that alone which knows
Be as a sword consumed before the sheath
By sightless lightning? — the intense atom glows
A moment, then is quenched in a most cold repose.

XXI

Alas! that all we loved of him should be,
But for our grief, as if it had not been,
And grief itself be mortal! Woe is me!
Whence are we, and why are we? of what scene
The actors or spectators? Great and mean
Meet massed in death, who lends what life must borrow.
As long as skies are blue, and fields are green,
Evening must usher night, night urge the morrow,
Month follow month with woe, and year wake year to sorrow.

XXII

He will awake no more, oh, never more!
'Wake thou,' cried Misery, 'childless Mother, rise
Out of thy sleep, and slake, in thy heart's core,
A wound more fierce than his, with tears and sighs.'
And all the Dreams that watched Urania's eyes,
And all the Echoes whom their sister's song
Had held in holy silence, cried: 'Arise!'
Swift as a Thought by the snake Memory stung,
From her ambrosial rest the fading Splendour sprung.

XXIII

She rose like an autumnal Night, that springs
Out of the East, and follows wild and drear
The golden Day, which, on eternal wings,
Even as a ghost abandoning a bier,
Had left the Earth a corpse. Sorrow and fear
So struck, so roused, so rapped Urania;
So saddened round her like an atmosphere
Of stormy mist; so swept her on her way
Even to the mournful place where Adonais lay.

XXIV

Out of her secret Paradise she sped,
Through camps and cities rough with stone, and steel,
And human hearts, which to her aery tread
Yielding not, wounded the invisible
Palms of her tender feet where'er they fell:
And barbéd tongues, and thoughts more sharp than they,

Rent the soft Form they never could repel,
Whose sacred blood, like the young tears of May,
Paved with eternal flowers that undeserving way.

XXV

In the death-chamber for a moment Death,
Shamed by the presence of that living Might,
Blushed to annihilation, and the breath
Revisited those lips, and Life's pale light
Flashed through those limbs, so late her dear delight.
'Leave me not wild and drear and comfortless,
As silent lightning leaves the starless night!
Leave me not!' cried Urania: her distress
Roused Death: Death rose and smiled, and met her vain caress.

XXVI

'Stay yet awhile! speak to me once again;
Kiss me, so long but as a kiss may live;
And in my heartless breast and burning brain
That word, that kiss, shall all thoughts else survive,
With food of saddest memory kept alive,
Now thou art dead, as if it were a part
Of thee, my Adonais! I would give
All that I am to be as thou now art!
But I am chained to Time, and cannot thence depart!

XXVII

'O gentle child, beautiful as thou wert,
Why didst thou leave the trodden paths of men
Too soon, and with weak hands though mighty heart
Dare the unpastured dragon [49] in his den?
Defenceless as thou wert, oh, where was then
Wisdom the mirrored shield, or scorn the spear?
Or hadst thou waited the full cycle, when
Thy spirit should have filled its crescent sphere,
The monsters of life's waste had fled from thee like deer.

XXVIII

'The herded wolves, bold only to pursue;
The obscene ravens, clamorous o'er the dead;
The vultures to the conqueror's banner true
Who feed where Desolation first has fed,
And whose wings rain contagion;—how they fled,
When, like Apollo, from his golden bow
The Pythian of the age [50] one arrow sped
And smiled!—The spoilers tempt no second blow,
They fawn on the proud feet that spurn them lying low.

XXIX

'The sun comes forth, and many reptiles spawn;
He sets, and each ephemeral insect then
Is gathered into death without a dawn,
And the immortal stars awake again;
So is it in the world of living men:
A godlike mind soars forth, in its delight
Making earth bare and veiling heaven, and when
It sinks, the swarms that dimmed or shared its light
Leave to its kindred lamps the spirit's awful night.'

---

[49] The world of harsh critics and unfeeling men.
[50] Byron, who slew the critics with his *English Bards and Scotch Reviewers*, as Apollo did the Python.

XXX

Thus ceased she: and the mountain shepherds came,
Their garlands sere, their magic mantles rent;
The Pilgrim of Eternity,[51] whose fame
Over his living head like Heaven is bent,
An early but enduring monument,
Came, veiling all the lightnings of his song
In sorrow; from her wilds Ierne [52] sent
The sweetest lyrist [53] of her saddest wrong,
And Love taught Grief to fall like music from his tongue.

XXXI

Midst others of less note, came one frail Form,[54]
A phantom among men; companionless
As the last cloud of an expiring storm
Whose thunder is its knell; he, as I guess,
Had gazed on Nature's naked loveliness,
Actaeon-like,[55] and now he fled astray
With feeble steps o'er the world's wilderness,
And his own thoughts, along that rugged way,
Pursued, like raging hounds, their father and their prey.

XXXII

A pardlike [56] Spirit beautiful and swift —
A Love in desolation masked; — a Power
Girt round with weakness; — it can scarce uplift
The weight of the superincumbent hour;
It is a dying lamp, a falling shower,
A breaking billow; — even whilst we speak
Is it not broken? On the withering flower
The killing sun smiles brightly: on a cheek
The life can burn in blood, even while the heart may break.

XXXIII

His head was bound with pansies overblown,
And faded violets, white, and pied, and blue;
And a light spear topped with a cypress cone,
Round whose rude shaft dark ivy-tresses grew
Yet dripping with the forest's noonday dew,
Vibrated, as the ever-beating heart
Shook the weak hand that grasped it; of that crew
He came the last, neglected and apart;
A herd-abandoned deer struck by the hunter's dart.

XXXIV

All stood aloof, and at his partial moan
Smiled through their tears; well knew that gentle band
Who in another's fate now wept his own,
As in the accents of an unknown land
He sung new sorrow; sad Urania scanned
The Stranger's mien, and murmured: 'Who art thou?'
He answered not, but with a sudden hand
Made bare his branded and ensanguined brow,
Which was like Cain's or Christ's — oh! that it should be so!

XXXV

What softer voice is hushed over the dead?
Athwart what brow is that dark mantle thrown?

---

[51] Byron, so called because of *Childe Harold's Pilgrimage* (see III, 70, 8).
[52] Ireland
[53] Thomas Moore
[54] Shelley
[55] Acteon, the hunter, after he had seen Artemis bathing, was changed into a stag and torn to pieces by his own hounds.
[56] leopard-like

What form leans sadly o'er the white death-bed,
In mockery of monumental stone,
The heavy heart heaving without a moan?
If it be He,[57] who, gentlest of the wise,
Taught, soothed, loved, honoured the departed one,
Let me not vex, with inharmonious sighs,
The silence of that heart's accepted sacrifice.

XXXVI

Our Adonais has drunk poison — oh!
What deaf and viperous murderer could crown
Life's early cup with such a draught of woe?
The nameless worm [58] would now itself disown:
It felt, yet could escape, the magic tone
Whose prelude held all envy, hate, and wrong,
But what was howling in one breast alone,
Silent with expectation of the song,
Whose master's hand is cold, whose silver lyre unstrung.

XXXVII

Live thou, whose infamy is not thy fame!
Live! fear no heavier chastisement from me,
Thou noteless blot on a remembered name!
But be thyself, and know thyself to be!
And ever at thy season be thou free
To spill the venom when thy fangs o'erflow:
Remorse and Self-contempt shall cling to thee;
Hot Shame shall burn upon thy secret brow,
And like a beaten hound tremble thou shalt — as now.

XXXVIII

Nor let us weep that our delight is fled
Far from these carrion kites that scream below;
He wakes or sleeps with the enduring dead;
Thou canst not soar where he is sitting now, —
Dust to the dust! but the pure spirit shall flow
Back to the burning fountain whence it came,
A portion of the Eternal, which must glow
Through time and change, unquenchably the same,
Whilst thy cold embers choke the sordid hearth of shame.

XXXIX

Peace, peace! he is not dead, he doth not sleep —
He hath awakened from the dream of life —
'Tis we, who lost in stormy visions, keep
With phantoms an unprofitable strife,
And in mad trance, strike with our spirit's knife
Invulnerable nothings. — *We* decay
Like corpses in a charnel; fear and grief
Convulse us and consume us day by day,
And cold hopes swarm like worms within our living clay.

XL

He has outsoared the shadow of our night;
Envy and calumny and hate and pain,
And that unrest which men miscall delight,
Can touch him not and torture not again;
From the contagion of the world's slow stain
He is secure, and now can never mourn
A heart grown cold, a head grown gray in vain;

[57] Leigh Hunt, Keats's close friend and benefactor.
[58] The critic of *The Quarterly Review.*

Nor, when the spirit's self has ceased to burn,
With sparkless ashes load an unlamented urn.

XLI

He lives, he wakes — 'tis Death is dead, not he;
Mourn not for Adonais. — Thou young Dawn,
Turn all thy dew to splendour, for from thee
The spirit thou lamentest is not gone;
Ye caverns and ye forests, cease to moan!
Cease, ye faint flowers and fountains, and thou Air,
Which like a mourning veil thy scarf hadst thrown
O'er the abandoned Earth, now leave it bare
Even to the joyous stars which smile on its despair!

XLII

He is made one with Nature: there is heard
His voice in all her music, from the moan
Of thunder, to the song of night's sweet bird;
He is a presence to be felt and known
In darkness and in light, from herb and stone,
Spreading itself where'er that Power may move
Which has withdrawn his being to its own;
Which wields the world with never-wearied love,
Sustains it from beneath, and kindles it above.

XLIII

He is a portion of the loveliness
Which once he made more lovely: he doth bear
His part, while the one Spirit's plastic stress
Sweeps through the dull dense world, compelling there,
All new successions to the forms they wear;
Torturing th' unwilling dross that checks its flight
To its own likeness, as each mass may bear;
And bursting in its beauty and its might
From trees and beasts and men into the Heaven's light.

XLIV

The splendours of the firmament of time
May be eclipsed, but are extinguished not;
Like stars to their appointed height they climb,
And death is a low mist which cannot blot
The brightness it may veil. When lofty thought
Lifts a young heart above its mortal lair,
And love and life contend in it, for what
Shall be its earthly doom, the dead live there
And move like winds of light on dark and stormy air.

XLV

The inheritors of unfulfilled renown
Rose from their thrones, built beyond mortal thought,
Far in the Unapparent. Chatterton [59]
Rose pale, — his solemn agony had not
Yet faded from him; Sidney,[60] as he fought
And as he fell and as he lived and loved
Sublimely mild, a Spirit without spot,
Arose; and Lucan [61] by his death approved:
Oblivion as they rose shrank like a thing reproved.

---

59 Thomas Chatterton (1752–1770), 'the marvelous boy,' who killed himself to escape poverty.

60 Sir Philip Sidney (1554–1586), who died from a battle-wound at thirty-two.

61 The Roman poet (A.D. 39–65), who killed himself at twenty-six to escape execution by Nero's order.

XLVI

And many more, whose names on Earth are dark,
But whose transmitted effluence cannot die
So long as fire outlives the parent spark,
Rose, robed in dazzling immortality.
'Thou art become as one of us,' they cry,
'It was for thee yon kingless sphere has long
Swung blind in unascended majesty,
Silent alone amid an Heaven of Song.
Assume thy wingéd throne, thou Vesper of our throng!'

XLVII

Who mourns for Adonais? Oh, come forth,
Fond wretch! and know thyself and him aright.
Clasp with thy panting soul the pendulous Earth;
As from a centre, dart thy spirit's light
Beyond all worlds, until its spacious might
Satiate the void circumference: then shrink
Even to a point within our day and night;
And keep thy heart light lest it make thee sink
When hope has kindled hope, and lured thee to the brink.

XLVIII

Or go to Rome, which is the sepulchre,
Oh, not of him, but of our joy: 'tis nought
That ages, empires, and religions there
Lie buried in the ravage they have wrought;
For such as he can lend, — they borrow not
Glory from those who made the world their prey;
And he is gathered to the kings of thought
Who waged contention with their time's decay,
And of the past are all that cannot pass away.

XLIX

Go thou to Rome, — at once the Paradise,
The grave, the city, and the wilderness;
And where its wrecks like shattered mountains rise,
And flowering weeds, and fragrant copses dress
The bones of Desolation's nakedness,
Pass, till the spirit of the spot shall lead
Thy footsteps to a slope of green access
Where, like an infant's smile, over the dead
A light of laughing flowers along the grass is spread;

L

And gray walls moulder round, on which dull Time
Feeds, like slow fire upon a hoary brand;
And one keen pyramid with wedge sublime,
Pavilioning the dust of him who planned
This refuge for his memory, doth stand
Like flame transformed to marble; and beneath,
A field is spread, on which a newer band
Have pitched in Heaven's smile their camp of death,
Welcoming him we lose with scarce extinguished breath.

LI

Here pause: these graves are all too young [62] as yet
To have outgrown the sorrow which consigned
Its charge to each; and if the seal is set,

[62] Shelley's son William, who died 7 June 1819, was buried there.

Here, on one fountain of a mourning mind,
Break it not thou! too surely shalt thou find
Thine own well full, if thou returnest home,
Of tears and gall. From the world's bitter wind
Seek shelter in the shadow of the tomb.
What Adonais is, why fear we to become?

LII

The One remains, the many change and pass;
Heaven's light forever shines, Earth's shadows fly;
Life, like a dome of many-coloured glass,
Stains the white radiance of Eternity,
Until Death tramples it to fragments.—Die,
If thou wouldst be with that which thou dost seek!
Follow where all is fled!—Rome's azure sky,
Flowers, ruins, statues, music, words, are weak
The glory they transfuse with fitting truth to speak.

LIII

Why linger, why turn back, why shrink, my Heart?
Thy hopes are gone before: from all things here
They have departed; thou shouldst now depart!
A light is passed from the revolving year,
And man, and woman; and what still is dear
Attracts to crush, repels to make thee wither.
The soft sky smiles,—the low wind whispers near:
'Tis Adonais calls! oh, hasten thither,
No more let Life divide what Death can join together.

LIV

That Light whose smile kindles the Universe,
That Beauty in which all things work and move,
That Benediction which the eclipsing Curse
Of birth can quench not, that sustaining Love
Which through the web of being blindly wove
By man and beast and earth and air and sea,
Burns bright or dim, as each are mirrors of
The fire for which all thirst; now beams on me,
Consuming the last clouds of cold mortality.

LV

The breath whose might I have invoked in song
Descends on me; my spirit's bark is driven,
Far from the shore, far from the trembling throng
Whose sails were never to the tempest given;
The massy earth and spheréd skies are riven!
I am borne darkly, fearfully, afar;
Whilst, burning through the inmost veil of Heaven,
The soul of Adonais, like a star,
Beacons from the abode where the Eternal are.

from *Hellas* [63]

Chorus

WORLDS on worlds are rolling ever
From creation to decay,

63 A lyrical drama inspired by the Greek war for independence from Turkey, *Hellas* was written at Pisa in the autumn of 1821; it was published at London in the spring of 1822. The modern Greeks, heirs of ancient glory, fighting for a new freedom, seemed to Shelley the heralds of a new Golden Age greater than any previous time.

Like the bubbles on a river
Sparkling, bursting, borne away.
But they are still immortal
Who, through birth's orient portal
And death's dark chasm hurrying to and fro,
Clothe their unceasing flight
In the brief dust and light
Gathered around their chariots as they go;
New shapes they still may weave,
New gods, new laws receive,
Bright or dim are they as the robes they last
On Death's bare ribs had cast.

A power from the unknown God,
A Promethean conqueror, came;
Like a triumphal path he trod
The thorns of death and shame.
A mortal shape to him
Was like the vapour dim
Which the orient planet animates with light;
Hell, Sin, and Slavery came,
Like bloodhounds mild and tame,
Nor preyed, until their Lord had taken flight;
The moon of Mahomet
Arose, and it shall set:
While blazoned as on Heaven's immortal noon
The cross leads generations on.

Swift as the radiant shapes of sleep
From one whose dreams are Paradise
Fly, when the fond wretch wakes to weep,
And Day peers forth with her blank eyes;
So fleet, so faint, so fair,
The Powers of earth and air
Fled from the folding-star [64] of Bethlehem:
Apollo, Pan, and Love,
And even Olympian Jove
Grew weak, for killing Truth had glared on them;
Our hills and seas and streams,
Dispeopled of their dreams,
Their waters turned to blood, their dew to tears,
Wailed for the golden years.

. . .

Chorus

The world's great age begins anew,
The golden years return,
The earth doth like a snake renew
Her winter weeds outworn:
Heaven smiles, and faiths and empires gleam,
Like wrecks of a dissolving dream.

A brighter Hellas rears its mountains
From waves serener far;
A new Peneus rolls his fountains
Against the morning star.
Where fairer Tempes bloom, there sleep
Young Cyclads on a sunnier deep.

A loftier Argo cleaves the main,
Fraught with a later prize;
Another Orpheus sings again,
And loves, and weeps, and dies.
A new Ulysses leaves once more
Calypso for his native shore.

Oh, write no more the tale of Troy,
If earth Death's scroll must be!
Nor mix with Laian [65] rage the joy
Which dawns upon the free:
Although a subtler Sphinx renew
Riddles of death Thebes never knew.

Another Athens shall arise,
And to remoter time
Bequeath, like sunset to the skies,
The splendour of its prime;
And leave, if nought so bright may live,
All earth can take or Heaven can give.

[64] The evening star which appears about the time the sheep are folded.

[65] Oedipus, son of Laius, king of Thebes, solved the riddle of the dread Sphinx who had afflicted the country, but he was fated to kill his father unknowingly and to marry Jocasta, his own mother.

Saturn and Love[66] their long repose
  Shall burst, more bright and good
Than all who fell, than One who rose,
  Than many unsubdued:
Not gold, not blood, their altar dowers,
But votive tears and symbol flowers.

Oh, cease! must hate and death return?
  Cease! must men kill and die?
Cease! drain not to its dregs the urn
  Of bitter prophecy.
The world is weary of the past,
Oh, might it die or rest at last!

Lines: 'When the lamp is shattered' [67]

I

  WHEN the lamp is shattered
The light in the dust lies dead —
  When the cloud is scattered
The rainbow's glory is shed.
  When the lute is broken,
Sweet tones are remembered not;
  When the lips have spoken,
Loved accents are soon forgot.

II

  As music and splendour
Survive not the lamp and the lute,
  The heart's echoes render
No song when the spirit is mute: —
  No song but sad dirges,
Like the wind through a ruined cell,
  Or the mournful surges
That ring the dead seaman's knell.

III

  When hearts have once mingled
Love first leaves the well-built nest;
  The weak one is singled
To endure what it once possessed.
  O Love! who bewailest
The frailty of all things here,
  Why choose you the frailest
For your cradle, your home, and your bier?

IV

  Its passions will rock thee
As the storms rock the ravens on high;
  Bright reason will mock thee,
Like the sun from a wintry sky.
  From thy nest every rafter
Will rot, and thine eagle home
  Leave thee naked to laughter,
When leaves fall and cold winds come.

A Dirge

ROUGH wind, that moanest loud
  Grief too sad for song;
Wild wind, when sullen cloud
  Knells all the night long;

Sad storm, whose tears are vain,
Bare woods, whose branches strain,
Deep caves and dreary main, —
  Wail, for the world's wrong!

---

[66] Saturn and Love were among the deities of a real or imaginary state of innocence and happiness. *All those who fell*, or the Gods of Greece, Asia, and Egypt; the *One who rose*, or Jesus Christ, at whose appearance the idols of the Pagan World were amerced of their worship; and *the many unsubdued*, or the monstrous objects of the idolatry of China, India, the Antarctic islands, and the native tribes of America, certainly have reigned over the understandings of men in conjunction or in succession, during periods in which all we know of evil has been in a state of portentous, and, until the revival of learning and the arts, perpetually increasing, activity. The Grecian gods seem indeed to have been personally more innocent, although it cannot be said, that as far as temperance and chastity are concerned, they gave so edifying an example as their successor. The sublime human character of Jesus Christ was deformed by an imputed identification with a Power, who tempted, betrayed, and punished the innocent beings who were called into existence by His sole will; and for the period of a thousand years, the spirit of this most just, wise, and benevolent of men has been propitiated with myriads of hecatombs of those who approached the nearest to His innocence and wisdom, sacrificed under every aggravation of atrocity and variety of torture. The horrors of the Mexican, the Peruvian, and the Indian superstitions are well known. [Shelley.]

[67] This and the following poem were written in 1822 and published in 1824.

John Keats

1795–1821

Keen, fitful gusts are whisp'ring

Keen, fitful gusts are whisp'ring here and there
Among the bushes half leafless, and dry;
The stars look very cold about the sky,
And I have many miles on foot to fare.
Yet feel I little of the cool bleak air,
Or of the dead leaves rustling drearily,
Or of those silver lamps that burn on high,
Or of the distance from home's pleasant lair:
For I am brimfull of the friendliness
That in a little cottage I have found;
Of fair-hair'd Milton's eloquent distress,
And all his love for gentle Lycid drown'd;
Of lovely Laura in her light green dress,
And faithful Petrarch gloriously crown'd.

[*Poems,* 1817]

On First Looking into Chapman's Homer [1]

Much have I travell'd in the realms of gold,
And many goodly states and kingdoms seen;
Round many western islands have I been
Which bards in fealty to Apollo hold.
Oft of one wide expanse had I been told
That deep-brow'd Homer ruled as his demesne;
Yet did I never breathe its pure serene
Till I heard Chapman speak out loud and bold:
Then felt I like some watcher of the skies
When a new planet swims into his ken;
Or like stout Cortez [2] when with eagle eyes
He star'd at the Pacific—and all his men
Look'd at each other with a wild surmise—
Silent, upon a peak in Darien.

[*Poems,* 1817]

ENDYMION [3]

Book I

[Proem]

A thing of beauty is a joy for ever:
Its loveliness increases; it will never
Pass into nothingness; but still will keep
A bower quiet for us, and a sleep
Full of sweet dreams, and health, and quiet breathing.
Therefore, on every morrow, are we wreathing
A flowery band to bind us to the earth,
Spite of despondence, of the inhuman dearth
Of noble natures, of the gloomy days,
Of all the unhealthy and o'er-darkened ways
Made for our searching: yes, in spite of all,
Some shape of beauty moves away the pall
From our dark spirits. Such the sun, the moon,
Trees old, and young, sprouting a shady boon
For simple sheep; and such are daffodils
With the green world they live in; and clear rills
That for themselves a cooling covert make

[1] Composed one autumn morning of 1815 after Keats and Cowden Clarke had spent the night reading Chapman's translation of Homer.

[2] Balboa was the real discoverer of the Pacific.

[3] Begun in the spring of 1817; on 18 April of that year he wrote to Reynolds: 'I cannot exist without Poetry ... half the day will not do — the whole of it — I began with a little, but habit has made me a Leviathan. I had become all in a Tremble from not having written anything of late — the Sonnet overleaf [*On the Sea*] did me good. I slept the better last night for it — this morning, however, I am nearly as bad again. Just now I opened Spenser, and the first lines I saw were these —

"The noble heart that harbours virtuous thought,
And is with child of glorious great intent,
Can never rest until it forth have brought
Th' eternal brood of glory excellent."

... I shall forthwith begin my *Endymion.*' His long story of the fair lad, Endymion, in love with the goddess of the moon, was finished 28 November 1817, and published in April 1818. It was dedicated to Thomas Chatterton.

'Gainst the hot season; the mid forest brake,
Rich with a sprinkling of fair musk-rose blooms:
And such too is the grandeur of the dooms
We have imagined for the mighty dead;
All lovely tales that we have heard or read:
An endless fountain of immortal drink,
Pouring unto us from the heaven's brink.

Nor do we merely feel these essences
For one short hour; no, even as the trees
That whisper round a temple become soon
Dear as the temple's self, so does the moon,
The passion poesy, glories infinite,
Haunt us till they become a cheering light
Unto our souls, and bound to us so fast,
That, whether there be shine, or gloom o'ercast,
They always must be with us, or we die.

. . .

Book IV

[Song of the Indian Maid [4]]

'O Sorrow,
Why dost borrow
The natural hue of health, from vermeil [5] lips? —
To give maiden blushes
To the white rose bushes?
Or is't thy dewy hand the daisy tips?

'O Sorrow,
Why dost borrow
The lustrous passion from a falcon-eye? —
To give the glow-worm light?
Or, on a moonless night,
To tinge, on syren shores, the salt sea-spry? [6]

'O Sorrow,
Why dost borrow
The mellow ditties from a mourning tongue? —
To give at evening pale
Unto the nightingale,
That thou mayst listen the cold dews among?

'O Sorrow,
Why dost borrow
Heart's lightness from the merriment of May? —
A lover would not tread
A cowslip on the head,
Though he should dance from eve till peep of day —
Nor any drooping flower
Held sacred for thy bower,
Wherever he may sport himself and play.

'To Sorrow,
I bade good-morrow,
And thought to leave her far away behind;
But cheerly, cheerly,
She loves me dearly;
She is so constant to me, and so kind:
I would deceive her
And so leave her,
But ah! she is so constant and so kind.

'Beneath my palm trees, by the river side,
I sat a weeping: in the whole world wide
There was no one to ask me why I wept,—
And so I kept
Brimming the water-lilly cups with tears
Cold as my fears.

'Beneath my palm trees, by the river side,
I sat a weeping: what enamour'd bride,
Cheated by shadowy wooer from the clouds,
But hides and shrouds
Beneath dark palm trees by a river side?

'And as I sat, over the light blue hills
There came a noise of revellers: the rills
Into the wide stream came of purple hue —
'T was Bacchus and his crew! [7]

---

[4] Endymion, seeking in vain the Moon-Goddess, whom he loves, comes in the forest upon the Indian maiden who is mourning the loss of her lover.

[5] vermilion

[6] sea-spray

[7] Amy Lowell, in her life of Keats, refuses to accept the common belief that this section on the Triumph of Bacchus was inspired by Titian's *Bacchus and Ariadne;* the sources she contends, are in Ovid, Diodorus Siculus, and Rabelais

The earnest trumpet spake, and silver thrills
From kissing cymbals made a merry din —
'T was Bacchus and his kin!
Like to a moving vintage down they came,
Crown'd with green leaves, and faces all on flame;
All madly dancing through the pleasant valley,
To scare thee, Melancholy!
O then, O then, thou wast a simple name!
And I forgot thee, as the berried holly
By shepherds is forgotten, when, in June,
Tall chesnuts keep away the sun and moon: —
I rush'd into the folly!

'Within his car, aloft, young Bacchus stood,
Trifling his ivy-dart,[8] in dancing mood,
With sidelong laughing;
And little rills of crimson wine imbrued
His plump white arms, and shoulders, enough white
For Venus' pearly bite:
And near him rode Silenus on his ass,
Pelted with flowers as he on did pass
Tipsily quaffing.

'Whence came ye, merry Damsels! whence came ye!
So many, and so many, and such glee?
Why have ye left your bowers desolate,
Your lutes, and gentler fate? —
"We follow Bacchus! Bacchus on the wing,
A conquering!
Bacchus, young Bacchus! good or ill betide,
We dance before him thorough kingdoms wide: —
Come hither, lady fair, and joined be
To our wild minstrelsy!"

'Whence came ye, jolly Satyrs! whence came ye!
So many, and so many, and such glee?
Why have ye left your forest haunts, why left
Your nuts in oak-tree cleft? —
"For wine, for wine we left our kernel tree;
For wine we left our heath, and yellow brooms,
And cold mushrooms;
For wine we follow Bacchus through the earth;
Great God of breathless cups and chirping mirth! —
Come hither, lady fair, and joined be
To our mad minstrelsy!"

'Over wide streams and mountains great we went,
And, save when Bacchus kept his ivy tent,
Onward the tiger and the leopard pants,
With Asian elephants:
Onward these myriads — with song and dance,
With zebras striped, and sleek Arabians' prance,
Web-footed alligators, crocodiles,
Bearing upon their scaly backs, in files,
Plump infant laughers mimicking the coil
Of seamen, and stout galley-rowers' toil:
With toying oars and silken sails they glide,
Nor care for wind and tide.

'Mounted on panthers' furs and lions' manes,
From rear to van they scour about the plains;
A three days' journey in a moment done:
And always, at the rising of the sun,
About the wilds they hunt with spear and horn,
On spleenful unicorn.

'I saw Osirian Egypt[9] kneel adown
Before the vine-wreath crown!
I saw parch'd Abyssinia rouse and sing
To the silver cymbals' ring!

[8] Thyrsus or wand; the ivy was sacred to Bacchus.

[9] Keats knew almost by heart Lemprière's *Classical Dictionary*, wherein the Egyptian god Osiris is said to correspond to Bacchus.

I saw the whelming vintage hotly pierce
Old Tartary the fierce!
The kings of Inde their jewel-sceptres vail,[10]
And from their treasures scatter pearled hail;
Great Brahma from his mystic heaven groans,
And all his priesthood moans;
Before young Bacchus' eye-wink turning pale.—
Into these regions came I following him,
Sick hearted, weary—so I took a whim
To stray away into these forests drear
Alone, without a peer:
And I have told thee all thou mayest hear.

'Young stranger!
I've been a ranger
In search of pleasure throughout every clime:
Alas, 't is not for me!
Bewitch'd I sure must be,
To lose in grieving all my maiden prime.

'Come then, Sorrow!
Sweetest Sorrow!
Like an own babe I nurse thee on my breast:
I thought to leave thee
And deceive thee,
But now of all the world I love thee best.

'There is not one,
No, no, not one
But thee to comfort a poor lonely maid;
Thou art her mother,
And her brother,
Her playmate, and her wooer in the shade."

. . .

When I have fears that I may cease to be [11]

When I have fears that I may cease to be
Before my pen has glean'd my teeming brain,
Before high-piled books, in charactery,
Hold like rich garners the full ripen'd grain;
When I behold, upon the night's starr'd face,
Huge cloudy symbols of a high romance,
And think that I may never live to trace
Their shadows, with the magic hand of chance;
And when I feel, fair creature of an hour,
That I shall never look upon thee more,
Never have relish in the faery power
Of unreflecting love;—then on the shore
Of the wide world I stand alone, and think
Till love and fame to nothingness do sink.

[10] lower (as a token of submission)
[11] Written in 1817; published in 1848.

Fragment of an Ode to Maia

WRITTEN ON MAY DAY, 1818 [12]

Mother of Hermes! and still youthful Maia! [13]
May I sing to thee
As thou wast hymned on the shores of Baiæ? [14]
Or may I woo thee
In earlier Sicilian? or thy smiles
Seek as they once were sought, in Grecian isles,
By bards who died content on pleasant sward,
Leaving great verse unto a little clan?
O, give me their old vigour, and unheard
Save of the quiet Primrose, and the span
Of heaven and few ears,
Rounded by thee, my song should die away
Content as theirs,
Rich in the simple worship of a day.

Lines on the Mermaid Tavern [15]

Souls of Poets dead and gone,
What Elysium have ye known,

[12] Published in 1848.
[13] The eldest and loveliest of the seven Pleiads, and goddess of the spring.
[14] Famous for its situation near Naples and for its baths. The worship of Maia extends, Keats implies, from these later Roman times back to the earlier days of Greece.
[15] Written in 1818; published in *Lamia, Isabella, The Eve of St. Agnes and Other Poems*, 1820.

Happy field or mossy cavern,
Choicer than the Mermaid Tavern?[16]
Have ye tippled drink more fine
Than mine host's Canary wine?
Or are fruits of Paradise
Sweeter than those dainty pies
Of venison? O generous food!
Drest as though bold Robin Hood
Would, with his maid Marian,
Sup and bowse[17] from horn and can.

I have heard that on a day
Mine host's sign-board flew away,
Nobody knew whither, till
An astrologer's old quill
To a sheepskin gave the story,
Said he saw you in your glory,
Underneath a new old sign
Sipping beverage divine,
And pledging with contented smack
The Mermaid in the Zodiac.

Souls of Poets dead and gone,
What Elysium have ye known,
Happy field or mossy cavern,
Choicer than the Mermaid Tavern?

Ode[18]

[*Written on the blank page before Beaumont and Fletcher's Tragi-Comedy 'The Fair Maid of the Inn.'*]

Bards of Passion and of Mirth,
Ye have left your souls on earth!
Have ye souls in heaven too,
Double lived in regions new?
Yes, and those of heaven commune
With the spheres of sun and moon;
With the noise of fountains wond'rous,
And the parle of voices thund'rous;
With the whisper of heaven's trees
And one another, in soft ease
Seated on Elysian lawns
Brows'd by none but Dian's fawns;
Underneath large blue-bells tented,
Where the daisies are rose-scented,
And the rose herself has got
Perfume which on earth is not;
Where the nightingale doth sing
Not a senseless, tranced thing,
But divine melodious truth;
Philosophic numbers smooth;
Tales and golden histories
Of heaven and its mysteries.

Thus ye live on high, and then
On the earth ye live again;
And the souls ye left behind you
Teach us, here, the way to find you,
Where your other souls are joying,
Never slumber'd, never cloying.
Here, your earth-born souls still speak
To mortals, of their little week;
Of their sorrows and delights;
Of their passions and their spites;
Of their glory and their shame;
What doth strengthen and what maim.
Thus ye teach us, every day,
Wisdom, though fled far away.

Bards of Passion and of Mirth,
Ye have left your souls on earth!
Ye have souls in heaven too,
Double-lived in regions new!

THE EVE OF ST. AGNES[19]

St. Agnes' Eve — Ah, bitter chill it was!
The owl, for all his feathers, was a-cold;
The hare limp'd trembling through the frozen grass,
And silent was the flock in woolly fold:
Numb were the Beadsman's fingers, while he told
His rosary, and while his frosted breath,
Like pious incense from a censer old,

[16] The Mermaid, in Bread Street, Cheapside, was the favorite rendezvous of men of letters during the latter part of the reign of Queen Elizabeth and the first part of the seventeenth century.

[17] drink

[18] Written in 1818; published in 1820.

[19] Begun early in 1819; published in 1820. The proverbially cold Eve of St. Agnes is 20 January. A virgin martyr of the Catholic Church, St. Agnes is the patron saint of young girls, who, so the tradition went, could obtain visions of their future husbands by performing certain rites upon the sacred evening.

Seem'd taking flight for heaven, without a death,
Past the sweet Virgin's picture, while his prayer he saith.

II

His prayer he saith, this patient, holy man;
Then takes his lamp, and riseth from his knees,
And back returneth, meagre, barefoot, wan,
Along the chapel aisle by slow degrees:
The sculptur'd dead, on each side, seem to freeze,
Emprison'd in black, purgatorial rails:
Knights, ladies, praying in dumb orat'ries,
He passeth by; and his weak spirit fails
To think how they may ache in icy hoods and mails.

III

Northward he turneth through a little door,
And scarce three steps, ere Music's golden tongue
Flatter'd to tears this aged man and poor;
But no — already had his deathbell rung:
The joys of all his life were said and sung:
His was harsh penance on St. Agnes' Eve:
Another way he went, and soon among
Rough ashes sat he for his soul's reprieve,
And all night kept awake, for sinners' sake to grieve.

IV

That ancient Beadsman heard the prelude soft;
And so it chanc'd, for many a door was wide,
From hurry to and fro. Soon, up aloft,
The silver, snarling trumpets 'gan to chide:
The level chambers, ready with their pride,
Were glowing to receive a thousand guests:
The carved angels, ever eager-eyed,
Star'd, where upon their heads the cornice rests,
With hair blown back, and wings put cross-wise on their breasts.

V

At length burst in the argent revelry,
With plume, tiara, and all rich array,
Numerous as shadows haunting faerily
The brain, new stuff'd, in youth, with triumphs gay
Of old romance. These let us wish away,
And turn, sole-thoughted, to one Lady there,
Whose heart had brooded, all that wintry day,
On love, and wing'd St. Agnes' saintly care,
As she had heard old dames full many times declare.

VI

They told her how, upon St. Agnes' Eve,
Young virgins might have visions of delight.
And soft adorings from their loves receive
Upon the honey'd middle of the night,
If ceremonies due they did aright;
As, supperless to bed they must retire,
And couch supine their beauties, lilly white;
Nor look behind, nor sideways, but require
Of Heaven with upward eyes for all that they desire.

VII

Full of this whim was thoughtful Madeline:
The music, yearning like a God in pain,

She scarcely heard: her maiden eyes divine,
Fix'd on the floor, saw many a sweeping train
Pass by — she heeded not at all: in vain
Came many a tiptoe, amorous cavalier,
And back retir'd; not cool'd by high disdain,
But she saw not: her heart was otherwhere:
She sigh'd for Agnes' dreams, the sweetest of the year.

VIII

She danc'd along with vague, regardless eyes,
Anxious her lips, her breathing quick and short:
The hallow'd hour was near at hand: she sighs
Amid the timbrels, and the throng'd resort
Of whisperers in anger, or in sport;
'Mid looks of love, defiance, hate, and scorn,
Hoodwink'd with faery fancy; all amort,[20]
Save to St. Agnes and her lambs unshorn,[21]
And all the bliss to be before to-morrow morn.

IX

So, purposing each moment to retire,
She linger'd still. Meantime, across the moors,
Had come young Porphyro, with heart on fire
For Madeline. Beside the portal doors,
Buttress'd from moonlight, stands he, and implores
All saints to give him sight of Madeline,
But for one moment in the tedious hours,
That he might gaze and worship all unseen;
Perchance speak, kneel, touch, kiss — in sooth such things have been.

X

He ventures in: let no buzz'd whisper tell:
All eyes be muffled, or a hundred swords
Will storm his heart, Love's fev'rous citadel:
For him, those chambers held barbarian hordes,
Hyena foemen, and hot-blooded lords,
Whose very dogs would execrations howl
Against his lineage: not one breast affords
Him any mercy, in that mansion foul,
Save one old beldame, weak in body and in soul.

XI

Ah, happy chance! the aged creature came,
Shuffling along with ivory-headed wand,
To where he stood, hid from the torch's flame,
Behind a broad hall-pillar, far beyond
The sound of merriment and chorus bland:
He startled her; but soon she knew his face,
And grasp'd his fingers in her palsied hand,
Saying, 'Mercy, Porphyro! hie thee from this place:
'They are all here to-night, the whole blood-thirsty race!

XII

'Get hence! get hence! there's dwarfish Hildebrand;
'He had a fever late, and in the fit
'He cursed thee and thine, both house and land:
'Then there's that old Lord Maurice, not a whit

[20] dead

[21] On the anniversary of the martyrdom of St. Agnes two lambs are blessed, to the singing of the *Agnus Dei*. The lambs are then shorn, and the wool made into cloth by nuns.

'More tame for his gray hairs — Alas me! flit!
'Flit like a ghost away.' — 'Ah, Gossip dear,
'We 're safe enough; here in this arm-chair sit,
'And tell me how' — 'Good Saints! not here, not here;
'Follow me, child, or else these stones will be thy bier.'

XIII

He follow'd through a lowly arched way,
Brushing the cobwebs with his lofty plume,
And as she mutter'd 'Well-a — well-a-day!'
He found him in a little moonlight room,
Pale, lattic'd, chill, and silent as a tomb.
'Now tell me where is Madeline,' said he,
'O tell me, Angela, by the holy loom
'Which none but secret sisterhood may see,
'When they St. Agnes' wool are weaving piously.'

XIV

'St. Agnes! Ah! it is St. Agnes' Eve —
'Yet men will murder upon holy days:
'Thou must hold water in a witch's sieve,
'And be liege-lord of all the Elves and Fays,
'To venture so: it fills me with amaze
'To see thee, Porphyro! — St. Agnes' Eve!
'God's help! my lady fair the conjuror plays
'This very night: good angels her deceive!
'But let me laugh awhile, I've mickle [22] time to grieve.'

[22] much

XV

Feebly she laugheth in the languid moon,
While Porphyro upon her face doth look,
Like puzzled urchin on an aged crone
Who keepeth clos'd a wond'rous riddle-book,
As spectacled she sits in chimney nook.
But soon his eyes grew brilliant, when she told
His lady's purpose; and he scarce could brook
Tears, at the thought of those enchantments cold,
And Madeline asleep in lap of legends old.

XVI

Sudden a thought came like a full-blown rose,
Flushing his brow, and in his pained heart
Made purple riot: then doth he propose
A stratagem, that makes the beldame start:
'A cruel man and impious thou art:
'Sweet lady, let her pray, and sleep, and dream
'Alone with her good angels, far apart
'From wicked men like thee. Go, go! — I deem
'Thou canst not surely be the same that thou didst seem.'

XVII

'I will not harm her, by all saints I swear,'
Quoth Porphyro: 'O may I ne'er find grace
'When my weak voice shall whisper its last prayer,
'If one of her soft ringlets I displace,
'Or look with ruffian passion in her face:
'Good Angela, believe me by these tears;
'Or I will, even in a moment's space,
'Awake, with horrid shout, my foemen's ears,

'And beard them, though they be more fang'd than wolves and bears.'

XVIII

'Ah! why wilt thou affright a feeble soul?
'A poor, weak, palsy-stricken, churchyard thing,
'Whose passing-bell may ere the midnight toll;
'Whose prayers for thee, each morn and evening,
'Were never miss'd.'—Thus plaining, doth she bring
A gentler speech from burning Porphyro;
So woful, and of such deep sorrowing,
That Angela gives promise she will do
Whatever he shall wish, betide her weal or woe.

XIX

Which was, to lead him, in close secrecy,
Even to Madeline's chamber, and there hide
Him in a closet, of such privacy
That he might see her beauty unespied,
And win perhaps that night a peerless bride,
While legion'd faeries pac'd the coverlet,
And pale enchantment held her sleepy-eyed.
Never on such a night have lovers met,
Since Merlin paid his Demon all the monstrous debt.[23]

XX

'It shall be as thou wishest,' said the Dame:
'All cates [24] and dainties shall be stored there
'Quickly on this feast-night: by the tambour frame [25]
'Her own lute thou wilt see: no time to spare,
'For I am slow and feeble, and scarce dare
'On such a catering trust my dizzy head.
'Wait here, my child, with patience; kneel in prayer
'The while: Ah! thou must needs the lady wed,
'Or may I never leave my grave among the dead.'

XXI

So saying, she hobbled off with busy fear.
The lover's endless minutes slowly pass'd;
The dame return'd, and whisper'd in his ear
To follow her; with aged eyes aghast
From fright of dim espial. Safe at last,
Through many a dusky gallery, they gain
The maiden's chamber, silken, hush'd, and chaste;
Where Porphyro took covert, pleas'd amain.[26]
His poor guide hurried back with agues in her brain.

XXII

Her falt'ring hand upon the balustrade,
Old Angela was feeling for the stair,
When Madeline, St. Agnes' charmed maid,
Rose, like a mission'd spirit, unaware:
With silver taper's light, and pious care,
She turn'd, and down the aged gossip led
To a safe level matting. Now prepare,
Young Porphyro, for gazing on that bed;
She comes, she comes again, like ring-dove fray'd [27] and fled.

XXIII

Out went the taper as she hurried in;
Its little smoke, in pallid moonshine died:

[23] Merlin, the magician of Arthur's court, was represented by one legend as the son of a demon. He paid the 'debt' of his existence when he was destroyed by Vivien, who used a spell that he had taught her.
[24] delicacies
[25] An embroidery-frame shaped like a drum.

[26] exceedingly
[27] frightened

She clos'd the door, she panted, all akin
To spirits of the air, and visions wide:
No uttered syllable, or, woe betide!
But to her heart, her heart was voluble,
Paining with eloquence her balmy side;
As though a tongueless nightingale should swell
Her throat in vain, and die, heart-stifled, in her dell.

XXIV

A casement high and triple-arch'd there was,
All garlanded with carven imag'ries
Of fruits, and flowers, and bunches of knot-grass,
And diamonded with panes of quaint device,
Innumerable of stains and splendid dyes,
As are the tiger-moth's deep-damask'd wings;
And in the midst, 'mong thousand heraldries,
And twilight saints, and dim emblazonings,
A shielded scutcheon blush'd with blood of queens and kings.

XXV

Full on this casement shone the wintry moon,
And threw warm gules [28] on Madeline's fair breast,
As down she knelt for heaven's grace and boon;
Rose-bloom fell on her hands, together prest,
And on her silver cross soft amethyst,
And on her hair a glory, like a saint:
She seem'd a splendid angel, newly drest,
Save wings, for heaven: — Porphyro grew faint:
She knelt, so pure a thing, so free from mortal taint.

[28] blood-red (a term in heraldry)

XXVI

Anon his heart revives: her vespers done,
Of all its wreathed pearls her hair she frees;
Unclasps her warmed jewels one by one;
Loosens her fragrant boddice; by degrees
Her rich attire creeps rustling to her knees:
Half-hidden, like a mermaid in sea-weed,
Pensive awhile she dreams awake, and sees,
In fancy, fair St. Agnes in her bed,
But dares not look behind, or all the charm is fled.

XXVII

Soon, trembling in her soft and chilly nest,
In sort of wakeful swoon, perplex'd she lay,
Until the poppied warmth of sleep oppress'd
Her soothed limbs, and soul fatigued away;
Flown, like a thought, until the morrow-day;
Blissfully haven'd both from joy and pain;
Clasp'd like a missal where swart Paynims pray; [29]
Blinded alike from sunshine and from rain,
As though a rose should shut, and be a bud again.

XXVIII

Stol'n to this paradise, and so entranced,
Porphyro gazed upon her empty dress,
And listen'd to her breathing, if it chanced
To wake into a slumberous tenderness;
Which when he heard, that minute did he bless,
And breath'd himself: then from the closet crept,

[29] As tightly shut as a prayer book among pagans.

Noiseless as fear in a wide wilderness,
And over the hush'd carpet, silent, stept,
And 'tween the curtains peep'd, where, lo! — how fast she slept.

XXIX

Then by the bed-side, where the faded moon
Made a dim, silver twilight, soft he set
A table, and, half anguish'd, threw thereon
A cloth of woven crimson, gold, and jet: —
O for some drowsy Morphean amulet!
The boisterous, midnight, festive clarion,
The kettle-drum, and far-heard clarinet,
Affray his ears, though but in dying tone: —
The hall door shuts again, and all the noise is gone.

XXX

And still she slept an azure-lidded sleep,
In blanched linen, smooth, and lavender'd,
While he from forth the closet brought a heap
Of candied apple, quince, and plum, and gourd;
With jellies soother [30] than the creamy curd,
And lucent syrops, tinct with cinnamon;
Manna and dates, in argosy transferr'd
From Fez; and spiced dainties, every one,
From silken Samarcand to cedar'd Lebanon.

XXXI

These delicates he heap'd with glowing hand
On golden dishes and in baskets bright
Of wreathed silver: sumptuous they stand
In the retired quiet of the night,
Filling the chilly room with perfume light. —

[30] softer

'And now, my love, my seraph fair, awake!
'Thou art my heaven, and I thine eremite: [31]
'Open thine eyes, for meek St. Agnes' sake,
'Or I shall drowse beside thee, so my soul doth ache.'

XXXII

Thus whispering, his warm, unnerved arm
Sank in her pillow. Shaded was her dream
By the dusk curtains: — 'twas a midnight charm
Impossible to melt as iced stream:
The lustrous salvers in the moonlight gleam;
Broad golden fringe upon the carpet lies:
It seem'd he never, never could redeem
From such a stedfast spell his lady's eyes;
So mus'd awhile, entoil'd in woofed phantasies.

XXXIII

Awakening up, he took her hollow lute, —
Tumultuous, — and, in chords that tenderest be,
He play'd an ancient ditty, long since mute,
In Provence call'd, 'La belle dame sans mercy:' [32]
Close to her ear touching the melody; —
Wherewith disturb'd, she utter'd a soft moan:
He ceased — she panted quick — and suddenly
Her blue affrayed eyes wide open shone:
Upon his knees he sank, pale as smooth-sculptured stone.

[31] hermit (here, 'devoted follower')
[32] The Beautiful Lady without Pity. The poem is by Alain Chartier, court poet of Charles II of France. Keats saw it in an English translation attributed to Chaucer. See Keats's own poem of this title, p. 839.

XXXIV

Her eyes were open, but she still beheld,
Now wide awake, the vision of her sleep:
There was a painful change, that nigh expell'd
The blisses of her dream so pure and deep
At which fair Madeline began to weep,
And moan forth witless words with many a sigh;
While still her gaze on Porphyro would keep;
Who knelt, with joined hands and piteous eye,
Fearing to move or speak, she look'd so dreamingly.

XXXV

'Ah, Porphyro!' said she, 'but even now
'Thy voice was at sweet tremble in mine ear,
'Made tuneable with every sweetest vow;
'And those sad eyes were spiritual and clear:
'How chang'd thou art! how pallid, chill, and drear!
'Give me that voice again, my Porphyro,
'Those looks immortal, those complainings dear!
'Oh leave me not in this eternal woe,
'For if thou diest, my Love, I know not where to go.'

XXXVI

Beyond a mortal man impassion'd far
At these voluptuous accents, he arose,
Ethereal, flush'd, and like a throbbing star
Seen mid the sapphire heaven's deep repose;
Into her dream he melted, as the rose
Blendeth its odour with the violet, —
Solution sweet: meantime the frost-wind blows
Like Love's alarum pattering the sharp sleet
Against the window-panes; St. Agnes' moon hath set.

XXXVII

'Tis dark: quick pattereth the flaw-blown sleet:
'This is no dream, my bride, my Madeline!'
'Tis dark: the iced gusts still rave and beat:
'No dream, alas! alas! and woe is mine!
'Porphyro will leave me here to fade and pine. —
'Cruel! what traitor could thee hither bring?
'I curse not, for my heart is lost in thine,
'Though thou forsakest a deceived thing; —
'A dove forlorn and lost with sick unpruned wing.'

XXXVIII

'My Madeline! sweet dreamer! lovely bride!
'Say, may I be for aye thy vassal blest?
'Thy beauty's shield, heart-shap'd and vermeil dyed?
'Ah, silver shrine, here will I take my rest
'After so many hours of toil and quest,
'A famish'd pilgrim, — sav'd by miracle.
'Though I have found, I will not rob thy nest
'Saving of thy sweet self; if thou think'st well
'To trust, fair Madeline, to no rude infidel.

XXXIX

'Hark! 'tis an elfin-storm from faery land,
'Of haggard seeming, but a boon indeed:
'Arise — arise! the morning is at hand; —

'The bloated wassaillers will never heed: —
'Let us away, my love, with happy speed;
'There are no ears to hear, or eyes to see, —
'Drown'd all in Rhenish and the sleepy mead:
'Awake! arise! my love, and fearless be,
'For o'er the southern moors I have a home for thee.'

XL

She hurried at his words, beset with fears,
For there were sleeping dragons all around,
At glaring watch, perhaps, with ready spears —
Down the wide stairs a darkling way they found. —
In all the house was heard no human sound.
A chain-droop'd lamp was flickering by each door;
The arras, rich with horseman, hawk, and hound,
Flutter'd in the besieging wind's uproar;
And the long carpets rose along the gusty floor.

XLI

They glide, like phantoms, into the wide hall;
Like phantoms, to the iron porch, they glide;
Where lay the Porter, in uneasy sprawl,
With a huge empty flaggon by his side:
The wakeful bloodhound rose, and shook his hide,
But his sagacious eye an inmate owns:
By one, and one, the bolts full easy slide: —
The chains lie silent on the footworn stones; —
The key turns, and the door upon its hinges groans.

XLII

And they are gone: aye, ages long ago
These lovers fled away into the storm.
That night the Baron dreamt of many a woe,
And all his warrior-guests, with shade and form
Of witch, and demon, and large coffin-worm,
Were long be-nightmar'd. Angela the old
Died palsy-twitch'd, with meagre face deform;
The Beadsman, after thousand aves told,
For aye unsought for slept among his ashes cold.

La Belle Dame sans Merci [33]

O WHAT can ail thee, knight-at-arms,
Alone and palely loitering?
The sedge has withered from the lake,
And no birds sing.

O what can ail thee, knight-at-arms,
So haggard and so woe-begone?
The squirrel's granary is full,
And the harvest's done.

I see a lilly on thy brow
With anguish moist and fever dew;
And on thy cheeks a fading rose
Fast withereth too.

I met a lady in the meads,
Full beautiful — a faery's child,
Her hair was long, her foot was light,
And her eyes were wild.

I made a garland for her head,
And bracelets too, and fragrant zone; [34]
She look'd at me as she did love,
And made sweet moan.

[33] Written in the spring of 1819; published by Leigh Hunt in *The Indicator*, 1820. The version printed here is an earlier one, first published in 1888. The title, but not the content, Keats owes to the poem by Alain Chartier (see note 32, p. 837).

[34] girdle

I set her on my pacing steed,
And nothing else saw all day long,
For sidelong would she bend, and sing
A faery's song.

She found me roots of relish sweet,
And honey wild, and manna dew,
And sure in language strange she said,
'I love thee true!'

She took me to her elfin grot,
And there she wept and sigh'd full sore,
And there I shut her wild, wild eyes
With kisses four.

And there she lulléd me asleep
And there I dream'd, ah woe betide!
The latest dream I ever dream'd
On the cold hill side.

I saw pale kings, and princes too,
Pale warriors, death-pale were they all;
They cried — 'La belle Dame sans Merci
Hath thee in thrall!'

I saw their starved lips in the gloam
With horrid warning gapéd wide,
And I awoke and found me here
On the cold hill's side.

And this is why I sojourn here
Alone and palely loitering,
Though the sedge is wither'd from the lake,
And no birds sing.

To Sleep [35]

O SOFT embalmer of the still midnight,
Shutting, with careful fingers and benign,
Our gloom-pleas'd eyes, embower'd from the light,
Enshaded in forgetfulness divine:
O soothest Sleep! if so it please thee, close
In midst of this thine hymn my willing eyes,
Or wait the 'Amen,' ere thy poppy throws
Around my bed its lulling charities.
Then save me, or the passed day will shine
Upon my pillow, breeding many woes, —
Save me from curious Conscience, that still lords
Its strength for darkness, burrowing like a mole;
Turn the key deftly in the oiled wards,
And seal the hushed Casket of my Soul.

[35] Written in 1819; published in 1848.

Ode on Melancholy [36]

I

No, no, go not to Lethe, neither twist
Wolf's-bane, tight-rooted, for its poisonous wine;
Nor suffer thy pale forehead to be kiss'd
By nightshade, ruby grape of Proserpine; [37]
Make not your rosary of yew-berries,
Nor let the beetle, nor the death-moth be
Your mournful Psyche,[38] nor the downy owl
A partner in your sorrow's mysteries;
For shade to shade will come too drowsily,
And drown the wakeful anguish of the soul.

II

But when the melancholy fit shall fall
Sudden from heaven like a weeping cloud,
That fosters the droop-headed flowers all,
And hides the green hill in an April shroud;
Then glut thy sorrow on a morning rose,
Or on the rainbow of the salt sand-wave,
Or on the wealth of globed peonies;
Or if thy mistress some rich anger shows,
Emprison her soft hand, and let her rave,
And feed deep, deep upon her peerless eyes.

[36] Written in the spring of 1819; published in 1820.
[37] Queen of the lower regions.
[38] The soul, sometimes represented as a butterfly.

III

She dwells with Beauty — Beauty that must die;
And Joy, whose hand is ever at his lips
Bidding adieu; and aching Pleasure nigh,
Turning to Poison while the bee-mouth sips:
Ay, in the very temple of delight
Veil'd Melancholy has her sovran shrine,
Though seen of none save him whose strenuous tongue
Can burst Joy's grape against his palate fine;
His soul shall taste the sadness of her might,
And be among her cloudy trophies hung.

Ode to a Nightingale [39]

I

My heart aches, and a drowsy numbness pains
My sense, as though of hemlock [40] I had drunk,
Or emptied some dull opiate to the drains
One minute past, and Lethe-wards had sunk:
'Tis not through envy of thy happy lot,
But being too happy in thine happiness, —
That thou, light-wingèd Dryad of the trees,
In some melodious plot
Of beechen green, and shadows numberless,
Singest of summer in full-throated ease.

II

O, for a draught of vintage! that hath been
Cool'd a long age in the deep-delved earth,
Tasting of Flora and the country green,
Dance, and Provençal song, and sunburnt mirth!
O for a beaker full of the warm South,
Full of the true, the blushful Hippocrene,[41]
With beaded bubbles winking at the brim,
And purple-stained mouth;
That I might drink, and leave the world unseen,
And with thee fade away into the forest dim:

III

Fade far away, dissolve, and quite forget
What thou among the leaves hast never known,
The weariness, the fever, and the fret
Here, where men sit and hear each other groan;
Where palsy shakes a few, sad, last gray hairs,
Where youth grows pale, and spectre-thin, and dies;
Where but to think is to be full of sorrow
And leaden-eyed despairs,
Where Beauty cannot keep her lustrous eyes,
Or new Love pine at them beyond to-morrow.

IV

Away! away! for I will fly to thee,
Not charioted by Bacchus and his pards,[42]
But on the viewless wings of Poesy,
Though the dull brain perplexes and retards:
Already with thee! tender is the night,
And haply the Queen-moon is on her throne,
Cluster'd around by all her starry Fays;
But here there is no light,

[39] Written in May 1819; first published in July 1819 in *Annals of the Fine Arts* and included in the 1820 volume. Haydon in a letter to Miss Mitford says: 'The death of his brother [in December 1818] wounded him deeply, and it appeared to me from that hour he began to droop. He wrote his exquisite "Ode to the Nightingale" at this time, and as we were one evening walking in the Kilburn meadows he repeated it to me . . . in a low, tremulous undertone which affected me extremely.'

[40] poison

[41] The fountain of the Muses on Mount Helicon.

[42] leopards

Save what from heaven is with the breezes blown
Through verdurous glooms and winding mossy ways.

V

I cannot see what flowers are at my feet,
Nor what soft incense hangs upon the boughs,
But, in embalmed darkness, guess each sweet
Wherewith the seasonable month endows
The grass, the thicket, and the fruit-tree wild;
White hawthorn, and the pastoral eglantine;
Fast fading violets cover'd up in leaves;
And mid-May's eldest child,
The coming musk-rose, full of dewy wine,
The murmurous haunt of flies on summer eves.

VI

Darkling I listen; and, for many a time
I have been half in love with easeful Death,
Call'd him soft names in many a mused rhyme,
To take into the air my quiet breath;
Now more than ever seems it rich to die,
To cease upon the midnight with no pain,
While thou art pouring forth thy soul abroad
In such an ecstasy!
Still wouldst thou sing, and I have ears in vain —
To thy high requiem become a sod.

VII

Thou wast not born for death, immortal Bird!
No hungry generations tread thee down;
The voice I hear this passing night was heard
In ancient days by emperor and clown:
Perhaps the self-same song that found a path
Through the sad heart of Ruth,[43] when, sick for home,
She stood in tears amid the alien corn;
The same that oft-times hath
Charm'd magic casements, opening on the foam
Of perilous seas, in faery lands forlorn.

VIII

Forlorn! the very word is like a bell
To toll me back from thee to my sole self!
Adieu! the fancy cannot cheat so well
As she is fam'd to do, deceiving elf.
Adieu! adieu! thy plaintive anthem fades
Past the near meadows, over the still stream,
Up the hill-side; and now 'tis buried deep
In the next valley-glades:
Was it a vision, or a waking dream?
Fled is that music: — Do I wake or sleep?

Ode on a Grecian Urn [44]

I

Thou still unravish'd bride of quietness,
Thou foster-child of silence and slow time,
Sylvan historian, who canst thus express
A flowery tale more sweetly than our rhyme:
What leaf-fring'd legend haunts about thy shape
Of deities or mortals, or of both,
In Tempe or the dales of Arcady?
What men or gods are these? What maidens loth?

---

[43] See *Ruth*, ii.

[44] Written in the spring of 1819; first published in January 1820 in *Annals of the Fine Arts* and included in the 1820 volume. The inspiration for the poem came partly from the Elgin Marbles, which Keats saw in the British Museum.

What mad pursuit? What struggle to escape?
What pipes and timbrels? What wild ecstasy?

II

Heard melodies are sweet, but those unheard
Are sweeter; therefore, ye soft pipes, play on;
Not to the sensual ear, but, more endear'd,
Pipe to the spirit ditties of no tone:
Fair youth, beneath the trees, thou canst not leave
Thy song, nor ever can those trees be bare;
Bold Lover, never, never canst thou kiss,
Though winning near the goal — yet, do not grieve;
She cannot fade, though thou hast not thy bliss,
For ever wilt thou love, and she be fair!

III

Ah, happy, happy boughs! that cannot shed
Your leaves, nor ever bid the Spring adieu;
And, happy melodist, unwearied,
For ever piping songs for ever new;
More happy love! more happy, happy love!
For ever warm and still to be enjoy'd,
For ever panting, and for ever young;
All breathing human passion far above,
That leaves a heart high-sorrowful and cloy'd,
A burning forehead, and a parching tongue.

IV

Who are these coming to the sacrifice?
To what green altar, O mysterious priest,
Lead'st thou that heifer lowing at the skies,
And all her silken flanks with garlands drest?
What little town by river or sea shore,
Or mountain-built with peaceful citadel,
Is emptied of this folk, this pious morn?
And, little town, thy streets for evermore
Will silent be; and not a soul to tell
Why thou art desolate, can e'er return.

V

O Attic shape! Fair attitude! with brede [45]
Of marble men and maidens overwrought,
With forest branches and the trodden weed;
Thou, silent form, dost tease us out of thought
As doth eternity: Cold Pastoral!
When old age shall this generation waste,
Thou shalt remain, in midst of other woe
Than ours, a friend to man, to whom thou say'st,
'Beauty is truth, truth beauty,' — that is all
Ye know on earth, and all ye need to know.

Ode to Psyche [46]

O Goddess! hear these tuneless numbers, wrung
By sweet enforcement and remembrance dear,
And pardon that thy secrets should be sung
Even into thine own soft-conched ear:
Surely I dreamt to-day, or did I see
The winged Psyche with awaken'd eyes?
I wander'd in a forest thoughtlessly,
And, on the sudden, fainting with surprise,
Saw two fair creatures, couched side by side

[45] embroidery (braid)

[46] Written in the spring of 1819; published in 1820. Keats wrote in a letter to George and Georgiana Keats: 'The following poem . . . is the first and the only one with which I have taken even moderate pains. I have for the most part dash'd off my lines in a hurry. This I have done leisurely — I think it reads the more richly for it . . . You must recollect that Psyche was not embodied as a goddess before the time of Apuleius the Platonist, who lived after the Augustan age, and consequently the goddess was never worshiped or sacrificed to with any of the ancient fervour — and perhaps never thought of in the old religion — I am more orthodox than to let a heathen Goddess be so neglected.'

In deepest grass, beneath the whisp'ring roof
Of leaves and trembled blossoms, where there ran
A brooklet, scarce espied:

'Mid hush'd, cool-rooted flowers, fragrant-eyed,
Blue, silver-white, and budded Tyrian,
They lay calm-breathing on the bedded grass;
Their arms embraced, and their pinions too;
Their lips touch'd not, but had not bade adieu,
As if disjoined by soft-handed slumber,
And ready still past kisses to outnumber
At tender eye-dawn of aurorean love:
The winged boy [47] I knew;
But who wast thou, O happy, happy dove?
His Psyche true!

O latest born and loveliest vision far
Of all Olympus' faded hierarchy!
Fairer than Phœbe's sapphire-region'd star,[48]
Or Vesper,[49] amorous glow-worm of the sky;
Fairer than these, though temple thou hast none,
Nor altar heap'd with flowers;
Nor virgin-choir to make delicious moan
Upon the midnight hours;
No voice, no lute, no pipe, no incense sweet
From chain-swung censer teeming;
No shrine, no grove, no oracle, no heat
Of pale-mouth'd prophet dreaming.

O brightest! though too late for antique vows,
Too, too late for the fond believing lyre,
When holy were the haunted forest boughs,
Holy the air, the water, and the fire;

[47] Cupid. For an account of the story of Cupid and Psyche, see Walter Pater's translation in *Marius the Epicurean*, William Morris's *The Earthly Paradise*, or the *Eros and Psyche* of Robert Bridges.

[48] The moon. Phoebe is Artemis.

[49] Venus, the Evening Star.

Yet even in these days so far retir'd
From happy pieties, thy lucent fans,[50]
Fluttering among the faint Olympians,
I see, and sing, by my own eyes inspir'd.
So let me be thy choir, and make a moan
Upon the midnight hours;
Thy voice, thy lute, thy pipe, thy incense sweet
From swinged censer teeming;
Thy shrine, thy grove, thy oracle, thy heat
Of pale-mouth'd prophet dreaming.

Yes, I will be thy priest, and build a fane
In some untrodden region of my mind,
Where branched thoughts, new grown with pleasant pain,
Instead of pines shall murmur in the wind:
Far, far around shall those dark-cluster'd trees
Fledge the wild-ridged mountains steep by steep;
And there by zephyrs, streams, and birds, and bees,
The moss-lain Dryads shall be lull'd to sleep;
And in the midst of this wide quietness
A rosy sanctuary will I dress
With the wreath'd trellis of a working brain,
With buds, and bells, and stars without a name,
With all the gardener Fancy e'er could feign,
Who breeding flowers, will never breed the same:
And there shall be for thee all soft delight
That shadowy thought can win,
A bright torch, and a casement ope at night,
To let the warm Love in!

To Autumn [51]

I

SEASON of mists and mellow fruitfulness,
Close bosom-friend of the maturing sun;

[50] translucent wings

[51] Written in September 1819; published in 1820.

Conspiring with him how to load and bless
With fruit the vines that round the thatch-eves run;
To bend with apples the moss'd cottage-trees,
And fill all fruit with ripeness to the core;
To swell the gourd, and plump the hazel shells
With a sweet kernel; to set budding more,
And still more, later flowers for the bees,
Until they think warm days will never cease,
For Summer has o'er-brimm'd their clammy cells.

II

Who hath not seen thee oft amid thy store?
Sometimes whoever seeks abroad may find
Thee sitting careless on a granary floor,
Thy hair soft-lifted by the winnowing wind;
Or on a half-reap'd furrow sound asleep,
Drows'd with the fume of poppies, while thy hook
Spares the next swath and all its twined flowers:
And sometimes like a gleaner thou dost keep
Steady thy laden head across a brook;
Or by a cyder-press, with patient look,
Thou watchest the last oozings hours by hours.

III

Where are the songs of Spring? Ay, where are they?
Think not of them, thou hast thy music too, —
While barred clouds bloom the soft-dying day,
And touch the stubble-plains with rosy hue;
Then in a wailful choir the small gnats mourn
Among the river sallows,[52] borne aloft
Or sinking as the light wind lives or dies;
And full-grown lambs loud bleat from hilly bourn;
Hedge-crickets sing; and now with treble soft
The red-breast whistles from a garden-croft;
And gathering swallows twitter in the skies.

LAMIA [53]

Part I

Upon a time, before the faery broods
Drove Nymph and Satyr from the prosperous woods,
Before king Oberon's bright diadem,
Sceptre, and mantle, clasp'd with dewy gem,
Frighted away the Dryads and the Fauns
From rushes green, and brakes, and cowslip'd lawns,
The ever-smitten Hermes empty left
His golden throne, bent warm on amorous theft:
From high Olympus had he stolen light,

[52] willows

[53] Written in 1819; published in 1820. In a note to the poem on its first publication Keats gave his source: 'Philostratus in his fourth book *de Vita Apollonii* [concerning the life of Apollonius], hath a memorable instance in this kind, which I may not omit, of one Menippus Lycius, a young man twenty-five years of age, that going betwixt Cenchreas and Corinth, met such a phantasm in the habit of a fair gentlewoman, which taking him by the hand, carried him home to her house, in the suburbs of Corinth, and told him she was a Phœnician by birth, and if he would tarry with her, he should hear her sing and play, and drink such wine as never any drank, and no man should molest him; but she, being fair and lovely, would live and die with him, that was fair and lovely to behold. The young man, a philosopher, otherwise staid and discreet, able to moderate his passions, though not this of love, tarried with her a while to his great content, and at last married her, to whose wedding, amongst other guests, came Apollonius; who, by some probable conjectures, found her out to be a serpent, a lamia; and that all her furniture was, like Tantalus' gold, described by Homer, no substance but mere illusions. When she saw herself described, she wept, and desired Apollonius to be silent, but he would not be moved, and thereupon she, plate, house, and all that was in it, vanished in an instant: many thousands took notice of this fact, for it was done in the midst of Greece.' (Burton's *Anatomy of Melancholy*, pt. III, sec. ii, memb. 1, subs. i).

On this side of Jove's clouds, to escape the sight
Of his great summoner, and made retreat
Into a forest on the shores of Crete.
For somewhere in that sacred island dwelt
A nymph, to whom all hoofed Satyrs knelt;
At whose white feet the languid Tritons poured
Pearls, while on land they wither'd and adored.
Fast by the springs where she to bathe was wont,
And in those meads where sometime she might haunt,
Were strewn rich gifts, unknown to any Muse,
Though Fancy's casket were unlock'd to choose.
Ah, what a world of love was at her feet!
So Hermes thought, and a celestial heat
Burnt from his winged heels to either ear,
That from a whiteness, as the lilly clear,
Blush'd into roses 'mid his golden hair,
Fallen in jealous curls about his shoulders bare.

From vale to vale, from wood to wood, he flew,
Breathing upon the flowers his passion new,
And wound with many a river to its head,
To find where this sweet nymph prepar'd her secret bed:
In vain; the sweet nymph might nowhere be found,
And so he rested, on the lonely ground,
Pensive, and full of painful jealousies
Of the Wood-Gods, and even the very trees.
There as he stood, he heard a mournful voice,
Such as once heard, in gentle heart, destroys
All pain but pity: thus the lone voice spake:
'When from this wreathed tomb shall I awake!
'When move in a sweet body fit for life,
'And love, and pleasure, and the ruddy strife
'Of hearts and lips! Ah, miserable me!'
The God, dove-footed, glided silently
Round bush and tree, soft-brushing, in his speed,
The taller grasses and full-flowering weed,
Until he found a palpitating snake,
Bright, and cirque-couchant [54] in a dusky brake.

She was a gordian [55] shape of dazzling hue,
Vermilion-spotted, golden, green, and blue;
Striped like a zebra, freckled like a pard,
Eyed like a peacock, and all crimson barr'd;
And full of silver moons, that, as she breathed,
Dissolv'd, or brighter shone, or interwreathed
Their lustres with the gloomier tapestries —
So rainbow-sided, touch'd with miseries,
She seem'd, at once, some penanced lady elf,
Some demon's mistress, or the demon's self.
Upon her crest she wore a wannish fire
Sprinkled with stars, like Ariadne's tiar: [56]
Her head was serpent, but ah, bitter-sweet!
She had a woman's mouth with all its pearls complete:
And for her eyes: what could such eyes do there
But weep, and weep, that they were born so fair?
As Proserpine still weeps for her Sicilian air.
Her throat was serpent, but the words she spake
Came, as through bubbling honey, for Love's sake,
And thus; while Hermes on his pinions lay,
Like a stoop'd falcon ere he takes his prey.

[54] lying coiled
[55] knotted
[56] A tiara, or crown, of seven stars, which Bacchus gave to Ariadne. After her death it became a constellation.

'Fair Hermes, crown'd with feathers, fluttering light,
'I had a splendid dream of thee last night:
'I saw thee sitting, on a throne of gold,
'Among the Gods, upon Olympus old,
'The only sad one; for thou didst not hear
'The soft, lute-finger'd Muses chaunting clear,
'Nor even Apollo when he sang alone,
'Deaf to his throbbing throat's long, long melodious moan.
'I dreamt I saw thee, robed in purple flakes,
'Break amorous through the clouds, as morning breaks,
'And, swiftly as a bright Phœbean dart,
'Strike for the Cretan isle; and here thou art!
'Too gentle Hermes, hast thou found the maid?'
Whereat the star of Lethe [57] not delay'd
His rosy eloquence, and thus inquired:
'Thou smooth-lipp'd serpent, surely high inspired!
'Thou beauteous wreath, with melancholy eyes,
'Possess whatever bliss thou canst devise,
'Telling me only where my nymph is fled,—
'Where she doth breathe!' 'Bright planet, thou hast said,'
Return'd the snake, 'but seal with oaths, fair God!'
'I swear,' said Hermes, 'by my serpent rod,
'And by thine eyes, and by thy starry crown!'
Light flew his earnest words, among the blossoms blown.
Then thus again the brilliance feminine:
'Too frail of heart! for this lost nymph of thine,
'Free as the air, invisibly, she strays
'About these thornless wilds; her pleasant days
'She tastes unseen; unseen her nimble feet
'Leave traces in the grass and flowers sweet;
'From weary tendrils, and bow'd branches green,
'She plucks the fruit unseen, she bathes unseen:
'And by my power is her beauty veil'd
'To keep it unaffronted, unassail'd
'By the love-glances of unlovely eyes,
'Of Satyrs, Fauns, and blear'd Silenus' sighs.
'Pale grew her immortality, for woe
'Of all these lovers, and she grieved so
'I took compassion on her, bade her steep
'Her hair in weïrd syrops, that would keep
'Her loveliness invisible, yet free
'To wander as she loves, in liberty.
'Thou shalt behold her, Hermes, thou alone,
'If thou wilt, as thou swearest, grant my boon!'
Then, once again, the charmed God began
An oath, and through the serpent's ears it ran
Warm, tremulous, devout, psalterian.[58]
Ravish'd, she lifted her Circean head,
Blush'd a live damask, and swift-lisping said,
'I was a woman, let me have once more
'A woman's shape, and charming as before.
'I love a youth of Corinth—O the bliss!
'Give me my woman's form, and place me where he is.
'Stoop, Hermes, let me breathe upon thy brow,
'And thou shalt see thy sweet nymph even now.'
The God on half-shut feathers sank serene,
She breath'd upon his eyes, and swift was seen
Of both the guarded nymph near-smiling on the green.
It was no dream; or say a dream it was,
Real are the dreams of Gods, and smoothly pass
Their pleasures in a long immortal dream.

[57] Hermes had as one of his duties the leading of the souls of the dead to Hades.

[58] musical

One warm, flush'd moment, hovering, it might seem
Dash'd by the wood-nymph's beauty, so he burn'd;
Then, lighting on the printless verdure, turn'd
To the swoon'd serpent, and with languid arm,
Delicate, put to proof the lythe Caducean [59] charm.
So done, upon the nymph his eyes he bent
Full of adoring tears and blandishment,
And towards her stept: she, like a moon in wane,
Faded before him, cower'd, nor could restrain
Her fearful sobs, self-folding like a flower
That faints into itself at evening hour:
But the God fostering her chilled hand,
She felt the warmth, her eyelids open'd bland,
And, like new flowers at morning song of bees,
Bloom'd, and gave up her honey to the lees.
Into the green-recessed woods they flew;
Nor grew they pale, as mortal lovers do.

Left to herself, the serpent now began
To change; her elfin blood in madness ran,
Her mouth foam'd, and the grass, therewith besprent,
Wither'd at dew so sweet and virulent;
Her eyes in torture fix'd, and anguish drear,
Hot, glaz'd, and wide, with lid-lashes all sear,
Flash'd phosphor and sharp sparks, without one cooling tear.
The colours all inflam'd throughout her train,
She writh'd about, convuls'd with scarlet pain:
A deep volcanian yellow took the place
Of all her milder-mooned body's grace;
And, as the lava ravishes the mead,
Spoilt all her silver mail, and golden brede;
Made gloom of all her frecklings, streaks and bars,
Eclips'd her crescents, and lick'd up her stars:
So that, in moments few, she was undrest
Of all her sapphires, greens, and amethyst,
And rubious-argent: of all these bereft,
Nothing but pain and ugliness were left.
Still shone her crown; that vanish'd, also she
Melted and disappear'd as suddenly;
And in the air, her new voice luting soft,
Cried, 'Lycius! gentle Lycius!' — Borne aloft
With the bright mists about the mountains hoar
These words dissolv'd: Crete's forests heard no more.

Whither fled Lamia, now a lady bright,
A full-born beauty new and exquisite?
She fled into that valley they pass o'er
Who go to Corinth from Cenchreas' shore;
And rested at the foot of those wild hills,
The rugged founts of the Peræan rills,
And of that other ridge whose barren back
Stretches, with all its mist and cloudy rack,
South-westward to Cleone. There she stood
About a young bird's flutter from a wood,
Fair, on a sloping green of mossy tread,
By a clear pool, wherein she passioned
To see herself escap'd from so sore ills,
While her robes flaunted with the daffodils.

Ah, happy Lycius! — for she was a maid
More beautiful than ever twisted braid,
Or sigh'd, or blush'd, or on spring-flowered lea
Spread a green kirtle to the minstrelsy:
A virgin purest lipp'd, yet in the lore
Of love deep learned to the red heart's core:
Not one hour old, yet of sciential brain
To unperplex bliss from its neighbour pain;
Define their pettish limits, and estrange

[59] Caduceus was the name of Hermes' magic wand.

Their points of contact, and swift counter-change;
Intrigue with the specious chaos, and dispart
Its most ambiguous atoms with sure art;
As though in Cupid's college she had spent
Sweet days a lovely graduate, still unshent,[60]
And kept his rosy terms in idle languishment.

Why this fair creature chose so faerily
By the wayside to linger, we shall see;
But first 'tis fit to tell how she could muse
And dream, when in the serpent prison-house,
Of all she list, strange or magnificent:
How, ever, where she will'd, her spirit went;
Whether to faint Elysium, or where
Down through tress-lifting waves the Nereids fair
Wind into Thetis' bower by many a pearly stair;
Or where God Bacchus drains his cups divine,
Stretch'd out, at ease, beneath a glutinous pine;
Or where in Pluto's gardens palatine[61]
Mulciber's columns gleam in far piazzian line.
And sometimes into cities she would send
Her dream, with feast and rioting to blend;
And once, while among mortals dreaming thus,
She saw the young Corinthian Lycius
Charioting foremost in the envious race,
Like a young Jove with calm uneager face,
And fell into a swooning love of him.
Now on the moth-time of that evening dim
He would return that way, as well she knew,
To Corinth from the shore; for freshly blew
The eastern soft wind, and his galley now
Grated the quaystones with her brazen prow
In port Cenchreas, from Egina isle
Fresh anchor'd; whither he had been awhile
To sacrifice to Jove, whose temple there
Waits with high marble doors for blood and incense rare.
Jove heard his vows, and better'd his desire;
For by some freakful chance he made retire
From his companions, and set forth to walk,
Perhaps grown wearied of their Corinth talk;
Over the solitary hills he fared,
Thoughtless at first, but ere eve's star appeared
His phantasy was lost, where reason fades,
In the calm'd twilight of Platonic shades.
Lamia beheld him coming, near, more near —
Close to her passing, in indifference drear,
His silent sandals swept the mossy green;
So neighbour'd to him, and yet so unseen
She stood: he pass'd, shut up in mysteries,
His mind wrapp'd like his mantle, while her eyes
Follow'd his steps, and her neck regal white
Turn'd — syllabling thus, 'Ah, Lycius bright,
'And will you leave me on the hills alone?
'Lycius, look back! and be some pity shown.'
He did; not with cold wonder fearingly,
But Orpheus-like at an Eurydice;
For so delicious were the words she sung,
It seem'd he had lov'd them a whole summer long:
And soon his eyes had drunk her beauty up,
Leaving no drop in the bewildering cup,
And still the cup was full, — while he, afraid
Lest she should vanish ere his lip had paid

[60] unharmed
[61] palatial

Due adoration, thus began to adore;
Her soft look growing coy, she saw his chain so sure:
'Leave thee alone! Look back! Ah, Goddess, see
'Whether my eyes can ever turn from thee!
'For pity do not this sad heart belie —
'Even as thou vanishest so shall I die.
'Stay! though a Naiad of the rivers, stay!
'To thy far wishes will thy streams obey:
'Stay! though the greenest woods be thy domain,
'Alone they can drink up the morning rain:
'Though a descended Pleiad, will not one
'Of thine harmonious sisters keep in tune
'Thy spheres, and as thy silver proxy shine?
'So sweetly to these ravish'd ears of mine
'Came thy sweet greeting, that if thou shouldst fade
'Thy memory will waste me to a shade: —
'For pity do not melt!' — 'If I should stay,'
Said Lamia, 'here, upon this floor of clay,
'And pain my steps upon these flowers too rough,
'What canst thou say or do of charm enough
'To dull the nice remembrance of my home?
'Thou canst not ask me with thee here to roam
'Over these hills and vales, where no joy is, —
'Empty of immortality and bliss!
'Thou art a scholar, Lycius, and must know
'That finer spirits cannot breathe below
'In human climes, and live: Alas! poor youth,
'What taste of purer air hast thou to soothe
'My essence? What serener palaces,
'Where I may all my many senses please,
'And by mysterious sleights a hundred thirsts appease?
'It cannot be — Adieu!' So said, she rose
Tiptoe with white arms spread. He, sick to lose
The amorous promise of her lone complain,
Swoon'd, murmuring of love, and pale with pain.
The cruel lady, without any show
Of sorrow for her tender favourite's woe,
But rather, if her eyes could brighter be,
With brighter eyes and slow amenity,
Put her new lips to his, and gave afresh
The life she had so tangled in her mesh:
And as he from one trance was wakening
Into another, she began to sing,
Happy in beauty, life, and love, and every thing,
A song of love, too sweet for earthly lyres,
While, like held breath, the stars drew in their panting fires.
And then she whisper'd in such trembling tone,
As those who, safe together met alone
For the first time through many anguish'd days,
Use other speech than looks; bidding him raise
His drooping head, and clear his soul of doubt,
For that she was a woman, and without
Any more subtle fluid in her veins
Than throbbing blood, and that the self-same pains
Inhabited her frail-strung heart as his.
And next she wonder'd how his eyes could miss
Her face so long in Corinth, where, she said,
She dwelt but half retir'd, and there had led
Days happy as the gold coin could invent
Without the aid of love; yet in content
Till she saw him, as once she pass'd him by,
Where 'gainst a column he lent thoughtfully
At Venus' temple porch, 'mid baskets heap'd
Of amorous herbs and flowers, newly reap'd

Late on that eve, as 'twas the night before
The Adonian feast; whereof she saw no more,
But wept alone those days, for why should she adore?
Lycius from death awoke into amaze,
To see her still, and singing so sweet lays;
Then from amaze into delight he fell
To hear her whisper woman's lore so well;
And every word she spake entic'd him on
To unperplex'd delight and pleasure known.
Let the mad poets say whate'er they please
Of the sweets of Faeries, Peris,[62] Goddesses,
There is not such a treat among them all,
Haunters of cavern, lake, and waterfall,
As a real woman, lineal indeed
From Pyrrha's pebbles[63] or old Adam's seed.
Thus gentle Lamia judg'd, and judg'd aright,
That Lycius could not love in half a fright,
So threw the goddess off, and won his heart
More pleasantly by playing woman's part,
With no more awe than what her beauty gave,
That, while it smote, still guaranteed to save.
Lycius to all made eloquent reply,
Marrying to every word a twinborn sigh;
And last, pointing to Corinth, ask'd her sweet,
If 'twas too far that night for her soft feet.
The way was short, for Lamia's eagerness
Made, by a spell, the triple league decrease
To a few paces; not at all surmised
By blinded Lycius, so in her comprized.
They pass'd the city gates, he knew not how,
So noiseless, and he never thought to know.

As men talk in a dream, so Corinth all,
Throughout her palaces imperial,
And all her populous streets and temples lewd,
Mutter'd, like tempest in the distance brew'd,
To the wide-spreaded night above her towers.
Men, women, rich and poor, in the cool hours,
Shuffled their sandals o'er the pavement white,
Companion'd or alone; while many a light
Flared, here and there, from wealthy festivals,
And threw their moving shadows on the walls,
Or found them cluster'd in the corniced shade
Of some arch'd temple door, or dusky colonnade.

Muffling his face, of greeting friends in fear,
Her fingers he press'd hard, as one came near
With curl'd gray beard, sharp eyes, and smooth bald crown,
Slow-stepp'd, and robed in philosophic gown:
Lycius shrank closer, as they met and past,
Into his mantle, adding wings to haste,
While hurried Lamia trembled: 'Ah,' said he,
'Why do you shudder, love, so ruefully?
'Why does your tender palm dissolve in dew?'—
'I'm wearied,' said fair Lamia: 'tell me who
'Is that old man? I cannot bring to mind
'His features:—Lycius! wherefore did you blind
'Yourself from his quick eyes?' Lycius replied,
''Tis Apollonius sage, my trusty guide
'And good instructor; but to-night he seems
'The ghost of folly haunting my sweet dreams.'

---

[62] In Persian mythology, one descended from fallen angels.

[63] After the flood Pyrrha and Deucalion were said to have re-peopled the world by casting over their shoulders stones from which sprang up human beings.

While yet he spake they had arrived before
A pillar'd porch, with lofty portal door,
Where hung a silver lamp, whose phosphor glow
Reflected in the slabbed steps below,
Mild as a star in water; for so new,
And so unsullied was the marble's hue,
So through the crystal polish, liquid fine,
Ran the dark veins, that none but feet divine
Could e'er have touch'd there. Sounds Æolian
Breath'd from the hinges, as the ample span
Of the wide doors disclos'd a place unknown
Some time to any, but those two alone,
And a few Persian mutes, who that same year
Were seen about the markets: none knew where
They could inhabit; the most curious
Were foil'd, who watch'd to trace them to their house:
And but the flitter-winged verse must tell,
For truth's sake, what woe afterwards befel,
'Twould humour many a heart to leave them thus,
Shut from the busy world of more incredulous.

Part II

Love in a hut, with water and a crust,
Is — Love, forgive us! — cinders, ashes, dust;
Love in a palace is perhaps at last
More grievous torment than a hermit's fast: —
That is a doubtful tale from faery land,
Hard for the non-elect to understand.
Had Lycius liv'd to hand his story down,
He might have given the moral a fresh frown,
Or clench'd it quite: but too short was their bliss
To breed distrust and hate, that make the soft voice hiss.
Beside, there, nightly, with terrific glare,
Love, jealous grown of so complete a pair,
Hover'd and buzz'd his wings, with fearful roar,
Above the lintel of their chamber door,
And down the passage cast a glow upon the floor.

For all this came a ruin: side by side
They were enthroned, in the even tide,
Upon a couch, near to a curtaining
Whose airy texture, from a golden string,
Floated into the room, and let appear
Unveil'd the summer heaven, blue and clear,
Betwixt two marble shafts: — there they reposed,
Where use had made it sweet, with eyelids closed,
Saving a tythe which love still open kept,
That they might see each other while they almost slept;
When from the slope side of a suburb hill,
Deafening the swallow's twitter, came a thrill
Of trumpets — Lycius started — the sounds fled,
But left a thought, a buzzing in his head.
For the first time, since first he harbour'd in
That purple-lined palace of sweet sin,
His spirit pass'd beyond its golden bourn
Into the noisy world almost forsworn.
The lady, ever watchful, penetrant,
Saw this with pain, so arguing a want
Of something more, more than her empery
Of joys; and she began to moan and sigh
Because he mused beyond her, knowing well
That but a moment's thought is passion's passing bell.
'Why do you sigh, fair creature?' whisper'd he:
'Why do you think?' return'd she tenderly:
'You have deserted me; — where am I now?
'Not in your heart while care weighs on your brow:

'No, no, you have dismiss'd me; and I go
'From your breast houseless: aye, it must be so.'
He answer'd, bending to her open eyes,
Where he was mirror'd small in paradise,
'My silver planet, both of eve and morn!
'Why will you plead yourself so sad forlorn,
'While I am striving how to fill my heart
'With deeper crimson, and a double smart?
'How to entangle, trammel up and snare
'Your soul in mine, and labyrinth you there
'Like the hid scent in an unbudded rose?
'Aye, a sweet kiss — you see your mighty woes.
'My thoughts! shall I unveil them? Listen then!
'What mortal hath a prize, that other men
'May be confounded and abash'd withal,
'But lets it sometimes pace abroad majestical,
'And triumph, as in thee I should rejoice
'Amid the hoarse alarm of Corinth's voice.
'Let my foes choke, and my friends shout afar,
'While through the thronged streets your bridal car
'Wheels round its dazzling spokes.' — The lady's cheek
Trembled; she nothing said, but, pale and meek,
Arose and knelt before him, wept a rain
Of sorrows at his words; at last with pain
Beseeching him, the while his hand she wrung,
To change his purpose. He thereat was stung,
Perverse, with stronger fancy to reclaim
Her wild and timid nature to his aim:
Besides, for all his love, in self despite,
Against his better self, he took delight
Luxurious in her sorrows, soft and new.
His passion, cruel grown, took on a hue
Fierce and sanguineous as 'twas possible
In one whose brow had no dark veins to swell.
Fine was the mitigated fury, like
Apollo's presence when in act to strike
The serpent — Ha, the serpent! certes, she
Was none. She burnt, she lov'd the tyranny,
And, all subdued, consented to the hour
When to the bridal he should lead his paramour.
Whispering in midnight silence, said the youth,
'Sure some sweet name thou hast, though, by my truth,
'I have not ask'd it, ever thinking thee
'Not mortal, but of heavenly progeny,
'As still I do. Hast any mortal name,
'Fit appellation for this dazzling frame?
'Or friends or kinsfolk on the citied earth,
'To share our marriage feast and nuptial mirth?'
'I have no friends,' said Lamia, 'no, not one;
'My presence in wide Corinth hardly known:
'My parents' bones are in their dusty urns
'Sepulchred, where no kindled incense burns,
'Seeing all their luckless race are dead, save me,
'And I neglect the holy rite for thee.
'Even as you list invite your many guests;
'But if, as now it seems, your vision rests
'With any pleasure on me, do not bid
'Old Apollonius — from him keep me hid.'
Lycius, perplex'd at words so blind and blank,
Made close inquiry; from whose touch she shrank,
Feigning a sleep; and he to the dull shade
Of deep sleep in a moment was betray'd.

It was the custom then to bring away
The bride from home at blushing shut of day,
Veil'd, in a chariot, heralded along

By strewn flowers, torches, and a marriage song,
With other pageants: but this fair unknown
Had not a friend. So being left alone,
(Lycius was gone to summon all his kin)
And knowing surely she could never win
His foolish heart from its mad pompousness,
She set herself, high-thoughted, how to dress
The misery in fit magnificence.
She did so, but 'tis doubtful how and whence
Came, and who were her subtle servitors.
About the halls, and to and from the doors,
There was a noise of wings, till in short space
The glowing banquet-room shone with wide-arched grace.
A haunting music, sole perhaps and lone
Supportress of the faery-roof, made moan
Throughout, as fearful the whole charm might fade.
Fresh carved cedar, mimicking a glade
Of palm and plantain, met from either side,
High in the midst, in honour of the bride:
Two palms and then two plantains, and so on,
From either side their stems branch'd one to one
All down the aisled place; and beneath all
There ran a stream of lamps straight on from wall to wall.
So canopied, lay an untasted feast
Teeming with odours. Lamia, regal drest,
Silently paced about, and as she went,
In pale contented sort of discontent,
Mission'd her viewless servants to enrich
The fretted splendour of each nook and niche.
Between the tree-stems, marbled plain at first,
Came jasper pannels; then, anon, there burst
Forth creeping imagery of slighter trees,
And with the larger wove in small intricacies.
Approving all, she faded at self-will,
And shut the chamber up, close, hush'd and still,
Complete and ready for the revels rude,
When dreadful guests would come to spoil her solitude.

The day appear'd, and all the gossip rout.
O senseless Lycius! Madman! wherefore flout
The silent-blessing fate, warm cloister'd hours,
And show to common eyes these secret bowers?
The herd approach'd; each guest, with busy brain,
Arriving at the portal, gaz'd amain,
And enter'd marveling: for they knew the street,
Remember'd it from childhood all complete
Without a gap, yet ne'er before had seen
That royal porch, that high-built fair demesne;
So in they hurried all, maz'd, curious and keen:
Save one, who look'd thereon with eye severe,
And with calm-planted steps walk'd in austere;
'Twas Apollonius: something too he laugh'd,
As though some knotty problem, that had daft
His patient thought, had now begun to thaw,
And solve and melt: — 'twas just as he foresaw.

He met within the murmurous vestibule
His young disciple. ' 'Tis no common rule,
Lycius,' said he, ' for uninvited guest
' To force himself upon you, and infest
' With an unbidden presence the bright throng

'Of younger friends; yet must I do this wrong,
'And you forgive me.' Lycius blush'd, and led
The old man through the inner doors broad-spread;
With reconciling words and courteous mien
Turning into sweet milk the sophist's spleen.

Of wealthy lustre was the banquet-room,
Fill'd with pervading brilliance and perfume:
Before each lucid pannel fuming stood
A censer fed with myrrh and spiced wood,
Each by a sacred tripod held aloft,
Whose slender feet wide-swerv'd upon the soft
Wool-woofed carpets: fifty wreaths of smoke
From fifty censers their light voyage took
To the high roof, still mimick'd as they rose
Along the mirror'd walls by twin-clouds odorous.
Twelve sphered tables, by silk seats insphered,
High as the level of a man's breast rear'd
On libbard's[64] paws, upheld the heavy gold
Of cups and goblets, and the store thrice told
Of Ceres' horn, and, in huge vessels, wine
Come from the gloomy tun with merry shine.
Thus loaded with a feast the tables stood,
Each shrining in the midst the image of a God.

When in an antichamber every guest
Had felt the cold full sponge to pleasure press'd,
By minist'ring slaves, upon his hands and feet,
And fragrant oils with ceremony meet
Pour'd on his hair, they all mov'd to the feast
In white robes, and themselves in order placed
Around the silken couches, wondering
Whence all this mighty cost and blaze of wealth could spring.

Soft went the music the soft air along,
While fluent Greek a vowel'd undersong
Kept up among the guests, discoursing low
At first, for scarcely was the wine at flow;
But when the happy vintage touch'd their brains,
Louder they talk, and louder come the strains
Of powerful instruments: — the gorgeous dyes,
The space, the splendour of the draperies,
The roof of awful richness, nectarous cheer,
Beautiful slaves, and Lamia's self, appear,
Now, when the wine has done its rosy deed,
And every soul from human trammels freed,
No more so strange; for merry wine, sweet wine,
Will make Elysian shades not too fair, too divine.
Soon was God Bacchus at meridian height;
Flush'd were their cheeks, and bright eyes double bright:
Garlands of every green, and every scent
From vales deflower'd, or forest-trees branch-rent,
In baskets of bright osier'd gold were brought
High as the handles heap'd, to suit the thought
Of every guest; that each, as he did please,
Might fancy-fit his brows, silk-pillow'd at his ease.

What wreath for Lamia? What for Lycius?
What for the sage, old Apollonius?

[64] leopard's

Upon her aching forehead be there hung
The leaves of willow and of adder's tongue;[65]
And for the youth, quick, let us strip for him
The thyrsus,[66] that his watching eyes may swim
Into forgetfulness; and, for the sage,
Let spear-grass and the spiteful thistle wage
War on his temples. Do not all charms fly
At the mere touch of cold philosophy?
There was an awful rainbow once in heaven:
We know her woof, her texture; she is given
In the dull catalogue of common things.
Philosophy will clip an Angel's wings,
Conquer all mysteries by rule and line,
Empty the haunted air, and gnomed mine —
Unweave a rainbow, as it erewhile made
The tender-person'd Lamia melt into a shade.

By her glad Lycius sitting, in chief place,
Scarce saw in all the room another face,
Till, checking his love trance, a cup he took
Full brimm'd, and opposite sent forth a look
'Cross the broad table, to beseech a glance
From his old teacher's wrinkled countenance,
And pledge him. The bald-head philosopher
Had fix'd his eye, without a twinkle or stir
Full on the alarmed beauty of the bride,
Brow-beating her fair form, and troubling her sweet pride.
Lycius then press'd her hand, with devout touch,
As pale it lay upon the rosy couch:
'Twas icy, and the cold ran through his veins;
Then sudden it grew hot, and all the pains
Of an unnatural heat shot to his heart.
'Lamia, what means this? Wherefore dost thou start?
'Know'st thou that man?' Poor Lamia answer'd not.
He gaz'd into her eyes, and not a jot
Own'd they the lovelorn piteous appeal:
More, more he gaz'd: his human senses reel:
Some hungry spell that loveliness absorbs;
There was no recognition in those orbs.
'Lamia!' he cried — and no soft-toned reply.
The many heard, and the loud revelry
Grew hush; the stately music no more breathes;
The myrtle sicken'd in a thousand wreaths.
By faint degrees, voice, lute, and pleasure ceased;
A deadly silence step by step increased,
Until it seem'd a horrid presence there,
And not a man but felt the terror in his hair.
'Lamia!' he shriek'd; and nothing but the shriek
With its sad echo did the silence break.
'Begone, foul dream!' he cried, gazing again
In the bride's face, where now no azure vein
Wander'd on fair-spaced temples; no soft bloom
Misted the cheek; no passion to illume
The deep-recessed vision: — all was blight;
Lamia, no longer fair, there sat a deadly white.
'Shut, shut those juggling eyes, thou ruthless man!
'Turn them aside, wretch! or the righteous ban
'Of all the Gods, whose dreadful images
'Here represent their shadowy presences,
'May pierce them on the sudden with the thorn
'Of painful blindness; leaving thee forlorn,
'In trembling dotage to the feeblest fright

[65] A variety of fern.
[66] The ivy-wreathed staff of Bacchus.

'Of conscience, for their long offended might,
'For all thine impious proud-heart sophistries,
'Unlawful magic, and enticing lies.
'Corinthians! look upon that grey-beard wretch!
'Mark how, possess'd, his lashless eyelids stretch
'Around his demon eyes! Corinthians, see!
'My sweet bride withers at their potency.'
'Fool!' said the sophist, in an under-tone
Gruff with contempt; which a death-nighing moan
From Lycius answer'd, as heart-struck and lost,
He sank supine beside the aching ghost.
'Fool! Fool!' repeated he, while his eyes still
Relented not, nor mov'd; 'from every ill
'Of life have I preserv'd thee to this day,
'And shall I see thee made a serpent's prey?'
Then Lamia breath'd death breath; the sophist's eye,
Like a sharp spear, went through her utterly,
Keen, cruel, perceant,[67] stinging: she, as well
As her weak hand could any meaning tell,
Motion'd him to be silent; vainly so,
He look'd and look'd again a level — No!
'A serpent!' echoed he; no sooner said,
Than with a frightful scream she vanished:
And Lycius' arms were empty of delight,
As were his limbs of life, from that same night.
On the high couch he lay! — his friends came round —
Supported him — no pulse, or breath they found,
And, in its marriage robe, the heavy body wound.

HYPERION[68]

A FRAGMENT

Book I

Deep in the shady sadness of a vale
Far sunken from the healthy breath of morn,
Far from the fiery noon, and eve's one star,
Sat gray-hair'd Saturn, quiet as a stone,
Still as the silence round about his lair;
Forest on forest hung about his head
Like cloud on cloud. No stir of air was there,
Not so much life as on a summer's day
Robs not one light seed from the feather'd grass,
But where the dead leaf fell, there did it rest.
A stream went voiceless by, still deadened more
By reason of his fallen divinity
Spreading a shade: the Naiad 'mid her reeds
Press'd her cold finger closer to her lips.

Along the margin-sand large foot-marks went,
No further than to where his feet had stray'd,
And slept there since. Upon the sodden ground
His old right hand lay nerveless, listless, dead,
Unsceptred; and his realmless eyes were closed;

[67] piercing

[68] Written in 1818–1819, and published as a fragment in 1820. On 22 September 1819 Keats wrote Reynolds that he had given up *Hyperion* — 'there were too many Miltonic inversions in it — Miltonic verse cannot be written but in an artful, or, rather, artist's humor.' He had designed a large epic in ten books, only two of which and a scrap of a third were finished. Keats's friend Woodhouse, in an interleaved and annotated copy of *Endymion*, wrote of *Hyperion:* 'The poem if completed would have treated of the dethronement of Hyperion, the former God of the Sun, by Apollo, — and incidentally of those of Oceanus by Neptune, of Saturn by Jupiter, etc., and of the war of the Giants for Saturn's reëstablishment, with other events, of which we have but very dark hints in the mythological poets of Greece and Rome.'

While his bow'd head seem'd list'ning to the Earth,
His ancient mother, for some comfort yet.

It seem'd no force could wake him from his place;
But there came one,[69] who with a kindred hand
Touch'd his wide shoulders, after bending low
With reverence, though to one who knew it not.
She was a Goddess of the infant world;
By her in stature the tall Amazon
Had stood a pigmy's height: she would have ta'en
Achilles by the hair and bent his neck;
Or with a finger stay'd Ixion's wheel.
Her face was large as that of Memphian sphinx,
Pedestal'd haply in a palace court,
When sages look'd to Egypt for their lore.
But oh! how unlike marble was that face:
How beautiful, if sorrow had not made
Sorrow more beautiful than Beauty's self.
There was a listening fear in her regard,
As if calamity had but begun;
As if the vanward clouds of evil days
Had spent their malice, and the sullen rear
Was with its stored thunder labouring up.
One hand she press'd upon that aching spot
Where beats the human heart, as if just there,
Though an immortal, she felt cruel pain:
The other upon Saturn's bended neck
She laid, and to the level of his ear
Leaning with parted lips, some words she spake
In solemn tenour and deep organ tone:
Some mourning words, which in our feeble tongue
Would come in these like accents; O how frail
To that large utterance of the early Gods!
'Saturn, look up! — though wherefore, poor old King?

[69] Thea, Hyperion's sister and wife.

'I have no comfort for thee, no not one:
'I cannot say, "O wherefore sleepest thou?"
'For heaven is parted from thee, and the earth
'Knows thee not, thus afflicted, for a God;
'And ocean too, with all its solemn noise,
'Has from thy sceptre pass'd; and all the air
'Is emptied of thine hoary majesty.
'Thy thunder, conscious of the new command,
'Rumbles reluctant o'er our fallen house;
'And thy sharp lightning in unpractis'd hands
'Scorches and burns our once serene domain.
'O aching time! O moments big as years!
'All as ye pass swell out the monstrous truth,
'And press it so upon our weary griefs
'That unbelief has not a space to breathe.
'Saturn, sleep on: — O thoughtless, why did I
'Thus violate thy slumbrous solitude?
'Why should I ope thy melancholy eyes?
'Saturn, sleep on! while at thy feet I weep.'

As when, upon a tranced summer-night,
Those green-rob'd senators of mighty woods,
Tall oaks, branch-charmed by the earnest stars,
Dream, and so dream all night without a stir,
Save from one gradual solitary gust
Which comes upon the silence, and dies off,
As if the ebbing air had but one wave;
So came these words and went; the while in tears
She touch'd her fair large forehead to the ground,
Just where her falling hair might be outspread
A soft and silken mat for Saturn's feet.
One moon, with alteration slow, had shed
Her silver seasons four upon the night,

And still these two were postured motionless,
Like natural sculpture in cathedral cavern;
The frozen God still couchant on the earth,
And the sad Goddess weeping at his feet:
Until at length old Saturn lifted up
His faded eyes, and saw his kingdom gone,
And all the gloom and sorrow of the place,
And that fair kneeling Goddess; and then spake,
As with a palsied tongue, and while his beard
Shook horrid with such aspen-malady:
'O tender spouse of gold Hyperion,
'Thea, I feel thee ere I see thy face;
'Look up, and let me see our doom in it;
'Look up, and tell me if this feeble shape
'Is Saturn's; tell me, if thou hear'st the voice
'Of Saturn; tell me, if this wrinkling brow,
'Naked and bare of its great diadem,
'Peers like the front of Saturn. Who had power
'To make me desolate? whence came the strength?
'How was it nurtur'd to such bursting forth,
'While Fate seem'd strangled in my nervous grasp?
'But it is so; and I am smother'd up,
'And buried from all godlike exercise
'Of influence benign on planets pale,
'Of admonitions to the winds and seas,
'Of peaceful sway above man's harvesting,
'And all those acts which Deity supreme
'Doth ease its heart of love in. — I am gone
'Away from my own bosom: I have left
'My strong identity, my real self,
'Somewhere between the throne, and where I sit
'Here on this spot of earth. Search, Thea, search!
'Open thine eyes eterne, and sphere them round
'Upon all space: space starr'd, and lorn of light;
'Space region'd with life-air; and barren void;
'Spaces, of fire, and all the yawn of hell. —
'Search, Thea, search! and tell me, if thou seest
'A certain shape or shadow, making way
'With wings or chariot fierce to repossess
'A heaven he lost erewhile: it must — it must
'Be of ripe progress — Saturn must be King.
'Yes, there must be a golden victory;
'There must be Gods thrown down, and trumpets blown
'Of triumph calm, and hymns of festival
'Upon the gold clouds metropolitan,
'Voices of soft proclaim, and silver stir
'Of strings in hollow shells; and there shall be
'Beautiful things made new, for the surprise
'Of the sky-children; I will give command:
'Thea! Thea! Thea! where is Saturn?'

This passion lifted him upon his feet,
And made his hands to struggle in the air,
His Druid locks to shake and ooze with sweat,
His eyes to fever out, his voice to cease.
He stood, and heard not Thea's sobbing deep;
A little time, and then again he snatch'd
Utterance thus. — 'But cannot I create?
'Cannot I form? Cannot I fashion forth
'Another world, another universe,
'To overbear and crumble this to naught?
'Where is another chaos? Where?' — That word
Found way unto Olympus, and made quake
The rebel three.[70] — Thea was startled up,

[70] Jupiter, Pluto, and Neptune, who had rebelled against Saturn, their father.

And in her bearing was a sort of hope,
As thus she quick-voic'd spake, yet full of awe.
'This cheers our fallen house: come to our friends,
'O Saturn! come away, and give them heart;
'I know the covert, for thence came I hither.'
Thus brief; then with beseeching eyes she went
With backward footing through the shade a space:
He follow'd, and she turn'd to lead the way
Through aged boughs, that yielded like the mist
Which eagles cleave upmounting from their nest.

Meanwhile in other realms big tears were shed,
More sorrow like to this, and such like woe,
Too huge for mortal tongue or pen of scribe:
The Titans fierce, self-hid, or prison-bound,
Groan'd for the old allegiance once more,
And listen'd in sharp pain for Saturn's voice.
But one of the whole mammoth-brood still kept
His sov'reignty, and rule, and majesty; —
Blazing Hyperion on his orbed fire
Still sat, still snuff'd the incense, teeming up
From man to the sun's God; yet unsecure:
For as among us mortals omens drear
Fright and perplex, so also shuddered he —
Not at dog's howl, or gloom-bird's hated screech,
Or the familiar visiting of one
Upon the first toll of his passing-bell,
Or prophesyings of the midnight lamp;
But horrors, portion'd to a giant nerve,
Oft made Hyperion ache. His palace bright
Bastion'd with pyramids of glowing gold,
And touch'd with shade of bronzed obelisks,
Glar'd a blood-red through all its thousand courts,
Arches, and domes, and fiery galleries;
And all its curtains of Aurorian clouds
Flush'd angerly: while sometimes eagle's wings,
Unseen before by Gods or wondering men,
Darken'd the place; and neighing steeds were heard,
Not heard before by Gods or wondering men.
Also, when he would taste the spicy wreaths
Of incense, breath'd aloft from sacred hills,
Instead of sweets, his ample palate took
Savour of poisonous brass and metal sick:
And so, when harbour'd in the sleepy west,
After the full completion of fair day, —
For rest divine upon exalted couch
And slumber in the arms of melody,
He pac'd away the pleasant hours of ease
With stride colossal, on from hall to hall;
While far within each aisle and deep recess,
His winged minions in close clusters stood,
Amaz'd and full of fear; like anxious men
Who on wide plains gather in panting troops,
When earthquakes jar their battlements and towers.
Even now, while Saturn, rous'd from icy trance,
Went step for step with Thea through the woods,
Hyperion, leaving twilight in the rear,
Came slope upon the threshold of the west;
Then, as was wont, his palace-door flew ope
In smoothest silence, save what solemn tubes,

Blown by the serious Zephyrs, gave of sweet
And wandering sounds, slow-breathed melodies;
And like a rose in vermeil tint and shape,
In fragrance soft, and coolness to the eye,
That inlet to severe magnificence
Stood full blown, for the God to enter in.

He enter'd, but he enter'd full of wrath;
His flaming robes stream'd out beyond his heels,
And gave a roar, as if of earthly fire,
That scar'd away the meek ethereal Hours
And made their dove-wings tremble. On he flared,
From stately nave to nave, from vault to vault,
Through bowers of fragrant and en-wreathed light,
And diamond-paved lustrous long ar-cades,
Until he reach'd the great main cupola;
There standing fierce beneath, he stamped his foot,
And from the basements deep to the high towers
Jarr'd his own golden region; and before
The quavering thunder thereupon had ceas'd,
His voice leapt out, despite of godlike curb,
To this result: 'O dreams of day and night!
'O monstrous forms! O effigies of pain!
'O spectres busy in a cold, cold gloom!
'O lank-ear'd Phantoms of black-weeded pools!
'Why do I know ye? why have I seen ye? why
'Is my eternal essence thus distraught
'To see and to behold these horrors new?
'Saturn is fallen, am I too to fall?
'Am I to leave this haven of my rest,
'This cradle of my glory, this soft clime,
'This calm luxuriance of blissful light,
'These crystalline pavilions, and pure fanes,
'Of all my lucent empire? It is left
'Deserted, void, nor any haunt of mine.
'The blaze, the splendor, and the sym-metry,
'I cannot see — but darkness, death and darkness.
'Even here, into my centre of repose,
'The shady visions come to domineer,
'Insult, and blind, and stifle up my pomp. —
'Fall! — No, by Tellus and her briny robes!
'Over the fiery frontier of my realms
'I will advance a terrible right arm
'Shall scare that infant thunderer, rebel Jove,
'And bid old Saturn take his throne again.' —
He spake, and ceas'd, the while a heavier threat
Held struggle with his throat but came not forth;
For as in theatres of crowded men
Hubbub increases more they call out 'Hush!'
So at Hyperion's words the Phantoms pale
Bestirr'd themselves, thrice horrible and cold;
And from the mirror'd level where he stood
A mist arose, as from a scummy marsh.
At this, through all his bulk an agony
Crept gradual, from the feet unto the crown,
Like a lithe serpent vast and muscular
Making slow way, with head and neck convuls'd
From over-strained might. Releas'd, he fled
To the eastern gates, and full six dewy hours
Before the dawn in season due should blush,
He breath'd fierce breath against the sleepy portals,

Clear'd them of heavy vapours, burst them wide
Suddenly on the ocean's chilly streams.
The planet orb of fire, whereon he rode
Each day from east to west the heavens through,
Spun round in sable curtaining of clouds;
Not therefore veiled quite, blindfold, and hid,
But ever and anon the glancing spheres,
Circles, and arcs, and broad-belting colure,[71]
Glow'd through, and wrought upon the muffling dark
Sweet-shaped lightnings from the nadir deep
Up to the zenith, — hieroglyphics old
Which sages and keen-eyed astrologers
Then living on the earth, with labouring thought
Won from the gaze of many centuries:
Now lost, save what we find on remnants huge
Of stone, or marble swart; their import gone,
Their wisdom long since fled. — Two wings this orb
Possess'd for glory, two fair argent wings,
Ever exalted at the God's approach:
And now, from forth the gloom their plumes immense
Rose, one by one, till all outspreaded were;
While still the dazzling globe maintain'd eclipse,
Awaiting for Hyperion's command.
Fain would he have commanded, fain took throne
And bid the day begin, if but for change.
He might not: — No, though a primeval God:
The sacred seasons might not be disturb'd.
Therefore the operations of the dawn
Stay'd in their birth, even as here 'tis told.
Those silver wings expanded sisterly,
Eager to sail their orb; the porches wide
Open'd upon the dusk demesnes of night;
And the bright Titan, phrenzied with new woes,
Unus'd to bend, by hard compulsion bent
His spirit to the sorrow of the time;
And all along a dismal rack of clouds,
Upon the boundaries of day and night,
He stretch'd himself in grief and radiance faint.
There as he lay, the Heaven with its stars
Look'd down on him with pity, and the voice
Of Cœlus, from the universal space,
Thus whisper'd low and solemn in his ear.
'O brightest of my children dear, earth-born
'And sky-engendered, Son of Mysteries
'All unrevealed even to the powers
'Which met at thy creating; at whose joys
'And palpitations sweet, and pleasures soft,
'I, Cœlus, wonder, how they came and whence;
'And at the fruits thereof what shapes they be,
'Distinct, and visible; symbols divine,
'Manifestations of that beauteous life
'Diffus'd unseen throughout eternal space:
'Of these new-form'd art thou, oh brightest child!
'Of these, thy brethren and the Goddesses!
'There is sad feud among ye, and rebellion
'Of son against his sire: I saw him fall,
'I saw my first-born [72] tumbled from his throne!
'To me his arms were spread, to me his voice
'Found way from forth the thunders round his head!
'Pale wox I, and in vapours hid my face.
'Art thou, too, near such doom? vague fear there is:
'For I have seen my sons most unlike Gods.

[71] One of the two enormous circles which encompass the celestial sphere at right angles to each other.

[72] Saturn

'Divine ye were created, and divine
'In sad demeanour, solemn, undisturb'd,
'Unruffled, like high Gods, ye liv'd and ruled:
'Now I behold in you fear, hope, and wrath;
'Actions of rage and passion; even as
'I see them, on the mortal world beneath,
'In men who die. — This is the grief, O Son!
'Sad sign of ruin, sudden dismay, and fall!
'Yet do thou strive; as thou art capable,
'As thou canst move about, an evident God;
'And canst oppose to each malignant hour
'Ethereal presence: — I am but a voice;
'My life is but the life of winds and tides,
'No more than winds and tides can I avail: —
'But thou canst. — Be thou therefore in the van
'Of circumstance; yea, seize the arrow's barb
'Before the tense string murmur. — To the earth!
'For there thou wilt find Saturn, and his woes.
'Meantime I will keep watch on thy bright sun,
'And of thy seasons be a careful nurse.' —
Ere half this region-whisper had come down,
Hyperion arose, and on the stars
Lifted his curved lids, and kept them wide
Until it ceas'd; and still he kept them wide:
And still they were the same bright, patient stars.
Then with a slow incline of his broad breast,
Like to a diver in the pearly seas,
Forward he stoop'd over the airy shore,
And plung'd all noiseless into the deep night.

Sonnet [73]

Written on a Blank Page in Shakespeare's Poems, facing 'A Lover's Complaint.'

Bright star, would I were stedfast as thou art —
Not in lone splendour hung aloft the night
And watching, with eternal lids apart,
Like nature's patient, sleepless Eremite,
The moving waters at their priestlike task
Of pure ablution round earth's human shores,
Or gazing on the new soft-fallen mask
Of snow upon the mountains and the moors —
No — yet still stedfast, still unchangeable,
Pillow'd upon my fair love's ripening breast,
To feel for ever its soft fall and swell,
Awake for ever in a sweet unrest,
Still, still to hear her tender-taken breath,
And so live ever — or else swoon to death.

[73] Written in the autumn of 1820, during the voyage to Italy which seemed to be Keats's last chance for life; published in 1848.

Walter Savage Landor 1775–1864

Rose Aylmer [1]

Ah, what avails the sceptred race,
Ah, what the form divine!
What every virtue, every grace!
Rose Aylmer, all were thine.
Rose Aylmer, whom these wakeful eyes
May weep, but never see,
A night of memories and of sighs
I consecrate to thee.

[1] This and the following poem were published in *Simonidea*, 1806. It was inspired by news of the death in India of Rose, the daughter of Henry, Baron Aylmer, who had been Landor's devoted friend during the poet's early years in Wales, 1795–1798.

Mother, I cannot mind my wheel

Mother, I cannot mind my wheel; [2]
My fingers ache, my lips are dry:
Oh! if you felt the pain I feel!
But oh, who ever felt as I?
No longer could I doubt him true —
All other men may use deceit;
He always said my eyes were blue,
And often swore my lips were sweet.

On Seeing a Hair of Lucretia Borgia [3]

Borgia, thou once wert almost too august
And high for adoration; now thou'rt dust;
All that remains of thee these plaits unfold,
Calm hair, meandering in pellucid gold.

Past ruin'd Ilion Helen lives [4]

Past ruin'd Ilion Helen lives,
Alcestis rises from the shades;
Verse calls them forth; 'tis verse that gives
Immortal youth to mortal maids.

Soon shall Oblivion's deepening veil
Hide all the peopled hills you see,
The gay, the proud, while lovers hail
These many summers you and me.

Dirce

Stand close around, ye Stygian set,
With Dirce in one boat conveyed,
Or Charon, seeing, may forget
That he is old, and she a shade.

A Fiesolan Idyl

Here, where precipitate Spring with one light bound
Into hot Summer's lusty arms expires,
And where go forth at morn, at eve, at night,
Soft airs that want the lute to play with 'em,
And softer sighs that know not what they want,
Aside a wall, beneath an orange-tree,
Whose tallest flowers could tell the lowlier ones
Of sights in Fiesole right above,
While I was gazing a few paces off
At what they seemed to show me with their nods,
Their frequent whispers and their pointing shoots,
A gentle maid came down the garden-steps
And gathered the pure treasure in her lap.
I heard the branches rustle, and stept forth
To drive the ox away, or mule, or goat, —
Such I believed it must be. How could I
Let beast o'erpower them? when hath wind or rain
Borne hard upon weak plant that wanted me,
And I (however they might bluster round)
Walkt off? 'Twere most ungrateful; for sweet scents
Are the swift vehicles of still sweeter thoughts,
And nurse and pillow the dull memory
That would let drop without them her best stores.
They bring me tales of youth and tones of love,
And 'tis and ever was my wish and way
To let all flowers live freely, and all die
(Whene'er their Genius bids their souls depart)
Among their kindred in their native place.
I never pluck the rose; the violet's head
Hath shaken with my breath upon its bank
And not reproacht me; the ever-sacred cup
Of the pure lily hath between my hands
Felt safe, unsoiled, nor lost one grain of gold.
I saw the light that made the glossy leaves

---

[2] The first four lines are a free translation of a fragment of Sappho.

[3] Published by Leigh Hunt in *The New Monthly Magazine*, July 1825.

[4] This and the following two poems were published in *Gebir, Count Julian, and other Poems*, 1831. It is one of the many poems 'To Ianthe,' Sophia Jane Swift, whom Landor met in 1800 and for whom thereafter he retained probably the deepest affection of his life.

More glossy; the fair arm, the fairer cheek
Warmed by the eye intent on its pursuit;
I saw the foot that, although half-erect
From its gray slipper, could not lift her up
To what she wanted. I held down a branch
And gathered her some blossoms, since their hour
Was come, and bees had wounded them, and flies
Of harder wing were working their way through
And scattering them in fragments under foot.
So crisp were some, they rattled unevolved;
Others, ere broken off, fell into shells,
For such appear the petals when detacht,
Unbending, brittle, lucid, white like snow,
And like snow not seen through, by eye or sun;
Yet every one her gown received from me
Was fairer than the first. I thought not so,
But so she praised them to reward my care.
I said, 'You find the largest.' 'This indeed,'
Cried she, 'is large and sweet.' She held one forth,
Whether for me to look at or to take
She knew not, nor did I; but taking it
Would best have solved (and this she felt) her doubt.
I dared not touch it; for it seemed a part
Of her own self; fresh, full, the most mature
Of blossoms, yet a blossom; with a touch
To fall, and yet unfallen. She drew back
The boon she tendered, and then, finding not
The ribbon at her waist to fix it in,
Dropt it, as loth to drop it, on the rest.

To Robert Browning [5]

There is delight in singing, tho' none hear
Beside the singer; and there is delight
In praising, tho' the praiser sit alone
And see the prais'd far off him, far above.
Shakespeare is not our poet, but the world's,
Therefore on him no speech! and brief for thee,
Browning! Since Chaucer was alive and hale,
No man hath walked along our roads with step
So active, so inquiring eye, or tongue
So varied in discourse. But warmer climes
Give brighter plumage, strong wing: the breeze
Of Alpine heights thou playest with, borne on
Beyond Sorrento and Amalfi, where
The Siren waits thee, singing song for song.

Remain, ah not in youth alone [6]

Remain, ah not in youth alone,
  Tho' youth, where you are, long will stay,
But when my summer days are gone,
  And my autumnal haste away.
'Can I be always by your side?'
  No; but the hours you can, you must,
Nor rise at Death's approaching stride,
  Nor go when dust is gone to dust.

You smiled, you spoke, and I believed [7]

You smiled, you spoke, and I believed,
By every word and smile deceived.
Another man would hope no more;
Nor hope I what I hoped before:
But let not this last wish be vain;
Deceive, deceive me once again!

[5] Published in *The Morning Chronicle*, 22 November 1845.

[6] This and the following poem were published in *Works* 1846.
[7] Also to 'Ianthe.'

I entreat you, Alfred Tennyson [8]

I ENTREAT you, Alfred Tennyson,
Come and share my haunch of venison.
I have too a bin of claret,
Good, but better when you share it.
Tho' 'tis only a small bin,
There's a stock of it within.
And as sure as I'm a rhymer,
Half a butt of Rudesheimer.
Come; among the sons of men is one
Welcomer than Alfred Tennyson?

[8] This and the two following poems were published in *Last Fruit off an Old Tree*, 1853.

Death stands above me

DEATH stands above me, whispering low
  I know not what into my ear:
Of his strange language all I know
  Is, there is not a word of fear.

On His Seventy-fifth Birthday

I STROVE with none; for none was worth my strife,
  Nature I loved, and next to Nature, Art;
I warmed both hands before the fire of life,
  It sinks, and I am ready to depart.

Alfred Lord Tennyson

1809–1892

Mariana [1]

'Mariana in the moated grange.'
—*Measure for Measure.*

WITH blackest moss the flower-plots
  Were thickly crusted, one and all:
The rusted nails fell from the knots
  That held the pear to the gable-wall.
The broken sheds look'd sad and strange:
  Unlifted was the clinking latch;
  Weeded and worn the ancient thatch
Upon the lonely moated grange.
    She only said, 'My life is dreary,
      He cometh not,' she said;
    She said, 'I am aweary, aweary,
      I would that I were dead!'

Her tears fell with the dews at even;
  Her tears fell ere the dews were dried;
She could not look on the sweet heaven,
  Either at morn or eventide.
After the flitting of the bats,
  When thickest dark did trance the sky,
  She drew her casement-curtain by,
And glanced athwart the glooming flats.
    She only said, 'The night is dreary,
      He cometh not,' she said;
    She said, 'I am aweary, aweary,
      I would that I were dead!'

Upon the middle of the night,
  Waking she heard the night-fowl crow:
The cock sung out an hour ere light:
  From the dark fen the oxen's low
Came to her: without hope of change,
  In sleep she seem'd to walk forlorn,
  Till cold winds woke the gray-eyed morn
About the lonely moated grange.
    She only said, 'The day is dreary,
      He cometh not,' she said;
    She said, 'I am aweary, aweary,
      I would that I were dead!'

About a stone-cast from the wall
  A sluice with blacken'd waters slept,
And o'er it many, round and small,
  The cluster'd marish-mosses crept.
Hard by a poplar shook alway,
  All silver-green with gnarled bark:
  For leagues no other tree did mark
The level waste, the rounding gray.
    She only said, 'My life is dreary,
      He cometh not,' she said;
    She said, 'I am aweary, aweary,
      I would that I were dead!'

[1] This and the three following poems were published in *Poems, chiefly Lyrical*, 1830. In Shakespeare's play Mariana, deserted by her lover, waits 'in the moated grange.'

And ever when the moon was low,
And the shrill winds were up and away,
In the white curtain, to and fro,
She saw the gusty shadow sway.
But when the moon was very low,
And wild winds bound within their cell,
The shadow of the poplar fell
Upon her bed, across her brow.
She only said, 'The night is dreary,
He cometh not,' she said;
She said, 'I am aweary, aweary,
I would that I were dead!'

All day within the dreamy house,
The doors upon their hinges creak'd;
The blue fly sung in the pane; the mouse
Behind the mouldering wainscot shriek'd,
Or from the crevice peer'd about.
Old faces glimmer'd thro' the doors,
Old footsteps trod the upper floors,
Old voices called her from without.
She only said, 'My life is dreary,
He cometh not,' she said;
She said, 'I am aweary, aweary,
I would that I were dead!'

The sparrow's chirrup on the roof,
The slow clock ticking, and the sound
Which to the wooing wind aloof
The poplar made, did all confound
Her sense; but most she loathed the hour
When the thick-moted sunbeam lay
Athwart the chambers, and the day
Was sloping toward his western bower.
Then, said she, 'I am very dreary,
He will not come,' she said;
She wept, 'I am aweary, aweary,
Oh God, that I were dead!'

Song

I

A SPIRIT haunts the year's last hours
Dwelling amid these yellowing bowers:
To himself he talks;
For at eventide, listening earnestly,
At his work you may hear him sob and sigh
In the walks;
Earthward he boweth the heavy stalks
Of the mouldering flowers:
Heavily hangs the broad sunflower
Over its grave i' the earth so chilly;
Heavily hangs the hollyhock,
Heavily hangs the tiger-lily.

II

The air is damp, and hush'd, and close,
As a sick man's room when he taketh repose
An hour before death;
My very heart faints and my whole soul grieves
At the moist rich smell of the rotting leaves,
And the breath
Of the fading edges of box beneath,
And the year's last rose.
Heavily hangs the broad sunflower
Over its grave i' the earth so chilly;
Heavily hangs the hollyhock,
Heavily hangs the tiger-lily.

[1830]

The Poet

THE poet in a golden clime was born,
With golden stars above;
Dower'd with the hate of hate, the scorn of scorn,
The love of love.

He saw thro' life and death, thro' good and ill,
He saw thro' his own soul.
The marvel of the everlasting will,
An open scroll,

Before him lay: with echoing feet he threaded
The secretest walks of fame:
The viewless arrows of his thoughts were headed
And wing'd with flame,

Like Indian reeds blown from his silver tongue,
And of so fierce a flight,
From Calpe [2] unto Caucasus they sung,
Filling with light

And vagrant melodies the winds which bore
Them earthward till they lit;
Then, like the arrow-seeds of the field flower,
The fruitful wit

Cleaving, took root, and springing forth anew
Where'er they fell, behold,
Like to the mother plant in semblance, grew
A flower all gold,

And bravely furnish'd all abroad to fling
The winged shafts of truth,
To throng with stately blooms the breathing spring
Of Hope and Youth.

So many minds did gird their orbs with beams,
Tho' one did fling the fire.
Heaven flow'd upon the soul in many dreams
Of high desire.

Thus truth was multiplied on truth, the world
Like one great garden show'd,
And thro' the wreaths of floating dark upcurl'd,
Rare sunrise flow'd.

And Freedom rear'd in that august sunrise
Her beautiful bold brow,
When rites and forms before his burning eyes
Melted like snow.

There was no blood upon her maiden robes
Sunn'd by those orient skies;
But round about the circles of the globes
Of her keen eyes

And in her raiment's hem was traced in flame
Wisdom, a name to shake
All evil dreams of power — a sacred name.
And when she spake,

Her words did gather thunder as they ran,
And as the lightning to the thunder
Which follows it, riving the spirit of man,
Making earth wonder,

So was their meaning to her words. No sword
Of wrath her right arm whirl'd,
But one poor poet's scroll, and with *his* word
She shook the world.

[1830]

The Mystic [3]

Angels have talked with him, and showed him thrones:
Ye knew him not: he was not one of ye,
Ye scorned him with an undiscerning scorn:
Ye could not read the marvel in his eye,
The still serene abstraction: he hath felt
The vanities of after and before;
Albeit, his spirit and his secret heart
The stern experiences of converse lives,
The linkéd woes of many a fiery change
Had purified, and chastened, and made free.
Always there stood before him, night and day,
Of wayward vary-coloured circumstance
The imperishable presences serene,
Colossal, without form, or sense, or sound,
Dim shadows but unwaning presences
Fourfacéd to four corners of the sky:

[2] Gibraltar

[3] Published in 1830, but omitted by Tennyson from later editions.

And yet again, three shadows, fronting one,
One forward, one respectant, three but one;
And yet again, again and evermore,
For the two first were not, but only seemed,
One shadow in the midst of a great light,
One reflex from eternity on time,
One mighty countenance of perfect calm,
Awful with most invariable eyes.
For him the silent congregated hours,
Daughters of time, divinely tall, beneath
Severe and youthful brows, with shining eyes
Smiling a godlike smile (the innocent light
Of earliest youth pierced through and through with all
Keen knowledges of low-embowéd eld)
Upheld, and ever hold aloft the cloud
Which droops lowhung on either gate of life,
Both birth and death: he in the centre fixt,
Saw far on each side through the grated gates
Most pale and clear and lovely distances.
He often lying broad awake, and yet
Remaining from the body, and apart
In intellect and power and will, hath heard
Time flowing in the middle of the night,
And all things creeping to a day of doom.
How could ye know him? Ye were yet within
The narrower circle; he had wellnigh reached
The last, which with a region of white flame,
Pure without heat, into a larger air
Upburning, and an ether of black blue,
Investeth and ingirds all other lives.

The Lady of Shalott [4]

Part I

On either side the river lie
Long fields of barley and of rye,
That clothe the wold and meet the sky;
And thro' the field the road runs by
To many-towered Camelot;
And up and down the people go,
Gazing where the lilies blow
Round an island there below,
The island of Shalott.

Willows whiten, aspens quiver,
Little breezes dusk and shiver
Thro' the wave that runs for ever
By the island in the river
Flowing down to Camelot.
Four gray walls, and four gray towers,
Overlook a space of flowers,
And the silent isle imbowers
The Lady of Shalott.

By the margin, willow-veil'd,
Slide the heavy barges trail'd
By slow horses; and unhail'd
The shallop flitteth silken-sail'd
Skimming down to Camelot:
But who hath seen her wave her hand?
Or at the casement seen her stand?
Or is she known in all the land,
The Lady of Shalott?

Only reapers, reaping early
In among the bearded barley,
Hear a song that echoes cheerly
From the river winding clearly,
Down to tower'd Camelot:
And by the moon the reaper weary,
Piling sheaves in uplands airy,
Listening, whispers ' 'Tis the fairy
Lady of Shalott.'

Part II

There she weaves by night and day
A magic web with colours gay.
She has heard a whisper say,

[4] This and the four following poems were first published in 1832. Partly owing to the excessive praise bestowed upon his first volume, the new *Poems* received some severe reviews, notably that by John Gibson Lockhart in *The Quarterly Review*, XLIX, April 1833, pp. 81–96. Stung by the unfavorable criticism — and saddened by Arthur Hallam's death in 1833 — Tennyson published almost nothing for ten years. Determined to perfect his mind and his art, he not only worked at new pieces, but carefully revised his earlier poems. A study of the various drafts of this poem, *Œnone*, and *The Palace of Art*, affords a remarkable lesson in the technique of verse. *The Lady of Shalott*, Tennyson's first published poem on an Arthurian subject, is based upon an Italian story of the *Donna di Scalotta*. The word 'Shalott,' substituted for the Italian name because of its softer sound, is the same as Malory's 'Astolat,' which Tennyson later used in *Lancelot and Elaine*.

A curse is on her if she stay
To look down to Camelot.
She knows not what the curse may be,
And so she weaveth steadily,
And little other care hath she,
The Lady of Shalott.

And moving thro' a mirror clear
That hangs before her all the year,
Shadows of the world appear.
There she sees the highway near
Winding down to Camelot:
There the river eddy whirls,
And there the surly village-churls,
And the red cloaks of market girls,
Pass onward from Shalott.

Sometimes a troop of damsels glad,
An abbot on an ambling pad,
Sometimes a curly shepherd-lad,
Or long-hair'd page in crimson clad,
Goes by to tower'd Camelot;
And sometimes thro' the mirror blue
The knights come riding two and two:
She hath no loyal knight and true,
The Lady of Shalott.

But in her web she still delights
To weave the mirror's magic sights,
For often thro' the silent nights
A funeral, with plumes and lights
And music, went to Camelot:
Or when the moon was overhead,
Came two young lovers lately wed;
'I am half sick of shadows,' said
The Lady of Shalott.

Part III

A bow-shot from her bower-eaves,
He rode between the barley-sheaves,
The sun came dazzling thro' the leaves,
And flamed upon the brazen greaves
Of bold Sir Lancelot.
A red-cross knight for ever kneel'd
To a lady in his shield,
That sparkled on the yellow field,
Beside remote Shalott.

The gemmy bridle glitter'd free,
Like to some branch of stars we see
Hung in the golden Galaxy.[5]
The bridle bells rang merrily
As he rode down to Camelot:
And from his blazon'd baldric slung
A mighty silver bugle hung,
And as he rode his armour rung,
Beside remote Shalott.

All in the blue unclouded weather
Thick-jewell'd shone the saddle-leather,
The helmet and the helmet-feather
Burn'd like one burning flame together,
As he rode down to Camelot.
As often thro' the purple night,
Below the starry clusters bright,
Some bearded meteor, trailing light,
Moves over still Shalott.

His broad clear brow in sunlight glow'd;
On burnish'd hooves his war-horse trode;
From underneath his helmet flow'd
His coal-black curls as on he rode,
As he rode down to Camelot.
From the bank and from the river
He flash'd into the crystal mirror,
'Tirra lirra,' by the river
Sang Sir Lancelot.

She left the web, she left the loom,
She made three paces thro' the room,
She saw the water-lily bloom,
She saw the helmet and the plume,
She look'd down to Camelot.
Out flew the web and floated wide;
The mirror crack'd from side to side;
'The curse is come upon me,' cried
The Lady of Shalott.

Part IV

In the stormy east-wind straining,
The pale yellow woods were waning,
The broad stream in his banks complaining,

[5] The Milky Way.

Heavily the low sky raining
Over tower'd Camelot;
Down she came and found a boat
Beneath a willow left afloat,
And round about the prow she wrote
The Lady of Shalott.

And down the river's dim expanse
Like some bold seër in a trance,
Seeing all his own mischance —
With a glassy countenance
Did she look to Camelot.
And at the closing of the day
She loosed the chain, and down she lay;
The broad stream bore her far away,
The Lady of Shalott.

Lying, robed in snowy white
That loosely flew to left and right —
The leaves upon her falling light —
Thro' the noises of the night
She floated down to Camelot:
And as the boat-head wound along
The willowy hills and fields among,
They heard her singing her last song,
The Lady of Shalott.

Heard a carol, mournful, holy,
Chanted loudly, chanted lowly,
Till her blood was frozen slowly,
And her eyes were darken'd wholly,
Turn'd to tower'd Camelot.
For ere she reach'd upon the tide
The first house by the water-side,
Singing in her song she died,
The Lady of Shalott.

Under tower and balcony,
By garden-wall and gallery,
A gleaming shape she floated by,
Dead-pale between the houses high,
Silent into Camelot.
Out upon the wharfs they came,
Knight and burgher, lord and dame,
And round the prow they read her name,
The Lady of Shalott.

Who is this? and what is here?
And in the lighted palace near
Died the sound of royal cheer;
And they cross'd themselves for fear,
All the knights at Camelot:
But Lancelot mused a little space;
He said, 'She has a lovely face;
God in his mercy lend her grace,
The Lady of Shalott.'

Œnone [6]

THERE lies a vale in Ida, lovelier
Than all the valleys of Ionian hills.
The swimming vapour slopes athwart the glen,
Puts forth an arm, and creeps from pine to pine,
And loiters, slowly drawn. On either hand
The lawns and meadow-ledges midway down
Hang rich in flowers, and far below them roars
The long brook falling thro' the clov'n ravine
In cataract after cataract to the sea.
Behind the valley topmost Gargarus [7]
Stands up and takes the morning: but in front
The gorges, opening wide apart, reveal
Troas and Ilion's column'd citadel,
The crown of Troas.
Hither came at noon
Mournful Œnone, wandering forlorn
Of Paris, once her playmate on the hills.
Her cheek had lost the rose, and round her neck
Floated her hair or seem'd to float in rest.
She, leaning on a fragment twined with vine,
Sang to the stillness, till the mountain-shade

[6] Œnone, a nymph of Mount Ida, in Troas, was the wife of Paris, son of King Priam of Troy. Asked to decide which of the three goddesses, Hera, Pallas Athena, or Aphrodite, was the most beautiful, Paris was tempted by offers of reward from each. In return for favoring Aphrodite, Paris was allowed to bring back to Troy from Sparta the loveliest of all women, Helen, wife of Menelaus. The Trojan War followed. After his mother's dream that he would someday bring destruction upon Troy, Paris had been abandoned as a baby in the nearby mountain range of Ida, where shepherds reared him.

[7] One of the highest peaks of Ida.

Sloped downward to her seat from the upper cliff.

'O mother Ida, many-fountain'd Ida,
Dear mother Ida, harken ere I die.
For now the noonday quiet holds the hill:
The grasshopper is silent in the grass:
The lizard, with his shadow on the stone,
Rests like a shadow, and the winds are dead.
The purple flower droops: the golden bee
Is lily-cradled: I alone awake.
My eyes are full of tears, my heart of love,
My heart is breaking, and my eyes are dim,
And I am all aweary of my life.

'O mother Ida, many-fountain'd Ida,
Dear mother Ida, harken ere I die.
Hear me, O Earth, hear me, O Hills, O Caves
That house the cold crown'd snake! O mountain brooks,
I am the daughter of a River-God,
Hear me, for I will speak, and build up all
My sorrow with my song, as yonder walls
Rose slowly to a music slowly breathed,[8]
A cloud that gather'd shape: for it may be
That, while I speak of it, a little while
My heart may wander from its deeper woe.

'O mother Ida, many-fountain'd Ida,
Dear mother Ida, harken ere I die.
I waited underneath the dawning hills,
Aloft the mountain lawn was dewy-dark,
And dewy-dark aloft the mountain-pine:
Beautiful Paris, evil-hearted Paris,
Leading a jet-black goat white-horn'd, white-hoov'd,
Came up from reedy Simois [9] all alone.

'O mother Ida, harken ere I die.
Far-off the torrent call'd me from the cleft:
Far up the solitary morning smote
The streaks of virgin snow. With down-dropt eyes
I sat alone: white-breasted like a star
Fronting the dawn he moved; a leopard skin
Droop'd from his shoulder but his sunny hair
Cluster'd about his temples like a God's:
And his cheek brighten'd as the foam-bow brightens
When the wind blows the foam, and all my heart
Went forth to embrace him coming ere he came.

'Dear mother Ida, harken ere I die.
He smiled, and opening out his milk-white palm
Disclosed a fruit of pure Hesperian gold,
That smelt ambrosially, and while I look'd
And listen'd, the full-flowing river of speech
Came down upon my heart.
'"My own Œnone,
Beautiful-brow'd Œnone, my own soul,
Behold this fruit, whose gleaming rind ingrav'n
'For the most fair,' would seem to award it thine,
As lovelier than whatever Oread haunt
The knolls of Ida, loveliest in all grace
Of movement, and the charm of married brows."

'Dear mother Ida, harken ere I die.
He prest the blossom of his lips to mine,
And added "This was cast upon the board,
When all the full-faced presence of the Gods
Ranged in the halls of Peleus; whereupon
Rose feud, with question unto whom 'twere due:
But light-foot Iris brought it yester-eve,
Delivering, that to me, by common voice
Elected umpire, Heré comes to-day,
Pallas and Aphrodité, claiming each
This meed of fairest. Thou, within the cave

---

[8] The walls of Troy, according to Ovid, rose to the music of Apollo.
[9] A stream near Troy.

Behind yon whispering tuft of oldest pine,
Mayst well behold them unbeheld, unheard
Hear all, and see thy Paris judge of Gods."

'Dear mother Ida, harken ere I die.
It was the deep midnoon: one silvery cloud
Had lost his way between the piney sides
Of this long glen. Then to the bower they came,
Naked they came to that smooth-swarded bower,
And at their feet the crocus brake like fire,
Violet, amaracus, and asphodel,
Lotos and lilies: and a wind arose,
And overhead the wandering ivy and vine,
This way and that, in many a wild festoon
Ran riot, garlanding the gnarled boughs
With bunch and berry and flower thro' and thro'.

'O mother Ida, harken ere I die.
On the tree-tops a crested peacock lit,
And o'er him flow'd a golden cloud, and lean'd
Upon him, slowly dropping fragrant dew.
Then first I heard the voice of her, to whom
Coming thro' Heaven, like a light that grows
Larger and clearer, with one mind the Gods
Rise up for reverence. She to Paris made
Proffer of royal power, ample rule
Unquestion'd, overflowing revenue
Wherewith to embellish state, "from many a vale
And river-sunder'd champaign clothed with corn,
Or labour'd mine undrainable of ore.
Honour," she said, "and homage, tax and toll,
From many an inland town and haven large,
Mast-throng'd beneath her shadowing citadel
In glassy bays among her tallest towers."

'O mother Ida, harken ere I die.
Still she spake on and still she spake of power,
"Which in all action is the end of all;
Power fitted to the season; wisdom-bred
And throned of wisdom — from all neighbour crowns
Alliance and allegiance, till thy hand
Fail from the sceptre-staff. Such boon from me,
From me, Heaven's Queen, Paris, to thee king-born,
A shepherd all thy life but yet king-born,
Should come most welcome, seeing men, in power
Only, are likest gods, who have attain'd
Rest in a happy place and quiet seats
Above the thunder, with undying bliss
In knowledge of their own supremacy."

'Dear mother Ida, harken ere I die.
She ceased, and Paris held the costly fruit
Out at arm's-length, so much the thought of power
Flatter'd his spirit; but Pallas where she stood
Somewhat apart, her clear and bared limbs
O'erthwarted with the brazen-headed spear
Upon her pearly shoulder leaning cold,
The while, above, her full and earnest eye
Over her snow-cold breast and angry cheek
Kept watch, waiting decision, made reply.

'"Self-reverence, self-knowledge, self-control,
These three alone lead life to sovereign power.
Yet not for power (power of herself
Would come uncall'd for) but to live by law,
Acting the law we live by without fear;
And, because right is right, to follow right
Were wisdom in the scorn of consequence."

'Dear mother Ida, harken ere I die.
Again she said: "I woo thee not with gifts.
Sequel of guerdon could not alter me

To fairer. Judge thou me by what I am,
So shalt thou find me fairest.
Yet, indeed,
If gazing on divinity disrobed
Thy mortal eyes are frail to judge of fair,
Unbias'd by self-profit, oh! rest thee sure
That I shall love thee well and cleave to thee,
So that my vigour, wedded to thy blood,
Shall strike within thy pulses, like a God's,
To push thee forward thro' a life of shocks,
Dangers, and deeds, until endurance grow
Sinew'd with action, and the full-grown will,
Circled thro' all experiences, pure law,
Commeasure perfect freedom."
'Here she ceas'd,
And Paris ponder'd, and I cried, "O Paris,
Give it to Pallas!" but he heard me not,
Or hearing would not hear me, woe is me!

'O mother Ida, many-fountain'd Ida,
Dear mother Ida, harken ere I die.
Idalian Aphrodité beautiful,
Fresh as the foam, new-bathed in Paphian[10] wells,
With rosy slender fingers backward drew
From her warm brows and bosom her deep hair
Ambrosial, golden round her lucid throat
And shoulder: from the violets her light foot
Shone rosy-white, and o'er her rounded form
Between the shadows of the vine-bunches
Floated the glowing sunlights, as she moved.

'Dear mother Ida, harken ere I die.
She with a subtle smile in her mild eyes,
The herald of her triumph, drawing nigh
Half-whisper'd in his ear, "I promise thee
The fairest and most loving wife in Greece."
She spoke and laugh'd: I shut my sight for fear:
But when I look'd, Paris had raised his arm,
And I beheld great Heré's angry eyes,
As she withdrew into the golden cloud,
And I was left alone within the bower;
And from that time to this I am alone,
And I shall be alone until I die.

'Yet, mother Ida, harken ere I die.
Fairest — why fairest wife? am I not fair?
My love hath told me so a thousand times.
Methinks I must be fair, for yesterday,
When I past by, a wild and wanton pard,[11]
Eyed like the evening star, with playful tail
Crouch'd fawning in the weed. Most loving is she?
Ah me, my mountain shepherd, that my arms
Were wound about thee, and my hot lips prest
Close, close to thine in that quick-falling dew
Of fruitful kisses, thick as Autumn rains
Flash in the pools of whirling Simois.

'O mother, hear me yet before I die.
They came, they cut away my tallest pines,[12]
My tall dark pines, that plumed the craggy ledge
High over the blue gorge, and all between
The snowy peak and snow-white cataract
Foster'd the callow eaglet — from beneath
Whose thick mysterious boughs in the dark morn
The panther's roar came muffled, while I sat
Low in the valley. Never, never more
Shall lone Œnone see the morning mist
Sweep thro' them; never see them overlaid
With narrow moon-lit slips of silver cloud,
Between the loud stream and the trembling stars.

'O mother, hear me yet before I die.
I wish that somewhere in the ruin'd folds,

[10] Idalium and Paphos were towns in Cyprus, where Aphrodite was worshiped particularly.

[11] leopard

[12] *I.e.*, to make ships for the journey of Paris to Sparta.

Among the fragments tumbled from the glens,
Or the dry thickets, I could meet with her
The Abominable,[13] that uninvited came
Into the fair Peleïan banquet-hall,
And cast the golden fruit upon the board,
And bred this change; that I might speak my mind,
And tell her to her face how much I hate
Her presence, hated both of Gods and men.

'O mother, hear me yet before I die.
Hath he not sworn his love a thousand times,
In this green valley, under this green hill,
Ev'n on this hand, and sitting on this stone?
Seal'd it with kisses? water'd it with tears?
O happy tears, and how unlike to these!
O happy Heaven, how canst thou see my face?
O happy earth, how canst thou bear my weight?
O death, death, death, thou ever-floating cloud,
There are enough unhappy on this earth,
Pass by the happy souls, that love to live:
I pray thee, pass before my light of life,
And shadow all my soul, that I may die.
Thou weighest heavy on the heart within,
Weigh heavy on my eyelids: let me die.

'O mother, hear me yet before I die.
I will not die alone, for fiery thoughts
Do shape themselves within me, more and more,
Whereof I catch the issue, as I hear
Dead sounds at night come from the inmost hills,
Like footsteps upon wool. I dimly see
My far-off doubtful purpose, as a mother
Conjectures of the features of her child
Ere it is born: her child! — a shudder comes
Across me: never child be born of me,
Unblest, to vex me with his father's eyes!

'O mother, hear me yet before I die.
Hear me, O earth. I will not die alone,
Lest their shrill happy laughter come to me
Walking the cold and starless road of death
Uncomforted, leaving my ancient love
With the Greek woman. I will rise and go
Down into Troy, and ere the stars come forth
Talk with the wild Cassandra,[14] for she says
A fire dances before her, and a sound
Rings ever in her ears of armed men.
What this may be I know not, but I know
That, wheresoe'er I am by night and day,
All earth and air seem only burning fire.'

[1832]

The Palace of Art[15]

I BUILT my soul a lordly pleasure-house,
Wherein at ease for aye to dwell.
I said, 'O Soul, make merry and carouse,
Dear soul, for all is well.'

A huge crag-platform, smooth as burnish'd brass
I chose. The ranged ramparts bright
From level meadow-bases of deep grass
Suddenly scaled the light.

Thereon I built it firm. Of ledge or shelf
The rock rose clear, or winding stair.

---

[13] Eris, goddess of discord.

[14] Priam's daughter, who was believed to be mad when she prophesied the fall of Troy.

[15] Upon first publication the poem carried the following introduction:

'I send you here a sort of allegory,
(For you will understand it) of a soul,
A sinful soul possess'd of many gifts,
A spacious garden full of flowering weeds,
A glorious Devil, large in heart and brain,
That did love Beauty only, (Beauty seen
In all varieties of mould and mind)
And Knowledge for its beauty; or if Good,
Good only for its beauty, seeing not
That Beauty, Good, and Knowledge are three sisters
That doat upon each other, friends to man,
Living together under the same roof,
And never can be sunder'd without tears.
And he that shuts Love out, in turn shall be
Shut out from Love, and on her threshold lie
Howling in outer darkness. Not for this
Was common clay ta'en from the common earth
Moulded by God, and temper'd with the tears
Of angels to the perfect shape of man.'

My soul would live alone unto herself
In her high palace there.

And 'while the world runs round and round,' I said,
'Reign thou apart, a quiet king,
Still as, while Saturn whirls, his stedfast shade
Sleeps on his luminous ring.'

To which my soul made answer readily:
'Trust me, in bliss I shall abide
In this great mansion, that is built for me,
So royal-rich and wide.'

. . .

Four courts I made, East, West and South and North,
In each a squared lawn, wherefrom
The golden gorge of dragons spouted forth
A flood of fountain-foam.

And round the cool green courts there ran a row
Of cloisters, branch'd like mighty woods,
Echoing all night to that sonorous flow
Of spouted fountain-floods.

And round the roofs a gilded gallery
That lent broad verge to distant lands,
Far as the wild swan wings, to where the sky
Dipt down to sea and sands.

From those four jets four currents in one swell
Across the mountain stream'd below
In misty folds, that floating as they fell
Lit up a torrent-bow.

And high on every peak a statue seem'd
To hang on tiptoe, tossing up
A cloud of incense of all odour steam'd
From out a golden cup.

So that she thought, 'And who shall gaze upon
My palace with unblinded eyes,
While this great bow will waver in the sun,
And that sweet incense rise?'

For that sweet incense rose and never fail'd,
And, while day sank or mounted higher,
The light aërial gallery, golden-rail'd,
Burnt like a fringe of fire.

Likewise the deep-set windows, stain'd and traced,
Would seem slow-flaming crimson fires
From shadow'd grots of arches interlaced,
And tipt with frost-like spires.

. . .

Full of long-sounding corridors it was,
That over-vaulted grateful gloom,
Thro' which the livelong day my soul did pass,
Well-pleased, from room to room.

Full of great rooms and small the palace stood,
All various, each a perfect whole
From living Nature, fit for every mood
And change of my still soul.

For some were hung with arras green and blue,
Showing a gaudy summer-morn,
Where with puff'd cheek the belted hunter blew
His wreathed bugle-horn.

One seem'd all dark and red — a tract of sand,
And some one pacing there alone,
Who paced for ever in a glimmering land,
Lit with a low large moon.

One show'd an iron coast and angry waves.
You seem'd to hear them climb and fall
And roar rock-thwarted under bellowing caves,
Beneath the windy wall.

And one, a full-fed river winding slow
By herds upon an endless plain,
The ragged rims of thunder brooding low,
With shadow-streaks of rain.

And one, the reapers at their sultry toil.
In front they bound the sheaves. Behind
Were realms of upland, prodigal in oil,
And hoary to the wind.

And one a foreground black with stones and slags,
Beyond, a line of heights, and higher
All barr'd with long white cloud the scornful crags,
And highest, snow and fire.

And one, an English home — gray twilight pour'd
On dewy pastures, dewy trees,
Softer than sleep — all things in order stored,
A haunt of ancient Peace.

Nor these alone, but every landscape fair,
As fit for every mood of mind,
Or gay, or grave, or sweet, or stern, was there
Not less than truth design'd.

. . .

Or the maid-mother by a crucifix,
In tracts of pasture sunny-warm,
Beneath branch-work of costly sardonyx
Sat smiling, babe in arm.

Or in a clear-wall'd city on the sea,
Near gilded organ-pipes, her hair
Wound with white roses, slept St. Cecily; [16]
An angel look'd at her.

Or thronging all one porch of Paradise
A group of Houris [17] bow'd to see
The dying Islamite, with hands and eyes
That said, We wait for thee.

Or mythic Uther's deeply-wounded son [18]
In some fair space of sloping greens
Lay, dozing in the vale of Avalon,
And watch'd by weeping queens.

Or hollowing one hand against his ear,
To list a foot-fall, ere he saw
The wood-nymph, stay'd the Ausonian king [19] to hear
Of wisdom and of law.

Or over hills with peaky tops engrail'd,
And many a tract of palm and rice,
The throne of Indian Cama [20] slowly sail'd
A summer fann'd with spice.

Or sweet Europa's mantle blew unclasp'd,
From off her shoulder backward borne:
From one hand droop'd a crocus: one hand grasp'd
The mild bull's golden horn.[21]

Or else flush'd Ganymede,[22] his rosy thigh
Half-buried in the Eagle's down,
Sole as a flying star shot thro' the sky
Above the pillar'd town.

Nor these alone: but every legend fair
Which the supreme Caucasian mind
Carved out of Nature for itself, was there,
Not less than life, design'd.

. . .

Then in the towers I placed great bells that swung,
Moved of themselves, with silver sound;
And with choice paintings of wise men I hung
The royal dais round.

For there was Milton like a seraph strong,
Beside him Shakespeare bland and mild;
And there the world-worn Dante grasp'd his song,
And somewhat grimly smiled.

And there the Ionian father [23] of the rest;
A million wrinkles carved his skin;
A hundred winters snow'd upon his breast,
From cheek and throat and chin.

[16] St. Cecilia, traditionally the inventor of the organ.

[17] The beautiful virgins who will, says the Koran, accompany the faithful Moslem or Islamite in paradise.

[18] King Arthur. See *Morte d'Arthur*, ll. 192 f. Avalon, in Celtic lore, is the Land of the Blessed, an island paradise in the western sea.

[19] Numa Pompilius, the second king of Rome, was supposedly taught the arts of legislation and government by Egeria, a wood-nymph.

[20] The god of love in Hindu mythology.

[21] Europa, princess of Phœnicia, was carried off to Crete by Zeus, in the form of a white bull.

[22] The beautiful Trojan boy carried off by the eagle of Zeus to become cupbearer to the gods.

[23] Homer

Above, the fair hall-ceiling stately-set
  Many an arch high up did lift,
And angels rising and descending met
    With interchange of gift.

Below was all mosaic choicely plann'd
  With cycles of the human tale
Of this wide world, the times of every land
    So wrought, they will not fail.

The people here, a beast of burden slow,
  Toil'd onward, prick'd with goads and stings;
Here play'd, a tiger, rolling to and fro
    The heads and crowns of kings;

Here rose, an athlete, strong to break or bind
  All force in bonds that might endure,
And here once more like some sick man declined,
    And trusted any cure.

But over these she trod: and those great bells
  Began to chime. She took her throne:
She sat betwixt the shining Oriels,
    To sing her songs alone.

And thro' the topmost Oriels' coloured flame
  Two godlike faces gazed below;
Plato the wise, and large-brow'd Verulam,[24]
    The first of those who know.

And all those names, that in their motion were
  Full-welling fountain-heads of change,
Betwixt the slender shafts were blazon'd fair
    In diverse raiment strange:

Thro' which the lights, rose, amber, emerald, blue,
  Flush'd in her temples and her eyes,
And from her lips, as morn from Memnon,[25] drew
    Rivers of melodies.

No nightingale delighteth to prolong
  Her low preamble all alone,
More than my soul to hear her echo'd song
    Throb thro' the ribbed stone;

Singing and murmuring in her feastful mirth,
  Joying to feel herself alive,
Lord over Nature, Lord of the visible earth,
    Lord of the senses five;

Communing with herself: 'All these are mine,
  And let the world have peace or wars,
'Tis one to me.' She — when young night divine
    Crown'd dying day with stars,

Making sweet close of his delicious toils —
  Lit light in wreaths and anadems,
And pure quintessences of precious oils
    In hollow'd moons of gems,

To mimic heaven; and clapt her hands and cried,
  'I marvel if my still delight
In this great house so royal-rich, and wide,
    Be flatter'd to the height.

'O all things fair to sate my various eyes!
  O shapes and hues that please me well!
O silent faces of the Great and Wise,
    My Gods, with whom I dwell!

'O God-like isolation which art mine,
  I can but count thee perfect gain,
What time I watch the darkening droves of swine
    That range on yonder plain.

'In filthy sloughs they roll a prurient skin,
  They graze and wallow, breed and sleep;
And oft some brainless devil enters in,
    And drives them to the deep.'[26]

[24] Francis Bacon

[25] The Egyptian statue from which music was said to be struck by the rays of the rising sun.

[26] See *St. Matthew*, viii, 32.

Then of the moral instinct would she prate
And of the rising from the dead,
As hers by right of full-accomplish'd Fate;
And at the last she said:

'I take possession of man's mind and deed.
I care not what the sects may brawl.
I sit as God holding no form of creed,
But contemplating all.'

. . .

Full oft the riddle of the painful earth
Flash'd thro' her as she sat alone,
Yet not the less held she her solemn mirth,
And intellectual throne.

And so she throve and prosper'd: so three years
She prosper'd: on the fourth she fell,
Like Herod, when the shout was in his ears,
Struck thro' with pangs of hell.[27]

Lest she should fail and perish utterly,
God, before whom ever lie bare
The abysmal deeps of Personality,
Plagued her with sore despair.

When she would think, where'er she turn'd her sight
The airy hand confusion wrought,
Wrote, 'Mene, mene,' and divided quite
The kingdom of her thought.[28]

Deep dread and loathing of her solitude
Fell on her, from which mood was born
Scorn of herself; again, from out that mood
Laughter at her self-scorn.

'What! is not this my place of strength,' she said,
'My spacious mansion built for me,
Whereof the strong foundation-stones were laid
Since my first memory?'

[27] See *Acts*, xii, 21–23.
[28] See *Daniel*, v.

But in dark corners of her palace stood
Uncertain shapes; and unawares
On white-eyed phantasms weeping tears of blood,
And horrible nightmares,

And hollow shades enclosing hearts of flame,
And, with dim fretted foreheads all,
On corpses three-months-old at noon she came,
That stood against the wall.

A spot of dull stagnation, without light
Or power of movement, seem'd my soul,
'Mid onward-sloping motions infinite
Making for one sure goal.

A still salt pool, lock'd in with bars of sand,
Left on the shore; that hears all night
The plunging seas draw backward from the land
Their moon-led waters white.

A star that with the choral starry dance
Join'd not, but stood, and standing saw
The hollow orb of moving Circumstance
Roll'd round by one fix'd law.

Back on herself her serpent pride had curl'd.
'No voice,' she shriek'd in that lone hall,
'No voice breaks thro' the stillness of this world:
One deep, deep silence all!'

She, mouldering with the dull earth's mouldering sod,
Inwrapt tenfold in slothful shame,
Lay there exiled from eternal God,
Lost to her place and name;

And death and life she hated equally,
And nothing saw, for her despair,
But dreadful time, dreadful eternity,
No comfort anywhere;

Remaining utterly confused with fears,
And ever worse with growing time,
And ever unrelieved by dismal tears,
And all alone in crime:

Shut up as in a crumbling tomb, girt round
With blackness as a solid wall,
Far off she seem'd to hear the dully sound
Of human footsteps fall.

As in strange lands a traveller walking slow,
In doubt and great perplexity,
A little before moon-rise hears the low
Moan of an unknown sea;

And knows not if it be thunder, or a sound
Of rocks thrown down, or one deep cry
Of great wild beasts; then thinketh, 'I have found
A new land, but I die.'

She howl'd aloud, 'I am on fire within.
There comes no murmur of reply.
What is it that will take away my sin,
And save me lest I die?'

So when four years were wholly finished,
She threw her royal robes away.
'Make me a cottage in the vale,' she said,
'Where I may mourn and pray.

'Yet pull not down my palace towers, that are
So lightly, beautifully built:
Perchance I may return with others there
When I have purged my guilt.'

[1832]

The Lotos-eaters[29]

'COURAGE!' he said, and pointed toward the land,
'This mounting wave will roll us shoreward soon.'
In the afternoon they came unto a land
In which it seemed always afternoon.
All round the coast the languid air did swoon,
Breathing like one that hath a weary dream.
Full-faced above the valley stood the moon;
And like a downward smoke, the slender stream
Along the cliff to fall and pause and fall did seem.

A land of streams! some, like a downward smoke,
Slow-dropping veils of thinnest lawn, did go;
And some thro' wavering lights and shadows broke,
Rolling a slumbrous sheet of foam below.
They saw the gleaming river seaward flow
From the inner land: far off, three mountain-tops,
Three silent pinnacles of aged snow,
Stood sunset-flush'd: and, dew'd with showery drops,
Up-clomb the shadowy pine above the woven copse.

The charmed sunset linger'd low adown
In the red West: thro' mountain clefts the dale
Was seen far inland, and the yellow down
Border'd with palm, and many a winding vale
And meadow, set with slender galingale;
A land where all things always seem'd the same!
And round about the keel with faces pale,
Dark faces pale against that rosy flame,
The mild-eyed melancholy Lotos-eaters came.

Branches they bore of that enchanted stem,
Laden with flower and fruit, whereof they gave
To each, but whoso did receive of them,
And taste, to him the gushing of the wave
Far far away did seem to mourn and rave

29 The poem is based upon a passage from Homer's *Odyssey*, IX, 82–97, which describes the coming of Ulysses and his mariners to the land of the lotos-eaters, upon the way home from the Trojan Wars. The fruit of the lotos-tree was an opiate, producing love of rest and forgetfulness of home. Ulysses escaped by tying his men to their boats.

On alien shores; and if his fellow spake,
His voice was thin, as voices from the grave;
And deep-asleep he seem'd, yet all awake,
And music in his ears his beating heart did make.

They sat them down upon the yellow sand,
Between the sun and moon upon the shore;
And sweet it was to dream of Fatherland,
Of child, and wife, and slave; but evermore
Most weary seem'd the sea, weary the oar,
Weary the wandering fields of barren foam.
Then some one said, 'We will return no more;'
And all at once they sang, 'Our island home
Is far beyond the wave; we will no longer roam.'

CHORIC SONG

I

There is sweet music here that softer falls
Than petals from blown roses on the grass,
Or night-dews on still waters between walls
Of shadowy granite, in a gleaming pass;
Music that gentlier on the spirit lies,
Than tir'd eyelids upon tir'd eyes;
Music that brings sweet sleep down from the blissful skies.
Here are cool mosses deep,
And thro' the moss the ivies creep,
And in the stream the long-leaved flowers weep,
And from the craggy ledge the poppy hangs in sleep.

II

Why are we weigh'd upon with heaviness,
And utterly consumed with sharp distress,
While all things else have rest from weariness?
All things have rest: why should we toil alone,
We only toil, who are the first of things,
And make perpetual moan,
Still from one sorrow to another thrown:
Nor ever fold our wings,
And cease from wanderings,
Nor steep our brows in slumber's holy balm;
Nor harken what the inner spirit sings,
'There is no joy but calm!'
Why should we only toil, the roof and crown of things?

III

Lo! in the middle of the wood,
The folded leaf is woo'd from out the bud
With winds upon the branch, and there
Grows green and broad, and takes no care,
Sun-steep'd at noon, and in the moon
Nightly dew-fed; and turning yellow
Falls, and floats adown the air.
Lo! sweeten'd with the summer light,
The full-juiced apple, waxing over-mellow,
Drops in a silent autumn night.
All its allotted length of days,
The flower ripens in its place,
Ripens and fades, and falls, and hath no toil,
Fast-rooted in the fruitful soil.

IV

Hateful is the dark-blue sky,
Vaulted o'er the dark-blue sea.
Death is the end of life; ah, why
Should life all labour be?
Let us alone. Time driveth onward fast,
And in a little while our lips are dumb.
Let us alone. What is it that will last?
All things are taken from us, and become
Portions and parcels of the dreadful Past.
Let us alone. What pleasure can we have
To war with evil? Is there any peace
In ever climbing up the climbing wave?
All things have rest, and ripen toward the grave
In silence; ripen, fall and cease:
Give us long rest or death, dark death, or dreamful ease.

V

How sweet it were, hearing the downward stream,
With half-shut eyes ever to seem
Falling asleep in a half-dream!
To dream and dream, like yonder amber light,
Which will not leave the myrrh-bush on the height;
To hear each other's whisper'd speech;
Eating the Lotos day by day,
To watch the crisping ripples on the beach,
And tender curving lines of creamy spray;
To lend our hearts and spirits wholly
To the influence of mild-minded melancholy;
To muse and brood and live again in memory,
With those old faces of our infancy
Heap'd over with a mound of grass,
Two handfuls of white dust, shut in an urn of brass!

VI

Dear is the memory of our wedded lives,
And dear the last embraces of our wives
And their warm tears: but all hath suffer'd change:
For surely now our household hearths are cold:
Our sons inherit us: our looks are strange:
And we should come like ghosts to trouble joy.
Or else the island princes over-bold
Have eat our substance, and the minstrel sings
Before them of the ten years' war in Troy,
And our great deeds, as half-forgotten things.
Is there confusion in the little isle?
Let what is broken so remain.
The Gods are hard to reconcile:
'Tis hard to settle order once again.
There *is* confusion worse than death,
Trouble on trouble, pain on pain,
Long labour unto aged breath,
Sore task to hearts worn out by many wars
And eyes grown dim with gazing on the pilot-stars.

VII

But, propt on beds of amaranth and moly,[30]
How sweet (while warm airs lull us, blowing lowly)
With half-dropt eyelid still,
Beneath a heaven dark and holy,
To watch the long bright river drawing slowly
His waters from the purple hill —
To hear the dewy echoes calling
From cave to cave thro' the thick-twined vine —
To watch the emerald-colour'd water falling
Thro' many a wov'n acanthus-wreath divine!
Only to hear and see the far-off sparkling brine,
Only to hear were sweet, stretch'd out beneath the pine.

VIII

The Lotos blooms below the barren peak:
The Lotos blows by every winding creek:
All day the wind breathes low with mellower tone:
Thro' every hollow cave and alley lone
Round and round the spicy downs the yellow Lotos-dust is blown.
We have had enough of action, and of motion we,
Roll'd to starboard, roll'd to larboard, when the surge was seething free,
Where the wallowing monster spouted his foam-fountains in the sea.
Let us swear an oath, and keep it with an equal mind,
In the hollow Lotos-land to live and lie reclined

---

[30] Amaranth was a legendary flower supposed never to fade; moly, a fabulous magic herb given by Hermes to Ulysses for protection against the charms of Circe, the enchantress.

On the hills like Gods together, careless of mankind.
For they lie beside their nectar, and the bolts are hurl'd
Far below them in the valleys, and the clouds are lightly curl'd
Round their golden houses, girdled with the gleaming world:
Where they smile in secret, looking over wasted lands,
Blight and famine, plague and earthquake, roaring deeps and fiery sands,
Clanging fights, and flaming towns, and sinking ships, and praying hands.
But they smile, they find a music centred in a doleful song
Steaming up, a lamentation and an ancient tale of wrong,
Like a tale of little meaning tho' the words are strong;
Chanted from an ill-used race of men that cleave the soil,
Sow the seed, and reap the harvest with enduring toil,
Storing yearly little dues of wheat, and wine and oil;
Till they perish and they suffer — some, 'tis whisper'd — down in hell
Suffer endless anguish, others in Elysian valleys dwell,
Resting weary limbs at last on beds of asphodel.
Surely, surely, slumber is more sweet than toil, the shore
Than labour in the deep mid-ocean, wind and wave and oar;
Oh rest ye, brother mariners, we will not wander more.

[1832]

St. Agnes' Eve [31]

Deep on the convent-roof the snows
  Are sparkling to the moon:
My breath to heaven like vapour goes:
  May my soul follow soon!
The shadows of the convent-towers
  Slant down the snowy sward,
Still creeping with the creeping hours
  That lead me to my Lord:
Make Thou my spirit pure and clear
  As are the frosty skies,
Or this first snowdrop of the year
  That in my bosom lies.

As these white robes are soil'd and dark,
  To yonder shining ground;
As this pale taper's earthly spark,
  To yonder argent round;
So shows my soul before the Lamb,
  My spirit before Thee;
So in mine earthly house I am,
  To that I hope to be.
Break up the heavens, O Lord! and far,
  Thro' all yon starlight keen,
Draw me, thy bride, a glittering star,
  In raiment white and clean.

He lifts me to the golden doors;
  The flashes come and go;
All heaven bursts her starry floors,
  And strows her lights below,
And deepens on and up! the gates
  Roll back, and far within
For me the Heavenly Bridegroom waits,
  To make me pure of sin.
The sabbaths of Eternity,
  One sabbath deep and wide —
A light upon the shining sea —
  The Bridegroom with his bride!

[31] Published in *The Keepsake*, 1837. See the introductory note to Keats's *The Eve of St. Agnes*, p. 831.

You ask me, why, tho' ill at ease [32]

You ask me, why, tho' ill at ease,
  Within this region I subsist,
  Whose spirits falter in the mist,
And languish for the purple seas.

[32] This and the five following poems were published in *Poems*, 1842, the edition that definitely established Tennyson's fame. They were written at various times during the ten years' interval between the volume of 1832 and the new one.

It is the land that freemen till,
That sober-suited Freedom chose,
The land, where girt with friends or foes
A man may speak the thing he will;

A land of settled government,
A land of just and old renown,
Where Freedom slowly broadens down
From precedent to precedent:

Where faction seldom gathers head,
But by degrees to fullness wrought,
The strength of some diffusive thought
Hath time and space to work and spread.

Should banded unions persecute
Opinion, and induce a time
When single thought is civil crime,
And individual freedom mute;

Tho' Power should make from land to land
The name of Britain trebly great —
Tho' every channel of the State
Should fill and choke with golden sand —

Yet waft me from the harbour-mouth,
Wild wind! I seek a warmer sky,
And I will see before I die
The palms and temples of the South.

Of old sat Freedom on the heights

Of old sat Freedom on the heights,
The thunders breaking at her feet:
Above her shook the starry lights:
She heard the torrents meet.

There in her place she did rejoice,
Self-gather'd in her prophet-mind,
But fragments of her mighty voice
Came rolling on the wind.

Then stept she down thro' town and field
To mingle with the human race,
And part by part to men reveal'd
The fullness of her face —

Grave mother of majestic works,
From her isle-altar gazing down,
Who, God-like, grasps the triple forks,
And, King-like, wears the crown:

Her open eyes desire the truth.
The wisdom of a thousand years
Is in them. May perpetual youth
Keep dry their light from tears;

That her fair form may stand and shine,
Make bright our days and light our dreams,
Turning to scorn with lips divine
The falsehood of extremes!

[1842]

Morte d'Arthur [33]

So all day long the noise of battle roll'd
Among the mountains by the winter sea;
Until King Arthur's table, man by man,
Had fall'n in Lyonnesse about their Lord,
King Arthur: then, because his wound was deep,
The bold Sir Bedivere uplifted him,
Sir Bedivere, the last of all his knights,
And bore him to a chapel nigh the field,
A broken chancel with a broken cross,
That stood on a dark strait of barren land.
On one side lay the Ocean, and on one
Lay a great water, and the moon was full.
Then spake King Arthur to Sir Bedivere:
'The sequel of to-day unsolders all
The goodliest fellowship of famous knights
Whereof this world holds record. Such a sleep
They sleep — the men I loved. I think that we
Shall never more, at any future time,
Delight our souls with talk of knightly deeds,

[33] This poem, which had been written at the latest by 1835, long before the plan for *The Idylls of the King* had been conceived, has its source in Malory's *Morte d'Arthur*, Book XXI. It was later incorporated in the last of the *Idylls*, 'The Passing of Arthur.'

Walking about the gardens and the halls
Of Camelot, as in the days that were.
I perish by this people which I made, —
Tho' Merlin [34] sware that I should come again
To rule once more — but let what will be, be,
I am so deeply smitten thro' the helm
That without help I cannot last till morn.
Thou therefore take my brand Excalibur,
Which was my pride: for thou rememberest how
In those old days, one summer noon, an arm
Rose up from out the bosom of the lake,
Clothed in white samite, mystic, wonderful,
Holding the sword — and how I row'd across
And took it, and have worn it, like a king:
And, wheresoever I am sung or told
In aftertime, this also shall be known:
But now delay not: take Excalibur,
And fling him far into the middle mere:
Watch what thou seëst, and lightly bring me word.'
  To him replied the bold Sir Bedivere:
'It is not meet, Sir King, to leave thee thus,
Aidless, alone, and smitten thro' the helm.
A little thing may harm a wounded man.
Yet I thy hest will all perform at full,
Watch what I see, and lightly bring thee word.'
  So saying, from the ruin'd shrine he stept
And in the moon athwart the place of tombs,
Where lay the mighty bones of ancient men,
Old knights, and over them the sea-wind sang
Shrill, chill, with flakes of foam. He, stepping down
By zig-zag paths, and juts of pointed rock,
Came on the shining levels of the lake.

[34] The magician and seer of Arthur's court.

  There drew he forth the brand Excalibur,
And o'er him, drawing it, the winter moon,
Brightening the skirts of a long cloud, ran forth
And sparkled keen with frost against the hilt:
For all the haft twinkled with diamond sparks,
Myriads of topaz-lights, and jacinth-work
Of subtlest jewellery. He gazed so long
That both his eyes were dazzled, as he stood,
This way and that dividing the swift mind,
In act to throw: but at the last it seem'd
Better to leave Excalibur conceal'd
There in the many-knotted waterflags,
That whistled stiff and dry about the marge.
So strode he back slow to the wounded King.
  Then spake King Arthur to Sir Bedivere:
'Hast thou perform'd my mission which I gave?
What is it thou hast seen? or what hast heard?'
  And answer made the bold Sir Bedivere:
'I heard the ripple washing in the reeds,
And the wild water lapping on the crag.'
  To whom replied King Arthur, faint and pale:
'Thou hast betray'd thy nature and thy name,
Not rendering true answer, as beseem'd
Thy fëalty, nor like a noble knight:
For surer sign had follow'd, either hand,
Or voice, or else a motion of the mere.
This is a shameful thing for men to lie.
Yet now, I charge thee, quickly go again
As thou art lief [35] and dear, and do the thing
I bade thee, watch, and lightly bring me word.'

[35] beloved

Then went Sir Bedivere the second time
Across the ridge, and paced beside the mere,
Counting the dewy pebbles, fix'd in thought;
But when he saw the wonder of the hilt,
How curiously and strangely chased, he smote
His palms together, and he cried aloud,
'And if indeed I cast the brand away,
Surely a precious thing, one worthy note,
Should thus be lost for ever from the earth,
Which might have pleased the eyes of many men.
What good should follow this, if this were done?
What harm, undone? deep harm to disobey,
Seeing obedience is the bond of rule.
Were it well to obey, then, if a king demand
An act unprofitable, against himself?
The King is sick, and knows not what he does.
What record, or what relic of my lord
Should be to aftertime, but empty breath
And rumours of a doubt? but were this kept,
Stored in some treasure-house of mighty kings,
Some one might show it at a joust of arms,
Saying, "King Arthur's sword, Excalibur,
Wrought by the lonely maiden of the Lake.
Nine years she wrought it, sitting in the deeps
Upon the hidden bases of the hills."
So might some old man speak in the aftertime
To all the people, winning reverence.
But now much honour and much fame were lost.'
So spake he, clouded with his own conceit,
And hid Excalibur the second time,
And so strode back slow to the wounded King.

Then spoke King Arthur, breathing heavily:
'What is it thou hast seen? or what hast heard?'
And answer made the bold Sir Bedivere:
'I heard the water lapping on the crag,
And the long ripple washing in the reeds.'
To whom replied King Arthur, much in wrath:
'Ah, miserable and unkind, untrue,
Unknightly, traitor-hearted! Woe is me!
Authority forgets a dying king,
Laid widow'd of the power in his eye
That bow'd the will. I see thee what thou art,
For thou, the latest-left of all my knights,
In whom should meet the offices of all,
Thou wouldst betray me for the precious hilt;
Either from lust of gold, or like a girl
Valuing the giddy pleasure of the eyes.
Yet, for a man may fail in duty twice,
And the third time may prosper, get thee hence:
But, if thou spare to fling Excalibur,
I will arise and slay thee with my hands.'
Then quickly rose Sir Bedivere, and ran,
And, leaping down the ridges lightly, plunged
Among the bulrush-beds, and clutch'd the sword,
And strongly wheel'd and threw it. The great brand
Made lightnings in the splendour of the moon,
And flashing round and round, and whirl'd in an arch,
Shot like a streamer of the northern morn,
Seen where the moving isles of winter shock
By night, with noises of the northern sea.
So flash'd and fell the brand Excalibur:
But ere he dipt the surface, rose an arm
Clothed in white samite, mystic, wonderful,
And caught him by the hilt, and brandish'd him

Three times, and drew him under in the mere.
And lightly went the other to the King.
Then spoke King Arthur, drawing thicker breath:
'Now see I by thine eyes that this is done.
Speak out: what is it thou hast heard, or seen?'
And answer made the bold Sir Bedivere:
'Sir King, I closed mine eyelids, lest the gems
Should blind my purpose, for I never saw,
Nor shall see, here or elsewhere, till I die,
Not tho' I live three lives of mortal men,
So great a miracle as yonder hilt.
Then with both hands I flung him, wheeling him;
But when I look'd again, behold an arm,
Clothed in white samite, mystic, wonderful,
That caught him by the hilt, and brandish'd him
Three times, and drew him under in the mere.'
And answer made King Arthur, breathing hard:
'My end draws nigh; 'tis time that I were gone.
Make broad thy shoulders to receive my weight,
And bear me to the margin; yet I fear
My wound hath taken cold, and I shall die.'
So saying, from the pavement he half rose,
Slowly, with pain, reclining on his arm,
And looking wistfully with wide blue eyes
As in a picture. Him Sir Bedivere
Remorsefully regarded thro' his tears,
And would have spoken, but he found not words,
Then took with care, and kneeling on one knee,
O'er both his shoulders drew the languid hands,
And rising bore him thro' the place of tombs.
But, as he walk'd, King Arthur panted hard,
Like one that feels a nightmare on his bed
When all the house is mute. So sigh'd the King,
Muttering and murmuring at his ear, 'Quick, quick!
I fear it is too late, and I shall die.'
But the other swiftly strode from ridge to ridge,
Clothed with his breath, and looking, as he walk'd,
Larger than human on the frozen hills.
He heard the deep behind him, and a cry
Before. His own thought drove him, like a goad.
Dry [36] clash'd his harness in the icy caves
And barren chasms, and all to left and right
The bare black cliff clang'd round him, as he based
His feet on juts of slippery crag that rang
Sharp-smitten with the dint of armed heels —
And on a sudden, lo! the level lake,
And the long glories of the winter moon.
Then saw they how there hove a dusky barge,
Dark as a funeral scarf from stem to stern,
Beneath them; and descending they were ware
That all the decks were dense with stately forms
Black-stoled, black-hooded, like a dream — by these
Three Queens with crowns of gold — and from them rose
A cry that shiver'd to the tingling stars,
And, as it were one voice, an agony
Of lamentation, like a wind, that shrills
All night in a waste land, where no one comes,
Or hath come, since the making of the world.
Then murmur'd Arthur, 'Place me in the barge,'
And to the barge they came. There those three Queens
Put forth their hands, and took the King, and wept.

[36] gratingly

But she, that rose the tallest of them all
And fairest, laid his head upon her lap,
And loosed the shatter'd casque, and chafed his hands,
And call'd him by his name, complaining loud,
And dropping bitter tears against his brow
Striped with dark blood: for all his face was white
And colourless, and like the wither'd moon
Smote by the fresh beam of the springing east;
And all his greaves and cuisses dash'd with drops
Of onset; and the light and lustrous curls —
That made his forehead like a rising sun
High from the daïs-throne — were parch'd with dust;
Or, clotted into points and hanging loose,
Mix'd with the knightly growth that fringed his lips.
So like a shatter'd column lay the King;
Not like that Arthur who, with lance in rest,
From spur to plume a star of tournament,
Shot thro' the lists at Camelot, and charged
Before the eyes of ladies and of kings.

Then loudly cried the bold Sir Bedivere,
'Ah! my Lord Arthur, whither shall I go?
Where shall I hide my forehead and my eyes?
For now I see the true old times are dead,
When every morning brought a noble chance,
And every chance brought out a noble knight.
Such times have been not since the light[37] that led
The holy Elders with the gift of myrrh.
But now the whole ROUND TABLE is dissolved
Which was an image of the mighty world;
And I, the last, go forth companionless,
And the days darken round me, and the years,
Among new men, strange faces, other minds.'

And slowly answered Arthur from the barge:
'The old order changeth, yielding place to new,
And God fulfils Himself in many ways,
Lest one good custom should corrupt the world.
Comfort thyself: what comfort is in me?
I have lived my life, and that which I have done
May He within Himself make pure! but thou,
If thou shouldst never see my face again,
Pray for my soul. More things are wrought by prayer
Than this world dreams of. Wherefore, let thy voice
Rise like a fountain for me night and day.
For what are men better than sheep or goats
That nourish a blind life within the brain,
If, knowing God, they lift not hands of prayer
Both for themselves and those who call them friend?
For so the whole round earth is every way
Bound by gold chains about the feet of God.
But now farewell. I am going a long way
With these thou seëst — if indeed I go —
(For all my mind is clouded with a doubt)
To the island-valley of Avilion;
Where falls not hail, or rain, or any snow,
Nor ever wind blows loudly; but it lies
Deep-meadow'd, happy, fair with orchard-lawns
And bowery hollows crown'd with summer sea,
Where I will heal me of my grievous wound.'

So said he, and the barge with oar and sail
Moved from the brink, like some full-breasted swan
That, fluting a wild carol ere her death,

[37] The Star of Bethlehem.

Ruffles her pure cold plume, and takes the flood
With swarthy webs. Long stood Sir Bedivere
Revolving many memories, till the hull
Look'd one black dot against the verge of dawn,
And on the mere the wailing died away.

Here ended Hall,[38] and our last light, that long
Had wink'd and threaten'd darkness, flared and fell:
At which the Parson, sent to sleep with sound,
And waked with silence, grunted 'Good!' but we
Sat rapt: it was the tone with which he read—
Perhaps some modern touches here and there
Redeem'd it from the charge of nothingness—
Or else we loved the man, and prized his work;
I know not: but we sitting, as I said,
The cock crew loud; as at that time of year
The lusty bird takes every hour for dawn:
Then Francis, muttering, like a man ill-used,
'There now—that's nothing!' drew a little back,
And drove his heel into the smoulder'd log,
That sent a blast of sparkles up the flue:
And so to bed; where yet in sleep I seem'd
To sail with Arthur under looming shores,
Point after point; till on to dawn, when dreams
Begin to feel the truth and stir of day,
To me, methought, who waited with a crowd,
There came a bark that, blowing forward, bore
King Arthur, like a modern gentleman
Of stateliest port; and all the people cried,
'Arthur is come again: he cannot die.'
Then those that stood upon the hills behind
Repeated—'Come again, and thrice as fair;'
And, further inland, voices echo'd—'Come
With all good things, and war shall be no more.'
At this a hundred bells began to peal,
That with the sound I woke, and heard indeed
The clear church-bells ring in the Christmas-morn.

[1842]

Ulysses[39]

It little profits that an idle king,
By this still hearth, among these barren crags,
Match'd with an aged wife, I mete and dole
Unequal laws unto a savage race,
That hoard, and sleep, and feed, and know not me.
I cannot rest from travel: I will drink
Life to the lees: all times I have enjoy'd
Greatly, have suffer'd greatly, both with those
That loved me, and alone; on shore, and when
Thro' scudding drifts the rainy Hyades[40]
Vext the dim sea: I am become a name;
For always roaming with a hungry heart
Much have I seen and known; cities of men
And manners, climates, councils, governments,
Myself not least, but honour'd of them all;
And drunk delight of battle with my peers,

---

[38] The *Morte d'Arthur* follows a shorter piece, *The Epic*, and is itself supposedly read by the poet 'Everard Hall' at 'Francis Allen's on the Christmas-eve.' One of the auditors is 'Parson Holmes.' In describing the reading, Tennyson gives a significant portrait of himself:

'—mouthing out his hollow oes and aes,
Deep-chested music.'

[39] The address of the aged Ulysses to his men, made long after his return to his 'island-home' of Ithaca, was suggested not by the *Odyssey*, as was *The Lotos-Eaters*, but by Dante's *Inferno*, xxvi, 90–142. Tennyson said that the poem, composed shortly after the death of Arthur Hallam, perhaps expressed the need of courageous going forward with life 'more simply than anything in *In Memoriam*.'

[40] A group of seven stars which were believed to herald the rainy season by their rising and setting.

Far on the ringing plains of windy Troy.
I am a part of all that I have met;
Yet all experience is an arch wherethro'
Gleams that untravell'd world, whose margin fades
For ever and for ever when I move.
How dull it is to pause, to make an end,
To rust unburnish'd, not to shine in use!
As tho' to breathe were life. Life piled on life
Were all too little, and of one to me
Little remains: but every hour is saved
From that eternal silence, something more,
A bringer of new things; and vile it were
For some three suns to store and hoard myself,
And this gray spirit yearning in desire
To follow knowledge like a sinking star,
Beyond the utmost bound of human thought.

This is my son, mine own Telemachus,
To whom I leave the sceptre and the isle —
Well-loved of me, discerning to fulfil
This labour, by slow prudence to make mild
A rugged people, and thro' soft degrees
Subdue them to the useful and the good.
Most blameless is he, centred in the sphere
Of common duties, decent not to fail
In offices of tenderness, and pay
Meet adoration to my household gods,
When I am gone. He works his work, I mine.

There lies the port; the vessel puffs her sail:
There gloom the dark broad seas. My mariners,
Souls that have toil'd, and wrought, and thought with me —
That ever with a frolic welcome took
The thunder and the sunshine, and opposed
Free hearts, free foreheads — you and I are old;
Old age hath yet his honour and his toil;
Death closes all: but something ere the end,
Some work of noble note, may yet be done,
Not unbecoming men that strove with Gods.
The lights begin to twinkle from the rocks:
The long day wanes: the slow moon climbs: the deep
Moans round with many voices. Come, my friends,
'Tis not too late to seek a newer world.
Push off, and sitting well in order smite
The sounding furrows; for my purpose holds
To sail beyond the sunset, and the baths
Of all the western stars, until I die.
It may be that the gulfs will wash us down:
It may be we shall touch the Happy Isles,
And see the great Achilles, whom we knew.
Tho' much is taken, much abides; and tho'
We are not now that strength which in old days
Moved earth and heaven; that which we are, we are;
One equal temper of heroic hearts,
Made weak by time and fate, but strong in will
To strive, to seek, to find, and not to yield.

[1842]

Locksley Hall

COMRADES, leave me here a little, while as yet 'tis early morn:
Leave me here, and when you want me, sound upon the bugle-horn.

'Tis the place, and all around it, as of old, the curlews call,
Dreary gleams about the moorland flying over Locksley Hall;

Locksley Hall, that in the distance overlooks the sandy tracts,
And the hollow ocean-ridges roaring into cataracts.

Many a night from yonder ivied casement, ere I went to rest,

Did I look on great Orion sloping slowly to the West.

Many a night I saw the Pleiads, rising thro' the mellow shade,
Glitter like a swarm of fire-flies tangled in a silver braid.

Here about the beach I wander'd, nourishing a youth sublime
With the fairy tales of science, and the long result of Time;

When the centuries behind me like a fruitful land reposed;
When I clung to all the present for the promise that it closed:

When I dipt into the future far as human eye could see;
Saw the Vision of the world, and all the wonder that would be.—

In the Spring a fuller crimson comes upon the robin's breast;
In the Spring the wanton lapwing gets himself another crest;

In the Spring a livelier iris changes on the burnish'd dove;
In the Spring a young man's fancy lightly turns to thoughts of love.

Then her cheek was pale and thinner than should be for one so young,
And her eyes on all my motions with a mute observance hung.

And I said, 'My cousin Amy, speak, and speak the truth to me,
Trust me, cousin, all the current of my being sets to thee.'

On her pallid cheek and forehead came a colour and a light,
As I have seen the rosy red flushing in the northern night.

And she turn'd—her bosom shaken with a sudden storm of sighs—
All the spirit deeply dawning in the dark of hazel eyes—

Saying, 'I have hid my feelings, fearing they should do me wrong;'
Saying, 'Dost thou love me, cousin?' weeping, 'I have loved thee long.'

Love took up the glass of Time, and turn'd it in his glowing hands;
Every moment, lightly shaken, ran itself in golden sands.

Love took up the harp of Life, and smote on all the chords with might;
Smote the chord of Self, that, trembling, pass'd in music out of sight.

Many a morning on the moorland did we hear the copses ring,
And her whisper throng'd my pulses with the fullness of the Spring.

Many an evening by the waters did we watch the stately ships,
And our spirits rush'd together at the touching of the lips.

O my cousin, shallow-hearted! O my Amy, mine no more!
O the dreary, dreary moorland! O the barren, barren shore!

Falser than all fancy fathoms, falser than all songs have sung,
Puppet to a father's threat, and servile to a shrewish tongue!

Is it well to wish thee happy?—having known me—to decline
On a range of lower feelings and a narrower heart than mine!

Yet it shall be: thou shalt lower to his level day by day,
What is fine within thee growing coarse to sympathise with clay.

As the husband is, the wife is: thou art mated with a clown,
And the grossness of his nature will have weight to drag thee down.

He will hold thee, when his passion shall have spent its novel force,
Something better than his dog, a little dearer than his horse.

What is this? his eyes are heavy: think not they are glazed with wine.
Go to him: it is thy duty: kiss him: take his hand in thine.

It may be my lord is weary, that his brain is overwrought:
Soothe him with thy finer fancies, touch him with thy lighter thought.

He will answer to the purpose, easy things to understand —
Better thou wert dead before me, tho' I slew thee with my hand!

Better thou and I were lying, hidden from the heart's disgrace,
Roll'd in one another's arms, and silent in a last embrace.

Cursed be the social wants that sin against the strength of youth!
Cursed be the social lies that warp us from the living truth!

Cursed be the sickly forms that err from honest Nature's rule!
Cursed be the gold that gilds the straiten'd forehead of the fool!

Well — 'tis well that I should bluster! — Hadst thou less unworthy proved —
Would to God — for I had loved thee more than ever wife was loved.

Am I mad, that I should cherish that which bears but bitter fruit?
I will pluck it from my bosom, tho' my heart be at the root.

Never, tho' my mortal summers to such length of years should come
As the many-winter'd crow that leads the clanging rookery home.

Where is comfort? in division of the records of the mind?
Can I part her from herself, and love her, as I knew her, kind?

I remember one that perish'd: sweetly did she speak and move:
Such a one do I remember, whom to look at was to love.

Can I think of her as dead, and love her for the love she bore?
No — she never loved me truly: love is love for evermore.

Comfort? comfort scorn'd of devils![41] this is truth the poet[42] sings,
That a sorrow's crown of sorrow is remembering happier things.

Drug thy memories, lest thou learn it, lest thy heart be put to proof,
In the dead unhappy night, and when the rain is on the roof.

Like a dog, he hunts in dreams, and thou art staring at the wall,
Where the dying night-lamp flickers, and the shadows rise and fall.

Then a hand shall pass before thee, pointing to his drunken sleep,
To thy widow'd marriage-pillows, to the tears that thou wilt weep.

Thou shalt hear the 'Never, never,' whisper'd by the phantom years,
And a song from out the distance in the ringing of thine ears;

And an eye shall vex thee, looking ancient kindness on thy pain.
Turn thee, turn thee on thy pillow: get thee to thy rest again.

---

[41] Alludes to the first two books of *Paradise Lost.*
[42] Dante in the *Inferno,* v, 121–123.

Nay, but Nature brings thee solace; for a tender voice will cry.
'Tis a purer life than thine; a lip to drain thy trouble dry.

Baby lips will laugh me down: my latest rival brings thee rest.
Baby fingers, waxen touches, press me from the mother's breast.

O, the child too clothes the father with a dearness not his due.
Half is thine and half is his: it will be worthy of the two.

O, I see thee old and formal, fitted to thy petty part,
With a little hoard of maxims preaching down a daughter's heart.

'They were dangerous guides the feelings — she herself was not exempt —
Truly, she herself had suffer'd' — Perish in thy self-contempt!

Overlive it — lower yet — be happy! wherefore should I care?
I myself must mix with action, lest I wither by despair.

What is that which I should turn to, lighting upon days like these?
Every door is barr'd with gold, and opens but to golden keys.

Every gate is throng'd with suitors, all the markets overflow.
I have but an angry fancy: what is that which I should do?

I had been content to perish, falling on the foeman's ground,
When the ranks are roll'd in vapour, and the winds are laid with sound.

But the jingling of the guinea helps the hurt that Honour feels,
And the nations do but murmur, snarling at each other's heels.

Can I but relive in sadness? I will turn that earlier page.
Hide me from my deep emotion, O thou wondrous Mother-Age!

Make me feel the wild pulsation that I felt before the strife,
When I heard my days before me, and the tumult of my life;

Yearning for the large excitement that the coming years would yield,
Eager-hearted as a boy when first he leaves his father's field,

And at night along the dusky highway near and nearer drawn,
Sees in heaven the light of London flaring like a dreary dawn;

And his spirit leaps within him to be gone before him then,
Underneath the light he looks at, in among the throngs of men:

Men, my brothers, men the workers, ever reaping something new:
That which they have done but earnest of the things that they shall do:

For I dipt into the future, far as human eye could see,
Saw the Vision of the world, and all the wonder that would be;

Saw the heavens fill with commerce, argosies of magic sails,
Pilots of the purple twilight, dropping down with costly bales;

Heard the heavens fill with shouting, and there rain'd a ghastly dew
From the nations' airy navies grappling in the central blue;

Far along the world-wide whisper of the south-wind rushing warm,
With the standards of the peoples plunging thro' the thunder-storm;

Till the war-drum throbb'd no longer, and the battle-flags were furl'd
In the Parliament of man, the Federation of the world.

There the common sense of most shall hold a fretful realm in awe,
And the kindly earth shall slumber, lapt in universal law.

So I triumph'd ere my passion sweeping thro' me left me dry,
Left me with the palsied heart, and left me with the jaundiced eye;

Eye, to which all order festers, all things here are out of joint:
Science moves, but slowly slowly, creeping on from point to point:

Slowly comes a hungry people, as a lion creeping nigher,
Glares at one that nods and winks behind a slowly-dying fire.

Yet I doubt not thro' the ages one increasing purpose runs,
And the thoughts of men are widen'd with the process of the suns.

What is that to him that reaps not harvest of his youthful joys,
Tho' the deep heart of existence beat for ever like a boy's?

Knowledge comes, but wisdom lingers, and I linger on the shore,
And the individual withers, and the world is more and more.

Knowledge comes, but wisdom lingers, and he bears a laden breast,
Full of sad experience, moving toward the stillness of his rest.

Hark, my merry comrades call me, sounding on the bugle-horn,
They to whom my foolish passion were a target for their scorn:

Shall it not be scorn to me to harp on such a moulder'd string?
I am shamed thro' all my nature to have loved so slight a thing.

Weakness to be wroth with weakness! woman's pleasure, woman's pain —
Nature made them blinder motions bounded in a shallower brain:

Woman is the lesser man, and all thy passions, match'd with mine,
Are as moonlight unto sunlight, and as water unto wine —

Here at least, where nature sickens, nothing. Ah, for some retreat
Deep in yonder shining Orient, where my life began to beat;

Where in wild Mahratta-battle[43] fell my father evil-starr'd; —
I was left a trampled orphan, and a selfish uncle's ward.

Or to burst all links of habit — there to wander far away,
On from island unto island at the gateways of the day.

Larger constellations burning, mellow moons and happy skies,
Breadths of tropic shade and palms in cluster, knots of Paradise.

Never comes the trader, never floats an European flag,
Slides the bird o'er lustrous woodland, swings the trailer from the crag;

Droops the heavy-blossom'd bower, hangs the heavy-fruited tree —
Summer isles of Eden lying in dark-purple spheres of sea.

There methinks would be enjoyment more than in this march of mind,
In the steamship, in the railway, in the thoughts that shake mankind.

[43] The Mahrattas are a Hindu people of India.

There the passions cramp'd no longer shall have scope and breathing space;
I will take some savage woman, she shall rear my dusky race.

Iron-jointed, supple-sinew'd, they shall dive, and they shall run,
Catch the wild goat by the hair, and hurl their lances in the sun;

Whistle back the parrot's call, and leap the rainbows of the brooks,
Not with blinded eyesight poring over miserable books —

Fool, again the dream, the fancy! but I *know* my words are wild,
But I count the gray barbarian lower than the Christian child.

I, to herd with narrow foreheads, vacant of our glorious gains,
Like a beast with lower pleasures, like a beast with lower pains!

Mated with a squalid savage — what to me were sun or clime?
I the heir of all the ages, in the foremost files of time —

I that rather held it better men should perish one by one,
Than that earth should stand at gaze like Joshua's moon in Ajalon! [44]

Not in vain the distance beacons. Forward, forward let us range,
Let the great world spin for ever down the ringing grooves of change.[45]

Thro' the shadow of the globe we sweep into the younger day:
Better fifty years of Europe than a cycle of Cathay.[46]

Mother-Age (for mine I knew not) help me as when life begun:
Rift the hills, and roll the waters, flash the lightnings, weigh the Sun.

O, I see the crescent promise of my spirit hath not set.
Ancient founts of inspiration well thro' all my fancy yet.

Howsoever these things be, a long farewell to Locksley Hall!
Now for me the woods may wither, now for me the roof-tree fall.

Comes a vapour from the margin, blackening over heath and holt,
Cramming all the blast before it, in its breast a thunderbolt.

Let it fall on Locksley Hall, with rain or hail, or fire or snow;
For the mighty wind arises, roaring seaward, and I go.[47]

[1842]

Break, break, break [48]

BREAK, break, break,
On thy cold gray stones, O Sea!
And I would that my tongue could utter
The thoughts that arise in me.

O well for the fisherman's boy,
That he shouts with his sister at play!
O well for the sailor lad,
That he sings in his boat on the bay!

And the stately ships go on
To their haven under the hill;
But O for the touch of a vanish'd hand,
And the sound of a voice that is still!

Break, break, break,
At the foot of thy crags, O Sea!
But the tender grace of a day that is dead
Will never come back to me.

[1842]

---

44 See *Joshua*, x, 12.
45 This line was composed after Tennyson's first ride on a railway train in 1830. He thought that the wheels ran in grooves.
46 China

47 The sequel to this poem, *Locksley Hall Sixty Years After*, was published in 1886.
48 The poem was inspired by the death of Arthur Hallam.

Songs from The Princess[49]

As thro' the land at eve we went,
And pluck'd the ripen'd ears,
We fell out, my wife and I,
O we fell out I know not why,
And kiss'd again with tears.
And blessings on the falling out
That all the more endears,
When we fall out with those we love
And kiss again with tears!
For when we came where lies the child
We lost in other years,
There above the little grave,
O there above the little grave,
We kiss'd again with tears.

The splendour falls on castle walls[50]
And snowy summits old in story:
The long light shakes across the lakes,
And the wild cataract leaps in glory.
Blow, bugle, blow, set the wild echoes flying,
Blow, bugle; answer, echoes, dying, dying, dying.

O hark, O hear! how thin and clear,
And thinner, clearer, farther going!
O sweet and far from cliff and scar
The horns of Elfland faintly blowing!
Blow, let us hear the purple glens replying:
Blow, bugle; answer, echoes, dying, dying, dying.

O love, they die in yon rich sky,
They faint on hill or field or river:
Our echoes roll from soul to soul,
And grow for ever and for ever.
Blow, bugle, blow, set the wild echoes flying,
And answer, echoes, answer, dying, dying, dying.

[49] *The Princess* was first published in 1847, but the second of this group of songs was added in 1848, and the first, fourth, and fifth in 1850. They are appropriate to the narrative, Tennyson indeed having added songs in 1850 to show, even more clearly than he had, that the real heroine of his satire upon a strictly feminist college was the little child who opens the heart of the princess to love and to womanly impulses.

[50] This song, full of Celtic magic, was suggested by the echoes of a bugle which Tennyson heard on the Lakes of Killarney in Ireland.

Tears, idle tears, I know not what they mean,[51]
Tears from the depth of some divine despair
Rise in the heart, and gather to the eyes,
In looking on the happy Autumn-fields,
And thinking of the days that are no more.

Fresh as the first beam glittering on a sail,
That brings our friends up from the underworld,
Sad as the last which reddens over one
That sinks with all we love below the verge;
So sad, so fresh, the days that are no more.

Ah, sad and strange as in dark summer dawns
The earliest pipe of half-awaken'd birds
To dying ears, when unto dying eyes
The casement slowly grows a glimmering square;
So sad, so strange, the days that are no more.

Dear as remember'd kisses after death,
And sweet as those by hopeless fancy feign'd
On lips that are for others; deep as love,
Deep as first love, and wild with all regret;
O Death in Life, the days that are no more.

Home they brought her warrior dead:
She nor swoon'd, nor utter'd cry:
All her maidens, watching, said,
'She must weep or she will die.'

Then they praised him, soft and low,
Call'd him worthy to be loved,
Truest friend and noblest foe;
Yet she neither spoke nor moved.

[51] James Knowles, in *The Nineteenth Century* for January 1893 (xxxiii, 164–188), records Tennyson's statement that this poem was written at Tintern Abbey when he watched the yellowing woods through the ruined windows. 'It is what I have always felt even from a boy, and what as a boy I called the "passion of the past."'

Stole a maiden from her place,
  Lightly to the warrior stept,
Took the face-cloth from the face;
  Yet she neither moved nor wept.

Rose a nurse of ninety years,
  Set his child upon her knee —
Like summer tempest came her tears —
  'Sweet my child, I live for thee.'

Ask me no more: the moon may draw the sea;
  The cloud may stoop from heaven and take the shape
  With fold to fold, of mountain or of cape;
But O too fond, when have I answer'd thee?
            Ask me no more.

Ask me no more: what answer should I give?
  I love not hollow cheek or faded eye:
  Yet, O my friend, I will not have thee die!
Ask me no more, lest I should bid thee live;
            Ask me no more.

Ask me no more: thy fate and mine are seal'd:
  I strove against the stream and all in vain:
  Let the great river take me to the main:
No more, dear love, for at a touch I yield;
            Ask me no more.

  'Now sleeps the crimson petal, now the white;[52]
Nor waves the cypress in the palace walk;
Nor winks the gold fin in the porphyry font:
The fire-fly wakens: waken thou with me.

  Now droops the milkwhite peacock like a ghost,
And like a ghost she glimmers on to me.

  Now lies the Earth all Danaë to the stars,
And all thy heart lies open unto me.

  Now slides the silent meteor on, and leaves
A shining furrow, as thy thoughts in me.

  Now folds the lily all her sweetness up,
And slips into the bosom of the lake:
So fold thyself, my dearest, thou, and slip
Into my bosom and be lost in me.'

  'Come down, O maid, from yonder mountain height:
What pleasure lives in height (the shepherd sang)
In height and cold, the splendour of the hills?
But cease to move so near the Heavens, and cease
To glide a sunbeam by the blasted Pine,
To sit a star upon the sparkling spire;
And come, for Love is of the valley, come,
For Love is of the valley, come thou down
And find him; by the happy threshold, he,
Or hand in hand with Plenty in the maize,
Or red with spirted purple of the vats,
Or foxlike in the vine; nor cares to walk
With Death and Morning on the silver horns,
Nor wilt thou snare him in the white ravine,
Nor find him dropt upon the firths of ice,
That huddling slant in furrow-cloven falls
To roll the torrent out of dusky doors:
But follow; let the torrent dance thee down
To find him in the valley; let the wild
Lean-headed Eagles yelp alone, and leave
The monstrous ledges there to slope, and spill
Their thousand wreaths of dangling water-smoke,
That like a broken purpose waste in air:
So waste not thou; but come; for all the vales
Await thee; azure pillars of the hearth

[52] This and the following song were read aloud by the Princess, who watched during the night by the wounded Prince. Her love for him breaks down her vows of isolation.

Arise to thee; the children call, and I
Thy shepherd pipe, and sweet is every sound,
Sweeter thy voice, but every sound is sweet;
Myriads of rivulets hurrying thro' the lawn,
The moan of doves in immemorial elms,
And murmuring of innumerable bees.'

IN MEMORIAM A. H. H.[53]

OBIIT MDCCCXXXIII

STRONG Son of God, immortal Love,
Whom we, that have not seen thy face,
By faith, and faith alone, embrace,
Believing where we cannot prove;

Thine are these orbs of light and shade;
Thou madest Life in man and brute;
Thou madest Death; and lo, thy foot
Is on the skull which thou hast made.

Thou wilt not leave us in the dust:
Thou madest man, he knows not why,
He thinks he was not made to die;
And thou hast made him: thou art just.

Thou seemest human and divine,
The highest, holiest manhood, thou:
Our wills are ours, we know not how;
Our wills are ours, to make them thine.

Our little systems have their day;
They have their day and cease to be:
They are but broken lights of thee,
And thou, O Lord, art more than they.

We have but faith: we cannot know;
For knowledge is of things we see;
And yet we trust it comes from thee,
A beam in darkness: let it grow.

Let knowledge grow from more to more,
But more of reverence in us dwell;
That mind and soul, according well,
May make one music as before,

But vaster. We are fools and slight;
We mock thee when we do not fear:
But help thy foolish ones to bear;
Help thy vain worlds to bear thy light.

Forgive what seem'd my sin in me,
What seem'd my worth since I began;
For merit lives from man to man,
And not from man, O Lord, to thee.

Forgive my grief for one removed,
Thy creature, whom I found so fair.
I trust he lives in thee, and there
I find him worthier to be loved.

Forgive these wild and wandering cries,
Confusions of a wasted youth;
Forgive them where they fail in truth,
And in thy wisdom make me wise.

I

I held it truth, with him[54] who sings
To one clear harp in divers tones,
That men may rise on stepping-stones
Of their dead selves to higher things.

But who shall so forecast the years
And find in loss a gain to match?
Or reach a hand thro' time to catch
The far-off interest of tears?

[53] Published in 1850. Arthur Henry Hallam, engaged to Tennyson's sister Emily and greatly beloved by Tennyson himself, died at Vienna on 15 September 1833. His body was brought by sea to England and buried at Clevedon, on the Bristol Channel, 3 January 1834. The various sections of the poem were written between the time of Hallam's death and the time of publication, without thought of any order or unity, or, indeed, of a future printing. They were later woven together to form a record of what Tennyson called 'The Way of the Soul,' working out its path through loss and grief, not to any formal 'philosophy' of the future life, but to the faith, as Professor Genung has it, 'that love is intrinsically immortal.' A. C. Bradley and others hold that the period actually covered in the poem is probably not quite three years, ending with the spring of 1836.

[54] Goethe, probably, but Tennyson was not too sure years later.

Let Love clasp Grief lest both be drown'd,
  Let darkness keep her raven gloss:
  Ah, sweeter to be drunk with loss,
To dance with death, to beat the ground,

Than that the victor Hours should scorn
  The long result of love, and boast,
  'Behold the man that loved and lost,
But all he was is overworn.'

II

Old Yew, which graspest at the stones
  That name the under-lying dead,
  Thy fibres net the dreamless head,
Thy roots are wrapt about the bones.

The seasons bring the flower again,
  And bring the firstling to the flock;
  And in the dusk of thee, the clock
Beats out the little lives of men.

O not for thee the glow, the bloom,
  Who changest not in any gale,
  Nor branding summer suns avail
To touch thy thousand years of gloom:

And gazing on thee, sullen tree,
  Sick for thy stubborn hardihood,
  I seem to fail from out my blood
And grow incorporate into thee.

III

O Sorrow, cruel fellowship,
  O Priestess in the vaults of Death,
  O sweet and bitter in a breath,
What whispers from thy lying lip?

'The stars,' she whispers, 'blindly run;
  A web is wov'n across the sky;
  From out waste places comes a cry,
And murmurs from the dying sun:

'And all the phantom, Nature, stands—
  With all the music in her tone,
  A hollow echo of my own,—
A hollow form with empty hands.'

And shall I take a thing so blind,
  Embrace her as my natural good;
  Or crush her, like a vice of blood,
Upon the threshold of the mind?

IV

To Sleep I give my powers away;
  My will is bondsman to the dark;
  I sit within a helmless bark,
And with my heart I muse and say:

O heart, how fares it with thee now,
  That thou should'st fail from thy desire,
  Who scarcely darest to inquire,
'What is it makes me beat so low?'

Something it is which thou hast lost,
  Some pleasure from thine early years.
  Break, thou deep vase of chilling tears,
That grief hath shaken into frost!

Such clouds of nameless trouble cross
  All night below the darken'd eyes;
  With morning wakes the will, and cries,
'Thou shalt not be the fool of loss.'

V

I sometimes hold it half a sin
  To put in words the grief I feel;
  For words, like Nature, half reveal
And half conceal the Soul within.

But, for the unquiet heart and brain,
  A use in measured language lies;
  The sad mechanic exercise,
Like dull narcotics, numbing pain.

In words, like weeds, I'll wrap me o'er,
  Like coarsest clothes against the cold:
  But that large grief which these enfold
Is given in outline and no more.

VI

One writes, that 'Other friends remain,'
  That 'Loss is common to the race'—
  And common is the commonplace,
And vacant chaff well meant for grain.

That loss is common would not make
My own less bitter, rather more:
Too common! Never morning wore
To evening, but some heart did break.

O father, wheresoe'er thou be,
Who pledgest now thy gallant son;
A shot, ere half thy draught be done,
Hath still'd the life that beat from thee.

O mother, praying God will save
Thy sailor, — while thy head is bow'd,
His heavy-shotted hammock-shroud
Drops in his vast and wandering grave.

Ye know no more than I who wrought
At that last hour to please him well;
Who mused on all I had to tell,
And something written, something thought;

Expecting still his advent home;
And ever met him on his way
With wishes, thinking, 'here to-day,'
Or 'here to-morrow will he come.'

O somewhere, meek, unconscious dove,
That sittest ranging golden hair;
And glad to find thyself so fair,
Poor child, that waitest for thy love!

For now her father's chimney glows
In expectation of a guest;
And thinking 'this will please him best,'
She takes a riband or a rose;

For he will see them on to-night;
And with the thought her colour burns;
And, having left the glass, she turns
Once more to set a ringlet right;

And, even when she turn'd, the curse
Had fallen, and her future Lord
Was drown'd in passing thro' the ford,
Or kill'd in falling from his horse.

O what to her shall be the end?
And what to me remains of good?
To her, perpetual maidenhood,
And unto me no second friend.

VII

Dark house, by which once more I stand
Here in the long unlovely street,[55]
Doors, where my heart was used to beat
So quickly, waiting for a hand,

A hand that can be clasp'd no more —
Behold me, for I cannot sleep,
And like a guilty thing I creep
At earliest morning to the door.

He is not here; but far away
The noise of life begins again,
And ghastly thro' the drizzling rain
On the bald street breaks the blank day.

. . .

IX

Fair ship, that from the Italian shore
Sailest the placid ocean-plains
With my lost Arthur's loved remains,
Spread thy full wings, and waft him o'er.

So draw him home to those that mourn
In vain; a favourable speed
Ruffle thy mirror'd mast, and lead
Thro' prosperous floods his holy urn.

All night no ruder air perplex
Thy sliding keel, till Phosphor,[56] bright
As our pure love, thro' early light
Shall glimmer on the dewy decks.

Sphere all your lights around, above;
Sleep, gentle heavens, before the prow;
Sleep, gentle winds, as he sleeps now,
My friend, the brother of my love;

My Arthur, whom I shall not see
Till all my widow'd race be run;
Dear as the mother to the son,
More than my brothers are to me.

X

I hear the noise about thy keel;
I hear the bell struck in the night:
I see the cabin-window bright;
I see the sailor at the wheel.

[55] Hallam, while he was studying law in London, lived at No. 67, Wimpole Street. [56] The morning star.

Thou bring'st the sailor to his wife,
And travell'd men from foreign lands;
And letters unto trembling hands;
And, thy dark freight, a vanish'd life.

So bring him: we have idle dreams:
This look of quiet flatters thus
Our home-bred fancies: O to us,
The fools of habit, sweeter seems

To rest beneath the clover sod,
That takes the sunshine and the rains,
Or where the kneeling hamlet drains
The chalice of the grapes of God;

Than if with thee the roaring wells
Should gulf him fathom-deep in brine:
And hands so often clasp'd in mine,
Should toss with tangle and with shells.

XI

Calm is the morn without a sound,
Calm as to suit a calmer grief,
And only thro' the faded leaf
The chestnut pattering to the ground:

Calm and deep peace on this high wold,
And on these dews that drench the furze,
And all the silvery gossamers
That twinkle into green and gold:

Calm and still light on yon great plain
That sweeps with all its autumn bowers,
And crowded farms and lessening towers,
To mingle with the bounding main:

Calm and deep peace in this wide air,
These leaves that redden to the fall;
And in my heart, if calm at all,
If any calm, a calm despair:

Calm on the seas, and silver sleep,
And waves that sway themselves in rest,
And dead calm in that noble breast
Which heaves but with the heaving deep.

. . .

XV

To-night the winds begin to rise
And roar from yonder dropping day:
The last red leaf is whirl'd away,
The rooks are blown about the skies;

The forest crack'd, the waters curl'd,
The cattle huddled on the lea;
And wildly dash'd on tower and tree
The sunbeam strikes along the world:

And but for fancies, which aver
That all thy motions gently pass
Athwart a plane of molten glass,
I scarce could brook the strain and stir

That makes the barren branches loud;
And but for fear it is not so,
The wild unrest that lives in woe
Would dote and pore on yonder cloud

That rises upward always higher,
And onward drags a labouring breast,
And topples round the dreary west,
A looming bastion fringed with fire.

. . .

XIX

The Danube to the Severn gave
The darken'd heart that beat no more;
They laid him by the pleasant shore,
And in the hearing of the wave.

There twice a day the Severn fills;
The salt sea-water passes by,
And hushes half the babbling Wye,[57]
And makes a silence in the hills.

The Wye is hush'd nor moved along,
And hush'd my deepest grief of all,
When fill'd with tears that cannot fall,
I brim with sorrow drowning song.

The tide flows down, the wave again
Is vocal in its wooded walls;

[57] A short distance above Clevedon the Wye flows into the Severn; Clevedon itself is near the junction of the Severn with the Bristol Channel. This section was written in Tintern Abbey.

My deeper anguish also falls,
And I can speak a little then.

. . .

XXVII

I envy not in any moods
The captive void of noble rage,
The linnet born within the cage,
That never knew the summer woods:

I envy not the beast that takes
His license in the field of time,
Unfetter'd by the sense of crime,
To whom a conscience never wakes;

Nor, what may count itself as blest,
The heart that never plighted troth
But stagnates in the weeds of sloth;
Nor any want-begotten rest.

I hold it true, whate'er befall;
I feel it, when I sorrow most;
'Tis better to have loved and lost
Than never to have loved at all.

XXVIII

The time draws near the birth of Christ: [58]
The moon is hid; the night is still;
The Christmas bells from hill to hill
Answer each other in the mist.

Four voices of four hamlets round,
From far and near, on mead and moor,
Swell out and fail, as if a door
Were shut between me and the sound:

Each voice four changes on the wind,
That now dilate, and now decrease,
Peace and goodwill, goodwill and peace,
Peace and goodwill, to all mankind.

This year I slept and woke with pain,
I almost wish'd no more to wake,
And that my hold on life would break
Before I heard those bells again:

But they my troubled spirit rule,
For they controll'd me when a boy;
They bring me sorrow touch'd with joy,
The merry merry bells of Yule.

XXIX

With such compelling cause to grieve
As daily vexes household peace,
And chains regret to his decease,
How dare we keep our Christmas-eve;

Which brings no more a welcome guest
To enrich the threshold of the night
With shower'd largess of delight
In dance and song and game and jest?

Yet go, and while the holly boughs
Entwine the cold baptismal font,
Make one wreath more for Use and Wont,
That guard the portals of the house;

Old sisters of a day gone by,
Gray nurses, loving nothing new;
Why should they miss their yearly due
Before their time? They too will die.

XXX

With trembling fingers did we weave
The holly round the Christmas hearth;
A rainy cloud possess'd the earth,
And sadly fell our Christmas-eve.

At our old pastimes in the hall
We gamboll'd, making vain pretence
Of gladness, with an awful sense
Of one mute Shadow watching all.

We paused: the winds were in the beech:
We heard them sweep the winter land;
And in a circle hand-in-hand
Sat silent, looking each at each.

Then echo-like our voices rang;
We sung, tho' every eye was dim,
A merry song we sang with him
Last year: impetuously we sang:

[58] The first Christmas after Hallam's death, in 1833. The scene is Tennyson's home at Somersby, in Lincolnshire.

We ceased: a gentler feeling crept
Upon us: surely rest is meet:
'They rest,' we said, 'their sleep is sweet,'
And silence follow'd, and we wept.

Our voices took a higher range;
Once more we sang: 'They do not die
Nor lose their mortal sympathy,
Nor change to us, altho' they change;

'Rapt from the fickle and the frail
With gather'd power, yet the same,
Pierces the keen seraphic flame
From orb to orb, from veil to veil.'

Rise, happy morn, rise, holy morn,
Draw forth the cheerful day from night:
O Father, touch the east, and light
The light that shone when Hope was born.

. . .

XXXV

Yet if some voice that man could trust
Should murmur from the narrow house,
'The cheeks drop in; the body bows;
Man dies: nor is there hope in dust:'

Might I not say? 'Yet even here,
But for one hour, O Love, I strive
To keep so sweet a thing alive:'
But I should turn mine eyes and hear

The moanings of the homeless sea,
The sound of streams that swift or slow
Draw down Æonian hills, and sow
The dust of continents to be;

And Love would answer with a sigh,
'The sound of that forgetful shore
Will change my sweetness more and more,
Half-dead to know that I shall die.'

O me, what profits it to put
An idle case? If Death were seen
At first as Death, Love had not been,
Or been in narrowest working shut,

Mere fellowship of sluggish moods,
Or in his coarsest Satyr-shape
Had bruised the herb and crush'd the grape,
And bask'd and batten'd in the woods.

. . .

XXXIX

Old warder of these buried bones,[59]
And answering now my random stroke
With fruitful cloud and living smoke,
Dark yew, that graspest at the stones

And dippest toward the dreamless head,
To thee too comes the golden hour
When flower is feeling after flower;
But Sorrow — fixt upon the dead,

And darkening the dark graves of men, —
What whisper'd from her lying lips?
My gloom is kindled at the tips,
And passes into gloom again.

. . .

L

Be near me when my light is low,
When the blood creeps, and the nerves prick
And tingle; and the heart is sick,
And all the wheels of Being slow.

Be near me when the sensuous frame
Is rack'd with pangs that conquer trust;
And Time, a maniac scattering dust,
And Life, a Fury slinging flame.

Be near me when my faith is dry,
And men the flies of latter spring,
That lay their eggs, and sting and sing
And weave their petty cells and die.

Be near me when I fade away,
To point the term of human strife,
And on the low dark verge of life
The twilight of eternal day.

[59] This section was written in 1868.

LI

Do we indeed desire the dead
 Should still be near us at our side?
 Is there no baseness we would hide?
No inner vileness that we dread?

Shall he for whose applause I strove,
 I had such reverence for his blame,
 See with clear eye some hidden shame
And I be lessen'd in his love?

I wrong the grave with fears untrue:
 Shall love be blamed for want of faith?
 There must be wisdom with great Death:
The dead shall look me thro' and thro'.

Be near us when we climb or fall:
 Ye watch, like God, the rolling hours
 With larger other eyes than ours,
To make allowance for us all.

LII

I cannot love thee as I ought,
 For love reflects the thing beloved;
 My words are only words, and moved
Upon the topmost froth of thought.

'Yet blame not thou thy plaintive song,'
 The Spirit of true love replied;
 'Thou canst not move me from thy side,
Nor human frailty do me wrong.

'What keeps a spirit wholly true
 To that ideal which he bears?
 What record? not the sinless years [60]
That breathed beneath the Syrian blue:

'So fret not, like an idle girl,
 That life is dash'd with flecks of sin.
 Abide: thy wealth is gather'd in,
When Time hath sunder'd shell from pearl.'

LIII

How many a father have I seen,
 A sober man, among his boys,
 Whose youth was full of foolish noise,
Who wears his manhood hale and green:

And dare we to this fancy give,
 That had the wild oat not been sown,
 The soil, left barren, scarce had grown
The grain by which a man may live?

Or, if we held the doctrine sound
 For life outliving heats of youth,
 Yet who would preach it as a truth
To those that eddy round and round?

Hold thou the good: define it well:
 For fear divine Philosophy
 Should push beyond her mark, and be
Procuress to the Lords of Hell.

LIV

Oh yet we trust that somehow good
 Will be the final goal of ill,
 To pangs of nature, sins of will,
Defects of doubt, and taints of blood;

That nothing walks with aimless feet;
 That not one life shall be destroy'd,
 Or cast as rubbish to the void,
When God hath made the pile complete;

That not a worm is cloven in vain;
 That not a moth with vain desire
 Is shrivell'd in a fruitless fire,
Or but subserves another's gain.

Behold, we know not anything;
 I can but trust that good shall fall
 At last — far off — at last, to all,
And every winter change to spring.

So runs my dream: but what am I?
 An infant crying in the night:
 An infant crying for the light:
And with no language but a cry.

LV

The wish, that of the living whole
 No life may fail beyond the grave,
 Derives it not from what we have
The likest God within the soul?

[60] Of Christ.

Are God and Nature then at strife,
  That Nature lends such evil dreams?
  So careful of the type she seems,
So careless of the single life;

That I, considering everywhere
  Her secret meaning in her deeds,
  And finding that of fifty seeds
She often brings but one to bear,

I falter where I firmly trod,
  And falling with my weight of cares
  Upon the great world's altar-stairs
That slope thro' darkness up to God,

I stretch lame hands of faith, and grope,
  And gather dust and chaff, and call
  To what I feel is Lord of all,
And faintly trust the larger hope.

LVI

'So careful of the type?' but no.
  From scarped cliff and quarried stone
  She cries, 'A thousand types are gone:
I care for nothing, all shall go.

'Thou makest thine appeal to me:
  I bring to life, I bring to death:
  The spirit does but mean the breath:
I know no more.' And he, shall he,

Man, her last work, who seem'd so fair,
  Such splendid purpose in his eyes,
  Who roll'd the psalm to wintry skies,
Who built him fanes of fruitless prayer,

Who trusted God was love indeed
  And love Creation's final law—
  Tho' Nature, red in tooth and claw
With ravine, shriek'd against his creed—

Who loved, who suffer'd countless ills,
  Who battled for the True, the Just,
  Be blown about the desert dust,
Or seal'd within the iron hills?

No more? A monster then, a dream,
  A discord. Dragons of the prime,
  That tare each other in their slime,
Were mellow music match'd with him.

O life as futile, then, as frail!
  O for thy voice to soothe and bless!
  What hope of answer, or redress?
Behind the veil, behind the veil.

LVII

Peace; come away: the song of woe
  Is after all an earthly song:
  Peace; come away: we do him wrong
To sing so wildly: let us go.

Come; let us go: your cheeks are pale;
  But half my life I leave behind:
  Methinks my friend is richly shrined;
But I shall pass; my work will fail.

Yet in these ears, till hearing dies,
  One set slow bell will seem to toll
  The passing of the sweetest soul
That ever look'd with human eyes.

I hear it now, and o'er and o'er,
  Eternal greetings to the dead;
  And 'Ave, Ave, Ave,' said,
'Adieu, adieu,' for evermore.

. . .

LXVII

When on my bed the moonlight falls,
  I know that in thy place of rest
  By that broad water of the west,
There comes a glory on the walls;

Thy marble bright in dark appears,
  As slowly steals a silver flame
  Along the letters of thy name,
And o'er the number of thy years.

The mystic glory swims away;
  From off my bed the moonlight dies;
  And closing eaves of wearied eyes
I sleep till dusk is dipt in gray:

And then I know the mist is drawn
  A lucid veil from coast to coast,
  And in the dark church like a ghost
Thy tablet glimmers to the dawn.

LXVIII

When in the down I sink my head,
Sleep, Death's twin-brother, times my breath;
Sleep, Death's twin-brother, knows not Death,
Nor can I dream of thee as dead:

I walk as ere I walk'd forlorn,
When all our path was fresh with dew,
And all the bugle breezes blew
Reveillée to the breaking morn.

But what is this? I turn about,
I find a trouble in thine eye,
Which makes me sad I know not why,
Nor can my dream resolve the doubt:

But ere the lark hath left the lea
I wake, and I discern the truth;
It is the trouble of my youth
That foolish sleep transfers to thee.

LXIX

I dreamed there would be Spring no more,
That Nature's ancient power was lost:
The streets were black with smoke and frost,
They chatter'd trifles at the door:

I wander'd from the noisy town,
I found a wood with thorny boughs:
I took the thorns to bind my brows,
I wore them like a civic crown:

I met with scoffs, I met with scorns
From youth and babe and hoary hairs:
They call'd me in the public squares
The fool that wears a crown of thorns:

They call'd me fool, they call'd me child:
I found an angel of the night;
The voice was low, the look was bright;
He look'd upon my crown and smiled:

He reach'd the glory of a hand,
That seem'd to touch it into leaf:
The voice was not the voice of grief,
The words were hard to understand.

. . .

LXXVIII

Again at Christmas [61] did we weave
The holly round the Christmas hearth;
The silent snow possess'd the earth,
And calmly fell our Christmas-eve:

The yule-clog sparkled keen with frost,
No wing of wind the region swept,
But over all things brooding slept
The quiet sense of something lost.

As in the winters left behind,
Again our ancient games had place,
The mimic picture's breathing grace,
And dance and song and hoodman-blind.

Who show'd a token of distress?
No single tear, no mark of pain:
O sorrow, then can sorrow wane?
O grief, can grief be changed to less?

O last regret, regret can die!
No — mixt with all this mystic frame,
Her deep relations are the same,
But with long use her tears are dry.

LXXIX

'More than my brothers are to me,' —
Let this not vex thee,[62] noble heart!
I know thee of what force thou art
To hold the costliest love in fee.

But thou and I are one in kind,
As moulded like in Nature's mint;
And hill and wood and field did print
The same sweet forms in either mind.

For us the same cold streamlet curl'd
Thro' all his eddying coves; the same
All winds that roam the twilight came
In whispers of the beauteous world.

At one dear knee we proffer'd vows,
One lesson from one book we learn'd,
Ere childhood's flaxen ringlet turn'd
To black and brown on kindred brows.

---

[61] That of 1834, the second Christmas after Hallam's death.

[62] Tennyson's brother Charles. The quotation repeats the last line of section IX.

And so my wealth resembles thine,
But he was rich where I was poor,
And he supplied my want the more
As his unlikeness fitted mine.

. . .

LXXXIII

Dip down upon the northern shore,
O sweet new-year delaying long;
Thou doest expectant nature wrong;
Delaying long, delay no more.

What stays thee from the clouded noons,
Thy sweetness from its proper place?
Can trouble live with April days,
Or sadness in the summer moons?

Bring orchis, bring the foxglove spire,
The little speedwell's darling blue,
Deep tulips dash'd with fiery dew,
Laburnums, dropping-wells of fire.

O thou new-year, delaying long,
Delayest the sorrow in my blood,
That longs to burst a frozen bud
And flood a fresher throat with song.

. . .

LXXXVI

Sweet after showers, ambrosial air,[63]
That rollest from the gorgeous gloom
Of evening over brake and bloom
And meadow, slowly breathing bare

The round of space, and rapt below
Thro' all the dewy-tassell'd wood,
And shadowing down the horned flood
In ripples, fan my brows and blow

The fever from my cheek, and sigh
The full new life that feeds thy breath
Throughout my frame, till Doubt and Death,
Ill brethren, let the fancy fly

From belt to belt of crimson seas
On leagues of odour streaming far,
To where in yonder orient star
A hundred spirits whisper 'Peace.'

LXXXVII

I past beside the reverend walls[64]
In which of old I wore the gown;
I roved at random thro' the town,
And saw the tumult of the halls;

And heard once more in college fanes
The storm their high-built organs make,
And thunder-music, rolling, shake
The prophet blazon'd on the panes;

And caught once more the distant shout,
The measured pulse of racing oars
Among the willows; paced the shores
And many a bridge, and all about

The same gray flats again, and felt
The same, but not the same; and last
Up that long walk of limes I past
To see the rooms in which he dwelt.

Another name was on the door:
I linger'd; all within was noise
Of songs, and clapping hands, and boys
That crash'd the glass and beat the floor;

Where once we held debate, a band
Of youthful friends, on mind and art,
And labour, and the changing mart,
And all the framework of the land;

When one would aim an arrow fair,
But send it slackly from the string;
And one would pierce an outer ring,
And one an inner, here and there;

And last the master-bowman, he,
Would cleave the mark. A willing ear

[63] This section answers the supplication of section LXXXIII. Note that it is all one sentence.

[64] Of Cambridge, where the friendship of Hallam and Tennyson had been formed at Trinity College. They were both members of the little group known as 'The Apostles,' mentioned in stanza 6 f.

We lent him. Who, but hung to hear
The rapt oration flowing free

From point to point, with power and grace
And music in the bounds of law,
To those conclusions when we saw
The God within him light his face,

And seem to lift the form, and glow
In azure orbits heavenly-wise;
And over those ethereal eyes
The bar of Michael Angelo.[65]

LXXXVIII

Wild bird, whose warble, liquid sweet,
Rings Eden thro' the budded quicks,[66]
O tell me where the senses mix,
O tell me where the passions meet,

Whence radiate: fierce extremes employ
Thy spirits in the darkening leaf,
And in the midmost heart of grief
Thy passion clasps a secret joy:

And I — my harp would prelude woe —
I cannot all command the strings;
The glory of the sum of things
Will flash along the chords and go.

. . .

XCV

By night [67] we linger'd on the lawn,
For underfoot the herb was dry;
And genial warmth; and o'er the sky
The silvery haze of summer drawn;

And calm that let the tapers burn
Unwavering: not a cricket chirr'd:
The brook alone far-off was heard,
And on the board the fluttering urn:

And bats went round in fragrant skies,
And wheel'd or lit the filmy shapes
That haunt the dusk, with ermine capes
And woolly breasts and beaded eyes;

[65] Tennyson wrote these lines from a recollection of Hallam's having said, after reading of the ridge of bone above the eyes of Michael Angelo, 'Alfred, look over my eyes; surely I have the bar of Michael Angelo!'
[66] hedge-rows
[67] In the summer of, presumably, 1835.

While now we sang old songs that peal'd
From knoll to knoll, where, couch'd at ease,
The white kine glimmer'd, and the trees
Laid their dark arms about the field.

But when those others, one by one,
Withdrew themselves from me and night,
And in the house light after light
Went out, and I was all alone,

A hunger seized my heart; I read
Of that glad year which once had been,
In those fall'n leaves which kept their green,
The noble letters of the dead:

And strangely on the silence broke
The silent-speaking words, and strange
Was love's dumb cry defying change
To test his worth; and strangely spoke

The faith, the vigour, bold to dwell
On doubts that drive the coward back,
And keen thro' wordy snares to track
Suggestion to her inmost cell.

So word by word, and line by line,
The dead man touch'd me from the past,
And all at once it seem'd at last
The living soul was flash'd on mine,

And mine in this was wound, and whirl'd
About empyreal heights of thought,
And came on that which is, and caught
The deep pulsations of the world,

Æonian music measuring out
The steps of Time — the shocks of Chance —
The blows of Death. At length my trance
Was cancell'd, stricken thro' with doubt.

Vague words! but ah, how hard to frame
In matter-moulded forms of speech,
Or ev'n for intellect to reach
Thro' memory that which I became:

Till now the doubtful dusk reveal'd
The knolls once more where, couch'd at ease,
The white kine glimmer'd, and the trees
Laid their dark arms about the field:

And suck'd from out the distant gloom
A breeze began to tremble o'er
The large leaves of the sycamore,
And fluctuate all the still perfume,

And gathering freshlier overhead,
Rock'd the full-foliaged elms, and swung
The heavy-folded rose, and flung
The lilies to and fro, and said

'The dawn, the dawn,' and died away;
And East and West, without a breath,
Mixt their dim lights, like life and death,
To broaden into boundless day.

XCVI

You say, but with no touch of scorn,
Sweet-hearted, you, whose light-blue eyes
Are tender over drowning flies,
You tell me, doubt is Devil-born.

I know not: one indeed I knew
In many a subtle question versed,
Who touch'd a jarring lyre at first,
But ever strove to make it true:

Perplext in faith, but pure in deeds,
At last he beat his music out.
There lives more faith in honest doubt,
Believe me, than in half the creeds.

He fought his doubts and gather'd strength,
He would not make his judgment blind,
He faced the spectres of the mind
And laid them: thus he came at length

To find a stronger faith his own;
And Power was with him in the night,
Which makes the darkness and the light,
And dwells not in the light alone,

But in the darkness and the cloud,
As over Sinaï's peaks of old,
While Israel made their gods of gold,
Altho' the trumpet blew so loud.[68]

. . .

XCIX

Risest thou thus, dim dawn,[69] again,
So loud with voices of the birds,
So thick with lowings of the herds,
Day, when I lost the flower of men;

Who tremblest thro' thy darkling red
On yon swoll'n brook that bubbles fast
By meadows breathing of the past,
And woodlands holy to the dead;

Who murmurest in the foliaged eaves
A song that slights the coming care,
And Autumn laying here and there
A fiery finger on the leaves;

Who wakenest with thy balmy breath
To myriads on the genial earth,
Memories of bridal, or of birth,
And unto myriads more, of death.

O wheresoever those may be,
Betwixt the slumber of the poles,
To-day they count as kindred souls;
They know me not, but mourn with me.

. . .

CIII

On that last night before we went [70]
From out the doors where I was bred,
I dream'd a vision of the dead,
Which left my after-morn content.

Methought I dwelt within a hall,
And maidens [71] with me: distant hills

[68] See *Exodus*, xix, 16–25; xxxii, 1–6.

[69] Probably of 15 September 1835, the second anniversary of Hallam's death.

[70] The stanza was one of those occasioned by the removal of the Tennysons from Somersby to High Beech, Epping Forest.

[71] Tennyson said that he 'rather believed' that these were 'the Muses, Arts, etc. — Everything that made life beautiful here, we may hope may pass on with us beyond the grave.' He again called them 'all the human powers and talents that do not pass with life but go along with it.' The 'hidden summits' are 'the high — the divine,' and the 'river' is 'life.'

From hidden summits fed with rills
A river sliding by the wall.

The hall with harp and carol rang.
They sang of what is wise and good
And graceful. In the centre stood
A statue veil'd, to which they sang;

And which, tho' veil'd, was known to me,
The shape of him I loved, and love
For ever: then flew in a dove
And brought a summons from the sea: [72]

And when they learnt that I must go
They wept and wail'd, but led the way
To where a little shallop lay
At anchor in the flood below;

And on by many a level mead,
And shadowing bluff that made the banks,
We glided winding under ranks
Of iris, and the golden reed;

And still as vaster [73] grew the shore
And rolled the floods in grander space,
The maidens gather'd strength and grace
And presence, lordlier than before;

And I myself, who sat apart
And watch'd them, wax'd in every limb;
I felt the thews of Anakim,[74]
The pulses of a Titan's heart;

As one would sing the death of war,
And one would chant the history
Of that great race, which is to be,
And one the shaping of a star; [75]

Until the forward-creeping tides
Began to foam, and we to draw
From deep to deep, to where we saw
A great ship lift her shining sides.

The man we loved was there on deck,
But thrice as large as man he bent
To greet us. Up the side I went,
And fell in silence on his neck:

Whereat those maidens with one mind
Bewail'd their lot; I did them wrong:
'We served thee here,' they said, 'so long,
And wilt thou leave us now behind?'

So rapt I was, they could not win
An answer from my lips, but he
Replying, 'Enter likewise ye
And go with us:' they enter'd in.

And while the wind began to sweep
A music out of sheet and shroud,
We steer'd her toward a crimson cloud
That landlike slept along the deep.

CIV

The time draws near the birth of Christ; [76]
The moon is hid, the night is still;
A single church below the hill
Is pealing, folded in the mist.

A single peal of bells below,
That wakens at this hour of rest
A single murmur in the breast,
That these are not the bells I know.

Like strangers' voices here they sound,
In lands where not a memory strays,
Nor landmark breathes of other days,
But all is new unhallow'd ground.

CV

To-night ungather'd let us leave
This laurel, let this holly stand:
We live within the stranger's land,
And strangely falls our Christmas-eve.

Our father's dust [77] is left alone
And silent under other snows:
There in due time the woodbine blows,
The violet comes, but we are gone.

---

[72] Of 'eternity,' according to Tennyson.

[73] Tennyson said this stanza imaged 'the great progress of the age, as well as the opening of another world.'

[74] See *Deuteronomy*, ix, 2.

[75] Refers, Tennyson said, to 'all the great hopes of science and men.'

[76] The Christmas of 1835, the third after Hallam's death.

[77] Tennyson's father died in March 1833 at Somersby.

No more shall wayward grief abuse
  The genial hour with mask and mime;
  For change of place, like growth of time,
Has broke the bond of dying use.

Let cares that petty shadows cast,
  By which our lives are chiefly proved,
  A little spare the night I loved,
And hold it solemn to the past.

But let no footstep beat the floor,
  Nor bowl of wassail mantle warm;
  For who would keep an ancient form
Thro' which the spirit breathes no more?

Be neither song, nor game, nor feast;
  Nor harp be touch'd, nor flute be blown;
  No dance, no motion, save alone
What lightens in the lucid east

Of rising worlds by yonder wood.
  Long sleeps the summer in the seed;
  Run out your measured arcs, and lead
The closing cycle rich in good.

CVI

Ring out, wild bells, to the wild sky,
  The flying cloud, the frosty light:
  The year is dying in the night;
Ring out, wild bells, and let him die.

Ring out the old, ring in the new,
  Ring, happy bells, across the snow:
  The year is going, let him go;
Ring out the false, ring in the true.

Ring out the grief that saps the mind,
  For those that here we see no more;
  Ring out the feud of rich and poor,
Ring in redress to all mankind.

Ring out a slowly dying cause,
  And ancient forms of party strife;
  Ring in the nobler modes of life,
With sweeter manners, purer laws.

Ring out the want, the care, the sin,
  The faithless coldness of the times;
  Ring out, ring out my mournful rhymes,
But ring the fuller minstrel in.

Ring out false pride in place and blood,
  The civic slander and the spite;
  Ring in the love of truth and right,
Ring in the common love of good.

Ring out old shapes of foul disease;
  Ring out the narrowing lust of gold;
  Ring out the thousand wars of old,
Ring in the thousand years of peace.

Ring in the valiant man and free,
  The larger heart, the kindlier hand;
  Ring out the darkness of the land,
Ring in the Christ that is to be.

CVII

It is the day when he was born,[78]
  A bitter day that early sank
  Behind a purple-frosty bank
Of vapour, leaving night forlorn.

The time admits not flowers or leaves
  To deck the banquet. Fiercely flies
  The blast of North and East, and ice
Makes daggers at the sharpen'd eaves,

And bristles all the brakes and thorns
  To yon hard crescent, as she hangs
  Above the wood which grides and clangs
Its leafless ribs and iron horns

Together, in the drifts that pass
  To darken on the rolling brine
  That breaks the coast. But fetch the wine,
Arrange the board and brim the glass;

Bring in great logs and let them lie,
  To make a solid core of heat;
  Be cheerful-minded, talk and treat
Of all things ev'n as he were by;

[78] Hallam was born on 1 February.

We keep the day. With festal cheer,
With books and music, surely we
Will drink to him, whate'er he be,
And sing the songs he loved to hear.

. . .

CXIV

Who loves not Knowledge? Who shall rail
Against her beauty? May she mix
With men and prosper! Who shall fix
Her pillars? Let her work prevail.

But on her forehead sits a fire:
She sets her forward countenance
And leaps into the future chance,
Submitting all things to desire.

Half-grown as yet, a child, and vain —
She cannot fight the fear of death.
What is she, cut from love and faith,
But some wild Pallas from the brain

Of Demons? fiery-hot to burst
All barriers in her onward race
For power. Let her know her place;
She is the second, not the first.

A higher hand must make her mild,
If all be not in vain; and guide
Her footsteps, moving side by side
With wisdom, like the younger child:

For she is earthly of the mind,
But Wisdom heavenly of the soul.
O friend, who camest to thy goal
So early, leaving me behind,

I would the great world grew like thee,
Who grewest not alone in power
And knowledge, but by year and hour
In reverence and in charity.

CXV

Now fades the last long streak of snow,
Now burgeons every maze of quick
About the flowering squares, and thick
By ashen roots the violets blow.

Now rings the woodland loud and long,
The distance takes a lovelier hue,
And drown'd in yonder living blue
The lark becomes a sightless song.

Now dance the lights on lawn and lea,
The flocks are whiter down the vale,
And milkier every milky sail
On winding stream or distant sea;

Where now the seamew pipes, or dives
In yonder greening gleam, and fly
The happy birds, that change their sky
To build and brood; that live their lives

From land to land; and in my breast
Spring wakens too; and my regret
Becomes an April violet,
And buds and blossoms like the rest.

CXVI

Is it, then, regret for buried time
That keenlier in sweet April wakes,
And meets the year, and gives and takes
The colours of the crescent prime?

Not all: the songs, the stirring air,
The life re-orient out of dust,
Cry thro' the sense to hearten trust
In that which made the world so fair.

Not all regret: the face will shine
Upon me, while I muse alone;
And that dear voice, I once have known,
Still speak to me of me and mine:

Yet less of sorrow lives in me
For days of happy commune dead;
Less yearning for the friendship fled,
Than some strong bond which is to be.

CXVII

O days and hours, your work is this,
To hold me from my proper place,
A little while from his embrace,
For fuller gain of after bliss:

That out of distance might ensue
  Desire of nearness doubly sweet;
  And unto meeting when we meet,
Delight a hundredfold accrue,

For every grain of sand that runs,
  And every span of shade that steals,
  And every kiss of toothed wheels,
And all the courses of the suns.

CXVIII

Contemplate all this work of Time,
  The giant labouring in his youth;
  Nor dream of human love and truth,
As dying Nature's earth and lime;

But trust that those we call the dead
  Are breathers of an ampler day
  For ever nobler ends. They say,
The solid earth whereon we tread

In tracts of fluent heat began,
  And grew to seeming-random forms,
  The seeming prey of cyclic storms,
Till at the last arose the man;

Who throve and branch'd from clime to clime,
  The herald of a higher race,
  And of himself in higher place,
If so he type this work of time

Within himself, from more to more;
  Or, crown'd with attributes of woe
  Like glories, move his course, and show
That life is not as idle ore,

But iron dug from central gloom,
  And heated hot with burning fears,
  And dipt in baths of hissing tears,
And batter'd with the shocks of doom

To shape and use. Arise and fly
  The reeling Faun, the sensual feast;
  Move upward, working out the beast
And let the ape and tiger die.

. . .

CXXI

Sad Hesper [79] o'er the buried sun
  And ready, thou, to die with him,
  Thou watchest all things ever dim
And dimmer, and a glory done:

The team is loosen'd from the wain,
  The boat is drawn upon the shore;
  Thou listenest to the closing door,
And life is darken'd in the brain.

Bright Phosphor, fresher for the night,
  By thee the world's great work is heard
  Beginning, and the wakeful bird;
Behind thee comes the greater light:

The market boat is on the stream,
  And voices hail it from the brink;
  Thou hear'st the village hammer clink,
And see'st the moving of the team.

Sweet Hesper-Phosphor, double name
  For what is one, the first, the last,
  Thou, like my present and my past,
Thy place is changed; thou art the same.

. . .

CXXIII

There rolls the deep where grew the tree.
  O earth, what changes hast thou seen!
  There where the long-street roars, hath been
The stillness of the central sea.

The hills are shadows, and they flow
  From form to form, and nothing stands;
  They melt like mist, the solid lands,
Like clouds they shape themselves and go.

But in my spirit will I dwell,
  And dream my dream, and hold it true;
  For tho' my lips may breathe adieu,
I cannot think the thing farewell.

---

[79] Mr. A. C. Bradley has pointed out that Hesper, the evening star, and Phosphor, the morning star — the 'planet of Love' in *Maud* — are one and the same, symbolical of that which endures throughout all change of place, and in which past and present are alike.

CXXIV

That which we dare invoke to bless;
  Our dearest faith; our ghastliest doubt;
  He, They, One, All; within, without;
The Power in darkness whom we guess;

I found Him not in world or sun,
  Or eagle's wing, or insect's eye;
  Nor thro' the questions men may try,
The petty cobwebs we have spun:

If e'er when faith had fall'n asleep,
  I heard a voice 'believe no more'
  And heard an ever-breaking shore
That tumbled in the Godless deep;

A warmth within the breast would melt
  The freezing reason's colder part,
  And like a man in wrath the heart
Stood up and answer'd, 'I have felt.'

No, like a child in doubt and fear:
  But that blind clamour made me wise;
  Then was I as a child that cries,
But, crying, knows his father near;

And what I am beheld again
  What is, and no man understands;
  And out of darkness came the hands
That reach thro' nature, moulding men.

CXXV

Whatever I have said or sung,
  Some bitter notes my harp would give,
  Yea, tho' there often seem'd to live
A contradiction on the tongue,

Yet Hope had never lost her youth;
  She did but look through dimmer eyes;
  Or Love but play'd with gracious lies,
Because he felt so fix'd in truth:

And if the song were full of care,
  He breathed the spirit of the song;
  And if the words were sweet and strong
He set his royal signet there;

Abiding with me till I sail
  To seek thee on the mystic deeps,
  And this electric force, that keeps
A thousand pulses dancing, fail.

CXXVI

Love is and was my Lord and King,
  And in his presence I attend
  To hear the tidings of my friend,
Which every hour his couriers bring.

Love is and was my King and Lord,
  And will be, tho' as yet I keep
  Within his court on earth, and sleep
Encompass'd by his faithful guard,

And hear at times a sentinel
  Who moves about from place to place,
  And whispers to the worlds of space,
In the deep night, that all is well.

CXXVII

And all is well, tho' faith and form
  Be sunder'd in the night of fear;
  Well roars the storm to those that hear
A deeper voice across the storm,

Proclaiming social truth shall spread,
  And justice, ev'n tho' thrice again
  The red fool-fury of the Seine [80]
Should pile her barricades with dead.

But ill for him that wears a crown,
  And him, the lazar, in his rags:
  They tremble, the sustaining crags;
The spires of ice are toppled down,

And molten up, and roar in flood;
  The fortress crashes from on high,
  The brute earth lightens to the sky,
And the great Æon sinks in blood,

And compass'd by the fires of Hell;
  While thou, dear spirit, happy star,
  O'erlook'st the tumult from afar,
And smilest, knowing all is well.

. . .

[80] The revolutions in France, the last of which had occurred in 1848.

CXXX

Thy voice is on the rolling air;
I hear thee where the waters run;
Thou standest in the rising sun,
And in the setting thou art fair.

What art thou then? I cannot guess;
But tho' I seem in star and flower
To feel thee some diffusive power,
I do not therefore love thee less:

My love involves the love before;
My love is vaster passion now;
Tho' mix'd with God and Nature thou,
I seem to love thee more and more.

Far off thou art, but ever nigh;
I have thee still, and I rejoice;
I prosper, circled with thy voice;
I shall not lose thee tho' I die.

CXXXI

O living will that shalt endure
When all that seems shall suffer shock,
Rise in the spiritual rock,[81]
Flow thro' our deeds and make them pure,

That we may lift from out of dust
A voice as unto him that hears,
A cry above the conquer'd years
To one that with us works, and trust,

With faith that comes of self-control,
The truths that never can be proved
Until we close with all we loved,
And all we flow from, soul in soul.

. . .

And rise, O moon, from yonder down,[82]
Till over down and over dale
All night the shining vapour sail
And pass the silent-lighted town,

The white-faced halls, the glancing rills,
And catch at every mountain head,
And o'er the friths that branch and spread
Their sleeping silver thro' the hills;

And touch with shade the bridal doors,
With tender gloom the roof, the wall;
And breaking let the splendour fall
To spangle all the happy shores

By which they rest, and ocean sounds,
And, star and system rolling past,
A soul shall draw from out the vast
And strike his being into bounds,

And, moved thro' life of lower phase,
Result in man, be born and think,
And act and love, a closer link
Betwixt us and the crowning race

Of those that, eye to eye, shall look
On knowledge; under whose command
Is Earth and Earth's, and in their hand
Is Nature like an open book;

No longer half-akin to brute,
For all we thought and loved and did,
And hoped, and suffer'd, is but seed
Of what in them is flower and fruit;

Whereof the man, that with me trod
This planet, was a noble type
Appearing ere the times were ripe,
That friend of mine who lives in God,

That God, which ever lives and loves,
One God, one law, one element,
And one far-off divine event,
To which the whole creation moves.

[81] See *I Corinthians*, x, 4.

[82] The epilogue, of which these stanzas are the last, celebrates the marriage of Tennyson's sister Cecilia to Edmund Lushington, 10 October 1842. The wedding-dance is ended and the poet has retired.

The Eagle[83]

He clasps the crag with crooked hands;
Close to the sun in lonely lands,
Ring'd with the azure world, he stands.

The wrinkled sea beneath him crawls;
He watches from his mountain walls,
And like a thunderbolt he falls.

[83] Published in *Poems*, seventh edition, 1851.

MAUD; A MONODRAMA[84]

Part I

I

I

I hate the dreadful hollow behind the little wood,
Its lips in the field above are dappled with blood-red heath,
The red-ribb'd ledges drip with a silent horror of blood,
And Echo there, whatever is ask'd her, answers 'Death.'

II

For there in the ghastly pit long since a body was found,
His who had given me life — O father! O God! was it well? —
Mangled, and flatten'd, and crush'd, and dinted into the ground:
There yet lies the rock that fell with him when he fell.

III

Did he fling himself down? who knows? for a vast speculation had fail'd,
And ever he mutter'd and madden'd, and ever wann'd with despair,
And out he walk'd when the wind like a broken worldling wail'd,
And the flying gold of the ruin'd woodlands drove thro' the air.

IV

I remember the time, for the roots of my hair were stirr'd
By a shuffled step, by a dead weight trail'd, by a whisper'd fright,
And my pulses closed their gates with a shock on my heart as I heard
The shrill-edged shriek of a mother divide the shuddering night.

V

Villainy somewhere! whose? One says, we are villains all.
Not he: his honest fame should at least by me be maintained:
But that old man, now lord of the broad estate and the Hall,
Dropt off gorged from a scheme that had left us flaccid and drain'd.

VI

Why do they prate of the blessings of Peace? we have made them a curse,
Pickpockets, each hand lusting for all that is not its own;
And lust of gain, in the spirit of Cain, is it better or worse
Than the heart of the citizen hissing in war on his own hearthstone?

VII

But these are the days of advance, the works of the men of mind,
When who but a fool would have faith in a tradesman's ware or his word?
Is it peace or war? Civil war, as I think, and that of a kind
The viler, as underhand, not openly bearing the sword.

VIII

Sooner or later I too may passively take the print
Of the golden age — why not? I have neither hope nor trust;

---

[84] Published in 1855. It grew out of — or rather was made as an 'explanation' of — the lines, 'O, that 't were possible,' *etc.*, printed in 1837 and now forming, with alteration, the fourth section of Part II of the poem. Tennyson himself was particularly fond of his 'little *Hamlet*,' and often read it aloud. The story of a young man, heir to madness, morbidly sensitive in a materialistic age, rescued by love, the loss of which drives him insane, is, in summary, a story of redemption — a redemption accomplished, as Tennyson said, in 'the unselfishness born of his great passion.' It has been suggested that the motto of *Maud* might well be the lines from *Locksley Hall* which Tennyson frequently copied for an autograph:

'Love took up the harp of Life, and smote on all the chords with might;
Smote the chord of Self, that, trembling, pass'd in music out of sight.'

May make my heart as a millstone, set my face as a flint,
Cheat and be cheated, and die: who knows? we are ashes and dust.

IX

Peace sitting under her olive, and slurring the days gone by,
When the poor are hovell'd and hustled together, each sex, like swine.
When only the ledger lives, and when only not all men lie;
Peace in her vineyard — yes! — but a company forges the wine.

X

And the vitriol madness flushes up in the ruffian's head,
Till the filthy by-lane rings to the yell of the trampled wife,
And chalk and alum and plaster are sold to the poor for bread,
And the spirit of murder works in the very means of life,

XI

And Sleep must lie down arm'd, for the villainous centre-bits [85]
Grind on the wakeful ear in the hush of the moonless nights,
While another is cheating the sick of a few last gasps, as he sits
To pestle a poison'd poison behind his crimson lights.

XII

When a Mammonite mother kills her babe for a burial fee,
And Timour [86]-Mammon grins on a pile of children's bones,
Is it peace or war? better, war! loud war by land and by sea,
War with a thousand battles, and shaking a hundred thrones.

[85] Tools used by burglars.
[86] Tamerlane, the fourteenth century conqueror, who was said to have had a thousand children crushed by his horsemen.

XIII

For I trust if an enemy's fleet came yonder round by the hill,
And the rushing battle-boat sang from the three-decker out of the foam,
That the smooth-faced snubnosed rogue would leap from his counter and till,
And strike, if he could, were it but with his cheating yardwand, home.——

XIV

What! am I raging alone as my father raged in his mood?
Must *I* too creep to the hollow and dash myself down and die
Rather than hold by the law that I made, nevermore to brood
On a horror of shatter'd limbs and a wretched swindler's lie?

XV

Would there be sorrow for *me?* there was *love* in the passionate shriek,
Love for the silent thing that had made false haste to the grave —
Wrapt in a cloak, as I saw him, and thought he would rise and speak
And rave at the lie and the liar, ah God, as he used to rave.

XVI

I am sick of the Hall and the hill, I am sick of the moor and the main.
Why should I stay? can a sweeter chance ever come to me here?
O, having the nerves of motion as well as the nerves of pain,
Were it not wise if I fled from the place and the pit and the fear?

XVII

Workmen up at the Hall! — they are coming back from abroad;
The dark old place will be gilt by the touch of a millionaire:

I have heard, I know not whence, of the singular beauty of Maud;
I play'd with the girl when a child; she promised then to be fair.

XVIII

Maud with her venturous climbings and tumbles and childish escapes,
Maud the delight of the village, the ringing joy of the Hall,
Maud with her sweet purse-mouth when my father dangled the grapes,
Maud the beloved of my mother, the moon-faced darling of all, —

XIX

What is she now? My dreams are bad. She may bring me a curse.
No, there is fatter game on the moor; she will let me alone.
Thanks, for the fiend best knows whether woman or man be the worse.
I will bury myself in myself, and the Devil may pipe to his own.

II

Long have I sigh'd for a calm: God grant I may find it at last!
It will never be broken by Maud, she has neither savour nor salt,
But a cold and clear-cut face, as I found when her carriage past,
Perfectly beautiful: let it be granted her: where is the fault?
All that I saw (for her eyes were downcast, not to be seen)
Faultily faultless, icily regular, splendidly null,
Dead perfection, no more; nothing more, if it had not been
For a chance of travel, a paleness, an hour's defect of the rose,
Or an underlip, you may call it a little too ripe, too full,
Or the least little delicate aquiline curve in a sensitive nose,
From which I escaped heart-free, with the least little touch of spleen.

III

Cold and clear-cut face, why come you so cruelly meek,
Breaking a slumber in which all spleenful folly was drown'd,
Pale with the golden beam of an eyelash dead on the cheek,
Passionless, pale, cold face, star-sweet on a gloom profound;
Womanlike, taking revenge too deep for a transient wrong
Done but in thought to your beauty, and ever as pale as before
Growing and fading and growing upon me without a sound,
Luminous, gemlike, ghostlike, deathlike, half the night long
Growing and fading and growing, till I could bear it no more,
But arose, and all by myself in my own dark garden ground,
Listening now to the tide in its broad-flung shipwrecking roar,
Now to the scream of a madden'd beach dragg'd down by the wave,
Walk'd in a wintry wind by a ghastly glimmer, and found
The shining daffodil dead, and Orion low in his grave.

IV

I

A million emeralds break from the ruby-budded lime
In the little grove where I sit — ah, wherefore cannot I be
Like things of the season gay, like the bountiful season bland,
When the far-off sail is blown by the breeze of a softer clime,
Half-lost in the liquid azure bloom of a crescent of sea,
The silent sapphire-spangled marriage ring of the land?

II

Below me, there, is the village, and looks how quiet and small!
And yet bubbles o'er like a city, with gossip, scandal, and spite;
And Jack on his ale-house bench has as many lies as a Czar;
And here on the landward side, by a red rock, glimmers the Hall;
And up in the high Hall-garden I see her pass like a light;
But sorrow seize me if ever that light be my leading star!

III

When have I bow'd to her father, the wrinkled head of the race?
I met her to-day with her brother, but not to her brother I bow'd:
I bow'd to his lady-sister as she rode by on the moor:
But the fire of a foolish pride flash'd over her beautiful face.
O child, you wrong your beauty, believe it, in being so proud;
Your father has wealth well-gotten, and I am nameless and poor.

IV

I keep but a man and a maid, ever ready to slander and steal;
I know it, and smile a hard-set smile, like a stoic, or like
A wiser epicurean, and let the world have its way:
For nature is one with rapine, a harm no preacher can heal;
The Mayfly is torn by the swallow, the sparrow spear'd by the shrike,
And the whole little wood where I sit is a world of plunder and prey.

V

We are puppets, Man in his pride, and Beauty fair in her flower;
Do we move ourselves, or are moved by an unseen hand at a game
That pushes us off from the board, and others ever succeed?
Ah yet, we cannot be kind to each other here for an hour;
We whisper, and hint, and chuckle, and grin at a brother's shame;
However we brave it out, we men are a little breed.

VI

A monstrous eft was of old the Lord and Master of Earth,
For him did his high sun flame, and his river billowing ran,
And he felt himself in his force to be Nature's crowning race.
As nine months go to the shaping an infant ripe for his birth,
So many a million of ages have gone to the making of man:
He now is first, but is he the last? is he not too base?

VII

The man of science himself is fonder of glory, and vain,
An eye well-practised in nature, a spirit bounded and poor;
The passionate heart of the poet is whirl'd into folly and vice.
I would not marvel at either, but keep a temperate brain;
For not to desire or admire, if a man could learn it, were more
Than to walk all day like the sultan of old in a garden of spice.

VIII

For the drift of the Maker is dark, an Isis hid by the veil.
Who knows the ways of the world, how God will bring them about?
Our planet is one, the suns are many, the world is wide.
Shall I weep if a Poland fall? shall I shriek if a Hungary fail? [87]

[87] Russia and Austria had completed the partition of Poland in 1846; in 1849 the Hungarians were defeated in their revolt against Austrian domination.

Or an infant civilisation be ruled with rod or with knout?
I have not made the world, and He that made it will guide.

IX

Be mine a philosopher's life in the quiet woodland ways,
Where if I cannot be gay let a passionless peace be my lot,
Far-off from the clamour of liars belied in the hubbub of lies;
From the long-neck'd geese of the world that are ever hissing dispraise
Because their natures are little, and, whether he heed it or not,
Where each man walks with his head in a cloud of poisonous flies.

X

And most of all would I flee from the cruel madness of love,
The honey of poison-flowers and all the measureless ill.
Ah Maud, you milkwhite fawn, you are all unmeet for a wife.
Your mother is mute in her grave as her image in marble above;
Your father is ever in London, you wander about at your will;
You have but fed on the roses and lain in the lilies of life.

V

I

A voice by the cedar tree
In the meadow under the Hall!
She is singing an air that is known to me,
A passionate ballad gallant and gay,
A martial song like a trumpet's call!
Singing alone in the morning of life,
In the happy morning of life and of May,
Singing of men that in battle array,
Ready in heart and ready in hand,
March with banner and bugle and fife
To the death, for their native land.

II

Maud with her exquisite face,
And wild voice pealing up to the sunny sky,
And feet like sunny gems on an English green,
Maud in the light of her youth and her grace,
Singing of Death, and of Honour that cannot die,
Till I well could weep for a time so sordid and mean,
And myself so languid and base.

III

Silence, beautiful voice!
Be still, for you only trouble the mind
With a joy in which I cannot rejoice,
A glory I shall not find.
Still! I will hear you no more,
For your sweetness hardly leaves me a choice
But to move to the meadow and fall before
Her feet on the meadow grass, and adore,
Not her, who is neither courtly nor kind,
Not her, not her, but a voice.

VI

I

Morning arises stormy and pale,
No sun, but a wannish glare
In fold upon fold of hueless cloud,
And the budded peaks of the wood are bow'd
Caught and cuff'd by the gale:
I had fancied it would be fair.

II

Whom but Maud should I meet
Last night, when the sunset burn'd
On the blossom'd gable-ends
At the head of the village street,
Whom but Maud should I meet?
And she touch'd my hand with a smile so sweet,
She made me divine amends
For a courtesy not return'd.

III

And thus a delicate spark
Of glowing and growing light
Thro' the livelong hours of the dark
Kept itself warm in the heart of my dreams,
Ready to burst in a colour'd flame;
Till at last when the morning came
In a cloud, it faded, and seems
But an ashen-gray delight.

IV

What if with her sunny hair,
And smile as sunny as cold,
She meant to weave me a snare
Of some coquettish deceit,
Cleopatra-like as of old
To entangle me when we met,
To have her lion roll in a silken net
And fawn at a victor's feet.

V

Ah, what shall I be at fifty
Should Nature keep me alive,
If I find the world so bitter
When I am but twenty-five?
Yet, if she were not a cheat,
If Maud were all that she seem'd,
And her smile were all that I dream'd,
Then the world were not so bitter
But a smile could make it sweet.

VI

What if tho' her eye seem'd full
Of a kind intent to me,
What if that dandy-despot, he,
That jewell'd mass of millinery,
That oil'd and curl'd Assyrian Bull
Smelling of musk and of insolence,
Her brother, from whom I keep aloof,
Who wants the finer politic sense
To mask, tho' but in his own behoof,
With a glassy smile his brutal scorn —
What if he had told her yestermorn
How prettily for his own sweet sake
A face of tenderness might be feign'd,
And a moist mirage in desert eyes,
That so, when the rotten hustings shake
In another month to his brazen lies,
A wretched vote may be gain'd.

VII

For a raven ever croaks, at my side,
Keep watch and ward, keep watch and ward,
Or thou wilt prove their tool.
Yea, too, myself from myself I guard,
For often a man's own angry pride
Is cap and bells for a fool.

VIII

Perhaps the smile and tender tone
Came out of her pitying womanhood,
For am I not, am I not, here alone
So many a summer since she died,
My mother, who was so gentle and good?
Living alone in an empty house,
Here half-hid in the gleaming wood,
Where I hear the dead at midday moan,
And the shrieking rush of the wainscot mouse,
And my own sad name in corners cried,
When the shiver of dancing leaves is thrown
About its echoing chambers wide,
Till a morbid hate and horror have grown
Of a world in which I have hardly mixt,
And a morbid eating lichen fixt
On a heart half-turn'd to stone.

IX

O heart of stone, are you flesh, and caught
By that you swore to withstand?
For what was it else within me wrought
But, I fear, the new strong wine of love,
That made my tongue so stammer and trip
When I saw the treasured splendour, her hand,
Come sliding out of her sacred glove,
And the sunlight broke from her lip?

X

I have play'd with her when a child;
She remembers it now we meet.

Ah well, well, well, I *may* be beguiled
By some coquettish deceit.
Yet, if she were not a cheat,
If Maud were all that she seem'd,
And her smile had all that I dream'd,
Then the world were not so bitter
But a smile could make it sweet.

VII

I

Did I hear it half in a doze
  Long since, I know not where?
Did I dream it an hour ago,
  When asleep in this arm-chair?

II

Men were drinking together,
  Drinking and talking of me;
'Well, if it prove a girl, the boy
  Will have plenty: so let it be.'

III

Is it an echo of something
  Read with a boy's delight,
Viziers nodding together
  In some Arabian night?

IV

Strange, that I hear two men,
  Somewhere, talking of me;
'Well, if it prove a girl, my boy
  Will have plenty: so let it be.'

VIII

She came to the village church,
And sat by a pillar alone;
An angel watching an urn
Wept over her, carved in stone;
And once, but once, she lifted her eyes,
And suddenly, sweetly, strangely blush'd
To find they were met by my own;
And suddenly, sweetly, my heart beat stronger
And thicker, until I heard no longer
The snowy-banded, dilettante,
Delicate-handed priest intone;
And thought, is it pride, and mused and sigh'd
'No surely, now it cannot be pride.'

IX

I was walking a mile,
More than a mile from the shore,
The sun look'd out with a smile
Betwixt the cloud and the moor,
And riding at set of day
Over the dark moor land,
Rapidly riding far away,
She waved to me with her hand.
There were two at her side,
Something flash'd in the sun,
Down by the hill I saw them ride,
In a moment they were gone:
Like a sudden spark
Struck vainly in the night,
Then returns the dark
With no more hope of light.

X

I

Sick, am I sick of a jealous dread?
Was not one of the two at her side
This new-made lord, whose splendour plucks
The slavish hat from the villager's head?
Whose old grandfather has lately died,
Gone to a blacker pit, for whom
Grimy nakedness dragging his trucks
And laying his trams in a poison'd gloom
Wrought, till he crept from a gutted mine
Master of half a servile shire,
And left his coal all turn'd into gold
To a grandson, first of his noble line,
Rich in the grace all women desire,
Strong in the power that all men adore,
And simper and set their voices lower,
And soften as if to a girl, and hold
Awe-stricken breaths at a work divine,
Seeing his gewgaw castle shine,
New as his title, built last year,
There amid perky larches and pine,

And over the sullen-purple moor
(Look at it) pricking a cockney ear.

II

What, has he found my jewel out?
For one of the two that rode at her side
Bound for the Hall, I am sure was he:
Bound for the Hall, and I think for a bride.
Blithe would her brother's acceptance be.
Maud could be gracious too, no doubt
To a lord, a captain, a padded shape,
A bought commission, a waxen face,
A rabbit mouth that is ever agape —
Bought? what is it he cannot buy?
And therefore splenetic, personal, base,
A wounded thing with a rancorous cry,
At war with myself and a wretched race,
Sick, sick to the heart of life, am I.

III

Last week came one to the county town,
To preach our poor little army down,
And play the game of the despot kings,
Tho' the state has done it and thrice as
well:
This broad-brimm'd hawker of holy things,
Whose ear is cramm'd with his cotton,
and rings
Even in dreams to the chink of his pence,
This huckster put down war! can he tell
Whether war be a cause or a consequence?
Put down the passions that make earth
Hell!
Down with ambition, avarice, pride,
Jealousy, down! cut off from the mind
The bitter springs of anger and fear;
Down too, down at your own fireside,
With the evil tongue and the evil ear,
For each is at war with mankind.

IV

I wish I could hear again
The chivalrous battle-song
That she warbled alone in her joy!
I might persuade myself then
She would not do herself this great wrong,
To take a wanton dissolute boy
For a man and leader of men.

V

Ah God, for a man with heart, head,
hand,
Like some of the simple great ones gone
For ever and ever by,
One still strong man in a blatant land,
Whatever they call him, what care I,
Aristocrat, democrat, autocrat — one
Who can rule and dare not lie.

VI

And ah for a man to arise in me,
That the man I am may cease to be!

XI

I

O let the solid ground
Not fail beneath my feet
Before my life has found
What some have found so sweet;
Then let come what come may,
What matter if I go mad,
I shall have had my day.

II

Let the sweet heavens endure,
Not close and darken above me
Before I am quite quite sure
That there is one to love me;
Then let come what come may
To a life that has been so sad,
I shall have had my day.

XII

I

Birds in the high Hall-garden
When twilight was falling,
Maud, Maud, Maud, Maud,
They were crying and calling.

II

Where was Maud? in our wood;
And I, who else, was with her,
Gathering woodland lilies,
Myriads blow together.

III

Birds in our wood sang
    Ringing thro' the valleys,
Maud is here, here, here
    In among the lilies.

IV

I kiss'd her slender hand,
    She took the kiss sedately;
Maud is not seventeen,
    But she is tall and stately.

V

I to cry out on pride
    Who have won her favour!
O Maud were sure of Heaven
    If lowliness could save her.

VI

I know the way she went
    Home with her maiden posy,
For her feet have touch'd the meadows
    And left the daisies rosy.[88]

VII

Birds in the high Hall-garden
    Were crying and calling to her,
Where is Maud, Maud, Maud?
    One is come to woo her.

VIII

Look, a horse at the door,
    And little King Charley snarling,
Go back, my lord, across the moor,
    You are not her darling.

XIII

I

Scorn'd, to be scorn'd by one that I scorn,
Is that a matter to make me fret?
That a calamity hard to be borne?
Well, he may live to hate me yet.
Fool that I am to be vext with his pride!
I past him, I was crossing his lands;
He stood on the path a little aside;
His face, as I grant, in spite of spite,
Has a broad-blown comeliness, red and
    white,
And six feet two, as I think, he stands;
But his essences turn'd the live air sick,
And barbarous opulence jewel-thick
Sunn'd itself on his breast and his hands.

II

Who shall call me ungentle, unfair,
I long'd so heartily then and there
To give him the grasp of fellowship;
But while I past he was humming an air,
Stopt, and then with a riding whip
Leisurely tapping a glossy boot,
And curving a contumelious lip,
Gorgonised me from head to foot
With a stony British stare.

III

Why sits he here in his father's chair?
That old man never comes to his place:
Shall I believe him ashamed to be seen?
For only once, in the village street,
Last year, I caught a glimpse of his face,
A gray old wolf and a lean.
Scarcely, now, would I call him a cheat;
For then, perhaps, as a child of deceit,
She might by a true descent be untrue;
And Maud is as true as Maud is sweet:
Tho' I fancy her sweetness only due
To the sweeter blood by the other side;
Her mother has been a thing complete,
However she came to be so allied.
And fair without, faithful within,
Maud to him is nothing akin:
Some peculiar mystic grace
Made her only the child of her mother,
And heap'd the whole inherited sin
On that huge scapegoat of the race,
All, all upon the brother.

IV

Peace, angry spirit, and let him be!
Has not his sister smiled on me?

[88] The English daisy is partly rose-colored.

XIV

I

Maud has a garden of roses
And lilies fair on a lawn;
There she walks in her state
And tends upon bed and bower,
And thither I climb'd at dawn
And stood by her garden-gate;
A lion ramps at the top,
He is claspt by a passion-flower.

II

Maud's own little oak-room
(Which Maud, like a precious stone
Set in the heart of the carven gloom,
Lights with herself, when alone
She sits by her music and books
And her brother lingers late
With a roystering company) looks
Upon Maud's own garden-gate:
And I thought as I stood, if a hand, as white
As ocean-foam in the moon, were laid
On the hasp of the window, and my Delight
Had a sudden desire, like a glorious ghost, to glide,
Like a beam of the seventh Heaven, down to my side,
There were but a step to be made.

III

The fancy flatter'd my mind,
And again seem'd overbold;
Now I thought that she cared for me,
Now I thought she was kind
Only because she was cold.

IV

I heard no sound where I stood
But the rivulet on from the lawn
Running down to my own dark wood;
Or the voice of the long sea-wave as it swell'd
Now and then in the dim-gray dawn;
But I look'd, and round, all round the house I beheld
The death-white curtain drawn;
Felt a horror over me creep,
Prickle my skin and catch my breath,
Knew that the death-white curtain meant but sleep,
Yet I shudder'd and thought like a fool of the sleep of death.

XV

So dark a mind within me dwells,
  And I make myself such evil cheer,
That if *I* be dear to some one else,
  Then some one else may have much to fear;
But if *I* be dear to some one else,
  Then I should be to myself more dear.
Shall I not take care of all that I think,
Yea, ev'n of wretched meat and drink,
If I be dear,
If I be dear to some one else.

XVI

I

This lump of earth has left his estate
The lighter by the loss of his weight;
And so that he find what he went to seek,
And fulsome Pleasure clog him, and drown
His heart in the gross mud-honey of town,
He may stay for a year who has gone for a week:
But this is the day when I must speak
And I see my Oread coming down,
O this is the day!
O beautiful creature, what am I
That I dare to look her way;
Think I may hold dominion sweet,
Lord of the pulse that is lord of her breast,
And dream of her beauty with tender dread,
From the delicate Arab arch of her feet
To the grace that, bright and light as the crest
Of a peacock, sits on her shining head,
And she knows it not: O, if she knew it,
To know her beauty might half undo it.

I know it the one bright thing to save
My yet young life in the wilds of Time,
Perhaps from madness, perhaps from
crime,
Perhaps from a selfish grave.

II

What, if she be fasten'd to this fool lord,
Dare I bid her abide by her word?
Should I love her so well if she
Had given her word to a thing so low?
Shall I love her as well if she
Can break her word were it even for me?
I trust that it is not so.

III

Catch not my breath, O clamorous heart,
Let not my tongue be a thrall to my eye,
For I must tell her before we part,
I must tell her, or die.

XVII

Go not, happy day,
From the shining fields,
Go not, happy day,
Till the maiden yields.
Rosy is the West,
Rosy is the South,
Roses are her cheeks,
And a rose her mouth
When the happy Yes
Falters from her lips,
Pass and blush the news
Over glowing ships;
Over blowing seas,
Over seas at rest,
Pass the happy news,
Blush it thro' the West;
Till the red man dance
By his red cedar-tree,
And the red man's babe
Leap, beyond the sea.
Blush from West to East,
Blush from East to West,
Till the West is East,
Blush it thro' the West.
Rosy is the West,
Rosy is the South,
Roses are her cheeks,
And a rose her mouth.

XVIII

I

I have led her home, my love, my only
friend.
There is none like her, none.
And never yet so warmly ran my blood
And sweetly, on and on
Calming itself to the long-wish'd-for end,
Full to the banks, close on the promised
good.

II

None like her, none.
Just now the dry-tongued laurels' pattering
talk
Seem'd her light foot along the garden
walk,
And shook my heart to think she comes
once more;
But even then I heard her close the door,
The gates of Heaven are closed, and she is
gone.

III

There is none like her, none.
Nor will be when our summers have de-
ceased.
O, art thou sighing for Lebanon
In the long breeze that streams to thy
delicious East,
Sighing for Lebanon,
Dark cedar, tho' thy limbs have here in-
creased,
Upon a pastoral slope as fair,
And looking to the South, and fed
With honey'd rain and delicate air,
And haunted by the starry head
Of her whose gentle will has changed my
fate,
And made my life a perfumed altar-flame;
And over whom thy darkness must have
spread
With such delight as theirs of old, thy
great

Forefathers of the thornless garden, there
Shadowing the snow-limb'd Eve from whom she came.

IV

Here will I lie, while these long branches sway,
And you fair stars that crown a happy day
Go in and out as if at merry play,
Who am no more so all forlorn,
As when it seem'd far better to be born
To labour and the mattock-harden'd hand,
Than nursed at ease and brought to understand
A sad astrology, the boundless plan
That makes you tyrants in your iron skies,
Innumerable, pitiless, passionless eyes,
Cold fires, yet with power to burn and brand
His nothingness into man.

V

But now shine on, and what care I,
Who in this stormy gulf have found a pearl
The countercharm of space and hollow sky,
And do accept my madness, and would die
To save from some slight shame one simple girl.

VI

Would die; for sullen-seeming Death may give
More life to Love than is or ever was
In our low world, where yet 'tis sweet to live.
Let no one ask me how it came to pass;
It seems that I am happy, that to me
A livelier emerald twinkles in the grass,
A purer sapphire melts into the sea.

VII

Not die; but live a life of truest breath,
And teach true life to fight with mortal wrongs.
O, why should Love, like men in drinking-songs,
Spice his fair banquet with the dust of death?
Make answer, Maud my bliss,
Maud made my Maud by that long loving kiss,
Life of my life, wilt thou not answer this?
'The dusky strand of Death inwoven here
With dear Love's tie, makes Love himself more dear.'

VIII

Is that enchanted moan only the swell
Of the long waves that roll in yonder bay?
And hark the clock within, the silver knell
Of twelve sweet hours that past in bridal white,
And died to live, long as my pulses play;
But now by this my love has closed her sight
And given false death her hand, and stol'n away
To dreamful wastes where footless fancies dwell
Among the fragments of the golden day.
May nothing there her maiden grace affright!
Dear heart, I feel with thee the drowsy spell.
My bride to be, my evermore delight,
My own heart's heart, my ownest own, farewell;
It is but for a little space I go:
And ye meanwhile far over moor and fell
Beat to the noiseless music of the night!
Has our whole earth gone nearer to the glow
Of your soft splendours that you look so bright?
I have climb'd nearer out of lonely Hell.
Beat, happy stars, timing with things below,
Beat with my heart more blest than heart can tell,
Blest, but for some dark undercurrent woe

That seems to draw — but it shall not be so:
Let all be well, be well.

XIX

I

Her brother is coming back to-night,
Breaking up my dream of delight.

II

My dream? do I dream of bliss?
I have walk'd awake with Truth.
O when did a morning shine
So rich in atonement as this
For my dark-dawning youth,
Darken'd watching a mother decline
And that dead man at her heart and mine:
For who was left to watch her but I?
Yet so did I let my freshness die.

III

I trust that I did not talk
To gentle Maud in our walk
(For often in lonely wanderings
I have cursed him even to lifeless things)
But I trust that I did not talk,
Not touch on her father's sin:
I am sure I did but speak
Of my mother's faded cheek
When it slowly grew so thin,
That I felt she was slowly dying
Vext with lawyers and harass'd with debt:
For how often I caught her with eyes all wet,
Shaking her head at her son and sighing
A world of trouble within!

IV

And Maud too, Maud was moved
To speak of the mother she loved
As one scarce less forlorn,
Dying abroad and it seems apart
From him who had ceased to share her heart,
And ever mourning over the feud,
The household Fury sprinkled with blood
By which our houses are torn:
How strange was what she said,
When only Maud and the brother
Hung over her dying bed —
That Maud's dark father and mine
Had bound us one to the other,
Betrothed us over their wine,
On the day when Maud was born;[89]
Seal'd her mine from her first sweet breath.
Mine, mine by a right, from birth till death.
Mine, mine — our fathers have sworn.

V

But the true blood spilt had in it a heat
To dissolve the precious seal on a bond,
That, if left uncancell'd, had been so sweet:
And none of us thought of a something beyond,
A desire that awoke in the heart of the child,
As it were a duty done to the tomb,
To be friends for her sake, to be reconciled;
And I was cursing them and my doom,
And letting a dangerous thought run wild
While often abroad in the fragrant gloom
Of foreign churches — I see her there,
Bright English lily, breathing a prayer
To be friends, to be reconciled!

VI

But then what a flint is he!
Abroad, at Florence, at Rome,
I find whenever she touch'd on me
This brother had laugh'd her down,
And at last, when each came home,
He had darken'd into a frown,
Chid her, and forbid her to speak
To me, her friend of the years before;
And this was what had redden'd her cheek
When I bow'd to her on the moor.

---

[89] See Part I, VII, p. 922.

VII

Yet Maud, altho' not blind
To the faults of his heart and mind,
I see she cannot but love him,
And says he is rough but kind,
And wishes me to approve him,
And tells me, when she lay
Sick once, with a fear of worse,
That he left his wine and horses and play,
Sat with her, read to her, night and day,
And tended her like a nurse.

VIII

Kind? but the deathbed desire
Spurn'd by this heir of the liar —
Rough but kind? yet I know
He has plotted against me in this,
That he plots against me still.
Kind to Maud? that were not amiss.
Well, rough but kind; why let it be so:
For shall not Maud have her will?

IX

For, Maud, so tender and true,
As long as my life endures
I feel I shall owe you a debt,
That I never can hope to pay;
And if ever I should forget
That I owe this debt to you
And for your sweet sake to yours;
O then, what then shall I say? —
If ever I *should* forget,
May God make me more wretched
Than ever I have been yet!

X

So now I have sworn to bury
All this dead body of hate,
I feel so free and so clear
By the loss of that dead weight,
That I should grow light-headed, I fear,
Fantastically merry;
But that her brother comes, like a blight
On my fresh hope, to the Hall to-night.

XX

I

Strange, that I felt so gay,
Strange, that *I* tried to-day
To beguile her melancholy;
The Sultan, as we name him, —
She did not wish to blame him —
But he vext her and perplext her
With his worldly talk and folly:
Was it gentle to reprove her
For stealing out of view
From a little lazy lover
Who but claims her as his due?
Or for chilling his caresses
By the coldness of her manners,
Nay, the plainness of her dresses?
Now I know her but in two,
Nor can pronounce upon it
If one should ask me whether
The habit, hat, and feather,
Or the frock and gipsy bonnet
Be the neater and completer;
For nothing can be sweeter
Than maiden Maud in either.

II

But to-morrow, if we live,
Our ponderous squire will give
A grand political dinner
To half the squirelings near;
And Maud will wear her jewels,
And the bird of prey will hover,
And the titmouse hope to win her
With his chirrup at her ear.

III

A grand political dinner
To the men of many acres,
A gathering of the Tory,
A dinner and then a dance
For the maids and marriage-makers,
And every eye but mine will glance
At Maud in all her glory.

IV

For I am not invited,
But, with the Sultan's pardon,

I am all as well delighted,
For I know her own rose-garden,
And mean to linger in it
Till the dancing will be over;
And then, oh then, come out to me
For a minute, but for a minute,
Come out to your own true lover,
That your true lover may see
Your glory also, and render
All homage to his own darling,
Queen Maud in all her splendour.

XXI

Rivulet crossing my ground,
And bringing me down from the Hall
This garden-rose that I found,
Forgetful of Maud and me,
And lost in trouble and moving round
Here at the head of a tinkling fall,
And trying to pass to the sea;
O Rivulet, born at the Hall,
My Maud has sent it by thee
(If I read her sweet will right)
On a blushing mission to me,
Saying in odour and colour, 'Ah, be
Among the roses to-night.'

XXII

I

Come into the garden, Maud,[90]
  For the black bat, night, has flown,
Come into the garden, Maud,
  I am here at the gate alone;
And the woodbine spices are wafted abroad,
  And the musk of the rose is blown.

II

For a breeze of morning moves,
  And the planet of Love [91] is on high,
Beginning to faint in the light that she loves
  On a bed of daffodil sky,
To faint in the light of the sun she loves,
  To faint in his light, and to die.

III

All night have the roses heard
  The flute, violin, bassoon;
All night has the casement jessamine stirr'd
  To the dancers dancing in tune;
Till a silence fell with the waking bird,
  And a hush with the setting moon.

IV

I said to the lily, 'There is but one
  With whom she has heart to be gay.
When will the dancers leave her alone?
  She is weary of dance and play.'
Now half to the setting moon are gone,
  And half to the rising day;
Low on the sand and loud on the stone
  The last wheel echoes away.

V

I said to the rose, 'The brief night goes
  In babble and revel and wine.
O young lord-lover, what sighs are those,
  For one that will never be thine?
But mine, but mine,' so I sware to the rose,
  'For ever and ever, mine.'

VI

And the soul of the rose went into my blood,
  As the music clash'd in the hall;
And long by the garden lake I stood,
  For I heard your rivulet fall
From the lake to the meadow and on to the wood,
  Our wood, that is dearer than all;

[90] This famous lyric is entirely missed if read, as it usually is, out of its context. It is not a flowery, romantic song, but the picture of an overwrought mind long in darkness, trembling now with passion before the coming of the light. The man's whole life is in this hour of dawn. The child-like, eager images of the flowers reveal delicately the touch of his affliction; but they also symbolize the love that has encompassed the whole of earth and now moves through everything. The wonderful eleventh stanza, with its climactic last line, is meaningless unless related to what has already transpired and what is yet to come.

[91] Venus

VII

From the meadow your walks have left so sweet
That whenever a March-wind sighs
He sets the jewel-print of your feet
In violets blue as your eyes,
To the woody hollows in which we meet
And the valleys of Paradise.

VIII

The slender acacia would not shake
One long milk-bloom on the tree;
The white lake-blossom fell into the lake
As the pimpernel dozed on the lea;
But the rose was awake all night for your sake,
Knowing your promise to me;
The lilies and roses were all awake,
They sigh'd for the dawn and thee.

IX

Queen rose of the rosebud garden of girls,
Come hither, the dances are done,
In gloss of satin and glimmer of pearls,
Queen lily and rose in one;
Shine out, little head, sunning over with curls,
To the flowers, and be their sun.

X

There has fallen a splendid tear
From the passion-flower at the gate.
She is coming, my dove, my dear;
She is coming, my life, my fate;
The red rose cries, 'She is near, she is near;'
And the white rose weeps, 'She is late;'
The larkspur listens, 'I hear, I hear;'
And the lily whispers, 'I wait.'

XI

She is coming, my own, my sweet;
Were it ever so airy a tread,
My heart would hear her and beat,
Were it earth in an earthy bed;
My dust would hear her and beat,
Had I lain for a century dead;
Would start and tremble under her feet,
And blossom in purple and red.

Part II

I

I

'The fault was mine, the fault was mine'—
Why am I sitting here so stunn'd and still,
Plucking the harmless wild-flower on the hill?—
It is this guilty hand!—
And there rises ever a passionate cry
From underneath in the darkening land—
What is it, that has been done?
O dawn of Eden bright over earth and sky,
The fires of Hell brake out of thy rising sun,
The fires of Hell and of Hate;
For she, sweet soul, had hardly spoken a word,
When her brother ran in his rage to the gate,
He came with the babe-faced lord;
Heap'd on her terms of disgrace,
And while she wept, and I strove to be cool,
He fiercely gave me the lie,
Till I with as fierce an anger spoke,
And he struck me, madman, over the face,
Struck me before the languid fool,
Who was gaping and grinning by:
Struck for himself an evil stroke;
Wrought for his house an irredeemable woe;
For front to front in an hour we stood,
And a million horrible bellowing echoes broke
From the red-ribb'd hollow behind the wood,
And thunder'd up into Heaven the Christless code,
That must have life for a blow.
Ever and ever afresh they seem'd to grow

Was it he lay there with a fading eye?
'The fault was mine,' he whisper'd, 'fly!'
Then glided out of the joyous wood
The ghastly Wraith of one that I know;
And there rang on a sudden a passionate cry,
A cry for a brother's blood:
It will ring in my heart and my ears, till I die, till I die.

II

Is it gone? my pulses beat —
What was it? a lying trick of the brain?
Yet I thought I saw her stand,
A shadow there at my feet,
High over the shadowy land.
It is gone; and the heavens fall in a gentle rain,
When they should burst and drown with deluging storms
The feeble vassals of wine and anger and lust,
The little hearts that know not how to forgive:
Arise, my God, and strike, for we hold Thee just,
Strike dead the whole weak race of venomous worms,
That sting each other here in the dust;
We are not worthy to live.

II

I

See what a lovely shell,
Small and pure as a pearl,
Lying close to my foot,
Frail, but a work divine,
Made so fairily well
With delicate spire and whorl,
How exquisitely minute,
A miracle of design!

II

What is it? a learned man
Could give it a clumsy name.
Let him name it who can,
The beauty would be the same.

III

The tiny cell is forlorn,
Void of the little living will
That made it stir on the shore.
Did he stand at the diamond door
Of his house in a rainbow frill?
Did he push, when he was uncurl'd,
A golden foot or a fairy horn
Thro' his dim water-world?

IV

Slight, to be crush'd with a tap
Of my finger-nail on the sand,
Small, but a work divine,
Frail, but of force to withstand,
Year upon year, the shock
Of cataract seas that snap
The three decker's oaken spine
Athwart the ledges of rock,
Here on the Breton strand!

V

Breton, not Briton; here
Like a shipwreck'd man on a coast
Of ancient fable and fear —
Plagued with a flitting to and fro,
A disease, a hard mechanic ghost
That never came from on high
Nor ever arose from below,
But only moves with the moving eye,
Flying along the land and the main —
Why should it look like Maud?
Am I to be overawed
By what I cannot but know
Is a juggle born of the brain?

VI

Back from the Breton coast,
Sick of a nameless fear,
Back to the dark sea-line
Looking, thinking of all I have lost;
An old song vexes my ear;
But that of Lamech [92] is mine.

VII

For years, a measureless ill,
For years, for ever, to part —

[92] See *Genesis*, iv, 23.

But she, she would love me still;
And as long, O God, as she
Have a grain of love for me,
So long, no doubt, no doubt,
Shall I nurse in my dark heart,
However weary, a spark of will
Not to be trampled out.

VIII

Strange, that the mind, when fraught
With a passion so intense
One would think that it well
Might drown all life in the eye,—
That it should, by being so overwrought,
Suddenly strike on a sharper sense
For a shell, or a flower, little things
Which else would have been past by!
And now I remember, I,
When he lay dying there,
I noticed one of his many rings
(For he had many, poor worm) and
thought
It is his mother's hair.

IX

Who knows if he be dead?
Whether I need have fled?
Am I guilty of blood?
However this may be,
Comfort her, comfort her, all things good,
While I am over the sea!
Let me and my passionate love go by,
But speak to her all things holy and high,
Whatever happen to me!
Me and my harmful love go by;
But come to her waking, find her asleep,
Powers of the height, Powers of the deep,
And comfort her tho' I die.

III

Courage, poor heart of stone!
I will not ask thee why
Thou canst not understand
That thou art left for ever alone:
Courage, poor stupid heart of stone.—
Or if I ask thee why,
Care not thou to reply:
She is but dead, and the time is at hand
When thou shalt more than die.

IV

I

O that 'twere possible [93]
After long grief and pain
To find the arms of my true love
Round me once again!

II

When I was wont to meet her
In the silent woody places
By the home that gave me birth,
We stood tranced in long embraces
Mixt with kisses sweeter sweeter
Than anything on earth.

III

A shadow flits before me,
Not thou, but like to thee:
Ah Christ, that it were possible
For one short hour to see
The souls we loved, that they might tell us
What and where they be.

IV

It leads me forth at evening,
It lightly winds and steals
In a cold white robe before me,
When all my spirit reels
At the shouts, the leagues of lights,
And the roaring of the wheels.

V

Half the night I waste in sighs,
Half in dreams I sorrow after
The delight of early skies;
In a wakeful doze I sorrow
For the hand, the lips, the eyes,
For the meeting of the morrow,
The delight of happy laughter,
The delight of low replies.

---

[93] See introductory note, p. 916.

VI

'Tis a morning pure and sweet,
And a dewy splendour falls
On the little flower that clings
To the turrets and the walls;
'Tis a morning pure and sweet,
And the light and shadow fleet;
She is walking in the meadow,
And the woodland echo rings;
In a moment we shall meet;
She is singing in the meadow
And the rivulet at her feet
Ripples on in light and shadow
To the ballad that she sings.

VII

Do I hear her sing as of old,
My bird with the shining head,
My own dove with the tender eye?
But there rings on a sudden a passionate
cry,
There is some one dying or dead,
And a sullen thunder is roll'd;
For a tumult shakes the city,
And I wake, my dream is fled;
In the shuddering dawn, behold,
Without knowledge, without pity,
By the curtains of my bed
That abiding phantom cold.

VIII

Get thee hence, nor come again,
Mix not memory with doubt,
Pass, thou deathlike type of pain,
Pass and cease to move about!
'Tis the blot upon the brain
That *will* show itself without.

IX

Then I rise, the eavedrops fall,
And the yellow vapours choke
The great city sounding wide;
The day comes, a dull red ball
Wrapt in drifts of lurid smoke
On the misty river-tide.

X

Thro' the hubbub of the market
I steal, a wasted frame,
It crosses here, it crosses there,
Thro' all that crowd confused and loud,
The shadow still the same;
And on my heavy eyelids
My anguish hangs like shame.

XI

Alas for her that met me,
That heard me softly call,
Came glimmering thro' the laurels
At the quiet evenfall,
In the garden by the turrets
Of the old manorial hall.

XII

Would the happy spirit descend,
From the realms of light and song,
In the chamber or the street,
As she looks among the blest,
Should I fear to greet my friend
Or to say 'Forgive the wrong,'
Or to ask her, 'Take me, sweet,
To the regions of thy rest'?

XIII

But the broad light glares and beats,
And the shadow flits and fleets
And will not let me be;
And I loathe the squares and streets,
And the faces that one meets,
Hearts with no love for me:
Always I long to creep
Into some still cavern deep,
There to weep, and weep, and weep
My whole soul out to thee.

V

I

Dead, long dead,
Long dead!
And my heart is a handful of dust,
And the wheels go over my head,
And my bones are shaken with pain,

For into a shallow grave they are thrust,
Only a yard beneath the street,
And the hoofs of the horses beat, beat,
The hoofs of the horses beat,
Beat into my scalp and my brain,
With never an end to the stream of passing feet,
Driving, hurrying, marrying, burying,
Clamour and rumble, and ringing and clatter,
And here beneath it is all as bad,
For I thought the dead had peace, but it is not so;
To have no peace in the grave, is that not sad?
But up and down and to and fro,
Ever about me the dead men go;
And then to hear a dead man chatter
Is enough to drive one mad.

II

Wretchedest age since Time began,
They cannot even bury a man;
And tho' we paid our tithes in the days that are gone,
Not a bell was rung, not a prayer was read;
It is that which makes us loud in the world of the dead;
There is none that does his work, not one;
A touch of their office might have sufficed,
But the churchmen fain would kill their church,
As the churches have kill'd their Christ.

III

See, there is one of us sobbing,
No limit to his distress;
And another, a lord of all things, praying
To his own great self, as I guess;
And another, a statesman there, betraying
His party-secret, fool, to the press;
And yonder a vile physician, blabbing
The case of his patient — all for what?
To tickle the maggot born in an empty head,
And wheedle a world that loves him not,
For it is but a world of the dead.

IV

Nothing but idiot gabble!
For the prophecy given of old [94]
And then not understood,
Has come to pass as foretold;
Nor let any man think for the public good,
But babble, merely for babble.
For I never whisper'd a private affair
Within the hearing of cat or mouse,
No, not to myself in the closet alone,
But I heard it shouted at once from the top of the house;
Everything came to be known.
Who told *him* we were there?

V

Not that gray old wolf, for he came not back
From the wilderness, full of wolves, where he used to lie;
He has gather'd the bones for his o'er-grown whelp to crack;
Crack them now for yourself, and howl, and die.

VI

Prophet, curse me the blabbing lip,
And curse me the British vermin, the rat;
I know not whether he came in the Hanover ship,[95]
But I know that he lies and listens mute
In an ancient mansion's crannies and holes:
Arsenic, arsenic, sure, would do it,
Except that now we poison our babes, poor souls!
It is all used up for that.

VII

Tell him now: she is standing here at my head;
Not beautiful now, not even kind;
He may take her now; for she never speaks her mind,
But is ever the one thing silent here.
She is not *of* us, as I divine;

[94] See *St. Luke*, xii, 2–3.

[95] The Norwegian rat, carried to England in the 18th century, was said by the Jacobites to have come with the House of Hanover in 1714, upon the accession of George I.

She comes from another stiller world of the dead,
Stiller, not fairer than mine.

VIII

But I know where a garden grows,
Fairer than aught in the world beside,
All made up of the lily and rose
That blow by night, when the season is good,
To the sound of dancing music and flutes:
It is only flowers, they had no fruits,
And I almost fear they are not roses, but blood;
For the keeper was one, so full of pride,
He linkt a dead man there to a spectral bride;
For he, if he had not been a Sultan of brutes,
Would he have that hole in his side?

IX

But what will the old man say?
He laid a cruel snare in a pit
To catch a friend of mine one stormy day;
Yet now I could even weep to think of it;
For what will the old man say
When he comes to the second corpse in the pit?

X

Friend, to be struck by the public foe,
Then to strike him and lay him low,
That were a public merit, far,
Whatever the Quaker holds, from sin;
But the red life spilt for a private blow —
I swear to you, lawful and lawless war
Are scarcely even akin.

XI

O me, why have they not buried me deep enough?
Is it kind to have made me a grave so rough,
Me, that was never a quiet sleeper?
Maybe still I am but half-dead;
Then I cannot be wholly dumb;
I will cry to the steps above my head
And somebody, surely, some kind heart will come
To bury me, bury me
Deeper, ever so little deeper.

Part III

I

My life has crept so long on a broken wing [96]
Thro' cells of madness, haunts of horror and fear,
That I come to be grateful at last for a little thing:
My mood is changed, for it fell at a time of year
When the face of night is fair on the dewy downs,
And the shining daffodil dies, and the Charioteer
And starry Gemini hang like glorious crowns
Over Orion's grave low down in the west,
That like a silent lightning under the stars
She seem'd to divide in a dream from a band of the blest,
And spoke of a hope for the world in the coming wars —
'And in that hope, dear soul, let trouble have rest,
Knowing I tarry for thee,' and pointed to Mars
As he glow'd like a ruddy shield on the Lion's breast.

II

And it was but a dream, yet it yielded a dear delight
To have look'd, tho' but in a dream, upon eyes so fair,
That had been in a weary world my one thing bright;
And it was but a dream, yet it lighten'd my despair

[96] This part was written just before the Crimean War.

When I thought that a war would arise in defence of the right,
That an iron tyranny now should bend or cease,
The glory of manhood stand on his ancient height,
Nor Britain's one sole God be the millionaire:
No more shall commerce be all in all, and Peace
Pipe on her pastoral hillock a languid note,
And watch her harvest ripen, her herd increase,
Nor the cannon-bullet rust on a slothful shore,
And the cobweb woven across the cannon's throat
Shall shake its threaded tears in the wind no more.

III

And as months ran on and rumour of battle grew,
'It is time, it is time, O passionate heart,' said I
(For I cleaved to a cause that I felt to be pure and true)
'It is time, O passionate heart and morbid eye,
That old hysterical mock-disease should die.'
And I stood on a giant deck and mix'd my breath
With a loyal people shouting a battle cry,
Till I saw the dreary phantom arise and fly
Far into the North, and battle, and seas of death.

IV

Let it go or stay, so I wake to the higher aims
Of a land that has lost for a little her lust of gold,
And love of a peace that was full of wrongs and shames,
Horrible, hateful, monstrous, not to be told;
And hail once more to the banner of battle unroll'd!
Tho' many a light shall darken, and many shall weep
For those that are crush'd in the clash of jarring claims,
Yet God's just wrath shall be wreak'd on a giant liar;
And many a darkness into the light shall leap,
And shine in the sudden making of splendid names,
And noble thought be freër under the sun,
And the heart of a people beat with one desire;
For the peace, that I deem'd no peace, is over and done,
And now by the side of the Black and the Baltic deep,
And deathful-grinning mouths of the fortress, flames
The blood-red blossom of war with a heart of fire.

V

Let it flame or fade, and the war roll down like a wind,
We have proved we have hearts in a cause, we are noble still,
And myself have awaked, as it seems, to the better mind;
It is better to fight for the good than to rail at the ill;
I have felt with my native land, I am one with my kind,
I embrace the purpose of God, and the doom assign'd.

Tithonus [97]

The woods decay, the woods decay and fall,
The vapours weep their burthen to the ground,

---

[97] Written in 1833, but not published until Thackeray obtained it for *The Cornhill Magazine*, February 1860. Tithonus, son of Laomedon, king of Troy, was the husband of Aurora, the goddess of the dawn. Aurora asked the gods to give Tithonus immortality, but she forgot to ask also for the gift of eternal youth. He had become desperately old and withered — for the gods cannot recall their gifts.

Man comes and tills the field and lies beneath,
And after many a summer dies the swan.
Me only cruel immortality
Consumes: I wither slowly in thine arms,
Here at the quiet limit of the world,
A white-hair'd shadow roaming like a dream
The ever-silent spaces of the East,
Far-folded mists, and gleaming halls of morn.

Alas! for this gray shadow, once a man—
So glorious in his beauty and thy choice,
Who madest him thy chosen, that he seem'd
To his great heart none other than a God!
I ask'd thee, 'Give me immortality.'
Then didst thou grant mine asking with a smile,
Like wealthy men who care not how they give.
But thy strong Hours indignant work'd their wills,
And beat me down and marr'd and wasted me,
And tho' they could not end me, left me maim'd
To dwell in presence of immortal youth,
Immortal age beside immortal youth,
And all I was, in ashes. Can thy love,
Thy beauty, make amends, tho' even now,
Close over us, the silver star, thy guide,
Shines in those tremulous eyes that fill with tears
To hear me? Let me go: take back thy gift:
Why should a man desire in any way
To vary from the kindly race of men,
Or pass beyond the goal of ordinance
Where all should pause, as is most meet for all?

A soft air fans the cloud apart; there comes
A glimpse of that dark world where I was born.
Once more the old mysterious glimmer steals
From thy pure brows, and from thy shoulders pure,
And bosom beating with a heart renew'd.
Thy cheek begins to redden thro' the gloom,
Thy sweet eyes brighten slowly close to mine,
Ere yet they blind the stars, and the wild team
Which love thee, yearning for thy yoke, arise,
And shake the darkness from their loosen'd manes,
And beat the twilight into flakes of fire.

Lo! ever thus thou growest beautiful
In silence, then before thine answer given
Departest, and thy tears are on my cheek.

Why wilt thou ever scare me with thy tears,
And make me tremble lest a saying learnt,
In days far-off, on that dark earth, be true?
'The Gods themselves cannot recall their gifts.'

Ay me! ay me! with what another heart
In days far-off, and with what other eyes
I used to watch—if I be he that watch'd—
The lucid outline forming round thee; saw
The dim curls kindle into sunny rings;
Changed with thy mystic change, and felt my blood
Glow with the glow that slowly crimson'd all
Thy presence and thy portals, while I lay,
Mouth, forehead, eyelids, growing dewy-warm
With kisses balmier than half-opening buds
Of April, and could hear the lips that kiss'd

Whispering I knew not what of wild and sweet,
Like that strange song I heard Apollo sing,
While Ilion like a mist rose into towers.

Yet hold me not for ever in thine East:
How can my nature longer mix with thine?
Coldly thy rosy shadows bathe me, cold
Are all thy lights, and cold my wrinkled feet
Upon thy glimmering thresholds, when the steam
Floats up from those dim fields about the homes
Of happy men that have the power to die,
And grassy barrows of the happier dead.
Release me, and restore me to the ground;
Thou seëst all things, thou wilt see my grave:
Thou wilt renew thy beauty morn by morn;
I earth in earth forget these empty courts,
And thee returning on thy silver wheels.

Milton [98]

ALCAICS

O MIGHTY-MOUTH'D inventor of harmonies,
O skill'd to sing of Time or Eternity,
God-gifted organ-voice of England,
Milton, a name to resound for ages;
Whose Titan angels, Gabriel, Abdiel,
Starr'd from Jehovah's gorgeous armouries,
Tower, as the deep-domed empyrëan
Rings to the roar of an angel onset —
Me rather all that bowery loneliness,
The brooks of Eden mazily murmuring,
And bloom profuse and cedar arches
Charm, as a wanderer out in ocean,
Where some refulgent sunset of India
Streams o'er a rich ambrosial ocean isle,
And crimson-hued the stately palm-woods
Whisper in odorous heights of even.

[98] Published in *The Cornhill Magazine*, December 1863, with three other similar attempts to secure the effect of classical meters in English. Alcaeus was a Greek lyric poet.

Northern Farmer [99]

OLD STYLE

I

WHEER 'asta beän saw long and meä liggin' [100] 'ere aloän?
Noorse? thourt nowt o' a noorse: whoy, Doctor 's abeän an' agoän:
Says that I moänt 'a naw moor aäle: but I beänt a fool:
Git ma my aäle, fur I beänt a-gawin' to breäk my rule.

II

Doctors, they knaws nowt, fur a [101] says what 's nawways true:
Naw soort o' koind o' use to saäy the things that a do.
I've 'ed my point o' aäle ivry noight sin' I beän 'ere.
An' I've 'ed my quart ivry market-noight for foorty year.

III

Parson 's a beän loikewoise, an' a sittin' 'ere o' my bed.
'The amoighty 's a taäkin o' you [102] to 'issén, [103] my friend,' a said,
An' a towd ma my sins, an's toithe [104] were due, an' I gied it in hond;
I done moy duty boy 'um, as I 'a done boy the lond.

IV

Larn'd a ma' beä. I reckons I 'annot sa mooch to larn.
But a cast oop, [105] thot a did, 'bout Bessy Marris's barne. [106]

[99] Published in *Enoch Arden, and Other Poems*, 1864. The dialect is that of the peasants whom Tennyson knew in Lincolnshire. He founded the poem solely upon the last words of a farm-bailiff, as reported by a great-uncle: 'God A'mighty little knows what He's about a-taking me An' Squire will be so mad an' all.'

[100] lying

[101] he

[102] *Ou* pronounced as in *sour*.

[103] himself

[104] tithe

[105] confessed

[106] child

Thaw a knaws I hallus voäted wi' Squoire an' choorch an' staäte,
An' i' the woost o' toimes I wur niver agin the raäte.[107]

V

An' I hallus coom'd to 's chooch afoor moy Sally wur deäd,
An' 'eärd 'um a bummin'[108] awaäy loike a buzzard-clock[109] ower my 'eäd,
An' I niver knaw'd whot a meän'd but I thowt a 'ad summut to saäy,
An' I thowt a said whot a owt to 'a said an' I coom'd awaäy.

VI

Bessy Marris's barne! tha knaws she laäid it to meä.
Mowt a beän, mayhap, for she wur a bad un, sheä.
'Siver, I kep 'um, I kep 'um, my lass, tha mun understond;
I done moy duty boy 'um as I 'a done boy the lond.

VII

But Parson a cooms an' a goäs, an' a says it eäsy an' freeä
'The amoighty's a taäkin' o' you to 'issén, my friend,' says 'eä.
I weänt saäy men be loiars, thaw summun[110] said it in 'äaste:
But 'e reäds wonn sarmin a weeäk, an' I 'a stubb'd Thurnaby waäste.

VIII

D'ya moind the waäste, my lass? naw, naw, tha was not born then;
Theer wur a boggle[111] in it, I often 'eärd 'um mysen;
Moäst loike a butter-bump,[112] for I 'eärd 'um about an' about,
But I stubb'd 'um oop wi' the lot, an' raäved an' rembled[113] 'um out.

IX

Keäper 's it wur;[114] fo' they fun 'um theer a-laäid of 'is faäce
Down i' the woild 'enemies[115] afoor I coom'd to the plaäce.
Noäks or Thimbleby — toäner[116] 'ed shot 'um as deäd as a naäil.
Noäks wur 'ang'd for it oop at 'soize[117] — but git ma my aäle.

X

Dubbut looök at the waäste: theer warn't not feeäd for a cow;
Nowt at all but bracken an' fuzz,[118] an' looök at it now —
Warnt worth nowt a haäcre, an' now theer 's lots o' feeäd,
Fourscoor yows[119] upon it an' some on it down i' seeäd.[120]

XI

Nobbut a bit on it 's left, an' I meän'd to 'a stubb'd it at fall,
Done it ta-year I meän'd, an' runn'd plow thruff it an' all,
If godamoighty an' parson 'ud nobbut let ma aloän,
Meä, wi' haäte hoonderd haäcre o' Squoire's, an' lond o' my oän.

XII

Do godamoighty knaw what a 's doing a-taäkin' o' meä?
I beänt wonn as saws 'ere a beän an' yonder a peä;
An' Squoire 'ull be sa mad an' all — a' dear a' dear!
And I 'a managed for Squoire coom Michaelmas thutty year.

XIII

A mowt 'a taäen owd Joänes, as 'ant not a 'aäpoth[121] o' sense,

---

107 tax (for charity)
108 buzzing
109 cockchafer
110 See *Psalms*, cxvi, 11.
111 goblin or spirit
112 bittern
113 plowed him up and threw him out

114 *I.e.*, the game-keeper's ghost.
115 anemones
116 one or the other
117 the assizes
118 furze
119 ewes
120 clover
121 halfpenny's worth

Or a mowt 'a taäen young Robins — a niver mended a fence:
But godamoighty a moost taäke meä an' taäke ma now
Wi' aäf the cows to cauve an' Thurnaby hoälms to plow!

XIV

Looök 'ow quoloty smoiles when they seeäs ma a passin' boy,
Says to thessén [122] naw doubt 'what a man a beä sewer-loy!' [123]
For they knaws what I beän to Squoire sin fust a coom'd to the 'All;
I done moy duty by Squoire an' I done moy duty boy hall.

XV

Squoire 's i' Lunnon, an' summun I reckons 'ull 'a to wroite,
For whoä 's to howd the lond ater meä thot muddles ma quoit;
Sartin-sewer I beä, thot a weänt niver give it to Joänes,
Naw, nor a moänt to Robins — a niver rembles the stoäns.

XVI

But summun 'ull come ater meä mayhap wi' 'is kittle o' steäm [124]
Huzzin' an' maäzin' [125] the blessed feälds wi' the Divil's oän teäm.
Sin' I mun doy I mun doy, thaw loife they says is sweet,
But sin' I mun doy I mun doy, for I couldn abeär to see it.

XVII

What atta stannin' theer fur, an' doesn bring ma the aäle?
Doctor 's a 'toättler,[126] lass, an a 's hallus i' the owd taäle; [127]
I weänt breäk rules fur Doctor, a knaws naw moor nor a floy;
Git ma my aäle I tell tha, an' if I mun doy I mun doy.

[122] themselves
[123] surely
[124] steam-boiler
[125] worrying and scaring
[126] teetotaler
[127] telling the same old story

Wages [128]

Glory of warrior, glory of orator, glory of song,
  Paid with a voice flying by to be lost on an endless sea —
Glory of Virtue, to fight, to struggle, to right the wrong —
  Nay, but she aim'd not at glory, no lover of glory she:
Give her the glory of going on, and still to be.

The wages of sin is death: if the wages of Virtue be dust,
  Would she have heart to endure for the life of the worm and the fly?
She desires no isles of the blest, no quiet seats of the just,
  To rest in a golden grove, or to bask in a summer sky:
Give her the wages of going on, and not to die.

The Revenge [129]

A BALLAD OF THE FLEET

I

At Flores in the Azores Sir Richard Grenville lay,
And a pinnace, like a flutter'd bird, came flying from far away:
'Spanish ships of war at sea! we have sighted fifty-three!'
Then sware Lord Thomas Howard: ''Fore God I am no coward;

[128] Published in *Macmillan's Magazine*, February 1868.
[129] Published in *The Nineteenth Century*, March 1878. According to Sir Walter Raleigh, the naval battle with the Spanish fleet was fought on 10 September 1591. Lord Thomas Howard, lying off the Azores to intercept the Spanish ships returning from the West Indies, received word that fifty-three warships were coming against him. The incident Tennyson describes followed.

But I cannot meet them here, for my ships are out of gear,
And the half my men are sick. I must fly, but follow quick.
We are six ships of the line; can we fight with fifty-three? '

II

Then spake Sir Richard Grenville: 'I know you are no coward;
You fly them for a moment to fight with them again.
But I've ninety men and more that are lying sick ashore.
I should count myself the coward if I left them, my Lord Howard,
To these Inquisition dogs and the devildoms of Spain.'

III

So Lord Howard past away with five ships of war that day,
Till he melted like a cloud in the silent summer heaven;
But Sir Richard bore in hand all his sick men from the land
Very carefully and slow,
Men of Bideford in Devon,
And we laid them on the ballast down below;
For we brought them all aboard,
And they blest him in their pain, that they were not left to Spain,
To the thumb-screw and the stake, for the glory of the Lord.

IV

He had only a hundred seamen to work the ship and to fight,
And he sailed away from Flores till the Spaniard came in sight,
With his huge sea-castles heaving upon the weather bow.
'Shall we fight or shall we fly?
Good Sir Richard, tell us now,
For to fight is but to die!
There'll be little of us left by the time this sun be set.'
And Sir Richard said again: 'We be all good English men.
Let us bang these dogs of Seville, the children of the devil,
For I never turn'd my back upon Don or devil yet.'

V

Sir Richard spoke and he laugh'd, and we roar'd a hurrah, and so
The little Revenge ran on sheer into the heart of the foe,
With her hundred fighters on deck, and her ninety sick below;
For half of their fleet to the right and half to the left were seen,
And the little Revenge ran on thro' the long sea-lane between.

VI

Thousands of their soldiers look'd down from their decks and laugh'd,
Thousands of their seamen made mock at the mad little craft
Running on and on, till delay'd
By their mountain-like San Philip that, of fifteen hundred tons,
And up-shadowing high above us with her yawning tiers of guns,
Took the breath from our sails, and we stay'd.

VII

And while now the great San Philip hung above us like a cloud
Whence the thunderbolt will fall
Long and loud,
Four galleons drew away
From the Spanish fleet that day,
And two upon the larboard and two upon the starboard lay,
And the battle-thunder broke from them all.

VIII

But anon the great San Philip, she bethought herself and went
Having that within her womb that had left her ill content;

And the rest they came aboard us, and they fought us hand to hand,
For a dozen times they came with their pikes and musqueteers,
And a dozen times we shook 'em off as a dog that shakes his ears
When he leaps from the water to the land.

IX

And the sun went down, and the stars came out far over the summer sea,
But never a moment ceased the fight of the one and the fifty-three.
Ship after ship, the whole night long, their high-built galleons came,
Ship after ship, the whole night long, with her battle-thunder and flame;
Ship after ship, the whole night long, drew back with her dead and her shame.
For some were sunk and many were shatter'd, and so could fight us no more —
God of battles, was ever a battle like this in the world before?

X

For he said 'Fight on! fight on!'
Tho' his vessel was all but a wreck;
And it chanced that, when half of the short summer night was gone,
With a grisly wound to be drest he had left the deck,
But a bullet struck him that was dressing it suddenly dead,
And himself he was wounded again in the side and the head,
And he said 'Fight on! fight on!'

XI

And the night went down, and the sun smiled out far over the summer sea,
And the Spanish fleet with broken sides lay round us all in a ring;
But they dared not touch us again, for they fear'd that we still could sting,
So they watch'd what the end would be.
And we had not fought them in vain,
But in perilous plight were we,
Seeing forty of our poor hundred were slain,
And half of the rest of us maim'd for life
In the crash of the cannonades and the desperate strife;
And the sick men down in the hold were most of them stark and cold,
And the pikes were all broken or bent, and the powder was all of it spent;
And the masts and the rigging were lying over the side;
But Sir Richard cried in his English pride,
'We have fought such a fight for a day and a night
As may never be fought again!
We have won great glory, my men!
And a day less or more
At sea or ashore,
We die — does it matter when?
Sink me the ship, Master Gunner — sink her, split her in twain!
Fall into the hands of God, not into the hands of Spain!'

XII

And the gunner said 'Ay, ay,' but the seamen made reply:
'We have children, we have wives,
And the Lord hath spared our lives.
We will make the Spaniard promise, if we yield, to let us go;
We shall live to fight again and to strike another blow.'
And the lion there lay dying, and they yielded to the foe.

XIII

And the stately Spanish men to their flagship bore him then,
Where they laid him by the mast, old Sir Richard caught at last,
And they praised him to his face with their courtly foreign grace;
But he rose upon their decks, and he cried:
'I have fought for Queen and Faith like a valiant man and true;
I have only done my duty as a man is bound to do:

With a joyful spirit I Sir Richard Grenville
die!'
And he fell upon their decks, and he died.

XIV

And they stared at the dead that had been
so valiant and true,
And had holden the power and glory of
Spain so cheap
That he dared her with one little ship and
his English few;
Was he devil or man? He was devil for
aught they knew,
But they sank his body with honour down
into the deep,
And they mann'd the Revenge with a
swarthier alien crew,
And away she sail'd with her loss and
long'd for her own;
When a wind from the lands they had
ruin'd awoke from sleep,
And the water began to heave and the
weather to moan,
And or ever that evening ended a great
gale blew,
And a wave like the wave that is raised
by an earthquake grew,
Till it smote on their hulls and their sails
and their masts and their flags,
And the whole sea plunged and fell on the
shot-shatter'd navy of Spain,
And the little Revenge herself went down
by the island crags
To be lost evermore in the main.

Merlin and the Gleam [130]

I

O young Mariner,
You from the haven
Under the sea-cliff,
You that are watching
The gray Magician
With eyes of wonder,
I am Merlin,
And *I* am dying,
I am Merlin
Who follow The Gleam.

II

Mighty the Wizard
Who found me at sunrise
Sleeping, and woke me
And learn'd me Magic!
Great the Master,
And sweet the Magic,
When over the valley,
In early summers,
Over the mountain,
On human faces,
And all around me,
Moving to melody,
Floated The Gleam.

III

Once at the croak of a Raven who
crost it,
A barbarous people,
Blind to the magic,
And deaf to the melody,
Snarl'd at and cursed me.
A demon vext me,
The light retreated,
The landskip darken'd,
The melody deaden'd,
The Master whisper'd
'Follow The Gleam.'

IV

Then to the melody,
Over a wilderness
Gliding, and glancing at
Elf of the woodland,
Gnome of the cavern,
Griffin and Giant,
And dancing of Fairies
In desolate hollows,
And wraiths of the mountain,
And rolling of dragons
By warble of water,

[130] Published in *Demeter, and Other Poems*, in 1889, when Tennyson was eighty years old. In Merlin, the magician of Arthur's court, living on in hope after the passing of Arthur and the Round Table, Tennyson symbolizes his own poetical career and the belief in the ideal that remains ever brighter with him.

Or cataract music
Of falling torrents,
Flitted The Gleam.

V

Down from the mountain
And over the level,
And streaming and shining on
Silent river,
Silvery willow,
Pasture and plowland,
Innocent maidens,
Garrulous children,
Homestead and harvest,
Reaper and gleaner,
And rough-ruddy faces
Of lowly labour,
Slided The Gleam —

VI

Then, with a melody
Stronger and statelier,
Led me at length
To the city and palace
Of Arthur the king;
Touch'd at the golden
Cross of the churches,
Flash'd on the Tournament,
Flicker'd and bicker'd
From helmet to helmet,
And last on the forehead
Of Arthur the blameless
Rested The Gleam.

VII

Clouds and darkness
Closed upon Camelot;
Arthur had vanish'd
I knew not whither,
The king who loved me,
And cannot die;
For out of the darkness
Silent and slowly
The Gleam, that had waned to a
    wintry glimmer
On icy fallow
And faded forest,
Drew to the valley
Named of the shadow,
And slowly brightening
Out of the glimmer,
And slowly moving again to a
    melody
Yearningly tender,
Fell on the shadow,
No longer a shadow,
But clothed with The Gleam.

VIII

And broader and brighter
The Gleam flying onward,
Wed to the melody,
Sang thro' the world;
And slower and fainter,
Old and weary,
But eager to follow,
I saw, whenever
In passing it glanced upon
Hamlet or city,
That under the Crosses
The dead man's garden,
The mortal hillock,
Would break into blossom;
And so to the land's
Last limit I came ——
And can no longer,
But die rejoicing,
For thro' the Magic
Of Him the Mighty,
Who taught me in childhood,
There on the border
Of boundless Ocean,
And all but in Heaven
Hovers The Gleam.

IX

Not of the sunlight,
Not of the moonlight,
Not of the starlight!
O young Mariner,
Down to the haven,
Call your companions,
Launch your vessel,
And crowd your canvas,
And, ere it vanishes

Over the margin,
After it, follow it,
Follow The Gleam.

Crossing the Bar [131]

Sunset and evening star,
And one clear call for me!
And may there be no moaning of the bar,
When I put out to sea,

But such a tide as moving seems asleep,
Too full for sound and foam,
When that which drew from out the boundless deep
Turns again home.

Twilight and evening bell,
And after that the dark!
And may there be no sadness of farewell,
When I embark;

For tho' from out our bourne of Time and Place
The flood may bear me far,
I hope to see my Pilot face to face
When I have crost the bar.

[131] Published in 1889. Only a few days before his death Tennyson requested that this lyric should conclude all editions of his poems.

Robert Browning

1812–1889

Porphyria's Lover [1]

The rain set early in to-night,
The sullen wind was soon awake,
It tore the elm-tops down for spite,
And did its worst to vex the lake:
I listened with heart fit to break.
When glided in Porphyria; straight
She shut the cold out and the storm,
And kneeled and made the cheerless grate
Blaze up, and all the cottage warm;
Which done, she rose, and from her form
Withdrew the dripping cloak and shawl,
And laid her soiled gloves by, untied
Her hat and let the damp hair fall,
And, last, she sat down by my side
And called me. When no voice replied,
She put my arm about her waist,
And made her smooth white shoulder bare,
And all her yellow hair displaced,
And, stooping, made my cheek lie there,
And spread, o'er all, her yellow hair,
Murmuring how she loved me — she
Too weak, for all her heart's endeavour,
To set its struggling passion free
From pride, and vainer ties dissever,
And give herself to me for ever.
But passion sometimes would prevail,
Nor could to-night's gay feast restrain
A sudden thought of one so pale
For love of her, and all in vain:
So, she was come through wind and rain.
Be sure I looked up at her eyes
Happy and proud; at last I knew
Porphyria worshipped me; surprise
Made my heart swell, and still it grew
While I debated what to do.
That moment she was mine, mine, fair,
Perfectly pure and good: I found
A thing to do, and all her hair
In one long yellow string I wound
Three times her little throat around,
And strangled her. No pain felt she;
I am quite sure she felt no pain.
As a shut bud that holds a bee,
I warily oped her lids: again
Laughed the blue eyes without a stain.
And I untightened next the tress
About her neck; her cheek once more
Blushed bright beneath my burning kiss:
I propped her head up as before,
Only, this time my shoulder bore

[1] First published in Fox's *Monthly Repository* in 1836; when reprinted in *Bells and Pomegranates* it was grouped with *Johannes Agricola in Meditation* as No. II of *Madhouse Cells*. It is the first of Browning's dramatic monologues.

Her head, which droops upon it still:
  The smiling rosy little head,
So glad it has its utmost will,
  That all it scorned at once is fled,
And I, its love, am gained instead!
Porphyria's love: she guessed not how
  Her darling one wish would be heard.
And thus we sit together now,
  And all night long we have not stirred,
And yet God has not said a word!

CAVALIER TUNES [2]

I. *Marching Along*

I

KENTISH Sir Byng stood for his King,
Bidding the crop-headed Parliament [3] swing:
And, pressing a troop unable to stoop
And see the rogues flourish and honest folk droop,
Marched them along, fifty-score strong,
Great-hearted gentlemen, singing this song.

II

God for King Charles! Pym [4] and such carles
To the Devil that prompts 'em their treasonous parles!
Cavaliers, up! Lips from the cup,
Hands from the pasty, nor bite take nor sup
Till you're—

CHORUS

Marching along, fifty-score strong,
Great-hearted gentlemen, singing this song.

III

Hampden to hell, and his obsequies' knell
Serve Hazelrig, Fiennes, and young Harry [5] as well!

[2] Published, with the three following poems, in *Bells and Pomegranates* III, under head of 'Dramatic Lyrics,' 1842.
[3] The Long Parliament (1640–1660), controlled by the Puritan roundheads.
[4] John Pym (1584–1643) was a leader against the King.
[5] Sir Henry Vane the younger, executed for treason after the accession of Charles II.

England, good cheer! Rupert [6] is near!
Kentish and loyalists, keep we not here

CHORUS

Marching along, fifty-score strong,
Great-hearted gentlemen, singing this song?

IV

Then, God for King Charles! Pym and his snarls
To the Devil that pricks on such pestilent carles!
Hold by the right, you double your might;
So, onward to Nottingham,[7] fresh for the fight,

CHORUS

March we along, fifty-score strong,
Great-hearted gentlemen, singing this song!

II. *Give a Rouse*

I

King Charles, and who'll do him right now?
King Charles, and who's ripe for fight now?
Give a rouse: here's, in hell's despite now,
King Charles!

II

Who gave me the goods that went since?
Who raised me the house that sank once?
Who helped me to gold I spent since?
Who found me in wine you drank once?

CHORUS

King Charles, and who'll do him right now?
King Charles, and who's ripe for fight now?
Give a rouse: here's, in hell's despite now,
King Charles!

[6] Rupert, Prince of Bavaria (1619–1682), nephew of Charles I.
[7] Where the first stand of the Royalists was made in August 1642.

III

To whom used my boy George quaff else,
By the old fool's side that begot him?
For whom did he cheer and laugh else,
While Noll's [8] damned troopers shot him?

CHORUS

King Charles, and who'll do him right now?
King Charles, and who's ripe for fight now?
Give a rouse: here's, in hell's despite now,
King Charles!

III. *Boot and Saddle*

I

Boot, saddle, to horse, and away!
Rescue my castle before the hot day
Brightens to blue from its silvery grey,

CHORUS

Boot, saddle, to horse, and away!

II

Ride past the suburbs, asleep as you'd say;
Many's the friend there, will listen and pray
'God's luck to gallants that strike up the lay —

CHORUS

Boot, saddle, to horse, and away!'

III

Forty miles off, like a roebuck at bay,
Flouts Castle Brancepeth the Roundheads' array:
Who laughs, 'Good fellows ere this, by my fay,

CHORUS

Boot, saddle, to horse, and away!'

IV

Who? My wife Gertrude; that, honest and gay,
Laughs when you talk of surrendering, 'Nay!
I've better counsellors; what counsel they?

CHORUS

Boot, saddle, to horse, and away!'

8 Oliver Cromwell's

My Last Duchess

FERRARA [9]

That's my last Duchess painted on the wall,
Looking as if she were alive. I call
That piece a wonder, now: Frà Pandolf's [10] hands
Worked busily a day, and there she stands.
Will't please you sit and look at her? I said
'Frà Pandolf' by design, for never read
Strangers like you that pictured countenance,
The depth and passion of its earnest glance,
But to myself they turned (since none puts by
The curtain I have drawn for you, but I)
And seemed as they would ask me, if they durst,
How such a glance came there; so, not the first
Are you to turn and ask thus. Sir, 't was not
Her husband's presence only, called that spot
Of joy into the Duchess' cheek: perhaps
Frà Pandolf chanced to say 'Her mantle laps
Over my lady's wrist too much,' or 'Paint
Must never hope to reproduce the faint
Half-flush that dies along her throat:' such stuff
Was courtesy, she thought, and cause enough
For calling up that spot of joy. She had
A heart — how shall I say? — too soon made glad,

9 A city in northern Italy.
10 Frà (Brother) Pandolph is an imaginary painter and — what is far more to the point here — a monk.

Too easily impressed; she liked whate'er
She looked on, and her looks went everywhere.
Sir, 't was all one! My favour at her breast,
The dropping of the daylight in the West,
The bough of cherries some officious fool
Broke in the orchard for her, the white mule
She rode with round the terrace — all and each
Would draw from her alike the approving speech,
Or blush, at least. She thanked men, — good! but thanked
Somehow — I know not how — as if she ranked
My gift of a nine-hundred-years-old name
With anybody's gift. Who'd stoop to blame
This sort of trifling? Even had you skill
In speech — (which I have not) — to make your will
Quite clear to such an one, and say, 'Just this
Or that in you disgusts me; here you miss,
Or there exceed the mark' — and if she let
Herself be lessoned so, nor plainly set
Her wits to yours, forsooth, and made excuse,
— E'en then would be some stooping; and I choose
Never to stoop. Oh sir, she smiled, no doubt,
Whene'er I passed her; but who passed without
Much the same smile? This grew; I gave commands; [11]
Then all smiles stopped together. There she stands
As if alive. Will't please you rise? We'll meet
The company below, then. I repeat,
The Count your master's known munificence
Is ample warrant that no just pretence
Of mine for dowry will be disallowed;
Though his fair daughter's self, as I avowed
At starting, is my object. Nay, we'll go
Together down, sir! Notice Neptune, though,
Taming a sea-horse, thought a rarity,
Which Claus of Innsbruck [12] cast in bronze for me!

[1842]

Soliloquy of the Spanish Cloister

I

Gr-r-r — there go, my heart's abhorrence!
Water your damned flower-pots, do!
If hate killed men, Brother Lawrence,
God's blood, would not mine kill you!
What? your myrtle-bush wants trimming?
Oh, that rose has prior claims —
Needs its leaden vase filled brimming?
Hell dry you up with its flames!

II

At the meal we sit together:
Salve tibi! [13] I must hear
Wise talk of the kind of weather,
Sort of season, time of year:
Not a plenteous cork-crop: scarcely
Dare we hope oak-galls, I doubt:
What's the Latin name for 'parsley'?
What's the Greek name for Swine's Snout?

III

Whew! We'll have our platter burnished,
Laid with care on our own shelf!
With a fire-new spoon we're furnished,
And a goblet for ourself,
Rinsed like something sacrificial
Ere 'tis fit to touch our chaps —
Marked with L. for our initial!
(He-he! There his lily snaps!)

[11] Professor Hiram Corson, in the preface to the third edition of his *Introduction to Browning*, tells of his asking Browning what this line meant: 'He [Browning] made no reply, for a moment, and then said, meditatively, "Yes, I meant that the commands were that she should be put to death." And then, after a pause, he added, with a characteristic dash of expression, as if the thought had just started in his mind, "Or he might have had her shut up in a convent."'

[12] An imaginary sculptor, supposedly from Innsbruck in the Tyrol, famous for its bronze work.

[13] Hail to thee (or 'Save thee!').

IV

Saint, forsooth! While brown Dolores
  Squats outside the Convent bank
With Sanchicha, telling stories,
  Steeping tresses in the tank,
Blue-black, lustrous, thick like horse-hairs,
  — Can't I see his dead eye glow,
Bright as 'twere a Barbary corsair's?
  (That is, if he'd let it show!)

V

When he finishes refection,
  Knife and fork he never lays
Cross-wise, to my recollection,
  As do I, in Jesu's praise.
I the Trinity illustrate,
  Drinking watered orange-pulp —
In three sips the Arian [14] frustrate;
  While he drains his at one gulp.

VI

Oh, those melons? If he's able
  We're to have a feast! so nice!
One goes to the Abbot's table,
  All of us get each a slice.
How go on your flowers? None double?
  Not one fruit-sort can you spy?
Strange! — And I, too, at such trouble,
  Keep them close-nipped on the sly!

VII

There's a great text in Galatians,[15]
  Once you trip on it, entails
Twenty-nine distinct damnations,
  One sure, if another fails:
If I trip him just a-dying,
  Sure of heaven as sure can be,
Spin him round and send him flying
  Off to hell, a Manichee? [16]

VIII

Or, my scrofulous French novel
  On grey paper with blunt type!
Simply glance at it, you grovel
  Hand and foot in Belial's gripe:
If I double down its pages
  At the woeful sixteenth print,
When he gathers his greengages,
  Ope a sieve and slip it in't?

IX

Or, there's Satan! — one might venture
  Pledge one's soul to him, yet leave
Such a flaw in the indenture
  As he'd miss till, past retrieve,
Blasted lay that rose-acacia
  We're so proud of! *Hy, Zy, Hine* . . .
'St, there's Vespers! *Plena gratiâ*
  Ave, Virgo! [17] Gr-r-r — you swine!

[1842]

Cristina [18]

I

She should never have looked at me
  If she meant I should not love her!
There are plenty . . . men, you call such,
  I suppose . . . she may discover
All her soul to, if she pleases,
  And yet leave much as she found them:
But I'm not so, and she knew it
  When she fixed me, glancing round them.

II

What? To fix me thus meant nothing?
  But I can't tell (there's my weakness)
What her look said! — no vile cant, sure,
  About 'need to strew the bleakness
Of some lone shore with its pearl-seed,
  That the sea feels' — no 'strange yearning
That such souls have, most to lavish
  Where there's chance of least returning.'

---

[14] A follower of Arius (A.D. 256–336), who denied the Trinity and the divinity of Christ as the Eternal Son of God.

[15] *Galatians*, iii, 10, which refers to *Deuteronomy*, xxviii, 15–68, is perhaps meant. Claim has also been made for *Galatians*, v, 19–21, with good reason.

[16] A follower of Mani, the Persian thinker who held the existence of two principles: light, or good, of which the soul is product; and darkness, or evil, from which the body springs.

[17] Hail, Mary, full of grace!

[18] Maria Christina (1806–1878), the daughter of Francis I, king of Sicily. In 1829 she married King Ferdinand VII of Spain. She was a complete coquette, crafty and dissolute.

III

Oh, we're sunk enough here, God knows!
  But not quite so sunk that moments,
Sure tho' seldom, are denied us,
  When the spirit's true endowments
Stand out plainly from its false ones,
  And apprise it if pursuing
Or the right way or the wrong way,
  To its triumph or undoing.

IV

There are flashes struck from midnights,
  There are fire-flames noondays kindle,
Whereby piled-up honours perish,
  Whereby swollen ambitions dwindle,
While just this or that poor impulse,
  Which for once had play unstifled,
Seems the sole work of a lifetime
  That away the rest have trifled.

V

Doubt you if, in some such moment,
  As she fixed me, she felt clearly,
Ages past the soul existed,
  Here an age 'tis resting merely,
And hence fleets again for ages,
  While the true end, sole and single,
It stops here for is, this love-way,
  With some other soul to mingle?

VI

Else it loses what it lived for,
  And eternally must lose it;
Better ends may be in prospect,
  Deeper blisses (if you choose it),
But this life's end and this love-bliss
  Have been lost here. Doubt you whether
This she felt as, looking at me,
  Mine and her souls rushed together?

VII

Oh, observe! Of course, next moment,
  The world's honours, in derision,
Trampled out the light for ever:
  Never fear but there 's provision
Of the devil's to quench knowledge
  Lest we walk the earth in rapture!
— Making those who catch God's secret
  Just so much more prize their capture!

VIII

Such am I: the secret's mine now!
  She has lost me, I have gained her;
Her soul's mine: and thus, grown perfect,
  I shall pass my life's remainder.
Life will just hold out the proving
  Both our powers, alone and blended:
And then, come the next life quickly!
  This world's use will have been ended.

[1842]

The Italian in England [19]

THAT second time they hunted me
From hill to plain, from shore to sea,
And Austria, hounding far and wide
Her blood-hounds through the country-side,
Breathed hot and instant on my trace,—
I made six days a hiding-place
Of that dry green old aqueduct
Where I and Charles, when boys, have plucked
The fire-flies from the roof above,
Bright creeping through the moss they love:
— How long it seems since Charles was lost!
Six days the soldiers crossed and crossed
The country in my very sight;
And when that peril ceased at night,
The sky broke out in red dismay
With signal-fires; well, there I lay
Close covered o'er in my recess,
Up to the neck in ferns and cress,
Thinking on Metternich our friend,[20]

---

[19] This and the five following poems were published in *Bells and Pomegranates* VII, under head of 'Dramatic Romances and Lyrics,' 1845. The incident, though typical of the Italian patriots hiding from Austrian oppression, is not historical. Mazzini greatly admired the poem, which was written after Browning's visit to Italy in 1844.

[20] Count Metternich of Austria was, of course, the enemy of Italian freedom.

And Charles's miserable end,[21]
And much beside, two days; the third,
Hunger o'ercame me when I heard
The peasants from the village go
To work among the maize; you know,
With us in Lombardy, they bring
Provisions packed on mules, a string
With little bells that cheer their task,
And casks, and boughs on every cask
To keep the sun's heat from the wine;
These I let pass in jingling line,
And, close on them, dear noisy crew,
The peasants from the village, too;
For at the very rear would troop
Their wives and sisters in a group
To help, I knew. When these had passed,
I threw my glove to strike the last,
Taking the chance: she did not start,
Much less cry out, but stooped apart,
One instant rapidly glanced round,
And saw me beckon from the ground;
A wild bush grows and hides my crypt;
She picked my glove up while she stripped
A branch off, then rejoined the rest
With that; my glove lay in her breast.
Then I drew breath; they disappeared:
It was for Italy I feared.

An hour, and she returned alone
Exactly where my glove was thrown.
Meanwhile came many thoughts; on me
Rested the hopes of Italy.
I had devised a certain tale
Which, when 'twas told her, could not fail
Persuade a peasant of its truth;
I meant to call a freak of youth
This hiding, and give hopes of pay,
And no temptation to betray.
But when I saw that woman's face,
Its calm simplicity of grace,
Our Italy's own attitude
In which she walked thus far, and stood,
Planting each naked foot so firm,
To crush the snake and spare the worm —
At first sight of her eyes, I said,
'I am that man upon whose head
They fix the price, because I hate
The Austrians over us: the State
Will give you gold — oh, gold so much! —
If you betray me to their clutch,
And be your death, for aught I know,
If once they find you saved their foe.
Now, you must bring me food and drink,
And also paper, pen and ink,
And carry safe what I shall write
To Padua, which you'll reach at night
Before the Duomo [22] shuts; go in,
And wait till Tenebrae [23] begin;
Walk to the third confessional,
Between the pillar and the wall,
And kneeling whisper, *Whence comes peace?*
Say it a second time, then cease;
And if the voice inside returns,
From Christ and Freedom; what concerns
The cause of Peace? — for answer, slip
My letter where you placed your lip;
Then come back happy we have done
Our mother service — I, the son,
As you the daughter of our land!'

Three mornings more, she took her stand
In the same place, with the same eyes:
I was no surer of sunrise
Than of her coming. We conferred
Of her own prospects, and I heard
She had a lover — stout and tall,
She said — then let her eyelids fall,
'He could do much' — as if some doubt
Entered her heart, — then, passing out,
'She could not speak for others, who
Had other thoughts; herself she knew:'
And so she brought me drink and food.
After four days, the scouts pursued
Another path; at last arrived
The help my Paduan friends contrived
To furnish me: she brought the news.

[21] Carlo Alberto, King of Sardinia from 1831 to 1849, who had come to terms with Austria. He had been very severe upon Mazzini's 'Young Italy' and other liberal societies. Finally in 1848 he assumed command of a revolt against Austria, but was defeated and forced to abdicate. He died in Oporto in 1849.

[22] The cathedral.

[23] Darkness, a religious office for the last three days of Holy Week. Fifteen lighted candles are set upon a stand, one being extinguished at the conclusion of each psalm, to represent the growing darkness that overspread the world at the time of the Crucifixion. The last candle is not put out, but is merely concealed for a few moments behind the altar, to show that over Christ death had no power.

For the first time I could not choose
But kiss her hand, and lay my own
Upon her head — 'This faith was shown
To Italy, our mother; she
Uses my hand and blesses thee.'
She followed down to the sea-shore;
I left and never saw her more.

How very long since I have thought
Concerning — much less wished for — aught
Beside the good of Italy,
For which I live and mean to die!
I never was in love; and since
Charles proved false, what shall now convince
My inmost heart I had a friend?
However, if I pleased to spend
Real wishes on myself — say, three —
I know at least what one should be.
I would grasp Metternich until
I felt his red wet throat distil
In blood thro' these two hands. And next,
— Nor much for that am I perplexed —
Charles, perjured traitor, for his part,
Should die slow of a broken heart
Under his new employers. Last
— Ah, there, what should I wish? For fast
Do I grow old and out of strength.
If I resolved to seek at length
My father's house again, how scared
They all would look, and unprepared!
My brothers live in Austria's pay
— Disowned me long ago, men say;
And all my early mates who used
To praise me so — perhaps induced
More than one early step of mine —
Are turning wise: while some opine
'Freedom grows license,' some suspect
'Haste breeds delay,' and recollect
They always said, such premature
Beginnings never could endure!
So, with a sullen 'All's for best,'
The land seems settling to its rest.
I think then, I should wish to stand
This evening in that dear, lost land,
Over the sea the thousand miles,
And know if yet that woman smiles
With the calm smile; some little farm
She lives in there, no doubt: what harm
If I sat on the door-side bench,
And, while her spindle made a trench
Fantastically in the dust,
Inquired of all her fortunes — just
Her children's ages and their names,
And what may be the husband's aims
For each of them. I'd talk this out,
And sit there, for an hour about,
Then kiss her hand once more, and lay
Mine on her head, and go my way.

So much for idle wishing — how
It steals the time! To business now.

Home-thoughts, from Abroad

I

Oh, to be in England
Now that April's there,
And whoever wakes in England
Sees, some morning, unaware,
That the lowest boughs and the brushwood sheaf
Round the elm-tree bole are in tiny leaf,
While the chaffinch sings on the orchard bough
In England — now!

II

And after April, when May follows,
And the whitethroat builds, and all the swallows!
Hark, where my blossomed pear-tree in the hedge
Leans to the field and scatters on the clover
Blossoms and dewdrops — at the bent spray's edge —
That's the wise thrush; he sings each song twice over,
Lest you should think he never could recapture
The first fine careless rapture!
And though the fields look rough with hoary dew,
All will be gay when noontide wakes anew

The buttercups, the little children's dower
— Far brighter than this gaudy melon-flower!

[1845]

Home-thoughts, from the Sea[24]

Nobly, nobly Cape Saint Vincent to the North-west died away;
Sunset ran, one glorious blood-red, reeking into Cadiz Bay;
Bluish mid the burning water, full in face Trafalgar lay;
In the dimmest North-east distance dawned Gibraltar grand and gray;
'Here and here did England help me: how can I help England?' — say,
Whoso turns as I, this evening, turn to God to praise and pray,
While Jove's planet rises yonder, silent over Africa.

[1845]

The Bishop Orders His Tomb at Saint Praxed's Church[25]

[ROME, 15—.]

Vanity, saith the preacher, vanity![26]
Draw round my bed: is Anselm keeping back?
Nephews — sons mine . . . ah God, I know not! Well —
She, men would have to be your mother once,
Old Gandolf[27] envied me, so fair she was!
What's done is done, and she is dead beside,
Dead long ago, and I am Bishop since,
And as she died so must we die ourselves,
And thence ye may perceive the world's a dream.
Life, how and what is it? As here I lie
In this state-chamber, dying by degrees,
Hours and long hours in the dead night, I ask
'Do I live, am I dead?' Peace, peace seems all.
Saint Praxed's ever was the church for peace;
And so, about this tomb of mine. I fought
With tooth and nail to save my niche, ye know:
— Old Gandolf cozened me, despite my care;
Shrewd was that snatch from out the corner South
He graced his carrion with, God curse the same!
Yet still my niche is not so cramped but thence
One sees the pulpit o' the epistle-side,[28]
And somewhat of the choir, those silent seats,
And up into the aery dome where live
The angels, and a sunbeam's sure to lurk:
And I shall fill my slab of basalt[29] there,
And 'neath my tabernacle[30] take my rest,
With those nine columns round me, two and two,
The odd one at my feet where Anselm stands:
Peach-blossom marble[31] all, the rare, the ripe
As fresh-poured red wine of a mighty pulse.

---

[24] The tradition is that these lines were written one April evening when Browning was on shipboard off the Bay of Trafalgar on his first voyage to Italy in 1838; they were more likely composed on a second voyage in August 1844.

[25] The church in Rome was named after St. Praxed, or Praxedes, a Christian virgin and saint of the first century who gave her wealth to the poor and to the persecuted Christians. Both the tomb and the Bishop are Browning's imaginary creations. Ruskin says of the poem: 'I know of no other piece of modern English, prose or poetry, in which there is so much told, as in these lines, of the Renaissance spirit, — its worldliness, inconsistency, pride, hypocrisy, ignorance of itself, love of art, of luxury, and of good Latin. It is nearly all that I said of the central Renaissance in thirty pages of the *Stones of Venice*, put into as many lines, Browning's being also the antecedent work. The worst of it is that this kind of concentrated writing needs so much ***solution*** before the reader can fairly get the good of it, that people's patience fails them, and they give the thing up as insoluble; though truly it ought to be to the current of common thought like Saladin's talisman, dipped in clear water, not soluble altogether, but making the element medicinal.' [*Modern Painters*, IV, chapter 20, section 34.] Prior to its publication in the 1845 volume, the poem appeared in ***Hood's Magazine***, March 1845 (III, 3: 237–239).

[26] See *Ecclesiastes*, i, 2.

[27] The Bishop's rival and predecessor.

[28] The right-hand side as one faces the altar; the left is the gospel-side.

[29] A dark, hard marble.

[30] canopy

[31] Very fine marble of pinkish shade.

— Old Gandolf with his paltry onion-stone,[32]
Put me where I may look at him! True peach,
Rosy and flawless: how I earned the prize!
Draw close: that conflagration of my church
— What then? So much was saved if aught were missed!
My sons, ye would not be my death? Go dig
The white-grape vineyard where the oil-press stood,
Drop water gently till the surface sink,
And if ye find . . . Ah God, I know not, I! . . .
Bedded in store of rotten fig-leaves soft,
And corded up in a tight olive-frail,[33]
Some lump, ah God, of *lapis lazuli,*[34]
Big as a Jew's head cut off at the nape,
Blue as a vein o'er the Madonna's breast . . .
Sons, all have I bequeathed you, villas, all,
That brave Frascati villa with its bath,
So, let the blue lump poise between my knees,
Like God the Father's globe on both his hands
Ye worship in the Jesu Church [35] so gay,
For Gandolf shall not choose but see and burst!
Swift as a weaver's shuttle fleet our years: [36]
Man goeth to the grave, and where is he?
Did I say basalt for my slab, sons? Black —
'Twas ever antique-black I meant! How else
Shall ye contrast my frieze to come beneath?
The bas-relief in bronze ye promised me,
Those Pans and Nymphs ye wot of, and perchance
Some tripod,[37] thyrsus, [38] with a vase or so,
The Saviour at his sermon on the mount,
Saint Praxed in a glory, and one Pan
Ready to twitch the Nymph's last garment off,
And Moses with the tables . . . but I know
Ye mark me not! What do they whisper thee,
Child of my bowels, Anselm? Ah, ye hope
To revel down my villas while I gasp
Bricked o'er with beggar's mouldy travertine [39]
Which Gandolf from his tomb-top chuckles at!
Nay, boys, ye love me — all of jasper, then!
'Tis jasper ye stand pledged to, lest I grieve.
My bath must needs be left behind, alas!
One block, pure green as a pistachio-nut,
There's plenty jasper somewhere in the world —
And have I not Saint Praxed's ear to pray
Horses for ye, and brown [40] Greek manuscripts,
And mistresses with great smooth marbly limbs?
— That's if ye carve my epitaph aright,
Choice Latin, picked phrase, Tully's [41] every word,
No gaudy ware like Gandolf's second line —
Tully, my masters? Ulpian [42] serves his need!
And then how I shall lie through centuries,
And hear the blessed mutter of the mass,
And see God made and eaten all day long,
And feel the steady candle-flame, and taste
Good strong thick stupefying incense-smoke!
For as I lie here, hours of the dead night,
Dying in state and by such slow degrees,
I fold my arms as if they clasped a crook,

[32] An inferior marble, likely to split into thin green layers as those of an onion.
[33] A basket for olives.
[34] Expensive blue stone.
[35] Il Gesu, the Jesuit church at Rome, where is the image here described.
[36] See *Job*, vii, 6.
[37] The three-legged stool on which the priestess of Apollo sat while giving out the oracular words at Delphi.
[38] A staff used by the drunken followers of Bacchus.
[39] A kind of cheap white limestone from Tivoli.
[40] *I.e.*, brown with age.
[41] Cicero's, *i.e.*, the purest Latin.
[42] Domitius Ulpianus (170–228), Roman jurist, with a style inferior — at least to Cicero's.

And stretch my feet forth straight as stone can point,
And let the bedclothes, for a mortcloth, drop
Into great laps and folds of sculptor's-work:
And as yon tapers dwindle, and strange thoughts
Grow, with a certain humming in my ears,
About the life before I lived this life,
And this life too, popes, cardinals and priests,
Saint Praxed at his sermon on the mount,
Your tall pale mother with her talking eyes,
And new-found agate urns as fresh as day,
And marble's language, Latin pure, discreet,
— Aha, ELUCESCEBAT [43] quoth our friend?
No Tully, said I, Ulpian at the best!
Evil and brief hath been my pilgrimage.
All *lapis,* all, sons! Else I give the Pope
My villas! Will ye ever eat my heart?
Ever your eyes were as a lizard's quick,
They glitter like your mother's for my soul,
Or ye would heighten my impoverished frieze,
Piece out its starved design, and fill my vase
With grapes, and add a vizor and a Term,[44]
And to the tripod ye would tie a lynx
That in his struggle throws the thyrsus down,
To comfort me on my entablature
Whereon I am to lie till I must ask
'Do I live, am I dead?' There, leave me, there!
For ye have stabbed me with ingratitude
To death — ye wish it — God, ye wish it! Stone —
Gritstone,[45] a-crumble! Clammy squares which sweat
As if the corpse they keep were oozing through —
And no more *lapis* to delight the world!
Well, go! I bless ye. Fewer tapers there,
But in a row: and, going, turn your backs
— Ay, like departing altar-ministrants,
And leave me in my church, the church for peace,
That I may watch at leisure if he leers —
Old Gandolf, at me, from his onion-stone,
As still he envied me, so fair she was!

[43] 'He was famous'; but the classic form dear to the Bishop was *Elucebat.*

[44] A combination of bust and quadrangular pedestal which tapers downward.

[45] A cheap sandstone.

Meeting at Night

I

THE grey sea and the long black land;
And the yellow half-moon large and low;
And the startled little waves that leap
In fiery ringlets from their sleep,
As I gain the cove with pushing prow,
And quench its speed in the slushy sand.

II

Then a mile of warm sea-scented beach;
Three fields to cross till a farm appears;
A tap at the pane, the quick sharp scratch
And blue spurt of a lighted match,
And a voice less loud, thro' its joys and fears,
Than the two hearts beating each to each!

[1845]

Parting at Morning

ROUND the cape of a sudden came the sea,
And the sun looked over the mountain's rim:
And straight was a path of gold for him,
And the need of a world of men for me.

[1845]

SAUL[46]

I

SAID Abner,[47] 'At last thou art come! Ere I tell, ere thou speak,
Kiss my cheek, wish me well!' Then I wished it, and did kiss his cheek.
And he, 'Since the King, O my friend, for thy countenance sent,
Neither drunken nor eaten have we; nor until from his tent
Thou return with the joyful assurance the King liveth yet,
Shall our lip with the honey be bright, with the water be wet.
For out of the black mid-tent's silence, a space of three days,
Not a sound hath escaped to thy servants, of prayer nor of praise,
To betoken that Saul and the Spirit have ended their strife,
And that, faint in his triumph, the monarch sinks back upon life.

II

Yet now my heart leaps, O beloved! God's child, with his dew
On thy gracious gold hair, and those lilies still living and blue
Just broken to twine round thy harp-strings, as if no wild heat
Were now raging to torture the desert!'

III

Then I, as was meet,
Knelt down to the God of my fathers, and rose on my feet,
And ran o'er the sand burnt to powder. The tent was unlooped;
I pulled up the spear that obstructed, and under I stooped;
Hands and knees on the slippery grass-patch, all withered and gone,
That extends to the second enclosure, I groped my way on
Till I felt where the foldskirts fly open. Then once more I prayed,
And opened the foldskirts and entered, and was not afraid
But spoke, 'Here is David, thy servant!' And no voice replied.
At the first I saw nought but the blackness; but soon I descried
A something more black than the blackness — the vast, the upright
Main prop which sustains the pavilion: and slow into sight
Grew a figure against it, gigantic and blackest of all.
Then a sunbeam, that burst thro' the tent-roof, showed Saul.

IV

He stood as erect as that tent-prop, both arms stretched out wide
On the great cross-support in the centre, that goes to each side;
He relaxed not a muscle, but hung there, as, caught in his pangs
And waiting his change, the king-serpent all heavily hangs,
Far away from his kind, in the pine, till deliverance come
With the spring-time, — so agonized Saul, drear and stark, blind and dumb.

V

Then I tuned my harp, — took off the lilies we twine round its chords
Lest they snap 'neath the stress of the noon-tide — those sunbeams like swords!
And I first played the tune all our sheep know, as, one after one,
So docile they come to the pen-door till folding be done.

[46] The first nine sections of the poem appeared in the 1845 volume; the enlarged version was published in ***Men and Women***, 1855. The later sections were written in Rome in 1852–1854. The poem is based upon ***I Samuel***, xvi, 14–23. Saul, king of Israel, in black melancholy, was told that he could be cured of his evil spirit by music. David, the shepherd-boy and harp-player, summoned to the King's tent, effects the cure. Alone with his sheep the boy tells of his glorious night, memorable for what Browning incorporates into the story, the Messianic announcement that climaxes the series of songs (he ***speaks*** lines 237–312, of course). Is it too much to hope that Browning's poem, in the very frame-work it now has, will inspire some future composer for the orchestra? At any rate, it should be read just as one listens to the developing themes of a symphony.

[47] Saul's cousin, and commander of the army.

They are white and untorn by the bushes, for lo, they have fed
Where the long grasses stifle the water within the stream's bed;
And now one after one seeks its lodging, as star follows star
Into eve and the blue far above us, — so blue and so far!

VI

— Then the tune, for which quails on the cornland will each leave his mate
To fly after the player; then, what makes the crickets elate
Till for boldness they fight one another: and then, what has weight
To set the quick jerboa [48] a-musing outside his sand house —
There are none such as he for a wonder, half bird and half mouse!
God made all the creatures and gave them our love and our fear,
To give sign, we and they are his children, one family here.

VII

Then I played the help-tune of our reapers, their wine-song, when hand
Grasps at hand, eye lights eye in good friendship, and great hearts expand
And grow one in the sense of this world's life. — And then, the last song
When the dead man is praised on his journey — 'Bear, bear him along
With his few faults shut up like dead flowerets! Are balm-seeds not here
To console us? The land has none left such as he on the bier.
Oh, would we might keep thee, my brother!' — And then, the glad chaunt
Of the marriage, — first go the young maidens, next, she whom we vaunt
As the beauty, the pride of our dwelling. — And then, the great march
Wherein man runs to man to assist him and buttress an arch
Nought can break; who shall harm them, our friends? — Then, the chorus intoned
As the Levites [49] go up to the altar in glory enthroned.
But I stopped here: for here in the darkness Saul groaned.

VIII

And I paused, held my breath in such silence, and listened apart;
And the tent shook, for mighty Saul shuddered: and sparkles 'gan dart
From the jewels that woke in his turban, at once with a start,
All its lordly male-sapphires, and rubies courageous at heart.
So the head: but the body still moved not, still hung there erect.
And I bent once again to my playing, pursued it unchecked,
As I sang, —

IX

'Oh, our manhood's prime vigour! No spirit feels waste,
Not a muscle is stopped in its playing nor sinew unbraced.
Oh, the wild joys of living! the leaping from rock up to rock,
The strong rending of boughs from the fir-tree, the cool silver shock
Of the plunge in a pool's living water, the hunt of the bear,
And the sultriness showing the lion is couched in his lair.
And the meal, the rich dates yellowed over with gold dust divine,
And the locust's-flesh steeped in the pitcher, the full draught of wine,
And the sleep in the dried river-channel where bulrushes tell
That the water was wont to go warbling so softly and well.
How good is man's life, the mere living! how fit to employ

[48] A small jumping rodent.

[49] priests

All the heart and the soul and the senses for ever in joy!
Hast thou loved the white locks of thy father, whose sword thou didst guard
When he trusted thee forth with the armies, for glorious reward?
Didst thou see the thin hands of thy mother, held up as men sung
The low song of the newly-departed, and hear her faint tongue
Joining in while it could to the witness, 'Let one more attest,
I have lived, seen God's hand thro' a lifetime, and all was for best'?
Then they sung thro' their tears in strong triumph, not much, but the rest.
And thy brothers, the help and the contest, the working whence grew
Such result as, from seething grape-bundles, the spirit strained true:
And the friends of thy boyhood — that boyhood of wonder and hope,
Present promise and wealth of the future beyond the eye's scope, —
Till lo, thou art grown to a monarch; a people is thine;
And all gifts, which the world offers singly, on one head combine!
On one head, all the beauty and strength, love and rage (like the throe
That, a-work in the rock, helps its labour and lets the gold go)
High ambition and deeds which surpass it, fame crowning them, — all
Brought to blaze on the head of one creature — King Saul!'

X

And lo, with that leap of my spirit, — heart, hand, harp and voice,
Each lifting Saul's name out of sorrow, each bidding rejoice
Saul's fame in the light it was made for — as when, dare I say,
The Lord's army, in rapture of service, strains through its array,
And upsoareth the cherubim-chariot — 'Saul!' cried I, and stopped,
And waited the thing that should follow. Then Saul, who hung propped
By the tent's cross-support in the centre, was struck by his name.
Have ye seen when Spring's arrowy summons goes right to the aim,
And some mountain, the last to withstand her, that held (he alone,
While the vale laughed in freedom and flowers) on a broad bust of stone
A year's snow bound about for a breastplate, — leaves grasp of the sheet?
Fold on fold all at once it crowds thunderously down to his feet,
And there fronts you, stark, black, but alive yet, your mountain of old,
With his rents, the successive bequeathings of ages untold —
Yea, each harm got in fighting your battles, each furrow and scar
Of his head thrust 'twixt you and the tempest — all hail, there they are!
— Now again to be softened with verdure, again hold the nest
Of the dove, tempt the goat and its young to the green on its crest
For their food in the ardours of summer. One long shudder thrilled
All the tent till the very air tingled, then sank and was stilled
At the King's self left standing before me, released and aware.
What was gone, what remained? All to traverse, 'twixt hope and despair;
Death was past, life not come: so he waited. Awhile his right hand
Held the brow, helped the eyes left too vacant forthwith to remand
To their place what new objects should enter: 'twas Saul as before.
I looked up and dared gaze at those eyes, nor was hurt any more
Than by slow pallid sunsets in autumn, ye watch from the shore,
At their sad level gaze o'er the ocean — a sun's slow decline
Over hills which, resolved in stern silence, o'erlap and entwine

Base with base to knit strength more intensely: so, arm folded arm
O'er the chest whose slow heavings subsided.

XI

What spell or what charm,
(For, awhile there was trouble within me) what next should I urge
To sustain him where song had restored him? — Song filled to the verge
His cup with the wine of this life, pressing all that it yields
Of mere fruitage, the strength and the beauty: beyond, on what fields,
Glean a vintage more potent and perfect to brighten the eye
And bring blood to the lip, and commend them the cup they put by?
He saith, 'It is good'; still he drinks not: he lets me praise life,
Gives assent, yet would die for his own part.

XII

Then fancies grew rife
Which had come long ago on the pasture, when round me the sheep
Fed in silence — above, the one eagle wheeled slow as in sleep;
And I lay in my hollow and mused on the world that might lie
'Neath his ken, though I saw but the strip 'twixt the hill and the sky:
And I laughed — 'Since my days are ordained to be passed with my flocks,
Let me people at least, with my fancies, the plains and the rocks,
Dream the life I am never to mix with, and image the show
Of mankind as they live in those fashions I hardly shall know!
Schemes of life, its best rules and right uses, the courage that gains,
And the prudence that keeps what men strive for.' And now these old trains
Of vague thought came again; I grew surer; so, once more the string
Of my harp made response to my spirit, as thus —

XIII

'Yea, my King,
I began — 'thou dost well in rejecting mere comforts that spring
From the mere mortal life held in common by man and by brute:
In our flesh grows the branch of this life, in our soul it bears fruit.
Thou hast marked the slow rise of the tree, — how its stem trembled first
Till it passed the kid's lip, the stag's antler; then safely outburst
The fan-branches all round; and thou mindedst when these too, in turn
Broke a-bloom and the palm-tree seemed perfect: yet more was to learn,
E'en the good that comes in with the palm-fruit. Our dates shall we slight,
When their juice brings a cure for all sorrow? or care for the plight
Of the palm's self whose slow growth produced them? Not so! stem and branch
Shall decay, nor be known in their place, while the palm-wine shall staunch
Every wound of man's spirit in winter. I pour thee such wine.
Leave the flesh to the fate it was fit for! the spirit be thine!
By the spirit, when age shall o'ercome thee, thou still shalt enjoy
More indeed, than at first when inconscious, the life of a boy.
Crush that life, and behold its wine running! Each deed thou hast done
Dies, revives, goes to work in the world; until e'en as the sun
Looking down on the earth, though clouds spoil him, though tempests efface,
Can find nothing his own deed produced not, must everywhere trace
The results of his past summer-prime, — so, each ray of thy will,
Every flash of thy passion and prowess, long over, shall thrill
Thy whole people, the countless, with ardour, till they too give forth
A like cheer to their sons, who in turn fill the South and the North

With the radiance thy deed was the germ of. Carouse in the Past!
But the license of age has its limit; thou diest at last:
As the lion when age dims his eyeball, the rose at her height
So with man — so his power and his beauty for ever take flight.
No! Again a long draught of my soul-wine! Look forth o'er the years!
Thou hast done now with eyes for the actual; begin with the seer's!
Is Saul dead? in the depth of the vale make his tomb — bid arise
A grey mountain of marble heaped four-square, till, built to the skies,
Let it mark where the great First King slumbers: whose fame would ye know?
Up above see the rock's naked face, where the record shall go
In great characters cut by the scribe, — Such was Saul, so he did;
With the sages directing the work, by the populace chid, —
For not half, they'll affirm, is comprised there! Which fault to amend,
In the grove with his kind grows the cedar, whereon they shall spend
(See, in tablets 'tis level before them) their praise, and record
With the gold of the graver, Saul's story, — the statesman's great word
Side by side with the poet's sweet comment. The river's a-wave
With smooth paper-reeds [50] grazing each other when prophet-winds rave:
So the pen gives unborn generations their due and their part
In thy being! Then, first of the mighty, thank God that thou art!'

XIV

And behold while I sang . . . But O Thou who didst grant me that day,
And before it not seldom hast granted thy help to essay,
Carry on and complete an adventure, — my shield and my sword
In that act where my soul was thy servant, thy word was my word, —
Still be with me, who then at the summit of human endeavour
And scaling the highest, man's thought could, gazed hopeless as ever
On the new stretch of heaven above me — till, mighty to save,
Just one lift of thy hand cleared that distance — God's throne from man's grave!
Let me tell out my tale to its ending — my voice to my heart
Which can scarce dare believe in what marvels last night I took part,
As this morning I gather the fragments, alone with my sheep,
And still fear lest the terrible glory evanish like sleep!
For I wake in the grey dewy covert, while Hebron [51] upheaves
The dawn struggling with night on his shoulder, and Kidron [52] retrieves
Slow the damage of yesterday's sunshine.

XV

I say then, — my song
While I sang thus, assuring the monarch, and ever more strong
Made a proffer of good to console him — he slowly resumed
His old motions and habitudes kingly. The right hand replumed
His black locks to their wonted composure, adjusted the swathes
Of his turban, and see — the huge sweat that his countenance bathes,
He wipes off with the robe; and he girds now his loins as of yore,
And feels slow for the armlets of price, with the clasp set before.
He is Saul, ye remember in glory, — ere error [53] had bent

[50] Papyrus, used by the ancients for writing-paper.

[51] A mountain in Judea, with the city of Hebron on it.
[52] A brook near Jerusalem.
[53] See *I Samuel*, xv. Saul disobeyed God's command to destroy all the Amalekites and their possessions.

The broad brow from the daily communion; and still, though much spent
Be the life and the bearing that front you, the same, God did choose,
To receive what a man may waste, desecrate, never quite lose.
So sank he along by the tent-prop till, stayed by the pile
Of his armour and war-cloak and garments, he leaned there awhile,
And sat out my singing, — one arm round the tent-prop, to raise
His bent head, and the other hung slack — till I touched on the praise
I foresaw from all men in all time, to the man patient there;
And thus ended, the harp falling forward. Then first I was 'ware
That he sat, as I say, with my head just above his vast knees
Which were thrust out on each side around me, like oak-roots which please
To encircle a lamb when it slumbers. I looked up to know
If the best I could do had brought solace: he spoke not, but slow
Lifted up the hand slack at his side, till he laid it with care
Soft and grave, but in mild settled will, on my brow: thro' my hair
The large fingers were pushed, and he bent back my head, with kind power —
All my face back, intent to peruse it, as men do a flower.
Thus held he me there with his great eyes that scrutinized mine —
And oh, all my heart how it loved him! but where was the sign?
I yearned — 'Could I help thee, my father, inventing a bliss,
I would add, to that life of the past, both the future and this;
I would give thee new life altogether, as good, ages hence,
As this moment, — had love but the warrant, love's heart to dispense!'

XVI

Then the truth came upon me. No harp more — no song more! outbroke —

XVII

'I have gone the whole round of creation: I saw and I spoke:
I, a work of God's hand for that purpose, received in my brain
And pronounced on the rest of his handwork — returned him again
His creation's approval or censure: I spoke as I saw:
I report, as a man may of God's work — all's love, yet all's law.
Now I lay down the judgeship he lent me. Each faculty tasked
To perceive him, has gained an abyss, where a dewdrop was asked.
Have I knowledge? confounded it shrivels at Wisdom laid bare.
Have I forethought? how purblind, how blank, to the Infinite Care!
Do I task any faculty highest, to image success?
I but open my eyes, — and perfection, no more and no less,
In the kind I imagined, full-fronts me, and God is seen God
In the star, in the stone, in the flesh, in the soul and the clod.
And thus looking within and around me, I ever renew
(With that stoop of the soul which in bending upraises it too)
The submission of man's nothing-perfect to God's all-complete,
As by each new obeisance in spirit, I climb to his feet.
Yet with all this abounding experience, this deity known,
I shall dare to discover some province, some gift of my own.
There's a faculty pleasant to exercise, hard to hoodwink,
I am fain to keep still in abeyance, (I laugh as I think)

Lest, insisting to claim and parade in it, wot ye, I worst
E'en the Giver in one gift. — Behold! I could love if I durst!
But I sink the pretension as fearing a man may o'ertake
God's own speed in the one way of love: I abstain for love's sake.
— What, my soul? see thus far and no farther? when doors great and small,
Nine-and-ninety flew ope at our touch, should the hundredth appal?
In the least things have faith, yet distrust in the greatest of all?
Do I find love so full in my nature, God's ultimate gift,
That I doubt his own love can compete with it? Here, the parts shift?
Here, the creature surpass the Creator, — the end, what Began? [54]
Would I fain in my impotent yearning do all for this man,
And dare doubt he alone shall not help him, who yet alone can?
Would it ever have entered my mind, the bare will, much less power,
To bestow on this Saul what I sang of, the marvellous dower
Of the life he was gifted and filled with? to make such a soul,
Such a body, and then such an earth for insphering the whole?
And doth it not enter my mind (as my warm tears attest)
These good things being given, to go on, and give one more, the best?
Ay, to save and redeem and restore him, maintain at the height
This perfection, — succeed with life's day-spring, death's minute of night?
Interpose at the difficult minute, snatch Saul the mistake,
Saul, the failure, the ruin he seems now, — and bid him awake
From the dream, the probation, the prelude, to find himself set
Clear and safe in new light and new life, — a new harmony yet
To be run, and continued, and ended — who knows? — or endure!
The man taught enough, by life's dream, of the rest to make sure;
By the pain-throb, triumphantly winning intensified bliss,
And the next world's reward and repose, by the struggles in this.

XVIII

'I believe it! 'T is thou, God, that givest, 't is I who receive:
In the first is the last, in thy will is my power to believe.
All's one gift: thou canst grant it moreover, as prompt to my prayer
As I breathe out this breath, as I open these arms to the air.
From thy will, stream the worlds, life and nature, thy dread Sabaoth:
I will? — the mere atoms despise me! Why am I not loth
To look that, even that in the face too? Why is it I dare
Think but lightly of such impuissance? What stops my despair?
This; — 'tis not what man Does which exalts him, but what man Would do!
See the King — I would help him but cannot, the wishes fall through.
Could I wrestle to raise him from sorrow, grow poor to enrich,
To fill up his life, starve my own out, I would — knowing which,
I know that my service is perfect. Oh, speak through me now!
Would I suffer for him that I love? So wouldst thou — so wilt thou!
So shall crown thee the topmost, ineffablest, uttermost crown —
And thy love fill infinitude wholly, nor leave up nor down

---

[54] There comes to mind here *A Death in the Desert*, where the poet's whole thought upon religion receives expression. Hardly suited to this present collection, it should, nevertheless, be read by anyone who wishes to know Browning.

One spot for the creature to stand in! It is by no breath,
Turn of eye, wave of hand, that salvation joins issue with death!
As thy Love is discovered almighty, almighty be proved
Thy power, that exists with and for it, of being Beloved!
He who did most, shall bear most; the strongest shall stand the most weak.
'Tis the weakness in strength, that I cry for! my flesh, that I seek
In the Godhead! I seek and I find it. O Saul, it shall be
A Face like my face that receives thee; a Man like to me,
Thou shalt love and be loved by, for ever: a Hand like this hand
Shall throw open the gates of new life to thee! See the Christ stand!'

XIX

I know not too well how I found my way home in the night.
There were witnesses, cohorts about me, to left and to right,
Angels, powers, the unuttered, unseen, the alive, the aware:
I repressed, I got through them as hardly, as strugglingly there,
As a runner beset by the populace famished for news —
Life or death. The whole earth was awakened, hell loosed with her crews;
And the stars of night beat with emotion, and tingled and shot
Out in fire the strong pain of pent knowledge: but I fainted not,
For the Hand still impelled me at once and supported, suppressed
All the tumult, and quenched it with quiet, and holy behest,
Till the rapture was shut in itself, and the earth sank to rest.
Anon at the dawn, all that trouble had withered from earth —
Not so much, but I saw it die out in the day's tender birth;
In the gathered intensity brought to the grey of the hills;
In the shuddering forests' held breath; in the sudden wind-thrills;
In the startled wild beasts that bore off, each with eye sidling still
Though averted with wonder and dread; in the birds stiff and chill
That rose heavily, as I approached them, made stupid with awe:
E'en the serpent that slid away silent, — he felt the new law.
The same stared in the white humid faces upturned by the flowers;
The same worked in the heart of the cedar and moved the vine-bowers:
And the little brooks witnessing murmured, persistent and low,
With their obstinate, all but hushed voices — 'E'en so, it is so!'

Love among the Ruins [55]

I

WHERE the quiet-coloured end of evening smiles
Miles and miles
On the solitary pastures where our sheep
Half-asleep
Tinkle homeward thro' the twilight, stray or stop
As they crop —
Was the site once of a city great and gay,
(So they say)
Of our country's very capital, its prince
Ages since
Held his court in, gathered councils, wielding far
Peace or war.

II

Now, — the country does not even boast a tree,
As you see,

[55] This and the sixteen following poems were published in *Men and Women*, 1855. It was written on 1 January 1852 at Paris. The scene is, however, the Roman Campagna.

To distinguish slopes of verdure, certain rills
From the hills
Intersect and give a name to, (else they run
Into one)
Where the domed and daring palace shot its spires
Up like fires
O'er the hundred-gated circuit of a wall
Bounding all,
Made of marble, men might march on nor be pressed,
Twelve abreast.

III

And such plenty and perfection, see, of grass
Never was!
Such a carpet as, this summer-time, o'erspreads
And embeds
Every vestige of the city, guessed alone,
Stock or stone —
Where a multitude of men breathed joy and woe
Long ago;
Lust of glory pricked their hearts up, dread of shame
Struck them tame;
And that glory and that shame alike, the gold
Bought and sold.

IV

Now, — the single little turret that remains
On the plains,
By the caper overrooted, by the gourd
Overscored,
While the patching houseleek's head of blossom winks
Through the chinks —
Marks the basement whence a tower in ancient time
Sprang sublime,
And a burning ring, all round, the chariots traced
As they raced,
And the monarch and his minions and his dames
Viewed the games.

V

And I know, while thus the quiet-coloured eve
Smiles to leave
To their folding, all our many-tinkling fleece
In such peace,
And the slopes and rills in undistinguished grey
Melt away —
That a girl with eager eyes and yellow hair
Waits me there
In the turret whence the charioteers caught soul
For the goal,
When the king looked, where she looks now, breathless, dumb
Till I come.

VI

But he looked upon the city, every side,
Far and wide,
All the mountains topped with temples, all the glades'
Colonnades,
All the causeys, bridges, aqueducts, — and then,
All the men!
When I do come, she will speak not, she will stand,
Either hand
On my shoulder, give her eyes the first embrace
Of my face,
Ere we rush, ere we extinguish sight and speech
Each on each.

VII

In one year they sent a million fighters forth
South and North,
And they built their gods a brazen pillar high
As the sky,

Yet reserved a thousand chariots in full
force —
Gold, of course.
Oh heart! oh blood that freezes, blood
that burns!
Earth's returns
For whole centuries of folly, noise and sin!
Shut them in,
With their triumphs and their glories and
the rest!
Love is best.

A Toccata of Galuppi's[56]

I

Oh Galuppi, Baldassaro, this is very sad
to find!
I can hardly misconceive you; it would
prove me deaf and blind;
But although I take your meaning, 'tis with
such a heavy mind!

II

Here you come with your old music, and
here's all the good it brings.
What, they lived once thus at Venice where
the merchants were the kings,
Where St. Mark's is, where the Doges used
to wed the sea with rings?

III

Ay, because the sea's the street there; and
'tis arched by . . . what you call
. . . Shylock's bridge[57] with houses on it,
where they kept the carnival:
I was never out of England — it's as if I
saw it all.

IV

Did young people take their pleasure when
the sea was warm in May?
Balls and masks begun at midnight, burning ever to mid-day,
When they made up fresh adventures for
the morrow, do you say?

V

Was a lady such a lady, cheeks so round
and lips so red, —
On her neck the small face buoyant, like a
bell-flower on its bed,
O'er the breast's superb abundance where
a man might base his head?

VI

Well, and it was graceful of them — they'd
break talk off and afford
— She, to bite her mask's black velvet —
he, to finger on his sword,
While you sat and played Toccatas, stately
at the clavichord?

VII

What? Those lesser thirds[58] so plaintive,
sixths diminished, sigh on sigh,
Told them something? Those suspensions,
those solutions — 'Must we die?'
Those commiserating sevenths — 'Life
might last! we can but try!'

VIII

'Were you happy?' — 'Yes.' — 'And are
you still as happy?' — 'Yes. And
you?'
— 'Then, more kisses!' — 'Did *I* stop
them, when a million seemed so few?'
Hark, the dominant's persistence, till it
must be answered to!

IX

So, an octave struck the answer. Oh, they
praised you, I dare say!
'Brave Galuppi! that was music! good
alike at grave and gay!
I can always leave off talking when I hear
a master play!'

---

[56] Baldassare Galuppi (1706–1785) was an Italian composer, chiefly of opera. During the latter part of his life he was organist at St. Mark's, Venice. The toccata, as the name implies (Italian *toccare*, to touch), is a 'touch-piece', built up of a rapid succession of notes, scale passages, *etc.*, played *staccato*. It is light, free, and rather more showy than profound. In the poem it typifies the life of Venice.

[57] The Rialto.

[58] This and the following technical terms in music are described, at least in their effect, by the phrases that follow them.

X

Then they left you for their pleasure: till in due time, one by one,
Some with lives that came to nothing, some with deeds as well undone,
Death stepped tacitly and took them where they never see the sun.

XI

But when I sit down to reason, think to take my stand nor swerve,
While I triumph o'er a secret wrung from nature's close reserve,
In you come with your cold music till I creep thro' every nerve.

XII

Yes, you, like a ghostly cricket, creaking where a house was burned:
'Dust and ashes, dead and done with, Venice spent what Venice earned.
The soul, doubtless, is immortal — where a soul can be discerned.

XIII

'Yours for instance: you know physics, something of geology,
Mathematics are your pastime; souls shall rise in their degree;
Butterflies may dread extinction, — you'll not die, it cannot be!

XIV

'As for Venice and her people, merely born to bloom and drop,
Here on earth they bore their fruitage, mirth and folly were the crop:
What of soul was left, I wonder, when the kissing had to stop?

XV

'Dust and ashes!' So you creak it, and I want the heart to scold.
Dear dead women, with such hair, too — what's become of all the gold
Used to hang and brush their bosoms? I feel chilly and grown old.

[1855]

A Woman's Last Word

I

Let's contend no more, Love,
Strive nor weep:
All be as before, Love,
— Only sleep!

II

What so wild as words are?
I and thou
In debate, as birds are,
Hawk on bough!

III

See the creature stalking
While we speak!
Hush and hide the talking,
Cheek on cheek!

IV

What so false as truth is,
False to thee?
Where the serpent's tooth is
Shun the tree —

V

Where the apple reddens
Never pry —
Lest we lose our Edens,
Eve and I.

VI

Be a god and hold me
With a charm!
Be a man and fold me
With thine arm!

VII

Teach me, only teach, Love!
As I ought
I will speak thy speech, Love,
Think thy thought —

VIII

Meet, if thou require it,
  Both demands,
Laying flesh and spirit
  In thy hands.

IX

That shall be to-morrow
  Not to-night:
I must bury sorrow
  Out of sight:

X

— Must a little weep, Love,
  (Foolish me!)
And so fall asleep, Love,
  Loved by thee.

[1855]

'*De Gustibus —*' [59]

I

Your ghost will walk, you lover of trees,
    (If our loves remain)
    In an English lane,
By a cornfield-side a-flutter with poppies.
Hark, those two in a hazel coppice —
A boy and a girl, if the good fates please,
    Making love, say, —
    The happier they!
Draw yourself up from the light of the moon,
And let them pass, as they will too soon,
    With the beanflowers' boon,
    And the blackbird's tune,
    And May, and June!

II

What I love best in all the world
Is a castle, precipice-encurled,
In a gash of the wind-grieved Apennine.
Or look for me, old fellow of mine,
(If I get my head from out the mouth
O' the grave, and loose my spirit's bands,
And come again to the land of lands) —
In a sea-side house to the farther South,
Where the baked cicala dies of drouth,
And one sharp tree — 'tis a cypress — stands,
By the many hundred years red-rusted,
Rough iron-spiked, ripe fruit-o'ercrusted,
My sentinel to guard the sands
To the water's edge. For, what expands
Before the house, but the great opaque
Blue breadth of sea without a break?
While, in the house, for ever crumbles
Some fragment of the frescoed walls,
From blisters where a scorpion sprawls.
A girl bare-footed brings, and tumbles
Down on the pavement, green-flesh melons,
And says there 's news to-day — the king
Was shot at, touched in the liver-wing,
Goes with his Bourbon [60] arm in a sling:
— She hopes they have not caught the felons.
    Italy, my Italy!
Queen Mary's saying serves for me —
    (When fortune's malice
    Lost her — Calais) —
Open my heart and you will see
Graved inside of it, 'Italy.' [61]
Such lovers old are I and she:
So it always was, so shall ever be!

[1855]

My Star [62]

All that I know
    Of a certain star
Is, it can throw
    (Like the angled spar)
Now a dart of red,
    Now a dart of blue;

[59] Within a short time after his removal to Italy, Browning's very themes and settings were reminiscent of his 'new country.' Mrs. Browning said that all a woman needed to be perfectly contented in this life was three things — life, love, and Italy — and she had the three! Browning left Italy upon her death in 1861. However, his last summer, that of 1889, he lived at Asolo, and died 12 December at his son's home in Venice.

[60] Ferdinand II, king of the Two Sicilies, was one of the Bourbons, against whom there was a popular revolt in Italy.

[61] When Calais was won from England by the French in 1558, the last year of her reign, Queen Mary in her grief said that the name 'Calais' would be found inscribed on her heart.

[62] For other tributes to Mrs. Browning, see *One Word More*, p. 1000, *Prospice*, p. 1015, and the lines from *The Ring and the Book*, p. 1016. When asked in later years for an autograph, Browning would write out this poem, saying that it was the only one he could remember.

Till my friends have said
They would fain see, too,
My star that dartles the red and the blue!
Then it stops like a bird; like a flower, hangs furled:
They must solace themselves with the Saturn above it.
What matter to me if their star is a world?
Mine has opened its soul to me; therefore I love it.

[1855]

Two in the Campagna [63]

I

I WONDER do you feel to-day
As I have felt since, hand in hand,
We sat down on the grass, to stray
In spirit better through the land,
This morn of Rome and May?

II

For me, I touched a thought, I know,
Has tantalized me many times,
(Like turns of thread the spiders throw
Mocking across our path) for rhymes
To catch at and let go.

III

Help me to hold it! First it left
The yellowing fennel, run to seed
There, branching from the brickwork's cleft,
Some old tomb's ruin: yonder weed
Took up the floating weft,

IV

Where one small orange cup amassed
Five beetles,—blind and green they grope
Among the honey-meal: and last,
Everywhere on the grassy slope
I traced it. Hold it fast!

V

The champaign with its endless fleece
Of feathery grasses everywhere!
Silence and passion, joy and peace,
An everlasting wash of air—
Rome's ghost [64] since her decease.

VI

Such life there, through such lengths of hours,
Such miracles performed in play,
Such primal naked forms of flowers,
Such letting nature have her way
While heaven looks from its towers!

VII

How say you? Let us, O my dove,
Let us be unashamed of soul,
As earth lies bare to heaven above!
How is it under our control
To love or not to love?

VIII

I would that you were all to me,
You that are just so much, no more.
Nor yours nor mine, nor slave nor free!
Where does the fault lie? What the core
Of the wound, since wound must be?

IX

I would I could adopt your will,
See with your eyes, and set my heart
Beating by yours, and drink my fill
At your soul's springs,—your part my part
In life, for good and ill.

X

No. I yearn upward, touch you close,
Then stand away. I kiss your cheek,
Catch your soul's warmth,—I pluck the rose
And love it more than tongue can speak—
Then the good minute goes.

---

[63] The large open country round the city of Rome.

[64] The Campagna is so called because it is marked with ancient ruins.

XI

Already how am I so far
  Out of that minute? Must I go
Still like the thistle-ball, no bar,
  Onward, whenever light winds blow,
Fixed by no friendly star?

XII

Just when I seemed about to learn!
  Where is the thread now? Off again!
The old trick! Only I discern —
  Infinite passion, and the pain
Of finite hearts that yearn.

[1855]

Love in a Life

I

Room after room,
I hunt the house through
We inhabit together.
Heart, fear nothing, for, heart, thou shalt find her —
Next time, herself! — not the trouble behind her
Left in the curtain, the couch's perfume!
As she brushed it, the cornice-wreath blossomed anew:
Yon looking-glass gleamed at the wave of her feather.

II

Yet the day wears,
And door succeeds door;
I try the fresh fortune —
Range the wide house from the wing to the centre.
Still the same chance! she goes out as I enter.
Spend my whole day in the quest, — who cares?
But 'tis twilight, you see, — with such suites to explore,
Such closets to search, such alcoves to importune!

[1855]

Life in a Love

Escape me?
Never —
Beloved!
While I am I, and you are you,
  So long as the world contains us both,
  Me the loving and you the loth,
While the one eludes, must the other pursue.
My life is a fault at last, I fear:
  It seems too much like a fate, indeed!
  Though I do my best I shall scarce succeed.
But what if I fail of my purpose here?
It is but to keep the nerves at strain,
  To dry one's eyes and laugh at a fall,
And baffled, get up and begin again, —
  So the chace takes up one's life, that 's all.
While, look but once from your farthest bound
  At me so deep in the dust and dark,
No sooner the old hope drops to ground
  Than a new one, straight to the self-same mark,
I shape me —
Ever
Removed!

[1855]

Memorabilia [65]

I

Ah, did you once see Shelley plain,
  And did he stop and speak to you
And did you speak to him again?
  How strange it seems and new!

II

But you were living before that,
  And also you are living after;
And the memory I started at —
  My starting moves your laughter.

---

[65] Browning was greatly influenced by Shelley's poetry, which he had loved from youth. He pays tribute, both in *Pauline* ('Sun-trader, life and light be thine forever!') and in a prose essay written in 1852. Browning was deeply affected by over-hearing a stranger remark one day in a London bookshop that he had seen and talked with Shelley. The stranger was amused at the startled expression on Browning's face.

III

I crossed a moor, with a name of its own
  And a certain use in the world no doubt,
Yet a hand's-breadth of it shines alone
  'Mid the blank miles round about:

IV

For there I picked up on the heather
  And there I put inside my breast
A moulted feather, an eagle-feather!
  Well, I forget the rest.

[1855]

The Last Ride Together [66]

I

I SAID — Then, dearest, since 'tis so,
Since now at length my fate I know,
Since nothing all my love avails,
Since all, my life seemed meant for, fails,
  Since this was written and needs must be —
My whole heart rises up to bless
Your name in pride and thankfulness!
Take back the hope you gave, — I claim
Only a memory of the same,
— And this beside, if you will not blame,
  Your leave for one more last ride with me.

II

My mistress bent that brow of hers;
Those deep dark eyes where pride demurs
When pity would be softening through,
Fixed me a breathing-while or two
  With life or death in the balance: right!
The blood replenished me again;
My last thought was at least not vain:
I and my mistress, side by side,
Shall be together, breathe and ride,
So, one day more am I deified.
  Who knows but the world may end to-night?

[66] Browning's love of horses and horsemanship will be remembered from one's reading of *How They Brought the Good News from Ghent to Aix.*

III

Hush! if you saw some western cloud
All billowy-bosomed, over-bowed
By many benedictions — sun's
And moon's and evening-star's at once —
  And so, you, looking and loving best,
Conscious grew, your passion drew
Cloud, sunset, moonrise, star-shine too,
Down on you, near and yet more near,
Till flesh must fade for heaven was here! —
Thus leant she and lingered — joy and fear!
  Thus lay she a moment on my breast.

IV

Then we began to ride. My soul
Smoothed itself out, a long-cramped scroll
Freshening and fluttering in the wind.
Past hopes already lay behind.
  What need to strive with a life awry?
Had I said that, had I done this,
So might I gain, so might I miss.
Might she have loved me? just as well
She might have hated, who can tell!
Where had I been now if the worst befell?
  And here we are riding, she and I.

V

Fail I alone, in words and deeds?
Why, all men strive and who succeeds?
We rode; it seemed my spirit flew,
Saw other regions, cities new,
  As the world rushed by on either side.
I thought, — All labour, yet no less
Bear up beneath their unsuccess.
Look at the end of work, contrast
The petty done, the undone vast,
This present of theirs with the hopeful past!
  I hoped she would love me; here we ride.

VI

What hand and brain went ever paired?
What heart alike conceived and dared?
What act proved all its thought had been?
What will but felt the fleshly screen?

We ride and I see her bosom heave.
There 's many a crown for who can reach.
Ten lines, a statesman's life in each!
The flag stuck on a heap of bones,
A soldier's doing! what atones?
They scratch his name on the Abbey-stones.
My riding is better, by their leave.

VII

What does it all mean, poet? Well,
Your brains beat into rhythm, you tell
What we felt only; you expressed
You hold things beautiful the best,
And pace them in rhyme so, side by side.
'Tis something, nay 'tis much: but then,
Have you yourself what 's best for men?
Are you — poor, sick, old ere your time —
Nearer one whit your own sublime
Than we who never have turned a rhyme?
Sing, riding 's a joy! For me, I ride.

VIII

And you, great sculptor — so, you gave
A score of years to Art, her slave,
And that 's your Venus — whence we turn
To yonder girl that fords the burn!
You acquiesce, and shall I repine?
What, man of music, you grown grey
With notes and nothing else to say,
Is this your sole praise from a friend,
'Greatly his opera's strains intend,
But in music we know how fashions end!'
I gave my youth; but we ride, in fine.

IX

Who knows what 's fit for us? Had fate
Proposed bliss here should sublimate
My being — had I signed the bond —
Still one must lead some life beyond,
Have a bliss to die with, dim-descried.
This foot once planted on the goal,
This glory-garland round my soul,
Could I descry such? Try and test!
I sink back shuddering from the quest.
Earth being so good, would heaven seem best?
Now, heaven and she are beyond this ride.

X

And yet — she has not spoke so long!
What if heaven be that, fair and strong
At life's best, with our eyes upturned
Whither life's flower is first discerned,
We, fixed so, ever should so abide?
What if we still ride on, we two
With life for ever old yet new,
Changed not in kind but in degree,
The instant made eternity, —
And heaven just prove that I and she
Ride, ride together, for ever ride?

[1855]

A Grammarian's Funeral [67]

Shortly after the revival of learning in Europe

Let us begin and carry up this corpse,
Singing together.
Leave we the common crofts,[68] the vulgar thorpes [69]
Each in its tether
Sleeping safe on the bosom of the plain,
Cared-for till cock-crow:
Look out if yonder be not day again
Rimming the rock-row!
That 's the appropriate country; there, man's thought,
Rarer, intenser,
Self-gathered for an outbreak, as it ought,
Chafes in the censer.
Leave we the unlettered plain its herd and crop;
Seek we sepulture
On a tall mountain, citied to the top,
Crowded with culture!

[67] This poem expresses the glorious spirituality of the Renaissance, as *The Bishop Orders His Tomb* portrays its decadent materialism. The speaker is one of a band of disciples of the dead scholar. The metre doubtless suggests the swaying march up the mountain as the master's body is borne to the appropriate country at sunrise.
[68] Enclosed farms.
[69] villages

All the peaks soar, but one the rest excels;
Clouds overcome it;
No! yonder sparkle is the citadel's
Circling its summit.
Thither our path lies; wind we up the heights:
Wait ye the warning?
Our low life was the level's and the night's;
He 's for the morning.
Step to a tune, square chests, erect each head,
'Ware the beholders!
This is our master, famous calm and dead,
Borne on our shoulders.

Sleep, crop and herd! sleep, darkling thorpe and croft,
Safe from the weather!
He, whom we convoy to his grave aloft,
Singing together,
He was a man born with thy face and throat,
Lyric Apollo!
Long he lived nameless: how should spring take note
Winter would follow?
Till lo, the little touch, and youth was gone!
Cramped and diminished,
Moaned he, 'New measures, other feet anon!
My dance is finished?'
No, that's the world's way: (keep the mountain-side,
Make for the city!)
He knew the signal, and stepped on with pride
Over men's pity;
Left play for work, and grappled with the world
Bent on escaping:
'What 's in the scroll,' quoth he, 'thou keepest furled?
Show me their shaping,
Theirs who most studied man, the bard and sage, —
Give!' — So he gowned him,
Straight got by heart that book to its last page:
Learned, we found him.
Yea, but we found him bald too, eyes like lead,
Accents uncertain:
'Time to taste life,' another would have said,
'Up with the curtain!' —
This man said rather, 'Actual life comes next?
Patience a moment!
Grant I have mastered learning's crabbed text,
Still there 's the comment.
Let me know all! Prate not of most or least,
Painful or easy!
Even to the crumbs I'd fain eat up the feast,
Ay, nor feel queasy.'
Oh, such a life as he resolved to live,
When he had learned it,
When he had gathered all books had to give!
Sooner, he spurned it.
Image the whole, then execute the parts —
Fancy the fabric
Quite, ere you build, ere steel strike fire from quartz,
Ere mortar dab brick!

(Here 's the town-gate reached: there 's the market-place
Gaping before us.)
Yea, this in him was the peculiar grace
(Hearten our chorus!)
That before living he'd learn how to live —
No end to learning:
Earn the means first — God surely will contrive
Use for our earning.
Others mistrust and say, 'But time escapes:
Live now or never!'
He said, 'What 's time? leave Now for dogs and apes!
Man has Forever.'

Back to his book then: deeper drooped his head:
  Calculus [70] racked him:
Leaden before, his eyes grew dross of lead:
  Tussis [71] attacked him.
'Now, master, take a little rest!'—not he!
  (Caution redoubled,
Step two abreast, the way winds narrowly!)
  Not a whit troubled
Back to his studies, fresher than at first,
  Fierce as a dragon
He (soul-hydroptic [72] with a sacred thirst)
  Sucked at the flagon.
Oh, if we draw a circle premature,
  Heedless of far gain,
Greedy for quick returns of profit, sure
  Bad is our bargain!
Was it not great? did not he throw on God,
  (He loves the burthen)—
God's task to make the heavenly period
  Perfect the earthen?
Did not he magnify the mind, show clear
  Just what it all meant?
He would not discount life, as fools do here,
  Paid by instalment!
He ventured neck or nothing—heaven's success
  Found, or earth's failure:
'Wilt thou trust death or not?' He answered 'Yes:
  Hence with life's pale lure!'
That low man seeks a little thing to do,
  Sees it and does it:
This high man, with a great thing to pursue,
  Dies ere he knows it.
That low man goes on adding one to one,
  His hundred 's soon hit:
This high man, aiming at a million,
  Misses an unit.

[70] The stone. [71] A cough.
[72] Soul-thirsty, the thirst increasing with drink.

That, has the world here—should he need the next,
  Let the world mind him!
This, throws himself on God, and unperplexed
  Seeking shall find him.
So, with the throttling hands of death at strife,
  Ground he at grammar;
Still, thro' the rattle, parts of speech were rife:
  While he could stammer
He settled *Hoti's* business—let it be!—
  Properly based *Oun*—
Gave us the doctrine of the enclitic *De*, [73]
  Dead from the waist down.
Well, here 's the platform, here 's the proper place:
  Hail to your purlieus,
All ye highfliers of the feathered race,
  Swallows and curlews!
Here 's the top-peak; the multitude below
  Live, for they can, there:
This man decided not to Live but Know—
  Bury this man there?
Here—here 's his place, where meteors shoot, clouds form,
  Lightnings are loosened,
Stars come and go! let joy break with the storm,
  Peace let the dew send!
Lofty designs must close in like effects:
  Loftily lying,
Leave him—still loftier than the world suspects,
  Living and dying.

[1855]

[73] Greek particles expressing fine shades of meaning. In a letter to the London *Daily News* on 21 November 1874, Browning wrote: 'In a clever article this morning you speak of "the doctrine of enclitic De"—"which, with all deference to Mr. Browning, in point of fact does not exist." No, not to Mr. Browning: but pray defer to Herr Buttmann, whose fifth list of "enclitics" ends with "the inseparable *De*"—or to Curtius, whose fifth list ends also with "*De* (meaning '*towards*' and as a demonstrative appendage)." That this is not to be confounded with the accentuated "De, meaning *but*" was the "doctrine" which the Grammarian bequeathed to those capable of receiving it.'

THE STATUE AND THE BUST [74]

There's a palace in Florence, the world knows well,
And a statue watches it from the square,
And this story of both do our townsmen tell.

Ages ago, a lady there,
At the farthest window facing the East
Asked, 'Who rides by with the royal air?'

The bridesmaids' prattle around her ceased;
She leaned forth, one on either hand;
They saw how the blush of the bride increased —

They felt by its beats her heart expand —
As one at each ear and both in a breath
Whispered, 'The Great-Duke Ferdinand.'

That selfsame instant, underneath,
The Duke rode past in his idle way,
Empty and fine like a swordless sheath.

Gay he rode, with a friend as gay,
Till he threw his head back — 'Who is she?'
— 'A bride the Riccardi brings home today.'

Hair in heaps lay heavily
Over a pale brow spirit-pure —
Carved like the heart of the coal-black tree,
Crisped like a war-steed's encolure [75] —
And vainly sought to dissemble her eyes
Of the blackest black our eyes endure.

And lo, a blade for a knight's emprise
Filled the fine empty sheath of a man, —
The Duke grew straightway brave and wise.

He looked at her, as a lover can;
She looked at him, as one who awakes:
The past was a sleep, and her life began.

Now, love so ordered for both their sakes,
A feast was held that selfsame night
In the pile which the mighty shadow makes.

(For Via Larga is three-parts light,
But the palace overshadows one,
Because of a crime which may God requite!

To Florence and God the wrong was done,
Through the first republic's murder there
By Cosimo and his cursed son.[76])

The Duke (with the statue's face in the square)
Turned in the midst of his multitude
At the bright approach of the bridal pair.

Face to face the lovers stood
A single minute and no more,
While the bridegroom bent as a man subdued —

---

[74] The statue is that of Ferdinand I (1549–1609), Grand Duke of Florence. In the Piazza della Santa of the Annunziata it stands, looking toward the palace of the Riccardi. The imaginary bust of the wife of the Riccardi is conceived of as looking from the palace window.

An American newspaper once received from a correspondent the following questions:

'1. When, how, and where did it happen? Browning's divine vagueness lets one gather only that the lady's husband was a Riccardi. 2. Who was the lady? who the duke? 3. The magnificent house wherein Florence lodges her préfet is known to all Florentine ball-goers as the Palazzo Riccardi. It was bought by the Riccardi from the Medici in 1659. From none of its windows did the lady gaze at her more than royal lover. From what window, then, if from any? Are the statue and the bust still in their original positions?'

These questions were found by Mr. Thomas J. Wise, who sent them to Browning. He received from Browning the following reply, written on 8 January 1887:

'Dear Mr. Wise, — I have seldom met with such a strange inability to understand what seems the plainest matter possible: "ball-goers" are probably not history-readers, but any guide-book would confirm what is sufficiently stated in the poem. I will append a note or two, however. 1. "This story the townsmen tell;" "when, how, and where," constitutes the subject of the poem. 2. The lady was the wife of Riccardi; and the duke, Ferdinand, just as the poem says. 3. As it was built by, and inhabited by, the Medici till sold, long after, to the Riccardi, it was not from the duke's palace, but a window in that of the Riccardi, that the lady gazed at her lover riding by. The statue is still in its place, looking at the window under which "now is the empty shrine." Can anything be clearer? My "vagueness" leaves what to be "gathered" when all these things are put down in black and white? Oh, "ball-goers"!'

[75] mane

[76] Cosimo de' Medici (1389–1464) and his grandson Lorenzo (1449–1492), who destroyed the republican government of Florence under their absolute rule.

Bowed till his bonnet brushed the floor —
For the Duke on the lady a kiss conferred,
As the courtly custom was of yore.

In a minute can lovers exchange a word?
If a word did pass, which I do not think,
Only one out of the thousand heard.

That was the bridegroom. At day's brink
He and his bride were alone at last
In a bed-chamber by a taper's blink.

Calmly he said that her lot was cast,
That the door she had passed was shut on her
Till the final catafalk [77] repassed.

The world meanwhile, its noise and stir,
Through a certain window facing the East
She could watch like a convent's chronicler.

Since passing the door might lead to a feast,
And a feast might lead to so much beside,
He, of many evils, chose the least.

'Freely I choose too,' said the bride —
'Your window and its world suffice,'
Replied the tongue, while the heart replied —

'If I spend the night with that devil twice,
May his window serve as my loop of hell
Whence a damned soul looks on paradise!

'I fly to the Duke who loves me well,
Sit by his side and laugh at sorrow
Ere I count another ave-bell.

''Tis only the coat of a page to borrow,
And tie my hair in a horse-boy's trim,
And I save my soul — but not to-morrow' —

[77] A funeral canopy, or hearse.

(She checked herself and her eye grew dim)
'My father tarries to bless my state:
I must keep it one day more for him.

'Is one day more so long to wait?
Moreover the Duke rides past, I know;
We shall see each other, sure as fate.'

She turned on her side and slept. Just so!
So we resolve on a thing and sleep:
So did the lady, ages ago.

That night the Duke said, 'Dear or cheap
As the cost of this cup of bliss may prove
To body or soul, I will drain it deep.'

And on the morrow, bold with love,
He beckoned the bridegroom (close on call,
As his duty bade, by the Duke's alcove)

And smiled ''T was a very funeral,
Your lady will think, this feast of ours, —
A shame to efface, whate'er befall!

'What if we break from the Arno bowers,
And try if Petraja,[78] cool and green,
Cure last night's fault with this morning's flowers?'

The bridegroom, not a thought to be seen
On his steady brow and quiet mouth,
Said, 'Too much favour for me so mean!

'But, alas! my lady leaves [79] the South;
Each wind that comes from the Apennine
Is a menace to her tender youth:

'Nor a way exists, the wise opine,
If she quits her palace twice this year,
To avert the flower of life's decline.'

Quoth the Duke, 'A sage and a kindly fear.
Moreover Petraja is cold this spring:
Be our feast to-night as usual here!'

[78] The Duke's villa near Florence.
[79] *I.e.*, is from.

And then to himself — 'Which night shall bring
Thy bride to her lover's embraces, fool —
Or I am the fool, and thou art the king!

'Yet my passion must wait a night, nor cool —
For to-night the Envoy arrives from France
Whose heart I unlock with thyself, my tool.

'I need thee still and might miss perchance.
To-day is not wholly lost, beside,
With its hope of my lady's countenance:

'For I ride — what should I do but ride?
And passing her palace, if I list,
May glance at its window — well betide!'

So said, so done: nor the lady missed
One ray that broke from the ardent brow,
Nor a curl of the lips where the spirit kissed.

Be sure that each renewed the vow,
No morrow's sun should arise and set
And leave them then as it left them now.

But next day passed, and next day yet,
With still fresh cause to wait one day more
Ere each leaped over the parapet.

And still, as love's brief morning wore,
With a gentle start, half smile, half sigh,
They found love not as it seemed before.

They thought it would work infallibly,
But not in despite of heaven and earth:
The rose would blow when the storm passed by.

Meantime they could profit in winter's dearth
By store of fruits that supplant the rose:
The world and its ways have a certain worth:

And to press a point while these oppose
Were simple policy; better wait:
We lose no friends and we gain no foes.

Meantime, worse fates than a lover's fate,
Who daily may ride and pass and look
Where his lady watches behind the grate!

And she — she watched the square like a book
Holding one picture and only one,
Which daily to find she undertook:

When the picture was reached the book was done,
And she turned from the picture at night to scheme
Of tearing it out for herself next sun.

So weeks grew months, years; gleam by gleam
The glory dropped from their youth and love,
And both perceived they had dreamed a dream;

Which hovered as dreams do, still above:
But who can take a dream for a truth?
Oh, hide our eyes from the next remove!

One day as the lady saw her youth
Depart, and the silver thread that streaked
Her hair, and, worn by the serpent's tooth,

The brow so puckered, the chin so peaked, —
And wondered who the woman was,
Hollow-eyed and haggard-cheeked,

Fronting her silent in the glass —
'Summon here,' she suddenly said,
'Before the rest of my old self pass,

'Him, the Carver, a hand to aid,
Who fashions the clay no love will change,
And fixes a beauty never to fade.

'Let Robbia's craft [80] so apt and strange
Arrest the remains of young and fair,
And rivet them while the seasons range.

'Make me a face on the window there,
Waiting as ever, mute the while,
My love to pass below in the square!

'And let me think that it may beguile
Dreary days which the dead must spend
Down in their darkness under the aisle,

'To say, "What matters it at the end?
I did no more while my heart was warm
Than does that image, my pale-faced friend."

'Where is the use of the lip's red charm,
The heaven of hair, the pride of the brow,
And the blood that blues the inside arm —

'Unless we turn, as the soul knows how,
The earthly gift to an end divine?
A lady of clay is as good, I trow.'

But long ere Robbia's cornice, fine,
With flowers and fruits which leaves enlace,
Was set where now is the empty shrine —

(And, leaning out of a bright blue space,
As a ghost might lean from a chink of sky,
The passionate pale lady's face —

Eyeing ever, with earnest eye
And quick-turned neck at its breathless stretch,
Some one who ever is passing by —)

The Duke had sighed like the simplest wretch
In Florence, 'Youth — my dream escapes!
Will its record stay?' And he bade them fetch

Some subtle moulder of brazen shapes —
'Can the soul, the will, die out of a man
Ere his body find the grave that gapes?

'John of Douay [81] shall effect my plan,
Set me on horseback here aloft,
Alive, as the crafty sculptor can,

'In the very square I have crossed so oft:
That men may admire, when future suns
Shall touch the eyes to a purpose soft,

'While the mouth and the brow stay brave in bronze —
Admire and say, "When he was alive
How he would take his pleasure once!"

'And it shall go hard but I contrive
To listen the while, and laugh in my tomb
At idleness which aspires to strive.'

So! While these wait the trump of doom,
How do their spirits pass, I wonder,
Nights and days in the narrow room?

Still, I suppose, they sit and ponder
What a gift life was, ages ago,
Six steps out of the chapel yonder.

Only they see not God, I know,
Nor all that chivalry of his,
The soldier-saints who, row on row,

Burn upward each to his point of bliss —
Since, the end of life being manifest,
He had burned his way thro' the world to this.

I hear you reproach, 'But delay was best,
For their end was a crime.' — Oh, a crime will do
As well, I reply, to serve for a test,

As a virtue golden through and through,
Sufficient to vindicate itself
And prove its worth at a moment's view!

[80] The term is here applied to the *kind* of work (terra-cotta relief covered with enamel) done by the great Della Robbia, for the last famous member of the craft, Girolamo, died in 1566.

[81] A sculptor from Bologna.

Must a game be played for the sake of pelf?
Where a button goes, 'twere an epigram [82]
To offer the stamp of the very Guelph.[83]

The true has no value beyond the sham:
As well the counter as coin, I submit,
When your table 's a hat, and your prize a dram.

Stake your counter as boldly every whit,
Venture as warily, use the same skill,
Do your best, whether winning or losing it,

If you choose to play! — is my principle.
Let a man contend to the uttermost
For his life's set prize, be it what it will!

The counter our lovers staked was lost
As surely as if it were lawful coin:
And the sin I impute to each frustrate ghost

Is, the unlit lamp and the ungirt loin,
Though the end in sight was a vice, I say.
You of the virtue (we issue join)
How strive you? *De te, fabula!* [84]

[1855]

'CHILDE ROLAND TO THE DARK TOWER CAME' [85]

[See Edgar's song in 'LEAR']

I

MY first thought was, he lied in every word,
  That hoary cripple, with malicious eye
  Askance to watch the working of his lie
On mine, and mouth scarce able to afford
Suppression of the glee, that pursed and scored
  Its edge, at one more victim gained thereby.

II

What else should he be set for, with his staff?
  What, save to waylay with his lies, ensnare
  All travellers who might find him posted there,
And ask the road? I guessed what skull-like laugh
Would break, what crutch 'gin write my epitaph
  For pastime in the dusty thoroughfare,

III

If at his counsel I should turn aside
  Into that ominous tract which, all agree,
  Hides the Dark Tower. Yet acquiescingly
I did turn as he pointed: neither pride
Nor hope rekindling at the end descried,
  So much as gladness that some end might be.

IV

For, what with my whole world-wide wandering,
  What with my search drawn out thro' years, my hope
  Dwindled into a ghost not fit to cope
With that obstreperous joy success would bring, —
I hardly tried now to rebuke the spring
  My heart made, finding failure in its scope.

---

[82] A matter for satire.
[83] Real money, with the stamp of the ruling faction.
[84] The story is about you!
[85] Written in a burst of creative inspiration on 2 January 1852 at Paris, where the Brownings were spending the winter. There has been long controversy over the meaning — or the 'no-meaning' — of this pictured drama, evolved from the single line of an old ballad quoted by Edgar when feigning madness in *King Lear* (III, 4). Browning more than once declared that there was no allegory; but one time, when asked if constancy to an ideal — 'He that endureth to the end shall be saved' — was not a sufficient understanding of his central purpose, he answered, 'Yes, just about that.' He denied then that he had ever said he wrote the poem only for its realistic imagery, without any moral purpose. (See J. W. Chadwick's testimony in 'An Eagle-Feather,' *The Christian Register*, 19 January 1888, Vol. 67, p. 37.) Certainly the poem implies, allegory or no allegory, the very essence of Browning's ideas.

Professor De Vane has shown that Browning's conception of the horrible in landscape was derived from Gerard de Lairesse's *The Art of Painting in All its Branches*, which the poet had practically memorized as a boy. A tower Browning saw in the Carrara mountains and the figure of a horse in a piece of tapestry in his home also contributed to the dream.

V

As when a sick man very near to death
Seems dead indeed, and feels begin and end
The tears and takes the farewell of each friend,
And hears one bid the other go, draw breath
Freelier outside, ('since all is o'er,' he saith,
'And the blow fallen no grieving can amend;')

VI

While some discuss if near the other graves
Be room enough for this, and when a day
Suits best for carrying the corpse away,
With care about the banners, scarves and staves:
And still the man hears all, and only craves
He may not shame such tender love and stay.

VII

Thus, I had so long suffered in this quest,
Heard failure prophesied so oft, been writ
So many times among 'The Band'—to wit,
The knights who to the Dark Tower's search addressed
Their steps—that just to fail as they, seemed best,
And all the doubt was now—should I be fit?

VIII

So, quiet as despair, I turned from him,
That hateful cripple, out of his highway
Into the path he pointed. All the day
Had been a dreary one at best, and dim
Was settling to its close, yet shot one grim
Red leer to see the plain catch its estray.[86]

IX

For mark! no sooner was I fairly found
Pledged to the plain, after a pace or two,
Than, pausing to throw backward a last view
O'er the safe road, 'twas gone; grey plain all round:
Nothing but plain to the horizon's bound.
I might go on; nought else remained to do.

X

So, on I went. I think I never saw
Such starved ignoble nature; nothing throve:
For flowers—as well expect a cedar grove!
But cockle, spurge, according to their law
Might propagate their kind, with none to awe,
You'd think; a burr had been a treasure-trove.

XI

No! penury, inertness and grimace,
In some strange sort, were the land's portion. 'See
Or shut your eyes,' said Nature peevishly,
'It nothing skills: I cannot help my case:
'Tis the Last Judgment's fire must cure this place,
Calcine[87] its clods and set my prisoners free.'

XII

If there pushed any ragged thistle-stalk
Above its mates, the head was chopped; the bents[88]
Were jealous else. What made those holes and rents
In the dock's[89] harsh swarth leaves, bruised as to baulk
All hope of greenness? 't is a brute must walk
Pashing[90] their life out, with a brute's intents.

XIII

As for the grass, it grew as scant as hair
In leprosy; thin dry blades pricked the mud

[86] wanderer

[87] Reduce to powder by heat.
[88] coarse grasses
[89] weed's
[90] crushing

Which underneath looked kneaded up with blood.
One stiff blind horse,[91] his every bone a-stare,
Stood stupified, however he came there:
Thrust out past service from the devil's stud!

XIV

Alive? he might be dead for aught I know,
With that red gaunt and colloped[92] neck a-strain,
And shut eyes underneath the rusty mane;
Seldom went such grotesqueness with such woe;
I never saw a brute I hated so;
He must be wicked to deserve such pain.

XV

I shut my eyes and turned them on my heart.
As a man calls for wine before he fights,
I asked one draught of earlier, happier sights,
Ere fitly I could hope to play my part.
Think first, fight afterwards — the soldier's art:
One taste of the old time sets all to rights.

XVI

Not it! I fancied Cuthbert's reddening face
Beneath its garniture of curly gold,
Dear fellow, till I almost felt him fold
An arm in mine to fix me to the place,
That way he used. Alas, one night's disgrace!
Out went my heart's new fire and left it cold.

XVII

Giles then, the soul of honour — there he stands
Frank as ten years ago when knighted first.
What honest men should dare (he said) he durst.
Good — but the scene shifts — faugh! what hangman's hands
Pin to his breast a parchment? His own bands
Read it. Poor traitor, spit upon and curst!

XVIII

Better this present than a past like that;
Back therefore to my darkening path again!
No sound, no sight as far as eye could strain.
Will the night send a howlet or a bat?
I asked: when something on the dismal flat
Came to arrest my thoughts and change their train.

XIX

A sudden little river crossed my path
As unexpected as a serpent comes.
No sluggish tide congenial to the glooms;
This, as it frothed by, might have been a bath
For the fiend's glowing hoof — to see the wrath
Of its black eddy bespate with flakes and spumes.

XX

So petty yet so spiteful! all along,
Low scrubby alders kneeled down over it;
Drenched willows flung them headlong in a fit
Of mute despair, a suicidal throng:
The river which had done them all the wrong,
Whate'er that was, rolled by, deterred no whit.

XXI

Which, while I forded, — good saints, how I feared
To set my foot upon a dead man's cheek,

---

[91] This was the picture inspired by the tapestry in Browning's house.
[92] ridge-marked

Each step, or feel the spear I thrust to seek
For hollows, tangled in his hair or beard!
— It may have been a water-rat I speared,
But, ugh! it sounded like a baby's shriek.

XXII

Glad was I when I reached the other bank.
Now for a better country. Vain presage!
Who were the strugglers, what war did they wage,
Whose savage trample thus could pad the dank
Soil to a plash? Toads in a poisoned tank,
Or wild cats in a red-hot iron cage —

XXIII

The fight must so have seemed in that fell cirque.
What penned them there, with all the plain to choose?
No foot-print leading to that horrid mews,
None out of it. Mad brewage set to work
Their brains, no doubt, like galley-slaves the Turk
Pits for his pastime, Christians against Jews.

XXIV

And more than that — a furlong on — why, there!
What bad use was that engine for, that wheel,
Or brake, not wheel — that harrow fit to reel
Men's bodies out like silk? with all the air
Of Tophet's tool, on earth left unaware,
Or brought to sharpen its rusty teeth of steel.

XXV

Then came a bit of stubbed ground, once a wood,
Next a marsh, it would seem, and now mere earth
Desperate and done with; (so a fool finds mirth,
Makes a thing and then mars it, till his mood
Changes and off he goes!) within a rood —
Bog, clay and rubble, sand and stark black dearth.

XXVI

Now blotches rankling, coloured gay and grim,
Now patches where some leanness of the soil's
Broke into moss or substances like boils;
Then came some palsied oak, a cleft in him
Like a distorted mouth that splits its rim
Gaping at death, and dies while it recoils.

XXVII

And just as far as ever from the end!
Nought in the distance but the evening, nought
To point my footstep further! At the thought,
A great black bird, Apollyon's [93] bosom-friend,
Sailed past, nor beat his wide wing dragon-penned
That brushed my cap — perchance the guide I sought.

XXVIII

For, looking up, aware I somehow grew,
'Spite of the dusk, the plain had given place
All round to mountains — with such name to grace
Mere ugly heights and heaps now stolen in view.
How thus they had surprised me, — solve it, you!
How to get from them was no clearer case.

XXIX

Yet half I seemed to recognise some trick
Of mischief happened to me, God knows when —
In a bad dream perhaps. Here ended, then,

[93] The angel of the bottomless pit; see *Revelation*, ix. 2.

Progress this way. When, in the very nick
Of giving up, one time more, came a click
As when a trap shuts — you're inside the den!

XXX

Burningly it came on me all at once,
This was the place! those two hills on the right,
Crouched like two bulls locked horn in horn in fight;
While to the left, a tall scalped mountain . . . Dunce,
Dotard, a-dozing at the very nonce,
After a life spent training for the sight!

XXXI

What in the midst lay but the Tower itself?
The round squat turret, blind as the fool's heart,
Built of brown stone, without a counterpart
In the whole world. The tempest's mocking elf
Points to the shipman thus the unseen shelf
He strikes on, only when the timbers start.

XXXII

Not see? because of night perhaps? — Why, day
Came back again for that! before it left,
The dying sunset kindled through a cleft:
The hills, like giants at a hunting, lay,
Chin upon hand, to see the game at bay, —
'Now stab and end the creature — to the heft!'

XXXIII

Not hear? when noise was everywhere! it tolled
Increasing like a bell. Names in my ears,
Of all the lost adventurers my peers, —
How such a one was strong, and such was bold,
And such was fortunate, yet each of old
Lost, lost! one moment knelled the woe of years.

XXXIV

There they stood, ranged along the hill-sides, met
To view the last of me, a living frame
For one more picture! in a sheet of flame
I saw them and I knew them all. And yet
Dauntless the slug-horn to my lips I set,
And blew. '*Childe Roland to the Dark Tower came.*'

[1855]

FRA LIPPO LIPPI [94]

I AM poor brother Lippo, by your leave!
You need not clap your torches to my face.
Zooks, what 's to blame? you think you see a monk!
What, it 's past midnight, and you go the rounds,
And here you catch me at an alley's end
Where sportive ladies leave their doors ajar?
The Carmine 's [95] my cloister: hunt it up,
Do, — harry out, if you must show your zeal,
Whatever rat, there, haps on his wrong hole,
And nip each softling of a wee white mouse,
Weke, weke, that 's crept to keep him company!
Aha, you know your betters! Then, you'll take
Your hand away that 's fiddling on my throat,
And please to know me likewise. Who am I?

[94] Fra Lippo Lippi (1406–1469), famous Florentine painter, the details and significance of whose life and work Browning derived chiefly from Vasari's *Lives of the Painters*. He is addressing the police, who have caught him returning in the early morning from one of his frequent escapades.

[95] The monastery of the Carmelite friars.

Why, one, sir, who is lodging with a friend
Three streets off — he 's a certain . . . how d' ye call?
Master — a . . . Cosimo of the Medici,[96]
In the house that caps the corner. Boh! you were best!
Remember and tell me, the day you're hanged,
How you affected such a gullet's-gripe!
But you, sir, it concerns you that your knaves
Pick up a manner nor discredit you:
Zooks, are we pilchards,[97] that they sweep the streets
And count fair prize what comes into their net?
He 's Judas to a tittle, that man is!
Just such a face! why, sir, you make amends.
Lord, I'm not angry! Bid your hang-dogs go
Drink out this quarter-florin to the health
Of the munificent House that harbours me
(And many more beside, lads! more beside!)
And all 's come square again. I'd like his face —
His, elbowing on his comrade in the door
With the pike and lantern, — for the slave that holds
John Baptist's head a-dangle by the hair
With one hand ('Look you, now,' as who should say)
And his weapon in the other, yet unwiped!
It 's not your chance to have a bit of chalk,
A wood-coal or the like? or you should see!
Yes, I'm the painter, since you style me so.
What, brother Lippo's doings, up and down,
You know them and they take you? like enough!
I saw the proper twinkle in your eye —
'Tell you, I liked your looks at very first.
Let 's sit and set things straight now, hip to haunch.

[96] Cosimo de' Medici (1389–1464), wealthy patron of arts and letters. See the reference to his palace in *The Statue and the Bust*.
[97] Cheap fish.

Here 's spring come, and the nights one makes up bands
To roam the town and sing out carnival,
And I've been three weeks shut within my mew,
A-painting for the great man, saints and saints
And saints again. I could not paint all night —
Ouf! I leaned out of window for fresh air.
There came a hurry of feet and little feet,
A sweep of lute-strings, laughs, and whifts of song, —
Flower o' the broom,
Take away love, and our earth is a tomb!
Flower o' the quince,
I let Lisa go, and what good in life since?
Flower o' the thyme — and so on. Round they went.
Scarce had they turned the corner when a titter
Like the skipping of rabbits by moonlight, — three slim shapes —
And a face that looked up . . . zooks, sir, flesh and blood,
That 's all I'm made of! Into shreds it went,
Curtain and counterpane and coverlet,
All the bed-furniture — a dozen knots,
There was a ladder! Down I let myself,
Hands and feet, scrambling somehow, and so dropped,
And after them. I came up with the fun
Hard by Saint Laurence,[98] hail fellow, well met, —
Flower o' the rose,
If I've been merry, what matter who knows?
And so as I was stealing back again
To get to bed and have a bit of sleep
Ere I rise up to-morrow and go work
On Jerome knocking at his poor old breast
With his great round stone to subdue the flesh,
You snap me of the sudden. Ah, I see!
Though your eye twinkles still, you shake your head —

[98] The church of San Lorenzo.

Mine 's shaved,—a monk, you say—the sting 's in that!
If Master Cosimo announced himself,
Mum 's the word naturally; but a monk!
Come, what am I a beast for? tell us, now!
I was a baby when my mother died
And father died and left me in the street.
I starved there, God knows how, a year or two
On fig-skins, melon-parings, rinds and shucks,
Refuse and rubbish. One fine frosty day
My stomach being empty as your hat,
The wind doubled me up and down I went.
Old Aunt Lapaccia trussed me with one hand,
(Its fellow was a stinger as I knew)
And so along the wall, over the bridge,
By the straight cut to the convent. Six words there,
While I stood munching my first bread that month:
'So, boy, you're minded,' quoth the good fat father
Wiping his own mouth, 'twas refection-time,—
'To quit this very miserable world?
Will you renounce' . . . The mouthful of bread? thought I;
By no means! Brief, they made a monk of me;
I did renounce the world, its pride and greed,
Palace, farm, villa, shop and banking-house,
Trash, such as these poor devils of Medici
Have given their hearts to—all at eight years old.
Well, sir, I found in time, you may be sure,
'Twas not for nothing—the good belly-ful,
The warm serge and the rope that goes all round,
And day-long blessed idleness beside!
'Let 's see what the urchin 's fit for'—that came next.
Not overmuch their way, I must confess.
Such a to-do! they tried me with their books:
Lord, they'd have taught me Latin in pure waste!
Flower o' the clove,
All the Latin I construe is, 'amo' I love!
But, mind you, when a boy starves in the streets
Eight years together, as my fortune was,
Watching folk's faces to know who will fling
The bit of half-stripped grape-bunch he desires,
And who will curse or kick him for his pains,—
Which gentleman processional and fine,
Holding a candle to the Sacrament
Will wink and let him lift a plate and catch
The droppings of the wax to sell again,
Or holla for the Eight[99] and have him whipped,—
How say I?—nay, which dog bites, which lets drop
His bone from the heap of offal in the street,—
Why, soul and sense of him grow sharp alike,
He learns the look of things, and none the less
For admonition from the hunger-pinch.
I had a store of such remarks, be sure,
Which, after I found leisure, turned to use.
I drew men's faces on my copy-books,
Scrawled them within the antiphonary's marge,
Joined legs and arms to the long music-notes,
Found eyes and nose and chin for A's and B's,
And made a string of pictures of the world
Betwixt the ins and outs of verb and noun,
On the wall, the bench, the door. The monks looked black.
'Nay,' quoth the Prior, 'turn him out, d' ye say?
In no wise. Lose a crow and catch a lark.

[99] The magistrates.

What if at last we get our man of parts,
We Carmelites, like those Camaldolese
And Preaching Friars,[100] to do our church up fine
And put the front on it that ought to be!'
And hereupon they bade me daub away.
Thank you! my head being crammed, the walls a blank,
Never was such prompt disemburdening.
First, every sort of monk, the black and white,
I drew them, fat and lean: then, folk at church,
From good old gossips waiting to confess
Their cribs of barrel-droppings, candle-ends,—
To the breathless fellow at the altar-foot,
Fresh from his murder, safe and sitting there
With the little children round him in a row
Of admiration, half for his beard and half
For that white anger of his victim's son
Shaking a fist at him with one fierce arm,
Signing himself with the other because of Christ
(Whose sad face on the cross sees only this
After the passion of a thousand years)
Till some poor girl, her apron o'er her head,
(Which the intense eyes looked through) came at eve
On tiptoe, said a word, dropped in a loaf,
Her pair of earrings and a bunch of flowers
(The brute took growling), prayed, and so was gone.
I painted all, then cried ''tis ask and have;
Choose, for more 's ready!'—laid the ladder flat,
And showed my covered bit of cloister-wall.
The monks closed in a circle and praised loud
Till checked, taught what to see and not to see,
Being simple bodies,—'That 's the very man!
Look at the boy who stoops to pat the dog!
That woman 's like the Prior's niece who comes
To care about his asthma: it 's the life!'
But there my triumph 's straw-fire flared and funked;
Their betters took their turn to see and say:
The Prior and the learned pulled a face
And stopped all that in no time. 'How? what 's here?
Quite from the mark of painting, bless us all!
Faces, arms, legs and bodies like the true
As much as pea and pea! it 's devil's-game!
Your business is not to catch men with show,
With homage to the perishable clay,
But lift them over it, ignore it all,
Make them forget there 's such a thing as flesh.
Your business is to paint the souls of men—
Man's soul, and it 's a fire, smoke . . . no, it 's not . . .
It 's vapour done up like a new-born babe—
(In that shape when you die it leaves your mouth)
It 's . . . well, what matters talking, it 's the soul!
Give us no more of body than shows soul!
Here 's Giotto,[101] with his Saint a-praising God,
That sets us praising,—why not stop with him?
Why put all thoughts of praise out of our heads
With wonder at lines, colours, and what not?
Paint the soul, never mind the legs and arms!
Rub all out, try at it a second time.
Oh, that white smallish female with the breasts,

[100] The Dominicans.

[101] Giotto di Bondone (1276–1337), painter, architect and sculptor.

She 's just my niece . . . Herodias, I would say,—
Who went and danced and got men's heads cut off!
Have it all out!' Now, is this sense, I ask?
A fine way to paint soul, by painting body
So ill, the eye can't stop there, must go further
And can't fare worse! Thus, yellow does for white
When what you put for yellow 's simply black,
And any sort of meaning looks intense
When all beside itself means and looks nought.
Why can't a painter lift each foot in turn,
Left foot and right foot, go a double step,
Make his flesh liker and his soul more like,
Both in their order? Take the prettiest face,
The Prior's niece . . . patron-saint—is it so pretty
You can't discover if it means hope, fear,
Sorrow or joy? won't beauty go with these?
Suppose I've made her eyes all right and blue,
Can't I take breath and try to add life's flash,
And then add soul and heighten them threefold?
Or say there 's beauty with no soul at all—
(I never saw it—put the case the same—)
If you get simple beauty and nought else,
You get about the best thing God invents:
That 's somewhat: and you'll find the soul you have missed,
Within yourself, when you return him thanks.
'Rub all out!' Well, well, there 's my life, in short,
And so the thing has gone on ever since.
I'm grown a man no doubt, I've broken bounds;
You should not take a fellow eight years old
And make him swear to never kiss the girls.
I'm my own master, paint now as I please—
Having a friend, you see, in the Corner-house!
Lord, it 's fast holding by the rings in front—
Those great rings serve more purposes than just
To plant a flag in, or tie up a horse!
And yet the old schooling sticks, the old grave eyes
Are peeping o'er my shoulder as I work,
The heads shake still—'It 's art's decline, my son!
You're not of the true painters, great and old;
Brother Angelico 's[102] the man, you'll find;
Brother Lorenzo[103] stands his single peer:
Fag on at flesh, you'll never make the third!'
Flower o' the pine,
You keep your mistr . . . manners, and I'll stick to mine!
I'm not the third, then: bless us, they must know!
Don't you think they're the likeliest to know,
They with their Latin? So, I swallow my rage,
Clench my teeth, suck my lips in tight, and paint
To please them—sometimes do, and sometimes don't;
For, doing most, there 's pretty sure to come
A turn, some warm eve finds me at my saints—
A laugh, a cry, the business of the world—
(*Flower o' the peach,*
Death for us all, and his own life for each!)

---

[102] Fra Angelico (1387–1455), a deeply spiritual painter, who brought the highest piety to his non-realistic art.

[103] Lorenzo Monaco, a painter belonging to the Order of the Camaldolese.

And my whole soul revolves, the cup runs over,
The world and life 's too big to pass for a dream,
And I do these wild things in sheer despite,
And play the fooleries you catch me at,
In pure rage! the old mill-horse, out at grass
After hard years, throws up his stiff heels so,
Although the miller does not preach to him
The only good of grass is to make chaff.
What would men have? Do they like grass or no —
May they or mayn't they? all I want 's the thing
Settled for ever one way. As it is,
You tell too many lies and hurt yourself:
You don't like what you only like too much,
You do like what, if given you at your word,
You find abundantly detestable.
For me, I think I speak as I was taught;
I always see the garden and God there
A-making man's wife: and, my lesson learned,
The value and significance of flesh,
I can't unlearn ten minutes afterwards.

You understand me: I'm a beast, I know.
But see, now — why, I see as certainly
As that the morning-star 's about to shine,
What will hap some day. We've a youngster here
Comes to our convent, studies what I do,
Slouches and stares and lets no atom drop —
His name is Guidi [104] — he'll not mind the monks —
They call him Hulking Tom, he lets them talk —
He picks my practice up — he'll paint apace,
I hope so — though I never live so long,
I know what 's sure to follow. You be judge!
You speak no Latin more than I, belike;
However, you're my man, you've seen the world
— The beauty and the wonder and the power,
The shapes of things, their colours, lights and shades,
Changes, surprises, — and God made it all!
— For what? do you feel thankful, ay or no,
For this fair town's face, yonder river's line,
The mountain round it and the sky above,
Much more the figures of man, woman, child,
These are the frame to? What 's it all about?
To be passed over, despised? or dwelt upon,
Wondered at? oh, this last of course! — you say.
But why not do as well as say, — paint these
Just as they are, careless what comes of it?
God's works — paint anyone, and count it crime
To let a truth slip. Don't object, 'His works
Are here already; nature is complete:
Suppose you reproduce her — (which you can't)
There 's no advantage! you must beat her, then.'
For, don't you mark? we're made so that we love
First when we see them painted, things we have passed
Perhaps a hundred times nor cared to see;
And so they are better, painted — better to us,
Which is the same thing. Art was given for that;
God uses us to help each other so,
Lending our minds out. Have you noticed, now,

[104] Tommaso Guidi (1401–1428), who was actually the master of Lippo, not his pupil.

Your cullion's[105] hanging face? A bit of chalk,
And trust me but you should, though! How much more,
If I drew higher things with the same truth!
That were to take the Prior's pulpit-place,
Interpret God to all of you! Oh, oh,
It makes me mad to see what men shall do
And we in our graves! This world 's no blot for us,
Nor blank; it means intensely, and means good:
To find its meaning is my meat and drink.
'Ay, but you don't so instigate to prayer!'
Strikes in the Prior: 'when your meaning 's plain
It does not say to folk — remember matins,
Or, mind you fast next Friday!' Why, for this
What need of art at all? A skull and bones,
Two bits of stick nailed crosswise, or, what 's best,
A bell to chime the hour with, does as well.
I painted a Saint Laurence six months since
At Prato, splashed the fresco in fine style:
'How looks my painting, now the scaffold 's down?'
I ask a brother: 'Hugely,' he returns —
'Already not one phiz of your three slaves
Who turn the Deacon[106] off his toasted side,
But 's scratched and prodded to our heart's content,
The pious people have so eased their own
When coming to say prayers there in a rage:
We get on fast to see the bricks beneath.
Expect another job this time next year,
For pity and religion grow i' the crowd —
Your painting serves its purpose!' Hang the fools!

— That is — you'll not mistake an idle word
Spoke in a huff by a poor monk, God wot,
Tasting the air this spicy night which turns
The unaccustomed head like Chianti wine!
Oh, the church knows! don't misreport me, now!
It 's natural a poor monk out of bounds
Should have his apt word to excuse himself:
And hearken how I plot to make amends.
I have bethought me: I shall paint a piece
. . . There 's for you! Give me six months, then go, see
Something in Sant' Ambrogio's![107] Bless the nuns!
They want a cast o' my office. I shall paint[108]
God in the midst, Madonna and her babe,
Ringed by a bowery flowery angel-brood,
Lilies and vestments and white faces, sweet
As puff on puff of grated orris-root
When ladies crowd to church at midsummer.
And then i' the front, of course a saint or two —
Saint John, because he saves the Florentines,
Saint Ambrose, who puts down in black and white
The convent's friends and gives them a long day,
And Job, I must have him there past mistake,
The man of Uz (and Us without the z,
Painters who need his patience). Well, all these
Secured at their devotions, up shall come
Out of a corner when you least expect,
As one by a dark stair into a great light,

105 low fellow's
106 St. Laurence was burned to death on a gridiron.

107 St. Ambrose's church in Florence.
108 The picture described is *The Coronation of the Virgin*, now in the Accademia di Belle Arti, Florence. The model for the Virgin was Lippo's mistress.

Music and talking, who but Lippo! I! —
Mazed, motionless and moon-struck — I'm the man!
Back I shrink — what is this I see and hear?
I, caught up with my monk's-things by mistake,
My old serge gown and rope that goes all round,
I, in this presence, this pure company!
Where 's a hole, where 's a corner for escape?
Then steps a sweet angelic slip of a thing
Forward, puts out a soft palm — ' Not so fast! '
— Addresses the celestial presence, ' nay —
He made you and devised you, after all,
Though he 's none of you! Could Saint John there draw —
His camel-hair make up a painting-brush?
We come to brother Lippo for all that,
Iste perfecit opus! '[109] So, all smile —
I shuffle sideways with my blushing face
Under the cover of a hundred wings
Thrown like a spread of kirtles when you're gay
And play hot cockles, all the doors being shut,
Till, wholly unexpected, in there pops
The hothead husband! Thus I scuttle off
To some safe bench behind, not letting go
The palm of her, the little lily thing
That spoke the good word for me in the nick,
Like the Prior's niece . . . Saint Lucy, I would say.
And so all 's saved for me, and for the church
A pretty picture gained. Go, six months hence!
Your hand, sir, and good-bye: no lights, no lights!
The street 's hushed, and I know my own way back,
Don't fear me! There's the grey beginning. Zooks!

[1855]

ANDREA DEL SARTO[110]

(CALLED ' THE FAULTLESS PAINTER ')

But do not let us quarrel any more,
No, my Lucrezia; bear with me for once:
Sit down and all shall happen as you wish.
You turn your face, but does it bring your heart?
I'll work then for your friend's friend, never fear,
Treat his own subject after his own way,
Fix his own time, accept too his own price,
And shut the money into this small hand
When next it takes mine. Will it? tenderly?
Oh, I'll content him, — but to-morrow, Love!
I often am much wearier than you think,
This evening more than usual, and it seems
As if — forgive now — should you let me sit
Here by the window with your hand in mine
And look a half-hour forth on Fiesole,
Both of one mind, as married people use,
Quietly, quietly the evening through,
I might get up to-morrow to my work
Cheerful and fresh as ever. Let us try.
To-morrow, how you shall be glad for this!
Your soft hand is a woman of itself,
And mine the man's bared breast she curls inside.
Don't count the time lost, neither; you must serve

109 'This fellow did the work.' The inscription runs along a scroll painted into the picture near Lippo's own image.

110 Andrea del Sarto (1486–1531), so called because he was 'the tailor's son,' was noted for his perfect technique. In 1512 he married Lucrezia del Fede, whom he addresses in the poem. Browning had been asked by John Kenyon, Mrs. Browning's cousin, to obtain for him a copy of the picture by Andrea in the Pitti Palace, representing the artist and his wife. Unable to secure a good copy, Browning sent the poem as a substitute interpretation. It draws heavily upon the account of Andrea in Vasari's *Lives of the Painters.*

For each of the five pictures we require:
It saves a model. So! keep looking so —
My serpentining beauty, rounds on rounds!
— How could you ever prick those perfect ears,
Even to put the pearl there! oh, so sweet —
My face, my moon, my everybody's moon,
Which everybody looks on and calls his,
And, I suppose, is looked on by in turn,
While she looks — no one's: very dear, no less.
You smile? why, there 's my picture ready made,
There 's what we painters call our harmony!
A common greyness silvers everything, —
All in a twilight, you and I alike
— You, at the point of your first pride in me
(That 's gone you know), — but I, at every point;
My youth, my hope, my art, being all toned down
To yonder sober pleasant Fiesole.
There 's the bell clinking from the chapel-top;
That length of convent-wall across the way
Holds the trees safer, huddled more inside;
The last monk leaves the garden; days decrease,
And autumn grows, autumn in everything.
Eh? the whole seems to fall into a shape
As if I saw alike my work and self
And all that I was born to be and do,
A twilight-piece. Love, we are in God's hand.
How strange now, looks the life he makes us lead;
So free we seem, so fettered fast we are!
I feel he laid the fetter: let it lie!
This chamber for example — turn your head —
All that 's behind us! You don't understand
Nor care to understand about my art,
But you can hear at least when people speak:
And that cartoon, the second from the door
— It is the thing, Love! so such things should be —
Behold Madonna! — I am bold to say.
I can do with my pencil what I know,
What I see, what at bottom of my heart
I wish for, if I ever wish so deep —
Do easily, too — when I say, perfectly,
I do not boast, perhaps: yourself are judge,
Who listened to the Legate's talk last week,
And just as much they used to say in France.
At any rate 'tis easy, all of it!
No sketches first, no studies, that 's long past:
I do what many dream of, all their lives,
— Dream? strive to do, and agonise to do,
And fail in doing. I could count twenty such
On twice your fingers, and not leave this town,
Who strive — you don't know how the others strive
To paint a little thing like that you smeared
Carelessly passing with your robes afloat, —
Yet do much less, so much less, Someone says,
(I know his name, no matter) — so much less!
Well, less is more, Lucrezia: I am judged.
There burns a truer light of God in them,
In their vexed beating stuffed and stopped-up brain,
Heart, or whate'er else, than goes on to prompt
This low-pulsed forthright craftsman's hand of mine.
Their works drop groundward, but themselves, I know,
Reach many a time a heaven that 's shut to me,
Enter and take their place there sure enough,
Though they come back and cannot tell the world.

My works are nearer heaven, but I sit here.
The sudden blood of these men! at a word —
Praise them, it boils, or blame them, it boils too.
I, painting from myself and to myself,
Know what I do, am unmoved by men's blame
Or their praise either. Somebody remarks
Morello's [111] outline there is wrongly traced,
His hue mistaken; what of that? or else,
Rightly traced and well ordered; what of that?
Speak as they please, what does the mountain care?
Ah, but a man's reach should exceed his grasp,
Or what 's a heaven for? All is silver-grey
Placid and perfect with my art: the worse!
I know both what I want and what might gain,
And yet how profitless to know, to sigh
'Had I been two, another and myself,
Our head would have o'erlooked the world!' No doubt.
Yonder 's a work now, of that famous youth
The Urbinate [112] who died five years ago.
('T is copied, George Vasari sent it me.)
Well, I can fancy how he did it all,
Pouring his soul, with kings and popes to see,
Reaching, that heaven might so replenish him,
Above and through his art — for it gives way;
That arm is wrongly put — and there again —
A fault to pardon in the drawing's lines,
Its body, so to speak: its soul is right,
He means right — that, a child may understand.
Still, what an arm! and I could alter it:
But all the play, the insight and the stretch —
Out of me, out of me! And wherefore out?
Had you enjoined them on me, given me soul,
We might have risen to Rafael, I and you!
Nay, Love, you did give all I asked, I think —
More than I merit, yes, by many times.
But had you — oh, with the same perfect brow,
And perfect eyes, and more than perfect mouth,
And the low voice my soul hears, as a bird
The fowler's pipe, and follows to the snare —
Had you, with these the same, but brought a mind!
Some women do so. Had the mouth there urged
'God and the glory! never care for gain.
The present by the future, what is that?
Live for fame, side by side with Agnolo! [113]
Rafael is waiting: up to God, all three!'
I might have done it for you. So it seems:
Perhaps not. All is as God over-rules.
Beside, incentives come from the soul's self;
The rest avail not. Why do I need you?
What wife had Rafael, or has Agnolo?
In this world, who can do a thing, will not;
And who would do it, cannot, I perceive:
Yet the will 's somewhat — somewhat, too, the power —
And thus we half-men struggle. At the end,
God, I conclude, compensates, punishes.
'Tis safer for me, if the award be strict,
That I am something underrated here,
Poor this long while, despised, to speak the truth.
I dared not, do you know, leave home all day,
For fear of chancing on the Paris lords.
The best is when they pass and look aside;

111 A peak of the Apennines, north of Florence.
112 Raphael (1483–1520), born at Urbino.
113 Michael Angelo (1475–1564).

But they speak sometimes; I must bear it all.
Well may they speak! That Francis,[114] that first time,
And that long festal year at Fontainebleau!
I surely then could sometimes leave the ground,
Put on the glory, Rafael's daily wear,
In that humane great monarch's golden look,—
One finger in his beard or twisted curl
Over his mouth's good mark that made the smile,
One arm about my shoulder, round my neck,
The jingle of his gold chain in my ear,
I painting proudly with his breath on me,
All his court round him, seeing with his eyes,
Such frank French eyes, and such a fire of souls
Profuse, my hand kept plying by those hearts,—
And, best of all, this, this, this face beyond,
This in the background, waiting on my work,
To crown the issue with a last reward!
A good time, was it not, my kingly days?
And had you not grown restless . . . but I know—
'T is done and past; 't was right, my instinct said;
Too live the life grew, golden and not grey,
And I'm the weak-eyed bat no sun should tempt
Out of the grange whose four walls make his world.
How could it end in any other way?
You called me, and I came home to your heart.
The triumph was—to reach and stay there; since
I reached it ere the triumph, what is lost?

[114] King Francis I, of France, who invited Andrea to paint for him at Fontainebleau. While at work there, Andrea suddenly went home to Italy, at the insistence of his wife. The story goes that he used money given to him by Francis, for purchasing pictures for the palace, to buy a house for Lucrezia.

Let my hands frame your face in your hair's gold,
You beautiful Lucrezia that are mine!
'Rafael did this, Andrea painted that;
The Roman's is the better when you pray,
But still the other's Virgin was his wife—'
Men will excuse me. I am glad to judge
Both pictures in your presence; clearer grows
My better fortune, I resolve to think.
For, do you know, Lucrezia, as God lives,
Said one day Agnolo, his very self,
To Rafael . . . I have known it all these years . . .
(When the young man was flaming out his thoughts
Upon a palace-wall for Rome to see,
Too lifted up in heart because of it)
'Friend, there 's a certain sorry little scrub
Goes up and down our Florence, none cares how,
Who, were he set to plan and execute
As you are, pricked on by your popes and kings,
Would bring the sweat into that brow of yours!'
To Rafael's!—And indeed the arm is wrong.
I hardly dare . . . yet, only you to see,
Give the chalk here—quick, thus the line should go!
Ay, but the soul! he 's Rafael! rub it out!
Still, all I care for, if he spoke the truth,
(What he? why, who but Michael Agnolo?
Do you forget already words like those?)
If really there was such a chance, so lost,—
Is, whether you're—not grateful—but more pleased.
Well, let me think so. And you smile indeed!
This hour has been an hour! Another smile?
If you would sit thus by me every night
I should work better, do you comprehend?
I mean that I should earn more, give you more.
See, it is settled dusk now; there 's a star;

Morello 's gone, the watch-lights show the wall,
The cue-owls speak the name [115] we call them by.
Come from the window, love,—come in, at last,
Inside the melancholy little house
We built to be so gay with. God is just.
King Francis may forgive me: oft at nights
When I look up from painting, eyes tired out,
The walls become illumined, brick from brick
Distinct, instead of mortar, fierce bright gold,
That gold of his I did cement them with!
Let us but love each other. Must you go?
That Cousin here again? he waits outside?
Must see you—you, and not with me? Those loans?
More gaming debts to pay? you smiled for that?
Well, let smiles buy me! have you more to spend?
While hand and eye and something of a heart
Are left me, work 's my ware, and what 's it worth?
I'll pay my fancy. Only let me sit
The grey remainder of the evening out,
Idle, you call it, and muse perfectly
How I could paint, were I but back in France,
One picture, just one more—the Virgin's face,
Not your's this time! I want you at my side
To hear them—that is, Michael Agnolo—
Judge all I do and tell you of its worth.
Will you? To-morrow, satisfy your friend.
I take the subjects for his corridor,
Finish the portrait out of hand—there, there,
And throw him in another thing or two
If he demurs; the whole should prove enough
To pay for this same Cousin's freak. Beside,
What 's better and what 's all I care about,
Get you the thirteen scudi [116] for the ruff!
Love, does that please you? Ah, but what does he,
The Cousin! what does he to please you more?

I am grown peaceful as old age to-night.
I regret little, I would change still less.
Since there my past life lies, why alter it?
The very wrong to Francis!—it is true
I took his coin, was tempted and complied,
And built this house and sinned, and all is said.
My father and my mother died of want.
Well, had I riches of my own? you see
How one gets rich! Let each one bear his lot.
They were born poor, lived poor, and poor they died:
And I have laboured somewhat in my time
And not been paid profusely. Some good son
Paint my two hundred pictures—let him try!
No doubt, there 's something strikes a balance. Yes,
You loved me quite enough, it seems to-night.
This must suffice me here. What would one have?
In heaven, perhaps, new chances, one more chance—
Four great walls in the New Jerusalem,
Meted on each side by the angel's reed,
For Leonard,[117] Rafael, Agnolo and me
To cover—the three first without a wife,
While I have mine! So—still they overcome
Because there 's still Lucrezia,—as I choose.

Again the Cousin's whistle! Go, my Love.

[1855]

[115] Italian *ciù*.

[116] Coins worth a little less than a dollar.

[117] Leonardo da Vinci (1452–1519).

CLEON[118]

'As certain also of your own poets have said' — [119]

CLEON the poet (from the sprinkled isles,
Lily on lily, that o'erlace the sea,
And laugh their pride when the light wave lisps 'Greece') —
To Protus in his Tyranny: much health!

They give thy letter to me, even now:
I read and seem as if I heard thee speak.
The master of thy galley still unlades
Gift after gift; they block my court at last
And pile themselves along its portico
Royal with sunset, like a thought of thee:
And one white she-slave from the group dispersed
Of black and white slaves (like the chequer-work
Pavement, at once my nation's work and gift,
Now covered with this settle-down of doves)
One lyric woman, in her crocus vest
Woven of sea-wools, with her two white hands
Commends to me the strainer and the cup
Thy lip hath bettered ere it blesses mine.

Well-counselled, king, in thy munificence!
For so shall men remark, in such an act
Of love for him whose song gives life its joy,
Thy recognition of the use of life;
Nor call thy spirit barely adequate
To help on life in straight ways, broad enough
For vulgar souls, by ruling and the rest.
Thou, in the daily building of thy tower, —
Whether in fierce and sudden spasms of toil,
Or through dim lulls of unapparent growth,
Or when the general work 'mid good acclaim
Climbed with the eye to cheer the architect, —
Didst ne'er engage in work for mere work's sake —
Hadst ever in thy heart the luring hope
Of some eventual rest a-top of it,
Whence, all the tumult of the building hushed,
Thou first of men mightst look out to the East:
The vulgar saw thy tower, thou sawest the sun.
For this, I promise on thy festival
To pour libation, looking o'er the sea,
Making this slave narrate thy fortunes, speak
Thy great words, and describe thy royal face —
Wishing thee wholly where Zeus lives the most,
Within the eventual element of calm.

Thy letter's first requirement meets me here.
It is as thou hast heard: in one short life
I, Cleon, have effected all those things
Thou wonderingly dost enumerate.
That epos[120] on thy hundred plates of gold
Is mine, — and also mine the little chant,
So sure to rise from every fishing-bark
When, lights at prow, the seamen haul their net.
The image of the sun-god on the phare,[121]
Men turn from the sun's self to see, is mine;
The Poecile,[122] o'er-storied its whole length,
As thou didst hear, with painting, is mine too.
I know the true proportions of a man
And woman also, not observed before;

[118] Cleon is an imaginary Greek poet replying to a letter from his equally imaginary friend and patron, Protus, a king. Cleon sums up the Greek culture and thought of the first century — both its strength and its inadequacy.

[119] See *Acts*, xvii, 28.

[120] Epic poem, engraved on gold plates.

[121] lighthouse

[122] The Portico at Athens.

And I have written three books on the soul,
Proving absurd all written hitherto,
And putting us to ignorance again.
For music, — why, I have combined the moods,[123]
Inventing one. In brief, all arts are mine;
Thus much the people know and recognize,
Throughout our seventeen islands. Marvel not.
We of these latter days, with greater mind
Than our forerunners, since more composite,
Look not so great, beside their simple way,
To a judge who only sees one way at once,
One mind-point, and no other at a time, —
Compares the small part of a man of us
With some whole man of the heroic age,
Great in his way — not ours, nor meant for ours.
And ours is greater, had we skill to know:
For, what we call this life of men on earth,
This sequence of the soul's achievements here
Being, as I find much reason to conceive,
Intended to be viewed eventually
As a great whole, not analysed to parts,
But each part having reference to all, —
How shall a certain part, pronounced complete,
Endure effacement by another part?
Was the thing done? — then, what 's to do again?
See, in the chequered pavement opposite,
Suppose the artist made a perfect rhomb,
And next a lozenge, then a trapezoid —
He did not overlay them, superimpose
The new upon the old and blot it out,
But laid them on a level in his work,
Making at last a picture; there it lies.
So, first the perfect separate forms were made,
The portions of mankind; and after, so,
Occurred the combination of the same.
Or where had been a progress, otherwise?
Mankind, made up of all the single men, —
In such a synthesis the labour ends.
Now mark me! those divine men of old time
Have reached, thou sayest well, each at one point
The outside verge that rounds our faculty;
And where they reached, who can do more than reach?
It takes but little water just to touch
At some one point the inside of a sphere,
And, as we turn the sphere, touch all the rest
In due succession: but the finer air
Which not so palpably nor obviously,
Though no less universally, can touch
The whole circumference of that emptied sphere,
Fills it more fully than the water did;
Holds thrice the weight of water in itself
Resolved into a subtler element.
And yet the vulgar call the sphere first full
Up to the visible height — and after, void;
Not knowing air's more hidden properties.
And thus our soul, misknown, cries out to Zeus
To vindicate his purpose in our life:
Why stay we on the earth unless to grow?
Long since, I imaged, wrote the fiction out,
That he or other god descended here
And, once for all, showed simultaneously
What, in its nature, never can be shown
Piecemeal or in succession; — showed, I say,
The worth both absolute and relative
Of all his children from the birth of time,
His instruments for all appointed work.
I now go on to image, — might we hear
The judgment which should give the due to each,
Show where the labour lay and where the ease,
And prove Zeus' self, the latent everywhere!
This is a dream: — but no dream, let us hope,

[123] scales

That years and days, the summers and the springs,
Follow each other with unwaning powers.
The grapes which dye thy wine are richer far
Through culture, than the wild wealth of the rock;
The suave plum than the savage-tasted drupe;[124]
The pastured honey-bee drops choicer sweet;
The flowers turn double, and the leaves turn flowers;
That young and tender crescent-moon, thy slave,
Sleeping above her robe as buoyed by clouds,
Refines upon the women of my youth.
What, and the soul alone deteriorates?
I have not chanted verse like Homer, no—
Nor swept string like Terpander,[125] no—nor carved
And painted men like Phidias and his friend:
I am not great as they are, point by point.
But I have entered into sympathy
With these four, running these into one soul,
Who, separate, ignored each others' art.
Say, is it nothing that I know them all?
The wild flower was the larger; I have dashed
Rose-blood upon its petals, pricked its cup's
Honey with wine, and driven its seed to fruit,
And show a better flower if not so large:
I stand myself. Refer this to the gods
Whose gift alone it is! which, shall I dare
(All pride apart) upon the absurd pretext
That such a gift by chance lay in my hand,
Discourse of lightly or depreciate?
It might have fallen to another's hand: what then?
I pass too surely: let at least truth stay!

[124] Fruit containing a stone (here the 'wild plum').
[125] Musician of the seventh century, B.C.; the 'father of Greek music.'

And next, of what thou followest on to ask.
This being with me as I declare, O king,
My works, in all these varicoloured kinds,
So done by me, accepted so by men—
Thou askest if (my soul thus in men's hearts)
I must not be accounted to attain
The very crown and proper end of life?
Inquiring theme how, now life closeth up,
I face death with success in my right hand:
Whether I fear death less than dost thyself
The fortunate of men? 'For' (writest thou)
'Thou leavest much behind, while I leave nought.
Thy life stays in the poems men shall sing,
The pictures men shall study; while my life,
Complete and whole now in its power and joy,
Dies altogether with my brain and arm,
Is lost indeed; since, what survives myself?
The brazen statue to o'erlook my grave,
Set on the promontory which I named.
And that—some supple courtier of my heir
Shall use its robed and sceptred arm, perhaps,
To fix the rope to, which best drags it down.
I go then: triumph thou, who dost not go!'

Nay, thou art worthy of hearing my whole mind.
Is this apparent, when thou turn'st to muse
Upon the scheme of earth and man in chief,
That admiration grows as knowledge grows?
That imperfection means perfection hid,
Reserved in part, to grace the after-time?
If, in the morning of philosophy,

Ere aught had been recorded, nay perceived,
Thou, with the light now in thee, couldst have looked
On all earth's tenantry, from worm to bird,
Ere man, her last, appeared upon the stage —
Thou wouldst have seen them perfect, and deduced
The perfectness of others yet unseen.
Conceding which, — had Zeus then questioned thee
'Shall I go on a step, improve on this,
Do more for visible creatures than is done?'
Thou wouldst have answered, 'Ay, by making each
Grow conscious in himself — by that alone.
All 's perfect else: the shell sucks fast the rock,
The fish strikes through the sea, the snake both swims
And slides, forth range the beasts, the birds take flight,
Till life's mechanics can no further go —
And all this joy in natural life is put
Like fire from off thy finger into each,
So exquisitely perfect is the same.
But 't is pure fire, and they mere matter are;
It has them, not they it: and so I choose
For man, Thy last premeditated work
(If I might add a glory to the scheme)
That a third thing should stand apart from both,
A quality arise within his soul,
Which, intro-active, made to supervise
And feel the force it has, may view itself,
And so be happy.' Man might live at first
The animal life: but is there nothing more?
In due time, let him critically learn
How he lives; and, the more he gets to know
Of his own life's adaptabilities,
The more joy-giving will his life become.
Thus man, who hath this quality, is best.

But thou, king, hadst more reasonably said:
'Let progress end at once, — man make no step
Beyond the natural man, the better beast,
Using his senses, not the sense of sense.'
In man there 's failure, only since he left
The lower and inconscious forms of life.
We called it an advance, the rendering plain
Man's spirit might grow conscious of man's life,
And, by new lore so added to the old,
Take each step higher over the brute's head.
This grew the only life, the pleasure-house,
Watch-tower and treasure-fortress of the soul,
Which whole surrounding flats of natural life
Seemed only fit to yield subsistence to;
A tower that crowns a country. But alas,
The soul now climbs it just to perish there!
For thence we have discovered ('t is no dream —
We know this, which we had not else perceived)
That there 's a world of capability
For joy, spread round about us, meant for us,
Inviting us; and still the soul craves all,
And still the flesh replies, 'Take no jot more
Than ere thou clombst the tower to look abroad!
Nay, so much less as that fatigue has brought
Deduction to it.' We struggle, fain to enlarge
Our bounded physical recipiency,
Increase our power, supply fresh oil to life,
Repair the waste of age and sickness: no,
It skills not! life 's inadequate to joy,
As the soul sees joy, tempting life to take.

They praise a fountain in my garden here
Wherein a Naiad sends the water-bow
Thin from her tube; she smiles to see it rise.
What if I told her, it is just a thread
From that great river which the hills shut up,
And mock her with my leave to take the same?
The artificer has given her one small tube
Past power to widen or exchange — what boots
To know she might spout oceans if she could?
She cannot lift beyond her first thin thread:
And so a man can use but a man's joy
While he sees God's. Is it, for Zeus to boast,
'See, man, how happy I live, and despair —
That I may be still happier — for thy use!'
If this were so, we could not thank our lord,
As hearts beat on to doing: 'tis not so —
Malice it is not. Is it carelessness?
Still, no. If care — where is the sign? I ask,
And get no answer, and agree in sum,
O king, with thy profound discouragement,
Who seest the wider but to sigh the more.
Most progress is most failure: thou sayest well.

The last point now: — thou dost except a case —
Holding joy not impossible to one
With artist-gifts — to such a man as I
Who leave behind me living works indeed;
For, such a poem, such a painting lives.
What? dost thou verily trip upon a word,
Confound the accurate view of what joy is
(Caught somewhat clearer by my eyes than thine)
With feeling joy? confound the knowing how
And showing how to live (my faculty)
With actually living? — Otherwise
Where is the artist's vantage o'er the king?
Because in my great epos I display
How divers men young, strong, fair, wise, can act —
Is this as though I acted? if I paint,
Carve the young Phoebus, am I therefore young?
Methinks I'm older that I bowed myself
The many years of pain that taught me art!
Indeed, to know is something, and to prove
How all this beauty might be enjoyed, is more:
But, knowing nought, to enjoy is something too.
Yon rower, with the moulded muscles there,
Lowering the sail, is nearer it than I.
I can write love-odes: thy fair slave's an ode.
I get to sing of love, when grown too grey
For being beloved: she turns to that young man,
The muscles all a-ripple on his back.
I know the joy of kingship: well, thou art king!

'But,' sayest thou — (and I marvel, I repeat,
To find thee trip on such a mere word) 'what
Thou writest, paintest, stays; that does not die:
Sappho survives, because we sing her songs,
And Aeschylus, because we read his plays!'
Why, if they live still, let them come and take
Thy slave in my despite, drink from thy cup,
Speak in my place. Thou diest while I survive?
Say rather that my fate is deadlier still,
In this, that every day my sense of joy
Grows more acute, my soul (intensified
By power and insight) more enlarged, more keen;
While every day my hairs fall more and more,

My hand shakes, and the heavy years increase —
The horror quickening still from year to year,
The consummation coming past escape,
When I shall know most, and yet least enjoy —
When all my works wherein I prove my worth,
Being present still to mock me in men's mouths,
Alive still, in the phrase of such as thou,
I, I the feeling, thinking, acting man,
The man who loved his life so over-much,
Sleep in my urn. It is so horrible,
I dare at times imagine to my need
Some future state revealed to us by Zeus,
Unlimited in capability
For joy, as this is in desire for joy,
— To seek which, the joy-hunger forces us:
That, stung by straitness of our life, made strait
On purpose to make prized the life at large —
Freed by the throbbing impulse we call death,
We burst there as the worm into the fly,
Who, while a worm still, wants his wings. But no!
Zeus has not yet revealed it; and, alas,
He must have done so, were it possible!

Live long and happy, and in that thought die:
Glad for what was! Farewell. And for the rest,
I cannot tell thy messenger aright
Where to deliver what he bears of thine
To one called Paulus; we have heard his fame
Indeed, if Christus be not one with him —
I know not, nor am troubled much to know.
Thou canst not think a mere barbarian Jew,
As Paulus proves to be, one circumcised,
Hath access to a secret shut from us?
Thou wrongest our philosophy, O king,
In stooping to inquire of such an one,
As if his answer could impose at all!
He writeth, doth he? well, and he may write.
Oh, the Jew findeth scholars! certain slaves
Who touched on this same isle, preached him and Christ;
And (as I gathered from a bystander)
Their doctrine could be held by no sane man.

[1855]

ONE WORD MORE [126]

TO E. B. B.

[*London, September,*] 1855

I

THERE they are, my fifty men and women
Naming me the fifty poems finished!
Take them, Love, the book and me together:
Where the heart lies, let the brain lie also.

II

Rafael [127] made a century of sonnets,
Made and wrote them in a certain volume
Dinted with the silver-pointed pencil
Else he only used to draw Madonnas:
These, the world might view — but one, the volume.
Who that one, you ask? Your heart instructs you.
Did she live and love it all her life-time?
Did she drop, his lady of the sonnets,[128]
Die, and let it drop beside her pillow
Where it lay in place of Rafael's glory,
Rafael's cheek so duteous and so loving —

[126] This poem, addressed to Mrs. Browning, was appended to *Men and Women*, 1855.

[127] Only four of Raphael's sonnets exist, and there is no certainty about the others ever having existed.

[128] Supposedly 'Margherita,' who figured in several of Raphael's paintings.

Cheek, the world was wont to hail a painter's,
Rafael's cheek, her love had turned a poet's?

III

You and I would rather read that volume,
(Taken to his beating bosom by it)
Lean and list the bosom-beats of Rafael,
Would we not? than wonder at Madonnas —
Her, San Sisto names, and Her, Foligno,
Her, that visits Florence in a vision,
Her, that 's left with lilies in the Louvre — [129]
Seen by us and all the world in circle.

IV

You and I will never read that volume.
Guido Reni, like his own eye's apple
Guarded long the treasure-book and loved it.[130]
Guido Reni dying, all Bologna
Cried, and the world cried too, 'Ours, the treasure!'
Suddenly, as rare things will, it vanished.

V

Dante once prepared to paint an angel: [131]
Whom to please? You whisper 'Beatrice.'
While he mused and traced it and retraced it,
(Peradventure with a pen corroded
Still by drops of that hot ink he dipped for,
When, his left-hand i' the hair o' the wicked,
Back he held the brow and pricked its stigma,
Bit into the live man's flesh for parchment,
Loosed him, laughed to see the writing rankle,
Let the wretch go festering through Florence) [132] —
Dante, who loved well because he hated,
Hated wickedness that hinders loving,
Dante standing, studying his angel, —
In there broke the folk of his Inferno.
Says he — 'Certain people of importance'
(Such he gave his daily dreadful line to)
'Entered and would seize, forsooth, the poet.'
Says the poet — 'Then I stopped my painting.'

VI

You and I would rather see that angel,
Painted by the tenderness of Dante,
Would we not? — than read a fresh Inferno.

VII

You and I will never see that picture.
While he mused on love and Beatrice,
While he softened o'er his outlined angel,
In they broke, those 'people of importance:'
We and Bice [133] bear the loss for ever.

VIII

What of Rafael's sonnets, Dante's picture?
This: no artist lives and loves, that longs not
Once, and only once, and for one only,
(Ah, the prize!) to find his love a language
Fit and fair and simple and sufficient —
Using nature that 's an art to others,
Not, this one time, art that 's turned his nature.
Ay, of all the artists living, loving,
None but would forego his proper dowry, —
Does he paint? he fain would write a poem, —
Does he write? he fain would paint a picture,

---

[129] These are, in order, the *Sistine Madonna*, at Dresden; the *Madonna of Foligno*, in the Vatican at Rome; the *Madonna del Granduca*, in the Pitti Palace, Florence; and *La Belle Jardinière* in the Louvre, Paris. The *Madonna del Granduca* is shown appearing to a worshiper in a vision.

[130] The book owned by Guido Reni, the artist, contained one hundred designs by Raphael, but no sonnets.

[131] At the close of the *Vita Nuova*, Dante says that on the first anniversary of Beatrice's death he wished to paint an angel in commemoration of her. He was interrupted, as he adds, 'by certain people of importance.'

[132] See *Inferno*, cantos 32–33.

[133] Beatrice

Put to proof art alien to the artist's,
Once, and only once, and for one only,
So to be the man and leave the artist,
Gain the man's joy, miss the artist's sorrow.

IX

Wherefore? Heaven's gift takes earth's abatement!
He who smites the rock [134] and spreads the water,
Bidding drink and live a crowd beneath him,
Even he, the minute makes immortal,
Proves, perchance, but mortal in the minute,
Desecrates, belike, the deed in doing.
While he smites, how can he but remember,
So he smote before, in such a peril,
When they stood and mocked — 'Shall smiting help us?'
When they drank and sneered — 'A stroke is easy!'
When they wiped their mouths and went their journey,
Throwing him for thanks — 'But drought was pleasant.'
Thus old memories mar the actual triumph;
Thus the doing savours of disrelish;
Thus achievement lacks a gracious somewhat;
O'er-importuned brows becloud the mandate,
Carelessness or consciousness, the gesture.
For he bears an ancient wrong about him,
Sees and knows again those phalanxed faces,
Hears, yet one time more, the 'customed prelude —
'How shouldst thou, of all men, smite, and save us?'
Guesses what is like to prove the sequel —
'Egypt's flesh-pots — nay, the drought was better.'

[134] For the story of Moses and the smiting of the rock, see *Exodus*, xvi–xix, and *Numbers*, xx.

X

Oh, the crowd must have emphatic warrant!
Theirs, the Sinai-forehead's cloven brilliance,
Right-arm's rod-sweep, tongue's imperial fiat.
Never dares the man put off the prophet.

XI

Did he love one face from out the thousands,
(Were she Jethro's daughter,[135] white and wifely,
Were she but the Æthiopian bondslave,) [136]
He would envy yon dumb patient camel,
Keeping a reserve of scanty water
Meant to save his own life in the desert;
Ready in the desert to deliver
(Kneeling down to let his breast be opened)
Hoard and life together for his mistress.

XII

I shall never, in the years remaining,
Paint you pictures, no, nor carve you statues,
Make you music that should all-express me;
So it seems: I stand on my attainment.
This of verse alone, one life allows me;
Verse and nothing else have I to give you.
Other heights in other lives, God willing:
All the gifts from all the heights, your own, Love!

XIII

Yet a semblance of resource avails us —
Shade so finely touched, love's sense must seize it.
Take these lines, look lovingly and nearly,
Lines I write the first time and the last time.[137]

[135] Zipporah, the wife of Moses.
[136] The Ethiopian wife of Moses (*Numbers*, xii, 1).
[137] In this poem alone Browning has written in unrhymed five-foot trochaics.

He who works in fresco, steals a hair-brush,
Curbs the liberal hand, subservient proudly,
Cramps his spirit, crowds its all in little,
Makes a strange art of an art familiar,
Fills his lady's missal-marge with flowerets.
He who blows thro' bronze, may breathe thro' silver,
Fitly serenade a slumbrous princess.
He who writes, may write for once as I do.

XIV

Love, you saw me gather men and women,
Live or dead or fashioned by my fancy,
Enter each and all, and use their service,
Speak from every mouth, — the speech, a poem.
Hardly shall I tell my joys and sorrows,
Hopes and fears, belief and disbelieving:
I am mine and yours — the rest be all men's,
Karshish,[138] Cleon, Norbert[139] and the fifty.
Let me speak this once in my true person,
Not as Lippo, Roland or Andrea,
Though the fruit of speech be just this sentence:
Pray you, look on these my men and women,
Take and keep my fifty poems finished;
Where my heart lies, let my brain lie also!
Poor the speech; be how I speak, for all things.

XV

Not but that you know me! Lo, the moon's self!
Here in London, yonder late in Florence,
Still we find her face, the thrice-transfigured.[140]
Curving on a sky imbrued with colour,
Drifted over Fiesole by twilight,
Came she, our new crescent of a hair's-breadth.
Full she flared it, lamping Samminiato,[141]
Rounder 'twixt the cypresses and rounder,
Perfect till the nightingales applauded.
Now, a piece of her old self, impoverished,
Hard to greet, she traverses the houseroofs,
Hurries with unhandsome thrift of silver,
Goes dispiritedly, glad to finish.

XVI

What, there 's nothing in the moon noteworthy?
Nay: for if that moon could love a mortal,
Use, to charm him (so to fit a fancy),
All her magic ('t is the old sweet mythos),[142]
She would turn a new side to her mortal,
Side unseen of herdsman, huntsman, steersman —
Blank to Zoroaster[143] on his terrace,
Blind to Galileo on his turret,
Dumb to Homer, dumb to Keats — him, even!
Think, the wonder of the moonstruck mortal —
When she turns round, comes again in heaven,
Opens out anew for worse or better!
Proves she like some portent of an iceberg
Swimming full upon the ship it founders,
Hungry with huge teeth of splintered crystals?
Proves she as the paved work of a sapphire
Seen by Moses when he climbed the mountain?
Moses, Aaron, Nadab and Abihu
Climbed and saw the very God, the Highest,[144]
Stand upon the paved work of a sapphire.
Like the bodied heaven in his clearness
Shone the stone, the sapphire of that paved work,

[138] 'Karshook,' the original reading, referred evidently to *Ben Karshook's Wisdom*, written in April 1854, but not included in *Men and Women*. Browning finally substituted 'Karshish' because of one of the 1855 poems, *An Epistle Containing the Strange Medical Experience of Karshish, the Arab Physician*.

[139] Character from *In a Balcony*. All the references are to poems published in the 1855 volume.

[140] They had seen the new moon in Florence; now in London, the last quarter.

[141] San Miniato, a church on the hill above Florence, opposite Fiesole.

[142] Of Endymion, celebrated in Keats's poem.

[143] Founder of the Persian religion and student of the stars.

[144] See *Exodus*, xxiv, 9–10.

When they ate and drank and saw God also!

XVII

What were seen? None knows, none ever shall know.
Only this is sure — the sight were other,
Not the moon's same side, born late in Florence,
Dying now impoverished here in London.
God be thanked, the meanest of his creatures
Boasts two soul-sides, one to face the world with,
One to show a woman when he loves her!

XVIII

This I say of me, but think of you, Love!
This to you — yourself my moon of poets!
Ah, but that 's the world's side, there 's the wonder,
Thus they see you, praise you, think they know you!
There, in turn I stand with them and praise you —
Out of my own self, I dare to phrase it.
But the best is when I glide from out them,
Cross a step or two of dubious twilight,
Come out on the other side, the novel
Silent silver lights and darks undreamed of,
Where I hush and bless myself with silence.

XIX

Oh, their Rafael of the dear Madonnas,
Oh, their Dante of the dread Inferno,
Wrote one song — and in my brain I sing it,
Drew one angel — borne, see, on my bosom!

R. B.

Ben Karshook's Wisdom [145]

I

'Would a man 'scape the rod?'
Rabbi Ben Karshook saith,
'See that he turn to God
The day before his death.'

'Ay, could a man inquire
When it shall come!' I say.
The Rabbi's eye shoots fire —
'Then let him turn to-day!'

II

Quoth a young Sadducee: [146]
'Reader of many rolls,
Is it so certain we
Have, as they tell us, souls?'

'Son, there is no reply!'
The Rabbi bit his beard;
'Certain, a soul have *I* —
We may have none,' he sneered.

Thus Karshook, the Hiram's-Hammer,[147]
The Right-hand Temple-column,
Taught babes in grace their grammar,
And struck the simple, solemn.

Abt Vogler [148]

(AFTER HE HAS BEEN EXTEMPORIZING UPON THE MUSICAL INSTRUMENT OF HIS INVENTION) [149]

I

Would that the structure brave, the manifold music I build,
Bidding my organ obey, calling its keys to their work,
Claiming each slave of the sound, at a touch, as when Solomon willed [150]

---

[145] Written 27 April 1854, and published in *The Keepsake*, an annual edited by Browning's friend, Miss Power, for whom he violated his usual custom of never contributing to magazines. 'Karshook' (Hebrew for 'thistle') is an imaginary character.

[146] Jews, largely aristocratic priests, who denied the Resurrection and the immortality of the soul.

[147] See *I Kings*, vii, 13–22. Hiram, king of Phoenicia, and skilled artisan in brass on Solomon's Temple, set up two pillars; the right one, Jachin, signified stability.

[148] This and the three following poems were published in *Dramatis Personae*, 1864.

[149] George Joseph Vogler (1749–1814), a Catholic priest, was noted as a musician and composer, and as the inventor of a small organ called the orchestrion. Browning's music teacher, John Relfe, had been a pupil of Vogler's.

[150] Jewish tradition credited Solomon with these powers because of a seal bearing 'the ineffable name' of God.

Armies of angels that soar, legions of demons that lurk,
Man, brute, reptile, fly, — alien of end and of aim,
Adverse, each from the other heaven-high, hell-deep removed, —
Should rush into sight at once as he named the ineffable Name,
And pile him a palace straight, to pleasure the princess he loved!

II

Would it might tarry like his, the beautiful building of mine,
This which my keys in a crowd pressed and importuned to raise!
Ah, one and all, how they helped, would dispart now and now combine,
Zealous to hasten the work, heighten their master his praise!
And one would bury his brow with a blind plunge down to hell,
Burrow awhile and build, broad on the roots of things,
Then up again swim into sight, having based me my palace well,
Founded it, fearless of flame, flat on the nether springs.

III

And another would mount and march, like the excellent minion he was,
Ay, another and yet another, one crowd but with many a crest,
Raising my rampired [151] walls of gold as transparent as glass,
Eager to do and die, yield each his place to the rest:
For higher still and higher (as a runner tips with fire,
When a great illumination surprises a festal night —
Outlining round and round Rome's dome [152] from space to spire)
Up, the pinnacled glory reached, and the pride of my soul was in sight.

[151] With ramparts.
[152] St. Peter's.

IV

In sight? Not half! for it seemed, it was certain, to match man's birth,
Nature in turn conceived, obeying an impulse as I;
And the emulous heaven yearned down, made effort to reach the earth,
As the earth had done her best, in my passion, to scale the sky:
Novel splendours burst forth, grew familiar and dwelt with mine,
Not a point nor peak but found and fixed its wandering star;
Meteor-moons, balls of blaze: and they did not pale nor pine,
For earth had attained to heaven, there was no more near nor far.

V

Nay more; for there wanted not who walked in the glare and glow,
Presences plain in the place; or, fresh from the Protoplast,[153]
Furnished for ages to come, when a kindlier wind should blow,
Lured now to begin and live, in a house to their liking at last;
Or else the wonderful Dead who have passed through the body and gone,
But were back once more to breathe in an old world worth their new:
What never had been, was now; what was, as it shall be anon;
And what is, — shall I say, matched both? for I was made perfect too.

VI

All through my keys that gave their sounds to a wish of my soul,
All through my soul that praised as its wish flowed visibly forth,
All through music and me! For think, had I painted the whole,
Why, there it had stood, to see, nor the process so wonder-worth:
Had I written the same, made verse — still effect proceeds from cause,

[153] The first and model creation.

Ye know why the forms are fair, ye hear how the tale is told;
It is all triumphant art, but art in obedience to laws,
Painter and poet are proud in the artist-list enrolled:—

VII

But here is the finger of God, a flash of the will that can,
Existent behind all laws, that made them and, lo, they are!
And I know not if, save in this, such gift be allowed to man,
That out of three sounds he frame, not a fourth sound, but a star.
Consider it well: each tone of our scale in itself is nought;
It is everywhere in the world—loud, soft, and all is said:
Give it to me to use! I mix it with two in my thought:
And, there! Ye have heard and seen: consider and bow the head!

VIII

Well, it is gone at last, the palace of music I reared;
Gone! and the good tears start, the praises that come too slow;
For one is assured at first, one scarce can say that he feared,
That he even gave it a thought, the gone thing was to go.
Never to be again! But many more of the kind
As good, nay, better perchance: is this your comfort to me?
To me, who must be saved because I cling with my mind
To the same, same self, same love, same God: ay, what was, shall be.

IX

Therefore to whom turn I but to thee, the ineffable Name?
Builder and maker, thou, of houses not made with hands!
What, have fear of change from thee who art ever the same?
Doubt that thy power can fill the heart that thy power expands?
There shall never be one lost good! What was, shall live as before;
The evil is null, is nought, is silence implying sound;
What was good shall be good, with, for evil, so much good more;
On the earth the broken arcs; in the heaven, a perfect round.

X

All we have willed or hoped or dreamed of good shall exist;
Not its semblance, but itself; no beauty, nor good, nor power
Whose voice has gone forth, but each survives for the melodist
When eternity affirms the conception of an hour.
The high that proved too high, the heroic for earth too hard,
The passion that left the ground to lose itself in the sky,
Are music sent up to God by the lover and the bard;
Enough that he heard it once: we shall hear it by-and-by.

XI

And what is our failure here but a triumph's evidence
For the fullness of the days? Have we withered or agonized?
Why else was the pause prolonged but that singing might issue thence?
Why rushed the discords in but that harmony should be prized?
Sorrow is hard to bear, and doubt is slow to clear,
Each sufferer says his say, his scheme of the weal and woe:
But God has a few of us whom he whispers in the ear;
The rest may reason and welcome: 'tis we musicians know.

XII

Well, it is earth with me; silence resumes her reign:
I will be patient and proud, and soberly acquiesce.
Give me the keys. I feel for the common chord[154] again,
Sliding by semitones, till I sink to the minor, — yes,
And I blunt it into a ninth, and I stand on alien ground,
Surveying a while the heights I rolled from into the deep;
Which, hark, I have dared and done, for my resting-place is found,
The C Major of this life: so, now I will try to sleep.

Rabbi Ben Ezra[155]

I

Grow old along with me!
The best is yet to be,
The last of life, for which the first was made:
Our times are in His hand
Who saith 'A whole I planned,
Youth shows but half; trust God: see all nor be afraid!'

II

Not that, amassing flowers,
Youth sighed 'Which rose make ours,
Which lily leave and then as best recall?'
Not that, admiring stars,
It yearned 'Nor Jove, nor Mars;
Mine be some figured flame which blends, transcends them all!'

III

Not for such hopes and fears
Annulling youth's brief years,
Do I remonstrate: folly wide the mark!
Rather I prize the doubt
Low kinds exist without,
Finished and finite clods, untroubled by a spark.

IV

Poor vaunt of life indeed,
Were man but formed to feed
On joy, to solely seek and find and feast:
Such feasting ended, then
As sure an end to men;
Irks care the crop-full bird? Frets doubt the maw-crammed beast?

V

Rejoice we are allied
To That which doth provide
And not partake, effect and not receive!
A spark disturbs our clod;
Nearer we hold of God
Who gives, than of His tribes that take, I must believe.

VI

Then, welcome each rebuff
That turns earth's smoothness rough,
Each sting that bids nor sit nor stand but go!
Be our joys three-parts pain!
Strive, and hold cheap the strain;
Learn, nor account the pang; dare, never grudge the throe!

VII

For thence, — a paradox
Which comforts while it mocks, —
Shall life succeed in that it seems to fail:
What I aspired to be,
And was not, comforts me:
A brute I might have been, but would not sink i' the scale.

---

[154] He wishes now to descend from the heights — by minors and complicated harmonies — until he strikes C major, which has no sharps or flats. The common chord, the keynote with a third and fifth, contains 'the rudiments of all music.'

[155] Rabbi Ben Ezra was a learned philosopher, physician, grammarian, astronomer, and poet of the twelfth century, whose ideas — highly congenial to Browning — are well set forth in the poem. There is an obvious but revealing comparison to be made with Fitzgerald's *Rubáiyát of Omar Khayyám*, first published in 1859.

VIII

What is he but a brute
Whose flesh has soul to suit,
Whose spirit works lest arms and legs want play?
To man, propose this test —
Thy body at its best,
How far can that project thy soul on its lone way?

IX

Yet gifts should prove their use:
I own the Past profuse
Of power each side, perfection every turn:
Eyes, ears took in their dole,
Brain treasured up the whole;
Should not the heart beat once 'How good to live and learn?'

X

Not once beat 'Praise be Thine!
I see the whole design,
I, who saw power, see now love perfect too:
Perfect I call Thy plan:
Thanks that I was a man!
Maker, remake, complete, — I trust what Thou shalt do!'

XI

For pleasant is this flesh;
Our soul, in its rose-mesh
Pulled ever to the earth, still yearns for rest;
Would we some prize might hold
To match those manifold
Possessions of the brute, — gain most, as we did best!

XII

Let us not always say
'Spite of this flesh to-day
I strove, made head, gained ground upon the whole!'
As the bird wings and sings,
Let us cry 'All good things
Are ours, nor soul helps flesh more, now, than flesh helps soul!'

XIII

Therefore I summon age
To grant youth's heritage,
Life's struggle having so far reached its term:
Thence shall I pass, approved
A man, for ay removed
From the developed brute; a god though in the germ.

XIV

And I shall thereupon
Take rest, ere I be gone
Once more on my adventure brave and new:
Fearless and unperplexed,
When I wage battle next,
What weapons to select, what armour to indue.[156]

XV

Youth ended, I shall try
My gain or loss thereby;
Leave the fire ashes, what survives is gold:
And I shall weigh the same,
Give life its praise or blame:
Young, all lay in dispute; I shall know, being old.

XVI

For note, when evening shuts,
A certain moment cuts
The deed off, calls the glory from the grey:
A whisper from the west
Shoots — 'Add this to the rest,
Take it and try its worth: here dies another day.'

XVII

So, still within this life,
Though lifted o'er its strife,
Let me discern, compare, pronounce at last,
'This rage was right i' the main,
That acquiescence vain:
The Future I may face now I have proved the Past.'

---

[156] put on

XVIII

For more is not reserved
To man, with soul just nerved
To act to-morrow what he learns to-day:
Here, work enough to watch
The Master work, and catch
Hints of the proper craft, tricks of the tool's true play.

XIX

As it was better, youth
Should strive, through acts uncouth,
Toward making, than repose on aught found made:
So, better, age, exempt
From strife, should know, than tempt
Further. Thou waitedest age: wait death nor be afraid!

XX

Enough now, if the Right
And Good and Infinite
Be named here, as thou callest thy hand thine own,
With knowledge absolute,
Subject to no dispute
From fools that crowded youth, nor let thee feel alone.

XXI

Be there, for once and all,
Severed great minds from small,
Announced to each his station in the Past!
Was I, the world arraigned,
Were they, my soul disdained,
Right? Let age speak the truth and give us peace at last!

XXII

Now, who shall arbitrate?
Ten men love what I hate,
Shun what I follow, slight what I receive;
Ten, who in ears and eyes
Match me: we all surmise,
They this thing, and I that: whom shall my soul believe?

XXIII

Not on the vulgar mass
Called 'work,' must sentence pass,
Things done, that took the eye and had the price;
O'er which, from level stand,
The low world laid its hand,
Found straightway to its mind, could value in a trice:

XXIV

But all, the world's coarse thumb
And finger failed to plumb,
So passed in making up the main account;
All instincts immature,
All purposes unsure,
That weighed not as his work, yet swelled the man's amount:

XXV

Thoughts hardly to be packed
Into a narrow act,
Fancies that broke through language and escaped;
All I could never be,
All, men ignored in me,
This, I was worth to God, whose wheel the pitcher shaped.

XXVI

Ay, note that Potter's wheel,[157]
That metaphor! and feel
Why time spins fast, why passive lies our clay,—
Thou, to whom fools propound,
When the wine makes its round,
'Since life fleets, all is change; the Past gone, seize to-day!'

XXVII

Fool! All that is, at all,
Lasts ever, past recall;
Earth changes, but thy soul and God stand sure:

[157] The metaphor, which recalls the *Rubáiyát*, likewise strongly suggested by the entire stanza, could have come independently, of course, from *Isaiah*, lxiv, 8, and also from *Jeremiah*, xviii, 1–6.

What entered into thee,
That was, is, and shall be:
Time's wheel runs back or stops: Potter and clay endure.

XXVIII

He fixed thee mid this dance
Of plastic circumstance,
This Present, thou, forsooth, wouldst fain arrest:
Machinery just meant
To give thy soul its bent,
Try thee and turn thee forth, sufficiently impressed.

XXIX

What though the earlier grooves
Which ran the laughing loves
Around thy base, no longer pause and press?
What though, about thy rim,
Skull-things in order grim
Grow out, in graver mood, obey the sterner stress?

XXX

Look not thou down but up!
To uses of a cup,
The festal board, lamp's flash and trumpet's peal,
The new-wine's foaming flow,
The Master's lips aglow!
Thou, heaven's consummate cup, what need'st thou with earth's wheel?

XXXI

But I need, now as then,
Thee, God, who mouldest men;
And since, not even while the whirl was worst,
Did I,—to the wheel of life
With shapes and colours rife,
Bound dizzily,—mistake my end, to slake Thy thirst:

XXXII

So, take and use Thy work:
Amend what flaws may lurk,
What strain o' the stuff, what warpings past the aim!
My times be in Thy hand!
Perfect the cup as planned!
Let age approve of youth, and death complete the same!

[1864]

CALIBAN UPON SETEBOS;[158]

OR,

NATURAL THEOLOGY IN THE ISLAND

'THOU THOUGHTEST THAT I WAS ALTOGETHER SUCH A ONE AS THYSELF'[159]

['WILL sprawl,[160] now that the heat of day is best,
Flat on his belly in the pit's much mire,
With elbows wide, fists clenched to prop his chin.
And, while he kicks both feet in the cool slush,
And feels about his spine small eft-things course,
Run in and out each arm, and make him laugh:
And while above his head a pompion-plant,[161]
Coating the cave-top as a brow its eye,
Creeps down to touch and tickle hair and beard,
And now a flower drops with a bee inside,
And now a fruit to snap at, catch and crunch,—
He looks out o'er yon sea which sunbeams cross

[158] Caliban, in Shakespeare's *Tempest*, was the half-monster son of the witch Sycorax, who worshiped a god called Setebos, a Patagonian divinity, whom Caliban discerns as a god of caprice. Not only is the poem a satire on the anthropomorphic idea of God, but it also is a hit at Calvinism and the doctrine of 'election.'

[159] *Psalms*, l, 21.

[160] Caliban usually speaks of himself in the third person.

[161] A kind of pumpkin vine.

And recross till they weave a spider-web
(Meshes of fire, some great fish breaks at times)
And talks to his own self, howe'er he please,
Touching that other, whom his dam called God.
Because to talk about Him, vexes — ha,
Could He but know! and time to vex is now,
When talk is safer than in winter-time.
Moreover Prosper and Miranda sleep
In confidence he drudges at their task,
And it is good to cheat the pair, and gibe,
Letting the rank tongue blossom into speech.]

Setebos, Setebos, and Setebos!
'Thinketh, He dwelleth i' the cold o' the moon.

'Thinketh He made it, with the sun to match,
But not the stars; the stars came otherwise;
Only made clouds, winds, meteors, such as that:
Also this isle, what lives and grows thereon,
And snaky sea which rounds and ends the same.

'Thinketh, it came of being ill at ease:
He hated that He cannot change His cold,
Nor cure its ache. 'Hath spied an icy fish
That longed to 'scape the rock-stream where she lived,
And thaw herself within the lukewarm brine
O' the lazy sea her stream thrusts far amid,
A crystal spike 'twixt two warm walls of wave;
Only, she ever sickened, found repulse
At the other kind of water, not her life,
(Green-dense and dim-delicious, bred o' the sun)
Flounced back from bliss she was not born to breathe,
And in her old bounds buried her despair,
Hating and loving warmth alike: so He.
'Thinketh, He made thereat the sun, this isle,
Trees and the fowls here, beast and creeping thing.
Yon otter, sleek-wet, black, lithe as a leech;
Yon auk, one fire-eye in a ball of foam,
That floats and feeds; a certain badger brown
He hath watched hunt with that slant white-wedge eye
By moonlight; and the pie[162] with the long tongue
That pricks deep into oakwarts for a worm,
And says a plain word when she finds her prize,
But will not eat the ants; the ants themselves
That build a wall of seeds and settled stalks
About their hole — He made all these and more,
Made all we see, and us, in spite: how else?
He could not, Himself, make a second self
To be His mate; as well have made Himself:
He would not make what he mislikes or slights,
An eyesore to Him, or not worth His pains:
But did, in envy, listlessness or sport,
Make what Himself would fain, in a manner, be —
Weaker in most points, stronger in a few,
Worthy, and yet mere playthings all the while,
Things He admires and mocks too, — that is it.
Because, so brave, so better though they be,
It nothing skills if He begin to plague.
Look now, I melt a gourd-fruit into mash,
Add honeycomb and pods, I have perceived,
Which bite like finches when they bill and kiss, —
Then, when froth rises bladdery, drink up all,

[162] magpie

Quick, quick, till maggots scamper through my brain;
Last, throw me on my back i' the seeded thyme,
And wanton, wishing I were born a bird.
Put case, unable to be what I wish,
I yet could make a live bird out of clay:
Would not I take clay, pinch my Caliban
Able to fly? — for, there, see, he hath wings,
And great comb like the hoopoe's to admire,
And there, a sting to do his foes offence,
There, and I will that he begin to live,
Fly to yon rock-top, nip me off the horns
Of grigs [163] high up that make the merry din,
Saucy through their veined wings, and mind me not.
In which feat, if his leg snapped, brittle clay,
And he lay stupid-like, — why, I should laugh;
And if he, spying me, should fall to weep,
Beseech me to be good, repair his wrong,
Bid his poor leg smart less or grow again,—
Well, as the chance were, this might take or else
Not take my fancy: I might hear his cry,
And give the manikin three sound legs for one,
Or pluck the other off, leave him like an egg,
And lessoned he was mine and merely clay.
Were this no pleasure, lying in the thyme,
Drinking the mash, with brain become alive,
Making and marring clay at will? So He.

'Thinketh, such shows nor right nor wrong in Him,
Nor kind, nor cruel: He is strong and Lord.
'Am strong myself compared to yonder crabs
That march now from the mountain to the sea;
'Let twenty pass, and stone the twenty-first,
Loving not, hating not, just choosing so.
'Say, the first straggler that boasts purple spots
Shall join the file, one pincer twisted off;
'Say, this bruised fellow shall receive a worm,
And two worms he whose nippers end in red;
As it likes me each time, I do: so He.

Well then, 'supposeth He is good i' the main,
Placable if His mind and ways were guessed,
But rougher than His handiwork, be sure!
Oh, He hath made things worthier than Himself,
And envieth that, so helped, such things do more
Than He who made them! What consoles but this?
That they, unless through Him, do nought at all,
And must submit: what other use in things?
'Hath cut a pipe of pithless elder-joint
That, blown through, gives exact the scream o' the jay
When from her wing you twitch the feathers blue:
Sound this, and little birds that hate the jay
Flock within stone's throw, glad their foe is hurt:
Put case such pipe could prattle and boast forsooth
'I catch the birds, I am the crafty thing,
I make the cry my maker cannot make
With his great round mouth; he must blow through mine!'
Would not I smash it with my foot? So He.

But wherefore rough, why cold and ill at ease?
Aha, that is a question! Ask, for that,
What knows,—the something over Setebos
That made Him, or He, may be, found and fought,

[163] crickets

Worsted, drove off and did to nothing, perchance.
There may be something quiet o'er His head,
Out of His reach, that feels nor joy nor grief,
Since both derive from weakness in some way.
I joy because the quails come; would not joy
Could I bring quails here when I have a mind:
This Quiet, all it hath a mind to, doth.
'Esteemeth stars the outposts of its couch,
But never spends much thought nor care that way.
It may look up, work up, — the worse for those
It works on! 'Careth but for Setebos
The many-handed as a cuttle-fish,
Who, making Himself feared through what He does,
Looks up, first, and perceives He cannot soar
To what is quiet and hath happy life;
Next looks down here, and out of very spite
Makes this a bauble-world to ape yon real,
These good things to match those as hips do grapes.
'Tis solace making baubles, ay, and sport.
Himself peeped late, eyed Prosper at his books
Careless and lofty, lord now of the isle:
Vexed, 'stitched a book of broad leaves, arrow-shaped,
Wrote thereon, he knows what, prodigious words;
Has peeled a wand and called it by a name;
Weareth at whiles for an enchanter's robe
The eyed skin of a supple oncelot; [164]
And hath an ounce sleeker than youngling mole,
A four-legged serpent he makes cower and couch,
Now snarl, now hold its breath and mind his eye,
And saith she is Miranda and my wife:
'Keeps for his Ariel a tall pouch-bill crane
He bids go wade for fish and straight disgorge;
Also a sea-beast, lumpish, which he snared,
Blinded the eyes of, and brought somewhat tame,
And split its toe-webs, and now pens the drudge
In a hole o' the rock and calls him Caliban;
A bitter heart that bides its time and bites.
'Plays thus at being Prosper in a way,
Taketh his mirth with make-believes: so He.

His dam held that the Quiet made all things
Which Setebos vexed only: 'holds not so.
Who made them weak, meant weakness He might vex.
Had He meant other, while His hand was in,
Why not make horny eyes no thorn could prick,
Or plate my scalp with bone against the snow,
Or overscale my flesh 'neath joint and joint,
Like an orc's [165] armour? Ay, — so spoil His sport!
He is the One now: only He doth all.

'Saith, He may like, perchance, what profits Him.
Ay, himself loves what does him good; but why?
'Gets good no otherwise. This blinded beast
Loves whoso places flesh-meat on his nose,
But, had he eyes, would want no help, but hate
Or love, just as it liked him: He hath eyes.
Also it pleaseth Setebos to work,

[164] The ounce, or snow leopard.

[165] A sea-monster.

Use all His hands, and exercise much craft,
By no means for the love of what is worked.
'Tasteth, himself, no finer good i' the world
When all goes right, in this safe summer-time,
And he wants little, hungers, aches not much,
Than trying what to do with wit and strength.
'Falls to make something: 'piled yon pile of turfs,
And squared and stuck there squares of soft white chalk,
And, with a fish-tooth, scratched a moon on each,
And set up endwise certain spikes of tree,
And crowned the whole with a sloth's skull a-top,
Found dead i' the woods, too hard for one to kill.
No use at all i' the work, for work's sole sake;
'Shall some day knock it down again: so He.

'Saith He is terrible: watch His feats in proof!
One hurricane will spoil six good months' hope.
He hath a spite against me, that I know,
Just as He favours Prosper, who knows why?
So it is, all the same, as well I find.
'Wove wattles [166] half the winter, fenced them firm
With stone and stake to stop she-tortoises
Crawling to lay their eggs here: well, one wave,
Feeling the foot of Him upon its neck,
Gaped as a snake does, lolled out its large tongue,
And licked the whole labour flat: so much for spite.
'Saw a ball flame down late (yonder it lies)
Where, half an hour before, I slept i' the shade:
Often they scatter sparkles: there is force!
'Dug up a newt He may have envied once
And turned to stone, shut up inside a stone.
Please Him and hinder this? — What Prosper does?
Aha, if He would tell me how! Not He!
There is the sport: discover how or die!
All need not die, for of the things o' the isle
Some flee afar, some dive, some run up trees;
Those at His mercy, — why, they please Him most
When . . . when . . . well, never try the same way twice!
Repeat what act has pleased, He may grow wroth.
You must not know His ways, and play Him off,
Sure of the issue. 'Doth the like himself:
'Spareth a squirrel that it nothing fears
But steals the nut from underneath my thumb,
And when I threat, bites stoutly in defence:
'Spareth an urchin that contrariwise,
Curls up into a ball, pretending death
For fright at my approach: the two ways please.
But what would move my choler more than this,
That either creature counted on its life
To-morrow and next day and all days to come,
Saying, forsooth, in the inmost of its heart,
'Because he did so yesterday with me,
And otherwise with such another brute,
So must he do henceforth and always.' — Ay?
'Would teach the reasoning couple what 'must' means!
'Doth as he likes, or wherefore Lord? So He.

'Conceiveth all things will continue thus,
And we shall have to live in fear of Him

[166] twigs

So long as He lives, keeps His strength: no change,
If He have done His best, make no new world
To please Him more, so leave off watching this, —
If He surprise not even the Quiet's self
Some strange day, — or, suppose, grow into it
As grubs grow butterflies: else, here are we,
And there is He, and nowhere help at all.

'Believeth with the life, the pain shall stop.
His dam held different, that after death
He both plagued enemies and feasted friends:
Idly! He doth His worst in this our life,
Giving just respite lest we die through pain,
Saving last pain for worst, — with which, an end.
Meanwhile, the best way to escape His ire
Is, not to seem too happy. Sees, himself,
Yonder two flies, with purple films and pink,
Bask on the pompion-bell above: kills both.
'Sees two black painful beetles roll their ball
On head and tail as if to save their lives:
Moves them the stick away they strive to clear.

Even so, 'would have Him misconceive, suppose
This Caliban strives hard and ails no less,
And always, above all else, envies Him.
Wherefore he mainly dances on dark nights,
Moans in the sun, gets under holes to laugh,
And never speaks his mind save housed as now:
Outside, 'groans, curses. If He caught me here,
O'erheard this speech, and asked 'What chucklest at?'
'Would, to appease Him, cut a finger off,
Or of my three kid yearlings burn the best,
Or let the toothsome apples rot on tree,
Or push my tame beast for the orc to taste:
While myself lit a fire, and made a song
And sung it, '*What I hate, be consecrate*
To celebrate Thee and Thy state, no mate
For Thee; what see for envy in poor me?'
Hoping the while, since evils sometimes mend,
Warts rub away, and sores are cured with slime,
That some strange day, will either the Quiet catch
And conquer Setebos, or likelier He
Decrepit may doze, doze, as good as die.

[What, what? A curtain o'er the world at once!
Crickets stop hissing; not a bird — or, yes,
There scuds His raven that has told Him all!
It was fool's play, this prattling! Ha! The wind
Shoulders the pillared dust, death's house o' the move,
And fast invading fires begin! White blaze —
A tree's head snaps — and there, there, there, there, there, there,
His thunder follows! Fool to gibe at Him!
Lo! 'Lieth flat and loveth Setebos!
'Maketh his teeth meet through his upper lip,
Will let those quails fly, will not eat this month
One little mess of whelks, so he may 'scape!]

[1864]

Prospice[167]

FEAR death? — to feel the fog in my throat,
The mist in my face,

---

[167] Written shortly after the death of Mrs. Browning. It appeared, prior to its inclusion in *Dramatis Personae*, in *The Atlantic Monthly* for June 1864.

When the snows begin, and the blasts denote
  I am nearing the place,
The power of the night, the press of the storm,
  The post of the foe;
Where he stands, the Arch Fear in a visible form,
  Yet the strong man must go:
For the journey is done and the summit attained,
  And the barriers fall,
Though a battle's to fight ere the guerdon be gained,
  The reward of it all.
I was ever a fighter, so — one fight more,
  The best and the last!
I would hate that death bandaged my eyes, and forbore,
  And bade me creep past.
No! let me taste the whole of it, fare like my peers
  The heroes of old,
Bear the brunt, in a minute pay glad life's arrears
  Of pain, darkness and cold.
For sudden the worst turns the best to the brave,
  The black minute's at end,
And the element's rage, the fiend-voices that rave,
  Shall dwindle, shall blend,
Shall change, shall become first a peace out of pain
  Then a light, then thy breast,
O thou soul of my soul! I shall clasp thee again,
  And with God be the rest!

[1864]

THE RING AND THE BOOK

from Book I. *The Ring and the Book*[168]

O lyric Love, half-angel and half-bird,
And all a wonder and a wild desire, —
Boldest of hearts that ever braved the sun,
Took sanctuary within the holier blue,
And sang a kindred soul out to his face, —
Yet human at the red-ripe of the heart —
When the first summons from the darkling earth
Reached thee amid thy chambers, blanched their blue,
And bared them of the glory — to drop down,
To toil for man, to suffer or to die, —
This is the same voice: can thy soul know change?
Hail then, and hearken from the realms of help!
Never may I commence my song, my due
To God who best taught song by gift of thee,
Except with bent head and beseeching hand —
That still, despite the distance and the dark,

[168] In 1860, during a stroll through Florence, Browning discovered on an open bookstall 'The Old Yellow Book', recording a Roman murder case of 1698. At once he saw a story behind the dry legal facts, but did nothing about writing it, offering it to others as the theme of a possible novel. But after Mrs. Browning's death, when he stood in need of work, he returned to it. Begun in the latter months of 1864, the poem was published in four volumes, the first appearing in November 1868, and the remaining three in successive months. There are twelve books, in all over 21,000 lines, recounting the murder story from strangely different points of view — that of three citizens, that of each of the principals, that of two lawyers, and that of the Pope who was himself the final court of appeals. The psychological interest is the amazing frailty of human testimony, the demonstration that the worth to God is

'. . . all the world's coarse thumb
And finger failed to plumb,
So passed in making up the main account.'

But the true glory of the poem is its own elevation and beauty, a detective novel transmuted into one of the moving spiritual productions of our literature.

Synopsis: — Count Guido Franceschini, a nobleman of Arezzo, marries Pompilia Comparini, a young girl of unknown parentage, in order to obtain her money, the amount of which has been exaggerated. Pompilia's supposed mother confesses — she and her husband Pietro having been badly treated by Guido — that Pompilia is not actually her child, but one substituted to defraud the Comparini's proper heirs. Straightway Guido plans to get rid of his low-born wife, by accusing her of infidelity. Pompilia persuades a young priest, Canon Giuseppe Caponsacchi, whose life had been raised from trivial boredom and insincerity by the sudden sight of her at a theatre — and whom Guido had meanly tried to entrap and accuse as his wife's 'lover' —, to carry her from the horrors of Guido's house to her own home. Guido pursues and has them arrested. Pompilia, denying the charge of adultery, is sent to a convent; Caponsacchi is banished for three years. About to have a child, Pompilia is allowed to go to her old home. The baby is born and all seems happier for her, until one night Guido and four ruffians break in, kill the Comparini, and mortally wound her. Guido is brought to trial while Pompilia lies dying.

The closing lines of the first book are an invocation to Mrs. Browning.

What was, again may be; some interchange
Of grace, some splendour once thy very thought,
Some benediction anciently thy smile:
—Never conclude, but raising hand and head
Thither where eyes, that cannot reach, yet yearn
For all hope, all sustainment, all reward,
Their utmost up and on,—so blessing back
In those thy realms of help, that heaven thy home,
Some whiteness which, I judge, thy face makes proud,
Some wanness where, I think, thy foot may fall!

from Book VI. *Giuseppe Caponsacchi*[169]

I have done with being judged.
I stand here guiltless in thought, word and deed,
To the point that I apprise you,—in contempt
For all misapprehending ignorance
O' the human heart, much more the mind of Christ,—
That I assuredly did bow, was blessed
By the revelation of Pompilia. There!
Such is the final fact I fling you, Sirs,
To mouth and mumble and misinterpret: there!
'The priest 's in love,' have it the vulgar way!
Unpriest me, rend the rags o' the vestment, do—
Degrade deep, disenfranchise all you dare—
Remove me from the midst, no longer priest
And fit companion for the like of you—
Your gay Abati[170] with the well-turned leg
And rose i' the hat-rim, Canons, cross at neck
And silk mask in the pocket of the gown,
Brisk bishops with the world's musk still unbrushed
From the rochet;[171] I'll no more of these good things:
There 's a crack somewhere, something that's unsound
I' the rattle!

For Pompilia—be advised,
Build churches, go pray! You will find me there,
I know, if you come,—and you will come, I know.
Why, there's a Judge weeping! Did not I say
You were good and true at bottom? You see the truth—
I am glad I helped you: she helped me just so.

But for Count Guido,—you must counsel there!
I bow my head, bend to the very dust,
Break myself up in shame of faultiness.
I had him one whole moment, as I said—
As I remember, as will never out
O' the thoughts of me,—I had him in arm's reach
There,—as you stand, Sir, now you cease to sit,—
I could have killed him ere he killed his wife,
And did not: he went off alive and well
And then effected this last feat—through me!
Me—not through you—dismiss that fear! 'T was you
Hindered me staying here to save her,—not
From leaving you and going back to him
And doing service in Arezzo. Come,
Instruct me in procedure! I conceive—
In all due self-abasement might I speak—

[169] Although this book has priority in the poem, the selections given will be perhaps better read after Book VII, *Pompilia*. Caponsacchi, summoned again before the Court, tells his story while Pompilia is dying in the hospital. His narrative is finished and he now concludes with a passionate revelation of the new life he has gained through her. Note the striking contrast between his and Pompilia's attitude towards Guido.

[170] Ecclesiastic

[171] vestment

How you will deal with Guido: Oh, not death!
Death, if it let her life be: otherwise
Not death,—your lights will teach you clearer! I
Certainly have an instinct of my own
I' the matter: bear with me and weigh its worth!
Let us go away—leave Guido all alone
Back on the world again that knows him now!
I think he will be found (indulge so far!)
Not to die so much as slide out of life,
Pushed by the general horror and common hate
Low, lower,—left o' the very ledge of things,
I seem to see him catch convulsively
One by one at all honest forms of life,
At reason, order, decency and use—
To cramp him and get foothold by at least;
And still they disengage them from his clutch.
'What, you are he, then, had Pompilia once
'And so forwent her? Take not up with us!'
And thus I see him slowly and surely edged
Off all the table-land whence life upsprings
Aspiring to be immortality,
As the snake, hatched on hill-top by mischance,
Despite his wriggling, slips, slides, slidders down
Hill-side, lies low and prostrate on the smooth
Level of the outer place, lapsed in the vale:
So I lose Guido in the loneliness,
Silence and dusk, till at the doleful end,
At the horizontal line, creation's verge,
From what just is to absolute nothingness—
Whom is it, straining onward still, he meets?
What other man deep further in the fate,
Who, turning at the prize of a footfall
To flatter him and promise fellowship,
Discovers in the act a frightful face—
Judas, made monstrous by much solitude!
The two are at one now! Let them love their love
That bites and claws like hate, or hate their hate
That mops and mows and makes as it were love!
There, let them each tear each in devil's-fun,
Or fondle this the other while malice aches—
Both teach, both learn detestability!
Kiss him the kiss, Iscariot! Pay that back,
That smatch o' the slaver blistering on your lip—
By the better trick, the insult he spared Christ—
Lure him the lure o' the letters, Aretine![172]
Lick him o'er slimy-smooth with jelly-filth
O' the verse-and-prose pollution in love's guise!
The cockatrice is with the basilisk![173]
There let them grapple, denizens o' the dark,
Foes or friends, but indissolubly bound,
In their one spot out of the ken of God
Or care of man, for ever and ever more!

Why, Sirs, what's this? Why, this is sorry and strange!—
Futility, divigation: this from me
Bound to be rational, justify an act
Of sober man!—whereas, being moved so much,
I give you cause to doubt the lady's mind:
A pretty sarcasm for the world! I fear
You do her wit injustice,—all through me!
Like my fate all through,—ineffective help!
A poor rash advocate I prove myself.
You might be angry with good cause: but sure
At the advocate,—only at the undue zeal
That spoils the force of his own plea, I think?

[172] Guido, *i.e.*, 'from Arezzo.'

[173] These fabulous monsters were believed to kill merely with a look.

My part was just to tell you how things stand,
State facts and not be flustered at their fume.
But then 't is a priest speaks: as for love,—no!
If you let buzz a vulgar fly like that
About your brains, as if I loved, forsooth,
Indeed, Sirs, you do wrong! We had no thought
Of such infatuation, she and I:
There are many points that prove it: do be just!
I told you,—at one little roadside-place
I spent a good half-hour, paced to and fro
The garden; just to leave her free awhile,
I plucked a handful of Spring herb and bloom:
I might have sat beside her on the bench
Where the children were: I wish the thing had been,
Indeed: the event could not be worse, you know:
One more half-hour of her saved! She 's dead now, Sirs!
While I was running on at such a rate,
Friends should have plucked me by the sleeve: I went
Too much o' the trivial outside of her face
And the purity that shone there—plain to me,
Not to you, what more natural? Nor am I
Infatuated,—oh, I saw, be sure!
Her brow had not the right line, leaned too much,
Painters would say; they like the straight-up Greek:
This seemed bent somewhat with an invisible crown
Of martyr and saint, not such as art approves.
And how the dark orbs dwelt deep underneath,
Looked out of such a sad sweet heaven on me—
The lips, compressed a little, came forward too,
Careful for a whole world of sin and pain.
That was the face, her husband makes his plea,
He sought just to disfigure,—no offence
Beyond that! Sirs, let us be rational!
He needs must vindicate his honour,—ay,
Yet shirks, the coward, in a clown's disguise,
Away from the scene, endeavours to escape.
Now, had he done so, slain and left no trace
O' the slayer,—what were vindicated, pray?
You had found his wife disfigured or a corpse,
For what and by whom? It is too palpable!
Then, here's another point involving law:
I use this argument to show you meant
No calumny against us by that title
O' the sentence,—liars try to twist it so:
What penalty it bore, I had to pay
Till further proof should follow of innocence—
Probationis ob defectum,[174]—proof?
How could you get proof without trying us?
You went through the preliminary form,
Stopped there, contrived this sentence to amuse
The adversary. If the title ran
For more than fault imputed and not proved,
That was a simple penman's error, else
A slip i' the phrase,—as when we say of you
'Charged with injustice'—which may either be
Or not be,—'t is a name that sticks meanwhile.
Another relevant matter: fool that I am!
Not what I wish true, yet a point friends urge:
It is not true,—yet, since friends think it helps,—
She only tried me when some others failed—

[174] For want of enough evidence.

Began with Conti, whom I told you of,
And Guillichini, Guido's kinsfolk both,
And when abandoned by them, not before,
Turned to me. That's conclusive why she turned.
Much good they got by the happy cowardice!
Conti is dead, poisoned a month ago:
Does that much strike you as a sin? Not much,
After the present murder, — one mark more
On the Moor's [175] skin, — what is black by blacker still?
Conti had come here and told truth. And so
With Guillichini; he 's condemned of course
To the galleys, as a friend in this affair,
Tried and condemned for no one thing i' the world,
A fortnight since by who but the Governor? —
The just judge, who refused Pompilia help
At first blush, being her husband's friend, you know.
There are two tales to suit the separate courts,
Arezzo and Rome: he tells you here, we fled
Alone, unhelped, — lays stress on the main fault,
The spiritual sin, Rome looks to: but elsewhere
He likes best we should break in, steal, bear off,
Be fit to brand and pillory and flog —
That 's the charge goes to the heart of the Governor:
If these unpriest me, you and I may yet
Converse, Vincenzo Marzi-Medici! [176]
Oh, Sirs, there are worse men than you I say!
More easily duped, I mean; this stupid lie,
Its liar never dared propound in Rome,
He gets Arezzo to receive, — nay more,
Gets Florence and the Duke to authorise!
This is their Rota's [177] sentence, their Granduke
Signs and seals! Rome for me henceforward — Rome,
Where better men are, — most of all, that man
The Augustinian of the Hospital, [178]
Who writes the letter, — he confessed, he says,
Many a dying person, never one
So sweet and true and pure and beautiful.
A good man! Will you make him Pope one day?
Not that he is not good too, this we have —
But old, — else he would have his word to speak,
His truth to teach the world: I thirst for truth,
But shall not drink it till I reach the source.

Sirs, I am quiet again. You see, we are
So very pitiable, she and I,
Who had conceivably been otherwise.
Forget distemperature and idle heat!
Apart from truth's sake, what 's to move so much?
Pompilia will be presently with God;
I am, on earth, as good as out of it,
A relegated priest; when exile ends,
I mean to do my duty and live long.
She and I are mere strangers now: but priests
Should study passion; how else cure mankind,
Who come for help in passionate extremes?
I do but play with an imagined life
Of who, unfettered by a vow, unblessed
By the higher call, — since you will have it so, —
Leads it companioned by the woman there.
To live, and see her learn, and learn by her,
Out of the low obscure and petty world —
Or only see one purpose and one will

[175] Othello's
[176] Governor of Arezzo, who heard the first trial.
[177] An ecclesiastical court of appeals.
[178] See *Pompilia*

Evolve themselves i' the world, change wrong to right:
To have to do with nothing but the true,
The good, the eternal — and these, not alone
In the main current of the general life,
But small experiences of every day,
Concerns of the particular hearth and home:
To learn not only by a comet's rush
But a rose's birth, — not by the grandeur, God —
But the comfort, Christ. All this, how far away!
Mere delectation, meet for a minute's dream! —
Just as a drudging student trims his lamp,
Opens his Plutarch, puts him in the place
Of Roman, Grecian; draws the patched gown close,
Dreams, 'Thus should I fight, save or rule the world!' —
Then smilingly, contentedly, awakes
To the old solitary nothingness.
So I, from such communion, pass content . . .

O great, just, good God! Miserable me!

Book VII. *Pompilia*[179]

I am just seventeen years and five months old,
And, if I lived one day more, three full weeks;
'T is writ so in the church's register,
Lorenzo in Lucina, all my names
At length, so many names for one poor child,
— Francesca Camilla Vittoria Angela
Pompilia Comparini, — laughable!
Also 't is writ that I was married there
Four years ago: and they will add, I hope,
When they insert my death, a word or two, —
Omitting all about the mode of death, —
This, in its place, this which one cares to know,
That I had been a mother of a son
Exactly two weeks. It will be through grace
O' the Curate, not through any claim I have;
Because the boy was born at, so baptized
Close to, the Villa, in the proper church:
A pretty church, I say no word against,
Yet stranger-like, — while this Lorenzo seems
My own particular place, I always say.
I used to wonder, when I stood scarce high
As the bed here, what the marble lion meant,
With half his body rushing from the wall,
Eating the figure of a prostrate man —
(To the right, it is, of entry by the door)
An ominous sign to one baptized like me,
Married, and to be buried there, I hope.
And they should add, to have my life complete,
He is a boy and Gaetan by name —
Gaetano, for a reason, — if the friar
Don Celestine[180] will ask this grace for me
Of Curate Ottoboni: he it was
Baptized me: he remembers my whole life
As I do his grey hair.

All these few things
I know are true, — will you remember them?
Because time flies. The surgeon cared for me,
To count my wounds, — twenty-two dagger-wounds,
Five deadly, but I do not suffer much —
Or too much pain, — and am to die to-night.

Oh how good God is that my babe was born,
— Better than born, baptized and hid away
Before this happened, safe from being hurt!
That had been sin God could not well forgive:

---

[179] Pompilia lies dying in the hospital; the time is 6 January 1698, four days after Guido's assault upon her.

[180] The monk who heard her confession and attended her in her last days. His tribute to her character is included in 'The Old Yellow Book,' wherein it much impressed Browning.

He was too young to smile and save himself.
When they took, two days after he was born,
My babe away from me to be baptized
And hidden awhile, for fear his foe should find, —
The country-woman, used to nursing babes,
Said 'Why take on so? where is the great loss?
'These next three weeks he will but sleep and feed,
'Only begin to smile at the month's end;
'He would not know you, if you kept him here,
'Sooner than that; so, spend three merry weeks
'Snug in the Villa, getting strong and stout,
'And then I bring him back to be your own,
'And both of you may steal to — we know where!'
The month — there wants of it two weeks this day!
Still, I half fancied when I heard the knock
At the Villa in the dusk, it might prove she —
Come to say 'Since he smiles before the time,
'Why should I cheat you out of one good hour?
'Back I have brought him; speak to him and judge!'
Now I shall never see him; what is worse,
When he grows up and gets to be my age,
He will seem hardly more than a great boy;
And if he asks 'What was my mother like?'
People may answer 'Like girls of seventeen' —
And how can he but think of this and that,
Lucias, Marias, Sofias, who titter or blush
When he regards them as such boys may do?
Therefore I wish some one will please to say
I looked already old though I was young;
Do I not . . . say, if you are by to speak . . .
Look nearer twenty? No more like, at least,
Girls who look arch or redden when boys laugh,
Than the poor Virgin that I used to know
At our street-corner in a lonely niche, —
The babe, that sat upon her knees, broke off, —
Thin white glazed clay, you pitied her the more:
She, not the gay ones, always got my rose.

How happy those are who know how to write!
Such could write what their son should read in time,
Had they a whole day to live out like me.
Also my name is not a common name,
'Pompilia,' and may help to keep apart
A little the thing I am from what girls are.
But then how far away, how hard to find
Will anything about me have become,
Even if the boy bethink himself and ask!
No father that he ever knew at all,
Nor ever had — no, never had, I say!
That is the truth, — nor any mother left,
Out of the little two weeks that she lived,
Fit for such memory as might assist:
As good too as no family, no name,
Not even poor old Pietro's name, nor hers,
Poor kind unwise Violante, since it seems
They must not be my parents any more.
That is why something put it in my head
To call the boy 'Gaetano' — no old name
For sorrow's sake; I looked up to the sky
And took a new saint [181] to begin anew.
One who has only been made saint — how long?
Twenty-five years: so, carefuller, perhaps,

[181] Gaetano, Archbishop of Teate, died in 1547, but was not canonized until 1671, by Pope Clement X.

To guard a namesake than those old saints grow,
Tired out by this time, — see my own five saints!

On second thoughts, I hope he will regard
The history of me as what someone dreamed,
And get to disbelieve it at the last:
Since to myself it dwindles fast to that,
Sheer dreaming and impossibility, —
Just in four days too! All the seventeen years,
Not once did a suspicion visit me
How very different a lot is mine
From any other woman's in the world.
The reason must be, 't was by step and step
It got to grow so terrible and strange:
These strange woes stole on tiptoe, as it were,
Into my neighbourhood and privacy,
Sat down where I sat, laid them where I lay;
And I was found familiarised with fear,
When friends broke in, held up a torch and cried
'Why, you Pompilia in the cavern thus,
'How comes that arm of yours about a wolf?
'And the soft length, — lies in and out your feet
'And laps you round the knee, — a snake it is!'
And so on.

Well, and they are right enough,
By the torch they hold up now: for first, observe,
I never had a father, — no, nor yet
A mother: my own boy can say at least
'I had a mother whom I kept two weeks!'
Not I, who little used to doubt . . . *I* doubt
Good Pietro, kind Violante, gave me birth?
They loved me always as I love my babe
(— Nearly so, that is — quite so could not be —)
Did for me all I meant to do for him,
Till one surprising day, three years ago,[182]
They both declared, at Rome, before some judge
In some court where the people flocked to hear,
That really I had never been their child,
Was a mere castaway, the careless crime
Of an unknown man, the crime and care too much
Of a woman known too well, — little to these,
Therefore, of whom I was the flesh and blood:
What then to Pietro and Violante, both
No more my relatives than you or you?
Nothing to them! You know what they declared.

So with my husband, — just such a surprise,
Such a mistake, in that relationship!
Everyone says that husbands love their wives,
Guard them and guide them, give them happiness;
'T is duty, law, pleasure, religion: well,
You see how much of this comes true in mine!
People indeed would fain have somehow proved
He was no husband: but he did not hear,
Or would not wait, and so has killed us all.
Then there is . . . only let me name one more!
There is the friend, — men will not ask about,
But tell untruths of, and give nicknames to,
And think my lover, most surprise of all!
Do only hear, it is the priest they mean,
Giuseppe Caponsacchi: a priest — love,
And love me! Well, yet people think he did.
I am married, he has taken priestly vows,

[182] In April or May 1694, after their return from Arezzo and an unsuccessful attempt to live there in the house of Guido, who detested them after he had once got his hands on Pietro's money.

They know that, and yet go on, say, the same,
'Yes, how he loves you!' 'That was love' — they say,
When anything is answered that they ask:
Or else 'No wonder you love him' — they say.
Then they shake heads, pity much, scarcely blame —
As if we neither of us lacked excuse,
And anyhow are punished to the full,
And downright love atones for everything!
Nay, I heard read-out in the public court
Before the judge, in presence of my friends,
Letters 't was said the priest had sent to me,
And other letters sent him by myself,
We being lovers!

Listen what this is like!
When I was a mere child, my mother . . . that 's
Violante, you must let me call her so
Nor waste time, trying to unlearn the word, . . .
She brought a neighbour's child of my own age
To play with me of rainy afternoons;
And, since there hung a tapestry on the wall,
We two agreed to find each other out
Among the figures. 'Tisbe, that is you,
'With half-moon on your hair-knot, spear in hand,
'Flying, but no wings, only the great scarf
'Blown to a bluish rainbow at your back:
'Call off your hound and leave the stag alone!'[183]
'— And there are you, Pompilia, such green leaves
'Flourishing out of your five finger-ends,
'And all the rest of you so brown and rough:
'Why is it you are turned a sort of tree?'[184]
You know the figures never were ourselves
Though we nicknamed them so. Thus, all my life, —
As well what was, as what, like this, was not, —
Looks old, fantastic and impossible:
I touch a fairy thing that fades and fades.
— Even to my babe! I thought, when he was born,
Something began for once that would not end,
Nor change into a laugh at me, but stay
For evermore, eternally quite mine.
Well, so he is, — but yet they bore him off,
The third day, lest my husband should lay traps
And catch him, and by means of him catch me.
Since they have saved him so, it was well done:
Yet thence comes such confusion of what was
With what will be, — that late seems long ago,
And, what years should bring round, already come,
Till even he withdraws into a dream
As the rest do: I fancy him grown great,
Strong, stern, a tall young man who tutors me,
Frowns with the others 'Poor imprudent child!
'Why did you venture out of the safe street?
'Why go so far from help to that lone house?
'Why open at the whisper and the knock?'

Six days ago when it was New Year's-day,
We bent above the fire and talked of him,
What he should do when he was grown and great.
Violante, Pietro, each had given the arm
I leant on, to walk by, from couch to chair
And fireside, — laughed, as I lay safe at last,
'Pompilia's march from bed to board is made,

[183] Refers to a figure of Diana.
[184] Daphne, a beautiful nymph, was changed into a laurel-tree when pursued by Apollo.

'Pompilia back again and with a babe,
'Shall one day lend his arm and help her walk!'
Then we all wished each other more New Years.
Pietro began to scheme—'Our cause is gained;
'The law is stronger than a wicked man:
'Let him henceforth go his way, leave us ours!
'We will avoid the city, tempt no more
'The greedy ones by feasting and parade,—
'Live at the other villa, we know where,
'Still farther off, and we can watch the babe
'Grow fast in the good air; and wood is cheap
'And wine sincere outside the city gate.
'I still have two or three old friends will grope
'Their way along the mere half-mile of road,
'With staff and lantern on a moonless night
'When one needs talk: they'll find me, never fear,
'And I'll find them a flask of the old sort yet!'
Violante said 'You chatter like a crow:
'Pompilia tires o' the tattle, and shall to bed:
'Do not too much the first day,—somewhat more
'To-morrow, and, the next, begin the cape
'And hood and coat! I have spun wool enough.'
Oh what a happy friendly eve was that!

And, next day, about noon, out Pietro went—
He was so happy and would talk so much,
Until Violante pushed and laughed him forth
Sight-seeing in the cold,—'So much to see
'I' the churches! Swathe your throat three times!' she cried,
'And, above all, beware the slippery ways,
'And bring us all the news by supper-time!'
He came back late, laid by cloak, staff and hat,
Powdered so thick with snow it made us laugh,
Rolled a great log upon the ash o' the hearth,
And bade Violante treat us to a flask,
Because he had obeyed her faithfully,
Gone sight-see through the seven,[185] and found no church
To his mind like San Giovanni—'There's the fold,
'And all the sheep together, big as cats!
'And such a shepherd, half the size of life,
'Starts up and hears the angel'[186]—when, at the door,
A tap: we started up: you know the rest.

Pietro at least had done no harm, I know;
Nor even Violante, so much harm as makes
Such revenge lawful. Certainly she erred—
Did wrong, how shall I dare say otherwise?—
In telling that first falsehood, buying me
From my poor faulty mother at a price,
To pass off upon Pietro as his child:
If one should take my babe, give him a name,
Say he was not Gaetano and my own,
But that some other woman made his mouth
And hands and feet,—how very false were that!
No good could come of that; and all harm did.
Yet if a stranger were to represent
'Needs must you either give your babe to me
'And let me call him mine for ever more,
'Or let your husband get him'—ah, my God,
That were a trial I refuse to face!
Well, just so here: it proved wrong but seemed right

[185] The seven *basilicae maiores* of Rome.
[186] Refers to model scenes of the Nativity set up at Christmas time in the churches.

To poor Violante — for there lay, she said,
My poor real dying mother in her rags,
Who put me from her with the life and all,
Poverty, pain, shame and disease at once,
To die the easier by what price I fetched —
Also (I hope) because I should be spared
Sorrow and sin, — why may not that have helped?
My father, — he was no one, any one, —
The worse, the likelier, — call him, — he who came,
Was wicked for his pleasure, went his way,
And left no trace to track by; there remained
Nothing but me, the unnecessary life,
To catch up or let fall, — and yet a thing
She could make happy, be made happy with,
This poor Violante, — who would frown thereat?

Well, God, you see! God plants us where we grow.
It is not that, because a bud is born
At a wild briar's end, full i' the wild beast's way,
We ought to pluck and put it out of reach
On the oak-tree top, — say, 'There the bud belongs!'
She thought, moreover, real lies were — lies told
For harm's sake; whereas this had good at heart,
Good for my mother, good for me, and good
For Pietro who was meant to love a babe,
And needed one to make his life of use,
Receive his house and land when he should die.
Wrong, wrong and always wrong! how plainly wrong!
For see, this fault kept pricking, as faults do,
All the same at her heart, — this falsehood hatched,
She could not let it go nor keep it fast.
She told me so, — the first time I was found
Locked in her arms once more after the pain,
When the nuns let me leave them and go home,
And both of us cried all the cares away, —
This it was set her on to make amends,
This brought about the marriage — simply this!
Do let me speak for her you blame so much!
When Paul, my husband's brother, found me out,
Heard there was wealth for who should marry me,
So, came and made a speech to ask my hand
For Guido, — she, instead of piercing straight
Through the pretence to the ignoble truth,
Fancied she saw God's very finger point,
Designate just the time for planting me,
(The wild briar-slip she plucked to love and wear)
In soil where I could strike real root, and grow,
And get to be the thing I called myself:
For, wife and husband are one flesh, God says,
And I, whose parents seemed such and were none,
Should in a husband have a husband now,
Find nothing, this time, but was what it seemed,
— All truth and no confusion any more.
I know she meant all good to me, all pain
To herself, — since how could it be aught but pain,
To give me up, so, from her very breast,
The wilding flower-tree-branch that, all those years,
She had got used to feel for and find fixed?
She meant well: has it been so ill i' the main?
That is but fair to ask: one cannot judge
Of what has been the ill or well of life,
The day that one is dying, — sorrows change
Into not altogether sorrow-like;

I do see strangeness but scarce misery,
Now it is over, and no danger more.
My child is safe; there seems not so much pain.
It comes, most like, that I am just absolved,
Purged of the past, the foul in me, washed fair,—
One cannot both have and not have, you know,—
Being right now, I am happy and colour things.
Yes, every body that leaves life sees all
Softened and bettered: so with other sights:
To me at least was never evening yet
But seemed far beautifuller than its day,
For past is past.

There was a fancy came,
When somewhere, in the journey with my friend,
We stepped into a hovel to get food;
And there began a yelp here, a bark there,—
Misunderstanding creatures that were wroth
And vexed themselves and us till we retired.
The hovel is life: no matter what dogs bit
Or cats scratched in the hovel I break from,
All outside is lone field, moon and such peace—
Flowing in, filling up as with a sea
Whereon comes Someone, walks fast on the white,
Jesus Christ's self, Don Celestine declares,
To meet me and calm all things back again.

Beside, up to my marriage, thirteen years
Were, each day, happy as the day was long:
This may have made the change too terrible.
I know that when Violante told me first
The cavalier,—she meant to bring next morn,
Whom I must also let take, kiss my hand,—
Would be at San Lorenzo the same eve
And marry me,—which over, we should go
Home both of us without him as before,
And, till she bade speak, I must hold my tongue,
Such being the correct way with girl-brides,
From whom one word would make a father blush,—
I know, I say, that when she told me this,
—Well, I no more saw sense in what she said
Than a lamb does in people clipping wool;
Only lay down and let myself be clipped.
And when next day the cavalier who came
(Tisbe had told me that the slim young man [187]
With wings at head, and wings at feet, and sword
Threatening a monster, in our tapestry,
Would eat a girl else,—was a cavalier)
When he proved Guido Franceschini,—old
And nothing like so tall as I myself,
Hook-nosed and yellow in a bush of beard,
Much like a thing I saw on a boy's wrist,
He called an owl and used for catching birds,—
And when he took my hand and made a smile—
Why, the uncomfortableness of it all
Seemed hardly more important in the case
Than,—when one gives you, say, a coin to spend,—
Its newness or its oldness; if the piece
Weigh properly and buy you what you wish,
No matter whether you get grime or glare!
Men take the coin, return you grapes and figs.
Here, marriage was the coin, a dirty piece
Would purchase me the praise of those I loved:
About what else should I concern myself?

So, hardly knowing what a husband meant,
I supposed this or any man would serve,
No whit the worse for being so uncouth:
For I was ill once and a doctor came
With a great ugly hat, no plume thereto,

[187] Perseus, at the rescue of Andromeda.

Black jerkin and black buckles and black sword,
And white sharp beard over the ruff in front,
And oh so lean, so sour-faced and austere! —
Who felt my pulse, made me put out my tongue,
Then oped a phial, dripped a drop or two
Of a black bitter something, — I was cured!
What mattered the fierce beard or the grim face?
It was the physic beautified the man,
Master Malpichi,[188] — never met his match
In Rome, they said, — so ugly all the same!

However, I was hurried through a storm,
Next dark eve of December's deadest day —
How it rained! — through our street and the Lion's-mouth
And the bit of Corso, — cloaked round, covered close,
I was like something strange or contraband, —
Into blank San Lorenzo, up the aisle,
My mother keeping hold of me so tight,
I fancied we were come to see a corpse
Before the altar which she pulled me toward.
There we found waiting an unpleasant priest
Who proved the brother, not our parish friend,
But one with mischief-making mouth and eye,
Paul, whom I know since to my cost. And then
I heard the heavy-church-door lock out help
Behind us: for the customary warmth,
Two tapers shivered on the altar. 'Quick —
'Lose no time!' — cried the priest. And straightway down
From . . . what's behind the altar where he hid —
Hawk-nose and yellowness and bush and all,
Stepped Guido, caught my hand, and there was I
O' the chancel, and the priest had opened book,
Read here and there, made me say that and this,
And after, told me I was now a wife,
Honoured indeed, since Christ thus weds the Church,
And therefore turned he water into wine,
To show I should obey my spouse like Christ.
Then the two slipped aside and talked apart,
And I, silent and scared, got down again
And joined my mother who was weeping now.
Nobody seemed to mind us any more,
And both of us on tiptoe found our way
To the door which was unlocked by this, and wide.
When we were in the street, the rain had stopped,
All things looked better. At our own house-door,
Violante whispered 'No one syllable
'To Pietro! Girl-brides never breathe a word!'
'— Well treated to a wetting, draggle-tails!'
Laughed Pietro as he opened — 'Very near
'You made me brave the gutter's roaring sea
'To carry off from roost old dove and young,
'Trussed up in church, the cote, by me, the kite!
'What do these priests mean, praying folk to death
'On stormy afternoons, with Christmas close
'To wash our sins off nor require the rain?'
Violante gave my hand a timely squeeze,

[188] Perhaps Marcello Malpighi (1628–1694), famous physician of Pope Innocent XII.

Madonna saved me from immodest speech,
I kissed him and was quiet, being a bride.

When I saw nothing more, the next three weeks,
Of Guido — 'Nor the Church sees Christ' thought I:
'Nothing is changed however, wine is wine
'And water only water in our house.
'Nor did I see that ugly doctor since
'The cure of the illness: just as I was cured,
'I am married, — neither scarecrow will return.'

Three weeks, I chuckled — 'How would Giulia stare,
'And Tecla smile and Tisbe laugh outright,
'Were it not impudent for brides to talk!' —
Until one morning, as I sat and sang
At the broidery-frame alone i' the chamber, — loud
Voices, two, three together, sobbings too,
And my name, 'Guido,' 'Paolo,' flung like stones
From each to the other! In I ran to see.
There stood the very Guido and the priest
With sly face, — the formal but nowise afraid, —
While Pietro seemed all red and angry, scarce
Able to stutter out his wrath in words;
And this it was that made my mother sob,
As he reproached her — 'You have murdered us,
'Me and yourself and this our child beside!'
Then Guido interposed 'Murdered or not,
'Be it enough your child is now my wife!
'I claim and come to take her.' Paul put in,
'Consider — kinsman, dare I term you so? —
'What is the good of your sagacity
'Except to counsel in a strait like this?
'I guarantee the parties man and wife
'Whether you like or loathe it, bless or ban.
'May spilt milk be put back within the bowl —
'The done thing, undone? You, it is, we look
'For counsel to, you fitliest will advise!
'Since milk, though spilt and spoilt, does marble good,
'Better we down on knees and scrub the floor,
'Than sigh, "the waste would make a syllabub!"[189]
'Help us so turn disaster to account,
'So predispose the groom, he needs shall grace
'The bride with favour from the very first,
'Not begin marriage an embittered man!'
He smiled, — the game so wholly in his hands!
While fast and faster sobbed Violante — 'Ay,
'All of us murdered, past averting now!
'O my sin, O my secret!' and such like.

Then I began to half surmise the truth;
Something had happened, low, mean, underhand,
False, and my mother was to blame, and I
To pity, whom all spoke of, none addressed:
I was the chattel that had caused a crime.
I stood mute, — those who tangled must untie
The embroilment. Pietro cried 'Withdraw, my child!
'She is not helpful to the sacrifice
'At this stage, — do you want the victim by
'While you discuss the value of her blood?
'For her sake, I consent to hear you talk:
'Go, child, and pray God help the innocent!'

I did go and was praying God, when came
Violante, with eyes swollen and red enough,

[189] A dish made from a mixture of wine and milk.

But movement on her mouth for make-believe
Matters were somehow getting right again.
She bade me sit down by her side and hear.
'You are too young and cannot understand,
'Nor did your father understand at first.
'I wished to benefit all three of us,
'And when he failed to take my meaning,—why,
'I tried to have my way at unaware—
'Obtained him the advantage he refused.
'As if I put before him wholesome food
'Instead of broken victual,—he finds change
'I' the viands, never cares to reason why,
'But falls to blaming me, would fling the plate
'From window, scandalize the neighbourhood,
'Even while he smacks his lips,—men's way, my child!
'But either you have prayed him unperverse
'Or I have talked him back into his wits:
'And Paolo was a help in time of need,—
'Guido, not much—my child, the way of men!
'A priest is more a woman than a man,
'And Paul did wonders to persuade. In short,
'Yes, he was wrong, your father sees and says;
'My scheme was worth attempting: and bears fruit,
'Gives you a husband and a noble name,
'A palace and no end of pleasant things.
'What do you care about a handsome youth?
'They are so volatile, and tease their wives!
'This is the kind of man to keep the house.
'We lose no daughter,—gain a son, that 's all:
'For 't is arranged we never separate,
'Nor miss, in our grey time of life, the tints
'Of you that colour eve to match with morn.
'In good or ill, we share and share alike,
'And cast our lots into a common lap,
'And all three die together as we lived!
'Only, at Arezzo,—that 's a Tuscan town,
'Not so large as this noisy Rome, no doubt,
'But older far and finer much, say folks,—
'In a great palace where you will be queen,
'Know the Archbishop and the Governor,
'And we see homage done you ere we die.
'Therefore, be good and pardon!'—'Pardon what?
'You know things, I am very ignorant:
'All is right if you only will not cry!'

And so an end! Because a blank begins
From when, at the word, she kissed me hard and hot,
And took me back to where my father leaned
Opposite Guido—who stood eyeing him,
As eyes the butcher the cast panting ox
That feels his fate is come, nor struggles more,—
While Paul looked archly on, pricked brow at whiles
With the pen-point as to punish triumph there,—
And said 'Count Guido, take your lawful wife
'Until death part you!'

All since is one blank,
Over and ended; a terrific dream.
It is the good of dreams—so soon they go!
Wake in a horror of heart-beats, you may—
Cry, 'The dread thing will never from my thoughts!'
Still, a few daylight doses of plain life,
Cock-crow and sparrow-chirp, or bleat and bell
Of goats that trot by, tinkling, to be milked;
And when you rub your eyes awake and wide,
Where is the harm o' the horror? Gone! So here.
I know I wake,—but from what? Blank, I say!

This is the note of evil: for good lasts.
Even when Don Celestine bade 'Search and find!
'For your soul's sake, remember what is past,
'The better to forgive it,'—all in vain!
What was fast getting indistinct before,
Vanished outright. By special grace perhaps,
Between that first calm and this last, four years
Vanish,—one quarter of my life, you know.
I am held up, amid the nothingness,
By one or two truths only—thence I hang,
And there I live,—the rest is death or dream,
All but those points of my support. I think
Of what I saw at Rome once in the Square
O' the Spaniards, opposite the Spanish House:[190]
There was a foreigner had trained a goat,
A shuddering white woman of a beast,
To climb up, stand straight on a pile of sticks
Put close, which gave the creature room enough:
When she was settled there he, one by one,
Took away all the sticks, left just the four
Whereon the little hoofs did really rest,
There she kept firm, all underneath was air.
So, what I hold by, are my prayer to God,
My hope, that came in answer to the prayer,
Some hand would interpose and save me—hand
Which proved to be my friend's hand: and,—best bliss,—
That fancy which began so faint at first,
That thrill of dawn's suffusion through my dark,
Which I perceive was promise of my child,
The light his unborn face sent long before,—
God's way of breaking the good news to flesh.

[190] The palace of the Spanish ambassador.

That is all left now of those four bad years.
Don Celestine urged 'But remember more!
'Other men's faults may help me find your own.
'I need the cruelty exposed, explained,
'Or how can I advise you to forgive?'
He thought I could not properly forgive
Unless I ceased forgetting,—which is true:
For, bringing back reluctantly to mind
My husband's treatment of me,—by a light
That 's later than my life-time,[191] I review
And comprehend much and imagine more,
And have but little to forgive at last.
For now,—be fair and say,—is it not true
He was ill-used and cheated of his hope
To get enriched by marriage? Marriage gave
Me and no money, broke the compact so:
He had a right to ask me on those terms,
As Pietro and Violante to declare
They would not give me: so the bargain stood:
They broke it, and he felt himself aggrieved,
Became unkind with me to punish them.
They said 't was he began deception first,[192]
Nor, in one point whereto he pledged himself,[193]
Kept promise: what of that, suppose it were?
Echoes die off, scarcely reverberate
For ever,—why should ill keep echoing ill,
And never let our ears have done with noise?
Then my poor parents took the violent way
To thwart him,—he must needs retaliate,—wrong,
Wrong, and all wrong,—better say, all blind!
As I myself was, that is sure, who else
Had understood the mystery: for his wife
Was bound in some sort to help somehow there.

[191] *I.e.*, the insight that comes now with death.
[192] By pretending that his income was more than it was.
[193] To support Pietro and Violante at Arezzo.

It seems as if I might have interposed,
Blunted the edge of their resentment so,
Since he vexed me because they first vexed him;
'I will entreat them to desist, submit,
'Give him the money and be poor in peace,—
'Certainly not go tell the world: perhaps
'He will grow quiet with his gains.'

Yes, say
Something to this effect and you do well!
But then you have to see first: I was blind.
That is the fruit of all such wormy ways,
The indirect, the unapproved of God:
You cannot find their author's end and aim,
Not even to substitute your good for bad,
Your straight for the irregular; you stand
Stupefied, profitless, as cow or sheep
That miss a man's mind; anger him just twice
By trial at repairing the first fault.
Thus, when he blamed me, 'You are a coquette,
'A lure-owl posturing to attract birds,
'You look love-lures at theatre and church,
'In walk, at window!'—that, I knew, was false:
But why he charged me falsely, whither sought
To drive me by such charge,—how could I know?
So, unaware, I only made things worse.
I tried to soothe him by abjuring walk,
Window, church, theatre, for good and all,
As if he had been in earnest: that, you know,
Was nothing like the object of his charge.
Yes, when I got my maid to supplicate
The priest, whose name she read when she would read
Those feigned false letters I was forced to hear
Though I could read no word of,—he should cease
Writing,—nay, if he minded prayer of mine,
Cease from so much as even pass the street
Whereon our house looked,—in my ignorance
I was just thwarting Guido's true intent;
Which was, to bring about a wicked change
Of sport to earnest, tempt a thoughtless man
To write indeed, and pass the house, and more,
Till both of us were taken in a crime.
He ought not to have wished me thus act lies,
Simulate folly,—but,—wrong or right, the wish,—
I failed to apprehend its drift. How plain
It follows,—if I fell into such fault,
He also may have overreached the mark,
Made mistake, by perversity of brain,
I' the whole sad strange plot, the grotesque intrigue
To make me and my friend unself ourselves,
Be other man and woman than we were!
Think it out, you who have the time! for me,—
I cannot say less; more I will not say.
Leave it to God to cover and undo!
Only, my dulness should not prove too much!
—Not prove that in a certain other point
Wherein my husband blamed me,—and you blame,
If I interpret smiles and shakes of head,—
I was dull too. Oh, if I dared but speak!
Must I speak? I am blamed that I forwent
A way to make my husband's favour come.
That is true: I was firm, withstood, refused . . .
—Women as you are, how can I find the words?

I felt there was just one thing Guido claimed
I had no right to give nor he to take;
We being in estrangement, soul from soul:
Till, when I sought help, the Archbishop smiled,
Inquiring into privacies of life,

— Said I was blameable — (he stands for God)
Nowise entitled to exemption there.
Then I obeyed, — as surely had obeyed
Were the injunction 'Since your husband bids,
'Swallow the burning coal he proffers you!'
But I did wrong, and he gave wrong advice
Though he were thrice Archbishop, — that, I know! —
Now I have got to die and see things clear.
Remember I was barely twelve years old —
A child at marriage: I was let alone
For weeks, I told you, lived my child-life still
Even at Arezzo, when I woke and found
First . . . but I need not think of that again —
Over and ended! Try and take the sense
Of what I signify, if it must be so.
After the first, my husband, for hate's sake,
Said one eve, when the simpler cruelty
Seemed somewhat dull at edge and fit to bear,
'We have been man and wife six months almost:
'How long is this your comedy to last?
'Go this night to my chamber, not your own!'
At which word, I did rush — most true the charge —
And gain the Archbishop's house — he stands for God —
And fall upon my knees and clasp his feet,
Praying him hinder what my estranged soul
Refused to bear, though patient of the rest:
'Place me within a convent,' I implored —
'Let me henceforward lead the virgin life
'You praise in Her you bid me imitate!'
What did he answer? 'Folly of ignorance!
'Know, daughter, circumstances make or mar
'Virginity, — 't is virtue or 't is vice.
'That which was glory in the Mother of God
'Had been, for instance, damnable in Eve
'Created to be mother of mankind.
'Had Eve, in answer to her Maker's speech
'"Be fruitful, multiply, replenish earth" —
'Pouted "But I choose rather to remain
'"Single" — why, she had spared herself forthwith
'Further probation by the apple and snake,
'Been pushed straight out of Paradise! For see —
'If motherhood be qualified impure,
'I catch you making God command Eve sin!
'— A blasphemy so like these Molinists',[194]
'I must suspect you dip into their books.'
Then he pursued ''T was in your covenant!'

No! There my husband never used deceit.
He never did by speech nor act imply
'Because of our souls' yearning that we meet
'And mix in soul through flesh, which yours and mine
'Wear and impress, and make their visible selves,
'— All which means, for the love of you and me,
'Let us become one flesh, being one soul!'
He only stipulated for the wealth;
Honest so far. But when he spoke as plain —
Dreadfully honest also — 'Since our souls
'Stand each from each, a whole world's width between,
'Give me the fleshy vesture I can reach
'And rend and leave just fit for hell to burn!' —
Why, in God's name, for Guido's soul's own sake
Imperilled by polluting mine, — I say,
I did resist; would I had overcome!

---

[194] Followers of Miguel de Molinos, a Spanish priest whose doctrines were condemned by the Pope in 1687.

My heart died out at the Archbishop's smile;
— It seemed so stale and worn a way o' the world,
As though 't were nature frowning — 'Here is Spring,
'The sun shines as he shone at Adam's fall,
'The earth requires that warmth reach everywhere:
'What, must your patch of snow be saved forsooth
'Because you rather fancy snow than flowers?'
Something in this style he began with me.
Last he said, savagely for a good man,
'This explains why you call your husband harsh,
'Harsh to you, harsh to whom you love. God's Bread!
'The poor Count has to manage a mere child
'Whose parents leave untaught the simplest things
'Their duty was and privilege to teach, —
'Goodwives' instruction, gossips' lore: they laugh
'And leave the Count the task, — or leave it me!'
Then I resolved to tell a frightful thing.
'I am not ignorant, — know what I say,
'Declaring this is sought for hate, not love.
'Sir, you may hear things like almighty God.
'I tell you that my housemate, yes — the priest
'My husband's brother, Canon Girolamo —
'Has taught me what depraved and misnamed love
'Means, and what outward signs denote the sin,
'For he solicits me and says he loves,
'The idle young priest with nought else to do.
'My husband sees this, knows this, and lets be.
'Is it your counsel I bear this beside?'
'— More scandal, and against a priest this time!
'What, 't is the Canon now?' — less snappishly —
'Rise up, my child, for such a child you are,
'The rod were too advanced a punishment!
'Let's try the honeyed cake. A parable!
'"Without a parable spake He not to them."[195]
'There was a ripe round long black toothsome fruit,
'Even a flower-fig, the prime boast of May:
'And, to the tree, said . . . either the spirit o' the fig,
'Or, if we bring in men, the gardener,
'Archbishop of the orchard — had I time
'To try o' the two which fits in best: indeed
'It might be the Creator's self, but then
'The tree should bear an apple, I suppose, —
'Well, anyhow, one with authority said
'"Ripe fig, burst skin, regale the fig-pecker —
'"The bird whereof thou art a perquisite!"
'"Nay," with a flounce, replied the restif[196] fig,
'"I much prefer to keep my pulp myself:
'"He may go breakfastless and dinnerless,
'"Supperless of one crimson seed, for me!"
'So back she flopped into her bunch of leaves.
'He flew off, left her, — did the natural lord, —
'And lo, three hundred thousand bees and wasps
'Found her out, feasted on her to the shuck:
'Such gain the fig's that gave its bird no bite!
'The moral, — fools elude their proper lot,
'Tempt other fools, get ruined all alike.
'Therefore go home, embrace your husband quick!

---

[195] *St. Matthew*, xiii, 34.
[196] stubborn

'Which if his Canon brother chance to see,
'He will the sooner back to book again.'

So, home I did go: so, the worst befell:
So, I had proof the Archbishop was just man,
And hardly that, and certainly no more.
For, miserable consequence to me,
My husband's hatred waxed nor waned at all,
His brother's boldness grew effrontery soon,
And my last stay and comfort in myself
Was forced from me: henceforth I looked to God
Only, nor cared my desecrated soul
Should have fair walls, gay windows for the world.
God's glimmer, that came through the ruin-top,
Was witness why all lights were quenched inside:
Henceforth I asked God counsel, not mankind.

So, when I made the effort, freed myself,
They said—'No care to save appearance here!
'How cynic,—when, how wanton, were enough!'
—Adding, it all came of my mother's life—
My own real mother, whom I never knew,
Who did wrong (if she needs must have done wrong)
Through being all her life, not my four years,
At mercy of the hateful,—every beast
O' the field was wont to break that fountain-fence,
Trample the silver into mud so murk
Heaven could not find itself reflected there,—
Now they cry 'Out on her, who, plashy pool,
'Bequeathed turbidity and bitterness
'To the daughter-stream where Guido dipt and drank!'

Well, since she had to bear this brand—let me!
The rather do I understand her now,—
From my experience of what hate calls love,—
Much love might be in what their love called hate.
If she sold . . . what they call, sold . . . me her child—
I shall believe she hoped in her poor heart
That I at least might try be good and pure,
Begin to live untempted, not go doomed
And done with ere once found in fault, as she.
Oh, and my mother, it all came to this?
Why should I trust those that speak ill of you,
When I mistrust who speaks even well of them?
Why, since all bound to do me good, did harm,
May not you, seeming as you harmed me most,
Have meant to do most good—and feed your child
From bramble-bush, whom not one orchard-tree
But drew bough back from, nor let one fruit fall?
This it was for you sacrificed your babe?
Gained just this, giving your heart's hope away
As I might give mine, loving it as you,
If . . . but that never could be asked of me!

There, enough! I have my support again,
Again the knowledge that my babe was, is,
Will be mine only. Him, by death, I give
Outright to God, without a further care,—
But not to any parent in the world,—
So to be safe: why is it we repine?
What guardianship were safer could we choose?

All human plans and projects come to nought,
My life, and what I know of other lives,
Prove that: no plan nor project! God shall care!

And now you are not tired? How patient then
All of you,—Oh yes, patient this long while
Listening, and understanding, I am sure!
Four days ago, when I was sound and well
And like to live, no one would understand.
People were kind, but smiled 'And what of him,
'Your friend, whose tonsure, the rich dark-brown hides?
'There, there!—your lover, do we dream he was?
'A priest too—never were such naughtiness!
'Still, he thinks many a long think, never fear,
'After the shy pale lady,—lay so light
'For a moment in his arms, the lucky one!'
And so on: wherefore should I blame you much?
So we are made, such difference in minds,
Such difference too in eyes that see the minds!
That man, you misinterpret and misprise—
The glory of his nature, I had thought,
Shot itself out in white light, blazed the truth
Through every atom of his act with me:
Yet where I point you, through the chrystal shrine,
Purity in quintessence, one dew-drop,
You all descry a spider in the midst.
One says, 'The head of it is plain to see,'
And one, 'They are the feet by which I judge,'
All say, 'Those films were spun by nothing else.'

Then, I must lay my babe away with God,
Nor think of him again, for gratitude.
Yes, my last breath shall wholly spend itself
In one attempt more to disperse the stain,
The mist from other breath fond mouths have made,
About a lustrous and pellucid soul:
So that, when I am gone but sorrow stays,
And people need assurance in their doubt
If God yet have a servant, man a friend,
The weak a saviour and the vile a foe,—
Let him be present, by the name invoked,
Giuseppe-Maria Caponsacchi!

There,
Strength comes already with the utterance!
I will remember once more for his sake
The sorrow: for he lives and is belied.
Could he be here, how he would speak for me!

I had been miserable three drear years
In that dread palace and lay passive now,
When I first learned there could be such a man.
Thus it fell: I was at a public play,
In the last days of Carnival last March,
Brought there I knew not why, but now know well.
My husband put me where I sat, in front;
Then crouched down, breathed cold through me from behind,
Stationed i' the shadow,—none in front could see,—
I, it was, faced the stranger-throng beneath,
The crowd with upturned faces, eyes one stare,
Voices one buzz. I looked but to the stage,
Whereon two lovers sang and interchanged
'True life is only love, love only bliss:
'I love thee—thee I love!' then they embraced.
I looked thence to the ceiling and the walls,—
Over the crowd, those voices and those eyes,—

My thoughts went through the roof and out, to Rome
On wings of music, waft of measured words,—
Set me down there, a happy child again,
Sure that to-morrow would be festa-day,
Hearing my parents praise past festas more,
And seeing they were old if I was young,
Yet wondering why they still would end discourse
With 'We must soon go, you abide your time,
'And,—might we haply see the proper friend
'Throw his arm over you and make you safe!'

Sudden I saw him; into my lap there fell
A foolish twist of comfits, broke my dream
And brought me from the air and laid me low,
As ruined as the soaring bee that 's reached
(So Pietro told me at the Villa once)
By the dust-handful. There the comfits lay:
I looked to see who flung them, and I faced
This Caponsacchi, looking up in turn.
Ere I could reason out why, I felt sure,
Whoever flung them, his was not the hand,—
Up rose the round face and good-natured grin
Of him who, in effect, had played the prank,
From covert close beside the earnest face,—
Fat waggish Conti, friend of all the world.
He was my husband's cousin,[197] privileged
To throw the thing: the other, silent, grave,
Solemn almost, saw me, as I saw him.

There is a psalm Don Celestine recites,
'Had I a dove's wings, how I fain would flee!'[198]
The psalm runs not 'I hope, I pray for wings,'—
Not 'If wings fall from heaven, I fix them fast,'—
Simply 'How good it were to fly and rest,
'Have hope now, and one day expect content!
'How well to do what I shall never do!'
So I said 'Had there been a man like that,
'To lift me with his strength out of all strife
'Into the calm, how I could fly and rest!
'I have a keeper in the garden here
'Whose sole employment is to strike me low
'If ever I, for solace, seek the sun.
'Life means with me successful feigning death,
'Lying stone-like, eluding notice so,
'Forgoing here the turf and there the sky.
'Suppose that man had been instead of this!'

Presently Conti laughed into my ear,
—Had tripped up to the raised place where I sat—
'Cousin, I flung them brutishly and hard!
'Because you must be hurt, to look austere
'As Caponsacchi yonder, my tall friend
'A-gazing now. Ah, Guido, you so close?
'Keep on your knees, do! Beg her to forgive!
'My cornet[199] battered like a cannon-ball.
'Good bye, I'm gone!'—nor waited the reply.

That night at supper, out my husband broke,
'Why was that throwing, that buffoonery?
'Do you think I am your dupe? What man would dare
'Throw comfits in a stranger lady's lap?
''Twas knowledge of you bred such insolence
'In Caponsacchi; he dared shoot the bolt,
'Using that Conti for his stalking-horse.

---

[197] Only in the sense that his brother had married Guido's sister.

[198] *Psalms*, lv, 6.

[199] Paper twisted into the shape of a cone.

'How could you see him this once and no more,
'When he is always haunting hereabout
'At the street-corner or the palace-side,
'Publishing my shame and your impudence?
'You are a wanton, — I a dupe, you think?
'O Christ, what hinders that I kill her quick?'
Whereat he drew his sword and feigned a thrust.

All this, now, — being not so strange to me,
Used to such misconception day by day
And broken-in to bear, — I bore, this time,
More quietly than woman should perhaps;
Repeated the mere truth and held my tongue.

Then he said, 'Since you play the ignorant,
'I shall instruct you. This amour, — commenced
'Or finished or midway in act, all 's one, —
''Tis the town-talk; so my revenge shall be.
'Does he presume because he is a priest?
'I warn him that the sword I wear shall pink[200]
'His lily-scented cassock through and through,
'Next time I catch him underneath your eaves!'

But he had threatened with the sword so oft
And, after all, not kept his promise. All
I said was, 'Let God save the innocent!
'Moreover, death is far from a bad fate.
'I shall go pray for you and me, not him;
'And then I look to sleep, come death or, worse,
'Life.' So, I slept.

There may have elapsed a week,
When Margherita, — called my waiting-maid,
Whom it is said my husband found too fair —
Who stood and heard the charge and the reply,
Who never once would let the matter rest
From that night forward, but rang changes still
On this the thrust and that the shame, and how
Good cause for jealousy cures jealous fools,
And what a paragon was this same priest
She talked about until I stopped my ears, —
She said, 'A week is gone; you comb your hair,
'Then go mope in a corner, cheek on palm,
'Till night comes round again, — so, waste a week
'As if your husband menaced you in sport.
'Have not I some acquaintance with his tricks?
'Oh no, he did not stab the serving-man
'Who made and sang the rhymes about me once!
'For why? They sent him to the wars next day.
'Nor poisoned he the foreigner, my friend,
'Who wagered on the whiteness of my breast, —
'The swarth skins of our city in dispute:
'For, though he paid me proper compliment,
'The Count well knew he was besotted with
'Somebody else, a skin as black as ink,
'(As all the town knew save my foreigner)
'He found and wedded presently, — "Why need
'"Better revenge?" — the Count asked. But what's here?
'A priest, that does not fight, and cannot wed,
'Yet must be dealt with! If the Count took fire
'For the poor pastime of a minute, — me —
'What were the conflagration for yourself,
'Countess and lady-wife and all the rest?
'The priest will perish; you will grieve too late;
'So shall the city-ladies' handsomest

[200] pierce

'Frankest and liberalest gentleman
'Die for you, to appease a scurvy dog
'Hanging's too good for. Is there no escape?
'Were it not simple Christian charity
'To warn the priest be on his guard, — save him
'Assured death, save yourself from causing it?
'I meet him in the street. Give me a glove,
'A ring to show for token! Mum's the word!'

I answered, 'If you were, as styled, my maid,
'I would command you: as you are, you say,
'My husband's intimate, — assist his wife
'Who can do nothing but entreat "Be still!"
'Even if you speak truth and a crime is planned,
'Leave help to God as I am forced to do!
'There is no other course, or we should craze,
'Seeing such evil with no human cure.
'Reflect that God, who makes the storm desist,
'Can make an angry violent heart subside.
'Why should we venture teach Him governance?
'Never address me on this subject more!'

Next night she said, 'But I went, all the same,
'— Ay, saw your Caponsacchi in his house,
'And come back stuffed with news I must outpour.
'I told him, "Sir, my mistress is a stone:
'"Why should you harm her for no good you get?
'"For you do harm her — prowl about our place
'"With the Count never distant half the street,
'"Lurking at every corner, would you look!
'"'Tis certain she has witched you with a spell.
'"Are there not other beauties at your beck?
'"We all know, Donna This and Monna That
'"Die for a glance of yours, yet here you gaze!
'"Go make them grateful, leave the stone its cold!"
'And he — oh, he turned first white and then red,
'And then — "To her behest I bow myself,
'"Whom I love with my body and my soul:
'"Only, a word i' the bowing! See, I write
'"One little word, no harm to see or hear!
'"Then, fear no further!" This is what he wrote.
'I know you cannot read, — therefore, let me!
'"*My idol!*"' . . .

But I took it from her hand
And tore it into shreds. 'Why join the rest
'Who harm me? Have I ever done you wrong?
'People have told me 't is you wrong myself:
'Let it suffice I either feel no wrong
'Or else forgive it, — yet you turn my foe!
'The others hunt me and you throw a noose!'

She muttered, 'Have your wilful way!' I slept.

Whereupon . . . no, I leave my husband out!
It is not to do him more hurt, I speak.
Let it suffice, when misery was most,
One day, I swooned and got a respite so.
She stooped as I was slowly coming to,
This Margherita, ever on my trace,
And whispered — 'Caponsacchi!'

If I drowned,
But woke afloat i' the wave with upturned eyes,

And found their first sight was a star! I turned —
For the first time, I let her have her will,
Heard passively, — 'The imposthume[201] at such head,
'One touch, one lancet-puncture would relieve, —
'And still no glance the good physician's way
'Who rids you of the torment in a trice!
'Still he writes letters you refuse to hear.
'He may prevent[202] your husband, kill himself,
'So desperate and all fordone is he!
'Just hear the pretty verse he made to-day!
'A sonnet from Mirtillo.[203] "*Peerless fair . . .*"
'All poetry is difficult to read,
'— The sense of it is, anyhow, he seeks
'Leave to contrive you an escape from hell,
'And for that purpose asks an interview.
'I can write, I can grant it in your name,
'Or, what is better, lead you to his house.
'Your husband dashes you against the stones;
'This man would place each fragment in a shrine:
'You hate him, love your husband!'

I returned,
'It is not true I love my husband, — no,
'Nor hate this man. I listen while you speak,
'— Assured that what you say is false, the same:
'Much as when once, to me a little child,
'A rough gaunt man in rags, with eyes on fire,
'A crowd of boys and idlers at his heels,
'Rushed as I crossed the Square, and held my head
'In his two hands, "Here's she will let me speak!
'"You little girl, whose eyes do good to mine,
'"I am the Pope, am Sextus, now the Sixth;
'"And that Twelfth Innocent, proclaimed to-day,[204]
'"Is Lucifer disguised in human flesh!
'"The angels, met in conclave, crowned me!" — thus
'He gibbered and I listened; but I knew
'All was delusion, ere folks interposed
'"Unfasten him, the maniac!" Thus I know
'All your report of Caponsacchi false,
'Folly or dreaming; I have seen so much
'By that adventure at the spectacle,
'The face I fronted that one first, last time:
'He would belie it by such words and thoughts.
'Therefore while you profess to show him me,
'I ever see his own face. Get you gone!'

'— That will I, nor once open mouth again, —
'No, by Saint Joseph and the Holy Ghost!
'On your head be the damage, so adieu!'

And so more days, more deeds I must forget,
Till . . . what a strange thing now is to declare!
Since I say anything, say all if true!
And how my life seems lengthened as to serve!
It may be idle or inopportune,
But, true? — why, what was all I said but truth,
Even when I found that such as are untrue
Could only take the truth in through a lie?
Now — I am speaking truth to the Truth's self:
God will lend credit to my words this time.

It had got half through April. I arose
One vivid daybreak, — who had gone to bed

[201] abscess
[202] anticipate
[203] One of the letters produced at the trial was signed with this name, drawn from pastoral poetry.

[204] Innocent XII was proclaimed pope on 12 July 1691 There has never been a Pope Sextus, the Sixth.

In the old way my wont those last three years,
Careless until, the cup drained, I should die.
The last sound in my ear, the over-night,
Had been something let drop on the sly
In prattle by Margherita, 'Soon enough
'Gaieties end, now Easter's past: a week,
'And the Archbishop gets him back to Rome, —
'Everyone leaves the town for Rome, this Spring, —
'Even Caponsacchi, out of heart and hope,
'Resigns himself and follows with the flock.'
I heard this drop and drop like rain outside
Fast-falling through the darkness while she spoke:
So had I heard with like indifference,
'And Michael's pair of wings will arrive first
'At Rome to introduce the company,
'Will bear him from our picture where he fights
'Satan, — expect to have that dragon loose
'And never a defender!' [205] — my sole thought
Being still, as night came, 'Done, another day!
'How good to sleep and so get nearer death!' —
When, what, first thing at daybreak, pierced the sleep
With a summons to me? Up I sprang alive,
Light in me, light without me, everywhere
Change! A broad yellow sun-beam was let fall
From heaven to earth, — a sudden drawbridge lay,
Along which marched a myriad merry motes,
Mocking the flies that crossed them and recrossed
In rival dance, companions new-born too.

[205] These lines refer to a fresco in the Church of San Francesco, at Arezzo.

On the house-eaves, a dripping shag of weed
Shook diamonds on each dull grey lattice-square,
As first one, then another bird leapt by,
And light was off, and lo was back again,
Always with one voice, — where are two such joys? —
The blessed building-sparrow! I stepped forth,
Stood on the terrace, — o'er the roofs, such sky!
My heart sang, 'I too am to go away,
'I too have something I must care about,
'Carry away with me to Rome, to Rome!
'The bird brings hither sticks and hairs and wool,
'And nowhere else i' the world; what fly breaks rank,
'Falls out of the procession that befits,
'From window here to window there, with all
'The world to choose, — so well he knows his course?
'I have my purpose and my motive too,
'My march to Rome, like any bird or fly!
'Had I been dead! How right to be alive!
'Last night I almost prayed for leave to die,
'Wished Guido all his pleasure with the sword
'Or the poison, — poison, sword, was but a trick,
'Harmless, may God forgive him the poor jest!
'My life is charmed, will last till I reach Rome!
'Yesterday, but for the sin, — ah, nameless be
'The deed I could have dared against myself!
'Now — see if I will touch an unripe fruit,
'And risk the health I want to have and use!
'Not to live, now, would be the wickedness, —
'For life means to make haste and go to Rome
'And leave Arezzo, leave all woes at once!'

Now, understand here, by no means mistake!
Long ago had I tried to leave that house
When it seemed such procedure would stop sin;
And still failed more the more I tried — at first
The Archbishop, as I told you, — next, our lord
The Governor, — indeed I found my way,
I went to the great palace where he rules,
Though I knew well 't was he who, — when I gave
A jewel or two, themselves had given me,
Back to my parents, — since they wanted bread,
They who had never let me want a nosegay, — he
Spoke of the jail for felons, if they kept
What was first theirs, then mine, so doubly theirs,
Though all the while my husband's most of all!
I knew well who had spoke the word wrought this:
Yet, being in extremity, I fled
To the Governor, as I say, — scarce opened lip
When — the cold cruel snicker close behind —
Guido was on my trace, already there,
Exchanging nod and wink for shrug and smile,
And I — pushed back to him and, for my pains,
Paid with . . . but why remember what is past?
I sought out a poor friar the people call
The Roman, and confessed my sin which came
Of their sin, — that fact could not be repressed, —
The frightfulness of my despair in God:
And, feeling, through the grate, his horror shake,
Implored him, 'Write for me who cannot write,
'Apprise my parents, make them rescue me!
'You bid me be courageous and trust God:
'Do you in turn dare somewhat, trust and write
'"Dear friends, who used to be my parents once,
'"And now declare you have no part in me,
'"This is some riddle I want wit to solve,
'"Since you must love me with no difference.
'"Even suppose you altered, — there's your hate,
'"To ask for: hate of you two dearest ones
'"I shall find liker love than love found here,
'"If husbands love their wives. Take me away
'"And hate me as you do the gnats and fleas,
'"Even the scorpions! How I shall rejoice!"
'Write that and save me!' And he promised — wrote
Or did not write; things never changed at all:
He was not like the Augustinian here!
Last, in a desperation I appealed
To friends, whoever wished me better days,
To Guillichini, that 's of kin,[206] — 'What, I —
'Travel to Rome with you? A flying gout
'Bids me deny my heart and mind my leg!'
Then I tried Conti, used to brave — laugh back
The louring thunder when his cousin scowled
At me protected by his presence: 'You —
'Who well know what you cannot save me from, —
'Carry me off! What frightens you, a priest?'
He shook his head, looked grave — 'Above my strength!
'Guido has claws that scratch, shows feline teeth;
'A formidabler foe than I dare fret:

[206] He was related to Guido.

'Give me a dog to deal with, twice the size!
'Of course I am a priest and Canon too,
'But . . . by the bye . . . though both, not quite so bold,
'As he, my fellow-Canon, brother-priest,
'The personage in such ill odour here
'Because of the reports — pure birth o' the brain —
'Our Caponsacchi, he's your true Saint George
'To slay the monster, set the Princess free,
'And have the whole High-Altar to himself:
'I always think so when I see that piece [207]
'I' the Pieve, that 's his church and mine, you know:
'Though you drop eyes at mention of his name!'

That name had got to take a half-grotesque
Half-ominous, wholly enigmatic sense,
Like any bye-word, broken bit of song
Born with a meaning, changed by mouth and mouth
That mix it in a sneer or smile, as chance
Bids, till it now means naught but ugliness
And perhaps shame.

— All this intends to say,
That, over-night, the notion of escape
Had seemed distemper, dreaming; and the name, —
Not the man, but the name of him, thus made
Into a mockery and disgrace, — why, she
Who uttered it persistently, had laughed,
'I name his name, and there you start and wince
'As criminal from the red tongs' touch!'— yet now,
Now, as I stood letting morn bathe me bright,
Choosing which butterfly should bear my news, —
The white, the brown one, or that tinier blue, —
The Margherita, I detested so,
In she came — 'The fine day, the good Spring time!
'What, up and out at window? That is best.
'No thought of Caponsacchi? — who stood there
'All night on one leg, like the sentry crane,
'Under the pelting of your water-spout —
'Looked last look at your lattice ere he leave
'Our city, bury his dead hope at Rome?
'Ay, go to looking-glass and make you fine,
'While he may die ere touch one least loose hair
'You drag at with the comb in such a rage!'

I turned — 'Tell Caponsacchi he may come!'

'Tell him to come? Ah, but, for charity,
'A truce to fooling! Come? What, — come this eve?
'Peter and Paul! But I see through the trick —
'Yes, come, and take a flower-pot on his head
'Flung from your terrace! No joke, sincere truth?'

How plainly I perceived hell flash and fade
O' the face of her, — the doubt that first paled joy,
Then, final reassurance I indeed
Was caught now, never to be free again!
What did I care? — who felt myself of force
To play with the silk, and spurn the horse-hair-springe.

'But — do you know that I have bade him come,
'And in your own name? I presumed so much,

[207] Vasari's picture of St. George killing the dragon was in the church of Santa Maria della Pieve, Arezzo.

'Knowing the thing you needed in your heart.
'But somehow—what had I to show in proof?
'He would not come: half-promised, that was all,
'And wrote the letters you refused to read.
'What is the message that shall move him now?

After the Ave Maria, at first dark,
'I will be standing on the terrace, say!'

'I would I had a good long lock of hair
'Should prove I was not lying! Never mind!'

Off she went—'May he not refuse, that's all—
'Fearing a trick!'

I answered, 'He will come.'
And, all day, I sent prayer like incense up
To God the strong, God the beneficent,
God ever mindful in all strife and strait,
Who, for our own good, makes the need extreme,
Till at the last He puts forth might and saves.
An old rhyme came into my head and rang
Of how a virgin, for the faith of God,
Hid herself, from the Paynims that pursued,
In a cave's heart; until a thunderstone,
Wrapped in a flame, revealed the couch and prey:
And they laughed—'Thanks to lightning, ours at last!'
And she cried 'Wrath of God, assert His love!
'Servant of God, thou fire, befriend His child!'
And lo, the fire she grasped at, fixed its flash,
Lay in her hand a calm cold dreadful sword
She brandished till pursuers strewed the ground,
So did the souls within them die away,
As o'er the prostrate bodies, sworded, safe,
She walked forth to the solitudes and Christ:
So should I grasp the lightning and be saved!

And still, as the day wore, the trouble grew
Whereby I guessed there would be born a star,
Until at an intense throe of the dusk,
I started up, was pushed, I dare to say,
Out on the terrace, leaned and looked at last
Where the deliverer waited me: the same
Silent and solemn face, I first descried
At the spectacle, confronted mine once more.

So was that minute twice vouchsafed me, so
The manhood, wasted then, was still at watch
To save me yet a second time: no change
Here, though all else changed in the changing world!

I spoke on the instant, as my duty bade,
In some such sense as this, whatever the phrase.

'Friend, foolish words were borne from you to me;
'Your soul behind them is the pure strong wind,
'Not dust and feathers which its breath may bear:
'These to the witless seem the wind itself,
'Since proving thus the first of it they feel.
'If by mischance you blew offence my way,
'The straws are dropt, the wind desists no whit,
'And how such strays were caught up in the street
'And took a motion from you, why inquire?
'I speak to the strong soul, no weak disguise.
'If it be truth,—why should I doubt it truth?—
'You serve God specially, as priests are bound,

'And care about me, stranger as I am,
'So far as wish my good, — that miracle
'I take to intimate He wills you serve
'By saving me, — what else can He direct?
'Here is the service. Since a long while now,
'I am in course of being put to death:
'While death concerned nothing but me, I bowed
'The head and bade, in heart, my husband strike.
'Now I imperil something more, it seems,
'Something that 's trulier me than this myself,
'Something I trust in God and you to save.
'You go to Rome, they tell me: take me there,
'Put me back with my people!'

He replied —
The first word I heard ever from his lips,
All himself in it, — an eternity
Of speech, to match the immeasurable depths
O' the soul that then broke silence — 'I am yours.'

So did the star rise, soon to lead my step,
Lead on, nor pause before it should stand still
Above the House o' the Babe, — my babe to be,
That knew me first and thus made me know him,
That had his right of life and claim on mine,
And would not let me die till he was born,
But pricked me at the heart to save us both,
Saying 'Have you the will? Leave God the way!'
And the way was Caponsacchi — 'mine,' thank God!
He was mine, he is mine, he will be mine.

No pause i' the leading and the light! I know,
Next night there was a cloud came, and not he:
But I prayed through the darkness till it broke
And let him shine. The second night, he came.

'The plan is rash; the project desperate:
'In such a flight needs must I risk your life,
'Give food for falsehood, folly or mistake,
'Ground for your husband's rancour and revenge' —
So he began again, with the same face.
I felt that, the same loyalty — one star
Turning now red that was so white before —
One service apprehended newly: just
A word of mine and there the white was back!

'No, friend, for you will take me! 'Tis yourself
'Risk all, not I, — who let you, for I trust
'In the compensating great God: enough!
'I know you: when is it that you will come?'

'To-morrow at the day's dawn.' Then I heard
What I should do: how to prepare for flight
And where to fly.

That night my husband bade
'— You, whom I loathe, beware you break my sleep
'This whole night! Couch beside me like the corpse
'I would you were!' The rest you know, I think —
How I found Caponsacchi and escaped.

And this man, men call sinner? Jesus Christ!
Of whom men said, with mouths Thyself mad'st once,
'He hath a devil'[208] — say he was Thy saint,

[208] See *St. John*, vii, 20 and viii, 48.

My Caponsacchi! Shield and show — unshroud
In Thine own time the glory of the soul
If aught obscure, — if ink-spot, from vile pens
Scribbling a charge against him — (I was glad
Then, for the first time, that I could not write) —
Flirted his way, have flecked the blaze!

For me,
'Tis otherwise: let men take, sift my thoughts
— Thoughts I throw like the flax for sun to bleach!
I did pray, do pray, in the prayer shall die,
Oh, to have Caponsacchi for my guide!
Ever the face upturned to mine, the hand
Holding my hand across the world, — a sense
That reads, as only such can read, the mark
God sets on woman, signifying so
She should — shall peradventure — be divine;
Yet 'ware, the while, how weakness mars the print
And makes confusion, leaves the thing men see,
— Not this man sees, — who from his soul, re-writes
The obliterated charter, — love and strength
Mending what's marred: 'So kneels a votarist,
'Weeds some poor waste traditionary plot
'Where shrine once was, where temple yet may be,
'Purging the place but worshipping the while,
'By faith and not by sight, sight clearest so, —
'Such way the saints work,' — says Don Celestine.
But I, not privileged to see a saint
Of old when such walked earth with crown and palm,
If I call 'saint' what saints call something else —
The saints must bear with me, impute the fault
To a soul i' the bud, so starved by ignorance,
Stinted of warmth, it will not blow this year
Nor recognize the orb which Spring-flowers know.
But if meanwhile some insect with a heart
Worth floods of lazy music, spendthrift joy —
Some fire-fly renounced Spring for my dwarfed cup,
Crept close to me, brought lustre for the dark,
Comfort against the cold, — what though excess
Of comfort should miscall the creature — sun?
What did the sun to hinder while harsh hands
Petal by petal, crude and colourless,
Tore me? This one heart gave me all the Spring!

Is all told? There's the journey: and where's time
To tell you how that heart burst out in shine?
Yet certain points do press on me too hard.[209]
Each place must have a name, though I forget:
How strange it was — there where the plain begins
And the small river mitigates its flow —
When eve was fading fast, and my soul sank,
And he divined what surge of bitterness,
In overtaking me, would float me back
Whence I was carried by the striding day —
So, — 'This grey place was famous once,' said he —
And he began that legend of the place
As if in answer to the unspoken fear,
And told me all about a brave man dead,

[209] *I.e.*, too hard for me to say nothing.

Which lifted me and let my soul go on!
How did he know too, — at that town's approach
By the rock-side, — that in coming near the signs
Of life, the house-roofs and the church and tower
I saw the old boundary and wall o' the world
Rise plain as ever round me, hard and cold,
As if the broken circlet joined again,
Tightened itself about me with no break, —
As if the town would turn Arezzo's self, —
The husband there, — the friends my enemies,
All ranged against me, not an avenue
To try, but would be blocked and drive me back
On him, — this other, . . . oh the heart in that!
Did not he find, bring, put into my arms
A new-born babe? — and I saw faces beam
Of the young mother proud to teach me joy,
And gossips round expecting my surprise
At the sudden hole through earth that lets in heaven.
I could believe himself by his strong will
Had woven around me what I thought the world
We went along in, every circumstance,
Towns, flowers and faces, all things helped so well!
For, through the journey, was it natural
Such comfort should arise from first to last?
As I look back, all is one milky way;
Still bettered more, the more remembered, so
Do new stars bud while I but search for old,
And fill all gaps i' the glory, and grow him —
Him I now see make the shine everywhere.
Even at the last when the bewildered flesh,
The cloud of weariness about my soul
Clogging too heavily, sucked down all sense, —
Still its last voice was, 'He will watch and care;
'Let the strength go, I am content: he stays!'
I doubt not he did stay and care for all —
From that sick minute when the head swam round,
And the eyes looked their last and died on him,
As in his arms he caught me and, you say,
Carried me in, that tragical red eve,
And laid me where I next returned to life
In the other red of morning, two red plates
That crushed together, crushed the time between,
And are since then a solid fire to me, —
When in, my dreadful husband and the world
Broke, — and I saw him, master, by hell's right
And saw my angel helplessly held back
By guards that helped the malice — the lamb prone,
The serpent towering and triumphant — then
Came all the strength back in a sudden swell,
I did for once see right, do right, give tongue
The adequate protest: for a worm must turn
If it would have its wrong observed by God.
I did spring up, attempt to thrust aside
That ice-block 'twixt the sun and me, lay low
The neutralizer of all good and truth.
If I sinned so, — never obey voice more
O' the Just and Terrible, who bids us — 'Bear!'
Not — 'Stand by, bear to see my angels bear!'
I am clear it was on impulse to serve God
Not save myself, — no — nor my child unborn!

Had I else waited patiently till now? —
Who saw my old kind parents, silly-sooth[210]
And too much trustful, for their worst of faults,
Cheated, brow-beaten, stripped and starved, cast out
Into the kennel: I remonstrated,
Then sank to silence, for, — their woes at end,
Themselves gone, — only I was left to plague.
If only I was threatened and belied,
What matter? I could bear it and did bear;
It was a comfort, still one lot for all:
They were not persecuted for my sake
And I, estranged, the single happy one.
But when at last, all by myself I stood
Obeying the clear voice which bade me rise,
Not for my own sake but my babe unborn,
And take the angel's hand was sent to help —
And found the old adversary athwart the path —
Not my hand simply struck from the angel's, but
The very angel's self made foul i' the face
By the fiend who struck there, — that I would not bear,
That only I resisted! So, my first
And last resistance was invincible.
Prayers move God; threats, and nothing else, move men!
I must have prayed a man as he were God
When I implored the Governor to right
My parents' wrongs: the answer was a smile.
The Archbishop, — did I clasp his feet enough,
Hide my face hotly on them, while I told
More than I dared make my own mother know?
The profit was — compassion and a jest.
This time, the foolish prayers were done with, right
Used might, and solemnized the sport at once.
All was against the combat: vantage, mine?
The runaway avowed, the accomplice-wife,
In company with the plan-contriving priest?
Yet, shame thus rank and patent, I struck, bare,
At foe from head to foot in magic mail,
And off it withered, cobweb-armoury
Against the lightning! 'T was truth singed the lies
And saved me, not the vain sword nor weak speech!

You see, I will not have the service fail!
I say, the angel saved me: I am safe!
Others may want and wish, I wish nor want
One point o' the circle plainer, where I stand
Traced round about with white to front the world.
What of the calumny I came across,
What o' the way to the end? — the end crowns all.
The judges judged aright i' the main, gave me
The uttermost of my heart's desire, a truce
From torture and Arezzo, balm for hurt
With the quiet nuns, — God recompense the good!
Who said and sang away the ugly past.
And, when my final fortune was revealed,
What safety while, amid my parents' arms,
My babe was given me! Yes, he saved my babe:
It would not have peeped forth, the bird-like thing,
Through that Arezzo noise and trouble: back
Had it returned nor ever let me see!
But the sweet peace cured all, and let me live
And give my bird the life among the leaves
God meant him! Weeks and months of quietude,

[210] naive

I could lie in such peace and learn so much —
Begin the task, I see how needful now,
Of understanding somewhat of my past, —
Know life a little, I should leave so soon.
Therefore, because this man restored my soul,
All has been right; I have gained my gain, enjoyed
As well as suffered, — nay, got foretaste too
Of better life beginning where this ends —
All through the breathing-while allowed me thus,
Which let good premonitions reach my soul
Unthwarted, and benignant influence flow
And interpenetrate and change my heart,
Uncrossed by what was wicked, — nay, unkind.
For, as the weakness of my time drew nigh,
Nobody did me one disservice more,
Spoke coldly or looked strangely, broke the love
I lay in the arms of, till my boy was born,
Born all in love, with nought to spoil the bliss
A whole long fortnight: in a life like mine
A fortnight filled with bliss is long and much.
All women are not mothers of a boy,
Though they live twice the length of my whole life,
And, as they fancy, happily all the same.
There I lay, then, all my great fortnight long,
As if it would continue, broaden out
Happily more and more, and lead to heaven:
Christmas before me, — was not that a chance?
I never realized God's birth before —
How he grew likest God in being born.
This time I felt like Mary, had my babe
Lying a little on my breast like hers.
So all went on till, just four days ago —
The night and the tap.
O it shall be success
To the whole of our poor family! My friends
. . . Nay, father and mother, — give me back my word!
They have been rudely stripped of life, disgraced
Like children who must needs go clothed too fine,
Carry the garb of Carnival in Lent:
If they too much affected frippery,
They have been punished and submit themselves,
Say no word: all is over, they see God
Who will not be extreme to mark their fault
Or He had granted respite: they are safe.

For that most woeful man my husband once,
Who, needing respite, still draws vital breath,
I — pardon him? So far as lies in me,
I give him for his good the life he takes,
Praying the world will therefore acquiesce.
Let him make God amends, — none, none to me
Who thank him rather that, whereas strange fate
Mockingly styled him husband and me wife,
Himself this way at least pronounced divorce,
Blotted the marriage-bond: this blood of mine
Flies forth exultingly at any door,
Washes the parchment white, and thanks the blow.
We shall not meet in this world nor the next,
But where will God be absent? In His face
Is light, but in His shadow healing too:
Let Guido touch the shadow and be healed!
And as my presence was importunate, —
My earthly good, temptation and a snare,

Nothing about me but drew somehow down
His hate upon me, — somewhat so excused
Therefore, since hate was thus the truth of him, —
May my evanishment for evermore
Help further to relieve the heart that cast
Such object of its natural loathing forth!
So he was made; he nowise made himself:
I could not love him, but his mother did.
His soul has never lain beside my soul;
But for the unresisting body, — thanks!
He burned that garment spotted by the flesh!
Whatever he touched is rightly ruined: plague
It caught, and disinfection it had craved
Still but for Guido; I am saved through him
So as by fire; to him — thanks and farewell![211]

Even for my babe, my boy, there's safety thence —
From the sudden death of me, I mean: we poor
Weak souls, how we endeavour to be strong!
I was already using up my life, —
This portion, now, should do him such a good,
This other go to keep off such an ill!
The great life; see, a breath and it is gone!
So is detached, so left all by itself
The little life, the fact which means so much.
Shall not God stoop the kindlier to His work,
His marvel of creation, foot would crush,
Now that the hand He trusted to receive
And hold it, lets the treasure fall perforce?
The better; He shall have in orphanage
His own way all the clearlier: if my babe
Outlive the hour — and he has lived two weeks —
It is through God who knows I am not by.
Who is it makes the soft gold hair turn black,
And sets the tongue, might lie so long at rest,
Trying to talk? Let us leave God alone!
Why should I doubt He will explain in time
What I feel now, but fail to find the words?
My babe nor was, nor is, nor yet shall be
Count Guido Franceschini's child at all —
Only his mother's, born of love not hate!
So shall I have my rights in after-time.
It seems absurd, impossible to-day;
So seems so much else not explained but known.

Ah! Friends, I thank and bless you every one!
No more now: I withdraw from earth and man
To my own soul, compose myself for God.

Well, and there is more! Yes, my end of breath
Shall bear away my soul in being true!
He is still here, not outside with the world,
Here, here, I have him in his rightful place!
'T is now, when I am most upon the move,
I feel for what I verily find — again
The face, again the eyes, again, through all,
The heart and its immeasurable love
Of my one friend, my only, all my own,
Who put his breast between the spears and me.
Ever with Caponsacchi! Otherwise
Here alone would be failure, loss to me —
How much more loss to him, with life debarred
From giving life, love locked from love's display,
The day-star stopped its task that makes night morn!

[211] Compare *Caponsacchi* on Guido (ll. 1887–1954, p. 1017f.).

O lover of my life, O soldier-saint,
No work begun shall ever pause for death!
Love will be helpful to me more and more
I' the coming course, the new path I must tread,
My weak hand in thy strong hand, strong for that!
Tell him that if I seem without him now,
That's the world's insight! Oh, he understands!
He is at Civita[212] — do I once doubt
The world again is holding us apart?
He had been here, displayed in my behalf
The broad brow that reverberates the truth,
And flashed the word God gave him, back to man!
I know where the free soul is flown! My fate
Will have been hard for even him to bear:
Let it confirm him in the trust of God,
Showing how holily he dared the deed!
And, for the rest, — say, from the deed, no touch
Of harm came, but all good, all happiness,
Not one faint fleck of failure! Why explain?
What I see, oh, he sees and how much more!
Tell him, — I know not wherefore the true word
Should fade and fall unuttered at the last —
It was the name of him I sprang to meet
When came the knock, the summons and the end.
'My great heart, my strong hand are back again!'
I would have sprung to these, beckoning across
Murder and hell gigantic and distinct
O' the threshold, posted to exclude me heaven:
He is ordained to call and I to come!
Do not the dead wear flowers when dressed for God?
Say, — I am all in flowers from head to foot!
Say, — not one flower of all he said and did,
Might seem to flit unnoticed, fade unknown,
But dropped a seed has grown a balsam-tree
Whereof the blossoming perfumes the place
At this supreme of moments! He is a priest;
He cannot marry therefore, which is right:
I think he would not marry if he could.
Marriage on earth seems such a counterfeit,
Mere imitation of the inimitable:
In heaven we have the real and true and sure.
'T is there they neither marry nor are given
In marriage but are as the angels: right,
Oh how right that is, how like Jesus Christ
To say that! Marriage-making for the earth,
With gold so much, — birth, power, repute so much,
Or beauty, youth so much, in lack of these!
Be as the angels rather, who, apart,
Know themselves into one, are found at length
Married, but marry never, no, nor give
In marriage; they are man and wife at once
When the true time is: here we have to wait
Not so long neither! Could we by a wish
Have what we will and get the future now,
Would we wish aught done undone in the past?
So, let him wait God's instant men call years;
Meantime hold hard by truth and his great soul,
Do out the duty! Through such souls alone
God stooping shows sufficient of His light
For us i' the dark to rise by. And I rise.

---

[212] Scene of Caponsacchi's banishment. Actually at this time, of course, he is speaking before the Judges at Rome.

from Book X. *The Pope*[213]

'Quis pro Domino?
'Who is upon the Lord's side?' asked the Count.
I, who write —
'On receipt of this command,
'Acquaint Count Guido and his fellows four
'They die to-morrow: could it be to-night,
'The better, but the work to do, takes time.
'Set with all diligence a scaffold up,
'Not in the customary place, by Bridge
'Saint Angelo, where die the common sort;
'But since the man is noble, and his peers
'By predilection haunt the People's Square,
'There let him be beheaded in the midst,
'And his companions hanged on either side:
'So shall the quality see, fear and learn.
'All which work takes time: till to-morrow, then,
'Let there be prayer incessant for the five!'

For the main criminal[214] I have no hope
Except in such a suddenness of fate.
I stood at Naples once, a night so dark
I could have scarce conjectured there was earth
Anywhere, sky or sea or world at all:
But the night's black was burst through by a blaze —
Thunder struck blow on blow, earth groaned and bore,
Through her whole length of mountain visible:
There lay the city thick and plain with spires,
And, like a ghost disshrouded, white the sea.
So may the truth be flashed out by one blow,
And Guido see, one instant, and be saved.
Else I avert my face, nor follow him
Into that sad obscure sequestered state
Where God unmakes but to remake the soul
He else made first in vain; which must not be.
Enough, for I may die this very night
And how should I dare die, this man let live?

Carry this forthwith to the Governor!

from Book XI. *Guido*[215]

You never know what life means till you die:
Even throughout life, 't is death that makes life live,
Gives it whatever the significance.
For see, on your own ground and argument,
Suppose life had no death to fear, how find
A possibility of nobleness
In man, prevented daring any more?
What 's love, what 's faith without a worst to dread?
Lack-lustre jewelry; but faith and love
With death behind them bidding do or die —
Put such a foil at back, the sparkle 's born!
From out myself how the strange colours come!
Is there a new rule in another world?
Be sure I shall resign myself: as here
I recognized no law I could not see,
There, what I see, I shall acknowledge too:
On earth I never took the Pope for God,
In heaven I shall scarce take God for the Pope.
Unmanned, remanned: I hold it probable—
With something changeless at the heart of me
To know me by, some nucleus that 's myself:
Accretions did it wrong? Away with them —
You soon shall see the use of fire!

---

[213] The Pope, venerable and holy as he draws near the time of his own death, is the final judge of Guido. The striking reason for his decision is here given as the climax of one of Browning's best characterizations.
[214] Guido

[215] Waiting in the condemned cell, Guido has continued his defiance; he hears now the summons to execution.

Till when,
All that was, is; and must for ever be.
Nor is it in me to unhate my hates, —
I use up my last strength to strike once more
Old Pietro in the wine-house-gossip-face,
To trample underfoot the whine and wile
Of beast Violante, — and I grow one gorge
To loathingly reject Pompilia's pale
Poison my hasty hunger took for food.
A strong tree wants no wreaths about its trunk,
No cloying cups, no sickly sweet of scent,
But sustenance at root, a bucketful.
How else lived that Athenian who died so,
Drinking hot bull's-blood, fit for men like me?
I lived and died a man, and take man's chance,
Honest and bold: right will be done to such.

Who are these you have let descend my stair?
Ha, their accursed psalm! Lights at the sill!
Is it 'Open' they dare bid you? Treachery!
Sirs, have I spoken one word all this while
Out of the world of words I had to say?
Not one word! All was folly — I laughed and mocked!
Sirs, my first true word, all truth and no lie,
Is — save me notwithstanding! Life is all!
I was just stark mad, — let the madman live
Pressed by as many chains as you please pile!
Do n't open! Hold me from them! I am yours,
I am the Granduke's — no, I am the Pope's!
Abate, — Cardinal, — Christ, — Maria, — God, . . .
Pompilia, will you let them murder me?

House [216]

I

Shall I sonnet-sing you about myself?
Do I live in a house you would like to see?
Is it scant of gear, has it store of pelf?
'Unlock my heart with a sonnet-key?'

II

Invite the world, as my betters have done?
'Take notice: this building remains on view,
Its suites of reception every one,
Its private apartment and bedroom too;

III

'For a ticket, apply to the Publisher.'
No: thanking the public, I must decline.
A peep through my window, if folk prefer;
But, please you, no foot over threshold of mine!

IV

I have mixed with a crowd and heard free talk
In a foreign land where an earthquake chanced:
And a house stood gaping, naught to balk
Man's eye wherever he gazed or glanced.

V

The whole of the frontage shaven sheer,
The inside gaped: exposed to day,
Right and wrong and common and queer,
Bare, as the palm of your hand, it lay.

VI

The owner? Oh, he had been crushed, no doubt!
'Odd tables and chairs for a man of wealth!
What a parcel of musty old books about!
He smoked, — no wonder he lost his health!

216 Published in *Pacchiarotto and Other Poems*, 1876.

VII

'I doubt if he bathed before he dressed.
A brasier? — the pagan, he burned perfumes!
You see it is proved, what the neighbours guessed:
His wife and himself had separate rooms.'

VIII

Friends, the goodman of the house at least
Kept house to himself till an earthquake came:
'Tis the fall of its frontage permits you feast
On the inside arrangement you praise or blame.

IX

Outside should suffice for evidence:
And whoso desires to penetrate
Deeper, must dive by the spirit-sense —
No optics like yours, at any rate!

X

'Hoity-toity! A street to explore,
Your house the exception! *"With this same key*
Shakespeare unlocked his heart," [217] once more!'
Did Shakespeare? If so, the less Shakespeare he!

Bad Dreams [218]

I

Last night I saw you in my sleep:
And how your charm of face was changed!
I asked, 'Some love, some faith you keep?'
You answered, 'Faith gone, love estranged.'

Whereat I woke — a twofold bliss:
Waking was one, but next there came
This other: 'Though I felt, for this,
My heart break, I loved on the same.'

Epilogue to Asolando

At the midnight in the silence of the sleep-time,
When you set your fancies free,
Will they pass to where — by death, fools think, imprisoned —
Low he lies who once so loved you, whom you loved so,
— Pity me?

Oh to love so, be so loved, yet so mistaken!
What had I on earth to do
With the slothful, with the mawkish, the unmanly?
Like the aimless, helpless, hopeless, did I drivel —
Being — who?

One who never turned his back but marched breast forward,
Never doubted clouds would break,
Never dreamed, though right were worsted, wrong would triumph,
Held we fall to rise, are baffled to fight better,
Sleep to wake.

No, at noonday in the bustle of man's work-time
Greet the unseen with a cheer!
Bid him forward, breast and back as either should be,
'Strive and thrive!' cry 'Speed, — fight on, fare ever
There as here!'

[1889]

[217] Lines 2–3 of Wordsworth's *Scorn not the Sonnet* (see p. 657).
[218] This and the following poem were published in *Asolando*, 1889.

Elizabeth Barrett Browning

1806–1861

The Cry of the Children [1]

φεῦ, φεῦ· τί προσδέρκεσθέ μ᾽ὄμμασιν, τέκνα;[2]
—*Medea*

I

Do ye hear the children weeping, O my brothers,
Ere the sorrow comes with years?
They are leaning their young heads against their mothers,
And *that* cannot stop their tears.
The young lambs are bleating in the meadows,
The young birds are chirping in the nest,
The young fawns are playing with the shadows,
The young flowers are blowing toward the west —
But the young, young children, O my brothers,
They are weeping bitterly!
They are weeping in the playtime of the others,
In the country of the free.

II

Do you question the young children in the sorrow,
Why their tears are falling so?
The old man may weep for his to-morrow
Which is lost in Long Ago;
The old tree is leafless in the forest,
The old year is ending in the frost,
The old wound, if stricken, is the sorest,
The old hope is hardest to be lost:
But the young, young children, O my brothers,
Do you ask them why they stand
Weeping sore before the bosoms of their mothers,
In our happy Fatherland?

III

They look up with their pale and sunken faces,
And their looks are sad to see,
For the man's hoary anguish draws and presses
Down the cheeks of infancy;
'Your old earth,' they say, 'is very dreary,
Our young feet,' they say, 'are very weak;
Few paces have we taken, yet are weary —
Our grave-rest is very far to seek:
Ask the aged why they weep, and not the children,
For the outside earth is cold,
And we young ones stand without, in our bewildering,
And the graves are for the old.'

IV

'True,' say the children, 'it may happen
That we die before our time:
Little Alice died last year, her grave is shapen
Like a snowball, in the rime.
We looked into the pit prepared to take her:
Was no room for any work in the close clay!
From the sleep wherein she lieth none will wake her,
Crying, "Get up, little Alice! it is day."
If you listen by that grave, in sun and shower,
With your ear down, little Alice never cries;
Could we see her face, be sure we should not know her,
For the smile has time for growing in her eyes:
And merry go her moments, lulled and stilled in
The shroud by the kirk-chime.

---

[1] First published in *Blackwood's Magazine*, August 1843. It was suggested by an official report on child labor.
[2] Alas, alas! why do you stare at me, children?

It is good when it happens,' say the children,
'That we die before our time.'

V

Alas, alas, the children! They are seeking
Death in life, as best to have:
They are binding up their hearts away from breaking,
With a cerement from the grave.
Go out, children, from the mine and from the city,
Sing out, children, as the little thrushes do;
Pluck you handfuls of the meadow-cowslips pretty,
Laugh aloud, to feel your fingers let them through!
But they answer, 'Are your cowslips of the meadows
Like our weeds anear the mine?
Leave us quiet in the dark of the coal-shadows,
From your pleasures fair and fine!

VI

'For oh,' say the children, 'we are weary,
And we cannot run or leap;
If we cared for any meadows, it were merely
To drop down in them and sleep.
Our knees tremble sorely in the stooping,
We fall upon our faces, trying to go;
And, underneath our heavy eyelids drooping
The reddest flower would look as pale as snow.
For, all day, we drag our burden tiring
Through the coal-dark, underground;
Or, all day, we drive the wheels of iron
In the factories, round and round.

VII

'For all day the wheels are droning, turning;
Their wind comes in our faces,
Till our hearts turn, our heads with pulses burning,
And the walls turn in their places:
Turns the sky in the high window, blank and reeling,
Turns the long light that drops adown the wall,
Turn the black flies that crawl along the ceiling:
All are turning, all the day, and we with all.
And all day, the iron wheels are droning,
And sometimes we could pray,
"O ye wheels" (breaking out in a mad moaning),
"Stop! be silent for to-day!"'

VIII

Ay! be silent! Let them hear each other breathing
For a moment, mouth to mouth!
Let them touch each other's hands, in a fresh wreathing
Of their tender human youth!
Let them feel that this cold metallic motion
Is not all the life God fashions or reveals:
Let them prove their living souls against the notion
That they live in you, or under you, O wheels!
Still, all day, the iron wheels go onward,
Grinding life down from its mark;
And the children's souls, which God is calling sunward,
Spin on blindly in the dark.

IX

Now tell the poor young children, O my brothers,
To look up to Him, and pray;
So the blesséd One who blesseth all the others,
Will bless them another day.
They answer, 'Who is God that He should hear us,
While the rushing of the iron wheels is stirred?

When we sob aloud, the human creatures near us
Pass by, hearing not, or answer not a word.
And *we* hear not (for the wheels in their resounding)
Strangers speaking at the door:
Is it likely God, with angels singing round Him,
Hears our weeping any more?

X

'Two words, indeed, of praying we remember,
And at midnight's hour of harm,
"Our Father," looking upward in the chamber,
We say softly for a charm.
We know no other words except "Our Father,"
And we think that, in some pause of angels' song,
God may pluck them with the silence sweet to gather,
And hold both within His right hand which is strong.
"Our Father!" If He heard us, He would surely
(For they call Him good and mild)
Answer, smiling down the steep world very purely,
"Come and rest with me, my child."

XI

'But, no!' say the children, weeping faster,
'He is speechless as a stone:
And they tell us, of His image is the master
Who commands us to work on.
Go to!' say the children, — 'up in Heaven,
Dark, wheel-like, turning clouds are all we find.
Do not mock us; grief has made us unbelieving:
We look up for God, but tears have made us blind.'
Do you hear the children weeping and disproving,
O my brothers, what ye preach?
For God's possible is taught by His world's loving,
And the children doubt of each.

XII

And well may the children weep before you!
They are weary ere they run;
They have never seen the sunshine, nor the glory
Which is brighter than the sun.
They know the grief of man, without its wisdom;
They sink in man's despair, without its calm;
Are slaves, without the liberty in Christdom,
Are martyrs, by the pang without the palm:
Are worn as if with age, yet unretrievingly
The harvest of its memories cannot reap, —
Are orphans of the earthly love and heavenly.
Let them weep! let them weep!

XIII

They look up with their pale and sunken faces,
And their look is dread to see,
For they mind you of their angels in high places,
With eyes turned on Deity.
'How long,' they say, 'how long, O cruel nation,
Will you stand, to move the world, on a child's heart, —
Stifle down with a mailed heel its palpitation,
And tread onward to your throne amid the mart?
Our blood splashes upward, O goldheaper,
And your purple shows your path!
But the child's sob in the silence curses deeper
Than the strong man in his wrath.'

SONNETS FROM THE PORTUGUESE [3]

I

I THOUGHT once how Theocritus had sung
Of the sweet years, the dear and wished-for years,
Who each one in a gracious hand appears
To bear a gift for mortals, old or young:
And, as I mused it in his antique tongue,
I saw, in gradual vision through my tears,
The sweet, sad years, the melancholy years,
Those of my own life, who by turns had flung
A shadow across me. Straightway I was 'ware,
So weeping, how a mystic Shape did move
Behind me, and drew me backward by the hair;
And a voice said in mastery, while I strove, —
'Guess now who holds thee?' — 'Death,' I said. But, there,
The silver answer rang — 'Not Death, but Love.'

III

UNLIKE are we, unlike, O princely Heart!
Unlike our uses and our destinies.
Our ministering two angels look surprise
On one another, as they strike athwart
Their wings in passing. Thou, bethink thee, art
A guest for queens to social pageantries,
With gages [4] from a hundred brighter eyes
Than tears even can make mine, to play thy part
Of chief musician. What hast *thou* to do
With looking from the lattice-lights at me,
A poor, tired, wandering singer, singing through
The dark, and leaning up a cypress-tree?
The chrism [5] is on thine head, — on mine, the dew, —
And Death must dig the level where these agree.

VII

THE face of all the world is changed, I think,
Since first I heard the footsteps of thy soul
Move still, oh, still, beside me, as they stole
Betwixt me and the dreadful outer brink
Of obvious death, where I, who thought to sink,
Was caught up into love, and taught the whole
Of life in a new rhythm. The cup of dole
God gave for baptism, I am fain to drink,
And praise its sweetness, Sweet, with thee anear.
The names of country, heaven, are changed away
For where thou art or shalt be, there or here;
And this . . . this lute and song . . . loved yesterday,
(The singing angels know) are only dear
Because thy name moves right in what they say.

XVI

AND yet, because thou overcomest so,
Because thou art more noble and like a king,
Thou canst prevail against my fears and fling
Thy purple round me, till my heart shall grow
Too close against thine heart henceforth to know
How it shook when alone. Why, conquering
May prove as lordly and complete a thing
In lifting upward, as in crushing low!
And as a vanquished soldier yields his sword

[3] These sonnets celebrate the love of Robert Browning and Elizabeth Barrett, who finally gave them one morning in 1847 to her husband, telling him to tear them up if he did not like them. Though they were meant to be private, Browning held that their high quality — 'the finest sonnets written in any language since Shakespeare' — demanded publication. They appeared in 1850. The title, recalling Camoëns, the Portuguese poet, was selected by Browning, because of his liking for his wife's earlier love poem, *Catarina to Camoëns*.

[4] pledges

[5] ointment

To one who lifts him from the bloody earth,
Even so, Belovéd, I at last record,
Here ends my strife. If *thou* invite me forth,
I rise above abasement at the word.
Make thy love larger to enlarge my worth.

XX

Belovéd, my Belovéd, when I think
That thou wast in the world a year ago,
What time I sate alone here in the snow
And saw no footprint, heard the silence sink
No moment at thy voice, but, link by link,
Went counting all my chains as if that so
They never could fall off at any blow
Struck by thy possible hand, — why, thus I drink
Of life's great cup of wonder! Wonderful,
Never to feel thee thrill the day or night
With personal act or speech, — nor ever cull
Some prescience of thee with the blossoms white
Thou sawest growing! Atheists are as dull,
Who cannot guess God's presence out of sight.

XXII

When our two souls stand up erect and strong,
Face to face, silent, drawing nigh and nigher,
Until the lengthening wings break into fire
At either curvéd point, — what bitter wrong
Can the earth do to us, that we should not long
Be here contented? Think. In mounting higher,
The angels would press on us and aspire
To drop some golden orb of perfect song
Into our deep, dear silence. Let us stay
Rather on earth, Belovéd, — where the unfit
Contrarious moods of men recoil away
And isolate pure spirits, and permit
A place to stand and love in for a day,
With darkness and the death-hour rounding it.

XXVI

I lived with visions for my company
Instead of men and women, years ago,
And found them gentle mates, nor thought to know
A sweeter music than they played to me.
But soon their trailing purple was not free
Of this world's dust, their lutes did silent grow,
And I myself grew faint and blind below
Their vanishing eyes. Then thou didst come — to be,
Belovéd, what they seemed. Their shining fronts,
Their songs, their splendours (better, yet the same,
As river-water hallowed into fonts),
Met in thee, and from out thee overcame
My soul with satisfaction of all wants:
Because God's gifts put man's best dreams to shame.

XLIII

How do I love thee? Let me count the ways.
I love thee to the depth and breadth and height
My soul can reach, when feeling out of sight
For the ends of Being and ideal Grace.
I love thee to the level of everyday's
Most quiet need, by sun and candle-light.
I love thee freely, as men strive for Right;
I love thee purely, as they turn from Praise.
I love thee with the passion put to use
In my old griefs, and with my childhood's faith.
I love thee with a love I seemed to lose
With my lost saints, — I love thee with the breath,
Smiles, tears, of all my life! — and, if God choose,
I shall but love thee better after death.

XLIV

BELOVÉD, thou hast brought me many flowers
Plucked in the garden, all the summer through
And winter, and it seemed as if they grew
In this close room, nor missed the sun and showers.
So, in the like name of that love of ours,
Take back these thoughts which here unfolded too,
And which on warm and cold days I withdrew
From my heart's ground. Indeed, those beds and bowers
Be overgrown with bitter weeds and rue,
And wait thy weeding; yet here 's eglantine,
Here 's ivy! — take them, as I used to do
Thy flowers, and keep them where they shall not pine.
Instruct thine eyes to keep their colours true,
And tell thy soul their roots are left in mine.

A Musical Instrument [6]

I

WHAT was he doing, the great god Pan,
  Down in the reeds by the river?
Spreading ruin and scattering ban,
Splashing and paddling with hoofs of a goat,
And breaking the golden lilies afloat
  With the dragon-fly on the river.

II

He tore out a reed, the great god Pan,
  From the deep cool bed of the river;
The limpid water turbidly ran,
And the broken lilies a-dying lay,
And the dragon-fly had fled away,
  Ere he brought it out of the river.

III

High on the shore sat the great god Pan,
  While turbidly flowed the river;
And hacked and hewed as a great god can,
With his hard bleak steel at the patient reed,
Till there was not a sign of the leaf indeed
  To prove it fresh from the river.

IV

He cut it short, did the great god Pan
  (How tall it stood in the river!),
Then drew the pith, like the heart of a man,
Steadily from the outside ring,
And notched the poor dry empty thing
  In holes, as he sat by the river.

V

'This is the way,' laughed the great god Pan
  (Laughed while he sat by the river),
'The only way, since gods began
To make sweet music, they could succeed.'
Then, dropping his mouth to a hole in the reed,
  He blew in power by the river.

VI

Sweet, sweet, sweet, O Pan!
  Piercing sweet by the river!
Blinding sweet, O great god Pan!
The sun on the hill forgot to die,
And the lilies revived, and the dragon-fly
  Came back to dream on the river.

VII

Yet half a beast is the great god Pan,
  To laugh as he sits by the river,
Making a poet out of a man:
The true gods sigh for the cost and pain, —
For the reed which grows nevermore again
  As a reed with the reeds in the river.

6 Published in 1860.

Emily Brontë

1818–1848

Remembrance [1]

Cold in the earth — and the deep snow piled above thee,
Far, far removed, cold in the dreary grave!
Have I forgot, my only Love, to love thee,
Severed at last by Time's all-severing wave?

Now, when alone, do my thoughts no longer hover
Over the mountains, on that northern shore,
Resting their wings where heath and fern-leaves cover
Thy noble heart for ever, ever more?

Cold in the earth — and fifteen wild Decembers
From those brown hills, have melted into spring:
Faithful, indeed, is the spirit that remembers
After such years of change and suffering!

Sweet Love of youth, forgive, if I forget thee,
While the world's tide is bearing me along;
Other desires and other hopes beset me,
Hopes which obscure, but cannot do thee wrong!

No later light has lightened up my heaven,
No second morn has ever shone for me;
All my life's bliss from thy dear life was given,
All my life's bliss is in the grave with thee.

But when the days of golden dreams had perished,
And even Despair was powerless to destroy,
Then did I learn how existence could be cherished,
Strengthened, and fed, without the aid of joy.

Then did I check the tears of useless passion —
Weaned my young soul from yearning after thine;
Sternly denied its burning wish to hasten
Down to that tomb already more than mine.

And, even yet, I dare not let it languish,
Dare not indulge in memory's rapturous pain;
Once drinking deep of that divinest anguish,
How could I seek the empty world again?

Song

The linnet in the rocky dells,
The moor-lark in the air,
The bee among the heather bells
That hide my lady fair:

The wild deer browse above her breast;
The wild birds raise their brood;
And they, her smiles of love caressed,
Have left her solitude!

I ween, that when the grave's dark wall
Did first her form retain,
They thought their hearts could ne'er recall
The light of joy again.

---

[1] This and the four following poems were published in 1846 in *Poems by Currer, Ellis, and Acton Bell* [the pen names taken respectively by Charlotte, Emily, and Anne Brontë.] The scene of Emily's poetry is the Yorkshire moors around Haworth, where she was born and reared in the church parsonage — the country of her novel, *Wuthering Heights*. Her verses were discovered in 1845, wholly by accident, by Charlotte, whereupon the sisters learned that each of the three had been writing secretly. The volume of 1846, brought out at their own expense, had a sale of two copies.

They thought the tide of grief would flow
  Unchecked through future years;
But where is all their anguish now,
  And where are all their tears?

Well, let them fight for honour's breath,
  Or pleasure's shade pursue —
The dweller in the land of death
  Is changed and careless too.

And, if their eyes should watch and weep
  Till sorrow's source were dry,
She would not, in her tranquil sleep,
  Return a single sigh!

Blow, west-wind, by the lonely mound,
  And murmur, summer-streams —
There is no need of other sound
  To soothe my lady's dreams.

[1846]

The Prisoner

A FRAGMENT

In the dungeon-crypts idly did I stray,
Reckless of the lives wasting there away;
'Draw the ponderous bars! open, Warder stern!'
He dared not say me nay — the hinges harshly turn.

'Our guests are darkly lodged,' I whisper'd, gazing through
The vault, whose grated eye showed heaven more grey than blue;
(This was when glad Spring laughed in awaking pride);
'Ay, darkly lodged enough!' returned my sullen guide.

Then, God forgive my youth; forgive my careless tongue;
I scoffed, as the chill chains on the damp flagstones rung:
'Confined in triple walls, art thou so much to fear,
That we must bind thee down and clench thy fetters here?'

The captive raised her face; it was as soft and mild
As sculptured marble saint, or slumbering unwean'd child;
It was so soft and mild, it was so sweet and fair,
Pain could not trace a line, nor grief a shadow there!

The captive raised her hand and pressed it to her brow:
'I have been struck,' she said, 'and I am suffering now;
Yet these are little worth, your bolts and irons strong;
And, were they forged in steel, they could not hold me long.'

Hoarse laughed the jailor grim: 'Shall I be won to hear;
Dost think, fond, dreaming wretch, that *I* shall grant thy prayer?
Or, better still, wilt melt my master's heart with groans?
Ah! sooner might the sun thaw down these granite stones.

'My master's voice is low, his aspect bland and kind,
But hard as hardest flint the soul that lurks behind;
And I am rough and rude, yet not more rough to see
Than is the hidden ghost that has its home in me.'

About her lips there played a smile of almost scorn:
'My friend,' she gently said, 'you have not heard me mourn;
When you my kindred's lives, *my* lost life, can restore,
Then may I weep and sue, — but never, friend, before!

'Still, let my tyrants know, I am not doomed to wear
Year after year in gloom, and desolate despair;

A messenger of Hope comes every night to me,
And offers for short life, eternal liberty.

'He comes with western winds, with evening's wandering airs,
With that clear dusk of heaven that brings the thickest stars.
Winds take a pensive tone, and stars a tender fire,
And visions rise, and change, that kill me with desire.

'Desire for nothing known in my maturer years,
When joy grew mad with awe, at counting future tears.
When, if my spirit's sky was full of flashes warm,
I knew not whence they came, from sun or thunder-storm.

'But, first, a hush of peace — a soundless calm descends;
The struggle of distress, and fierce impatience ends;
Mute music soothes my breast — unuttered harmony,
That I could never dream, till Earth was lost to me.

'Then dawns the Invisible; the Unseen its truth reveals;
My outward sense is gone, my inward essence feels:
Its wings are almost free — its home, its harbour found,
Measuring the gulf, it stoops — and dares the final bound.

'Oh! dreadful is the check — intense the agony —
When the ear begins to hear, and the eye begins to see;
When the pulse begins to throb, the brain to think again;
The soul to feel the flesh, and the flesh to feel the chain.

'Yet I would lose no sting, would wish no torture less;
The more that anguish racks, the earlier it will bless;
And robed in fires of hell, or bright with heavenly shine,
If it but herald death, the vision is divine!'

She ceased to speak, and we, unanswering, turned to go —
We had no further power to work the captive woe:
Her cheek, her gleaming eye, declared that man had given
A sentence, unapproved, and overruled by Heaven.

Then like a tender child whose hand did just enfold
Safe in its eager grasp a bird it wept to hold,
When pierced with one wild glance from the troubled hazel eye,
It gushes into tears and lets its treasure fly,

Thus ruth and selfish love, together striving, tore
The heart all newly taught to pity and adore;
If I should break the chain, I felt my bird would go;
Yet I must break the chain, or seal the prisoner's woe.

[1846]

Sympathy

There should be no despair for you
While nightly stars are burning,
While evening pours its silent dew,
And sunshine gilds the morning.
There should be no despair — though tears
May flow down like a river:
Are not the best beloved of years
Around your heart for ever?

They weep, you weep, — it must be so;
  Winds sigh as you are sighing,
And Winter sheds its grief in snow
  Where Autumn's leaves are lying:
Yet, these revive, and from their fate
  Your fate cannot be parted:
Then, journey on, if not elate,
  Still *never* broken-hearted!

[1846]

The Old Stoic

Riches I hold in light esteem,
  And Love I laugh to scorn;
And lust of fame was but a dream,
  That vanished with the morn:

And if I pray, the only prayer
  That moves my lips for me
Is, 'Leave the heart that now I bear,
  And give me liberty!'

Yes, as my swift days near their goal,
  'Tis all that I implore; —
In life and death a chainless soul,
  With courage to endure.

[1846]

A little while, a little while [2]

A little while, a little while,
  The weary task is put away,
And I can sing and I can smile,
  Alike, while I have holiday.

Where wilt thou go, my harassed heart —
  What thought, what scene invites thee now?
What spot, or near or far apart,
  Has rest for thee, my weary brow?

There is a spot, 'mid barren hills,
  Where winter howls and drives the rain;
But, if the dreary tempest chills,
  There is a light that warms again.

The house is old, the trees are bare,
  Moonless above bends twilight's dome;
But what on earth is half so dear —
  So longed for — as the hearth of home?

The mute bird sitting on the stone,
  The dank moss dripping from the wall,
The thorn-trees gaunt, the walks o'er-grown, —
  I love them — how I love them all!

Still, as I mused, the naked room,
  The alien firelight died away;
And from the midst of cheerless gloom,
  I passed to bright, unclouded day.

A little and a lone green lane,
  That opened on a common wide;
A distant, dreamy, dim blue chain
  Of mountains circling every side;

A heaven so clear, an earth so calm,
  So sweet, so soft, so hushed an air;
And, deepening still the dream-like charm,
  Wild moor-sheep feeding everywhere:

That was the scene, I knew it well;
  I knew the turfy pathway's sweep,
That, winding o'er each billowy swell,
  Marked out the tracks of wandering sheep.

Could I have lingered but an hour,
  It well had paid a week of toil;
But Truth has banished Fancy's power:
  Restraint and heavy task recoil.

Even as I stood with raptured eye,
  Absorbed in bliss so deep and dear,
My hour of rest had fleeted by,
  And back came labour, bondage, care.

The Night-wind

In summer's mellow midnight,
  A cloudless moon shone through
Our open parlour window,
  And rose-trees wet with dew.

[2] This, like the four following poems, was published posthumously in *Wuthering Heights and Agnes Grey* (new edition of 1850), with a memoir by Charlotte Brontë. Charlotte says that it was written in Emily's sixteenth year when she was away at school and 'the leisure of the evening play-hour brought back in full tide the thoughts of home.' The date may have been somewhat later.

I sat in silent musing;
  The soft wind waved my hair;
It told me heaven was glorious,
  And sleeping earth was fair.

I needed not its breathing
  To bring such thoughts to me;
But still it whispered lowly,
  'How dark the woods will be!

'The thick leaves in my murmur
  Are rustling like a dream,
And all their myriad voices
  Instinct with spirit seem.'

I said, 'Go, gentle singer,
  Thy wooing voice is kind:
But do not think its music
  Has power to reach my mind.

'Play with the scented flower,
  The young tree's supple bough,
And leave my human feelings
  In their own course to flow.'

The wanderer would not heed me;
  Its kiss grew warmer still:
'Oh, come!' it sighed so sweetly;
  'I'll win thee 'gainst thy will.

'Were we not friends from childhood?
  Have I not loved thee long?
As long as thou, the solemn night,
  Whose silence wakes my song.

'And when thy heart is resting
  Beneath the church-aisle stone,
I shall have time for mourning,
  And *thou* for being alone.'

'Ay — there it is! it wakes to-night [3]
  Deep feelings I thought dead;
Strong in the blast — quick gathering light —
  The heart's flame kindles red.

'Now I can tell by thine altered cheek,
  And by thine eyes' full gaze,
And by the words thou scarce dost speak,
  How wildly fancy plays.

'Yes — I could swear that glorious wind
  Has swept the world aside,
Has dashed its memory from thy mind
  Like foam-bells from the tide:

'And thou art now a spirit pouring
  Thy presence into all:
The thunder of the tempest's roaring,
  The whisper of its fall:

'An universal influence,
  From thine own influence free;
A principle of life — intense —
  Lost to mortality.

'Thus truly, when that breast is cold,
  Thy prisoned soul shall rise;
The dungeon mingle with the mould —
  The captive with the skies.
Nature's deep being, thine shall hold,
Her spirit all thy spirit fold,
  Her breath absorb thy sighs.
Mortal! though soon life's tale is told,
  Who once lives, never dies!'

[1850]

The Visionary

SILENT is the house: all are laid asleep:
One alone looks out o'er the snow-wreaths deep,
Watching every cloud, dreading every breeze
That whirls the 'wildering drift, and bends the groaning trees.

Cheerful is the hearth, soft the matted floor;
Not one shivering gust creeps through pane or door;
The little lamp burns straight, its rays shoot strong and far:
I trim it well, to be the wanderer's guiding-star.

[3] In these stanzas a louder gale has roused the sleeper on her pillow: the wakened soul struggles to blend with the storm by which it is swayed. [Charlotte Brontë.]

Frown, my haughty sire! chide, my angry dame!
Set your slaves to spy; threaten me with shame:
But neither sire nor dame, nor prying serf shall know
What angel nightly tracks that waste of frozen snow.

What I love shall come like visitant of air,
Safe in secret power from lurking human snare;
Who loves me, no word of mine shall e'er betray,
Though for faith unstained my life must forfeit pay.

Burn then, little lamp; glimmer straight and clear —
Hush! a rustling wing stirs, methinks, the air:
He for whom I wait thus ever comes to me;
Strange Power! I trust thy might; trust thou my constancy.

[1850]

Stanzas

Often rebuked, yet always back returning
To those first feelings that were born with me,
And leaving busy chase of wealth and learning
For idle dreams of things which cannot be:

To-day, I will seek not the shadowy region:
Its unsustaining vastness waxes drear;
And visions rising, legion after legion,
Bring the unreal world too strangely near.

I'll walk, but not in old heroic traces,
And not in paths of high morality,
And not among the half-distinguished faces,
The clouded forms of long-past history.

I'll walk where my own nature would be leading:
It vexes me to choose another guide:
Where the grey flocks in ferny glens are feeding;
Where the wild wind blows on the mountain-side.

What have those lonely mountains worth revealing?
More glory and more grief than I can tell:
The earth that wakes *one* human heart to feeling
Can centre both the worlds of Heaven and Hell.

[1850]

No coward soul is mine [4]

No coward soul is mine,
No trembler in the world's storm-troubled sphere:
I see Heaven's glories shine,
And Faith shines equal, arming me from Fear.

O God within my breast,
Almighty, ever-present Deity!
Life, that in me has rest,
As I, undying Life, have power in Thee!

Vain are the thousand creeds
That move men's hearts: unutterably vain;
Worthless as withered weeds,
Or idlest froth amid the boundless main,

To waken doubt in one
Holding so fast by Thy infinity,
So surely anchored on
The steadfast rock of Immortality.

[4] The following are the last lines my sister Emily ever wrote. [Charlotte Brontë.] The first draft, however, was composed nearly three years before her death.

With wide-embracing love
Thy Spirit animates eternal years,
Pervades and broods above,
Changes, sustains, dissolves, creates, and rears.

Though earth and moon were gone,
And suns and universes ceased to be,
And Thou wert left alone,
Every existence would exist in Thee.

There is not room for Death,
Nor atom that his might could render void:
Thou — THOU art Being and Breath,
And what THOU art may never be destroyed.

[1850]

Tell me, tell me, smiling child

TELL me, tell me, smiling child,
What the past is like to thee?
'An Autumn evening, soft and mild,
With a wind that sighs mournfully.'

Tell me, what is the present hour?
'A green and flowery spray,
Where a young bird sits gathering its power
To mount and fly away.'

And what is the future, happy one?
'A sea beneath a cloudless sun, —
A mighty, glorious, dazzling sea,
Stretching into infinity.'

Arthur Hugh Clough[1]

1819–1861

I have seen higher, holier things than these[2]

I HAVE seen higher, holier things than these,
And therefore must to these refuse my heart,
Yet am I panting for a little ease;
I'll take, and so depart.

Ah, hold! the heart is prone to fall away,
Her high and cherished visions to forget,
And if thou takest, how wilt thou repay
So vast, so dread a debt?

How will the heart, which now thou trustest, then
Corrupt, yet in corruption mindful yet,
Turn with sharp stings upon itself! Again,
Bethink thee of the debt!

— Hast thou seen higher, holier things than these,
And therefore must to these thy heart refuse?
With the true best, alack, how ill agrees
That best that thou would'st choose!

The Summum Pulchrum[3] rests in heaven above;
Do thou, as best thou may'st, thy duty do:
Amid the things allowed thee live and love;
Some day thou shalt it view.

[1] The Oxford University Press is publishing a new and complete edition of Clough's poems, edited from the manuscripts. The text of 1869, with its many posthumous poems, omitted — for reasons hardly forceful to-day — much material that shows the author's gift for humor and satire. His narrative and humorous verse has hitherto been overshadowed by his 'poems of doubt' and meditation. The text printed here is that of the new Oxford edition, and contains several previously unpublished lines, as well as alterations of the 1869 text (these last not indicated). Unfortunately no anthology can do justice to Clough's long poems. His long-vacation story, *The Bothie of Tober-na-vuolich*, is not represented here at all.

[2] The first three stanzas are dated 16 May and the last two 13 November 1841(?). In *Ambarvalia* the poem formed part ten of 'Blank Misgivings of a Creature moving about in Worlds not realised.' In 1869, the editors entitled it 'Τὸ καλόν'. This and the two following poems were published in *Ambarvalia*, 1849.

[3] Highest Beauty

My wind is turned to bitter north [4]

My wind is turned to bitter north,
  That was so soft a south before;
My sky, that shone so sunny bright,
  With foggy gloom is clouded o'er:
My gay green leaves are yellow-black,
  Upon the dark autumnal floor;
For love, departed once, comes back
  No more again, no more.

A roofless ruin lies my home,
  For winds to blow and rains to pour;
One frosty night befell, and lo,
  I find my summer days are o'er:
The heart bereaved, of why and how
  Unknowing, knows that yet before
It had what e'en to Memory now
  Returns no more, no more.

Qua Cursum Ventus [5]

As ships, becalmed at eve, that lay
  With canvass drooping, side by side,
Two towers of sail at dawn of day
  Are scarce long leagues apart descried;

When fell the night, upsprung the breeze,
  And all the darkling hours they plied,
Nor dreamt but each the self-same seas
  By each was cleaving, side by side:

E'en so — but why the tale reveal
  Of those, whom year by year unchanged,
Brief absence joined anew to feel,
  Astounded, soul from soul estranged?

At dead of night their sails were filled,
  And onward each rejoicing steered —
Ah, neither blame, for neither willed,
  Or wist, what first with dawn appeared!

To veer, how vain! On, onward strain,
  Brave barks! In light, in darkness too,
Through winds and tides one compass guides —
  To that, and your own selves, be true.

But O blithe breeze! and O great seas,
  Though ne'er, that earliest parting past,
On your wide plain they join again,
  Together lead them home at last.

One port, methought, alike they sought,
  One purpose hold where'er they fare, —
O bounding breeze, O rushing seas!
  At last, at last, unite them there!

[4] Written about 1845.
[5] Written 1845–1847. The title comes from Virgil's *Aeneid*, iii, 269.

Amours de Voyage [6]

[*from* Canto ii]

Dulce it is, and *decorum,* no doubt, for the country to fall, — to
Offer one's blood an oblation to Freedom, and die for the Cause; yet
Still, individual culture is also something, and no man
Finds quite distinct the assurance that he of all others is called on,
Or would be justified even, in taking away from the world that
Precious creature, himself. Nature sent him here to abide here;
Else why send him at all? Nature wants him still, it is likely;
On the whole, we are meant to look after ourselves; it is certain
Each has to eat for himself, digest for himself, and in general
Care for his own dear life, and see to his own preservation;
Nature's intentions, in most things uncertain, in this are decisive;
Which, on the whole, I conjecture the Romans will follow, and I shall.

[*from* Canto v]

Whither depart the souls of the brave that die in the battle,
Die in the lost, lost fight, for the cause that perishes with them?

[6] The poem was begun and largely written in the summer of 1849, when Clough was at Rome during the siege by the French army. It is a satirical narrative, full of lively description, written in the form of letters, chiefly those of the 'hero,' Claude. He is a young man whose introspective irresolution is as amusing as it is enervating — *il doutait de tout, même de l'amour!* The metre of the poem continues the experiment with hexameters which Clough had made the previous year in *The Bothie.* First published in *The Atlantic Monthly,* February–May, 1858.

Are they upborne from the field on the slumberous pinions of angels
Unto a far-off home, where the weary rest from their labour,
And the deep wounds are healed, and the bitter and burning moisture
Wiped from the generous eyes? or do they linger, unhappy,
Pining and haunting the grave of their by-gone hope and endeavour?
All declamation, alas! though I talk, I care not for Rome, nor
Italy; feebly and faintly, and but with the lips, can lament the
Wreck of the Lombard youth, and the victory of the oppressor.
Whither depart the brave? — God knows; I certainly do not.

Say not the struggle nought availeth [7]

Say not the struggle nought availeth,
The labour and the wounds are vain,
The enemy faints not, nor faileth,
And as things have been things remain.

If hopes were dupes, fears may be liars;
It may be, in yon smoke concealed,
Your comrades chase e'en now the fliers,
And, but for you, possess the field.

For while the tired waves, vainly breaking,
Seem here no painful inch to gain,
Far back, through creeks and inlets making,
Came silent, flooding in, the main,

And not by eastern windows only,
When daylight comes, comes in the light,
In front, the sun climbs slow, how slowly,
But westward, look, the land is bright.

[7] Written at Rome in 1849, during the siege by the French. It was published posthumously, as were the four following poems, in 1862.

[8] The MS. is signed, 'London November ? 1849 (after Chamouni)', and bears the title given above. The title usually given, '*Ite Domum saturae, venit Hesperus,*' was supplied by Clough's editors.

Les Vaches [8]

The skies have sunk, and hid the upper snow,
(Home, Rose, and home, Provence and La Palie)
The rainy clouds are filing fast below,
And wet will be the path, and wet shall we.
Home, Rose, and home, Provence and La Palie.

Ah dear, and where is he, a year agone,
Who stepped beside and cheered us on and on?
My sweetheart wanders far away from me,
In foreign land or o'er a foreign sea.
Home, Rose, and home, Provence and La Palie.

The lightning zigzags shoot across the sky,
(Home, Rose, and home, Provence and La Palie)
And through the vale the rains go sweeping by;
Ah me, and when in shelter shall we be?
Home, Rose, and home, Provence and La Palie.

Cold, dreary cold, the stormy winds feel they
O'er foreign lands and foreign seas that stray.
(Home, Rose, and home, Provence and La Palie)
And doth he e'er, I wonder, bring to mind
The pleasant huts and herds he left behind?
And doth he sometimes in his slumbering see
The feeding kine, and doth he think of me,
My sweetheart wandering whersoe'er it be?
Home, Rose, and home, Provence and La Palie.

The thunder bellows far from snow to snow,
(Home, Rose, and home, Provence and La Palie)
And loud and louder roars the flood below.
Heigho! but soon in shelter shall we be.
Home, Rose, and home, Provence and La Palie.

Or shall he find before his term be sped,
Some comelier maid that he shall wish to wed?
(Home, Rose, and home, Provence and La Palie)
For weary is work, and weary day by day
To have your comfort miles on miles away.
Home, Rose, and home, Provence and La Palie.

Or may it be 'tis I shall find my mate,
And he returning see himself too late?
For work we must, and what we see, we see,
And God he knows, and what must be, must be,
When sweethearts wander far away from me.
Home, Rose, and home, Provence and La Palie.

The sky behind is brightening up anew,
(Home, Rose, and home, Provence and La Palie)
The rain is ending, and our journey too;
Heigho! aha! for here at home are we:—
In, Rose, and in, Provence and La Palie.

It fortifies my soul to know [9]

It fortifies my soul to know
That, though I perish, Truth is so:
That, howsoe'er I stray and range,
Whate'er I do, Thou dost not change.
I steadier step when I recall
That, if I slip, Thou dost not fall.

[9] In the 1869 edition the poem was entitled 'With Whom is no variableness, neither shadow of turning.' The MS. is in a notebook Clough was using in 1850.

Green fields of England [10]

Green fields of England! whereso'er
Across this watery waste we fare,
Your image at our hearts we bear,
Green fields of England, everywhere.

Sweet eyes in England, I must flee
Past where the waves' last confines be,
Ere your loved smile I cease to see,
Sweet eyes in England, dear to me.

Dear home in England, safe and fast
If but in thee my lot lie cast,
The past shall seem a nothing past
To thee, dear home, if won at last;
Dear home in England, won at last.

The Latest Decalogue [11]

Thou shalt have one God only; who
Would be at the expense of two?
No graven images may be
Worshipped, except the currency:
Swear not at all; for, for thy curse
Thine enemy is none the worse:
At church on Sunday to attend
Will serve to keep the world thy friend:
Honour thy parents; that is, all
From whom advancement may befall:
Thou shalt not kill; but needst not strive
Officiously to keep alive:
Do not adultery commit;
Advantage rarely comes of it:
Thou shalt not steal; an empty feat,
When it's so lucrative to cheat:
Bear not false witness; let the lie
Have time on its own wings to fly:
Thou shalt not covet; but tradition
Approves all forms of competition.

[10] Written on a voyage to America in November 1852 and sent home in a letter to Blanche Smith, later Clough's wife.

[11] The last four lines have not been printed in former editions.

The sum of all is, thou shalt love,
If any body, God above:
At any rate shall never labour
More than thyself to love thy neighbour.

When the dews are earliest falling [12]

When the dews are earliest falling,
When the evening glen is grey,
Ere thou lookest, ere thou speakest,
My beloved,
I depart, and I return to thee, —
Return, return, return.

Dost thou watch me while I traverse
Haunts of men, beneath the sun —
Dost thou list while I bespeak them
With a voice whose cheer is thine?
O my brothers! men, my brothers,
You are mine, and I am yours;
I am yours to cheer and succour,
I am yours for hope and aid:
Lo, my hand to raise and stay you,
Lo, my arm to guard and keep,
My voice to rouse and warn you,
And my heart to warm and calm:
My heart to lend the life it owes
To her that is not here,
In the power of her that dwelleth
Where you know not — no, nor guess not —
Whom you see not; unto whom, —
Ere the evening star hath sunken,
Ere the glow-worm lights its lamp,
Ere the weariest workman slumbers, —
I return, return, return.

Easter Day [13]

NAPLES, 1849

Through the the great sinful streets of Naples as I past,
With fiercer heat than flamed above my head
My heart was hot within me; till at last
My brain was lightened when my tongue had said —
Christ is not risen!

Christ is not risen, no —
He lies and moulders low;
Christ is not risen!

What though the stone were rolled away, and though
The grave found empty there? —
If not there, then elsewhere;
If not where Joseph laid Him first, why then
Where other men
Translaid Him after, in some humbler clay.
Long ere to-day
Corruption that sad perfect work hath done,
Which here she scarcely, lightly had begun:
The foul engendered worm
Feeds on the flesh of the life-giving form
Of our most Holy and Anointed One.
He is not risen, no —
He lies and moulders low;
Christ is not risen!

Ashes to ashes, dust to dust;
As of the Unjust, also of the Just —
Christ is not risen!

What if the women, ere the dawn was grey,
Saw one or more great angels, as they say
(Angels, or Him himself)? Yet neither there, nor then,
Nor afterward, nor elsewhere, nor at all,
Hath He appeared to Peter or the Ten;
Nor, save in thunderous terror, to blind Saul;
Save in an after-Gospel and late Creed,
He is not risen, indeed, —
Christ is not risen!

[12] Published in 1863. The title '*Wirkung in der Ferne*' was given by editors.

[13] The manuscript dates the poem August 1849, the year after Clough had resigned from Oriel College, Oxford, for conscience' sake (see Arnold's *Thyrsis*, p. 1104). Published in *Letters and Remains*, 1865.

Or, what if e'en, as runs the tale, the Ten
Saw, heard, and touched, again and yet again?
What if at Emmaüs' inn, and by Capernaum's Lake,
Came One, the bread that brake —
Came One that spake as never mortal spake,
And with them ate, and drank, and stood, and walked about?
Ah! 'some' did well to 'doubt'!
Ah! the true Christ, while these things came to pass,
Nor heard, nor spake, nor walked, nor dreamt alas!
He was not risen, no —
He lay and mouldered low,
Christ was not risen!

As circulates in some great city crowd
A rumour changeful, vague, importunate, and loud,
From no determined centre, or of fact
Or authorship exact,
Which no man can deny
Nor verify;
So spread the wondrous fame;
He all the same
Lay senseless mouldering, low:
He was not risen, no —
Christ was not risen!

Ashes to ashes, dust to dust;
As of the unjust, also of the just —
Yea, of that Just One, too!
This is the one sad Gospel that is true —
Christ is not risen!

Is He not risen, and shall we not rise?
Oh, we unwise!
What did we dream, what wake we to discover?
Ye hills, fall on us, and ye mountains, cover!
In darkness and great gloom
Come ere we thought it is *our* day of doom;
From the cursed world, which is one tomb,
Christ is not risen!

Eat, drink, and play, and think that this is bliss:
There is no heaven but this;
There is no hell,
Save earth, which serves the purpose doubly well,
Seeing it visits still
With equallest apportionment of ill
Both good and bad alike, and brings to one same dust
The unjust and the just
With Christ, who is not risen.

Eat, drink, and die, for we are souls bereaved:
Of all the creatures under heaven's wide cope
We are most hopeless, who had once most hope,
And most beliefless, that had most believed.
Ashes to ashes, dust to dust;
As of the unjust, also of the just —
Yea, of that Just One too!
It is the one sad Gospel that is true —
Christ is not risen!

Weep not beside the tomb,
Ye women, unto whom
He was great solace while ye tended Him;
Ye who with napkin o'er this head
And folds of linen round each wounded limb
Laid out the sacred dead;
And thou that bar'st Him in thy wondering womb;
Yea, Daughters of Jerusalem, depart,
Bind up as best ye may your own sad bleeding heart:

Go to your homes, your living children tend,
Your earthly spouses love;
Set your affections *not* on things above,
Which moth and rust corrupt, which quickliest come to end:
Or pray, if pray ye must, and pray, if pray ye can,

For death; since dead is He whom ye deemed more than man,
Who is not risen: no —
But lies and moulders low —
Who is not risen!

Ye men of Galilee!
Why stand ye looking up to heaven, where Him ye ne'er may see,
Neither ascending hence, nor hither returning again?
Ye ignorant and idle fishermen!
Hence to your huts, and boats, and inland native shore,
And catch not men, but fish;
Whate'er things ye might wish,
Him neither here nor there ye e'er shall meet with more.
Ye poor deluded youths, go home,
Mend the old nets ye left to roam,
Tie the split oar, patch the torn sail:
It was indeed 'an idle tale' —
He was not risen!

And, oh, good men of ages yet to be,
Who shall believe *because* ye did not see —
Oh, be ye warned, be wise!
No more with pleading eyes,
And sobs of strong desire,
Unto the empty vacant void aspire,
Seeking another and impossible birth
That is not of your own, and only mother earth.
But if there is no other life for you,
Sit down and be content, since this must even do:
He is not risen!
One look, and then depart,
Ye humble and ye holy men of heart;
And ye! ye ministers and stewards of a Word
Which ye would preach, because another heard —
Ye worshippers of that ye do not know,
Take these things hence and go: —
He is not risen!

Here, on our Easter day
We rise, we come, and lo! we find Him not,
Gardener nor other, on the sacred spot:
Where they have laid Him is there none to say?
No sound, nor in, nor out — no word
Of where to seek the dead or meet the living Lord.
There is no glistering of an angel's wings,
There is no voice of heavenly clear behest:
Let us go hence, and think upon these things
In silence, which is best.
He is not risen? No —
But lies and moulders low.
Christ is not risen.

Easter Day

II

So in the sinful streets, abstracted and alone,
I with my secret self held communing of mine own.
So in the southern city spake the tongue
Of one that somewhat overwildly sung;
But in a later hour I sat and heard
Another voice that spake — another graver word.
Weep not, it bade, whatever hath been said,
Though He be dead, He is not dead.
In the true creed
He is yet risen indeed;
Christ is yet risen.

Weep not beside His tomb,
Ye women unto whom
He was great comfort and yet greater grief;
Nor ye, ye faithful few that wont with Him to roam,
Seek sadly what for Him ye left, go hopeless to your home;
Nor ye despair, ye sharers yet to be of their belief;
Though He be dead, He is not dead,

Nor gone, though fled,
Not lost, though vanished;
Though He return not, though
He lies and moulders low;
In the true creed
He is yet risen indeed;
Christ is yet risen.

Sit if ye will, sit down upon the ground,
Yet not to weep and wail, but calmly look around.
Whate'er befell,
Earth is not hell;
Now, too, as when it first began
Life yet is life, and man is man.
For all that breathe beneath the heaven's high cope,
Joy with grief mixes, with despondence hope.
Hope conquers cowardice, joy grief:
Or at the least, faith unbelief.
Though dead, not dead;
Not gone, though fled;
Not lost, not vanished.
In the great gospel and true creed,
He is yet risen indeed;
Christ is yet risen.

Dipsychus[14]

[*from* scene iv]

Dipsychus

O LET me love my love unto myself alone,
And know my knowledge to the world unknown;
No witness to the vision call,
Beholding, unbeheld of all;
And worship thee, with thee withdrawn, apart,
Whoe'er, whate'er thou art,
Within the closest veil of mine own inmost heart.

. . .

Where are the great, whom thou would'st wish to praise thee?
Where are the pure, whom thou would'st choose to love thee?
Where are the brave, to stand supreme above thee,
Whose high commands would rouse, whose chiding raise thee?
Seek, seeker, in thyself; submit to find
In the stones, bread; and life in the blank mind.

(Written in London, standing in the Park,
An evening in July, just before dark.)

Spirit

As I sat at the café, I said to myself,
They may talk as they please about what they call pelf,
They may sneer as they like about eating and drinking,
But help it I cannot, I cannot help thinking
How pleasant it is to have money, heigh ho!
How pleasant it is to have money.

I sit at my table *en grand seigneur,*
And when I have done, throw a crust to the poor;
Not only the pleasure, one's self, of good living,
But also the pleasure of now and then giving.
So pleasant it is to have money, heigh ho!
So pleasant it is to have money.

It was but last winter I came up to Town,
But already I'm getting a little renown;
I make new acquaintance where'er I appear;
I am not too shy, and have nothing to fear.

[14] Begun at Venice, the scene of the poem, in 1850 and never finished. Fragments of it were printed in 1862, and a highly 'edited' text in *Letters and Remains*, 1865. The new Oxford edition contains the first full reproduction of the MS. The story is that of a sensitive modern 'Faust' tempted and won by his 'Mephistopheles', or the Spirit of the World — a medley of meditation, description, and satire which contains much of Clough's best work.

So pleasant it is to have money, heigh ho!
So pleasant it is to have money.

I drive through the streets, and I care not a d–mn;
The people they stare, and they ask who I am;
And if I should chance to run over a cad,
I can pay for the damage if ever so bad.
So pleasant it is to have money, heigh ho!
So pleasant it is to have money.

We stroll to our box and look down on the pit,
And if it weren't low should be tempted to spit;
We loll and we talk until people look up,
And when it's half over we go out and sup.
So pleasant it is to have money, heigh ho!
So pleasant it is to have money.

The best of the tables and best of the fare —
And as for the others, the devil may care;
It isn't our fault if they dare not afford
To sup like a prince and be drunk as a lord.
So pleasant it is to have money, heigh ho!
So pleasant it is to have money.

We sit at our tables and tipple champagne;
Ere one bottle goes, comes another again;
The waiters they skip and they scuttle about,
And the landlord attends us so civilly out.
So pleasant it is to have money, heigh ho!
So pleasant it is to have money.

It was but last winter I came up to Town,
But already I'm getting a little renown;
I get to good houses without much ado,
Am beginning to see the nobility too.
So pleasant it is to have money, heigh ho!
So pleasant it is to have money.

O dear! what a pity they ever should lose it!
For they are the gentry that know how to use it;
So grand and so graceful, such manners, such dinners,
But yet, after all, it is we are the winners.
So pleasant it is to have money, heigh ho!
So pleasant it is to have money.

Thus I sat at my table *en grand seigneur,*
And when I had done threw a crust to the poor;
Not only the pleasure, one's self, of good eating,
But also the pleasure of now and then treating.
So pleasant it is to have money, heigh ho!
So pleasant it is to have money.

They may talk as they please about what they call pelf,
And how one ought never to think of one's self,
And how pleasures of thought surpass eating and drinking —
My pleasure of thought is the pleasure of thinking
How pleasant it is to have money, heigh ho!
How pleasant it is to have money.

(Written in Venice, but for all parts true,
'Twas not a crust I gave him, but a sou.)

[*from* scene v] [15]

Dipsychus

I DREAMT a dream; till morning light
A bell rang in my head all night,

[15] Dipsychus, already having yielded his virtue, finds increasing confusion in his moral world. Lines 18–27, 46–49, 75–78, 108–119, of this scene are published for the first time in the new Oxford edition of Clough.

Tinkling and tinkling first, and then
Tolling; and tinkling — tolling again.
So brisk and gay, and then so slow!
O joy and terror! mirth and woe!
Ting, ting, there is no God; ting, ting, —
Dong, there is no God; dong,
There is no God; dong, dong!

Ting, ting, there is no God; ting, ting;
Come dance and play, and merrily sing —
Ting, ting a ding; ting, ting a ding!
O pretty girl who trippest along,
Come to my bed — it isn't wrong.
Uncork the bottle, sing the song!
Ting, ting a ding: Dong; dong.
Wine has dregs; the song an end;
(A silly girl is a poor friend)
And age and weakness who shall mend?
Dong! There is no God! Dong!

Ting, ting a ding! Come dance and sing!
Staid Englishman, who toil and slave
From your first breeching to your grave,
And seldom spend and always save,
And do your duty all your life
By your young family and wife;
Come, be't not said you ne'er had known
What earth can furnish you alone.
The Italian, Frenchman, German even,
Have given up all thoughts of heaven;
And you still linger — oh, you fool! —
Because of what you learnt at school.
You should have gone at least to college,
And got a little ampler knowledge.
Ah well, and yet — dong, dong, dong:
Do, if you like, as now you do;
If work's a cheat, so's pleasure too.
And nothing's new and nothing's true;
Dong, there is no God; dong!

O Rosalie, my precious maid,
I think thou thinkest love is true;
And on thy fragrant bosom laid,
I almost could believe it too.
O in our nook, unknown, unseen,
We'll hold our fancy like a screen,
Us and the dreadful fact between.
And it shall yet be long, aye, long,
The quiet notes of our low song
Shall keep us from that sad dong, dong.
Hark! hark! hark! O voice of fear!
It reaches us here, even here!
Dong, there is no God; dong.

Ring ding, ring ding, tara, tara,
To battle, to battle — haste, haste —
To battle, to battle — aha, aha!
On, on to the conqueror's feast.
From east and west, and south and north,
Ye men of valour and of worth,
Ye mighty men of arms, come forth,
And work your will, for that is just;
And in your impulse put your trust,
Beneath your feet the fools are dust.
Alas! alas! O grief and wrong,
The good are weak, the wicked strong;
And O my God, how long, how long?
Dong, there is no God! dong.

Ring, ting; to bow before the strong,
There is a rapture too in this;
Speak, outraged maiden, in thy wrong, —
Did terror bring no secret bliss?
Were boys' shy lips worth half a song
Compared to the hot soldier's kiss?
Work for thy master, work, thou slave —
He is not merciful, but brave.
Be't joy to serve, who free and proud
Scorns thee and all the ignoble crowd;
Take that, 'tis all thou art allowed,
Except the snaky hope that they
May sometime serve who rule to-day.
When, by hell-demons, shan't they pay?
O wickedness, O shame and grief,
And heavy load, and no relief!
O God, O God! and which is worst,
To be the curser or the curst,
The victim or the murderer? Dong.
Dong, there is no God; dong.

Ring ding, ring ding, tara, tara,
Away, and hush that preaching — fagh!
Ye vulgar dreamers about peace,
Who offer noblest hearts, to heal,
The tenderest hurts honour can feel,
Paid magistrates and the Police!
O piddling merchant justice, go,
Exacter rules than yours we know;

Resentment's rule, and that high law
Of whoso best the sword can draw.
Ah well, and yet — dong, dong, dong.
Go on, my friends, as now you do;
Lawyers are villains, soldiers too;
And nothing's new and nothing's true.
Dong, there is no God; dong.

O Rosalie, my lovely maid,
I think thou thinkest love is true;
And on thy faithful bosom laid,
I almost could believe it too.
The villainies, the wrongs, the alarms,
Forget we in each other's arms.
No justice here, no God above;
But where we are, is there not love?
What? what? thou also go'st? For how
Should dead truth live in lovers' vow.
What, thou? thou also lost? Dong!
Dong; there is no God; dong.

I had a dream, from eve to light
A bell went sounding all the night.
Gay mirth, black woe, thin joys, huge pain:
I tried to stop it, but in vain.
It ran right on, and never broke;
Only when day began to stream
Through the white curtains to my bed,
And like an angel at my head
Light stood and touched me — I awoke,
And looked, and said, 'It is a dream.'

. . .

Spirit

'There is no God,' the wicked saith,
'And truly it's a blessing,
For what He might have done with us
It's better only guessing.'

'There is no God,' a youngster thinks,
'Or really, if there may be,
He surely didn't mean a man
Always to be a baby.'

'There is no God, or if there is,'
The tradesman thinks, ''twere funny
If He should take it ill in me
To make a little money.'

'Whether there be,' the rich man says,
'It matters very little,
For I and mine, thank somebody,
Are not in want of victual.'

Some others, also, to themselves,
Who scarce so much as doubt it,
Think there is none, when they are well,
And do not think about it.

But country folks who live beneath
The shadow of the steeple;
The parson and the parson's wife,
And mostly married people;

Youths green and happy in first love,
So thankful for illusion;
And men caught out in what the world
Calls guilt, in first confusion;

And almost every one when age,
Disease, or sorrows strike him,
Inclines to think there is a God,
Or something very like Him.

Whate'er you dream with doubt possest

WHATE'ER you dream with doubt possest,
Keep, keep it snug within your breast,
And lay you down and take your rest;
Forget in sleep the doubt and pain,
And when you wake, to work again.
The wind it blows, the vessel goes,
And where and whither, no one knows.

'Twill all be well: no need of care;
Though how it will, and when, and where,
We cannot see, and can't declare.
In spite of dreams, in spite of thought,
'Tis not in vain, and not for nought,
The wind it blows, the ship it goes,
Though where and whither, no one knows.

Matthew Arnold

1822–1888

SONNETS

Quiet Work [1]

One lesson, Nature, let me learn of thee,
One lesson which in every wind is blown,
One lesson of two duties kept at one
Though the loud world proclaim their enmity

Of toil unsever'd from tranquillity!
Of labour, that in lasting fruit outgrows
Far noisier schemes, accomplish'd in repose,
Too great for haste, too high for rivalry!

Yes, while on earth a thousand discords ring,
Man's fitful uproar mingling with his toil,
Still do thy sleepless ministers move on,

Their glorious tasks in silence perfecting;
Still working, blaming still our vain turmoil,
Labourers that shall not fail, when man is gone.

To a Friend

Who prop, thou ask'st, in these bad days, my mind? —
He [2] much, the old man, who, clearest-soul'd of men,
Saw The Wide Prospect,[3] and the Asian Fen,
And Tmolus hill,[4] and Smyrna bay, though blind.

Much he,[5] whose friendship I not long since won,
That halting slave, who in Nicopolis
Taught Arrian, when Vespasian's brutal son
Clear'd Rome of what most shamed him. But be his [6]

My special thanks, whose even-balanced soul,
From first youth tested up to extreme old age,
Business could not make dull, nor passion wild;

Who saw life steadily, and saw it whole;
The mellow glory of the Attic stage,
Singer of sweet Colonus, and its child.[7]

[1849]

Shakespeare [8]

Others abide our question. Thou art free.
We ask and ask — Thou smilest and art still,
Out-topping knowledge. For the loftiest hill,
Who to the stars uncrowns his majesty,

Planting his steadfast footsteps in the sea,
Making the heaven of heavens his dwelling-place,
Spares but the cloudy border of his base
To the foil'd searching of mortality;

And thou, who didst the stars and sunbeams know,
Self-school'd, self-scann'd, self-honour'd, self-secure,
Didst tread on earth unguess'd at. — Better so!

All pains the immortal spirit must endure,
All weakness which impairs, all griefs which bow,
Find their sole speech in that victorious brow.

[1849]

---

[1] This and the six following poems were published in *The Strayed Reveller, and Other Poems*, 1849. [2] Homer

[3] Europe (from Εὐρώπη, *the wide prospect*).

[4] A mountain range not far from Smyrna, 'one of the birthplaces of Homer.'

[5] Epictetus, the Stoic philosopher, banished from Rome by the Emperor Domitian in A.D. 89.

[6] Sophocles'

[7] In his *Oedipus at Colonus* Sophocles describes his native village near Athens.

[8] Arnold had written to his friend Arthur Hugh Clough in 1847, 'I keep saying, Shakspeare, Shakspeare, you are as obscure as life is.'

In Harmony with Nature

TO A PREACHER

'In harmony with Nature?' Restless fool,
Who with such heat dost preach what were to thee,
When true, the last impossibility —
To be like Nature strong, like Nature cool!

Know, man hath all which Nature hath, but more,
And in that *more* lie all his hopes of good.
Nature is cruel, man is sick of blood;
Nature is stubborn, man would fain adore;

Nature is fickle, man hath need of rest;
Nature forgives no debt, and fears no grave;
Man would be mild, and with safe conscience blest.

Man must begin, know this, where Nature ends;
Nature and man can never be fast friends.
Fool, if thou canst not pass her, rest her slave!

[1849]

The Forsaken Merman

Come, dear children, let us away;
Down and away below!
Now my brothers call from the bay,
Now the great winds shoreward blow,
Now the salt tides seaward flow;
Now the wild white horses play,
Champ and chafe and toss in the spray.
Children dear, let us away!
This way, this way!

Call her once before you go —
Call once yet!
In a voice that she will know:
'Margaret! Margaret!'
Children's voices should be dear
(Call once more) to a mother's ear;
Children's voices, wild with pain —
Surely she will come again!
Call her once and come away;
This way, this way!
'Mother dear, we cannot stay!
The wild white horses foam and fret.'
Margaret! Margaret!

Come, dear children, come away down;
Call no more!
One last look at the white-wall'd town,
And the little grey church on the windy shore;
Then come down!
She will not come though you call all day;
Come away, come away!

Children dear, was it yesterday
We heard the sweet bells over the bay?
In the caverns where we lay,
Through the surf and through the swell,
The far-off sound of a silver bell?
Sand-strewn caverns, cool and deep,
Where the winds are all asleep;
Where the spent lights quiver and gleam,
Where the salt weed sways in the stream,
Where the sea-beasts, ranged all round,
Feed in the ooze of their pasture-ground;
Where the sea-snakes coil and twine,
Dry their mail and bask in the brine;
Where great whales come sailing by,
Sail and sail, with unshut eye,
Round the world for ever and aye?
When did music come this way?
Children dear, was it yesterday?

Children dear, was it yesterday
(Call yet once) that she went away?
Once she sate with you and me,
On a red gold throne in the heart of the sea,
And the youngest sate on her knee.
She comb'd its bright hair, and she tended it well,
When down swung the sound of a far-off bell.
She sigh'd, she look'd up through the clear green sea;
She said: 'I must go, for my kinsfolk pray

In the little grey church on the shore to-day.
'Twill be Easter-time in the world — ah me!
And I lose my poor soul, Merman! here with thee.'
I said: 'Go up, dear heart, through the waves;
Say thy prayer, and come back to the kind sea-caves!'
She smiled, she went up through the surf in the bay.
Children dear, was it yesterday?

Children dear, were we long alone?
'The sea grows stormy, the little ones moan;
Long prayers,' I said, 'in the world they say;
Come!' I said; and we rose through the surf in the bay.
We went up the beach, by the sandy down
Where the sea-stocks bloom, to the white-wall'd town;
Through the narrow paved streets, where all was still,
To the little grey church on the windy hill.
From the church came a murmur of folk at their prayers,
But we stood without in the cold blowing airs.
We climb'd on the graves, on the stones worn with rains,
And we gazed up the aisle through the small leaded panes.
She sate by the pillar; we saw her clear:
'Margaret, hist! come quick, we are here!
Dear heart,' I said, 'we are long alone;
The sea grows stormy, the little ones moan.'
But, ah, she gave me never a look,
For her eyes were seal'd to the holy book!
Loud prays the priest; shut stands the door.
Come away, children, call no more!
Come away, come down, call no more!

Down, down, down!
Down to the depths of the sea!
She sits at her wheel in the humming town,
Singing most joyfully.
Hark what she sings: 'O joy, O joy,
For the humming street, and the child with its toy!
For the priest, and the bell, and the holy well;
For the wheel where I spun,
And the blessed light of the sun!'
And so she sings her fill,
Singing most joyfully,
Till the spindle drops from her hand,
And the whizzing wheel stands still.
She steals to the window, and looks at the sand,
And over the sand at the sea;
And her eyes are set in a stare;
And anon there breaks a sigh,
And anon there drops a tear,
From a sorrow-clouded eye,
And a heart sorrow-laden,
A long, long sigh;
For the cold strange eyes of a little Mermaiden
And the gleam of her golden hair.

Come away, away children;
Come children, come down!
The hoarse wind blows coldly;
Lights shine in the town.
She will start from her slumber
When gusts shake the door;
She will hear the winds howling,
Will hear the waves roar.
We shall see, while above us
The waves roar and whirl,
A ceiling of amber,
A pavement of pearl.
Singing: 'Here came a mortal,
But faithless was she!
And alone dwell for ever
The kings of the sea.'

But, children, at midnight,
When soft the winds blow,
When clear falls the moonlight,
When spring-tides are low;
When sweet airs come seaward

From heaths starr'd with broom,
And high rocks throw mildly
On the blanch'd sands a gloom;
Up the still, glistening beaches,
Up the creeks we will hie,
Over banks of bright seaweed
The ebb-tide leaves dry.
We will gaze, from the sand-hills,
At the white, sleeping town;
At the church on the hill-side—
And then come back down.
Singing: 'There dwells a loved one,
But cruel is she!
She left lonely for ever
The kings of the sea.'

[1849]

In Utrumque Paratus [9]

If, in the silent mind of One all-pure,
At first imagined lay
The sacred world; and by procession sure
From those still deeps, in form and colour drest,
Seasons alternating, and night and day,
The long-mused thought to north, south, east, and west,
Took then its all-seen way;

O waking on a world which thus-wise springs!
Whether it needs thee count
Betwixt thy waking and the birth of things
Ages or hours—O waking on life's stream!
By lonely pureness to the all-pure fount
(Only by this thou canst) the colour'd dream
Of life remount!

Thin, thin the pleasant human noises grow,
And faint the city gleams;
Rare the lone pastoral huts—marvel not thou!
The solemn peaks but to the stars are known,
But to the stars, and the cold lunar beams;
Alone the sun arises, and alone
Spring the great streams.

But, if the wild unfather'd mass no birth
In divine seats hath known;
In the blank, echoing solitude if Earth,
Rocking her obscure body to and fro,
Ceases not from all time to heave and groan,
Unfruitful oft, and at her happiest throe
Forms, what she forms, alone;

O seeming sole to awake, thy sun-bathed head
Piercing the solemn cloud
Round thy still dreaming brother-world outspread!
O man, whom Earth, thy long-vext mother, bare
Not without joy—so radiant, so endow'd
(Such happy issue crown'd her painful care)—
Be not too proud!

O when most self-exalted most alone,
Chief dreamer, own thy dream!
Thy brother-world stirs at thy feet unknown,
Who hath a monarch's hath no brother's part;
Yet doth thine inmost soul with yearning teem.
—Oh, what a spasm shakes the dreamer's heart!
'I, too, but seem.'

[1849]

[9] *I.e.*, 'Prepared for either' of the explanations of creation here set forth.

RESIGNATION [10]

TO FAUSTA [11]

To die be given us, or attain!
Fierce work it were, to do again.
So pilgrims, bound for Mecca, pray'd
At burning noon; so warriors said,

[10] This poem, which concluded the poems of 1849, is, as Herbert Paul says, 'part of Arnold's life and character [at least at twenty-six]—We cannot think of him without it.'

[11] Arnold's elder sister Jane, later Mrs. W. E. Forster.

Scarf'd with the cross, who watch'd the miles
Of dust which wreathed their struggling files
Down Lydian mountains; so, when snows
Round Alpine summits, eddying, rose,
The Goth, bound Rome-wards; so the Hun,
Crouch'd on his saddle, while the sun
Went lurid down o'er flooded plains
Through which the groaning Danube strains
To the drear Euxine; — so pray all,
Whom labours, self-ordain'd, enthrall;
Because they to themselves propose
On this side the all-common close
A goal which, gain'd, may give repose.
So pray they; and to stand again
Where they stood once, to them were pain;
Pain to thread back and to renew
Past straits, and currents long steer'd through.

But milder natures, and more free —
Whom an unblamed serenity
Hath freed from passions, and the state
Of struggle these necessitate;
Whom schooling of the stubborn mind
Hath made, or birth hath found, resign'd —
These mourn not, that their goings pay
Obedience to the passing day.
These claim not every laughing Hour
For handmaid to their striding power;
Each in her turn, with torch uprear'd,
To await their march; and when appear'd,
Through the cold gloom, with measured race,
To usher for a destined space
(Her own sweet errands all forgone)
The too imperious traveller on.
These, Fausta, ask not this; nor thou,
Time's chafing prisoner, ask it now!

We left, just ten years since, you say,
That wayside inn we left to-day.[12]
Our jovial host, as forth we fare,
Shouts greeting from his easy chair.
High on a bank our leader stands,
Reviews and ranks his motley bands,
Makes clear our goal to every eye —
The valley's western boundary.
A gate swings to! our tide hath flow'd
Already from the silent road.
The valley-pastures, one by one,
Are threaded, quiet in the sun;
And now beyond the rude stone bridge
Slopes gracious up the western ridge.
Its woody border, and the last
Of its dark upland farms is past —
Cool farms, with open-lying stores,
Under their burnish'd sycamores;
All past! and through the trees we glide,
Emerging on the green hill-side.
There climbing hangs, a far-seen sign,
Our wavering, many-colour'd line;
There winds, upstreaming slowly still
Over the summit of the hill.
And now, in front, behold outspread
Those upper regions we must tread!
Mild hollows, and clear heathy swells,
The cheerful silence of the fells.
Some two hours' march with serious air,
Through the deep noontide heats we fare;
The red-grouse, springing at our sound,
Skims, now and then, the shining ground;
No life, save his and ours, intrudes
Upon these breathless solitudes.
O joy! again the farms appear.
Cool shade is there, and rustic cheer;
There springs the brook will guide us down,
Bright comrade, to the noisy town.
Lingering, we follow down; we gain
The town, the highway, and the plain.
And many a mile of dusty way,
Parch'd and road-worn, we made that day;
But, Fausta, I remember well,
That as the balmy darkness fell
We bathed our hands with speechless glee,
That night, in the wide-glimmering sea.

---

[12] Those who have been long familiar with the English Lake-Country will find no difficulty in recalling, from the description in the text, the roadside inn at Wythburn on the descent from Dunmail Raise towards Keswick; its sedentary landlord of thirty years ago, and the passage over the Wythburn Fells to Watendlath. [Arnold.] The first 'expedition' was made in 1833, as a stone marker standing by the roadside, just across from the inn, affirms

Once more we tread this self-same road,
Fausta, which ten years since we trod;
Alone we tread it, you and I,
Ghosts of that boisterous company.
Here, where the brook shines, near its head,
In its clear, shallow, turf-fringed bed;
Here, whence the eye first sees, far down,
Capp'd with faint smoke, the noisy town;
Here sit we, and again unroll,
Though slowly, the familiar whole.
The solemn wastes of heathy hill
Sleep in the July sunshine still;
The self-same shadows now, as then,
Play through this grassy upland glen;
The loose dark stones on the green way
Lie strewn, it seems, where then they lay;
On this mild bank above the stream,
(You crush them!) the blue gentians gleam.
Still this wild brook, the rushes cool,
The sailing foam, the shining pool!
These are not changed; and we, you say,
Are scarce more changed, in truth, than they.

The gipsies, whom we met below,
They, too, have long roam'd to and fro;
They ramble, leaving, where they pass,
Their fragments on the cumber'd grass.
And often to some kindly place
Chance guides the migratory race,
Where, though long wanderings intervene,
They recognise a former scene.
The dingy tents are pitch'd; the fires
Give to the wind their wavering spires;
In dark knots crouch round the wild flame
Their children, as when first they came;
They see their shackled beasts again
Move, browsing, up the gray-wall'd lane.
Signs are not wanting, which might raise
The ghosts in them of former days —
Signs are not wanting, if they would;
Suggestions to disquietude.
For them, for all, time's busy touch,
While it mends little, troubles much.
Their joints grow stiffer — but the year
Runs his old round of dubious cheer;
Chilly they grow — yet winds in March,
Still, sharp as ever, freeze and parch;
They must live still — and yet, God knows,
Crowded and keen the country grows;
It seems as if, in their decay,
The law grew stronger every day.
So might they reason, so compare,
Fausta, times past with times that are.
But no! — they rubb'd through yesterday
In their hereditary way,
And they will rub through, if they can,
To-morrow on the self-same plan,
Till death arrive to supersede,
For them, vicissitude and need.

The poet, to whose mighty heart
Heaven doth a quicker pulse impart,
Subdues that energy to scan
Not his own course, but that of man.
Though he move mountains, though his day
Be pass'd on the proud heights of sway,
Though he hath loosed a thousand chains,
Though he hath borne immortal pains,
Action and suffering though he know —
He hath not lived, if he lives so.
He sees, in some great-historied land,
A ruler of the people stand,
Sees his strong thought in fiery flood
Roll through the heaving multitude,
Exults — yet for no moment's space
Envies the all-regarded place.
Beautiful eyes meet his — and he
Bears to admire uncravingly;
They pass — he, mingled with the crowd,
Is in their far-off triumphs proud.
From some high station he looks down,
At sunset, on a populous town;
Surveys each happy group, which fleets,
Toil ended, through the shining streets,
Each with some errand of its own —
And does not say: *I am alone.*
He sees the gentle stir of birth
When morning purifies the earth;
He leans upon a gate and sees
The pastures, and the quiet trees.
Low, woody hill, with gracious bound,

Folds the still valley almost round;
The cuckoo, loud on some high lawn,
Is answer'd from the depth of dawn;
In the hedge straggling to the stream,
Pale, dew-drench'd, half-shut roses gleam;
But, where the farther side slopes down,
He sees the drowsy new-waked clown
In his white quaint-embroider'd frock
Make, whistling, tow'rd his mist-wreathed flock —
Slowly, behind his heavy tread,
The wet, flower'd grass heaves up its head.
Lean'd on his gate, he gazes — tears
Are in his eyes, and in his ears
The murmur of a thousand years.
Before him he sees life unroll,
A placid and continuous whole —
That general life, which does not cease,
Whose secret is not joy, but peace;
That life, whose dumb wish is not miss'd
If birth proceeds, if things subsist;
The life of plants, and stones, and rain,
The life he craves — if not in vain
Fate gave, what chance shall not control,
His sad lucidity of soul.

You listen — but that wandering smile,
Fausta, betrays you cold the while!
Your eyes pursue the bells of foam
Wash'd, eddying, from this bank, their home.
Those gipsies, so your thoughts I scan,
Are less, the poet more, than man.
They feel not, though they move and see;
Deeper the poet feels; but he
Breathes, when he will, immortal air,
Where Orpheus and where Homer are.
In the day's life, whose iron round
Hems us all in, he is not bound;
He leaves his kind, o'erleaps their pen,
And flees the common life of men.
He escapes thence, but we abide —
Not deep the poet sees, but wide.

The world in which we live and move
Outlasts aversion, outlasts love,
Outlasts each effort, interest, hope,
Remorse, grief, joy; — and were the scope
Of these affections wider made,
Man still would see, and see dismay'd,
Beyond his passion's widest range,
Far regions of eternal change.
Nay, and since death, which wipes out man,
Finds him with many an unsolved plan,
With much unknown, and much untried,
Wonder not dead, and thirst not dried,
Still gazing on the ever full
Eternal mundane spectacle —
This world in which we draw our breath,
In some sense, Fausta, outlasts death.
Blame thou not, therefore, him who dares
Judge vain beforehand human cares;
Whose natural insight can discern
What through experience others learn;
Who needs not love and power, to know
Love transient, power an unreal show;
Who treads at ease life's uncheer'd ways —
Him blame not, Fausta, rather praise!
Rather thyself for some aim pray
Nobler than this, to fill the day;
Rather that heart, which burns in thee,
Ask, not to amuse, but to set free;
Be passionate hopes not ill resign'd
For quiet, and a fearless mind.
And though fate grudge to thee and me
The poet's rapt security,
Yet they, believe me, who await
No gifts from chance, have conquer'd fate.
They, winning room to see and hear,
And to men's business not too near,
Through clouds of individual strife
Draw homeward to the general life.
Like leaves by suns not yet uncurl'd;
To the wise, foolish; to the world,
Weak; — yet not weak, I might reply,
Not foolish, Fausta, in His eye,
To whom each moment in its race,
Crowd as we will its neutral space,
Is but a quiet watershed
Whence, equally, the seas of life and death are fed.

Enough, we live! — and if a life,
With large results so little rife,
Though bearable, seem hardly worth
This pomp of worlds, this pain of birth;

Yet, Fausta, the mute turf we tread,
The solemn hills around us spread,
This stream which falls incessantly,
The strange-scrawl'd rocks, the lonely sky,
If I might lend their life a voice,
Seem to bear rather than rejoice.
And even could the intemperate prayer
Man iterates, while these forbear,
For movement, for an ampler sphere,
Pierce Fate's impenetrable ear;
Not milder is the general lot
Because our spirits have forgot,
In action's dizzying eddy whirl'd,
The something that infects the world.

Memorial Verses [13]

APRIL, 1850

GOETHE in Weimar sleeps, and Greece,
Long since, saw Byron's struggle cease.
But one such death remain'd to come;
The last poetic voice is dumb—
We stand to-day by Wordsworth's tomb.

When Byron's eyes were shut in death,
We bow'd our head and held our breath.
He taught us little; but our soul
Had *felt* him like the thunder's roll.
With shivering heart the strife we saw
Of passion with eternal law;
And yet with reverential awe
We watch'd the fount of fiery life
Which served for that Titanic strife.

When Goethe's death was told, we said:
Sunk, then, is Europe's sagest head.
Physician of the iron age,
Goethe has done his pilgrimage.
He took the suffering human race,
He read each wound, each weakness clear;
And struck his finger on the place,
And said: *Thou ailest here, and here!*
He look'd on Europe's dying hour
Of fitful dream and feverish power;
His eye plunged down the weltering strife,
The turmoil of expiring life—
He said: *The end is everywhere,*
Art still has truth, take refuge there!
And he was happy, if to know
Causes of things, and far below
His feet to see the lurid flow
Of terror, and insane distress,
And headlong fate, be happiness.[14]

And Wordsworth!—Ah, pale ghosts, rejoice!
For never has such soothing voice
Been to your shadowy world convey'd,
Since erst, at morn, some wandering shade
Heard the clear song of Orpheus come
Through Hades, and the mournful gloom.
Wordsworth has gone from us—and ye,
Ah, may ye feel his voice as we!
He too upon a wintry clime
Had fallen—on this iron time
Of doubts, disputes, distractions, fears.
He found us when the age had bound
Our souls in its benumbing round;
He spoke, and loosed our heart in tears.
He laid us as we lay at birth
On the cool flowery lap of earth,
Smiles broke from us and we had ease;
The hills were round us, and the breeze
Went o'er the sun-lit fields again;
Our foreheads felt the wind and rain.
Our youth return'd; for there was shed
On spirits that had long been dead,
Spirits dried up and closely furl'd,
The freshness of the early world.

Ah! since dark days still bring to light
Man's prudence and man's fiery might,
Time may restore us in his course
Goethe's sage mind and Byron's force;
But where will Europe's latter hour
Again find Wordsworth's healing power?
Others will teach us how to dare,
And against fear our breast to steel;
Others will strengthen us to bear—

[13] Published in *Fraser's Magazine*, June 1850. Wordsworth, long a neighbor and friend of the Arnold family at Fox How, Ambleside, died 23 April 1850. In a letter to Clough, Arnold said that the poem was written at the request of Wordsworth's son-in-law, Edward Quillinan, and 'in the grand style.'

[14] Lines 29–33 are practically a translation of Virgil *Georgics*, ii, 490–492.

But who, ah! who, will make us feel?
The cloud of mortal destiny,
Others will front it fearlessly —
But who, like him, will put it by?

Keep fresh the grass upon his grave
O Rotha,[15] with thy living wave!
Sing him thy best! for few or none
Hears thy voice right, now he is gone.

EMPEDOCLES ON ETNA [16]

from ACT II

Evening. The Summit of Etna

EMPEDOCLES

FULNESS of life and power of feeling, ye
Are for the happy, for the souls at ease,
Who dwell on a firm basis of content!
But he, who has outlived his prosperous days —
But he, whose youth fell on a different world
From that on which his exiled age is thrown —
Whose mind was fed on other food, was train'd
By other rules than are in vogue to-day —
Whose habit of thought is fix'd, who will not change,
But, in a world he loves not, must subsist
In ceaseless opposition, be the guard
Of his own breast, fetter'd to what he guards,
That the world win no mastery over him —
Who has no friend, no fellow left, not one;
Who has no minute's breathing space allow'd
To nurse his dwindling faculty of joy —
Joy and the outward world must die to him,
As they are dead to me.

A long pause, during which EMPEDOCLES *remains motionless, plunged in thought. The night deepens. He moves forward and gazes round him, and proceeds:* —

And you, ye stars,
Who slowly begin to marshal,
As of old, in the fields of heaven,
Your distant, melancholy lines!
Have you, too, survived yourselves?
Are you, too, what I fear to become?
You, too, once lived;
You too moved joyfully
Among august companions,
In an older world, peopled by Gods,
In a mightier order,
The radiant, rejoicing, intelligent Sons of Heaven.
But now, ye kindle
Your lonely, cold-shining lights,
Unwilling lingerers
In the heavenly wilderness,
For a younger, ignoble world;
And renew, by necessity,
Night after night your courses,
In echoing, unnear'd silence,
Above a race you know not —
Uncaring and undelighted,
Without friend and without home;
Weary like us, though not
Weary with our weariness.

No, no, ye stars! there is no death with you,
No languor, no decay! languor and death,

---

[15] A small stream near Grasmere, where Wordsworth is buried.

[16] First published in *Empedocles on Etna, and Other Poems*, 1852. For reasons that Arnold details in his important Preface to the *Poems* of 1853 — an essay that is vital to any study of his poetry — *Empedocles* was 'withdrawn from circulation before fifty copies were sold.' It was restored in 1867 in its complete form 'at the request of a man of genius, whom it had the honour and the good fortune to interest, — Mr. Robert Browning.' It is the drama of the Greek poet and philosopher of the fifth century B.C., living on in Sicily, when 'the calm, the cheerfulness, the disinterested objectivity have disappeared: the dialogue of the mind with itself has commenced; modern problems have presented themselves; we hear already the doubts, we witness the discouragement, of Hamlet and of Faust.' The time of the action covers one day. Empedocles, an exile, is carried in a litter up Mount Etna. His friends, Pausanias and the youth Callicles, fearful of what may happen, arrange that Callicles shall follow at a distance and play upon his harp those songs which may heal the mood of the heart-sick philosopher. Scene 2 of Act I is a talk at noon-day, in which Empedocles bravely tries to enhearten Pausanias with a high Stoic philosophy — partly Arnold's own — and send his friend back to live in a world in which he himself no longer has any place. Act II opens at evening, with Empedocles alone upon the summit. Far below Callicles sings the story of Typho imprisoned under Etna for his revolt against Zeus, and then another song — whereupon the closing scene begins.

They are with me, not you! ye are alive —
Ye, and the pure dark ether where ye ride
Brilliant above me! And thou, fiery world,
That sapp'st the vitals of this terrible mount
Upon whose charr'd and quaking crust I stand —
Thou, too, brimmest with life! — the sea of cloud,
That heaves its white and billowy vapours up
To moat this isle of ashes from the world,
Lives; and that other fainter sea, far down,
O'er whose lit floor a road of moonbeams leads
To Etna's Liparëan sister-fires
And the long dusky line of Italy —
That mild and luminous floor of waters lives,
With held-in joy swelling its heart; I only,
Whose spring of hope is dried, whose spirit has fail'd,
I, who have not, like these, in solitude
Maintain'd courage and force, and in myself
Nursed an immortal vigour — I alone
Am dead to life and joy, therefore I read
In all things my own deadness.

A long silence. He continues: —

Oh, that I could glow like this mountain!
Oh, that my heart bounded with the swell of the sea!
Oh, that my soul were full of light as the stars!
Oh, that it brooded over the world like the air!

But no, this heart will glow no more; thou art
A living man no more, Empedocles!
Nothing but a devouring flame of thought —
But a naked, eternally restless mind!

After a pause: —

To the elements it came from
Everything will return —
Our bodies to earth,
Our blood to water,
Heat to fire,
Breath to air.
They were well born, they will be well entomb'd —
But mind? . . .

And we might gladly share the fruitful stir
Down in our mother earth's miraculous womb;
Well would it be
With what roll'd of us in the stormy main;
We might have joy, blent with the all-bathing air,
Or with the nimble, radiant life of fire.

But mind, but thought —
If these have been the master part of us —
Where will *they* find their parent element?
What will receive *them*, who will call *them* home?
But we shall still be in them, and they in us,
And we shall be the strangers of the world,
And they will be our lords, as they are now;
And keep us prisoners of our consciousness,
And never let us clasp and feel the All
But through their forms, and modes, and stifling veils.
And we shall be unsatisfied as now;
And we shall feel the agony of thirst,
The ineffable longing for the life of life
Baffled for ever; and still thought and mind
Will hurry us with them on their homeless march,
Over the unallied unopening earth,
Over the unrecognizing sea; while air
Will blow us fiercely back to sea and earth,
And fire repel us from its living waves.
And then we shall unwillingly return
Back to this meadow of calamity,
This uncongenial place, this human life;
And in our individual human state
Go through the sad probation all again,
To see if we will poise our life at last,

To see if we will now at last be true
To our own only true, deep-buried selves,
Being one with which we are one with the whole world;[17]
Or whether we will once more fall away
Into some bondage of the flesh or mind,
Some slough of sense, or some fantastic maze
Forged by the imperious lonely thinking-power.
And each succeeding age in which we are born
Will have more peril for us than the last;
Will goad our senses with a sharper spur,
Will fret our minds to an intenser play,
Will make ourselves harder to be discern'd.
And we shall struggle awhile, gasp and rebel—
And we shall fly for refuge to past times,
Their soul of unworn youth, their breath of greatness;
And the reality will pluck us back,
Knead us in its hot hand, and change our nature
And we shall feel our powers of effort flag,
And rally them for one last fight—and fail;
And we shall sink in the impossible strife,
And be astray for ever.

Slave of sense
I have in no wise been;—but slave of thought? . . .
And who can say: I have been always free,
Lived ever in the light of my own soul?—
I cannot; I have lived in wrath and gloom,
Fierce, disputatious, ever at war with man,
Far from my own soul, far from warmth and light.
But I have not grown easy in these bonds—
But I have not denied what bonds these were.
Yea, I take myself to witness,
That I have loved no darkness,
Sophisticated no truth,
Nursed no delusion,
Allow'd no fear!

And therefore, O ye elements! I know—
Ye know it too—it hath been granted me
Not to die wholly, not to be all enslaved.
I feel it in this hour. The numbing cloud
Mounts off my soul; I feel it, I breathe free.

Is it but for a moment?
—Ah, boil up, ye vapours!
Leap and roar, thou sea of fire!
My soul glows to meet you.
Ere it flag, ere the mists
Of despondency and gloom
Rush over it again,
Receive me, save me!
[*He plunges into the crater.*

CALLICLES (*from below*)

Through the black, rushing smoke-bursts,
Thick breaks the red flame;
All Etna heaves fiercely
Her forest-clothed frame.

Not here, O Apollo!
Are haunts meet for thee.
But, where Helicon breaks down
In cliff to the sea,

Where the moon-silver'd inlets
Send far their light voice
Up the still vale of Thisbe,
O speed, and rejoice!

On the sward at the cliff-top
Lie strewn the white flocks,
On the cliff-side the pigeons
Roost deep in the rocks.

In the moonlight the shepherds,
Soft lull'd by the rills,
Lie wrapt in their blankets
Asleep on the hills.

—What forms are these coming
So white through the gloom?

[17] See *The Buried Life*, p. 1096.

What garments out-glistening
The gold-flower'd broom?

What sweet-breathing presence
Out-perfumes the thyme?
What voices enrapture
The night's balmy prime? —

'Tis Apollo comes leading
His choir, the Nine.
— The leader is fairest,
But all are divine.

They are lost in the hollows!
They stream up again!
What seeks on this mountain
The glorified train? —

They bathe on this mountain,
In the spring by their road;
Then on to Olympus,
Their endless abode.

— Whose praise do they mention?
Of what is it told? —
What will be for ever;
What was from of old.

First hymn they the Father
Of all things; and then,
The rest of immortals,
The action of men.

The day in his hotness,
The strife with the palm;
The night in her silence,
The stars in their calm.

SWITZERLAND [18]

1. *Meeting*

AGAIN I see my bliss at hand,
The town, the lake are here;
My Marguerite smiles upon the strand,
Unalter'd with the year.

I know that graceful figure fair,
That cheek of languid hue;
I know that soft, enkerchief'd hair,
And those sweet eyes of blue.

Again I spring to make my choice;
Again in tones of ire
I hear a God's tremendous voice:
'Be counsell'd, and retire.'

Ye guiding Powers who join and part,
What would ye have with me?
Ah, warn some more ambitious heart,
And let the peaceful be!

[1852]

2. *Parting*

YE storm-winds of Autumn!
Who rush by, who shake
The window, and ruffle
The gleam-lighted lake;
Who cross to the hill-side
Thin-sprinkled with farms,
Where the high woods strip sadly
Their yellowing arms —
Ye are bound for the mountains!
Ah! with you let me go
Where your cold, distant barrier,
The vast range of snow,
Through the loose clouds lifts dimly
Its white peaks in air —
How deep is their stillness!
Ah, would I were there!

But on the stairs what voice is this I hear,
Buoyant as morning, and as morning clear?
Say, has some wet bird-haunted English lawn
Lent it the music of its trees at dawn?
Or was it from some sun-fleck'd mountain-brook
That the sweet voice its upland clearness took?
Ah! it comes nearer —
Sweet notes, this way!

[18] The general title for this group of love lyrics was given in 1853. (The date of first publication is appended to each separate poem.) The final arrangement of the group, with the titles here used, was made in 1885. What situation, if any, gave rise to the poems is not known, although letters to Clough, written in 1848 and 1849, point to a possible 'Marguerite.' Far more clear in detail is the scenery of the Bernese Oberland about Thun, situated on the Aar river, at the end of the Lake of Thun.

Hark! fast by the window
The rushing winds go,
To the ice-cumber'd gorges,
The vast seas of snow!
There the torrents drive upward
Their rock-strangled hum;
There the avalanche thunders
The hoarse torrent dumb.
—I come, O ye mountains!
Ye torrents, I come!

But who is this, by the half-open'd door,
Whose figure casts a shadow on the floor?
The sweet blue eyes — the soft, ash-colour'd hair —
The cheeks that still their gentle paleness wear —
The lovely lips, with their arch smile that tells
The unconquer'd joy in which her spirit dwells —
Ah! they bend nearer —
Sweet lips, this way!

Hark! the wind rushes past us!
Ah! with that let me go
To the clear, waning hill-side,
Unspotted by snow,
There to watch, o'er the sunk vale,
The frore mountain-wall,
Where the niched snow-bed sprays down
Its powdery fall.
There its dusky blue clusters
The aconite spreads;
There the pines slope, the cloud-strips
Hung soft in their heads.
No life but, at moments,
The mountain-bee's hum.
— I come, O ye mountains!
Ye pine-woods, I come!

Forgive me! forgive me!
Ah, Marguerite, fain
Would these arms reach to clasp thee!
But see! 'tis in vain.

In the void air, towards thee,
My stretch'd arms are cast;
But a sea rolls between us —
Our different past!

To the lips, ah! of others
Those lips have been prest,
And others, ere I was,
Were strain'd to that breast;

Far, far from each other
Our spirits have grown;
And what heart knows another?
Ah! who knows his own?

Blow, ye winds! lift me with you!
I come to the wild.
Fold closely, O Nature!
Thine arms round thy child.

To thee only God granted
A heart ever new —
To all always open,
To all always true.

Ah! calm me, restore me;
And dry up my tears
On thy high mountain-platforms,
Where morn first appears;

Where the white mists, for ever,
Are spread and upfurl'd —
In the stir of the forces
Whence issued the world.

[1852]

3. *A Farewell*

My horse's feet beside the lake,
Where sweet the unbroken moonbeams lay,
Sent echoes through the night to wake
Each glistening strand, each heath-fringed bay.

The poplar avenue was pass'd,
And the roof'd bridge that spans the stream;
Up the steep street I hurried fast,
Led by thy taper's starlike beam.

I came! I saw thee rise! — the blood
Pour'd flushing to thy languid cheek.
Lock'd in each other's arms we stood,
In tears, with hearts too full to speak.

Days flew; — ah, soon I could discern
A trouble in thine alter'd air!
Thy hand lay languidly in mine,
Thy cheek was grave, thy speech grew rare.

I blame thee not! — this heart, I know,
To be long loved was never framed;
For something in its depths doth glow
Too strange, too restless, too untamed.

And women — things that live and move
Mined by the fever of the soul —
They seek to find in those they love
Stern strength, and promise of control.

They ask not kindness, gentle ways —
These they themselves have tried and known;
They ask a soul which never sways
With the blind gusts that shake their own.

I too have felt the load I bore
In a too strong emotion's sway;
I too have wish'd, no woman more,
This starting, feverish heart away.

I too have long'd for trenchant force,
And will like a dividing spear;
Have praised the keen, unscrupulous course,
Which knows no doubt, which feels no fear.

But in the world I learnt, what there
Thou too wilt surely one day prove,
That will, that energy, though rare,
Are yet far, far less rare than love.

Go, then! — till time and fate impress
This truth on thee, be mine no more!
They will! — for thou, I feel, not less
Than I, wast destined to this lore.

We school our manners, act our parts —
But He, who sees us through and through,
Knows that the bent of both our hearts
Was to be gentle, tranquil, true.

And though we wear out life, alas!
Distracted as a homeless wind,
In beating where we must not pass,
In seeking what we shall not find;

Yet we shall one day gain, life past,
Clear prospect o'er our being's whole;
Shall see ourselves, and learn at last
Our true affinities of soul.

We shall not then deny a course
To every thought the mass ignore;
We shall not then call hardness force,
Nor lightness wisdom any more.

Then, in the eternal Father's smile,
Our soothed, encouraged souls will dare
To seem as free from pride and guile,
As good, as generous, as they are.

Then we shall know our friends! — though much
Will have been lost — the help in strife,
The thousand sweet, still joys of such
As hand in hand face earthly life —

Though these be lost, there will be yet
A sympathy august and pure;
Ennobled by a vast regret,
And by contrition seal'd thrice sure.

And we, whose ways were unlike here,
May then more neighbouring courses ply;
May to each other be brought near,
And greet across infinity.

How sweet, unreach'd by earthly jars,
My sister! to maintain with thee
The hush among the shining stars,
The calm upon the moonlit sea!

How sweet to feel, on the boon air,
All our unquiet pulses cease!
To feel that nothing can impair
The gentleness, the thirst for peace —

The gentleness too rudely hurl'd
On this wild earth of hate and fear;
The thirst for peace a raving world
Would never let us satiate here.

[1852]

4. *Isolation. To Marguerite*

We were apart; yet, day by day,
I bade my heart more constant be.
I bade it keep the world away,
And grow a home for only thee;
Nor fear'd but thy love likewise grew,
Like mine, each day, more tried, more true.

The fault was grave! I might have known,
What far too soon, alas! I learn'd —
The heart can bind itself alone,
And faith may oft be unreturn'd.
Self-sway'd our feelings ebb and swell —
Thou lov'st no more; — Farewell! Farewell!

Farewell! — and thou, thou lonely heart,
Which never yet without remorse
Even for a moment didst depart
From thy remote and spheréd course
To haunt the place where passions reign —
Back to thy solitude again!

Back! with the conscious thrill of shame
Which Luna felt, that summer-night,
Flash through her pure immortal frame,
When she forsook the starry height
To hang over Endymion's sleep
Upon the pine-grown Latmian steep.

Yet she, chaste queen, had never proved
How vain a thing is mortal love,
Wandering in Heaven, far removed.
But thou hast long had place to prove
This truth — to prove, and make thine own:
'Thou hast been, shalt be, art, alone.'

Or, if not quite alone, yet they
Which touch thee are unmating things —
Ocean and clouds and night and day;
Lorn autumns and triumphant springs;
And life, and others' joy and pain,
And love, if love, of happier men.

Of happier men — for they, at least,
Have *dream'd* two human hearts might blend
In one, and were through faith released
From isolation without end
Prolong'd; nor knew, although not less
Alone than thou, their loneliness.

[1857]

5. *To Marguerite — (continued)*[19]

Yes! in the sea of life enisled,
With echoing straits between us thrown,
Dotting the shoreless watery wild,
We mortal millions live *alone.*
The islands feel the enclasping flow,
And then their endless bounds they know.

But when the moon their hollows lights,
And they are swept by balms of spring,
And in their glens, on starry nights,
The nightingales divinely sing;
And lovely notes, from shore to shore,
Across the sounds and channels pour —

Oh! then a longing like despair
Is to their farthest caverns sent;
For surely once, they feel, we were
Parts of a single continent!
Now round us spreads the watery plain —
Oh might our marges meet again!

Who order'd, that their longing's fire
Should be, as soon as kindled, cool'd?
Who renders vain their deep desire? —
A God, a God their severance ruled!
And bade betwixt their shores to be
The unplumb'd, salt, estranging sea.

[1852]

[19] Original title: 'To Marguerite, in Returning a Volume of the Letters of Ortis.'

6. *Absence*

In this fair stranger's eyes of grey
Thine eyes, my love! I see.
I shiver; for the passing day
Had borne me far from thee.

This is the curse of life! that not
A nobler, calmer train
Of wiser thoughts and feelings blot
Our passions from our brain;

But each day brings its petty dust
Our soon-choked souls to fill,
And we forget because we must
And not because we will.

I struggle towards the light; and ye,
Once-long'd-for storms of love!
If with the light ye cannot be,
I bear that ye remove.

I struggle towards the light—but oh,
While yet the night is chill,
Upon time's barren, stormy flow,
Stay with me, Marguerite, still!

[1852]

7. *The Terrace at Berne*

(Composed Ten Years after the Preceding)

Ten years!—and to my waking eye
Once more the roofs of Berne appear;
The rocky banks, the terrace high,
The stream!—and do I linger here?

The clouds are on the Oberland,
The Jungfrau snows look faint and far;
But bright are those green fields at hand,
And through those fields comes down the Aar,

And from the blue twin-lakes it comes,
Flows by the town, the churchyard fair;
And 'neath the garden-walk it hums,
The house!—and is my Marguerite there?

Ah, shall I see thee, while a flush
Of startled pleasure floods thy brow,
Quick through the oleanders brush,
And clap thy hands, and cry: *'Tis thou!*

Or hast thou long since wander'd back,
Daughter of France! to France, thy home;
And flitted down the flowery track
Where feet like thine too lightly come?

Doth riotous laughter now replace
Thy smile; and rouge, with stony glare,
Thy cheek's soft hue; and fluttering lace
The kerchief that enwound thy hair?

Or is it over?—art thou dead?—
Dead!—and no warning shiver ran
Across my heart, to say thy thread
Of life was cut, and closed thy span!

Could from earth's ways that figure slight
Be lost, and I not feel 'twas so?
Of that fresh voice the gay delight
Fail from earth's air, and I not know?

Or shall I find thee still, but changed,
But not the Marguerite of thy prime?
With all thy being re-arranged,
Pass'd through the crucible of time;

With spirit vanish'd, beauty waned,
And hardly yet a glance, a tone,
A gesture—anything—retain'd
Of all that was my Marguerite's own?

I will not know! For wherefore try,
To things by mortal course that live,
A shadowy durability,
For which they were not meant, to give?

Like driftwood spars, which meet and pass
Upon the boundless ocean-plain,
So on the sea of life, alas!
Man meets man—meets, and quits again.

I knew it when my life was young;
I feel it still, now youth is o'er.
—The mists are on the mountain hung,
And Marguerite I shall see no more.

[1867]

Longing [20]

COME to me in my dreams, and then
By day I shall be well again!
For then the night will more than pay
The hopeless longing of the day.

Come, as thou cam'st a thousand times,
A messenger from radiant climes,
And smile on thy new world, and be
As kind to others as to me!

Or, as thou never cam'st in sooth,
Come now, and let me dream it truth;
And part my hair, and kiss my brow,
And say: *My love! why sufferest thou?*

Come to me in my dreams, and then
By day I shall be well again!
For then the night will more than pay
The hopeless longing of the day.

Self-dependence [21]

WEARY of myself, and sick of asking
What I am, and what I ought to be,
At this vessel's prow I stand, which bears me
Forwards, forwards, o'er the starlit sea.

And a look of passionate desire
O'er the sea and to the stars I send:
'Ye who from my childhood up have calm'd me,
Calm me, ah, compose me to the end!

'Ah, once more,' I cried, 'ye stars, ye waters,
On my heart your mighty charm renew;
Still, still let me, as I gaze upon you,
Feel my soul becoming vast like you!'

From the intense, clear, star-sown vault of heaven,
Over the lit sea's unquiet way,
In the rustling night-air came the answer:
'Wouldst thou *be* as these are? *Live* as they.

'Unaffrighted by the silence round them,
Undistracted by the sights they see,
These demand not that the things without them
Yield them love, amusement, sympathy.

'And with joy the stars perform their shining,
And the sea its long moon-silver'd roll;
For self-poised they live, nor pine with noting
All the fever of some differing soul.

'Bounded by themselves, and unregardful
In what state God's other works may be,
In their own tasks all their powers pouring,
These attain the mighty life you see.'

O air-born voice! long since, severely clear,
A cry like thine in mine own heart I hear:
'Resolve to be thyself; and know that he,
Who finds himself, loses his misery!'

A Summer Night

IN the deserted, moon-blanch'd street,
How lonely rings the echo of my feet!
Those windows, which I gaze at, frown,
Silent and white, unopening down,
Repellent as the world;—but see,
A break between the housetops shows
The moon! and, lost behind her, fading dim
Into the dewy dark obscurity
Down at the far horizon's rim,
Doth a whole tract of heaven disclose!

And to my mind the thought
Is on a sudden brought
Of a past night, and a far different scene.

[20] First published in 1852, and later made the fifth poem in a group called *Faded Leaves*. The lyrics were inspired by Frances Lucy Wightman, whom Arnold married in June 1851.

[21] This and the three following poems were also published with *Empedocles on Etna*, in 1852.

Headlands stood out into the moonlit deep
As clearly as at noon;
The spring-tide's brimming flow
Heaved dazzlingly between;
Houses, with long white sweep,
Girdled the glistening bay;
Behind, through the soft air,
The blue haze-cradled mountains spread away,
That night was far more fair —
But the same restless pacings to and fro,
And the same vainly throbbing heart was there,
And the same bright, calm moon.

And the calm moonlight seems to say:
Hast thou then still the old unquiet breast,
Which neither deadens into rest,
Nor ever feels the fiery glow
That whirls the spirit from itself away,
But fluctuates to and fro,
Never by passion quite possess'd
And never quite benumb'd by the world's sway? —
And I, I know not if to pray
Still to be what I am, or yield and be
Like all the other men I see.

For most men in a brazen prison live,
Where, in the sun's hot eye,
With heads bent o'er their toil, they languidly
Their lives to some unmeaning taskwork give,
Dreaming of nought beyond their prison-wall.
And as, year after year,
Fresh products of their barren labour fall
From their tired hands, and rest
Never yet comes more near,
Gloom settles slowly down over their breast:
And while they try to stem
The waves of mournful thought by which they are prest,
Death in their prison reaches them,
Unfreed, having seen nothing, still unblest.

And the rest, a few,
Escape their prison and depart
On the wide ocean of life anew.
There the freed prisoner, where'er his heart
Listeth, will sail;
Nor doth he know how there prevail,
Despotic on that sea,
Trade-winds which cross it from eternity.
Awhile he holds some false way, undebarr'd
By thwarting signs, and braves
The freshening wind and blackening waves.
And then the tempest strikes him; and between
The lightning-bursts is seen
Only a driving wreck,
And the pale master on his spar-strewn deck
With anguish'd face and flying hair
Grasping the rudder hard,
Still bent to make some port he knows not where,
Still standing for some false, impossible shore.
And sterner comes the roar
Of sea and wind, and through the deepening gloom
Fainter and fainter wreck and helmsman loom,
And he too disappears, and comes no more.

Is there no life, but these alone?
Madman or slave, must man be one?

Plainness and clearness without shadow of stain!
Clearness divine!
Ye heavens, whose pure dark regions have no sign
Of languor, though so calm, and, though so great,
Are yet untroubled and unpassionate;
Who, though so noble, share in the world's toil,
And, though so task'd, keep free from dust and soil!
I will not say that your mild deeps retain
A tinge, it may be, of their silent pain

Who have long'd deeply once, and long'd in vain —
But I will rather say that you remain
A world above man's head, to let him see
How boundless might his soul's horizons be,
How vast, yet of what clear transparency!
How it were good to abide there, and breathe free;
How fair a lot to fill
Is left to each man still!

[1852]

The Buried Life

LIGHT flows our war of mocking words, and yet,
Behold, with tears mine eyes are wet!
I feel a nameless sadness o'er me roll.
Yes, yes, we know that we can jest,
We know, we know that we can smile!
But there's a something in this breast,
To which thy light words bring no rest,
And thy gay smiles no anodyne.
Give me thy hand, and hush awhile,
And turn those limpid eyes on mine,
And let me read there, love! thy inmost soul.

Alas! is even love too weak
To unlock the heart, and let it speak?
Are even lovers powerless to reveal
To one another what indeed they feel?
I knew the mass of men conceal'd
Their thoughts, for fear that if reveal'd
They would by other men be met
With blank indifference, or with blame reproved;
I knew they lived and moved
Trick'd in disguises, alien to the rest
Of men, and alien to themselves — and yet
The same heart beats in every human breast!

But we, my love! — doth a like spell benumb
Our hearts, our voices? — must we too be dumb?

Ah! well for us, if even we,
Even for a moment, can get free
Our heart, and have our lips unchain'd;
For that which seals them hath been deep-ordain'd!

Fate, which foresaw
How frivolous a baby man would be —
By what distractions he would be possess'd,
How he would pour himself in every strife,
And well-nigh change his own identity —
That it might keep from his capricious play
His genuine self, and force him to obey
Even in his own despite his being's law,
Bade through the deep recesses of our breast
The unregarded river of our life
Pursue with indiscernible flow its way;
And that we should not see
The buried stream, and seem to be
Eddying at large in blind uncertainty,
Though driving on with it eternally.

But often, in the world's most crowded streets,
But often, in the din of strife,
There rises an unspeakable desire
After the knowledge of our buried life;
A thirst to spend our fire and restless force
In tracking out our true, original course;
A longing to inquire
Into the mystery of this heart which beats
So wild, so deep in us — to know
Whence our lives come and where they go.
And many a man in his own breast then delves,
But deep enough, alas! none ever mines.
And we have been on many thousand lines,
And we have shown, on each, spirit and power;
But hardly have we, for one little hour,
Been on our own line, have we been ourselves —
Hardly had skill to utter one of all
The nameless feelings that course through our breast,
But they course on for ever unexpress'd.
And long we try in vain to speak and act

Our hidden self, and what we say and do
Is eloquent, is well — but 'tis not true!
And then we will no more be rack'd
With inward striving, and demand
Of all the thousand nothings of the hour
Their stupefying power;
Ah yes, and they benumb us at our call!
Yet still, from time to time, vague and forlorn,
From the soul's subterranean depth upborne
As from an infinitely distant land,
Come airs, and floating echoes, and convey
A melancholy into all our day.

Only — but this is rare —
When a belovéd hand is laid in ours,
When, jaded with the rush and glare
Of the interminable hours,
Our eyes can in another's eyes read clear,
When our world-deafen'd ear
Is by the tones of a loved voice caress'd —
A bolt is shot back somewhere in our breast,
And a lost pulse of feeling stirs again.
The eye sinks inward, and the heart lies plain,
And what we mean, we say, and what we would, we know.
A man becomes aware of his life's flow,
And hears its winding murmur; and he sees
The meadows where it glides, the sun, the breeze.

And there arrives a lull in the hot race
Wherein he doth for ever chase
That flying and elusive shadow, rest.
An air of coolness plays upon his face,
And an unwonted calm pervades his breast.
And then he thinks he knows
The hills where his life rose,
And the sea where it goes.

[1852]

The Future

A WANDERER is man from his birth.
He was born in a ship
On the breast of the river of Time;
Brimming with wonder and joy
He spreads out his arms to the light,
Rivets his gaze on the banks of the stream.

As what he sees is, so have his thoughts been.
Whether he wakes,
Where the snowy mountainous pass,
Echoing the screams of the eagles,
Hems in its gorges the bed
Of the new-born clear-flowing stream;
Whether he first sees light
Where the river in gleaming rings
Sluggishly winds through the plain;
Whether in sound of the swallowing sea —
As is the world on the banks,
So is the mind of the man.

Vainly does each, as he glides,
Fable and dream
Of the lands which the river of Time
Had left ere he woke on its breast,
Or shall reach when his eyes have been closed.
Only the tract where he sails
He wots of; only the thoughts,
Raised by the objects he passes, are his.

Who can see the green earth any more
As she was by the sources of Time?
Who imagines her fields as they lay
In the sunshine, unworn by the plough?
Who thinks as they thought,
The tribes who then roam'd on her breast,
Her vigorous, primitive sons?

What girl
Now reads in her bosom as clear
As Rebekah read, when she sate
At eve by the palm-shaded well?
Who guards in her breast
As deep, as pellucid a spring
Of feeling, as tranquil, as sure?

What bard,
At the height of his vision, can deem
Of God, of the world, of the soul,
With a plainness as near,
As flashing as Moses felt

When he lay in the night by his flock
On the starlit Arabian waste?
Can rise and obey
The beck of the Spirit like him?

This tract which the river of Time
Now flows through with us, is the plain.
Gone is the calm of its earlier shore.
Border'd by cities and hoarse
With a thousand cries is its stream.
And we on its breast, our minds
Are confused as the cries which we hear,
Changing and shot as the sights which we see.

And we say that repose has fled
For ever the course of the river of Time.
That cities will crowd to its edge
In a blacker, incessanter line;
That the din will be more on its banks,
Denser the trade on its stream,
Flatter the plain where it flows,
Fiercer the sun overhead.
That never will those on its breast
See an ennobling sight,
Drink of the feeling of quiet again.

But what was before us we know not,
And we know not what shall succeed.

Haply, the river of Time—
As it grows, as the towns on its marge
Fling their wavering lights
On a wider, statelier stream—
May acquire, if not the calm
Of its early mountainous shore,
Yet a solemn peace of its own.

And the width of the waters, the hush
Of the grey expanse where he floats,
Freshening its current and spotted with foam
As it draws to the Ocean, may strike
Peace to the soul of the man on its breast—
As the pale waste widens around him,
As the banks fade dimmer away,
As the stars come out, and the night-wind
Brings up the stream
Murmurs and scents of the infinite sea.

[1852]

Philomela [22]

Hark! ah, the nightingale—
The tawny-throated!
Hark, from that moonlit cedar what a burst!
What triumph! hark!—what pain!

O wanderer from a Grecian shore,
Still, after many years, in distant lands,
Still nourishing in thy bewilder'd brain
That wild, unquench'd, deep-sunken, old-world pain—
Say, will it never heal?
And can this fragrant lawn
With its cool trees, and night,
And the sweet, tranquil Thames,
And moonshine, and the dew,
To thy rack'd heart and brain
Afford no balm?

Dost thou to-night behold,
Here, through the moonlight on this English grass,
The unfriendly palace in the Thracian wild?
Dost thou again peruse
With hot cheeks and sear'd eyes
The too clear web, and thy dumb sister's shame?
Dost thou once more assay
Thy flight, and feel come over thee,
Poor fugitive, the feathery change
Once more, and once more seem to make resound
With love and hate, triumph and agony,
Lone Daulis, and the high Cephissian vale?
Listen, Eugenia—
How thick the bursts come crowding through the leaves!
Again—thou hearest?
Eternal passion!
Eternal pain!

[22] This and the two following poems were published in *Poems*, 1853. Philomela was dishonored by Tereus, king of Thrace, husband of her sister Procne. Her tongue was cut out that she might not betray the crime, but she wove the story into a piece of tapestry which she gave her sister. Procne, after killing her son Itys, or Itylus, and serving him as food to the father, took flight with Philomela. Pursued by Tereus, the sisters prayed for deliverance and were turned into birds; Philomela became a nightingale, Procne a swallow. Arnold reverses the roles of the sisters.

Requiescat

Strew on her roses, roses,
And never a spray of yew!
In quiet she reposes;
Ah, would that I did too!

Her mirth the world required;
She bathed it in smiles of glee.
But her heart was tired, tired,
And now they let her be.

Her life was turning, turning,
In mazes of heat and sound.
But for peace her soul was yearning,
And now peace laps her round.

Her cabin'd, ample spirit,
It flutter'd and fail'd for breath.
To-night it doth inherit
The vasty hall of death.

[1853]

THE SCHOLAR-GIPSY [23]

Go, for they call you, shepherd, from the hill;
Go, shepherd, and untie the wattled cotes! [24]
No longer leave thy wistful flock unfed,
Nor let thy bawling fellows rack their throats,
Nor the cropp'd herbage shoot another head.
But when the fields are still,
And the tired men and dogs all gone to rest,
And only the white sheep are sometimes seen
Cross and recross the strips of moon-blanch'd green,
Come, shepherd, and again begin the quest!

Here, where the reaper was at work of late —
In this high field's dark corner, where he leaves
His coat, his basket, and his earthen cruse,
And in the sun all morning binds the sheaves,
Then here, at noon, comes back his stores to use —
Here will I sit and wait,
While to my ear from uplands far away
The bleating of the folded flocks is borne,
With distant cries of reapers in the corn —
All the live murmur of a summer's day.

Screen'd is this nook o'er the high, half-reap'd field,
And here till sun-down, shepherd! will I be.
Through the thick corn the scarlet poppies peep,
And round green roots and yellowing stalks I see
Pale pink convolvulus in tendrils creep;
And air-swept lindens yield
Their scent, and rustle down their perfum'd showers
Of bloom on the bent grass where I am laid,
And bower me from the August sun with shade;
And the eye travels down to Oxford's towers.

And near me on the grass lies Glanvil's book —

[23] 'There was very lately a lad in the University of Oxford, who was by his poverty forced to leave his studies there; and at last to join himself to a company of vagabond gypsies. Among these extravagant people, by the insinuating subtlety of his carriage, he quickly got so much of their love and esteem as that they discovered to him their mystery. After he had been a pretty while exercised in the trade, there chanced to ride by a couple of scholars, who had formerly been of his acquaintance. They quickly spied out their old friend among the gypsies; and he gave them an account of the necessity which drove him to that kind of life, and told them that the people he went with were not such impostors as they were taken for, but that they had a traditional kind of learning among them, and could do wonders by the power of imagination, their fancy binding that of others: that himself had learned much of their art, and when he had compassed the whole secret, he intended, he said, to leave their company, and give the world an account of what he had learned.' — Glanvil's *Vanity of Dogmatizing*, 1661. [Arnold.]

[24] sheep-folds

Come, let me read the oft-read tale again!
The story of the Oxford scholar poor,
Of pregnant parts and quick inventive brain,
Who, tired of knocking at preferment's door,
One summer-morn forsook
His friends, and went to learn the gipsy-lore,
And roam'd the world with that wild brotherhood,
And came, as most men deem'd, to little good,
But came to Oxford and his friends no more.

But once, years after, in the country-lanes,
Two scholars, whom at college erst he knew,
Met him, and of his way of life enquired;
Whereat he answer'd, that the gipsy-crew,
His mates, had arts to rule as they desired
The workings of men's brains,
And they can bind them to what thoughts they will.
'And I,' he said, 'the secret of their art,
When fully learn'd, will to the world impart;
But it needs heaven-sent moments for this skill.'

This said, he left them, and return'd no more.—
But rumours hung about the country-side,
That the lost Scholar long was seen to stray,
Seen by rare glimpses, pensive and tongue-tied,
In hat of antique shape, and cloak of grey,
The same the gipsies wore.
Shepherds had met him on the Hurst in spring;
At some lone alehouse in the Berkshire moors,
On the warm ingle-bench, the smock-frock'd boors
Had found him seated at their entering,

But, 'mid their drink and clatter, he would fly.
And I myself seem half to know thy looks,
And put the shepherds, wanderer! on thy trace;
And boys who in lone wheatfields scare the rooks
I ask if thou hast pass'd their quiet place;
Or in my boat I lie
Moor'd to the cool bank in the summer-heats,
'Mid wide grass meadows which the sunshine fills,
And watch the warm, green-muffled Cumner hills,
And wonder if thou haunt'st their shy retreats.

For most, I know, thou lov'st retired ground!
Thee at the ferry Oxford riders blithe,
Returning home on summer-nights, have met
Crossing the stripling Thames at Bablock-hithe,
Trailing in the cool stream thy fingers wet,
As the punt's rope chops round;
And leaning backward in a pensive dream,
And fostering in thy lap a heap of flowers
Pluck'd in shy fields and distant Wychwood bowers,
And thine eyes resting on the moonlit stream.

And then they land, and thou art seen no more!—

Maidens, who from the distant hamlets come
To dance around the Fyfield elm in May,
Oft through the darkening fields have seen thee roam,
Or cross a stile into the public way.
Oft thou hast given them store
Of flowers — the frail-leaf'd, white anemony,
Dark bluebells drench'd with dews of summer eves,
And purple orchises with spotted leaves —
But none hath words she can report of thee.

And, above Godstow Bridge, when hay-time's here
In June, and many a scythe in sunshine flames,
Men who through those wide fields of breezy grass
Where black-wing'd swallows haunt the glittering Thames,
To bathe in the abandon'd lasher[25] pass,
Have often pass'd thee near
Sitting upon the river bank o'ergrown;
Mark'd thine outlandish garb, thy figure spare,
Thy dark vague eyes, and soft abstracted air —
But, when they came from bathing, thou wast gone!

At some lone homestead in the Cumner hills,
Where at her open door the housewife darns,
Thou hast been seen, or hanging on a gate
To watch the threshers in the mossy barns.
Children, who early range these slopes and late
For cresses from the rills,
Have known thee eying, all an April-day,
The springing pastures and the feeding kine;
And mark'd thee, when the stars come out and shine,
Through the long dewy grass move slow away.

In autumn, on the skirts of Bagley wood —
Where most the gipsies by the turf-edged way
Pitch their smoked tents, and every bush you see
With scarlet patches tagg'd and shreds of grey,
Above the forest-ground called Thessaly —
The blackbird, picking food,
Sees thee, nor stops his meal, nor fears at all;
So often has he known thee past him stray,
Rapt, twirling in thy hand a wither'd spray,
And waiting for the spark from heaven to fall.

And once, in winter, on the causeway chill
Where home through flooded fields foot-travellers go,
Have I not pass'd thee on the wooden bridge,
Wrapt in thy cloak and battling with the snow,
Thy face tow'rd Hinksey and its wintry ridge?
And thou hast climb'd the hill,
And gain'd the white brow of the Cumner range;
Turn'd once to watch, while thick the snowflakes fall,
The line of festal light in Christ-Church hall[26] —
Then sought thy straw in some sequester'd grange.

But what — I dream! Two hundred years are flown

[25] A pool below a dam.

[26] The great dining-hall of Christ Church College, Oxford.

Since first thy story ran through Oxford halls,
And the grave Glanvil did the tale inscribe
That thou wert wander'd from the studious walls
To learn strange arts, and join a gipsy-tribe;
And thou from earth art gone
Long since, and in some quiet churchyard laid—
Some country-nook, where o'er thy unknown grave
Tall grasses and white flowering nettles wave,
Under a dark, red-fruited yew-tree's shade.

—No, no, thou hast not felt the lapse of hours!
For what wears out the life of mortal men?
'Tis that from change to change their being rolls;
'Tis that repeated shocks, again, again,
Exhaust the energy of strongest souls
And numb the elastic powers.
Till having used our nerves with bliss and teen,[27]
And tired upon a thousand schemes our wit,
To the just-pausing Genius we remit
Our worn-out life, and are—what we have been.

Thou hast not lived, why should'st thou perish, so?
Thou hadst *one* aim, *one* business, *one* desire;
Else wert thou long since number'd with the dead!
Else hadst thou spent, like other men, thy fire!
The generations of thy peers are fled,
And we ourselves shall go;
But thou possessest an immortal lot,
And we imagine thee exempt from age
And living as thou liv'st on Glanvil's page,
Because thou hadst—what we, alas! have not.

For early didst thou leave the world, with powers
Fresh, undiverted to the world without,
Firm to their mark, not spent on other things;
Free from the sick fatigue, the languid doubt,
Which much to have tried, in much been baffled, brings.
O life unlike to ours!
Who fluctuate idly without term or scope,
Of whom each strives, nor knows for what he strives,
And each half lives a hundred different lives;
Who wait like thee, but not, like thee, in hope.

Thou waitest for the spark from heaven! and we,
Light half-believers of our casual creeds,
Who never deeply felt, nor clearly will'd,
Whose insight never has borne fruit in deeds,
Whose vague resolves never have been fulfill'd;
For whom each year we see
Breeds new beginnings, disappointments new;
Who hesitate and falter life away,
And lose to-morrow the ground won to-day—
Ah! do not we, wanderer! await it too?

Yes, we await it!—but it still delays,
And then we suffer! and amongst us one,[28]
Who most has suffer'd, takes dejectedly
His seat upon the intellectual throne;

[27] care, sorrow

[28] Goethe

And all his store of sad experience he
Lays bare of wretched days;
Tells us his misery's birth and growth and signs,
And how the dying spark of hope was fed,
And how the breast was soothed, and how the head,
And all his hourly varied anodynes.

This for our wisest! and we others pine,
And wish the long unhappy dream would end,
And waive all claim to bliss, and try to bear;
With close-lipp'd patience for our only friend,
Sad patience, too near neighbour to despair—
But none has hope like thine!
Thou through the fields and through the woods dost stray,
Roaming the country-side, a truant boy,
Nursing thy project in unclouded joy,
And every doubt long blown by time away.

O born in days when wits were fresh and clear,
And life ran gaily as the sparkling Thames;
Before this strange disease of modern life,
With its sick hurry, its divided aims,
Its heads o'ertax'd, its palsied hearts, was rife—
Fly hence, our contact fear!
Still fly, plunge deeper in the bowering wood!
Averse, as Dido did with gesture stern
From her false friend's approach in Hades turn,[29]
Wave us away, and keep thy solitude!
Still nursing the unconquerable hope,
Still clutching the inviolable shade,
With a free, onward impulse brushing through,
By night, the silver'd branches of the glade—
Far on the forest-skirts, where none pursue,
On some mild pastoral slope
Emerge, and resting on the moonlit pales
Freshen thy flowers as in former years
With dew, or listen with enchanted ears,
From the dark dingles, to the nightingales!

But fly our paths, our feverish contact fly!
For strong the infection of our mental strife,
Which, though it gives no bliss, yet spoils for rest;
And we should win thee from thy own fair life,
Like us distracted, and like us unblest.
Soon, soon thy cheer would die,
Thy hopes grow timorous, and unfix'd thy powers,
And thy clear aims be cross and shifting made;
And then thy glad perennial youth would fade,
Fade, and grow old at last, and die like ours.

Then fly our greetings, fly our speech and smiles!
—As some grave Tyrian trader, from the sea,
Descried at sunrise an emerging prow
Lifting the cool-hair'd creepers stealthily,
The fringes of a southward-facing brow
Among the Ægæan isles;
And saw the merry Grecian coaster come,
Freighted with amber grapes, and Chian wine,

[29] See *Aeneid*, vi, 450–471.

Green, bursting figs, and tunnies steep'd in brine —
And knew the intruders on his ancient home,

The young light-hearted masters of the waves —
And snatch'd his rudder, and shook out more sail;
And day and night held on indignantly
O'er the blue Midland [30] waters with the gale,
Betwixt the Syrtes [31] and soft Sicily,
To where the Atlantic raves
Outside the western straits; and unbent sails
There, where down cloudy cliffs, through sheets of foam,
Shy traffickers, the dark Iberians [32] come;
And on the beach undid his corded bales.

[1853]

THYRSIS [33]

A Monody, *to commemorate the author's friend,* Arthur Hugh Clough, *who died at Florence,* 1861.

How changed is here each spot man makes or fills!
In the two Hinkseys nothing keeps the same;
The village street its haunted mansion lacks,
And from the sign is gone Sibylla's [34] name,
And from the roofs the twisted chimney-stacks —
Are ye too changed, ye hills?
See, 'tis no foot of unfamiliar men
To-night from Oxford up your pathway strays!
Here came I often, often, in old days —
Thyrsis and I; we still had Thyrsis then.

Runs it not here, the track by Childsworth Farm,
Past the high wood, to where the elm-tree crowns
The hill behind whose ridge the sunset flames?
The signal-elm, that looks on Ilsley Downs,
The Vale, the three lone weirs, the youthful Thames? —
This winter-eve is warm,
Humid the air! leafless, yet soft as spring,
The tender purple spray on copse and briers!
And that sweet city with her dreaming spires,
She needs not June for beauty's heightening,

Lovely all times she lies, lovely to-night! —
Only, methinks, some loss of habit's power
Befalls me wandering through this upland dim.
Once pass'd I blindfold here, at any hour;
Now seldom come I, since I came with him.
That single elm-tree bright
Against the west — I miss it! is it gone?
We prized it dearly; while it stood, we said,

30 Mediterranean

31 Shoals in the Gulf of Sidra, on the northern coast of Africa.

32 Early inhabitants of the Spanish peninsula.

33 The poem was not published until April 1866 in *Macmillan's Magazine*, but, as Arnold's note says, 'Throughout . . . there is reference to the preceding piece, *The Scholar-Gipsy*.' Clough had resigned his fellowship in Oriel College, Oxford, in 1848, largely because of his inability to profess conformity to the Thirty-nine Articles of the Anglican Church. He had been at Oxford during the entire period of Arnold's own residence there. In January 1862, shortly after the news had come from Florence, Arnold wrote Mrs. Clough: 'I shall go alone [to Oxford] after Easter; — and there, among the Cumner hills where we have so often rambled, I shall be able to think him over as I could wish. Here [in London, where Arnold was a busy, harassed Inspector of Schools] all impressions are half impressions, and every thought is interrupted.'

34 Not a pagan allusion, but the Christian name of the old Hinksey ale-house keeper!

Our friend, the Gipsy-Scholar, was not dead;
While the tree lived, he in these fields lived on.

Too rare, too rare, grow now my visits here,
But once I knew each field, each flower, each stick;
And with the country-folk acquaintance made
By barn in threshing-time, by new-built rick.
Here, too, our shepherd-pipes we first assay'd.
Ah me! this many a year
My pipe is lost, my shepherd's holiday!
Needs must I lose them, needs with heavy heart
Into the world and wave of men depart;
But Thyrsis of his own will went away.

It irk'd him to be here, he could not rest.
He loved each simple joy the country yields,
He loved his mates; but yet he could not keep,
For that a shadow lour'd on the fields,
Here with the shepherds and the silly sheep.
Some life of men unblest
He knew, which made him droop, and fill'd his head.
He went; his piping took a troubled sound
Of storms that rage outside our happy ground;[35]
He could not wait their passing, he is dead.

So, some tempestuous morn in early June,
When the year's primal burst of bloom is o'er,
Before the roses and the longest day—
When garden-walks and all the grassy floor
With blossoms red and white of fallen May
And chestnut-flowers are strewn—
So have I heard the cuckoo's parting cry,
From the wet field, through the vext garden-trees,
Come with the volleying rain and tossing breeze:
The bloom is gone, and with the bloom go I!

Too quick despairer, wherefore wilt thou go?
Soon will the high Midsummer pomps come on,
Soon will the musk carnations break and swell,
Soon shall we have gold-dusted snapdragon,
Sweet-William with his homely cottage-smell,
And stocks in fragrant blow;
Roses that down the alleys shine afar,
And open, jasmine-muffled lattices,
And groups under the dreaming garden-trees,
And the full moon, and the white evening-star.

He hearkens not! light comer, he is flown!
What matters it? next year he will return,
And we shall have him in the sweet spring-days,
With whitening hedges, and uncrumpling fern,
And blue-bells trembling by the forest-ways,
And scent of hay new-mown.
But Thyrsis never more we swains shall see;
See him come back, and cut a smoother reed,

[35] Only partly true. Clough's poetry does reflect his troubled faith, but it reveals far more his powers as a humorist, satirist, and story-teller. Arnold's elegy has, indeed, put emphasis—as he himself realized and confessed—upon only one side of his friend.

And blow a strain the world at last shall heed—
For Time, not Corydon,[36] hath conquer'd thee!

Alack, for Corydon no rival now!—
But when Sicilian shepherds lost a mate,
Some good survivor with his flute would go,
Piping a ditty sad for Bion's fate;[37]
And cross the unpermitted ferry's flow,
And relax Pluto's brow,
And make leap up with joy the beauteous head
Of Proserpine, among whose crowned hair
Are flowers first open'd on Sicilian air,
And flute his friend, like Orpheus, from the dead.

O easy access to the hearer's grace
When Dorian shepherds sang to Proserpine!
For she herself had trod Sicilian fields,[38]
She knew the Dorian water's gush divine,
She knew each lily white which Enna yields,
Each rose with blushing face;
She loved the Dorian pipe, the Dorian strain.
But ah, of our poor Thames she never heard!
Her foot the Cumner cowslips never stirr'd;
And we should tease her with our plaint in vain!

Well! wind-dispersed and vain the words will be,
Yet, Thyrsis, let me give my grief its hour
In the old haunt, and find our tree-topp'd hill!
Who, if not I, for questing here hath power?
I know the wood which hides the daffodil,
I know the Fyfield tree,
I know what white, what purple fritillaries
The grassy harvest of the river-fields,
Above by Ensham, down by Sandford, yields,
And what sedged brooks are Thames's tributaries;

I know these slopes; who knows them if not I?—
But many a dingle on the loved hill-side,
With thorns once studded, old, white-blossom'd trees,
Where thick the cowslips grew, and far descried
High tower'd the spikes of purple orchises,
Hath since our day put by
The coronals of that forgotten time;
Down each green bank hath gone the ploughboy's team,
And only in the hidden brookside gleam
Primroses, orphans of the flowery prime.

Where is the girl, who by the boatman's door,
Above the locks, above the boating throng,
Unmoor'd our skiff when through the Wytham flats,
Red loosestrife and blond meadow-sweet among
And darting swallows and light water-gnats,
We track'd the shy Thames shore?
Where are the mowers, who, as the tiny swell
Of our boat passing heaved the river-grass,
Stood with suspended scythe to see us pass?—
They all are gone, and thou art gone as well!

[36] In Virgil's *Eclogues* Corydon defeated Thyrsis in a verse-contest.

[37] Refers to the lament written by Moschus for Bion, pastoral poet of Sicily.

[38] Proserpine had been seized by Pluto while she was gathering flowers at Enna in Sicily, and carried off to be queen of the lower regions.

Yes, thou art gone! and round me too the night
In ever-nearing circle weaves her shade.
I see her veil draw soft across the day,
I feel her slowly chilling breath invade
The cheek grown thin, the brown hair sprent with grey;
I feel her finger light
Laid pausefully upon life's headlong train; —
The foot less prompt to meet the morning dew,
The heart less bounding at emotion new,
And hope, once crush'd, less quick to spring again.

And long the way appears, which seem'd so short
To the less practised eye of sanguine youth;
And high the mountain-tops, in cloudy air,
The mountain-tops where is the throne of Truth,
Tops in life's morning-sun so bright and bare!
Unbreachable the fort
Of the long-batter'd world uplifts its wall;
And strange and vain the earthly turmoil grows,
And near and real the charm of thy repose,
And night as welcome as a friend would fall.

But hush! the upland hath a sudden loss
Of quiet! — Look, adown the dusk hill-side,
A troop of Oxford hunters going home,
As in old days, jovial and talking, ride!
From hunting with the Berkshire hounds they come.
Quick! let me fly, and cross
Into yon farther field! — 'Tis done; and see,
Back'd by the sunset, which doth glorify
The orange and pale violet evening-sky,
Bare on its lonely ridge, the Tree! the Tree!

I take the omen! Eve lets down her veil,
The white fog creeps from bush to bush about,
The west unflushes, the high stars grow bright,
And in the scatter'd farms the lights come out.
I cannot reach the signal-tree to-night,
Yet, happy omen, hail!
Hear it from thy broad lucent Arno-vale[39]
(For there thine earth-forgetting eyelids keep
The morningless and unawakening sleep
Under the flowery oleanders pale),

Hear it, O Thyrsis, still our tree is there! —
Ah, vain! These English fields, this upland dim,
These brambles pale with mist engarlanded,
That lone, sky-pointing tree, are not for him;
To a boon southern country he is fled,
And now in happier air,
Wandering with the great Mother's[40] train divine
(And purer or more subtle soul than thee,
I trow, the mighty Mother doth not see)
Within a folding of the Apennine,

Thou hearest the immortal chants of old! —
Putting his sickle to the perilous grain

---

[39] The River Arno flows through Florence, where Clough is buried in the Protestant Cemetery.

[40] Cybele (identified with Rhea in Cretan worship) was the goddess of nature, the 'Mother of the Gods' venerated on Mt. Ida.

In the hot cornfield of the Phrygian king,
For thee the Lityerses-song again
Young Daphnis with his silver voice doth sing;[41]
Sings his Sicilian fold,
His sheep, his hapless love, his blinded eyes —
And how a call celestial round him rang,
And heavenward from the fountain-brink he sprang,
And all the marvel of the golden skies.

There thou art gone, and me thou leavest here
Sole in these fields! yet will I not despair.
Despair I will not, while I yet descry
'Neath the mild canopy of English air
That lonely tree against the western sky.
Still, still these slopes, 'tis clear,
Our Gipsy-Scholar haunts, outliving thee!
Fields where soft sheep from cages pull the hay,
Woods with anemones in flower till May,
Know him a wanderer still; then why not me?

A fugitive and gracious light he seeks,
Shy to illumine; and I seek it too.
This does not come with houses or with gold,
With place, with honour, and a flattering crew;
'Tis not in the world's market bought and sold.
But the smooth-slipping weeks
Drop by, and leave its seeker still untired;
Out of the heed of mortals he is gone,
He wends unfollow'd, he must house alone;
Yet on he fares, by his own heart inspired.

Thou too, O Thyrsis, on like quest wast bound,
Thou wanderedst with me for a little hour!
Men gave thee nothing; but this happy quest,
If men esteem'd thee feeble, gave thee power,
If men procured thee trouble, gave thee rest.
And this rude Cumner ground,
Its fir-topped Hurst, its farms, its quiet fields,
Here cam'st thou in thy jocund youthful time,
Here was thine height of strength, thy golden prime!
And still the haunt beloved a virtue yields.

What though the music of thy rustic flute
Kept not for long its happy, country tone;
Lost it too soon, and learnt a stormy note
Of men contention-tost, of men who groan,
Which task'd thy pipe too sore, and tired thy throat —
It fail'd, and thou wast mute!
Yet hadst thou always visions of our light,
And long with men of care thou couldst not stay,
And soon thy foot resumed its wandering way,
Left human haunt, and on alone till night.

41 Daphnis, the ideal Sicilian shepherd of Greek pastoral poetry, was said to have followed into Phrygia his mistress Piplea, who had been carried off by robbers, and to have found her in the power of the king of Phrygia, Lityerses. Lityerses used to make strangers try a contest with him in reaping corn, and to put them to death if he overcame them. Hercules arrived in time to save Daphnis, took upon himself the reaping-contest with Lityerses, overcame him, and slew him. The Lityerses-song connected with this tradition was, like the Linus-song, one of the early plaintive strains of Greek popular poetry, and used to be sung by corn-reapers. Other traditions represented Daphnis as beloved by a nymph who exacted from him an oath to love no one else. He fell in love with a princess, and was struck blind by the jealous nymph. Mercury, who was his father, raised him to Heaven, and made a fountain spring up in the place from which he ascended. At this fountain the Sicilians offered yearly sacrifices. [Arnold.]

Too rare, too rare, grow now my visits here!
'Mid city-noise, not, as with thee of yore,
Thyrsis! in reach of sheep-bells is my home.
—Then through the great town's harsh, heart-wearying roar,
Let in thy voice a whisper often come,
To chase fatigue and fear:
Why faintest thou? I wander'd till I died.
Roam on! The light we sought is shining still.
Dost thou ask proof? Our tree yet crowns the hill,
Our Scholar travels yet the loved hill-side.

Stanzas from the Grande Chartreuse [42]

Through Alpine meadows soft-suffused
With rain, where thick the crocus blows,
Past the dark forges long disused,
The mule-track from Saint Laurent goes.
The bridge is cross'd, and slow we ride,
Through forest, up the mountain-side.

The autumnal evening darkens round,
The wind is up, and drives the rain;
While, hark! far down, with strangled sound
Doth the Dead Guier's stream complain,
Where that wet smoke, among the woods,
Over his boiling cauldron broods.

Swift rush the spectral vapours white
Past limestone scars with ragged pines,
Showing—then blotting from our sight!—
Halt—through the cloud-drift something shines!
High in the valley, wet and drear,
The huts of Courrerie appear.

Strike leftward! cries our guide; and higher
Mounts up the stony forest-way.
At last the encircling trees retire;
Look! through the showery twilight grey
What pointed roofs are these advance?—
A palace of the Kings of France?

Approach, for what we seek is here!
Alight, and sparely sup, and wait
For rest in this outbuilding near;
Then cross the sward and reach that gate.
Knock; pass the wicket! Thou art come
To the Carthusians' world-famed home.

The silent courts, where night and day
Into their stone-carved basins cold
The splashing icy fountains play—
The humid corridors behold!
Where, ghostlike in the deepening night,
Cowl'd forms brush by in gleaming white.

The chapel, where no organ's peal
Invests the stern and naked prayer—
With penitential cries they kneel
And wrestle; rising then, with bare
And white uplifted faces stand,
Passing the Host from hand to hand;

Each takes, and then his visage wan
Is buried in his cowl once more.
The cells!—the suffering Son of Man
Upon the wall—the knee-worn floor—
And where they sleep, that wooden bed,
Which shall their coffin be, when dead!

The library, where tract and tome
Not to feed priestly pride are there,
To hymn the conquering march of Rome,
Nor yet to amuse, as ours are!
They paint of souls the inner strife,
Their drops of blood, their death in life.

The garden, overgrown—yet mild,
See, fragrant herbs are flowering there!
Strong children of the Alpine wild
Whose culture is the brethren's care;
Of human tasks their only one,
And cheerful works beneath the sun.

[42] Published in *Fraser's Magazine*, April 1855. Founded in the eleventh century, the Grande Chartreuse, located in the French Alps near Grenoble, was the principal monastery of the Carthusian monks.

Those halls, too, destined to contain
Each its own pilgrim-host of old,
From England, Germany, or Spain —
All are before me! I behold
The House, the Brotherhood austere!
— And what am I, that I am here?

For rigorous teachers seized my youth,
And purged its faith, and trimm'd its fire,
Show'd me the high, white star of Truth,
There bade me gaze, and there aspire.
Even now their whispers pierce the gloom:
What dost thou in this living tomb?

Forgive me, masters of the mind!
At whose behest I long ago
So much unlearnt, so much resign'd —
I come not here to be your foe!
I seek these anchorites, not in ruth,
To curse and to deny your truth;

Not as their friend, or child, I speak!
But as, on some far northern strand,
Thinking of his own Gods, a Greek
In pity and mournful awe might stand
Before some fallen Runic stone —
For both were faiths, and both are gone.

Wandering between two worlds, one dead,
The other powerless to be born,
With nowhere yet to rest my head,
Like these, on earth I wait forlorn.
Their faith, my tears, the world deride —
I come to shed them at their side.

Oh, hide me in your gloom profound,
Ye solemn seats of holy pain!
Take me, cowl'd forms, and fence me round,
Till I possess my soul again;
Till free my thoughts before me roll,
Not chafed by hourly false control!

For the world cries your faith is now
But a dead time's exploded dream;
My melancholy, sciolists vow,
Is a pass'd mode, an outworn theme —
As if the world had ever had
A faith, or sciolists been sad!

Ah, if it *be* pass'd, take away,
At least, the restlessness, the pain;
Be man henceforth no more a prey
To these out-dated stings again!
The nobleness of grief is gone —
Ah, leave us not the fret alone!

But — if you cannot give us ease —
Last of the race of them who grieve
Here leave us to die out with these
Last of the people who believe!
Silent, while years engrave the brow;
Silent — the best are silent now.

Achilles ponders in his tent,
The kings of modern thought are dumb;
Silent they are, though not content,
And wait to see the future come.
They have the grief men had of yore,
But they contend and cry no more.

Our fathers water'd with their tears
This sea of time whereon we sail,
Their voices were in all men's ears
Who pass'd within their puissant hail.
Still the same ocean round us raves,
But we stand mute, and watch the waves.

For what avail'd it, all the noise
And outcry of the former men? —
Say, have their sons achieved more joys,
Say, is life lighter now than then?
The sufferers died, they left their pain —
The pangs which tortured them remain.

What helps it now, that Byron bore,
With haughty scorn which mock'd the smart,
Through Europe to the Ætolian[43] shore
The pageant of his bleeding heart?
That thousands counted every groan,
And Europe made his woe her own?

What boots it, Shelley! that the breeze
Carried thy lovely wail away,
Musical through Italian trees

[43] Grecian. Byron died at Missolonghi on the shores of Aetolia.

Which fringe thy soft blue Spezzian bay?[44]
Inheritors of thy distress
Have restless hearts one throb the less?

Or are we easier, to have read,
O Obermann![45] the sad, stern page,
Which tells us how thou hidd'st thy head
From the fierce tempest of thine age
In the lone brakes of Fontainebleau,
Or chalets near the Alpine snow?

Ye slumber in your silent grave! —
The world, which for an idle day
Grace to your mood of sadness gave,
Long since hath flung her weeds away.
The eternal trifler breaks your spell;
But we — we learnt your lore too well!

Years hence, perhaps, may dawn an age,
More fortunate, alas! than we,
Which without hardness will be sage,
And gay without frivolity.
Sons of the world, oh, speed those years;
But, while we wait, allow our tears!

Allow them! We admire with awe
The exulting thunder of your race;
You give the universe your law,
You triumph over time and space!
Your pride of life, your tireless powers,
We laud them, but they are not ours.

We are like children rear'd in shade
Beneath some old-world abbey wall,
Forgotten in a forest-glade,
And secret from the eyes of all.
Deep, deep the greenwood round them waves,
Their abbey, and its close of graves!

But, where the road runs near the stream,
Oft through the trees they catch a glance
Of passing troops in the sun's beam —
Pennon, and plume, and flashing lance!
Forth to the world those soldiers fare,
To life, to cities, and to war!

And through the wood, another way,
Faint bugle-notes from far are borne,
Where hunters gather, staghounds bay,
Round some fair forest-lodge at morn;
Gay dames are there, in sylvan green;
Laughter and cries — those notes between!

The banners flashing through the trees
Make their blood dance and chain their eyes;
That bugle-music on the breeze
Arrests them with a charm'd surprise.
Banner by turns and bugle woo:
Ye shy recluses, follow too!

O children, what do ye reply? —
'Action and pleasure, will ye roam
Through these secluded dells to cry
And call us? — but too late ye come!
Too late for us your call ye blow,
Whose bent was taken long ago.

'Long since we pace this shadow'd nave;
We watch those yellow tapers shine,
Emblems of hope over the grave,
In the high altar's depth divine;
The organ carries to our ear
Its accents of another sphere.

'Fenced early in this cloistral round
Of reverie, of shade, of prayer,
How should we grow in other ground?
How can we flower in foreign air?
— Pass, banners, pass, and bugles, cease;
And leave our desert to its peace!'

East London [46]

'Twas August, and the fierce sun overhead
Smote on the squalid streets of Bethnal Green,
And the pale weaver, through his windows seen
In Spitalfields, look'd thrice dispirited.

[44] Shelley was drowned in the Gulf of Spezzia, by the shores of which he had spent his last days.

[45] Étienne Pivert de Senancour, whose writings, particularly *Obermann*, were much read by Arnold. See Arnold's two poems upon him, *Stanzas in Memory of the Author of 'Obermann'* and *Obermann Once More.*

[46] This and the six following poems were published in *New Poems*, 1867.

I met a preacher[47] there I knew, and said:
'Ill and o'erwork'd, how fare you in this scene?'—
'Bravely!' said he; 'for I of late have been
Much cheer'd with thoughts of Christ, *the living bread.*'

O human soul! as long as thou canst so
Set up a mark of everlasting light,
Above the howling senses' ebb and flow,

To cheer thee, and to right thee if thou roam—
Not with lost toil thou labourest through the night!
Thou mak'st the heaven thou hop'st indeed thy home.

West London

CROUCH'D on the pavement, close by Belgrave Square,[48]
A tramp I saw, ill, moody, and tongue-tied.
A babe was in her arms, and at her side
A girl; their clothes were rags, their feet were bare.

Some labouring men, whose work lay somewhere there,
Pass'd opposite; she touch'd her girl, who hied
Across, and begg'd, and came back satisfied.
The rich she had let pass with frozen stare.

Thought I: 'Above her state this spirit towers;
She will not ask of aliens, but of friends,
Of sharers in a common human fate.

'She turns from that cold succour, which attends
The unknown little from the unknowing great,
And points us to a better time than ours.'

[1867]

[47] The Reverend William Tyler, noted for his work among the poor.
[48] A fashionable part of London.

Austerity of Poetry

THAT son of Italy[49] who tried to blow,
Ere Dante came, the trump of sacred song
In his light youth amid a festal throng
Sate with his bride to see a public show.

Fair was the bride, and on her front did glow
Youth like a star; and what to youth belong—
Gay raiment, sparkling gauds, elation strong.
A prop gave way! crash fell a platform! lo,

'Mid struggling sufferers, hurt to death, she lay!
Shuddering, they drew her garments off—and found
A robe of sackcloth next the smooth, white skin.

Such, poets, is your bride, the Muse! young, gay,
Radiant, adorn'd outside; a hidden ground
Of thought and of austerity within.

[1867]

Calais Sands[50]

A THOUSAND knights have rein'd their steeds
To watch this line of sand-hills run,
Along the never-silent Strait,
To Calais glittering in the sun;

To look tow'rd Ardres' Golden Field[51]
Across this wide aërial plain,
Which glows as if the Middle Age
Were gorgeous upon earth again.

Oh, that to share this famous scene,
I saw, upon the open sand,
Thy lovely presence at my side,
Thy shawl, thy look, thy smile, thy hand!

[49] Giacopone da Todi, a poet of the thirteenth century.
[50] This poem is said to commemorate an event in Arnold's courtship of Frances Lucy Wightman, whose father for a time opposed any match and forbade any meeting of the two.
[51] The 'Field of the Cloth of Gold.'

How exquisite thy voice would come,
My darling, on this lonely air!
How sweetly would the fresh sea-breeze
Shake loose some band of soft brown hair!

Yet now my glance but once hath roved
O'er Calais and its famous plain;
To England's cliffs my gaze is turn'd,
On the blue strait mine eyes I strain.

Thou comest! Yes! the vessel's cloud
Hangs dark upon the rolling sea.
Oh, that yon sea-bird's wings were mine,
To win one instant's glimpse of thee!

I must not spring to grasp thy hand,
To woo thy smile, to seek thine eye;
But I may stand far off, and gaze,
And watch thee pass unconscious by,

And spell thy looks, and guess thy thoughts,
Mixt with the idlers on the pier.—
Ah, might I always rest unseen,
So I might have thee always near!

To-morrow hurry through the fields
Of Flanders to the storied Rhine!
To-night those soft-fringed eyes shall close
Beneath one roof, my queen! with mine.

[1867]

Dover Beach

The sea is calm to-night.
The tide is full, the moon lies fair
Upon the straits;—on the French coast the light
Gleams and is gone; the cliffs of England stand,
Glimmering and vast, out in the tranquil bay.
Come to the window, sweet is the night-air!
Only, from the long line of spray
Where the sea meets the moon-blanch'd land,
Listen! you hear the grating roar
Of pebbles which the waves draw back, and fling,
At their return, up the high strand,
Begin, and cease, and then again begin,
With tremulous cadence slow, and bring
The eternal note of sadness in.

Sophocles long ago
Heard it on the Ægæan, and it brought
Into his mind the turbid ebb and flow
Of human misery;[52] we
Find also in the sound a thought,
Hearing it by this distant northern sea.

The Sea of Faith
Was once, too, at the full, and round earth's shore
Lay like the folds of a bright girdle furl'd.
But now I only hear
Its melancholy, long, withdrawing roar,
Retreating, to the breath
Of the night-wind, down the vast edges drear
And naked shingles[53] of the world.

Ah, love, let us be true
To one another! for the world, which seems
To lie before us like a land of dreams,
So various, so beautiful, so new,
Hath really neither joy, nor love, nor light,
Nor certitude, nor peace, nor help for pain;
And we are here as on a darkling plain
Swept with confused alarms of struggle and flight,
Where ignorant armies clash by night.

[1867]

Palladium[54]

Set where the upper streams of Simois[55] flow
Was the Palladium, high 'mid rock and wood;
And Hector was in Ilium, far below,
And fought, and saw it not—but there it stood!

---

[52] See *Antigone*, ll. 583 f.

[53] Beaches covered with stones.

[54] A statue of Pallas Athena, supposed to have fallen from heaven during the building of Troy. Upon it depended the city's safety.

[55] This and the Xanthus were the two rivers of Troy.

It stood, and sun and moonshine rain'd their light
On the pure columns of its glen-built hall.
Backward and forward roll'd the waves of fight
Round Troy — but while this stood, Troy could not fall.

So, in its lovely moonlight, lives the soul.
Mountains surround it, and sweet virgin air;
Cold plashing, past it, crystal waters roll;
We visit it by moments, ah, too rare!

We shall renew the battle in the plain
To-morrow; — red with blood will Xanthus be;
Hector and Ajax will be there again,
Helen will come upon the wall to see.

Then we shall rust in shade, or shine in strife,
And fluctuate 'twixt blind hopes and blind despairs,
And fancy that we put forth all our life,
And never know how with the soul it fares.

Still doth the soul, from its lone fastness high,
Upon our life a ruling effluence send.
And when it fails, fight as we will, we die;
And while it lasts, we cannot wholly end.

Rugby Chapel [56]

NOVEMBER 1857

COLDLY, sadly descends
The autumn-evening. The field
Strewn with its dank yellow drifts
Of wither'd leaves, and the elms,
Fade into dimness apace,
Silent; — hardly a shout
From a few boys late at their play!
The lights come out in the street,
In the school-room windows; — but cold,
Solemn, unlighted, austere,
Through the gathering darkness, arise
The chapel-walls, in whose bound
Thou, my father! art laid.

There thou dost lie, in the gloom
Of the autumn evening. But ah!
That word, *gloom,* to my mind
Brings thee back, in the light
Of thy radiant vigour, again;
In the gloom of November we pass'd
Days not dark at thy side;
Seasons impair'd not the ray
Of thy buoyant cheerfulness clear.
Such thou wast! and I stand
In the autumn evening, and think
Of bygone autumns with thee.

Fifteen years have gone round
Since thou arosest to tread,
In the summer-morning, the road
Of death, at a call unforeseen,
Sudden. For fifteen years,
We who till then in thy shade
Rested as under the boughs
Of a mighty oak, have endured
Sunshine and rain as we might,
Bare, unshaded, alone,
Lacking the shelter of thee.

O strong soul, by what shore
Tarriest thou now? For that force,
Surely, has not been left vain!
Somewhere, surely, afar,
In the sounding labour-house vast
Of being, is practised that strength,
Zealous, beneficent, firm!

Yes, in some far-shining sphere,
Conscious or not of the past,
Still thou performest the word
Of the Spirit in whom thou dost live —
Prompt, unwearied, as here!

[56] Arnold's father, Dr. Thomas Arnold, the great headmaster of Rugby School, died suddenly on 12 June 1842. He was buried in the school chapel. In a letter of August 1867, Arnold says: 'I knew, my dearest mother, that the Rugby Chapel Poem would give you pleasure: often and often it had been in my mind to say it to you, and I have foreborn because my own saying of my things does not please me. It was Fitzjames Stephen's thesis, maintained in the *Edinburgh Review* [cvii (1858), pp. 172–193 — a review of *Tom Brown's School-days*], of Papa's being a narrow bustling fanatic, which moved me first to the poem. I think I have done something to fix the true legend about Papa, as those who knew him best feel it ought to run —.'

Still thou upraisest with zeal
The humble good from the ground,
Sternly repressest the bad!
Still, like a trumpet, dost rouse
Those who with half-open eyes
Tread the border-land dim
'Twixt vice and virtue; reviv'st,
Succourest! — this was thy work,
This was thy life upon earth.

What is the course of the life
Of mortal men on the earth? —
Most men eddy about
Here and there — eat and drink,
Chatter and love and hate,
Gather and squander, are raised
Aloft, are hurl'd in the dust,
Striving blindly, achieving
Nothing; and then they die —
Perish; — and no one asks
Who or what they have been,
More than he asks what waves,
In the moonlit solitudes mild
Of the midmost Ocean, have swell'd,
Foam'd for a moment, and gone.

And there are some, whom a thirst
Ardent, unquenchable, fires,
Not with the crowd to be spent,
Not without aim to go round
In an eddy of purposeless dust,
Effort unmeaning and vain.
Ah yes! some of us strive
Not without action to die
Fruitless, but something to snatch
From dull oblivion, nor all
Glut the devouring grave!
We, we have chosen our path —
Path to a clear-purposed goal,
Path of advance! — but it leads
A long, steep journey, through sunk
Gorges, o'er mountains in snow.
Cheerful, with friends, we set forth —
Then, on the height, comes the storm.
Thunder crashes from rock
To rock, the cataracts reply,
Lightnings dazzle our eyes.
Roaring torrents have breach'd
The track, the stream-bed descends
In the place where the wayfarer once
Planted his footstep — the spray
Boils o'er its borders! aloft
The unseen snow-beds dislodge
Their hanging ruin; alas,
Havoc is made in our train!
Friends, who set forth at our side,
Falter, are lost in the storm.
We, we only are left!
With frowning foreheads, with lips
Sternly compress'd, we strain on,
On — and at nightfall at last
Come to the end of our way,
To the lonely inn 'mid the rocks;
Where the gaunt and taciturn host
Stands on the threshold, the wind
Shaking his thin white hairs —
Holds his lantern to scan
Our storm-beat figures, and asks:
Whom in our party we bring?
Whom we have left in the snow?

Sadly we answer: We bring
Only ourselves! we lost
Sight of the rest in the storm.
Hardly ourselves we fought through,
Stripp'd, without friends, as we are.
Friends, companions, and train,
The avalanche swept from our side.

But thou would'st not *alone*
Be saved, my father! *alone*
Conquer and come to thy goal,
Leaving the rest in the wild.
We were weary, and we
Fearful, and we in our march
Fain to drop down and to die.
Still thou turnedst, and still
Beckonedst the trembler, and still
Gavest the weary thy hand.

If, in the paths of the world,
Stones might have wounded thy feet,
Toil or dejection have tried
Thy spirit, of that we saw
Nothing — to us thou wast still
Cheerful, and helpful, and firm!
Therefore to thee it was given
Many to save with thyself;

And, at the end of thy day,
O faithful shepherd! to come,
Bringing thy sheep in thy hand.

And through thee I believe
In the noble and great who are gone;
Pure souls honour'd and blest
By former ages, who else —
Such, so soulless, so poor,
Is the race of men whom I see —
Seem'd but a dream of the heart,
Seem'd but a cry of desire.
Yes! I believe that there lived
Others like thee in the past,
Not like the men of the crowd
Who all round me to-day
Bluster or cringe, and make life
Hideous, and arid, and vile;
But souls temper'd with fire,
Fervent, heroic, and good,
Helpers and friends of mankind.

Servants of God! — or sons
Shall I not call you? because
Not as servants ye knew
Your Father's innermost mind,
His, who unwillingly sees
One of his little ones lost —
Yours is the praise, if mankind
Hath not as yet in its march
Fainted, and fallen, and died!

See! In the rocks of the world
Marches the host of mankind,
A feeble, wavering line.
Where are they tending? — A God
Marshall'd them, gave them their goal.
Ah, but the way is so long!
Years they have been in the wild!
Sore thirst plagues them, the rocks,
Rising all round, overawe;
Factions divide them, their host
Threatens to break, to dissolve.
— Ah, keep, keep them combined!
Else, of the myriads who fill
That army, not one shall arrive;
Sole they shall stray; in the rocks
Stagger for ever in vain,
Die one by one in the waste.

Then, in such hour of need
Of your fainting, dispirited race,
Ye, like angels, appear,
Radiant with ardour divine!
Beacons of hope, ye appear!
Languor is not in your heart,
Weakness is not in your word,
Weariness not on your brow.
Ye alight in our van! at your voice,
Panic, despair, flee away.
Ye move through the ranks, recall
The stragglers, refresh the outworn,
Praise, re-inspire the brave!
Order, courage, return.
Eyes rekindling, and prayers,
Follow your steps as ye go.
Ye fill up the gaps in our files,
Strengthen the wavering line,
Stablish, continue our march,
On, to the bound of the waste,
On, to the City of God.

[1867]

Dante Gabriel Rossetti

1828–1882

The Blessed Damozel[1]

The blessed damozel leaned out
  From the gold bar of Heaven;
Her eyes were deeper than the depth
  Of waters stilled at even;
She had three lilies in her hand,
  And the stars in her hair were seven.

Her robe, ungirt from clasp to hem,
  No wrought flowers did adorn,
But a white rose of Mary's gift,
  For service meetly worn;
Her hair that lay along her back
  Was yellow like ripe corn.

[1] Written in 1847 and first published in the short-lived magazine of the Pre-Raphaelite Brotherhood, *The Germ*. The revised version is given here.

Herseemed she scarce had been a day
  One of God's choristers;
The wonder was not yet quite gone
  From that still look of hers;
Albeit, to them she left, her day
  Had counted as ten years.

(To one, it is ten years of years.
  . . . Yet now, and in this place,
Surely she leaned o'er me — her hair
  Fell all about my face. . . .
Nothing: the autumn-fall of leaves.
  The whole year sets apace.)

It was the rampart of God's house
  That she was standing on;
By God built over the sheer depth
  The which is Space begun;
So high, that looking downward thence
  She scarce could see the sun.

It lies in Heaven, across the flood
  Of ether, as a bridge.
Beneath, the tides of day and night
  With flame and darkness ridge
The void, as low as where this earth
  Spins like a fretful midge.

Around her, lovers, newly met
  'Mid deathless love's acclaims,
Spoke evermore among themselves
  Their heart-remembered names;
And the souls mounting up to God
  Went by her like thin flames.

And still she bowed herself and stooped
  Out of the circling charm;
Until her bosom must have made
  The bar she leaned on warm,
And the lilies lay as if asleep
  Along her bended arm.

From the fixed place of Heaven she saw
  Time like a pulse shake fierce
Through all the worlds. Her gaze still strove
  Within the gulf to pierce
Its path; and now she spoke as when
  The stars sang in their spheres.

The sun was gone now; the curled moon
  Was like a little feather
Fluttering far down the gulf; and now
  She spoke through the still weather.
Her voice was like the voice the stars
  Had when they sang together.

(Ah sweet! Even now, in that bird's song,
  Strove not her accents there,
Fain to be hearkened? When those bells
  Possessed the mid-day air,
Strove not her steps to reach my side
  Down all the echoing stair?)

'I wish that he were come to me,
  For he will come,' she said.
'Have I not prayed in Heaven? — on earth,
  Lord, Lord, has he not pray'd?
Are not two prayers a perfect strength?
  And shall I feel afraid?

'When round his head the aureole clings,
  And he is clothed in white,
I'll take his hand and go with him
  To the deep wells of light;
As unto a stream we will step down,
  And bathe there in God's sight.

'We two will stand beside that shrine,
  Occult, withheld, untrod,
Whose lamps are stirred continually
  With prayer sent up to God;
And see our old prayers, granted, melt
  Each like a little cloud.

'We two will lie i' the shadow of
  That living mystic tree
Within whose secret growth the Dove
  Is sometimes felt to be,
While every leaf that His plumes touch
  Saith His Name audibly.

'And I myself will teach to him,
  I myself, lying so,
The songs I sing here; which his voice
  Shall pause in, hushed and slow,
And find some knowledge at each pause,
  Or some new thing to know.'

(Alas! We two, we two, thou say'st!
Yea, one wast thou with me
That once of old. But shall God lift
To endless unity
The soul whose likeness with thy soul
Was but its love for thee?)

'We two,' she said, 'will seek the groves
Where the lady Mary is,
With her five handmaidens, whose names
Are five sweet symphonies,
Cecily, Gertrude, Magdalen,
Margaret and Rosalys.

'Circlewise sit they, with bound locks
And foreheads garlanded;
Into the fine cloth white like flame
Weaving the golden thread,
To fashion the birth-robes for them
Who are just born, being dead.

'He shall fear, haply, and be dumb:
Then will I lay my cheek
To his, and tell about our love,
Not once abashed or weak:
And the dear Mother will approve
My pride, and let me speak.

'Herself shall bring us, hand in hand,
To Him round whom all souls
Kneel, the clear-ranged unnumbered heads
Bowed with their aureoles:
And angels meeting us shall sing
To their citherns and citoles.

'There will I ask of Christ the Lord
Thus much for him and me: —
Only to live as once on earth
With Love, — only to be,
As then awhile, for ever now
Together, I and he.'

She gazed and listened and then said,
Less sad of speech than mild, —
'All this is when he comes.' She ceased.
The light thrilled towards her, fill'd
With angels in strong level flight.
Her eyes prayed, and she smil'd.

(I saw her smile.) But soon their path
Was vague in distant spheres:
And then she cast her arms along
The golden barriers,
And laid her face between her hands,
And wept. (I heard her tears.)

The Woodspurge

THE wind flapped loose, the wind was still,
Shaken out dead from tree and hill:
I had walked on at the wind's will, —
I sat now, for the wind was still.

Between my knees my forehead was, —
My lips, drawn in, said not Alas!
My hair was over in the grass,
My naked ears heard the day pass.

My eyes, wide open, had the run
Of some ten weeds to fix upon;
Among those few, out of the sun,
The woodspurge flowered, three cups in one.

From perfect grief there need not be
Wisdom or even memory:
One thing then learnt remains to me, —
The woodspurge has a cup of three.

[*Poems,* 1870]

THE HOUSE OF LIFE [2]

A SONNET is a moment's monument, —
Memorial from the Soul's eternity
To one dead deathless hour. Look that it be,
Whether for lustral rite or dire portent,
Of its own arduous fulness reverent:
Carve it in ivory or in ebony,
As Day or Night may rule; and let Time see
Its flowering crest impearled and orient.

[2] Rossetti began writing the sonnets which form this sequence as early as 1848. It was not given its final order until 1881. The title derives from the fact that in astrology the heavens are divided into houses, the most important of which is the house of human life.

A Sonnet is a coin: its face reveals
The soul,—its converse, to what Power 'tis due:—
Whether for tribute to the august appeals
Of Life, or dower in Love's high retinue,
It serve; or, 'mid the dark wharf's cavernous breath,
In Charon's palm it pay the toll to Death.

Bridal Birth

As when desire, long darkling, dawns, and first
The mother looks upon the newborn child,
Even so my Lady stood at gaze and smiled
When her soul knew at length the Love it nursed.
Born with her life, creature of poignant thirst
And exquisite hunger, at her heart Love lay
Quickening in darkness, till a voice that day
Cried on him, and the bonds of birth were burst.

Now, shielded in his wings, our faces yearn
Together, as his fullgrown feet now range
The grove, and his warm hands our couch prepare:
Till to his song our bodiless souls in turn
Be born his children, when Death's nuptial change
Leaves us for light the halo of his hair.

Lovesight

When do I see thee most, beloved one?
When in the light the spirits of mine eyes
Before thy face, their altar, solemnize
The worship of that Love through thee made known?
Or when in the dusk hours, (we two alone,)
Close-kissed and eloquent of still replies
Thy twilight-hidden glimmering visage lies,
And my soul only sees thy soul its own?

O love, my love! if I no more should see
Thyself, nor on the earth the shadow of thee,
Nor image of thine eyes in any spring,—
How then should sound upon Life's darkening slope
The ground-whirl of the perished leaves of Hope,
The wind of Death's imperishable wing?

The Lovers' Walk

Sweet twining hedgeflowers wind-stirred in no wise
On this June day; and hand that clings in hand:—
Still glades; and meeting faces scarcely fann'd:—
An osier-odoured stream that draws the skies
Deep to its heart; and mirrored eyes in eyes:—
Fresh hourly wonder o'er the Summer land
Of light and cloud; and two souls softly spann'd
With one o'erarching heaven of smiles and sighs:—

Even such their path, whose bodies lean unto
Each other's visible sweetness amorously,—
Whose passionate hearts lean by Love's high decree
Together on his heart for ever true,
As the cloud-foaming firmamental blue
Rests on the blue line of a foamless sea.

The Birth-bond

HAVE you not noted, in some family
Where two were born of a first marriage-bed,
How still they own their gracious bond, though fed
And nursed on the forgotten breast and knee? —
How to their father's children they shall be
In act and thought of one goodwill; but each
Shall for the other have, in silence speech,
And in a word complete community?

Even so, when first I saw you, seemed it, love,
That among souls allied to mine was yet
One nearer kindred than life hinted of.
O born with me somewhere that men forget,
And though in years of sight and sound unmet,
Known for my soul's birth-partner well enough!

Genius in Beauty

BEAUTY like hers is genius. Not the call
Of Homer's or of Dante's heart sublime, —
Not Michael's [3] hand furrowing the zones of time, —
Is more with compassed mysteries musical;
Nay, not in Spring's or Summer's sweet footfall
More gathered gifts exuberant Life bequeaths
Than doth this sovereign face, whose love-spell breathes
Even from its shadowed contour on the wall.

As many men are poets in their youth,
But for one sweet-strung soul the wires prolong
Even through all change the indomitable song;
So in likewise the envenomed years, whose tooth
Rends shallower grace with ruin void of ruth,
Upon this beauty's power shall wreak no wrong.

[3] Michelangelo's

Silent Noon

YOUR hands lie open in the long fresh grass, —
The finger-points look through like rosy blooms:
Your eyes smile peace. The pasture gleams and glooms
'Neath billowing skies that scatter and amass.
All round our nest, far as the eye can pass,
Are golden kingcup-fields with silver edge
Where the cow-parsley skirts the hawthorn-hedge.
'Tis visible silence, still as the hour-glass.

Deep in the sun-searched growths the dragon-fly
Hangs like a blue thread loosened from the sky: —
So this wing'd hour is dropt to us from above.
Oh! clasp we to our hearts, for deathless dower,
This close-companioned inarticulate hour
When twofold silence was the song of love.

Love-sweetness

SWEET dimness of her loosened hair's downfall
About thy face; her sweet hands round thy head
In gracious fostering union garlanded;
Her tremulous smiles; her glances' sweet recall

Of love; her murmuring sighs memorial;
  Her mouth's culled sweetness by thy kisses shed
  On cheeks and neck and eyelids, and so led
Back to her mouth which answers there for all: —

What sweeter than these things, except the thing
  In lacking which all these would lose their sweet: —
  The confident heart's still fervour: the swift beat
And soft subsidence of the spirit's wing,
Then when it feels, in cloud-girt wayfaring,
  The breath of kindred plumes against its feet?

Heart's Haven

Sometimes she is a child within mine arms,
  Cowering beneath dark wings that love must chase, —
  With still tears showering and averted face,
Inexplicably filled with faint alarms;
And oft from mine own spirit's hurtling harms
  I crave the refuge of her deep embrace, —
  Against all ills the fortified strong place
And sweet reserve of sovereign countercharms.

And Love, our light at night and shade at noon,
  Lulls us to rest with songs, and turns away
  All shafts of shelterless tumultuous day.
Like the moon's growth, his face gleams through his tune;
And as soft waters warble to the moon,
  Our answering spirits chime one roundelay.

Mid-rapture

Thou lovely and belovéd, thou my love;
  Whose kiss seems still the first; whose summoning eyes,
  Even now, as for our love-world's new sunrise,
Shed very dawn; whose voice, attuned above
All modulation of the deep-bowered dove,
  Is like a hand laid softly on the soul;
  Whose hand is like a sweet voice to control
Those worn tired brows it hath the keeping of: —

What word can answer to thy word, — what gaze
  To thine, which now absorbs within its sphere
  My worshipping face, till I am mirrored there
Light-circled in a heaven of deep-drawn rays?
  What clasp, what kiss mine inmost heart can prove,
  O lovely and belovéd, O my love?

Sleepless Dreams

Girt in dark growths, yet glimmering with one star,
  O night desirous as the nights of youth!
  Why should my heart within thy spell, forsooth,
Now beat, as the bride's finger-pulses are
Quickened within the girdling golden bar?
  What wings are these that fan my pillow smooth?
  And why does Sleep, waved back by Joy and Ruth,
Tread softly round and gaze at me from far?

Nay, night deep-leaved! And would Love feign in thee
  Some shadowy palpitating grove that bears

Rest for man's eyes and music for his ears?
O lonely night! art thou not known to me,
A thicket hung with masks of mockery
And watered with the wasteful warmth of tears?

Willowwood

I

I SAT with Love upon a woodside well,
Leaning across the water, I and he;
Nor ever did he speak nor looked at me,
But touched his lute wherein was audible
The certain secret thing he had to tell:
Only our mirrored eyes met silently
In the low wave; and that sound came to be
The passionate voice I knew; and my tears fell.

And at their fall, his eyes beneath grew hers;
And with his foot and with his wing-feathers
He swept the spring that watered my heart's drouth.
Then the dark ripples spread to waving hair,
And as I stooped, her own lips rising there
Bubbled with brimming kisses at my mouth.

II

And now Love sang: but his was such a song,
So meshed with half-remembrance hard to free,
As souls disused in death's sterility
May sing when the new birthday tarries long.
And I was made aware of a dumb throng
That stood aloof, one form by every tree,
All mournful forms, for each was I or she,
The shades of those our days that had no tongue.

They looked on us, and knew us and were known;
While fast together, alive from the abyss,
Clung the soul-wrung implacable close kiss;
And pity of self through all made broken moan
Which said, 'For once, for once, for once alone!'
And still Love sang, and what he sang was this:—

III

'O ye, all ye that walk in Willowwood,
That walk with hollow faces burning white;
What fathom-depth of soul-struck widowhood,
What long, what longer hours, one life-long night,
Ere ye again, who so in vain have wooed
Your last hope lost, who so in vain invite
Your lips to that their unforgotten food,
Ere ye, ere ye again shall see the light!

Alas! the bitter banks in Willowwood,
With tear-spurge wan, with blood-wort burning red:
Alas! if ever such a pillow could
Steep deep the soul in sleep till she were dead,—
Better all life forget her than this thing,
That Willowwood should hold her wandering!'

IV

So sang he: and as meeting rose and rose
Together cling through the wind's well-away,
Nor change at once, yet near the end of day
The leaves drop loosened where the heart-stain glows,—
So when the song died did the kiss unclose;
And her face fell back drowned, and was as grey

As its grey eyes; and if it ever may
Meet mine again I know not if Love knows.

Only I know that I leaned low and drank
A long draught from the water where she sank,
Her breath and all her tears and all her soul:
And as I leaned, I know I felt Love's face
Pressed on my neck with moan of pity and grace,
Till both our heads were in his aureole.

Soul's Beauty

Under the arch of Life, where love and death,
Terror and mystery, guard her shrine, I saw
Beauty enthroned; and though her gaze struck awe,
I drew it in as simply as my breath.
Hers are the eyes which, over and beneath,
The sky and sea bend on thee, — which can draw,
By sea or sky or woman, to one law,
The allotted bondman of her palm and wreath.

This is that Lady Beauty, in whose praise
Thy voice and hand shake still, — long known to thee
By flying hair and fluttering hem, — the beat
Following her daily of thy heart and feet,
How passionately and irretrievably,
In what fond flight, how many ways and days!

Lost Days

The lost days of my life until to-day,
What were they, could I see them on the street
Lie as they fell? Would they be ears of wheat
Sown once for food but trodden into clay?
Or golden coins squandered and still to pay?
Or drops of blood dabbling the guilty feet?
Or such spilt water as in dreams must cheat
The undying throats of Hell, athirst alway?

I do not see them here; but after death
God knows I know the faces I shall see
Each one a murdered self, with low last breath.
'I am thyself, — what hast thou done to me?'
'And I — and I — thyself,' (lo! each one saith,)
'And thou thyself to all eternity!'

My Sister's Sleep[4]

She fell asleep on Christmas Eve:
At length the long-ungranted shade
Of weary eyelids overweigh'd
The pain nought else might yet relieve.

Our mother, who had leaned all day
Over the bed from chime to chime,
Then raised herself for the first time,
And as she sat her down, did pray.

Her little work-table was spread
With work to finish. For the glare
Made by her candle, she had care
To work some distance from the bed.

Without, there was a cold moon up,
Of winter radiance sheer and thin;
The hollow halo it was in
Was like an icy crystal cup.

Through the small room, with subtle sound
Of flame, by vents the fireshine drove
And reddened. In its dim alcove
The mirror shed a clearness round.

[4] This poem does not refer to either of Rossetti's sisters Written in 1847; printed in *The Germ*, 1850.

I had been sitting up some nights,
And my tired mind felt weak and blank;
Like a sharp strengthening wine it drank
The stillness and the broken lights.

Twelve struck. That sound, by dwindling years
Heard in each hour, crept off; and then
The ruffled silence spread again,
Like water that a pebble stirs.

Our mother rose from where she sat:
Her needles, as she laid them down,
Met lightly, and her silken gown
Settled: no other noise than that.

'Glory unto the Newly Born!'
So, as said angels, she did say;
Because we were in Christmas Day,
Though it would still be long till morn.

Just then in the room over us
There was a pushing back of chairs,
As some who had sat unawares
So late, now heard the hour, and rose.

With anxious softly-stepping haste
Our mother went where Margaret lay,
Fearing the sounds o'erhead — should they
Have broken her long watched-for rest!

She stooped an instant, calm, and turned;
But suddenly turned back again;
And all her features seemed in pain
With woe, and her eyes gazed and yearned.

For my part, I but hid my face,
And held my breath, and spoke no word:
There was none spoken; but I heard
The silence for a little space.

Our mother bowed herself and wept:
And both my arms fell, and I said,
'God knows I knew that she was dead,'
And there, all white, my sister slept.

Then kneeling, upon Christmas morn
A little after twelve o'clock
We said, ere the first quarter struck,
'Christ's blessing on the newly born!'

The Staff and Scrip[5]

'Who owns these lands?' the Pilgrim said.
'Stranger, Queen Blanchelys.'
'And who has thus harried them?' he said.
'It was Duke Luke did this:
God's ban be his!'

The Pilgrim said: 'Where is your house?
I'll rest there, with your will.'
'You've but to climb these blackened boughs
And you'll see it over the hill,
For it burns still.'

'Which road, to seek your Queen?' said he.
'Nay, nay, but with some wound
You'll fly back hither, it may be,
And by your blood i' the ground
My place be found.'

'Friend, stay in peace. God keep your head,
And mine, where I will go;
For He is here and there,' he said.
He passed the hill-side, slow,
And stood below.

The Queen sat idle by her loom:
She heard the arras stir,
And looked up sadly: through the room
The sweetness sickened her
Of musk and myrrh.

Her women, standing two and two,
In silence combed the fleece.
The Pilgrim said, 'Peace be with you,
Lady;' and bent his knees.
She answered, 'Peace.'

---

[5] Based upon a tale (No. 25) in the *Gesta Romanorum*, a collection of Latin stories popular in the Middle Ages. The poem was contributed to *The Oxford and Cambridge Magazine* (1856), which Rossetti's friend William Morris was helping to edit.

Her eyes were like the wave within;
  Like water-reeds the poise
Of her soft body, dainty thin;
  And like the water's noise
    Her plaintive voice.

For him, the stream had never well'd
  In desert tracts malign
So sweet; nor had he ever felt
  So faint in the sunshine
    Of Palestine.

Right so, he knew that he saw weep
  Each night through every dream
The Queen's own face, confused in sleep
  With visages supreme
    Not known to him.

'Lady,' he said, 'your lands lie burnt
  And waste: to meet your foe
All fear: this I have seen and learnt.
  Say that it shall be so,
    And I will go.'

She gazed at him. 'Your cause is just,
  For I have heard the same:'
He said: 'God's strength shall be my trust.
  Fall it to good or grame,
    'Tis in His name.'

'Sir, you are thanked. My cause is dead.
  Why should you toil to break
A grave, and fall therein?' she said.
  He did not pause but spake:
    'For my vow's sake.'

'Can such vows be, Sir—to God's ear,
  Not to God's will?' 'My vow
Remains: God heard me there as here,'
  He said with reverent brow,
    'Both then and now.'

They gazed together, he and she,
  The minute while he spoke;
And when he ceased, she suddenly
  Looked round upon her folk
    As though she woke.

'Fight, Sir,' she said; 'my prayers in pain
  Shall be your fellowship.'
He whispered one among her train,—
  'To-morrow bid her keep
    This staff and scrip.'

She sent him a sharp sword, whose belt
  About his body there
As sweet as her own arms he felt.
  He kissed its blade, all bare,
    Instead of her.

She sent him a green banner wrought
  With one white lily stem,
To bind his lance with when he fought.
  He writ upon the same
    And kissed her name.

She sent him a white shield, whereon
  She bade that he should trace
His will. He blent fair hues that shone,
  And in a golden space
    He kissed her face.

Right so, the sunset skies unseal'd,
  Like lands he never knew,
Beyond to-morrow's battle-field
  Lay open out of view
    To ride into.

Next day till dark the woman pray'd:
  Nor any might know there
How the fight went: the Queen has bade
  That there do come to her
    No messenger.

Weak now to them the voice o' the priest
  As any trance affords;
And when each anthem failed and ceas'd,
  It seemed that the last chords
    Still sang the words.

Lo, Father, is thine ear inclin'd,
  And hath thine angel pass'd?
For these thy watchers now are blind
  With vigil, and at last
    Dizzy with fast.

'Oh what is the light that shines so red?
'Tis long since the sun set;'
Quoth the youngest to the eldest maid:
''Twas dim but now, and yet
The light is great.'

Quoth the other: ''Tis our sight is dazed
That we see flame i' the air.'
But the Queen held her brows and gazed,
And said, 'It is the glare
Of torches there.'

'Oh what are the sounds that rise and spread?
All day it was so still;'
Quoth the youngest to the eldest maid:
'Unto the furthest hill
The air they fill.'

Quoth the other; ''Tis our sense is blurr'd
With all the chants gone by.'
But the Queen held her breath and heard,
And said, 'It is the cry
Of Victory.'

The first of all the rout was sound,
The next were dust and flame,
And then the horses shook the ground:
And in the thick of them
A still band came.

'Oh what do ye bring out of the fight,
Thus hid beneath these boughs?'
'Even him, thy conquering guest to-night,
Who yet shall not carouse,
Queen, in thy house.'

'Uncover ye his face,' she said.
'O changed in little space!'
She cried, 'O pale that was so red!
O God, O God of grace!
Cover his face.'

His sword was broken in his hand
Where he had kissed the blade.
'O soft steel that could not withstand!
O my hard heart unstayed,
That prayed and prayed!'

His bloodied banner crossed his mouth
Where he had kissed her name.
'O east, and west, and north, and south,
Fair flew my web, for shame,
To guide Death's aim!'

The tints were shredded from his shield
Where he had kissed her face.
'Oh, of all gifts that I could yield,
Death only keeps its place,
My gift and grace!'

Then stepped a damsel to her side,
And spoke, and needs must weep:
'For his sake, lady, if he died,
He prayed of thee to keep
This staff and scrip.'

That night they hung above her bed,
Till morning wet with tears.
Year after year above her head
Her bed his token wears,
Five years, ten years.

That night the passion of her grief
Shook them as there they hung.
Each year the wind that shed the leaf
Shook them and in its tongue
A message flung.

And once she woke with a clear mind
That letters writ to calm
Her soul lay in the scrip; to find
Only a torpid balm
And dust of palm.

They shook far off with palace sport
When joust and dance were rife;
And the hunt shook them from the court;
For hers, in peace or strife,
Was a Queen's life.

A Queen's death now: as now they shake
To gusts in chapel dim,—
Hung where she sleeps, not seen to wake,
(Carved lovely white and slim,)
With them by him.

Stand up to-day, still armed, with her,
  Good knight, before His brow
Who then as now was here and there,
  Who had in mind thy vow
    Then even as now.

The lists are set in Heaven to-day,
  The bright pavilions shine;
Fair hangs thy shield, and none gainsay;
  The trumpets sound in sign
    That she is thine.

Not tithed with days' and years' decease
  He pays thy wage He owed,
But with imperishable peace
  Here in His own abode,
    Thy jealous God.

Sister Helen [6]

'Why did you melt your waxen man,[7]
    Sister Helen?
To-day is the third since you began.'
'The time was long, yet the time ran,
    Little brother.'
  (O Mother, Mary Mother,
Three days to-day, between Hell and Heaven!)

'But if you have done your work aright,
    Sister Helen,
You'll let me play, for you said I might.'
'Be very still in your play to-night,
    Little brother.'
  (O Mother, Mary Mother,
Third night, to-night, between Hell and Heaven!)

'You said it must melt ere vesper-bell,
    Sister Helen;
If now it be molten, all is well.'
'Even so, — nay, peace! you cannot tell,
    Little brother.'
  (O Mother, Mary Mother,
O what is this, between Hell and Heaven?)

'Oh the waxen knave was plump to-day,
    Sister Helen;
How like dead folk he has dropped away!'
'Nay now, of the dead what can you say,
    Little brother?'
  (O Mother, Mary Mother,
What of the dead, between Hell and Heaven?)

'See, see, the sunken pile of wood,
    Sister Helen,
Shines through the thinned wax red as blood!'
'Nay now, when looked you yet on blood,
    Little brother?'
  (O Mother, Mary Mother,
How pale she is, between Hell and Heaven!)

'Now close your eyes, for they're sick and sore,
    Sister Helen,
And I'll play without the gallery door.'
'Aye, let me rest, — I'll lie on the floor,
    Little brother.'
  (O Mother, Mary Mother,
What rest to-night, between Hell and Heaven?)

'Here high up in the balcony,
    Sister Helen,
The moon flies face to face with me.'
'Aye, look and say whatever you see,
    Little brother.'
  (O Mother, Mary Mother,
What sight to-night, between Hell and Heaven?)

'Outside it 's merry in the wind's wake,
    Sister Helen;
In the shaken trees the chill stars shake.'
'Hush, heard you a horse-tread as you spake,
    Little brother?'
  (O Mother, Mary Mother,
What sound to-night, between Hell and Heaven?)

[6] First printed in a German publication, *The Düsseldorf Artists' Annual* (1854), which issued an English number under the supervision of Rossetti's friend Mrs. Mary Howitt.

[7] According to a medieval superstition melting and torturing a waxen image of a person would bring suffering and death upon him.

'I hear a horse-tread, and I see,
Sister Helen,
Three horsemen that ride terribly.'
'Little brother, whence come the three,
Little brother?'
(*O Mother, Mary Mother,*
Whence should they come, between Hell and Heaven?)

'They come by the hill-verge from Boyne Bar,
Sister Helen,
And one draws nigh, but two are afar.'
'Look, look, do you know them who they are,
Little brother?'
(*O Mother, Mary Mother,*
Who should they be, between Hell and Heaven?)

'Oh, it's Keith of Eastholm rides so fast,
Sister Helen,
For I know the white mane on the blast.'
'The hour has come, has come at last,
Little brother!'
(*O Mother, Mary Mother,*
Her hour at last, between Hell and Heaven!)

'He has made a sign and called Halloo!
Sister Helen,
And he says that he would speak with you.'
'Oh tell him I fear the frozen dew,
Little brother.'
(*O Mother, Mary Mother,*
Why laughs she thus, between Hell and Heaven?)

'The wind is loud, but I hear him cry,
Sister Helen,
That Keith of Ewern's like to die.'
'And he and thou, and thou and I,
Little brother.'
(*O Mother, Mary Mother,*
And they and we, between Hell and Heaven!)

'Three days ago, on his marriage-morn,
Sister Helen,
He sickened, and lies since then forlorn.'
'For bridegroom's side is the bride a thorn,
Little brother?'
(*O Mother, Mary Mother,*
Cold bridal cheer, between Hell and Heaven!)

Three days and nights he has lain abed,
Sister Helen,
And he prays in torment to be dead.'
'The thing may chance, if he have prayed,
Little brother!'
(*O Mother, Mary Mother,*
If we have prayed, between Hell and Heaven!)

'But he has not ceased to cry to-day,
Sister Helen,
That you should take your curse away.'
'*My* prayer was heard,—he need but pray,
Little brother!'
(*O Mother, Mary Mother,*
Shall God not hear, between Hell and Heaven?)

'But he says, till you take back your ban,
Sister Helen,
His soul would pass, yet never can.'
'Nay then, shall I slay a living man,
Little brother?'
(*O Mother, Mary Mother,*
A living soul, between Hell and Heaven!)

'But he calls for ever on your name,
Sister Helen,
And says that he melts before a flame.'
'My heart for his pleasure fared the same,
Little brother.'
(*O Mother, Mary Mother,*
Fire at the heart, between Hell and Heaven!)

'Here's Keith of Westholm riding fast,
Sister Helen,
For I know the white plume on the blast.'

'The hour, the sweet hour I forecast,
Little brother!'
(*O Mother, Mary Mother,*
Is the hour sweet, between Hell and Heaven?)

'He stops to speak, and he stills his horse,
Sister Helen;
But his words are drowned in the wind's course.'
'Nay hear, nay hear, you must hear perforce,
Little brother!'
(*O Mother, Mary Mother,*
What word now heard, between Hell and Heaven!)

'Oh he says that Keith of Ewern's cry,
Sister Helen,
Is ever to see you ere he die.'
In all that his soul sees, there am I,
Little brother!'
(*O Mother, Mary Mother,*
The soul's one sight, between Hell and Heaven!)

'He sends a ring and a broken coin,
Sister Helen,
And bids you mind the banks of Boyne.'
'What else he broke will he ever join,
Little brother?'
(*O Mother, Mary Mother,*
No, never joined between Hell and Heaven!)

'He yields you these and craves full fain,
Sister Helen,
You pardon him in his mortal pain.'
'What else he took will he give again,
Little brother?'
(*O Mother, Mary Mother,*
Not twice to give, between Hell and Heaven!)

'He calls your name in an agony,
Sister Helen,
That even dead Love must weep to see.'
'Hate, born of Love, is blind as he,
Little brother!'
(*O Mother, Mary Mother,*
Love turned to hate, between Hell and Heaven!)

'Oh, it's Keith of Keith now that rides fast,
Sister Helen,
For I know the white hair on the blast.'
'The short short hour will soon be past,
Little brother!'
(*O Mother, Mary Mother,*
Will soon be past, between Hell and Heaven!)

'He looks at me and he tries to speak,
Sister Helen,
But oh! his voice is sad and weak!'
'What here should the mighty Baron seek,
Little brother?'
(*O Mother, Mary Mother,*
Is this the end, between Hell and Heaven?)

'Oh his son still cries, if you forgive,
Sister Helen,
The body dies but the soul shall live.'
'Fire shall forgive me as I forgive,
Little brother!'
(*O Mother, Mary Mother,*
As she forgives, between Hell and Heaven!)

'Oh he prays you, as his heart would rive,
Sister Helen,
To save his dear son's soul alive.'
'Fire cannot slay it, it shall thrive,
Little brother!'
(*O Mother, Mary Mother,*
Alas, alas, between Hell and Heaven!)

'He cries to you, kneeling in the road,
Sister Helen,
To go with him for the love of God!'
'The way is long to his son's abode,
Little brother.'
(*O Mother, Mary Mother,*
The way is long, between Hell and Heaven!)

'A lady's here, by a dark steed brought,
Sister Helen,
So darkly clad, I saw her not.'
'See her now or never see aught,
Little brother!'
(*O Mother, Mary Mother,*
What more to see, between Hell and Heaven!)

'Her hood falls back, and the moon shines fair,
Sister Helen,
On the Lady of Ewern's golden hair.'
'Blest hour of my power and her despair,
Little brother!'
(*O Mother, Mary Mother,*
Hour blest and bann'd, between Hell and Heaven!)

'Pale, pale her cheeks, that in pride did glow,
Sister Helen,
'Neath the bridal-wreath three days ago.'
'One morn for pride and three days for woe,
Little brother!'
(*O Mother, Mary Mother,*
Three days, three nights, between Hell and Heaven!)

'Her clasped hands stretch from her bending head,
Sister Helen;
With the loud wind's wail her sobs are wed.'
'What wedding-strains hath her bridal-bed,
Little brother?'
(*O Mother, Mary Mother,*
What strain but death's, between Hell and Heaven!)

'She may not speak, she sinks in a swoon,
Sister Helen,—
She lifts her lips and gasps on the moon.'
'Oh! might I but hear her soul's blithe tune,
Little brother!'
(*O Mother, Mary Mother,*
Her woe's dumb cry, between Hell and Heaven!)

'They've caught her to Westholm's saddle-bow,
Sister Helen,
And her moonlit hair gleams white in its flow.'
'Let it turn whiter than winter snow,
Little brother!'
(*O Mother, Mary Mother,*
Woe-withered gold, between Hell and Heaven!)

'O Sister Helen, you heard the bell,
Sister Helen!
More loud than the vesper-chime it fell.'
'No vesper-chime, but a dying knell,
Little brother!'
(*O Mother, Mary Mother,*
His dying knell, between Hell and Heaven!)

'Alas! but I fear the heavy sound,
Sister Helen;
Is it in the sky or in the ground?'
'Say, have they turned their horses round,
Little brother?'
(*O Mother, Mary Mother,*
What would she more, between Hell and Heaven?)

'They have raised the old man from his knee,
Sister Helen,
And they ride in silence hastily.'
'More fast the naked soul doth flee,
Little brother!'
(*O Mother, Mary Mother,*
The naked soul, between Hell and Heaven!)

'Flank to flank are the three steeds gone,
Sister Helen,
But the lady's dark steed goes alone.'

'And lonely her bridegroom's soul hath flown,
Little brother.'
(*O Mother, Mary Mother,*
The lonely ghost, between Hell and Heaven!)

'Oh, the wind is sad in the iron chill,
Sister Helen,
And weary sad they look by the hill.'
'But he and I are sadder still,
Little brother!'
(*O Mother, Mary Mother,*
Most sad of all, between Hell and Heaven!)

'See, see, the wax has dropped from its place,
Sister Helen,
And the flames are winning up apace!'
'Yet here they burn but for a space,
Little brother!'
(*O Mother, Mary Mother,*
Here for a space, between Hell and Heaven!)

'Ah! what white thing at the door has cross'd,
Sister Helen?
Ah! what is this that sighs in the frost?'
'A soul that's lost as mine is lost,
Little brother!'
(*O Mother, Mary Mother,*
Lost, lost, all lost, between Hell and Heaven!)

Sudden Light[8]

I HAVE been here before,
But when or how I cannot tell:
I know the grass beyond the door,
The sweet keen smell,
The sighing sound, the lights around the shore.

You have been mine before,—
How long ago I may not know:
But just when at that swallow's soar
Your neck turned so,
Some veil did fall,—I knew it all of yore.

Then, now,—perchance again! . . .
O round mine eyes your tresses shake!
Shall we not lie as we have lain
Thus for Love's sake,
And sleep, and wake, yet never break the chain?

The Portrait[9]

THIS is her picture as she was:
It seems a thing to wonder on,
As though mine image in the glass
Should tarry when myself am gone.
I gaze until she seems to stir,—
Until mine eyes almost aver
That now, even now, the sweet lips part
To breathe the words of the sweet heart:—
And yet the earth is over her.

Alas! even such the thin-drawn ray
That makes the prison-depths more rude,—
The drip of water night and day
Giving a tongue to solitude.
Yet only this, of love's whole prize,
Remains; save what in mournful guise
Takes counsel with my soul alone,—
Save what is secret and unknown,
Below the earth, above the skies.

In painting her I shrined her face
Mid mystic trees, where light falls in
Hardly at all; a covert place
Where you might think to find a din
Of doubtful talk, and a live flame
Wandering, and many a shape whose name

[8] Originally included in *Sonnets and Songs Towards a Work to be called 'The House of Life'* in *Poems*, 1870.

[9] One of the earliest of Rossetti's poems, this was written possibly before 1847. Published in *Poems*, 1870. It is not, of course, concerned with Miss Siddal, whom he married, after a ten-years' courtship, in 1860.

Not itself knoweth, and old dew,
And your own footsteps meeting you,
And all things going as they came.

A deep dim wood; and there she stands
As in that wood that day: for so
Was the still movement of her hands
And such the pure line's gracious flow.
And passing fair the type must seem,
Unknown the presence and the dream.
'Tis she: though of herself, alas!
Less than her shadow on the grass
Or than her image in the stream.

That day we met there, I and she
One with the other all alone;
And we were blithe; yet memory
Saddens those hours, as when the moon
Looks upon daylight. And with her
I stooped to drink the spring-water,
Athirst where other waters sprang;
And where the echo is, she sang,—
My soul another echo there.

But when that hour my soul won strength
For words whose silence wastes and kills,
Dull raindrops smote us, and at length
Thundered the heat within the hills.
That eve I spoke those words again
Beside the pelted window-pane;
And there she hearkened what I said,
With under-glances that surveyed
The empty pastures blind with rain.

Next day the memories of these things,
Like leaves through which a bird has flown,
Still vibrated with Love's warm wings;
Till I must make them all my own
And paint this picture. So, 'twixt ease
Of talk and sweet long silences,
She stood among the plants in bloom
At windows of a summer room,
To feign the shadow of the trees.

And as I wrought, while all above
And all around was fragrant air,
In the sick burthen of my love
It seemed each sun-thrilled blossom there
Beat like a heart among the leaves.
O heart that never beats nor heaves,
In that one darkness lying still,
What now to thee my love's great will
Or the fine web the sunshine weaves?

For now doth daylight disavow
Those days,— nought left to see or hear.
Only in solemn whispers now
At night-time these things reach mine ear,
When the leaf-shadows at a breath
Shrink in the road, and all the heath,
Forest and water, far and wide,
In limpid starlight glorified,
Lie like the mystery of death.

Last night at last I could have slept,
And yet delayed my sleep till dawn,
Still wandering. Then it was I wept:
For unawares I came upon
Those glades where once she walked with me:
And as I stood there suddenly,
All wan with traversing the night,
Upon the desolate verge of light
Yearned loud the iron-bosomed sea.

Even so, where Heaven holds breath and hears
The beating heart of Love's own breast,—
Where round the secret of all spheres
All angels lay their wings to rest,—
How shall my soul stand rapt and awed,
When, by the new birth borne abroad
Throughout the music of the suns,
It enters in her soul at once
And knows the silence there for God!

Here with her face doth memory sit
Meanwhile, and wait the day's decline,
Till other eyes shall look from it,
Eyes of the spirit's Palestine,
Even than the old gaze tenderer:
While hopes and aims long lost with her
Stand round her image side by side,
Like tombs of pilgrims that have died
About the Holy Sepulchre.

The Burden of Nineveh[10]

In our Museum[11] galleries
To-day I lingered o'er the prize[12]
Dead Greece vouchsafes to living eyes,—
Her Art for ever in fresh wise
From hour to hour rejoicing me.
Sighing I turned at last to win
Once more the London dirt and din;
And as I made the swing-door spin
And issued, they were hoisting in
A wingéd beast from Nineveh.

A human face the creature wore,
And hoofs behind and hoofs before,
And flanks with dark runes fretted o'er.
'Twas bull, 'twas mitred Minotaur,
A dead disbowelled mystery;
The mummy of a buried faith
Stark from the charnel without scathe,
Its wings stood for the light to bathe,—
Such fossil cerements as might swathe
The very corpse of Nineveh.

The print of its first rush-wrapping,
Wound ere it dried, still ribbed the thing.
What song did the brown maidens sing,
From purple mouths alternating,
When that was woven languidly?
What vows, what rites, what prayers preferr'd,
What songs has the strange image heard?
In what blind vigil stood interr'd
For ages, till an English[13] word
Broke silence first at Nineveh?

Oh, when upon each sculptured court,
Where even the wind might not resort,—
O'er which Time passed, of like import
With the wild Arab boys at sport,—
A living face looked in to see:—
Oh seemed it not—the spell once broke—
As though the carven warriors woke,
As though the shaft the string forsook,
The cymbals clashed, the chariots shook,
And there was life in Nineveh?

[10] Contributed to *The Oxford and Cambridge Magazine*, 1856.
[11] The British Museum, London.
[12] The Elgin Marbles.
[13] Excavations were carried on at Nineveh by the English in 1845–1851.

On London stones our sun anew
The beast's recovered shadow threw.
(No shade that plague of darkness knew,
No light, no shade, while older grew
By ages the old earth and sea.)
Lo thou! could all thy priests have shown
Such proof to make thy godhead known?
From their dead Past thou liv'st alone;
And still thy shadow is thine own
Even as of yore in Nineveh.

That day whereof we keep record,
When near thy city gates the Lord
Sheltered his Jonah[14] with a gourd,
This sun, (I said) here present, pour'd
Even thus this shadow that I see.
This shadow has been shed the same
From sun and moon,—from lamps which came
For prayer,—from fifteen days of flame,
The last, while smouldered to a name
Sardanapalus'[15] Nineveh.

Within thy shadow, haply, once
Sennacherib[16] has knelt, whose sons
Smote him between the altar-stones:
Or pale Semiramis her zones
Of gold, her incense brought to thee,
In love for grace, in war for aid: . . .
Ay, and who else? . . . till 'neath thy shade
Within his trenches newly made
Last year the Christian knelt and pray'd—
Not to thy strength—in Nineveh.[17]

Now, thou poor god, within this hall
Where the blank windows blind the wall
From pedestal to pedestal,
The kind of light shall on thee fall
Which London takes the day to be:
While school-foundations in the act
Of holiday, three files compact,

[14] See *Jonah*, iv. After Jonah was delivered from the fish, God sent him to Nineveh (see lines 126–127). God created the gourd to shadow Jonah from the sun.
[15] The last king of Assyria.
[16] Another king of Assyria.
[17] During the excavations, the Tiyari workmen held their services in the shadow of the great bulls. (Layard's *Nineveh*, ch. ix.) [Rossetti.]

Shall learn to view thee as a fact
Connected with that zealous tract:
'Rome,—Babylon and Nineveh.'

Deemed they of this, those worshippers,
When, in some mythic chain of verse
Which man shall not again rehearse,
The faces of thy ministers
Yearned pale with bitter ecstasy?
Greece, Egypt, Rome,—did any god
Before whose feet men knelt unshod
Deem that in this unblest abode
Another scarce more unknown god
Should house with him, from Nineveh?

Ah! in what quarries lay the stone
From which this pillared pile has grown,
Unto man's need how long unknown,
Since thy vast temples, court and cone,
Rose far in desert history?
Ah! what is here that does not lie
All strange to thine awakened eye?
Ah! what is here can testify
(Save that dumb presence of the sky)
Unto thy day and Nineveh?

Why, of those mummies in the room
Above, there might indeed have come
One out of Egypt to thy home,
An alien. Nay, but were not some
Of these thine own 'antiquity?'
And now,—they and their gods and thou
All relics here together,—now
Whose profit? whether bull or cow,
Isis or Ibis, who or how,
Whether of Thebes or Nineveh?

The consecrated metals found,
And ivory tablets, underground,
Winged teraphim [18] and creatures crown'd,
When air and daylight filled the mound,
Fell into dust immediately.
And even as these, the images
Of awe and worship,—even as these,—
So, smitten with the sun's increase,
Her glory mouldered and did cease
From immemorial Nineveh.

[18] idols or images

The day her builders made their halt,
Those cities of the lake of salt
Stood firmly 'stablished without fault,
Made proud with pillars of basalt,
With sardonyx and porphyry.
The day that Jonah bore abroad
To Nineveh the voice of God,
A brackish lake lay in his road,
Where erst Pride fixed her sure abode
As then in royal Nineveh.

The day when he, Pride's lord [19] and Man's,
Showed all the kingdoms at a glance
To Him before whose countenance
The years recede, the years advance,
And said, Fall down and worship me:—
'Mid all the pomp beneath that look,
Then stirred there, haply, some rebuke,
Where to the wind the Salt Pools shook,
And in those tracts, of life forsook,
That knew thee not, O Nineveh!

Delicate harlot! On thy throne
Thou with a world beneath thee prone
In state for ages sat'st alone;
And needs were years and lustres flown
Ere strength of man could vanquish thee:
Whom even thy victor foes must bring,
Still royal, among maids that sing
As with doves' voices, taboring
Upon their breasts, unto the King,—
A kingly conquest, Nineveh!

. . . Here woke my thought. The wind's slow sway
Had waxed; and like the human play
Of scorn that smiling spreads away,
The sunshine shivered off the day:
The callous wind, it seemed to me,
Swept up the shadow from the ground:
And pale as whom the Fates astound,
The god forlorn stood winged and crown'd:
Within I knew the cry lay bound
Of the dumb soul of Nineveh.

[19] Satan

And as I turned, my sense half shut
Still saw the crowds of kerb and rut
Go past as marshalled to the strut
Of ranks in gypsum quaintly cut.
It seemed in one same pageantry
They followed forms which had been erst;
To pass, till on my sight should burst
That future of the best or worst
When some may question which was first,
Of London or of Nineveh.

For as that Bull-god once did stand
And watched the burial-clouds of sand,
Till these at last without a hand
Rose o'er his eyes, another land,
And blinded him with destiny: —
So may he stand again; till now,
In ships of unknown sail and prow,
Some tribe of the Australian plough
Bear him afar, — a relic now
Of London, not of Nineveh!

Or it may chance indeed that when
Man's age is hoary among men, —
His centuries threescore and ten, —
His furthest childhood shall seem then
More clear than later times may be:
Who, finding in this desert place
This form, shall hold us for some race
That walked not in Christ's lowly ways,
But bowed its pride and vowed its praise
Unto the God of Nineveh.

The smile rose first, — anon drew nigh
The thought: . . . Those heavy wings spread high
So sure of flight, which do not fly;
That set gaze never on the sky;
Those scriptured flanks it cannot see;
Its crown, a brow-contracting load;
Its planted feet which trust the sod: . . .
(So grew the image as I trod:)
O Nineveh, was this thy God, —
Thine also, mighty Nineveh?

Christina Rossetti

1830–1894

GOBLIN MARKET[1]

MORNING and evening
Maids heard the goblins cry:
'Come buy our orchard fruits,
Come buy, come buy:
Apples and quinces,
Lemons and oranges,
Plump unpecked cherries,
Melons and raspberries,
Bloom-down-cheeked peaches,
Swart-headed mulberries,
Wild free-born cranberries,
Crab-apples, dewberries,
Pine-apples, blackberries,
Apricots, strawberries; —
All ripe together
In summer weather, —
Morns that pass by,
Fair eves that fly;
Come buy, come buy:
Our grapes fresh from the vine,
Pomegranates full and fine,
Dates and sharp bullaces,
Rare pears and greengages,
Damsons and bilberries,
Taste them and try:
Currants and gooseberries,
Bright-fire-like barberries,
Figs to fill your mouth,
Citrons from the South,
Sweet to tongue and sound to eye;
Come buy, come buy.'

Evening by evening
Among the brookside rushes,
Laura bowed her head to hear,
Lizzie veiled her blushes:
Crouching close together

[1] Christina Rossetti's first published volume, *Goblin Market and other Poems*, appeared in 1862. All the poems printed here, except the last, are from that book.

In the cooling weather,
With clasping arms and cautioning lips,
With tingling cheeks and finger tips.
'Lie close,' Laura said,
Pricking up her golden head:
'We must not look at goblin men,
We must not buy their fruits:
Who knows upon what soil they fed
Their hungry thirsty roots?'
'Come buy,' call the goblins
Hobbling down the glen.
'Oh,' cried Lizzie, 'Laura, Laura,
You should not peep at goblin men.'
Lizzie covered up her eyes,
Covered close lest they should look;
Laura reared her glossy head,
And whispered like the restless brook:
'Look, Lizzie, look, Lizzie,
Down the glen tramp little men.
One hauls a basket,
One bears a plate,
One lugs a golden dish
Of many pounds weight.
How fair the vine must grow
Whose grapes are so luscious;
How warm the wind must blow
Through those fruit bushes.'
'No,' said Lizzie: 'No, no, no;
Their offers should not charm us,
Their evil gifts would harm us.'
She thrust a dimpled finger
In each ear, shut eyes and ran:
Curious Laura chose to linger
Wondering at each merchant man.
One had a cat's face,
One whisked a tail,
One tramped at a rat's pace,
One crawled like a snail,
One like a wombat prowled obtuse and furry,
One like a ratel tumbled hurry skurry.
She heard a voice like voice of doves
Cooing all together:
They sounded kind and full of loves
In the pleasant weather.

Laura stretched her gleaming neck
Like a rush-imbedded swan,
Like a lily from the beck,
Like a moonlit poplar branch,
Like a vessel at the launch
When its last restraint is gone.

Backwards up the mossy glen
Turned and trooped the goblin men,
With their shrill repeated cry,
'Come buy, come buy.'
When they reached where Laura was
They stood stock still upon the moss,
Leering at each other,
Brother with queer brother;
Signalling each other,
Brother with sly brother.
One set his basket down,
One reared his plate;
One began to weave a crown
Of tendrils, leaves, and rough nuts brown
(Men sell not such in any town);
One heaved the golden weight
Of dish and fruit to offer her:
'Come buy, come buy,' was still their cry.
Laura stared but did not stir,
Longed but had no money:
The whisk-tailed merchant bade her taste
In tones as smooth as honey,
The cat-faced purr'd,
The rat-paced spoke a word
Of welcome, and the snail-paced even was heard;
One parrot-voiced and jolly
Cried 'Pretty Goblin' still for 'Pretty Polly';—
One whistled like a bird.

But sweet-tooth Laura spoke in haste:
'Good folk, I have no coin;
To take were to purloin:
I have no copper in my purse,
I have no silver either,
And all my gold is on the furze
That shakes in windy weather
Above the rusty heather.'
'You have much gold upon your head,'
They answered all together:
'Buy from us with a golden curl.'
She clipped a precious golden lock,
She dropped a tear more rare than pearl,

Then sucked their fruit globes fair or red:
Sweeter than honey from the rock,
Stronger than man-rejoicing wine,
Clearer than water flowed that juice;
She never tasted such before,
How should it cloy with length of use?
She sucked and sucked and sucked the more
Fruits which that unknown orchard bore;
She sucked until her lips were sore;
Then flung the emptied rinds away
But gathered up one kernel stone,
And knew not was it night or day
As she turned home alone.

Lizzie met her at the gate
Full of wise upbraidings:
'Dear, you should not stay so late,
Twilight is not good for maidens;
Should not loiter in the glen
In the haunts of goblin men.
Do you not remember Jeanie,
How she met them in the moonlight,
Took their gifts both choice and many,
Ate their fruits and wore their flowers
Plucked from bowers
Where summer ripens at all hours?
But ever in the moonlight
She pined and pined away;
Sought them by night and day,
Found them no more but dwindled and grew grey;
Then fell with the first snow,
While to this day no grass will grow
Where she lies low:
I planted daisies there a year ago
That never blow.
You should not loiter so.'
'Nay, hush,' said Laura:
'Nay, hush, my sister:
I ate and ate my fill,
Yet my mouth waters still;
To-morrow night I will
Buy more: ' and kissed her:
'Have done with sorrow;
I'll bring you plums to-morrow
Fresh on their mother twigs,
Cherries worth getting;
You cannot think what figs
My teeth have met in,
What melons icy-cold
Piled on a dish of gold
Too huge for me to hold,
What peaches with a velvet nap,
Pellucid grapes without one seed:
Odorous indeed must be the mead
Whereon they grow, and pure the wave they drink
With lilies at the brink,
And sugar-sweet their sap.'

Golden head by golden head,
Like two pigeons in one nest
Folded in each other's wings,
They lay down in their curtained bed:
Like two blossoms on one stem,
Like two flakes of new-fall'n snow,
Like two wands of ivory
Tipped with gold for awful kings.
Moon and stars gazed in at them,
Wind sang to them lullaby,
Lumbering owls forbore to fly,
Not a bat flapped to and fro
Round their nest:
Cheek to cheek and breast to breast
Locked together in one nest.

Early in the morning
When the first cock crowed his warning,
Neat like bees, as sweet and busy,
Laura rose with Lizzie:
Fetched in honey, milked the cows,
Aired and set to rights the house,
Kneaded cakes of whitest wheat,
Cakes for dainty mouths to eat,
Next churned butter, whipped up cream,
Fed their poultry, sat and sewed;
Talked as modest maidens should:
Lizzie with an open heart,
Laura in an absent dream,
One content, one sick in part;
One warbling for the mere bright day's delight,
One longing for the night.

At length slow evening came:
They went with pitchers to the reedy brook;

Lizzie most placid in her look,
Laura most like a leaping flame.
They drew the gurgling water from its deep;
Lizzie plucked purple and rich golden flags,
Then turning homewards said: ‘The sunset flushes
Those furthest loftiest crags;
Come, Laura, not another maiden lags,
No wilful squirrel wags,
The beasts and birds are fast asleep.’
But Laura loitered still among the rushes
And said the bank was steep.

And said the hour was early still,
The dew not fall’n, the wind not chill:
Listening ever, but not catching
The customary cry,
‘Come buy, come buy,’
With its iterated jingle
Of sugar-baited words:
Not for all her watching
Once discerning even one goblin
Racing, whisking, tumbling, hobbling;
Let alone the herds
That used to tramp along the glen,
In groups or single,
Of brisk fruit-merchant men.

Till Lizzie urged, ‘O Laura, come;
I hear the fruit-call but I dare not look:
You should not loiter longer at this brook:
Come with me home.
The stars rise, the moon bends her arc,
Each glowworm winks her spark,
Let us get home before the night grows dark:
For clouds may gather
Though this is summer weather,
Put out the lights and drench us through;
Then if we lost our way what should we do?’

Laura turned cold as stone
To find her sister heard that cry alone,
That goblin cry,
‘Come buy our fruits, come buy.’
Must she then buy no more such dainty fruit?
Must she no more such succous pasture find,
Gone deaf and blind?
Her tree of life drooped from the root:
She said not one word in her heart’s sore ache;
But peering thro’ the dimness, nought discerning,
Trudged home, her pitcher dripping all the way;
So crept to bed, and lay
Silent till Lizzie slept;
Then sat up in a passionate yearning,
And gnashed her teeth for baulked desire, and wept
As if her heart would break.

Day after day, night after night,
Laura kept watch in vain
In sullen silence of exceeding pain.
She never caught again the goblin cry:
‘Come buy, come buy;’—
She never spied the goblin men
Hawking their fruits along the glen:
But when the noon waxed bright
Her hair grew thin and grey;
She dwindled, as the fair full moon doth turn
To swift decay and burn
Her fire away.

One day remembering her kernel-stone
She set it by a wall that faced the south;
Dewed it with tears, hoped for a root,
Watched for a waxing shoot,
But there came none;
It never saw the sun,
It never felt the trickling moisture run:
While with sunk eyes and faded mouth
She dreamed of melons, as a traveller sees
False waves in desert drouth
With shade of leaf-crowned trees,
And burns the thirstier in the sandful breeze.

She no more swept the house,
Tended the fowls or cows,

Fetched honey, kneaded cakes of wheat,
Brought water from the brook:
But sat down listless in the chimney-nook
And would not eat.

Tender Lizzie could not bear
To watch her sister's cankerous care
Yet not to share.
She night and morning
Caught the goblins' cry:
'Come buy our orchard fruits,
Come buy, come buy:'—
Beside the brook, along the glen,
She heard the tramp of goblin men,
The voice and stir
Poor Laura could not hear;
Longed to buy fruit to comfort her,
But feared to pay too dear.
She thought of Jeanie in her grave,
Who should have been a bride;
But who for joys brides hope to have
Fell sick and died
In her gay prime,
In earliest Winter time,
With the first glazing rime,
With the first snow-fall of crisp Winter time.

Till Laura dwindling
Seemed knocking at Death's door:
Then Lizzie weighed no more
Better and worse;
But put a silver penny in her purse,
Kissed Laura, crossed the heath with clumps of furze
At twilight, halted by the brook:
And for the first time in her life
Began to listen and look.

Laughed every goblin
When they spied her peeping:
Came towards her hobbling,
Flying, running, leaping,
Puffing and blowing,
Chuckling, clapping, crowing,
Clucking and gobbling,
Mopping and mowing,
Full of airs and graces,
Pulling wry faces,
Demure grimaces,
Cat-like and rat-like,
Ratel- and wombat-like,
Snail-paced in a hurry,
Parrot-voiced and whistler,
Helter skelter, hurry skurry,
Chattering like magpies,
Fluttering like pigeons,
Gliding like fishes,—
Hugged her and kissed her:
Squeezed and caressed her:
Stretched up their dishes,
Panniers, and plates:
'Look at our apples
Russet and dun,
Bob at our cherries,
Bite at our peaches,
Citrons and dates,
Grapes for the asking,
Pears red with basking
Out in the sun,
Plums on their twigs;
Pluck them and suck them,
Pomegranates, figs.'—

'Good folk,' said Lizzie,
Mindful of Jeanie:
'Give me much and many:'—
Held out her apron,
Tossed them her penny.
'Nay, take a seat with us,
Honour and eat with us,'
They answered grinning:
'Our feast is but beginning.
Night yet is early,
Warm and dew-pearly,
Wakeful and starry:
Such fruits as these
No man can carry;
Half their bloom would fly,
Half their dew would dry,
Half their flavour would pass by.
Sit down and feast with us,
Be welcome guest with us,
Cheer you and rest with us.'—
'Thank you,' said Lizzie: 'But one waits
At home alone for me:
So without further parleying,
If you will not sell me any

Of your fruits though much and many,
Give me back my silver penny
I tossed you for a fee.' —
They began to scratch their pates,
No longer wagging, purring,
But visibly demurring,
Grunting and snarling.
One called her proud,
Cross-grained, uncivil;
Their tones waxed loud,
Their looks were evil.
Lashing their tails
They trod and hustled her,
Elbowed and jostled her,
Clawed with their nails,
Barking, mewing, hissing, mocking,
Tore her gown and soiled her stocking,
Twitched her hair out by the roots,
Stamped upon her tender feet,
Held her hands and squeezed their fruits
Against her mouth to make her eat.

White and golden Lizzie stood,
Like a lily in a flood, —
Like a rock of blue-veined stone
Lashed by tides obstreperously, —
Like a beacon left alone
In a hoary roaring sea,
Sending up a golden fire, —
Like a fruit-crowned orange-tree
White with blossoms honey-sweet
Sore beset by wasp and bee, —
Like a royal virgin town
Topped with gilded dome and spire
Close beleaguered by a fleet
Mad to tug her standard down.

One may lead a horse to water,
Twenty cannot make him drink.
Though the goblins cuffed and caught her,
Coaxed and fought her,
Bullied and besought her,
Scratched her, pinched her black as ink,
Kicked and knocked her,
Mauled and mocked her,
Lizzie uttered not a word;
Would not open lip from lip
Lest they should cram a mouthful in:
But laughed in heart to feel the drip
Of juice that syrupped all her face,
And lodged in dimples of her chin,
And streaked her neck which quaked like curd.
At last the evil people
Worn out by her resistance
Flung back her penny, kicked their fruit
Along whichever road they took,
Not leaving root or stone or shoot;
Some writhed into the ground,
Some dived into the brook
With ring and ripple,
Some scudded on the gale without a sound,
Some vanished in the distance.

In a smart, ache, tingle,
Lizzie went her way;
Knew not was it night or day;
Sprang up the bank, tore thro' the furze,
Threaded copse and dingle,
And heard her penny jingle
Bouncing in her purse, —
Its bounce was music to her ear.
She ran and ran
As if she feared some goblin man
Dogged her with gibe or curse
Or something worse:
But not one goblin skurried after,
Nor was she pricked by fear;
The kind heart made her windy-paced
That urged her home quite out of breath with haste
And inward laughter.

She cried 'Laura,' up the garden,
'Did you miss me?
Come and kiss me.
Never mind my bruises,
Hug me, kiss me, suck my juices
Squeezed from goblin fruits for you,
Goblin pulp and goblin dew.
Eat me, drink me, love me;
Laura, make much of me:
For your sake I have braved the glen
And had to do with goblin merchant men.'

Laura started from her chair,
Flung her arms up in the air,

Clutched her hair:
'Lizzie, Lizzie, have you tasted
For my sake the fruit forbidden?
Must your light like mine be hidden,
Your young life like mine be wasted,
Undone in mine undoing
And ruined in my ruin,
Thirsty, cankered, goblin-ridden?'—
She clung about her sister,
Kissed and kissed and kissed her:
Tears once again
Refreshed her shrunken eyes,
Dropping like rain
After long sultry drouth;
Shaking with aguish fear, and pain,
She kissed and kissed her with a hungry mouth.

Her lips began to scorch,
That juice was wormwood to her tongue,
She loathed the feast:
Writhing as one possessed she leaped and sung,
Rent all her robe, and wrung
Her hands in lamentable haste,
And beat her breast.
Her locks streamed like the torch
Borne by a racer at full speed,
Or like the mane of horses in their flight,
Or like an eagle when she stems the light
Straight toward the sun,
Or like a caged thing freed,
Or like a flying flag when armies run.

Swift fire spread through her veins, knocked at her heart,
Met the fire smouldering there
And overbore its lesser flame;
She gorged on bitterness without a name:
Ah! fool, to choose such part
Of soul-consuming care!
Sense failed in the mortal strife:
Like the watch-tower of a town
Which an earthquake shatters down,
Like a lightning-stricken mast,
Like a wind-uprooted tree
Spun about,
Like a foam-topped waterspout
Cast down headlong in the sea,
She fell at last;
Pleasure past and anguish past,
Is it death or is it life?

Life out of death.
That night long Lizzie watched by her,
Counted her pulse's flagging stir,
Felt for her breath,
Held water to her lips, and cooled her face
With tears and fanning leaves:
But when the first birds chirped about their eaves,
And early reapers plodded to the place
Of golden sheaves,
And dew-wet grass
Bowed in the morning winds so brisk to pass,
And new buds with new day
Opened of cup-like lilies on the stream,
Laura awoke as from a dream,
Laughed in the innocent old way,
Hugged Lizzie but not twice or thrice;
Her gleaming locks showed not one thread of grey,
Her breath was sweet as May
And light danced in her eyes.

Days, weeks, months, years
Afterwards, when both were wives
With children of their own;
Their mother-hearts beset with fears,
Their lives bound up in tender lives;
Laura would call the little ones
And tell them of her early prime,
Those pleasant days long gone
Of not-returning time:
Would talk about the haunted glen,
The wicked, quaint fruit-merchant men,
Their fruits like honey to the throat
But poison in the blood;
(Men sell not such in any town:)
Would tell them how her sister stood
In deadly peril to do her good,
And win the fiery antidote:
Then joining hands to little hands
Would bid them cling together,
'For there is no friend like a sister
In calm or stormy weather;

To cheer one on the tedious way,
To fetch one if one goes astray,
To lift one if one totters down,
To strengthen whilst one stands.'

A Birthday

My heart is like a singing bird
Whose nest is in a watered shoot;
My heart is like an apple-tree
Whose boughs are bent with thickset fruit;
My heart is like a rainbow shell
That paddles in a halcyon sea;
My heart is gladder than all these
Because my love is come to me.

Raise me a dais of silk and down;
Hang it with vair [2] and purple dyes;
Carve it in doves, and pomegranates,
And peacocks with a hundred eyes;
Work it in gold and silver grapes,
In leaves, and silver fleurs-de-lys;
Because the birthday of my life
Is come, my love is come to me.

Remember

Remember me when I am gone away,
Gone far away into the silent land;
When you can no more hold me by the hand,
Nor I half turn to go yet turning stay.
Remember me when no more day by day
You tell me of our future that you planned:
Only remember me; you understand
It will be late to counsel then or pray.
Yet if you should forget me for a while
And afterwards remember, do not grieve:
For if the darkness and corruption leave
A vestige of the thoughts that once I had,
Better by far you should forget and smile
Than that you should remember and be sad.

[2] A kind of squirrel fur used in the fourteenth century on costly dresses.

Up-hill

Does the road wind up-hill all the way?
Yes, to the very end.
Will the day's journey take the whole long day?
From morn to night, my friend.

But is there for the night a resting-place?
A roof for when the slow dark hours begin.
May not the darkness hide it from my face?
You cannot miss that inn.

Shall I meet other wayfarers at night?
Those who have gone before.
Then must I knock, or call when just in sight?
They will not keep you standing at that door.

Shall I find comfort, travel-sore and weak?
Of labour you shall find the sum.
Will there be beds for me and all who seek?
Yea, beds for all who come.

Song

When I am dead, my dearest,
Sing no sad songs for me;
Plant thou no roses at my head,
Nor shady cypress tree:
Be the green grass above me
With showers and dewdrops wet;
And if thou wilt, remember,
And if thou wilt, forget.

I shall not see the shadows,
I shall not feel the rain;
I shall not hear the nightingale
Sing on as if in pain:
And dreaming through the twilight
That doth not rise nor set,
Haply I may remember,
And haply may forget.

In an Artist's Studio[3]

ONE face looks out from all his canvases,
One selfsame figure sits or walks or leans:
We found her hidden just behind those screens,
That mirror gave back all her loveliness.
A queen in opal or in ruby dress,
A nameless girl in freshest summer-greens,
A saint, an angel — every canvas means
The same one meaning, neither more nor less.
He feeds upon her face by day and night,
And she with true kind eyes looks back on him,
Fair as the moon and joyful as the light:
Not wan with waiting, not with sorrow dim;
Not as she is, but was when hope shone bright;
Not as she is, but as she fills his dream.

[*New Poems,* 1895]

[3] That of her brother Dante Gabriel Rossetti.

William Morris

1834–1896

THE DEFENCE OF GUENEVERE[1]

BUT, knowing now that they would have her speak,
She threw her wet hair backward from her brow,
Her hand close to her mouth touching her cheek,

As though she had had there a shameful blow,
And feeling it shameful to feel ought but shame
All through her heart, yet felt her cheek burned so,

She must a little touch it; like one lame
She walked away from Gauwaine, with her head
Still lifted up; and on her cheek of flame

The tears dried quick; she stopped at last and said:
'O knights and lords, it seems but little skill
To talk of well-known things past now and dead.

'God wot I ought to say, I have done ill,
And pray you all forgiveness heartily!
Because you must be right such great lords — still

'Listen, suppose your time were come to die,
And you were quite alone and very weak;
Yea, laid a dying while very mightily

'The wind was ruffling up the narrow streak
Of river through your broad lands running well:
Suppose a hush should come, then some one speak:

'"One of these cloths is heaven, and one is hell,
Now choose one cloth for ever, which they be,
I will not tell you, you must somehow tell

'"Of your own strength and mightiness; here, see!"
Yea, yea, my lord, and you to ope your eyes,
A foot of your familiar bed to see

'A great God's angel standing, with such dyes,

[1] This and the three following poems are from *The Defence of Guenevere and other Poems,* 1858, the first volume of verse published by Morris.

Not known on earth, on his great wings, and hands,
Held out two ways, light from the inner skies

'Showing him well, and making his commands
Seem to be God's commands, moreover, too,
Holding within his hands the cloths on wands;

'And one of these strange choosing cloths was blue,
Wavy and long and one cut short and red;
No man could tell the better of the two.

'After a shivering half-hour you said,
"God help! heaven's colour, the blue;" and he said, "hell."
Perhaps you then would roll upon your bed,

'And cry to all good men that loved you well,
"Ah Christ! if only I had known, known, known;"
Launcelot went away, then I could tell,

'Like wisest man how all things would be, moan,
And roll and hurt myself, and long to die,
And yet fear much to die for what was sown.

'Nevertheless you, O Sir Gauwaine, lie,
Whatever may have happened through these years,
God knows I speak truth, saying that you lie.'

Her voice was low at first, being full of tears,
But as it cleared, it grew full loud and shrill,
Growing a windy shriek in all men's ears,

A ringing in their startled brains, until
She said that Gauwaine lied, then her voice sunk,
And her great eyes began again to fill,

Though still she stood right up, and never shrunk,
But spoke on bravely, glorious lady fair!
Whatever tears her full lips may have drunk,

She stood, and seemed to think, and wrung her hair,
Spoke out at last with no more trace of shame,
With passionate twisting of her body there:

'It chanced upon a day that Launcelot came
To dwell at Arthur's court: at Christmas-time
This happened; when the heralds sung his name,

'"Son of King Ban of Benwick," seemed to chime
Along with all the bells that rang that day,
O'er the white roofs, with little change of rhyme.

'Christmas and whitened winter passed away,
And over me the April sunshine came,
Made very awful with black hail-clouds, yea

'And in the Summer I grew white with flame,
And bowed my head down—Autumn, and the sick
Sure knowledge things would never be the same,

'However often Spring might be most thick

Of blossoms and buds, smote on me, and I grew
Careless of most things, let the clock tick, tick,

'To my unhappy pulse, that beat right through
My eager body; while I laughed out loud,
And let my lips curl up at false or true,

'Seemed cold and shallow without any cloud.
Behold my judges, then the cloths were brought:
While I was dizzied thus, old thoughts would crowd,

'Belonging to the time ere I was bought
By Arthur's great name and his little love,
Must I give up for ever then, I thought,

'That which I deemed would ever round me move
Glorifying all things; for a little word,
Scarce ever meant at all, must I now prove

'Stone-cold for ever? Pray you, does the Lord
Will that all folks should be quite happy and good?
I love God now a little, if this cord

'Were broken, once for all what striving could
Make me love anything in earth or heaven.
So day by day it grew, as if one should

'Slip slowly down some path worn smooth and even,
Down to a cool sea on a summer day;
Yet still in slipping was there some small leaven

'Of stretched hands catching small stones by the way,
Until one surely reached the sea at last,
And felt strange new joy as the worn head lay

'Back, with the hair like sea-weed; yea all past
Sweat of the forehead, dryness of the lips,
Washed utterly out by the dear waves o'ercast

'In the lone sea, far off from any ships!
Do I not know now of a day in Spring?
No minute of that wild day ever slips

'From out my memory; I hear thrushes sing,
And wheresoever I may be, straightway
Thoughts of it all come up with most fresh sting;

'I was half mad with beauty on that day,
And went without my ladies all alone,
In a quiet garden walled round every way;

'I was right joyful of that wall of stone,
That shut the flowers and trees up with the sky,
And trebled all the beauty: to the bone,

'Yea right through to my heart, grown very shy
With weary thoughts, it pierced, and made me glad;
Exceedingly glad, and I knew verily,

'A little thing just then had made me mad;
I dared not think, as I was wont to do,
Sometimes, upon my beauty; if I had

'Held out my long hand up against the blue,
And, looking on the tenderly darken'd fingers,
Thought that by rights one ought to see quite through,

'There, see you, where the soft still light yet lingers,
Round by the edges; what should I have done,
If this had joined with yellow spotted singers,

'And startling green drawn upward by the sun?
But shouting, loosed out, see now! all my hair,
And trancedly stood watching the west wind run

'With faintest half-heard breathing sound—why there
I lose my head e'en now in doing this;
But shortly listen—In that garden fair

'Came Launcelot walking; this is true, the kiss
Wherewith we kissed in meeting that spring day,
I scarce dare talk of the remember'd bliss,

'When both our mouths went wandering in one way,
And aching sorely, met among the leaves;
Our hands being left behind strained far away.

'Never within a yard of my bright sleeves
Had Launcelot come before—and now, so nigh!
After that day why is it Guenevere grieves?

'Nevertheless you, O Sir Gauwaine, lie,
Whatever happened on through all those years,
God knows I speak truth, saying that you lie.

'Being such a lady could I weep these tears
If this were true? A great queen such as I
Having sinn'd this way, straight her conscience sears;

'And afterwards she liveth hatefully,
Slaying and poisoning, certes never weeps,—
Gauwaine be friends now, speak me lovingly.

'Do I not see how God's dear pity creeps
All through your frame, and trembles in your mouth?
Remember in what grave your mother sleeps,

'Buried in some place far down in the south,
Men are forgetting as I speak to you;
By her head sever'd in that awful drouth

'Of pity that drew Agravaine's fell blow,
I pray your pity! let me not scream out
For ever after, when the shrill winds blow

'Through half your castle-locks! let me not shout
For ever after in the winter night
When you ride out alone! in battle-rout

'Let not my rusting tears make your sword light!
Ah! God of mercy how he turns away!
So, ever must I dress me to the fight,

'So—let God's justice work! Gauwaine, I say,
See me hew down your proofs: yea all men know
Even as you said how Mellyagraunce one day,

'One bitter day in *la Fausse Garde,* for so
All good knights held it after, saw—
Yea, sirs, by cursed unknightly outrage; though

'You, Gauwaine, held his word without a flaw,
This Mellyagraunce saw blood upon my bed—
Whose blood then pray you? is there any law

'To make a queen say why some spots of red
Lie on her coverlet? or will you say,
"Your hands are white, lady, as when you wed,

'"Where did you bleed?" and must I stammer out—"Nay,

I blush indeed, fair lord, only to rend
My sleeve up to my shoulder, where there lay

'"A knife-point last night:" so must I defend
The honour of the lady Guenevere?
Not so, fair lords, even if the world should end

'This very day, and you were judges here
Instead of God. Did you see Mellyagraunce
When Launcelot stood by him? what white fear

'Curdled his blood, and how his teeth did dance,
His side sink in? as my knight cried and said,
"Slayer of unarm'd men, here is a chance!

'"Setter of traps, I pray you guard your head,
By God I am so glad to fight with you,
Stripper of ladies, that my hand feels lead

'"For driving weight; hurrah now! draw and do,
For all my wounds are moving in my breast,
And I am getting mad with waiting so."

'He struck his hands together o'er the beast,
Who fell down flat, and grovell'd at his feet,
And groan'd at being slain so young—"at least."

'My knight said, "Rise you, sir, who are so fleet
At catching ladies, half-arm'd will I fight,
My left side all uncovered!" Then I weet,

'Up sprang Sir Mellyagraunce with great delight
Upon his knave's face; not until just then
Did I quite hate him, as I saw my knight

'Along the lists look to my stake and pen
With such a joyous smile, it made me sigh
From agony beneath my waist-chain, when

'The fight began, and to me they drew nigh;
Ever Sir Launcelot, kept him on the right,
And traversed warily, and ever high

'And fast leapt caitiff's sword, until my knight
Sudden threw up his sword to his left hand,
Caught it, and swung it; that was all the fight.

'Except a spout of blood on the hot land;
For it was hottest summer; and I know
I wonder'd how the fire, while I should stand,

'And burn, against the heat, would quiver so,
Yards above my head; thus these matters went;
Which things were only warnings of the woe

'That fell on me. Yet Mellyagraunce was shent,
For Mellyagraunce had fought against the Lord;
Therefore, my lords, take heed lest you be blent

'With all this wickedness; say no rash word
Against me, being so beautiful; my eyes,
Wept all away to grey, may bring some sword

'To drown you in your blood; see my breast rise,
Like waves of purple sea, as here I stand;
And how my arms are moved in wonderful wise,

'Yea also at my full heart's strong command,
See through my long throat how the words go up
In ripples to my mouth; how in my hand

'The shadow lies like wine within a cup
Of marvellously colour'd gold; yea now
This little wind is rising, look you up,

'And wonder how the light is falling so
Within my moving tresses: will you dare,
When you have looked a little on my brow,

'To say this thing is vile? or will you care
For any plausible lies of cunning woof,
When you can see my face with no lie there

'For ever? am I not a gracious proof—
"But in your chamber Launcelot was found"—
Is there a good knight then would stand aloof,

'When a queen says with gentle queenly sound:
"O true as steel come now and talk with me,
I love to see you step upon the ground

'"Unwavering, also well I love to see
That gracious smile light up your face, and hear
Your wonderful words, that all mean verily

'"The thing they seem to mean: good friend, so dear
To me in everything, come here to-night,
Or else the hours will pass most dull and drear;

'"If you come not, I fear this time I might
Get thinking over much of times gone by,
When I was young, and green hope was in sight;

'"For no man cares now to know why I sigh;
And no man comes to sing me pleasant songs
Nor any brings me the sweet flowers that lie

'"So thick in the gardens; therefore one so longs
To see you, Launcelot; that we may be
Like children once again, free from all wrongs

'"Just for one night." Did he not come to me?
What thing could keep true Launcelot away
If I said "come"? there was one less than three

'In my quiet room that night, and we were gay;
Till sudden I rose up, weak, pale, and sick,
Because a bawling broke our dream up, yea

'I looked at Launcelot's face and could not speak,
For he looked helpless too, for a little while;
Then I remember how I tried to shriek,

'And could not, but fell down; from tile to tile
The stones they threw up rattled o'er my head,
And made me dizzier; till within a while

'My maids were all about me, and my head
On Launcelot's breast was being soothed away
From its white chattering, until Launcelot said—

'By God! I will not tell you more to-day.
Judge any way you will—what matters it?
You know quite well the story of that fray,

'How Launcelot still'd their bawling, the mad fit
That caught up Gauwaine — all, all, verily,
But just that which would save me; these things flit.

'Nevertheless you, O Sir Gauwaine, lie,
Whatever may have happen'd these long years,
God knows I speak truth, saying that you lie!

'All I have said is truth, by Christ's dear tears.'
She would not speak another word, but stood
Turn'd sideways; listening, like a man who hears

His brother's trumpet sounding through the wood
Of his foes' lances. She lean'd eagerly,
And gave a slight spring sometimes, as she could

At last hear something really; joyfully
Her cheek grew crimson, as the headlong speed
Of the roan charger drew all men to see,
The knight who came was Launcelot at good need.

Shameful Death

There were four of us about that bed;
The mass-priest knelt at the side,
I and his mother stood at the head,
Over his feet lay the bride;
We were quite sure that he was dead,
Though his eyes were open wide.

He did not die in the night,
He did not die in the day,
But in the morning twilight
His spirit pass'd away,
When neither sun nor moon was bright,
And the trees were merely grey.

He was not slain with the sword,
Knight's axe, or the knightly spear,
Yet spoke he never a word
After he came in here;
I cut away the cord
From the neck of my brother dear.

He did not strike one blow,
For the recreants came behind,
In a place where the hornbeams grow,
A path right hard to find,
For the hornbeam boughs swing so,
That the twilight makes it blind.

They lighted a great torch then,
When his arms were pinion'd fast,
Sir John the knight of the Fen,
Sir Guy of the Dolorous Blast,
With knights threescore and ten,
Hung brave Lord Hugh at last.

I am threescore and ten,
And my hair is all turn'd grey,
But I met Sir John of the Fen
Long ago on a summer day,
And am glad to think of the moment when
I took his life away.

I am threescore and ten,
And my strength is mostly pass'd,
But long ago I and my men,
When the sky was overcast,
And the smoke roll'd over the reeds of the fen,
Slew Guy of the Dolorous Blast.

And now, knights all of you,
I pray you pray for Sir Hugh,
A good knight and a true,
And for Alice, his wife, pray too.

[1858]

The Haystack in the Floods

Had she come all the way for this,
To part at last without a kiss?
Yea, had she borne the dirt and rain
That her own eyes might see him slain
Beside the haystack in the floods?

Along the dripping leafless woods,
The stirrup touching either shoe

She rode astride as troopers do;
With kirtle kilted to her knee,
To which the mud splash'd wretchedly;
And the wet dripp'd from every tree
Upon her head and heavy hair,
And on her eyelids broad and fair;
The tears and rain ran down her face.
By fits and starts they rode apace,
And very often was his place
Far off from her; he had to ride
Ahead, to see what might betide
When the roads cross'd; and sometimes, when
There rose a murmuring from his men,
Had to turn back with promises;
Ah me! she had but little ease;
And often, for pure doubt and dread
She sobb'd, made giddy in the head
By the swift riding; while, for cold,
Her slender fingers scarce could hold
The wet reins; yea, and scarcely, too,
She felt the foot within her shoe
Against the stirrup: all for this,
To part at last without a kiss
Beside the haystack in the floods.

For when they near'd that old soak'd hay,
They saw across the only way
That Judas, Godmar, and the three
Red running lions dismally
Grinn'd from his pennon, under which,
In one straight line along the ditch,
They counted thirty heads.

So then,
While Robert turn'd round to his men,
She saw at once the wretched end,
And, stooping down, tried hard to rend
Her coif the wrong way from her head,
And hid her eyes; while Robert said:
'Nay, love, 'tis scarcely two to one,
At Poictiers where we made them run
So fast — why, sweet my love, good cheer.
The Gascon frontier is so near,
Nought after this.'

But, 'O,' she said,
'My God! my God! I have to tread
The long way back without you; then
The court at Paris; those six men; [2]
The gratings of the Chatelet;
The swift Seine on some rainy day
Like this, and people standing by,
And laughing, while my weak hands try
To recollect how strong men swim.
All this, or else a life with him,
For which I should be damned at last,
Would God that this next hour were past!'

He answer'd not, but cried his cry,
'St. George for Marny!' cheerily;
And laid his hand upon her rein.
Alas! no man of all his train
Gave back that cheery cry again;
And, while for rage his thumb beat fast
Upon his sword-hilts, some one cast
About his neck a kerchief long,
And bound him.

Then they went along
To Godmar; who said: 'Now, Jehane,
Your lover's life is on the wane
So fast, that, if this very hour
You yield not as my paramour,
He will not see the rain leave off —
Nay, keep your tongue from gibe and scoff,
Sir Robert, or I slay you now.'

She laid her hand upon her brow,
Then gazed upon the palm, as though
She thought her forehead bled, and — 'No.'
She said, and turn'd her head away,
As there were nothing else to say,
And everything were settled: red
Grew Godmar's face from chin to head:
'Jehane, on yonder hill there stands
My castle, guarding well my lands:
What hinders me from taking you,
And doing that I list to do
To your fair wilful body, while
Your knight lies dead?'

A wicked smile
Wrinkled her face, her lips grew thin,
A long way out she thrust her chin:

[2] The six Judges who, while Jehane is confined in the Chatelet prison in Paris, will try her as a witch.

'You know that I should strangle you
While you were sleeping; or bite through
Your throat, by God's help — ah!' she said,
'Lord Jesus, pity your poor maid!
For in such wise they hem me in,
I cannot choose but sin and sin,
Whatever happens: yet I think
They could not make me eat or drink,
And so should I just reach my rest.'
'Nay, if you do not my behest,
O Jehane! though I love you well,'
Said Godmar, 'Would I fail to tell
All that I know.' 'Foul lies,' she said.
'Eh? lies my Jehane? by God's head,
At Paris folks would deem them true!
Do you know, Jehane, they cry for you,
"Jehane the brown! Jehane the brown!
Give us Jehane to burn or drown!" —
Eh — gag me Robert! — sweet my friend,
This were indeed a piteous end
For those long fingers, and long feet,
And long neck, and smooth shoulders sweet;
An end that few men would forget
That saw it — So, an hour yet:
Consider, Jehane, which to take
Of life or death!'

So, scarce awake,
Dismounting, did she leave that place,
And totter some yards: with her face
Turn'd upward to the sky she lay,
Her head on a wet heap of hay,
And fell asleep: and while she slept,
And did not dream, the minutes crept
Round to the twelve again; but she,
Being waked at last, sigh'd quietly,
And strangely childlike came, and said:
'I will not.' Straightway Godmar's head,
As though it hung on strong wires, turn'd
Most sharply round, and his face burn'd.

For Robert — both his eyes were dry,
He could not weep, but gloomily
He seem'd to watch the rain; yea, too,
His lips were firm; he tried once more
To touch her lips; she reach'd out, sore
And vain desire so tortured them,
The poor grey lips, and now the hem
Of his sleeve brush'd them.

With a start
Up Godmar rose, thrust them apart;
From Robert's throat he loosed the bands
Of silk and mail; with empty hands
Held out, she stood and gazed, and saw,
The long bright blade without a flaw
Glide out from Godmar's sheath, his hand
In Robert's hair; she saw him bend
Back Robert's head; she saw him send
The thin steel down; the blow told well,
Right backward the knight Robert fell,
And moan'd as dogs do, being half dead,
Unwitting, as I deem: so then
Godmar turn'd grinning to his men,
Who ran, some five or six, and beat
His head to pieces at their feet.

Then Godmar turn'd again and said:
'So, Jehane, the first fitte is read!
Take note, my lady, that your way
Lies backward to the Chatelet!'
She shook her head and gazed awhile
At her cold hands with a rueful smile,
As though this thing had made her mad.

This was the parting that they had
Beside the haystack in the floods.

[1858]

The Sailing of the Sword

Across the empty garden-beds,
When the Sword went out to sea,
I scarcely saw my sisters' heads
Bowed each beside a tree.
I could not see the castle leads,
When the Sword went out to sea.

Alicia wore a scarlet gown,
When the Sword went out to sea,
But Ursula's was russet brown:
For the mist we could not see
The scarlet roofs of the good town,
When the Sword went out to sea.

Green holly in Alicia's hand,
  When the Sword went out to sea;
With sere oak-leaves did Ursula stand;
  O! yet alas for me!
I did but bear a peel'd white wand,
  When the Sword went out to sea.

O, russet brown and scarlet bright,
  When the Sword went out to sea,
My sisters wore; I wore but white:
  Red, brown, and white, are three;
Three damozels; each had a knight,
  When the Sword went out to sea.

Sir Robert shouted loud, and said,
  When the Sword went out to sea,
'Alicia, while I see thy head,
  What shall I bring for thee?'
'O, my sweet lord, a ruby red:'
  The Sword went out to sea.

Sir Miles said, while the sails hung down,
  When the Sword went out to sea,
'Oh, Ursula! while I see the town,
  What shall I bring for thee?'
'Dear knight, bring back a falcon brown:'
  The Sword went out to sea.

But my Roland, no word he said
  When the Sword went out to sea:
But only turn'd away his head,—
  A quick shriek came from me:
'Come back, dear lord, to your white maid;'
  The Sword went out to sea.

The hot sun bit the garden-beds,
  When the Sword came back from sea;
Beneath an apple-tree our heads
  Stretched out toward the sea;
Grey gleam'd the thirsty castle-leads,
  When the Sword came back from sea.

Lord Robert brought a ruby red,
  When the Sword came back from sea;
He kissed Alicia on the head:
  'I am come back to thee;
'Tis time, sweet love, that we were wed,
  Now the Sword is back from sea!'

Sir Miles he bore a falcon brown,
  When the Sword came back from sea;
His arms went round tall Ursula's gown,—
  'What joy, O love, but thee?
Let us be wed in the good town,
  Now the Sword is back from sea!'

My heart grew sick, no more afraid,
  When the Sword came back from sea;
Upon the deck a tall white maid
  Sat on Lord Roland's knee;
His chin was press'd upon her head,
  When the Sword came back from sea!

[1858]

An Apology [3]

Of Heaven or Hell I have no power to sing,
I cannot ease the burden of your fears,
Or make quick-coming death a little thing,
Or bring again the pleasure of past years,
Nor for my words shall ye forget your tears,
Or hope again for aught that I can say,
The idle singer of an empty day.

But rather, when aweary of your mirth,
From full hearts still unsatisfied ye sigh,
And, feeling kindly unto all the earth,
Grudge every minute as it passes by,
Made the more mindful that the sweet days die—
Remember me a little then I pray,
The idle singer of an empty day.

The heavy trouble, the bewildering care
That weighs us down who live and earn our bread,
These idle verses have no power to bear;
So let me sing of names remembered,
Because they, living not, can ne'er be dead,
Or long time take their memory quite away
From us poor singers of an empty day.

[3] This poem and the following song are from *The Earthly Paradise*, 1868–1870, a collection of stories in verse — two for each month, one drawn from a classical and one from a medieval source.

Dreamer of dreams, born out of my due time,
Why should I strive to set the crooked straight?
Let it suffice me that my murmuring rhyme
Beats with light wing against the ivory gate,[4]
Telling a tale not too importunate
To those who in the sleepy region stay,
Lulled by the singer of an empty day.

Folk say, a wizard to a northern king
At Christmas-tide such wondrous things did show,
That through one window men beheld the spring,
And through another saw the summer glow,
And through a third the fruited vines a-row,
While still, unheard, but in its wonted way,
Piped the drear wind of that December day.

So with this Earthly Paradise it is,
If ye will read aright, and pardon me,
Who strive to build a shadowy isle of bliss
Midmost the beating of the steely sea,
Where tossed about all hearts of men must be;
Whose ravening monsters mighty men shall slay,
Not the poor singer of an empty day.

Song from *Ogier the Dane*

Haec

In the white-flowered hawthorn brake,
Love, be merry for my sake;
Twine the blossoms in my hair,
Kiss me where I am most fair —
Kiss me, love! for who knoweth
What thing cometh after death?

[4] The palace of Morpheus, god of sleep, has a gate of ivory.

Ille

Nay, the garlanded gold hair
Hides thee where thou art most fair;
Hides the rose-tinged hills of snow —
Ay, sweet love, I have thee now!
Kiss me, love! for who knoweth
What thing cometh after death?

Haec

Shall we weep for a dead day,
Or set Sorrow in our way?
Hidden by my golden hair,
Wilt thou weep that sweet days wear?
Kiss me, love! for who knoweth
What thing cometh after death?

Ille

Weep, O Love, the days that flit,
Now, while I can feel thy breath;
Then may I remember it
Sad and old, and near my death.
Kiss me, love! for who knoweth
What thing cometh after death?

The Day is Coming[5]

COME hither lads, and hearken, for a tale there is to tell,
Of the wonderful days a-coming when all shall be better than well.

And the tale shall be told of a country, a land in the midst of the sea,
And folk shall call it England in the days that are going to be.

There more than one in a thousand in the days that are yet to come
Shall have some hope of the morrow, some joy of the ancient home.

For then — laugh not, but listen, to this strange tale of mine —
All folk that are in England shall be better lodged than swine.

[5] From *Chants for Socialists*, 1885.

Then a man shall work and bethink him, and rejoice in the deeds of his hand,
Nor yet come home in the even too faint and weary to stand.

Men in that time a-coming shall work, and have no fear
For to-morrow's lack of earning and the hunger-wolf anear.

I tell you this for a wonder, that no man then shall be glad
Of his fellow's fall and mishap to snatch at the work he had.

For that which the worker winneth shall then be his indeed,
Nor shall half be reaped for nothing by him that sowed no seed.

O strange new wonderful justice! But for whom shall we gather the gain?
For ourselves and for each of our fellows, and no hand shall labour in vain.

Then all *mine* and all *thine* shall be *ours,* and no more shall any man crave
For riches that serve for nothing but to fetter a friend for a slave.

And what wealth then shall be left us when none shall gather gold
To buy his friend in the market, and pinch and pine the sold?

Nay, what save the lovely city, and the little house on the hill,
And the wastes and the woodland beauty, and the happy fields we till.

And the homes of ancient stories, the tombs of the mighty dead;
And the wise men seeking out marvels, and the poet's teeming head;

And the painter's hand of wonder; and the marvellous fiddle-bow,
And the banded choirs of music: — all those that do and know.

For all these shall be ours and all men's, nor shall any lack a share
Of the toil and the gain of living in the days when the world grows fair.

Ah! such are the days that shall be! But what are the deeds of to-day,
In the days of the years we dwell in, that wear our lives away?

Why, then, and for what are we waiting? There are three words to speak.
WE WILL IT, and what is the foeman but the dream-strong wakened and weak?

O why and for what are we waiting? while our brothers droop and die,
And on every wind of the heavens a wasted life goes by.

How long shall they reproach us where crowd on crowd they dwell,
Poor ghosts of the wicked city, the gold-crushed hungry hell?

Through squalid life they laboured, in sordid grief they died,
Those sons of a mighty mother, those props of England's pride.

They are gone; there is none can undo it, nor save our souls from the curse;
But many a million cometh, and shall they be better or worse?

It is we must answer and hasten, and open wide the door
For the rich man's hurrying terror, and the slow-foot hope of the poor.

Yea, the voiceless wrath of the wretched, and their unlearned discontent,
We must give it voice and wisdom till the waiting-tide be spent.

Come, then, since all things call us, the living and the dead
And o'er the weltering tangle a glimmering light is shed.

Come, then, let us cast off fooling, and put by ease and rest
For the CAUSE alone is worthy till the good days bring the best.

Come, join in the only battle wherein no man can fail,
Where whoso fadeth and dieth, yet his deed shall still prevail.

Ah! come, cast off all fooling, for this, at least we know:
That the Dawn and the Day is coming, and forth the Banners go.

Algernon Charles Swinburne

1837–1909

Before the beginning of years[1]

BEFORE the beginning of years
There came to the making of man
Time, with a gift of tears;
Grief, with a glass that ran;
Pleasure, with pain for leaven;
Summer, with flowers that fell;
Remembrance fallen from heaven,
And madness risen from hell;
Strength without hands to smite;
Love that endures for a breath;
Night, the shadow of light,
And life, the shadow of death.

And the high gods took in hand
Fire, and the falling of tears,
And a measure of sliding sand
From under the feet of the years;
And froth and drift of the sea;
And dust of the labouring earth;
And bodies of things to be
In the houses of death and of birth;
And wrought with weeping and laughter,
And fashioned with loathing and love
With life before and after
And death beneath and above,
For a day and a night and a morrow,
That his strength might endure for a span
With travail and heavy sorrow,
The holy spirit of man.

From the winds of the north and the south
They gathered as unto strife;
They breathed upon his mouth,
They filled his body with life;
Eyesight and speech they wrought
For the veils of the soul therein,
A time for labour and thought,
A time to serve and to sin;
They gave him light in his ways,
And love, and a space for delight,
And beauty and length of days,
And night, and sleep in the night.
His speech is a burning fire;
With his lips he travaileth;
In his heart is a blind desire,
In his eyes foreknowledge of death;
He weaves, and is clothed with derision;
Sows, and he shall not reap;
His life is a watch or a vision
Between a sleep and a sleep.

[1] One of the choruses in *Atalanta in Calydon*, 1865.

Hymn to Proserpine[2]

(After the Proclamation in Rome of the Christian Faith)

Vicisti, Galilæ[3]

I HAVE lived long enough, having seen one thing, that love hath an end;
Goddess and maiden and queen, be near me now and befriend.
Thou art more than the day or the morrow, the seasons that laugh or that weep;
For these give joy and sorrow; but thou, Proserpina, sleep.

[2] This and the three following poems were published in *Poems and Ballads*, 1866.

[3] The Roman Emperor Julian, who had renounced Christianity, is purported to have said on his deathbed 'Thou hast conquered, Galilean.'

Sweet is the treading of wine, and sweet the feet of the dove;
But a goodlier gift is thine than foam of the grapes or love.
Yea, is not even Apollo, with hair and harpstring of gold,
A bitter God to follow, a beautiful God to behold?
I am sick of singing: the bays burn deep and chafe; I am fain
To rest a little from praise and grievous pleasure and pain.
For the Gods we know not of, who give us our daily breath,
We know they are cruel as love or life, and lovely as death.
O Gods dethroned and deceased, cast forth, wiped out in a day!
From your wrath is the world released, redeemed from your chains, men say.
New Gods are crowned in the city; their flowers have broken your rods;
They are merciful, clothed with pity, the young compassionate Gods.
But for me their new device is barren, the days are bare;
Things long past over suffice, and men forgotten that were.
Time and the Gods are at strife; ye dwell in the midst thereof,
Draining a little life from the barren breasts of love.
I say to you, cease, take rest; yea, I say to you all, be at peace,
Till the bitter milk of her breast and the barren bosom shall cease,
Wilt thou yet take all, Galilean? but these thou shalt not take,
The laurel, the palms and the pæan, the breasts of the nymphs in the brake;
Breasts more soft than a dove's, that tremble with tenderer breath;
And all the wings of the Loves, and all the joy before death;
All the feet of the hours that sound as a single lyre,
Dropped and deep in the flowers, with strings that flicker like fire.
More than these wilt thou give, things fairer than all these things?
Nay, for a little we live, and life hath mutable wings.
A little while and we die; shall life not thrive as it may?
For no man under the sky lives twice, outliving his day.
And grief is a grievous thing, and a man hath enough of his tears:
Why should he labour, and bring fresh grief to blacken his years?
Thou hast conquered, O pale Galilean; the world has grown grey from thy breath;
We have drunken of things Lethean, and fed on the fullness of death.
Laurel is green for a season, and love is sweet for a day;
But love grows bitter with treason, and laurel outlives not May.
Sleep, shall we sleep after all? for the world is not sweet in the end;
For the old faiths loosen and fall, the new years ruin and rend.
Fate is a sea without shore, and the soul is a rock that abides;
But her ears are vexed with the roar and her face with the foam of the tides.
O lips that the live blood faints in, the leavings of racks and rods!
O ghastly glories of saints, dead limbs of gibbeted Gods!
Though all men abase them before you in spirit, and all knees bend,
I kneel not neither adore you, but standing, look to the end.
All delicate days and pleasant, all spirits and sorrows are cast
Far out with the foam of the present that sweeps to the surf of the past:
Where beyond the extreme sea-wall, and between the remote sea-gates,
Waste water washes, and tall ships founder, and deep death waits:
Where, mighty with deepening sides, clad about with the seas as with wings,
And impelled of invisible tides, and fulfilled of unspeakable things,

White-eyed and poisonous-finned, shark-toothed and serpentine-curled,
Rolls, under the whitening wind of the future, the wave of the world.
The depths stand naked in sunder behind it, the storms flee away;
In the hollow before it the thunder is taken and snared as a prey;
In its sides is the north-wind bound; and its salt is of all men's tears;
With light of ruin, and sound of changes, and pulse of years:
With travail of day after day, and with trouble of hour upon hour;
And bitter as blood is the spray; and the crests are as fangs that devour:
And its vapour and storm of its steam as the sighing of spirits to be;
And its noise as the noise in a dream; and its depth as the roots of the sea:
And the height of its heads as the height of the utmost stars of the air:
And the ends of the earth at the might thereof tremble, and time is made bare.
Will ye bridle the deep sea with reins, will ye chasten the high sea with rods?
Will ye take her to chain her with chains, who is older than all ye Gods?
All ye as a wind shall go by, as a fire shall ye pass and be past;
Ye are Gods, and behold, ye shall die, and the waves be upon you at last.
In the darkness of time, in the deeps of the years, in the changes of things,
Ye shall sleep as a slain man sleeps, and the world shall forget you for kings.
Though the feet of thine high priests tread where thy lords and our forefathers trod,
Though these that were Gods are dead, and thou being dead art a God,
Though before thee the throned Cytherean [4] be fallen, and hidden her head,
Yet thy kingdom shall pass, Galilean, thy dead shall go down to thee dead.

[4] Venus rose from the foam at Cythera.

Of the maiden thy mother men sing as a goddess with grace clad around;
Thou art throned where another was king; where another was queen she is crowned.
Yea, once we had sight of another: but now she is queen, say these.
Not as thine, not as thine was our mother, a blossom of flowering seas,
Clothed round with the world's desire as with raiment, and fair as the foam,
And fleeter than kindled fire, and a goddess, and mother of Rome.
For thine came pale and a maiden, and sister to sorrow; but ours,
Her deep hair heavily laden with odour and colour of flowers,
White rose of the rose-white water, a silver splendour, a flame,
Bent down unto us that besought her, and earth grew sweet with her name.
For thine came weeping, a slave among slaves, and rejected; but she
Came flushed from the full-flushed wave, and imperial, her foot on the sea.
And the wonderful waters knew her, the winds and the viewless ways,
And the roses grew rosier, and bluer the sea-blue stream of the bays.
Ye are fallen, our lords, by what token? we wist that ye should not fall.
Ye were all so fair that are broken; and one more fair than ye all.
But I turn to her still, having seen she shall surely abide in the end;
Goddess and maiden and queen, be near me now and befriend.
O daughter of earth, of my mother, her crown and blossom of birth,
I am also, I also, thy brother; I go as I came unto earth.
In the night where thine eyes are as moons are in heaven, the night where thou art,
Where the silence is more than all tunes, where sleep overflows from the heart,
Where the poppies are sweet as the rose in our world, and the red rose is white,

And the wind falls faint as it blows with the fume of the flowers of the night,
And the murmur of spirits that sleep in the shadow of Gods from afar
Grows dim in thine ears and deep as the deep dim soul of a star,
In the sweet low light of thy face, under heavens untrod by the sun,
Let my soul with their souls find place, and forget what is done and undone.
Thou are more than the Gods who number the days of our temporal breath;
For these give labour and slumber; but thou; Proserpina, death.
Therefore now at thy feet I abide for a season in silence. I know
I shall die as my fathers died, and sleep as they sleep; even so.
For the glass of the years is brittle wherein we gaze for a span;
A little soul for a little bears up this corpse which is man.
So long I endure, no longer; and laugh not again, neither weep.
For there is no God found stronger than death; and death is a sleep.

The Garden of Proserpine

Here, where the world is quiet;
  Here, where all trouble seems
Dead winds' and spent waves' riot
  In doubtful dreams of dreams;
I watch the green field growing
For reaping folk and sowing,
For harvest-time and mowing,
  A sleepy world of streams.

I am tired of tears and laughter,
  And men that laugh and weep;
Of what may come hereafter
  For men that sow to reap:
I am weary of days and hours,
Blown buds of barren flowers,
Desires and dreams and powers
  And everything but sleep.

Here life has death for neighbour,
  And far from eye or ear
Wan waves and wet winds labour,
  Weak ships and spirits steer;
They drive adrift, and whither
They wot not who make thither;
But no such winds blow hither,
  And no such things grow here.

No growth of moor or coppice,
  No heather-flower or vine,
But bloomless buds of poppies,
  Green grapes of Proserpine,
Pale beds of blowing rushes
Where no leaf blooms or blushes
Save this whereout she crushes
  For dead men deadly wine.

Pale, without name or number,
  In fruitless fields of corn,
They blow themselves and slumber
  All night till light is born;
And like a soul belated,
In hell and heaven unmated,
By cloud and mist abated
  Comes out of darkness morn.

Though one were strong as seven,
  He too with death shall dwell,
Nor wake with wings in heaven,
  Nor weep for pains in hell;
Though one were fair as roses,
His beauty clouds and closes;
And well though love reposes,
  In the end it is not well.

Pale, beyond porch and portal,
  Crowned with calm leaves, she stands
Who gathers all things mortal
  With cold immortal hands;
Her languid lips are sweeter
Than love's who fears to greet her
To men that mix and meet her
  From many times and lands.

She waits for each and other,
  She waits for all men born;
Forgets the earth her mother,
  The life of fruits and corn;
And spring and seed and swallow
Take wing for her and follow

Where summer song rings hollow
  And flowers are put to scorn.

There go the loves that wither,
  The old loves with wearier wings;
And all dead years draw thither,
  And all disastrous things;
Dead dreams of days forsaken,
Blind buds that snows have shaken,
Wild leaves that winds have taken,
  Red strays of ruined springs.

We are not sure of sorrow,
  And joy was never sure;
To-day will die to-morrow;
  Time stoops to no man's lure;
And love, grown faint and fretful,
With lips but half regretful
Sighs, and with eyes forgetful
  Weeps that no loves endure.

From too much love of living,
  From hope and fear set free,
We thank with brief thanksgiving
  Whatever gods may be
That no life lives for ever;
That dead men rise up never;
That even the weariest river
  Winds somewhere safe to sea.

Then star nor sun shall waken,
  Nor any change of light:
Nor sound of waters shaken,
  Nor any sound or sight:
Nor wintry leaves nor vernal,
Nor days nor things diurnal;
Only the sleep eternal
  In an eternal night.

[1866]

A Leave-taking

Let us go hence, my songs; she will not hear.
Let us go hence together without fear;
Keep silence now, for singing-time is over
And over all old things and all things dear.
She loves not you nor me as all we love her.
Yea, though we sang as angels in her ear,
  She would not hear.

Let us rise up and part; she will not know.
Let us go seaward as the great winds go,
Full of blown sand and foam; what help is there?
There is no help, for all these things are so,
And all the world is bitter as a tear.
And how these things are, though ye strove to show,
  She would not know.

Let us go home and hence; she will not weep,
We gave love many dreams and days to keep,
Flowers without scent, and fruits that would not grow,
Saying, 'If thou wilt, thrust in thy sickle and reap.'
All is reaped now; no grass is left to mow;
And we that sowed, though all we fell on sleep,
  She would not weep.

Let us go hence and rest; she will not love.
She shall not hear us if we sing hereof,
Nor see love's ways, how sore they are and steep.
Come hence, let be, lie still: it is enough.
Love is a barren sea, bitter and deep;
And though she saw all heaven in flower above,
  She would not love.

Let us give up, go down; she will not care.
Though all the stars made gold of all the air,
And the sea moving saw before it move
One moon-flower making all the foam-flowers fair;
Though all those waves went over us, and drove
Deep down the stifling lips and drowning hair,
  She would not care.

Let us go hence, go hence; she will not see.
Sing all once more together: surely she,
She too, remembering days and words that were,

Will turn a little toward us, sighing; but we,
We are hence, we are gone, as though we had not been there.
Nay, and though all men seeing had pity on me,
She would not see.

[1866]

The Triumph of Time

(Stanzas 33–38)

I WILL go back to the great sweet mother,
Mother and lover of men, the sea.
I will go down to her, I and none other,
Close with her, kiss her and mix her with me;
Cling to her, strive with her, hold her fast;
O fair white mother, in days long past
Born without sister, born without brother,
Set free my soul as thy soul is free.

O fair green-girdled mother of mine,
Sea, that art clothed with the sun and the rain,
Thy sweet hard kisses are strong like wine,
Thy large embraces are keen like pain.
Save me and hide me with all thy waves,
Find me one grave of thy thousand graves,
Those pure cold populous graves of thine
Wrought without hand in a world without stain.

I shall sleep, and move with the moving ships,
Change as the winds change, veer in the tide;
My lips will feast on the foam of thy lips,
I shall rise with thy rising, with thee subside;
Sleep, and not know if she be, if she were,
Filled full with life to the eyes and hair,
As a rose is fulfilled to the roseleaf tips
With splendid summer and perfume and pride.

This woven raiment of nights and days,
Were it once cast off and unwound from me,
Naked and glad would I walk in thy ways,
Alive and aware of thy ways and thee;
Clear of the whole world, hidden at home,
Clothed with the green and crowned with the foam,
A pulse of the life of thy straits and bays,
A vein in the heart of the streams of the sea.

Fair mother, fed with the lives of men,
Thou art subtle and cruel of heart, men say.
Thou hast taken, and shalt not render again;
Thou art full of thy dead, and cold as they.
But death is the worst that comes of thee;
Thou art fed with our dead, O Mother, O sea,
But when hast thou fed on our hearts? or when,
Having given us love, hast thou taken away?

O tender-hearted, O perfect lover,
Thy lips are bitter, and sweet thine heart.
The hopes that hurt and the dreams that hover,
Shall they not vanish away and apart?
But thou, thou art sure, thou art older than earth;
Thou art strong for death and fruitful of birth;
Thy depths conceal and thy gulfs discover;
From the first thou wert; in the end thou art.

[1866]

Hertha [5]

I AM that which began;
Out of me the years roll;
Out of me God and man;
I am equal and whole;
God changes, and man, and the form of them bodily; I am the soul.

---

[5] Published in *Songs before Sunrise*, 1871. Hertha is the Germanic goddess of the earth, whom Swinburne uses to personify the life force.

Before ever land was,
Before ever the sea,
Or soft hair of the grass,
Or fair limbs of the tree,
Or the flesh-coloured fruit of my branches,
I was, and thy soul was in me.

First life on my sources
First drifted and swam;
Out of me are the forces
That save it or damn;
Out of me man and woman, and wild-beast and bird; before God was, I am.

Beside or above me
Nought is there to go;
Love or unlove me,
Unknow me or know,
I am that which unloves me and loves; I am stricken, and I am the blow.

I the mark that is missed
And the arrows that miss,
I the mouth that is kissed
And the breath in the kiss,
The search, and the sought, and the seeker, the soul and the body that is.

I am that thing which blesses
My spirit elate;
That which caresses
With hands uncreate.
My limbs unbegotten that measure the length of the measure of fate.

But what thing dost thou now,
Looking Godward, to cry
'I am I, thou art thou,
I am low, thou art high'?
I am thou, whom thou seekest to find him; find thou but thyself, thou art I.

I the grain and the furrow,
The plough-cloven clod
And the ploughshare drawn thorough,
The germ and the sod,
The deed and the doer, the seed and the sower, the dust which is God.

Hast thou known how I fashioned thee,
Child, underground?
Fire that impassioned thee,
Iron that bound,
Dim changes of water, what thing of all these hast thou known of or found?

Canst thou say in thine heart
Thou hast seen with thine eyes
With what cunning of art
Thou wast wrought in what wise,
By what force of what stuff thou wast shapen, and shown on my breast to the skies?

Who hath given, who hath sold it thee,
Knowledge of me?
Hath the wilderness told it thee?
Hast thou learnt of the sea?
Hast thou communed in spirit with night? have the winds taken counsel with thee?

Have I set such a star
To show light on thy brow
That thou sawest from afar
What I show to thee now?
Have ye spoken as brethren together, the sun and the mountains and thou?

What is here, dost thou know it?
What was, hast thou known?
Prophet nor poet
Nor tripod nor throne
Nor spirit nor flesh can make answer, but only thy mother alone.

Mother, not maker,
Born, and not made;
Though her children forsake her,
Allured or afraid,
Praying prayers to the God of their fashion, she stirs not for all that have prayed.

A creed is a rod,
And a crown is of night;
But this thing is God,
To be man with thy might,

To grow straight in the strength of thy spirit, and live out thy life as the light.

I am in thee to save thee,
As my soul in thee saith;
Give thou as I gave thee,
Thy life-blood and breath,
Green leaves of thy labour, white flowers of thy thought, and red fruit of thy death.

Be the ways of thy giving
As mine were to thee;
The free life of thy living,
Be the gift of it free;
Not as servant to lord, nor as master to slave, shalt thou give thee to me.

O children of banishment,
Souls overcast,
Were the lights ye see vanish meant
Alway to last,
Ye would know not the sun overshining the shadows and stars overpast.

I that saw where ye trod
The dim paths of the night
Set the shadow called God
In your skies to give light;
But the morning of manhood is risen, and the shadowless soul is in sight.

The tree many-rooted
That swells to the sky
With frondage red-fruited,
The life-tree am I;
In the buds of your lives is the sap of my leaves: ye shall live and not die.

But the Gods of your fashion
That take and that give,
In their pity and passion
That scourge and forgive,
That are worms that are bred in the bark that falls off; they shall die and not live.

My own blood is what stanches
The wounds in my bark;
Stars caught in my branches
Make day of the dark,
And are worshiped as suns till the sunrise shall tread out their fires as a spark.

Where dead ages hide under
The live roots of the tree,
In my darkness the thunder
Makes utterance of me;
In the clash of my boughs with each other ye hear the waves sound of the sea.

That noise is of Time,
As his feathers are spread
And his feet set to climb
Through the boughs overhead,
And my foliage rings round him and rustles, and branches are bent with his tread.

The storm-winds of ages
Blow through me and cease,
The war-wind that rages,
The spring-wind of peace,
Ere the breath of them roughens my tresses, ere one of my blossoms increase.

All sounds of all changes,
All shadows and lights
On the world's mountain-ranges
And stream-riven heights,
Whose tongue is the wind's tongue and language of storm-clouds or earth-shaking nights;

All forms of all faces,
All works of all hands
In unsearchable places
Of time-stricken lands,
All death and all life, and all reigns and all ruins, drop through me as sands

Though sore be my burden
And more than ye know,
And my growth have no guerdon
But only to grow,
Yet I fail not of growing for lightnings above me or death-worms below.

These too have their part in me,
As I too in these;
Such fire is at heart in me,
Such sap is this tree's,
Which hath in it all sounds and all secrets
of infinite lands and of seas.

In the spring-coloured hours
When my mind was as May's,
There brake forth of me flowers
By centuries of days,
Strong blossoms with perfume of manhood,
shot out from my spirit as rays.

And the sound of them springing
And smell of their shoots
Were as warmth and sweet singing
And strength to my roots;
And the lives of my children made perfect
with freedom of soul were my fruits.

I bid you but be;
I have need not of prayer;
I have need of you free
As your mouths of mine air;
That my heart may be greater within me,
beholding the fruits of me fair.

More fair than strange fruit is
Of faiths ye espouse;
In me only the root is
That blooms in your boughs;
Behold now your God that ye made you, to
feed him with faith of your vows.

In the darkening and whitening
Abysses adored,
With dayspring and lightning
For lamp and for sword,
God thunders in heaven, and his angels are
red with the wrath of the Lord.

O my sons, O too dutiful
Toward Gods not of me,
Was not I enough beautiful?
Was it hard to be free?
For behold, I am with you, am in you and
of you; look forth now and see.

Lo, winged with world's wonders,
With miracles shod,
With the fires of his thunders
For raiment and rod,
God trembles in heaven, and his angels are
white with the terror of God.

For his twilight is come on him,
His anguish is here;
And his spirits gaze dumb on him,
Grown grey from his fear;
And his hour taketh hold on him striken,
the last of his infinite year.

Thought made him and breaks him,
Truth slays and forgives;
But to you, as time takes him,
This new thing it gives,
Even love, the beloved Republic, that feeds
upon freedom and lives.

For truth only is living,
Truth only is whole,
And the love of his giving
Man's polestar and pole;
Man, pulse of my centre, and fruit of my
body, and seed of my soul.

One birth of my bosom;
One beam of mine eye;
One topmost blossom
That scales the sky;
Man, equal and one with me, man that is
made of me, man that is I.

Ave atque Vale [6]

In Memory of Charles Baudelaire

Nous devrions pourtant lui porter quelques fleurs;
Les morts, les pauvres morts, ont de grandes douleurs,
Et quand Octobre souffle, émondeur des vieux arbres
Son vent mélancolique à l'entour de leurs marbres,
Certe, ils doivent trouver les vivants bien ingrats.
—Les Fleurs du Mal

[6] Written in 1867 under the shock of what proved to be a false report of the death of the author of *The Flowers of Evil*. Published in *Poems and Ballads*, Second Series, 1878.

SHALL I strew on thee rose or rue or laurel,
Brother, on this that was the veil of thee?
Or quiet sea-flower moulded by the sea,
Or simplest growth of meadow-sweet or sorrel,
Such as the summer-sleepy Dryads weave,
Waked up by snow-soft sudden rains at eve?
Or wilt thou rather, as on earth before,
Half-faded fiery blossoms, pale with heat
And full of bitter summer, but more sweet
To thee than gleanings of a northern shore
Trod by no tropic feet?

For always thee the fervid languid glories
Allured of heavier suns in mightier skies;
Thine ears knew all the wandering watery sighs
Where the sea sobs round Lesbian [7] promontories,
The barren kiss of piteous wave to wave
That knows not where is that Leucadian grave
Which hides too deep the supreme head of song.
Ah, salt and sterile as her kisses were,
The wild sea winds her and the green gulfs bear
Hither and thither, and vex and work her wrong,
Blind gods that cannot spare.

Thou sawest, in thine old singing season, brother,
Secrets and sorrows unbeheld of us:
Fierce loves, and lovely leaf-buds poisonous,
Bare to thy subtler eye, but for none other
Blowing by night in some unbreathed-in clime;
The hidden harvest of luxurious time,
Sin without shape, and pleasure without speech;
And where strange dreams in a tumultuous sleep
Make the shut eyes of stricken spirits weep;
And with each face thou sawest the shadow on each,
Seeing as men sow men reap.

O sleepless heart and sombre soul unsleeping,
That were athirst for sleep and no more life
And no more love, for peace and no more strife!
Now the dim gods of death have in their keeping
Spirit and body and all the springs of song,
Is it well now where love can do no wrong,
Where stingless pleasure has no foam or fang
Behind the unopening closure of her lips?
Is it not well where soul from body slips
And flesh from bone divides without a pang
As dew from flower-bell drips?

It is enough; the end and the beginning
Are one thing to thee, who art past the end.
O hand unclasped of unbeholden friend,
For thee no fruits to pluck, no palms for winning,
No triumph and no labour and no lust,
Only dead yew-leaves and a little dust.
O quiet eyes wherein the light saith nought,
Whereto the day is dumb, nor any night
With obscure finger silences your sight,
Nor in your speech the sudden soul speaks thought,
Sleep, and have sleep for light.

[7] Baudelaire in his *Lesbos* describes the island as mourning for the death of Sappho, who cast herself into the sea from the heights of Leucas.

Now all strange hours and all strange loves are over,
Dreams and desires and sombre songs and sweet,
Hast thou found place at the great knees and feet
Of some pale Titan-woman [8] like a lover,
Such as thy vision here solicited,
Under the shadow of her fair vast head,
The deep division of prodigious breasts,
The solemn slope of mighty limbs asleep,
The weight of awful tresses that still keep
The savour and shade of old-world pine-forests
Where the wet hill-winds weep?

Hast thou found any likeness for thy vision?
O gardener of strange flowers, what bud, what bloom,
Hast thou found sown, what gathered in the gloom?
What of despair, of rapture, of derision,
What of life is there, what of ill or good?
Are the fruits grey like dust or bright like blood?
Does the dim ground grow any seed of ours,
The faint fields quicken any terrene root,
In low lands where the sun and moon are mute
And all the stars keep silence? Are there flowers
At all, or any fruit?

Alas, but though my flying song flies after,
O sweet strange elder singer, thy more fleet
Singing, and footprints of thy fleeter feet,
Some dim derision of mysterious laughter
From the blind tongueless warders of the dead,
Some gainless glimpse of Proserpine's veiled head,
Some little sound of unregarded tears
Wept by effaced unprofitable eyes,
And from pale mouths some cadence of dead sighs —
These only, these the hearkening spirit hears,
Sees only such things rise.

Thou art far too far for wings of words to follow,
Far too far off for thought or any prayer.
What ails us with thee, who art wind and air?
What ails us gazing where all seen is hollow?
Yet with some fancy, yet with some desire,
Dreams pursue death as winds a flying fire,
Our dreams pursue our dead and do not find.
Still, and more swift than they, the thin flame flies,
The low light fails us in elusive skies,
Still the foiled earnest ear is deaf, and blind
Are still the eluded eyes.

Not thee, O never thee, in all time's changes,
Not thee, but this the sound of thy sad soul,
The shadow of thy swift spirit, this shut scroll
I lay my hand on, and not death estranges
My spirit from communion of thy song —
These memories and these melodies that throng
Veiled porches of a Muse funereal —
These I salute, these touch, these clasp and fold
As though a hand were in my hand to hold,
Or through mine ears a mourning musical
Of many mourners rolled.

---

[8] A reference to Baudelaire's poem, *La Géante.*

I among these, I also, in such station
As when the pyre was charred, and piled the sods,
And offering to the dead made, and their gods,
The old mourners had, standing to make libation,
I stand, and to the gods and to the dead
Do reverence without prayer or praise and shed
Offering to these unknown, the gods of gloom,
And what of honey and spice my seed-lands bear,
And what I may of fruits in this chilled air,
And lay, Orestes-like,[9] across the tomb
A curl of severed hair.

But by no hand nor any treason stricken,
Not like the low-lying head of Him, the King,
The flame that made of Troy a ruinous thing,
Thou liest, and on this dust no tears could quicken
There fall no tears like theirs that all men hear
Fall tear by sweet imperishable tear
Down the opening leaves of holy poets' pages.
Thee not Orestes, not Electra mourns;
But bending us-ward with memorial urns
The most high Muses that fulfil all ages
Weep, and our God's heart yearns.

For, sparing of his sacred strength, not often
Among us darkling here the lord of light
Makes manifest his music and his might
In hearts that open and in lips that soften
With the soft flame and heat of songs that shine.
Thy lips indeed he touched with bitter wine,
And nourished them indeed with bitter bread;
Yet surely from his hand thy soul's food came,
The fire that scarred thy spirit at his flame
Was lighted, and thine hungering heart he fed
Who feeds our hearts with fame.

Therefore he too now at thy soul's sunsetting,
God of all suns and songs, he too bends down
To mix his laurel with thy cypress crown,
And save thy dust from blame and from forgetting.
Therefore he too, seeing all thou wert and art,
Compassionate, with sad and sacred heart,
Mourns thee of many his children the last dead,
And hallows with strange tears and alien sighs
Thine unmelodious mouth and sunless eyes,
And over thine irrevocable head
Sheds light from the under skies.

And one weeps with him in the ways Lethean,
And stains with tears her changing bosom chill:
That obscure Venus[10] of the hollow hill,
That thing transformed which was the Cytherean,
With lips that lost their Grecian laugh divine
Long since, and face no more called Erycine
A ghost, a bitter and luxurious god.

[9] In the opening scene of Aeschylus' *Choëphoroe* Orestes, at the tomb of his father Agamemnon, offers as a sacrifice to the dead a lock of his hair, symbol of mourning and votive dedication.

[10] The Venus of the Venusberg. Behind these verses lies the Tannhäuser legend.

Thee also with fair flesh and singing spell
Did she, a sad and second prey, compel
Into the footless places once more trod,
And shadows hot from hell.

And now no sacred staff shall break in blossom,
No choral salutation lure to light
A spirit sick with perfume and sweet night
And love's tired eyes and hands and barren bosom.
There is no help for these things; none to mend
And none to mar; not all our songs, O friend,
Will make death clear or make life durable.
Howbeit with rose and ivy and wild vine
And with wild notes about this dust of thine
At least I fill the place where white dreams dwell
And wreathe an unseen shrine.

Sleep; and if life was bitter to thee, pardon,
If sweet, give thanks; thou hast no more to live;
And to give thanks is good, and to forgive.
Out of the mystic and the mournful garden
Where all day through thine hands in barren braid
Wove the sick flowers of secrecy and shade,
Green buds of sorrow and sin, and remnants grey,
Sweet-smelling, pale with poison, sanguine-hearted,
Passions that sprang from sleep and thoughts that started,
Shall death not bring us all as thee one day
Among the days departed?

For thee, O now a silent soul, my brother,
Take at my hands this garland, and farewell.
Thin is the leaf, and chill the wintry smell,
And chill the solemn earth, a fatal mother,
With sadder than the Niobean [11] womb,
And in the hollow of her breasts a tomb.
Content thee, howsoe'er, whose days are done;
There lies not any troublous thing before,
Nor sight nor sound to war against thee more,
For whom all winds are quiet as the sun,
All waters as the shore.

THE HEPTALOGIA [12]

or

THE SEVEN AGAINST SENSE

A Cap with Seven Bells

I. *John Jones*

At the Piano

LOVE me and leave me; what love bids retrieve me? can June's fist grasp May?
Leave me and love me; hopes eyed once above me like spring's sprouts, decay;
Fall as the snow falls, when summer leaves grow false — cards packed for storm's play!

Nay, say Decay's self be but last May's elf, wing shifted, eye sheathed —
Changeling in April's crib rocked, who lets

[11] Niobe's children were slain by Apollo and Diana because she had expressed pride in having more offspring than their mother, Latona.

[12] These seven 'specimens of modern poets' were published in 1880. The three given here are the parodies of Browning, Rossetti, and Swinburne himself.

'scape rills locked fast since frost breathed —
Skin cast (think!) adder-like, now bloom bursts bladder-like, — bloom frost bequeathed?

Ah, how can fear sit and hear as love hears it grief's heart's cracked grate's screech?
Chance let the gate sway that opens on hate's way and shews on shame's beach
Crouched like an imp sly change watch sweet love's shrimps lie, a toothful in each.

Time feels his tooth slip on husks wet from Truth's lip, which drops them and grins —
Shells where no throb stirs of life left in lobsters since joy thrilled their fins —
Hues of the prawn's tail or comb that makes dawn stale,[13] so red for our sins!

Years blind and deaf use the soul's joys as refuse, heart's peace as manure,
Reared whence, next June's rose shall bloom where our moons rose last year, just as pure:
Moons' ends match roses' ends: men by beasts' noses' ends mete sin's stink's cure.

Leaves love last year smelt now feel dead love's tears melt — flies caught in time's mesh!
Salt are the dews in which new time breeds new sin, brews blood and stews flesh;
Next year may see dead more germs than this weeded and reared them afresh.

Old times left perish, there's new time to cherish; life just shifts its tune;
As, when the day dies, earth, half afraid, eyes the growth of the moon;
Love me and save me, take me or waive me; death takes one so soon!

[13] 'Whose youth and freshness
Wrinkles Apollo's, and makes stale the morning.'
— Shakespeare. [Swinburne.]

II. *Sonnet for a Picture*

That nose is out of drawing. With a gasp,
She pants upon the passionate lips that ache
With the red drain of her own mouth, and make
A monochord of colour. Like an asp,
One lithe lock wriggles in his rutilant grasp.
Her bosom is an oven of myrrh, to bake
Love's white warm shewbread to a browner cake.
The lock his fingers clench has burst its hasp.
The legs are absolutely abominable.
Ah! what keen overgust of wild-eyed woes
Flags in that bosom, flushes in that nose?
Nay! Death sets riddles for desire to spell,
Responsive. What red hem earth's passion sews,
But may be ravenously unripped in hell?

III. *Nephelidia*

From the depth of the dreamy decline of the dawn through a notable nimbus of nebulous moonshine,
Pallid and pink as the palm of the flag-flower that flickers with fear of the flies as they float,
Are they looks of our lovers that lustrously lean from a marvel of mystic miraculous moonshine,
These that we feel in the blood of our blushes that thicken and threaten with throbs through the throat?
Thicken and thrill as a theatre thronged at appeal of an actor's appalled agitation,
Fainter with fear of the fires of the future than pale with the promise of pride in the past;
Flushed with the famishing fullness of fever that reddens with radiance of rathe recreation,
Gaunt as the ghastliest of glimpses that

gleam through the gloom of the gloaming when ghosts go aghast?
Nay, for the nick of the tick of the time is a tremulous touch on the temples of terror,
Strained as the sinews yet strenuous with strife of the dead who is dumb as the dust-heaps of death:
Surely no soul is it, sweet as the spasm of erotic emotional exquisite error,
Bathed in the balms of beatified bliss, beatific itself by beatitude's breath.
Surely no spirit of sense of a soul that was soft to the spirit and soul of our senses
Sweetens the stress of suspiring suspicion that sobs in the semblance and sound of a sigh;
Only this oracle opens Olympian, in mystical moods and triangular tenses —
'Life is the lust of a lamp for the light that is dark till the dawn of the day when we die.'
Mild is the mirk and monotonous music of memory, melodiously mute as it may be,
While the hope in the heart of a hero is bruised by the breach of men's rapiers, resigned to the rod;
Made meek as a mother whose bosom-beats bound with the bliss-bringing bulk of a balm-breathing baby,
As they grope through the grave-yard of creeds, under skies growing green at a groan for the grimness of God.
Blank is the book of his bounty beholden of old, and its binding is blacker than bluer:
Out of blue into black is the scheme of the skies, and their dews are the wine of the bloodshed of things;
Till the darkling desire of delight shall be free as a fawn that is freed from the fangs that pursue her,
Till the heart-beats of hell shall be hushed by a hymn from the hunt that has harried the kennel of kings.

James Thomson

1834–1882

THE CITY OF DREADFUL NIGHT [1]

PROEM

Lo, thus, as prostrate, 'In the dust I write
My heart's deep languor and my soul's sad tears.'
Yet why evoke the spectres of black night
To blot the sunshine of exultant years?
Why disinter dead faith from mouldering hidden?
Why break the seals of mute despair unbidden,
And wail life's discords into careless ears?

Because a cold rage seizes one at whiles
To show the bitter old and wrinkled truth
Stripped naked of all vesture that beguiles,
False dreams, false hopes, false masks and modes of youth;
Because it gives some sense of power and passion
In helpless impotence to try to fashion
Our woe in living words howe'er uncouth.

Surely I write not for the hopeful young,
Or those who deem their happiness of worth,
Or such as pasture and grow fat among
The shadows of life and feel nor doubt nor dearth,
Or pious spirits with a God above them
To sanctify and glorify and love them,
Or sages who foresee a heaven on earth.

[1] Written between 1870 and 1874; published in *The National Reformer*, 1874. In 1880 the four installments were collected into a volume bearing the name of the poem for its title.

For none of these I write, and none of these
Could read the writing if they deigned to try:
So may they flourish, in their due degrees,
On our sweet earth and in their unplaced sky.
If any cares for the weak words here written,
It must be some one desolate, Fate-smitten,
Whose faith and hope are dead, and who would die.

Yes, here and there some weary wanderer
In that same city of tremendous night,
Will understand the speech, and feel a stir
Of fellowship in all-disastrous fight;
'I suffer mute and lonely, yet another
Uplifts his voice to let me know a brother
Travels the same wild paths though out of sight.'

O sad Fraternity, do I unfold
Your dolorous mysteries shrouded from of yore?
Nay, be assured; no secret can be told
To any who divined it not before:
None uninitiate by many a presage
Will comprehend the language of the message,
Although proclaimed aloud for evermore.

I

The City is of Night; perchance of Death,
But certainly of Night; for never there
Can come the lucid morning's fragrant breath
After the dewy dawning's cold grey air;
The moon and stars may shine with scorn or pity;
The sun has never visited that city,
For it dissolveth in the daylight fair.

Dissolveth like a dream of night away;
Though present in distempered gloom of thought
And deadly weariness of heart all day.
But when a dream night after night is brought
Throughout a week, and such weeks few or many
Recur each year for several years, can any
Discern that dream from real life in aught?

For life is but a dream whose shapes return,
Some frequently, some seldom, some by night
And some by day, some night and day: we learn,
The while all change and many vanish quite,
In their recurrence with recurrent changes
A certain seeming order; where this ranges
We count things real; such is memory's might.

A river girds the city west and south,
The main north channel of a broad lagoon,
Regurging with the salt tides from the mouth;
Waste marshes shine and glister to the moon
For leagues, then moorland black, then stony ridges;
Great piers and causeways, many noble bridges,
Connect the town and islet suburbs strewn.

Upon an easy slope it lies at large,
And scarcely overlaps the long curved crest
Which swells out two leagues from the river marge.
A trackless wilderness rolls north and west,
Savannahs, savage woods, enormous mountains,
Bleak uplands, black ravines with torrent fountains;
And eastward rolls the shipless sea's unrest.

The city is not ruinous, although
Great ruins of an unremembered past,

With others of a few short years ago
More sad, are found within its precincts vast.
The street-lamps always burn; but scarce a casement
In house or palace front from roof to basement
Doth glow or gleam athwart the mirk air cast.

The street-lamps burn amidst the baleful glooms,
Amidst the soundless solitudes immense
Of rangéd mansions dark and still as tombs.
The silence which benumbs or strains the sense
Fulfils with awe the soul's despair unweeping:
Myriads of habitants are ever sleeping,
Or dead, or fled from nameless pestilence!

Yet as in some necropolis you find
Perchance one mourner to a thousand dead,
So there; worn faces that look deaf and blind
Like tragic masks of stone. With weary tread,
Each wrapt in his own doom, they wander, wander,
Or sit foredone and desolately ponder
Through sleepless hours with heavy drooping head.

Mature men chiefly, few in age or youth,
A woman rarely, now and then a child:
A child! If here the heart turns sick with ruth
To see a little one from birth defiled,
Or lame or blind, as preordained to languish
Through youthless life, think how it bleeds with anguish
To meet one erring in that homeless wild.

They often murmur to themselves, they speak
To one another seldom, for their woe
Broods maddening inwardly and scorns to wreak
Itself abroad; and if at whiles it grow
To frenzy which must rave, none heeds the clamour,
Unless there waits some victim of like glamour,
To rave in turn, who lends attentive show.

The City is of Night, but not of Sleep;
There sweet sleep is not for the weary brain;
The pitiless hours like years and ages creep,
A night seems termless hell. This dreadful strain
Of thought and consciousness which never ceases,
Or which some moments' stupor but increases,
This, worse than woe, makes wretches there insane.

They leave all hope behind who enter there:[2]
One certitude while sane they cannot leave,
One anodyne for torture and despair;
The certitude of Death, which no reprieve
Can put off long; and which, divinely tender,
But waits the outstretched hand to promptly render
That draught whose slumber nothing can bereave.[3]

. . .

XIV

Large glooms were gathered in the mighty fane,
With tinted moongleams slanting here and there;

[2] 'Leave all hope, ye who enter!' Dante saw those words written above the gate to hell. (*Inferno*, Canto III, l. 9.)

[3] Though the Garden of thy life be wholly waste, the sweet flowers withered, the fruit-trees barren, over its wall hang ever the rich dark clusters of the Vine of Death, within easy reach of thy hand, which may pluck them when it will. [Thomson.]

And all was hush: no swelling organ-strain,
No chant, no voice or murmuring of prayer;
No priests came forth, no tinkling censers fumed,
And the high altar space was unillumed.

Around the pillars and against the walls
Leaned men and shadows; others seemed to brood
Bent or recumbent in secluded stalls.
Perchance they were not a great multitude
Save in that city of so lonely streets
Where one may count up every face he meets.

All patiently awaited the event
Without a stir or sound, as if no less
Self-occupied, doomstricken, while attent.
And then we heard a voice of solemn stress
From the dark pulpit, and our gaze there met
Two eyes which burned as never eyes burned yet:

Two steadfast and intolerable eyes
Burning beneath a broad and rugged brow;
The head behind it of enormous size.
And as black fir-groves in a large wind bow,
Our rooted congregation, gloom-arrayed,
By that great sad voice deep and full were swayed:—

O melancholy Brothers, dark, dark, dark!
O battling in black floods without an ark!
O spectral wanderers of unholy Night!
My soul hath bled for you these sunless years,
With bitter blood-drops running down like tears:
Oh, dark, dark, dark, withdrawn from joy and light!

My heart is sick with anguish for your bale;
Your woe hath been my anguish; yea, I quail
And perish in your perishing unblest.
And I have searched the highths and depths, the scope
Of all our universe, with desperate hope
To find some solace for your wild unrest.

And now at last authentic word I bring,
Witnessed by every dead and living thing;
Good tidings of great joy for you, for all:
There is no God; no Fiend with names divine
Made us and tortures us; if we must pine,
It is to satiate no Being's gall.

It was the dark delusion of a dream,
That living Person conscious and supreme,
Whom we must curse for cursing us with life;
Whom we must curse because the life He gave
Could not be buried in the quiet grave,
Could not be killed by poison or by knife.

This little life is all we must endure,
The grave's most holy peace is ever sure,
We fall asleep and never wake again;
Nothing is of us but the mouldering flesh,
Whose elements dissolve and merge afresh
In earth, air, water, plants, and other men.

We finish thus; and all our wretched race
Shall finish with its cycle, and give place
To other beings, with their own time-doom:
Infinite æons ere our kind began;
Infinite æons after the last man
Has joined the mammoth in earth's tomb and womb.

We bow down to the universal laws,
Which never had for man a special clause
Of cruelty or kindness, love or hate:

If toads and vultures are obscene to sight,
If tigers burn with beauty and with might,
Is it by favour or by wrath of Fate?

All substance lives and struggles evermore
Through countless shapes continually at war,
By countless interactions interknit:
If one is born a certain day on earth,
All times and forces tended to that birth,
Not all the world could change or hinder it.

I find no hint throughout the Universe
Of good or ill, of blessing or of curse;
I find alone Necessity Supreme;
With infinite Mystery, abysmal, dark,
Unlighted ever by the faintest spark
For us the flitting shadows of a dream.

O Brothers of sad lives! they are so brief;
A few short years must bring us all relief:
Can we not bear these years of labouring breath?
But if you would not this poor life fulfil,
Lo, you are free to end it when you will,
Without the fear of waking after death.—

The organ-like vibrations of his voice
Trilled through the vaulted aisles and died away;
The yearning of the tones which bade rejoice
Was sad and tender as a requiem lay:
Our shadowy congregation rested still
As brooding on that 'End it when you will.'

. . .

XX

I sat me weary on a pillar's base,
And leaned against the shaft; for broad moonlight
O'erflowed the peacefulness of cloistered space,
A shore of shadow slanting from the right:
The great cathedral's western front stood there,
A wave-worn rock in that calm sea of air.

Before it, opposite my place of rest,
Two figures faced each other, large, austere;
A couchant sphinx in shadow to the breast,
An angel standing in the moonlight clear;
So mighty by magnificence of form,
They were not dwarfed beneath that mass enorm.

Upon the cross-hilt of a naked sword
The angel's hands, as prompt to smite, were held;
His vigilant, intense regard was poured
Upon the creature placidly unquelled,
Whose front was set at level gaze which took
No heed of aught, a solemn trance-like look.

And as I pondered these opposéd shapes
My eyelids sank in stupor, that dull swoon
Which drugs and with a leaden mantle drapes
The outworn to worse weariness. But soon
A sharp and clashing noise the stillness broke,
And from the evil lethargy I woke.

The angel's wings had fallen, stone on stone,
And lay there shattered; hence the sudden sound:
A warrior leaning on his sword alone
Now watched the sphinx with that regard profound;
The sphinx unchanged looked forthright, as aware
Of nothing in the vast abyss of air.

Again I sank in that repose unsweet,
Again a clashing noise my slumber rent;

The warrior's sword lay broken at his feet:
An unarmed man with raised hands impotent
Now stood before the sphinx, which ever kept
Such mien as if with open eyes it slept.

My eyelids sank in spite of wonder grown;
A louder crash upstartled me in dread:
The man had fallen forward, stone on stone,
And lay there shattered, with his trunkless head
Between the monster's large quiescent paws,
Beneath its grand front changeless as life's laws.

The moon had circled westward full and bright,
And made the temple-front a mystic dream,
And bathed the whole enclosure with its light,
The sworded angel's wrecks, the sphinx supreme:
I pondered long that cold majestic face
Whose vision seemed of infinite void space.

XXI

Anear the centre of that northern crest
Stands out a level upland bleak and bare,
From which the city east and south and west
Sinks gently in long waves; and thronéd there
An Image sits, stupendous, superhuman,
The bronze colossus of a wingéd Woman,
Upon a graded granite base foursquare.

Low-seated she leans forward massively,
With cheek on clenched left hand, the forearm's might
Erect, its elbow on her rounded knee;
Across a clasped book in her lap the right
Upholds a pair of compasses; she gazes
With full set eyes, but wandering in thick mazes
Of sombre thought beholds no outward sight.

Words cannot picture her; but all men know
That solemn sketch the pure sad artist [4] wrought
Three centuries and threescore years ago,
With phantasies of his peculiar thought:
The instruments of carpentry and science
Scattered about her feet, in strange alliance
With the keen wolf-hound sleeping undistraught;

Scales, hour-glass, bell, and magic-square above;
The grave and solid infant perched beside,
With open winglets that might bear a dove,
Intent upon its tablets, heavy-eyed;
Her folded wings as of a mighty eagle,
But all too impotent to lift the regal
Robustness of her earth-born strength and pride;

And with those wings, and that light wreath which seems
To mock her grand head and the knotted frown
Of forehead charged with baleful thoughts and dreams,
The household bunch of keys, the housewife's gown
Voluminous, indented, and yet rigid
As if a shell of burnished metal frigid,
The feet thick-shod to tread all weakness down;

The comet hanging o'er the waste dark seas,
The massy rainbow curved in front of it
Beyond the village with the masts and trees;

[4] Albrecht Dürer

The snaky imp, dog-headed, from the Pit,
Bearing upon its batlike leathern pinions
Her name unfolded in the sun's dominions,
The 'MELENCOLIA' that transcends all wit.

Thus has the artist copied her, and thus
Surrounded to expound her form sublime,
Her fate heroic and calamitous;
Fronting the dreadful mysteries of Time,
Unvanquished in defeat and desolation,
Undaunted in the hopeless conflagration
Of the day setting on her baffled prime.

Baffled and beaten back she works on still,
Weary and sick of soul she works the more,
Sustained by her indomitable will:
The hands shall fashion and the brain shall pore,
And all her sorrow shall be turned to labour,
Till Death the friend-foe piercing with his sabre
That mighty heart of hearts ends bitter war.

But as if blacker night could dawn on night,
With tenfold gloom on moonless night unstarred,
A sense more tragic than defeat and blight,
More desperate than strife with hope debarred,
More fatal than the adamantine Never
Encompassing her passionate endeavour,
Dawns glooming in her tenebrous regard:

The sense that every struggle brings defeat
Because Fate holds no prize to crown success;
That all the oracles are dumb or cheat
Because they have no secret to express;
That none can pierce the vast black veil uncertain
Because there is no light beyond the curtain;
That all is vanity and nothingness.

Titanic from her high throne in the north,
That City's sombre Patroness and Queen,
In bronze sublimity she gazes forth
Over her Capital of teen and threne,[5]
Over the river with its isles and bridges,
The marsh and moorland, to the stern rock-ridges,
Confronting them with a coëval mien.

The moving moon and stars from east to west
Circle before her in the sea of air;
Shadows and gleams glide round her solemn rest.
Her subjects often gaze up to her there:
The strong to drink new strength of iron endurance,
The weak new terrors; all, renewed assurance
And confirmation of the old despair.

William Blake

He came to the desert of London town
Grey miles long;
He wandered up and he wandered down,
Singing a quiet song.

He came to the desert of London town,
Mirk miles broad;
He wandered up and he wandered down,
Ever alone with God.

There were thousands and thousands of human kind
In this desert of brick and stone:
But some were deaf and some were blind,
And he was there alone.

At length the good hour came; he died
As he had lived, alone:
He was not missed from the desert wide,
Perhaps he was found at the Throne.

[*A Voice from the Nile and other Poems*, 1884]

[5] sorrow and lamentation

Sunday up the River[6]

AN IDYLL OF COCKAIGNE[7]

I

I LOOKED out into the morning,
  I looked out into the west:
The soft blue eye of the quiet sky
  Still drooped in dreamy rest;

The trees were still like clouds there,
  The clouds like mountains dim;
The broad mist lay, a silver bay
  Whose tide was at the brim.

I looked out into the morning,
  I looked out into the east:
The flood of light upon the night
  Had silently increased;

The sky was pale with fervour,
  The distant trees were grey,
The hill-lines drawn like waves of dawn
  Dissolving in the day.

I looked out into the morning;
  Looked east, looked west, with glee:
O richest day of happy May,
  My Love will spend with me!

IV

The church bells are ringing:
  How green the earth, how fresh and fair!
The thrushes are singing:
  What rapture but to breathe this air!

The church bells are ringing:
  Lo, how the river dreameth there!
The thrushes are singing:
  Green flames wave lightly everywhere!

The church bells are ringing:
  How all the world breathes praise and prayer!
The thrushes are singing:
  What Sabbath peace doth trance the air!

X

Were I a real Poet, I would sing
Such joyous songs of you, and all mere truth;
As true as buds and tender leaves in Spring,
As true as lofty dreams in dreamful youth;
That men should cry: How foolish every one
Who thinks the world is getting out of tune!
Where is the tarnish in our golden sun?
Where is the clouding in our crystal moon?
The lark sings now the eversame new song
With which it soared through Eden's purest skies;
This poet's music doth for us prolong
The very speech Love learnt in Paradise;
This maiden is as young and pure and fair
As Eve agaze on Adam sleeping there.

[6] Reprinted from *Fraser's Magazine* (1869) in the 1880 volume, *The City of Dreadful Night and other Poems.*
[7] The land of cockneys; also an imaginary country of idleness and luxury.

George Meredith

1828–1909

MODERN LOVE[1]

I

BY this he knew she wept with waking eyes:
That, at his hand's light quiver by her head,
The strange low sobs that shook their common bed,
Were called into her with a sharp surprise,
And strangled mute, like little gaping snakes,
Dreadfully venomous to him. She lay
Stone-still, and the long darkness flowed away
With muffled pulses. Then, as midnight makes
Her giant heart of Memory and Tears

[1] The sequence of poems entitled *Modern Love* was published in 1862. It is autobiographical.

Drink the pale drug of silence, and so beat
Sleep's heavy measure, they from head to feet
Were moveless, looking through their dead black years,
By vain regret scrawled over the blank wall.
Like sculptured effigies they might be seen
Upon their marriage-tomb, the sword [2] between;
Each wishing for the sword that severs all.

II

It ended, and the morrow brought the task.
Her eyes were guilty gates, that let him in
By shutting all too zealous for their sin:
Each sucked a secret, and each wore a mask.
But, oh, the bitter taste her beauty had!
He sickened as at breath of poison-flowers:
A languid humour stole among the hours,
And if their smiles encountered, he went mad,
And raged deep inward, till the light was brown
Before his vision, and the world, forgot,
Looked wicked as some old dull murder-spot.
A star with lurid beams, she seemed to crown
The pit of infamy: and then again
He feinted on his vengefulness, and strove
To ape the magnanimity of love,
And smote himself, a shuddering heap of pain.

IV

All other joy of life he strove to warm,
And magnify, and catch them to his lip:
But they had suffered shipwreck with the ship,
And gazed upon him sallow from the storm.
Or if Delusion came, 'twas but to show
The coming minute mock the one that went.
Cold as a mountain in its star-pitched tent,
Stood high Philosophy, less friend than foe:
Whom self-caged Passion, from its prison-bars,
Is always watching with a wondering hate.
Not till the fire is dying in the grate,
Look we for any kinship with the stars.
Oh, wisdom never comes when it is gold,
And the great price we pay for it full worth:
We have it only when we are half earth.
Little avails that coinage to the old!

VIII

Yet it was plain she struggled, and that salt
Of righteous feeling made her pitiful.
Poor twisting worm, so queenly beautiful!
Where came the cleft between us? whose the fault?
My tears are on thee, that have rarely dropped
As balm for any bitter wound of mine:
My breast will open for thee at a sign!
But, no: we are two reed-pipes, coarsely stopped:
The God [3] once filled them with his mellow breath;
And they were music till he flung them down,
Used! used! Hear now the discord-loving clown
Puff his gross spirit in them, worse than death!
I do not know myself without thee more:
In this unholy battle I grow base:
If the same soul be under the same face,
Speak, and a taste of that old time restore!

XVII

At dinner, she is hostess, I am host.
Went the feast ever cheerfuller? She keeps
The Topic over intellectual deeps
In buoyancy afloat. They see no ghost.
With sparkling surface-eyes we ply the ball:
It is in truth a most contagious game:
HIDING THE SKELETON, shall be its name.
Such play as this the devils might appal!

[2] In the days of chivalry chastity between lovers was considered insured by the presence of a naked sword.

[3] Apollo

But here's the greater wonder; in that we
Enamoured of an acting nought can tire,
Each other, like true hypocrites admire;
Warm-lighted looks, Love's ephemerioe,
Shoot gaily o'er the dishes and the wine.
We waken envy of our happy lot.
Fast, sweet, and golden, shows the marriage-knot.
Dear guests, you now have seen Love's corpse-light shine.

XXI

We three are on the cedar-shadowed lawn;
My friend being third. He who at love once laughed
Is in the weak rib by a fatal shaft
Struck through, and tells his passion's bashful dawn
And radiant culmination, glorious crown,
When 'this' she said: went 'thus': most wondrous she.
Our eyes grow white, encountering; that we are three,
Forgetful; then together we look down.
But he demands our blessing; is convinced
That words of wedded lovers must bring good.
We question; if we dare! or if we should!
And pat him, with light laugh. We have not winced.
Next, she has fallen. Fainting points the sign
To happy things in wedlock. When she wakes,
She looks the star that thro' the cedar shakes:
Her lost moist hand clings mortally to mine.

XXIX

Am I failing? For no longer can I cast
A glory round about his head of gold.
Glory she wears, but springing from the mould;
Not like the consecration of the Past!
Is my soul beggared? Something more than earth
I cry for still: I cannot be at peace
In having Love upon a mortal lease.
I cannot take the woman at her worth!
Where is the ancient wealth wherewith I clothed
Our human nakedness, and could endow
With spiritual splendour a white brow
That else had grinned at me the fact I loathed?
A kiss is but a kiss now! and no wave
Of a great flood that whirls me to the sea.
But, as you will! we'll sit contentedly,
And eat our pot of honey on the grave.

XXX

What are we first? First, animals; and next
Intelligences at a leap; on whom
Pale lies the distant shadow of the tomb,
And all that draweth on the tomb for text.
Into which state comes Love, the crowning sun:
Beneath whose light the shadow loses form.
We are the lords of life, and life is warm.
Intelligence and instinct now are one.
But nature says: 'My children most they seem
When they least know me: therefore I decree
That they shall suffer.' Swift doth young Love flee,
And we stand wakened, shivering from our dream.
Then if we study Nature we are wise.
Thus do the few who live but with the day:
The scientific animals are they.—
Lady, this is my sonnet to your eyes.

XLIII

Mark where the pressing wind shoots javelin-like,
Its skeleton shadow on the broad-backed wave!
Here is a fitting spot to dig Love's grave;
Here where the ponderous breakers plunge and strike,
And dart their hissing tongues high up the sand:
In hearing of the ocean, and in sight

Of those ribbed wind-streaks running into white.
If I the death of Love had deeply planned,
I never could have made it half so sure,
As by the unblest kisses which upbraid
The full-waked sense; or failing that, degrade!
'Tis morning: but no morning can restore
What we have forfeited. I see no sin:
The wrong is mixed. In tragic life, God wot,
No villain need be! Passions spin the plot:
We are betrayed by what is false within.

XLVI

At last we parley: we so strangely dumb
In such a close communion! It befell
About the sounding of the Matin-bell,
And lo! her place was vacant, and the hum
Of loneliness was round me. Then I rose,
And my disordered brain did guide my foot
To that old wood where our first love-salute
Was interchanged: the source of many throes!
There did I see her, not alone. I moved
Toward her, and made proffer of my arm.
She took it simply, with no rude alarm;
And that disturbing shadow passed reproved.
I felt the pained speech coming, and declared
My firm belief in her, ere she could speak.
A ghastly morning came into her cheek,
While with a widening soul on me she stared.

XLVIII

Their sense is with their senses all mixed in,
Destroyed by subtleties these women are!
More brain, O Lord, more brain! or we shall mar
Utterly this fair garden we might win.
Behold! I looked for peace, and thought it near.
Our inmost hearts had opened, each to each.
We drank the pure daylight of honest speech.
Alas! that was the fatal draught, I fear.
For when of my lost Lady came the word,
This woman, O this agony of flesh!
Jealous devotion bade her break the mesh,
That I might seek that other like a bird.
I do adore the nobleness! despise
The act! She has gone forth, I know not where.
Will the hard world my sentience of her share?
I feel the truth; so let the world surmise.

XLIX

He found her by the ocean's moaning verge,
Nor any wicked change in her discerned;
And she believed his old love had returned,
Which was her exultation, and her scourge.
She took his hand, and walked with him, and seemed
The wife he sought, though shadow-like and dry.
She had one terror, lest her heart should sigh,
And tell her loudly she no longer dreamed.
She dared not say, 'This is my breast: look in.'
But there's a strength to help the desperate weak.
That night he learned how silence best can speak
The awful things when Pity pleads for Sin.
About the middle of the night her call
Was heard, and he came wondering to the bed.
'Now kiss me, dear! it may be, now!' she said.
Lethe had passed those lips, and he knew all.

L

Thus piteously Love closed what he begat:
The union of this ever-diverse pair!
These two were rapid falcons in a snare,
Condemned to do the flitting of the bat.
Lovers beneath the singing sky of May,

They wandered once; clear as the dew on flowers:
But they fed not on the advancing hours:
Their hearts held cravings for the buried day.
Then each applied to each that fatal knife,
Deep questioning, which probes to endless dole.
Ah, what a dusty answer gets the soul
When hot for certainties in this our life!—
In tragic hints here see what evermore
Moves dark as yonder midnight ocean's force,
Thundering like ramping hosts of warrior horse,
To throw that faint thin line upon the shore!

Juggling Jerry[4]

Pitch here the tent, while the old horse grazes:
By the old hedge-side we'll halt a stage.
It's nigh my last above the daisies:
My next leaf'll be man's blank page.
Yes, my old girl! and it's no use crying:
Juggler, constable, king, must bow.
One that outjuggles all's been spying
Long to have me, and he has me now.

We've travelled times to this old common:
Often we've hung our pots in the gorse.
We've had a stirring life, old woman!
You, and I, and the old grey horse.
Races, and fairs, and royal occasions,
Found us coming to their call:
Now they'll miss us at our stations:
There's a Juggler outjuggles all!

Up goes the lark, as if all were jolly!
Over the duck-pond the willow shakes.
Easy to think that grieving's folly,
When the hand's firm as driven stakes!
Ay, when we're strong, and braced, and manful,
Life's a sweet fiddle: but we're a batch
Born to become the Great Juggler's han'ful:
Balls he shies up, and is safe to catch.

Here's where the lads of the village cricket:
I was a lad not wide from here:
Couldn't I whip off the ball from the wicket?
Like an old world those days appear!
Donkey, sheep, geese, and thatched ale-house—I know them!
They are old friends of my halts, and seem,
Somehow, as if kind thanks I owe them:
Juggling don't hinder the heart's esteem.

Juggling's no sin, for we must have victual:
Nature allows us to bait for the fool.
Holding one's own makes us juggle no little;
But, to increase it, hard juggling's the rule.
You that are sneering at my profession,
Haven't you juggled a vast amount?
There's the Prime Minister, in one Session,
Juggles more games than my sins'll count.

I've murdered insects with mock thunder:
Conscience, for that, in men don't quail.
I've made bread from the bump of wonder:
That's my business, and there's my tale.
Fashion and rank all praised the professor:
Ay! and I've had my smile from the Queen:
Bravo, Jerry! she meant: God bless her!
Ain't this a sermon on that scene?

I've studied men from my topsy-turvy
Close, and, I reckon, rather true.
Some are fine fellows: some, right scurvy:
Most, a dash between the two.
But it's a woman, old girl, that makes me
Think more kindly of the race:
And it's a woman, old girl, that shakes me
When the Great Juggler I must face.

We two were married, due and legal:
Honest we've lived since we've been one.

[4] Published in *Modern Love and Poems of the English Roadside,* 1862.

Lord! I could then jump like an eagle:
You danced bright as a bit o' the sun.
Birds in a May-bush we were! right merry!
All night we kiss'd, we juggled all day.
Joy was the heart of Juggling Jerry!
Now from his old girl he's juggled away.

It's past parsons to console us:
No, nor no doctor fetch for me:
I can die without my bolus;
Two of a trade, lass, never agree!
Parson and Doctor! — don't they love rarely,
Fighting the devil in other men's fields!
Stand up yourself and match him fairly:
Then see how the rascal yields!

I, lass, have lived no gipsy, flaunting
Finery while his poor helpmate grubs:
Coin I've stored, and you won't be wanting:
You sha'n't beg from the troughs and tubs.
Nobly you've stuck to me, though in his kitchen
Many a Marquis would hail you Cook!
Palaces you could have ruled and grown rich in,
But your old Jerry you never forsook.

Hand up the chirper! ripe ale winks in it;
Let's have comfort and be at peace.
Once a stout draught made me light as a linnet.
Cheer up! the Lord must have his lease.
May be — for none see in that black hollow —
It's just a place where we're held in pawn,
And, when the Great Juggler makes as to swallow,
It's just the sword-trick — I ain't quite gone!

Yonder came smells of the gorse, so nutty,
Gold-like and warm: it's the prime of May.
Better than mortar, brick and putty,
Is God's house on a blowing day.
Lean me more up the mound; now I feel it:
All the old heath-smells! Ain't it strange?
There's the world laughing, as if to conceal it,
But He's by us, juggling the change.

I mind it well, by the sea-beach lying,
Once — it's long gone — when two gulls we beheld,
Which, as the moon got up, were flying
Down a big wave that sparked and swelled.
Crack, went a gun: one fell: the second
Wheeled round him twice, and was off for new luck:
There in the dark her white wing beckon'd: —
Drop me a kiss — I'm the bird dead-struck!

The Lark Ascending[5]

He rises and begins to round,
He drops the silver chain of sound,
Of many links without a break,
In chirrup, whistle, slur and shake,
All intervolved and spreading wide,
Like water-dimples down a tide
Where ripple ripple overcurls
And eddy into eddy whirls;
A press of hurried notes that run
So fleet they scarce are more than one,
Yet changeingly the trills repeat
And linger ringing while they fleet,
Sweet to the quick o' the ear, and dear
To her beyond the handmaid ear,
Who sits beside our inner springs,
Too often dry for this he brings,
Which seems the very jet of earth
At sight of sun, her music's mirth,
As up he wings the spiral stair,
A song of light, and pierces air
With fountain ardour, fountain play,
To reach the shining tops of day,
And drink in everything discerned

[5] This and the following poem were published in *Poems and Lyrics of the Joy of Earth,* 1883.

An ecstasy to music turned,
Impelled by what his happy bill
Disperses; drinking, showering still,
Unthinking save that he may give
His voice the outlet, there to live
Renewed in endless notes of glee,
So thirsty of his voice is he,
For all to hear and all to know
That he is joy, awake, aglow,
The tumult of the heart to hear
Through pureness filtered crystal-clear,
And know the pleasure sprinkled bright
By simple singing of delight,
Shrill, irreflective, unrestrained,
Rapt, ringing, on the jet sustained
Without a break, without a fall,
Sweet-silvery, sheer lyrical,
Perennial, quavering up the chord
Like myriad dews of sunny sward
That trembling into fulness shine,
And sparkle dropping argentine;
Such wooing as the ear receives
From zephyr caught in choric leaves
Of aspens when their chattering net
Is flushed to white with shivers wet;
And such the water-spirit's chime
On mountain heights in morning's prime,
Too freshly sweet to seem excess,
Too animate to need a stress;
But wider over many heads
The starry voice ascending spreads,
Awakening, as it waxes thin,
The best in us to him akin;
And every face to watch him raised,
Puts on the light of children praised,
So rich our human pleasure ripes
When sweetness on sincereness pipes,
Though nought be promised from the seas,
But only a soft-ruffling breeze
Sweep glittering on a still content,
Serenity in ravishment.

For singing till his heaven fills,
'Tis love of earth that he instils,
And ever winging up and up,
Our valley is his golden cup,
And he the wine which overflows
To lift us with him as he goes:
The woods and brooks, the sheep and kine
He is, the hills, the human line,
The meadows green, the fallows brown,
The dreams of labour in the town;
He sings the sap, the quickened veins;
The wedding song of sun and rains
He is, the dance of children, thanks
Of sowers, shout of primrose-banks,
And eye of violets while they breathe;
All these the circling song will wreathe,
And you shall hear the herb and tree,
The better heart of men shall see,
Shall feel celestially, as long
As you crave nothing save the song.
Was never voice of ours could say
Our inmost in the sweetest way,
Like yonder voice aloft, and link
All hearers in the song they drink.
Our wisdom speaks from failing blood,
Our passion is too full in flood,
We want the key of this wild note
Of truthful in a tuneful throat,
The song seraphically free
Of taint of personality,
So pure that it salutes the suns
The voice of one for millions,
In whom the millions rejoice
For giving their one spirit voice.

Yet men have we, whom we revere,
Now names, and men still housing here,
Whose lives, by many a battle-dint
Defaced, and grinding wheels on flint,
Yield substance, though they sing not, sweet
For song our highest heaven to greet:
Whom heavenly singing gives us new,
Enspheres them brilliant in our blue,
From firmest base to farthest leap,
Because their love of Earth is deep,
And they are warriors in accord
With life to serve, and pass reward,
So touching purest and so heard
In the brain's reflex of yon bird:
Wherefore their soul in me, or mine,
Through self-forgetfulness divine,
In them, that song aloft maintains,
To fill the sky and thrill the plains

With showerings drawn from human stores,
As he to silence nearer soars,
Extends the world at wings and dome,
More spacious making more our home,
Till lost on his aërial rings
In light, and then the fancy sings.

Lucifer in Starlight

On a starred night Prince Lucifer uprose.
Tired of his dark dominions swung the fiend
Above the rolling ball in cloud part screened,
Where sinners hugged their spectre of repose.
Poor prey to his hot fire of pride were those.
And now upon his western wing he leaned,
Now his huge bulk o'er Afric's sands careened,
Now the black planet shadowed Arctic snows.
Soaring through wider zones that pricked his scars
With memory of the old revolt from Awe,
He reached a middle height, and at the stars,
Which are the brain of heaven, he looked, and sank.
Around the ancient track marched, rank on rank,
The army of unalterable law.

Dirge in Woods [6]

A wind sways the pines,
And below
Not a breath of wild air;
Still as the mosses that glow
On the flooring and over the lines
Of the roots here and there.
The pine-tree drops its dead;
They are quiet, as under the sea.
Overhead, overhead
Rushes life in a race,
As the clouds the clouds chase;
And we go,
And we drop like the fruits of the tree,
Even we,
Even so.

[6] Published, together with the following, in *A Reading of Earth*, 1888.

Meditation under Stars

What links are ours with orbs that are
So resolutely far:
The solitary asks, and they
Give radiance as from a shield:
Still as the death of day,
The seen, the unrevealed.
Implacable they shine
To us who would of Life obtain
An answer for the life we strain,
To nourish with one sign.
Nor can imagination throw
The penetrative shaft: we pass
The breath of thought, who would divine
If haply they may grow
As Earth; have our desire to know;
If life comes there to grain from grass,
And flowers like ours of toil and pain;
Has passion to beat bar,
Win space from cleaving brain;
The mystic link attain,
Whereby star holds on star.

Those visible immortals beam
Allurement to the dream:
Ireful at human hungers brook
No question in the look.
For ever virgin to our sense,
Remote they wane to gaze intense:
Prolong it, and in ruthlessness they smite
The beating heart behind the ball of sight:
Till we conceive their heavens hoar,
Those lights they raise but sparkles frore,
And Earth, our blood-warm Earth, a shuddering prey
To that frigidity of brainless ray.

Yet space is given for breath of thought
Beyond our bounds when musing: more
When to that musing love is brought,

And love is asked of love's wherefore.
'Tis Earth's, her gift; else have we nought:
Her gift, her secret, here our tie.
And not with her and yonder sky?
Bethink you: were it Earth alone
Breeds love, would not her region be
The sole delight and throne
Of generous Deity?

To deeper than this ball of sight
Appeal the lustrous people of the night.
Fronting yon shoreless, sown with fiery sails,
It is our ravenous that quails,
Flesh by its craven thirsts and fears distraught.
The spirit leaps alight,
Doubts not in them is he,
The binder of his sheaves, the same, the right:
Of magnitude to magnitude is wrought,
To feel it large of the great life they hold:
In them to come, or vaster intervolved,
The issues known in us, our unsolved solved:
That there with toil Life climbs the self-same Tree,
Whose roots enrichment have from ripeness dropped.
So may we read and little find them cold:
Let it but be the lord of Mind to guide
Our eyes; no branch of Reason's growing lopped;
Nor dreaming on a dream; but fortified
By day to penetrate black midnight; see,
Hear, feel, outside the senses; even that we,
The specks of dust upon a mound of mould,
We who reflect those rays, though low our place,
To them are lastingly allied.

So may we read, and little find them cold:
Not frosty lamps illumining dead space,
Not distant aliens, not senseless Powers.
The fire is in them whereof we are born;
The music of their motion may be ours.
Spirit shall deem them beckoning Earth and voiced
Sisterly to her, in her beams rejoiced.
Of love the grand impulsion, we behold
The love that lends her grace
Among the starry fold.
Then at new flood of customary morn,
Look at her through her showers,
Her mists, her streaming gold,
A wonder edges the familiar face:
She wears no more that robe of printed hours;
Half strange seems Earth, and sweeter than her flowers.

Francis Thompson

1859–1907

THE HOUND OF HEAVEN[1]

I FLED Him, down the nights and down the days;
I fled Him, down the arches of the years;
I fled Him, down the labyrinthine ways
Of my own mind; and in the mist of tears
I hid from Him, and under running laughter.
Up vistaed hopes I sped;
And shot, precipitated,
Adown Titanic glooms of chasméd fears,
From those strong Feet that followed, followed after.
But with unhurrying chase,
And unperturbéd pace,
Deliberate speed, majestic instancy,
They beat — and a Voice beat
More instant than the Feet —
'All things betray thee, who betrayest Me.'

[1] Written in 1890; published in *Poems*, 1893.

I pleaded, outlaw-wise,
By many a hearted casement, curtained red,
Trellised with intertwining charities;
(For, though I knew His love Who followéd,
Yet was I sore adread
Lest, having Him, I must have naught beside);
But, if one little casement parted wide,
The gust of His approach would clash it to.
Fear wist not to evade, as Love wist to pursue.
Across the margent of the world I fled,
And troubled the gold gateways of the stars,
Smiting for shelter on their clangéd bars;
Fretted to dulcet jars
And silvern chatter the pale ports o' the moon.
I said to dawn, Be sudden; to eve, Be soon;
With thy young skiey blossoms heap me over
From this tremendous Lover!
Float thy vague veil about me, lest He see!
I tempted all His servitors, but to find
My own betrayal in their constancy,
In faith to Him their fickleness to me,
Their traitorous trueness, and their loyal deceit.
To all swift things for swiftness did I sue;
Clung to the whistling mane of every wind.
But whether they swept, smoothly fleet,
The long savannahs of the blue;
Or whether, Thunder-driven,
They clanged his chariot 'thwart a heaven
Plashy with flying lightnings round the spurn o' their feet: —
Fear wist not to evade as Love wist to pursue.
Still with unhurrying chase,
And unperturbéd pace,
Deliberate speed, majestic instancy,
Came on the following Feet,
And a Voice above their beat —
'Naught shelters thee, who wilt not shelter Me.'

I sought no more that after which I strayed
In face of man or maid;
But still within the little children's eyes
Seems something, something that replies;
They at least are for me, surely for me!
I turned me to them very wistfully;
But, just as their young eyes grew sudden fair
With dawning answers there,
Their angel plucked them from me by the hair.
'Come then, ye other children, Nature's — share
With me' (said I) 'your delicate fellowship;
Let me greet you lip to lip,
Let me twine with you caresses,
Wantoning
With our Lady-Mother's vagrant tresses,
Banqueting
With her in her wind-walled palace,
Underneath her azured daïs,
Quaffing, as your taintless way is,
From a chalice
Lucent-weeping out of the dayspring.
So it was done:
I in their delicate fellowship was one —
Drew the bolt of Nature's secrecies.
I knew all the swift importings
On the wilful face of skies;
I knew how the clouds arise
Spuméd of the wild sea-snortings;
All that's born or dies
Rose and drooped with — made them shapers
Of mine own moods, or wailful or divine —
With them joyed and was bereaven.
I was heavy with the even,
When she lit her glimmering tapers
Round the day's dead sanctities.
I laughed in the morning's eyes.
I triumphed and I saddened with all weather,

Heaven and I wept together,
And its sweet tears were salt with mortal mine;
Against the red throb of its sunset-heart
I laid my own to beat,
And share commingling heat;
But not by that, by that, was eased my human smart.
In vain my tears were wet on Heaven's grey cheek.
For ah! we know not what each other says,
These things and I; in sound *I* speak—
Their sound is but their stir, they speak by silences.
Nature, poor stepdame, cannot slake my drouth;
Let her, if she would owe me,
Drop yon blue bosom-veil of sky, and show me
The breasts o' her tenderness:
Never did any milk of hers once bless
My thirsting mouth.
Nigh and nigh draws the chase,
With unperturbéd pace,
Deliberate speed, majestic instancy;
And past those noiséd Feet
A voice comes yet more fleet—
Lo! naught contents thee, who content'st not Me.

Naked I wait Thy love's uplifted stroke!
My harness piece by piece Thou hast hewn from me,
And smitten me to my knee;
I am defenceless utterly.
I slept, methinks, and woke,
And, slowly gazing, find me stripped in sleep.
In the rash lustihead of my young powers,
I shook the pillaring hours
And pulled my life upon me; grimed with smears,
I stand amid the dust o' the mounded years—
My mangled youth lies dead beneath the heap.
My days have crackled and gone up in smoke,
Have puffed and burst as sun-starts on a stream.
Yea, faileth now even dream
The dreamer, and the lute the lutanist;
Even the linked fantasies, in whose blossomy twist
I swung the earth a trinket at my wrist,
Are yielding; cords of all too weak account
For earth with heavy griefs so overplussed.
Ah! is Thy love indeed
A weed, albeit an amaranthine weed,
Suffering no flowers except its own to mount?
Ah! must—
Designer infinite!—
Ah! must Thou char the wood ere Thou canst limn with it?
My freshness spent its wavering shower i' the dust;
And now my heart is as a broken fount,
Wherein tear-drippings stagnate, spilt down ever
From the dank thoughts that shiver
Upon the sighful branches of my mind.
Such is; what is to be?
The pulp so bitter, how shall taste the rind?
I dimly guess what Time in mists confounds;
Yet ever and anon a trumpet sounds
From the hid battlements of Eternity;
Those shaken mists a space unsettle, then
Round the half-glimpséd turrets slowly wash again.
But not ere him who summoneth
I first have seen, enwound
With glooming robes purpureal, cypress-crowned;
His name I know, and what his trumpet saith.
Whether man's heart or life it be which yields
Thee harvest, must Thy harvest fields
Be dunged with rotten death?

Now of that long pursuit
Comes on at hand the bruit;
That Voice is round me like a bursting sea:
'And is thy earth so marred,

Shattered in shard on shard?
Lo, all things fly thee, for thou fliest Me!
Strange, piteous, futile thing!
Wherefore should any set thee love apart?
Seeing none but I makes much of naught' (He said),
'And human love needs human meriting:
How hast thou merited —
Of all man's clotted clay the dingiest clot?
Alack thou knowest not
How little worthy of any love thou art!
Whom wilt thou find to love ignoble thee
Save Me, save only Me?
All which I took from thee I did but take,
Not for thy harms,
But just that thou might'st seek it in My arms.
All which thy child's mistake
Fancies as lost, I have stored for thee at home;
Rise, clasp My hand, and come!'
Halts by me that footfall:
Is my gloom, after all,
Shade of His hand, outstretched caressingly?
'Ah, fondest, blindest, weakest,
I am He whom thou seekest!
Thou dravest love from thee, who dravest Me.'

Thomas Hardy

1840–1928

Hap

If but some vengeful god would call to me
From up the sky, and laugh: 'Thou suffering thing,
Know that thy sorrow is my ecstasy,
That thy love's loss is my hate's profiting!'

Then would I bear it, clench myself, and die,
Steeled by the sense of ire unmerited;
Half-eased in that a Powerfuller than I
Had willed and meted me the tears I shed.

But not so. How arrives it joy lies slain,
And why unblooms the best hope ever sown?
— Crass Casualty obstructs the sun and rain,
And dicing Time for gladness casts a moan. . . .
These purblind Doomsters had as readily strown
Blisses about my pilgrimage as pain.

[*Wessex Poems,* 1898]

In a Wood

from *The Woodlanders*[1]

Pale beech and pine so blue,
Set in one clay,
Bough to bough cannot you
Live out your day?
When the rains skim and skip,
Why mar sweet comradeship,
Blighting with poison-drip
Neighbourly spray?

Heart-halt and spirit-lame,
City-opprest,
Unto this wood I came
As to a nest;
Dreaming that sylvan peace
Offered the harrowed ease —
Nature a soft release
From men's unrest.

But, having entered in,
Great growths and small
Show them to men akin —
Combatants all.

[1] Though Hardy so identifies the poem, it does not appear in the novel issued in 1887.

Sycamore shoulders oak,
Bines the slim sapling yoke,
Ivy-spun halters choke
Elms stout and tall.

Touches from ash, O wych,
Sting you like scorn!
You, too, brave hollies, twitch
Sidelong from thorn.
Even the rank poplars bear
Lothly a rival's air,
Cankering in black despair
If overborne.

Since, then, no grace I find
Taught me of trees,
Turn I back to my kind,
Worthy as these.
There at least smiles abound,
There discourse trills around,
There, now and then, are found
Life-loyalties.

[*Wessex Poems*, 1898]

The Impercipient

(*At a Cathedral Service*)

THAT with this bright believing band
I have no claim to be,
That faiths by which my comrades stand
Seem fantasies to me,
And mirage-mists their Shining Land,
Is a strange destiny.

Why thus my soul should be consigned
To infelicity,
Why always I must feel as blind
To sights my brethren see,
Why joys they've found I cannot find,
Abides a mystery.

Since heart of mine knows not that ease
Which they know; since it be
That He who breathes All's Well to these
Breathes no All's-Well to me,
My lack might move their sympathies
And Christian charity!

I am like a gazer who should mark
An inland company
Standing upfingered, with, 'Hark! hark!
The glorious distant sea!'
And feel, 'Alas, 'tis but yon dark
And wind-swept pine to me!'

Yet I would bear my shortcomings
With meet tranquillity,
But for the charge that blessed things
I'd liefer not have be.
O, doth a bird deprived of wings
Go earth-bound wilfully!

* * *

Enough. As yet disquiet clings
About us. Rest shall we.

[*Wessex Poems*, 1898]

A Broken Appointment

You did not come,
And marching Time drew on, and wore me numb.—
Yet less for loss of your dear presence there
Than that I thus found lacking in your make
That high compassion which can overbear
Reluctance for pure lovingkindness' sake
Grieved I, when, as the hope-hour stroked its sum,
You did not come.

You love not me,
And love alone can lend you loyalty;
—I know and knew it. But, unto the store
Of human deeds divine in all but name,
Was it not worth a little hour or more
To add yet this: Once you, a woman, came
To soothe a time-torn man; even though it be
You love not me?

[*Poems of the Past and the Present*, 1902]

The Darkling Thrush

I LEANT upon a coppice gate
When Frost was spectre-gray,

And Winter's dregs made desolate
  The weakening eye of day.
The tangled bine-stems scored the sky
  Like strings of broken lyres,
And all mankind that haunted nigh
  Had sought their household fires.

The land's sharp features seemed to be
  The Century's corpse outleant,
His crypt the cloudy canopy,
  The wind his death-lament.
The ancient pulse of germ and birth
  Was shrunken hard and dry,
And every spirit upon earth
  Seemed fervourless as I.

At once a voice arose among
  The bleak twigs overhead
In a full-hearted evensong
  Of joy illimited;
An aged thrush, frail, gaunt, and small,
  In blast-beruffled plume,
Had chosen thus to fling his soul
  Upon the growing gloom.

So little cause for carolings
  Of such ecstatic sound
Was written on terrestrial things
  Afar or nigh around,
That I could think there trembled through
  His happy good-night air
Some blessed Hope, whereof he knew
  And I was unaware.

[*Poems of the Past and the Present,* 1902]

In Tenebris

I

'Percussus sum sicut foenum, et aruit cor meum.'
—*Ps.* ci.[2]

WINTERTIME nighs;
But my bereavement-pain
It cannot bring again:
  Twice no one dies.

  Flower-petals flee;
But, since it once hath been,
No more that severing scene
  Can harrow me.

  Birds faint in dread:
I shall not lose old strength
In the lone frost's black length:
  Strength long since fled!

  Leaves freeze to dun;
But friends can not turn cold
This season as of old
  For him with none.

  Tempests may scath;
But love can not make smart
Again this year his heart
  Who no heart hath.

  Black is night's cope;
But death will not appal
One who, past doubtings all,
  Waits in unhope.

[*Poems of the Past and the Present,* 1902]

The Dead Quire

I

BESIDE the Mead of Memories,
Where Church-way mounts to Moaning
    Hill,
The sad man sighed his phantasies:
    He seems to sigh them still.

II

''Twas the Birth-tide Eve, and the ham-
    leteers
Made merry with ancient Mellstock zest,
But the Mellstock quire of former years
    Had entered into rest.

[2] 'My heart is smitten, and withered like grass . . .' (*Psalm* 102:4 in King James Version). This poem is the first of a series of three on 'darkness'; in each case the epigraph is taken respectively from one of the Psalms included in the Catholic Office of the Tenebrae. This office comprises the Matins and Lauds of Maundy Thursday, Good Friday, and Saturday before Easter, the ritual dirge and mourning for the dead Christ.

III

'Old Dewy lay by the gaunt yew tree,
And Reuben and Michael a pace behind,
And Bowman with his family
By the wall that the ivies bind.[8]

IV

'The singers had followed one by one,
Treble, and tenor, and thorough-bass;
And the worm that wasteth had begun
To mine their mouldering place.

V

'For two-score years, ere Christ-day light,
Mellstock had throbbed to strains from these;
But now there echoed on the night
No Christmas harmonies.

VI

'Three meadows off, at a dormered inn,
The youth had gathered in high carouse,
And, ranged on settles, some therein
Had drunk them to a drowse.

VII

'Loud, lively, reckless, some had grown,
Each dandling on his jigging knee
Eliza, Dolly, Nance, or Joan —
Livers in levity.

VIII

'The taper flames and hearthfire shine
Grew smoke-hazed to a lurid light,
And songs on subjects not divine
Were warbled forth that night.

IX

'Yet many were sons and grandsons here
Of those who, on such eves gone by,
At that still hour had throated clear
Their anthems to the sky.

X

'The clock belled midnight; and ere long
One shouted, "Now 'tis Christmas morn;
Here's to our women old and young,
And to John Barleycorn!"

XI

'They drink the toast and shout again:
The pewter-ware rings back the boom,
And for a breath-while follows then
A silence in the room.

XII

'When nigh without, as in old days,
The ancient quire of voice and string
Seemed singing words of prayer and praise
As they had used to sing:

XIII

'*While shepherds watch'd their flocks by night,* —
Thus swells the long familiar sound
In many a quaint symphonic flight —
To, *Glory shone around.*

XIV

'The sons defined their fathers' tones,
The widow his whom she had wed,
And others in the minor moans
The viols of the dead.

XV

'Something supernal has the sound
As verse by verse the strain proceeds,
And stilly staring on the ground
Each roysterer holds and heeds.

[8] Hardy once listed 'old church and dance music' among his hobbies; his father and grandfather before him were accomplished rural musicians, and this family love and knowledge of music is reflected in many of Hardy's novels. 'Old Dewy' of this stanza, for instance, memorializes the musician of *Under the Greenwood Tree*. Mrs. Hardy records that the cemetery described here is modeled on that of Stinsford Churchyard, where the elder Hardys were buried.

XVI

'Towards its chorded closing bar
Plaintively, thinly, waned the hymn,
Yet lingered, like the notes afar
Of banded seraphim.

XVII

'With brows abashed, and reverent tread,
The hearkeners sought the tavern door:
But nothing, save wan moonlight, spread
The empty highway o'er.

XVIII

'While on their hearing fixed and tense
The aerial music seemed to sink,
As it were gently moving thence
Along the river brink.

XIX

'Then did the Quick pursue the Dead
By crystal Froom that crinkles there;
And still the viewless quire ahead
Voiced the old holy air.

XX

'By Bank-walk wicket, brightly bleached,
It passed, and 'twixt the hedges twain,
Dogged by the living; till it reached
The bottom of Church Lane.

XXI

'There, at the turning, it was heard
Drawing to where the churchyard lay:
But when they followed thitherward
It smalled, and died away.

XXII

'Each headstone of the quire, each mound,
Confronted them beneath the moon;
But no more floated therearound
That ancient Birth-night tune.

XXIII

'There Dewy lay by the gaunt yew tree,
There Reuben and Michael, a pace behind,
And Bowman with his family
By the wall that the ivies bind. . . .

XXIV

'As from a dream each sobered son
Awoke, and musing reached his door:
'Twas said that of them all, not one
Sat in a tavern more.'

XXV

— The sad man ceased; and ceased to heed
His listener, and crossed the leaze [4]
From Moaning Hill towards the mead —
The Mead of Memories.

[*Time's Laughingstocks*, 1909]

Channel Firing [5]

THAT night your great guns, unawares,
Shook all our coffins as we lay,
And broke the chancel window-squares,
We thought it was the Judgment-day

And sat upright. While drearisome
Arose the howl of wakened hounds:
The mouse let fall the altar-crumb,
The worms drew back into the mounds,

The glebe cow drooled. Till God called, 'No;
It's gunnery practice out at sea
Just as before you went below;
The world is as it used to be:

'All nations striving strong to make
Red war yet redder. Mad as hatters
They do no more for Christés sake
Than you who are helpless in such matters.

'That this is not the judgment-hour
For some of them's a blessed thing,
For if it were they'd have to scour
Hell's floor for so much threatening. . . .

[4] pasture
[5] This prophetic poem was published in *The Fortnightly Review* (May 1914) three months before the outbreak of World War I.

'Ha, ha. It will be warmer when
I blow the trumpet (if indeed
I ever do; for you are men,
And rest eternal sorely need).'

So down we lay again. 'I wonder,
Will the world ever saner be,'
Said one, 'than when He sent us under
In our indifferent century!'

And many a skeleton shook his head.
'Instead of preaching forty year,'
My neighbour Parson Thirdly said,
'I wish I had stuck to pipes and beer.'

Again the guns disturbed the hour,
Roaring their readiness to avenge,
As far inland as Stourton Tower,
And Camelot, and starlit Stonehenge.

[*Satires of Circumstance*, 1914]

The Convergence of the Twain

(*Lines on the loss of the 'Titanic'*)

I

In a solitude of the sea
Deep from human vanity,
And the Pride of Life that planned her, stilly couches she.

II

Steel chambers, late the pyres
Of her salamandrine fires,
Cold currents thrid, and turn to rhythmic tidal lyres.

III

Over the mirrors meant
To glass the opulent
The sea-worm crawls — grotesque, slimed, dumb, indifferent.

IV

Jewels in joy designed
To ravish the sensuous mind
Lie lightless, all their sparkles bleared and black and blind.

V

Dim moon-eyed fishes near
Gaze at the gilded gear
And query: 'What does this vaingloriousness down here?' . . .

VI

Well: while was fashioning
This creature of cleaving wing,
The Immanent Will that stirs and urges everything

VII

Prepared a sinister mate
For her — so gaily great —
A Shape of Ice, for the time far and dissociate.

VIII

And as the smart ship grew
In stature, grace, and hue,
In shadowy silent distance grew the Iceberg too.

IX

Alien they seemed to be:
No mortal eye could see
The intimate welding of their later history,

X

Or sign that they were bent
By paths coincident
On being anon twin halves of one august event,

XI

Till the Spinner of the Years
Said 'Now!' And each one hears,
And consummation comes, and jars two hemispheres.

[*Satires of Circumstance*, 1914]

A Singer Asleep

(*Algernon Charles Swinburne,* 1837–1909)

I

In this fair niche [6] above the unslumbering sea,
That sentrys up and down all night, all day,
From cove to promontory, from ness to bay,
The Fates have fitly bidden that he should be
  Pillowed eternally.

II

— It was as though a garland of red roses
Had fallen about the hood of some smug nun
When irresponsibly dropped as from the sun,
In fulth of numbers freaked with musical closes,
Upon Victoria's formal middle time
  His leaves of rhythm and rhyme.

III

O that far morning of a summer day
When, down a terraced street whose pavements lay
Glassing the sunshine into my bent eyes,
I walked and read with a quick glad surprise
  New words, in classic guise, —

IV

The passionate pages of his earlier years,
Fraught with hot sighs, sad laughters, kisses, tears;
Fresh-fluted notes, yet from a minstrel who
Blew them not naïvely, but as one who knew
  Full well why thus he blew.

V

I still can hear the brabble and the roar
At those thy tunes, O still one, now passed through
That fitful fire of tongues then entered new!
Their power is spent like spindrift on this shore;
  Thine swells yet more and more.

VI

— His singing-mistress verily was no other
Than she the Lesbian, she the music-mother
Of all the tribe that feel in melodies;
Who leapt, love-anguished, from the Leucadian steep
Into the rambling world-encircling deep
  Which hides her where none sees.

VII

And one can hold in thought that nightly here
His phantom may draw down to the water's brim,
And hers come up to meet it, as a dim
Lone shine upon the heaving hydrosphere,
And mariners wonder as they traverse near,
  Unknowing of her and him.

VIII

One dreams him sighing to her spectral form:
'O teacher, where lies hid thy burning line;
Where are those songs, O poetess divine
Whose very orts [7] are love incarnadine?'
And her smile back: 'Disciple true and warm,
  Sufficient now are thine.' . . .

---

[6] Swinburne is buried at Bonchurch on the Isle of Wight. Hardy had been an admirer of Swinburne since the publication of *Poems and Ballads* (1866) and felt that they had shared similar fates at the hands of a prudish public.

[7] Fragments left from a meal. Only fragments of Sappho's poems remain.

IX

So here, beneath the waking constellations,
Where the waves peal their everlasting
strains,
And their dull subterrene reverberations
Shake him when storms make mountains
of their plains —
Him once their peer in sad improvisations,
And deft as wind to cleave their frothy
manes —
I leave him, while the daylight gleam de-
clines
Upon the capes and chines.

[*Satires of Circumstance*, 1914]

Rain on a Grave

Clouds spout upon her
Their waters amain
In ruthless disdain, —
Her who but lately
Had shivered with pain
As at touch of dishonour
If there had lit on her
So coldly, so straightly
Such arrows of rain:

One who to shelter
Her delicate head
Would quicken and quicken
Each tentative tread
If drops chanced to pelt her
That summertime spills
In dust-paven rills
When thunder-clouds thicken
And birds close their bills.

Would that I lay there
And she were housed here!
Or better, together
Were folded away there
Exposed to one weather
We both, — who would stray there
When sunny the day there,
Or evening was clear
At the prime of the year.

Soon will be growing
Green blades from her mound,
And daisies be showing
Like stars on the ground,
Till she form part of them —
Ay — the sweet heart of them,
Loved beyond measure
With a child's pleasure
All her life's round.

[*Satires of Circumstance*, 1914]

The Voice

Woman much missed, how you call to me,
call to me,
Saying that now you are not as you were
When you had changed from the one who
was all to me,
But as at first, when our day was fair.

Can it be you that I hear? Let me view
you, then,
Standing as when I drew near to the town
Where you would wait for me: yes, as I
knew you then,
Even to the original air-blue gown!

Or is it only the breeze, in its listlessness
Travelling across the wet mead to me here,
You being ever dissolved to wan wistless-
ness,
Heard no more again far or near?

Thus I; faltering forward,
Leaves around me falling,
Wind oozing thin through the thorn from
norward,
And the woman calling.

[*Satires of Circumstance*, 1914]

The Oxen[8]

Christmas Eve, and twelve of the clock.
'Now they are all on their knees,'

[8] It is a folk belief that at the hour of Christ's birth the oxen kneel as they did in the stable at Bethlehem.

An elder said as we sat in a flock
  By the embers in hearthside ease.

We pictured the meek mild creatures where
  They dwelt in their strawy pen,
Nor did it occur to one of us there
  To doubt they were kneeling then.

So fair a fancy few would weave
  In these years! Yet, I feel,
If someone said on Christmas Eve,
  'Come; see the oxen kneel,

'In the lonely barton [9] by yonder coomb
  Our childhood used to know,'
I should go with him in the gloom,
  Hoping it might be so.

[*Moments of Vision*, 1917]

On Sturminster Foot-bridge

(*Onomatopœic*) [10]

RETICULATIONS creep upon the slack stream's face
  When the wind skims irritably past,
The current clucks smartly into each hollow place
That years of flood have scrabbled in the pier's sodden base;
  The floating-lily leaves rot fast.

On a roof stand the swallows ranged in wistful waiting rows,
  Till they arrow off and drop like stones
Among the eyot-withies at whose foot the river flows:
And beneath the roof is she who in the dark world shows
  As a lattice-gleam when midnight moans.

[*Moments of Vision*, 1917]

In Time of 'The Breaking of Nations' [11]

I

ONLY a man harrowing clods
  In a slow silent walk
With an old horse that stumbles and nods
  Half asleep as they stalk.

II

Only thin smoke without flame
  From the heaps of couch-grass;
Yet this will go onward the same
  Though Dynasties pass.

III

Yonder a maid and her wight
  Come whispering by:
War's annals will fade into night
  Ere their story die.

[*Moments of Vision*, 1917]

Afterwards

WHEN the Present has latched its postern behind my tremulous stay,
  And the May month flaps its glad green leaves like wings,
Delicate-filmed as new-spun silk, will the neighbours say,
  'He was a man who used to notice such things'?

If it be in the dusk when, like an eyelid's soundless blink,
  The dewfall-hawk comes crossing the shades to alight
Upon the wind-warped upland thorn, a gazer may think,
  'To him this must have been a familiar sight.'

[9] farmyard

[10] Hostile critics cited this poem among others as evidence of Hardy's atrocious 'ear' for meter, not recognizing that he, in this case, was attempting to convey by the rhythm the impression of a clucking of ripples into riverside holes when blown upon by an upstream wind.

[11] 'Jeremiah li. 20' [Hardy]. Mrs. Hardy records that though this poem was occasioned by the bloodier battles of World War I, its genesis and the image of this stanza recall an afternoon in the garden in 1870, reading Tennyson, when news of the battle of Gravelotte in the Franco-Prussian War came.

If I pass during some nocturnal blackness, mothy and warm,
  When the hedgehog travels furtively over the lawn,
One may say, 'He strove that such innocent creatures should come to no harm,
  But he could do little for them; and now he is gone.'

If, when hearing that I have been stilled at last, they stand at the door,
  Watching the full-starred heavens that winter sees,
Will this thought rise on those who will meet my face no more,
  'He was one who had an eye for such mysteries'?

And will any say when my bell of quittance is heard in the gloom,
  And a crossing breeze cuts a pause in its outrollings,
Till they rise again, as they were a new bell's boom,
  'He hears it not now, but used to notice such things'?

[*Moments of Vision,* 1917]

Last Words to a Dumb Friend

Pet was never mourned as you,
Purrer of the spotless hue,
Plumy tail, and wistful gaze
While you humoured our queer ways,
Or outshrilled your morning call
Up the stairs and through the hall—
Foot suspended in its fall—
While, expectant, you would stand
Arched, to meet the stroking hand;
Till your way you chose to wend
Yonder, to your tragic end.

Never another pet for me!
Let your place all vacant be;
Better blankness day by day
Than companion torn away.
Better bid his memory fade,
Better blot each mark he made,
Selfishly escape distress
By contrived forgetfulness,
Than preserve his prints to make
Every morn and eve an ache.

From the chair whereon he sat
Sweep his fur, nor wince thereat:
Rake his little pathways out
Mid the bushes roundabout;
Smooth away his talons' mark
From the claw-worn pine-tree bark,
Where he climbed as dusk embrowned,
Waiting us who loitered round.

Strange it is this speechless thing,
Subject to our mastering,
Subject for his life and food
To our gift, and time, and mood;
Timid pensioner of us Powers,
His existence ruled by ours,
Should—by crossing at a breath
Into safe and shielded death,
By the merely taking hence
Of his insignificance—
Loom as largened to the sense,
Shape as part, above man's will,
Of the Imperturbable.

As a prisoner, flight debarred,
Exercising in a yard,
Still retain I, troubled, shaken,
Mean estate, by him forsaken;
And this home, which scarcely took
Impress from his little look,
By his faring to the Dim
Grows all eloquent of him.

Housemate, I can think you still
Bounding to the window-sill,
Over which I vaguely see
Your small mound beneath the tree,
Showing in the autumn shade
That you moulder where you played.

[*Late Lyrics and Earlier,* 1922]

Gerard Manley Hopkins[1] 1844–1889

Heaven-Haven

A nun takes the veil

I HAVE desired to go
Where springs not fail,
To fields where flies no sharp and sided hail
And a few lilies blow.

And I have asked to be
Where no storms come,
Where the green swell is in the havens dumb,
And out of the swing of the sea.

The Habit of Perfection[2]

ELECTED Silence, sing to me
And beat upon my whorlèd ear,
Pipe me to pastures still and be
The music that I care to hear.

Shape nothing, lips; be lovely-dumb:
It is the shut, the curfew sent
From there where all surrenders come
Which only makes you eloquent.

Be shellèd, eyes, with double dark
And find the uncreated light:
This ruck and reel which you remark
Coils, keeps, and teases simple sight.

Palate, the hutch of tasty lust,
Desire not to be rinsed with wine:
The can must be so sweet, the crust
So fresh that come in fasts divine!

Nostrils, your careless breath that spend
Upon the stir and keep of pride,
What relish shall the censers send
Along the sanctuary side!

O feel-of-primrose hands, O feet
That want the yield of plushy sward,
But you shall walk the golden street
And you unhouse and house the Lord.[3]

And, Poverty, be thou the bride
And now the marriage feast begun,
And lily-coloured clothes provide
Your spouse not laboured-at nor spun.

The Wreck of the Deutschland

To the
happy memory of five Franciscan Nuns
exiles by the Falk Laws
drowned between midnight and
morning of Dec. 7th, 1875[4]

PART THE FIRST

I

THOU mastering me
God! giver of breath and bread;
World's strand, sway of the sea;
Lord of living and dead;
Thou hast bound bones and veins in me, fastened me flesh,
And after it almost unmade, what with dread,
Thy doing: and dost thou touch me afresh?
Over again I feel thy finger and find thee.

---

[1] Father Hopkins' poems were not brought together into one volume and published until his friend Robert Bridges issued *Poems of Gerard Manley Hopkins* in 1918. The text used here is that of the third edition (Oxford, 1948), with additional poems and notes edited by W. H. Gardner.

[2] Written in 1866, while Hopkins was undergoing conversion from the Anglican to the Roman Catholic Church.

[3] Remove the Host from, and replace in, the tabernacle of the altar.

[4] In the early morning of December 6th, the steamer *Deutschland* lost her propeller in a gale and drove aground on a sand bar, the Kentish Knock, near the mouth of the Thames. Despite a clear day following, it was thirty hours before her distress signals were answered; in consequence, many passengers died from the intense cold and prolonged exposure in the rigging as the vessel slowly broke up. Details in the second part of the poem are drawn directly from contemporary newspaper accounts, while Hopkins assured Bridges that what referred to himself, in the first part especially, was 'strictly and literally true and did all occur . . .' The poem was written after a seven-year silence consequent

2

I did say yes
O at lightning and lashed rod;
Thou heardst me truer than tongue confess
Thy terror, O Christ, O God;
Thou knowest the walls, altar and hour and night:
The swoon of a heart that the sweep and the hurl of thee trod
Hard down with a horror of height:
And the midriff astrain with leaning of, laced with fire of stress.

3

The frown of his face
Before me, the hurtle of hell
Behind, where, where was a, where was a place?
I whirled out wings that spell[5]
And fled with a fling of the heart to the heart of the Host.
My heart, but you were dovewinged, I can tell,
Carrier-witted, I am bold to boast,
To flash from the flame to the flame then, tower from the grace to the grace.

4

I am soft sift
In an hourglass — at the wall
Fast, but mined with a motion, a drift,
And it crowds and it combs to the fall;
I steady as a water in a well, to a poise, to a pane,
But roped with, always, all the way down from the tall
Fells or flanks of the voel,[6] a vein
Of the gospel proffer, a pressure, a principle, Christ's gift.

5

I kiss my hand
To the stars, lovely-asunder
Starlight, wafting him out of it; and
Glow, glory in thunder;
Kiss my hand to the dappled-with-damson west:
Since, tho' he is under the world's splendour and wonder,
His mystery must be instressed,[7] stressed;
For I greet him the days I meet him, and bless when I understand.

6

Not out of his bliss
Springs the stress felt
Nor first from heaven (and few know this)
Swings the stroke dealt —
Stroke and a stress that stars and storms deliver,
That guilt is hushed by, hearts are flushed by and melt —
But it rides time like riding a river
(And here the faithful waver, the faithless fable and miss).

7

It dates from day
Of his going in Galilee;
Warm-laid grave of a womb-life grey;
Manger, maiden's knee;
The dense and the driven Passion, and frightful sweat;
Thence the discharge of it, there its swelling to be,
Though felt before, though in high flood yet —
What none would have known of it, only the heart, being hard at bay,

---

upon Hopkins' entering the Jesuit Order; it is both the first of his mature work and the first to use his 'sprung rhythm.'

[5] at that time

[6] Welsh for bald or bare hill. Near St. Beuno's College, Wales, a Jesuit school where Hopkins wrote the poem, is a mountain called 'The Voel.'

[7] A word of Hopkins' own coinage; as used here, meaning 'to be felt vividly and deeply in every fiber of one's being, under the influence of nature or God's Grace; forcibly borne in upon the mind made receptive by humility and faith.'

8

Is out with it! Oh,
We lash with the best or worst
Word last! How a lush-kept plush-
capped sloe
Will, mouthed to flesh-burst,
Gush! — flush the man, the being with
it, sour or sweet,
Brim, in a flash, full! — Hither then,
last or first,
To hero of Calvary, Christ,'s feet —
Never ask if meaning it, wanting it,
warned of it — men go.

9

Be adored among men,
God, three-numberèd form;
Wring thy rebel, dogged in den,
Man's malice, with wrecking and
storm.
Beyond saying sweet, past telling of
tongue,
Thou art lightning and love, I found it,
a winter and warm;
Father and fondler of heart thou hast
wrung:
Hast thy dark descending and most art
merciful then.

10

With an anvil-ding
And with fire in him forge thy will
Or rather, rather then, stealing as
Spring
Through him, melt him but master
him still:
Whether at once, as once at a crash
Paul,
Or as Austin,[8] a lingering-out swéet
skíll,
Make mercy in all of us, out of us all
Mastery, but be adored, but be adored
King.

[8] St. Augustine

PART THE SECOND

11

'Some find me a sword; some
The flange and the rail; flame,
Fang, or flood' goes Death on drum,
And storms bugle his fame.
But wé dream we are rooted in earth —
Dust!
Flesh falls within sight of us, we, though
our flower the same,
Wave with the meadow, forget that
there must
The sour scythe cringe,[9] and the blear
share come.

12

On Saturday sailed from Bremen,
American-outward-bound,
Take settler and seamen, tell men
with women,
Two hundred souls in the round —
O Father, not under thy feathers nor
ever as guessing
The goal was a shoal, of a fourth the
doom to be drowned;
Yet did the dark side of the bay of
thy blessing
Not vault them, the millions of rounds
of thy mercy not reeve even
them in?

13

Into the snows she sweeps,
Hurling the haven behind,
The Deutschland, on Sunday; and so
the sky keeps,
For the infinite air is unkind,
And the sea flint-flake, black-backed in
the regular blow,
Sitting Eastnortheast, in cursed quarter,
the wind;
Wiry and white-fiery and whirlwind-
swivellèd snow
Spins to the widow-making unchilding
unfathering deeps.

[9] bend, sink

14

She drove in the dark to leeward,
She struck — not a reef or a rock
But the combs of a smother of sand: night drew her
Dead to the Kentish Knock;
And she beat the bank down with her bows and the ride of her keel:
The breakers rolled on her beam with ruinous shock;
And canvas and compass, the whorl [10] and the wheel
Idle for ever to waft her or wind her with, these she endured.

15

Hope had grown grey hairs,
Hope had mourning on,
Trenched with tears, carved with cares,
Hope was twelve hours gone;
And frightful a nightfall folded rueful a day
Nor rescue, only rocket and lightship, shone,
And lives at last were washing away:
To the shrouds they took, — they shook in the hurling and horrible airs.

16

One stirred from the rigging to save
The wild woman-kind below,
With a rope's end round the man, handy and brave —
He was pitched to his death at a blow,
For all his dreadnought breast and braids of thew:
They could tell him for hours, dandled the to and fro
Through the cobbled foam-fleece, what could he do
With the burl [11] of the fountains of air, buck and the flood of the wave?

17

They fought with God's cold —
And they could not and fell to the deck
(Crushed them) or water (and drowned them) or rolled
With the sea-romp over the wreck.
Night roared, with the heart-break hearing a heart-broke rabble,
The woman's wailing, the crying of child without check —
Till a lioness arose breasting the babble,
A prophetess towered in the tumult, a virginal tongue told.

18

Ah, touched in your bower of bone
Are you! turned for an exquisite smart,
Have you! make words break from me here all alone,
Do you! — mother of being in me, heart.
O unteachably after evil, but uttering truth,
Why, tears! is it? tears; such a melting, a madrigal start!
Never-eldering revel and river of youth,
What can it be, this glee? the good you have there of your own?

19

Sister, a sister calling
A master, her master and mine! —
And the inboard seas run swirling and hawling; [12]
The rash smart sloggering brine

[10] propeller

[11] Usually used by Hopkins in the sense of 'roundness,' 'fulness'; perhaps here, 'bubbling up.'

[12] So spelled in all three manuscript versions.

Blinds her; but she that weather sees one thing, one;
Has one fetch[13] in her: she rears herself to divine
Ears, and the call of the tall nun
To the men in the tops and the tackle rode over the storm's brawling.

20

She was first of a five and came
Of a coifèd sisterhood.
(O Deutschland, double a desperate name!
O world wide of its good!
But Gertrude,[14] lily, and Luther, are two of a town,
Christ's lily and beast of the waste wood:
From life's dawn it is drawn down,
Abel is Cain's brother and breasts they have sucked the same.)

21

Loathed for a love men knew in them,
Banned by the land of their birth,
Rhine refused them. Thames would ruin them;
Surf, snow, river and earth
Gnashed: but thou art above, thou Orion of light;
Thy unchancelling[15] poising palms were weighing the worth,
Thou martyr-master: in thy sight
Storm flakes were scroll-leaved flowers, lily showers — sweet heaven was astrew in them.

22

Five! the finding and sake[16]
And cipher of suffering Christ.
Mark, the mark is of man's make
And the word of it Sacrificed.
But he scores it in scarlet himself on his own bespoken,
Before-time-taken, dearest prizèd and priced —
Stigma, signal, cinquefoil token
For lettering of the lamb's fleece, ruddying of the rose-flake.

23

Joy fall to thee, father Francis,
Drawn to the Life that died;
With the gnarls of the nails in thee, niche of the lance, his
Lovescape[17] crucified
And seal of his seraph-arrival! and these thy daughters
And five-livèd and leavèd favour and pride,
Are sisterly sealed in wild waters,
To bathe in his fall-gold mercies, to breathe in his all-fire glances.

24

Away in the loveable west,
On a pastoral forehead of Wales,
I was under a roof[18] here, I was at rest,
And they the prey of the gales;
She to the black-about air, to the breaker, the thickly
Falling flakes, to the throng that catches and quails
Was calling 'O Christ, Christ, come quickly':
The cross to her she calls Christ to her, christens her wild-worst Best.

25

The majesty! what did she mean?
Breathe, arch and original Breath.

[13] stratagem, device

[14] German saint and mystic (*c.*1256–*c.*1302) whose convent was near Luther's birthplace, Eisleben.

[15] A 'chancel' is a sanctuary; hence, for his own purposes God — the hunter, Orion — has deprived these nuns of their refuge in Germany.

[16] emblems of, reminders of, as in 'namesake' or 'keepsake'

[17] A Hopkins coinage; here, the pattern of the five wounds of Christ, hence the stigmata received by St. Francis; the 'pattern' of love, love in its essence.

[18] See n. 6.

Is it love in her of the being as her lover had been?
Breathe, body of lovely Death.
They were else-minded then, altogether, the men
Woke thee with a *we are perishing* in the weather of Gennesareth.[19]
Or is it that she cried for the crown then,
The keener to come at the comfort for feeling the combating keen?

26

For how to the heart's cheering
The down-dugged ground-hugged grey
Hovers off, the jay-blue heavens appearing
Of pied and peeled May!
Blue-beating and hoary-glow height; or night, still higher,
With belled fire and the moth-soft Milky Way,
What by your measure is the heaven of desire,
The treasure never eyesight got, nor was ever guessed what for the hearing?

27

No, but it was not these.
The jading and jar of the cart,
Time's tasking, it is fathers that asking for ease
Of the sodden-with-its-sorrowing heart,
Not danger, electrical horror; then further it finds
The appealing of the Passion is tenderer in prayer apart:
Other, I gather, in measure her mind's
Burden, in wind's burly and beat of endragonèd seas.

28

But how shall I . . . make me room there:
Reach me a . . . Fancy, come faster —
Strike you the sight of it? look at it loom there,
Thing that she . . . there then! the Master,
Ipse, the only one, Christ, King, Head:
He was to cure the extremity where he had cast her;
Do, deal, lord it with living and dead;
Let him ride, her pride, in his triumph, despatch and have done with his doom there.

29

Ah! there was a heart right
There was single eye!
Read the unshapeable shock night
And knew the who and the why;
Wording it how but by him that present and past,
Heaven and earth are word of, worded by? —
The Simon Peter of a soul! to the blast
Tarpeian-fast, but a blown beacon of light.

30

Jesu, heart's light,
Jesu, maid's son,
What was the feast[20] followed the night
Thou hadst glory of this nun? —
Feast of the one woman without stain.
For so conceivèd, so to conceive thee is done;
But here was heart-throe, birth of a brain,
Word, that heard and kept thee and uttered thee outright.

[19] The Sea of Galilee; the reference is to the storm on the Sea which Christ miraculously calmed.

[20] December 8th is the Feast of the Immaculate Conception of the Blessed Virgin Mary.

31

Well, she has thee for the pain, for the
Patience; but pity of the rest of them!
Heart, go and bleed at a bitterer vein for the
Comfortless unconfessed of them—
No not uncomforted: lovely-felicitous Providence
Finger of a tender of, O of a feathery delicacy, the breast of the
Maiden could obey so, be a bell to, ring of it, and
Startle the poor sheep back! is the shipwrack then a harvest, does tempest carry the grain for thee?

32

I admire thee, master of the tides,
Of the Yore-flood, of the year's fall;
The recurb and the recovery of the gulf's sides,
The girth of it and the wharf of it and the wall;
Stanching, quenching ocean of a motionable mind;
Ground of being, and granite of it: past all
Grasp God, throned behind
Death with a sovereignty that heeds but hides, bodes but abides;

33

With a mercy that outrides
The all of water, an ark
For the listener; for the lingerer with a love glides
Lower than death and the dark;
A vein for the visiting of the past-prayer, pent in prison,
The-last-breath penitent spirits—the uttermost mark
Our passion-plungèd giant risen,
The Christ of the Father compassionate, fetched in the storm of his strides.

34

Now burn, new born to the world,
Doubled-naturèd name,
The heaven-flung, heart-fleshed, maiden-furled
Miracle-in-Mary-of-flame,
Mid-numbered He in three of the thunder-throne!
Not a dooms-day dazzle in his coming nor dark as he came;
Kind, but royally reclaiming his own;
A released shower, let flash to the shire, not a lightning of fire hard-hurled.

35

Dame, at our door
Drowned, and among our shoals,
Remember us in the roads, the heaven-haven of the Reward:
Our King back, oh, upon English souls!
Let him easter in us, be a dayspring to the dimness of us, be a crimson-cresseted east,
More brightening her, rare-dear Britain, as his reign rolls,
Pride, rose, prince, hero of us, high-priest,
Our hearts' charity's hearth's fire, our thoughts' chivalry's throng's Lord.

Spring

Nothing is so beautiful as spring—
When weeds, in wheels, shoot long and lovely and lush;
Thrush's eggs look little low heavens, and thrush
Through the echoing timber does so rinse and wring

The ear, it strikes like lightnings to hear him sing;
The glassy peartree leaves and blooms, they brush
The descending blue; that blue is all in a rush
With richness; the racing lambs too have fair their fling.

What is all this juice and all this joy?
A strain of the earth's sweet being in the beginning
In Eden garden.—Have, get, before it cloy,
Before it cloud, Christ, lord, and sour with sinning,
Innocent mind and Mayday in girl and boy,
Most, O maid's child, thy choice and worthy the winning.

The Windhover:

To Christ our Lord[21]

I CAUGHT this morning morning's minion, king-
dom of daylight's dauphin, dapple-dawn-drawn Falcon, in his riding
Of the rolling level underneath him steady air, and striding
High there, how he rung[22] upon the rein of a wimpling wing
In his ecstasy! then off, off forth on swing,
As a skate's heel sweeps smooth on a bow-bend: the hurl and gliding
Rebuffed the big wind. My heart in hiding
Stirred for a bird,—the achieve of, the mastery of the thing!

Brute beauty and valour and act, oh, air, pride, plume, here
Buckle![23] AND the fire that breaks from thee then, a billion
Times told lovelier, more dangerous, O my chevalier!

No wonder of it: shéer plód makes plough down sillion[24]
Shine, and blue-bleak embers, ah my dear,
Fall, gall themselves, and gash gold-vermilion.

Pied Beauty[25]

GLORY be to God for dappled things—
For skies of couple-colour as a brinded[26] cow;
For rose-moles all in stipple upon trout that swim;
Fresh-firecoal chestnut-falls; finches' wings;
Landscape plotted and pieced—fold, fallow, and plough;
And áll trádes, their gear and tackle and trim.

All things counter, original, spare, strange;
Whatever is fickle, freckled (who knows how?)
With swift, slow; sweet, sour; adazzle, dim;
He fathers-forth whose beauty is past change:
Praise him.

Peace

WHEN will you ever, Peace, wild wood-dove, shy wings shut,
Your round me roaming end, and under be my boughs?

[21] Hopkins considered this sonnet his best poem, hence the dedication. In this, as in other of his sonnets (e.g., 'Felix Randal,' 'Carrion Comfort,' and 'No worst, there is none,' below), the unusual structure of the lines is an attempt to capture the sense of *length* or *quantity* in the lines of Italian sonnets which, Hopkins felt, was too often lacking in the strict iambic pentameter of English sonnets.

[22] A term used in both falconry and the show-ring for horses; to circle or spiral in sweeping curves.

[23] Here used in the ambivalent senses both imperatively and intransitively of the verb.

[24] side of a furrow

[25] In a 'curtal sonnet' like this and 'Peace' (below), the six plus four lines (with another half line at the end) are meant to be similar in proportion to those of an Italian sonnet, eight plus six.

[26] brindled

When, when, Peace, will you, Peace? I'll not play hypocrite
To own my heart: I yield you do come sometimes; but
That piecemeal peace is poor peace. What pure peace allows
Alarms of wars, the daunting wars, the death of it?

O surely, reaving [27] Peace, my Lord should leave in lieu
Some good! And so he does leave Patience exquisite,
That plumes to Peace thereafter. And when Peace here does house
He comes with work to do, he does not come to coo,
He comes to brood and sit.

The Bugler's First Communion

A BUGLER boy from barrack (it is over the hill
There)—boy bugler, born, he tells me, of Irish
Mother to an English sire (he
Shares their best gifts surely, fall how things will),

This very very day came down to us after a boon he on
My late being there begged of me, overflowing
Boon in my bestowing,
Came, I say, this day to it—to a First Communion.

Here he knelt then ín regimental red.
Forth Christ from cupboard fetched, how fain I of feet
To his youngster take his treat!
Low-latched in leaf-light housel [28] his too huge godhead.

There! and your sweetest sendings, ah divine,
By it, heavens, befall him! as a heart Christ's darling, dauntless;
Tongue true, vaunt- and tauntless;
Breathing bloom of a chastity in mansex fine.

Frowning and forefending angel-warder
Squander the hell-rook ranks sally to molest him;
March, kind comrade, abreast him;
Dress his days to a dexterous and starlight order.

How it dóes my heart good, visiting at that bleak hill,
When limber liquid youth, that to all I teach
Yields tender as a pushed peach,
Hies headstrong to its wellbeing of a self-wise self-will!

Then though I should tread tufts of consolation
Dáys áfter, só I in a sort deserve to
And do serve God to serve to
Just such slips of soldiery Christ's royal ration.

Nothing élse is like it, no, not all so strains
Us: fresh youth fretted in a bloomfall all portending
That sweet's sweeter ending;
Realm both Christ is heir to and thére réigns.

O now well work that sealing sacred ointment!
O for now charms, arms, what bans off bad
And locks love ever in a lad!
Let mé though see no more of him, and not disappointment

Those sweet hopes quell whose least me quickenings lift,
In scarlet or somewhere of some day seeing
That brow and bead of being,
An our day's God's own Galahad. Though this child's drift

[27] depriving of
[28] Here, the consecrated wafer of the Eucharist.

Seems by a divíne doom chánnelled, nor do I cry
Disaster there; but may he not rankle and roam
In backwheels[29] though bound home? —
That left to the Lord of the Eucharist, I here lie by;

Recorded only, I have put my lips on pleas
Would brandle[30] adamantine heaven with ride and jar, did
Prayer go disregarded:
Forward-like, but however, and like favourable heaven heard these.

Felix Randal

FELIX RANDAL the farrier, O he is dead then? my duty all ended,
Who have watched his mould of man, big-boned and hardy-handsome
Pining, pining, till time when reason rambled in it and some
Fatal four disorders, fleshed there, all contended?

Sickness broke him. Impatient he cursed at first, but mended
Being anointed and all; though a heavenlier heart began some
Months earlier, since I had our sweet reprieve and ransom
Tendered to him. Ah well, God rest him all road ever he offended!

This seeing the sick endears them to us, us too it endears.
My tongue had taught thee comfort, touch had quenched thy tears,
Thy tears that touched my heart, child, Felix, poor Felix Randal;

How far from then forethought of, all thy more boisterous years,
When thou at the random[31] grim forge, powerful amidst peers,
Didst fettle for the great grey drayhorse his bright and battering sandal!

Brothers

How lovely the elder brother's
Life all laced in the other's,
Lóve-laced! — what once I well
Witnessed; so fortune fell.
When Shrovetide, two years gone,
Our boys' plays brought on
Part was picked for John,
Young Jóhn, then fear, then joy
Ran revel in the elder boy.
Their night was come now; all
Our company thronged the hall;
Henry, by the wall,
Beckoned me beside him:
I came where called, and eyed him
By meanwhiles; making mý play
Turn most on tender byplay.
For, wrung all on love's rack,
My lad, and lost in Jack,
Smiled, blushed, and bit his lip;
Or drove, with a diver's dip,
Clutched hands down through clasped knees —
Truth's tokens tricks like these,
Old telltales, with what stress
He hung on the imp's success.
Now the other was bráss-bóld:
Hé had no work to hold
His heart up at the strain;
Nay, roguish ran the vein.
Two tedious acts were past;
Jack's call and cue at last;
When Henry, heart-forsook,
Dropped eyes and dared not look.
Eh, how áll rúng!
Young dog, he did give tongue!
But Harry — in his hands he has flung
His tear-tricked cheeks of flame
For fond love and for shame.

---

[29] Hopkins' coinage, apparently analogous to eddies which move contrary to the main current.
[30] shake

[31] Built with irregularly shaped stones.

Ah Nature, framed in fault,
There's comfort then, there's salt;
Nature, bad, base, and blind,
Dearly thou canst be kind;
There dearly thén, deárly,
I'll cry thou canst be kind.

Spring and Fall:

to a young child

Márgarét, are you gríeving
Over Goldengrove unleaving?
Leáves, líke the things of man, you
With your fresh thoughts care for, can you?
Áh! ás the heart grows older
It will come to such sights colder
By and by, nor spare a sigh
Though worlds of wanwood leafmeal[32] lie;
And yet you wíll weep and know why.
Now no matter, child, the name:
Sórrow's spríngs áre the same.
Nor mouth had, no nor mind, expressed
What heart heard of, ghost guessed:
It ís the blight man was born for,
It is Margaret you mourn for.

The Leaden Echo and the Golden Echo

(Maidens' song from St. Winefred's Well)[33]

THE LEADEN ECHO

How to kéep — is there ány any, is there none such, nowhere known some, bow or brooch or braid or brace, láce, latch or catch or key to keep
Back beauty, keep it, beauty, beauty, beauty, . . . from vanishing away?
Ó is there no frowning of these wrinkles, rankèd wrinkles deep,
Dówn? no waving off of these most mournful messengers, still messengers, sad and stealing messengers of grey?
No there's none, there's none, O no there's none,
Nor can you long be, what you now are, called fair,
Do what you may do, what, do what you may,
And wisdom is early to despair:
Be beginning; since, no, nothing can be done
To keep at bay
Age and age's evils, hoar hair,
Ruck and wrinkle, drooping, dying, death's worst, winding sheets, tombs and worms and tumbling to decay;
So be beginning, be beginning to despair.
O there's none; no no no there's none:
Be beginning to despair, to despair,
Despair, despair, despair, despair.

THE GOLDEN ECHO

Spare!
There ís one, yes I have one (Hush there!);
Only not within seeing of the sun,
Not within the singeing of the strong sun,
Tall sun's tingeing, or treacherous the tainting of the earth's air,
Somewhere elsewhere there is ah well where! one,
Óne. Yes I cán tell such a key, I dó know such a place,
Where whatever's prized and passes of us, everything that's fresh and fast flying of us, seems to us sweet of us and swiftly away with, done away with, undone,
Úndone, done with, soon done with, and yet dearly and dangerously sweet
Of us, the wimpled-water-dimpled, not-by-morning-matchèd face,
The flower of beauty, fleece[34] of beauty, too too apt to, ah! to fleet,

[32] Both words are Hopkins' own coinage, the one from the Old English *wann*, bloodless, weak, pale; the other by analogy with *piecemeal*.

[33] An uncompleted poetic drama based on the Welsh legend of St. Winefred's death defending her chastity, and the miraculously healing spring which her father, St. Beuno, caused to flow at the site of the murder.

[34] Elsewhere used to mean 'the velvetiness of rose petals, or of a child's skin, etc.'

Never fleets móre, fastened with the tenderest truth
To its own best being and its loveliness of youth: it is an everlastingness of, O it is an all youth!
Come then, your ways and airs and looks, locks, maiden gear, gallantry and gaiety and grace,
Winning ways, airs innocent, maiden manners, sweet looks, loose locks, long locks, lovelocks, gaygear, going gallant, girlgrace —
Resign them, sign them, seal them, send them, motion them with breath,
And with sighs soaring, soaring síghs deliver
Them; beauty-in-the-ghost, deliver it, early now, long before death
Give beauty back, beauty, beauty, beauty, back to God, beauty's self and beauty's giver.
See; not a hair is, not an eyelash, not the least lash lost; every hair
Is, hair of the head, numbered.
Nay, what we had lighthanded left in surly the mere mould
Will have waked and have waxed and have walked with the wind what while we slept,[35]
This side, that side hurling a heavyheaded hundredfold
What while we, while we slumbered.
O then, weary then whý should we tread? O why are we so haggard at the heart, so care-coiled, care-killed, so fagged, so fashed, so cogged, so cumbered,
When the thing we freely fórfeit is kept with fonder a care,
Fonder a care kept than we could have kept it, kept
Far with fonder a care (and we, we should have lost it) finer, fonder
A care kept. — Where kept? Do but tell us where kept, where. —
Yonder. — What high as that! We follow, now we follow. — Yonder, yes yonder, yonder,
Yonder.

[35] In a letter to Bridges, Hopkins glossed these lines, 'The seed that we so carelessly and freely flung into the dull furrow, and then forgot it, will have come to ear meantime . . .'

(Carrion Comfort) [36]

Not, I'll not, carrion comfort, Despair, not feast on thee;
Not untwist — slack they may be — these last strands of man
In me ór, most weary, cry *I can no more*. I can;
Can something, hope, wish day come, not choose not to be.
But ah, but O thou terrible, why wouldst thou rude on me
Thy wring-world right foot rock? lay a lionlimb against me? scan
With darksome devouring eyes my bruisèd bones? and fan,
O in turns of tempest, me heaped there; me frantic to avoid thee and flee?

Why? That my chaff might fly; my grain lie, sheer and clear.
Nay in all that toil, that coil, since (seems) I kissed the rod,
Hand rather, my heart lo! lapped strength, stole joy, would laugh, chéer.
Cheer whom though? the hero whose heaven-handling flung me, fóot tród
Me? or me that fought him? O which one? is it each one? That night, that year
Of now done darkness I wretch lay wrestling with (my God!) my God.

No worst, there is none

No worst, there is none. Pitched past pitch of grief,
More pangs will, schooled at forepangs, wilder wring.

[36] Bridges gave the title to this sonnet found posthumously in Hopkins' papers; he believed it to be the one which Hopkins once described as 'written in blood.'

Comforter, where, where is your comforting?
Mary, mother of us, where is your relief?
My cries heave, herds-long; huddle in a main, a chief
Woe, world-sorrow; on an age-old anvil wince and sing —
Then lull, then leave off. Fury had shrieked 'No ling-
ering! Let me be fell: force[37] I must be brief.'
  O the mind, mind has mountains; cliffs of fall
Frightful, sheer, no-man-fathomed. Hold them cheap
May who ne'er hung there. Nor does long our small
Durance deal with that steep or deep. Here! creep,
Wretch, under a comfort serves in a whirlwind: all
Life death does end and each day dies with sleep.

I wake and feel the fell of dark

I WAKE and feel the fell of dark, not day.
What hours, O what black hoürs we have spent
This night! what sights you, heart, saw; ways you went!
And more must, in yet longer light's delay.
  With witness I speak this. But where I say
Hours I mean years, mean life. And my lament
Is cries countless, cries like dead letters sent
To dearest him that lives alas! away.

  I am gall, I am heartburn. God's most deep decree
Bitter would have me taste: my taste was me;
Bones built in me, flesh filled, blood brimmed the curse.
  Selfyeast of spirit a dull dough sours. I see
The lost are like this, and their scourge to be
As I am mine, their sweating selves; but worse.

[37] perforce

That Nature is a Heraclitean Fire and of the comfort of the Resurrection[38]

CLOUD-PUFFBALL, torn tufts, tossed pillows | flaunt forth, then chevy on an air-
built thoroughfare: heaven-roysterers, in gay-gangs | they throng; they glitter in marches.
Down roughcast, down dazzling whitewash, | wherever an elm arches,
Shivelights[39] and shadowtackle in long lashes lace, lance, and pair.
Delightfully the bright wind boisterous ropes, wrestles, beats earth bare
Of yestertempest's creases; | in pool and rut peel parches
Squandering ooze to squeezed | dough, crust, dust; stanches, starches
Squadroned masks and manmarks | treadmire toil there
Footfretted in it.[40] Million-fuelèd, | nature's bonfire burns on.
But quench her bonniest, dearest | to her, her clearest-selvèd spark
Man, how fast his firedint, | his mark on mind, is gone!
Both are in an unfathomable, all is in an enormous dark
Drowned. O pity and indig|nation! Manshape, that shone

[38] Heraclitus, a Greek philosopher (*c.*500 B.C.), taught that all things are in a state of flux, that even matter is constantly changing; to fire, which he considered an immaterial substance, he attributed the origin of all things. Hopkins considered this poem a 'sonnet' (see n. 21) with 'codas.'

[39] A strip or beam of light visible because of the motes or 'shives' dancing in it.

[40] After the storm, man's ruts and footmarks squeezed into the mud are obliterated by the wind which dries, stirs up, and blows away the dust.

Sheer off, disseveral,[41] a star, | death blots black out; nor mark
Is any of him at all so stark
But vastness blurs and time | beats level.
Enough! the Resurrection,
A heart's-clarion! Away grief's grasping, | joyless days, dejection.
Across my foundering deck shone
A beacon, an eternal beam. | Flesh fade, and mortal trash
Fall to the residuary worm; | world's wildfire, leave but ash:
In a flash, at a trumpet crash,
I am all at once what Christ is, | since he was what I am, and
This Jack, joke, poor potsherd, | patch, matchwood, immortal diamond,
Is immortal diamond.

Thou art indeed just, Lord

Justus quidem tu es, Domine, si disputem tecum: verumtamen justa loquar ad te: Quare via impiorum prosperatur? &c.[42]

Thou art indeed just, Lord, if I contend
With thee; but, sir, so what I plead is just.
Why do sinners' ways prosper? and why must
Disappointment all I endeavour end?
Wert thou my enemy, O thou my friend,
How wouldst thou worse, I wonder, than thou dost
Defeat, thwart me? Oh, the sots and thralls of lust
Do in spare hours more thrive than I that spend,
Sir, life upon thy cause. See, banks and brakes
Now, leavèd how thick! lacèd they are again
With fretty chervil, look, and fresh wind shakes
Them; birds build — but not I build; no, but strain,
Time's eunuch, and not breed one work that wakes.
Mine, O thou lord of life, send my roots rain.

[41] Hopkins' coinage, equivalent to 'separate and aloof,' 'individualized.'
[42] *Jeremiah* 12:1. The first three lines of the sonnet paraphrase the Latin. In a letter to Bridges, Hopkins said of the poem, 'Observe, it must be read *adagio molto* and with great stress.'

Robert Bridges

1844–1930

Elegy[1]

Clear and gentle stream!
Known and loved so long,
That hast heard the song
And the idle dream
Of my boyish day;
While I once again
Down thy margin stray,
In the selfsame strain
Still my voice is spent,
With my old lament
And my idle dream,
Clear and gentle stream!

Where my old seat was
Here again I sit,
Where the long boughs knit
Over stream and grass
A translucent eaves:
Where back eddies play
Shipwreck with the leaves,
And the proud swans stray,
Sailing one by one
Out of stream and sun,
And the fish lie cool
In their chosen pool.

Many an afternoon
Of the summer day
Dreaming here I lay;

[1] All the poems printed here, except the last, appeared in *Shorter Poems,* which Bridges issued in five books between 1890 and 1894.

And I know how soon,
Idly at its hour,
First the deep bell hums
From the minster tower,
And then evening comes,
Creeping up the glade,
With her lengthening shade,
And the tardy boon
Of her brightening moon.

Clear and gentle stream!
Ere again I go
Where thou dost not flow,
Well does it beseem
Thee to hear again
Once my youthful song,
That familiar strain
Silent now so long:
Be as I content
With my old lament
And my idle dream,
Clear and gentle stream.

Elegy

The wood is bare: a river-mist is steeping
The trees that winter's chill of life bereaves:
Only their stiffened boughs break silence, weeping
Over their fallen leaves;

That lie upon the dank earth brown and rotten,
Miry and matted in the soaking wet:
Forgotten with the spring, that is forgotten
By them that can forget.

Yet it was here we walked when ferns were springing,
And through the mossy bank shot bud and blade: —
Here found in summer, when the birds were singing,
A green and pleasant shade.

'Twas here we loved in sunnier days and greener;
And now, in this disconsolate decay,
I come to see her where I most have seen her,
And touch the happier day.

For on this path, at every turn and corner,
The fancy of her figure on me falls:
Yet walks she with the slow step of a mourner,
Nor hears my voice that calls.

So through my heart there winds a track of feeling,
A path of memory, that is all her own:
Whereto her phantom beauty ever stealing
Haunts the sad spot alone.

About her steps the trunks are bare, the branches
Drip heavy tears upon her downcast head;
And bleed from unseen wounds that no sun stanches,
For the year's sun is dead.

And dead leaves wrap the fruits that summer planted:
And birds that love the South have taken wing
The wanderer, loitering o'er the scene enchanted,
Weeps, and despairs of spring.

A Passer-by

Whither, O splendid ship, thy white sails crowding,
Leaning across the bosom of the urgent West,
That fearest nor sea rising, nor sky clouding,
Whither away, fair rover, and what thy quest?
Ah! soon, when Winter has all our vales opprest,
When skies are cold and misty, and hail is hurling,

Wilt thóu glíde on the blue Pacific, or rest
In a summer haven asleep, thy white sails furling.

I there before thee, in the country that well thou knowest,
Already arrived am inhaling the odorous air:
I watch thee enter unerringly where thou goest,
And anchor queen of the strange shipping there,
Thy sails for awnings spread, thy masts bare;
Nor is aught from the foaming reef to the snow-capped, grandest
Peak, that is over the feathery palms more fair
Than thou, so upright, so stately, and still thou standest.

And yet, O splendid ship, unhailed and nameless,
I know not if, aiming a fancy, I rightly divine
That thou hast a purpose joyful, a courage blameless,
Thy port assured in a happier land than mine.
But for all I have given thee, beauty enough is thine,
As thou, aslant with trim tackle and shrouding,
From the proud nostril curve of a prow's line
In the offing scatterest foam, thy white sails crowding.

There is a hill

There is a hill beside the silver Thames,
Shady with birch and beech and odorous pine:
And brilliant underfoot with thousand gems
Steeply the thickets to his floods decline.
Straight trees in every place
Their thick tops interlace,
And pendant branches trail their foliage fine
Upon his watery face.

Swift from the sweltering pasturage he flows:
His stream, alert to seek the pleasant shade,
Pictures his gentle purpose, as he goes
Straight to the caverned pool his toil has made.
His winter floods lay bare
The stout roots in the air:
His summer streams are cool, when they have played
Among their fibrous hair.

A rushy island guards the sacred bower,
And hides it from the meadow, where in peace
The lazy cows wrench many a scented flower,
Robbing the golden market of the bees:
And laden barges float
By banks of myosote;
And scented flag and golden flower-de-lys
Delay the loitering boat.

And on this side the island, where the pool
Eddies away, are tangled mass on mass
The water-weeds, that net the fishes cool,
And scarce allow a narrow stream to pass;
Where spreading crowfoot mars
The drowning nenuphars,
Waving the tassels of her silken grass
Below her silver stars.

But in the purple pool there nothing grows,
Not the white water-lily spoked with gold;
Though best she loves the hollows, and well knows
On quiet streams her broad shields to unfold:
Yet should her roots but try
Within these deeps to lie,

Not her long reaching stalk could ever hold
Her waxen head so high.

Sometimes an angler comes, and drops his hook
Within its hidden depths, and 'gainst a tree
Leaning his rod, reads in some pleasant book,
Forgetting soon his pride of fishery;
And dreams, or falls asleep,
While curious fishes peep
About his nibbled bait, or scornfully
Dart off and rise and leap.

And sometimes a slow figure 'neath the trees,
In ancient-fashioned smock, with tottering care
Upon a staff propping his weary knees,
May by the pathway of the forest fare:
As from a buried day
Across the mind will stray
Some perishing mute shadow, — and unaware
He passeth on his way.

Else, he that wishes solitude is safe,
Whether he bathe at morning in the stream:
Or lead his love there when the hot hours chafe
The meadows, busy with a blurring steam;
Or watch, as fades the light,
The gibbous moon grow bright,
Until her magic rays dance in a dream,
And glorify the night.

Where is this bower beside the silver Thames?
O pool and flowery thickets, hear my vow!
O trees of freshest foliage and straight stems,
No sharer of my secret I allow:
Lest ere I come the while
Strange feet your shades defile;
Or lest the burly oarsman turn his prow
Within your guardian isle.

On a Dead Child

Perfect little body, without fault or stain on thee,
With promise of strength and manhood full and fair!
Though cold and stark and bare,
The bloom and the charm of life doth awhile remain on thee.

Thy mother's treasure wert thou; — alas! no longer
To visit her heart with wondrous joy; to be
Thy father's pride; — ah, he
Must gather his faith together, and his strength make stronger.

To me, as I move thee now in the last duty,
Dost thou with a turn or gesture anon respond;
Startling my fancy fond
With a chance attitude of the head, a freak of beauty.

Thy hand clasps, as 'twas wont, my finger, and holds it:
But the grasp is the clasp of Death, heartbreaking and stiff;
Yet feels to my hand as if
'Twas still thy will, thy pleasure and trust that enfolds it.

So I lay thee there, thy sunken eyelids closing, —
Go lie thou there in thy coffin, thy last little bed! —
Propping thy wise, sad head,
Thy firm, pale hands across thy chest disposing.

So quiet! doth the change content thee? — Death, whither hath he taken thee?
To a world, do I think, that rights the disaster of this?
The vision of which I miss,

Who weep for the body, and wish but to
warm thee and awaken thee?

Ah! little at best can all our hopes avail us
To lift this sorrow, or cheer us, when
in the dark,
Unwilling, alone we embark,
And the things we have seen and have
known and have heard of, fail us.

The Philosopher to his Mistress

Because thou canst not see,
Because thou canst not know
The black and hopeless woe
That hath encompassed me:
Because, should I confess
The thought of my despair,
My words would wound thee less
Than swords can hurt the air:

Because with thee I seem
As one invited near
To taste the faery cheer
Of spirits in a dream;
Of whom he knoweth nought
Save that they vie to make
All motion, voice and thought
A pleasure for his sake:

Therefore more sweet and strange
Has been the mystery
Of thy long love to me,
That doth not quit, nor change,
Nor tax my solemn heart,
That kisseth in a gloom,
Knowing not who thou art
That givest, nor to whom.

Therefore the tender touch
Is more; more dear the smile:
And thy light words beguile
My wisdom overmuch:
And O with swiftness fly
The fancies of my song
To happy worlds, where I
Still in thy love belong.

To L. B. C. L. M.

I love all beauteous things,
I seek and adore them;
God hath no better praise,
And man in his hasty days
Is honoured for them.

I too will something make
And joy in the making;
Altho' to-morrow it seem
Like the empty words of a dream
Remembered on waking.

The hill pines were sighing

The hill pines were sighing,
O'ercast and chill was the day:
A mist in the valley lying
Blotted the pleasant May.

But deep in the glen's bosom
Summer slept in the fire
Of the odorous gorse-blossom
And the hot scent of the brier.

A ribald cuckoo clamoured,
And out of the copse the stroke
Of the iron axe that hammered
The iron heart of the oak.

Anon a sound appalling,
As a hundred years of pride
Crashed, in the silence falling:
And the shadowy pine-trees sighed.

The Winnowers

Betwixt two billows of the downs
The little hamlet lies,
And nothing sees but the bald crowns
Of the hills, and the blue skies.

Clustering beneath the long descent
And grey slopes of the wold,

The red roofs nestle, over-spent
  With lichen yellow as gold.

We found it in the mid-day sun
  Basking, what time of year
The thrush his singing has begun,
  Ere the first leaves appear.

High from his load a woodman pitched
  His faggots on the stack:
Knee-deep in straw the cattle twitched
  Sweet hay from crib and rack:

And from the barn hard by was borne
  A steady muffled din,
By which we knew that threshéd corn
  Was winnowing, and went in.

The sunbeams on the motey air
  Streamed through the open door,
And on the brown arms moving bare,
  And the grain upon the floor.

One turns the crank, one stoops to feed
  The hopper, lest it lack,
One in the bushel scoops the seed,
  One stands to hold the sack.

We watched the good grain rattle down,
  And the awns fly in the draught;
To see us both so pensive grown
  The honest labourers laughed:

Merry they were, because the wheat
  Was clean and plump and good,
Pleasant to hand and eye, and meet
  For market and for food.

It chanced we from the city were,
  And had not gat us free
In spirit from the store and stir
  Of its immensity:

But here we found ourselves again.
  Where humble harvests bring
After much toil but little grain,
  'Tis merry winnowing.

I never shall love the snow again

I NEVER shall love the snow again
    Since Maurice died:
With corniced drift it blocked the lane
And sheeted in a desolate plain
    The country side.

The trees with silvery rime bedight
    Their branches bare.
By day no sun appeared; by night
The hidden moon shed thievish light
    In the misty air.

We fed the birds that flew around
    In flocks to be fed:
No shelter in holly or brake they found.
The speckled thrush on the frozen ground
    Lay frozen and dead.

We skated on stream and pond; we cut
    The crinching snow
To Doric temple or Arctic hut;
We laughed and sang at nightfall, shut
    By the fireside glow.

Yet grudged we our keen delights before
    Maurice should come.
We said, In-door or out-of-door
We shall love life for a month or more,
    When he is home.

They brought him home; 'twas two days late
    For Christmas day:
Wrapped in white, in solemn state,
A flower in his hand, all still and straight
    Our Maurice lay.

And two days ere the year outgave
    We laid him low.
The best of us truly were not brave,
When we laid Maurice down in his grave
    Under the snow.

My delight and thy delight

MY delight and thy delight
Walking, like two angels white,
In the gardens of the night:

My desire and thy desire
Twining to a tongue of fire,
Leaping live, and laughing higher;
Thro' the everlasting strife
In the mystery of life.

Love, from whom the world begun,
Hath the secret of the sun.

Love can tell, and love alone,
Whence the million stars were strewn,
Why each atom knows its own,
How, in spite of woe and death,
Gay is life, and sweet is breath:

This he taught us, this we knew,
Happy in his science true,
Hand in hand as we stood
Neath the shadows of the wood,
Heart to heart as we lay
In the dawning of the day.

[*New Poems,* 1899]

A. E. Housman

1859–1936

A SHROPSHIRE LAD[1]

II

Loveliest of trees, the cherry now
Is hung with bloom along the bough,
And stands about the woodland ride
Wearing white for Eastertide.

Now, of my threescore years and ten,
Twenty will not come again,
And take from seventy springs a score,
It only leaves me fifty more.

And since to look at things in bloom
Fifty springs are little room,
About the woodlands I will go
To see the cherry hung with snow.

IV

Reveille

Wake: the silver dusk returning
  Up the beach of darkness brims,
And the ship of sunrise burning
  Strands upon the eastern rims.

Wake: the vaulted shadow shatters,
  Trampled to the floor it spanned,
And the tent of night in tatters
  Straws the sky-pavilioned land.

Up, lad, up, 'tis late for lying:
  Hear the drums of morning play;
Hark, the empty highways crying
  'Who'll beyond the hills away?'

Towns and countries woo together,
  Forelands beacon, belfries call;
Never lad that trod on leather
  Lived to feast his heart with all.

Up, lad: thews that lie and cumber
  Sunlit pallets never thrive;
Morns abed and daylight slumber
  Were not meant for man alive.

Clay lies still, but blood's a rover;
  Breath's a ware that will not keep.
Up, lad: when the journey's over
  There'll be time enough to sleep.

[1] Housman published two slender but important collections of verse. The first, *A Shropshire Lad,* was issued in 1896; the second, *Last Poems,* in 1922. After his death, in 1936, came a final volume, *More Poems,* issued by his brother. The sixty-three lyrics of the first were composed in one stretch of eighteen months, 1894–5, many of them, Housman wrote, from his most prolific period when he suffered from a 'relaxed sore throat . . . the first five months of 1895 . . .' But several of the poems in the later two volumes also date from this time.

VIII

'Farewell to barn and stack and tree,
  Farewell to Severn shore.
Terence,[2] look your last at me,
  For I come home no more.

'The sun burns on the half-mown hill,
  By now the blood is dried;
And Maurice amongst the hay lies still
  And my knife is in his side.

'My mother thinks us long away;
  'Tis time the field were mown.
She had two sons at rising day,
  To-night she'll be alone.

'And here's a bloody hand to shake,
  And oh, man, here's good-bye;
We'll sweat no more on scythe and rake,
  My bloody hands and I.

'I wish you strength to bring you pride,
  And a love to keep you clean,
And I wish you luck, come Lammastide,
  At racing on the green.

'Long for me the rick will wait,
  And long will wait the fold,
And long will stand the empty plate,
  And dinner will be cold.'

IX

On moonlit heath and lonesome bank
  The sheep beside me graze;
And yon the gallows used to clank
  Fast by the four cross ways.

A careless shepherd once would keep
  The flocks by moonlight there,[3]
And high amongst the glimmering sheep
  The dead man stood on air.

They hang us now in Shrewsbury jail:
  The whistles blow forlorn,
And trains all night groan on the rail
  To men that die at morn.

There sleeps in Shrewsbury jail to-night,
  Or wakes, as may betide,
A better lad, if things went right,
  Than most that sleep outside.

And naked to the hangman's noose
  The morning clocks will ring
A neck God made for other use
  Than strangling in a string.

And sharp the link of life will snap,
  And dead on air will stand
Heels that held up as straight a chap
  As treads upon the land.

So here I'll watch the night and wait
  To see the morning shine,
When he will hear the stroke of eight
  And not the stroke of nine;

And wish my friend as sound a sleep
  As lads' I did not know,
That shepherded the moonlit sheep
  A hundred years ago.

XII

When I watch the living meet,
  And the moving pageant file
Warm and breathing through the street
  Where I lodge a little while,

If the heats of hate and lust
  In the house of flesh are strong,
Let me mind the house of dust
  Where my sojourn shall be long.

In the nation that is not
  Nothing stands that stood before;
There revenges are forgot,
  And the hater hates no more;

Lovers lying two and two
  Ask not whom they sleep beside,

[2] Housman proposed the title *Poems by Terence Hearsay* for his first volume; at a friend's suggestion, he changed it to *A Shropshire Lad*, but occasional references to Terence remain, as here and in LXII.
[3] 'Hanging in chains was called keeping sheep by moonlight' [Housman].

And the bridegroom all night through
  Never turns him to the bride.

XIII

WHEN I was one-and-twenty
  I heard a wise man say,
'Give crowns and pounds and guineas
  But not your heart away;
Give pearls away and rubies
  But keep your fancy free.'
But I was one-and-twenty,
  No use to talk to me.

When I was one-and-twenty
  I heard him say again,
'The heart out of the bosom
  Was never given in vain;
'Tis paid with sighs a plenty
  And sold for endless rue.'
And I am two-and-twenty,
  And oh, 'tis true, 'tis true.

XVIII

OH, when I was in love with you,
  Then I was clean and brave,
And miles around the wonder grew
  How well did I behave.

And now the fancy passes by,
  And nothing will remain,
And miles around they'll say that I
  Am quite myself again.

XIX

To an Athlete Dying Young

THE time you won your town the race
We chaired you through the market-place;
Man and boy stood cheering by,
And home we brought you shoulder-high.

Today, the road all runners come,
Shoulder-high we bring you home,
And set you at your threshold down,
Townsman of a stiller town.

Smart lad, to slip betimes away
From fields where glory does not stay
And early though the laurel grows
It withers quicker than the rose.

Eyes the shady night has shut
Cannot see the record cut,
And silence sounds no worse than cheers
After earth has stopped the ears:

Now you will not swell the rout
Of lads that wore their honours out,
Runners whom renown outran
And the name died before the man.

So set, before its echoes fade,
The fleet foot on the sill of shade,
And hold to the low lintel up
The still-defended challenge-cup.

And round that early-laurelled head
Will flock to gaze the strengthless dead,
And find unwithered on its curls
The garland briefer than a girl's.

XXVI

ALONG the field as we came by
A year ago, my love and I,
The aspen over stile and stone
Was talking to itself alone.
'Oh who are these that kiss and pass?
A country lover and his lass;
Two lovers looking to be wed;
And time shall put them both to bed,
But she shall lie with earth above,
And he beside another love.'

And sure enough beneath the tree
There walks another love with me,
And overhead the aspen heaves
Its rainy-sounding silver leaves;
And I spell nothing in their stir,
And now perhaps they speak to her,
And plain for her to understand
They talk about a time at hand
When I shall sleep with clover clad,
And she beside another lad.

XXVII

'Is my team ploughing,
That I was used to drive
And hear the harness jingle
When I was man alive?'

Ay, the horses trample,
The harness jingles now;
No change though you lie under
The land you used to plough.

'Is football playing
Along the river shore,
With lads to chase the leather,
Now I stand up no more?'

Ay, the ball is flying,
The lads play heart and soul;
The goal stands up, the keeper
Stands up to keep the goal.

'Is my girl happy,
That I thought hard to leave,
And has she tired of weeping
As she lies down at eve?'

Ay, she lies down lightly,
She lies not down to weep:
Your girl is well contented.
Be still, my lad, and sleep.

'Is my friend hearty,
Now I am thin and pine,
And has he found to sleep in
A better bed than mine?'

Yes, lad, I lie easy,
I lie as lads would choose;
I cheer a dead man's sweetheart,
Never ask me whose.

XXXI

ON Wenlock Edge[4] the wood's in trouble;
His forest fleece the Wrekin heaves;
The gale, it plies the saplings double,
And thick on Severn snow the leaves.

'Twould blow like this through holt and hanger
When Uricon[5] the city stood:
'Tis the old wind in the old anger,
But then it threshed another wood.

Then, 'twas before my time, the Roman
At yonder heaving hill would stare:
The blood that warms an English yeoman,
The thoughts that hurt him, they were there.

There, like the wind through woods in riot,
Through him the gale of life blew high;
The tree of man was never quiet:
Then 'twas the Roman, now 'tis I.

The gale, it plies the saplings double,
It blows so hard, 'twill soon be gone:
To-day the Roman and his trouble
Are ashes under Uricon.

XXXV

ON the idle hill of summer,
Sleepy with the flow of streams,
Far I hear the steady drummer
Drumming like a noise in dreams.

Far and near and low and louder
On the roads of earth go by,
Dear to friends and food for powder,
Soldiers marching, all to die.

East and west on fields forgotten
Bleach the bones of comrades slain,
Lovely lads and dead and rotten;
None that go return again.

Far the calling bugles hollo,
High the screaming fife replies,
Gay the files of scarlet follow:
Woman bore me, I will rise.

---

[4] Wenlock Edge and the 'Wrekin' in the line below are long hills or ridges in Shropshire.

[5] Uriconium (or Viroconium), now Wroxeter on the Severn, near Shrewsbury, was anciently a Roman legionary fortress against the Welsh hill tribes.

XL

Into my heart an air that kills
  From yon far country blows:
What are those blue remembered hills,
  What spires, what farms are those?

That is the land of lost content,
  I see it shining plain,
The happy highways where I went
  And cannot come again.

XLII

The Merry Guide

Once in the wind of morning
  I ranged the thymy wold;
The world-wide air was azure
  And all the brooks ran gold.

There through the dews beside me
  Behold a youth that trod,
With feathered cap on forehead,
  And poised a golden rod.

With mien to match the morning
  And gay delightful guise
And friendly brows and laughter
  He looked me in the eyes.

O whence, I asked, and whither?
  He smiled and would not say,
And looked at me and beckoned
  And laughed and led the way.

And with kind looks and laughter
  And nought to say beside
We two went on together,
  I and my happy guide.

Across the glittering pastures
  And empty upland still
And solitude of shepherds
  High in the folded hill,

By hanging woods and hamlets
  That gaze through orchards down
On many a windmill turning
  And far-discovered town,

With gay regards of promise
  And sure unslackened stride
And smiles and nothing spoken
  Led on my merry guide.

By blowing realms of woodland
  With sunstruck vanes afield
And cloud-led shadows sailing
  About the windy weald,

By valley-guarded granges
  And silver waters wide,
Content at heart I followed
  With my delightful guide.

And like the cloudy shadows
  Across the country blown
We two fare on for ever,
  But not we two alone.

With the great gale we journey
  That breathes from gardens thinned,
Borne in the drift of blossoms
  Whose petals throng the wind;

Buoyed on the heaven-heard whisper
  Of dancing leaflets whirled
From all the woods that autumn
  Bereaves in all the world.

And midst the fluttering legion
  Of all that ever died
I follow, and before us
  Goes the delightful guide,

With lips that brim with laughter
  But never once respond,
And feet that fly on feathers,
  And serpent-circled wand.

XLVIII

Be still, my soul, be still; the arms you bear are brittle,
  Earth and high heaven are fixt of old and founded strong.
Think rather,—call to thought, if now you grieve a little,

The days when we had rest, O soul, for they were long.

Men loved unkindness then, but lightless in the quarry
I slept and saw not; tears fell down, I did not mourn;
Sweat ran and blood sprang out and I was never sorry:
Then it was well with me, in days ere I was born.

Now, and I muse for why and never find the reason,
I pace the earth, and drink the air, and feel the sun.
Be still, be still, my soul; it is but for a season:
Let us endure an hour and see injustice done.

Ay, look: high heaven and earth ail from the prime foundation;
All thoughts to rive the heart are here, and all are vain:
Horror and scorn and hate and fear and indignation —
Oh why did I awake? when shall I sleep again?

LII

Far in a western brookland
That bred me long ago
The poplars stand and tremble
By pools I used to know.

There, in the windless night-time,
The wanderer, marvelling why,
Halts on the bridge to hearken
How soft the poplars sigh.

He hears: no more remembered
In fields where I was known,
Here I lie down in London
And turn to rest alone.

There, by the starlit fences,
The wanderer halts and hears
My soul that lingers sighing
About the glimmering weirs.

LIV

With rue my heart is laden
For golden friends I had,
For many a rose-lipt maiden
And many a lightfoot lad.

By brooks too broad for leaping
The lightfoot boys are laid;
The rose-lipt girls are sleeping
In fields where roses fade.

LXII

'Terence, this is stupid stuff:
You eat your victuals fast enough;
There can't be much amiss, 'tis clear,
To see the rate you drink your beer.
But oh, good Lord, the verse you make,
It gives a chap the belly-ache.
The cow, the old cow, she is dead;
It sleeps well, the horned head:
We poor lads, 'tis our turn now
To hear such tunes as killed the cow.
Pretty friendship 'tis to rhyme
Your friends to death before their time
Moping melancholy mad:
Come, pipe a tune to dance to, lad.'

Why, if 'tis dancing you would be,
There's brisker pipes than poetry.
Say, for what were hop-yards meant,
Or why was Burton built on Trent?
Oh many a peer of England brews
Livelier liquor than the Muse,
And malt does more than Milton can
To justify God's ways to man.[6]
Ale, man, ale's the stuff to drink
For fellows whom it hurts to think:
Look into the pewter pot
To see the world as the world's not.

---

[6] This allusion to *Paradise Lost* was engraved around the edge of a large silver loving cup presented to Housman by his students when he left University College, London, for Cambridge. Housman was a connoisseur of fine wines, but he owned to preferring good beer or ale.

And faith, 'tis pleasant till 'tis past:
The mischief is that 'twill not last.
Oh I have been to Ludlow fair
And left my necktie God knows where,
And carried half-way home, or near,
Pints and quarts of Ludlow beer:
Then the world seemed none so bad,
And I myself a sterling lad;
And down in lovely muck I've lain,
Happy till I woke again.
Then I saw the morning sky:
Heigho, the tale was all a lie;
The world, it was the old world yet,
I was I, my things were wet,
And nothing now remained to do
But begin the game anew.

Therefore, since the world has still
Much good, but much less good than ill,
And while the sun and moon endure
Luck's a chance, but trouble's sure,
I'd face it as a wise man would,
And train for ill and not for good.
'Tis true, the stuff I bring for sale
Is not so brisk a brew as ale:
Out of a stem that scored the hand
I wrung it in a weary land.
But take it: if the smack is sour,
The better for the embittered hour;
It should do good to heart and head
When your soul is in my soul's stead;
And I will friend you, if I may,
In the dark and cloudy day.

There was a king reigned in the East:
There, when kings will sit to feast,
They get their fill before they think
With poisoned meat and poisoned drink.
He gathered all that springs to birth
From the many-venomed earth;
First a little, thence to more,
He sampled all her killing store;
And easy, smiling, seasoned sound,
Sate the king when healths went round.
They put arsenic in his meat
And stared aghast to watch him eat;
They poured strychnine in his cup
And shook to see him drink it up:
They shook, they stared as white's their shirt:
Them it was their poison hurt.
—I tell the tale that I heard told.
Mithridates, he died old.

LAST POEMS[7]

VII

In valleys green and still
Where lovers wander maying
They hear from over hill
A music playing.

Behind the drum and fife,
Past hawthornwood and hollow,
Through earth and out of life
The soldiers follow.

The soldier's is the trade:
In any wind or weather
He steals the heart of maid
And man together.

The lover and his lass
Beneath the hawthorn lying
Have heard the soldiers pass,
And both are sighing.

And down the distance they
With dying note and swelling
Walk the resounding way
To the still dwelling.

IX

The chestnut casts his flambeaux, and the flowers
Stream from the hawthorn on the wind away,
The doors clap to, the pane is blind with showers.

[7] See n. 1.

Pass me the can, lad; there's an end of May.

There's one spoilt spring to scant our mortal lot,
One season ruined of our little store.
May will be fine next year as like as not:
Oh ay, but then we shall be twenty-four.

We for a certainty are not the first
Have sat in taverns while the tempest hurled
Their hopeful plans to emptiness, and cursed
Whatever brute and blackguard made the world.

It is in truth iniquity on high
To cheat our sentenced souls of aught they crave,
And mar the merriment as you and I
Fare on our long fool's-errand to the grave.

Iniquity it is; but pass the can.
My lad, no pair of kings our mothers bore;
Our only portion is the estate of man:
We want the moon, but we shall get no more.

If here to-day the cloud of thunder lours
To-morrow it will hie on far behests;
The flesh will grieve on other bones than ours
Soon, and the soul will mourn in other breasts.

The troubles of our proud and angry dust
Are from eternity, and shall not fail.
Bear them we can, and if we can we must.
Shoulder the sky, my lad, and drink your ale.

XII

THE laws of God, the laws of man,
He may keep that will and can;
Not I: let God and man decree
Laws for themselves and not for me;
And if my ways are not as theirs
Let them mind their own affairs.
Their deeds I judge and much condemn,
Yet when did I make laws for them?
Please yourselves, say I, and they
Need only look the other way.
But no, they will not; they must still
Wrest their neighbour to their will,
And make me dance as they desire
With jail and gallows and hell-fire.
And how am I to face the odds
Of man's bedevilment and God's?
I, a stranger and afraid
In a world I never made.
They will be master, right or wrong;
Though both are foolish, both are strong.
And since, my soul, we cannot fly
To Saturn nor to Mercury,
Keep we must, if keep we can,
These foreign laws of God and man.

XXV

The Oracles

'TIS mute, the word they went to hear on high Dodona[8] mountain
When winds were in the oakenshaws and all the cauldrons tolled,
And mute's the midland navel-stone beside the singing fountain,
And echoes list to silence now where gods told lies of old.

I took my question to the shrine that has not ceased from speaking,
The heart within, that tells the truth and tells it twice as plain;
And from the cave of oracles I heard the priestess shrieking
That she and I should surely die and never live again.

Oh priestess, what you cry is clear, and sound good sense I think it;

[8] Site of the shrine of Zeus, in Epirus; it and that of Apollo at Delphi were the two most famous 'oracles' in Greece.

But let the screaming echoes rest, and froth your mouth no more.
'Tis true there's better boose than brine, but he that drowns must drink it;
And oh, my lass, the news is news that men have heard before.

The King with half the East at heel is marched from lands of morning;
Their fighters drink the rivers up, their shafts benight the air.
And he that stands will die for nought, and home there's no returning.
The Spartans on the sea-wet rock sat down and combed their hair.

XXXV

When first my way to fair I took
Few pence in purse had I,
And long I used to stand and look
At things I could not buy.

Now times are altered: if I care
To buy a thing, I can;
The pence are here and here's the fair,
But where's the lost young man?

—To think that two and two are four
And neither five nor three
The heart of man has long been sore
And long 'tis like to be.

XLI

Fancy's Knell

When lads were home from labour
At Abdon under Clee,
A man would call his neighbour
And both would send for me.
And where the light in lances
Across the mead was laid,
There to the dances
I fetched my flute and played.

Ours were idle pleasures,
Yet oh, content we were,
The young to wind the measures,
The old to heed the air;
And I to lift with playing
From tree and tower and steep
The light delaying,
And flute the sun to sleep.

The youth toward his fancy
Would turn his brow of tan,
And Tom would pair with Nancy
And Dick step off with Fan;
The girl would lift her glances
To his, and both be mute:
Well went the dances
At evening to the flute.

Wenlock Edge was umbered,
And bright was Abdon Burf,
And warm between them slumbered
The smooth green miles of turf;
Until from grass and clover
The upshot beam would fade,
And England over
Advanced the lofty shade.

The lofty shade advances,
I fetch my flute and play:
Come, lads, and learn the dances
And praise the tune to-day.
To-morrow, more's the pity,
Away we both must hie,
To air the ditty,
And to earth I.

MORE POEMS[9]

I

Easter Hymn

If in that Syrian garden, ages slain,
You sleep, and know not you are dead in vain,
Nor even in dreams behold how dark and bright
Ascends in smoke and fire by day and night

[9] See n. 1.

The hate you died to quench and could but fan,
Sleep well and see no morning, son of man.

But if, the grave rent and the stone rolled by,
At the right hand of majesty on high
You sit, and sitting so remember yet
Your tears, your agony and bloody sweat,
Your cross and passion and the life you gave,
Bow hither out of heaven and see and save.

XXXVI

Here dead lie we because we did not choose
To live and shame the land from which we sprung.
Life, to be sure, is nothing much to lose;
But young men think it is, and we were young.

Rudyard Kipling[1]

1865–1936

Recessional[2]

1897

God of our fathers, known of old,
Lord of our far-flung battle-line,
Beneath whose awful Hand we hold
Dominion over palm and pine—
Lord God of Hosts, be with us yet,
Lest we forget—lest we forget!

The tumult and the shouting dies;
The Captains and the Kings depart:
Still stands Thine ancient sacrifice,
An humble and a contrite heart.
Lord God of Hosts, be with us yet,
Lest we forget—lest we forget!

Far-called, our navies melt away;
On dune and headland sinks the fire:
Lo, all our pomp of yesterday
Is one with Nineveh and Tyre!
Judge of the Nations, spare us yet,
Lest we forget—lest we forget!

If, drunk with sight of power, we loose
Wild tongues that have not Thee in awe,
Such boastings as the Gentiles use,
Or lesser breeds without the Law—
Lord God of Hosts, be with us yet,
Lest we forget—lest we forget!

For heathen heart that puts her trust
In reeking tube and iron shard,
All valiant dust that builds on dust,
And guarding, calls not Thee to guard,
For frantic boast and foolish word—
Thy mercy on Thy People, Lord!

[*The Five Nations*, 1903]

Epitaphs of the War

1914–18

EQUALITY OF SACRIFICE

A. 'I was a Have.' B. 'I was a "have-not."'
(*Together.*) 'What hast thou given which I gave not?'

THE COWARD

I could not look on Death, which being known,
Men led me to him, blindfold and alone.

[1] The text and order of the poems here follow *Rudyard Kipling's Verse: Definitive Edition* (Doubleday and Company, 1945); though this ordering is not chronological, it has the authority of Kipling's own grouping.

[2] A month after observing the smugly complacent attitude of many Englishmen during Queen Victoria's Diamond Jubilee, Kipling first published this solemn hymn of warning in the London *Times* of July 17, 1897.

A DEAD STATESMAN

I COULD not dig: I dared not rob:
Therefore I lied to please the mob.
Now all my lies are proved untrue
And I must face the men I slew.
What tale shall serve me here among
Mine angry and defrauded young?

SALONIKAN GRAVE [3]

I HAVE watched a thousand days
Push out and crawl into night
Slowly as tortoises.
Now I, too, follow these.
It is fever, and not the fight —
Time, not battle, — that slays.

Danny Deever

'WHAT are the bugles blowin' for?' said Files-on-Parade.
'To turn you out, to turn you out,' the Colour-Sergeant said.
'What makes you look so white, so white?' said Files-on-Parade.
'I'm dreadin' what I've got to watch,' the Colour-Sergeant said.
For they're hangin' Danny Deever, you can hear the Dead March play,
The Regiment's in 'ollow square — they're hangin' him to-day;
They've taken of his buttons off an' cut his stripes away,
An' they're hangin' Danny Deever in the mornin'.

'What makes the rear-rank breathe so 'ard?' said Files-on-Parade.
'It's bitter cold, it's bitter cold,' the Colour-Sergeant said.
'What makes that front-rank man fall down?' said Files-on-Parade.
'A touch o' sun, a touch o' sun,' the Colour-Sergeant said.
They are hangin' Danny Deever, they are marchin' of 'im round,
They 'ave 'alted Danny Deever by 'is coffin on the ground;
An' 'e'll swing in 'arf a minute for a sneakin' shootin' hound —
O they're hangin' Danny Deever in the mornin'!

''Is cot was right-'and cot to mine,' said Files-on-Parade.
''E's sleepin' out an' far to-night,' the Colour-Sergeant said.
'I've drunk 'is beer a score o' times,' said Files-on-Parade.
''E's drinkin' beer alone,' the Colour-Sergeant said.
They are hangin' Danny Deever, you must mark 'im to 'is place,
For 'e shot a comrade sleepin' — you must look 'im in the face;
Nine 'undred of 'is county an' the Regiment's disgrace,
While they're hangin' Danny Deever in the mornin'.

'What's that so black agin the sun?' said Files-on-Parade.
'It's Danny fightin' 'ard for life,' the Colour-Sergeant said.
'What's that that whimpers over'ead?' said Files-on-Parade.
'It's Danny's soul that's passin' now,' the Colour-Sergeant said.
For they're done with Danny Deever, you can 'ear the quickstep play,
The Regiment's in column, an' they're marchin' us away;
Ho! the young recruits are shakin', an' they'll want their beer to-day,
After hangin' Danny Deever in the mornin'!

[*Barrack-Room Ballads*, 1890]

The Widow at Windsor

'AVE you 'eard o' the Widow at Windsor
With a hairy gold crown on 'er 'ead?

[3] Between 1915 and 1918, Salonica became the base for Allied operations in the Balkans; at one time, 300,000 men were stationed there, thousands dying from disease before the successful issue of the campaign.

She 'as ships on the foam — she 'as millions at 'ome,
An' she pays us poor beggars in red.[4]
(Ow, poor beggars in red!)
There's 'er nick on the cavalry 'orses,
There's 'er mark on the medical stores —
An' 'er troopers you'll find with a fair wind be'ind
That takes us to various wars.
(Poor beggars! — barbarious wars!)
Then 'ere's to the Widow at Windsor,
An' 'ere's to the stores an' the guns,
The men an' the 'orses what makes up the forces
O' Missis Victorier's sons.
(Poor beggars! Victorier's sons!)

Walk wide o' the Widow at Windsor,
For 'alf o' Creation she owns:
We 'ave bought 'er the same with the sword an' the flame,
An' we've salted it down with our bones.
(Poor beggars! — it's blue with our bones!)
Hands off o' the sons o' the Widow,
Hands off o' the goods in 'er shop,
For the Kings must come down an' the the Emperors frown
When the Widow at Windsor says 'Stop!'
(Poor beggars! — we're sent to say 'Stop!')
Then 'ere's to the Lodge o' the Widow,
From the Pole to the Tropics it runs —
To the Lodge that we tile[5] with the rank an' the file,
An' open in form with the guns.
(Poor beggars! — it's always they guns!)

We 'ave 'eard o' the Widow at Windsor,
It's safest to leave 'er alone:
For 'er sentries we stand by the sea an' the land
Wherever the bugles are blown.
(Poor beggars! — an' don't we get blown!)
Take 'old o' the Wings o' the Mornin',
An' flop round the earth till you're dead;
But you won't get away from the tune that they play
To the bloomin' old rag over'ead.
(Poor beggars! — it's 'ot over'ead!)
Then 'ere's to the Sons o' the Widow,
Wherever, 'owever they roam.
'Ere's all they desire, an' if they require
A speedy return to their 'ome.
(Poor beggars! — they'll never see 'ome!)

[*Barrack-Room Ballads,* 1890]

Shillin' a Day[6]

My name is O'Kelly, I've heard the Revelly
From Birr[7] to Bareilly, from Leeds to Lahore,
Hong-Kong and Peshawur,
Lucknow and Etawah,
And fifty-five more all endin' in 'pore.'
Black Death and his quickness, the depth and the thickness
Of sorrow and sickness I've known on my way,
But I'm old and I'm nervis,
I'm cast from the Service,
And all I deserve is a shillin' a day.
(*Chorus*) Shillin' a day,
Bloomin' good pay —
Lucky to touch it, a shillin' a day!

[4] A 'red' or a 'red 'un' was slang for a coin, usually a sovereign. But because of the low pay of the enlisted man in the British Army and the numerous deductions often made from it, few were the months when the soldier was not in debt to the paymaster, that is, 'in the red.'

[5] Technically, to 'tile' or 'tyle' is to protect a Masonic lodge from intrusion.

[6] The usual pension of the retired soldier. This poem appeared for the first time in the British edition of *Barrack-Room Ballads,* two years after the American issue.

[7] A town in central Ireland; with the exception of Leeds and Hong Kong, the remaining place names mentioned here are Indian, chiefly in the central provinces in which there was much Moslem resistance in the 1857 Mutiny.

Oh, it drives me half crazy to think of the days I
Went slap for the Ghazi,[8] my sword at my side,
When we rode Hell-for-leather
Both squadrons together,
That didn't care whether we lived or we died.
But it's no use despairin', my wife must go charin'
An' me commissairin', the pay-bills to better,
So if me you be'old
In the wet and the cold,
By the Grand Metropold, won't you give me a letter?
(*Full chorus*) Give 'im a letter —
'Can't do no better,
Late Troop-Sergeant-Major an' — runs with a letter!
Think what 'e's been,
Think what 'e's seen.
Think of his pension an' —
GAWD SAVE THE QUEEN!

[*Barrack-Room Ballads*, 1892]

'*Follow Me 'Ome*'

THERE was no one like 'im, 'Orse or Foot,
Nor any o' the Guns I knew;
An' because it was so, why, o' course 'e went an' died,
Which is just what the best men do.

So it's knock out your pipes an' follow me!
An' it's finish up your swipes an' follow me!
Oh, 'ark to the big drum callin',
Follow me — follow me 'ome!

'Is mare she neighs the 'ole day long,
She paws the 'ole night through,
An' she won't take 'er feed 'cause o' waitin' for 'is step,
Which is just what a beast would do.

'Is girl she goes with a bombardier
Before 'er month is through;
An' the banns are up in church, for she's got the beggar hooked,
Which is just what a girl would do.

We fought 'bout a dog — last week it were —
No more than a round or two;
But I strook 'im cruel 'ard, an' I wish I 'adn't now,
Which is just what a man can't do.

'E was all that I 'ad in the way of a friend,
An' I've 'ad to find one new;
But I'd give my pay an' stripe for to get the beggar back,
Which it's just too late to do!

So it's knock out your pipes an' follow me!
An' it's finish up your swipes an' follow me!
Oh, 'ark to the fifes a-crawlin'!
Follow me — follow me 'ome!

Take 'im away! 'E's gone where the best men go.
Take 'im away! An' the gun-wheels turnin' slow.
Take 'im away! There's more from the place 'e come.
Take 'im away, with the limber an' the drum.

For it's 'Three rounds blank' an' follow me,
An' it's 'Thirteen rank' an' follow me;
Oh, passin' the love o' women,
Follow me — follow me 'ome!

[*The Seven Seas*, 1896]

[8] A 'ghazi' is a Moslem fanatically dedicated to exterminating unbelievers by the sword.

Chant-Pagan

English Irregular, Discharged

Me that 'ave been what I've been —
  Me that 'ave gone where I've gone —
Me that 'ave seen what I've seen —
  'Ow can I ever take on
With awful old England again,
An' 'ouses both sides of the street,
And 'edges two sides of the lane,
And the parson an' gentry between,
An' touchin' my 'at when we meet —
  Me that 'ave been what I've been?

Me that 'ave watched 'arf a world
'Eave up shiny with dew,
Kopje[9] on kop to the sun,
An' as soon as the mist let 'em through
Our 'elios winkin' like fun —
Three sides of a ninety-mile square,
Over valleys as big as a shire —
'Are ye there? Are ye there? Are ye there?'
An' then the blind drum of our fire . . .
An' I'm rollin' 'is lawns for the Squire,
Me!

Me that 'ave rode through the dark
Forty mile, often, on end,
Along the Ma'ollisberg[10] Range,
With only the stars for my mark
An' only the night for my friend,
An' things runnin' off as you pass,
An' things jumpin' up in the grass,
An' the silence, the shine an' the size
Of the 'igh, unexpressible skies —
I am takin' some letters almost
As much as a mile to the post,
An' 'mind you come back with the change!'
Me!

Me that saw Barberton took
When we dropped through the clouds on their 'ead,
An' they 'ove the guns over and fled —
Me that was through Di'mond 'Ill,
An' Pieters an' Springs an' Belfast —
From Dundee to Vereeniging all —
Me that stuck out to the last
(An' five bloomin' bars on my chest) —
I am doin' my Sunday-school best,
By the 'elp of the Squire an' 'is wife
(Not to mention the 'ousemaid an' cook),
To come in an' 'ands up an' be still,
An' honestly work for my bread,
My livin' in that state of life
To which it shall please God to call
Me!

Me that 'ave followed my trade
In the place where the Lightnin's are made;
'Twixt the Rains and the Sun and the Moon —
Me that lay down an' got up
Three years with the sky for my roof —
That 'ave ridden my 'unger an' thirst
Six thousand raw mile on the hoof,
With the Vaal and the Orange for cup,
An' the Brandwater Basin for dish, —
Oh! it's 'ard to be'ave as they wish
(Too 'ard, an' a little too soon),
I'll 'ave to think over it first —
Me!

I will arise an' get 'ence —
I will trek South and make sure
If it's only my fancy or not
That the sunshine of England is pale,
And the breezes of England are stale,
An' there's somethin' gone small with the lot.
For *I* know of a sun an' a wind,
An' some plains and a mountain be'ind,
An' some graves by a barb-wire fence,
An' a Dutchman I've fought 'oo might give
Me a job were I ever inclined
To look in an' offsaddle an' live
Where there's neither a road nor a tree —

[9] In the Afrikaans dialect of the South African Boers, 'kopje' is the diminutive of 'kop,' that is, a small hill.

[10] The Magalies Berg is a long ridge just north of Pretoria. This, and the place names in the next stanza are all connected with the Boer War, the beginning and end of which are marked by Dundee and Vereeniging.

But only my Maker an' me,
And I think it will kill me or cure,
So I think I will go there an' see.
Me!

[*The Five Nations*, 1903]

Harp Song of the Dane Women

'The Knights of the Joyous Venture'—Puck of Pook's Hill [11]

What is a woman that you forsake her,
And the hearth-fire and the home-acre,
To go with the old grey Widow-maker?

She has no house to lay a guest in—
But one chill bed for all to rest in,
That the pale suns and the stray bergs nest in.

She has no strong white arms to fold you,
But the ten-times-fingering weed to hold you—
Out on the rocks where the tide has rolled you.

Yet, when the signs of summer thicken,
And the ice breaks, and the birch-buds quicken,
Yearly you turn from our side, and sicken—

Sicken again for the shouts and the slaughters.
You steal away to the lapping waters,
And look at your ship in her winter-quarters.

You forget our mirth, and talk at the tables,
The kine in the shed and the horse in the stables—
To pitch her sides and go over her cables.

Then you drive out where the storm-clouds swallow,
And the sound of your oar-blades, falling hollow,
Is all we have left through the months to follow.

Ah, what is Woman that you forsake her,
And the hearth-fire and the home-acre,
To go with the old grey Widow-maker?

[11] *Puck of Pook's Hill* (1906) is a collection of 'children's stories' intended for adults, making concrete episodes from English history; the story with which this poem is connected deals with the unsettled century atfer the Norman Conquest.

A St. Helena Lullaby

'A Priest in Spite of Himself'—Rewards and Fairies [12]

'How far is St. Helena from a little child at play?'
What makes you want to wander there with all the world between?
Oh, Mother, call your son again or else he'll run away.
(*No one thinks of winter when the grass is green!*)

'How far is St. Helena from a fight in Paris street?'
I haven't time to answer now—the men are falling fast.
The guns begin to thunder, and the drums begin to beat.
(*If you take the first step, you will take the last!*)

'How far is St. Helena from the field of Austerlitz?'
You couldn't hear me if I told—so loud the cannon roar.
But not so far for people who are living by their wits.
(*'Gay go up' means 'Gay go down' the wide world o'er!*)

'How far is St. Helena from an Emperor of France?'
I cannot see—I cannot tell—the Crowns they dazzle so.

[12] *Rewards and Fairies* (1910) is an extension of the plan of the Puck stories (see n. 11); here the story deals with the time of Napoleon's rise to power, years before the bitter final exile to **St. Helena**.

The Kings sit down to dinner, and the Queens stand up to dance.
(*After open weather you may look for snow!*)

'How far is St. Helena from the Capes of Trafalgar?'
A longish way — a longish way — with ten year more to run.
It's South across the water underneath a falling star.
(*What you cannot finish you must leave undone!*)

'How far is St. Helena from the Beresina ice?'[13]
An ill way — a chill way — the ice begins to crack.
But not so far for gentlemen who never took advice.
(*When you can't go forward you must e'en come back!*)

'How far is St. Helena from the field of Waterloo?'
A near way — a clear way — the ship will take you soon.
A pleasant place for gentlemen with little left to do.
(*Morning never tries you till the afternoon!*)

'How far from St. Helena to the Gate of Heaven's Grace?'
That no one knows — that no one knows — and no one ever will.
But fold your hands across your heart and cover up your face,
And after all your trapesings, child, lie still!

[13] In the retreat from Moscow, Napoleon's army forced the passage of the Beresina River in White Russia (November 26–28, 1812) with enormous losses.

Road-Song of the Bandar-Log

'Kaa's Hunting' — The Jungle Book[14]

Here we go in a flung festoon,
Half-way up to the jealous moon!
Don't you envy our pranceful bands?
Don't you wish you had extra hands?
Wouldn't you like if your tails were — *so* —
Curved in the shape of a Cupid's bow?
Now you're angry, but — never mind,
Brother, thy tail hangs down behind!

Here we sit in a branchy row,
Thinking of beautiful things we know;
Dreaming of deeds that we mean to do,
All complete, in a minute or two —
Something noble and grand and good,
Won by merely wishing we could.
Now we're going to — never mind,
Brother, thy tail hangs down behind!

All the talk we ever have heard
Uttered by bat or beast or bird —
Hide or fin or scale or feather —
Jabber it quickly and all together!
Excellent! Wonderful! Once again!
Now we are talking just like men.
Let's pretend we are . . . Never mind!
Brother, thy tail hangs down behind!
This is the way of the Monkey-kind!

Then join our leaping lines that scumfish through the pines,
That rocket by where, light and high, the wild-grape swings.
By the rubbish in our wake, and the noble noise we make,
Be sure — be sure, we're going to do some splendid things!

[14] In the story of 'Kaa's Hunting' from *The Jungle Book* (1894) Kaa, the python, rescues Mowgli from the monkey people — the 'Bandar-Log'; monkeys, for Kipling, were the symbol for the ultimate in conceit and planlessness.

Walter de la Mare[1]

1873–

All That's Past

VERY old are the woods;
And the buds that break
Out of the briar's boughs,
When March winds wake,
So old with their beauty are —
Oh, no man knows
Through what wild centuries
Roves back the rose.

Very old are the brooks;
And the rills that rise
Where snow sleeps cold beneath
The azure skies
Sing such a history
Of come and gone,
Their every drop is as wise
As Solomon.

Very old are we men;
Our dreams are tales
Told in dim Eden
By Eve's nightingales;

We wake and whisper awhile,
But, the day gone by,
Silence and sleep like fields
Of amaranth lie.

[*The Listeners,* 1912]

The Listeners

'Is there anybody there?' said the Traveller,
Knocking on the moonlit door;
And his horse in the silence champed the grasses
Of the forest's ferny floor:
And a bird flew up out of the turret,
Above the Traveller's head:
And he smote upon the door again a second time;
'Is there anybody there?' he said.
But no one descended to the Traveller;
No head from the leaf-fringed sill
Leaned over and looked into his grey eyes,
Where he stood perplexed and still.
But only a host of phantom listeners
That dwelt in the lone house then
Stood listening in the quiet of the moonlight
To that voice from the world of men:
Stood thronging the faint moonbeams on the dark stair,
That goes down to the empty hall,
Hearkening in an air stirred and shaken
By the lonely Traveller's call.
And he felt in his heart their strangeness,
Their stillness answering his cry,
While his horse moved, cropping the dark turf,
'Neath the starred and leafy sky;
For he suddenly smote on the door, even
Louder, and lifted his head: —
'Tell them I came, and no one answered,
That I kept my word,' he said.
Never the least stir made the listeners,
Though every word he spake
Fell echoing through the shadowiness of the still house
From the one man left awake:
Ay, they heard his foot upon the stirrup,
And the sound of iron on stone,
And how the silence surged softly backward,
When the plunging hoofs were gone.

[*The Listeners,* 1912]

[1] The bibliography of De La Mare's published poetry is complex because in the successive reprinting and re-ordering of collections, he has extensively revised texts of many of his poems. Moreover, he frequently uses the same title for radically different poems, and prints very early work along with late. With each poem here, the original date and volume in which it appeared is indicated; with the exception of the last poem, however, the text and order follow the versions in the two-volume *Collected Poems, 1901–1918* (1920) and *Poems, 1919 to 1934* (1936).

The Ghost

Peace in thy hands,
Peace in thine eyes,
Peace on thy brow;
Flower of a moment in the eternal hour,
Peace with me now.

Not a wave breaks,
Not a bird calls,
My heart, like a sea,
Silent after a storm that hath died,
Sleeps within me.

All the night's dews,
All the world's leaves,
All winter's snow
Seem with their quiet to have stilled in life's dream
All sorrowing now.

[*The Listeners,* 1912]

An Epitaph

Here lies a most beautiful lady,
Light of step and heart was she;
I think she was the most beautiful lady
That ever was in the West Country.
But beauty vanishes; beauty passes;
However rare — rare it be;
And when I crumble, who will remember
This lady of the West Country?

[*The Listeners,* 1912]

The Song of the Mad Prince

Who said, 'Peacock Pie'?
The old King to the sparrow:
Who said, 'Crops are ripe'?
Rust to the harrow:
Who said, 'Where sleeps she now?
Where rests she now her head,
Bathed in eve's loveliness'? —
That's what I said.

Who said, 'Ay, mum's the word';
Sexton to willow:
Who said, 'Green dusk for dreams,
Moss for a pillow'?
Who said, 'All Time's delight
Hath she for narrow bed;
Life's troubled bubble broken'? —
That's what I said.

[*Peacock Pie,* 1913]

The Old Angler

Twilight leaned mirrored in a pool
Where willow boughs swept green and hoar,
Silk-clear the water, calm and cool,
Silent the weedy shore:

There in abstracted, brooding mood
One fishing sate. His painted float
Motionless as a planet stood;
Motionless his boat.

A melancholy soul was this,
With lantern jaw, gnarled hand, vague eye;
Huddled in pensive solitariness
He had fished existence by.

Empty his creel; stolen his bait —
Impassively he angled on,
Though mist now showed the evening late
And daylight well-nigh gone.

Suddenly, like a tongueless bell,
Downward his gaudy cork did glide;
A deep, low-gathering, gentle swell
Spread slowly far and wide.

Wheeped out his tackle from noiseless winch,
And furtive as a thief, his thumb,
With nerve intense, wound inch by inch
A line no longer numb.

What fabulous spoil could thus unplayed
Gape upward to a mortal air? —
He stoops engrossed; his tanned cheek greyed;
His heart stood still: for there,

Wondrously fairing, beneath the skin
Of secretly bubbling water seen,
Swims — not the silver of scale and fin —
But gold immixt with green.

Deeply astir in oozy bed,
The darkening mirror ripples and rocks:
And lo — a wan-pale, lovely head,
Hook tangled in its locks!

Cold from her haunt — a Naiad slim.
Shoulder and cheek gleamed ivory white;
Though now faint stars stood over him,
The hour hard on night.

Her green eyes gazed like one half-blind
In sudden radiance; her breast
Breathed the sweet air, while gently twined,
'Gainst the cold water pressed,

Her lean webbed hands. She floated there,
Light as a scentless petalled flower,
Water-drops dewing from her hair
In tinkling beadlike shower.

So circling sidelong, her tender throat
Uttered a grieving, desolate wail;
Shrill o'er the dark pool lapsed its note,
Piteous as nightingale.

Ceased Echo. And he? — a life's remorse
Welled to a tongue unapt to charm,
But never a word broke harsh and hoarse
To quiet her alarm.

With infinite stealth his twitching thumb
Tugged softly at the tautened gut,
Bubble-light, fair, her lips now dumb,
She moved, and struggled not;

But with set, wild, unearthly eyes
Pale-gleaming, fixed as if in fear,
She couched in the water, with quickening sighs,
And floated near.

In hollow heaven the stars were at play;
Wan glow-worms greened the pool-side grass;
Dipped the wide-bellied boat. His prey
Gazed on; nor breathed. Alas! —

Long sterile years had come and gone;
Youth, like a distant dream, was sped;
Heart, hope, and eyes had hungered on. . . .
He turned a shaking head,

And clumsily groped amid the gold,
Sleek with night dews, of that tangling hair,
Till pricked his finger keen and cold
The barb imbedded there.

Teeth clenched, he drew his knife — 'Snip, snip,' —
Groaned, and sate shivering back; and she,
Treading the water with birdlike dip,
Shook her sweet shoulders free:

Drew backward, smiling, infatuate fair,
His life's disasters in her eyes,
All longing and folly, grief, despair,
Daydreams and mysteries.

She stooped her brow; laid low her cheek,
And, steering on that silk-tressed craft,
Out from the listening, leaf-hung creek,
Tossed up her chin, and laughed —

A mocking, icy, inhuman note.
One instant flashed that crystal breast,
Leaned, and was gone. Dead-still the boat:
And the deep dark at rest.

Flits moth to flower. A water-rat
Noses the placid ripple. And lo!
Streams a lost meteor. Night is late,
And daybreak zephyrs flow. . . .

And he — the cheated? Dusk till morn,
Insensate, even of hope forsook,
He muttering squats, aloof, forlorn,
Dangling a baitless hook.

[*The Veil*, 1921]

The Stranger

In the nook of a wood — where a pool freshed with dew
Glassed, daybreak till evening, blue sky glimpsing through,
Then a star; or a slip of a moon, silver-white,
Thridding softly aloof the quiet of night —
Was a thicket of flowers.

Willow-herb, mint, pale speedwell and rattle,
Water hemlock and sundew — to the wind's tittle-tattle
They nodded, dreamed, swayed, in jocund delight,
In beauty and sweetness arrayed, still and bright.
By turn scampered rabbit; trotted fox; bee and bird
Paused droning, sang shrill, and the fair water stirred.
Plashed a frog, or some brisk little flickering fish —
Gudgeon, stickleback, minnow — set the ripples a-swish.

A lone pool, a pool grass-fringed, crystal-clear:
Deep, placid, and cool in the sweet of the year;
Edge-parched when the sun to the Dog Days drew near;
And, with winter's bleak rime, hard as glass, robed in snow,
The whole wild-wood sleeping, and nothing a-blow
But the wind from the North — bringing snow. . . .

That is all. . . .
Save that one long, sweet, June night-tide straying,
The harsh hemlock's pale umbelliferous bloom
Tenting nook, dense with fragrance and secret with gloom,
In a beaming of moon-coloured light faintly raying,
On buds orbed with dew phosphorescently playing —
Came a Stranger — still-footed, feat-fingered, clear face,
Unhumanly lovely — and supped in that place.

[*Poems for Children*, 1930]

The End

'This is the end': the anguished word
Scarce stirred the air. She bowed her head.
No sign I made that heart had heard;
I, too, was weary and sped.

Above us loomed the night-black tree;
Beneath, a valley in shadow lay;
A waning moon beyond the sea
Cast a faint sickly ray.

Once, 'Oh, have courage!' had been my cry;
Now mutely aghast I gazed into
A face distorted, caught the sigh
That shook her through and through.

No, no. Why further should we roam,
Since every road man journeys by
Ends on a hillside far from home
Under an alien sky;

Where souls disconsolate and sick
That Valley scan, each treads alone,
And a Sea whose menace leaves the quick
Colder than churchyard stone?

[*O Lovely England*, 1953]

Wilfred Owen[1]

1893–1918

Arms and the Boy

Let the boy try along this bayonet-blade
How cold steel is, and keen with hunger of blood;
Blue with all malice, like a madman's flash;
And thinly drawn with famishing for flesh.

Lend him to stroke these blind, blunt bullet-heads
Which long to nuzzle in the hearts of lads,
Or give him cartridges of fine zinc teeth,
Sharp with the sharpness of grief and death.

For his teeth seem for laughing round an apple.
There lurk no claws behind his fingers supple;
And God will grow no talons at his heels,
Nor antlers through the thickness of his curls.

Greater Love

Red lips are not so red
As the stained stones kissed by the English dead.
Kindness of wooed and wooer
Seems shame to their love pure.
O Love, your eyes lose lure
When I behold eyes blinded in my stead!

Your slender attitude
Trembles not exquisite like limbs knife-skewed,
Rolling and rolling there
Where God seems not to care;
Till the fierce Love they bear
Cramps them in death's extreme decrepitude.

Your voice sings not so soft,—
Though even as wind murmuring through raftered loft,—
Your dear voice is not dear,
Gentle, and evening clear,
As theirs whom none now hear,
Now earth has stopped their piteous mouths that coughed.

Heart, you were never hot,
Nor large, nor full like hearts made great with shot;
And though your hand be pale,
Paler are all which trail
Your cross through flame and hail:
Weep, you may weep, for you may touch them not.

Insensibility

I

Happy are men who yet before they are killed
Can let their veins run cold.
Whom no compassion fleers
Or makes their feet
Sore on the alleys cobbled with their brothers.
The front line withers,
But they are troops who fade, not flowers
For poets' tearful fooling:
Men, gaps for filling:
Losses who might have fought
Longer; but no one bothers.

II

And some cease feeling
Even themselves or for themselves.

[1] The first selection of Owen's poetry was made posthumously by his friend, Siegfried Sassoon, in 1920. Later, Edmund Blunden was given access to the surviving papers, manuscripts, letters, and notebooks; in 1931 he brought out a complete edition of the poems, with notes and a long biographical memoir, which has been several times reprinted. The text here follows the edition published by New Directions in 1949.

Dullness best solves
The tease and doubt of shelling,
And Chance's strange arithmetic
Comes simpler than the reckoning of their shilling.
They keep no check on armies' decimation.

III

Happy are these who lose imagination:
They have enough to carry with ammunition.
Their spirit drags no pack,
Their old wounds save with cold can not more ache.
Having seen all things red,
Their eyes are rid
Of the hurt of the colour of blood for ever.
And terror's first constriction over,
Their hearts remain small-drawn.
Their senses in some scorching cautery of battle
Now long since ironed,
Can laugh among the dying, unconcerned.

IV

Happy the soldier home, with not a notion
How somewhere, every dawn, some men attack,
And many sighs are drained.
Happy the lad whose mind was never trained:
His days are worth forgetting more than not.
He sings along the march
Which we march taciturn, because of dusk,
The long, forlorn, relentless trend
From larger day to huger night.

V

We wise, who with a thought besmirch
Blood over all our soul,
How should we see our task
But through his blunt and lashless eyes?
Alive, he is not vital overmuch;
Dying, not mortal overmuch;
Nor sad, nor proud,
Nor curious at all.
He cannot tell
Old men's placidity from his.

VI

But cursed are dullards whom no cannon stuns,
That they should be as stones;
Wretched are they, and mean
With paucity that never was simplicity.
By choice they made themselves immune
To pity and whatever moans in man
Before the last sea and the hapless stars;
Whatever mourns when many leave these shores;
Whatever shares
The eternal reciprocity of tears.

Dulce et Decorum Est

Bent double, like old beggars under sacks,
Knock-kneed, coughing like hags, we cursed through sludge,
Till on the haunting flares we turned our backs,
And towards our distant rest began to trudge.
Men marched asleep. Many had lost their boots,
But limped on, blood-shod. All went lame, all blind;
Drunk with fatigue; deaf even to the hoots
Of gas-shells dropping softly behind.

Gas! Gas! Quick, boys! — An ecstasy of fumbling,
Fitting the clumsy helmets just in time,
But someone still was yelling out and stumbling
And floundering like a man in fire or lime. —
Dim through the misty panes and thick green light,

As under a green sea, I saw him drowning.

In all my dreams before my helpless sight
He plunges at me, guttering, choking, drowning.

If in some smothering dreams, you too could pace
Behind the wagon that we flung him in,
And watch the white eyes writhing in his face,
His hanging face, like a devil's sick of sin;
If you could hear, at every jolt, the blood
Come gargling from the froth-corrupted lungs,
Bitter as the cud
Of vile, incurable sores on innocent tongues, —
My friend, you would not tell with such high zest
To children ardent for some desperate glory,
The old Lie: Dulce et decorum est
Pro patria mori.[2]

Futility

Move him into the sun —
Gently its touch awoke him once,
At home, whispering of fields unsown.
Always it woke him, even in France,
Until this morning and this snow.
If anything might rouse him now
The kind old sun will know.

Think how it wakes the seeds, —
Woke, once, the clays of a cold star.
Are limbs, so dear-achieved, are sides,
Full-nerved — still warm — too hard to stir?
Was it for this the clay grew tall?
— O what made fatuous sunbeams toil
To break earth's sleep at all?

[2] 'Sweet and fitting is it to die for one's country,' from Horace, *Odes*, III, 2.

Anthem for Doomed Youth

What passing-bells for these who die as cattle?
Only the monstrous anger of the guns.
Only the stuttering rifles' rapid rattle
Can patter out their hasty orisons.
No mockeries for them from prayers or bells,
Nor any voice of mourning save the choirs, —
The shrill, demented choirs of wailing shells;
And bugles calling for them from sad shires.

What candles may be held to speed them all?
Not in the hands of boys, but in their eyes
Shall shine the holy glimmers of good-byes.
The pallor of girls' brows shall be their pall;
Their flowers the tenderness of silent minds,
And each slow dusk a drawing-down of blinds.

Strange Meeting[3]

It seemed that out of battle I escaped
Down some profound dull tunnel, long since scooped
Through granites which titanic wars had groined.
Yet also there encumbered sleepers groaned,
Too fast in thought or death to be bestirred.
Then, as I probed them, one sprang up, and stared
With piteous recognition in fixed eyes,
Lifting distressful hands as if to bless.

[3] Probably written in the last months of his life, this poem is Owen's most brilliant example of the use of assonance and dissonance to suggest, within the controlling form of poetry, the shock, the phantasmagorical quality of modern war.

And by his smile, I knew that sullen hall,
By his dead smile I knew we stood in Hell.
With a thousand pains that vision's face was grained;
Yet no blood reached there from the upper ground,
And no guns thumped, or down the flues made moan.
' Strange friend,' I said, ' here is no cause to mourn.'
' None,' said the other, ' save the undone years,
The hopelessness. Whatever hope is yours,
Was my life also; I went hunting wild
After the wildest beauty in the world,
Which lies not calm in eyes, or braided hair,
But mocks the steady running of the hour,
And if it grieves, grieves richlier than here.
For by my glee might many men have laughed,
And of my weeping something had been left,
Which must die now. I mean the truth untold,
The pity of war, the pity war distilled.
Now men will go content with what we spoiled.
Or, discontent, boil bloody, and be spilled.
They will be swift with swiftness of the tigress,
None will break ranks, though nations trek from progress.
Courage was mine, and I had mystery,
Wisdom was mine, and I had mastery;
To miss the march of this retreating world
Into vain citadels that are not walled.
Then, when much blood had clogged their chariot-wheels
I would go up and wash them from sweet wells,
Even with truths that lie too deep for taint.
I would have poured my spirit without stint
But not through wounds; not on the cess of war.
Foreheads of men have bled where no wounds were.
I am the enemy you killed, my friend.
I knew you in this dark; for so you frowned
Yesterday through me as you jabbed and killed.
I parried; but my hands were loath and cold.
Let us sleep now. . . .'

David Herbert Lawrence[1]

1885–1930

Piano

Softly, in the dusk, a woman is singing to me;
Taking me back down the vista of years, till I see
A child sitting under the piano, in the boom of the tingling strings
And pressing the small, poised feet of a mother who smiles as she sings.

In spite of myself, the insidious mastery of song
Betrays me back, till the heart of me weeps to belong

[1] The texts of the first four poems follow *Collected Poems* (first published in London, 1928). For this edition, Lawrence revised many of the poems, but in those reprinted here, nothing was changed but some small matters of punctuation. Lawrence defended the form of his poetry as depending more on his feeling for the length of a line than on regular stresses. In a preface added to *New Poems* (1918), he praised Whitman and the use of ' free verse ' for his kind of poetry. That which attempts to capture the fleeting present cannot have ' finish '; it is of the ' moment, the quick of all change and haste and opposition: the moment, the immediate present, the Now.'

To the old Sunday evenings at home, with winter outside
And hymns in the cosy parlour, the tinkling piano our guide.

So now it is vain for the singer to burst into clamour
With the great black piano appassionato. The glamour
Of childish days is upon me, my manhood is cast
Down in the flood of remembrance, I weep like a child for the past.

[*New Poems*, 1918]

The North Country

In another country, black poplars shake themselves over a pond,
And rooks and the rising smoke-waves scatter and wheel from the works beyond:
The air is dark with north and with sulphur, the grass is a darker green,
And people darkly invested with purple move palpable through the scene.

Soundlessly down across the counties, out of the resonant gloom
That wraps the north in stupor and purple travels the deep, slow boom
Of the man-life north imprisoned, shut in the hum of the purpled steel
As it spins to sleep on its motion, drugged dense in the sleep of the wheel.

Out of the sleep, from the gloom of motion, soundlessly, somnambule
Moans and booms the soul of a people imprisoned, asleep in the rule
Of the strong machine that runs mesmeric, booming the spell of its word
Upon them and moving them helpless, mechanic, their will to its will deferred.

Yet all the while comes the droning inaudible, out of the violet air,
The moaning of sleep-bound beings in travail that toil and are will-less there
In the spellbound north, convulsive now with a dream near morning, strong
With violent achings heaving to burst the sleep that is now not long.

[*New Poems*, 1918]

Gloire de Dijon [2]

When she rises in the morning
I linger to watch her;
She spreads the bath-cloth underneath the window
And the sunbeams catch her
Glistening white on the shoulders,
While down her sides the mellow
Golden shadow glows as
She stoops to the sponge, and her swung breasts
Sway like full-blown yellow
Gloire de Dijon roses.

She drips herself with water, and her shoulders
Glisten as silver, they crumple up
Like wet and falling roses, and I listen
For the sluicing of their rain-dishevelled petals.
In the window full of sunlight
Concentrates her golden shadow
Fold on fold, until it glows as
Mellow as the glory roses.

Icking.

[*Look! We have Come Through!*, 1917]

Snake [3]

A snake came to my water-trough
On a hot, hot day, and I in pyjamas for the heat,
To drink there.

[2] The collection from which this poem comes records the turbulent but ultimately happy first years of Lawrence with Frieda von Richthofen Weekley after their elopement in 1912. This poem records a morning of their first summer which they spent in Icking, Bavaria.

[3] The event recorded here took place in the first summer of the two years (1920–1922) which Law-

In the deep, strange-scented shade of the great dark carob-tree
I came down the steps with my pitcher
And must wait, must stand and wait, for there he was at the trough before me.

He reached down from a fissure in the earth-wall in the gloom
And trailed his yellow-brown slackness soft-bellied down, over the edge of the stone trough
And rested his throat upon the stone bottom,
And where the water had dripped from the tap, in a small clearness,
He sipped with his straight mouth,
Softly drank through his straight gums, into his slack long body,
Silently.

Someone was before me at my water-trough,
And I, like a second comer, waiting.

He lifted his head from his drinking, as cattle do,
And looked at me vaguely, as drinking cattle do,
And flickered his two-forked tongue from his lips, and mused a moment,
And stooped and drank a little more,
Being earth-brown, earth-golden from the burning bowels of the earth
On the day of Sicilian July, with Etna smoking.

The voice of my education said to me
He must be killed,
For in Sicily the black, black snakes are innocent, the gold are venomous.

And voices in me said, If you were a man
You would take a stick and break him now, and finish him off.

But must I confess how I liked him,
How glad I was he had come like a guest in quiet, to drink at my water-trough
And depart peaceful, pacified, and thankless,
Into the burning bowels of this earth?

Was it cowardice, that I dared not kill him?
Was it perversity, that I longed to talk to him?
Was it humility, to feel so honoured?
I felt so honoured.

And yet those voices:
If you were not afraid, you would kill him!

And truly I was afraid, I was most afraid,
But even so, honoured still more
That he should seek my hospitality
From out the dark door of the secret earth.

He drank enough
And lifted his head, dreamily, as one who has drunken,
And flickered his tongue like a forked night on the air, so black,
Seeming to lick his lips,
And looked around like a god, unseeing, into the air,
And slowly turned his head,
And slowly, very slowly, as if thrice adream,
Proceeded to draw his slow length curving round
And climb again the broken bank of my wall-face.

And as he put his head into that dreadful hole,
And as he slowly drew up, snake-easing his shoulders, and entered farther,
A sort of horror, a sort of protest against his withdrawing into that horrid black hole,
Deliberately going into the blackness, and slowly drawing himself after,
Overcame me now his back was turned.

---

rence and Frieda spent in Taormina, Sicily. All his life, Lawrence feared reptiles as poisonous, yet held some of the ancient reverence for them as symbols: witness his novel, *The Plumed Serpent,* 1926.

I looked round, I put down my pitcher,
I picked up a clumsy log
And threw it at the water-trough with a clatter.

I think it did not hit him,
But suddenly that part of him that was left behind convulsed in undignified haste,
Writhed like lightning, and was gone
Into the black hole, the earth-lipped fissure in the wall-front,
At which, in the intense still noon, I stared with fascination.

And immediately I regretted it.
I thought how paltry, how vulgar, what a mean act!
I despised myself and the voices of my accursed human education.

And I thought of the albatross,[4]
And I wished he would come back, my snake.

For he seemed to me again like a king,
Like a king in exile, uncrowned in the underworld,
Now due to be crowned again.

And so, I missed my chance with one of the lords
Of life.
And I have something to expiate;
A pettiness.

Taormina.

[*Birds, Beasts and Flowers,* 1923]

City-Life[5]

When I am in a great city, I know that I despair.

[4] A recollection of Coleridge's *Rime of the Ancient Mariner.*

[5] The remaining poems were mostly written in the very last years of Lawrence's life as he faced imminent death from tuberculosis. All were left in manuscript, some in more than one form; those reprinted here follow the preferred version of Richard Aldington and Giuseppe Orioli, editors of the posthumous *Last Poems,* 1932.

I know there is no hope for us, death waits, it is useless to care.

For oh the poor people, that are flesh of my flesh,
I, that am flesh of their flesh,
when I see the iron hooked into their faces
their poor, their fearful faces
I scream in my soul, for I know I cannot
take the iron hooks out of their faces, that make them so drawn,
nor cut the invisible wires of steel that pull them
back and forth, to work,
back and forth to work,
like fearful and corpse-like fishes hooked and being played
by some malignant fisherman on an unseen shore
where he does not choose to land them yet, hooked fishes of the factory world.

Bavarian Gentians[6]

Not every man has gentians in his house
in soft September, at slow, sad Michaelmas.

Bavarian gentians, big and dark, only dark
darkening the day-time torch-like with the smoking blueness of Pluto's gloom,
ribbed and torch-like, with their blaze of darkness spread blue
down flattening into points, flattened under the sweep of white day
torch-flower of the blue-smoking darkness, Pluto's dark-blue daze,
black lamps from the halls of Dis, burning dark blue,
giving off darkness, blue darkness, as Demeter's pale lamps give off light,
lead me then, lead me the way.

[6] Aldington feels that this poem, written in the fall of 1929 after Lawrence's last visit with Frieda to her mother in Bavaria, marks Lawrence's first acceptance of the fact of his own approaching death.

Reach me a gentian, give me a torch!
let me guide myself with the blue, forked torch of this flower
down the darker and darker stairs, where blue is darkened on blueness
even where Persephone goes, just now, from the frosted September
to the sightless realm where darkness is awake upon the dark
and Persephone herself is but a voice
or a darkness invisible enfolded in the deeper dark
of the arms Plutonic, and pierced with the passion of dense gloom,
among the splendour of torches of darkness, shedding darkness on the lost bride and her groom.

Lucifer

ANGELS are bright still, though the brightest fell.
But tell me, tell me, how do you know
he lost any of his brightness in the falling?
In the dark-blue depths, under layers and layers of darkness
I see him more like the ruby, a gleam from within
of his own magnificence
coming like the ruby in the invisible dark, glowing
with his own annunciation, towards us.

The Ship of Death

Now it is autumn and the falling fruit
and the long journey towards oblivion.

The apples falling like great drops of dew
to bruise themselves an exit from themselves.

And it is time to go, to bid farewell
to one's own self, and find an exit
from the fallen self.

II

Have you built your ship of death, O have you?
O build your ship of death, for you will need it.

The grim frost is at hand, when the apples will fall
thick, almost thundrous, on the hardened earth.

And death is on the air like a smell of ashes!
Ah! can't you smell it?
And in the bruised body, the frightened soul
finds itself shrinking, wincing from the cold
that blows upon it through the orifices.

III

And can a man his own quietus make
with a bare bodkin? [7]

With daggers, bodkins, bullets, man can make
a bruise or break of exit for his life;
but is that a quietus, O tell me, is it quietus?

Surely not so! for how could murder, even self-murder
ever a quietus make?

IV

O let us talk of quiet that we know,
that we can know, the deep and lovely quiet
of a strong heart at peace!

How can we this, our own quietus, make?

V

Build then the ship of death, for you must take
the longest journey, to oblivion.

[7] *Hamlet,* III, i, 75–6.

And die the death, the long and painful death
that lies between the old self and the new.

Already our bodies are fallen, bruised, badly bruised,
already our souls are oozing through the exit
of the cruel bruise.

Already the dark and endless ocean of the end
is washing in through the breaches of our wounds,
already the flood is upon us.

Oh build your ship of death, your little ark
and furnish it with food, with little cakes, and wine
for the dark flight down oblivion.

VI

Piecemeal the body dies, and the timid soul
has her footing washed away, as the dark flood rises.

We are dying, we are dying, we are all of us dying
and nothing will stay the death-flood rising within us
and soon it will rise on the world, on the outside world.

We are dying, we are dying, piecemeal our bodies are dying
and our strength leaves us,
and our soul cowers naked in the dark rain over the flood,
cowering in the last branches of the tree of our life.

VII

We are dying, we are dying, so all we can do
is now to be willing to die, and to build the ship
of death to carry the soul on the longest journey.

A little ship, with oars and food
and little dishes, and all accoutrements
fitting and ready for the departing soul.
Now launch the small ship, now as the body dies
and life departs, launch out, the fragile soul
in the fragile ship of courage, the ark of faith
with its store of food and little cooking pans
and change of clothes,
upon the flood's black waste
upon the waters of the end
upon the sea of death, where still we sail
darkly, for we cannot steer, and have no port.

There is no port, there is nowhere to go
only the deepening blackness darkening still
blacker upon the soundless, ungurgling flood
darkness at one with darkness, up and down
and sideways utterly dark, so there is no direction any more.
and the little ship is there; yet she is gone.
She is not seen, for there is nothing to see her by.
She is gone! gone! and yet
somewhere she is there.
Nowhere!

VIII

And everything is gone, the body is gone
completely under, gone, entirely gone.
The upper darkness is heavy as the lower,
between them the little ship
is gone.

It is the end, it is oblivion.

IX

And yet out of eternity a thread
separates itself on the blackness,

a horizontal thread
that fumes a little with pallor upon the dark.

Is it illusion? or does the pallor fume
A little higher?
Ah wait, wait, for there's the dawn,
the cruel dawn of coming back to life
out of oblivion.

Wait, wait, the little ship
drifting, beneath the deathly ashy grey
of a flood-dawn.

Wait, wait! even so, a flush of yellow
and strangely, O chilled wan soul, a flush of rose.

A flush of rose, and the whole thing starts again.

X

The flood subsides, and the body, like a worn sea-shell
emerges strange and lovely.
And the little ship wings home, faltering and lapsing
on the pink flood,
and the frail soul steps out, into the house again
filling the heart with peace.
Swings the heart renewed with peace
even of oblivion.

Oh build your ship of death. Oh build it!
for you will need it.
For the voyage of oblivion awaits you.

Shadows

And if tonight my soul may find her peace
in sleep, and sink in good oblivion,
and in the morning wake like a new-opened flower
then I have been dipped again in God, and new-created.

And if, as weeks go round, in the dark of the moon
my spirit darkens and goes out, and soft strange gloom
pervades my movements and my thoughts and words
then I shall know that I am walking still
with God, we are close together now the moon's in shadow.

And if, as autumn deepens and darkens
I feel the pain of falling leaves, and stems that break in storms
and trouble and dissolution and distress
and then the softness of deep shadows folding, folding
around my soul and spirit, around my lips
so sweet, like a swoon, or more like the drowse of a low, sad song
singing darker than the nightingale, on, on to the solstice
and the silence of short days, the silence of the year, the shadow,
then I shall know that my life is moving still
with the dark earth, and drenched
with the deep oblivion of earth's lapse and renewal.

And if, in the changing phases of man's life
I fall in sickness and in misery
my wrists seem broken and my heart seems dead
and strength is gone, and my life
is only the leavings of a life:
and still, among it all, snatches of lovely oblivion, and snatches of renewal
odd, wintry flowers upon the withered stem, yet new, strange flowers
such as my life has not brought forth before, new blossoms of me —

then I must know that still
I am in the hands of the unknown God,
he is breaking me down to his own oblivion
to send me forth on a new morning, a new man.

William Butler Yeats[1]

1865–1939

To the Rose upon the Rood of Time[2]

RED Rose, proud Rose, sad Rose of all my days!
Come near me, while I sing the ancient ways:
Cuchulain[3] battling with the bitter tide;
The Druid, grey, wood-nurtured, quiet-eyed,
Who cast round Fergus[4] dreams, and ruin untold;
And thine own sadness, whereof stars, grown old
In dancing silver-sandalled on the sea,
Sing in their high and lonely melody.
Come near, that no more blinded by man's fate,
I find under the boughs of love and hate,
In all poor foolish things that live a day,
Eternal beauty wandering on her way.

Come near, come near, come near — Ah, leave me still
A little space for the rose-breath to fill!
Lest I no more hear common things that crave;
The weak worm hiding down in its small cave,
The field-mouse running by me in the grass,
And heavy mortal hopes that toil and pass;
But seek alone to hear the strange things said
By God to the bright hearts of those long dead,
And learn to chaunt a tongue men do not know.
Come near; I would, before my time to go,
Sing of old Eire and the ancient ways:
Red Rose, proud Rose, sad Rose of all my days.

[*The Rose,* 1893]

The Lake Isle of Innisfree[5]

I WILL arise and go now, and go to Innisfree,
And a small cabin build there, of clay and wattles made:
Nine bean-rows will I have there, a hive for the honeybee,
And live alone in the bee-loud glade.

And I shall have some peace there, for peace comes dropping slow,
Dropping from the veils of the morning to where the cricket sings;
There midnight's all a glimmer, and noon a purple glow,
And evening full of the linnet's wings.

I will arise and go now, for always night and day
I hear lake water lapping with low sounds by the shore;
While I stand on the roadway, or on the pavements grey,
I hear it in the deep heart's core.

[1890] [*The Rose,* 1893]

[1] Yeats frequently revised his own work, especially the earlier poems; the text used here, however, follows *The Collected Poems of W. B. Yeats,* 2nd ed., 1951.

[2] In Rosicrucian symbolism, the cross (rood) represents the struggle and opposition, the pain and self-sacrifice of life, while the rose represents the transfiguring ecstasy when that 'cross' blossoms with the rose of love, harmony, and beauty. But in addition to this and the usual religious associations, Yeats also used the rose as a complex symbol for Ireland, for love (Maude Gonne), and for the Platonic 'Intellectual Beauty.'

[3] Pronounced Cu hoo' lin; the great legendary hero of the Irish Ulster Cycle whom Yeats repeatedly uses in his poems and plays to represent heroic loneliness, exaltation, and defeat. After the unwitting slaying of his own son, Cuchulain's anger was diverted by the Druids into battle with the sea.

[4] An elder contemporary of Cuchulain, King of all Ireland, who was displaced or (in Yeats' versions) gave up the kingship to become a poet and Druidic wizard.

[5] A small island in Lough Gill, a western Irish lake in County Sligo near which Yeats spent much of his boyhood. The dream of finding a retreat there had been inspired by Thoreau's *Walden* (note the reference to bean-rows), and the immediate occasion for the poem was a wave of nostalgia Yeats felt in London's crowded streets.

The Man Who Dreamed of Faeryland

He stood among a crowd at Dromahair;[6]
His heart hung all upon a silken dress,
And he had known at last some tenderness,
Before earth took him to her stony care;
But when a man poured fish into a pile,
It seemed they raised their little silver heads,
And sang what gold morning or evening sheds
Upon a woven world-forgotten isle
Where people love beside the ravelled seas;
That Time can never mar a lover's vows
Under that woven changeless roof of boughs:
The singing shook him out of his new ease.

He wandered by the sands of Lissadell;[7]
His mind ran all on money cares and fears,
And he had known at last some prudent years
Before they heaped his grave under the hill;
But while he passed before a plashy place,
A lug-worm with its grey and muddy mouth
Sang that somewhere to north or west or south
There dwelt a gay, exulting, gentle race
Under the golden or the silver skies;
That if a dancer stayed his hungry foot
It seemed the sun and moon were in the fruit:
And at that singing he was no more wise.

He mused beside the well of Scanavin,
He mused upon his mockers: without fail
His sudden vengeance were a country tale,
When earthy night had drunk his body in;
But one small knot-grass growing by the pool
Sang where — unnecessary cruel voice —
Old silence bids its chosen race rejoice,
Whatever ravelled waters rise and fall
Or stormy silver fret the gold of day,
And midnight there enfold them like a fleece
And lover there by lover be at peace.
The tale drove his fine angry mood away.

He slept under the hill of Lugnagall;
And might have known at last unhaunted sleep
Under that cold and vapour-turbaned steep,
Now that the earth had taken man and all:
Did not the worms that spired about his bones
Proclaim with that unwearied, reedy cry
That God has laid His fingers on the sky,
That from those fingers glittering summer runs
Upon the dancer by the dreamless wave.
Why should those lovers that no lovers miss
Dream, until God burn Nature with a kiss?
The man has found no comfort in the grave.

[*The Rose*, 1893]

He Thinks of His Past Greatness When a Part of the Constellations of Heaven[8]

I HAVE drunk ale from the Country of the Young[9]
And weep because I know all things now:
I have been a hazel-tree, and they hung

---

[6] A western Irish village near Lough Gill. All the local place names from this region mentioned in the poem were associated with the mythological past, especially with the great battle in which a quasi-divine race of invaders just preceding the Celts finally conquered the original inhabitants. They became the ancestors of the Irish fairies.

[7] Also the estate of the Gore-Booths, friends of Yeats.

[8] Originally entitled 'Mongan Thinks of His Past Greatness'; Mongan was a legendary wizard who went through several reincarnations.

[9] Mythical land of the gods and the happy dead; setting of Yeats' *Wanderings of Oisin* (1889).

The Pilot Star and the Crooked Plough [10]
Among my leaves in times out of mind:
I became a rush that horses tread:
I became a man, a hater of the wind,
Knowing one, out of all things, alone, that his head
May not lie on the breast nor his lips on the hair
Of the woman that he loves, until he dies.
O beast of the wilderness, bird of the air,
Must I endure your amorous cries?

[*Wind Among the Reeds,* 1899]

Pardon, old fathers [11]

PARDON, old fathers, if you still remain
Somewhere in ear-shot for the story's end,
Old Dublin merchant 'free of the ten and four' [12]
Or trading out of Galway into Spain;
Old country scholar, Robert Emmet's friend,
A hundred-year-old memory to the poor; [13]
Merchant and scholar who have left me blood
That has not passed through any huckster's loin,
Soldiers that gave, whatever die was cast:
A Butler or an Armstrong [14] that withstood
Beside the brackish waters of the Boyne
James and his Irish when the Dutchman crossed; [15]

[10] The hazel tree Yeats considered the Irish mythical equivalent of the tree of life; the pilot star and the crooked plough are respectively the Pole Star and the Constellation of Ursa Major, representing direction or guidance, and difficulty, thus equivalent to the rose and the cross (n. 2). The hazel and the plough, together with the sun, were primary symbols of the mythological Irish gods.

[11] Appearing as the introductory poem of the volume, these lines were prompted by Yeats' growing anger with churlish, ignorant Dublin, and with the way the best energies of his friends were being expended fruitlessly in the Irish cause.

[12] Yeats' eighteenth-century ancestor, Benjamin Yeats, had been a prominent Dublin importer, one of the few exempted from the usual customs fees. County Galway, in western Ireland, was also once a center of a flourishing Spanish trade.

[13] John Yeats, son of Benjamin and contemporary of the Irish patriot, Robert Emmet (17-8–1803), was a distinguished scholar at Trinity College and a highly regarded rector in western County Sligo.

[14] Old and socially prominent Irish families connected by marriage to the Yeats.

[15] On July 12, 1690, the 'Dutchman' William of Orange (since 1688 William III of England) and his Protestant forces decisively defeated the exiled King James II and his Catholic Irish supporters in a battle fought over the Irish river.

Old merchant skipper [16] that leaped overboard
After a ragged hat in Biscay Bay;
You most of all, silent and fierce old man,
Because the daily spectacle that stirred
My fancy, and set my boyish lips to say,
'Only the wasteful virtues earn the sun';
Pardon that for a barren passion's sake,
Although I have come close on forty-nine,
I have no child, I have nothing but a book,
Nothing but that to prove your blood and mine.

[*Responsibilities,* 1914]

The Cold Heaven [17]

SUDDENLY I saw the cold and rook-delighting heaven
That seemed as though ice burned and was but the more ice,
And thereupon imagination and heart were driven
So wild that every casual thought of that and this
Vanished, and left but memories, that should be out of season
With the hot blood of youth, of love crossed long ago;
And I took all the blame out of all sense and reason,
Until I cried and trembled and rocked to and fro,
Riddled with light. Ah! when the ghost begins to quicken,
Confusion of the death-bed over, is it sent
Out naked on the roads, as the books say, and stricken
By the injustice of the skies for punishment?

[*Responsibilities,* 1914]

[16] Yeats' maternal grandfather, William Pollexfen, who owned a fleet of ships and was partner in a prosperous milling concern.

[17] Inspired by memories of Yeats' bitter disappointment when Maude Gonne married John MacBride.

The Wild Swans at Coole[18]

THE trees are in their autumn beauty,
The woodland paths are dry,
Under the October twilight the water
Mirrors a still sky;
Upon the brimming water among the stones
Are nine-and-fifty swans.

The nineteenth autumn has come upon me
Since I first made my count;
I saw, before I had well finished,
All suddenly mount
And scatter wheeling in great broken rings
Upon their clamorous wings.

I have looked upon those brilliant creatures,
And now my heart is sore.
All's changed since I, hearing at twilight,
The first time on this shore,
The bell-beat of their wings above my head,
Trod with a lighter tread.

Unwearied still, lover by lover,
They paddle in the cold
Companionable streams or climb the air;
Their hearts have not grown old;
Passion or conquest, wander where they will,
Attend upon them still.

But now they drift on the still water,
Mysterious, beautiful;
Among what rushes will they build,
By what lake's edge or pool
Delight men's eyes when I awake some day
To find they have flown away?

[1916] [*Wild Swans at Coole,* 1919]

[18] Coole Park was the Galway estate in western Ireland of Lady Augusta Gregory, Yeats' friend and collaborator in the Abbey Theater. After meeting Lady Gregory in 1896, Yeats spent many summers at her home.

In Memory of Major Robert Gregory[19]

I

Now that we're almost settled in our house[20]
I'll name the friends that cannot sup with us
Beside a fire of turf in th' ancient tower,
And having talked to some late hour
Climb up the narrow winding stairs to bed:
Discoverers of forgotten truth
Or mere companions of my youth,
All, all are in my thoughts to-night being dead.

II

Always we'd have the new friend meet the old
And we are hurt if either friend seem cold,
And there is salt to lengthen out the smart
In the affections of our heart,
And quarrels are blown up upon that head;
But not a friend that I would bring
This night can set us quarrelling,
For all that come into my mind are dead.

III

Lionel Johnson[21] comes the first to mind,
That loved his learning better than mankind,
Though courteous to the worst; much falling he
Brooded upon sanctity
Till all his Greek and Latin learning seemed

[19] Lady Gregory's son had joined the R.A.F. in the First World War, and had been killed over Italy in 1918.

[20] A few years before, Yeats had bought an ancient ruined Norman tower at Ballylee, near Lady Gregory's Galway estate. With the initial help and advice of Robert Gregory (see stanza x), he had slowly refitted it as a home.

[21] English poet (1867–1902), classical scholar, aesthete, convert to Roman Catholicism, friend of Yeats' youth; his life ended pathetically in chronic alcoholism.

A long blast upon the horn that brought
A little nearer to his thought
A measureless consummation that he dreamed.

IV

And that enquiring man John Synge[22] comes next,
That dying chose the living world for text
And never could have rested in the tomb
But that, long travelling, he had come
Towards nightfall upon certain set apart
In a most desolate stony place,
Towards nightfall upon a race
Passionate and simple like his heart.

V

And then I think of old George Pollexfen,[23]
In muscular youth well known to Mayo men
For horsemanship at meets or at racecourses,
That could have shown how pure-bred horses
And solid men, for all their passion, live
But as the outrageous stars incline
By opposition, square and trine;[24]
Having grown sluggish and contemplative.

VI

They were my close companions many a year,
A portion of my mind and life, as it were,
And now their breathless faces seem to look
Out of some old picture-book;
I am accustomed to their lack of breath,
But not that my dear friend's dear son,
Our Sidney[25] and our perfect man,
Could share in that discourtesy of death.

VII

For all things the delighted eye now sees
Were loved by him: the old storm-broken trees
That cast their shadows upon road and bridge;
The tower set on the stream's edge;
The ford where drinking cattle make a stir
Nightly, and startled by that sound
The water-hen must change her ground;
He might have been your heartiest welcomer.

VIII[26]

When with the Galway foxhounds he would ride
From Castle Taylor[27] to the Roxborough side
Or Esserkelly plain, few kept his pace;
At Mooneen he had leaped a place
So perilous that half the astonished meet
Had shut their eyes; and where was it
He rode a race without a bit?
And yet his mind outran the horses' feet.

IX

We dreamed that a great painter had been born
To cold Clare[28] rock and Galway rock and thorn,
To that stern colour and that delicate line
That are our secret discipline
Wherein the gazing heart doubles her might.

[22] Irish playwright (1871–1909) of peasant life drawn into the Irish Renaissance by Yeats; his best play, *The Playboy of the Western World* (1907), produced at the Abbey Theater under the auspices of Yeats and Lady Gregory, involved Yeats in a bitter controversy with Irish extremists who thought the play traduced Irish morality.

[23] Yeats' favorite maternal uncle; the Pollexfens were prominent in the western Irish counties, Sligo and Mayo.

[24] In astrology, when two planets are 120° apart in the zodiac, they are in 'trine' (a favorable 'aspect'); in 'opposition' when 180° apart; 'square' when 90° apart.

[25] Sir Philip Sidney (1554–1586), considered by his contemporaries as the ideal Renaissance gentleman.

[26] This stanza was inserted at Lady Gregory's request.

[27] The place names in this stanza are from the region around the southern part of the county, near the homes of Lady Gregory and Yeats.

[28] The county adjoining Galway to the south; in the Dublin Municipal Gallery hang two paintings of scenes in this region by young Gregory.

Soldier, scholar, horseman, he,
And yet he had the intensity
To have published all to be a world's delight.

X

What other could so well have counselled us
In all lovely intricacies of a house
As he that practised or that understood
All work in metal or in wood,
In moulded plaster or in carven stone?
Soldier, scholar, horseman, he,
And all he did done perfectly
As though he had but that one trade alone.

XI

Some burn damp faggots, others may consume
The entire combustible world in one small room
As though dried straw, and if we turn about
The bare chimney is gone black out
Because the work had finished in that flare.
Soldier, scholar, horseman, he,
As 'twere all life's epitome.
What made us dream that he could comb grey hair?

XII

I had thought, seeing how bitter is that wind
That shakes the shutter, to have brought to mind
All those that manhood tried, or childhood loved
Or boyish intellect approved,
With some appropriate commentary on each;
Until imagination brought
A fitter welcome; but a thought
Of that late death took all my heart for speech.

[1918] [*Wild Swans at Coole,* 1919]

The Second Coming [29]

TURNING and turning in the widening gyre [30]
The falcon cannot hear the falconer;
Things fall apart; the centre cannot hold;
Mere anarchy is loosed upon the world,
The blood-dimmed tide is loosed, and everywhere
The ceremony of innocence is drowned;
The best lack all conviction, while the worst
Are full of passionate intensity.

Surely some revelation is at hand;
Surely the Second Coming [31] is at hand.
The Second Coming! Hardly are those words out
When a vast image out of *Spiritus Mundi* [32]
Troubles my sight: somewhere in sands of the desert
A shape with lion body and the head of a man,
A gaze blank and pitiless as the sun,
Is moving its slow thighs, while all about it
Reel shadows of the indignant desert birds.
The darkness drops again; but now I know
That twenty centuries of stony sleep
Were vexed to nightmare by a rocking cradle,
And what rough beast, its hour come round at last,
Slouches towards Bethlehem to be born?

[1919] [*Michael Robartes and the Dancer,* 1921]

[29] Behind the disquiet and uneasy foreboding in this poem lies most immediately the rioting and looting in Ireland as the extremists of the Revolutionary movement broke loose in 1919 from the restraint of the older leaders.

[30] A circular or spiral movement; besides the more conventional uses of this word lies Yeats' special conception of the cyclic movements of man's experience, the pattern of birth, growth, and dissolution — in turn superseded by a new pattern.

[31] Fused with the Christian conception of Christ's return is Yeats' private conviction that a regular historical cycle of 2000 years was nearing its end, to give birth to a new era, not necessarily better than the preceding.

[32] Literally, 'World Spirit'; for Yeats, a kind of race memory or repository of vital symbols to which man's mind had access in moments of intuitive vision.

Sailing to Byzantium [33]

I

THAT is no country for old men. The young
In one another's arms, birds in the trees
— Those dying generations — at their song,
The salmon-falls, the mackerel-crowded seas,
Fish, flesh, or fowl, commend all summer long
Whatever is begotten, born, and dies.
Caught in that sensual music all neglect
Monuments of unageing intellect.

II

An aged man is but a paltry thing,
A tattered coat upon a stick, unless
Soul clap its hands and sing, and louder sing
For every tatter in its mortal dress,
Nor is there singing school but studying
Monuments of its own magnificence;
And therefore I have sailed the seas and come
To the holy city of Byzantium.

III

O sages standing in God's holy fire
As in the gold mosaic [34] of a wall,
Come from the holy fire, perne in a gyre,[35]
And be the singing-masters of my soul.
Consume my heart away; sick with desire
And fastened to a dying animal
It knows not what it is; and gather me
Into the artifice of eternity.

IV

Once out of nature I shall never take
My bodily form from any natural thing,
But such a form as Grecian goldsmiths make
Of hammered gold and gold enamelling
To keep a drowsy Emperor awake;
Or set upon a golden bough to sing [36]
To lords and ladies of Byzantium
Of what is past, or passing, or to come.

[1926] [*The Tower,* 1928]

The Tower [37]

I

WHAT shall I do with this absurdity —
O heart, O troubled heart — this caricature,
Decrepit age that has been tied to me
As to a dog's tail?
Never had I more
Excited, passionate, fantastical
Imagination, nor an ear and eye
That more expected the impossible —
No, not in boyhood when with rod and fly,
Or the humbler worm, I climbed Ben Bulben's back [38]
And had the livelong summer day to spend.
It seems that I must bid the Muse go pack,

[33] In the revised version of his prose '*Summa Theologica*' — *A Vision* (1937), Yeats wrote, 'I think if I could be given a month of Antiquity and leave to spend it where I chose, I would spend it in Byzantium a little before Justinian opened St. Sophia [A.D. 537] . . . I think that in early Byzantium, maybe never before or since in recorded history, religious, aesthetic and practical life were one, that architect and artificers . . . spoke to the multitude and the few alike.' For Yeats, Byzantium stood for the unity of all aspects of life, the perfection of craftsmanship, the 'mystical mathematics' of perfection of form in all artistic creation. But it was in the past, like Egypt, and therefore part of the mysteries of the dead.

[34] Byzantine iconography conventionally portrayed saints and holy figures against a gold background.

[35] A 'perne' is a spindle or spool; hence in Yeats' special sense, to move in a circular or spiral pattern (cf. n. 30).

[36] 'I have read somewhere that in the Emperor's palace at Byzantium was a tree made of gold and silver, and artificial birds that sang' [Yeats]. But 'golden bough' also carries connotations of the branch used in ancient religious mysteries, as described in Sir J. G. Frazer's influential anthropological study, *The Golden Bough.*

[37] Cf. n. 20. For Yeats, this ancient tower, which he had converted into a dwelling, became a dominant symbol, a link with the past of Ireland, an image of past conflicts and wars, an emblem of aristocracy and decay; it represented for him personally a kind of 'ivory tower,' a sanctuary where the poet — part hermit, part sage and scholar, part fool — might explore the 'winding stairs' of his own mind, the experiences of himself and history.

[38] A low mountain in County Sligo, scene of much of Yeats' childhood, and site of many Irish legends.

Choose Plato and Plotinus[39] for a friend
Until imagination, ear and eye,
Can be content with argument and deal
In abstract things; or be derided by
A sort of battered kettle at the heel.

II

I pace upon the battlements and stare
On the foundations of a house, or where
Tree, like a sooty finger, starts from the earth;
And send imagination forth
Under the day's declining beam, and call
Images and memories
From ruin or from ancient trees,
For I would ask a question of them all.

Beyond that ridge lived Mrs. French,[40] and once
When every silver candlestick or sconce
Lit up the dark mahogany and the wine,
A serving-man, that could divine
That most respected lady's every wish,
Ran and with the garden shears
Clipped an insolent farmer's ears
And brought them in a little covered dish.

Some few remembered still when I was young
A peasant girl[41] commended by a song,
Who'd lived somewhere upon that rocky place,
And praised the colour of her face,
And had the greater joy in praising her,
Remembering that, if walked she there,
Farmers jostled at the fair
So great a glory did the song confer.

And certain men, being maddened by those rhymes,
Or else by toasting her a score of times,
Rose from the table and declared it right
To test their fancy by their sight;
But they mistook the brightness of the moon
For the prosaic light of day—
Music had driven their wits astray—
And one was drowned in the great bog of Cloone.

Strange, but the man who made the song was blind;
Yet, now I have considered it, I find
That nothing strange; the tragedy began
With Homer that was a blind man,
And Helen has all living hearts betrayed.
O may the moon and sunlight seem
One inextricable beam,
For if I triumph I must make men mad.

And I myself created Hanrahan[42]
And drove him drunk or sober through the dawn
From somewhere in the neighbouring cottages.
Caught by an old man's juggleries
He stumbled, tumbled, fumbled to and fro
And had but broken knees for hire
And horrible splendour of desire;
I thought it all out twenty years ago:

Good fellows shuffled cards in an old bawn;[43]
And when that ancient ruffian's turn was on
He so bewitched the cards under his thumb
That all but the one card became
A pack of hounds and not a pack of cards,

---

[39] Yeats, as a student of the mystical and occult, was much interested in the third-century neoplatonist Plotinus who transformed the idealist philosophy of Plato into mystical terms. The essence of his philosophy was the desire to escape from the material world, including his own body.

[40] 'The persons mentioned are associated by legend, story and tradition with the neighbourhood of Thoor Ballylee . . . where the poem was written. Mrs. French lived at Peterswell in the eighteenth century and was related to Sir Jonah Barrington, who described the incident of the ears . . .' [Yeats].

[41] The following story had been told to Yeats by an old peasant woman who knew both the girl, Mary Hynes, and the blind poet, Raftery, a famous wandering Galway bard who died about 1835. Cf. Yeats' own feelings for, and poems on, the beautiful Maude Gonne.

[42] Yeats published *Stories of Red Hanrahan* in 1904. Hanrahan was a lusty old gambler, a daemon-driven poet and schoolmaster who lived in the neighborhood of Yeats' tower. As Yeats handles his story, he becomes a symbol of one torn between the desires of the man and the unappeasable desires of the poet.

[43] In Ireland, an enclosure of mud or stone walls about a dwelling; hence the fortified outworks and outbuildings of a castle.

And that he changed into a hare.
Hanrahan rose in frenzy there
And followed up those baying creatures towards —

O towards I have forgotten what — enough!
I must recall a man that neither love
Nor music nor an enemy's clipped ear
Could, he was so harried, cheer;
A figure that has grown so fabulous
There's not a neighbour left to say
When he finished his dog's day:
An ancient bankrupt master of this house.

Before that ruin came, for centuries,
Rough men-at-arms, cross-gartered to the knees
Or shod in iron, climbed the narrow stair,
And certain men-at-arms there were
Whose images, in the Great Memory stored,
Come with loud cry and panting breast
To break upon a sleeper's rest
While their great wooden dice beat on the board.

As I would question all, come all who can;
Come old, necessitous, half-mounted man;
And bring beauty's blind rambling celebrant;
The red man the juggler sent
Through God-forsaken meadows; Mrs. French,
Gifted with so fine an ear;
The man drowned in a bog's mire,
When mocking Muses chose the country wench.

Did all old men and women, rich and poor,
Who trod upon these rocks or passed this door,
Whether in public or in secret rage
As I do now against old age?
But I have found an answer in those eyes
That are impatient to be gone;
Go therefore; but leave Hanrahan,
For I need all his mighty memories.

Old lecher with a love on every wind,
Bring up out of that deep considering mind
All that you have discovered in the grave,
For it is certain that you have
Reckoned up every unforeknown, unseeing
Plunge, lured by a softening eye,
Or by a touch or a sigh,
Into the labyrinth of another's being;

Does the imagination dwell the most
Upon a woman won or a woman lost?
If on the lost, admit you turned aside
From a great labyrinth out of pride,
Cowardice, some silly over-subtle thought
Or anything called conscience once;
And that if memory recur, the sun's
Under eclipse and the day blotted out.

III

It is time that I wrote my will;
I choose upstanding men
That climb the streams until
The fountain leap, and at dawn
Drop their cast at the side
Of dripping stone; I declare
They shall inherit my pride,
The pride of people that were
Bound neither to Cause nor to State,
Neither to slaves that were spat on,
Nor to the tyrants that spat,
The people of Burke and of Grattan [44]
That gave, though free to refuse —
Pride, like that of the morn,
When the headlong light is loose,
Or that of the fabulous horn,
Or that of the sudden shower
When all streams are dry,
Or that of the hour
When the swan must fix his eye
Upon a fading gleam,
Float out upon a long

[44] Edmund Burke (1729–97) and Henry Grattan (1746–1820), famous Irish patriots and statesmen.

Last reach of glittering stream
And there sing his last song.
And I declare my faith:
I mock Plotinus' thought
And cry in Plato's teeth,
Death and life were not
Till man made up the whole,
Made lock, stock and barrel
Out of his bitter soul,
Aye, sun and moon and star, all.
And further add to that
That, being dead, we rise,
Dream and so create
Translunar Paradise.
I have prepared my peace
With learned Italian things
And the proud stones of Greece,
Poet's imaginings
And memories of love,
Memories of the words of women,
All those things whereof
Man makes a superhuman
Mirror-resembling dream.

As at the loophole there
The daws chatter and scream,
And drop twigs layer upon layer.
When they have mounted up,
The mother bird will rest
On their hollow top,
And so warm her wild nest.

I leave both faith and pride
To young upstanding men
Climbing the mountain-side,
That under bursting dawn
They may drop a fly;
Being of that metal made
Till it was broken by
This sedentary trade.

Now shall I make my soul,
Compelling it to study
In a learned school
Till the wreck of body,
Slow decay of blood,
Testy delirium
Or dull decrepitude,
Or what worse evil come —
The death of friends, or death
Of every brilliant eye
That made a catch in the breath —
Seem but the clouds of the sky
When the horizon fades;
Or a bird's sleepy cry
Among the deepening shades.

[1925] [*The Tower,* 1928]

Leda and the Swan[45]

A SUDDEN blow: the great wings beating still
Above the staggering girl, her thighs caressed
By the dark webs, her nape caught in his bill,
He holds her helpless breast upon his breast.

How can those terrified vague fingers push
The feathered glory from her loosening thighs?
And how can body, laid in that white rush,
But feel the strange heart beating where it lies?

A shudder in the loins engenders there
The broken wall, the burning roof and tower
And Agamemnon dead.[46]
Being so caught up,
So mastered by the brute blood of the air,
Did she put on his knowledge with his power
Before the indifferent beak could let her drop?

[1923] [*The Tower,* 1928]

[45] In the Greek myth, Leda was ravished by the god Zeus appearing in the form of a swan. From the eggs born of this union were produced the twins Castor and Pollux, great warriors, and Helen, beautiful cause of the Trojan War.

[46] Agamemnon had married Helen's half-sister, Clytemnestra; before the beginning of the Trojan War, he had made a propitiatory sacrifice of their daughter to insure success. Upon his return from the war, Clytemnestra and her lover murdered Agamemnon partly in revenge.

Among School Children

I

I WALK through the long schoolroom questioning;[47]
A kind old nun in a white hood replies;
The children learn to cipher and to sing,
To study reading-books and histories,
To cut and sew, be neat in everything
In the best modern way — the children's eyes
In momentary wonders stare upon
A sixty-year-old smiling public man.

II

I dream of a Ledaean body,[48] bent
Above a sinking fire, a tale that she
Told of a harsh reproof, or trivial event
That changed some childish day to tragedy —
Told, and it seemed that our two natures blent
Into a sphere from youthful sympathy,
Or else, to alter Plato's parable,[49]
Into the yolk and white of the one shell.

III

And thinking of that fit of grief or rage
I look upon one child or t'other there
And wonder if she stood so at that age —
For even daughters of the swan can share
Something of every paddler's heritage —
And had that colour upon cheek or hair,
And thereupon my heart is driven wild:
She stands before me as a living child.

IV

Her present image floats into the mind —
Did Quattrocento finger[50] fashion it
Hollow of cheek as though it drank the wind
And took a mess of shadows for its meat?
And I though never of Ledaean kind
Had pretty plumage once — enough of that,
Better to smile on all that smile, and show
There is a comfortable kind of old scarecrow.

V

What youthful mother, a shape upon her lap
Honey of generation had betrayed,
And that must sleep, shriek, struggle to escape
As recollection or the drug decide,
Would think her son, did she but see that shape
With sixty or more winters on its head
A compensation for the pang of his birth,
Or the uncertainty of his setting forth?

VI

Plato thought nature but a spume that plays
Upon a ghostly paradigm of things;[51]
Solider Aristotle played the taws
Upon the bottom of a king of kings;[52]
World-famous golden-thighed Pythagoras[53]
Fingered upon a fiddle-stick or strings

---

[47] Yeats as Irish Senator (1922–28) was involved with the reform of the educational system.

[48] Maude Gonne, whom Yeats liked to identify with Helen, daughter of Leda and Zeus.

[49] Yeats is here combining the myth of the birth of Helen (see n. 45) with the parable explaining the nature of love in Plato's *Symposium*. According to the parable, originally each human was complete in itself — a double being in one body. But the gods, jealous of man's happiness and fearful of his presumption, clove this 'integer' asunder, and ever since the parts have been seeking reunion.

[50] Painters, like Botticelli or da Vinci whom Yeats admired greatly, of the fifteenth century, apex of the Italian Renaissance.

[51] Plato held that what is commonly called reality is but a partial and imperfect manifestation of an ideal reality.

[52] Though he was Plato's pupil, Aristotle is generally more concerned with the present reality; he was tutor to Alexander the Great.

[53] Yeats was greatly interested in this sixth-century B.C. Greek philosopher because of his connections with mysticism and the occult. Pythagoras' doctrine included the transmigration of souls or reincarnation. He discovered the laws of vibrating strings upon which harmony is based and evolved the idea that the 'reality' of the world is to be found, not in its matter, but in the mathematical relationships which govern its order and 'harmony.' Around him grew up many legends, including the idea that he possessed a golden thigh or hip.

What a star sang and careless Muses heard:
Old clothes upon old sticks to scare a bird.

VII

Both nuns and mothers worship images,
But those the candles light are not as those
That animate a mother's reveries,
But keep a marble or a bronze repose.
And yet they too break hearts — O Presences
That passion, piety or affection knows,
And that all heavenly glory symbolise —
O self-born mockers of man's enterprise;

VIII

Labour is blossoming or dancing where
The body is not bruised to pleasure soul,
Nor beauty born out of its own despair,
Nor blear-eyed wisdom out of midnight oil.
O chestnut-tree, great-rooted blossomer,
Are you the leaf, the blossom or the bole?
O body swayed to music, O brightening glance,
How can we know the dancer from the dance?

[1926] [*The Tower,* 1928]

A Dialogue of Self and Soul

I

My Soul. I summon to the winding ancient stair;
Set all your mind upon the steep ascent,
Upon the broken, crumbling battlement,
Upon the breathless starlit air,
Upon the star that marks the hidden pole;
Fix every wandering thought upon
That quarter where all thought is done:
Who can distinguish darkness from the soul?

My Self. The consecrated blade upon my knees
Is Sato's ancient blade,[54] still as it was,
Still razor-keen, still like a looking-glass
Unspotted by the centuries;
That flowering, silken, old embroidery, torn
From some court-lady's dress and round
The wooden scabbard bound and wound,
Can, tattered, still protect, faded adorn.

My Soul. Why should the imagination of a man
Long past his prime remember things that are
Emblematical of love and war?
Think of ancestral night that can,
If but imagination scorn the earth
And intellect its wandering
To this and that and t'other thing,
Deliver from the crime of death and birth.

My Self. Montashigi, third of his family, fashioned it
Five hundred years ago, about it lie
Flowers from I know not what embroidery —
Heart's purple — and all these I set
For emblems of the day against the tower
Emblematical of the night,
And claim as by a soldier's right
A charter to commit the crime once more.

My Soul. Such fullness in that quarter overflows
And falls into the basin of the mind
That man is stricken deaf and dumb and blind,
For intellect no longer knows
Is from the *Ought,* or *Knower* from the *Known* —

[54] An old Samurai sword, given to Yeats in Portland, Oregon, in 1920 by Junzo Sato, a fellow member in a secret society. Yeats kept it wrapped in silk embroidery from Lady Gregory's court gown, making a complex symbol of life and ceremonious order.

That is to say, ascends to Heaven;
Only the dead can be forgiven;
But when I think of that my tongue's a stone.

II

My Self. A living man is blind and drinks his drop.
What matter if the ditches are impure?
What matter if I live it all once more?
Endure that toil of growing up;
The ignominy of boyhood; the distress
Of boyhood changing into man;
The unfinished man and his pain
Brought face to face with his own clumsiness;
The finished man among his enemies? —
How in the name of Heaven can he escape
That defiling and disfigured shape
The mirror of malicious eyes
Casts upon his eyes until at last
He thinks that shape must be his shape?
And what's the good of an escape
If honour find him in the wintry blast?

I am content to live it all again
And yet again, if it be life to pitch
Into the frog-spawn of a blind man's ditch,
A blind man battering blind men;
Or into that most fecund ditch of all,
The folly that man does
Or must suffer, if he woos
A proud woman not kindred of his soul.

I am content to follow to its source
Every event in action or in thought;
Measure the lot; forgive myself the lot!
When such as I cast out remorse
So great a sweetness flows into the breast
We must laugh and we must sing,
We are blest by everything,
Everything we look upon is blest.

[1927] [*The Winding Stair*, 1933]

Byzantium [55]

The unpurged images of day recede;
The Emperor's drunken soldiery are abed;
Night resonance recedes, night-walkers' song
After great cathedral gong;
A starlit or a moonlit dome disdains
All that man is,
All mere complexities,
The fury and the mire of human veins.

Before me floats an image, man or shade,
Shade more than man, more image than a shade;
For Hades' bobbin bound in mummy-cloth
May unwind the winding path;
A mouth that has no moisture and no breath
Breathless mouths may summon;
I hail the superhuman;
I call it death-in-life and life-in-death.

Miracle, bird or golden handiwork,
More miracle than bird or handiwork,
Planted on the star-lit golden bough,
Can like the cocks of Hades crow,
Or, by the moon embittered, scorn aloud
In glory of changeless metal
Common bird or petal
And all complexities of mire or blood.

At midnight on the Emperor's pavement [56] flit
Flames that no faggot feeds, nor steel has lit,
Nor storm disturbs, flames begotten of flame,
Where blood-begotten spirits come
And all complexities of fury leave,
Dying into a dance,
An agony of trance,
An agony of flame that cannot singe a sleeve.

---

[55] Cf. nn. 33–6 above.
[56] Yeats had specifically in mind the marble pavement of the Forum of Constantine in Byzantium.

Astraddle on the dolphin's[57] mire and blood,
Spirit after spirit! The smithies break the flood,
The golden smithies of the Emperor!
Marbles of the dancing floor
Break bitter furies of complexity,
Those images that yet
Fresh images beget,
That dolphin-torn, that gong-tormented sea.

[1930] [*The Winding Stair,* 1933]

Crazy Jane Talks with the Bishop[58]

I MET the Bishop on the road
And much said he and I.
'Those breasts are flat and fallen now,
Those veins must soon be dry;
Live in a heavenly mansion,
Not in some foul sty.'

'Fair and foul are near of kin,
And fair needs foul,' I cried.
'My friends are gone, but that's a truth
Nor grave nor bed denied,
Learned in bodily lowliness
And in the heart's pride.

'A woman can be proud and stiff
When on love intent;
But Love has pitched his mansion in
The place of excrement;
For nothing can be sole or whole
That has not been rent.'

[1931] [*Words for Music Perhaps,* 1932]

[57] Symbol both for sexual love and for the soul; sometimes the dolphin is pictured in art as carrying the soul on its back to paradise.

[58] Crazy Jane is a character used in several of Yeats' poems; she was 'more or less founded' on an old County Galway woman whom Yeats knew—'the local satirist and a really terrible one.'

Lapis Lazuli[59]

(*For Harry Clifton*)

I HAVE heard that hysterical women say
They are sick of the palette and fiddle-bow,
Of poets that are always gay,
For everybody knows or else should know
That if nothing drastic is done
Aeroplane and Zeppelin will come out,
Pitch like King Billy bomb-balls[60] in
Until the town lie beaten flat.

All perform their tragic play,
There struts Hamlet, there is Lear,
That's Ophelia, that Cordelia;
Yet they, should the last scene be there,
The great stage curtain about to drop,
If worthy their prominent part in the play,
Do not break up their lines to weep.
They know that Hamlet and Lear are gay;
Gaiety transfiguring all that dread.
All men have aimed at, found and lost;
Black out; Heaven blazing into the head:
Tragedy wrought to its uttermost.
Though Hamlet rambles and Lear rages,
And all the drop-scenes drop at once
Upon a hundred thousand stages,
It cannot grow by an inch or an ounce.

On their own feet they came, or on ship-board,
Camel-back, horse-back, ass-back, mule-back,
Old civilisations put to the sword.
Then they and their wisdom went to rack:
No handiwork of Callimachus,[61]

[59] Suggested by a Chinese carving which had been given Yeats, depicting a mountain with temples, trees, paths, and an ascetic or pupil about to ascend. 'Ascetic, pupil, hard stone, eternal theme of the sensual east' [Yeats].

[60] Either a reference to German (Kaiser Wilhelm) bombing of London in the First World War, or King William III's bombardments of Irish towns in 1690–91 in the war against James II.

[61] An Athenian sculptor of the fifth century B.C., with a reputation for flawless precision. Yeats once wrote, 'With Callimachus pure Ionic revives again . . . and upon the only example of his work known to us, a marble chair, a Persian is represented, and may one not discover a Persian symbol in that bronze lamp, shaped like a palm, known to us by a description in Pausanias? But he was an archaistic workman, and those who set him to work brought back public life to an older form.' (*A Vision.*)

Who handled marble as if it were bronze,
Made draperies that seemed to rise
When sea-wind swept the corner, stands;
His long lamp-chimney shaped like the stem
Of a slender palm, stood but a day;
All things fall and are built again,
And those that build them again are gay.

Two Chinamen, behind them a third,
Are carved in lapis lazuli,
Over them flies a long-legged bird,
A symbol of longevity;
The third, doubtless a serving-man,
Carries a musical instrument.

Every discoloration of the stone,
Every accidental crack or dent,
Seems a water-course or an avalanche,
Or lofty slope where it still snows
Though doubtless plum or cherry-branch
Sweetens the little half-way house
Those Chinamen climb towards, and I
Delight to imagine them seated there;
There, on the mountain and the sky,
On all the tragic scene they stare.
One asks for mournful melodies;
Accomplished fingers begin to play.
Their eyes mid many wrinkles, their eyes,
Their ancient, glittering eyes, are gay.

[1936] [*Last Poems,* 1936–1939]

News for the Delphic Oracle

I

THERE all the golden codgers lay,
There the silver dew,
And the great water sighed for love,
And the wind sighed too.
Man-picker Niamh [62] leant and sighed
By Oisin on the grass;
There sighed amid his choir of love
Tall Pythagoras.[63]
Plotinus [64] came and looked about,
The salt-flakes on his breast,
And having stretched and yawned awhile
Lay sighing like the rest.

II

Straddling each a dolphin's [65] back
And steadied by a fin,
Those Innocents re-live their death,
Their wounds open again.
The ecstatic waters laugh because
Their cries are sweet and strange,
Through their ancestral patterns dance,
And the brute dolphins plunge
Until, in some cliff-sheltered bay
Where wades the choir of love
Proffering its sacred laurel crowns,
They pitch their burdens off.

III

Slim adolescence that a nymph has stripped,
Peleus on Thetis [66] stares.
Her limbs are delicate as an eyelid,
Love has blinded him with tears;
But Thetis' belly listens.
Down the mountain walls
From where Pan's cavern is
Intolerable music falls.
Foul goat-head, brutal arm appear,
Belly, shoulder, bum,
Flash fishlike; nymphs and satyrs
Copulate in the foam.

[*Last Poems,* 1936–1939]

---

[62] Pronounced Nee av. In the Irish myths which Yeats used for his *Wanderings of Oisin* (1889), Niamh was the daughter of the King of the Country of the Young (abode of the gods and the happy dead). Coming to Ireland, she 'picked' Oisin (pronounced U sheen) as her lover and carried him back with her.

[63] Cf. n. 53. He was said to have derived his moral doctrines from Delphi, and his name means 'mouthpiece of Delphi.'

[64] Cf. n. 39. Yeats conceives him as having achieved his wish, escape from the mortal body, by swimming through the briny 'sea of life.'

[65] Cf. n. 57.

[66] According to Greek mythology, it was prophesied that a son of the goddess Thetis would prove more powerful than his father; Zeus, who loved her, fearing for his life therefore married her to the mortal Peleus. The son born was Achilles.

John Kinsella's Lament for Mrs. Mary Moore

A BLOODY and a sudden end,
  Gunshot or a noose,
For Death who takes that man would keep,
  Leaves what man would lose.
He might have had my sister,
  My cousins by the score,
But nothing satisfied the fool
  But my dear Mary Moore,
None other knows what pleasures man
  At table or in bed.
What shall I do for pretty girls
  Now my old bawd is dead?

Though stiff to strike a bargain,
  Like an old Jew man,
Her bargain struck we laughed and talked
  And emptied many a can;
And O! but she had stories,
  Though not for the priest's ear,
To keep the soul of man alive,
  Banish age and care,
And being old she put a skin
  On everything she said.
What shall I do for pretty girls
  Now my old bawd is dead?

The priests have got a book that says
  But for Adam's sin
Eden's Garden would be there
  And I there within.
No expectation fails there,
  No pleasing habit ends,
No man grows old, no girl grows cold,
  But friends walk by friends.
Who quarrels over halfpennies
  That plucks the trees for bread?
What shall I do for pretty girls
  Now my old bawd is dead?

[1938] [*Last Poems,* 1936–1939]

The Circus Animals' Desertion

I

I SOUGHT a theme and sought for it in vain,
I sought it daily for six weeks or so.
Maybe at last, being but a broken man,
I must be satisfied with my heart, although
Winter and summer till old age began
My circus animals were all on show,
Those stilted boys, that burnished chariot,
Lion and woman and the Lord knows what.

II

What can I but enumerate old themes?
First that sea-rider Oisin[67] led by the nose
Through three enchanted islands, allegorical dreams,
Vain gaiety, vain battle, vain repose,
Themes of the embittered heart, or so it seems,
That might adorn old songs or courtly shows;
But what cared I that set him on to ride,
I, starved for the bosom of his faery bride?

And then a counter-truth filled out its play,
The Countess Cathleen[68] was the name I gave it;
She, pity-crazed, had given her soul away,
But masterful Heaven had intervened to save it.
I thought my dear must her own soul destroy,
So did fanaticism and hate enslave it,
And this brought forth a dream and soon enough

---

[67] Cf. n. 62. Yeats here is reviewing nostalgically some of his more important and controversial poems and plays.

[68] A play by Yeats, 1892. Cathleen is a symbol both for Ireland and for Maude Gonne, struggling for the oppressed and starving people. By presenting Cathleen as bargaining her soul to the devil for the relief of her suffering people, Yeats stirred up a storm of protest from the pious patriots.

This dream itself had all my thought and love.

And when the Fool and Blind Man stole the bread
Cuchulain fought the ungovernable sea;[69]
Heart-mysteries there, and yet when all is said
It was the dream itself enchanted me:
Character isolated by a deed
To engross the present and dominate memory.
Players and painted stage took all my love,
And not those things that they were emblems of.

III

Those masterful images because complete
Grew in pure mind, but out of what began?
A mound of refuse or the sweepings of a street,
Old kettles, old bottles, and a broken can,
Old iron, old bones, old rags, that raving slut
Who keeps the till. Now that my ladder's gone,
I must lie down where all the ladders start,
In the foul rag-and-bone shop of the heart.

[*Last Poems,* 1936–1939]

[69] Cf. n. 3. In Yeats' play, *On Baile's Strand* (1904), the Fool and the Blind Man play a kind of chorus to the main action, as symbolic shadows or anti-selfs to Cuchulain and King Conchubar at whose direction Cuchulain's anger and grief over his dead son was diverted into battle with the sea.

Edith Sitwell[1]

1887–

Spring

When spring begins, the maids in flocks
Walk in soft fields, and their sheepskin locks

Fall shadowless, soft as music, round
Their jonquil eyelids and reach the ground.

Where the small fruit-buds begin to harden
Into sweet tunes in the palace garden,

They peck at the fruit-buds' hairy herds
With their lips like the gentle bills of birds.

. . .

But King Midas heard the swan-bosomed sky
Say, 'All is surface and so must die.'
And he said: 'It is spring; I will have a feast
To woo eternity; for my least

Palace is like a berg of ice;
And the spring winds, for birds of paradise,

With the leaping goat-footed waterfalls cold,
Shall be served for me on a dish of gold

By a maiden fair as an almond-tree,
With hair like the waterfalls' goat-locks; she

Has lips like that jangling harsh pink rain,
The flower-bells that spirt on the trees again.'

In Midas's garden the simple flowers
Laugh, and the tulips are bright as the showers,

[1] The dates of publication, especially of the earlier poems, do not necessarily represent the order of composition; the order and the texts reprinted here follow *Collected Poems of Edith Sitwell,* 1954.

For spring is here; the auriculas,
And the Emily-colored primulas [2]
Bob in their pinafores [3] on the grass
As they watch the gardener's daughter pass.

Then King Midas said, 'At last I feel
Eternity conquered beneath my heel

Like the glittering snake of Paradise —
And you are my Eve!' — but the maiden flies

Like the leaping goat-footed waterfalls
Singing their cold, forlorn madrigals.

[*Bucolic Comedies*, 1923]

Waltz [4]

'Daisy and Lily,
Lazy and silly,
Walk by the shore of the wan grassy sea [5] —
Talking once more 'neath a swan-bosomed tree.[6]
Rose castles,
Tourelles,[7]
Those bustles
Where swells
Each foam-bell of ermine,[8]
They roam and determine
What fashions have been and what fashions will be —
What tartan leaves born,
What crinolines worn.
By Queen Thetis,[9]
Pelisses
Of tarlatine blue,
Like the thin plaided leaves that the castle crags grew;
Or velours d'Afrande:
On the water-gods' land
Her hair seemed gold trees on the honey-cell sand
When the thickest gold spangles, on deep water seen,
Were like twanging guitar and like cold mandoline,
And the nymphs of great caves,
With hair like gold waves
Of Venus, wore tarlatine.
Louise and Charlottine
(Boreas' daughters)
And the nymphs of deep waters,
The nymph Taglioni,[10] Grisi the ondine,
Wear plaided Victoria and thin Clementine
Like the crinolined waterfalls;
Wood-nymphs wear bonnets, shawls;
Elegant parasols
Floating were seen.
The Amazons wear balzarine [11] of jonquille
Beside the blond lace of a deep-falling rill;
Through glades like a nun
They run from and shun
The enormous and gold-rayed rustling sun;
And the nymphs of the fountains
Descend from the mountains
Like elegant willows
On their deep barouche pillows,
In cashmere Alvandar, barège Isabelle,
Like bells of bright water from clearest wood-well.
Our élégantes favoring bonnets of blond,
The stars in their apiaries,
Sylphs in their aviaries,
Seeing them, spangle these, and the sylphs fond,

---

[2] 'Emily' seems to Dame Edith a 'countrified, old-fashioned' name; pink primulas remind her of pink-cheeked country girls.

[3] Frilled flowers bending in the wind.

[4] Earlier, one of a pair of poems, and sub-titled 'Sylph's Song.' This and other poems in the volume *Façade* were technical experiments with patterns in sound. Collaborating with Dame Edith, Sir William Walton wrote music to accompany their recitation.

[5] A sea the color of faded summer grass, appearing at a distance like a grassy plain.

[6] One covered thickly with snow.

[7] Literally, 'turrets.'

[8] Like flower bells made of thick foam.

[9] In Greek mythology, a goddess beloved of Zeus, but married to the mortal King Peleus, the mother of Achilles.

[10] Historically, a famous woman dancer of the nineteenth century; similarly, Grisi was a renowned operatic soprano. 'Ondine' means 'water-nymph' or 'sprite.'

[11] A light dress fabric of mixed cotton and wool.

From their aviaries fanned
With each long fluid hand
The manteaux espagnoles,[12]
Mimic the waterfalls
Over the long and the light summer land.

. . .

So Daisy and Lily,
Lazy and silly,
Walk by the shore of the wan grassy sea,
Talking once more 'neath a swan-bosomed tree.
Rose castles,
Tourelles,
Those bustles!
Mourelles [13]
Of the shade in their train follow.
Ladies, how vain — hollow —
Gone is the sweet swallow —
Gone, Philomel!' [14]

[*Façade,* 1922]

Harvest

to Stephen Spender [15]

I, AN old woman whose heart is like the Sun
That has seen too much, looked on too many sorrows,
Yet is not weary of shining, fulfilment, and harvest,
Heard the priests that howled for rain and the universal darkness,
Saw the golden princes sacrificed to the Rain-god,
The cloud that came and was small as the hand of Man.
And now in the time of the swallow, the bright one, the chatterer,
The young women wait like the mother of corn for the lost one —
Their golden eyelids are darkened like the great rain-clouds.
But in bud and branch the nature of Fate begins
— And love with the Lion's claws and the Lion's hunger
Hides in the brakes in the nihilistic Spring.
Old men feel their scolding heart
Reproach the veins that for fire have only anger.
And Christ has forgiven all men — the thunder-browed Caesar,
That stone-veined Tantalus [16] howling with thirst in the plain
Where for innocent water flows only the blood of the slain,
Falling forever from veins that held in their noonday
The foolish companion of summer, the weeping rose.
We asked for a sign that we have not been forsaken —
And for answer the Abraham-bearded Sun, the father of all things,
Is shouting of ripeness over our harvest forever.
And with the sound of growth, lion-strong, and the laughing Sun,
Whose great flames stretch like branches in the heat
Across the firmament, we almost see
The great gold planets spangling the wide air
And earth —
O sons of men, the firmament's belovèd,
The Golden Ones of heaven have us in care —
With planetary wisdom, changeless laws,
Ripening our lives and ruling hearts and rhythms,
Immortal hungers in the veins and heart
Born from the primal Cause

[12] Spanish loose robes or negligees.

[13] A word coined (?) by Dame Edith by analogy with 'tourelle' above; from the French 'muraille — a wall.' Also, by suggestion, the poisonous plant 'morelle,' a variety of the deadly nightshade, and 'morella,' an obsolete term for a dress or curtain fabric.

[14] In Greek mythology, a maiden ravished by her brother-in-law, Tereus, and turned into a nightingale.

[15] Modern English poet (b. 1900). There is a biographical sketch of him at the end of this volume.

[16] In Greek mythology, a king punished by the gods for his wickedness; he was inflicted with great thirst and hunger, then placed in a stream of Hades which always receded from him as he stooped to drink, and under trees whose branches always withdrew as he reached to pluck the fruit.

That keeps the hearts and blood of men and beasts ever in motion,
The amber blood of the smooth-weeping tree
Rising towards the life-giving heat of the Sun. . . .
For is not the blood — the divine, the animal heat
That is not fire — derived from the solar ray?
And does not the Beast surpass all elements
In power, through the heat and wisdom of the blood
Creating other Beasts — the Lion a Lion, the Bull a Bull,
The Bear a Bear — some like great stars in the rough
And uncreated dark — or unshaped universes
With manes of fire and a raging sun for heart?
Gestation, generation, and duration —
The cycles of all lives upon the earth —
Plants, beasts, and men, must follow those of heaven;
The rhythms of our lives
Are those of the ripening, dying of the seasons,
Our sowing and reaping in the holy fields,
Our love and giving birth — then growing old
And sinking into sleep in the maternal
Earth, mother of corn, the wrinkled darkness.
So we, ruled by those laws, see their fulfilment.
And I who stood in the grave-clothes of my flesh
Unutterably spotted with the world's woes
Cry, 'I am Fire. See, I am the bright gold
That shines like a flaming fire in the night — the gold-trained planet,
The laughing heat of the Sun that was born from darkness —
Returning to darkness — I am fecundity, harvest.'
For on each country road,
Grown from the needs of men as boughs from trees,
The reapers walk like the harvesters of heaven —
Jupiter and his great train, and the corn-goddess,
And Saturn marching in the Dorian mode.[17]
We heard in the dawn the first ripe-bearded fire
Of wheat (so flames that are men's spirits break from their thick earth),
Then came the Pentecostal Rushing of Flames, God in the wind that comes to the wheat,
Returned from the Dead for the guilty hands of Caesar
Like the rose at morning shouting of red joys
And redder sorrows fallen from young veins and heart-springs,
Come back for the wrong and the right, the wise and the foolish,
Who like the rose care not for our philosophies
Of life and death, knowing the earth's forgiveness
And the great dews that come to the sick rose:
For those who build great mornings for the world
From Edens of lost light seen in each other's eyes,
Yet soon must wear no more the light of the Sun
But say farewell among the morning sorrows.
The universal language of the Bread —
(O Thou who are not broken, or divided —
Thou who art eaten, but like the Burning Bush
Art not consumed — Thou Bread of Men and Angels) —

[17] In classical Greece, one of three principal modes of music; it was considered suitable especially for choral music, virile and grave in its nature, inspiring the nobler and more heroic virtues.

The Seraphim rank on rank of the ripe wheat—
Gold-bearded thunders and hierarchies of heaven
Roar from the earth: 'Our Christ is arisen, He comes to give a sign from the Dead.'

[*Green Song and Other Poems*, 1944]

Heart and Mind

Said the Lion to the Lioness—'When you are amber dust—
No more a raging fire like the heat of the Sun
(No liking but all lust)—
Remember still the flowering of the amber blood and bone,
The rippling of bright muscles like a sea,
Remember the rose-prickles of bright paws,
Though we shall mate no more
Till the fire of that sun the heart and the moon-cold bone are one.'

Said the Skeleton lying upon the sands of Time—
'The great gold planet that is the mourning heat of the Sun
Is greater than all gold, more powerful
Than the tawny body of a Lion that fire consumes
Like all that grows or leaps . . . so is the heart
More powerful than all dust. Once I was Hercules
Or Samson, strong as the pillars of the seas:
But the flames of the heart consumed me, and the mind
Is but a foolish wind.'

Said the Sun to the Moon—'When you are but a lonely white crone,
And I, a dead King in my golden armor somewhere in a dark wood,
Remember only this of our hopeless love:
That never till Time is done
Will the fire of the heart and the fire of the mind be one.'

[*Green Song and Other Poems*, 1944]

The Coat of Fire

Amid the thunders of the falling Dark
In the Tartarean darkness of the fog
I walk, a Pillar of Fire,
On pavements of black marble, hard
And wide as the long boulevard
Of Hell . . . I, in whose veins the Furies wave
Their long fires, move where purgatories, heavens, hells, and worlds
Wrought by illusion hide in the human breast
And tear the enclosing heart . . . And the snow fell
(Thin flakes of ash from Gomorrah) on blind faces
Turned to the heedless sky. . . . A dress has the sound
Of Reality, reverberates like thunder.
And ghosts of aeons and of equinoxes
(Of moments that seemed aeons, and long partings)
Take on the forms of fashionable women
With veils that hide a new Catastrophe, and under
Is the fall of a world that was a heart. Some doomed to descend
Through all the hells and change into the Dog
Without its faithfulness, the Crocodile
Without its watchfulness, and then to Pampean mud.[18]
In the circles of the city's hells beneath the fog
These bear, to light them, in the human breast,
The yellow dull light from the raging human dust,
The dull blue light from the brutes, light red as rust

[18] Pertaining to the vast plains or pampas of South America; pampas clay is either an ossiferous, bluish clay or reddish, argillaceous earth.

Of blood from eyeless weeping ghosts, light black as smoke
From hell.[19] And those breasts bear
No other light. . . . They circle in the snow
Where in the dust the apterous
Fates turned insects whisper, 'Now abandon
Man the annelida. Let all be wingless
That hang between the abyss and Abaddon.[20]
The Catastrophes with veils and trains drift by,
And I to my heart, disastrous Comet, cry,
'Red heart, my Lucifer, how fallen art thou,
And lightless, I!'
The dresses sweep the dust of mortality
And roll the burden of Atlas' woe, changed to a stone,
Up to the benches where the beggars sway —
Their souls alone as on the Judgment Day —
In their Valley of the myriad Dry Bones under world-tall houses.
Then with a noise as if in the thunders of the Dark
All sins, griefs, aberrations of the world rolled to confess,
Those myriad Dry Bones rose to testify:

'See her, the Pillar of Fire!
The aeons of Cold
And all the deaths that Adam has endured
Since the first death cannot outfreeze our night!'
And where is the fire of love that will warm our hands?
There is only this conflagration
Of all the sins of the world! To the dust's busyness
She speaks of the annihilation
Of every form of dust, burned down to Nothingness!
To the small lovers, of a kiss that seems the red
Lightning of Comets firing worlds — and of a Night
That shall outburn all nights that lovers know —
The last red Night before the Judgment Day!
O Pillar of Flame, that drifts across the world to Nowhere!
The eyes are seas of fire! All forms, all sights,
And all sensations are on fire! The storms
Of blood, a whirlpool of the flame! The ears, all sounds
Of all the world, a universe of fire! All smells, a ravening
Raging cyclone of wild fire! The nose, burned quite away!
The tongue is on fire, all tastes on fire, the mind
Is red as noon upon the Judgment Day!
The tears are rolling, falling worlds of fire!
With what are these on fire? With passion, hate,
Infatuation, and old age, and death,
With sorrow, longing, and with laboring breath.
And with despair and life are these on fire!
With the illusions of the world, the flames of lust,
And raging red desire![21]
A Pillar of Fire is she in the empty dust,
And will not change those fires into warmth for our hands,
Said the beggars, lolling and rocking
The heedless world upon a heaving shoulder.

[*Song of the Cold* (Am. ed., 1948)]

---

[19] Dame Edith notes that the three preceding lines contain 'references to the Tibetan *Book of the Dead.*'

[20] The bottomless pit of the book of Revelation.

[21] The preceding fourteen lines have reference to Buddha's Fire Sermon, according to Dame Edith. In this sermon, Buddha likens the passions and senses of the body to consuming fire; the wise man, therefore, conceives an aversion for things known through the mind and the senses.

Thomas Stearns Eliot

1888–

The Love Song of J. Alfred Prufrock

S'io credesse che mia risposta fosse
A persona che mai tornasse al mondo,
Questa fiamma staria senza piu scosse.
Ma perciocche giammai di questo fondo
Non torno vivo alcun, s'i'odo il vero,
Senza tema d'infamia ti rispondo.[1]

LET us go then, you and I,
When the evening is spread out against the sky
Like a patient etherised upon a table;
Let us go, through certain half-deserted streets,
The muttering retreats
Of restless nights in one-night cheap hotels
And sawdust restaurants with oyster-shells:
Streets that follow like a tedious argument
Of insidious intent
To lead you to an overwhelming question . . .
Oh, do not ask, 'What is it?'
Let us go and make our visit.

In the room the women come and go
Talking of Michelangelo.

The yellow fog that rubs its back upon the window-panes,
The yellow smoke that rubs its muzzle on the window-panes
Licked its tongue into the corners of the evening,
Lingered upon the pools that stand in drains,
Let fall upon its back the soot that falls from chimneys,
Slipped by the terrace, made a sudden leap,
And seeing that it was a soft October night,
Curled once about the house, and fell asleep.

And indeed there will be time[2]
For the yellow smoke that slides along the street,
Rubbing its back upon the window-panes;
There will be time, there will be time
To prepare a face to meet the faces that you meet;
There will be time to murder and create,
And time for all the works and days[3] of hands
That lift and drop a question on your plate;
Time for you and time for me,
And time yet for a hundred indecisions,
And for a hundred visions and revisions,
Before the taking of a toast and tea.

In the room the women come and go
Talking of Michelangelo.

And indeed there will be time
To wonder, 'Do I dare?' and, 'Do I dare?'
Time to turn back and descend the stair,
With a bald spot in the middle of my hair —
[They will say: 'How his hair is growing thin!']
My morning coat, my collar mounting firmly to the chin,
My necktie rich and modest, but asserted by a simple pin —
[They will say: 'But how his arms and legs are thin!']

---

[1] From Dante's *Inferno,* XXVII, 61–6; as Dante and Virgil pass through that part of Hell devoted to the punishment of evil counsellors, Guido da Montefeltro replies to a question: 'If I believed that my reply were to a person who should ever return to the world, this flame would stand without more quiverings; but inasmuch as, if I hear truth, never did any one return alive from this depth, I answer thee without fear of infamy.'

[2] Andrew Marvell, in his poem, 'To His Coy Mistress,' argues first wittily, then with gravity, that in this short life there is no time for indecisions and procrastinations; the poem begins, 'Had we but world enough, and time . . .'

[3] *Works and Days* is the title of a poem by the Greek poet, Hesiod (8th cent. B.C.), in which he urges his brother to make the most of his farming.

Do I dare
Disturb the universe?
In a minute there is time
For decisions and revisions which a minute will reverse.

For I have known them all already, known them all: —
Have known the evenings, mornings, afternoons,
I have measured out my life with coffee spoons;
I know the voices dying with a dying fall [4]
Beneath the music from a farther room.
So how should I presume?

And I have known the eyes already, known them all —
The eyes that fix you in a formulated phrase,
And when I am formulated, sprawling on a pin,
When I am pinned and wriggling on the wall,
Then how should I begin
To spit out all the butt-ends of my days and ways?
And how should I presume?

And I have known the arms already, known them all —
Arms that are braceleted and white and bare
[But in the lamplight, downed with light brown hair!] [5]
Is it perfume from a dress
That makes me so digress?
Arms that lie along a table, or wrap about a shawl.
And should I then presume?
And how should I begin?

. . .

Shall I say, I have gone at dusk through narrow streets
And watched the smoke that rises from the pipes
Of lonely men in shirt-sleeves, leaning out of windows? . . .

I should have been a pair of ragged claws
Scuttling across the floors of silent seas.

. . .

And the afternoon, the evening, sleeps so peacefully!
Smoothed by long fingers,
Asleep . . . tired . . . or it malingers,
Stretched on the floor, here beside you and me.
Should I, after tea and cakes and ices,
Have the strength to force the moment to its crisis?
But though I have wept and fasted, wept and prayed,
Though I have seen my head [grown slightly bald] brought in upon a platter,[6]
I am no prophet — and here's no great matter;
I have seen the moment of my greatness flicker,
And I have seen the eternal Footman hold my coat, and snicker,
And in short, I was afraid.

And would it have been worth it, after all,
After the cups, the marmalade, the tea,
Among the porcelain, among some talk of you and me,
Would it have been worth while,
To have bitten off the matter with a smile,
To have squeezed the universe into a ball [7]

[4] An echo of Duke Orsino's opening speech in Shakespeare's *Twelfth Night,* where he describes an overheard strain of music as having a 'dying fall,' and praises it as the 'food of love.'

[5] Perhaps an echo of an image found in Donne's metaphysical love poetry, as in 'The Relique,' where the poet affirms that if anyone digs up his grave, he will spy 'A bracelet of bright hair about the bone . . .'

[6] Pleased with the dancing of Salome, Herod had John the Baptist beheaded at the request of her mother, and the head brought in on a platter (Matt. 14:3–11, or Mark 6:17–28).

[7] Cf. Marvell again: 'Let us roll all our strength and all / Our sweetness up into one ball, / And tear our pleasures with rough strife / Thorough the iron gates of life.'

To roll it toward some overwhelming question,
To say: 'I am Lazarus, come from the dead,[8]
Come back to tell you all, I shall tell you all' —
If one, settling a pillow by her head,
Should say: 'That is not what I meant at all.
That is not it, at all.'

And would it have been worth it, after all,
Would it have been worth while,
After the sunsets and the dooryards and the sprinkled streets,
After the novels, after the teacups, after the skirts that trail along the floor —
And this, and so much more? —
It is impossible to say just what I mean!
But as if a magic lantern threw the nerves in patterns on a screen:
Would it have been worth while
If one, settling a pillow or throwing off a shawl,
And turning toward the window, should say:
'That is not it at all,
That is not what I meant, at all.'

. . .

No! I am not Prince Hamlet, nor was meant to be;
Am an attendant lord,[9] one that will do
To swell a progress, start a scene or two,
Advise the prince; no doubt, an easy tool,
Deferential, glad to be of use,
Politic, cautious, and meticulous;
Full of high sentence, but a bit obtuse;
At times, indeed, almost ridiculous —
Almost, at times, the Fool.[10]

I grow old . . . I grow old . . .
I shall wear the bottoms of my trousers rolled.

Shall I part my hair behind? Do I dare to eat a peach?
I shall wear white flannel trousers, and walk upon the beach.
I have heard the mermaids singing, each to each.

I do not think that they will sing to me.

I have seen them riding seaward on the waves
Combing the white hair of the waves blown back
When the wind blows the water white and black.

We have lingered in the chambers of the sea
By sea-girls wreathed with seaweed red and brown
Till human voices wake us, and we drown.

[*Prufrock,* 1917]

Gerontion

Thou hast nor youth nor age
But as it were an after dinner sleep
Dreaming of both.[11]

Here I am, an old man in a dry month,
Being read to by a boy, waiting for rain.
I was neither at the hot gates [12]
Nor fought in the warm rain
Nor knee deep in the salt marsh, heaving a cutlass,
Bitten by flies, fought.
My house is a decayed house,
And the jew squats on the window sill, the owner,
Spawned in some estaminet [13] of Antwerp,
Blistered in Brussels, patched and peeled in London.
The goat [14] coughs at night in the field overhead;

[8] Brought back to life by Jesus in the miracle recorded by John 11.

[9] As Rosencrantz and Guildenstern in Shakespeare's *Hamlet,* or the fop Osric.

[10] Though there is no Fool in *Hamlet,* Eliot is thinking of the other Shakesperian tragedies, like *Lear,* where the Fool is often perceptive, but ineffectual and the butt of ridicule.

[11] From Shakespeare's *Measure for Measure,* where the Duke counsels contempt for the world to Claudio who is about to be executed (III, i, 32–4). The poem's title means 'a little old man.'

[12] A literal translation of the Greek Thermopylae, historic site of Greek defenses against the invading Persians.

[13] café

[14] Traditional symbol of lust.

Rocks, moss, stonecrop, iron, merds.[15]
The woman keeps the kitchen, makes tea,
Sneezes at evening, poking the peevish gutter.
I an old man,
A dull head among windy spaces.

Signs are taken for wonders. 'We would see a sign!'
The word within a word, unable to speak a word,[16]
Swaddled with darkness. In the juvescence [17] of the year
Came Christ the tiger [18]

In depraved May, dogwood and chestnut, flowering judas,
To be eaten, to be divided, to be drunk
Among whispers; by Mr. Silvero
With caressing hands, at Limoges [19]
Who walked all night in the next room;

By Hakagawa, bowing among the Titians;
By Madame de Tornquist, in the dark room
Shifting the candles; Fräulein von Kulp
Who turned in the hall, one hand on the door.
Vacant shuttles
Weave the wind. I have no ghosts,
An old man in a draughty house
Under a windy knob.

After such knowledge, what forgiveness? Think now
History has many cunning passages, contrived corridors
And issues, deceives with whispering ambitions,
Guides us by vanities. Think now
She gives when our attention is distracted
And what she gives, gives with such supple confusions
That the giving famishes the craving.[20] Gives too late
What's not believed in, or if still believed,
In memory only, reconsidered passion. Gives too soon
Into weak hands, what's thought can be dispensed with
Till the refusal propagates a fear. Think
Neither fear nor courage saves us. Unnatural vices
Are fathered by our heroism. Virtues
Are forced upon us by our impudent crimes.
These tears are shaken from the wrath-bearing tree.[21]

The tiger springs in the new year. Us he devours. Think at last
We have not reached conclusion, when I
Stiffen in a rented house. Think at last
I have not made this show purposelessly
And it is not by any concitation [22]
Of the backward devils.
I would meet you upon this honestly.
I that was near your heart was removed therefrom
To lose beauty in terror, terror in inquisition.
I have lost my passion: why should I need to keep it
Since what is kept must be adulterated?
I have lost my sight, smell, hearing, taste and touch:
How should I use them for your closer contact?

These with a thousand small deliberations
Protract the profit of their chilled delirium,
Excite the membrane, when the sense has cooled,

[15] dung
[16] John I:I: 'In the beginning was the Word, and the Word was with God, and the Word was God.' The 'Word of God' was made completely manifest in Christ.
[17] springtime
[18] Suggestive of William Blake's 'The Tyger,' which begins, 'Tyger! Tyger! burning bright . . .' Cf. Christ's words in Matt. 10:34, 'Think not that I am come to send peace on earth: I came not to send peace, but a sword.'
[19] French center of fine porcelain making.
[20] An echo of Enobarbus' description (Shakespeare, *Antony and Cleopatra,* II, ii, 243–6) of Cleopatra — 'Other women cloy / The appetites they feed, but she makes hungry / Where most she satisfies.'
[21] The tree of knowledge of good and evil, the fruit of which Adam and Eve tasted, and by extension the tree or cross on which Christ died.
[22] agitation, stirring up

With pungent sauces, multiply variety
In a wilderness of mirrors. What will the spider[23] do,
Suspend its operations, will the weevil
Delay? De Bailhache, Fresca, Mrs. Cammel, whirled
Beyond the circuit of the shuddering Bear[24]
In fractured atoms. Gull against the wind, in the windy straits
Of Belle Isle,[25] or running on the Horn,
White feathers in the snow, the Gulf claims,
And an old man driven by the Trades
To a sleepy corner.

Tenants of the house,
Thoughts of a dry brain in a dry season.

[*Poems,* 1920]

Sweeney Among the Nightingales[26]

ὤμοι, πέπληγμαι καιρίαν πληγὴν ἔσω.[27]

Apeneck Sweeney spreads his knees
Letting his arms hang down to laugh,
The zebra stripes along his jaw
Swelling to maculate giraffe.

The circles of the stormy moon
Slide westward toward the River Plate,[28]
Death and the Raven[29] drift above
And Sweeney guards the hornèd gate.[30]

Gloomy Orion and the Dog[31]
Are veiled; and hushed the shrunken seas;
The person in the Spanish cape
Tries to sit on Sweeney's knees

Slips and pulls the table cloth
Overturns a coffee-cup,
Reorganized upon the floor
She yawns and draws a stocking up;

The silent man in mocha brown
Sprawls at the window-sill and gapes;
The waiter brings in oranges
Bananas figs and hothouse grapes;

The silent vertebrate in brown
Rachel *née* Rabinovitch
Contracts and concentrates, withdraws;
Tears at the grapes with murderous paws;

She and the lady in the cape
Are suspect, thought to be in league;
Therefore the man with heavy eyes
Declines the gambit, shows fatigue,

Leaves the room and reappears
Outside the window, leaning in,
Branches of wistaria
Circumscribe a golden grin;

The host with someone indistinct
Converses at the door apart,
The nightingales are singing near
The Convent of the Sacred Heart,[32]

And sang within the bloody wood
When Agamemnon cried aloud,
And let their liquid siftings fall
To stain the stiff dishonoured shroud.

[*Poems,* 1920]

---

[23] symbol for death

[24] In Cicero's *Somnium Scipionis* (or *Dream of Scipio*), preserved for medieval readers by the influential commentary of Macrobius, Scipio is instructed in how to win heavenly bliss, but warned that the wicked are kept whirling about the earth after death. Chaucer uses the image both at the beginning of his ' Parliament of Fowls ' and at the end of *Troilus and Criseyde*. The ' Bear ' is the constellation of Ursa Major, or the Big Dipper.

[25] Between Labrador and Newfoundland.

[26] Sweeney as a character in this and other Eliot poems represents brute man, unredeemed by any recognizably human values. The nightingales of the title and at the end of the poem are an oblique recollection of the Greek story of Philomela, raped by her brother-in-law, Tereus, who cut out her tongue to prevent her outcry; she nevertheless made it known to her sister, and when Tereus drew his sword on them, all were turned into birds, Philomela into a nightingale.

[27] When Agamemnon returned from the Trojan War, his faithless wife Clytemnestra and her lover Aegisthus murdered him. This line, Agamemnon's cry in Aeschylus' tragedy, *Agamemnon,* can be translated, ' Ay me! I have been smitten deep with a mortal blow.'

[28] The estuary between Argentina and Uruguay.

[29] A bird of ill omen, a symbol of death; it is also a constellation in the southern skies.

[30] That one of the twin gates of sleep through which issues in dreams the true shades of death.

[31] Two constellations; Orion was slain when attempting to win his love by violence, revived, then slain again accidentally by Diana, goddess of chastity, who set him among the stars.

[32] Possibly an association (with symbolic overtones) with the actual convent of that name near London and the hospital where Florence Nightingale founded her home for nurses. In any case, the associations throughout the lines here are non-logical, for Agamemnon was killed in his bath.

THE WASTE LAND

[Possibly the most influential poem so far in the twentieth century, *The Waste Land* first appeared in the October, 1922, issue of *The Criterion,* a quarterly journal just founded which Eliot edited. Not until it appeared in book form a few months later did Eliot add the notes which now usually accompany the poem. In these notes, Eliot expresses his great debt to Jesse L. Weston's *From Ritual to Romance* (1920) and Sir James G. Frazer's *The Golden Bough* (1890–1915), both influential anthropological studies of primitive myth and religious ritual.

In her book, Miss Weston attempts to demonstrate the connection between the Grail legend embedded in the Arthurian stories, and the ancient fertility and vegetation rites of the Near East. These rites became the basis for various mystery cults in which the original ceremonies came to represent the initiation of youth into the 'mysteries' of the source of spiritual as well as physical well-being. It is Miss Weston's contention that these cults were spread to the West by Levantine traders, later to be absorbed into and transformed by Christian symbolism. Generally, in the Grail legend, an ancient Fisher King, wounded (and sexually impotent), rules over a 'waste land' whose barrenness is related to the condition of the king. He cannot be cured, nor his land redeemed, until the perfect knight, inspired by a vision, usually of a chalice, passes many trying adventures and temptations to reach the 'Chapel Perilous.' If he there survives the most dangerous temptations of all, he may ask the questions about the mysterious lance and cup which will bring healing.

The central volumes of Frazer's study examine the elements of the myths of the Near Eastern fertility gods, Adonis, Attis, and Osiris—their seasonal wounding, death, and rebirth. In all this material it is important to note, for the purpose of understanding the poem, the influence these cults had on Christianity (the wounding, death, and resurrection of Christ in the spring); the connection between the idea of the Fisher King and the title — 'fishers of men' — which Christ bestowed upon the Apostles; the use of the anagram 'Ichthys' (Greek for fish) and the form of the fish in Christian symbolism; and the ancient use of the fish as a phallic symbol. According to Miss Weston, the bleeding lance and the chalice of the Grail legend are medieval Christian identifications of ancient sexual symbols with the lance which pierced Christ's side and with the Communion Cup; the search for the Grail is the medieval transformation of the ancient mystery-cult initiatory ceremonies.

In Eliot's adaptation of these ideas for the theme and structure of his poem, he presents the modern age as a 'waste land,' emotionally, spiritually, and culturally barren; it is a time of 'death,' awaiting, desperately, the coming of 'spiritual rain' and 'rebirth.' The ancient prophets have degenerated into fortunetellers (like Mme. Sosostris), the Levantine adventurers into currant-merchants (Mr. Eugenides); the pervasive imagery of sexual barrenness, impotence, or perversion at all levels represents the sterility of the times; the numerous quotations or echoes from the great world literature of the past suggest by contrast the cultural and spiritual emptiness of the present. Through this material, Eliot moves, not by connected logical discourse, but by a logic of free association; and the 'I' who speaks through much of the poem is not only the old seer Tiresias with whom he identifies himself at one point, but 'Everyman' at every level of society, seeking — more or less impotently, more or less consciously — a salvation-giving 'vision of the Grail.' In the following notes to the poem, those which Eliot himself furnished are so identified.]

'Nam Sibyllam quidem Cumis ego ipse oculis meis vidi in ampulla pendere, et cum illi pueri dicerent: Σίβυλλα τί θελεις; respondebat illa: ἀποθανεῖν θέλω.' [33]

For Ezra Pound
il miglior fabbro.

I. The Burial of the Dead [34]

April is the cruellest month, breeding
Lilacs out of the dead land, mixing
Memory and desire, stirring
Dull roots with spring rain.
Winter kept us warm, covering
Earth in forgetful snow, feeding

[33] In the *Satyricon* of Petronious, a guest at a banquet gives this scoffing account of the once great counsellor of Aeneas and the speaker of wisdom to a nation: 'Yes, and I myself with my own eyes saw the Sibyl of Cumae hanging in a cage; and when the boys cried at her: "Sibyl, what do you want?", she used to reply, "I want to die."' The dedication (just below) to Eliot's friend and critic, the American poet Ezra Pound, makes use of the praise of one poet for another in Dante's *Purgatorio,* XXVI — 'the better craftsman.'

[34] In the ancient fertility myths, the god was buried in order that he might be reborn in the spring; in this section of the poem the irony lies in the presence of many examples of 'death' but with little or no hope of 'rebirth.'

A little life with dried tubers.
Summer surprised us, coming over the Starnbergersee[35]
With a shower of rain; we stopped in the colonnade,
And went on in sunlight, into the Hofgarten,
And drank coffee, and talked for an hour.
Bin gar keine Russin, stamm' aus Litauen, echt deutsch.[36]
And when we were children, staying at the archduke's,
My cousin's, he took me out on a sled,
And I was frightened. He said, Marie,
Marie, hold on tight. And down we went.
In the mountains, there you feel free.
I read, much of the night, and go south in the winter.

What are the roots that clutch, what branches grow
Out of this stony rubbish? Son of man,[37]
You cannot say, or guess, for you know only
A heap of broken images, where the sun beats,
And the dead tree gives no shelter, the cricket no relief,[38]
And the dry stone no sound of water. Only
There is shadow under this red rock,[39]
(Come in under the shadow of this red rock),
And I will show you something different from either
Your shadow at morning striding behind you
Or your shadow at evening rising to meet you;
I will show you fear in a handful of dust.

Frisch weht der Wind
Der Heimat zu
Mein Irisch Kind,
Wo weilest du?[40]

'You gave me hyacinths first a year ago;
'They called me the hyacinth girl.'
—Yet when we came back, late, from the Hyacinth garden,
Your arms full, and your hair wet, I could not
Speak, and my eyes failed, I was neither
Living nor dead, and I knew nothing,
Looking into the heart of light, the silence.
Oed' und leer das Meer.[41]

Madame Sosostris, famous clairvoyante,
Had a bad cold, nevertheless
Is known to be the wisest woman in Europe,
With a wicked pack of cards.[42] Here, said she,

[35] A lake and fashionable summer resort for the wealthy near Munich, Germany; the Hofgarten is a park with open-air restaurants.

[36] 'I am no Russian, but a true German woman from Lithuania,' i.e. from one of the German families settled in the Slavic fringes of Germany.

[37] 'Cf. Ezekiel II, i' [Eliot]. 'And He said unto me, Son of Man, stand upon thy feet, and I will speak unto thee.' The whole chapter is an exhortation of God's to the prophet to preach to the erring ones and bring them back to the fold.

[38] 'Cf. Ecclesiastes XII, v' [Eliot]. Warning of the coming of death, the Preacher says, 'Also when they shall be afraid of that which is high, and fears shall be in the way, and the almond tree shall flourish, and the grasshopper shall be a burden, and desire shall fail: because man goeth to his long home, and the mourners go about the streets . . .' And he concludes, 'Then shall the dust return to the earth as it was: and the spirit shall return unto God who gave it. Vanity of vanities, saith the preacher: all is vanity. . . . Fear God, and keep his commandments: for this is the whole duty of man. For God shall bring every work into judgment, with every secret thing, whether it be good, or whether it be evil.'

[39] Cf. Isaiah 32:1–2: 'Behold, a king shall reign in righteousness . . . And a man shall be as an hiding place from the wind, and a covert from the tempest; as rivers of water in a dry place, as the shadow of a great rock in a weary land.'

[40] Eliot notes that this comes from Wagner's *Tristan und Isolde*, I, 5–8. At the opening of the opera, a young sailor sings, 'Fresh blows the wind to the homeland; my Irish child, where do you tarry?' Most immediately the line is an evocation of adolescent love, but the wider reference Eliot also has in mind is the passionate love of Tristan and Isolde themselves, and the connection of their story with the Arthurian legends.

[41] Again Eliot points to the opera, III, 24; Tristan is dying, and to the question if Isolde's ship has yet appeared, the lookout replies, 'Waste and empty the sea.'

[42] 'I am not familiar with the exact constitution of the Tarot pack of cards, from which I have obviously departed to suit my own convenience. The Hanged Man, a member of the traditional pack, fits my purpose in two ways: because he is associated in my mind with the Hanged God of Frazer, and because I associate him with the hooded figure in the passage of the disciples to Emmaus in Part V. The Phoenician Sailor and the Merchant appear later; also the 'crowds of people,' and Death by Water is executed in Part IV. The Man with Three Staves (an authentic member of the Tarot pack) I associate, quite arbitrarily, with the Fisher King himself.' [Eliot] The Tarot cards (78 in number, 22 of them emblematical) are probably very ancient. They are still used for games and fortune telling.

Is your card, the drowned Phoenician Sailor,[43]
(Those are pearls that were his eyes. Look!)[44]
Here is Belladonna, the Lady of the Rocks,[45]
The lady of situations.
Here is the man with three staves, and here the Wheel,[46]
And here is the one-eyed merchant,[47] and this card,
Which is blank, is something he carries on his back,[48]
Which I am forbidden to see. I do not find
The Hanged Man.[49] Fear death by water.
I see crowds of people, walking round in a ring.
Thank you. If you see dear Mrs. Equitone,
Tell her I bring the horoscope myself:
One must be so careful these days.

Unreal City,[50]
Under the brown fog of a winter dawn,
A crowd flowed over London Bridge, so many,
I had not thought death had undone so many.[51]
Sighs, short and infrequent, were exhaled,[52]
And each man fixed his eyes before his feet.
Flowed up the hill and down King William Street,[53]
To where Saint Mary Woolnoth kept the hours
With a dead sound on the final stroke of nine.[54]
There I saw one I knew, and stopped him, crying: 'Stetson!
'You who were with me in the ships at Mylae![55]
'That corpse you planted last year in your garden,[56]
'Has it begun to sprout? Will it bloom this year?
'Or has the sudden frost disturbed its bed?
'Oh keep the Dog far hence, that's friend to men,
'Or with his nails he'll dig it up again![57]

[43] Evocative of the Near Eastern fertility gods, whose images were sometimes thrown into the water to mark the end of summer. The Phoenicians were both worshippers of such gods, and great traders — representative of the mercantile genius of materialistic civilizations, yet, according to Miss Weston, carriers of the religious mysteries to the West.

[44] From Ariel's song over the King believed drowned in Shakespeare's *Tempest* (I, ii). In *The Tempest* (ideas from which are repeatedly echoed in this poem as a leading motif), Ferdinand's father, the King, and his companions are apparently drowned, and while Ferdinand sits weeping on the shore, he hears this song of Ariel's which continues, 'Nothing of him that doth fade / But doth suffer a sea-change / Into something rich and strange.' But Prospero, an exiled ruler himself, has arranged all this so that Ferdinand may fall in love with his daughter (an innocent love of the kind impossible in the waste land) and so that the King (who has helped do Prospero a grievous injury) may be made repentant — a 'death by water' that transformed him into 'something rich and strange.' Pearls — symbols of purity — and an image of baptism have their thematic relevance here.

[45] Belladonna means literally 'beautiful lady' but it is also the name of a numbing poisonous drug, and this is a lady of 'situations.' But though 'Rocks' suggest the quality of the waste land, there is also an implied ironic reference to one of the Madonnas painted by da Vinci.

[46] An authentic Tarot card, symbolizing fortune, or the will of the gods.

[47] The card of The Fool depicts a one-eyed man; cf. Mr. Eugenides, the Smyrna currant merchant of line 209.

[48] The ancient Levantine merchants used to carry the religious mysteries; Mr. Eugenides brings not only currants but a hint of sexual perversion.

[49] In most primitive religions, such as those of the Near East which influenced Christianity, there is a hanged or maimed god.

[50] Eliot calls attention at this point to Baudelaire's poem, 'The Seven Old Men' (no. 93 in *Fleurs du mal*), which begins, 'Swarming city, city full of dreams, / Where the spectre in full day walks with the passer-by.' Baudelaire describes a visit to the slums through foul, yellow fog, where he met in succession seven old men, evil-eyed, bent, hostile; 'these seven hideous monsters had the look of eternal beings.'

[51] As Dante enters the Gate of Hell ('Inferno III, 55–7' [Eliot]) he sees a crowd of lost souls wailing, neither praise- nor blame-worthy — just empty lives — of whom he says, '. . . so long a train / of people that I should never have believed / that death had undone so many.'

[52] Again Eliot calls attention to Dante's *Inferno* (IV, 25–7); in the first circle of Hell, Dante comes upon those virtuous souls who are unsaved because they lived before the time of Christ. They are described, 'No plaint could be heard, except of sighs, / which caused the eternal air to tremble.'

[53] Leading from London Bridge past the church of St. Mary Woolnoth and the Bank of England.

[54] 'A phenomenon which I have often noticed' [Eliot].

[55] In a war between two ancient commercial powers, Rome defeated Phoenician Carthage in the naval battle of Mylae, 260 B.C.; Eliot suggests here that all wars are alike.

[56] A suggestion of the buried fertility god.

[57] 'Cf. the Dirge in Webster's *White Devil*' [Eliot]. In this famous Jacobean tragedy of lust, passion, and betrayal, a maddened mother sings a dirge over the grave of her murdered son (V, iv) which concludes, 'But keep the wolf far thence, that's foe to man, / For with his nails he'll dig them up again.' By substituting 'friend' for 'foe' and 'Dog' for 'wolf,' Eliot seems to invoke the association of Sirius (the Dog Star) which heralded the rising of the Nile, the rebirth of the buried fertility

'You! hypocrite lecteur! — mon semblable,
— mon frère!' [58]

II. A Game of Chess [59]

The Chair she sat in, like a burnished throne,
Glowed on the marble, where the glass
Held up by standards wrought with fruited vines
From which a golden Cupidon peeped out
(Another hid his eyes behind his wing)
Doubled the flames of sevenbranched candelabra
Reflecting light upon the table as
The glitter of her jewels rose to meet it,
From satin cases poured in rich profusion;
In vials of ivory and coloured glass
Unstoppered, lurked her strange synthetic perfumes,
Unguent, powdered, or liquid — troubled, confused
And drowned the sense in odours; stirred by the air
That freshened from the window, these ascended
In fattening the prolonged candle-flames,
Flung their smoke into the laquearia,[60]

---

god, and the return of spring. But the association is clearly ironic here.

[58] Eliot directs attention to Baudelaire's preface to his *Fleurs du mal.* After describing human vices as animals, and boredom as the ugliest of all, Baudelaire concludes, 'You know him, reader . . . Hypocrite reader! — my double — my brother!'

[59] Both suggestive of the idle pastime of the bored (see l. 137) and evocative once more of the passions of Jacobean tragedy through association with Thomas Middleton. There is his play, *A Game of Chess,* or more especially, a scene in his tragedy, *Women beware Women* (to which Eliot refers specifically at l. 138) where a mother's attention is distracted by a game of chess while her daughter-in-law is seduced. But such an evocation only points up the barren similarity of the two situations counterpointed in this section, however widely apart they are socially. This contrast with the past and its great literature is further emphasized in the opening description, which is rich in echoes from Enobarbus' description of Cleopatra's first meeting with Antony (Shakespeare's '*Antony and Cleopatra,* II, ii' [Eliot]), or of the Phoenician Queen Dido's palace in Virgil's *Aeneid* — stories of passions which were great, but also desperate.

[60] The gilded spaces or 'coffers' between exposed crossbeams of a ceiling; from the 'Aeneid, I, 726' [Eliot]. The passage referred to — 'lighted lamps hang from the fretted ceiling of gold, and flaming torches drive out the night' — describes the scene in which Dido, Queen of Carthage, gives a great feast for Aeneas and is smitten with love for him. When he leaves Carthage, she kills herself.

Stirring the pattern on the coffered ceiling.
Huge sea-wood fed with copper
Burned green and orange, framed by the coloured stone,
In which sad light a carvèd dolphin swam.
Above the antique mantel was displayed
As though a window gave upon the sylvan scene [61]
The change of Philomel, by the barbarous king [62]
So rudely forced; yet there the nightingale [63]
Filled all the desert with inviolable voice
And still she cried, and still the world pursues,
'Jug Jug' to dirty ears.
And other withered stumps of time
Were told upon the walls; staring forms
Leaned out, leaning, hushing the room enclosed.
Footsteps shuffled on the stair.
Under the firelight, under the brush, her hair
Spread out in fiery points [64]
Glowed into words, then would be savagely still.

'My nerves are bad to-night. Yes, bad. Stay with me.
'Speak to me. Why do you never speak. Speak.
'What are you thinking of? What thinking? What?
'I never know what you are thinking. Think.'

I think we are in rats' alley [65]
Where the dead men lost their bones.

---

[61] Eliot calls attention to the echo of Milton's *Paradise Lost,* IV, 140, which begins the description of the paradisiacal garden and the innocently blissful Adam and Eve, with their as yet pure and uncarnal love for each other.

[62] See 'Ovid, *Metamorphoses,* VI, Philomela' [Eliot]. The story is given in n. 26.

[63] 'Cf. Part III, l. 204' [Eliot].

[64] Shelley has a similar description in his 'Ode to the West Wind' — 'Like the bright hair uplifted from the head / Of some fierce Maenad . . .' Maenads were semi-human followers of Dionysus (Greek god of fertility), and they danced themselves into a frenzy in the orgiastic rites of that god.

[65] 'Cf. Part III, l. 195' [Eliot].

'What is that noise?'
The wind under the door.[66]
What is that noise now? What is the wind doing?'
Nothing again nothing.
'Do
'You know nothing? Do you see nothing? Do you remember
'Nothing?'

I remember
Those are pearls that were his eyes.
'Are you alive, or not? Is there nothing in your head?'[67]
But

O O O O that Shakespeherian Rag —[68]
It's so elegant
So intelligent
'What shall I do now? What shall I do?'
'I shall rush out as I am, and walk the street
'With my hair down, so. What shall we do to-morrow?
'What shall we ever do?'
The hot water at ten.
And if it rains, a closed car at four.
And we shall play a game of chess,
Pressing lidless eyes and waiting for a knock upon the door.[69]

When Lil's husband got demobbed,[70] I said —
I didn't mince my words, I said to her myself,
HURRY UP PLEASE ITS TIME[71]
Now Albert's coming back, make yourself a bit smart.
He'll want to know what you done with that money he gave you
To get yourself some teeth. He did, I was there.
You have them all out, Lil, and get a nice set,
He said, I swear, I can't bear to look at you.
And no more can't I, I said, and think of poor Albert,
He's been in the army four years, he wants a good time,
And if you don't give it him, there's others will, I said.
Oh is there, she said. Something o' that, I said.
Then I'll know who to thank, she said, and give me a straight look.
HURRY UP PLEASE ITS TIME
If you don't like it you can get on with it, I said.
Others can pick and choose if you can't.
But if Albert makes off, it won't be for lack of telling.
You ought to be ashamed, I said, to look so antique.
(And her only thirty-one.)
I can't help it, she said, pulling a long face,
It's them pills I took, to bring it off, she said.
(She's had five already, and nearly died of young George.)
The chemist[72] said it would be all right, but I've never been the same.
You are a proper fool, I said.
Well, if Albert won't leave you alone, there it is, I said,
What you get married for if you don't want children?
HURRY UP PLEASE ITS TIME
Well, that Sunday Albert was home, they had a hot gammon,
And they asked me in to dinner, to get the beauty of it hot —

[66] 'Cf. Webster, "Is the wind in that door still?"' [Eliot]. In Webster's play, *The Devil's Law Case,* a man is wounded in a duel, and while he lies dying from the infected wound, the brother of his heir bribes the doctors and attempts to finish him off. But the blow, by opening the wound, insures its healthful drainage. The doctors find him still breathing, and one of them asks the question quoted above, meaning, 'Does he still live?' (III, ii.)

[67] 'Cf. Part I, l. 37, 48' [Eliot].

[68] ragtime; a reference to Ariel's song, with both meaning and music vulgarized into the cheap rhymes below

[69] 'Cf. the game of chess in Middleton's *Women beware Women*' [Eliot], and n. 59.

[70] Slang for 'to be demobilized,' i.e. released from the army.

[71] This is the usual warning of closing time in English pubs.

[72] i.e. the druggist who sold the abortifacient 'pills'

Hurry up please its time
Hurry up please its time
Goonight Bill. Goonight Lou. Goonight May. Goonight.
Ta ta. Goonight. Goonight.
Good night, ladies, good night, sweet ladies, good night, good night.[73]

III. The Fire Sermon

The river's tent is broken: the last fingers of leaf
Clutch and sink into the wet bank. The wind
Crosses the brown land, unheard. The nymphs are departed.
Sweet Thames, run softly, till I end my song.[74]
The river bears no empty bottles, sandwich papers,
Silk handkerchiefs, cardboard boxes, cigarette ends
Or other testimony of summer nights. The nymphs are departed.
And their friends, the loitering heirs of city directors;
Departed, have left no addresses.
By the waters of Leman [75] I sat down and wept . . .
Sweet Thames, run softly till I end my song,
Sweet Thames, run softly, for I speak not loud or long.
But at my back in a cold blast I hear [76]

[73] Echo both of the popular song, 'Good-night, Ladies,' and more bitingly, of the song the mad Ophelia sings (*Hamlet,* IV, v) among snatches of bawdry before her 'death by water'; note the reference to death and burial (of her father) in Ophelia's passage, and to the adulterous Queen Gertrude as a 'sweet lady.'

[74] See 'Spenser, *Prothalamion*' [Eliot]; through the series of vulgar 'love' affairs along the banks of the modern Thames which constitute this section of the poem runs the echo of this fine marriage song by Edmund Spenser, wīth its suggestions of the age of Elizabeth, nymphs, country swains, and other pastoral conventions, in contrast to the sordid, ugly city life of the present.

[75] Specifically, a lake in Switzerland; but suggestive also of the Elizabethan word for 'lover.' Note also the echo in the line of Psalm 137: 'By the rivers of Babylon, there we sat down, yea, we wept, when we remembered Zion. . . . How shall we sing the Lord's song in a strange land?'

[76] Cf. n. 2. In Marvell's 'To His Coy Mistress,' possibly the most striking image is 'But at my back I always hear / Time's wingèd chariot hurrying near: / And yonder all before us lie / Deserts of vast eternity,' an association invoked again in l. 196.

The rattle of the bones, and chuckle spread from ear to ear.
A rat crept softly through the vegetation
Dragging its slimy belly on the bank
While I was fishing in the dull canal
On a winter evening round behind the gashouse
Musing upon the king my brother's wreck [77]
And on the king my father's death before him.
White bodies naked on the low damp ground
And bones cast in a little low dry garret,
Rattled by the rat's foot only, year to year.
But at my back from time to time I hear
The sound of horns and motors, which shall bring [78]
Sweeney to Mrs. Porter in the spring.
O the moon shone bright on Mrs. Porter
And on her daughter
They wash their feet in soda water [79]
Et O ces voix d'enfants, chantant dans la coupole! [80]

[77] 'Cf. *The Tempest,* I, ii' [Eliot]; see also n. 44. Ferdinand, recounting the events since the shipwreck, says, 'Sitting on a bank, / Weeping again the king my father's wrack . . .' But by changing 'father' to 'brother,' Eliot extends the association in the same way he had at the end of Part I.

[78] 'Cf. Marvell, *To His Coy Mistress*' and 'Day, *Parliament of Bees:* "When of the sudden, listening, you shall hear, / A noise of horns and hunting, which shall bring / Actaeon to Diana in the spring, / Where all shall see her naked skin . . ."' [Eliot]. The twelve pastoral eclogues of the seventeenth-century poet, John Day, satirize human follies in the persons of bees; the scene described in this passage is to be painted on the ceiling of the home of the vain-glorious reveller. While hunting, Actaeon came upon the naked Diana and her maidens bathing, and for this sacrilege, he was turned into a stag and killed by his own dogs.

[79] Sweeney is an ape-like vulgarian whom Eliot has used in several poems (see n. 26). 'I do not know the origin of the ballad from which these lines are taken: it was reported to me from Sydney, Australia' [Eliot]. The refrain of the American version of 'Pretty Red Wing' begins, 'Oh the moon shone bright on pretty Red Wing.' The version sung by Australian troops in the First World War celebrated a brothel operated by a Mrs. Porter, though the parts washed by her and her daughter were not feet. There is yet another obscene version involving the loves of an Indian maid sung by schoolboys.

[80] See 'Verlaine, *Parsifal*' [Eliot]. In some versions of the Grail legend, Parsifal is the pure knight who cures the king. In the last line of the sonnet by the French poet, Paul Verlaine, Parsifal, during the ceremony of the foot-washing which precedes the healing of the king, hears a choir: 'And O, the voices of children singing in the choir-loft.' The ceremonial reference is to the washing of the feet of the Apostles by Christ.

Twit twit twit
Jug jug jug jug jug jug
So rudely forc'd.
Tereu [81]

Unreal City
Under the brown fog of a winter noon
Mr. Eugenides, the Smyrna merchant
Unshaven, with a pocket full of currants
C.i.f. London: documents at sight,[82]
Asked me in demotic French [83]
To luncheon at the Cannon Street Hotel
Followed by a weekend at the Metropole.[84]

At the violet hour, when the eyes and back
Turn upward from the desk, when the human engine waits
Like a taxi throbbing waiting,
I Tiresias,[85] though blind, throbbing between two lives,
Old man with wrinkled female breasts, can see
At the violet hour, the evening hour that strives
Homeward, and brings the sailor home from sea,[86]
The typist home at teatime, clears her breakfast, lights
Her stove, and lays out food in tins.
Out of the window perilously spread [87]
Her drying combinations touched by the sun's last rays,
On the divan are piled (at night her bed)
Stockings, slippers, camisoles, and stays.
I Tiresias, old man with wrinkled dugs
Perceived the scene, and foretold the rest —
I too awaited the expected guest.
He, the young man carbuncular, arrives,
A small house agent's clerk, with one bold stare,
One of the low on whom assurance sits
As a silk hat on a Bradford [88] millionaire.
The time is now propitious, as he guesses,
The meal is ended, she is bored and tired,
Endeavours to engage her in caresses
Which still are unreproved, if undesired.
Flushed and decided, he assaults at once;
Exploring hands encounter no defence;
His vanity requires no response,
And makes a welcome of indifference.
(And I Tiresias have foresuffered all
Enacted on this same divan or bed;
I who have sat by Thebes [89] below the wall
And walked among the lowest of the dead.)
Bestows one final patronising kiss,
And gropes his way, finding the stairs unlit . . .

She turns and looks a moment in the glass,

---

[81] Poetic representations of the song of the nightingale, with associations of Philomela and her ravisher, King Tereus.

[82] 'The currants were quoted at a price "carriage and insurance free to London"; and the Bill of Lading etc. were to be handed to the buyer upon payment of the sight draft' [Eliot]. Eliot's years in a London bank familiarized him with the terms of commerce.

[83] Originally, demotic script signified the vulgarized form of Egyptian writing; hence, by extension, 'popular, or illiterate.'

[84] The Cannon Street Hotel in London, a popular businessmen's hotel; the Metropole, a luxury hotel at the shore resort of Brighton, frequented by pairs wanting a quiet week end together.

[85] 'Tiresias, although a mere spectator and not indeed a "character," is yet the most important personage in the poem, uniting all the rest. Just as the one-eyed merchant, seller of currants, melts into the Phoenician Sailor, and the latter is not wholly distinct from Ferdinand Prince of Naples, so all the women are one woman, and the two sexes meet in Tiresias. What Tiresias *sees,* in fact, is the substance of the poem. The whole passage from Ovid is of great anthropological interest . . .' [Eliot]. Eliot then quotes from *Metamorphoses* III. Seven years of his life, Tiresias had spent as a woman. In a dispute among the gods as to whether man or woman received more pleasure from love, Tiresias was called upon to arbitrate, but because he sided with Zeus, Hera struck him blind. In compensation, Zeus gave him the gift of foresight. As the blind seer he appears in Sophocles' tragedies, *Antigone* and *Oedipus Tyrannus,* to explain the cause of the curse that had made Thebes a waste land, and to warn the wicked King Creon.

[86] 'This may not appear as exact as Sappho's lines, but I had in mind the "longshore" or "dory" fisherman, who returns at nightfall' [Eliot]. The 149th fragment of Sappho, famous Greek poetess, contains the apostrophe to the evening star: 'Hesperus, you bring home all things that the shining morning scattered; you bring the sheep, you bring the goat, you bring the child to the mother.' Many English poets have echoed this passage, for instance Byron or especially R. L. Stevenson who concludes his *Requiem,* 'Here he lies where he longed to be; / Home is the sailor, home from sea, and the hunter home from the hill.'

[87] An ironic parody of the famous lines from Keats' 'Ode to a Nightingale,' the nightingale whose song was: 'The same that oft-times hath / Charmed magic casements, opening on the foam / Of perilous seas, in faery lands forlorn.'

[88] An English industrial town where many rich made fortunes in war profits.

[89] The home of Tiresias, where he warns in vain against Creon's brutal policy of leaving the enemy slain without ceremonious burial.

Hardly aware of her departed lover;
Her brain allows one half-formed thought to pass:
'Well now that's done: and I'm glad it's over.'
When lovely woman stoops to folly [90] and
Paces about her room again, alone,
She smoothes her hair with automatic hand,
And puts a record on the gramophone.

'This music crept by me upon the waters' [91]
And along the Strand, up Queen Victoria Street.[92]
O City city, I can sometimes hear
Beside a public bar in Lower Thames Street,
The pleasant whining of a mandoline
And a clatter and a chatter from within
Where fishmen lounge at noon: where the walls
Of Magnus Martyr hold
Inexplicable splendour of Ionian white and gold.[93]

The river sweats [94]
Oil and tar
The barges drift
With the turning tide
Red sails
Wide
To leeward, swing on the heavy spar.
The barges wash
Drifting logs
Down Greenwich reach [95]
Past the Isle of Dogs.
Weialala leia
Wallala leialala

Elizabeth and Leicester [96]
Beating oars
The stern was formed
A gilded shell
Red and gold
The brisk swell
Rippled both shores
Southwest wind
Carried down stream
The peal of bells
White towers
Weialala leia
Wallala leialala

'Trams and dusty trees.
Highbury bore me. Richmond and Kew [97]
Undid me. By Richmond I raised my knees
Supine on the floor of a narrow canoe.'

[90] The first line, as Eliot notes, of the song in chapter 24 of Oliver Goldsmith's *Vicar of Wakefield;* the Vicar's daughter, who has been 'vilely seduced,' sings, 'When lovely woman stoops to folly / And finds too late that men betray, / What charm can soothe her melancholy, / What art can wash her guilt away? / The only art her guilt to cover, / To hide her shame from every eye, / To give repentance to her lover / And wring his bosom — is to die.'

[91] See '*The Tempest,* as above' [Eliot]; from Ferdinand's account of Ariel's song.

[92] In the commercial district of the City of London, near St. Paul's Cathedral and the Bank of England, along with King William Street and Cannon Street (above). The Strand used to be faced by the great houses of Elizabethan nobles but, like the others, it has now been completely taken over by commerce. Lower Thames Street along the river, narrow and congested, is in the fish market district.

[93] The Church of St. Magnus Martyr, rebuilt by Sir Christopher Wren in 1676, stands near London Bridge. 'The interior of St. Magnus Martyr is to my mind one of the finest among Wren's interiors. . . .' [Eliot].

[94] 'The Song of the (three) Thames-daughters begins here. From line 292 to 306 inclusive they speak in turn. [See] *Götterdämmerung,* III, i: the Rhine-daughters' [Eliot]. In the third act of Wagner's opera, *The Twilight of the Gods,* the three Rhine maidens bewail the theft of the gold which they guarded at the bottom of the river and the consequent loss of beauty of the river. The meter of their song is followed here in the poem, and the refrain is literally echoed.

[95] The Reach marks the beginning of the Thames Estuary, while the Isle of Dogs is a center of shipbuilding and piers for the great ocean-going steamers.

[96] See 'Froude, *Elizabeth,* Vol. I, ch. iv, letter of De Quadra to Philip of Spain: "In the afternoon we were in a barge, watching the games on the river. (The queen) was alone with Lord Robert and myself on the poop, when they began to talk nonsense, and went so far that Lord Robert at last said, as I was on the spot there was no reason why they should not be married if the queen pleased"' [Eliot]. Eliot is citing the letter of the Spanish ambassador quoted in J. A. Froude's *The Reign of Elizabeth.* At one time the affair of Queen Elizabeth and Lord Robert Leicester was the scandal of the court, and he was later suspected of murdering his wife so that nothing would stand in the way of marriage to the queen. In Eliot's lines, note once more the echoes of the description of Cleopatra's barge from Shakespeare's play.

[97] Eliot cites a passage in Dante's *Purgatorio,* V, 133. 'La Pia,' born in Siena, married a nobleman who later imprisoned her near the malarial Maremma marshes to kill her. She asks Dante, 'Remember me, who am La Pia; / Siena made me, Maremma unmade me: / 'Tis known to him who, first plighting troth, / Had wedded me with his gem.' Highbury, Richmond, and Kew are residential suburbs and parks near London.

'My feet are at Moorgate, and my heart
Under my feet. After the event
He wept. He promised 'a new start.'
I made no comment. What should I resent?'

'On Margate Sands.[98]
I can connect
Nothing with nothing.
The broken fingernails of dirty hands.
My people humble people who expect
Nothing.'
la la

To Carthage then I came[99]

Burning burning burning burning[100]
O Lord Thou pluckest me out[101]
O Lord Thou pluckest

burning

IV. Death by Water

Phlebas the Phoenician,[102] a fortnight dead,
Forgot the cry of gulls, and the deep sea swell
And the profit and loss.
A current under sea
Picked his bones in whispers.[103] As he rose and fell
He passed the stages of his age and youth
Entering the whirlpool.
Gentile or Jew
O you who turn the wheel and look to windward,
Consider Phlebas, who was once handsome and tall as you.

V. What the Thunder Said[104]

After the torchlight red on sweaty faces
After the frosty silence in the gardens
After the agony in stony places
The shouting and the crying
Prison and palace and reverberation
Of thunder of spring over distant mountains[105]
He who was living is now dead
We who were living are now dying
With a little patience

Here is no water but only rock
Rock and no water and the sandy road
The road winding above among the mountains
Which are mountains of rock without water
If there were water we should stop and drink
Amongst the rock one cannot stop or think
Sweat is dry and feet are in the sand
If there were only water amongst the rock
Dead mountain mouth of carious teeth that cannot spit
Here one can neither stand nor lie nor sit
There is not even silence in the mountains
But dry sterile thunder without rain
There is not even solitude in the mountains

---

[98] Moorgate, a slum area near the Bank of England; Margate, a coastal resort popular for the week end.

[99] See 'St. Augustine's *Confessions:* "to Carthage then I came, where a cauldron of unholy loves sang all about mine ears"' [Eliot]. The passage comes from the great Church Father's account of his wild and profligate youth.

[100] 'The complete text of the Buddha's Fire Sermon (which corresponds in importance to the Sermon on the Mount) from which these words are taken, will be found translated in the late Henry Clarke Warren's *Buddhism in Translation* . . .' [Eliot]. In this sermon, Buddha likens the passions, the desires, the senses of the body to consuming fire; the wise man, therefore, conceives an aversion for things known through the mind or the senses.

[101] 'From St. Augustine's *Confessions* again. The collocation of these two representatives of eastern and western asceticism, as the culmination of this part of the poem, is not an accident' [Eliot]. Having suffered the loss of his concubine, Augustine praises God for being 'continually ready to pluck me out of the mire, and to wash me thoroughly.' 'Death by fire' *could* be restorative, too, like 'death by water.'

[102] The Phoenician Sailor 'which is your card' of l. 47 — the drowned fertility god as well as a Levantine merchant.

[103] An oblique reference once more to Ariel's song about the supposedly drowned king in *The Tempest:* 'Of his bones are coral made.'

[104] 'In the first part of Part v three themes are employed: the journey to Emmaus, the approach to the Chapel Perilous (see Miss Weston's book) and the present decay of eastern Europe' [Eliot].

[105] In the preceding lines there is a general evocation of the Passion — the betrayal of Christ in the Garden, the imprisonment and trial before Pilate, the Crucifixion and the reverberation of the earthquake which marked the end.

But red sullen faces sneer and snarl
From doors of mudcracked houses
                                        If there were water
   And no rock
   If there were rock
   And also water
   And water
   A spring
   A pool among the rock
   If there were the sound of water only
   Not the cicada
   And dry grass singing
   But sound of water over a rock
   Where the hermit-thrush [106] sings in the pine trees
   Drip drop drip drop drop drop drop
   But there is no water

   Who is the third who walks always beside you? [107]
When I count, there are only you and I together
But when I look ahead up the white road
There is always another one walking beside you
Gliding wrapt in a brown mantle, hooded
I do not know whether a man or a woman
—But who is that on the other side of you?

   What is that sound high in the air [108]
Murmur of maternal lamentation
Who are those hooded hordes swarming
Over endless plains, stumbling in cracked earth
Ringed by the flat horizon only
What is the city over the mountains
Cracks and reforms and bursts in the violet air
Falling towers
Jerusalem Athens Alexandria
Vienna London
Unreal

   A woman drew her long black hair out tight [109]
And fiddled whisper music on those strings
And bats with baby faces in the violet light
Whistled, and beat their wings
And crawled head downward down a blackened wall
And upside down in air were towers
Tolling reminiscent bells, that kept the hours
And voices singing out of empty cisterns and exhausted wells.

   In this decayed hole among the mountains
In the faint moonlight, the grass is singing
Over the tumbled graves, about the chapel
There is the empty chapel, only the wind's home.
It has no windows, and the door swings,
Dry bones can harm no one.
Only a cock stood on the rooftree [110]
Co co rico co co rico
In a flash of lightning. Then a damp gust
Bringing rain

[106] In a note to this line, Eliot quotes an ornithologist's praise of its song — 'Its notes . . . in purity and sweetness of tone and exquisite modulation . . . are unequalled.' Eliot adds, 'Its "water-dripping song" is justly celebrated.'

[107] The account of the despairing journey of the two disciples to Emmaus after the Crucifixion, and the appearance of Christ to them (though they do not recognize him until afterwards) appears in Luke 24. The preceding lines of the poem have imaged, among other things, the barren despair of the disciples, while of the succeeding lines Eliot adds in a note, 'The following lines were stimulated by the account of one of the Antarctic expeditions (I forget which, but I think one of Shackleton's): it was related that the party of explorers, at the extremity of their strength, had the constant delusion that there was *one more member* than could actually be counted.'

[108] In a note to the next eleven lines, Eliot quotes in German a passage from *Blick ins Chaos* (*A Glance at Chaos*, 1920) by the Nobel Prize winner Hermann Hesse; the passage translated reads: 'Already half of Europe, already at least half of Eastern Europe, is on the way to Chaos, traveling drunken in an illusion of holy ecstasy along the edge of the abyss, and celebrates this by singing, singing drunken hymns, as Dmitri Karamasoff [a character in Dostoevsky's *The Brothers Karamazov*] sang. Over these songs the insulted burgher laughs, the saint and the seer hear them with tears.'

[109] These climactic, hallucinatory images of the next several lines seem suggested by the final approach to the Chapel Perilous, the initiatory rites to the mysteries discussed in Miss Weston's book, the chapel (ll. 386–7) where the last and most dangerous temptations beset the venturing knight — ultimately the greatest temptation in the Christian calendar of sins, despair.

[110] The crowing of a cock was popularly supposed to be the signal for spirits to depart. There are also suggestions of the cock who crowed after Peter's denial of Christ.

Ganga[111] was sunken, and the limp leaves
Waited for rain, while the black clouds
Gathered far distant, over Himavant.
The jungle crouched, humped in silence.
Then spoke the thunder
Da
Datta: what have we given?[112]
My friend, blood shaking my heart
The awful daring of a moment's surrender
Which an age of prudence can never retract
By this, and this only, we have existed
Which is not to be found in our obituaries
Or in memories draped by the beneficent spider[113]
Or under seals broken by the lean solicitor
In our empty rooms
Da
Dayadhvam: I have heard the key[114]
Turn in the door once and turn once only
We think of the key, each in his prison
Thinking of the key, each confirms a prison
Only at nightfall, aethereal rumours
Revive for a moment a broken Coriolanus[115]
Da
Damyata: The boat responded
Gaily, to the hand expert with sail and oar
The sea was calm, your heart would have responded
Gaily, when invited, beating obedient
To controlling hands

I sat upon the shore
Fishing, with the arid plain behind me[116]
Shall I at least set my lands in order?
London Bridge is falling down falling down falling down[117]
Poi s'ascose nel foco che gli affina[118]
Quando fiam uti chelidon[119] — O swallow swallow
Le Prince d'Aquitaine à la tour abolie[120]
These fragments I have shored against my ruins

111 The river Ganges of India; Himavant (below) is a mountain peak in the Himalayas on India's northern border, where the Ganges has its source (and a region, incidentally, which is the stronghold of Buddhism). Miss Weston relates many of the elements of the fertility myths she discusses to Indian rituals propitiating the rain god.

112 ' "Datta, dayadhvam, damyata" (Give, sympathise, control). The fable of the meaning of the Thunder is found in the *Brihadaranyaka-Upanishad,* 5, I. . . .' [Eliot]. In the passage referred to, three sons, students with their father of Brahmin, three times ask their father to speak; each time he utters the single syllable 'Da' which they successively, and rightly, interpret as above. However, Eliot for his purposes changes the meaning of 'datta' (to give alms) into the surrender of self, and extends the meaning of 'damyata' (self-control) to others.

113 'Cf. Webster, *The White Devil,* v, vi: ". . . they'll remarry / Ere the worm pierce your winding-sheet, ere the spider / Make a thin curtain for your epitaphs" ' [Eliot]. See also n. 57.

114 Eliot refers to Dante's *Inferno,* XXXIII, 46, which is sometimes translated, 'And below I heard the outlet of the horrible tower locked up,' though modern commentators insist on 'nailed up.' Dante meets Ugolino in the lowest circle of hell, gnawing on the head of his enemy. After a series of betrayals and counter-betrayals, Ugolino and four of his sons and grandsons had been imprisoned and left to starve. In the same note, Eliot connects this with a philosophical statement of human isolation: 'Also F. H. Bradley, *Appearance and Reality,* p. 346. "My external sensations are no less private to myself than are my thoughts or my feelings. In either case my experience falls within my own circle, a circle closed on the outside; and, with all its elements alike, every sphere is opaque to the others which surround it. . . . In brief, regarded as an existence which appears in a soul, the whole world for each is peculiar and private to that soul." '

115 In Shakespeare's play of this name, Coriolanus is an arrogant Roman general, tragically caught in a conflict between his loyalty, and his wounded pride and vanity. In the end he betrays both Rome and Rome's enemies, and thus is linked in his isolation and betrayal to Ugolino.

116 'Weston: *From Ritual to Romance;* chapter on the Fisher King' [Eliot].

117 From the nursery rhyme: 'London Bridge is falling down, falling down, falling down, / London Bridge is falling down, my fair lady. / Take the key and lock her up, lock her up, lock her up, / Take the key and lock her up, my fair lady.'

118 '*Purgatorio,* XXVI, 148' [Eliot]. In Dante's journey through Purgatory, he meets the Provençal poet, Arnaut Daniel, who is gladly suffering his present torments that he may enter Heaven; after speaking, 'Then he dived back into that fire which refines them.'

119 'When shall I be like the swallow'; Eliot cites the source, the late Latin poem *Pervigilium Veneris (Eve of St. Venus),* and adds, 'Cf. Philomela in Parts II and III.' The poem is an account of the rejoicing of nature at the advent of spring, though the poet is melancholy; even the nightingale (Philomela) sings despite her terrible memories: 'She is singing: I am silent. When will spring awake in me? / When shall I be like the swallow and from dumb distress be free?' But the happy creatures of nature chant the refrain, 'Are ye loveless or love-lorn? Yours be love tomorrow morn!'

120 'Gerard de Nerval, Sonnet *El Desdichado*' [Eliot]. The poem ('The Disinherited'), a series of images of melancholy, begins: 'I am the gloomy one, — the widower, — the unconsoled, / The Prince of Acquitaine at the ruined tower.'

Why then Ile fit you. Hieronymo's mad againe.[121]
Datta. Dayadhvam. Damyata.
Shantih shantih shantih [122]

Journey of the Magi

'A COLD coming we had of it,
Just the worst time of the year
For a journey, and such a long journey:
The ways deep and the weather sharp,
The very dead of winter.' [123]
And the camels galled, sore-footed, refractory,
Lying down in the melting snow.
There were times we regretted
The summer palaces on slopes, the terraces,
And the silken girls bringing sherbet.
Then the camel men cursing and grumbling
And running away, and wanting their liquor and women,
And the night-fires going out, and the lack of shelters,
And the cities hostile and the towns unfriendly
And the villages dirty and charging high prices:
A hard time we had of it.
At the end we preferred to travel all night,
Sleeping in snatches,
With the voices singing in our ears, saying
That this was all folly.

Then at dawn we came down to a temperate valley,
Wet, below the snow line, smelling of vegetation;
With a running stream and a water-mill beating the darkness,
And three trees on the low sky,[124]
And an old white horse [125] galloped away in the meadow.
Then we came to a tavern with vine-leaves over the lintel,
Six hands at an open door dicing for pieces of silver,[126]
And feet kicking the empty wine-skins.
But there was no information, and so we continued
And arrived at evening, not a moment too soon
Finding the place; it was (you may say) satisfactory.

All this was a long time ago, I remember,
And I would do it again, but set down
This set down
This: were we led all that way for
Birth or Death? There was a Birth, certainly,
We had evidence and no doubt. I had seen birth and death,
But had thought they were different; this Birth was
Hard and bitter agony for us, like Death, our death.
We returned to our places, these Kingdoms,
But no longer at ease here, in the old dispensation,[127]
With an alien people clutching their gods.
I should be glad of another death.

[*Collected Poems 1909–1935*]

[121] 'Kyd's *Spanish Tragedy*' [Eliot] . In this Elizabethan early melodrama of revenge, by Thomas Kyd, Hieronymo is a Spanish counsellor driven mad at times by the treacherous murder of his son. He devises a play to trap the murderers, and when retainers of the king come to request presentation, he replies, 'Why then, I'll fit you' — i.e. 'I'll accommodate you,' with, of course, ironic double meaning. At the end, successful in his revenge, to avoid confessing he bites off his own tongue, which provides an association with the story of Philomela. The popular subtitle of the play was 'Hieronimo's mad againe.'

[122] 'Repeated as here, a formal ending to an Upanishad. "The Peace which passeth understanding" is our equivalent to this word' [Eliot]. The *Upanishads* (cf. n. 112) are ancient Sanskrit essays on man and the universe, part of the sacred literature of India.

[123] From a sermon of an Elizabethan churchman whom Eliot admired, Lancelot Andrewes (1555–1626), bishop and ranking member of the translators of the 'King James' Bible.

[124] Anticipatory of the three crosses of Calvary.

[125] In Revelation, 6:2, a white horse is the first of the four horses revealed in the vision of the Apocalypse, later (19:11) identified as the mount of him who 'was called Faithful and True, and in righteousness he doth judge and make war' — i.e. a form of Christ.

[126] A premonitory fusion of the images of the Roman soldiers gambling for Christ's garments, and Judas' pieces of silver

[127] i.e. life under the old codes, like the Mosaic laws, before the coming of Christ and the new law of love.

LITTLE GIDDING

['Little Gidding' is the fourth of the *Four Quartets* (brought together in one volume in 1943); the others are 'Burnt Norton,' 'East Coker,' and 'The Dry Salvages.' All four titles are names of locations associated in one way or another with Eliot's family, or with Eliot's own life. Thus, Eliot's devout Anglicanism has prompted an interest in the historical Little Gidding, a small seventeenth-century Anglican community. Founded by Nicholas Ferrar, it was a retreat for pious devotion and mystic contemplation.

Structurally, the *Four Quartets* bear comparison with the great string quartets of Beethoven. Eliot has been much interested in the analogies between music and poetry, especially with respect to rhythm and structure, the relationships of themes and counterthemes stated, developed, varied, and counterpointed. Each of the four poems displays the usual five-movement structure of a string quartet. There is the statement of theme and countertheme in 'fugue' form in the first movement, with progressive development in the second and third movements, often with 'modulations' between 'minor' and 'major keys.' The fourth, usually short, often functions as a kind of lyrical interlude, while the whole quartet is brought to a vigorous resolution in the last movement. But in addition, while each of the four poems in the group may be compared to a quartet, they are also part of a larger whole, also conceived in quartet terms. 'Little Gidding,' therefore, not only exhibits these characteristics within itself, but simultaneously serves as the resolution of the whole series.

From another point of view, it may be noted that each of the four poems is dominated by imagery of one of the four elements, air, earth, water and fire; for 'Little Gidding,' it is fire, both the consuming fire of the passions which ravages man, and the purifying fire of purgatory. Ultimately, this is also the fire of the mystically ravishing vision, for the central theme of the quartets is the anguished search of the penitent sinner for salvation. This is most completely realized in the rare moment of mystic unity with God when all worldly senses and passions are subsumed in a divine ecstasy, when the world of 'time' is transcended in a still moment of Eternity. In his development of this theme, Eliot follows the theological and psychological analysis of the mystical union made by the sixteenth-century Spanish mystic, St. John of the Cross. St. John describes the first stage as an 'Active Night' when the penitent must voluntarily purge himself of all sensory delights and affections, leading to an overwhelming consciousness of sinfulness and unworthiness, a state bordering upon despair. Follows then a respite, but after this purgation of the senses must follow the second 'Dark Night' of the soul, a final purgation of the soul itself, with neither physical nor spiritual desire, with the understanding dark, the memory empty, a passive waiting for the operation of God's grace which will bring the final, complete vision. As St. John explains metaphorically, the closer we come to the blinding radiance, the more man's sight is darkened; 'If a man wishes to be sure of the road he travels on, he must close his eyes and walk in the dark.'

Few men, to be sure, have the complete experience, but on a lower level, all life can be considered from this viewpoint. Simply stated, the idea of this experience is the source of the basic antitheses which Eliot uses in 'Little Gidding' — light and dark, fire and ice; of the basic paradoxes, losing everything to find everything, enduring the greatest sorrow to gain the greatest joy, finding the beginning in the end, dying into life.

The major theme of 'Little Gidding,' then, as of all four poems, is redemption. Subordinate but still important themes drawn from a view of history and from the experience of art are mentioned in the explanatory notes.]

I

MIDWINTER spring is its own season
Sempiternal though sodden towards sundown,
Suspended in time, between pole and tropic.
When the short day is brightest, with frost and fire,
The brief sun flames the ice, on pond and ditches,
In windless cold that is the heart's heat,
Reflecting in a watery mirror
A glare that is blindness in the early afternoon.
And glow more intense than blaze of branch, or brazier,
Stirs the dumb spirit: no wind, but pentecostal fire
In the dark time of the year. Between melting and freezing
The soul's sap quivers. There is no earth smell
Or smell of living thing. This is the spring time
But not in time's covenant. Now the hedgerow
Is blanched for an hour with transitory blossom

Of snow, a bloom more sudden
Than that of summer, neither budding nor fading,
Not in the scheme of generation.
Where is the summer, the unimaginable
Zero summer? [128]

If you came this way,[129]
Taking the route you would be likely to take
From the place you would be likely to come from,
If you came this way in may time, you would find the hedges
White again, in May, with voluptuary sweetness.
It would be the same at the end of the journey,
If you came at night like a broken king,[130]
If you came by day not knowing what you came for,
It would be the same, when you leave the rough road
And turn behind the pig-sty to the dull façade
And the tombstone. And what you thought you came for
Is only a shell, a husk of meaning
From which the purpose breaks only when it is fulfilled
If at all. Either you had no purpose
Or the purpose is beyond the end you figured
And is altered in fulfilment. There are other places
Which also are the world's end, some at the sea jaws,
Or over a dark lake, in a desert or a city —
But this is the nearest, in place and time,
Now and in England.

If you came this way,
Taking any route, starting from anywhere,
At any time or at any season,
It would always be the same: you would have to put off
Sense and notion. You are not here to verify,
Instruct yourself, or inform curiosity
Or carry report. You are here to kneel
Where prayer has been valid. And prayer is more
Than an order of words, the conscious occupation
Of the praying mind, or the sound of the voice praying.
And what the dead had no speech for, when living,
They can tell you, being dead: the communication
Of the dead is tongued with fire beyond the language of the living.
Here, the intersection of the timeless moment
Is England and nowhere. Never and always.

II

Ash on an old man's sleeve
Is all the ash the burnt roses leave.
Dust in the air suspended
Marks the place where a story ended.
Dust inbreathed was a house —
The wall, the wainscot and the mouse.
The death of hope and despair,
This is the death of air.

There are flood and drouth
Over the eyes and in the mouth,
Dead water and dead sand
Contending for the upper hand.
The parched eviscerate soil
Gapes at the vanity of toil,
Laughs without mirth.
This is the death of earth.

---

[128] i.e. the ecstatic, timeless moment of vision.

[129] Literally, the road to Little Gidding; symbolically, the road to vision and salvation.

[130] Defeated and harried by the Parliamentary forces under Fairfax and Cromwell, King Charles I at length had to escape from his headquarters at Oxford, in disguise and with only two companions, to make his way to the Scots' forces in the north. On the night of May 2, 1646, he reached Little Gidding, but because of his known fondness for the community, he was forced to remove immediately. For his refusal to betray his principles and the Anglican Church to the demands of Parliament, Charles has been called a 'martyr' by his modern sympathizers, and it is useful to remember Eliot's avowed royalism in politics and Anglo-Catholicism in religion. The allusion to Charles in this line points up the subordinate but important theme of history in the poem.

Water and fire succeed
The town, the pasture and the weed.
Water and fire deride
The sacrifice that we denied.
Water and fire shall rot
The marred foundations we forgot,
Of sanctuary and choir.
This is the death of water and fire.

In the uncertain hour before the morning
Near the ending of interminable night [131]
At the recurrent end of the unending
After the dark dove with the flickering tongue
Had passed below the horizon of his homing
While the dead leaves still rattled on like tin
Over the asphalt where no other sound was
Between three districts whence the smoke arose
I met one walking, loitering and hurried
As if blown towards me like the metal leaves
Before the urban dawn wind unresisting.
And as I fixed upon the down-turned face
That pointed scrutiny with which we challenge
The first-met stranger in the waning dusk
I caught the sudden look of some dead master
Whom I had known, forgotten, half recalled
Both one and many; in the brown baked features [132]
The eyes of a familiar compound ghost
Both intimate and unidentifiable.
So I assumed a double part, and cried
And heard another's voice cry: 'What! are *you* here?'
Although we were not. I was still the same,
Knowing myself yet being someone other —
And he a face still forming; yet the words sufficed
To compel the recognition they preceded.
And so, compliant to the common wind,
Too strange to each other for misunderstanding,
In concord at this intersection time
Of meeting nowhere, no before and after,
We trod the pavement in a dead patrol.
I said: 'The wonder that I feel is easy,
Yet east is cause of wonder. Therefore speak:
I may not comprehend, may not remember.'
And he: 'I am not eager to rehearse
My thought and theory which you have forgotten.
These things have served their purpose: let them be.
So with your own, and pray they be forgiven
By others, as I pray you to forgive
Both bad and good. Last season's fruit is eaten
And the fullfed beast shall kick the empty pail.
For last year's words belong to last year's language
And next year's words await another voice.
But, as the passage now presents no hindrance

[131] Historically, it may be recalled that this quartet was written during the years of the great fire raids on London and other English cities, and while Eliot was serving as an air-raid warden.

[132] In Canto xv of the *Inferno,* Dante and Virgil meet a troop of spirits condemned for unnatural acts, who glance at them 'as in the evening men are wont . . .' One with 'baked aspect' accosts Dante who recognizes his old master, Brunetto Latini, and exclaims, 'Are you here . . . ?' As they walk along, they speak of, among other things, writing, reputation, and teachers and scholars condemned to this circle of Hell. The handling of the dialogue here follows Dante's practice, and the form of this whole section is a close approximation of the *terza rima* in which *The Divine Comedy* is written.

To the spirit unappeased and peregrine[133]
Between two worlds become much like each other,
So I find words I never thought to speak
In streets I never thought I should revisit
When I left my body on a distant shore.
Since our concern was speech, and speech impelled us
To purify the dialect of the tribe[134]
And urge the mind to aftersight and foresight,
Let me disclose the gifts reserved for age
To set a crown upon your lifetime's effort.
First, the cold friction of expiring sense
Without enchantment, offering no promise
But bitter tastelessness of shadow fruit
As body and soul begin to fall asunder.
Second, the conscious impotence of rage
At human folly, and the laceration
Of laughter at what ceases to amuse.
And last, the rending pain of re-enactment
Of all that you have done, and been; the shame
Of motives late revealed, and the awareness
Of things ill done and done to others' harm
Which once you took for exercise of virtue.
Then fools' approval stings, and honour stains.
From wrong to wrong the exasperated spirit
Proceeds, unless restored by that refining fire[135]
Where you must move in measure, like a dancer.'
The day was breaking. In the disfigured street
He left me, with a kind of valediction,
And faded on the blowing of the horn.[136]

III

There are three conditions which often look alike
Yet differ completely, flourish in the same hedgerow:
Attachment to self and to things and to persons, detachment
From self and from things and from persons; and, growing between them, indifference
Which resembles the others as death resembles life,
Being between two lives — unflowering, between
The live and the dead nettle. This is the use of memory:
For liberation — not less of love but expanding
Of love beyond desire, and so liberation
From the future as well as the past. Thus, love of a country
Begins as attachment to our own field of action
And comes to find that action of little importance
Though never indifferent. History may be servitude,
History may be freedom. See, now they vanish,
The faces and places, with the self which, as it could, loved them,
To become renewed, transfigured, in another pattern.

Sin is Behovely, but
All shall be well, and
All manner of things shall be well.[137]
If I think, again, of this place,
And of people, not wholly commendable,

---

[133] In English, 'foreign' or 'alien,' but carrying with it its Latin root-meaning of 'wanderer, pilgrim'

[134] A comparison is sometimes suggested to Stephen Mallarmé, 'Le Tombeau d'Edgar Poe': 'Donner un sens plus pur aux mots de la tribu.'

[135] Eliot has asserted he had in mind the Arnaut Daniel episode in Dante's *Purgatorio,* XXVI; see n. 118.

[136] Cf. *Hamlet,* I, i, 157: the ghost 'faded on the crowing of the cock.' Literally, of course, Eliot recalls the sounding of the 'all clear' after an air raid.

[137] These three lines are a refrain from Juliana of Norwich (1343–1443), an anchoress who wrote *XVI Revelations of Divine Love.*

Of no immediate kin or kindness,
But some of peculiar genius,
All touched by a common genius,
United in the strife which divided them;
If I think of a king at nightfall,[138]
Of three men, and more, on the scaffold
And a few who died forgotten
In other places, here and abroad,
And of one who died blind and quiet,[139]
Why should we celebrate
These dead men more than the dying?
It is not to ring the bell backward
Nor is it an incantation
To summon the spectre of a Rose.[140]
We cannot revive old factions
We cannot restore old policies
Or follow an antique drum.
These men, and those who opposed them
And those whom they opposed
Accept the constitution of silence
And are folded in a single party.
Whatever we inherit from the fortunate
We have taken from the defeated
What they had to leave us — a symbol:
A symbol perfected in death.
And all shall be well and
All manner of thing shall be well
By the purification of the motive
In the ground of our beseeching.

IV

The dove descending breaks the air [141]
With flame of incandescent terror
Of which the tongues declare
The one discharge from sin and error.
The only hope, or else despair
  Lies in the choice of pyre or pyre —
  To be redeemed from fire by fire.

  Who then devised the torment? Love.
Love is the unfamiliar Name
Behind the hands that wove
The intolerable shirt of flame [142]
Which human power cannot remove.
  We only live, only suspire
  Consumed by either fire or fire.

V

What we call the beginning is often the end
And to make an end is to make a beginning.
The end is where we start from. And every phrase
And sentence that is right (where every word is at home,
Taking its place to support the others,
The word neither diffident nor ostentatious,
An easy commerce of the old and the new,
The common word exact without vulgarity,
The formal word precise but not pedantic,
The complete consort dancing together)
Every phrase and every sentence is an end and a beginning,
Every poem an epitaph.[143] And any action
Is a step to the block, to the fire, down the sea's throat
Or to an illegible stone: and that is where we start.
We die with the dying:
See, they depart, and we go with them.
We are born with the dead:
See, they return, and bring us with them.
The moment of the rose and the moment of the yew-tree [144]
Are of equal duration. A people without history

[138] Cf. n. 130; in the line below, the three men on the scaffold may recall the Earl of Strafford, Archbishop Laud, and King Charles, all executed by Parliamentary order.

[139] John Milton, partisan of the Roundheads against the King, who finished his *Paradise Lost* in blindness and enforced retirement after the Restoration.

[140] Mystically, the symbol for the divine radiance; cf. the use of the same symbol by Yeats, or Dante. The rose was also a Royalist symbol.

[141] The Third Person of the Trinity, the Holy Spirit, is conventionally represented symbolically as a descending dove, but there is here also the grimly ironic parallel of dropping fire bombs.

[142] Suggestive of the myth of Hercules. His death was brought about by a shirt smeared with blood, meant to win back his love, but proving to have an agonizing poison in it. Cf. Eliot's use of the paradox that it is the love of God which torments us, but to make us more worthy, as in the opening lines of this stanza.

[143] A lesser but still important theme throughout the quartets is the pain, the struggle, and the consummation in the creation of poetry.

[144] symbol of death

Is not redeemed from time, for history is a pattern
Of timeless moments. So, while the light fails
On a winter's afternoon, in a secluded chapel
History is now and England.
With the drawing of this Love and the voice of this Calling [145]

We shall not cease from exploration
And the end of all our exploring
Will be to arrive where we started
And know the place for the first time.
Through the unknown, remembered gate
When the last of earth left to discover
Is that which was the beginning;
At the source of the longest river
The voice of the hidden waterfall
And the children in the apple-tree [146]
Not known, because not looked for
But heard, half-heard, in the stillness
Between two waves of the sea.
Quick now, here, now, always—
A condition of complete simplicity
(Costing not less than everything)
And all shall be well and
All manner of thing shall be well
When the tongues of flame are in-folded
Into the crowned knot of fire
And the fire and the rose are one.

[145] A translation from the Middle English of the fourteenth-century mystical work, *The Cloud of Unknowing,* sometimes ascribed on very uncertain evidence to either Richard Rolle or Walter Hilton.

[146] A hint of the River of Life leading back to the child-like Adam and Eve in the Garden, at the 'beginning' of life, and, in the sense of the Fall, at the 'end.'

Cecil Day Lewis

1904–

Chorus

[from *NOAH AND THE WATERS*] [1]

SINCE you have come thus far,
Your visible past a steamer's wake continually fading
Among the receding hours tumbled, and yet you carry
Souvenirs of dead ports, a freight of passion and fear,
Remembrance of loves and landfalls and much deep-sea predicament
Active upon the heart:—consider by what star
Your reckoning is, and whether conscious a course you steer
Or whether you rudderless yaw, self-mutinied, all at sea.

You have come far
To the brink of this tableland where the next step treads air,
Your thoughts like antennæ feeling doubtfully towards the future,
Your will swerving all ways to evade that unstable void;
High stakes, hard falls, comfortless contacts lie before,
But to sidestep these is to die upon a waterless plateau;
You must uncase and fly, for ahead is your thoroughfare.

Consider Noah's fate,
Chosen to choose between two claims irreconcilable,
Alive on this island, old friends at his elbow, the floods at his feet.
Whether the final sleep, fingers curled about

[1] A play (1936) in prose and verse, 'something in the tradition of the mediæval morality plays . . . its drama derives largely from the weight and imminence of the issue it represents . . . This issue is the choice that must be made by Noah between clinging to his old life and trusting himself to the Flood' [Day Lewis]. Day Lewis transposes the biblical story to modern England and makes it a parable of the Marxist class war which he sees as about to engulf the modern capitalist world. This choral speech occurs half way through the play as the issues have been made clear and Noah must soon decide whether to stand by his fellows in the old order, or cast his lot with the rising 'flood.'

The hollow comfort of a day worn smooth as holy relics;
Or trusting to walk the waters, to see when they abate
A future solid for sons and for him the annealing rainbow.

It is your fate
Also to choose. On the one hand all that habit endears:
The lawn is where bishops have walked; the walled garden is private
Though your bindweed lust overruns it; the roses are sweet dying;
Soil so familiar to your roots you cannot feel it effete.
On the other hand what dearth engenders and what death
Makes flourish: the need and dignity of bearing fruit, the fight
For resurrection, the exquisite grafting on stranger stock.

Stand with us here and now
Consider the force of these waters, the mobile face of the flood
Trusting and terrible as a giant who turns from sleep. Think how
You called them symbols of purity and yet you daily defiled them:
They failed you never; for that they were always the disregarded.
Ubiquitous to your need they made the barley grow
Or bore you to new homes; they kept you hale and handsome.
Of all flesh they were the sign and substance. All things flow.

Stand with us now
Looking back on a time you have spent, a land that you know.
Ask what formed the dew and dressed the evening in awe;
What hands made buoyant your ships, what shaped the impatient prow,
Turned sea-shells and dynamos and wheels on river and railroad:
Truth's bed and earth's refreshment—one everywhere element
In the tissue of man, the tears of his anger, the sweat of his brow.

Then look with Noah's eyes
On the waters that wait his choice. Not only are they insurgent
Over the banks and shallows of their birthplace, but they rise
Also in Noah's heart: their rippling fingers erase
The ill-favoured façade of his present, the weird ancestral folly,
The maze of mirrors, the corrupting admirers, the silted lies.
Now must he lay his naked virtue upon their knees.

Then turn your eyes
Upon that unbounded prospect and your dwindling island of ease,
Measuring your virtue against its challenger, measuring well
Your leap across the gulf, as the swallow-flock that flies
In autumn gathers its strength on some far-sighted headland.
Learn the migrant's trust, the intuition of longer
Sunlight: be certain as they you have only winter to lose,
And believe that beyond this flood a kinder country lies.

Tempt me no more

Tempt me no more; for I
Have known the lightning's hour,
The poet's inward pride,
The certainty of power.

Bayonets are closing round.
I shrink; yet I must wring
A living from despair
And out of steel a song.

Though song, though breath be short,
I'll share not the disgrace

Of those that ran away
Or never left the base.

Comrades, my tongue can speak
No comfortable words,
Calls to a forlorn hope,
Gives work and not rewards.

Oh keep the sickle sharp
And follow still the plough:
Others may reap, though some
See not the winter through.

Father, who endest all,
Pity our broken sleep;
For we lie down with tears
And waken but to weep.

And if our blood alone
Will melt this iron earth,
Take it. It is well spent
Easing a saviour's birth.

[*Magnetic Mountain,* 1933]

Word over All

Now when drowning imagination clutches
At old loves drifting away,
Splintered highlights, hope capsized — a wrecked world's
Flotsam, what can I say
To cheer the abysmal gulfs, the crests that lift not
To any land in sight?
How shall the sea-waif, who lives from surge to surge, chart
Current and reef aright?

Always our time's ghost-guise of impermanence
Daunts me: whoever I meet,
Wherever I stand, a shade of parting lengthens
And laps around my feet.
But now, the heart-sunderings, the real migrations —
Millions fated to flock
Down weeping roads to mere oblivion — strike me
Dumb as a rooted rock.

I watch when searchlights set the low cloud smoking
Like acid on metal: I start
At sirens, sweat to feel a whole town wince
And thump, a terrified heart,
Under the bomb-strokes. These, to look back on, are
A few hours' unrepose:
But the roofless old, the child beneath the debris —
How can I speak for those?

Busy the preachers, the politicians weaving
Voluble charms around
This ordeal, conjuring a harvest that shall spring from
Our hearts' all-harrowed ground.
I, who chose to be caged with the devouring
Present, must hold its eye
Where blaze ten thousand farms and fields unharvested,
And hearts, steel-broken, die.

Yet words there must be, wept on the cratered present,
To gleam beyond it:
Never was cup so mortal but poets with mild
Everlastings have crowned it.
See wavelets and wind-blown shadows of leaves on a stream
How they ripple together,
As life and death intermarried — you cannot tell
One from another.

Our words like poppies love the maturing field,
But form no harvest:
May lighten the innocent's pang, or paint the dreams
Where guilt is unharnessed.

Dark over all, absolving all, is hung
Death's vaulted patience:
Words are to set man's joy and suffering there
In constellations.

We speak of what we know, but what we have spoken
Truly we know not —
Whether our good may tarnish, our grief to far
Centuries glow not.
The Cause shales off, the Humankind stands forth
A mightier presence,
Flooded by dawn's pale courage, rapt in eve's
Rich acquiescence.

[*Word over All*, 1943]

TWO SONGS

Written to Irish Airs[2]

'Love Was Once Light As Air'
(Air: *Dermott*)

Love was once light as air
Brushed over all my thoughts and themes;
Love once seemed kind as air
When the dewfall gleams.
Now he's another thing —
Naked light, oh hard to bear,
Too much discovering
With his noonday beams.

Long had I sought for you,
Long, long by subtle masks delayed:
Fair shapes I thought were you
On my green heart played.
Now love at his height informs
All that was so vague to view,
Shall not those slighter forms
In his noon hour fade?
Fade they then fast as snow
When April brings the earth to light,
One shape — alas 'tis so —
Still lingers white:
One heart-wrung phantom still,
One I would not tell to go,
Shadows my noontime still
And haunts my night.

[2] These two poems are written to be set to old Irish melodies; 'St. Patrick's Day,' for instance, was a popular eighteenth-century Irish patriotic song.

'Oh Light Was My Head'
(Air: *St. Patrick's Day*)

Oh light was my head as the seed of a thistle
And light as the mistletoe mooning an oak,
I spoke with the triton, I skimmed with the nautilus,
Dawn was immortal as love awoke.
But when a storm began to blow
My thistle was dashed, my tree laid low,
My folk of the wave went down to their deep, so I
Frown on a thistledown floating capriciously,
Scorn as mere fishes the folk of the sea,
Agree the renowned golden bough[3] is a parasite,
Love but a gallous-eyed ghost for me.

Ah, fooled by the cock at the cool of the morning
And fooled by the fawning mirage of the day,
I say that I'm truly well rid of this featherwit —
Reason has tethered it down in clay.
But when the light begins to go,
When shadows are marching heel and toe,
When day is a heap of ashes, I know that I'll

[3] In certain ancient religious mysteries, involving fertility rites, a runaway slave might attempt to break a bough from a sacred tree in the consecrated grove; if successful, this gave him the right to fight the guardian priest, and to succeed to the office if he killed the priest. Anthropologically, this has important analogies to the oak and mistletoe (a parasitic plant) venerated by the Celtic Druids referred to in line 2 above.

Ride to love's beam like a barque at her anchorage,
Glide on the languorous airs of the past,
For fast as the pride of our reason is waning,
Old follies returning grow wise at last.

[*Poems, 1943–1947,* 1948]

One and One

I REMEMBER, as if it were yesterday,
Watching that girl from the village lay
The fire in a room where sunlight poured,
And seeing, in the annexe beyond, M. play
A prelude of Bach on his harpsichord.

I can see his face now, heavy and numb
With resignation to the powers that come
At his touch meticulous, smooth as satin,
Firm as hammers: I can hear the air thrum
With notes like sun-motes in a twinkling pattern.

Her task there fetched from the girl the innate
Tingling response of glass to a note:
She fitted the moment, too, like a glove,
Who deft and submissive knelt by the grate
Bowed as if in the labour of love.

Their orbits touched not: but the pure submission
Of each gave value and definition
To a snapshot printed in that morning's sun.
From any odd corner we may start a vision
Proving that one and one make One.

[*Poems in Wartime,* 1940]

Wystan Hugh Auden[1] 1907–

Musée des Beaux Arts[2]

ABOUT suffering they were never wrong,
The Old Masters: how well they understood
Its human position; how it takes place
While someone else is eating or opening a window or just walking dully along;
How, when the aged are reverently, passionately waiting
For the miraculous birth, there always must be
Children who did not specially want it to happen, skating
On a pond at the edge of the wood:
They never forgot
That even the dreadful martyrdom must run its course
Anyhow in a corner, some untidy spot
Where the dogs go on with their doggy life and the torturer's horse
Scratches its innocent behind on a tree.

In Brueghel's *Icarus,*[3] for instance: how everything turns away
Quite leisurely from the disaster; the ploughman may
Have heard the splash, the forsaken cry,
But for him it was not an important failure; the sun shone
As it had to on the white legs disappearing into the green
Water; and the expensive delicate ship that must have seen

[1] Except for the last one, the order of the poems printed here follows *The Collected Poetry of W. H. Auden,* 1945, though this violates the chronology of their original publication.

[2] Museum of Fine Arts, a picture gallery. The poem is written as a meditation inspired by a walk through such a gallery.

[3] 'The Fall of Icarus,' a famous painting by Pieter Brueghel (1525?–1569) in the Royal Museum, Brussels; in a Greek legend of symbolic significance, Icarus was the son of Daedalus who, by flying too near the sun on the wings devised by his father, melted the wax which held the wings together and fell, drowning in the Icarian Sea. In Brueghel's picture, the drowning of Icarus is but a very inconspicuous event — a hardly noticeable pair of legs above the water — in a scene depicting the world going indifferently about its work.

Something amazing, a boy falling out of the sky,
Had somewhere to get to and sailed calmly on.

[*Another Time,* 1940]

Something Is Bound to Happen

Doom is dark and deeper than any sea-dingle.
Upon what man it fall
In spring, day-wishing flowers appearing,
Avalanche sliding, white snow from rock-face,
That he should leave his house,
No cloud-soft hand can hold him, restraint by women;
But ever that man goes
Through place-keepers, through forest trees,
A stranger to strangers over undried sea,
Houses for fishes, suffocating water,
Or lonely on fell as chat,
By pot-holed becks
A bird stone-haunting, an unquiet bird.

There head falls forward, fatigued at evening,
And dreams of home,
Waving from window, spread of welcome,
Kissing of wife under single sheet;
But waking sees
Bird-flocks nameless to him, through doorway voices
Of new men making another love.

Save him from hostile capture,
From sudden tiger's spring at corner;
Protect his house,
His anxious house where days are counted
From thunderbolt protect,
From gradual ruin spreading like a stain;
Converting number from vague to certain,
Bring joy, bring day of his returning,
Lucky with day approaching, with leaning dawn.

[*Poems* (Am. Ed., 1934)]

In Memory of W. B. Yeats[4]

(*d. Jan. 1939*)

I

He disappeared in the dead of winter:
The brooks were frozen, the airports almost deserted,
And snow disfigured the public statues;
The mercury sank in the mouth of the dying day.
O all the instruments agree
The day of his death was a dark cold day.

Far from his illness
The wolves ran on through the evergreen forests,
The peasant river was untempted by the fashionable quays;
By mourning tongues
The death of the poet was kept from his poems.

But for him it was his last afternoon as himself,
An afternoon of nurses and rumours;
The provinces of his body revolted,
The squares of his mind were empty,
Silence invaded the suburbs,
The current of his feeling failed: he became his admirers.

Now he is scattered among a hundred cities
And wholly given over to unfamiliar affections;
To find his happiness in another kind of wood
And be punished under a foreign code of conscience.
The words of a dead man
Are modified in the guts of the living.

But in the importance and noise of to-morrow
When the brokers are roaring like beasts on the floor of the Bourse,

[4] A biographical sketch of the great Irish poet appears at the end of this volume.

And the poor have the sufferings to which they are fairly accustomed,
And each in the cell of himself is almost convinced of his freedom;
A few thousand will think of this day
As one thinks of a day when one did something slightly unusual.
O all the instruments agree
The day of his death was a dark cold day.

2

You were silly like us: your gift survived it all;
The parish of rich women, physical decay,
Yourself; mad Ireland hurt you into poetry.[5]
Now Ireland has her madness and her weather still,
For poetry makes nothing happen: it survives
In the valley of its saying where executives
Would never want to tamper; it flows south
From ranches of isolation and the busy griefs,
Raw towns that we believe and die in; it survives,
A way of happening, a mouth.

3

Earth, receive an honoured guest;
William Yeats is laid to rest:
Let the Irish vessel lie
Emptied of its poetry.

Time that is intolerant
Of the brave and innocent,
And indifferent in a week
To a beautiful physique,

Worships language and forgives
Everyone by whom it lives;
Pardons cowardice, conceit,
Lays its honours at their feet.

Time that with this strange excuse
Pardoned Kipling and his views,
And will pardon Paul Claudel,[6]
Pardons him for writing well.

In the nightmare of the dark
All the dogs of Europe bark,
And the living nations wait,
Each sequestered in its hate;

Intellectual disgrace
Stares from every human face,
And the seas of pity lie
Locked and frozen in each eye.

Follow, poet, follow right
To the bottom of the night,
With your unconstraining voice
Still persuade us to rejoice;

With the farming of a verse
Make a vineyard of the curse,
Sing of human unsuccess
In a rapture of distress;

In the deserts of the heart
Let the healing fountain start,
In the prison of his days
Teach the free man how to praise.

[*Another Time,* 1940]

September 1, 1939[7]

I SIT in one of the dives
On Fifty-second Street[8]
Uncertain and afraid
As the clever hopes expire
Of a low dishonest decade:
Waves of anger and fear
Circulate over the bright
And darkened lands of the earth,
Obsessing our private lives;
The unmentionable odour of death.
Offends the September night.

[5] His involvement in the Irish nationalist movement was very important in the development of Yeats' mature poetry.

[6] A reference to the later unpopularity of Kipling's 'imperialism' and to the Catholic apologetics of Paul Claudel (1868–1955), a distinguished French writer.

[7] The day Hitler's German army invaded Poland, beginning World War II.

[8] Auden had come to New York to live in 1939.

Accurate scholarship can
Unearth the whole offence
From Luther until now
That has driven a culture mad,
Find what occurred at Linz,[9]
What huge imago[10] made
A psychopathic god:
I and the public know
What all schoolchildren learn,
Those to whom evil is done
Do evil in return.

Exiled Thucydides[11] knew
All that a speech can say
About Democracy,
And what dictators do,
The elderly rubbish they talk
To an apathetic grave;
Analysed all in his book,
The enlightenment driven away,
The habit-forming pain,
Mismanagement and grief:
We must suffer them all again.

Into this neutral air
Where blind skyscrapers use
Their full height to proclaim
The strength of Collective Man,
Each language pours its vain
Competitive excuse:
But who can live for long
In an euphoric dream;
Out of the mirror they stare,
Imperialism's face
And the international wrong.

Faces along the bar
Cling to their average day:
The lights must never go out,
The music must always play,
All the conventions conspire
To make this fort assume
The furniture of home;
Lest we should see where we are,
Lost in a haunted wood,
Children afraid of the night
Who have never been happy or good.

The windiest militant trash
Important Persons shout
Is not so crude as our wish:
What mad Nijinsky wrote
About Diaghilev[12]
Is true of the normal heart;
For the error bred in the bone
Of each woman and each man
Craves what it cannot have,
Not universal love
But to be loved alone.

From the conservative dark
Into the ethical life
The dense commuters come,
Repeating their morning vow;
'I *will* be true to the wife,
I'll concentrate more on my work,'
And helpless governors wake
To resume their compulsory game:
Who can release them now,
Who can reach the deaf,
Who can speak for the dumb?

Defenceless under the night
Our world in stupor lies;
Yet, dotted everywhere,
Ironic points of light
Flash out wherever the Just
Exchange their messages:
May I, composed like them
Of Eros[13] and of dust,
Beleaguered by the same
Negation and despair,
Show an affirming flame.

[*Another Time*, 1940]

---

[9] Austrian town where Hitler spent most of his boyhood.

[10] A term from psychology in which Auden was much interested; Auden supposes that the psychological student of history will eventually discover what 'image' or conception of his parent buried in the subconscious mind of Hitler produced his pathological character.

[11] Fifth-century B.C. Greek historian and general, exiled after the failure of his expedition against the Spartans; his objective examination of the issues involved in the Peloponnesian War was often cast in the form of the public speeches delivered in argumentation, e.g. as those by Pericles.

[12] Vaslav Nijinsky (1892–1950) was the greatest male dancer produced by the Russian ballet; his later life was spent in insane asylums. Sergei Diaghilev (1872–1929) was the great impresario of the ballet troupe; his attempt to dominate Nijinsky's life, as he did the others', was broken when Nijinsky married and left the troupe. What Nijinsky wrote in his diary is quoted in lines 65–6 below.

[13] God of love; erotic love.

Perhaps

O LOVE, the interest itself in thoughtless Heaven,
Make simpler daily the beating of man's heart; within,
There in the ring where name and image meet,

Inspire them with such a longing as will make his thought
Alive like patterns a murmuration of starlings,
Rising in joy over wolds, unwittingly weave.

Here too on our little reef display your power,
This fortress perched on the edge of the Atlantic scarp,
The mote between all Europe and the exile-crowded sea;

And make us as *Newton* was who, in his garden watching
The apple falling towards *England,* became aware
Between himself and her of an eternal tie.

For now that dream which so long had contented our will,
I mean, of uniting the dead into a splendid empire,
Under whose fertilising flood the *Lancashire*[14] moss

Sprouted up chimneys, and *Glamorgan* hid a life
Grim as a tidal rock-pool's in its glove-shaped valleys,
Is already retreating into her maternal shadow;

Leaving the furnaces gasping in the impossible air,
That flotsam at which *Dumbarton* gapes and hungers;
While upon wind-loved *Rowley* no hammer shakes

The cluster of mounds like a midget golf-course, graves
Of some who created these intelligible dangerous marvels,
Affectionate people, but crude their sense of glory.

Far-sighted as falcons, they looked down another future;
For the seed in their loins were hostile though afraid of their pride,
And, tall with a shadow now, inertly wait.

In bar, in netted chicken-farm, in lighthouse,
Standing on these impoverished constricted acres,
The ladies and gentlemen apart, too much alone,

Consider the years of the measured world begun,
The barren virtuous marriage of stone and water.
Yet, O, at this very moment of a hopeless sigh,

When, inland, they are thinking their thoughts but watching these islands
As children in *Chester* look to *Moel Fammau*[15] to decide
On picnics by the clearness or withdrawal of her treeless crown.

Some possible dream, long coiled in the ammonite's slumber
Is uncurling, prepared to lay on our talk and reflection
Its military silence, its surgeon's idea of pain;

And out of the future into actual history,

[14] A heavily industrialized county in northwest England; similarly, below, Glamorgan is an extremely important coal producing and heavy industry region in south Wales, Dumbarton an industrial town on the Clyde near Glasgow, and Rowley, a once rural village near Birmingham, now overgrown with manufacturing. Auden at one time lived in Birmingham.

[15] The highest (1820 ft.) hill in the Welsh Clwydian range, just west of the city of Chester.

As when *Merlin*,[16] tamer of horses, and his lords to whom
Stonehenge was still a thought, the *Pillars* passed

And into the undared ocean swung north their prow,
Drives through the night and star-concealing dawn
For the virgin roadsteads of our hearts an unwavering keel.

[*Look, Stranger!*, 1935]

Spring 1940

O SEASON of repetition and return,
Of light, and the primitive visions of light
Opened in little ponds disturbing
The blind water that conducts excitement,

How lucid the image in your shining well
Of a limpid day, how eloquent your streams
Of lives without language, the cell manoeuvres and the molecular bustle.

O hour of images when we sniff the herb
Of childhood and forget who we are and dream
Like whistling boys of the vast spaces
Of the Inconsistent racing towards us

With all its appealing private detail. But
Our ways are revealing; crossing the legs
Or resting the cheek in the hand, we
Hide the mouths through which the Disregarded

Will always enter. For we know we're not boys
And never will be: part of us all hates life,
And some are completely against it.
Spring leads the truculent sailors into

The park, and the plump little girls, but none
Are determined like the tiny brains who found
The great communities of summer:
Only on battlefields, where the dying

With low voices and not very much to say
Repair the antique silence the insects broke
In an architectural passion,
Can night return to our cooling fibres.

O not even war can frighten us enough,
That last attempt to eliminate the Strange
By uniting us all in a terror
Of something known, even that's a failure

Which cannot stop us taking our walks alone,
Scared by the unknown unconditional dark,
Down the avenues of our longing:
For however they dream they are scattered,

Our bones cannot help reassembling themselves
Into the philosophic city where dwells
The knowledge they cannot get out of;
And neither a Spring nor a war can ever

So condition his ears as to keep the song
That is not a sorrow from the Double Man.
O what weeps is the love that hears, an
Accident occurring in his substance.

[*New Year Letter*, 1941]

Petition

SIR, no man's enemy, forgiving all
But will its negative inversion, be prodigal:
Send to us power and light, a sovereign touch

[16] The legendary Welsh wizard connected with the Arthurian story; among the feats ascribed to him was the magical transportation of the great rocks which form the Druidic ruins at Stonehenge from Ireland to mark the graves of Britons slain in battle there. The legendary ancestors of the Celts of Britain were the Trojans, who after the Homeric battle emigrated to the west through the Pillars of Hercules (i.e. the Straits of Gibraltar).

Curing the intolerable neural itch,
The exhaustion of weaning, the liar's quinsy,
And the distortions of ingrown virginity.
Prohibit sharply the rehearsed response
And gradually correct the coward's stance;
Cover in time with beams those in retreat
That, spotted, they turn though the reverse were great;
Publish each healer that in city lives
Or country houses at the end of drives;
Harrow the house of the dead; look shining at
New styles of architecture, a change of heart.

[*Poems,* 1930]

Herman Melville [17]

(*For Lincoln Kirstein*) [18]

Towards the end he sailed into an extraordinary mildness,
And anchored in his home and reached his wife
And rode within the harbour of her hand,
And went across each morning to an office
As though his occupation were another island.

Goodness existed: that was the new knowledge
His terror had to blow itself quite out
To let him see it; but it was the gale had blown him
Past the Cape Horn of sensible success
Which cries: 'This rock is Eden. Shipwreck here.'
But deafened him with thunder and confused with lightning:
—The maniac hero hunting like a jewel
The rare ambiguous monster that had maimed his sex,
Hatred for hatred ending in a scream,
The unexplained survivor [19] breaking off the nightmare—
All that was intricate and false; the truth was simple.

Evil is unspectacular and always human,
And shares our bed and eats at our own table,
And we are introduced to Goodness every day,
Even in drawing-rooms among a crowd of faults;
He has a name like Billy [20] and is almost perfect
But wears a stammer like a decoration:
And every time they meet the same thing has to happen;
It is the Evil that is helpless like a lover
And has to pick a quarrel and succeeds,
And both are openly destroyed before our eyes.

For now he was awake and knew
No one is ever spared except in dreams;
But there was something else the nightmare had distorted—
Even the punishment was human and a form of love:
The howling storm had been his father's presence [21]
And all the time he had been carried on his father's breast.

---

[17] The famous American novelist (1819–1891); after his great creative period in the middle of the nineteenth century which produced *Moby-Dick* and its 'maniac hero' Ahab, Melville virtually ceased to write, eventually took a job in the New York customs house, and only at the very end of his life wrote the fine novelette, *Billy Budd* (published posthumously, 1924). This has often been interpreted as a 'testament of acceptance,' a recognition of the power of goodness in the world, as contrasted with Ahab's heroic defiance of a god of wrath (symbolized by the white whale) and Melville's own life-long search for belief outside conventional orthodoxy.

[18] b. 1907; patron of the theater arts, especially the ballet.

[19] Ishmael, narrator of *Moby-Dick,* who is left floating alone in the sea after the catastrophe in which the whale sinks the ship, destroying captain and crew.

[20] Billy Budd, in the story an example of almost pre-lapsarian innocence and perfection, who yet has a slight stammer to mark his imperfect humanity. Claggart, a minor officer aboard the ship and as depraved as Billy is good, falsely accuses the young sailor of inciting to mutiny; Billy, helpless to refute the accusation verbally, instinctively strikes and kills his accuser. The Captain, though convinced of Billy's essential innocence, is forced to hang him for striking a superior in time of war.

[21] Psychological explanations of Melville's life usually emphasize the traumatic effect of his father's bankruptcy, insanity, and death while Melville was still a boy.

Who now had set him gently down and left him.
He stood upon the narrow balcony and listened:
And all the stars above him sang as in his childhood
'All, all is vanity,' but it was not the same;
For now the words descended like the calm of mountains —
— Nathaniel[22] had been shy because his love was selfish —
But now he cried in exultation and surrender
'The Godhead is broken like bread. We are the pieces.'

And sat down at his desk and wrote a story.

[*Another Time*, 1940]

As I walked out one evening

As I walked out one evening,
Walking down Bristol Street,
The crowds upon the pavement
Were fields of harvest wheat.

And down by the brimming river
I heard a lover sing
Under an arch of the railway:
'Love has no ending.

I'll love you, dear, I'll love you
Till China and Africa meet,
And the river jumps over the mountain
And the salmon sing in the street.

I'll love you till the ocean
Is folded and hung up to dry,
And the seven stars go squawking
Like geese about the sky.[23]

[22] Nathaniel Hawthorne who was Melville's closest friend in the 1850's; for obscure reasons, the friendship did not survive the intensity which Melville brought to it.
[23] The Pleiades, the seven daughters of Atlas; in one version of the myth, they were chased by Orion the hunter, and he and they were turned into their respective constellations.

The years shall run like rabbits,
For in my arms I hold
The Flower of the Ages,
And the first love of the world.'

But all the clocks in the city
Began to whirr and chime:
'O let not Time deceive you,
You cannot conquer Time.

In the burrows of the Nightmare
Where Justice naked is,
Time watches from the shadow
And coughs when you would kiss.

In headaches and in worry
Vaguely life leaks away,
And Time will have his fancy
Tomorrow or today.

Into many a green valley
Drifts the appalling snow;
Time breaks the threaded dances
And the diver's brilliant bow.

O plunge your hands in water,
Plunge them in up to the wrist;
Stare, stare in the basin
And wonder what you've missed.

The glacier knocks in the cupboard,
The desert sighs in the bed,
And the crack in the tea-cup opens
A lane to the land of the dead.

Where the beggars raffle the banknotes
And the Giant is enchanting to Jack,
And the Lily-white Boy is a Roarer,
And Jill goes down on her back.

O look, look in the mirror,
O look in your distress;
Life remains a blessing
Although you cannot bless.

O stand, stand at the window
As the tears scald and start;
You shall love your crooked neighbor
With your crooked heart.'

It was late, late in the evening,
The lovers they were gone;
The clocks had ceased their chiming,
And the deep river ran on.

[*Another Time,* 1940]

Look, stranger, on this island now

Look, stranger, on this island now
The leaping light for your delight discovers,
Stand stable here
And silent be,
That through the channels of the ear
May wander like a river
The swaying sound of the sea.

Here at the small field's ending pause
When the chalk wall falls to the foam and its tall ledges
Oppose the pluck
And knock of the tide,
And the shingle scrambles after the sucking surf,
And the gull lodges
A moment on its sheer side.

Far off like floating seeds the ships
Diverge on urgent voluntary errands,
And the full view
Indeed may enter
And move in memory as now these clouds do,
That pass the harbour mirror
And all the summer through the water saunter.

[*Look, Stranger!,* 1935]

O for doors to be open and an invite with gilded edges

—'O for doors to be open and an invite with gilded edges
To dine with Lord Lobcock and Count Asthma on the platinum benches,
With the somersaults and fireworks, the roast and the smacking kisses'—
Cried the cripples to the silent statue,
The six beggared cripples.

—'And Garbo's and Cleopatra's wits to go astraying,
In a feather ocean with me to go fishing and playing,
Still jolly when the cock has burst himself with crowing'—
Cried the cripples to the silent statue,
The six beggared cripples.

—'And to stand on green turf among the craning yellow faces
Dependent on the chestnut, the sable, and Arabian horses,
And me with a magic crystal to foresee their places'—
Cried the cripples to the silent statue,
The six beggared cripples.

—'And this square to be deck and these pigeons sails to rig,
And to follow the delicious breeze like a tantony pig[24]
To the shaded feverless islands where the melons are big'—
Cried the cripples to the silent statue,
The six beggared cripples.

—'And these shops to be turned to tulips in a garden bed,
And me with my crutch to thrash each merchant dead
As he pokes from a flower his bald and wicked head'—
Cried the cripples to the silent statue,
The six beggared cripples.

[24] Short for St. Anthony, patron saint of swineherds. Conventionally he is represented as accompanied or followed by a pig; hence, 'tantony pig,' an obsequious follower.

—'And a hole in the bottom of heaven, and Peter and Paul
And each smug surprised saint like parachutes to fall,
And every one-legged beggar to have no legs at all'—
Cried the cripples to the silent statue,
The six beggared cripples.

[*Look, Stranger!*, 1935]

Advent

[from *FOR THE TIME BEING*]

III

Chorus[25]

ALONE, alone, about a dreadful wood
Of conscious evil runs a lost mankind,
Dreading to find its Father lest it find
The Goodness it has dreaded is not good:
Alone, alone, about our dreadful wood.

Where is that Law for which we broke our own,
Where now that Justice for which Flesh resigned
Her hereditary right to passion, Mind
His will to absolute power? Gone. Gone.
Where is that Law for which we broke our own?

The Pilgrim Way has led to the Abyss.
Was it to meet such grinning evidence
We left our richly odoured ignorance?
Was the triumphant answer to be this?
The Pilgrim Way has led to the Abyss.

We who must die demand a miracle.
How could the Eternal do a temporal act,
The Infinite become a finite fact?
Nothing can save us that is possible:
We who must die demand a miracle.

[25] *For the Time Being* (1944) is a Christmas 'oratorio' in which Auden ironically presents a modern celebration of the birth of Christ. This chorus is from the opening pages.

The Flight into Egypt[26]

[from *FOR THE TIME BEING*]

I

Joseph

Mirror, let us through the glass
No authority can pass.

Mary

Echo, if the strong should come,
Tell a white lie or be dumb.

Voices of the Desert

It was visitors' day at the vinegar works
In Tenderloin Town when I tore my time;
A sorrowful snapshot was my sinful wage:
Was that why you left me, elusive bones?
Come to our bracing desert
Where eternity is eventful,
For the weather-glass
Is set at Alas,
The thermometer at Resentful.

Mary

The Kingdom of the Robbers lies
Between Time and our memories;

Joseph

Fugitives from Space must cross
The waste of the Anonymous.

Voices of the Desert

How should he figure my fear of the dark?
The moment he can he'll remember me,
The silly, he locked in the cellar for fun,
And his dear little doggie shall die in his arms.
Come to our old-world desert
Where everyone goes to pieces;
You can pick up tears
For souvenirs
Or genuine diseases.

[26] These are the concluding sections of the 'oratorio' (see n. 25).

Joseph

Geysers and volcanoes give
Sudden comical relief;

Mary

And the vulture is a boon
On a dull hot afternoon.

Voices of the Desert

All Father's nightingales knew their place,
The gardens were loyal: look at them now.
The roads are so careless, the rivers so rude,
My studs have been stolen; I must speak to the sea.
Come to our well-run desert
Where anguish arrives by cable,
And the deadly sins
May be bought in tins
With instructions on the label.

Mary

Skulls recurring every mile
Direct the thirsty to the Nile;

Joseph

And the jackal's eye at night
Forces Error to keep right.

Voices of the Desert

In a land of lilies I lost my wits,
Nude as a number all night I ran
With a ghost for a guest along green canals;
By the waters of waking I wept for the weeds.
Come to our jolly desert
Where even the dolls go whoring;
Where cigarette-ends
Become intimate friends,
And it's always three in the morning.

Joseph and Mary

Safe in Egypt we shall sigh
For lost insecurity;
Only when her terrors come
Does our flesh feel quite at home.

II

Recitative

Fly, Holy Family, from our immediate rage,
That our future may be freed from our past; retrace
The footsteps of law-giving
Moses, back through the sterile waste,

Down to the rotten kingdom of Egypt, the damp
Tired delta where in her season of glory our
Forefathers sighed in bondage;
Abscond with the Child to the place

That their children dare not revisit, to the time
They do not care to remember; hide from our pride
In our humiliation;
Fly from our death with our new life.

III

Narrator

Well, so that is that. Now we must dismantle the tree,
Putting the decorations back into their cardboard boxes —
Some have got broken — and carrying them up to the attic.
The holly and the mistletoe must be taken down and burnt,
And the children got ready for school. There are enough
Left-overs to do, warmed-up, for the rest of the week —
Not that we have much appetite, having drunk such a lot,
Stayed up so late, attempted — quite unsuccessfully —
To love all of our relatives, and in general
Grossly overestimated our powers. Once again

As in previous years we have seen the actual Vision and failed
To do more than entertain it as an agreeable
Possibility, once again we have sent Him away,
Begging though to remain His disobedient servant,
The promising child who cannot keep His word for long.
The Christmas Feast is already a fading memory,
And already the mind begins to be vaguely aware
Of an unpleasant whiff of apprehension at the thought
Of Lent and Good Friday which cannot, after all, now
Be very far off. But, for the time being, here we all are,
Back in the moderate Aristotelian city
Of darning and the Eight-Fifteen, where Euclid's geometry
And Newton's mechanics would account for our experience,
And the kitchen table exists because I scrub it.
It seems to have shrunk during the holidays. The streets
Are much narrower than we remembered; we had forgotten
The office was as depressing as this. To those who have seen
The Child, however dimly, however incredulously,
The Time Being is, in a sense, the most trying time of all.
For the innocent children who whispered so excitedly
Outside the locked door where they knew the presents to be
Grew up when it opened. Now, recollecting that moment
We can repress the joy, but the guilt remains conscious;
Remembering the stable where for once in our lives
Everything became a You and nothing was an It.
And craving the sensation but ignoring the cause,
We look round for something, no matter what, to inhibit
Our self-reflection, and the obvious thing for that purpose
Would be some great suffering. So, once we have met the Son,
We are tempted ever after to pray to the Father;
'Lead us into temptation and evil for our sake.'
They will come, all right, don't worry; probably in a form
That we do not expect, and certainly with a force
More dreadful than we can imagine. In the meantime
There are bills to be paid, machines to keep in repair,
Irregular verbs to learn, the Time Being to redeem
From insignificance. The happy morning is over,
The night of agony still to come; the time is noon:
When the Spirit must practise his scales of rejoicing
Without even a hostile audience, and the Soul endure
A silence that is neither for nor against her faith
That God's Will will be done, that, in spite of her prayers,
God will cheat no one, not even the world of its triumph.

IV

Chorus

He is the Way.
Follow Him through the Land of Unlikeness;
You will see rare beasts, and have unique adventures.

He is the Truth.
Seek Him in the Kingdom of Anxiety;

You will come to a great city that has expected your return for years.

He is the Life.
Love Him in the World of the Flesh;
And at your marriage all its occasions shall dance for joy.

The Shield of Achilles[27]

She looked over his shoulder
For vines and olive trees,
Marble, well-governed cities
And ships upon wine-dark seas;
But there on the shining metal
His hands had put instead
An artificial wilderness
And a sky like lead.

A plain without a feature, bare and brown,
No blade of grass, no sign of neighborhood,
Nothing to eat and nowhere to sit down;
Yet, congregated on that blankness, stood
An unintelligible multitude,
A million eyes, a million boots, in line,
Without expression, waiting for a sign.

Out of the air a voice without a face
Proved by statistics that some cause was just
In tones as dry and level as the place;
No one was cheered and nothing was discussed,
Column by column, in a cloud of dust,
They marched away, enduring a belief
Whose logic brought them, somewhere else, to grief.

She looked over his shoulder
For ritual pieties,
White flower-garlanded heifers,
Libation and sacrifice:
But there on the shining metal
Where the altar should have been
She saw by his flickering forge-light
Quite another scene.

Barbed wire enclosed an arbitrary spot
Where bored officials lounged (one cracked a joke)
And sentries sweated for the day was hot;
A crowd of ordinary decent folk
Watched from outside and neither moved nor spoke
As three pale figures were led forth and bound
To three posts driven upright in the ground.

The mass and majesty of this world, all
That carries weight and always weighs the same,
Lay in the hands of others; they were small
And could not hope for help, and no help came;
What their foes liked to do was done; their shame
Was all the worst could wish: they lost their pride
And died as men before their bodies died.

She looked over his shoulder
For athletes at their games,
Men and women in a dance
Moving their sweet limbs,
Quick, quick, to music;
But there on the shining shield
His hands had set no dancing-floor
But a weed-choked field.

A ragged urchin, aimless and alone,
Loitered about that vacancy; a bird
Flew up to safety from his well-aimed stone:
That girls are raped, that two boys knife a third,
Were axioms to him, who'd never heard
Of any world where promises were kept
Or one could weep because another wept.

[27] In the *Iliad,* after Patroclus wearing Achilles' armor is lost, Achilles' mother, Thetis, goes to the armorer of the gods for new equipment. The description of the making of the shield is a famous passage in Homer.

The thin-lipped armorer
 Hephaestos hobbled away;
Thetis of the shining breasts
 Cried out in dismay
At what the God had wrought
 To please her son, the strong
Iron-hearted man-slaying Achilles
 Who would not live long.

[*Shield of Achilles*, 1955]

Louis MacNeice

1907–

Bagpipe Music

It's no go the merrygoround, it's no go the rickshaw,
All we want is a limousine and a ticket for the peepshow.
Their knickers are made of crêpe-de-chine, their shoes are made of python,
Their halls are lined with tiger rugs and their walls with heads of bison.

John MacDonald found a corpse, put it under the sofa,
Waited till it came to life and hit it with a poker,
Sold its eyes for souvenirs, sold its blood for whiskey,
Kept its bones for dumb-bells to use when he was fifty.

It's no go the Yogi-Man, it's no go Blavatsky,[1]
All we want is a bank balance and a bit of skirt in a taxi.

Annie MacDougall went to milk, caught her foot in the heather,
Woke to hear a dance record playing of Old Vienna.
It's no go your maidenheads, it's no go your culture,
All we want is a Dunlop[2] tyre and the devil mend the puncture.

The Laird o' Phelps spent Hogmanay[3] declaring he was sober,
Counted his feet to prove the fact and found he had one foot over.
Mrs. Carmichael had her fifth, looked at the job with repulsion,
Said to the midwife 'Take it away; I'm through with overproduction.'

It's no go the gossip column, it's no go the Ceilidh,[4]
All we want is a mother's help and a sugar-stick for the baby.

Willie Murray cut his thumb, couldn't count the damage,
Took the hide of an Ayrshire cow and used it for a bandage.
His brother caught three hundred cran[5] when the seas were lavish,
Threw the bleeders back in the sea and went upon the parish.

It's no go the Herring Board, it's no go the Bible,
All we want is a packet of fags when our hands are idle.

It's no go the picture palace, it's no go the stadium,
It's no go the country cot with a pot of pink geraniums,
It's no go the Government grants, it's no go the elections,

[1] Elena Petrovna Blavatsky (1831–1891), one of the founders and the leading light of the Theosophical Society; the Society was devoted to religious mysticism and occult or arcane learning, especially of India, Egypt, and the Jewish Cabbala. MacNeice here uses Indian Yogi and Theosophy to represent the neurotic desire to 'escape.'

[2] a large English rubber company

[3] Scottish for New Year's Eve celebration

[4] Pronounced 'keh li'; a Gaelic word for a visit, a gossiping session.

[5] A standard measure for fresh caught herrings, fixed by the governmental Fisheries Board (see two lines below) at thirty-seven and a half gallons—about 750 fish.

Sit on your arse for fifty years and hang your hat on a pension.

It's no go my honey love, it's no go my poppet;
Work your hands from day to day, the winds will blow the profit.
The glass is falling hour by hour, the glass will fall for ever,
But if you break the bloody glass you won't hold up the weather.

[*Earth Compels,* 1938]

Prayer before Birth

I AM not yet born; O hear me.
Let not the bloodsucking bat or the rat or the stoat or the club-footed ghoul come near me.

I am not yet born, console me.
I fear that the human race may with tall walls wall me.
with strong drugs dope me, with wise lies lure me,
on black racks rack me, in blood-baths roll me.

I am not yet born; provide me
With water to dandle me, grass to grow for me, trees to talk
to me, sky to sing to me, birds and a white light
in the back of my mind to guide me.

I am not yet born; forgive me
For the sins that in me the world shall commit, my words
when they speak me, my thoughts when they think me,
my treason engendered by traitors beyond me,
my life when they murder by means of my
hands, my death when they live me.

I am not yet born; rehearse me
In the parts I must play and the cues I must take when
old men lecture me, bureaucrats hector me, mountains
frown at me, lovers laugh at me, the white
waves call me to folly and the desert calls
me to doom and the beggar refuses
my gift and my children curse me.

I am not yet born; O hear me,
Let not the man who is beast or who thinks he is God come near me.

I am not yet born; O fill me
With strength against those who would freeze my
humanity, would dragoon me into a lethal automaton,
would make me a cog in a machine, a thing with
one face, a thing, and against all those
who would dissipate my entirety, would
blow me like thistledown hither and
thither or hither and thither
like water held in the
hands would spill me.

Let them not make me a stone and let them not spill me.
Otherwise kill me.

[*Springboard,* 1944]

The Sunlight on the Garden

THE sunlight on the garden
Hardens and grows cold,
We cannot cage the minute
Within its nets of gold,
When all is told
We cannot beg for pardon.

Our freedom as free lances
Advances towards its end;
The earth compels, upon it
Sonnets and birds descend;
And soon, my friend,
We shall have no time for dances.

The sky was good for flying
Defying the church bells
And every evil iron
Siren and what it tells:
The earth compels,
We are dying, Egypt, dying [6]

And not expecting pardon,
Hardened in heart anew,
But glad to have sat under
Thunder and rain with you,
And grateful too
For sunlight on the garden.

[*Earth Compels,* 1938]

Brother Fire

WHEN our brother Fire was having his dog's day
Jumping the London streets with millions of tin cans
Clanking at his tail, we heard some shadow say
'Give the dog a bone'—and so we gave him ours;
Night after night we watched him slaver and crunch away
The beams of human life, the tops of topless towers.

Which gluttony of his for us was Lenten fare
Who mother-naked, suckled with sparks, were chill
Though cotted in a grill of sizzling air
Striped like a convict—black, yellow and red;
Thus were we weaned to knowledge of the Will
That wills the natural world but wills us dead.

O delicate walker, babbler, dialectician Fire,
O enemy and image of ourselves,
Did we not on those mornings after the All Clear,
When you were looting shops in elemental joy
And singing as you swarmed up city block and spire,
Echo your thought in ours? 'Destroy! Destroy!'

[*Springboard,* 1944]

[6] A recollection of Antony's dying words to Cleopatra (Shakespeare, *Antony and Cleopatra,* IV, XV).

Stephen Spender[1]

1909–

My parents kept me from children who were rough

MY parents kept me from children who were rough
Who threw words like stones and who wore torn clothes.
Their thighs showed through rags. They ran in the street
And climbed cliffs and stripped by the country streams.

I feared more than tigers their muscles like iron
Their jerking hands and their knees tight on my arms.
I feared the salt coarse pointing of those boys
Who copied my lisp behind me on the road.

[1] Spender has over the years occasionally revised some of his poetry, especially the earlier work; the text here follows *Collected Poems,* 1955.

They were lithe, they sprang out behind hedges
Like dogs to bark at my world. They threw mud
While I looked the other way, pretending to smile.
I longed to forgive them, but they never smiled.

[*Poems*, 1933]

What I expected

WHAT I expected, was
Thunder, fighting,
Long struggles with men
And climbing.
After continual straining
I should grow strong;
Then the rocks would shake,
And I rest long.

What I had not foreseen
Was the gradual day
Weakening the will
Leaking the brightness away,
The lack of good to touch,
The fading of body and soul
— Smoke before wind,
Corrupt, unsubstantial.

The wearing of Time,
And the watching of cripples pass
With limbs shaped like questions
In their odd twist,
The pulverous grief
Melting the bones with pity,
The sick falling from earth —
These, I could not foresee.

Expecting always
Some brightness to hold in trust,
Some final innocence
Exempt from dust,
That, hanging solid,
Would dangle through all,
Like the created poem,
Or faceted crystal.

[*Poems*, 1933]

I think continually of those who were truly great

I THINK continually of those who were truly great.
Who, from the womb, remembered the soul's history
Through corridors of light where the hours are suns,
Endless and singing. Whose lovely ambition
Was that their lips, still touched with fire,
Should tell of the Spirit, clothed from head to foot in song.
And who hoarded from the Spring branches
The desires falling across their bodies like blossoms.

What is precious, is never to forget
The essential delight of the blood drawn from ageless springs
Breaking through rocks in worlds before our earth.
Never to deny its pleasure in the morning simple light
Nor its grave evening demand for love.
Never to allow gradually the traffic to smother
With noise and fog, the flowering of the Spirit.

Near the snow, near the sun, in the highest fields,
See how these names are fêted by the waving grass
And by the streamers of white cloud
And whispers of wind in the listening sky.
The names of those who in their lives fought for life,
Who wore at their hearts the fire's centre.
Born of the sun, they travelled a short while toward the sun,
And left the vivid air signed with their honour.

[*Poems*, 1933]

The Landscape near an Aerodrome

More beautiful and soft than any moth
With burring furred antennae feeling its huge path
Through dusk, the air liner with shut-off engines
Glides over suburbs and the sleeves set trailing tall
To point the wind. Gently, broadly, she falls,
Scarcely disturbing charted currents of air.

Lulled by descent, the travellers across sea
And across feminine land indulging its easy limbs
In miles of softness, now let their eyes trained by watching
Penetrate through dusk the outskirts of this town
Here where industry shows a fraying edge.
Here they may see what is being done.

Beyond the winking masthead light
And the landing ground, they observe the outposts
Of work: chimneys like lank black fingers
Or figures, frightening and mad: and squat buildings
With their strange air behind trees, like women's faces
Shattered by grief. Here where few houses
Moan with faint light behind their blinds,
They remark the unhomely sense of complaint, like a dog
Shut out, and shivering at the foreign moon.

In the last sweep of love, they pass over fields
Behind the aerodrome, where boys play all day
Hacking dead grass: whose cries, like wild birds,
Settle upon the nearest roofs
But soon are hid under the loud city.

Then, as they land, they hear the tolling bell
Reaching across the landscape of hysteria,
To where, larger than all those batteries
And charcoaled towers against that dying sky,
Religion stands, the Church blocking the sun.

[*Poems,* 1933]

An Elementary School Class Room in a Slum

Far far from gusty waves these children's faces.
Like rootless weeds, the hair torn round their pallor.
The tall girl with her weighed-down head. The paper-
seeming boy, with rat's eyes. The stunted, unlucky heir
Of twisted bones, reciting a father's gnarled disease,
His lesson from his desk. At back of the dim class
One unnoted, sweet and young. His eyes live in a dream
Of squirrels' game, in tree room, other than this.

On sour cream walls, donations. Shakespeare's head,
Cloudless at dawn, civilized dome riding all cities.
Belled, flowery, Tyrolese valley. Open-handed map
Awarding the world its world. And yet, for these
Children, these windows, not this world, are world,
Where all their future's painted with a fog,
A narrow street sealed in with a lead sky,
Far far from rivers, capes, and stars of words.

Surely, Shakespeare is wicked, the map a bad example

With ships and sun and love tempting them to steal —
For lives that slyly turn in their cramped holes
From fog to endless night? On their slag heap, these children
Wear skins peeped through by bones and spectacles of steel
With mended glass, like bottle bits on stones.
All of their time and space are foggy slum.
So blot their maps with slums as big as doom.

Unless, governor, teacher, inspector, visitor,
This map becomes their window and these windows
That shut upon their lives like catacombs,
Break O break open till they break the town
And show the children to green fields, and make their world
Run azure on gold sands, and let their tongues
Run naked into books, the white and green leaves open
History theirs whose language is the sun.

[*The Still Centre,* 1939]

To a Spanish Poet

(*to Manuel Altolaguirre*) [2]

You stared out of the window on the emptiness
Of a world exploding;
Stones and rubble thrown upwards in a fountain
Blown to one side by the wind.
Every sensation except being alone
Drained out of your mind.
There was no fixed object for the eye to fix on.
You became a child again
Who sees for the first time how the worst things happen.

[2] A Spanish Republican poet whom Spender met while he was a newspaper correspondent covering the Spanish Civil War.

Then, stupidly, the stucco pigeon
On the gable roof that was your ceiling,
Parabolized before your window
Uttering (you told me later!) a loud coo.
Alone to your listening self, you told the joke.
Everything in the room broke.
But you remained whole,
Your own image unbroken in your glass soul.

Having heard this all from you, I see you now
— White astonishment haloing irises
Which still retain in their centres
Black laughter of black eyes.
Laughter reverberant through stories
Of an aristocrat lost in the hills near Malaga
Where he had got out of his carriage
And, for a whole week, followed, on foot, a partridge.
Stories of that general, broken-hearted
Because he'd failed to breed a green-eyed bull.

But reading the news, my imagination breeds
The penny-dreadful fear that you are dead.

Well, what of this journalistic dread?

Perhaps it is we — the living — who are dead
We of a world that revolves and dissolves
While we set the steadfast corpse under the earth's lid.
The eyes push irises above the grave
Reaching to the stars, which draw down nearer,
Staring through a rectangle of night like black glass,
Beyond these daylight comedies of falling plaster.

Your heart looks through the breaking ribs —
Oiled axle through revolving spokes.
Unbroken blood of the swift wheel.
You stare through centrifugal bones
Of the revolving and dissolving world.

[*The Still Centre,* 1939]

Dylan Thomas

1914–1953

The force that through the green fuse drives the flower

The force that through the green fuse drives the flower
Drives my green age; that blasts the roots of trees
Is my destroyer.
And I am dumb to tell the crooked rose
My youth is bent by the same wintry fever.

The force that drives the water through the rocks
Drives my red blood; that dries the mouthing streams
Turns mine to wax.
And I am dumb to mouth unto my veins
How at the mountain spring the same mouth sucks.

The hand that whirls the water in the pool
Stirs the quicksand; that ropes the blowing wind
Hauls my shroud sail.
And I am dumb to tell the hanging man
How of my clay is made the hangman's lime.

The lips of time leech to the fountain head;
Love drips and gathers, but the fallen blood
Shall calm her sores.
And I am dumb to tell a weather's wind
How time has ticked a heaven round the stars.

And I am dumb to tell the lover's tomb
How at my sheet goes the same crooked worm.

[*Eighteen Poems,* 1934]

Especially when the October wind

Especially when the October wind
With frosty fingers punishes my hair,
Caught by the crabbing sun I walk on fire
And cast a shadow crab upon the land,
By the sea's side, hearing the noise of birds,
Hearing the raven cough in winter sticks,
My busy heart who shudders as she talks
Sheds the syllabic blood and drains her words.

Shut, too, in a tower of words, I mark
On the horizon walking like the trees
The wordy shapes of women, and the rows
Of the star-gestured children in the park.
Some let me make you of the vowelled beeches,
Some of the oaken voices, from the roots
Of many a thorny shire tell you notes,
Some let me make you of the water's speeches.

Behind a pot of ferns the wagging clock
Tells me the hour's word, the neural meaning
Flies on the shafted disk, declaims the morning
And tells the windy weather in the cock.
Some let me make you of the meadow's signs;
The signal grass that tells me all I know
Breaks with the wormy winter through the eye.
Some let me tell you of the raven's sins.

Especially when the October wind
(Some let me make you of autumnal spells,
The spider-tongued, and the loud hill of Wales)
With fists of turnips punishes the land,
Some let me make you of the heartless words.
The heart is drained that, spelling in the scurry
Of chemic blood, warned of the coming fury.
By the sea's side hear the dark-vowelled birds.

[*Eighteen Poems,* 1934]

Light breaks where no sun shines

Light breaks where no sun shines;
Where no sea runs, the waters of the heart
Push in their tides;
And, broken ghosts with glow-worms in their heads,
The things of light
File through the flesh where no flesh decks the bones.

A candle in the thighs
Warms youth and seed and burns the seeds of age;
Where no seed stirs,
The fruit of man unwrinkles in the stars,
Bright as a fig;
Where no wax is, the candle shows its hairs.

Dawn breaks behind the eyes;
From poles of skull and toe the windy blood
Slides like a sea;
Nor fenced, nor staked, the gushers of the sky
Spout to the rod
Divining in a smile the oil of tears.

Night in the sockets rounds,
Like some pitch moon, the limit of the globes;
Day lights the bone;
Where no cold is, the skinning gales unpin
The winter's robes;
The film of spring is hanging from the lids.

Light breaks on secret lots,
On tips of thought where thoughts smell in the rain;
When logics die,
The secret of the soil grows through the eye,
And blood jumps in the sun;
Above the waste allotments the dawn halts.

[*Eighteen Poems,* 1934]

And death shall have no dominion

And death shall have no dominion.
Dead men naked they shall be one
With the man in the wind and the west moon;
When their bones are picked clean and the clean bones gone,
They shall have stars at elbow and foot;
Though they go mad they shall be sane,
Though they sink through the sea they shall rise again;
Though lovers be lost love shall not;
And death shall have no dominion.

And death shall have no dominion.
Under the windings of the sea
They lying long shall not die windily;
Twisting on racks when sinews give way,
Strapped to a wheel, yet they shall not break;
Faith in their hands shall snap in two,
And the unicorn evils run them through;
Split all ends up they shan't crack;
And death shall have no dominion.

And death shall have no dominion.
No more may gulls cry at their ears
Or waves break loud on the seashores;
Where blew a flower may a flower no more
Lift its head to the blows of the rain;
Though they be mad and dead as nails,
Heads of the characters hammer through daisies;
Break in the sun till the sun breaks down,
And death shall have no dominion.

[*Twenty-five Poems,* 1936]

After the funeral

(*In memory of Ann Jones*)

After the funeral, mule praises, brays,
Windshake of sailshaped ears, muffle-toed tap
Tap happily of one peg in the thick

Grave's foot, blinds down the lids, the teeth in black,
The spittled eyes, the salt ponds in the sleeves,
Morning smack of the spade that wakes up sleep,
Shakes a desolate boy who slits his throat
In the dark of the coffin and sheds dry leaves,
That breaks one bone to light with a judgment clout,
After the feast of tear-stuffed time and thistles
In a room with a stuffed fox and a stale fern,
I stand, for this memorial's sake, alone
In the snivelling hours with dead, humped Ann
Whose hooded, fountain heart once fell in puddles
Round the parched worlds of Wales and drowned each sun
(Though this for her is a monstrous image blindly
Magnified out of praise; her death was a still drop;
She would not have me sinking in the holy
Flood of her heart's fame; she would lie dumb and deep
And need no druid [1] of her broken body).
But I, Ann's bard on a raised hearth, call all
The seas to service that her wood-tongued virtue
Babble like a bellbuoy over the hymning heads,
Bow down the walls of the ferned and foxy woods
That her love sing and swing through a brown chapel,
Bless her bent spirit with four, crossing birds.
Her flesh was meek as milk, but this skyward statue
With the wild breast and blessed and giant skull
Is carved from her in a room with a wet window
In a fiercely mourning house in a crooked year.
I know her scrubbed and sour humble hands
Lie with religion in their cramp, her threadbare
Whisper in a damp word, her wits drilled hollow,
Her fist of a face died clenched on a round pain;
And sculptured Ann is seventy years of stone.
These cloud-sopped, marble hands, this monumental
Argument of the hewn voice, gesture and psalm,
Storm me forever over her grave until
The stuffed lung of the fox twitch and cry Love
And the strutting fern lay seeds on the black sill.

[*Map of Love,* 1939]

[1] The Celtic Druids were both priests and poets; Thomas is saying in effect, 'Ann Jones has really no need of lamenting poetry from a bard like me.'

A Refusal to Mourn the Death, by Fire, of a Child in London

Never until the mankind making
Bird beast and flower
Fathering and all humbling darkness
Tells with silence the last light breaking
And the still hour
Is come of the sea tumbling in harness

And I must enter again the round
Zion of the water bead
And the synagogue of the ear of corn
Shall I let pray the shadow of a sound
Or sow my salt seed
In the least valley of sackcloth to mourn

The majesty and burning of the child's death.
I shall not murder

The mankind of her going with a grave truth
Nor blaspheme down the stations of the breath
With any further
Elegy of innocence and youth.

Deep with the first dead lies London's daughter,
Robed in the long friends,
The grains beyond age, the dark veins of her mother,
Secret by the unmourning water
Of the riding Thames.
After the first death, there is no other.

[*Deaths and Entrances,* 1946]

Poem in October

It was my thirtieth year to heaven
Woke to my hearing from harbour and neighbour wood
And the mussel pooled and the heron
Priested shore
The morning beckon
With water praying and call of seagull and rook
And the knock of sailing boats on the net webbed wall
Myself to set foot
That second
In the still sleeping town and set forth.

My birthday began with the water-[2]
Birds and the birds of the winged trees flying my name
Above the farms and the white horses
And I rose
In rainy autumn
And walked abroad in a shower of all my days.
High tide and the heron dived when I took the road
Over the border
And the gates
Of the town closed as the town awoke.

A springful of larks in a rolling
Cloud and the roadside bushes brimming with whistling
Blackbirds and the sun of October
Summery
On the hill's shoulder,
Here were fond climates and sweet singers suddenly
Come in the morning where I wandered and listened
To the rain wringing
Wind blow cold
In the wood faraway under me.

Pale rain over the dwindling harbour
And over the sea wet church the size of a snail
With its horns through mist and the castle
Brown as owls
But all the gardens
Of spring and summer were blooming in the tall tales
Beyond the border and under the lark full cloud.
There could I marvel
My birthday
Away but the weather turned around.

It turned away from the blithe country
And down the other air and the blue altered sky
Streamed again a wonder of summer
With apples
Pears and red currants
And I saw in the turning so clearly a child's
Forgotten mornings when he walked with his mother
Through the parables
Of sun light
And the legends of the green chapels

And the twice told fields of infancy
That his tears burned my cheeks and his heart moved in mine.

[2] In Welsh, 'Dylan' means the 'tide' or 'water'; it is also the name of the Welsh god of the waves.

These were the woods the river and sea
Where a boy
In the listening
Summertime of the dead whispered the truth of his joy
To the trees and the stones and the fish in the tide.
And the mystery
Sang alive
Still in the water and singingbirds.

And there could I marvel my birthday
Away but the weather turned around.
And the true
Joy of the long dead child sang burning
In the sun.
It was my thirtieth
Year to heaven stood there then in the summer noon
Though the town below lay leaved with October blood.
O may my heart's truth
Still be sung
On this high hill in a year's turning.

[*Deaths and Entrances,* 1946]

In my craft or sullen art

In my craft or sullen art
Exercised in the still night
When only the moon rages
And the lovers lie abed
With all their griefs in their arms,
I labour by singing light
Not for ambition or bread
Or the strut and trade of charms
On the ivory stages
But for the common wages
Of their most secret heart.

Not for the proud man apart
From the raging moon I write
On these spindrift pages
Nor for the towering dead
With their nightingales and psalms
But for the lovers, their arms
Round the griefs of the ages,
Who pay no praise or wages
Nor heed my craft or art.

[*Deaths and Entrances,* 1946]

Fern Hill

Now as I was young and easy under the apple boughs
About the lilting house and happy as the grass was green,
The night above the dingle starry,
Time let me hail and climb
Golden in the heydays of his eyes,
And honoured among wagons I was prince of the apple towns
And once below a time I lordly had the trees and leaves
Trail with daisies and barley
Down the rivers of the windfall light.

And as I was green and carefree, famous among the barns
About the happy yard and singing as the farm was home,
In the sun that is young once only,
Time let me play and be
Golden in the mercy of his means,
And green and golden I was huntsman and herdsman, the calves
Sang to my horn, the foxes on the hills barked clear and cold,
And the sabbath rang slowly
In the pebbles of the holy streams.

All the sun long it was running, it was lovely, the hay
Fields high as the house, the tunes from the chimneys, it was air
And playing, lovely and watery
And fire green as grass.
And nightly under the simple stars
As I rode to sleep the owls were bearing the farm away,
All the moon long I heard, blessed among stables, the nightjars
Flying with the ricks, and the horses
Flashing into the dark.

And then to awake, and the farm, like a wanderer white
With the dew, come back, the cock on his shoulder: it was all
Shining, it was Adam and maiden,
The sky gathered again
And the sun grew round that very day.
So it must have been after the birth of the simple light [3]
In the first, spinning place, the spellbound horses walking warm
Out of the whinnying green stable
On to the fields of praise.

And honoured among foxes and pheasants by the gay house
Under the new made clouds and happy as the heart was long,
In the sun born over and over,
I ran my heedless ways,
My wishes raced through the house high hay
And nothing I cared, at my sky blue trades, that time allows
In all his tuneful turning so few and such morning songs
Before the children green and golden
Follow him out of grace,

Nothing I cared, in the lamb white days, that time would take me
Up to the swallow thronged loft by the shadow of my hand,
In the moon that is always rising,
Nor that riding to sleep
I should hear him fly with the high fields
And wake to the farm forever fled from the childless land.
Oh as I was young and easy in the mercy of his means,
Time held me green and dying
Though I sang in my chains like the sea.

[*Deaths and Entrances,* 1946]

[3] A recollection of Genesis 1:2–3.

Chaucer Glossary

Words whose meaning can easily be guessed by the context or by pronunciation are not glossed. The notes contain words or expressions which have a particular medieval significance.

abrayde awoke
abye to pay for
achaat buying
achatours buyers
affyle his tonge polish his speech
agayns when you meet
ageyn against
al although
alday always
alderbest best of all
ale-stake the sign of an ale-house
algate in any case
amblere an ambling horse
anlas dagger
anon instantly
antiphoner anthem-book
apayd satisfied
apparence apparition, false-seeming
apyked trimmed
arace to tear away
areste to stop
artow art thou
arwes arrows
aspye spy
assoilling absolution
asterte to escape
attempree moderate
auter altar
avaunt boast
aventure chance
avys opinion
bachelere young aspirant to knighthood
batailed battlemented
bawdrick belt worn over the shoulder
beggestere beggar-woman
bekke nod
bemes trumpets
bet quickly
beye to buy
bicched bones cursed dice
bihight promised
biknewe acknowledged
bisette set to work
bismotered stained
bisyde near
bit bids
bityde to happen
(a)-blakeberied a-blackberrying
blankmanger creamed fowl, with eggs and spices
boist box
bokeler buckler
boles bulls
borwe to borrow
bote remedy
bourde jest
bracer a guard for the arm in archery
brast burst
braun brawn (meat)
breech breeches
bren bran
breste to break
bretful full to the brim
breyde to start
brook to enjoy
bugle-horn a drinking vessel made of the horn of the wild ox
bulle a papal edict sealed with a lump of metal called a bull
bulte to sift
burdoun bass melody
burel unlearned
burgeys burgess
but unless
but-if unless
caas case
caityf captive
can knew
cardiacle pain in the heart
carf carved
carl fellow
carpe to joke
cas accident
casten planned
catapuce spurge
catel property
ceint girdle
celle a subordinate house of a monastery
centaure centaury
ceruce ointment made with white lead
chapman merchant
chere behavior
chese to choose
chevisaunce monetary arrangement
chiertee fondness
chivachye military expedition
clepen to call
clergeon little school-boy
clerk student
cloisterer monk in his cloister
cloutes rags
cod bag
cofre box
coillons testicles
colde disastrous
colerik of a bilious temperament
col-fox black-fox
colours rhetorical ornaments
colpons shreds
complexioun disposition, dependent on the humors
composicioun arrangement
conne to learn
conscience tender feeling
conseil a secret
contek strife
cop tip
cope cloak
corages dispositions
cordial heart stimulant
cors body
coude knew
countour accountant
courtepy upper coat
couthe known, knew
covyne trickery
coy shy
crulle curled
cure care
curious careful
cut a straw or stick used in drawing lots or 'cuts'
dalliance amorous talk or play
daun master (Latin *dominus*)
daunce (the olde) the old game
daunger control
daungerous overbearing
dawes days
dees dice
defenden to forbid
degree rank
deliver active
delve to dig
demen to judge
departed divided
depeint painted
despeyred in despair
despitous scornful
devyse to relate
deye dairy-woman
deyntee value
deys dais
digne worthy, haughty
disport pleasantry
doome decree, judgment
dormant (table) a side-table permanently in place
drecched troubled
drede doubt
dreynt drowned
dronkelewe drunken
drough drew
duren to remain
dyke to make ditches
echoon each one
eek, eke also
eft again
endelong along
endyte to write
engyned tortured
envyned with a good cellar
erme to grieve
erst first
esed entertained
estatlich dignified

evene lengthe medium height
everichon everyone
ey egg
facultee profession
fadme fathom
falding coarse woolen cloth
faren fared
farsed stuffed
faste by close by
feendly fiendish
ferne distant
ferre further
ferthing small portion
fetis, fetys elegant
fey faith
fille fell
finde to provide for
fithele fiddle
floytinge playing the flute
for-dronke dead drunk
forlete to give up
for-pyned wasted away from torment
for-sleuthen to waste in idleness
forster forester
forward agreement
forwrapped wrapped up
fother a cart-load
fowles birds
franchyse nobleness
francklin, frankeleyn a substantial farmer
fraternitee guild
frayneth beseeches
free generous
fruytesteres female fruit-sellers
fume vapor rising from the stomach
fumetere fumitory
fumositee fumes caused by drunkenness
fustian coarse cloth
gabbe to lie
Galianes medicines (? named after the physician Galen)
galingale a spice
gamed it pleased
gargat throat
gat-tothed with widely spaced teeth — a sign of lasciviousness
gaude trifle
gauded fitted with beads, in the rosary
gaytres (*beryies*) berries of the buckthorn
gerner garner
gipoun short coat
gipser wallet
giternes guitars
glade to make glad
go to walk
gobet fragment
goliardeys buffoon
graunt mercy many thanks
grave buried
grette greeted
greyn grain; possibly a pearl
grope to test
grote a four-penny piece
ground texture
gruf on his face
grys gray fur
habergeoun coat of mail
halke nook
halse to beseech
halwes shrines of saints
han to have
hardily certainly
harlot rogue
harre hinge
hasard dice-play
haunt skill
hauteyn lofty
hawe yard (literally *hedge*)
heed head
heig high
hele well-being
heled hidden
hem them
hende noble
henne hence
hente to obtain, seize
herberwe harbor, inn
herde shepherd
herien to praise
herne corner
herteless cowardly
heryinge praising
heste command
hight commanded
hir their
holt wood
homicyde murderer
honest honorable
hoot hot
hors horses
housbondrye economy
hyne farm worker
ilke same
infect invalidated
jape trick
jet fashion
jordanes chamber-pots
kinde, kynde nature
kitte cut
knarre a chunky fellow
knowes knees
kyn kine
kythe to show
laas cord
large coarsely
latoun an alloy made of zinc and copper
laude praise
layes short, romantic narrative poems
lazar leper
leed cauldron above a furnace
leef lief
leet caused
lemes flames
lere to learn
lese loose
lesinges lies
lest delight
lette to wait; hindered
letuaries prescriptions
lever rather
lewed ignorant, rude
leyser leisure
licour sap
liefe loved one; dear
lighte cheered; illuminated
likerous lecherous, gluttonous
limitour a friar licensed to beg within certain limits
lissed soothed
list pleased
lith limb
litharge ointment made from protoxide of lead
lodemenage pilotage
londe country
losengeour flatterer
lough laughed
love-dayes days appointed for settlement of disputes by arbitration
lust delight
luxurie lechery
male wallet
mary marrow
mase an astounding thing
maugree in spite of
maunciple a buyer for the lawyers in the Inns of Court
maystou mayest thou
mede field; reward
medlee varicolored
mercenarie hireling
merciable merciful
mery pleasant
messe-dayes mass-days
mete food
mette dreamed
mewe coop
mister trade
mistriste to mistrust
miteyn glove
mo more
moot should
mormal a running sore
mortreux a stew
morwe morning
moste might
mottelee particolored costume
mountance amount
mowe may
namely especially
namo no more
narette do not impute
nas was not (*ne was*)
natheles nevertheless
neet cattle
ner nearer
nighter-tale night time
nones occasion
noot know not
nose-thirles nostrils
not-heed cropped head
nouthe (*as*) just now
nyce foolish
observe to favor
on-lyve alive
oon (*alwey after*) uniformly good
ordinaunce arrangement
orisoun prayer
orlogge clock
ounces bunches
outher either
out-rydere an inspector of the property of the monastery
oweth owneth
pace to pass
pardoner one who sold indulgences
parfourned performed
parisshens parishioners
parten to depart
parvys church porch, especially at St. Paul's, London, a meeting place for lawyers
pas walk
patente letter of privilege, royal or ecclesiastical
peire set (of beads)
pers dark blue or red
persoun parson
peyne to take pains
piled thin
pinche at to find fault with
pinched pleated
plat plainly
pleyn full
pleyne to complain
pomely dappled
poraille poor people

post pillar
poudre-marchant flavoring powder
predicacioun preaching
preve proof
pricasour a hard rider
pricking riding
propre own
prow profit
pryme nine A.M.
prys reputation
pulled plucked
purchasour conveyancer
purfled decorated
pyned tortured
quell to kill
queynte strange
quik alive
raughte reached
ravisedest didst draw
recche to interpret
redily at once
reed counsel
remes realms
repreve shame
rethor rhetorician
reve steward
reweth have pity
reysed gone on a military expedition
rote harp
rouncy nag
roundel(s) poem with an intricate pattern
ryden out to go on knightly service
saffron with to color
salue to hail
sangwin red
sangwyn jolly, robust
saugh saw
sautry psaltery
sawcefleem covered with pimples
say saw
scalled scabby
scarsly economically
scathe pity
science knowledge
scoleye to attend school
seche to seek
seigh saw
seintuarie a consecrated object
sely innocent
semen to seem
sendal a thin silk
sentence significance
sethe to boil
sewed pursued
seynd smoked
shapen to plan
shaply fit
sheeldes French crowns
shene bright
shent scolded
shente injured
sho she
shoop, shopen planned
shrewe to curse
shrewe wicked person
sikerly surely
snewed snowed
snibben to rebuke
solas pleasure
solempne important
som-del somewhat
somnour summoner, an officer who summoned culprits before an ecclesiastical court
soothyly truly
sop in wyn bread or cake dipped in wine
sote sweet
souded confirmed
souning tending toward
spreyned sprinkled
spyced conscience nice conscience
stape in age advanced in years
stepe bulging
sterlinges silver coins
sterve to die
steven voice
stewe fish-pond
stewes brothels
stinte to stop
stirte started, rushed
stoor farm stock
storven died
stot cob
streit strict
streite limited
streyneth constrains
strike hank
sursanure a wound healing only on the outside
swal swelled
sweven dream
swich such
swinken to work
swowne to swoon
swythe quickly
syketh sighs
sythes times
tabard a rough coat worn by laborers
tables backgammon
taille credit
takel weapons
talen to tell stories
talent desire
tapicer upholsterer
targe small shield
temple one of the colleges of law in London
terme (in) in set phrases
than then
thee to prosper
thennes thence
thilke that
tho then; those
thretty thirty
tide time
til to
tombesteres female tumblers
tool weapon
toon toes
to-swinke to work too much
to-tere to tear asunder
tregetoures jugglers
tretee treaty
tretys well-proportioned
triacle a remedy (treacle)
trouthe troth
tukked tucked
tweye two
twinne to depart from
tythe taxes due the church
unbrent unburnt
undern nine to twelve A.M.
unkindely against nature
unnethes scarcely
upright flat on the back
usage custom
vavasour a sub-vassal
venerye hunting
verray true
vertu power
viage voyage
vigilye the eve of a festival of the church
vileinye rudeness
virelay ballad with returning rime
vitaille victuals
voyded expelled
wafereres confectioners
wanton playful
war aware
wardrobe privy
warisshed healed
waryce to save
wastel-breed fine white bread
waytea after demanded
webbe weaver
welked withered
wende would have supposed
werre war
werte wart
whelkes pustules
widwe widow
wight man
wike week
wimpel covering for the head
wink to shut the eyes
wis surely
withholde engaged
wlatsom loathsome
wonder wondrous
wone custom
woning dwelling
wood crazy
worm snake
wortes herbs
worthy distinguished
wot know
wreye to reveal
wrighte artisan
wys (to make it) to make a fuss
yaf gave
y-chaped mounted
y-corven cut
ydel vain
yë eyes
yeddinges songs
yeldhalle guildhall
yemen yeomen
yerde stick
yerne briskly
yeve to give
Ypocras spiced wine

Biographies

Matthew Arnold (1822–1888) defined poetry as a 'criticism of life.' In his own poetry, issued chiefly between 1849 and 1869, one may trace the disillusion and doubt of the young man breaking away from the earnestness of his schoolmaster father and adjusting himself to the world by his own methods. Arnold was the son of Dr. Thomas Arnold, headmaster of Rugby. He went from that school to Balliol College, Oxford, then became a Fellow of Oriel. In 1851 he was appointed Inspector of Schools, a post whose exacting duties he fulfilled for more than thirty years with patience and wisdom because he felt that the future of England depended upon the education of the masses. His first volume of poems, *The Strayed Reveller,* appeared in 1849; *Empedocles on Etna,* 1852; *Poems,* 1853; *Merope,* 1858; *New Poems,* 1867; a collective edition in 1869. Most of his prose work was published after 1860: *On Translating Homer,* 1861; *Essays in Criticism,* First Series, 1865; Second Series, 1888; *Celtic Literature,* 1867; *Culture and Anarchy,* 1869; *Literature and Dogma,* 1873; *Discourses in America,* 1885. From 1857–1867 he was Professor of Poetry at Oxford. In his books and on the lecture platform — audiences crowded to hear him in England and America — Arnold preached the necessity for culture which he defined as 'setting ourselves to ascertain what perfection is and to make it prevail.' Without culture, he felt, England and America must be overwhelmed by the wave of vulgarity which was destroying civilization.

Wystan Hugh Auden (1907–   ), by virtue of his imperious talent and self-assurance, became the accepted leader of a brilliant group of young English writers who first achieved prominence in the early 'thirties. Born in York and educated in an English public school, he was already the center of a serious literary circle by the time he graduated from Oxford. After a short career in teaching, he settled in London until 1939 when he came to New York. In 1946 he became an American citizen. In the catastrophic decade of the Great Depression, the Spanish Civil War, and the emergence of terrifying Fascist dictatorships he and his friends (the poets Spender, Day Lewis, and MacNeice, and the novelist, Christopher Isherwood) rejected the cynicism or nihilism characteristic of so much of the writing in the 'twenties. Their sympathies lay with the radical activities in which they participated. In 1937, for instance, Auden drove an ambulance in Republican Spain. The work of these writers, Auden included, showed a strong political consciousness in the widest meaning of the word 'political,' although all of them with their deep sense of the humane values of individualism refused to write the mere propaganda of Marxist dogma. Auden afterwards became an Anglo-Catholic, though his writing continued to show a strong satiric vein. Besides his collaboration with Isherwood in the plays *The Dog Beneath the Skin* (1935) and *The Ascent of F.6* (1936), his work includes *Poems* (1930), *Spain* (1937), *Another Time* (1940), *The Double Man* (1941), *The Age of Anxiety* (1947), *Nones* (1951), and *The Shield of Achilles* (1955).

William Blake (1757–1827) was the son of a small London shopkeeper. He never went to school but was apprenticed at the age of ten to James Basire, engraver to the Society of Antiquaries. Blake as a boy was deeply impressed by his father's religion, Swedenborgianism, and though in later life he rejected some of its doctrines, he continued to believe in its allegory and mysticism and to feel himself under direct daily guidance from heaven. When he had completed his apprenticeship he tried to earn his living as an engraver, a dealer in engravings, and a teacher of drawing. In 1782 he married Catherine Boucher, the illiterate daughter of a market gardener. She believed unshakeably in his genius and fostered it wisely. Unable to get his work published in the usual manner Blake was inspired, by the spirit, he said, of his dead brother, to invent a new manner of printing. The words and pictures of each page were engraved in relief on copper and the printed sheets partly colored by hand. The *Songs of Innocence* were produced in this way in 1789. *The Book of Thel* appeared in the same year, and *Songs of Experience* in 1794. Blake was assisted by various friends, chief among them John Flaxman, and a tiresome wealthy patron, William Hayley, until in 1804 he decided to work no more for the world but only in the service of the Eternal. Some of his most magnificent work as an artist and engraver dates from this time, but the poems of this period most of his contemporaries found unintelligible. He died almost unknown and was buried in a pauper's grave.

Robert Bridges (1844–1930) went from Eton and Oxford into the practice of medicine where he attained distinguished success. He was a Fellow of the Royal College of Physicians and a member of the staff in two London hospitals. In 1882 he deliberately abandoned medicine for poetry. Much of his earlier work was issued from the private press of his friend Mr. Henry Daniel, Provost of Worcester College, including his sonnet-sequence *The Growth of Love* and *Shorter Poems* in five books. In addition to his verse writing Bridges utilized his extensive learning and his keen critical sense in the organization of the Society for Pure English and in the discovery and fostering of poetic talent in others, notably Gerard Manley Hopkins. In 1912 Oxford gave him his first public recognition with an honorary doctorate in letters and the publication of his poetry in the Oxford Poets. In 1913 Bridges was appointed Poet Laureate. In his eighty-fifth year he published his great philosophic poem *The Testament of Beauty.*

Emily Brontë (1818–1848) was the daughter of Patrick Brontë, rector of Haworth on the lonely Yorkshire moors. The father composed poetry as well as sermons, and the whole family — Branwell, the talented dissipated brother, Emily, and Charlotte and Anne, her elder and younger sisters — were interested in writing from their early youth. After some not altogether happy English schooling Charlotte and Emily went to Brussels for a year or two to equip themselves for the teaching of French by which they hoped to earn their living. In 1846 Charlotte accidentally discovered some of the verses which Emily had for years been writing in secret and was struck by their power. After days of argument against Emily's proud reserve she prevailed upon her to attempt publication. The three sisters joined their work — though the elder and younger were in no way Emily's poetic equals — and in 1846 published *Poems* by Currer, Ellis, and Acton Bell. The literary ambitions of their childhood were rekindled and all three sisters began to work on novels. Emily's *Wuthering Heights* was published in 1847. In 1848 she died of consumption against which she had struggled proudly to the end, refusing sympathy or care, reluctant to abandon so soon the life which, despite its narrow material limits, was to her strong mystic soul and powerful imagination rich in interest and beauty.

Elizabeth Barrett Browning (1806–1861) was already well known for her poetry when she married Robert Browning in 1846. She had published an *Essay on Mind, with Other Poems* (1826), *Prometheus Bound and Miscellaneous Poems* (1833), *The Seraphim and Other Poems* (1838), *Poems* (1844) including 'The Cry of the Children.' The poetical record of Browning's impetuous courtship she kept in *Sonnets from the Portuguese,* so named by him to disguise the intimacy of their autobiographical relation. These were first published in the second edition of her collected *Poems* (2 vols., 1850). From her Florentine home Mrs. Browning watched, hopefully, the signs of the dawn of Italian independence. This enthusiasm is manifested in her *Casa Guidi Windows* (1851). The extremely popular *Aurora Leigh,* a romance in verse, appeared in 1857. *Poems before Congress* is dated 1860 and *Last Poems* was issued posthumously in 1862. After her death in Florence, where they had spent most of their fifteen years of married life, Browning could not bring himself to live longer in that city and returned to England.

Robert Browning (1812–1889) was privately educated far beyond the attainments of the average public-school boy. Though his first poem, *Pauline* (1833), was issued anonymously, he was soon known to the literary circle in London as the coming poet. The indifference of the public to his *Paracelsus* (1835) and *Sordello* (1840), as well as the comparative failure of *Strafford,* a tragedy brought out at Covent Garden by his friend Macready, the actor, prevented any general recognition of his talents until the 1850's. In 1846, after a romantic courtship, he married Elizabeth Barrett, a poet whose name was far better known than his. For the sake of her health they lived in Italy, for the most part in Florence. After her death in 1861 Browning returned to London where he now took his place, with Tennyson, as a leading poet of the day. In 1850 he had published *Christmas Eve and Easter Day;* in 1855, *Men and Women;* and in 1864, *Dramatis Personæ.* The book which brought him most acclaim, particularly from the men at the universities, was *The Ring and the Book* (1868–1869). His remaining works, from *Balaustion's Adventures* (1871) to *Asolando* (1889), lack the clarity and emotional depth of the poetry composed during the life-time and under the influence of his wife. During his last years a veritable Browning cult, devoted to explaining the difficulties of his verse, grew up in England and America. *Asolando* was published on the day of his death, which took place in the home of his son in Venice. He was buried in Westminster Abbey on the last day of the year.

Robert Burns (1759–1796), the eldest of seven children, was the son of an Ayrshire peasant. He set to work early as a farm laborer and from 1784–1788 farmed eighteen acres in partnership with his brother Gilbert. It was at this time that he wrote 'The Jolly Beggars,' 'The Cotter's Saturday Night,' many of his lyrics, and the satires on 'Death and Dr. Hornbook' and 'Holy Willie's Prayer.' In 1786 Burns decided to emigrate to Jamaica. To obtain the passage-money he published the Kilmarnock edition of his early poems. It made him famous and took him for a time to Edinburgh where both drawing-rooms and taverns were delighted with the charm of his manner and the wit and ease of his talk. The second edition of his poems (1787) brought him £500 and enabled him to settle on a small farm at Ellisland and to marry Jean Armour, one of his many loves. He also received an exciseman's place which he nearly lost at one time by expressing his sympathy with the French Revolution. All this time Burns was constantly writing songs. He contributed scores of them to the successive volumes of Johnson's *Scots Musical Museum* and to Thomson's *Scottish Airs.* In 1791 his farm failed and Burns moved to Dumfries. The town offered him too many opportunities of indulging his fondness for drink and good company, and he went rapidly down the path of dissipation.

George Noel Gordon, Lord Byron (1788–1824), was born in London and came into the title when he was ten years old. He was educated at Harrow and Trinity College, Cambridge, where, in 1807, he printed his *Hours of Idleness.* To the severe criticism they received in *The Edinburgh Review* he replied in 1809 with *English Bards and Scotch Reviewers.* From 1809–1811 he travelled abroad visiting Portugal, Spain, Greece, and the Levant. In 1812 he published the first two cantos of *Childe Harold* and 'awoke to find himself famous.' He was courted by men of letters and by ladies of fashion, chief among them the brilliant Lady Caroline Lamb who sometimes sought him disguised as a page. In 1815 Byron married Anne Isabella Milbanke, an heiress, who separated from him in 1816 after she had learned of his incestuous relations with his half-sister Augusta. Embittered by the strictures of what he regarded as a hypocritical society, Byron left England never to return. In company part of the time with the Shelleys he travelled to Switzerland and Venice which, with Ravenna, Pisa, and Genoa, became his headquarters. Additional cantos of *Childe Harold* appeared in 1816 and 1818; between 1819 and 1821, the first five cantos of *Don Juan.* In 1819 began Byron's connection with Teresa, Countess Guiccioli, who lived with him for a time in Venice and whom he followed to Ravenna when she procured a separation from her husband. While there and at Pisa he wrote his dramas and the later cantos of *Don Juan.* In 1822 Byron and Leigh Hunt joined in the production of *The Liberal* magazine which published many of Byron's poems. In 1823 Byron, whose passion for liberty never faded, set out to join the Greek insurgents and died of fever at Missolonghi.

Thomas Campion (1567–1620), poet and musician, tried his hand at a variety of other professions. He studied at Peterhouse, Cambridge, without taking a degree, and at Gray's Inn without being called to the bar. His degree in medicine he took probably at a Continental university. Five of his poems appeared without signature in the 1591 edition of Sidney's *Astrophel and Stella,* and ten years later he issued, with Philip Rosseter, *A Book of Airs* for which he wrote half the musical settings as well as all the lyrics. In 1602 he published *Observations in the Art of English Poesy* directed 'against the vulgar and unartificial custom of riming.' Although he rhymed most excellently himself Campion wished to restore English poetry to the dignity of the unrhymed, quantitative classical verse. He wrote masques, and the words and music for four more *Books of Airs.*

Thomas Carew (1595?–1639?) took his B.A. at Merton College, Oxford, and then went through the motions of studying law at the Middle Temple. He served for three years under Sir Dudley Carleton, English ambassador to Venice and The Hague, but was dismissed for slandering Sir Dudley and his wife. He accompanied Lord Herbert of Cherbury when he went as ambassador to France in 1619. In 1628 Charles I made him a Gentleman of the Privy Chamber and then Sewer, an office which supported him for the rest of his life. Carew was one of the 'sons of Ben (Jonson)' and a great admirer of Donne. The collection of his verse published as *Poems* in 1640 was enlarged in the second and third editions.

Geoffrey Chaucer (1340?–1400) was the son of John Chaucer, a vintner of London. In 1357 he was employed in the service of Lionel, afterwards Duke of Clarence. He entered military service in 1359 and served in France, where he was taken prisoner but shortly ransomed. He married Philippa, probably daughter of Sir Payne Roet and sister of John of Gaunt's third wife. Chaucer evidently enjoyed John of Gaunt's patronage. Philippa died probably in 1387. Chaucer held various positions at court and in the king's service. In 1372–1373 he was sent on a mission to Genoa and Florence where he may have met Boccaccio and Petrarch. In 1374 he was appointed controller of customs in the port of London. He went on secret service to Flanders in 1376 and 1377 and was probably attached to embassies to France and Lombardy in 1378. In 1389 he was made clerk of the king's works. He received pensions from Edward III, John of Gaunt, Richard II, and Henry IV. He was buried in Westminster Abbey. Chaucer's writings fall into three periods: the period of French influence (before 1372) to which belong *The Book of the Duchess* and his translation of part of *The Romance of the Rose;* the period of Italian influence (1372–1386) when he abandoned the octasyllabic couplet for the seven line stanza and wrote *The House of Fame, The Parliament of Foules, Troilus and Criseyde,* and *The Legend of Good Women;* and the period from 1387–1400 in which he used the heroic couplet and wrote *The Canterbury Tales.*

Arthur Hugh Clough (1819–1861) was the *Thyrsis* of Matthew Arnold's poem. Their friendship began at Rugby and ripened at Oxford where Clough was a member of Balliol and then a Fellow and Tutor of Oriel. In 1848 scrupulous honor caused him to resign his post because his faith in the orthodox religious beliefs which were conventionally demanded of an Oxford fellow was growing steadily fainter. The world looked for a manifesto of his theological position and he published *The Bothie of Tober-na-Vuolich,* concealing its serious purpose under its hexameters and the gay exterior of a 'long vacation pastoral.' Clough went to Italy, was in Rome during its siege by the French in 1849, and there wrote *Amours de Voyage.* In 1850 he began in Venice his *Dipsychus,* not published until after his death. Clough in 1849 became head of University Hall, in London, a residence for students of University College. In 1852 he resigned with the intention of settling in Cambridge, Massachusetts, but was recalled to England to an appointment in the Education Office, which enabled him to marry Miss Blanche Smith. Ill health sent him abroad in 1861 and he died in Florence.

Samuel Taylor Coleridge (1772–1834), son of the vicar of Ottery St. Mary, Devon, was educated at Christ's Hospital, where he began his lifelong friendship with Charles Lamb, and at Jesus College, Cambridge, which he left without taking a degree. In 1794 he met Robert Southey and the pair devoted themselves to 'Pantisocracy,' a form of communism which they intended to realize on the banks of the Susquehanna. Coleridge in 1795 married, without much eagerness, Southey's sister-in-law Sara Fricker. He could not bring himself to do the hack work which might have brought him a steady income and his family were almost wholly supported by his patrons and friends, chief among them Southey. In 1796 Coleridge started a newspaper, *The Watchman,* which lasted for only ten numbers. He lectured on contemporary political problems, preached in Unitarian pulpits, and was about to enter the ministry when he was granted an annuity by Josiah and Thomas Wedgwood. Between 1797 and 1801, when he was living in close intimacy with Wordsworth, Coleridge wrote most of his greatest poetry, 'Kubla Khan,' 'Christabel,' and 'The Ancient Mariner,' one of the *Lyrical Ballads* which the poets published together in 1798. The next year Coleridge went with Wordsworth to Germany and on his return settled near him in Cumberland. He fell deeply in love with the sister of Wordsworth's wife but a divorce from Mrs. Coleridge was impossible. A period followed of wretchedness, neglect of his family, wanderings abroad, and a more and more continual resort to the opium which he had begun taking some years before. Yet at this time he produced some of his finest criticism in the form of public lectures dealing with the English poets, chiefly Shakespeare and Milton. In 1816 he put himself under the care of a physician, James Gillman, with whom he lived in Highgate, London, for the rest of his life. He improved physically and published much of his work, including the *Biographia Literaria* (1817), which contains many of his critical principles and which did much to introduce German philosophy to English thinkers; also a revised edition of his periodical essays *The Friend,* and *Aids to Reflection* (1825).

William Collins (1721–1759) was the son of a Chichester hatter who wished to make a clergyman of him. The young man's tastes, however, did not lie in that direction. He was sent to Winchester, where he began his lifelong friendship with Joseph Warton, and to Magdalen College, Oxford. He took his B.A. in 1743. He then went to London where he frequented the company of literary men and the greenrooms of theaters, constantly in debt, constantly planning great literary projects which were never executed, now and then writing poetry. The *Persian Eclogues* were published while he was still an undergraduate, the *Odes on Descriptive and Allegorical Subjects* in 1747, and the long *Ode on the Popular Superstitions of the Highlands of Scotland* after his death. Toward the latter part of his life Collins's mind began to weaken from a deficiency, said Samuel Johnson, who knew him well, 'rather of his vital than intellectual powers.' He tried travel in France but without avail. He was for a time in an asylum for the insane and died in his sister's house in Chichester.

Abraham Cowley (1618–1667) was the son of a wealthy citizen of London, king's scholar at Westminster, and scholar and Fellow of Trinity College, Cambridge. At the age of ten he composed an epical romance and at twelve an epic, both published in 1633. A pastoral drama and a Latin comedy appeared in 1638, and in 1641 *The Cutter of Coleman Street,* a comedy directed against the Puritans. Ejected from Cambridge in that year as the result of the Civil War, he went first to Oxford and thence to Paris where he became cipher-secretary to Queen Henrietta Maria and was employed on delicate diplomatic missions. He came to England in 1656, probably as a Royalist spy though he was ostensibly studying medicine at Oxford. At the Restoration he expected preferment but received only a gift from the Duke of Buckingham of a small estate where he spent his remaining years. Cowley enjoyed a high literary reputation among his contemporaries and was at one time President of the newly formed Royal Society for the advancement of science. His principal poetic works, in addition to those already mentioned, are *The Mistress,* a cycle of love poems (1647), *Miscellanies* (1656), odes on the Restoration and against Cromwell (1660–1661), and *Verses on Several Occasions* (1663).

William Cowper (1731–1800), son of a rector of Great Berkhampstead, was educated at a private school (where he was bullied) and at Westminster School. He was then articled to a solicitor and called to the bar in 1754. He suffered from fits of depression, chiefly the result of a sensitive spirit struggling against the doctrine of eternal damnation. When he was offered a clerkship in the House of Lords in 1763 nervousness developed his depression into mania and he tried to commit suicide. From his madness he was cured but he lived thereafter in retirement. In 1765 he became a boarder in the house of Morley Unwin at Huntingdon where the cheerful, simple life perfectly suited him. After Unwin's death he removed, with Mary, Unwin's widow, to Olney where he came under the influence of Newton, an evangelical curate, who stirred up again his religious terrors. His marriage with Mrs. Unwin was prevented by another outbreak of madness. In 1779 Newton's influence was withdrawn and Cowper entered upon the most peaceful period of his life and began to write much poetry. One happy influence Newton had had: he induced Cowper to collaborate in the collection of *Olney Hymns* published in 1779. His contributions included 'Hark, my soul! it is the Lord' and 'God moves in a mysterious way.' At the suggestion of Mrs. Unwin he wrote *Table Talk* and other satires published in 1782. *'John Gilpin'* and *The Task* (1785) were written at the suggestion of his friend Lady Austen, whose vivacity and generosity did much to cheer his melancholy and to whom he wrote many of his charming letters. In 1786 he moved with Mrs. Unwin to Weston-

Underwood where the next few years were made happy by friendships, by the popular admiration for his poetry, and by his work on a translation of Homer published in 1791. The illness and death (1796) of Mrs. Unwin, however, left Cowper shattered in mind and body.

Richard Crashaw (1613?–1649), son of a violently anti-Catholic Anglican divine, became an ardent convert to the Roman Church. He was educated at Charterhouse and at Pembroke Hall, Cambridge. In 1634, the year in which he took his B.A., he published his first volume of poetry, *Epigrammatum Sacrorum Liber.* In 1635 he became a Fellow of Peterhouse where he remained until the Parliamentary sympathies of the University during the Civil War forced him to flee to the Continent. It was probably in 1645 that he was converted to Catholicism. In the next year he went to Paris and seems to have been introduced to Queen Henrietta Maria by his friend Abraham Cowley, her secretary. She preferred him to the attention of Cardinal Palotto, governor of Rome, who gave him a post in his household and subsequently had him admitted *beneficiatus* in the Church of Our Lady of Loretto where he died shortly after his arrival. Crashaw's principal poetic work was the *Steps to the Temple* (1646), a collection of religious poems to which is attached a secular section, the 'Delights of the Muses.' His 'Hymn to St. Teresa' belongs to the period before he became a Roman Catholic. The posthumous *Carmen Deo Nostro* (1652) includes new works and reprints many of the best of his earlier poems.

Samuel Daniel (1562–1619), the son, possibly, of a music-master, entered Magdalen Hall, Oxford, in 1579. After travelling in Italy he became tutor to William Herbert, son of Sidney's sister, the Countess of Pembroke, whose literary circle at Wilton House he called 'my best school.' Later he was tutor to Lady Anne Clifford, daughter of the Countess of Cumberland, and another learned lady, the Countess of Bedford, presented him, on James's accession to the throne, to the favor of Queen Anne. For her he wrote masques and in her household he held various offices until 1618 when he retired to his farm in Somerset. 'Well-languaged Daniel's' works include *The Complaint of Rosamond,* a Senecan tragedy *Cleopatra, Musophilus, or A Defense of all Learning,* a prose *Defense of Rhyme* in reply to Campion, and a long poetic history of the *Civil Wars.*

Cecil Day Lewis (1904–   ), a slightly older member of the group at Oxford that included Auden, Spender, and MacNeice, was born in Ireland but came to England shortly before his mother's death when he was four. By the time he was six, he was already writing verse, and at Wadham College, he was a full-fledged associate of the Auden 'circle.' After his marriage in 1928, he supported himself by teaching until 1935; after that he devoted himself to writing poetry and criticism, editing, and political activity, supporting himself largely by his income from pseudonymously written and very successful detective novels. With Auden, Isherwood, Spender, and MacNeice, he believed in the necessity of political action and shared their strong sympathy with the radical activities preceding World War II, although his poetry (which he liked to think of as revolutionary in technique, also) is rather more programmatic than theirs. Like them, too, he admired and learned from Hopkins, Wilfred Owen, Yeats, and Eliot, however different his political and intellectual sympathies. His work includes, besides his novels and critical essays, *Transitional Poems* (1929), *The Magnetic Mountain* (1933), *A Time to Dance and Other Poems* (1935), *Word Over All* (1943), *Poems, 1943–1947* (1948), the drama in verse and prose, *Noah and the Waters* (1936), and the travel narrative in verse, *An Italian Visit* (1953).

Walter de la Mare (1873–   ), after attending St. Paul's Cathedral Choir School, went in 1889 directly into the London offices of the Anglo-American Oil Company where he spent the next eighteen years. But the literary bent given an impetus at school nevertheless found an outlet in several stories published under the pseudonym of Walter Ramal in various magazines. His first volume, *Songs of Childhood,* was published in 1902, still under the pseudonym, but by 1908 he felt sufficiently assured to leave the oil company and devote himself to the life of a professional man of letters. Since then, his output has been large and consistently fine: poetry for both adults and children including *The Listeners,* 1912, *Peacock Pie,* 1913, *The Veil,* 1921, and *Winged Chariot,* 1951; novels, among them *Memoirs of a Midget,* 1921; anthologies; dramas and short stories for all ages; and collections of observations and criticism. Even at eighty, there is little slackening, as the volume, *O Lovely England,* 1953, attests. Much, if not all of his work, is characterized by a grave, melancholy, dream-like quality; his poetry seems to embody the 'secret quest of a soul burdened with a sense of loneliness.' Whether intended ostensibly for children or for adults, his poems in their illusory simplicity are neither childish nor founded on the evasions of fantasy, but at their best, they have the intense reality of vision.

John Donne (1572–1631), greatest of the metaphysical poets, was the son of a London ironmonger and of a daughter of John Heywood, the writer. His mother carefully supervised Donne's early education. In 1584 he was entered at Hart Hall, Oxford, and later transferred to Cambridge but seems not to have taken a degree at either university, probably because as a Roman Catholic he could not take the required oaths. He was admitted to Lincoln's Inn but was diverted from the study of the law by an 'immoderate desire of humane learning and languages.' He cared greatly for the writing of poetry and for the study of divinity. He was a volunteer with the Earl of Essex on the expedition to Cadiz in 1596 and to the Azores in 1597; on his return he became secretary to Sir Thomas Egerton, Lord Keeper of the Great Seal, but lost favor with him in 1601 by a secret marriage with his niece Anne More. Unable to find other employment and with a rapidly growing family, Donne spent years in poverty until he was persuaded to take orders in the Anglican Church. He was ordained in 1615 when the brilliance of his sermons brought him rapid advancement. In 1621 he was made Dean of St. Paul's and he frequently preached before Charles I. With a very few exceptions none of Donne's poems was published during his lifetime but they were widely circulated in manuscript.

Michael Drayton (1563–1631), born in Warwickshire, was brought up as a page in the house of Sir Henry Goodere at Polesworth. Sir Henry's younger daughter, Anne, is the 'Idea' of the sonnets. In 1597 Drayton published *England's Heroical Epistles,* imaginary letters in verse by historical personages, but lack of money forced him to turn to hack play-writing and in the next five years he collaborated in not fewer than twenty-three plays for Henslowe. The patronage of Sir William Aston set him free to return to the patriotic verse he cared for. In 1619 he published a revised edition of his shorter poems and in 1622 he finally completed *Poly-Olbion,* a long topographical poem celebrating the glories and beauties of England. Toward the close of his life he turned to lighter themes. *Nymphidia* was published in 1627 and the *Muses' Elysium* in 1630.

John Dryden (1631–1700) was born at the vicarage of Aldwinkle in Northamptonshire. He was educated at Westminster and Trinity College, Cambridge. He had a small competence and is said to have attached himself to his wealthy cousin Sir Gilbert Pickering, Cromwell's chamberlain. In 1663 he married Lady Elizabeth Howard, eldest daughter of the Earl of Berkshire. In 1658 Dryden wrote his 'Heroic Stanzas' on the death of Cromwell; in 1660 'Astræa Redux' on the return of Charles II. His (prose) *Wild Gallant* was acted in 1663, *The Rival Ladies* in 1664, *The Indian Emperor* in 1665. In 1667 Dryden published *Annus Mirabilis.* In 1668 he was appointed poet laureate and in 1670 historiographer. Between 1668 and 1681 he wrote heroic dramas such as *Tyrannic Love, The Conquest of Granada, Amboyna, Aurengzebe, All for Love* (a version of the story of Antony and Cleopatra), and such comedies as *The Spanish Friar, Marriage-à-la-Mode,* and *The Mock Astrologer.* From 1673 to the Revolution Dryden, as champion of the High Church party, engaged in literary warfare with the Whigs. Much of his critical work appeared in the form of apologetic prefaces to his plays but the *Essay of Dramatic Poesy* was published separately in 1668. In 1680 began the period of his didactic poems, *Absalom and Achitophel, The Medal, MacFlecknoe, Religio Laici, The Hind and the Panther.* At the Revolution Dryden, who had been converted to Catholicism, refused to take the oaths and was deprived of the laureateship and of a place in the Customs which he had held since 1683. The last part of his life was occupied with translations from the classics and with paraphrases of Chaucer, Boccaccio, and Ovid. He was buried in Westminster Abbey in Chaucer's grave.

William Dunbar (1465?–1530?), a Scot, was possibly an M.A. of St. Andrew's, certainly for a time a Franciscan friar. He executed various diplomatic missions for James IV, in one of which he was wrecked off the coast of Zealand. In 1500 James granted him a pension. He accompanied the embassy to negotiate the marriage between James and Margaret Tudor, and his first long poem, *The Thistle and the Rose,* was written in 1503 to celebrate the wedding. In 1511 he described Queen Margaret's visit to the North of Scotland in *The Queen's Progress at Aberdeen.* His other works are *The Golden Targe,* a dream allegory of love; 'The Lament for the Makers'; ballads; and various satires, chief among them 'The Dance of the Seven Deadly Sins.' Dunbar is supposed by some to have fallen at Flodden in 1513; others think that he wrote the *Orisone* after 1517.

Thomas Stearns Eliot (1888–), though born in St. Louis, comes from a New England family distinguished for centuries by the educators and divines it has produced. Eliot was possibly the most brilliant member of the brilliant Harvard Class of 1910; after a year at the Sorbonne he returned to Harvard to write a doctoral dissertation in philosophy, meantime studying Sanskrit and Pali. Without taking his degree, he migrated to Oxford for another year's reading. His marriage to an Englishwoman, a brief experience teaching school, and work first in a London bank, then as literary editor of Faber and Faber, English publishers, preceded his naturalization as a British subject in 1927. In the meantime he had begun to establish an international reputation as the foremost English critic, essayist, and poet of the time: *The Waste Land* (1922) was almost immediately recognized as a foundation-stone of postwar literature, while his critical and philosophical opinions, expressed in his essays and in *The Criterion,* the magazine he began editing also in 1922, influenced a generation of readers and writers. He has admired the French symbolists, Dante, Dryden, the Elizabethan damatists, and the metaphysical poets, as well as his friend and mentor, Ezra Pound. From all these he has learned much, but his poetry has never been derivative. Among other things, it depends upon juxtaposition and contrast, an elimination of colorless connectives, an evocation of traditional aesthetic and ethical standards to criticize implicitly modern civilization which he sees as chaotic, barren, and sterile. In his own search for order and identification with a meaningful tradition, he turned to Anglo-Catholicism, the implications and values of which he has explored in his later poetry, *Ash-Wednesday* (1930), and the *Four Quartets* (1935–1943), in such poetic dramas as *Murder in the Cathedral* (1935) and *The Cocktail Party* (1950), and in such essays as *The Idea of a Christian Society* (1940) and *Notes Towards the Definition of Culture* (1949). In 1948, he was awarded the Nobel Prize for Literature.

Oliver Goldsmith (1730–1774), the second son of an Irish clergyman, was entered at Trinity College, Dublin, in 1744 as a sizar but ran away to

Cork in consequence of 'personal chastisement' from his tutor. He returned, however, and graduated B.A. in 1749. He presented himself for ordination but was rejected, and then studied medicine at Edinburgh and at Leyden and during 1755–1756 wandered about France and Italy. He reached London in destitution in 1756 and supported himself with difficulty as a physician in Southwark, as an usher in a school in Peckham, and as a hack writer on Griffiths' *Monthly Review.* He published in 1759 his *Enquiry into the Present State of Polite Learning,* edited *The Bee,* and contributed to various periodicals. He was also employed by John Newberry the bookseller, in whose *Public Ledger* appeared the 'Chinese Letters' subsequently republished as *The Citizen of the World.* About this time Goldsmith made the acquaintance of Thomas Percy, the ballad enthusiast, later Bishop of Dromore, and of Samuel Johnson of whose Club he was one of the original members. The manuscript of his *Vicar of Wakefield* (1766) was sold by Johnson for Goldsmith for £60 and the proceeds saved him from arrest for debt. His long poem *The Traveller,* which appeared in 1764, was enthusiastically received by the public, as was *The Deserted Village,* published in 1770. Goldsmith's first comedy, *The Good-natured Man,* was produced in 1768; his second, *She Stoops to Conquer,* in 1773, with enormous success. He died the next year and was buried in the Temple church-yard. The Club erected a monument to him in Westminster Abbey.

Thomas Gray (1716–1771) was born in London and educated at Eton, with Horace Walpole, and at Peterhouse, Cambridge. He accompanied Walpole on a tour of the Continent in 1739, but they quarrelled in 1741 and returned home separately. Their friendship was renewed in 1744. Gray then resided at Cambridge, removing from Peterhouse to Pembroke College in 1756 because of a practical joke played upon him by undergraduates. In 1742 he wrote his odes 'On Spring,' 'On a Distant Prospect of Eton College,' 'On Adversity,' and began the 'Elegy in a Country Churchyard,' over which he worked until 1751. In 1757 Walpole published Gray's 'Progress of Poetry' and 'The Bard,' which led to his general recognition as the foremost poet of the day and to the offer of the laureateship which Gray declined. Gray was, with the possible exception of Milton, the most learned of the English poets. His studies embraced the classics, ancient history and the history of England, genealogy, heraldry, Old English and Middle English poetry, Norse and Welsh verse, zoölogy, botany, painting, architecture, and music. In his later years he devoted attention to Icelandic and Celtic verse and in imitation of this wrote 'The Fatal Sisters' and 'The Descent of Odin.' In 1768 he was appointed Professor of History and Modern Languages at Cambridge. A journey among the English Lakes which he made in 1769 is commemorated in the *Journal* (1775) which, with his letters, is his most important prose.

Thomas Hardy (1840–1928) was born in a little hamlet in Dorset, one of the southern English counties in the district he was to make collectively famous as 'Wessex.' The England where he spent his formative years was the old agricultural England — little changed since Elizabethan times — which was later to be the inspiration of his novels and his poetry. Hardy came of a once important family which had come down in the world, but his father, a small land-owner and builder, was a skilled musician, and his mother was an omnivorous reader. Hardy attended a village school, studied a little Latin, Greek, and French, fiddled at country dances. At sixteen he was apprenticed to an architect in Dorchester, and in 1861 went to London to continue his architectural studies. There, as earlier, he wrote verses which for many years found no publisher. In 1867 he left London, settled in Weymouth, and, while still practicing his profession, began to write novels. His first real success was his fourth attempt, *Far from the Madding Crowd,* published serially in 1874. For the next twenty years Hardy lived the life of a popular novelist, although his *Tess of the D'Urbervilles* had to be bowdlerized before any magazine would print it, and *Jude the Obscure* was greeted with a flood of abusive letters and the attempt by a bishop to stop its circulation in lending libraries. Hardy thereupon ceased writing novels altogether; 'Perhaps I can express more fully in verse ideas and emotions which run counter to the inert crystallized opinion — hard as a rock — which the vast body of men have vested interests in supporting.' His volumes of verse run from *Wessex Poems* in 1898 to *Winter Words* in the year of his death, and include his epic drama of the Napoleonic wars, *The Dynasts,* one of the most ambitious achievements in modern English poetry. In his last years the much abused novelist was honored as no English man of letters has been since Tennyson.

Robert Henryson (1430?–1506?), one of the greatest of the Scotch Chaucerians, was probably the Master Robert Henryson who was incorporated a member of Glasgow University in 1462 and was at the time 'licentiate in arts and bachelor in degrees.' He was probably also a clerical schoolmaster attached to Dunfermline Abbey. He wrote, in addition to short poems, thirteen *Moral Fables of Æsop the Phrygian, Orpheus and Eurydice,* and *The Testament of Cresseid,* written for the most part in Chaucer's seven-line stanza and for centuries attributed to Chaucer himself. It continues Chaucer's story, making Cresseid lose her beauty and die in misery.

George Herbert (1593–1633), younger brother of Lord Herbert of Cherbury and son to that Magdalen Herbert on whom Donne wrote his Ninth Elegy, believed that poetry should be turned from the service of profane to that of heavenly love. While an undergraduate at Trinity College, Cambridge, he began to write religious verse. He took his B.A. in 1612, his M.A. in 1616, and then began the study of divinity. In 1619 he was made Public Orator of the University, and the association into which this brought him with royalty and the great of the land distracted him for a time from ecclesiastical to courtly ambitions. In 1627, however, he resigned his oratorship, and in 1630 was ordained and instituted as rector of Bemerton near Salisbury. In 1629 he had married Jane Danvers. Music was Herbert's favorite recreation. He had 'a very good hand on the lute' and set to music many of his own lyrics and sacred poems. In his last illness he entrusted the manuscript of his poems to his friend Nicholas Ferrar, desiring that 'if he can think it may turn to the advantage of any dejected poor soul, let it be made public; if not, let him burn it.' Ferrar published *The Temple* in 1633.

Robert Herrick (1591–1674) published his two books of verse in one volume (1648). *Noble Numbers* is a collection of short religious poems; *Hesperides* sings of 'may-poles, hock-carts, wassails, wakes,' and Herrick's life mingled diverse elements in the same pleasant incongruity. He was born in London and for ten years apprenticed to his uncle, a goldsmith. He went at twenty-two — a very late age in the seventeenth century — to St. John's College, Cambridge, but transferred to Trinity Hall where he was graduated B.A. in 1617. During the next nine years he spent most of his time in London in a circle of poets and wits. He was one of the 'Tribe of Ben.' In 1629 he was installed as vicar of Dean Prior in Devon, where he lived till 1647 sometimes in love with his country life, sometimes very weary of it. He was ejected from his living by the Puritans but restored to it in 1662 and remained there till his death.

Thomas Hoccleve (1370?–1450?) was for many years a clerk in the office of the Privy Seal. It was for his poetry, however, that Henry IV granted him an annuity. According to his own account in his autobiographical poems Hoccleve spent a gay youth, married for love when he was middle-aged and poor, and was cared for in his old age at Southwark Priory, Hampshire. Poetically Hoccleve was a disciple of Chaucer. He wrote ballades, roundels, and other short pieces, *The Letters of Cupid,* translated from Christine de Pisan; *La Male Regle,* an autobiographical poem; *The Regiment of Princes;* the *Complaint* and the *Dialogue,* both autobiographical; and *Ars Sciendi Mori.*

Gerard Manley Hopkins (1844–1889) was converted to Rome during his undergraduate years. This was the central event of his life and his brilliance and popularity — he was called the 'Star of Balliol' — made the occurrence sensational in Oxford. When he was received into the Society of Jesus, he burned his poems and 'resolved to write no more, as not belonging to his profession.' In the winter of 1875 when five Franciscan nuns perished in the wreck of the *Deutschland* off the English coast, at the instance of his rector he memorialized their death in a poem. This is the first of the poems in which he worked out the new ideas of rhythm which is their most notable trait. In 1884 he was elected to a fellowship in the revived Catholic University at Dublin where the remaining five years of his life were spent. Although his vows permitted him little contact with the world, Father Hopkins exercised an influence over his poet friends, Coventry Patmore, Richard Watson Dixon, and Robert Bridges. It was Bridges who, recognizing with accurate judgment that Hopkins's innovations would not be comprehended in the '90's and 1900's, waited till 1918 before releasing them to the world.

Alfred Edward Housman (1859–1936) attended an English public school and went thence to Oxford where he failed in his final examinations in classics and philosophy. For ten years he lived in London as a clerk in the Patent Office. Long and diligent study of the classics made him an accurate and distinguished scholar. He was appointed Professor of Latin at University College, London. Ten years later he removed to Cambridge as Professor of Latin and Fellow of Trinity. He was a contributor to classical journals, an editor of the little known Latin poet Manilius, and a devastating critic of less profound scholars. He published two small volumes of verse, *A Shropshire Lad* (1896) and *Last Poems* (1922). *The Collected Poems of A. E. Housman* was issued in 1939.

Ben Jonson (1573?–1637) was of Border descent but was born probably in London. He was educated at Westminster School and worked for a time at the trade of his step-father, bricklaying. He enlisted for military service in Flanders and on his return became associated with a company of actors. By 1597 he was attached to Henslowe's company as a player and playwright. He killed a fellow-actor in a duel but escaped death by claiming benefit of clergy. He became a Roman Catholic during his imprisonment but abjured twelve years later. His *Every Man in His Humour,* with Shakespeare in the cast, was performed by the Lord Chamberlain's company in 1598; *Every Man Out of His Humour* in 1599, *Cynthia's Revels* 1600, *The Poetaster* 1601. His first extant tragedy, *Sejanus,* was given by Shakespeare's company at the Globe in 1603. In 1604 he was temporarily imprisoned for his share in *Eastward Ho,* a play reflecting on the Scots and incidentally on King James. In 1605 Jonson produced his first court masque 'of Blacknesse' and from that time on was constantly producing masques for the court. His satirical comedy *Volpone* was acted in 1606, *Epicœne, or the Silent Woman* in 1609, *The Alchemist* 1610, *Cataline* 1611, *Bartholomew Fair* 1614, *The Devil is an Ass* 1616. Though he was not formally appointed the first poet laureate, the essentials of the position were conferred on Jonson in 1616 when a pension was granted him by James I. In the same year he published a folio volume of his collected *Works,* a practice then unusual enough to cause much laughter at his expense. Two years later he made a journey to Scotland where Drummond of Hawthornden made notes of his lively, opinionated talk which show why it so much delighted his contemporaries. The group of young poets which it drew about him were known as the Tribe of Ben. In 1631 Jonson quarrelled with Inigo Jones after the production of the masque *Chloridia* and lost court patronage. His last masque was produced in 1634. Beside his dramas Jonson wrote

Epigrams and *The Forrest* (1616); *Underwoods,* a collection of lyrics (1640); and the prose *Timber; or Discoveries* (1641).

JOHN KEATS (1795–1821) asked to have engraved upon his tombstone, 'Here lies one whose name was writ in water,' so little did he feel that the extraordinary poetic productions of his short life had fulfilled his high poetic ambitions. Keats was the son of a London livery-stable keeper but received unusually good schooling and was encouraged in his taste for reading by his teacher Charles Cowden Clark. Left an orphan at fifteen he was apprenticed to a surgeon and in 1815 licensed to practice. But his whole interest was in letters, and on the night when Clark introduced him to the works of Edmund Spenser he definitely decided to devote himself to poetry. Through Clark he met Leigh Hunt, Lamb, Hazlitt, and other literary men, and the artists Haydon and Joseph Severn. In 1817 he published his first volume of *Poems,* to which the world paid no attention at all. When *Endymion* appeared in 1818 the reviewers attacked it savagely, especially those who were politically opposed to Leigh Hunt and erroneously regarded Keats as his disciple. Contrary to the legend long current, Keats was not hounded to death by the cruelty of these critics. He was better aware than they of his poetic weaknesses and was working steadily to acquire the equipment he felt essential for a poet in the nineteenth century. 'The road lies through application, study, and thought. I will pursue it,' he wrote in one of the remarkable letters which contain his theory of poetry. In the two years after *Endymion* Keats wrote almost all his greatest lyrics and began work on *Hyperion.* In July 1820 appeared his third volume, *Lamia, Isabella, The Eve of St. Agnes, and Other Poems.* About this time he fell passionately in love with the attractive, shallow Fanny Brawne, but neither his financial condition nor his health would permit him to marry. He had contracted consumption which grew steadily worse. In September 1820 Severn took him to Italy but even that climate could not help him. He died a few months later in Rome.

RUDYARD KIPLING (1865–1936), early known for his stories and ballads of native and British military life in India, actually spent only thirteen youthful years there. Though he was born in Bombay, from the age of six to seventeen he was in England at school, and by the time he was twenty-four, he had left India permanently. Preceded to England by *Plain Tales from the Hills* and *Departmental Ditties,* he achieved in less than eighteen months of intensive work after his arrival in London an extraordinary reputation. In 1892, his marriage to an American led to his settling for an unhappy four years near her family in Brattleboro, Vermont. Perhaps because of his trouble there, certainly because of the deaths of a young daughter and of his son in the First World War, Kipling began to turn from the popular Indian material to subjects of a new gravity. After 1900, his reputation declined, but it is now increasingly asserted that there was no real falling off in Kipling's skill and power; rather, it seems, his audience failed to follow him in his new interests, while a shift in political temper made his authoritarian view of Empire unpopular. But this view always depended upon an austere conception of duty, of government for the benefit, if not always with the consent, of the governed. Leaving politics aside, however, Mr. T. S. Eliot is probably right in calling Kipling the most accomplished writer of 'verse' (by which he intends no invidious comparison with 'poetry') that England has ever produced.

WALTER SAVAGE LANDOR (1775–1864), son of a Warwickshire physician, was educated at Rugby and Trinity College, Oxford, whence he was rusticated, his intractable temper having involved him in trouble as it did frequently throughout his life. He married in 1811 Julia Thuillier with whom he quarrelled in 1835, lived in Italy (Como, Pisa, Florence) from 1815–1835, Bath from 1838–1858, and the last part of his life in Florence, where he was on intimate terms with the Brownings. Like them he was passionately interested in Italy's struggle for freedom from the dominance of Austria. Landor's principal prose work took the form of *Imaginary Conversations* published in 1824–1853. Verse he wrote from boyhood till old age. Boythorn in Dickens' *Bleak House* is a genial caricature of some of Landor's peculiarities.

DAVID HERBERT LAWRENCE (1885–1930) was born in the coal-mining region of Nottinghamshire. His mother, with her lower middle-class education, taught him to despise his coal-mining father, but his own education, his experience as a factory clerk and as a teacher, and his dawning aspiration to write led him to despise the bourgeois success and gentility his mother had marked out for him. *Sons and Lovers* (1913), his first important novel, only slightly fictionalizes this autobiographical material. But more generally, his whole controversial career as a writer, his elopement with the aristocratic German wife (Frieda von Richthofen Weekley) of a former teacher of Lawrence's, and his wandering life through Europe, Ceylon, Australia, Mexico, and New Mexico can be looked upon as a continuous rebellion against his personal background and brutalizing industrial civilization. Gradually Lawrence came to consider himself almost the 'Messiah' of a new way of life, which combined elements of vitalism, primitivism, and theosophy. Denying the value of mechanized civilization and the conscious reason (sterile rationalism to him), he preached a kind of instinctive, spontaneous response to life, a reliance on the deepest impulses, the 'feeling of the blood' in man — a doctrine in which sex played, for the scandalized public, a notorious but actually an almost religious part. For many critics this prophetic, tractarian strain constitutes a major flaw in his later novels, though in his poetry it shows only in an occasional esoteric symbol or polemical phrase. But both his prose and poetry show the same reliance on spontaneous invention, the same disdain for conventional form. As the leader of a 'cult,' however, Lawrence has prompted rather more devotion or hostility than discriminating criticism. Never as robust as he wished himself to be in the role of hero, he contracted both malaria and dysentery in Mexico in 1925, bringing on a fatally virulent form of his latent tuberculosis from which he died five years later. He is buried on his ranch near Taos, New Mexico.

Richard Lovelace (1618–1657) was described by a contemporary as 'an approv'd both soldier, gentleman, and lover,' and by another as 'one of the handsomest men of England.' He was born heir to great estates in Kent and was educated at Charterhouse School and Gloucester Hall, Oxford. He obtained the favor of a great lady attendant upon Queen Henrietta Maria and at her request was granted his M.A. in his second year. Thereupon he immediately took up his residence at court. He served in the Scottish expeditions of 1639 and 1640. In 1642 he presented to the House of Commons the Kentish Petition in favor of the Bishops, the liturgy, and common prayer. For this he was imprisoned for seven weeks in the Gate House, whose stone walls did not a prison make. During the Civil War he served with the King's army in England and with the French army in Holland, where he was wounded at the siege of Dunkirk. These expeditions were the occasion of the farewells to Lucasta. Lucasta may have been Lucy Sacheverell; she may have been a Lucas; or she may have been a creature of Lovelace's imagination. In 1648 he took part in the Royalist risings in Kent, was again imprisoned, and again moved to poetry. After his release in 1649 he collected his poems into a volume, *Lucasta.* His other volume was published by his brother after his death.

Louis MacNeice (1907–), born in Ireland and educated in England, was an Oxford contemporary of Auden, Spender, and Day Lewis. Trained in classics and philosophy, he has taught at the Universities of Birmingham and London; to his credit are some excellent translations from classical Greek, reviews and critical essays, as well as several volumes of poetry. Like Spender, he served as a fire-warden in London during the war. He is frequently grouped with his friends in discussions of the brilliant young writers who first attracted attention around 1930; like them, he was searching for something affirmative in which to believe, as contrasted with the attitude of many writers in the 'twenties. Acknowledging the youthful enthusiasms of his undergraduate years, he wrote (in *Modern Poetry,* 1938), 'My evolution during this period was typical, I think . . . My ideology was built up on *Ulysses,* "The Waste Land," and D. H. Lawrence. As the two former are essentially negative works, my positive creed was inevitably Lawrentian.' The 'Lawrentian' period passed, but he continued to insist, 'The good poet has a definite attitude to life; most good poets, I fancy, have more than that — they have beliefs (though their beliefs need not be *explicit* in their work).' He once said that the system of capitalism must end, but distrusting all parties and dogma, including Marxism, and though admiring the work of his friends Auden and Spender, he went his own way with stubborn independence, developing his own style and eschewing overt political commentary. Nevertheless, satire is a frequent note in his poetry.

Christopher Marlowe (1564–1593), son of a prosperous shoe-maker in Canterbury, was educated at the King's School there and at Corpus Christi College, Cambridge. He took his B.A. in 1584, his M.A. in 1587, and between those dates apparently spent some time abroad in secret government service. In London as one of the 'university wits' he knew the leading men of letters of his day who admired and quoted him. He attached himself to the Lord Admiral's theatrical company which produced most of his plays. Most notable of these are *Tamburlaine, Dr. Faustus, The Jew of Malta,* and *Edward II.* Marlowe held and propagated atheistical opinions and a warrant was issued for his arrest in 1593. He was killed at a tavern in Deptford as the result, apparently, of a quarrel about the score but it is possible that he was a government agent and that his murder had a political complexion.

Andrew Marvell (1621–1678) was born at Winstead near Hull and educated at Hull Grammar School and Trinity College, Cambridge. While there he was converted to Roman Catholicism by Jesuits but shortly reconverted by his father, an Anglican rector. He was graduated B.A. in 1639 but remained at Cambridge for further study. In 1641 his father's death made it necessary for him to earn his living. He had a clerkship in a business house in Hull and was then abroad for about four years, probably as a tutor. In 1651 he became tutor to the daughter of the Lord General Fairfax of Nun Appleton House in Yorkshire, famous for its beautiful garden whence came the impulse for many of Marvell's poems. In 1653 he was made tutor to a ward of Cromwell's, William Dutton, with whom he lived at Eton in the house of John Oxenbridge. Oxenbridge, who had made several trips to the Bermudas, probably provided the inspiration for the Bermuda poem. In 1657 Marvell was appointed assistant to Milton, who was then Latin secretary to the Council of State, and in 1659 he was elected to Richard Cromwell's Parliament. He was re-elected in 1660 and 1661 and during his whole term of membership was assiduous in writing to his constituents at Hull news letters which are valuable historic documents. The Restoration moved Marvell to satiric verse attacking the ministers and even Charles II himself. Most of his poems were not published until 1681; the satires after the Revolution, in 1689.

George Meredith (1828–1909) was born into a family of Portsmouth naval outfitters, a fact which all his life he carefully concealed. He was sent at fourteen to Neuwied, a remarkable school in Germany where two years' training stamped in him a passion for liberty and sowed a love of German romanticism evident in much of his earlier work. On his return to England Meredith went through the form of reading law, but he knew that he was going to write and he went about it promptly with fugitive contributions to journals, and, in 1851, a volume of *Poems. Modern Love,* 1862, tells the story of his marriage to the daughter of Thomas Love Peacock. At first rapturously happy, it ended in misery when she fled to Italy with her lover. In 1864 Meredith married Marie Vulliamy. His novels, chief of which are *Richard Feverel, Harry Richmond, Beauchamp's Career, The Egoist, Diana of the Crossways,* were admired at once by men of letters but only gradually accepted by the public. His poetry was unappreciated during his lifetime and many of the early volumes were published at his own expense. His books include *Poems and Lyrics of the Joy of Earth,* 1883; *A Reading of Earth,* 1888; *A Reading of Life,* 1901.

John Milton (1608–1674) was born in Cheapside, London. His father was a scrivener and composer of music. The boy was educated at St. Paul's School and Christ's College, Cambridge, where he became B.A. in 1629 and M.A. in 1632. After leaving the University he adopted no profession but lived for the next five years at Horton in Bucks with his father, reading the classics and preparing himself for his vocation as a poet. At this time he wrote *L'Allegro, Il Penseroso, Comus,* and *Lycidas.* During the twenty years that elapsed between this and his composition of *Paradise Lost* Milton wrote almost no poetry. From 1638–1639 he travelled abroad, chiefly in Italy, and on his return became tutor to his nephews, Edward and John Philips. He married, probably in 1642, Mary Powell. Their relations were not happy and in 1643 Milton published a pamphlet on divorce. Three others followed. In 1644 he published the treatise *Of Education* and the *Areopagitica* on the liberty of the press. In 1647, his circumstances having become easier on his father's death, he gave up teaching. In 1649 he was appointed Latin Secretary to the newly formed Council of State, a post which he retained until the Restoration though his increasing blindness, which became total in 1652, made it necessary for him to employ assistance. In 1652 his wife died, leaving three daughters, and in 1656 Milton married Catharine Woodcock, who died two years later. At the Restoration he was arrested and fined, and though released he lost the greater part of his fortune. He turned again to poetry and began the composition of *Paradise Lost.* He married his third wife, Elizabeth Minshull (who survived him), in 1663 and moved to what is now Bunhill Row in London, where he spent the remainder of his life. *Paradise Lost* was published in 1667 (twelve books in 1674); *Paradise Regained* and *Samson Agonistes* in 1671.

Thomas Moore (1779–1852), the son of a Dublin grocer, went to London at twenty-one without money or connections. Within a year he had made so many distinguished friends that his translation of the *Odes of Anacreon* was published under the patronage of the Prince Regent. Moore was handsome, charming, and sang so divinely that his verses seemed even better than they really were. In 1803 he was appointed registrar for the naval court of Bermuda but though he delighted in the beauty of the Islands he found the work dull, hired a deputy to perform it, and went to visit in the United States. There, like so many other British travellers, he found the realities of democracy quite different from those of his imagination and vented his disappointment in satirical *Epistles, Odes, and Other Poems* (1806). In 1807 he published the first volume of *Irish Melodies,* words of his own set to Irish airs adapted for him by his friend Sir John Stevenson. The Irish nationalism of the songs was more picturesque than violent and they were as enormously popular in England as in Ireland. For more than twenty-five years (1807–1834) Moore continued to add to the collection. In 1817 his *Lalla Rookh* — four poetic oriental romances in a prose setting — lifted him to the very crest of the wave of celebrity and fashion. He was admired not only by noble lords and great ladies but by men of letters. After Byron's death he was asked to be his official biographer and performed the delicate task (1830) to the perfect satisfaction of the poet's friends, though his book is scarcely frank or comprehensive enough for the satisfaction of posterity. Moore's later writing included satiric political verse, an unsuccessful poem with an oriental setting, *The Loves of the Angels* (1823), and an historical novel *The Epicurean* (1827).

William Morris (1834–1896) was born at Walthamstow near London, the son of a prosperous billbroker. He went to school at Marlborough and then to Exeter College, Oxford. There he read assiduously, formed a close friendship with Burne-Jones, and became the center of a little group of students more interested in literature and art than in the university curriculum. Inheriting a considerable fortune when he came of age, he founded and endowed *The Oxford and Cambridge Magazine* to which he contributed a number of poems and stories. In 1861 he established the famous firm of Morris and Company, artists and decorators. For them he designed wall-papers and tapestries and rediscovered old crafts of dyeing and weaving. He revived printing as a fine art at his Kelmscott Press. Dissatisfied with the conditions of modern industrialism, he became an active Socialist, founded *The Commonweal* (1885) as the organ of the Socialist League, and wrote for it *The Dream of John Ball* and *News from Nowhere.* Driven out by intrigue from the Socialist organization he busied himself in his last years with a series of prose romances, a way of escape from a hostile world into the *Glittering Plain* and the *Wood beyond the World.* He died at sixty-two, someone has said, simply of being William Morris and trying to pack into one life the work of half a dozen men. Poetry was only part of Morris's activity, but it was a very important part. *The Defence of Guenevere* was published in 1858, *The Life and Death of Jason* in 1867, followed by *The Earthly Paradise* (1868–1870). Then came *Love is Enough* (1873), *Sigurd the Volsung* (1877), and, in 1891, *Poems by the Way.*

Wilfred Owen (1893–1918), after only three years at London University, took a private tutoring position in 1913 near Bordeaux because of the climate and poor health. But in 1915 he nevertheless returned to England to volunteer for the Army. From December 1916 until June 1917 he served with the Manchester Regiment during some of the grimmest months of trench warfare. Invalided home suffering from shock, he happened to meet Siegfried Sassoon, by now a famous poet of the war. From this time, too, dates Owen's maturity as a poet. A youthful devotion to Keats was succeeded by a resolve to voice the agonies of war in public protest. Found among his papers after his death was a fragmentary preface for a collection of his poems; in it he asserted that his book was not to be about 'heroes.' Rather, 'The subject of it is War, and the pity of War.' Not in consolation of those now enduring it, he added, but in the hope that it might warn a future generation. He came to regard the ethic of Christ as irrefutable; man might ignore it, but not compromise with it. Hence his feeling, as in 'Strange Meeting,' for friend and enemy alike as common sufferers in a desolation not of their own making. But in this travail, he felt, his place was with his fellows. At the end of August 1918 he rejoined his regiment and became commander of his company. For gallantry in an action of October 1st, he was decorated with the Military Cross. On November 4th, seven days before the Armistice, he was killed attempting to lead his men across the Sambre Canal.

Alexander Pope (1688–1744) was the son of a Roman Catholic linen-draper of London. He was a hunch-back and once described his life as one long disease, but his wit and poetic powers were precocious. He early attracted the attention of men of letters; Wycherley introduced him to London life. His *Pastorals* were published in 1709. In 1711 his *Essay on Criticism* made him known to Addison's circle, and his 'Messiah' was published in *The Spectator* in 1712. 'The Rape of the Lock' appeared in Lintot's *Miscellanies* in the same year. 'Windsor Forest' (1713) appealed to the Tories by its reference to the Peace of Utrecht and won for Pope the friendship of Swift. He drifted away from Addison's 'Little Senate' and became a member of the 'Scriblerus Club' which included Swift and Gay. Through the first half of the eighteenth century Pope was the dominating figure in English poetry. In 1715 he issued the first volume of his translation of Homer's *Iliad,* completed in 1720 and supplemented five years later by a translation of the *Odyssey.* The success of these translations added considerably to his fortune and enabled him to buy the lease of a house at Twickenham and live the rest of his life there in comfortable independence. At about the time he went to Twickenham he formed a strong attachment for Martha Blount, with whom his intimacy continued throughout his life, and for Lady Mary Wortley Montagu, whom in later years he assailed with bitterness. His other important poetic works include *Eloisa to Abelard* (1717), *The Dunciad* (1728), *Moral Essays* (1731–1735), *An Essay on Man* (1732–1734), and *Satires* with a prefatory 'Epistle to Dr. Arbuthnot' (1735).

Sir Walter Raleigh (1552?–1618), son of a Devonshire gentleman, was educated at Oriel College, Oxford. He served as a soldier in France and the Low Countries, helped to suppress an insurrection in Ireland, and engaged in expeditions to the Americas. He obtained the favor of Queen Elizabeth but forfeited it and was committed to the Tower (1592) for his marriage with Elizabeth Throgmorton. In 1603 he was charged with conspiring against James I and condemned to death, but his sentence was commuted and again he was sent to the Tower. There he lived with his wife and son till 1616, when he was released to undertake an expedition to the Oronoco in search of gold. On the failure of the expedition and at the demand of the Spanish ambassador he was arrested and executed at Westminster. Much of Raleigh's poetry is lost but about thirty short pieces survive. His prose works include *A Report of the Truth of the Fight about the Isles of the Azores,* 1591, containing the story of Sir Richard Grenville's encounter with the Spanish fleet; *The Discovery of the Empire of Guiana,* 1596; and the first book of a *History of the World,* 1614.

Christina Georgina Rossetti (1830–1894), sister of Dante Gabriel Rossetti, was the first of the associates of the Pre-Raphaelite Brotherhood to receive the public's approval. She contributed to *The Germ,* and published as her first mature work in book form *Goblin Market and other Poems* in 1862. Fourteen other volumes of verse (most important of which are *The Prince's Progress,* 1866, and *A Pageant and other Poems,* 1881), short stories, and pious exhortations appeared before her death. Religious scruples kept her from marrying the man she loved and that renunciation was responsible for much of her finest poetry. The burden of her song is love. It is also the anticipated joy of the life everlasting. She speaks of heavenly sights with the certainty and clear perception with which worldly poets speak of nature's beauty.

Dante Gabriel Rossetti (1828–1882) was born in London, the eldest son of an Italian scholar, patriot, and exile. At an early age he decided to become a painter and joined with John Millais and Holman Hunt in forming the Pre-Raphaelite Brotherhood, a little group of artists and writers who declared their faith in a return to the simplicity, significance, and truth to nature of the early Italian school of art. They published a short-lived magazine, *The Germ,* to which Rossetti contributed both prose and verse. About 1855 he came in touch with William Morris, Burne-Jones, and Swinburne, over all of whom his influence was great. Before his meeting with this Oxford group Rossetti had fallen in love with a milliner's assistant who became his model and to whose beauty much of his loveliest work in painting and in poetry owes its inspiration. Their marriage was deferred over a period of nearly ten years because of her delicate health and Rossetti's constant financial embarrassments. Their married life was short and troubled. She was attacked by tuberculosis and died from an over-dose of laudanum taken during her husband's absence. In a passion of remorse Rossetti placed in her coffin the manuscript volume of poems he had prepared for publication. When failing eyesight threatened to close his career as a painter he turned again to poetry. Urged by his friends he permitted the grave to be opened; the manuscript was recovered and published in 1870 as *Poems by Dante Gabriel Rossetti.* A furious attack upon Rossetti as the arch-representative of the 'Fleshly School of Poetry' hastened the decline into which he was sinking. To alleviate his suffering he took chloral and his last years were a tragic alternation of feverish activity and collapse bordering on insanity. A late flowering of poetic power produced *Ballads and Sonnets* in the year before his death.

SIR WALTER SCOTT (1771–1832), son of Walter Scott, an Edinburgh lawyer, was educated at Edinburgh High School and University. He was apprenticed to his father and called to the bar in 1792. His interest in the old Border tales and ballads had early been awakened and was stimulated by Percy's *Reliques* and by the study of the older romantic poetry of France and Italy and the modern Germans. He devoted much of his leisure to the exploration of the Border country. In 1802–1803 appeared the three volumes of his *Minstrelsy of the Scottish Border,* a collection of ballads with imitations in a separate section, and in 1805 his first considerable original poem, *The Lay of the Last Minstrel. Marmion* followed in 1808 and *The Lady of the Lake* in 1810. In 1813 Scott was offered the laureateship but declined it in favor of Southey. The fame of Byron as a narrative poet made it seem wise for Scott to turn his attention to the historical novel. He published *Waverley* in 1814 and in the next eleven years produced twenty novels. Their success was phenomenal but not until 1827 did Scott publicly admit his authorship. He prospered materially, however, added to the lands and treasures of his estate at Abbotsford on the Tweed where he had built himself a Gothic castle, and in 1820 was made a baronet. Scott had secretly entered into partnership with an Edinburgh firm of printers, the Ballantynes. In 1825 the London publishing house of Constable went bankrupt, carrying the Ballantynes down with them. The losses amounted to £130,000 and Scott, who might legally have confined his responsibility to a small fraction of that sum, quixotically determined to clear the debt. Thenceforth he worked heroically, writing sometimes twelve hours a day, and shortening his life in his efforts to satisfy the creditors who were finally paid off at his death with the sums realized on the sale of his copyrights.

WILLIAM SHAKESPEARE (1564–1616) was the eldest son of John Shakespeare, variously described as a yeoman, a glover, a butcher, and a wool-dealer, of Stratford-on-Avon, who rose through a succession of municipal offices to be in 1568 bailiff, or mayor, of the town. Although in financial straits he applied in 1596 for a grant of arms which was authorized three years later. William was undoubtedly educated at the free grammar school in Stratford. He married in 1582 Anne, probably daughter of Richard Hathaway of Shottery. About 1586 he went to London where he was probably first engaged in some subordinate capacity at one of the two theaters then existing and afterwards became a member of the Lord Chamberlain's (after the accession of James I, the King's) company of players. His earliest work as a dramatist probably dates from 1591 and is to be found in the three parts of *Henry VI.* His long poems *Venus and Adonis* and *Lucrece* were published in 1593 and 1594, and the *Sonnets* were probably begun at about the same time. Before 1600 most of his historical plays and comedies were written, between 1600 and 1609 the tragedies, and in the next years the dramatic romances. After that he seems to have spent his time chiefly at Stratford where he had purchased, in 1597, Newplace, the largest house in the town. He died there and is buried in Stratford Church.

PERCY BYSSHE SHELLEY (1792–1822) upset the tradition of the solid squirearchy from which he sprang by revolting against the fagging system at Eton, and by publishing at Oxford a pamphlet on *The Necessity of Atheism.* He and his close friend Thomas Jefferson Hogg were thereupon expelled from University College. The anger of Shelley's father was at last appeased so far that he gave him a small allowance and permission to live where he chose. A quixotic desire to rescue his sisters' school friend, Harriet Westbrook, from what he deemed parental and religious tyranny moved Shelley to elope with her to Edinburgh. Longing to devote himself to the advancement of liberal causes, he turned his energies first to that of Catholic emancipation, going on to free speech, vegetarianism, an attack on the Christian church as the ally of obscurantism and oppression, and a vast admiration for William Godwin's theories of political justice. In 1813 he set forth in his long poem *Queen Mab* his interpretation of history and hopes for a future era of love and freedom. In the next year he met Godwin's daughter Mary, a highly intelligent girl of seventeen, deeply interested in the causes Shelley cared for and for which Harriet, since the birth of her first child, no longer even pretended enthusiasm. Shelley eloped with Mary to Switzerland and a few years later Harriet drowned herself. During these years Shelley had been gradually transferring his interests from social reform to poetry. *Alastor* was published in 1816, the *Hymn to Intellectual Beauty* in 1817. In 1818 Shelley and Mary went to Italy where he continued his studies in Greek, Italian, and English poetry, wrote *The Cenci* (1819), *The Witch of Atlas* (1820), *Prometheus Unbound* (1820), a prose *Defence of Poetry* (posthumously published), saw much of Byron in Venice and Pisa, and conceived for the young Countess Emilia Viviani a Platonic passion expressed in *Epipsychidion*

(1821). In 1822 Shelley and his friend Edward Williams were caught in a storm while sailing in the Gulf of Spezzia, and drowned.

Sir Philip Sidney (1554–1586) embodied for his contemporaries the renascence ideal of the gentleman. Of high birth, charming in appearance and manners, he was distinguished as a courtier, diplomat, soldier, and man of letters. He was the son of Sir Henry Sidney, thrice Lord Deputy of Ireland, and of a sister of Robert Dudley, Earl of Leicester. He was educated at Shrewsbury, where he began his lifelong friendship with Fulke Greville, at Christ Church, Oxford, and at Cambridge. For three years he travelled on the Continent. About 1576 he first met, while she was still a child, Penelope Devereux, daughter of the Earl of Essex, believed to be the Stella of his sonnets. Five years later she married Lord Rich against her will, and the misfortune of this marriage seems to have increased Sidney's love for her. Sidney was much at court and Elizabeth sent for him on several important diplomatic missions. In 1583 he married the daughter of Sir Francis Walsingham. In 1585 he sailed for the Netherlands, where he had been appointed governor of Flushing, and a few months later took part in the relief of Zutphen where he received a fatal bullet wound in the thigh. He was buried in St. Paul's Cathedral amid national mourning. Like his sister, the Countess of Pembroke, Sidney was a friend and patron of poets. Spenser's dedication to him of the *Shepheardes Calender* was only one of many. He himself wrote a *Defence of Poesie,* a prose romance, the *Arcadia,* and much poetry, including the sonnet sequence *Astrophel and Stella.*

Edith Sitwell (1887–) and her two literary brothers, Osbert and Sacheverell, come from an old and titled English family. Together, they formed a deliberately eccentric trio, at every opportunity controverting stuffy convention with elegant dignity. After a private education, she first attracted attention in 1916 when she helped found *Wheels,* meant to be an annual anthology. Though the anthology survived no more than a few issues, she went on to achieve her own unique reputation for a poetic style, brilliant and brittle in an almost surrealist sense. For a while she lived in Paris, where she was a friend of that other great stylist in language, Gertrude Stein. An excellent musician in her own right, she adapted many musical techniques to her poetic virtuosity; carrying this even further, she wrote poetry to be recited to music, most notably her collaboration with Sir William Walton in *Façade.* A woman of decided opinions, she thrived on controversy, but this did not interfere with her generosity to young artists. Her technical brilliance, her arbitrarily personal use of language, her objectivity and concreteness partly obscured for a long time a vein of feeling almost mystical, a sense of 'metaphysical horror.' But as with so many English poets who went through the fire raids on London during the War — Spender or MacNeice or Thomas, for example — her more recent volumes, *Street Song* (1942), *Green Song and Other Poems* (1944), or *The Canticle of the Rose* (1949), show a constant deepening and intensification of experience in her verse. Honorary degrees and the title of Dame mark the recognition of her significance to English poetry.

John Skelton (1460?–1529) typifies the transition from medieval England to the England of the new learning and the new national life. He was born in Norfolk and educated probably at Cambridge. By 1493 he had received from both universities the academic title of poet laureate. He was tutor to Prince Henry, later Henry VIII, and then rector of Diss in Norfolk, but continued his connection with the court where he flourished in the favor of the King till his antagonism against Wolsey became too violent. 'Colin Clout,' 'Speak, Parrot,' and 'Why Come Ye Not to Court?' contain bitter personal attacks upon the Cardinal and the evil effects of his dominance. Skelton was obliged to seek sanctuary with the Abbot of Westminster, where he remained virtually a prisoner till his death. His prolific work includes 'The Bowge of Court'; 'A Garland of Laurel'; 'Philip Sparrow,' the lament of a young lady whose sparrow has been killed by a cat; 'The Tuning of Elinor Rumming,' a tale of an ale wife and her customers; and a morality play, *Magnificence.* His short, two-beat lines rhyming in no set order have been called 'Skeltonian verse' or 'Skeltoniads.'

Stephen Spender (1909–), youngest of the remarkable group of Oxford poets that included Auden, Day Lewis, and MacNeice, left University College in 1931 without graduating. Orphaned at an early age, he spent much of his shy and self-conscious youth on the Continent, especially in Germany (1929–1932) with the novelist Christopher Isherwood. Like the others, he was both a pronounced individualist and yet deeply sympathetic to Socialist aims in the 1930's. His spiritual autobiography, *World within World* (1951), is for the mid-twentieth century a representative account of the travail of a young mind deeply sensitive to humane values; with many reservations about Communist dogma, he yet nominally joined the Party after the outbreak of the Spanish Civil War. In the face of the Great Depression and the threat of catastrophic war contained in the rise of totalitarian dictatorships all over the world, such an action seemed the only positive alternative to the ineffectual complacency of the western democracies. He made a number of visits to Spain as a correspondent and as a delegate (without illusions, however) to the Madrid International Writer's Congress, the only English writer to defy the lack of a visa to do so. Nevertheless, his talent has remained almost purely lyrical. (He has frequently been compared to Shelley.) Besides his poetry, he has written short stories, a novel, a play, and a good deal of criticism of increasing perceptivity. During World War II, while serving as a fire-warden in London, he helped Cyril Connolly found and edit the brilliant magazine, *Horizon.*

Edmund Spenser (1552?–1599) was born in London and educated at the Merchant Taylors' School and as a sizar at Pembroke Hall, Cambridge. As early as 1569 he contributed a number of epigrams and sonnets to Van der Noodt's *Theatre of Voluptuous Worldlings*. In his youth also were written the first two of the four Platonic *Hymns in Honour of Love and Beauty*. In 1579 he obtained a place in the household of the Earl of Leicester where he made the acquaintance of Sir Philip Sidney, to whom he dedicated his *Shepheardes Calender* published in 1580. In the same year he began his *Faerie Queene*. In 1580 also Spenser was appointed secretary to Lord Grey, Lord Deputy of Ireland, and in 1586 became one of the 'undertakers' for the settlement of Munster and acquired Kilcolman Castle in County Cork. Here he settled and occupied himself successfully with literary work though he always regarded Ireland as a place of exile. His well-informed prose *View of the Present State of Ireland* was probably written in 1596. Two years later Kilcolman was burned in an insurrection of the natives and Spenser was compelled to flee with his wife and four children to Cork. He died in London and was buried in Westminster Abbey near the grave of his admired Chaucer.

Henry Howard, Earl of Surrey (1517?–1547), son of Thomas Howard, afterwards third duke of Norfolk, came on both sides of royal blood. At thirteen he was made companion to Henry Fitzroy, Duke of Richmond, illegitimate son of Henry VIII, with whom he lived at Windsor Palace and with whom he travelled to France in 1532. On their return Richmond was married to Surrey's sister and Surrey to the Lady Frances Vere. Surrey aided his father in overthrowing the power of Thomas Cromwell and in the subjection of Scotland. He was with the army during the war with France, was wounded before Montreuil, and was commander of Boulogne. When barely thirty years old he was condemned and executed on a malicious charge of plotting to succeed Henry VIII on the throne. Like Wyatt, Surrey studied the Italian poets, especially Petrarch, and with Wyatt he shares the merit of bringing the sonnet from Italy to England. In his translation of the *Aeneid* he introduced into English the use of blank verse.

Algernon Charles Swinburne (1837–1909) began his education at Eton where he read prodigiously and laid the foundation of his wide knowledge of literature, ancient and modern. He went on to Balliol, at Oxford, where he neglected his studies, offended convention by his outspoken republicanism, and angered the authorities by his irregular habits. He was finally withdrawn from college. In 1860 he published his first work, two poetic plays, dedicated to Rossetti, and in 1865 he dedicated to Landor *Atalanta in Calydon*. With the appearance of *Poems and Ballads* in 1866 (later series 1878, 1889) Swinburne became over night the most talked-of figure in British letters. This was due not so much to the book itself as to a furious review of an advance copy. For years the name of Swinburne was to all sober-minded Englishmen a synonym for a scandalous sensualist. In *Songs before Sunrise* (1871) he shifted his theme to the cause of human liberty. For the next ten years he published steadily, poetry, drama, and prose, till his feverish activity, combined with his irregular habits of life, brought him to the verge of collapse. He was rescued by his friend Watts-Dunton who took him to his home in a London suburb and kept him there for thirty years under a gentle restraint. Though Swinburne's life was lengthened it was at the expense of his genius. His later work was by no means of the early calibre.

Alfred, Lord Tennyson (1809–1892), the third son of the rector of Somersby, entered Trinity College, Cambridge, in 1828. A group of serious-minded undergraduates calling themselves 'The Apostles' adopted him as their poet. Arthur Hallam, leading spirit of the society, became Tennyson's friend and a dominant influence in his life. Tennyson won the Chancellor's Medal for English verse in 1829. In 1827 *Poems by Two Brothers* had included verse by him and his two brothers, Charles and Frederick. *Poems, Chiefly Lyrical* (1830) and *Poems* (1833) met with a mildly favorable and an occasionally sneering reception from the reviewers in the quarterlies. Meanwhile Tennyson's dear friend Hallam had died in Vienna, bringing upon the poet a grief which was not finally consoled until he published in 1850 his monody, *In Memoriam*. Made silent by his sorrow and his irritation at the critics' thrusts, Tennyson published no book until the two volumes in 1842 which are the foundation of his fame. The public received kindly his poetical satire of rights-for-women, *The Princess* (1847), and every reader from the Queen to her humblest subject found in *In Memoriam* consolation and guidance among the perplexities of modern life. *Maud* (1855) seemed, because of its 'morbid' subject, a temporary lapse, but the first four of the *Idylls of the King* (1859) and *Enoch Arden* (1864) were recognized popularly as the fulfillment of his genius, though the skepticism of the critics increased as the new idylls appeared: in 1869 *The Holy Grail;* in 1871 *The Last Tournament;* in 1872 *Gareth and Lynette*. In 1850, on the death of Wordsworth, Tennyson had been chosen poet laureate, from which date until the mid-'70's he dominated the literary scene. Every distinguished visitor to the country made, as a matter of course, a pilgrimage to 'Aldworth,' his home in Surrey, or to Farringford in the Isle of Wight. No English poet has ever been so admired as a public figure. In the last years of his life he turned to the stage at the behest of Henry Irving, and wrote a number of historical dramas on English themes. In 1884 he was made a baron. His funeral in Westminster Abbey was an occasion of state.

Dylan Thomas (1914–1953) was a poet in the authentic Welsh bardic tradition — both in the intensity of his lyricism and in the often cryptic quality of statement. After a grammar school education at the Welsh seaport of Swansea, he tried his hand at newspaper reporting and hack journalism. But by the time he was seventeen he had already published poetry, and his *Eighteen Poems* was issued when he was only twenty. Dame Edith Sitwell was one of the first to recognize and encourage his unique talent, and by the time of his sudden death in New York when he was only thirty-nine, he had already achieved a remarkable reputation — with his poetry, with experiments in fiction and playwrighting, and by his extensive lecture tours reading his own and others' poetry. His brief but turbulent life is matched by the violent and vivid quality of his poetry. Of a later generation than the group around Auden and Spender, he shows little concern with economic or political questions in his verse. He does, however, besides his own knowledge of the Bible and Welsh poetic lore, share with them antecedents in Freud, Joyce, and Hopkins. He has been called both a 'language-juggler' and a 'language-lover' and his work is more expressive of states of feeling than visual perception; he had a seemingly inexhaustible talent for image-making both prose and poetic. Besides his early poems, his work includes *Twenty-five Poems* (1936), *New Poems* (1942), the autobiographical reminiscence, *Portrait of the Artist as a Young Dog* (1940), and the posthumous play, *Under Milk Wood.*

FRANCIS THOMPSON (1859–1907), son of a Lancashire doctor, was a strange, impractical man, unable to deal with the ordinary details of existence. He spent seven years at a Roman Seminary but the authorities decided that he was unfitted for the priesthood. His father sent him to Manchester to study medicine. In four years he did not succeed in passing a single examination. He tried to enlist but he was already a drug addict and was rejected on the grounds of health. With neither hope nor expectation for the future he travelled to London, where he sank gradually into the worst kind of destitution, selling newspapers, fetching cabs, hawking pencils, saved from the last inroads of consumption only by his drug. In 1887 Wilfrid Meynell, editor of a Roman Catholic magazine, *Merry England,* was impressed by a tattered manuscript of poems left in his letter-box and a year later discovered the author. Under his friendly care Thompson was gradually won back to health and civilization, and under his patronage were published *Poems,* 1893; *Sister Songs,* 1895; and *New Poems,* 1896. 'To be the poet of the return to Nature is somewhat, but I would be the poet of the return to God,' was Thompson's wish.

JAMES THOMSON (1700–1748), born at Ednam on the Scottish border, the son of a minister, was educated at Edinburgh University. He began early to write verse that showed his fondness for the rustic scene. He came to London in 1725 and under stress of poverty wrote 'Winter,' the first of his *Seasons* which appeared successively 1726–1730 and were the precursors of the romantic poetry of nature. He made the acquaintance of Arbuthnot, Gay, and Pope, found patrons, and eventually, through the influence of Lord Littleton, received a sinecure, the Surveyor-Generalship of the Leeward Islands. He travelled in France and Italy as tutor to Charles Richard Talbot, son of the Solicitor-General, and in 1734–1736 published his long poem *Liberty,* in which Liberty herself narrates the vicissitudes of her progress through the ages in Greece, Rome, and Britain. He produced a series of tragedies, including *Sophonisba* and *Tancred and Sigismunda,* and, with David Mallet, the masque of *Alfred. The Castle of Indolence,* written in Thomson's pleasant home in Richmond, was published in 1748.

JAMES THOMSON (1834–1882), the child of poor parents, was born in Port Glasgow and educated at the Royal Caledonian Asylum in London. He became an army schoolmaster but was discharged in 1862 for a breach of discipline. A passionate early love affair was cut short by the death of the beautiful girl whom he hoped to marry. Thomson made friends with Charles Bradlaugh, the radical, wrote for *The National Reformer,* and took an active part in the propaganda of free thought. He lived in London a life of sadness and isolation, aggravated by insomnia and his addiction to drink, and died in University College Hospital. His chief poem, 'The City of Dreadful Night,' was contributed to *The National Reformer* in 1874. It was republished with other poems in 1880. *Vane's Story and Other Poems* (1881) shows that Thomson could also write in happier mood though he reverts to gloom and terror in *Insomnia* (1882). Most of his important prose papers were collected in *Essays and Phantasies* (1881) and *Satires and Profanities* (1884). He wrote under the initials B.V. — Bysshe Vanolis, an expression of his admiration for Shelley and Novalis.

HENRY VAUGHAN (1622–1695) considered himself a poetic disciple of George Herbert. He was born in Brecknockshire, South Wales, and his enthusiastic Welsh patriotism caused him to sign himself 'Silurist,' Siluria being the old Roman name of his district. To his teacher, the Rev. Matthew Herbert, he always felt indebted for exciting his enthusiasm for literature. From Herbert's tuition Vaughan went to Jesus College, Oxford, probably about 1638. He did not take a degree but went to London to study law, made literary acquaintances, and began to write poetry. The outbreak of the Civil War interrupted his legal studies and he retired to Wales where he turned to the study of medicine. He may have been for a time a lieutenant with the Royalist troops; certainly after the War he settled in 'Siluria' for the rest of a long pleasant life as a country doctor. His first volume of religious poems, *Silex Scintillans,* was published in 1650, with a second part added in 1655.

EDMUND WALLER (1606–1687) inherited Beaconsfield in Buckinghamshire. He was educated at Eton and King's College, Cambridge. In 1631 he married a London heiress who died three years later. He entered Parliament early and was at first a brilliant and active member of the opposition. Later he became a Royalist and in 1643 was the leader in a plot ('Waller's plot') to seize London for Charles I. For this he was imprisoned, fined, and banished but, on betraying his associates, spared execution. He made his peace with Cromwell in 1651 and returned to England. He was received again into royal favor on the Restoration and was once more a member of Parliament. The eighteenth century gave Waller rather more credit than he deserved for the development of the heroic couplet, deeming him, with Denham, the founder of the school of correct verse.

William Wordsworth (1770–1850) was born at Cockermouth, Cumberland, and spent most of his life in the Lake District. After attending the grammar school at Hawkshead he entered St. John's College, Cambridge, in 1787. The most important parts of his undergraduate training were really his long vacations in the Lake Country, in France, and in Switzerland. After taking his B.A. he went to France late in 1791. There he fell in love with the daughter of a Royalist surgeon in Blois who bore him a daughter. Poverty and the war kept Wordsworth and Annette Vallon apart for nine years and at the end of that time they no longer wished to marry. The enthusiastic hopes of the imminent regeneration of society which his year in Revolutionary France had raised in Wordsworth's heart were shattered by the English declaration of war and the excesses of the Reign of Terror. He went through a period of perplexity and despair. In 1795 his outlook began to brighten. He went to live with his beloved sister Dorothy, whose sympathy and poetic sensitiveness did much for his verse. In 1793 he had published his first poems, *An Evening Walk* and *Descriptive Sketches,* and in 1795 a legacy of £900 made it possible for him to devote all his energies to poetry. In the same year began his long friendship with Samuel Taylor Coleridge. With the Coleridges the Wordsworths lived for a year in close intercourse at Alfoxden and Stowey in Somerset, and there Wordsworth planned his vast work *The Recluse,* of which he finished only a part. Together in 1798 the poets published the *Lyrical Ballads.* The important Preface setting forth a new theory of poetry was not added until 1800. In 1798–1799 the Wordsworths went with Coleridge to Germany and then settled at Grasmere where Wordsworth spent the remainder of his life, first at Dove Cottage and later at Rydal Mount. In 1802 he married Mary Hutchinson to whom five children were born. In 1805 the first draft of *The Prelude* to *The Recluse* was finished but was not published until after his death. A volume of *Poems,* including the odes to 'Duty' and 'On Intimations of Immortality' appeared in 1807; *The Excursion,* another section of *The Recluse,* in 1814; his collected Works in 1815; the *Ecclesiastical Sonnets* in 1822; and in 1842 a final volume. In 1843 Wordsworth succeeded Southey as poet laureate.

Sir Thomas Wyatt (1503?–1542) was educated at St. John's College, Cambridge. In 1521 he married Elizabeth, daughter of Lord Cobham. Henry VIII recognized his ability and sent him on diplomatic missions to France and, in 1527, to Italy. There he was impressed by the work of the Italian poets, especially Petrarch, in translating whom he produced the first group of sonnets in English. He also translated and wrote short poems imitative of French forms. Wyatt was suspected of being a lover of Anne Boleyn before her marriage with the King, and it may have been for this that he was temporarily imprisoned in the Tower of London in 1536. Restored to favor he served as a member of the Privy Council and as ambassador to Spain. He was charged with treason during his residence there and again sent to the Tower in 1541, but cleared himself and was pardoned. In 1542 he was in Parliament and was to have been made Commander of the Fleet.

William Butler Yeats (1865–1939) has been called both the greatest poet of Ireland and the greatest poet in English of this century. His early years as a student and a young man were divided between London and Ireland, especially the Sligo region of his mother's parents, where he developed much of his feeling for the history, folklore, and legends of the Irish past. Growing up in a rationalist home, his naturally religious bent found an outlet in his dabblings with the then current fascination in the occult, particularly Theosophy and Rosicrucianism. This interest—at least as a possible way of dealing with and structuring experience—returned in later years when he discovered accidentally that his wife was a medium. Much of his earliest poetry shows a cloying staleness of image and diction, a romantic and cloudy 'escapism' which is directly attributable not only to late nineteenth-century aestheticism, but as well to the esoteric vagueness derived from his interest in mysticism. But a significant change is marked by his involvement in the Irish Republican movement. (Eventually, he was to become a member of the Irish Senate, 1922–8.) Besides his early admiration for some of the Irish leaders, known through his father, decisive influences here were his passionate love for Maude Gonne, a fiery patriot, and his collaboration with Lady Gregory in the spectacular renascence of Irish drama. As a result of these experiences, his poetry gradually became more immediate and direct. By the end of his life, he had achieved a fine compression, a due regard for opposed tensions, a luminosity which displays an extraordinary vitality and perception of all life. He is, consequently, that singular phenomenon, a lyric poet who achieved greatness only in old age. He was awarded the Nobel Prize for Literature in 1923.

Index of Titles

For obvious reasons no titles are included here which merely repeat the first line of the poem.

T

U

Index of First Lines

G

H

I

N

O

P

Q

R

S

T

Y